ISBN 978-1-5281-3899-4
PIBN 10931309

THE NEW INTERNATIONAL YEAR BOOK

A COMPENDIUM OF THE WORLD'S PROGRESS

FOR THE YEAR

1912

EDITOR

FRANK MOORE COLBY, M.A.

ASSOCIATE EDITOR

ALLEN LEON CHURCHILL

NEW YORK

DODD, MEAD AND COMPANY

1913

PREFACE

The New International Year Book differs in scope from other annual publications. It is intended to be an encyclopædia of the year. It therefore includes departments which are not to be found in any other single annual volume. It is enabled to do so first by its large size and second by its exclusion of information not pertaining to the year or not derived from the latest sources available. Among the departments that are either not to be found or are less fully treated in other annual publications, are Biography, Agriculture, Political History, Societies and Religious Bodies. American subjects are, of course, far more fully treated than in any of the British annuals. At the same time owing to its international scope it necessarily devotes more attention to foreign affairs than do the other American publications. The plan of the work requires that the text shall be new each year and no part of it carried forward and merely revised. There has been a slight deviation from this rule in the present volume in that the paragraphs on Manufactures in a few of the articles on the States in the 1911 volume have been in part repeated in order to admit of comparison with the statistics of manufactures for the other States which are now for the first time included in this volume. The Presidential Campaign, marking as it did a new turn in American political history, required unusually full treatment. Nearly fifty pages have been given to it and especial pains have been taken to insure comprehensiveness and impartiality. Among other subjects which have required special attention are the Titanic Disaster and the question of Safety at Sea; the Balkan War, which is treated under the title Turkey and the Balkan Peoples; Railway Accidents; Electoral Reform; Minimum Wage; Workingmen's Compensation; Syndicalism; Surgery; Synthesis of Rubber; Panama Canal; Aqueducts; City Planning.

Frank Moore Colby.

EDITOR

FRANK MOORE COLBY, M. A.

ASSOCIATE EDITOR

ALLEN LEON CHURCHILL

LIST OF CONTRIBUTORS

AGRICULTURE, HORTICULTURE, FOODS, IRRIGATION, BOTANY, FORESTRY, ETC.

ALFRED CHARLES TRUE, PH. D.,
UNITED STATES DEPARTMENT OF AGRICULTURE, AND

EDWIN WEST ALLEN, PH. D.,
UNITED STATES DEPARTMENT OF AGRICULTURE; ASSISTED BY EXPERTS IN THE DEPARTMENT OF AGRICULTURE AT WASHINGTON.

ANTHROPOLOGY AND ETHNOLOGY

CLARK WISSLER, PH. D.,
AMERICAN MUSEUM OF NATURAL HISTORY, AND
ROBERT H. LOWIE, PH. D.,
AMERICAN MUSEUM OF NATURAL HISTORY.

ARCHÆOLOGY

OLIVER SAMUEL TONKS, PH. D.,
PROFESSOR OF ART IN VASSAR COLLEGE.

ARCHITECTURE

A. D. F. HAMLIN, M. A.,
PROFESSOR OF THE HISTORY OF ARCHITECTURE, AND EXECUTIVE HEAD, SCHOOL OF ARCHITECTURE, COLUMBIA UNIVERSITY.

ASTRONOMY

T. W. EDMONDSON, PH. D.,
PROFESSOR OF MATHEMATICS, NEW YORK UNIVERSITY.

CHEMISTRY

JAMES LEWIS HOWE, PH. D.,
PROFESSOR OF CHEMISTRY AT WASHINGTON AND LEE UNIVERSITY.

CHEMISTRY, INDUSTRIAL, AND EXPOSITIONS

MARCUS BENJAMIN, PH. D.,
EDITOR FOR THE UNITED STATES NATIONAL MUSEUM.

DRAMA

CLAYTON HAMILTON,
DRAMATIC CRITIC FOR THE "BOOKMAN."

ECONOMIC AND POLITICAL SCIENCE

FRANK HAMILTON HANKINS, PH. D.
ASSISTANT PROFESSOR OF ECONOMICS AND SOCIOLOGY, CLARK COLLEGE.

EDUCATION

MILO B. HILLEGAS, PH. B.,
ASSISTANT PROFESSOR OF ELEMENTARY EDUCATION, TEACHERS COLLEGE, COLUMBIA UNIVERSITY.

ELECTRICAL ENGINEERING

WILLIAM E. WICKENDEN, B. S.,
ASSISTANT PROFESSOR OF ELECTRICAL ENGINEERING, MASSACHUSETTS INSTITUTE OF TECHNOLOGY.

EXPLORATION AND POLAR RESEARCH

CYRUS C. ADAMS,
MEMBER OF THE STAFF OF THE AMERICAN GEOGRAPHICAL SOCIETY, GEOGRAPHICAL WRITER FOR THE NEW YORK "SUN."

FOREIGN GAZETTEER

EDWARD LATHROP ENGLE AND
ALLAN EVA ENGLE.

GEOLOGY

DAVID HALE NEWLAND,
ASSISTANT STATE GEOLOGIST, NEW YORK.

INTERNATIONAL ARBITRATION

CLINTON ROGERS WOODRUFF, LL. B.,
SECRETARY OF THE NATIONAL MUNICIPAL LEAGUE AND OF THE MOHONK CONFERENCE, AND PRESIDENT OF THE BOARD OF PERSONAL REGISTRATION, PHILADELPHIA.

LIBRARY PROGRESS

M. R. HAINES,
MANAGING EDITOR OF THE "LIBRARY JOURNAL."

LITERATURE, ENGLISH AND AMERICAN

EDWIN E. SLOSSON, PH. D.,
LITERARY EDITOR, "THE INDEPENDENT."

LITERATURE, FRENCH

ALBERT SCHINZ, PH. D.,
PROFESSOR OF FRENCH LITERATURE, BRYN MAWR COLLEGE.

LITERATURE, GERMAN

AMELIA VON ENDE,
CONTRIBUTOR TO NEW YORK EVENING "POST" AND "NATION."

MANUFACTURES, CIVIL ENGINEERING, TECHNOLOGY, AERONAUTICS, AND FIRE PROTECTION

HERBERT TREADWELL WADE.

MEDICINE

ALBERT WARREN FERRIS, A. M., M. D.,
SENIOR RESIDENT PHYSICIAN, GLEN SPRINGS, WATKINS, N. Y.; FORMER PRESIDENT, NEW YORK STATE COMMISSION IN LUNACY; FORMER ASSISTANT IN NEUROLOGY, COLUMBIA UNIVERSITY; FORMER ASSISTANT IN MEDICINE, NEW YORK UNIVERSITY AND BELLEVUE HOSPITAL MEDICAL COLLEGE; ASSISTED BY

DAVID G. YATES, M. D.,
SURGEON, NEW YORK CHILDREN'S HOSPITAL; SURGEON, DEMILT DISPENSARY.

MILITARY PROGRESS

C. DEW. WILLCOX,
LIEUTENANT-COLONEL, U. S. A., PROFESSOR OF MODERN LANGUAGES, U. S. MILITARY ACADEMY.

MILITARY STATISTICS, FOREIGN

HERBERT TREADWELL WADE.

MUSIC

ALFRED REMY, M. A.,
PROFESSOR OF HARMONY AND COUNTERPOINT, INTERNATIONAL CONSERVATORY, NEW YORK.

NAVAL PROGRESS AND BATTLESHIPS

H. F. BRYAN,
COMMANDER, U. S. N.

PAINTING AND SCULPTURE

FLORENCE N. LEVY,
EDITOR, "AMERICAN ART ANNUAL."

PHILOLOGY

CHARLES KNAPP, PH. D.,
PROFESSOR OF CLASSICAL PHILOLOGY, BARNARD COLLEGE, COLUMBIA UNIVERSITY; AND

LOUIS H. GRAY, PH. D.,
ASSOCIATE EDITOR OF THE "ORIENTALISCHE BIBLIOGRAPHIE."

PHILOSOPHY

FRANK THILLY, A. M., PH. D., LL. D.,
PROFESSOR OF PHILOSOPHY, SAGE SCHOOL OF PHILOSOPHY, CORNELL UNIVERSITY.

PHYSICS

W. W. STIFLER, PH. D.,
LECTURER IN PHYSICS, COLUMBIA UNIVERSITY.

PSYCHOLOGY, PSYCHICAL RESEARCH, AND PSYCHOTHERAPY

MADISON BENTLEY, B. S., PH. D.,
HEAD OF THE DEPARTMENT OF PSYCHOLOGY, UNIVERSITY OF ILLINOIS; AND

CHRISTIAN A. RUCKMICH,
INSTRUCTOR IN PSYCHOLOGY, CORNELL UNIVERSITY.

RAILWAYS

WILLIAM E. HOOPER,
ASSOCIATE EDITOR, "RAILWAY AGE GAZETTE."

SANITARY ENGINEERING AND MUNICIPAL ACTIVITIES

MOSES NELSON BAKER, C. E.,
EDITOR OF THE "ENGINEERING NEWS."

SPORTS

CHARLES A. TAYLOR,
MEMBER OF THE STAFF OF THE NEW YORK "TRIBUNE"; AND

ARTHUR BARTLETT MAURICE,
EDITOR OF THE "BOOKMAN."
(Article Football)

UNIVERSITIES AND COLLEGES

MILO B. HILLEGAS, PH. D.,
ASSISTANT PROFESSOR OF ELEMENTARY EDUCATION, TEACHERS COLLEGE, COLUMBIA UNIVERSITY.

WEIGHTS AND MEASURES
(Metric System; Recent Progress)

CH.-ED. GUILLAUME,
ADJUNCT DIRECTOR OF THE INTERNATIONAL BUREAU OF WEIGHTS AND MEASURES.

ZOOLOGY AND BIOLOGY

AARON L. TREADWELL, PH. D.,
PROFESSOR OF BIOLOGY, VASSAR COLLEGE.

ILLUSTRATIONS

MAPS

NOTE: Cross references in SMALL CAPITALS indicate that the allusion is to a separate article; cross references in *italics* denote that the reference is to a subdivision of a main article. A cross reference in *italics*, standing alone in an article, carries the reference to another subdivision of the same article. The letters q. v. (*quod vide*=Latin "which see") in parentheses following a word, indicate that the subject is treated under its own name elsewhere in the vo ume.

NOTE: In certain tables in this work it will be found, by addition, that the totals do not correspond to the sum of the items. This is the result of the omission or inclusion of certain small items which are not mentioned in the table, but are included in the totals. This is a usage frequently employed in the compilation of government statistics, from which sources the greater number of the tables in the YEAR BOOK are taken.

THE NEW INTERNATIONAL YEAR BOOK

ABYSSINIA. An independent empire of eastern Africa. Area variously estimated at from 308,000 to 432,000 square miles. The population consists of Semitic Abyssinians, Gallas and Somalis, Negroes, Falashas, and non-natives—in all between nine and eleven millions. Addis Abbeba, the capital, has from 30,000 to 35,000 inhabitants; Harar, 50,000; Aksum, 5000. The Alexandrian is the national church, and education is in the hands of Coptic teachers. Cattle- and sheep-raising and a primitive sort of agriculture are the main industries. The forests yield rubber and valuable timbers. Gold-mining tracts extend along the banks of the Baro River, and coal has been found. Imports through Jibuti in 1909, about £811,566; in 1910, £950,147. Exports by way of Jibuti average £335,000. Imports through Zeila, the Sudan, and Italian colonies, about £192,795 in 1909; exports average about £40,000. American cotton goods and arms and ammunition, provisions, wearing apparel, and hardware are the chief imports; coffee, hides and skins, wax, ivory, rubber, civet, gum-arabic, and glue the main exports. Miles of railway in Abyssinia, 111; of telegraph, 1056. Progress was being made during the year on the extension of the Addis Abbeba-Diré Dawa extension of the Dijbuta line to Diré Dawa.

Menelek II. (born 1844) has been emperor since 1889; but owing to his incapacity the government has been administered since 1910 by his grandson, Lidj Jeassu (born 1897).

ACADEMY, French (Académie Française). The French Academy is the first of the five academies constituting the Institute of France. It consists of forty members and is the final authority on questions relating to the niceties of the French language and of grammar, rhetoric, and poetry, and of the classification of French classics. Two new members were elected in 1912: Gen. Louis Lyautey to succeed Jules Henri Poincaré and Emile Boutroux to succeed Hippolyte Langlois de Vogüé. There was one vacancy in the academy at the end of the year.

ACCIDENTS. See Employers' Liability, Insurance, Railway Accidents, etc.

ACCIDENTS AND DISEASES. See Labor Legislation.

ACCIDENTS, COAL MINE. See Coal.

ACCIDENTS, Compensation for. See Labor Legislation.

ACCIDENTS, Physician's Duty to Report. See Labor Legislation.

ADAM, John Noble. An American merchant and public official, died February 9, 1912. He was born in Peebles, Scotland, in 1842, and was educated in a parochial school in Edinburgh. He was apprenticed to business in Edinburgh from 1854 to 1864. He was engaged in business in that city from 1865 to 1872. In the latter year he came to the United States and engaged in business in New Haven, Conn., where he remained until 1881, when he removed to Buffalo. He was very successful and in 1903 was enabled to retire with a large fortune. He then began to devote himself to politics. He was a candidate for mayor in 1905 and was elected by the largest majority ever given to a mayor in Buffalo. His administration attracted attention throughout the country. It was conducted on a sound basis and was considered a model of municipal government. He was several times mentioned as possible candidate for governor of the State on the Democratic ticket.

ADEN. A British dependency in southwestern Arabia; a part of the Bombay Presidency. Its area is 75 square miles and that of the attached island of Perim 5 square miles; population (1911), 46,165. The area of the protectorate extends over some 9000 square miles (estimated population, 100,000). The town of Aden is an important coaling and trading station, strongly fortified. Exports consist of coffee, gums, skins, and hides, cotton goods, feathers, spices, etc.; and were valued in 1909-10 at £2,621,780 by sea and £102,594 by land; treasure, £545,341. Imports (1909-10), £2,956,055 by sea, £163,693 by land; treasure, £524,706. The settlement is presided over by a resident (1912, Brig.-Gen. J. A. Bell) subject to the Bombay government.

Besides Perim, the island of Sokotra (1382 square miles, 12,000 inhabitants) and the Kuria Muria Islands (five in number) are attached to Aden.

ADMINISTRATION. See United States.

ADVANCEMENT OF SCIENCE, American Association for the. The sixty-fourth meeting of this association convened in Cleveland, O., December 30, under the presidency of Dr. Charles Edward Pickering. A number of other societies, most of them affiliated with the association, met at the same time. These included, among others, the American Mathematical Society, the Entomological Society of America, the American Microscopical Society, the American Psychological Association, the American Association of Anatomists, the American Physiological Society and the American Society of Naturalists. Addresses of welcome were delivered by Mayor Baker of Cleveland, Dr. Charles F. Thwing, president of the

Western Reserve University, and Dr. F. M. Comstock, acting-president of the Case School of Applied Science. Responses were made by President Pickering. The annual address was delivered by the retiring president, Dr. Charles Edward Bessey. The address was entitled: "Some of the Next Steps in Botanical Science." The annual addresses of the retiring vice-presidents were as follows: Geological and Geographical Section, "Significance of the Pleistocene Mollusks," Vice-President Shimek; Section of Mathematics and Astronomy, "The Spectroscopic Determination of Stellar Philosophies, Considered Practically," Vice-President Frost; Section of Zoölogy, Section F, "Is it Worth While?" Vice-President Nachtrieve; Section of Botany, "The Scope of State Natural History Surveys," Vice-President Newcomb; Section of Physics, "Unitary Theories in Physics," Vice-President Millikan; Section of Physiology and Experimental Medicine, "On the Function of Individual Cells in Nerve Centres," Vice-President Porter; Section of Education, "Educational Diagnosis," Vice-President Thorndike; Section of Anthropology and Psychology, "The Study of Man," Vice-President Ladd; Section of Social and Economic Science, "Comparative Measurements of the Changing Cost of Living," Vice-President Norton. Other noteworthy addresses delivered at the meeting include the following: "Across the United States with the European Geographers," by Dr. W. Humphreys of the United States Weather Bureau; "A Summary of the Study of Agricultural Instruction in Rural Schools," President Benjamin M. Davis of the American Nature Study Society; "The Relation of Climate to Horticulture," President W. T. Macoun of the Society for Horticultural Science. A number of symposiums and sessions were held by the various sections and affiliated societies. The following officers were elected for 1913: president, E. B. Wilson, Columbia University; vice-presidents, Section A, Frank Schlesinger, Allegheny Observatory; Section B, A. D. Cole, Ohio State University; Section C, A. A. Noyes, Massachusetts Institute of Technology; Section D, O. P. Hood, United States Bureau of Mines; Section E, J. S. Diller, United States Geological Survey; Section F, A. G. Mayer, Carnegie Institution of Washington; Section G, H. C. Cowles, University of Chicago; Section H, W. B. Pillsbury, University of Michigan; Section L, P. P. Claxton, United States Commissioner of Education; general secretary, H. W. Springsteen, Western Reserve University. The next meeting will be held at Atlanta, Ga., in December, 1913, and January, 1914.

ADVANCEMENT OF SCIENCE, British Association for. See Biology.

ADVENTISTS, Seventh-Day. The chief tenets of this body are a belief in the literal, personal second appearing of Christ, yet without ever setting a time for that event, and the observance of the seventh day of the week as the Sabbath. Their total communicants throughout the world are 108,975. They have 116 organized conferences, 93 mission fields, 2799 churches, 89 advanced educational institutions, 613 primary schools, total enrollment, 23,541; 37 publishing houses and branches, 102 sanitariums and branches, publish 125 periodicals, issue publications in 71 languages, are operating in about 85 countries, and employ over 10,000 evangelistic and institutional laborers, thus constituting every eleventh member an active laborer. Total contributions for 1911 were $2,363,088.29, a per capita of $21.68. Total funds for evangelistic work since the organization of the central governing body known as the General Conference, in 1863, aggregate over twenty-three million dollars. Total investments, in institutions, churches, etc., exceed thirteen million dollars.

In the year 1894 active work was begun in non-Christian lands, and has been continued until the present, so that a segregation of the work conducted in non-Christian and non-Protestant lands from the foregoing figures, indicates the following: Mission work is carried forward in 67 countries, at 140 main stations, and 145 sub-stations, with a total foreign force of 586, and 974 native helpers, a total force of 1560 laborers. There are 413 churches, 17,565 adherents, 7454 pupils in 205 schools, taught by 364 foreign and native teachers. Publications are issued in 64 languages, and work is conducted orally in 73 languages. Total income for 1911 from the foreign field was $135,234.87, a per capita of $7.69.

The headquarters of the denomination is in Washington, D. C., in which place will be held in May, 1913, the next quadrennial session, which will commemorate fifty years of organized work by the denomination. At this gathering delegates and representatives will assemble from all over the world.

ADULTERATION. See Food and Nutrition.

AEHRENTHAL, Alois Lexa von, Count. Premier and foreign minister to the Austro-Hungarian Empire, died February 17, 1912. He was born in 1854 and was educated at the Universities of Bonn and Prague. In 1877 he entered the diplomatic service and after occupying various subordinate positions in Paris and St. Petersburg and in the foreign ministry at Vienna he was made minister to Rumania in 1888. In 1889 he was transferred as ambassador to St. Petersburg and in 1906 he became premier and foreign minister. The most notable event of his career in public life was the annexation of Bosnia and Herzegovina in October, 1908. This was carried out largely through his efforts and with such force and diplomacy that it won for him the title of the "Bismarck of Austria." The two provinces had been under a protectorate of Austria since the Treaty of Berlin in 1878, and, although the taxes had been collected by Austrian officials, Turkey had enjoyed a nominal suzerainty. The success of Japan in the Russo-Japanese War, which destroyed to a large extent the power of Russia as a military force in Europe, opened the way for a bold stroke on the part of Austria, which had hitherto been deterred from actual seizure of these provinces through fear of Russia. It was said that von Aehrenthal, by secret negotiations, made sure of the support of the German Emperor and arranged with Prince Ferdinand of Bulgaria to share the burden of the seizure by acting simultaneously with him in proclaiming his kingship and the independence of his state. Although the seizure of the provinces filled Europe with amazement, no power dared or cared to move first and the event was accomplished without serious trouble. At the time of the seizure of the provinces von Aehrenthal was regarded as a close ally of the heir to the throne, the Archduke Francis

Ferdinand, who had been a strong advocate of the seizure of the Turkish provinces. In 1910, however, von Aehrenthal placed himself at the head of the peace party in Austria-Hungary, insisting in particular upon a pacifying attitude towards Italy. The archduke, who was regarded as the head of the war party, became bitterly offended, and just after the outbreak of the war between Italy and Turkey a ministerial crisis arose over the attitude which Austria should hold toward Italy. The quarrel was laid before the Emperor Francis Joseph for decision and von Aehrenthal placed his resignation in the emperor's hands. The emperor gave unqualified support to the peace policy and it marked a triumph for von Aehrenthal. It was, however, his last triumph. He was already in broken health and the strain of the struggle with the archduke completed the wreck. Within a few days he was obliged to take to his bed and never left it until the time of his death.

AERONAUTICS. The navigation of the air by aeroplane, dirigible balloon, and aerostat or spherical non-dirigible balloon is as usual discussed under the broad title of aeronautics in the YEAR BOOK. In the record for 1912 much important progress was to be noted, yet many of the sensational features of previous years were absent. Steady advances were manifested, especially in aviation and the development of the hydro-aeroplane, while a new record for spherical balloons was made in the international race held in Germany.

AVIATION

In the period from 1908 when Europe was thrilled by the wonderful achievements of Wilbur Wright, whose untimely death was a sad event of the year under discussion, and by the Rheims Aviation Meet of 1909, the development of the aeroplane had proceeded steadily, and by 1912 aviation had passed beyond the point where a few daring enthusiasts were willing to risk their lives on machines designed without a thorough knowledge of the various elements involved and frequently imperfectly constructed. Furthermore, spectacular exhibitions too often accompanied by feats of useless and reckless daring, had been supplanted by more serious long distance competitions, and the military applications of the aeroplane were being not only considered, but under practical test by the armies and navies of the great powers in some cases in actual war. In fact it was to the military and naval services that inventors and manufacturers largely looked for the sale of their machines, as aside from such support there was little other practical application that assured immediate commercial returns. Accordingly the most striking features connected with aviation during the year 1912 have been in the development and use of aeroplanes by the various military services, and to this must be added the growth of interest in the hydro-aeroplane and its consequent improvement.

The military aeroplane is now recognized as an essential implement of war and not only did it find practical application in actual warfare by the fighting armies in 1912, but the equipment and training of aerial battalions was proceeding apace. So far as design and construction were concerned this fact tended towards conservatism and a progressive development, as the requirements for military service were not essentially different from what would be demanded under other conditions. For example, the transport of passengers, either for observation or to drop explosives, was considered an essential of the military aeroplane, and this, of course, is one of the main functions of any machine for mechanical flight. Furthermore, it must carry some armament, as bombs for dropping or guns for attacking dirigibles and weight-carrying possibilities go also with the future commercial vehicle. The militray developments in their special relations to the armies and navies of the world will be found discussed at length under MILITARY PROGRESS and NAVAL PROGRESS.

The year's development in the case of the hydro-aeroplane was of special significance and interest, for its use promised to become more general and there seemed to be a strong probability that its employment for sport might find a field comparable to that of yachting or at least ice boating. The hydro-aeroplanes as built in 1912 afforded good sport without undue danger and did not require any elaborate aerodrome or chosen field for rising or landing. In fact at the Paris Aero-exposition nearly all of the aeroplanes exhibited were arranged so that floats could be adapted for use over water, while in America it was reported that the most active demand was for such types of aeroplanes.

PROBLEMS OF DESIGN AND CONSTRUCTION. Perhaps the most important technical problem in connection with aeroplane design during the year was the attempt to obtain automatic inherent stability independent of the action of the aviator. This problem was not solved, but the operation of an aeroplane remained in the same condition as that of the bicycle where the rider instinctively preserves his balance by changing the direction of the wheel. Similar methods of regulation were required for the aeroplane. Some form of gyroscope was advocated to accomplish this regulation mechanically, and in fact the gyroscopic action of the rotary motor was considered available for this purpose. Other experiments such as the oil pump and inertia weights, devices of Esnault, Pelterie, and others, were also undertaken, and even a pendulum or the pendular mounting of the motor on a swinging crossframe were proposed.

In the strength of the aeroplane and its materials, important developments were being made. Here progress was satisfactory, as wood was being eliminated and the higher grades of steel were extensively employed. At the Paris Aviation Exposition in October, of 45 representative machines exhibited, 10 had the frame work entirely of steel, 21 of wood and steel, and 14 of wood, while in 1911 wooden construction was observed in the majority of machines. This improvement in construction was shown in the Hanriot monoplane, where the entire skeleton was composed of steel tubing which was solidly welded together in one piece by the oxy-acetylene process. The use of steel and aluminum for propellers had not proved so successful, as it was found difficult to join the blades to the boss so firmly as to resist the centrifugal stress developed by the rapidly rotating propeller, but towards the end of the year it was proposed to press the blades and boss from a single piece of steel tubing, and this plan was said to have many favorable fea-

(3) Paulhan (Curtiss biplane, Curtiss motor), 86.3 points. (4) Robinson (Curtiss biplane, Curtiss motor), 71.9 points. Colliex, who had developed the Voison *Canard* during the previous year, made a number of good flights, but met with an accident with both of two machines. There was also shown at Monaco one monoplane of Deperdussin, piloted by Lorenzo, which made a successful flight with a passenger, but did not participate in the competition. The flights of the hydro-aeroplanes were observed by naval representatives of a number of governments.

Aerostation

International Balloon Race, Bennett Cup Summary. The competition for the Gordon-Bennett Cup for spherical balloons in 1912 resulted in the breaking of the world's record of 1211 miles made by M. Émile Dubonnet January 7-8 in the balloon *Condor III.*, and a new record of 1361 miles by the French balloon *Picardie*. Twenty balloons participated in the contest which was started at Stuttgart, Germany, on October 27. The cup which was held by Germany by virtue of the success of the balloon *Berlin II.* with Lieutenant Hans Gericke, pilot, in 1911, was won by France for the first time. The following is a summary of the eight balloons which accomplished over 745 miles each: *Picardie* (France)—M. Maurice Bienaimé, pilot; M. Rumpelmayer, aide; landed near Moscow, Russia, October 29, distance 2191 kilometers (1361⅝ miles). *Ile de France* (France)—Alfred Lablanc, pilot; landed near Moscow, Russia, October 29, distance 2001 kilometers (1243⅝ miles). *Uncle Sam* (United States)—H. E. Honeywell, pilot; landed near Dukchty, Russia, October 29, distance 1056 miles. *Frankfurt* (Austria)—F. H. Lenhart, pilot; landed at Rosenofskoy, Russia, October 28, distance 1769 kilometers (1100 miles). *Zurich* (Switzerland)—Victor de Beauclair, pilot landed in Russia October 28, distance 1523 kilometers (946½ miles). *Reichsflugverein* (Germany)—Otto Korn, pilot; landed near Dukchty, Russia, October 28, distance 1385 kilometers (860¾ miles). *Minckelers* (Belgium)—F. Gérard, pi t; landed near Riga, Russia, October 28, distance 1291 kilometers (802⅜ miles). *Honeymoon* (England)—Jean de Francia, pilot; landed at Breslau, Germany, October 28, distance 1253 kilometers (778¾ miles).

The other competitors with less distances to their credit were:

Busley, Austria; *Azurea*, Switzerland; *Hamburg III.*, Germany; *Andromeda*, Italy; *Graf. Zeppelin*, Denmark; *Belgica II.*, Belgium; *Libia*, Italy; *Million Population Club*, America; *Bearn*, France; *Astarte*, Austria; *Helvetia*, Switzerland; and *Dusseldorf II.*, loaned by Germans to America.

The *Dusseldorf II.*, which was loaned by Germans to the United States to replace a balloon destroyed previous to the competition, was piloted by John Watts with Arthur T. Attherholt as aide, and made a distance of about 1000 miles, landing at Pskov in Russia. This balloon was protested against and was duly ruled out of the race.

While trying out his new balloon *Berlin II.* preliminary to the Gordon-Bennett race, on October 20, Lieut. Hans Gericke, the well-known German aeronaut and the winner of the Bennett race at St. Louis in 1911, fell to his death with his aide, Lieutenant Strahler, as a result of his balloon bursting. Lieutenant Gericke started out from Bitterfeld, and while above Spansberg, Saxony, at an elevation of about 6000 feet, approached a thunder shower and was caught by a sudden upward current which carried the balloon to a height of 15,000 feet in a very short period of time, as shown by the recording instruments. Either on account of the rapid expansion of the gas, or because it was struck by lightning, the balloon burst and the two men fell to their deaths at a terrific speed.

The National Balloon Race was held at Kansas City and was won by the balloon *Uncle Sam*, which subsequently participated in the International Balloon Race in Germany. This race was started on July 27 and with the exception of the *Uncle Sam*, which was in the air for two days, the other competitors landed on July 28. A summary follows: *Uncle Sam*—H. E. Honeywell, pilot; landed at Manassas, Va., distance 885 miles. *Kansas City*—John Watts, pilot; landed at Bellville, Mich., distance 625 miles. *Drifter*—Albert Holz, pilot; landed at New Berlin, Wis., distance 425 miles. *Million Population Club II.*—P. McCullogh, pilot; landed at Spring Green, Wis., distance 370 miles. *Million Population Club I.*—J. Berry, pilot; landed at Nord, Ill., distance 355 miles. *Goodyear*—G. M. Bumbaugh, pilot; landed at Pola, Ill., distance 330 miles. *Cole*—E. J. Custer, pilot; landed at McGregor, Iowa, distance 325 miles.

The various legal questions connected with aeronautics continue to arise and demand more or less complete solution from time to time. An international conference on legal questions of the use of the air met at Paris, but adjourned without coming to any definite conclusions. The prefect of police of the Department of the Seine found it necessary during the year to forbid the landing of aeroplanes within the limits of the city of Paris and also to prohibit their rising or descending from ground nearer that 1640 feet to any inhabited building except an authorized aerodrome within the limits of the department.

Fatalities of the Year. The record of fatalities during 1912 contained an unusually large number of officers and men of the aviation corps of the different armies. In the United States one of the most notable accidents was that in which Miss Harriett Quimby, with A. P. Willard, was thrown from her 70 horsepower Blériot monoplane on July 1 at the Boston meeting. Miss Quimby had distinguished herself as the first aviatress to fly across the English Channel and had made a record for herself in numerous flights. While the fatalities of the year in number exceeded those of previous years, yet when the total mileage was considered it would be found that there had been a great gain in safety and that conditions of construction and operation were better understood. There was a tendency to discourage sensational performances at public exhibitions, and the accidents that did occur were due to more normal circumstances.

AEROPLANE. See Aeronautics.

AEROPLANE CATAPULT. See Naval Progress, *Aviation*.

AEROSTATION. See Aeronautics.

AESTHETICS. See Psychology.

AFGHANISTAN. A central Asian monarchy, practically under British domination, and having foreign relations only with the British-Indian government. Capital, Kabul, with about 70,000 inhabitants. Area, about 225,000 square miles. The inhabitants, estimated at 5,000,000, belong mostly to the Sunni sect of the Mohammedans. The important industries are agriculture and stock-raising. The chief products and exports are cereals, lentils, fruits, live animals, raw wool, silk, carpets, and camels'-hair goods. Commercial relations are sustained with India and Russia. According to Indian statistics the imports into Afghanistan amounted in 1911 to £774,396, and the exports to £610,102. The trade with Russia is estimated at about 4,000,000 roubles imports and an approximate value exports. An indeterminable revenue is derived mainly from taxation on production, and its collection is marked by oppression and extortion. The loosely organized government is headed by an ameer (1912, Habib Ullah Khan; born 1872, succeeded his father 1901), who is granted a subsidy of Rs. 180,000 by the Indian government. His will is theoretically absolute and a condition of feudalism prevails.

ARMY. A standing army organized on a modern basis, with improved methods of training, was maintained under the command of the ameer's brother, Sardar Nasrullah Khan. Service is nominally obligatory, but to obtain the necessary strength only about one man in eight is called to the colors. This gives an establishment of about 27,000 infantry and 7000 cavalry, apart from a well-trained force of artillery armed with modern guns. There are irregular troops, including some 25,000 mounted men and a smaller force of infantry which would be joined with the regular army to give a war strength of about 80,000 horse and 60,000 foot. The manufacture of military supplies at Kabul, where small arms and ordnance shops were maintained, was carried on during the year, and the facilities for military transport and the improvement of the roads were advanced.

HISTORY. In the early summer a large number of the tribesmen of Khost, including the Ghilzais, revolted, and the ameer was slow in proceeding against them, being apparently afraid to trust his own troops. He was criticized for his inactivity, which was attributed by some to a desire on his part to pose as a champion of Pan-Islamism, the rebels being Mohammedans. Finally, the revolt was put down chiefly through the efforts of the Mullahs, and the governor of Khost was imprisoned at Kabul. Pacificatory measures were taken and the chief grievances were removed. Forced labor was forbidden and the taxes were reduced or abolished.

AFRICA. See articles on the various countries; also EXPLORATION. For recent books on Africa, see LITERATURE, ENGLISH AND AMERICAN, *Travel* and *Contemporary History*.

AFRICAN LANGUAGES See ANTHROPOLOGY.

AFRICAN METHODIST EPISCOPAL CHURCH. See COLORED METHODISTS.

AFRICAN METHODIST EPISCOPAL UNION CHURCH. See COLORED METHODISTS.

AGRICULTURAL BANKS. See AGRICULTURAL CREDIT.

AGRICULTURAL BOYS' AND GIRLS' CLUBS. See AGRICULTURAL EDUCATION.

AGRICULTURAL CREDIT. Within the past two years keen interest has developed in this country in the provision of credit facilities for farmers. This has been largely due to the active propaganda by former Governor Herrick, present ambassador to France, and Mr. David Lubin, organizer of the International Institute of Agriculture. Various investigations of the subject were in progress during the year. The Southern Commercial Congress sent a small body of representatives to study the subject in Europe. It also developed plans for a committee consisting of two members from each State of the Union to study European systems. This committee will attend the meeting of the International Institute of Agriculture in Rome in May, 1913. The American Bankers' Association in 1911 directed that an inquiry on this subject be made. At the same time the Department of State was interested and coöperated with the bankers' committee. Under the immediate direction of Ambassador Herrick a thoroughgoing investigation of systems of agricultural credit in various European countries was made and the results submitted to the government at Washington. So general became the interest in the subject that all three political parties embodied a plank in their platforms recomending the establishment of some system of agricultural credit suitable to American conditions. Finally in October President Taft took the first executive step in the direction of establishing such credit facilities in a letter to the governors. He urged that this be made a subject of consideration at the Congress of Governors in December. This was done. He expressed his belief that the coöperative credit societies of Germany, known as Raiffeisen banks, might be adapted to American conditions. He pointed out that the 12,000,000 farmers of this country pay interest charges estimated at $510,-000,000 per year. They are charged at the rate of 8½ per cent., as compared with 3½ per cent. to 4½ per cent. paid by French and German farmers. He thought it possible that such coöperative farmers' banks having been instituted, Congress might be induced to create also national land mortgage banks similar to the land credit banks of Germany and France.

PLANS PROPOSED. Among the various plans proposed for organizing rural credit are the following: 1. Extend the scope of national banking privileges by permitting banks to make loans on real estate, and develop the interest of State banks in farmers' business; 2. Establish government agricultural banks, or let the government guarantee private agricultural banks; 3. Provide for the organization of coöperative credit societies after one or more of the European plans.

With reference to the first of these plans it was pointed out that more than 2000 national banks are now located in towns of less than 6000 population and are therefore accessible to farmers. Similarly, several thousand State banks which are not hampered by loan restrictions are available. It is declared that farmers have not as yet strongly felt the need of better facilities. They now generally receive book credit from merchants and implement dealers. The rapid development of manufacturing and commerce, together with the prosperity and individual character of our agriculture, has turned the attention of bankers to the development of facilities for trade and industry. Now that a great increase in the use of machinery and fertilizers, a tendency toward larger farms and the introduction of modern business methods into agriculture are becoming prominent, it is argued that the banks will soon devise schemes to increase agricultural credit. That there was some truth in these contentions was shown by the organization of the first land-credit bank at Joliet, Ill. This was patterned after the Crédit Foncier of France. It planned to lend to farmers on long time at moderate rates of interest. The borrower was to have the privilege of paying interest and part of the principle every six months. The bank was to issue collateral trust bonds secured by farm mortgages and its capital of $250,000. It was believed that these collateral trust bonds would become a common and much desired form of investment. Loans were to be made for as long as twenty years. The scheme showed that a loan of $1000 bearing interest at 5½ per cent. could be paid off in forty semi-annual installments, diminishing gradually from $57 to $24, and totaling $1600. The second set of schemes was not widely advocated and was generally believed to be impracticable in this country. It was not believed desirable for the government itself to reënter the banking field in such manner nor to guarantee private banks, as is done by the government in Egypt.

EUROPEAN PLANS. The European schemes are of two general sorts: First, coöperative credit societies composed of peasant farmers, such as the Raiffeisen system of Germany; and second, land-credit banks formed by larger farmers, such as the Landschaften system of Germany, or by a banking corporation, as the Crédit Foncier of France. The former loan directly small sums for short periods to members only. The latter convert land mortgages into negotiable long-term bonds of convenient denominations for the general investor.

The Raiffeisen and Schültze-Delitzch banks of Germany are formed on a strictly coöperative basis, no one but members being allowed to borrow, though non-members may make deposits. The former are organized by small farmers in rural communities and the latter by artisans and small tradesmen in towns and cities. They restrict their area of operations narrowly, including no greater territory than constitutes a neighborhood. This is necessary because all members assume unlimited liability for the debts of the banks. The capital is secured from savings, from loans, from the provincial bank of the district or from the central bank, and from certain small reserve funds. Thus in 1909 the total working capital of the 3000 Raiffeisen societies of Germany was 1,935,500,000 marks, of which 88.8 per cent. was provided by the savings and deposits of the farmers and the local public. The administration of these banks is simple, democratic, and practically gratuitous. They make loans in small amounts for short periods varying from a few months to a few years. Their average rate of interest is between 4 per cent. and 5 per cent., and the average credit advanced per member is 500 marks. They sometimes demand mortgage or collateral security, but rely chiefly on personal integrity, most loans being made on two-name paper. Their loans to members in 1909 on current accounts, similar to the Scotch cash credit, amounted to $101,000,000 and those for fixed periods to about $258,000,000. It is claimed that neither debtors nor creditors of these societies have lost anything since they first started in 1849. Local societies are organized into provincial banks and these in turn into a national federation with a central bank at its head. Societies similar to these coöperative credit groups are found in nearly every European country. Thus the Irish Agricultural Organization Society has over 200 affiliated credit banks.

The Landschaften is a somewhat similar system for the benefit of the larger land owners. They lend only to members, securing their funds by the issue of bonds in convenient denominations secured by mortgages on land and by the general assets of the association. There is, moreover, the unlimited liability of all the members. Like the former, these banks are not run for profit and pay no dividends. Their rate of interest has for many recent years been below 4½ per cent. Their bonds sell freely on the German stock exchanges, with very slight variations in value.

The Crédit Foncier is a second form of land credit bank, similar in some respects to the Landschaften system. It serves as intermediary between land owners wishing to borrow on mortgages and persons with money to invest. Its function is the conversion of mortgages into negotiable form. Its method, therefore, consists in employing a body of experts to decide when loans should be made and to what amount and to issue against all mortgage loans negotiable bonds. These bonds have become such a favorite form of investment that the money market of the world has been made available for the French land owner. Their recent rate of interest on mortgage loans has been 4.3 per cent. The charter of the French institution limits its rate of profit to .6 of one per cent. These mortgage loans are made for long periods of time, averaging more than fifty years. The scheme provides for amortization, the semi-annual or annual payments covering both interest and a portion of the principle. Thus, on a loan at 4.3 per cent. interest running for 75 years the annual payment equals 4.48 per cent.; on one running 60 years the rate would be 4.66 per cent.; for 50 years, 4.88 per cent.; for 40 years, 5.25 per cent., and for 10 years, 12.4 per cent. The total loans of the Crédit Foncier December 31, 1911, equaled 6,147,000,000 francs. Most of this, however, represented loans on urban real estate.

JEWISH AGRICULTURAL AND INDUSTRIAL AID SOCIETY. This was an organization begun in 1911. It had headquarters at 174 Second Avenue, New York. It organized three "credit unions" in 1911 and five in 1912. Each union provides $500 capital by selling shares of $5 each to members; the aid society then lends to the union $1000 at 2 per cent. interest. Loans cannot exceed $100, nor extend beyond six months. Most loans are made on two-name paper. Up to the fall of 1912 these unions had a membership of 240 and outstanding loans of $17,755.

AGRICULTURAL EDUCATION. The remarkable development in agricultural education in the United States during the past sixteen years is brought out by the following figures: In 1896 the institutions for agricultural education in the United States numbered 70; 61 State colleges of agriculture and 9 agricultural schools. At the present time there are 67 State colleges of agriculture, 42 privately endowed colleges giving instruction in agriculture, and upwards of 2500 secondary and elementary schools in which agriculture is taught, making in all about 2600 colleges and schools. This number does not include the many rural elementary schools in which some of the facts concerning agriculture are now taught as required by law or by official regulation in about one-third of the States. This period has also witnessed the development of almost the entire system of extension teaching in agriculture, with the exception only of farmers' institutes and the organization of numerous agricultural associations whose functions were primarily educational. The past year has been one of greater material progress in agricultural education than any of those which have preceded it.

IN FOREIGN COUNTRIES. Several agricultural schools were established and various phases of itinerant instruction and demonstration work in agriculture were inaugurated or extended. In Egypt private contributions amounting to about $300,000 were made for the support of the school of agriculture at Ghizeh and three other agricultural schools, as well as for the establishment of new agricultural schools. The government also expended $41,500 in this work. A department for special instruction in the wool and sheep industry was added to the curriculum of Sidney Technical College, New South Wales; a training farm for boys without means who wish to prepare for farming was provided for at Booborowie, South Australia; and plans were approved for the establishment of agricultural high schools at North Bundaleer and at Moorak, South Australia. An official report shows that there were 219 agricultural and forestry schools in operation in Austria in 1911; and 7 agricultural colleges, with an annual budget of $192,000, and 32 agricultural schools, costing $865,000 a year, in Hungary. The 1912 session of the Manitoba legislature separated the College of Agriculture from the University of Manitoba.

Following tentative experiments about four years ago, several European countries have seriously undertaken to give instruction in agriculture to soldiers in garrisons. In the four years Germany has given agricultural instruction in nearly every garrison in the empire. This instruction is usually given in winter, for one or two hours a week. France and Italy are other countries in which soldiers are instructed in agriculture, while Roumania reduces to one year the military service of graduates of elementary agricultural schools and others who can pass an examination equivalent to a year's work in these schools.

The Royal Agricultural College at Cirencester, England, incorporated its collegiate work with that of the University of Bristol, the plan being for students in agriculture and forestry to spend the first year in general science work at Bristol and the second and third years at Cirencester.

Many of the provincial agricultural schools in Italy established and equipped demonstration farms. By royal decree the higher council of agricultural, industrial, and commercial instruction was superseded by a council for agricultural instruction of fourteen members appointed by the minister of agriculture.

A new school of agriculture was established at San Francisco de Borja, Mexico, and a poultry school near the City of Mexico.

In Spain a large tract of land with extensive buildings was acquired for the site for an agricultural institute of instruction and experimentation.

EDUCATIONAL CONVENTIONS. The year 1912 was the fiftieth anniversary of the passage of the land-grant act of 1862, providing for the establishment of State agricultural and mechanical colleges in the United States, and the twenty-fifth anniversary of the Hatch act of 1887, providing for an agricultural experiment station in each State. The occasion was celebrated by the Association of American Agricultural Colleges and Experiment Stations at its annual convention in Atlanta, November 13-15, by the presentation of several historical papers.

At the annual convention of the National Education Association held in Chicago, July 6-12, one general session was devoted to the general topic, "Rural Life Conditions and Rural Education." The department of rural and agricultural education devoted one session to papers on the "Redirection of Rural Education," one to consideration of a report of its committee on a course of study in agriculture for high schools, and a third to a joint session with the School Garden Association of America, at which there were papers and discussions on rural and city school gardens, home gardens and experimental plats, and forestry in rural schools. A second meeting of the School Garden Association of America and the annual meeting of the American Nature Study Society ere held in Cleveland during Convocation week.

The first conference of the International Association of Poultry Instructors and Investigators was held in London July 18-24, with twenty-seven countries represented. A permanent organization was effected, with E. Browen, of London, as president, and Dr. Raymond Pearl, of Orono, Me., as secretary.

At an educational conference held in connection with the Royal International Horticultural Exhibition, Chealsea, England, May 23, papers on horticultural education in their respective countries were presented by Dean L. H. Bailey, of New York State College of Agriculture, Ithaca, N. Y.; K. Weinhausen, of Berlin, and Prof. A. Buyssens, of the School of Horticulture, Vilvorde, Belgium.

Over 200 delegates representing the agricultural committees of bankers' associations in 22 States met at Minneapolis and St. Paul August 7-8 to discuss agricultural education and improvement. A silver trophy offered to the State committee making the largest contribution for agricultural education and improvement was awarded to the committee of North Dakota, which reported financing the better-farming association of that State to the extent of $45,000, besides giving $5000 for farmers' institutes and $5000 for corn-growing contests, in which over 11,000 men and boys participated.

UNITED STATES OFFICE OF EXPERIMENT STATIONS. This office, as heretofore, represented the United States Department of Agriculture in its relations with agricultural colleges and schools, published the official statistics and organization lists of the State agricultural colleges and experiment stations, issued annual reports of progress in agricultural education and farmers' institutes, edited a chapter on agricultural education each month in the *Experiment Station Record*, and issued other educational publications as follows: Bulletins—"Agricultural Schools in Arkansas," "Some Types of Children's Garden Work," "Proceedings of the American Association of Farmers' Institute Workers"; Farmers' Institute Lectures—"Farm Homes," "The Peanut," "Farm Home Grounds"; circulars—"Report of Committee on Instruction in Agriculture," "A Working Erosion Model for Schools"; reprint—"The Occupation of the Agricultural College Graduate."

Special studies were made of the eleven agricultural schools in Georgia and of other isolated schools and types of instruction in agriculture in California, Oregon, New York, and elsewhere.

UNITED STATES BUREAU OF EDUCATION. A specialist in rural education was added to the staff of the bureau, statistics of the agricultural and mechanical colleges were published, and bulletins were issued relating to courses of study for rural schools teachers, agricultural education in secondary schools, teaching language through agriculture and domestic science, the readjustment of a rural high school to the needs of the community, and a bibliography of education in agriculture and home economics.

GRADUATE SCHOOL OF AGRICULTURE. The fifth session of this school was held in July, under the auspices of the Association of American Agricultural Colleges and Experiment Stations, at the Michigan Agricultural College, East Lansing, Mich. The faculty included Dr. A. C. True, director of the United States Office of Experiment Stations, as dean; forty-eight specialists in the regular courses of the school, and six speakers at special conferences. Three members of the faculty were from European institutions, viz.: Dr. E. J. Russell, director of the Rothamsted Experiment Station, England; Dr. F. H. A. Marshall, of Cambridge University, England; and Dr. Oscar Loew, of the Munich Hygienic Institute, Germany. One hundred and eighty students were enrolled.

THE AGRICULTURAL COLLEGES. The agricultural colleges continued their rapid advance in the enrollment of students, the erection of buildings and the securing of more liberal funds. For example, New York State College of Agriculture was given appropriations aggregating $907,000, including the following large items: Forestry building, $100,000; agronomy wing, $100,000; animal husbandry laboratory, $91,000; livestock judging pavilion, $38,000; current expenses, $265,000; extension work, $50,000. At the same institution the following buildings were being constructed: Agricultural auditorium, $130,000; poultry building, $90,000; home economics building, $150,000.

Among other examples of material prosperity the following biennial appropriations for agricultural colleges are noteworthy: Georgia, $250,000; North Carolina, $220,000; North Dakota, $200,000; New Jersey, $100,000 for an agricultural building and $29,000 for other improvements; New Mexico, $30,000 for a science hall; Rhode Island, $75,000 for a science building; South Dakota, $100,000 for an agricultural building; Washington, $150,000 for an agricultural building. The Massachusetts Agricultural College erected a $75,000 dairy building, the Missouri College a $60,000 agricultural-chemistry building, and the Minnesota College a large agricultural-engineering building. The new agricultural building at the University of California was dedicated November 20, and Dr. Thomas F. Hunt was installed as dean of the College of Agriculture. Fires destroyed the main building of the Texas Agricultural and Mechanical College, causing a loss of $100,000, and the main building and the dormitory of the Maryland Agricultural College, valued at $250,000.

The principal lines of development in the work of the agricultural colleges were in providing better facilities for the training of teachers of agriculture and in strengthening the extension work in agriculture. Larger specific appropriations for extension work, both federal and State, made it possible to employ additional men and women for the extension departments of the colleges and to inaugurate several new features of extension work, chief among which was the county and district system of advisory bureaus for farmers, in which the United States Department of Agriculture, the State agricultural colleges, and other agencies coöperated. One of the largest of the coöperative extension enterprises was the boys' and girls' agricultural club movement. Over 90,000 boys were engaged, North and South, in the corn, Kafir corn, and cotton club work, in which the United States Department of Agriculture coöperated, and there were over 40,000 other boys in the North who were members of corn clubs, wheat clubs, or potato clubs, or were engaged in other agricultural contests. In the Southern corn club work several boys secured yields of over 200 bushels per acre, while in the North many yields ran over 100 bushels. Illinois reported over 50 yields running above 100 bushels, and Ohio 91 such yields. Ohio sent 225 prize winners on a free trip to Washington. There were also more than 23,000 members of girls' canning and poultry clubs in 12 Southern States. Each member of a canning club cultivated 1-10 acre of tomatoes, kept account of labor, expenses and income, and from these computed net profits. The lowest average net profit per 1-10 acre for all of the girls in a State was $14.57, while the highest was $40.00. One girl raised 5928 pounds of tomatoes on her plot, while another filled 1525 quart cans of tomatoes from hers.

SECONDARY SCHOOLS. The number of colleges and schools offering secondary courses in agriculture increased in nearly all parts of the United States. New State schools of agriculture were established in Colorado, Nebraska, and New York, the legislature of the latter State making provision for an agricultural school on Long Island. A school of agriculture was organized in connection with the Chautauqua Institute, Chautauqua, N. Y., on a 110-acre farm adjoining the institute grounds. A grant of $250,000 by the General Education Board was made to the George Peabody College for Teachers at Nashville, Tenn., for the establishment of the Seaman A. Knapp School of Country Life, which will give special attention to the training of teachers for

CORN CLUB BOYS FROM BALTIMORE COUNTY, MARYLAND, VISITING THE SECRETARY OF AGRICULTURE

ROSEDALE SCHOOL GARDEN, CLEVELAND, OHIO

AGRICULTURAL EDUCATION

rural schools. This grant was made contingent upon the raising of an equal sum by the institution.

In Louisiana the legislature increased the appropriation for agricultural schools from $25,000 to $50,000. A $40,000 science building was erected at the Minnesota School of Agriculture, Crookston.

Many public high schools established courses in agriculture during the year and many others announced their intention of inaugurating similar work as soon as satisfactorily trained teachers could be found. The system of giving bonuses to schools employing teachers of agriculture, as inaugurated in about a dozen States, gave much satisfaction. It was found that under this system better trained teachers were employed, better equipment provided, and better supervision was possible. Progress was also made in the development of elementary courses in agriculture in the rural elementary schools. This was particularly true where boys' and girls' contests and exhibitions were conducted.

AGRICULTURAL EXPERIMENT STATIONS. Extension of the Work. In the fiscal year 1911 the appropriation under the Adams act of 1906 reached its maximum of $15,000 to each State, giving an annual aggregate of $720,000 to be devoted exclusively to original research on agricultural problems. The Hatch fund is also supporting a large amount of experimental work. Progress is being made in confining the work of the stations to more thorough investigations by an elimination of the simple tests and demonstrations, as well as the dissemination of general agricultural information. This is being helped by the rapid organization of extension divisions in the agricultural colleges, which are taking over the informational functions hitherto performed by the stations. There is a growing tendency to make permanent State appropriations for station work and larger amounts are being given by the States for local experiments. In California a citrus-fruit substation has been located at Riverside; in Massachusetts a substation for cranberry culture has been established at East Wareham; in Missouri a poultry station has been established at Mountain Grove; in Oregon and South Dakota dry-farming substations have been provided for; in Texas a substation for tobacco culture has been established. In Ohio, South Dakota, and Wisconsin provision has been made for county experiment farms and for the experimental use of farms connected with public institutions. In Utah demonstration farms located on sage-brush lands have shown that such lands can be profitably handled under dry-farming methods, with the result that these lands are being largely taken up for agricultural purposes.

Federal and State Stations. Agricultural experiment stations maintained in whole or in part by federal funds now exist in every State and Territory, including Alaska, Hawaii, Porto Rico, and Guam. There are also stations in the Philippines under the insular government. In 1911 the stations employed 1567 persons in the work of administration and inquiry, as compared with 628 in 1897. Likewise, in 1897 the stations had a total income of $1,129,833, of which $720,000 was derived from the Hatch act, while in 1911 their total income was $3,062,425, of which $1,440,000 was received from the United States and the Hatch and Adams acts. The value of the additions to station equipment in 1911 aggregated $939,705, of which $448,708 was for buildings. In addition to this, the Office of Experiment Stations in 1911 had an appropriation of $424,000, including $30,000 each for Alaska, Hawaii, and Porto Rico stations; $15,000 for the Guam station; $15,000 for nutrition investigations; $100,000 for irrigation investigations; $100,000 for drainage investigations, and $10,000 for investigations of farmers' institutes and agricultural schools, together with $4727 derived from the sale of agricultural products at the insular experiment stations. In Alabama, Connecticut, Hawaii, Louisiana, Missouri, New Jersey, New York, North Carolina, and Virginia separate stations are maintained wholly or in part by State funds and in a number of States substations are maintained. Excluding substations, the total number of stations in the United States is 65, of which 54 receive federal funds. In 1911 the stations published 566 annual reports, bulletins, and circulars, which were supplied to over 1,000,000 addresses on the regular mailing lists. The correspondence with farmers is enormous and constantly increasing.

Office of Experiment Stations. This office has general supervision of the federal funds granted to the stations, annually inspects them, approves projects of investigation under the Adams act, and gives the stations advice and assistance in a great variety of ways. The annual report of this office contains summary descriptions of the work of each station, detailed statistics of the agricultural colleges and experiment stations, and articles on the progress of agricultural education, farmers' institutes, and extension work in this country and abroad. The review of the world's literature of agricultural science in the *Experiment Station Record* is increasingly comprehensive. Two volumes of this journal are now issued annually, containing over 7500 abstracts. The 26 volumes thus far issued contain references to over 90,000 articles, besides editorials, special articles, and notes. Two general indexes covering 25 volumes have been issued. The card index of the literature of the American stations issued by this office now contains over 32,000 cards and is being widely used by students. Copies of this index are deposited in the libraries of the agricultural colleges, experiment stations, and State departments of agriculture. The special investigations in charge of this office, for which its income in 1912 aggregates $335,060, are in five main lines: (1) Maintenance of experiment stations in Alaska, Hawaii, Porto Rico, and Guam; (2) agricultural education (q. v.); (3) food and nutrition (q. v.); (4) irrigation (q. v.); (5) drainage (q. v.). See also Agricultural Education.

Recent Experiments. The soil investigations of the Illinois station have so far resulted in increasing the yield of staple crops that farmers and business men are convinced that by proper management soil fertility can be maintained and increased, and the principles advocated by the station are being applied to practice by leading farmers throughout the State. The Missouri station has determined that nitrogen and phosphorus are the limiting elements of plant food in Missouri soils and that the majority of Missouri uplands respond to an application of these elements. The Ohio station found that there is a direct relation between the supply of available phosphorus in the soil and the phosphorus content of wheat. The Wisconsin station found that bacterial activity in the soil may so change the nature of substances in solution in soil water as to exert an influence on evaporation.

The Missouri station has shown that maintaining young heifers on a high plane of nutrition does not affect their milking qualities and that the size of the cow may be permanently increased by liberal feeding when young. In experiments to determine the efficiency of mitigated cultures of human tubercle bacilli as a vaccine against bovine tuberculosis, it was found that vaccinated cattle contracted the disease when exposed to infected animals even under the favorable conditions of outdoor life. The fecal excretions of tuberculous cattle were a much more important source of infection to swine than foods contaminated with the saliva of tuberculous cattle. Not only a very large percentage of the pigs fed behind tuberculous cattle became diseased but some of the pigs showed well-developed tubercular lesions in less than four weeks of exposure. The Indiana station has shown that an excess of soft fats and a large average of fat globules in cream materially increase the moisture absorbing and retaining property of butter, while the acidity of cream, the size of butter granules, the temperature of the wash water, the use of the dry or wet salting method do not appreciably affect the moisture content of the butter. The results of twenty years' spraying work with Bordeaux mixture on late potatoes by the Vermont station showed an average gain of 105 bushels per acre.

In Alaska the experiments with cattle and sheep on the island of Kodiak were seriously interefered with by the eruption of Mt. Katmai, 95 miles distant. Ashes covered the pastures to an average depth of 14 inches, making it necessary to remove the cattle to the State of Washington for the winter. It has been ascertained that the volcanic ash contains no substance deleterious to plants, and experiments are being made in plowing the land and seeding to grasses, clover, and grains. At Rampart several farms of alfalfa survived the winter and made good growth the following summer. The breeding of varieties of barley better adapted to the climate at Rampart promises to be a success. Winter rye proved hardier than winter wheat in that locality. At Fairbanks considerable quantities of potatoes and hay were produced and brought high prices in the local market.

In Hawaii the work of the station has resulted in making the pineapple industry second in importance in the Territory, and the area devoted to pineapples is being rapidly increased. Breeding experiments to secure a strain of pineapples less subject to the deleterious effects of manganese in the soil are being continued. The demonstration farms established on the islands of Hawaii, Maui, Kauai, and Oahu are collecting much information which will aid in diversifying the agriculture of the Territory.

In Porto Rico experiments with citrus fruits, mangoes, cocoanuts, yams, yantias, dasheens, and sweet potatoes are giving valuable results. The improvement of the livestock of the island by the importation of horses, cattle, and poultry is making good progress. The calves obtained from half-bred Zebu bulls are much larger, hardier, and make more rapid growth than pure native-bred calves.

In Guam the pineapples and avocados introduced from Hawaii are doing well. Continued cultivation is giving better results with corn, sorghum, Kafir corn, Para grass, and other food and forage plants. A preliminary survey of the insect fauna of the island has been made.

Outside of the United States stations have recently been established at Linz, Austria; La Rioja, Argentina; Therezina, Brazil; Forts Resolution, Smith, and Providence, Canada; Rosthern, Saskatchewan, Canada; Wilmer, British Columbia; Kentville, Nova Scotia; San José, Costa Rica; Carcassonne, France; Kissidongon and Mamon, French Guinea; Bettiah Estate, Bengal, India; Gwibi, Rhodesia; Burgos and Pontevedra, Spain. Special stations have also been established for cacao at São Antonio, Brazil; for rubber at Issororo, British Guiana; for viticulture at Toulouse, France, and Madrid, Spain; for forestry at Chimmitz, Hungary; for beet culture at Rovigo, Italy; for mulberries at Ascoli, Italy; for agricultural chemistry, vegetable pathology, and entomology at Fort-de-France, Martinique; for cotton at Port Herald, Nyasaland; for olives at Tortosa, Spain. Greece has established a ministry of agriculture and commerce and the Grecian agricultural society has established experiment stations. The agricultural work carried on by the ministry of public works of Peru has been reorganized and a central agronomic station established at Santa Beatriz, near Lima.

AGRICULTURAL LEGISLATION. FEDERAL LEGISLATION. Agricultural measures received unusual consideration from Congress during 1912. After several years' effort to obtain legislation to protect this country from the introduction of dangerous insects and plant diseases through the importation of infested nursery stock and similar products, a plant quarantine act was adopted and became effective October 1. Under its provisions a permit must now be obtained from the Secretary of Agriculture to import nursery stock, as well as a certificate of inspection in the country of export. Subsequent interstate movements of the nursery stock must also be reported to the secretary. A similar procedure may also be required as to imported fruits, vegetables, seeds, etc., in case their unrestricted entry becomes prejudicial. If deemed necessary in order to check the introduction of a new pest, the Secretary of Agriculture may exclude entirely importations likely to transmit it, and may quarantine any State or section as regards interstate shipments. A foreign quarantine has already been declared against the white pine blister rust and potato wart, against Hawaiian products because of the Mediterranean fruit fly, and against certain New England evergreens and other material likely to disseminate the gipsy and brown-tail moths. The administration of this act is entrusted to a federal horticultural board, composed of officials of the federal Department of Agriculture, but the inspection work is wholly in the hands of the State authorities.

A standard apple barrel, containing 7056 cubic inches, has been established, as well as standard grades for apples on the basis of variety, size, and quality. After July 1, 1913, the shipment in interstate commerce of barrels will subject the sender to prosecution for misbranding, unless the fruit and barrels conform to the requirements. The importation into the United States of grain and grass seed deemed adulterated or otherwise unfit for seeding purposes has been prohibited after February 24, 1913.

The so-called Lever bill, carrying an ultimate appropriation of about $3,500,000 per annum to the States for the maintenance of agricultural extension work through their agricultural colleges, passed the House of Representatives in August and was favorably reported in December by the Senate committee on agriculture and forestry. There was also pending in the Senate the Page bill, which not only provides federal aid for extension work but also for instruction in secondary schools in agriculture, industrial training, and home economics, the training of teachers in these subjects and the maintenance of branch experiment stations, with an ultimate expenditure of about $15,000,000 per annum.

A resolution establishing a commission to investigate the workings of coöperative rural credit unions and land mortgage banks in foreign countries was adopted by the Senate. Favorable committee reports were made on bills to provide for grain inspection and to prevent gambling in agricultural commodities. Determined efforts to secure a reduction of the revenue tax of 10 cents a pound on colored oleomargarine were being sharply contested by the dairy interests.

State Legislation. In about two-thirds of the States no sessions of the legislatures were held in 1912 and the amount of legislation in others was comparatively small.

Arizona and New Mexico on attaining statehood enacted complete irrigation codes, and the former also passed a pure food law. Maryland and Virginia revised their fertilizer and drainage laws, and Maryland and New York provided for seed inspection. In New York after July 1, 1913, food products must be sold in standard containers or labeled to show the net weight or volume; and Massachusetts required sales by weight of such commodities as potatoes. Important changes in the system of taxing lands suitable for forestry were initiated in New York. Land deemed suitable for forest growth by the State Conservation Commission may now be assessed during maintenance as forests on the basis of the land value alone, and if handled under the supervision of the commission may be exempted entirely for 35 years. A stumpage tax of 5 per cent. is levied on the timber upon cutting. In Massachusetts an amendment to the constitution giving to the legislature authority to enact similar laws was adopted by a large popular vote. New York also authorized its counties, towns, and villages to acquire and operate forests and its counties to employ agricultural advisers. An unsuccessful attempt was made to require stallion registration in that State, but $5000 was obtained for promoting horse breeding in the State. The Massachusetts cattle bureau was converted into a bureau of animal industry.

Foreign Legislation. The Canadian government nearly trebled its appropriations for agriculture granting for 1912-13 nearly $4,500,000. Of this sum, $1,500,000 is to be used for acquiring terminal grain-elevators under what is known as the Canadian grain act of 1912, which also regulates the grading, storing, transporting, and marketing of grain. Provision was made for extending the rural mail service; $500,000 was granted for allotment to the provinces for use in encouraging agriculture, and increased aid was given to the system of experimental farms.

In Great Britain a division of horticulture was established in the Board of Agriculture and Fisheries, and a number of agricultural research institutions were located under the development act of 1908. A commissioner of agriculture was provided for Wales, and a Welsh agricultural council was under consideration. The French pure food laws were extensively revised. The system of agricultural instruction was also reorganized, and commissions were authorized to study and combat plant and animal parasites and to classify useful and injurious birds. A law granting subsidies to breeding associations, agricultural societies, and others interested in livestock improvement was enacted in Denmark. Russia readjusted its tariff rates to encourage the importation and manufacture of agricultural machinery. Uruguay took similar action as to imported seeds and agricultural implements, and Nicaragua as to commercial fertilizers.

AGRICULTURAL TRAINING FOR FACTORY CHILDREN. See Child Labor.

AGRICULTURE. The year 1912 was an anniversary year for American agricultural institutions. It was the semi-centennial of the establishment of the federal Department of Agriculture at Washington, and of the Morrill act donating public lands for the establishment and maintenance of agricultural colleges in all the States and Territories. It was likewise the fiftieth anniversary of the homestead act, which provided for cutting up the public domain into farms and its settlement by farmers who live on the land. It is a strange coincidence that these three measures of such vital and far-reaching importance to the agriculture of this country, and which had been for some time national issues, should have been passed and signed by President Lincoln within a few weeks of each other, at a time when the country, in the midst of a great civil war, was struggling to maintain the Union. Twenty-five years later, in 1887, the act was passed making provision for a system of agricultural experiment stations, and hence the year 1912 marked the twenty-fifth anniversary of its birth.

These are the most important events in the history of American agriculture. They have resulted in the largest and most influential movement in education, the most highly developed department of agriculture, and the most comprehensive and efficient system of experiment stations to be found in any country. They have placed agriculture on a new basis, as an enlightened and progressive industry, and have marvelously improved its efficiency and its ability to meet the demands of a stead-

PRODUCTION OF THE MORE IMPORTANT CROPS IN 1911 AND 1912, BY COUNTRIES

Countries	Wheat 1911 (Bushels)	Wheat 1912 (Bushels)	Rye 1911 (Bushels)	Rye 1912 (Bushels)	Oats 1911 (Bushels)	Oats 1912 (Bushels)	Barley 1911 (Bushels)	Barley 1912 (Bushels)	Corn 1911 (Bushels)	Corn 1912 (Bushels)
United States	621,338,000	730,267,000	33,119,000	35,664,000	922,298,000	1,418,337,000	160 [illegible]0	223,824,000	2,531,488,000	3,124,746,000
Canada	204,414,000	205,685,000	2,694,000	3,086,000	371,000,000	381,502,000	40,631,000	43,895,000	17,173,200	[illegible]0
Mexico	....	....	....	....	....	....	....	....	....	....
*Argentina	213,000,000	198,342,000	......	....	75,590,000	79,924,000	15,870,000	....	27,675,000	[illegible]0
Chile	38,850,000	40,403,000	....	....	2,065,000	2,756,000	--	16,100,000	216,735	1,181,000
Uruguay	10,284,000	8,815,000	....	....	....	2,067,000	....	....	118,200	1 [illegible]0
Austria	53,258,500	69,640,000	112,204,500	117,114,000	156,630,000	167,423,000	74,580,000	78,384,000	14,960,000	11,810,000
Hungary, Croatia and Slav.	194,035,000	184,365,000	54,372,000	56,693,000	96,427,500	76,893,000	76,115,000	7[illegible]0	161,426,000	215,925,000
Belgium	14,718,600	16,336,000	23,108,000	22,520,000	41,417,000	35,208,000	4,602,000	4,232,000	--	....
Bulgaria	72,408,000	45,403,000	14,780,000	12,402,000	20,277,000	12,058,000	20,375,000	18,400,000	57,924,000	55,118,000
Denmark	4,764,500	3,745,000	19,745,000	18,386,000	51,071,500	52,708,000	24,693,000	2[illegible]0	....	....
Finland	....	....	....	....	....	....	....	....	--	....
France	322,375,000	334,871,000	48,156,000	50,936,000	350,818,000	375,642,000	49,863,000	50,646,000	26,772,000	24,045,000
Germany	149,370,000	160,227,000	427,775,700	456,608,000	530,764,400	586,999,000	149,290,000	159,927,000	....	....
[illegible]e	....	3,673,000	....	....	....	....	....	4,140,000	3,973,000	3,973,000
Italy	193,739,400	165,720,000	[illegible]0	5,285,000	41,223,000	28,306,000	10,900,000	8,403,000	93,914,000	92,516,000
Montenegro	....	....	....	....	....	....	....	....	--	....
Netherlands	5,687,000	4,591,000	17,325,000	16,339,000	18,543,300	14,814,000	3,670,000	3,956,000	....	....
Norway	....	294,000	....	787,000	....	11,300,000	....	3,266,000	....	....
Portugal	--	10,652,000	....	2,953,000	....	10,335,000	....	8,740,000	7,875,000	7,874,000
Rumania	96,324,200	89,400,000	4,988,000	3,622,000	28,656,000	21,359,000	26,418,000	21,160,000	131,449,000	88,445,000
Russia, [illegible]ope; R[illegible]sia, [illegible]sia	509,190,000	727,011,000	762,109,000	1,043,982,000	858,356,000	1,067,585,000	411,225,000	464,125,000	82,286,000	79,964,000
Servia	....	13,957,000	....	1,376,000	....	4,479,000	....	4,140,000	26,535,000	25,197,000
Spain	157,733,000	112,416,000	31,562,000	25,755,000	34,048,500	24,461,000	89,939,200	58,605,000	27,172,000	25,984,000
Sweden	6,875,000	2[illegible]00	24,295,000	22,810,000	73,633,000	80,613,000	15,358,000	14,260,000	....	....
Switzerland	3,631,600	[illegible]0	1,801,000	1,772,000	4,944,000	4,203,000	462,300	414,000	128,500	118,000
Turkey, Europe; Turkey, Asia	--	154,266,000	....	14,567,000	....	29,627,000	....	138,000,000	45,276,000	43,307,000
[illegible]d [illegible]m	64,830,000	56,564,000	....	236,000	194,270,000	191,542,000	60,220,000	59,800,000	....	....
B[illegible]sh I[illegible]lies	372,000,000	366,370,000	....	....	....	....	....	110,400,000	137,795,000	129,921,000
[illegible]us	....	....	....	....	....	....	....	....	....	....
Japan	20,716,000	....	....	....	4,644,000	....	94,668,000	....	3,483,000	....
Persia	....	....	....	....	....	....	....	....	....	....
Algeria	36,104,500	27,507,000	3,350	....	11,538,000	12,287,000	47,662,000	33,138,000	554,000	369,000
Egypt	38,311,700	28,943,000	....	....	....	....	11,962,000	11,500,000	67,958,000	68,693,000
Sudan	....	....	....	....	....	....	....	....	....	....
Tunis	8,695,000	4,225,000	....	....	3,795,000	2,067,000	9,430,000	4,823,000	....	....
U. S. Africa	....	....	....	....	....	....	....	....	....	....
Australia	75,880,000	88,152,000	....	146,920	--	35,828,000	....	3,680,000	9,173,000	11,034,000
New Zealand	....	....	....	....	....	....	....	....	....	....

* Data for countries in the southern hemisphere represent esti[illegible] on the crops harvested 1912-13.

ily growing population. The anniversary of these events was observed by the Association of American Agricultural Colleges and Experiment Stations at its annual convention in Atlanta in November.

CROP PRODUCTION IN THE UNITED STATES. The year 1912 was the most productive of all agricultural years in the United States. The crops of corn, hay, potatoes, oats, barley, rye, flaxseed, and beet sugar were the largest ever raised, while the cotton crop, it is estimated, is the second largest. Rice and buckwheat have only been exceeded once, and wheat and tobacco are third in size. All of the cereals showed increases over 1911, which was a year of low production, the average increase being 30 per cent. Hay increased 52.7 per cent., potatoes 41.5 per cent., corn 25.2 per cent., wheat 15.9 per cent., oats 53.7 per cent., and barley 40.2 per cent. over 1911. The prices at the farm were generally good, and will continue the prosperity that farmers have enjoyed in recent years. The total value of all crops was $6,137,000,000, an amount which is vastly above the highest previous mark, that of 1911. The farm value of the dairy products is estimated at about $830,000,000, an amount which exceeded the value of the cotton lint and nearly equaled that of the hay crop; while the products of the poultry industry were worth at the farm about $570,000,000. The latter value has been exceeded in two former years. Wool production has apparently been exceeded in two former years, yet in 1912 it amounted to 318,548,000 pounds. This wool had a farm value of about $55,500,000, or about 6 per cent. below the average value of the wool clip of the five preceding years.

The animals sold from the farm and the animals slaughtered on it together numbered about 111,000,000 for 1912, and had a value of about $1,930,000,000. This is the highest value of animals sold and slaughtered since about 1900, except in 1909 and 1911. The total value of the animal products in 1912 is estimated at about $3,395,000,000. This is a larger value than that of 1911, but is about $150,000,000 below the value for 1910, which is the only year which exceeded 1912.

The grand total for the production of farm products, crop and animal, in 1912, is estimated at $9,532,000,000, the highest value yet reached by a half billion dollars. It is more than twice the value of farm production in 1899, according to the census, and is about one-eighth more than in 1909.

FOREIGN TRADE IN AGRICULTURAL PRODUCTS. For the fourth time the value of agricultural exports of the United States exceeded a billion dollars, or enough to pay the expenses of the national government. The billion-dollar mark was reached in 1907, when the value of agricultural exports amounted to $1,054,000,000. That amount has not since been equaled, but the exports of 1908 and 1911 exceeded a billion dollars in value, and in 1912 the amount fell short of the record mark by only $4,000,000.

Cotton represents the largest agricultural export, and showed a marked increase in 1912. Wheat flour still maintains a high relative position, the exports of wheat and the flour which it represented amounting to 80,000,000 bushels in 1912. Apples are supporting an increased export trade, which now amounts to about $10,000,000; while prunes and raisins show steady increases, representing several million dollars a year. On the other hand, beef and its products have greatly declined in the export trade. Packinghouse products have declined in value of exports since 1906, when they reached their highest value, $208,000,000, and have declined still more in quantity because of increasing prices, but they showed a value in 1912 of $164,000,000. Their value has increased since 1910. The export of forest products marked the highest value ever reached, $108,000,000, due partly to high prices and partly to increased volume.

Imports of agricultural products in the United States are steadily increasing in value, reaching the highest point in 1912, when they amounted to $784,000,000. Notable increases occurred in coffee, sugar, molasses, tobacco, wool, and packinghouse products, in which hides and skins were very prominent. Since 1908 the balance in the foreign trade in agricultural products has not kept up to its former figure, but this is not due to diminished export values but to a greater increase of imports. Notwithstanding this, the balance in favor of exports of farm products was $278,000,000 in 1912, and this was higher than the amounts for 1909 and 1910.

WORLD'S PRODUCTION OF CROPS. In general, European crops in 1912 suffered from a cool and backward season, and later from very rainy and otherwise unfavorable weather at the time of harvest. This is true for practically every country excepting Italy, in which a serious drought during the growing season reduced crop production. The untoward weather conditions influenced both yield and quality, but in general the quantity produced more than met expectations. The reductions in yield have been marked enough, however, to increase perceptibly the requirements of all grain import countries, and this condition was reflected in a brisk export movement of wheat in the United States during the fall of the year, more particularly during the month of October. The wet weather at the time of the European harvest was particularly injurious to oats and barley and the hay crops, which were to a large extent discolored by rain while standing on the fields awaiting stacking or thrashing.

England suffered from the most blighting spring drought that has afflicted that country for a decade. Throughout Great Britain the season was decidedly unfavorable. Following the severe drought of 1911, the rainfall in 1912 was so heavy and prolonged as to do much damage to crops. All cereals suffered severely, potatoes were badly affected by disease, hay was of poor quality, and pastures were flooded.

A severe drought prevailed in South Africa, including Natal, Transvaal, and the Orange Free State, seriously affecting the agricultural and grazing interests. Deaths of sheep from lack of grass ran into hundreds of thousands, many cattle were sacrificed, and a large portion of the growing crops were a total failure.

WORLD'S PRODUCTION OF RUBBER. The total world production of wild and plantation rubber for the year ended June 30, 1912, amounted, according to the statistics of Hecht, to 93,669 tons, as compared with 79,302 tons in the previous year and 76,026 tons in 1909-10. The consumption in 1911-12 is given as 99,564 tons, as contrasted with 74,082 tons in 1910-11. Experiments in rubber growing in Hawaii, conducted by the Federal Experiment Station, have given very encouraging results. Rubber of a high quality has been produced, only 10 per cent. below Para rubber. The high price of labor in the islands is regarded as the most serious drawback. Several plantations on a considerable scale have been established. The production of rubber synthetically is one of the notable accomplishments of chemistry during the year. See CHEMISTRY, INDUSTRIAL.

WORLD'S PRODUCTION OF SILK. According to statistics of the Silk Merchants' Union of Lyons, France, the world's production of raw silk was approximately as follows: Western Europe 9,557,038 lbs., Levant and Central Asia 6,206,012 lbs., extreme Orient 36,717,986 lbs.; grand total 52,481,036 lbs., as compared with 54,002,227 lbs. in 1910.

FOREIGN STATISTICS AND DEVELOPMENT. Revised statistics of the census of England and Wales show that in 1911 78 per cent. of the population was living under urban and only 22 per cent. under rural conditions, while 60 years ago the population was about evenly divided between town and country. There was an increase of over 36,000 acres in the arable area, and a decrease of 115,400 acres in the area under permanent grass. Statistics presented at the British Association show that the United Kingdom produces rather more than one-half of its total food supply exclusive of sugar and such beverages as tea and coffee, which cannot be grown. Only in the case of wheat was a large falling off noted; barely one-fifth of the total wheat consumed is produced in the country. The development of agriculture in the valley of the Amazon is contemplated in a decree of the Brazilian government which proposes concessions to certain agricultural or breeding undertakings located there, in the form of exemption of import duties on machinery and materials, premiums on land sown to foodstuffs, and on the production of preserved milk, meat, etc., for five years. Notable progress was made in Uruguay during 1911 in the conversion of land formerly devoted to stock-raising into cereal production. To encourage this movement the government is arranging a plan to lend money to farmers who may have had a poor crop or desire to hold for a better market. Two American dry-farming experts have been engaged by the government, who are teaching modern methods by lectures and demonstrations. Other agricultural specialists are being engaged. An agricultural defense bureau was organized at the close of 1911, with divisions for economic entomology and plant pathology, and the director was sent to the United States to study methods of organization and work. Inspection against the importation of diseases and insects in seeds, plants, etc., is provided. Coffee growing has been started in Paraguay, the experimental plantations having shown it to be a suitable crop. The individual holdings are small as yet. It is estimated that half a million trees will soon be in bearing in the Department of Altos.

The Grecian government is making a determined effort to promote the agriculture of Greece, which is in a very backward condition. Foreign agricultural experts are being employed to organize in different branches of agriculture, the government has undertaken the drainage of large marshes which cannot be left to local initiative, and an effort is being made by the Ministry of Agriculture and Commerce to increase the cultivation of cotton and to improve its quality. A factory for making artificial fertilizers has been opened. A report of the Department of Agriculture for British East Africa indicates a hopeful outlook for the agricultural development of that country, there being a large influx of money for developments in many branches of farming, a continued influx of settlers, and an increase of land values and of exports. There has been a marked increase in the acreage of rubber, sisal, sem sem, and other tropical crops, and marked progress is noted in animal husbandry, especially in the raising of pure-bred and graded wool sheep.

A movement is said to be on foot in the Philippines for the government to engage in rice growing on a wholesale scale. Since 1898 it is reported $82,000,000 has been sent out of the country to purchase rice. In the fiscal year 1912, $10,000,000 worth of rice was imported. The crop the past year was the shortest of recent years. A campaign has been carried on to generalize the use of Indian corn, or maize, as a food substitute for rice. The animal importation of rice into the islands has varied in the past thirteen years from 100,000 to 250,000 tons. To produce this quantity would necessitate an increase in the area planted to rice of about 600,000 acres, or improvement in present methods which would give a corresponding increased production. The principal exports from the Philippines in the fiscal year 1912 were copra $16,514,749, hemp $16,281,830, sugar $10,400,575, and cigars $2,660,000.

FARM TENDENCY. The census returns show that there has been an uninterrupted increase in the proportion of tenancy in the United States for the last thirty years. In 1880 out of each 100 farms 25 were operated by tenants, by 1890 the number had risen to 28, by 1900 to 35, and by 1910 to 37. The rate of increase, however, seems to be decreasing, as indicated by the last census, there being actual decreases in the proportion of tenant farms in some of the geographical divisions, the proportion varying in many cases with the value of land per acre, the value of farms as units, or the character of farming.

A special committee appointed to inquire into the condition of tenant farmers in Great Britain and consider needed legislation, submitted a report to Parliament during the year. It was found that a large number of estates are being broken up and sold, the reason assigned being apprehension among the landowners as to the probable tendency of legislation and taxation in regard to land, and a belief that land at present is let at rates below its economic value. The committee recommended that the twelve months' notice of termination which has been customary should be extended to two years, and that a scheme of state-aided purchase should be instituted.

ECONOMICS OF PRODUCTION AND DISTRIBUTION. The cost of producing crops on irrigated and non-irrigated lands is the subject of an inquiry by the Bureau of Statistics of the United States Department of Agriculture, 73 farms being considered in the case of wheat, 104 of oats, 119 of alfalfa, and 7 of potatoes. The cost per bushel of wheat was 22.9 cents on irrigated land and 26.3 cents on non-irrigated; oats 11.2 cents on irrigated and 9 cents on non-irrigated; alfalfa $2.54 per ton on irrigated and $1.54 on non-irrigated; and potatoes 25.3 cents per bushel on irrigated and 39.2 cents on non-irrigated.

The Canadian Conservation Commission has issued a report which deals, among other things, with an agricultural survey made of 1212 farms in the various provinces. One object was to determine whether the fertility of the land was being conserved. There was found to be hardly any systematic conservation of fertility outside of Ontario, but that in most of the provinces the farmers are living on the accumulated capital provided by nature, thereby leaving their lands poorer. The yield of crops per acre in Canada on the whole was pronounced unsatisfactory. Already the effect of the soil-robbing system is apparent in Manitoba; not a single farmer reported an increase in yield per acre, and 46 per cent. reported an actual decrease. In Ontario about half the farmers follow a systematic rotation, but elsewhere the percentage was found to be very small. The indication of certain superior farms as "illustration farms," and provision for extending aid and supervision to them, was decided upon. It was stated that if all the farmers would follow the systems and methods of 10 per cent. of the farms examined, production would be doubled in ten years.

The purchasing power of an acre has been calculated by the Bureau of Statistics of the United States Department of Agriculture, which has had the subject under investigation for several years. The money value of one acre of produce in 1911 averaged about $15.48, as compared with $15.50 in 1910, $15.99 in 1909, and $9.58 in 1899. An investigation of prices of about 85 articles generally purchased by farmers indicated that such articles averaged in price in 1911 about 1.1 per cent. higher than in 1910, 2.6 per cent. higher than in 1909, and about 15.3 per cent. higher than in 1899. Taking into consideration the variation in the price of things which farmers buy and sell, it appears that the purchasing power of one acre of crops in 1911 was 1.2 per cent. less than in 1910, 5.7 per cent. less than in 1909, and 41.6 per cent. greater than in 1899. On this basis 1909 stands as the most prosperous of recent years and apparently the most prosperous for farmers in the past fifty years for which there are records.

Increasing study is being given to the problems of distribution of farm products, and it is recognized that this subject must be given the same attention which agricultural production has received. Large crops mean as a rule low prices for the producers without a corresponding reduction in favor of the consumer, and each year sees an enormous waste of perishable food products at the farm because no practicable means have as yet been devised for placing them in the hands of the hungry thousands perhaps a few hundred miles away. The organizing of better and more economical means of shipping and of more direct dealing between the producer and the consumer has been unusually active the past year. Systems of auto-truck lines have been inaugurated in several sections of the central West, which make regular collections of farm produce for delivery to the local markets. The cost of transportation on small lots is much cheaper than the farmer could do it. This promises soon to be a regular feature of many communities. A recent study of the marketing of grain from the Pacific Coast region shows that it is carried 18,000 miles by sea to the English miller cheaper than by the 2000 mile haul across the mountains to milling centres in the Mississippi Valley. For instance, the total ocean freight rate and marine insurance on wheat from Sacramento to England is estimated at from 16¾ cents to 22½ cents per bushel, and 39 cents to Chicago. The aproximate cost of marketing wheat in England from country shipping points in the Pacific Northwest, including commission, warehouse, and freight charges, is estimated at from 18.6 cents to 40.5 cents per bushel, and of barley from 14.7 to 34 cents per bushel.

Agricultural Credit. There is a recognized need of better facilities for raising money to carry on farming operations in the United States, and provision of some form of agricultural credit has been one of the live questions of the year. A special investigation of conditions, made by the United States Department of Agriculture, developed the fact that a large proportion of the farm owners and tenants are able to give good security, but less than half of these can secure needed short-time loans and advances because of insufficient opportunity to borrow. Long-time loans are even more difficult to obtain. Sources of credit of any kind other than the country stores are often lacking. Interest on loans for purchasing farm property was found to range usually from 6 to 8 per cent., with commission of 2 to 5 per cent. The latter, with renewals after three to five years adds materially to the interest rate. All three political parties adopted a rural credit plank in their platforms. Through the ambassadors and ministers President Taft conducted an investigation of the subject of agricultural credit in Europe, and in October published a letter to the governors of the States, embodying a report on this subject and recommending that the matter be considered by the States; and a special conference of governors was held in Washington early in December.

In connection with the Southern Commercial Congress at Nashville in the spring, a conference on rural credit was held, at which strong arguments were made to show the need of correcting the financial weakness of the rural life in this country as compared with the industrial and commercial life, by building up rural credit on European experience. This congress arranged for the appointment of a select committee from the various States of the Union to go to Europe in the summer of 1913 for the purpose of studying coöperative credit systems there, with a view to formulating a system to meet the needs of American agriculture. Some of the Canadian provinces have planned to send delegates with this committee.

A concrete scheme for the formation of a system of land banks in the United Kingdom was presented before the British Association at the 1912 meeting. The system proposed was to be self-supporting and free from state control. It would be confined at first to assisting farmers in the purchase of their holdings, and later extended to the purchase of livestock, seeds, fertilizers, and the selling of farm produce.

In Uruguay, by an act passed in January, 1912, a section of rural credit, with an initial capital of $500,000, was established in the Bank of the Republic (the central bank of Uruguay), and the formation of local rural credit banks was authorized. This is one of the steps toward breaking up the large estates into smaller farms, and is intended to aid the small landholder and to encourage colonization schemes. Rural credit banks are being extended in Jamaica; and the provision of land banks is under consideration by the Parliament of South Africa, on the plan of the land bank in the Transvaal, which has proved a great success. See AGRICULTURAL CREDIT.

INCREASING AGRICULTURAL EFFICIENCY. An interesting development in extending expert assistance to the farmers is the provision of what are variously known as county agents, county administration men, agricultural commissioners, and farm bureaus. In these the county, or an even smaller area, is usually the unit. In some cases they are maintained by the county entirely, in others in part by the agricultural college, and in others through coöperation with the United States Department of Agriculture. In De Kalb County, Ill., for example, an organization was formed, a guaranty fund of $10,000 raised, and a professor from the State university employed for a period of three years as agricultural commissioner, who will devote his whole time to aiding the farmers in developing and improving their methods, conferring with them, and conducting demonstrations. In a number of States funds have been provided to enable the agricultural colleges to furnish a limited number of such men and exercise supervision over them, the county sharing the expense. At the last session of Congress $300,000 was appropriated for carrying on such work through the Department of Agriculture. There are now about 75 county agents in various parts of the country and others are being established as fast as means and competent men can be had. In every case the work in the State is conducted in coöperation with the agricultural college or experiment station.

This movement is in line with the object aimed at by the National Soil Fertility League, that is, to provide for better and more profitable systems of farming, which will conserve the soil fertility, and to improve the efficiency of production. During the past year it has been aided by donations from two large business concerns. Sears, Roebuck and Co., a Chicago mail-order house, has provided $1,000,000 for experts to advise and demonstrate in each of 100 counties throughout the country. The International Harvester Company has set aside $1,000,000 to be used in conducting a campaign of agricultural extension among farmers, under the direction of Prof. P. G. Holden, formerly of the Iowa State College. The resources of this large concern and its 40,000 dealers throughout the country will be directed toward the success of the enterprise. The Chicago board of trade has also announced a similar plan to devote $1,000,000 to the improvement of agricultural practice through practical aid extended to farmers through county agents. The general education board, which has for several years financed agricultural demonstration in the South, has recently announced that it will extend this assistance to Northern States. Allotments have been made for work in New York and Maine.

The railroads and bankers' associations of the country are also interesting themselves in the matter of greater efficiency in agricultural production. It is stated that about three-fourths of the mileage of railroads in the United States is operated by companies which are making organized efforts to promote the agricultural development of their territory. In addition to exploitation of the country which they serve, they are conducting demonstration farms, coöperative experiments, employing agricultural experts for the advice of the farmer, and publishing and distributing literature. The State and national bankers' associations have entered actively into this effort, as in the case of North Dakota, where a better-farming association was financed to the extent of $45,000, $5000 contributed for farmers' institutes, and $5000 for holding local corn-growing contests.

A novel departure the past year was the issuing of farm proclamations by the governors of three States. The governor of Virginia designated August 14 as "Forage Day," and urged the farmers to meet in their county court-houses to discuss the growing of alfalfa and other forage crops. Specialists were in attendance at many of the meetings. Early in September the governors of Ohio and Minnesota issued special proclamations setting aside the week of September 16-21 as "Seed-Corn Week," and urging the farmers to select their corn for next year's planting, laying special emphasis on the necessity for early selection.

To induce immigrants coming from foreign rural communities to settle on the land, Mr. M. G. Kahn, of New York, has presented 13,000 acres of land in New Jersey for perpetual use, to be let rent-free in 10-acre lots to such immigrants.

The Boy Scouts' headquarters at London has initiated garden work for the members, and garden clubs have been formed. A farm colony for Boy Scouts has also been established in England by the gift of a farm of about 100 acres. Five acres are allotted to each group of eight boys, which they conduct with the advice of experts for their own profit. There are about fifty boys in residence, who engage in every branch of agriculture. The colony is expected to direct their attention to farming, and to be self-supporting when started.

The establishment of a coöperative farm for women is under consideration in England, the first proposed colony to be on a tract of 223 acres in Sussex. The purpose is to train young women who are desirous of emigrating to English over-sea possessions, and to furnish an opportunity to an increasing number of women who wish to engage in farming, but lack experience and facilities.

IMPORTANT EVENTS. The Scottish board of agriculture was recently created by the government. Prof. Bryner Jones, principal of the agricultural department of the University College of Wales, has been appointed as first commissioner of agriculture for Wales. He will advise the British board of agriculture on the agricultural work of the country and on the prospective grants from the Development fund to Wales.

The Republic of China has established a department of agriculture and forestry on modern lines. The new department has begun the publication of a quarterly agricultural journal (in Chinese), and a national meteorological service will be established.

R. N. Lyne, director of agriculture in Portuguese East Africa, has been appointed director of the new agricultural department of Ceylon.

The Italian government has instituted a consulting commission for agriculture, composed of sixteen members. The object of the commission is to study and suggest methods for intensifying agricultural production and protection from fraud in the commerce of agricultural products. It will take over the duties of the present Œnologic Commission in relation to the wine industry, and of the commissions for the poultry and oil industries.

A commission to examine the wheat supply of France was organized under an order issued in June by the minister of commerce and industry.

In Western Australia the state government has decided to undertake the manufacture of agricultural implements and machinery.

It is announced that Prince von Liechtenstein has established an institute for plant breeding at Eisgrub, in Moravia. Prof. Eric von Tschermak, professor of plant breeding at the agricultural high school at Vienna, will be director of the institute.

Prof. A. D. Hall, director of the Rothamsted Station since 1902, has resigned to devote his attention entirely to the work of the development commission, of which he has been agricultural representative since its inception.

Dr. J. C. Willis has resigned as director of the Royal Botanic Gardens, Peradeniya, Ceylon, to accept the directorship of the botanic gardens at Rio Janeiro.

Dr. William Trelease, director of the Missouri Botanical Gardens since 1889, has resigned, and has been succeeded by Dr. George T. Moore.

MEETINGS AND CONVENTIONS. The annual meeting of the Southern Commercial Congress, held at Nashville, Tenn., in the spring of 1912, was devoted to the presentation of facts showing the educational and agricultural recovery of the South during the past half century, and the discussion of measures for future advancement. It advocated a commission to standardize drainage laws, and favored a complete survey by the government of all swamp and overflowed lands and the preparation of plans for their drainage.

A National Drainage Congress was held at New Orleans in April, the first meeting after the organization of the new body. It advocated a plan for the drainage of the swamp lands of the country (largely held in private ownership) by the general government, on a partial reimbursement plan.

The National Irrigation Congress held its twenty-first meeting at Salt Lake City, Utah, at the end of September, celebrating the sixty-fifth anniversary of the beginning of American irrigation.

The International Dry Farming Congress was held at Lethbridge, Alberta, Canada, October 21 to 25.

An international congress for rice culture was held at Berecelli, Italy, in October, with an exposition of irrigation and rice culture. It was expected that the exposition would be the most important one of its kind ever held in Europe.

An international congress of electroculture was held at Rheims, France, in October. Among other topics on the programme were the influence of atmospheric and dynamic electricity on the nitrification of the soil, on fertilizers, on the germination of seeds, growth of plants, action on injurious insects and fungi, protection from hail, etc.

An international association of poultry instructors and investigators has been formed, which held its first conference in London during July, twenty-seven countries being represented. A central bureau of information is to be maintained, which will be located in London for the present.

The extent to which agricultural problems are commanding the attention of various branches of science was well illustrated at the meeting of the American Association for the Advancement of Science at Washington in the closing days of 1911. Likewise at the 1912 meeting of the British Association for the Advancement of Science, held at Dundee, in September, agriculture formed the subject of a full section for the first time. Agriculture was also well represented at the Eighth International Congress of Applied Chemistry, in New York, there being a long list of papers relating to investigation in agricultural chemistry, animal nutrition, soils, fertilizers, factors influencing plant growth, dairying, etc.

The Tenth International Congress of Agriculture will be held at Ghent, June 8-13, 1913, in connection with the International Exposition. The Third International Congress of the Association of Agricultural Women will be held at the same place immediately following the Congress of Agriculture.

LITERATURE. The following are among the recent books which have appeared: L. L. Van Slyke, *Fertilizers and Crops, or the Science and Practice of Plant Feeding* (New York, 1912); E. T. Russell, *Soil Conditions and Plant Growth* (New York, Bombay, and Calcutta, 1912); Eugene Grubb and W. S. Guilford, *The Potato* (New York, 1912); C. G. Elliott, *Engineering for Land Drainage* (New York, 1912); *Abridged Agricultural Records* (a compilation of the findings of the U. S. Department of Agriculture and the agricultural experiment stations) (Washington, 1912); *Agricultural Opportunities in Various Sections of the Country* (U. S. Department of Commerce and Labor, 1912); George Walker Fiske, *The Challenge of the Country. A Study of Country Life Opportunities* (New York, 1912); C. E. Marshall, *Microbiology for Agricultural and Domestic Science Students* (London, 1912); Wilfrid Sadler, *Bacteria as Friends and Foes of the Dairy Farmer* (London, 1912); H. Sangier, *Agricultural Credit in France* (Paris, 1911); *Systems of Rural Coöperative Credit* (U. S. Senate, 1912); *Agricultural Credit* (U. S. Senate, 1912); T. N. Carver, *Principles of Rural Economics* (Boston and London, 1911); J. L. Coulter, *Coöperation Among Farmers* (New York, 1911); I. B. Green, *Law for the American Farmer* (New York, 1911).

AIRSHIP NO. 1. See NAVAL PROGRESS, *Aviation*.

AIRSHIPS. See AERONAUTICS.

AKRON. See AERONAUTICS.

ALABAMA. POPULATION. According to the Census Bureau statistics issued in 1912, out of a total population of 2,138,093 in 1910, the foreign born whites numbered 18,956, compared with 14,338 in 1900. The largest proportion of these, 3599, came from Germany; from Italy, 2695; from England, 2348. In the city of Birmingham, with a total population of 132,685, the foreign-born population numbered 5700. Of these, 1360 came from Italy. There were in 1910, 908,202 negroes in the State, with 151,410 mulattoes. The negroes in 1890 numbered 678,489 and the mulattoes, 77,420.

AGRICULTURE. The acreage, value, and production of the principal crops in 1911-12 are shown in the following table:

		Acreage	Prod. Bu.	Value
Corn	1912	3,150,000	54,180,000	$42,120,000
	1911	3,000,000	54,000,000	42,120,000
Wheat	1912	30,000	318,000	359,000
	1911	30,000	345,000	414,000
Oats	1912	260,000	5,200,000	3,224,000
	1911	283,000	5,434,000	3,586,000
Rye	1912	1,000	12,000	16,000
	1911	1,000	10,000	12,000
Rice	1912	300	9,000	8,000
	1911	300	6,000	4,000
Potatoes	1912	15,000	1,215,000	1,094,000
	1911	15,000	1,170,000	1,381,000
Hay	1912	209,000	a 261,000	3,811,000
	1911	209,000	293,000	3,750,000
Tobacco	1912	300	b 225,000	79,000
	1911	200	140,000	35,000
Cotton	1912	......	......	......
	1911	......	c 1,600,000	......

a Tons. b Pounds. c Bales.

The agricultural statistics of the Thirteenth Census, dated April 15, 1910, were published in 1912. According to these figures the number of all farms in the State in 1910 was 262,901, compared with 223,220 in 1900. The land in farms was 20,732,312 acres, approximately the same as in 1900. The improved land in farms was 9,693,581 acres, a gain of about 1,000,000 acres in the decade. The average number of acres per farm was 78.9, compared with 92.7 in 1900. The total value of farm property, including land, buildings, implements and machinery, domestic animals, poultry, and bees, was $370,138,429, compared with $179,399,882 in 1900. The average value of all property per farm was $1408 and the average value of land per acre was $10.46. The farms operated by owners and managers numbered 104,575 and those operated by tenants, 158,326. Of the farms operated by owners and managers, 74,504 were free from mortgage, while 27,457 were mortgaged. The native white farmers numbered 151,214; the foreign-born whites, 1244, and the negroes and other non whites, 110,443. The total value of the domestic animals, poultry, and bees in 1910 was $65,594,834, compared with $36,105,799, in 1900. The cattle numbered 932,428 valued at $13,469,626; horses and colts, 135,636, valued at $13,651,284; mules, 247,146, valued at $31,577,217; swine, 1,266,733, valued at $4,356,520; sheep and lambs, 142,930, valued at $299,919. Poultry of all kinds numbered 5,028,104, valued at $1,807,239.

MINERAL PRODUCTION. Alabama ranks third among the States in the production of iron ore. There were mined in the State in 1911 3,955,,582 long tons, compared with 4,801,275 long tons in 1910. The value in 1911 was $4,876,106, compared with a value in 1910 of $6,083,722. The greater part of the iron produced in the State is hematite.

The production of coal in the State in 1911 was 15,018,965 short tons, with a value of $19,077,489. This was a decrease of 1,092,497 short tons from the production of 1910. The coal mines of the State were practically free from labor troubles in 1911.

MANUFACTURES. The Census of 1910 included statistics of manufactures in the State. The most important results are given in the table below: Lumber and timber products were the greatest in value and in the number of wage-earners employed. The value of the lumber and timber product was $26,058,000, and the wage-earners employed in the industry numbered 22,409. In the manufacturing connected with cotton goods the value of the product was $22,212,000 and the wage-earners numbered 12,731. In the iron and steel industry the product was valued at $21,236,000, and the men employed numbered 3783. Other industries employing over 1000 wage-earners were coke, oil, cottonseed and cake, fertilizers, printing and publishing, and brick and tile. The total number of wage-earners engaged in the industries of the State in 1909 was 72,148. Of these 65,686 were male and 6462 female. There were 3653 persons under 16 years of age employed. Of these 1380 were females. The prevailing hours of labor were from 60 to 72 a week. Of the total, 44.5 per cent. worked 60 hours a week, 25.7 per cent. more than 60 and less than 72, and 10.3 per cent., 54 hours a week. The chief manufacturing city in the State was Birmingham, where 8999 wage-earners were employed and the value of the product was $24,122,214. Other important manufacturing centres were Bessemer, Montgomery, Mobile, and Anniston.

	Number or Amount 1909	1904	1899
Number of establishments	3,398	1,882	2,000
Persons engaged in manufactures	81,972	67,884	(1)
Proprietors and firm members	3,769	1,948	(1)
Salaried employees	6,055	3,763	2,259
Wage earners (average number)	72,148	62,173	52,711
Primary horse-power	357,837	293,185	173,208
Capital	$173,180,000	$105,383,000	$60,166,000
Expenses	129,153,000	94,252,000	59,097,000
Services	33,849,000	25,745,000	16,971,000
Salaries	6,565,000	3,867,000	2,059,000
Wages	27,284,000	21,878,000	37,998,000
Materials	83,443,000	60,458,000	37,998,000
Miscellaneous	11,861,000	8,049,000	4,128,000
Value of products	145,962,000	109,170,000	72,110,000
Value added by manufacture (value of products less cost of materials)	62,519,000	48,712,000	34,112,000

1 Figures not available.

EDUCATION. The enumeration taken in July, 1912, showed the number of persons of school age in the State as 727,297, of whom 399,273 were white and 328,024 colored. The total enrollment in all the schools of the State was 298,648 white and 146,457 colored. The enrollment shows a slight decrease from 1911, both in white and colored pupils. The number of teachers employed in 1912 was as follows: White male teachers, 2886; female, 5086; colored male teachers, 937; colored female teachers, 906. The average yearly salary of male white teachers was $410; of female white teachers, $334; of colored male teachers, $175; colored female teachers, $155. The total disbursement for educational purposes in 1912 was $3,703,711. Efforts were made during the year to improve the elementary schools of the State by a closer supervision, by the grading of schools, and by the vitalizing of school work. Considerable progress was made.

CHARITIES AND CORRECTIONS. The institutions under the control of the State include the Alabama Hospital for the Insane at Tuscaloosa, the Alabama Boys' Industrial School at Birmingham, the Alabama Mercy Home at Birmingham, and the State Prison at Montgomery. There is no board or commission directly in charge of the charitable and correctional institutions of the State.

POLITICS AND GOVERNMENT. There was no meeting of the legislature in 1912, as its sessions are quadrennial. The last was held in 1911 and the next regular session will begin January 10, 1915. However, the condition of the State's finances during 1912 indicated that it would be necessary to call the legislature in extraordinary session during 1913. The chief matter for consideration will be an adjustment of the revenue laws. The term of Governor O'Neal does not expire until 1915, so there was no election for governor in 1912. The State Democratic primary was held on April 1 and Charles Henderson was nominated for president of the State railroad commission; John H. Wallace, game and fish commissioner, and John W. Abercrombie, Congressman-at-large. The State Democratic convention of April 17 renominated Justices Sayre and McClellan for the supreme court. All of these nominees were subsequently elected in November.

An important constitutional amendment was adopted in the November election, which provided that the legislature may put officers of Jefferson County on salaries instead of fees as at present. This is expected to effect a very large annual saving to the people of the largest county in the State.

The fact that Mr. Oscar W. Underwood, Democratic leader of the House of Representatives from Alabama, was one of the leading candidates for the Democratic presidential nomination, gave unusual interest to political happenings in the State. The Democratic delegates were naturally pledged to Mr. Underwood and voted for him throughout the Democratic convention until his name was withdrawn. A dispute as to the Republican delegates in the Ninth District of the State was one of the most discussed contests decided by the National Republican committee. This contest is described fully in the article PRESIDENTIAL CAMPAIGN. The delegates were finally given to President Taft, and the Republican delegates in the other districts were given to the President practically without dispute. The Republican convention was held on March 7. The Progressive Republicans refused to accept the delegates chosen at this convention, and on May 11 held a State convention with 300 delegates present. At this convention a platform was adopted and Mr. Roosevelt was endorsed for the presidency. Twelve delegates to the national convention were elected, each with half a vote. It was decided to hold State primaries in which State officers would be nominated after the national convention. The Democratic State convention met on April 17, and the delegates, as noted above, were instructed for Mr. Underwood for President. The result of the presidential vote in the State in the election of November 9 was as follows: Wilson, 82,439; Roosevelt, 22,689; Taft, 9731.

INDUSTRIAL PROGRESS. The most important industrial event of the year was the coming of the Alabama Interstate Power Company, backed by English capital, which will develop the water power of Alabama on an enormous scale. The entire project will cost about $50,000,000. Work was well under way during 1912 on the initial plant at Lock 12 on the Coosa River, which will cost about $3,500,000. Electric power from this plant will be carried to Birmingham and Montgomery.

STATE GOVERNMENT. Governor, Emmett O'Neal; lieutenant-governor, W. D. Seed; secretary of State, Cyrus B. Brown; auditor, C. B. Smith; adjutant-general, J. B. Scully; attorney-general, R. C. Brickell; treasurer, John Purifoy; superintendent of education, H. J. Willingham; commissioner of agriculture, R. F. Kolb; ex-officio commissioner of insurance, Cyrus B. Brown—all Democrats.

JUDICIARY. Supreme Court — Chief justice, J. R. Dowdell; associate justices, Ormond Somerville, A. D. Sayre, J. C. Anderson, Edward de Graffinried, J. J. Mayfield, and Thomas McClellan; clerk, R. F. Ligon, jr.—all Democrats.

STATE LEGISLATURE, 1913. Senate, Democrats, 44; Republicans, 10; House, Democrats, 95; Republicans, 4; joint ballot, Democrats, 135; Republicans, 14. Democratic majority, Senate, 30; House, 91; joint ballot, 121.

The representatives in Congress will be found in the section *Congress*, article UNITED STATES.

ALABAMA, UNIVERSITY OF. A State university of higher learning at Tuscaloosa, Ala., founded in 1831. The total number of students enrolled in the various departments of the university in the year 1911-12 was 1175, which includes 550 enrolled in the summer school. The members of the faculty numbered 100. The faculty of the summer school numbered 30. The institution is supported largely by the State, and had no notable benefactions during the year. The volumes in the library numbered 40,000. President, George H. Denney, LL. D.

ALASKA. POPULATION. While there was a small increase in the number of residents in Alaska who were engaged in industries of a permanent character in 1912, there was apparently a considerable decrease in the population of the Territory as a whole. The total population in 1910 was 64,356, including natives. The native population has remained comparatively stationary in the two years since 1910. A moderate decline in the white population in the last two years is due, in part, to diminished activity in placer mining in the interior valleys, and, to some extent, to the withdrawal of much of the public lands and natural resources from development. The Territory includes sixteen towns, one of which was added during 1912.

MINERAL PRODUCTION. The most notable event in the mining industry in the Territory during 1912 was an increase in the output of copper ore in the Chitina and Prince William Sound regions. Preparations were also made for a very large gold quartz development in the Juneau district. The entire mineral production in 1911 was valued at $20,650,000. The gold production in 1911 was $16,853,256, compared with $16,126,749 in 1910. The output from siliceous ores was $4,226,687, compared with $4,105,459 in 1910. The production from placer mines was valued at $12,540,000 in 1911. About three-fourths of the gold production comes from the placer mines, but the tendency in Alaska is for the relative output from the deep mines to increase. The Fairbanks Camp in the Yukon Basin continued to lead all other placer gold districts in the Territory in production, but the output decreased from $6,100,000 in 1910 to $4,500,000 in 1911. The production of the Innoko-Iditarod regions of the Yukon Basin increased from $825,000 in 1910 to approximately $3,000,000 in 1911. The Seward Peninsula production was about $3,100,000 as against $3,530,000 in 1910.

The production of silver in Alaska in 1911 was 460,231 fine ounces, compared with 157,850 fine ounces in 1910. Of the total production, 320,114 fine ounces were obtained from copper ores, 110,288 from placer gold, and the small remainder from siliceous ores of the lode gold mines.

The copper production in 1911 showed a remarkable increase. The output in that year was 22,314,889 pounds, compared with 4,311,026 pounds in 1910. The large increase in 1911 was due to the entrance of the Copper River district into the producing list. The total mine production for 1911 was 27,267,878 pounds. A considerable portion of this had not been smelted at the close of the year. The copper produced from the Copper River district came entirely from one mine, the Bonanza. Other properties are being developed and in some cases encouraging results are reported. There was practically no output of coal in Alaska in 1911. The greater part of the coal used in the Territory was imported. The importations amounted to 71,452 tons. No practical steps were undertaken during the year for the opening of the coal fields.

The necessity for adequate coal reserves on the Pacific Coast, and especially in Alaska, for the needs of the navy department resulted in an appropriation of $75,000 from Congress for mining and testing Alaska coal. This work was undertaken by the Department of the Interior through the agency of the Bureau of Mines. It was hoped that some investigation of the Matanuska coal fields would be possible, but the season had so far advanced when the appropriation became available that work was necessarily confined to the Bering field where a coal mine was opened and coal for experimental use by the navy under practical working conditions was mined and transported to tidewater. The Alaska coal leasing bill, which was favorably reported by the Senate committee on public lands in the second session of the Sixty-second Congress, proposes to give to all of the entrymen interested in still pending entries and who are not involved in pending criminal proceedings, or have not been found guilty of criminal acts in connection with their claims, a preference right to lease the lands in which they are respectively interested. During 1912 considerable progress was made in the disposition of these claims. The criminal cases resulting from alleged coal frauds in Alaska were expedited during the year and set for trial so that the innocence or guilt of the defendants may be promptly and definitely determined.

An end was made to the controversy over what has been known for years as the Cunningham coal claims of Alaska by the action in September of Secretary Fisher in finally cancelling them. In rendering his decision on this question, which had come to him through appeal, he said that "the findings of fact and the conclusions both of law and fact of the commissioner as expressed in his opinion of these cases are correct." After the decision was announced the registrar and receiver of the Land Office at Juneau, Alaska, by order of the acting commissioner of the General Office, placed on record the cancellation for fraud in the Cunningham claims. But money which had already been paid to the United States is forfeited and can be restored only by act of Congress.

Agriculture. Successful work was carried on during 1912 at the Experiment stations in the Territory. As the result of an unusually long summer in 1911, vegetables, particularly potatoes, matured well, except at interior points. Grain breeding at the Rampart station promises success and tests were made during the year of the several hybrid varieties of barley already developed. At the Sitka station the hybrids obtained by the crossing of several cultivated varieties of strawberry with the wild strawberry of the Alaska coast were more successful than before. Work at the Kodiak station in the breeding of cattle and sheep met with signal success during the year, but the grazing in the part of Kodiak Island where the station is situated was damaged by a heavy fall of volcanic ashes in the summer of 1912. See Agricultural Experiment Stations.

Commerce. The merchandise shipments, including precious metals and copper, increased materially during 1912. The total commerce between Alaska and the United States and between the Territory and foreign countries aggregated $62,680,507 for the fiscal year 1912. Merchandise shipments from Alaska to the United States aggregated in value $18,809,270, as against $15,736,510 in 1911. There was a large increase in the shipment of material required in the canning of fish, an industry which has greatly expanded in recent years. Dredging machinery to a considerable value was also shipped into the Territory. The total shipments, including copper and precious metals, from Alaska to the United States, were valued at $20,776,756, being an increase of nearly $7,000,000 over 1911. Of the large increase more than $4,000,000 was in copper ore and nearly $3,000,000 in canned salmon.

Fisheries. Ccording to a review made in 1912, there were 17,932 persons engaged in all branches of the fisheries of Alaska during the calendar year 1911. The total investment in all branches of the fisheries in that year, exclusive of that in the vessel fisheries for off-shore cod and halibut was $22,617,387. Of this amount, $19,931,215 was invested in the salmon canning business and $623,126 in salting and mild-curing salmon. Other large investments were in the halibut fishery, in the herring fishery, and in the cod fishery. At the end of 1912 there were five private and two government hatcheries in operation.

Education. The number of public schools for natives of Alaska maintained during 1912 was 86, with an enrollment of 4018 and an average daily attendance of 1805. The field force of the Alaska school service consists of five superintendents, 110 teachers, 7 physicians, 7 nurses, 2 contract physicians, and 2 hospital attendants. Of the appropriation for education, $24,926 was expended for the medical relief of natives. Adequate provision for the medical relief of natives of Alaska is an urgent duty, and the Secretary of the Interior in his annual report asks for liberal appropriations therefor.

TRANSPORTATION. The importance of wagon roads and trails to the development of the Territory is manifest. Valuable work was carried on during the year by the board of road commissioners, although the season was an unfavorable one for road work in most parts of the Territory on account of heavy and incessant rains in the late summer and fall. An act creating a legislative assembly in the Territory of Alaska, passed during the last session of Congress, provided for the creation of a railroad commission to conduct an examination into the transportation question in Alaska and to report its conclusions to Congress at the beginning of the second session of the Sixty-second Congress. There was practically no building of railroads during the year. Traffic on the Copper River Railroad was suspended for several weeks as the result of washouts.

The Secretary of the Interior in his annual report of 1911 recommended to Congress as necessary for the immediate relief of Alaska the construction by the federal government of a central trunk-line railroad from tidewater through the Matanuska coal fields to the Tanana or Yukon rivers; more liberal appropriations for aids to navigation such as lights and buoys; more liberal appropriations for the construction of roads and trails; and the adoption of a form of territorial government better adapted to the remote situation and the peculiar local conditions of the Territory. The last of these recommendations is the only one upon which action was taken by Congress. A territorial legislature with limited jurisdiction was created. A government railroad was not authorized, but a provision was inserted in the territorial government bill authorizing the appointment of a commission consisting of an army engineer, a navy engineer, a representative of the Geological Survey, and a civil engineer who had had practical experience in the construction and operation of railroads. This commission was appointed and proceeded to Alaska, where it engaged in a personal examination of the Territory with a view to making a comprehensive report to Congress.

On February 2 the President sent to Congress a message largely devoted to the government and development of Alaska. He urged the construction of a government railroad and the establishment of a commission form of government. One-half of this commission should be elected and the other half appointed by the President. He proposed a leasing system for government coal and phosphate lands in Alaska.

LEGISLATION. A measure was introduced into Congress to provide a form of self-government for Alaska. This bill created a legislature for the Territory to be composed of two houses, elected from the four judicial districts of the Territory. Each district is represented in the legislature by two senators and four representatives. The senators are to hold office for four years and are chosen alternately every two years. The members of the lower house hold office for two years only. The legislature, under this measure, would consist of a senate of eight and a lower house of sixteen members. This body was given no right to dispose of any of the public domain and was not empowered to legislate upon certain measures, which were reserved for Congress. On almost all ordinary matters, however, the right was given to this legislature to act. Its enactments were made subject to veto by the governor of the Territory, who could be overruled by a two-thirds' vote of the legislature. The acts of the legislature were to be transmitted at every session to the President, who was to submit them to Congress, which has the right to nullify any of these acts. Until they are thus nullified, however, they have the force of laws. This measure was presented to take the place of the bill introduced in 1910, which provided practically for a commission form of government with a commission appointed by the President. This measure failed to pass Congress.

ALBERTA. A province of the Dominion of Canada (since September 1, 1905). Capital, Edmonton (population, 1911 census, 24,900; estimated in 1912 at over 53,000). Area, 255,285 square miles; population (1911 census), 374,663. Lieutenant-governor (in 1912 and since September 1, 1905), George Hedley Vicars Bulyea. There are an executive council (responsible ministry of four members) and a legislative assembly (41 members elected for five years). Premier in 1912, Arthur L. Sifton. See CANADA.

ALBERT, CHARLES STANLEY. An American clergyman and editor, died January 28, 1912. He was born in Hanover, Pa., in 1837 and graduated from Hanover College in 1867. He studied theology at the Mt. Airy Theological Seminary, graduating in 1870. In the same year he was ordained to the Lutheran ministry. He filled pastorates in several cities until 1894, when he became editor of the *Augsburg Teacher*. He filled many positions in the Lutheran Church and was editor of many of its publications. He was also author of a number of booklets.

ALCOHOL. A systematic investigation, instituted by the Bavarian government, into the relation between alcoholism and criminality, brought to light some interesting data. In 1910, 8864 convictions were obtained against persons violating the law, whose derelictions were directly referable to intoxication or to chronic alcoholism. One hundred and ninety of these individuals were chronic alcoholics, and 14 per cent. of all those convicted were under the influence of drink when committing the offenses charged against them. Over half these offenses were crimes against the person—the infliction of dangerous bodily injuries seeming to be a special predilection of drinkers. Every third offense of this character could be referred to alcoholism. Only a small proportion of crimes against property were committed under the influence of drink. The vital connection between insanity and alcohol is illustrated anew by statistics from Kansas, a Prohibition State. Whereas in almost every part of the world the increasing ratio of mental disease is causing alarm, in Kansas the proportion of insanity is apparently steadily declining. In 1904 commitments to the asylums for the insane amounted to 56.2 per hundred thousand of the population. In 1910 the number had fallen to 42.3 and in 1911 to 38.3 per 100,000. The members of the State board of control and the asylum officials credit this satisfactory condition of affairs to the stricter enforcement of the prohibition laws and the consequent diminution in the quantity of alcohol consumed. They pointed out that alienists attribute at least 10 per cent. of all cases of insanity to alcohol, directly, and indirectly the drug is an important factor in the causation of a much higher percentage of cases, so that the Kansas statistics agree fairly well with those of the alienist statistician. See INSANITY.

The life insurance companies of England make a careful study of the relation of alcohol to longevity. For example, the report of the Sceptre Life Association contains an instructive comparison between the mortality of its abstaining and non-abstaining policyholders. In 1911, in the general section, the mortality was 77.78 per cent. of the expected; that is, there were 105 out of 135 expected deaths. In the temperance section the mortality was only 51.11 per cent. of the expected deaths, or sixty-nine out of 135. For the last twenty-eight years the percentage of actual to expected deaths has been in the general section, 79.7; in the temperance section, 52.45. Both classes of policyholders are of the same social status, engaged in the same occupations, and have passed the same medical examination. The conclusion is therefore drawn that total abstinence tends to longevity. However, no account is taken of the fact that total abstainers are apt to be more careful in all their ways of life than the average citizen. They are more thrifty, pay more attention to hygiene, etc., and these factors must play some part in their longevity.

Late in 1912 Col. L. Mervin Maus, U. S. A., chief surgeon of the Eastern Division of the army, published an article upon the use of alcohol among officers and officials of the military, naval, and civil services of the United States. He classes alcohol with the narcotics as equally dangerous, and states that, taken in "moderation," it lowers the general intelligence, perception, judgment, caution, and power of rapid action, lowers also one's moral standards and lessens self-restraint, while it produces unreliability, untruthfulness, dishonesty, and crime. He cites Lord Kitchener as forbidding his men to use spirits in the Sudan campaign, also Lord Roberts as opposed to its use, and points to the Boers, who, totally abstaining from spirits and beer, showed remarkable efficiency. He quotes Sir Frederick Treves as saying at Ladysmith, "The drinking men fell out and dropped as regularly as if they were labeled with the big letter D on their backs." Colonel Maus urges that total abstinence be a requirement in the election of all civil officers, and for all appointments to important positions or to the positions of heads of bureaus in any department of government and in any place of importance and responsibility.

WOOD ALCOHOL. During the Christmas holidays of 1911 161 inmates of the Berlin municipal lodging house were taken violently ill and 71 of them died. An investigation showed that wood alcohol, sold in neighboring saloons for ordinary whisky, was the cause. The incident gave rise to widespread discussion and to new attempts to add to our rather small stock of knowledge as to the underlying cause of its extreme toxicity, under certain circumstances, and to its behavior in the animal metabolism. Investigations at the Institute for the Fermentation Industries at Berlin, demonstrated that methyl alcohol is slowly digested by animals and more slowly eliminated, so that repeated small doses are apt to accumulate in the system and produce severe toxic symptoms. These facts have not heretofore been duly appreciated. Considerable difference of opinion also exists as to whether the toxic action of wood alcohol is due to the alcohol itself or to some of the contaminating substances almost invariably present in it; as fusel i, acetone, etc. To guard against the possibility of such fatalities as those referred to above, the Austrian board of health issued an ordinance more strictly limiting the use of wood alcohol in the industrial arts, and prohibiting absolutely its employment in the preparation of all articles of food.

The New York health board, at its meeting on January 23, adopted a new section of the sanitary code, which prohibits the sale or use of wood alcohol in any food or drink or in any preparation or mixture intended for external use by man, such as hair tonics, face lotions, etc. See LIQUORS.

ALDRICH BANK PLAN. See BANKS AND BANKING.

ALESIA. See ARCHÆOLOGY.

ALEUTIANS. See ANTHROPOLOGY.

ALFALFA. The alfalfa crop of 1912 was affected by climatic conditions in the same manner as the hay crop in general. The season in most countries favored a good growth, but was unfavorable to the production of good hay on account of rainy weather at hay-making time and while the quantity of hay secured was satisfactory, the quality left much to be desired. The rainy weather with which most European countries had to contend was especially detrimental to the making of alfalfa hay, as the crop is not so readily cured as the grasses. In the United States and Argentina, the two principal alfalfa-growing countries of the world, the season was much more favorable to hay production than in Europe. Statistics on alfalfa are not regularly published for all countries and the world's production is not generally estimated. Certain data given at random indicate in a general way the importance of the crop in different countries and regions. In many countries, especially the United States and Argentina, the acreage is on the increase. Argentina has about 15,000,000 acres in alfalfa, but only about 10 per cent. of the area is cut for hay, the rest being used for grazing purposes. France grows about 2¾ million acres and produces from 5 to 6 million tons of hay. The acreage of Germany in 1912 was reported as 608,000 acres and that of the United Kingdom as 56,374 acres. In Hungary about 30,000 acres are grown for seed production, while the area devoted to hay production amounts to over 500,000 acres.

No data covering acreage and production in the United States other than the Census figures given in the YEAR BOOK for 1911 are available. The crop is growing in favor and importance wherever its culture is profitable. In many of the States east of the Mississippi River, in which alfalfa culture is comparatively recent, the crop is grown not only as an important source of forage and hay for consumption on the farm, but it is also produced for the hay markets of the larger eastern cities, where its value is being more and more appreciated.

In experiments conducted in New Zealand during the past year alfalfa was successfully used as a soil binder in the reclamation of sandy lands.

ALGER, PHILIP ROUNSEVILLE. An American naval officer and mathematician, died February 23, 1912. He was born in Boston in 1859 and graduated from the United States Naval Academy in 1880. He served on the China and Mediterranean stations, and from 1888 to 1891 was on duty at the Navy Department in Washington. From 1891 to 1899 he was professor of mathematics and from 1899 to 1907 was head of the department of mechanics at the United States Naval Academy. This chair was abolished in 1907. He was a member of the Special Naval Board of Ordnance and was secretary and treasurer of the United States Naval Institute. From 1903 to the time of his death he was the editor of the *Proceedings* of the Institute. He was the author of *Exterior Ballistics* (1904); *Elastic Strength of Guns* (1906), and *Hydromechanics* (1902). He also contributed numerous articles on naval ordnance to technical magazines.

ALGERIA. A north African country, called a colony but actually an integral part of the French Republic. Algiers is the capital.

AREA AND POPULATION. Area by departments, European and native population (1911 census), and total density per square kilometer, are shown below.

The principal towns are: Algiers, with (1911) 172,397 inhabitants; Oran, 123,086; Constantine, 65,173; Bône, 42,039; Tlemçen, 39,874; Blidah, 35,461; Sidi bel Abbes, 30,942.

Department	Sq.kms.	Europeans	Natives	D.
Algiers	54,540	271,767	1,421,819	31
Constantine	87,302	155,654	1,945,443	24
Oran	65,897	319,089	892,212	19
Algeria proper	207,739	746,510	4,259,474	24
Southern Territories	367,550	5,533	481,052	1
Total	575,289*	752,043	4,740,526	10

* 222,119 square miles.

PRODUCTION. The country is largely agricultural. In the table below will be found the areas devoted to principal crops and the yield in 1911 and 1912, with the average yield per hectare (1912):

	Hectares 1911	Hectares 1912	Quintals 1911	Quintals 1912	Qs. per ha.
Wheat	1,337,411	1,462,714	9,959,934	7,395,012	5.1
Barley	1,360,500	1,388,212	40,399,613	7,160,292	5.2
Oats	181,411	192,460	1,755,092	1,792,713	9.3
Corn	8,941	12,412	85,573	94,964	7.7
Rye	636	154	851	1,036	6.7
Vines*	150,486	148,548	8,443,368	....	56.1
Tobacco	8,547	10,137	88,120	....	10.3
Cotton	900	......	....	....	....

* Yield in hectoliters.

Fruits, olive oil, timber, cork, and livestock are also produced for export. Silk culture is practiced. The mines yield iron, zinc, lead, silver, copper, mercury, coal, and petroleum. The phosphate industry is progressing. The fisheries products are of appreciable value. Livestock (1911): 226,764 horses, 192,484 mules, 279,315 donkeys, 1,113,952 cattle, 8,528,610 sheep, 3,861,847 goats, 110,012 swine.

COMMERCE AND COMMUNICATIONS. The table below shows the imports for consumption and exports of domestic produce in thousands of francs:

	1907	1908	1909	1910
Imports	448,200	449,300	462,000	512,000
Exports	338,500	319,200	359,200	513,300

Principal articles of export in 1911, values in thousands of francs:

Article	Value	Article	Value
Wine	207,698	Cork	9,784
Cereals	80,492	Vegetables	9,718
Animals	34,193	Wool	8,184
Fruits	15,902	Skins	7,837
Iron ore	12,000	Esparto	7,166
Phosphates	10,977	Flour	6,031
Tobacco	10,047	Fibre	4,677
Zinc	9,925	Olive oil	4,489

Principal countries of origin and destination, 1910 trade, values in thousands of francs:

	Imps.	Exps.		Imps.	Exps.
France	437,896	410,367	Germany	4,401	10,593
Belgium	1,091	10,375	Russia	1,116	3,438
Neth'ds	1,729	7,772	Fr. Cols.	4,633	21,211
G. Brit.	13,885	19,610	Morocco	14,407	8,421
Spain	6,179	4,627	U. S.	3,569	2,748
Italy	2,855	7,644	Brazil	9,109	1
Aus.-Hy.	2,805	3,705	Others	8,247	2,752
			Total	511,967	513,267

Vessels entered (1910 trade), 5003, of 5,691,063 tons. Merchant marine (January 1, 1911), 980 vessels, of 31,771 tons (steamers, 105, of 21,246 tons). Railways in operation Decmeber 31, 1911, 3297 kilometers of main and 150 kilometers of local lines; telegraph lines 15,199 kms., wires 39,652.

FINANCE. The budget for 1912, as voted December 29, 1911, appears below:

Revenue	1000 fr.	Expenditures	1000 fr.
Direct taxes	13,928	Debts	23,473
Domains	8,271	Administration	2,106
Indirect taxes	44,133	Interior	26,158
Monopolies, etc.	9,691	Native adm.*	5,794
Various	2,715	Finance	9,639
Receipts d'ordre	28,569	Posts and tels.	12,162
Extraordinary	37,859	Public works	19,113
		Agriculture, etc.	8,583
Total	145,167	Other	273
		Extraordinary	37,859
		Total	145,156

* Administration.

Southern Territories: 6,523,301 francs revenue, 6,513,284 francs expenditure (budget 1912).

Algeria is administered by a governor-general—in 1912, M. Lutaud.

ALIENS. See IMMIGRATION.

ALLITSEN, FRANCES. An English composer, died October 2, 1912. She was born in London, where she studied at the Guildhall School of Music. She made her début in concert singing in Grosvenor Hall, London, in July, 1872. Among her more important works are *Sonata for the Piano* (1881); *Ouverture Slavonique* (1884); *A Dramatic Scene*, and *Cleopatra*. She also wrote over a hundred songs and duets.

ALMA-TADEMA, SIR LAURENCE. An English artist, died June 25, 1912. He was born in 1836 in the village of Dronryp, near Leeuwarden, Netherlands. His father, Pieter Tadema, a notary, died when the artist was four years old. It was intended that the son should be a notary as his father had been, but his artistic talent was so apparent that before he was sixteen years old he was sent to Antwerp, where he became a student under Gustav Wappers. He entered the academy at Antwerp in 1852. In the same year he painted a portrait of himself which attracted much attention. In 1860 another picture, "The Bargain," was favorably received. From the Academy of Wappers he went to the atelier of Henri Leys, and in 1859 he assisted Leys in painting the frescoes in the Hotel de Ville at Antwerp.

Alma-Tadema's first great success was his picture "The Education of Clovis," painted in 1861 and exhibited in Antwerp the same year. This was the first of the famous series of Merovingian pictures, of which the most widely known was the "Fredegonda" in 1878. In 1862 he received his first gold medal at Amsterdam. In the following year he married a French woman, Marie Pauline Girard, and lived at Brussels until 1869, when she died. In the same year he exhibited two pictures at the Royal Academy and in the following year three more, including "Un Jongleur." He removed to London in 1870 and from that year until the time of his death made his home in that city. He had already achieved international fame, and in addition to the honors received in Holland and Belgium, had received medals of the Paris Salon of 1864 and the Exposition Universelle of 1867. In the year following his removal to London he married Laura Epp. From his arrival in England, Alma-Tadema's career was marked with unbroken success. In 1879 he became a member of the Royal Academy and in 1899, on Queen Victoria's birthday, he was knighted. His most famous pictures were those which portrayed scenes in ancient history, especially the history of Greece and Rome. He made a profound study of archæology, and his pictures, aside from their artistic value, are remarkably faithful in depicting customs and architecture of the times to which they relate. Among his best-known pictures are "Clothilde at the Tomb of Her Grandchildren"; "How the Egyptians Amused Themselves 3000 Years Ago"; "Tarquinius Superbus"; "The Vintage"; "A Roman Emperor"; "The Conversion of Paula"; "The Finding of Moses," and "Caracalla and Geta." His work is peculiarly successful in defining the texture of marble and bronze. His drawing is good, his coloring faithful, but he has been charged with a merely intellectual appeal and a lack of any deep feeling.

ALSACE-LORRAINE. See GERMANY.

ALSOP CLAIM. See ARBITRATION, INTERNATIONAL.

ALTERNATORS. See DYNAMO-ELECTRIC MACHINERY.

ALTITUDE RECORDS. See AERONAUTICS.

ALUMINUM. The consumption of aluminum in the United States in 1911, according to the United States Geological Survey, was 46,125,000 pounds. Bauxite ore, the present source of metallic aluminum, is mined in Arkansas, Georgia, Alabama, and Tennessee, the output from these States combined amounting in 1911 to 1,555,618 long tons, valued at $750,649, an increase of about 5 per cent. in both quantity and value, compared with the figures for 1910. The use of aluminum and its alloys in automobiles, dirigible balloons, and aeroplanes, is constantly increasing. In the form of magnalium it is used in the beams of analytical balances, and other new alloys are being constantly brought to public attention. The metal is also employed in paper decorations and for wrapping, and is finding a host of applications in the smaller articles of everyday use and ornamentation.

ALZEY. See ARCHÆOLOGY.

AMBROSE CHANNEL. See DOCKS AND HARBORS.

AMERICAN ASSOCIATIONS AND SOCIETIES. For organizations whose official title begins with the word American, see under the titles of the subjects with which they are concerned.

AMERICAN ECONOMIC ASSOCIATION. See POLITICAL ECONOMY.

AMERICANIST CONGRESS, INTERNATIONAL. See ANTHROPOLOGY.

AMERICAN PEACE SOCIETIES. See ARBITRATION.

AMERICAN PRISON ASSOCIATION. See PENOLOGY.

AMERICAN SOCIOLOGICAL SOCIETY. See SOCIOLOGY.

AMERICAN SUGAR REFINING COMPANY. See TRUSTS.

AMERICAN TELEPHONE COMPANY. See TRUSTS.

AMERICAN TOBACCO COMPANY. See TRUSTS.

AMHERST COLLEGE. The number of students enrolled in the several departments of the college in the autumn of 1912 was 430. The faculty numbered 49. The most interesting event in the history of the college during the year was the election of Dr. Meiklejohn (q. v.) to succeed President Harris. (See also UNIVERSITIES AND COLLEGES.) The most noteworthy benefaction of the year was $157,160 for the Pratt Dormitory. The amount of productive funds of the college in 1911-12 was $2,473,837. In the library were about 106,000 volumes. President, Alexander Meiklejohn, Ph. D.

AMMONIA, SULPHATE OF. See FERTILIZERS.

AMPHIBIA. See ZOÖLOGY.

AMUNDSEN, ROALD. See POLAR RESEARCH.

ANÆMIA, MINERS'. See HOOKWORM.

ANÆSTHESIA. A French surgeon, Dr. Descarpentries, has introduced a new method of producing general anæsthesia, namely, by the intramuscular injection of ether. He has performed over 150 operations, major and minor, under this anæsthetic without complications, even in children and elderly persons. Successive doses of the anæsthetic proportioned to the weight of the patient (about 0.5 c. c. to the pound) are injected slowly into the gluteal muscles, care being taken to avoid striking the bone or piercing small blood vessels. Complete anæsthesia is induced in 15 to 20 minutes and consciousness returns slowly in about an hour after the last injection; sensation returns somewhat later. Alcoholic subjects seem to be especially amenable to this method. The first injection is very painful for a moment, and it is the practice of Descarpentries to give a preliminary inhalation of ethyl chloride or chloroform to obviate this, and sometimes to supplement the ether. The intramuscular method seems likely to be useful in operations upon the head, face, and respiratory passages, when an anæsthetist might impede the surgeon, and in country and military surgery, where an assistant is often lacking.

The intramuscular method is an outgrowth of intravenous anæsthesia, which has been noticed in previous numbers of the YEAR BOOK. By the intravenous route, ether, dissolved in normal salt solution in the proportion of 1.20, is thrown directly into a large vein. The danger of producing thrombosis or embolism has caused this method to be received with considerable reserve, although a total of 498 cases are on record with only two deaths; one from unknown causes and one from embolism.

LOCAL ANÆSTHESIA. Finsterer obtained complete anæsthesia of the entire abdominal viscera by what he calls "paravertebral blocking" of the spinal nerves. He introduces a long hypodermic needle close to the spinous process of the first lumbar vertebra, 3 cm. from the median line, and injects the nerve at its exit from the spinal canal, using a solution of novocain. The second and third lumbar nerves are treated in the same manner. Anæsthesia is complete in fifteen minutes, but when an abdominal operation is to be performed the skin has to be anæsthetized separately. This technic is, in comparison with spinal anæsthesia, harmless, but a good deal of skill is required to reach the proper points.

ANDRÉE, RICHARD. A German geographer and ethnographer, died February, 1912. He was born in 1835 at Braunschweig. He studied natural history at Leipzig and from 1859 to 1863 worked as foundryman in Bohemia for the purpose of obtaining information in relation to the German-Czech race conflicts. From 1891 to 1903 he was editor of the *Globus*. He became in 1902 professor at the University of Munich. His writings in relation to his observations in Bohemia are from the point of view of the German nationalist. They include *Nationalitätsverhaltnisse und Sprachgrenze in Böhmen* (1870), and *Tschechische Gänge* (1872). His later works comprise *Zur Volkskunde der Juden* (1881); *Die Metalle bei den Naturvolkern* (1884); *Die Masken in der Volkerkunde* (1886); *Die Flutsagen* (1891); *Braunschweiger Volkskunde* (1896); *Aufl. von Scobel* (1899), and *dazu Geographisches Handbuch von Scobel* (1899).

ANDREWS, WILLIAM SWAIN. An American soldier, lawyer, and public official, died December 29, 1912. He was born in Texas in 1841, the son of Stephen Pearl Andrews, the famous Abolitionist. He attended school in New York City and at the age of 18 he went on the stage, where, for a time, he acted with Edwin Booth. He went to the Civil War as lieutenant of zouaves and was later transferred to the signal corps under General Burnside. At the close of the war he returned to the stage and was on the stage of the Ford Theatre on the night of the assassination of President Lincoln. In 1868 and again in 1881 he was elected to the New York State Assembly and during the second term was speaker of that body. He secured the passage of the first pure-food law enacted in New York and was also responsible for the organization of the Society for the Prevention of Cruelty to Children. He was at one time collector of internal revenue of New York and in 1876, 1884, and 1888 was secretary of the Democratic national committee. During the Tilden campaign he was editor of the New York *Star*. In 1893-4 he was commissioner of street-cleaning in New York and in 1896 was made commissioner of records.

ANGLO-AMERICAN ARBITRATION. See ARBITRATION, INTERNATIONAL.

ANGOLA. A west African Portuguese colony, with an estimated area of 500,000 square miles and a population of between three and four millions. St. Paul de Loanda is the capital. Tropical agricultural products are exported. The rubber supply is failing. The trade is mainly with Portugal. In 1909 the imports were valued at 5,674,861 and the exports at 5,485,085 milreis; transit, 326,349 milreis. Vessels entered, 1741, of 1,005,000 tons. Revenue (estimate) in 1909-10, 2,321,373 milreis; expenditure, 3,171,373. Work on the railway line from Lobito Bay, in the southwest frontier of Belgian Congo, which is to connect with the Central African system, is progressing. Total length of lines open for traffic in 1911, 821 kilometers. The colony is administered by a governor-general (in 1912, N. de Mattos).

ANIMAL DISEASES. See VETERINARY SCIENCE.

ANIMAL PSYCHOLOGY. See PSYCHOLOGY.

ANKYLOSTOMIASIS. See HOOKWORM DISEASE.

ANNAM. A French protectorate on the China Sea; a part of the French colony of Indo-China (q. v.) Hué is the capital, with 65,000 inhabitants, and Bin-Dinh the largest town (74,400). The trade is included with that of French Indo-China. Raw silk, cattle, and agricultural and forest products are exported. There are valuable mineral deposits imperfectly developed. The native king (1912, Duy-Tan) is the nominal head of the government. He succeeded in 1907 at the age of eight and was placed under a council of regency. Internal affairs are actually administered by the French resident (1912, M. Mahé).

ANNELIDA. See ZOÖLOGY.

ANNIVERSARIES. See EXPOSITIONS.

ANSHUTZ, THOMAS POLLOCK. An American painter and instructor in art, died June 16, 1912. He was born in Newport, Ky., in 1851. He studied painting at the National Academy of Design in New York City until 1865, and afterwards at the Pennsylvania Academy of Fine Arts. He received instruction in Paris in 1892-3 under Doucet and Bouguereau. Although he achieved distinction with his paintings, he was best known as a teacher of painting. He was a member of the Pennsylvania Academy of Fine Arts from 1882 until the time of his death. Many of the most notable artists of the day received instruction at his hands. His paintings received honorable mention at the Art Club in Philadelphia, the silver medal at the St. Louis Exposition in 1904, the Walter Lippincott prize in Philadelphia in 1909, the gold medal of honor at the Pennsylvania Academy of Fine Arts in the same year, and a gold medal at the South American Exposition at Buenos Ayres in 1910. He was a charter member and president of the Philadelphia Sketch Club and was an associate of the National Academy of Design.

ANTARCTIC EXPLORATION. See POLAR EXPLORATION.

ANTHRACITE COAL. See COAL.

ANTHRACITE COAL TRUST. See TRUSTS.

ANTHRACITE CONCILIATION BOARD. See ARBITRATION AND CONCILIATION, INDUSTRIAL.

ANTHRACITE MINERS. See ARBITRATION AND CONCILIATION, INDUSTRIAL.

ANTHROPOLOGY. In 1912 there has been an unusual tendency toward the publication of textbooks briefly summarizing the present state of our knowledge with respect to anthropology. Thus, Marett has given an epitome of ethnological principles in his *Anthropology;* Sollas in his important book on *Ancient Hunters and their Modern Representatives* has presented a valuable outline of European archæology, while briefer treatises emphasizing the physical traits of early man have been published by both Keith and Duckworth; Ranke offers a revised edition of his famous book, *Der Mensch;* Obermaier gives a full treatment of prehistoric European culture in *Der Mensch der Vorzeit;* Weule has written a very brief sketch of descriptive ethnography; and G. F. Wright presents an argument against excessive estimates of man's antiquity.

In ethnology the old struggle between the evolutionary and historical schools continues, as evidenced by Andrew Lang's rejoinder to Goldenweiser and Lowie on the subject of totemism, Lang still regarding totemism as a phenomenon essentially everywhere alike. However, such British ethnologists as Rivers and Marett now admit the method of historical analysis, and Rivers employs it in an interesting way to account for conventionalized art forms. Conventionalization, he argues, cannot be merely the result of inexactness in copying a realistic object, nor of technical factors alone, for such factors do not explain why, say, a human figure becomes conventionalized in one case into a lozenge and elsewhere into a spiral. Such instances become intelligible, however, from the interaction between two different tribes, one of which has developed a naturalistic art, while the other has originated a definite geometrical style.

While there is thus a movement toward the use of historical principles even in quarters where formerly schematic representations of cultural evolution were the rule, there has also developed a noteworthy difference among adherents of historical methods. This is due to the fact that Graebner, the chief advocate of such methods in Germany, practically eliminates the psychological element by defining as the sole object of ethnology the complete determination of how cultural features have been diffused from tribe to tribe, this diffusion, moreover, having never taken place, according to Graebner, by the adoption of single elements, but always wholesale, so that he does not hesitate to separate distinct strata in the culture of any particular group. Apart from this last-named feature, which most other students reject, Graebner's point of view appears narrow and formal to fellow-adherents of historical methods, who insist on the necessity of intensive consideration of psychological factors. This, for example, is where Rivers and Boas part company with Graebner. Graebner has been specially criticized for denying that similarities of culture can be explained by anything but historical contact. Against this view a number of critics have argued that certain similarities can be explained by the universal likeness of the human mind, which will react similarly to similar stimuli, especially where the number of possible reactions is limited by the nature of the case. Lowie has further contended that many so-called similarities that Graebner accounts for by historical contact are really no more than superficial analogies and thus present no problem whatever. That is to say, phenomena that at first appeared to be identical have frequently turned out, on closer examination, to be radically different. Before raising the question at all, how two widely separated peoples have come to possess some common trait, we must, therefore, be sure that the traits are genuinely homologous and not merely analogous.

ANTIQUITY OF MAN AND PHYSICAL ANTHROPOLOGY. In October, 1911, an interesting skeleton was unearthed in Ipswich, England. Its position resembled the contracted posture characteristic of neolithic burials, but Professor Keith is of opinion that it might have been assumed without intentional arrangement. The teeth found in no way differ from those of neolithic man, and from the fragments of the skull Keith concludes that the head did not differ much from that of modern Europeans except for the single Neanderthaloid trait that the maximum width of the skull is situated rather far back. The tibia, however, also resembles the Neanderthal type in lacking the sharp anterior crest or shin of modern man. If the skeleton does not represent a burial and if the loam at this point is part of the original mantel of bowlder clay, the man of Ipswich represents the earliest human form found next to the Heidelberg man, being in that case even somewhat older than the Galley Hill find. Unfortunately the geological age of both the Galley Hill and the Ipswich man has not been satisfactorily determined, for if of the same age, they would indicate the contemporaneous existence of two different types of man,—one with Neanderthaloid and one with modern traits.

A sensational find was made toward the close of the year in Sussex, England, of which only preliminary accounts are available. It consists of parts of a skull, believed to be that of a woman, and there is said to be evidence that its owner lacked the power of speech. Some authorities are reported to regard the skull as representing a very primitive type different from that of the Neanderthal man and find in its characteristics confirmation of the hypothesis just referred to, that two distinct species of humanity coexisted in Pleistocene times. However, in this case also there has not yet been a satisfactory determination of the geological antiquity of the skull. See article GEOLOGY.

In a recent article Boule describes his conception of Neanderthal man as a type below the average stature of the modern European, with an enormous head, a short and thick trunk and very stout limbs.

An interesting archæological find of upper Aurignacian level consists of bas-reliefs of female figures in rock shelters of the Dordogne district. The figures show a curious development of steatopygy and resemble anatomically the modern Bushman type.

Professor Wright has put forward a critique of the arguments for the great antiquity of the human species and heroically defends the now quite discredited view that a space of fifteen thousand years suffices to account for the development of man and of human culture.

Loth has investigated the muscular system of the Negro and arrived at the conclusion that there are racial differences between the soft parts of Caucasians and Negroes and that such differences also exist between Negroes and Mongolians, the Negroes occupying a morphologically lower position.

Ethnography

AMERICAN. *Blackfoot.* Many of the religious conceptions of an important Plains tribe are discussed by Wissler in his *Ceremonial Bundles of the Blackfoot Indians.* The Blackfoot have developed a conception, apparently almost peculiar to them, that the medicine bundle secured by an individual through a supernatural revelation may be transferred to a second individual who offers an appropriate amount of property as a token of his gratitude. The benefits of practically every supernatural communication could be purchased in this way, the only exceptions being doctors' formulæ and certain individual experiences by which a man secured a presence within himself on which his life depended. Thus there arose a definite system with religious, social, and economic functions. To own and transfer many bundles is believed to result in long life, health, and happiness, secures social position, and is a good investment inasmuch as medicine bundles are readily convertible into property often much greater in amount than that originally offered by the seller. The purchase is effected through the offices of a middleman hired by the bundle owner. The buyer is regarded as the ceremonial "son" of the seller. A peculiarity of the Blackfoot bundle is its non-hereditary character. In general a bundle is transferred to a stranger, and even when a son does receive the bundle of his deceased father the customary transfer procedure is imperative. Foremost among Blackfoot bundles is that associated with the beaver. Its ritual includes a tobacco-planting ceremony analogous to that of the Crow Indians and is intimately related with the Sun Dance performance. There are indications that the Beaver bundle is the oldest, and as the mode of procedure in the rituals of the several bundles is strikingly uniform it seems that the other bundles have all been patterned on the Beaver medicine. The Medicine Pipe bundle is believed to have been handed down by the Thunder and must be opened at the sound of the first thunder in the spring. The Hako of the Pawnee, with its variants among the Teton, Arikara, and other tribes, is more in the nature of an adoption ceremony and does not seem to be genetically related to the Medicine Pipe ritual of the Blackfoot. In almost all the ceremonials of the Blackfoot incense is burned on an altar, the surface of which is worked out in symbolic designs by the use of colored earth. This is suggestive of the dry sand paintings of the Arapaho, Cheyenne, and southwestern tribes, but the combination of dry painting with an incense altar seems confined to the Blackfoot. Uhlenbeck has published a new series of Blackfoot texts.

Crow. Lowie has discussed the *Social Life of the Crow Indians.* The clan with maternal descent forms the unit of organization. Marriages within one's clan were not considered proper, and any transgressor was derided for having married his "sister." The clans, of which there were at least thirteen, were grouped together, mostly in pairs, but the larger resulting units were of a rather loose character and cannot be considered exogamous phratries, as Curtis is inclined to do. While the paternal clan had little or nothing to do with one's marrying possibilities, it was important in other ways. Personal names were generally given by a clansman of the child's father, and nicknames were given to an individual on the basis of actions performed by his father's fellow-clansfolk. Further, there was a curious relationship obtaining among all those whose fathers were fellow-clansmen; any member in this group might play practical jokes on any other member and had the privilege of twitting him publicly with any foolish or contemptible deed he had done. Both in the definition of this "joking relationship" and in the exogamous clan system with maternal descent the Crow resemble their closest linguistic allies, the Hidatsa, but differ from all other branches of the Siouan family, among which definite social units are either lacking or have descent traced through the father. The government of the Crow was not unlike that of neighboring tribes. Those who had performed at least one of each of a number of definitely recognized deeds of valor formed a sort of aristocracy, and one of their number directed the movements of the camp. For the annual buffalo hunt one of the military societies was appointed as a constabulary force to prevent the premature startling of the herd. A man's war record largely determined his social prestige. Occasional disputes as to which of two men had actually performed some heroic deed were settled by an ordeal, which is noteworthy on account of the rarity of this institution among the American Indians.

Southeast. Swanton has published some of his studies of southeastern tribes. Most important among these are the Natchez, who are now shown to have spoken a Muskhogean language and to have possessed a culture in many ways typical of the entire area, yet not without unique traits, such as the custom of strangling the relatives of a deceased person of prominence at his funeral. The Natchez probably acquired their clan system after settlement among the Creek. They built mounds for their temples, which suggest a kinship with the Mississippi and Ohio cultures. The power of the chiefs seems to have been much greater than usual. Of the tribes still partly in existence the Chitimacha are the most primitive. They used wooden mortars and pestles similar to those found in the Woodland area of the United States, practised pottery, and are still skilful basket-makers. There was formerly a caste of noblemen who married only in their own class. Society was also divided into a number of totemic clans with descent through the mother. At the time of puberty a boy was subjected to a several days' fast in a temple, which no woman was permitted to approach. Each boy also underwent confinement for the purpose of securing a personal guardian spirit. Among the Gulf tribes the Biloxi were known as the solitary instance of a people with Siouan affiliations, but Swanton has discovered a second tribe of that family, the Ofo or Ofoyoula. Their dialect is closely related to that of the Biloxi, both languages showing kinship with Tutelo and other East Siouan groups and in a somewhat more remote way with the more northern representatives of the family, such as the Dakota.

California. Mason has contributed a study of *The Ethnology of the Salinan Indians* of southwestern California. Though geographically closer to the Chumash, who represent the southwestern Californian culture area, the Salinan were only in a moderate degree influenced by their southern neighbors and may be treated as slightly aberrant members of the central Californian culture g up. They depend on acorns as the staple food, lack a gentile organization, and reveal but a weak development of war and ritualistic practices. Nevertheless, a number of similarities with the Chumash and Costanoan might lead to a grouping together of the three coastal stocks into one sub-area. Among these parallels are the use of communal houses, the greater importance of wealth and chieftainship, and the ceremonial smoking of tobacco. A noteworthy Salinan trait is the administration of Jimson weed to boys in connection with a definite puberty ceremony.

Mexico. Numerous Cora texts published by Preuss afford a conception of the religion of this interesting tribe. Cora mythology is characterized by three principal deities, the Sun god, the Moon or Earth goddess, and the Morning Star, to which must be added an indefinite number of lesser beings representing the four quarters, as well as certain animals and plants. Most of the cosmological conceptions are symbolically represented, on a small scale, on the dance site of the tribe and on the inside of a sacred gourd decorated with patterns in beadwork. There are three principal ceremonies, all connected with the growth of cultivated plants. One of them is a sowing festival celebrated in the spring, while the others are harvest feasts revolving about the fresh corn cobs and roasted maize. In addition to these there are performances intended to produce rain and to remove disease, and in one village there is a feast for the promotion of the children's welfare. A peculiarity of the Cora as well as of the neighboring Huichol is the predominance of songs in their ceremonial activities, the chanting being continued throughout entire nights even without the accompaniment of dances or other ceremonial activities.

South America. In collaboration with Messrs. Holmes, Willis, Wright, and Fenner, Dr. Aleš Hrdlička has published a bulletin entitled *Early Man in South America*, as a critique of the claims frequently made, that osseous human remains of geologic antiquity have been found in South America. The verdict of the authors is purely negative, and the sources of error are pointed out.

Nordenskiöld, on the basis of South American studies, joins Graebner in the contention that American cultures have been influenced by those of Asiatic and Melanesian origin, though this view runs counter to that of most Americanists. See OCEANIA.

Leland Locke, after investigating specimens of old Peruvian *quipus* or "knot records," concludes that the quipu was not employed to record historical events other than dates and numerical data; that distances of the knots from the main cord were used roughly to locate the orders, which were on a decimal scale; that the colors used had no special significance, but were chosen according to the maker's fancy or convenience, though a rough color scheme is not excluded.

ASIA. As one of the results of the Riabouschinsky expedition Dr. Jochelson announces that the language of the Aleutians is an old Eskimo dialect, while that of the Kamtchatkans is of the same morphological type as some North American Indian languages. The mythology of the Kamtchatkans and Aleutians is that of the Northwest Coast Indians.

Dr. Laufer has published a monograph on *Jade; a study in Chinese archæology and religion.* While primarily of interest to sinologues, this book contains matter of general ethnological importance, especially in a discussion of the Chinese stone age. Laufer rejects for one thing the utterances of Chinese philosophers as to the use of stone in the old days corresponding to our European palæolithic epoch and followed by a neolithic era. Such remarks are pure speculations and are in line with a tendency to evolutionary theorizing among Chinese thinkers. In the present state of our knowledge it is not yet justifiable to speak of a stone age of China, and still less of a stone age of the Chinese as different from the more primitive aboriginal populations of the empire. The stone implements so far found are all polished, many of them with great elegance, so that they would be classed as neolithic. They are scattered in certain parts of the country and are generally rare. Two types occur, a cruder type in river beds or immediately beneath the surface, and a superior type in graves. It is, however, not certain that a chronological difference exists between the two, for the more elaborate forms may have been confined to ceremonial usage contemporaneously with the general use of the cruder implements for everyday purposes. No so-called stone work-shops have hitherto been discovered in China, and there is nothing to show that what stone implements have been found belong to a very ancient period of time. It is also important to note that Chinese records do not ascribe the occasional finds of stone tools to the ancestors of the Chinese, but view them with superstitious fear. As between ascribing certain stone finds to the Chinese or non-Chinese tribes, the more probable supposition seemes to be that the latter were the manufacturers.

Some data on the Lolo, one of the aboriginal tribes inhabiting parts of the Chinese provinces of Szechuan, Yun-nan, and Kueichou, have been published by Herbert Müller. The Lolo do not form either a cultural or a physical unit, but belong together linguistically, all groups speaking tongues of Tibeto-Burman type. The Lolo of Kienchang in southern Szechuan are divided into two endogamous castes, the Nosu and Lesu, to which there is in some districts added a third class largely composed of captives and occupying the position of slaves. Even where the slave class is lacking, however, the social status of the castes differs, members of the Nosu devoting themselves exclusively to war, the chase, and horse-breeding, and leaving agriculture and other occupations to the Lesu. The Nosu differ from the rest of the population in their coiffures and the wearing of sandals. Culturally the Lolo present a primitive type. Metallurgy was originally unknown to them and pottery still is. Their own industries seem to be limited to the felting of garments, woodwork, tanning of skins, and the preparation of a varnish. Felted raincoats form the most characteristic articles of clothing. Their weapons consist of a long lance, a sword of Tibetan form, a small but strong bow and poisoned arrows resting point upward in a three-part quiver of possibly old Chinese pattern. The leather armor is of elaborate make, consisting of two large plates for the back and chest and a series of smaller plates, all of thick leather varnished yellow on the inside and red without. Lolo culture in general seems to indicate a fusion of a distincty primitive with a distinctly high civilization.

Oceania. In reporting the results of explorations in the Bismarck Archipelago, Friederici develops some important ideas on the old problem of the connection between Oceanian and New World cultures, which has recently received considerable attention from Graebner. Friederici personally inclines to the view that the Malayo-Polynesian culture had representatives who reached the shores of America, though he regards the proof as insufficient. Among the parallels emphasized by him are the taboo against uttering one's own name, which occurs in his own field from Geelvink Bay to the Solomon Islands, and the use of mnemotechnic strings by both the Borrial of northwestern New Britian and the ancient Peruvians. Friederici insists, however, that even if Polynesians crossed the Pacific this must have taken place in relatively recent times and their influence cannot be accounted very great. Friederici insists that many parallels may be due to independent development due to the similarity of conditions, and thus takes a view decidedly opposed to that of Graebner. His position coincides very closely, however, with that of Dr. Dixon as expressed in the vice-presidential address at the Washington meeting of the American Association for the Advancement of Science (in *Science*, XXXV., pp. 46-55). Dixon does not deny that certain curious coincidences may be due to historical contact, but is equally convinced that American Indian culture is essentially of independent growth. From another point of view this conclusion has also been reached by Lowie (see above).

Torres Straits. Under the heading of "Arts and Crafts" (Vol. IV. of the *Reports of the Cambridge Anthropological Expedition to Torres Straits*), Professor Haddon, with the aid of several collaborators, has published a monograph on the material culture of the area. Generally speaking, the Torres Straits Islanders were horticulturists, but the Muralry people and their closest relatives are rather nomadic, depending upon wild fruit rather than on the cultivation of the soil. Owing to the absence of large game there was practically no hunting, but both sexes indulged in the quest for sea animals, the men specializing in the search for dugong and turtle while the women and children collected shellfish and fish imprisoned on the reefs. Basketry and plaitwork are the most important arts practised; the absence of string bags, so characteristic of New Guinea and Australia, is noteworthy. The dwellings differed considerably in the several groups of islands. Thus, in the east a round thatched hut was constructed, while the northern type of house was invariably built on piles and that of other islands represented the gable roof form. Bows and arrows, stone-headed clubs, and, in the west, the javelin and spear-thrower are the most characteristic weapons. The last-mentioned is known to have been borrowed from the Australians. Among the most typical art products of the Straits are masks and effigies. Some of these are carved out of a single block of wood, but the most remarkable ones are of turtle-shell. These may represent either the human face or a complete animal, which may or may not be combined with a human face. The artistic skill exemplified in the construction of these elaborate masks also appears in the ornamentation of various articles of daily use. The extensive and faithful representation of animal forms is especially noteworthy. In the field of art there is very close relationship with the culture of the adjacent mainland of New Guinea and of the islands at the mouth of the Fly River.

Neuhauss, in a new work on German New Guinea, records observations on the Pygmies of that territory. The Pygmies no longer constitute distinct tribes, but there are many reversions to the Pygmy type in different regions, notably in the vicinity of Saddle Mountain. The Pygmies must be carefully distinguished from pathologically stunted Papuans. A short-trunked, long-limbed person, even if only 142 cm. in height, must be considered a dwarfish Papuan. On the other hand, men below 150 (and women below 140) cm. who have a long trunk and short extremities, a convex upper lip, a lobeless ear, and a relatively considerable tendency toward brachycephaly are p a y representatives of the Pygmy race. Neuhauss also classifies the remaining populations of German New Guinea. The Papuans are old inhabitants, though more recent arrivals than the Pygmies, but the Melanesians are fairly recent intruders from the north and east, who occupied the coast or neighboring islands and have driven the Papuans into the interior without much racial blending taking place. Although there are many exceptions, the Melanesians are generally a coastal people. Politically they have gained a position of ascendancy and levy tribute from the Papuan natives, whom they dominate partly through their superiority as navigators, which enables them to cover large extents of territory.

Africa. A number of valuable special studies have been published on African ethnography, of which may be mentioned a study of Thonga social life by Junod. The Thonga are a Bantu tribe extending from the neighborhood of St. Lucia Bay on the Natal coast northward up to the Sable River. Junod describes with great detail the initiation rites by which every fourth or fifth year all boys from ten to sixteen are admitted into the tribe. After running the gauntlet between two rows of initiated men who whip them, the boys are stripped of clothing and circumcised, whereupon they are secluded for three months in a carefully enclosed elliptical place tabooed to women, who are killed if by chance they catch sight of the leaves covering the wounds of the newly initiated. The novices are subjected to various trials of endurance and learn esoteric formulæ in addition to receiving practical instructions as to methods of hunting game. Toward the close of the probationary period they drink a medicine for purification and are taught to perform a masked dance, the masks forming a very high helmet protruding like a beak in front. During the last night the novices are not allowed to sleep, but are led to a pool to wash, receive a final admonition and return in a grand procession to the capital of the tribal chief, where they are now recognized as full-fledged members of the tribe. A girls' puberty ceremony is not common to all the Thonga, but does occur among the northern groups. Several girls are secluded for a month, during which period they are obliged to take a daily bath in a pool, must submit to maltreatment on the part of their guardians, and receive instructions as to sexual matters.

Meinhof has made a comparative study of a number of African languages: Ful as probably the oldest of Hamitic tongues; Haussa as a West African dialect of Hamitic that has been influenced by Sudanese; Shilh as a representative of Berber speech; Bedauye as the northernmost of East African Hamitic languages; Somali; Masai; and the Nama dialect of Hottentot. In addition to important results of a purely linguistic character, such as the discovery of "polarity," viz. the tendency for masculine nouns to assume plurals of feminine form and vice versa, Meinhof arrives at conclusions of more general ethnological interest. All the languages dealt with appear to him as members of the Hamitic stock. All of them differ fundamentally in structure from the Sudanese languages, so that whatever resemblances occur must be due to recent borrowing. On the other hand, there are remote affinities with the Semitic and affinities still more remote with Indo-Germanic languages. Certain resemblances exist between the Hamitic and Bantu stocks, but the latter also display traits shared with the Sudanese dialects.

Pöch has expressed interesting views as to the famous Rhodesian antiquities to which some investigators have ascribed an Asiatic origin. According to Pöch, the stone ruins are not the remains of habitations but of fortifications, and the geological conditions of southern Rhodesia, where granite blocks of various sizes abound, invite such stone structures even among the Bantu of to-day, so that the theory of an alien origin appears unnecessary.

The Duke of Mecklenburg has published a popular account of his second trip to Africa, indicating some significant discoveries. The main body of the expedition proceeded from the mouth of the Congo to the Ubangi confluence, then up the Ubangi to Ft. de Possel, and thence northward through the Ubangi-Shari district to the Lake Chad region. In Bagirmi stone axes and hammer-like implements were discovered. The aborigines of this region have no cattle of their own, but secure milk from the immigrant Arabs and Fulbe. Special attention was paid to the interesting variations in Sudanese architecture, the circular ground plan common in the region being associated with all kinds of superstructures. Thus, the Gabri of the Benue district have bee-hive huts carefully thatched in the upper half, but with the lower part of the walls formed merely of long grass stalks descending irregularly toward the ground; the typical Bagirmi huts are walled with mats; and the Massa of the central Logone have thatched roofs and clay walls. Most peculiar of all are the houses of the Musgum living between the Logone and Shari Rivers, which are pointed conical clay structures, the outside of which is decorated with curious bosses arranged to form a regular and distinctive pattern. The Musgum women wear flat discs in the upper and lower lips, causing a beak-like projection that suggests the appearance of the similarly deformed women of several South American and East African tribes. A detachment of the expedition under Drs. Schultze and Mildbraed ascended the Ssanga and Djah Rivers, exploring southeastern Kamerun and marching thence to the coast. In the southeast they discovered Pygmies speaking a language distinct from that of the neighboring tribes, while the coastal Pygmies spoke merely the Mabea dialect of Bantu. The Pygmies are the elephant hunters of the region. They employ neither bows and arrows nor pitfalls on the hunt, but rely exclusively on long thrusting-spears. Another detachment under Dr. Schubotz traversed the Uele district toward the Nile, and made important observations on the Azande and Mangbettu. The Azande are divided into two sharply separated groups, the Abungura, who inhabit round huts with conical tops; and the Abandja, who dwell in rectangular houses with thatched pyramidal roofs and whitewashed clay walls decorated with paintings.

Congresses, Societies, Expeditions. The XVIII international Americanist Congress met in London from May 27 to June 1, the United States being represented by Professors MacCurdy and Boas and Dr. Hrdlička. The agitation for a general anthropological congress not limited to the discussion of American problems was continued during the session. In September an international Congress of Anthropology and Archæology convened in Geneva. The first International Eugenics Congress met in London from July 24 to July 30. The Amercian Anthropological Association and the American Folk-Lore Society met in Cleveland, O., from December 30, 1912 to January 2, 1913. Professor Dixon was elected president, and Professor Kroeber ranking vice-president of the Anthropological Association, and all other officers were reëlected. The Folk-Lore Society reëlected last year's officers. In the interests of the Bureau of American Ethnology Dr. Swanton has continued his investigations of the Southeastern Indians now resident in Oklahoma and Dr. Michelson has been engaged in studying several Algonkin languages. Doctor Hrdlicka, of the United States National Museum, visited the Upper Yenisei region of Siberia. The American Museum of Natural History equipped expeditions to the Northern Blackfoot and Western Sioux (Dr. Wissler); Ute, Crow, and Eastern Sioux (Dr. Lowie); to the Menomini (Mr. Skinner); and began an archæological reconnaissance of the lower Rio Grande district (Mr. Nelson). Professor Dixon of Harvard has been in India in order to study some of the aboriginal populations there. Professor Starr of Chicago has made a trip to West Africa. Under the auspices of the Geological Survey of Canada Dr. Goldenweiser has investigated the social organization and religion of the Iroquois, while Mr. Waugh has devoted himself to the material culture of these tribes: Dr. Radin began work on the Ojibwa; and Mr. Barbeau continued field-work among the Wyandot. Dr. Fewkes, by the coöperation of the Bureau of American Ethnology and Mr. George G. Heye, was enabled to resume his archæological researches in the

West Indies. The International School of American Archæology and Ethnology in Mexico continued its linguistic and archæological studies throughout the year, the work of the first half of the year being under the supervision of Professor Boas. Among his collaborators were Doctors Radin and Mason. Professor Moorehead of Phillips Academy, Andover, Mass., conducted an archæological survey of Maine.

ANTI-BOYCOTT ASSOCIATION, AMERICAN. See BOYCOTT.

ANTIGUA. A presidency of the Leeward Islands (q. v.). United with it are the islands of Barbuda and Redonda. Negroes form the bulk of the population. St John, the capital (also the capital of the Leeward Islands colony), had (in 1911) 7910 inhabitants. There are no rivers and few springs in Antigua and droughts are frequent. Sugar, cotton, and pineapples are raised, the land under cultivation approximating 52,414 acres. In 1911, 11,075 tons of sugar and 5380 puncheons of molasses were produced. Trade (exclusive of internal) and finance statistics are shown below for four years:

	1907-8	1908-9	1909-10	1910-11
Imports..	£164,587	£175,587	£139,496	£170,033
Exports..	172,410	179,106	114,122	196,184
Revenue.	50,619	51,502	48,583	52,326
Exp'd'ure	46,967	49,964	49,204	53,495
Shipping*	567,678	722,862	643,966	644,705

* Tonnage entered and cleared.

Total customs revenue (1910-11), £31,782. Public debt (1910), £129,900. The governor of the colony is the administrator of Antigua. See LEEWARD ISLANDS.

ANTIQUITY OF MAN. See ANTHROPOLOGY.

ANTI-SALOON LEAGUE. See LIQUOR REGULATION.

ANTISEPTICS. See LISTER, JOSEPH, BARON.

ANTI-VIVISECTION. See VIVISECTION.

ANTWERP, PORT OF. See DOCKS AND HARBORS.

APPALACHIAN FOREST RESERVE See FORESTRY.

APPLES. See HORTICULTURE.

APPOINTMENTS. See NAVAL PROGRESS, *Great Britain. General Progress.*

AQUEDUCTS. The Catskill aqueduct to supply Greater New York, and the Los Angeles aqueduct in California, continued to be the most important projects in this department of engineering. Both were reaching completion at the end of the year and both involved extensive distribution systems. In Europe no structures comparable with these were in progress, and outside of some work in Great Britain little of importance was to be recorded.

CATSKILL AQUEDUCT. During 19'2 progress on the great project for the Catskill water supply to the Greater City of New York was made, and it had reached a point where much of the work was being carried on above the surface of the ground. The huge siphon passing 1100 feet below the Hudson River at Storm King was concreted and many of the sections of the aqueduct proper which range from 12 to 17 feet in diameter were finished. In New York City the deep water pressure tunnel was being excavated in the rock from the various shafts which had been sunk at short intervals through the city. The Ashokan dam was practically completed at the end of the year, and progress had been made on the great Kensico dam, forming the storage reservoir for the city supply, the completion of which it was expected would not occur until 1920. The Kensico dam, which is 300 feet in height above the lowest part of its foundation, is almost 2000 feet in length, and was being built across the valley of the Bronx River just above the village of Valhalla. It was designed to impound a body of water 5 miles long by 4¼ broad at the widest point, or about 2218 acres with an irregular shore line at a height 15 feet below the top of the dam. The Catskill aqueduct was to empty into this lake near the northern end and the outlet will be at the centre of the western side, along which will be built a large by-pass through which water can enter the main supply aqueduct of the City of New York without passing through the reservoir. The Kensico dam is estimated to contain about 1,000,000 cubic yards of masonry, and the accompanying table has been prepared to show how it compares in size and massive construction with other similar works:

	Cubic yards
Kensico (estimated, in dam itself)..	1,000,000
Croton (New York City water supply), familiarly known as "New Croton"	855,000
Assouan (Egypt)	704,000
Ashokan (Board of Water Supply New York City), under construction 1912	550,000
Tansa (Bombay, India, Water Works)	408,500
McCall's Ferry (Pennsylvania)......	300,000
Mochne (Germany)	353,200
Roosevelt (Arizona)	340,000
Gillepe (Belgium)	325,000
Wachusett (Boston water supply)...	266,700
Cataract (Australia)	146,300

The Kensico dam was to be constructed with broad sloping buttresses of granite supporting the down stream face, divided into 22 panels of rough granite masonry with massive cut stones for the borders of the panels. This material was being obtained from a quarry but a few hundred yards distant from the dam, and was particularly available for this purpose. The dam was designed with expansion joints to provide for the action of frost and water and with drainage wells which carry off the inevitable leakage that must take place in such a structure. The dam itself was to be surmounted by a roadway 28 feet in breadth and was not to include the spillway, as this was to be built in a gully on the eastern hill, that lent itself to such a specific purpose. At the end of the year the excavations for the dam foundation were practically finished, and the preparations were being made for laying the cyclopean masonry which will form the bulk of the inside of the great dam. The construction is unique in that the rock required for the masonry and for the crushed stone is found on the site, so that work can be prosecuted with great economy. Wherever possible electric power is used, which is supplied by contract from high-tension lines.

LOS ANGELES AQUEDUCT. This huge project,

the progress of which has been noted in previous issues of the YEAR BOOK, in 1912 was rapidly nearing completion. During the year attention was directed particularly to the large inverted steel siphons used for crossing deep canyons and broad valleys. These steel pipes, which are among the largest ever constructed, range in length from 611 to 15,696 feet and vary in diameter from 8 ft. 6 in to 11 ft., being constructed of steel ranging from ¼ in. to 1⅛ in. in thickness, the thickness of course depending upon the pressure in the section where the siphons are required. For the shallower depressions where the pressure is light, reinforced concrete was used in building the siphons, but if the head is great, as in the case of the siphon crossing the Jawbone Canyon, where it amounts to 850 feet, the thickest steel is required. This particular siphon has a length of 8095.51 feet, but this is not the longest, as in the Antelope Valley, an arm of the Mojave Desert 35 miles from the nearest railway, 15,596 feet of steel pipe 10 feet in diameter were being laid, connecting at either end with concrete pipes designed to resist a lower pressure. At the lowest point in this siphon two 24-inch double disk Rensselaer gate-valves were placed, both for cleaning and for regulating the pressure, as in case of accident, to the main aqueduct the flow could be diverted into the canyons with less damage than at the point of failure. The nine-mile siphon exclusive of the piers cost $18.47 per linear foot or at the rate of $5.18 per hundred weight, while in the case of the siphon crossing the Soledad Canyon even cheaper costs were effected. Here two sections were riveted together and a 12-foot length was hoisted into its position on the line. The estimated cost of the entire project was $24,500,000 and the work, prosecuted by the Los Angeles Water Board itself, was being efficiently and economically carried on.

MANCHESTER AQUEDUCT. The project of increasing the water supply of Manchester by the construction of a third pipe line from Lake Thirlmere made satisfactory progress during the year, and the northern and middle sections were completed, and the various siphons were in course of being tested. On the southern section the pipe-laying was almost finished, as were the various crossings of railways, canals, etc. A notable subway 600 feet long and 14 ft. 6 in. in diameter had been built under the Manchester Ship Canal to carry the steel pipes, and this also was virtually completed at the end of the year.

GLASGOW. The project for increasing the water supply of Glasgow from Loch Arklet was nearing completion, and the tunnel leading to Loch Katrine was completely driven through during the year, the inlet basin at the west end being about half-finished. The project involved a large dam, a system of diverting pipes and other controlling works, and was reaching such completion that the use of the works in 1913 was anticipated.

ARABIA. See TURKEY.

ARBITRATION, INTERNATIONAL. The treaties of general arbitration signed August 3, 1911, between the United State and Great Britain and France (see YEAR BOOK 1911), which were so widely debated while pending before the Senate, were formally ratified by that body on March 7, 1912, by a vote of 76 to 3, but only after they were amended by a vote of 42 to 40 by striking out the following: "It is further agreed, however, that in cases in which the parties disagree as to whether or not a difference is subject to arbitration under Art. I. of this treaty, that question shall be submitted to the Joint High Commission of Inquiry; and if all or all but one of the members of the Commission agree and report that such difference is within the scope of Art. I., it shall be referred to arbitration in accordance with the provisions of this treaty." In the opinion of the advocates of these treaties the Senate's amendments deprived them of much of their special merits, but the treaties even as amended are important steps in advance because for the first time they make the legal character of a question the test of its arbitrability. Previous treaties have left arbitrability to the capricious judgment of the disputants at the very time when their dispute was hottest.

The year 1912 has seen few new treaties of arbitration negotiated. This was largely due to the fact that the 154 existing treaties pretty well cover the ground. The World Peace Foundation has prepared the following chronological summary of these treaties: 1899, 3; 1901, 1; 1902, 12; 1903, 6; 1904, 26; 1905, 23; 1906, 4; 1907, 5; 1908, 22; 1909, 32; 1910, 18; 1911, 10; 1912, 1. Gross total, 163. Duplicated supersessions, 9. Net total, 154. Notwithstanding that the field has been so widely covered and that the Spanish-American countries are so busily building up an extensive network of bipartite treaties, there is a general impression that there has been a slight recession in the movement for international arbitration, an impression which is strengthened by the fact that the trustees of the Nobel prize fund are of the opinion that nothing occurred during 1912 of sufficient merit in this realm or that of the peace movement to justify the award of the Nobel Peace Prize. Another fact to the same effect has been the prevalence of war—first between Italy and Turkey, and later between the Balkan States and Turkey. These, however, are generally recognized as wars which could not be arbitrated any more than could the late Civil War in the United States.

The French Ministry of Foreign Affairs has established a bureau to deal with questions of international arbitration and the periodic Hague conferences. This bureau's duties are "the conclusion of treaties of arbitration with certain states and the search for the formulas best adapted to the circumstances" in the case of all states.

There has been steady progress in the arrangements between the United States and Great Britain to carry out the provisions of the North Atlantic Fisheries arbitration award of the Hague Court and to adjust the pecuniary claims between the two nations. This work does not seem to have been impeded in any way by the fate of the treaty with Great Britain or by the Panama affair. An agreement was reached November 15 between the American government and that of Great Britain as to the composition of the tribunal for the arbitration of these claims. Sir Charles Fitzpatrick, Chief Justice of Canada, will represent Great Britain, and Chandler P. Anderson, counselor of the Department of State, will represent the United States. The third member of the tribunal will be chosen by these two, and will not be a citizen of either the United States or of Great Britain. Cecil J. B. Hurst, of the British Foreign Office, will be chief counsel for Great Britain, and Edmund L. Newcombe, Canadian Deputy Minister of Justice, will be associated with him. Severo Mallet-Prevost, of New York, will be chief counsel for the United States. Robert Lansing, one of the counsel for the United States in the fisheries arbitration and the Alaska boundary arbitration, will be associated with him. The amount claimed on both sides amounts to about four million dollars, and a schedule of these claims has already been agreed upon. The treaty (that of July 20, 1912) under which this tribunal is created provides that all outstanding claims between the two countries shall be submitted to arbitration, and a supplemental schedule may be submitted to the tribunal before it meets early in the year 1913. For an account of the question with Great Britain concerning the Panama Canal tolls, see PANAMA CANAL.

UNITED STATES AND CANADA. The International Joint Commission between the United States and Canada met in Washington January 11, 1912, in accordance with the treaty between the United States and Great Britain, signed January 11, 1909, and proclaimed May 13, 1910. In the words of Commissioner Tawney "the treaty has provided a means for frank, direct and constant relations between the two great neighboring peoples who inhabit the greater part of the North American continent and who must live in amicable relations to realize the ultimate ideal of an Anglo-Saxon civilization. This commission constitutes the medium for this direct communication, and to it, by the express terms of the treaty, may be referred for consideration and settlement all questions of differences that may arise between the peoples living along one common frontier . . . . it expressly authorizes, clothes this commission with jurisdiction to consider and determine all questions of difference, without reservations or qualifications of any kind . . . This may be called a miniature Hague Tribunal of our own; just for us English-speaking nations of the continent of North America." The American Commissioners are: James A. Tawney, Frank Sherwin Streeter, and George Turner. The Canadian Commissioners are: T. Chase Casgrain, Henry A. Powell, and Charles A. McGrath.

THE ALSOP CLAIMS. Early in September, 1912, these claims were paid, and what some years ago threatened the amicable relations between the United States and Chile was settled finally with only passing comment. The Alsops did business in Peru, Bolivia, and Chile, dealing in guano, hides, and minerals. These three nations a generation ago were involved in a war in the progress of which property of this country was destroyed. The first two countries named settled the claims against them, but Chile refused on the ground that the claims had to do with certain lands which had been subsequently ceded by Bolivia to Chile. The American government proposed arbitration by the Hague Tribunal, but this was not welcomed by the Chilean government, which finally consented, however, to refer the claims to the good offices of Edward VII., King of England, as arbitrator. On the King's death the dispute was submitted to his successor, George V. In August acting on the report of Lord Desart, Lord Robson, and Mr. Hurst, whom he had designated to study the case, King George pronounced his award, assigning a sum about one-third as much as the original amount of the claim to the Alsops in full settlement. In commenting upon this satisfactory outcome of the only outstanding disputed question with Chile, *The Outlook* said: "The case is generally interesting as being one of the few nowadays for which the good offices of the International Court of Arbitration at the Hague were not successfully invoked. Chile, though evidently willing to have the matter settled by arbitration, would not accede to our government's request to submit the case to the Hague court. Doubtless the Chileans thought that they might come off with better grace by submitting to more old-fashioned and more elastic arbitral methods. At all events, Latin-American pride seemed ruffled at a suggestion of the Hague's supposedly sterner justice. The old order naturally persists, especially among emotional peoples."

OTHER LATIN-AMERICAN QUESTIONS. The Hague Tribunal on May 3, 1912, rendered an arbitral award in regard to the claim of the Canevaro Brothers, in which it decided that the Peruvian government should pay to the claimants the sum of £39,811, 8s., 1d., with interest in the sum of £9338, 17s., 1d. The Chamizal district near El Paso, Tex., has long been in dispute between Mexico and the United States. About two years ago it was decided to arbitrate the ownership of the disputed land and to mark a boundary. A joint commission was organized and has been at work for over a year, and this troublesome question will in all likelihood be satisfactorily and definitely settled at an early date. A commission appointed March 30, 1911, to determine the Bolivia-Peru boundary question presented its report in July, 1912. Another commission for the settlement of a similar question has been appointed. On December 20, 1912, the American state department was advised that the Ecuadorean government had appointed an arbitrator in the dispute between tnat government and the Guayaquil and Quito Railway Company. This railroad, an American corporation, in 1911 had rendered extensive service to the Ecuadorean government on account, especially during a revolution. Ecuador made no provision to pay, but kept on using the service. The United States interposed its good offices and in 1912, at the request of Ecuador, both governments named arbitrators to pass upon the claims under the terms of the railroad contract. The Santo Domingo-Haiti boundary line uncertainty has been temporarily cleared up by the United States which has indicated a provisional line without prejudice to the rights of either and arranged for the determination of the *de jure* line. On January 21, 1912, a treaty of peace between Argentina and the United States of Colombia was signed, in which practically every question involving sovereign rights in international disputes, except those which may conflict with provisions of the constitution of either country, may be settled by arbitration. The United States is preparing a protocol submitting to arbitration the claim of John Celestine Landreau against Peru, arising out of contracts and transactions in connection with the discovery and exploitation of guano that had been under discussion since 1874.

EUROPEAN QUESTIONS. On November 11, 1912, the Hague Tribunal rendered a decision in the long-standing indemnity dispute between Turkey and Russia, dating back to the war of

1877-1878. The decision was favorable to Turkey and involved the question of additional interest on the war indemnity. The Turko-Italian War resulted in a question between Italy and France relative to the seizure of the French mail steamers *Carthage* and *Manouba* in January. On March 6, 1912, it was agreed to leave the matter to the Hague court and the case comes up for trial in March, 1913. (See FRANCE, *History*.) The stopping of the *Tavignano* at about the same time caused the appointment of a commission of inquiry, which reported in July to the principals a decision which will be reviewed by the Hague court in connection with the other case.

PRESIDENT TAFT AS A PACIFIST. In the view of the American Peace Society, President Taft has been more than a moralizing philosopher. In the words of its organ, *The Advocate of Peace*, "he has attempted and accomplished large concrete things for the cause of international peace. The expansion of the Bureau of Trade Relations has been not only a means of industrial advance, but of international goodwill. When confronted with the acute situation growing out of the question of Japanese competition with our laborers of the Pacific States, he not only avoided the 'competition' by means of a treaty with Japan, but doubled our exports to that country in three years, and brightened perceptibly the chances of an unlimited arbitration treaty between the two countries. By influencing American bankers to participate in the Hukuang loan, and subsequently in the reform of Chinese currency, the friendship of China for the Untied States was promoted, our exports to that country increased 50 per cent. in two years, and international goodwill increased among the concert of great powers in China. It was President Taft's hand that preserved the independence of Liberia and brought back to life that interesting little waif of ours. During the Taft régime Venezuela has sloughed off Castro and enjoyed a fuller measure of peace. Zelaya has fortunately been deposed in Nicaragua and the Emery claim settled. The Alsop case has been disposed of and the troubles of a generation with Chile ended. American leadership has shown Nicaragua the way to financial integrity, and Honduras is about to accept our guidance in its business affairs, as has Santo Domingo. The boundary dispute between Panama and Costa Rica has been settled through the influence of the United States. The whole Central American situation has been spared further encroachments of Zelayaism by our government's recent stand for orderly government in that section. A 'United States of Central America' is appreciably nearer because of the Taft policy of Pan-American friendship and goodwill. President Taft's self-restraint before the turmoils of the Republic of Mexico has subserved the interests of 40,000 of our people residing in that country and been an inspiration to all Christian civilization. In conjunction with Argentina and Brazil he has been able to prevent war between Haiti and Santo Domingo, and to stop the onrush of civil war in Honduras. War in Cuba has been forestalled by vigorous warnings from our government. The fisheries dispute with Great Britain, dragging down through two generations, has been settled at the Hague. The Passamaquoddy Bay dispute has been arbitrated, and the seal fisheries disputes between our country, Great Britain, Japan, and Russia have at last been settled without a hint of arms. Three tantalizing cases have been satisfactorily settled with Venezuela. A boundary dispute between our country and Mexico has been referred to a commission. A treaty of arbitration covering ancient pecuniary claims between the United States and Great Britain has been ratified. The Taft administration has been indefatigable in promoting the International Court of Prize and the International Court of Arbitral Justice, the former a supreme court of war and the latter a supreme court of peace, both of which are all but established."

INTERNATIONAL CONGRESS OF CHAMBERS OF COMMERCE. The fifth congress, which met in Boston, September 24-26, 1912, and was attended by upwards of 500 foreign delegates, was in some aspects converted into a great arbitration congress. A thorough-going resolution was offered by the president, Mr. Canon-Legrand, declaring not only for the highest possible extension of international arbitration and the establishment of the court, but for the union of nations to avert the atrocity of war. French, English, German, and American voices seconded the resolution; and when it was passed amidst tumultuous applause, all present rose to their feet in the inspiration of the moment, and many sprang to their chairs and waved their hats. The meeting was regarded as highly significant and as a most important step toward the promotion of coöperation between the great commercial bodies of all nations and as advancing the cause of international peace.

UNIVERSAL PEACE CONGRESS. The nineteenth congress was held at Geneva September 23 to 28. In point of numbers it compared favorably with most of the preceding sessions, the enrollment reaching something over 500 (270 delegates and the rest individual members). Twenty countries were represented, namely, the United States, Germany, France, Austria, Russia, Italy, Spain, Great Britain, the Netherlands, Belgium, Denmark, Finland, Hungary, Norway, Sweden, Poland, Portugal, Switzerland, Turkey, and Egypt. There were twenty-nine delegates from the United States. As pointed out by the *Advocate of Peace*, "the composition of the congress, the size of the delegations from the European countries, and the general spirit of the meetings were a striking testimony to the deep and growing hold which the movement is taking on the Old World. The delegates were for the most part thoroughly serious and capable men and women, having a clear conception of the aims of the movement and sincerely and courageously consecrated to their realization. In this aspect of it the congress impressed us as one of the most notable ever held. The devotion and courage of the European pacifists seemed to us to have been deepened and intensified by the discouraging events of the past year." The congress did its work, as heretofore, through committees made up of representatives of the different countries. Each national delegation was allowed two representatives on each of the committees. These committees examined in advance all the important topics on the program and presented resolutions for discussion and adoption. These resolutions covered a great variety of subjects and made an extended programme. Prominent on the agenda were the subjects of limitation of armaments, arbitration treaties, a court of arbitral justice, the use of airships in war, the enforcement of arbitral awards, the causes of war, commercial boycott as a means of preventing wars, peace education, propaganda work, and a number of questions of current politics, namely, Alsace-Lorraine, Tripoli and Morocco, Egypt. There was considerable confusion at numerous sessions because of marked difference of opinion concerning Italian, Moroccan, and Egyptian questions.

The Seventeenth Conference of the Interparliamentary Union was held at Geneva, September 18 to 20 in conjunction with the Peace Congress. The enrollment reached 160. In former conferences the attendance has been three or four times that number. There were only four representatives from the United States group, namely, Senator T. E. Burton, Congressman Richard Bartholdt, Frank Plumley, and William D. B. Ainey, as against fifteen or twenty in other years. The absence of the Italian representatives, because of the war in Tripoli, also contributed seriously to the reduction of numbers. It was noteworthy that the men present were very largely those who are doing the real work of the Union in the different countries. The discussions dealt directly with the phases of the movement for which the Union has most stood—arbitration treaties, the court of arbitral justice, limitation of armaments. An effort was made to widen the scope of the labors of the Union, and it is probable that international relations generally will hereafter be included in the programme. Dr. A. Gobat, for years the executive secretary, a delegate from Switzerland, served as acting president.

THE WORLD CONFERENCES FOR PROMOTING CONCORD BETWEEN ALL DIVISONS OF MANKIND (G. Spiller, 63 South Hill Park, London, N. W., secretary) has issued a statement declaring among other matters that the present national congress secretariats and committees are requested to continue to act, and will be, if possible, extended to all countries; the national and local secretariats and committees should encourage their government, municipalities, associations, and clubs, etc., to admit no discrimination on the ground of race and color; they should organize annually one national and many local inter-racial conferences or public meetings; they should approach ministers of education, and other cabinent ministers subsidizing education, to permeate the teaching with racial concord; they should endeavor to win over the churches and other humanitarian organizations to the cause of inter-racial amity, and induce them to arrange for regular annual addresses on the subject; they should collect for the central executive an album containing at least 100 photographs of educated men and women of their country or people.

THE CONGRESS OF JURISTS provided for at the Third International American Conference at Rio de Janeiro, August 23, 1906, composed of one representative from each of the signatory states for the purpose of preparing a draft of a code of public international law and a draft of a code of private international law to regulate the relations between American nations was held in Rio de Janeiro, June 26, 1912. There were present delegates from fourteen states. Dr. Epitacio Pessoa of Brazil was chosen permanent president. A committee on permanent regulations reported that in view of the magnitude and difficulty of the task, the attempt to proceed immediately to the adoption of codes was impractical, but agreed to recommend the appointment of two special committees respectively to report drafts on extradition and the execution of foreign judgments. The draft prepared by the first committee was approved, but there was disagreement as to the second. The congress then provided for six sub-committees to prepare codes, four dealing with public international law and two with private international law, and to meet again at Rio de Janeiro in June, 1914, to hear the reports of these committees.

The Eighteenth Annual Lake Mohonk Conference on International Arbitration was held May 15-17 with President Nicholas Murray Butler as chairman. The international delegates were especially numerous. The founder of these conferences, Albert K. Smiley, died in November, 1912, at Redlands, Cal., in his eighty-fifth year. Under his thoughtful and effective leadership these conferences have exercised a wide influence on the movement for international arbitration and justice. In the judgment of competent observers no one man in his generation accomplished more for it. He lived to see the principle of arbitration well established. The conferences will be continued by his brother and coadjutor, Daniel Smiley.

THE AMERICAN ASSOCIATION FOR INTERNATIONAL CONCILIATION (407 West 117th street New York City) has issued the following leaflets during 1912: Special Bulletin: "War Practically Preventable, and Agreements for Universal Peace," by Rev. Michael Clune, June, 1912; "The International Mind," opening address at the Lake Mohonk Conference on International Arbitration, by Nicholas Murray Butler, June, 1912; "The Irrationality of War. On Science as an Element in the Developing of International Good Will and Understanding," by Sir Oliver Lodge, July, 1912; "The Interest of the Wage-earner in the Present Status of the Peace Movement": address delivered at the Lake Mohonk Conference on International Arbitration, by Charles Patrick Neill, August, 1912; "The Relation of Social Theory to Public Policy," by Franklin H. Giddings, September, 1912; "The Double Standard in Regard to Fighting," by George M. Stratton, October, 1912; "As to Two Battleships," contributions to the debate upon the Naval Appropriation Bill in the House of Representatives, November, 1912; "The Cosmopolitan Club Movement," by Louis P. Lochner, December, 1912; "The Spirit of Self-Government:" address delivered at the 144th Anniversary Banquet of the Chamber of Commerce of the State of New York, by Elihu Root, January, 1913. A small edition of a monthly bibliography of articles having to do with international matters has also been published and distributed to libraries, magazines, and newspapers.

Leaflets issued previously included papers by Baron d'Estournelles de Constant, George Trumbull Ladd, Elihu Root, Barrett Wendell, Charles E. Jefferson, Seth Low, William James, Andrew Carnegie, Philander C. Knox, Pope Pius X., Heinrich Lammasch, Norman Angell, and others.

THE WORLD PEACE FOUNDATION (formerly the International School of Peace), 290 Beacon street, Boston, has issued the following pamphlets during 1912: No. 4, part I., "Concerning Sea Power," by David Starr Jordan; part II., "Heroes of Peace," by Edwin D. Mead;

part III., "International Good Will as a Substitute for Armies and Navies," by William C. Gannett. No. 5, part I, "The Drain of Armaments," by Arthur W. Allen; part II., "The Truth About Japan," by John G. De Forest; part III., "The Cosmic Roots of Love," by Henry M. Simmons; part IV., "World Scouts," by Albert Jay Nock; part V., "The Right and Wrong of the Monroe Doctrine," by Charles F. Dole. No. 6, part I., "The World Peace Foundation: Its Present Activities"; part II., "Neutralization: America's Opportunity," by Erving Winslow; part III., "William T. Stead and His Peace Message," by James A. Macdonald; part IV., "Educational Organizations Promoting International Friendship," by Lucia Ames Mead; part V., "Revised List of Arbitration Treaties," compiled by Denys P. Myers. No. 7, part I., "Heroes of the Sea," by W. M. Thackeray; part II., "The Forces that Make for Peace," by William J. Bryan. A full report of the activities of the Foundation was published in July as No. 6, part I.

The American Society for Judicial Settlement of International Disputes held its third annual conference in Washington, D. C., December 20-21, 1912. The first conference (Washington, 1910) was devoted to the subject of the advantages of, and the best way to secure, a true international court of justice. The second conference was devoted largely to the momentous question of the proposed arbitration treaties with Great Britain and France, and at the third conference the general subject of an international court and the essentials of the law to be applied therein were considered, as was also the subject of the sanctions of international law. Governor Baldwin of Connecticut presided. The Society during 1912, published the following leaflets: "The Proposed Arbitration Treaties With Great Britain and France," by William Howard Taft (February, 1912); "Non-Justiciable Disputes and the Peace Treaties," by Omer F. Hershey (May, 1912); "The International Grand Jury," by William I. Hull (August, 1912); "The Court of Arbitral Justice," by James Brown Scott (November, 1912).

The Fourth Central American Conference was held at Managua, Nicaragua, January 1-20, 1912, with representatives from Costa Rica, Salvador, Gautemala, Honduras, and Nicaragua present. *The Pan-American Bulletin* gives as the purpose of these annual conferences "to consider the most efficient and proper means of bringing uniformity in the economic and fiscal interests of Central America."

The Fourth American National Peace Congress will be held in St. Louis May 1, 2, 3, under the auspices of the Business Men's League of that city. The preceding congresses have been held as follows: New York, 1907; Chicago, 1909; Baltimore, 1911.

The Institute of International Law held an annual session at Christiania, Norway, August 24-31, 1912. A proposal was made by Alejandro and James Brown Scott to establish an American Institute of International Law.

The American Society of International Law held its sixth annual meeting at Washington April 25-27. The programme was devoted to the organization and procedure for the Third Hague Conference which is to meet on or about 1915. The Honorable Elihu Root presided.

Church Peace League. The federal council of the Churches of Christ in America, at its quadrennial conference in Chicago, December 9, adopted the following plank, submitted by Rev. Charles E. Beals, Field Secretary of the American Peace Society: "The Council favors the organization of a church peace league in America, the annual observance of peace Sunday by the churches, and the memorializing of the Third Hague Conference in behalf of the establishment of a permanent court of international justice and the adoption of such other measures as shall render war unnecessary and impossible. It calls upon Christian men and women to unite in a demand that the teaching and spirit of Jesus be applied in international relations by our national Congress and Department of State."

ARBITRATION AND CONCILIATION, Industrial. It has come to be generally recognized that more efficient means of insuring industrial peace must be developed in the United States and Great Britain and on the continent of Europe. Various plans are in vogue designed to achieve this end, including trade agreements, various forms of arbitration and conciliation through representatives of both parties or through government officials, profit sharing, and welfare work. The necessity for continued industrial peace increases with the growing complexity of economic life. The increasing division of labor involves an increase of mutual dependence. The welfare of the public at large comes more and more to rest not only upon the various forms of public service utilities, but ever upon an increasing number of manufacturing, mining, and agricultural pursuits. Moreover, with the increase of class consciousness in the laboring population, accompanied as it is by the development of trade unionism, strikes tend to become wider in scope and therefore much more injurious to public convenience and welfare. There are those who hold that permanent industrial peace is impossible under the present organization of industry because of the necessary opposition between the interests of employer and employee. The one seeking profit fears his returns will diminish with every increase of wages or shortening of hours. At the same time, the doctrine that the public interest predominates over the interest of either employer or employee has been so widely accepted that both the latter parties have been forced by public opinion to effect reasonable agreements much more frequently than heretofore. Appeal must be made not to force, but to the sense of justice of the community. The tendency of thought therefore is toward either some form of compulsory arbitration enforced by the political sovereign or some form of public investigation with reliance upon public opinion to compel the disputants to accept the judgment of impartial arbitrators. Compulsory arbitration has met with considerable success in Australia and New Zealand. Compulsory investigation by an impartial board whose findings are enforced by public opinion is embodied in the Canadian Trades Disputes Investigation act. A similar law has been enacted in Wisconsin. Moreover, the Boston Chamber of Commerce in December took steps toward securing the enactment of such a law in Massachusetts. An inquiry by the British board of trade showed that European countries are now endeavoring to prohibit strikes in the public utilities or in the public services.

THE CLOAK AND SUIT INDUSTRY. One of the most unique forms of trade agreement yet effected in this country is that which followed the great strike in the ladies' garment industry of New York City. This industry includes about 2000 establishments employing 50,000 workers and representing $40,000,000 of capital; its annual output approximates $250,000,000. Under the agreement effected between the associated employers and the workers' union not only has peace been preserved, but conditions of workers have steadily improved. The union is definitely recognized and preference is given its members, though the closed shop is not maintained. This agreement provided for a grievance board of five representatives of the employers' association and five of the International Ladies' Garment Workers' Union. This meets weekly to settle all disputes as to wages and hours. Appeal may be made from this board to a permanent board of arbitration of three prominent citizens. In addition there is a joint board of sanitary control with representatives of the employer, the employed, and the public. This board has greatly reduced the danger from fire, has abolished basement shops and is steadily raising the sanitary conditions of the establishments. By the fall of 1912, 319 shops had been certificated as meeting all of 28 conditions laid down by the board. In addition a campaign of education by bulletins and lectures with reference to sanitary conditions is carried on. See STRIKES.

RAILWAY ENGINEERS. Late in 1911 the engineers of fifty-two eastern railroads, numbering about 30,000, made a demand for increased pay, uniform classification of service, and uniform working rules. Their demand being refused a referendum was held in January which showed 93 per cent. of the men ready to strike. Through the intervention of the commissioners, Neill and Knapp, under the Erdman act, the dispute was submitted to a board of arbitration composed of Oscar S. Straus, of New York, Charles R. Van Hise, president of Wisconsin University, Albert Shaw, of New York, Frederick W. Judson, of St. Louis, Otto M. Eidlitz, of New York, Daniel Willard, president of the Baltimore and Ohio Railroad, and P. H. Morrissey, representing the railway engineers. This board began hearings in July and rendered its decision in November. The award dated back to May 1, and holds until May 1, 1913. Advances in pay were granted, but not as extensive as the men demanded. The total annual increase in the engineer's wages of all the roads was estimated to be augmented by something over $2,000,000, whereas the original demands would have made a total increase of over $7,000,000. The larger and better roads were little affected, but on some small roads very extensive changes were made. The arbitration board reported in favor of a compulsory adjustment of disputes on public utilities by States or national wage commissions because of the fundamental importance of these industries to the welfare of all persons and all other industries. Mr. Morrissey did not assent to the rates fixed by the board because in his view they were based on unreliable statistics and because he objected to the principle of compulsory arbitration. This was believed to be the most important case of industrial arbitration from the viewpoint of public welfare since the great coal strike of 1902. The railroads involved operate 40 per cent. of the total mileage in the United States, covering the area east of Chicago and north of Virginia.

In May the firemen of these same roads put forward a demand for increased wages, for new rules as to hours and overtime, and for extra firemen on freight locomotives. Their demands were modified on December 18 to include extra firemen on only 2000 engines. Moreover, they preferred to arbitrate under the Erdman act rather than strike.

ANTHRACITE MINERS. The superiority of conciliatory methods to open hostility in effecting trade agreements was forcibly illustrated by the work of the anthracite conciliation board. This board was established by the commission which settled the strike of 1912. It is composed of six members, three representing each side. An award by majority is final. In case of the tie a federal circuit judge acts as umpire. This has brought about three successive agreements of three years each, the last expiring April 1, 1912. It also deals with grievances. During the first three years it dealt with 145 grievances and in the six years 1906-12 with 48. Altogether 25 cases were referred to the umpire. The agreement provides that no strike or lockout shall be declared during the deliberation of the board, but this rule has not been rigidly observed. Early in the year efforts were made to effect a new agreement. The anthracite miners, numbering about 175,000, demanded a 20 per cent. increase of wages, a one-year contract, a minimum scale of $3.50 per day for miners and $2.75 per day for laborers, and minor concessions. The coal operators refused. Agreement was finally reached early in May on the basis of a 10 per cent. increase in wages, but with the abolition of the sliding scale whereby wages were correlated with prices; the net gain to the miners was about 5½ per cent. Though the miners at first refused to accept this agreement and there was some rioting and mob violence leading to three deaths at the hands of the State constabulary, nevertheless their convention May 14 assented, largely because the union membership had fallen to less than 30,000 and union funds amounted to less than $200,000. The settlement was at once followed by an increase in the wholesale price of coal of 25 cents per ton. This increase would net the companies over and above the increase of wages an amount estimated at $4,000,000 to $6,000,000 a year. This occasioned universal public objection and caused investigations to be begun by many public authorities all over the eastern part of the country, including the United States district-attorney for Pennsylvania.

There was a similar cessation of work in bituminous mining in April, more than 2,000,000 men being idle. Adjustment of demands was made by conciliatory methods, an increase of five cents per ton being given.

CANADA. The Industrial Disputes Investigation act of 1907 has gained in favor. Growing out of a coal strike it was made to include not only mines but steam and electric railways, steamships, telephone and telegraph lines, and lighting and power works. The act requires that before a strike or lockout investigation must be made by a board to which each side appoints one member, these two choosing a chairman. In case of disagreement the government appoints the chairman. This board tries conciliation first; if this fails it investigates and publishes the facts and its decisions. Public opinion is relied on for enforcement, the disputants having legal right to cease operations. In more than five years up to December there had been 132 boards, of which 53 were in railways and 40 in mining. There had resulted only 15 strikes, only 4 of which were on railways. The act has thus been of great service to employers, employees, and the public.

AUSTRALASIA. The states of the Australian Commonwealth and New Zealand have thus far been most successful in dealing with trade disputes. They have developed two methods. One of these involves the use of wage boards and the other a resort to industrial courts. These two institutions are combined also. The Australian legislation is designed not only to preserve peace, but also to prevent sweating, by the establishment of a fair and reasonable level of wages. (See MINIMUM WAGE.) Therefore collective bargaining is encouraged; this has led in New South Wales to the legal incorporation of unions under prescribed conditions imposing legal responsibility on their funds. Indeed as a rule preference is given to the trade union because of its importance in enforcing collective responsibility. In New Zealand cases are taken up first by boards of conciliation, from which appeal may be made to the Industrial Court. Similarly in Victoria appeals may be made from wage boards to the Court of Industrial Appeals. Court decrees have sometimes been enforced by criminal processes, but usually the imposition of a fine is the penalty. It is reported that 80 per cent. of such fines are collected. The employers who at first were opposed have come quite generally to approve this legislation. On the other hand labor has for several years manifested discontent with it, probably because the gains in wages and conditions in recent years have been very small as compared with earlier years. Discontent is especially marked where unions are strongest. It is claimed that these acts have prevented the losses of strikes and lockouts for both employers and employees; the unnecessary and often cruel sufferings of women and children of strikers; and one of the causes of sickness, crime, and poverty among unskilled workers.

ARBUCKLE, JOHN. An American merchant and philanthropist, died March 27, 1912. He was born in Scotland in 1838 and was brought to the United States by his parents when he was still a child. His education was obtained in the public schools of Allegheny, Pa., where his family had settled. In 1871 he removed to New York City, where with his brother, Charles, he established the firm of Arbuckle Brothers. The specialty of the house was at first coffee sold in packages, and a large business was soon built up. Shortly afterwards John Arbuckle conceived the idea of selling sugar in the same manner and entered into an agreement with the late Henry O. Havemeyer by which the latter was to provide sugar. Such a large business was built up by retailing sugar in this manner that the American Sugar Refining Company decided to enter into the business itself and refused to supply it to Mr. Arbuckle. The latter thereupon began refining raw sugar and this precipitated a bitter fight with the sugar trust which continued for many years. In order to injure the Arbuckle coffee business the sugar trust began selling coffee in packages. In 1901 a compromise was arrived at, and while Mr. Arbuckle remained in the business of selling sugar, the sugar trust gave up the business of selling coffee. He became one of the foremost sugar makers of the United States and was perhaps the best-known coffee merchant engaged in business. In his later years he became much interested in philanthropic work and was particularly interested in making life easier for the working girl. A farm of 800 acres at New Paltz, N. Y., was used to give tired men and women from New York and Brooklyn outdoor work. In addition to his sugar and coffee enterprises he was engaged in the wrecking business and spent many years in working on a system for floating sunken ships. He put into successful operation a scheme for raising sunken vessels and driving out water by compressed air. Among the vessels which he raised by this plan were the United States cruiser *Yankee* and the United States collier *Nero*. John Arbuckle is said to have left a fortune of at least $20,000,000.

ARCHÆOLOGICAL INSTITUTE OF AMERICA. The annual meeting of this institute was held at Granville, O., December 26-31, 1912. The meeting of the American Philological Association was held in conjunction with it. In his report, President Francis W. Kelsey gave a sketch of the growth of the institute since 1902. He suggest the formation of a Committee on Egyptian Archæology to coördinate with the existing Committee on Medieval and Renaissance Studies. He also suggested the investigation of the possibility of procuring funds for the establishment of an American school in Peking, and the formation of a committee on museums, consisting of experts who will hold themselves in readiness to render assistance to affiliated societies in this part of their work. The council of the institute took favorable action on all these suggestions. On December 31, the absorption of the School of Classical Studies in Rome with the American Academy became complete and the school passed finally out of its subordinate relation to the institute. The movement to procure endowment for the school in Jerusalem made such progress during the year as to indicate that the institute will be relieved of further expense. During 1912 the demand came to the institute for several series of extension courses of lectures on archæological subjects, and the success of these courses was so great that ten similar courses have been arranged for 1913. Harry L. Wilson, of Johns Hopkins University, was elected president of the institute.

ARCHÆOLOGY. SYRIA AND PALESTINE. To the south of the "Street called Straight" in Damascus a series of streets forming concentric semicircles has been found, which is supposed to have enclosed the site of a theatre of Roman times. The houses within the semicircles are constructed on the top and sides of a great pile of rubbish. Among other discoveries made upon this site is to be mentioned that of a complete piece of the outer wall of an ancient temple. The wall is well preserved throughout its fifty feet of length and varies from twenty-seven to thirty feet in height. An inscription connected with the temple has been recovered; it mentions two men, Menedoros and Zenonos, as stewards of the temple, and is dated in the year 349 A. D. For some reason the name of Diocletian has been erased from the text of the inscription. Near Marash, in northern Syria, Garstang has discovered a royal monument of the Hittites. This monument is a slab of dolerite 1.20m. in height, by .66m. in breadth, by .34m. in thickness, and it bears upon the face of it in relief a man clad in the Hittite costume and holding a triangular shaped bow against his shoulder. The figure is posed upon the back of an animal with a short tail, while above the figure is a winged rosette, a sign of royal rank. The monument dates in the ninth century B. C. The same scholar, Garstang, has finished his search of the site of Sakhtje Genzi. By using sectional cuttings it has been possible to show that the strata penetrated date from the XVIIIth. to the XXVIth. dynasties of Egypt. This is especially valuable for the determination of Hittite chronology. In the course of the work on this site the temple and several Hittite houses were found.

EGYPT. Work on the great rock-cut temple of Abu-Simbel was brought to a close last season. In the course of clearing away the sand from the front of the entrance a wide terrace was brought to view, whereon was discovered a small temple in which stood an altar having two obelisks in front of it and a shrine beside it. The shrine contained a scarabœus and an ape, while upon the altar were four more apes. Across the whole breadth of the terrace was discovered a row of statues consisting of figures of the pharaoh alternating with those of the sacred hawk of the sun. These statues acting as standards emphasize tremendously the size of the great rock-cut colossi of the façade of the temple. The colossi themselves have been repaired by driving liquid cement into the fissures which time has caused in them.

At Abydos the Egyptian Exploration Fund is continuing its work. At present the Osireion, the underground temple devoted to the mysteries of Osiris, has received the most attention, where the secret entrance to the building is being sought. During the campaign a previously undisturbed tomb was opened. It was built of unbaked bricks and dated from Roman times. In it were twelve sandstone sarcophagi, each containing a mummy with the blue and gold painting upon the wrappings still fresh. In another place was discovered a XIIth. dynasty burial wherein was a woman's skeleton with bracelets of cowry shells and carnelian beads and a ring with five scarabs. Near by lay a silver nose ring, ornaments of shell, glass beads, and copper, and iron rings. In addition to accomplishing this work Naville, who is in charge of the excavations, partially unearthed a mastaba behind the temple of Seti. Its walls, of carefully joined blocks of quartzite, are nearly thirteen feet in thickness, and the structure dates, so the excavator thinks, before the reign of Menaptah, in whose reign it was previously supposed to belong. It is hoped that the building may prove to be the legendary tomb of Osiris.

Some thirty-five miles to the south of Cairo near the village of Tarkhan an extensive cemetery has been discovered dating from the earliest historic period down to the Pyramid period. Although many graves have been destroyed, about 600 have been found extending over an area of a mile in the desert. The cemetery is bound to be, so it is held, one of the standard sources for our knowledge of the early historic age of Egypt. The date of this most northerly settlement known for this early age is given by a tomb which was found to contain pottery of a pre-Menite king, and by another tomb containing pottery of Narmer-Mena. It is believed that the presence of so large a cemetery, belonging for the most part to a time before the time of Mena, argues that a chief town of this time must have been in the region of the present Kafr Ammar. This town antedated the founding of Memphis and seems to have been settled a few generations before the reign of Menes. If it was founded as the capital of the dynastic race before that of Memphis then it shows a stage in the conquest of the land by the kings of Abydos. Of especial interest is the unusual state of preservation exhibited by the wood and cloth found in the burials. Thus the linen in the earliest tombs was still fresh and strong, and large sheets from XIth. dynasty tombs were as sweet as if just woven; while pieces of wood used in the coffins were still as sound as when buried. The wood employed for this purpose was that which previously had been built into houses, as is shown by the fact that not only were many pierced along the edge so that they might be so lashed together in the dwelling that they might slide past one another when they shrank or expanded, but also by the fact that some were charred on the inside and weathered on the outside as they would have been had an old house been consumed by fire. So remarkable was the preservation of the burials in this cemetery that even the palm fibre and rush webbing of the bed frames were intact. Among the small finds, besides about 300 alabaster vessels and pottery, were four sealings of Narma-Mena, a king hitherto unknown.

At El-Gerzeh a pre-dynastic grave containing iron beads was opened. At Gurna the Germans have located three, and possibly four, chapels belonging to the XXth. or the XXIst. dynasties. Under these was found a building of Thothmes IV. In addition to this a number of tombs were opened in one of which were the sarcophagi of the great grandson and the granddaughter of Takelothis I. The work of the English at Heliopolis has demonstrated that the town had been deserted since the Persian invasion in 525 B. C. Darius evidently destroyed the city since he looked upon it as the key to Memphis. The temple enclosure was found to be three-quarters of a mile in length and surrounded by two walls forty to fifty feet in thickness, dating from the XIXth. dynasty. The great surprise came in the discovery, in the northwest corner, of an earth fortress of the same type as that at Tel el Yehudiyeh (see YEAR BOOK for 1907) which has been attributed by Petrie to the Hyksos invaders. The fort is of the same size and shape here as there, being a rounded square a quarter of a mile across and having a wall over 100 feet in thickness.

Early in the summer of 1912, the palace of Amenhotep III. at Memphis was laid bare. It was then found that the rows of houses in which the officials of the palace lived were inside the palace walls. A number of frescoes were discovered, among which may be mentioned those representing ducks in flight and pigeons rising from marshes of lotus and papyrus. Also at Memphis has been found a huge sphinx of alabaster. The monument lay between the two famous colossi and measured twenty-six feet in length and fourteen in height. It dates about 1300 B. C. At the northern gate of the temple of Ptah another sphinx of red granite, over eleven feet in length and seven in height, came to light. On it was an inscription of Rameses II. Near by was also found a life-sized, and perfect, group in red granite representing the same king and the god Ptah standing. Deep under the north gate was recovered a lintel of Amenemhat III., which indicates that he was the builder of the gate. Herodotus ascribes the gate to the same king under the Greek name Mœris. During the past season a greater part of the Ethiopian city at Meroë has been plotted and excavated. The palace, when excavated, was found to be equipped with a very elaborate system of baths of the plunge variety. The walls were decorated with rows of colored tiles ornamented with reliefs all in place. A small but perfect Roman temple was discovered as well as many statues in a new style of art apparently strongly influenced by Greek art, but marked by African peculiarities. Thus a "Venus" in the attitude of the "Medici" shows marked steatopygy.

Among the papyri discovered at Oxyrhynchus is a fragment of 400 lines from a satyr play by Sophocles. The play, which bears the name of the *Ichneutæ*, or the *Trackers*, deals with the exploits of Hermes, namely, his theft of Apollo's cattle and his invention of the lyre.

Asia Minor. In the island of Cos two hoards of coins have been discovered, the first comprising twenty-one drachmas dating from the third century B. C., and the second ten copper coins of the same date. At Miletus and Didyma the work is drawing to a close. Remains of a prehistoric settlement have been found on Kilitepe and the Hellenistic wall has been further searched and the general plan of the city made clearer. It is now known that the regular size of a block, or *insula*, was 29 x 55.50m., and the normal width of the streets was from 4.40 to 4.50m. Particularly interesting among the discoveries was that of a fine Corinthian structure in the southern market-place dedicated to Laodice, who was perhaps the wife of Antiochos II. The work on the baths of Faustina is finished. At Didyma the sacred way and the limits of the ancient town have been examined. More than half of the great temple has now been laid bare. All the columns are standing to the height of several meters. At both sides in the wall of the pronaos low, barrel-vaulted passages lead down to the Adyton, 4.50m. below. At Tchalef, the Hittite capital of the fourteenth century B. C., gigantic foundations, supposed to belong to the palace, have been excavated, and 170 almost perfect reliefs have been recovered. One represented a figure resembling Herakles.

The Americans at Sardis have this year cleared up the temple of Artemis. This meant that in the later part of the work a depth of fifty feet of earth had to be removed. In this part, however, the building was well preserved and presents an imposing appearance. The temple is a little over 100m. long and a little less than 50m. wide. It is octostyle pseudodipteral with twenty columns on the side. The cella contains two rooms of different sizes and on different levels. It is now believed that the east end of the fourth century temple was unfinished when it was so injured that it became necessary to take down most of its columns. This may have been at the time of the earthquake in the year 17 A. D. Near the temple was found an inscription 138 lines long, containing a letter from Augustus to the people of Sardis. Probably the most important discovery of the year was that of an inscription eight lines in length written in both Aramaic and in Lydian. This document is dated by a year in the reign of Artaxerxes and is almost perfectly preserved. By it a key to the Lydian tongue is afforded. Many tombs were opened this season, but they present no remarkable difference from those of last year.

Greece. During 1912, most of the excavations on old sites were continued. While the work has been rewarded with valuable results no site except that excavated by the Americans at Sardis has afforded anything of spectacular nature. In Athens the Greek Archæological Society has continued the work in the neighborhood of the Pnyx, and has opened a number of graves of different dates throughout the city. At New Phaleron seventy graves of the archaic period have been opened, and from them pottery of the Phaleron, Corinthian, and so-called Proto-Corinthian styles have been recovered These graves for the most part were those of children. At Anavysos, near Thorikos, tombs were excavated which contained styles of pottery running from the geometric to the black-figured styles; at Sunium investigation of the rubbish connected with the old temple of Athena has brought to light a number of votive offerings of the archaic period, including a lead figure of Apollo, a marble statuette of the so-called island type, and several scarabs.

From the Greek islands of the Ægean interesting results have been obtained. In Samos excavations have been continued on the site of the Heræum. Since no traces of internal supports were found, the assumption has been made that the building was hypæthral, or open to the sky. Although the temple was in the process of construction throughout the sixth century B. C., it was apparently never brought to completion. The columns were of both marble and poros, and in one case the two materials were so combined that a marble capital was superposed upon a poros shaft. Seventy column bases of the finest type of archaic work, belonging to the pre-Persian building were discovered in the foundations of the later structure. An interesting discovery in the neighborhood of the temple was an hemicycle containing a base of a statue inscribed with the name of M. Tullius Cicero.

Crete continues to offer its quota of material. At Gortyna the circular building into which the famous "Gortyn Code" was built has been cleared enough to prove that the building was an odeum restored by the Emperor Trajan. In the course of the work two new blocks of the inscription have been recovered. Near the basilica the excavators have uncovered a nymphæum which included a fountain of three basins and much sculpture. This building dated from the early imperial times, but continued to stand in place until the seventh century A. D., as is shown by an inscription of that date recording its restoration. The continuation of the work of the Italians at Hagia Triada has resulted in the discovery of an interesting and well-preserved shrine of the "Late Minoan III." period, and a large number of inscribed tablets, mostly accounts. At the same place a prehistoric town has been brought to light, having in its midst the "Lesser Palace." The oldest part of the town was to the west where the houses were located very closely together. In this locality many domestic utensils were recovered. The excavators also uncovered a small temple, which is of peculiar interest owing to the fact that its façade is supported by three columns resembling those shown in the panels at Cnossos. In eastern Crete, at Vrokastro, the Americans have been at work on a part of the geometric hill-town. The burial places revealed three types of interment, rock-cut tholoi, bone-chambers, and rock-shelters. The pottery was strongly reminiscent of the Minoan style, although together with it was found purely geometric ware. The inhabitants practiced both inhumation and cremation. Objects of bronze as well as iron were found in the burials. At Thasos the lower portion of a statue has been found at Osmanieh (Limena) which is of particular interest because it is the work of Philiscus the son of Polycharmus (see Pliny, *N. H.*, XXXVI, 34, 35). The fragment belonged to a statue of Artemis Polo.

In northern Greece, Pagasæ (see YEAR BOOK for 1911) has again proved a profitable site. From one of the southwest towers as many as 230 grave stelæ and fragments (almost all of them painted) have been recovered. One of the paintings represents two men, one standing and one seated, and is considered to be the best yet found on this site. As it will be remembered, this whole series was used in repairing the town wall probably in the year 191 B. C. The stelæ themselves date from the period reaching from the year 350 to *circa* 250 B. C. The temple of Athena at Gonnus, mentioned last year, has yielded a number of new inscriptions, architectural details, and small objects. At Halos in Phthiotis the English have opened ten cist-graves which contained inhumation burials and geometric pottery similar to that found in the island of Skyros. The largest of the tumuli in the locality when opened was found to contain sixteen burned pyres covered with stones and containing together with burned human remains, geometric pottery, iron swords, knives, spears, and bronze fibulæ, etc. The occurrence of burning and cremation at a distance of only half an hour, both of them in connection with geometric pottery is at present confusing. At Seskio, in Thessaly, five important geometric graves have been excavated, while at Dranitsa, in Dolopia, the remains of thirty-one bodies were found in a large chamber-tomb of the geometric period.

At Tanagra, in Bœotia, 150 graves dating from the sixth to the first century, B. C., were opened. The oldest graves were found to be pits containing ashes or shafts, containing unburned bones, although pithoi and terra-cotta sarcophagi were also in use in the sixth century. These early graves contained many objects—one grave alone having as many as 175 aryballi in it. The later graves consisted of large tiles, stone slabs and even earthen pipes. At Halae two members of the American school opened about 200 graves dating from the geometric period down to Roman times. Since the burials have never been disturbed the results are valuable for dating the wares found in the graves. Of particular interest was the discovery of plates decorated with Bœotian geometric designs on a white ground found in connection with a black-figured lekythos. At Thebes three more rooms in the so-called "Palace of Kadmos" were excavated. One very interesting find in the court was that of a potter's kiln dating from Mycenæan times. The kiln was circular in plan divided vertically by a wall and had a pierced floor of baked earth. At Thespiæ the common grave of those who fell at Delion in 424 has been opened.

Near Elatea upon a rising piece of ground an entire prehistoric village has been uncovered. The site was occupied from remote times. Thus in the lowest stratum the excavators found finely polished stone implements together with articles of bronze, which showed that the period was one of transition from stone to bronze. There is a marked resemblance between these bronzes and those dating from the Early Minoan in Crete. In the next stratum the finds belonged only to the Bronze Age. The Bronze Age period is marked by stone buildings; and among the remains of these numerous fragments of vases were discovered which were originally decorated with a coating of black color on which again geometric designs were executed in white. In the upper stratum were found objects of the same date as the Late Minoan of Crete. At Elassona, in Macedonia, two prehistoric settlements have been found similar to those in Thessaly. In one of these were vases of the so-called Late Minoan II. period.

THE PELOPONNESOS. The Austrians have continued at Palæopolis the work which they inaugurated in 1910. Here two baths and a mausoleum of Roman times have been examined, and graves of Greek, Roman, and Christian times have been opened. It is interesting to note that the only whole inscription in the place to come down intact is one found in connection with a Christian burial and containing a curse. At Agos the foundations of a temple 100 meters long with the base of the cult-statue still in place have been cleared out. An examination of near-by Byzantine walls brought to light pieces of statuary, a score of inscriptions, and over 200 pieces of entablatures from buildings in the market place. At Skala, in the Inachos valley, a Mycenæan cemetery has been found. At Kynouria a small temple to Apollo Tyritos has been discovered. Two inscriptions on bronze plates making mention of a "temple of the Great God" found on the hill of Palaio-Katuna has led to the belief that this place is the site of Thisoa.

In the Island of Corfu Doerpfeld continues his work referred to in last year's report. The "Gorgon" temple has been further examined and the great altar has been laid bare. In Cephalonia a large number of tombs of Hellenistic date containing vases, coins, and jewelry have been opened.

AFRICA. At Bonah (Hippo), in Tunis, two superposed Roman villas have been excavated. In both the mosaic floors were preserved, in one case to the extent of an area of thirty yards. This one portrays a hunting scene, while another is decorated with a fishing scene. At Mactar, also in Tunis, the remains of three buildings have been brought to light. In one the mosaic floors were preserved in three rooms. From the sunken vessel *Mahdia* more objects have been recovered, including among other things a low relief representing Asklepios and Hygeia, together with a great deal of pottery, and many objects of bronze. These include a bust of Athena, masks, heads of animals, and household utensils. The finding of human and animal bones shows that the wreck of the vessel was attended by a loss of life.

ITALY. At Ostia work has been carried on industriously since last year. Something over 1600 yards of the "Via Decumana" have been exposed and many of the public buildings of the town have been cleaned out. With the excavation of the intervening spaces, the most important portion of the town is now exposed as a connected whole. In the theatre the excavators have discovered a fine statue of Venus which appears to be a copy of some Hellenistic work. The baths, originally excavated in the year 1888, have been further examined and their beautiful pavements, showing marine subjects in black on white ground, have been laid bare. It is interesting to note in connection with the remark of Clement of Alexander, to the effect that the Romans had the custom of placing a shrine to Fortune in a portion of the house not usually mentioned, that actually in that apartment of the firemen's quarters just such a shrine with an inscription to Fortune was discovered. In connection with the firemen another inscription has been recovered which shows that these men received corn free from the city. In their barracks was found a watering trough for horses. The barracks of the *vigiles* have been completely cleared as well as the area behind the theatre where remains of a Christian church came to light. The palæstra has been examined and the great cisterns beneath it show the excellence of the public buildings. Here also were found five furnaces for heating. The structure had almost perfectly preserved mosaic floors. Since no traces of anything earlier than 266 B. C. have come to light, it is believed that the town was founded at that time. Excavations at San Pietro Montagnon, near Padua, have brought to light strata of pre-Roman remains. These contained objects in bronze, as human figures, horses, rings, etc., together with an enormous number of terra-cotta cups and saucers.

At Pompeii work has been carried on with particularly successful results. The "Street of Abundance" has been shown to have been for the most part a business thoroughfare, for the windows on the ground floor are wide as shop windows should be. Balconies were found to be frequent on this street. The most spectacular of all the finds in this locality was that of a wine shop in just the condition which it presented on the fatal day in the year 79 A. D., when the town was covered by the eruption of Vesuvius. The top of the counter, or bar, is of glazed white tiles and pierced with openings in which rested the wine-jars. In the corner of the shop were amphoræ of various sizes to hold the supply of wines. On the counter rested an ivory, or bone, cash-box still containing gold and silver coins, while near by were scattered copper coins showing how precipitately the place was deserted. Among the finds were a pair of jars in the form of cocks with the beaks serving as spouts, while at the back of the shop was an arrangement used for heating the various drinks served. This heater consisted of a copper boiler which rested over a hole in the masonry and it was supplied with a lid chained to it so that no absent-minded person might mislay it. How sudden must have been the overthrow of the city is shown by the presence of the remains of people, men and women, who were overcome while in the shop. Further evidence of the unexpectedness of the eruption is afforded by the discovery of the fine palace of one Obellius Firmus, for just before the door of the house lay the six bodies of Obellius, his wife, two little children, and two other persons—probably servants. The little children had fallen, clasped in each other's arms, and the parents had met their death clasping each other's hands. A number of frescoes have been uncovered on the walls of various houses. One in particular represents the carrying of the image of Cybele in procession. The goddess is surrounded by worshippers while four men are inserting poles in holes in the stage on which the goddess is placed preparatory to carrying it away. Another fresco shows the unusual scene of a girl being punished. She is represented as kneeling with her face buried in the lap of another female, while a third figure holds a rod over her bared back. On the opposite wall of the room is painted a woman who raises her hand in surprise at the punishment. On the street walls of a number of the houses were found notices referring to politics. The most interesting (at this present time of the suffrage movement) is one dealing with the part played by women in Roman elections. It reads: "Aselinas and Smyrine say 'Vote for Fuscunas as your alderman.'"

Recent excavations for foundations near the Monte Testaccio, in Rome, have brought to light a strong-box which had been destroyed by a fire of such violence that many of the coins in it were fused. Some 770, however, have been identified, and these run from the time of Antonius Pius to that of Gallienus. The ancient buildings cleared by the excavations proved to be granaries. Many pieces of jars and fragments of marble and terra-cotta decorations, together with some inscriptions, have also been recovered.

FRANCE. At Alesia the walls of the fortifications reared by Vercingetorix in his last stand against Cæsar have been excavated. The ramparts were found to be built in alternating sections of earthwork and wooden beams, and the whole structure faced with rough stonework. The wooden beams had decayed, but their locations were clearly marked. The square spikes used in holding the beams in place were found still *in situ*. At Sos (Lot-et-Garonne) excavations have brought to light the remains of a pre-Roman city which was defended by strong ramparts of tremendous blocks of stone. It is believed on the strength of this evidence that this is the town of the Sotiates which so stoutly resisted Cæsar in the year 56 B. C. Subterranean passages and mines synchronous with the Romans agree with Cæsar's description of this town. Digging has also brought to light Latin inscriptions, and tombs from which were recovered a terra-cotta head, some coins of the colony of Nîmes, and a spear head. A portion of a colonnade, probably belonging to a villa, was also found.

GERMANY. Excavations on the site of the Roman fort at Alzey demonstrate that it varies from other forts found in Germany in that it was built of stone instead of wood and earth. Ashes seem to indicate that the fort was destroyed by fire. Its date is given by coins discovered there as probably about 330 A. D. Near Ober-Grombach the foundations of a country villa of Roman times have been recovered.

ENGLAND. Recent excavations at Chester in the process of extending the infirmary have encountered the cemetery of the XXth. Legion. Some of the graves had Roman roofing-tiles bearing the stamp of the legion. One of the graves contained three urns, in one of which was a metal mirror, which seems to show that the burial was that of a woman. In the course of the excavations bronze coins of the time of Antoninus Pius and of Commodus came to light, together with Roman sandals, tiles, and bottles. At Watergate Hanger, West Marden, a Roman villa has been excavated. In the building was one large room and several small ones, three having tesselated pavements. Near to the villa was uncovered a building which may have been the cottage of some one connected with the estate.

ARCHBALD, ROBERT W. See UNITED STATES, *Congress*.

ARCHITECTURE. The year 1912 appears, in general, to have been a year of normal architectural activity, unbroken by any widespread disturbance, financial, industrial, or political. The influence of the Tripolitan and Balkan wars has been confined to regions of minor importance architecturally; while in the United States uninterrupted peace and prosperity have completed the final recovery from the "panic" of 1907, and resulted in the production of new buildings exceeding in value those of any year since 1905.

CITY PLANNING. The interest in city planning and its development both as an art and a science has continued unabated on both sides of the Atlantic; congresses have been numerous, the most important of these having been held in October at Düsseldorf, Germany, where competitive designs were exhibited for an extensive replanning of that interesting city. An account of the recent aspects of the subject will be found in the article CITY PLANNING.

REINFORCED CONCRETE. While the use of reinforced concrete or ferro-concrete has been further extended and broadened in engineering works, its strictly architectural applications have generally been confined to the more utilitarian parts of the construction. Massive or monolithic concrete, on account of its unsatisfactory texture and color, has not come into use for the exteriors of monumental buildings, at least to any appreciable extent; but for bridges, viaducts, embankment walls, and many similar purposes in which architecture and engineering play an equal or nearly equal part, it is proving an invaluable material. In the United States also, as to some extent in Europe, concrete has during the past year been widely used in the building of small residences, either in the "massive" or "poured concrete" form, or by the use of concrete blocks molded at the site of the building and laid up as masonry. At Rungis in France, a church was erected by a new process of combining separately cast units of concrete. The new triple-domed Catholic cathedral at St. Louis, Mo., by Barnet, Haynes, and Barnet, was largely constructed of concrete; and at Camden, N. J., the dome of the Linden Baptist church, by Truscott and Moses, was built of slabs of concrete carried by ribs of timber. Concrete also entered largely into the construction of the handsome new railway station at Leipzig, Germany.

EUROPEAN ARCHITECTURE: ITALY. From a sentimental point of view the most interesting architectural event in Europe was the completion and dedication in April of the historic Campanile of St. Mark's at Venice, whose leisurely but thorough reconstruction has occupied nearly the entire ten years since its fall in 1902. It is a faithful reproduction of the original design. The most difficult detail of the task was the piecing together of the hundreds of fragments of the sculptures of Sansovino (*cir.* 1530 A. D.) in the Loggetta at the base of the tower; this has been accomplished with remarkable success. Rome witnessed the final completion of the colossal Victor Emanuel monument, which has been in process of construction for thirty years; and which, with the possible exception of the Taj Mahal at Agra, is the most costly monument ever erected to any human being. It is magnificent and yet somewhat disappointing in its lack of unity and concentration of interest.

GERMANY. The architects of Germany appear to have been full of business in 1912. For many important works, the architects were selected by competition, a procedure more in favor there than in America. There was observable, as in other recent years, an oscillation of tendencies between the "Moderne Kunst" or "Art Nouveau" style, and a somewhat baroque version of Palladian design. The majority of the churches show a restless striving after novelty, resulting in a very unecclesiastical eccentricity; one of the least bizarre examples was the Protestant Christ Church at Mannheim, a domical edifice in the Baroque style. The majority of the new school buildings, though excellently planned, show the same apparent cult of the ugly, both in mass and detail; a pleasing exception is the new Reformgymnasium at Tempelhof by Köhler and Kranz. In contrast to the schools and churches the theatres and railway stations of the year's product were almost without exception dignified and appropriate in design. Of the former, the most interesting is the municipal theatre group at Stuttgart. This dignified group, on classic lines, comprises a large and a small theatre, with restaurants, offices, rehearsal rooms, etc., admirably combined in a harmonious design by Max Lettmann. Among railway buildings may be mentioned the new station at Leipzig, already referred to, another at Mülheim in Alsace, and the new elevated railway in Hamburg which, with its artistic terminal and way stations, exemplifies the admirable German practice in the artistic treatment of engineering works. Another example of this is seen in the new bridge over the Rhine at Cologne. German civic architecture is illustrated by the new police department buildings by Theo. Fischer, a baroque *Verkehrsministerium* by K. Hocheder, and a new tax office, with ugly roof and dormers, all in Munich. German achievements of the year in this line have been less interesting on the whole than in business buildings, which displayed less of "art nouveau" eccentricity than usual. Among notable examples may be mentioned the Tietz department store (Cremer and Wolfstein) at Berlin, with a fine glass-roofed court, and the Wertheim store on the Königsstrasse by Keyser and Von Grossheim, the new Hahn establishment by W. Schelbach, and a number of sumptuous restaurant buildings erected by various brewing companies (Pschorrhaus, Berliner Saal, etc)—all these in Berlin; and the Lindwurmhof (a business block), the Gewerbeschau or Industrial Exhibition group, and a large block of municipal tenements around a large court, all at Munich.

From Vienna and Austria in general there is nothing specially calling for mention.

FRANCE. There is little building of great importance to report. A few interesting edifices in Paris deserve mention. The Singer-Polignac tenements by G. Vaudoyer in the 13th *arrondissement* (ward) of Paris, containing 64 apartments of from two to four rooms each, renting from $45 to $80 yearly, with many arrangements worthy of study by tenement house reformers in this country; the new Hôpital de la Pitié by J. Rochet; a very extensive and thoroughly modern group of buildings for this great municipal hospital; the extension of the Carnavalet Museum by R. Foucault; and the Apollo Concert Hall in the Rue de Clichy, with a reversible floor on trunnions, which can be turned over to provide at will a clear floor for dancing or a sloping floor with seats for concerts. At Nantes a design by M. Déverin has been adopted for a new Hôtel de Ville to be incorporated with the existing medieval château or castle of that city. The French architectural societies have been earnestly discussing the whole question of officialism in the profession, especially the appointment of government architects, their relation to the non-official ranks of the profession, and the employment and compensation of architects specially employed on government works.

GREAT BRITAIN. There has been the usual architectural activity. The most important event of the year in London was the completion of the great Methodist Memorial Hall in Westminister by Lanchester and Rickards, which has been in course of construction for a number of years, and which was dedicated and opened on October 3. It is a vast and impressive edifice crowned by a square dome of 90 feet span, and containing the central administrative offices of the Wesleyan Methodist body in Great Britain, with a great auditorium, conference rooms, etc. Next to this in importance, possibly surpassing it in the popular interest awakened, has been the publication of Sir Aston Webb's design for a new façade for Buckingham Palace, which has been severely criticised by some and as warmly defended by others. It is at least an improvement over the front as originally erected by Blore in 1837. Another controversy which has divided public opinion both in Liverpool and in the profession at large has been the proposed remodeling of the podium or terrace of St. George's Hall in that city, to provide a setting for a projected monument to Edward VII.

Work has continued on the County Council Hall in London, and on the Aldwych improvements; extensive additions to the Law Courts have been completed, from designs by Sir Henry Tanner; and the first steps taken towards the extension of the Guildhall, although as yet no final design has been adopted. New government offices have been begun at the corner of Great George Street, and a design by T. Edwin Cooper has been selected in a competition for new offices for the Port of London Authority: an imposing block with a lofty central tower, on an irregular lot. The work on Liverpool Cathedral has been continued, and the restored Winchester Cathedral, substantially completed in 1911, was dedicated with a thanksgiving service on St. Swithin's day, 819 years after its original dedication in 1093. At Cambridge new buildings were completed for the Museum of Archæology and Ethnology, by T. G. Jackson, and for Queens, Emmanuel, and Sidney-Sussex colleges; at Oxford for Lady Margaret Hall (R. Blomfield), Merton College (B. Champneys), Hertford and Balliol colleges; at Selby Abbey, the new south transept was completed and dedicated (J. Oldred Scott); and at Dublin the competition for new buildings for University College was awarded to Doolin and Butler for an interesting design externally treated in a Greco-Roman or Pompeiian style. The great building for the National Museum of Wales at Aberystwyth, by Dunbar Smith and Cecil Brewer, was advanced towards completion, and the Edinburgh College of Art was finished. Various memorials to King Edward VII. have been projected or designed: *e. g.*, by C. L. Lutyens and B. Mackennal for Green Park, London; and one for Edinburgh by Albert Hodge and G. W. Browne. A new church in Brixton, Christ Church, by Beresford Pite—on a conspicuous site, is an extraordinarily incoherent design, which does not atone by picturesqueness for its lack of harmony of mass and line.

THE UNITED STATES. Uninterrupted prosperity is reflected in a general increase in the recorded municipal building permits of the leading cities. Permits for new buildings in Greater New York alone aggregated over $203,000,000 (estimated cost of buildings) besides those for $11,000,000 of alterations, a total increase of 15 per cent. over 1911. New York thus stands far and away in the lead of all cities in the world in the number and cost of new buildings. Of the above vast sum $30,000,000 were for the erection of apartment houses and tenements, and $60,000,000 for business buildings, offices, "loft buildings," stores, and factories. Over against this advance must be set the retrograde step taken by Congress in the repeal of the Tarsney act, under which, in the past fifteen years, many admirable government buildings have been designed by non-official architects selected by competition. The resignation of the efficient supervising architect of the treasury, a warm advocate of the Tarsney act, followed this repeal.

Tendencies in style have not materially changed. Civic and governmental buildings, and the larger museums and libraries were generally in some version of the classic styles, with a noticeable tendency to the use of colossal colonnades, often carried to an absurdly illogical excess, as in the Normal School at San Diego, Cal., by W. S. Hebbard, and in the topheavy State Education Building by H. F. Hornbostel, recently dedicated at Albany, N. Y. In commercial buildings of the skyscraper type, classic and Gothic models divided the public favor, *e. g.*, the Union Central Building at Cincinnati, with a columnar treatment of the upper part, and the ultra-Gothic Woolworth Building by Cass Gilbert in New York. The latter is the tallest inhabited structure in the world, 756 feet high, with 57 stories; externally of white glazed terra-cotta, and somewhat disappointing in the thinness of its detail and its weakness of silhouette and composition. Western buildings showed more freedom and originality of design, both in large and small buildings. On the Pacific Coast architectural interest centred especially in the two exhibitions projected in connection with the opening of the Panama Canal in 1915; the Panama-Pacific (international) at San Francisco, for which a board of architects was appointed, selected partly from California and partly from the East; and the Panama-California (State) at San Diego. Work on both of these, nominally begun in 1911, was continued during the year. An important competition for a new city hall for San Francisco resulted in the adoption of the design of Bakewell & Brown, of that city, an imposing composition with a fine central dome. The government appointed Mr. A. W. Lord, of New York, architect for the various administrative and other buildings to be erected at Panama and along the canal by the Canal Commission.

It is impossible to mention even a tithe of the interesting and important buildings begun or completed during the past year in the United States. In New York the vast but externally disappointing Grand Central Terminal was well advanced towards completion; the imposing new Municipal Office Building was externally completed; the Woolworth Building, the fine Bankers' Trust Building (Trowbridge & Livingston), and the marble United States Rubber Company Building (Carrère & Hastings) were completed; two huge hotels, the Vanderbilt (Warren & Wetmore) and the McAlpin (F. M. Andrews), were opened, and the fine new Central Library in Brooklyn (R. F. Almirall) begun. Notable buildings in Boston were the great Copley-Plaza Hotel (H. J. Hardenburgh, C. H. Blackall), a new U. S. Customs House (Peabody & Stearns), the Brigham Hospital (Codman & Despradelle), extensive dormitories for Harvard University (Shepley, Rutan & Coolidge), a huge department store by D. H. Burnham, a public causeway over the Charles River dam, and several large banks, clubs, etc., representing all together a cost of between twenty and thirty millions. Among many buildings in Chicago and the Middle West a few were: The Insurance Exchange, by D. H. Burnham, the Gothic North American Building by Holabird & Roche, the Telephone Building by the same, and a number of strongly designed warehouses (by G. C. Nimmons, H. Shaw, etc.), at Chicago; at St. Louis, the new Public Library (Cass Gilbert), and Church of the Ascension by Mariner & La Beaume; at Minneapolis, the New Museum and Music Hall (McKim, Mead & White) was begun, and a high school by C. H. Johnston completed; at Pittsburgh progress was made on the Western Pennsylvania University buildings and those for the Carnegie Technical Schools. From the further West: The L. C. Smith Building at Seattle by Gaggin & Gaggin, 34 stories high; at Tacoma, Wash., the N. Pacific R. R. station by Reed & Stem and the Woodmen of the World Building (Holabird & Roche); at San Francisco, St. Ignatius R. C. Church by J. I. Devlin, the Union Savings Bank by Bliss & Faville, and many business buildings. Many interesting buildings in the compiler's list, at Washington, D. C., Buffalo, Baltimore, Cleveland, Montreal, Toronto, and other cities must be omitted for lack of space.

Other Countries. In Haarlem, Holland, a very impressive and interesting church, St. Bavon's, has been completed (J. T. J. Cuypers), and at Amsterdam a new Exchange by H. P. Berlage. Competitions have been held or announced for a senate palace at Bucharest (Rumania), for a palace of justice at Athens, and for law courts and a royal palace at Sofia (Bulgaria), and for a new municipal palace at Rangoon (Burma). At Ghent (Belgium) a splendid new railroad station has been completed and buildings begun for a great exhibition to be held in 1913. At Constantinople a new bridge over the Golden Horn has been built by German engineers. In India (and in Great Britain) the approaching transfer of the capital to Delhi has aroused earnest discussion as to the style of the new buildings and the planning of the new capital district. South Africa reports continued building activity; a design was adopted for the Rhodes Memorial at Cape Town, by H. Baker; Johannesburg is being transformed by new structures, and a new registration act was in process of drafting for the regulation of the practice of architecture.

For the necrology of architects see Necrology. Consult also Archæology, City Planning, and Municipal Government.

ARCTIC EXPLORATIONS. See Polar Exploration.

ARGENTINA. A South American federal republic. Capital, Buenos Ayres.

Area and Population. The republic consists of fourteen provinces, ten territories, and the federal district. The area, according to the most recent planimetric calculation, is 2,806,400 square kilometers (1,083,551 square miles). The census of 1895 showed 3,954,911 inhabitants (exclusive of an estimated 90,000 not enumerated). The estimate of December 31, 1910, was 7,121,822 (including some 30,000 uncivilized Indians). Outside of the federal district (city of Buenos Ayres), the population had the greatest density in the province of Tucumán, 13 per square kilometer; Santa Fé, 7; Buenos Ayres (province) and Entre Rios, each 6; Corrientes, 4.7. Estimated population of the larger cities: In 1912, Buenos Ayres, 1,383,663; Santa Fé, 48,928; in 1911, Rosario, 208,990; in 1910, La Plata, 95,000; Cordoba, 95,000; Avellaneda, 87,000; Tucumán, 66,000; Mendoza, 39,000.

Immigration and Emigration. 1909, 278,148 and 137,508; 1910, 289,640 and 97,854; 1911, 225,772 and 120,709. The immigrants in 1911 included 118,723 Spaniards, 58,185 Italians, 13,605 Turks, 9713 Russians, 4016 French, 5023 Austro-Hungarians, 3593 Germans, and 1730 British.

Education. Of the children of school age in 1911, about 45 per cent. were reported in attendance, and of these only about ·13 per cent. could read and write. Of the total population over six years old, about 50 per cent. are illiterate. For 1911, primary schools (public and private) were reported at 7183, with 22,456 teachers and 746,725 pupils. The government maintains for secondary education 27 national colleges (10,227 students). Normal schools number 62 (5954 students). There are some 20 schools for special and technical instruction. For higher and professional education, three national universities are maintained at Buenos Ayres, Cordoba, and La Plata, and provincial universities at Paraná and Santa Fé (total 438 professors and 7317 students). The 1911 government expenditure on education was 19,241,252 pesos

INDUSTRIES. Agriculture and stock-raising continue to be Argentina's chief source of wealth. Mining has made little progress. The leading industrial business is meat-packing, in the River Platte region. Manufactures include flour, butter, cheese, sugar, beer, and wine. The area under cultivation in 1909-10 was about 19,500,000 hectares, of which 5,836,500 were wheat, 3,005,000 corn, 1,455,600 linseed, 4,706,530 alfalfa, 572,000 oats, about 2,100,000 cultivated grass. Other crops include grapes, sugar-cane, barley, potatoes, millet, and beans. Area of wheat harvested in 1910-11, 4,953,000 hectares, yielding 39,730,000 metric quintals (8 qs. per ha.); under crop in 1911-12, 6,897,000 hectares, with estimated yield of 46,109,000 quintals (6.7 qs. per ha.). Area of oats harvested in 1910-11, 650,000 hectares, yielding 6,850,000 quintals (10.5 qs. per ha.); under crop in 1911-12, 1,031,000 hectares, with estimated yield of 8,773,000 quintals (8.5 qs. per ha.). Estim ated area sown for 1912-13: Wheat, 6,868,000 hectares; oats, 1,190,000; flax, 1,745,000 (against 1,630,000 in 1911-12). The estimated production of raw sugar for 1912-13 was 1,430,000 quintals, against 1,801,000 in the previous year. See IRRIGATION.

Livestock (1910): 29,124,229 cattle, 7,537,765 horses, 750,167 mules and asses, 67,383,952 sheep, 3,946,750 goats, and 1,404,281 swine. As a sheep-raising country, Argentina ranks second, Australia being first, with (in 1910), 92,047,015; Russia had (in 1909) 62,371,579, including goats; United States (1909), 57,216,000; United Kingdom (1911), 30,479,807; Uruguay (1908), 26,286,296.

COMMERCE. Imports and exports, exclusive of corn and bullion, have been valued as follows, in gold pesos (one peso=96.447 cents):

	1901	1906	1909	1910	1911
Imports.	113,960	269,971	302,756	351,771	366,811
Exports.	167,716	292,254	397,351	372,626	324,698

In 1909 coin and bullion amounting to 67,454,000 pesos were imported and 1,247,000 exported; in 1910, 37,028,000 and 1,670,000; in 1911, 12,764,000 and 3,009,000. Leading classified imports in 1910 and 1911, in thousands of pesos: Textiles and manufactures, 68,365 and 69,698; iron and steel and manufactures, 43,119 and 43,086; vehicles and railway equipment, 35,095 and 36,865; building materials, 29,237 and 33,789; earthenware, earths, stones, coal, etc., 30,926 and 33,202; food products, 27,141 and 29,337; oil, grease, etc., 13,892 and 15,890; metals and manufactures (other than iron and steel), 12,870 and 15,480; wines, liquors, and other beverages, 14,951 and 13,799; agricultural implements and machinery, 18,922 and 13,692; chemicals, drugs, etc., 12,290 and 12,178; timber, woods, straw, and manufactures, 8671 and 10,401; paper and manufactures, 8308 and 8670; electrical apparatus, 5742 and 6684; tobacco, 6082 and 5892. The textile import in 1911 was subdivided: Cotton, 35,576; wool, 14,249; silk, 5865; other, 14,007. Iron and steel: Primary and relatively primary material, 22,885; manufactures, 20,200.

Agentine exports are classified under six heads, as follows (in thousands of pesos):

	1909	1910	1911
Agricultural products...	230,504	196,582	139,764
Pastoral products.......	153,548	161,007	168,395
Forest products.........	8,927	10,565	12,255
Fish and game..........	752	1,429	1,663
Mineral products........	743	540	565
Miscellaneous	2,876	2,505	2,055
Total	397,351	372,626	324,698

Classified agricultural exports in 1910 and 1911, in thousands of pesos: Raw products, 186,317 and 129,711; elaborated products, 5109 and 4827; by-products, 5155 and 5225;—Pastoral exports: ordinary animal products, 135,033 and 137,383; elaborated products, 18,286 and 17,640; live animals, 5056 and 9460; by-products, 2631 and 3911. Leading exports, in thousands of pesos:

	1900	1909	1910	1911
Wheat	48,628	106,039	72,202	80,675
Wool	27,992	59,921	58,848	50,494
Cowhides	13,445	28,978	30,711	34,440
Linseed	10,674	43,713	44,604	33,580
Frozen and chilled beef	2,459	21,066	25,371	31,284
Rendered tallow and grease.....	....	.....	9,537	11,768
Oats	....	.....	8,143	11,666
Sheepskins	7,473	8,484	8,657	7,761
Quebracho:				
Logs	2,398	4,380	5,604	6,897
Extract	598	4,226	4,429	4,980
Frozen mutton....	4,513	5,320	6,008	6,873
Wheat flour	1,718	5,595	4,947	4,739
Bran	1,163	4,483	4,522	4,612
Corn	11,934	58,274	60,261	2,767
Jerked beef	1,980	1,325	1,033	1,662
Bristles	....	.....	1,335	1,581
Canned meat	....	.....	1,208	1,541
Whale oil	....	.....	889	1,206
Meat extract	230	2,892	3,047	1,031

The most noteworthy features of the above figures for 1911, as compared with 1910, are the decline of wool exports by 8,354,000 pesos and of corn by 57,494. Trade by countries, in thousands of pesos:

Countries	Imports 1910	Imports 1911	Exports 1910	Exports 1911
Great Britain..	109,377	108,637	80,792	91,841
Germany	61,129	65,862	45,055	43,073
United States..	48,419	52,353	25,324	24,300
France	33,651	38,027	37,762	39,692
Italy	31,776	29,346	10,475	13,587
Belgium	19,599	19,485	30,481	35,626
Spain	10,911	11,279	2,870	2,178
Brazil	9,104	8,461	17,542	17,874
Austria-Hung'y	3,466	4,304	1,868	2,398
Uruguay	2,262	3,070	1,534	2,341
Netherlands ..	2,517	2,978	4,301	6,440
For orders.....	.....	.....	103,783	36,357
Total, including other..	351,771	366,811	372,626	324,698

The exports "for orders" are not recorded at the Argentine ports as for specific countries, but are subject to cable or other orders as to final destination. Nearly all of these shipments ultimately reach the western European countries and in about the same proportion as the direct shipments given above.

SHIPPING. Entered at the ports in 1910: 31,701 steamers, of 20,351,382 tons, 30,868 sail, of 2,260,515 tons; total, 62,569 vessels, of 22,557,897 tons. Merchant marine in 1911: 161 steamers, of 80,447 tons net, and 185 sail, of 57,350 tons net.

COMMUNICATIONS. A creditable development is observed in Argentina's railways. At the end of 1909 the total length in operation was 25,181 kilometers; 1910, 28,636; and on December 31, 1911, 31,799 kilometers (19,759 miles). About 5360 kilometers belong to the government. At the beginning of 1912 Argentina had a mileage of 10,820 of 5 ft. 6in. gauge, 1426 miles of 4 ft. 8½ in. gauge and 5736 miles of the meter gauge, giving a total mileage of nearly 18,000. The Buenos Ayres Great Southern operated 3384 miles of this amount, and in 1912 had 309 miles under construction, including the extension of the Neuguem line towards the Andes, leaving about 70 miles to complete to the Chilean frontier. The Great Southern was active during the year, extending and improving its track in and about the city of Buenos Ayres. The Buenos Ayres and Pacific Railway opened during the year a direct line from Justo Darect, in the province of San Luis, to La Paz, in the province of Mendozo, shortening the trans-Andean route. Telegraphs (1910), 61,005 kilometers of line, with 161,476 kilometers of wire and 2825 offices; telephones, 33,400, with 94,300 kilometers of wire; post offices, 2995.

FINANCE. The unit of value is the gold peso, worth 96.5 cents; the paper peso, under the conversion law of 1899, is current at 0.44 of the gold peso. Revenue increased from 205,341,838 pesos paper in 1905 (gold revenue being reduced to paper) to 254,232,013 in 1908, 274,526,578 in 1909, and 304,679,200 in 1910. The budget for 1912 showed estimated receipts 89,281,681 pesos gold and 128,751,718 paper, equivalent to 331,664,629 pesos paper; estimated expenditure, 29,909,343 pesos gold and 248,764,942 paper, or 316,740,722 paper. The estimated receipts included: Customs, 79,200,000 gold; port dues, etc., 8,750,000 gold; excise, 57,780,000 paper; posts and telegraphs, 16,500,000 paper, stamps, 16,500,000 paper; public works, 10,700,000 paper. Estimated expenditure for 1912, compared with the estimates submitted to the Congress for 1913: Congress, 5,178,580 and 5,178,580 pesos paper; interior, 45,588,047 and 45,066,287; foreign affairs 5,089,472 and 5,028,308; finance, 19,703,218 and 21,073,964; public debt, 76,608,169 and 79,446,194; justice and instruction, 53,079,657 and 49,800,000; war, 29,123,262 and 29,123,262; marine, 28,227,400 and 26,358,076; agriculture, 15,291,156 and 15,700,598; public works, 8339,760 and 8,754,360; pensions, 12,512,000 and 12,512,000; military acquisitions, 18,000,000 and 10,300,000; total, 316,740,722 and 308,741,629.

Debt, December 31, 1911: Foreign, 303,719,786 pesos gold; interior, 161,367,000 gold and 139,656,940 paper; floating, 34,064,123 paper. Outstanding paper money, 685,150,000 pesos.

ARMY. The army of Argentina is recruited by compulsory service which under the statutes of 1905 and 1907 require personal service between the ages of 20 and 45; 10 years in the standing army and its reserve; 10 years in the national guard and 5 years in the territorial forces. A peace strength of about 18,000 is maintained, but in 1912 the peace establishments of the standing army and its departments were published, showing that 15,540 conscripts were required for 1912, or a decrease of about 3000 as compared with 1911. On a war basis about 250,000 men would be raised by utilizing the reserves and the national guard, of which, however, but a fraction have received military training. The active army was organized into 18 battalions of infantry, including two of mounted infantry, 10 regiments of cavalry, 5 regiments of field artillery, 3 regiments of mountain artillery and 4 battalions of engineers.

NAVY. The Argentine programme of naval construction provides for two large battleships and twelve destroyers and authorizes the construction of a third large battleship and four additional destroyers if it should be needed as a setoff to Brazilian naval development. The new battleships, the *Rivadavia* and the *Moreno*, each of 28,000 tons, were launched in 1911, the former at Quincy, Mass., on August 26, and the latter at Camden, N. J., on September 23. Neither was completed near the close of 1912. Orders also were placed for the twelve destroyers, four each in Germany, France, and England. The German boats were completed in 1912 and joined the Argentine fleet; the French boats were under trial; the English boats were completed, but in October were sold by their builders to the Greek government, without being turned over to Argentina.

Near the end of 1912 the fleet in commission included the following: Four armored cruisers, of 27,400 aggregate tons (*Garibaldi, San Martin, General Belgrane*, and *Pueyrredón*, built in 1896-98); two armored coast-guards, of 4600 tons (1890 and 1891); one coast-guard, of 4200 tons (*Almirante Brown*, 1880); two coast-guards, of 3070 tons (1874 and 1875); three protected cruisers, of 11,440 tons (*Veinte y cinco de Mayo, Nueve de Julio*, and *Buenos Aires*, 1890-95); two torpedo cruisers, of 1776 tons (1890 and 1893); two armored river gunboats, of 2000 tons (*Rosario* and *Paraná*, 1908); seven torpedo-boat destroyers, of 5000 tons (*Misiones, Corrientes*, and *Entre Rios* 1896; *Jujuy, La Plata, Cordobá*, and *Catamarca*, 1912); 12 first-class torpedo boats, of 969 tons; 9 second-class torpedo boats, of 144 tons; one submarine; six transports, of 29,243 tons. See NAVAL PROGRESS, and BATTLESHIPS.

GOVERNMENT. Argentina (officially La Nación Argentina), is one of the five American republics having the federal form of government; the others are the United States, Mexico, Venezuela, and Brazil. The Argentine constitution resembles that of the United States. The Senate has 30 members, elected indirectly for nine years, two from each province and the Federal District; the Chamber of Deputies, 120 members, elected by direct vote for four years. The president is chosen by an electoral college for a six-year term and is ineligible for the next term. He is assisted by a responsible ministry of eight members. President, for the term ending October 12, 1916, Roque Sáenz Peña; vice-president, Victorino de la Plaza.

HISTORY. The difficulty which had arisen with Italy in 1911, over questions of quarantine regulations, and which caused the Italian government to issue a decree prohibiting Italian emigration to Argentina, was removed in the summer of 1912 by the signing of a sanitary convention between the two countries, specifying the preventive measures which each should take against cholera and yellow fever respectively. The Italian government then announced that it would withdraw its decree as to emigration. During January and February the country was disturbed by a serious railway strike, but order was maintained and a settlement finally effected. Work on the survey of the Chilean-Argentine boundary was continued and substantial progress was made in the delimitation of the Bolivian-Argentine frontier.

ARID LANDS. See IRRIGATION.

ARIZONA. POPULATION. According to the Census Bureau statistics issued in 1912, out of the total population of 204,254 in 1910, 46,824 were foreign-born whites, as compared with 22,395 in 1900. The largest number of these, 29,438, came from Mexico; from England, 3500; and from other European countries in smaller numbers. In 1910, there were 2009 negroes and 448 mulattoes in the State. In 1890 the negroes numbered 1357 and the mulattoes, 425.

AGRICULTURE. The acreage, value and production of the principal crops in 1911-12 are shown in the following table:

		Acreage	Prod. Bu.	Value
Corn	1912	16,000	528,000	$528,000
	1911	15,000	495,000	480,000
Wheat	1912	23,000	707,000	778,000
	1911	27,000	800,000	760,000
Oats	1912	6,000	268,000	188,000
	1911	6,000	252,000	151,000
Potatoes	1912	1,000	125,000	156,000
	1911	1,000	95,000	133,000
Hay	1912	113,000	a 384,000	4,608,000
	1911	130,000	a 502,000	6,024,000

a Tons.

MINERAL PRODUCTION. The gold production of the State in 1911, was valued at $3,430,503, compared with a value of $3,149,366 in 1910. The output of 1911 was the largest of recent years and the increase was due chiefly to increased output from siliceous gold ores in Mohave county and from copper ores in Cochise county. The output of silver in the State in 1911 was 3,276,571 fine ounces, compared with 2,556,528 ounces in 1910. Of the total silver output in 1911, copper ores supplied 2,136,121 ounces; lead ores, 635,363 ounces, dry or siliceous ores, 414,981; and the lead-zinc and zinc ores nearly equal parts of the bulk of the small remainder.

The production of copper in the State for 1911, was 303,202,532 pounds of blister copper, compared with 297,250,538 pounds in 1910. This was the largest output in the history of the State and continued Arizona in the first place among copper-producing States. At the close of 1911 the copper output was 3,494,333,111 pounds or 21.38 per cent. of the total output of the country, thus giving Arizona third rank among the copper-producing States. There were nine copper-smelting plants in operation during the year.

MANUFACTURES. The Thirteenth Census included statistics relating to the manufactures of the State, and its principal results are given in the table below. These figures are for the calendar year 1909. In general, this table brings out the fact that the manufacturing industries of Arizona, as a whole, showed a considerable development in the last five years. The percentage of increase, as will be seen, is 84. Of the persons engaged in manufactures, by far the larger number are found employed, in the smelting and refining of copper, which is the leading manufacturing industry of the State. In this are employed 3129 wage earners. No other industry employs any considerable number of men except those engaged in work for railroad companies in general shop construction of cars and repairs. These number 1089. In lumber and timber products 831 men were employed, and in printing and publishing, 268. Other industries of the State are flour mills and grist mills, lumber and timber products, and ice manufacture. Of the total number of persons employed in the various industries, 5.9 per cent. were proprietors and officials, 4.6 per cent. clerks, and 89.4 per cent. wage earners.

The following table gives a summary of the results of the census for the calendar years 1909 and 1904.

	Number or Amount 1909	1904
Number of establishments	311	169
Persons engaged in manufactures	7,202	5,217
Proprietors and firm members	261	133
Salaried employees	500	291
Wage earners (average number)	6,441	4,793
Primary horsepower	39,140	21,412
Capital	$32,873,000	$14,396,000
Expenses	41,131,000	20,244,000
Services	6,303,000	4,441,000
Salaries	798,000	472,000
Wages	5,505,000	3,969,000
Materials	33,600,000	14,595,000
Miscellaneous	1,228,000	1,208,000
Value of products	50,257,000	28,083,000
Value added by manufacture (value of products less cost of material)	16,657,000	13,488,000

FINANCE. The receipts for the fiscal year ended June 30, 1912, amounted to $1,192,350, and the disbursements to $1,300,858. There was a balance on hand on June 30, 1911, of $519,959, leaving a balance at the end of the fiscal year, 1912, of $411,441. The chief revenue was from taxes, and the total amount collected by taxation in 1912 was $617,731. The chief expenditures are for the support of State institutions, for education and for the State government. The bonded indebtedness of the State at the end of the fiscal year was $946.672.

CHARITIES AND CORRECTIONS. The charitable and correctional institutions of the State with their populations in 1912 are as follows: State Prison at Florence, 383; State Industrial School at Benson, 96; State Insane Asylum at Phœnix, 270; Home for Aged and Infirm Arizona Pioneers at Prescott, 33; the Florence Crittendon Home at Phœnix, 6. At the State Prison a new building was in process of construction. This is to provide for a library, schoolroom, recreation room, and store-room. The State Industrial School is to be removed to Old Fort Grant near Willcox which was donated to the State by the United States government. The school work is to be reorganized and a trades school added. Several important measures were enacted at the legislative session of 1912. Among those was a child labor law in a form approved by the National Child Labor Committee. A parole law was also passed. This provided for an indeterminate sentence and for a board of commissioners of paroled prisoners. An act was passed making it a felony for a parent to fail to provide his or her minor child with necessaries and making it a felony for a husband to abandon his wife or to fail to provide for her. Another measure provided for the commitment of destitute, homeless, and depraved women, and neglected, abandoned, and homeless children to the Florence Crittendon Home at Phœnix. A measure was passed providing for the care, maintenance, and instruction of blind children under school age.

POLITICS AND GOVERNMENT. The State legislature met in 1912 and the most important measures enacted are noted in the paragraph *Legislation* below.

Arizona became formally one of the States of the Union on February 14, when the President signed the proclamation of admission. On the same day George W. H. Hunt was inaugurated as governor. In his first message to the legislature he urged an amendment to the State constitution, providing for the recall of judicial officers. This was the provision in the constitution of the State as originally prepared, which led to its veto by President Taft. An amended constitution which left out this provision was passed by Congress and accepted by the President. The legislature passed this measure, it was signed by the governor, and was adopted by the people on November 5. On March 26 the legislature elected as United States Senators from Arizon Marcus A. Smith, Democrat, and Henry F. Ashurst, Democrat. They had been previously chosen at the primary election. Arizona furnished one of the most important of the disputed cases before the Democratic national committee at the national convention. This contest turned on the outcome of the election held in Maricopa and Cochise counties. Its details are discussed from the standpoint of both the contesting parties in the article PRESIDENTIAL CAMPAIGN. The disputed delegates were awarded to President Taft. The delegates elected at the Democratic State convention were pledged to Governor Wilson. The result of the vote for President on November 9 was as follows: Wilson, 10,324; Roosevelt, 6949; Taft, 3021. An amendment providing for woman suffrage was carried at this election.

A movement was undertaken in October to invoke the recall against Governor Hunt as a result of dissatisfaction with his prison reform policies. He advocated the honor system and a liberal use of the executive parole and he met with great opposition which resulted in an attempt to bring about his recall. Petitions to this effect were circulated throughout the State, but the movement came to nothing. Petitions were also circulated to bring about the recall of State Senators M. G. Cunniff and Homer Wood in Yavapai County. Mr. Cunniff was president of the Senate. These senators were attacked because of their opposition to woman suffrage and several other measures which were considered at the session of the legislature.

LEGISLATION. The first session of the State legislature passed several measures of unusual importance. Among these was the creation of a tax commission; an act fixing eight hours of labor for miners, hoisting engineers and smelting men; an act regulating child labor; an act providing for indeterminate prison sentences, and an act prohibiting the employment of teachers in the public schools, who were suffering from tuberculosis. At a special session of the legislature other measures of importance were passed. These included a white-slave act; an act denying corporations the right to contribute in political campaigns; an act denying State officials the right to use, and the railroads the right to issue, passes; an act known as the three-cent fare bill, regulating the transport of passengers by common carirers; a compulsory workmen's compensation act (see EMPLOYERS' LIABILITY), an act providing for an inheritance tax; a pure-food act; an act providing for publicity of campaign expenditures before and after election; a general registration act, and a primary law for elections.

STATE GOVERNMENT. Governor, George W. P. Hunt! secretary of State and lieutenant-governor, Sidney P. Osborn; treasurer, David Johnson; auditor, J. C. Callaghan; adjutant-general, Charles Harris; attorney-general, George P. Bullard; superintendent of education, C. O. Case; commissioner of insurance, Sidney P. Osborn—all Democrats.

JUDICIARY. Supreme Court — Chief justice, Alfred Franklin; associate justices, D. L. Cunningham, Henry D. Ross; clerk, J. P. Dillon—all Democrats.

STATE LEGISLATURE, 1913. Senate, Democrats, 19; Republicans, 4; House, Democrats, 31; Republicans, 4; joint ballot, Democrats, 50; Republicans, 8. Democratic majority, Senate, 15; House, 27; joint ballot, 42.

The representatives in Congress will be found in the section *Congress*, article UNITED STATES. See also EXPLORATION.

ARKANSAS. POPULATION. According to the Census Bureau statistics issued in 1912, out of a total population in 1910 of 1,574,449, the foreign-born whites numbered 16,909, compared with 14,186 in 1900. Of these, the largest number, 5813, came from Germany; from Italy, 1699; from England, 1517; and from Ireland, 1077. Other European countries were represented by smaller numbers. There were in 1910 442,891 negroes in the State and 81,371 mulattoes. The negroes in 1890 numbered 309,117 and the mulattoes 39,630.

AGRICULTURE. The acreage, value, and production of the principal crops in 1911-12 are shown in the following table:

		Acreage	Prod. Bu.	Value
Corn	1912	2,475,000	50,490,000	$33,828,000
	1911	2,390,000	49,712,000	35,793,000
Wheat	1912	94,000	940,000	884,000
	1911	96,000	1,008,000	907,000
Oats	1912	175,000	3,482,000	1,741,000
	1911	205,000	4,100,000	2,173,000
Rye	1912	1,000	10,000	10,000
	1911	1,000	10,000	9,000
Rice	1912	90,800	3,405,000	3,201,000
	1911	71,600	2,792,000	2,289,000
Potatoes	1912	25,000	1,750,000	1,610,000
	1911	26,000	1,430,000	1,644,000
Hay	1912	286,000	a 352,000	4,224,000
	1911	200,000	a 230,000	2,990,000
Tobacco	1912	800	b 520,000	94,000
	1911	800	b 480,000	57,000
Cotton	1912	....	746,802	....
	1911	....	c 915,000	....

a Tons. b Pounds. c Bales.

The Thirteenth Census statistics of agriculture, dated April 15, 1910, were published in 1912. According to these figures the number of all farms in the State in 1910 was 214,678, compared with 178,694 in 1900. The land in farms was 17,416,075 acres, a gain of about 1,000,000 acres in the decade. The improved land in farms was 8,076,254 acres, compared with 6,953,735 acres in 1900. The average acres per farm was 81.1, compared with 93.1 in 1900. The total value of farm property, including land, buildings, implements and machinery, domestic animals, poultry, and bees, was $400,089,303, compared with $181,416,001 in 1900. The average value of all property per farm was $1864, compared with $1015 in 1900. The average value of land per acre in 1910 was $14.13, compared with $6.92 in 1900. The farms operated by owners and managers numbered 107,412 and those operated by tenants, 107,266. Of the farms operated by owners and managers, 82,321 were free from mortgage and 22,374 were mortgaged. The native white farmers numbered 148,627; foreign-born whites, 2478; and negro and other non-whites, 63,593. The total value of domestic animals, poultry, and bees was $74,058,292, compared with $37,483,771 in 1900. The cattle numbered 1,028,071, valued at $15,460,666; horses and colts, 254,716, valued at $23,152,209; mules, 222,200, valued at $27,128,027; swine, 1,518,947, valued at $5,170,924; sheep and mules, 144,189, valued at $327,984. Poultry of all kinds numbered 5,788,570, valued at $2,063,432.

Mineral Production. The production of coal in the State in 1911 amounted to 2,106,789 short tons, valued at $3,396,849. This shows an increase over the output of 1910 of 200,831 short tons in quantity and $417,636 in value. It was, however, 270,000 tons less than the output of 1909, and nearly 570,000 tons less than that of 1907. The increase was caused chiefly by the competition of fuel oil and natural gas and of the more cheaply mined coals of other States.

In 1911 there were produced in the State 664 short tons of zinc, valued at $75,696, and 64 short tons of lead, valued at $5760.

Manufactures. The Thirteenth Census statistics for the calendar year 1909 were compiled in 1912. A summary of the results of this census is shown below.

Of the 2925 manufacturing establishments in the State, the largest proportion is included in those concerned with the manufacture of lumber and timber products. There were of these in 1909, 1697 establishments. No other manufacturing industry approaches this in number of establishments. The printing and publishing industry includes 295 plants, bread and other bakery products, 133, and flour and gristmill products, 113. The number of persons engaged in manufactures in the State at the time of this census was 44,457 over the age of 16, and 525 under that age. The male employees numbered 43,793, and female, 694. The prevailing hours of labor in all industries were 60 per week, 15.5 per cent. of the total number of employees being employed in establishments where the hours are less than 60 a week, and only 6.8 in those where they were more. Although Arkansas is not one of the leading States in value of its manufactures, the following table shows considerable increase over the figures of the previous census:

	Number or Amount 1909	1904	of Inc. 1904-09
Number of establishments	2,925	1,907	53.4
Persons engaged in manufactures	51,730	37,557	37.7
Proprietors and firm members	3,455	2,140	61.4
Salaried employees	3,293	2,328	41.5
Wage earners (average number)	44,982	33,089	35.9
Primary horsepower	173,088	109,509	58.1
Capital	$70,174,000	$46,306,000	51.5
Expenses	64,830,000	45,301,000	43.1
Services	22,574,000	16,854,000	33.9
Salaries	3,461,000	2,310,000	49.8
Wages	19,113,000	14,544,000	31.4
Materials	34,935,000	21,799,000	60.3
Miscellaneous	7,321,000	6,648,000	10.1
Value of products	74,916,000	53,865,000	39.1
Value of products less cost of material	39,981,000	32,066,000	24.7

Education. The total school population of the State, ages 6 to 21 years, on June 30, 1912, was 603,226. Of these 427,723 were white and 175,503 were colored. There were enrolled in the public schools of the State 409,756 children, of whom 300,015 were white and 109,731 were colored. The average daily attendance in the public schools was 261,747. The number of teachers employed was 10,175. Of these 8227 were white and 1948 were colored. During 1912 282 new schoolhouses were erected at a total value of $1,014,109. The total number of schoolhouses in the State at the end of the year was 6333 and the total value of school property was $10,131,828. The expenditures for the maintenance of schools during the year was $3,837,549. There were 93 State high schools in 1911-12 and 60 unaided high schools. The total enrollment in the high schools was 9622. The development of the public school system of the State during the last few years has been remarkable. In 1900 the value of all school property was approximately $2,500,000, and in 1912 more than $10,000,000. In the twelve years since 1900 the school population has increased more than 118,000, or nearly 25 per cent., and the annual school revenues have nearly trebled in value. The number of teachers employed has increased from less than 7000 to more than 10,000. The legislature of 1911 passed several important enactments relating to education. Among these was the creation of a State board of education with general administrative powers, an act making possible State aid to high schools and an act providing liberal appropriations for the maintenance of the State University, State Normal School, the four Agricultural schools, and the Deaf Mute and Blind schools.

Finance. The receipts for the fiscal years 1911-12 were $6,899,247 and the expenditures were $6,734,915. The balance on hand at the end of the fiscal year was $800,770. The chief source of income of the State is the direct tax on all property. The chief expenditures are for schools and charitable institutions. The State debt amounts to $1,250,500.

Politics and Government. On March 27, 1912, a Democratic primary election for State officers was held, resulting in the defeat of George W. Donaghey by Congressman Joe T. Robinson. It is customary in Arkansas to give an official a second term, and generally he gets it without opposition. Governor Donaghey was running for a third term as governor. The only man who has succeeded in being elected governor of Arkansas three times was the late United States Senator Jeff Davis. The nomination in the Democratic primary in Arkansas is paramount to election.

All except two of the delegates to the national Republican convention were pledged to President Taft. There was a contest in the State which was taken up by the national committee. The contest hinged upon the methods used in the election of delegates at the district and State conventions. The Roosevelt delegates declared they had been excluded from the convention halls and from participation in the convention. After hearing the contest the national committee gave the delegates to President Taft.

The Democratic State convention on April 12 selected delegates pledged to Champ Clark of Missouri to the Democratic national convention.

The State elections in Arkansas are held on

the second Tuesday in September, instead of the same day as the presidential elections, as is the case in most of the other States. The State is always Democratic by a large majority and in this election the Democratic candidate for governor, Congressman Joe T. Robinson, was elected by a plurality of 63,386 over Roland, his Republican opponent. The vote was: Robinson, 109,826; Roland, 46,240, and Mikel (Socialist), 13,384. The Progressive party had no candidate for governor. Under the initiative and referendum amendment the people in the general State election of September 9 voted on four acts and five amendments to the constitution. These were Act No. 1, to reduce the rate of taxation and revise the revenue laws; Act No. 2, to provide State-wide Prohibition; Act No. 3, to amend the election laws of the State; Act No. 4, to create a textbook commission; amendment No. 11, providing for the "Grandfather Clause"; amendment No. 12, to exempt capital invested in cotton mills from taxation for a period of ten years; amendment No. 13, limiting the pay of legislators to sixty days; amendment No. 14, providing for the recall of State officers; amendment No. 15, permitting municipalities to issue bonds. Of these nine acts and amendments, all except amendment No. 13 failed to receive the majority required by law. The acts are required to receive only a majority, but the amendments are required to receive a majority of the vote of the candidate in the election who received the highest vote. Amendment No. 15 received a majority, but not a majority of the highest vote cast for governor. The Supreme Court held that according to the constitution only three amendments can be submitted at one time, and ruled against this amendment without taking up the question of whether it received a sufficient number of votes to be adopted. When the Democrats wrested the government of Arkansas from the Carpet-baggers a constitutional convention was held and because of the outrageous misuse of the bond-issuing power in Arkansas by the Carpet-bag government, the constitution was made to prohibit the issuance of bonds by municipalities. The majority is now in favor of this privilege and already a campaign looking to submitting a bond amendment to the people at the next general election has been started.

The total vote for President in Arkansas was: Wilson, 68,838; Taft, 24,297; Roosevelt, 22,673. In April, Peter Stewart, a Socialist, was elected mayor of Hartford. He was the first Socialist mayor elected in the State. On December 16, 1912, Governor Donaghey paroled 360 State convicts. This was intended as a blow at the convict lease system which is employed in Arkansas. As the result of this action, three county convict camps in which convicts were leased to contractors were wiped out of existence. The lease to convict contractors working on the railroad expired on January 1, 1913, and as only enough convicts to work the State farm remained, the leases could not be renewed. In a statement Governor Donaghey declared he had consistently fought the convict lease system, but had found little or no support in the legislature. He declared that conditions in the convict camps were very bad and sought in this way to remedy conditions and recommended that the legislature of 1913 put a stop to the convict lease system by legislation. On January 3 United States Senator Jeff Davis died suddenly at his home in Little Rock.

STATE GOVERNMENT. Governor, J. T. Robinson; lieutenant-governor, W. C. Rodgers; secretary of State, Earle W. Hodges; treasurer, John W. Crockett; auditor and insurance commissioner, J. M. Oathout; attorney-general, W. M. Moose; superintendent of education, Geo. B. Cook; commissioner of agriculture, J. H. Page; commissioner of public lands, R. G. Dye—all Democrats.

JUDICIARY. Supreme Court—Chief justice, Edgar A. McCulloch; justices, F. G. Smith, C. D. Wood, William F. Kirby, and Jesse C. Hart; clerk of the court, P. D. English—all Democrats.

STATE LEGISLATURE, 1913. Senate, Democrats, 34; Republicans, 1; House, Democrats, 96; Republicans, 4; joint ballot, Democrats, 130; Republicans, 5. Democratic majority, Senate, 33; House, 92; joint ballot, 125.

The representatives in Congress will be found in the section *Congress*, article UNITED STATES.

ARKANSAS, UNIVERSITY OF. A State institution of higher learning at Fayetteville, Ark., founded in 1871. The number of students enrolled in the several departments of the university in 1912 was about 500. The faculty numbered 80. In June, 1912, President J. M. Tillman resigned, and Professor J. H. Reynolds, head of the department of history and political science, was elected acting president until a permanent president is secured. Professor A. H. Purdue, State geologist and head of the department of geology, was given leave of absence to become State geologist of Tennessee; Dr. N. F. Drake of Stanford University to fill Professor Purdue's place. A $45,000 building for the department of education is being erected from the Peabody educational fund. The income of the university is about $225,000 per year. The number of bound volumes in the library is 20,000, and of pamphlets, 19,000.

ARMAMENT. See BATTLESHIPS.

ARMIES. See MILITARY PROGRESS and articles on countries.

ARMOR. See BATTLESHIPS and MILITARY PROGRESS.

ARROWROCK DAM AND RESERVOIR. See DAMS.

ART. See PAINTING; SCULPTURE; ARCHITECTURE, and MUSIC.

ARTIFICIAL GEMS. See CHEMISTRY, INDUSTRIAL.

ARTILLERY. See MILITARY PROGRESS.

ART MUSEUMS. See MUSEUMS.

ART NOUVEAU. See ARCHITECTURE.

ASBESTOS. The production of asbestos in 1911 was, according to the report of the United States Geological Survey, the largest in the history of the industry. The total amounted to 7604 short tons, valued at $119,935. This is still less than 8 per cent. of the production of Canada, which supplies the bulk of asbestos used in the factories of the United States. In 1911, four States (Georgia, Vermont, Virginia, and Wyoming) produced this mineral. Vermont ranked first in the production and Georgia second. The imports of asbestos in the United States in 1911, chiefly as noted above from Canada, amounted to 57,124 long tons, valued at $1,318,539. The total exports from Canada amounted to 75,120 short tons. Considerable quantities were imported from Italy, Russia, and Great Britain.

ASHANTI. See GOLD COAST.

ASIA. See ANTHROPOLOGY, EXPLORATIONS, and articles on countries.

ASIA MINOR, EXCAVATIONS IN. See ARCHÆOLOGY.

ASPHALT. There was a greatly increased production of asphalt materials in 1911, chiefly as a result of the movement throughout the United States for better roads. The total production for the year was 360,004 short tons, valued at $3,820,751, compared with 260,080 short tons, valued at $3,080,067 in 1910. The asphalt produced included bituminous rock, 51,328 short tons; refined bitumen, 29,305 short tons; maltha, 8574 short tons; gilsonite, 30,236 short tons; oil asphalt, 234,951 short tons; grahamite, 5000 short tons. The States in which asphalt in these varieties is produced are California, Utah, Oklahoma, and Texas. In California were produced in 1911 190,945 short tons of all varieties; in Oklahoma, including Illinois and Kentucky, 82,387 short tons; in Texas, 55,826 short tons, and in Utah, 30,846 short tons. The imports of asphalt in 1911 amounted to 165,288 short tons, valued at $789,236, compared with 186,311 short tons, valued at $785,963, in 1910.

The chief countries producing asphalt are the United States, Trinidad, Germany, France, Italy, Spain, Austria, Russia, and Venezuela. The United States imported from Trinidad in 1911 111,630 tons, and the total exports from Trinidad to all countries was 179,718 short tons.

ASQUITH, H. H. See GREAT BRITAIN.

ASSOCIATION OF AMERICAN UNIVERSITIES. See UNIVERSITIES AND COLLEGES.

ASSUAN DAM. See DAMS; IRRIGATION.

ASSYRIOLOGY. See ARCHÆOLOGY.

ASTOR, JOHN JACOB. An American capitalist, died at sea April 15, 1912. He was born at Rhinebeck, N. Y., in 1864, the son of William Astor. He was educated by private tutors and later took a scientific course at Harvard University, graduating in 1888 with the degree of B. S. For the two years following his graduation he traveled in unfrequented parts of Europe and in the partially unexplored regions of the Rocky Mountains. Soon after his father's death in 1892 he took over the management of the great Astor estates left by William Astor and began extensive building operations which added greatly to his fortune. These include the Astor, Netherland, St. Regis, and Knickerbocker hotels in New York City. Throughout his life he was greatly interested in mechanics and invented several appliances. Among these were a patent bicycle brake and a pneumatic road improver. He also invented improvements on marine turbines and in 1902 gave to the world his rights in these patents. In 1906 he invented a fuel machine for the utilization of peat deposits. In 1910 he obtained a patent on a device for swivel chairs.

John Jacob Astor obtained the title of colonel as a member of the staff of Governor Morton. On the outbreak of the Spanish-American War he offered his services to the government and equipped a battery, which was presented to the government without cost. This battery did efficient service in the Philippines. Colonel Astor was commissioned inspector-general of volunteers with the rank of lieutenant-colonel. He served with General Shafter's army during the entire time that it was in Cuba and participated in the battle of Santiago. He was detailed by General Shafter to deliver the official terms of surrender to the Secretary of War, and was mustered out of service on November 1, 1898. Colonel Astor was director of many financial institutions and railways. He was one of the founders of the New Theatre and was active in the Hudson-Fulton celebration in New York City. He was also a member of many clubs and patriotic societies. He was the author of *A Journey in Other Worlds* (1890), and *A Romance of the Future* (1894). Colonel Astor was one of the victims of the *Titanic* disaster.

ASTRA-TORRES. See NAVAL PROGRESS, *Aviation.*

ASTRONOMY. No especially striking discoveries in observational astronomy marked the year 1912, though all departments of astronomical research showed steady and satisfactory progress. One new star, *Nova Geminorum, No. 2*, was discovered and was under observation by many astronomers during the greater part of the year; it bid fair to rival *Nova Persei*, which blazed forth in 1901, in its rapid fluctuations of brightness and in the surprising changes in the character of its spectrum. Further important advances in our knowledge of the sun were reported from the Mount Wilson Solar Observatory. The Königstuhl Observatory, at Heidelberg, still continued to report the greatest share of the discoveries of new minor planets, though its preëminence in that respect is beginning to be disputed by other observatories, notably by those at Simeïs (Russia) and Johannesburg (South Africa). Although, as stated in the YEAR BOOK for 1911, the recent series of long-duration solar eclipses has come to an end, expeditions were fitted out for the purpose of observing the two eclipses which occurred during the year; the results from these expeditions may be considered as practically negligible, the second eclipse—visible in Brazil—being a complete failure on account of unfavorable weather conditions.

THE SUN. Mr. C. G. Abbot, in the *Report of the Smithsonian Astrophysical Observatory*, gave as the general mean for the solar constant, as determined from observations made by himself and Mr. Fowle at sea-level at Washington and at altitudes of more than a mile and nearly three miles on Mount Wilson and Mount Whitney, respectively, 1.922 calories (15° C.) per sq. cm. per minute. The solar radiation was found to be relatively greater in the infra-red region of the spectrum than in the ultra-violet, and it was suggested that this is possibly because the shorter radiations from the deeper layers of the solar atmosphere are selectively absorbed during their passage through the upper layers. It was estimated that the sources from which we receive solar radiations have temperatures between 5000° and 7000° abs. C. and mostly between 6000° and 7000°. Evidence of the existence of an irregular variation in the solar radiation was found; its amplitude is from 3 to 10 per cent., and its period is between five and ten days. In order to settle this important question, Mr. Abbot conducted a series of observations at Bassour, in Algeria, during the summers of 1911 and 1912, while one of his colleagues at the same time made observations at Mount Wilson.

Very little sun-spot activity was recorded during the year, the only notable spots being one of fairly large size and circular form which persisted from June 17 to 28, and a group containing two intense nuclei which made its appearance during the early part of October; but in neither case did the spots approach in magnitude the most striking of those observed during the recent period of maximum solar activity.

Professor Dyson, the English Astronomer Royal, drew attention to a possible relationship between the six principal lines in the spark spectrum of radium as determined by Runge and Precht, and certain lines recorded by himself and Lockyer in the spectrum of the chromosphere observed at various eclipses of 1898, 1900, 1901, and 1905.

Professor C. L. Doolittle gave the results of a series of determinations of the aberration constant derived from latitude observations at the Sayre and Flower observatories extending over a period of thirty-two years. The value of the aberration constant finally obtained was 20.525", with a possible error of .0043", and the corresponding value of the solar parallax was 8.780".

SOLAR ECLIPSES. Two eclipses of the sun occurred in 1912. Neither of them was of great importance, although in both cases expeditions were sent out for the purpose of observation. The first took place on April 17 and was visible along a line stretching from northern Portugal across France to Belgium. A certain amount of popular interest was aroused in it on account of the conflicting predictions which had been made concerning its character. Owing to the proximity of the apex of the moon's shadow to the surface of the earth, it had been predicted as a total eclipse by some astronomers and an annular eclipse by others. Actually, it was viewed as a total eclipse in Portugal and as an annular eclipse in France and Belgium, where observers had a splendid view of the phenomenon known as Baily's beads. The duration of totality was so short—barely a second—that the eclipse was not considered likely to add much to our knowledge of the sun. The corona as viewed in Portugal was reported to be of the minimum type associated with the periods of quiescent solar activity, such as that which prevails at the present time. The second eclipse, which occurred on October 10, was visible in Brazil, and several expeditions were fitted out for its observation, but owing to the fact that the bases chosen were in the centre of a widespread rain area, no results were obtained.

MOUNT WILSON SOLAR OBSERVATORY. In his annual report to the Carnegie Institution of the work accomplished at this observatory during 1911, Professor W. S. Adams, the acting director, gave a summary of the principal results obtained by himself and other members of the staff. Among the more important of these results may be mentioned the following:

Mr. C. E. St. John, who has been engaged for some time in the investigation of sun-spot spectra, has determined the probable system of circulation of calcium vapor in sun-spots and the regions surrounding them. In studying the radial motions of the spot-vapors, a phenomenon first discovered by Evershed, he has found that all the vapors of the reversing layer and chromosphere are involved in the movements. Of the high-level vapors of the chromosphere, viz., calcium, hydrogen, magnesium, and sodium, the calcium invariably has an inward radial motion across the penumbræ of the spots, the hydrogen generally, and the magnesium and sodium frequently. The radial motion in the case of calcium is occasionally found combined with a rotary motion which gives rise to a vortical structure similar to that discovered in connection with the magnetic fields of sun-spots (see YEAR BOOKS for 1908 and 1911). The weaker or low-level lines of calcium, magnesium and sodium and the lines of the reversing layer show displacements in the opposite direction, indicating an outflow of the low-lying vapors, the highest velocity of outflow being associated with the lowest levels.

In furtherance of the coöperative plan for spectroscopic observations of the rotation of the sun adopted by the International Union for Coöperation in Solar Research at the Mount Wilson conference in September, 1910, Professor Adams completed a new series of observations, the results of which showed almost complete agreement with those of his previous investigation in 1908. Measurements upon spectra of the two opposite edges of the sun in three different regions of the spectrum, one of which, for purposes of comparison, was selected in common by all the observers taking part in the investigation, gave values for the equator and latitude 15° about 1 per cent. less than the values obtained in 1908, while between latitude 30° and the sun's pole the values were practically identical with those previously found. The general results fail to indicate any variation of the sun's rate of rotation, unless it be of long period. One of the most striking results brought out by these observations was the fact that the lines of different elements give different values of the rotation velocity. Thus the lines of lanthanum and cyanogen give low velocities, while certain lines of hydrogen, manganese and iron give comparatively high velocities. These observations are in substantial agreement with other evidence which we possess regarding the differences of level in the solar atmosphere, and indicate that the period of rotation increases as the surface of the sun is approached, or that the outer layers of the solar atmosphere rotate much more rapidly than those which lie close to the photosphere.

Other important investigations, notably of the Zeeman effect for iron, titanium, and a number of other metals, and of the displacements of the lines of the arc, spark, and furnace spectra of iron and titanium, were completed; and it is expected that these investigations will furnish material for important deductions regarding the physical condition of the stars. Much work was done by Mr. St. John on the question of the existence of free oxygen in the solar atmosphere, in the course of which he proved that the great a and B and A oxygen bands present in their solar spectrum are of purely terrestrial origin.

JUPITER. Mention was made in the YEAR BOOK for 1911 of the remarkable change in longitude experienced by the Great Red Spot, amounting to nearly eight degrees. This westward drift continued until the summer of 1912, when it became temporarily suspended; between June, 1911, and April, 1912, it amounted to twenty degrees, equivalent to about 22,000 miles per year. M. Quénisset described other remarkable changes which had occurred on the planet during the recent opposition. The great northern equatorial band was observed to be much less pronounced and more irregular than in 1910 and 1911, while the north temperate band was much darker and broader than before, being nearer to the north pole of the planet. The south tropical spot was darker and better defined than in 1911, but had shrunk somewhat in size. Professor E. E. Barnard reported some interesting observations of the dark belt discovered by Molesworth in the latitude of the Red Spot in 1901. This peculiar feature of the planet's surface, which appears to have an accelerative effect on the motion of the Red Spot whenever they come together, underwent an extraordinary diminution in length from 115° in June, 1911, to 63° in the summer of 1912. It has a rotation period of 9 hours 55 min. 19 sec., or about 22 sec. shorter than the Red Spot, and whenever it has come into conjunction with it previously, as in 1902, 1904, 1906, 1908 and 1910, it has flowed northward over the bright tropical zone of the planet after skirting the southern border of the Spot.

Lunar Petrography. In an interesting article on "The Selective Absorption of Light on the Moon's Surface and Lunar Petrography," published in the *Astrophysical Journal*, Professor R. W. Wood continued his photographic researches into the constitution of the surface of the moon. He had previously shown that, when the moon is photographed by means of light of the shortest wave-lengths capable of traversing the earth's atmosphere, certain features are brought out which cannot be seen or photographed with visible light. The most conspicuous object thus detected was the area in the vicinity of the lunar crater Aristarchus, which shows as a dark patch on a photograph taken by means of ultra-violet light, but is invisible on an ordinary photograph. Professor Wood showed how by combining photographs taken by light from three or more regions of the spectrum it may be possible to begin the study of the petrography of the lunar surface.

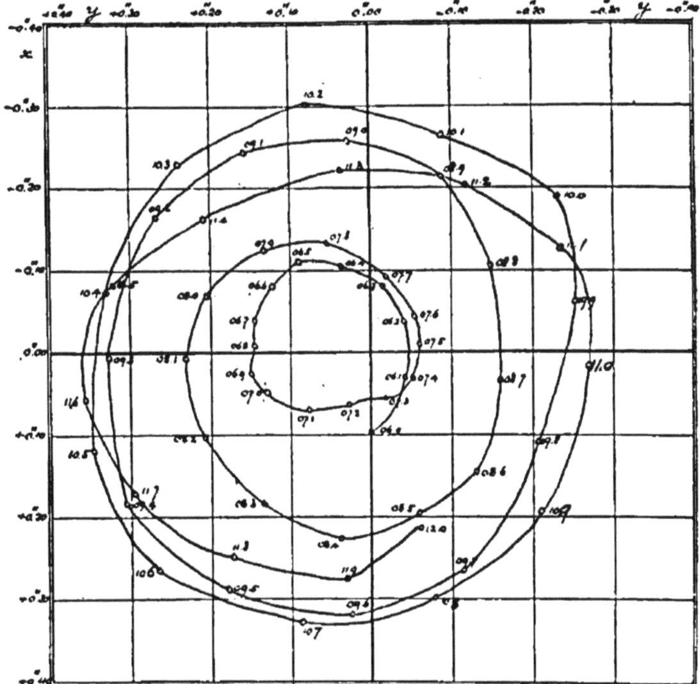

Wandering of the Pole, 1906-1911.
From the *Astronomische Nachrichten*

A yellow image, corresponding very closely to the visual image, is taken through a deep orange screen, the violet image is obtained by giving a very short exposure without any screen, and an ultra-violet image is obtained by using a screen of silvered uviol glass. For comparison, various rock specimens and sulphur deposits were photographed through the screens, and the general conclusion reached was that the patch is probably material which was at some time ejected from the crater by a volcanic blast, and consists of sulphur deposits or perhaps ash containing sulphur. By extending the range of the photographs to other regions of the spectrum in which anomalies in reflecting power are shown by other mineral substances, data should be obtainable for a petrographic survey of the lunar surface.

NEW STARS. A new star of the fourth magnitude was discovered on March 12 in the constellation *Gemini* by Herr Enebo of Domaas, Norway. It was close to *Nova Geminorum, No. 1*, discovered by Professor Turner in 1903. In the course of a few days its brightness decreased to the fifth magnitude, while its spectrum was similar to those of *Novæ Aurigæ* and *Persei* in the earlier stages. On the examination of plates taken before the discovery of the *nova*, it was found at Heidelberg that a star of brighter than magnitude 12 had occupied the same place on March 7, while two Harvard plates taken on March 11 showed the *nova* as a star of the fifth magnitude, although it could not be detected on two plates taken on the preceding day. There was a recrudescence of brightness on March 24, accompanied by a diminution in the redness of the star, and a second increase in brilliancy occurred on April 9. On April 19 its brightness was about 7, and the spectrum changed from an absorption to an emission spectrum, a change similar to that noticed in the case of *Nova Persei*. The magnitude became fairly stationary about the end of May, its value being about 8, with a slight brightening about June 7. The oscillations in brightness were somewhat similar to those of *Nova Persei* in 1901, but of smaller amplitude and longer period.

From observations at the Yerkes Observatory, in December, 1910, and January, 1911, Slocum found that the parallax of *Nova Lacertæ*, discovered by Espin in 1910, was .018", indicating that the outburst producing the *nova* occurred about 180 years ago.

VARIATION OF LATITUDE. It was first demonstrated by Küstner of Berlin in 1888 that observatories do not maintain absolutely invariable distances from the north pole of the earth. When it is considered that the maximum departure of the pole from its mean position is not more than half a second of arc, or less than fifty feet measured on the earth's surface, it is not surprising that the announcement was at first received with some suspicion, but, startling though the fact was, it was speedily confirmed by other observers. The immediate consequence of its discovery was the establishment of an International Latitude Service, whose duty it is to detect and record the sequence of changes in the position of the pole. Four stations, in Japan, California, Maryland, and Sicily, were chosen nearly on the same parallel and dividing it as nearly as possible into four equal quadrants. It is clear that if the pole is tipped toward one of the stations the latitude of that station will be increased while that of the station situated on the opposite side of the earth will be correspondingly diminished. In general it may be said that this is the case, but in a few years it became evident that, in addition to the actual motion of the pole, other causes were at work tending to change the latitude, for there were times when a small but decided increase of latitude was noticed at all four stations. The reality of these small variations of latitude was first suspected by Kimura in 1902, and accordingly this term in the variation has been called the "Kimura term." Various explanations of the Kimura term have been offered, but up to now it has baffled investigators. One explanation has been that it is due to anomalous refraction caused by an inclination of the atmospheric strata, but no such inclination has been observed, at least over any extended area. Shinjo suggested that the difference in temperature between the sun side and the shade side of the observing station could be sufficiently great to produce a pressure-gradient large enough to be responsible for the greater part of the term. In the *Astronomische Nachrichten*, Ross considered that the effect represented by the term was a physical one caused by a progressive change of the zenith point throughout the night at a rate varying with the season. For the further elucidation of the term, he suggested the installation of two special latitude stations on the equator 180° apart and at high altitudes.

In the *Astronomische Nachrichten*, Albrecht summarized the results secured by the International Latitude Service in 1911. It is shown that the maximum departure of the pole from its mean position occurred in that year, and that the spiral curve showing the wandering of the pole has now begun to coil up towards its centre. The accompanying chart, copied from the same journal, shows the wandering of the pole during the period from 1906 to 1911.

STELLAR AND NEBULAR PARALLAXES. Professor A. S. Flint published a list of the parallaxes of 124 stars chiefly between the magnitudes 1.5 and 2.5. Professor Max Wolf, of Heidelberg, basing his calculations on the assumption that many of the spiral nebulæ are of intrinsically the same dimensions, determined the distances of eight nebulæ from their parallaxes, and their diameters from the measured angular diameters combined with the distances. The distances of the nebulæ selected for discussion range from 33,000 to 578,000 light years, and their diameters from 900 to 2200 light years.

MINOR PLANETS. For the fourth year in succession, the number of minor planets announced as new failed to reach the century. Of the seventy-six planets reported, no fewer than ten were actually photographed in 1911, though they were not recognized as new at the time. One of these, which received the provisional designation MF*a*, was discovered at the Lowell Observatory at Flagstaff, Ariz., by Lampland, while the remaining nine, designated by the letters MF*b* to MF*g*, NK, NK*a*, and NK*b*, were observed by Wood at the Johannesburg Observatory. The remaining sixty-six were provisionally designated by the letters NO to QB, with the addition of OG*a* and OK*a*. This year, only twenty were announced from the Königstuhl Observatory at Heidelberg by Professor Max Wolf (3), and his assistants Kaiser (12), Massinger (3), Voigt (1), and Helffrich (1). Of the remaining forty-six, seventeen were credited to Metcalf (Winchester, Mass.), ten to Beljawsky (Simeïs), six to Wood and van der Spuy (Johannesburg), four to Wood, three each to Mme. Beljawsky (Simeïs), and Palisa (Vienna), and one each to Baillaud (Paris), Bernard (Yerkes), and Rheden (Vienna). Six of the above minor planets were found to be identical with others previously known, so that the number of new asteroids not certainly identified with the discoveries of former years was seventy.

Permanent numbers were assigned to the following minor planets:

Number	Temporary Designation	Discoverer	Date of Discovery
715	LX	Wood	1911, Apl. 22
716	MD	Palisa	" Jul. 30
717	MJ	Kaiser	" Aug. 26
718	MS	Palisa	" Sep. 29
719	MT	Palisa	" Oct. 3
720	MW	Kaiser	" Oct. 18
721	MZ	Kaiser	" Oct. 18
722	NA	Palisa	" Oct. 18
723	NB	Palisa	" Oct. 21
724	NC	Palisa	" Oct. 21
725	ND	Palisa	" Oct. 21
726	NM	Metcalf	" Nov. 22
727	NT	Massinger	1912, Feb. 11
728	NU	Palisa	" Feb. 16
729	OD	Metcalf	" Feb. 9
730	OK	Palisa	" Apl. 10
731	OQ	Massinger	" Apl. 15
732	OR	Massinger	" Apl. 15

The names, *Albert*, *Transvaalia*, *Berkeley*, *Erida*, and *Mireille* were given to 594, 715, 716, 718, and 719 respectively.

In the YEAR BOOK for 1911, mention was made of the discovery of a new minor planet, whose rapidly increasing right ascension at opposition suggested some resemblance to Eros, and hence its possible use in determining the solar parallax. This was the planet MT, discovered by Palisa on October 3, 1911. Soon after discovery, and before a sufficiently large number of observations for an accurate determination of its orbit had been obtained, the planet was lost sight of, but fortunately it was picked up later. Calculations based on the earliest set of observations indicated that the planet had a period of about two and a half years, and its perihelion distance was found to be about 1.15 or almost the same as that of Eros, but the eccentricity of its orbit was nearly twice as great as that of the planet discovered by Witt in 1898. The next opposition will occur in March, 1913, but, as the planet will at that time be near aphelion, it will be unfavorably situated for observation; indeed, most of its oppositions take place when it is in the same unfavorable position. Later observations gave an increased value for the period, viz. about five years, and aphelion was found to lie beyond the orbit of Jupiter. As the planet aproaches even nearer to the earth than Eros, and its diameter is probably not more than four or five miles, it is expected that the perturbations which the comparatively massive earth will produce in its orbit will provide data for a determination of the mass of the earth.

COMETS. The periodic comets due to return to perihelion in 1912 were Wolf's (1884 III.), De Vico-Swift's (1894 IV.) and Tuttle's (1858 IV.). The first named came to light in 1911, when it was first detected by its original discoverer, Professor Max Wolf, at Heidelberg. An account of it will be found in the YEAR BOOK for 1911. It passed through perihelion on February 11, 1912. De Vico-Swift's Comet has a period of about 6.4 years, and was due to pass through perihelion in December, but its return to the heavens had not been reported by the end of the year. Tuttle's Comet (1912 b) has a period of about 13.7 years, and was last seen in 1899. Originally discovered by Méchain in 1790, it was rediscovered by Tuttle in 1858 and was seen again in 1871, 1885, and 1899. It was first detected during this return by Schaumasse at Nice on October 18, when it was a body of magnitude 11.5. Owing to planetary perturbations during its last cycle due to its close approach to Jupiter, the time of revolution of the comet in its orbit has been shortened by about 70 days, and perihelion passage took place on October 25 when the comet was about 97.6 million miles from the sun.

Only two new comets were discovered during the year. These were: Gale's Comet (1912 a). This comet was discovered by Gale at Waratah, New South Wales, on September 8. When first detected, it was a round object of the fifth magnitude and about two minutes in diameter; it possessed a nucleus but no tail. Perihelion passage occured on October 4. On September 13 the comet was visible to the naked eye, the nucleus being star-shaped with an even coma of about four minutes in diameter surrounding it. It had then a fan-shaped tail with two branches extending about 5 degrees and making an angle of 60 degrees with each other. It remained visible until about the beginning of November, the angle between its tails increasing to more than 90 degrees. One striking peculiarity of this comet is the great inclination of the plane of its orbit to the ecliptic. Borrelly's Comet (1912 c) was discovered by Borrelly at Marseilles on November 2. It was reported as presenting the appearance of a round nebulosity of the tenth magnitude with a very indistinct nucleus and no tail. When it passed through perihelion on October 22, it was distant about 102 million miles from the sun.

Fayet announced that Schaumasse's Comet (1911 h), discovered on November 30, 1911, is a periodic comet with a period of about seven years.

BOOKS. Among the more important books published in 1912 are: Turner, *The Great Star Map*; Chambers, *Astronomy*; Symonds, *Nautical Astronomy*; Dreyer, *A Short Account of Sir William Herschel's Life and Works*; Kayser, *Handbuch der Spectroscopie, Bd. VI.*; Klinkerfues, *Theoretische Astronomie*. See CARNEGIE INSTITUTION.

ASTRO-PHYSICS. See ASTRONOMY.

ATHENS, EXCAVATION IN. See ARCHÆOLOGY.

ATHLETICS, TRACK AND FIELD. James Thorpe of the Carlisle Indian School by the wonderful showing he made in 1912 stamped himself as the greatest all-round athlete the world has ever seen. Others whose performances on the track and field made the year a most noteworthy one in the establishment of new records were James E. Meredith of Mercersburg Academy, who ran 800 meters in 1:51 9-10, and a half mile in 1:52½; Howard Drew, the negro sprinter, who equalled the American record of 9⅗ seconds for 100 yards and the world's record of 7⅕ seconds for 70 yards indoors; Donald Lippincott of the University of Pennsylvania, who equalled the world's record of 10⅗ seconds for the 100 meters; Marc Wright of Dartmouth, who cleared the bar in the pole vault at a height of 13 feet 2¼ inches; Abel Kiviat of the Irish-American A. C., who ran 1500 meters in 3:55⅘ and a mile in 4:15⅗; Hannes Kolehmainen of Finland, who ran 5000 meters in 14:36⅗; and George Horine of California, who in the running high jump cleared 6 feet 6⅛ inches. See OLYMPIC GAMES.

The following All-American athletic team for the season of 1912 was selected by James E. Sullivan, secretary-treasurer of the A. A. U.: Seventy-yard run, H. P. Drew, Springfield (Mass.) High School; 100-yard run, Ralph Craig, Detroit Y. M. C. A.; 220-yard run, A. T. Meyer, Irish-American A. C.; 440-yard run, C. D. Reidpath, Syracuse University; 600-yard run, M. W. Sheppard, Irish-American A. C.; 880-yard run, J. E. Meredith, Mercersburg Academy; one-mile run, A. R. Kiviat, Irish-American A. C.; two-mile run, T. S. Berna, Cornell University; 120-yard hurdles, F. W. Kelly, University of Southern California; 220-yard hurdles, J. J. Eller, Irish-American A. C.; running broad jump, A. L. Gutterson, Boston A. A.; running high jump, G. L. Horine, Olympic Club, San Francisco; pole vault, H. S. Babcock, New York A. C.; standing high jump, Platt Adams, New York A. C.; standing broad jump, Ben Adams, New York A. C.; three standing broad jumps, L. Goehring, Mohawk A. C., New York; ten-mile run, H. J. Smith, New York City; marathon race, Gaston Strobino, South Paterson (N. J.) A. C.; one-mile walk, R. B. Gifford, McCaddin Lyceum, Brooklyn; running hop, step and jump, C. E. Brickley, Harvard University; shot-put, P. M'Donald, Irish-American A. C.; shot-put (both hands), Ralph Rose, Olympic Club, San Francisco; 56-pound weight for distance, P. Ryan, Irish-American A. C.; hammer, M. M'Grath, Irish-American A. C.; discus, J. H. Duncan, Bradhurst Field Club; javelin, H. G. Lott, Mohawk A. C., New York; five-mile run, H. L. Scott, South Paterson A. C.; all-around, James Thorpe, Carlisle Indian School; cross-country, W. J. Kramer, Long Island A. C., Brooklyn.

The senior championships of the A. A. U. were held at Pittsburgh, September 21, the Irish-American A. C. winning with a total of 67 points as against 34 points scored by the New York A. C. Other teams entered and their scores were: Boston A. A., 20; Springfield (Mass.) High School, 5; McCaddin Lyceum, Brooklyn, 5; University of Missouri, 5; Mohawk A. C., 5; Shannahan C. C., 3; unattached, 9. Among the unattached contestants was Hannes Kolehmainen, the Finnish runner, who won the 5-mile race. In the junior championships the New York A. C. was the victor by the narrow margin of 1 point, its total score being 31. The Irish-American A. C. finished second. The senior indoor championships were won by the Irish-American A. C. (70) with the New York A. C. (45) second. In the junior events the New York A. C. (24) finished first and the Irish-American A. C. (16), second. The all-around championship was won by James Thorpe of the Carlisle Indian School, who scored 7476 points out of a possible 10,000 in ten events. This is a new American record, the best previous performance having been that of M. J. Sheridan who in '907 made 7385 points.

The thirty-seventh annual track and field meet of the Intercollegiate Association of Amateur Athletes of America was held at Franklin Field, Philadelphia, May 30 and June 1. Five new records were made. C. D. Reidpath of Syracuse ran 440 yards in 48 seconds; J. P. Jones of Cornell ran 800 yards in 1:53⅘; Paul Withington of Harvard ran 2 miles in 9:24⅘; R. A. Gardner of Yale cleared the bar in the pole vault at a height of 13 feet 1 inch, and Thomas Beatty of Columbia put the 16-lb. shot 48 feet 10¾ inches.

Pennsylvania won the meet with a total of 28 points. Cornell was second with 17⅔ points and Michigan third with 15 points. Other colleges scoring points were: Harvard, 13; Columbia, 13; Syracuse, 12; Dartmouth, 11½; Yale, 10; Wesleyan, 7; Brown, 6; Princeton, 5; Bowdoin, 2; Rutgers, 2; Massachusetts Institute of Technology, 1.

The University of California won the annual meet of the Conference Colleges of the West, held at Lafayette, Ind., June 1, scoring 41⅓ points. The University of Missouri, which won the 1911 championship, finished second with 29½ points. The totals for the other colleges were: Illinois, 26; Chicago, 15; Wisconsin, 12½; Colorado, 10; Minnesota, 8; Northwestern, Ames and Oberlin, 5 each; Wabash, 4⅓; Iowa, Purdue and Earlham, 1 each; Depauw, ½. California also won the Pacific Coast College meet.

In the New England Intercollegiate championships held at Springfield, Mass., May 17 and 18, Dartmouth was the victor with a total of 46 points. Brown was second with 23 and the M. I. T. third with 16. Other scores were: Bates, 12; Wesleyan, 10; Colby and Vermont, 8 each; Maine, 6⅓; Bowdoin, 6; Holy Cross, 5; Williams (winner in 1911), 5; Worcester P. I., 5; Trinity, 2½; Amherst, 1.

The English championships were held at London, June 22. G. H. Patchings of South Africa and T. R. Nicolson of Scotland made the best individual showings. Patchings won the 100 yard dash, was second in the 440-yards and third in the 220 yards while Nicolson won the 16-lb. hammer throw and was third in the shot-put. P. Kirwan of the Irish-American A. C., New York, for the second successive year won the broad jump.

ATLANTA, GA. See SEWAGE PURIFICATION.

ATLANTIC CITY See NEW JERSEY, *Politics and Government.*

ATLANTIC FLEET. See UNITED STATES, *Navy.*

ATMOSPHERE. See CHEMICAL PROGRESS, and METEOROLOGY.

ATOMIC WEIGHTS AND MEASURES. See CHEMISTRY.

ATOPHAN (PHENYL-QUINOLIN-CARBOXYLIC-ACID). This is a complex substance having the chemical formula $C_{16}H_{11}O_2N$. It is prepared by warming together pyroracemic acid, benzaldehyd, and anilin in alcoholic solution. The drug crystallizes in small, colorless needles, having a melting point of 208° to 209° C. It is insoluble in water, but readily soluble in alkalies, hot alcohol, and boiling glacial acetic acid. Atophan has the property of increasing uric acid elimination. Under moderate doses of the drug the normal average daily output of uric acid may be doubled or trebled, and it is therefore introduced as a substitute for the salicylates in rheumatic conditions and gout. It is said to be particularly efficient in acute attacks of gout, arthritis, and articular rheumatism, but less valuable in chronic types of these diseases.

AUCKLAND ISLANDS. A dependency of New Zealand (q. v.).

AUGUSTA, GA. See CITY PLANNING.

AUSTIN, HENRY. An American lawyer and writer, died October 17, 1912. He was born in Boston in 1848. He held various editorial positions in Boston, New York, Baltimore and

New Orleans, and was at one time associated with Edward Bellamy and others. He wrote many poems, which were collected in a volume entitled *Vagabond Verses*. He also wrote *The Story of Government*, and *A History of Tammany*, as well as several volumes of fiction.

AUSTRALIA, COMMONWEALTH OF. A self-governing dependency of the United Kingdom from January 1, 1901, consisting of six federated states, the Northern Territory, and the Federal Capital Territory. The temporary seat of the federal government is Melbourne, the capital of Victoria. The permanent capital will be in the Yass-Canberra district of the Federal Capital Territory within the state of New South Wales. See CITY PLANNING.

AREA AND POPULATION. The estimated area and the population according to the censuses of March 31, 1901, and April 3, 1911, are as follows:

	Sq. m.	Pop.'01	Pop.'11
New South Wales..	*310,372	*1,354,846	1,646,724
Victoria	87,884	1,201,070	1,315,551
Queensland	670,500	498,129	605,813
South Australia.....	380,070	358,346	408,558
Western Australia..	975,920	184,124	282,114
Tasmania	26,215	172,475	191,211
Northern Territory..	523,620	4,811	3,310
Federal Capital Territory...........(about 900)		.....	1,714
Commonwealth....	2,974,581	3,773,801	4,455,005

* Including the Federal Capital Territory.

The census returns do not include full-blooded aborigines. Such of these, however, as were in the employ of whites, or were living in contiguity to the settlements of whites were enumerated, numbering in 1911 19,939. The total number of aboriginal natives is unknown. A general opinion has prevailed that there are about 150,000, but an estimate made in 1908 by the Queensland chief protector of aborigines is only about 74,000.

The 1911 census showed 2,313,035 males and 2,141,970 females, or 107.99 males per 100 females. Persons of non-European race numbered 52,353, or 1.175 per cent. of the total; these included 37,789 full-bloods (34,838 Asiatic, 2524 Polynesian) and 14,554 half-castes (10,113 Australian, 3852 Asiatic). The following figures show the population specified as to birthplace in 1901 and 1911 respectively: Australasia, 2,934,091 and 3,699,540 (Commonwealth, 2,908,303 and 3,667,672); Europe, 753,832 and 664,671; Asia, 47,014 and 36,442; Africa, 2869 and 4958; America, 12,507 and 11,278; Polynesia, 10,363 and 3410.

Classification by religion in 1911 was: Christian, 4,274,414; non-Christian, 36,785; indefinite, 14,673; no religion, 10,016; object to state, 83,003; unspecified, 36,114. The Christians included: Church of England, 1,710,443; Roman Catholic, 921,425; Presbyterian, 558,336; Methodist, 547,806; Protestant (undefined), 109,861; Baptist, 97,074; Catholic (undefined), 75,379; Congregational, 74,046; Lutheran, 72,395; Jews numbered 17,287.

The figures for conjugal conditions are: Never married, 2,783,543; married, 1,469,622; widowed, 191,743; divorced, 4500; not stated, 5597.

A remarkable feature of the distribution of population in Australia is the tendency to accumulate in towns, especially in the capital cities. In every state the population of the capital far exceeds that of any other town therein and, with suburbs, ranges between 21 and 46 per cent. of the entire population of the state. The following table shows: *a* population of the capital cities, April 3, 1911; *b* and *c* their populations including suburbs (that is approximately within a ten-mile radius of the post office) in 1901 and 1911 respectively; *d* the percentage of the 1911 population with suburbs on the total of the state:

	a	b	c	d
Sydney, N.S.W..	112,921	487,932	629,503	38.19
Melbourne, Vict.	103,593	496,079	588,971	44.82
Brisbane, Qld...	35,491	119,428	139,480	23.03
Adelaide, S. Aus.	42,294	162,261	189,646	46.06
Perth, W. Aus..	35,767	36,274	106,792	37.86
Hobart, Tas.....	27,526	34,604	39,937	20.87
Total	357,592	1,336,578	1,694,329	38.05

The total increase in population from 1901 to 1911 was 681,204 (18.05 per cent.), of which the metropolitan increase was 357,751 and the increase in the rest of the country 323,453. Of the metropolitan increase 234,463 is credited to Sydney and Melbourne. It must be noted further that most of the increase outside the metropolitan areas—323,435—was in towns rather than in the rural districts; many rural counties actually showed a decrease from 1901 to 1911. It is apparent that this distribution of population marks an unsound economic condition.

Population of the other largest towns, within a ten-mile radius, April 3, 1911: Newcastle, N. S. W., 62,406; Ballarat, Vict., 52,551; Bendigo, Vict., 41,757; Parramatta, N. S. W. (five-mile radius and excluding a portion thereof lying within the Sydney ten-mile radius), 34,558; West Maitland, N. S. W., 33,787; Geelong, Vict., 33,518; Broken Hill, N. S. W., 31,386; Kalgoorlie, W. Aust., 31,324; Launceston, Tas., 25,227; Rockhampton, Qld., 20,915; Bulli, N. S. W., 20,873; Toowoomba, Qld. (five-mile radius), 19,776.

The increase of population in Australia is due far more to excess of births over deaths than to immigration. From 1901 to 1910 inclusive the natural increase, or excess of births over deaths, was 619,259, while during the same period the net immigration, or excess of arrivals over departures, was only 40,485. Statistics for 1911: Arrivals, 141,909; departures, 72,609; net immigration, 69,300:—Births, 122,193 (birth rate, 27.21); deaths, 47,869 (death rate, 10.66); excess of births over deaths, 74,324; marriages, 39,482 (marriage rate, 8.79). The percentage of illegitimate to total births in 1910 was 5.84. Estimated population December 31, 1910, 4,425,083; December 31, 1911, 4,568,707.

The Northern Territory was under the jurisdiction of South Australia from 1863 to January 1, 1911, when it was transferred to the Commonwealth. In 1905 the Commonwealth assumed the administration of Papua (q. v.).

The Federal Capital Territory was taken over by the Commonwealth from New South Wales January 1, 1911. The Commonwealth also acquired certain territory at Jervis Bay, together with the right to construct and operate a railway from the new capital thereto. The area of the Federal Capital Territory is approximately 900 square miles, or 576,000 acres, of which it will be necessary to reserve from occupation the catchment area of the Cotter

River, 170 square miles, or 108,800 acres. An area of about 12 square miles, or 7680 acres, has been set apart for the city site, and it is proposed to reserve a further area of about 100,000 acres for parks, roads, military college (opened June 27, 1911), and other public purposes, leaving 359,520 acres available for profitable occupation. The site of the city is 204 miles distant from Sydney, 429 from Melbourne, 912 from Adelaide, and 929 from Brisbane. For the railway to Jervis Bay a route has been selected about 96 miles in length. In 1911 the Commonwealth government invited competitive designs for laying out the capital city, and 149 designs were received. The first premium was awarded to Walter Burley Griffin, Chicago; second premium, Eliel Saarinen, Helsingfors; third premium, D. Alf Agache, Paris. See CITY PLANNING.

EDUCATION. According to the 1911 census, persons able to read and write English numbered 3,650,030; read only, 15,009; able to read and write a foreign language only, 26,210; read only, 2647; not stated, 95,727. Public instruction is under the control of the separate states. Primary instruction is free and compulsory. The following statistics relate to 1910:

	N. S. W.	Vict.	Qld.	S. Aust.
State schools	3,105	2,036	1,189	733
" teachers	5,791	5,028	2,606	1,316
Enrollment...	218,539	206,263	89,695	52,929
Av. att'dance	157,498	145,968	69,439	37,549
Expenditure:				
Maintenance..	£979,775	£788,246	£323,372	£177,827
Buildings...	£191,188	£118,556	£ 50,668	£ 44,025
Priv. schools	774	641	159	185
" teachers	3,602	2,067	761	683
Enrollment...	59,247	54,740	16,320	11,334
Av. att'dance	49,351	44,000	13,950	9,408

	W. Aust.	Tas.	Cmlth.
State schools.......	455	390	7,908
" teachers......	967	799	16,507
Enrollment	32,664	27,820	627,910
Average attendance	27,442	17,974	455,870
Expenditure:			
Maintenance......	£172,470	£74,907	£2,516,597
Buildings	£ 47,637	£16,957	£ 469,031
Private schools.....	119	140	2,018
" teachers......	407	420	7,940
Enrollment	9,400	7,653	158,694
Average attendance	7,563	5,600	129,872

In 1910 the net cost of primary education, including buildings, was £2,985,628, or £6 11s. per pupil in average attendance, as compared with £4 9s. 3d. in 1901. There are a number of superior and technical schools. In 1910 the four universities, Sydney, Melbourne, Adelaide, and Tasmania (at Hobart), had 233 teachers and 3272 students. The University of Queensland, at Brisbane, was opened in 1911.

MINERALS. It was the discovery of gold in payable quantities (in New South Wales and Victoria in 1851) that first attracted population to Australia and thus laid the foundation of the state, but the value of mineral production is now considerably less than that of the agricultural or the pastoral industry. The following table shows the value of the most important minerals, and the total for all minerals, produced in 1910, and the grand total of production from the beginning of mining in Australia to the end of that year; comparative figures are also given for 1909 and 1901:

	Gold £	Coal £	Copper £	Sil. ld.† £
N. S. W..	802,211	3,009,657	486,257	2,110,040
Victoria ..	2,442,745	189,254	450	2,090
Queensl'd.	1,874,955	322,822	932,489	123,086
S. Aust.*..	49,711	....	307,316	907
W. Aust..	6,246,848	113,699	95,928	20,210
Tasmania..	157,370	48,609	566,972	247,576
Cmlth. ...	11,553,840	3,684,041	2,389,412	2,508,909
1909	12,604,509	3,083,696	2,332,988	2,329,164
1901	14,005,732	2,602,770	2,208,590	2,367,687

*Including Northern Territory. †Silver and lead.

	Zinc £	Tin £	Total £	Gd. Total £
N. S. W...	1,289,634	228,156	8,449,919	206,740,724
Vict.	....	3,706	2,629,701	290,998,207
Qld.	....	243,271	3,708,547	96,067,380
S. Aus.* ...	....	31,113	472,568	32,130,167
W. Aust. ..	147	45,129	6,522,263	101,463,422
Tasmania .	....	399,393	1,432,193	33,800,780
Cmlth.	1,289,781	950,768	23,215,191	761,200,680
1909	1,041,524	979,888	23,045,162	737,985,489
1901	†149,207	432,576		

*Incl. Northern Ter. †N. S. W., 1899.

Totals in the foregoing table are exclusive of returns relating to building stone, slates, cement, etc. To the end of 1910 the total output of gold, the most important mining product, was valued at £525,645,357. Further figures for gold for 1901, 1903 (the year of greatest output), and 1911 (subject to slight revision), and the total production from the beginning of mining to the end of 1911:

	1901 £	1903 £	1911 £	Total £
N. S. W..	737,164	1,080,029	769,353	58,760,346
Vict.	3,102,753	3,259,482	2,140,855	289,663,989
Qld.	2,541,764	2,839,801	1,640,323	73,739,851
S. Aust. .	16,613	26,650	15,000	892,810
W. Aust..	7,235,652	8,770,719	5,823,075	103,850,486
Tas.	295,176	254,403	132,108	7,245,982
N. Ter...	76,609	61,600	30,910	2,043,017
Cmth. ...	14,005,732	16,294,684	10,551,624	536,196,981

The greatest yields of gold in each state have been as follows: New South Wales, £2,660,946 in 1852; Victoria, £12,214,976 in 1856; Queensland, £2,871,578 in 1900; South Australia, £76,025 in 1904; Western Australia, £8,770,719 in 1903; Tasmania, £327,545 in 1899; Northern Territory, £111,945 in 1881.

AGRICULTURE. The acreage under crop (exclusive of grasses), and under artificially sown grasses was as follows in the year 1910-11: New South Wales, 3,386,017 and 1,055,303; Victoria, 3,925,070 and 991,195; Queensland, 667,113 and 140,196; South Australia (including Northern Territory), 2,746,694 and 26,416; Western Australia, 855,024 and 8348; Tasmania, 286,920 and 493,233; Commonwealth, 11,893,838 and 2,714,691, as compared with 10,972,299 and 2,457,856 in 1909-10 and 9,433,455 and 2,144,858 in 1905-6. Area and production of the leading crops in 1910-11:

	Wheat		Oats	
	Acres	Bu.	Acres	Bu.
N. S. W...	2,128,826	27,913,547	77,991	1,702,706
Vict.	2,398,089	34,813,019	392,681	9,699,127
Qld.	106,718	1,022,378	2,537	50,469
S. Aust....	2,104,717	24,344,740	77,674	1,136,618
W. Aust...	581,862	5,897,540	61,918	776,233
Tasmania .	52,242	1,120,744	63,887	2,063,303
N. Ter.....	2	20	....	....
Cmlth. ..	7,372,456	95,111,983	676,688	15,428,456
1909-10. ...	6,586,236	90,413,597	698,448	14,734,868
1900-01	5,666,614	48,353,402	470,308	12,043,310

	Corn Acres	Corn Bu.	Hay Acres	Hay Tons
N. S. W.	213,217	7,594,130	638,577	843,044
Vict.	20,151	982,103	832,669	1,292,410
Qld.	180,862	4,460,306	98,558	151,252
S. Aust.	619	6,375	440,177	595,064
W. Aust.	46	718	175,432	178,891
Tas.	......	....	72,992	115,190
N. Ter.	19	449	....	....
Cmlth.	414,914	13,044,081	2,258,405	3,175,851
1909-10	364,585	10,770,648	2,228,029	3,153,196
1900-01	346,505	9,354,971	1,517,963	1,218,089

It is of interest to note that in Australia a very large proportion of the hay crop is cereal grasses, mainly wheat and oats. Thus, of the 638,577 acres of hay in New South Wales, 422,972 were wheaten, and of the 832,669 acres in Victoria, 575,791 were oaten. Crop values for the Commonwealth, 1910-11 (exclusive of the value of straw in the case of cereal crops): Wheat, £16,458,187 (£2 4s. 8d. per acre); oats, £1,709,378 (£2 10s. 6d.); corn, £1,805,548 (£4 7s. 0d.); hay, £8,502,932 (£3 15s. 4d.); barley, £400,054 (£3 13s. 10d.); potatoes, £1,940,857 (£12 16s. 2d.); green forage, £1,709,000 (£2 17s. 7d.). Sugar output in 1910-11: Queensland, 207,264 tons; New South Wales, 18,828 tons; total, 226,092 tons, against 147,403 in 1910-11 and 172,242 in 1905-6.

	Horses	Cattle	Sheep	Swine
N. S. W.	650,636	3,140,307	45,560,969	321,632
Vict.	472,080	1,547,569	12,882,665	333,281
Qld.	593,813	5,113,699	20,331,838	152,212
S. Aust.	249,326	384,862	6,267,477	96,386
W. Aust.	134,114	825,040	5,158,516	57,628
Tas.	41,388	201,854	1,788,310	63,715
N. Ter.	24,509	513,383	57,240	998
Cmlth.	2,165,866	11,744,714	92,047,015	1,025,850
1909	2,022,917	11,040,391	91,676,281	765,137
1900	1,609,654	8,640,225	70,602,995	*931,309

* In 1901.

Cattle (including calves) slaughtered in 1910, 1,363,074, against 1,177,791 in 1909 and 1,110,157 in 1901. Sheep (including lambs) slaughtered in 1910, 15,679,915, against 13,386,856 in 1909 and 8,972,169 in 1901. Australia has more sheep than any other country in the world; Argentina ranks second with 67,383,952 in 1910. Estimated wool production, stated as in the grease, was 792,868,466 lbs., valued at about £32,000,000 in 1910; 1909, 718,037,132 lbs., about £28,000,000; 1906, 577,673,431 lbs.

MANUFACTURES. For statistical purposes a manufactory is defined as any factory, workshop, or mill where four or more persons are employed or power is used. The following table, relating to 1910, shows the number of manufactories, the average number of employees, salaries and wages paid (exclusive of amounts drawn by working proprietors), and value of output:

	Mft.	Empl.	Wages	Output
N. S. W.	4,823	99,746	£ 8,691,386	£ 49,615,643
Vict	4,873	102,176	7,600,932	36,660,854
Qld.	1,563	33,944	2,830,704	15,792,109
S. Aust.	1,278	27,010	2,323,398	11,184,695
W. Aust.	680	14,107	1,683,657	4,533,611
Tas.	605	9,848	744,882	2,983,762
Cmlth.	13,822	286,831	23,874,959	120,770,674
1909	13,197	266,418	21,105,456	107,409,733
1906	11,575	228,560	*13,207,159	....

* Exclusive of Qld. and S. Aust.

COMMERCE. The following table shows: Total exports; domestic exports, or exports of Australian produce; reëxports, or exports of foreign produce; total exports:

Year	Tot. Imp.	Dom. Exp.	Re-exp.	Tot. Exp.
1901	£42,433,811	£47,741,776	£1,954,396	£49,696,172
1906	44,744,912	66,299,871	3,437,889	69,737,763
1909	51,171,896	62,843,711	2,475,125	65,318,836
1910	60,014,351	71,836,195	2,654,955	74,491,150
Specie and bullion included in figures above:				
1901	£ 934,864	£14,423,298	£ 846,921	£15,270,219
1906	2,330,917	15,584,836	2,125,097	17,709,933
1909	1,056,375	7,580,158	1,100,126	8,680,284
1910	1,331,960	3,587,201	1,048,076	4,635,277

Imports and exports are thus classified: *a* animal foodstuffs; *b* vegetable foodstuffs; *c* non-alcoholic beverages; *d* spirits and alcoholic liquors; *e* tobacco; *f* live animals; *g* animal non-foodstuff substances; *h* vegetable substances and non-manufactured fibres; *i* apparel, textiles, etc.; *j* oils, fats, etc.; *k* paints, etc.; *l* stones and minerals, used industrially; *m* specie; *n* metals (unmfd.) and ores; *o* metals (partly mfd.); *p* metals (mfd.), including machinery; *q* leather and rubber and their manufactures; *r* wood and wicker; *s* earthenware, glass, cements, etc.; *t* paper; *u* jewelry and fancy goods; *v* instruments (scientific, etc.); *w* drugs, chemicals, and fertilizers; *x* miscellaneous: *y* total. Trade by classes in thousands of pounds sterling:

	Total Imp. 1909	Total Imp. 1910	Dom. Exp. 1909	Dom. Exp. 1910	Total Exp. 1909	Total Exp. 1910
a	751	874	5,474	8,791	5,495	8,815
b	2,742	1,944	8,440	11,884	8,642	12,077
c	1,410	1,646	4	6	86	97
d	1,497	1,654	134	138	165	175
e	616	769	77	67	129	124
f	114	337	206	307	207	312
g	337	371	28,970	33,129	28,793	33,136
h	997	1,120	196	279	216	293
i	14,766	17,439	79	77	284	278
j	1,337	1,597	1,423	2,193	1,462	2,231
k	416	481	5	6	11	14
l	164	470	875	943	878	946
m	54	374	4,267	1,200	5,366	2,247
n	1,233	1,222	10,324	10,342	10,331	10,350
o	741	1,036	8	9	40	42
p	10,372	12,075	208	221	414	483
q	1,080	1,303	525	577	577	637
r	2,060	2,583	1,033	1,021	1,063	1,058
s	792	1,015	14	13	27	30
t	2,099	2,457	59	58	121	133
u	1,204	1,428	142	135	205	283
v	413	445	7	7	63	61
w	1,744	2,186	211	244	258	295
x	4,234	5,188	164	189	304	368
y	51,172	60,014	62,844	71,836	65,319	74,491

Estimated value of imports entered for consumption: 1909, £49,439,926; 1910, £58,268,574. Leading pastoral and agricultural exports in 1909 and 1910 respectively include: Wool in the grease, 529,020,213 lbs. and 587,093,269 lbs.; scoured and washed wool, 74,082,419 and 78,178,300 (total value for the two years, £25,483,110 and £28,777,283); tallow (net), £1,229,541 and £1,888,796; frozen mutton and lamb, £1,231,035 and £2,161,513; frozen beef, £733,210 and £1,179,146; hides, £423,348 and £406,047; wheat, 31,549,498 and 47,761,895 bu.; flour, 129,969 and 139,946 tons. Domestic exports of gold and silver coin and bullion in 1909 and 1910: Gold—coin, £4,267,070 and £1,199,679; bullion and gold contained in matte, £3,548,268 and £2,480,584;—silver—bullion and silver in matte, £659,332 and £753,090.

Total imports and total exports by countries in thousands of pounds sterling:

	Imports 1909	Imports 1910	Exports 1909	Exports 1910
Great Britain	31,172	36,646	30,917	37,698
United States	5,003	6,495	2,599	1,599
Germany	3,331	3,779	6,395	7,340
British India	1,794	2,669	2,020	1,535
New Zealand	2,195	2,204	2,342	2,343
Belgium	968	1,243	4,754	5,949
Ceylon	740	770	1,217	631
Japan	602	718	1,883	657
Canada	508	649	80	100
Straits Settlements	490	588	445	545
Norway	431	550	1	2
Java	1,057	539	311	345
France	410	502	6,481	8,551
Total, incl. other	51,172	60,014	65,319	74,491

Tonnage entered and cleared in over-sea trade: 1909, 4,361,194 and 4,155,557; 1910, 4,607,820 and 4,725,326.

COMMUNICATIONS. The following table shows the railway mileage, exclusive of sidings and crossovers, June 30, 1911 (*a* government lines; *b* private lines available for general traffic; *c* total open for general traffic; *d* private lines used for special purposes only; *e* grand total.

	a	b	c	d	e
N. S. W.	3,761	141	3,902	125	4,027
Vict.	3,523	14	3,537	37	3,574
Qld.	3,868	501	4,369	21	4,390
S. Aust.	1,935	.....	1,935	58	1,993
W. Aust.	2,376	277	2,653	555	3,208
Tasmania	470	166	636	39	675
N. Ter.	146	.....	146	.....	146
Cmlth.	16,079	1,099	17,178	835	18,013
1910	15,467	949	16,416	1,016	17,432

Mileage (government) under construction, June 30, 1911, 2634; authorized, 1645. Cost of construction and equipment of government lines to June 30, 1911, £152,855,231; for the year ended on that date, percentage of working expenses to gross earnings, 61.94, compared with 61.70 in 1910 and 58.87 in 1906. The authorized transcontinental line will connect the railways of the eastern and southern districts of Australia with the Western Australian lines, the terminals being Port Augusta (S. Aust.) and Kalgoorlie (W. Aust.) This line will be built on standard gauge, 4 feet, 8½ inches, and it was believed that all the railways of the Commonwealth so far as it is possible will be brought to this basis. The length will be 1100 miles. A proposal for another transcontinental line is to extend the main northern line from Adelaide, which at present terminates at Oodnadatta, as far as Pine Creek, the southern terminal of the Northern Territory line from Darwin. The route now followed by the telegraph line is 1140 miles long. Telegraphs, exclusive of railway telegraphs, December 31, 1910: Lines, 44,100 miles; wire, 96,825; offices, 3883. Post offices in 1910, 5506 (5256 in 1906); in addition, receiving offices, 2328 (2145).

FINANCE. The table top of adjoining column gives the Commonwealth revenue and expenditure for the year ended June 30, 1911.

Not included in this expenditure is the subsidy paid to the states, which in the fiscal year 1911 was £5,603,191; 1910, £8,492,436; 1909, £7,930,395. Commonwealth notes issued and unredeemed, March 27, 1912, £10,048,472; gold reserve, £4,841,536. Revenue for fiscal year 1911-12, £20,546,361; expenditure, £14,-721,938.

Revenue		Expenditure	
Customs	£10,507,080	Posts	£ 3,559,785
Excise	2,473,364	Treasury	†1,960,318
Posts	3,906,015	Defense	1,395,798
Land tax	1,370,344	T'de & cus.	1,051,497
Total*	18,806,237	Total*	13,158,529
1910	15,540,669	1910	7,499,516
1909	14,350,793	1909	6,420,398

* Including other items. † Of which, £1,874,-568 for invalid and old-age pensions.

State consolidated revenue and expenditure for year ended June 30, 1911, and outstanding debt on that date:

	Revenue	Expend.	Debt
N. S. W.	£13,839,139	£13,807,538	£95,523,926
Victoria	9,204,503	9,194,157	* 57,983,764
Queensland	5,320,008	5,314,737	44,613,197
S. Australia	4,181,472	4,181,472	† 34,224,653
W. Australia	3,850,439	3,734,448	23,703,953
Tasmania	970,092	1,016,963	11,077,790
Total	37,365,653	37,249,315	‡ 267,127,283
1910	36,956,812	35,373,254	257,623,663
1906	31,273,984	29,864,490	238,427,820

* Includes an advance of £750,000 from S. Aust. to Vict. † Includes Northern Ter. debt, £3,657,-385, and debt on Port Augusta-Oodnadatta railway, £2,240,011. ‡ Against which, sinking fund £5,442,379.

In the fiscal year 1911, the aggregate state revenue from railways and tramways was £19,-176,212; expenditure thereon, £12,137,748. Aggregate state loan expenditure in the fiscal year 1911, £11,926,123 (of which £6,884,430 for railways and tramways; total to end of that year, £200,988,517 (£159,204,321).

ARMY. On June 30, 1912 expired the first twelve-month's operation of the Australian Defense acts of 1909 and 1910, which provided for compulsory enrollment and training of cadets and a national guard. There were enrolled during the year a strength of 92,276 cadets, but of these only 60,418 had made the regulation number of drills, so that there resulted enormous prosecutions and the infliction of fines and penalties of additional service. Some 19,000 young men, who had attained the requisite age, were passed into the Citizen Defence Force from the senior cadets, while 15,-809 junior cadets who received physical culture drill were passed as physically fit. During 1912 the government was devoting $500,000 to the provision of proper drill halls and other facilities, as their lack was interfering somewhat with the complete carrying out of the scheme. The plan of organization of the military force of the Commonwealth resulted from Lord Kitchener's report which recommended an army of 80,000 on a peace basis, divided into a garrison of 40,000 and a mobile force of 40,000. Before the requisite legislation was enacted this plan was amended by Senator Pearce so that the law increased the establishment and provided for 93 infantry battalions, 28 light cavalry regiments, 224 guns, 14 engineer companies, and departmental troops. This force will be formed from trained men from 19 to 25 years of age, who have undergone cadet training and in time of war the total strength will be increased to 107,000, while all Australia was to be divided into 215 territorial districts, every two towns or three country areas forming an infantry battalion. It was reported that during the year over 89,000 men were under arms.

NAVY. War vessels in commission at the end of 1912 included the cruisers *Encounter* and *Protector* and the gunboats *Gayundah* and *Paluma* (all of which are used as training ships), the training-ship *Tingera*, the torpedo-boat destroyers *Warrego*, *Yarra*, and *Parramatta*, and the torpedo boats *Countess of Hopetoun* and *Childers*.

In 1911 the Commonwealth government adopted a programme of naval construction covering a period of twenty-two years and providing for a fleet of 8 battle-cruisers, 10 protected-cruisers, 18 destroyers, 12 submarines, and other vessels. At the end of 1912, the battle-cruiser *Australia* (launched October 25, 1911) was completing at Clydebank; the protected cruiser *Melbourne* (launched May 30, 1912) was completing at Birkenhead, and the protected-cruiser *Sydney* at Glasgow; the protected-cruiser *Brisbane* was building at Sydney, N. S. W.

GOVERNMENT. The legislative power is vested in a parliament of two houses, the Senate (36 members, 6 from each state), and the House of Representatives (75, in proportion to state population). Members of both houses are elected by universal adult suffrage. The executive power is vested in the British sovereign acting through his appointee, the governor-general, who is assisted by a responsible ministry, the executive council. The governor-general in 1912 was Baron Denman, who succeeded the Earl of Dudley, July 31, 1911. Ministry in 1912 (from April 29, 1910): Prime minister and treasurer, Andrew Fisher; attorney-general, William Morris Hughes; external affairs, Josiah Thomas (from October 14, 1911); home affairs, King O'Malley; postmaster-general, Charles Edward Frazer (from October 14, 1911); defense, George Foster Pearce; trade and customs, Frank Gwynne Tudor; without portfolio, vice-president of the executive council, Gregor McGregor; honorary ministers, Edward Findley and Ernest Alfred Roberts (from October 23, 1911).

Each state has a parliament elected, like the federal parliament, by universal adult suffrage. Members of the upper and of the lower house respectively, are as follows: New South Wales, 62 and 90; Victoria, 34 and 65; Queensland, 44 and 72; South Australia, 18 and 40; Western Australia, 30 and 50; Tasmania, 18 and 30. The governor of each state is appointed by the Crown and is assisted by a responsible ministry. The governors and prime ministers respectively in 1912 were: New South Wales, Baron Chelmsford, and J. S. T. McGowen; Victoria, Sir John Michael Fleetwood Fuller and W. A. Watt; Queensland, Sir William MacGregor and D. F. Denham; South Australia, Admiral Sir Day Hort Bosanquet and A. H. Peake; Western Australia, Sir Gerald Strickland and J. Scaddan; Tasmania, Maj-Gen. Sir Harry Barron and Sir N. E. Lewis. Sir Gerald Strickland was appointed to succeed Baron Chelmsford as governor of New South Wales in 1913, and Sir Harry Barron to succeed Strickland in Western Australia. A. E. Solomon succeeded Sir N. E. Lewis as premier of Tasmania.

HISTORY

THE LABOR PARTY'S PROGRAMME. At an important conference of the Labor party at Hobart in January the party platform as amended contained the following planks: (1) Maintenance of a "White" Australia; (2) a graduated tax on unimproved land; (3) effective federation; (4) the "new" protection; (5) nationalization of monopolies; (6) amendment of the Arbitration act; (7) navigation law; (8) Commonwealth passenger and freight steamships; (9) restriction of public borrowing; (10) establishment of a general insurance department; (11) Commonwealth sugar refining. The conference declared that legislative action had been taken on the following planks of their 1908 platform: (1) "White" Australia; (2) old age and invalid pensions; (3) graduated tax on unimproved land; (4) citizen army with compulsory training; (5) a Commonwealth bank; and (6) electoral reform. Thus they had carried into effect more or less completely the greater part of their previous programme. It remained to proceed further along those lines and to deal with these additional policies. As to the "new" protection and the nationalization of monopolies, they depended on the referenda of 1911, which resulted adversely, by a large majority, but the conference decided unanimously to appeal again to the people at the next general election. To explain briefly the chief planks in the amended platform: The first, that which relates to a "White" Australia means, as the term implies, a reservation of all territory belonging to the Commonwealth for exclusive settlement by people of European origin. The practical and immediate object, now that the Commonwealth has the Northern Territory (taken over from South Australia at the beginning of 1911) is the settlement and development of the land by whites. The plan formulated by the government to this end comprises the sending out of expeditions to explore and test the capacities of the territory, the establishment of a leasehold system for land settlement and development and the provision for a settlers' bank whence capital, for land improvement, may be had on favorable terms. As to the land tax it has been in effect since 1910 and, according to the Labor party, has been successful in its object of reducing the large estates, and checking the evils of absentee ownership. They therefore favor its continuance. The term "effective federation" means an increase of the federal power in order to admit of the nationalization of monopolies. The fourth plank, concerning the "new" protection, has been explained in previous issues of this YEAR BOOK. Briefly, the object of the "new" protection is to keep the native market for native manufacturers by adequate customs duties, provided that they pay fair wages, ask fair prices, and do not enter into "combines." This principle was embodied in the Excise Tariff act of 1906 which, after causing much confusion in industrial affairs and after long and costly litigation, was pronounced unconstitutional by the High Court (in 1908), as regulating the territorial trade and industry of the states, as discriminating between states and parts of states, and as dealing with other matters than taxation. The contemplated amendment to the Arbitration and Conciliation act was to prohibit lawyers from appearing before the courts on behalf either of the unions or the employers.

PARLIAMENT. The Commonwealth Parliament was opened on June 19, by the governor-general, Lord Denman. The principal subject of his speech was the birth-rate. It was admitted to be altogether too low for a young country. There had been a marked increase in immigration to which the land tax had largely contributed, but the increase of the population was still too small. The government was now planning to bestow a maternity grant on the mothers of children born in the Commonwealth. A motion of censure was brought on June 20 by Mr. Deakin declaring that the government deserved censure for failing to realize its national and constitutional obligations, for neglecting its duty to secure industrial peace and uphold the law, for mal-administration and excessixe partisanship, and for its reckless financial policy. It was defeated by a vote of 35 to 25. The maternity bill was passed during the session and went into effect in October. It provided for the payment of a bonus up to a maximum of £5 for every child born of white parentage in the Commonwealth. Other important subjects before Parliament were the encouragement of immigration, the opening of the leasehold lands in the Northern Territory, the plan for a preferential tariff agreement with Canada and the proposals for an arrangement with New Zealand for the joint defense of the Pacific. Owing to the friction between the federal and New South Wales governments, the latter refused to renew the lease of the Government House at Sydney after October 31. This caused much indignation among the citizens of Sydney and upon the departure of Lord Denman on October 7, the mayor delivered an address in which the government was blamed for its action.

MISCELLANEOUS. The trans-Australian railroad to connect Port Augusta in South Australia with Kalgoorlie and to open communication between Western Australia and the other states was formally begun on September 20, Lord Denman turning the first sod at Port Augusta. A body of cadets of the newly organized army visited England in March and were entertained by official corporations in London and other cities. See MINIMUM WAGE, and ARBITRATION AND CONCILIATION, INDUSTRIAL.

AUSTRALIAN ANTARCTIC EXPEDITION. See POLAR EXPLORATION.

AUSTRALIAN CAPITAL COMPLETION. See CITY PLANNING.

AUSTRIA-HUNGARY. The Austro-Hungarian monarchy consists of the Austrian empire, the Hungarian kingdom, and the territory of Bosnia and Herzegovina. The capital of Austria is Vienna, and of Hungary, Budapest. In these cities the common legislature (the Delegations) convenes alternately. The sovereign resides at Vienna.

AREA AND POPULATION. The table below shows the area and population of Austria by crownlands, of Hungary by divisions, of Bosnia, and of Herzegovina. The figures for area are shown in square miles, calculated from square kilometers as given in the latest available official reports. The population is shown according to the final figures for population present (*ortsanwesende Bevölkerung*) of the censuses of December 31, 1900, and December 31, 1910. It must be noted, however, that for Bosnia and Herzegovina the population figures are those of the censuses of April 22, 1895, and October 10, 1910, and hence the totals given for the monarchy cannot be quite exact. Moreover, the figure for the population present in the monarchy in 1900 is 45,405,267, as Bosnia and Herzegovina were not annexed until October 5, 1908.

	Sq.m.	Pop. 1900	Pop. 1910
Lower Austria....	7,654.4	3,100,493	3,531,814
Upper Austria....	4,626.3	810,246	853,006
Salzburg	2,761.9	192,763	214,737
Styria	8,658.4	1,356,494	1,444,157
Carinthia	3,987.0	367,324	396,200
Carniola	3,841.7	508,150	525,995
Trieste with ter..	36.8	178,599	229,510
Görz and Gradisca .	1,126.7	232,897	260,721
Istria	1,913.6	345,050	403,566
Tyrol	10,301.7	852,712	946,613
Vorarlberg	1,004.6	129,237	145,408
Bohemia	20,056.6	6,318,697	6,769,548
Moravia	8,579.7	2,437,706	2,622,271
Silesia	1,987.3	680,422	756,949
Galicia	30,307.8	7,315,939	8,025,675
Bukowina	4,031.4	730,195	800,098
Dalmatia	4,954.0	593,784	645,666
Austrian Empire	115,831.8	26,150,708	28,571,934
Rt. bank Danube.	17,216.6	2,923,401	3,084,404
Left bank Danube.	12,699.2	2,049,611	2,175,924
Bet. Danube and Theiss	13,947.5	3,284,233	3,769,658
Right bank Theiss	13,293.8	1,674,241	1,769,681
Left bank Theiss..	16,724.3	2,336,104	2,594,924
Bet. Theiss and Maros	14,014.3	2,054,712	2,141,769
Transylvania	22,101.5	2,476,998	2,678,367
Fiume with ter...	7.7	38,955	49,806
Hungary	109,004.9	16,838,255	18,264,533
Croatia & Slavonia	16,422.4	2,416,304	2,621,954
Hung. Kingdom.	125,427.3	19,254,559	20,886,487
Austria-Hungary	241,259.0	45,405,267	49,458,421
Bosnia	16,239.4	1,348,581	1,631,006
Herzegovina	3,528.6	219,511	267,038
Civil population.	......	1,568,092	1,898,044
Military	......	22,944	33,758
Total B. & H.	19,767.9	* 1,591,036	† 1,931,802
Monarchy	261,027.0	46,996,303	51,390,223

* Census of April 22, 1895. † Census of October 10, 1910.

Of the Austrian population in 1910, 14,034,022 were male and 14,537,912 female. The 1910 census showed the inhabitants of Austria to be divided according to religion as follows: Roman Catholic, 22,530,169; Greek Catholics, 3,417,223; Jewish, 1,313,687; Greek Oriental, 606,764; Evangelical (Augsburg), 444,307; Evangelical (Helvetian), 144,379; Old Catholic, 21,288; other, 13,634; without confession, 20,789.

In Austria, among the civil population, there were in 1910: Marriages, 214,600; births and deaths, 944,948 and 624,240 (each including stillbirths). In Hungary, among the population civil and military: Marriages, 179,510; births and deaths, 758,467 and 506,286 (each including stillbirths). In Bosnia and Herzegovina: Marriages, 20,651; births and deaths, 77,343 and 52,010 (each including stillbirths). Emigration from Austria-Hungary: 1908, 101,275 (of whom 56,214 from Austria); 1909, 272,266 (143,532); 1910, 278,240 (148,638). Population present of the larger cities (census of December 31, 1910): In Austria, Vienna, 2,031,498; Prague, 223,741; Trieste (with territory), 229,510; Lemberg, 206,113; Graz, 151,781; Cracow, 151,886; Brünn, 125,737; Czernowitz, 87,128; Pilsen, 81,165; Königliche Weinberge, 77,093;

Zizkow, 72,195; Pola, 70,145; Linz, 67,817; Przemysl, 54,069; Innsbruck, 53,194; Smichow, 51,815;—in Hungary, Budapest, 880,371; Szeged, 118,328; Szabadka (Maria-Theresiopel, 94,610; Debreczen, 92,729; Zágráb (Agram), 79,038; Pozsony (Pressburg), 78,223; Temesvár, 72,555; Kecskemét, 66,834; Nagy-Várad (Grosswardein), 64,169; Arad, 63,166; Hódmező-Vásárhely, 62,445; Kolozsvár (Klausenburg), 60,808; Ujpest (Neupest), 55,197; Miskolcz, 51,459. Sarajevo in Bosnia had in, 1910, 51,919 inhabitants, and Mostar in Herzegovina 16,392.

EDUCATION. Throughout the monarchy elementary instruction is free and compulsory. In Austria there were, at the end of 1909, 23,450 elementary schools (including 1208 private), with 105,370 teachers and 4,454,238 pupils; children of school age, 4,744,521; training colleges, 133. In 1912 gymnasia numbered 316 (105,002 students); realschulen, 149 (49,065). There are many technical, professional, and special schools. The state maintains eight universities, which in 1911-12 were reported to have 1920 teachers and 29,742 students. The eight government technical high schools had, in 1911, 833 teachers and 11,174 students.

In Hungary there were, in 1909-10, 19,206 primary schools, with 46,340 teachers and 2,903,817 pupils; children of school age, 3,112,600; 95 training colleges, with 10,174 students; 197 gymnasia, with 3787 teachers and 63,338 students; 43 realschulen, with 978 and 14,424. There are many technical and professional schools. The three universities maintained by the state had, in 1910, 610 professors, etc., and 10,040 students.

AGRICULTURE. Area in hectares (2.471 acres) of principal crops harvested in Austria in 1910 and 1911, with production in metric quintals (220.46 pounds) and yield per hectare in 1911:

Crops	Hectares 1910	Hectares 1911	Quintals 1910	Quintals 1911	Qs. per ha.
Wheat	1,213,579	1,215,090	15,673,315	16,026,388	13.2
Rye	2,060,980	2,021,345	27,671,921	26,446,569	13.1
Barley	1,101,525	1,096,677	14,722,147	16,201,813	14.8
Oats	1,833,018	1,878,058	20,631,564	22,700,639	12.1
Corn	311,773	300,813	4,416,782	3,041,344	10.0
S. Beet	253,731	247,115	70,618,000	42,498,000	172.0

Various yields in 1910, not given above, in thousands of quintals: Beets (other than sugar beets), 41,510; potatoes, 133,664; hempseed, 127; mixed grains, 726; buckwheat, 1300; millet, 395; pulse, 2631; flaxseed, 169; hops, 165; cabbage, 8397; clover hay, 45,795; mixed fodder, 6750; hay, 101,169. Wine production in 1910, 2,547,000 hectoliters. Silkworm eggs placed for hatching in 1912, 10,245 hectograms; estimated production of cocoons, 2,110,000 kilograms, against 2,162,113 kgs. produced in 1911.

Production in 1912: Wheat, 18,952,639 quintals (15.0 qs. per ha.); rye, 29,748,033 (14.6); barley, 17,065,756 (16.0); oats, 24,300,998 (13.0); corn, 3,875,179 (12.8). Planted to sugar beets in 1912, 262,612 hectares.

Livestock in 1910 included 9,159,808 cattle, 2,428,586 sheep, and 6,431,966 swine.

For Hungary the harvested area of the principal crops in 1911 and 1912, their production, and the yield per hectare in 1911 are shown below:

Crops	Hectares 1911	Hectares 1912	Quintals 1911	Quintals 1912	Qs. per ha.
Wheat	3,708,399	3,820,988	51,919,122	50,176,446	14.0
Rye	1,185,937	1,207,750	13,800,299	14,398,031	11.6
Barley	1,171,659	1,128,749	16,708,600	15,891,585	14.3
Oats	1,173,657	1,103,291	13,948,693	11,155,771	11.9
Corn	2,878,772	2,883,189	41,004,415	54,850,169	14.2
Flax	....	9,592	....	....	...
S. beet	....	172,326	19,500,000	15,000,000	...
Vines	....	328,168	....	....	...
Tobacco	....	47,581	....	....	...

In 1910, 1,242,000 hectares were planted to potatoes, yielding 133,664,000 quintals. Silkworm eggs placed for hatching in 1912, 20,071 hectograms; estimated production of cocoons, 1,694,000 kilograms, against 1,878,276 kgs. produced in 1911.

Livestock in Hungary proper, according to a census taken in the spring of 1911, with percentage of increase or decrease as compared with the figures of the 1895 census: Horses, 2,000,611 (1.4 per cent.); mules and asses, 18,765 (15.8 decrease); cattle (including 155,192 buffaloes), 6,183,424 (6.1 increase); sheep, 7,696,881 (2.3); swine, 6,415,197 (0.5 decrease); goats, 331,383 (15.7 increase). While the increase in the number of cattle was not proportionate to the increase of population, there was a great improvement in the quality of the stock; the breed known as "spotted" cattle, introduced with a view to improving the stock, increased from 1,347,826 in 1895 to 3,590,808 in 1911. The decrease in swine was due to the prevalence of disease during the preceding ten years. During the twelve months preceding the census there were born 1,672,678 calves, of which 824,932 were kept for breeding, 241,975 sold for breeding, 15,568 slaughtered for home consumption, 540,604 slaughtered for selling, and 49,599 died.

The foregoing figures do not include the livestock of Croatia and Slavonia. Results of the census of March 24, 1911, with percentage of increase or decrease since 1895: Horses, 350,036 (12.4 per cent.); mules and asses, 3173 (9.0 decrease); cattle, 1,134,664 (24.9 increase); swine, 1,163,493 (31.8); sheep, 850,161 (42.7); goats, 95,592 (326.4).

MINING AND METALS. In Austria the total value of mining products (exclusive of salt, petroleum, etc.) in 1909 was 317,501,821 kronen and in 1910 315,484,476 kronen; furnace products, 137,235,740 and 143,951,194. Quantity and value of the more important minerals in 1910: Coal, 13,773,985 metric tons (139,437,987 kronen); lignite, 25,132,855 (136,116,897); salt, 345,629 (45,065,081); graphite, 33,131 (1,388,052); iron ore, 2,627,583 (23,604,359); silver ore, 23,629 (4,165,951); lead ore, 22,841 (4,090,528); mercury ore, 100,899 (2,373,634); zinc ore, 34,637 (2,282,855). Metal production in 1910 included: Raw iron, 1,504,786 metric tons (valued at 120,233,559 kronen); zinc, 12,458 (6,640,618); lead, 15,476 (5,610,206); mercury, 603 (3,423,455); copper, 1468 (2,018,073). Silver produced was valued at 4,320,021 kronen and gold 580,393.

In Hungary in 1910 the value of the coal output was 16,679,000 kronen; lignite, 71,494,000; raw iron, 40,987,000; iron ore, 13,628,000; gold, 9,960,000; silver, 1079.

COMMERCE. The total special trade in 1911 exceeded that in any previous year, although the value of exports was less than in 1910 or 1907. The following table shows, in thousands of kronen, the trade of the common customs territory. Imports of merchandise for home consumption, of total merchandise, of coin and bullion, and total imports:

Years	Mdse. Home Consump.	Total Mdse.	Coin and B.	Total Imports
1895	1,444,986	1,487,052	107,659	1,594,711
1900	1,696,358	1,748,968	44,898	1,793,866
1905	2,146,133	2,213,145	55,982	2,269,127
1907	2,501,974	2,587,147	43,839	2,630,986
1909	2,746,331	2,821,261	237,101	3,058,362
1910	2,852,852	2,929,734	43,099	2,972,833
1911	3,191,712	....	41,414	....

Exports of domestic merchandise, of total merchandise, of coin and bullion, and total exports have been as follows, in thousands of kronen:

Years	Domestic Mdse.	Total Mdse.	Coin and B.	Total Exports
1895	1,483,620	1,568,118	50,362	1,618,480
1900	1,942,003	2,061,705	66,546	2,128,251
1905	2,243,780	2,390,722	59,533	2,450,255
1907	2,457,286	2,658,085	79,456	2,737,541
1909	2,318,868	2,475,053	128,342	2,603,395
1910	2,418,606	2,587,641	80,931	2,618,572
1911	2,404,303	....	132,915	....

Values, in thousands of kronen, of the leading classes of imports for consumption and exports of domestic produce are shown in the following table. The letters indicate: *a* Cotton and its manufactures; *b* wool and its manufactures; *c* cereals, pulse, flour, etc.; *d* coal and other fuel; *e* vegetables, fruits, etc. (exclusive of southern fruits); *f* animal products; *g* iron and steel and their manufactures; *h* other common metals and their manufactures; *i* machines, apparatus, etc.; *j* electrical machinery, apparatus, etc.; *k* vehicles and vessels; *l* instruments, watches, etc.; *m* silk and silk goods; *n* flax, hemp, jute, etc., and their manufactures; o colonial produce; *p* leather and its manufactures; *q* chemicals, by-products, etc.; r minerals; *s* tobacco; *t* rubber and its manufactures; *u* sugar; *v* cattle and draught animals; *w* apparel, etc.; *x* wood manufactures; *y* glass and glassware; *z* paper and its manufactures; *aa* southern fruits; *ab* comestibles; *ac* beverages; *ad* gums and resins; *ae* turners' and carvers' materials; *af* earthenware; *ag* literary and artistic articles.

	Imports 1909	Imports 1910	Imports 1911	Exports 1909	Exports 1910	Exports 1911
a	326,944	363,610	379,280	64,121	87,324	101,142
b	264,987	274,280	249,694	99,047	102,543	103,327
c	220,652	107,349	126,671	118,158	116,189	102,199
d	217,083	200,682	218,566	340,949	348,571	370,388
e	156,085	162,181	226,937	82,023	98,896	114,718
f	154,017	174,545	215,052	240,194	232,404	230,887
g	58,288	57,659	65,556	35,833	47,816	56,817
h	113,446	120,448	138,597	69,806	82,543	85,464
i	91,548	106,110	118,472	23,856	30,144	32,575
j	20,781	26,221	31,778	9,237	9,525	10,191
k	14,095	18,094	21,148	9,060	14,778	13,53[illegible]
l	54,456	57,311	60,701	12,907	13,638	14,975
m	106,794	121,665	121,094	45,522	41,051	44,591
n	74,982	76,444	96,178	55,441	59,134	61,001
o	71,512	85,583	108,492	24	15	27
p	68,978	79,438	91,390	66,816	68,811	67,092
q	76,931	81,400	84,133	47,596	49,404	51,311
r	50,486	56,454	62,935	45,497	45,230	42,772
s	50,290	54,916	58,720	11,639	13,507	14,724
t	49,138	69,278	55,334	19,064	20,076	19,995
u	142	162	233	240,642	241,019	216,566
v	10,495	10,539	30,853	111,266	97,545	49,503
w	23,008	24,712	25,822	81,219	86,491	89,880
x	22,301	27,008	33,368	66,940	78,111	80,719
y	7,158	8,027	9,917	71,010	74,156	71,170
z	22,113	35,773	35,737	57,248	60,147	59,156
aa	39,620	47,498	52,296	4,204	4,042	3,829
ab	31,343	36,653	47,413	9,708	8,916	8,542
ac	11,652	12,748	13,563	35,201	34,611	35,590
ad	20,475	25,691	27,501	7,778	10,017	8,388
ae	21,027	26,393	27,222	3,187	4,048	3,723
af	7,575	9,049	9,845	20,567	23,355	24,230
ag	57,736	57,734	61,434	27,465	27,665	29,432

In 1909 and 1910 imports of raw materials, in millions of kronen, amounted to 1604.4 and 1582.3; pa tia y manufactured materials, 435.0 and [illegible]; manufactures, 706.9 and 794.6;—exports of raw materials, 875.5 and 870.3; partially manufactured, 406.0 and 434.9; manufactures, 1037.4 and 1113.4.

Trade (special) by countries, in thousands of kronen:

Countries	Imports 1910	Imports 1911	Exports 1910	Exports 1911
Germany	1,153,882	1,263,204	1,062,483	1,038,217
United States.	236,920	289,760	81,352	58,452
Great Britain.	228,534	229,448	224,433	216,279
British India..	214,038	219,739	68,624	51,574
Russia........	167,212	209,215	90,999	96,199
Italy..........	131,022	141,629	229,390	222,133
France........	112,376	112,417	76,166	74,955
Switzerland...	84,732	85,366	104,852	112,096
Rumania......	52,163	78,150	102,929	123,974
Brazil.........	59,203	75,376	10,762	11,693
Belgium.......	48,648	50,217	24,116	22,128
Bulgaria......	11,817	42,612	17,304	37,356
Egypt.........	33,735	35,419	35,112	39,917
Turkey........	52,008	33,182	128,757	93,504
Total, including other.	2,852,852	3,191,712	2,418,606	2,404,303

SHIPPING. Entered at the ports in 1910, 190,105 vessels, of 28,235,486 tons (sail, 20,315, of .791,467 tons); cleared, 189,986 vessels, of 28,335,345 tons (sail, 20,229, of 786,247 tons). Under the Austro-Hungarian flag: Entered, 177,305 vessels, of 25,993,866 tons; cleared, 177,237, of 26,094,641 tons. Merchant marine at the beginning of 1911: 510 steamers, of 522,970 tons, and 16,185 sail, of 49,159 tons.

COMMUNICATIONS. Railways in operation in 1911 aggregated 46,088 kilometers, of which 23,070 kms. were in Austria, 21,062 in Hungary, and 1956 in Bosnia and Herzegovina. Of the Austrian lines, about seven-tenths, and of the Hungarian, about four-fifths, are owned or operated by the state. The electrification of the Vienna and Pressburg lines (63 miles in length) took place during 1912, the city portions being worked on the direct-current system and the country portions by alternating current. Telegraphs (1911): Austria, 6970 offices, with 46,952 kms. of line and 235,493 kms. of wire; Hungary, 4592 offices, 25,068 kms. line and 144,124 kms. wire; Bosnia and Herzegovina, 173 offices, 4102 kms. line, and 12,778 kms. wire. Telephone stations (1910): Austria, 110,882; Hungary, 59,885; Bosnia and Herzegovina, 780. Post offices (1910): Austria, 9461; Hungary, 6152; Bosnia and Herzegovina, 172; abroad, 36.

FINANCE. The standard of value is gold, and the monetary unit the kronen, par value 20.263 cents. The cost of administering the common affairs of the monarchy is borne by both governments in a proportion agreed to by their parliaments and sanctioned by the emperor-king. The agreement renewed for ten years in 1907 provides that the net proceeds of the common customs be applied to the common expenditure, and the remaining expenditure be satisfied by Austria in the proportion of 63.6 per cent. and by Hungary 36.4 per cent. The expenditure of the monarchy in 1908 was 514,376,180 kronen (ordinary 394,372,164, extraordinary 120,004,016); in 1909, 643,578,124 kronen (440,391,996 and 203,186,128). Net customs receipts in the two years, 169,931,455 kr. and 197,379,735 kr. The net expenditure, therefore, was 344,444,725 kr. in 1908 and 445,-598,389 in 1909; this expenditure, for 1908, was satisfied by Austria in the sum of 219,066,840 kr. and Hungary 125,377,885 kr.;—for 1909, Austria 283,400,575 kr. and Hungary 162,197,814 kr. Estimated expenditure for 1911, 457,903,864 kr.; for 1913, 503,974,188 kr. (of which 6,024,019 extraordinary). Estimated net customs receipts for 1913, 197,704,169 kr. Estimated departmental expenditures for 1913: Foreign affairs, 18,954,716 kr.; war, 479,511,979 (including marine, 74,757,210); finance, 5,143,953 (including pensions, 4,605,000). By the terms under which the union of Austria and Hungary was effected in 1867, no debts are contracted by the monarchy; the total general debt, contracted before that time, amounted on January 1, 1912, to 5,179,043,911 kr. Distinct from this are large debts contracted by both Austria and Hungary since 1868.

In Austria, revenue and expenditure have been as follows, in thousands of kronen:

	1907	1908	1909	1910
Revenue...	2,253,052	2,388,384	2,883,648	2,895,492
Exp'diture	2,209,093	2,373,894	2,795,703	2,901,364

The budget for 1912 showed estimated revenue of 2,916,685,263 kr. (2,770,393,164 ordinary and 146,597,180 extraordinary); estimated expenditure, 2,916,685,263 kr. (2,668,097,637 ordinary and 248,607,626 extraordinary). The larger items of estimated revenue: Railways, 822,584,010 kr.; excise, 391,947,100; direct taxes, 379,790,000; tobacco monopoly, 318,258,100; posts and telegraphs, 201,305,500. The larger estimated expenditures: Railways, 637,566,780 kr. ordinary and 124,617,930 kr. extraordinary; finance, 861,085,365 and 5,441,700 (including 505,797,962 for public debt); common expense of the monarchy, 338,107,811 and 8,080,126; posts and telegraphs, 162,072,820 and 17,211,720; worship and public instruction, 105,117,244 and 8,196,440; public works, 87,139,930 and 26,085,310; justice, 88,091,286 and 1,247,000; national defense, 100,426,715 and 1,080,595. Provisional estimates for 1913 were 3,137,202,566 kr. revenue and 3,137,481,539 kr. expenditure. On January 1, 1912, the consolidated debt was 6,711,294,746 kr.; floating debt, 350,333,568 kr.; total, 7,061,628,314 kr. (not including Austria's part in the common debt).

In Hungary, revenue and expenditure have been as follows, in thousands of kronen:

	1907	1908	1909	1910
Revenue...	1,395,711	1,531,368	1,750,783	2,074,549
Exp'diture	1,399,477	1,616,245	1,721,564	1,901,666

In 1910 ordinary revenue amounted to 1,543,102,641 kr.; ordinary expenditure, 1,418,776,584; total expenditure included 149,444,732 kr. for sinking fund. The 1912 budget showed estimated revenue 1,852,747,661 kr. (1,667,091,211 ordinary, 185,656,450 extraordinary); estimated expenditure, 1,852,694,998 kr. (including 1,580,378,496 kr. ordinary and 168,877,261 kr. for sinking fund). Larger items of estimated ordinary revenue for 1912: Railways, 427,000,000 kr.; direct taxes, 287,010,000; excise. 270,630,000; tobacco monopoly, 185,267,000; posts and telegraphs, 95,545,000. Larger estimated ordinary expenditures, 1912: Ministry of commerce, 430,221,650 kr.; ministry of finance, 249,592,018; Hungarian debt, 219,642,197; ministry of the interior, 101,112,054; part in the common expense of the monarchy, 101,563,468; ministry, worship and public instruction, 95,093,039; ministry of agriculture, 70,140,526; debt of the monarchy, 60,619,340; ministry of national defense, 62,117,366. Debt in 1910 (not including Hungary's part in the common debt), 5,317,327,796 kr.; in addition, arrears, etc., 927,998,323 kr.; total, 6,245,326,119 kr.

Army. On July 5, 1912, a new army bill was officially promulgated designed to increase the personnel, which on a peace strength had been fixed at 305,000 in 1889. The term of service with the colors was reduced from three to two years and the total period of service was increased from ten to twelve years. For cavalry and horse artillery three years with the colors and seven years in the reserve were retained, a proviso which was adopted for the *Landwehr* cavalry. In general, the two years' service was not to be completely established until 1917, but it was to be introduced gradually. The new recruit contingents voted were for the "Common" army, 159,500; Austrian *Landwehr*, 26,996; *Honved*, 25,000; as against 103,000, 20,000, and 12,500 in previous years, working up to the increased strength gradually. See below under *History*

For the *Ersatz* reserve the initial period of training was determined at ten weeks instead of eight, and there were to be three subsequent yearly trainings, not exceeding a total period of four weeks. The entire service will cover twelve years.

	Present (1912)	1917	Increase
Common army............	305,914	336,000	30,000
Austrian Landwehr........	48,084	55,600	7,500
Hungarian Honved........	32,770	51,000	18,000
Total	386,768	442,600	55,500

In 1912 the active army of Austria-Hungary was composed of 17 army corps, comprising 8 cavalry divisions and 36 infantry divisions, with a *Landwehr* division attached to each. In March, 1912, the 2 corps on the Italian frontier were increased and various changes of garrison were made. Four new brigades and 2 additional cavalry divisions were formed at Budapest and Lemberg and 40 sections of machine guns were formed for attachment to infantry battalions. There were in the active army in 1912, 106 regiments of the line, 4 of Tyrolese Rifles, and 26 battalions of Regular Rifles, making a total of 468 battalions, 15 regiments of dragoons, 11 of Uhlans, and 16 of Hussars, making a total of 250 squadrons. The organization of the artillery gives to each army corps 130 field guns, 24 howitzers, and 24 guns for the *Landwehr* division, making in all 178 guns, while on a peace basis the heavy artillery was organized into 28 4-gun batteries of siege howitzers. There were also 40 mountain batteries and 6 fortress artillery regiments.

Navy. Number and displacement of warships of 1500 or more tons, and of torpedo craft of 50 or more tons, built and building, December 1, 1912: Dreadnoughts (battleships having a main battery of all big guns; that is, 11 inches or more in calibre): built, one (*Viribus Unitis*) of 20,010 tons; building, three of 60,030 tons. Predreadnoughts (battleships of about 10,000 or more tons whose main batteries are of more than one calibre): built, 6 of 74,613 tons; building, none. Coast-defense vessels (including smaller battleships and monitors): built, 6 of 41,700 tons; building, none. Battle cruisers: none built or building. Armored cruisers: built, 3 of 18,580 tons; building, none. Cruisers (unarmored warships of 1500 or more tons): built, 4 of 10,332 tons; building, 3 of 10,449 tons. Torpedo-boat destroyers: built, 12 of 4728 tons; building, 6 of 4722 tons. Torpedo boats: built, 40 of 6500 tons; building, 12 of 2928 tons. Submarines: built, 6 of 1686 tons; building, 7 of 4473 tons. Total tonnage: built, 178,149; building, 82,602. Excluded from the foregoing: Ships over 20 years old unless reconstructed and rearmed within five years; torpedo craft over 15 years old; transports, colliers, repair ships, torpedo-depot ships, and other auxiliaries.

The third of the four dreadnoughts was launched November 30, 1912, being christened *Prinz Eugen;* the first is the *Viribus Unitis* (commissioned October 6, 1912), and the second the *Kaiser Franz Josef* (to be completed in the summer of 1913). Primary armament of each of the four, twelve 12-inch guns. Provision was made in the 1912 budget for a total active personnel of 17,277 men. See NAVAL PROGRESS.

GOVERNMENT. Austria and Hungary have each a representative parliament and a responsible ministry appointed by the sovereign. Croatia and Slavonia and each crownland of Austria have separate diets. The common administration is directed, under the constitutional compromise of 1867, by the emperor-king, acting through three ministers, for foreign affairs, finance, and war, who are responsible to the Delegations. These bodies, of 60 members each, represent the Austrian and Hungarian parliaments and convene each year alternately at Vienna and at Budapest. They examine the requirements of the common services and advise the parliaments as to necessary appropriations. The common government deals with finance relating to the monarchy as a whole, foreign affairs, the diplomatic, postal, and telegraphic services, the army, the navy, and certain state monopolies. The sovereign in 1912 was Franz Joseph I., who was born August 18, 1830, and became emperor of Austria December 2, 1848, and king of Hungary June 8, 1867. His nephew, the Archduke Franz Ferdinand, born December 18, 1863, is the heir-presumptive. Common ministry at the beginning of 1912: Premier and minister for foreign affairs, Aloys (Count) Lexa von Aehrenthal (appointed 1906); finance, Stephan (Baron) Burián de Rajecz (1903); war, Gen. Moritz (Ritter) von Auffenberg (1911). Count Lexa von Aehrenthal died February 17 and was succeeded by Leopold (Count) Berchtold, Baron von und zu Ungarschütz. On February 20, 1912, Baron Burián de Rajecz was succeeded by Dr. Leon (Ritter) von Biliński. General von Auffenberg resigned December 9, 1912, and was succeeded by the under secretary, Gen. A. (Ritter) von Krobatin. The navy department is a section of the war ministry; at its head in 1912 was Admiral Rudolf (Count) Montecuccoli.

The Austrian ministry in 1912 (formed November 3, 1911): Premier, Karl (Count) Stürgkh; interior, Dr. Karl (Baron) Heinold von Udynski; worship and public instruction, Dr. Max (Ritter) Hussarek von Heinlein; finance, Wenzel (Ritter) von Zaleski; commerce, Dr. Rudolf Schuster von Bonnott; railways, Zdenko (Baron) von Forster; agriculture, Fr. Zenker; national defense, Gen. Friedrich (Baron) von Georgi; public works, Ottokar Trnka; justice, Dr. Viktor (Ritter) von Hochenburger; without portfolio, Dr. Ladislas (Ritter) von Dlugosz.

The Hungarian ministry (formed April 17, 1912): Premier and minister of the interior, Dr. Ladislas de Lukács; finance, J. de Teleszky; commerce, Ladislas Beöthy de Bessenyö; agriculture, Count Serényi de Kis-Serény; worship and public instruction, Count Zichy; justice, Dr. Ferencz Székely; national defense, Lieutenant Field Marshal Baron Hazai; for Croatia and Slavonia, G. Josipovich. See BOSNIA AND HERZEGOVINA.

HISTORY

THE REICHSRATH. The Austrian government programme at the beginning of 1912 included the budget and provisions for new taxes to cover the deficit, the new military law, the construction of canals and waterways, appropriations for local railway lines and for certain public works, and various measures of social legislation, including workingmen's insurance, an increase of the salaries of civil servants, and a reform of the discipline of the service. When the Reichsrath had adjourned at the beginning of July it had made noteworthy progress in carrying out these plans, despite the difficulties arising from the rivalry of races and from the external political situation. The military reforms which had been urged for twenty years were at length voted (see *New Military Law*), and a statute of functionaries passed the Lower House (see *Statute of Functionaries*). These measures imposed new burdens on the revenues and radical fiscal reforms were required. The Reichsrath did not, however, deal thoroughly with the matter. It admitted the new expenses, but did not accept the new taxes, except provisionally and in part. The essential points in the financial situation were set forth by the former minister of finance, Baron Plener, in the summer. He pointed out that the deficit for 1912 amounted to 112,000,000 or 118,000,000 crowns, and that the public debt had increased by 1,746,000,000 crowns, during the last few years as the result of bond issues which had been so frequent that the market was overstocked and the profit to the government slight. Radical reforms were necessary, but the Reichsrath temporized, contenting itself with provisional arrangements.

THE NEW MILITARY LAW. The military law passed the Austrian Reichsrath after some difficulties, on June 26, and was at length forced through the Hungarian parliament, despite the prolonged obstructive tactics of the minority (see below, *Hungarian Cabinet Crisis*). The German element in the empire had long favored the reform, for the army not only expressed the unity of the state but afforded the basis for the alliance with Germany, and a strong army was required to maintain the national prestige. The measure was especially desired by the emperor, who intervened personally on its behalf. The rivalry between the Poles and the Ruthenians threatened at one time to prevent its passage. In Galicia, the Poles, who outnumbered the Ruthenians, controlled the local government, and the Ruthenians complaining of their oppression demanded autonomy for eastern Galicia. In accordance with the usual practice of the national parties, the Ruthenians threatened to obstruct parliamentary procedure unless the government conceded their demands. When the government promised to do so, the Poles took offense and in their turn began to hamper the government. Upon the assurance of the emperor that he trusted the patriotism of both races, and on his appeal to the Poles for a friendly settlement of affairs in Galicia, the opposition ceased and the law was voted. The law of 1889, which the present measure superseded, fixed the contingent of army recruits at 103,100 for a period of ten years. Though the need of an increase and of a new military organization was manifest in 1899 if Austria-Hungary was to hold her place among her neighbors, the distracted state of the country at that time prevented the desired changes. The new law fixes for a period of twelve years the Austro-Hungarian contingent at 159,000 and increases equally the landwehrs of Austria and Hungary. To lessen the burden on the people, the term of service for the great majority of recruits is reduced from three to two years, the three-year term being retained only for the cavalry and other mounted troops. Naval service was to last four years. These inequalities in the length of service occasioned criticism and the government promised to consider plans for their removal. Important changes were made in the code of military justice, which had become altogether antiquated, having been in force for more than a century. Naturally the financial question raised by these heavy additions to the expenses was a very serious one, and time was required to work out an answer. The minister of war submitted a programme demanding an appropriation of 250,000,000 crowns, but the minister of finance refused, in view of the state of the treasury, to present the demand to the parliaments. The question was adjourned.

STATUTE OF FUNCTIONARIES. During the session that terminated in July, the Reichsrath made progress with the measure for reforming the rules of the civil service and increasing the remuneration of officials. It passed the lower house and was submitted to the upper house. The important point at issue was the right of public functionaries to form unions. The Socialists, who had a hundred votes in the assembly, won others to their side on behalf of this right, and the new measure gave civil servants complete liberty of action in regard to unions, containing provisions on this subject and on the subject of coalition, of which the government disapproved. The latter threatened to refuse to submit the law to the royal sanction if these were not changed. It was argued that they would destroy discipline and play into the hands of the syndicalists. It was expecteu that the upper house would modify these provisions and that the civil servants would welcome the measure, nevertheless, because of the improvement in their material condition for which it provided.

HUNGARIAN CABINET CRISIS. The crisis in the cabinet arising from the difficulties over the army question led to the resignation of Count Khuen-Héderváry early in March, and serious difficulties in the way of forming a new cabinet soon developed. There was much distrust in Hungary of the policy of the war office, and the war minister, General von Auffenberg, was fiercely attacked in the Hungarian press for his alleged designs on Hungary. The imperial government on the other hand was determined to control the Hungarian contingent of the dual army, and in this was supported by a portion of the public. Count Khuen-Héderváry, to whom the crown entrusted negotiations for opening the way to a new cabinet, found the solution of the difficulty impossible. Both the Justh and Kossuth groups determined to obstruct the measure unless the Hungarian government would commit itself to universal suffrage. Count Héderváry, by way of compromise with the Kossuth group, promised to introduce a resolution accepting the principle that the reservists could not be made to serve with the colors in time of peace unless parliament had granted the annual levy. This, however, was offered without the crown's assent, and the imperial government refused to accept it, whereupon the Héderváry cabinet resigned (March 7), but was asked to retain office temporarily. The relations between Austria and Hungary were at a deadlock, the emperor threatening to abdicate if the principle of imperial control over the Hungarian forces were denied. Toward the end of March Count Héderváry declared that while the Hungarian government's views had not altered, it could not act upon them, since such a course would result in the emperor's abdication. The resignation of the ministry was recalled, but, further difficulties arising, it resigned again on April 17. Dr. de Lukács was then chosen as minister-president to succeed Count Khuen-Héderváry, and it was understood that he would find means of coming to terms with the Kossuth party; but he was soon at odds with the opposition over the military and franchise questions. The Justh group declared that his policy was no more favorable to universal suffrage than that of his predecessor. In May the suffrage agitation led to rioting in Budapest. On June 4 the army bill was at length carried through by the strong measures of Count Stephen Tisza, who had been elected president of the lower house. Finding it impossible to proceed on account of the disturbances in the house, he summoned the police to keep order. Members of the opposition used the most violent language and M. de Justh was particularly bitter and abusive, denouncing Count Tisza as a scoundrel and usurper. On June 7 the violent scenes of the previous session were repeated and culminated finally in an attempt on the life of Count Tisza. After the opposition had taken their seats, despite the ruling of Count Tisza that they should be excluded, they were surrounded by 150 constables, and upon their continued refusals were removed, one by one. After they had gone, Count M. Kovács, who had remained behind, shouted that a member of the opposition was still there and fired several shots at Count Tisza from a revolver. The bullets struck in the woodwork of the presidential tribune at which he was sitting. Kovács was immediately attacked by the other members and carried out unconscious. Popular demonstrations against the government occurred and it was clear that public opinion was decidedly against the arbitrary methods employed by the government. The feeling against Count Tisza was so strong that he did not venture for some time to go out into the streets. When he did appear in public, on June 15, he was surrounded by a mob and narrowly escaped violence. The police were obliged to intervene.

On the reopening of the parliament on September 17 the riotous scenes were repeated. The opposition deputies blew on horns, beat drums and cymbals, fought with their rivals and with the police. On the following day, when they attempted to renew the pandemonium, the sitting was suspended and the police summoned, whereupon the opposition members left the house. The session was then reopened and the government majority voted the exclusion of the opposition deputies. After voting the Delegation the house adjourned.

RACE QUESTIONS. The conflict between the Germans and Czechs in Bohemia had for four years checked the activities of the Bohemian Diet, thrown the administration into confusion, and resulted in a financial deficit which prevented the payment of salaries of many classes of public officers and the carrying out of necessary public works. An adjustment of some sort was absolutely necessary if the functions of government were to be performed and negotiations toward a compromise were carried on in the summer of 1912. The government used all possible means to prevent their failure. The chief features of the proposed compromise were as follows: The Czechs, while maintaining their traditional principles of an undivided Bohemia, were to concede to the Germans a certain measure of administration, as the price of political peace. In the German districts judicial and administrative officers were to be of that race, and the rule as to the two languages was to be determined by local law for the officials of the autonomous districts and by imperial law for the state officers. The Bohemian budget would be divided between the two nationalities and there would be two sets of rules for civil servants. The law was to protect the rights of that race which in any locality was in a minority. By July the prospect for the restoration of peace in Bohemia seemed promising. Another race difficulty was the recent movement of the southern Slavs, that is, the Croats, Slovenians, and Serbs, for separation from Austria and Hungary and the creation of a southern Slavic empire, thus turning the dual into a triple monarchy. This movement had gathered force ever since the annexation of Bosnia and Herzegovina. Croatia has long desired to cut loose from Hungary and absorb the Croats of Istria and Dalmatia. The Slovenians prefer a union with the Croats to inclusion in the Austrian kingdom, and the Serbs of Austria and those on the Servian frontier would, in spite of their present rivalry, welcome the new arrangement. Bosnia-Herzegovina would also form a part of the new federation. Though the realization of this purpose seemed far off, the movement has gained strength from the economic development of those countries, which tends to make them more independent financially. In Croatia the Hungarian government has had to repress agitation with violent measures. Croats, Serbs, and Slovenians have protested against these measures of oppression, and the Diet of Bosnia has expressed its sympathy with their kinsfolk in Austria and Hungary. The events in the neighboring Turkish provinces added to the danger and the development was naturally watched with interest in Montenegro and Servia. In 1912 this southern Slavic movement was in fact one of the most serious questions before the state.

DISTURBANCES IN CROATIA. At the end of February serious disturbances occurred at Agram, where the feeling ran high against the government and against Hungary. Much damage was done to property and a number of policemen were wounded. Many arrests followed. The immediate cause of the outbreak was the arrest of a former opposition deputy, who was condemned to three months' imprisonment for having signed his client's name to an election petition. Throughout the Slav provinces of the south the feeling against Hungary was very bitter. Early in April the appointment of the new ban, M. Cuvaj, as royal commissioner for Croatia and Slavonia, with dictatorial powers, was announced. In his proclamation he declared that the activity of the Diet was suspended and the arrangement for the Diet, elections was stopped. Restrictions were placed on the press and the right of free assembly was provisionally suspended. The previous Diet had been dissolved at the end of January, owing to its conflict with the government, and it was feared that the new Diet would be no more practicable than the old one. The Czech parties at a meeting at Prague on April 8 expressed sympathy with the Serbs and Croats for their defense of their national rights against the Magyar government of force, and declared their belief that the struggles of Czechs, Serbs, and Croats would ultimately lead to an independent Czech kingdom in the north and an independent Croatia in the south.

There was bitter opposition against the arbitrary rule in Croatia and members of the Reichsrath in April were inclined to urge the Austrian government to intervene on behalf of Croatia against the new ban. An attempt was made to assassinate the ban on June 8 by a Bosnian law-student of Agram University, who fired at him on the street and mortally wounded his companion, M. Hervoitch, a prominent Croatian official. A trial for alleged conspiracy at Agram in the summer had features in common with the Agram high treason trial of 1909, and was characterized by the press as equally farcical. A number of youths were involved, and in August one of them was sentenced to death, seven were sentenced to varying terms of imprisonment, and four were acquitted. The sentence aroused much indignation in Croatia and was regretted by a portion of the Austrian press. Appeal was taken to a higher court.

FOREIGN AFFAIRS. Count Aehrenthal, the foreign minister, died at Vienna on February 17. Almost up to the moment of his death there had been a bitter campaign against him in which many many persons of great political influence were said to be concerned. The ground of the attacks was his failure to give adequate return to Germany for her support during the annexation crisis, and his opposition to the chief of the general staff in his efforts to strengthen Austrian defenses in view of the increasing number of Italian troops on the Austrian border. He resigned in January on account of illness, and in the following month, there being no hope of his recovery, his resignation was accepted. He was succeeded by Count Berchtold, the first Hungarian to hold the office in more than thirty years. On April 30 the latter made an outspoken declaration as to the imperial foreign policy before the Hungarian delegation committee. After affirming his loyalty to the principles of Count Aehrenthal, he declared that they would maintain unswervingly the triple alliance, and that their friendly relations with the German empire and with Italy remained unchanged. The extension of the Italian naval campaign to the Ægean and the closing of the Dardanelles had caused much alarm and the government brought to the attention of Turkey the disadvantages involved in closing the straits. It was hoped that the measure would be repealed when danger to the Dardanelles had ceased. The emperor received visits from the Russian Grand Duke Andrew Vladimirovich in February, the Emperor William of Germany in March, and King Nicholas of Montenegro and King Ferdinand of Bulgaria in June. Count Berchtold conferred with the German chancellor at Buchlau in September, with the King of Italy and his foreign minister at Rome in October, and with the German and Italian ambassadors at Budapest in November. For further details as to Austro-Hungarian diplomacy, see TURKEY AND THE BALKAN PEOPLES.

MISCELLANEOUS. Hungarian Socialists proclaimed on May 22 a general strike for the following day as a demonstration for universal suffrage. Some disorders occurred at Budapest on account of the government's prohibition of open air meetings.

AUTOMOBILES. The remarkable increase in the use of automobiles which has characterized the years since their practical perfection, continued in 1912. According to figures compiled by *The Automobile*, the total number of cars registered at the end of 1912 was 1,010,483. This figure, however, includes duplicate registrations amounting to 15,345. The largest number of motor vehicles registered in any State was in New York, 105,546. California follows with 88,699; Illinois, 68,073; Ohio, 63,066; Pennsylvania, 59,357; Indiana, 54,334; and Massachusetts, 51,229. The smallest number registered was in Nevada, 900. The registration in 1911 was in round numbers, 677,000, showing that the registration nearly doubled in 1912. The total number of motor vehicles of all kinds produced in 1912 was 378,261, compared with a production of 209,957 in 1911. The production of various classes of cars in 1912 was as follows: Gasoline cars, 340,746; gasoline trucks, 27,909; electric cars, 8013; steam cars, 850; electric trucks, 743.

The increased popularity of low-priced cars is shown by the fact that there were produced in 1912 177,563 cars to sell at $1250 and less. Cars made to sell from $1250 to $2000 numbered 100,444. Cars made to sell between $2000 and $3000 numbered 68,891, and those amounting to more than $3000, 31,362.

There were exported in the first eleven months of 1912 23,089 automobiles, valued at $23,998,351. The largest number were exported to Canada, 6864; to the United Kingdom, 4371; to British Oceania, 3112; to South America, 1859. The number imported during the same period was 1795, valued at $1,974,496.

The increase in the use of motor trucks continued in 1912. There were manufactured in 1912 27,909 gasoline motor trucks, compared with 8500 in 1911. There were 743 electric trucks made, compared with 553 in 1911. In 1912 there were produced 200 gasoline fire trucks, compared with 105 in 1911.

RACING EVENTS. Ralph de Palma is clearly entitled to be called the champion driver of 1912. He started in more road races and is credited with more victories than any other driver. He won the Vanderbilt Cup race, the light car race at Santa Monica, the Elgin National Trophy race and the Elgin free-for-all contest. "Teddy" Tetzlaff ranked second to de Palma in number of wins, capturing the Santa Monica free-for-all, the Tacoma heavy car race and the Tacoma free-for-all event. Other drivers of the year deserving special mention are "Joe" Dawson, who in a National car averaged 78.72 miles an hour for 500 miles, a new record for sustained speed on a specially built course, and "Bob" Burman, who in a Blitzen Benz made a new world's record for one mile of 47.85 seconds on a circular dirt track at Brighton Beach.

A noteworthy feature of the year's sport was that no fatal accidents occurred in the twenty principal races. One driver, David L. Bruce-Brown, however, was killed while training at Milwaukee and his mechanic was so badly injured that he died a week after the accident. Bruce-Brown was the winner of the Grand Prize race in 1910 and 1911.

The premier racing honors were won by foreign cars much to the disappointment of the American manufacturers. In the Grand Prize, the Elgin, the Vanderbilt, the Santa Monica, and the Tacoma races, foreign machines were the victors. Two cars showed marked superiority in road events. These were the Fiat and the Mercedes. The Fiat finished first four times and second once in twelve starts, while the Mercedes captured three firsts and one third in the same number of starts. Tetzlaff drove a Fiat car and de Palma a Mercedes.

A summary of the principal racing events in the United States follows: Vanderbilt Cup Race, 299.54 miles, won by de Palma in a Mercedes, 4 hours, 20 minutes, 31.54 seconds, average 69 miles per hour; H. Hughes second in a Mercer; S. Wishart third in a Mercedes. Elgin National Trophy, 254 miles, won by de Palma, 3 hours, 43 minutes, 26 seconds, average 68.4 miles per hour; R. Mulford second in a Knox; Merz third in a Stutz. Elgin Free-for-all, 305 miles, won by de Palma, 4 hours, 28 minutes, 36 seconds, average 70.01 miles per hour; Bergdoll in a Benz second, Mulford in a Knox third. Grand Prize, 409.79 miles, won by Bragg in a Fiat, 5 hours, 59 minutes, 25 seconds, average 69.3 miles per hour; Bergdoll in a Benz second, Anderson in a Stutz third. Santa Monica Free-for-all, 303 miles, won by Tetzlaff, average 78.5 miles, per hour; Bragg second in a Fiat, Bruce-Brown third in a Benz.

In the Grand Prix Race at Dieppe, France, Bouillet covered 956.63 miles in 13 hours, 58 minutes, 23½ seconds, an average of 68 miles per hour. Zuccarelli won the Grand Prix race for light cars, 402.4 miles, at Le Mans, France. His time was 6 hours, 12 minutes, 22 seconds. The event for heavy cars was captured by Goux, whose time for the same distance was 5 hours, 31 minutes, 54 seconds.

The most important new records made in 1912 follow: Speedway, 3 kilometers, Bragg in a Fiat, 1 minute, 54.83 seconds; 100 miles, Tetzlaff in a Fiat, 1 hour, 13 minutes, 37.25 seconds; 150 miles, same driver and car, 1:49:52.84; 200 miles, same driver and car, 2:25:59.52;

250 miles, same driver and car, 3:7:13.94; 300 miles, same driver and car, 3:48:49.3; 350 miles, same driver and car, 4:25:15.27; 400 miles, same driver and car, 5:4:14.23; 450 miles, same driver and car, 5:44:4:54; 500 miles, same driver and car, 6:21:6.03. One mile circular track—1 mile, Burman in a Blitzen Benz II., 47.85 seconds; 2 miles, Oldfield in a Christie, 1:35:89; 3 miles, Disbrow in a Simplex, 2:27.81; 4 miles, same driver and car, 3:17.02; 5 miles, same driver and car, 4:6.58; 10 miles, same driver and car,8:17.02; 15 miles, 13:3; 20 miles, same driver and car, 17:57.4; 25 miles, same driver and car,22:26.6; 75 miles, Wishart in a Mercer, 1:15:52.5; 100 miles, same driver and car, 1:40:51; 150 miles, same driver and car, 2:30:51; 200 miles, same driver and car, 3:28:4.5.

AUTOMOBILE FIRE APPARATUS. See FIRE PROTECTION.

AVERY, ROBERT. An American soldier and lawyer, died October 1, 1912. He was born in Tunkhannock, Pa., in 1839 and was educated at Wyoming Seminary. At the outbreak of the Civil War he went to the front as captain in the 102d New York Infantry in 1863. He was promoted to be lieutenant-colonel and was brevetted lieutenant-colonel of volunteers on March 13, 1865, for gallant services at Chancellorsville, where he commanded the right wing of the Second Army Corps and where he was shot through the neck. For services on Lookout Mountain he was brevetted colonel and brigadier-general. In the latter battle he lost his right leg. After the war he was sent to Raleigh, N. C., as judge advocate to assist in the work of reconstruction. In 1870 he was admitted to the bar and practiced law in New York City. He was a director in several industrial corporations and in railroads.

AVIATION. See AERONAUTICS; MILITARY PROGRESS and NAVAL PROGRESS.

AVIETTES. See AERONAUTICS.

AYCOCK, CHARLES BRANTLEY. Former governor of North Carolina, died April 4, 1912. He was born in Fremont, N. C. He studied law and engaged in its practice at Goldsboro, N. C. From 1893 to 1898 he was United States district attorney. In 1901 he was elected governor of the State, serving in that office until 1905.

AYME, LOUIS HENRI. An American public official and scientist, died May 16, 1912. He was born in New York City in 1855 and graduated from Columbia College in 1874. He studied medicine for a short time and then became scientific assistant on the United States Transit of Venus Expedition to New Zealand in 1874. From 1880 to 1884 he was United States consul at Merida, Yucatan, Mexico, and in the two years following was ethnologist of the Smithsonian Institution in Oaxaca, Mexico. From 1886 to 1891 he was on the staff of the Chicago *Inter Ocean* and served for the next five years on the staffs of several Chicago papers. In 1898 he was appointed consul at Guadaloupe and in 1908 at Para, Brazil. In the latter year he became consul-general at Lisbon, Portugal. He was well known as an archæologist and was a member of many American and foreign learned societies. He was the author of *Notes on Mitla* (1882), and in 1890 was associate editor of *Elliott's Magazine*, Chicago. He contributed scientific and archæological articles to many magazines.

BACILLUS CARRIER. See TYPHOID FEVER.

BACON, FRANCIS. An American surgeon, died April 26, 1912. He was born in 1831 and graduated from the Yale Medical School in 1851. In the following year he distinguished himself in a yellow fever epidemic which broke out in Galveston and he himself was stricken with the disease. At the outbreak of the Civil War he became surgeon of the Second Connecticut Volunteers. He served throughout the war and was promoted to be medical director of the Army of the Potomac and afterwards to the same position in the Department of the Gulf. From 1865 to 1877 he occupied the chair of surgery in the Yale Medical School. He was an authority on yellow fever.

BACON, HENRY. An American artist, died March 14, 1912. He was born in Haverhill, Mass., in 1839, and later removed with his family to Providence and afterwards to Philadelphia. He enlisted in the Federal army at the age of 18, and became field artist for *Leslie's Weekly*. He served in the war until he was wounded. After its close he went to Paris to take up the study of art. He remained in that city for twenty years, studying under Frère and Cabanal. Several of his pictures were hung in the salon. After leaving Paris he went to London and for several years lived in Chelsea in the house once occupied by Thomas Carlyle. Although he was successful in oil painting, his watercolor pictures brought him first into prominence. For several years he spent his winters in Cairo, Egypt, making excursions with caravans into the desert, gathering material for the watercolor pictures of caravan life and desert scenes which chiefly made him famous. Some of his pictures are in the collections of J. P. Morgan and Henry Walters. One of his best-known pictures is that of "General Gates and the Boys of Boston Common," which hangs in the Adams House in Boston.

BAGDAD RAILWAY. See TURKEY.

BAHAMAS. The most northerly of the British West Indian colonies; a chain of about 20 inhabited islands and numerous islets and rocks. Total area, 4403½ square miles; population (1911), 55,944 (of whom 13,554 in the island of New Providence.) Nassau is the capital. Sponges are the principal export (£110,740 in 1910), the export of salt herring declined from £2470 in 1890 to £96 in 1910; preserved fruits (£9219 in 1910), pineapples, oranges, and grapefruit are other products. Area planted (1910) to sisal, over 20,000 acres; export, 6,296,687 pounds, valued at £42,057.

	1907	1908	1909	1910
Imports ...	£372,937	£369,490	£343,489	£329,014
Exports* ..	226,819	183,558	165,116	188,286
Revenue ..	89,694	81,862	77,578	84,386
Expenditure	79,790	99,655	92,858	85,315
Shipping† ..	1,929,077	1,334,314	1,304,660	1,722,340

* Of colonial produce. † Tonnage entered and cleared.

Customs revenue (1910-11), £69,334. Public debt (March 31, 1911), £55,639. Governor and commander-in-chief (1912) Sir William Grey-Wilson (since 1904).

BALANCE OF TRADE. See UNITED STATES, *Commerce*.

BALDWIN, SIMEON E. See CONNECTICUT.

BALFOUR, A. J. See GREAT BRITAIN, *History*.

BALKAN QUESTION. See TURKEY AND THE BALKAN PEOPLES.

BALKAN STATES, THE. See BULGARIA; GREECE; MONTENEGRO; RUMANIA; SERVIA; and TURKEY.

BALKAN WAR. See TURKEY AND THE BALKAN PEOPLES.

BALLOONS. See AERONAUTICS.

BALTIMORE. See MARYLAND, *Politics and Government.*

BALTIMORE HIGH PRESSURE FIRE SERVICE. See FIRE PROTECTION.

BANANA FOOD PRODUCTS. See HORTICULTURE.

BANG, HERMAN JOACHIM. A Danish author, died in January, 1912. He was born in the Island of Seeland in 1857. He was educated at the Academy of Sorö and at Copenhagen. He was the author of many popular novels, short stories, and romances. Among the best known of his writings are the following: *Haa blöse Slägter* (1880); *Fädra* (1883, dramatized as *Ellen Urne,* 1885); *Excentriske Noveller* (1885); *Stille Eksistenser* (1886); *Tine* (1889); *Under Aaget,* a collection of novels (1890); *Teatret* (1892); *Ludvigsbakke* (1896); *Udvalgte Fortællinger* (1899); *Liv og Död* (1900), and *Mikæl* (1903).

BANK CLEARINGS. See FINANCIAL REVIEW.

BANKERS' ASSOCIATION, AMERICAN. See BANKS AND BANKING.

BANKING PENSIONS. See OLD AGE PENSIONS.

BANKING REFORM. See CURRENCY REFORM.

BANKS, STATE. See STATE BANKS.

BANKS AND BANKING. In addition to the matter found in this article, which deals primarily with the condition of all banks in the United States and with the subject of banking reform, there will be found elsewhere articles as follows: NATIONAL BANKS; STATE BANKS; SAVINGS BANKS; POSTAL SAVINGS BANKS; LOAN AND TRUST COMPANIES; AGRICULTURAL CREDIT; CURRENCY REFORM; CLEARING HOUSE; and FINANCIAL REVIEW.

RESOURCES AND LIABILITIES. The aggregate resources of 25,194 banks about June 14, 1912, as reported by the Comptroller of the Currency, were $24,986,000,000. The reporting banks included 7372 national, 13,381 State, 630 mutual savings, 1292 stock savings, 1410 loan and trust companies, 1110 private banks. The aggregate resources represented an increase of $5,403,000,000 over 1908, or an increase of 27.5 per cent. The aggregate was distributed among the various classes of banks as follows: National, 41.2 per cent.; State, 15.6 per cent.; mutual savings, 15.6 per cent.; stock savings, nearly 4 per cent.; loan and trust companies, 20.4 per cent., and private banks, less than 1 per cent. The resources included loans and discounts of $13,953,000,000. Of these, 24 per cent. represented loans secured by real estate and 31 per cent. those secured by other collateral. National banks were credited with 42.7 per cent. of all loans and discounts, State banks with 18 per cent., and loan and trust companies with 19 per cent. The resources also included bonds and other securities to the value of $5,359,000,000. The principal item under liabilities was individual and savings deposits, aggregating $17,024,000,000. Of these, 34.2 per cent. were in national banks, 17.2 ped cent. in State banks, 21.2 per cent. in mutual savings banks, and 21.6 per cent. in loan and trust companies. Compared with 1908, loans and discounts had increased 33.8 per cent. and individual deposits 33.1 per cent.

The geographical distribution of the banks was as follows: New England States 1983, with total resources of $3,077,000,000; Eastern States 2901, with $10,441,000,000 resources; Southern States 6096, with $2,355,000,000 resources; Middle Western States 8383, with $6,150,000,000 resources; Western States 5003, with $1,179,000,000 resources; Pacific States 1721, with $1,726,000,000 resources, and Island possessions 35, with $76,0.0,000 resources. There were six States with aggregate banking resources of more than $1,000,000,000 each: Massachusetts, New York, Pennsylvania, Ohio, Illinois, and California. The aggregate resources of the 929 banks of New York State were $6,680,000,000. There were eight States with more than 1000 banks each: Pennsylvania, Texas, Ohio, Illinois, Minnesota, Iowa, Missouri, and Kansas.

The individual and savings deposits of Massachusetts banks aggregated $2,284,000,000; of New York banks, $6,479,000,000; of Pennsylvania banks, $2,176,000,000; of Illinois banks, $1,401,000,000; of Ohio banks, $1,077,000,000, and of California banks, $1,085,000,000.

BANKING POWER. The banking power of 28,995 United States banks, partly estimated, was $22,548,000,000. This represented an increase of nearly $5,000,000,000 in four years. The banking power as thus estimated is based on capital, surplus, deposits, and circulation.

NEW YORK CITY DEPOSITS. The investigations of the Pujo committee (see MONEY TRUST) showed that the deposits of 19,000 country banks, with New York City banks, on November 1 amounted to $483,373,000; these banks had themselves made call loans in New York City amounting to $240,480,000. During the preceding four months these out-of-town deposits had diminished by $67,000,000, whereas the out-of-town direct call loans had increased by about $100,000,000. This phenomenon was explained by the high money rate prevailing in the fall. Since this is an annual change, the explanation seemed correct. The New York banks pay 2 per cent. on deposit accounts; they then use these deposits to make call loans. This situation proved of first importance for the general stability of credit at the time of the panic of 1907. Thousands of interior banks made a call for the immediate return of their deposits. Although the New York banks were able to satisfy this demand to the extent of at least $75,000,000 within a few days, nevertheless the credit facilities at New York shrank by several hundred million dollars. Thus at the very time when credit was most needed it diminished by an enormous sum at the very centre of financial operations. There were those who blamed this situation upon the operations of the stock exchange. They even advocated either the closing of that exchange, or the prohibition of call loans, or of deposits by interior banks with New York banks. On the other hand, it was argued that the deposit of reserves by interior banks with central reserve city banks was essential to the credit operations of the country; that the call loan market was an advantage in that it provided a use for money at low rates that would otherwise be idle; that the interior banks would suffer most by prohibitions mentioned, and that the true remedy is in the provision of an elastic bank-note system whereby bank credits may be made to expand and contract with the volume of business.

BANKING AND CURRENCY REFORM. For many years, and particularly since the panic of 1907, there has been general insistence in business, banking, and academic circles that a reform of banking and currency systems is imperative. The Aldrich-Vreeland act of 1908, in addition to establishing a temporary means for meeting most obvious needs, created the National Monetary Commission, which was authorized to make a thorough investigation of banking and currency methods throughout the world and to recommend legislation. It was quite generally agreed that the principal defects in the American financial system were the lack of elasticity in bank-note issues and the lack of coöperation or central control. The lack of elasticity has been due to the fact that bank notes are issued only on the basis of United States bonds. There is thus a lack of correlation between the increase and decrease of bank currency and the rise and fall of business demands, whether seasonal as for crop movements, or extraordinary as in times of panic. Indeed, national bank issues have often been perversely elastic, expanding in times of easy money and contracting in times of money stringency. It has, therefore, been argued that American bank notes should be issued on the basis of general banking assets, as is almost universally the case elsewhere. Thus commercial paper representing actual business transactions and securities representing sound industrial values would be made available for the issue of bank credit to meet legitimate business needs. Experience elsewhere shows that, the need having been satisfied, the notes return for retirement.

The lack of coöperation or central control has resulted in undue shrinkage of credit in times of panic, improper banking methods, undue tendencies to speculation, and lack of means of regulating the importation and exportation of gold. The more than 25,000 banks have been operating under a system of individualism which has imposed upon each the necessity of protecting its own credit. The banking reserves, amounting to more than $1,500,000,000, have been widely scattered and have not been available to meet real business needs in time of urgent stringency. With every decline in confidence there has been a scramble for gold reserve everywhere, so that the power to extend credit has disappeared just when most needed. It has been argued, therefore, that some scheme for pooling reserves should be devised so that the united strength of all the banks could be brought to bear upon weak points. Moreover, it is believed that something comparable to the control exerted by the city clearing house over its members should be developed in the nation at large. Such control is exerted in European countries by the central banks and in Canada by the few large banks over their many branches.

THE ALDRICH BANK PLAN. *Organization.* On January 8 the scheme of banking and currency reform elaborated by the National Monetary Commission was presented to Congress. Under various tentative forms this scheme had been presented to the country in 1911 and became known as the Aldrich plan. Late in 1911 it received the unqualified indorsement of the American Bankers' Association and of banking associations in about two-thirds of the States. The discussion of it in 1912 was continuous but somewhat overshadowed by the political campaign. This plan was designed to meet the weaknesses above outlined and to adapt to American conditions the best features of European central banks. It provided for three sets of organizations, each resting upon the one below, culminating in the National Reserve Association. Local banks, at least ten in number, with combined capitalization, including surplus of at least $3,000,000, were to form local associations having corporate powers. All banks, whether national or State, including trust companies, meeting certain conditions were made eligible to membership in the local associations by purchasing stock equal to 20 per cent. of their capital in the National Reserve Association. Exactly and only this number of shares must be purchased and they were not transferable. The functions of the local associations would be to choose directors for themselves and for the next grade of organization, known as district associations, supervise members somewhat as clearing houses do, and at times guarantee commercial paper to be rediscounted by the central association. The method of choosing directors was elaborate, being ostensibly designed to prevent centralization of control. There were two methods of voting. One by the banks individually, each bank one vote, the other on the basis of shares in the National Reserve Association. Three-fifths of the directors of the local associations were to be chosen by the first method and two-fifths by the second. This would give the small banks a predominant influence in such elections.

The numerous local associations thus formed were to be grouped into fifteen district associations, the number to be altered as conditions demanded. The number of directors of such associations was to be double the number of local associations included in the district. Each local board of directors was to choose one director for the district. Two-thirds of the remaining directors were to be chosen by the second method noted above, each bank voting according to the number of its shares. The other directors were to be chosen by these five-sixths and were to represent agricultural, commercial, and industrial interests. The managers and deputy managers of the district associations were to be appointed by the executive committee of the national associations. The district associations were to choose the national directors, facilitate domestic exchanges, and otherwise to act as the agents of the central body and facilitate its coöperation with the local banks.

The principal feature of the whole scheme was the National Reserve Association, having a capital of at least $200,000,000. Its directors were to number forty-six; of these one was to be chosen by the board of each of the fifteen district associations. A second group of fifteen similarly chosen were to represent the agricultural, commercial, industrial, and other than banking interests of the district, and were not to be officers or directors of banks or other financial institutions. Nine additional directors were to be chosen by voting representatives chosen by the boards of directors of the various branches, each casting votes equal to the shares in the National Reserve Association held by the banks in the branch association which he represented. Finally there were to be seven ex-officio members: The governor, two deputy governors, the Secretary of the Treasury, the Secretary of Agriculture, the Secretary of C mmerce and Labor, and the Comptroller of the Currency. The important body of the national board of directors was to be an executive committee of nine members, including the governor, the two deputy governors, the Comptroller of the Currency, and five other directors. The governor was removable only by a two-thirds vote of the board of directors for cause. The national association was given an extensive group of powers and duties, including control of branches; power to establish branches abroad; to act as the fiscal agent of the government; to buy and sell government and State securities of foreign governments, and gold coin and bullion; to deal in bills of exchange, both foreign and domestic; to fix the rate of domestic exchange; to discount bills of exchange arising out of commercial transactions and indorsed by a depository bank and made at least thirty days previously, provided the total amount thus rediscounted for any bank should not exceed the capital of such bank, and also provided that notes and bills bearing the signature or indorsement of any one person or firm should not aggregate more than 10 per cent. of the capital and surplus of the applying bank.

Elasticity. The Aldrich plan aimed to secure the desired elasticity in note issues and the extension of credit by a new system of note issue, new regulations for the rediscounting of commercial paper, and the reserve regulations of the national association. It provided that all note issues in excess of $900,000,000, but less than $1,200,000,000, not covered by an equal amount of legal money on hand, should be taxed at the rate of 1½ per cent. annually; and all issues exceeding the latter amount at the rate of 5 per cent. An important part of the plan was the retirement of the existing bond secured circulation of the national banks. It was provided that the National Reserve Association should purchase at not less than par the 2 per cent. bonds now held by national banks to secure their circulation. The association thereupon was to assume responsibility for redeeming the notes issued thereon, replacing them with its own notes. National banks were not required, however, to sell their bonds; but if they retired any part of their notes they could not reissue them. The bonds thus purchased by the Reserve Association were to be exchanged for a new series of 3 per cent. fifty-year government bonds bearing an annual tax of 1½ per cent. The government was to have the option of retiring these bonds or of purchasing them at par for postal savings banks. It was believed that these features in connection with the discount characteristics of the plan would make the note issues responsive to business needs.

The plan provided that the great amount of legal money now held in the thousands of individual banks as a necessary legal reserve would be deposited with the National Reserve Association; instead of being idle, as it is now for the most part, it would thus become available for the rediscounting of paper presented by the member banks. These latter could rediscount their paper in several different ways, either directly or under the guarantee of their local association. Whenever any bank thus secured credit with the central association it was to be allowed to count such credit as a part of its legal reserve. In addition, association notes, which would soon replace national bank notes, were to count also as legal reserve. In this manner the individual banks would find their ability to care for the business paper of their respective communities at least doubled.

As to reserves, the plan provided that all demand obligations, including deposits of banks and the government, as well as outstanding notes, should be covered by a reserve of 50 per cent. in gold or other legal money. The remaining 50 per cent. might be represented by bills of exchange and discounted paper. If the amount of gold in the reserves should fall below 33 1-3 per cent. of the note issues no more notes were to be issued. Moreover, if the gold and legal money held in reserve ever fell below 50 per cent. of outstanding notes a tax of 1½ per cent. annually upon each 2½ per cent. or fraction thereof of such deficiency was imposed.

The National Reserve Association was not to be a profit-making institution. The plan provided that stockholders or member banks should receive a 4 per cent. cumulative dividend. Profit beyond 4 per cent. was to be divided as follows: One-half to the surplus of the association itself; ¼ to the United States government by way of compensation for the use of government deposits, and ¼ to the stockholders or member banks until they should have received 5 per cent. in all. If there was an excess of profits beyond this latter amount this was to be divided equally between the government and the Reserve Association until the latter's surplus equaled 20 per cent. of the capital, after which all this excess was to go to the government.

Advantages. The advantages claimed in the Aldrich plan may be indicated by the defects of the present condition which it sought to remedy: No plan for concentration or mobilization of reserves for use in times of stress; lack of means for replenishing reserves or for increasing lending power in times of stress; the inelastic bond-secured notes; no coöperation among banks, especially outside of clearing-house cities; no effective agency for exchanges between different parts of the country, especially in times of financial distress; no effective agency for handling foreign exchanges, especially in times of panic; lack of standardized commercial paper, leading to the accumulation of reserves in central reserve cities, thus causing speculation there and checking agricultural, industrial, and commercial development elsewhere; the inequality of credit facilities in different parts of the country; need of greater uniformity, steadiness, and reasonableness of rates of discount; need of elastic credit for crop movements; the need of uniform banking standards, especially as to capitalization, reserve, examinations, and reports; the need of American banks abroad to develop our trade; inability of national banks adequately to serve farmers because they cannot lend on real estate; and the existence of the independent Treasury, causing fluctuations in the money supply and leading to favoritism in the distribution of government funds to depository banks.

Disadvantages. The principal source of opposition to the Aldrich plan, in so far as it was expressed, was due to the fear that the National Reserve Association would obtain a dominating position in American finance and industry. It was pointed out that, though the manner of election of directors was designed to place the small banks in a position of special power, not only would the majority of directors be bankers but, as at present, small banks would be largely controlled by reserve city banks upon which they are dependent for extensions of credit. It was held that the plan did not sufficiently safeguard against the acquisition of control by purchases of stock by large banks or by holding companies. Thus the whole institution would not only become a bankers' bank but might gradually come under the control of the larger banking institutions centralized in Wall Street. This fear was aggravated by certain findings of the Pujo committee (see TRUSTS, *Money Trust*), revealing the tremendous power in a system of interlocking directorates and other forms of combination. It was argued that the scheme would not be acceptable to the American people until provision was made for greater security against control by any centralized financial group, for greater representation of agricultural, industrial, and commercial interests, and for greater responsibility to the public. President Taft in his annual message declared that the government might be given a larger representation in the executive committee without any danger of injecting politics into its management. It was also widely believed that the plan did not adequately guard against the possibilities of inflation. It was argued that one of the chief causes of our periodic industrial depressions is the over-expansion of business credit and the undue enlargement of productive agencies. Since the Aldrich plan provided that the notes of the Reserve Association could be counted as reserve by member banks, as could also the credit of such banks with the central association, it was argued by some that not only would banks be able to double their credits but even to multiply them many fold. Consequently, in the effort to provide elasticity to meet the exceptional needs of a crisis, it was held that the formulators of this plan had gone to the extent of laying the basis of an unprecedented era of speculation to be followed by a collapse equally monumental. Those favoring the plan made much of the argument that it was really an extension of the principles of the clearing-house which had often proved of highest importance in times of panic. Opponents, however, contended that the clearing-house advantages could be secured by some scheme of coöperation among the banks of different sections, preferably by admitting country banks to membership in the clearing-house associations of nearby cities; it would not thus be necessary to go the full extent of centralization. In this manner, which would be comparable to the Aldrich plan with the Central Reserve Association, the advantages of coöperation could be secured without the manifest dangers of centralization.

BANKS, NATIONAL. See NATIONAL BANKS.

BAPTISTS. According to the *American Baptist Year Book* for 1912, the total number of communicants in the Baptist denomination in 1912, in North America was 5,637,953 and the total number in the world was 6,482,046. In the United States the denomination is divided loosely into two main bodies, the northern and the southern. In addition to the regular Baptist denomination there are several other bodies, of which the most important are the following: General Baptists, 33,600 communicants, 545 churches, 550 ministers; United Baptists, 13,698 communicants, 196 churches, 260 ministers; Primitive Baptists, 10,311 communicants, 2922 churches, 1500 ministers.

In addition there are several small bodies, including the Seventh Day Baptists, The Two Seed in the Spirit Baptists, Church of God and Saints of Christ.

The Northern Baptists have 1,211,426 communicants with 9715 churches and 8223 ministers. The regular Southern Baptists have 2,304,724 communicants with 22,795 churches and 14,635 ministers.

Among the general societies supported by the denomination are the American Baptist Foreign Mission Society, which has general charge of the foreign missions, the American Baptist Publication Society, the American Baptist Home Mission Society, which has charge of the home missions, the Woman's American Baptist Foreign Mission Society and the American Baptist Education Society. The missions are carried on in nearly all the fields into which missionaries are sent. Under the auspices of the denomination are 98 colleges, 10 theological seminaries and 96 academies, seminaries, institutions and training schools.

The Northern Baptist convention and the Southern Baptist Convention are bodies which have general charge of the different activities of the denomination. The Northern Baptist convention met at Des Moines, May 22-29, 1912. The most important question under discussion at this meeting was that of education, especially collegiate education. As a result of the investigations made, the convention accepted definitely and vigorously the duty of furnishing to those for whom it is responsible an adequate and distinctly Christian education. A radical and far-reaching programme was proposed, beginning, under the direction of a permanent commission on religious and moral education, in the home and Sunday-school, and extending to every institution of learning which bears the denominational name. The Baptist Education Society was combined with the Education board of the convention. A forward movement calling for the raising of $3,000,000 for the missionary interests of the denomination was instituted with great enthusiasm. A new plan of comity and coöperation between the Northern and Southern conventions was taken into consideration. See BAPTISTS, FREE.

BAPTISTS, FREE. The General Conference of Free Baptists is the national representative body of the Free Baptist denomination. It was incorporated in 1892, and receives as its members delegates from State organizations which in turn are made up of delegates from local associations; and these are composed of delegates from local churches. The General Conference since it incorporated has administered all the missionary and denominational activities of Free Baptists, home and foreign missions, education, and internal and interdenominational relations. Since 1904 negotiations have been conducted through joint committees with the Baptist Societies, the American Baptist Foreign Mission Society, the American Baptist Home Mission Society, and the American Baptist Publication Society, with reference to uniting the missionary and denominational activities of the Free Baptists with those of the Baptists. These negotiations culminated in the adoption of an agreement, popularly called the "Basis of Union," the provisions of which went into effect October 1, 1911, by which the General Conference transferred the greater part of its invested funds and all of its missionary and publication interests to these societies, using them as their own missionary agencies. This union of funds and functions naturally leads to the consideration of union, and its actual accomplishment, between the constituent bodies and the local churches, so that during the year closing, both East and West, many other forms of union, affecting associations and churches, have taken place, or are in process.

The Free Baptists have been organized in about 1400 churches, with about 80,000 church members. Their numbers are largest in the New England States, particularly Maine and New Hampshire and a few Western States, such as Michigan and Wisconsin, although they have churches scattered through New York State, Ohio, Indiana, Illinois, Nebraska, Iowa, and Kansas.

The Morning Star, which was founded in 1826, as the organ of the Free Baptists, was consolidated with *The Watchman*, of Boston, October 1, 1911. The Sunday School lesson sheets and Star Quarterlies have been incorporated in the publications of the American Baptist Publication Society. The foreign mission field of the Free Baptists, opened in 1835, in Bengal, India, usually manned by about twenty resident missionaries, has become one of the missionary fields of the American Baptist Foreign Mission Society.

BAR ASSOCIATION, AMERICAN. The annual meeting of this association was held in Milwaukee, on August 19, 1912. From the standpoint of popular interest the most important incident of the meeting was the action of the association on the election of William H. Lewis, Butler R. Wilson, and William R. Morris, all negro lawyers, as members of the association. The executive committee voted to elect all three in 1911 and Mr. Lewis and Mr. Wilson were elected at the annual meeting in 1911. It was alleged that no member of the executive committee who voted upon the election of Mr. Wilson and Mr. Lewis had any knowledge of the race of the candidate when so voting. On January 4, 1912, the committee having learned the race of Mr. Lewis, a resolution was passed to the effect that as the committee acted in ignorance the Lewis election be reconsidered and rescinded and his name be restored to the list of nominees to be acted upon by the general council in 1912. It was well known that this action of the committee was the result of protests made by lawyers in the southern States against the election of colored members. Mr. Lewis was an assistant attorney-general of the United States and had been proposed for membership by Attorney-General Wickersham. Following the action of the executive committee as noted above, Mr. Wickersham vigorously protested and threatened to leave the association if it rescinded the election of Mr. Lewis. At a meeting on August 12, 1912, resolutions similar to those affecting Mr. Lewis were passed in regard to Mr. Wilson and Mr. Morris. The committee, defending its action, declared that it had not rejected any of the three mentioned persons for membership in the association or assumed to determine the advisability of electing to such membership a colored man otherwise qualified, but inasmuch as the settled practice of the association has been to elect only white men as members, the committee felt itself constrained to reserve the important question of electing colored men for determination by the association itself, and to that end, the committee regarded it as its duty to rescind its earlier action. The association voted that Mr. Lewis, Mr. Wilson, and Mr. Morris might retain their membership in the association, but that hereafter no member should be elected until the fact that they were colored had been made known to all members. Shortly after the meeting, Mr. Lewis, Mr. Wilson, and Mr. Morris resigned as members.

The address of the president, S. S. Gregory, was devoted to a résumé of new laws relating to government, trust regulation, judicial procedure, and kindred subjects during the year. Among the other important addresses delivered were the following: "New Nationalism," Frank B. Kellog, of Minnesota; "Procedure in our American Judicial System," Frederick M. Judson, of St. Louis; "Recent Movement Toward the Realization of High Ideals in the Legal Profession," Charles A. Boston, of New York; "Judges," by Henry D. Estabrook, of New York; "The Courts and the Constitution," by Senator George Sutherland, of Utah.

Reports of committees, including those of the special committee to suggest remedies and formulate proposed laws to prevent delay and unnecessary cost in litigation, the committee on uniform State laws, the committee on international law, and the committee on patent, trademark, and copyright law. In conjunction with the meeting of the Bar Association were held meetings of the Association of American Law Schools and the American Institute of Criminal Law and Criminology. The officers elected at the meeting were as follows: President, Frank B. Kellog; secretary, George Whitelock; treasurer, Frank E. Wadhams. Each State and Territory is represented by one vice-president and one member of the general council. The membership of the association is about 6000. The next meeting wi be held in August, 1913.

BARBADOS. The most easterly of the Caribbees; a British colony. Its area is 166 square miles, and its population (1911), 171,-892. Many laborers have been drawn to the canal zone, which together with emigrants to Pará (Brazil) and the United States accounts for the decrease in population since 1891, when it was 182,306. Bridgetown is the capital. The area under sugar-cane, the island's most important product, is estimated at 64,000 acres, There were in operation 332 sugar-works in 1910, producing 39,899 hogsheads of sugar and 77,722 puncheons of molasses. The export of cotton to Great Britain in 1910 was 589,118 pounds, valued at £35,942.

*	1907-8	1908-9	1909-10	1910-11
	£	£	£	£
Imports	1,271,530	1,225,870	1,119,343	1,345,194
Exports ...	935,256	947,178	888,086	1,088,830
Revenue ..	209,817	189,805	195,803	213,297
Expend ...	188,296	198,865	199,624	211,949
Shipping† ..	1,736,363	2,073,765	2,437,086	3,395,085

* Commerce is for calendar years, finance for fiscal years. † Tonnage entered and cleared.

Customs revenue (1909-10), £127,313. Public debt (March 31, 1910), £422,900 (sinking fund, £85,740). Governor in 1912, Sir Leslie Probyn (since 1911).

BARBUDA. See ANTIGUA.

BARGE CANAL. See CANALS.

BARLEY. The year 1912 was not favorable to the production of good barley crops in most countries growing this cereal, although record yields which largely discounted shortages elsewhere were secured in Russia and the United States. In nearly all European countries the growth of the crop was retarded by a backward season and still more injury was done by continued heavy rains in August and September, which interfered with harvesting and threshing. While in many regions the yield was satisfactory in spite of these conditions, the quality of the grain suffered much, a large proportion of the crop being stained or discolored as a result of the wet weather. The quantity of barley suitable for brewing purposes was inadequate to meet the requirements of Europe, the shortage being greatest in Germany, Austria, and France. Russia produced in 1912 464,124,715 bushels, an excess of more than 50,000,000 over the yield of 1911. The Roumanian yield was about 21,160,000 bushels, or over 5,000,000 bushels less than the preceding crop. In Italy, where a severe drought during the growing season proved injurious, the yield amounted to about 8,403,000 bushels, or about 20 per cent. less than the yield of the year before. The production of Spain was estimated at approximately 59,000,000 bushels, or about two-thirds of the crop of 1911. Estimates placed the French yield at about 51,000,000 bushels, or about 780,000 bushels more than the year before. Canada produced about 44,000,000 bushels, or over 3,000,000 bushels more than in 1911, due to some extent to an increase in acreage.

In the United States a production for the year of 223,824,000 bushels exceeded the yield of 1911 by 63,584,000 bushels. This crop was the first to exceed 200,000,000 bushels. The season was so favorable that the average acre yield of 29.7 bushels also stood out clearly as a record. The area devoted to the crop in 1912 was 7,530,000 acres, as against 7,627,000 acres in 1911. The price paid farmers on December 1, 1912, was only 50.5 cents per bushel, as compared with 86.9 cents on December 1, 1911, and on this basis the total value of the crop was given by the Department of Agriculture at $112,957,000, or 18.5 per cent. above the five-year average. The leading States in barley production and their yields were as follows: Minnesota, 42,018,000 bushels; California, 41,760,000 bushels; North Dakota, 35,162,000 bushels; Wisconsin, 24,843,000 bushels; South Dakota, 23,062,000 bushels, and Iowa, 11,570,000 bushels. All other States produced less than 10,000,000 bushels. The highest average yield per acre for any State was 45 bushels, which was produced in Utah.

BARNARD COLLEGE. See COLUMBIA UNIVERSITY.

BAROTSELAND. See RHODESIA.

BARR, ROBERT. An English novelist, died October 22, 1912. He was born in Glasgow, Scotland, in 1850, but removed to Canada early in his youth. He graduated from the Normal School at Toronto and for a time held the position of headmaster of the Windsor (Canada) Public School. In 1876 he removed to Detroit, where he joined the editorial staff of the *Free Press*, for which he wrote under the name of "Luke Sharp." Five years later he went to England. In 1892 he organized with Jerome K. Jerome the *Idler* magazine and was its editor for twenty years. He wrote many novels and short stories and was widely known as a writer in England and America. Among his best-known publications are: *In a Steamer Chair* (1892); *The Face and the Mask, Revenge*, and *In the Midst of Alarms* (1894); *A Woman Intervenes* (1896); *The Mutable Many* (1897); *The Countess Tekla* (1899); *Stranleigh's Millions* (1908); *Cardillac* (1909); *The Sword Maker* (1910).

BARTON, CLARA. An American philanthropist, died April 12, 1912. She was born in North Oxford, Worcester county, Mass., in 1821, and received her early education in the public schools. At the age of sixteen she began to teach, and after a few years entered and was graduated from the Liberal Institute at Clinton, N. Y. She afterwards resumed teaching and continued this for about ten years. She organized a system of public schools in Bordentown, N. J. In connection with her efforts to bring about the release of her brother, who had been captured by Federal troops in the Civil War, she came in contact with the wounded soldiers. She at once conceived the plan of organizing relief for the wounded. She announced in the papers of Worcester, Mass., that she would receive contributions and see to it personally that they were distributed. The answers which came to her appeals were so liberal that it was necessary to secure a warehouse in Washington to hold the stores that were accumulated. There was much opposition to the idea of women going to the front at that time, but she managed to make her way through to the headquarters of General Butler in Virginia. She first accomplished the release of her brother, who was still a prisoner, and then began the active work of nursing the wounded. She continued it almost throughout the war, and in 1864 was appointed by General Butler head nurse in the hospitals of the Army of the James. During the last year of the war she was entrusted by President Lincoln with the task of looking after the correspondence of the relatives of prisoners who were missing after the exchanges had been made. In 1865 she supervised the laying out of the grounds of the national cemetery at Andersonville.

During travel abroad in 1869 she first became acquainted with the Red Cross movement. At Geneva she was shown the treaty which had been signed by most of the civilized nations except the United States. By the provisions of this treaty those who wore the badge of the Red Cross were allowed to go on battlefields to care for the wounded. Miss Barton became greatly interested in this treaty and began at once to advocate its adoption by the United States. At the time of the outbreak of the Franco-German War she was at Bern and was invited by the officials of the Red Cross to engage in the work of that organization during the war. She went at once to Strassburg and became active in nursing and helping wounded soldiers. During this work she learned the importance of having trained helpers and ready supplies. For her services she received the Iron Cross of Merit from the German emperor. She afterwards went to Paris and was in that city during the Commune and after. Through her methods in handling the half-starved mobs that thronged the streets she came to have great influence over them. For her work in Europe she received many honors. The Servian Red Cross Medal was presented to her by Queen Natalie of Servia. She was awarded the Geneva Medal of Honor from the Comité International.

When she returned to the United States and endeavored to have the government become a signatory to the Red Cross treaty she found it unwilling to do so, and for several years she pressed upon the government officials her convictions in the matter. In 1881 she went to Washington in the attempt to persuade President Garfield to advocate action by the government. After an interview with Mr. Blaine, at that time Secretary of State, a meeting was held on March 21, 1881, in Washington, which resulted in the formation of the American Red Cross Association to take the place of the informal committee which had existed since 1877. Miss Barton was chosen president of the association. The Red Cross, under her leadership, took an active part in furnishing assistance in practically all the great disasters which came to the United States and other countries in that period. During the first year of the organization came the Michigan forest fires, and in the following year floods along the Mississippi and destructive cyclones engaged the resources of the association. In 1883 aid was furnished during the war in the Balkans. In the next year relief went to the Ohio and Mississippi valleys on account of the floods there. In 1889 aid was given to the sufferers from the Johnstown flood and in the Russian famines in 1891-2. After the Armenian massacres in 1896 Miss Barton organized relief expeditions and went to Constantinople herself. She actively engaged in relief work in the Spanish-American War. The last work in which she took personal part was after the flood at Galveston and after exertions continuing for more than six weeks she suffered a nervous breakdown. At this time she lacked but one year of being 80 years of age. In the organization of the American Red Cross she insisted that the association should be independent of any State organizations or of sanitary or Christian commissions. This desire to keep the control of the Red Cross completely separate from other associations led to much criticism which began in 1903 and finally led to Miss Barton's retirement from its head. On May 4, 1904, she resigned the presidency. She was the author of *The History of the Red Cross* (1882; published by the Government); *American Relief Expedition to Asia Minor* (1896); *History of the Red Cross in Peace and War* (1898); *The Story of the Red Cross* (1904); and *Story of My Childhood* (1907).

BASEBALL. The highest honors in baseball in 1912 were won by the Boston team of the American League, familiarly known as the Boston Red Sox. This aggregation of players captured the American League pennant with the greatest ease, despite the fact that the Philadelphia Athletics had practically the same team as in 1911, when they won the world's championship for the second successive year.

The series between the Red Sox and the New York Giants, winners of the National League flag, to decide the 1912 world's championship, was the most exciting ever played. Eight games were necessary, Boston winning four and New York three. One game resulted in a tie score. The total attendance at the championship series was 250,037, while the receipts aggregated $490,833. These figures broke all previous records. A composite score of the games shows that the Red Sox players outfielded the Giants, but were weaker than the New Yorkers in batting. It was the errors made at critical times by the Giants that led to their defeat. The scores of the games follow: Boston, 4, New York, 3; Boston 6, New York, 6; Boston, 1, New York, 2; Boston, 3, New York, 1; Boston, 2, New York, 1; Boston, 2, New York, 5; Boston, 4, New York, 11; Boston, 3, New York, 2.

A noteworthy feature of the American League pennant race was the excellent showing made by the Washington team, which nosed out the Philadelphia Athletics for second place. At the beginning of the season, the Washingtons were regarded by the majority of experts as doomed to finish in the second division, but the pitching of Johnson and the all-round work of Gandil, Foster, and Milan kept the team hovering between second and third places during the last half of the season. The final standing of the American League teams was: Boston won 105, lost 47; Washington won 91, lost 61; Philadelphia won 90, lost 62; Chicago won 78, lost 76; Cleveland won 75, lost 78; Detroit won 69, lost 84; St. Louis won 53, lost 101; New York won 50, lost 102. The leading pitcher of the American League was Joseph Wood, of Boston, and the leading batter was again Tyrus Cobb, of Detroit, whose average was .410.

In the National League the New York Giants began the season in much better physical condition than their rivals, with the result that they rolled up a commanding lead in the first weeks of the campaign. During this early season spurt, "Rube" Marquard, the Giant pitcher, won 19 straight games, a new record for modern baseball. A bad slump struck the team later on, however, and for a time it seemed as though Chicago and Pittsburgh might drag the Giants out of first place. The New Yorks rallied in season, nevertheless, and finished the campaign with 103 victories as against 48 defeats. The standing of the other clubs follows: Pittsburgh won 93, lost 59; Chicago won 92, lost 59; Cincinnati won 75, lost 78; Philadelphia won 73, lost 79; St. Louis won 63, lost 90; Brooklyn won 58, lost 95; Boston won 52, lost 101. Hendrix of the Pittsburgh team was the leading pitcher in point of number of games won, and Zimmerman of Chicago was the leading batter. According to the ranking of the secretary of the league, based on the number of runs for which each pitcher was responsible, or, in other words, runs earned off the pitching solely, the leading pitcher of the league was Tesreau of the New York Giants. The average number of runs in 9-inning games chargeable to him was 1.96. Mathewson, also of the Giants, ranked second with 2.12, and Rucker of Brooklyn, third, with 2.20.

The pennant winners in the more important minor leagues in 1912 were: International, Toronto; American Association, Minneapolis; Southern, Birmingham; Tri-State, Harrisburg; Pacific Coast, Oakland; Connecticut, New Haven; New York State, Utica; New England, Lawrence.

Williams made the best showing among the colleges, winning 11 games and losing 3. Princton ranked second with 18 victories and 6 defeats. The scores in Williams's principal games were: Williams 2, Princton 0; Williams 6, Yale 1; Williams 4, Dartmouth 1, and Williams 2, Dartmouth 0; Williams 6, Holy Cross 1; Williams 8, Cornell 5; Williams 6, Wesleyan 1, and Williams 3, Wesleyan 2; Williams 8, Amherst 2, and Williams 0, Amherst 2; Williams 6, Harvard 7.

Princeton defeated Georgetown 3-1 and 5-4; Brown 2-1; Cornell 2-0; Pennsylvania 8-0 and 3-2; Michigan 6-3; Harvard 5-1; Lafayette 3-2; Amherst 11-1; Yale 4-2, and 19-6. Princeton was defeated by Penn State 1-4; Holy Cross 4-6; Cornell 2-3; Williams 0-2; Yale 1-6.

Yale defeated Cornell 4-1 and 2-1; Columbia 4-0; Holy Cross 8-2; Georgetown 6-3 and 17-0; Amherst 12-3; Princeton 6-1; Dartmouth 6-5; Harvard 9-6 and 5-2. Yale was defeated by Georgetown 2-3; Holy Cross 4-9; Brown 1-3 and 2-8; Princeton 2-4 and 6-19; Cornell 0-3.

Harvard defeated Columbia 8-5; Amherst 3-2; Lafayette 6-1; Pennsylvania 2-1; Williams 8-6; Holy Cross 7-3. Harvard was defeated by Georgetown 1-5; Bates 2-3; Holy Cross 5-7; Dartmouth 5-9; Brown 4-5 and 1-2; Princeton 1-5; Yale 6-9 and 2-5.

BASKETBALL. Columbia for the second successive year won the intercollegiate championship with 8 victories and 2 defeats. Dartmouth finished second, winning 7 games and losing 3. The standing of the other teams was: Pennsylvania won 6, lost 4; Cornell won 5, lost 5; Princeton won 3, lost 7; Yale won 1, lost 9. Columbia defeated Princeton 29-16, and 23-16; Yale 22-20, 20-8 and 18-14; Dartmouth 18-17; Pennsylvania 15-10 and 22-20. Columbia was defeated by Dartmouth 18-30 and by Cornell 7-19. Dartmouth defeated Yale 37-16 and 14-12; Cornell 19-16 and 18-10; Pennsylvania 19-18; Princeton 42-12; Columbia 30-18. Dartmouth was defeated by Columbia 17-18, by Pennsylvania 18-21; and by Princeton 38-43. Pennsylvania won victories over Yale 21-13 and 27-11; Cornell 23-21 and 23-18; Dartmouth 21-18; Princeton 34-21. Pennsylvania lost to Dartmouth 18-19; Columbia 10-15 and 20-22; Princeton 29-30. Cornell defeated Princeton 37-26 and 32-18; Columbia 19-7; Yale 33-17 and 27-13. Cornell lost to Dartmouth 16-19 and 10-18; Pennsylvania 21-23 and 18-23. Yale's only victory was over Princeton, 19-18. The total number of points made by each team follows: Dartmouth 252; Cornell 233; Pennsylvania 226; Princeton 224; Columbia 192; Yale 145. The total number of points scored against these teams was: Columbia 170; Dartmouth 184; Cornell 186; Pennsylvania 194; Princeton 299; Yale 239.

BASUTOLAND. A British dependency in southern Africa, northeast of the Cape of Good Hope Province. Its area is 11,716 square miles, and its population (1911 preliminary) 405,-932 (1411 whites). Maseru, the capital, had 841 natives and 500 whites. The soil is excellent for grain cultivation, the abundant native pastures furnish food for enormous herds, and the climate is well suited to Europeans. The chief products are wool, wheat, mealies, and kaffir corn. The South African Railway operates a branch line from Marseilles to a point near Maseru within the Basutoland border.

*	1907-8	1908-9	1909-10	1910-11
Imports.	£238,500	£239,830	£258,994	£.......
Exports.	248,500	193,122	349,884	....
Revenue	116,529	108,638	119,974	145,500
Expenditure..	126,603	126,921	127,437	134,888

* Commerce is for calendar, finance for fiscal years.

The paramount chief is Letsie. The governor-general for the Union of South Africa administers the territory (which is not, however, a part of the Union), through a resident-commissioner (Sir Herbert Cecil Sloley in 1912).

BATHTUB TRUST. See TRUSTS.

BATTLESHIPS. GREAT BRITAIN. The four ships of the *Orion* class (*Orion*, *Monarch*, *Thunderer*, *Conqueror*) are now in commission. The *Orion*, the first completed, rolled so deeply in a heavy sea that her bilge keels had to be enlarged. She developed a much more serious defect, in common with the *Dreadnought* and all the single-masted ships, the *Neptune*, *Hercules*, *Colossus*, *Lion*, *Monarch*, *Thunderer*, and *Princess Royal*, viz., the heat from the funnels made the fire-control station and the navigation-bridge untenable. The necessary extensive (and expensive) alterations have already been made on some of these ships.

Of the four ships of the *King George V.* class (*King George V.*, *Centurion*, *Ajax*, and *Audacious*), the first two having been completed, the *Ajax* and *Audacious* are due for completion in 1913. The ships are fitted with anti-rolling tanks. The *King George V.* carries a single pole-mast and a signal mast.

Four ships of the *Iron Duke* class (26,400 tons; *Iron Duke*, *Marlborough*, *Delhi*, *Benbow*) have been laid down this year. They will be improved *George V.'s*, and the first British dreadnought battleships to have a torpedo-defense battery of 6-inch guns. The 6-inch guns are, for the most part, placed behind armor. The class will be further strengthened by internal subdivision against torpedo attack; and by internal armor over the vital parts. Oil fuel, as well as coal, is to be carried.

Of the four battleships of the 1912 programme, the *Queen Elizabeth* and the *Warspite* have been laid down, and the *Valiant* and the *Barham* ordered. Each of these ships will carry eight 15-inch guns in four turrets on the centre-line, and sixteen 6-inch guns in a central casemate: Displacement, 27,000 tons; speed, 25 knots; turbine engines to develop between 50,000 and 60,000 horsepower. They will be provided with funnel and deck protection against aërial craft, and will be the most costly battleships yet designed.

GERMANY. There are five ships of the turbine-driven *Kaiser* class: *Kaiser*, *Friedrich der Grosse*, *Kaiserin*, *König Albert*, *Prinz Regent Luitpold*. The *Kaiser* and the *Friedrich der Grosse* are in commission; the other three will be completed in 1913. The forward turret and the two after-turrets are on the centre line, No. 4 turret being superposed so as to fire over No. 5. Turrets Nos. 3 and 4 are in broadside, but *en échelon*. It is understood this this is now the standard disposition.

UNITED STATES. The *Wyoming* and *Arkansas* are now in commission; the *New York*, *Texas*, *Nevada*, and *Oklahoma* are under construction. Bids for the *Pennsylvania* will be opened on February 18, 1913. Exclusive of

TYPICAL BATTLESHIPS AND BATTLE CRUISERS,

Particulars		*King George V.* British Battleship	*Kaiser.* German Battleship	*Conte di Cavour.* Italian Battleship
Number of ships in class		4	5	5
Where built		Portsmouth Dock Yard.	Imperial Yard, Kiel.	Spezia Dock Yard.
Laid down		Jan. 16, 1911	October, 1909	August 10, 1910
Launched		Oct. 18, 1911	March 22, 1911	August 10, 1911
Completed		Nov. 16, 1912	October, 1912	January, 1914
Length, between perpendiculars	in feet	555	564½	557
Length, over all	in feet	596	....	....
Beam	in feet	89	95¼	92
Maximum beam	in feet	....	....	....
Maximum draft	in feet	....	....	....
Mean draft	in feet	27½	27¼	28
Displacement, in tons		....	24,500	21,500
Designed displacement, in tons		23,600	....	....
Designed horsepower		31,000	25,000	24,000
Designed speed, by knots		21	21	22
Speed on trials, by knots		....	23.6	....
Maximum speed on trials, by knots		....	....	....
Armor, belt	in inches	12	13	9½ to 4½
" above belt	in inches	9¾	9	6
" battery	in inches	....	7.5	....
" deck	in inches	2¾	1¼	1¾
" turret guns	in inches	12	12	9½
" torpedo defense guns	in inches	4	....	5
Armament		10—13.5-inch 16—4-inch	10—12-inch 14— 6-inch 12— 3.4-inch	13—12-inch 20— 4.7-inch 14— 3-inch
Torpedo tubes	in pounds	5—21-inch	5—19.5-inch	3
Weight of 11-inch shell	in pounds	....	....	....
Weight of 12-inch shell	in pounds	....	981	920
Weight of 13.5-inch shell	in pounds	1,400	....	....
Weight of 14-inch shell	in pounds	....	....	....
Weight of broadside	in pounds	14,000	9,810	11,950
Weight of ahead fire	in pounds	5,600	5,886	4,596
Weight of astern fire	in pounds	5,600	7,848	4,596
Weight of 11-inch gun	in tons	....	....	....
Weight of 12-inch gun	in tons	....	51.5	....
Weight of 13.5-inch gun	in tons	86	....	....
Weight of 14-inch gun	in tons	....	....	....
Motive power		Parsons Turbines	Parsons Turbines	Parsons Turbines
Fuel		Coal and oil	Coal and oil	Coal and oil
Coal capacity, normal, in tons		900	1,000	1,000
Coal capacity, maximum, in tons		2,700	3,600	2,500
Complement, officers and men		....	....	999
Total cost, in dollars		9,489,675	11,322,253	12,652,900
Cost per ton, in dollars		402	466	575

armor and armament, the limit of cost set by Congress in the naval appropriation bill of August 22, 1912, is $7,425,000. Present plans contemplate: Length on designer's waterline, 600 feet; length over all, 608 feet; breadth, 97½ feet; draft, 28 feet, 10 inches; displacement, 31,400 tons; speed on four-hour trial, 21 knots; armament, twelve 14-inch guns, twenty-two 5-inch guns, four submerged torpedo tubes; heavy armor; motive power, reciprocating engines or turbine, to be decided when bids are opened; to burn oil exclusively.

FRANCE. The three ships of the *Bretagne* class (*Bretagne, Provençe,* and *Lorraine*) were laid down this year. Characteristics: Displacement, 23,500 tons; speed, 20 knots; Parsons turbines in four groups, one group to a shaft; four torpedo tubes, 18-inch; Bullivant torpedo nets; armament, ten 14.5-inch guns in five centre-line turrets, twenty-two 5.5-inch guns, four turret guns fire ahead and four astern, and all ten fire abeam, with a very wide arc of train. Two ships are to be laid down in May, 1913. The displacement now contemplated is 25,700, though it may ultimately be increased to 27,000 tons, to afford better protection than that of the *Barts* and *Bretagnes*. It is now thought that these ships will be armed with twelve 14.5-inch guns in three centre-line turrets. The nominal speed will be 20 knots under easy conditions, and 21 knots are to be exceeded on trial.

JAPAN. The battleship *Fuso,* building at Kure, launched March 11, 1912, will displace about 30,000 tons; her main armament is not known. It is given as ten 13.5-inch guns, and also as ten 15-inch guns, with a secondary battery of sixteen 6-inch guns. Speed, 22½ knots, with 45,000 horsepower turbines.

ITALY. The *Dante Alighieri* is now in commission. At full power her engines worked up to 35,000 horsepower and her speed on a series of runs over the measured mile gave a mean of 24.5 knots. At four-fifths horsepower a shaft power of 21,000 was developed, giving 21 knots speed. For political reasons it was decided to make the *Duilio* and *Doria* (laid down in 1912) sister ships to the *Cavour*. It is said that the *Morosini* and *Dandolo*, projected, will be of 29,000 tons, 48,000 indicated horsepower, 25 knots speed, and will each carry ten 14-inch or 15-inch guns and twenty-two 6-inch guns.

AUSTRIA. The *Viribus Unitis* is the first of the four ships of her class to be completed. Of the others, the *Tegetthoff* was launched on March 21, 1912, and the *Prinz Eugen* on November 30, 1912; the fourth, not yet named, was laid down in July, 1911.

RUSSIA. The *Sevastopol, Petropavlovsk, Poltava,* and *Gangut,* all launched in 1911, are still under construction in St. Petersburg under the supervision of Messrs. John Brown and Company, Clydebank. The *Emperor Alexander III., Empress Marie,* and *Catherine II.,* building at Nicolaieff on the Black Sea, were

H. B. M. BATTLE CRUISER "PRINCESS ROYAL"

IN COMMISSION 1912

MAIN BATTERY EIGHT 13.5-INCH GUNS—SECONDARY BATTERY SIXTEEN 4-INCH GUNS

COMPLETED OR NEARING COMPLETION IN 1912.

Viribus Unitis. Austrian Battleship	*Jean Bart.* French Battleship	*Wyoming.* American Battleship	*Princess Royal.* British Battle Cruiser	*Moltke.* German Battle Cruiser	*Kongo.* Japanese Battle Cruiser
4	4	2	3	2	4
Stabilimento Tecnico, Trieste	Brest Dock Yard.	Philadelphia Cramps	Vickers, Barrow.	Blohm & Voss Hamburg.	Vickers, Barrow.
April, 1910	Nov. 10, 1910	Feb. 9, 1910	May 2, 1910	April, 1909	Jan. 17, 1911
June 24, 1911	Sept. 22, 1911	May 25, '11	August, 1910	April, 1910	May, 1912
Sept. 26, 1912	August, 1913	Oct., 1912	June, 1912	March, 1912	July, 1913
495.4	541½	554	660	610	....
....	....	562	700	....	704
89	88½	93¼	88.5	....	88.5
....	....	....	....	96¾	92
....	29½	....	....	....	....
26	....	28½	28	27	27.5
20,000	23,026	27,243	26,350	22,640	27,500
....	....	26,000	....	....	....
25,000	29,000	28,000	70,000	50,000	68,000
20	20	20.5	28	25.5	27
21.2	....	21.223	....	28.07	....
....	....	22.045	34.7	29.70	....
11	11	11	9¾	8	10
....	7	....	....	5	7
....	....	6½	3	....	....
2	2.76; 1.9; 1.2	3	....	2½	2
12	10.6	12 to 8	9	8	10
....	....	....	....	....	....
12—12-inch	12—12-inch	12—12-inch	8—13.5-inch	10—11-inch	8—14-inch
12— 6-inch	22—5.5-inch	21— 5-inch	16— 4-inch	12— 5.9-inch	16— 6-inch
18— 3-inch	....	....	....	....	....
4	4—18-inch	2—21-inch	2—21-inch	4—19.5-inch	8—21-inch
....	....	....	....	760	....
992	970	850	....	....	....
....	....	....	1,250	....	....
....	....	....	....	....	1,700
11,772	9,700	10,200	10,000	7,600	13,600
5,952	7,760	....	5,000	4,552	6,800
5,952	7,760	....	2,500	6,080	6,800
....	....	....	....	40	....
54.3	55	52	....	....	....
....	....	....	76	....	....
....	....	....	....	....	83
Parsons Turbines	Parsons Turbines	Parsons Turbines	Parsons Turbines	Parsons Turbines	Parsons or Curtis Turbines
Coal and oil	Coal and oil	Coal and oil	Coal and oil	Coal and oil	Coal and oil
900	900	1,650	1,000	1,000	1,000
2,000	2,700	2,500	3,500	3,100	4,000
1,070	1,166	1,043	....	....	....
12,287,912	13,042,220	....	9,800,644	10,494,899	12,166,250
614	566	....	372	463	442

laid down on October 30, 1911. Supposed characteristics: Displacement, 22,500 tons; designed indicated horsepower, 25,000; speed, 21 knots; armament, twelve 12-inch guns and twelve 6-inch guns. They are due for launching in 1913.

BRAZIL. The original main armament of the *Rio de Janeiro* was to have been twelve 14-inch guns, all on the centre line. It has been officially announced that this plan has been changed, and that she will have fourteen 12-inch guns in seven centre-line turrets.

ARGENTINA. The *Moreno* and *Rivadavia*, due for completion in 1912, are still under construction.

BRITISH BATTLE CRUISERS. The position of the battle cruiser with reference to the battleship is best shown in England. Until 1911 no British battleship of the *Dreadnought* type was given a designed speed of more than 21 knots. The *Iron Duke* class, laid down in 1912, will make 22.0 knots. The designed speed of the battle cruiser has risen from 25 knots in the *Indomitable* class (eight 12-inch guns, sixteen 4-inch guns) to 28 knots in the *Princess Royal* class (eight 13.5-inch, sixteen 4-inch guns). England will therefore soon be in the position of six years ago, when the newest battleship, the *Dreadnought*, was as fast as the armored cruisers, the *Cressy* class, completed some four or five years before her. As the battleships of the 1912-13 programme are to make 25 knots, how can the name "battle cruiser," which is understood to connote abnormal speed, be rightly given to the 25-knot *Indomitables*? The British battle cruiser *Tiger*, laid down on June 20, 1912, and due for completion March 31, 1914, will displace 30,000 tons (estimated), develop 110,000 indicated horsepower (estimated), have a designed speed of 31 knots, and be armed with eight big guns and sixteen 6-inch guns.

BAVARIA. See LUITPOLD, KARL JOSEPH WILHELM.

BAVARIAN ELECTIONS. See GERMANY.

BECHUANALAND PROTECTORATE. A British dependency in the south of Africa, considered administratively as a part of the crown colony of British Bechuanaland until the annexation of that colony (November 15, 1895) to the (then) Cape Colony. Thereafter the protectorate was administered as a separate territory by a resident-commissioner (1912, Lieut.-Col. F. W. Panzera), under the direction of the high commissioner for South Africa, from the headquarters at Mafeking (Cape of Good Hope province). The area is estimated at 275,000 square miles; population (census 1911), 125,350 (1692 whites). The chief of the Bamangwato is Khama, and his chief town is Serowe; of the Bakwena, Sechele, residing at Molepolole; of the Bangwaketsi, Gaseitsiwe, at Kanye; of the Bakhatla, Linchwe, at Mochudi; of the Batawana, Mathibe, at Lake N'gami; of the Bamalete, Baitlothe, at Ramoutsa. The railway from Capetown to Rhodesia (with an extension beyond the Victoria Falls) traverses the protectorate. Estimated revenue (1911-12), £46,600; estimated expenditure, £68,551. The annual deficit is made up by the imperial government.

BEECHER, WILLIS JUDSON. An American theologian and educator, died May 8, 1912. He was born in Hampden, Ohio, in 1838 and graduated from Hamilton College in 1858. He studied theology at the Auburn Theological Seminary, graduating in 1854. In the same year he was ordained to the Presbyterian ministry. He was pastor at Ovid, N. Y., in 1864-65. In the latter year he was appointed professor of moral science and belles lettres at Knox College, which chair he held until 1869 when he resigned to become pastor of the First Church of Christ at Galesburg, Illinois, and remained here until 1871. In that year he was appointed professor of Hebrew language and literature at the Auburn Theological Seminary. He continued in this position until 1908. In 1902 he was Stone lecturer at the Charleston Theological Seminary. He was president of the Society of Biblical Literature and Exegesis in 1904. He wrote several works on theological subjects, among them *Prophets and the Promise* (1905); *The Teaching of Jesus Concerning the Future Life* (1908); *The Dated Events of the Old Testament* (1907). He also contributed many articles to newspapers, magazines, and reviews.

BEEF TRUST. See TRUSTS.

BEER. See LIQUORS.

BEERNAERT, AUGUSTE MARIE FRANÇOIS. A Belgian public official and philanthropist, died October 6, 1912. He was born at Ostend in 1829. He studied law and in 1853 began its practice in Brussels. He soon attracted attention by his gifts as a speaker. He took an active part in politics and in 1873 was appointed Minister of Public Works in the cabinet of Malou. In 1884 when the latter again took office Beernaert became minister of agriculture, commerce, and art, and on the resignation of Malou a few months later succeeded him as premier. He was one of the earliest and foremost advocates of international arbitration and was probably a member of more arbitral tribunals than any other man of his time. The reforms in the Belgian Congo were largely due to his efforts. He was for more than forty years the head of the powerful Catholic party in the Belgian Parliament. In 1909 he was, with M. d'Estournelles de Constant, awarded the Nobel prize for peace. Shortly before his death he presided over the Interparliamentary Congress at Geneva.

BEET SUGAR. See SUGAR.

BEHRENS, SIEGFRIED. An American musician, died November 5, 1912. He was born in Hamburg, Germany, in 1839. He took up the study of the piano at ten years of age. In 1856 he came to the United States with a reputation as a performer of wonderful promise. His first position was that of instructor in music at a school near West Point. In 1867 he was appointed operatic conductor with the Strakosch-Gottschalk-Patti Opera Company. When still but 24 years of age he was selected as a conductor of the Caroline Richings English Opera Company and continued with it until that organization consolidated with the Parepa Rosa Company. When the Metropolitan Opera Company at New York decided to begin the production of grand opera in Philadelphia at the Old Academy of Music, Behrens was selected as manager of the company and conductor. He had a profound knowledge of musical subjects and a remarkable memory for technical and personal matters relating to musicians.

BELASCO, DAVID. See DRAMA.

BELGIAN CONGO. See CONGO, BELGIAN.

BELGIAN EXPOSITION. See EXPOSITIONS.

BELGIAN HARBOR IMPROVEMENT. See DOCKS AND HARBORS.

BELGIUM. A constitutional monarchy of western Europe, lying between France and the Netherlands and bordering on the North Sea. The capital is Brussels.

AREA AND POPULATION. The area and population by provinces, according to the census taken December 31, 1910, and compared with the figures for 1831, with the number of inhabitants per square kilometer in 1910, are as follows:

	Sq. kms.	1831	1910	Per km.
Antwerp	2,832	349,942	968,677	342
Brabant	3,283	561,828	1,469,677	448
West Flanders	3,234	608,226	874,135	270
East Flanders	3,000	742,973	1,120,335	373
Hainaut	3,722	613,179	1,232,867	331
Liège	2,895	375,030	888,341	307
Limbourg	2,408	160,090	275,691	114
Luxembourg	4,418	160,762	231,215	52
Namur	3,660	213,784	362,846	99
Total Belgium	29,451*	3,785,814	7,423,784	252

* 11,371 square miles.

Of the total population in 1910, 3,680,790 were males and 3,742,994 were females. The census of 1900 returned 6,693,548 (3,324,834 males and 3,368,714 females); 1880, 5,520,009; 1850, 4,426,205. Since 1856 the population shows an augmentation of 63.90 per cent., a development by no means equal throughout the provinces, as shown by the following details: Antwerp, 122.95 per cent.; Brabant, 96.26; West Flanders, 39.88; East Flanders, 44.19; Hainaut, 60.31; Liège, 76.38; Limburg, 43.81; Luxemburg, 19.33; Namur, 26.79. In the table below will be seen the population in 1900, the population in 1910, the augmentation during the decade due to excess of births over deaths, and that due to excess of immigration over emigration for the kingdom, by provinces (+ = excess of immigration, — = excess of emigration):

	1910	1900	Ex. Births	Emigration
Antwerp	819,159	968,677	137,121	+12,397
Brabant	1,263,535	1,469,677	122,357	+83,785
West Flanders	805,236	874,135	105,206	—36,307
East Flanders	1,029,971	1,120,335	130,091	—39,727
Hainaut	1,142,954	1,232,867	78,161	+11,752
Liège	826,175	888,341	60,537	+ 1,629
Limburg	240,796	275,691	43,027	— 8,132
Luxemburg	219,210	231,215	19,596	— 7,591
Namur	346,512	362,846	21,467	— 5,133
Tot. Belgium	6,693,548	7,423,784	717,563	+12,673

Population (census of 1910) of Antwerp, 301,766 (with suburbs, 398,255); of Brussels, 177,078 (720,347); Ghent, 166,445 (210,428); Liège, 167,521 (242,357). These four cities, with their environs, contain 21.16 per cent. of the population of the kingdom; but the appearance of "urbanization" induced by these figures is offset by the fact that the dependent communes cover areas with boundaries widely separated from the urban centres. Within these confines are areas devoted to agriculture. Some of the more important urban communes, with their population (census 1910), are: Mechlin, 59,142; Bruges, 53,285; Borgerhout, 49,333; Verviers, 46,948; Seraing, 41,015; Ostend, 42,207; Louvain, 42,123; Tournai, 36,982; Courtrai, 35,689; Alost, 35,125; Saint-Nicolas, 34,774; Namur, 32,362; Berchem, 30,274; Charleroi, 28,177; Mons, 27,828; Jumet, 27,956; Roulers, 25,026.

Movement of the population 1910: 176,413 living births, 165,576 legitimate and 10,837 illegitimate; 8008 still-births, 709 illegitimate; 58,776 marriages; 1089 divorces; 112,826 deaths, 58,605 males and 54,221 females. Of the deaths, 9141 were due to tuberculous affections (7217 pulmonary); 10,592 to organic diseases of the heart, 10,265 to senile debility; there were 3525 violent deaths (1051 suicides—822 men, 229 women).

EDUCATION. In 1910 there were 7525 primary schools (21,313 teachers and 929,347 pupils), 54 primary normal schools (4725 students), 4722 schools for adults (240,019 scholars), 3112 infant schools (271,237 children). University population: Ghent, 1172; Liège, 2790; Brussels, 1318; Louvain, 2600—total, 7880.

AGRICULTURE. Under cultivation in the kingdom (a previous census, 1910 statistics not yet being available), 2,607,514 hectares (including 721,938 fallow, under brush, and otherwise irregularly productive), of which 1,818,156 under sown crops and grasses, and 67,419 under orchards, gardens, vineyards, etc. The following table gives areas planted to main crops in 1911 and 1912, in hectares; the production, in quintals; and the average yield per hectare in 1911:

	Hectares 1911	Hectares 1912	Quintals 1911	Quintals 1912	Qs. per har
Wheat	153,000	166,600	3,978,000	4,158,600	26.0
Rye	255,000	260,000	5,865,000	5,720,000	23.0
Barley	34,500	34,000	1,000,500	918,000	29.0
Oats	245,000	255,500	6,002,500	5,110,000	24.5
Flax	19,000	21,000	....	126,600†	...
Beets *	60,800	66,000	14,760,000	19,000,000	242.8
Tobacco	4,000	3,900	100,000	100,000	25.0

* Sugar beets. † Seed; fibre, 168,800 quintals.

The incessant August and September rains in 1912 affected both the tobacco and the sugar-beet crops; so that, while the yield in weight will not be materially affected, the quality has suffered. The autumn sowings were benefited by a warm, sunny October.

Estimated number of cattle December 31, 1909, 1,856,833; horses, 255,229; swine, 1,116,500.

MINING AND METALS, ETC. Number of quarries in operation in 1910, 1522, with 35,711 employees; value of products, 66,418,720 francs. Coal mines, 133 (143,701 employees); 23,916,560 metric tons, valued at 348,877,000 francs (14.59 francs per ton) Value of iron ore (1910), 566,950 fr.; blende, 139,600 fr.; galena, 26,450 fr. Furnace products, 1,852,090 metric tons, valued at 120,161,000 fr.; manufactured iron, 299,500 tons, 39,494,000 fr.; cast steel ingots, 1,892,160 tons, 161,606,000 fr.; worked steel ingots, blooms and billets, 1,074,210 tons, 98,634,000 fr.; finished steel, 1,534,550 tons, 192,220,000 fr.; zinc ingots, 181,745 tons, 103,541,000 fr.; pig-lead, 40,715 tons, 13,464,000 fr.; silver from lead 264,655 kilos, 27,754,000 fr.

Sugar mills numbered (1900), 92; production, 271,282 tons. Sugar refineries, 22; production, 114,538 tons. Manufactured tobacco, 10,761 tons. Breweries, 3349; production, 1,601,858 kiloliters. Distilleries, 125; 71,087 (50° G. L.).

COMMERCE. The table below gives a résumé (in millions of francs) of the trade during the last years of four decades:

		1880	1890	1900	1910
Imports	(general)	2,710.4	3,189.2	3,594.4	6,551.7
"	(special)	1,680.9	1,672.1	2,215.8	4,265.0
Exports	(general)	2,226.2	2,948.1	3,297.5	5,694.6
"	(special)	1,216.7	1,437.0	1,922.9	3,407.4

A few of the important imports, with values in thousands of francs in 1910, follow—cereals, etc. (582,666), wool and woolens (442,139), minerals (197,462), seeds (171,178), timber (150,494), cotton, etc. (148,489), flax, etc. (143,034), raw hides (139,296), coal (107,478), rough diamonds (98,447), resins, etc. (96,301), iron ore, etc. (92,520), machinery (80,458), dyes, etc. (68,213), coffee (63,699), live animals (53,334). Exports—wool, yarn and mfrs. (436,450), iron and steel (224,287), machinery, etc. (180,762), cereals (163,170), raw flax (121,136), vegetable fibre, yarn and mfrs. (113,439), seeds (111,509), cut diamonds (99,057), zinc (91,960), raw hides (91,441), coal (88,636), paints, etc. (85,087), glass and glassware (84,496), cotton mfrs. (78,478), resins, etc. (53,010), manures (50,277), sugar (45,151), live animals (42,647).

France furnished imports to the value (1910) of 747.2 millions of francs and received exports valued at 669.1 millions; Germany, 576.1 and 881.4; Great Britain, 516.8 and 457.6; Russia, 364.1 and 67.0; Netherlands, 293.1 and 327.9; Argentina, 278.1 and 128.6; United States, 231.2 and 117.1. During the year 10,943 vessels, of 15,101,171 tons entered, and 10,929 of 15,074,061 tons, cleared. Merchant marine, 97 steamers (184,261 tons) and 4 sailing vessels (3183 tons).

COMMUNICATIONS. Railways in operation, December 31, 1910, by the state, 4330 kilometers (of which 4072 are state-owned); by companies, 349—a total length of 4679 kilometers throughout the kingdom. In view of the present agitation over the numbers of annual victims of railway accidents in the United States, it is of interest to note that out of 193,069,662 passengers carried over the Belgian lines during 1910, the total number of persons killed and injured was 1147, of whom 165 were suicides, persons walking illegally upon the tracks, etc. The total number of victims from 1835 to the end of 1910, out of 3,999,925,826 persons carried, was 42,989, of whom 6037 were suicides, etc.—an average of 10.75 accidents to one million passengers. Of the persons killed in 1910, 11 were passengers and 77 employes of the railways (443 and 3238 from 1835-1910); of those injured, 359 were passengers and 535 employees (7616 and 25,655). The light railways in Belgium amounted to 2450 miles with 444 miles under construction. Electrification had progressed actively and 360 miles of existing line were so worked, while 150 miles of that under construction was designed for electric operation. The Neckerpoel Station at Malines was being reconstructed during the year. Telegraph lines (end of 1910), 7582 kilometers; wires, 39,884 (not including semi-private lines along waterways, etc.). There are 11 wireless stations.

FINANCE. The franc (worth 19.3 cents), is the unit of value. The table of revenue and expenditure below is in thousands of francs (1912 budget):

	1835	1900	1909	1912
Rev. ordinary....	89,171	494,106	645,107	703,883*
" extraordinary	1,904	48,672	150,109	......
Total	91,075	542,778	795,216	......
Exp. ordinary....	85,614	479,056	634,450	708,081†
" extraordinary	1,490	95,102	151,747	......
Total	87,104	574,158	786,197	......

* Direct taxes, 73,166,000 francs; customs, 57,803,650; excise, 81,138,300; registration, 77,253,000; revenue-earning administrations, 371,925,730; domains, dividends, interest, etc., 31,635,090; repayments, etc., 8,458,324.

† Service of the debt, 198,711,930; civil list, 5,479,090; justice, 30,636,400; foreign affairs, 4,990,846; interior, 7,792,915; sciences and arts, 40,679,402;; colonies, 1,262,700; industry and labor, 26,764,217; railways, posts, telegraphs, 255,728,463; war, 67,976,440; gendarmerie, 10,379,460; finance, 24,385,900; agriculture and public works, 30,446,746; repayments, etc., 2,826,000.

The total consolidated debt in 1835 was 96,841,080 francs; in 1870, 682,880,914; in 1900, 2,050,898,151; in 1910, 3,703,403,693; on January 1, 1912, the total consolidated debt was 3,734,354,038.

GOVERNMENT. The king is the executive, assisted by a ministry of eight members, responsible to a chamber of representatives and appointed by the king. The legislative power is exercised conjointly by the king and a parliament made up of two houses—a senate and an elective chamber of representatives. The reigning sovereign in 1912 was Albert, son of the late Prince Philippe of Saxe-Coburg and Gotha, born 1875. Prince Leopold (born 1901), is heir-apparent. The ministry, as constituted November 12, 1912, was as follows: Premier and minister of war, Baron de Broqueville; Justice, H. Carton de Wiart; Foreign Affairs, J. Davignon; Interior, Paul Berryer; Science and Arts, P. Poullet; Finance, M. Levie; Agriculture and Public Works, G. Helleputte; Industry and Labor, Armand Hubert; Railways, A. van de Vyvere; Marine, Posts, and Telegraphs, M. Seghers; Colonies, J. Renkin.

ARMY. During 1912 further progress was made in the reorganization of the army on a basis of personal service as provided by the law of December 14, 1909, which provided for a strength of 42,800 men on a peace basis and 180,000 on a war footing, the annual quota being obtained by the enlistment of one son in each family. In 1912 there were with the colors 3540 officers and 41,120 men exclusive of officials and gendarmes. Progress was being made with the plans for the fortification of Antwerp, for other works, and for an aviation school. The organization of the forces was as follows: Cavalry—2 regiments of chasseurs, 2 of guides, and 4 of lancers, each composed of 4 active squadrons and 1 in reserve, and also the mounted troops of the gendarmerie, numbering about 1700 men. Artillery—4 brigades each of 2 regiments of 6 field batteries with 12 reserve field batteries and ammunition columns and 4 horse batteries. Engineers—1 regiment of 3 battalions, a reserve battalion and 5 companies of technical troops. The infantry included 14 regiments of the line and 1 regiment of genadiers, organized into 4 battalions of 4 companies each, 3 battlions for active service and 1 a reserve battalion. There were further a regiment of carabineers of 6 battalions, 4 active and 2 reserve, and 3 regiments of chasseurs-à-pied. It was believed that within a few months Belgium would be able to place in the field a field army of about 300,000 men without counting the territorial army.

HISTORY

NATIONAL DEFENSE. Sharp criticism was directed against the government during the closing months of 1911 for its neglect of Belgian defenses. The subject was much discussed after the threatened crisis in the Franco-German negotiations over the Moroccan affair in September. It was pointed out that the country was utterly unprepared to resist an invasion at that time. And if Germany, as might have happened, had thrown her forces into Belgium in order to turn the flanks of her enemy, there would have been no means of preventing it and Belgium would have failed completely to do her share in maintaining her own integrity. Belgian neutrality is guaranteed by the other powers, but that guarantee is based on the assumption that she will put forth some efforts on her own behalf. The discussion continued into 1912, and drew out many vigorous protests from leading politicians of all groups and from military authorities against this neglect of the Belgian frontiers. In the course of a debate in the Chamber, members of the opposition taxed the government with its unpreparedness. The matters brought out in the debate confirmed the critics in their opinion that Belgium would have been in no position to do her part had matters taken a different turn in 1911. The government was believed by many to lean towards Germany. It was accused of a lack of patriotism and the French-speaking element was further incensed by its attempt to make the Flemish language paramount to French. If Belgium is to preserve her independence, she must, it was argued, organize her defenses. "Neither the improvident nor the pusillanimous will be defended by any one," said a prominent speaker, "they will simply be placed under somebody else's tutelage. We have known in our history what it was to be under the tutelage of foreigners, and the painful recollection survives. That remembrance explains the profound grief and resentment with which the nation realizes that the country was not prepared to defend its integrity during the critical months of July, August, and September last year." M. Vandervelde, the Socialist leader, figured prominently in the discussion and took the same general position as to the national duty of a Socialist that was taken by Herr Bebel in Germany the year before. The latter had declared that if war were forced on Germany the German Socialists would fight for their country like other Germans. M. Vandervelde said that if Belgium were attacked the Belgian Socialists would fight in her defense. He declared if his party came into power it would address itself to this problem and place the defenses of Belgium on a firm basis.

ELECTIONS. The Clerical party which has

been in power for twenty-eight years had seen its majority cut down from 72 in 1900 to six in the last Parliament. The opposition appeared to be steadily gaining ground, and as the elections approached was hopeful of completely overthrowing the weakened government. To accomplish this it was necessary for Socialists and Liberals to join hands. A Socialist-Liberal alliance was formed in 1911 looking to the reversal of the government's policy on the school question and to the reform of the suffrage. The school question was the chief issue in the elections, which were held on June 2, 1912. The Socialists and Liberals were strongly opposed to the government's proposal that the church schools should have the same subsidies as the others. The Clericals, on the other hand, argued for the public support of a religious education, pointing to the labor troubles in Great Britain and the outbreak of crime in France as the fruits of the opposite system. The result of the elections was an unexpected and decisive victory for the government, giving the Clericals a new lease of power with an increased majority. The Catholic majority in the Chamber was increased from six to eighteen. Partial elections to the Senate on June 4 indicated also a Catholic majority. The constitution of parties in the new Chamber in which the number of seats had recently been increased from 166 to 186, was as follows: Clerical, 101; Liberals, 45; Socialists, 38; Christian Democrats, 2. Various reasons were assigned for this outcome. It was explained in part by the fear of the Liberals that their new allies, the Socialists, would carry them too far. They were with them in their attacks on the Church, but they were not with them in their attacks on property. The moderate Liberals were naturally loath to arm with power a party that sought ultimately the nationalization of the means of production. They agreed with the Socialists in wishing to abolish the system of plural voting. In Belgium there is universal suffrage for citizens over twenty-five, but special qualifications entitle certain classes to additional votes. Certain property qualifications give the citizen one additional vote, and certain educational qualifications give him two additional votes. It was chiefly owing to these conditions that the Clericals had remained so long in power, and it was not likely that they would bring in a measure of electoral reform to their own undoing. It was therefore only by a Socialist-Liberal alliance that such a measure could be carried. But many of the Liberals enjoyed the advantage of the plural vote, and the more moderate among them, though theoretically opposed to the system, hesitated to relinquish this advantage which might be very useful against the Socialists if the present alliance did not last. Another reason assigned for the defeat of the allied parties was their anticlerical teachings. See also SOCIALISM.

PLANS OF THE OPPOSITION. The opposition groups, who had gained steadily on their rivals for the last ten years and who had counted on an easy victory, were much discouraged by the results. Not only were the Clericals entrenched in power for six years, but, since the Liberals could not hope to secure a majority by themselves, and since an alliance with the Socialists redounded to the advantage of their adversaries, there seemed little hope of breaking the power of the Clericals so long as the present electoral system continued. The opposition therefore set out to secure a constitutional amendment abolishing plural voting. Some of the Clericals favored this, being enthusiasts for universal suffrage including votes for women, but party discipline seemed likely to prevent their breaking the ranks. As to woman suffrage, the Liberals were strongly opposed to it and the Socialists, though in favor of it, decided in their party congress to defer the question for the present. The principle, "one man, one vote," found its strong support among the Socialists, the Liberals, and the Labor party. The last-named decided upon the extreme measure of a general strike to force the government to grant constitutional revision, if it did not of itself take that action after the opening of Parliament. The trades unions began to gather funds for the purpose. Many of the Liberals declared that they would support such a strike if it occurred, and the movement found adherents even among the *bourgeoisie*. Parliament opened on November 12, and M. Schollaert was elected president of the Chamber. The programme of the ministry comprised elaborate plans of social legislation and national defense, including old age pensions, compulsory school attendance, improvement in technical training, and an extension of the compulsory military system. A ministry of marine was constituted.

NIEDERFULLBACH FOUNDATION. The difficulty over the Niederfullbach Foundation, which had been in the courts since the death of King Leopold, entered on a new phase in May, when the Coburg government took up the question. A report of the Coburg government denied the jurisdiction of Belgian courts over the "Foundation," and demanded that Belgium should restore the properties. It urged the government to appeal to the Bundesrath, to negotiate with the Brussels government on the subject. The interest of Coburg in the affair lay in the fact that it would derive a revenue from the taxes upon the foundation.

BELLOC, HILAIRE. See LITERATURE, ENGLISH AND AMERICAN.

BENEFACTIONS. See GIFTS AND BEQUESTS.

BENGAZI. See TRIPOLI.

BENSON, E. F. See LITERATURE, ENGLISH AND AMERICAN.

BENT, SAMUEL ARTHUR. An American lawyer and author, died November 22, 1912. He was born in Boston in 1841 and graduated from Yale College in 1861. After studying law he was admitted to the bar in 1865. From 1872 to 1874 he was American editor of the Swiss (Geneva) *Times* and Galignani's (Paris) *Messenger*. From 1878 to 1886, he was superintendent of schools in Nashua, N. H. He was secretary and treasurer of the Bostonian Society from 1890 to 1899 and several times served on the Boston School Committee. He was greatly interested in historical matters and wrote *Familiar Short Sayings of Great Men* (1882); *Hints on Language* (1883); and *Notes to the Golden Legend* (1886).

BERCHTOLD, COUNT LEOPOLD. See AUSTRIA-HUNGARY and TURKEY AND THE BALKAN PEOPLES.

BEREA COLLEGE. An institution of higher learning at Berea, Ky., founded in 1855. Its chief educational work is carried on among "mountain whites." The enrollment in the several departments in the autumn of 1912 was as follows: College, 95; normal, 96; model school,

214; academy, 233; vocational school, 117; foundation school, 222. The larger portion of the normal school students were absent during the fall term teaching among the mountains. The faculty in all departments numbered about 50. Among the new appointments for 1912 were those of Rev. Charles F. Hubbard, D. D., professor of Latin and oean of the college; Professor Frank E. Howard, Ph. D., professor of education in the normal department; and Frank Montgomery, M. S., instructor in animal husbandry and investigator in mountain agriculture. There were no noteworthy benefactions received during the year. The productive funds of the college amount to $1,040,000, and the income to $65,000. There are about 27,000 volumes in the library. President, William Goodell Frost, Ph. D., D. D.

BERGSON, HENRI. See PHILOSOPHY.

BERIBERI. Little calls attention to the fact that beriberi is very prevalent in Newfoundland, and is satisfied that it is due to the fine (overmilled) white flour. Although often complicated by starvation, exposure, and scurvy, many cases are clearly of the neuritic type. The symptoms vary in severity from numbness and tingling of the legs and arms (paræsthesia) to night blindness, retention of urine, sensory and motor paralysis, involvement of the nerves of the heart, œdema, and death. Little has proved clinically that such cases recover on a diet of whole wheat flour, and his findings reinforce the milled rice theory of the causation of beriberi in the East. But he shows also that it is not any particular grain that is at fault, but the removal of the pericarp in milling.

At the annual meeting of the Far Eastern Association of Tropical Medicine at Hongkong beriberi occupied a prominent place in the discussions. The views of American, English, French, and Japanese investigators were nearly unanimous in favor of the dietetic, as opposed to the infectious, origin of the disease. While rice polishings or an extract thereof have been found almost a specific in the cure of the malady, numerous attempts to isolate the active principle were unsuccessful. Chamberlain and Vedder, army sanitarians in the Philippines, reported that they had found the disease common in nurslings, the children of mothers suffering from beriberi. The symptoms resembled somewhat those observed in adults, and began with vomiting followed after a few days by great restlessness, sleeplessness, continual whining, and still later by dyspnœa, rapid pulse and œdema of the face and extremities. Still later oliguria and aphonia developed in many cases. To these infants was given extract of rice polishing in 20-drop doses every two hours while awake. Improvement began within twenty-four hours, and in a week all the symptoms disappeared except the aphonia, which often lasted for two months.

BERLIN. See ARCHITECTURE.

BERMUDA. A group of islands (about 300) lying about 500 miles to the east of Cape Hatteras. Area, about 19 sq. miles; population (1911 census), 18,994 (12,303 colored). Hamilton (the capital) had 2627 inhabitants; St. George's, 1079. During the year ending May, 1912, about 20,000 tourists entered the colony. Nearly three-fourths of the area is unfit for cultivation. The remainder is utilized for the production of early spring table crops, for export to the United States. There are no railways.

	1907	1908	1909	1910
Imports	£410,596	£392,522	£440,648	£517,074
Exports	140,598	105,392	183,884	106,508
Revenue	67,538	57,068	68,921	78,593
Expenditure..	59,172	53,586	67,093	68,392
Shipping*.....	829,376	742,068	850,316	688,315

* Tonnage entered and cleared.

Customs revenue (1910), £64,999; public debt, £45,500. The governor, Lieut.-Gen. Sir Walter Kitchener, died March 29, 1912, and Gen. Sir George Mackworth Bullock was appointed April 4, 1912.

BESSEMER PROCESS. See METALLURGY.

BETA. See NAVAL PROGRESS, *Aviation*.

BEVERIDGE, ALBERT J. See PRESIDENTIAL CAMPAIGN and INDIANA.

BIBLE SOCIETY, AMERICAN. An organization founded in 1816 for the encouragement of a wider circulation of the Holy Scriptures without note or comment. The ninety-seventh year of the society was a successful one. Its work continually expanded and its one hindrance was a lack of funds. One of the most important developments of the work of the society is that connected with its "home" agencies. These continued without interruption in 1911-12 with many marks of success. These agencies circulated during the year 646,625 Scriptures. The agency among the colored people of the South reached the largest circulation ever attained, 41,267 copies. Other agencies are the Northwestern Agency, covering the States of Illinois, Indiana, Michigan, Wisconsin, Minnesota, Iowa, Nebraska, North Dakota, and South Dakota; the South Atlantic Agency, embracing the States of Virginia, West Virginia, North Carolina, South Carolina, Georgia, and Florida; the Western Agency, embracing the States of Missouri, Kansas, Colorado, Idaho, Montana, Utah, Wyoming, New Mexico, and Arizona; the Southwestern Agency, embracing the States of Texas, Oklahoma, Louisiana, and Arkansas; the Pacific Agency, including the States of California, Oregon, Nevada, and Washington; and the Central Agency, including within its field the States of Ohio, Kentucky, Tennessee, Alabama, and Mississippi. The "foreign" agencies of the society are in the West Indies, Venezuela, Mexico, Central America, Brazil, Siam, China, Japan, Korea, and the Philippines. The total issues at home and abroad during the year were 3,691,-201 volumes. These issues consist of 430,093 Bibles, 670,728 Testaments, and 2,590,375 portions of the Scriptures. This is the largest distribution made in any year of the history of the society. Of the total issues, 1,837,356 volumes were issued from the Bible House in New York, and 1,853,845 by the society's agents abroad. The total issues of the society for ninety-six years of its existence amount to 94,219,105 volumes. New translations of the Scriptures included one in the Ibanag dialect of the Philippines. This translation was of the New Testament. The society also coöperated with the British and Foreign Bible Society in a revision of the Tagalog New Testament. The American Bible Society joined with the American Baptist Foreign Mission Society in bringing out the Old Testament in Panayan. There were other translations of portions of the Scriptures in dialects of the Philippine Islands. The Book of Acts was brought out in addition to Mark, Luke, and John as the beginning of the Kurdish New Testament. Translation was also carried on in Chinese and the Siamese languages.

Mr. James Wood, since 1896 a member of the board of managers, and for the last eight years a vice-president of the society, was elected its president to succeed Theophilus A. Brouwer, who died June 15, 1911. The principal receipts of the society in 1911-12 were as follows: From individuals, $25,528; from churches, $60,783; from auxiliaries, $13,769, making a total of $100,081. The receipts from legacies were $224,701, and the income from trusts and available investments was $121,184. The society received from the sale of its books $238,522. The total receipts available for current work amounted to $691,347. The total expenditures for the year amounted to $734,494.

BICYCLING. See CYCLING.

BIEBERSTEIN, BARON ADOLF MARSCHALL VON. A German diplomat, died September 24, 1912. He was born in Karlsruhe, in the Grand Duchy of Baden, in 1842. He was educated at the Frankfurt Gymnasium and at the University of Heidelberg. He entered the diplomatic service and up to the retirement of Bismarck in 1890 his career was unmarked by any unusual occurrence. In 1890 he was made secretary of state for foreign affairs in particular charge of the details of commercial treaties. During his term of office he brought about many treaties with foreign nations, most of which, with slight modifications, are still in force. He was appointed Prussian minister of state in 1894. He had already gained such a reputation for skill and diplomacy that in 1897 the emperor in recognition of his abilities appointed him ambassador to Turkey. He held this office for more than thirteen years and greatly enhanced his reputation. During his stay in Constantinople he was frequently called to Berlin for conferences with the emperor in regard to matters which had to do not only with German policy in Turkey but with the general foreign policy of the country. It was generally understood that he would have succeeded Count von Bülow as imperial chancellor but for the fact that a man of Bieberstein's calibre was needed in Constantinople to maintain the domination of Germany in Turkey. As the result of his skillful diplomatic manœuvring he gained for Germany the supremacy in Turkey once held by England. Most of what he accomplished, however, was undone by the revolution of the Young Turks and the Turco-Italian War.

Von Bieberstein is said to have inspired the emperor to write the telegram of sympathy to President Krüger of the Transvaal at the outbreak of the Boer War. It was said, too, that he was chosen by the emperor to see that peace developments at The Hague should not take a course that might embarrass German plans. During The Hague conference, von Bieberstein's position was often in marked opposition to that of the British delegates. In June, 1912, he was made German ambassador to Great Britain. At that time his reputation was greater than that of any other German diplomat. His transfer was heralded as proof of the German decision to change its foreign policy toward both England and Turkey.

BIJAGOZ. See PORTUGUESE GUINEA.

BILLIARDS. The billiard performances of 1912 were disappointing as far as the professional matches were concerned, but the showing made by the amateurs was excellent. Among the amateurs the player who stands out most prominently is Mortier, the winner of the international 18.2 balk line tournament held at Paris from March 21 to April 3, Mortier's grand average was 17.33, his best single average 40, and his highest run 178. The comparison of these figures with those registered by William F. Hoppe, who again won the 18.2 balk line professional championship, is interesting. Hoppe's grand average was 18.80, his best single average 29 7-17, and his highest run 122. Hoppe's best showing during the year was made in his 18.2 balk line match with George Sutton in February, when he established an average of 29.45. O. C. Morningstar made the record run of the year, 167 in the tournament held in November. Another amateur deserving of mention is J. F. Poggenburg, who ranked next to Mortier in performance figures. Poggenburg was able to finish not better than eighth in the Paris tournament, but won the American international championship after a tie with Charles F. Conklin. Poggenburg's best grand average was 13.31, his best single average 28.57, and his highest run 149.

In the American amateur chapionships Morris D. Brown was the victor, with an average of 12.12 and a high run of 88. The entries in this tournament included Percy Collins, Poggenburg, Conklin, J. Mayer, Dr. W. G. Douglas, and Dr. W. E. Uffenheimer. The class B championship was again won by George P. B. Clarke and the class C championship by Clyde B. Terry. The increasing popularity of the three-cushion game has led the amateurs to arrange a championship tournament this year (1913). In the professional three-cushion matches of 1912 Alfred de Oro lost his championship title to John W. Carney, who in turn bowed to the prowess of John D. Horgan. De Oro, after losing his title as champion in pool, now known as pocket billards, to Edward Ralph in April, regained it by defeating Ralph in November. An amateur tournament also was held, which was won by Arthur B. Hyman.

BINGHAM, HENRY HARRISON. A member of Congress from Pennsylvania, died March 23, 1912. He was born in Philadelphia in 1841 and graduated at Jefferson College in 1862. He studied law for a short time, but deferred this to enlist in the Federal army as lieutenant in in the 140th Pennsylvania Volunteers. He was three times wounded in action. In 1866 he was mustered out of service after having been brevetted for distinguished gallantry major, lieutenant-colonel, colonel, and brigadier-general. He received a medal of honor for special gallantry on the field of battle. In 1867 he was appointed postmaster of Philadelphia, and resigned in 1872 to become clerk of courts, to which office he had been elected by the people, and was reëlected in 1875. He took a prominent part in politics and was a delegate at nearly all the Republican national conventions from 1876 to 1904. He was elected to the 46th Congress and was reëlected to successive Congresses, including the 62d. His term of service in the House of Representatives exceeded that of any other member and he was popularly known as "the father of the House."

BIOGRAPHY. See FRENCH LITERATURE, GERMAN LITERATURE, and LITERATURE, *English and American.*

BIOLOGICAL CHEMISTRY. See CHEMISTRY.

BIOLOGY. For morphology of animals see ZOÖLOGY; of plants, see BOTANY. See also ENTOMOLOGY, FISH AND FISHERIES, and ORNITHOLOGY.

HEREDITY. The year 1912 was marked by no strikingly new methods of attack on biological problems such as those of a decade or more ago, when the rediscovery of Mendel's law started an immense amount of work on heredity and allied subjects. (See YEAR BOOK for 1907.) There was, however, no decrease in the interest in these subjects, as was indicated by the large number of publications dealing with them. Most writers have apparently accepted the doctrine of unit characters, which may in inheritance be separated and recombined as if they were separate entities, though a few have protested against this assumption as contrary to fact. If the offspring of a cross exhibit a blending rather than a selection of one or the other of opposed characters, it would seem as if the hypothesis should be modified. Precisely this blending is claimed by Cunningham, who in experiments on crosses between the silky and the jungle fowl got results which led him to doubt if recessive characters derived from crosses are ever pure, as they should be if the Mendelian assumption is accurate. Cunningham thinks that the Mendelians are too anxious to discover, or invent, factors whose segregation would agree with the observed results, and suggested the desirability of research in the investigation of the divisibility of "real" characters. Morgan, continuing his work on fruit flies, found new illustrations of sex limited inheritance (see YEAR BOOK for 1911), while Strong, in breeding ring doves, found that blond males and white females gave blond hybrids which were mostly male, while the offspring of the reciprocal cross gave blond and white in about equal numbers, indicating that white is a sex limited character. Strong thought that the male is heterozygous for sex, while the female is homozygous. Davenport, reviewing the results obtained by experimental breeders, on the one hand, and by students of centrosomes on the other, in the matter of sex limited inheritance, concluded that these converging lines of attack demonstrate results which "constitute one of the greatest advances made in biology during the present decade, if not in the history of science." Davenport found his results so nearly in agreement with those obtained by other workers that he was able to state as definite laws: (1) The male carries two sex chromosomes and the female one; (2) determiners for secondary sex characters are centred in the sex chromosomes; (3) aside from secondary sex characters whose determiners are located in the sex chromosomes are others whose development is especially influenced or modified, probably by secretions of the sex glands. Pearl, in a lengthy paper on the inheritance of fecundity in the domestic fowl, stated that fecundity in this animal is inherited strictly in accordance with Mendelian laws, and that individual variations in fecundity depend upon two separately inherited physiological factors, L_1 and L_2, high fecundity appearing only when both are present in the same individual. One factor, L_2, is sex limited in that it does not appear in any gamete which carries the female sex determiner. In determining fecundity, the male is as important as the female, so that mere selection of females alone would never lead to a racial increase in fecundity. Pearl suggested further that the diminishing birth rate in man might conceivably be explained on the assumption of the loss of one or more of the genes upon the presence of which high fecundity depends. Jordan, discussing human heredity, gave reasons for believing that left-handedness, a tendency to tuberculosis, and nephritis are probably inherited according to Mendel's laws. A further suggestion made by Jordan was that possibly finger print patterns might be inherited in the same fashion, which, if true, would be of importance in deciding questions of disputed parentage.

While perhaps the majority of workers believe that whatever be the material carrier of heredity qualities, they are situated in the chromatin of the sex cells, others have objected that in the spermatozoon the middle piece carrying the centrosome enters during fertilization and may contain some of this heredity material. In a series of remarkable experiments Lillie was able, using the centrifuge, to remove any part or all of the middle piece of the spermatozoon of an annelid *Nereis*, during the act of fertilization, while the head continued to enter the egg and produced a perfectly normal sperm pronucleus with a normal centrosome. Since the head of the spermatozoon is practically nothing but chromatin, and since in these cases only the head entered, yet produced perfectly normal division, it would seem as if the head is really the important portion of the spermatozoon. That a centrosome appeared in connection with this nucleus, though normally coming in with the middle piece, indicates that the centrosome is not a permanent organ, but is formed anew at each division by some forces at work in the egg. Wilson, writing from the point of view of the cytologist, took a strong position concerning the reality of unit characters. The existence of such characters, which may be independently combined, disassociated, and recombined, he regarded as definitely proved. These unit characters are dependent upon separate material bodies or substances, and these substances are the chromosomes. A unit character may be due to the coöperation of several unit factors, and different unit characters appear as unit factors are added to, or subtracted from, a given combination in the zygote. These unit factors play their specific rôle only as they form part of a still more general apparatus of ontogenetic reaction that is constituted by the organism as a whole. Thus it is not possible to speak of characters as borne by "determiners." They appear as responses of the germinal organization operating as a unit system. Wilson compared the results of combining these factors with the action of a chemist in altering the quality of a protein by addition, subtraction, or substitution of one or more side chains. Wilson thought that the chromosomes furnish a material basis for carriers of these factors.

EUGENICS. Much work was done in the investigation of eugenic problems during the year, though especially from the sociological point of view it was urged that environment rather than heredity is responsible for human character, thus continuing the old controversy of Eugenics *versus* Euthenics. Davenport, at Cold Spring Harbor, in addition to his own investigation, has for the last two summers conducted a training course in methods of eugenic investigation at the biology laboratory of the Brooklyn Institute. The first international eugenics congress was held in London from July 24th to July 30th, with Leonard Darwin as president. See EUGENICS.

MUTATION. As was stated in the YEAR BOOK for 1911, Davis believed that *Œnothera lamarckiana*, which furnished most of the evidence on which de Vries based his mutation hypothesis, is really a hybrid, and the mutants appearing in its cultures are really the reappearance of component species. In 1912 Davis published later results of his experiments which seemed to indicate that by combining *Œ. biennis* and *Œ. grandiflora* he was able to produce forms taxonomically belonging to *Œ. lamarckiana*. If this be true, de Vries's mutants are really variants due to the mixing of different protoplasm, and *Œ. lamarckiana* is really heterozygous rather than homozygous. On the other hand, Swarczewsky, comparing the mutations of various species of *Œnothera*, concluded that *Œ. biennis* exhibits mutations similar to those of *Œ. lamarckiana*, indicating that the mutations of the latter are older than the species and must not be regarded as arising from a splitting of hybrids. Osborn, from the standpoint of the paleontologist, declared against the idea that species ordinarily arise through mutation, and stated that all absolutely new characters which we have traced to their beginnings in fossil mammals arise gradually and continuously. Discontinuity in inheritance, which is what is observed by the morphologist, does not prove discontinuity in origin, and all paleontological evidence is against the latter assumption.

SELECTION. Davenport questioned whether in evolution advance can ever be made by personal selection, and decided that this must still remain an open question. Swamping by intercrossing, he declared, occurs very rarely, if at all. A new character depending on many determiners may appear, but no true blend occurs, and the original characters may again segregate. Castle, however, thought that in some characters, as coat color in rats, it is possible to permanently modify the character by selection in each generation. As a result of this selection the mean shifts in each generation thus opposed to the pure line concept. Alexander Graham Bell reported that in his flock of sheep in Nova Scotia he had been able by selection to produce a race of six-nippled sheep in which there was a marked tendency toward the production of twins.

INHERITANCE OF ACQUIRED CHARACTERS. Przibram in an article, "Die Umwelt des Keimplasmas," stated that the question as to whether characters appearing in response to environmental changes will appear in their offspring under similar conditions, must now be answered in the affirmative, and as to the method of this transference there are three possibilities: (1) New characters may arise because of germinal variation; (2) they may arise first in the soma and by it be impressed on the germ plasm; (3) both soma and germ plasm may be simultaneously affected by the same external stimulus. To decide this question Przibram proposed a coöperative inquiry as to how far external agencies could directly affect germ plasm. That is, how far can light, heat, etc., penetrate the body and act directly on the germ plasm? Secerov, working with salamanders, found that photographic paper enclosed in a tube and put in the body of a salamander in the position occupied by the sex organs would, if the animal was exposed to light, be affected by the light rays. Congdon determined the rectal temperature of rats and found certain variations under certain conditions, but reached no definite conclusions as to the possibility of the sex organs varying in temperature. This would seem more probable in the male than in the female, as the male organs are more exposed.

SEX DETERMINATION. The most important theories concerning the determination of sex are on the one hand, those that regard sex as determined by the environment of the developing embryo, and on the other hand those that consider sex is determined not later than the time of the fertilization of the egg, probably by the presence of a peculiar chromosome or combination of chromosomes. Guyer (see YEAR BOOK for 1910) thought he had found an accessory chromosome in the spermatogenesis of man, indicating a chromosomal determination in the human species. Gutherz, in 1912, studying similar material, was unable to find any trace of an accessory chromosome, so that the question as to determination of sex in man must be regarded as still an open one. Miss King, continuing experiments on the question of sex determination in amphibians, treated the eggs of toads with hypertonic solutions of sugar and salt. The proportion of females developing from these eggs was slightly greater than in the control, indicating that perhaps the egg may be heterozyous in regard to sex. Extraction of water also tended to produce a larger proportion of females. Miss King concluded from her results that in the toad there is no evidence for a chromosomal control of sex. In earlier years Geoffrey Smith had discovered that crabs infested with a parasitic crustacean, *Sacculina*, would change their secondary sex characters from male to female. Smith continued these observations in 1912, and his results indicated that the roots of the parasite elaborate from the blood of the host a pigmented yolk substance similar in every way to the yolk material formed by the ovary when ripening. Thus the parasite produces changes by acting in exactly the same fashion as does the developing ovary. Riddle reported that C. O. Whitman had been able to control sex and color in pigeons. He used light and dark colored birds as respective parents, and removed eggs as fast as laid to other birds, thus forcing them to their maximum egg production. All of first several pairs of eggs produced dark male hybrids. All of last several pairs produced light female hybrids. In between is a period in which he was not able to predict the result of any crossing. Whitman did not use Mendelian phraseology, but stated in such terms, one may say that he was able to shift, control, or determine, experimentally, the dominance of sex and color.

The whole literature of the subject of sex determination was reviewed by Hertwig in

Biologisches Centralblatt. Hertwig apparently concluded that there are male and female producing spermatozoa, and that the chromosomes may have a determing action, but considered that these may be modified or destroyed in their action by environmental conditions.

VITALISM AND MECHANISM. Schäfer, as president of the British Association for the Advancement of Science, at its meeting in Belfast, discussed in a part of his presidential address the question as to the origin of life from non-living, and apparently regarded it as not impossible that such a process may be eventually carried on experimentally, though his assertions were too guarded and conservative to warrant the interpretation given them in the public press. Schäfer evidently considered it possible that a process of origin of new living matter may be going on at the present time, though if it is going on at all it is quite as likely to be taking place on land as in the sea. The geologist would have no evidence of this process, nor is it probable that the microscopist would be able to see the organisms that arose in this way. Under the title "The Mechanistic Conception of Life," Loeb published in 1912 a collection of essays relating to his thesis that life is really a chemical and physical process and that we may hope to eventually explain it in chemical and physical terms. We must, he said, either produce living matter artificially or we must find the reason why it is impossible.

Loeb thinks that activation of the egg by the spermatozoon is now practically reduced to a physico-chemical process, the sperm starting the egg to develop by accelerating the oxidations. The life of the individual begins, therefore, when the oxidations in the egg are accelerated. Death follows if the oxidations cease. He resolves all animal activities into tropisms, and maintains that here we have a strictly scientific basis for all our so-called higher mental and ethical processes. "We eat, drink, and reproduce not because this is desirable, but because, machine-like, we are compelled to do so. . . . We struggle for justice and truth since we are instinctively compelled to see our fellow beings happy. Not only is the mechanistic conception of life compatible with ethics: it seems the only conception of life which can lead to an understanding of the source of ethics."

Jennings showed that Driesch's vitalism theory is opposed to the experimental method, because it is impossible, according to it, to predict the action of the entelechy. Even though one may have determined the action of a given set of physical compounds, one would have no certainty that the action would be the same at a subsequent time, because a different entelechy might be in control.

BIPLANE. See AERONAUTICS.

BIRD PROTECTION. See ORNITHOLOGY.

BIRMINGHAM, ENG. See CITY PLANNING.

BISMARCK ARCHIPELAGO. A German possession, part of the German New Guinea protectorate. Area, with the Solomon Islands, 22,046 square miles; population, 250,000. The islands are administered by a commissioner residing at Rabaul. See ANTHROPOLOGY.

BIRTHRATE. See VITAL STATISTICS.

BLACKFOOT INDIANS. See ANTHROPOLOGY.

BLACKLISTING. See LABOR LEGISLATION.

BLAIR, CHARLES AUSTIN. An American jurist, died August 30, 1912. He was born in Jackson, Mich., in 1854, and graduated from the University of Michigan in 1876. He studied law and in 1878 was admitted to the bar. In 1882 he was elected city attorney of Jackson, and in 1895-6 he served as prosecuting attorney of Jackson county. In 1903-4 he was attorney-general of the State. In the latter year he was appointed associate justice of the supreme court of Michigan.

BLAKE, EDWARD. A Canadian statesman, died March 1, 1912. He was born in Middlesex county, Ontario, in 1833, and was educated in Upper Canada College and Toronto University. After studying law he was called to the bar in 1856. At the time of the confederation of the Provinces in 1867 he was elected both to the Canadian House of Commons and to the Provincial Legislature. He was at once offered the leadership of the Provincial Opposition, but at that time declined. He accepted the leadership, however, two years later and on the defeat of the Provincial Conservatives in 1871 became Liberal prime minister of Ontario. In the year following it was made illegal to sit in both the Federal and Provincial Parliaments, and Blake retired from the Provincial Parliament. In 1873 as the result of an exposure, which he had done much to bring about, the federal administration of Sir John MacDonald collapsed under the Pacific Railway scandal. Mr. Blake became a member of the Liberal cabinet, which was formed by Alexander Mackenzie. He was obliged to retire in a few months on account of ill health, and in 1875 returned to the cabinet as Minister of Justice. In that capacity he was responsible for the formation of the Supreme Court of Canada, the first presidency of which he declined. On the return of Sir John MacDonald to power in 1878 Mr. Mackenzie retired, and Mr. Blake thereafter was the leader of the beaten Liberal party. In 1887 he resigned the leadership to Sir Wilfrid Laurier. While impaired health was given as the cause it was known to be a fact that Mr. Blake was uneasy about the lengths to which some of his colleagues were pushing their advocacy of closer trade relations with the United States. Some of these had adopted the cry of "unrestricted reciprocity." He refused nomination at the general election of 1891 and after the Liberals had lost that election he published a farewell letter criticising the platform of the party, especially as to its stand on reciprocity. This letter had great influence in turning Canadian sentiment against reciprocity. In 1892 Mr. Blake, on the invitation of Justin M'Carthy, entered the Parliament of Great Britain as a member of the Nationalist party. He was given a seat from South Longford. He became in 1894 a member of the executive committee of the party, and in the same year was appointed a member of the Royal Commission on the Financial Relations between Great Britain and Ireland. He was returned without opposition at the elections of 1895, 1900, and 1906. In 1907 he gave up his seat and from that year until the time of his death lived a retired life in Canada.

BLAST FURNACES. See COKE, COPPER, IRON, LEAD, METALLURGY.

BLIND, CARE OF THE. See CHARITY.

BLODGETT, JOHN TAGGART. An American jurist, died March 4, 1912. He was born in

Belmont, Mass., in 1859 and graduated from Brown University in 1880. After studying law he was admitted to the Rhode Island bar in 1883. He was appointed ju ge of the United States circuit court in 1885dand in 1895 was appointed judge of the United States circuit court of appeals. In 1890 he was United States commissioner for the district of Rhode Island and in 1892 was chief supervisor of elections in that State. He was appointed associate justice of the Supreme Court of the State in 1900.

BLUE BLACK BLOC. See GERMANY, *History*.

BLYDEN, EDWARD WILMOT. An American negro author and lecturer, died February, 1912. He was born in St. Thomas, West Indies, in 1832 and after studying theology became a Presbyterian minister. For a time he was president of Liberia College. He was later appointed Liberian secretary of state for the Interior and Liberian minister at London. He wrote several books on the negro in Africa.

BOAS, EMIL LEOPOLD. An American steamship director and philanthropist, died May 3, 1912. He was born in Doerlitz, Germany, in 1854 and was educated in Breslau and Berlin. In 1878 he removed to the United States, where in New York he engaged in the banking business as representative of the firm of his uncle in Berlin. At that time this firm's office represented the Hamburg-American line of steamships and thus Mr. Boas formed a connection which finally led to his becoming resident director of this line in the United States in 1892. For his services in behalf of commerce between the United States and Europe he received many decorations from the European government. He took an active part in philanthropic and economic questions and was a member of most of the important organizations dealing with these subjects in the United States.

BOHEMIA. See AUSTRIA-HUNGARY, *Area and Population*, and *History*.

BOILERS. See STEAM ENGINES.

BOISE, OTIS BARDWELL. An American teacher of music, died December 2, 1912. He was born in Oberlin, Ohio, in 1844 and was educated in the public schools of Cleveland. He studied music in Leipzig and after the completion of his studies in that city settled in New York City, as a teacher of composition in the New York Conservatory and organist in the Fifth Avenue Presbyterian Church. He spent 1876 and 1877 in Europe, and resumed teaching in New York City in 1878. After seven years spent in business from 1881 to 1888 he again resumed professional work. In 1901 he was appointed head of the department of harmony and composition at the Peabody Conservatory of Music in Baltimore. He was the author of *Harmony Made Practical* (1900), and *Music and Its Masters* (1901).

BOKHARA. A Russian vassal state (83,000 square miles, about 1,500,000 inhabitants) in Central Asia. Capital Bokhara.

BOLAMA. See PORTUGUESE GUINEA.

BOLIVIA. An interior South American republic. Sucre, the seat of the supreme court, is called the capital; but the president resides at La Paz, where the Congress convenes and the foreign diplomats are stationed.

AREA, POPULATION, ETC. The area is officially estimated at 1,379,014 square kilometers (532,437 square miles) or, including territory within disputed boundaries, 1,458,034 square kilometers (562,947 square miles). No census has been taken since that of 1900, which showed 1,744,568 inhabitants; but the estimated population in 1912 was 2,450,000. Of the inhabitants in 1900 50.9 per cent. were returned as Indian, 26.7 mestizo, 12.7 white, 0.21 negro, and 9.4 unclassified. The great elevated plateau of western and central Bolivia contains most of the larger towns. Municipal populations are reported as follows: La Paz, 94,568; Cochabamba, 28,650; Potosí, 25,000; Sucre, 23,500; Oruro, 23,800; Santa Cruz, 21,500. In 1910 elementary schools, public and private, numbered 717 (1299 teachers and 46,000 pupils); 18 secondary schools (126 and 1631); 17 institutions for superior instruction (65 and 680). The number of pupils in all educational institutions in 1911 is reported at 84,288. The State religion is Roman Catholicism.

PRODUCTION AND COMMERCE. The less sparely peopled portion of Bolivia is distinctively a mining country. Crops include corn, rice, barley, and potatoes, but they are of little commercial importance. In the north rubber is produced in considerable quantities. The principal minerals now in exploitation are tin, silver, bismuth, and copper. In output of tin ore Bolivia ranks next after the Federated Malay States. Livestock (1910): Cattle, 734,535; horses, 96,867; sheep, 1,454,729; mules, 44,635; asses, 174,090; goats, 473,370; swine, 114,147; llamas, 428,209; alpacas, 112,033.

Imports and exports have been as follows:

	1906	1907	1908	1909	1910	1911
Imports	31,997	34,562	33,069	36,937	48,802	58,371
Exports	50,757	45,902	58,924	63,764	74,567	82,631

Classified imports in 1911: Animal substances, 9,081,844 bolivianos; vegetable substances, 12,497,512; mineral substances, 19,992,494; textiles and their manufactures, 7,219,180; paper, 1,607,052; drugs and chemicals, 577,157; beverages, 2,191,838; machinery, apparatus, etc., 2,554,661; vehicles, 561,275; arms and explosives, 2,026,414; unclassified, 61,980; total, 58,371,409. Classified exports in 1911: Mineral substances, 62,532,010 bolivianos; vegetable substances, 19,409,725; animal substances, 298,022; live animals, 102,389; animales disecados, 8500; manufactured products, 51,113; products nacionalizados, 101,814; various, 37,599; total, 82,631,172. Principal specific exports in 1911 (values for 1910 in parenthesis): Tin, 60 per cent. barilla, 37,073 metric tons, valued at 52,639,603 bolivianos (38,548 tons, 37,006,504 bolivianos in 1910); silver, 5,379,253 bolivianos (5,269,942); bismuth, 50 per cent. barilla, 415 tons, 2,106,162 bolivianos (1,923,417); copper, 80 per cent. barilla, 2950 tons, 1,426,943 (1,786,952); wolfram barilla, 297,272 tons, 231,188 (141,629); zinc, 9798 tons, 372,490 (435,009); unconcentrated bismuth, 140,639 tons, 111,889 (43,178); rubber, 3646 tons, 18,921,192 (3007 tons, 26,825,231 bolivianos); coca, 252 tons, 511,051 (420,105); cueros vacunos, 324 tons, 259,182 (218,163).

COMMUNICATIONS. Railways in operation in 1911 aggregated 1022 kilometers (635 miles). A large railway extension has been undertaken, and the mileage was greatly increased during 1912. It was expected that the Viacha-La Paz line would be completed in February, 1913. The work was well advanced in 1912 on the Oruro-Cochabamba, Unywni-Tupiza, Mulatos-Potosí, and other lines. Telegraph lines (reported

1911), 5007 kilometers (3111 miles); offices, 161. Post offices, over 200.

Trade by countries, in thousands of bolivianos:

	Imports		Exports	
	1910	1911	1910	1911
Great Britain	16,312	12,470	46,296	59,582
Germany	8,473	10,311	15,424	10,993
United States	5,501	9,865	160	627
Chile	7,921	9,837	695	411
Belgium	3,541	4,064	3,812	3,760
Argentina	1,587	3,220	400	454
France	1,083	2,832	5,153	6,751
Peru	2,593	2,759	10	22
Italy	901	1,420	4	...
Brazil	486	843	2,467	5
Total, incl. other	48,802	58,371	74,567	82,631

FINANCE. The monetary standard is gold, pursuant to the law of September 14, 1906; monetary unit, the boliviano, par value 38.932 cents (12.5 to the pound sterling). Estimated ordinary revenue and expenditure: 1909, 13,300,000 and 16,454,625 bolivianos; 1910, 13,540,000 and 13,887,435; 1911, 13,141,175 and 17,805,859; 1912, 17,237,100 and 17,356,552. Estimated receipts for 1912 included: Import duties, 7,668,000 bs.; export duties, 3,687,100; taxes, 2,548,000. Estimated expenditures: Foreign affairs and worship 948,489 bs.; interior, 3,114,179; commerce and finance, 4,795,135; justice and industry, 1,270,102; war and colonization, 4,983,416; instruction and agriculture, 1,871,609. The foreign debt on June 29, 1912, amounted to £1,937,805, having been reduced by £27,545 in a year. Internal debt in 1912, 4,208,069 bs.; floating debt, 2,034,989 bs.

GOVERNMENT. The president, who with two vice-presidents, is elected for a term of four years, is assisted by a cabinet of six ministers. Congress consists of the Senate (16 members) and the Chamber of Deputies (75). The president in 1912 was Eliodoro Villazón (for the term beginning August 12, 1909); first vice-president, Macario Pinilla.

BOLL-WEEVIL. See COTTON.

BOLLER, ALFRED PANCOAST. An American engineer, died December 10, 1912. He was born in Philadelphia in 1840 and graduated from the Rensselaer Polytechnic Institute in 1861. After acting as engineer with several railway and other corporations, he became in 1865 chief engineer for the Hudson River Railroad. This position he left to engage in the iron business with Samuel Milliken as New York agents for the Phœnix Iron Company. In 1870 he became vice-president and engineer for the Phillipsburg Manufacturing Company and retained this position for twenty years. During the same period he was consulting engineer for railroads in Haiti and Cuba as well as chief engineer for the Manhattan Railroad Company and consulting engineer for the department of public works of New York City. In 1898 he entered into partnership with Henry W. Hodge, forming the firm of Boller & Hodge. He was one of the most eminent engineers in the United States.

BONAH. See ARCHÆOLOGY.

BONBRIGHT, DANIEL. An American educator, died November 27, 1912. He was born in Youngstown, Pa., in 1831, and graduated from Yale College in 1850. From 1854 to 1856 he was a tutor at Yale, and in the two years following studied at the universities of Berlin, Bonn, and Göttingen. In 1858 he became professor of the Latin language and literature at Northwestern University. He was appointed dean of the faculty of liberal arts at that university in 1899, serving until 1902. From 1900 to 1902 he was acting-president of Northwestern University.

BONES, GRAFTING OF. See HYGIENE, INTERNATIONAL CONGRESS OF.

BONNOT, M. See FRANCE, *History*.

BOOHER CONVICT LABOR BILL. See PENOLOGY.

BOOTH, WILLIAM. Commander-in-chief of the Salvation Army, died August 20, 1912. He was born in Nottingham, England, in 1829, the son of a carpenter, who, by dint of strict economy, contrived to give his son educational advantages and send him to a private theological tutor for preparation for the Methodist ministry. At 23 years of age William Booth became pastor of a small chapel in Nottingham. Although he was not at this time a gifted speaker and did not seem especially qualified for evangelical work, he plunged into this field with great zeal. Shortly after his admission to the ministry, he traveled over England on itinerant preaching tours and during one of these met Catherine Mumford, to whom he became engaged. For many years he endeavored to make money enough to justify their marriage, but this did not take place until 1856. Mrs. Booth was in many ways no less remarkable than her husband. She had the same religious zeal and a kindred instinct for organization. For five years after their marriage they lived the precarious existence of revivalists. Finally they found themselves in London in the darkest part of the slums in the vicinity of Whitechapel and Shoreditch. Here William Booth conceived the idea of bringing light into the hopeless lives of those who dwelt in this part of London. He laid a plan of campaign before the Methodist New Connection Church, but this body found it too radical. Thereupon Booth, who now had three small children and his wife to support, cut loose from orthodoxy and set about preaching to the people of the slums in his own way. Those whom he chose to lead were not only of the very poor, but the very criminal, the lowest dregs of the great city.

In 1865 he settled with his family in Mile End Waste, one of the blackest corners of East End, London. Here he began the work of saving souls by a new method. His first tabernacle was a second-hand tent, erected in a disused burying-ground, on Mile End Road. This he called the Christian Mission, and in this place the Salvation Army was born.

During the years of his ministry in Whitechapel, Booth came more and more to fit his evangelical methods to the temper and understanding of the people who listened to him. He saw that the love of show and parade attracted the inhabitants of those mean streets and he began to introduce features of display. Finally, in 1878, from a number of faithful adherents, whom he had redeemed from the slums, he organized the Salvation Army, a band of not more than one hundred, and to these he gave uniforms, flags to carry, and drums and cornets for music. The first appearance of this little band on the streets of Whitechapel was attended by a riotous demonstration on the part of the lookers-on, in many cases the police siding with the roughs and arresting the Salvationists for obstructing the highways. When reports of this method of evangelizing reached

WILLIAM BOOTH
FOUNDER AND HEAD OF THE SALVATION ARMY
Died August 20, 1912

the ears of the clergy in the fashionable congregations they bitterly denounced the "vulgar sensationalism" and "irreverent trumpery" of this Salvation Army. In spite of this double opposition, Booth continued steadfastly in his work and before a year had passed, there were 127 officers in the Salvation Army, and 81 corps had been established throughout England. The military form of government was prescribed, and Booth gave himself the title of "General," while the officers below him were given titles with rank corresponding to that in the regular army.

Before the Salvation Army was four years old, General Booth and his wife began a long series of social reforms and charities, which, with the Salvation Army of to-day, stand as their monuments. One of the first of these reforms was the prison-gate mission. This consisted in the establishment of pickets of the army, who should stand at the portals of the prisons and give counsel and aid to criminals who had served their terms and were being turned out of the prisons. Food stations, supported by voluntary contributions, distributed meat to the starving, training schools were established where those who were regenerated could learn honesty and self-reliance and could be fitted to be officers of the Army.

Opposition to the work of General Booth among members of the clergy continued until 1884, when Queen Victoria made public a message which she had sent to him, warmly commending his work. After that Canon Farrar, who had been among its bitterest opponents, gave his approbation to General Booth's movement, and cordial support was also given by Cardinal Manning.

With the growth of the Army came the development of General Booth's insistence upon what came to be practically a military despotism. This devlopment came with the increase of the Army's forces and the widening of its influences. From the beginning, General Booth, first at the head of his large family of active workers, and then as supreme in command, directed every move, received all reports from subordinates, and appointed himself custodian of all funds. Title to all property owned by the Salvationists in all parts of the world either stood in his name or was held in trust by him. The insistence on the supreme control over the affairs of the Army resulted in what was probably the greatest grief of his life, the breach between himself and his son, Ballington Booth, who had been given command of the Salvation Army in America. Ballington Booth, with his wife, Maude Ballington Booth, threw himself into the work in the United States with great energy, but he found himself hampered by the dictatorship of his father. General Booth in turn declared his son too independent and not at all amenable to discipline from London. Early in 1906 General Booth peremptorily recalled Ballington Booth, from his command in America. Ballington Booth, instead of obeying, seceded from the Army in the spring of 1906 and established another organization called "The Volunteers of America." He issued a statement in which he declared that General Booth had drawn upon the funds of the American Army to keep up the exchequer in Canada and elsewhere, that he had spoken slightingly of American, and that his orders directed to the commander in America had all been prejudicial to the organization in the United States. General Booth and his son were estranged until the former's death.

General Booth traveled in the interest of the Salvation Army all over the world. He visited the United States and Canada five times. He made two tours of India and three journeys to Australia and South Africa. He also spent some time in Japan where he was given an audience with the Emperor. He was received also by most of the royalties on the continent of Europe.

In addition to his work as active head of the Salvation Army, General Booth wrote and published several books. The best of these was *Darkest England and the Way Out*, published in 1890. In this book he set forth his theory for the care and cure of the congested criminal classes in the slums of the great cities through farm colonies. These theories were put into practice by the Salvation Army with more or less success. The best known of his other works are, *Love, Marriage and the Home*, *The Training of Children; Religion for Every Day; Letters to My Soldiers*, and *Salvation Soldiery Visions*. He also founded the *War Cry*, the official paper of the Salvation Army, and many other periodicals which are published under Army auspices. The last four years of General Booth's life were clouded by the failure of his eyesight and weakened health. For a year before he died he was practically without the use of his eyes. Shortly after his death a paper which he had prepared and sealed many years before, was opened and it was found that he had named as his successor, Herbert Bramwell Booth, who for many years had been his father's chief aid in the conduct of the affairs of the Salvation Army.

BOOTS AND SHOES. The boot and shoe industry in 1912 was fairly prosperous, all things considered, and business was steady through the year, with prices advancing with those of leather. Calf shoes were in most active demand during the year and were the favorite variety. The agitation in connection with the proposed change of tariff continued, and with the election of a Democratic President and continued Democratic majorities in Congress, it was believed that an attempt would be made to reduce or repeal the duty on shoes. When the duty on hides was abolished in 1909 the tariff on boots and shoes was reduced to 15 per cent. if the uppers were made of kid and 10 per cent. if the uppers were made of calf or side leather. It was conceded that the superiority of American shoe factories, both in equipment and labor, was such as to make the industry independent of protection, except on the score of wages, which were reported 50 per cent. cheaper in Europe than in the United States. American superintendents and foremen had been called to Europe to organize and superintend plants in which American machinery had been set up, and the shoe manufacturers in the United States feared that they would be unable to compete with European labor and maintain the present schedules of prices. It had been argued that when the duty on hides was repealed that shoes would become cheaper, but this prediction had not been realized, as notwithstanding the free importation of hides their price had steadily appreciated.

The question of substitution in the sale of boots and shoes continued to be discussed during the year, and in several State legislatures, as well as in Congress, bills of the "Pure

Food" variety were introduced, requiring the stamping on the sole of shoes where substitutes for leather were used in any part. The shoe trade opposed such legislation, both on account of the stringency of the penalties proposed and on account of the fact that it would tend to increase the price of the lower grade of shoes, in which substitutes for leather were satisfactorily used in certain parts. They claimed that it was not adulteration or fraud, and that the effect would be to increase the price of the cheaper grades of shoes, where durability was one of the most essential elements in their commercial success.

In 1912 Haverhill, Mass., shipped 571,991 cases of shoes as compared with 530,592 cases in 1911. Brockton, Mass., however, showed a decrease in production, and the shipments, amounting to 678,966 cases, as compared with 785,534 cases in 1911, were the lowest since 1904. The value of this production, $47,527,620, was a decrease of $6,470,842.50 over 1911, and a decrease in labor cost of $1,468,741.50. In Lynn, Mass., the shoe output for the year was estimated in cost of $30,000,000. See LEATHER.

BORAH, WILLIAM E. See PRESIDENTIAL CAMPAIGN.

BORDEN, R. L. See CANADA.

BORMANN, EDWARD. A German humorist and poet, died May 1912. He was born in Leipzig in 1851 and was educated in the Polytechnic School in Dresden and at the universities of Leipzig and Bonn. His first literary work was a series of humorous sketches in dialect contributed to the *Fliegende Blätter*. He was also the author of a book of humorous songs in High German. He wrote also many volumes of poems and stories.

BORNET, JEAN BAPTISTE EDOUARD. A French botanist, died January, 1912. He was born in Guerigny in 1828. He studied medicine in Paris, but his chief tastes were for botany, and he carried on studies, especially in fungi, under the direction of Tulasne and Leveillé. He afterwards accompanied Thuret to Cherbourg, where his attention was devoted chiefly to the study of marine algæ, with which he deals in several of his books. His works, in some of which he collaborated with Thuret, include: *Recherches sur la structure de l'éphèbe pubescens* (1852); *Recherches sur la fécondation des Floridées* (1867); *Recherches sur les gonidies des Lichens* (1873); *Notes algologiques, recueil d'observations sur les Algues* (1876-80); *Revisions des Nostocacées hétérocystées*, in collaboration with Flahault (1886).

BORRELLY'S COMET. See ASTRONOMY.

BOSNIA AND HERZEGOVINA. Provinces, formerly Ottoman, annexed to the Austro-Hungarian monarchy October 5, 1908. Area: Bosnia, 16,240 square miles; Herzegovina, 3529; total, 19,769. Population according to the census of October 10, 1910 (results of the census of April 22, 1895, in parentheses): Bosnia, 1,631,006 (1,348,581); Herzegovina, 267,038 (219,511); total civil population, 1,898,044 (1,568,092); in addition, the military population numbered 33,758 (22,944), making the total number of inhabitants 1,931,802 in 1910, against 1,591,036 in 1895. The civil population in 1910 consisted of 994,852 males (52.41 per cent.) and 903,192 females (47.59). Population according to religion: Servian Orthodox, 825,338 (43.48 per cent.); Mohammedans, 612,090 (32.25); Roman Catholics, 434,190 (22.88); Jews, 11,857 (0.62); Greek Catholics, 8136 (0.43); Evangelicals (Augsburg), 5849 (0.31); Evangelicals (Helvetian), 488 (0.03); others, 96; total, 1,898,044. Movement of the civil population, 1911: Marriages, 20,763; births and deaths (each including stillbirths), 76,911 and 49,840; excess of births, 27,071. Population of Sarajevo, the capital, in 1910, 51,919; Mostar, 16,392; Banjaluka, 14,800; Tuzla, 11,333; Bjelina, 10,061; Srebrenica, 7215; Brčka, 6647; Travnik, 6517.

In 1910 there were 458 elementary schools (306 general, 143 religious, and 9 private), with 41,130 pupils, against 434 schools and 38,950 pupils in 1909. There are secondary, normal, commercial, and technical schools. In 1910 Mohammedan mektebs numbered 1970, with 2032 teachers and 64,805 pupils; in addition, 94 reformed mektebs, with 7719 pupils.

The soil is fertile, but agriculture is not highly developed. The following yields are officially reported for 1910, in metric quintals (220.46 pounds): Wheat, 727,018; rye, 100,033; barley, 824,565; spelt, 56,016; oats, 772,555; millet, 85,132; beans, 64,858; corn, 2,553,219; potatoes, 1,373,830; hay, 9,332,290; clover, 97,527; apples, 49,030; pears, 50,025; cherries, 14,258; plums, 302,400. Reported number of livestock (1910): 221,971 horses, 1,308,930 cattle, 1,393,068 goats, 2,499,422 sheep, and 527,270 swine.

Mineral output (1910): Lignite, 706,659 metric tons; iron ore, 32,721; manganese ore, 4000; chrome ore, 320. Output of metals (1910): Raw iron, 48,811 tons (valued at 3,485,070 kronen); rolled iron, 27,363 tons (4,367,220 kr.); iron castings, 5091 tons (1,058,824 kr.); lead, 18 tons (7320 kr.). Salt production, 23,579 tons (2,617,291 kr.).

Bosnia and Herzegovina are included in the Austro-Hungarian customs territory; the imports from and exports to Austria-Hungary and foreign countries in 1910 were estimated at 144,538,617 kr. and 135,458,446 kr., respectively. Railways, January 1, 1911, 1956 kilometers; telegraphs, 4102 kms. of line and 12,778 kms. of wire, with 173 offices; post offices, about 175.

Estimated revenue and expenditure for 1911, 79,129,475 kr. and 79,535,715 kr., respectively. The existing constitution bears date of February 17, 1910. There is an elective diet competent to deal with provincial finance, taxation, police, railways, public works, and law, subject to Austro-Hungarian veto. The administrative authority is entrusted to the Austro-Hungarian minister of finance (in 1912, from February 20, Dr. Leon (Ritter) von Biliński).

BOSS, LEWIS. An American astronomer, died October 5, 1912 He was born in Providence, R. I., in 1846 and graduated from Dartmouth College in 1870. From 1872 to 1876 he was assistant on the United States Northern Boundary Commission. In the latter year he was appointed director of the Dudley Observatory and professor of astronomy at Union College. The former position he held until the time of his death. In 1878 he was a member of the government expedition to observe the total eclipse in Colorado, and in 1882 was chief of the government expedition to observe the transit of Venus at Santiago, Chile. He was superintendent of weights and measures in New York from 1893 to 1906. During this period he was for a short time editor and manager of the Albany *Express*. In 1906 he was appointed director of the department of meridian astronomy at the Carnegie Institution of Washington. He was editor of the *Astronomical Journal* in 1909. He received medals and prizes for astronomical work from several foreign scientific societies. He was the author of *Declinations of Fixed Stars* (1878); *Catalogue of 8241 Stars* (1890), and the following monograms: *The Solar System, and related papers* (1888); *Prize Essay on the Physical Nature of Comets* (1881); *179 Southern Stars* (1898); *Solar Motion and Related Researches* (1901); *Positions and Motions of 627 Standard Stars* (1903); *Preliminary General Catalogue of 6188 Stars* (1910); *Catalogue of 1059 Standard Stars* (1910). His catalogues of stars are considered standard among astronomers.

BOSTON, MASS. See DOCKS AND HARBORS.

BOSTON OPERA COMPANY. See MUSIC.

BOSTON AND MAINE RAILROAD. See RAILWAYS.

BOSTON PORT IMPROVEMENT. See DOCKS AND HARBORS.

BOSTON SYMPHONY ORCHESTRA. See MUSIC.

BOSTON UNIVERSITY. An institution of higher learning in Boston under the auspices of the Methodist Episcopal Church, founded in 1869. The enrollment in all the departments of the university in the autumn of 1912 was 1425. The faculty numbered 150. There were no noteworthy changes in the faculty during the year and no noteworthy benefactions were received. The amount of productive funds of the university is about $2,500,000. There are about 40,000 volumes in the library. President, Lemuel Herbert Murlin, D. D.

BOTANY. Judged by the output of literature and the reports of meetings, the year 1912 was an active one for botanists. The American Association for the Advancement of Science met at Cleveland, O., December 30, 1912. The address of the retiring president, Dr. C. E. Bessey, of the University of Nebraska, was on "Some of the Next Steps in Botanical Science." A number of affiliated botanical societies met at the same place. The British Association for the Advancement of Science met at Dundee, Scotland, and the section devoted to botany was well attended. Ecology and hybridism in plants were the principal topics discussed. The German Association of Scientists and Physicians met at Münster and the French Association for the Advancement of Science at Nîmes in September. At the latter meeting a special programme was arranged on the subject of fungicides. The Australasian Association met at Melbourne in January, 1913.

Among the botanists who died during the past year were: Prof. Eduard Strasburger, of the University of Bonn; E. Griffin, professor of botany at the National School of Agriculture; Grignon, France; Thomas Durand, director of the Botanic Garden at Brussels; Dr. M. B. Thomas, Wabash College; Dr. W. A. Buckhout, State College, Pa.; and W. R. Smith, for many years superintendent of the National Botanic Garden, Washington, D. C.

The subject of restrictive legislation against the spread of plant diseases and other pests has received attention, and the laws of the twenty or more countries already having such provisions have been strengthened in many respects. A national quarantine against plant diseases and insect pests was provided in an act of Congress approved August 20, 1912. Under this law the importation of potatoes from regions known to be infested with the fungus *Chrysophlyctis endobiotica* and of species of pine capable of carrying the blister blight, *Peridermium pini*, has been prohibited. Canada has extended her import regulations to prevent the entrance of the potato disease mentioned. Restrictive regulations regarding plant importations were adopted by Chile and Uruguay during 1912.

Among papers of taxonomic interest which appeared during the year were several numbers of the *North American Flora*, issued from the New York Botanic Garden; four parts of *Das Pflanzenreich*, published by Engelmann in Leipzig; and several numbers of the *Contributions from the National Herbarium*. Dr. W. Trelease published an *Account of The Black Oaks*, and Miller and Standley a *Study of the North American Species of Nymphæa*. Dr. C. E. Bessey published a revision of his *Outlines of Plant Phyla*, in which 14 phyla are recognized with 652 families of plants.

PLANT BREEDING. The activity in this line of botanical investigation has been quite marked. Dr. Hugo de Vries, in continuing his investigations on *Œnothera*, visited the type locality of *Œ. grandiflora* in Alabama, studying the species in its original habitat. He found several characteristic types of the species, some of which have not been described. Zeijlstra claims that *Œ. nanella*, one of the forms described by de Vries as a mutant, is dwarfed by reason of the presence of bacteria. When bacteria are absent the plant develops normally according to his claim. Heribert-Nilsson believes that mutants of *Œ. lamarckiana* described by de Vries are only the segregations of characters observed in a natural hybrid, and that the species is not an elementary one. Gates reports a series of forms of *Œ. biennis* parallel with those described for *Œ. lamarckiana*. Heckel has described a number of experiments with various species of *Solanum* from South America, and in *S. immite* within a single year a mutant resembling S. *tuberosum* was secured by the superabundant application of fertilizers. East and Hayes claim that crossing produces heterozygosis in all characters in which the parent plants differ, while inbreeding tends to result in homozygosis. Harris found from an extended study of beans that the effects produced by starvation were inherited only to a very limited extent. Pearl and Bartlett have shown that chemical characters in maize, as low protein, low oil, etc., are inherited as Mendelian unit characters.

STUDIES OF SOIL ORGANISMS. Jensen has made a study of the soil fungi in this country, and reports on the presence of 132 species and varieties isolated from soils. Miss Dale found a marked similarity in the soil fungus flora in England to that described by Jensen, many of the genera and some of the species being identical. A large number of investigations were reported on nitrogen transformation and assimilation by soil organisms with and without symbiosis with other species of plants, and the known number of organisms taking part in this important activity has been considerably increased. Other studies have been concerned with the breaking down of materials found in the soil, and Kellerman and McBeth found that not only bacteria, but certain fungi were important agents in the destruction of cellulose. The investigations of Bottomley on *Myrica* and of Spratt on *Eleagnus* and *Alnus* have shown the polymorphism of the organism *Pseudomonas radicicola*, through which nitrogen assimilation in leguminous and other plants takes place. Von Faver has described bacteria from excrescences on leaves of tropical *Rubiaceæ* which he claims assimilate nitrogen from the air. A recent investigation into the symbiosis in lichens is thought to show that under certain conditions the alga receives a portion of its carbohydrates from material secured by the fungus from its substratum.

PLANT PHYSIOLOGY. Palladin and his co-workers have continued their investigations on respiratory chromogens and found that methylene blue accelerated respiration of plants in the presence of oxygen. Stoklasa demonstrated the photochemical synthesis of carbohydrates under the influence of ultraviolet rays. Spöhr has shown a reduction of nitrates into nitrites and ammonia with the liberation of oxygen under the ultraviolet rays. Herlitzka claims that spectroscopic differences are observable in the chlorophyll in leaves and in solutions and thinks that they are present in leaves in colloidal form. Politis, from a study of anthocyanin, has concluded that this coloring material is not derived from the cell sap, but from bodies he calls "cyanoplasts.' When their degeneration takes place the coloring matter becomes diffused in the cell sap. Cailletet claims that ferns and other plants accustomed to grow in damp shady places obtain a considerable portion of their carbon from their substratum. A somewhat similar claim is also made for lichens. Parkin has confirmed the observation that sucrose is the first sugar formed in the process of photosynthesis. The subject of nitrogen nutrition of plants continues to receive much attention. Puriewitsch claims that the amino acids are the best sources from which plants may obtain the nitrogen required for protein synthesis, and Loew believes that most plants can utilize nitrates in the absence of light and that transportation to the leaves is not necessary for metabolism. Hydrocyanic acid in germinating seeds of flax and sorghum has been found by Ravenna and Vecchi. Mirande has reported it in the *Calycanthaceæ*, and Petrie has found it in 29 species of Australian plants exclusive of grasses. The synthesis of fats, according to Ivanow, is brought about by the action of lipase on glycerins and fatty acids. The rôle of various substances in the plant economy has been given further study. Bernardini and Morelli claim that magnesium plays an important part in plant development through its combining with phosphorus. Weevers claims that potassium is connected with the formation of protoplasm and also with the synthesis and metabolism of proteids. Stoklasa believes that potassium is indispensable to the building up of carbohydrates as well as to other important functions of the plant. Ivanow claims that phosphates accelerate respiration in plants. Montemartini and Javillier have shown that manganese in small quantity stimulates plant activities, but Kelley found that when present in larger amounts oxidation is produced and the ability of plants to absorb phosphoric acid is lowered.

PLANT DISEASES. Considerable attention has been turned to the injury of plants by causes other than parasites. In France an investigation was made by a commission to determine the cause of the dying of trees and other plants in parks, and it was found due to tar-laden dust arising from tarred roads. The amount of injury was in proportion to the amount of phenol in the compound used and the distance from the roads and amount of travel. The cause and control of chlorosis are still being sought. Gile found that more than 2 per cent. of calcium carbonate in the soil caused chlorosis in pineapples. Chlorosis in maize and in grapevines has been investigated in France and Italy, and a number of causes are mentioned, among them a lack of iron, sulphur, etc., and a superabundance of lime. Anderson found that the failure of apple, pear, and cherry trees to produce fruit in the neighborhood of cement works was due to the alkalinity of the dust interfering with pollination. Floyd found that certain citrus tree troubles could be produced by the use of organic fertilizers. Among the diseases due to fungi the chestnut bark disease is perhaps receiving most attention in this country at this time. First recognized in 1904, in Brooklyn, N. Y., it has spread along the eastern seaboard, and it is now known to be present in at least ten States. In Pennsylvania a commission has been created to study and combat it, an appropriation of $275,000 having been made for that purpose. Congress has granted $80,000 to the U. S. Department of Agriculture to investigate its cause and means for control. The fungus was named *Diaporthe parasitica*, but it appears to differ from a harmless saprophyte common in Europe mainly in its parasitic habit. During the past summer a saprophytic form of the fungus was found in this country. It is claimed that no morphological differences are apparent between the two forms. The black canker or ink disease of chestnut trees in southern Europe, so called from the characteristic exudation accompanying it, is quite distinct from the trouble in this country.

The white-pine blister blight continues to demand attention, and it has been conclusively shown that a single inspection of pine seedlings will not determine the presence of the fungus. The importation into this country of all pine seedlings belonging to the group of white pines has been prohibited. In England and elsewhere in Europe the black wart disease of potatoes (*Chrysophlyctis endobiotica*) continues to be destructive. Its known range now includes much of England, parts of Scotland and Wales, and Germany and Austria, as well as Newfoundland, Miquelon, and probably Nova Scotia. In Germany the most serious disease of the potato is the leaf roll, a trouble of uncertain origin, and a commission has been appointed to study it. Wollenweber, Appel, and others are studying the relation of *Fusarium* to this and other potato diseases. Jones and others have reported on the life history of the fungus *Phytophthora parasitica*, the cause of the late rot of the potato. A new dry rot of the potato, due to *Fusarium trichothecoides*, has been described within the year. An investigation by Schuster in Germany has shown about a half dozen species of bacteria capable of producing potato diseases. The subject of rusts of grains and other plants continues to be investigated, and Arthur, Kern, Clinton, Hecke, Dietel,

Eriksson, Olive, and others have contribuated to our knowledge regarding some of the phases in the life history of this group of fungi. Eriksson claims that the hollyhock rust adds more proof to his mycoplasma theory of rust transmission, while Beckwith claims that in the case of grain rusts the fungus is carried over in the seed as mycelium or spores. Bolley has presented additional evidence regarding his theory that soil-borne fungi and not soil depletion are the cause of diminishing yields of grain and other crops. Among fruit diseases reported upon, Brooks and Miss De Meritt describe the apple leaf spots, particularly the forms caused by *Sphæropsis malorum*. Ewart claims that the bitter pit of apples is due to local poisoning of the pulp cells, either as a result of spraying or absorption by the tree. The fungus *Glœosporium malicorticis* is reported by Jackson as causing a serious canker disease of apple trees in Oregon. From the same State is reported a bacterial disease of cherries, due to *Pseudomonas cerasus*.

A new peach disease is reported by Güssow as occurring in New York and Canada in the vicinity of Niagara Falls. The grape downy mildew was very destructive in France in 1911 and somewhat less so in 1912. Studies have been made of means for its control. A new disease of the persimmon due to *Glœosporium kaki* is reported in Japan. Taubenhaus has proved by inoculation experiments that many of the *Glœosporia* described from different host plants are the same species. An additional report has been made from the laboratory of Dr. E. F. Smith on the crown-gall disease, due to *Bacterium tumefaciens*, and analogies between this disease of plants and cancer in animals have been pointed out.

THE CONTROL OF PLANT DISEASES. Extensive experiments are in progress in this country and elsewhere to find some fungicides superior to Bordeaux mixture. For many diseases, especially those affecting fruit trees, a lime-sulphur mixture is proving very valuable, as it is not only a fungicide, but destroys insects at the same time. For some diseases, however, its use can not be recommended. For these Bordeaux mixture should be used even if some injury follows its corrosive action. In England and Italy very dilute mixtures of Bordeaux mixture have been found efficient in controlling plant diseases and they are without some of the objectionable features of the stronger mixture. Vermorel and Dantony have shown that the wetting power, and hence the efficiency, of fungicides depend upon the surface tension of the film deposited on the leaf and that the addition of a small quantity of gelatin to the mixture increases its covering power to a remarkable degree. In France combined treatments with liquid sprays and powdered sulphur have been very successfully used for the prevention of the downy and powdery mildews of grapes. The value of spraying potatoes with Bordeaux mixture when little or no disease is present has been shown at the Vermont Agricultural Experiment Station, where in 20 years' experiments gains were made of 18 per cent. when no disease was noticeable and 215 per cent. when diseases were severe. The average gain was 205 bushels per acre. Stewart and French have found that neither lime-sulphur compound nor lead benzoate could be substituted for Bordeaux mixture in spraying potatoes. In Germany a machine has been devised for the treatment of smutted grain with hot air, that is said to rapidly and effectually destroy a smut and free the seed from that source of infection.

BIBLIOGRAPHY. Among the more important books and longer contributions to appear during 1912 were: Three new periodicals, *Journal of Economic Botany* (published by the Pomona College, Pomona, Cal.), *Mycologisches Zentralblatt* (Jena), and *Zeitschrift für Gärungsphysiologie* (Berlin). E. Bourcart, *Les Maladies des Plantes;* O. Brefeld, *Untersuchungen Gesammtgebiete der Mykologie;* J. M. Coulter, C. R. Barnes, and H. C. Cowles, *Text Book of Botany;* Vol. II.; J. M. Coulter, W. E. Castle, E. W. East, W. L. Tower, and C. B. Davenport, *Heredity and Eugenics;* J. Eriksson, translated by Anna Molander, *Fungoid Diseases of Plants;* L. R. Jones, N. J. Giddings, and B. J. Lutman. *Investigations of the Potato Fungus Phytophthora Infestans;* A. Lister and Gulielma Lister, *Monograph Mycetozoa;* G. Massee, *British Fungi and Lichens;* C. McIlvaine, and R. K. Macadam, revised by C. F. Millspaugh, *One Thousand American Fungi;* A. Nathanson, *Allgemeine Botanik;* W. Palladin, *Plant Physiology* (German Edition); E. G. Pringsheim, *Die Reizbewegungen der Pflanzen;* E. F. Smith, *Bacteria in Relation to Plant Diseases;* E. F. Smith, Nellie A. Brown, and Lucia McCulloch, *The Structure and Development of Crown Gall, a Plant Cancer;* R. E. Smith and Elizabeth H. Smith, *California Plant Diseases.*

BOTANY. See CARNEGIE INSTITUTION.

BOTHA, GENERAL LOUIS. See SOUTH AFRICA, UNION OF.

BOURBON. See RÉUNION.

BOVEY, HENRY TAYLOR. An English scientist, died February, 1912. He was born in Devonshire in 1853. He received his education in private schools and at Cambridge University. After traveling for several years he adopted the profession of civil engineering and became assistant engineer on the Mersey docks and harbor works. In 1887 he was appointed professor of civil engineering in applied mechanics at McGill University, and on the establishment of a department of applied science in that institution, was made dean. He was one of the founders of the Canadian Society of Civil Engineers and was in 1900 its president. Among his writings on scientific subjects are *Applied Mechanics* (1882); *Theory of Structures and Strength of Materials* (1893); *Hydraulics* (1895), together with many papers for various scientific societies. He received the degrees of D. C. L. and LL. D., from McGill University and Queen's College.

BOWDOIN COLLEGE. An institution of higher education at Brunswick, Me., founded in 1794. The students in all departments of the college in the autumn of 1912 numbered 393 and the faculty numbered 82, including the faculty of the medical school. During the year the changes in the faculty included the addition of an instructor in music, one in biology, and one in the department of economics. A new building for the gymnasium, funds for which were raised by subscription from the alumni and others, approached completion at the beginning of the collegiate year. The productive funds of the college amounted to $2,-149,485 and the income in 1911-12 to $127,839. There were 103,035 volumes in the library.

President, William De Witt Hyde, D. D., S. T. D.

BOWLING. The twelfth annual tournament of the American Bowling Congress was held at Chicago in March. The individual championship was won by L. Sutton, of Rochester, N. Y. (679). M. Hotchkiss, of Detroit (674), finished second, and W. Elivert, of Toledo (664), third. The two-men team contest was won by the Owen-Sutton combination, with a score of 1259. In the five-men team event the Brunswick All-Stars of New York were the victors, with a total of 2904 pins.

The sixth annual tournament of the National Bowling Association was held at Paterson, N. J., in March. The winners and scores yere: Individual, Leo Lucke, Brooklyn (699); two-men team, Lindsey-Johnson, New Haven (1301); five-men team, Grand Centrals, Rochester (2997). The five-men score breaks the record of 2969 pins made by the Bonds of Cleveland in 1911. Other new records of the year were made by Louis Vieletich, of Kansas, whose high individual score at the A. B. C. tournament was 280, and by James Smith, of Buffalo, who rolled up a total of 771 for three games in the Canadian tournament held at Toronto. Smith also averaged 228 8-9 for nine games at the same tournament.

BOWYER, JOHN MARSHALL. A rear-admiral, retired of the United States navy, died March 15, 1912. He was born in Cass county, Ind., in 1853 and graduated from the United States Naval Academy in 1874. He rose through various grades, becoming lieutenant-colonel in 1899, commander in 1903 and captain in 1907. At the outbreak of the Spanish-American War he was appointed executive officer of the *Princeton* and with this vessel did patrol duty about the western end of Cuba. He took part in the suppression of the Philippine insurrection and in the Boxer outbreak in North China. From 1901 to 1905 he acted as assistant superintendent of a gun factory in the Navy Yard at Washington and as head of the Department of Yards and Docks. In 1905 he commanded the U. S. S. *Columbia*. He was the senior officer in command of the *Columbia* at Colon and the *Marblehead* at Panama in 1906 at the time of the troubles attendant upon the separation of Panama from Colombia. In 1907 he commanded the battleship *Illinois* and made the cruise to the Pacific and around the world with the Atlantic fleet. From 1909 to 1911 he was superintendent of the United States Naval Academy. He received medals for service in various campaigns. He was made rear-admiral in 1911 and retired in the same year.

BOXING. The year 1912 was a record year in boxing in the fact that eight champions were defeated. One of those to relinquish his laurels was "Abe" Attell, who for twelve years had held the featherweight championship. He was defeated by Johnny Kilbane, of Cleveland, in a 20-round battle at Los Angeles. Another champion to bow to Father Time was Ad Wolgast, of Michigan, who had won the lightweight title from "Battling" Nelson. Wolgast was beaten by Willie Ritchie, of San Francisco, in 16 rounds on a foul. Besides the Americans who lost their titles six foreign champions went down to defeat. They were "Jim" Sullivan, middleweight champion of England, who was knocked out by Billy Papke, of the United States; Jack Harrison, middleweight champion of Great Britain, who was knocked out by Eddie McGoorty, of the United States; Dave Smith, middleweight champion of Australia, who also was knocked out by Eddie McGoorty, of the United States; Georges Carpentier, middleweight champion of France, who was defeated by both Billy Papke and Frank Klaus, of the United States; "Digger" Stanley, bantamweight champion of Great Britain, who was knocked out by Charles Ledoux, of France; Matt Wells, lightweight champion of Great Britain, who was defeated by Freddie Welsh, a former holder of the title. The men who defeated Smith, Carpentier, Harrison, and Stanley were non-residents and the titles therefore did not change hands. Sullivan retired from the ring.

The following is a list of the present world's champions: Heavyweight, Jack Johnson; lightweight, Willie Ritchie; featherweight, Johnny Kilbane, and bantamweight, Johnny Coulon. The middleweight and welterweight titles are open.

Two new classes were added in 1912 by the State Commission of New York and a change also was made in the division of weights. The additional classes are the paperweight for boys of 108 pounds or under, and the commission weight for men over 158 pounds and under 175 pounds.

During the year 46 clubs received licenses in New York State and the provision that each shall pay a tax of 5 per cent. of the gross receipts netted the State nearly $60,000. Boxing inspectors also were appointed for each club to see to it that the commission's rules were enforced.

The boxing championships of the Amateur Athletic Union were held at Boston on April 9. The results of the final bouts were: 105-pound class, James Lynch, of Cambridge, defeated Patsy Green, of Cambridge; 115-pound class, Tommy Reagan, of East Boston, defeated George Pritchard, of Forest Hill; 125-pound class, John Cooper, of Chelsea, defeated Edward Desmond, of Boston; 135-pound class, Al. Wambgans, of New Orleans, defeated Mike Sullivan, of East Boston; 145-pound class, Charles Askins, of Boston, defeated W. P. Widdicombe, of Fort McKinley, Me.; 158-pound class, A. Sheridan, of New York, defeated B. A. Lavalle, of Somerville; heavyweight class, John Silveris, of Beverly, defeated Thomas Kelly, of Roxbury.

The winners at the English Amateur Boxing championships were: Bantamweight, W. W. Allen, the titleholder; featherweight, G. R. Baker; lightweight, R. Marriott; middleweight, E. V. Chandler; heavyweight, R. Smith.

BOYCOTT. DANBURY HATTERS' CASE. This case grew out of a strike in 1902 by the union hatters in the employ of Loewe and Company in Danbury, Conn. The purpose was to maintain a closed shop. The American Federation of Labor assisted the United Hatters of North America and the American Anti-Boycott Association carried on the fight in behalf of the employers. In 1908 the United States Supreme Court declared the boycott illegal under the anti-trust law, and ordered the company to sue for damages. In 1910 a jury in the United States Circuit Court of Connecticut placed the damages at $74,000, which sum would be trebled under the provisions of the Sherman act. This fine was levied upon the individual members of the union. Upon appeal to the United States Circuit Court of Appeals a decision was secured in 1911 declaring this manner of levying the fine unwarranted. The case was then retried in the United States District Court at Hartford, where a jury rendered a verdict in 1912 awarding $80,000 damages to Loewe and Company. Steps were then taken by the defense to appeal the case once more. On the basis of this decision various suits have been begun against trade unions. Late in 1912 suit was begun against the United Mine Workers for damages of $750,000. None of these suits have been terminated. The American Federation of Labor has been most outspoken in its opposition to the interpretation of the Sherman act, which renders trade unions illegal, and especially to that portion of these boycott decisions which has made unions liable for damages.

BOY SCOUTS. See AGRICULTURE.

BOY SCOUTS OF AMERICA. An organization founded in 1908 for the general purpose of training boys between the ages of 12 and 18 in self-reliance, manhood, and good citizenship. A member of the organization is pledged "to do his duty to God and his country and to obey the scout law; to help other people at all times; to keep himself physically strong, mentally awake, and morally straight." The movement has had an extraordinary success since its beginning. At the head of each band of scouts is the scout-master, who must be a person of influence and possess qualities which boys respect. He has general charge of the organization and training of boy scouts. During 1912, 4520 new scout-masters were commissioned, making a total of over 6000 men who have voluntarily given their services as scout-masters and assistants. An interesting tabulation of the occupation of scout-masters is furnished in the second annual report of the organization for 1912. It shows that out of a total of 1500 there were 463 clergymen, 150 clerks, 110 teachers, 76 students, 74 superintendents of schools. Others included lawyers, mechanics, and managers. Out of the 1500, 956 were college graduates. In nationality, 1232 were American, 104 English, and 124 foreigners of other nationalities. Badges are awarded to the boy scouts for excellence in service.

The most important event of the year 1911-12 was the visit of Lieutenant-General Sir Robert Baden-Powell to the United States. General Baden-Powell was the originator of the boy scout movement in England. He visited twenty of the most important scout centres of the United States and delivered lectures on the movement. During his visit the annual meeting of the national organization was held in New York City. In the summer of 1912 important summer schools for scout-masters were conducted in different parts of the country. The officers of the Boy Scouts of America in 1912 were as follows: Honorary president, Hon. William H. Taft; honorary vice-president, Col. Theodore Roosevelt; president, Colin H. Livingstone, Washington, D. C.; chief scout, Ernest Thompson Seton; national scout commissioners, Daniel Carter Beard, Adjutant-General William Verbeck, of New York, and Col. Peter S. Bomus, of New York.

BRADLEY, JOHN EDWIN. An American educator, died October 7, 1912. He was born in Lee, Mass., in 1839 and graduated from Williams College in 1865. For three years following he was principal of the high school in Pittsfield, Mass. From 1868 to 1886 he was principal of the high school in Albany, N. Y. In the latter year he became superintendent of the city schools of Minneapolis, holding this position until 1892, when he was elected president of Illinois College He retained this office until 1900. He was a member of several educational associations and was a member of the National Congregational Council for several years, and of the International Congregational Council in 1899 and 1908. In 1900 he was vice-president of the Ecumenical International Council, New York. He was the author of *Science and Industry; School Incentives; Healthfulness of Intellectual Pursuits; Unconscious Education; Work and Play*, and *Talks with Students.*

BRAGG, EDWARD STUYVESANT. An American soldier and public official, died June 20, 1912. He was born in Unadilla, N. Y., in 1827. He studied for three years at Geneva (now Hobart College) and then began the study of law. He was admitted to the bar in 1848 and soon after removed to Fond du Lac, Wis. From 1854 to 1856 he was district attorney of Fond du Lac county. He was delegate to the Charleston Convention in 1860. He supported Stephen A. Douglas for the presidency. At the outbreak of the Civil War he entered the Union army as captain of the 6th Wisconsin Infantry. He served with distinction throughout the war, rising to the rank of brigadier-general. He participated in nearly all the campaigns of the Army of the Potomac. After the war he returned to Fond du Lac, where in 1866 he was postmaster. In the following year he was elected State senator. In 1866 and 1868 he was delegate to the National Convention and was again a delegate to the Democratic National Convention in 1872. He was elected to Congress in 1877 and served until 1883. In the following year as chairman of the Democratic National Convention he seconded the nomination of Grover Cleveland. In this speech he used the phrase which afterwards became famous in reference to Cleveland, "We love him for the enemies he has made." In 1885 he was elected to Congress for one term. He was appointed minister to Mexico in 1888. He was prominently mentioned as a presidential candidate by the delegates to the Indianapolis Convention of the Gold Democrats in 1896. In 1900 he supported McKinley. He was appointed consul-general at Havana in 1902 by President Roosevelt. In a letter to his wife, written from Havana, he said that "Uncle Sam might as well try to make a whistle out of a pig's tail as to try to make something out of the Latin race." This letter was published and caused much irritation in Cuba, and General Bragg was transferred to the consul-generalship at Hongkong. Here he remained until 1906 when he retired in consequence of ill health. Shortly afterwards a pension of $50 a month was given him by Congress. General Bragg was, in his time, one of the most efficient debaters in public life.

BRASTOW, LEWIS ORSMOND. An American theologian and educator, died August 10, 1912. He as born in Brewer, Me., in 1834, and graduated from Bowdoin College in 1857. He studied theology at the Bangor Theological Seminary and was ordained to the Congregational ministry in 1861. He acted as chaplain of the 12th regiment of Vermont Volunteer Infantry in the Civil War, and also as pastor in the St. Johnsbury, Vermont, Congregational Church from 1861 to 1873. He was pastor at Burlington, Vt., from 1873 to 1884. In 1885 he was appointed professor of practical theology at the Yale Divinity School, holding this chair until 1907. He was the author of *Representative Modern Preachers* (1904), and *The Modern Pulpit* (1906). He also contributed articles on theological subjects to magazines and newspapers.

BRAZIL, United States of. A South American republic. Capital, Rio de Janeiro.

Area and Population. The area is not known with accuracy but is estimated at 8,550,000 square kilometers (3,301,155 square miles). Still more uncertain is the number of inhabitants. The censuses of 1890 and 1900 disclosed 14,333,915 and 17,318,556, respectively. The estimate of December 31, 1908, placed the population at 20,515,000; this figure includes the inhabitants (about 70,000) of the Acre territory, acquired from Bolivia in 1902. No census was taken in 1910 on account of lack of funds. An unofficial estimate in 1912 was 24,000,000. Recent estimates of municipal populations (necessarily not very accurate): Rio de Janeiro, 1,000,000 (probably too high); São Paulo, 400,000; Bahia, 350,000; Recife (Pernambuco), 113,000; Belem do Pará, 100,000; Porto Alegre, 100,000; Manáos, 80,000; Fortaleza (Ceará), 60,000; Curityba, 60,000; Nichtheroy, 50,000; Santos, 50,000.

Immigration in 1910, 88,564; in 1911, 135,967 (Rio de Janeiro, 72,970; Santos, 53,067). Of the total in 1911, 47,493 were Portuguese, 27,141 Spaniards, 22,914 Italians, 14,013 Russians, 6319 Turks, and 4251 Germans. The total number of immigrants recorded from 1820 to 1911 was 2,967,153; of these, 1,277,785 were Italians, 781,140 Portuguese, 367,221 Spaniards, 109,572 Germans, and 82,512 Russians.

Education. In Brazil, as in most of Latin America, the greater part of the population is illiterate. But in recent years primary instruction has made considerable progress. In 1910 there were 12,221 primary schools, with 634,539 pupils (352,418 boys, 282,121 girls). Of the schools, 2695 were private, 2608 municipal, and 6918 government. Secondary schools in 1909 numbered 327, with 30,258 pupils. Various institutions offer some opportunity for technical and professional instruction.

Production. Agriculture is the principal source of wealth, but vast areas of the country are unsettled and even unexplored. The principal crop is coffee, grown chiefly in the state of São Paulo, but also in Espirito Santo, Minas Geraes, and Rio de Janeiro. The price of coffee is maintained by the imposition of an additional tax on exports over a certain amount, by the encouragement of consumption abroad, and, in São Paulo, by the prohibition of further extension of coffee plantations. The great cacao crop is produced almost entirely in the state of Bahia, which also leads in tobacco. Other important crops are sugar, produced especially in Pernambuco, cotton, rice, corn, yerba maté, and bananas. Rubber, gathered in the Amazon valley, ranks next to coffee in export value. Cattle-raising is carried on extensively in Matto Grosso, Minas Geraes, Rio de Janeiro, and São Paulo. There is some production of gold, manganese, monazite sand, and gems, but the country's mineral resources are little developed. The leading manufacture is cotton fabrics.

Commerce. Imports and exports of merchandise were valued at $235,574,837 and $310,006,438 in 1910, against $179,690,125 and $308,331,829 in 1909. The leading imports include iron and steel manufactures, machinery, railway materials, cotton goods, flour, coal, wine, arms and ammunition, codfish, kerosene, jerked beef, and paper. In 1910 the principal exports included: Coffee, 9,723,738 bags of 60 kilos, valued at $127,212,875 (against 16,880,696 bags, $161,922,682, in 1909); rubber, 38,547 metric tons, $124,400,714 (39,207 tons, $91,578,388, in 1909); yerba maté, 59,360 tons, $9,575,550; hides, 34,059 tons, $8,626,966; tobacco, 34,149 tons, $8,048,925; cacao, 29,158 tons, $6,824,139; sugar, 58,824 tons; cotton, 11,160 tons; skins, 2696 tons. In 1910 the United Kingdom supplied imports and received exports valued at $67,061,000 and $73,441,000, respectively; Germany, $37,456,000 and $36,286,000; United States, $30,254,000 and $112,184,000; France, $22,268,000 and $26,117,000; Argentina, $20,133,000 and $11,618,000; Portugal, $13,104,000 and $834,000; Belgium, $10,655,000 and $5,612,000.

Shipping. Foreign entrances, 1909: 5016 vessels, of 12,422,515 tons (6,239,330 British); 1910: 5509, of 13,591,515 tons. Brazilian entrances in 1910: 16,834 vessels, of 7,813,659 tons. In 1911 the merchant marine consisted of 238 steamers, of 130,582 tons net, and 290 sailing vessels, of 60,728 tons net.

Communications. According to the president's message, as reported in 1912 by the Pan-American Union, Brazil had, at the end of 1911, 22,128 kilometers (13,750 miles) of railway, as compared with 21,370 kilometers (13,279 miles) at the end of 1910. Among the important extensions in 1911 was one from Pirapora to Belem, connecting the latter city with Rio de Janeiro, distant by rail 3650 kilometers (2268 miles). Railways reported under construction at the beginning of 1911 aggregated about 3750 kilometers (2330 miles). The practical completion was to be recorded of the Madeira Mamore line, built to connect the navigation of the Amazon, where it is interrupted by rapids. A contract was let during the year to a German syndicate for the Santa Katarina Railway, while the Brazilian North-Eastern Railways, operated on a meter gauge, had under construction 186 miles of line. The railway line connecting the towns of Araguara and Pio-Preto in the state of São Paulo, a distance of 143 miles, was opened early in July, 1912. The Southern São Paulo, running from Santos to Santa Juquia, had 100 miles of line under construction. Telegraphs in 1909: Lines, 36,199 miles; wire, 73,124 miles; offices, 2070; post offices, 3246.

Finance. The gold milreis is valued at 54.6 cents; the paper milreis fluctuates between 31.5 and 33.5 cents. The 1911 budget showed estimated revenue of 85,048,526 milreis gold and 299,908,400 milreis paper; estimated expenditure, 69,100,356 gold and 394,186,258 paper. The 1912 budget: Estimated revenue, 91,790,776 milreis gold and 318,350,000 paper; estimated expenditure, 56,868,562 gold and 382,924,976 paper. The budget submitted to the congress for 1913 showed estimated revenue of 125,792,000 milreis gold and 345,243,000 paper; estimated expenditure, 80,861,000 gold and 431,374,000 paper. Public debt, December 31, 1911: Foreign, £82,903,120 and 300,000,000 francs; internal, 620,525,600 milreis paper; floating, 256,546,647 milreis paper; paper money in circulation, 612,519,626 milreis. A presidential decree of April 24, 1912, authorized a bond issue up to approximately $35,000,000.

NAVY. In 1912 the Brazilian navy included: Two dreadnoughts (*Minas Geraes* and *São Paulo*), aggregating 38,500 tons; one old battleship (*Riachuelo*), 5700; two armored coast guards (*Deodoro* and *Floriano*), 6320; two monitors, 940; two scout cruisers (*Rio Grande* and *Bahia*), 6200; one protected cruiser (*Barroso*) 3450; two second-class cruisers, 5840; three torpedo cruisers, 3090; one old gunboat, 800; one old destroyer, 500; ten modern destroyers, 6500; two schoolships, 4000. In addition, there were several old torpedo boats, river gunboats, transports, and dispatch boats. Brazil's third dreadnought, the *Rio de Janeiro*, 27,500 tons, which was begun in February, 1910, at Elswick, was not completed in 1912. Owing to changes in design, there has been considerable delay in her construction. Three armored gunboats for river patrol duty were ordered in January, 1912.

ARMY. The reorganization of the Brazilian army under the law of 1908 was completed in 1912 and a peace strength of about 28,000 men was secured, which it was proposed to increase to 30,000. Service is compulsory from the ages of 21 to 44—two years with the colors, seven in the reserve, seven in the second line, four in the national guard, and four in its reserve. The organization of the permanent army consisted of 15 regiments of infantry, each of 3 battalions; 12 regiments of light infantry, 15 machine-gun companies, 9 regiments of cavalry and 3 independent regiments, 10 squadrons for infantry brigades, scouting troops for the cavalry, 45 4-gun batteries, 5 6-gun howitzer batteries, 9 4-gun horse batteries, 6 4-gun mountain batteries, siege artillery, 15 ammunition columns, and engineering and transport troops. The republic is divided into 13 military inspection districts, in 4 of which "strategic brigades" were organized.

GOVERNMENT. The president is elected for four years by direct vote and is not eligible for the succeeding term. He is assisted by a cabinet of seven ministers appointed by and responsible to himself. The congress consists of two houses, the Senate and the Chamber of Deputies. Senators, numbering 63, are elected by direct vote for nine years, three for each state and the federal district. The deputies, 212 in number, are elected for three years. The president in 1912 was Marshal Hermes da Fonseca, who was elected March 2 and inaugurated November 15, 1910.

HISTORY. There were election disturbances in the state of Bahia in January which required the calling out of the federal troops to restore order. Threatened disorders in the state of Para led also to government intervention in October. The death of Baron Rio Branco (q. v.), Brazil's most famous minister for foreign affairs, through whose efforts the territories of the republic had been greatly increased, withdrew an influential figure from South American politics. He was succeeded as foreign minister by Dr. Lauro Miller. A treaty of commerce and navigation was concluded with Bolivia. A fish commission to protect the Brazilian whale industry was created in July. Legislation for improving the condition of the Brazilian Indians was enacted. For the question with the United States in connection with the Brazilian coffee valorization syndicate, see COFFEE VALORIZATION, and UNITED STATES, *Foreign Affairs*. See also IRRIGATION.

BREAD. See FOOD AND NUTRITION.

BREEDING. See STOCK-RAISING, and BIOLOGY.

BRETHREN, CHURCH OF THE (also known as Dunkers or Dunkards). A religious denomination which had its origin in Germany in 1708. It includes a considerable body of Christians in the United States. Bodies of worshippers settled first near Germantown, Pa., whence they spread to various sections of the country. The faith and practice of the denomination are not generally known outside of the communities in which they live. There are three groups, the Conservatives, Progressives, and Old Order. The first are the most numerous, numbering about 95,000 communicants, 3066 ministers and 938 organized churches in the United States, and about 20 in foreign countries. This body maintains ten colleges and one of the largest denominational printing houses in the West at Elgin, Ill. During the year this body found it necessary to close the work hitherto carried on in France and Switzerland, but arrangements were made to add to the forces in Denmark and Sweden. Four new missionaries were added to the workers in India. Missions are carried on in China, and these were greatly hindered in 1912 by the revolution in that country. An orphanage was opened during the year in China and a girls' school will be opened soon. The denomination maintains about 50 missionaries in foreign countries. The national conference of the denomination was held in York, Pa., in the early part of June. The conference for 1913 will be held at Winona Lake, Indiana, in June. The Progressive Brethren in 1912 numbered about 20,000 communicants, with 220 churches and 185 ministers. They maintain a college and publishing house at Ashland, Ohio. The Old Order numbers about 4000 communicants, 75 churches and 225 ministers. A small body known as the Seventh Day German Baptists numbers about 240 communicants, 14 churches and 9 ministers. It is found in the vicinity of Ephrata, Pa.

BREWING INDUSTRY. See EMPLOYERS' LIABILITY.

BRIDGES. There were no extraordinary developments in bridge construction during the year 1912. A large number of works which embodied few if any new features of engineering design were in course of construction. As was to be expected, reinforced concrete in one form or another was gaining in use, and this material figured in a larger proportion of the smaller bridges as well as some of notable size. In the United States, excepting a few large railway bridges and the completion of the St. Louis bridge, little out of the ordinary run of construction and erection was to be noted. A bridge across the Hudson River from Manhattan Island to the New Jersey shore continued under discussion during the year, and meetings were held by commissioners looking towards the evolution of a plan for such a structure. The great growth of automobile traffic between New York City and New Jersey, both pleasure and commercial, stimulated this discussion, as such traffic could not be handled by any tunnel or tunnels, which if railway transportation alone was concerned, would be far more economical and feasible. The National government has always regarded very zealously the channel of the Hudson River, and the location of piers in this stream would be such as to require a great width of span. The height of an appropriate structure would also involve considerable expense on the New York side on account of the cost of approaches, but various locations in the upper part of New York City were proposed where this concern would not be insurmountable. During the year progress was made on the great Hell Gate bridge, connecting Long Island with the mainland of New York, and this structure promised to be an important addition to the notable group of bridges around New York City. In Canada progress was being made with the piers for the new Quebec bridge, and the adopted designs of the structure continued to be discussed.

St. Louis Municipal Bridge. The municipal or free bridge, the fourth to be built across the Mississippi River at St. Louis, was reaching completion at the end of 1912, including the approaches on the west side of the river, which involved a viaduct for both railway and highway. This involved a steel superstructure of the plate girder type, with a maximum grade on the highway of 3.443 per cent. and on the railway of 1.385 per cent. This approach was built through the city by cutting a right-of-way 100 feet in width through the settled portion, with extra space for a station building, between 4th Street and Broadway. The total length of the approach is about half a mile, and the estimated cost for foundations, superstructure, right-of-way, etc., was about a million and a quarter dollars.

Galveston Causeway. During the year there was completed the earth, steel, and concrete structure crossing the two-mile stretch on Galveston Bay and connecting the island on which the city is built to the mainland of Texas. This work has been in course of construction since 1909, and represents the final work in the campaign which was designed to render the city independent of the storms and tidal waves from the Gulf of Mexico, that had caused such great damage to the city in years past. The causeway, 12,642 feet in length, carries the tracks for the railway lines entering the city and a driveway on which trolley cars are operated, in addition to accommodations for vehicles and pedestrians. The causeway proper amounts to 10,170 feet, protected by concrete piling and concrete slabs, and the two sections of this are united by an arch bridge construction, 100 feet of which is taken up by a roller-lift bridge. This bridge, which is carried on a massive concrete pivot pier 78 x 553 feet in plan, weighs 3,283,000 pounds, of which 1,400,000 is steel and the remainder is 300 cubic yards of concrete which is used as a counterbalance. The bridge is balanced so perfectly that it is operated by a 50 horsepower electric motor, two of which, along with a 50 horsepower gasoline engine with dynamo and storage batteries, are located in a concrete power house on the west side of the causeway. The arched bridge portion of the causeway consists of 28 concrete arches, each with a 70-foot span and 9-foot elevation, supported on reinforced concrete piers founded on 30-foot piles driven into the clay bed of the river. The double-track railway on top of the causeway is laid with 90-pound rails and equipped with an elaborate and modern block signal system. The cost of the entire project was estimated at about $2,000,000.

Canada. The most striking bridge construction of the year was possibly to be found in Canada, where progress was being made on the foundations for the great Quebec bridge, but there were also a high level bridge at Edmondton across the Saskatchewan River and a bridge for the Grand Trunk Railway across the Pembina River which had one 240-foot span and two 220-foot spans, besides approaches. Bridges built with steel piers and girders across the McCleod River, 1000 feet in length and 118 feet high; across the Battle River, 2272 feet in length and 184 feet high, and the Clover Bar Bridge, 1665 feet in length and 137 feet high, were all in course of construction.

Great Britain. Bridge construction in the United Kingdom during 1912 was limited, and aside from a few lift bridges, as that over the Trent River and two for Dublin, most of the work was of ferro-concrete construction, a bridge at Waterford being the largest structure of reinforced concrete in the United Kingdom. It had 12 spans 45 feet each, with a lifting span of 90 feet, and was 48 feet in width. This bridge, as well as reinforced structures for the Stour near Ballingdon and the Wallsend bridge, were reaching completion at the end of 1912.

A large suspension bridge with a principal span of 414 feet was built in novel form over the Danube at Passau. On one side of the river chains were anchored directly to the cliff, while on the opposite bank the usual form of tower was built.

Mersey Suspension Bridge. A suspension bridge of 2700 feet span over the Mersey River at Liverpool, England, was one of the propositions made during the year. This bridge was designed to accommodate automobile and street car traffic and would be 2700 feet in length on the main span, towers 500 feet high (200 feet in height above high-water mark), depth of girders 50 feet, weight of girders 2100 tons, width between girders 50 feet, width between towers 300 feet, and weight of cables (410 square inches in each) 6400 tons. The total cost was estimated by L. H. Chase, who was responsible for the proposition, at not to exceed $4,000,000, exclusive of the land and legal expenses. A novel feature of the design was to employ a spiral incline instead of long approaches on each shore. This spiral was to have an external diameter of 300 feet and an internal diameter of 200 feet, with a building occupying the space inside the helix.

Constantinople Pontoon Bridge. During 1912 a new pontoon bridge at Constantinople, crossing the Golden Horn and connecting Galata with Stamboul, was opened. This structure takes the place of a former floating bridge built forty years previously across the Golden Horn, which at this point is 1542 feet in width. The particular form of construction was dictated by motives of economy in which the length of span, depth of water, nature of the bottom and necessity for providing for steamships of large draught in the vicinity figured. Work was begun in 1910 and abutments were built on either shore 1530 feet apart. The pontoons are arranged in two rows parallel to the longitudinal axis of the bridge, and the roadway is a continuous structure built upon them 82 feet in width between the railings with two footways of 18 feet and a central driveway 46 feet in width. There are two clear openings 39 feet in width with a clear headway of 17 1-2 feet, while, when the middle opening span is swung clear, a passage of 205 feet is given for vessels. This middle span is swung around through 180°, propellers driven by electric machinery being the motive power.

CHINESE BRIDGES. A cantilever bridge that had been three years in course of construction across the Yellow River near Tsinanfu on the line of the Tientsin-Pukow River in China was completed during 1912 by the Maschinenfabrik Augsburg-Nürnburg, of Germany. This bridge is a cantilever structure 4100 feet in length, composed of nine spans of 300 feet each and a three-span cantilever structure comprising anchor arms of 420 feet and a cantilever span of 540 feet. Eight of the bridge spans are on the north bank and one on the south bank of the river. The bridge is designed to carry ultimately two standard railway tracks, but one track was laid at the time of its construction and the trusses were proportioned for that weight, it being the intention to provide duplicate trusses outside of the original parts when the strength incidental to the double tracking was required. False-work was used in the construction of the approach and anchor spans, but the channel spans required cantilever erection on account of the soft bottom and changing conditions of the river, which varies greatly in flood times. This also involved difficulties in constructing the piers which are of concrete with stone facing founded on reinforced-concrete piles driven in open cylinders or cofferdams, except in the case of the river piers. The river at low-water width is about 1300 feet across, but at times of flood it spreads out over a vast area embraced between high-water dikes. The superstructure is made up of trusses of the subdivided Warren type with parallel cords, except that the top cord of the cantilever is upcurved towards the main piers to get extra depth. On the cantilever span the roadway is level with the rail-level in mid-channel 144 feet above low-water. The trusses are spaced 31 feet apart. Each cantilever arm is one-sixth of the span length and the suspended span is two-thirds the cantilever span length, or 360 feet, the closure of the suspended span being made on October 9, and the bridge opened on December 1. The cost of the bridge was stated at between $2,400,000 and $2,850,000.

Another Chinese bridge of importance was that on the Antung-Mukden Railway, across the River Yalu, with six 300-foot spans, one of which opened, was also under construction during the year, at an estimated cost of $1,200,000.

INDIA. Important bridge building was reported from India during the year, where progress was being made on the foundation of the Sara Ghat bridge across the Lower Ganges. The structure consists of 15 bow string girders 350 feet long and 52 feet deep. At Allahabad the Bengal and North-Western Railway was building a bridge with 40 spans of 150 feet. It had made considrable progress during the year, while the Jumna bridge on the East Indian Railway at the same place, which has 14 through spans of 213 feet 9 inches, was being widened. A double-leaf rolling lift bridge of 225 feet span was being built over the Pambam channel.

AFRICA. In Africa several important bridges were under construction in Egypt, while in Nigeria an important bridge at Jebba on the Largos Railway, was under construction, the northern channel crossing being already completed, while a 7-span structure was being built across the southern channel. A notable masonry bridge 1466 feet in length and consisting of 27 arches was building at Constantine in Algeria during the year. The arches making up this bridge are from 28 to 98 feet in span, with one of 230 feet, and the bridge itself forms a half-circle. It was being built with two masonry ribs with girders across them and a ferro-concrete slab floor. A steel arch of 525 feet span over the Sauanga River was also under construction.

BRINKLEY, FRANK. An English editor, died October 28, 1912. He was born in 1844. He removed to Japan and in 1867 commanded the Royal Artillery. He was principal instructor at the Marine Artillery College at Tokyo in 1871, and later was appointed professor of mathematics at the Imperial Engineering College, Tokyo. In 1881 he became editor and proprietor of the *Japan Daily Mail*. He was adviser to the Japanese government and was Japanese correspondent of the *London Times*. In recognition of his service to the government, the Japanese Order of Sacred Treasure was conferred upon him. Among his published writings are, *Japan* (1901), and *Japan and China* (1903). He also compiled an unabridged Japanese-English Dictionary. He wrote the article on "Japan" for the *Encyclopædia Britannica*.

BRISSON, HENRI. A French statesman and writer, died April 14, 1912. He was born in Bourges in 1835. After studying law in Paris he was called to the bar in 1859. His most important work in his earlier days, however, was in journalism. He was one of the famous group of Liberal and Republican writers which included Jules Ferry, Charles Floquet, and Louis Blanc. These writers became famous for their attacks on the Empire in the columns of *Le Temps*. In 1868 Brisson founded *La Revue Politique*, but this was soon suppressed by the military authorities. In 1869 he made his first attempt to enter politics as a candidate for a Paris division but he was defeated. He was elected in 1871 one of the deputies for Paris to the National Assembly. He became identified with the extreme Left He took a notable part in the proceedings of the Assembly and at the beginning of the session of 1881 was elected president of the Chamber of Deputies. To this position he was reëlected nineteen times during the next thirty-two years, although there were intervals when others occupied the chair. In 1885 he was appointed prime minister and minister of justice. He at once found himself in complications as the result of a coalition of the Right and the extreme Left over the votes for the occupation of Tongking and for the execution of the treaty of Tien-tsin. The ministry, having refused to accept the decision of a special commission which advised the abandonment of all territories occupied by France or under French protection in China, found its majority reduced to two or three votes. The position of Brisson was further compromised by the fact that he was a candidate for the presidency to succeed Grévy. Grévy was reëlected for a second term, Brisson receiving only 68 votes. He with his cabinet then resigned. It is said one of his greatest ambitions was to become president of France and that he did not abandon this ambition up to the time of his death. In the elections of 1889 he defeated the Boulangist candidate and was throughout the whole Boulangist episode one of the strongest adversaries of that movement. As one of the members of the Assembly he was one of the first to initiate the political campaign against the religious orders and constantly took a prominent part in the debates in the Chamber. In 1893 he presided over the Panama Inquiry Commission. From 1894 to 1898 he was president of the Chamber. In 1898 he was again appointed prime minister. France was then in the midst of the throes resulting from the Dreyfus affair. Among the members of Brisson's cabinet were Delcassé, Bourgeois, Cavaignac, and Lockroy. On July 7, Cavaignac, as minister of war, delivered the famous speech which conveyed the impression that the Dreyfus affair was finally closed. It soon appeared, however, that the authenticity of the documents upon which this information was based was questioned, and on July 9, General Picquart addressed his celebrated letter to Brisson denouncing the documentary evidence as false. The events which followed led to the fall of the ministry. From that period until the time of his death M. Brisson was chiefly known as a Radical politician. From 1905 he was president of the Chamber. His views were particularly strong on questions concerning the church and state. Although brought up in the Catholic faith he became a pronounced freethinker.

BRITISH ASSOCIATION FOR THE ADVANCEMENT OF SCIENCE. See BIOLOGY.

BRITISH COAL MINERS' STRIKE. See STRIKES.

BRITISH COLUMBIA. A province of the Dominion of Canada (since July 1, 1871). Capital, Victoria (population, 1911 census, 31,660). Area, 355,855 square miles; population, 1911 census, 392,480. Lieutenant-governor (in 1912, appointed 1909), Thomas W. Patterson. There are an executive council (responsible ministry) of seven members and an elective legislative assembly of forty-two members. Premier in 1912, Sir Richard McBride. See CANADA.

The provincial general election gave the Conservatives a decisive majority. An important factor was the great personal popularity of the premier, Sir William McBride. The extensive programme of railway building held the people together. Not a Liberal secured a seat and only two Socialists won against the Conservatives. The delegation to the Dominion House of Commons continued to be solidly Conservative.

BRITISH EAST AFRICA PROTECTORATE. The territory lying between the Umba and the Juba rivers, from German East Africa to Italian Somaliland and Abyssinia, and inland to Uganda; a British dependency. Area (estimated), about 200,000 sq. miles, inclusive of coast territory leased from the sultan of Zanzibar. Population (1901), about 4,000,000; estimated population in 1910, of the administrative districts only, 2,295,336. Mombasa, the largest town and chief port, has a population of about 30,000 (230 Europeans). Nairobi (14,000 inhabitants, of whom 700 are Europeans and 3171 Indians) is the administrative headquarters and the central station of the Uganda Railway. At Kilmdini improvements are in progress that will make it the finest harbor on the east African coast and the centre of trade for equatorial Africa. In 1910, of the 389,598 acres (6216 freehold, 383,382 lease) classed as productive, 369,746 were devoted to grazing, 19,852 to crops. Cattle, sheep, and ostriches are raised. The crops include grains, cocoanuts, cotton, sisal, rubber, tobacco, coffee, and fruits. The worked mines yield carbonate of soda, limestone, graphite, and gold. The cost of construction of the Uganda (Mombasa-Victoria) Railway (585 miles) to March 31, 1911, was approximately £5,683,297. Two branches were under construction in 1912, one to Magadi Lake and the other from Nairobi towards Port Holi. On the line from Jinja at the Ripon Falls, Victoria Nyanza Lake to Kakindu on the Nile, navigation was opened. Four steamers are operated on Victoria Nyanza in connection with the railway. Railway passengers carried (1910-11), 403,224; tons of goods, 77,478; revenue, £300,116; expenditure, £201,596. The telegraph system, exclusive of the lines in Uganda, has 2263 miles of line (the railway line has three wires).

	1907-8	1908-9	1909-10	1910-11
Imports	£799,717	£797,158	£775,246	£1,000,346*
Exports	515,052	436,313	590,057	962,911†
Revenue	474,760	485,668	503,039	609,585‡
Exp'diture	691,677	703,103	669,404	682,041
Gr't-in-aid	152,975	138,000	133,500	130,000
Ship'ing§	1,995,940	1,838,159	1,914,153	1,364,740

* Agricultural implements, £29,265; apparel, £25,065; cotton goods, £261,141; cereals, £80,654; machinery, £24,840; p[illegible], £77,351; sugar, £33,332; tobacco, £22,[illegible].

† Copra, £30,608; grain, £59,156; hides and skins, £62,258; ivory, £21,975; rubber, £31,963.

‡ Uganda Railway, £283,617; licenses and taxes, £162,734; customs, £78,123; posts and telegraphs, £22,725; fines and court fees, £19,857; government property, £18,351.

§ Tonnage entered at Mombasa and Kilindini.

The import figures are exclusive of railway material, government stores, and specie. The United Kingdom supplied imports to the value (1910-11) of £359,556, and received exports valued at £354,525; British possessions, £250,276 and £85,986; Germany, £105,154 and £185,222; the United States, £70,022 and £132,419; the Netherlands, £67,313 imports; France, £112,658 exports.

The governor (appointed 1911) was, in 1912, Col. Sir Percy Girouard.

BRITISH GUIANA. A British colony on the northeast coast of South America. Area, 90,500 square miles; the interior is unbroken forest. The census of 1911 gave returns as follows: 6901 aborigines, 126,517 East Indians, 114,780 negroes, 2622 Chinese, 706 Africans, 10,084 Portuguese, and 3037 other Europeans; a total of 296,041 (153,717 males, 142,324 females). The unenumerated aborigines inhabiting the unsettled parts of the country are roughly estimated at 10,000. Population (1891) of Georgetown, the capital, 57,528. Cotton and coffee, once important products, have declined; sugar production is now the main industry. There are 44 sugar plantations, with a combined area of 156,666 acres (73,324 under sugar-cane, 5196 under plantains, etc., and the remainder unproductive). The export in 1910-11 was 100,954 tons of sugar (in great part Demerara crystals), 2,515,176 pf. gallons of rum, 179,163 gallons of molasses, and

2930 tons of molascuit. Rice is grown in the lowlands, on about 36,000 acres (export in 1910-11, 8,472,214 pounds). Batatas, timber, and charcoal are also exported. Rubber is cultivated.

Gold and diamond diggers, about 10,000; gold exports (1910-11), 55,543 ounces; diamond export, 3009 carats. About half the trade is with Great Britain and a third with the United States. Railway lines: Georgetown to Rosignol, 60½ miles; Vreeder Hoop to Greenwich Park, 15; branch line to the gold diggings, 18¾. There are telegraph, telephone, and cable systems.

	1907-8 (In £)	1908-9 (In £)	1909-10 (In £)	1910-11 (In £)
Imports*.	1,765,358	1,838,947	1,774,457	1,749,766 ‡
Exports*.	1,711,543	2,104,176	1,985,337	1,820,198 ¶
Revenue.	546,882	540,058	540,269	563,100
Exp'diture	519,706	539,196	546,711	542,757
Shipping†	786,880	961,384	897,864	1.006,199

* Trade is inclusive of transit (£97,998 in 1910-11) and bullion and specie. † Tonnage entered and cleared. ‡ Flour, £185,318; manures, £150,065; textiles, £143,440; machinery, £57,161; oils, £56,414; currency, £57,464, etc. ¶ Raw sugar, £1,040,464; gold bullion, £198,119; batatas, £139,623; spirits, rum, £95,215; rice, etc., £50,603; timber, etc., £35,538; molascuit, £21,930; molasses, £7541; charcoal, £8488; diamonds, £6161; etc.

Customs revenue (1910-11), £329,578. Public debt, March 31, 1911, £887,115. Sir F. M. Hodgson (appointed 1909) was governor in 1912 (Charles T. Cox, acting).

BRITISH HONDURAS. A British crown colony on the east coast of Central America. Area, 8598 square miles; population (1911 census), 40,510. Belize, the capital, had (1911) 10,478 inhabitants; Stann Creek, 2640; Corozal, 1789; Orange Walk, 856. Valuable forests are alternated with stretches of rich arable land on which oil-bearing nuts, vanilla, etc., grow wild in great profusion. Wood-cutting is the main occupation of the people; output 1910: 10,175,571 superficial feet of mahogany, 711,237 of cedar, and 3669 tons of logwood. The fruit export (1910) included 441,181 bunches of bananas, 3,514,101 plantains, and 4,871,321 cocoanuts; other products are sapodilla gum (2,790,890 pounds in 1910), rubber (16,835 pounds), and sponges and tortoise-shell (2703 pounds). Specie export, £15,475. Total imports in 1910 amounted to $2,819,217; exports, $2,344,380; revenue (1910-11), $459,295; expenditures, $542,810; customs revenue, $258,118; tonnage entered and cleared, 979,427; public debt, $168,815. Col. Sir E. J. E. Swayne was governor in 1912 (W. Collet, acting).

BRITISH INDIA. See INDIA, BRITISH

BRITISH NEW GUINEA. See PAPUA.

BRITISH NEW GUINEA. See EXPLORATION.

BRITISH NORTH BORNEO. The northern part of the island of Borneo, forming together with adjacent islands, a British protectorate, under the jurisdiction of the British North Borneo Company. Area, 31,000 square miles. The 1911 census returns about 208,000 inhabitants, mainly Bruneis, Illanuns, Bajaus, and Sulus on the coast, Dusuns, Muruts, etc., in the interior—peaceable in the main, but occasionally engaging in head-hunting expeditions. The Europeans number 355, and the Chinese 26,000. The exports go almost entirely to Singapore and China, and consist of timber in considerable quantities, tobacco (nearly three million dollars' worth in 1908), rubber, cocoanuts, sago, coffee, pepper, cattle, cutch, etc. The chartered company does not engage in trade. Coal is worked, iron ore and oil have been discovered. British, Mexican, and other dollars having ceased to be legal tender, the Straits Settlements dollar (worth $0.56776) is now the standard coin. Completed railways, 120 miles. Imports (1910), 3,801,306 S. S. dollars; exports, 4,609,021; shipping entered and cleared, 316,499 tons; revenue proper, 1,752,791 dollars; land sales, 143,932; expenditure, 815,207. The company administers the country through a resident governor (F. R. Ellis in 1912). Sandakan (administration headquarters), Jesselton, Lahat Datu, Tawao, and Kudat are the principal towns or stations.

BRUNEI (3000 square miles, 30,000 inhabitants), on the northwest coast, is under British protection.

BRITISH SOLOMON ISLANDS PROTECTORATE. The southern islands of the group, under British protection, have a total area estimated (March 31, 1911) at 14,800 square miles (according to the *Handbook of the British Solomon Islands Protectorate*, 1911); and an estimated population of 150,000 natives and 443 foreigners (252 British). Head-hunters and cannibals exist among the native tribes. The climate is unhealthy. The British resident-commissioner (C. M. Woodford in 1912) has his headquarters at Tulagi. Imports (1910-11). £103,147; exports, £88,890 (copra, pearl, and tortoise-shell, etc.); revenue, £14,130; expenditure, £9493.

BRITISH SOMALILAND. A British protectorate on the Gulf of Aden. Area, about 68,000 square miles; population (1911), 302,859, largely wandering tribes of Mohammedans. Berbera, Bulhar, and Zeila are the chief ports. Livestock constitutes the wealth of the country. Imports amounted in 1910-11 to £267,183; exports, £247,333; revenue, £30,862; expenditure, £99,224; grant-in-aid, £101,000. Administrator (1912), H. A. Byatt.

BRITISH TRADE UNION CONGRESS. See TRADE UNIONS.

BRITISH WEST AFRICA. See articles on NORTHERN NIGERIA, SOUTHERN NIGERIA, GOLD COAST, SIERRA LEONE, and GAMBIA.

BROOKLYN RAPID TRANSIT COMPANY. See RAPID TRANSIT.

BROWN, JUSTUS MORRIS. An American soldier, died December 21, 1912. He was born in Clarement County, Ohio, in 1840. He studied medicine at the University of Pennsylvania and in 1862 was appointed assistant surgeon in the United States army. He served through the war, reaching the rank of captain and assistant surgeon. After the close of the war he was promoted through various ranks until in 1901 he was made colonel and assistant surgeon-general. In 1903 he was retired at his own request after 40 years of service. By act of Congress he was advanced to the rank of brigadier-general, retired, in 1904. He received brevets of captain and major in 1865 for faithful and meritorious services during the war.

BROWNE, WILLIAM HAND. An American writer, educator and librarian, died December 13, 1912. He was born in Baltimore in 1828. He graduated from the medical department of the University of Maryland in 1850. In 1879 he was appointed librarian and assistant professor of English literature at Johns Hopkins University and in 1891 was made full professor of English literature and held this chair until 1910, when he became professor emeritus. He was author of, *Maryland, the History of a Palatinate; George Calvert and Cecilius Calvert, Barons Baltimore; Life of Alexander H. Stephens* (with Colonel R. M. Johnston). He compiled the *Clarendon Dictionary of the English Language* and *Selections from the Early Scottish Poets.* He was the translator of several works from Latin and from French and German. In 1867-8 he edited the *Southern Review* and from 1870 to 1875 the *Southern Magazine.* He was the editor also of *The Archives of Maryland,* and other historical works.

BROWNING, ROBERT WIEDEMANN BARRETT. Son of Robert and Elizabeth Barrett Browning, died July 7, 1912. He was born in 1849 and lived the greater part of his life in Italy. He adopted art as a profession and for several years studied at Antwerp. He then returned to Italy and lived with his father in the Palazzo Rezzonico, Venice, where on December 12, 1889, Robert Browning died. The son afterwards erected a home on a piece of ground at Asolo where his father had hoped to build his Pippa's Tower. His most notable literary venture was the publication in 1899 of the *Love Letters of Robert and Elizabeth Browning.*

BROWN UNIVERSITY. The total number of students enrolled in all departments of the university in the autumn of 1912 was 934. Of these, 634 were men in the undergraduate department, 211 were in the women's college, and 89 were graduate students. The faculty numbered 84. Among the important changes in the faculty during the year were the following: President W. H. P. Faunce was on leave of absence during the year and Professor W. G. Everett was appointed acting-president. Professor Alexander Meiklejohn (q. v.) resigned the chair of logic to become p esident of Amherst College. Professor A. H. Jones was appointed to fill the vacancy as professor of logic. Professor Meiklejohn was also dean of the university, and Professor O. E. Randall was made dean in his place. Professors J. I. Manatt, H. T. Fowler, L. T. Damon, and C. von Klenze were on leave of absence during the year. Dr. S. S. Colvin was appointed professor of educational psychology. The movement to raise the million dollar endowment fund of the university was successfully completed in June, 1912. The payments on the fund will not be completed for two years. The income of the university from investments for the year 1911-12 was $123,730; from other sources, $118,571. There were about 195,000 volumes in the library. President, W. H. P. Faunce, D. D.

BRUNEI. See BRITISH NORTH BORNEO.

BRUSH, GEORGE JARVIS. An American mineralogist and educator, died Feburary 6, 1912. He was born in Brooklyn in 1831 and was educated privately. He studied chemistry and mineralogy at the Sheffield Scientific School and in 1850 went to Louisville as assistant to Professor Silliman in the university in that city. In 1852-3 he was assistant in chemistry at the University of Virginia, and for three years following 1853 he studied in Europe. In 1855 he was appointed professor of metallurgy at the Sheffield Scientific School. He held this chair until 1871. For a portion of this time he acted also as professor of mineralogy and later was made professor of this branch alone. He held this chair until 1898 when he was appointed professor emeritus. He was director of the Sheffield Scientific School from 1872 to 1898. He was a member of many learned and scientific societies in the United States and foreign countries. He wrote extensively on mineralogical subjects.

BRYAN, WILLIAM J. See PRESIDENTIAL CAMPAIGN.

BRYN MAWR COLLEGE. An institution for the higher education of women at Bryn Mawr, Pa., founded in 1885. The students enrolled in the college on November 1, 1912, numbered 442. Of these, 69 were graduate students, and 373 undergraduates. The faculty numbered 61. New additions made to the faculty at the beginning of the year included the fol owing: Don Roscoe Joseph, M. D., was appointed associate professor of physiology; Clarence Henry Haring, was appointed associate in history; James Fulton Ferguson, Ph. D., was appointed associate in ancient history and in Latin; Thomas Clachar Brown, Ph. D., was appointed associate in geology; James Ryals Conner, Ph. D., was appointed associate in mathematics; Roger Frederic Brunel, Ph. D., was appointed associate in chemistry. Important benefactions received during the year included a legacy of $750,000 from Carola Woerishoffer, a graduate of the college in the class of 1907. This sum has been set aside by the board of directors as a special endowment fund. The sum of $25,000 was collected and presented by the class of 1905 for the purpose of building an infirmary for the college. This infirmary was approaching completion at the end of the year. The endowment fund of the college amounted at the end of the year 1911-12 to $1,890,334. The library contained 67,209 volumes. President, M. C. Thomas, Ph. D., LL. D.

BUBONIC PLAGUE. See PORTO RICO, and PLAGUE.

BUCHHOLZ, CHARLES WALDEMAR. An American engineer, died October 20, 1912. He was born in Hettin, Prussia, in 1843 and received his education as an engineer in that country. In 1861 he removed to the United States, where he entered the navy as an ensign. He afterwards resigned and took up the practice of engineering. From 1877 to 1880 he was chief assistant engineer of the Madeira and Mamore Railroad in Brazil. He was afterwards for many years chief engineer of the Erie Railroad. In 1907 he retired from active service on this road but continued to be consulting engineer. In addition to his work for the Erie and other railroads he was president and chief engineer of the Quaker City Elevated Railroad, an enterprise which resulted in failure. Mr. Buchholz was at one time spoken of as consulting engineer for the Panama Canal. He was one of the leading engineers of the United States.

BUCKHOUT, WILLIAM A. An American educator, died December 3, 1912. He was born at Oswego, N. Y., in 1848 and graduated from the Pennsylvania State College in 1868. In the same year he was appointed instructor in natural science in that institution. In 1871 he became professor of botany and horticulture and served in this capacity until his death. He became widely known through his research work in connection with the department of agriculture of Pennsylvania. He was a Fellow of the American Association for the Advancement of Science.

BUCK STOVE COMPANY CASE. See BOYCOTT.

BUCKWHEAT. The data relating to the yields of buckwheat in 1912 in the principal buckwheat growing countries indicated a normal world's production. Russia produced 57,178,000 bushels; Canada, 10,924,000 bushels, and the United States, 19,249,000 bushels. France grows annually over a million acres, and produces normally about 25,000,000 bushels. The crop is also grown in Germany and other European countries, but statistics are not available. This year the culture of the crop and particularly the harvest was seriously interfered with in Europe by wet weather. In the United States the production of buckwheat during recent years has shown a tendency to increase. The crop of 1912 was the largest since 1868 and was about 20 per cent. above the 5-year average. The farm value per bushel on December 1, 1912, as given by the Department of Agriculture was 66.1 cents and on this basis the total value of the crop was $12,720,000, which exceeded the 5-year average by more than 12 per cent., and which has been exceeded since 1869 only by the value of the crop of 1911, the difference being only $15,000, due to the higher bushel value of 72.6 cents. Among the twenty-four States reporting buckwheat yields in 1912 Pennsylvania ranked first with 7,405,000 bushels, New York second with 6,593,000 bushels, Michigan third with 1,088,000 bushels, and West Virginia fourth with 888,000 bushels. The average yield per acre for the entire country was 22.9 bushels as compared with 21.1 bushels in 1911. The highest average acre-yield for any State in 1912 was 31 bushels, produced in New Hampshire, which had an area of only 1000 acres.

BUDGETS. See MUNICIPAL GOVERNMENT.

BUILDING OPERATIONS. The table in the next column prepared by the United States Geological Survey shows the building operations in a number of the leading cities of the country in 1910-11. Of the 51 cities included in this table 28 showed a decrease and 23 an increase in 1911. The total increase was $29,762,561; the total decrease was $62,672,039, a net decrease of $32,909,478 or 4.48 per cent. In 1910 29 of these cities showed an increase and 22 a decrease, the net decrease in that year being $7,824,566 or 4.90 per cent. The greatest decrease in 1911 was in New York City, $18,371,910. The greatest increase was in Cincinnati, O., $4,635,670, or 57.57 per cent.

BUILDINGS, TALL. See TALL BUILDINGS.

BUKOWINA. See AUSTRIA-HUNGARY, *Area and Population.*

BULGARIA. One of the "Balkan states"; a constitutional monarchy of Europe. Formerly a principality under the suzerainty of Turkey. Capital, Sofia.

AREA AND POPULATION. Area and population (December 31, 1910) are shown below:

	Area Sq. kil.	Sq. m.	Pop. 1910
Bulgaria, Northern	63,751.1	24,614	3,095,735
Eastern Rumelia	32,594.4	12,585	1,241,778
Total Bulgaria	96,345.5	37,199	4,337,513

The population in 1900 numbered 3,744,283,

BUILDING OPERATIONS, 1910-11

City.	1910 Number of permits or buildings.	1910 Cost.	1911 Number of permits or buildings.	1911 Cost.
Baltimore, Md.	2,841	11,771,680	*2,150	*8,901,198
Boston, Mass.	3,608	20,869,671	3,547	19,379,396
Brooklyn, N. Y.	9,892	39,233,098	9,223	37,218,384
Buffalo, N. Y.	3,494	9,232,000	3,402	10,364,000
Chicago, Ill.	23,255	101,098,700	12,586	103,272,000
Cincinnati, O.	4,050	8,052,870	11,228	12,688,540
Cleveland, O.	7,460	13,948,413	7,860	16,994,677
Columbus, O.	2,363	5,133,591	2,694	4,668,277
Denver, Col.	2,683	11,319,955	2,410	6,084,260
Detroit, Mich.	5,498	17,415,950	6,667	19,012,670
Indianapolis	5,112	8,194,311	4,941	8,349,477
Jersey City	1,522	6,932,570	2,012	5,506,342
Kan. City, Mo.	3,147	12,819,690	3,736	12,818,103
Los Angeles	10,738	21,684,100	12,498	23,004,185
Louisville, Ky.	2,468	3,996,792	2,447	5,625,527
Memphis, Tenn.	3,419	6,280,498	3,213	5,859,146
Milwa'kee, Wis.	4,086	9,797,580	4,360	12,299,375
Minneapolis	6,225	14,363,830	6,026	13,735,285
Newark, N. J.	3,001	13,394,812	*2,460	*10,975,334
New Orleans	2,530	4,483,730	†2,282	†3,155,150
New York	6,877	154,075,625	6,496	135,703,715
Oakland, Cal.	3,968	6,913,643	3,946	7,132,566
Omaha, Neb.	1,538	6,250,988	1,372	5,426,863
Philadelphia	16,383	37,866,565	16,215	40,030,985
Pittsburgh, Pa.	3,903	12,753,664	4,392	11,963,257
Portland, Ore.	6,523	20,886,202	7,686	19,152,370
Pro'dence, R.I.	2,306	4,935,300	2,755	5,524,200
Richmond, Va.	1,397	4,012,822	1,528	6,018,699
Roch'ter, N. Y.	3,456	10,082,528	3,680	9,389,775
St. Louis, Mo.	9,419	19,600,063	8,152	18,607,556
St. Paul, Minn.	3,809	10,053,006	2,033	6,909,240
San Francisco	5,690	20,508,556	6,079	20,915,474
Wash'ton, D.C.	5,847	16,278,658	4,678	14,464,548
Worc'ter, Mass.	1,514	3,919,652	1,545	4,716,163
Total	212,467	784,112,998	206,124	701,203,520

* Figures supplied by the Bureau of Statistics, Department of Commerce and Labor. The number of permits or buildings was estimated. † Public buildings were not included.

of whom 2,887,684 were Bulgarians and 530,275 Turks; in 1910 the Bulgarians numbered 4,293,853 and the Turks 23,632. Sofia had, in 1910, 102,812 inhabitants; Varna, 47,981; Ruschuk, 36,255; Slivno, 25,142; Shumla, 22,225; Plevna, 23,049. Philippopolis, the capital of Eastern Rumelia, had, in 1910, 47,981 inhabitants. Movement of population 1909: 38,917 marriages, 172,583 living births, 1544 stillbirths, 113,304 deaths; surplus of births over deaths, 59,279. The national religion is the Orthodox Greek, but the Bulgarian Church is not included in the Orthodox communion. In 1909-10 there were reported to be 3786 elementary schools with 8697 teachers and 430,011 pupils (262,394 boys and 167,717 girls.)

PRODUCTION. The following table shows main crops, area in hectares devoted to each in 1911 and 1912; yields in quintals, and average yield per hectare in 1912.

COMMERCE AND COMMUNICATIONS. In the table below will be found imports and exports in thousands of leva:

	1908	1909	1910	1911
Imports	130,150	160,430	177,357	199,345
Exports	112,357	111,434	129,052	184,634

In thousands of leva the details of the 1910 trade are as follows: Imports—textiles, etc., 49,383; metals, etc., 23,299; machinery, etc., 19,777; colonial products, 10,348; skins, etc., 9188; timber, etc., 6993; chemical products, 5538; resins and oils, 5109; paper, etc., 3772. Exports—cereals, 80,811; animal products, 13,002; textiles, etc., 10,037; animals, 7324; perfumes, 5555; skins, 4038; colonial products, 2056; metals, etc., 1127; woodenwares, 656; etc. In the order of their import importance

	Hectares		Quintals		Qs.
	1911	1912	1911	1912	ha.
Wheat	1,118,409	1,120,500	19,596,528	17,350,000	15.5
Rye	220,721	215,000	3,751,176	3,150,000	14.7
Barley	251,178	260,000	4,425,593	4,000,000	15.4
Oats	180,797	160,000	2,967,735	1,750,000	10.9
Corn	631,935	650,000	7,770,420	14,000,000	21.5
Rice	2,319	3,000	30,238	30,000	10.0
Flax	485	600	....	....	....
Beets*	2,967	3,000	620,000	450,000†	20.90
Vines.	60,000	60,000	550,995‡	....	....
Tobacco	12,135	10,600	106,472	80,000†	8.8
Cotton	....	700	....	1,500†	....

* Sugar beets. † Estimate. ‡ Most.

the countries of origin and destination were Austria-Hungary, Germany, Great Britain, Turkey, France, Belgium, Italy, etc.

Total railway lines constructed and in operation in 1910, 1,891,800 kms., of which 1,888,-920 kms. operated by the state. Four lines of railway were under construction in Bulgaria during the opening months of the year, previous to the outbreak of the war. Until 1908, 435,-555 kms. of the foregoing belonged to Turkey and to the Compagnie Orientale, but were in that year bought by the Bulgarian government. The value of all lines is given (1909) as 225,-530,645 leva; of rolling stock, at 24,942,487. Net receipts (1909), 19,187,200; net expenditures, 13,873,687.

FINANCE. A table showing revenue and expenditure for three years in leva (1 lev=19.3 cents):

	1910	1911	1912*
Revenue	173,389,493	178,445,300	190,273,440
Expenditure	163,451,041	178,395,443	188,929,057

*1912 estimate.

In 1911 the revenue from customs amounted to 63,230,000 leva; direct taxes, 39,949,000; transport, 30,420,000; domains, etc., 12,080,-000; imports, 10,710,000; licenses, 9,450,000; fines, 1,031,000. Expenditure for public debt, 40,440,000; war, 39,642,000; public works, 30,-382,000; instruction, 23,508,000; interior, 10,-460,000; commerce and agriculture, 10,083,000! finance, 8,443,000; foreign affairs, 6,452,000; justice, 5,836,000. On Januray 1, 1911, the public debt stood at 555,590,213 leva.

NAVY. At the opening of the war with Turkey the navy contained 6 first-class torpedo boats (*Smély*, *Hrabry*, *Derzky*, *Choumny*, *Letiachty*, and *Stroghy*) of 100 tons each; one cruiser (*Nadejda*) of 735; two yachts, one transport; two second-class torpedo boats of 20 tons each; and some small craft.

ARMY. During 1912 an opportunity was afforded to test the efficiency and training of the army of Bulgaria. The expectations of military critics who had observed the organization, training, and equipment of this force during the ten years preceding the outbreak of hostilities in the Balkan War, were more than realized. The army is recruited from a contingent of about 80,000 young men who become available each year and of these 24,000 are usually embodied in the standing army, which on a peace basis was maintained with about 3500 officers and 61,000 men. Military service is compulsory from the age of 20 for a period of 25 years and in case of war the young men may be summoned at the age of 17. In the active army 2 years are spent in the Infantry and 3 years in the other arms of the service, though in practice this had been reduced somewhat. There was service in the reserve of the active army for 18 years in the infantry and for 16 years in the other arms, with an annual training period of from 14 to 18 days. In the first Ban of the militia 4 years' service is required in the infantry and 5 years in the other arms, with from 7 to 21 days a year training. In the second Ban of the militia 2 years with from 3 to 7 days' training is required for all arms of the service. The system of organization and recruitment with its feature of a large reserve was designed to put a strength of 380,000 officers and men with about 425 guns into the field upon mobilization. How far this was realized during the year will be found discussed in the articles on MILITARY PROGRESS and TURKEY AND THE BALKAN PEOPLES.

GOVERNMENT. The executive authority is vested in a king (since October 5, 1908). Ferdinand I., king of the Bulgarians, was born at Vienna, February 26, 1861, son of Prince Augustus of Saxe-Coburg and Gotha. Prince Boris (born January 30, 1894) is the eldest son of the king's first marriage, in 1893, to Princess Marie Louise of Parma.

The ancient Bulgars were of Finnic stock; the modern Bulgarians are made up of Slavic, Teutonic, and Mongoloid elements, amalgamated with Mussulman and Greek. Their language belongs to the southern Slavic group and the Cyrillic alphabet is used.

By the constitution of 1879 (amended 1893 and 1911), the legislative authority was vested in a single chamber, the Sobranje, whose members are elected by universal manhood suffrage (one member to every 20,000 of the population). The king acts through a council of ministers nominated by himself. The ministry as constituted March 29, 1911, was composed in 1912 as follows: Iv. Ev. Guechov, premier and minister for foreign affairs; T. Theodorov, finance; M. Pelev, instruction; P. Abrachev, justice; Gen. W. Nikyphorov, war; Chr. Theodorov, commerce, industry, and labor; D. Christov, agriculture and state domains; D. Yablansky, public works; A. Franghia, railways, posts, and telegraphs; interior and public sanitation, vacant.

HISTORY

In February the treaty with Russia concerning reimbursement for the cost of Russian occupation of Eastern Rumelia was signed. It provided for the payment of 10,680,250 roubles in bi-annual installments of 250,000 roubles each, without interest, until the debt should be liquidated. The treaty was submitted to the Sobranje for ratification. On August 15, 1812, Bulgaria celebrated at the ancient capital Tirnovo the twenty-fifth anniversary of the accession of Prince Ferdinand of Saxe-Coburg-Gotha, who in 1908 was proclaimed king and has since been recognized in that capacity by the European powers. The extraordinary advance of Bulgaria under his rule as shown by the events of 1912 makes a brief review of her recent history desirable. In the closing months of 1912 the splendid successes of Bulgaria in the Balkan War proved that a new and vigorous national state had developed in eastern Europe. Twenty-five years before when Ferdinand assumed the duties of government Bulgaria, newly liberated from the Turks, was regarded as an insignificant principality and a catspaw of Russia. At that time (1887) only a year had passed since his predecessor, Prince Alexander, had been punished for his attempt to pursue the aim of national independence by enforced abdication and transportation to Russian soil. Russia denounced the union with Eastern Rumelia, urged the Turks to reconquer what they had lost, recalled her representatives from Bulgaria, and forbade the meeting of the Sobranje. Russophile uprisings and conspiracies were only put down by the ruthless methods of Stambouloff. In the disordered conditions which Prince Ferdinand found, he fell in with the high-handed policy of Stambouloff as the lesser of the two evils, though he saw the need of coming to terms with Russia as soon as circumstances permitted. Stambouloff was virtually dictator, and during the first years of his reign, Prince Ferdinand's situation was precarious. Russia declared him a usurper; Turkey refused to acknowledge him, and Austria withheld her support. The Orthodox bishops refused to do him homage and were expelled by Stambouloff. Brigandage attributed to Russian influence was common and a Russian officer attempted a military raid on Burgas. A political ally of Stambouloff was assassinated at Sofia, and the Bulgarian representative at Constantinople was murdered. Stambouloff brought to light a military conspiracy under Major Panitza and the latter was executed. The severity and arbitrary nature of Stambouloff's course caused the prince much anxiety and finally he broke openly with Stambouloff, who resigned in 1894. A year afterwards the latter was murdered in Sofia by Macedonian avengers of Major Panitza's death. From this time Prince Ferdinand sought the friendship of Russia. On February 14, 1896, the conversion of the heir-apparent, Prince Boris, to the Orthodox faith, secured Russia's good will. Soon afterwards Turkey and the other powers recognized Prince Ferdinand and his position became secure. Russian influence was again paramount, but was not exerted in internal affairs. The fear of the Bulgarian people, however, that the designs of Russia would result in arrangements prejudicial to the interests of the Bulgars in Macedonia offered a serious difficulty. A revolt in Macedonia in 1903 was suppressed with great cruelty. The rivalry there between Greeks and Bulgars was another element of danger. When the opportunity for independence presented itself in 1908 the popular demand for it could not be disregarded, and at Tirnovo on October 5 of that year, Prince Ferdinand proclaimed the independence of Bulgaria and assumed the royal title. Since then the aim of his policy has been the maintenance of friendly relations with Russia and Austria.

BULGARIA AND TURKEY. The incessant quarrels between Bulgars and Turks in Macedonia had several times brought the two countries to the verge of war. The popular demand for the liberation of Macedonia from the Turk grew more pressing in the summer of 1912, especially after the Kotchana massacre (see TURKEY, paragraphs on *History*). For the events preceding the war and for an account of the war itself, see TURKEY AND THE BALKAN PEOPLES.

BULL MOOSE. See PRESIDENTIAL CAMPAIGN.

BURNHAM, DANIEL HUDSON. An American architect, died June 1, 1912. He was born in Henderson, N. Y., in 1846 and moved with his parents to Chicago in 1856. He was educated in private schools in that city and studied under private instructors in Waltham, Mass. He studied architecture in Chicago and in 1872 became senior member of the firm of Burnham and Root. This firm in 1891 became E. H. Burnham & Company. He first attained eminence as an architect in the designing of skyscrapers. He with his partner John Wellborn Root designed "The Rookery" in Chicago, and this was followed by designs for the Masonic Temple, the Great Northern Hotel, Railway Exchange, Marshall Field's department store, and other well-known buildings. He also designed buildings in San Francisco, Buffalo, Cleveland, Philadelphia, Pittsburgh, and Detroit. The Columbian Exposition of 1893 first directed his attention forcibly to the building of cities. The chief architect of the Exposition was Mr. Root, but he died when the work was well under way and Mr. Burnham became supervising architect of the Exposition. As the designer of the exposition buildings and the organizer and controlling operator of all the forces which carried out that undertaking, he achieved an international reputation. He began to receive appeals from cities for plans to increase their beauty. He became chairman of the National Committee for the beautifying of Washington, the other members of which were C. F. McKim, Augustus St. Gaudens, and Frederick Law Olmstead, Jr. Under the plans prepared by this commission the work of beatifying the national capital is now being carried on. One of Burnham's personal contributions to the scheme is the new Union Station in Washington. He was also chairman of the committee which prepared plans for beautifying the city of Cleveland, and after the San Francisco earthquake he perfected a scheme for remodeling the plan of the city, which, however, was not undertaken. The United States government sent Mr. Burnham to the Philippines to reconstruct the cities of Manila and Baguio. Plans prepared by him are being carried out in Chicago. He was a Follow of the American Institute of Architects and was its president in 1894.

BURTSELL, RICHARD LALOR. An American Roman Catholic priest, died Feburary 4, 1912. He was born in New York City in 1841 and after studying at Fordham University and in Rome was appointed assistant to Monsignor Preston, rector of St. Anne's Church in New York City. He was soon appointed rector of the Church of the Epiphany. Dr. Burtsell came into prominence in 1890 when he was deposed by Archbishop Corrigan on account of his espousal of the cause of Dr. Edward McGlynn in the famous controversy which led to Dr. McGlynn's excommunication. The Archbishop made charges to Propaganda at Rome and these were sustained. Dr. Burtsell was removed from his parish and sent to Rondout. The Church of the Epiphany endeavored to have Dr. Burtsell restored to his pastorate and in 1893 a petition signed by 50,000 residents of New York City was presented to Monsignor Satolli, the papal delegate in Washington. Monsignor Satolli replied that the only course was a personal appeal to the Pope. In 1894 Dr. Burtsell went to Rome and asked the Pope to leave the final decision to Monsignor Satolli. There was no result from this intercession, and in 1898 Dr. Burtsell was made an irremovable rector by Archbishop Corrigan. In 1901 he was appointed rural dean for Ulster and Sullivan counties. This was taken to signify a complete reconciliation with the church authorities. Dr. Burtsell accompanied Cardinal Farley on his visit to Rome to receive the cardinal's hat in 1911. He was appointed a domestic prelate at that time.

BURT, Silas Wright. An American soldier and civil service reformer, died December 1, 1912. He was born in Albany, N. Y., in 1830 and graduated from Union College in 1849. He studied engineering and from 1849 to 1854 was civil engineer. He served as colonel and assistant inspector-general in New York State from 1861 to 1868. During the Civil War he was engaged in raising, organizing, and equipping volunteers for the Civil War. He was special deputy naval officer at the port of New York from 1869 to 1878 and was naval officer from 1878 to 1883. From 1883 to 1885 he was chief examiner of the State civil service. He was again naval officer of the port from 1885 to 1889. In 1895 he was appointed a member of the civil service commission of New York and served in this capacity until 1900 and was its president in this year. He was one of the founders of the Civil Service Reform Association of New York and of the National Civil Service Reform League.

BUSINESS CONDITIONS IN 1912. See Financial Review.

BUTLIN, Sir Henry Trentham. An English physician, died January 24, 1912. He was born in 1845 in Camborne, Cornwall, and was educated by private tutors. He received his professional education at St. Bartholomew's Hospital, where he became house surgeon in 1868. After the expiration of his term in this position he practiced for some time in the country, but in 1870 returned to London where he obtained a fellowship in the College of Surgeons in 1871. He rapidly became one of the most eminent surgeons in England. He served in various important positions in St. Bartholomew's Hospital, acting as chief surgeon from 1892 to 1902. In 1909 he was elected president of the Royal College of Surgeons and retained this position until within several months of his death. He made a careful investigation into the subject of cancer and in November, 1911, delivered two lectures on the parasite of cancer, which may be described as the latest attempt at the solution of the problem. He first brought forward the theory that the cancer cell is a parasite, in 1905, and the lectures in 1911 were in amplification of that theory.

BUTT, Archibald Clavering. An American soldier, died at sea, April 15, 1912. He was born in Georgia in 1871 and was educated at Sewanee University, Tenn. He engaged in newspaper work and was for a time Washington correspondent for five newspapers in the South. He afterwards became secretary of the American Legation in the City of Mexico. He then resumed newspaper work and wrote several novels based on his Mexican experiences. He entered the army as captain in one of the volunteer regiments that served in the Philippines at the time of the Spanish-American War. He was in the Quartermaster's Department and rendered service of remarkable efficiency. On his return from the Philippines he entered the regular army and served in Cuba during the occupation of Havana by the American army. He was then detailed as personal aid to President Roosevelt and he also served President Taft in this position. He was promoted to be a major in 1911. He was one of the victims of the wreck of the steamship *Titanic*, on which he was returning from a brief visit abroad. From the testimony of witnesses, Major Butt conducted himself with the greatest unselfishness and heroism previous to the sinking of the *Titanic*.

BUTTE DAM. See Dams.

BUTTER. See Dairying.

BYERS, Margaret (Morrow). An Irish educator, died February 21, 1912. She was educated privately and for a short time taught school. She married Rev. John Byers and made her home in Belfast. She became deeply interested in the conditions of Irish women and began efforts for their improvement. She founded and became director of Victoria College, which was prominent in pioneer educational work. The institution began as a secondary school before college education for women had been discussed. In 1878 she worked for the inclusion of girls in the benefits of the Irish Intermediate act. In 1881 the Royal University of Ireland offered its examination and degrees to women. Mrs. Byers was the first Ulster woman to receive an honorary degree from a university. She was a member of the first senate of the Queen's University of Belfast. In conjunction with other women she founded in 1874 the Belfast Women's Temperance Association and Christian Workers' Union out of which was developed the Belfast Prison Gate Mission for Women and the Victoria Homes for the reclamation and training of neglected and destitute girls. She was the first president of the Irish Women's Temperance Union. She was the author of many papers on different phases of the progress of girls' education in Ireland and on Irish industrial schools and temperance. She received the degree of LL. D. from the University of Dublin.

BYRD, Adam Monroe. An American public official, formerly congressman from Mississippi, died June 21, 1912. He was born in Sumter county, Ala., in 1859, and when eight years of age removed to Mississippi, where he was educated in the common schools and at Cooper Institute, Daleville, Miss. He studied law at the Columbian University, taking his degree in 1884. From 1887 to 1889 he was superintendent of education in Neshoba county, Mississippi. He was a member of the State senate in 1889, 1890 and 1892, and of the House of Representatives in 1895. In 1897 he was appointed judge of the 6th chancery district of Mississippi and was reappointed in 1901. He was elected to Congress in 1903 and was successively reëlected until 1911, representing the 5th Mississippi district.

CABINET. See UNITED STATES.

CALGARY. See MUNICIPAL GOVERNMENT; COMMISSION PLAN; GARBAGE AND REFUSE DISPOSAL.

CALICE, COUNT. An Austrian diplomat, died August 29, 1912. He was born in 1831. He entered the diplomatic service and from 1880 to 1906 was representative of Austria in Turkey, and he held a place of great influence in Constantinople. He played an important part in nearly all the crises of the period in which he was ambassador and was a strong supporter of the Near Eastern p. icy of Counts Kalnoky and Goluchowski. Hisl influence was felt especially during the peace negotiations between Turkey and Greece in 1897, and when Austria and Russia agreed upon a programme of reforms for Macedonia he was the chief author of the Austro-Hungarian suggestions. He was identified also with the February and October programmes of 1903 and the reforms to which they led. Soon after the accession of Baron von Aehrenthal as premier, Count Galice retired from official life. Earlier in his diplomatic career he was successively consul and consul-general at Liverpool, consul-general and minister-resident in China, Japan and Siam, and minister to Rumania, and from 1877 to 1880 was one of the principal heads of the department at the Austrian Foreign Office.

CALIFORNIA. POPULATION. According to the Census Bureau statistics issued in 1912, out of a total population in the State in 1910 of 2,377,549 the foreign-born whites numbered 517,355, compared with 316,505 in 1900. The largest number, 76,208, came from Germany; from Italy, 63,549; from Ireland, 52,440; from Canada, 41,311; from England, 48,606; from Mexico, 33,384; from Sweden, 26,395; and from Portugal, 22,570. In the City of San Francisco, with a population of 416,912, the foreign-born whites numbered 130,892. Of these 24,121 came from Germany, and 23,127 from Ireland.

AGRICULTURE. The acreage, value, and production of tue principal crops in 1911-12 are shown in the following table:

		Acreage	Prod. Bu.	Value
Corn	1912	52,000	1,924,000	$1,635,000
	1911	51,000	1,836,000	1,652,000
Wheat	1912	370,000	6,290,000	5,850,000
	1911	480,000	8,640,000	7,603,000
Oats	1912	200,000	7,800,000	4,290,000
	1911	210,000	7,140,000	4,213,000
Rye.	1912	8,000	141,000	127,000
	1911	8,000	126,000	116,000
Rice	1912	1,400	70,000	64,000
	1911	150	6,000	4,000
Potatoes ..	1912	78,000	10,140,000	6,591,000
	1911	72,000	9,720,000	8,748,000
Hay	1912	2,500,000	a 3,825,000	52,402,000
	1911	700,000	a 1,225,000	13,352,000

a Tons.

MINERAL PRODUCTION. The total output of the metal mines of the State in 1911, according to the United States Geological Survey, was valued at $25,174,677, a decrease of $1,-845,728 from the value of the product of 1910. The total decrease was due mainly to the curtailment of the output of copper because of litigation over the smelter fumes question. The value of the production of gold in 1911 was $19,738,908, an increase over the value of the output of 1910 of $23,468. The output of silver amounted to 1,270,445 fine ounces, valued at $673,336, a decrease of 569,640 fine ounces in quantity and $320,310 in value from 1910. The output of lead in 1911 was 1,398,-111 pounds, valued at $62,915, a decrease of 1,-472,866 pounds in quantity and $63,408 in value from 1910.. The output of zinc, of which none was produced in 1910, was 2,807,035, valued at $160,001. There were 522 producing gold mines in the State, 11 silver mines, 31 silver-lead, and 30 copper mines, in 1911. There was produced from the placer mines of the State in 1911 gold to the value of $8,986,527 and 39,541 ounces of silver.

The output of copper in 1911 was 35,835,-651 pounds of blister copper, compared with 45,-760,200 pounds in 1910. The reduction in output was due to the necessity of eliminating from the smelter smoke ingredients injurious to vegetation. This resulted in the shutting down of all but one of the smelters in the copper-producing districts. At the close of 1911 California had produced about 480,970,000 pounds of copper or 2.9 per cent. of the output of the country since 1845. In 1911 it ranked sixth among the States producing copper. Five plants treated copper ores in 191 , although several were operated for only a short period.

The increased production of petroleum in the State, which has been a marked feature of its mineral history in recent years, continued in 1911, when 81,134,391 barrels were obtained from the wells of the State, compared with a production of 73,010,560 barrels in 1910. California far surpassed all other States in the production of petroleum. The value of her product in 1911 was $38,719,080. The price per barrel was lower than in 1910, 47.7 cents, compared with a price of 49 cents in 1910. The largest producing field in 1911 was the Kern field which yielded 45,921,712 barrels. From the Fresno fields were obtained 18,483,751 barrels. Explorations carried on in 1911 showed the probable existence of other large fields, which were still undeveloped.

MANUFACTURES. The Thirteenth Census statistics are for the calendar vear 1909 and were compiled in 1912. A summary of the results of the census will be found below:

	Number or Amount 1909	Number or Amount 1904	P.C. of Inc'se 1904-9
Number of establishments	7,659	6,839	12.0
Persons engaged in manufactures. ..	141,576	120,040	17.9
Proprietors and firm members...	8,077	7,402	9.1
Salaried employees	18,203	12,283	48,2
Wage earners (average numb.)	115,296	100,355	14.9
Primary horsepower.	329,100	210,359	56.4
Capital	$537,134,000	$282,647,000	90.0
Expenses	476,154,000	321,928,000	47.9
Services	107,097,000	79,056,000	35.5
Salaries	22,955,000	14,399,000	59.4
Wages	84,142,000	64,657,000	30.1
Materials	325,238,000	215,726,000	50.8
Miscellaneous	43,819,000	27,146,000	61.4
Value of products...	529,761,000	367,218,000	44.3
Value of prod'ts less cost of materials	204,523,000	151,492,000	35.0

Although agriculture and mining are the principal industries in California, it will be seen from this table that the State showed a marked growth in manufactures during the period between the last census and the present one. Of the 7659 manufacturing establishments, those devoted to printing and publishing ranked first in number, 1240. Manufactories of bread and bakery products numbered 864; lumber and timber products, 644; foundry and machine shop products, 543; copper, tin, and sheet iron products, 233. The total number of persons engaged in all industries of the State at the time of this census was 141,576. Of these, 123,929 were male, and 17,647 were female. Of the total number of persons engaged in these industries, 9.6 per cent. were proprietors and officials, 8.9 per cent. clerks, and 81.4 per cent. wage earners. The prevailing hours of labor in the State averaged from 54 to 60 a week; 21.1 per cent. of the total were employed in establishments where a week of less than 54 hours prevailed, and 8.8 per cent. in establishments where the prevailing hours were more than 60 a week. The largest number of wage earners were found in San Francisco, where the average number was 28,244; in Los Angeles, 17,327, and in Oakland, 6905. The number of employees in San Francisco decreased about 10,000 in the five year 1904-1909.

EDUCATION. The students enrolled in the public schools of the State in 1912 numbered 423,824. Of these 356,945 were in the elementary schools, 47,420 in the high schools, 9713 in the kindergarten schools, and 3164 in the normal schools. The total enrollment in 1911 was 394,752. The teachers employed in the State in 1912 numbered 13,820, of whom 10,674 were teachers in the elementary schools. The total expenditures for education in 1911 amounted to $225,604,155. The expenditures for 1912 exceeded that amount by a considerable sum. The total number of elementary school buildings, including primary and grammer schools, was 4081. The average amount paid to teachers in the elementary schools per annum was: For men, $1010.18, and for women, $726.94. There were 229 high schools maintained in 55 counties. The total enrollment in the high schools was 47,420.

FINANCE. There was a balance in the treasury at the beginning of the fiscal year, June 30, 1911, of $7,453,602. The cash receipts during the year ending June 30, 1912 were $39,323,132. The disbursements amounted to $36,620,818. There was a balance on hand at the end of the fiscal year of $9,903,533. The chief receipts are from county taxation and from the taxation of franchises and corporations. The chief expenditures are for education, expenses of the State institutions, and the administration of the State offices.

POLITICS AND GOVERNMENT. The year 1912 was one of great political excitement in the State. Governor Johnson was one of the most aggressive supporters of Mr. Roosevelt and his nomination as vice-president on the Progressive ticket made him one of the most prominent figures in the contest. The fact that women were for the first time to vote in the presidential campaign gave added zest to the contest in the State. The presidential primary, employed for the first time in the history of the State, made still another feature of political interest. The Progressive sentiment in California had been very strong since the organization of the Progressive movement and it was anticipated that in the presidential primary election held on May 14, Colonel Roosevelt would carry the State. Two days before the election President Taft issued an appeal for the votes of women. This appeal was based solely on the achievements of his administration. It included a short review of the most important acts of the administration, and he appealed to the Republican men and women who exercised the franchise, to consider fairly and well his achievements, especially those which affected California. At the presidential primary election Mr. Roosevelt carried the State by a plurality of nearly 70,000 over Mr. Taft and by a plurality of more than 25,000 over Mr. Taft and Senator La Follette combined. The total vote was as follows: Roosevelt, 138,563; Taft, 69,345; La Follette, 45,876. The total vote cast in the primary was 253,784. This may be compared with a vote in the presidential election of 1908, which was 214,398. Mr. Taft did not carry a single county in the State. Mr. Roosevelt ran second in only one county, which voted for Senator La Follette by a small margin.

The contest for two delegates to the National Convention which formed one of the most discussed cases before the National Committee, will be found treated in the article PRESIDENTIAL CAMPAIGN under the head of *Disputed Contests*. These delegates were finally given, by the decision of the committee, to President Taft. In the Democratic primaries Champ Clark defeated Governor Wilson by even greater majority than Mr. Roosevelt obtained over President Taft. Primary elections for representatives to the State and national legislatures were held on September 3. In these elections the Progressive party was again successful by large majorities. More than 80 of the 100 nominees for the State legislature who were elected, were pledged to vote for Roosevelt electors in the legislative convention. The California law provides that the legislative nominees shall constitute a State convention which names candidates for presidential electors. As a result of this election, the Progressive party was given official place on the ballot, while it was necessary for the regular Republican candidates to be nominated by petition. The head of the Progressive movement, Meyer Lissner, announced, however, on September 7 that the Progressives would waive their right to nominate electors when the convention met on September 24 and would place the Roosevelt electors on ballot by petition.

In accordance with this decision it was necessary for the Taft electors to be nominated by petition. This was neglected until it was too late, and those who wished to vote for President Taft in the election were practically disfranchised. As a result, most of the Republican voters who did not wish to vote the Progressive ticket apparently cast their votes for Governor Wilson. The result of the election on November 5 was so close that it required an official count before it could be determined. The count disclosed that Mr. Roosevelt had a plurality of 164 votes.. The total vote was as follows: Wilson, 283,441; Roosevelt, 283,605; Taft, 3943; Debs, Socialist, 69,869. Two Roosevelt electors received fewer votes than Wilson electors, and the electoral vote was therefore eleven for Roosevelt and two for Wilson. The Progressives elected all the representatives to Congress with the exception of 2. A great increase in the total vote in 1912 compared with 1908 is due to the increased number voting as a result of woman suffrage. It is worthy of note that Mr. Roosevelt apparently did not carry the preponderance of the votes of the women in the State in spite of the fact that he was the only one of the candidates who openly advocated woman suffrage.

OTHER EVENTS. On February 26 the Supreme Court of the State decided in favor of the Southern Pacific Railroad in a case involving a claim to California land valued at more than $1,000,000. Clarence Darrow, chief counsel for the McNamara brothers in the trial in which they were convicted of blowing up the building of the *Los Angeles Times* in 1911, was indicted for bribery on January 27. It was alleged that he had instigated the bribery of a juror in the case to vote for an acquittal of the defendants. Mr. Darrow, after a long trial, was acquitted of the charge on August 17.

On March 23 the legislature rejected the proposed local option amendment to the State constitution.

LEGISLATION. The legislature met in two extra sessions in 1912. Important measures were passed in both these sessions. In the first the following laws were enacted: (1) A measure providing for the registration of voters. (2) An act providing for the confinement and care of persons so addicted to the intemperate use of narcotics or stimulants as to have lost the power of self-control. (3) An act providing for the organization of a State railroad commission, and defining its powers, duties, etc. (4) An act amending the law as to primary elections. This contained in particular one feature which provides for the order in which names are to be printed on the ballots so that as far as possible, each candidate shall have his name at the head of the list on equal terms with all the others. A presidential primary act was passed (see *Politics and Government* above). Other measures provided for the organization and management of municipal water districts, and various acts were passed amending the banking laws of the State. Measures were passed providing for the recall of elective officers of counties and subdivisions thereof; for the initiative and referendum in counties; for the recall of officers of cities and towns; and for the initiative and referendum in cities and towns. Other measures relating to elections regulated election ballots and provided for the appointment of a registrar of voters in counties by the board of supervisors thereof.

At the second session was passed an elaborate act providing for the protection of horticulture, and to prevent the introduction into the State of insects, diseases, or animals injurious to fruit or fruit trees, bushes or vegetables. Constitutional amendments were passed for submission to the people regulating the deposit of moneys belonging to the State and providing for the publication of free text-books.

STATE GOVERNMENT. Governor, H. W. Johnson, Prog.; Lieutenant-Governor, A. J. Wallace; Secretary of State, F. C. Jordan; Treasurer, E. D. Roberts; Comptroller, A. B. Nye; Adjutant-General, Edwin A. Forbes; Attorney-General, U. S. Webb; Superintendent of Education, Edward Hyatt; Commissioner of Insurance, E. C. Cooper; Commissioner of Agriculture, R. L. Telfer—all Republicans, except Governor.

JUDICIARY. Supreme Court: Chief Justice, W. H. Beatty; Associate Justices, H. A. Melvin, Lucien Shaw, F. M. Angellotti, M. C. Sloss, F. W. Henshaw, W. G. Lorigan; Clerk, B. G. Taylor—all Republicans.

STATE LEGISLATURE. 1913. Democrats, Senate, 12; House, 25; joint ballot, 37. Republicans, Senate, 1; House, 8; joint ballot, 9; Progressives, Senate, 27; House, 46; joint ballot, 73; Socialist, House, 1; joint ballot, 1. Progressive majority, Senate, 14; House, 12; joint ballot, 26.

The representatives in Congress will be found in the article CONGRESS, section *United States*.

CALIFORNIA, UNIVERSITY OF. An institution of higher learning at Berkeley, Cal., founded in 1860. The students enrolled in the university in the autumn of 1912 numbered 6659, of whom 1871 were summer session students. The faculty numbered 407. Among the important additions to the faculty during the year were the following: I. W. Howerth, professor of education and director of university extension; T. F. Hunt, professor of agriculture and director of experiment station; G. N. Lewis, p ess r of physical chemistry; F. R. Marshall, professor of animal industries; J. T. Nance, professor of military science and tactics; C. L. Seeger, professor of music; W. C. Bray, assistant professor of chemistry; W. W. Bonns, assistant professor of pomology and plant physiologist; C. G. Chinard, associate professor of French; J. V. Cooke, assistant professor of pathology and director of laboratory of animal experimentation; J. E. Dougherty, assistant professor of poultry husbandry; F. S. Foote, Jr., associate professor of railroad engineering; S. J. Holmes, associate professor of zoölogy; Mary L. Kissell, associate professor of domestic art; W. A. Morris, associate professor of English history; P. E. Smith, assistant professor of anatomy; R. C. Tolman, assistant professor of chemistry. The important benefactions of the year included gifts from Mrs. Phoebe A. Hearst of collections and of moneys for maintenance for the Museum of Anthropology, and a rich collection of occidental and oriental manuscripts, early printed books, rare bindings, etc.; from Miss Annie M. Alexander, a gift of $10,500 for the support of the Museum of Vertebrate Zoölogy; from Ernest V. Cowell, a bequest of $750,000, one-third of which is to be used for a gymnasium, one-third for a stadium, and one-third for a hospital. A number of other smaller benefactions were also received. The endowments of the university amounted to about $4,350,000. The total income from all sources for the year 1911-12, not including gifts, was about $1,800,000. The volumes in the library numbered about 250,000. The most important event in the academic year was the reorganization of the agricultural department in the autumn of 1912. Dr. Thomas Forsyth Hunt, formerly of the Pennsylvania State College, took office on October 1 as professor of agriculture, director of the Agriculture Experiment Station, and dean of the College of Agriculture. The Regents of the university have taken steps to establish one of the foremost agricultural colleges and experiment stations in the United States with important outlying stations in other parts of California. Dr. Herbert John Webber, formerly professor of plant breeding at Cornell University was called to the same professorship at California University. Dr. John Washington Gilmore, president of the College of Hawaii, was appointed professor of agronomy. President, Benjamin Ide Wheeler.

CALIFORNIA FIGS. See HORTICULTURE.

CAMBODIA. A French protectorate on the Gulf of Siam; part of the French colony of Indo-China (q. v.). The capital is Pnom-Penh, with 50,000 inhabitants; other towns are Kampot and Khsach-Kandal. A large part of the country is covered with forest. The natives cultivate cotton, rice, betel, tobacco, indigo, cardamons, coffee, cacao, etc.; they also raise cattle and buffaloes. The great lakes are fished in primitive fashion. The most of the trade goes through Saigon (Cochin-China). Sisonath is the native king. The French resident superior was M. Outrey in 1912.

CAMBRIDGE. See ARCHITECTURE.

CAMEROON. See KAMERUN.

CAMORRA. See ITALY.

CAMPAIGN, PRESIDENTIAL. See PRESIDENTIAL CAMPAIGN.

CAMPANILE. See ARCHITECTURE.

CANADA, DOMINION OF. A British self-governing dependency between the United States and the Arctic Ocean. Capital, Ottawa, Ontario.

AREA AND POPULATION. The following table shows by provinces and territories: (1) Area in square miles, by planimetric calculation, inclusive of 125,765 square miles of water, but excluding the territorial seas, the Gulf of St. Lawrence, and the Canadian portion of the Great Lakes; (2) population according to the census of 1901; (3) population according to the final returns of the census of April 2, 1911; (4) increase per cent. between 1901 and 1911:

Provinces	Area	1901	1911	Inc.
Alberta	255,285	73,022	374,663	413.1
Brit. Columbia.	355,855	178,657	392,480	119.7
Manitoba	73,732	255,211	455,614	78.5
New Brunswick	27,985	331,120	351,889	6.3
Nova Scotia...	21,428	459,574	492,338	7.1
Ontario	260,862	2,182,947	2,523,274	15.6
Pr. Edward Isl.	2,184	103,259	93,728	* 9.2
Quebec	351,873	1,648,898	2,002,712	21.5
Saskatchewan..	251,700	91,279	492,432	439.5
Yukon (ter.)..	207,076	27,219	8,512	* 68.7
Northwest Territories	1,921,685	20,129	17,196	* 15.8
Canada	3,729,665	5,371,315	7,204,838	34.1

* Decrease.

The rural population in 1911 was 3,924,394 and the urban 3,280,444, the former figure showing an increase in ten years of 574,878, or 17.16 per cent., and the latter 1,258,645, or 62.25 per cent. The increase over 1901 by provinces was: Alberta, 180,327 rural and 121,314 urban; British Columbia, 100,318 and 113,505; Manitoba, 70,511 and 129,892; New Brunswick, decrease 1493 rural and increase 22,262 urban; Nova Scotia, decrease 23,981 rural and increase 56,745 urban; Ontario, decrease 52,184 rural and increase 392,511 urban; Prince Edward Island, decrease 9546 rural and increase 15 urban; Quebec, increase 39,951 and 313,863 respectively; Saskatchewan, 287,338 and 113,815; Yukon, decrease 13,430 and 5277; Northwest Territories (population wholly rural), decrease 2933. These figures indicate particularly the rapid development of Alberta and Saskatchewan and, in the older parts of the Dominion, the trend of population from country to town.

In 1911 the population comprised 3,821,067 males (53.03 per cent.) and 3,383,771 females (46.97 per cent.); single, 2,369,160 males (32.88), 1,941,354 females (26.94); married, 1,1331,564 (18.48), and 1,251,182 (17.37); widowed, 80,121 (1.24), and 179,598 (2.49); divorced, 839 and 691.

Population of the Dominion capital and the provincial capitals in 1911: Ottawa, 87,062; Edmonton, Alb., 24,900; Victoria, B. C., 31,660; Winnipeg, Man., 136,035; Fredericton, N. B., 7208; Halifax, N. S., 46,619; Toronto, Ont., 376,538; Charlottetown, P. E. I., 11,198; Quebec, Que., 78,190; Regina, Sask., 30,132; Dawson, Yukon (ter.), 3013. Other cities: Montreal, Que., 470,480; Vancouver, B. C., 100,401; Hamilton, Ont., 81,969; London, Ont., 46,300; Calgary, Alb., 43,704; St. John, N. B., 42,511; Brantford, Ont., 23,132; Kingston, Ont., 18,874.

Immigrants in years ending March 31: 1910, 208,794 (of whom 59,790 from the United Kingdom and 103,984 from the United States); 1911, 311,084 (123,013 and 121,451); 1912, 354,237 (138,121 and 133,710). The immigrants from the United States are practically all farmers and farm laborers and come principally from the Western States.

EDUCATION. Public instruction is controlled by the separate provincial governments. Primary education is free and, except in Quebec and Manitoba, compulsory.

Alberta. Statistics for 1909 and 1910 respectively: Schools, 970 and 1195; pupils enrolled, 46,048 and 55,307; average attendance, 22,225.06 and 29,611.45; teachers, 1323 and 1610; expenditure on school buildings and grounds, $769,201 and $1,062,987; teachers' salaries, $758,816 and $908,045 (average in 1910, $704.97). Total expenditure in 1910, $3,362,393.

British Columbia. Years ending June 30, 1910 and 1911: Schools, 211 each; pupils enrolled, 39,822 and 45,125; average attendance, 28,094.16 (70.54 per cent.) and 32,163.24 (71.27 per cent.); teachers, 1037 and 1179; expenditure, $1,917,236 and $2,641,522 (education proper, $612,053 and $715,734).

Manitoba. For 1910: Enrollment, 76,247; attendance, 43,885 (57.55 per cent.); teachers, 2774; expenditure, $4,000,671.

New Brunswick. During the year ending June 30, 1911, there were enrolled in the public schools 68,951 pupils, compared with 68,154 in 1910. For terms ending June 30, 1910 and 1911: Schools, 1860 and 1885; pupils enrolled, 62,994 and 63,073; average attendance, 42,418 (67.33 per cent.) and 41,597 (65.95); teachers, 1974 and 1975.

Nova Scotia. Years ending July 31, 1910 and 1911: Schools (common and high), 2579 and 2639; pupils enrolled, 102,035 and 102,910; average attendance, 65,629 (70 per cent.) and 61,250 (68.1 per cent.); teachers, 2723 and 2799. Enrollment in common schools, 93,378 and 94,234; high schools, 8657 and 8676; technical schools, 2183 and 2410; government night schools, 123 and 66; grand total, 104,341 and 105,386; expenditure, $1,265,233 and $1,379,332.

Ontario. For 1909 and 1910: 1. Elementary schools, 6380 and 6408; pupils enrolled, 456,302 and 459,145; average attendance, 60.17 per cent. and 60.84 per cent.; teachers, 10,274 and 10,518; expenditure, $8,141,423 and $9,343,202; average of teachers' salaries, male $660 and $711, female $449 and $483. 2. Secondary schools, 145 and 146; pupils enrolled, 31,101 and 32,612; average attendance, 20,791 and 20,389 (62.52 per cent.); teachers, 820 and 853; expenditure, $1,621,637 and $1,636,166; average of teachers' salaries, $1195 and $1259. The total enrollment in elementary and secondary schools, including kindergartens and night schools, was 508,563 in 1909 and 512,345 in 1910.

Prince Edward Island. Years ending September 30, 1910 and 1911: Schools, 478 and 478; pupils enrolled, 17,933 and 17,397; average attendance, 11,632 (64.8 per cent.) and 10,511 (60.4); teachers, 591 and 591; expenditure, $181,572 and $181,177 (of which government $127,548 and $126,438). The average of teachers' salaries ranged in the several classes from $149 to $410 in 1911.

Quebec. Years ending September 30, 1910 and 1911: Elementary: Schools, 5720 and 5905; pupils enrolled, 218,914 and 226,438; average attendance, 162,928 (74.42 per cent.) and 167,-168 (73.82); teachers, 6901 and 7134. Model: Schools, 661 and 671; pupils enrolled, 100,492 and 106,386; average attendance, 82,514 (82.11 per cent.) and 86,758 (81.55); teachers, 2988 and 3186. Secondary: Academies and Roman Catholic classical colleges, 255 and 242; pupils enrolled, 61,740 and 63,439; teachers, 3133 and 3214. Total, including normal schools, night schools, universities, etc.: Schools, 6760 and 6934; enrollment, 394,945 and 410,422; average attendance, 78.23 and 77.53 per cent.; teachers, 14,000 and 14,597. Of the teachers, in the latter year, 3272 were male and 11,325 female; 8532 were lay teachers and 6065 were in religious orders. Aggregate contributions for education in 1909-10, $6,210,530; in 1910-11, $6,794,333.

Saskatchewan. Years ending December 31, 1909 and 1910: Elementary schools, 1692 and 1912; pupils enrolled, 53,969 and 63,964; average attendance, 28,202 (52.25 per cent.) and 33,731 (52.80); teachers, 2294 and 2672; expenditure, $3,032,999 and $3,586,036 (of which $1,044,011 and $1,208,651 teachers' salaries). There are 13 high schools, a normal school, and a training school for teachers for foreign-speaking communities.

AGRICULTURE. In 1911, the area under field crops was 32,404,110 acres, which yielded a value, computed at local market prices, of $558,-099,600, a record figure. Of the total, 22,704,028 acres were under grain crops. The principal crop, wheat, was the largest on record. The following table compares the yield of the leading crops in 1911 with the yield in 1901, and for 1911 shows the acreage and the value (all figures in thousands):

Crops	1000 bu. 1901	1000 bu. 1911	1911 1000 ac.	1911 1000 $
Wheat	55,572	215,851	10,374	138,567
Oats	151,497	348,188	9,220	126,812
Barley	22,224	40,641	1,404	23,004
Rye	2,317	2,694	143	2,086
Peas	12,349	4,536	287	4,648
Buckwheat	4,547	8,156	359	5,232
Mixed grains....	.....	16,679	560	10,127
Flaxseed	.....	7,867	683	11,855
Beans	861	1,156	61	2,219
Corn for husking	25,876	18,773	316	12,172
Potatoes	55,363	66,023	159	29,358
Turnips, etc.....	76,076	84,933	227	19,541
Hay and		1000 tons		
clover	7,853	12,694	7,903	146,596
Fodder corn.....	.....	2,577	285	12,469
Sugar beets.....	.....	177	21	1,165
Alfalfa	.....	228	102	2,249

Crops in 1912 are reported as follows, in metric measure: Wheat, 3,949,029 hectares, 55,-979,230 quintals; oats, 3,729,895 ha., 58,835,238 qs.; barley, 572,703 ha., 9,556,819 qs.; rye, 60,-176 ha., 783,875 qs.; corn, 118,511 ha., 3,611,-514 qs.; flaxseed, 678,972 ha., 5,370,533 qs.; sugar beets, 7689 ha., 1,850,620 qs. These figures for 1912 show increased production as compared with those for 1911 except in the case of wheat and corn.

Livestock estimates June, 1911: Horses on farms, 2,266,400; milch cows, 2,876,600; other cattle, 4,210,000; sheep, 2,389,300; swine, 2,792,-200. See AGRICULTURE, AND AGRICULTURAL LEGISLATION.

HOMESTEADS. Ordinary homestead entries and preëmptions in 1910 and 1911:

Provinces	Homesteads 1910	Homesteads 1911	Pre-emptions 1910	Pre-emptions 1911
Manitoba	3,132	2,944	.....	.....
Saskatchewan	26,878	20,681	10,795	6,714
Alberta	18,013	14,960	7,557	3,869
British Columbia...	234	324	.....	.....
Total	48,257	38,909	18,352	10,583

Purchased homesteads in 1910, 1863; in 1911, 1514. Entries for South African volunteer homesteads, 2186 and 2064.

MINING. The value of Canada's mineral production increased from $16,763,353 in 1890 to $64,420,983 in 1900 and $106,823,623 in 1910. In 1911 the output declined to $103,220,994. The following table shows for calendar years the value of the principal mineral products and of the total product, in thousands of dollars:

	1901	1906	1910	1911
Silver	3,265	5,659	17,580	17,355
Nickel	4,595	8,949	11,181	10,230
Gold	24,129	11,502	10,206	9,781
Copper	6,097	10,720	7,094	6,887
Lead	2,249	3,089	1,216	828
Pig iron*	1,212	1,857	1,651	613
Coal	12,699	19,732	30,910	26,468
Cement	660	3,171	6,412	7,645
Bricks	2,400	4,103	5,992	6,595
Asbestos	1,260	2,036	2,556	2,922
Building stone.....	1,650	1,830	3,650	1,329
Gypsum	340	643	934	993
Petroleum	1,008	762	389	357
Total metals.....	41,940	41,950	49,439	46,105
" non-metals.	23,865	37,337	57,385	57,116
Grand total......	65,805	79,287	106,824	103,221

* From Canadian ore.

About half of the coal is now produced in Nova Scotia, two-fifths of the gold in Yukon, more than one-third of the nickel in Ontario, almost all of the silver in Ontario, and of the asbestos in Quebec.

FISHERIES. In the year ending March 31, 1911, the total catch was valued at $29,965,433, against $29,629,170 in 1909-10. Value by provinces in 1909-10 and 1910-11: Alberta, $82,562 and $82,460; British Columbia, $10,314,755 and $9,163,235; Manitoba, $1,003,405 and $1,302,799; New Brunswick, $4,676,315 and $4,134,144; Nova Scotia, $8,081,111 and $10,119,243; Ontario, $2,-177,813 and $2,026,121; Prince Edward Island, $1,197,556 and $1,153,708; Quebec, $1,808,436 and $1,692,475; Saskatchewan, $173,580 and $172,903; Yukon (ter.), $82,562 and $82,460. The most valuable fish taken in the year 1910-11: Salmon, $7,205,871; cod, $5,921,248; lobsters, $3,784,099; herring, $2,278,842; halibut, $1,251,839; haddock, $1,218,759; whitefish, $983,-594; trout, $825,290. Persons employed in the fishing industry in 1909-10 and 1910-11, 90,357 and 93,588; vessels, 1750 and 1680; boats, 41,-170 and 38,977; capital invested, $17,357,932 and $19,019,870.

MANUFACTURES. As a part of the Fifth Census, a census of manufactures was taken in June, 1911, for the calendar year 1910. The following table shows the chief general results as compared with figures for 1900 (*a* number of establishments, *b* capital, *c* employees on salaries, *d* salaries, *e* employees on wages, *f* wages, *g* value of raw and partly manufactured materials, *h* products):

	1900	1910	Increase Total	Increase P. C.
a	14,650	19,218	4,568	31.18
b	$446,916,487	$1,247,583,609	$800,667,122	179.15
c	30,691	44,077	13,386	43.61
d	$ 23,676,146	$43,779,715	$20,103,569	84.92
e	308,482	471,126	162,644	52.72
f	$89,573,204	$197,228,701	$107,655,497	120.19
g	$266,527,858	$601,509,018	$334,981,160	125.68
h	$481,053,375	$1,165,975,639	$684,922,264	142.38

The returns for 1910 compared with those for 1905 show the increase per cent. of capital 47.36, of employees on salaries 20.77, of salaries 42.49, of employees on wages 32.32, of wages 46.77, and of products 62.31.

Groups of industries, number of establishments, capital, and value of products in 1910:

	Estab.	Capital	Produce
Food	6,985	$133,344,823	$245,669,321
Textiles	1,444	108,787,407	135,902,441
Iron and steel..	824	123,561,319	113,640,610
Timber, lumber, and re-mfrs...	4,999	259,889,715	184,630,376
Leather & mfrs.	399	48,788,803	62,850,412
Paper & printing	773	62,677,612	46,458,053
Beverages & liq.	260	43,237,757	28,936,782
Chemicals, etc...	178	26,926,124	27,798,833
Clay, glass, stone.	771	45,859,507	25,781,860
Metals & mfrs., exc. steel......	341	67,133,540	73,241,796
Tobacco & mfrs.	173	21,659,935	25,329,323
Land vehicles....	465	49,397,096	69,712,114
Water vehicles...	172	10,351,765	6,575,417
Miscellaneous ...	1,011	235,148,103	104,618,560
Hand trades.....	423	11,120,403	14,829,741
Total	19,218	$1,247,583,609	$1,165,975,639

Capital and value of products by provinces in 1910: Alberta, $29,518,346 and $18,788,826; British Columbia, $123,027,521 and $65,204,235; Manitoba, $47,941,540 and $53,673,609; New Brunswick, $36,125,012 and $35,422,302; Nova Scotia, $79,596,341 and $52,706,184; Ontario, $595,394,608 and $579,810,225; Prince Edward Island, $2,013,365 and $3,136,470; Quebec, $326,946,925 and $350,901,656; Saskatchewan, $7,019,951 and $6,332,132; total, $1,247,583,609 and $1,165,975,639.

The number of kinds of industries in 1900 was 264, with 14,650 establishments; in 1905, 274, with 15,796 establishments; and in 1910, 300, with 19,218 establishments.

COMMERCE. The following table shows imports of merchandise for home consumption, of total merchandise, of coin and bullion, and total imports, value in dollars, in years ended March 31:

Yrs.	Mdse. Home Consump.	Total Mdse.	Coin and B.	Total Imports
1910	369,815,427	385,835,103	6,017,589	391,852,692
1911	451,745,108	462,041,330	10,206,210	472,247,540
1912	521,448,309	533,286,663	26,033,881	559,320,544

For the same years, exports of domestic merchandise, of total merchandise, of coin and bullion, and total exports:

	Domest. Mdse.	Total Mdse.	Coin and B.	Total Exports
1910	279,247,551	298,763,993	2,594,536	301,358,529
1911	274,316,553	290,000,210	7,196,155	297,196,365
1912	290,223,857	307,716,151	7,601,099	315,317,250

In the fiscal year 1911, dutiable imports of merchandise, $291,818,801; free, $170,222,529; import duties, $73,312,368; in 1912, $343,370,082, $189,916,581 and $87,576,037 respectively.

Principal imports for consumption by classes, in thousands of dollars, in the fiscal year 1912 (1911 in parentheses): Metals, minerals, and their manufactures, 123,375 (105,727), including iron and steel 96,140 (81,771); coal, coke, etc., 41,338 (32,264); cotton and manufactures, 30,983 (32,876); wool and manufactures, 26,677 (26,383); sugar, molasses, etc., 18,152 (17,481); settlers' effects, 15,145 (14,073); wood and manufactures, 20,620 (17,237); fruits, 15,314 (11,955); breadstuffs, 13,483 (10,284); drugs, chemicals, etc., 12,582 (12,178); carriages, automobiles, etc., 11,754 (7258); oils, 8912 (7869); hides and skins except furs, 8904 (8105); rubber and manufactures, 8103 (6951); silk and manufactures, 7431 (6930); tea, 6707 (5655); leather and manufactures, 6387 (5332); paper and manufactures, 6348, (5537); tobacco, 5701 (4816); spirits and wines, 5604 (4538); books, etc., 5327 (4589).

The following table shows by great classes domestic exports and total exports in the years ending March 31, 1911 and 1912 (*a* produce of mine; *b* produce of fisheries; *c* produce of forest; *d* animals and their produce; *e* agricultural produce; *f* manufactures; *g* miscellaneous; *h* total merchandise; *i* coin and bullion; *j* grand total):

	1911 Dom. exps.	1911 Total	1912 Dom. exps.	1912 Total
a	$42,787,561	$43,078,440	$41,324,516	$41,510,582
b	15,675,544	15,789,859	16,704,678	16,815,192
c	45,439,057	45,597,599	40,892,674	41,104,887
d	52,244,174	53,053,837	48,210,654	49,220,897
e	82,601,284	90,059,113	107,143,375	115,454,486
f	35,283,118	40,432,526	35,836,284	42,508,985
g	285,815	1,988,836	111,676	1,101,122
h	274,316,553	290,000,210	290,223,857	307,716,151
i	....	7,196,155	....	7,601,099
j	274,316,553	297,196,365	290,223,857	315,317,250

The leading export is grain, details of which (domestic exports) in thousands of bushels (*b*) and thousands of dollars (*d*) are shown below for fiscal years; also, wheat flour, in thousands of barrels (*b*) and thousands of dollars (*d*):

Years	Wheat	Oats	Barley	All grain	Wheat flour
1905—b.........	14,700	2,367	1,041	19,748	1,321
d.........	12,387	862	515	15,125	5,878
1910—b.........	49,741	3,402	2,045	56,867	3,064
d.........	52,609	1,567	1,108	56,751	14,860
1911—b.........	45,802	5,432	1,545	53,841	3,949
d.........	45,521	2,145	831	49,536	13,855
1912—b.........	64,466	8,881	2,062	76,001	3,739
d.........	62,591	3,820	1,824	68,428	16,034

Other important domestic exports, in thousands of dollars, in the fiscal year 1912 (1911 in parentheses): Lumber, 32,367 (36,136); cheese, 20,889 (20,740); silver, 15,908 (15,010); live animals, 4720 (9599); meats, 9313 (9002), of which, bacon, 7520 (8019); flaxseed, 2842 (6095); wood manufactures, 6022 (6661), of which wood pulp, 5094 (5716); wood for pulp, 5698 (6093); copper, 5646 (5575); gold, 7193 (5344); hides and skins except furs, 5004 (4608); furs, 3842 (4278); codfish, 4271 (4389); salmon, 4312 (4092); paper, 3867 (3912); nickel, 3744 (3842); lobsters, 3648 (3265); apples, green or ripe, 5104 (1757); asbestos, 2098 (2076); coal, 4338 (6014); hay, 6374 (2723); agricultural implements, 5699 (5903).

For years ended March 31, the following table shows by principal countries imports for consumption (including merchandise and coin and bullion) and total exports:

Countries	Imports 1911	Imports 1912	Exports 1911	Exports 1912
United States	284,934	356,354	119,397	120,535
Great Britain	109,936	116,907	136,965	151,853
France	11,564	11,745	2,782	2,124
Germany	10,047	11,090	2,663	3,815
South America	7,334	10,533	5,150	4,825
West Indies	9,036	8,491	6,567	6,901
Belgium	3,614	3,686	2,773	3,732
Switzerland	3,103	3,458	23	20
China & Japan	3,106	3,113	1,150	902
Netherlands	1,821	2,424	1,397	1,783
Newfoundland	1,818	1,842	3,875	4,284
Spain	1,155	1,273	38	115
Italy	962	1,147	379	285
Portugal	186	260	88	70
Australia	512	432	3,926	3,947
Other	12,821	14,727	10,033	10,126
Total	461,951	547,482	297,196	315,317

For fiscal years, imports for consumption and total exports by provinces, in thousands of dollars:

	Imports 1911	Imports 1912	Exports 1911	Exports 1912
Alberta	9,136	13,722	365	58
Brit'h Columbia	38,164	49,155	23,017	20,273
Manitoba	34,625	42,460	3,135	3,303
New Brunswick	11,464	11,899	28,273	28,980
Nova Scotia	16,748	18,848	20,001	23,569
Ontario	203,215	234,952	93,965	108,555
Pr. Edward Isl.	649	706	436	583
Quebec	135,931	160,451	123,726	123,105
Saskatchewan	10,909	14,236	4,057	4,622
Yukon (ter.)	1,058	953	221	2,275
British prepaid postal parcels	53	100		
	461,951	547,482	297,196	315,317

SHIPPING. The shipping figures given below for fiscal years are exclusive of the coasting trade:

	Entered Vessels	Entered Tons	Cleared Vessels	Cleared Tons
Sea-going				
1901	13,752	7,514,732	12,953	7,028,330
1902	15,339	7,603,034	14,967	7,128,454
1911	15,235	11,919,339	14,709	10,377,847
1912	16,642	12,768,191	16,224	11,821,414
On Inland Waters				
1901	20,814	5,720,575	20,313	5,766,171
1902	23,585	7,595,741	23,822	7,698,175
1911	23,820	13,286,102	23,668	11,846,257
1912	23,235	14,496,915	24,013	13,886,607

In 1912 British vessels entered from sea numbered 2409, of 6,026,767 tons; Canadian, 2845, of 1,517,879 tons; foreign, 3312, of 2,021,130 tons. Of the total entrances from sea, 9247, of 11,854,795 tons, were steam, 7395, of 913,396 tons, sail.

COMMUNICATIONS. The total single-track railway mileage in operation increased from 13,151 on June 30, 1890, to 17,657 in 1900, 20,487 in 1905, 24,731 in 1910, and 25,400 on June 30, 1911. The following figures are for the fiscal years 1910 and 1911 respectively: Gross earnings, $173,956,217 and $188,733,494; working expenses, $120,405,440 and $131,034,785; net earnings, $53,550,777 and $57,698,709. Mileage in operation by provinces in 1911: Alberta, 1494; British Columbia, 1842; Manitoba, 3466; New Brunswick, 1548; Nova Scotia, 1354; Ontario, 8322; Prince Edward Island, 269; Quebec, 3882; Saskatchewan, 3121; Yukon (ter.), 102. Capital expenditure for construction of government railways to March 31, 1911, $261,414,695; capital expenditure for canals, to 1911, $99,311,890. Electric railways (total computed as single track), June 30, 1911, 1587 miles. During the year nearly 400 miles of contracts were let by the Canadian Pacific Railway, and work on most of these was in active progress. These contracts include the Waybourne to Lethbridge line, of 100 miles; the Swift Current extension, 80 miles; the Waybourne to Stirling line, 25 miles, and the Suffield line, 30 miles. Extensions were being made on the Vancouver Island system and active surveys on the western part of the main line, with the view of revising and improving the grades, were in progress. The expenditures for new work during the year were expected to amount to $20,000,000.

Progress continued on the Grand Trunk Pacific Railway, and especially on the eastern or government section. The line from Winnipeg to Cochrane was practically completed at the end of the year, while the section from Moncton to the New Brunswick boundary was finished and rails had been laid nearly 500 miles west from that boundary. Similar progress had been made west of the Ontario boundary, where about 400 miles of rails had been laid. The eastern section also includes the new Quebec bridge, which was somewhat behind the rest of the work, and provision was made for a train ferry until its completion. It was estimated that the expenditures for construction of the eastern portion would amount to over $25,000,000 in 1912. The western section which was being built by the company, had been constructed as far as Tête Jaune Cache by the middle of the year on its way from Prince Rupert to Hazelton. At the end of the year the branches to Moose Jaw, Brandon, Calgary, Battleford, Prince Albert, and the Alberta coal fields were either completed or nearly finished. The Grand Trunk Pacific shares a Union Station at Winnipeg with the Canadian Northern, and this structure was opened in June.

The third of the great transcontinental lines was the Canadian Northern Company, which on its route to the Pacific had over 1000 miles of construction in hand. This line crosses the Rocky Mountains at Yellowhead and then deflects from the Grand Trunk so as to reach Vancouver for its western terminal. At this place there were to be elaborate terminal arrangements, and the line was in progress eastward to meet the construction now carried on in the mountains. The Canadian Northern for its Montreal terminal will work in connection with the Canadian Northern Tunnel and Terminal Company, and use a three-mile double-track tunnel under Mount Royal, in Montreal, so as to gain access to the city and to the wharves. Construction all along the line and especially between Port Arthur and Montreal was reported well in hand, and at the close of the year ending June 30, 1912, it was reported that 586 miles had been added to the system, giving a total average mileage for the year of 3888.

During the year the Algoma Central Railway Company's main line had reached Hobon on the Canadian Pacific, 221 miles north of Sault Ste. Marie. The Kettle Valley Railway in British Columbia was building from Cold Water westward to Hope Mountain, while progress was recorded on the Kootenay Central and on the Pacific and Great Eastern. Work on the Hudson's Bay Railway was begun from Le Pas to Spitlock and a further length had been contracted for. Port Nelson was definitely decided upon as the Hudson Bay terminus in place of Fort Churchill. In the maritime provinces the Atlantic-Quebec and Western Railway was completed.

In 1911, the government telegraphs comprised 4807 miles of line, with 603 offices; chartered companies, 33,905 miles of line and 173,546 miles of wire, with 3249 offices. Post offices in 1911, 13,324.

Finance. Dominion expenditure and revenue for fiscal years ending March 31 (except 1902, which ended June 30) are shown in the table below, in dollars. The various items are indicated as follows: *a* expenditure chargeable to Consolidated Fund, *b* expenditure chargeable to Capital, *c* railway subsidies, *d* other charges, *e* total disbursements; *f* revenue on account of Consolidated Fund; *g* other revenue; *h* total revenue; *i* difference between receipts and expenditures; *j* sinking funds; *k* net difference between receipts and expenditures, i. e., net excess of expenditure (except in 1912, when there was a net excess of receipts).

	1902	1910	1911	1912
a	50,759,392	79,411,747	87,774,198	98,161,441
b	10,078,638	29,756,353	30,852,963	30,939,576
c	2,093,939	2,048,097	1,284,892	859,400
d	1,038,831	4,179,577	2,949,197	7,181,665
e	63,970,800	115,395,774	122,861,250	137,142,082
f	58,050,790	101,503,711	117,780,410	136,108,217
g	1,543	112,765	103,918	....
h	58,052,333	101,616,476	117,884,328	136,108,217
i	5,918,462	13,779,298	4,976,922	1,033,865
j	2,569,381	1,441,031	1,203,416	1,156,456
k	3,349,081	12,338,267	3,773,506	122,591

Principal source of Consolidated Fund receipts in the year ended March 31, 1912: Taxes, $105,847,804 (customs $85,051,872, excise $19,261,662, Chinese revenue, $1,534,270); railways, $11,034,166; posts, $10,492,394; Dominion lands, $3,775,857; interest on investments, $1,281,317; public works, $354,065; canals, $263,717. Leading items of expenditure chargeable against Consolidated Fund: Collection of revenue, $28,256,780 (including railways and canals $12,330,463, posts $9,172,035, customs $2,443,846, and Dominion lands $2,277,100); charges on public debt, $12,706,853 (interest $12,259,397, management $447,457); sinking funds, $1,156,456; subsidies to provinces, $10,281,045; public works, $10,344,487; militia and defense, $7,580,600; civil government, $4,777,678; legislation, $2,439,807. Of the expenditure chargeable to capital ($30,939,576), $21,110,352 was for the National Transcontinental Railway, $4,116,385 for various public works, $2,560,938 for canals, and $1,710,449 for intercolonial and connected railways. Net public debt at end of fiscal years: 1890, $237,533,212; 1900, $265,493,807; 1910, $336,268,546; 1911, $340,042,052; 1912, $339,919,461. The gross public debt on March 31, 1911 and 1912, respectively, was $474,941,487 and $508,338,592, while total assets were $134,899,435 and $168,419,131.

Savings Banks. On March 31, 1912, the 1172 post office savings banks had 147,919 open accounts, with deposits and interest $43,563,764 (average account, $294.51). On the same date, the 18 government savings banks (of which 13 in Nova Scotia) had deposits and interest $14,655,564. Total, $58,219,328, against $58,094,331 March 31, 1911.

Army. Every citizen of Canada between the ages of 18 and 60 is liable to military service under the provisions of the Canadian Militia act of 1904, but up to 1912 there was no necessity for compulsion and the system of cadet and volunteer training flourished so that compulsory service was quite unnecessary. The permanent force which approximates to a regular army was the chief means of instruction, while it was proposed to develop the Kingston Military College into a staff college and have associated with it military colleges in other parts of the Dominion. Progress was being made with the general scheme of reorganization determined on in the preceding years, and at the end of the year, 1912, the established strength of the Canadian active militia for 1912 was reported as follows: Officers, 5202; non-commissioned officers and men, 58,532; making a total of 63,734, with 15,471 horses. On December 31, 1912, the strength of the permanent corps was: Officers, 215; non-commissioned officers and men, 2709, making a total of 2924.

Navy. The department of the Naval Service was created by a law which became effective May 4, 1910. Up to the end of 1912 no ships of fighting value had been acquired except the first-class cruiser *Niobe* (11,000 tons), and the second-class cruiser *Rainbow* (3600 tons). On July 29, 1911, during the gale and fog, the *Niobe* sustained damage by grounding off Cape Sable, N. S. She was repaired at Halifax. In October, 1912, a floating dock, with 27,500 tons' lifting capacity, arrived in the St. Lawrence from Barrow, to be placed at the eastern end of Montreal harbor. There are 24 small vessels for fishing protection, lighthouse and revenue service, etc. In August, 1911, the king approved of the Canadian naval forces receiving the style "The Royal Canadian Navy." See discussion of naval policy under *History* below, and Naval Progress.

Government. The executive government and authority are vested in the king and exercised in his name by a governor-general aided by a privy council, or responsible ministry, which includes 15 heads of departments. Parliament consists of the Senate (87 members nominated for life by the governor-general) and the House of Commons. The latter body is elected by popular vote for five years unless sooner dissolved. Its membership for the period beginning 1911 was 221; under the reapportionment necessitated by the 1911 census, the next Commons will have 231 members (Quebec having a constant representation of 65). Representation by provinces: Alberta, 4 senators and 12 commoners; British Columbia, 3 and 11;

Manitoba, 4 and 15; New Brunswick, 10 and 11; Nova Scotia, 10 and 16; Ontario, 24 and 82; Prince Edward Island, 4 and 3; Quebec, 24 and 65; Saskatchewan, 4 and 15; Yukon (ter.), one commoner; total, 87 and 231. The governor-general in 1912 was Prince Arthur, Duke of Connaught and Strathearn (brother of Edward VII.), who was appointed March 6, and assumed office October 13, 1911. The ministry of Sir Wilfrid Laurier, who as a Liberal had been prime minister since 1896, was succeeded October 10, 1911, by a Conservative ministry under the premiership of Robert Laird Borden; its composition in 1912 was as follows: Prime minister, R. L. Borden; minister of trade and commerce, George Eulas Foster; interior, Dr. William James Roche; public works, Robert Rogers; railways and canals, Francis Cochrane; finance, William Thomas White; postmaster-general, Louis Philippe Pelletier; minister of marine and fisheries, and of the naval service, John Douglas Hazen; justice, Charles Joseph Doherty; militia and defense, Col. Samuel Hughes; secretary of state, Louis Coderre; minister of labor, Thomas Wilson Crothers; inland revenue and mines, Wilfred Bruno Nantel; customs, Dr. John Dowsley Reid; agriculture, Martin Burrell; ministers without portfolios, George Halsey Perley, Albert Edward Kemp, James Alexander Lougheed. Leader of the opposition in the Commons, Sir Wilfrid Laurier.

Each province has an elected legislature and an executive (lieutenant-governor) appointed by the governor-general and aided by a responsible ministry. See articles on the several provinces.

History

Parliament. Parliament was opened on January 10 and closed on April 1. Conflict between the two houses prevented the passage of several measures, the Senate insisting on certain amendments which the House of Commons would not accept. Among the measures thus held up were the highways subsidy bill and the tariff commission bill, the latter providing for a board of three commissioners to be appointed by the governor-general in council to inquire into the industrial conditions of the country. A grain act amending the law regulating storage and distribution of wheat was passed during the session. (See Agriculture.) On February 27 a bill was brought in to extend the limits of Manitoba to Hudson's Strait and to transfer Ungava to Quebec; to Ontario was granted a strip of territory to admit of railway communication with Nelson River or Fort Churchill and Manitoba was to provide terminal facilities with freedom from taxation. The federal subsidy to Manitoba was increased from $833,000 to $1,349,346. Very early in the new administration there was evidence of a breach between the Quebec Nationalists and the Borden government. The Nationalist leaders, having used every effort in vain to force the government into establishing Roman Catholic schools in Keewatin, now began a savage attack on the ministry for refushing to extend the Quebec school system to the new territory added to Manitoba. The Nationalists argued that there was as good reason for establishing separate schools in this territory as in establishing them in the Northwest Territories where, in 1875, before the new provinces of Alberta and Saskatchewan were created, such schools had been established. The government's attitude toward the marriage question (see below), also alienated the Nationalists. In parliamentary circles at the close of the year the chief subject of discussion was the question of naval defense. See paragraph below on *Naval Policy*.

The Marriage Law. Early in the year, a bill concerning civil and religious marriage was introduced in Parliament. It provided that a marriage performed by a competent authority could not be invalidated by any law or canonical decree or custom of any province. Parliament submitted to the Supreme Court the questions whether such a law was within the competence of Parliament, and whether the Quebec law invalidates a marriage not contracted before a Roman Catholic priest, though otherwise legally binding. The subject came to public attention in the famous Hebert case in Quebec. A marriage celebrated by a Protestant minister in 1907 was afterwards annulled by the archbishop, in accordance with the Papal decree of *Ne Temere*, and his action was ratified by the Superior Court. On February 22, however, the decision was reversed on appeal, the judge declaring that any officer qualified to perform marriage can legally unite people of any religious faith. The question involved was whether the authority of the *Ne Temere* decree was binding in Quebec. According to this judgment the *Ne Temere* decree has no civil effect, and in general, the canon law of the Roman Catholic Church is not binding on the state. Appeal was taken from this decision to the Imperial Privy Council. The decision of the Supreme Court on the questions submitted by Parliament pronounced the latter body incompetent to pass a general marriage law for the whole Dominion, declaring the solemnization, including the form and ceremony, to be within the exclusive legislative competence of the several provinces; but that the law of Quebec does not invalidate marriages not contracted before a Roman Catholic priest. The decision of the Imperial Privy Council on July 21 confirmed the judgment of the Supreme Court, denying the competence of Parliament in the matter.

Naval Policy. There was much discussion during the year of the government's naval policy, especially on the occasion of the official visit of Mr. Borden and six of his colleagues to London at the end of June. The chief purpose of the visit was to confer with the British admiralty as to the best means of coöperating with the imperial government in the defense of the empire. During the naval conference in London between the Canadian and imperial ministries there was evidence of strong popular feeling on the subject of Canadian naval policy. The public became more insistent on Canada's assumption of responsiblity for naval defense. It was said that Canada was lagging behind New Zealand and Australia. It was loudly demanded that Canada should do her share. The new Conservative government decided to submit to Parliament, when it assembled in November, certain emergency proposals in regard to the navy. In October, after this determination was made known, Mr. F. D. Monk, the Nationalist member of the cabinet, resigned his portfolio of public works, having steadily insisted that before the government took action on the navy it should order a referendum. The

Conservative party came into power on the understanding, in the words of Mr. Borden, that it would "consult with the British government in order to ascertain whether or not the conditions existing were or were not so grave as to require immediate and effective aid." If necessary, aid would be given, and if Parliament would not concur, the matter would be referred to the people. As to a permanent policy, when that had been developed and explained, the subject would be referred to the people. On December 5, Mr. Borden set forth the government's policy in an address to the House of Commons at Ottawa. The main features were: The contribution of three dreadnoughts, at a cost of $35,000,000, to be built in the United Kingdom to form a part of the battle line of the British navy, and to be directed and maintained by the British admiralty. Later, if a Canadian navy is decided upon, these vessels may be returned to Canada by the admiralty. Concerning Canada's voice in imperial naval affairs, an arrangement was proposed whereby a Canadian minister should take part in the proceedings of the British committee of imperial defense. The greater cost of construction in Canada, estimated at $12,000,000, was the reason for having the vessels built in the United Kingdom, but the admiralty was ready to order a number of smaller vessels to be built in Canadian yards. Mr. Borden declared that the three new dreadnoughts were to be the "largest and strongest ships of war that science can build or money supply." In the course of his address he read a memorandum from the admiralty which set forth the needs of the British navy and dwelt especially on the recent German policy of naval expansion. In general the attitude of the Liberal opposition was that there was no emergency which called for this departure from the principle of a strictly Canadian navy. On the other hand, the government contended that the situation was sufficiently grave to demand immediate action.

Sir Wilfrid Laurier offered an amendment on December 12, declaring for a Canadian navy with fleets on each coast, to be manned and maintained by Canada, and for Canadian shipyards. He objected to the policy of turning over the vessels to be equipped, manned, and maintained by the British admiralty. The matter was still under discussion when Parliament adjourned, December 18, to meet on January 14, 1913. See NAVAL PROGRESS.

THE LANGUAGE QUESTION. Complaints of inefficiency and of discrimination against the English language in the bi-lingual schools of Ontario led to investigation of the subject by a government commission, which reported in the autumn that these charges were well founded. It declared that in over thirty of these schools the Roman Catholic catechism was taught in violation of the rules, that teachers lacked the requisite training, that French was used in many schools more extensively than English, and that many teachers could not speak English with any facility. Lack of funds accounted largely for these defects. New regulations were made after the publication of the report providing for more thorough teaching of English in the bi-lingual schools. They required additional inspection, the withholding of state aid if satisfactory English teaching was not provided, that teaching in English should be begun on entering school, and that French should be used as the language of instruction only in the first form.

An important Congress of the French Language was held in the summer and one of its chief purposes was to protect the French interests as regards these schools in Ontario. It was proposed that the 3,000,000 French of North America should unite for their rights and religion. It was declared that the life and unity of the French race depended upon the preservation of their language, and their right to speak and conserve it had long been recognized as an unwritten law. They protested against "the cynically brutal" attempt to assimilate the French of Ontario. The congress passed resolutions to the effect that: (1) French people in Quebec wishing to migrate should be encouraged to settle in the west and form colonies; (2) the French of Quebec and Ontario should unite for their common interests; (3) that all pupils of French schools in America should pray for the French schools in Ontario; (4) that the French press should denounce the reduction in the schools of Ontario and the double inspection; (5) that the French of Alberta should insist on a better status for French in the bi-lingual schools there; (6) that in any bi-lingual school the language instruction should be that of the majority and that pupils should be permitted to choose the language for written examinations; (7) that in Quebec the teaching of English should be improved. In the autumn there was considerable opposition in Ontario to the new school regulations.

MISCELLANEOUS. On June 30, Regina, the capital of Saskatchewan, with a population of 17,000, was struck by a cyclone which inflicted serious loss of life and damage to property. Thirty deaths were reported and 150 persons were said to have been injured. Many buildings were completely destroyed. The damage was roughly estimated at $6,000,000. On April 9 Canada signed a trade agreement with the West Indies and South America, to go into effect January 1, 1913. An agreement between representatives of Canada and the West Indies was signed in April, whereby mutual trade preferences were to be given and arrangements made for improving steamship and cable communication.

For notes of other matters relating to Canada not described here see MUNICIPAL GOVERNMENT; CITY PLANNING; ARBITRATION AND CONCILIATION, INDUSTRIAL; EMPLOYERS' LIABILITY; EXPLORATION.

CANADIAN CONSERVATION COMMISSION. See AGRICULTURE.

CANADIAN NORTHERN RAILWAY. See CANADA.

CANADIAN PACIFIC RAILWAY. See CANADA.

CANADIAN RECIPROCITY. See PAPER, and PRESIDENTIAL CAMPAIGN.

CANADIAN SURVEY. See EXPLORATION.

CANALEJAS Y MENDEZ, JOSÉ. Prime minister of Spain, assassinated November 12, 1912. He was born in 1859. His public career began at the age of eighteen, when he delivered a course of lectures at the Academy of Jurisprudence in Madrid. The following year he made addresses before political meetings in many of the larger Spanish cities, promulgating strongly liberal ideals of jurisprudence and government. At the age of 25 he was sent to the Cortes from the District of Soria and he took his seat in that body among the advanced Liberals. During the existence of the ephemeral republic which followed the resignation of King Amadeo of Savoy he served as subsecretary of the president. He had taken a prominent part in the overthrow of the monarchy and his identification with the cause of the republic gained for him an unpopularity with the crown and its representatives which it took him years to outlive. In spite of this he rose rapidly. He served as minister of finance and justice in several cabinets although he was not welcome at the Royal Palace. He formed the Radical Party which was made up largely of advocates of State socialism and this further widened the cleavage between him and the rulers of the government. It was not until 1900, however, that he became an important national figure. General Azcárraga was prime minister and headed a reactionary and clerical ministry. The Cortes was the scene of frequent hostile demonstrations against the government and this was accentuated by outbreaks in Barcelona. Canalejas urged in the Cortes that war must be waged on Clericalism. Immediately the Socialists and Republicans who had not hitherto dared openly to voice their convictions rallied around him and hailed him as the man of the hour.

In 1902 he accepted the portfolio of agriculture in the cabinet of Premier Sagasta and in this office he introduced many reforms for the working classes. This added largely to his popularity among the Liberals. He demanded that the new cabinet should meet formally and sign a document setting forth in unmistakable language the position of the ministers on all political issues of the day. He denounced the tenant system of land-holding and the concentration of lands into fewer and fewer hands. In 1904 in an oration which is memorable in Spain, he defended the Parliamentary immunity which the Conservatives were trying to have suspended in order to further their reactionary designs.

In 1905 King Alfonso, who had hitherto been hostile in his attitude toward Canalejas and looked upon him as a dangerous man, heard the latter make an address at the Academy of Jurisprudence. Upon hearing this speech the king revised his opinion, and to this change in his attitude was due largely the election of Canalejas as president of the Cortes in 1906 while the Liberals were in power and during the ministries of Morot and Lopez. From this time there began a cordial friendship between King Alfonso and Canalejas which lasted unbroken until the latter's death. King Alfonso in 1910 created a sensation when he asked Canalejas to become premier and form a ministry. It was the first time that such an advanced Radical had been elevated to the premiership. Canalejas had a difficult task in assembling a cabinet and he once resigned, but was induced to reconsider and before long secured a firm hold on the conduct of public affairs. His trouble was due chiefly to his programme for the separation of church and state and his efforts to accomplish this eventually brought about a rupture of the relations between the Vatican and the Spanish government. He had not been premier long before a royal order was issued whereby non-Catholic religious organizations were permitted to display emblems on the walls of their churches. Next the premier, acting in full accord with the king, introduced into the Cortes a measure which aimed to reduce the number of Catholic religious orders in the country each of which was free from taxation. This greatly offended the Vatican and precipitated the final struggle. Negotiations followed between the Pope and the government and after a bitter controversy during which a bill was introduced in the Cortes forbidding the organization of any new religious organization, the Council recalled its ambassador to Rome. Canalejas was then left in control of the situation. There were many demonstrations by Catholics throughout the country and the prime minister even went so far as to suppress meetings held by them. On December 23, 1910, the entrance of any new religious organization into Spain was forbidden for two years or until the Concordat of 1851 was revised. Following this there were passed government acts which authorized religious societies without admitting the validity of perpetual vows, but prohibiting them from holding real estate except what was necessary for their actual requirements. All congregations were liable to taxation and no foreigners were permitted to organize religious bodies until they took the oath of allegiance and became Spanish citizens. Negotiations with Rome were resumed and the associations bill was submitted to the Cortes without any reference to the wishes of the Pope, on May 8, 1911.

On April 1, 1911, Canalejas resigned the premiership as the result of an attempt to revise the decision in the case of Ferrer, the anarchist philosopher who was sentenced to death for his part in the revolutionary uprising at Barcelona. He was directed by the king, however, to form a new ministry and thus remained in power.

The troubles in Morocco in 1911 brought much trouble to the premier owing to the sharp division of public opinion. As to the conduct of the campaign, the Republicans and Socialists opposed his programme. The doctrine of anti-militarism was preached throughout the country and in August, 1911, Spain suffered from a long series of strikes, involving railroads, mines and industries. Canalejas charged that the Radicals, Socialists, and Anarchists were at the bottom of the plots to bring about trouble and he again showed his fearlessness by putting down disorder. On November 12, 1912, he was shot and killed by an anarchist in the streets of Madrid. For events of 1912, see SPAIN, *History*.

Canalejas was a conspicuous figure in public life for thirty-five years and was undoubtedly one of the strongest figures in Spanish political history in modern times. He showed great wisdom and patriotism and in spite of inborn Radicalism was cautious and moderate in action. He had undertaken economic reforms in Spain which promised to lift that country to the level of most European nations. These included the building of railroads and the development of industries in all parts of the country. He was a man of wealth, but of simple habits. His leisure time was spent with his books or in hunting. In 1897 just previous to the outbreak of the Spanish-American War he visited New York for the ostensible purpose of learning the opinion of the American people and the administration in regard to the existing situation in Cuba.

CANALS. The construction of the Panama Canal which made more than its usual progress in 1912 was naturally the most important event in the construction of artificial waterways throughout the world. This will be found treated elsewhere in the YEAR BOOK under its own title. (See PANAMA CANAL.) No other works throughout the world were comparable with this project, but at the same time important extensions and improvements were in progress. These are briefly summarized in the following paragraphs:

NEW YORK BARGE CANAL. During 1912 the progress of construction on the New York State barge canal system continued and at the end of the year the value of the work completed was approximately $54,000,000, or more than 60 per cent. of the total construction. So great was the progress that speculation was aroused whether the barge canal could be constructed within the appropriation of $101,000,000, the sum authorized in 1903 for the improvement of the Erie, Champlain, and Oswego canals, and that of $7,000,000, appropriated in 1909 for the improvement of the Cayuga and Seneca Canal. Up to October 1, 1912, the work placed under contract amounted to $77,029,116, and the work actually completed amounted to $50,684,369. Plans were prepared during the year for the remainder of the contracts so that the entire waterway would be ready for navigation by the year 1915. In his annual report for 1912 the State engineer stated that the work could not be completed within the original appropriations and that further action should be taken by the Assembly to provide for the completion along the original lines.

In 1912 a break of considerable size occurred in the canal at Irondequoit Creek where the barge canal followed the alignment of the old canal. This break interfered with navigation for about six weeks and required the construction of a temporary trough and some modifications in the plans for the work at this point.

CAPE COD CANAL. During 1912 work actively progressed on the Cape Cod Canal between Cape Cod and Buzzards Bay which involved the construction of 8 miles of canal from shore line to shore line or of 13 miles from the 30-foot depth contour in Barnstable Bay to the same depth in Buzzards Bay. This involved the dredging of approach channels 300 feet wide in the former bay and 25 feet in width in the latter. The canal has a depth at mean low water of 25 feet and the banks where constructed through sand will have a slope of 1 to 3. In soft or exposed places the banks are to be rip-rapped from 6 feet vertically below low-water to 6 feet above high-water. There was also in course of construction a 3000-foot breakwater to protect the eastern terminus of the canal.

During the year 1912 about 2,600,000 cubic yards of material were excavated and removed. The breakwater at the Sandwich end was carried to its full length, 3000 feet from the shore, and at the end of the year was substantially completed with the exception of some dressing of the slope. During the year the placing of rip-rap on the banks to protect them from wave action of passing vessels was begun and was completed for a length of about 1 1-2 miles at the easterly end. The re-locating of the old Colony Railroad was completed and there was but one railroad crossing on the canal and that was at Buzzards Bay. An additional highway bridge at Sagamore similar to that at Bourne was finished during the year and the various changes in the highways were adopted by the local authorities with the object of giving a continuous east and west highway on both sides of the canal. These new highways, with the exception of one small piece, were completed. At the end of the year it was estimated that a greater rate of progress than previously would be maintained and the canal completed in the year 1914.

The equipment at work on the canal and channels included 4 steam shovels and a 16-inch suction dredge inland, 2 dipper dredges in Barnstable Bay, and 3 dipper dredges in Buzzards Bay.

WELLAND CANAL. The improvement of this important waterway was in progress, and the completion of the entire project was estimated to cost some $45,000,000 and result in a saving of eight hours' time in the trip between Port Colburne and Fort Dalhousie, as the number of locks was being reduced from 22 to 7. The depth of water in the canal was being increased from 15 to 25 feet and to 30 feet in the locks. The canal itself was being widened from 150 to 200 feet.

CANADIAN SAULT SAINTE MARIE CANAL. Progress was made during the year on the new lock for the short canal between Lake Superior and Lake Huron on the Canadian side at Sault Sainte Marie. This lock was 1715 feet in length, or 1350 feet between the inner gates, and 50 feet in width. It had a depth of 24 1-2 feet as against 18 feet in the older locks, but this increase would only be useful after the dredging of the lock channels to a depth of 21 feet, which had been maintained. The new Canadian lock was to cost almost $10,000,000.

During the year 1912, 22,778 ships of 65,736,-807 net tons register passed through the canals at Sault Sainte Marie, of which number 14,-916 of 30,947,133 net tons used the United States canal and 7861 vessels of 25,789,674 tons used the Canadian canal. The total freight movement was 72,472,676 net tons, of which 32,-824,815 tons were carried through the United States canal and 39,647,861 tons through the Canadian canal. These figures indicate that while more vessels used the American canal, yet a larger class of vessels carrying a greater portion of freight was using the Canadian canal.

PROPOSED GERMAN CANAL. A commission appointed to consider the construction of a canal so as to render communication between interior cities and some German port independent of Holland reported during the year. This project was considered of great commercial importance, as much of the trade of Germany has had to pass through Dutch seaports. It was proposed to start a canal at Wesel on the Rhine and extend it in a northerly direction between that river and the Netherlands frontier, joining the Ems a few miles above its mouth. The estimated cost of the project was about $55,000,000, and in addition to the commercial advantages of the waterway it would assist in reclaiming a large area of fen land through which it would pass. An alternative proposition was to start a canal at Cologne on the Rhine and by constructing a channel 23 feet deep make it possible for seagoing ships to reach that city. The objections to this plan were both the great number of roads and railways to be crossed and the great cost of its execution.

Canalization of the Main River. Since this river was first made navigable from its junction with the Rhine and Frankfort in 1886, various improvements had been made so that by 1912 it was in regular use for boats of 1500 tons, drawing 8 feet, as far as Hanau. It was proposed to extend the canal from that city to Aschaffenburg at an estimated expense of about $7,000,000. The river traffic since its canalization has increased annually, and the harbor facilities at Frankfort were considered quite inadequate to meet the demands of the traffic. It was decided to extend the present basin at an expense of about $17,000,000, which includes the cost of the land required.

At Berlin two new basins were to be added to increase the extent of harbor accommodations.

Improvement of the Seine. In 1912 nothing had been accomplished to protect Paris from floods, which in previous years had occasioned great damage. It was proposed to raise the quays and facilitate the flow of water through the city by widening the narrow parts of the river and deepening it between Suresnes and Bougival, at an estimated cost of about $7,000,000. The damage of the previous great inundation involving an expenditure of about $400,000 had been made good, but no advance was made in the various schemes previously suggested for dredging and improving the river, both in view of flood and to increase its commercial availability.

CANARY ISLANDS. A Spanish possession made up of islands lying off the northwest coast of Africa. Santa Cruz (Teneriffe) is the seat of government and Las Palmas the leading town. Area, 2808 square miles; population, 403,908.

CANCER. Among the interesting developments of the year in cancer investigation were the experiments of Wasserman and his colleagues with the combination of selenium and eosin. Working on the principles of chemotherapy already laid down by Ehrlich, these observers obtained remarkable results in the cure of experimental tumors of mice. The problem was primarily that of finding a substance which had a greater affinity and toxicity for parasitic cells than for the normal cells of the host. Starting with the accidental observation that salts of the rare metals selenium and tellurium, when brought into contact with tumors, are taken up selectively by the tumor cells, they set out to discover h w these metals might be introduced into tumors in living animals and exert their specific toxic action. A compound of selenium and eosin was finally evolved which, injected daily into mice afflicted with cancer, caused a softening of the tumor by the third day, and total absorption often by the tenth day. When the tumors were large there occurred severe, even fatal, intoxication, attributed to the rapid absorption of the products of tissue disintegration. The animals which recovered were observed for months, and in cases where the tumor totally disappeared under the influence of the injections no recurrence took place. But where the tumors were not completely destroyed rapid recurrence was the rule. These experiments were performed with four different varieties of carcinoma and one of sarcoma, none of which is curable by any other form of treatment yet devised. Experiments with two spontaneous tumors in mice also produced complete cures. These experiments show that selenium-eosin has a definite affinity for mouse-cancer cells, being deposited about the muclei and producing complete disintegration of the cells. The investigators take pains, however, to point out that the extreme toxicity of selenium combined with the harmful effects of rapid absorption of disintegrating tumors makes the treatment too hazardous to try upon human beings. They say that their work "merely establishes an essential scientific fact, namely, that the existing view that it may be possible to have chemical substances specifically pass out of the vessels into a tumor and destroy it, is untenable. We wish most particularly, in order to prevent false hopes and excitement among persons with tumors, to emphatically point out that at the present time we have no evidence that this substance will act in the same way with human cancers. We have not yet investigated this question. It may well seem not impossible that an essential beginning has been made and a solid foundation established, extension of which along these lines may yield progress in human therapy."

While noteworthy, Wasserman's experiments and their results must not be taken as settling firmly the parasitic theory of cancerous disease. The trend of thought based on all authoritative investigation is away from cancer infectivity. Other efforts along the same lines of investigation were made by Neuberg, Caspari, and Lohe, who worked on the hypothesis that the greater autolytic power of tumor tissue as compared with normal tissue must be due either to a direct increase of certain ferments or to a defect in protective elements, and tried to produce an active autolysis *in vitro* by the addition of colloids of a number of the heavy metals. These investigators tried to obtain salts and other compounds of heavy metals in such form as to be nontoxic for the host and yet to exercise a direct action on the tumor. They employed organic chemical compounds of a rather complex nature (the exact composition of which they refuse to divulge) of the heavy metals, such as lead, silver, arsenic, antimony, vanadium, mercury, copper, gold, etc. Cobalt and silver were found to yield the most marked effects.

The reaction following intravenous injection is described as most striking and rapid. Within a minute afterward the tumor may become hyperemic and a condition of stasis so extreme may develop that at times a serous exudate oozes from the surface. Hemorrhages may occur within the tumor, which in twenty-four hours becomes soft and fluctuating. Primary and transplanted carcinomas of mice, rat sarcomas, and an adenocarcinoma of a dog all yielded readily to the treatment and disappeared completely.

Of the many investigations dealing with the essential nature of malignant tumors those of Peyton Rous, of New York, were most significant. This investigator proved conclusively that sarcoma may be produced by injecting the fluid obtained from a tumor after it has been freed from every trace of tumor cells. This result is interpreted as due to a living virus so small that it passes through rather coarse filters, though it is not impossible that some non-living substance produced by the cells in the animal body may be involved. At any rate, this is so far the only demonstration that a growth corresponding in every characteristic to a malignant tumor can be propagated by cell-free material, except possibly the remarkable thyroid proliferations that occur epidemically in fish hatcheries, and as to the real nature of which there is some doubt.

To this evidence in favor of the infective theory of the causation of cancer may be added that derived from the study of plant tumors by Erwin F. Smith, of the bureau of plant industry in the United States Department of Agriculture. Smith is convinced that the disease of plants known as crown-gall is in reality a plant cancer. The growth is cellular and infiltrative in character; it sends out long strands of new tissue in the course of which secondary growths may develop having the same structure as the parent growth, so that when the primary growth is in the stem secondary growths in the leaf do not have the structure of the leaf but of the stem. These growths differ from animal cancer in that discontinuous metastasis does not seem to occur, metastatic growths being connected with the primary growth by strands of new tissue, but Smith points out that since plants lack a rapid circulation discontinuous metastasis can hardly be expected. The disease is caused by a definite bacterium *(Bacterium tumefaciens)*, discovered by Smith, which occurs in the cells of the growths and produces typical crown-galls when inoculated into certain plants. Smith believes that this bacterium stimulates the cells to rapid and indefinite proliferation, and that the facts discovered in regard to crown-gall or plant cancer have a direct bearing on human cancer. A similar growth in the sugar beet shows a similar analogy in structure and development to human and animal cancer.

If the view advanced by Smith is accepted, to him will belong the credit of having discovered the precise cause of a cancerous growth; but on account of the absence of complete analogy between the structure of plants and that of animals, the question whether crown-gall is a cancer or not in the ordinary sense of the word must for the present remain unsettled. See *Bulletins 213* and *255*, Bureau of Plant Industry, United States Department of Agriculture.

The electro-therapeutic treatment of cancer has received a new impetus within the past year in consequence of the visit to this country of de Keating-Hart, of Paris, and of his demonstration at the New York Skin and Cancer Hospital of the two methods evolved by him, viz., fulguration and thermo-radiotherapy. Dr. Bainbridge, who as secretary of the committee on scientific research of the Skin and Cancer Hospital has tested many proposed surgical and non-surgical methods of treating cancer, is now giving a thorough test to both of the de Keating-Hart methods. In a paper read before the American Electro-therapeutic Association in September, Bainbridge gave a preliminary report of this work, stating that while it is yet too early to make definite predictions concerning the value of the methods there is enough of good in them to warrant the careful test to which they are being subjected by him and his staff.

Fulguration (de Keating-Hart). This consists in the application, from a specially constructed apparatus, of long sparks (ten to twelve centimeters) of a unipolar current, of high frequency, high tension, and relatively low amperage. After as thorough surgical removal as possible of the macroscopic evidences of cancer the wound is "bombarded" with the fulguration sparks. The application is made by means of a special electrode, in the form of a sound, consisting of a smooth, metallic mandrel, or obturator, which works snugly within an insulated tube of hard rubber. By means of bellows a current of carbon dioxid, or sterilized cooled air, is driven through the rubber tube, the purpose of this being to prevent a rise in the temperature of the column of air within the electrode and to remove coagulable liquids from the immediate field of contact. The length of the spark is controlled by the withdrawal to a greater or less degree of the metallic obturator. The electrode is kept in constant motion during the fulguration process in order to prevent burning at any given point. The dosage, or duration of application of the sparks upon a given point, may be generally stated as "ten minutes of fulguration for an area of ten square centimeters." From this it will be seen that the de Keating-Hart fulguration is distinctly not a destructive method. In this regard it is to be distinguished from the so-called "destructive fulguration," "high-frequency cauterization," "high-frequency desiccation," and other methods in which short sparks of a bipolar current of high-frequency, low tension, and relatively high amperage are employed.

The theory upon which the de Keating-Hart fulguration method has been developed is that "the *unipolar long spark of high frequency and high tension acts not upon the neoplasm but upon the soil on which the neoplasm has developed.*" In other words, it is "in no sense a destroyer of tissue, but a *modifier* of trophic nerve centres."

Thermo-radiotherapy is based upon the premise that, "other conditions being equal, the radiosensitiveness of tissues depends upon their temperature." It consists, therefore, in the application of X-rays immediately after or coincidentally with the warming of the tissues by fulguration or other means. Heat is usually applied, according to the nature and location of the tumor, (1) by the injection into the neoplasm (sarcoma) of hot physiological salt solution; (2) by irrigations with warm fluids (in cancer of rectum, vagina, stomach); (3) by passing a high-frequency current through needles thrust into the skin or through a flat electrode placed on the surface of the tumor (in tumors of woody consistency). In order to obviate the danger of X-ray dermatitis in the treatment of deep-seated tumors, the surface over the tumor is cooled by means of cracked ice wrapped in cotton, or by blowing air upon the surface which is first dampened.

Whereas it is claimed by de Keating-Hart that cancer may be cured and recurrence prevented by fulguration, thermo-radiotherapy is employed solely as a palliative measure.

CAPE COD CANAL. See Canals.

CAPE COLONY. See CAPE OF GOOD HOPE PROVINCE.

CAPE OF GOOD HOPE PROVINCE. One of the four original provinces of the Union of South Africa (see SOUTH AFRICA, UNION OF). Capetown, the capital, had, according to the census of 1911, with suburbs, 161,579 (85,442 whites); Capetown municipality had 67,159 (29,863 whites). Kimberley and Beaconsfield, 44,433 (17,507 whites): Kimberley municipality, 29,525 (13,598); Beaconsfield municipality, 14,294 (3404); Kenilworth, 614. Port Elizabeth, 30,688; with suburbs, 37,063 (20,007 whites). East London, 20,867; with suburbs, 24,606 (14,899 whites). Grahamstown, 13,830; Paarl, 11,018; Simonstown, 4751; Vryburg, 2461; Mafeking, 2296. Of the total population, Europeans form about one-quarter and the colored races three-quarters; one-fifth of the population is urban. For area, population, production, and trade, see SOUTH AFRICA, UNION OF. Of the total population, 1,735,491 (859,716 males) were unable to read or write. Protestants outnumbered those of other sects, and Catholics, Mohammedans, and Jews followed in the order named; over one million were classed as of no religion. The amount of public revenue for the eleven months ending May 30, 1910, was £7,747,332; the expenditure, £7,611,298; customs revenue, £1,248,322; public debt outstanding May 30, 1910, £48,240,891. Administrator (1912), Sir N. F. de Waal.

CAPE VERDE ISLANDS. A Portuguese colony off the west coast of Africa, having a total area of 1475 square miles and a population (1909) of 147,424. Praia (São Thiago) is the capital.

CAR CONSTRUCTION. See RAILWAYS.

CAREY, ASA BACON. An American soldier, died April 4, 1912. He was born in Windham county, Conn., in 1835 and graduated from the United States Military Academy in 1858. In the same year he was appointed second lieutenant in the 7th Infantry. At the beginning of the Civil War he was made first lieutenant in the 13th Infantry and in the same year was appointed to be captain. He was promoted to be major and paymaster in 1867, lieutenant-colonel and deputy paymaster in 1895, colonel and assistant paymaster-general in 1898 and brigadier-general and paymaster-general in 1899. In the same year he was retired by operation of law. In 1862 he was brevetted major for gallantry and meritorious services in the campaign against the Indians in New Mexico. He received a brevet for lieutenant-colonel for services against the Navajo Indians in 1865. He was the author of *Legislative History of the Pay Department of the United States Army*.

CAREY ACT. See IRRIGATION, and LANDS, PUBLIC.

CARINTHIA. See AUSTRIA-HUNGARY, *Area and Population*.

CARLETON, WILL. An American poet, died December 18, 1912. He was born in Hudson, Michigan in 1845 and graduated from Hillsdale College in 1869. For several years after leaving college he engaged in newspaper work in Detroit, Chicago, Boston, and New York. Nearly his whole life was given up to the writing of poetry, chiefly in the ballad form and his writings met with a large sale. He was well known as a writer and lecturer. For several years prior to his death he was editor of *Everywhere*, a monthly magazine. Among his best known works are: *Farm Ballads; Farm Legends; Farm Festivals; Young Folks' Rhymes; City Ballads; City Legends; City Festivals; Songs of Two Centuries; Poems for Young Americans; A Thousand Thoughts; Correct Affinities*, and *Ghosts, or Dreams?*

CARNEGIE, ANDREW. See GIFTS AND BEQUESTS.

CARNEGIE FOUNDATION. See UNIVERSITIES AND COLLEGES.

CARNEGIE INSTITUTE OF TECHNOLOGY. An institution for higher technical education in Pittsburgh, Pa., founded by Andrew Carnegie in 1900. Until 1912 it was known as the "Carnegie Technical Schools." In that year it was incorporated under the present title. The enrollment for 1912-13 was 2700 students from 37 States and 21 foreign countries. The institute consists of four separate schools, each with its own faculty, building, and student body. These are the School of Applied Science, School of Applied Design, School of Applied Industries, and the Margaret Morrison Carnegie School for Women. In connection with the institute is operated Camp Louise Carnegie, which is situated near Pittsburgh on the Allegheny River. This is a 750-acre engineering camp where students in certain courses are stationed for their field work. The endowment of the institute, contributed wholly by Mr. Carnegie, amounts to $7,000,000, and about $4,000,000 has been spent for building and equipment. Director, Arthur Arton Hamerschlag, Sc. D., LL. D.

CARNEGIE INSTITUTION OF WASHINGTON. Investigations were carried on throughout the year in all departments of research into which the work of this institution is divided. During the year many specialists were invited to become associated with each of the departments for limited periods of time. Eight such specialists were connected with the departments during 1912 by direct appointment of the executive committee.

DEPARTMENT OF BOTANICAL RESEARCH. The work of this department centres in the Desert Laboratory, Tucson, Ariz., but the work was extended through 1912 to include certain parts of the desert of Northern Africa. In the early winter of 1911-12 Dr. Cannon carried on investigations in the deserts of Algeria, and during the winter of 1911-12 Director MacDougall in the Libyan desert. Studies were continued at the Desert Laboratory, at the Carmel Laboratory on the Carmel coast, at the Salton Sea, and at various substations, where observations were made on the phenomena presented by plants under varying conditions. The desiccation of the Salton Sea, now under observation, presents many instructive conditions which are being carefully studied in their climatic, biological, and physical aspects. One of the most important investigations undertaken during the year was that of a comprehensive study of the cactus plants. In this study Professor N. L. Britton, director of the New York Botanical Garden, and Dr. J. N. Rose, of the Smithsonian Institution, coöperated.

DEPARTMENT OF EXPERIMENTAL EVOLUTION. The advances made by this department during the year were chiefly along the lines of study in cytology, in the chemistry of pigmentation, in the factors of mutation, and in the problems of human heredity. These studies were carried on by the aid of experiments with plants and animals and by the aid of data concerning human traits and their transmission through successive generations. The director of the institution, Dr. Woodward, gave much of his time to studies in human heredity. In this he made use of his connection with the Eugenics Record Office, whose work was liberally supported by Mrs. E. H. Harriman and Mr. John D. Rockefeller.

DEPARTMENT OF ECONOMICS AND SOCIOLOGY. The work of this department has now reached such a stage of advancement that the time of its completion depends mainly on the amount of leisure the collaborators may obtain for consecutive attention to their several contributions to the *Economic History of the United States.*

GEOPHYSICAL LABORATORY. This department issued during the year twenty-six publications. Two of the most notable of these were *High Temperature Gas Thermometry* and *The Methods of Petrographic-Microscopic Research.* Among the more interesting of the investigations of the laboratory are those of the physics and chemistry of active volcanoes, which were carried on during the summer of 1912. Members of the staff descended into the crater of Kilauea and collected considerable quantities of gas as it emerged from the liquid lavas of the crater.

DEPARTMENT OF HISTORICAL RESEARCH. This department is chiefly concerned with the preparation of publications, and the most important issued during the year was the *Guide to the Manuscript Material Relating to American History in German State Archives,* prepared by Professor Marion D. Learned. Two other volumes, *Guide to the Materials for American History, to 1873, in the Public Record Office of Great Britain* and *Guide to the Materials for the History of the United States in the Principal Archives* of Mexico were in press at the end of the year. Progress was made on materials for American history in the archives of Paris. Search was also made in several other European cities for sources of American history. The work of editing the series of *Letters of Delegates to the Continental Congress* was continued during the year, as was labor on the compilation of *European Treaties Having a Bearing on United States History.*

DEPARTMENT OF MARINE BIOLOGY. Investigations were carried on chiefly by the vessel *Anton Dohrn* in the Gulf and West Indian region. During February and March, 1912, a temporary laboratory was established at Montego Bay, Jamaica, where important researches were conducted. In May the director and three collaborators visited the Bahamas, making a successful cruise of 517 miles with the *Anton Dohrn.* Many papers of interest and value were issued from this department during the year.

DEPARTMENT OF MERIDIAN ASTROMETRY. Particular attention was given in this department to studies of stellar motion, for which the extensive data accumulated by the department are furnishing evidence. Special attention was also given to the reduction of meridian observations made in 1911 in São Luis, Argentina.

NUTRITION LABORATORY. Many interesting studies were carried on by this laboratory during the year. One of the most interesting of these was that of the metabolism of a subject who underwent a prolonged fast extending to thirty-one days, without food, and who drank only distilled water during that period. Another noteworthy investigation was that of metabolism during severe muscular work. Many important papers were published in the journals of the laboratory during 1912.

DEPARTMENT OF TERRESTRIAL MAGNETISM. Satisfactory progress was made by this department during the year in its magnetic survey of the globe. By means of the non-magnetic ship *Carnegie* it is now easier to make a magnetic survey of the ocean areas than of the land areas. On February 3, 1912, the *Carnegie* reached Manila after a circuit of the Indian Ocean. From Manila she proceeded to Suva, thence to Tahiti, and at the end of the year 1912 was *en route* to Coronel, Chile. Unexpectedly large errors were found in the best magnetic charts of the Indian Ocean and in some parts of the Pacific Ocean. Observations by this department were carried on simultaneously on land areas embracing portions of five continents in about twenty different countries. Many noteworthy series of transcontinental stations have been completed. The first volume of researches of the department, giving the results of land observations from the time of its establishment in 1905 to the end of the year 1910, was in press at the end of the year. The final computations of the ocean observations made during the various cruises of the *Galilee* and the *Carnegie* were well advanced for a second volume during the year. Many improvements in instrumental appliances were made in response to needs and suggestions arising from the extensive experience of the department on land and sea. One of the most important of these new appliances is that called an "earth inductor," which permits the measurement of the dip of the magnetic needle with decreased labor.

SOLAR OBSERVATORY. Effective progress was made during the year in many branches of solar and stellar research. The new tower telescope was completed and important auxiliary apparatus has been added to the equipment of the 60-inch reflector. This 150-foot tower telescope with its spectrograph and spectroheliograph was tested and found to be quite up to expectations. Two research associates, Professor Kapteyn, of Gröningen, and Professor Stormer, of Christiania, took part in the work of the observatory during the year. The total amount of the expenditures of the institution in 1912 was $1,147,937. The total receipts amounted to $1,240,308. At a meeting of the board of trustees held on December 13, 1912, appropriations amounting to $1,318,773 were authorized for 1913. The president of the institution is Robert S. Woodward. The chairman of the board of trustees is John S. Billings, the vice-president is Elihu Root, and the secretary Cleveland H. Dodge.

CARNEGIE PEACE ENDOWMENT. See PEACE ENDOWMENT, CARNEGIE.

CARNIOLA. See AUSTRIA-HUNGARY, *Area and Population.*

CAROLINE ISLANDS. A German possession lying north of New Guinea and forming part of the German New Guinea Protectorate. Area (Caroline, Pelew, and Marianne or Ladrone islands, excepting Guam), about 600 square miles; population, about 55,000. Capitals, Ponapé and Yap. Imports (1910), £117,-

DR. ALEXIS CARREL

RECIPIENT OF THE NOBEL PRIZE IN MEDICINE, 1912

750; exports, £502,100; revenue (1912, with New Guinea), £78,000; expenditure, £138,000.

CARREL, Alexis. A French chemist, awarded in 1912 the Nobel prize in medicine. He was born in Lyons, France, in 1873 and was educated at the University of Lyons, receiving the degree of B. L. in 1890 and B. S. in 1891. His medical degree he did not receive until 1900. For some years after his graduation he was connected with the University of Illinois and while there published a monograph on cancerous goitre. This was a careful study of an affection hitherto considered rare, but shown by his investigations to be relatively frequent. He came to the United States and worked at the Hull physiological laboratory of the University of Chicago. In the latter half of 1905 two papers, written in collaboration with Dr. C. G. Guthrie, attracted wide attention from those who were watching for new lines of investigation in medicine. The first of these was entitled *Anastomosis and the Transplantation of Blood Vessels*, and *Transplantation of Veins and Organs*. These papers opened up a new field of research, and they were followed in 1906 by a paper on *Amputation of the Thigh and its Replantation* by the same men. This paper showed the possibility of having the whole series of structures in the leg grow together after complete separation. In the meantime Dr. Carrel had become attached to the Rockefeller Institute and he there continued his studies in the transplantation of veins and organs. He showed in an article entitled *The Heterotransplantation of Blood Vessels Preserved in Cold Storage*, published in 1907, that it was possible to preserve portions of veins and arteries in such condition by cold storage that the ordinary death changes did not occur in them and that they could be grafted on to arteries or veins successfully. In 1908 he published a description of the successful transplantation of kidneys from one animal to another, and in 1910-11 other papers were written and published showing further developments in the work of transplanting and repairing blood vessels. In the latter year he published a paper entitled *Cultivation in Vitro of Thyroid*. This was a demonstration of the growth of the cells of the various organs when placed upon proper nutritive media in glass or other vessels. Dr. Carrel's work in 1912 related to the preservation of life in cold storage. He demonstrated that portions of the heart of warm-blooded animals might be stimulated into activity for a long time after the death of the animal if kept under conditions in which exhausted material was removed and more nutritious material supplied. The publication of these results attracted wide attention.

CARRINGTON, Henry Beebee. An American soldier, died October 26, 1912. He was born in Wallingford, Conn., in 1824, and graduated from Yale College in 1845. He studied law at the Yale Law School and practiced until 1861. He had taken great interest in military affairs and from 1857 to 1861 he was adjutant-general of Ohio. In May, 1861, he was appointed colonel of the 18th United States Infantry and in the following year was made brigadier-general of volunteers. He was commander of the District of Indiana and organized and sent to the front 120,000 volunteers from that State. It was largely through his efforts that the disloyal "Sons of Liberty" were exposed. After the war he was engaged in active service in the West. He opened a wagon route to Montana through Wyoming in 1866, commanded the Rocky Mountain District, planned and built Fort Phil Kearney, was in active service with the Sioux Indians and was wounded in a skirmish with them. He retired from active service in 1870 on account of disability. In 1875 he was granted access by Great Britain and France to all archives pertaining to the American revolutionary war and he surveyed and mapped the important battlefields. In 1889 he made a treaty with the Flathead Indians in Montana and removed them to the western part of the State. In 1890 he took a detailed census of the "Six Nations" of New York, and the "Cherokees" of North Carolina. He wrote *Russia as a Nation; American Classics; Land of Massacre and Indian Operations on the Plains, 1866-1890; Battles of the American Revolution; Battle Maps and Charts of the American Revolution; The Six Nations; Beacon Lights of Patriotism; Washington, the Soldier*, and *Lafayette and American Independence*. He edited Rev. S. F. Smith's poems of *Home and Country*. He contributed many articles on educational and historical subjects to magazines, and delivered many addresses on these subjects.

CARTWRIGHT, Sir Richard. A Canadian statesman, died September 24, 1912. He was born in Kingston, Ontario, in 1835. He early showed an interest in politics and at the age of 28 was elected to the United Assembly of the Canadian Provinces as a member for Lenox. When the confederation came about in 1867 he was elected a member of parliament from the same place. At that time he was a Tory, in accordance with the traditions of his family, but when Sir John McDonald fell into trouble on account of the Pacific Railway scandal, Cartwright threw in his lot with the Reform party and in 1873 was made minister of finance in the cabinet formed by Alexander McKenzie. Five years later Sir John McDonald was again in power and Cartwright lost both his portfolio and his seat in parliament. At a bye-election, however, he was returned to the house as a member for Central Huron. He was in and out of parliament through the long eclipse of the Liberal party and he never slackened in the zeal of his campaign against protection. When the Liberals were successful after ten years of failure, Cartwright, after the abdication of Mr. Blake, stood second in power in the Liberal party. He was given the portfolio of trade and commerce in the new cabinet, formed by Sir Wilfrid Laurier, and in that capacity was largely responsible for the fiscal policy of Canada from 1896 until the defeat of his party at the polls in September, 1911.

CATHOLIC UNIVERSITY OF AMERICA. An institution of higher learning at Washington, D. C., under the auspices of the Roman Catholic Church, founded in 1889. The number of students enrolled in the several departments of the university in the autumn of 1912 was about 500. The members of the faculty numbered 56. There were no noteworthy changes in the faculty during the year. A chair of Old Testament was founded with a gift of $50,000, presented by Mr. James J. Ryan, of Philadelphia. Five scholarships, amounting to $25,000, were founded by Dr. Max Pam to combat socialism. The productive funds of the university amount to $1,300,000 and the income to about $108,000. The volumes in the library numbered 80,000. Rector, Thomas J. Shahan.

CATSKILL AQUEDUCT AND WATER SUPPLY. See AQUEDUCTS.

CAUSEWAY. See BRIDGES.

CAVALRY. See MILITARY PROGRESS.

CAYENNE. See FRENCH GUIANA.

CAYMAN ISLANDS. A British possession, administratively attached to Jamaica but governed locally by a commissioner (1912, G. S. S. Hirst) with headquarters at Georgetown. Three islands constitute the dependency: Grand Cayman (about 93 sq. miles; population, 1911 census, 4128), Little Cayman (4⅝ sq. miles, 136 inhabitants), and Cayman Brac (15⅝ sq. miles, 1300 inhabitants). Turtle hunting is the chief occupation of the natives; an average of 5000 yearly are exported after being fattened. Cocoanuts, cattle and ponies, and turtle shell are also exported.

CELLS. See BOTANY; BIOLOGY.

CELTIC PHILOLOGY. See PHILOLOGY, MODERN.

CEMENT. The total quantity of cement produced in the United States in 1911 was 79,547,958 barrels, valued at $66,705,136. This included Portland, natural, and puzzolan cement. The production in 1910 was 77,785,141 barrels, valued at $68,752,092, showing an increase for 1911 of 1,762,817 barrels and a decrease of $2,046,956 in value. The increase in quantity was the smallest recorded in thirteen years, and the fact that the total value showed an actual decrease indicated that trade conditions in the cement industry were not as satisfactory in 1911 as in 1910. The Portland cement produced in 1911, as reported to the United States Geological Survey, amounted to 78,528,637 barrels, valued at $66,248,817, an increase of about 2,000,000 barrels over the production of 1910 and a decrease of about $2,000,000 in value. The average price per barrel in 1911 was slightly less than 84.4 cents, as compared with 89.1 cents in 1910.

The natural cement produced in 1911 was 926,091 barrels, valued at $378,533, and the puzzolan cement amounted to 93,230 barrels, valued at $77,786. In the production of Portland cement Pennsylvania by far exceeded any other State. There were, in 1911, 25 producing plants in this State, from which came 26,864,679 barrels, valued at $19,258,253. Indiana ranks second, 7,407,830 barrels, valued at $5,937,241; California third with 6,317,701 barrels, valued at $8,737,150. Other States producing more than 1,000,000 barrels were Kansas, Illinois, New Jersey, Missouri, Michigan, New York, Iowa, and Ohio. For the statistics of cement production in these States see paragraph *Mineral Production* under them.

In 1911 there were 115 plants recorded as having produced Portland cement, as compared with 111 plants in 1910. The total number of rotary kilns in the producing plants was 916, as compared with 902 in 1910. There were imported, in 1911, 164,670 barrels of cement, as compared with 306,863 barrels in 1910. The imports have steadily fallen off since 1907, when 2,033,438 barrels were imported. The exports of Portland cement in 1911 were 3,135,409 barrels, valued at $4,632,215, or, approximately, $1.47 per barrel.

The natural cement produced in the United States comes chiefly from New York, Pennsylvania, Illinois, Indiana, Ohio, Minnesota, and Kansas. A small quantity also comes from Georgia and Texas. New York and Pennsylvania produced 429,832 barrels.

Puzzolan cement is produced in Alabama, New York, Ohio, and Pennsylvania. There were only four plants producing this cement in 1911.

PORTLAND CEMENT. The use of Portland cement as a building material has grown so rapidly in recent years that its effect on the building stone and clay product industries was beginning to be felt, and in certain lines this competition, it was thought, would become even greater in the future. The following table, compiled by Edwin C. Eckel, an authority on building stones and clays, indicates the production of these materials in the decade 1900-1910.

Year	Stone	Clay products	Portland cement
1900......	$41,211,243	$ 96,212,345	$ 9,280,525
1901......	52,071,708	110,211,587	12,532,360
1902......	60,494,733	122,169,531	20,864,078
1903......	63,690,026	131,062,421	27,713,319
1904......	64,382,910	131,023,248	23,355,119
1905......	69,294,955	149,697,188	33,245,867
1906......	72,147,140	161,032,722	52,466,186
1907......	77,125,025	158,942,369	53,992,551
1908......	72,029,816	133,197,762	43,547,679
1909......	76,786,617	166,321,213	52,858,354
1910......	82,757,343	170,115,974	68,205,800

This indicates that while the total stone output was doubled in the period and the clay product output had increased 76 per cent., the production of Portland cement has increased 635 per cent.

CENSUS, THIRTEENTH. See UNITED STATES CENSUS BUREAU.

CENTENARIES. See EXPOSITIONS.

CENTRAL AMERICA. See articles on Central American countries.

CENTRAL AMERICAN CONFERENCE. See ARBITRATION, INTERNATIONAL.

CENTRAL BANK. See BANKS AND BANKING.

CEREBRO-SPINAL MENINGITIS. See MENINGITIS.

CEYLON (anciently TAPROBANE). The island of "dusky leaves" *(Támraparní)*. An island in the Indian Ocean; a British crown colony. Area, 25,332 sq. miles; population, according to the census of March 10, 1911, 4,106,350—an increase of 14.7 per cent. over that of 1901. There were 8555 Europeans, 26,857 Burghers or Eurasians, 2,714,616 Sinhalese, 1,089,354 Tamils, 266,454 Moors, 13,089 Malays, 12,198 various. More than half the people (2,479,118) are Buddhists; Hindus, 932,696; Christians, 408,984; Mohammedans, 283,582; various, 1155. Colombo, the capital, had 211,284 inhabitants; Negombo, 13,045; Moratuwa, 27,256; Kalutara, 13,005; Kandy, 29,928; Jaffna, 40,441; Galle, 39,936; Matara, 13,851.

Plantation laborers number about 530,279 (in large part Indian coolies). Acreage under cocoanuts, 942,621; rice, 680,574; other grains, 101,708; tea, 580,845; rubber, 186,634; cinnamon, 47,292; cacao, 43,358; tobacco, 16,241; coffee, 1512; cinchona, 263. There are 1986 gem quarries and pearl banks leased to an English company; the plumbago mines and pits (609) yielded (1910) about 632,275 cwts., valued (estimate) at Rs. 9,484,125.

Commercial and financial statistics appear below, in rupees:

	1908	1909	1910
Imports	130,291,908	133,782,127	164,864,703a
" U. K.	34,259,049	33,076,095	42,874,524
Exports	130,170,406	146,899,631	173,717,722b
" U. K.	63,887,326	72,320,809	80,063,196
Revenue	35,572,849	39,332,861	43,741,758
Expenditure...	35,032,055	33,882,957	36,467,708
Shipping*	13,877,141	14,013,507	15,038,445
" Br.	9,522,449	9,248,994	9,755,605

a Rice from India (Rs. 47,064,866), textiles and coal from the United Kingdom, etc.

b Cocoanut products, Rs. 38,313,348; cinnamon, Rs. 2,724,506; cacao, Rs. 2,861,760. Pounds of tea exported (no value given), 182,070,094 in 1910 (2,392,963 lbs. in 1884, 85,376,322 in 1894, 157,929,-333 lbs. in 1904).

* Tonnage entered and cleared.

A large part of the trade is with British colonies. Public debt, July, 1911, £5,962,700. The railways are all owned and operated by the government; total mileage, 576⅝. The line from Madawachchi to Talai Mannar (about 65½ miles) at the northwestern end of Mannar Island (expected to be completed at the end of 1912) will be connected with the Indian railways by steamers landing at Danishkodi, the terminus of the Indian line. Dock and harbor improvements are in progress. Governor (1912), Col. Sir H. E. McCallum.

Tributary to the Ceylon government are the MALDIVE ARCHIPELAGO (a group of 17 islands, with a population roughly estimated at 30,-000) and the LACCADIVE ISLANDS.

CHAMBERS OF COMMERCE, CONGRESS OF. See ARBITRATION, INTERNATIONAL.

CHAMPLAIN MEMORIAL LIGHTHOUSE. See LIGHTHOUSES.

CHARITY. See PUBLIC CHARITIES.

CHARTER REFORM. See MUNICIPAL GOVERNMENT.

CHARTS, ERRORS IN. See CARNEGIE INSTITUTION.

CHATHAM ISLANDS. A dependency of New Zealand (q. v.).

CHAUTAUQUA INSTITUTION. A system of popular education founded at Chautauqua, N. Y., in 1874, by John H. Vincent and Lewis Miller. The thirty-ninth annual assembly of this institution was held at Chautauqua from June 27 to August 25, 1912. The attendance was not as large as in 1911 on account of weather conditions and the withdrawal of certain railroad rates. The summer schools, however, had the largest year in the history of the institution. In the Chautauqua summer schools two appointments of great importance in the educational life of the institution were those of Prof. Shailer Mathews, dean of the Divinity School of the University of Chicago, as director of religious work and head of the School of Religious Teaching, and of Mr. Earl Barnes, of Philadelphia, as head of the School of Psychology and Pedagogy. In coöperation with Cornell University a Chautauqua School of Practical Agriculture, the first summer school of its kind in the country, was inaugurated and operated during the summer of 1912 on the institution farm of 112 acres. A number of interesting conferences were held during the summer. Four of the weeks were devoted to "Child Welfare," "Business and the Public Welfare," "Recognition Week," and "The Awakened Church." In each of these weeks there were a number of main addresses and individual lectures and conferences dealing with the main theme. A political symposium was conducted, with addresses by Attorney-General Wickersham, the Hon. Eugene W. Chafin, and the Hon. William J. Bryan. Contributions are made only once during the summer sessions of the institution. This was called "old first night gift." In 1912 this amounted to over $8000, $5000 of which was devoted to the new music studio erected to the memory of the late William H. Sherwood, for twenty-two years the head of the piano department of the summer schools; $2000 for the summer school fellowship fund, and $1000 for permanent scholarships. The officers of the institution for 1912 were John H. Vincent, chancellor; George E. Vincent, president; Arthur E. Bestor, director; Clement Studebaker, president of trustees, and Fred W. Hyde, treasurer.

CHEESE. See DAIRYING.

CHEMICAL COMPOUNDS, NEW. See CHEMICAL PROGRESS.

CHEMICAL SOCIETY, AMERICAN. A society for the discussion of subjects indicated by its title, founded in 1876. During 1912 the membership greatly increased and at the end of the year numbered over 6200. The only meeting of the society which was held in 1912 was in conjunction with the Eighth International Congress of Applied Chemistry in New York City, September 4-12, and all preparation of papers was dispensed with in order to assure the success of that congress. The officers of the society for 1912-13 were as follows: President, A. D. Little; secretary, Charles L. Parsons; treasurer, A. P. Hallock; editors, W. A. Noyes, *Journal of the American Chemical Society;* A. M. Patterson, *Chemical Abstracts;* M. C. Whitaker, *Journal of Industrial and Engineering Chemistry.*

CHEMICAL TARIFF. See TARIFF.

CHEMISTRY. While it is true that the science of chemistry is progressing to-day more rapidly than ever before in its history, it is also true that "remarkable discoveries" are few in number. The general trend of investigation consists in applying the new and refined methods, especially of physical chemistry, to old material. In this investigation we often find the same line of work leading on the one hand to strictly theoretical conclusions and abstractions, and on the other to most concrete industrial applications. Thus the study of the equilibrium of gases, especially at the very high temperatures of the electric furnace, and the disturbance of this equilibrium at various temperatures by different catalytic agents, is really the foundation of the successful production of synthetic ammonia from nitrogen and hydrogen, and of the manufacture of lime saltpetre from the air and limestone, now practiced on such an immense scale in Norway. These industries in turn have the most important influence upon the whole field of agriculture. Again, the study of the equilibrium between various salts and their aqueous solutions might seem purely of theoretical interest, yet this study may have important applications in pointing to possible discoveries of potash in the United States, and a consequent emancipation of the American farmer from a foreign fertilizer syndicate. See CHEMISTRY, INDUSTRIAL.

The attention of the American public has

been turned to the applications of chemistry to an unusual degree the past year, owing to the meeting in this country in September of the Eighth International Congress of Applied Chemistry, and it is a noteworthy fact that a very considerable proportion of the papers presented at that congress were on theoretical chemistry, while many of the others were on applications of theoretical chemistry to the problems of industrial chemistry. More than ever is it becoming difficult to draw a line between theoretical and applied or industrial chemistry, and many references which might equally well be considered here are passed over to the article on Industrial Chemistry. See CHEMISTRY, INDUSTRIAL.

ATOMIC WEIGHTS. The annual report of the International Committee on Atomic Weights is this year much briefer than usual and no changes have been made in the Atomic Weight Table for 1913, except that *holmium*, one of the rare-earth metals, for the first time makes its appearance. Hitherto there have been no sufficiently reliable determinations of its atomic weight to justify its admission to the table. The splitting of tellurium by Flint, by the fractional precipitation of its chloride, still remains unconfirmed, though the work has been repeated by Harcourt and Baker, and also by Pellini. Further work on the subject is promised by Flint during the present year. Nothing further has been published regarding *canadium*, the supposed new metal of the platinum group reported last year, except the suggestion that it may be identical with *amarillium*, another platinum metal reported in 1903, and long since consigned to the haven of lost elements. Hönigschmid, using several grams of radium, has found its atomic weight to be 225.95, but Ramsay and Gray, with smaller quantities, have found 226.36, which is in close agreement with previous work. The latter figure is also closer to the theoretical probability.

INERT GASES. Four years ago Ramsay published results of experiments which tended to show that when niton (radium emanation) acts on water, neon is formed. Many chemists have been inclined to assume that this neon was in reality derived from the atmosphere, and not from the niton. Now Ramsay has found that the gas given off from a solution of thorium nitrate, which had been sealed with niton in a glass tube for two years, consisted of nearly one-third neon and the balance helium. As there was scarcely a trace of argon present, the neon could not have come from the atmosphere, and it is highly probable that the neon was derived from the decomposition of the niton. Confirmatory of this is the fact that the gas from King's Well, at Bath, contains 78 times as much argon, 188 times as much neon, and 73 times as much helium as the atmosphere. This water is strongly radio-active, and it would seem that the only probable source of the neon is the decomposition of the niton. A redetermination by Ramsay of the wave-lengths of sound in relatively large quantities of neon, krypton, and xenon confirms the monatomic character of these gases. No efforts to induce the inert gases to enter into combination with other elements have thus far been attended with success, but Schrader has found that *actinium A, B,* and *C,* as well as the *B* and *C* decomposition products of radium and thorium, are less volatile in an oxygen atmosphere than in hydrogen and some other gases. Russell also finds that while *radium C* volatilizes from a quartz surface in the presence of oxygen only near 1200°C., it volatilizes completely in hydrogen at 360°. Both chemists infer that this may be due to the formation of a compound with oxygen which is far less volatile than the element itself, which would be formed in a hydrogen atmosphere. Russell has also found that even at temperatures as high as 1150°C. the rate of disintegration of radium (and also of its disintegration products) is unaffected by the temperature, showing that in these reactions, if the breaking up of atoms can be considered a reaction, we are dealing with a change which is entirely outside of our control as far as heat is concerned, in spite of the fact that heat is given off by the change.

OTHER ELEMENTS. Silver mirrors are formed by the deposition of metallic silver upon glass from ammoniacal solution by the addition of such reducing agents as formaldehyde, milk-sugar, tartrates, etc. Similiar mirrors are formed by electric discharge from silver kathodes in various rarified gases ("kathodic dusting"). The electric conductivity of a silver mirror is while being formed very low, and then suddenly increases, but never attains a value equal to that of ordinary metallic silver. The question of the condition in which this silver exists has been investigated by Kohlschütter, who finds that both under the microscope and the ultra-microscope this silver is amorphous and homogeneous, and that it may be considered as being in a state of colloidal division. The firmness with which the precipitated silver adheres to the glass is due to the fact that silver hydroxide is first absorbed by the glass surface and then the reducing agent is in turn absorbed. It follows, as is found in practice, that the nature of the glass and the nature of the solution both affect very materially the character of the deposit, owing to the effect of surface tension on absorption, and of electrolytes on the precipitation of colloids. A study by Brunck of the properties of metallic tantalum, now obtainable in a pure condition, has suggested its use for many laboratory purposes in the place of the now very expensive platinum. Unattacked by acid or alkaline solutions, it can be used for kathodes in electrolysis, and, with a thin plating of platinum, for anodes. Without this plating, a thin layer of non-conducting oxide, probably Ta_2O_5, is formed. Tantalum is also suggested for weights, while tungsten is proposed by Ruder for the same purpose. Tungsten can be used for acid-proof dishes, tubes, and filtering gauze, as well as for resistance furnaces. Sir William Crookes finds that while platinum is not volatile at 900° C., at 1300° C. it loses appreciably in weight, the metal being sublimed. Under the same conditions iridium loses even more, a volatile oxide being formed. Rhodium, on the other band, is hardly appreciably volatile.

By the action of 11·14 per cent. ozone on symmetrical butylene, C_4H_8, Harries obtains not only the volatile monomeric ozonide $C_4H_8.O_3$, and the non-volatile dimeric $(C_4H_8.O_3)_2$, but also two similar products, $C_4H_8.O_4$ and $(C_4H_8.O_4)_2$, in which the group O_4 is present and which Harries calls "oxozonides." If, however, the ozone is first led through a solution of caustic soda and also through concentrated sulphuric acid, only the ozonides are formed. From this he concludes that ordinary 11-14 per cent. ozone consists of about two-thirds common ozone (O_3), and one-third oxozone, the formula of which is O_4.

ATMOSPHERE. The normal amount of carbon dioxide in the atmosphere is considered to be 3 parts in 10,000, but an analysis by Müntz and Lainé of air collected on the Charcot Antarctic Expedition shows only from 1.447 to 2.553 parts, with an average of about 2 parts. This small amount, hardly two-thirds of the normal quantity, is accounted for by the temperature of the water of the southern ocean, which is generally below 0°C., thus reducing the dissociation temperature of the dissolved bicarbonates. This shows that, contrary to the ideas of Gay-Lussac, the movement of the atmosphere is not sufficient to cause a uniform distribution of the constituents. The composition of the higher layers of the atmosphere has been considered by Wegener, and is held by him to be very different from that of the lower strata. At the altitude of 40 kilometers half of the oxygen has disappeared, while the nitrogen has correspondingly increased. Above this the oxygen and nitrogen rapidly decrease, helium is at a maximum (4 per cent.), and hydrogen rapidly increases. Wegener considers that there is evidence of a gas much lighter than hydrogen, which he calls "geo-coronium," in the highest layers of the atmosphere. This begins to appear at about 50 kilometers, and above 200 kilometers is the chief constituent, while at 500 kilometers hydrogen has nearly disappeared, leaving geo-coronium as practically the sole constituent gas. Wegener's views are based on changes of density of the atmosphere, as shown by the suspension of the Krakatoa dust-clouds, diffuse reflection of light, and also of sound, the glow of meteors and spectra of the aurora and of meteor trails, and also the analogy of the sun's atmosphere. Geocoronium resembles the sun's coronium and is identified with Mendeléef's speculative element of the atomic weight 0.4.

COMBUSTION OF CARBON. The question as to whether the first product in the combustion of carbon is carbon monoxide (CO), which is further oxidized to the dioxide (CO_2) if an excess of oxygen is present, or whether the dioxide is first formed and reduced to the monoxide if the carbon is in excess, has long been an unsolved problem. Perhaps the latter view is the one more commonly held, but it rests on little experimental evidence. More recently Rhead and Wheeler have approached the subject from the standpoint of determining the velocity of the various reactions between carbon and oxygen at different temperatures. They find that some CO is produced by the oxidation of carbon at low temperatures under conditions which do not admit of its being formed by reduction from CO_2, and, on the other hand, CO_2 is undoubtedly produced at low temperatures in quantities which cannot be altogether accounted for on the supposition that CO is first formed and then oxidized to CO_2. It thus appears that when carbon burns it is oxidized simultaneously to both CO and CO_2, a conclusion which accounts for the results obtained by previous experimenters on both sides. When CO burns it is ordinarily considered that the reaction is merely the addition of oxygen, as $CO+O=CO_2$, but this has been several times called in question, especially because even at high temperatures a trace at least of water appears to be necessary that the reaction may take place. Now Wieland finds that moist CO is oxidized to CO_2 by palladium black, even in the absence of oxygen. This can be accounted for by the union of CO with water to formic acid $CO+H_2O=HCOOH$; and the subsequent splitting of formic acid into CO_2 and hydrogen, $HCOOH=CO_2+H_2$, both reactions taking place under the influence of palladium, which absorbs the hydrogen liberated. This formation of formic acid, even when CO burns at a high temperature, was confirmed by directing a CO flame against ice, when formic acid was found in the resulting water. In the ordinary combustion of carbon monoxide the hydrogen formed by the decomposition of the formic acid is at once oxidized to water, and this immediately reacts with another molecule of the carbon monoxide.

NEW COMPOUNDS. An interesting derivative of hydrazoic acid, HN_3, has been prepared by Darzens, by the action of cyanogen bromide on the sodium salt, NaN_3. Double decomposition readily ensues, with the formation of $NC.N_3$, which Darzens calls carbon pernitride, but which would be better named cyanogen trinitride. It is a colorless oil which crystallizes at 36° C., and explodes with great violence when heated or exposed to shock. The existence of other compounds of carbon and nitrogen than cyanogen is indicated by the work of Lidoff. In numerous reactions where CO_2 is formed and nitrogen evolved, as in the oxidation of urea by sodium hypobromite, a certain quantity of nitrogen appears to be lost, and this is due, according to Lidoff, to the formation of oxidized cyanogen. The compound CNO, oxan, is formed in many reactions, but best by heating a mixture of CNBr and CNI to 160° C. with silver oxide, or by passing NO_2 over carbon at temperatures below 300° C. This gas unites with bases to form oxanates, as K_2CNO_3, but in no case could oxan or any oxanates be obtained in pure condition. It seems probable that peroxan, CNO_2, and peroxanates are also formed in some of these reactions, as well as isooxan, NCO. That a volatile compound of boron and hydrogen is formed when magnesium boride is dissolved in water, has been long known, but the quantity obtained is so small and it is so unstable that it has hitherto never been separated in a pure form and its composition has not been definitely determined. Two compounds have now been isolated by Stock from this reaction, one B_4H_{10}, and the other probably B_6H_{12}. The former boils at 16° C., ignites in contact with the air, and is quickly decomposed by water; the other is even more unstable and boils at a higher temperature. Other hydrides of boron appear to be formed, but none of a simpler formula, which is quite unexpected, as it would be supposed from analogy that there would be a hydride of the formula BH_3. An interesting substantiation of Franklin's theory of the ammono-salts (in which ammonia corresponds to water) is furnished by Ruff's work on the action of ammonia on titanium tetrabromide. $TiBr_4.8NH_3$ is first formed, and on washing with liquid ammonia this is more or less ammonolysed, giving a product which contains titanium amide, $Ti(NH_2)_4$. This by the action of potassamide, KNH_2, is converted into a potassium ammono-titanate, KN.Ti.NH, and a new titanium nitride, Ti_3N_4. This nitride is hydrolysed by water with formation of ammonia and titanic acid, and on heating is converted into TiN, the nitride of trivalent titanium, also new. The potassium in the ammono-titanate appears to be replaceable by chlorine, indicating the amphoteric character of the TiN_2 group. Many years ago Hadow found that when bromine was added to a solution of potassium plato-cyanide, which is in solid form beautifully fluorescent, but in solution colorless, a brown salt is formed with a metallic appearance. This Hadow considered to be a double salt, in which one-fifth of the molecules are oxidized to a bromo-platicyanide, the composition being $5K_2Pt(CN)_4.Pt(CN)_4Br_2$. In recent work Levy finds Hadow's view was correct except that only one-sixth of the salt is oxidized instead of one-fifth. He also finds that the plato-cyanide can be oxidized by other agents and that the group $(7K_2Pt(CN)_4)$ is capable of acting as a weakly positive bivalent base. More interesting were the results obtained on oxidizing the plato-cyanide with hydrogen peroxide, especially when the latter was used in the form of "perhydrol." Simple and double salts of the type $M_1Pt(CN)_4$ were obtained. This formula may be written $MCN.Pt(CN)_3$ and in it the platinum appears to be trivalent. This in a way confirms the work of Wöhler two years ago in preparing oxides of trivalent platinum.

THE COBALT-NITRATE TEST. The colors given when various white oxides are heated with cobalt nitrate have long been used in qualitative analysis for the recognition of these oxides, and at least the zinc-cobalt green and the aluminum-cobalt blue have had some use as pigments. While many have endeavored to determine the nature of these colored substances, and the idea that they are solid solutions is not new, Burgstaller is the first to offer what seems a satisfactory explanation of the colors. Noting that the colors in question are blue, red, or green, he considers that in the blue and red we are dealing with solid solutions which show the usual colors of cobalt in solution. In the green we have the blue solution of cobalt in a substratum of yellow zinc oxide. While at ordinary temperatures zinc oxide is white, when heated it is yellow, and Burgstaller considers that the presence of the cobalt hinders the usual transformation to the white modification on cooling.

INORGANIC ISOMERISM. Perhaps the most notable work of the year in chemistry has been the development of Werner's work on inorganic isomerism. In the review of last year some of this work was described, but in the past twelve months it has been carried considerably further. In the case of the diethylenediamin compounds of cobalt, which can be represented by the formula $(^{A}_{B}Co\ en_2).C$, and in which *en* is the bivalent ethylenediamin, $C_2H_4(NH_2)_2$, six isomers are possible according to Werner's theory—viz., we may have within the coördinated group the A and B, or the A and C, or the B and C, and in each of these three cases the A and B (or A and C, or B and C) may be either on opposite sides of the cobalt atom, giving the *trans* form, or on the same side, the *cis* form. In the case where A, B, and C are respectively NO_2, Cl, and SCN, all six of these isomers have actually been prepared. When one of the groups within the complex is replaced by another, it by no means follows that the same position will be occupied by the replacing group as was occupied by the group it replaces. There may be a decided rearrangement, a *trans* form being converted into a *cis* form. A new theory is suggested by Werner to account for such rearrangements within the complex, as follows: The substituting group is drawn into the complex by the attraction of the central cobalt (or other) atom, but this attraction will be stronger in some directions than in others, depending on the nature and position of the groups already in the complex. The substituting group will enter the complex in that position in which the attraction is the strongest. Now since the central atom possesses only six coördination valences, one group must pass out of the complex, and this will be the one for which the central atom has the least attraction, and it may or may not be the one which was occupying the position which the entering group has taken. This theory is capable of applications outside of the 'complex' compounds of inorganic chemistry, for molecular rearrangements are quite frequent in the reactions of organic chemistry, and it is quite possible that some of these at least may be accounted for by an extension of this theory. Molecular rearrangements are thus not to be considered anomalous, but represent the ordinary course of reaction.

INORGANIC OPTICAL ISOMERISM. Further work by Werner on this subject, which was first brought out in 1911, has established even more strongly the possibility of optical isomerism in the complex inorganic compounds. The preparation of numerous compounds of the types, $(^{A}_{B}Co\ en_2).X$ and $(^{A}_{A}Co\ en_2).X$, in both dextrorotary and levorotary forms, has been accomplished, the racemic (inactive mixture) form generally being resolved into the optical isomers by the use of bromo-camphorsuphonates, a method of familiar use in organic chemistry. Compounds have also been prepared in which the univalent groups, A and B, are replaced by a single bivalent group, such as the oxalate and carbonate radical. These show a very high rotation. Most striking is the preparation of active compounds of the type $(Co\ en_3).Cl_3$, where the central atom is surrounded by three identical bivalent groups, the coördinated group $(Co\ en_3)$ being in fact asymmetrical. The corresponding chromium and rhodium compounds have been formed, and the rotation of the chromium compounds, $(Cr\ en_3).X_3$ is found to be less than that of the similar cobalt compounds, while that of the rhodium isomers is about the same as that of the corresponding chromium salts, but opposite in sign. This shows that the nature of the optical activity depends upon the special nature of the central metallic atom. The levorotary form of tri-αα-dipyridyl ferric chloride has also been prepared by Werner. It has a very high rotation and shows that inorganic optical isomerism is not confined to ethylenediamin compounds. In all these cases of optical isomerism, however, the active complex is a cation and contains nitrogen. That these are not necessary conditions, Werner has shown by resolving salts of the blue chrom-oxalic acid into dextrorotary and levorotary forms. This was accomplished by the use of the strychnin salts. These salts show an extraordinarily large rotation and go over rapidly into the racemic (inactive) form. Here the active complex is an anion and contains no nitrogen. It would appear that optical activity is a general property, and may be found wherever there is an asymmetrical central atom with a valence as high as four.

PEPTIDS. The field of organic chemistry is so immense that it is difficult to make selections for notice, but mention may be made of work upon the polypeptids, since these possess a peculiar interest and importance in their relation to protoplasm and to nutrition. While on the one hand albumin can be broken down into mixtures of various amino-acids, on the other hand the masterly work of Fischer and his associates has enabled the building up from amino-acids of many polypeptids, which represent in a simple form what the vastly more intricate albumin molecules must be. Naturally the subject has attracted many workers, and much progress has been made. How complicated the subject is may be judged from work of Abderhalden, who has prepared all six of the possible tripeptids which contain the three amino-acids, glycocoll, d-alanin, and l-leucin. The six are as follows:

Glycyl-d-alanyl-l-leucin,
Glycyl-l-leucyl-d-alanin,
d-Alanyl-glycyl-l-leucin,
d-Alanyl-l-leucyl-glycin,
l-Leucyl-glycyl-d-alanin,
l-Leucyl-d-alanyl-glycin.

These possess different optical rotation and different properties. When one considers that in the building up of protein substances at least 16 different amino-acids have their part, one appreciates the enormous number of structural isomers that are possible.

ARTIFICIAL SYNTHESIS OF FOOD-STUFFS. The problem of artificial synthesis of food-stuffs has attracted much attention, and Abderhalden shows that experiments indicate that a dog can be nourished for weeks exclusively on salts, water, oxygen, grape-sugar, fatty-acids, glycerol, and amino-acids, and yet gain in body weight. All of these organic substances can be prepared synthetically, so that the problem of the artificial preparation of food-stuffs may be considered as settled. The economical production of these materials is another matter. Kober and Sugiura have attacked the problem of the decomposition products of protein substances from the standpoint of the structure of their salts, especially with copper. They have studied the reaction between copper oxide and a large number of polypeptids, and distinguish three types of reaction. First, those in which a deep blue is obtained, like that of the copper ammoniates. This is given by all simple dipeptids made from mono-amino-acids. The second type is that in which a bluish-red color appears, and is given by the tripeptids of mono-amino-acids and the amides of dipeptids. This is called the semi- or partial-biuret reaction. The third type is the true biuret reaction, which gives a purple-red color and is obtained from tetrapeptids and amides of tripeptids. A peculiar interest attaches to this work from the standpoint of general chemistry, for there seems to be structurally in these compounds a coördinated grouping, and the three types are dependent on whether two, three, or four nitrogen atoms are coördinated with the copper atom, and here again Werner's theory may be invoked for explanation.

CHEMISTRY, BUREAU OF. See FOOD AND NUTRITION.

CHEMISTRY, INDUSTRIAL. The announcement of the synthesis of rubber (see RUBBER, SYNTHESIS OF) may be considered the great distinctive event in industrial chemistry during 1912. Interest in synthetic chemistry has been largely increased not only by this discovery, but also in consequence of the president's address before the British Association, in September, in which belief was expressed that in the laboratory by means of chemical combinations life might be produced. Of remarkable interest to chemists in the United States was the gathering from all parts of the world of representatives of industrial chemistry, at the Eighth International Congress of Applied Chemistry. A summary of the more important announcements, similar to those given in recent issues of the YEAR BOOK, follows.

ORGANIZATIONS. The American Chemical Society, with a membership of over 6100, and now the largest body of chemists in the world, held no meetings during the year. The summer meeting was abandoned in order that the members might attend the Congress of Applied Chemistry, and the time of the winter meeting has been changed to spring. The president is Arthur D. Little, a chemical engineer in Boston, Mass. The sixth presentation of the Perkin gold medal of the associated chemical and electro-chemical societies of America was made on January 19 to Mr. Herman Frasch, for his contributions to industrial chemistry, notably those in connection with petroleum refining. The president is Dr. Leo H. Baekeland, of New York City.

The American Institute of Chemical Engineers held its summer meeting in New York, on September 5, at the same time as the Congress of Applied Chemistry, but only formal business was considered, and the papers presented were read before the congress. The annual meeting was held in Detroit, Mich., on December 4-7.

The thirty-first annual meeting of the Society of Chemical Industry was held in New York City on September 3. The council announced the membership as 4285, as compared with 4300 last year. Dr. Rudolph Messel, the retiring president, was succeeded by Prof. Marston T. Bogert, of Columbia University, who is the fourth American chemist to fill that office. Among his predecessors were C. F. Chandler (1899), W. H. Nichols (1904), and Ira Remsen (1909). The medal of the society was awarded to Sir William Crookes, for his epoch-making discoveries in physical chemistry and the rare metals.

The eighth International Congress of Applied Chemistry was opened in Washington, D. C., by William H. Nichols, president, who, after announcing that the patron, President Taft, owing to an accident, would be unable to preside, introduced Edward W. Morley, honorary president, who made the address of welcome which was responded to by representatives of foreign nations. In the afternoon a reception was given at the White House, where Mr. Taft addressed the Congress, followed by a garden party in the White House grounds. The formal opening for reading of papers took place in New York City and continued until September 13. Most of the meetings were held in the lecture-rooms of Columbia University and those of the College of the City of New York. Papers were presented before the following sections: "Analytical Chemistry," W. F. Hillebrand;* "Inorganic Chemistry," Charles L. Parsons;* "Metallurgy and Mining," Joseph W. Richards;* "Explosives," Charles E. Munroe;* "Silicate Industries," A. S. Cushman;* "Organic Chemistry," M. T. Bogert;* "Coal Tar Colors and Dyestuffs," H. A. Metz;* "Industry and Chemistry of Sugar," W. D. Horne;* "India Rubber and Other Plastics," L. H. Baekeland;* "Fuels and Asphalt," D. T. Day;* "Fats, Fatty Oils, and Soaps," David Wesson;* "Paints, Drying Oils, and Varnishes," M. Toch;* "Starch, Cellulose, and Paper," A. D. Little;* "Fermentation," Francis Wyatt;* "Agricultural Chemistry," Frank K. Cameron;* "Hygiene," W. P. Mason;* "Pharmaceutical Chemistry," J. P. Remington;* "Bromatology," W. D. Bigelow;* "Physiological Chemistry and Pharmacology," John J. Abel;* "Photochemistry," W. D. Bancroft;* "Electrochemistry," William D. Walker;* "Physical Chemistry," W. R. Whitney;* "Law and Legislation Affecting Chemical Industry," Edward D. White;* and "Political Economy and Conservation of Natural Resources," J. A. Holmes.* In all more than 600 papers were presented, which were collected and published in 24 volumes, aggregating over 5000 pages, with illustrations, also four volumes devoted to additional papers and discussions appeared subsequent to the congress. Four international lectures were delivered by eminent members of the chemical profession from each nation represented, in the four official languages, French, German, Italian, and English. They were: "The Part Played by Infinitely Small Quantities of Chemicals in Biological Chemistry," by Gabriel Bertrand of Paris, France; "The Latest Achievements and Problems of the Chemical Industry," by C. Duisberg of Elberfeld, Germany; "The Photochemistry of the Future," by Giacomo Ciamician of Bologna, Italy, and "The Permanent Fireproofing of Cotton Goods," by W. H. Perkin of Manchester, England. Twenty-five hundred members of the congress were present at the meeting. Subsequent to the congress factory visits and excursions were made, one of which extended to the Pacific Coast, and all along the route local committees were organized to receive and entertain the guests, and to facilitate their visits to manufacturing plants. The next (the ninth) congress will be held in St. Petersburg, Russia, in 1915, over which Paul Walden of the Polytechnical School of Riga, was chosen to preside. *The Journal of Industrial and Engineering Chemistry* for October, and *Metallurgical and Chemical Engineering* for September 12, give extended summaries of the congress.

METALS. The diseases of metals previously referred to (see YEAR BOOKS for 1909, p. 152, and for 1911, p. 150) are now found to extend to aluminum. Sheets of aluminum that had been obtained by cold rolling and then transformed into boilers, cooking-utensils, and other hollow vessels, showed corrosions and efflorescences, discontinuous, but mostly disposed in certain directions, straight on the flat bottoms of the vessels and curved on their sides, but always coincident with the direction of the lamination. The explanation offered was that in consequence of the formation of layers (by hammering) two neighboring layers of the plate may assume different degrees of hardness and also of electric tension, and in the presence of saline solutions these behave like two different metals in an electrolyte; the most hammered layer plays the part of a positive electrode and loses its metal. The methods proposed as remedies are first to do away with the danger caused by hammering, by a proper degree of reheating, and second to avoid contact with water.

METALLURGY. A new process for the electrolytic recovery of zinc is reported from Japan. Zinc ore is dissolved in the electrolyte, and from this liquid zinc is precipitated by electrolysis. A defect of the process heretofore has been the spongy form of the zinc which adhered to the cathode. To prevent this, carbon was tried instead of lead in the anode. The carbon was coarse and dissolved in the zinc sulphate, and the zinc which gathered on the cathode was then found to be refined to a degree rarely surpassed by the imported metal.

FUEL. Somewhat startling was the proposal made on March 24 by Sir William Ramsay at the Smoke Abatement Exhibition held in London, that coal be no longer mined, but burned in the seams as it lies, the heat being used to generate power, which then could be transmitted by means of electricity to places where it was needed for use.

He claimed that there is nothing to prevent a bore-hole from being put down until the coal-stratum is reached, and concentric tubes being used to set the coal on fire (by electricity) and to blow air down to enable the coal to burn. When sufficient heat has been engendered the amount of air sent down might be restricted. Coal with plenty of air gives off carbon dioxide. When half-burned it gives carbon monoxide, which is used for gas-engines. If steam were blown in it would give a mixture of hydrogen and carbonic oxide, or water-gas, which also is used for gas-engines. Bring the gas-engines to the mouth of the pit or bore-hole and produce the power there. You would thus have 30 per cent. of the energy of the coal available as against 15 per cent. available in fuel-engines. That energy might be transformed into electricity at the mouth of the bore-hole, and it could be distributed through the country.

In June, W. A. Bone, of Leeds University, described a process for gas heating based on the fact that hot surfaces promote the combustion of gases in contact with them. An explosive mixture of gas and air in the proportions for complete combustion is caused to burn without flame in contact with the surface of a red-hot porous solid, such as a block made of particles of fire brick and bound together by some suitable means. This process may be used for cooking purposes, also it is adaptable to the heating of furnaces, the raising of steam in multitubular boilers, the melting of metals, as for instance type metal, and other purposes. Schnabel of Germany and Lucke of New York had previously recommended similar processes.

A process for the utilization of peat, invented by F. H. Nixon, of London, consists of cutting

* Presiding officer of the section.

Courtesy of The Scientific American, N. Y.

SIR WILLIAM RAMSAY'S PROPOSED METHOD FOR OBTAINING POWER DIRECT FROM COAL

BURNING COAL IN THE EARTH TO PRODUCE GAS, WHICH IS UTILIZED IN INTERNAL COMBUSTION ENGINES TO GENERATE ELECTRIC POWER

the turf, after it has been air-dried, into corrugated blocks, which are sprayed with petroleum so as to form firelighters. The blocks are given a coating of highly inflammable material which strengthens them and prevents them from breaking. It is claimed that this process overcomes the obstacles associated hitherto with the combination of peat and petroleum which have been connected mainly with the employment of a briquetting machine that is not only difficult to work, but also expresses too much of the petroleum from the finished blocks.

NITROGEN. According to Sir William Ramsay, Scandinavia, Italy, Germany, Switzerland, Austria, and Russia now possess factories for preparing nitrates from the atmosphere, chiefly for purposes of agriculture, *i. e.*, making fertilizers, but also for making explosives. A company for the manufacture of ammonium sulphate from the atmosphere by the method of the Austrian engineer, Serpek, has been formed by French and Norwegian capitalists, and the construction of a plant at Arendal, Norway, is reported.

POTASH. The limited supply of potash, controlled almost entirely by the German Potash Syndicate, has led to the search for sources of that chemical in the United States, and the discovery of a deposit at Searles Lake in the northwestern part of San Bernardino County in California, is announced by the United States Geological Survey. The importance of the deposit is due to the occurrence of the potassium salts in soluble form in a natural saturated brine, under conditions especially favorable to its separation and recovery by solar evaporation. The bed is estimated to be at least sixty feet thick, and covers eleven square miles. A conservative estimate places the amount of potassium oxide at 4,000,000 short tons, but the available tonnage may well be expected to exceed 10,000,000 tons, which would supply the country at its present rate of consumption for thirty years.

ARTIFICIAL DIAMONDS. No satisfactory method for artificially making large diamonds has as yet been found, but among the methods that seem to promise results is the following, which was published in April. It has been found that illuminating gas is decomposed on exposure to mercury vapor, and when allowed to act on metallic amalgams of mercury the carbon in the gas is liberated in an amorphous form and in crystals, or diamonds. As the diamonds thus obtained are extremely small, the inventor placed diamond dust in a tube in which gas was dissolved, to act as "mother crystals." The newly formed crystals adhere to this dust, and the result is a larger, but small, stone. The amalgam used is sodium. It is placed in a glass tube containing a small quantity of diamond dust, and illuminating gas is passed through the tube for four weeks. The brilliants which are thus manufactured appear to possess all the attributes of the genuine diamond, but they are diminutive in size.

ILLUMINATING GAS. The centennial anniversary of the introduction of the use of gas as an illuminant was celebrated in Philadelphia, Pa., on April 18 and 19. A symposium was organized under the auspices of the American Philosophical Society, the Franklin Institute, the American Chemical Society, and the American Gas Institute, at which the following addresses were presented: "By-Products in Gas Manufacture," by Charles E. Munroe; "The Commercial and Financial Aspects of the Gas Industry," by George B. Cortelyou; "The Technic of Gas Manufacture," by Alfred E. Forstell; "Gas as an Illuminant," by Van Rensselaer Lansingh; and "The Use of Gas for Heat and Power," by Edward B. Rosa. A limited edition of these addresses has been issued in book form. A loan exhibition of articles, models, appliances, books, and pictures having an historical interest, was held at the same time in the hall of the Franklin Institute.

FIBRES. The demand for artificial silk is on the increase. The raw material used in its production is cotton. Its chemical nature does not change after manufacture, and, except for some additional process to render it brilliant or incombustible, it is still nothing but cotton. Therefore, the only difference between artificial silk and cotton fabrics lies in the weaving process, mechanical for cotton stuffs, chemical for artificial silk stuffs. Three processes are in general use, the Chardonnet, the viscose, and the one called vegetable casein (*caséine végétale*). Of these the viscose process seems to be the most desirable, as it is the cheapest. Recently patents have been taken out for an artificial silk, the base of which is spun glass—spun at one-eighteenth of a hair's diameter. This almost imperceptible filament, to which are added certain chemical products producing brilliancy and suppleness, is stronger and more solid than any of the other artificial silks. It can be twisted, braided, or woven with extraordinary facility, and constitutes a real advance in that industry, the product of which the Germans call "glanstoff" and the French "artificial silk." It is uninflammable, unaffected by humidity, and indestructible by acids or by alcohol. Two new fibres are on trial, the first being paper yarns made from pine fibres, which are very cheap. The pine fibre has to be made into paper before spinning, and it is not intended to supplant either cotton or wool for the finer yarns. It forms a strong, coarse yarn, which can be readily dyed any shade and will take on also a high polish, while it is moth and insect proof, and not subject to mildew. The second fibre is obtained by dredging in the shallow seas of the Spencer Gulf, South Australia, where it is found embedded in sand, from which it is separated by washing. From a chemical and microscopical examination the fibre appears to be a land plant which has been submeregd by an incursion of the sea, thereby undergoing a process of natural retting. While the fibre is rather brittle and deficient in tensile strength, it is possible to use it in conjunction with wool or shoddy. As it comes to market it is particularly rich in sodium and magnesium chlorides, and yields a large amount of mineral residue on burning, it has properties which should render it uninflammable. The dyeing affinities of the fibre are peculiar. It has a strong attraction for basic colors, which dye it without a mordant, thus making it very similar to jute, while it evinces only a slight attraction for the substantial cotton colors and for those of the sulphur group.

A metallic yarn new this year, consists of a core of any suitable substance coated chemically with a metallic layer. The layer is strongly adherent, and the metal particles are protected from oxidation and the action of gas. It can be produced in all shades of gold, and also in silver and copper in any of the modern art shades. Having a smooth surface, it is admirably adapted for working in with other threads, and in combination with artificial silk it can be woven into tissues sparkling with the iridescence of the rainbow. The newest substitute for wool is the banana fibre. This material is much like jute and hemp. The Chinese were the first to use it, and the supply available is almost without limit. One feature of the cloth produced from this fibre is that it is suitable for use in tropical climates. A new jute substitute made from paper yarn and cotton waste by a German firm, is in demand. The new substitute, called "textilose," offers many advantages over jute for packing dry, powery substances such as cement. The nature of the material prevents any dust escaping from the bag. A chemical process, somewhat similar to the mercerization of cotton, is being successfully applied in Barmen to spun worsted yarns. The yarn is run into a bath of sodium bisulphite, a chemical which exerts a shrinking action upon wool. This action is resisted by mechanical tension, and the process is continued for some five minutes at a high temperature, until the wool assumes a gelatinous or rubber-like elasticity. The yarn is removed to a weak mineral acid solution, boiled under relaxing tension for an hour, and is finally rinsed and dried. Norgine, a new product made from kelp, is used in the textile industry for stiffening and dressing purposes, and gives very satisfactory results. It is not used as a substitute for potato starch, dextrine, etc.; only as an admixture in starch to give the goods a softer and more flexible feel. Norgine is therefore considered as a ligament or aglutinant. The seaweed from which it is made comes from Sweden. A by-product of norgine is iodine.

PAPER. As sources for paper pulp the kaoliang or tall millet, so extensively grown in Manchuria, is recommended, and a series of experiments made in Dalny show that 77 per cent. of the raw material is available for that purpose. A pulp factory is proposed near Naples, Italy, to utilize esparto grass or alfa from Tripoli. Following the reference to bamboo as a paper stock (see YEAR BOOK, 1911, p. 166) the government of Burma will grant unusual concessions to those who desire to establish paper mills, and will use that material for pulp. Bamboo paper napkins are reported from Hongkong. The bark from hemlock, formerly of no value, is now used in the northwestern States for making tanning extract. A new paper cloth invented in Germany is described as follows: A thin sheet of pulp having been deposited on a felt, a piece of cotton or linen cloth of the same size is laid thereon, and this again is covered by a second sheet of pulp, with which the cloth mixes so intimately that the whole forms one solid and compact sheet. The process is inexpensive, while the applicability of paper cloth thus made to a variety of purposes is obvious. It is called "sandwich paper."

GLASS. A new form of glass called "siloxyd glass," recommended as an improvement over quartz glass, is made by adding to raw quartz solutions of oxides of zircon, titanium, and other metals difficult to fuse, or silicates of same to silicic acid, the resulting mixture yielding on fusion a transparent glassy substance which fuses at 1750°C. The advantages claimed for this material over ordinary quartz glass are that its strength is 30 to 50 per cent. greater tested by bending, and 10 to 30 per cent. more tested by pressure, and that it is less brittle, because the devitrification is only about half that of quartz glass. It is also more resistant to basic metallic oxides. The advantages claimed for siloxyd glass give to this material a wide range of usefulness, especially for apparatus used in the acid industry and for laboratory purposes where socket pipes, tee pipes for acid conduits, evaporating basins, concentrating dishes, cooling vessels, special boxes, conical pipes, condensation utensils, balls for acid towers, etc., are required. Most of the articles used for such purposes have been made of platinum, as no quality of glass that would meet the requirements had been produced.

An unsmashable glass called "triplex" glass has been invented in France. It is made as follows: Two sheets of glass are taken and one face of each is covered with a thin layer of gelatin; the sheets, gelatin faces opposite, are placed together, with a very thin sheet of celluloid between. The whole is subjected to hydraulic pressure to make the combination solid. The composite sheet as it comes from the press is as transparent as ordinary glass. When struck, as by a hammer or spike, it may be cracked, but it cannot be broken into bits. The glass is pulverized at the point of shock and in its neighborhood, involving a great absorption of energy. This glass may be of great service in carriages, automobiles, public conveyances, and railways, for besides the direct shock the return shock often determines the breakage of glass in most accidents, and most serious wounds are due to broken glass.

COLOR PHOTOGRAPHY. The reproduction of actual colors in a photograph has, until recently, been attended with difficulty, owing to the lack of sensitiveness in autochrome plates in comparison with ordinary plates. Efforts to strengthen the sensitiveness of the autochrome plate have been made in two ways: First, by substituting for natural light an artificial light strong enough to reduce the time of exposure to a fraction of a second; second, by hypersensitizing the plate through the use of certain coloring agents of the cyanide group. For the first method flash powders are employed, notably a mixture of two parts of magnesium and one part of potassium perchlorate. The substitution of this powder for daylight has marked a new step in the production of a photograph in color. The results are as favorable as those obtained in daylight, and the time of exposure can be regulated to a fraction of a second. In using this process the light entering the camera must be filtered through a screen different from that ordinarily employed in autochrome photography, and without it the colors reproduced would not be true to nature. The second method of overcoming lack of sensitiveness consists in hypersensitizing the plates themselves by impregnating them with cyanide coloring agents known by the names of pinachrome, pinacyanol, and pinaverdol. Until recently autochrome plates after sensitizing required the use of still another different taking screen, but with the solution now used for this process the magnesium screen may be employed. After sensitizing the plate, it must be dried very quickly, as slight delay in the drying will in-

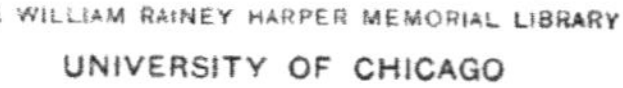

THE WILLIAM RAINEY HARPER MEMORIAL LIBRARY
UNIVERSITY OF CHICAGO

jure the colors. The plate is placed vertically to dry in an air-tight container sealed against light, and bolding a receiver containing sulphuric acid or calcium chloride.

PERFUMERY. Peter M. Short, an English chemist, has succeeded in manufacturing from petroleum an essence which is said to be a perfect substitute for attar of roses. While experimenting with liquid air to produce a candle from paraffin by freezing, he found that certain free agents remained floating at the top. These he investigated and found a substance which imitates attar of roses.

MISCELLANEOUS. A new oil has made its appearance in Europe that is extracted from tomato seeds. Especially in Italy is it possible to obtain this oil in considerable quantities, owing to the extensive cultivation of the tomato there. From a chemical standard the tomato-seed oil is classed as a dry-seed oil of the type of cottonseed oil. It will find, therefore, an immediate employment in soap-making and in all industries where cottonseed or similar oils are used.

New sources for the supplying of wood oil to paint manufacturers are notable in the oil obtainable from the kukui nut (*Aleurites moluccana*, or candlenut) which grows abundantly in Hawaii and the Philippines. These nuts yield an oil having the same properties as wood oil. If the nuts can be gathered and the oil extracted profitably, this oil should compete in the American market with Chinese wood oil.

The production of gas from peat having a low water content (up to about 20 per cent.) for use in suction gas (sauggas) engines has already met with considerable success in Germany, but recently successful efforts have been made to utilize peat with a water content 50 to 60 per cent. and thus do away with the process of drying.

A substitute for wood from straw is made in Europe, as follows: The straw waste is first split longitudinally, by a special cutting device to destroy the resiliency in the stalk. The ripped material is then placed in the machine together with certain ingredients, being laid upon a traveling plate. The latter is kept at a uniform temperature by means of steam, so as to cook the straw and the associated substances. When this stage has been carried to the requisite degree intense pressure is applied, the results of which are to compress the fibres of straw closely and tightly together, forming a homogeneous mass. A pressure of between two and three tons to the square inch is required in order to produce the best results, and the fabric issues from the machine in continuous lengths of the required thickness and width to be sawn as desired.

W. H. Warren and M. R. Grose, of Worcester, Mass., describe a new baking powder prepared from maple-sugar "sand," a waste product in the production of maple syrup. It has the following composition: Calcium bimalate, 57 parts; sodium bicarbonate, 25 parts; starch, 18 parts.

A substitute fertilizer called "phonolith" is now being manufactured in Germany. Its composition is: Water, 2 per cent.; silicic acid, 50 per cent.; oxide of iron, 7 per cent.; clay, 18 per cent.; lime, 4 to 5 per cent.; magnesia, 1 per cent.; potash, 8 to 10 per cent., and soda, 6 to 8 per cent.

LITERATURE. *The Chemical World, a monthly Journal of Chemistry and Chemical Engineering*, began publication in London, England, with the issue for January, 1912.

CHESS. A. K. Rubenstein, the Russian champion, captured the highest honors in chess in 1912 by winning the international matches held at San Sebastian, Wilna, and Poestyen, and tying O. S. Duras, of Prague, in the Breslau match. This showing makes it probable that some time this year Rubenstein will be pitted against Dr. Emanuel Lasker, the world's champion. Other international winners were Alexander A. Alechine, of St. Petersburg, at Stockholm, and Rudolph Spielmann, of Munich, at Abbazia, where the play was restricted to "king's gambit." No important tournaments were held in the United States, although the *American Chess Bulletin* arranged a king's gambit correspondence tournament, open to players of the United States and Canada. The tournament began in November, 1912, and will end in May, 1913. Columbia for the second successive year won the intercollegiate tournament, capturing 10½ games and losing 1½. Harvard finished second, with 8½ to 3½. Princeton won 3 games and lost 9, and Yale won 2 and lost 10. The Triangular College League tournament resulted in a tie between Cornell and Pennsylvania. Brown, the other contestant, failed to win a game.

CHESTERTON, G. K. See LITERATURE, ENGLISH AND AMERICAN.

CHICAGO CIVIL SERVICE COMMISSION. See MUNICIPAL GOVERNMENT.

CHICAGO OPERA COMPANY. See MUSIC.

CHICAGO RAPID TRANSIT. See RAPID TRANSIT.

CHICAGO, UNIVERSITY OF. An institution of higher learning at Chicago, Ill., founded in 1892. The total number of students enrolled in all departments of the university in the autumn of 1912 was 3362. The faculty numbered 337. The total benefactions received during the year amounted to $1,087,178. Among these was a gift by Mr. Julius Rosenwald of $250,000 toward the building fund of the university. Mr. Rosenwald so conditioned the gift as to necessitate the securing of $500,000 from other friends of the university. The productive funds of the university in 1911-12 amounted to $17,226,573. There were in the library 371,351 books and 195,000 pamphlets. President, Harry Pratt Judson.

CHILD LABOR. NATIONAL CONFERENCE The eighth annual conference of the National Child Labor Committee was held in Louisville, Ky., in February. The general subject was "Child Labor and Education." A number of educators were present by special invitation. The main features of the present programme of child labor reform, as night work in glass factories, employment of small children in fruit, vegetable, fish, and oyster canneries, night messenger service, and regulation of street trades, were touched upon, but special attention was given to industrial training and vocational guidance. Evening schools for young children who work from eight to 12 hours during the day were unanimously condemned as cruel and inhuman. Continuation schools for children from 14 to 16, even to 21, years were variously advocated as a means of raising the industrial efficiency of the next generation. One speaker held that the high schools and even the eighth grade have little or no economical value to-day, as pupils go out from them into automatic work with no real preparation for life. Mrs. Florence Kelley advocated compulsory half-time schools for minors above 16 years.

In the discussion of vocational guidance it was brought out that there are 42,000 children licensed each year in New York City, most of whom earn less than the cost of their own support and yet work in "blind-alley" trades where they receive no training for the future. It was emphasized that there is great danger that vocational guides may become too explicit in their directions instead of supplying information as to conditions and opportunities. It was also pointed out as possible evils that employment bureaus may be formed by schools only to degenerate into agencies for finding jobs; that encouragement might be given to short cuts in industrial training, and that attention of the child may be directed toward industry too early. Miss Helen T. Woolley gave an account of a study under her direction at Cincinnati, which is to continue over five years, of two groups of children, one in industry and the other in school. The hope was expressed that vocational guidance would result in changing the character of the school curriculum so that children would wish to stay and parents would wish to have them stay in school to the end. One speaker held that a desirable result would be the conviction that most industries are not suited for children under any condition. Dr. Samuel M. Lindsay declared that federal aid to education is a necessary step in the solution of the child-labor problem. He declared that 20 per cent. of the white voting population in some States is illiterate; that many of the poorer sections of the country cannot meet the increased demands for vocational training, and therefore outside aid for the better equipment and of school houses and educational opportunities is imperative. The rejuvenation of the rural school was advocated as a necessary step in raising the status of rural child labor and checking the movement of country youth to the city and the mill community. The importance of industrial training and the great social cost of child labor led to a resolution calling upon the educators of the country to revolutionize school methods and curriculums so as to raise the standards of attendance and also provide practical vocational opportunities for all. In emphasizing the social cost of child labor several of the speakers emphasized the deterioration of the factory population of England, as shown by the reductions in the standards for army recruits in 1885 and again in the British-Boer War. The extension of medical inspection of schools to mills was advocated. One remedy for the exploitation of children, advocated by Rev. John A. Ryan, was the legal minimum wage (q. v.). He declared that many children are exploited through the fact that their wage does not compensate for energy expended, with the result that growth and intelligence are stunted and vitality diminished. The United States commissioner of education, P. P. Claxton, proposed as a substitute for child labor that the children of the mill communities be given agricultural training. This would raise the wages of the adult workers in the mills and enormously increase the welfare not only of children but of mill communities in general.

Annual Report. The report of the general secretary of the National Child Labor Committee showed that during the year 1912 investigations had been conducted into the administration of child labor laws in twelve States; into textile mills in four States; into canneries in two States; into truck gardens and berry-fields in two States; into the night-messenger service in Pennsylvania and the District of Columbia; into the employment of children on the stage in two States and the District of Columbia; into tenement home work in Massachusetts and New York; into coal mines of Pennsylvania, and into the street trades in Michigan, Ohio, and District of Columbia. Special attention had been given to tenement home work in New York City. In addition to the forty-one articles for the making of which in tenements licenses may be had, the inspectors of the committee found the following kinds of work and articles: Crocheting of twelve different commodities; dolls' cloths of many varieties; teddy-bear legs; play suits for children; beading moccasins and bags; embroideries of all kinds; ribbon rosettes; roses and fancy bows; passementeries; Irish crochet, including lace, collars, cuffs, buttons, and medallions; millinery ornaments; braiding hat straws; glove stitching; coil winding; making lamp shades, brushes, belts, garters, suspenders, bead necklaces, kimonos, and hatpins. The prohibtion of tenement manufacturing and the creation of minimum wage boards were recommended.

Legislation. The fight for advancing child labor legislation has largely taken the form in recent years of efforts to secure the passage of a model or uniform law. This law has been agreed to by the National Child Labor Committee, the American Bar Association, and the United States Commission on Uniform Laws. It prohibits the employment of children under 14, forbids night work and dangerous occupations for children under 16, and requires educational and medical certification. It forbids the employment of children under 18, and in some cases under 21, in trades considered exceptionally dangerous. It prohibits the employment of girls under 21 in coal mines or quarries, and the employment of minors in saloons, barrooms, or night-messenger service. It forbids street-trading to boys under 10 and girls under 16, and otherwise regulates the street trades. The hours of employment are limited to 8 per day and 48 per week, between 7 A. M. and 7 P. M. for boys under 16 and girls under 18.

In 1912 new laws were enacted in twelve States. Arizona adopted the model law above outlined. Kentucky limited to 60 hours per week the employment of women under 21 in all gainful occupations, except domestic service and nursing; two additional factory inspectors, both women, were authorized. Louisiana exempted stage children from the child labor law. The Maryland law approximated the model law, but permitted children of 12 to be employed in canneries, stores, places of amusement, and the transmission of merchandise and messages. At the same time a compulsory school attendance law was passed and the factory inspection department reorganized. Massachusetts established a 56-hour week for women and children in mercantile workshops; established a minimum wage commission, and appointed a commission of three to investigate the condition of widowed mothers having dependent children. Minnesota thoroughly revised her child labor law, following closely the model law. Boys under 18 were forbidden employment as night messengers between 10 P. M. and 5 A. M.; such employment was totally prohibited for girls under 21; and exemption of stage children under official authorization was established. A vigorous campaign was carried on by the commission in Mississippi, through the distribution of reports and a weekly press service. A law was finally secured following closely the model law, though exempting canneries in the country but not those on the coast. Mississippi became the first State in which cotton manufacturing is a principal industry in which children under 16 have a legal 8-hour day in such mills. This law prohibited the night work of boys under 16 and of girls under 18. New Jersey limited the employment of all females to 10 hours a day in manufacturing or mercantile establishments, bakeries, laundries, and restaurants. New York established a 54-hour week for women and children employed in all manufacturing industries, except canneries, and perfected official supervision of children seeking employment certificates. Rhode Island prohibited the employment of boys under 21 in messenger service between 10 P. M. and 5 A. M. South Carolina forbade the employment of children under 18 at night or under 14 during the day as messengers in cities of 5000 population and over. Virginia limited the hours of all females and boys under 14 to ten per day in mercantile establishments in towns of 2000 or more.

NEW YORK. The New York Factory Investigating Commission appointed to inquire into the conditions of labor and other aspects of modern factory life studied among other things the conditions of child labor in the New York canneries and city tenements. For a number of years efforts have been made to bring the canneries under some form of effective public control. An apparently successful effort a few years ago was defeated by official decisions declaring sheds attached to the canneries not to be factories within the meaning of the law, since no machinery was installed in them. The experts of the Investigating Commission found numbers of children, some as young as 3 or 4 years, 102 were 8 or under, and nearly 1000 under 14, employed in these sheds in stringing beans, husking corn, and otherwise assisting in the preparing of fruit and vegetables for canning, without any restrictions as to hours. Women were shown to have worked as many as 115 to 120 hours in one week. They described in a most realistic manner the hardships of such children and the social loss involved in allowing them to grow up in ignorance and without definite vocational training. There was thus secured the widest publicity for abuses which the reformers have long sought to remedy. The inquiry brought out the fact that more than half the canners employed no children at all and that a few of them made good profits without working women excessive hours. Thus restrictive legislation in behalf of the workers would protect them and the more conscientious employers at the same time. Much concrete evidence bearing on the employment of children in home work in New York City was being gathered at the close of the year.

ENGLAND. The London County Council promulgated the following rules for the regulation of street trades. No child under 14 who is liable for full time school attendance may be employed on school days more than 3½ hours in any one day, nor between 8 A. M. and 5 P. M., nor before 6:30 A. M. or after 8:30 P. M.; on other than school days such may not be employed more than 8 hours in any one day nor before 6:30 A. M. or after 9 P. M. No girl under 16 shall be employed in any street trade. No boy under 16 may be thus employed, except between the hours of 6 A. M. and 9 P. M., and all such must be exempt from school attendance and procure and wear a badge constituting a license. An elaborate set of rules was formulated to govern the issue and withdrawal of badges and the punishments for altering, lending, selling, or pawning same.

SCOTLAND. A council on child welfare was formed through a federation of public, religious, and philanthropic agencies and individuals interested in the promotion of the welfare of children. Its organization consists of a central committee operating through local councils and executive committees. It will aim to provide means for perfecting child life in all aspects up to the age of 21. Much attention will be given to the collection and dissemination of information. It will arrange conferences and coöperate in every way with existing agencies.

See CHILDREN'S BUREAU; WIDOWS' PENSIONS; WOMEN IN INDUSTRY; MINIMUM WAGE; SWEATING.

LITERATURE. Among the new books of the year were. E. N. Clopper, *Child Labor in City Streets;* Arthur Holmes, *The Conservation of the Child;* William F. Ogburn, *Progress and Uniformity in Child Labor Legislation;* Dunlop and Denmon, *English Apprenticeship and Child Labor: A History; Report of the Commission on Minimum Wage Boards, by the Massachusetts Commission;* D. H. Whitehouse, *Problems of Boy Life;* S. P. Breckinridge and E. Abbott, *The Delinquent Child and the Home.*

The National Child Labor Committee began in June the publication of a quarterly, *The Child Labor Bulletin.*

CHILDREN, ILLITERACY OF. See ILLITERACY.

CHILDREN'S BUREAU. On April 2, the House of Representatives passed the Peters bill authorizing the establishment of a federal children's bureau in the Department of Commerce and Labor, this bill having previously passed the Senate. Shortly thereafter President Taft named Miss Julia C. Lathrop of Chicago as the chief of the new bureau. During the five preceding years the National Child Labor Committee had carried on an agitation for the creation of such a bureau, the idea having originated with Miss Lillian D. Wald of New York City. It was opposed on constitutional grounds and as an unauthorized invasion of the rights of the States. The law specifies that "the said bureau shall investigate and report upon all matters pertaining to the welfare of children and child life, and shall especially investigate the questions of infant mortality, the birthrate, physical degeneracy, orphanage, juvenile delinquency and juvenile courts, desertion and illegitimacy, dangerous occupations, accidents and diseases of the children of the working-class, employment, legislation affecting the children in the several States and Territories, and such other facts as have a bearing upon the welfare, efficiency, character, and training of children." On many of the subjects here indicated information is almost if not quite wholly lacking; what is at hand is in a chaotic condition, and almost all the various activities for child welfare lack coördination. Having no administrative powers, the main function of the bureau will be to secure information and make it available to the States and all parties interested. The first pamphlet of the bureau stated that the first work would consist in the compilation of existing material and the publication of a statistical handbook. The bureau will collate material from the current literature of all countries; will prepare digests of legislation; will make an original investigation of infant mortality; will aid in securing registration of births, and will issue popular pamphlets on the subjects within its scope.

The first subject taken up by the new bureau was an investigation of infant mortality or the death of children under 1 year of age. Preliminary work had been completed by December 20. The plan was very comprehensive, including housing, feeding, care of infants, milk supply, industrial and economic condition of parents, sanitary conditions of the neighborhood, and other factors in the hygienic environment. The investigation was to begin in smaller towns surrounding the larger cities of New England, Pennsylvania, and Michigan, these being the only States where birth registration is complete. Statistics presented by Dr. Cressy L. Wilbur showed that deaths of babies under 1 year of age in the poorer districts of a principal American city were 373 per 1000; on the other hand, in the better residence quarters the death rate was 156. Estimating that 300,000 babies die annually in the United States, these figures warranted the conclusion that, could good conditions be provided for all, at least 150,000 babies would be saved annually. It was thought that even more than this number could be saved, since the infant death rate in New Zealand is only 68 per 1000. See CHILD LABOR.

CHILDREN'S COURT. See JUVENILE COURT.

CHILD WELFARE. See EDUCATION.

CHILE. A republic on the Pacific coast of South America. Capital, Santiago.

AREA AND POPULATION. Chile has an estimated area of 757,366 square kilometers (292,419 square miles), including Tacna province (23,958 sq. kms., 9250 sq. miles), claimed by Peru. The census of November 27, 1907, disclosed 3,249,279 inhabitants (Tacna, 28,748). In 1912 figures were published showing the population by provinces, as officially calculated for December 31, 1910. The total was 3,415,060, distributed as follows (in parentheses are shown the provincial areas in square kilometers): Aconcagua, 132,730 (14,000); Antofagasta, 118,718 (120,718); Arauco, 62,259 (5068); Atacama, 65,118 (79,531); Bíobío, 100,495 (13,863); Cautín, 161,935 (16,524); Chiloé, 91,657 (22,255); Colchagua, 159,421 (9973); Concepción, 225,054 (8579); Coquimbo, 178,731 (36,509); Curicó, 108,120 (7885); Linares, 111,773 (10,279); Llanquihue, 113,285 (91,676); Magallanes (ter.), 23,650 (171,438); Malleco, 113,020 (8555); Maule, 115,568 (7281); Ñuble, 169,858 (9059); O'Higgins, 94,257 (5617); Santiago, 546,599 (15,260); Tacna, 42,925 (23,958); Talca, 132,730 (10,006); Tarapacá, 115,940 (46,957); Valdivia, 131,751 (23,285); Valparaíso, 299,466 (23,285); total, 3,415,060 (757,366). Population of the larger cities (1907 census): Santiago, 332,724; Valparaíso, 162,447; Concepción, 55,330; Iquique, 40,171; Talca, 38,040; Chillán, 34,269; Antofagasta, 32,496; Viña del Mar, 26,262. Immigration is small (2543 in 1910). In 1910, marriages 19,326, births 130,052, stillbirths 3471, deaths 106,073; excess of births 23,979.

EDUCATION. Primary instruction is gratuitous, but not compulsory. Public primary schools at the end of 1911 numbered 2896, with 375,274 pupils enrolled and an average attendance of 58.76 per cent. Private schools receiving state aid had an enrollment of 52,315, with average attendance 32,683. In 1910 private schools without state assistance had 30,385 pupils enrolled. In 1911: 41 lyceums for boys, enrollment 12,052, average attendance 10,797; 36 lyceums for girls, enrollment 8277, attendance 6789; 15 normal schools, with 2322 students; 277 manual training schools. The University of Chile had 2002 students, and the Catholic University 683. The state religion is Roman Catholicism, but religious toleration prevails.

AGRICULTURE. Figures published in 1912 by the Chilean bureau of statistics show the following estimated production of the principal cereals and foodstuffs: Wheat, 496,022 metric tons; barley, 53,562; oats, 27,006; corn, 31,002; beans, 37,026; carobs, 7486; potatoes, 202,481. Estimated wine production, 990,644 hectoliters. The pastoral industry is developing, notably in wool production in the south.

MINING. The country's prosperity is largely due to the production of enormous quantities of sodium nitrate in the northern provinces of Antofagasta and Tarapacá. This valuable fertilizer is exported to many countries. Coal is mined (898,971 metric tons in 1909), though not in sufficient quantity to supply the domestic demand. Copper, for which Chile was once famous, shows a tendency to regain its former importance (in 1909, 42,726 metric tons, valued at about $9,939,300). See the export values of mineral products in the section *Commerce*.

COMMERCE. Imports and exports, special trade, in thousands of pesos gold:

	1908	1909	1910	1911
Imports......	267,264	262,082	297,486	348,990
Exports......	319,149	306,430	317,213	330,621

The leading imports include cotton and woolen goods, iron and steel manufactures, and coal. Principal exports in 1911, in thousands of pesos gold: Nitrate, 262,649; copper, 18,687; hides and leather, 8983; wool, 7696; calcium borate, 6231; iodine, 5140; meat, 3769; nuts, 1858; barley, 1853; beans, 1834; oats, 1590; wheat, 1384; whale oil, 1164; bran, 1150; flour, 827.

Imports and exports, special trade, 1911, in thousands of pesos gold, by principal countries: Great Britain, 111,768 and 145,913; Germany, 89,579 and 71,780; United States, 43,222 and 53,577; France, 18,991 and 16,069; Belgium, 10,567 and 9532; Argentina, 21,410 and 3284; Peru, 20,344 and 1074; Italy, 8681 and 979; Netherlands, 274 and 9429; Spain, 3600 and 5511; Australia, 6056 and 63.

SHIPPING. Entered at the ports in the foreign trade, 1911, 4115 vessels of 11,309,296 tons (steam, 3626 of 10,449,368 tons); cleared, 3418 of 9,303,926 tons (steam, 3021 of 3,593,069 tons). Entered coastwise, 11,018 vessels of 15,939,724 tons (steam, 10,484 of 15,797,835 tons); cleared, 10,547 of 18,292,445 tons (steam, 10,979 of 17,620,939 tons). Merchant marine, 1911: 84 steamers of 69,604 tons net and 91 sail of 52,918 tons net.

COMMUNICATIONS. The length of railways in operation is reported at 5804 kilometers, of which 2706 kms. are state lines and 3098 private; under construction, 2243 kms. Since this report was made, a considerable amount (exact figures not available) of the railway under construction has been completed. The Chile longitudinal railway, a meter gauge line over 350 miles in length, was almost completed in 1912. This work included the Espino tunnel and the Andean section, which was the last of five tunnels through the mountains on a section where 44 miles of rack road are required. Other lines under construction or completed during 1912 were the following: Paloma-San Marcos, Copiapo-Lagunas, Vallimar-Algarrobal, San Bernardo-Volcan, Malipilla-San Antonio, Rancagua-Donihua, Alcomes-Pichilimu, and Curico-Hualam and also the Chilean Northern Railway, the Pueblo Hundido-Pintados line, joining the Chanaral and Iquique railways, of which 719 kilometers were under construction, had 390 kilometers completed in 1912. The Chilean railways aggregated over 5000 miles in length. Telegraph lines (1910), 22,334 miles, of which 16,513 state; post offices, about 1100.

FINANCE. The monetary unit is the peso, worth 36.5 cents. The value of the paper peso is about 22 cents. Revenue, 1910, 82,764,423 pesos gold and 152,975,645 paper; expenditure, 60,677,704 pesos gold and 234,143,253 paper. The chief sources of revenue were: Nitrate export duties, 79,665,417 pesos gold; state railways, 47,760,751 paper; import duties, 44,436,032 paper; surtax on imports, 29,608,792 paper. Estimate expenditure, 1912, 81,070,927 pesos gold and 280,894,118 paper; 1913, 55,746,850 gold and 268,596,590 paper. Chief departmental estimates, 1912: Finance, 35,876,488 pesos gold and 16,572,749 paper; marine, 16,986,459 and 14,725,348; war, 674,684 and 33,115,000; industry and public works, 24,256,843 and 113,707,948; interior, 1,103,183 and 42,728,561; public instruction, 542,640 and 43,240,683. Debt (December 31, 1910): Foreign, 336,781,600 pesos gold; internal, 6,093,800 gold and 179,465,191 paper.

ARMY. The Chilean army was in course of reorganization during the year 1912 and it was expected that this would be completed by the end of 1913. The establishment of the active army was fixed for 1912 at 17,860, including a permanent staff of 8000. There were in addition 2500 men in the coast artillery and 1737 in the gendarmerie. The organization included 10 regiments of infantry, 8 regiments of cavalry, 20 batteries of field artillery, 1 mountain battery, 2 battalions of mounted infantry, and a corps of engineers. The active army is supposed to be raised to 150,000 war strength by including a portion of the national guard.

NAVY. The Chilean navy in 1912 included: Two battleships, aggregating 15,600 tons (*Capitán Prat*, built in 1892, and *O'Higgins*, 1897); one armored cruiser, 7000 tons (*Esmeralda*, 1896); four protected cruisers, 14,500 tons (built 1890-99); two torpedo cruisers, 1470 tons; seven torpedo-boat destroyers, 2270 tons; five first-class torpedo boats, 728 tons, and several auxiliary vessels, transports, etc. The keel of a 28,600-ton dreadnought, the *Almirante Latorre*, was laid down at Elswick December 1, 1911. The construction of a second dreadnought, the *Almirante Cochrane*, was decided upon in 1912. Contracts for six destroyers and two submarines were let in 1911, and the first of the destroyers was launched September 28, 1912.

GOVERNMENT. The president is elected by indirect vote for five years and is assisted by a council of state and a responsible ministry. The legislative body consists of the Senate (37 members, elected for six years) and the Chamber of Deputies (108, for three years). The president in 1912 was Ramón Barros Luco, inaugurated December 23, 1910. Ministry, formed August 10, 1912: Premier and minister of the interior, Guillermo Barros; foreign affairs, worship, and colonization, Antonio Huneeus; justice and public instruction, Enrique Villegas; finance, Manuel Rivas; war and marine, Claudio Vicuña; industry and public works, Oscar Viel.

For events connected with arbitration in Chile in 1912 see ARBITRATION, INTERNATIONAL.

CHINA. A successful revolution, followed by the abdication of the infant emperor, transformed the Chinese Empire into the Chinese Republic, February 12, 1912. The capital is Peking.

AREA AND POPULATION. The country has a total estimated area of 4,278,143 square miles, and consists of the following: China proper, or "the eighteen provinces"; the three provinces comprising Manchuria; Sinkiang province (which includes East Turkestan); and the dependencies of Mongolia and Tibet. The population is unknown. Of China proper there have been many censuses, or government estimates, the results of some of these being: 1761, 190,257,000; 1812, 360,440,000; 1842, 413,021,000; 1860, 260,925,000; 1882, 381,309,000; 1885, 377,636,000. Chinese censuses hitherto have been enumerations of households, whence the number of persons is computed by multiplying by the average number in a household (exclusive of children under six years of age). For the census taken in 1910 averages varied in different provinces from 3.1 to 5.8 per household; in Chihli it was 5.5 (but in Peking city 5.8); in some provinces the average was not ascertained, or at least not published. The mean of the ascertained averages was 4.8, and this figure has been used in calculating the population of provinces for which no specific average is given. The problem is further complicated by incompleteness of returns from Shansi and Szechwan. The figure for the latter province given below is not shown by the census, but is the number reported by the viceroy to the Peking authorities; judged from the partial returns of the census, the figure is plausible. The population figures for China proper, excepting the one for

Szechwan, are those published in 1912 by W. W. Rockhill as his interpretation of the 1910 census. Mr. Rockhill, American ambassador at Constantinople and formerly American minister at Peking, has published monographs on Chinese population summarizing the extant data; in 1904 he placed the population of China proper at less than 275,000,000, and in 1912 said that, although the new information furnished by the 1910 census is insufficient for definite conclusions, it tends to confirm the opinion that the population of China is much smaller than we have been led to believe and that in the last century it has been increasing very slowly, if at all. In the last column of the table are given the estimates of the Maritime Customs in its report published in 1912.

	Sq. m.	Census '10	M. C. est.
Anhwei	54,826	14,077,683	36,000,000
Chekiang	36,680	13,942,655	11,800,000
Chihli	115,830	22,970,654	29,400,000
Fukien	46,332	8,556,678	20,000,000
Honan	67,954	22,375,516	*
Hunan	83,398	20,583,187	22,000,000
Hupeh	71,428	21,256,144	34,000,000
Kansu	125,483	3,807,883	*
Kiangsi	69,498	16,254,374	24,534,000
Kiangsu	38,610	15,379,042	23,980,000
Kwangsi	77,220	5,426,356	8,000,000
Kwangtung	99,970	23,696,366	32,000,000
Kweichow	67,182	9,266,914	*
Shansi	81,853	9,422,871	*
Shantung	55,984	25,813,685	38,000,000
Shensi	75,290	6,726,064	*
Szechwan	218,533	54,505,600	78,711,000
Yünnan	146,718	8,049,673	7,571,000
China proper	1,532,789	†302,111,334	420,996,000
Shengking	54,761	5,830,819	....
Kirin	105,019	5,349,287	....
Heilungkiang	202,703	1,562,254	....
Manchuria	362,483	†12,742,360	17,000,000
Total China proper and Manchuria	....	314,853,644	437,996,000
Sinkiang	550,579	1,768,560	
Tibetan Marches (of Szechwan and Yünnan)	....	195,496	
Mongolia	1,076,292	1,800,000(?)	
Tibet	‡756,000	2,000,000(?)	
Total	4,278,143	329,617,750	

* Honan, Kansu, Kweichow, Shansi, and Shensi, 55,000,000. †Not including infants under six. ‡Including Kuku-nor and Tsaidam.

The annual estimates of the Maritime Customs (those for 1912 are given above) are widely quoted and often regarded as authoritative. But in respect of more than half of the provinces, they are beyond all doubt gross exaggerations; they are based on no known authority and, in any serious attempt to deduce an approximate figure for the population of China, are negligible factors.

The census of Peking taken in 1908 by the Ministry of the Interior disclosed 126,008 households; this indicates, on the basis of 5.8 persons to the household, a population of 730,846 (of whom 458,252 in the Tartar city, and 272,594 in the Chinese), the number being exclusive of infants under six. The 1910 census gives Peking a population of 805,110. The excess of males is notable, adult males numbering 500,819, adult females 256,638, and children (6 to 16) 47,653. If we estimate the proportion of infants under 6 at two per cent., the total of all persons in Peking is about 821,000.

For the treaty ports, the Maritime Customs' estimates probably represent the actual population more accurately than they do for the provinces; these estimates in 1912 for the larger treaty ports: Canton, 900,000; Hankow, 826,000; Tientsin, 800,000; Shanghai, 651,000; Foochow, 654,000; Chungking, 598,000; Soochow, 500,000; Ningpo, 350,000; Hangchow, 350,000; Nanking, 267,000; Changsha, 250,000; Chinkiang, 184,000; Antung, 161,000; Wuhu, 122,000; Amoy, 114,000; Wenchow, 100,000; Shansi, 90,000; Swatow, 66,000; Kongmoon, 62,000; Newchwang, 61,000. The Maritime Customs placed the numbers of foreigners living in the treaty ports in 1911 at 153,522, of whom 78,306 Japanese, 51,221 Russian, 10,256 British, 3470 American, 3224 Portuguese, 2758 German, and 1925 French.

Education. There are three classes of schools —the old-style schools, the mission schools, and the public schools—conducted more or less under western methods. The old-style schools are private institutions, whose curriculum is confined practically to the Chinese classics. Examination in the classics as the test for government employment was abolished by the decree of September 3, 1905, which also provided for an elaborate educational system based on that of Japan. In 1912 the Ministry of Public Instruction stated that it does not publish statistics of educational conditions.

Industries. China proper, though a distinctively agricultural country, is rich in minerals. Its coal deposits are among the richest in the world, but exploitation has not attained a great development. Tin, iron, antimony, lead, zinc, copper, and salt are worked, tin (in Yünnan) and iron being the most important. The principal crops include wheat, barley, corn, millet, beans, and peas, in the north; in the south, rice, cotton, and sugar. Tea and silk cocoons are products of extreme importance, the former in the west and south, the latter in every province. There is a large silk manufacture, but it is feared that, unless easily remediable defects are attended to, Chinese pongees will have to yield place in European markets to much inferior imitation makes.

Large amounts of opium have been produced, especially in Szechwan, but the output, pursuant to government decree, and the importation from India, through the coöperation of the Indian government, are being contracted. An agreement between China and Great Britain signed May 8, 1911, provides that the consolidated opium duty (import and likin) be raised from hk. tls. 110 to hk. tls. 350 per picul (133 1-3 pounds), that the export of opium from India to China shall cease before 1917, if clear proof be given of the complete absence of production of native opium in China, and that Indian opium shall not be conveyed into any province of China which has suppressed the cultivation and import of native opium. Imports of native opium recorded at the customs in 1911 amounted to 3384 piculs, against 19,875 piculs in 1910. It was reported that no opium was under cultivation in Szechwan in 1911; in that year the amount passing Ichang downwards was 688 piculs, against 28,530 piculs in 1910. The poppy is replaced with wheat, and Szechwan promises to regain her position as one of China's granaries.

The net importation of foreign opium into China in 1911 was 27,808 piculs, valued at hk. tls. 48,256,745, as compared with 35,358 piculs, valued at hk tls. 55,410,850 in 1910, and 48,917 piculs, hk tls. 35,744,979, in 1909. Restricted traffic in the drug has provoked speculation, and prices have trebled and quadrupled; thus, in 1907, the date of the first restriction agreement, which was superseded by the more stringent one of 1911, the Hongkong value of new Benares opium was 915 dollars (Mexican) per chest (about 160 pounds), whereas in 1911 it was 3800 dollars. See paragraph below on *Opium Question*.

COMMERCE. The total foreign trade of 1909 was the greatest recorded up to that time; it was exceeded, however, by the trade of 1910, and the latter by that of 1911. Values are stated in haikwan, or maritime customs, taels. This unit fluctuates with the price of silver; in 1907 it was worth about 79 cents, in 1908 65.5 cents, in 1909 63.4 cents, and during 1910 and 1911 it averaged 66 and 65 cents respectively. The following table shows the values in haikwan taels of total imports, imports for consumption, total exports, and exports of Chinese produce:

Year	Imports Total	Imports Net	Exports Total	Exports Chinese
1902	..325,546,311	315,363,905	224,363,990	214,181,584
1905	..461,194,532	447,100,791	241,981,938	227,888,197
1907	..429,071,662	416,401,369	277,050,990	264,380,697
1909	..430,048,606	418,158,067	350,883,353	338,992,814
1910	..476,553,402	462,964,894	394,421,836	380,833,328
1911	..482,576,127	471,503,943	388,410,350	377,338,166

Principal imports in 1910 and 1911, in thousands of haikwan taels: Cotton goods, 65,878 and 89,295; cotton yarn, 65,304 and 51,172; opium, 55,411 and 48,257; sugar, 22,441 and 22,602; rice, 31,320 and 18,699; iron, 9252 and 13,180; dyes, etc., 9720 and 12,313; tobacco, 9418 and 10.711; fish, 8959 and 10,063; flour, 8708 in 1911; coal, etc., 8196 and 8468; machinery, 6897 and 6793; wood, 6001 and 5842; paper, 4181 and 5606; matches, 5275 and 5298; leather, 4740 and 4810; woolen goods, 4116 and 4287.

Leading exports in 1910 and 1911, in thousands of haikwan taels: Raw silk, 80,242 and 74,510; beans and beancake, 36,681 and 48,190; tea, 35,931 and 38,335; cotton, 28,352 and 21,608; silk manufactures, 10,072 and 13,166; hides and skins, 19,930 and 16,519; straw goods, 11,921 and 15,418; oils, 13,092 and 14,631; sesame, 14,377 and 11,739; wool, 5191 and 7648; tin, 6246 and 6436; wheat, 6286 in 1911; peanuts, 3120 and 4563; silks, 4417 and 4339; cattle, 4553 and 4205; paper, 3506 and 3582; fireworks, 4075 and 3480; tobacco, 3512 and 3231; fruits, 3217 in 1911, medicines, 3003 and 3155. The export of silk in 1911 amounted to 96,094 piculs (against 110.184 in 1910), exclusive of cocoons 20,925 piculs, refuse cocoons 38,240, wild raw 33,831, waste 117,937, and waste yarn 144. Tea export: Black, 734,180 piculs; green, 299,237; brick, 416,656; tablet, 9073; dust, 3657; total, 1,462,803, against 1,560,800 in 1910. Imports of coin and bullion in 1911 amounted to hk. tls. 65,120,036, and exports hk. tls. 25,267,603. Partly through a decline in price due to competition between the Standard Oil Company and the Royal Dutch-Shell combination, the importation of kerosene advanced from 74,508,657 gals. in 1910 to 235,898,240 gals. in 1911.

The following table shows imports (including reëxports) and domestic exports by countries, in thousands of haikwan taels:

Countries	Imports 1910	Imports 1911	Exports 1910	Exports 1911
Hongkong	172,466	148,249	108,723	103,670
Great Britain....	70,949	89,997	18,703	17,295
Japan	76,756	79,506	61,606	62,049
United States ...	24,799	40,823	32,289	33,966
British India.....	43,958	37,034	4,535	5,810
Germany	21,368	22,457	13,342	14,096
Russia	16,047	17,266	45,962	50,718
Belgium	11,551	10,867	6,541	6,772
Straits, etc........	8,309	7,736	5,618	5,660
Dutch E. Indies..	5,756	6,725	1,433	1,451
Macao	7,411	6,508	4,657	4,745
Fr. Indo-China ..	5,981	3,383	2,112	1,331
France	2,761	3,018	38,830	39,102
Korea	2,382	2,510	2,629	3,490
Netherlands	1,198	1,417	7,184	6,503
Austria-Hungary	1,776	1,353	1,647	2,270
Sweden	313	846	27	47
Italy	508	675	10,827	9,346
Canada	1,158	553	1,571	1,283
Total incl. other..	476,553	482,576	380,833	377,338
Re-exports	13,589	11,072	13,589	11,072
Net imports	462,965	471,504	....	....
Gross exports....	......	....	394,422	388,410

SHIPPING. Entries and clearances combined in both the foreign and the coasting trade (tonnage in thousands):

Flag	1910 Vessels	1910 Tons	1911 Vessels	1911 Tons
Chinese, Shipping	36,909	14,147	31,258	12,830
Chinese, Junks....	109,166	5,451	99,570	5,052
British	28,000	34,253	28,885	34,712
Japanese	31,197	18,908	21,259	19,173
Other	14,538	16,023	12,426	14,005
Total	219,810	88,777	193,398	85,772
Steam	96,196	82,337	89,533	80,084
Sail	123,614	6,439	103,865	5,688

Statistics of the carrying trade from and to foreign countries in 1911 (tonnage in thousands):

Flag	Entries No.	Entries Tons	Clearances No.	Clearances Tons
British	4,687	4,886	4,753	5,028
Japanese	2,215	2,883	2,143	2,805
Chinese	27,091	1,986	26,333	1,988
German	743	1,311	769	1,406
French	459	556	467	590
Russian	480	363	533	406
American	311	285	319	295
Norwegian	257	259	264	266
Total, incl. other	36,418	12,834	35,748	13,085
1910	36,282	12,765	33,785	12,545

COMMUNICATIONS. Rivers and canals in China are of more importance to commerce than are roads, which, though numerous, are generally in poor condition. An imperial edict of May 9, 1911, announced the government's intention to nationalize privately-owned main railroad lines. This order, which contributed to the unrest that came to a head in the rebellion of the following October, had special reference to the two great lines under construction, the Canton-Hankow and the Szechwan-Hupeh. About the beginning of 1912 the reported length of railway open to traffic was 5822 1-2 miles; under construction, 2205 miles (the latter figure includes lines on which work had been begun even though subsequently suspended or abandoned).

The separate lines are as follows: (1) Chinese

Eastern Railway (Russian control); A Manchouli-Harbin-Suifenho, 950 miles; *b* Harbin-Kwanchengtze (Changchun), 131. Branch, Angangki-Tsitsihar, 17. (2) South Manchurian Railway (Japanese control): Kwanchengtze-Dairen, 437 1-2. Branches: Kwanchengtze-Kirin (Chinese control), 30 opened, 50 under construction; Mukden-Antung, 189; Suchiatun-Fushun Collieries, 39; Yentai-Taikang Collieries, 10; Tashikiao-Yingkow (Newchwang), 13; Liushutun branch, 3 1-2; Choushuitze-Port Arthur, 31 1-2. The foregoing lines and the Kowpangtze-Yingkow branch (57) and the Shanhaikwan-Mukden section of the Imperial Railways are in Manchuria—total, about 2182 miles. (3) Imperial-Railways of North China: Peking - Tientsin - Sinminia - Mukden, 522. Branches: Peking-Tungchow, 12; Peking-Lukowkiao (junction with Hankow Railway), 4; Tangku-Chinwangtao, 6; Lienshan-Hulutao Harbor, under construction, 7; Kowpangtze-Yinkow, 57. (4) Peking-Kalgan Railway: Peking-Kalgan, 124; Kalgan-Tienchen-Tatungfu-Suiyüan, of which Kalgan-Tienchen, 55 miles, completed and Tatungfu-Suiyüan, 165 miles, under construction. Branch: Peking-Mentowkow, 16 1-2. (5) Peking-Hankow Railway: Peking-Hankow, 755. Branches: Liangsiang-Toli, 12; Liuliho-Chaokiachwang, 10; Kaoyihsien-Lincheng, 10 (these three branches to local coal mines): Kaopeitien-Siling (imperial tombs), 26; Paotingfu branch, 3; Chochow-Yüchow, 12. (6) Tientsin-Pukow (Kiangsu) Railway: Northern section (German), Tientsin-Tsinan-Tsinanfu-Hanchwang, 390; southern section (British), Pukow-Linhwaikwan-Süchowfu-Likwoyi, 236 (though running November 29, 1911, between Tientsin and Pukow, which is across the Yangtse from Nanking). (7) Shantung Railway (German control): Tsingtau-Tsinan, 256. Branch, Changtien-Poshan, 28. (8) Shansi Railways: Taiyüanfu-Shihkiachwang (the Chengtai Railway), 151; Yütze-Taikuhsien-Pingyaohsien, under construction, 40. (9) Taokow-Sinsiang-Tsinghwachen, 96. Branch, Fawangchen-Jameisen, 7. (10) Kaifeng-Chengchow-Honanfu, 140. (11) Honanfu-Tungkwan, under construction, 166—to reach Sianfu, 240 miles from Honanfu. (12) Tichshanfu-Hwangshihkang (Tayeh Mines Railway, Hupeh), 17. (13) Szechwan-Hupeh Railway: Kwangshui, on the Peking-Hankow line in Hupeh, to Kweichowfu, in Szechwan, via Ichang, under construction, 800. (14) Canton-Hankow Railway, total length 739 miles, of which open 73 miles. Canton-Yingiak and 30 miles Chuchow-Changsha. Branches; Canton-Fatshan-Samshui, 32; Chuchow-Pingsiang, 65. (15) Canton-Kowloon, 112 (89 1-2 Chinese, 22 1-2 British). (16) Sinhung Railway, in Kwangtung, 55 miles, of which 40 open. (17) Yünnan Railway (French): Laokai, on the Tongking frontier, to Yünnanfu, *via* Mengtze, 291 miles, an extension of the French Indo-Chinese line from Hanoi. (18) Swatow-Chaochowfu 24. (19) Amoy-Changchowfu, 10 open, 23 under construction. (20) Kiukiang-Nanchang, 82, of which 20 open from Kiukiang. (21) Anhwei Railway, 150 from Wuhu, none of which open, and construction suspended. (22) Kiangsu-Chekiang Railway: Shanghai-Kashing-Hangchow, 118; Hangchow-Ningpo, under construction, 100. (23) Shanghai-Nangkin Railway: Shanghai - Soochow - Chinkiang - Nanking, 193. Branches: Shanghai-Woosung 10; Nanking City Railway, 7 1-2. Total miles open at beginning of 1912, 5822 1-2; under construction, 2205.

FINANCE. A comprehensive statement of actual revenue and expenditure is not available. Under the empire probably a considerable part of the revenue found its way into the private purse of the provincial collectors. Whether or not such peculation flourishes under the republic, it is certain that the financial straits of the government in recent years continued in 1912. The budget for 1911 showed estimated revenue hk. tls. 297,000,000 and estimated expenditure hk. tls. 351,000,000; for 1912, hk. tls. 297,000,000 and hk. tls. 576,520,000.

Exact records are made and reported for the receipts from the Maritime Customs. These have been: 1908, hk. tls. 32,901,895; 1909, 35,539,917; 1910, 35,571,879. In 1911, they amounted to hk. tls. 36,179,225, of which hk. tls. 29,656,393 were derived from foreign trade and hk. tls. 6,523,432 from home trade. In detail: Duties on imports (including opium), hk. tls. 14,742,801; duties on exports of native produce, 12,622,759 (to foreign countries 8,135,021, to Chinese ports 4,487,738); coast trade duties (including opium), 2,035,694; tonnage dues, 1,346,385; transit dues inwards, 1,289,991, and outwards, 578,039; opium likin, 3,564,150; total, hk. tls. 36,197,825, as compared with hk. tls. 35,571,879 in 1910, 36,068,595 in 1906, and 30,007,044 in 1902. Opium import duties in 1911 amounted to hk. tls. 1,391,632; these duties in 1911 (exclusive of opium) was hk. tls. 4,955,788, against 4,052,022 in 1910, the increase being due largely to the raising of the consolidated tax from hk. tls. per picul to hk. tls. 350 on May 8, 1911. The increase in import 353,692, was due to larger importations of kerosene and cottons; a decrease in export duties, hk. tls. 374,607 is attributed to the combined effects of flood, famine, and revolution. See below, paragraph *Foreign Loan*.

The public debt, January 1, 1911, stood as follows: £59,892,171, 377,783,388 francs; 12,470,000 yen; $2,220,000; Shanghai tls. 3,270,000; hk. tls. 421,499,998 (the 1901 indemnity to the Powers); the total amounting to $658,669,498.

ARMY. The difficult task of organizing the army of the Chinese Republic in 1912 was in the hands of Major Brissand-Desmaillet of the French army. An active and a reserve army independent of the provincial militia was being organized with the guard division as the pattern and the tactical school. The plan of organization involved 5 years spent in the active army and then its graduates would pass into the reserve. Attention was also being paid to plans for the reorganization of the militia, but the entire scheme or reorganization, so far as its execution was concerned, was rather in an elementary condition. A school of aviation was established under an American instructor at Canton and war material, much of it of German origin, was being provided. An opportunity to view the Chinese army was given on October 10, at Peking, when 11,500 troops of all arms took part in a review on the anniversary of the Revolution. The Republican Guard, the Imperial Guard, gendarmerie, reserve troops, Imperial and Republican Guard Cavalry and Republican and Imperial Guard Artillery, paraded to the number of about 11,500 and made a good appearance, the Republican Guard being of the best physique. The Republican Guard Artillery had on parade 12 Japanese mountain guns, and 12 Skoda 75 mm. (2.95 in.) Q. F. field guns, 1910 model.

NAVY. Since the war with Japan in 1895, the Chinese navy has not included an armored ship. Aside from small craft, the only serviceable vessels are six cruisers. Of these, four (one of 4300 tons and three of about 3000 tons each) were built in 1897 and 1898; the fifth, the *Ying Swei*, of 2400 tons, was launched at Barrow, July 14, 1911, and the sixth, the *Chao Ho*, of 2400 tons, at Elswick, October 23, 1911. A seventh cruiser, of the same type as the *Ying Swei*, was launched at the yard of the New York Shipbuilding Company, May 4, 1912. A river gunboat was launched at Kiel, in 1911, and a gunboat of 780 tons, the *Yung Fung*, was nearing completion at Nagasaki, at the end of 1912. There is a considerable number of torpedo boats, river gunboats, etc.

GOVERNMENT. The rule of the Manchu dynasty, which began in 1644, came to an end with the abdication of the emperor, Pu-yi, February 12, 1912. The emperor Tsai-t'ien (reign title, Kuang-hsü), died August 14, 1908, and was succeeded on November 14 following, by his brother's son Pu-yi (reign title, Hsüan-t'ung), who was born February 11, 1906. The emperor's father, Prince Chun, was regent. A constitution drawn up by the Senate was sanctioned by an edict of November 3, 1911. On November 1 Yuan Shih-kai, who had been summoned by the regent, was granted the powers of a dictator, and on December 6 the regent abdicated. On December 29 the Nanking (Republican) Assembly elected Sun Yat Sen president of the republic of China. After the emperor's abdication, the Nanking Assembly, on February 15, 1912, elected Yuan Shih-kai provisional president of the republic, Sun Yat Sen retiring in his favor. Yuan was formally installed at Peking, on March 10, and a cabinet was formed with Tang Shao-yi as premier. Tang was succeeded in June by Lu Chêng-hsiang. In November, 1912, a new ministry was formed, as follows: Premier and minister of the interior, Chao Ping-chuan; foreign affairs, Liang Yü-hao; finance, Cheu Hsüeh-hsi; war, Tüan Chih-jui; marine, Liu-Küan-su; education, Fan Yüan-lien; justice, Hsü Shih-ying; agriculture and forests, Ch'en Chen-hsien; industry and commerce, Liu K'üei-yi; posts and communications, Chu Ch'i-ch'ien.

HISTORY

THE PROVISIONAL GOVERNMENT. Dr. Sun Yat Sen, who it will be remembered was elected president of the new republic at Nanking, at the close of 1911, formed a cabinet which comprised some of the ablest men of the empire, among others, Wang Chung-hui, a graduate of Yale University. In a message issued at the beginning of the year, the new president assailed the Manchu dynasty for its tyranny and demanded the opening of the country to foreign trade and promised to maintain treaty obligations. Before the close of 1911, the powers had agreed upon a plan for the protection of the railway line from Peking to the sea. Early in January, United States troops were ordered from Manila for that purpose and a large reinforcement of British troops was ordered from Honkong to Canton. In January a renewal of hostilities seemed imminent, the negotiations between the revolutionaries and the government having come to a standstill. The movement to bring about the abdication of the emperor steadily gained force in China and by the middle of the month it was clear that it was not only supported by popular opinion, but by almost the whole body of princes. The Manchus, however, were much concerned as to their future treatment and earnestly desired the continuance of Yuan Shih-kai in office as he had rendered loyal service to the throne. Negotiations looking to abdication were going on throughout the early part of January. These provided for generous treatment of the emperor and his court as well as of the Manchus generally. Much excitement was caused by an attempt, on January 16, to assassinate Yuan Shih-kai, while returning from an audience at the palace. Three bombs were thrown at him in the street but though some twenty persons were wounded he himself was not hurt.

On January 18, it was announced that an agreement had been reached between the Imperialists and the Republicans for the abdication of the emperor and the selection of Yuan Shih-kai as president in place of Sun Yat Sen, who would retire in his favor. Soon afterwards much alarm was caused by the report that Sun Yat Sen had repudiated his promise and would insist on the transfer of the imperial authority directly to the provisional republican government at Nanking. The terms of abdication, however, were finally agreed upon. They included the annual grant of 4,000,000 taels to the emperor, and the provision that he should reside first in the Forbidden City, and ultimately in the Summer Palace, and that he should receive such honors as are accorded to a foreign sovereign visiting China. An imperial bodyguard was to be provided by the republic. The private property of the emperor and princes was to be respected. So also was the rank of princes and hereditary nobles, whose order of succession should be maintained. On February 12, the Manchu dynasty, which had held the throne for 267 years, formally abdicated and proclaimed a republic. Three edicts were issued on that day announcing the change. The first, after briefly reviewing the history of the revolution, declares that the form of government shall be a constitutional republic and that plenary powers are given to Yuan Shih-kai to establish a provisional republican government, and to confer with the Nanking government as to measures for carrying out this purpose with harmony. This decree was signed by Yuan Shih-kai and six members of the cabinet. The second decree pronounces the terms of abdication satisfactory, and the third urges the people and the officials to maintain peace. The decrees were received with satisfaction and proclamations of the change in government were posted in public places. Official notice was given to the legations, which were requested to make them known to their respective governments. The ancient flag of China, the yellow dragon, was abolished and a new flag adopted, which was composed of five stripes, crimson, yellow, white, blue, and black, symbolizing the five races of the republic, namely, Mongols, Chinese, Manchus, Mohammedans, and Tibetans.

On February 15, Yuan Shih-kai was chosen president, and on February 20, Gen. Li Yuan Heng was chosen vice-president. On February 27, Yuan Shih-kai received delegates from the Nanking Assembly, who extended to him the invitation to come to Nanking and assume office. Yuan Shih-kai accepted the invitation, saying that he would proceed to Nanking as soon as circumstances permitted. The situation was temporarily complicated by an outbreak on February 29, of the troops of the Third Division, which had hitherto been regarded as trustworthy. Reports of widespread disaffection throughout the North occasioned much alarm, but martial law was declared at Peking and order soon restored. On March 10, Yuan Shih-kai took the oath of office as provisional president, and it was announced that the new cabinet would be formed under the premiership of Tang Shao-yi. At a formal meeting of the Assembly at Nanking, Sun Yat Sen and the provisional government laid down their office. On the following day the Assembly agreed to transfer the seat of the government to Peking. The first cabinet was made up of the members of the Nanking and Peking governments, under the premiership of Tang Shao-yi, who held also the portfolio of the minister of communications. The members of the cabinet were remarkable for their knowledge and experience, almost all of them having special acquaintance with European affairs and having traveled abroad. It was then decided that the Advisory Council of Nanking upon removal to Peking should continue to act as a National Assembly until the meeting of the new parliament, which was to take place before October.

Soon after the establishment of the republic, much anxiety was caused by the sudden mutiny of 1500 troops at Nanking on April 11. Loyal troops, however, were soon hurried to the district and after some fighting order was restored. The loss of life was placed at from 200 to 300. The Advisory Council was formally opened at Peking on April 29. The new president, Yuan Shih-kai, in the address outlined some of the reforms essential to the country's welfare. He urged the strengthening of friendship with foreign states, the necessity of reforming land taxation and mining regulations, including the currency system of introducing uniform weights and measures, improving education, legal procedure, and means of communication, and advocating the employment of foreign experts in finance, agriculture, and forestry. In June the foreign minister, Lu Cheng-hsiang, was appointed premier and his nomination was approved by the Advisory Council on June 29. The appointment was generally acceptable, both to the Chinese themselves, and to the foreign legations. In September, Liang Men-Tung was appointed foreign minister, the premier having relinquished the portfolio.

DIFFICULTIES OF THE NEW RÉGIME. The new government was endangered by the separatist tendencies of the southern provinces, the reactionary spirit in the North, where the monarchist sentiment was strong, and above all by the growing ascendancy of the army. The commanders of the military forces in the provinces began to assert political authority and it was feared that the military power would soon dominate the government as it had done in Turkey. The danger was enhanced by the uncertainty and inequality of the soldiers' pay, owing to the financial embarrassment of the government. The assistance which Yuan Shih-kai had expected from the foreign powers had not been forthcoming. He could not command foreign loans unless he could assure foreign capitalists of such a degree of control over expenditures as would stir up opposition in the provinces. (See below *Foreign Loan.*) The execution of two generals who had been in the revolutionary movement and who were now charged with attempting to incite another revolution led to an attack on the government in the Assembly. The trial was by court-martial and the procedure was summary. The government's opponents argued that at Hankow where the trial took place the civil authorities should have had jurisdiction, as the military administration had been dissolved. The Advisory Assembly petitioned Yuan Shih-kai for further explanation and upon receiving it pronounced it unsatisfactory and demanded the attendance of the premier and war minister at its session. This Yuan Shih-kai refused. The criticism of the government for the executions, though emphatic at first, soon subsided. Dr. Sun Yat Sen visited Peking in the latter part of August and was received with popular enthusiasm. He argued for a strong central government, loyal support of the president, and the sinking of party differences. Much was said in the European press about the weakness of the new government owing to dissensions among the party groups. Doctor Morrison, who had lately been appointed Chinese adviser, described the conditions in more favorable terms. He pointed out that the three party groups in the Advisory Council, though they differed in their programmes, were all republicans. He denied that their differences were of a kind that would lead to civil war or disrupt the national unity. The leading and most powerful party had no such tendency. Its aims were merely: The establishment of a party cabinet instead of a coalition government; the reform of the administration; the enforcement of conscription; the spread of education; the equality of the sexes; and a policy of colonization.

At the end of the year elections were being held under a recent law of the National Council, providing for a permanent constitutional government. The new legislature or National Assembly was to be bi-cameral, consisting of an upper house whose members were to be chosen indirectly by the provincial assemblies and to serve six years, one-third retiring every two years, and a lower house whose members were to be elected by popular vote, the qualifications for the suffrage being: The payment of a direct tax of $2.00 or more, or the ownership of immovable property to the value of $500 or more, or the possession of certain educational qualifications. The ratio of representation was one for every 800,000 inhabitants, but no province was to have less than ten representatives. The number of qualified voters as appeared from reports published at the close of the year was very small. Some estimates placed it at 2,000,000.

FOREIGN LOAN. On March 14, the Chinese government secured a joint loan from British and Belgian capitalists. This led to a protest from the ministers of Great Britain, France, Germany, and the United States, on the ground that it violated prior agreements with the "four nations" banks who had offered a loan to the government without security and had received an option to finance the government up to the end of August. The Chinese government agreed to cancel the Belgian arrangement. Negotiations were subsequently begun with the four nations for a loan of £60,000,000, but difficulties arose concerning the safeguards which the latter required. These guarantees involved the strengthening of the central government, but this conflicted with the aspiration of the provinces for a greater measure of self-government. The further objection was raised by many of the Chinese that it tended toward foreign domination. The British government, many years ago, refused to lend its sanction to any loans except such as were made through the Hongkong and Shanghai Bank, and the allied German corporation, the Deutsch-Asiatische Bank. Over the loans thus negotiated the British and German governments assumed control. These loans were examined by the authorities and were subject to certain conditions to insure safety. The government also stood behind the banks. Later, by the inclusion of the French banks in the consortium, this dual control became a triple control and still later the United States was added. To the four powers having this privilege, Russia and Japan were added in June, 1912, on the understanding that the loan should contain no terms injurious to their special interests. During the summer of 1912, negotiations were carried on with this six-power group of bankers for a loan, whose figure was placed by the press at £60,000,000, but they were impeded by the fact that the conditions imposed were regarded by many of the Chinese as humiliating to the new government. There were, moreover, opportunities of making arrangements with outside bankers who would not exact such conditions. In some quarters it was argued that the consortium was a monopoly and even if it had been justified in the past it was not now that China had at last acquired a stable government. While the negotiations with the six-power group were pending, other negotiations with a London company, Messrs. C. Birch Crisp, resulted in the authorization of a loan of £10,000,000, whereupon the six-power group declared that they could not proceed with the matter so long as such separate arrangements were pending. The loan with the London syndicate was concluded on August 30. The London foreign office was notified on September 4. Inquiries into the state of Chinese finance seemed to indicate that almost all the proceeds of the new loan would have to be paid out immediately to meet arrears. The British government, through its minister at Peking expressed its disapproval of the loan and argued that it would do little to relieve necessities as the foreign liabilities at the close of 1912 would exceed the £10,000,000. The conditions which the six-power group had sought to impose and which checked the negotiations were made known toward the end of September. They involved the control of expenditure through the appointment of a foreign auditor as in previous cases, who was to insure the proper application of the funds and to cause annual statements to be issued, and, secondly, foreign supervision of the collection of the revenues. The latter condition was declared by the Chinese government to be an infringement of its sovereign rights. On this point the negotiators could not agree.

The new loan, officially entitled the "Chinese government 5 per cent. Gold Loan for 1912," was for £5,000,000, only half the amount authorized and issued at 95 per cent. Payment of both interest and principal were made a first charge on the surplus revenues of the salt tax (*gabelle*), which were estimated at about £3,610,000. It was to run for 40 years. It was floated on September 26. As to the various objections to the loan, and particularly the British government's opposition, Mr. Crisp made a public statement in the latter part of September to the effect that his examination of Chinese conditions did not bear out the contentions of the foreign office, that the loan would be repudiated. On the contrary, he had gathered from Doctor Mirrison, the Chinese adviser, and from other sources that conditions were widely different from what the foreign office supposed. He did not believe that the loan would be repudiated and he found that his confidence was shared by other financiers. He and his associates believed the transaction would be remunerative and would also do something toward the restoration of British prestige in China. The powers objected to the loan on the ground that the revenues on which it was secured were already hypothecated to other services. On November 5 the Chinese government announced that other revenues would be applied to the service on the loan and on the following day negotiations with the six-power group were reopened. It was announced on December 12 that the six-power group would issue a loan on terms favorable to China and would allow Crisp and Co., and other British firms to participate.

MONGOLIA. At the close of 1911 there were repeated rumors of a Russian design to annex Mongolia. The Chinese revolution had aroused a separatist movement in the eastern half of Mongolia, where the Chinese authorities were superseded by Mongolian dignitaries. In the western half the Chinese functionaries refused to leave and the natives were unable to remove them. Early in January, Russia informed the Chinese government that Outer Mongolia must be recognized as independent so far as its internal affairs were concerned and that Russia would aid the natives in maintaining order and in constructing a railway from Kiakhta to Urga. The Chinese government was to retain control of the external affairs, but was not to maintain military forces in the territory. Russia had previously warned the imperial government against the aggressive policy of China in Mongolian affairs, and reminded it of Russia's privileges in Mongolia as regarded railways and mines. Russia professed no desire for the separation of Mongolia from China, but insisted on Mongolian autonomy under Chinese sovereignty. It was finally announced early in January that the Russian government was not aiming at a protectorate in Mongolia, as was suspected, but was merely acting as an intermediary accepted by both countries in the difficulty arising over the Mongolian movement for autonomy which followed the Chinese revolution. Later in the year Russia was clearly determined to recognize Outer Mongolia as an autonomous state, and on November 3, the Russian representative at Urga concluded a treaty between Russia and Mongolia, whereby the former was to aid Mongolia in maintaining autonomy, to support her right to a national army, and to exclude Chinese troops and colonists. At the same time it was reported that Chinese troops were advancing into Mongolia. Many believed eventually that Outer and Inner Mongolia would be divided between Russia and Japan. On September 18 China decided that it would accept the Russian proposals as to Outer Mongolia, but would resist aggression in Inner Mongolia. Early in October, Chinese troops were reported to have massacred large numbers of Mongolians to check the tendency to join Outer Mongolia.

TIBET. As a result of the revolution in China the garrison at Lhasa mutinied, and the amban abdicated. There were revolts among the natives elsewhere and in June the Dalai Lama returned to Lhasa. The Chinese government dispatched an expedition to Tibet, but was obliged to recall it under pressure from Great Britain. The latter government had sent a memorandum on August 17, warning China against the apparent design to turn nominal authority over Tibet into actual sovereignty, as violating the Anglo-Chinese Treaty of 1906. A force of Chinese troops, 2000 strong, were reported to have been ambushed in eastern Tibet early in October, but later to have fought their way out. Chinese successes were reported in Litang. A new province was officially proclaimed under the title of Hsikangseng and comprising western Szechwan and eastern Tibet.

THE OPIUM QUESTION. As noted in the preceding YEAR BOOK the agreement of 1907 between British and Chinese governments for the annual reduction of the imports of opium from India into China having expired in 1911, a new agreement was signed in May of that year providing that "the export of opium from India to China shall cease in less than seven years if clear proof is given to the satisfaction of the British minister at Peking of the complete absence of the production of native opium in China." The 1907 agreement looked to the extinction of the Indian opium trade with China in ten years. The trade in 1907 amounted to 51,000 chests and it was to be decreased by 5100 chests annually, subject, however, to China's discontinuance of the poppy cultivation to a corresponding extent. In 1911 the Indian trade had fallen to 31,016 chests and in 1912 it was placed at 21,260. Meanwhile according to the report of an expert employed by the British foreign office to investigate China's progress in carrying out her part of the agreement the decreases in poppy cultivation ranged from 75 per cent. in some of the provinces to less than 25 per cent. in others. After the renewal of the agreement in May, 1911, the disturbed political conditions greatly hindered the Chinese government in carrying out its programme for the suppression of opium production, and it was evident in 1912 that China was failing to curtail poppy cultivation to the extent stipulated by that agreement. The area of poppy cultivation was reported to have greatly increased and at the same time the provincial governments were refusing to admit Indian opium. Official British protests were made repeatedly against this one-sided state of affairs, but though the Chinese government gave assurances that the provincial authorities would be ordered to recall their restrictions on Indian opium there was little change in the situation. In October the British government informed the Chinese authorities that while allowance would be made for China's difficulties in the matter, the question of withdrawing from the agreement of May, 1911, might have to be reconsidered.

The International Conference, held at Shanghai, in 1909, at the invitation of the United States, passed the series of important resolutions, noted in our previous records, asking the governments represented to pledge themselves to measures for the prevention of the abuse of opium. A second conference was held at The Hague, in December, 1911, and remained in session till January, 1912. It prepared a convention of twenty-five articles relating to the control of the production and distribution of raw opium and the gradual reduction of the manufacture and sale of prepared opium. The convention was signed by the representatives of the following powers: United States, Germany, France, China, Great Britain, Italy, Persia, Japan, The Netherlands, Russia, Portugal, and Siam. For recent books on China see LITERATURE, ENGLISH AND AMERICAN, *Travel* and *Contemporary History*. See also ANTHROPOLOGY.

CHINESE IMMIGRATION. See IMMIGRATION AND EMIGRATION.

CHISHOLM, HUGH J. An American capitalist, died July 8, 1912. He was born in Niagara-on-the-Lake, Canada, in 1847. When but thirteen years of age he became a train newsboy on the Grand Trunk Railway, at the same time studying in evening classes in the Business College of Toronto. He gradually secured control of news routes on the trains of the Grand Trunk road to Portland, Me. His business grew to great magnitude. He became interested in the wood pulp business and began the manufacture of indurated fibre. He later organized several large paper and pulp manufactories, including the Rumford Falls Power Company. Here he established a community of model homes for mill operatives, known as Strathglass Park. He was one of the organizers of the International Paper Company and became its president in 1907. He was also president or director in various other important corporations.

CHOSEN. See KOREA.

CHRISTIAN ENDEAVOR, UNITED SOCIETY OF. An interdenominational society for young people, founded in Portland, Me., in 1889. The conventions of the society are held biennially and no convention was held during 1912. No statistics for membership were gathered, but the membership for 1909 was about 4,000,000 in 79,077 societies. The next international convention will be held July 4-14, 1913, in Los Angeles, Cal. The officers of the society in 1912 were as follows: President, Francis B. Clark, D. D.; general secretary, William Shaw; editorial secretary, Amos R. Wells; treasurer, H. N. Lathrop; and interstate secretary, Karl Lehmann.

CHRISTIANS. This denomination reported in 1912, 104,027 communicants; 1203 churches; 1314 ministers. Each church is independent in its local affairs, but for the conduct of general work the churches and ministers are organized into conferences, and these are represented by delegates in the American Christian Convention, which meets once in four years. The convention has charge of the general enterprises of the church. It includes the Christian Publishing Association, the Mission Board of the Christian Church, which are incorporated bodies, and the departments of education, finance, sunday school, and Christian endeavor. The publishing house prints books, tracts, and sunday school literature, and issues the *Herald of Gospel Liberty*, the oldest religious paper in the United States. The Mission Board issues a monthly magazine, *The Christian Missionary*, and prosecutes missionary and church extension work in Japan, Porto Rico, and continental United States. The denomination has eight colleges, one preparatory school, and one theological seminary. It maintains a home for aged ministers at Lakemont, N. Y., and an orphanage at Elon College, N. C.

CHRISTIAN SCIENTISTS. See RELIGIOUS DENOMINATIONS.

CHRISTMAS ISLANDS. See STRAITS SETTLEMENTS.

CHROMETITE. See METEOROLOGY.

CHURCH, ALFRED JOHN. An English clergyman and writer, died April 27, 1912. He was born in London in 1829 and was educated in King's College, London, and Lincoln College, Oxford. From 1857 to 1870 he was assistant master in Merchant Taylor's School, London, and from 1870 to 1872 was head master of Henley Grammar School. From 1873 to 1880 he was head master of Retford Grammar School. He was professor of Latin in the University College, London, from 1880 to 1888 and from 1892 to 1897 was rector of Ashley, Gloucestershire. He wrote many books, chiefly for boys. Among these are, *Stories from Homer, Virgil, Greek Tragedians, Livy, and Herodotus; Two Thousand Years Ago; Fall of Carthage*, etc. Other works include a book of reminiscences, *Memories of Men and Books* (1908). In collaboration with Rev. George A. Brodribb, he translated *Tacitus*.

CHURCH PEACE LEAGUE. See ARBITRATION, INTERNATIONAL.

CHURCH STATISTICS. See RELIGIOUS DENOMINATIONS.

CHURTON, EDWARD TOWNSON. Former Anglican bishop of Nassau, died May, 1912. He was born in 1841 and was educated at Eton, and at Oriel College, Oxford. He was ordained in 1886 and officiated as vicar at Charlton and at Dover. From 1886 to 1900 he was bishop of Nassau. He resigned the office in the latter year. Among his published writings are: *The Island Missionary of the Bahamas; The Missionary's Foundation of Christian Doctrine* (1890); *Retreat Addresses* (1893); *Sanctuary of Missions* (1898); *Foreign Missions* (1901), and *The Use of Penitence* (1905).

CIGARS AND CIGARETTES. See TOBACCO.

CINCINNATI SYMPHONY ORCHESTRA. See MUSIC.

CIRCULATION OF NATIONAL BANKS. See NATIONAL BANKS.

CITRUS FRUITS. See HORTICULTURE.

CITY BUDGET. See MUNICIPAL GOVERNMENT.

CITY CHARTERS. See MUNICIPAL GOVERNMENT.

CITY MANAGER PLAN. See MUNICIPAL GOVERNMENT.

CITY PLANNING, or the art of laying out cities to serve the comfort, convenience, and higher aspirations of the public, is a thing of the twentieth century. True, there have been noble isolated examples of city planning scattered through the centuries and countries of the world, but not until within a few years past has city planning become a part of the national thought and life of any country, with the exception of Germany. In that country a school of city planners has existed for decades and has left its imprint in periodicals, in books, and to a considerable extent in the planning and replanning of cities. The coöperation of German governing bodies with the most enlightened elements in the artistic and scientific circles of the empire has made Germany the world's leader in this field. The contrast is great with democratic nations like our own. For an interesting account of the conditions that make it possible for Germany and Austria to carry out far-reaching plans of municipal improvement see the article by Otto Wagner in the *Architectural Record* for May, 1912.

UNITED STATES. The first awakening to the æsthetic possibilities of city planning in this country dates from the World's Columbian Exposition in 1893. With the memory of that exposition and of other noble groupings of public buildings, and the arrangements of parks, water fronts, and monuments, as seen on visits to Europe, the architects and landscape architects of the United States began to see visions. Then came the revivification of the Washington-L'Enfant plan of our federal capital as a further stimulus. Soon civic associations throughout the country grasped the idea that cities should be planned instead of permitted to spread outwards and grow in a haphazard fashion. These bodies then began to employ landscape architects to report on improvements in their city plan. At this juncture too much stress was unfortunately laid on the æsthetics of city planning and the movement was handicapped by the widespread use of such terms as "the city beautiful." This term, together with the costliness of the new city plans often proposed, created more public opposition to than support of the new movement; all the more so because the public was thus led to believe that city planning was simply a costly æsthetic fad which must be denied until public improvements of a more solid and necessary kind had been secured. As a consequence, although city planning or improvement reports have been made for many cities of the United States, in a few cases at an expense of thousands of dollars, few cities have yet officially adopted any considerable part of the plans recommended. One reason for shelving or pigeon-holing so many carefully wrought plans, aside from the "city beautiful" handicap already mentioned, is that most of these reports and plans were made at the instance of voluntary organizations, having no official connection with the responsible city government.

Such radical changes as have been proposed stand little chance of being executed unless they originate with some municipal body or officer who is an integral part of the city government. Hartford, Conn., has an official City Plan Commission, which made its fifth annual report in 1912. Somewhat similar commissions were authorized by the New Jersey legislature in 1911, and one, for Newark, was created in that year. In addition, the Board of Public Works of Newark has a city planning engineer, who submitted a comprehensive report for street and park plan improvements in 1912. In Philadelphia there is a city planning engineer in the Bureau of Surveys. Los Angeles and a number of other cities now have city planning commissions. Cleveland, O., voted bonds in 1912 for a library, which will be the fourth building in its official group or civic centre scheme, worked out some years ago by a commission of consulting experts. San Francisco voted $8,800,000 of bonds early in 1912 for a new city hall and to provide land for a new civic centre. In December, 1912, a large popular majority declared in favor of the erection of an auditorium, library, opera house (at private expense), State building, and other structures in the civic centre, and at the same time an official city planning commission was authorized, the members to serve without pay. At Augusta, Ga., a plaza was projected in 1912, opposite the union passenger station; a proposed post office building and Carnegie library will flank the plaza on either side. In New York City a site for a new court house was chosen in 1912 which, it is hoped, will yet be a part of a new civic centre, including perhaps a post office, State office building, and possibly other structures. This site is only a short distance from the City Hall, Brooklyn Bridge, Hall of Records, and the large and monumental Municipal Office Building now under construction. In Pittsburgh the mayor has appointed a city planning commission and a municipal art commission. The Forest Hills (L. I.) "garden city" has advanced towards readiness for occupancy. A fine plan for the development of Seattle, prepared by Virgil Bague, was defeated by popular vote.

It will be noted that so far as actual construction work is concerned the specific examples thus far cited for the United States do not go beyond groups of public buildings or civic centres. Little else has yet been accomplished, except that a goodly number of cities have created or extended park and parkway systems and some have cut new or widened old streets in order to facilitate the movement of traffic.

City planning and replanning on a comprehensive scale has proceeded far on paper, but has not yet got much beyond it in the United States. It involves many complex problems and, oftentimes, huge expense. The solution of these problems and the meeting of the expense would be greatly aided if it were possible to apply in the United States what has been so successfully used in Europe, the principle of excess condemnation, or the taking of more land by the city than is needed for the specific improvement and the resale of the land at its enhanced value after the improvement has been made. There appears to be a strong belief in legal circles that excess condemnation has no warrant under the existing constitutions of most of our States, if indeed it would not be against the federal Constitution. In the absence of power to utilize excess condemnation much more might be accomplished than is generally undertaken by making use of the well-established principle of assessments for benefits, or the putting upon such real estate as is increased in value by street, park, and other improvements a large part of the expenditure involved. This policy was ably advocated by Nelson P. Lewis in a paper entitled "How to Pay the Bills for City Planning," read before the City Planning Conference held at Boston, Mass., in May, 1912. These conferences, it may be added, are perhaps contributing more largely than any other single activity to a solution of American city planning problems. They have been participated in from the start by building and landscape architects, engineers, housing reformers, sociologists, and city officials, and the four volumes of *Proceedings* may be consulted with profit. The conferences have been notable for the minor place which has been given in them to æsthetic considerations, except as these grow out of the fitting of form to function. The physical or utilitarian, legal, and financial aspects of city planning and the intimate relations between city planning and housing reform have been the dominant features of the conferences. Another factor making for progress is the recent establishment of courses in city planning at a number of universities.

Canada. In a general way Canada has shared in the city planning movement of the United States, responding to many of the same stimuli and taking a part in the work of propaganda and physical achievement. On May 4, 1912, an act of the Ontario legislature came into force which gives the Ontario Railway and Municipal Board power to pass on all plans for laying out vacant lands within the city of Toronto. All plans for outlying lands must conform to a general plan to be prepared by the city and which may cover the territory five miles in any direction from the city limits. No land development plan may be registered, nor any lots sold therefrom, until the plan has been approved by the board named. Some of the rapidly growing cities of the Canadian Northwest are alive to city planning and are taking advantage of the unique opportunity afforded by the fact that they are being created after the city planning movement was in full swing. Calgary, Alberta, has an official city planning commission, with a paid full-time secretary, and in 1912 invited competitive plans for a civic centre.

Great Britain. Town planning (the current term there) in Great Britain owes its first great impetus to what has become widely known as the garden city movement, or the laying out of entirely new towns or town additions with a view to giving people of small and moderate incomes a chance to live in comfortable detached or semi-detached, or at best not over-large, two-storied tenement-houses, surrounded with garden plots. The street plan, open spaces, public buildings, and other elements of a well-planned city were all given proper attention. These garden cities were private undertakings and left untouched the replanning of built-up areas and also the planning of new areas where the land owners had no interest in progressive city planning.

In 1909 Parliament passed the housing and town planning act, which gave all municipalities large powers over city planning, more particularly as regards the laying out of new areas. These powers, however, are subject to the jurisdiction of a central body known as the Local Government Board. Under the act municipal authorities can, on approval of the board, lay out vacant land in accordance with a carefully planned scheme, which appears to be largely the work of the local town or borough engineering department. Up to November, 1912, 124 local authorities had schemes in various stages of progress. Birmingham had prepared and submitted to the board for approval plans for one area of 2320 acres and for another area of 1442 acres, and Rochdale had got equally far with an area of 43 acres. Apparently no final approvals had been made by the board up to November. A total of 17 applications, from 13 local authorities, had been granted to the extent of permission to prepare and submit schemes. A dozen or so other applications for authority to prepare plans were awaiting action. Two of these, both involving rural districts, embraced nearly 6000 acres each. Altogether, the "schemes and proposals for schemes" before the board involved a total of more than 52,000 acres of land, not including a larger number of schemes in preliminary stages.

A summer school of town planning was held at the Hampstead Garden Suburb in August, 1912, under the auspices of the University of London. A second one will be held August 2-9, 1913. A scheme for a 400-acre extension to the suburb is now before the Local Government Board and adds to the attractiveness of this locality for summer school purposes.

The Surveying and Housing World (London) is a weekly journal which contains a large amount of news regarding British town planning projects, including reproductions of maps of new schemes. *The Town Planning Review*, published by the department of civic design, school of architecture, University of Liverpool, is a scholarly illustrated quarterly which contains essays and news articles and notes on city planning in Great Britain, on the continent of Europe, and in the United States and Canada.

AUSTRALIA. *Capital Competition.* A notable event in city planning in 1912 was the award of prizes in the competition for a plan for the proposed new capital of the Australian Commonwealth. In a world-wide competition the first prize of £1750 ($8500) was awarded to Walter Burley Griffin, architect and landscape architect, Chicago, Ill.; second prize of £750 to Eliel Saarinen, architect, Helsingfors, Finland; third prize of £5000 to Prof. D. A. Agache, architect, Paris, France. Honorable mention was made of plans submitted by Harold Van Buren Magonigle, architect, New York City, and of a London competitor. In a minority report it was recommended that the first prize should go to three collaborators of Sydney, N. S. W.; the second to Arthur C. Comey, landscape architect, Cambridge, Mass., and the third to a Swedish civil engineer and two collaborators. The premiated plans became the property of the government, to be used as it sees fit.

Competitors for the prizes were supplied with contour maps and photographic views of the site and its vicinity, a variety of local data, and a statement of the requirements to be met in the way of government buildings, streets, transportation, etc. As illustrating the scope of city planning in general, as well as of this competition, it may be noted that in examining each scheme submitted the judges considered the following main heads and a number of subheads not given: (1) General conditions, including location, width, and grades of roads; railways, tramways, firebreaks, and "allocation of districts for specific purposes," as residences, etc. (2) Hygiene, including sewerage and drainage, sunlight and air facilities, prevailing winds, and aspect. (3) Architectural and general effect, including ornamental waters and parks. (4) Expansion, and (5) economy. (6) Miscellaneous, including places of amusement and sports, arboreal treatment, and factory buildings.

The site selected in 1908 for the new capital is located in the Yass-Canberra district of New South Wales in a federal district of 900 square miles. The site has an area of five square miles, exclusive of suburbs, and is 170 miles southwest of Sydney, 300 miles northeast of Melbourne, and 170 miles from the east coast. The average elevation is 2000 feet above sea level, but the site includes mountain peaks, one of which is 6000 feet high. A sluggish stream named the Molonglo River flows through the site, and one of the suggestions to competitors was to provide attractive water areas by damming and diking this stream. A varied topography, an entire absence of either habitations or railways, and the general requirements laid down gave the competitors a remarkably free hand and a unique opportunity to apply all the latest and best principles of the art of city planning. How this was done by Mr. Griffin is shown, in part, by the accompanying general plan of the first premiated design, reproduced by permission from *Engineering News* of July 4, 1912, which contains a lengthy article on the first design, prepared with the coöperation of Mr. Griffin. It will be noted that the federal government centre is located on either side of an axial line which connects the summits of Mt. Ainslie, within the city, and Mt. Bimberi, 30 miles distant, the latter having an elevation of 6230 feet and therefore being a commanding feature in the distant landscape. An ornamental waterway lies in front of the main government buildings and across this are public gardens, from which leads a wide parkway. On quite another radial line, but at no great angle with the first, and across the ornamental waterway, is the municipal government centre, and beyond that is the manufacturing centre. On still other radial lines extending out from the government centre are the residential section and a large suburban and semi-agricultural section, both on the same side of the water as the government centre. The market centre is on yet another radial line, and close by it are the union railway station and the military post. The ornamental waterway is flanked on either hand by lakes of irregular size. The water areas as well as other features of the layout insure quiet and dignity to the government centre. A large group of university buildings occupies a choice location near the municipal centre. The plan as a whole is made up of a number of centres, polygonal in shape, from which extend radial lines of main communication. These lines, combined with the polygonal form of the centres, give rectangular city blocks and avoid the curved streets and triangular blocks incident to the radial-circumferential plan. The whole street plan is based on the assumption that local street railways will be provided to such an extent that necessary walking will be reduced to a few blocks in any direction. It will be noted that the steam railway also gives ready access to all parts of the city except the small residential section, presumably intended for high-cost houses, but that it is kept at a respectable distance from the government centre.

Those who have had the privilege of hearing Mr. Griffin explain his plans have been impressed with the careful analysis and synthesis displayed in his studies. He was born at Mayward, Ill., in 1876, and is a graduate of the University of Illinois. His professional work has been chiefly architectural, but he has done some previous town planning and landscape work on

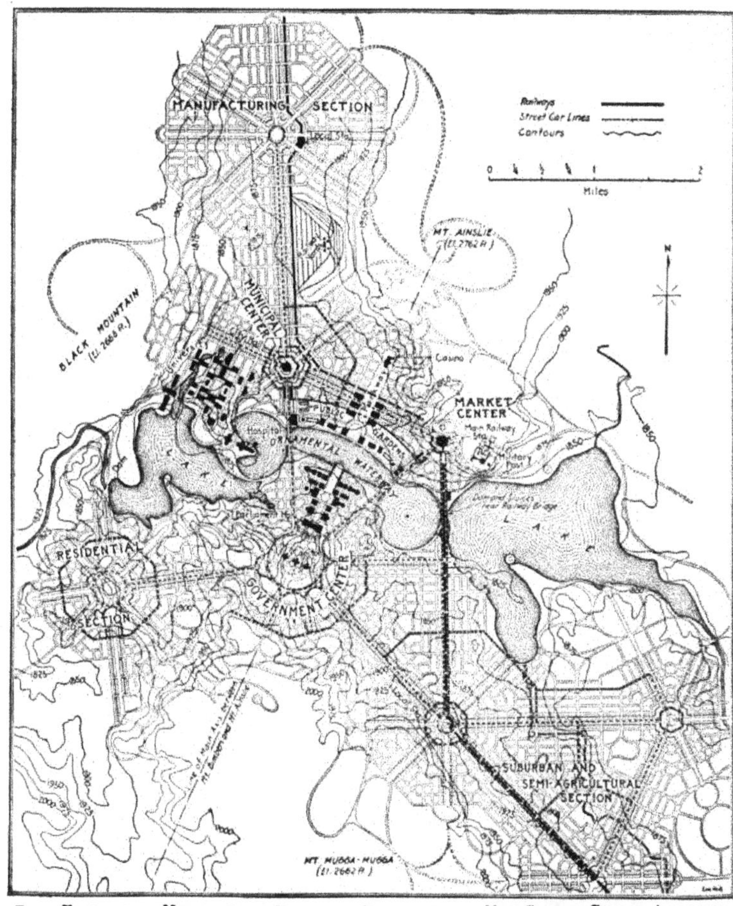

From Engineering News. First Premiated Design for the New Capital City of Australia. (*Designed by Walter B. Giffin, Chicago, Ill.*)

a small scale, including the planning of Idalia, Fla., and a design for a modern Shanghai, China.

In the Australian capital competition 137 separate designs were submitted, of which 11 were thrown out because of informalities. The 126 remaining designs were submitted by the minister for home affairs to a federal capital design board, consisting of J. M. Coane, as chairman, James A. Smith, and John Kirkpatrick, the two first named being engineers and the last one an architect. Mr. Coane made the minority report already mentioned. Both reports were published in the summer of 1912 as a public document of the commonwealth of Australia, consisting chiefly of photographic reproductions of the designs selected by the majority and minority. The minister named approved the plans early in 1912, but in the August following word reached this country that he had appointed a departmental board to prepare an official plan based on the premiated designs and suggestions to be obtained from the unsuccessful designs as well. Unfortunately, the authorities refused to make the terms of the competition conform to the requirements of the British and Australian Institutes of Architects, with the result that no architect of note from either of the countries most directly concerned took part in the contest.

CIVIC FEDERATION, National. The

annual meeting of the federation was held in Washington, on March 5, 6, and 7, 1912. Henry B. F. McFarland, former commissioner of the District of Columbia delivered the address of welcome, Cardinal Gibbons addressed the federation on industrial peace, and the annual address was given by the president, Seth Low. This was in general a review of the labor conditions. Other important addresses delivered were those on "Government Mediation in Railroad Labor Disputes," by M. A. Knapp, of the Interstate Commerce Commission; "The Case of the Federal Employee," by Samuel Gompers; "Pension for Federal Employees," by Franklin Mac Veagh, Secretary of the Treasury; "Civic Federation and the Trust Problem," by Talcott Williams.

The officers elected at the meeting in 1912 were as follows: President, Seth Low; vice-presidents, Samuel Gompers, Ellison Smythe, Benjamin Ide Wheeler; treasurer, Isaac N. Seligman; chairman of the executive council, Ralph M. Easley.

CIVIL SERVICE. FEDERAL CIVIL SERVICE. According to the figures compiled by the civil service commission in 1911, the total number of positions under the federal civil service in that year was 391,350. This total included 28,191 in the employ of the Isthmian Canal. The total number in the civil service in Washington was 33,811 and the total number outside of Washington 329,348.

Several important measures regarding federal civil service were taken in 1912. One of these was the action of President Taft in taking an important step toward bringing all government employees under the civil service on October 15, when he made the announcement that all fourth-class postmasters were to be placed under civil service rules and thus taken out of the "spoils system." In 1908, President Roosevelt placed under civil service rules the fourth-class postmasters of the States north of the Ohio and east of the Mississippi rivers. These numbered nearly 14,000. There still remained outside the civil service rules over 36,000. These are the postmasters who are included in President Taft's order. The result of the order promulgated by President Roosevelt was so satisfactory that about 20,000 fourth-class postmasters in the States south of the Ohio and west of the Mississippi signed a petition to be transferred to the merit system. President Taft had already put himself on record as advocating the inclusion in that system not only of the fourth-class postmasters, but all postmasters and all other federal officials, including collectors of customs, collectors of internal revenue, naval customs officers, surveyors, assayers, receivers, and public land agents. Legislation by Congress, however, is required to give the President power to add first, second, and third-class postmasters to the civil service list.

On December 7, 1912, the President by executive order placed in the classified service all artisan and supervisory artisan positions under the jurisdiction of the Department of the Navy. These positions numbered about 20,000.

In his message sent to Congress on December 3 President Taft renewed his previous recommendations to Congress for legislation making permanent the non-competitive system of appointment in the consular and diplomatic services. These now rest on executive order.

MUNICIPAL CIVIL SERVICE. On December 3, the voters of Los Angeles rejected by a large majority the new city charter, which contained the most advanced civil service provisions yet proposed in the United States. These placed practically every city official and employee, except elective officers and members of the civil service commission, within the classified service.

In San Francisco the jurisdiction of the civil service commission was increased and the merit system extended to include the county service by the adoption of an amendment to the city charter on December 10.

The National Civil Service Reform League held its annual meeting in Milwaukee, December 5 and 6, 1912. The principal adress was delivered by President Charles W. Eliot. Other important papers read at the meeting were the "Competitive System for Higher City Officers," by Hon. William Dudley Foulke; "Methods of Removal in the Chicago and Illinois Services," by Mr. Robert Catherwood, and the "Illinois System of Removals in the Civil Service," by Hon. William B. Hale. See MUNICIPAL GOVERNMENT.

CLANCY, JOHN. An Irish Roman Catholic bishop, died October 19, 1912. He was born in Sooey, county Sligo, in 1856, and was educated at the Marist Brothers' School and afterwards at St. Patrick's College, Maynooth. From 1883 to 1895 he was professor of rhetoric and English literature in Maynooth College. He was consecrated bishop of Elphin in the latter year.

CLANCY PROCESS. See METALLURGY.

CLARK, CHAMP. See PRESIDENTIAL CAMPAIGN.

CLARKE, WILLIAM NEWTON. An American scholar and educator, died January 15, 1912. He was born in Cazenovia, N. Y., in 1841, and graduated from Madison, now Colgate University, in 1861. He studied theology at the Hamilton Theological Seminary, graduating in 1863. In the same year he was ordained to the Baptist ministry and became pastor at Keene, N. H. He occupied several pastorates in the years following, including churches at Newton Centre, Mass., and Montreal. In 1883 he was appointed professor of New Testament Interpretation at the Toronto Baptist College. From 1887 to 1890 he was pastor at Hamilton, N. Y. In the latter year he became professor of Christian theology at Colgate University and in 1908 was appointed professor of ethics and apologetics in the same institution. He was the author of *Commentary on the Gospel of Mark* (1881); *Outline of Christian Theology* (1898); *What Shall We Think of Christianity?* (1899); *A Study of Christian Missions* (1900); *The Christian Doctrine of God* (1909), and *Sixty Years with the Bible* (1909).

CLARK UNIVERSITY. An institution established originally for post-graduate work, in Worcester, Mass., in 1889. It includes, in addition to other departments, a collegiate department. The number of students enrolled in the several departments of the university in the autumn of 1912, was 90, and the faculty numbered 24. There were no noteworthy changes in the faculty during the year and no important benefactions were received. The endowment, including that for the collegiate department, amounts to $3,973,800. There were about 60,000 volumes in the library. President, G. Stanley Hall, Ph. D., LL. D.

CLASSICS. See PHILOLOGY, *Classical.*

CLASSICAL PHILOLOGY. See PHILOLOGY, CLASSICAL.

CLAYTON-BULWER TREATY. See PANAMA CANAL.

CLAY-WORKING INDUSTRIES. The two main divisions included under the heading clay-working industries are the manufacture of brick and tile, and of pottery. In 1911, while there was a decreased value in the product of brick and tile, pottery showed an increase. The total value of the product of the clay-working industries in 1911 was $162,236,181, compared with $170,115,974 in 1910. The decrease in value of the brick and tile industry was $8,613,675, and the increase in the value of the pottery industry was $733,882. In the brick and tile industry decreases were shown in both the quantity and value of common brick, in the quantity of vitrified paving brick, in the value of fancy or ornamental brick, in the quantity and value of fire brick and in the value of drain tile and architectural terra-cotta. Increases were recorded in the value of vitrified paving brick and some other varieties of special brick. A decrease in the common brick output may be partly accounted for by the increased use of hollow brick or tile for the construction of large buildings and even of dwelling houses. The leading State in the value of the clay-working industries is Ohio, which ranked first among the States in 1911, with a product valued at $32,663,895. The brick and tile product was valued at $17,888,630, and the pottery at $14,776,265. Pennsylvania ranked second, with a product valued at $20,270,033; New Jersey, third, with a total value of $18,178,228; Illinois, fourth, $14,330,014; New York, fifth, $10,184,376. Other States in the clay-working industries which had a large value were California, Georgia, Indiana, Kansas, Kentucky, Missouri, and West Virginia. All the States produced clay products of some value.

The total value of the imports of clay products in the United States in 1911 was $10,804,749 (pottery of all kinds, $10,638,616; brick, $166,133). The imports in 1910 were valued at $11,353,341. The exports in 1911 were valued at $3,665,720 (brick, $2,264,354; pottery, $1,401,366).

CLEAVES, HENRY BRADSTREET. An American public official, former governor of Maine, died June 22, 1912. He was born in Bridgeton, Me., in 1840, and received an academic education. He enlisted in the Civil War in the 23d Maine Infantry, and after the expiration of his term of enlistment reënlisted in the 30th Maine Infantry. He was promoted through various non-commissioned grades to the rank of first lieutenant. He returned to Bridgeton at the close of the war and studied law. In 1868 he was admitted to the bar, practicing in Portland. In 1876-77 he was a member of the State legislature. He was city solicitor of Portland in 1877, and from 1880 to 1885 was attorney-general of the State. During his service in this office he was instrumental in securing the passage by the legislature of the right to levy a franchise tax upon railroad and telegraph corporations. He was elected governor of the State in 1892, and was reëlected in 1894.

CLEVELAND, O. See CITY PLANNING, and ARCHITECTURE.

CLIMATE. See METEOROLOGY.

CLOAK AND SUIT INDUSTRY. See ARBITRATION, AND CONCILIATION, *Industrial.*

CLOSED SHOP. See STRIKES.

CLOTHING STRIKE. See STRIKES.

CLOUSTON, SIR EDWARD SEABORNE. A Canadian financier and philanthropist, died November 23, 1912. He was born in Moose Factory, Canada, in 1849, and was educated in the schools of Montreal. He entered the bank of Montreal in 1865, and rising through various grades became in 1890 general manager of that bank. He was governor of McGill University, Royal Victoria Hospital, Montreal General Hospital, and the Western Hospital in the same city. He was president of the Canadian Bankers' Association, and director of the Art Association of Montreal. He was created a baronet in 1908.

COAL. The total coal production of the United States in 1911 was 496,221,168 short tons, valued at $626,366,876. Of this amount, 80,771,488 long tons, equivalent to 90,464,067 short tons, was anthracite. The production in 1911 showed a decrease from 501,596,378 short tons in 1910. The decrease may be attributed entirely to the depressed condition of the iron and steel trade in 1911. This was reflected in the decreased production of coke. The total decrease in the production of bituminous coal was 11,354,041 short tons. More than half this decrease was made up by the increase in the production of anthracite in Pennsylvania, which showed a gain of 5,388,242 long tons.

Coal was produced in thirty States and the Territory of Alaska in 1911, but in four, Idaho, Nevada, Alaska, and North Carolina, the aggregate output was less than 3000 tons. Of the ten States in which the production increased, only two, Pennsylvania and Virginia, are eastern States. The chief decreases were in the coke production States and in those States which profited by the strike of 1910.

For amount of production in the various States, see articles on States.

MINERS EMPLOYED. The total number of men employed in the coal mines of the United States in 1911 was 722,335, of whom 172,585 were employed in the anthracite mines of Pennsylvania, and 549,750 in the bituminous and lignite mines. The coal mining industry as a whole was not disturbed by serious labor troubles in 1911. In the bituminous regions, where operations are conducted under agreements with the Mine Workers' Union, the compacts extend from April 1 to March 31 of the "even" years. In the "odd" years, as in 1911, the difficulties are local and generally short-lived. In the anthracite region of Pennsylvania operations were conducted without serious interruptions under the second three-year extension of the awards of the Strike Commission.

COAL MINING ACCIDENTS. Statistics of accidents in the coal mines and in other branches of the mining and quarrying industry in 1911 were compiled under the direction of the director of the United States Bureau of Mines. These returns show that 2719 men were killed in the coal mines in 1911, a decrease from 2840 in 1910. The most prolific cause of accidents was falls of roof and coal, 1321 deaths, or 48.6 per cent. of the total. In only two States, Alabama and Tennessee, were deaths from explosions of dust and gas more numerous than those from falls. The total deaths from explosions was 371. Mine cars and haulage motors killed 393. Premature blasts and powder explosions killed 134, and 63 men met their deaths in shaft accidents. The death rate per thousand employees was 3.76.

Coal Consumption. Practically the entire output of both anthracite and bituminous coal in the United States is consumed within the country. The total quantity of coal exported in 1911 was 19,524,603 short tons. The consumption of coal of domestic production was 476,696,485 tons. Imports in 1911 amounted to 1,385,956 tons. The quantity of coal consumed in the manufacture of coke at the mines in 1911 was 42,217,167 short tons.

World Production of Coal. The world's production of coal in 1911 was 1,303,763,496 short tons. Of this the United States produced 38.1 per cent. Great Britain produced 304,518,927 short tons; Germany, 258,223,763 short tons; Austria, 43,375,550; France, 25,570,053; Belgium, 25,490,842. Other countries producing more than 10,000,000 tons were Japan, China, and India. The figures for these three countries as well as for Austria-Hungary are for 1910.

Production in 1912. The production of coal in the United States in 1911-12 is given in the table below which is taken from the *Engineering and Mining Journal*. It will be noted that there was in 1912 a largely increased production over 1911. Nearly all the large producing States had increased production. This applies to bituminous coal. The figures for anthracite coal show a decreases of 6,000,000 tons.

States	1911 Short tons	1912 Short tons
Bituminous:		
Alabama	15,040,267	18,500,000
Arkansas	1,950,000	2,120,000
California	5,000	2,500
Colorado	10,197,595	11,306,968
Georgia	165,830	150,000
Illinois	50,336,559	(b) 57,685,700
Indiana	14,209,661	(c) 14,940,628
Iowa	(b) 7,729,674	(b) 6,820,828
Kansas	6,390,207	6,850,000
Kentucky	13,929,450	15,479,500
Maryland	4,166,236	(a) 4,500,000
Michigan	1,476,074	(a) 1,550,000
Missouri	3,760,607	3,710,992
Montana	2,913,397	(d) 3,143,799
New Mexica	3,148,158	3,369,201
North Dakota	468,700	545,000
Ohio	30,342,039	(a) 32,700,000
Oklahoma	3,074,242	3,450,000
Oregon	45,000	48,200
Pennsylvania	144,754,163	150,000,000
Tennessee	6,451,208	(a) 6,522,000
Texas	1,974,593	(a) 2,000,000
Utah	2,501,471	3,088,356
Virginia	6,864,667	(a) 8,000,000
Washington	3,550,906	3,650,000
West Virginia	59,920,207	(a) 60,000,000
Wyoming	6,755,196	7,522,294
Total bituminous	402,121,307	427,655,966
Anthracite:		
Colorado	65,500	60,545
New Mexico	41,200	47,892
Pennsylvania	90,419,856	84,200,000
Total anthracite..	90,526,556	84,308,437
Grand total	492,647,863	511,964,403

(a) Estimated. (b) Fiscal year ending June 30. (c) Year ending September 30.

For note on the chemistry of coal, see Chemistry, Industrial.

COAL LANDS. See Alaska.

COAL MINERS. See Arbitration and Conciliation, *Industrial*.

COAL-MINING, Substitute for. See Chemistry, Industrial.

COAST FORTIFICATIONS. See United States, *Army*.

COAST TRADE. See United States, Commerce.

COBALT-NITRATE TEST. See Chemistry.

COCHIN-CHINA. The southernmost division of the French colony of Indo-China (q. v.). Saigon is the capital, with 64,845 inhabitants; Cholon has 191,655. River and coast fishing, stock-raising, and agriculture are carried on. Irrigation and drainage works are in process of construction. J. M. Gourbeil was governor in 1912, on leave; M. Destenay, *ad int.*

COFFEE TRUST. See Trusts.

CŒLENTERATES. See Zoölogy.

COFFEE VALORIZATION. See Trusts.

COINAGE. See United States.

COINS, FOREIGN, Value of. The table on the next page (160) gives the value of foreign coins in United States currency in December, 1912.

COKE. The most striking feature in connection with the making of coke in the United States in 1911 was that while the total production of retort and oven coke decreased, the number of retort or by-product ovens increased over 10 per cent., and the increase in the number of these ovens in operation was larger than in any year since their operation in the United States, except the increase of 1904 over 1903. The decrease in the production of coke was largely the result of the depression in the iron trade. The total production in 1911 was 35,551,489 short tons, valued at $84,130,849, the smallest output in both quantity and value, except in the panic year 1908, since 1905. It may be compared to the production of 1910, which was 41,705,810 short tons, the largest production in any one year. The value of the product in 1910 was $99,742,701. The average price in 1911 was $2.37, as compared with $2.39 in 1910.

The production in 1911 included 27,703,644 tons of oven coke, valued at $56,832,952, and of 7,847,845 tons of retort or by-product coke, valued at $27,297,897. In 1910 the production of oven coke was 32,570,876 tons and that of retort or by-product coke was 7,138,734 tons. Thus, while the output of oven coke decreased 6,866,432 tons that of by-product coke increased 709,111 tons. The coal consumed in the manufacture of coke in 1911 amounted to 53,278,248 short tons, valued at $64,112,084. As the value of the coke produced was $84,130,489, the difference between the value of the coal used and the coke produced, $20,018,765, less the cost of manufacture, expense of administration, etc., represented the profit on the coke-making operations. The total number of ovens in operation in 1911 was 103,879 compared with 104,440 in 1910. Of the 103,879 ovens in existence at the close of 1911, 40,399 were idle throughout the year. The number of ovens idle in 1910 was 8373. The number of ovens in blast during the whole or parts of 1911 was 63,480, of which 59,160 were beehive or partial combustion ovens, and 4320 were retort or distillation ovens. At the close to the year there were 2254 ovens in the course of construction. Of these, 698 were by-product recovery ovens. Counting each bank of ovens as a separate establishment, there were in 1911, 570 establishments, against 578 in 1910. In 1911, 19 plants were abandoned

Country	Standard	Monetary Unit	Value in U. S. Gold Dollar	Remarks
Argentina	Gold	Peso	$0.96,5	Currency: depreciated paper, convertible at 44 per cent. of face value.
Austria-Hungary	Gold	Crown	.20,3	Member of Latin Union; gold is the actual standard.
Belgium	Gold	Franc	.19,3	12½ bolivianos equal 1 pound sterling.
Bolivia	Gold	Boliviano	.38,9	
Brazil	Gold	Milreis	.54,6	Currency: Government paper, convertible at $0.32,44 to the milreis.
British Colonies in Australia and Africa	Gold	Pound sterling	4.86,65	
Canada	Gold	Dollar	1.00,0	
Central American States:				
Brit. Honduras	Gold	Dollar	1.00,0	
Costa Rica	Gold	Colon	.46,5	
Guatemala	Silver	Peso	.45,1	Currency, inconvertible paper, exchange rate 16 to 18 pesos—$1.00.
Honduras	Silver	Peso	.45,1	Currency, bank notes, exchange rate March 20, 1912, $0.41,5.
Nicaragua	Silver	Peso	.45,1	Currency, inconvertible paper, exchange rate 16¾ to 17 pesos—$1.00.
Salvador	Silver	Peso	.45,1	Currency, convertible into silver on demand.
Chile	Gold	Peso	.36,5	Currency: inconvertible paper; exchange rate, approximately, $0.22,30.
China	Silver	Tael: Shanghai	.67,6	
		Haikwan	.75,3	
		Canton	.73,8	
Colombia	Gold	Dollar	1.00,0	Currency: inconvertible paper; exchange rate, approximately, $1.02 paper to $1 gold.
Denmark	Gold	Crown	.26,8	
Ecuador	Gold	Sucre	.48,7	
Egypt	Gold	Pound (100 piasters)	4.94,3	The actual standard is the British pound sterling, which is legal tender for 97½ piasters.
Finland	Gold	Mark	.19,3	
France	Gold	Franc	.19,3	Member of Latin Union; gold is the actual standard.
Germany	Gold	Mark	.23,8	
Great Britain	Gold	Pound sterling	4.86,65	
Greece	Gold	Drachma	.19,3	Member of Latin Union; gold is the actual standard.
Hayti	Gold	Gourde	.96,5	Currency: inconvertible paper; exchange rate, approximately, $0.29,41.
India	Gold	Pound sterling*	4.86,65	(15 rupees equal 1 pound sterling.)
Italy	Gold	Lira	.19,3	Member of Latin Union; gold is the actual standard.
Japan	Gold	Yen	.49,8	
Mexico	Gold	Peso	.49,8	
Netherlands	Gold	Florin	.40,2	
Newfoundland	Gold	Dollar	1.01,4	
Norway	Gold	Crown	.26,8	
Panama	Gold	Balboa	1.00,0	
Persia	Gold	Kran	.17,4	This is the value of the gold kran. Currency is silver circulating above its metallic value; exchange value of silver kran, approximately, $0.08,85.
Peru	Gold	Libra	4.86,6½	
Philippine Islands	Gold	Peso	.50,0	
Portugal	Gold	Milreis	1.08,0	Currency: inconvertible paper; exchange rate, approximately, $0.98,60.
Rumania	Gold	Leu	.19,3	
Russia	Gold	Ruble	.51,5	
Santo Domingo	Gold	Dollar	1.00,0	
Servia	Gold	Dinar	.19,3	
Siam	Gold	Tical	3.70,8	Valuation is for the gold peseta; currency is silver circulating above its metallic value; exchange value, approximately, $0.17,94.
Spain	Gold	Peseta	.19,3	
Straits Settlements	Gold	Dollar	.56,77	
Sweden	Gold	Crown	.26,8	
Switzerland	Gold	Franc	.19,3	Member of Latin Union; gold is the actual standard.
Turkey	Gold	Piaster	.04,4	100 piasters equal to the Turkish £.
Uruguay	Gold	Peso	1.03,4	
Venezuela	Gold	Bolivar	.19,3	

* The sovereign is the standard coin of India, but the rupee ($0.32,44 1-3) is the current coin at 15 to the sovereign.

and dismantled and 10 new ones were constructed.

Of the States producing coke, Pennsylvania stands first. The production in 1911 was 21,923,935 short tons. There were in the State 279 establishments making coke, and 54,904 ovens. Alabama ranks second as a producer of coke, the product in 1911 amounting to 2,761,521 short tons, from 44 establishments with 10,121 ovens. West Virginia ranked third, with 2,291,049 short tons, and 138 establishments, with 19,876 ovens. Other States producing coke in large quantities are Colorado, New York, Virginia, Tennessee, Ohio, and Kentucky. The statistics of production in these States will be found in the paragraphs *Mineral Production* under them.

BY-PRODUCTS OF COKE. As mentioned above, the manufacture of by-products of coke is each year increasing in importance. The total value of these products from the manufacture of coke in retort ovens in 1911 was $10,033,961, or a little more than one-third of the value of the coke produced. The by-products recovered in 1911 consisted of 33,274,861,000 feet of surplus gas, 69,410,599 gallons of tar, 72,920,056 pounds of ammonium sulphate or its equivalent, 23,180,118 pounds of anhydrous ammonia, and 4,660,596 gallons of ammonia liquor.

The imports of coke in the United States in 1911 amounted to 77,923 short tons, valued at $234,455, compared with 172,716 tons, valued at $625,130, in 1910. The exports amounted to 102,383 short tons, valued at $3,215,990.

The production of coke in the United States in 1912 is shown in the table below. The figures are those of the *Engineering and Mining Journal*. There was a considerable increase in the output in 1912.

	Short tons		Short tons
Alabama ..	3,050,000	Pennsylvania	28,492,275
Colorado ...	969,688	Tennessee ...	345,000
Georgia	47,200	Utah	347,356
Illinois	1,684,000	Virginia	1,101,000
Kansas	8,000	Washington .	40,000
Kentucky .	89,100	West Virginia	2,300,000
Montana ...	68,400	Other States	2,500,000
New Mexico	400,180		
Ohio	321,000	Total	41,803,199
Oklahoma .	40,000		

COLD STORAGE. See STOCK-RAISING AND MEAT PRODUCTION, and FOOD AND NUTRITION.

COLGATE UNIVERSITY. An institution of higher learning at Hamilton, N. Y., founded in 1819. The total enrollment in 1912 was 408 for the college and 54 in the theological seminary. The faculty numbered 44. A noteworthy event during the year was the creation of the office of vice-president, which was filled by Professor M. S. Read. There were no important benefactions received during the year. The productive funds of the college amounted to about $2,000,000 and the income to about $150,000. The volumes in the library numbered 61,000. President, Elmer Burritt Bryan.

COLLEGES. See UNIVERSITIES AND COLLEGES.

COLLEGES, AGRICULTURAL. See AGRICULTURAL EDUCATION.

COLLINS, LOREN WARREN. An American jurist, died September 27, 1912. He was born in Lowell, Mass., in 1838. In 1854 he removed to Minnesota and served throughout the Civil War in the 7th Minnesota Regiment, and was brevetted captain for gallantry in service. After the war he studied law and was admitted to the bar. He was for ten years county attorney of Stearns County, Minn. He was a member of the State legislature from 1881 to 1883. In the latter year he was appointed judge of the 7th judicial district of Minnesota. In 1887 he was appointed associate justice of the supreme court of the State. He resigned this position in 1904.

COLLISIONS. See RAILWAY ACCIDENTS.

COLLYER, ROBERT. A Unitarian clergyman and writer, died November 30, 1912. He was born in Keighley, Yorkshire, England, in 1823. As a youth he worked for nine years as a blacksmith in Yorkshire and the greater part of his early education was acquired by reading from books which were propped up on the forge before him. Previous to his working as a smith he had been put, at the age of 8, at work in a cotton-mill, where his experiences enabled him in later years to write effectively against child labor. At the age of 18 years he had versed himself sufficiently in the principles of Wesleyanism to be able to fill the pulpit in the local Methodist Church. When he was 27 years of age he removed to the United States. He worked at his early trade of blacksmith near Philadelphia for nine years, after which he went to Chicago as a preacher. During these years he had experienced a theological change. The principles of Methodism became incompatible to him and he joined the Unitarian Church. As a minister in this denomination he worked among missions in Chicago and finally took charge of Unity Church in 1860. He remained in this pastorate for nineteen years. His work following the great fire in Chicago added greatly to his reputation and to the esteem in which he was held in that city. He combated the idea that the fire was a Divine retribution and inspired the people of the stricken city with new energy. In 1879 he was called to the pastorate of the Church of the Messiah in New York City, and it is in this church that he always considered that the chief work of his life had been done. He remained in the active performance of the duties of pastor until he was well past 70, although he had several times offered to resign in favor of a younger man. In 1903 he was made pastor emeritus of the church. Dr. Collyer served in the Civil War as a nurse. He was one of the most striking figures in the life of New York City. He took an active and at times an aggressive part in philanthropic and charitable enterprises and he was notably effective as a speaker even in his last years. In 1910 he accepted the degree of D. D. from the Meadville Theological College. He had up to this time refused this degree on the ground that he was not a college graduate. Dr. Collyer's published works included: *Nature and Life* (1864); *The Life That Now Is* (1871); *The Simple Truth—A Home Book* (1878); *Talks to Young Men* (1888), and *Things New and Old* (1893).

COLOMBIA. A northwestern republic of South America. Capital, Bogotá.

AREA, POPULATION, ETC. On account of unsettled boundaries in the southeast, there are various estimates of area, ranging from 435,100 to 465,700 square miles. According to data reported from the national census board, the population on March 4, 1912, was 5,031,-

850. It was stated that this figure did not include the inhabitants of the recently established commissaries of Vapues, Putumayo, and Caquetá or the uncivilized Indians in some of the remote forests. Reported population in 1912 of towns over 18,000: Bogotá, 121,257; Medellin, 71,004; Barranquilla, 48,907; Cartagena, 36,632; Manizales, 34,720; Sonsón, 29,-346; Pasto, 27,760; Cali, 27,747; Aguadas, 26,-423; Ibagué, 24,693; Palmira, 24,312; Neiva, 21,852; Montería, 21,521; Yarumal, 21,250; Cúcuta, 20,364; Bucaramanga, 19,755; Miraflores, 19,150; Lorica, 19,005; Popayán, 18,-724; Cartago, 18,628; Pereira, 18,428; Andes, 18,391; Salamina, 18,195; Fredonia, 18,176. Primary instruction is gratuitous but not compulsory. There are several normal schools and a few establishments for professional education. Pupils and students attending 3877 institutions in 1900 were reported at 239,987.

INDUSTRIES AND COMMERCE. The people are engaged chiefly in agriculture and mining. In portions of the country cattle-raising is important. Leading products include bananas, coffee, cacao, sugar-cane, cotton, rubber, and cereals. There are large mineral resources, especially in Antioquia, including copper, lead, zinc, mercury, iron, platinum, and salt. The famous emerald mines of Muzo are leased by the government to an English syndicate. Manufactures are little developed.

Imports and exports have been valued as follows:

	1908	1909	1910	1911
Imp'ts	.$13,513,892	$12,117,927	$17,025,637	$18,108,863
Exp'ts	.$14,998,744	$16,040,198	$17,625,153	$22,375,799

The leading imports include flour, cotton goods, sugar, petroleum, iron and steel manufactures, and lard. Principal exports in 1911: Coffee, $9,475,448; gold, $3,751,632; bananas, $2,172,000; hides, $1,779,790; Panama hats, $1,-088,821; rubber, $900,886; ivory nuts, $739,-419; platinum, $345,896; tobacco, $332,935. Over half the total exports go to the United States.

COMMUNICATIONS. The railways form no continuous system but consist of various short lines engaged in local traffic. The total length at the end of 1911 was reported at 1000 kms., and extensions on several lines were under way. The railways in 1911 transported 1,-350,548 passengers and 383,930 tons of freight; the gross receipts were $2,758,281. Telegraph, 19,062 kms. of line. Post offices, about 500.

FINANCE. The gold dollar, or peso, is equivalent to the United States dollar, the silver peso fluctuates with the price of silver, and the paper peso is legally current at one cent. The budget for 1910 balanced at $10,831,500; for 1911, revenue $9,570,500, expenditure $10,-831,500; for 1913, each $12,500,000. Of the estimated 1913 receipts, customs were placed at $8,250,000; mines and salt, $1,636,000; stamps, $400,000; posts and telegraphs, $410,-000. Estimated expenditure for the ministry of war, $2,661,379; public debt, $2,551,554; interior, $1,264,515; posts and telegraphs, $1,-029,681; finance, $1,070,591. The foreign debt is reported at £2,666,400 (also the government guarantees railway bonds, £492,000, and interest on railway bonds, £1,480,000); internal debt (1910), $3,290,169. There is an enormous outstanding paper currency.

GOVERNMENT. The president is elected by the Congress for a (constitutional) term of four years and is assisted by a cabinet of seven ministers. The Congress is composed of the Senate (35 members elected indirectly) and the House of Representatives (92 members elected by direct vote). The president in 1912 was Carlos E. Restrepo, elected July 15 and inaugurated August 7, 1910. First and second designados (vice-presidents), Marco Suárez and José María González Valencia, respectively.

The United States vice-consul, William B. MacMaster, died under circumstances indicating violence, and the United States government ordered an investigation. Attempts had several times been recently made on his life and his relations with Colombian officials had been strained. The investigation brought out facts tending to prove that he had been murdered.

COLON, MUNICIPAL IMPROVEMENTS IN. See PANAMA CANAL.

COLORADO. POPULATION. According to the Census Bureau statistics issued in 1912, out of a total population in 1910 of 799,024, the foreign-born whites numbered 126,851, compared with 90,475 in 1900. The largest number, 17,070, came from Germany; from Italy, 14,368; from Russia, 13,610; from Austria, 13,153; from Sweden, 12,445; from Canada, 8727; and from Ireland, 8709. Other European countries were represented by smaller numbers. The negroes in the State in 1910 numbered 11,-453 and the mulattoes 3638. In 1890 the negroes numbered 6215 and the mulattoes 2159.

MANUFACTURES. The Thirteenth Census included statistics of manufactures in the State. These are for the calendar year 1909 and were compiled in 1912. The general results will be found in the table below. The industries in which the largest capital is invested are those connected with slaughtering and meat packing, the value of whose products was $9,-657,000. The wage earners employed in these industries numbered 659. Second in value of production were flour-mill and grist-mill products, $7,868,000; printing and publishing, $6,-962,000, giving employment to 2366 wage earners. The largest number of wage earners were employed in the industries connected with cars and general shop construction. These numbered 3993. The value of the product of these industries was $6,559,000. The only other industries whose product was valued at more than $5,000,000 were those connected with foundry and machine shop products. The value of these was $5,907,000. The wage earners in the State in 1909 numbered 28,067, of whom 25,957 were male and 2110 were female. The wage earners under 16 years of age numbered 165, of whom 16 were females. The prevailing hours of labor for more than one-half the wage earners employed ranged from 54 to 60 a week. Of the total number of wage earners 22.7 per cent. were employed in establishments where the prevailing hours were less than 54 a week, and 22.9 per cent. in establishments where the prevailing hours were more than 60 a week. There are only four cities in the State in which manufactories are important: Denver, with 12,-058 wage earners and the value of the manufactured product in that city was $51,538,547. In Pueblo were 1320 wage earners, in Colorado Springs, 516, and in Trinidad, 220. The following table shows the growth of manufactures in the five-year period, 1904 to 1909, together with the percentage of increase:

	Number or amount. 1909	1904	P. C. of inc. 1904-1909
Number of establishments	2,034	1,606	26.6
Persons engaged in manufactures	34,115	25,888	31.8
Proprietors and firm members.	1,722	1,398	23.2
Salaried employees	4,326	2,677	61.6
Wage earners (average number)	28,067	21,813	28.7
Primary horsepower.	154,615	124,901	23.8
Capital	$162,668,000	$107,664,000	51.1
Expenses	114,690,000	88,282,000	29.9
Services	25,560,000	18,649,000	37.1
Salaries	5,648,000	3,549,000	59.1
Wages	19,912,000	15,100,000	31.9
Materials	80,491,000	63,114,000	27.5
Miscellaneous	8,639,000	6,519,000	32.5
Value of products...	130,044,000	100,144,000	29.9
Value added by manufacture (value of products less cost of materials)......	49,553,000	37,030,000	33.8

MINERAL PRODUCTION. The production of gold in 1911 was valued at $19,001,975, a decrease of $1,505,083 from the output of 1910. The production of Cripple Creek, which in 1911 was $10,562,653, decreased $439,600. The output of Ouray county decreased $242,889, following a decrease of $848,978 in 1910. Of the total ore mined and sold or treated, dry or siliceous ores made up 79 per cent. and yielded $17,907,034 of the gold, or 94 per cent. of the total gold output. Nearly 2 per cent. came from placer mines and nearly 2 per cent. from lead ores, the remainder of the gold production being derived from copper, zinc, and lead-zinc ores. The total output of the placer mines of the State in 1911 was $319,759. The silver production of the State in 1911 was 7,330,168 fine ounces against 8,509,598 ounces in 1910. Leadville showed a decrease of 314,719 ounces and yielded 41 per cent. of the State output in 1911. Dry or siliceous ores yielded 5,096,026 ounces in 1911, or nearly 70 per cent. of the total output; lead ores, $1,265,594; lead-zinc ores, $476,049; copper ores, $342,550, and the small remainder came from copper-lead and zinc ores.

The production of copper in the State in 1911 was 9,791,861 pounds, as compared with 9,307,497 pounds in 1910. The State ranks ninth among copper-producing States. The total recorded output from the beginning of the industry is 213,543,924 pounds. The main production of the metal is derived from the treatment of mixed ores, in which copper is of minor importance. These included lead-silver ores and pyritic ores rich in gold and silver.

COAL. The production of coal in the State in 1911 was 10,157,383 short tons, valued at $14,747,764. Colorado is the principal coal-producing State west of the Mississippi River and ranks seventh among all the States. The production in 1910 was the maximum in the history of coal mining in the State, 11,973,736 short tons. The decreased production in 1911 was due to an unusually mild winter in 1910-11, the decreased consumption of locomotive fuel and the resumption of mining in the coal-producing States of the Mississippi Valley. The number of men employed in the coal mines of the State in 1911 was 14,273.

PETROLEUM. There were produced in 1911, 226,926 barrels of petroleum, compared with 239,794 barrels in 1910. The largest production was in the Florence field, 187,341 barrels. From the Boulder fields were obtained 37,973 barrels.

AGRICULTURE. The acreage, value, and production of the principal crops in 1911 and 1912 are shown in the following table.

		Acreage	Prod. Bu.	Value
Corn	1912	420,000	8,736,000	$ 4,368,000
	1911	378,000	5,222,000	4,073,000
Wheat	1912	453,000	10,968,000	8,006,000
	1911	438,000	8,274,000	6,950,000
Oats	1912	290,000	12,412,000	4,717,000
	1911	290,000	10,150,000	4,872,000
Rye	1912	25,000	488,000	268,000
	1911	21,000	252,000	176,000
Potatoes ..	1912	85,000	8,075,000	3,311,000
	1911	90,000	3,150,000	3,118,000
Hay	1912	870,000	(a) 1,905,000	16,574,000
	1911	707,000	(a) 1,414,000	16,150,000

(a) Tons.

EDUCATION. The total school population of the State between the ages of 6 and 21 in 1912 was 227,187. Of these 114,589 were male and 112,598 female. The total enrollment in the schools was 177,428. Of these, 89,932 were male and 87,426 were female. The enrollment in the high schools of the State was 16,377, the enrollment in grade schools below high schools was 112,582, and the enrollment in rural schools was 48,469. The average monthly salary for male teachers was $102.45 and for female teachers, $69.01. The disbursements for school purposes in 1912 were as follows: For teachers' salaries, $3,836,166; for current expenses, $1,232,254; for sites and building improvements, $1,262,794; for library purposes, $13,252; for redemption of bond, $203,758; for interest on bonds, $183,099. The Superintendent of Education recommends for legislative enactment measures making the term of office of State and county superintendents four years. Recommendation is also made for a law for the medical examination of school children by specialists and trained nurses.

FINANCE. The report of the State treasurer for the biennial period ending November 30, 1912, showed a balance in the treasury on December 1, 1910, of $3,309,320. The receipts for the two-year period were $8,237,909 and the disbursements amounted to $7,383.035, leaving a balance in the treasury on December 1, 1912, of $4,164,195. The chief source of revenue was from taxation. The principal expenditures were for education and the support of State institutions.

CHARITIES AND CORRECTIONS. The charitable and correctional institutions under the control of the State included the Boys' Industrial School, the Dependent Children's Home, the Insane Asylums, Home for the Mute and Blind, Soldiers' and Sailors' Home, and the State Penitentiary and Reformatory.

POLITICS AND GOVERNMENT

The legislature did not meet in 1912 as the sessions are biennial and the last was held in 1911.

CONVENTIONS AND ELECTIONS. The Republican State convention which met on March 26 elected delegates to the national convention pledged to President Taft, who had about 700 delegates, and there were about 200 for Mr. Roosevelt. The Democratic State convention for the election of delegates sent delegates pledged to Governor Wilson. On August 1, the Progressive party convened at Denver and chose a complete State ticket headed by E. P. Costigan. In the primaries on September 10, C. C. Parks was nominated as Republican candidate for governor. The Democrats nominated as their candidate for governor, E. M. Ammon. In the election held on November 5, Wilson received 114,223 votes; Taft, 58,386; Roosevelt, 72,306; and Debs, 16,418 votes. In the contest for governor, Ammon, the Democratic candidate, received 101,293 votes, Costigan, Progressive, 63,035, and Parks, Republican, 54,724. The Democrats elected all the Congressmen, including two Congressmen-at-large.

A number of important measures were voted upon. These included a measure prohibiting the sale of intoxicating liquors, a measure regulating the employment of women, and an act establishing a public service commission. These measures were all presented under the laws providing for initiative and referendum. In addition, a number of other amendments to the constitution were voted upon, but these were relatively unimportant.

On May 21 one of the most closely contested municipal elections ever held in Denver, resulted in the election of Henry J. Arnold as mayor. Mr. Arnold headed the Citizens' ticket. He was opposed by a Republican candidate, United States Marshal D. C. Bailey, and a Democratic candidate, John B. Hunter. Mr. Arnold's plurality was over 20,000.

State Government. Governor, E. M. Ammon; Lieutenant-Governor, B. F. Montgomery; Secretary of State, James B. Pearce; Treasurer, M. A. Leddy; Auditor, R. Kenehan; Attorney-General, Fred Farrar; Superintendent of Public Instruction, Mary C. Bradford, all Democrats.

Judiciary. Supreme Court: Chief Justice, George W. Musser, Dem.; Justices, S. H. White, Dem.; W. A. Hill, Dem.; M. S. Bailey, Dem.; William H. Gabbert, Rep.; Tully Scott, Dem.; James E. Garrigues, Rep.; Clerk, James R. Killian, Dem.

State Legislature, 1913. Democrats, Senate, 24; House, 48; joint ballot, 72. Republicans, Senate, 11; House, 17; joint ballot, 28. Democratic majority, Senate, 13; House, 31; joint ballot, 44.

The representatives in Congress will be found in the section *Congress*, article United States.

COLORADO, University of. A State institution of higher education at Boulder, Col., founded in 1876. The total enrollment in the several departments of the university in the year 1911-12 was 1306. The faculty numbered 217. Among the important events in the history of the university during the year were the establishment of a school of social and home service, inauguration of the university extension department, and the appointment of Loran Osborn, Ph. D., as director, the establishment of an electrical testing laboratory, and the appointment of a research assistant in charge, the establishment of a school of pharmacy, the establishment of a hygienic laboratory, and the appointment of Dr. A. R. Peebles as professor of preventive and experimental medicine. For the establishment of the electrical testing laboratory there was given the sum of $10,000. The income of the university is $250,000 annually. There are 63,487 volumes in the library.

COLORATION. See Entomology.

COLOR PHOTOGRAPHY. See Chemistry, Industrial.

COLUMBIA, District of. See United States.

COLUMBIA UNIVERSITY. The total number of students receiving instruction in all departments of the university in the autumn of 1912 was 9002. Of these, 3602 were in attendance at the summer session of 1912. The remainder, 6148, were distributed in the different departments of the college as follows: Columbia College, 819; Barnard College, 590; college of architecture, 129; college of music, 20; schools of mines, engineering and chemistry, 634; school of law, 457; school of journalism, 336; school of pedagogy, 1045; school of pharmacy, 420; school of practical arts, 227; graduate school (non-professional), 1399. In addition, there are enrolled in extension and similar courses, 1741 students. Among the changes in the faculty during the collegiate year 1911-12 was the retirement of John W. Burgess, Ph. D., professor of political science and constitutional law, and dean of the faculty of political science, philosophy and pure science, and fine arts. Professor Burgess was the oldest professor on the rolls of the university. George N. Olcott, associate professor of Latin, died on March 3, 1912. Note of the establishment of the school of journalism and other items of interest in the administration of the university during the year will be found in the article on Universities and Colleges.

COLUMBUS, O. See Sewage Purification.

COMAN, Henry Benjamin. An American jurist, died January 10, 1912. He was born in Morrisville, N. Y., in 1858, and was educated in the public schools and at the Cazenovia Seminary. After studying law he was admitted to the bar in 1880. Until 1890 he was clerk in the office of the surrogate in Madison county. He afterwards took up private practice and in 1899 received an appointment to the office of the attorney-general in Albany. In the year following he was appointed deputy attorney-general with the special assignment to enforce the franchise tax law. He became first deputy attorney-general in 1901 and in 1902 was defeated for the office of attorney-general on the Republican ticket. In 1907 he was appointed justice of the supreme court of the State.

COMBUSTION OF CARBON. See Chemical Progress.

COMETS. See Astronomy.

COMMERCE. For foreign trade see United States and articles on foreign countries; for internal trade see United States and articles on industries, and Financial Review.

COMMERCE COURT. See Railways.

COMMISSION FORM OF GOVERNMENT. See Municipal Government.

COMMISSION ON INDUSTRIAL RELATIONS. See Labor Legislation.

COMMISSION PLAN. See Municipal Government.

COMMITTEES. National. See Presidential Campaign.

COMORO ISLANDS. See MAYOTTE.

COMPENSATION FOR WORKMEN. See WORKMEN'S COMPENSATION.

COMPOUNDS. See CHEMISTRY.

COMPRESSED AIR ILLNESS. See OCCUPATIONAL DISEASES.

COMPULSORY ARBITRATION. See ARBITRATION AND CONCILIATION, INDUSTRIAL.

CONCERTS. See MUSIC.

CONCRETE. See CEMENT, and TALL BUILDINGS.

CONCRETE, REINFORCED. See ARCHITECTURE.

CONDENSED MILK. See DAIRYING.

CONGO, BELGIAN. A central African colony of Belgium (the former Congo Free State). Boma (Bas-Congo) is the capital. All the statistics given below are from the official report of the Belgian colonial minister.

AREA AND POPULATION. The colony covers (January 1, 1912), an area of 2,365,000 square kilometers (913,127 square miles); white population, 4003 (2432 Belgians). No official estimate of native population is given; other sources vary from nine to twenty millions. Besides Boma, important towns are Matadi, Banana, Leopoldville, Stanleyville, Kambove, Niangara, Bandundu, etc.

PRODUCTION. The chief products of the country are shown in the list of exports, rubber leading in importance. The Kilo gold mine, situated in the Ituri basin, not far from Lake Albert, has 8 experts and 1750 negro workers, and produced (1910) 876 kgs. of gold.

Sale of crown lands in 1910, about 14 hectares at a total price of 241,528 francs; crown lands rented in 1910, 4062 hectares, rental 18,345 francs. A large proportion of these lands is in the Katanga district.

COMMERCE. Total imports (general trade) in 1910, 43,979,000 francs; special trade, 36,846,508. Exports, details and totals for four years, are shown below (general trade), with values in thousands of francs:

Articles	1907	1908	1909	1910
Rubber	57,330	40,144	60,171	76,030
Palm oil	1,741	1,376	1,095	2,016
Palm nuts	2,522	2,056	2,199	3,101
Ivory	11,034	9,597	10,354	9,361
Various	4,914	3,694	4,195	5,091
Total exports	77,541	56,867	78,014	95,599

Exports, special trade (1910), 66,602,298 francs (rubber, 51,015,649; ivory, 6,056,475; palm nuts, 2,657,164; raw gold, 2,514,022; palm oil, 1,797,594; white copal, 1,314,348; cacao, 1,071,372; etc.). The principal countries of origin and destination are in the order named, Belgium, Great Britain, France, Germany, Netherlands, Angola, Denmark, Portugal, Uganda, etc. Tonnage entered and cleared (1910), 627,997.

RAILWAYS. On January 1, 1912, the various railway lines, with holdings, were as follows: Congo Railway Company, 400 kilometers; Stanleyville-Ponthierville, 125; Kindu-Kongolo, 355; Lualaba-Tanganika, 300 (approximate length under construction); Rhodesian frontier-Elisabethville and Elisabethville-Bukama, 275 in operation and 168 under construction; Boma-la Lukula, 80.

FINANCE AND GOVERNMENT. Financial statistics appear in the table below in thousands of francs for four years (1911 and 1912 budgets):

	1909	1910	1911	1912
Revenue	34,570	33,517	40,870	45,368
Expenditure	34,470	40,371	*59,658	†66,539

* Including 12,222,443 francs extraordinary.
† 16,818,660 francs extraordinary.

The total public debt amounts to 214,909,700 francs.

The governor-general in 1912 was F. Fuchs.

HISTORY. In the closing weeks of 1911 a serious insurrection broke out in an extensive portion of the Welle district, where the Wallendu massacred a large part of the natives who were loyal to the whites. A body of troops some 300 strong were hurried into the region and very severe repressive measures were taken. In June the various societies and agencies that were concerned with the improvement of the Congo presented to Sir Edward Grey a memorandum, which, while admitting that many improvements had been introduced in the administration since Belgium assumed control, asserted that the native races were still as insecure as ever as regards the ownership of land. They had no lands, according to Belgian law, outside the arbitrarily assigned boundaries of their villages. This status had already been admitted by the British government to be contrary to the spirit of the treaties that define the international position of the Congo State. It was therefore the government's right to press for measures that would insure security of tenure for the natives. Congo reformers felt much alarm at the proposal of Belgium to establish vast state rubber plantations for revenue purposes. When questioned on this subject, M. Renkin, the Belgian minister for the colonies, declared that the government had not decided to carry this out on a large scale, but was considering whether it should not reduce the number of plantations instead of increasing them, and should conduct such enterprises as remained in its hands chiefly as examples for the benefit of private enterprise. It was required that every laborer's contract should be countersigned by a legislator. There were instances of abuse and the government was trying to reduce them to the minimum.

CONGO FREE STATE. See CONGO, BELGIAN.

CONGO, FRENCH. See FRENCH EQUATORIAL AFRICA.

CONGREGATIONALISTS. The Congregationalists are the eighth largest religious body in the United States. Congregationalism in its churches is found in their relation to each other, under—first, a group of churches in annual session, which is called, "Association"; second, all the churches of a State meeting annually, called "Conference"; third, a National Council, the constituency of which is formed by delegates in triennial sessions from associations and conferences. The chief organization, under the auspices of which the benevolent and missionary work of the churches is carried on, are: The American Board of Commissioners for Foreign Missions; the Congregational Education Society; the Congregational Church Building Society; the Congregational Home Missionary Society; the American Missionary Association; the Congregational Sunday School and Publishing Society; the Congregational Board of Ministerial Relief; the Woman's Foreign Mission Boards, and the Woman's Federation and Auxiliaries for Home Missionary Work. For fellowship, culture, and inspiration, clubs are maintained, of which there are about fifty in the United States. A license to preach is granted in some States by local associations, and in other States by ministerial associations.

The theological seminaries known as Congregational are Yale (undenominational), opened in 1822; Bangor, Me., 1816; Andover, Cambridge, Mass., 1807; Hartford, Conn., 1834; Oberlin, Ohio, 1835; Chicago, Ill., 1855; Pacific, Berkeley, Cal., 1869; Talladega, Ala., 1872; Atlanta, Ga., 1901. In these institutions are 392 undergraduates, and 127 instructors. Forty colleges were founded by Congregationalists; in these are enrolled 22,962 students. The instructors number 2030. In their libraries there are 1,862,491 volumes. The amount of productive funds is $37,553,224.55. On January 1, 1912, Congregationalists reported 738,861 members in the United States. At that date there were reported 6048 churches, and 6116 ministers. The Sunday schools enrolled 664,629 members. For home expenses the amount was $9,356,122. The total of contributions was $2,454,340, which was distributed as follows: Foreign missions, $518,325; education, $59,311; church building, $81,315; home missions, $346,593; American Missionary Association, $144,190; Sunday school work, $66,703; ministerial aid, $36,935; additional Congregational work, $523,513; undenominational, $677,455. World-wide Congregationalism, 14,424 churches and chapels; 1,389,882 members, and 1,550,799 members in Sunday schools.

The National Council was organized at Oberlin, Ohio, November 17, 1871. This body as well as local and State bodies does not legislate for the churches. It is simply advisory. Whatever of wisdom there is in its resolutions and recommendations is readily accepted by the churches. There is a tendency toward centralization, especially in missionary and benevolent service. That a greater efficiency might be secured a commission on apportionment of beneficence was created at Boston, 1910, with a view to developing a systematic method of gathering and assigning the contributions of the churches for missionary service. Ministerial and religious education is receiving a large consideration, the object being to advance the intellectual culture of the ministry, to elevate the standard, and to cultivate a more scientific understanding and application of biblical literature and teaching, especially in the interest of the young. The commission of nineteen, appointed at Boston, 1910, will report to the next session of National Council, recommending—that the National Council meet once in two years; that delegates to the council serve for two successive sessions; that the moderator be elected at the end of each session; that the committee on nominations be made permanent; that the council nominate a majority of the corporation members of the American board; that the delegates to National Council constitute a voting body in the interest of home and foreign benevolence; that a home board of missions be created as a uniting bond between the home societies, whose board of managers shall coördinate and supervise the work of the missionary organization at home; that the secretaryship be enlarged in its functions.

The fifteenth triennial session of National Council will be held in Kansas City, Mo., October 22-31, 1913. The officers are: Moderator, Rev. Nehemiah Boynton, D. D., Brooklyn, N. Y.; secretary and editor, Rev. Asher Anderson, D. D., Boston, Mass.; treasurer and registrar, Rev. Joel S. Ives, Hartford, Conn.

CONGREGATIONAL METHODIST CHURCH. There were in this denomination in 1912, 15,229 communicants, 333 churches, and 337 ministers. In general, the polity of the church agrees with that of the Methodist Episcopal Church. Its greatest strength is in the Southern States. A publishing house is maintained at Ellisville, Miss. The official organ of the denomination is *The Messenger*. The only educational institution under the auspices of the denomination is the Atlanta Bible School.

CONGRESS OF APPLIED CHEMISTRY, INTERNATIONAL. See METALLURGY.

CONGRESS OF HYGIENE. See HYGIENE, CONGRESS OF.

CONGRESS OF JURISTS. See ARBITRATION, INTERNATIONAL.

CONGRESS OF THE UNITED STATES. See UNITED STATES.

CONNECTICUT. POPULATION. According to the Census Bureau statistics issued in 1912, of the total population in 1910 of 1,114,756 the foreign-born whites numbered 328,759 compared with 237,396 in 1900. The largest number, 58,456, came from Ireland; from Italy, 56,946; from Russia, 54,095; from Germany, 31,122; from Austria, 24,762; from England, 22,417, and from Sweden, 18,195. In the city of Bridgeport, with a population of 102,054 in 1910, the foreign-born whites numbered 36,180. In New Haven, with a population of 133,605, they numbered 42,784. In 1910 the negroes in the State numbered 15,174, and the mulattoes 3746. In 1890 the negroes numbered 12,302, and the mulattoes, 3081.

AGRICULTURE. The acreage, value, and production of the principal crops in 1911 and 1912 are shown in the following table:

		Acreage	Prod. Bu.	Value
Corn	1912	60,000	3,000,000	$ 2,310,000
	1911	59,000	2,862,000	2,875,000
Oats	1912	11,000	338,000	166,000
	1911	11,000	386,000	216,000
Rye	1912	7,000	122,000	112,000
	1911	8,000	148,000	138,000
Potatoes	1912	28,000	2,461,000	1,920,000
	1911	23,000	1,955,000	2,053,000
Hay	1912	379,000	(a) 436,000	9,810,000
	1911	490,000	(a) 539,000	12,666,000
Tobacco	1912	17,500	(b) 29,750,000	7,170,000
	1911	17,000	(b) 27,625,000	5,663,125

(a) Tons. (b) Pounds.

MANUFACTURES. The Thirteenth Census statistics are for the calendar year 1909 and were compiled in 1912. Connecticut is pre-eminently a manufacturing State, and the growth and concentration of its population have been closely related to the increase and importance of its manufacturing industries. This State ranks twelfth in value of its manufactured products. The table below gives a summary of the results of the census:

	Numer or Amount 1909	1904	P. C. of Inc. 1904-9
Number of establishments	4,251	3,477	22.3
Persons engaged in manufactures....	233,871	198,046	18.1
Proprietors and firm members...	3,468	2,918	18.8
Salaried employees	19,611	.13,523	45.0
Wage earners (average No.)...	210,792	181,605	16.1
Primary horsepower.	400,275	304,204	31.6
Capital	$517,547,000	$373,284,000	38.6
Expenses	429,904,000	328,610,000	30.8
Services	135,756,000	104,983,000	29.3
Salaries	25,637,000	17,040,000	50.5
Wages	110,119,000	87,943,000	25.2
Materials	257,259,000	191,302,000	34.5
Miscellaneous	36,889,000	32,325,000	14.1
Value of products..	490,272,000	369,082,000	32.8
Value of products less cost of materials..	233,013,000	177,780,000	31.1

In addition it may be noted that of the 4251 establishments, 403 were devoted to foundry and machine shop products, 393 to lumber and timber products, 431 to bread and other bakery products, and 363 to printing and publishing. The value of the brass and bronze products in 1909 was $66,933,000; of foundry and machine shop products $65,535,000; of cotton goods, including cotton small wares, $24,232,000. All these products showed a marked increase in the period of 1904-1909. The total number of persons engaged in manufactures in the State in 1909 was 233,871. Of these, 176,478 were male, and 57,393 were female. The number of wage-earners under 16 years of age was 5421. The great majority of wage-earners in the State employed in the manufacturing industries worked from 54 to 60 hours a week; only 8.4 per cent. of the total number being employed in establishments where the prevailing hours are less than 54 a week. The chief manufacturing city is Bridgeport, where 25,775 wage-earners were employed; second is New Haven, with 23,547, followed by Waterbury, 20,170, Hartford, 14,627, and New Britain, 13,513.

Education. The school children in the State, in 1912, numbered 255,652. The enrollment in the public schools was 197,852 and the average daily attendance, 155,735. There were 1455 schools and 5491 teachers. The average monthly salary of women teachers was $57.87. The total expenditure for schools during the fiscal year was $6,122,367, of which $3,250,671 was expended for teachers' wages.

Finance. The receipts for the fiscal year 1912 amounted to $9,915,417, which includes $4,000,000 of bonds sold during the year. The expenditures during the same period were $8,105,750, including $1,450,000, which was paid for a temporary loan. The balance on hand at the end of the fiscal year amounted to $1,809,667. The chief receipts were from taxation of railroads, from State taxation, and from the inheritance tax. The chief expenditures were for the courts, for education, for the maintenance of highways, for the militia, and for the support of humane institutions. The State debt amounts to $7,064,100.

Politics and Government

There was no session of the State legislature in 1912 as that body meets biennially and the last session was held in 1911. Elections were held for governor and other State officials on November 5. The Republican State convention for the election of delegates to the national convention met in New Haven on April 17. The four delegates-at-large and a majority of the ten district delegates were instructed to vote for President Taft. The entire delegation did vote for him at Chicago. The four delegates-at-large were: Charles F. Brooker, national committeeman, Charles Hopkins Clark, J. Henry Roraback, chairman of the Republican State committee, and Frank B. Weeks, former governor. Mr. Brooker was chosen chairman of the delegation. The Democrats at their convention for the election of delegates to their national convention, held May 1 and 2 at Bridgeport, pledged the votes of Connecticut to Governor Baldwin. The four delegates-at-large were: W. O. Burr of Hartford, Bryan F. Mahan of New London, William Kennedy of Naugatuck, and David E. Fitzgerald of New Haven. Mr. Kennedy was chosen chairman. The delegation voted for Governor Baldwin at Baltimore several times, and then scattered. The first State convention of the Progressive party was held on July 30 at Hartford. Forty-nine delegates to Chicago were chosen. Resolutions were adopted instructing the Connecticut delegation to vote for Mr. Roosevelt at the convention of the Progressive party, also in favor of direct primaries in National and State elections, presidential primaries for delegates to the national convention, election of United States Senators by direct vote, the initiative, referendum and recall and other measures advocated by the party.

On September 11 the Republicans met at Hartford in State convention for the nomination of governor and other State officers, and an entirely new ticket was put in the field, headed by Judge John P. Studley of New Haven, as candidate for governor, who was nominated over Dr. George H. Knight of Salisbury and Judge Silas A. Robinson of Middletown. Their platform, among other things, called for home rule for cities, a workmen's compensation act, and a commission for the improvement of agricultural conditions. On the following day the Democrats held their convention for the nomination of State officers in the same hall, and Governor Baldwin was renominated. Their platform called for the initiative and referendum, direct primaries, popular election of Senators, workmen's compensation and home rule for cities. The Progressive party met in convention on September 26 and nominated for governor Herbert Knox Smith, former commissioner of corporations. In the election on November 5, Governor Wilson received 74,561 votes, President Taft 68,324, Mr. Roosevelt 34,129, Debs, Socialist, 10,056 and Chafin, Prohibition, 2096. The vote for governor was: For Baldwin, 78,264; for Studley, 67,531; for Smith, 31,020; for Beardsley, Socialist, 10,236, and for Bossette, Prohibition 2096. The Democrats elected representatives to Congress in all five districts.

Augustine Lonergan of Hartford, defeated Charles C. Bissell of Suffield, in the first; Bryan F. Mahan of New London, defeated William A. King of Windham, in the second; Thomas F. Reilly of Meriden (reëlected), defeated John Q. Tilson of New Haven, in the third; Jeremiah Donovan of Norwalk, defeated Ebenezer J. Hill of Norwalk, in the fourth, and William Kennedy of Naugatuck, defeated State Comptroller Thomas D. Bradstreet of Thomaston, in the fifth. Mr. Bradstreet had been nominated to succeed Dr. George H. Knight of Salisbury, who fell dead on the platform while addressing a Republican convention at his own home early in the campaign. The previous Congressional delegation had stood four Republicans and one Democrat. The State legislature stands: Senate, 21 Democrats, 14 Republicans; House, 130 Republicans, 120 Democrats, 6 Progressives, and 2 Progressive Republicans; total, 258. No United States Senator is to be elected this year. A constitutional amendment adopted since the last session requires the regular legislative session, which opens on the Wednesday after the first Monday in January, to terminate by the first Wednesday after the first Monday of June in the same year. The session of 1911 lasted from January 5 until September 26.

State Government. Governor, Simeon E. Baldwin, Dem.; Lieutenant-Governor, Lyman T. Tingier, Dem.; Secretary of State, Albert L. Phillips, Dem.; Treasurer, Edward S. Roberts, Dem.; Attorney-General, John H. Light, Rep.; Commissioner of Insurance, Burton Mansfield, Dem.

Judiciary. Supreme Court: Chief Justice, Frederick B. Hall, Rep.; Associate Justices, S. O. Prentice, Rep.; George W. Wheeler, Dem.; John M. Thayer, Dem.; Alberto T. Roraback, Rep.; Clerk, George A. Conant, Rep.

State Legislature, 1913. Republicans, Senate, 21; House, 120; joint ballot, 141. Democrats, Senate, 14; House, 132; joint ballot, 146. Progressives, House, 6; joint ballot, 6. Republican majority, Senate, 7. Democratic majority, House, 6.

The representatives in Congress will be found in the section *Congress*, article United States.

CONNELL, Richard E. A member of Congress from New York, died October 30, 1912. He was born in Poughkeepsie, N. Y., in 1857 and was educated in parochial and public schools in that city. He engaged in newspaper work as a reporter and from 1891 to the time of his death was editor of the Poughkeepsie *News-Press*. He was active in Democratic politics and from 1892 to 1894 was police commissioner of Poughkeepsie. He was elected to the 62d Congress in 1911. In 1900 he was a delegate to the Democratic national convention at Kansas City.

CONSERVATION. See Irrigation, Forestry, Lands, Public Drainage, Alaska.

CONSULAR SERVICE. See Civil Service.

CONSUMPTION. See Tuberculosis.

CONTRIBUTIONS, Political. See Presidential Campaign Contributions.

CONVENTIONS, National Political. See Presidential Campaign.

CONVICT LEASING SYSTEM. See Arkansas, and Penology.

COOLIDGE, John Bacon. An American chemist and dentist, died February 5, 1912. He was born in 1821. As a boy, he learned the shoemaker's trade, at the same time studying medicine and dentistry. After the Civil War he opened a dental office in Boston, afterwards taking a degree at the New York Medical College. He was the first dentist in the United States to use nitrous oxide gas as an anæsthetic. He gave an exhibition of the use of this gas in 1864. With Dr. Weatherby, a Boston dentist, he established the Boston Dental College in 1867. This later was merged with the Tufts Dental School. In this school Dr. Coolidge was secretary for fifteen years, and for 27 years was professor of chemical dentistry and dental art mechanism. He invented many of the instruments now in use by modern dentists.

COOPER, Philip Henry. A rear-admiral, retired, of the United States navy, died December 29, 1912. He was born in Camden, N. Y., in 1844 and graduated from the United States Naval Academy in 1863. He was appointed ensign in the same year and served on the *Constellation* until 1865. He participated in the battle of Mobile Bay and in the siege of Fort Morgan. He was executive officer of the *Richmond* at the surrender of the ram, *Webb*, on the Mississippi River. From 1865 to 1867 he served on the *Powhatan*. He was instructor in the United States Naval Academy in 1868-69. In 1870-71 he took part in the Tehuantepec surveying expedition. After commanding several vessels he was appointed superintendent of the Naval Academy in 1894, serving until 1898. He took part in the Spanish-American War as commander of the *Chicago*. In 1902-3 he was superintendent of the second naval district and in 1903 was squadron commander of the Asiatic Station and commander-in-chief of this station in 1904. He retired in that year.

COÖPERATIVE CREDIT SOCIETIES. See Agricultural Credit.

COÖPERATIVE MARKETING. See Horticulture.

COPPER. In the following article the production of copper is dealt with as a whole. The statistics of production in the several States will be found in the paragraph *Mineral Production* under those States. The statistics are those gathered by the United States Geological Survey.

The production of copper in 1911 by smelters from copper-bearing material from the United States was 1,097,232,741 pounds, valued at $137,154,092 as compared with 1,080,159,509 pounds, valued at $137,180,257 in 1910. The production in 1911 was the largest in the history of the industry, surpassing that of 1910 by about 1.5 per cent. The increase in the production in 1911 was due chiefly to the entrance of new producers into the field, as several of the older districts made smaller productions, the decrease generally being due to curtailment on account of the unsatisfactory condition of the copper metal market. The average price of copper for the year, 12.5 cents a pound, was slightly below that of 1910 and was the lowest yearly average price since 1902. Near the close of the year, however, the price of copper was notably better, the average for December being 13.71 cents a pound. The market conditions continued to improve until the average price for 1912 rose to about 17 cents per pound, the highest price since the panic of 1907. Among the new companies which contributed to the output in 1911 were the Miami Copper Company, Arizona, the Ray Consolidated Copper Company, Arizona, the Chino Copper Company, New Mexico, and the Bonanza mine of the Copper River district, Alaska. The production from the Yerington district, Nevada, began early in 1912. Several of the older districts voluntarily curtailed their output and there was a material reduction in the Shasta County, Cal., district on account of the "smelter fume" difficulties. During the year 44 copper-smelting and refining plants treated material from the United States. Of these, 39 were domestic plants and fire were foreign. Three were in British Columbia and two in Mexico.

Twenty-one States and Territories contributed to the copper production of 1911. The three leading States, Arizona, Montana, and Michigan, produced 72 per cent. of the total output in 1911 as compared with 74 per cent. in 1910, while the six leading States, including Utah, Nevada, and California, produced over 90 per cent. of the total output in 1911 as compared with over 96 per cent. in 1910. Arizona continued in 1911 to be the largest producer of copper. There were mined in that State 306,141,538 pounds, compared with 297,491,151 pounds in 1910. This was the largest production in the history of copper mining in the State. Montana ranked second with 272,847,705 pounds, compared with 284,808,533 pounds in 1910. Michigan, the third State in rank, produced in 1911, 219,840,201 pounds as compared with 222,683,461 in 1910. In Utah were produced 146,960,827 pounds in 1911 compared with 127,597,072 pounds in 1910. In Nevada 67,377,518 pounds were produced, compared with 64,359,398 pounds in 1910. In California were produced 36,316,136 pounds compared with 48,700,756 pounds in 1910. The production in Alaska showed a remarkable increase. In 1911 the production was 27,267,878 compared with 4,241,689 pounds in 1910. The table below shows the production of copper by States in the years 1910-1911 in pounds:

State	1910	1911
Alaska	4,311,026	22,314,889
Arizona	297,250,538	303,202,532
California	45,760,203	35,835,651
Colorado	9,307,497	9,791,861
Idaho	6,877,515	4,514,116
Michigan	221,462,984	218,185,236
Montana	283,078,473	271,814,491
New Mexico	3,784,609	2,860,400
Nevada	64,494,640	65,561,015
Oregon	22,022	125,943
South Dakota	43	1,607
Utah	125,185,455	142,340,215
Washington	65,021	195,503
Wyoming	217,127	130,499
Eastern States and unapportioned	18,342,359	20,358,791
Total	1,080,159,509	1,097,232,749

Yield of Copper From Ores. There were mined in 1911 29,944,942 tons of copper, copper-lead, and copper-zinc ores. This ore contained 1,095,716,597 pounds of recoverable copper, or an average of 1.826 per cent., as compared with 1.88 per cent. for 1910. In 1911 copper ores produced 1,095,131,104 pounds of copper, and the copper-lead and copper-zinc ores produced 585,179 pounds. There were 4,355,680 tons of smelting ore, which yielded 407,570,198 pounds of copper, and 25,632,585 tons of concentrating ore which yielded 687,560,906 pounds. The highest grade of ore was produced in Alaska, where the average yield was 19.77 per cent. copper.

Consumption and Uses. The apparent consumption of refined new copper in the United States in 1911, was 681,700,000 pounds, as compared with 732,400,000 pounds in 1910. Adding to this 214,207,000 pounds of secondary copper and copper in alloys produced during the year, it gives a total of 895,900,000 of new and old copper which was available for domestic consumption. While no systematic attempt was made in 1911 to ascertain the proportion of the copper output used in the industries, some idea may be gained from the form in which the output of the refineries was cast. The following table shows the appróximate quantity of copper cast and the different forms during 1911:

Forms in which cast	Total	Percentage.
Wire bars	731,029,349	50
Ingots and ingot bars	409,786,682	29
Cakes	143,716,125	10
Cathodes	135,499,770	9
Other forms	25,774,328	2
Total	1,445,806,254	100

Exports and Imports. The imports of copper in unmanufactured form into the United States in 1911 were 334,604,538 pounds. The largest quantity was brought from Mexico. Other large exporters to the United States were Peru, Canada, Spain, and Great Britain. The exports of metallic copper from the United States in 1911 amounted to 786,553,208 pounds. Of this the largest amount was taken by the Netherlands, 230,693,649. Germany followed with 190,428,008 pounds; France, 135,038,893 pounds; and Great Britain, 108,061,603 pounds.

World Production. The world production of copper in 1911 was 1,958,201,285 pounds, compared with 1,903,297,003 in 1910. In 1911 the smelter output of the United States was 56 per cent. of the world's production, as compared with 56.75 per cent. in 1910. The following table, compiled by Henry R. Merton & Co., Ltd., showed the world's production by countries in 1910-11, with the figures reduced to pounds. The official figures for the production of the United States and Canada are inserted.

The production of copper in the United States in 1912 was 1,242,836,024 pounds, a slight increase over tne production of 1911. The production in the copper-producing States in 1912 will be found in the following table, taken from the *Engineering and Mining Journal*. There was a remarkable increase in production in Alaska, also suostantial increases in Arizona, Michigan, and Montana. Utah had a decreased production, as did California:

State	In Pounds	State	In Pounds
Alaska	33,600,000	Nevada	81,816,000
Arizona	357,773,703	New Mexico.	26,174,000
California	29,867,430	Utah	136,372,157
Colorado	6,800,000	Washington.	1,233,009
Idaho	5,038,000	East and South	18,915,616
Michigan	231,629,486	Other States	4,492,623
Montana	309,125,000		
		Totals	1,242,836,024

(Copper extracted from ore or contained in the ore produced.)

Countries	1910	1911
Germany	55,335,460	49,162,580
England	1,102,300	1,102,300
Italy	7,275,180	5,731,960
Norway	23,368,760	20,943,700
Austria	4,850,120	5,511,500
Russia	50,044,420	57,319,600
Sweden	4,409,200	4,409,200
Spain and Portugal	112,655,060	116,843,800
Turkey	1,322,760	2,204,600
Hungary	220,460	220,460
Servia	10,802,540	19,400,480
Total Europe	271,386,260	282,850,180
Canada	56,598,074	55,848,665
Mexico	131,614,620	125,300,820
Newfoundland	2,425,060	2,645,520
United States	1,080,159,509	1,097,232,700
Total North America	1,270,797,263	1,280,727,705
Argentina	661,380	2,204,600
Bolivia	5,511,500	3,968,280
Chile	78,924,680	66,358,460
Peru	41,005,560	57,099,140
Cuba	7,716,100	9,920,700
Total Central and South America	133,819,220	139,551,180
Cape Colony	9,920,700	15,652,660
Namaqualand	5,511,500	....
Other Africa	18,518,640	22,486,920
Total Africa	33,950,840	38,139,580
Japan	102,954,820	123,237,140
Australia	90,388,600	93,695,500
Grand total	1,903,297,003	1,958,201,285

The world production of copper in 1912 was 1,004,844 metric tons, according to the figures compiled by the *Engineering and Mining Journal*. In this compilation the figures are based upon crude copper, that is, the smelters' production. The production in the copper-producing countries in 1912 is given in the following table:

Country	Met. Tons	Country	Met. Tons
United States	563,747	Japan	54,000
Mexico	71,982	Russia	35,900
Canada	33,577	Germany	23,000
Cuba	4,000	Africa	20,000
Australasia	46,100	Spain and Portugal	58,000
Peru	27,600	Other countries	31,000
Chile	35,938	Totals	1,004,844

COPYRIGHT. A copyright convention between the United States and Hungary was signed at Budapest, on January 30, 1912; ratifications were exchanged on September 16, and the convention went into effect on October 16. It provided that authors who are citizens or subjects of one of the two countries, or their assigns shall enjoy in the other country the same rights for liberty, artistic, dramatic, musical, and photographic works as are enjoyed by the natives. On July 1, the British copyright law, which was described in the preceding YEAR BOOK, went into effect. During the fiscal year ending June 30, 1912, the registrations in the United States numbered 120,931, of which 29,286 were for books, 22,580 for periodicals, 26,777 for musical compositions, 17,639 for pictorial illustrations, and 13,498 for photographs.

CORA INDIANS. See ANTHROPOLOGY.

CORBETT, JAMES FRANCIS. Roman Catholic bishop of Sale, Victoria, died May, 1912. He was born in Limerick, Ireland, in 1840, and was educated in France. For several years after his admission to the priesthood he devoted himself to missionary duties in Limerick and was for many years secretary to the Roman Catholic archbishop of Melbourne. He was consecrated first bishop of Sale at St. Kilda in 1887.

CORDIALS. See LIQUORS.

CORN. The corn corp of the world in 1912 was estimated at 4,371,055,000 bushels, as compared with 3,461,093,000 bushels in 1911 and with 3,757,591,000 bushels, the average production for the five years 1906-1910. Of the 24 countries reporting yields, 15 are corn-surplus countries, the leading ones given in the order of their importance being the United States, Argentina, Hungary, British India, Rumania, and Russia, which produce about 95 per cent. of the world's annual crop. The corn importing countries which also produce this cereal are France, Austria, Italy, Switzerland, Spain, and Portugal, and while in some of these countries the production is small the annual yield of Italy ranks with that of Hungary. The large crop of the United States in 1912 and the satisfactory yields in other leading corn-producing countries brought the world's production for the year well above the average. In many sections of southeastern Europe the crop suffered from adverse climatic conditions which depressed both yield and quality. In the entire corn-growing region of Europe, except in Italy and Turkey, where drought proved injurious, the corn crop was retarded by cool, cloudy weather and by continued heavy rains, which in addition to reducing the yield prevented to a large extent the proper ripening of the late varieties and an adequate drying of the ears so that they might be stored with safety against heating and moulding. In some sections the entire plant was used from the fields as forage in order to save as much of the crop as conditions would permit. In Italy, where drought injured all cereals, corn was the best crop of the year, but the yield was below the average annual production of the country. The Turkish crop was also reduced by drought, but the total yield was nearly normal. The yields of Rumania, Bulgaria, and Austria were below the yields secured in 1911.

In the United States a late spring delayed planting and poor seed corn in some parts resulted in an unsatisfactory stand, but in general during the summer conditions were so favorable that the crop made an excellent growth. Suitable weather in September hastened maturity, and when towards the close of the month killing frosts occurred over a large portion of the corn belt the injury done was much less than had been expected. Although the early frosts gave rise to a considerable quantity of soft corn of poor storing quality, the production of sound and marketable grain was far greater than in any previous year. The total production was placed by the Department of Agriculture at 3,124,746,000 bushels, and the area devoted to the crop at 107,083,000 acres, as compared with 2,531,488,000 bushels grown on 105,825,000 acres in 1911. This was by far the largest crop ever produced and the first time the three-billion bushel mark was passed. The yield represented about three-fourths of the entire world's production. The bountiful harvest evidently had the effect of lowering the market price, for the farm value per bushel on December 1, 1912, was only 48.7 cents, as compared with 61.8 cents on December 1, 1911. On this basis the total value of the immense crop was $1,520,454,000, which was surpassed by the corn crop values of 1908 and 1911. The acreage of corn in 1912 was also the highest on record. The average yield per acre was reported as 29.2 bushels, as against 23.9 bushels the preceding year, and the highest since 1906. The best yields by States were the following: Iowa, 432,021,000 bushels; Illinois, 426,320,000 bushels; Missouri, 243,904,000 bushels; Indiana, 199,364,000 bushels; Nebraska, 182,616,000 bushels; Ohio, 174,410,000 bushels; Kansas, 174,225,000 bushels; Texas, 153,300,000 bushels; Kentucky, 109,440,000 bushels, and Oklahoma, 101,878,000 bushels. Illinois had an acreage of 10,658,000 and Iowa of 10,047,000 acres, while Missouri, ranking next, had only 7,622,000 acres. The production of Iowa was the largest ever produced by that State or by any State. The average acre-yield ranged from 13 bushels in Florida to 50 in Connecticut. Among the leading States Iowa stood first, with an average yield of 43 bushels per acre, and Ohio second, with 42.8 bushels.

While the United States produces about three-fourths of the world's crop, it furnishes only about one-third of the quantity entering into international trade. The exports for the year ending June 30, 1912, amounted to 40,038,795 bushels, and for the preceding year to 63,761,458 bushels. On March 1, 1912, about 884,069,000 bushels, or 39.4 per cent. of the previous year's crop, remained in farmers' hands, as compared with 1,165,378,000 bushels, or 40.4 per cent. of the crop of 1910, held on farms March 1, 1911. The supply of old corn on the farms at the time the 1912 crop was harvested was estimated at about 70,000,000 bushels, a smaller quantity than is usually carried over. The surplus for distribution from the supply of 1912 was estimated at 240,000,000 bushels.

CORNELL UNIVERSITY. The total registration in all departments of the university in 1912 was 4468, divided as follows: College of Arts and Sciences, 1032; New York State Veterinary College, 118; New York State Agricultural College, 1181; College of Law, 295; College of Mechanical Engineering, 917; College of Civil Engineering, 513; College of Architecture, 133; Department of the Graduate School, 279. The faculty numbers 696, which includes emeritus professors, professors, associate professors, lecturers, instructors, and assistant instructors. President Schurman was given leave of absence on his appointment as minister to Greece (see UNITED STATES, *Diplomatic Service*). The following professors died during the year: George William Jones, William Albert Finch, John Craig, and Ralph Stockman Tarr. Prof. H. S. Williams retired as emeritus professor. The following professors resigned: J. W. Jenks, to accept the position of financial adviser to China; Prof. E. W. Kemmerer, and Prof. B. M. Duggar. Prof. A. S. Johnson was called to the head of the department of economics from Stanford University; Prof. W. E. Lunt was appointed to the new professorship of modern European history; Prof. E. G. Montgomery was called to the chair of farm crops, and E. N. Spring to the second chair in forestry. Among the donations received during the year 1911-12 was an endowment fund for the promotion of studies in German culture made by Mr. Jacob H. Schiff. Out of this fund was established the Jacob H. Schiff Fellowship in German and the Jacob H. Schiff Lectureship (non-resident) for the promotion of studies in German culture. Mrs. Florence Rand Lang during the year completed her gift of $60,000 to the university. Col. Oliver H. Payne gave $180,000 for the Medical College in New York City. The Fraser scholarships in law were made possible by a gift of $3000 by Mr. William Metcalf, Jr. The number of volumes in the library was 409,700, with 62,000 additional pamphlets. The productive funds of the university amounted to $9,525,000 and the income to about $1,385,000. Acting-president in 1912-13, Prof. Thomas Frederick Crane.

CORPORATION PENSIONS. See WELFARE WORK.

CORPORATIONS. See TRUSTS, and TAXATION.

CORPORATION TAX. See TAXATION.

CORROSION OF METALS. See CHEMISTRY, INDUSTRIAL.

CORTELYOU, GEORGE W. See PRESIDENTIAL CAMPAIGN CONTRIBUTIONS.

COSTA RICA. A Central American republic between Nicaragua and Panama. Capital, San José.

AREA, POPULATION, ETC. Estimated area, 18,691 square miles (48,410 square kms.). The population December 31, 1911, is reported at 388,266; by provinces: San José, 121,162; Alajuela, 91,707; Cartago, 59,968; Heredia, 42,659; Guanacaste, 33,810; Puntarenas, 20,040; Limón, 18,920. The enumeration, however, is incomplete, as it does not include the districts of Pacuarito, Río Hondo, Cimarrones, Madre de Dios Florida, La Germania, Pocora Este, El Cario, and El Peje, or the towns of Florencia, Aguas Zarzas, Tres Amigos, and Kopper de San Carlos. The city of San José has 31,668 inhabitants. In 1910 immigrants numbered 11,233; emigrants, 7236; births, 15,847; deaths, 9723. In 1911, births and deaths, 16,839 and 9483. Pupils in primary and secondary schools, about 32,000; teachers, over 1000.

PRODUCTION AND COMMERCE. The people are engaged chiefly in agriculture, which is carried on successfully. Besides the principal crops, bananas and coffee, the products include corn, sugar, beans, rice, and cacao.

Imports and exports in 1910: 16,984,378 and 18,009,385 colones respectively; in 1911, 19,079,917 and 19,191,808. The leading imports are cotton fabrics, rice, flour, and iron and steel goods. Chief exports in 1910 and 1911: Bananas, 9,097,285 and 9,309,586; coffee, 5,916,181 and 6,109,542; gold and silver in bars, 1,744,487 and 2,517,372; woods, 169,079 and 193,732; hides and skins, 269,719 and 188,542; rubber, 219,957 and 180,784; cacao, 88,556 and 185,806. By far the greater part of both imports and exports passes through the port of Limón. The United States supplies nearly one-half of the imports and receives over one-half of the exports, Great Britain and Germany ranking second and third.

COMMUNICATIONS. The Atlantic port Limón is connected by rail with the Pacific port Puntarenas, by way of San José. Length of railways, 604 kms. (431 miles). Telegraphs: 128 offices, 2437 kms. of wire. Post offices, 190.

FINANCE. The standard of value is gold; the monetary unit, the colon, par value 46.536 cents. Revenue and expenditure for fiscal years, in colones:

	1909-10	1910-11	1911-12
Revenue	9,280,584	11,471,967	9,707,269
Expenditure	9,280,584	8,858,572	9,801,956

Of the 1911-12 revenue, 5,829,653 colones were derived from customs and 2,322,446 from liquors. The larger departmental expenditures: Finance, 3,800,644 colones; public works, 1,705,816; war, 1,240,542; public instruction, 1,081,331; government, 754,542. Debt, December 31, 1910: Foreign, £1,617,200; internal, 27,974,408 colones. A new foreign loan (French) of 35,000,000 francs, announced in October, 1911, was issued in 1912, proceeds to apply on internal debt.

GOVERNMENT. The president, elected for four years, is assisted by a cabinet of five members. The congress consists of a single chamber of 43 representatives. Both president and representatives are elected by indirect vote. The president in 1912 was Ricardo Jiménez, who was inaugurated May 8, 1910, succeeding Cleto González Víquez.

COST OF FOOD. See FOOD AND NUTRITION.

COST OF LIVING. See PRICES.

COTTON. The Bureau of Statistics of the United States Department of Agriculture on December 17, 1912, estimated the cotton crop of the United States for 1912 at 13,820,000 bales of 500 pounds each. The crop, together with the seed, it is believed, will be worth $860,000,000. The International Institute of Agriculture about the same date estimated the cotton production of the United States, India, Egypt, and Japan at over 1o,000,000 bales, an amount about 4 per cent. less than last year's crop. According to the United States Bureau of the Census, on December 13, 1912, there had been ginned of the American crop 12,424,853 running bales, excluding linters. On the same date in 1911, 88.5 per cent. of the total crop had been ginned. These statistics include Sea Island cotton as follows: Florida, 19,505 bales; Georgia, 34,537 bales, and South Carolina, 4702 bales.

The estimated crop and the amount ginned on December 13, 1912, by States, were as follows:

State	Est'd crop (500-lb bales)	Reported ginned (running bales)
United States	13,820,000	12,424,853
Alabama	1,330,000	1,223,336
Arkansas	854,000	700,874
Florida	68,000	52,882
Georgia	1,701,000	1,666,899
Louisiana	435,000	364,112
Mississippi	1,109,000	884,992
North Carolina	878,000	820,249
Oklahoma	1,039,000	904,347
South Carolina	1,184,000	1,127,480
Tennessee	280,000	231,341
Texas	4,850,000	4,370,540
All other States	92,000	77,800

Of the States listed as "all others," Virginia is estimated to have produced 24,000 bales, Missouri 59,000, and California 9000 bales. Cotton is grown in other States, but in such small quantities as not to be included in the estimates.

The final report of the Bureau of the Census on the crop of 1911 showed there were produced 16,205,097 bales of 500 pounds each. This total included 546,769 bales of linters and 119,252 bales of Sea Island cotton. The production by States was:

States	500-lb bales	States	500-lb bales
Unit'd States	16,205,097	North Carolina	1,101,104
Alabama	1,753,484	Oklahoma	1,060,133
Arkansas	971,311	South Carolina	1,677,204
Florida	84,977	Tennessee	478,249
Georgia	2,838,571	Texas	4,437,876
Louisiana	399,525	All others	154,137
Mississippi	1,248,521		

The world's production of cotton for mill consumption for 1911 showed a decided increase over that of 1910, a gain of about 3,500,000 bales being recorded. The contributions of the different countries to the supply of 1911 and 1910, according to the United States Census, were as follows:

Country	1911 500-lb bales	1910 500-lb bales
Total	22,297,000	18,711,000
United States	15,546,000	11,483,000
British India	2,514,000	3,082,000
Egypt	1,450,000	1,506,000
Russia	1,200,000	900,000
China	625,000	775,000
Brazil	320,000	310,000
Peru	128,000	128,000
Mexico	124,000	105,000
Turkey	100,000	135,000
Persia	80,000	90,000
Other countries	210,000	195,000

The world's consumption for the year ended August 31, 1912, was 20,402,000 bales of 500 pounds net weight. The number of active consuming spindles is estimated at 140,996,000. The United States contributed 69.7 per cent. of the world's cotton supply in its crop of 1911. The exports of cotton for the year ended June 30, 1912, were 10,675,445 bales, valued at $565,849,271, and the imports for the same period were 109,780,071 pounds (equal to 219,560 bales of 500 pounds each), valued at $20,217,581. As usual, a large proportion of the imported cotton came from Egypt and was purchased for special purposes.

Data regarding the 1912 crop in other lands are very meager and conflicting, most of the available estimates baving been made before the crop was ginned. Aside from the estimate of the Institute of Agriculture at Rome of a crop of 18,000,000 bales for the United States, India, Egypt, and Japan, reports from Egypt indicate a crop of 1,550,000 bales and India 2,113,600 bales of 500 pounds each. From German East Africa 5000 bales are expected to be marketed, and from Togoland 2500 bales. In the province of Adana, Asiatic Turkey, a crop of 100,000 bales is estimated. In the Italian province of Eritrea 3500 bales were produced. A recent review of the cotton industry of Lancashire showed that while the demand for raw cotton increased 70 per cent. on the continent of Europe from 1892 to 1910, and there was an increased consumption of 90 per cent. in the United States, the demand in Great Britain fell off more than 4 per cent. To meet this situation the British Cotton-Growing Association, with a capital of $2,000,000, is attempting to foster cotton culture in Africa, the West Indies, and other British dependencies. In 1908 the association marketed 16,713 bales, and in 1911

27,673 bales, indicating a gradual increase. In September, 1912, Lagos and Northern Nigeria had marketed 8853 and 2301 bales, respectively, as compared with 5274 and 500 in 1911. In Uganda the production has increased from about 200 bales in 1907 to over 2000 bales in 1911. The situation in Nyasaland and Southern Nigeria is not promising, transportation problems being very perplexing. From the British West Indies in 1911 there were exported 6197 bales of cotton, valued at $989,375. In the French colonies the production has shown a slight increase, the crop of 1910 being reported as 1566 bales and that of 1911 as 2048 bales. An attempt of the French Cotton Association to grow cotton in Madagascar during the past year failed by reason of drought and insect depredations. The Russian government is attempting to become independent for her cotton supplies, and an appropriation of $100,000 was made in 1912 for the development and improvement of cotton cultivation in Transcaucasia and Central Asia. The government has also undertaken the extension of irrigation projects and is arranging special credit organizations for the benefit of cotton growers. In the consular district of Batum over 75,000 acres were planted to cotton in 1911. Under the auspices of the Portuguese government the first cotton in Portuguese East Africa was grown in 1911; 200 bales of American long staple upland cotton, valued at from 11 to 16 cents a pound, were produced from 120 acres. Japan is trying to develop cotton culture in Korea, but the crop of 1911 was reported as only 900 tons, as compared with 2200 tons in 1910. An attempt to grow Egyptian cotton in Siam was a failure. Statistics regarding the production of cotton in China are difficult to obtain, but it is believed that China produces four-fifths of the cotton required by its people. An attempt has been begun to grow cotton in Argentina, but the scarcity of labor will prove a serious obstacle to its extension. The Egyptian government has established markets for the purchase of cotton throughout the country, where the producer can be assured correct grading and weighing. Cotton-testing laboratories were established at Havre, France, and Shanghai, China, to determine the moisture in cotton offered for sale. Similar laboratories have been in operation in other localities of Europe and America for some time. An experimental cotton warehouse built of reinforced concrete was erected in Manchester, England, during 1912. It is believed this type of warehouse will greatly reduce storage charges.

WORK OF THE U. S. DEPARTMENT OF AGRICULTURE. The preparation and distribution of the official cotton grades has been continued and these types are now distributed in twenty-five States and also in England, Germany, France, Italy, India, Brazil, and Mexico, 131 sets being sold during the past year. Improved facilities have made it possible to reduce the price of these sets to $25. Investigations are in progress on improved methods of ginning and handling cotton, the moisture in baled cotton, and the effect of diseases, especially the root rot, on the quality of fibre. The farmers' coöperative demonstration work in the boll-weevil infested region has been continued, 13,641 demonstrators reporting upon 109,999 acres of cotton. On these farms the yield of cotton was more than 75 per cent. greater than for the entire States. Nearly 5000 boys were enrolled in cotton clubs organized during the year, each boy being expected to grow at least two acres. The experiments in acclimatizing and breeding Egyptian cotton at Yuma, Ariz., have proved so successful that coöperative plantings in other similar regions were begun, and about 800 acres were planted to this crop in Arizona and California. The department has verified in California the discovery of the Hawaii Experiment Station in 1909, that cotton can be readily grown from cuttings, thus making it possible to perpetuate desirable strains without the possibility of deterioration through planting of seed. Considerable assistance was rendered by the department in arranging uniform regulations for the various State quarantines against the spread of the Mexican cotton boll-weevil and in testing cultural and other means for its control. This serious pest occupied about 1400 square miles in the United States in 1892 and 271,000 square miles in 1912, its average annual advance for the last six years having been over about 27,000 square miles. During 1912 the bollworm continued its eastward advance in Alabama and Florida, and 5 counties in western Florida and 25 in Alabama, or about one-third of the latter State, are now infested. The U. S. Bureau of Entomology reports 49 species of insect enemies of the boll-weevil, and it is claimed that 40 per cent. of the natural means of control is due to other insects. A weevil enemy of Caravonica cotton is reported in German East Africa, the habits and injury caused being very similar to those of the Mexican boll-weevil.

COTTON TARIFF. See TARIFF.

COULLIÉ, PETER HECTOR. A Roman Catholic cardinal, archbishop of Lyons, died September 11, 1912. He was born in Paris in 1839 and served as archbishop of Lyons for several years previous to his elevation to the cardinalate by Pope Leo XIII. in 1897.

COUNTERMINE, JOHN DONKAN. An American clergyman and writer, died December, 1912. He was born in Schenectady, N. Y., in 1850, and graduated from Union College in 1873. He studied at the Princeton Theological Seminary, graduating in 1876, and took a special course in philosophy, science, and literature at Omaha University. He was ordained to the Presbyterian ministry in 1876, and held several pastorates in New York City and Albany and in Kansas. He was pastor of the First Church of Topeka, Kansas, from 1897 to 1904. In the latter year he resigned to enter evangelistic work and continued this until 1910, when he was appointed professor of Old Testament History and Criticism and New Testament Exegesis and Comparative Religions in the Philadelphia training school for Christian workers. He was at the same time pastor of the Fourth Reformed Protestant Church in Philadelphia. He was the author of *The Religious Belief of Shakespeare* (1906); and *Daybreak Everywhere* (1907). He also contributed to the religious and secular press.

COUNTRY LIFE MOVEMENT. See AGRICULTURE.

COUNTY HIGHWAY IMPROVEMENTS IN CALIFORNIA AND NEW JERSEY. See ROADS AND PAVEMENTS.

COURT TENNIS. See TENNIS.

COX, Charles Finney. An American scientist and railway official, died January, 1912. He was born in Richmond county, N. Y., in 1846 and graduated from Oberlin College in 1869. He engaged in railroad work and became treasurer of several important railroads. He was a Fellow of the New York Academy of Sciences, and acted as its president in 1908-9. He was also president of the New York Microscopical Society in 1888, and was one of the founders and chief promoters of the New York Botanical Gardens. As a result of his important contributions to microscopical botany and zoölogy he was elected a Fellow of the Royal Microscopical Society of London. His most important published work is *Protoplasm and Life*.

CRAIG, John. An American horticulturist, died August 11, 1912. He was born in Lakeville, Quebec, Canada, in 1864. In 1885 he was horticulturist at the Iowa State College and in 1888 was appointed assistant horticulturist at the Iowa Experiment Station. From 1890 to 1897 he was horticulturist of the Dominion Experiment Station at Ottowa, Canada. He returned to the Iowa State College in 1898 and in the following year was appointed professor of horticulture and forestry in that institution. In 1893 he was appointed professor of horticulture at Cornell University. From 1904 to the time of his death he was editor of *The National Nurseryman*. He was the author of *Practical Agriculture* (1901), and contributed to the *Cyclopædia of American Horticulture*.

CRANE, Richard Teller. An American manufacturer, died January 8, 1912. He was born in 1832 and spent his early life chiefly in manual labor. He learned and worked at the machinist's trade in Paterson, Brooklyn, and New York until 1855, when he removed to Chicago, where he soon started in business in a brass foundry. He was later joined by his brother, Charles S. Crane, in the firm of R. T. Crane and Brother. This developed into one of the largest manufacturing industries in its line in the United States. Crane attracted wide attention by his writings in opposition to college education for men.

CREDIT BANKS. See Agricultural Credit.

CRÉDIT FONCIER. See Agricultural Credit.

CRETE. An island in the Mediterranean Sea; an autonomous state under the suzerainty of Turkey. Area, 3327 square miles; population (census of April 17, 1911): 307,812 Christians, 27,852 Mohammedans, 487 Jews, 7850 Europeans—total, 344,001. Canea, the capital, has 24,399 inhabitants; Candia, 25,185; Retbymo, 9086. Greek is the language of the people. The chief products for export are wheat and fruit, wool, soap, olive oil, carobs, vallonea, and cheese. The trade (mostly with Greece and Turkey) amounted in 1910 to 19,650,000 drachmas imports and 17,477,000 exports. Tonnage entered, 1,811,865. Revenue (1909-10), 6,024,729; expenditure, 8,567,251. Debt, 5,317,226 drachmas. No successor was appointed to the retiring high-commissioner, M. Zaimis, in 1911, and the ultimate disposition of the island was indefinitely postponed; but in October, 1912, following upon her declaration of war with Turkey, Greece sent a representative to govern the island in the name of the king of Greece. See below.

History. Disturbed conditions in Crete continued during the early part of 1912. In February riots occurred leading to the murder of a number of Moslems. The consuls of the protecting powers protested in a note to the Cretan government against the attitude of the insurgent parties and declared that if certain measures that were apparently contemplated were taken, for example, the sending of deputies to Athens or the dismissal of Mohammedan employees, and if the persecution of the Mohammedans continued, the powers would take the necessary steps to prevent such acts. The powers insisted on the maintenance of the *status quo*, but would certainly take measures unfavorable to Cretan aspirations if the Cretes were unable to govern themselves peacefully. Additional warships were sent into Cretan waters. The extremists gained the upper hand in the Cretan Assembly, which voted to send the deputies to Athens. The Assembly then voted to abolish the present government. A "constituent" Assembly was formed to carry on the administration. This amounted to the replacing of the executive government by a revolutionary authority. The president of the Assembly was vested with the entire civil and military power. The government offices were seized by the military. The crisis came to an end on March 15 with the election of a permanent commission by the Assembly. The commission was to comprise eighty-one members, of whom five selected from the different parties were to form an executive body.

Nineteen of the deputies elected to represent Crete in the Greek Chamber were intercepted by a British cruiser on April 28 and detained at Suda Bay till the beginning of June when the Greek Chamber was prorogued. But about forty other deputies succeeded in reaching Athens with the avowed intention of taking seats at the new session of the Chamber. M. Venezelos, the Greek premier, refused to admit them, saying that he had promised the powers to exclude the deputies, and thereby had averted the reoccupation of the island on which the powers had determined if the deputies were admitted. The approaches to the Chamber were guarded and the Cretan deputies were detained till after the session had closed. A filibustering expedition of the Cretans against Samos was disapproved of by the Greek government and came to nothing. On the approach of the war with Turkey, however, Greece changed her attitude and in her ultimatum to the Ottoman government included a demand for the admission of the delegates. One of her first acts after the outbreak of the war was to admit the Cretan delegates to the Assembly (October 14). M. Stephen Dragoumis, premier of Greece in 1910, was appointed governor-general of Crete. See Turkey and the Balkan Peoples. For archæological discoveries in Crete in 1912, see Archæology.

CRICKET. The Philadelphia Cricket Club visited England in August and made an excellent showing, winning five matches, losing three, and drawing one. The Philadelphians scored victories over Reigate Priory, Royal Artillery, Stoke Poges, The Mote, and Blackheath. They lost to Mr. J. R. Tilden's XI., Folkestone, and Sutton. Another tour which attracted considerable interest in cricket circles was that taken by the Australians in the United States, Canada, and Bermuda. Seven matches were played, of which the Australians won five, drew one, and lost one. The only team to defeat the inraders was the Gentlemen of Philadelphia. The Australians won victories over New York XV., Gentlemen of Philadelphia (second match), All-Bermuda, Winnipeg XV., and British Columbia XV. The Rosedale Club of Toronto, in a trip to Philadelphia, lost to Germantown, Morristown-Frankford, and Gentlemen of Philadelphia, but defeated the Philadelphia Club and drew with Merion. The Germantown Club visited Canada, where it scored victories over Toronto, Ottawa, and Rosedale, and was defeated by Montreal. In the forty-second annual match between the United States and Canada the United States won. England was the victor in the triangular contest with Australia and South Africa. Cambridge turned the tables on Oxford in their annual match, while Eton again defeated Harrow.

The Richmond County Club won the championship of the New York and New Jersey Cricket Association with seven victories, three draws, and no defeats. The Metropolitan District League laurels went to the Brooklyn Club in Class A and to Bensonhurst in Class B. A new record for the United States and Canada was established in 1912 by F. J. Higgins of Los Angeles, who scored seven centuries.

CRIME. See PENOLOGY.

CRIMINOLOGY. See PENOLOGY.

CRITICISM. See FRENCH LITERATURE, GERMAN LITERATURE, and LITERATURE, ENGLISH AND AMERICAN.

CROATIA AND SLAVONIA. See AUSTRIA-HUNGARY, *Area and Population*.

CROP PRODUCTION. See AGRICULTURE.

CROSS-COUNTRY RUNNING AND MARATHONS. The Senior Metropolitan Cross-Country Championship run, the principal event of the kind in the United States, was held at New York City. William J. Kramer of the Long Island A. C. for the fourth successive year was the individual winner, his time for the six miles being 34 minutes 37⅗ seconds. T. Johannson of the Irish-American A. C. finished second and F. Bellars of the New York A. C. third. The team scores were: Irish-American A. C., 42; New York A. C., 64; Long Island A. C., 73. T. F. Barden, unattached, won the National A. A. U. cross-country championship, his time being 35 minutes 27 seconds. M. D. Huysman of the Irish-American A. C. finished second and M. Hughes of the New York A. C. third. The winning club was the Morningside A. C.

Harvard broke Cornell's long string of victories by winning the intercollegiate cross-country run held at Ithaca, N. Y., November 23. John Paul Jones of Cornell, however, captured the individual honors for the third successive year. His time was 32 minutes 29½ seconds. Taber of Brown finished second, and Copeland of Harvard third. The score and order at the finish of the colleges entered were: Harvard, 32; Cornell, 48; Dartmouth, 87; Brown, 117; Pennsylvania, 154; Massachusetts Institute of Technology, 156; Syracuse, 174; Princeton, 199; Yale, 209; College of the City of New York, 312. In dual cross-country runs Harvard defeated Yale and Cornell, Princeton defeated Columbia, Cornell defeated Pennsylvania, Yale defeated Princeton, and Pennsylvania defeated Carlisle.

The results of the principal amateur Marathons held in 1912 follow: Boston A. A., 25 miles, won by M. Ryan of the Irish-American A. C. of New York, in 2 hours 21 minutes 18⅕ seconds, a new record for the course; Missouri A. C., 25 miles, won by Joseph Erxleben of the Missouri A. C., in 2 hours 36 minutes 30 seconds; modified Marathon, New York, 12½ miles, won by Louis Scott of the South Paterson A. C., in 1 hour 8 minutes 28⅗ seconds; London Marathon, 26 miles, won by J. Corkery of the Irish-Canadian A. C., in 2 hours 26 minutes 55⅕ seconds. The National A. A. U. 10-mile championship was won by Harry Smith, unattached, his time being 53 minutes 51⅗ seconds.

The American Professional Championship Marathon, held at Newark, N. J., was won by W. Kolehmainen, whose time, 2 hours 29 minutes 35⅕ seconds, established a new world's record. Kolehmainen also won the Powderhall Marathon at Edinburgh and the 12-mile indoor race at New York City. The Paris Marathon was won by Hans Holmer, who finished second to Kolehmainen in the American professional event. See ATHLETICS, TRACK AND FIELD, and OLYMPIC GAMES.

CROTHERS, AUSTIN LANE. An American public official, former g e n of Maryland, died May 25, 1912. He was born in Cecil county, Md., in 1860, and was educated at the University of Maryland and after studying law was admitted to the bar. From 1891 to 1895 he was State's attorney for Cecil county and from 1897 to 1901 was a member of the State Senate. He was defeated for reëlection to the Senate in 1902 and 1906. In 1908 he was appointed judge of the circuit court, but being elected governor of the State in that same year, he resigned the former office. He served from 1908 to 1912.

CROW INDIANS. See ANTHROPOLOGY.

CROWN POINT MEMORIAL LIGHTHOUSE. See LIGHTHOUSES.

CRUDE OIL. See PETROLEUM.

CRUISERS. See BATTLESHIPS.

CRUSTACEA. See ZOÖLOGY.

CRYSTALLINE SCHISTS. See GEOLOGY.

CUBA. A West Indian island republic. The capital is Havana.

AREA, POPULATION, ETC. The area is 44,164 square miles comprised in six provinces—Havana, Pinar del Río, Matanzas, Santa Clara, Camagüey, and Oriente. Estimated population June 30, 1911, 2,223,284, of whom 1,961,-896 natives and 261,388 foreigners; 1912, 2,271,762. The census of September 30, 1907, disclosed a population of 2,048,980, as compared with 1,572,797 in 1899. Of the total inhabitants in 1907, 69.75 per cent. were white, 16.40 mulatto, 13.28 black, and 0.57 yellow. Immigration in 1910, 32,606, of whom 28,380 Spanish; in 1911, 38,053, of whom 32,104 Spanish, 1360 North American, and 932 British. The larger cities are Havana (estimated population, 320,000), Santiago de Cuba, Cienfuegos, Matanzas, Puerto Príncipe, and Cárdenas.

Enrollment in the public schools in February, 1911, 152,658 (attendance, 105,774); in private schools, 24,434.

PRODUCTION. Sugar-cane and tobacco are the staple crops. Large quantities of fruits and vegetables are raised. The output of raw sugar for the year 1911-12 was estimated at over 1,850,000 tons; the output in 1910-11 was 1,460,391 tons, in 1909-10 1,804,349, in 1899-1900 283,051. From sugar-cane are also produced large quantities of molasses and spirits. The cultivation of tobacco is most important in Pinar del Río and makes possible the important industry of cigar and cigarette manufacture. Reported tobacco yield in 1909, 494,358 bales (of about 120 pounds); in 1910, 639,598. Cattle-raising is carried on extensively in some parts of the country, especially in Camagüey. Livestock June 30, 1910: Cattle, 3,098,179; horses, 572,901; mules, 59,994; asses, 2414. There are large mineral resources, especially in Oriente, including iron, copper, manganese, lead, zinc, gold, and salt. The mineral output in 1910 was valued at $4,374,719.

COMMERCE. The values of the imports and exports of merchandise are reported as follows: 1908, 86,368,767 and 98,840,091; 1909, 83,856,835 and 115,637,321; 1910, 98,239,539 and 144,036,697. Imports and exports of precious metals: 1908, 1,150,376 and 4,245,769; 1909, 2,934,536 and 1,926,546; 1910, 5,206,588 and 2786. The leading imports are breadstuffs, meats, cotton goods, machinery, iron and steel, and vegetables. Principal exports in 1910: Sugar, $108,782,000; tobacco, $27,874,000; iron ore, $3,925,000; fruits, $2,098,000. Reported trade by countries in 1911: United States imports $60,015,000, exports $106,853; other America, $9,159,000 and $3,642,000; United Kingdom, $13,309,000 and $5,697,000; Spain, $9,205,000 and $460,000; France, $6,203,000 and $1,307,000; Germany, $7,235,000 and $3,642,000; other Europe, $5,352,000 and $809,000; other, $2,399,000 and $726,000; total, $113,267,000 and $123,136,000.

Entered at the ports in the foreign trade, 1911: 1573 vessels, of which 1462 steam; coastwise, 1623 vessels, 1448 steam. Merchant marine, 1911: 41 steamers, of 32,315 tons, and 121 sail, of 11,964 tons.

COMMUNICATIONS. Railways in operation at the beginning of 1911 aggregated 3433 kilometers (2133 miles); telegraphs, 8151 kms. (5848 miles) of line, with 9952 rms. (6184 miles) of wire and 171 offices; wireless telegraph stations, 10; post offices, 487.

FINANCE. In 1910, revenue and expenditure amounted to $41,614,694 and $40,593,392. The balance in the treasury was $1,960,331. Customs in 1910 yielded $24,838,030. For the fiscal year 1912-13, the revenue was estimated at $37,940,000 and the expenditure $33,974,147. Branches of estimated revenue: Customs, $26,434,000; excise, $3,900,000; lottery, $3,700,000; direct taxes, $1,113,000; posts and telegraphs, $1,076,000; consular dues, $500,000; other, $1,217,000; total, $37,940,000. Estimated expenditures: Administration, $10,117,394; public instruction, $4,782,653; sanitary service, $3,784,987; public debt, $3,710,500; public works, $3,704,625; finance, $3,329,504; justice, $2,038,220; executive, $1,000,540; foreign affairs, $717,224; agriculture, industry, and commerce, $488,400; total, $33,974,147.

GOVERNMENT. The president is elected by indirect vote for four years and is assisted by a cabinet of eight members. The legislature is bicameral, consisting of the Senate (twenty-four members, four for each province) and the House of Representatives (eighty-three). The president in 1912 was Gen. José Miguel Gómez, inaugurated January 28, 1909; vice-president, Alfredo Zayas. On November 1, 1912, Gen. Mario G. Menocal and Enrique José Varona, the Conservative candidates, were elected president and vice-president respectively. Each of the provinces is administered by an elective governor.

HISTORY. Internal troubles became manifest in Cuba early in the year, and led to warnings by the United States that intervention might follow if the disorders assumed a revolutionary character. On May 22 a serious revolt of the negroes was reported, and on May 25 the United States Senate authorized the government to intervene in certain contingencies. Meanwhile the government was making naval preparations on an extensive scale. By the latter part of May a fleet of eight battleships, with a hospital ship and several tugs, was concentrated at Key West. President Taft assured the president of Cuba that this was due merely to the desire to act promptly if it should be necessary to protect American life and property, and that these precautions had nothing to do with any purpose of intervention. It was announced on June 14 that the government forces had attacked and routed the chief body of rebels under the command of their generals, Estenoz and Ivonet, near Jara Huerca. The rebels were completely routed and suffered heavy loss. They left all their ammunition and provisions in the hands of the government troops. The American marines were ordered home on July 25. In connection with a demand for immediate settlement of American claims, an assault was made by a reporter on the American chargé d'affaires, but upon the protest of the United States an apology was tendered. (See UNITED STATES, *Foreign Affairs*.) The campaign for the first presidential election since the withdrawal of the United States troops began in April. The Conservative candidate was General Juan Mario Menocal, and the Liberal, Vice-President Alfredo Zayas. The election was held at the beginning of November and passed off without disturbance.

It was given out in 1912 that the questions at issue between Cuba and the governments of England, France, and Germany would be settled by friendly negotiations. Claims dating from the Spanish régime had in the past caused strained relations with those governments, especially with that of France.

CUMBERLAND PRESBYTERIAN CHURCH. The denominational body now known under this title is that portion of the larger denomination of the same name whose General Assembly in 1906 voted to combine with the Presbyterian Church in the United States. The present members of the Cumberland Presbyterian Church refused to abide by this decision and organized into a separate body. During the years from 1906 to the present time litigation has been carried on between representatives of this body and the Presbyterian Church in the United States in regard to the possession of the properties of the former Cumberland Presbyterian Church. This litigation is being conducted in a number of States. During 1912 the Cumberlands lost in the Supreme Court of Oklahoma. The report to the effect that the Cumberlands had lost in the United States Supreme Court in 1911 was erroneous. To the close of 1912 no case had yet reached the United States Supreme Court except on the question of jurisdiction, on which question the decision was in favor of the Unionists. From the best statistics available the total number of churches is 1457, and the total membership, estimated, 110,000.

CUMMINS, SENATOR. See PRESIDENTIAL CAMPAIGN.

CUNNINGHAM COAL CLAIMS. See ALASKA.

CUPPLES, SAMUEL. An American manufacturer and philanthropist, died January 7, 1912. He was born in Harrisburg, Pa., in 1831 and was educated in the public schools. He began his business career as a boy in a grocery store in Pittsburgh in 1843 and in 1846 be removed to Cincinnati. In 1851 he engaged in the manufacture of wooden ware in St. Louis. This grew to be one of the largest enterprises in the country. He took an active interest in educational matters and is said to have done more than any other man to build up the public schools of Missouri. He promoted the St. Louis Manual Training School, on which most of the manual training schools of the country are modeled. His gifts to educational institutions amounted to millions of dollars. One of his largest gifts was that of property valued at $3,500,000 to Washington University, St. Louis.

CURAÇAO. A Netherlands West Indian colony, 436 sq. miles, composed of the islands of Curaçao (212 sq. m.), Bonaire (Buen Ayre), Aruba, St. Martin, St. Eustations, and Saba. Total population December 31, 1910, 54,469 (24,297 males, 30,172 females). Export of phosphate: Curaçao, 3571 cubic meters; Aruba, 33,542. Raw gold export (Aruba), 59,421 kilos. Total imports (1910), 3,162,310 guilders; exports. 1,716,886; tonnage entered, 2578; revenue (estimate 1912), 690,000 guilders; expenditure, $1,107,000; subvention, 417,000. Dr. Th. I. A. Nugens, governor in 1912.

CURRENCY REFORM. The agitation for a revision of banking and currency laws, which had been a conspicuous feature of public discussion during all the years following the 1907 panic, continued in scientific and financial circles during 1912, but was pushed into the background so far as the general public was concerned by the excitement of the political campaign. Even the American Bankers' Association, which had unqualifiedly and by unanimous vote approved the Aldrich plan at the New Orleans meeting in 1911, did not reindorse it nor appoint a committee to further it or any other plan of currency revision at the Detroit convention in September, 1912. The principal reason for this was the desire of the bankers to avoid making any proposals for banking and currency reform issues of the political campaign which at that time was at its height. It was argued that wise legislation would be more probable if the subject did not become a matter of partisan politics. The bankers' association therefore contented itself with merely declaring its willingness to cooperate in devising a satisfactory financial system.

Though banking reform did not figure as an issue in the campaign, the various party platforms contained planks with reference to it. The Republican platform did not mention the Aldrich plan, but declared revision to be necessary in order to prevent money panics, to "promote the prosperity of the country by producing constant employment," and to aid in crop movements; it held that reform should safeguard the individual banks against domination by sectional, financial, or political interests. The Democratic platform was of much the same tenor, with the addition of open "opposition to the Aldrich plan or the establishment of a central bank." The Progressive party also disapproved the Aldrich plan, but demanded currency reform and protection from Wall Street control. It also stated, "We believe the present method of issuing notes through private agencies is harmful and unscientific. The issue of currency is financially a governmental function." This last proposal was condemned by some as a reversion to the doctrines of the Greenback party. It did not figure, however, as an actual political issue of importance in the presidential campaign. For full discussion see BANKS AND BANKING.

CURTISS. See NAVAL PROGRESS, *Aviation*.

CURTISS TURBINE. See STEAM TURBINE.

CUTTING, WILLIAM BAYARD. An American lawyer and philanthropist, died March 1, 1912. He was born in New York in 1850 and graduated from Columbia University in 1869. He studied law and was admitted to the bar in 1871. From that time until his death he practiced law in New York City. He took an active interest in social questions and was prominent in reform politics. He was civil service commissioner in New York City under Mayor Low and was also president of the tenement house commission. He was a director in many financial institutions. He was also a trustee or director of Columbia University, New York Botanical Gardens, and the Museum of Natural History.

CYCLING. Frank J. Kramer of East Orange retained his title as professional sprint champion, although Alfred Gouillet, the winner of the Western series of races, tied the champion in total number of points. Gouillet, however, refused to meet Kramer in a deciding race. Kramer, in the Eastern series, scored five firsts, one second, and one third. Alfred Grenda took second place in the East with one first, three seconds, and one fourth. Gouillet scored five firsts and two seconds. Fogler made the next best showing, with two seconds, three thirds, and one fourth. George Wiley captured the professional paced championship, scoring twenty firsts, 10$\frac{1}{2}$ seconds, and 2$\frac{1}{2}$ thirds. The amateur championship was won by Donald McDougall, who captured five firsts and one fourth. McDougall also won the 1-mile amateur sprint at the World's Championship meet held at Newark. Other winners at this meet were: 100 kilometers, motor-paced professional race, George Wiley; 1-mile professional sprint, Frank J. Kramer.

Among the new records established in 1912 were: $\frac{1}{3}$ mile, against time, unpaced, 33 seconds, by A. J. Clarke; $\frac{2}{3}$ mile, 1 minute 11$\frac{1}{5}$ seconds, by Alfred Gouillet; $\frac{3}{4}$ mile, 1 minute 24$\frac{3}{5}$ seconds, by A. Gouillet; 1 mile, 1 minute 5 seconds, by A. Gouillet; $\frac{1}{3}$ mile, amateur, unpaced, 38 seconds, by E. L. Young; $\frac{1}{2}$ mile, 56$\frac{1}{5}$ seconds, by E. L. Young; 150 miles, amateur competition, 8 hours 26 minutes 27 seconds, by Joseph G. Kopsky.

The annual six-day race was held in Madison Square Garden December 9 to 14. The winning team was Rutt and Fogler. Moran and Fogler won the Boston six-day race.

CYPRUS. An island in the easternmost basin of the Mediterranean, nominally a part of the Ottoman Empire, but ceded for administrative purposes to Great Britain in 1878. It covers 3584 square miles and its population by districts (1911) is as follows: Nicosia, 81,497; Famagusta, 58,530; Larnaca, 29,737; Limassol, 46,084; Papho, 38,508; Kyrenia, 19,752—total, 274,108. The Mohammedans form about 25.9 per cent. of the population, the remainder being nearly all Christians of the native Cypriote Church. Nicosia, the capital, had, in 1911, 16,052 inhabitants. Elementary schools of all classes, 583 (187 Mohammedan, 396 Christian); with a total enrollment of about 30,779 (5675 Mohammedans).

Agriculture, the chief industry, has been greatly retarded by reason of the lack of water; the rivers, nearly all mountain torrents, dry up in summer, and the rainfall is deficient. A plan for storing water for irrigation is in process of realization. The large numbers of goats, together with frequent forest fires, are a hindrance to the development of otherwise valuable forests. Cereal, carobs, the famous Cyprus wine, cheese, fruit, vegetables, and livestock are exported. The imports in 1910 were valued, exclusive of specie, at £588,480 (from Great Britain, £118,203; from British colonies, £2116; from other countries, £468,161; the exports at £651,068 (to Great Britain, £138,839; to British colonies, £994; to other countries, £511,235). Shipping entered and cleared (1910), 742,485 (British, 105,451). Revenue (1910-11), £286,848; expenditure, £251,520. Government grant (1911-12), £50,000 (1910-11, £40,000). A sum of £92,800 is payable annually to Turkey, but this is appropriated to the interest on the guaranteed loan of 1855. British high-commissioner in 1912, Major Sir H. J. Goold-Adams.

On account of riotous movements in the town of Limasol during May the high-commissioner announced at the beginning of June that an armed force of British troops would occupy it until further notice and would disperse any gathering held for the purpose of breaking peace. A number of rioters were arrested and the police force was strengthened for fear of attempts at rescue. Additional British troops were quartered in the city during the summer. A deputation of Greek members of the Legislative Council visited London in July to plead for redress of grievances.

DAHLGREN, Charles Bunker. An American soldier, died January 10, 1912. He was born in 1839, a son of the late Rear-Admiral John A. Dahlgren. He served with his father in the blockade of Charleston and after the war was assistant at the Washington Navy Yard. He wrote a number of books dealing with naval warfare.

DAHN, Felix Sophus Julius. A German historian, novelist, and poet, died January 3, 1912. He was born in Hamburg in 1834 and studied in the universities of Munich and Berlin. He devoted himself chiefly to history and law. He became *privat docent* in Munich in 1857 and professor of law in that university in 1864. He afterwards occupied the same position at Würzburg, Königsberg, and Breslau. He filled the chair of history and law at the latter institution from 1888 until the time of his death. His works on historical subjects are important, but he is best known as novelist and poet. *Der Kampf um Rom* in four volumes passed through more than thirty editions. Among his other works his epic poem, *Sind Götter?* and *Moltke als Erzieher* are well known. He also wrote a number of dramas. His novels are of the historical type and cover periods from prehistoric times to the Crusades.

DAHOMEY. A French West African colony. Capital, Porto Novo, with 40,000 inhabitants; other towns are: Abomey (10,732), Ouidah or Whydah (13,000), Grand Popo (2115), and Cotonou (1954). A railway (748 kilometers), which, when completed, will connect Cotonou with the Niger at a point near Karimana, is finished as far as Savé (261 kms.). Construction was under way in 1912. The line has three main sections: Cotonou to Paouignan, 194 kms.; Paouignan to Parakou, 246; Parakou to the Niger, 250. A branch from Cotonou (58 kms.) runs to Ouidah (Whydah) and Segboroué. The chief products and exports are palm kernels (export 1909, 8,353,252 francs), palm oil (6,452,109), corn (712,713), live animals (151,378), copra (99,420), cotton (130,078). Ch. Noufflard was lieutenant-governor in 1912. See French West Africa.

DAIRYING. The farm value of the dairy products of the United States in 1912 was estimated to be about $830,000,000. A severe drought prevailed in the early summer throughout the East, but copious rains later improved pastures so that the output of butter in creameries was larger than for several years previous. The price of butter increased about 11 per cent. over 1911, and the price of milk 5 per cent. The imports of butter and butter substitutes into the United States during the fiscal year ended June 30, 1912, amounted to 1,025,668 pounds, valued at $237,154. The exports amounted to 6,092,235 pounds, valued at $1,468,432. The cheese imports totaled 46,542,007 pounds, valued at $8,807,249. The cheese exports amounted to 6,337,559 pounds, valued at $898,035.

As in 1911, the cost of milk production averaged so high as to drive many men out of the dairy business. The New York and New Jersey Experiment Stations report that it cost about 4 cents per quart to make milk. The Minnesota Experiment Station found the cost of producing milk in Minnesota was so high that the income received from milk and butter was not sufficient to cover the cost of production on most farms. In a five-year test at the Connecticut Experiment Station it was concluded that even from a good herd milk could not be produced at a profit at 4 cents per quart. The Ohio Experiment Station found that it cost 6¼ cents per quart to produce milk in Ohio, and the cost of delivering was 3½ cents per quart, making a total cost of milk in Ohio at 9¾ cents, which allowed for no profit to the producer. A Boston firm estimated that the cost of delivering a quart of milk to the consumer was 4.4 cents, to which must be added 0.37 cent for shrinkage. The average price to the producer for milk delivered in Boston was 3.9 cents per quart, making a net cost per quart when delivered to the consumer of 8.67 cents. The New York State Food Commission found that the cash margin between cost price and retail selling price was as follows: Fresh milk, 71.5 per cent.; creamery butter, 16.9 per cent.; whole milk cheese, 28.13 per cent., and condensed milk, 22.7 per cent. During the year the previous high yields of milk of the Guernsey, Brown Swiss, Ayrshire, and Holstein breeds have been exceeded. The largest yield was that of Creamelle Vale, a Holstein cow, which produced 29,625 pounds of milk in one year.

An act of Congress August 10, 1912, provided that the sanitary regulations for slaughtering and canning meat be extended to cover renovated butter factories. Outbreaks of typhoid fever, septic sore throat, and other milk-borne diseases have stimulated the health authorities to continue their efforts in the sanitary regulation of the milk supply.

Dr. Delepine has made a statistical study of the tuberculous milk recently in the city of Manchester, England, and finds that the quantity of such milk has been reduced to nearly one-third of that of fourteen years ago. Infantile mortality, though still high, has considerably decreased in that time, which in part is attributed to the reduction in the amount of tuberculous milk.

In view of the fact that tubercle bacilli are found in butter and cheese, it has been advocated that a certified butter made from pasteurized cream should be put on the market, and that it would probably pay as soon as the public could be taught the value of using a sanitary product. There is a steadily expanding demand at all seasons of the year for the highest grade of unsalted butter at the largest distributing markets. As defects in cream are more noticeable in fresh than in salted butter, none but the best cream and methods of butter making can be employed in the production of the unsalted product. This is an additional reason for the pasteurization of a larger percentage of the cream which is made into butter. Experiments with ozone in the preservation of milk have not proved satisfactory; many bacteria were destroyed, but not enough to be efficient for preservation. Several new patents have been granted by the French government for the sterilization of milk by ultra-violet rays. In one case the milk is quickly raised to a temperature of 60° C., then submitted to the action of ultra-violet rays by exposure to radiations of a quartz vapor mercury lamp, working at 3 amperes and 220 volts. A new product known as "Syntho" and resembling cream is found on the Chicago market, and is made by emulsifying melted beef tallow in milk. A method of making a synthetic milk has also been reported from Germany. A decision of importance to the dairy interests was made by the Appellate Division of the New York Supreme Court, which declared that the sale of oleo is illegal when the color of the substitute resembles butter. This is a reversal of the decision of the lower courts.

The dairy industry is expanding in Canada, but not enough butter is produced to supply the home demand. During the year over 2,000,000 pounds of butter were imported to Canada from New Zealand. There was a decline in exports of cheese and cream from Canada to the United States. An excessive hot and dry summer in the United Kingdom caused a greater reduction in the number of cows kept, so that the amount of milk and milk products produced was very much reduced. The local government board of England and Wales has issued an order allowing the use of boric acid, borax, or hydrogen peroxid as a preservative of cream containing more than 35 per cent. fat, but no preservative can be added to market milk or thin cream, nor can any thickening substance be added to cream. The production of condensed and powdered milk is assuming great importance in New Zealand, which now sends about 200,000 pounds each year to the United Kingdom, besides other shipments to Australia and the South Sea Islands. The New Zealand method of evaporating milk to the powdered form has been introduced into Australia, where a great development of this industry is expected.

The following treatises on dairying have been published during the year: *Report of the Commission on Milk Standards Appointed by the New York Milk Committee* (Pub. Health and Mar. Hosp. Serv. U. S., Pub. Health Rpts., 27 (1912), No. 19, pp. 673-691; reprinted as Reprint No. 78); E. V. Wilcox, *Production and Inspection of Milk* (Hawaii Sta. [Spec. Bul.], 1912, July 31); T. P. Cooper, *The Cost of Producing Minnesota Dairy Products, 1904-1908* (Minnesota Sta. Bul. 124; U. S. Dept. Agr., Bur. Statis. Bul. 88); B. Marquart, *Lehrbuch des Milchvieh-Kontrollwesens* (Berlin); G. A. Witt, *Die heittechnischen Einrichtungen der Käserei* (Bern); A. Monvoisin, *Le Lait, son Analyse, son Utilization* (Paris); J. P. Sheldon, *Dairying: A Book for All Who Are Engaged in the Production and Management of Milk* (London); C. Porcher, *Le Lait desséché* (Lyon); W. G. Savage, *Milk and the Public Health* (London); M. J. Rosenau, *The Milk Question* (Boston); M. A. O'Callaghan, *Dairying in Australasia;* W. Sadler, *Bacteria as Friends and Foes of the Dairy Farmer* (London); K. Storen, *Dairying* (Christiania); J. Michels, *Market Dairying and Milk Products* (Wauwatosa, Wis.).

DALE, Thomas Henry. Former congressman from Pennsylvania, died August 21, 1912. He was born in Daleville, Pa., in 1846 and was educated in the public schools of that town and at Wyoming Seminary. He enlisted in the volunteers at the outbreak of the Civil War. From 1870 to 1901 he was engaged in the wholesale produce and coal business in Scranton. He afterwards became president of the Anthracite Trust Company, and several other corporations. He was elected prothonotary of Lackawanna County in 1882, 1885, and 1888, and was elected to the 59th Congress in 1905.

DALEN, Gustaf. See Nobel Prize.

DALRYMPLE-HAY, Sir John Charles. An English admiral, died January 28, 1912. He was born in Edinburgh in 1821. After a year spent at Rugby he entered the navy in 1834, and after an eighteen months' cruise on the African station he went for three months to the Pacific. He next served in the *Benbow* in the Mediterranean. As lieutenant he served in China, for a portion of the time as flag-lieutenant to Sir Thomas Cochrane, who, in 1846, promoted him to the command of the *Wolverine*. His next service was again in China, where in 1849 he did excellent service against pirates. In that year he defeated Sha-ping-tzai, a noted pirate who had assembled a fleet of sixty-four large junks in the Tongking River. These junks were nearly all destroyed. As a result of this service Hay was promoted to the rank of captain in 1850. In 1854 he commanded the *Victory* at Portsmouth, and in the two years following served in the Black Sea and on the North America and West Indies station. In 1861 he succeeded to the baronetcy, and in the following year was returned to parliament as a Liberal Conservative. He retained his seat for three years, but was defeated in 1865. In 1866 he was made rear-admiral, and in the same year he again returned to parliament. He held this seat until April, 1880, when he was defeated. In July of the same year he occupied a seat which had become vacant. As a result of the so-called Childers retirement scheme, which came into force in 1870, Admiral Hay was obliged to retire from active service at the age of 49. In 1873 he became a vice-admiral on the retired list and in 1878 was made full admiral. For sixteen years after his retirement he continued to sit in the House of Commons, where he took an active part in questions relating to the navy. In 1885 he did not seek reëlection, and from that year until the time of his death lived in retirement. He received the degree of honorary D. C. L. from Oxford, and honorary LL. D. from Glasgow universities. He was a Fellow of the Royal Society and vice-president of the Institute of Naval Architects. He wrote *The Flag List and Its Prospects* (1870); *Ashanti and the Gold Coast* (1873); *Our Naval Deficiencies* (1883); *Piracy in the China Sea* (1889), and a volume of reminiscences entitled *Lines from My Log-Books* (1898).

DAMASCUS. See ARCHÆOLOGY.

DAMS. The failures of dams with great loss of life and damage throughout the United States directed attention in 1912 to the necessity for State regulation of their construction and maintenance. There were on the statute books laws to provide for the supervision of dams and reservoirs in the following twenty-seven States: Colorado, Connecticut, Florida, Georgia, Idaho, Indiana, Kansas, Maine, Massachusetts, Michigan, Montana, Nebraska, Nevada, New Jersey, New Mexico, New York, Oklahoma, Oregon, Pennsylvania, Rhode Island, South Carolina, South Dakota, Tennessee, Texas, Utah, Vermont, and Wyoming. The statutes in these various States represented widely differing methods and extent of supervision and control. Fifteen provide for State supervision and twelve place the control in the hands of local officers. In Colorado the preliminary approval of plans and specifications of dams and reservoirs must be made by a State engineer and the construction supervised, a permit for use not being granted until a certificate for operation is obtained. In New York during the year an active inspection of various dam sites was made, and in other States efforts towards the p pe inspection and regulation of dams and reesorvoirs were under way. It was found that poor engineering and faulty construction were responsible for a number of the failures, and civil engineers were paying increased attention to the problems of construction, especially the foundations of dams and endeavoring to eliminate the false economy by which many builders were attempting to reduce the cost.

ARROWROCK DAM. Plans for what was to be the highest masonry dam in the world were prepared for the United States Reclamation Service in connection with the Arrowrock reservoir for the Boise project. This dam was to be located in the canyon of the Boise River about twenty miles above the City of Boise, Idaho, and was to rise to a height of 350 feet, with a concrete masonry spillway. It was to be 1050 feet in length on the top and its foundations would go down some eighty or ninety feet below the bed of the river at their lowest points. The dam was to be of the gravity type, curved in plan, built of concrete by the officials of the United States Reclamation Service. There was provided in the plans as a spillway a concrete weir about 400 feet in length discharging into a channel passing around the north end of the dam and into a creek below. During the construction the diversion works were to consist of two crib cofferdams across the Boise River, with a channel about 490 feet in length and a cross-sectional area of about 670 square feet.

BUTTE DAM. Another gravity type of dam was designed for the Rio Grande project, New Mexico-Texas, at Elephant Butte, New Mexico. The top of this dam, which was to extend about 1200 feet in length and carry a roadway, was to be 200 feet above the original river bed. The dam, with a dike about 1¼ miles northwest, was to form a reservoir with a capacity of 2,600,000 acre-feet. The dam was to be of concrete in which were to be imbedded rough stones of various sizes up to about four cubic yards each, and the foundations were to be made in rock excavations. This work also was to be done by government forces of the Reclamation Service and the detailed specifications provided for a structure of massive design and construction.

FAILURE OF OHIO RIVER DAM NO. 26. The corps of engineers of the United States army during the year was actively engaged in the improvement of the entire Ohio River by the construction of locks and movable dams with a view to securing a navigable depth of nine feet. Dam No. 26, across the Ohio River below Gallipolis, was completed during the year and on August 8, 1912, one day after the water was let in behind it, it was destroyed and a loss estimated at $60,000 was caused. This dam consisted of a lock, two bear-trap dams, and a 600-foot section of movable Chanoine wickets which were built on a concrete base resting on the shale bottom of the river. This shale foundation proved defective and the concrete bases were shoved off and the wickets carried down stream.

ASSUAN DAM. This great structure to control the waters of the Nile was completed during the year and formally opened on December 23 in the presence of Lord Kitchener, the Khedive, and other distinguished guests. After the dam had been built it was found desirable to increase its height and strengthen the structure and this last work had been in progress since 1909. Sir Benjamin Baker, the original engineer, decided that the original structure, which was finished in 1903, could be raised to increase the amount of water stored at Assuan and accordingly plans were prepared which provided for increasing the height of the masonry crest by 16.4 feet and the water level by 23 feet, as well as thickening the dam by 16 feet. The storage capacity thus obtained was increased from 35,300 million cubic feet to 81,190 million cubic feet and the estimated cost of the structure was £1,500,000. The contract was placed in 1907. The new masonry was built in front of the old, leaving an interval into which cement grouting could be run when the temperature of both masses had become the same. The new dam has a thickness at the top of 36 feet, as compared with 23 feet for the older structure and carries a driveway of

29 feet 6 inches in width, as against a former width of 18 feet 4 inches. Heavy locks and control works were installed, and the additions from an engineering standpoint were in keeping with the monumental character of the original work. Raising the level of water covered quite a few archæological remains, and these were all carefully studied and excavated, inscriptions being copied and records and measurements made.

KLINGENBERG DAM. A massive masonry dam in which architectural features were introduced, was under construction during the year at Klingenberg, in Saxony. This dam was 1,033.5 feet in length, 131.2 feet high and 113.5 feet thick at the base. It spans the valley of the Wild Weisseritz and was to impound the water for a distance of 2½ miles back. The stone used in the construction is gneiss, obtained from a nearby quarry, and 156,954 cubic yards were required in the construction. The architectural features were designed by Prof. Hans Poelzig, of Breslau, and involved supporting the lower masonry by buttresses, a central tower with a turreted effect, and a suggestion of arches along the extent of the dam.

See also AQUEDUCTS for description of *Kensico Dam*.

DANBURY HATTERS' CASE. See BOYCOTT.

DANISH WEST INDIES. Three West Indian islands (St. Croix, 84 square miles, 15,467 inhabitants; St. Thomas, 33 and 10,678; St. John, 21 and 941), which compose a colony of Denmark. Negroes form the majority of the population, and the cultivation of sugarcane is the chief industry. Governor in 1912, L. C. Helwez-Larsen; government seat, Charlotte Amalie (St. Thomas).

DARTMOUTH COLLEGE. The total number of students enrolled in the various departments of the college in the autumn of 1912 was about 1300. The faculty numbered 137. The noteworthy changes in the faculty during the year included the appointments of E. G. Bill, assistant professor of mathematics, E. R. Greene, assistant professor of French, and Rev. Benjamin T. Marshall, Phillips professor of Biblical history and literature. There were no noteworthy benefactions during the year. The productive funds of the college amounted to $3,715,804 and the income to $176,281. The volumes in the library numbered about 125,000. President, Ernest Fox Nichols, LL. D.

DARWIN, SIR GEORGE HOWARD. An English scientist, second son of Charles Darwin, died December 7, 1912. He was born in Down, Kent, in 1845 and was educated privately and at Trinity College, Cambridge. He studied law and became a barrister in 1874, but returned to Cambridge and devoted himself to the study of mathematical science, especially the mechanics of tides and the form of the earth. In this field he became known as an authority. He read and published numerous scientific papers. Among these were several relating to the marriage of first cousins. He also wrote on *Harmonic Analysis of Tide Observations*, *Effects of Tidal Friction on the Earth*, and on the moon and periodic orbits. He also made studies in evolution and these studies he said at one time led him to doubt whether biologists had been correct in looking for continuous transformation of species. He thought that judging by analogy they should rather expect to find slight continuous changes in species occurring during a long period, followed by a somewhat sudden transformation into a new species or by rapid extinction. In 1906 he attended the two hundredth anniversary of the birth of Benjamin Franklin in the United States. In 1899 he was made president of the Royal Astronomical Society and six years later was president of the British Association.

DAVENPORT, HOMER CALVIN. An American cartoonist, died May 2, 1912. He was born in Silverton, Ore., in 1867, and was reared on a farm in that State. He had no school education nor did he ever study art. His early days included employment as a jockey, as a railroad fireman and as a clown in a circus. He had a remarkable taste for caricature from his boyhood and he developed this by constant practice and close observation. For a time he worked on the *Portland Oregonian* and then went to San Francisco, where in 1892 he secured employment on the *Examiner* in that city. Three years later he was brought by W. R. Hearst, the owner of the paper, to New York, and began to draw the cartoons for the *New York Journal*, which made him famous. His drawings during the campaign for the first election of President McKinley created wide attention, especially his caricatures of Mark Hanna and his conception of the trusts. He traveled widely and made pictures of many famous men, including William E. Gladstone. During the successive political campaigns he drew pictures which attracted wide attention. He had great interest in full-blooded Arabian horses and imported a considerable number to the United States. He delivered lectures on the general subject of humane treatment of dumb animals. He was the author of *Davenport's Cartoons; The Bell of Silverton, and Other Short Stories of Oregon*, and *The Dollar or the Man?*

DAWSON, THOMAS CLELAND. An American diplomat, died May 1, 1912. He was born in Hudson, Wis., in 1865, and graduated from Hanover College in 1883. He studied law at Harvard University and at Cincinnati Law School. For several years he was engaged in journalism and after his admission to the bar practiced law from 1886 to 1889 in Des Moines, Ia. In 1890 he again entered journalism as legislative correspondent of the *Iowa Daily Register*. He later became city editor of that paper. From 1891 to 1897 he practiced law at Council Bluffs, Ia., and from 1891 to 1894 was attorney-general of the State. In 1897 he was appointed secretary of the United States Legation to Brazil, and five times acted as chargé d'affaires of the legation. He was consul-general of the United States to Santo Domingo from 1904 to 1907, and was minister to Colombia from 1907 to 1909, and to Chile from 1909 to 1910. In 1910 he was appointed chief of the Division of Latin-American Affairs in the United States State Department. Mr. Dawson won a remarkable reputation as a pacifier in disputes between Latin-American countries. He did especially efficient work in Santo Domingo and in Panama following the separation of that republic from Colombia. He did important work also in Nicaragua and Honduras. In 1911 he was peace commissioner to Honduras, and in June of that year represented the United States at the centennial celebration of Venezuelan independence. Mr. Dawson was offered the post of ambassador to Brazil, but declined.

DEATH RATE. See VITAL STATISTICS.

DEBT. See articles on countries.

DEEP SEA EXPLORATION. See CARNEGIE INSTITUTION.

DELAWARE. POPULATION. According to the Census Bureau statistics issued in 1912, out of a total population of 202,322 in 1910, the foreign-born whites numbered 17,420, compared with 13,729 in 1900. The largest proportion of these, 3984, came from Ireland; from Russia, 3428; from Italy, 2893; from Germany, 2572, and from England, 1555. Other European countries were represented by smaller numbers. In 1910 the negroes in the State numbered 31,181 and the mulattoes, 3706. In 1890 the negroes numbered 28,386 and the mulattoes, 3549.

AGRICULTURE. The acreage, value, and production of the principal crops in 1911-1912 are shown in the following table:

		Acreage	Prod. Bu.	Value
Corn	1912	195,000	6,630,000	$3,381,000
	1911	195,000	6,630,000	4,044,000
Wheat	1912	111,000	1,942,000	1,864,000
	1911	113,000	1,887,000	1,698,000
Oats	1912	4,000	122,000	55,000
	1911	4,000	120,000	56,000
Rye	1912	1,000	14,000	11,000
	1911	1,000	15,000	14,000
Potatoes	1912	11,000	1,100,000	770,000
	1911	11,000	660,000	634,000
Hay	1912	72,000	a 96,000	1,440,000
	1911	72,000	a 63,000	1,418,000

a Tons.

MANUFACTURES. The Thirteenth Census included statistics for the manufacturing industries of the State. These are for the calendar year 1909 and the general results will be found in the table below. The largest number of men employed in any single industry are those engaged in the tanning of leather. These number 3045. The manufacture of foundry and machine shop products gave employment to 2210 wage earners; the paper and wood pulp industry to 1525; canning and preserving to 1369; shipbuilding to 1239, and lumber and timber production to 1174. These are the only industries giving employment to more than 1000 men, with the exception of those employed by the railroads in the car shops and elsewhere, who numbered 2210. Of all the persons engaged in the manufacturing industries of the State, 5.8 per cent. were officials, 5.7 per cent. clerks, and 88.6 per cent. wage earners. Of the clerks employed, 81.8 per cent. were male and 18.2 were female, and of the wage earners, 82.4 per cent. were male and 17.6 per cent. were female. Of the total number employed 97.5 per cent. were sixteen years old and over, and 2.5 per cent. were under sixteen. The largest number of women and children are employed in the canning and preserving industry. For the great majority of the wage earners employed in the manufacturing industries of the State the prevailing hours of labor range from fifty-four to sixty hours per week, or from nine to ten hours a day, only 8 per cent. of the total being employed in establishments working less than nine hours a day, and only 4.5 per cent. being employed in establishments working more than ten hours a day.

The following table gives a summary of the results of the census for the calendar years 1909 and 1904:

	Number of amount 1909	1904
Number of establishments	736	631
Persons engaged in manufactures	23,984	20,567
Proprietors and firm members	722	641
Salaried employees	2,024	1,451
Wage earners (average number)	21,238	18,475
Primary horsepower	52,779	49,490
Capital	$60,906,000	$50,926,000
Expenses	46,958,000	37,362,000
Services	12,618,000	9,787,000
Salaries	2,322,000	1,629,000
Wages	10,296,000	8,158,000
Materials	30,938,000	24,884,000
Miscellaneous	3,402,000	2,691,000
Value of products	52,840,000	41,160,000
Value added by manufacture (value of products less cost of materials)	21,902,000	16,276,000

FINANCE. The report of the State treasurer for the fiscal year 1912 shows: Cash balance at beginning of year, $49,986.91; cash receipts for year (including balance), $893,558.49; cash expenditures for year, $801,210.85; cash balance at close of year, $92,347.64.

The total bonded debt is $826,785, and the total assets are $2,004,583.49.

The chief sources of revenue are railroads—State tax, $112,000; corporations—organization tax, $105,693.01; corporations—annual franchise tax, $62,551.25.

The chief expenditures are for educational purposes, $254,078.19; charities and eleemosynary institutions, $94,981.49; public health, $31,814.88; executive department of government, $54,658.21 (salary and expenses of State officers, etc.); department of justice, $42,611.67 (salaries of jurges, attorney-general, and expenses of department, etc.).

POLITICS AND GOVERNMENT. There was no session of the legislature in 1912, as the sessions are biennial and the last was held in 1911.

CONVENTIONS AND ELECTIONS. There was an election for governor and other State officers, and representatives to Congress on November 5. The Republican State convention for the election of delegates to the national convention was held on April 16. The convention indorsed President Taft, but sent the six delegates to Chicago unpledged and free to act on personal judgment. A vigorous debate occurred in the convention over a proposal to increase the negro representation on the State committee, the negroes demanding that the committee be increased from 12 to 16 members, four to be negroes. The proposal was defeated. The delegates elected to the Democratic State convention were pledged to Governor Wilson. The first Progressive convention held in the State convened on July 31. Six delegates were elected to the Progressive convention in Chicago. The platform denounced the action of the managers and delegates to the Chicago convention and said: "We emphatically condemn those delegates from Delaware who assisted in the perpetration of this fraud on popular government." The platform also condemned the Senators from Delaware for their support of Senator Lorimer. The Republican State convention for the nomination of State officers and representatives to Congress met at Dover on August 20. Charles R. Miller of Wilmington was nominated for governor and George H. Hall of Milford for representative to Congress. On September 10 the Democratic nominees to the convention nominated Thomas W. Monaghan for governor and on the following day the Progressive party nominated George B. Hynson. A division occurred in the Progressive party as the result of the assumption of leadership by representatives of the former régime of Senator Addicks. J. Frank Allee was one of the leaders. This was so displeasing to the followers of Mr. Roosevelt in Wilmington, where a large majority of the Progressive party existed in Delaware, that they bolted from the Progressive State convention held on September 11, and formed another party under the title of the National Progressive party. Instead of indorsing George H. Hall, the Republican nominee for Congress, the National Progressives nominated John G. Townsend, Jr., of Selbyville. They accepted the three Roosevelt electors nominated by the original Progressive convention. This made four candidates for Congressman in Delaware, including the regular Republican nominee, the Democratic nominee, the egu ar Progressive nominee, and the Nationak Prbgressive nominee. The vote on November 5 resulted in the election of Mr. Miller, Republican candidate for governor. His vote was 22,745, while for Mr. Monaghan, the Democratic candidate, were cast 21,460, and for Hynson, Progressive, 3019 votes. The vote for President was as follows: Wilson, 22,631; Taft, 15,997; Roosevelt, 8886; and Debs, 556. The candidate of the Prohibition party for governor, John Heyd, received 622 votes, and Rearick, Socialist, 555 votes.

OTHER EVENTS. On February 13 President Taft withdrew the nomination of Cornelius P. Swain to be United States marshal for the district of Delaware. This action was due to an investigation of alleged political corruption in Delaware. The withdrawal was the result of a request by Senator Du Pont to Attorney-General Wickersham. Mr. Swain's nomination was once confirmed by the Senate, but the action was reconsidered on receipt of the complaint from Willard Saulsbury of the national Democratic committee for Delaware. Mr. Saulsbury alleged that Swain was unfit for public office because he had been implicated in buying votes in Sussex County. The specific charge was that Swain had taken $3000 from the office of T. Coleman Du Pont of Wilmington to Bridgeville, where it was used for corrupt purposes in the election of 1904. As a result of these charges, which implicated Senator Du Pont, the latter asked for an investigation by a committee of the Senate. No action had been taken on this at the end of the year.

DELEGATES, CONTESTS FOR. See PRESIDENTIAL CAMPAIGN.

DELTA. See NAVAL PROGRESS, *Aviation*.

DEMOCRATIC NATIONAL CONVENTION. See PRESIDENTIAL CAMPAIGN.

DEMOCRATIC PARTY. See PRESIDENTIAL CAMPAIGN, UNITED STATES, and articles on States.

DENATURED ALCOHOL. See ALCOHOL.

DENMARK. A constitutional European monarchy situated north of Germany. Copenhagen is the capital.

AREA AND POPULATION. The area and population by insular and mainland divisions, according to the census taken February 1, 1911, compared with the figures for population in 1906, are shown in the following table:

	Sq. Miles	Pop. 1906	Pop. 1911
Islands:			
Seeland	2,895	1,026,119	1,096,897
Bornhohn	227	41,031	42,885
Lolland-Falster	692	108,029	115,658
Fyn	1,341	289,346	303,179
Jutland:			
Southeast Jutland..	2,827	462,445	482,264
Southwest Jutland...	4,144	338,224	364,620
North Jutland......	2,920	334,005	351,573
Total Denmark proper.	15,046	2,588,919	2,757,076
Faroe Islands.........	540	16,348	18,000
Total	15,586	2,605,267	2,775,076

The males in 1911 numbered 1,337,900 and the females 1,419,176 (1,257,765 and 1,331,154 in 1906). The rural population in 1911 numbered 1,647,350, as compared with 1,565,585, an increase of 81,765; the urban, 1,109,726, as compared with 1,023,334, a gain of 86,392. Copenhagen (København), covering 28 square miles, had (1911) 462,161 inhabitants; Frederiksberg, 97,237; Aarhus, 61,755; Odense, 42,-237; Aalborg, 33,449; Horsens, 23,843; Randers, 22,970; Esbjerg, 18,208; Vejle, 17,261; Fredericia, 14,228; Kolding, 14,219; Helsingör, 13,783; Svendborg, 12,667; Nyköbing, 11,010; Viborg, 10,885.

PRODUCTION. Agriculture and dairying are the principal industries. About 80 per cent. of the total area is productive; less than one-half the p ducti e area is under crop, the remainder being forest, pasture, and meadow. The table below gives area (in hectares) and production (in quintals) of the main crops in 1911 and 1912, with yield per hectare in 1911:

	Hectares 1911	Hectares 1912	Quintals 1911	Quintals 1912	Qs. ha.
Wheat ..	40,512	40,512	1,216,157	1,018,777	30.0
Rye	276,009	276,009	5,007,279	4,670,173	18.1
Barley....	233,714	233,714	5,018,129	5,676,095	21.4
Oats	402,939	402,939	7,332,941	7,647,923	18.1
Beets* ..	24,900	30,300	7,304,799	8,035,279	293.4
Tobacco .	65	66	1,170	....	18.0

* Sugar beets.

The 1912 autumn sowings were retarded by a late harvest and wet weather.

Livestock estimate, July, 1910: 535,018 horses, 2,253,982 cattle, 726,829 sheep, 40,257 goats, 1,467,822 swine.

Beet-sugar production (1910), 100,510 tons (8 mills); there were 28 distilleries (15,010,000 liters 100°), and 22 margarine, etc., factories (34,320 tons output). Fisheries products were valued at £769,126.

COMMERCE, ETC. The general and special trade by great classes in 1910 is shown below (in thousands of kroner):

	Imports Gen.	Imports Spec.	Exports Gen.	Exports Spec.
Provisions	204,400	173,857	466,083	434,537
Raw products....	259,373	243,678	63,192	45,194
Manures, etc.	65,175	62,963	6,912	4,462
Fuel	45,058	40,561	5,867	8
Other*	60,401	56,020	6,020	1,173
	634,407	577,166	548,074	485,374

* Includes goods for personal and household use.

Principal exports (special trade), values in thousands of kroner: Provisions, eggs, etc., 368,026; animals, 51,797; beverages, 13,078; cereals, etc., 10,789; metals and hardware,

5230; colonial goods, 1747; wood and woodenwares, 787; textile mfrs., 552.

Principal countries of origin and destination, general trade, values in thousands of kroner:

	Imports		Exports	
	1909	1910	1909	1910
Germany	256,039	241,556	133,051	124,511
United Kingdom	113,502	117,232	329,567	341,418
Sweden	58,274	56,304	39,542	23,139
United States	86,196	51,692	31,126	4,844
Russia	83,248	49,219	29,838	7,992
France	16,261	15,843	1,026	2,736
Netherlands	22,094	14,502	2,099	3,291
Belgium	10,417	8,290	1,981	2,100

Total general (1911): 705,500,000 kroner imports and 626,761,000 kroner exports; total special, 623,314,000 imports and 536,647,000 exports.

Vessels entered in the 1911 trade, 35,873, of 4,015,804 tons (coasting, 98,112, of 1,876,909); cleared, 36,238, of 1,513,632 (98,001, of 1,831,-221). Merchant marine (January 1, 1912), 3562 vessels, of 513,081 tons.

Railways in operation at end of 1910, 2120 miles (1212 miles state-owned).

ARMY. The contingent of recruits required for the Danish army in 1912 was the same as in the previous year, namely, 8000 infantry, 600 cavalry, 1600 artillery, and 300 engineers. From the various recruits a force is maintained with the colors of over 11,000 men, the establishment consisting of about 830 officers and 13,000 men on a peace footing. The organization consists of 52 battalions of infantry (31 line and 21 reserve), 12 squadrons of cavalry, 24 field batteries, 18 coast batteries (12 line and 6 reserve), and 12 companies of engineers. These formations are maintained on a skeleton basis, but they were arranged so that Denmark can mobilize 83,000 men, of whom 58,500 would be infantry, 5000 cavalry, 6800 field artillery, and 8600 fortress artillery, forming an effective force of about 70,000. In 1912 the permanent staff consisted of 12 generals, 92 superior officers, 630 junior officers, and 1663 non-commissioned officers. Military service was obligatory on all able-bodied men who had attained the age of 22.

NAVY. The fleet, maintained for purposes of coast defense, is composed of three monitors carrying, each, two 9.4-inch and four 6-inch guns, and one carrying one 9.4 and three 4.7; three torpedo gunboats; 14 first-class torpedo boats 3 submarines; besides an old battleship, a cruiser, and some small craft.

FINANCE. The budget for the financial year 1912-13 estimated the revenue at 97,838,034 kroner (taxes and duties, 83,586,400) and the expenditure at 101,745,054 (war, 19,766,655; worship and instruction, 14,873,788; interior, 13,059,811; marine, 11,159,013; debt, 9,366,866; justice, 9,707,000; finance, 7,635,918). The debt stood (March 31, 1912) at 351,978,008 (external, 270,467,250; internal, 81,510,758).

GOVERNMENT. The king is the executive, assisted by a ministry of eight members, appointed by him and responsible to the parliament or rigsdag. This body is made up of an upper house of 54 and a lower of 114 members. Reigning sovereign (1912), Christian Charles Frederick Albert Alexander William, born September 26, 1870; married, April 26, 1898, to Alexandrine, Duchess of Mecklenburg (born December 24, 1879); was proclaimed king (Christian X.) May 15, 1912, upon the death (May 14) of his father, King Frederick VIII. Heir-apparent, Prince Christian Frederick Francis Michael (born March 11, 1899). The ministry (constituted July 5, 1910) was in 1912 composed as follows: K. Berntsen, premier and minister for defense; C. W. (Count) von Ahlefeldt-Laurvig, foreign affairs; A. Nielsen, agriculture; J. Appel, worship and instruction; T. Larsen, public works; J. Jensen-Sönderup, interior; N. T. Neergaard, finance; O. H. V. B. Muus, commerce, etc.; F. T. von Bülow, justice.

HISTORY. A debate on the foreign policy of the government occurred in the middle of February. The foreign minister, Count Ahlefeldt, asserted that the policy of Denmark in foreign affairs consisted in absolute neutrality towards foreign powers and no special intimacy with any one. A vote on this speech resulted in an expression of agreement with these principles by all the parties in the parliament. The King of Denmark died suddenly on the street at Hamburg on the night of May 14. He was walking alone, and his identity was not discovered until after the body had been taken to the mortuary. (See FREDERICK VIII.) He was succeeded by his eldest son, Christian, who was born September 26, 1870. On the opening of the parliament on October 7 the speech from the throne announced that a bill would be submitted for the amendment of the constitution with a view to making both houses more truly representative. Bills were also promised for the amelioration of social conditions, including a measure for the relief of indigent widows and widowers. The prime minister introduced the constitutional reform bill on October 23. This provided for woman suffrage and for their election to the Folkething. The age limit was reduced from 30 to 25 years. The term of parliament was increased from three to four years. It was also provided that of the 66 members of the Landsthing, 54 should be chosen by the communal bodies and these in turn should choose the remaining 12. The admission of members by privilege or by the nomination of the king was abolished.

DENT, CLINTON THOMAS. An English surgeon, died September, 1912. He was born in 1850 and was educated at Trinity College, Cambridge. He became one of the most eminent surgeons in England and was vice-president of the College of Surgeons, senior surgeon of St. Joseph's Hospital, and chief surgeon of the Metropolitan police force. He was, in addition, well known as a traveler and mountain climber. Among his published works are: *Explorations in the Caucasus; Above the Snow Line*, and many writings on Alpine and medical subjects in magazines.

DENTAL SCHOOLS. See UNIVERSITIES AND COLLEGES.

DE PAUW UNIVERSITY. An institution of higher learning at Greencastle, Ind., founded in 1837. The total enrollment in the autumn of 1912 was 1115. The faculty numbered 53. The most important event in the history of the university during the year was the resignation of President Francis J. McConnell, LL. D., as president of the university and the election of Rev. George Richmond Grose, D. D., as his successor. Dr. McConnell was elected bishop in the Methodist Episcopal Church. The university received a bequest of

$250,000 from Simeon Smith, of Bloomfield, Ind. The productive funds of the university at the end of the year 1911-12 amounted to $562,817, and the income for the year to $83,-972. The library contained 30,000 volumes.

DERAILMENTS. See RAILWAY ACCIDENTS.

DESCLAUZAS, MARIE. A French actress, died in April, 1912. She was born in Paris in 1840. Her first appearance on the stage was made in Rheims, but she soon returned to Paris and her experience was, for the most part, identified with that city, except for a time spent in Russia, where she was very popular. She visited America and was successful in the operettas of Offenbach and Lecocq. She also played in Brussels, where she created the part of Mlle. Lange in *La fille de Madame Angot.* Among other plays in which she appeared with great success in Paris were *Sapho, L'Abbé Constantin*, and *Musotte.* In her later years she was a member of the Gymnase.

DESIGN, NATIONAL ACADEMY OF. See PAINTING.

DESPRADELLE, CONSTANT DÉSIRÉ. An American architect, died September 4, 1912. He was born in Burgoyne, France, in 1862, and graduated at the École des Beaux Arts in 1882. For several years following he studied architecture at that school. He won several important prizes in architectural composition and in 1890 was appointed architect *diplomé* of the French government. From 1889 to 1893 he was inspector of State buildings and national palaces in France. In the latter year he was appointed Rotch professor of architectural design at the Massachusetts Institute of Technology and at the same time became a member of the firm of Codman and Despradelle. He received one of the first five awards in the Phoebe A. Hearst competition for the University of California in 1899 and was given the first gold medal at the Salon in Paris for the design of a monument, "The Beacon of Progress," to glorify the American nation. Two of these drawings were purchased by the French government for the Luxembourg. In 1906 he was appointed consulting architect of the Museum of Fine Arts, in Boston. In 1910 he became corresponding member of the Institute of France, Académie des Beaux Arts. He was a member of many American and foreign architectural societies.

DESTROYERS. See NAVAL PROGRESS, *Great Britain, United States, Germany, General Progress.*

DETAILLE, JEAN BAPTISTE EDOUARD. A French painter, died December 24, 1912. He was born in Paris in 1848. He studied painting under Meissonier and his earlier works reflected the influence of that master. He secured a medal in 1869 with a painting called "Repose During Drill in Camp St. Maur." He took part in the Franco-Prussian War and during its progress made sketches of scenes incident to camp and campaign life. In 1877 he exhibited the famous picture "Salute to the Wounded." Another well-known canvas is "Movement of Troops." "The Passing Regiment," painted in 1875, is familiar through reproductions. This is the property of the Corcoran Art Gallery in Washington. In the Metropolitan Museum in New York are three of his works, including "The Defense of Campaigny." This was considered by the artist his best work. The Vanderbilt collection in New York has also three of his paintings. He was a chevalier of the Legion of Honor.

DETROIT. See MICHIGAN.

DEWITT, DAVID MILLER. An American public official, formerly member of Congress from New York, died June 24, 1912. He was born in Paterson, N. J., in 1837, and graduated from Rutgers College in 1858. In the same year he was admitted to the bar. From 1862 to 1868 he was district-attorney of Ulster county, N. Y. In 1873 he was elected to the 43d Congress, serving one term. He was a member of the New York Assembly in 1883, and in 1885-6 served as surrogate of Ulster county. He was the author of *The Impeachment and Trial of Andrew Johnson* (1903), and *The Assassination of Abraham Lincoln and Its Expiation* (1909).

DIAMONDS. See METEOROLOGY; GEMS; and INTERNATIONAL METRIC CARAT.

DIAMONDS, ARTIFICIAL. See CHEMISTRY, INDUSTRIAL.

DIAZ, FELIX. See MEXICO, *History.*

DICKENS, ALFRED TENNYSON. The oldest surviving son of Charles Dickens, died January 2, 1912. He was born in London in 1845 and attended school at Boulogne and afterwards in England. When he was 20 years of age he went to Australia on the advice of his father and remained there for the greater period of his life. In 1909 he delivered a lecture in Australia on reminiscences of his father and later repeated this lecture in England, and in 1911 came to the United States for the purpose of giving lectures in various cities. Ill health compelled him to shorten his tour and he died suddenly in New York City.

DICK PATENT CASE. See TRUSTS.

DICTOGRAPH. This instrument during 1912 figured in many criminal trials, notably that of the McNamara brothers (q. v.), and was responsible for convictions in a number of cases. The instrument consists of the adoption of an ordinary telephone circuit with a sensitive granular carbon transmitter with a diaphragm somewhat greater than usually employed, so as to increase the reproduction of the sound at the receiving end of the line. Such a transmitter, small and inconspicuous, would be placed in the room where suspected persons would hold conferences or conversations and wires were led to a recording station, where a stenographer recorded the spoken words for use of the authorities. In large auditoriums a number of transmitters were used to reproduce the sounds at different parts of the hall, and a similar device with a loud speaking telephone receiver was installed in the waiting rooms of various railway stations; likewise, in business offices the dictograph was being used in connection with a phonograph, where dictation could be recorded on a cylinder for subsequent transcription by a typist. The use of the dictograph has not involved many new principles, but there have been worked out practically a number of ideas that have led to the perfection of previous devices.

DIERX, LÉON. A French poet, died June, 1912. He was born on the island of Réunion in 1838. He studied at the Central School of Arts and Manufactures at Paris and then returned to his native island as engineer. He afterwards devoted himself to the study and writing of poetry. He was given a small office in the ministry of public instruction which enabled him to live. He joined a group of poets known as Parnassians, which included Coppée, Sully-Prudhomme, and others. In 1898 he was elected *Prince des poets* by the poets of the new generation. His published works include: *Poèmes et poésies* (1864); *Les Lèvres closes* (1867); *Poésies complètes* (1872), and the dramas, *La rencontre* (1875) and *Les Amants* (1879).

DIESEL ENGINE. See INTERNAL COMBUSTION MOTORS; FUEL OIL.

DIETETICS. See FOOD AND NUTRITION.

DIPHTHERIA. The persistence of the bacillus of diphtheria in the throats and noses of patients symptomatically recovered from an attack, as well as their frequent occurrence in well persons who have been in contact with diphtheria patients, is a serious drawback in the eradication of this disease. Such bacilli are as virulent as those found in the height of an attack and constitute a constant source of dissemination and an extremely difficult problem for the sanitarian. Antitoxin cures the disease clinically, but has little or no effect on the diphtheria carrier.

Hewlett and Nankivell studied the subject from every angle and concluded that of the current methods of dealing with carriers complete isolation has been most successful. Local and internal treatment were unsatisfactory. With a view of reaching the deeper tonsillar crypts not touched by local treatment, iodin was given until iodism resulted, but without success. As it had been found that with the disappearance of the diphtheria bacilli, an increase in the non-virulent organisms in the throat occurred, inoculation of the throat with such organisms was attempted in two cases, without result. The best results were obtained finally from the preparation of a vaccine from the *Bacillus diphtheriæ;* cultures of the bacteria were grown on serum or blood-agar; the growth was collected, washed repeatedly in normal salt solution and centrifuged; the bacteria were then ground in intense cold and passed through a Berkefeld filter. The resulting filtrate was diluted with sterile salt solution. Of five diphtheria patients injected with this vaccine while a membrane was still in the throat, four showed no bacilli after two weeks and one showed none after a month. In thirteen chronic carriers injections of the vaccine were followed by disappearance of the bacteria in a comparatively short time. In six patients the bacteria failed to disappear altogether. During the course of the investigation Hewlett and Nankivell found that scarlet fever patients who at the same time harbor the diphtheria bacillus are likely to become carriers, while those with diphtheria subsequently becoming infected with scarlet fever do not become carriers. Another investigator, Petruschky, used injections of bacteria killed with chloroform and washed. He was successful with seven chronic diphtheria carriers and was able to establish active immunity by the injection of 0.1 c. c. of a suspension of dead bacteria, followed four or five days later by the same quantity of a suspension ten times stronger. He emphasizes that such injections may be given for protective purposes, including the immunization of chronic carriers and school children carrying diphtheria bacilli in their throats.

DIRECT ELECTION OF SENATORS. See ELECTORAL REFORM.

DIRECT PRIMARIES. See ELECTORAL REFORM.

DIRIGIBLE BALLOONS. See AERONAUTICS.

DISEASES, INDUSTRIAL. See LABOR LEGISLATION.

DISEASES, OCCUPATIONAL. See OCCUPATIONAL DISEASES.

DISTILLED SPIRITS. See LIQUORS.

DISTRIBUTION OF ADMIRALTY BUSINESS. See NAVAL PROGRESS, *Great Britain, General Progress.*

DISTRIBUTION OF FARM PRODUCTS. See AGRICULTURE.

DISTRICT OF COLUMBIA. See UNITED STATES.

DIVERS, EDWARD. An English chemist and educator, died April 8, 1912. He was born in London in 1837 and was educated at the Royal College of Chemistry and at Queen's College, Galway, Ireland. In 1870 he was lecturer on medical jurisprudence in the Middlesex Hospital Medical School. He was appointed professor of chemistry in the Imperial College of Engineering in Japan in 1873 and in 1882 was chosen principal of this institution. In 1902 he was vice-president of the Chemical Society and in the latter year was president of the Chemical Section of the British Association. He was president of the Society of Chemical Industry in 1905. He published many memoirs on chemical subjects.

DIVORCE. Ever since the publication of the report of the Bureau of Labor covering divorces in the United States from 1887 to 1906 and summarizing the statistics for 1867-1906, the discussion of the divorce problem has been extensive. That report showed that nearly one million divorces have been granted in twenty years; during the same period the annual number increased 160 per cent., while population increased only 50 per cent. In 1900 about 8 per cent. of all marriages were terminated by divorce, warranting the estimate that by 1912 at least 10 per cent. were thus terminated. The increasing rate is not confined to the United States, but is found in England, Germany, France, other European countries, Australia, and Japan. Contrary to popular notion, hasty marriage is not a chief cause; for marriages broken by divorces have more frequently than not lasted seven years. Moreover, desire to marry another is not often a cause. Divorce colonies, such as that at Reno, Nev., receive only a very small proportion of all those seeking divorces. While divorces arousing the greatest publicity are those of the well-to-do, the vast majority of divorces are among the middle and laboring classes. Although the ostensible grounds for 95 per cent. of all divorces are cruelty, drunkenness, infidelity, desertion, failure to support, and imprisonment for crime, it is not now generally believed by students of the problem that the increasing rate is an index of growing immorality. The foregoing six causes are only the legal grounds and do not indicate the true sociological conditions accounting for the phenomenon. Professor E. A. Ross in his *Changing America*, published early in the year, points out that divorce is a symptom of social conditions. It is caused primarily in his opinion by changes in the economic status of women, especially the removal of many household economic activities of former days into the factory. Women are less valuable partners in the home; and they are now more able to support themselves independently. Professor Ross concludes also that intellectual changes, especially the liberation of modern thought, the growth of the ideas of democracy and individual liberty, have been potent factors in increasing divorce. The remedy is to be found not in repressing and prohibition, but in education of youth for marriage and the cultivation of rational standards of individual responsibility for racial and social welfare.

ENGLAND. The most important event of the year on the subject of divorce was the report of the Royal Commission on Divorce and Matrimonial Causes. This commission consisted of twelve distinguished persons, including two women, and spent three years in its investigations. The development of the law of divorce in England has not kept pace with that of other western nations. Previous to 1857 for more than 250 years the only manner of divorce was by act of Parliament. In that year a law established a civil court sitting at London for the hearing of divorce cases for England and Wales. As previously, however, the expenses were still prohibitive for all but fairly well-to-do persons. As to the legal basis for divorce the law recognized only the so-called scriptural ground, adultery. Moreover the sex line was drawn, a double standard of morality being maintained. It was no doubt the excessive expenses of divorce proceedings that explains the very low divorce rate which has existed in England. Counting both separations and divorces the total has been less than one per cent. of all marriages, a rate found only in Austria, Canada, Italy, and Scotland. It is contended that a low divorce rate is no guarantee of high sexual morality; it is believed that easier divorce will even improve morals by greatly lessening bigamy and adultery; and it will have the very desirable result of terminating many unions that have proved intolerable. The objects therefore sought by the commission were an extension of the grounds for divorce, equalization of the legal privileges of the sexes, and a lessening of the expenses involved in divorce proceedings in order to bring legal relief within the reach of the poorer classes.

The report, submitted in November, revealed a division of opinion. The majority of the commission, nine in number, including the chairman, Lord Gorell, and the two women members, recommended extensive changes in the law designed to make divorce much easier. They would place the two sexes on a basis of legal equality as regards the grounds for divorce, these grounds to include adultery, desertion for at least three years, cruelty, incurable insanity after five years' confinement, habitual drunkenness found to be incurable after three years, and imprisonment under a commuted death sentence. They recommended that divorce cases be heard by a judge alone, that is, without jury, he being authorized also to close court and prohibit publication of details. They would increase facilities for hearing cases of poor people through the country, rather than in London alone, as at present. Moreover, they recommended that no report on divorce cases be allowed until the case is completed and that the publication of the portraits of the parties involved be forbidden. It was the opinion of the majority that the evidence accumulated by their investigation showed that an extension of the grounds for divorce would raise rather than lower the standard of morality; and that the present difficulties, legal and financial, of securing a divorce produced considerable sexual immorality, especially among the poor. The minority report, signed by the Archbishop of York and two others, declared that only adultery constituted a sufficient ground for divorce. It did, however, favor equality of legal rights for both sexes. It favored local divorce courts, but not on the scale recommended in the majority report. Both majority and minority agreed in recommending that laws be enacted making possible the nullification of marriage in cases of unsound mind, of epilepsy and recurrent insanity, of venereal disease in communicable form, when a woman is in a condition that renders marriage a fraud upon the husband, or of willful refusal to perform the duties of marriage.

The line of division between the majority and minority as to the grounds for divorce was due to different attitudes toward the marriage contract. The minority took the position that marriage is sacramental in character and is essentially indissoluble, and therefore it recognized only that ground for divorce having New Testament sanction. The majority, however, proceeded on the assumption that marriage is a legal bond and that the state may rightly allow other grave causes than adultery for its dissolution. It held that the existing device of legal separation on grounds of cruelty, willful desertion, and drunkenness puts an end *de facto* to married life. Moreover, mere separation is unnatural, leads to evil consequences, and is inadequate in those cases where continued married life has become practically impossible.

It seems certain that, should the recommendations of the majority become law, the divorce rate in England and Wales would increase for a time.

DIXON, J. M. See PRESIDENTIAL CAMPAIGN.

DOBSON, AUSTIN. See LITERATURE, ENGLISH AND AMERICAN.

DOCKS AND HARBORS. The problem of providing proper pier facilities for the commerce of New York was agitated during the year and attracted the attention of municipal authorities and commercial bodies. The War Department, whose engineers are charged with the maintenance of the river channels, expressed its unwillingness to permit further encroachments on the fairway by the lengthening of existing piers, and was not disposed to give assurances that the present temporary extensions would be made permanent. The demands of commerce required piers over 1000 feet in length to accommodate such ships as the Hamburg-American line and the Cunard Company were building, while the proper and economic distribution of the commerce of the port also needed attention. It was proposed that the pier-head line from the Battery to Pier 30 should be straightened and accommodations be made for twenty piers from 950 to 1040 feet in length, and that in the future piers constructed above this point should extend to the pier-head line, and if greater length was required they should be excavated from the land. Various schemes were proposed for freight railways connecting the piers and for the development of the South Brooklyn wharves, but despite much valuable and constructive planning little of a positive nature was actually accomplished.

AMBROSE CHANNEL. To June 30, 1912, $5,080,237.68 had been expended in building four dredges and excavating 61,586,673 cubic yards of sand, mud, and concrete from the Ambrose Channel, New York harbor, which at the end of the fiscal year was about 96 per cent. completed. This channel has a depth of 40 feet at mean low water, with widths of from 1850 to 2000 feet throughout its entire length, excepting a few shoal spots where soundings show occasional depths of between 39 and 40 feet. It is easily navigable at mean low tides for ships of 37 feet draught going at moderate speed, and has a maximum high water capacity of 44 feet. This channel was completely buoyed and lighted so that the largest vessels could enter it at all hours of the night, some steamers even making the passage in heavy fog. This channel had been restricted during its construction to the use of vessels of 29 feet draught or over, or of 600 feet length or over, but in 1909 regulations were issued permitting its use by day or night by all steamers not having tows, regardless of size. The necessity for some permanent restriction was suggested, owing to the fact that tows, sailing vessels, or craft not under complete control would interfere with the safe and legitimate use of the channel by the vessels for which it was intended primarily.

PORT OF BOSTON. In 1911 the Massachusetts State legislature passed a bill appropriating $25,000,000 for the development of the port of Boston and a board of port directors was appointed. The first improvement was the remodeling of the commonwealth docks in the heart of the city at an expense of $2,500,000, to accommodate the passenger service established by the Hamburg-American steamship line with Europe, which was to be put in operation early in 1913. It was also proposed to build a large dry dock capable of accommodating transatlantic steamers of great size, and developing the port according to a consistent scheme in which communication with the railways was to be an important feature. On December 24 an appropriation of $3,000,000 was made for this purpose by the port directors, and a dry dock 1180 feet long, 175 feet wide, founded on a ledge of solid rock which is about 1300 feet in length and varies in width from 200 to 500 feet, will be built. This ledge previously has been a permanent obstacle in the way of desired pier extension, but will be particularly useful in connection with the new dry dock. This new dock will afford accommodations for the largest vessels, which the dredging of the channel and the construction of new piers make it possible to accommodate in the course of the improvement.

PORT OF LONDON. Work was begun during the year on the new dock adjoining the Victoria and Albert dock, which was the first portion of the extensive scheme of improvement to be taken up. The area of the dock was to be 65 acres, with a depth of 35 feet. The lock was to be 850 feet in length and 120 feet in width, with a depth of 45 feet over the sill at high water. The amount of the contract was $7,000,000. A graving, or dry dock, 1000 feet in length and 110 feet in width, was also a feature of this improvement. At Tilbury a contract was let for a jetty 1000 feet long and 50 feet in width, to be connected with the dock system of railways and equipped with the most modern type of cranes and appliances for handling cargo. This arrangement will afford two docks which together will cover an area of 50,000 square feet and will be used by vessels discharging part of their cargo either into barges or railway cars without entering the dock. Progress was made in dredging the channel of the Thames, and five large dredges with 21 steam hoppers of from 500 to 1000 cubic yards capacity and a suction dredger were at work, while a careful survey and examination of this work was being made by the engineering staff. The aim was to secure a 30-foot channel at low water as far as Albert dock.

LIVERPOOL. Work was in progress during the year on the great Gladstone dock, 1020 feet long, or 137 feet longer than the *Olympic*, with an entrance 120 feet in width and a depth of 35 feet of water at the lowest high-water tide. This dock was being built with a vestibule, or half-tide dock, of 14¾ acres, which was to form access also to a second dock capable of accommodating vessels 1100 feet in length, construction of which was contemplated some time in the future. The entrance to this vestibule was to be 870 feet in length, with a sill 30 feet below old dock sill. To maintain a deep-water entrance from the sea, the Mersey requires continual dredging, and in 1912 some 18½ million tons of material were excavated. Various engineering works were in progress and in general the improvement of the port has been successful, the stone revetment on Taylor's Bank seeming to serve satisfactorily.

DOVER. The new sea wall, extending from the shore to the turret at the east end of the old Admiralty pier, and the reclamation of the foreshore between this wall and the existing pier, a length of 2300 feet, and 30 feet in width at its greatest part, was completed during the year. On the area thus reclaimed a new marine railway station will be built, with foundations of reinforced concrete piles driven through the newly deposited material to the solid chalk of the bed of the sea. The new station will afford accommodations for railway, custom house, and post office, and four lines of railway, with electric cranes for the speedy removal of baggage and freight to and from the railway cars and the boats. The Admiralty naval basin was found to be lacking in safety, owing to the strong currents that run through it and the great swell that is experienced in rough weather. This basin, which cost some $17,000,000, requires extensive dredging on account of the sand and mud brought in by the tide.

THE HUMBER. The large Immingham dock of the Great Central Railway Company was opened during the year on the south side of the Humber, about six miles above its mouth. This dock was built to develop the export of coal from Derbyshire and Yorkshire and the mines in central England, and had an equipment of electric hoists capable of delivering into vessels 400 tons an hour. There was storage room for 100,000 tons of coal and 100 miles of siding. This dock also was designed for the importation of timber and general merchandise and has a water area of 55½ acres. The lock itself is 840 feet long, 90 feet wide, and 28 feet at low water on the sill and 48 feet at high water. A central pair of gates divide it into two compartments and there are two jetties at the entrance approach which extend 650 feet. One of these will be used for passengers and the other for coal vessels that do not require to enter the dock. A graving dock 750 feet in length, 56 feet wide, and 27 feet over the sill was built adjacent to the dock entrance. Other docks and piers were being constructed on the river, which was to receive improvement in the way of dredging.

ROSYTH. Less progress than was to be expected was made on the new naval dock and harbor in 1912.

BELGIUM. The improvement of the harbors along the coast was being actively undertaken by the Belgian Department of Public Works during the year, and new projects were determined on. At Zeebrugge the jetty was to be prolonged a distance of 1½ miles towards Ostend by reinforced concrete construction. A dock for the use of steam trawlers was also being constructed at a cost of $50,000, and at Blankenberghe various improvements were to be undertaken. At La Panne a new fishery port was to be built. To maintain the channels to the port of Ostend an annual appropriation of about $400,000, apart from new works, is required.

ANTWERP. A commission to consider the improvement of the Scheldt, with special reference to the construction of a new cut six miles in length across a sharp bend in the river below the city, published its report early in 1912. The commission advises that the cut, known as the Grande Coupure scheme, be discarded and that the river channel should be rectified by reducing to normal and easy curves the more tortuous parts, and also by construction of a lock at Kruisschaus, which would afford access to a long channel 400 feet in width, after which a series of docks would be constructed. The estimated cost of this work was between $8,000,000 and $9,000,000.

UNITED STATES NAVAL DRY DOCKS. Dry dock No. 4, at New York, after various vicissitudes of construction since 1905, was finally completed and officially accepted during the year. The final contract provided for a dry dock with a length of 694 ft. 6 in. from coping at head to caisson when in outer gate seat, a width at elevation on top of keel blocks of 112 feet, and a depth over the sill at mean high water of 35 feet. In building this dock reinforced concrete carried on pneumatic caisson piers similar to those used for the foundations of high buildings was employed. This dock was able to accommodate the largest battleships in the United States navy or contemplated. Work also progressed during the year on the Puget Sound dock, which was to have a length of 827 ft. 6 in. and a width of 110 feet at the keel blocks, corresponding to that of the locks of the Panama Canal. It was virtually completed at the end of the year. Progress on the Pearl Harbor dry dock at Honolulu, under construction for the United States Navy Department, was delayed both on account of the changes in plan to accommodate vessels up to 1000 feet in length, the limit of the Panama Canal locks, and on account of the difficulty in using the coral rock as a foundation for the structure. This coral work, which when mixed with the cement is the aggregate for the concrete and the walls, did not produce a mixture sufficiently strong. Hence a large amount of aggregate was required from the Pacific coast of the United States.

The size and distribution of docks was a matter that was intimately connected with the construction of large battleships. The docks under construction at Pearl Harbor, and the Puget Sound and the New York dock, while large enough to dock ships of 800 and 600 feet in length, respectively, were so far apart that the question of injuries to large battleships away from their immediate vicinity presented many difficulties; in fact, these three docks and the one at Norfolk were the only ones capable of accommodating the larger battleships in the United States navy, and two 1000-foot docks, one on the Atlantic and one on the Pacific coast, were recommended by the Secretary of the Navy in his report.

At the end of the year the Seattle Construction and Dry Dock Company was completing its new floating dry dock, with a lifting capacity of 12,000 tons. The new dock was 468 feet long, 110 feet wide over all, and 85 feet wide between towers. The dock was to be placed in a basin dredged to a depth of 50 feet at low tide, and affording ample facilities for the largest class of vessels entering port.

A new floating dock for the use of the British admiralty at Portsmouth was constructed during the year by Cammell, Laird & Co. of Birkenhead, and was successfully floated on August 14. The over-all dimensions of this dock are 650 feet in length and 144 feet in width, with a clear width at the top of the side towers of 113 feet. The side towers are 60 feet high from the bottom of the pontoon. The total displacement when submerged to take in a ship of 36 feet draught is 49,000 tons. This great dock was two years in building and has a capacity for vessels up to 32,000 tons. It has a complete equipment, including power plant, machine shops, traveling cranes, flying gangways, telephone, and other facilities. On September 3 in the Medway the first-class battleship *St. Vincent*, of 19,250 tons displacement, was successfully docked. On October 2 the large battle cruiser *Lion*, of 26,350 tons displacement, was successfully raised from a draught of 31 feet 6 inches.

A dock of almost similar construction was built for the Chatham Dock Yard, and one hardly smaller for the Vickers Canadian Works at Montreal. English makers also made a dock of 5100 tons capacity for Largos, one of 37,500 tons for Sourabaya, and a dock of 1500 tons capacity for the British admiralty for lifting submarines.

For municipal ownership of docks, see MUNICIPAL GOVERNMENT.

DOCK WORKERS' STRIKE. See STRIKES.

DOMINICA. A presidency of the Leeward Islands (q. v.). Most of the inhabitants are descendants of the original French settlers and speak a *patois*. Roseau, the capital, had (1911) 6577 inhabitants. The island is fertile; coffee, sugar, spices, oils, timber, fruits, etc., are exported.

Customs revenue (1910-11), £22,441; debt, £47,295. Administrator (1912), W. Douglas Young.

	1907-8	1908-9	1909-10	1910-11
Imports.	£121,650	£153,114	£128,779	£147,322
Exports.	124,294	112,013	102,339	112,111
Revenue	39,865	41,147	39,521	42,133
Expenditure..	31,486	37,178	41,860	39,603
Shipping* ...	508,631	746,640	713,227	694,985

* Tonnage entered and cleared.

DOMINICAN REPUBLIC, or SANTO DOMINGO. An independent state occupying the eastern part of the island of Haiti. Capital, Santo Domingo.

AREA AND POPULATION. The estimated area is 18,756 square miles. The population, mostly of mixed Spanish and negro origin, is about 675,000, according to an official estimate published in 1912. For 1910 there are reported 3594 marriages, 28,235 births, and 6576 deaths. Principal towns: Santo Domingo, with about 20,000 inhabitants; Puerto Plata, 17,500; Macorís, 15,000; Santiago, 12,000. Public schools in 1910 numbered 526, with 18,812 pupils.

PRODUCTION AND COMMERCE. The leading crops include sugar, cacao, tobacco, coffee, and bananas. Statistics of production are not published. There is a considerable output of honey, and cattle-raising is important. Mining is not developed.

Imports and exports have been valued as follows:

	1908	1909	1910	1911
Imports ..	$4,767,775	$4,425,913	$6,257,691	$6,949,662
Exports ..	9,398,487	8,113,690	10,849,623	11,004,906

Leading imports, in thousands of dollars, in 1910 and 1811: Cotton manufactures, 1481 and 1617; iron and steel, 863 and 998; rice, 497 and 540; meat and dairy products, 416 and 415; wheat flour, 411 and 407; oils, 338 and 321. Principal exports: Raw sugar, 5591 and 4160; cacao, 2850 and 3902; leaf tobacco, 958 and 1421; coffee, 324 and 319; bananas, 289 and 195; beeswax, 149 and 165; cattle hides, 124 and 104; drug and dye materials, 81 and 102. Trade with principal countries, in thousands of dollars:

	Imports		Exports	
	1910	1911	1910	1911
United States	3,739	4,120	7,661	5,761
Germany	1,087	1,266	2,094	2,947
United Kingdom	715	776	142	764
France	210	213	724	1,081
Spain	123	152	...	...
Italy	102	139	22	9
Other	202	282	206	445
Total	6,258	6,950	10,850	11,005

Entered at the ports in the foreign trade in 1911, 607 vessels, of 478,796 tons (333, of 446,151 steam), and cleared 573, of 420,746 (315, of 396,740 steam). Merchant marine, 11 sailing vessels, of 1541 tons.

COMMUNICATIONS. Puerto Plata is connected by rail with Santiago and Moca, and Sánchez with La Vega; a branch connects Macorís with Jina, and Salcedo with Cabullas. Length of railways, 282 kms. (175 miles); in addition, private lines for the larger sugar plantations, 362 kms. (225 miles). A line is projected to connect Santo Domingo with Cibao, 129 kms. (80 miles). Telegraphs, about 2300 kms., with over 50 offices. Post offices, 81.

FINANCE. Revenue and expenditure in 1910, $4,705,738 and $4,645,287. Customs receipts in 1910, $3,203,427; in 1911, $3,485,687. Of the latter amount, $3,162,729 was import duties, $225,455 export duties, and $97,502 fees, fines, etc. A treaty between the Dominican Republic and the United States authorized a loan of $20,000,000 for the conversion of the debt and established an American receivership of customs, from April 1, 1905. Obligations are met promptly.

GOVERNMENT. The president is elected by indirect vote for six years and is assisted by a cabinet of seven members. The legislative body consists of the Senate (12 members) and the Chamber of Deputies (24). Gen. Ramón Cáceres was installed in 1906 to complete his predecessor's term and was inaugurated for a full term July 1, 1908. He was shot and killed by an assassin November 19, 1911. On December 2 Eladio Victoria, a senator, was elected provisional president by the congress, and president February 2, 1912. He was inaugurated February 28. Political unrest was soon apparent. The new president was charged with being little more than the tool of the ambitious and aggressive minister of war, his nephew, Alfredo M. Victoria. Revolutionary outbreaks ensued, and late in November President Victoria resigned. The revolutionists demanded that Archbishop Adolfo Alejandro Nouel serve as provisional president until the constitution could be revised and general elections held. Accordingly, the archbishop was elected December 2, for two years, and early in the month he assumed the executive duties in the hope of restoring peace. See UNITED STATES, *Foreign Relations*.

DONNET-LEVEQUE. See NAVAL PROGRESS, *Aviation*.

DOVER, PORT OF. See DOCKS AND HARBORS.

DRAINAGE. UNITED STATES. The increasing activity in the development of land by drainage has continued through the year 1912, the greatest activity being in the South Atlantic States and the lower Mississippi Valley. The work is ordinarily done by drainage districts formed under the general laws of the States, sometimes by special legislative acts. Almost the entire area of wet lands has passed into private ownership, and that to which the United States still holds title is virtually held in trust for the States. The Federal government lends no financial aid in drainage work, save in the control of the Mississippi river and some of its main tributaries. The United States Department of Agriculture has a force of engineers investigating technical drainage problems, and frequently gives advisory assistance with respect to certain projects, occasionally conducting surveys and preparing the plans. The cost of the improvements is assessed against the land, generally in proportion to the benefits to be received.

Plans have been made for draining a number of districts in the Coastal Plain of Virginia, North and South Carolina, and Georgia, and the excavation of ditches has begun for several large districts on the borders of the Dismal Swamp and between Albemarle and Pamlico sounds. The largest single swamp area is the Everglades of Florida, sloping uniformly southward from Lake Okeechobee. The State is digging five canals intended to lower the level of the lake and prevent it from overflowing, which is one source of the inundation of that vast prairie. Along the Gulf Coast of Louisiana are more than 10,000 sq. m. of lands too low for gravity drainage. These are being reclaimed by individual enterprise, in tracts of several thousand acres. Dikes are built entirely surrounding each tract, a network of ditches is excavated, and machinery is installed to pump the seepage and rain water over the embankment. In Texas, a drainage survey has been completed of all Jefferson County, approximately 700,000 acres, and indications are that similar work will be done by adjacent counties. Construction work is in progress for two districts embracing several hundred thousand acres in southwest Missouri and northeast Arkansas, and plans have been completed for other large districts in Arkansas and Mississippi. In the spring of 1912 occurred the most severe flood that has been recorded for the Mississippi river, below the Ohio. The levees broke in several places, and some 8350 sq. m. were overflowed. However, had the levees been completed to the full height and cross-section planned (the work has progressed continuously), it is probable that the flood would have been confined between the embankments and there would have been no considerable loss of life and property. See MISSISSIPPI FLOODS.

The extension of the use of tile drains to improve the productiveness of farm lands already under cultivation, continues unabated. The greatest activity in this line is in Illinois, Indiana, Iowa, Minnesota, and Wisconsin. Underdrainage is quite rapidly coming to be practiced in New York, Maryland, and Kentucky, and to a less extent in Kansas, Mississippi, Alabama, Georgia, the Carolinas, and Virginia. The continued irrigation of lands in the arid region has developed the need for artificial drainage there. Natural drainage being deficient, the water applied in excess of that used by the vegetation and that directly evaporated, accumulates in the depressions of a relatively impervious substratum until the plane of saturation rises to the lower points of the ground surface, or it flows along upon the substratum until it reaches the surface at a lower elevation. To prevent the resultant swampy condition, deep drains are usually efficient to intercept the underflow, sometimes with wells down to a waterbearing stratum deeper than it is economical to place the drains.

EGYPT. Work was begun in 1912 on the project to drain 950,000 feddans (978,500 acres) in the delta of Lower Egypt, at a cost estimated at $12,500,000. The work is being done by the Egyptian government, which owns 90 per cent. of the land, and will be completed in four years. The project comprises two separate drainage systems, some miles apart, which will be built coincidentally. The West Behera system will drain 480,000 feddans, including Lake Mariout. About two-thirds of the whole area is classed as cultivated, but none is highly productive. The lake covers 35,000 feddans, is 1 meter deep, and its surface is 3 meters below sea level. The drainage pumps will hold the ground water about 5.6 meters below sea level. The Gharbid system will drain 470,000 feddans, half of which now produces rice; the balance yields nothing. The drainage water will be pumped into Lake Borollos. In both systems the ditches will be 6 meters deep, and the water will be maintained 5 feet below the land surface. No plot of ground will be more than 1¼ miles from a drain owned and maintained by the government. This project, in importance to Egypt, is second only to the Assuan Dam. Egypt's prosperity is almost entirely dependent upon the cotton crop, and it is estimated that upon the completion of this drainage project the cotton yield will be increased 50 per cent. over that for 1911. Moreover, cotton is raised only every second year, alternating with wheat or maize, so it is probable Egypt will soon produce enough cereals for her needs instead of importing 200,000 tons of wheat yearly, as now. As an experiment, about 600 feddans of the drained land have been given in 5-feddan lots to landless peasants. For 3 years the holders will have the land practically free, doing reclamation work; during the next 10 years they will pay a moderate rental; then they will have title to the land for life, and it will descend in the family if the government approves. See DAMS.

OTHER COUNTRIES. In India there has begun the dredging of the Jhelum River between Sopar and the Baramulla rapids, using hydroelectric power developed for the railway projected to be built into the Kashmir Valley. The surface of Woolar Lake is to be lowered 10 feet, thereby reclaiming 55,000 acres of swamp land and reducing the severity of floods at Srinagar. Dipper dredges removing the packed boulders forming the bed of the rapids have met with difficulty and work there is held in abeyance, but suction dredges are working in the channel above the rapids. Authoritative opinion holds there is no danger of reducing the winter supply of water for the irrigation canals now under construction, which would seriously affect the great wheat-growing districts of the Punjab. Russia plans to reclaim by pumping 378 acres on the Caspian Sea near Baku, for drilling oil wells. This land has been sold for $5700 per acre. If this is successful, 700 acres more will be similarly reclaimed. In Cuba, 200 square leagues known as Cienega de Zapata have been granted to a company, with the obligation to sanitate and reclaim the land in 8 years. Activity in drainage continues in Norway, Germany, and the Netherlands, and is developing in Algeria, China, and Australia.

DRAMA. The theatre season of 1912, in both America and England, was made notable mainly by two movements which were diametrically opposed to each other in purpose and in method. One of these movements was romantic and the other realistic.

The romantic movement expressed itself in several plays which were localized in the fabulous and eye-enchanting East. The appearance of these plays cannot be taken as an evidence of any active interest in the actual life of the Orient; it was an evidence, rather, of a desire to escape the tyranny of fact by seeking the unusual and the remote. These plays laid their emphasis on plot instead of character, and told their stories mainly to the eye. The first of these pieces to captivate both London and New York was *Kismet*, by Edward Knoblauch. It was a picturesque romance set in the fabled Bagdad of one thousand and one years ago, and dealt with the multifarious adventures of the beggar Hajj upon his day of days. Action was the dominant note of this hurrying and many-mooded narrative; there was never any lull in the luxuriance of incident; and the story was illustrated by a sumptuous investiture of scenic decoration which delighted the eye and drenched the mind with all the glamour of the gorgeous East. But even more artistic was the pantomime called *Sumurun*, which was produced by Max Reinhardt of Berlin and imported successively to London and New York. *Kismet* was pictorial in its appeal, but *Sumurûn* carried still further the conception of the modern drama as an art that is mainly visual instead of auditory, for it was imagined as a bit of decoration. Divested of dialogue, the Reinhardt pantomime could not attempt to set forth a "criticism of life," instead, it exhibited to the eye a continuously seductive pattern of lines and colors, forms and shadows, while the ear was allured by incidental music. The scenery was very simple: the backgrounds were devoid of perspective lines and were rendered in monochrome, so that they stopped the eye and flung into vivid relief the costumes of the actors. The pantomime told a savage story reminiscent of the *Arabian Nights*.

Later in the year, the locus of the romantic drama was moved still further eastward, from Arabia to China. An ancient Chinese drama entitled *The Flower of the Palace of Han*, which was written between 1260 and 1368 A. D., by Ma Tchen-Yuen, was presented in New York, and proved mildly interesting as a curiosity. The Century Theatre production of *The Daughter of Heaven*, a panoramic play of modern China, by Pierre Loti and Judith Gautier, adapted into English by George Egerton, was a disappointment as a work of art and must be noted as the most colossal failure of the year. The piece was not at all dramatic, and, in the English version was lacking even in literary merit. It was lavishly produced, but the sumptuous scenery served more as an incumbrance to the story than as an illustration of it. Finer, from the artistic standpoint, was *The Yellow Jacket*, by J. Harry Benrimo and George C. Hazleton, Jr. This was an imaginary Chinese play acted in accordance with the traditional conventions of the Chinese theatre. Considerable humor was evoked by a tactful exhibition of the crudities of the Chinese method of handling the stage, which is almost identical with the method of our own Elizabethan dramatists; and the piece itself was charmingly poetic. As an æsthetic adventure, *The Yellow Jacket* was one of the very finest achievements of the year.

Closely related to these fantastic Oriental dramas were two other plays which emphasized the contrast at the present day between the life of the Orient and the life of the Occident. *The Bird of Paradise*, by Richard Walton Tully, was set in the Hawaiian Islands. A drunken beach-comber was dragged upward to civilization by marrying an American girl, and a promising young American physician was dragged downward to savagery by marrying a native princess. *The Typhoon*, a melodrama of the Sardou type, written by a Hungarian playwright, Menyhert Lengyel, was adapted into English by Emil Nyitray and Byron Ongley. A Japanese student in Berlin, who is engaged upon a secret mission for his country, kills a German woman, who has been his mistress. In order that the hero may fulfill his mission, his fellow-countrymen in Berlin depute another and less important member of the student colony to assume the guilt of the murder and take the consequences.

The other notable dramatic movement of the year was, as has been stated, a realistic movement. It expressed itself emphatically in a very remarkable group of British plays, nearly all of which were written by authors formerly unknown. These plays were sedulously localized in actuality. The authors laid their emphasis on character instead of plot; and, eschewing the adventitious aid of pictorial appeal, they addressed their message to the ear, through the literary medium of dialogue. The greatest of these plays was *The Pigeon*, by John Galsworthy. It offered a sympathetic exhibition of the social status of the despised and rejected of this world and discussed the delicate problem of organized charity. Like all of this author's dramas, *The Pigeon* was deliberately inconclusive; it asked questions, but forbore to answer them. In *The New Sin*, by Basil MacDonald Hastings, the hero is so situated that he can accomplish nothing by continuing to live, but can confer a material benefit upon a dozen of his fellow beings by merely ceasing to exist; and the play propounds a tensely interesting struggle between his theoretical right to live and his practical duty to die. *Hindle Wakes*, which was written in the Lancashire dialect by Stanley Houghton, exhibits the effect on several selected characters of a single incident that is assumed to have happened before the play begins. A working girl and the son of her employer have gone away together over the mid-August holidays. Their escapade is discovered by their parents, and by the young man's fiancée and her father. These people force the young man to agree to marry the girl whom he has wronged; but in the final scene the girl refuses him, on the ground that she does not love him, and that she herself is just as responsible as he for what has happened. *Rutherford & Son*, by Githa Lowerby, is a sturdy exhibition of the power of one man of extraordinary strength and narrowness of mind to crush the life-spirit out of every one who comes in contact with him. This uneventful but impressive drama is set in the living-room of a Northumbrian family; and the dialogue is written in the North Country dialect. Somewhat analogous to these plays is *A Scrape o' the Pen*, a scarcely successful attempt by Graham Moffat to repeat the impression that he made the year before with *Bunty Pulls the Strings*.

Of plays contributed during the year by the acknowledged leaders of the British drama, the palm must be accorded to *Fanny's First Play*, by George Bernard Shaw. This brilliantly witty composition illustrates the theme that the so-called "principles" of ordinary people are merely habits of the mind and will be powerless to aid them to cope with a novel situation. The play itself is enclosed within a prologue and an epilogue in which the author satirizes four of the best-known dramatic critics of London. Two plays by Sir Arthur Pinero were produced in 1912; but neither of them approached the lofty standard which has been set by this playwright in the past. *Preserving Mr. Panmure* was remarkable mainly for the technical skill with which the author toyed with a theme that in itself was trivial. *The Mind-the-Paint Girl* was a more important composition. It discussed the advantages and disadvantages of those marriages which have frequently occurred in recent years between London show-girls and young scions of the peerage. It was designed as a *genre* study of the conditions of life in and about a typical musical-comedy theatre. It was admirably written; but only one of its four acts attained the tensity of drama. *Lady Patricia*, by Rudolf Besier, was also a little disappointing. It was a fanciful satire of pre-Raphaelite affectation. The dialogue was written with literary skill; but the drama was too thin in substance and too symmetrical in structure. Alfred Sutro contributed *The Perplexed Husband*, an entertaining satire of the woman-suffrage movement. *Milestones*, which was written by Arnold Bennett in collaboration with Edward Knoblauch, was one of the most successful plays of the London season and was only a little less successful in New York. It owed its popularity to its unique idea. All three acts were set in the same room; but the first act was dated 1860, the second 1885, and the third 1912. The story followed the fortunes of two families through three successive generations, and showed how in every generation there had been a struggle between the radicalism of youth and the conservatism of age.

Of continental playwrights who were represented on the New York stage in 1912 the most important were August Strindberg, Maurice Donnay, Edmond Rostand, Henry Bernstein, and Arthur Schnitzler. Mme. Simone produced, in English, *The Return from Jerusalem* of Donnay and *The Lady of Dreams* (*La Princesse Lointaine*) of Rostand, both of which had been noted for many years in France. Strindberg's *The Father* was the first of his plays to be produced professionally in America, and it created a profound impression, in spite of the morbid horror of its study of incipient insanity. *The Attack* (*L'Assaut*) of Bernstein was constructed in accordance with his usual formula and was replete with moments of suspense and of surprise; but the material was less vital than that of his previous plays. Schnitzler's clever series of dialogues entitled *Anatol* may be recorded as the season's portion of "caviare to the general."

Turning to plays of American authorship, it must be noted that very little work of genuine importance was accomplished in 1912 by the recognized American playwrights. The best American play of the year was *Kindling*, by a new author named Charles Kenyon. This was a profoundly sincere and sympathetic study of the emotions of the desperate poor, and was significant, not merely as a play, but also as a social document. The heroine was a poor woman condemned to live in an insanitary tenement who stole a hundred dollars in order to escape to a homestead in Wyoming so that her unborn child might have a better chance to live. The play experienced a commercial failure when it was presented in New York; but it was immediately resurrected by a disinterested group of authors who had been impressed by its merits, and was subsequently played for over forty weeks upon the road. Augustus Thomas, the acknowledged leader of the American dramatists, produced two disappointing pieces during the course of the year. These were entitled *The Model* and *Mere Man*. Both of them suffered from the fact that the author discussed too many unrelated themes during the course of the dialogue. *The Talker*, by Marion Fairfax, exhibited the harm that may be wrought by so-called "advanced" ideas upon the minds of idle women who are lacking in culture. A. E. Thomas contributed an ingratiating sentimental comedy called *The Rainbow*, which told very prettily the story of a father's love for his seventeen-year-old daughter, from whom he had been separated since her babyhood. *A Rich Man's Son*, by James Forbes, was less humorous and human than his former efforts. Edward Sheldon, however, showed an advance in *The High Road*, which exhibited for the first time an endeavor to look at life in the large and to draw a complete portrait of a character; but the piece, though admirable in material, was straggling in structure. George M. Cohan came forward with a brisk comedy entitled *Broadway Jones*, wherein a young man whose character has been all but ruined by the fast life of New York is made an estimable citizen by the simple process of settling down in the little country town where he was born. The Cohan touch was also evident in the American revision of *Hawthorne of the U. S. A.*, a romantic farce originally written by the London playwright, James Bernard Fagan. In this piece a young American adventurer averts a revolution in the Balkans by buying off the insurgent soldiers with money he has won at Monte Carlo, and ultimately marries the princess of the little state that he has saved.

Among the American farces of the year may be mentioned *Ready Money*, by James Montgomery, *Officer 666* by Augustin MacHugh, *Never Say Die*, by William Collier and W. H. Post, and *Stop Thief*, by Carlyle Moore. The first two were transferred successfully from New York to London. Of these the best is *Ready Money*. The theme of this piece is that anyone may easily make money if people think that he already has it; and the hero, who is utterly without resources, successfully floats a mining venture by the expedient of flashing a roll of counterfeit bank notes before the eyes of prospective investors.

The most exciting melodrama of the season was *Within the Law*, by Bayard Veiller. A shopgirl who has been wrongfully convicted of robbery and sent to jail, resolves after her release to be revenged on her prosecutors. She organizes a gang of criminals and cleverly handles them so that their depredations are kept always within the letter of the law. The drama deals with the efforts of the police to undermine her campaign by tempting one of her gang to an overt violation of the statutes. This piece was deficient in characterization, but it was admirably plotted. Its overwhelming success soon led to the production of several other melodramas dealing with criminals and detectives and police. Of these the most interesting were *The Argyle Case* by Harriet Ford and Harvey J. O'Higgins, and *The Conspiracy*, by John Emerson and Robert Baker.

David Belasco made three productions during the course of the year. Once again he demonstrated his superlative ability to lend an air of verisimilitude to compositions which in themselves were artificial. *The Governor's Lady*, by Alice Bradley, told a sentimental story of an ambitious man who put aside his faithful wife of many years in order that he might be free to marry a younger woman who could help him in his climbing. In the last act the man and his wife met by accident in a Childs restaurant and were reconciled. The act was utterly untrue to nature, but it allowed Mr. Belasco an opportunity to set a restaurant upon the stage. *The Case of Becky*, by Edward Locke, was a melodrama built upon the theme of dual personality. The heroine, who was normally a charming girl, suffered frequently from lapses to a secondary personality,—that of an impish hoyden,—but was eventually cured by means of hypnotism. *Years of Discretion*, by Frederic Hatton and Fanny Locke Hatton, was a conventional comedy that was lifted into life by exquisite acting and careful stage direction.

Several new theatres were opened in New York during the course of the year, but the only one that need be noted as inaugurating a new policy is The Little Theatre, which was erected by Mr. Winthrop Ames. This house seats only 299 people, and it is the policy of the manager to offer intimate productions of unusual works of art for the benefit of the tasteful few. The edifice itself is a gem of architecture and is easily the most beautiful playhouse in America. To Mr. Ames belongs the credit of having produced at this theatre such admirable works as *The Pigeon* and *Rutherford & Son*. He was also the first manager to put into practice the idea of a children's theatre, by offering at daily matinées a dramatization of *Snow White and the Seven Dwarfs*, the famous fairy tale of the Brothers Grimm. Shortly afterward, George C. Tyler erected a cozy theatre for children on the roof of the Century Theatre, and followed Mr. Ames' policy of giving daily matinées. His first production was a little play by Mrs. Frances Hodgson Burnett entitled *Racketty-Packetty House*. Both of these pieces were enthusiastically welcomed; and the idea of a children's theatre seems at last to have become an established fact. See FRENCH LITERATURE; GERMAN LITERATURE, and LITERATURE, ENGLISH AND AMERICAN.

DREADNOUGHT. See BATTLESHIPS.

DREDGING. See DOCKS AND HARBORS, and PANAMA CANAL.

DRY DOCKS. See DOCKS AND HARBORS.

DUBLIN. See ARCHITECTURE.

DUFFIELD, HENRY MARTYN. American soldier and lawyer, died July 13, 1912. He was born in Detroit, Mich., in 1842, and graduated from Williams College in 1861. He enlisted as a private in the 9th Michigan Infantry in the same year and rose through the ranks of service until he became assistant and acting provost marshal-general of the Army of the Cumberland. In 1865 he was admitted to the bar and practiced law in Detroit. From 1881 to 1887 he was city counsellor of that city. He was appointed brigadier-general of volunteers in 1898 in the Spanish-American War. In 1903 he served as umpire of the German-Venezuelan Arbitration Commission. He was prominent in American politics and attended every national convention from 1876. He was a member of several military societies.

DULUTH. See MUNICIPAL GOVERNMENT, *Commission Plan.*

DULUTH COMMISSION PLAN. See MUNICIPAL GOVERNMENT.

DUNBAR, RALPH O. American jurist, died September 19, 1912. He was born in Schuyler county, Ill., in 1845. He removed with his parents to Oregon when he was one year of age. He was educated at Willamette University and in 1867 removed to Olympia, Wash. In 1869 he was admitted to the bar. He practiced at Yakima City for several years and then removed to Goldendale. In 1879 he was elected a member of the Territorial legislature and in 1885 was speaker of that body. He was appointed associate justice of the supreme court of the State in 1889 for the term expiring 1913.

DUNCAN, JOSEPH WILSON. An American soldier, died May 14, 1912. He was born in a tent in an army camp on the bank of the Nueces River, Texas, in 1853. He was educated in the public schools of Nashville, Tenn., and Columbian College (now George Washington University). He served for a time as an engineer of the geological survey of the Yellowstone, and in 1873 was appointed second lieutenant of the 21st Infantry. He went through the various stages of promotion until he became colonel in 1903. His services include participation in the Indian wars in 1877-78, and 1890-91. In the Spanish-American War he took part in the battle of San Juan Hill and in the siege of Santiago de Cuba. He served in the Philippines in 1899-1902 and in 1905-6. In 1906 he commanded the forces engaged in the so-called battle of the Lava Cone, in which he practically annihilated a body of rebellious Moros, after a severe fight in which over 100 Americans were killed. General Duncan was severely criticised because the women of the Moros were killed in the assault made by the American soldiers. It was claimed, however, that the women fought so viciously that they had to be treated as the men were. From 1907-11 General Duncan was a member of the general staff when he was sent to Texas to prevent filibustering along the Mexican border. He was several times brevetted for gallantry in action and was promoted to be brigadier-general for his services in the Philippines.

DUNCAN, WILLIAM BUTLER. An American capitalist, died June 20, 1912. He was born in Edinburgh, Scotland, in 1830, and while he was still a youth accompanied his father to the United States. The latter engaged in banking business in New York City. Mr. Duncan graduated from Brown University in 1860 and at once entered the business of banking. In 1865 he became head of the banking firm of Duncan, Sherman & Co., of New York City. Turning his attention to railroads he was from 1874 to 1878 president of the Mobile and Ohio Railroad Company. He was also connected at various times with important financial interests as officer and director, and he became one of the leading figures in the financial and social life of New York City. His collection of rare editions of books and autograph copies was a notable one. He was vice-president of the New York Chamber of Commerce and president of the Pilgrims of the United States, and of The Pilgrim Society of America. He was a member of the National Academy of Design, the Metropolitan Museum of Art, and the American Museum of Natural History.

DUTCH EAST INDIES. The colonial possessions of the Netherlands, lying between Australia and the Asiatic continent. Capital, Batavia.

AREA AND POPULATION. The Dutch East Indies consist of two main divisions: (1) Java

(16 residencies) and Madoera (1 residency); and (2) the outposts (17 provinces). Area and population (for the outposts approximate) of Java, Madoera, and the outpost provinces at end of 1905:

	Sq. m.	Pop.
Java	48,686	28,604,719
Madoera	2,090	1,493,289
Outposts		
Island of Sumatra:		
Sumatra, West Coast	31,788	....
Padang Highlands	.....	403,431
Padang Lowlands	.....	905,040
Tapanoeli	.....	413,301
Benkoelen	9,437	204,269
Lampong Districts	11,338	156,518
Palembang	53,718	796,352
Sumatra, East Coast	35,481	568,417
Atjeh	20,550	582,175
Riouw*	16,379	112,216
Banka	4,473	115,189
Billiton	1,869	36,858
Borneo, West District	56,061	450,929
Borneo, South and East Dists	157,587	782,726
Island of Celebes †:		
Celebes	49,600	415,499
Menado	22,177	436,436
Amboina †	19,870	299,004
Ternate †	176,598	370,902
Timor	17,782	308,600
Bali and Lombok	4,063	523,535
Total	739,559	37,979,377

* Consists of Indragiri in Sumatra and the Riouw and Lingga archipelagoes. † Included in Ternate are a part of eastern Celebes island, Dutch New Guinea, and a part of the Moluccas; the rest of the Moluccas are in Amboina. Dutch New Guinea extends to 141° E., with estimated area 152,428 square miles and estimated population 262,000.

The native population (exclusive of New Guinea) numbered 37,020,460 (Java and Madoera, 29,715,908); Europeans, 80,910; Chinese, 563,449; Arabs, 29,588; Orientals other than natives, 22,970. Batavia had 138,551 inhabitants; Semarang, 96,600; Pekalongan, 41,710; Djokjakarta, 118,378; Padang, 91,440; Palembang, 60,985; Bandjermasin, 16,708.

COMMERCE. Government and private trade, merchandise and specie, are given for three years (in florins):

Imports	1908	1909	1910
Government:			
Merchandise	7,667,549	6,718,507	10,014,463
Specie	8,850,000	5,500,000	2,640,000
Private:			
Merchandise	243,544,983	260,287,611	315,331,656
Specie	20,499,027	9,130,140	17,308,683
Total	280,561,559	281,636,258	345,294,802
Exports	**1908**	**1909**	**1910**
Government:			
Merchandise	16,856,649	16,754,694	29,461,209
Specie	....	....	....
Private:			
Merchandise	452,823,332	437,982,299	422,084,962
Specie	1,034,623	357,201	1,051,660
Total	470,714,604	455,094,194	452,597,831

Of the trade other than government in 1910, 233,743,330 florins imports (219,493,063 mdse., 14,250,267 specie) and 259,452,610 florins exports (259,009,535 mdse., 443,075 specie) are attributable to Java and Madoera. Principal exports follow, quantities in metric tons (figures in parenthesis represent the export from Java and Madoera): Coffee from government plantations 1096 tons (1096); from private estates 14,735 (9800); sugar, 1,317,049 (1,316,946); rice, 61,822 (52,032); arrack, 3,554,000 liters (3,553,000); rattans, 44,190 (422); black pepper, 21,495 (9584); skins, 7932 (5744); tobacco, 61,236 (38,012); indigo, 54 (54); nutmegs, 2580 (317); dammar, 9808 (1984); kapok (Java cotton), 9186 (8377); tea, 15,337 (15,337); copra, 248,148 (107,992); tin from government mines, 15,678 (14,214); other tin, 2343 (2278); cinchona, 7235 (7119) from private and 564 (564) from government plantations. Merchant marine (1910), 12,669 vessels, of 621,292 cubic meters capacity (11,785, of 292,579, native craft). Vessels entered (1910), 6582, of 11,907,000 cubic meters capacity. Railways in operation (1910), 2553 kilometers (Java and Madoera, 2230; Sumatra, 323). A government line (152 miles) connects the p t of Padang with Fort de Kock and has three short branches. The Deli Railway is a private line on the northeast coast in the tobacco-growing district and radiates in several directions from Medan (about 80 miles).

PRODUCTION. Area (1910) under rice, 3,274,264 bahoes (1 baho=1¾ acres), production, 84,286,647 piculs; sugar cane, 213,856 (sugar production, 20,459,495 piculs); tobacco, 213,532; indigo, 17,940; other cultures, 3,213,941. Government coffee plantations (Java), 72,192 bahoes (production, 32,067 piculs); production from emphyteutic lands, 172,336; from private estates, 13,818; native culture (total Dutch East Indies), 79,914 piculs. Tobacco: 830,568 kilos from government plantations, 8,064,555 from emphyteutic plantations, and 436,409 from private estates. Tea (Java), 15,055,083 kilos; indigo (1906), 289,527 kilos; cacao (1910), 1,180,849.

Tin from the government mines at Banka in 1910-11, 270,170 piculs; from private mines (as Billiton and Riouw), 73,110. Coal production (1910), 542,947 metric tons; petroleum, 1,491,382 tons. Gold, silver, diamonds, copper, and manganese are mined.

FINANCE, ETC. Estimated revenue (1910), 220,834,112 florins (actual 1909, 197,237,032); expenditure, 226,804,203 (201,278,893). Budget, 1911: 228,738,000 florins; 1912, 265,862,000. A. W. F. Idenburg was governor-general in 1912.

ARMY. The colonial force maintained by voluntary recruitment has an effective strength of 36,861 officers and men, of which 12,841 are Europeans. Auxiliary troops are supplied by the feudatory chiefs and a territorial militia of little value is maintained. Plans have been adopted for the mobilization of this force for war purposes.

DUTCH EXPOSITION. See EXPOSITIONS, *Holland*.

DUTCH GUIANA, or SURINAM. A colony of the Netherlands (between 46,000 and 49,000 square miles) on the northern coast of South America. Population (1910): 913 Europeans, 7804 Dutch East Indians, 19,683 British East Indians, 52,369 indigenous, 3643 other; total (exclusive of negroes in interior forests), 86,233. Of these, 36,480 are classed as without occupation. Immigrants employed under contract on plantations December 31, 1910, 11,561. Sugar production (1910) 12,015,100 kilos; molasses, 164,100 liters; rum, 797,800 liters; cacao, 1,683,000 kilos; coffee, 202,300; corn, 1,323,000; rice, 1,993,700; bananas, 202,300 bunches. Gold yield 1,081,476 grams, valued at 1,481,622 guilders (or florins); gold export,

1,446,073 guilders. Total imports (1910), 424,-698 gl.; exports, 8,345,447. Tonnage entered, 210,998; cleared, 213,391. Revenue and expenditure (provisional) in 1911, 6,489,000 and 7,308,-000 guilders, respectively; subvention, 818,000. R. D. Fock, governor in 1912.

DUTCH WEST INDIES. See CURAÇAO and DUTCH GUIANA.

DYKES, JAMES OSWALD. A Scotch theologian and educator, died January 1, 1912. He was born in Port Glasgow, Scotland, in 1835, and was educated at Edinburgh University and New College. He also studied at Heidelberg and Erlangen. In 1859 he was ordained and became an assistant at St. George's Church, Edinburgh, 1861. Three years later he resigned on account of ill health and spent three years in Melbourne, Australia. From 1869 to 1888 he was minister of the Regent Square Church, London. Under his ministry this church became one of the leading non-conformist churches in London. In 1888 Dr. Dykes was chosen principal of the Presbyterian College and at the same time became Barbour Professor of Divinity in that institution. This position he retained until 1907 when he resigned and became principal emeritus. He was the author of *Beatitudes of the Kingdom* (1872); *Laws of the Kingdom* (1873); *From Jerusalem to Antioch* (1874); *Law of the Ten Words* (1884); *The Gospel According to St. Paul* (1888); *The Christian Minister and His Duties* (1908), and *The Divine Worker in Creation and Providence* (1909).

DYNAMIC GEOLOGY. See GEOLOGY.

DYNAMITERS, TRIAL OF. See TRADE UNIONS.

DYNAMO-ELECTRIC MACHINERY. In the field of electric generators the developments of 1912, as in 1911, tended toward larger sizes and higher speeds rather than distinct new types. Steam turbine-alternators reached the enormous capacity of 25,000 kilowatts, equivalent to 33,500 horsepower, in striking contrast to the units of 100 kilowatts which were installed in the first generating station in New York just thirty years previous, and which were at that time known as the "Jumbo" type because of their great capacity. In 1912 alternators of 20,000 kilowatts were built for operation at 1800 revolutions per minute, and machines of 5000 kilowatts for 3600 revolutions per minute. In these developments America has led Europe, the 20,000 kilowatt unit appearing there for the first time in 1912. In the realm of water-wheel generators a similar development in capacity has occurred, reaching a maximum of 17,000 kilowatts. The difficulties in designing large direct-current generators for steam-turbine drive were partially overcome. Direct-connected units of 1500 kilowatts and 600 volts and geared units of 1000 kilowatts were produced. The demand for automobile-lighting generators capable of giving constant voltage at variable speeds greatly stimulated inventive activity in this line. One unique type is a shunt generator having the armature and brush gear mounted on a sleeve which winds along the shaft against a spring, varying the surface of the armature which is active according to the speed, so that a constant voltage is maintained over a speed range from 800 to 3800 revolutions per minute. Ingenious work was done in developing electrical devices which may serve as generators for automobile lighting and ignition, and as motors for self-starting in conjunction with a storage battery.

Important progress continued in rectifying and converting apparatus. Synchronous converters of 7500 kilowatts with a maximum capacity of 10,000 kilowatts were put in operation. The high-power mercury-arc rectifier operating in a steel tube entered the commercial field in Germany, but remained in the development stage in America. A very ingenious device was brought out by a Swiss company which compensates for the poor power factor of induction motors. It consists of a phase advancer or small rotary armature, to which current is supplied through a commutator. A stationary field is created, which reacts on the windings to create a current leading to that of the source from which the armature is magnetized by 90° in phase. This current feeds back into the induction motor to which the device is attached and corrects its power factor very successfully.

EARTHQUAKES. The record of earthquakes for the past year was not specially notable in regard to numbers or magnitude of the disturbances. Fewer disasters attended their occurrence than usual, at least as compared with the formidable list that marked the period from 1906 to 1910, beginning with the San Francisco shock. The seismograph stations, of which a number have been established in different parts of the country, registered many disturbances from more or less distant sources. These were centred chiefly in northern Alaska, in the Cordilleran region of Mexico and South America, and in the eastern Mediterranean region. Some of the more prominent ones are here noted: A severe shock occurred on January 31 in the vicinity of Prince William Sound; reports from Valdez described it as the heaviest ever felt in that place. It continued for about one minute and was followed by nine minor tremors. The glaciers on the nearby mountains sent forth tremendous reverberating noises from avalanches along their courses. A prolonged but not damaging earthquake was felt on May 14 in the West Indies, notably at Antigua, St. Kitts, and Guadeloupe. The principal shock of the year noticeable within the limits of the United States took place June 12 in South Carolina and Georgia. The cities of Columbia, Augusta, and Savannah appear to have experienced its full effects, which were sufficient to cause the houses to rock slightly and lighter objects to sway perceptibly. Little damage resulted. A second Alaskan 'quake was reported on July 7 in the vicinity of Fairbanks. The only very severe disaster of the year happened on August 10 in European Turkey. Reports indicated a focus near the Dardanelles, from which it extended northward as far as Adrianople with decreasing violence; Gallipoli on the straits was practically laid to the ground and many of the villages along the northern and southern shores of the Sea of Marmora were seriously damaged. The loss of life was variously estimated, but according to the more moderate figures it probably reached 3000, with twice that number of injured. On August 18 a slight shock occurred in northern Arizona; it was felt at Williams, Holbrook, and other places, and was registered by seismographs many hundred miles away. Minor disturbances were reported in Chile on or about September 30, nearly coincident with predictions of cataclysmic earthquakes, and caused a veritable panic among the lower classes. There were no serious consequences. A rather heavy shock was felt in the City of Mexico on November 19, but involved little damage.

SEISMOLOGY. In a recently issued treatise by Davison, earthquakes are divided into two classes: volcanic and tectonic. Those connected with volcanic energy are stated to be less important and destructive than the second class, which are related to differential movements of the rocks known as faults. It is thought that the fractures developed by folding may give rise to some earthquakes, but the more potent cause is abrupt displacement. This violent disarrangement of the strata is the culmination of intermittent stress, and the friction generated by the sliding of one rock-mass over another produces a series of vibrations which, propagated outward in all directions, appear at the surface as earth waves. As a general rule, the centre of the disturbance is not more than a few miles from the surface.

EASTERN FLEET. See NAVAL PROGRESS, *Great Britain, General Progress.*

ECHELON CLOUDS. See METEOROLOGY.

ECONOMIC ASSOCIATION, AMERICAN. The twenty-fifth annual meeting of the association was held in Boston December 27-31. The chief subjects dealt with were wages, banking reform, cost of living, agricultural economics and the economics of price regulation. Among the important papers read were the following: "Theory of the Minimum Wage," Henry R. Seager; "Rising Cost of Living," Irving Fisher of Yale University; "Banking Reform," by E. W. Kemmerer of Princeton University; "Economic Theory," by Simon N. Patten of the University of Pennsylvania; "Economics of Governmental Price Regulation," J. M. Clark of Amherst College, and Chester W. Wright of Chicago University. The presidential address was delivered by Frank A. Fetter and was entitled "Population or Prosperity." In connection with the meeting of the association were held meetings of the American Historical Association, the American Political Science Association, the American Sociological Society, the American Statistical Association, and the American Association for Labor Legislation. The officers elected for 1912 were: President, Frank A. Fetter, Princeton University; secretary, Thomas M. Carver, Harvard University. The association numbers about 2500 members.

ECONOMICS, SOCIAL. See SOCIAL ECONOMICS.

ECUADOR. An equatorial South American republic on the Pacific coast. Capital, Quito.

AREA AND POPULATION. The area is reported at 299,600 square kilometers (115,676 square miles); including the Galápagos islands, 307,243 square kilometers (118,627 square miles). The population, chiefly of Indian blood, is estimated at 1,500,000, though it is not unlikely that this figure is somewhat too large. The larger towns are Guayaquil (80,000), Quito (70,000), Cuenca (40,000), Riobamba (18,000).

EDUCATION. In his message of August 10, 1912, acting President Marín reported the number of public, municipal, and private schools at 1590, with 98,413 pupils and 2326 teachers. Higher education is carried on at the universities of Quito, Guayaquil, and Cuenca, and the law school at Loja; these institutions have 74 professors and over 600 students. The established religion is Roman Catholicism.

INDUSTRIES. Agriculture is the chief source of wealth. Valuable minerals exist, but have been little exploited. The most important article of manufacture is the Panama hat. Ecuador is one of the foremost cacao producers of the world. Besides this crop there are cultivated coffee, rice, sugar-cane, and tobacco.

COMMERCE. Imports and exports have been valued as follows, in thousands of sucres:

	1906	1907	1908	1909	1910	1911
Imports..	17,012	19,670	20,555	18,704	16,048	16,477
Exports..	21,965	22,907	26,559	24,879	27,333	28,062

The leading imports are cotton goods, foodstuffs, hardware, and machinery. Principal exports in 1910 and 1911, in thousands of sucres: Cacao, 15,792 and 21,057; vegetable ivory, 3339 and 4768; Panama hats, 2517 and 2584; rubber, 2012 and 2066; coffee, 1471 and 1536; gold, 498 and 1240; hides, 515 and 528. Trade by principal countries, in thousands of sucres:

	Imports		Exports	
	1910	1911	1910	1911
United Kingdom....	4,968	5,124	2,282	2,343
United States......	4,509	4,629	8,181	8,399
Germany	3,148	3,232	4,496	4,616
France	1,053	1,081	9,588	9,844

COMMUNICATIONS. About 350 miles of railway were in operation in 1911, of which 297 miles were completed in the Guayaquil-Quito line. Work on the line from Bahía de Caraquez to Quito, begun in July, 1909, continued in 1912. A line from Manta to Santa Ana was begun June 30, 1911, and in the summer of 1912 construction trains were running to Montecristi. Telegraphs (1912), 3318 miles, with 60 offices; telephones, 328 miles.

NAVY. The navy includes one destroyer, one torpedo boat, three launches, one transport, and an auxiliary vessel.

FINANCE. The unit of value is the sucre, worth 48.655 cents (one-tenth of a sovereign). Revenue and expenditure in 1909 amounted to 15,877,684 and 15,564,882 sucres respectively; in 1910, 23,984,710 (including loans 10,416,258) and 22,047,254. Import duties in 1910 were 5,172,990 sucres, and export duties 2,922,221. Of the 1910 expenditure, 8,690,392 sucres were for the public debt, 4,231,887 for war and marine, 1,701,964 for interior and police, and 1,164,774 for public instruction. Estimated revenue and expenditure for 1913 balanced at 18,971,324 sucres. Public debt, June 30, 1910, 43,511,024 sucres; a loan of 3,000,000 sucres was negotiated in January, 1911.

ARMY. During 1912 no important changes were made in the military organization of the republic and the forces continued on the same basis, with progress being made in the enrollment of the organization of the first and second reserves, which supplement the small standing army maintained under the law of 1902.

GOVERNMENT AND HISTORY. The constitution of the republic bears date of December 23, 1906. The president is elected by direct vote for four years and is assisted by a cabinet of five members. The legislative body consists of two houses, the Senate (32 members) and the House of Representatives (48). For the term beginning August 31, 1911, Emilio Estrada was inaugurated president in succession to Gen. Eloy Alfaro. Estrada died December 21, 1912, and was succeeded by Carlos Freile Zaldumbide, president of the Senate, as acting president. There began immediately a revolutionary movement, headed apparently by the friends of General Alfaro, which quickly developed into a fierce struggle, marked by acts of infamous barbarity. General Montero, a revolutionary leader, was proclaimed president by the army, but early in 1912 he was killed. Alfaro also was killed, and his body savagely mutilated. The speaker of the House of Representatives, Francisco Andrade Marin, became acting president. On March 31, 1912, Gen. Leonidas Plaza was elected president; he was inaugurated on Francisco Andrade Marín, became acting president in 1901-5 and was commander of the government forces which opposed the revolutionary outbreak of 1912. See ARBITRATION, INTERNATIONAL.

EDUCATION IN THE UNITED STATES. STATISTICS FOR ELEMENTARY SCHOOLS. The public elementary schools enrolled 16,898,791 and private schools 1,441,137 pupils in 1910. About seventy-one per cent. of the population 5 to 18 years of age were enrolled in the public elementary schools. It costs, on an average, $22.67 per pupil to support these schools. This is by far the lowest per capita cost in the entire educational system. Each student in the public high schools costs $47.13, each student in public normal schools $158.48, and each one in college costs $303.48. The investment for buildings, grounds, and equipment for each child in the public elementary schools was about $65. The corresponding investment for high schools was $275, and for colleges and universities $1100. The estimated expense for the public elementary schools for 1910-11 was $383,127,609, and for private schools $43,231,110. About seventy-two per cent. of the public school funds are raised by local taxation, though in some of the southern States only fifty-eight per cent. of the income is from local taxes. There are in the public elementary schools an average of thirty-five pupils to each teacher, while in the public high schools there are twenty-two students per teacher, and in colleges there is one instructor to each eight students.

STATISTICS FOR HIGH SCHOOLS. The Bureau of Education reports that during the year ending June, 1911, 10,234 public and 1979 private high schools enrolled an aggregate of 1,115,326 students, 88 per cent. of whom were in the public high schools. In addition it was estimated that there were at least 100,000 other secondary students in preparatory departments of colleges and universities, in normal schools and in certain manual and industrial schools. 44.23 per cent. of the high school students were boys. The schools employed 25,138 men and 32,102 women instructors. Of the 55,083 boys and 81,359 girls who graduated during the year, 47 per cent of the boys and 27 per cent. of the girls had declared their intention of entering college, and 5746 boys and 14,505 girls had prepared for admittance to normal schools or other higher institutions. Among the entire number of high school students only 6.8 per cent. seem to be preparing for college. The students were distributed among the classes as follows: First year 41.90 per cent.; second year 26.75 per cent.; third year 18.34 per cent; fourth year 13.01 per cent. It should be noted in connection with the low per cent. in the fourth year that only 88.31 per cent. of the students are in four year high schools. If all the schools offered four-year courses, there would be an increase in the students of the fourth year, and a consequent lowering of the per cents. in the other years.

The increases in the number of high school students during the past twenty years and particularly during the past ten years has been remarkable. The following table presents the facts regarding the number of students in high schools for each 1000 of population in 1910, the per cent. increase in high school enrollment, the per cent. increase in population, and the ratio between the per cent. increase in high school enrollment, and the per cent. increase in population for twenty years, 1890 to 1910, and also for ten years, 1900 to 1910.

Divisions	Enrollment in high schools for each 1000 population 1910	Per Cent. Increase				Ratio of per cent. increase enrollment to per cent. increase population	
		High school enrollment		Population			
		20 Yrs.	10 Yrs.	20 Yrs.	10 Yrs.	20 Yrs.	10 Yrs.
United States	12	259	72	47	22	5.5	3.3
North Atlantic	14	214	67	49	23	4.4	2.9
South Atlantic	7(10)*	217	80	37	17	5.9	4.7
South Central	7 (9)*	316	93	55	22	5.8	4.2
North Central	15	250	54	34	14	7.4	4.[illegible]
Western	16	681	184	126	67	5.4	2.8

* Numbers in parentheses are for white population.

A marked change seems to have taken place in the purpose students have in attending high schools. Over 18 per cent. of all the high school students in 1890 were taking courses that prepared for college. In 1900 the proportion had fallen to 14.53 per cent. and in 1911 only about 7 per cent. were taking college preparatory work. Mr. Willard J. Fisher in *Science* (November 1, 1912) comments on this change as follows: "Since 1890 the problem of the secondary school has changed from that of a fitting school to one of a decidedly non-fitting school—some bigots would say a decidedly *unfitting* school; a school in which only 6.8 per cent. of the pupils anticipate college work of any sort. This being the case, the colleges and universities can not lead the way in the fashion of 1892 and the committee of ten; the problems of secondary education can be solved only in the schools." It is interesting to see what difference this apparent change in the students' purpose, and the vigorous criticism of the public high school have made in the popularity of various subjects. There has been an increasing per cent. of the students taking the following subjects. In each case the subject is followed by the per cent. of students taking it in 1910. English Literature (57.05). Algebra (56.92). Rhetoric (56.59). Latin (49.59). Geometry (30.87). German (23.60). French (11.70). The following subjects show a decreasing popularity: Physical geog aphy (19.14). Civil government (15.99). Physiology (15.76). Physics (14.79). Chemistry (7.13). Trigonometry (2.18). Geology (1.35). Psychology (1.35). Greek (1.31). Astronomy (.88). The following subjects were not tabulated as early as 1905: Botany (16.34). Zoölogy (7.88). Agriculture (4.55). Domestic economy (4.14). Spanish (.65).

ILLITERACY. In the entire population above ten years of age illiteracy declined from 10.7 per cent. in 1900 to 7.7 per cent. in 1910. For further details of the report on this subject issued in 1912 by the United States Census Bureau, see the article ILLITERACY. The different methods of collecting the data make it impossible to compare directly the illiteracy in the United States with that found in other countries. The Bureau of Education gives the following comparative statistics for France, Germany, Great Britain, the United States, and certain European countries:

Country	Year	Per cent. of illiterates	Basis of estimate
France	1906	11.4	Population over 10 years of age.
German Empire	1905	.03	Army recruits.
Great Britain	1904	1.5	Marriage regis.
United States	1910	7.7	Population over 10 years of age.
Denmark	...	.2	Army recruits.
The Netherlands	...	1.4	Army recruits.
Sweden	...	.3	Army recruits.
Switzerland	...	.5	Army recruits.
Austria	1900	28.2	
Hungary	1900	40.0	
Italy	1901	48.0	
Spain	1900	58.7	
Russia	1897	70.0	

ELEMENTARY EDUCATION IN CERTAIN FOREIGN COUNTRIES. The data presented in the following table were taken from the report of the United States Commissioner of Education. They should be regarded as indications of conditions rather than as accurate statistics. For ease in making comparisons the corresponding statistics of the United States are given.

PUBLIC SCHOOL ADMINISTRATION. The criticisms which have been directed against the public schools during the past few years were repeated in 1912. As in previous years they were based on the belief that the schools have courses of study overcrowded with "mummified and antiquated subjects," which have no relation to life, and as a consequence the methods employed in teaching tend to destroy rather than encourage initiative on the part of the child. There has been nothing new in the criticisms, neither has there been much that is new in the schools' methods of remedying the defects. The efforts of school officers and bodies of citizens have been directed toward a more thorough understanding of the factors that affect the efficiency of the schools. To this end there has been an increasing number of school investigations or surveys. The most important work of this sort was that undertaken in New York City by the board of estimate in 1911, and completed in June, 1912. The investigation cost about $100,000 and was conducted by Prof. Paul Hanus of Harvard University with a group of assistants. The report of the investigation has not as yet been made public except that part of it which had to do with certain phases of the administration of the schools. This part of the report was written by Prof. E. C. Moore of Yale and was rejected by the board of estimate on the ground that it contained unsubstantiated statements. The issue of the report was awaited with much interest on account of the high professional standing of those participating in this investigation.

The Training School for Public Service connected with the New York Bureau of Municipal Research has conducted investigations of surveys in Dobbs Ferry, Syracuse, and certain counties in Maryland. Its most important undertaking was a collaboration with the Wisconsin State board of public affairs in studying rural school conditions and needs in Wisconsin. Investigators examined the conditions in twenty-seven counties in widely separated parts of the State, and they made a more detailed study of the conditions in 131 schools in thirteen counties. The report which was published in August sets forth in clear and concise form the conditions observed, both favorable and unfavorable. The final chapter is devoted to the discussion of fifteen suggested administrative and legislative remedies. A

Country	Date	Enrollment	Per cent. of population	Teachers	Expenditures Total	Expenditures Per capita of population
Austria-Hungary:						
Austria	1908	4,242,628	14.85	97,399	a$27,451,081	a$1.00
Hungary	1907-8	3,271,773	16.27	43,203	18,404,200	.91
Belgium	1909	923,286	12.4	20,865	7,798,146	1.04
Bulgaria	1907-8	430,111	10.0	9,398	2,270,313	.54
Denmark	1909	363,661	14.0	......	....	.....
France	1908-9	5,629,906	14.3	154,586	b58,497,743	b1.49
Germany Empire	1905	10,224,125	17.0	166,579	124,420,918	2.05
Great Britain and Ireland	1909	6,045,089	16.90	161,796	110,784,545	3.09
Greece	1907	241,433	9.2	4,346	1,291,574	.49
Italy	1909	3,002,168	8.75	60,323	26,252,585	.76
Netherlands	1909-10	904,142	15.3	26,073	13,583,917	2.30
Norway	1908	369,993	15.5	8,106	3,496,708	1.45
Russia	1909	5,738,289	3.65	.....	....	.....
Sweden	1909	784,974	14.33	19,351	11,315,229	2.06
Spain	1907	2,000,000	11.9	.....	5,000,000	.25
Switzerland	1909	529,590	14.15	12,022	4,246,987	1,13
Japan	1908-9	5,996,139	12.1	134,337	26,815,959	.54
United States	1910	17,813,852	19.38	523,210	426,250,434	4.64

a 1906-7.
b In 1907-8 for public schools only, enrolling 4,603,773 pupils, or 82.2 per cent. of the total enrollment.

similar investigation is planned for the high schools and normal schools of Wisconsin.

Two State superintendents of public instruction resigned in 1912: E. T. Fairchild of Kansas, to become the president of the New Hampshire College of Agriculture and Mechanic Arts, and J. T. Eggleston of Virginia to become rural school specialist in the Bureau of Education.

Two events have served to call particular attention to the educational work of New York State. On January 1, 1912, the new system of rural school supervision became operative. The legislature of 1910 abolished the office of school commissioner, and in its place created the office of district superintendent, the change to take effect in 1912. The law created a board of school directors in each supervisory district consisting of two members from each town, to be chosen at the general election. The sole duty of this board is to elect the superintendent of schools. The salary of the superintendent is $1200, with a maximum expense allowance of $300, both to be paid by the State. The tenure of office is five years. To be eligible to this office one must hold a life certificate to teach in any school in the State, and in addition must pass an examination in the teaching of agriculture. Superintendents must devote their whole time to the duties of their office, and they are required to forward detailed weekly reports to the commissioner of education. It is too early to form any just estimate of the efficiency of the system, but it seems to be fulfilling expectations. The boards of school directors made earnest efforts to secure the best available individuals for superintendents; 206 of the 207 required superintendents were selected before February. Of these, 62 were college graduates, 92 were graduates of State normal schools, 35 held life certificates, and 28 held teachers' permanent certificates. All had had experience in teaching.

On October 15, 16, and 17 a notable group of educators met in Albany to take part in the dedication of the New York State Education building. This building cost nearly $5,000,000, and is said to be the most splendid and commodious building devoted wholly to education in the world. It will house the various offices of the education department, including the State library and the State museum. In the various addresses there were frequent references to the great credit due to Commissioner Andrew S. Draper, under whose leadership this vast undertaking was begun and completed.

Stratton D. Brooks resigned the superintendency of the Boston schools to become president of the University of Oklahoma. He was succeeded by Dr. Franklin B. Dyer, who resigned the superintendency of the Cincinnati schools. Randall J. Condon, superintendent of the Providence schools, went to the superintendency in Cincinnati. Both Boston and Cincinnati were reported to have raised the salary of their superintendents from $6000 to $10,000. Superintendent J. G. Callicut of Tocama became the new superintendent of Indianapolis.

This year marked the twenty-fifth anniversary of Dr. William H. Maxwell's connection with the administration of the New York City schools. A large company of prominent citizens met in Carnegie Hall to pay tribute to the man and the results of his work. Doctor Maxwell was presented with a chest containing a silver service. The translation of the Latin inscription on the chest is as follows: "William Henry Maxwell for twenty-five years city superintendent of schools in Brooklyn and New York; given on account of his unique service, his loyalty, his zeal, and his courage."

VOCATIONAL EDUCATION. The demand for vocational education remains insistent. Progress has been in the same general direction as in the preceding year. Some new schools have been established, but school officers have been studying the results in the schools already working, and at the same time making a thorough study of the local conditions which vocational education must meet. There is a very great scarcity both of those who are able to direct the work and of those qualified to teach vocational subjects. The demand is for a new type of teacher, one who has, in addition to a liberal training, experience and skill in the industry he attempts to teach. Such men and women are not attracted by the salaries offered ordinary teachers. There is very general agreement among the advocates of vocational education that the federal and State governments must assist the communities in the establishment and maintenance of such schools. Their fundamental argument is that this type of education is expensive and that our workmen move from place to place so freely that the commmunity which is at the expense of educating the workman has no assurance that it will ever profit by the investment. There is every indication that popular opinion favors such federal aid. There has, however, been a diversity of opinion as to how large an appropriation is needed, in what manner it shall be used and how its administration may be safeguarded. On February 26 Senator Carrol Page introduced Senate Bill No. 3 which is now known as the Page Vocational bill. This bill as modified would eventually appropriate in round numbers $14,500,000 annually. This sum would be divided as follows: $3,000,000 for the encouraging of instruction in agriculture, the trades and industries, and home economics; a like sum for the support of institutions in which only trades and industries and home economics shall be taught; $3,000,000 for agricultural high schools; $3,000,000 for extension work by the State agricultural colleges; $1,000,000 for demonstration and experimental work at the agricultural high schools, the work to be under the direction of the State agricultural colleges; $1,500,000 for the preparation of teachers for the schools contemplated by the bill. The administration of this appropriation is divided between the Secretary of the Interior and the Secretary of Agriculture. In general, the provisions of the bill make it necessary for the State and community to add two dollars to each dollar received from the government. The appropriation for the training of teachers is to be available at once, but the other sums are not to be available until July, 1916. The bill has the cordial support of many educational organizations. There are some who believe that the type of education proposed is still in such an experimental stage that we are not ready to employ economically any large amount of money. They see danger also in the divided authority over the administration of the funds. Whether the bill in its present form becomes a law or not, the fact remains that this bill

NEW YORK STATE EDUCATION BUILDING, ALBANY, N. Y.

represents the most advanced thought on the subject.

WIDER USE OF SCHOOL PLANT. It was estimated that in 1910 a total of $1,357,751,103 was invested in the State school systems. The average number of days that the school plants were in use for school purposes varied from 100 in New Mexico to 193 in Rhode Island. The average for the entire country was 157.5 days. These facts have been receiving very thoughtful attention from many sources, and as a result there is a strong agitation for a wider use of the school plant. This purpose is being accomplished in two ways: first, by a more economical use of the school plant for educational purposes, and second by allowing the buildings to be used for civic purposes and as social centres. The most conspicuous example of an economical use of school property is in Gary, Ind., where the pupils are organized into two groups, one group working in the classrooms while the other group is at work either in the laboratories or shops, or is on the playgrounds. This arrangement is said to double the capacity of school buildings. All-the-year schools are becoming increasingly popular. There are lecture courses for adults and also evening industrial and commercial courses. There is, however, a growing opposition to evening courses for those who have left school and entered the industries before they have the education required by the State. It is held that attendance at school after a day's work is a hardship and results in injury to the health; therefore such pupils should be freed from labor for a few hours each week at the expense of the employer and given more definite instruction in the schools. Such, in effect, is the law of New York State. Los Angeles, Milwaukee, Denver, Salt Lake, Grand Rapids, Worcester, and other cities use the school houses as polling places. During the presidential campaign, New York City opened school houses to the different parties for political meetings.

It is, however, in making school houses civic and social centres that the greatest progress has been made. Seven hundred and seventy-eight clubs of various characters were operated in the school houses of New York last year. A recent Wisconsin law orders that "where the citizens of any community are organized into a non-partisan, non-sectarian, non-exclusive association for the presentation and discussion of public questions the school board shall accommodate them in some school building and provide free of charge, light, heat, and janitor service." So important have these activities become that the architecture of school houses is changing, and the newer buildings contain provisions that were unknown in the earlier structures.

SECRET SOCIETIES IN HIGH SCHOOLS. The secret societies in high schools are a development of the past 35 years. This development took place with little attention on the part of school authorities, who generally were inclined to encourage rather than discourage the students in their efforts to organize. If arguments were needed to justify the existence of such societies, they were based on the social and educational possibilities of self-directed organization. Since 1900, however, school superintendents, high school principals, and teachers have been waging a determined warfare against these societies. Their fundamental arguments are that such organizations are undemocratic and that the weak school spirit found in public high schools, unlike the strong college spirit, is unable to prevent a snobbishness that is extremely injurious to the welfare of both student and school. In the past five years the legislatures of thirteen States have passed laws against such societies. In at least twelve other States many of the most important cities have regulations which provide either for the suspension or expulsion of students joining secret societies, or make the students who become members ineligible to membership in any of the school organizations, such as musical and dramatic clubs, athletic and debating teams, etc. The courts before whom the question has been argued have shown a strong tendency to uphold the school boards. The States having prohibitive laws are: California, Indiana, Iowa, Kansas, Massachusetts, Michigan, Minnesota, Mississippi, Nebraska, Ohio, Oregon, Vermont, and Washington.

CHILD WELFARE. The year has seen a pronounced increase in the attention given to the welfare of children. The studies that have been made regarding the health of school children are tending to give a more accurate conception of the magnitude of the task before the schools. Prof. Thomas D. Wood, M. D., in an address before the National Council of Education, estimated that at least five per cent. of pupils in the public schools have now, or have had, tubercular diseases of the lungs, twenty-five per cent. have suffered from defective vision, and thirty per cent. have enlarged tonsils, adenoids, or enlarged cervical glands which need attention. In all, about seventy-five per cent. of the school children in this country need attention for physical defects which are partially or wholly remediable. Congress has established, in the Department of Commerce and Labor, a children's bureau, the purpose of which is to "investigate and report upon all matters pertaining to the welfare of children and child life, and . . . to especially investigate the questions of infant mortality, the birth rate, orphanage, juvenile courts, desertion, dangerous occupations, accidents and diseases of children, employment, legislation affecting children in the several States and Territories, and such other facts as have a bearing upon the welfare of children." Miss Julia C. Lathrop of Hull House, Chicago, was chief of the bureau at a salary of $5000. Eleven of the fourteen States whose legislatures met in 1912 improved their child labor laws. The investigations bearing on the number of children who either fail to pass in school or who leave before completing the course tended to emphasize attention to the dullards, but now attention is also given to the unusually bright children. See WELFARE WORK.

BIBLIOGRAPHY. Among the important publications of the year are the following: Mabel Carney, *Country Life and the Country School*. *Vocational Education in Chicago and Other Cities* (report of a committee of the Chicago Commercial Club); Elwood P. Cubberley, *Improvement of Rural Schools;* Irving King, *Social Aspects of Education;* Maria Montessori, translated from the Italian by Anna E. George, *The Montessori Method;* Julius Sachs, *The American Secondary School and Some of Its Problems;* Edward L. Thorndike, *Educa-*

tion; Harland Updegraff, *A Study of Expenses of City School Systems.*

EDWARD VII., MEMORIALS TO. See ARCHITECTURE.

EFFICIENCY, MUNICIPAL. See MUNICIPAL GOVERNMENT.

EGYPT. A northeast African khediviate virtually under the control of Great Britain, nominally under Turkish suzerainty. Cairo is the capital. Area (estimate), 400,000 square miles (exclusive of the Sudan, of which only 12,013 square miles are cultivated and settled); population (1907), 11,189,978, not including nomadic Bedouins.

EDUCATION. Lord Kitchener's remarks on recent changes in the educational system will be of interest as having a wider application than originally intended. He says in part: "In 1910 an important and very interesting experiment was commenced, viz.: The handing over of local education to the recently constituted provincial councils. This new departure has introduced a much-needed elasticity and diversity into the system. It is premature at present to give any definite opinion on the result while the experiment is still in a somewhat indeterminate and provisional stage.

"As might have been expected, a considerable amount of divergence is apparent in the policy carried out by the different councils. In some there has been a tendency towards providing secondary education, instead of the very necessary elementary vernacular industrial and agricultural schools which are so much required in the provinces. One of the worst features of the elementary education hitherto supplied has been that it was restricted so largely to the cultivation of memory. An instruction that is merely 'bookish' leaves some of the most useful faculties of the mind undeveloped. Manual exercises train the eye to accuracy in observation, the hand to skill in execution, and the mind to a sense of the importance of truthfulness in work. What seems most required for progress in this direction is to evolve the best type of rural school, adapted to the special practical needs of agricultural districts, and when this has been done we may confidently hope to see a considerable increase in the number of boys educated. It must not be forgotten that any hasty or unthought-out development of education in rural districts, unless it is carefully adapted to rural necessities, may imperil the agricultural interests on which the prosperity of the country so largely depends. A rural exodus in Egypt would be an economic and social disaster of considerable magnitude."

AGRICULTURE. The newly organized department of agriculture began working regularly from the beginning of 1911. The area planted to cotton in 1910 was stated at 1,642,610 feddans, and in 1911 at 1,711,228—an increase of 68,618 feddans. Production, in 1911, of cleaned cotton, 3,318,529 metric quintals; estimated 1912 production, 3,602,327. Amount of sugar-cane treated in 1909-10, 515,839 tons (sugar yield 553,346 metric quintals); 472,344 in 1910-11 (493,942); 1911-12 estimate, 570,000 (580,000).

Much hardship has resulted from the dearth of cattle for plowing in the Delta, disease having carried off a quarter of a million of these animals in the seven years past. Increase of cotton pests, due to improper drainage and the wholesale destruction of birds, has wrought havoc. Legislation has been passed for the protection of bird-life, and a commission was recently appointed to devise means for the suppression or better control of the cotton worm and boll-worm. The government has taken measures for the distribution of improved cotton seed; the amount sold in the spring of 1912 was about 40,000 ardebs, or about one-tenth of the seed required for the total area sown. See AGRICULTURAL EDUCATION.

The areas under cereals in 1911, according to the department of Direct Taxes, are shown in the following table, with total yield in ardebs and estimated yield per feddan:

	Feddans	Ardebs*	Ar. per f.
Wheat	1,237,821	6,882,000	5.56
Barley	370,143	2,124,000	5.74
Rice	227,109	1,321,000	5.82
Corn	1,772,686	12,320,000	6.95

* The ardeb varies, that of wheat being 150 kilograms; barley, 120; unhusked rice, 291; corn, 140.

IRRIGATION, ETC. The raising of the Assuan dam progressed steadily in 1911; the completion of the grouting up of the space between the new and the old work was scheduled for February, 1912, and the termination of the whole work for the end of the year. To quote again Lord Kitchener: "The monumental work of the raised dam and the immense benefits accruing by the increased irrigation of the country will repay the expenditure many times over. Other completed improvements include the giving of Seifi (summer) water to Upper Egypt, and the abolition of the basin system, which for so long has restricted the full yield of the land. Now that abundant irrigation water is assured, no effort should be spared to enable the inhabitants of Egypt to obtain the fullest advantage from their magnificent soil and climate; and the question of drainage, which has long been discussed, becomes one of vital importance. Measures have been approved for a large and comprehensive scheme of drainage in the provinces of Behera and Gharbieh, the result aimed at being the lowering of the water in the drains to a depth of from 1½ to 2 meters below the surface of the soil. . . The fellah remains the same as he has always been, one of the best and most hard-working types of humanity, somewhat conservative, like most cultivators, and hardly realizing the changes that have taken place around him. It is difficult for a people who have, through many ages, always striven for more water for their cultivation, to realize that too much of a good thing may be detrimental. It is, however, an incontestable fact that a considerable portion of the irrigation water now supplied is not only wasted, but does actual harm to the crops. [Hence] the urgent necessity for drainage works." See also DRAINAGE.

COMMERCE AND COMMUNICATIONS. The year 1911 witnessed a considerable increase in imports—£E27,227,118—as compared with the previous year—£E23,553,000. The total amount of exports in 1911, including cigarettes, was £E28,599,000, compared with £E28,044,000 in 1910. The total export of cotton fell from £E24,241,000 in 1910 to £E22,988,000 in 1911, the United Kingdom taking over £E1,000,000 less than in the previous year. Trade with the principal countries of origin and destination is shown in thousands of pounds Egyptian (£E1=$4.943.):

	Imports		Exports	
	1910	1911	1910	1911
United Kingdom	7,311	8,557	14,343	13,958
British possessions*	169	257	10	10
British Possessions†	967	1,095	82	111
France‡	2,703	2,839	2,480	2,316
Turkey	2,905	2,808	1,892§	2,071§
Austria-Hungary	1,647	1,988	1,435	1,443
Germany	1,262	1,500	3,088	3,117
Italy	1,169	1,461	1,659¶	1,789¶

* British possessions in the Mediterranean. † British possessions in the Far East. ‡ With Algeria. § United States. ¶ Russia.

State railways, 2904 kilometers. The Marg, Khanka, Abou-Zaabel line and the Ashmoun-Barrage line were opened for traffic in 1911; land was acquired for the Zifta-Zagazig line, the new Zifta station was completed, and satisfactory progress was made with the new bridges of Mansura, Assiut, and Embabeh; the new station at Alexandria was under way. The three light railways are the Egyptian Delta Light Railway, 952 kilometers; the Chemins de Fer de la Basse-Egypte .109; the Fayum Light Railway, 169. The 40 kilometers of standard gauge between Cairo and Helouan (Egyptian Delta Light Railway Company) are being put into condition to operate.

Telegraph lines, 5913 kilometers (wires), 20,-503) The extension of the Marsa-Matruh line from Sidi-Barani to Bagbag has been completed.

Army. The Egyptian army, in which all male inhabitants under the law are liable for service—6 years in the army, 5 years in the police, and 4 years in reserve—was maintained in 1912 at a peace strength of about 9000 officers and men, although there were available for conscription about 150,000 young men. The result is that the recruits are carefully selected and the various organizations carefully trained. The command of Egyptian troops in 1912 continued to be vested in Lieutenant-General Sir Reginald Wingate, who was also governor-general of the Sudan, and 188 British officers were attached to the Egyptian army. The effective war schedule was about 18,000, including 800 cavalry, 600 in the camel corps, 200 in Arab battalions, 1250 well-trained artillery, and 10,000 infantry. In May, 1912, Lord Kitchener, in a report, stated that while there was no change in the military condition of Egypt, arrangements had been made for concentrating troops in the Sudan at suitable points for effective action, and it was necessary to raise an equatorial battalion for the garrisoning of Mongalla, Bahr-el-Ghazal, and the upper Nile provinces. The British government in 1911 maintained 6063 officers and men in Egypt under the command of Major-General the Hon. J. H. G. Byng, C. B., to the maintenance of which the Egyptian government contributed £150,000. This force included 1 cavalry regiment, 1 horse battery, 1 mountain battery, 1 company Royal Engineers, 4 infantry battalions, the third battalion Coldstream Guards, and other details.

Finance and Government. The financial condition of the country is best shown by excerpts from the report of the financial adviser (Sir Paul Harvey) on the budget of 1912: "The financial situation is satisfactory. The crisis of 1907, with its inevitable reaction on public revenues, found the government engaged in heavy expenditure on great works of public utility. The indifferent cotton crops of 1908 and 1909, moreover, had a depressing effect on the revenue. This period is now over, and the corner has been turned. The series of [recent] failures in the banking and business community are due to causes antecedent to the present year. The failure of the Bank of Egypt was due, in a word, to an unsound system of business and finance initiated many years ago. The other failures may be ranked as a result, however, long deferred, of the speculative movement which came to an end with the crisis of 1907. The essential sources of the country's wealth and prosperity remain unaffected."

The revenue in 1911 amounted to £E16,793,-000 (customs, £E2,169,000; railway receipts £E3,729,000; tobacco, £E1,669,000); expenditure, £E14,872,000. The budget for 1912 shows £E15,900,000 revenue and £15,400,000 expenditure.

The total outstanding capital of the debt, December 31, 1910, was £94,972,200; charge on account of interest and sinking fund, £E3,571,-000; paid off during the year £350,540; making a total capital December 31, 1911, of £94,621,-660 and an annual charge of £E3,561,000.

Reigning Khedive in 1912, Abbas (II.) Hilmi. The British agent, consul-general, and minister plenipotentiary is Field Marshal Viscount Kitchener of Khartum, the real ruler of Egypt. No sittings of the international commission of judicial reform were held in 1911, but the modification of Article 12 of the Mixed Civil Code received the assent of the powers, by which a new legislative assembly with power to legislate for foreigners was established. Dissatisfaction has been expressed at headquarters with the policy of the provincial councils in devoting the full amount of their expenditure to education and neglecting their other duties toward the community—the establishment of better communications, bridges, drains, and improved sanitation. Plague increased in 1911, the number of cases being 1656, as compared with 1238 in 1910; the mortality increased from 50 to 60 per cent. The white slave traffic is becoming an important issue, but, as the trade is carried on by foreigners, subject only to their own governments, the Egyptian government and police are powerless to cope adequately with the evil. The sum of £E15,700 was granted in 1911 for the restoration of mosques and other Arab and Coptic monuments.

History

Lord Kitchener's Administration. During the first nine months of his administration as British agent and consul-general in Egypt, Lord Kitchener made three tours of the provinces to study local conditions and to discuss with persons acquainted with the facts the effect of the measures for improving the condition of the rural population. He was received everywhere with popular enthusiasm as the "friend of the fellahin." The chief aim of his policy was to promote the welfare of the agricultural population. To this end a number of important legislative measures were undertaken. His plans embraced laws for improving the public health, expediting the administration of justice, and protecting the fellahin from usury and other forms of economic injustice. An important step in reform was the extension of the savings bank system to the country districts. Usury was made a penal offense. A plan was proposed for the exemption of small holdings up to five acres from seizure for debt. A system of justices of the peace was instituted in the rural districts where "cantonal tribunals" were to have jurisdiction over a certain range of questions that especially concerned the peasantry and depended on local customs. The sentences imposed could not exceed a fine of £5 or 24 hours' imprisonment. On July 4, Lord Kitchener left Cairo for England. The nine months of his régime were marked by more peaceful conditions in native politics. The rival factions were disposed to compromise and the bitterness between Copts and Moslems seemed less acute. Interest was apparently drawn away from party politics to the new measures of social and economic amelioration.

OTHER EVENTS. In the spring of 1912 a punitive expedition was led against the Anuaks on the Sudanese-Abyssinian frontier for their attacks on the Nuers, a tribe under British protection. In the middle of March, after traversing the Nuer country, the column fell in with the enemy, who resisted stubbornly, killing over forty, including several officers, but were defeated and driven into the forest. The general session was opened by the khedive on March 25. Among the measures to improve the condition of the country which the khedive announced in his speech, were the improvement of irrigation, creation of a department of agriculture, extension of education, and extension of the postal savings bank to the rural districts. An appeal having been made to the g vernment to abolish the press law, which, during recent months, had suspended a number of newspapers, the government declared that the law would fall into disuse just as soon as the reasons for its existence disappeared. At a meeting of the Nationalist party Mahomed Farid Bey, the leader of the party, delivered a speech which the government held to be seditious. Farid immediately fled from the country, and action was brought against the directors of two native journals who, having published his speech, were accused of complicity. They were sentenced to three months' imprisonment. Sentence was recorded against Farid on April 10 of one year's imprisonment at hard labor.

Three Egyptians accused of conspiring against the lives of the khedive, the prime minister, and Lord Kitchener, were tried and found guilty in August. One was sentenced to fifteen years' hard labor, and the others to fifteen years' imprisonment, the maximum penalty in each case. A fourth prisoner, accused of complicity in the crime, was liberated. Appeal from the sentence by the counsel for the three prisoners was denied by the upper court. Several arrests were made early in September for seditious activity.

The king and queen of England visited Egypt in January on their return from India. The khedive visited their majesties at Windsor in June.

EGYPT. DRAINAGE OF THE DELTA. See DRAINAGE.

EGYPTIAN EXPLORATION FUND. See ARCHÆOLOGY.

EICHBERGITE. See METEOROLOGY.

EIGHT-HOUR DAY. See LABOR LEGISLATION, *Hours*.

ELATEA. See ARCHÆOLOGY.

ELDER, CYRUS. An American lawyer and author, died December 14, 1912. He was born in Somerset, Pa., in 1843, and was educated in public and private schools at Utica, O. In 1856 he was admitted to the bar and in the same year was a delegate to the Republican national convention. He served in 1861-2 in the Civil War and in the following year settled in law practice in Johnstown, Pa. He was solicitor for many important steel corporations, and organized the Bessemer Steel Company, Limited. In the Johnstown flood his wife lost her life, and he was made secretary of the flood finance committee and had much to do with reorganizing the city. He was president of the Cambria public library and was editor of the *Industrial League Bulletin* and the *Farmers' and Mechanics' Almanac*, which were protectionist publications. He wrote also *Dreams of a Free Trade Paradise*, and *Man and Labor*. He also published several books of poems and a small book called *My Testament*, in which he strongly favored cremation.

ELECTION DAY, EMPLOYMENT ON. See LABOR LEGISLATION, *Miscellaneous*.

ELECTORAL REFORM. The various plans for the improvement of the electorate which have been advocated within the last few years, were discussed with renewed interest in 1912, on account of the attention given to them in political discussion, and by the candidates for the presidential office. With these plans there will be included in this discussion the initiative and referendum, although they are more properly related to legislation than to elections. Other devices which have been called "short cuts to good government" are provisions for direct primaries, the direct election of senators, legislation against corrupt practices in elections, and movements for an improved and simpler form of ballot. In most of the States in which the legislatures were in session in 1912, measures relating to these questions were either passed or failed to pass. In other States, elections were held on constitutional amendments providing for some or all of them. With the initiative and referendum is usually included a provision for the recall, although in most cases the recall is applied only in municipal elections.

INITIATIVE AND REFERENDUM. The Republican platform contained no indorsement of the initiative, referendum, and recall. President Taft's attitude toward these devices was in general that they were related to the States rather than to the national government, and that while they might be effective in some cases, he was not willing to give them his indorsement until they had undergone a further test. The Democratic platform contained no direct allusion to the initiative, referendum, and recall, but Governor Wilson's attitude toward the questions may be considered as being that of his party. In his academic writings before he had entered political life he had severely denounced them, but his political experiences had converted him to the belief that they were efficient methods for improving the electorate. Largely through his efforts while he was governor, the initiative, referendum, and recall were made a part of the laws of New Jersey. Governor Wilson did not give any particular emphasis to the defense of these measures during the campaign.

No specific plank indorsing the initiative, referendum, and recall was included in the National Progressive platform, but in many of his addresses Mr. Roosevelt praised and defended them, altnough making the reservation that there might be cases in which they might be abused. Although there was more or less discussion of these measures during the campaign by presidential candiuates and others, it was generally assumed that they did not enter largely into national questions, but related rather to the government of States.

The initiative, referendum, and recall were adopted in Idaho at the election on November 5. Vote was taken on the constitutional amendment submitted to the people by the legislature in 1911. A similar amendment was adopted by the voters of Nevada. The vote for the initiative, referendum, and recall was nearly 9 to 1. The new constitution of Ohio contains provisions for the initiative, referendum, and recall (see OHIO). Votes were taken on a constitutional amendment providing for these measures in Wyoming and it was carried. In Arizona, the initiative, referendum, and recall were included in the constitution adopted in 1911, and these were enacted into laws by the legislature which met in 1912. Other States which adopted the measures during the year were North Dakota and Nebraska. The question is to be submitted to the voters of Wisconsin in 1913. The Mississippi legislature discussed legislation looking to the submission of the initiatve, referendum, and recall to the vote of the people of the State. The recall principle met with much opposition, and was finally rejected. A resolution was adopted providing for an amendment to the constitution incorporating the provisions for the initiative and referendum, and this amendment was submitted to a vote in the election on November 5. The amendment was lost, although it received a total of 25,-153 votes against 13,383 votes. Under the constitution, however, it had to receive a majority of all the votes cast in the election, and the total vote cast by presidential electors was 64,-948. Something over 26,000 voters did not vote either for or against it. The legislature of 1914 will undoubtedly submit the proposition again.

The States which have no provision for the initiative and referendum are: Alabama, Connecticut, Delaware, Florida, Georgia, Illinois, Indiana, Iowa, Kentucky, Maryland, Massachusetts, Michigan, New Hampshire, New York, North Carolina, North Dakota, Pennsylvania, Rhode Island, South Carolina, Tennessee, Texas, Utah, Vermont, Virginia, West Virginia, and Wisconsin.

In Illinois, although the initiative, referendum, and recall are not provided for by statute, there is a species of initiative enforced in the State by means of which certain questions of public policy are submitted at elections. The recall exists in cities and villages which have adopted the commission form of government. In Iowa there is also a recall provision in the law providing for the commission plan of city government. This is true also of Massachusetts. In this State the legislature of 1912 adopted an amendment authorizing the referendum. This is to be referred for action to the legislature of 1913 before it can be submitted to the voters for adoption or rejection. In Michigan, while there are no statutory provisions for the initiative, referendum, and recall, the towns and cities which have the commission form of government are authorized to adopt them. Although there has been no legislation in New Hampshire relating to the initiative, referendum, and recall, the referendum is used in submitting proposed amendments to the constitution for ratification by the voters of the State. This has been the practice from the first adoption of the constitution. In rare instances, matters of legislation have been referred to popular vote before they become operative, one instance being the license law relating to the sale of intoxicating liquors. In North Dakota the legislature of 1912 passed an amendment to the constitution, referring the initiative, referendum, and recall to the people. It is now required that the legislature which meets in 1913 shall adopt or pass one or more of these amendments. If such action shall be taken the amendments so adopted will be submitted to the voters at the general election to be held in November, 1914. In North Dakota cities governed by the commission form of government are given the power to use the initiative, referendum, and recall. In Pennsylvania, measures will be introduced into the legislature of 1913 providing for the initiative, referendum, and recall; the recall to be applied to all city, county, and State officers, except the judiciary. In Utah an amendment was adopted in 1900 providing for the initiative and referendum, but the legislature has failed to pass the necessary measures to place this provision of the constitution in force. In West Virginia the city of Parkersburg has a provision for the recall of officials in its charter.

An important decision was handed down by the United States Supreme Court on February 19, 1912. This was the first judgment of the court made upon the constitutionality of the initiative and referendum. The decision in general was that only Congress, and not the supreme court, could object to the initiative and referendum. See WASHINGTON.

THE RECALL. As noted above, the recall of officers by election, held after the presentation of a petition signed by a proportionate number of those voting in the previous election, has found its use almost entirely in the cases of cities which have the commission form of government. The only instance of its usage in 1912 was in the case of Seattle, where the mayor was recalled and another election held (see WASHINGTON). A wider use of the recall was one of the most discussed features of the campaign if 1912, as the result of the advocacy by Mr. Roosevelt, in his speech before the Ohio constitutional convention, of a plan of recall of judicial decisions under certain conditions. Mr. Roosevelt's proposal was amplified in other speeches, especially in a speech made in New York City shortly after the Columbus address. These speeches are summarized in the article PRESIDENTIAL CAMPAIGN. This plan found no support in the platforms or campaign utterances of the Democratic and Republican parties. The Republican platform contained a plank which insisted on the necessity of upholding the courts, and was in effect a denunciation of the principle of the recall of judicial decisions. The Democratic platform contained no mention of the proposal. The plank in the platform of the National Progressive party, advocating the measure was as follows: The Progressive party demands such restriction of the power of the courts as shall leave to the people the ultimate authority to determine the fundamental questions of social welfare and public policy. To secure this end it pledges itself to provide: (1) That when an act passed under the police power of the State is held unconstitutional under the State constitution by the courts, the people, after an ample interval for deliberation, shall have an opportunity to vote on the question whether they desire the act to become law, notwithstanding such decision. (2) That every decision of the highest appellate court of the State declaring an act of the legislature unconstitutional on the ground of its violation of the federal Constitution, shall be subject to the same review by the United States Supreme Court as is now accorded to decisions sustaining such legislation.

President Taft, in several speeches delivered during the campaign, denounced the principle of the recall of judges and judicial decisions as a most dangerous fallacy, and one that struck at the roots of the government. Governor Wilson, too, found no merit in the plan. Two States provide for the recall of judges under certain conditions. These are California, in which an amendment providing for such recall was passed in 1911, and Arizona, where the legislature in 1912 passed the recall measure which had in 1911 caused President Taft to veto the resolution providing for the admission of Arizona and New Mexico as States. See Arizona.

Direct Primaries. The principle of direct primary elections for the choice of State officers, representatives to Congress, and delegates to conventions, received general support from all three candidates for the presidency in 1912. Chief interest centred in the presidential preferential primaries held in several of the States. This is discussed in the paragraph below. Nearly all the States have some form of provision for primary elections. In the few in which it does not exist, measures will undoubtedly be enacted providing for them within a few years. In States which have the direct primaries for local officers, the tendency is to extend them to the selection of all officers, and to the election of delegates to the presidential conventions. The complaint against direct primaries most frequently heard is that they destroy party organization; that no method can be devised by which party lines can be maintained and that nothing can prevent opposition party men from voting at a primary election because they cannot be identified. As a result of this condition it is possible for a man of the opposition party in the minority in the State or district to force the nomination of an unpopular man upon the majority and thus secure the election of a popular man in the minority party. These objections have so far not been fully met by advocates of the direct primaries.

Another serious complaint made against them is that there has been and will be manipulation by which an unfit man is selected simply by multiplying the number of candidates. In several States the law has been corrected to prevent this. The usual method is the so-called "second choice plan." Wisconsin was the first of the States to pass such a plan. It was adopted in 1912 by Minnesota, and forms a part of the laws of Idaho, Washington, and North Dakota. The general theory of this plan is one of elimination. It strives to obtain approximately at least the majority nominees. The elimination is upon the theory of the elimination made by delegates in a convention, when the delegates drop their favorite, who has received the smallest number of votes among the candidates, and express their second choice by voting for one of the remaining candidates. This action is repeated until some candidate has a majority in the convention. In Minnesota the primary laws provide that if any candidate receives a majority he shall be declared the nominee and the second choice vote shall not be taken into consideration. If no candidate receives a majority, the elimination process is invoked. This is done by dropping the candidate who has the smallest number of first choice votes to his credit and adding the second choice votes cast by his supporters to the first choice votes of the remaining candidates for whom they were cast. If no condidate then has a majority, the process is repeated until some candidate has a majority or only two candidates remain. This general principle applies to the second choice plan in other States. For obvious reasons this provision is not made applicable to non-partisan offices. The names of the two highest candidates on the non-partisan primary ballot are placed on the general election ballot as the nominees, thereby giving the voter his second choice vote at the general election.

In addition to the "second choice plan," the law in Minnesota was extended to all State officers, United States senators, and justices of the State supreme court. Justices of the supreme court, all judges of municipal district and probate courts, county superintendents of schools, and all city officials in cities containing 50,000 inhabitants or more, are to become candidates without party designation and are voted for upon a separate non-partisan ballot and are in all particulars to be nominated and elected in a compulsory non-partisan manner. Thus the entire judiciary, educational officers, and all city officials of the large cities of the State are taken absolutely out of politics. In this respect Minnesota takes a position more radical than hitherto taken by any other State of the Union. A direct primary law was passed by the legislature of Kentucky in 1912. The new constitution of Ohio provides for direct primaries (see Ohio). The Massachusetts legislature also passed a direct primary law in 1912. Several measures relating to the direct primaries and direct elections were introduced into the legislature of Vermont, which convened in the autumn of 1912.

The States which have no provision for direct primaries are: Delaware, Indiana, New Mexico, North Carolina, Rhode Island, Vermont, and West Virginia.

Many of these primary laws include provisions for direct election of United States senators. In most of the southern States primary elections have been in operation for many years. In some cases, however, they are not the result of legal enactments, but are held by direction of State committees of the political parties. In Tennessee the primary is voluntary. The Democrats operate under a primary plan and the Republicans under the old convention system. In Texas the primary for senator is advisory, although the legislature always elects the candidate nominated. In practically all the southern States a victory in the primaries is equivalent to election, as the Democratic party carries the dominant vote. As most of the State legislatures did not meet in 1912, there was little important legislation relating to direct primary laws.

Direct Election of Senators. The provision for direct election of senators is usually combined in some form with the direct primary laws. The passage by the 62nd Congress of a constitutional amendment providing for direct election of senators in all the States will, when it is ratified by two-thirds of the States, secure a uniform system for the direct election of senators. This amendment is in the form of a joint resolution. In its original form it provided that the control of elections should be taken from the federal government, where it is now secured, by Section 4, of Article 1, of the State constitution. This was defeated in the previous session of Congress by the vote of southern senators, who expressed a fear of negro domination if there should be federal control of the elections. The joint resolution was reintroduced in the first session of the 62nd Congress and was passed by the House of Representatives by a vote of 296 to 16. The Senate also passed this resolution with an amendment providing that the control of elections shall remain in the hands of the federal government. The provision did not emerge from conference in time to be passed at this session of Congress. It was passed, however, at a succeeding session (see Congress). Three States voted favorably on the amendment in 1912.

The direct election of senators in some form is provided for in the following States: Arizona, California, Illinois, Iowa, Kansas, Maryland, Minnesota, Missouri, Montana, Nebraska, Nevada, New Jersey, Ohio, Oklahoma, Oregon, South Dakota, Texas, Virginia, Wisconsin, and Wyoming.

The original purpose of the plan of senatorial primaries for the direct election of senators was the elimination of the possibility of corruption in the State legislatures. It had, of course, the further object of securing practically the election of senators by direct vote of the people. These primaries as first held were comparatively inexpensive to candidates, but in the last few years there have been notable examples of lavish expenditures of money in the senatorial primaries. An instance of this is in the case of the election of Senator Stephenson of Wisconsin, who admitted the expenditure of $107,000 in the senatorial primaries. Attempts were made in the different States by the passage of corrupt practices acts to remedy this condition, and the corrupt practices act passed by Congress in 1911 limits the expenditure in these elections to $10,000.

Corrupt Practices. Several of the States passed stringent corrupt practices acts in 1912, and doubtless there would have been more had the legislatures of more States been in session. One of the most stringent laws is that passed by the Minnesota legislature. This act denies to the candidate the right to give anything of value to a voter. This includes things as trivial as a cigar or a drink of liquor. Indiana enacted a corrupt practices act at the last session of the legislature. Other States having corrupt practices acts are as follows: Iowa, Louisiana, Maine, Maryland, Massachusetts, Missouri, New Jersey, New Mexico, New York, North Dakota, Ohio, Oklahoma, Oregon, Tennessee, Virginia, Washington, West Virginia, and Wyoming.

Presidential Preferential Primaries. The plan for indicating a choice for presidential candidate by popular vote received its first application in 1912. In 1911, the legislatures of several States had authorized the holding of such primaries. These States were New Jersey, Wisconsin, Nebraska, North Dakota, Washington, and California. In addition to these the legislatures of Illinois, Maryland, Massachusetts, Ohio, and South Dakota authorized the holding of presidential primaries in 1912. In most cases a special session of the legislature was convened for this purpose. Certain of the southern States, including South Carolina and Louisiana, provided for presidential primaries by formal statutes, and in Pennsylvania delegates to the national convention are elected by direct primaries and candidates for delegates are permitted to print on the ballot the name of the candidate for President whom they wish to support. This amounts in effect to a presidential preferential primary.

The platform of the Democratic party contained a plank directing the national committee to incorporate in the call for the next nominating convention a requirement that all expressions of preference for presidential candidates shall be given and the selection of delegates and alternates made through a primary election conducted by the party organizations in each State where such expression and election are not provided for by State law. The Republican platform contained no formal reference to the presidential primaries. President Taft during the campaign expressed himself in favor of these primaries when they were held under proper conditions. Preferential primaries otherwise held, he characterized as "soap-box primaries" (see Presidential Campaign). The platform of the National Progressive party contained no plank formally advocating presidential primaries, but throughout the campaign it was one of the leading issues with Mr. Roosevelt and the other Progressive candidates. Upon the results of the presidential primaries held in the various States Mr. Roosevelt based his assertion that he was the people's choice.

Presidential preferential primaries or primaries which were equivalent were held in the States of California, Illinois, Maryland, Massachusetts, Nebraska, New Hampshire, New Jersey, North Dakota, Ohio, Oregon, Pennsylvania, South Dakota, and Wisconsin. These elections are treated in detail in the article Presidential Campaign and in the articles on the several States. It may be noted here that the total Republican direct primary vote cast in these States was 2,284,163, while the Republican vote cast in these States in the presidential election of 1908 was 3,372,713, that is to say, there were about 1,000,000 less votes cast in the presidential primaries in 1912 than were cast in the presidential campaign four years previous. It is probable that this form of primary will have become general in the States before the next presidential election.

For measures of electoral reform in foreign countries in 1912, see BELGIUM, FRANCE, GREAT BRITAIN, and other countries, paragraphs on *History*.

ELECTORAL VOTE. See PRESIDENTIAL CAMPAIGN.

ELECTRICAL INDUSTRIES. Throughout 1912 the electrical industries in America fully sustained the records of expansion set in previous years viz, about 15 per cent. The comparative estimates of the manufactures and value of electric service for 1911 and 1912, as formulated by a leading electrical journal, are as follows:

	1911	1912
Electrical manufactures..	$325,000,000	$350,000,000
Electric railway earnings	575,000,000	625,000,000
Central station earnings..	375,000,000	450,000,000
Telephone earnings......	310,000,000	350,000,000
Telegraph earnings	75,000,000	85,000,000
Isolated plant service....	125,000,000	125,000,000
Misc. electric service.....	100,000,000	125,000,000
Total	$1,885,000,000	$2,110,000,000

An important aspect of this development was the growing tendency toward concentration. It is estimated that 90 per cent. of the electrical manufactures were produced by three concerns. More than 60 per cent. of the telephone earnings and more than 50 per cent. of the telegraph earnings were made by the Bell companies. The central stations are largely independent, but the percentage controlled by a few large syndicates has increased greatly during 1912. See also DYNAMO-ELECTRIC MACHINERY.

ELECTRICAL POWER, TRANSMISSION OF. See TRANSMISSION OF ELECTRICAL POWER.

ELECTRIC BATTERIES. The developments in the field of electric batteries in 1912 were mainly commercial. One new type was reported, the nickel-iron cell of Gouin. The positive electrode consists of perforated tubes of nickel, filled with specially prepared hydroxides of nickel, mixed with powdered graphite. These tubes are reinforced with twisted nickel wires and are nested horizontally in a nickel frame. The negative grids consist of thin iron wire plaited into flat ribbons, carrying protoxides of iron. The inventor claims that it rivals the Edison cell in lightness and life and is on a par with the lead cell in first cost.

The greatest advances of the battery are in the vehicle field. It is conservatively estimated that there are now in America 80,000 electric storage-battery vehicles, of which about 26,000 were produced in 1912. The projected production of electric vehicles for 1913 is 40,000, and the value of the storage batteries for the new cars will probably amount to $25,000,000. A number of important installations of stand-by batteries were made on city distribution systems, the discharge capacity in some cases being as high as 44,000 amperes. See DYNAMO-ELECTRIC MACHINERY.

ELECTRIC LIGHT AND POWER. See MUNICIPAL OWNERSHIP.

ELECTRIC LIGHTING. In the field of incandescent lamps, 1912 was marked by the complete decline of the carbon filament. The metallized carbon type was largely adopted by central stations for free renewals. Its general performance is much more economical than that of the carbon lamp, though somewhat more fragile and of shorter useful life. Steady improvements in the tungsten filament and reductions of price have greatly increased its use. The earlier lamps, especially those of high power, showed a tendency to blacken the bulb which greatly reduced the available period of service. A bulb-blackening preventive has been applied with great success. A severe test of tungsten lamps made in subway trains showed that but 15 per cent. of the lamps failed electrically or through breakage in 1000 hours of burning. The use of miniature lamps for automobile lighting and the local illumination of machinery was very greatly extended. Important developments were made in long-life flame arcs. By proper restriction of the air supply in conjunction with the purging of the gas in the arc chamber from fumes it is possible to obtain a life per trim of 120 hours or more, with good efficiency and well-sustained candle-power. These results make the flame arc an important factor in street-lighting, where in the past the expense of the frequent renewals has been a great handicap. The fluorescent rhodamine reflector has been successful in correcting the color of light from the glass-tube mercury arc. Green rays absorbed by the reflector are converted into red and the combined spectrum is approximately white.

The high-pressure quartz-tube mercury arc, which was used to some extent in Europe in preceding years, reached the commercial stage in America in 1912. While not white, the light of these lamps is much better balanced in color than that from the glass tube arcs, and is very satisfactory for out-door illumination. Lamps of this type have a high efficiency of about 4 candle-power per watt, and the quartz tubes give a life of from 1000 to 2000 hours, after which the lamps fail through loss of vacuum. The tubes can then be renewed at a cost of from $6 to $12. It is confidently expected that improvements in the art of quartz working will lower the cost and increase the life of the tubes to the point where the renewal cost of such lamps per annum will be much less than the present cost of trimming street arcs. In such a case the quartz tube lamp should assume great importance in street lighting. The first installation for the purpose was made in Chicago. The radiation from the quartz-tube lamp is rich in actinic rays, making it a powerful and efficient sterilizing agent. One lamp can sterilize 500 cubic meters of water per day if the water is caused to flow in a thin sheet over an area on which the radiation is concentrated. This process has been commercially established in Chicago and in St. Petersburg, Russia. European inventors have brought out a number of types of 3-phase, alternating current arc lamps. In general these have three electrodes, each capable of lateral and longitudinal motion, so that three symmetrical arcs are maintained. Such lamps are claimed to give an efficiency of 10 candle-power per watt and to be very long-burning and low in renewal cost.

Methods of illumination in which the lamps are wholly or partially concealed and the light derived from white ceilings and walls gained greatly in favor. These indirect methods are less efficient than the direct. Their advantages are largely the elimination of glare and the pleasing architectural effects which they make possible. Artificial methods of producing the color quality of daylight have reached a commercial development. In general these take the form of a composite screen of colored glass which absorbs from the artificial light those rays which are in excess of daylight proportions. This filtration process as applied to the tungsten filament lamp yields an efficiency of about 13 per cent., hence is rather costly for general use.

ELECTRIC RAILWAYS. The most significant developments in electric railroading in 1912 related to the high-voltage direct current system. The aggregate mileage in America equipped for such operation reached and exceeded 1000 route-miles, and the rolling stock comprises over 500 motor cars and locomotives. The standard trolley voltages for this system are 1200, 1500 and 2400, the latter adopted for the first time in 1912 for the Butte, Anaconda and Pacific Railway. The motive power in the latter case is to consist of pairs of 1200-volt motors in series. The largest high-voltage, direct-current system yet projected is involved in the accepted plans for the electrification of the suburban railways of Melbourne, Australia. This system includes 250 miles of track and will require 500 motor cars and a number of large locomotives. A voltage of 1500 was chosen after an exhaustive investigation of all proposed systems. Important extensions were made in the single-phase system of the New Haven Railroad. This company announced its intention of extending this form of operation to the four-track division between Boston and Providence in 1913. The estimated cost is $7,000,000.

A number of very important projects of electrification of suburban systems were inaugurated in European cities in 1912. Among these are the unification of the surface tram system in Paris and its electrification with direct-current equipment, using conduits in the central districts and trolleys in the suburbs. The Western State Railroad of France has undertaken the electrification of its Paris suburban system. A beginning was made on the electrification of all the city and suburban lines of Berlin with the single-phase system at 15,000 volts and 16⅔ cycles. This task was made necessary by the present congested state of the system, and, when complete, will practically double the traffic capacity of the existing trackage. The work will cost about $31,000,000, and will require four years for its completion. Electrification plans have been announced for the suburban sections of the London and Northwestern and the London and Southwestern systems, in which the use of direct-current systems is contemplated. The direct-current system at 1100 volts was installed on a number of the city lines in Budapest.

The use of the light-weight storage battery car has been much extended. This system is employed in some cases with three-car trains operated from a single point by the multiple unit system. Large storage battery cars have appeared as rivals of the gasoline-electric cars on branch lines of standard railroads.

ELECTRIC STEEL FURNACE. See METALLURGY.

ELECTROCULTURE. See AGRICULTURE.

ELECTRO-METALLURGY. See METALLURGY.

ELECTRO-THERAPEUTIC TREATMENT. See CANCER.

ELEMENTARY SCHOOLS. See EDUCATION.

ELEMENTS. See CHEMISTRY.

EL-GERZEH. See ARCHÆOLOGY.

EMPLOYERS, WELFARE OF. See WELFARE WORK.

EMPLOYERS' LIABILITY. Since the enactment of the Workmen's Compensation act in Great Britain in 1897 such legislation has become practically universal among western nations. The old liability laws imposed obligations on the employer only in case the injured worker could break down the common-law defenses of assumed risk, contributory negligence, and the fellow-servant rule. Experience showed that under such conditions the injured worker often failed to receive any financial relief whatever and was frequently forced to assume a heavy financial burden in litigation only to lose finally because of inability to carry his case to higher courts. Gradually the common-law defenses were broken down. The new legislation aims to give compensation for injury according to some definite plan without imposing litigation expenses on the worker. See WORKMEN'S COMPENSATION.

In the last two years workmen's compensation laws have been passed in the States of Arizona, California, Kansas, Maryland, Massachusetts, Michigan, Minnesota, New Hampshire, New Jersey, Ohio, Rhode Island, Washington, and Wisconsin; and federal laws extended the compensation act of 1908 to artisans and laborers in hazardous work under the Bureau of Mines and the Forestry Service. The State laws are drawn up on the basis of one of several distinct plans. They provide either for direct compensation by the employer, as in New Jersey, or for insurance by the employer under more or less State supervision. Such insurance may be compulsory, as in Washington, or optional, as in Massachusetts, Minnesota, and Ohio. Moreover, this insurance may be wholly in the hands of the State authorities, as in Washington and Ohio, or left to private companies under State scrutiny, as in Massachusetts and New Jersey. In Ohio the State insurance fund is a general one for all industries, but in Washington there is a separate fund for each industry. The Washington law is the only one thus far enacted which has been an out-and-out compulsory law. The reason for this is that the State courts have refused to uphold the constitutionality of such legislation with coercive features. A New York law enacted in 1910 applying to a specified list of dangerous occupations was thus declared unconstitutional. Consequently with the exception noted the States have made compensation laws optional. The success of an optional law is increased greatly by making it easier for the employer to accept it than to remain under the employers' liability law: this may be done by presuming all who do not give express notice to the contrary to have accepted the act, as in New Jersey, and by lower costs. These laws have quite uniformly removed the common-law defenses, but in Massachusetts these defenses are all restored to any employer accepting the compensation plan, and in Kansas and New Jersey willful neglect on the part of the worker is made a bar to compensation. A compensation law may apply to all trades, as in California, New Jersey, and Ohio, or only to a specified list deemed particularly hazardous. The development of compensation legislation has seemed to favor the adoption of some plan of mutual insurance for employers. This scheme has the advantage of spreading the loss due to industrial accidents over a large body; and at the same time guarantees to the worker his compensation regardless of the financial status of his employer. Insurance schemes may be contributory or noncontributory, depending on whether the workers are or are not required to contribute to the fund. Most States have made provision for an administrative board to have charge of the enforcement of the compensation act; such was not the case in New Jersey. Where a board is provided it is usually authorized to adjust all claims; in New Jersey such adjustment was left to the courts.

OHIO PLAN. The compensation law passed by the legislature in 1911 was tested in the courts in 1912, although the legislature had previously secured a prejudgment from the State Supreme Court that the law was constitutional. Against the law it was argued in the first place that it was an unwarranted exercise of the police power. This the court denied. In the second place it was argued that the law took private property without due process of law. This the court held to be unfounded as the act is not coercive, but optional. In similar manner the court denied that the act deprives any party of freedom of contract or impairs the obligation of contract, nor does the law make any arbitrary discrimination, but acts uniformly on all persons brought within its scope. As this decision indicates, the Ohio law is optional. It provides for the creation of an insurance fund to which employers shall contribute 90 per cent. and employees 10 per cent. The law provides that if any employer accepts the plan his employees must accept it also; if, however, the employer rejects it he loses the protection of the common-law doctrine. The board of three commissioners appointed to administer the law drew up a tentative schedule of insurance rates; this schedule was to be subject to revision at the end of six months. The law aroused very lively competition on the part of the liability companies, which was met in part by a campaign of education by the commissioners. The latter have endeavored to induce employers to improve their plants by providing maximum and minimum rates for each industry.

NEW YORK LAW. Following the declaration by the New York Court of Appeals in 1911 that the Wainwright compensation act was unconstitutional, the friends of such legislation were divided between those who favored a constitutional amendment, those who favored the passage of an optional law, and those who favored another compulsory act of wider scope. Various bills were thus presented to the legislature; one was based on the Washington compulsory State insurance law; one was based on the Ohio optional insurance law; and a third was a scheme of optional compensation without the idea of mutual insurance. None of these were passed. The legislature, however, adopted a proposed amendment which, if approved by the next legislature and by popular vote in November, 1913, will become a part of the State constitution. Among other things this resolution says: "Nothing contained in this constitution shall be construed to limit the power of the legislature to enact laws for the protection of the lives, health, or safety of employees; or for the payment, either by employers, or by employers and employees or otherwise, either directly or through a State or other system of insurance or otherwise, of compensation for injuries to employees or for death of employees resulting from such injuries, without regard to fault as a cause thereof, except where the injury is occasioned by the willful intention of the injured employee or results solely from the intoxication of the injured employee while on duty."

WASHINGTON LAW. One of the most advanced compensation laws was that enacted in Washington in 1911, and upheld as constitutional in October, 1911. This law is based on the principle of insurance, the administration of which is in the hands of State authorities. Moreover, it is compulsory. Employers are divided into classes according to degrees of risk to workers and rates of assessment are then apportioned to the estimated risk. These rates are fixed in the law, but the Industrial Insurance Commission which has charge of the administration is authorized to levy upon the various classes of employers only so frequently as actual needs may require. The summary for the year ending September showed 5750 firms listed and assessed; 130,000 employers; 11,896 accidents reported; 6984 claims allowed; 2256 claims disallowed or suspended; 2656 claims still unadjusted. The commission received $980,446 for the accident fund and paid out on claims $445,528. It invested as a reserve to guarantee compensations $245,985 and had a cash balance of $290,933. In addition the commission paid for its own expenses out of legislative appropriations $107,000, or about 10 per cent. of the total funds handled. This ratio of expenses was believed to be extremely low. Results of the first year's experience showed that the rates of assessment provided in the law were much larger than necessary. A few appeals were taken from the commission to the courts; and 43 suits were begun against employers who defaulted in their payments.

OTHER PLANS. During 1912 the States of Arizona, Maryland, Michigan, and Rhode Island adopted the principle of workmen's compensation in place of the older principle of employer's liability. The Arizona law provides compulsory compensation for a list of especially dangerous occupations. The Michigan law applies to all employees but farm and domestic servants and casual workers. It is semi-optional, the employers having the choice of various methods of payment, the yearly choice of employers to be filed with an industrial accident board. The members of this board are to serve for six years at an annual salary of $3500. An employee must give express notice if he does not wish to come under the law. The law provides for medical benefit for not more than three weeks; for death payments amounting to 50 per cent. of wages, but not to exceed $10 per week for not more than 300 weeks; for payment in case of total incapacity of 50 per cent. of wages for not longer than 500 weeks; and in case of partial incapacity of one-half of the loss of wages for not more than 300 weeks; the payment in the case of certain bodily members to be according to a fixed legal scale. The employer is allowed four methods of paying the compensation: Self insurance, a liability insurance company, a mutual employer's company, or an accident fund administered by the State commissioner of insurance.

The Maryland law is purely optional. If the employer chooses to accept the compensation idea he may insure in a liability company or, if he has as many as 1500 employees, in a mutual benefit fund. The State commissioner of insurance has charge of the administration of the law. The rates of compensation in the Maryland and Rhode Island laws are almost identical with those provided in the Michigan act above described. The Rhode Island law is also similar to the Michigan law in that it is semi-optional. It, however, contains the beneficent provision that unless the employee expressly states otherwise he is presumed to accept the law.

The legislatures of 1911 and 1912 created ten commissions for the investigation of employers' liability and workmen's compensation; moreover, some of the commissions previously appointed have not yet reported. The Michigan and Maryland commissions preceded the legislation already described. The commissions of Pennsylvania, Colorado, North Dakota, Minnesota, Delaware, Texas, Connecticut, and West Virginia are expected to report early in 1913. The Missouri commission was compelled to give up its work because of an adverse opinion by the attorney-general as to the legality of the appropriation for its maintenance. The Iowa commission made a special investigation of the working of the different systems of compensation in operation in New Jersey, Ohio, and Wisconsin. The Nebraska commission met with special difficulty in the matter of compensation for agricultural laborers. The Pennsylvania commission drew up a compensation bill providing compensation, not only during the customary 300 weeks in case of total permanent disability, but also at lessened amount during life.

Federal Commission. The United States Employers' Liability and Workmen's Compensation Commission's bill, promoted by the American Association for Labor Legislation and the National Civic League and introduced in Congress by Senator Sutherland on February 20, provided compulsory compensation for accidents or deaths, except when caused by willful neglect, for all except casual employees of interstate railways. The bill provided for adjustment of claims either directly by employer and employee, or by an adjustment committee chosen by the employer and employees, or by a federal adjuster. The latter would be a permanent official appointed and removable by the United States District Court and having certain powers to summon witnesses and take testimony. Medical benefit to the amount of $200 was provided. Periodic readjustment of compensation on the basis of medical examination was also provided for. The death benefit was made equal to 40 per cent. of the wages in case a widow survives; 50 per cent. for a period not to exceed eight years in case a widow and one or more children under 16 years of age survive; 25 per cent. in case no widow, but one child survives, with an addition of 10 per cent. for each additional child up to a total of 50 per cent. If the deceased should leave no widow or children but dependent parents the compensation would be 25 per cent. of wages if one and 40 per cent. if both survive. Various other special compensations are provided for the various possible dependents. In case of permanent total disability the compensation would be 50 per cent. of wages for life. In case of pe manent partial disability compensation would be 50 per cent. of wages for periods varying from 72 months for the loss of one arm to 5 months for the loss of the fourth finger. The bill provided that these monthly payments might be commuted for a lump sum after the lapse of 6 months. In all cases the wages were to be computed on a basis of 26 days in a month, but no wages were to be considered as above $100 a month or as below $50.

It must be understood that the United States had already provided in 1908 compensation for artisans and laborers employed in certain branches of the government service. The amounts of compensation paid under this law from August 1, 1908, to October 1, 1912, slightly exceeded $1,100,000. During the first year 1689 claims were granted and during the second year 2499.

Constitutionality of Federal Law. There has been much debate over the question whether Congress has the authority to enact a general workmen's compensation law. Considerable light was thrown on this question by the decisions of the United States Supreme Court handed down January 15, 1912, in various cases involving the constitutionality of the federal employers' liability act as amended April 5, 1910. In these cases the Supreme Court unanimously concluded that the congressional power to regulate commerce includes power to force interstate common carriers to assume liability for accidents to employees. The court declared that no person has any property or vested interest in any rule of the common law; consequently Congress may take away the common-law doctrines behind which employers had defended themselves against liability and may substitute therefor the principle of employers' responsibility. This applies to the fellow-servant doctrine, to the principle of contributory negligence and the doctrine of assumption of risk. Moreover, the court held that any enactment of Congress on this subject would take precedence of conflicting State laws. In addition the power of Congress in this matter is not restricted to interstate common carriers, but may be extended to all persons or corporations engaged in interstate commerce. This decision was thought by many to form a basis for a much broader workmen's compensation law than that provided in the bill presented by the federal commission as above outlined. Although that bill, applied to nearly one and one-half million railway employees, legislation applying to the great corporations likewise carrying on interstate trade would extend federal protection to additional millions of workers.

Canadian Plan. After twenty-one months' work the Canadian Workmen's Compensation Commission submitted a partial report in July. On the whole this commission favored the establishment of a mutual insurance fund. It found that employers desired that the workmen be required to pay 10 per cent. of the cost of an insurance scheme, whereas the representatives of labor on the other hand insisted that the employers should bear the entire cost. Before submitting its recommendations for legislation the commission expected to gather additional information on this question and to work out many problems of administration.

THE BREWING INDUSTRY PLAN. During recent years a number of the larger employers of labor, including the United Steel Corporation, the International Harvester Company, and various railroads, have instituted voluntary compensation schemes. None of these, however, were as liberal as the plan drawn up by a joint committee representing the Brewers' Association and the International Union of United Brewery Workers of America. A comprehensive plan providing for accident prevention, accident compensation, and old-age pensions was agreed to. Penalties are provided for those employers who fail to install safety appliances as recommended by a board of directors and award. The fund for the payment of benefits will be provided by each employer paying 1.5 per cent. of the amount of his pay-roll and each employee 0.5 per cent. of the amount of his wages. Complete recognition of the union is shown by the fact that the higher officials of the union are included in the scheme. The benefits include first aid for all injuries. In case of partial disability the compensation equals 65 per cent. of wages after the first week, unless disability continues more than four weeks, in which case compensation is given for the first week also. In case of total disability not resulting in death the workman will receive 65 per cent. of his wages for five years, in weekly amounts of not less than $5 nor more than $20. In case of death the dependents will receive a sum equal to 300 times 65 per cent. of the deceased's wages, but not more than $3400. For the retirement pensions plan, see WORKINGMEN'S INSURANCE.

ENGLAND. See GREAT BRITAIN.

ENGLISH PHILOLOGY. See PHILOLOGY.

ENTOMOLOGY. GIPSY MOTHS, ETC. The gipsy moth problem continued to attract attention during 1912, and L. H. Worthley, an employee of the Bureau of Entomology, was sent to Europe in January to investigate possible parasites of this insect. The entomologist of the Dominion of Canada reported that much damage had been done by both gipsy and brown-tail moths in Nova Scotia and New Brunswick and that gipsy moth eggs and larvæ had been found on nursery stock imported from Japan. Much alarm was also felt in the United States over the possible importation of this pest from Europe on fruit and ornamental trees. To guard against the further spread the federal government established a quarantine against certain areas in all of the New England States except Vermont, forbidding the transportation of deciduous trees, florists' stock and Christmas trees from the quarantined area to other parts of the country unless properly inspected and determined to be free from gipsy and brown-tail moths. The gipsy moth quarantine covered also logs, tan bark, railroad ties, and similar products.

Calosoma sycophanta, a beetle imported from Europe, where it eats gipsy moth larvæ, was reported to have secured a good foothold in Massachusetts, though as it requires about three years to develop sufficiently to be easily noticed it has not yet done much toward exterminating the pests. Britton reported that in Connecticut the Stonington colony of gipsy moth is apparently exterminated, as none have been seen since 1910, and only a few are to be found at Wallingford. The brown-tail was reported as spreading southward in the State.

In the vicinity of Boston and along the Connecticut shore the leopard moth was reported as especially troublesome. This is chiefly a town and city insect, not spreading into the country, where it is possible that woodpeckers keep it in check by eating the boring larvæ.

HOUSE FLIES, ETC. The house fly problem also attracted much attention during 1912, numerous "swat the fly" campaigns having been inaugurated. No very satisfactory or practicable methods for trapping the insects seems to have yet been found, and the practice of destroying all breeding places seems to be the most feasible method of elimination, though this would be more successfully carried on in the city than in the country, where breeding places are so much more numerous. Grasshoppers did much damage in Colorado and Minnesota during 1912, and in the latter State a mixture of sodium arsenate and molasses devised especially for destroying grasshoppers proved to be fatal to many flies. The suggestion was made that a mixture of eight ounces of sodium arsenate, with one pint of molasses in twenty gallons of water, would, if sprayed over piles of horse manure in which flies are breeding, be efficient in killing off the larvæ. No mention was made of the possible effect of this poison on the value of the manure as fertilizer.

Observations reported in 1912 apparently make it certain that the stable fly, *Stomoxys calcitrans*, is responsible for the transmission of infantile paralysis. This fly should not be, as happened in some cases in the public press, confused with the house or "typhoid" fly, *Musca domestica*.

The total appropriation for the United States Bureau of Entomology for the year beginning July, 1912, was $691,840.

COLORATION. The Davy prize was awarded in 1912 to a paper by Pictet, "Recherches experimentales sur les mechanismes du melanisme et de l'albinism chez les lepidoptères." In this paper Pictet showed that wing color is due either to pigmentation or to structures producing interference phenomena, the two being in inverse ratio to one another. Melanism appears if there is much pigment in the scales, or if the pigment becomes more opaque or if the scales either increase in size or become more numerous. Albinism appears if the conditions are opposite to those just mentioned. He regarded melanism as a sign of vigor and health, while albinism indicates an enfeeblement of organs. Lovell, as the result of experiments on insect vision, concluded that while insects will visit green flowers in search of honey, just as they will visit other inconspicuous places, they are much more apt to visit conspicuous flowers, indicating a well-developed sense of sight.

Fiebrig, in an elaborate paper, gave his results on a study of insect sleep, in which he showed that insects do assume a sleeping posture, frequently an "upside down" one, comparable to that assumed by mammals, holding themselves firmly to plant stems by their mandibles. The wings and legs are relaxed and have no supporting function during this period.

At this time light and other stimuli affect the insects in much the same way as they do in other animals.

It was reported during the year that hickory trees in the eastern United States are being killed by a beetle, *Scolytus quadrispinosus*, which excavates tunnels under the bark. The only remedy seems to be to mark infected trees in the summer, and some time between October and March, when the y ung are under the bark, to kill the trees and burn the bark. If not too seriously infected the portion attacked may be cut out and burned instead of cutting the entire tree. A walnut weevil was reported from Connecticut, whose attacks can be prevented in large part by spraying with lead arsenate. Experiments reported by the United States Bureau of Entomology indicated that a single thorough application of lead arsenate applied to apple trees just after the petals have fallen, is sufficient to control the codling moth, though unless very carefully done this is not as efficacious as the usual two-spraying method. There was a temporary decrease owing to climatic conditions in the number of boll weevils in Texas, but this gives no reason to believe that the improvement is more than temporary. The insect appeared for the first time in Florida in 1912.

The second International Congress of Entomology met at Oxford, England, in August, under the presidency of Professor E. B. Poulton.

ERICHSEN, MYLIUS. See POLAR EXPLORATION.

ERITREA. An Italian colony on the west shore of the Red Sea. Estimated area, 45,800 sq. miles; population, 279,000. Asmara is the capital. Salt is an important product, being sent to southern Abyssinia, where it is the monetary currency. Imports 1910, 16,372,830 lire (17,225,720 in 1909); exports, 7,277,865 (6,845,026); transit, 3,857,351 (3,152,380). Tonnage entered, 183,532 (171,155). The railway from Massowah to Asmara was finished in 1911; it will be extended to Keren and Agordat. Estimated revenue (1910-11), 8,977,750 lire (state contribution, 6,350,000); expenditure, 7,223,700 (military administration, 3,988,200). Giuseppe Salvago (Marquis) Raggi was governor in 1912.

ESPIONAGE. See GERMANY.

ETHICAL CULTURE, SOCIETIES FOR. The first society was founded in 1876 by Felix Adler, in New York, for the purpose of uniting people of varying religious beliefs or none, in the ordinary acceptance of the term, upon a basis of a devotion to the moral ideal. The movement extended to other cities, and now societies of ethical culture are found in nearly all the larger cities in the United States. The most important events in the history of the society during the year were, first, the Moral Education Congress, which was originated by the International Ethical Union held in August at The Hague, and second, the dedication of the meeting-house of the Ethical Society of St. Louis, which took place in the early part of October. There was also greatly renewed activity in the work of the Chicago Society for Ethical Culture. This was due to the new leadership of Mr. Horace Bridges of London, who took charge in October. The Philadelphia Society for Ethical Culture started during the year, the movement for a new meeting-house, and an active correspondence bureau, established in Madison, Wis., has had considerable success in disseminating literature in connection with the society's propaganda for moral education in public schools. The president of the New York Society is Dr. Felix Adler.

ETHICS. See PHILOSOPHY.

ETHIOPIA. See ABYSSINIA.

ETHNOGRAPHY. See ANTHROPOLOGY.

ETHNOLOGY. See ANTHROPOLOGY.

ETTOR, J. J. See STRIKES.

EUGENICS. A noteworthy event of the year was the meeting of the first International Eugenics Congress at the University of London, July 12-30 under the presidency of Major Leonard Darwin. The general spirit of the congress was conservative. It was called to afford a chance for a free interchange of views and not to determine a definite propaganda. It did not put forward a platform or even unite on any general proposition in regard to the eugenics movement. But while this indeterminate course was unsatisfactory to the more radical and enthusiastic members, it was generally approved. The congress accomplished its main purpose of stimulating interest in the study and giving it an international character. Much was done in 1912, not only toward securing wide public discussion of eugenics but in removing wrong popular impressions arising either from misrepresentations or from the exaggerations of extremists. Important bodies which gave their attention to it in the United States during the year were the American Medico - Psychological Association, which favored strong measures for the prevention of insanity, the National Association for the Study of the Feeble-Minded, and the Association for the Study of Epilepsy. Prevention was the main theme of discussion and there was a general tendency to favor it. The subject of prevention was also discussed by the National Conference of Charities and Corrections in connection with the treatment of defectives. A school was opened in Boston for the practical instruction of parents and teachers in the subject of eugenics. See BIOLOGY, and SOCIOLOGY.

EVANGELICAL ASSOCIATION. A religious denomination which has its chief strength among the German-born citizens of the United States. In general, it has the doctrine and polity of American Methodism, but is modified in the direction of greater democracy. Communicants are found in nearly all parts of the northern section of the United States and Canada. There is a considerable strength also in the West and South. Missionary work is carried on among Italian immigrants. There were in 1912 109,506 communicants, 1665 churches, and 978 ministers. For administrative purposes there are twenty-four districts. In the Sunday schools there are about 175,000 pupils. The Young People's Alliance, connected with the church, numbers 50,000 members. A publishing house is maintained at Cleveland, O., and several philanthropic institutions and hospitals in Chicago, Philadelphia, and in cities throughout the Middle West. The chief educational institution is Northwestern College at Naperville, Ill.

EVANS, EDWARD C. An American clergyman, writer and educator, died October 23, 1912. He was born in Wrexham, North Wales, in 1844. In 1869 he removed to the United States and entering Princeton University, graduated in 1876. In the following year he was

Marquand Classical Fellow at Oxford University. He later studied at Princeton Theological Seminary and then accepted a professorship at Lake Forest University. From 1879 to 1882 he was pastor of the Welsh C. M. Church in Remsen, N. Y. He was well known as a preacher and writer. He received the degree of D. D. from Hamilton College in 1910.

EVANS, ROBLEY DUNGLISON. A rear-admiral, retired, of the United States navy, died January 3, 1912. He was born in Floyd county, Va., in 1846. After the death of his father in 1855 he went to live with his uncle, Alexander H. Evans, in Washington, D. C. He there attended Gonzaga College. In 1859 he was appointed to the United States Naval Academy and in the following year began his studies at Annapolis, graduating in 1863. He saw active service in the Civil War on the frigate *Powhatan* under Admiral Lardner and under the same officer in the East Gulf. Afterwards, under Admiral Porter, he participated in the assault upon and capture of Fort Fisher. He was severely wounded in the assault made by the defenders of the fort against their besiegers. After spending several months in the hospital he was, at his own request, restored to the active list. He was promoted by Congress for conspicuous gallantry and soon afterwards sailed for China on the *Delaware*, the flagship of Rear-Admiral Rowan. On his return to the United States he was assigned to ordnance duty until 1870, when he was stationed at Annapolis for two years. He was then sent to the Mediterranean as navigating officer of the *Shenandoah*. Upon the threatened outbreak of war between the United States and Spain in 1874, he returned and was appointed executive officer of the *Congress*. On this ship he returned to the Mediterranean and remained there until the *Congress* was sent to Philadelphia at the opening of the Centennial in 1876. In the years immediately following he served as commander of the training-ship and in the Washington Navy Yard and as a member of the first advisory board whose reports resulted in the foundation of the new navy. Upon his recommendation steel was adopted for the construction of United States battleships. He worked for a short time in the steel works at Pittsburgh, testing and inspecting steel. In 1891 he was assigned to the command of the *Yorktown* and was ordered to Valparaiso. Here an incident took place which won him the sobriquet "Fighting Bob." Previous to the entry of the *Yorktown* into the harbor of Valparaiso, a Chilean mob had assaulted the sailors of the cruiser *Baltimore*. This brought about a delicate diplomatic situation, especially as some Chilean refugees had taken shelter on board the *Yorktown*. The Chilean government was informed that the refugees would be protected on the *Yorktown* at all costs. Evans's gig was stoned by the Chileans; whereupon he demanded a suitable apology from the commander of the Chilean war vessel, a portion of whose crew had perpetrated the act, and supported the request by a notification that if the apology was not forthcoming within twenty-four hours the guns of the *Yorktown* would be trained upon the Chilean man-of-war. An apology immediately followed. Returning from Chile, Evans was sent to the Bering Sea to prevent unlawful sealing. At that time there was friction between Great Britain and the United States over the sealing industry and there was talk of possible war. Evans enforced his instructions so resolutely that of 108 vessels that had been warned against proceeding to the sealing grounds, 98 were prevented from violating the law. Practically no seals were killed in that year. In his five months' duty Evans sailed 63,000 miles. In 1893 he was made a captain and was given command of the cruiser *New York*. At the outbreak of the Spanish war in 1898 he was in command of the *Iowa*, which was part of Rear-Admiral Sampson's fleet, which shut Cervera up in the harbor of Santiago. In the battle which followed Cervera's dash for freedom, the *Iowa* took a prominent part and was largely instrumental in the destruction of the *Maria Teresa*, Cervera's flagship. The *Iowa* also engaged the *Vizcaya*, the *Cristobal Colon* and the *Oquendo*. When the *Vizcaya* was run aground Evans sent boats to rescue her crew and received her commander and other officers on board the *Iowa*. He always insisted that the credit of the victory belonged to Admiral Sampson. In 1901 he was made rear-admiral. He commanded the fleet in the Far East in 1904. In 1907 he was given the signal honor of commanding the great battleship fleet which left Hampton Roads, December 16, for its cruise around the world. When the fleet reached San Francisco, Admiral Evans retired from its command, chiefly as the result of ill health. He was retired August 18, 1908, after receiving the thanks of the Navy Department for the manner in which he handled the fleet. Admiral Evans wrote two books of reminiscences, and *A Sailor's Log* (1901).

EVERETT, WILLIAM HENRY. A rear-admiral, retired, of the United States navy, died June 10, 1912. He was born in New York in 1847 and graduated from the United States Naval Academy in 1868. In the following year he was made ensign. He was promoted through various grades until he became captain in 1904. In 1906 he was made rear-admiral and retired at his own request.

EVERGLADES. See EXPLORATION; FLORIDA, and DRAINAGE.

EWERS, EZRA PHILETUS. An American soldier, died January 16, 1912. He was born in Wayneport, N. Y., in 1837. He enlisted as a private in the 19th Infantry and was promoted to be first lieutenant in that regiment in 1864. In 1866 he was transferred to the 37th Infantry and in the same year was made captain. He served afterwards with the 5th Infantry and with the 9th Infantry. He was promoted to be lieutenant-colonel in 1897 and brigadier-general of volunteers in 1898. He was honorably discharged from the volunteer service in 1899 and in the same year was appointed colonel of the 10th United States Infantry. In 1901 he was retired by operation of law and was advanced to the rank of brigadier-general in 1904. He was brevetted for gallantry in action in the Civil War.

EXHIBITIONS, ART. See PAINTING AND SCULPTURE.

EXPERIMENTAL PSYCHOLOGISTS, ASSOCIATION OF. See PSYCHOLOGY.

EXPLORATION. (For Arctic and Antarctic, see POLAR EXPLORATION.)

NORTH AMERICA. Dr. Carl Lumholtz has published the results of his studies in 1909 and 1910 of the economic possibilities of the arid and little-known country east of the Colorado River in southern Arizona and the Altar dis-

By courtesy of D. Appleton & Co.

ROBLEY D. EVANS

REAR-ADMIRAL, UNITED STATES NAVY

trict of the State of Sonora, Mexico. Most of this region, he says, will remain suitable only for cattle- and horse-raising, but considerable areas can be brought under cultivation. He refers to the extensive valley south of the Mexican boundary running east and west and passing beyond Sonoyta, the great plains northeast and southeast of Pinacate, and most of the flat valleys where water may be found at depths of from fifty to several hundred feet and brought to the surface for irrigation. The western part of the region includes a great auriferous belt, stretching southward from California and Nevada. The extraordinary adaptation of plant and animal life to arid conditions is very interesting. The rainfall is only about three inches a year, but he saw no plant, bush or tree suffering from drought and the juicy pulp of the cacti is sufficient to quench thirst. He made a careful study of the Papago Indians, who speak a dialect of the Piman language.

In August the United States and Canada completed the delimitation of their boundary line along the 141st meridian from near Mt. St. Elias to the Arctic Ocean, 600 miles. The survey has been in progress for years and advanced slowly because the working season is very short, and the transportation of outfit and supplies is difficult. Mr. Henry G. Bryant, president of the Geographical Society of Philadelphia, spent three months in the summer exploring the St. Augustine River, which enters the Gulf of St. Lawrence in the Canadian Labrador. The course of this river was unknown before Mr. Bryant traced it to its source on the Height of Land 141 miles from the point where it enters the Gulf. His survey resulted in a good map of this important river. The party led by Prof. Herschell C. Parker ascended Mt. McKinley to an altitude of about 20,000 feet. They were only about 300 feet from the summit when a very hard storm compelled them to give up the attempt. The party mapped a large area and demonstrated the possibility of reaching the top of the mountain by the northern route. The region of the Everglades in south Florida has been almost unknown because the country is extremely difficult to penetrate, and many cypress swamps abound. Parts of this region are now being drained and many settlers are going there. Prof. Harshberger of the University of Pennsylvania visited the Everglades in the summer and studied their botanical features and economic prospects. Drainage canals will eventually reclaim this swampy region. The lands need only thorough drainage and the application of mineral fertilizers to produce large returns. A great variety of food crops thrive and new settlements are constantly starting. It will be long, however, before the vast area is entirely reclaimed. See FLORIDA.

AFRICA. Dr. D. T. MacDougal and Mr. Godfrey Sykes of the Desert Laboratory of the Carnegie Institution of Washington examined some features of Egyptian deserts in January-March to determine their most obvious biological and physical conditions. The main work was in the Libyan Desert following the railroad from the Nile to the Oasis of Kharga, thence by caravan to Dahkla, Farafra, and Baharia, returning to the Nile at Minia. Distances of forty miles were traversed without the sight of a single plant, dead or alive. Lizards, beetles, rodents, birds, and gazelles were seen in places far from water, and must have depended upon the little moisture in their food. The quantity of water consumed by men and animals seemed to be less than that required in American deserts. More extended cultivation will in most cases depend upon engineering enterprise and efficiency in irrigation. The present size of the oases may be increased by a unified control of the water supply, and it is probable that exploratory borings might tap supplies that would help to form oases.

Italian topographers are at work preparing a map of Tripolitania, the country which Italy has acquired from Turkey. No authoritative map of this part of North Africa has existed, but the Italians intend to push the work of completely mapping the country. The Austrian-Uganda Expedition has ascended the extinct volcano Elgon. This famous mountain, about sixty miles northeast of Victoria Nyanza, was first brought to notice by the British explorer Joseph Thomson, who found on the lower slopes many artificial caves inhabited by natives. The crater lies between the two peaks of the mountain, the higher of which is 14,192 feet above the sea.

ASIA. The results of the exploration of the Kamchatka River, the largest river in the peninsula of that name, have been published in St. Petersburg. Mr. Lebedef says that the upper part of the river is swift and full of rapids. From the River Sheroma to Mashuri, about sixty miles, it is navigable in small boats, and the velocity is less than four miles an hour. Below Mashuri, the river is navigable for light draft barges to Nizhne-Kamclatsk. Below this point the stream is 200 yards wide and is navigable by vessels drawing not more than five feet of water. At its mouth the river is 360 yards wide, with a depth of eighteen feet and a discharge of about 39,400 cubic feet a second. The river is fed chiefly by melted snow and ice and only to a small extent by rivers.

The most important exploration recently carried on in Siberia is that of B. M. Shitkof in the Yalmal Peninsula between the Kara Sea and the Gulf of Ob, the interior of which had been almost unknown. He used twelve men and 480 reindeers in the work. The interior consists of slightly elevated tundras broken by the depression of the river valleys and lakes, which are very numerous. Conifers extend about to 67° N., beyond which are only dwarf willow and birch. Grass is found in some areas, and parts of the tundra are gay with flowers. Strong winds mark the spring months. The maxima and minima of temperature in May were +37.6° and —77° F.; in June, +28.4° and —78° F. The late ice reached a thickness of seven feet, but the snow cover on the level tundra was generally less than a foot deep. The Samoyedes on the peninsula own large herds of reindeer, but have been little influenced by civilization.

The expedition sent out by India in 1911 to punish the Abors who murdered English and Indian explorers was unable to follow the natives into their most remote mountain fastnesses; neither did the expedition entirely solve the problem of the identity of the Sangpo River of Tibet with the Dihong-Brahmaputra, as the expedition was unable to advance far enough north, though it explored a part of the hitherto unknown stretch of the river. There is no doubt, however, that the two rivers are identical. Several large, snowy peaks were discovered on the main Himalayan Divide, including one very fine peak of over 25,000 feet.

AUSTRALASIA AND OCEANIA. The Hon. Miles Staniford Smith, administrator of the territory of Papua (British New Guinea), has carried out extensive explorations in the western part of the territory, embracing 54,000 square miles which have hitherto been almost unknown. Three-fourths of this region is drained by the Kikor River and its tributaries. It is an elevated plateau consisting of limestone beds, running up to the volcanic or the limestone rocks of the ranges, the whole plateau consisting of alternate ranges and valleys, making the country very rough. The rainfall is excessively heavy, much of it sinking into the limestone. Rivers disappear and come to the surface again on the other side of a range, so that there is a large system of underground drainage. The sparse population is not homogeneous, but seems to be a mixture of Papuan and Melanesian elements. The natives are settled in substantial buildings on their cultivated lands. They are cannibals and their weapons are the bow and arrow and spear. They largely employ the stone adze and ax in their work. The climate is cool and bracing, owing to the high elevation. Large bodies of good coal were found on the borders of the plateau.

About forty miles off the north coast of Mindanao, Philippine Islands, the German survey ship *Planet* found a depth of 32,078 feet, a new record in ocean depths. In other words, the depth where the sounding was taken is 6.07 miles, exceeding by 482 feet the greatest depth hitherto known. In 1901 the United States survey ship *Nero* made a sounding to the southeast of the Island of Guam of 31,596 feet, which beat the world's record for sea depths up to that time. The *Challenger* expedition originated the practice of designating all areas with a depth exceeding 18,000 feet as "deeps," and giving a distinctive name to each of them. Some fifty of these deeps are now known.

EXPOSITIONS. During the year no important expositions were held in the United States.

PUT-IN-BAY. The design by J. H. Friedlander, with whom is associated A. D. Seymour, Jr., of New York, was accepted by the commission having in charge the celebration of the centennial of Commodore Perry's victory on Lake Erie, to be held from July 4 to October 5, 1913. The design consists of a Doric column forty-five feet high, with a spectators' gallery and a light in the top. It is to stand on a plaza 525 feet long, the length of the neck of land at Put-in-Bay, already chosen as the proper site, and sixty feet wide. At one end of the plaza is to be a historical museum, and at the other a memorial building typifying the 100 years of peace with Great Britain. The celebration will include a naval display by the United States and Great Britain. It is planned to bring American and British gunboats, torpedo boats, and torpedo-boat destroyers through the Welland Canal to Lake Erie. For this purpose a temporary abrogation of the clause in the treaty of Ghent barring warships from the waters of the Great Lakes is being sought. The old *Niagara*, Perry's flagship, sunk in Erie harbor, is to be raised and made fit to participate.

SAN FRANCISCO. Material progress has been made in the preparations for the great Panama-Pacific International Exposition to be held in San Francisco from February 20 to December 4, 1915, to celebrate the opening of the Panama Canal. The buildings will be "the loftiest and the most impressive ever constructed" and "the decorative plan will produce an artistic effect never surpassed." As viewed from San Francisco Bay, three main groups of exposition palaces will be seen rising against the amphitheatre of the hills. A central group with the Palace of Fine Arts on the west and Palace of Machinery on the east will extend 4500 feet east and west. Its towers, exclusive of the main tower in the Court of Honor, will rise 130 to 175 feet in height. The domes in the centre of the exhibit palaces will tower 144 feet. West of the central group will be the Palace of Fine Arts building and nearest the Golden Gate there will rise tier upon tier in terraces the palaces and pavilions of the foreign nations, while closer to the water will be the buildings of the States. The dominating theme of the exposition, from an architectural viewpoint, will be the huge tower of the Administration Building, 425 feet high, and flanked on either side by the gilded domes, towers, and minarets of other buildings. The prevailing color tone of the exposition, and there will be one throughout, will suggest a gold, although possibly it may be best described as a tawny buff, several shades removed from white. The domes will glisten with gold, and at night will be played upon by searchlights.

A "Commission Extraordinary to Europe," composed of John Hays Hammond, Gen. Clarence R. Edwards, Admiral Sidney A. Staunton, R. B. Hale, and W. T. Sisson, visited twenty-four countries in Europe for the purpose of interesting participation, and already a number of representatives of foreign governments have visited San Francisco for the purpose of selecting sites for special buildings. Many State commissions have also visited San Francisco for a similar purpose. Numerous conventions have already signified their intention of meeting in San Francisco in 1915. Other interesting features announced are that the Greeks of the United States will reproduce in white marble on Telegraph Hill, which overlooks San Francisco Bay and is adjacent to the exposition site, the famous Parthenon of Athens. The three caravels, reproductions of the Columbus vessels, now in Jackson Park, Chicago, are to be repaired and brought to San Francisco by the Knights of Columbus.

SAN DIEGO. (See YEAR BOOK, 1911, p. 247.) The Panama-California Exposition will be held in San Diego, Cal., from Jan. 1 to Dec. 31, 1915. Building operations were begun in December, 1911, and the Administration Building was completed in April, 1912. Designs for other buildings have been accepted and sites for many State and county buildings designated. Grading and improvement of the grounds is going on at a rapid rate. Thousands of trees and shrubs have been set out, including a citrous grove where seventeen varieties of these fruit trees have been placed, and an irrigation system has been installed. The entire site of 615 acres in Balboa Park has been enclosed with a woven wire fence eight feet high, and, in all, nearly three miles in length. This fence will be covered with vines and present the appearance of a wall of living green. It is planned to have all the buildings completed by January 1, 1914, in order that the floral features may have an entire year for their development.

An international conference of manufacturers and merchants representing twenty-six governments was held in Berlin on October 7 to discuss an international agreement as to measures which should be taken in future to regulate and control international exhibitions. The limitation of the number of exhibitions, rules for the awarding of medals, and the publication of an international code of regulations were considered. Subsequent to the Franco-British Exhibition held in London in 1908 and the Japanese-British Exhibition held in 1910, statistics show that trade relations between the countries mentioned were substantially stimulated, British exports increasing largely.

JAPAN. In March announcement was made on the authority of the vice-minister of agriculture and commerce of Japan that the purpose of holding an international world's fair in Tokyo in 1917 had been altogether abandoned.

HOLLAND. The centenary of Holland's liberation from the French will be observed during 1913 by a series of special exhibitions and centenary celebrations to be held in many cities and towns throughout Holland. Amsterdam will have a "nautical exhibition." At Leeuwarden an exhibition of Frisian art is being organized. Middelburg's exhibition will show Dutch costumes, together with Dutch furniture and art objects. Utrecht is to have an exhibition of the early Netherland school of painting; while Zaltbommel's exhibit will be of Delft ware. Nijmegen is to show Roman antiquities excavated there, and at Muiden, near Amsterdam, is to be shown an ancient Dutch castle. Monnikendam's contribution will be a "Waterlandisch Huis."

BELGIUM. A universal and international exposition similar to those held in Antwerp (1894), Brussels (1910), and Liège (1905) will be opened in Ghent on April 27 and continued till November 15, 1913. A site covering 280 acres has been selected and the buildings are in an advanced state of completion. Germany, France, Great Britain, including Canada, New Zealand, and India, Argentina, Brazil, Chile, Peru, China, and Japan have engaged space.

NORWAY. A national exposition will be held in Christiania from May 15 till September 30, 1914, to celebrate the centenary of Norway's adoption of its constitution on May 17, 1814. The scope of the exposition will be large, but exhibitions will be restricted to citizens of Norway.

INTERNATIONAL CONGRESSES. Among the important international congresses held in the United States during the year were: The Waterways Congress, Philadelphia, May 23-28; Eighth International Congress of Applied Chemistry, Washington, September 4, and New York, September 6-13; conferences in connection with the Third International Rubber and Allied Trades Exposition, New York, September 23-October 3; Fifteenth International Congress on Hygiene and Demography, Washington, September 23-28; and International Congress of Chambers of Commerce, September 24-28.

EXPRESS COMPANIES. See PARCELS POST.

FACTORY INSPECTORS. See LABOR LEGISLATION.

FACTORY INVESTIGATION COMMISSION. See CHILD LABOR, and SWEATING.

FAIRBAIRN, ANDREW MARTIN. An English scholar and educator, died February 9, 1912. He was born in 1838 near Edinburgh, and was educated at the universities of Edinburgh and Berlin, and at the Evangelical Union Theological Academy, Glasgow. He spent the first forty years of his life in Scotland, for twelve years as minister of the parish at Bathgate near Edinburgh. During this time he devoted himself to the study of theology. From 1872 to 1877 he was pastor of the Congregational Church in Aberdeen, and from 1877 to 1886 was principal of Airedale College. He developed a remarkable capacity for organization which manifested itself in the part which he took in the foundation and development of Mansfield College, a non-residential college at Oxford, which was designed not only to train students for the ministry in the Congregational and other Free Church bodies, but to be the centre of Free Church life in the University. After persistent efforts this college was founded in 1886, with Fairbairn as its principal. As the result of his efforts the college became at once a success. With its chapel open to all members of the university it became the centre of University Free Church life. Its theological students are either connected with the ordinary colleges or are attached to the university through the non-collegiate body. Dr. Fairbairn remained the principal from 1886 to 1909, when he was made principal emeritus. In addition to his work as minister and principal, he was from 1878 to 1882 Muir lecturer at the University of Edinburgh; from 1892 to 1894 Gifford lecturer at the University of Aberdeen; and from 1891 to 1892 was Lyman Beecher lecturer at Yale University. In 1898-9 he went to India and delivered the Haskell lectures. He was a member of many of the governing bodies of theological institutions in Scotland and Wales. He was one of the most eminent theologians of his day. Among his published writings are: *Studies in the Philosophy of Religion and History* (1876); *Studies in the Life of Christ* (1881); *The City of God* (1882); *Religion in History and in Modern Life* (1884); *Christ in Modern Theology* (1893); *Christ in the Centuries* (1893); *Catholicism, Roman and Anglican* (1899); *The Philosophy of the Christian Religion* (1902); *Studies in Religion and Theology; The Church in Idea and in History.*

FALKLAND ISLANDS. A British colony, composed of a group of islands in the south Atlantic. They are East Falkland (3000 sq. miles), West Falkland (2300) and about 100 smaller islands (about 1200). Population (1911), 2272 (1371 males, 901 females); with South Georgia, 3275 (2370 males, 905 females); population per square mile, 0.3. Stanley (800 inhabitants) is the only town. Sheep-farming is the sole industry, and the exports are wool, hides and skins, horns, hoofs, and live sheep. In 1911 there were about 3300 horses, 6000 cattle, 706,170 sheep, 100 swine. The 1910 imports were valued at £94,-294, and the exports at £308,930. Shipping entered and cleared, 325,583 tons. Revenue, £26,-773; expenditure, £17,405. There are no roads outside the town limits. W. L. Allardyce was governor in 1912.

South Georgia is a dependency of the Falkland Islands. It is a group of islands aggregating 1000 sq. miles, and is the headquarters for seven whaling stations, whose output of oil for the season ending March 31, 1911, was upwards of 150,000 barrels. Other dependencies are the South Orkneys and the Sandwich group.

FARLEY, Joseph Pearson. An American soldier, died April 6, 1912. He was born in Washington, D. C., in 1839, and graduated from the United States Military Academy in 1861. He served throughout the Civil War, rising to the rank of captain. In the years following the war he was promoted through various grades until he was made major-general in 1903. In the same year he was retired after forty years of service. From 1865 to 1867 he was assistant professor of drawing at West Point. He was a member of various statutory boards, ordnance boards, and gun-testing boards. He was the author of *West Point in the Early 60's* (1902), and *Three Rivers: A Retrospect of War and Peace* (1910). He contributed articles on arms and explosives to technical journals.

FARNSWORTH, Wilson Amos. An American missionary, died June 5, 1912. He was born in Greene, N. Y., in 1822, and graduated from Middlebury College in 1848. In 1852 he graduated from Andover Theological Seminary and was ordained to the Congregational ministry in the same year. He was a missionary of the American Board in Asia Minor for more than fifty years and at the time of his death was the oldest missionary on the board.

FEDERAL AID FOR ROADS. See Roads and Pavements.

FEDERAL CAPITAL TERRITORY. See Australia.

FEDERAL EMPLOYERS' LIABILITY ACT, Constitutionality of. See Employers' Liability.

FEDERATED MALAY STATES, The. A British protectorate composed of four states in the Malay Peninsula, as follows (import and export values in Straits Settlements dollars):

	Area Sq. miles	Pop. 1911	Imps. 1910	Exps. 1910
Perak	7,900	494,128	21,784,361	44,084,758
Selangor	3,200	294,014	24,315,540	46,732,071
Negri Semb.	2,600	130,201	870,477	7,978,071
Pahang	14,000	117,933	2,140,973	4,048,025
Total	27,700	1,036,271	49,111,351	102,840,990

The total length of the Federated Malay States railways in operation is 537 miles—23 in Province Wellesley (see Penang), 205½ in Perak, 102 in Selangor, 154 in the Nigri Sembilan, 31 in Pahang, and 21 in Malacca (qq.v.). In addition the F. M. S. Railways Co. operates 120½ miles of line in Johore.

The total revenue in 1910 amounted to 26,553,018 dollars; the expenditures to 23,598,610 (1 Straits Settlements dollar =$0.56776).

In 1909 a federal council was created by an agreement between the high commissioner and the four native rulers, to consist of the high commissioner as president, the chief secretary, the sultans of Perak, Selangor, and Pahang, the yam tuan of the Negri Sembilan, the four British residents, and four unofficial members nominated by the high commissioner. The first meeting was held December 11, 1909, at Kuala Kangsar. Kuala Lumpur is the administrative headquarters.

The high commissioner in 1912 was Sir Arthur Young (governor of the Straits Settlements), and the chief secretary, E. L. Brockman. See Perak, Selangor, Negri Sembilan, Pahang.

FEMALE POPULATION IN THE UNITED STATES. See Sex Distribution.

FENCING. The nineteenth annual intercollegiate tournament was won by the United States Military Academy. The United States Naval Academy finished second and Cornell, the winner in 1911, third. The standing of the various teams entered was: U. S. Military Academy won 41 bouts, lost 4; U. S. Naval Academy won 29, lost 16; Cornell won 28, lost 17; Harvard won 17, lost 28; Columbia won 11, lost 34; Pennsylvania won 9, lost 36. The individual championship went to H. A. Raynor of the U. S. Military Academy, who won 15 straight bouts. In dual matches the U. S. Military Academy defeated Yale 7—2, Cornell 6—3, and Columbia 8—1; the U. S. Naval Academy defeated Harvard 5—4, Pennsylvania 7—2, Columbia 7—2, and Yale 8—1; Pennsylvania defeated Harvard 5—4, Columbia 7—2 and 5—4, Yale 5—4, and Princeton 5½—3½; Cornell defeated Columbia 6—3; Yale defeated Harvard 6—3; Harvard defeated Columbia 6—3; Williams defeated Springfield Training School 8—1.

In the national championships held by the Amateur Fencers' League, S. Hall of the Fencers' Club of New York won with the foils, A. Z. V. Post of the same club, with the duelling swords, and C. A. Bill of the New York A. C., with the sabres. The women's championship with the foils was won by Miss Adelaide Baylis of New York City. The foils team championship was captured by the Fencers' Club of New York, which defeated the Boston A. A. in the final round by 5 bouts to 2. The New York A. C. won the sabre team championship, the Fencers' Club finishing second. An international tournament was held at Ostend, France, in July. A summary follows: Foil teams—France first, Belgium second, Great Britain third; sabre teams—Belgium first, France second, Italy third. See Olympic Games.

FERMENTED LIQUORS. See Liquors.

FERMORITE. See Meteorology.

FERRO-CONCRETE. See Architecture.

FERTILITY. See Soils.

FERTILIZERS. There was great activity during 1912 along many lines bearing on the fertilizer industry, but more especially in the extension of the manufacture and use of fertilizers and in the development of new sources of fertilizing materials.

Extension of the Use of Fertilizers. There is not only a steady growth in the use of fertilizers in regions which have hitherto extensively employed them, but there is a rapid extension of their use to regions which have heretofore used them to only a limited extent or not at all. Russia trebled its use of fertilizers in the five years, 1907 to 1911. Its consumption of fertilizers (largely imported) was, however, only 362,600 tons in 1911, or about one-fortieth of that of Germany per acre of cultivated land. Australia doubled its consumption of fertilizers in the nine years ending with 1910, in which 290,000 tons are reported to have been used. Spain, generally considered backward agriculturally, is now increasing its manufacture and use of commercial fertilizers, but more particularly in the intensively cultivated orange-growing regions of Valencia. Japan and China, although furnishing the most notable examples in the world of the maintenance of high productiveness of the soil without resource to commercial fertilizers, show an increase in recent years in the use of fertilizers, which, however, is still small in the case of China, but has reached relatively large proportions in Japan, 10 per cent. (in value) of the total imports of the latter in 1911 being fertilizers, mainly bean cakes, nitrate of soda, sulphate of ammonia, and rock phosphate. Under governmental encouragement and instruction the use of fertilizers is steadily increasing in Denmark, Hungary, South Africa, and the Philippines. The use of fertilizers, especially on sugar plantations, is already large in Hawaii, Java, and Cuba and is increasing each year. The manufacture of fertilizers in England and western European countries has for many years been large and is steadily growing to meet increasing home consumption and export. Increase in the use of fertilizers, coincident with improvement of methods of farming, has been especially rapid in the United States during the last ten years. The late wet spring of 1912 caused a falling off in the consumption of fertilizers in the Southern States, but it is probable that this was only a local and temporary setback and that the complete statistics for the year (not now available) will show a substantial increase in both production and consumption of fertilizers in the United States for the year.

The production and consumption of the raw materials supplying nitrogen, phosphoric acid, and potash furnish an index of the progress in the fertilizer industry.

Nitrogen. There is no evidence of a falling off in the world's production and consumption of the principal sources of nitrogen in fertilizers, namely, nitrate of soda. The imports into the United States apparently declined in 1912, but this was probably due to excess of supply held over from the previous year and an increase in production and consumption of sulphate of ammonia. The world's consumption of nitrate of soda is stated to have been 2,624,000 short tons in 1911, one-half to three-fourths of which was used as fertilizer.

The world's consumption of sulphate of ammonia (used mainly as fertilizer) was 451,000 tons in 1900, and 1,155,000 tons in 1911, Germany being the greatest producer (440,000 tons), as well as consumer (418,000 tons). The United States stands next to Germany in consumption (212,300 tons). There was a sharp decline in imports by the United States of sulphate of ammonia in 1911 and 1912, due to increased domestic production.

It is estimated that the synthetic processes of preparing nitrogen compounds from the air produced 27,500 tons of Norwegian calcium nitrate and 85,900 tons of calcium cyanamid in 1911. This by no means represents the capacity of the factories already erected, in course of construction, or planned. With the improvement of synthetic processes constantly going on, the erection of new factories abroad and in this country for the manufacture of the synthetic compounds, and the improvement of technic and extension of mining of Chilean nitrate, an abundant future supply of nitrogen fertilizers at a reduced price seems assured.

PHOSPHATES. The world's consumption of phosphates in 1911 was 6,235,000 tons, of which America, the greatest consumer as well as producer, used 1,817,000 tons. These phosphates were used almost exclusively in the manufacture of superphosphates, of which the world's production in 1911 was 10,565,000 tons. The two great centres of phosphate mining are the United States, which marketed 3,418,672 short tons in 1911, and Tunis, which produced 1,416,000 tons in that year.

POTASH. The mining of potash salts has been especially active since the new German potash law went into effect. Nearly 11,000,000 tons of potash salts of various kinds were mined in 1911. This represents a large increase over the production in 1910. It is estimated that the world's consumption of actual potash (K_2O) for strictly agricultural purposes was about 935,000 tons in 1911. The greatest consumer, Germany, used 464,565 tons, the United States standing next with a consumption of 261,337 tons. The largest consumer of potash per acre of cultivated land is Holland, followed in order by Germany, Belgium, the United States, and France.

DEVELOPMENT OF NEW FERTILIZER RESOURCES. There was continued activity in this line during 1912. The result of investigations by the United States Bureau of Soils, coöperating with the United States Geological Survey, showed an extension of the already enormous deposits of phosphates in the United States and the possibilities of production of potash from the Pacific Coast kelps. Dry kelps were found to contain from 20 to 30 per cent. of potash (calculated as chlorid) and 0.15 to 0.3 per cent. of iodine. Commercial success in obtaining potash from this source depends upon the cheapening of methods of harvesting the kelp and extracting the potash and iodine. Various silicates of potash have been shown to occur in great abundance in the United States and elsewhere, but it has been demonstrated that these silicates, especially the feldspars, are poor sources of potash fertilizer in untreated condition, and the commercial success of methods of treatment to extract the potash or to convert it into more ready available forms has not yet been demonstrated, although the prospect of success in this direction is good. Potash salts of commercial value were found in the basin of Searles Lake and a company has been formed to exploit the deposit. Other possible sources of potash were explored without success. No nitrate deposits of commercial value have yet been found in the United States.

In Europe there was renewed activity in development of the Galician potash deposits, and borings for potash were made in the region of Belport on the French frontier nearest the great German deposits with the hope of discovering a continuation of those deposits in French territory.

SCIENTIFIC INVESTIGATIONS. The more strictly scientific investigations relating to fertilizers resulted in no especially striking discoveries in 1912, but tended to emphasize certain facts of far-reaching importance, namely, that many substances, for example, sulphur, manganese, iron, boron, etc. (the so-called catalytic fertilizers of Bertrand and others) as well as lime and magnesia, play a more important rôle in the nutrition of plants than has heretofore been assigned them, and that very small variations in the proportion of the fertilizing constituents may modify profoundly the nutritive value of the soil solution; i. e., it is necessary for normal plant growth to maintain a certain balance of these constituents (the so-called law of physiological ratios of Mazé). That very small amounts of fertilizing constituents may have a very great influence upon the growth of plants is shown by the recent work of the United States Bureau of Soils with certain organic constituents occurring in minute amounts in the soil, and by the experiments of Hiltner and others showing that spraying or painting small amounts of substances on the leaves of plants may affect their growth as much as the addition of larger amounts to the soil.

LITERATURE. The literature bearing on fertilizers issued during 1912 was large. Many valuable papers dealing with the chemical phases of the subject were presented at the Eighth International Congress of Applied Chemistry at New York. A review of progress in the fertilizer industry by G. Wichern appeared in *Chemiker Zeitung*, 36 (1912), Nos. 37, 39, 43, 46, 47, 51, 52. An exhaustive report by United States Consul T. H. Norton on the utilization of atmospheric nitrogen was published as Bulletin 52, United States Department of Commerce and Labor, Bureau of Manufactures, Special Agent Series. *The American Fertilizer Handbook* for 1912 contained as in previous years a large amount of useful information about fertilizers and the fertilizer business. The more important treatises on the subject were: L. L. Van Slyke, *Fertilizers and Crops*; J. E. Halligan, *Soil Fertility and Fertilizers*; A. C. Stillwell, *A Chapter on Fertilizers*; A. Rogers and A. B. Amber, *On Industrial Chemistry*, and E. and M. Lambert, *Annuaire Statistique des Engrais et Produits Chimiques destinés à l'agriculture.*

FESTIVALS. See MUSIC.

FETTEROLF, ADAM H. An American educator, died December 2, 1912. He was born at Perkiomen, Pa., in 1841, and was educated at Freeland Seminary, now Ursinus College. When he was twenty years of age he was chosen professor of mathematics in this institution. Five years later he was made its president, and purchasing the interest of the owner became proprietor. Five years later he sold the seminary to Ursinus College. He then removed to Bucks county, Pa., where he became one of the owners and president of Andalusia College. He continued in this post until 1880, when he was elected president of Girard College, Philadelphia. He received the degrees of LL. D. from Lafayette College and Ph. D. from Delaware College. He was a member of several learned societies.

F. F. I. See NAVAL PROGRESS, AVIATION.

FIBRES. See CHEMISTRY, INDUSTRIAL.

FICTION. See FRENCH LITERATURE; GERMAN LITERATURE; and LITERATURE, ENGLISH AND AMERICAN.

FIFE, DUKE OF (WILLIAM GEORGE DUFF). Brother-inlaw of King George V.; died January 29, 1912. He was born November 10, 1849, the only son of James, fifth Earl of Fife, and Lady Agnes Hay, daughter of the Earl of Erroll. At his birth he inherited the titles of Baron Braca and Viscount Macduff. He was known under the latter title until the death of his father, Earl of Fife. He was educated at Eton, where he remained from 1863 to 1866. As Viscount Macduff he was elected to Parliament for the division of Moray and Nairn in 1874, serving until 1879, when through his father's death he became Earl of Fife in the peerage of Ireland and Baron Skene in the peerage of the United Kingdom. From 1872 to 1902 he was lord-lieutenant of the county of Elgin. In 1882 he served on a special mission to the King of Saxony. In 1885 he was created Earl of Fife in the United Kingdom. He showed strong instincts for business and was associated with others in banking and other financial enterprises which were successful. Among these was the foundation of the Chartered Company of South Africa, of which he was one of the founders and vice-president. After the Jameson Raid in 1896 he resigned his seat on the board of this company. From his early youth Viscount Macduff enjoyed the personal friendship of the Prince of Wales, afterwards King Edward VII. It was, however, with general surprise that the announcement was received in 1889 of the betrothal of the Prince of Wales's eldest daughter, Princess Louise, to the Earl of Fife. The marriage received the approval of Queen Victoria and was solemnized in St. James's Palace on July 27, 1889. The Earl of Fife was immediately elevated to the dignity of Duke of Fife and Marquis of Macduff in the United Kingdom. As a result of the delicate health of Princess Louise, which prevented her appearing in public to a great extent, the Duke of Fife himself was less known than otherwise would have been the case. In addition to being the director in several banks, he was a keen supporter of the Volunteer movement. In 1900 he was made lord-lieutenant of the newly created County of London and in that capacity became president of the County of London Territorial Force Association. The death of the Duke of Fife was the direct result of the wreck, on December 13, 1911, of the steamship *Delhi*, on which he, with the Princess Royal and their daughters, was traveling to Egypt. The vessel ran ashore about three miles south of Cape Spartel. Through the assistance of French sailors the passengers were safely landed, but only after great hardships. After his arrival in Egypt the Duke fell ill and died. He left two daughters, Princess Alexandra, born May 17, 1891, and Princess Maud, born April 3, 1893.

FIJI ISLANDS. A group of south Pacific islands; a British crown colony. The principal inhabited islands are Viti Levu (4112 sq. miles), Vanua Levu (2432), Taviuni (217), Kadavu (124), Koro (58), Gau (45), and Ovalau (43). Total area, including the dependency of Rotumah (14), is 7435 sq. miles; total population (1911) 139,541 (80,008 males, 59,533 females), of whom 87,096 Fijians, 40,286 (26,073 males) Indians, 3707 Europeans. The Indian immigrant population (sugar-plantation laborers) is over 40,000. Sugar, copra, and fruit (particularly pineapples) are the chief products and exports. Total imports (1910), £870,120; exports, £1,005,818 (sugar, £669,432; copra, £258,914; fruit, £47,301). There is no railway. Suva, the capital, has cable communication with Brisbane and with Canada.

Revenue, £211,952; expenditure, £236,661. Public debt, £104,115. Sir Henry May was governor in 1912.

FILCHNER, DR. See POLAR EXPLORATION.

FILTRATION. See WATER PURIFICATION.

FINANCIAL REVIEW. The following article gives a general summary of business conditions during the year. Other articles related to topics here discussed are the following: BANKS AND BANKING; NATIONAL BANKS; STATE BANKS; LOAN AND TRUST COMPANIES; SAVINGS BANKS; POSTAL SAVINGS BANKS; PRICES; TARIFF; TRUSTS; INSURANCE; UNITED STATES STEEL CORPORATION; AGRICULTURAL CREDIT. See also LABOR and various articles there referred to.

GENERAL BUSINESS CONDITIONS. Recent financial history really begins with the recovery during the latter part of 1908 and all of 1909 from the serious panic and industrial depression begining in October, 1907. Recovery was checked during 1910 and the year 1911 was one of only moderate business prosperity. In comparison therewith the year 1912 was a year of notable industrial and commerical activity. Even during the first half of the year before the bountiful crops were assured a strong optimistic tone prevailed, and during the second half this continued, although money became relatively scarce and dear. The year was at the same time notable for great political excitement during the early months and a pronounced political change in the November election. But the business world, contrary to all precedent, viewed these political changes calmly and appeared indifferent to probable tariff changes. The agricultural production of the year established new high records and constituted a firm basis for confidence in the general situation. It was $9,532,000,000, an increase of 13.24 per cent. over 1911. The farm value of corn exceeded a billion and a half dollars; the total value of winter and spring wheat exceeded half a billion; and that of oats approached half a billion. The crops of barley, potatoes, rye, and hay were the largest in our history. The cotton crop was exceeded only by that of 1911 in amount, its value including cotton seed, $986,920,000, exceeding all other years. The iron and steel industry likewise achieved an unprecedented volume. The iron ore shipments from Lake Superior exceeded 48,000,000 tons, which was nearly 50 per cent. in excess of those of 1911 and about 5,000,000 tons above the record of 1910. Eleven new blast furnaces with 1,200,000 tons annual capacity were started and seven more with 900,000 tons were under construction. Moreover, there was an addition of more than 3,000,000 tons of annual capacity to the open hearth steel mills under construction at the close of the year. The number of unfilled orders on the books of the United States Steel Corporation increased from 5,379,000 tons in January to 7,852,000 tons in November, in spite of nearly capacity production. Other companies also had an unprecedented number of orders, some having contracted to the limit of their capacity even for the second half of 1913. The total pig iron production was about 29,500,000 tons, rising from 2,057,911 tons in January to 2,689,933 tons for October, and 2,630,850 tons for November; the October record was the largest monthly record yet made. Building operations exceeded those of 1911 by about 6.6 per cent. Bank clearings showed an increase of 9 per cent. over 1911, and exceeded the previous maximum made in 1909 by nearly 5 per cent. In foreign trade both imports and exports exceeded those of all previous years. Imports totaled $1,800,000,000 or about $240,000,000 in excess of the previous record made in 1910; exports totaled $2,400,000,000 or $300,000,000 more than the previous maximum reached in 1911. Immigration which has come to be an index of business prosperity was 567,110 in the first ten months, or nearly 80 per cent. more than in the same period of 1911. The year was not a good one from the stock exchange viewpoint. In the early months prices were low and the market was dull; later, prices rose and activity increased only to be badly disturbed by the Balkan War, which led to European liquidation of American securities and a consequent lack of expected gold imports. Prices of securities fell further following the decision of the Supreme Court in the Union Pacific-Southern Pacific case (see TRUSTS). Banks on the other hand experienced great prosperity. Railway traffic was enormous, especially in October and November, when car shortage was extensive. Railway earnings surpassed all previous records and the roads in turn bought more freely of rails and rolling stock. Gross receipts increased about 8 per cent. over 1911, and net earnings about 5 per cent. Freight cars built numbered 152,429, or more than double the number built in 1911 and slightly exceeding the ten-year average. Locomotives built numbered 4915, of which 512 were for export. The total was more than in any year since 1907. New railway construction, however, was only 2997 miles, or the least for any of the past 14 years. Textile manufacturers experienced a moderate degree of prosperity in spite of very unusual labor disturbances and extensive agitation for the reduction of the cotton and wool tariff schedules. (See TARIFF.) Prices of commodities continued to advance, reaching a level at least 50 per cent. above that of 1896. This tended to reduce profits; the upward movement, however, was checked somewhat by abundant crops promising cheaper food. Wages also advanced, but from many quarters came the complaint that labor was scarce.

According to the New York *Journal of Commerce* dividend and interest payments for January, 1913, would make an entirely new record. It estimated dividend payments to total $100,215,822, distributed as follows: Railroads, $33,953,800; industrials, $49,288,183; street railways, $8,509,839; and bank and trust companies, $8,500,000. Interest payments were estimated to aggregate $144,012,678, distributed as follows: Railroads, $99,300,000; industrials, $25,200,000; street railways, $6,800,000; government, $3,247,678; and Greater New York, $9,465,000. The grand total of $244,264,500 was 7.6 per cent. greater than similar disbursements January, 1912. The increase was due in part to the large issues of bonds and notes during the year by railroad and industrial organizations and in part to increased earnings due to higher prices.

STATISTICS. In the accompanying table are noted some of the more important statistical items for the United States in 1912, with the percentage of change from 1911; the percentage of increase and decrease being shown by plus and minus signs respectively.

Item	Value	Per cent
Corn	$1,520,454,000	− 2.9
Winter Wheat	323,572,000	−14.6
Spring Wheat	231,708,000	+41.3
Total Wheat	555,280,000	+ 2.2
Oats	452,469,000	+ 9.1
Barley	112,957,000	−18.8
Rye	23,636,000	−14.1
Buckwheat	12,720,000	− .1
Total six cereals	$2,677,516,000	− .9
Flaxseed	$32,202,000	− 8.7
Potatoes	212,550,000	− 9.3
Hay	856,695,000	+ 9.1
Tobacco	104,063,000	+22.0
Rice	23,423,000	+28.3
Cotton, including seed	960,000,000	+ 2.4
Total above	$4,866,449,000	+ 1.4
Bank clearings	$172,276,149,104	+ 9.0
Imports of merchandise (estimated)	$1,817,000,000	+18.6
Exports of merchandise (estimated)	$2,425,000,000	+15.9
Total trade (estimated)	$4,242,000,000	+17.0
Circulation December 1	$3,337,277,820	+ 2.0
Building expenditure	$900,000,000	+ 6 0
New York stock sales	131,050,000	+ 3.5
New York bond sales	$677,000,000	−23.8
Business failures, number	13,832	+ 9.3
Failure liabilities	$197,995,457	+ 5.2
Railways built, miles	2,997	− 2.2
Railway receiverships, miles	4,001	+46.0
Railway foreclosures, miles	661	−52.0
Pig-iron, output, tons	29,240,000	+23.7
Iron-ore shipments, tons	48,000,000	+46.0
Total coal product, tons	540,000,000	+10.0
Anthracite shipments, tons	64,000,000	− 8.5
Labor strikers	475,000	+89.3
Gold produced, value	$91,685,168	− 5.3
Silver produced, ounces	62,369,974	+ 3.2

STOCK EXCHANGE. On the whole the year was considered a bad one by stock brokers. Although there was a considerable accumulation of banking funds in reserve centres in the early months a general lethargy prevailed reflecting the conservatism of the business world. With the prospect of abundant crops and the great increase in foreign trade resulting in high probability of gold importation from Europe, greatly increased activity was shown in April and May. This was followed, however, by a dull stock exchange summer but with rising prices in September. This upward movement was checked by the outbreak of the Balkan War and the panicky conditions into which the European exchanges were thrown. American stocks and bonds held abroad were unloaded to an amount estimated at $50,000,000 or more; this caused total stock transactions for October to exceed those of other months, except March and April, but resulted in sharp declines in values. Following Democratic success at the polls an outburst of activity advanced prices by 2 to 4 points. But in December the dissolution of the Union Pacific merger resulted in heavy liquidation; this was followed by slight recovery. During the later months the discount rate was 6 per cent. and the call loan rate very sensitive, going as high as 20 per cent. The total transactions on the New York stock exchange were 131,051,000 shares of stock and $677,354,000 of bonds. The stock transactions were the smallest in number since 1908 with the exception of 1911.

STOCK HOLDINGS. An inquiry made in November brought out some interesting statistics as to the distribution of the securities listed on the New York, Boston, Chicago, Philadelphia, Baltimore, and Washington stock exchanges. Leading companies whose stocks were not listed were also canvassed. Two hundred and seventy-four companies with aggregate capital of $8,098,000,000 reported a total of 861,729 stock holders, having an average holding of $9393. There were included 48 railroads with $3,482,000,000 aggregate capital and 274,000 stock holders; 95 industrial companies with $2,983,000,000 capital and 374,000 stock holders; 99 public utility companies with $1,091,000,000 capital and 109,000 stock holders; 21 mining companies with $305,000,000 capital and 59,500 stock holders; and 11 oil companies with $236,448,000 capital and 44,500 stock holders. The number of women stock holders was shown to be increasing; 193 of the above companies with 385,000 stock holders reported 156,800 women stock holders. In addition the Pennsylvania Railroad had 35,846 women stock holders. The total number of stock holders was the largest in the Pennsylvania Railroad, 74,541; and in the Steel Corporation, 104,822.

Statistics bearing on foreign holdings of American securities were secured. They showed that American railroad securities are decreasing in favor and American industrials are increasing. Between 1900 and 1912 there was a decline in the proportion of the securities of reporting roads held abroad from 34.5 per cent. to 13.1 per cent.; even the total amount of foreign holdings had declined in spite of great additions to the capital of the roads involved. Companies with aggregate capital of $5,311,000,000 reported that 9.6 per cent of their securities were held abroad. The percentage for railroads was 13.8; for industrials 8.8; for public utilities 3.4; for mining companies 6.2; and for oil companies 1.7. English investors had 63.6 per cent. of all foreign holdings; French 6.1 per cent.; German 8.5 per cent.; and Dutch 18.6 per cent. The statistics showed that between 20 and 25 per cent. of the capital of American corporations whose stocks are active in the markets were held by brokers in speculative accounts. Such holdings were much less than a decade ago.

BUILDINGS. The amount of building expenditures in 1912 of all cities, as reported by *Bradstreet's*, was $908,000,000, a gain of 6.8 per cent. over 1911. On the basis of the same cities the total was greater than in any preceding year, except 1909. The approximation to the 1909 record was due to cities outside of New York; in the latter the expenditures exceeded those of 1911 by 15 per cent. and those of 1910 by 7 per cent., but were 17 per cent. less than those of 1909. The month of December showed more than normal activity on account of mild open weather, the total for that month exceeded that of December, 1911, by 32 per cent. in 126 cities. The largest monthly record yet made was that of April, 1912, when $99,561,000 of building expenditures were recorded.

BANK CLEARINGS. The amount of bank clearings is considered an indication of the volume of business. By this test the year 1912 was a year of unprecedented trade. Nearly all the principal cities showed increases over preceding years, most of them, excepting New York, showing totals never before reached. These totals were explained by the large crops, the enlargement of pay rolls through increased wages and greater numbers of employees, the increased readiness to pay obligations, and the splendid volume of demand for goods. Of 122 cities with total clearing of $172,376,000,000, according to *Bradstreet's*, only ten showed totals smaller than in 1911. Moreover, each month, except June, showed larger clearings than the corresponding months of the preceding year. The total for 1912 exceeded that of 1911 by 9 per cent.; that of 1910 by 6.8 per cent.; and that of 1909, the previous maximum, by 4.8 per cent. The clearings by months in millions of dollars were as follows: Januray, $14,965; February, $12,771; March, $14,319; April, $14,-837; May, $14,701; June, $13,508; July, $13,-836; August, $13,088; September, $12,940; October, $16,987; November, $15,211; and December, $15,201. The clearings for October surpassed all previous monthly records; as did also those for the fourth quarter. The total clearings for New York were $100,744,000,000, or about 60 per cent. of the total. Those of some other cities were: Chicago, $15,380,795,541; Boston, $8,962,808,530; Philadelphia, $8,166,-286,613; St. Louis, $4,027,580,800; Pittsburgh, $2,798,990,214; Kansas City, $2,713,027,916; San Francisco, $2,677,561,952; Baltimore, $1,-957,475,681; Cincinnati, $1,369,215,000; Minneapolis, $1,182,232,466; Los Angeles, $1,168,-941,700; Cleveland, $1,150,397,652; Detroit, $1,-127,975,160; New Orleans, $1,058,354,962; Omaha, $860,681,557; Louisville, $724,894,243; Milwaukee, $724,683,441; Atlanta, $691,941,-254; Seattle, $602,430,660; Portland, Ore., $597,087,865; St. Paul, $579,166,753; Buffalo, $579,088,538; Denver, $487,848,305; Providence, $442,694,200; Indianapolis, $434,525,978; Richmond, $429,787,122; Memphis, $421,302,287; Washington, D. C., $391,776,791; Fort Worth, $386,933,076; St. Joseph, $383,062,742; Salt Lake City, $369,452,285; Columbus, $322,964,-400; Albany, $314,379,325; and Nashville, $308,-279,450.

CANADA. The total clearings for sixteen Canadian cities were $9,010,000,000, or 22.6 per cent. increase over 1911. The clearings were at the minimum of $602,000 in February, rising to over $800,000 in May, falling to $698,000 in September, but rising again to $866,000 in October and $876,000 in November. The clearings for principal cities were as follows: Montreal, $2,845,000,000; Toronto, $2,170,-000,000; Winnipeg, $1,537,800,000; Vancouver, B. C., $645,118,000; Calgary, $275,492,000; Ottawa, $244,123,000; and Edmonton, $220,727,-000.

FAILURES. (a) *Commercial. Bradstreet's* record showed a total of 13,832 commercial failures in the United States in 1912, being an increase of 9.3 per cent. over 1911. By geographical divisions they were distributed as follows: New England, 1489; Middle States, 4611; Western States, 2403; Northwestern States, 831; Southern States, 3144; Far Western States, 1354. The total number was greater than in any year since 1896, excepting 1908. This was explained in part by the fact that the number of business concerns, 1,673,000, was 44 per cent. greater than in 1900; and by the effects of a late spring, lower values of cotton in the South on account of the large crop, and minor disturbances. The percentage of failures to the number in business was .82, as compared with .77 in 1911, .72 in 1910, .76 in 1909, and .94 in 1908. The total liabilities were $198,-000,000; the total assets were almost exactly one-half that amount. The total of liabilities exceeded only slightly the totals of 1911 and 1910, and was much below the total of 1908, and only slightly more than one-half the total of 1907. There were an unusual number of large failures, this being largely responsible for the great total. There were about 250 failures, each having liabilities of at least $100,000 and with a total of $88,000,000. The largest single failure was an automobile concern; other large failures were in the automobile, iron and steel, cement, cotton and wool, lumber, building, and brewing industries.

The Canadian failures numbered 1310, as compared with 1401 in 1911; 1469 in 1910; 1588 in 1909; and 1715 in 1908. The total liabilities were $12,261,000, being smaller than in any year since 1907. The total assets were $5,593,000.

(b) *Financial.* Banks were generally prosperous in 1912. Banking suspensions totaled 48, as compared with 61 in 1911, 44 in 1910, 40 in 1909, and 132 in 1908. There were suspensions of banks as follows: National, 4; State, 16; savings, 2; private, 23; and loan and trust companies, 3. The total liabilities of all suspended institutions were $18,937,000, to which private banks contributed 32 per cent., loan and trust companies 30 per cent., State banks 21 per cent., national banks 11 per cent., and savings banks one-third of 1 per cent. The total was the smallest in any year since 1902, and in 20 years was the smallest except in 1902 and 1900. The liabilities constituted only 4 per cent. of all failure liabilities in 1912, as compared with 14 per cent. in 1911 and 52 per cent. in 1907. The total assets were $5,249,000, bearing a favorable ratio to the liabilities.

(3) *Railway Receiverships and Foreclosures.* In 1912 11 unimportant roads with 525 miles of lines, and total funded indebtedness of $4,815,300, and total outstanding stocks of $14,813,190 were sold under foreclosure. These figures compared very favorably with those of the three years preceding, but exceeded the mileage and total securities of roads sold in 1906-7-8. The principal roads involved were the Chicago, Peoria, and St. Louis, with 255 miles of line, funded debt of $3,730,000 and stocks of $7,350,000. Roads placed in the hands of receivers were 13 in number with a total mileage of 3784 miles, with funded debt of $107,354,854 and total stock of $74,757,643. In addition to these, the Tennessee Central with 284 miles of road, $12,367,900 funded debt, and $7,941,450 stock, went into the hands of a receiver on December 31. The number of roads and mileage exceeded the figures of 1909-10-11, but the total of bonds and stocks was exceeded in 1911. The principal road involved was the Père Marquette with 2331 miles, $63,672,000 bonds, and $26,-186,000 stock. Other principal roads were the Kansas City, Mexico, and Orient with 764 miles, $21,146,000 bonds and $25,000,000 stock; and the Denver, Northwest, and Pacific with 211 miles, $11,288,000 bonds, $10,940,000 stocks. For an account of these failures, see RAILWAYS.

CANADA. The year was one of marked prosperity in Canadian provinces, as shown by a wheat crop of more than 200,000,000 bushels, total value of farm products exceeding half a billion dollars, and an influx of about 400,000 immigrants. The growth of industry and population in the eastern section was above the normal and in Manitoba, Saskatchewan, and Alberta it was very extraordinary. These sections experienced a great increase of population, bountiful crops, and phenomenal rises in the value of real estate. Building construction was consequently unusually active. The cities of Winnipeg, Medicine Hat, Edmondton, and Calgary had virtual booms. The bank clearings of Winnipeg increased 21 per cent. over 1911, and those of Edmondton, 82 per cent. Railroad building in the Canadian west and northwest was very considerable, several new outlets for the products of these sections being under way, including extensions by the Canadian Northern, Grand Trunk Pacific, the Canadian Pacific, and the Hudson's Bay railways. Montreal held its position of first rank as a manufacturing centre, with Toronto second and growing more rapidly than its larger rival. Foreign trade exceeded $1,000,000,000 in value, exports being about $680,000,000, and imports about $331,000,000. For construction work Canada annually borrows about $200,000,000 of British capital. This investment of foreign money was seriously interfered with in later months by the Balkan War. The result was a checking of construction, a sharp decline in available bank reserves, and tightness of money.

GREAT BRITAIN. London comment on 1912 showed that it was a year of good trade but had politics. There was an unusual amount of labor unrest; the coal strike of seven weeks' duration in the spring was a severe blow to manufacturing and transportation (see MINIMUM WAGE); the dockers' strike in the summer interfered with foreign traffic (see STRIKES AND LOCKOUTS). Great political excitement prevailed throughout the year; the Balkan War was a factor of first importance in the later months. Nevertheless foreign trade responded to the worldwide upward movement, there being an increase in the first eleven months of 9 per cent. in the value of imports, 7 per cent. in exports, and 9 per cent. in reëxports. Railway traffic increased in the second half year so as to more than offset the effects of labor disputes. Bank clearings at London to December 11 showed an increase of 8.5 per cent. over 1911. The London *Economist* reported issues of new capital to December 14 to the amount of £202,000,000, or the largest in a decade except in 1909. The Bank of England took a rather serious view of the general situation owing partly to a belief that much overcapitalization had prevailed. Its discount rate was lowered to 3 per cent. in May, raised to 4 per cent. late in August, and to 5 per cent. after the Balkan War began. In general the discount rate ranged nearly 1 per cent. higher than in 1911. Excessive hoarding on the continent due to the possibility of war was a factor in this result.

CONTINENTAL EUROPE. On the continent the conspicuous feature of the year was the Balkan War. This introduced doubt and hesitation into what would otherwise have been a year of extraordinary prosperity. There was some drain of gold by the Allies previous to the outbreak of hostilities; and thereafter hoarding of gold in France, Austria, and central Europe was estimated at thirty-five million pounds or more. Everywhere, and particularly in Austria and the war zone, the fourth quarter was one of great scarcity of money, of excitement, strain, and declining security values.

In *Germany* unprecedented records were made in railway receipts, volume of foreign trade, steamship tonnage under construction, the production of pig iron, coal, coke and lignite, and bank clearings. The money market was easy in January and early in February, making possible the repayment of the large American loans contracted in 1911. Security prices rose in January but fell slowly thereafter until midsummer. This decline was due to the repayment of American loans and the flotation of large Prussian and German loans exhausting the reserves of the money market. A recovery in September was followed by greater decline in October and November, due to the war scare and a very tight money market. The total loss in values of stocks listed on the Berlin exchange during October exceeded half a billion dollars. American securities in considerable volume were unloaded. The rate of the Reichsbank was reduced from 5 to 4 1-2 per cent. in June owing to temporary ease of the money situation, but it was compelled to advance its rate to 5 per cent. on October 24, and to 6 per cent. on November 14. The extraordinary condition of German credit appears clearly from the fact that in Berlin the private rate of discount rose from 4 5-8 to 6 per cent., while in London it fell from 5 to 4 3-4 per cent. The markets for money and securities were therefore much depressed at the close of the year, but the general economic situation was good. Record crops had been produced; both exports and imports gained over 1911; the ocean-carrying trade was in an unusually prosperous state; freight movements were very large, and an unprecedented car shortage existed in October and November; shipyards had a record output and also maximum orders at the year's close; railway earnings attained new maxima.

In *France* the year was one of moderate prosperity. As shown by the few available statistics foreign trade varied little from that of 1911; the Paris bourse, like the stock exchanges of all countries, had its ups and downs; crops were considerably better than in 1911, but not abnormal because of excessive rainfall; and the money market tightened sharply in the closing months. Imports for the first eight months totaled $1,019,000,000 in value, or slightly less than for same period in 1911. About 60 per cent. of imports were raw materials, 24 per cent. were foodstuffs, and 16 per cent. were manufactures. The exports for the eight months aggregated $821,760,000 or $64,-000,000 more than for these months in 1911. Business conditions up to October were better than in 1910 or 1911. Prices of securities rose until about June 1, when trading became less active. In the late summer, however, occurred a period of over-speculation in Russian industrials and certain copper and other mining stocks. Following the outbreak of the Balkan War the Bank of France took the very exceptional course of advancing its rate from 3 1-2 to 4 per cent. This is believed to have stimulated the hoarding which was already noticeable and to have reacted unfavorably on the availability of gold and credit in all European banking centres.

FINCH, WILLIAM ALBERT. An American lawyer and educator, died March 31, 1912. He was born in Newark, N. J., in 1855, and graduated from Cornell University in 1880. In the same year he was admitted to the bar and until 1891 practiced at Ithaca, N. Y. In that year he was appointed professor of law in Cornell University. He held this position until the time of his death. He was regarded as an authority on the law of real property and he published *Finch's Selected Cases on the Law* *of Property and Land*, and *The Law of Property and Land—A Syllabus* (1900).

FINLAND. A Russian grand duchy on the Gulf of Bothnia. Capital, Helsingfors.

AREA AND POPULATION. Area in square kilometers and population December 31, 1910, are given below by governments:

	Sq. kms.	Pop.
Nyland	11,872	376,218
Åbo-Björneborg	24,171	499,332
Tavastehus	21,584	342,321
Viborg	43,055	521,469
St.-Michel	22,840	198,829
Kuopio	42,730	333,777
Wasa	41,711	514,940
Uleåborg	165,641	328,311
Total	373,604*	3,115,197

*Of which, 47,829 sq. kilometers internal waters.

The total area in square kilometers is equivalent to 144,249 square miles. The population was 33 per square kilometer in Nyland (greatest density), and 2 in Uleåborg (the least), and the average density for the country was 9. Evangelicals numbered 3,057,627, Greek Orthodox 52,004, Baptists 4467, Methodists 676, Roman Catholics 423. Speaking Finnish as their native tongue were 2,565,742, Swedish, 344,364, Russian 7339, German 1794, Lapp 1660, other tongues 298. Number of marriages (1910), 18,781; births, 95,363; deaths, 51,007; still-births, 2379. Of the 2,712,562 adults listed as actively prusuing occupations, 1,555,357 were engaged in agriculture. Helsingfors had 147,-218 inhabitants, Åbo 49,691, Viborg 49,007, Tammerfors 44,147, Nikolaistad 21,819, Björneborg 17,466, Uleåborg 10,114, Kuopio 15,845.

Education is on a much higher plane than in Russia. Primary instruction is free and compulsory between the ages of seven and fifteen. Secondary schools are well attended, and special schools of agriculture are maintained, devoting particular attention to stock-raising and dairying.

PRODUCTION AND COMMERCE. Cereal crops are grown; also roots and forage plants. The timber industry is unimportant. Iron ore is mined and pig and bar iron are produced for export.

The trade bv countries of origin and destination, with values in thousands of marks (gold) is shown below for 1911:

	Imps.	Exps.		Imps.	Exps.
Germany	173,400	46,600	France	6,400	27,100
Russia	137,500	89,000	Spain	2,200	8,700
U. K.	61,700	88,100	Other	5,200	7,700
Denmark	23,100	11,700			
Swe.& Nor.	21,600	14,500	Tot. '11	444,500	319,600
Neth., etc.	13,400	26,500	Tot. '10	384,100	288,100

Principal articles of export, 1911 trade, values in thousands of marks—timber, 160,-500; paper and pulp, 57,400; butter, 34,000; hides and leather, 12,200; wooden wares, 6500; fish, 5300; cotton textiles, 4300; iron, 2300. Vessels entered (1911), 9599 of 2,690,475 tons; cleared, 9509 of 2,648,285. Merchant marine (January 1, 1912), 2959 sailing, (327,625 tons) and 487 steamers (72,013.)

COMMUNICATIONS. Railways in operation January 1, 1912, 3763 kilometers. The Russian government has decreed that all new lines are to be constructed in conformity with Russian lines, and that existing lines are to be so altered as to permit the use on them of Russian rolling stock. With the completion of the Kaskö-Kristinestad line will be begun extensions of present lines to form a continuous route from Nikolaistad to St. Petersburg. The projected alterations and extensions were decided upon, not by the Finnish Diet, but by Russia; though the Finnish railways are for the most part owned by the (Finnish) state.

FINANCE. The revenue for the year 1911 amounted to 159,421,716 marks (1 mark=19.3 cents); of which 69,033,168 was derived from state domains and forests, railways, canals, etc.; 62,660,151 from indirect taxes (customs 53,-050,218, and excise 9,609,933); 7,402,091 from posts, 6,450,758 from direct taxes, 3,790,329 from stamps, etc. Expenditure, 159,950,052 marks, of which 75,918,101 for communications, 17,180,055 for worship and instruction, 13,526,-102 for civil administration, 12,178,917 military contribution, 8,473,672 debt charge, 7,125,419 for agriculture, etc.; 6,665,794 for commerce and industry; etc. The 12,178,917 marks military contribution goes into the Russian treasury. The debt stood January 1, 1912, at 176,313,484 marks.

GOVERNMENT. Until the present régime Finland enjoyed the autonomy guaranteed her in the reign of Alexander I. Latterly the Russification system has been applied to an increasing number of departments, until the schools, the press, the law, and the legislature have all been invaded. By the end of 1912 the constitution was virtually annulled (see succeeding paragraphs). The Diet (200 members elected by universal suffrage for three years), formerly possessed of large powers in civil administration, has latterly been little more than a figurehead. The Russian sovereign is the grand duke. There is a resident governor-general (1912, F. A. Seyn), and a secretary of state (Lieut.-Gen. A. [Baron] Langhoff), residing at St. Petersburg.

HISTORY

THE CONSTITUTIONAL HISTORY QUESTION. For more than a dozen years the apparent design of Russia to assimilate Finland to the rest of the empire without regard to her constitutional rights has aroused the bitter opposition of the Finns and occasioned protests from their sympathizers throughout the world. Further measures in pursuance of this policy were taken by the imperial government in the opening months of 1912, but before giving an account of them it may be well to review briefly the recent history of Russia's relations with Finland. In the latter country it was generally assumed that the grant of Alexander I. in 1809 established the grand duchy as a separate state with inalienable rights against the pretensions of Russia. On the other hand, Russian opinion regarded the promise of Alexander as no more binding than that of Peter the Great to the Baltic provinces and held that Finland was merely an autonomous province of the empire. It had been the policy of Russia to promise to respect the national institutions of her newly acquired territories and later step by step to proceed in her course of centralization and assimilation without regard to her agreement. That this did not happen to the Finns was due to their steady and vigorous insistence on their own rights. Alexander II. expressly recognized the legislative authority of the Finnish Diet over a wide range of fundamental matters and by his own declaration governed Finland as a constitutional ruler. Since 1869 therefore the Finns have obeyed the czar as the constitutional grand duke of Finland, apart from his capacity as autocrat of all the Russias. Enjoying virtual independence Finland developed along her own lines and her national institutions had nothing in common with those of Russia. Russian sovereignty was practically limited to matters pertaining to the imperial family, foreign relations, and the army and navy. Customs tariffs divided the two countries, and they had no common bank or currency system or other institution expressing a community of interest. The czar, in his capacity of grand duke, had for his adviser a secretary of state for Finland, who must be a Finn. The Finnish Senate, at Helsingfors, under the presidency of a Russian governor-general, directed the internal affairs of the country, as a national ministry in the name of the grand duke. In questions concerning both Finnish and imperial interests the secretary of state for Finland referred each subject to the proper Russian minister and the two addressed a conjoint report thereon to the czar, but the Finns did not regard this as involving the supremacy of the Russian ministerial council over Finnish officials. This view was contested by Russian statesmen, and by the act of June 2, 1908, it was provided that all Finnish administrative questions should be first submitted to the Russian ministerial council, which would decide whether or not they concerned the general interests of the empire. The main issue between the two governments, however, concerned not administrative, but legislative independence, to which Finland could show a clearer title. The Finns and their sympathizers took their stand on the principle that the authority of the Finnish Diet could not be curtailed without its own consent. If, therefore, the Russian government wished to establish a different system of legislation for matters affecting the common interests of Finland and the empire, the consent of the Diet at Helsingfors must first be obtained. The Finns absolutely denied Russia's right to disregard this rule on the score of imperial sovereignty. On the other hand, Russian nationalist sentiment demanded complete subordination of Finland to the imperial government.

Imperial Restrictions. By the law of February 15, 1899, proclaimed during the high-handed régime of Governor-General Boubrikov, Russia required that all matters of legislation that concerned the common interest should be referred to the czar, who with the advice of the imperial council, should decide whether they affected the general interests of the empire, and should be removed from the jurisdiction of the Finnish Diet. It also provided that the governor-general, the secretary of state, and certain Finnish senators, appointed by the throne should participate in the proceedings of the Finnish Diet. This was bitterly opposed, not only in Finland, but in other countries, where the so-called Russification of Finland aroused much sympathy, and led to many public protests. During the stormy days of the Russian revolution, this act was provisionally superseded (November 4, 1905), and for a while Finland was left to her own devices. The decrees providing for the new Russian Duma did not provide for any Finnish representation in that body and the grand duchy was for the time being in a position of political isolation. But the growth of Russian nationalist sentiment on the one hand, and the uncompromising attitude of the Finn leaders on the other, soon brought matters once more to a crisis. The Stolypin government was aggressively nationalist in its policy, and the third Duma had a nationalist majority. A new law, curtailing Finland's legislative independence, was passed on June 30, 1910. This provided that thenceforth laws of general interest must, at the instance of the czar alone, and after consulting the Finnish Diet, follow the usual Russian legislative procedure, that is, be voted by the Duma and the imperial council. Two representatives from Finland were to attend the sessions of the Duma. A few months after the promulgation of this law the Finnish Diet, in extraordinary session, denied its validity and refused to send deputies to the Duma. The law of June 30, 1910, attempts to enumerate the matters of general interest which fall within the competence of the Duma, but their range is very wide and, the principle being admitted, there is nothing to prevent their indefinite extension in the future. They include not only the right of the Duma to regulate Finland's financial relations to the empire, the military service, the rights of Russian subjects in Finland, etc., but even the rights of meeting and association, and questions of education and the press. The Duma contained, however, many friends of Finland, who vigorously opposed the passage of the law. It was evident that Russian public opinion was divided on the subject, and that Finland could rely on a considerable minority in the Duma for support when the question was reopened.

Further Measures. In January and February, 1912, the Russian government definitely applied the principle of the law of 1910. Two laws pertaining to Finland were passed by the Duma, and sanctioned by the czar as laws of general interest. The first of these (January 24, 1912) abolished the obligation of personal military service on the part of the Finns and in lieu thereof required an annual payment of 20,000,000 markkas. Finland had long contended that her national army could not leave her own territory and that principle was laid down in a law passed in 1878, which forbade the national troops to serve outside Finland, even in time of war. The imperial government could not admit that principle, but on the other hand was loth to force Finns into the service against their consent, both on account of the difficulty of such a policy, and on account of its bad effect on the morale of the army. The law of February 2, 1912, bestowed on Russian subjects living in Finland the same rights as those possessed by the Finns themselves. This was regarded by the Finns as a further step toward Russification, for it was feared that the Russian government would appoint these Russian residents to office in the Finnish administration and thus gradually denationalize the service. In a small country, where there were only about 8000 public functionaries, it was pointed out that it would be easy to turn over a majority of the offices to Russian bureaucrats. The Finns saw in this measure the

STATISTICS OF FIRES IN EUROPEAN CITIES IN 1911

Place	Area Square miles	Population	Number of Alarms	Total No. of Fires	Confined to Building or place of Origin	Total Loss	No. of Fires per thousand Population	Loss per Capita	Loss per Fire
Birmingham	21	840,372	1,035	817	790	$ 444,295	.97	$ .53	$ 544
London	..	7,252,963	6,868	4,403	...	3,945,015	.67	.54	896
Belfast	25.8	385,000	204	186	...	359,135	.48	.93	1,931
Dublin	12.4	309,272	247	165	165	42,435	.53	.13	257
Aberdeen	10.5	163,877	177	157	157	61,050	.96	.37	389
Edinburgh	41.25	320,313	554	470	454	212,070	1.47	.66	451
Marseilles	87.7	553,500	613	591	573	700,320	1.07	1.27	1,185
Paris	30	2,846,986	5,060	4,342	...	1,717,385	1.52	.60	396
Berlin	24.4	2,083,391	3,509	2,935	2,892	......	1.41	..	...
Dresden	26.09	548,300	608	455	455	......	.83	..	...
Hamburg	32	955,822	2,255	1,463	1,460	170,595	1.53	.18	117
Florence	..	232,860	252	232	...	51,929	1.00	.22	224
Milan	..	619,256	1,169	875	...	284,587	1.41	.46	325
St. Petersburg	123.	1,907,708	2,716	1,095	...	1,772,706	.57	.93	1,619
Moscow	35.5	1,575,583	1,181	1,103	1,043	2,298,341	.70	1.46	2,084
Vienna	..	2,031,498	2,334	2,014	...	170,086	.99	.08	84
Vancouver	13	125,000	546	186	181	326,444	1.49	2.61	1,755

designs of the Nationalists and recalled the late Premier Stolypin's attempt to introduce courses in the Finnish tongue in the University of St. Petersburg, with a view to fitting Russians for service in the Finnish civil service. Whether the law would be applied in a moderate spirit, or in accordance with the extreme views of the Nationalists, remained to be seen. M. Stolypin's successor to the premiership, M. Kokovtsov, was generally regarded as more inclined to a moderate attitude toward the Finns, and it was observed that he had gone no further with Stolypin's project for the annexation of the two parishes of the Finnish p ince at Vyborg. Stolypin had decided on this measure a few weeks before his death, and so late as April 19, 1912 a member of the imperial council declared that "Russia has no need of the approval of the alien populations. We have not taken them to give them pleasure, but because they were necessary to us." Conservative journals, like the *Novoye Vremya*, attacked M. Kokovtsov for his remissness in this matter.

FIRE DRILLS. See FIRE PROTECTION.

FIRE PREVENTION. See FIRE PROTECTION.

FIRE PROTECTION. During the year 1912, the committee on statistics and origin of fires of the National Board of Underwriters published a report, giving the record of fire losses in the United States and foreign countries, in continuance of their investigations, begun in the previous year. As a result, they were able to show returns for a larger number of European cities than previously, and to make a comparison between the per capita losses for two successive years. The summary of these statistics is given herewith:

Country	No. of Cities Reporting Loss 1910	No. of Cities Reporting Loss 1911	Population 1910	Population 1911	Per Capita Loss 1910	Per Capita Loss 1911
U. S.	297	298	29,996,723	31,210,084	$2.39	$2.62
England	11	12	2,335,847	9,898,317	.44	.53
France	8	3	4,392,529	3,518,493	.92	.81
Germany	13	8	5,616,822	2,306,354	.19	.21
Ireland	2	2	657,680	694,272	.45	.58
Scotland	..	2	......	484,190	..	.56
Italy	..	6	......	1,373,995	..	.31
Russia	..	2	......	3,483,291	..	1.17
Austria	..	1	......	2,031,498	..	.08
Canada	..	1	......	125,000	..	2.61

This report brings out the interesting fact that in no one of the foreign cities does the

STATISTICS OF FIRES IN AMERICAN CITIES IN 1911

Place	Area Square miles	Population	Number of Alarms	Total No. of Fires	Confined to Building or place of Origin	Total Loss	No. of Fires per thousand Population	Loss per Capita
New York	326.8	5,076,976	16,023	14,574	...	$12,470,806	2.87	$2.45
Chicago	195.5	2,300,000	12,861	9,130	8,650	5,954,601	3.97	2.59
Philadelphia	129.5	1,575,000	4,213	3,878	3,779	2,154,051	2.46	1.37
St. Louis	61.37	710,000	4,148	3,715	3,657	2,349,289	5.23	3.31
Boston	37.04	685,000	4,618	3,606	3,588	2,232,267	5.26	3.26
Cleveland	46	600,000	2,463	2,108	1,988	644,918	3.51	1.07
Baltimore	33	565,000	1,663	1,606	1,596	525,141	2.84	.93
Pittsburgh	40.67	550,000	1,800	1,785	...	947,905	3.25	1.72
Detroit	41.5	485,000	2,584	2,371	...	1,225,243	4.89	2.53
Buffalo	42	425,000	1,915	1,832	1,807	1,044,716	4.31	2.46
San Francisco	38.87	430,000	1,704	1,704	1,558	841,380	3.96	1.96
Cincinnati	53	378,728	1,711	1,623	1,599	1,391,413	4.28	3.67
Newark	23.5	360,000	1,055	956	904	859,556	2.66	2.39
New Orleans	196.25	345,000	576	555	495	406,765	1.61	1.18
Washington	70	350,000	1,228	1,139	1,080	653,515	3.26	1.87
Los Angeles	121	330,000	1,537	1,352	1,292	918,209	4.10	2.78

per capita loss approach five dollars, while in the United States, in 1911, there were 34 such cities, in nine of which the loss exceeded ten dollars, reaching a maximum in the case of Bangor, Me., where it was $137.43. That the lesson of adequate fire protection seems to be hard to learn, is shown by the fact that Bangor, Me., and Atchison, Kan., in 1910, as well as in 1911, suffered losses in excess of five dollars.

As a basis of more detailed comparison, the statistics on page 227 for foreign cities may be cited from this report and campared with similar cities in the United States.

Americar Fire Losses in 1912. The losses by fire in the United States and Canada during the year 1912, as recorded by *The Journal of Commerce and Commercial Bulletin*, of New York, aggregated $225,320,900, as compared with $234,337,250 in 1911, and $234,470,650 in 1910. The losses during January and February were particularly heavy, aggregating $64,254,-800, and were in large measure due to the severe winter and the prevalence of high winds. The aggregate amount of improved and insured property destroyed was relatively larger than in the preceding years.

The fire losses in the United States and Canada during the thirty-six years ended with 1912, aggregated $5,406,666,325, or an annual average of $150,185,181. From the accompanying table giving the losses by years during the years 1877-1912, it will be noted that the tendency is almost steadily upward as regards the country's fire waste, and it was considered impossible to determine to what extent the strenuous efforts to reduce fire risks and thereby diminish the losses in general are offset by the new factors oi our civilization that go to produce new fire hazards:

1912	$225,320,900	1894	$128,246,400
1911	234,337,250	1893	156,445,875
1910	234,470,650	1892	151,516,000
1909	203,649,200	1891	143,764,000
1908	238,562,250	1890	108,993,700
1907	215,671,250	1889	123,046,800
1906	459,010,000	1888	110,885,600
1905	175,193,800	1887	120,283,000
1904	252,554,050	1886	104,924,700
1903	156,195,700	1885	102,818,700
1902	149,260,850	1884	110,149,600
1901	164,347,450	1883	110,149,000
1900	163,362,250	1882	84,505,000
1899	136,773,200	1881	81,280,000
1898	119,650,500	1880	74,643,400
1897	110,319,650	1879	77,703,700
1896	115,655,500	1878	64,315,900
1895	129,835,700	1877	68,265,800
Total for 36 years			$5,406,666,325

A carefully compiled record, also made by the *Journal of Commerce*, summarizing the fires credited with causing a property loss of $10,000 or over in each instance shows that there were no less than 3640 such fires during 1912. This compares with 3410 fires in 1911 and 3225 in 1910.

Fire Prevention. On October 9, which was the forty-first anniversary of the great Chicago fire, the celebration of Fire Prevention Day took place quite generally throughout the United States. In Illinois, Iowa, and New York official proclamations were issued by the governors, calling for the observance of the day, and recommending that public and private consideration be given to this important subject. In several western States there was an even more practical movement, whereby individual householders endeavored to put their premises in order so as to eliminate as far as possible all danger of fire.

Private Fire Departments and Drills. During 1912, great attention was paid to the organization of private fire departments in large manufacturing establishments and the training of employees to deal promptly with fire, through organized fire brigades, and also to train the great mass of workers, especially where large numbers of women are employed, to leave the premises by prearranged methods of exit in orderly discipline. The necessity for this work was emphasized in a number of fatal fires in manufacturing plants, previous to 1912, and the development of this work usually under trained experts was rending such drills remarkably effective. In some States training and drills of employees can be ordered by responsible State or city officials, but in the main the organization is effected by employers themselves with the assistance oftentimes of outside experts. If the plant is a large one, the system is correspondingly elaborate and the fire brigade is trained not only to answer various stations, but to handle the fire-fighting equipment so that any incipient blaze can be promptly checked before the arrival of the city fire apparatus. In several cases, such fire organization has been able to deal promptly with fires that otherwise would have occasioned serious loss, not to mention possible panic and the movement is endorsed, not only as an insurance measure, but on the score of economy, as it gives a feeling of assurance to the operatives and enables the work to be performed more effectively.

High Pressure Systems. During 1912 there was put in service, at San Francisco, a high pressure fire system, made possible by a bond issue of $5,400,000, voted in 1908, when the lessons of the 1906 conflagration were being carefully considered. This scheme provides protection for about 5000 acres, or the larger part of the built-up area of the city, starting at Twin Peaks, a point 758 feet above the water front, and eventually covering the entire city. At Twin Peaks there is a two-compartment storage reservoir of 11,000,000 gallons capacity, and at Ashbury Heights and at Clay and Jones Streets there are distributing or pressure regulating tanks at elevations of 462 feet and 388 feet, supplying respectively the upper and lower zones. In addition there are two salt water pumping stations, each with four units of 2700 gallons per minute capacity, and water-front connections for two fire boats of 10,000 gallons capacity. This gives a storage capacity of 12,-000,000 gallons of fresh water and a total pumping capacity of 41,600 gallons of salt water per minute. From the distributing reservoirs adequate water and pressure is secured throughout the protected district and various means of safeguarding supply and distribution, and preventing possible interruption from earthquake or other causes have been devised, the geological formation of the region having been most carefully considered. The pumps for the reservoirs are centrifugal electrically driven, but those on the water-front are 3-stage centrifugal driven by Curtis steam turbines. These stations are fireproof buildings with storage capacity for fresh water and crude oil, which is used for fuel under the boilers. The pipe line is cast iron and the aggregate length is about 70 miles. This new system gives San Francisco excellent fire protection, and were a higher standard of building, as regards fireproof construction, observed, it would be in an enviable position. Soon after the system had been placed in successful use it was recommended that it should be extended to the grounds of the Panama-Pacific Exposition.

The Baltimore high pressure fire system, which had been under construction since 1909, was completed during 1912, and on June 7 was formally and successfully tested. This system is unique in employing lap-welded steel pipe with bolted flange joints and portable hydrant heads, whose hose outlets are controlled by regulating valves so that each hose stream may be independently regulated. The district protected by the mains of the system covers about 170 acres and is bounded by Pratt, Eutaw, Franklin, Howard, Saratoga, Gay, Baltimore, and South streets. The total length of mains in the city is distributed as follows: 30-inch main, .66 miles; 24-inch, .025 mile; 16-inch, 3.24 miles; 10-inch, 5.30 miles. There are 16-inch mains three blocks apart in both directions with 10-inch mains in all other streets and 8-inch mains used as hydrant branches. The hydrants number 226, spaced about 170 feet apart, and there is a fire-boat connection at the water-front. The pumps supplying the system are steam driven reciprocating displacement pumps. Three are Allis-Chalmers twin horizontal Corliss simple non-condensing crank and fly wheel pumps, each with cylinders 22 inches in diameter, 36 inches stroke, and plungers 13⅝, with a total discharge capacity of 12,770 gallons per minute, against a pump pressure of 242 pounds, and one a Epping-Carpenter horizontal duplex direct acting compound non-condensing pump, 14 and 25 x 12 x 16, capable of delivering 1000 gallons per minute at 32 revolutions.

MOTOR APPARATUS. During the year considerable progress was made with motor fire apparatus, and in almost all cases where new equipment was required, automobile hose wagons, combination engines, hook and ladder trucks, or water towers were supplied. In New York City, the leading development was a front drive tractor, for use with the ordinary steam fire engine, supplanting the horse draft gear at the front wheels. The New York fire department did not feel convinced of the efficiency of gasoline propelled pumping engines, although it maintained one, and believed that the same fire engine should not be displaced, but equipped with more motors in place of horses. Early in the year a fire engine supplied with a four-cylinder gasoline motor geared to the front wheels was installed at a busy station, and during a test of several months it performed most satisfactorily. This resulted in contracts being awarded for 28 of these engines, at a total expense of about a quarter of a million dollars, said to be the largest single contract for fire apparatus ever made.

The New York fire department received several aerial motor trucks with gasoline-electric motor propulsion, the current being supplied to motors at each of the four wheels from a generator, direct connected to a gasoline engine, the power plant being located behind the front wheels and under the driver's seat. Various other combinations of gas-electric motors, electric storage batteries, and gasoline engines with direct transmission were in use in various fire departments, and extension ladders up to 85 feet in length were being supplied to many of the larger fire departments.

As will be seen from the accompanying table, the largest fires during the year 1912 were those at Houston, Tex., which destroyed a number of cotton compresses and other property, causing an estimated loss of $4,500,000, and the fire in New York City, which destroyed the Equitable Life Assurance Society's building, with a loss of $3,000,000, but which, however, did not involve much insurance.

During 1912 there were no less than twenty-eight fires which caused a property damage of half a million dollars or over. These large fires are given below:

Houston, Tex., cottonseed oil plant	$ 625,000
New York City, Equitable Life Building	3,000,000
New York City, terminal warehouse	1,100,000
Newark, N. J., furniture store & other	500,000
Halifax, N. S., sugar refinery	1,000,000
Philadelphia, Pa., millinery factory and other	1,100,000
Chicago, Ill., grain elevator	600,000
Houston, Tex., cotton compresses and other	4,500,000
Toronto, Ont., car barns and other	500,000
Providence, R. I., rubber warehouse	575,000
Houston, Tex., several business houses	625,000
Flint, Mich., deaf and dumb school	600,000
Schenley, Pa., whisky warehouse	800,000
Keasbey, N. J., brick works and asphalt plant	940,000
Moose Jaw, Sask., electric power plant	500,000
Telluride, Col., stamp mill	500,000
Chicoutimi, Que., various	1,200,000
Ray, Ariz., business section of town	500,000
Saskatoon, Sask., department store	500,000
North Adams, Mass., theatre, hotel, and stores	600,000
Vancouver, B. C., several wholesale stores	1,750,000
New Iberia, La., sugar plant	500,000
Ronan, Mont., business section of town	500,000
Ocean Park, Cal., hotel, casino and stores	1,125,000
Cleveland, O., wholesale grocery house	500,000
Benicia, Cal., arsenal	1,000,000
Philadelphia, Pa., wharves and railroad property	1,000,000
Bayonne, N. J., steamers and oil works	500,000

The interest in the subject of fire protection and fire prevention manifested during the year, was evidenced by the publication not only of many magazine articles in the lay as well as in the engineering and insurance press, but of several important books. These included *Fire Prevention*, by ex-Chief Edward F. Croker, New York City Fire Department, *Fire Prevention and Fire Protection*, by J. K. Freitag, and *Fire Protection*, by P. J. McKeon, all of which were substantial contributions to the subject.

During the year the Forest Service of the United States Department of Agriculture, published an interesting bulletin on forest fires, dealing with their causes, extent, and effects, and giving a summary of the recorded destruction and losses. This was prepared by Fred G. Plummer, geographer, and was a valuable contribution to the literature on this subject, as in addition to statistics and description, it discussed the various meteorological phenomena observed in connection with great forest fires in the United States and Canada. See FORESTRY.

FISH AND FISHERIES. The United States Bureau of Fisheries, in its various laboratories, carried on the usual amount of research during the year. A comparatively new line of work is the investigation of the fresh-water mussels as a source of supply for button material, and also as providing fresh-water pearls. Lefevre and Curtis continued their work on the development of the mussel, with attention to the problem of artificially rearing the animals in the Mississippi river, and various explorations of other rivers in the Appalachian system were conducted. The fiscal year of the bureau ends in June, but the report of the commissioner, giving statistics as to the distribution of fish and the value of the fisheries for the year, was not available at the time of preparing this report. An unofficial statement as to the value of the swordfisheries was that 1,014,350 pounds were landed at Boston in 1912, having a value of $93,370. The American Fisheries Society met in Denver, September 3-5. The meeting for 1913 is to be held in Boston with Dr. Charles H. Townsend of the New York Aquarium, as president. Fish collections were made during the year in Panama, and by Eigenmann in Colombia, S. A. It is believed that the fish fauna of the Panama region is completely represented in the collections, of which the one sent in 1912 was the second. Thompson studied the dorsal fin of the rockling, *Motella*, and concluded that it is not used as a lure, because it is situated too far behind the mouth, and because it is doubtful if the prey has sufficiently clear vision to see it. It is abundantly supplied with sense cells, and p a y is a sense organ.

Hussakoff reported on the spawning habits of the sea lamprey, whose breeding season on Long Island, N. Y., is apparently in May and early June. Nests two to three feet in diameter are built anywhere in the rivers. The larger stones are carried out by the sucker-shaped mouth. Both sexes work at nest building, and copulation takes place at frequent intervals for several hours. Apparently the lampreys die after egg laying, being exhausted by the labor of preparing the nest, and the subsequent sex activity. They pay very little attention to observers standing near the nest, and apparently have very feeble senses of sight and hearing.

The second specimen of living lungfish ever brought to the United States was sent to the American Museum of Natural History from Africa. It was shipped in a ball of dried mud into which it had burrowed.

C. Tate Regan published in 1912 a volume on the *Fresh Water Fishes of the British Islands*, which was regarded by reviewers as of very great value to anyone interested in the British fishes. For fisheries in foreign countries, see articles on countries.

FISHERIES AWARD. See ARBITRATION, INTERNATIONAL.

FISK UNIVERSITY. An institution for the higher education of the colored race at Nashville, Tenn., founded in 1866. The total number of students enrolled in the various departments of the university in the autumn of 1912 was 312. The teachers numbered 32, and the workers 12. The most notable incident in the history of the university during the year was the resignation of President George A. Gates. A successor had not been chosen at the end of the year. The sum of $25,000 was given by Mr. J. Pierpont Morgan toward an endowment of the university. The income from all sources is $50,000 a year. The library contains about 10,000 volumes.

FLAX. The world's commercial crop of flaxseed in 1912, as in previous years, was produced by the United States, Argentina, Russia, British India, and Canada. In total production the United States ranked first, with 28,073,000 bushels, while Argentina, in the harvest completed early in the year, produced 25,116,700 bushels, and Canada 21,143,400 bushels. The annual yield of Russia for recent years has ranged from 20,000,000 to 23,000,000 bushels, and British India has an average annual yield of about 15,000,000 bushels, the range from year to year being, however, quite wide. The production of 1912 in the United States has never been equaled and was over 44 per cent. above the five-year average and more than double the short crop of 1910. The farm value on December 1, 1912, was 114.7 cents per bushel, as compared with 182.1 and 231.7 cents for that date in 1911 and 1910 respectively. On this basis the crop is valued by the Department of Agriculture at $32,202,000, or well above the average value of the five preceding years. The highest yields by States in 1912 were as follows: North Dakota, 12,086,000 bushels; Montana, 5,520,000 bushels; South Dakota, 5,323,000 bushels, and Minnesota, 4,121,000 bushels. In Montana the production has more than doubled since 1910, while in many of the older flaxseed-producing States the crop no more than holds its own. The flaxseed crop of Canada more than doubled in both acreage and yield from 1911 to 1912. The average annual Canadian production for the five years 1905-1909 was only 1,445,000 bushels.

Statistics regarding flax culture for fibre are rather meager. The principal flax fibre region is a belt about 350 miles wide and extending from the southern part of the Baltic Sea eastward across Russia to the Siberian border. While seed production there receives only secondary consideration the region is nevertheless one of the p incipa flaxseed-producing sections of the worldr In Europe the flax fibre crop of 912 was fairly good, but wet weather interfered to some extent with the harvesting and retting.

FLEET REORGANIZATION. See NAVAL PROGRESS, *England, France, General Progress.*

FLORIDA. POPULATION. According to the Census Bureau statistics issued in 1912, out of a total population of 752,619 in 1910, the foreign-born whites numbered 33,842, compared with 19,257 in 1900. The largest number, 10,778, came from Cuba and other West Indies; from Italy, 4535; from Spain, 4157; from England, 2917; from Germany, 2441. Other European countries were represented by smaller numbers. In 1910 the negroes numbered 308,669, and the mulattoes, 49,511. In 1890 the negroes numbered 166,180 and the mulattoes 19,757.

MANUFACTURES. The Thirteenth Census included statistics of manufactures in the State. These are for the calendar year 1909 and were compiled in 1912. The most important results are given in the table below. The industry in which the value of the product was greatest was tobacco manufactures, $21,575,000 and in this industry there were employed 12,280 men. Lumber and timber products were valued at $20,863,000 and gave employment to the largest number of men, 19,227. In the turpentine and resin industry were employed 18,143 persons and the value of the product was $11,938,000. These are the only industries in which over 10,000 men were employed and in which the product was valued at more than $10,000,000. The number of wage earners in the State in 1909 was 56,532, of whom 53,520 were male and 3512 were female. Of the wage earners, 941 were under 16 years of age, and of these 41 were females. The prevailing hours of labor showed considerable diversity. Of the total number employed, 53.5 per cent. were in establishments where the prevailing hours were from 54 to 60 hours per week, and 30.6 per cent. in establishments where they were less than 54 a week, while 15.9 per cent. were in establishments where they were more than 60 a week. The largest number of wage earners, 8996, were in Tampa. In Key West were employed 2431, in Jacksonville 1988, and in Pensacola 961. The principal results of the census are shown in the following table, with corresponding figures for 1904 and the per cent. of increase between 1904 and 1909:

	Number or Amount 1909	1904	P. C. of Inc. 1904-09
Number of establishments	2,159	1,418	52.8
Persons engaged in manufactures	64,810	46,985	37.9
Proprietors and firm members	2,712	1,769	53.3
Salaried employees	4,625	3,125	48.0
Wage earners (average number)	57,473	42,091	36.5
Primary horsepower	89,816	43,413	106.9
Capital	$65,291,000	$32,972,000	98.0
Expenses	63,218,000	40,577,000	55.8
Services	27,937,000	18,437,000	51.5
Salaries	4,955,000	2,670,000	85 6
Wages	22,982,000	15,767,000	45 8
Materials	26,128,000	16,532,000	58 0
Miscellaneous	9,153,000	5,608,000	63.2
Value of products	72,890,000	50,298,000	44.9
Value added by manufacture (value of products less cost of materials)	46,762,000	33,766,000	38.5

AGRICULTURE. The acreage, value, and production of the principal crops in 191 and 1912 are shown in the following table:

		Acreage	Prod. Bu.	Value
Corn	1912	655,000	8,515,000	$6,727,000
	1911	636,000	9,286,000	7,429,000
Oats	1912	43,000	740,000	518,000
	1911	43,000	580,000	435,000
Rice	1912	600	15,000	14,000
	1911	700	18,000	14,000
Potatoes	1912	11,000	1,023,000	1,125,000
	1911	10,000	900,000	1,305,000
Hay	1912	43,000	a 54,000	977,000
	1911	18,000	a 23,000	426,000
Tobacco	1912	3,100	b 2,604,000	781,000
	1911	2,600	b 2,444,000	684,320
Cotton	1912	......	52,895	......
	1911	......	c 73,000	......

a Tons. b Pounds. c Bales.

EDUCATION. The total enrollment of the schools of the State in 1911-12 was 157,161. Of these, 99,517 were white and 57,644 were colored. The average daily attendance was 110,364. Of these, 69,252 were white and 41,112 were colored. The teachers employed numbered 4284, of whom 3281 were white and 1003 were colored. Of the white teachers, 734 were males and 2547 were females. Of the negro teachers, 232 were males and 771 females. The average monthly salary paid to teachers was $47.85. The average monthly salary of white male teachers was $72.40; of white female teachers, $48.37; male negro teachers, $39.95; and female negro teachers $28.12. The total expenditures for school purposes in 1911-12 amounted to $2,327,394. The total value of the public school property in the State was $3,136,886. There are 83 high schools in the State.

FINANCE. There was a balance in the State treasury on January 1, 1911, of $180,143. The total receipts during the year were $1,188,162, and the total disbursements were $1,031,906, leaving a balance on December 31, 1911, of $336,399. The chief receipts were from taxes, from general license tax, from corporation taxes, and from the sale of fertilizer stamps. The chief disbursements were for the departments of State, administration of State government, education, and State institutions. The public debt of the State consists solely in refunding bonds, all of which are held by the educational funds of the State, which amounts to $601,567.

CHARITIES AND CORRECTIONS. The institutions supported by the State include the Deaf, Dumb, and Blind Institute, the Confederate Soldiers' Home, the State asylums for the insane, and State prisons.

POLITICS AND GOVERNMENT

There was no meeting of the State legislature in 1912, as the sessions are biennial and the last was held in 1911.

CONVENTIONS AND ELECTIONS. On April 30 the Democratic presidential primary was carried for Mr. Underwood. Only the Democrats nominated by primary election, the Republicans, Progressives, Socialists, and Prohibitionists nominating their tickets in convention. There was a Democratic primary election for State officers and representatives to Congress. The Democrats nominated Park M. Trammell for governor. The Republicans in convention nominated William R. O'Neal. The vote on November 5, for President was as follows: Wilson, 36,416; Taft, 4279; Roosevelt, 4535; and Debs, 4806. It will be noted that the Socialist vote was greater than that cast for either President Taft or Mr. Roosevelt. For governor Mr. Trammell received 38,977 votes and Mr. O'Neal 2646. The Progressive candidate for governor, Hodges, received 2314 votes, Cox, Socialist, 3467 votes, and Bigham, Prohibitionist, 1061 votes.

OTHER EVENTS. On January 22, the city of Key West celebrated the formal opening of the Key West extension to the Florida East Coast Railway. Representatives were present from Italy, Mexico, Portugal, Costa Rica, the Dominican Republic, Ecuador, Guatemala, Salvador, and Uruguay. The United States armored cruisers Washington and North Carolina, and the scout cruisers, Salem and Birmingham, represented the United States navy. A Portuguese cruiser participated in the celebration.

As a result of certain reports published by the Department of Agriculture an investigation was authorized by the House of Representatives in the matter of the draining of the Florida Everglades. The engineers connected with this work were charged with having misapplied funds, and Mr. Elliott, chief engineer of the drainage division of the department, was dismissed. Representative Clark of Florida, on whose motion the investigation was begun, issued a statement in which he charged that the officers of the government made it possible for loan sharks to sell lands under from 2 to 10 feet of water, thereby bringing discredit upon the federal government and the State, while enriching unscrupulous real estate boomers. Mr. Clark declared in a speech in the house that he could prove "that the Secretary of Agriculture told me in the presence of reputable witnesses that he suppressed a circular letter that gave the facts, at the instance of persons engaged in selling lands in the everglades of Florida." See EXPLORATION.

As a result of the controversy over the Everglades matter, the house committee on expenditures in the Department of Agriculture made an investigation of the work of the department in relation to the drainage of the Everglades. The report consisted of two parts, one expressing the views of the majority and the other, those of the minority. In general, the report of the majority of the committee was as follows: The waste lands of the United States consist of two great classes. One of these is lands which cannot be cultivated for lack of water. These are being reclaimed by a process of reclamation. The other lands are those which are entirely, or largely submerged by water, and are therefore useless in their present condition. Some of these can be reclaimed by drainage. These swamp lands have been allowed to pass through the hands of the federal government into those of the several States, which are less able to deal with such enormous undertakings as are involved in the drainage of these lands than the government would be. The States are also less competent to cope with the great powers of special private interests, which see in such lands opportunities for speculative enterprise. Companies were organized for the purpose of exploiting these lands. These companies seized upon certain statements issued under the approval of the Drainage Division of the Department of Agriculture and circulated them in order to stimulate the sale of these lands before they had been drained. These statements, it appeared, had been made by the official in charge of the field investigations carried on by the department, but had not been critically examined by the authorities of the department. Upon learning of the use to which these statements had been put, the Department of Agriculture held up the report from which they had been taken. As a consequence, there was an immediate protest from the people who were interested in these lands. The investigation of the committee apparently showed that Mr. Wright, the government official, from whom these statements had come, was financially interested in these lands several years ago. Mr. Wright had for some time ceased to be connected with the government service. In regard to the relation which Assistant Secretary Hays held to the affair, the committee was divided. The majority cited facts which appeared to indicate that Mr. Hays knew about the transactions of Mr. Wright, and that he himself, though not profiting financially by any transactions in the lands, took part in the negotiations concerning them. The minority report, on the contrary, defended Mr. Hays, and cited testimony which tended to show that he did not know of Mr. Wright's connection, and that he was in no wise culpable.

As a result of the inquiry made into the matter of the Florida Everglades by the Department of Agriculture, C. G. Elliott, former chief of the drainage investigation in the department, Allison D. Morehouse, assistant chief, Ray P. Teele, formerly assistant chief of irrigation investigation, and Frank E. Singleton, an accountant, were indicted. The first two had been dismissed by Secretary Wilson, and the third had resigned.

STATE GOVERNMENT, 1912. Governor, P. Trammell; Secretary of State, H. C. Crawford; Treasurer, J. C. Luning; Comptroller, W. V. Knott; Attorney-General, Park M. Trammell; Auditor, Ernest Amos; Adjutant-General, J. C. R. Foster; Superintendent of Public Instruction, W. N. Sheats; Commissioner of Agriculture, W. A. McRea—all Democrats.

JUDICIARY. Supreme Court: Chief Justice, J. B. Whitfield; Justices W. A. Hocker, R. F. Taylor, T. M. Shackleford, and R. S. Cockrell; Clerk, Milton H. Mabry—all Democrats.

STATE LEGISLATURE, 1913. The legislature is: Senate, Democrats, 32; House, Democrats, 71.

The representatives in Congress will be found in the section *Congress*, article UNITED STATES.

FLORIDA, UNIVERSITY OF. A State institution of higher learning at Gainesville, Fla., founded in 1905. The registration in the several departments of the university in 1911-12 was 302. The faculty numbered about 60. During the year a gift of $1500 was received from the general education board for a chair of secondary education, and $2750 was given by the southern education board for the chair of elementary education. The Southern Railway gave a scholarship of $200 to the college of agriculture. There has been received from the Peabody Board of Trust, $40,000, for a building to be known as the George Peabody Hall for the Department of Education. This building is now in process of erection. The State legislature of 1912 appropriated $105,000 for permanent improvements. Out of this fund there have been constructed the following buildings: college of agriculture, language and history building for the college of liberal arts, and the university commons. The sum of $6000 has been expended on the university library, bringing the total number of books on file up to about 30,000 volumes. President, A. A. Murphree, LL. D.

FLOUR. See FOOD AND NUTRITION.

FLY. See ENTOMOLOGY.

FLYING PAY. See NAVAL PROGRESS, AVIATION.

FOOD AND NUTRITION. FOOD INSPECTION. A total of 1459 violations of the United States Food and Drugs Act of 1906 were reported for prosecution in 1912, an increase of 25 per cent. over the previous year. Of these 991 were criminal cases. The first jail sentences for violation of the act were inflicted, and there was a tendency on the part of the courts to impose larger fines for first offenses. Decrees of forfeiture and condemnation were entered against 294 shipments of adulterated and misbranded foods and drugs, and 103 shipments of filthy or decomposed products were destroyed.

The Referee Board of Consulting Scientific Experts, p pu a y known as the Remsen board, submitted othdirrlconclusions as to the use of copper salts in the greening of vegetables, finding that the consumption of even small quantities of copper may have a deleterious action and must be considered injurious to health. The use of copper salts in foods under the jurisdiction of the act was thereupon prohibited after January 1, 1913. Other decisions were also promulgated by the Department of Agriculture, authorizing the use of saccharin, previously prohibited in foods, as a drug if properly labeled, prohibiting the sale of absinthe, restricting the use of the terms sweet oil, maraschino cherries, and candied citron, prescribing the labeling of vinegars, and limiting the amount of liquids and other extraneous material in canned goods.

An amendment to the Food and Drugs Act, adopted August 23, specifically extended its scope to claims as to the curative or therapeutic effect of drugs and medicines.

The resignation of Dr. H. W. Wiley, who as chief chemist of the Department of Agriculture had been prominently associated with the passage and enforcement of pure-food legislation, occurred in April, and was followed late in December by the appointment of Dr. Carl L. Alsberg, a scientist of the department, as his successor.

A pure-food law was enacted by the new State of Arizona. This leaves New Mexico as the only State without such a law, although in Arkansas, Delaware, and West Virginia no special appropriations are available. Additional legislation relative to the labeling of goods to show the net weight or volume was adopted in New York, and also a law requiring an annual bacteriological inspection of all shellfish grounds as to their sanitary condition.

Cost of Food. Although there were considerable fluctuations in food prices throughout the year the general tendency was still upward. *Bradstreet's* for December showed an average increase of 15 per cent. over the corresponding period in 1902, and 6.2 per cent. over that on December 1, 1911. Breadstuffs were apparently somewhat cheaper, but livestock, fruits, and provisions showed considerable increases. Comprehensive data gathered by the United States Bureau of Labor were in general accord with these findings. Round steak was found to have risen 13.61 per cent., lard 11.3, wheat flour 10.7, eggs 11.8, butter 15.3, and sugar 6 per cent. over the previous year. For the ten years the increases ranged from 8.5 per cent. on sugar to 26.1 per cent. on eggs, 32.9 per cent. on milk, 33.3 per cent. on butter, 39 per cent. on wheat flour, 53.9 per cent. on lard, 84 per cent. on round steak, 86 per cent. on pork chops, and 111.9 per cent. on potatoes.

The high prices and their causes were subjects of much speculation and inquiry, and led to a great diversity of conclusions. Data collected by the United States consular service and others, however, indicated that the problem extended in varying degree to every civilized country, and while complex in many of its phases was the result in part at least of progress toward a higher plane of living. Such remedies as were attempted in this country aimed usually either to increase the production of foodstuffs and other raw materials or to effect economies in the distribution of commodities. The establishment of public market places for the direct sale of farm products met with favor in many localities, and there was also much interest in the formation of coöperative associations both for selling and purchasing goods, such as have been quite successful in European countries. Late in December women's clubs and similar organizations in Philadelphia, Chicago, New York, and other cities, were holding special sales of eggs and other foodstuffs in the hope of effecting reductions in prices.

Nutrition Studies. Many of the principal studies of the year dealt with problems connected with the more effective utilization of food products and the preservation of quality in perishable goods. For instance, corn meal and Kafir-corn meal were tested with reference to a wider use as human food, and it was found that the latter could readily replace half the wheat flour in many recipes. Bacteriological studies of dried and frozen eggs showed the need of strict compliance with sanitary methods in their manufacture, but that when properly handled these products are both wholesome and valuable.

An exhaustive study of cold-storage methods by a Massachusetts State commission revealed many benefits from the practice, in spite of the slow but inevitable deterioration in quality noted. The commission recommended a systematic inspection of warehouses, the prohibition of storage for more than one year or the restorage of goods, and the labeling of all storage products.

Much attention was given to the canning and preserving of foods. Cinnamon and cloves were found to have considerable preservative action, whereas pepper and ginger had very little. The practice of partially filling cans with food and then adding water was shown to be needless, and it was demonstrated that with most food products substantial uniformity in the weights of canned and package goods were readily attainable. The action of canned goods on tin containers was found in the case of shrimps, asparagus, spinach, string beans, and pumpkins to be due to the presence of volatile alkalis or amino acids.

The relation of foods to certain diseases was another leading subject of inquiry. Nelson, of the New Jersey experiment stations, reported that the floating or "fattening" of oysters in brackish water possessed the advantages of ridding the oysters of much of the mechanically entangled slime and other dirt and improved the keeping and cooking qualities, and concluded that the practice is not injurious, but even desirable if the water in which the oysters are floated is pure. On the other hand, Stiles, of the United States Department of Agriculture, found that epidemics of typhoid fever due to the ingestion of polluted sea food were in most cases traceable to floating in polluted waters, and many oyster sections showing sewage contamination were closed by State authorities during the year. A third investigator reported good results by floating oysters in an artificial sea water.

Studies as to the danger of transmitting typhoid fever by green vegetables showed that rainfall alone did not wholly free plants from infected material, and that the typhoid bacillus could survive even unfavorable conditions long enough for such crops as lettuce and radish to mature. Legislation was recommended to prohibit the sale of these products from farms unprovided with proper sanitary facilities.

Additional evidence was adduced to show the relationship between the excessive use of polished rice and such diseases as beriberi and polyneuritis. A substance named "torulin," which seemed to prevent polyneuritis, was isolated from a number of foodstuffs, and in the Philippine Islands the substitution of vegetables for a part of the polished rice in the diet reduced the attacks of beriberi (q. v.). Such data as were accumulated during the year tended to cast doubt on the theory as to the connection of pellagra with the use of corn. The claim that breads, especially white bread, tend to cause dental caries was found to be true only as regards farinaceous foods in general.

Numerous studies of the proteins were reported, particularly as to their utilization by the body. The proteins from legumes and cotton-seed were found to be much less completely utilized than those of cereals, and those of meat powders slightly less so than those of fresh meat.

The principal scientific gathering of the year was the Fifteenth Congress of Hygiene and Demography, held at Washington, D. C., September 23-28, with President Taft as honorary president. One of its nine sections was devoted especially to the hygiene of food production, distribution, and consumption, and the extensive exhibits assembled in connection with the congress included a large amount of illustrative material along these lines. The Graduate School of Home Economics held its fourth session July 1-26, at the Michigan Agricultural College, in close affiliation with the Graduate School of Agriculture.

BOOKS OF THE YEAR. Some of the more important books to appear in 1912 were the following: W. H. Jordan, *Principles of Human Nutrition—A Study in Practical Dietetics* (New York); E. A. Locke, *Food Values—Practical Tables for Use in Private Practice and Public Institutions* (New York and London); E. Braun, *Economy and System in the Bakery* (Cincinnati); J. A. Murray, *The Economy of Food* (London); G. Reymann, *Diatetische Kost Vorschriften, zum Gebrauch in gesunden und kranken Tagen* (Lauterecken); W. Tibbles, *Foods—Their Origin, Composition and Manufacture* (London); E. P. Cathcart, *The Physiology of Protein Metabolism* (New York, Bombay, and Calcutta); and P. G. Stiles, *Nutritional Physiology*. See CARNEGIE INSTITUTION.

FOOD RIOTS. See PRICES.

FOOT AND MOUTH DISEASE. See VETERINARY SCIENCE.

FOOTBALL. A number of radical changes in the rules, which seem, in the main, to have had the effect of improving materially the game, made the football season of 1912 a conspicuous one. The most important of these changes were: (1) The shortening of the actual playing field from 110 yards to 100 yards, and the addition of two end zones behind the goal posts, each zone 10 yards in length and the width of the playing field, in which zones the forward pass could be executed legitimately; (2) the abolition of the onside kick; (3) the shortening of the intermission between the first and second and the third and fourth periods; (4) the changing of the value of a touchdown from 5 points to 6 points, thus making a touchdown converted into a goal count 7 points instead of 6 as formerly; and (5) giving the attacking team four downs instead of three to gain the ten yards required to retain possession of the ball. Another and even more radical change—that of widening the playing field from its present 160 feet to 210 feet—was considered by the rules committee, but rejected for the reason that there would not be space for a field of such width within the stadiums already constructed.

Not only were there fewer casualties in the football season of 1912 than in any season since 1901, but such casualties as there were were confined almost entirely to games in which the contesting teams were of inferior rank and inadequate condition. No serious accident marred the meetings of the higher class elevens—a happy condition which must be ascribed, in part at least, to the changes in the rules.

The Harvard University eleven, containing fine material, and splendidly coached in the new game, was the undisputed leader of the season. To Princeton, the champion of the previous year, second place was ascribed, and Yale was placed third. There was very little question of the preëminence of these three teams, but a number of surprises made the ranking of the other elevens more difficult. Dartmouth had an excellent eleven, holding Harvard to a 0—3 score, and sustaining its only bad defeat at the hands of Princeton. The unexpected reverse that Carlisle met at the hands of Pennsylvania stamps the Indian team as having been below the class of the leaders. The University of Pennsylvania had one of those in-and-out elevens which seem to be becoming a habit at that institution, losing by small scores to Swarthmore and Lafayette, and being badly beaten by Brown and Penn State. Of all the elevens in the East, Penn State is the hardest to rank. The team went through the season of 1912 without being defeated or tied, and was scored on only once. But it met no opponent of the caliber of Harvard, Princeton, or Yale. Cornell's season was even more disastrous than Pennsylvania's, the Ithaca eleven losing seven games and winning but three. A southern contestant of promise and achievement was Vanderbilt, which rolled up an impressive point total, and coming north to play Harvard, met honorable defeat, holding the 1912 leaders to a small score.

None of the Middle Western elevens showed anything like impressive strength. Michigan played three games against eastern opponents, losing to the weak Syracuse and Pennsylvania elevens by close scores, and winning from the still weaker Cornell eleven. As an indication of comparative sectional strength, it may be noted that Syracuse, victor over Michigan by a score of 18—7, was beaten by Princeton 65—0. In the Middle Western Conference League Wisconsin was first with five victories and no defeats, and Chicago second with six victories and one defeat.

The results from the principal games played in the East follow: Harvard defeated Princeton 16—6, Yale 20—0, Brown 30—10, and Dartmouth 3—0. Princeton, losing to Harvard, tied Yale 6—6, and defeated Dartmouth 22—7. Yale, beaten by Harvard, and emphatically outplayed by Princeton, despite the tie score, won from Brown 10—0. Pennsylvania, as usual, won her Thanksgiving Day game with Cornell 7—2, and in the annual contest between the services, Annapolis won from West Point for the third consecutive year.

While the much-discussed "All American" eleven is to a large extent a matter of personal choice, a consensus of the selections of some thirty critics of the game picks out the following men as the best in their positions in the East for the season of 1912: Ends, Bomeisler (Yale) and Felton (Harvard); tackles, Storer (Harvard) and Englehorn (Dartmouth); guards, Shenk (Princeton) and Brown (Navy); centre, Ketcham (Yale); quarter-back, Pazzetti (Lehigh); half-backs, Brickley (Harvard) and Baker (Princeton); full-back, Thorpe (Carlisle).

The championship of the Intercollegiate Soccer League was won by Yale, which went through its season with five victories and no defeats.

Pennsylvania, Harvard and Haverford were tied for second place, and Columbia and Cornell were respectively fifth and sixth. The winners in other American Soccer leagues were: New York District League, Newark; New Jersey League, West Hudson; Metropolitan District Association, St. George; Connecticut League, Park City; Southern California League, Rangers; Northwestern League, Black Diamonds. The annual match between Leland Stanford University and the University of California was won by the former by a score of 4—2; and in England Cambridge defeated Oxford by 3 goals to 1.

FORAGE DAY. See the article on AGRICULTURE.

FORD, ISAAC NELSON. An American newspaper correspondent, died August 9, 1912. He was born in Buffalo, N. Y., in 1848, and graduated from Brown University in 1870. He entered journalism by joining the staff of the New York *Tribune* in 1870, and remained in the service of that journal as office editor, editorial writer, book reviewer, and correspondent until the time of his death. He made many journeys in Canada, the United States, the West Indies, Mexico, and Central and South America. In 1895 he became London correspondent of the New York *Tribune*, and in this capacity traveled extensively throughout Europe. He was the author of *Tropical America* (1893), and a contributor to magazines and periodicals.

FOREST FIRES. See FORESTRY; FIRE PROTECTION.

FORESTRY. The coöperative plan entered into by the United States Forest Service and various State authorities for the control of forest fires has worked out very successfully, and the country has been spared the heavy loss of life and property that characterized 1910. The lumber manufacturers of Montana, Idaho, Oregon, Washington, and California are also coöperating in preserving the forests from fire. Only about 76,000,000 feet of standing timber is reported as destroyed by fire in the northwest during 1912. Extensive forest fires swept parts of the Yukon Valley, Alaska, early in the summer, destroying much timber. On the Colorado plateau considerable loss is reported. Investigations by the forest service seem to indicate that lightning plays a much greater part in causing forest fires than had hitherto been believed. By recent legislation, the railroads in western Canada are held responsible for fires starting within 300 yards of their right of way, and must assume costs and damages for losses to a distance of 10 miles, when fires spread from their lands. In British Columbia, every owner of forest land is obliged to pay 1½ cents per acre and 2½ cents per thousand feet of timber, and the crown lands contribute 2 cents per acre, to a fund which the government supplements by like amounts to be used for fire protection.

For the year ending June 30, 1912, the exports of forest products of all kinds from the United States were valued at $108,083,382, while the imports for the same period amounted to $172,611,580, a gain of $5,000,000 in exports and $10,000,000 in imports. Of the imports, rubber was the principal item, valued at $102,941,901, followed by lumber and other forms of wood, including pulp wood, $34,664,114, and wood pulp, $14,218,922. The lumber production for the United States for 1911, according to the United States Census, was 37,003,207,000 feet board measure, a reduction of little more than 3,000,000,000 feet from the production of 1910. Of the 1911 production, 78.1 per cent. was of soft woods and 21.9 per cent. hard woods. Washington led in its timber cut, with 4,064,754,000 feet, followed by Louisiana, with 3,550,456,000 feet, and Mississippi, with 2,041,615,000 feet. The following additional States each contributed more than a billion feet to the total output: Oregon, North Carolina, Arkansas, Wisconsin, Texas, Minnesota, Michigan, West Virginia, Virginia, Alabama, California, and Pennsylvania. The combined output of lumber of the southern States in 1911 amouted to 68 per cent. of the total. North Dakota is the only State not reporting any lumber production. The output of lath and shingles for the same period was: lath, 2,971,110,000; shingles, 12,113,867,000.

NATIONAL FOREST SERVICE. The exterior boundaries of the National Forests have assumed a fairly stable condition. There were, on June 30, 1912, 163 National Forests, whose gross area embraced 187,406,376 acres, the additions during the year being 238,384 acres, and the eliminations 3,440,251 acres, a net reduction of 3,201,867 acres. Within these forest areas are 22,379,213 acres of alienated land, leaving as the net area of all National Forests, on June 30, 1912, 165,027,163 acres. The distribution of the net area by States was as follows:

State, etc.	Net area Acres	State, etc.	Net area Acres
Arizona	12,462,257	New Mexico..	8,819,408
Arkansas	1,208,782	North Dakota	6,414
California	20,890,945	Oklahoma ...	61,480
Colorado	13,277,374	Oregon	13,658,679
Florida	308,410	South Dakota	1,156,884
Idaho	17,977,454	Utah	7,287,716
Kansas	155,736	Washington...	9,836,146
Michigan	84,711	Wyoming	8,369,023
Minnesota	846,627	Alaska	26,643,260
Montana	16,127,358	Porto Rico....	32,975
Nebraska	520,905		
Nevada	5,294,619	Total	165,027,163

A plan for the exchange of school lands lying within the National Forests for lands of equal area or value elsewhere has been perfected, and applications are pending for the exchange of land held by individuals and companies on a basis of equal value. The systematic classification of agricultural lands within the National Forests begun in 1909, was greatly extended in 1912, work being in progress in four of the six forest districts, the United States Bureau of Soils coöperating. The cost of administration, protection, and permanent improvements in the National Forests for 1912 was $5,217,827.51, or a trifle over 2½ cents per acre. The receipts were: timber sold, $1,089,702.04; grazing, $968,842.26; and special uses, $98,812.27; with a total of all receipts of $2,109,256.91, an increase of $140,263.49 over those of 1911. The free use of timber on National Forests to the value of $196,335.41 was permitted.

The Weeks law, by which forest areas are to be secured in the Appalachian and White mountains, has been in force for a year, and by purchase or condemnation, 257,228 acres were in process of acquisition, at an average price of $5.95 per acre. The first purchase in the White Mountains under this law was authorized June 19, 1912, when 30,365 acres were accepted, the Geological Survey having favorably reported upon their desirability for protection of the streams in that region.

The reforestation work of the Forest Service has been continued, and tentative plans have been adopted for the direct seeding or planting of 30,000 acres in the different National Forests each year. Extensive operations in seed collection and nursery work have been carried on to supply the necessary materials. An investigation of the fire-killed timber in Idaho and Montana showed that fire-killed Douglas fir timber was almost if not quite as strong as that of the same grade cut from the live tree. An experiment station has been established in the Manti forest, Utah, for the study of problems of grazing and water run-off, especially in relation to heavy storms. The investigations of forest products and wood utilization have been considerably extended at the laboratories at Madison, Wis., and Chicago, Ill. Track tests in p g ess since 1902 have shown that, almost withoutr exception, treating ties increases their durability 2 or 3 times. Wood distillation and tapping experiments with western pines have been extensively carried on, and it has been found that the yellow pine of Arizona and California yields a product that readily serves the purposes for which ordinary turpentine is used.

LEGISLATION, ETC. A recent compilation has shown that 14 States have enacted special legislation regarding taxation, forest management, etc., while in 34 States such lands are taxed the same as other property. By a recent law, New York exempts from taxation for 35 years, all tracts of 1 to 100 acres planted to forest trees at the rate of 800 per acre. In Minnesota 30,000 acres of prairie land have been planted to forest trees under the law granting a bounty for such plantings. The Pennsylvania Forestry Commission set out more than 2,000,000 seedlings during 1912. The State forest reserves of Pennsylvania now include over 985,000 acres. Massachusetts has begun the reforestation of the Little River and Ludlow watersheds. Wisconsin added about 36,000 acres to its State forests, the total area of which, in 1912, was about 400,000 acres. San Diego, Cal., is said to own 7000 acres of land which is being planted according to a definite forest plan. Twelve counties in Indiana have organized for the care and planting of forest trees. The chestnut bark blight disease continues to spread and is now known to occur in 10 States, from Massachusetts to Virginia. The International Paper Company, which is said to control 147,000 acres in New Hampshire and Vermont, has adopted a cutting plan of 0.2 cord per acre, which is about the amount of the natural regeneration. In Hawaii a rubber plantation expected to tap 40,000 planted trees in 1912, and a yield of 6000 pounds of rubber is estimated. The governor of Hawaii, by proclamation, has added to a number of the forest reserves in those islands, and the Molokai Reserve of 44,674 acres was created.

FOREIGN COUNTRIES. An English association for the encouragement of forestry was formed within the year, and an advisory committee on forestry in Scotland has been appointed. Recent reports show that about 18 per cent. of the area of Belgium is in forest as follows: state 76,000 acres, municipalities, 411,000 acres; other public institutions, 518,800 acres, and private holdings, 818,350 acres. About 8 per cent. of the area of Holland is in forests, an increase of nearly one-third in the past 30 years. The state forests comprise about 200,000 acres. The forest area of Germany is said to be 34,500,000 acres, or about 27 per cent. of the area of the country. From the Prussian forest domain a net revenue of $5 per acre is estimated. In Baden the net revenue for wood alone is said to have been $7.40 per acre in 1909. The state forests of Bavaria, which comprise 2,150,000 acres, are valued at $50 per acre, and the net revenue for 1911 was $3,222,145. Sweden is said to have 72,800,000 acres in forest, 78.2 per cent. of which is privately owned and 21.8 per cent. state forest. The maximum production of forest products of Sweden was reached in 1900, since which time there has been a rapid decline. Experiments in Sweden have shown that burning over heath lands had a favorable effect in reforestation, as less seed was required to get a good stand. Recent reports state that there are in Asiatic Russia, 1,363,240 square miles in forest, and in European Russia, 461,375 square miles, or a total of 35 per cent. of the total land area of the empire. An attempt is being made to develop the forest resources in the Ural Mountains, by the construction of railroads and introduction of modern methods of foresty. In Italy legislation has been recently enacted creating an independent administration of the state forests, providing for reforestation and proper forest management. Newly planted areas are exempt from taxation for 15 years if in coppice and 40 years if high forest. The teak forests of Siam produced for export in 1911 timber valued at $2,820,914. The minister of finance of Japan reports for 1911 a total area in forests of 51,900,000 acres, about half of which are state forests. The timbered area of Sakhalin is estimated at 8,500,000 acres, and that of Formosa at 12,000,000 acres. An extensive experiment in reforesting the bare hills near Port Arthur in Manchuria has been begun. In 1910 an attempt was made to develop forest management in Siberia, and 21 districts with 57 officials were created to look after a forest area estimated at 500,000,000 acres. Queensland, Australia, has about 4,000,000 acres in forest reserves and about 40,000,000 acres that have not been fully examined. An immediate revision of the forestry laws of Chile is contemplated.

FORESTRY SCHOOLS, PERSONNEL, ETC. The committee appointed in 1911 by the conference of forest schools has reported upon the standardization of instruction in forestry in the United States, and outlined a course of higher grade instruction, requirements for admission, etc. Their report says that there are 24 institutions in this country that give courses leading to a degree in forestry, and about 40 others which include forestry in their courses of instruction. A State college of forestry has been established in connection with Syracuse University, New York, and Dr. H. P. Baker appointed dean. The department of forestry at Cornell has been considerably extended and courses are now offered leading to degrees. Walter Mulford and S. N. Spring have been added to the faculty, and appropriations were made of $100,000 for a forestry building. A forestry department has been provided for in the University of Idaho through the coöperation of the lumber and timber interests in the State. The Washington School of Forestry has added a course in logging engineering. The Yale School of Forestry has secured a tract of pine forest in New Hampshire to be used for teaching silviculture and forest operations. The Harvard Forest School posesses over 2000 acres of timbered land that it proposes using as a working laboratory. E. A. Sterling, for several years forester of the Pennsylvania Railroad, and F. G. Miller, dean of the College of Forestry of the University of Washington, have resigned to engage in commercial work. Dr. H. Stoetzer, director of the Forest Academy at Eisenach, and Dr. J. L. von Liburnau, through whose efforts the Austrian Experiment Station was founded, have died.

Among the recent books treating of some phases of forestry may be mentioned: S. B. Elliott, *Important Timber Trees of the United States;* C. O. Hanson, *Forestry for Woodmen;* R. C. Hawley and A. F. Hawes, *Forestry in New England;* J. Nisbet, *The Elements of British Forestry;* W. Noyes, *Wood and Forest;* S. J. Record, *Economic Woods of the United States;* C. K. Schneider, *Illustriertes Handbuch der Laubholzkunde.*

FORMOSA, or TAIWAN. An island off the Chinese coast, a dependency of Japan. Capital, Dai-Hoku (or Tai-pei). Area, 2324 square ri (13,841 square miles.) Legal population December 31, 1908, 2,984,590; total estimated population in 1912, 3,443,679 (1,806,048 male, 1,637,631 female). Estimated resident population of the larger towns December 31, 1910: Dai-Hoku, 91,309; Dainan (Tainan), 57,622; Kagi (Chia-i), 22,218; Rokko (Lu-Kong), 19,036; Kiilung (Keelung), 17,110; Shinchiku (Hsin-Chu), 16,064; Gilan (Ilan), 15,803; Shokwa (Chang-Hua), 15,506; Taku (Takow), 12,161; Daichiu (Taichu), 11,296; Toko (Tonkong), 10,178. The census of 1905 showed that 97.62 per cent. of the inhabitants in the administrative area were illiterate, but the Japanese are developing an educational system.

The agricultural products include rice, tea, sugar, sweet potatoes, ramie, and jute. Camphor is worked in the forests as a government monopoly. The mineral products include gold, coal, silver, copper, sulphur, and petroleum. Gold production in 1908 and 1909, 51,778 and 50,811 ounces; silver, 32,791 and 49,813 ounces; copper, 86,347 and 115,671 kwan; sulphur, 525,017 and 576,632 kwan; coal, 151,887 and 180,515 tons. Exclusive of the large trade with Japan, imports and exports of merchandise were valued in 1910 at 19,853,000 and 12,080 yen respectively; in 1911, 19,555,000 and 13,176,000. Railways, 467 kilometers (290 miles); telegraphs, 2283 kms. of line and 5591 kms. of wire; telephones, 1107 kms. of line and 12,210 kms. of wire; post offices, 135. Revenue and expenditure (provisional accounts) amounted to 55,338,350 and 41,201,533 yen respectively in the fiscal year 1911. The budget for the fiscal year 1912 balanced at 43,651,651 yen; for 1913, 45,325,508 yen. Formosa is administered by a governor-general (in 1912, Lieut.-Gen. Count Sakuma Samata).

FORTIFIED WINES. See LIQUORS.

FOSTER, DAVID JOHNSON. Former congressman from Vermont, died March 21, 1912. He was born in Barnet, Vt., in 1807, and graduated from Dartmouth College in 1880. He studied law and was admitted to the bar in 1883. Beginning practice in Burlington, he was elected State's attorney in 1886, serving until 1890. From 1892 to 1894 he was a member of the State Senate and from 1894 to 1898 was commissioner of State taxes. He was elected to the Fifty-seventh Congress in 1901 and was reëlected to the succeeding congresses, including the Sixty-first.

FOUNDATIONS. The use of the freezing process which has been applied in various kinds of excavation where a damp and loose subsoil was encountered was described during the year, in its application to a building foundation, the method consisting of excavating within a sheet-pile enclosure by sinking freezing pipes five inches in diameter vertically around the site of the excavation. These pipes were sunk to a distance of 23 feet below the bottom of the proposed excavation, and were connected with brine pipes and a refrigerating plant. By freezing the material excavation was possible so that the material and moisture and water in the centre could be removed and the floor covered with a thick bed of concrete placed under water. The frozen material prevented the water entering the excavation, and the site was pumped out and the side walls were completed.

One of the most important foundations of the year was that of the new Adams Express Company building in New York, in which pneumatic caissons were used, set, sunk, and concreted by the aid of locomotive cranes. This building, 32 stories in height and of 202 x 107 feet area, is supported on 24 piers sunk through quicksand, gravel, and hard pan to rock at a maximum depth of about 70 feet below the Broadway curb. Rectangular wooden caissons varying from 9½ x 9½ to 9 x 34 feet were employed. The use of the cranes presented features of interest and was attended with great success. See also BRIDGES and TALL BUILDINGS.

FOURTH OF JULY ACCIDENTS. See TETANUS.

FRANCE. A republic in western Europe. Area and population by departments below. Capital, Paris.

AREA AND POPULATION. According to the census of March 5, 1911, the area in hectares was 53,646,374 hectares, which is equivalent to 536,464 sq. kilometers, or 207,129 sq. miles. The area as calculated in 1901 excludes the foreshore, the estuaries, and certain barren regions, and amounts to 52,944,198 hectares. The population was 39,601,509.

Marriages in 1911, provisional figures, 307,788 (307,710 in 1910); divorces, 13,058 (12,975); living births, 742,114 (774,399); stillbirths, 33,840 (36,009), deaths, 776,983 (702,972)—an excess of 71,418 births over deaths in 1910 and a deficit in 1911 of 34,869.

Some of the principal cities with their communal population in 1911: Paris, 2,888,110; Marseilles, 550,619; Lyons, 523,796; Bordeaux, 261,678; Lille, 217,807; Toulouse, 149,576; Saint-Etienne, 148,656; Nice, 142,940; Nantes, 170,535; Le Havre, 130,159; Rouen, 124,987; Nancy, 119,949; Reims, 115,178; Toulon, 104,582; Amiens, 93,207; Limoges, 92,181, Brest, 90,540; Nimes, 80,437; Dijon, 76,847; Orléans, 72,096; Tours, 73,398; Versailles, 60,458; Avignon, 49,304; Cherbourg, 43,731; Angoulême, 38,211; Rochefort, 35,010; Saint-Nazaire, 38,267; Pau, 37,149.

EDUCATION. In 1911 the conscription list carried 301,467 men of the class of 1910. Degree of instruction of 18,093 of these, unknown. Of the other 283,374, 2.79 per cent. could neither read nor write. 1.31 per cent. could read only, 27.44 per cent. could read and write; 65.98 per cent. had acquired a more extensive primary education, and 2.30 per cent. were graduates of secondary institutions.

Infant schools (1910-11), 3967 (2691 public and 1156 private lay schools, and 10 public and

110 private clerical schools); total teachers, 8615 (219 clerical). Children in lay schools, 603,747; in clerical schools, 17,175—total, 620,922 (315,822 boys, 305,100 girls). Primary schools, including superior primary schools (1910-11), 82,488 (619 clerical); teachers, 156,981 (2055 clerical); pupils, 5,654,794 (5,579,502 in lay and 75,292 in clerical schools). Primary normal schools (1910-11), 166 (166 in 1911-12); teachers, 1720 (1726); students, 9326 (9358). State expenditure for primary instruction (1909), 212,608,176 francs.

Secondary public schools (1911-12): 344 lycées and colleges for boys (97,512 students) and 129 for girls (30,788); 56 secondary courses for girls (5503 pupils). Students in universities January 15, 1912, 41,194.

AGRICULTURE. Of the productive area (1909), 23,615,220 hectares were under crops (including sown meadows), 4,837,610 under natural meadows, 1,577,220 under forage plants, 3,627,330 under pasture, 1,686,942 under vines, 1,220,150 under industrial plants, truck gardens, etc., 9,329,193 under woods and forests; 3,843,520 hectares were fallow or uncultivated; 3,218,579 not included in any of the foregoing. The leading crops, with their area (in hectares) and yield (in quintals) for 1911 and 1912 (the latter, subject to slight revision) and the yield per hectare in 1911, are as follows:

	Hectares 1911	Hectares 1912	Quintals 1911	Quintals 1912	Qs. ha.
Wheat	6,443,360	6,555,500	87,727,100	91,182,600	13.6
Rye	1,174,420	1,211,865	11,875,000	13,039,000	10.1
Barley	771,935	751,150	10,856,570	11,381,340	14.1
Oats	3,991,490	3,997,250	50,693,500	54,519,700	12.7
Flax*	24,028	22,355	126,079a	....	5.2
Beets†	242,930	245,385	42,357,640	63,841,100	174.4
Vines‡	1,683,113	1,678,941	44,885,500	59,339,035	26.7
Tobacco*	15,937	4,036	183,404	....	11.5

* In the principal producing departments. † Sugar beets. ‡ In the important producing departments. Production above given in hectoliters. a Seed.

Other important crops (1910): Potatoes, 1,546,990 hectares, 85,230,900 quintals, value 885,074,670 francs; dry beans, 122,370 ha., 1,275,720 qs., 52,673,670 fr.; forage beets, 665,460 ha., 214,094,450 qs., 404,829,590 fr.; truck-garden products, 111,070 ha., 203,820,050 fr. Quintals of corn produced (1911), 4,283,000. In 1912, 33,133 hectograms of silk-worm eggs were placed to be hatched, against 35,431 hectograms in 1911. The cocoons obtained amounted to 6,233,942 kilograms, against 5,109,426 in 1911. Average yield of cocoons per hectogram of eggs, 188.1 kg. (144.2 in 1911.) Livestock statistics follow (December 31):

	1910	1911	*
Horses	3,197,720	3,236,110	+ 38,390
Mules	192,740	194,040	+ 1,300
Donkeys	360,710	360,950	+ 240
Cattle	14,532,030	14,552,430	+ 20,400
Sheep	17,110,760	16,425,330	—685,430
Goats	1,417,710	1,424,180	+ 6,470
Pigs	6,900,230	6,719,570	—180,660

* Increase + or decrease —.

For notes on agricultural education in France, see AGRICULTURE EDUCATION.

MINING, ETC. The kind and number of mines in operation in 1909, the number of workers employed, the production in metric tons, and the value in francs, are shown below in first part of table; in second part, metal works in operation, workers, production, and value:

Ores	No.	Workers	Tons	Francs
Coal and Anthr.	296	187,242	37,115,891	568,726,505
Lignite		3,506	724,195	7,192,299
Peat	2803	......	78,593	960,255
Iron	99	17,228	11,889,990	53,117,346
Lead and silver	35		13,794	2,825,855
Zinc	3	7,326	50,911	4,537,896
Gold	5		96,903	5,862,347
Copper	3		458	26,384
Iron Pyrites	8		273,221	4,512,996
Manganese	25		9,378	267,774
Antimony	6		28,105	1,919,913
Arsenic	1		2,141	176,286
Tungsten	1		50	150,000
Tin	1		22	55,500
Bit. schist*	84		119,721	550,262
As. limestone†			44,826	652,217
Boghead		803	4,507	180,250
Sulphur		34	2,936	50,029
Salt (rock)	59	203	708,806	10,328,643
" (sea)		...	404,255	7,052,569
Quarries	...	131,686	49,271,000	249,995,000
Total		348,068	100,839,703	919,140,326
Metal Works	**No.**	**Workers**	**Tons**	**Francs**
Smelting works..	56	15,405	3,573,800	293,054,000
Puddling works..	110	17,148	557,700	98,078,000
Steel works......	102	59,528	2,040,300	436,879,000
Other ‡	33	4,792	97,906	74,730,000

* Bituminous schist. † Asphaltic limestone. ‡ Gold, silver, lead, platinum, zinc, copper, nickel, aluminum, and antimony.

Value of silk produced (exclusive of ribbons) in 1909, 452,855,000 francs; 1910, 471,297,000 francs. Sugar works (1909-10), 244; tons of beets treated, 6,246,845; refined sugar produced, 733,901,598 kilograms. Alcohol (pure) produced in 1910, 2,391,219 hectoliters; denatured alcohol, 640,609 hectoliters. Value of the fisheries products (1908), 129,646,083 francs.

COMMERCE. Imports and exports (special trade), values in thousands of francs (A—foodstuffs, B—raw materials, C—manufactured articles, D—by parcels post):

	Imports 1910	Imports 1911	Exports 1910	Exports 1911
A	1,413,031	1,989,832	858,199	725,240
B	4,345,671	4,638,979	1,930,847	1,919,170
C	1,414,630	1,531,856	2,960,951	3,039,761
D	......	......	483,808	487,906
Total.	7,173,332	8,160,667	6,233,805	6,172,077

Countries of origin and destination, special commerce, values in thousands of francs:

	Imports 1910	Imports 1911	Exports 1910	Exports 1911
U. K......	930,344	1,020,827	1,275,138	1,246,980
Germany..	860,477	965,086	804,013	819,061
U. S.......	614,123	883,138	456,039	396,595
Belgium ..	469,749	533,001	1,003,650	1,002,503
Algeria ...	446,643	457,540	438,930	484,628
Russia	337,325	412,641	87,534	55,461
Argentina..	302,914	364,875	162,843	171,917
Spain	195,271	227,745	140,655	137,610
Italy	188,913	187,877	344,194	288,274
Brazil	167,166	155,061	68,813	78,332
Switzerland	138,912	142,153	385,518	402,949
Turkey ...	96,117	100,177	72,927	82,156
Aus.-Hun..	88,614	86,180	45,961	46,208
Other	2,336,764	2,624,366	947,590	939,403
Total ...	7,173,332	8,160,667	6,233,805	6,172,077

A glance at those articles of special commerce valued at over one hundred million francs will show their growth or diminution in importance during six consecutive years (values in millions of francs):

Imports	1905	1906	1907	1908	1909	1910
Raw wool...	446.1	533.1	580.4	459.0	634.4	658.9
Raw cotton..	311.4	358.9	440.7	389.9	494.7	469.8
Coal	217.8	361.2	429.1	391.2	442.1	400.7
Oil seeds....	192.6	231.2	272.8	253.7	292.1	379.7
Silk	267.2	345.2	441.5	279.9	331.5	346.3
Rubber (raw)	98.3	120.3	109.4	115.2	208.8	320.1
Cereals	151.7	221.3	225.6	97.0	152.9	301.3
Wines	108.8	102.5	104.4	116.5	123.8	296.5
Machinery ..	130.1	148.4	224.2	221.8	216.2	247.5
Skins, etc...	179.7	199.6	153.1	153.3	199.3	206.9
Timber	166.9	172.6	183.5	187.7	183.2	165.9
Copper	108.1	164.7	155.3	138.9	122.6	130.6
Coffee	94.6	101.8	103.6	104.3	112.3	126.4
Minerals	105.2	99.4	99.3	87.9	86.2	107.4
Flax	80.4	87.4	82.9	79.6	81.2	82.4
Exports	**1905**	**1906**	**1907**	**1908**	**1909**	**1910**
Wools	260.2	273.0	266.2	228.6	337.7	341.4
Silk	275.0	307.8	355.6	270.2	316.9	332.8
Cottons	254.5	306.7	352.2	281.1	332.0	328.2
Wines	247.6	196.9	228.1	196.8	214.4	243.3
Rubber	53.7	68.0	57.8	68.0	130.6	236.5
Woolens	193.4	224.0	245.5	196.1	212.1	212.5
Silks	148.3	172.3	197.3	133.9	164.0	183.6
Clothing	145.2	140.9	150.4	123.8	145.5	173.1
A. de P.*...	175.2	184.0	218.2	183.9	178.3	172.7
Raw cotton..	46.5	54.1	67.5	66.7	95.6	172.7
Auto's	100.5	137.9	144.4	127.3	146.6	161.9
Chemicals ..	114.7	120.3	132.5	122.0	147.8	159.2
Skins (raw).	140.3	153.1	122.3	115.7	141.5	133.7
" (worked).	133.2	122.2	106.3	102.2	102.2	111.9
Paper	74.5	77.6	83.2	84.8	93.4	110.8
Metals	111.1	114.8	118.8	110.0	99.1	102.4
Machinery ...	71.3	82.5	94.0	92.5	90.7	99.3

* Articles de Paris, viz.—fancy stationery, toys, brushes, lorgnettes, fans, buttons, parasols, etc., made in Paris.

SHIPPING. The number of ships, French and foreign, with their aggregate tonnage, entered and cleared, exclusive of coasting, during the years 1910 and 1911, are given herewith:

	1910		1911.	
	No.	Tons	No.	Tons
Entered:				
French	7,529	6,753,520	7,690	7,138,790
Foreign	20,167	21,928,942	20,493	22,728,220
Total	27,696	28,682,462	28,183	29,867,010
Cleared:				
French	7,020	6,253,688	6,946	6,623,511
Foreign	13,894	15,666,870	13,860	15,931,835
Total	20,914	21,920,558	20,806	22,555,346

COMMUNICATIONS. Railways in operation December 31, 1911, 40,632 kilometers of main and 9617 kms. of local line. An important cut-off to shorten the through distance from Paris to Milan was under construction during the year on the line between Frasne and Villorbe, connecting France and Switzerland. This new line, 15½ miles in length, included five tunnels, one of which was 3¾ miles in length. An important project was the conversion of the section of the Midi line between Toulouse and Bayonne with its numerous branches, aggregating some 310 miles, for operation by electricity provided by hydro-electric power plants in the Pyrenees Mountains. Two hundred and seven miles of the lines around Limoges in the department of Haute Vienne were also being electrified, and a beginning was made of the electrification of the suburban lines of the Western State Railway to Auteuil, Versailles, St. Germain, and Argenteuil. The section of the Paris Nord-Sud line from Porte Clichy to La Fourche was opened in January, 1912. Telegraph lines, 182,794 kms.; wires, 690,636. Urban telephone lines, 43,286 kms.; wires, 858,132; interurban lines, 103,080; wires, 480,650. Post offices (1910), 14,016.

Merchant marine January 1, 1911, 17,621 vessels, of 1,451,648 tons (1726 steamers, of 815,567.)

FINANCE. The monetary unit is the franc, worth 19.3 cents. The 1912 budget as voted estimated the revenue for the year at 4,495,849,566 francs (including revenue returnable from Algeria, 2,480,900 francs); the expenditure at 4,497,963,139 francs. Sources of revenue: 3,136,996,425 from taxes; 953,225,785 from monopolies and state industrial enterprises; 68,218,850 from state domains; 69,441,485 from divers sources (indemnities, repayments, annuities, salés, prison labor, etc.); 153,000,000 from special sources; 114,967,021 *recettes d'ordre* (from colonial railways, fines, fees, etc.); 2,480,000 from Algeria. Expenditure: 1,286,084,002 for the public debt, 19,972,948 for public services, 2,539,705,705 for the ministries, 605,873,584 for costs of administration and collection of taxes, 46,326,900 for reimbursement, restitution, etc. The total public debt stood, January 1, 1911, at 31,162,001,387 francs, and the floating debt at 1,305,898,400.

ARMY. During 1912 there were but few changes in the general organization of the French army, but it was realized that the new German army act was likely to result in a general increase in numbers. By virtue of decrees of January, 1912, the minister of war was assisted by the secretary-general, who, under the minister's authority, was given the supreme direction of the administration of the army, while a council of directors, which includes the secretary-general and the chief of the army general staff, was established. The chief of the general staff (General Joffre) was designated as the officer in command of the principal groups of armies in case of war. The French army is recruited by compulsory service, and men serve two years in the active army, eleven years in the reserve, six years in the territorial army and six years in its reserve. Much interest attached to the annual contingent of recruits due to the declining birth-rate. The contingent of men, which averaged 215,000 in 1896-1905, amounted to 214,449 in 1911. This was for the combatant contingent of the home army and was 15,080 less than in 1910. The French army was expected to furnish on a war footing a first line effective strength of 2,500,000, and with the two classes of the active army and eleven classes of the reserve 2,000,000 more could be placed in the field. On the day of mobilization it was stated an efficient force of nearly 1,400,000 could be assembled, including the standing army and 800,000 men recently discharged and available. The army estimates for 1912 amounted to 940,500,000 francs, the increase being due in large part to an increase of pay in the recent reorganization of the artillery.

The active army continued its organization with twenty army corps exclusive of the garrisons at Paris and Tunis, and headquarters were located at Lille, Amiens, Rouen, Le Mans, Orléans, Chalons-sur-Marne, Besançon, Bourges, Tours, Rennes, Nantes, Limoges, Clermont-Ferrand, Lyons, Marseilles, Montpelier, Toulouse,

Bordeaux, Algiers, and Nancy. The total establishments given in the estimates of 1912 were as follows: Active army, 28,743 officers and 555,900 men; gendarmerie and Republic Guards, 667 officers and 24,265 men; Colonial troops in France, 1047 officers and 25,844 men, making a total of 31,367 officers and 606,009 men. In the active army there were in Algeria and Tunis in 1912, 21,868 officers and 71,147 men. This active army was composed of about 590 battalions of infantry, 30 battalions of chasseurs, 12 foreign, 24 zouaves, 24 Algerian tirailleurs, 1 Saharan tirailleurs, and 5 African light infantry, or an aggregate of about 685 battalions. A law was passed in 1912 increasing the cavalry so that there were to be 32 regiments of dragoons, 23 of chasseurs, 14 of hussars, 12 of cuirassiers, 4 of chasseurs d'Afrique, and 6 of spahis, also 2 squadrons for the Sahara, and squadrons in Senegal, Indo-China, and other colonies. The artillery, whose reorganization and rearmament were still in progress, was to comprise 42 coast and 47 fortress batteries, 619 field batteries, 21 Rimailho 6-inch field howitzer batteries, 14 mountain batteries, and 16 horse batteries, in addition to which there were outside of France and Corsica 8 coast, 15 field, and 4 mountain batteries. There were 26 battalions of engineers and 3 railway companies, with other technical corps including aeronautic troops and a military train of 20 squadrons. The French army reserve includes 245 three-battalion regiments of infantry (with a skeleton formation of officers and men) and 30 battalions of chasseurs, 40 regiments of cavalry, 41 squadrons, and 216 batteries. In the territorial army there were 145 infantry regiments, 7 battalions of chasseurs, 42 squadrons, about 100 batteries, 20 battalions of engineers, men of the customs and forest service, zouaves in Algeria, and other troops.

The scheme of service is two years in the active army, eleven years in the reserve, six years in the territorial army, and six years in its reserve. The reservists and territorial troops are called out for periodical training. The strength of the first line of the French army on a war basis was estimated at 2,500,000, with the two classes of the active army and eleven classes of the reserve. Then would come a second line of 2,000,000 more which could be placed in the field. It was estimated that at a time of mobilization a force of 1,400,000 troops could be assembled on an effective basis. See Aeronautics.

Navy. On December 1, 1912, the number and displacement of warships, built and building, of 1500 or more tons, and of torpedo craft of more than 50 tons, were as follows: 7 battleships (dreadnought type), having a main battery of all big guns (11 inches or over in calibre), of 161,644 aggregate tons—all building; 20 battleships (predreadnought type), with main batteries of more than one calibre, of 286,005 tons—built; 2 coast-defense vessels (smaller battleships and monitors), of 15,400 tons—built; 10 cruisers (designed for speed at some expense of armament and armor protection), of 49,978—built; 75 torpedo-boat destroyers, of 29,816 tons—built, and 9, of 6860 tons—building; 157 torpedo boats, of 15,370 tons—built; 76 submarines, of 27,803 tons—built, and 13, of 7456—bulding. Total vessels built, 361, of 630,769 tons; building, 29, of 175,960 tons—in all, 390 vessels, of 806,729 tons. Excluded from the foregoing are ships over twenty years old, unless reconstructed and rearmed within five years; torpedo craft over fifteen years old; transports, colliers, repair ships, torpedo depot ships, or other auxiliaries. Personnel, 60,188 officers and men. See Naval Progress.

A new bill passed February 13, 1912, by the Chamber of Deputies, provides for a home fleet to consist of 28 battleships divided into 4 squadrons each and 4 vessels in reserve; in addition each squadron to include 2 second cruisers and 12 destroyers, with 2 cruisers and 4 destroyers in reserve. The fleet for foreign service is to contain ten principal vessels, with the necessary auxiliaries. There are to be 94 vessels, together with mine-layers and mine-raisers, in the submarine flotilla. To complete this programme by the time fixed (January 1, 1919), 16 new battleships are to be constructed at the rate of two a year (1910-1917). The *Courbet* and the *Jean Bart* (launched 1911, to be completed 1913), the *France* and the *Paris* (launched 1912, to be completed 1914) have 23,100 tons displacement and twelve 12-inch guns. The *Bretagne*, the *Provence*, and the *Lorraine* were laid down in 1912 and are to be completed 1915—two belonging to the regular programme and the third being designed to replace the lost *Liberté*, destroyed by explosion in 1911. The submersible *Vendémiaire* was sunk in a collision June 8, 1912, and her crew lost.

Government. Under the present constitution the president is the executive, assisted by a cabinet responsible to the Chamber. The legislative power is vested in a parliament or assembly, composed of a senate and a chamber of deputies. President in 1912, Armand Fallières (elected January 17, 1906). The cabinet, constituted January 12, 1912, was as follows: Raymond Poincaré, premier and minister for foreign affairs; A. Briand, justice; L. L. Klotz, finance; M. Steeg, interior; M. Millerand, war; M. Delcassé, marine; M. Guist'hau, instruction, etc.; J. Dupuy, public works, etc.; F. David, commerce and industry; M. Pams, agriculture; M. Lebrun, colonies; L. Bourgeois, labor, etc.

History

Attacks on the Caillaux Ministry. Parliament was deeply absorbed during the closing weeks of 1911 and the early part of 1912 in a discussion of the history of the Franco-German negotiations which had resulted in a French protectorate over Morocco at the expense of a large part of the French Congo. The bargain was condemned by French public men as requiring too heavy a compensation from France. From the report of the investigation made by the French Senate, it appeared that M. Cambon in negotiating with the German foreign minister received instructions that had not come to the knowledge of the French foreign minister or formed the subject of deliberation at a ministerial council. This created a very painful impression on the public mind. There were other signs of weakness in the ministerial majority. It was criticised for its inertia, and many believed that unless it dealt vigorously with important measures like electoral reform, national insurance, and the income tax it would lose the little prestige that remained to it. But the chief point against it was this belief that the prime minister, by underhand dealings with German officials during the Moroccan negotiations, had prejudiced French official diplomacy. Sen-

ARMAND FALLIÈRES
Retiring President of the French Republic, 1912

RAYMOND POINCARÉ
Premier, 1912

FRANCE

sational charges to this effect were made by the French press, which alleged that M. Caillaux, while minister of finance, interfered in the French foreign policy by negotiating himself with Germany concerning the Congo-Kamerun railway scheme, independently of the ministry and of the French embassy at Berlin. It was further charged that he, as prime minister, had secretly resumed these negotiations after the incident of Agadir, that he received a representative from Germany without informing the French foreign minister, and that he even agreed in secret to an understanding with Germany on principles that would lead to acquiescence in the loss of Alsace-Lorraine and to the dissolution of the triple accord. The senate committee, though its inquires did not substantiate these charges in detail, brought out the fact that M. de Selves had not been informed of all the negotiations between Paris and Berlin. When asked the direct question M. de Selves declared that he could not answer because he stood between two duties, the duty of telling the whole truth and the duty of maintaining the solidarity of the ministry. It therefore appeared that while M. de Selves, as foreign minister, and M. Jules Cambon, as ambassador to Berlin, were negotiating with Germany, secret negotiations were at the same time being conducted by the prime minister, M. Caillaux, and others in the government. On January 10, M. Caillaux announced that he would not continue in power, attributing this decision to his difficulty in finding a new minister of marine The fall of the cabinet, however, was due to dissensions of long standing and arising chiefly from the cause above mentioned.

THE NEW MINISTRY. The formation of the new cabinet was enstrusted to M. Raymond Poincaré. It was completed on January 13, and announced the next morning as follows: M. Poincairé, president of the council (prime minister) and minister for foreign affairs; M. Briand, minister of justice and vice-president of the council; M. Steeg, minister of the interior; M. Millerand, minister of war; M. Klotz, minister of finance; M. Delcassé, minister of marine; M. Guist'hau, minister of public instruction; M. Lebrun, minister for the colonies; M. Pams, minister of agriculture; M. Fernand David, minister of commerce; M. Jean Dupuy, minister of public works; M. Bourgeois, minister of labor. The high intellectual standing and the political experience of the ministers were the subject of much remark. Two of them, M. Léon Bourgeois and M. Briand, had been prime ministers. M. Millerand had made a distinguished record as member of the Waldeck-Rousseau ministry, and M. Delcassé had been for many years the centre of European attention as foreign minister. M. Poincaré was born in 1860 and entered politics in 1887 as a member of the Chamber of Deputies. He served in the first Dupuy cabinet as minister of public instruction, and in the succeeding Dupuy cabinets as finance minister. In the third Ribot ministry he served again as minister of instruction and in the Sarrien cabinet again as minister of finance. He had previously twice declined the office of minister of foreign affairs, which portfolio he now assumed in addition to the premiership. The ministerial declaration of policy was read on January 16. It laid great emphasis on the strong national feelings and aspirations of the government, whose first task was to be the carrying through of the treaty with Germany. It declared that this treaty would soon be completed and that without doubt an understanding would be reached with Spain. It announced the government's intention to remain faithful to the alliances and friendships of France, and to cultivate steadily cordial relations with other nations. Progress it declared was essentially "order in motion." The condition precedent of all republican democracy was self-discipline. It next proceeded to the important question of electoral reform, declaring that the last general election had shown the need of far-reaching changes in the electoral system. The government promised to carry a measure of reform that should reflect the aims of the Republican majority and accord with the work done by the parliamentary commission on universal suffrage. The measure would secure a more exact representation for political parties and give those who are elected "the freedom that is required for the subordination of local interests in all cases to the national interests." This plain reference to the proportional representation and the restoration of the *scrutin de liste* was received with enthusiasm by the Chamber as a whole. The government received nearly a unanimous vote of confidence, namely, 440 against 6.

The Senate committe in its report on the Franco-German treaty declared that no other course than the ratification of the treaty was compatible with the interests of France, and referred to the great prestige which had been gained as a result of the negotiations. It further said that recognition of the French protectorate in Morocco would come as the fruition of the government's policy during a period of ten years. The committee's report was adopted by a large majority on January 24. With it was passed a resolution deploring secret treaties and the addition of secret clauses to treaties altering their sense. On February 27 the Chamber by a vote of 541 to 76 finally adopted the budget in the form in which it had left the Senate. On March 30 it passed a bill extending the provisions of the eight-hour law of 1905 to all classes of miners and slate quarrymen.

The senatorial elections of January 7 made little change in the relative strength of the respective groups. The distribution of seats was as follows: Radicals and Radical Socialists, 48; Progressists, 23; Democrats, 20; Conservatives, 5; Socialists, 4.

ELECTORAL REFORM. The Electoral Reform measure offered by the government substituted for the scheme proposed by the universal suffrage committee a plan based on the *scrutin de liste* applying to considerable areas and providing for minority representation. It was the main concern of the parliament for several months. After much discussion and criticism it passed the Chamber on July 12 by a vote of 339 to 217. In effect it was a compromise between proportional representation and the present majority system. Its chief principles were the *scrutin de liste* with minority representation, the electoral quotient in enlarged electoral areas, and the assignment of any remaining seats to the *liste* that contained the largest number of votes. By electoral quotient was meant the number of voters in a department divided by the number of deputies assigned to it. Each *liste*, i. e., party ticket, was to have the number of seats determined by dividing the total vote for the *liste* by the electoral quotient. Vacancies were to be filled by candidates on the same *liste* who had received the largest number of votes in the preceding election. It was to take as the electoral area the *Département*, assigning one seat for every 20,000 French inhabitants, or for fractions over 20,000. The bill thus provided that the number of deputies should rest on the basis of population and not as the committee proposed, on the number of registered electors. It enlarged the electoral basis by grouping departments. The Republican party was divided on the subject, some 200 Radicals opposing the government measure, and looking for a chance to overthrow the ministry by a Socialist alliance. A vigorous campaign was carried on against it after the adjournment, MM. Clemenceau and Combes being the chief opponents. In the Senate the measure was submitted to a committee which in November reported in favor of the *scrutin de liste*, but against the representation of minorities.

MUNICIPAL ELECTIONS. Municipal elections in Paris and the provinces early in May pointed to the growing strength of the Collectivist Socialists. The Moderates and the opoposition generally held their own, while the Radicals suffered losses.

THE FRANCO-GERMAN TREATY. The debate on the Franco-German treaty in the Senate began on February 5, on the question whether the Senate committee appointed to investigate the treaty should have power to inquire into the secret negotiations and into any engagements that were unknown to parliament, and to fix the responsibilities which might have been incurred by such negotiations and engagements. In the course of the discussion M. Caillaux was charged with offering certain guarantees as the foundation of a Franco-German *entente*. These guarantees were that France would not oppose henceforth the project of the Bagdad railway; that the shares of that railway company as well as German government stock were to be admitted to quotation on the Bourse; that Germany was to have her turn at the presidency of the Ottoman debt, which was now held alternately by France and England; that nearly all the French Congo was to be ceded to Germany, that a French colony on the Pacific was to be ceded, and that Germany and France were to conclude an agreement concerning European affairs which entailed most serious consequences, among others, the renunciation by France of any claim to a revision of the treaty of Frankfort of 1871. One of the senators declared that he would not vote for a treaty which filled good Frenchmen with vexation and filled Germans with joy. France contended that the treaty should be passed as a necessity of French foreign policy and protested against the secret negotiations and engagements. As to the Gession of the French Congo, it was characterized as the first instance of departure by France from her policy of not ceding territory without consulting by plebiscite the persons immediately concerned.

Some of the arguments of prominent French statesmen on the treaty negotiations of 1911 were as follows: M. Pichon held that the French government should not have consented to negotiate so long as the German gunboat *Panther* was at Agadir. It should have trusted to the patriotism of the country which was ready to support it in a firm attitude. He criticised the government also for not associating Great Britain and Spain in the negotiations and he quoted from the speeches of Sir Edward Grey and Mr. Lloyd-George to prove the firm support that Great Britain was ready to give to France in this emergency. M. Ribot declared that France had a right to establish order in Morocco and that the government should not have acted as if Germany were the only interested power. He regarded the Agadir incident as a sad blunder of German diplomacy from which France ought to have profited. He was loudly applauded when he declared that if he had been minister of foreign affairs at that time he would not have allowed the French ambassador, M. Jules Cambon, to have returned to Berlin while the German gunboat remained at Agadir. M. Clemenceau said he would not vote for a treaty that had been extorted under the guns of German warships and without the participation of the friends of France in the negotiations. He said that to reject the treaty would, to be sure, be a leap in the dark, but that a leap into the unknown was better than a leap into what they knew too well. The treaty which had been adopted on December 20 by the Chamber, was finally adopted by the Senate on February 10 by a vote of 212 to 42.

TREATY WITH MOROCCO. A French commission was sent to Fez to secure from the sultan a treaty recognizing the French protectorate, and the treaty was signed on March 30. It conformed in essential features to the treaty of Bardo with Tunis. It made a special exception of Tangier, and the Spanish sphere whose future administration was to be determined and whose limits were to be fixed later. The sultan was reluctant to exclude this sphere, but M. Regnault, the French commissioner, had received precise instructions to reserve Tangier and the future Spanish sphere from the operation of the treaty.

The text of the treaty was published early in April. It provided that the sultan should not for the future contract, directly or indirectly, any public or private loan or grant any concession without the authorization of the French government. It recognized the right of the French government to occupy any part of Moroccan territory where such occupation was necessary for the maintenance of order or the security of commerce, the sole condition being that the French government should first notify the Maghzen. The French resident-general was to be the sole intermediary between the sultan and the representatives of foreign powers, and French diplomatic and consular agents were charged with the interests of the natives as against foreigners. The treaty provided for the reorganization of the finances and for the support of the sultan in maintaining his authority. It proclaimed freedom of religion.

TREATY WITH SPAIN. A Franco-Spanish commission for the settlement of the Moroccan question was appointed in the latter part of February. The negotiations turned on the rectification of the frontiers, the sultan's sovereignty over the Spanish zone, the collection of customs, the control of the Spanish section of the proposed Fez to Tangier railway, and the question of compensation to France out of Spanish territory for her concessions to Germany. France claimed such compensation on the ground that by ceding territory in the Congo to Germany she had virtually raised the German "mortgage" on Morocco, which was prejudicial to the interests of Spain as well as of France. Spain admitted the principle, and the question turned on the nature and extent of the compensation. After long discussions, in which the friendly offices of Great Britain were sought at intervals, the treaty was prepared at the end of October. Spain ceded the greater part of her southern zone and gained in exchange a large extension of her northern zone to include Mount Ghani, commanding Alcazar. She engaged, however, not to fortify this position. Of the southern zone she retained only the strip of coast on which the town of Ifni was situated. Spain was to retain the collection of customs in her zone, but was to pay an annual sum proportionate thereto toward the liquidation of the Moroccan debt. Other provisions were the internationalization of the Tangier-Fez railway and the choice of the sultan's representative or khalifa from a list submitted by Spain, and the appointment of a Spanish resident general as his coadjutor.

NAVAL POLICY. The new naval programme which had been formed in 1911 was submitted to the Chamber on February 12, and was carried by a vote of 452 to 53. It provided for the construction of 28 battleships by 1920. The general naval policy of France was set forth at that time by M. Delcassé, minister of marine, as aiming at the creation of a strong enough navy to proceed anywhere and to constitute a superior force in those waters in which France had vital interests. At present and for a long time to come the Mediterranean waters are and will remain the most important sea for French naval progress. He said that France should proceed on this principle and not on the principle of any particular number of ships merely because some other power was laying down a similar number.

NAVAL CONCENTRATION. In June the government decided to transfer the Atlantic squadron to the Mediterranean, and on September 10 that decision was definitely announced. M. Delcassé, the minister of marine, ordered the six vessels which constituted the squadron at Brest to sail to Toulon on October 15 and join the Mediterranean fleet. The latter would then comprise 18 battleships and six large armored cruisers. This was explained in the French press as due to the belief that a single powerful fleet was a better protection than divided forces, and that the Brest squadron of six old vessels would be of little use in the Atlantic, but might in the event of war be valuable in the Mediterranean. It was urged that in no sense was it an aggressive movement, but a mere return to the situation of 1909. Nevertheless it was associated in the public mind with the recent increase of the Italian and Austro-Hungarian navies, and in Austria there was bitter comment on it as a proof of an offensive and defensive alliance between France and Great Britain.

THE MOTOR-CAR BANDITS. A succession of atrocious crimes, beginning toward the end of November, 1911, became the subject of excited discussion not only in France, but all over the world, owing to the peculiar methods and the extraordinary boldness of the criminals. On December 21, 1911, a bank messenger was shot and robbed in the Rue Ordener. On February 27, three men in a motor car killed a policeman near the Saint Lazare railway station, while he was trying to stop them, and the motor car was subsequently found half destroyed by fire. On the following night the house of a lawyer at Pontoise was entered by a man who rode up to it in a motor car. During March several attempts were made to break into garages and steal machines. These outrages were followed by a far more serious one on the morning of March 25, when four men held up a motor car near Montgeron, on the road from Paris to Fontainebleau, and killed one of the chauffeurs and wounded the other. The robbers immediately jumped into the car and disappeared. Two hours later they drew up before the bank at Chantilly, on the other side of Paris, nearly 40 miles away from the scene of the first murder. Meanwhile two more men had joined them. Four of the robbers entered the bank and shot and killed the cashier and a clerk and wounded another employee. They seized all the cash, amounting to some 40,000 francs, as well as some securities, leaped into the car, and rode at full speed toward Paris, firing at everyone who tried to stop them or who looked at them too closely. A little more than an hour later, the car having sustained some injury, it was abandoned near Asnières, and the bandits disappeared without leaving any trace. The failure of the police to capture the perpetrators of this series of robberies and murders caused much consternation, and led to a summons of the ministers in council for a discussion of measures to promote the efficiency of the police and detective service.

The band of criminals who had terrorized Paris for a period of six months was at last rounded up on April 28 at a suburb, Choisy-le-Roi, eight or nine miles to the south of the city, where Bonnot, the ringleader of the band, with one of his accomplices, was traced to a motor-car garage. A regular siege was set up by the police and a company of troops, and a fusillade on both sides lasted for four hours, when the building was finally blown up with dynamite. Bonnot was captured alive, but so severely wounded that he died on reaching the hospital. His confederate, Dubois, was found dead in the building. This event followed the murder of the assistant-chief detective, named Jouin, on April 24, by Bonnot, who escaped, and the police suspected that he and some of his confederates were making one of the suburbs their headquarters. Two police officers were wounded in the attack on the garage. Bonnot was born in 1876 of a respectable family, but in youth fell under anarchist influences and was involved subsequently in many strikes. He began a series of robberies in 1909 and finally organized a band of criminals whose movements he directed with uncommon skill and energy. His confederate, Dubois, was a veteran of the French Foreign Legion, who had subsequently taken up the trade of a motor car mechanic.

Another sensational incident occurred on May 14, when the hiding place of two other members of the band of criminals, Garnier and Vallet, at Nogent-sur-Marne was stormed by soldiers and police under the chief of police, M. Guichard. The attack was begun on the night of May 14 and lasted until early morning, when, as in the previous instance, the house was shattered by an explosive and the officers of law rushed in. Both criminals were killed.

MISCELLANEOUS. To the long list of naval disasters in recent years was added another serious accident on June 8, when a submarine was run down by a battleship near Cherbourg, causing the loss of the crew of 23 men and two officers. In consequence of anti-militarist declarations at the annual congress of the Teachers' Union in August the government ordered their dissolution by September 10, and on that date most of them complied under protest. A few deferred their action on the ground that it was impossible to call meetings until after the holidays, and one of them, the Union of the Seine, decided to defy the government's order. The government began proceedings against it, but at the same time announced certain reforms to secure teachers against arbitrary treatment and to improve their salaries.

For notes on other subjects relating to France, see AGRICULTURE; FINANCIAL REVIEW; LABOR LEGISLATION; AERONAUTICS; SOCIALISM, etc.

FRANCO-GERMAN TREATY. See FRANCE, *History*.

FRATERNAL INSURANCE. See INSURANCE.

FRATERNITIES IN HIGH SCHOOLS. See EDUCATION.

FREDERICK VIII. King of Denmark, died May 15, 1912. He was born at Copenhagen in 1843, the eldest son of Christian IX. and of Princess Louise of Hesse-Cassel. He received his education at an ordinary grammar school. On the death of King Frederick VII. in 1863 and the accession of King Christian IX. difficulties with Austria and Prussia came to a head, and Prince Frederick, as he then was, took part in the war of 1864, which cost Denmark the duchies of Schleswig-Holstein and Lauenburg and which produced permanent ill-feeling against Germany. Upon the death of Queen Louise in 1898, however, Prince Frederick was able to take steps toward a better understanding with Germany. On the death of King Christian in January, 1906, Prince Frederick succeeded him as Frederick VIII. Shortly after his accession he made visits to England and Iceland. In the latter country he aroused great enthusiasm by appointing a mixed commission to consider the vexed question of home rule. The effort to bring this about, however, did not succeed. At the time of his accession Frederick VIII. was not particularly popular, but his great political energy, his genial eloquence and the simplicity of his life won for him before he died the hearty respect and confidence of his subjects. He was one of the most democratic of European rulers and was frequently to be seen upon the streets of Copenhagen unattended. In 1910 he suffered a severe attack of illness. This returned in 1912 and he went to Nice for the benefit of his health. Returning apparently recovered, he stopped in Hamburg. In the evening he went for a stroll about the streets and was found dead by passers-by. His body was for some time unidentified, as there were no marks of royalty upon his clothing. Frederick VIII. was related to many important royal families of Europe. He was the brother of Queen Alexandra and of the King of Greece; his wife is a sister of the German Emperor and of the Empress Marie of Russia; he was a brother-in-law of the Duke of Cumberland, son of the last King Henry, and was father of King Haakon of Norway, who married Princess Maud of Wales; he was father-in-law of Prince Charles of Sweden, a brother of the present king of that country, and he was a son-in-law of King Charles XV. of Sweden. His death threw into mourning nearly all the principal non-Catholic reigning houses in Europe.

FREE BAPTISTS. See BAPTISTS, FREE.

FREER, PAUL CASPAR. An American chemist and public official, died April 18, 1912. He was born in Chicago in 1862 and took his degree in medicine from the Rush Medical College in 1882. He afterwards studied at the University of Munich, receiving the degree of Ph. D. in 1887. In the same year he became assistant in Owens College, Manchester, and in a few months was appointed assistant and instructor in Tufts College. Here he remained until 1889, when he was appointed professor of general chemistry at the University of Michigan. He occupied this chair until 1903. From 1901 to 1905 he was superintendent of the government laboratories at Manila, P. I. He was director of the Bureau of Science at Manila from 1905 to the time of his death, at the same time acting as dean of the Philippine Islands Medical School. He was editor of the Philippine *Journal of Science* and was the author of *A General Inorganic Descriptive Chemistry* (1895), and *The Elements of Chemistry* (1896), and over fifty pamphlets on chemical subjects published in the United States and Germany.

FRENCH EQUATORIAL AFRICA (formerly FRENCH CONGO). A French possession in equatorial Africa, on the west coast, composed of the Gabun Colony (capital, Libreville), the Middle Congo Colony (Brazzaville), and the Ubangi-Shari-Chad Colony (Fort-de-Possel). From the old area of 669,280 square miles, must be deducted, roughly, 170,270 square miles ceded under the convention of November 14, 1911, to Germany by France; and to it must be added about 6450 square miles ceded to France by Germany from the Kamerun country. The area ceded to Germany carries a population of about one million out of the original ten million (the estimated population in 1906). The products and exports are rubber, ivory, timber, palm kernels and oil, cacao, etc. Gold, copper, and iron are mined. Imports (1910), 13,190,677 francs; exports, 24,630,872 (11,119,319 and 17,453,933 in 1909). Revenue and expenditure balanced (1909) at 6,137,000 francs. A commissioner-general (M. Merlin in 1912) residing at Brazzaville is administrator-in-chief. KANEM and WADAI are French dependencies.

FRENCH ESTABLISHMENTS IN OCEANIA. A southern Pacific French colony, consisting of widely scattered groups and single islands. Area (estimated), 3065 square kilometers; population, 30,563. Capital, Papeete (3617 inhabitants), on Tahiti. Imports and exports (1910), 5,659,367 and 6,031,289 francs, respectively. Adrien Bonhoure was governor in 1912.

FRENCH GUIANA (CAYENNE). A colony (French) and penal settlement on the northern coast of South America. It covers 88,240 square kilometers (34,069 square miles) and had a population in 1911 of 49,000. Cayenne, the chief town and only seaport, had (1906) 12,426 inhabitants. Gold-mining (placer) is the chief occupation of the people. Imports and exports in 1910 were valued at 12,233,000 and 11,567,000 francs respectively. Governor (1912), F. E. Levecque.

FRENCH GUINEA. A French West

African colony. Capital, Konakry, with (1909) 6583 inhabitants; Kankan, the chief commercial centre, has 11,666; Boké, 2097; Kindia, 2083; Dubreka, 1408. The railway from Konakry to Kouroussa (588 kilometers) was completed and in operation January 1, 1911. Transport from and into the interior is by caravan, the best porters being Soussous and Malinkés. The route from Konakry to the Niger, known as the Leprince route, is via Kindia, Timbo, and Kouroussa. Rubber is the principal export, and is gathered over all the colony; but the principal sources are the Foutah-Djallon, the Faranah region, and other circles of Upper Guinea. Rice is grown, grazing is widely practiced. The mineral resources are believed to be considerable. Lieutenant-governor in 1912, C. Guy. See French West Africa.

FRENCH INDIA. Five French dependencies in India, covering 513 square kilometers, with 277,723 inhabitants in 1906 and 282,472 in 1911. Density per sq. km. (1906), 541.4. The towns are Pondichéry (the capital), Karikal, Mahé, Chandernagar, and Yanaon. The imports and exports (1910) were valued at 8,351,443 and 37,466,013 francs, respectively. Chief exports, oil seeds, raw cotton, and pulse. Railway from Pondichéry to Villäpuram and Peralam to Karikal, 30 kilometers. P. L. A. Duprat was governor in 1912.

FRENCH INDO-CHINA. A dependency of France in southeastern Asia, made up of five states and a strip of territory leased from China, as follows:

	Sq. Kilometers	Pop 1906	D.†
Annan	159,890	5,513,681	34 5
Cambodia	175,450	1,193,534	6.8
Cochin-China	56,965	2,870,514	50.4
Tongking	119,750	5,896,510	49.3
Laos	290,000	663,727	2.3
Kwangchow-Wan*	1,000	177,097	177.0
Total	803,055	16,315,063	20.3

*Leased territory. †Density per square kilometer.

Total population in 1911, 16,090,220. Hanoi (in Tongking) is the capital, with (1911) 113,676 inhabitants; Cholon had 191,655, Bin-Dinh 75,000, Saïgon 64,845, Pnom-Penh 54,621, Hué 50,000, Vien-tiane 20,000, Haïphong 27,000.

The railway from Saïgon to Mytho (the oldest railway in the country) is being extended to Cantho (60 miles). Other lines are the Haïphong-Laoki-Yünanfu (291 miles), the line from Hanoi to the Chinese frontier (308), Tourane-Hué-Quang-tri and Tourane-Faïfu (130), Saïgon-Khat-Hoa-Langbian (83). The Yünnan Railway was completed in 1910.

Trade statistics are returned for the colony as a whole, and are given below in francs:

	1909	1910	1911
Imports	249,753,677	238,686,288	244,143,000
Exports	273,034,618	290,546,912	250,147,000

The general budget balanced for 1912 at 38,317,000 francs; the budget of Tongking at 8,341,017; Annam, 3,250,462; Cambodia, 4,232,416; Cochin-China, 7,321,817; Laos, 898,729; Kwangchow-Wan, 218,950; total, 59,580,391. Governor (1912), A. Sarraut.

FRENCH LITERATURE. As compared with last year, the 1912 literature impresses one as even more earnest in its pursuits. Almost no light productions; but everywhere moral and even religious preoccupations prevail; of which Bergsonianism, which is synonymous with intuitive idealism, is only one manifestation. See an illustrative article, "Le mysticisme littéraire," by Ségur, in *La Revue*, August 15, 1912.

Theatre. If no absolutely first-class play was produced, on the other hand there were an unusually great number of plays of average merit. We first mention such as betray cleverness without proclaiming anything else except power to amuse the theatre-goer: *En garde*, by Capus and Véber, the well-known theory of Capus, that excitement and effort drive happiness away; the lazy alone are happy. Gavault's *L'idée de Françoise* is optimistic; *L'habit vert*, by Flers and Caillavet, is a very successful satire on the French Academy. Tristan Bernard's *On naît esclave* is amusing; it shows how the masters are really the servants of their servants. Bernstein's *Assaut* is a clever melodrama in the manner of that author, and was played admirably by Guitry: jealousy against a self-made man, and finally the hero comes out vindicated. Among the plays which claim to be more philosophical are: The sensational *La Flambée*, by Kistemaekers (now played in this country under the title *The Spy*): an officer of the army is bankrupt through speculation; he is then offered solvency if he will betray army secrets to the enemy; he kills the spy on the spot and all his friends come to the rescue to free him from the consequences of the murder—it is "la flambée patriotique." Bourget and Beaunier put on the stage the *Crise*, brought about by the politicians of a republic, an arraignment of modern politics. Two better plays, though not the best of the two authors, are Hervieu's *Bagatelle* and Bataille's *Les flambeaux:* the first takes up the same theme as Musset in *On ne badine pas avec l'amour;* while in the second we see a great scholar, an admirable man, who yields one day to human passion, which has sorrowful consequences; however, he rallies at the end in a most pathetic and beautiful death. The following are more original in their conception: Brieux's *La foi*, in which a man who loses his faith then sees the awful social consequences of a population without religion, p etends to believe, then again is disgusted,r and in dying tells what he conceives to be the truth— was not much liked. L. Bénièro (the author of *Papillon dit lyonnais*) has another interesting idea; he shows in *Crédulité* the curious effects, sometimes sad, sometimes comical, of superstitious beliefs taking hold of some members of a family; "Molièresque" has been an adjective used to praise the play. The Théâtre Antoine has had a long season with L. Népoty's *Les petits;* it shows the family spirit badly broken up by remarriage. *Esther, princesse d'Israël*, by Sebastien Leconte and A. Dumas, is an anti-Racinian play showing a fanatic and cruel Esther, cunning, and seeking the throne in order to gratify her thirst for the blood of the enemies of the Jews. A. DuBois writes also an anti-Racinian play, *Bérénice*—here again the heroine is not the sweet lover of the seventeenth century tragedy, but a shrewd diplomat who tries to induce Titus to give freedom of conscience to the Jews. An exotic play by P. Anthelm, *L'honneur japonais*, and a play dealing with the problem of colonization, *Les sauterelles*, by E. Fabre (the plague of poor magistrates), must also be quoted. Sarah Bernhardt appeared in a new play, *La reine Elizabeth.* The *Hélène de Sparte*, by Verhaeren, was played for the first time in Paris, and the *Belami*, from Maupassant's novel, proved no great success. An interesting reconstitution of Molière's life was made for the Maison de Molière by Donnay.

Shakespeare continues to be played carefully by the Compagnie française du théâtre de Shakespeare. During 1912 they gave *The Merry Wives of Windsor.* The Odéon gave a good *Troilus and Cressida.* Lope de Véga's *Étoile de Séville* is another sign of interest in the theatre of other nations. As to Shaw's *Mrs. Warren's Profession*, it surprised the Parisians, who wondered at such frank brutality in an English play.

Here we must mention two books: Avine, *La Renaissance du théâtre breton et l'œuvre de l'abbé Bayon;* and G. Polti, *Les Trente-six situations dramatiques.*

POETRY. Here especially (as is natural) the idealistic, at times religious, tendency is notable; not exclusively, however, our modern world allowing too much freedom to temperamental differences for any philosophical conviction to remain unrepresented. Verhaeren, after years of poetry devoted to the *forces tumultueuses* of civilization, lets a great pantheistic inspiration run through his *Blés mouvants.* Francis Jammes continues the publication of his *Géorgiques chrétiennes*, for which he was offered a prize of 3000 francs by the Academy. Religious also are the *Carmina sacra* of Louis le Cardonnel, the symbolist. Bergsonian, religious, and almost mystical is H. Franck's *La danse devant l'arche*, the ark of alliance, symbol of man's need of truth from beyond this finite universe. Franck died recently, very young. Space allows us to mention only the titles of many books, all more or less betraying the same return to conservative and classical ideals, both in thought and form: de Bouhélier, *Romance de l'homme;* Reynac, *Naissance du Verbe;* Ranette, *Clartés au crépuscle;* Lebey, *Sur une route de peupliers;* Even, *Flâneries rustiques et marines;* Thaly, *Les Chansons d'outre-mer*, and *Jardin des Tropiques* (the Antilles); Valentin, *Je dirai sur la route;* Colomb, *L'écrin*, and *Les combats;* perhaps above the others in value are Jacques Césanne's *Eternel poème* (sorrow, described in turn with sarcasm, humor, or gravity, and the only thing is to accept); and J. Gasquet's *Le paradis retrouvé* (broad and humanitarian optimism). Very little really light poetry, as A. Jaron's *Amusettes*, could be quoted. Three women deserve mention here: Cécile Périn, author of *Les pas légers* (see YEAR BOOK for 1911), broadens her horizon, and in *Variations du cœur pensif* wants "*Oh! tout aimer et tout connaître*"; Mme. de Rohan, in *Souffles d'Océan* sings the beauties of various countries, with preference the Orient; Mme. L. Berger sings of women, "Les vestales," "Les Druidesses," "Charlotte Corday," "Mme. de Lamballe"—and women's dresses. Two books, each of a single poem—a thing seldom seen nowadays—have won some distinction for their authors: Chantavoine's *La vie*, an "épopée familière"; and G. de Vesmes's *Le songe de la vie*, an episode of the Crusades. From among those who preach a destructive philosophy, two only are prominent: A. Londre's *Les poèmes effrénés* yields to wild enthusiasm for life in its violent forms; he is haughty, proud, and assured of the ultimate victory of man over inanimate matter; it is futurism without the name. R. Randau is still more violent in his *Autour des feux de la brousse*, asking a return to nature, but not the nature of the civilized peasant, but of the man in the wilderness:

> "Prends ta pensée au poing comme on tire un sabre
> Et massacre l'idée avec la pamoison."

Two groups of poets have published collective works, claiming to represent the vanguard of modern thought: "Les loups," whose ideas have been indicated in last year's account, and who publish under the patronage of Jean Richepin, author of the preface, an *Anthologie de la jeune poésie française;* there are sixteen of them; but they are by no means so aggressive as their name would lead us to believe. The other group is that of the *Anthologie de l'Effort* (*L'Effort* is a periodical), containing poems by many of the best names, such as Duhamel, Ghéon, Spire Bazalgette (new translations from Whitman). There is a strong tendency among them to use the *vers libre.* The name of Baudelaire is heard at times, and surely inspired Ivan Gilkin in *La nuit*, and F. Bénoit in *Foire aux paysages.* Banville, rather neglected of late, has been honored by an edition under the auspices of Ch. Morice. And Mistral comes before the public with *Les Olivades*, translated by himself from the Provençal original.

One of the best known of the poets of to-day died, Pierre Quillard. And Léon Dierx, for many years the "Prince des Poètes," also died. In his place Paul Fort, the author of the *Ballades françaises*, was elected "Prince."

Here belongs the mention of A. Séché's *Les accents de la satire dans la poésie contemporaine.* He treats of Rostand, Tailhade, Pochon, Bruant, Jean Rictus, etc.

FICTION. The earnestness of effort and the endeavor not to waste one's talent are impressive. Let us first take the works of the masters: Anatole France's *Les dieux ont soif* is a keen study of the peculiar hypnosis produced, during the French Revolution, on generous, idealistic minds, making them irresponsible, bloodthirsty monsters. P. Loti's *Pélerin d'Angkor* is not only a fascinating picture of Indo-China but interesting as a sort of return of Loti to the spiritualistic beliefs of Christianity. Romain Rolland has brought to an end, in the tenth volume, the story of *Jean-Christophe; La nouvelle journée* snows the hero, after having overcome his grief for the death of Olivier, born to life again by a new love, and then dying, not yet recognized by the world as a great artist, but having fulfilled his mission.

There are not as many social novels as usual: Acker, in *Deux cahiers*, compares the women of the past with those of the new generation. Boylesve's *Madeleine, jeune femme*, is a sequel to last year's book; the young woman brought up according to old-fashioned principles is now saved from temptations by the ideas imposed on her (hence one does not know whether Boylesve believes in old-fashioned education; this book seems to contradict the former one). Boulenger's *Marché aux fleurs* combats an idea really abandoned to-day, the idea of not consulting the girl's heart in marriage. Marcel Prévost continues his "series" with *Lettres à Françoise naman*, discussing modern education (very suggestive), and Pierre Mille's *Caillou et Titi* is a study of children's minds. Bauduin has an unpleasant picture of the peasants marching to ruin through alcoholism in *Les campagnes en marche*. Henry Bordeaux, in *La neige sur les pas*, discusses the "pardon" for a sinner in matrimonial affairs, in his usual orthodox fashion. *Les Fabrecé*, by Paul Margueritte, is one of the strongest books of the year; it is a sort of "Rougon-Macquardt series" in one volume: the family spirit passing from generation to generation and producing sometimes evils, but much more frequently blessings. *Les rafales*, by J.-H. Rosny, *aîné*, is the first of a series of pictures of bourgeois life: a second-rate business man attempts new methods, is ruined, and lacks the energy to start again; then his wife, one of those admirable French women, courageous and energetic when circumstances require it, steps in and saves the situation. *A l'affût*, by G. Rageot, is a powerful, rapid drama: it tells the vengeance of a forester against his employer who has brought shame on him. Here we may place a number of psychological novels that deserve mention: The most successful of the year, because the French Academy awarded it a 10,000-franc prize, is André Lafon's *L'élève Gilles*, the story of a boy, sensitive, not stupid, having no sensational adventures, told in a terse manner, and in the style of *Marie Claire*. H. Régnier's *L'Amphisbène* is in the ordinary style of the author: the heroine writes to her former husband, now a good friend of hers, the whole story of her new love. A. Bailly in *Les chaînes du passé* comes back to the self-analyzing hero of the *Disciple*, by Bourget. A. Beaunier's *L'homme qui a perdu son moi* describes the scholar who loses his own self because taken up so entirely by the object of his studies. G. Rageot's *La renommée* shows the disastrous results that fame can have in a family, on husband, wife, and child (very unreal, however). Binet-Valmer's novels have always some flavor of their own; this time the author of *Lucien* studies in *Le plaisir* the everlasting enmity between man and woman waged in love. Three authors have criticisms of what may be called the "smart set" of Paris: P. Valdagne, *Les leçons de Lisbeth Lottin*; J. L. Vauroyer, *La maîtresse de l'amie*, and H. Duvernois, *Le veau gras*. Character sketches are attempted very brilliantly: the young woman during the honeymoon by the exquisite master, A. Lichtenberger, in *La petite madame*; the tramp, by M. Audibert, in *Pilleraud*; the second-rate actor (combination of Daudet and Zola style), by A. Arnoux, in *Didier Flaboche*; the victim of hazing, by M. Yell, in *Cauët*. There are political novels: Delzens, *Le maître des foules*; O. Aubrey (pseudonym of a former president of the cabinet), *Sœur Anne*; and especially the beautiful *Frontières du cœur*, by Victor Margueritte, the author of *Une époque*: a French girl marries a German physician, they are perfectly happy, but a war breaks out, and both come to feel that something now is between them that prevents them from ever being one again; *Herr Professor Knatschke*, by Hansi (J. J. Waltz), is a bitter satire of an Alsatian against the conquerors. The problem of colonization has, as last year, inspired some of the best novels; first of all, *La fête Arabe*, by the brothers Tharaud; Colonel Baratier, *Épopées Africaines*; Jean d'Estray, *Then-si, la petite amie exotique*; R. Randau, *Le commandant et la Foulbé*; Ch. Géniaux, *Le choc des races* (in Tunis). Among exotic novels, J. Clary, *L'île du soleil couchant* (Japan). Novels that betray the revival of religious preoccupations are: L. Barry, *Au delà du bonheur*; L. Cathlin, *Le prêtre*; and R. Claude, *L'extase*. Two scientific novels of interest are J. H. Rosny, *aîné*, *La mort de la terre*, which describes humanity having reached the extremes of civilization and dying from thirst, the globe being absolutely dried out; and M. Renard, *Le Péril bleu*, an amusing fancy of the Wells order. One of the most interesting attempts at renewing the novel is that by Pierre Hamp, *Le rail*, in which men are considered absolutely independently from what we call human qualities, and are studied merely as organs of a great modern railroad company. J. Lorédan's *Un grand procès de sorcellerie au XVII. siècle* is a most fascinating historical novel. Some amusing books are: T. Bernard, *Mathilde et ses mitaines*; Fisher, *L'inconduite de Lucie*; Foley, *Perrette en escapade*; P. A. Schayé, *Journal de Cloud Barbaut*.

WOMEN'S NOVELS. This year we look in vain for the anti-man novel, except in Louise Compain's *La vie tragique de Geneviève*, a sort of *Uncle Tom's Cabin*, where the woman has taken the place of the negro. All the others seem to have grown tired, for a while at least, of wandering in lands of fancy for women; in Mme. Camille Marbo's well-received book, *Celle qui défiait l'amour*, the heroine who defies love is punished. The same attitude is found in Jehan Yvray and others. What is Mme. Jacques Morel's (Mme. Pottier) *Feuilles mortes*, which was awarded the 5000 francs prize of "La vie heureuse," except the old theme of *La Nouvelle Héloïse*? Even Mme. Daniel Lesueur, the author of the fierce *Nietzschéenne*, gives up the "fight," and in *Le tournant des jours* studies a type of the artistic woman. The other famous women writers publish novels where the woman question plays no part: Marcel Tinayre, *Madeleine au miroir*; Delarue-Madrus, *L'inexpérimentée*; Miriam Harry, *La divine chanson*, inspired by the poetry of the Oriental countries. Finally, a delightful book, rather for children, Mme. Georges Renard, *Les bêtes qui ne le sont pas*, depicting life on a farm.

SHORT STORY. Once more the "Prix Goncourt" was awarded this year to a volume of short stories; it went to A. Savignon, who lives in England, on the southern coast, whence he sends articles to English magazines and papers; his volume, *Les filles d'Ouëssant*, describes the very primitive customs of the islands. Marguerite Audoux in *Valsérine* offers sketches of boys and girls in the same manner as in *Marie Claire*. Bourget has seven stories in his *Envers du Décor*, not different from what he writes generally. R. Dervieu, in *Petites filles d'une grande nuit*, delights in discovering the rascality of people generally considered saintly. *Le village dans la Pinède*, by G. Mourey, tells stories of humble people in Provence. Léon Lafage has found the accents of a Daudet for his stories of Quercy contained in *Le bel écu de Jean Clochepin*.

We must also mention a lively discussion regarding the short story, started in the fall by the men of the younger generation; they think that this "genre" has become vulgar by the influence of the "feuilleton" and propose to restore it and to elect a "Prince de la nouvelle" as they elect a "Prince des poètes." They accuse even such men as Schwob, Rosny, Maupassant, Daudet and Marguerittes of having yielded to the temptation to write for the masses.

HISTORY OF LITERATURE AND CRITICISM. Scholars are working more diligently than ever, but on special periods or subjects. Only three general works need be mentioned, and none of them of the highest value. Strowski has a *Tableau de la Littérature en France au XIX. siècle* (short); Léo Clarétie gives the last (5) volume of his popular *History of French Literature;* while Abry, Audic, and Crouzet give a *Histoire illustrée de la Littérature Française,* interesting because they take as a criterion of importance the success of a book with the public. (In France, too, the country of intelligent criticism!) Striking is the lack of important work in the field of the Middle Ages. After Luchaire's posthumous *La société Française au temps de Philippe Auguste* (which is not strictly literature) we must come down to the Renaissance, where keen interest is shown, especially in the line of editing important texts. The first volume of Lefranc's *Rabelais* came out; an excellent edition of Calvin's *Institution chrétienne* (1541) by the same; he also completed Léopold Monod's *Le caractere de Calvin d'après ses lettres.* Further, the *Vie d'un héros, Agrippa d'Aubigné,* by S. Rocheblave, must be mentioned. In the seventeenth century we have to record the discovery of *Racine MSS.,* in Russia by the Abbé Bonnet (some still doubt their authenticity); a valuable edition of *La Princesse de Clèves,* with introduction by Dorchain; and the well-informed books by Magne on *Voiture et l'Hôtel de Rambouillet,* which show that tradition had idealized perhaps too much the "refined" society: the Marquise, however, comes out very well from this searching study. In the eighteenth century Rousseau (whose bi-centenary has been celebrated all over the world, and not without violent protest, especially from political opponents of the present government) easily leads the list of men who have inspired students in literature; we can only name from all that literature: Faguet's two volumes *(Rousseau contre Molière* and *Rousseau penseur),* Fabre, Bouvier, Tiersot *(Rousseau as a Musician),* Plan *(Rousseau raconté par les gazettes de son temps),* etc. The *Revue de Métaphysique et de Morale* devoted a whole number to the glorification of Rousseau, while the *Revue critique des idées et des livres* devoted one entire issue "contre la glorification de Rousseau." F. Gaussy continues his studies on Voltaire by *Voltaire seigneur de village* (in Ferney). Delafaye has a *Vie et œuvre de Palissot;* Harmant (pseudonym) a *Histoire de Mme. de Genlis,* which is remarkably well informed. A new edition of *Mirabeau,* by Lumet, "*Les écrits,*" is about all that concerns the time of the Revolution. For romanticism, Pellissier's *Le réalisme du romantisme* is the only general work. But we have also: Beaunier, *Chateaubriand;* Comte d'Antioche, *Chateaubriand, ambassadeur à Londres;* Léon Séché, *Les amitiés de Lamartine; Journal d'Italie,* by Stendhal, published by Arbalet; *Stendhal et les commentateurs,* by Mélia; *Vigny,* by Baldensperger; *Théophile Gautier,* by Larguier; *H. de Balzac,* by Lumet; the third volume of W. Karénine considerable work on George Sand; *Sainte Beuve, étude médicopsychologique,* by Dr. Voizard; and *Cénacle de Joseph Delorme,* by L. Séché; *Les pamphlets contre V. Hugo,* by Bersaucourt; *Sur Barbey d'Aurevilly,* by Laurentie; *Une étape de la conversion d'Huysmans,* by Du Fresnois; *Le Baile (maître) Alphonse Daudet,* by Baptiste Bonet; memoirs on Daudet by a Provençal friend.

Let us mention also here the *Mémoires de Jean Richepin;* Bourget, *Pages de critique et de doctrine;* Bertaud, *Les romanciers du nouveau siècle.* Niceforo, *Le génie de l'argot.* A. Dauzat, *Défense de la langue française.*

Among various events to be recorded: The celebration of the bi-centenary of Rousseau, already alluded to; the centenary of Eugénie and Maurice de Guérin; the fiftieth anniversary of *Salammbô;* the inauguration of the statue of Verlaine in the Luxembourg. The "Nobel prize" for literature went to Maeterlinck; the "Association syndicale des critiques" conferred a gold medal on Berret's *Moyen-Age dans la Légende des Siècles* (see YEAR BOOK, 1911). Elections in the French Academy: The philosopher Boutroux and General Liautey. The deaths which have not been recorded elsewhere: Gabriel Monod and the éditeur Lemerre. Finally, let us mention the donation to the French Academy of the Château de Nohant, made famous by George Sand; and of the so-called "Désert" in Ermenonville, made famous by the stay of Rousseau in that locality at the end of his life.

FRENCH SOMALI COAST. A French protectorate on the Gulf of Aden. Official report gives area 120,000 square kilometers and population 208,061. Jibuti, the capital, has about 11,000 inhabitants. Imports (1910), 21,024,712 francs; exports, 33,566,887. There are 81 miles of railway in the country (the railway from Jibuti into Abyssinia, which has a total length of 193 miles). The local budget balanced (1909) at 1,373,000 francs. M. Pascal was governor in 1912.

FRENCH WEST AFRICA. A French African possession composed of the following colonies and territories (area, population, and density), according to *Gotha* and purporting to be for 1910:

	Sq. kms.	Pop.	D.
Senegal	191,600	1,172,096	6
French Guinea	239,000	1,822,090	8
Ivory Coast	325,200	1,132,812	3.5
Dahomey	107,000	825,450	8
Upper Senegal and Niger	782,700	4,472,991	6
Mauritania (ter.)	893,700	600,000	0.7
Military Territory of the Niger	1,383,700	1,074,121	0.8
Total	3,922,900	11,100,000	2.8

The *Annuaire du Government Général de l'Afrique Occidentale Française* (pub. 1911) gives the following areas: Senegal, 192,000 sq. kilometers; Fr. Guinea, 231,702; Ivory Coast, 315,000; Dahomey, 107,000; Upper Senegal and Niger, 2,000,000, with the Saharian zone of influence, 819,000 for the administered districts; Military Territory, 1,300,000; Mauritania, 350,000. Total European population in 1911, 7358; aboriginals, 11,336,000.

The products and exports are peanuts, rubber, palm kernels, palm oil, gum arabic, live animals, etc. Imports and exports of the colonies in 1910 and the increase over the 1909 trade are seen below (values in francs):

	Imports		Exports	
	1910	Increase	1910	Increase
Senegal	82,607,568	14,695,829	64,254,179	5,089,262
U. S. & N.	7,036,901	4,694,709	8,996,934	5,836,438
Fr. G. ..	29,562,772	6,642,249	18,306,405	1,062,296
I. Coast.	16,049,454	4,857,212	15,749,700	3,961,848
D'y	17,838,753	3,622,757	17,886,254	1,535,640
Total...	153,095,448	34,512,256	125,193,472	15,361,452

For railways see the articles on the separate colonies and territories. The total budget balanced (1909) at 87,865,000 francs and the debt stood (Jan. 1, 1910) at 156,277,000. Dakar, in Senegal, is the capital. See the articles under separate titles. Governor-general (1912), W. Merland-Ponty.

FRIENDS, Religious Society of. The "Hicksite" branch has been more than ordinarily active during the past year. Its biennial general conference was held at Chautauqua August 27-September 3. In conjunction with the other branch of Friends the Whittier fellowship movement has taken form and a guest-house opened at Hampton Falls, N. H., in the Whittier neighborhood. The general conference advancement committee and the advancement committee of Baltimore Yearly Meeting have been doing unusually good work. The Philadelphia Yearly Meeting has established a central bureau with a secretary in charge, the particular labor being to look after the philanthropic and First-day school interests of the society. The society has during the year practically enlarged its endowment fund for two colored schools in the South in which it is interested, to the extent of about $60,000, and has been spending an unusual amount in the various lines of its activities. In 1913 it will hold its biennial summer school at George School, about twenty-five miles from Philadelphia. This will make the fourth in the series. The school lasts two weeks and takes up a comprehensive study of sociological and religious topics by practical class work and lectures by experts. Considerable labor has been employed in strengthening the weak spots in the society; and a few meetings which had been discontinued have been revived. The society has also been branching out in places where it has never had meetings, by organizing associations and holding meetings for the delivery of the Friendly message and the promulgation of the Quaker faith.

FUEL. See Chemistry, Industrial.

FULGURATION. See Cancer.

FUNGICIDES. See Botany.

FUNK, Isaac Kaufmann. An American author and publisher, died April 4, 1912. He was born in Clifton, O., in 1839, and graduated at Wittenberg College in 1860. He studied theology at the Wittenberg Theological Seminary in 1861. In the same year he entered the ministry of the Lutheran Church. Until 1872 he occupied pastorates in Carey, O., and Brooklyn, N. Y., but after a trip through Europe, Egypt, and Palestine he entered journalism and the publishing business. In 1872-3 he was associate editor of *The Christian Radical*, and from 1873 to 1875 of *The Union Advocate*. He founded in 1876 *The Metropolitan Pulpit*, and in the following year *The Complete Preacher*, which was merged in 1878 with *The Homiletic Monthly*. The name of this was changed in 1885 to *The Homiletic Review*, under which it is still known. In 1887 Dr. Funk entered into partnership with Adam Willis Wagnalls, founding the publishing house known for many years as Funk and Wagnalls, and which was later incorporated as The Funk and Wagnalls Company. He took an aggressive interest in prohibition and in 1880 established *The Voice* as a campaign paper. This was conducted for many years. In 1880 he founded *The Literary Digest*. His firm gave especial attention to the publication of important books of reference. Among these were *The Pulpit Commentary*, *The Jewish Encyclopædia*, *The Schaff-Herzog Encyclopædia of Religious Knowledge*, *A Standard Bible Dictionary*, and *The Encyclopædia of Social Reform*. The most important of these publications is probably *A Standard Dictionary of the English Language*, of which the first edition was issued in November, 1894, and a revised and enlarged edition in 1903. Dr. Funk took an active part in the preparation of this dictionary, as lexicography was his favorite pursuit. In his later years he became much interested in the investigation of psychic and spiritualistic phenomena, but was never a believer in spiritualism in the accepted meaning of the term. His published works include *The Next Step in Evolution* (1902); *The Widow's Mite, and Other Psychic Phenomena* (1904), and *The Psychic Riddle* (1907).

FURNESS, Christopher, First Baron of Grantley. An English ship owner and builder, died November 10, 1912. He was born in West Hartlepool, England, in 1852, and was educated privately. He succeeded his father, John Furness, as head of the steamship line of Furness, Withy & Company. He was, in addition, interested in many other important enterprises. In 1907 he effected the consolidation of the British Maritime Trust and the Chesapeake and Ohio Steamship Company. He was the chief promoter of the Cargo Fleet Iron Company. From 1891 to 1895 and again from 1900 to 1910 he was Liberal member of Parliament from Hartlepool. He was reëlected in 1910, but was unseated on petition. In 1908 he created much discussion among labor men and employees by the terms of an ultimatum which he delivered to the employees of the shipping concern of which he was the head. The men were on strike for larger wages and they were told by Furness that if they thought they could carry on the works the firm was willing to sell out to them at a price to be fixed by assessors; or, if they preferred, the firm was willing to admit its workmen to partnership on a profit-sharing basis. The trade union accepted the proposal for a year as an experiment. The plan was considered a success by the company, which paid the men 9 per cent. The men, however, were dissatisfied and did not continue the arrangement. Sir Christopher Furness was knighted in 1895, and was created first Baron of Grantley in 1910.

FURNESS, Horace Howard. An American Shakespearean scholar, died August 13, 1912. He was born in Philadelphia in 1833 and graduated from Harvard College in 1854. The two years following his graduation were spent in Europe. Returning to Philadelphia, he studied law and in 1859 was admitted to the bar. His contributions to legal subjects were important, but the chief work of his life was the study of Shakespeare's works and the preparation of his *Variorum Shakespeare*. This he began early in his life and continued until the time of his death. The first volume, *Romeo and Juliet*, was issued in 1871, and this was followed by *Macbeth* (1873); *Hamlet* (1877); *King Lear* (1880); *Othello* (1886); *Merchant of Venice* (1888); *As You Like It* (1890); *The Tempest* (1892); *Midsummer Night's Dream* (1895); *Winter's Tale* (1898); *Much Ado About Nothing* (1899); *Twelfth Night* (1901); *Love's Labor Lost* (1904); *Antony and Cleopatra* (1907).

Dr. Furness's interest in Shakespeare began when he heard Fanny Kemble interpret some of the characters in his youth. He then began to make a study of Shakespeare and his writings, and came to be known as the greatest Shakespearean authority in the United States and one of the greatest in the world. He also began a collection of Shakespearean relics, which he continued until his death. This is the most notable Shakespearean collection in the United States. It contains not only relics of Shakespeare himself, but of the many actors and actresses who have become eminent in Shakespearean rôles. Associated with him in his editorial work were his wife, herself the author of a concordance of Shakespeare's *Poems*, and his son, Horace Howard Furness, Jr. The *Variorum Shakespeare* has been received as a monument of scholarship. Dr. Furness received honorary degrees from Yale, Columbia, and Cambridge Universities. He was a member of many foreign and American learned societies. In addition to his writings on Shakespeare he wrote several articles on homeopathy and spiritualism. In the years immediately preceding his death he and his son made a study of monkeys, with important and interesting results.

FUTRELLE, JACQUES. An American author, died at sea April 15, 1912. He was born in Pike county, Ga., in 1875, and was educated in public and private schools. From 1890 to 1892 he was engaged in newspaper work. For two years following he acted as theatrical manager and from 1904 to 1906 was a member of the editorial staff of the *Boston American*. He was the author of *The Chase of the Golden Plate* (1906); *The Thinking Machine* (1907); *The Simple Case of Susan* (1908); *Elusive Isabel* (1909), and *The Diamond Master* (1909). Mr. Futrelle was one of the victims of the *Titanic* disaster.

GAIRDNER, JAMES. An English historian, died November 4, 1912. He was born in Glasgow, Scotland, in 1828, and was educated at Edinburgh University. In 1846 he became clerk in the Public Record office of Edinburgh and two years later was appointed assistant keeper of the records. Even before this time he had begun his association with the great work of his life, a monumental edition of the *Letters and Papers of the Reign of Henry VIII.*, and continued editing this work until the time of his death. He edited for the master of the rolls, *Memorials of Henry VII.*, and *Letters and Papers of the Reigns of Richard III. and Henry VII.* In 1879 he was appointed editor of *The Letters and Papers of the Reign of Henry VIII.*, and under his editorship Volumes 5 to 21 were completed. He also edited the *Paston Letters*, 1872 to 1875. He was editor of several volumes for the Camden Society and was the author of a volume on *England* in the series *Early Chroniclers of Europe*. He wrote a *Life of Richard III.* (1878); *The English Church in the Sixteenth Century to the Death of Mary* (1902); *Lollardy and the Reformation in England* (1908). He also contributed many articles to the *Dictionary of National Biography* and the *English Historical Review*.

GALE'S COMET. See ASTRONOMY.

GALSWORTHY, JOHN. See LITERATURE, ENGLISH AND AMERICAN.

GALVESTON CAUSEWAY. See BRIDGES.

GAMBIA. A British crown colony (69 sq. miles, population about 9000) and protectorate (3550 sq. miles, about 152,000 inhabitants) on the west African river Gambia. The inhabitants are mostly pagan and Mohammedan negroes of the Jollof, Mandingo, Sarahouli, Fullah, Jolah, and other tribes. The capital of the colony is Bathurst, on St. Mary's Island. The cultivation of peanuts is the principal industry. Imports (1910), £578,983. Imports of cotton goods in 1910, £130,611; kola nuts, £65,534; rice, £46,087; sugar, £9708; spirits, £7129; specie, £208,544, etc. About 49 per cent. of imports come from England. Exports (1910, £535,447. Exports of peanuts (mostly to France) in 1910, £387,943; hides, £11,310; palm kernels, £5640; specie, £112,194; etc. Revenue (1910), £82,880; expenditure, £63,301. Lieut.-Col. Sir H. L. Galway was governor in 1912.

GAMMA. See NAVAL PROGRESS, AVIATION.

GARBAGE AND REFUSE DISPOSAL. With the exception of the United States, the universal practice among cities which have abandoned primitive methods of garbage disposal is to mix the garbage with ashes and other more or less combustible refuse and burn the mixture in refuse destructors. These are operated under forced draft at a high temperature and in many instances, especially where soft coal is used as domestic fuel, the heat of combustion is utilized to raise steam for electric and other power. This type of destructor, which originated in Great Britain and is extensively used in that country, has been coming into use in the United States during the past five years, in place of the older type of crude furnaces which burn garbage only and require large quantities of extra fuel for the purpose.

During 1912 San Francisco began the construction of a large destructor, and Seattle continued carrying out its plan to build five 60-ton-per-day plants, located in different parts of the city. The first of the Seattle destructors was put in operation in February, 1908; the second in August, 1911, and the third was put under construction early in 1912. (See *Engineering News*, July 4, 1912, for illustrated description.) A number of cities in the Canadian Northwest were also building destructors in 1912. As a rule, the destructors built in the United States have not utilized the heat of combustion other than about the plant itself. This has been largely due to the opposition and influence of electric light and power companies, but probably it has also been due in no small part to the fact that there is as yet little experience to prove that it would pay to install and operate electric generating plants under conditions prevailing in American cities. During 1912 the city of Minneapolis began supplying current to light a considerable number of arc street lamps from power derived from a garbage incinerator of the American type. At

Calgary, Alberta, two refuse destructors were being built in 1912. It was proposed to use the heat from one destructor in a municipal asphalt paving plant and from the other to warm a sewage treatment plant during the severe winter weather of that section.

In nearly all the larger cities of the United States garbage is treated by the reduction process for the sake of the resulting grease and fertilizer base. With the exception of Cleveland and Columbus, O., these reductions plants are owned and operated by private companies. The companies generally receive a bonus from the cities, but the two municipal plants just named report a profit.

Piggeries, or hog ranches, as they are called in the West, appear to be becoming more numerous of late. A few years ago they were generally regarded as a makeshift, certain to be a nuisance and likely to breed tuberculosis, trichinæ, and hog cholera. Little is now heard about danger from trichinæ, and in general it now appears that if reasonable sanitary precautions are taken a municipal garbage piggery or hog ranch is no more offensive to human beings and no more dangerous to the animals themselves than any other equally large collection of hogs. A wise precaution, which seems to be taken but seldom, is to cook the garbage thoroughly before it is fed to hogs, thus insuring the destruction of any possible infectious bacteria in the garbage, just as the skimmed milk of many creameries is now pasteurized before it is fed to hogs or to calves. Feeding city garbage to hogs is practiced in a number of places in New England, in some places in the Middle West, and in California.

The garbage of Los Angeles is collected by the city and hauled to a well-designed shipping station. There it is dumped into railway cars supplied by a contractor, hauled twenty miles over an electric railway line into the country, and fed to some twenty thousand hogs, under a subcontract system. Hog-breeding is practiced on an extensive scale. The pigs are immunized against hog cholera while quite young and the losses from that disease are said to have fallen to a very low figure since immunization was begun. In 1912 the Los Angeles County Board of Health ordered the feeding of Los Angeles garbage to hogs stopped, but the city attorney has questioned the authority of the board in the premises. The garbage of the adjoining city of Pasadena was also being fed to hogs in 1912, the hog ranch being located on or near the city sewage farm, near a rapidly growing residence section. It was reported that Pasadena had contracted for an American type of garbage furnace.

Early in 1912 there was made public a lengthy report on "City Waste Studies in Ohio." The studies were made in 1909-10 by engineers of the Ohio State Board of Health, but the report was not completed until 1911. See *Modern Destructor Practice*, by W. Francis Goodrich (London and Philadelphia, 1912), for an exposition of the British type of refuse destructor and an account of its use throughout the world. The book also gives some information regarding other types of garbage burners and contains a few paragraphs on American garbage-reduction works. A symposium on garbage and refuse disposal was presented by a dozen or so engineers and health officers at the annual meeting of the American Public Health Association at Washington, D. C., in September, 1912, and will presumably be printed in the *Journal* of the association during 1913.

GARDEN CITY MOVEMENT. See CITY PLANNING, *Great Britain*.

GARDNER, JAMES TERRY. An American engineer and capitalist, died September 10. 1912. He was born in Troy, N. Y., in 1842, and was educated as an engineer at the Rensselaer Polytechnic Institute and the Sheffield Scientific School. He was employed during the Civil War by the Unitd States government as inspector of the harbor defenses of San Francisco, and he later served on the United States Geological Survey. From 1876 to 1883 he was director of the New York State Geological Survey and during the same period served on the State board of health. In the latter part of his life he entered business and became vice-president of several large coal companies.

GAS ENGINES. See INTERNAL COMBUSTION MOTORS.

GAS, ILLUMINATING. See CHEMISTRY, INDUSTRIAL.

GAS, NATURAL. The output of natural gas in 1911 was slightly less than that of 1910, the respective figures being 508,353,244,000 cubic feet and 509,155,309,000 cubic feet. The value of the product in 1911, however, was greater than that of 1910 by nearly $4,000,000. The value of the 1911 product was, in round numbers, $74,000,000. The increase in demand for natural gas by consumers of all kinds, according to the officials of the United States Geological Survey, makes the supply of gas a matter of great seriousness. In Ohio and Indiana the yield has diminished so rapidly as to stop the investment of further capital necessary for increased production. An important feature bearing on the production of gas was the excessive demand for it in Kansas City, Mo., and a commission was appointed to investigate the probable duration of the supply of that city, which reported that a supply of natural gas sufficient for the needs of the city was not possible for longer than three or four years.

Pennsylvania was the greatest consumer of natural gas in 1911, with an output of 154,475,376,000 cubic feet; Ohio was second, with 112,123,029,000 cubic feet; West Virginia third, with 80,868,645,000 cubic feet, and Kansas fourth, with 77,861,243,000 cubic feet. On December 31, 1911, there were 10,809 productive wells in Pennsylvania, 4755 in West Virginia, 4717 in Ohio, 2633 in Indiana, and 2004 in Kansas. The total number of productive wells in the United States on that date was 28,428.

During the last few years the separation of the more volatile g ades of gasoline from natural gas issuing from oil wells has become a profitable industry. There was in 1911 an output of 7,425,839 gallons of gasoline from this source, with an estimated value of $531,704.

GAS TURBINES. See INTERNAL COMBUSTION MOTORS.

GATES, GEORGE AUGUSTUS. An American educator, died November 20, 1912. He was born in Topsham, Vt., in 1851, and graduated from Dartmouth College in 1873. After studying from 1878 to 1880 in Germany he entered the Andover Theological Seminary. He was ordained to the Congregational ministry and from 1880 to 1887 was pastor at Upper Montclair, N. J. In the latter year he was elected president of Iowa College and remained in this position until 1901, when he became pastor of the First Church at Cheyenne, Wyo. From 1902 to 1909 he was president of Pomona College. He was elected president of Fisk University for colored students at Nashville, Tenn., in 1909. He was considered one of the foremost leaders in the higher education of the negro race. He resigned the presidency of Fisk University on account of ill health in 1912. He wrote an exposure of school-book trust methods, entitled *A Foe to American Schools*, in 1897.

GEMS, ARTIFICIAL. See CHEMISTRY, INDUSTRIAL.

GEMS AND PRECIOUS STONES. The precious stones mined in the United States in 1911 were valued at $343,692, compared with a value in 1910 of $295,380. The diamonds mined were valued at $2700; emeralds, $9500; sapphires, $215,313; turquoises, $44,751. The important feature of the gem-mining industry of the United States, according to the United States Geological Survey, was the result of the prospecting in 1911 at the Turner emerald mine near Shelby, N. C. The quality of some of the gems and the value of the gem material found in this deposit with a small amount of development work are promising, for the output included gems valued at $100 to $200 per carat and was equal in quality to the average run of emeralds from South America. The largest emerald so far discovered in North Carolina measured about 1 x ¾ x ½ inch. Most of the American diamonds came from Arkansas and California. The most important find of the year in Arkansas was an 8⅛-carat white diamond, the largest diamond so far found in the State. Another white diamond of 3 44-64 carats was also found. Much interest was aroused in the moss agates found in Montana, some of which are remarkable for their resemblance to landscapes. The cut gems consist of stones suitable for use in brooches, stickpins, watch fobs, and other ornaments. The gems cut from this stone command good prices, bringing anywhere from $1 to $200 or $300 each.

GEOGRAPHICAL SOCIETY, AMERICAN. To celebrate the sixtieth anniversary of its foundation and the completion of its new home at Broadway and 156th Street, New York City, the society organized a transcontinental excursion and invited as its foreign guests forty-three eminent European geographers delegated by the leading foreign geographical societies and universities. The excursion left New York on August 22, under the direction of Prof. W. M. Davis, and returned to that city on October 17, having spent eight weeks in visiting the Yellowstone National Park, Crater Lake, the leading Pacific Coast cities, the Grand Cañon of the Colorado, the North Carolina Appalachians, and other regions affording many geographical types for their observation. Over sixty American geographers were with the excursion in different sections of the journey, and thus the foreign guests saw a considerable part of the United States under scientific guidance. The society will publish a memorial volume, which will include papers by the foreign members of the excursion. The society has rearranged its book collections to make them best available for study. It gave a two months' exhibition of 700 photographs illustrating the scenery and various activities of many of the Western and Southern States. Its annual *Bulletin* contains over 1100 pages, including an analytical index which is a guide to the best geographical periodicals and maps of the year. Its lecture course was largely attended. It coöperated in fitting out the Crocker Land Expedition to the American Arctic, which is to sail north in the summer of 1913.

GEOGRAPHIC SOCIETY, NATIONAL. A society founded in 1888 with the object of collecting and diffusing geographic knowledge chiefly through its official organ, *The National Geographic Magazine*. It maintains research work both independently and in connection with other organizations and institutions. During 1912, in coöperation with Yale University, the society maintained a large expedition in Peru under the direction of Dr. Hiram Bingham. In the early part of the summer Mr. George C. Martin, geologist of the United States Geological Survey, was sent by the society to Alaska to make an investigation of the eruption of Mt. Katmai and neighboring volcanoes. This work is preliminary to an extended study of the belt of volcanoes in Alaska which will be systematically undertaken in 1913. The society also assisted W. E. Clyde Todd of the Carnegie Museum of Pittsburgh in making a biological survey of the region east of Hudson Bay. The membership of the society is about 150,000. The officers in 1912 were as follows: President, Henry Gannett; vice-president, O. H. Tittmann; secretary, O. P. Austin; treasurer, John Joy Edson; director and editor, Gilbert H. Grosvenor; assistant editor, John Oliver La Gorce.

GEOLOGY. The contributions to geology in the year 1912 may be said to include much of real interest and value, if nothing of extraordinary character. Progress conformed to the normal course that it has followed in the last few years. An important factor for the promotion of the science has been, of course, the work carried on by governmental surveys, State and national, with their staffs of experts, who cover practically all fields of research after a more or less systematic plan. The material that is thus annually assembled for publication is of enormous volume and of the widest scope. Among the works of very general appeal which appeared during the year under such auspices may be mentioned the geological map of North America, issued by the United States Geological Survey under coöperation with the surveys of Canada and Mexico. The map includes the latest developments in exploration and stratigraphic classification, and is prepared on a scale of one inch to about 80 miles. It is accompanied by a very comprehensive index that has been compiled by Bailey Willis. This volume is really a summary of the results accomplished in mapping the various sections of the continent, with views as to the correlation of these results. The work will no doubt find wide appreciation as a standard of reference in this field.

PRE-CAMBRIAN LIFE. That the abundant and varied life forms present in the lowermost Paleozoic strata comprising the Cambrian system do not represent the first beginnings of life on the globe has long been known to geologists, although the records supplied by the earlier formations have been of the scantiest kind. A very general explanation for the scarcity of fossils in the oldest strata is found in the various vicissitudes to which they have been sub-

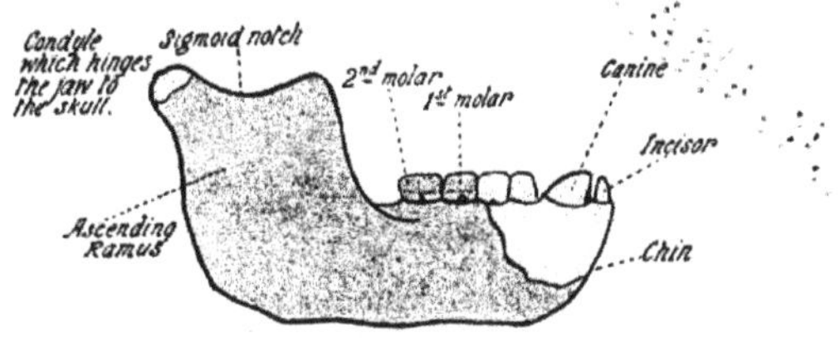

JAW OF EOANTHROPUS DAWSONI

Courtesy of the Popular Science Monthly

RECONSTRUCTION OF EOANTHROPUS DAWSONI ("SUSSEX MAN")

DRAWN UNDER THE DIRECTION OF DR. W. P PYCRAFT OF THE BRITISH MUSEUM FOR THE ILLUSTRATED LONDON NEWS

jected incidental to their great age. The Pre-Cambrian sediments in most sections have undergone profound changes from heat and pressure that have obscured, if not obliterated, any evidences of organic life they may have contained. Nevertheless, discoveries of fossils in these strata have been reported from time to time. One of the more recent finds was made by A. C. Lawson in the vicinity of Stelprock Lake, west of Port Arthur, Ontario, Canada. The fossils occurred in limestones that are placed by that authority in the Lower Huronian division, just above the Keewatin of the Archean, from which the limestones are separated by an erosion interval. If this determination of position should prove correct, the discovery is perhaps the most important of its kind yet made, as it spans a tremendous gap in the records of life history on the globe. A description of the fossils has been given by Walcott, who finds that they are related to the sponges, or rather combine characters possessed by both the sponge and coral families. They are quite unlike the fauna found by him in the Pre-Cambrian of Montana and are placed in the new genus Antikokania. They consist of globose, cylindrical or pear-shaped forms, built up of radiating tubes, of hexagonal outline in some specimens. Though of primitive character, they still must be considerably removed from the first stages in the development of life on the earth.

Early Man. The discovery of some primitive human remains in southern England aroused both geological and anthropological interest as one of the well-authenticated instances in which man has been revealed in the surroundings of a past geological period. The discovery was made in a gravel pit in Sussex and consisted of the upper part of a skull and one-half of a lower jaw, together with numerous animal remains, including those of the Pliocene elephant, mastodon, hippopotamus, beaver, and horse. Very primitive flints (eoliths) were also found in the vicinity. The fossil associates would seem to indicate the late Tertiary period, preceding the Glacial epoch, an earlier date than that assigned to any similar discovery hitherto made in Europe. It should be mentioned, however, that the flints resembled those usually referred to the Middle Pleistocene, or Chellean stage, of human culture. Professor Keith and Dr. A. S. Woodward, who examined the skull, agreed that it represented a type of man more primitive than the Neanderthal and Heidelberg types. Compared with the Heidelberg type, which is supposed to have existed in the early Pleistocene, there are some features in common, but the general aspect of Sussex man is more ape-like. The skull is, however, more human than simian, its distinctive features being a flattened form and thickened walls. It is not a close relative of any other type thus far found, but apparently belongs to a more or less distinct branch of the human family, not in direct line of ancestry to the present race.

At a meeting of the British association Professor Keith discussed the evidences as to the antiquity of man, and favored the view that in the distant past there was not one kind but several very different kinds of man, all of which have become extinct except that branch which has given rise to modern man. From the imperfect records afforded by the few bones that have so far been uncovered, it seems probable that man began to take on his human characters near the beginning of the Pliocene period. Neanderthal man existed toward the end of the Pleistocene, while the Heidelberg type was of earlier date, possibly near the beginning of that period. To this latter stage also belonged the Java representative, Pithecanthropus. These represented two distinct types, neither of which was the direct ancestor of modern man. With the new discovery of the Sussex skull we have record of a third type which goes back much farther, in fact to the Pliocene Tertiary. The evidences show that man took on human characteristics near the beginning of the Pliocene, which Prof. Keith is inclined to place roundly at a million and a half years ago.

Dynamic Geology. As a continuation of his interesting experiments on the behavior of rocks under extreme pressures, Prof. F. D. Adams sought to determine the probable depth in the earth's interior at which rocks under the hydrostatic pressure of their superincumbent load would yield by flowage, thus closing all cavities. This zone of flowage has been estimated to occur at various depths; the conclusion reached by Van Hise, which has been most generally followed perhaps, indicated 12,000 meters. Two samples of rock were selected for experiment, one the Solenhofen limestone and the other Westerly granite, as representative of widespread types. These were subjected to pressures up to more than 100 tons to the square inch, at normal temperatures and under conditions of heat. It was found that granite at ordinary temperatures, under cubic compression such as obtains in the earth's crust, sustains a load of nearly 100 tons to the square inch, or more than seven times greater than the pressure that serves to crush it at the surface. With the gradient of temperature corresponding to the depth, it would appear that granite may resist flowage and closing of its cavities to a depth at least of 11 miles. Aside from its theoretic interest with regard to problems like those connected with isostatic adjustment, the work has an imporant economic bearing with reference to the extension of mineral veins in depth. This class of ore-deposits, as well as that arising from replacement, is dependent upon the agency of underground waters whose circulation is restricted necessarily to the zone where open cavities and pore-spaces occur. In view of the experiments, it would appear that such veins and replacements may be found within a range of at least 11 miles from the surface, or to a much greater depth than it is possible to follow them by any method of mining now employed.

In a study of the stratigraphical features known as conformity and unconformity, W. O. Crosby gives a clear explanation of their nature and meaning, with illustrations drawn from the coastal plain of eastern North America. The essential factor, as well as the chief interest, in unconformity pertains to the dynamic relations as expressed by erosion. Strata which are unconformable bear evidence of a double interchange between land and sea. The relation implies a considerable time break or hiatus, and thus arises somewhat incidentally the great value of unconformity in stratigraphic demarcation and classification. Conformity, on the other hand, signifies that deposition was essentially continuous, that no true hiatus and consequently no period of erosion intervened during the accumulation of the strata that are conformable. Deposition may be infinitely slow, as in the great oceanic depression, but any apparent gap arising from such cause does not necessarily imply an unconformity. Localized erosion, like that due to shifting currents, is also not related to true unconformity. Examples of conformable and unconformable conditions of different character are to be found in the Atlantic coast province among the stratified formations which range in age from the Cretaceous to the present. The Cretaceous sediments were deposited on the eroded surface of older formations that had been profoundly deformed and metamorphosed before their submergence. This great unconformity is the joint product of deformation and erosion, and has greater importance than the numerous unconformities that occur later in the series and that are characterized by erosion alone. For the former type, in which the beds are discordant, Crosby proposes the name clino-unconformity; for the latter class, with accordant dip and strike, he proposes the term para-unconformity.

VOLCANISM. The underlying principles of volcanic activity have been considered by Daly, who views the earth as made up in its outer part of a siliceous shell that is overlain by the sedimentary mantle and underlain at a depth of 40 kilometers by a basaltic substratum. In the process of eruption this basaltic material forces its way through fissures into the outer part, where important changes begin to take place. The increase of volume in the magma affords energy for expanding the fissures, the superheat brings about more or less assimilation of the country rocks, and the gases occluded in the molten material will concentrate in the upper levels and under the roof of the bathylithic chamber. Various phases of volcanic action may then occur. Fissure eruptions are characterized by a superheated magma, always of basaltic nature; they involve thus the substratum rock alone, without assimilation of the acid country rocks. This phase may be conditioned by a narrow feeding channel. A second phase is called eruption through local foundering, which is conceived as taking place when the magma is of great proportions and superheated sufficiently to allow extensive assimilation of the overlying solid material. This assimilation alters the composition, giving rise to differentiation which results in the collecting of the siliceous rock varieties at the top. The upper portions may overflow and produce a rock mass somewhat similar to a fissure eruption, but differing in its acid character. The rhyolite sheet in Yellowstone Park is thus explained. The third phase is the central eruption, exemplified by modern volcanoes. In this the gases play an important rôle, assisting in opening the vent by abrasive and melting action, and through reactions between themselves liberating the energy to maintain the eruption of the rock through the vent. Bathyliths are the result of main abyssal injections. Plutonic stocks and bosses are the cupolas in bathylithic roofs. Sheets, dikes, and laccoliths are satellitic and soon lose their thermal and hydrostatic communication with the main abyssal injection. The hypothesis is, of course, largely speculative, inasmuch as the data with which it deals are very obscure or even beyond the horizon of direct observation; it represents, however, an interesting attempt to develop a reasonable explanation on the basis of generally accepted geological principles.

CRYSTALLINE SCHISTS. The origin of the foliated crystalline rocks has long engaged the attention of geologists, and one of the later contributions on the subject is by Trueman. The paper is especially valuable for its review and critical tests of previous work. A two-fold derivation of gneisses is recognized, according as they have received their foliation during consolidation from a molten state, in which case they are classed as primary, or as their foliation has been developed by secondary processes, which is regarded as the more common condition. The recognition of primary gneisses is rather a matter of field than laboratory study. A more common problem is presented to geologists in the separation of the sedimentary derivatives from the igneous members in the secondary class. The criteria that may be used in its solution include texture, chemical analysis, and the presence of certain minerals, which have a limited range of occurrence or possess different characters when found in the two groups.

Of much more general importance than might be inferred from its title perhaps is *The Geology of the Lake Superior Region*, a work in which Van Hise and Leith have brought together the results of long-continued investigation by themselves and their predecessors in this very remarkable section of old crystalline rocks. There is perhaps no other similar area anywhere that has received so thorough a study or that has gained so prominent a place in the literature relating to the Pre-Cambrian formations. Its interest lies in the great variety of the rocks, which are representative of all the stratigraphic divisions from the Archean to the Cambrian systems, in the metamorphic and structural features which the rocks exhibit; and in the extensive mineral resources of the region, especially those of copper and iron. The different aspects of the subject are fully and clearly treated by the authors who have been foremost among the interpreters in this classic field. Among the broader features of the geology of the region, as now made known, are the dominance of igneous formations in the basal or Archean portion, the rocks of which show evidence of uplift and profound erosion at a very early period. Upon this eroded basement were deposited the Lower Huronian strata, of terrestrial and marine origin. Then successively came the Middle and Upper Huronian, mainly of marine deposits, separated by a great unconformity. The Keweenawan system of terrestrial accumulations followed after another time gap. The iron ore deposits within the region are estimated to contain nearly two billions of tons and up to 1910 had produced about one-fourth of that amount. In regard to their origin the earlier theories enunciated by Van Hise have been largely revised in the light of more detailed study; the view is now held that the deposits were formed largely by chemical precipitation in sea water. The iron is supposed to have been abstracted from volcanic rocks either through magmatic solutions which poured into the sea or from the action of the saline waters upon submarine volcanic flows.

After deposition as stratified beds the iron deposits were uplifted and broken by regional forces exposing them to oxidation and the concentrating action of ground waters which have enriched the ores to the present state. The copper ores in the Keweenawan beds are also considered to have been derived from volcanic sources, in particular from the basaltic intrusions found within the stratified series.

ORE DEPOSITS. Among the contributions to mining geology may be noticed Weed's *Geology and Ore Deposits of the Butte District, Montana*, one of the series of monographs on the more important mineral districts issued by the United States Geological Survey. This volume will appeal to students on account of the historic relation which its subject bears to the development of knowledge in regard to mineral veins. The principle of secondary enrichment, perhaps the most signal feature in the recent progress of applied geology in America, was first clearly enunciated in connection with the Butte mines. In practical value the volume has suffered not a little from its delayed appearance, as the field studies were completed as far back as 1905. This has, perhaps, been a help from the scientific standpoint, for it shows evidences of mature reasoning in the treatment of the very complicated problems which are involved. The Butte district, it may be noted, ranks first among the copper districts of the world. In the last 20 years, the period of its greatest activity, it has contributed about five and a half billions of pounds of copper, besides important quantities of silver and some gold.

PETROLEUM. A novel explanation of the origin of petroleum was proposed by Murray Stuart in a paper on the Burma oil-fields, included in the reports of the Indian geological survey. According to the usual theory petroleum results from the distillation of organic matter in deeply buried rocks under the influence of heat and pressure. The alternative proposed by Stuart is that the oil originates from decomposition of vegetal débris at the surface, chiefly in lagoons or swamps where the decomposition is facilitated by bacterial action. The oil would rise to the surface as formed, and if the lagoons were subsequently drained it would become commingled with mud and sand of the outflowing stream. By experiment it has been found that fine muds and clay have the property of carrying down or precipitating oil when mixed with water. In that way a sedimentary deposit of the fine materials with the mechanically entangled oil might accumulate on the beds of streams and after the lapse of time become consolidated by burial under a load of overlying sediment. The theory has been worked out with especial reference to the Burma oil-pools, but the author holds that it may be applicable to other fields as well

GEOPHYSICAL LABORATORY. See CARNEGIE INSTITUTION.

GEORGETOWN UNIVERSITY. An institution for higher education, under the auspices of the Roman Catholic Church, at Washington, D. C., founded 1789. The number of students enrolled in the various departments of the university in the autumn of 1912 was 1124. The faculty numbered 173. The most noteworthy event in the history of the university during the year was the appointment of the Rev. Alphonsus J. Donlon as president, to succeed Rev. Joseph J. Himmel, who had held that office from 1908 and was obliged to resign on account of ill health. The following noteworthy benefactions were received during the year: To the Georgetown University Hospital, $45,000 from Mrs. E. Francis Riggs; for a wing for maternity cases, $15,000 from Dr. George M. Kober. From Dr. Kober was also received a gift for the medical library. The volumes in the library numbered 121,000.

GEORGE WASHINGTON UNIVERSITY. An institution of higher learning in Washington, D. C., formerly known as Columbian University, founded in 1821. The enrollment in all departments of the university in the autumn of 1912 was 1270. The faculty numbered 185. There were no noteworthy changes in the faculty during the year, and no important benefactions were received. The endowment amounted to about $125,000. The total receipts for 1911-12 amounted to $141,724. There were 44,500 volumes in the library. The president is Charles H. Stockton.

GEORGIA. POPULATION. According to the Census Bureau statistics issued in 1912, out of a total population in 1910 of 2,609,121 the foreign-born whites numbered 15,072, compared with 12,021 in 1900. The greatest proportion of these, 3224, came from Russia; from Germany, 3025; from England, 1650. Other European countries were represented by smaller numbers. In 1910 the negroes in the State numbered 1,176,987 and the mulattoes, 204,205. In 1890 the negroes numbered 858,815 and the mulattoes, 85,133. It will be noted that the negroes and mulattoes form a majority of the population of the State.

AGRICULTURE. The acreage, value, and production of the principal crops in 1911 and 1912 are shown in the following table:

		Acreage		Prod. Bu.	Value
Corn	1912	3,910,000		53,958,000	$45,864,000
	1911	3,692,000		59,072,000	49,030,000
Wheat	..1912	132,000		1,228,000	1,498,000
	1911	145,000		1,740,000	1,984,000
Oats	1912	364,000		7,571,000	4,921,000
	1911	404,000		8,686,000	6,480,000
Rye	1912	11,000		101,000	141,000
	1911	12,000		114,000	157,000
Rice	1912	900		27,000	24,000
	1911	1,450		39,000	30,000
Potatoes	.1912	12,000		936,000	814,000
	1911	12,000		864,000	950,000
Hay	1912	234,000	(a)	316,000	5,372,000
	1911	87,000	(a)	117,000	1,989,000
Tobacco	.1912	1,400	(b)	1,162,000	349,000
	1911	1,200	(b)	1,080,000	302,400
Cotton	...1911	....	(c)	2,560,000	....

(a) Tons. (b) Pounds. (c) Bales.

The iron ore produced in the State in 1911 was 207,279 long tons, compared with 313,878 long tons in 1910. The value of the product in 1911 was $315,704, compared with a value of the product in 1910 of $482,659.

MANUFACTURES. The Thirteenth Census statistics for the calendar year 1909 were compiled in 1912. Although Georgia is an agricultural rather than a manufacturing State, it has been for the past 60 years one of the leading and most progressive industrial States of the South. The increase in the five-year period, 1904-1909, is shown in the table given below:

	Number or Amount 1909	1904	P. C. of inc. 1904-'09
Number of establishments	4,792	3,219	48.9
Persons engaged in manufactures..	118,036	102,365	15.3
Proprietors and firm members.	5,141	3,512	46.4
Salaried empl'es	8,307	6,104	36.1
Wage earners (average number)	104,588	92,749	12.8
Prim'y horsepower	298,241	220,419	35.3
Capital	$202,778,000	$135,211,000	50.0
Expenses	176,165,000	129,151,000	36.4
Services	43,867,000	33,320,000	31.7
Salaries	9,062,000	5,927,000	52.9
Wages	34,805,000	27,393,000	27.1
Materials	116,970,000	83,625,000	39.9
Miscellaneous....	15,328,000	12,206,000	25.6
Value of products.	202,863,000	151,040,000	34 3
Value of products less cost of materials	85,893,000	67,415,000	27.4

In addition to the data included in that table it may be noted that the industries devoted to lumber and timber products rank first in number, 1828. Manufactories of turpentine and rosin numbered 592; printing and publishing, 442; oil, cottonseed, and cake, 142; and cotton goods, including cotton small ware, 116. The cotton industry had the largest value of product, $48,037,000; lumber and timber products, $24,632,000; oil, cottonseed, and cake, products, $23,641,000, and fertilizers, $16,800,000. The total number of persons engaged in the manufacturing industries of the State in 1909 was 118,036. Of these 100,245 were male, and 17,791 female. Employees under 16 years of age numbered 6041. The prevailing hours of labor in the State ranged from 60 to 72 a week with the majority of those employed. Of all the wage-earners, 23.2 per cent. were employed in establishments where the prevailing hours were less than 60 a week and 1.4 per cent. where they were more than 72 a week.

Education. Children of school age in the State in 1912 numbered 735,471. The total enrollment was 565,071 and the average attendance, 352,059. The teachers numbered 13,024. The expenditures for common schools amounted to $5,966,345. Of the total number of pupils enrolled, 342,129 were white and 22,942 colored. The attendance by white pupils was 221,381 and by colored, 130,678. The average monthly salary of white male teachers was $64, and white female teachers, $43.93; colored male teachers, $26.52, and colored female teachers, $20.56. The total number of schools was 7968, of which 4933 were for white pupils and 3035 for colored. The total expenditure for common schools in 1911 was $5,065,229.

Finance. There was a balance in the State treasury at the beginning of the fiscal year 1911 of $618,923. The total receipts for the fiscal year ending December 31, 1911, were $5,558,447, and the total disbursements were $5,450,284, leaving a balance at the end of the fiscal year of $727,076. The chief sources of revenue are general tax, railroad tax, railroad rentals, and license fees. The chief expenditures are for education, for the maintenance of State institutions, and for the expenses of the State government. The outstanding bonds of the State at the end of the fiscal year were valued at $6,834,202.

Politics and Government. The legislature met in 1912 and passed no unusual measure.

Conventions and Elections. The Republican State convention for the choosing of delegates to the national convention met at Atlanta on February 14. The Taft forces were in control and although there were contesting Roosevelt delegates from several congressional districts they were not allowed to enter the hall. All the delegates chosen were pledgd to vote for President Taft. The convention also gave the President a strong indorsement of his administration. Early in May, mass meetings were held throughout the State and delegates were elected to a convention to nominate Roosevelt delegates to the national convention. This was brought about largely through the efforts of Ormsby McHarg, who made a tour throughout the State advising voters that the convention held previously was illegal and that none of the delegates chosen would be seated in Chicago. This convention met and elected Roosevelt delegates. The regular Taft delegates, however, were seated by the national committee.

On July 17 the National Progressive party held a convention in the State. Dissensions arose among the delegates, and as a result two delegations from Georgia went to the National were seated by the national committee.

At the Democratic primary, held on May 1, Mr. Underwood defeated Governor Wilson by more than 8000 votes. The delegates to the Democratic national convention, therefore, went pledged to vote for Mr. Underwood. At a Democratic primary held on August 21, Senator Bacon was renominated and John M. Slaton was chosen as Democratic candidate for governor. In the election held on November 3, Governor Wilson received 93,171 votes, Mr. Roosevelt, 22,010, President Taft, 5190, and Debs, Socialist, received 1014 votes. The Democrats elected all the representatives in Congress.

On January 25 Joseph M. Brown was inaugurated governor of the State to serve until July 1, 1913, when John M. Slaton, nominated as noted above on August 21, will succeed him.

State Government. Governor, Joseph M. Brown (after July 1, 1913. J. M. Slaton); Secretary of State, Philip Cook; Treasurer, William J. Speer; Comptroller and ex officio Commissioner of Insurance, W. A. Wright; Attorney-General, Thomas S. Felder; Adjutant-General, W. G. Obear; Superintendent of Education, M. J. Brittain; Commissioner of Agriculture, J. D. Psico—all Democrats.

Judiciary. Supreme Court: Chief Justice, William H. Fish; Beverly D. Evans, Presiding Justice; Associate Justices, J. H. Lumpkin, M. W. Beck, Samuel C. Atkinson and Horace M. Holden; Clerk, Z. D. Harrison—all Democrats.

State Legislature, 1913. Democrats, Senate, 43; House, 183; joint ballot, 226. Republicans, Senate, 1; House, 1; joint ballot, 2. Democratic majority, Senate, 42; House, 182; joint ballot, 224.

The representatives in Congress will be found in the section *Congress*, article United States.

GEORGIA, University of. An institution of higher learning at Athens, Ga., founded in 1785. The total enrollment in the various departments of the university in the autumn of 1912 was 700. The faculty numbered 65. Among the new members of the faculty in 1912 were Professor L. R. Geissler, in the chair of psychology, and Professor R. E. Curtis, in the chair of business administration. Several important additions were made to the faculty in the department of agriculture during the year. Among the gifts received were $12,500 from the Phelps-Stokes Fund, and $40,000 from the Peabody Trust Fund, for the erection of the Peabody Educational building. The productive funds of the university amounted to about $370,000, and the annual income to about $220,000. There were 40,000 volumes in the library and 10,000 pamphlets. Chancellor, David C. Borrow, A. M.

GERMAN ANTARCTIC EXPEDITION. See POLAR EXPLORATION.

GERMAN EAST AFRICA. A protectorate of Germany bordering on the Indian Ocean, between the British East Africa Protectorate and Portuguese East Africa. Area, as officially estimated, 995,000 square kilometers (384,170 square miles). The native population is unknown, but has been unofficially estimated at 7,000,000. White population, January 1, 1911, 4227, of whom 3113 German. There are government schools, and teaching is also carried on by the nine Evangelical and six Roman Catholic missions.

Products of the German plantations include coffee, cacoa, vanilla, tobacco, rubber, sugar, cotton, cocoanuts, and cardamoms. There are various mineral deposits, and many gems are found. Imports and exports, in thousands of marks: 1905, 17,655 and 9950; 1909, 33,942 and 13,120; 1910, 38,659 and 20,805. Exports in 1909 and 1910 included: Rubber, 2768 and 6195 thousand marks; sisal, 2333 and 3011; copra, 798 and 1909; ivory, 960 and 703; wax, 659 and 672; coffee, 887 and 838; hides and skins, 2030 and 2889; gold ore, 240 and 843; earth nuts, 233 and 596.

Railways, December 31, 1911: Northern (formerly the Usumbara), from Tanga to Kilimanjaro, 352 kilometers; Central, which is being built from Dar-es-Salaam to Ujiji, on Lake Tanganyika, via Tabora, 713 kilometers and 134 kilometers under construction; total in operation, 1065 kilometers. In January, 1912, the Central railway was opened to traffic as far as Tabora, 847 kilometers, and before the end of the year the railroad was over 150 kilometers beyond that town. Post and telegraph offices (1910), 42 and 30.

Estimated revenue for 1911-12 and 1912-13 respectively: Colonial revenue, 11,062,045 and 15,703,605 marks; imperial contribution, 3,543,790 and 3,618,307; loans, 17,615,000 and 17,250,000; total, 32,219,835 and 36,571,912. The estimated expenditures for the two years balanced the above totals and included the amounts of the loans as extraordinary. Governor (1912), Baron von Rechenberg; seat of government, the port Dar-es-Salaam (population about 26,000).

GERMAN EVANGELICAL SYNOD OF NORTH AMERICA. A religious denomination, founded in 1840, as the Evangelical Association of the West. Its present name was adopted in 1877. It represents in doctrine the Prussian Union of 1877. Its strength is greatest in the central and north central States, although it is found in nearly all of the States of the Union. In 1912 the communicants numbered 254,995, the ministers 1058, and congregations 1343. The church property was valued at $13,429,739. For the maintenance of churches there was spent $1,218,253 and for benevolent purposes $227,873. Missions are sustained in India, where the communicants and adherents of the denomination numbered about 3500. The official organs of the denomination are *Der Friedensbote* and *The Messenger of Peace*, both published in the Eden Publishing House at St. Louis. The denomination sustains Elmhurst College at Elmhurst, Ill., and the Eden Theological Seminary at St. Louis. Charitable institutions are maintained for orphans, superannuated ministers, and the widows and orphans of deceased ministers. Nine instituions are engaged in deaconness work of the Kaiserswerth model.

GERMANIC PHILOLOGY. See PHILOLOGY.

GERMAN LITERATURE. The older generation of German writers is gradually being removed by death or is lapsing into silence and leaving the field to the youth it once opposed. It is quite evident that this youth rules the book market. The number of biographical and appreciative, rather than critical, monographs on writers still in their prime and capable of further development, is increasing. Complete uniform editions are also being published. All these publication have an air of finality which previous generations reserved for a time when an author's creative work was well-nigh ended. The old lament that the German poet comes into his own only after he is dead, is a thing of the past. The distinctions that have poured upon Gerhart Hauptmann, and at the occasion of his fiftieth birthday, the complete edition of his works, the new edition of Dr. Paul Schlenther's biography, originally published when the poet was only thirty-six, and finally the awarding of the Nobel prize, can also be considered a victory for his generation. But since he is the most perfect expression of the spirit of his race and his age, the honors bestowed upon him are well deserved. Arthur Schnitzler, the novelist and dramatist, who with due allowance for his Austrian temperament can be called another embodiment of the *Zeitgeist*, has also reached the half-century mark and been honored with a complete edition of his works. He has had an American success, too, the long run of *The Affairs of Anatol* in New York. But in his native Vienna, Schnitzler has experienced an official rebuff, his play *Professor Bernhardi* having been barred from public production. This incident is one of three within the year to remind German authors that censorship is not abolished. The other cases occurred in Munich, where an unpublished play by a new author, Leonor Goldschmied, was not even allowed a public reading, and the performance of Franz Dülberg's *Korallenkettlin*, a drama published some years ago, was prohibited. The latter work was finally produced in Bremerhaven, without disapproval on the part of the audience or interference from the authorities. Thus it would seem as if the ultramontane party in Austria and in Bavaria were responsible for the measures taken in Vienna and in Munich. Otherwise the year passed very quietly. No book published in 1912 could be called a work of the first literary importance, or met with a sensational success. The decline of the best seller, which was noted a year ago, is very marked; even the list of books most in demand has disappeared from the columns of literary magazines.

DRAMA. For Gerhart Hauptmann the year was marked by the performance at the little theatre of Lauchstedt, hallowed by Goethe tradition, of *Gabriel Schillings Flucht*, a psychological drama written six years ago and not originally intended for public production. Max Halbe's comedy *Der Ring des Gauklers*, and Max Dreyer's domestic drama *Die Frau des Kommandeurs*, proved once more the futility of their efforts to repeat previous successes. Herbert Eulenberg, on the contrary, who had long in vain courted a stage success, surprised his critics with his *Belinde*, which was awarded the "Schiller Volkspreis." Walter von Molo, a young Austrian, made a successful début wtih a four-act play, *Die Mutter*. Another newcomer challenging attention is Gerdt von Bassewitz, the author of the tragedy *Judas*. A woman dramatist came into great prominence, Hanna Rademacher, whose historical drama *Johanna von Neapel*, was received with great favor. Hermann Bahr is risking his reputation by being too prolific: his plays of the year are *Das Tänzchen* and *Das Prinzip*. Oscar Blumenthal's *Waffengang* is identical in style and calibre with the numerous plays produced in the thirty-five years of his career. Ludwig Fulda's *Seeräuber* will not enhance the author's reputation. Ludwig Thoma's *Magdalena* proved to be a Bavarian peasant tragedy of almost cold-blooded realism. Josef Schanderl's *Nachtrab* is a delightful Munich comedy. Wilhelm Weigand's *Könige* and *Psyche's Erwachen* have great poetical qualities and Franz Dülberg's *Cardenio* presents a novel version of a story previously dramatized by Immermann and others. Leo Birinski's *Narrentanz*, founded like his *Moloch* upon the Russian revolution, has not been taken seriously by the critics. Frank Wedekind is being more and more generally accepted as a serious representative of the intellectual and moral fermentation going on in modern Germany, even his Faustian *Franziska*, a recently published play which he calls a "Mysterium," having been favorably noticed.

POETRY. There have been few noteworthy books of verse this year. Ernst Lissauer's *Der Strom* stands foremost, being full of striking images and remarkably condensed in feeling and form. A volume of posthumous verse by Wilhelm Holzamer is a precious legacy, for his untimely death cut short the development of rare gifts. Hanns von Gumppenberg's *Schauen und Sinnen* is a book containing many a line of genuine lyric sweep. Alfons Paquet's *Held Namenlos* shows his strong sense for the romance of reality. Two books of verse have come from Carl Meissner: *Der schwarze Wag* reflects with some bitterness the limitations of provincial life; *Im Schauen der Dinge* is based upon a more philosophical acceptance of life. A new edition of Maria Janitschek's poems is distingushed by the symbolistic quality and the rhapsodic ring with which she struck a new note some years ago. Maria Stona's new volume of poems, *Flammen und Fluten*, also proves that she has lost none of the intensity and the tenderness of her earlier lyrics. Ricarda Huch is the peer of her sisters; her new book, *Gedichte*, reflects an artistic temperament held in leash by the unerring taste of a rarely cultured mind. A monumental anthology is Bruno Wille's work in two volumes: *Die Waltdichter fremder Zunge und Schätze aus ihren Werken von dem Veden bis Tolstoi*.

FICTION. That this year of honor to Gerhart Hauptmann should terminate with the publication of his novel *Atlantis*, which appeared simultaneously in Germany and America, is in a manner to be regretted, as the work is inferior in construction and in style to his *Fool in Christ*. But it has a strong psychological interest and in the medical knowledge with which it describes the effects of a shipwreck upon the mind of the hero, is typical of the modern German tendency of welding science and art. A noteworthy achievement is George Hermann's story *Die Nacht des Doktor Herzfeld*, which also incidentally touches with commendable discretion upon a recent medical discovery of great importance. Hermann Stegemann, an Alsatian writer of great power, has published two novels, *Thomas Ringwald* and *Die Himmelspacher*, both remarkable for the virile wholesome type of their heroes and for his plastic visualization of dramatic conflicts. Wilhelm Scharrelmann, a most sympathetic reader of the child-soul, has written a touching and truthful story of child-life in tenement lodgings: *Piddl Hundertmark*. Gerhard Ouckama Knoop, one of the most striking individualities in German fiction, has chosen a Dutch landscape for the background of a story of rapid rise to wealth and rank, and as rapid decline: *Die Hochmögenden*. Walter Harlan's *Catrejn's Irrfahrt* is a story of old Flanders. Rudolf Hans Bartsch, the Austrian novelist, has written a delightful novel based upon the life of Franz Schubert, *Schwammerl*, the very title suggesting its local atmosphere and intimate charm. His compatriot Wilhelm Fisher-Graz traces the development of a girl of humble birth to noble womanhood in a story, *Aus der Tiefe*, of which the scene is Steiermark during Napoleon's campaign. Max Dauthendey, the poet, makes his début as novelist with *Raubmenschen*, a powerful story of a German's experience in Mexico. A young Swiss writer of promise is hailed in Alexander Castell, whose novel *Bernards Versuchung*, has a touch of Gallic worldliness and grace. The new book by Emil Strauss, *Der nackte Mann*, presents scenes of court and town life and has a most sympathetic aristocratic heroine. It would seem as if the experiences of Louise of Saxony had directed the attention of some writers to this type of womanhood and the tragedy of lives hedged in by the conventions of their caste, for Kurt Aram in his *Baronin Gorn*, and Adolf Paul in his *Dornröschen* also treat this theme. Oscar A. H. Schmitz, in a somewhat exaggerated and highly colored manner, presents a picture of manners and morals in that numerous class of modern Germany, which has emancipated itself from the code of the bourgeoisie and apes Bohemia, in a novel called *Wenn wir Frauen erwachen*. A Jewish writer, who by his novels and dramas has been steadily attracting more and more attention, Schalom Asch, has written a story of the recent Russian revolution, *Die Jüngsten*. The far too prolific Georg von Omptada has two books to his credit: *Die Tochter des grossen Georgi*, a story of actor life, and *Der zweite Schuss*, a novel dealing with the problem of honor. Among women novelists, Franziska Mann occupies a place of her own: *Frau Sophie und ihre Kinder*, is a noteworthy example of her sympathetic insight into the woman- and child-soul. Elisabeth Stewart has succeeded in telling with absorbing interest a story of life in a provincial parish fifty years ago: *Un-*

vergessene Menchen. Among the numerous volumes of short stories Carl Hauptmann's *Nächte* is typical for his sympathetic understanding of eccentric characters and unusual conflicts. Arthur Schnitzler's *Masken und Wunder* is admirable for his artistic handling of daring problems. Hermann Hesse's *Umwege* tells of plain people who go a roundabout way to their predestined simple goal. Anna Croissant-Rust delightfully blends humor and pathos in her record of human lives, called *Arche Noah.* But the most charming collection of short tales and sketches of everyday life is Walter Harlan's book entitled *Familienszenen.* There is a rare literary flavor about *Die goldene Fratze,* a volume of short stories by the Swiss writer, Jakob Schaffner, and about Richard Huldschiner's *Narren der Liebe.*

HUMOR. TRAVELS. ESSAYS. The year's best book of humor is Rudolf Presber's volume entitled *Das goldene Lachen.* In the travel books of the German market, America is beginning to pay a more and more important part. Arthur Holitscher's *Amerika-heute und morgen* is a most thoughtful record of experiences and impressions. Kurt Aram entitles his book *Mit hundert Mark nach Amerika.* Alfons Pacquet's *Li* is a fascinating account of travels outside of the tourist's beaten track in Siberia, China, and Japan. A book of clever reflections and keen observations in W. Fred's *Impressionen,* bearing the appropriate sub-title "notes of an itinerant journalist." Alpine literature has received a noteworthy addition in Alfred Steinitzer's sumptuously illustrated book, *Der Alpinismus in Bildern.* A selection of the writings of Ferdinand Gregorovius has been published, called *Wanderjahre in Italien.* Hermann Bahr seems to have collected a multitude of scraps from his workshop in the three books entitled *Essays, Austriaca,* and *Inventur,* which are of varying calibre and interest. Karl Schaffler's *Essays* are rich in æsthetical suggestions. Otto Pniower's *Dichtung und Dichter* is an interesting commentary on contemporaneous literature. Felix Poppenberg's *Maskenzüge* is a most fascinating volume of impressions of men, women, art, and nature.

LITERATURE. Books on literature have been very numerous in the year's output, but few of them are of permanent interest. Karl Bleibtreu has written a *Geschichte der deutchen Nationalliteratur von Goethe's Tode bis zur Gegenwart,* and Georg Witkowski covers about the same ground in *Die Entwicklung der deutschen Literatur seit 1830.* Eduard Engle has written a *Geschichte der französischen Literatur von Anfang bis zur Gegenwart.* Willamowitz-Möllendorf has collaborated with others on a monumental work called *Die griechische und romische Literatur und Sprache.* A posthumous volume by Heinrich Bulthaupt contains his *Literarische Vorträge.* A noteworth addition to Goethe literature is *Goethe und die Antike,* by Ernst Maass. There is also a new revised edition of Georg Witkowski's *Goethe,* and of Johannes Scherr's *Shiller und seine Zeit.*

BIOGRAPHY. MEMOIRS. HISTORY. Psychological interest is mainly responsible for the continual stream of books on Friedrich Hebbel and Heinrich von Kleist. Notable among them are Walter Block-Wunschmann's *Friedrich Hebbel, ein Lebensbuch,* and Julius Hart's *Kleistbuch.* Nietzsche-literature has been increased by Elisabeth Förstar Nietzsche's record of the poet-philosopher's youth: *Der junge Nietzsche,* and by Prof. Richard M. Meyer's work, *Nietzsche, sein leben und seine Warke.* Dr. Emil Reicke presents a sympathetic study of *Malvida von Meysenburg,* the remarkable woman who by her friendship for Herzen, Wagner, Nietzsche, and Romain Rolland, has inscribed herself indelibly in the intellectual annals of the century. An important contribution to Bismarck-literature is Emil Ludwig's *Bismarck,* a remarkable record and interpretation. Noteworthy memoirs are Paul Heyse's *Jugenderinnerungen und Bekenntnisse* and Johannes Trojan's *Erinnerungen.* Additions to the history of Germany are Prof. Wilhelm Stolze's book, *Die Gründung des deutschen Reiches im Jahre 1870,* a book of reminiscences by Sigmund Münz, called *Von Bismarck bis Bülow.* Dr. Bernhard Rogge's recollections: *Bei der Garde* and Dr. Theodor Schiemane's year-book *Deutschland und die grosse Politik anno 1911.* Of new editions must be noted Johannes Scherr's *1848, ein weltgaschichtliches Drama,* and *1870-1, vier Bücher deutscher Geschichte.*

PHILOSOPHY. RELIGION. FOLKLORE. ART., etc. A notable contribution to the literature of philosophy is Dr. Hans Driesch's *Ordnungslehre.* Of the seriousness with which German thinkers seek a new reading of life there are many evidences, among them Dr. Alfred Weber's *Religion und Kultur,* Arthur Bonus's *Religiöse Spannungen,* and Dr. Gottfried Traub's *Staatschristentum oder Volskirche,* and *Ich suchte dich Gott.* Of curious human and historical interest is Dr. Max Kemmerich's book *Aus der Geschichte der menschlichen Dummheit,* dealing with superstitions surviving in parts of Bavaria. An enterprise of great cultural importance is the collection of Norse sagas and stories entitled "Thule," of which the latest volume is a book of Greenland stories by Erich von Mendelssohn: *Grönländer und Färinger Geschichten.* A book which stands perhaps unique in the literature of folklore is Dr. Barthold Rein's volume of well-lore: *Der Brunnen im Volksleben.* Among the numerous books on art are some interpretations combining technical knowledge with literary flavor; foremost among them Julius Meyer-Gräfe's book on *Hogarth,* and his works on the Impressionists, on some English masters, Hans von Marées, Cézanne, Van Gogh and others. Karl Schaffler, one of Germany's ablest critics, is the author of a book on *Max Liebermann.* A volume of unique and timely interest is Franz Feldhaus's *Lionardo der Techniker und Erfinder,* dealing with Lionardo's achievements as a mechanical genius and especially his experiments with flying-machines, in which he anticipated our dirigibles and aeroplanes. An interesting interpretation of the "Upanishads" is presented in a unique form in *Das hohe Ziel der Erkenntniss,* by the late Omar al Raschid Bey, a German scholar naturalized in Turkey. Gustav F. Steffen is a writer on economics, whose work is attracting attention and who in *Die Grundlagen der Soziologie* oners a new conception of this science. Prof. Werner Sombart, whose book *Die Juden und das Wirtschaftsleben,* is being translated into English, created no little excitement by *Die Zukunft der Juden,* in which in the interest of preserving unadulterated the valuable qualities of the Jewish race he declares against intermarriage and assimilation.

NEW EDITIONS AND TRANSLATIONS. New

editions of the German classics are almost too numerous to mention. Those most frequently reëdited are Goethe, Schiller, Kleist, Heine, and Hebbel, but there have also been new editions of Kant, Lessing, Körner, Börne, Holderlin, Brentano, E. T. A. Hoffmann, Immermann, and others. Of the more recent writers those who are available in complete editions are Hermann Conradi, Richard Dehmel, Otto Julius Bierbaum, Detlev von Liliencron, Gerhart Hauptmann, and Arthur Schnitzler. There is a new edition of the Bible revised from Luther's text by Hermann Hesse. There is also a facsimile reprint of the "Bible of Mayence," the "zweiundvierzigzeilige Bibel von Johannes Gutenberg," Proof of the reviving interest in historical documents of the Middle Ages is the new edition of the memoirs of Hans von Schweinichen, a knight-errant of Silesia; *Memorial-Buch der Fahrten und Taten des schlesischen Ritters, Hans von Schweinichen*, covering the latter half of the sixteenth century. Translations from the world's literature are also very numerous. One of the most interesting is the new edition of the *Decameron*, translated by Albert Wesselski and illustrated by reproductions of the woodcuts of the Venice edition of 1492. An edition of the complete works of Poe translated by Theodor and Gisela Etzel is remarkable for the illustrations by Alfred Kubin, whose weird drawings prove him to be a spiritual brother of Poe.

DEATHS. Death has removed Alfred Freiherr von Berger, poet, dramatist and critic, and director of the Burgtheater of Vienna, Felix Dahn, poet and novelist, Josef Ettlinger, critic and founder of the *Literarische Echo* and the *Freie Volksbühne*, Rochus Freiherr von Liliencron, one of the most versatile scholars of Germany, Anton von Perfall, the novelist, Arthur Pfungst, poet and founder of the *Monistenbund*, Albert Träger, poet, and Irma von Troll-Borostyani, novelist and advocate of woman's rights.

GERMAN MUSIC. See MUSIC.

GERMAN NAVY LAW. See NAVAL PROGRESS, *England, General Progress*.

GERMAN NEW GUINEA. A protectorate of Germany including Kaiser-Wilhelms-Land (the northeastern part of New Guinea island) and the Bismarck Archipelago. Officially estimated area, 240,000 square kilometers (92,664 square miles). The native population is estimated at about 530,000; white (January 1, 1911), 723, of whom 578 German. Imports and exports in 1909, 2,666,000 and 2,459,000 marks; in 1910, 3,891,000 and 3,623,000. Of the 1910 imports, 2,915,000 marks were attributed to the Bismarck Archipelago, and of the exports 3,224,000; of the totals, 1,686,000 marks imports were from 2,370,000 marks exports to Germany. Vessels entered (1910), 437, of 408,000 tons. The budget for 1911-12 balanced at 2,183,421 marks (including imperial subvention 759,597); for 1911-13, 2,764,128 (subvention 1,207,543). Governor (1912), Dr. Hall; seat of government (formerly Herbertshöhe), Rabaul, in Neu-Pommern.

Attached to German New Guinea are the other German Pacific dependencies (Caroline, Palau, Mariana, and Marshall islands), except Samoa and Kiaochow. These dependencies have an estimated area of 2572 square kilometers (956 square miles), with about 53,000 inhabitants; whites (January 1, 1911), 320, of whom 194 German. Imports and exports, in 1910, of the East Caroline Islands, 318,000 and 211,000 marks; West Caroline, Palau, and Marianas, 740,000 and 1,453,000; Marshall Islands, 1,297,000 and 9,378,000. Imports of the German Pacific possessions (including Samoa, but excluding Kiaochow), were 65,464,000 marks in 1909 and 69,375,000 in 1910; exports, 54,732,000 and 60,561,000. The German Solomon Islands are included with Kaiser-Wilhelms-Land.

GERMAN NEW GUINEA. See ANTHROPOLOGY.

GERMAN SAMOA. A protectorate of Germany in the South Pacific, consisting of the two largest of the Samoan Islands (Savaii (652.9 square miles) and Upolu (335.5), together with Manono (3.3) and Apolima (1.8); total area, 993.5 square miles. Population, about 37,500; of whom native Samoans number about 34,000; whites (January 1, 1911), 490, of whom 284 German. Imports and exports in 1909, 3,338,000 and 3,022,000 marks; in 1910, 3,462,000 and 3,534,000. The export is almost wholly copra, 3,022,000 marks in 1909 and 3,534,000 in 1910; Cacao, 406,000 and 555,000. The budget for 1911-12 balanced at 932,155 marks; 1912-13, 949,815. The estimates for these years included no imperial subvention. Governor (1912), Dr. Schultze; seat of government, Apia, in Upolu.

GERMAN SOLOMON ISLANDS. A German possession included with Kaiser-Wilhelms-Land. It includes the island of Bougainville.

GERMAN SOUTHWEST AFRICA. A protectorate of Germany between Angola and the Cape Province. Area, as officially estimated, 835,100 square kilometers (322,432 square miles). Colored population, about 82,000; whites (January 1, 1911), 13,962, of whom 11,140 Germans. The most important industry is stock-raising; livestock in 1910 included 121,139 cattle, 343,989 sheep, and 327,095 goats; in 1911, sheep for shearing 32,200, sheep for slaughter 381,000. Valuable diamond fields are worked in the neighborhood of Lüderitzbucht; diamond output in the year ended March 31, 1911, 814,322 carats. Imports and exports in thousands of marks: 1905, 23,632 and 216; 1907, 32,396 and 1616; 1909, 34,713 and 22,071; 1910, 44,344 and 34,692. Leading exports in 1909 and 1910: Diamonds, 15,026 and 26,869 thousand marks; copper ore, 4655 and 5697; lead, 982 and 861; hides, 135 and 145. In 1909 and 1910, imports from Germany, 26,390,000 and 34,455,000 marks; exports to Germany, 18,158,000 and 28,674,000. Railways at the end of 1911: Otavi railway, 671 kilometers; Swakopmund-Windhuk railway, 382; North-South railway, 311 (and 195 under construction); Lüderitzbucht railway, 545; 1909 kilometers (1186 miles), in operation and 195 kilometers (121 miles) under construction. Early in 1912 the line between Windhoek and Keetmanshoop was completed, connecting the Northern and Southern systems of railway. Post offices, 68. The budget for 1911-12 balanced at 43,998,022 marks, including 11,415,858 marks imperial subvention and 9,000,000 marks loans; for 1912-13, 46,019,312 marks, including 13,828,346 marks subvention and 9,000,000 marks loan. Governor (1912), Dr. Seitz; seat of government, Windhuk.

GERMANY. The German Empire, *das Deutsche Reich*, extending from France to Russia, consists of twenty-five federated states and the imperial territory (Reichsland) of Alsace-Lorraine. Capital, Berlin.

AREA AND POPULATION. The area in square kilometers and equivalent square miles, according to the most recent calculations, and the population, according to the census of December 1, 1910, are shown by states in the following table (*k* kingdom, *g* grand duchy, *d* duchy, *p* principality, *ft* free town, r Reichsland):

	Sq. km.	Sq. mi.	Pop. '10
Prussia (k)	348,779 9	134,663.9	40,165,219
Bavaria (k)	75,870.2	29.293.5	6,887,291
Württemberg (k)	19,507.3	7,531.8	2,437,574
Saxony (k)	14,992.9	5,788.8	4,806,661
Baden (g)	15,070.3	5,818.6	2,142,833
Mecklenburg-Schwerin (g)	13,126.9	5,068.3	639,958
Hesse (g)	7,688.4	2,969.5	1,282,051
Oldenburg (g)	6,429.1	2,482 3	483,042
Brunswick (d)	3,672.0	1,417.8	494,339
Saxe-Weimar (g)	3,610.0	1,393.8	417,149
Mecklenburg-Strelitz (g)	2,929.5	1,131.1	106,442
Saxe-Meiningen (d)	2,468,3	952.8	278,762
Anhalt (d)	2,299.4	887.8	331,128
Saxe-Coburg-Gotha (d)	1,976.8	763,2	257,177
Saxe-Altenburg (d)	1,323.5	511.0	216,128
Lippe (p)	1,215.2	469.4	150,937
Waldeck (p)	1,121.0	432.8	61,707
Schwarzburg-Rudolstadt (p)	941.0	363.0	100,702
Schwarzburg-Sondershausen (p)	862.2	332.9	89,917
Reuss Younger Line (p)	826.7	319.2	152,752
Hamburg (f t)	414.5	160.0	1,014.664
Schaumburg-Lippe (p)	340.3	131.4	46,652
Reuss Elder Line (p)	316.3	122.1	72,769
Lübeck (f t)	297.7	114.9	116.599
Bremen (f t)	256.4	99.0	299,526
Alsace-Lorraine (r)	14,521.8	5,606.9	1,874,014
Total	540,857.6	208,825.2	64,925,993

Total 1820	26,294,000	1880	45,234,061
Total 1850	35,397,000	1890	49,428,470
Total 1860	37,747,000	1900	56,367,178
Total 1870	40,818,000	1905	60,641,000

Of the population present in 1910, 30,040,-166 were males, and 32,885,827 females. On June 30, 1911, the estimated population of the empire was 65,429,000, and of the Zoolgebiet 65,671,000; 1912, 66,303,000 and 66,547,000. In 1871, the year of the empire's establishment, the population was 41,058,792, and the average annual increase to 1880 was 1.08 per cent.; from 1880 to 1890, 0.89; from 1890 to 1900, 1.31; and from 1900 to 1910, 1.41. In 1871 the population per square kilometer was 75.9 (196.6 per square mile); in 1910, 1200 (310.8).

The foreign population at the 1910 census was 1,259,873 (716,994 males, 542,879 females), of whom 634,983 Austrians, 144,175 Dutch, 137,697 Russians, 104,204 Italians, 68,257 Swiss, 32,079 Hungarians, 26,233 Danes, 19,140 French, 18,319 British, and 17,572 Americans.

Evangelicals numbered 39,991,421 (61.6 per cent.); Roman Catholics, 23,821,453 (36.7); other Christians, 283,946; Jews, 615,021; others, 214,152.

Communal population of the larger cities (including the military) according to the census of December 1, 1910: Berlin, 2,071,257; (Greater Berlin, 3,710,000); Hamburg, 932,-116; Leipzig, 626,267; Munich, 608,375; Dresden, 551,697; Cologne, 516,527; Breslau, 514,-765; Frankfort-on-the-Main, 414,576; Düsseldorf, 358,728; Nuremberg, 333,142; Charlottenburg, 305,978; Hannover, 302,375; Essen, 294,-653;; Chemnitz, 287,807; Stuttgart, 286,218; Magdeburg, 279,629; Bremen, 247,437; Königsberg, 245,994; Stettin, 237,419; Neukölln (formerly Rixdorf), 237,289; Duisburg, 229,483; Dortmund, 214,226; Kiel, 211,627; Mannheim, 202,115; Halle, 180,843; Strassburg, 178,891; Berlin-Schöneberg, 172,823; Altona, 172,628; Danzig, 170,337; Elberfeld, 170,195; Gelsenkirchen, 169,513; Barmen, 169,214; Posen, 156,-691; Aachen, 156,143; Cassel, 153,196.

In 1910 the marriage rate per thousand inhabitants was 7.7, birth, 30.7, death, 17.1, living births, 29.8; stillbirths, 2.9 per cent.; illegitimate births, 9.1 per cent. Movement of the population from 1907 to 1910:

	1907	1908	1909	1910
Marriages	503,964	500,620	494,127	496,396
Births*	2,060,973	2,076,660	2,038,357	1,982,836
Stillbirths	61,040	61,607	60,079	58,057
Deaths*	1,178,349	1,197,098	1,154,296	1,103,723

* Including stillbirths.

In spite of the fact that the average annual increase in the first decade of the century (1.41 per cent.) was greater than in the preceding decade (1.31), and that the death rate declined from 19.0 in 1907 to 17.1 in 1910, it is believed that the rate of population increase is no longer advancing; the marriage rate declined from 8.1 in 1907 to 7.7 in 1910, and the birth rate from 33.2 to 30.7. The movement in the death rate is similar to that of other countries where modern medical science is widely applied. The movement in the marriage rate, and more particularly in the birth rate, reflects a condition normal in a population tending rapidly cityward. Also, in a civilized community the birth rate shows, within certain limits, an inverse relation to the diffusion of artificial refinements. The falling birth rate, long conspicuous in France, is just beginning to be noticeable in Germany.

In 1910 German emigrants numbered 25,531; in 1911, 22,690, of whom 18,900 to the United States, 511 to Canada, 363 to Brazil, and 2554 to other American countries.

AGRICULTURE. In 1907, 27.95 per cent. of the population were supported by agriculture, against 34.9 per cent. in 1895. The area harvested, in thousands of hectares, and the yield in metric quintals, in 1911 and 1912, with yield per hectare in 1911, are shown below:

	Hectares 1911	Hectares 1912	Quintals 1911	Quintals 1912	Qs. ha.
Wheat	1,974	1,926	40,663,350	43,606,240	20.6
Rye	6,136	6,268	108,661,160	115,982,890	17.7
Barley	1,585	1,590	31,599,150	34,819,740	19.9
Oats	4,328	4,387	77,041,010	85,201,830	17.8

Harvest area of potatoes in 1910 and 1911, 3,296,219 and 3,321,479 ha., yield 434,683,950 and 343,742,250 qs.; meadow hay, 5,965,017 and 5,934,798 ha., yield 28,250,115 and 19,975,324 metric tons; vines, 112,506 and 110,053 ha., yield 846,139 and 2,922,886 hectoliters of must (2,020,620 in 1909). Tobacco production in 1910 was 288,542 qs.; in 1911, 292,047; hops, 204,110 and 106,277. The sugar beet is an important crop. For Prussia, the harvest area in 1911 and 1912 was 350,287 and 426,327 ha.; yield, 59,961,440 and 129,632,150 qs.

Latest livestock statistics available are for

1907: Horses, 4,345,047; mules and asses, 11,-291; cattle, 20,630,544; sheep, 7,703,710; swine, 22,146,532; goats, 3,533,970; fowls, 77,103,045. Slaughter in 1911: Oxen, 559,698; bulls, 424,-369; cows, 1,768,949; calves over three months, 982,284; calves up to three months, 4,577,982; sheep, 2,232,187; swine, 18,541,694; goats, 493,-566; horses, 151,529; dogs, 6553.

See AGRICULTURAL EDUCATION.

MINERALS AND METALS. Included in the figures for Germany's mineral and metal production are those of the Grand Duchy of Luxemburg. The following table shows the principal mining products and the total of all mining products, in thousands of metric tons, valued in thousands of marks:

	1909		1910	
	1000 t.	1000 m.	1000 t.	1000 m.
Coal	148,788.1	1,519,222	152,827.8	1,526,604
Lignite ...	68,657.6	178,980	69,547.3	178,618
Rock salt..	1,369.8	6,242	1,424.1	6,440
Pot. salts..	7,042.0	81,655	8,311.7	91,357
Iron ore....	25,504.5	97,981	28,709.7	106,809
Zinc ore ..	723.6	42,834	718.3	45,185
Lead ore ..	159.9	14,462	148.5	14,064
Copper ore	798.6	22,967	926.0	23,406
Total	253,572.7	1,980,469	263,167.8	2,008.708

As compared with 2,008,708 marks in 1910, the total value of mining products in 1905 was 1,417,719,000; in 1901, 1,313,873,000; in 1891, 775,701. The output of salts in 1910 (exclusive of rock salt and potash salts) was 1,769,500 tons, valued at 115,497 marks (of which common salt 669,100 tons, 19,262,000 marks, and potassium chloride, 741,300 tons, 72,984,000 marks).

Important reduction products, in thousands of metric tons, valued in thousands of marks:

	1919		1910	
	1000 t.	1000 m.	1000 t.	1000 m.
Pig iron	12,644.9	691,564	14,793.6	802,851
Zinc	219.8	94,972	221.4	99,399
Lead	167.9	43,991	159.9	42,042
Copper	31.2	38,655	34.9	42,389
Silver	.....	28,137	....	30,654
Gold	.....	14,145	....	12,919
Sulph. acid.	1,434.7	41,349	1,616.3	44,344

COMMERCE. Imports for consumption and exports of domestic products are shown below in thousands of marks:

	1909	1910	1911
Imports:			
Merchandise	8,520,125	8,934,126	9,544,777
Coin and bullion.....	340,285	375,866	266,845
Total	8,860,410	8,309,992	9,811,622
Exports:			
Merchandise	6,592,242	7,474,661	8,101,812
Coin and bullion.....	266,451	169,537	118,090
Total	6,858,693	7,644,198	8,219,902

Principal imports of merchandise for consumption in 1911, in millions of marks (figures in parentheses for 1910): Cereals, 1181.3 (887.0): cotton, 643.8 (601.2); hides and skins, 643.8 (545.2); wool, 485.0 (504.3); chemicals and drugs, 325.8 (205.1); timber, etc., 305.5 (288.1); coal, 265.6 (243.6); coffee, 251.7 (176.6); copper, 233.5 (216.2); live animals, 228.1 (263.9); fruits, 212.6 (176.2); silk, 207.0 (181.7); rubber and gutta-percha, 193.8 (296.6); iron, 190.0 (170.9); eggs, 171.4 (163.2); copra, etc., 164.3 (170.9); wheaten products, 150.6 (102.8); butter, 127.6 (90.5); leaf tobacco, 116.5 (104.1); woolen yarn, 113.8 (119.5); fish, 113.0 (106.9); oil cake, 104.3 (92.8); flax and hemp, 99.2 (70.2); cotton yarn, 98.9 (102.1); linseed, 94.4 (100.8); tin, 92.1 (70.5); iron manufactures, 89.3 (81.7); rice, 88.2 (80.3); animal fats, 87.7 (69.4); silk goods, 80.6 (81.5); machinery, 71.0 (64.3); wine, 68.5 (71.6); furs, etc., 67.1 (59.5); jute, 62.2; zinc, 60.4; lead, 55.6; cacao, 55.5; cotton goods, 51.5 (56.5); petroleum, 50.1 (56.8).

Principal exports of domestic produce in 1911, in millions of marks (figures in parentheses for 1910): Iron manufactures, 1014.2 (810.3); machinery, 544.4 (459.9); chemicals and drugs, 505.0 (450.3); coal, 507.8 (444.6); cotton goods, 391.5 (374.8); cereals, 291.8 (314.7); woolen goods, 262.7 (263.3) dyes, colors, etc., 250.6 (246.3); paper, 227.7 (217.4); sugar, 227.7 (196.3); electrical apparatus, 208.0 (218.2); leather, 205.6 (192.0); silk goods, 201.8 (184.1); hides and skins, 164.4 (149.1); ships, 160.3 (123.8); copper manufactures, 150.0 (140.0); furs, etc., 137.2 (167.9); wool, 116.6 (115.2); apparel, 112.5 (103.8); glass and glassware, 108.4 (99.2); books, maps, etc., 98.4 (97.1); pottery, 95.7 (85.3); toys, 90.6 (86.1); woolen yarn, 88.1 (77.5); leather manufactures, 81.7 (78.5); cotton, 78.1 (87.7); musical instruments, 72.3 (62.8); wooden manufactures, 63.2; cotton yarn, 59.2; gold and silver manufactures, 52.9 (49.6).

Special trade in merchandise with countries commercially most important, in millions of marks:

	1910	1911	1910	1911
Russia	1322.2	1562.8	537.3	612.4
United States	1187.6	1343 5	632.7	639.3
United Kingdom .	766.6	808.8	1102.0	1139.7
Austria Hungary .	759.2	739.1	826.6	917.8
France	508.8	524 4	543.4	598.6
British India	404.0	440.3	89.8	99 5
Argentina	357.2	369.9	240.2	253 9
Belgium	325.6	340.0	390.7	412.7
Brazil	278.9	320.0	121.7	152.0
British Australia..	267.9	248.2	63.3	79 7
Netherlands	258 5	297.7	498.7	533 1
Dutch East Indies.	187.5	184.4	49.8	611.1
Switzerland	173 9	179.6	452.6	482.4
Sweden	163.8	183.0	190.5	191.6
Denmark	158 1	180.2	224.7	218.0
Chile	154.6	158.3	64.8	83.4
Spain	140.2	164.1	71.6	85 4
British W. Africa	108.8	106.7	15.2	13.7
China	94.7	103.3	66.5	71 8
Egypt	93.6	99 5	34.2	42.8
Rumania	68.9	107.8	65.7	91.4
Norway	49.7	54.1	119.9	124 3
Finland	26.2	34.6	73.8	75.4
Turkey	67.1	70.0	104.7	112 5
Mexico	23.7	31.0	46.9	45.1

Imports from the German protectorates in 1910 and 1911, in millions of marks: 49.9 and 43.1; exports thereto, 49.0 and 50.3.

SHIPPING. Entries and clearances, with registered tonnage, in 1910:

	Entered		Cleared	
	Vessels	1000 tons	Vessels	1000 tons
German	86,810	17,766	87,387	17,967
Foreign	24,987	12,164	25,184	12,236
Total	111,797	29,931	112,571	30,202
	Steamers ent.		Steamers cl.	
German	57,008	15,289	57,087	15,531
Foreign	15,367	11,231	15,458	11,274
Total	72,375	26,521	72,545	26,804

The merchant marine, January 1, 1912, included 4732 sea-going vessels, of 3,023,725 tons, of which 2009, of 2,513,666 tons were steamers. With Hamburg was registered a tonnage of 1,676,326; Bremen, 893,387; Prussia, 312,713; Lübeck, 50,455; Oldenburg, 54,220; Mecklenburg, 36,554.

COMMUNICATIONS. Railways in operation March 31, 1912 (normal gauge, narrow gauge, and totals in kilometers):

	Norm. g.	Nar. g.	Total
Owned or operated by:			
Prussia and Hesse	38,119	240	38,359
Bavaria	7,924	115	8,039
Saxony	2,814	508	3,322
Württemberg	1,917	101	2,088
Baden	1,743	28	1,771
Mecklenburg	1,099	....	1,099
Oldenburg	652	....	652
Prussia (Royal Military Ry.)	71	....	71
Imperial government in Alsace-Lorraine	2,022	78	2,100
Government railways	56,431	1,070	57,501
Private railways	3,561	1,145	4,706
Total in 1912	59,992	2,215	62,207
Total in 1911	59,259	2,178	61,437
Total in 1909	58,537	2,087	60,624

The foregoing totals for 1912, in miles:

Government railways	35,065	665	35,729
Private railways	2,213	711	2,924
Total	37,278	1,376	38,654

During 1912 the Berlin Elevated Railways were being extended from Christianstrasse to Weserstrasse, a distance of 5½ miles. In Leipzig the new station was under construction and a portion was opened on May 1. It is to serve as a union station for all lines centring at this point and is to be put in service for that purpose in 1913. Extensions and additions to the lines connecting the German and Belgian railways were opened on July 1, the new lines aggregating 87 miles in length.

Telegraphs are owned by the imperial government, except in Bavaria and Württemberg; these kingdoms, under certain limitations, operate their own telegraphs and posts. Total telegraph offices (1911), 46,444 (45,116 in 1910); line, 228,560 kilometers (224,794); wire, 706,248 kilometers (676,091). Total post offices (1911), 40,987 (40,816 in 1910).

FINANCE. The monetary unit is the mark, worth 23.821 cents. The imperial budget adopted for the year ended March 31, 1912 (law of April 7, 1911), balanced at 2,924,790,000 marks (including extraordinary revenue and expenditure balancing at 216,975,817 marks). The budget for the year ended March 31, 1913 (law of May 28, 1912) balanced at 2,886,135,087 marks (including extraordinary revenue and expenditure balancing at 134,473,100 marks). Of the extraordinary estimated revenue for 1912-13, loans accounted for 130,674,439 marks; of the extraordinary estimated expenditure, 82,570,000 marks were for the navy. Larger sources of estimated ordinary revenue, 1912-13: Customs, excise, stamps, etc., 1,734,570,093 marks (customs 660,308,000, spirits excise 195,046,000, sugar 143,500,000, beer 122,100,000, stamps of the empire 187,741,500); posts and telegraphs, 791,381,000; railways, 141,780,000; matricular contributions of the several states (exclusive of their contributions from spirits excise), 51,940,794 (Prussia 33,498,900). Larger estimated expenditures, including ordinary (permanent and transitory) and extraordinary, 1912-13: Military administration, 827,795,405 marks (against 815,670,790 estimated for 1911-12); posts and telegraphs, 714,009,235 (684,696,385); administration of the navy, 470,433,623 (458,033,086); debts of the empire, 240,032,521 (285,748,054); pensions, 143,411,248 (153,798,446); interior, 123,017,171 (140,843,167); administration of railways, 124,343,651 (122,499,005).

In October, 1911, the interest-bearing debt of the empire was 4,823,656,700 marks, having decreased 72,976,800 marks since 1910. Non-interest-bearing debt: Treasury bonds, 300,000,000 (having increased 54,000,000 since 1910); paper money, 120,000,000. Total debt, 5,243,656,700 marks (the decrease from 1910 being 18,976,800). A war fund of 120,000,000 marks in gold is kept at Spandau.

ARMY. Under the terms of the Quinquennial law, voted by the Reichstag in March, 1911, increases in the strength of the German army were being made with the idea of securing a peace strength of 515,221 in 1915-16, this being an increase of 9428 over the law of 1905. On March 22, 1912, the Reichstag, however, took up proposals for a still further increase of the army and its reorganization, which became law on June 14. This law of 1912 increases the peace strength to 544,211, to be distributed as follows: Prussia, 420,939; Bavaria, 60,351; Saxony, 41,625; Württemburg, 21,296. Adding non-commissioned officers and the one year volunteers this would give a total strength of over 658,200 men. The new law provided for the formation of two army corps (to be known as the 20th and 21st) with headquarters in East Prussia and Alsace-Lorraine respectively and the creation of 18 new infantry battalions and large increases to the machine-gun companies. Various steps in the reorganization were to be accelerated and the two new corps were formally constituted on October 1, 1912. As a result, at the end of the year the German army was organized in 25 army corps and 3 Bavarian corps, and on October 1, 1912, consisted of 648 battalions of infantry, 510 squadrons of cavalry, 633 batteries of field and horse artillery, 42 battalions of foot artillery, 31 battalions of pioneers, 18 of transportation troops, and 25 battalions of train. During the following two years it was proposed to increase this organization to 651 battalions, 516 squadrons, 633 batteries, 49 battalions of foot artillery, 33 battalions of pioneers, 18 of transportation troops, and 25 of train. Service in the German army is compulsory, every citizen with certain exceptions being liable for service from his 19th to his 45th year, spending 7 years in the regular army, either with the colors or in its reserve, 5 years in the first levy of the Landwehr, 10 years in the second levy and finally with the Landwehr home defense army, until the end of his 55th year. This general plan is modified in the case of the cavalry and the horse artillery, which requires 3 years of uninterrupted service with the colors instead of 2 as in other arms of the service, while the Ersatz Reserve is maintained from the surplus of recruits over those required for the regular army.

From October 1, 1912, when the reorganization became effective, the effective strength of the German army was 655,714 men, of whom 27,037 were officers, 2361 medical officers, 810 veterinary surgeons, 1154 paymasters, 2 band inspectors, 1193 armorers, 92,347 under officers and 531,004 privates. The men were distributed into four contingents, 412,346 being Prussians, 39,834 Saxons, 20,244 Württembürgers and 58,580 Bavarians. The number of horses was 126,480. These figures may be compared with those of the 1911 budget, which provided for 626,489 men, of whom 507,253 were privates, 25,650 officers, and 86,453 under officers. The number of horses was 118,246. See MILITARY PROGRESS.

NAVY. Number and displacement of warships of 1500 or more tons, and of torpedo craft of 50 or more tons, built and building, December 1, 1912: Dreadnoughts (battleships having a main battery of all big guns, that is, 11 inches or more in calibre): built, 10 of 212,380 tons; building, 7 of 172,330 tons. Predreadnoughts (battleships of about 10,000 or more tons, whose main batteries are of more than one calibre): built, 20 of 242,800 tons; building, none. Coast-defense vessels (including smaller battleships and monitors): built, 3 of 12,203 tons; building, none. Battle cruisers (armored cruisers having guns of largest calibre in main battery): built, 3 of 64,364 tons; building, 3 of 75,000 tons. Armored cruisers: built, 9 of 94,245 tons; building, none. Cruisers (unarmored warships of 1500 or more tons): built, 68 of 135,636 tons; building, 5 of 27,065 tons. Torpedo-boat destroyers: built, 119 of 63,014 tons; building, 12 of 8280 tons. Torpedo boats: built, 9 of 1600 tons; building, none. Submarines: built, 26 of 11,740 tons; building, 6 of 3600 tons. Total tonnage: built, 837,982; building, 286,275. Excluded from the foregoing: Ships over 20 years old, unless reconstructed and rearmed within five years; torpedo craft over 15 years old; transports, colliers, repair ships, torpedo depot ships, and other auxiliaries.

Of the ten dreadnoughts built, two were completed in 1909, two in 1910, three in 1911, and three in 1912; those completed in 1912 are the *Oldenburg* (launched June 30, 1910), the *Kaiser* (March 22, 1911), and the *Friedrich der Grosse* (June 10, 1911). The 1909 and 1910 dreadnoughts carry twelve 11-inch guns, but the three completed in 1911 and the *Oldenburg* carry twelve 12-inch guns. Each of these eight ships is able to fire only eight of the twelve big guns on either broadside. The *Kaiser* and the *Friedrich der Grosse* carry ten 12-inch guns, but their distribution permits all to fire on either broadside (like the British *Neptune* class). Of the seven dreadnoughts building at the end of 1912, three are sister ships to the *Kaiser* and will be completed in 1913; these three are the *Kaiserin* (launched November 11, 1911), the *Prinzregent Luitpold* (February 17, 1912), and the *König Albert* (April 27, 1912).

The three battle cruisers built are the *Von der Tann*, the *Moltke*, and the *Goeben;* the latter, launched March 28, 1911, and completed in 1912, was reported to have attained a speed on May 20 of 30.5 knots. A fourth battle cruiser, the *Seydlitz*, was launched March 30, 1912, and will probably be completed in 1913.

Reported officers and men in 1912, 68,122, including two admirals of the fleet, four admirals, 13 vice-admirals, 21 rear-admirals and 335 captains and commanders. See NAVAL PROGRESS and BATTLESHIPS.

GOVERNMENT. The executive authority is vested in the king of Prussia under the title of German emperor. In 1912 the emperor was William II., who was born January 27, 1859, and succeeded to the throne June 15, 1888. Heir-apparent, Prince Frederick William, born May 6, 1882. The imperial ministers act under the general supervision of the imperial chancellor, who is appointed by the emperor without reference to the political majority of the legislative body and is directly responsible to him. The legislature consists of the Bundesrath (58 members chosen by the governments of the several states) and the Reichstag (397 members elected for five years by popular vote). Imperial chancellor (and Prussian premier) in 1912, Theobald von Bethmann-Hollweg (from July, 1909). The imperial ministers, or secretaries of state, were: Alfred von Kiderlin-Waechter (died December 30, 1912); interior, Klemens Delbrück; navy, Grand Admiral Alfred von Tirpitz; justice, Hermann Lisco; treasury, Dr. Kühn; posts and telegraphs, Reinhold Kraetke, colonies, Wilhelm Solf.

HISTORY

NATIONALIZATION. On February 8, the federal council adopted a new nationalization bill, whose chief purpose was to render the loss of German nationality more difficult and its recovery easier. Under existing law a German subject lost his nationality after ten years' residence abroad unless his name was placed on the consular registers. The new law provided that German nationality should not be lost unless the German subject becomes naturalized in a foreign country or fails in his military obligations in Germany. A national defense league (*Wehrverein*) similar in purpose to the navy league and devoted to the development of the army was established in Berlin, on January 28, under the leadership of General Keim.

THE ELECTIONS. The attitude of the government was distinctly set forth on the eve of the elections. It declared that the tasks before the new Reichstag were to continue the social policy of the government and to maintain the army and navy in a state of the highest efficiency. The Social Democratic party having proved itself an obstacle to these ends was a peril to the country and ought to be defeated. On the other hand, the Social Democrats were regarded as the party of peace and their triumph was hoped for by many as a check on any aggressive tendency and as an aid to a better understanding between Germany and the other foreign powers. Nevertheless, the Socialists were influenced by the rising tide of nationalism and there was no sign of the bitter and unconditional hostility toward armaments that had formerly been noticeable. The Social Democracy of late years has been more and more inclined to compromise under the influence of the movement known as Revisionism, and there was a tendency for the National Liberals, the Socialists, the South German Populists, and the Prussian Radicals to draw together in a great coalition against the "Blue-Black" government, with the general object of securing a wider democracy. The Blue-Black *bloc*, which had ruled parliament for three years, was criticised for its policy of protectionism and reaction and for exploiting the country in the interests of the Agrarians and Conservatives at the expense of the small manufacturers, merchants, tradesmen, and working people. The constant increase in the cost of living was attributed largely to the prohibitive duties on agricultural imports. The Moroccan crisis of 1911 made a deep impression on the mind of the electors. On the one hand, the government was condemned for having brought the nation to the verge of war without its knowledge. In many quarters this heightened the force of the demand for giving the representatives of the people a voice in foreign affairs. On the other hand, the Moroccan affair was attributed less to the fault of the government than to the unwarrantable interference of Great Britain. Anglophobia prevailed among the middle classes, while among the Prussian Conservatives, and the Right Wing of the National Liberals and the Pan-Germans there was constant talk of the "dog-in-the-manger" attitude of Great Britain. Observers declared that at no time in recent years, not even during the Boer War, was there such violent hatred of England in Germany. In general, it was not expected that the elections would result in any change in the policy of armaments, but it was thought that they might, in the long run, effect some constitutional improvement tending to restraint of the government and its Conservative supporters in its foreign policy. The movement for the curtailment of *Junker* leadership in imperial affairs and for increased parliamentary control over them was especially strong throughout the southern German states, where the Liberals and Radicals both worked toward this end. As to the Catholic Centre, it was weakened somewhat in popular support by the resentment of the Protestants against the recent course of the Vatican, notably in the "Borromæus Encyclical," the anti-modernist oath imposed on priests and professors, and the decree of October, 1911, *Motu Proprio*, which denied civil jurisdiction over ecclesiastics.

The elections were held on January 12. Second ballots were taken on January 19, 20 and 25. Complete returns, according to the revised figures, were as follows (the figures in parentheses indicating the losses or gains of the respective parties, compared with the old Reichstag): Centre 90 (loss 13); Conservatives, 45 (loss 13); Free Conservatives, 13 (loss 12); Socialists, 110 (gain 57); National Liberals, 44 (loss 7); Radicals, 41 (loss 8); Poles, 18 (loss 2); Anti-Semites, 11 (loss 10). The remaining 25 seats were divided among other small party groups. The enormous gain for the Socialists greatly exceeded expectations, the most sanguine prophecies looking only to 100 or 105 seats. Throughout the empire they received 4,238,000 votes, an increase of more than a million over the last elections. They thus became the most important party in the Reichstag. The Centre received 2,012,900, a loss of 166,753; the National Liberals 1,671,297, a gain of 34,249; the Radicals 1,556,549, a gain of 322,614; the Conservatives (combined) 1,515,-003. The Blue-Black *bloc* composed of the Centre and Conservatives could no longer be relied upon by the government as a sufficient support. It was thenceforth necessary to reinforce it from the groups of the Left, as for example, the Radicals or National Liberals. The election showed a tendency to align parties more distinctly according to the issues of reaction and progress. On the one hand were the forces representing modern democratic advance, and on the other, the conservative element, supported by the powerful bureaucratic agrarian and financial interests. One side was composed of the Socialists, Radicals, and National Liberals; the other of the different Conservative bodies, the Roman Catholic Centre, and the Poles, and other small groups that usually support the Centre. It was evident that henceforth the *bloc* must be supplemented by recruits from the Right Wing of the National Liberals. The blow at the Centre was especially severe, for they not only lost in numbers, but suffered serious diminution of prestige from their defeat in Cologne.

SIGNIFICANCE OF THE ELECTIONS. The chief result of the elections was a change in the balance of power in the Reichstag, preparing the way for a *bloc* of the parties of the Left, though a weak one. For several years public men of progressive tendencies in Germany have believed that the only way of withstanding the reactionary parties was by an alliance of Liberals and Socialists. But all attempts to bring this about were thwarted by party jealousies. The late Dr. Theodor Barth, editor of *The Nation*, toiled incessantly and with great ability to unite the parties of the Left, but his efforts were not successful. During the last two years, however, political events tended to force the parties of the Left together in self-defense. The coalition of the Centre and Conservatives caused a rejection of the succession duties, and the fall of von Bülow. The Liberals and Socialists were agreed in theory on the question of the succession duties, and both sections of the Liberals, namely, the Liberal Democrats and the National Liberals, finding the government coalition against them, naturally were inclined to a Socialist alliance. The Liberals and Socialists were also in accord on the questions of Prussian electoral reform, customs reform, necessary changes in the constitution, and, in general, as to measures of a progressive tendency. A Socialist Liberal alliance, moreover, was shown to be practicable in the case of the Grand Duchy of Baden, where for several years the two parties had acted together with success. At the 1912 elections, therefore, the Liberals and Socialists went to the polls with strong determination to defeat the Blue-Black *bloc*. At the first ballot they did not join upon common candidates, but left the way open to an alliance later. At the second ballot they joined forces under the rallying cry "A solid front against the Right," and for the first time proved by their success that solidification of the parties of the Left was possible. This demonstration of the power of the progressive element in German politics made a strong impression upon political observers.

BAVARIAN ELECTIONS. The elections of February 5 for the Landtag were another indication of the growing strength of the parties of the Left. In the preceding Landtag the Clericals of Centre had an overwhelming majority of 98 votes out of 163. This vote was supplemented by the 16 votes of the Conservatives and Agrarians. The Liberals and Socialists formed a direct electoral alliance, and, as in the elections for the Reichstag, bent all their energies to overthrowing the parties of the Right. Their efforts were so far successful as to cut down materially the reactionary majority. The figures were as follows: Centre, 86 (formerly 98); Conservatives and Agrarians, 4 (formerly 16); Liberals, 37 (formerly 26); Socialists, 30 (formerly 22); Agrarian League, 6 (formerly 3). On the eve of the elections the ministry resigned, but the prince regent deferred his acceptance of the resignation. Since it was known that the elections had so seriously cut down the Clerical majority, the prince regent summoned Baron von Hertling to form a new cabinet. In this ministry none of the members of the former ministry held office. This change attracted much attention as indicating for the first time a recognition on the part of the German government of a parliamentary régime. Hitherto in Bavaria, as well as in other German states, the ministers were regarded as officers of state like any others, and quite independent of the wishes of the majority in parliament. The change in the cabinet after the elections was regarded by many as breaking the tradition in that it substituted for the former ministry, which was the old-fashioned ministry of functionaries, a new ministry under the leader of the parliamentary majority.

PARLIAMENT. The new Reichstag was opened on February 7. In a speech from the throne the chancellor declared it to be the aim of his policy to maintain the order of the empire and state unhampered, improve the general welfare and increase and strengthen the prestige of the nation. He referred to the important measures adopted for a whole generation to meet the needs of social improvement, and said that the same social spirit must continue to control legislation. He declared that the finances of the empire had reached a more stable footing. Bills for the maintenance and the strengthening of the military and land forces would be presented. He pointed to the recent agreement with France as a fresh proof of the readiness of Germany to settle international disputes amicably. The Reichstag was adjourned on May 22 to meet at the end of November. Its chief work during the first session was the voting of the defense bills. (See paragraph *Defense Bills.*) There was no opposition to them on principle save on the part of the Social Democrats, but the majority was divided on the question of providing the financial means. The increases called for an expenditure of 150,000,000 marks annually on the average for a period of five years. Herr Wermuth, secretary for the treasury, demanded that new revenues be provided to meet these new expenditures. On this question the alignment of parties was precisely what it had been in June, 1909, when the rejection of the succession tax had overthrown the von Bülow government. The Liberals opposed any tax that would fall upon the mass of the population, such as taxes on consumption or on the means of transportation, and demanded taxes on acquired wealth and especially on successions. The Conservatives, supported by the Centre, opposed a succession tax in any form. The majority, comprising Socialists, Liberals, and National Liberals, were solidly in favor of a succession tax as the only solution of the problem. The Centre, however, proposed a means of evading the difficulty. They argued that it was not necessary to create new sources of revenue except for a trifling fraction of the expenditures, since under the able administration of the finance minister, Herr Wermuth, the budget excess for this year would be sufficient. This view finally prevailed, despite the vigorous protest of Herr Wermuth, who pointed out that the excess of one or even two years should not be taken as proof that the following years would show the same favorable balance. Upon the adoption of this policy, Herr Wermuth resigned and was succeeded by Herr Kuehn, the under secretary. Specifically, the plan proposed to meet the new military and naval expenditures provisionally out of the current budget surplus and to cover any deficit by abolishing the rebate duty on spirits. This arrangement was not acceptable to the Liberals and a compromise was reached just before the close of the session, whereby it was provided that a law imposing a general tax on acquired wealth, "which shall take account of the different forms of such wealth," should be presented to the Reichstag before April 30, 1913, and that six months after it went into effect the reduction of the consumption duty on sugars contemplated by the law of July 15, 1909, was to become operative. It was added, however, that this reduction was to go into effect "at the latest on October 1, 1916." The lowering of the sugar duty, which was a tax on consumption, was desired by the Liberals, who of course also favored a tax on acquired wealth, but the wording of the resolution left the way open to long delays. In effect it guaranteed nothing, and made it possible to defer the reduction of the sugar duty till October 1, 1916. The Liberals introduced a resolution demanding that the project for a succession tax established in 1909 should go into effect on January 1, 1913. This the government accepted, but declared that it would give the previous proposal the precedence. The army and navy bills and the spirits bill were finally passed. Such was the situation at the close of the session. It was expected that the fiscal problem, which for three years had been the chief subject before the Reichstag, would form the main business of the autumn session.

Toward the end of the spring session the Kaiser's Strassburg speech, in which he was reported to have threatened to revoke the new constitution of Alsace-Lorraine if matters did not mend (see below paragraph *Alsace-Lorraine*), revived the old question of imperial encroachments and a "personal régime" and threatened to bring back the stormy scenes of November, 1908. Times had changed, however. Chancellor von Bülow wished to govern as a constitutional chancellor. Now the Reichstag had to deal with a chancellor who was long accustomed to the "personal régime" and who stood by the kaiser through thick and thin. There was, however, some energetic language on the subject, but the discussion was brief and availed nothing. Nevertheless the new Reichstag made some progress along the lines indicated by the government's critics in November, 1908. It increased its strength and fortified itself to some extent against imperial aggression by changes in the rules. It modified its organization in two important points: In the first place it assumed the right to address "petty questions" to the government, as in the British parliament; and in the second place it assumed the right to follow its interpellations with motions declaring that the sense of the assembly was or was not in accord with the government. It made use of the first of these new powers in the session, but not of the second. An anti-duelling resolution was adopted by the Reichstag, in which there was much criticism of the war ministry for its dismissal of a Catholic officer of the army who had refused to fight a duel to "maintain his honor." Catholics and Socialists were especially emphatic in their condemnation. The war minister, while deprecating the practice of duelling, declared it to be inevitable.

ALSACE-LORRAINE. On May 7 the Alsace-Lorraine Diet passed a vote of censure on the government's decision to suspend its orders at the factory of Grafenstadt on account of the director's alleged hostility to the empire. A week later the emperor in an address at Strassburg declared that if affairs did not improve in Alsace-Lorraine he would disregard the constitution and annex the country to Prussia. This led to Socialist attacks in the Reichstag and interpellations. The chancellor defended the emperor's course. The new constitution established in the autumn of 1911 had been welcomed by the people. The Democratic character of the first chamber of the new Alsace-Lorraine legislature, however, offended the reactionaries in the empire, who declared that the constitution had brought about an intolerable situation. The attitude of the chamber in this Grafenstadt affair and its previous action in suppressing the funds placed at the emperor's disposal (though it subsequently restored them) aggravated their hostility. They therefore supported the kaiser when he showed especial favor at Strassburg to the public official, Under Secretary of State Mandel, in whom the Alsace-Lorraine chamber had voted lack of confidence on account of the Grafenstadt affair; and they approved his alleged threat as to making the Reichsland a Prussian province.

FOREIGN POLICY. The meeting of czar and kaiser at Port Baltic on July 4 led, as usual, to much discussion in the press. The official *communiqué* which followed the interview contained a passage which tended to reassure those who lived in constant alarm over the aggressive designs of Germany. It declared: "There could be no question either of non-agreements, because there was no particular occasion for them, or of producing alterations of any kind in the grouping of the European powers, the value of which for the maintenance of equilibrium and of peace has already been proved." It was taken as significant that Germany should thus reaffirm the principle of the balance of power. It tended to strengthen confidence in her policy. See FRANCE, *History*, and TURKEY AND THE BALKAN PEOPLES.

THE QUESTION OF THE JESUITS. One of the first acts of the new Clerical ministry in Bavaria under Baron von Hertling was to issue a decree relieving the Jesuits from the restrictions imposed upon them by that portion of the law of 1872 which was still unrepealed, and forbade their performing any spiritual function. The government had declared that this did not prohibit their celebrating low mass, holding public meetings, etc. This law against the Jesuits was declared by Baron von Hertling to be an "odious law of exceptions" and he urged that it be repealed as soon as possible. The indignation of the Protestants was strongly aroused. The imperial chancellor, von Bethmann-Hollweg, tried to quiet public clamor by declaring himself in a general way oposed to the Bavarian minister's construction of the law, but at the same time he conferred with the latter and they finally decided to carry the question to the Federal Council, which was to pronounce authoritatively on the meaning of the law. The Bavarian bishops in an address to the council made an energetic demand for the repeal of the law. Catholic sentiment was deeply aroused and the Catholic Congress at Aix-la-Chapelle in August made this issue the leading feature of their programme. The matter was pending before the Federal Council in the summer, but it was slow to take action on account of the political difficulties involved—the risk of offending Protestant sentiment on the one hand and of alienating the government's Clerical supporters on the other. The Catholics complained that while the Jesuits, the loyal servants of the church, were oppressed and muzzled by laws of exceptions, the Socialists, foes of both church and state, were left free to propagate their subversive doctrines as they chose. Liberals and Socialists were on principle opposed to any law of exceptions, but the rivalry of parties, and especially the hostility between Socialists and Clericals, made their action in this matter problematical.

On November 26 the decision of the council, though gently worded, was in spirit essentially adverse to the position taken by Baron von Hertling. There was much indignant comment on it in the Clerical press, and in the Reichstag at the beginning of December the Clerical Centre openly attacked the government and declared a complete lack of confidence in the ministry of von Bethmann-Hollweg. Some saw in this a presage of the dissolution of the Blue-Black *bloc*, but others were not disposed to regard it seriously.

DEFENSE BILLS. On May 21 the Reichstag passed the army bill and the navy law amendment bill. As to the financial arrangements, they postponed the reduction of sugar duties. The Reichstag committee decided on the reintroduction of the death duty proposals next year. The increases of the German military and naval effectives came up for discussion in April. The policy was regarded with alarm in England and France. The augmentation was said to be greater than at any time since the Franco-German War. In 1911 the law of the quinquennium provided for an increase of 11,000 men and it was supposed that this would suffice for another five years, but within a year from its passage came this far greater increase, adding 29,000 more men, not counting the under officers. This was attributed by the Germans themselves to the incident of Agadir, which had revealed the fact that France was not sufficiently afraid of war. According to German public opinion, the empire had not derived from the Moroccan affair the advantages to which it was entitled. The military strength of Germany in future must be sufficient to prevent any such failure. The new measure provided for the formation of two new army corps to protect the Franco-Prussian frontier. The naval bill amended the existing naval programme by providing for three additional battleships and two additional cruisers, to be ready by 1920. It also provided for an increase of the personnel by 1600 men and for the more immediate effectiveness of the fleet.

The increased expenditure on defense was to be met out of the budget surplus and by reducing the percentage of the brandy excise to be allotted to the states.

NAVY LEAGUE. Early in April the German Navy League published its annual report. This showed a total membership at the end of 1911 of 1,054,404, and an increase in the league's funds. The twelfth annual meeting of the league was held on June 9 at Weimar. The new programme for agitating on behalf of the naval defense was adopted with enthusiasm. Grand-Admiral von Köster in his address demanded more large cruisers and a great increase of personnel. He said that they would not be going too fast if by 1917 five additional cruisers were built and 5000 men were added to the personnel. He criticised the present provisions of the navy law.

ESPIONAGE TRIALS. The trials in recent years of German subjects in Great Britain for espionage, and of British subjects in Germany, have attracted much notice in the press and have tended to increase the national jealousies. An important trial of this nature began on January 31, when Mr. Bertrand Stewart, who had been arrested in Bremen on August 2, was brought to trial before the Imperial Supreme Court at Leipzig. The charge was that during the year 1911 he had endeavored to obtain knowledge of military secrets. After a four-days' session the court found Mr. Stewart guilty and sentenced him to detention in a fortress for three years and six months, which period, however, was reduced by four months on account of the long imprisonment. There were extenuating circumstances in the case and the sentence was regarded in Great Britain as too severe. It was pointed out that much lighter sentences had been imposed by British courts when German offenders of the same class were brought before them. It was, however, realized in Great Britain that the system of jurisprudence under which the case was tried was altogether alien to the English, especially in the importance attached by the German judge to the unsupported testimony of informers.

OTHER EVENTS. On January 24 Prussia celebrated the two-hundredth anniversary of the birth of Frederick the Great. In March the kaiser visited Vienna and Venice on his way to Corfu. In July occurred his interview with the czar (see RUSSIA, *History*), and in September he visited Switzerland. As to labor conditions, see STRIKES and the various articles on LABOR.

HIGH COST OF FOOD. In Germany, as in other countries, there was much concern over the increased price of food products, and in some places there was popular agitation of the subject. The Federal Council in February suspended the import duties on potatoes till May 1. The Socialists conducted a vigorous campaign for lower prices. In the autumn there was bitter complaint of the high price of meat and in September many of the town councils demanded that the frontiers be opened to the importation of cattle and that the duties on cattle feed be abolished. The government took the stand that it was a general economic phenomenon throughout the world and refused to modify the tax system. In Prussia, however, some slight concessions were made. (See below, paragraph on *Prussia*.)

THE OIL MONOPOLY. Toward the end of the year the government introduced its project for a monopoly of the petroleum industries in Germany, urging as an argument the need of new sources of revenue from which to provide for the relief of veterans of the wars of 1864, 1866, and 1870. This did not look to a state monopoly, properly speaking, but to a monopolistic organization, with the collaboration of several of the large banks, which should operate under state supervision. It was designed not only as a source of revenue but as a competitor of the American Standard Oil Company, which virtually controlled the German market. It encountered considerable opposition in the Reichstag, but was finally referred to a commission. The matter was still unsettled at the close of the year.

PRUSSIA. The Prussian Diet was opened on January 15, but adjourned until after the elections. Herr von Bethmann-Hollweg in a speech from the throne again abstained from any reference to the Prussian franchise. The government programme, as announced by him, included, besides the measures of financial reform, a proposed plan for new legislation dealing with water works, fisheries, internal colonization, compulsory attendance at continuation schools in rural districts, etc. Motions for the reform of the Prussian electoral system were rejected by the Diet May 23. In order to destroy the influence of the six Socialist deputies who, despite the three-class electoral system, had succeeded in securing seats, the Landtag adopted a very rigorous rule, whereby the president could exclude deputies and have them removed by the police. This was applied in the case of Socialist Deputy Borchardts, who was twice dragged out by the police, although he showed the officer the article in the penal code punishing with hard labor anyone preventing a deputy from performing his parliamentary duties. The president made a criminal charge against him and his companion, Leinert, who was also thrown out ,and the majority in the Landtag voted the suspension of parliamentary immunity. This course on the part of the reactionary majority was interpreted by their opponents as a desperate defense against the encroachments of the populace whom these Socialists represented and who would endeavor to force their way into parliament in spite of the obstacles interposed by the present electoral system. The reactionaries were determined to oppose the slightest modification of that system.

In October, in consequence of the agitation over the high price of meat, the Prussian government decided to modify some of the meat regulations, though it did not accede to the demand that the provisions excluding frozen meat be repealed.

For notes on Germany on subjects not dealt with here, see KIDERLEN-WÄCHTER, ALFRED VON; ARCHITECTURE; GREAT BRITAIN, *History*.

GIBRALTAR. A narrow peninsula extending southward from the southwest coast of Spain; a British crown colony, naval and coaling station, and *entrepôt* of the British trade with the Arabian states of north Africa. Area, 1⅞ sq. miles; population, exclusive of the military, 19,120. Practically a free port. It gives no trade returns. Revenue (1910), £80,929; expenditure, £76,410; total tonnage entered and cleared, 10,940,218 (6,562,085 British). Gen. Sir Archibald Hunter was governor and commander-in-chief in 1912.

GIFTS AND BEQUESTS. The following list of gifts and bequests in 1912 is compiled from the record kept by the *Chicago Daily Tribune*. The total amount given in gifts and bequests during the year amounted to the immense total of $241,821,719, as compared with $126,499,918 in 1911. It must be taken into consideration that the total for 1912 includes only published donations. It is probable that the entire amount given, if it were known, would be twice the sum. Of the total amount, $177,923,076 represents gifts and $63,898,643 represents bequests. The total amount given may be classified as follows: To charities of various kinds, $184,747,555; educational institutions, $35,207,907; religious bodies, $10,847,756; art museums, galleries, and municipal improvements, $8,906,501; and libraries, $2,112,000. The sum contributed by women amounted to $17,787,287 of which $12,252,037 was by bequests and $5,535,250 by gifts.

Andrew Carnegie again contributed the largest individual sum, a total of $130,403,000. Of this, $125,000,000 was distributed through the Carnegie Corporation of New York. Mr. Carnegie gave to the Carnegie Technical Schools of Pittsburgh $2,000,000 and to the Teachers' Foundation Fund $2,000,000. His other gifts were to libraries, colleges, and for miscellaneous purposes. He proposed a pension of $25,000 for former presidents of the United States, but it did not meet with favor. John D. Rockefeller made no unusually large gifts during the year. The total amount distributed by him was $227,000, chiefly for colleges and hospitals. Mrs. Russell Sage made gifts totaling $428,500. Included in this was $150,000 with which was purchased Marsh Island, Louisiana, which is to form a refuge for migratory birds. (See ORNITHOLOGY.) The sums given by J. Pierpont Morgan aggregated $591,700. The largest gift made by Mr. Morgan was one of $200,000 to Trinity College. His other gifts were made to hospitals, colleges, and various relief funds. Julius Rosenwald of Chicago gave to charities, to institutions, and to schools, $760,000. Miss Helen Gould gave to the New York Y. M. C. A. and Y. W. C. A. $271,000.

Academy of Arts and Sciences, will by Francis Amory, $25,000.

Adam, J. N., Buffalo, N. Y., will to charity, $100,000.

Adams, Ivers W., Ashburnham, Mass., gift to town, $25,000.

Agassiz, G. B., Boston, Mass., gift to Harvard University, $25,000.

Aldrichs, W. K., Harrisburg, Pa., will to church, $50,000.

Alfred University, gift by various donors, $100,000.

Allegheny College, gifts by various donors, $500,000.

Allen, Elio T., Kenosha, Wis., gift to charity, $10,000.

Allentown, Pa., college for women, gift by various donors, $16,000.

American Museum of Safety, gift by Elbert G Gary, $5000; gift by unnamed donor, $5000.

Amory, Francis, Boston, Mass., bequest to Lying-in Hospital, $500,000; to Harvard University, $50,000; Academy of Arts and Sciences, $25,000.

Ancient Order of Hibernians, Chicago, gift to Catholic Church Extension Society, $38,000.

Anderson, Lars, gift of memorial bridge to Massachusetts, $200,000.

Andrei, Henrietta B., New York, will to schools, $7500.

Armour, George, Princeton, N. J., gift to St. Paul's School, Concord, N. H., $50,000.

Armour Institute, Chicago, Ill., gift by various donors, $33,345.

Armstrong, Henry B., Poughkeepsie, N. Y., to charity, $200,000.

Art Institute, Chicago, Ill., by D. H. Burnham, $50,000.

Artman, E. R., Philadelphia, Pa., to charity, $100,000.

Ashburnham, Mass., by Ivers W. Adams, $25,000.

Associated Jewish Charities, by Simon Mandel, $21,000.

Astor, Vincent, New York, to Titanic Relief fund, $10,000.

Athletic Club, Philadelphia, Pa., gift by J. P. Crozer, $50,000.

Ayres, J. B., Normal, Ill., gift to Illinois Western University, $10,000.

Babcock J. L., Petersburg, Fla., to University of Michigan, $5000.

Bacon, Francis, New Haven, Conn., to charity, $115,000; to Yale College, $400,000; to Yale University, $500,000.

Bain, Magdalena, Kenosha, Wis., to Pontifical College, Columbus, O., $20,000; to church, $20,000.

Baker, George F., New York, gift to Cornell University, $2,000,000.

Baker, Henry M., Concord, N. H., to charity, $5000 will to Dartmouth College, $5000; will to library, $10,000.

Bamberger, Henry, Philadelphia, Pa., to charity, $450,000.

Baptist Theological Seminary, gift by Mrs. Charles Lovelace, $5000.

Barnum, Agnes, St. Louis, Mo., to charity, $11,500; to church, 102,000

Barry, J. D., New York, to charity, $10,000.

Bartlett, Mr. and Mrs. A. L., Olean, N. Y., gift to church, $25,000.

Bartlett, Francis P., Boston, Mass., gift to Museum of Fine Arts, $1,481,000.

Bates College, by unnamed donor, $10,000.

Bath, Me., gift of city hall by various donors, $100,000.

Belfield, T. B., Philadelphia, Pa., to church, $25,000.

Belknap, Mrs. M. B., Louisville, Ky., gift to Lincoln Institute, $10,000.

Beloit College, gift by Mrs. R. H. Sage, $50,000; by Dana Sherrill, $30,000.

Bennett, Benjamin F., Baltimore, Md., gift to Goucher College, $60,000.

Berea College, by J. L. Maxwell, $5000; by Katharine Knapp, $10,000; gift by unnamed donor, $5000.

Bernard, G. T., Jamestown, N. Y., gift to City of New Bedford, Mass., $6000.

Bethea, Solomon, Dixon, Ill., to Dixon Hospital, $75,000.

Bethel, U. N., Montclair, N. J., gift to education, $10,000.

Bethell, Mary E., Sacramento, Cal., to charity, $6000.

Bible Teachers' Training School, gift by Mrs. J. E. Kennedy, $100,000.

Blackburn College, by Ann Brethner, $22,000.

Blanchard, Frederick, Tyngsboro, Mass., gift to library, $5000.

Blodgett, Mrs. J. J., New York, gift to St. John's Cathedral, $200,000.

Boardman, Mrs. J. D., estate of, Middletown, gift to Y. M. C. A., $5000.

Borden, Matthew C. D., Fall River, Mass., gift to Yale University, $250,000.

Boston, Mass., Public Library, by Katherine Knapp, $10,000.

Bowdoin College, by Georgiana B. Gannett, $6000; gift by Mary E. W. Perry, Middletown, R. I., $10,000.

Boursell, R. L., Rondout, N. Y., to charity, $9500.

Boyd, R. F., Nashville, Tenn., to charity, $7000.

Boyne, S. W., New York, to church, $52,672; to colleges, $200,000; to charities, $74,360.

Brady, James B., New York, gift to charity, $550,000; gift to Johns Hopkins Hospital, $220,000.

Brady, A. N., Albany, N. Y., gift to Maternity Hospital, $100,000.

Brainerd, Ciprian, gift to Yale University, $65,000.

Brandeis, Emil, Omaha, Neb., to charity, $5000.

Brethner, Ann, Peoria, Ill., to Blackburn College, $22,000.

Britton, Dora, Saybrook, Ill., gift to church, $40,000.

Brookins, R. S., St. Louis, Mo., to Washington University, $250,000.

Brooks, Mrs. S. H., Memphis, Tenn., gift of art gallery to city, $100,000.

Brown, Elizabeth N., Philadelphia, Pa., gift to charity, $50,000.

Brown, W. L., Evanston, Ill., gift to charity, $180,000.

Brown University, gift by various donors, $534,500; gift by Robert Knight, $25,000; from Hazard estate, $25,000; gift by John D. Rockefeller, $25,000; gift by Henry F. Leppitt, $5000; gift by Samuel Nickerson, $25,000; gift by William E. Lincoln, $5000; gift by unnamed donor, Providence, R. I., $5000; gift by Harriet F. Safe, $5000; gift by James M. Duane, $25,000; gift by unnamed donor, $25,000 gift by Elmer L. Corthell, $5000; gift by Mrs. William Goddard, $25,000; gift by Henry K. Porter, $25,000; gift by J. D. Rockefeller, Jr., $25,000; unnamed donor, $10,000; gift by Henry A. Laughlin, $25,000; gift by Samuel P. Cobb, $25,000; gift by William Gammell, $25,000; gift by various donors, $7500; gift by Jesse H. and Eliza G. Radeke, $25,000; gift by Henry D. Sharpe, $25,000; gift by Edgar L. Marston, $16,000; gift by Stephen O. Metcalf, $25,000; by J. B. F. Herreshoff, $10,000.

Browne, Alanson D., St. Louis, Mo., gift to William Jewell College, $100,000; to Missouri Baptist Sanitarium, $200,000.

Browne, Mrs. N. B., Concordia, Kas., gift to town, $60,000.

Bryn Mawr College, will by Emma C. Woerrishoff, $750,000.

Buckingham, May, gift to charity, $102,000.

Buckley, Ernest R., Chicago, Ill., will to town of Tomah, Wis., $20,000.

Buckley, Mrs. L. L., Concordia, Kan., will to National Suffrage Association, $30,0000.

Burgess, Caroline A., Philadelphia, Pa., will to charity, $10,000; will to church, $6000.

Burnham, D. H., Chicago, Ill., will to Art Institute, '$50,000.

Busch, Adolphus, St. Louis, Mo., gift to charity, $5000; conditional gift to opera house, $50,000.

Butterfield, Caroline F., New York, will to charities, $30,000.

Byers, Martha L., Pittsburgh, Pa., will to Yale University, $10,000.

Cabot, A. T., Brookline, Mass., to Harvard University, $500,000; to Boston Art Museum, $100,000.

California University, gift by Jane K. Lather, $550,000.

Caldwell, Jennie E., Bloomington, Ill., to maternal home, $500,000.

Cancer hospital, by Cornelia Storrs, $1,000,000.

Carnegie, Andrew, gift to library, Somerville, Mass., $80,000; gift to Titanic relief fund, $5000; gift to endowment fund Yale forestry school, $100,000; gift of library to Winfield, Kas., $15,000; gift of library to Centralia, Wash, $15,000; gift to Ripon College, $25,000; gift of library to Muskogee, Okla., $50,000; gift of branch libraries to Nashville, Tenn., $50,000; gift of library to Winchester, Ky., $15,000; gift for tuberculosis home at Farmingdale, N. J., $10,000; gift of library to Mayfield, Ky., $20,000; gift to Christian College, Columbus, Mo., $25,000; gift of library to Enfield, Conn., $20,000; gift of library to San Francisco, Cal., $750,000; gift of library to Columbus, Kas., $10,000; transfer to Carnegie New York Foundation, $125,000,000; gift of library to Crowley, La., $15,000; gift to Wells College, $18,000; gift of branch library to Minneapolis, Minn., $125,000; gift to Carnegie technical schools, $2,000,000; gift of library to New Rochelle, N. Y., $20,000; additional gift to Carnegie Foundation, $2,000,000.

Carnegie Foundation, additional gift by Andrew Carnegie, $2,000,000.

Carnegie Technical schools, gift by Andrew Carnegie, $2,000,000.

Carroll, Catharine, New York, will to church, $20,000.

Carroll, D. H., Baltimore, Md., will to charities, $400,000.

Carson, Robert N., will for girls' home, $6,000,000.

Carson, William, Eureka, Cal., to charity, $20,000; to church, $32,500.

Carthell, Elmer L., Providence, R. I., gift to Brown University, $5000.

Cartwright, M. H., Nashville, Tenn., to charity, $6000.

Carver, Anna H., Philadelphia, Pa., to Herzog Theological Hall, $25,000; will to charity, $190,000.

Casenove, Sarah E., Boston, Mass., to charity, $60,000.

Catholic Church Extension Society, gift by Ancient Order of Hibernians, $38,000.

Catholic University, gift by Patrick Garian, $10,000.

Centralia, Wash., gift of library, by Andrew Carnegie, $15,000.

Central College, by J. L. Jamison, $5000.

Chaffee, Mrs. Z., Providence, R. I., gift to Y. M. C. A., $5000.

Chandler, Helen, Camden, N. J., will to missions, $30,000.

Chandler, J. A., Albany, N. Y., will to charity, $5000.

Chase, Valora, Waterville, Me., will to town, $5000.

Chattanooga, Tenn., gift to missions by various donors, $40,000.

Chattanooga University, gifts by various donors, $200,000.

Chelsea, Mass., gift to church by unnamed donor, $10,000.

Chicago, Ill., gift to public school by Julius Rosenwald, $10,000.

Chicago Children's Benefit, tag day, $55,000.

Chicago Hebrew Institute, gift by Julius Rosenwald, $50,000.

Chicago United Charities, will by Richard T. Crane, $100,000.

Chicora College, S. C., gift by various donors, $35,000.

Children's Hospital, Philadelphia, Pa., gift by Mrs. Richard Dale, $20,000; by various donors, $180,000.

Chinese donors, Chicago, Ill., to Chinese relief fund, $8853.

Chinese relief fund, gift by various donors, Chicago, Ill., $13,131; gift of Chinese donors, Chicago, Ill., $8853; gift by various donors, Boston, Mass., $23,374; gift by various donors, $10,000; gift by Mrs. Russell Sage, $6000.

Christian Church hospital, Kansas City, Mo., gift by P. A. Long, $85,000; gift by various donors, $200,000.

Christian College, Columbia, Mo., gifts by Andrew Carnegie, $25,000.

Churchill, E. H., Joliet, Ill., gift to Peru, Ind., $50,000.

Cincinnati, O., gift to charity, by unnamed donor, $5000.

City College, New York, gift by Adolph Lewisohn, $50,000.

Clay, Mary, Philadelphia, Pa., will to charity, $6900.

Cleeman, L. C., Philadelphia, Pa., will to University of Pennsylvania, $50,000.

Cleveland, O., to hospitals, by C. Morris, $1,000,000.

Clifford, Mrs. G. H., Rockland, Me., to charity, $25,000.

Cloth, Caroline, Memphis, Tenn., to charity, $70,000; to church, $15,000.

Cobb, Samuel P., gift to Brown University, $25,000.

Cockruns, Helen, Fairbury, Ill., to church, $16,000.

Coggeshall, Mary J., Des Moines, Ia., gift to National Suffrage Association, $15,000.

Colby College, by William H. Dexter, $10,000.

Colby, Mary J., Franklin, N. H., to charity, $92,000.

Colorado College, gift by Mrs. A. D. Juilliard, $100,000.

Colored Y. M. C. A., Cincinnati, O., gift by Julius Rosenwald, $25,000; gift by unnamed donor, $25,000.

Colored Y. M. C. A. of New York, gift by Julius Rosenwald, $25,000.

Collins, Ellen, New York, to charity, $25,000.

Colt, Samuel P. Providence, R. I., gift to Y. M. C. A., $10,000.

Columbia Club, Aledo, Ill., gift to Filiam and Vashti College, $60,000.

Columbia Medical School, gift by Mrs. Russell Sage, $25,000.

Columbia University, gift by A. W. Openhym, $91,666.

Columbus, Kan., gift of library by Andrew Carnegie, $10,000.

Conklin, N. W., New York, gift to Western Theological Seminary, $100,000.

Conn, Bernard, Philadelphia, Pa., gift to Villa Nova College, $100,000.

Connecticut, Wesleyan University, gift by various donors, $900,000.

Convent of the Holy Child, gift by Mrs. T. F. Ryan, $250,000.

Converse, E. C., New York, gift to Harvard University, $125,000.

Cook, W. L., Philadelphia, Pa., to charity, $7000.

Coolidge, T. J., Boston, Mass., gift to Harvard University, $50,000.

Cooper Union, will by Henry Iden, $100,000; will by T. G. Sellew, $10,000.

Cooper, William, New York, gift to Music Conservatory, $5000.

Corkery, Mary A., Chicago, Ill., will to church, $5000.

Cornell University, gift by George F. Baker, $2,000,000; gift by Mrs. John Craig, $5000; gift by Jacob H. Schiff, $100,000.

Council of Grain Exchanges, gift by Sears, Roebuck & Co., $1,000,000.

Cousens, Harriet S., Newton, Mass., to charity, $6000; to Pomona College, $5000.

Craig, Mrs. John, New York, gift to Cornell University, $5000.

Crane, Charles R., Chicago, Ill., gift to Crane Nursery, $16,000.

Crane, Richard T., Chicago, Ill., for Home for Helpless and Motherless Children, $1,000,000; to Chicago United Charities, $100,000; to other charities, $35,000; for employees' pension, $1,000,000.

Crestman, J. M., Iris, Miss., gift to charity, $50,000.

Crozer, J. P., Philadelphia, Pa., gift to athletic club, $50,000.

Cudahy, Michael, gift to University of California, $10,000.

Culling, Mrs. Brockhaltz, Newport, R. I., will to charity, $180,000.

Cupples, Samuel, St. Louis, Mo., conditional bequest to college, $1,000,000.

Curley, John, New York, to charities, $84,664.

Curtis, C. H. K., Philadelphia, Pa., gift of organ to Portland, Me., city hall, $60,000.

Curtis, Frank M., gift of park to New Kensington, Pa., $10,000.

Cutting, Sarah A., Berkeley, Cal., to school, $24,000.

Dale, Mrs. Richard, Philadelphia, Pa., gift to Children's Hospital, $20,000.

Daly, Katherine E., New York, to charity, $85,790.

Dartmouth College, gift by Wallace Robinson, $100,000; by T. W. Woodman, $5000; by Emily H. Hitchcock, $70,000; by Henry M. Baker, $5000.

Davis, Joshua H., Minneapolis, Minn., to charity, $15,000; to Windom Institute, $5000.

Dawes, Edward L., New Brighton, Pa., gift to charity, $30,000.

Deaconness' fund, Chicago, Ill, gift by unnamed donor, $25,000.

Deering, Charles, Chicago, Ill., gift to charity, $50,000.

DeForest, Marion, N. Y., to church, $10,000; to charity, $15,000.

Delgado, Isaac, New Orleans, La., will to charities, $800,000; to found training school for boys, $200,000.

Delaney, H. S., Baltimore, Md., gift to Goucher College, $60,000.

Demuth, Harriett, New York, to charity, $10,000.

De Muth, Louis, New York, to charities $6000.

Denver, Col., gift by unnamed donor, to Jewish Hospital, $25,000.

De Pauw University, gift by Simeon Smith, $250,000; gift by various donors, $300,000.

DePeyster, Katherine, New York, to Historical Society, $395,501.

Dexter, William H., Worcester, Mass., will to church, $6500; to Colby College, $10,000; to Worcester Academy, $40,000.

Dimock, Henry F., New York, to Yale University, $1,867,229.

Dix, Henry A., Millville, N. J., gift to hospital, $10,000.

Dodge, C. P., Colorado Springs, Colo., gift to Y. M. C. A., $5000.

Donohoe, Annie, San Francisco, Cal., to Vallejo, Y. M. Institute, $100,000.

Dorty, Adea A., New York, will to charity, $119,500.

Douglas Hospital, Philadelphia, Pa., gift by various donors, $12,024.

Douw, D. Matilda, New York, to missionary societies, $50,000.

Downey, Eliza, Philadelphia, Pa., to charity, $5400.

Drexel, Mrs. Joseph, Philadelphia, Pa., to charity, $45,000; to church, $40,000; to St. Joseph Seminary, $10,000; to University of Pennsylvania, $80,000; to Washington Catholic University, $10,000.

Dropsie College, by Elizabeth A. Lazarus, $50,000.

Drumm, Andrew, Kansas City, Mo., gift for Home for Boys, $550,000.

Duane, James M., New York, gift to Brown University, $25,000.

Dunham, Sarah R., Hartford, Conn., to hospital, $5000.

DuPont, Pierre S., Philadelphia, Pa., gift to William Penn Charter School, $20,000.

Durham, N. C., gift of hospital to city by George W. Watts, $100,000.

Dynan, Elizabeth, Cambridge, Mass., to charity, $5400.

Dyersburg, Tenn., gift for hospital by various donors, $20,000.

Earl, Hannah M., Albany, N. Y., to Troy orphan asylum, $20,000.

Eastman, George, Rochester, N. Y., gift to University of Rochester, $500,000.

Eaton, Cornelia, New York, to Presbyterian Hospital, $15,000.

Educational Alliance, will by Isidor Straus, $200,000.

Educational institutions, will by Georgette E. Wolfe, $15,000.

Edwards, R. E., Kinsley, Kas., gift to Fairmont College, $10,000.

Eggleston, Mrs. W. C., New York, to Yale University, $100,000.

Eli, H. B., Webster, Ia., gift to Iowa Wesleyan College, $17,000.

Ellis, Rudolph, Philadelphia, Pa., gift to charity, $100,000.

Emergency Hospital, Washington, D. C., gift by Mrs. G. Staterbury, $10,000.

Emporia College, gift by Thomas Potter, $20,000.

Enfield, Conn., gift of library by Andrew Carnegie, $20,000.

Epworth Home, gift by N. W. Harris, $5000; gift by J. B. Hobbs, $5000.

Equitable Life Assurance Company, New York, gift to fire victim families, $20,000.

Esker, Mrs. J. H., Nashville, Tenn., gift to church, $119,500.

Evangelical Baptist Church, Cleveland, O., gift by John D. Rockefeller, $5500.

Evans, Harriet S., Philadelphia, Pa., to charity, $45,000; to church, $15,000.

Evanston, Ill., Hospital, gift by James A. Patten, $75,000.

Evanston Woman's Club, gift by James A. Patten, $15,000.

Fairmont College, gift by R. E. Edwards, $10,000.

Farmingdale, N. J., gift for tuberculosis home by Andrew Carnegie, $10,000.

Farquhar, A. B., York, Pa, gift of park to city, $20,000.

Farwell, Mrs. J. V., Lake Forest, Ill., to church, $7500; to charity, $7000.

Faxon, Henry H., Quincy, Mass., gift to charity, $20,000.

Federated Hebrew Charities, gift by Moses Goldenberg, $20,000.

Filiam and Vashti College, gift by Columbia Club, Aledo, Ill., $60,000.

Fisk University, gift by J. P. Morgan, $25,000.

Foote, B. B., New Haven, Conn., to charities, $2,020,000.

Forest Park, St. Louis, gift by unnamed donor, $5000.

Foster, James H., Scotland, Ill., to church, $363,000.

Fox, Charles K., Haverhill, Mass., to Gould Academy, $100,000.

Foy, Theresa, New York, to charities, $27,000.

Freeman, Edward C., Lebanon, Pa., will to church, $10,000.

Frick, H. C., New York, gift to Sailors' Home, $25,000.

Friend, Frank R., St. Paul, Minn., to charity, $50,000.

Funk, Isaac K., New York, to Wittenberg College, $10,000.

Gamble, Mr. and Mrs. D. B., Cincinnati, O., gift to Smith College, $23,000.

Gammell, William, Providence, R. I., gift to Brown University, $25,000.

Gannett, Georgiana B., Brookline, Mass., will to Bowdoin College, $6000.

Garrett, Anna, Philadelphia, Pa., will to church, $6000.

Garrett, Elizabeth A., Philadelphia, Pa., will to charity, $600,000.

Gartos, Lilia, New York, will to charity, $22,500.

Garvan, Patrick, Hartford, Conn., will to Catholic University, $10,000.

Gary, Elbert H., New York, gift to American Museum of Safety, $5000.

German Wallace College, gift by Mrs. James Wallace, $25,000; by unnamed donor, $10,000.

Georgetown University, by Charles B. Kinney, $20,000.
Gibson, Mary K., Philadelphia, Pa., gift to Home for Children, $50,000.
Girls' Home, gift by Robert N. Carson, $6,000,000; gift by Mrs. Frederick Vanderbilt, $150,000.
Glenwood Training School, gift by Julius Rosenwald, $12,500.
Goddard, Mrs. William, Providence, R. I., gift to Brown University, $5000.
Goldenberg, Moses, Baltimore, Md., gift to federated Hebrew charities, $20,000.
Goldenberg, Sarah, New York, will to charity, $9000.
Golding, Samuel, New York, to charity, $10,000; to National Academy of Design, $10,000.
Gome, Elizabeth, Philadelphia, Pa., to charity, $5000.
Good, Frances H., Philadelphia, Pa., to charity, $5000.
Goodwin, William W., Cambridge, Mass., to Harvard University, $16,000.
Göttingen University, gift by J. Pierpont Morgan, $50,000.
Gottstein, Karol, Seattle, Wash., will to charity, $15,000.
Goucher College, gift by various donors, $61,500; gift by Benjamin F. Bennett, $60,000; gift by H. S. Delaney, $60,000.
Gould, Helen, New York, gift to Portsmouth (Va.) Y. M. C. A., $10,000; gift to tuberculosis hospital, St. Louis, $10,000; gift to Y. W. C. A., $250,000.
Gould Academy, will by Charles K. Fox, $100,000.
Graham, Lizzie, Winfield, Kas., will to Southwest College, $14,000.
Grand Prairie Seminary, gift by W. A. Rankin, $10,000.
Greaves, Hannah, Philadelphia, Pa., will to charity, $7000.
Guggenheim, Benjamin, New York, to education, $20,000; to charities, $105,000.
Haldron, Thomas W., Philadelphia, Pa., to charity, $20,000.
Hall, E. H., Boston, Mass., to charity, $15,000; to Harvard University, $15,000.
Hall, J. J., St. Paul, Minn., gift to Luther College, Deborah, Ia., $50,000.
Hamilton College, gift by unnamed donor, $100,000.
Hanley, James, Providence, R. I., to charity, $26,500.
Hanover Library, Hanover, N. H., by Emily H. Hitchcock, $50,000.
Harkins, Bishop, Providence, R. I., gift to charity, $12,000.
Harriman, Mary A., New York, gift to Sailors' Home, New York, $5000.
Harris, Henry B., New York, to charity, $9000.
Harris, N. W., Chicago, gift to Epworth Home, $5000.
Harris, Mr. and Mrs. N. W., Chicago, gift to Mt. Holyoke College, $25,000.
Harrity, W. F., Philadelphia, Pa., to charity, $200,000.
Hart, Charles, Philadelphia, Pa., to church, $5000.
Hartford Theological Seminary, gift by Mrs. J. S. Kennedy, $350,000; conditional gift by unnamed donor, $100,000.
Harvard University, gift by George H. Leatherbee, $20,000; by E. H. Hall, $15,000; gift by various donors, $40,000; by G. B. Agassiz, $25,000; by unnamed donor, $10,000; by A. L. Lowell, $70,000; by A. T. Cabot, $500,000; by T. J. Coolidge, $50,000; will by Francis Amory, $50,000; by Morris Loeb, $500,000; gift of library building by P. A. B. Widener, $1,000,000; gift by Class of 1912, $200,000; by William W. Goodwin, $16,000; gift by E. C. Converse, $125,000; by Albert L. Rotch, $50,000; gift by unnamed donor, $10,000.
Harvard University Art Fund, by various donors, $150,000.
Hasbrouck, Melinda, New York, to charity, $10,000.
Hawkins, William, Philadelphia, Pa., to charity, $50,000.
Hayden, Thomas F., St. Louis, Mo., to charity, $70,000; to church, $30,000; to Kenwick Seminary, $10,000.
Hazard Estate, Providence, R. I., to Brown University, $25,000.
Hebrew Free School, Boston, Mass., gift by various donors, $50,000.
Hebrew Guardian Society, gift by Adolph Lewisohn, $100,000.
Hebrew Technical School, New York, gift by various donors, $50,000.
Heilbron, Sigmund, Philidelphia, Pa., to charity, $8250.
Henzy, Anne B., Philadelphia, Pa., to charity, $75,000.
Herely, Michael P., Philadelphia, Pa., will to charity, $5000; to church $15,000.
Herreshoff, J. B. F., New York, gift to Brown University, $10,000.
Herrman, Nathan, New York, to charity, $100,000.
Herzog Theological Hall, by Anna H. Carver, $25,000.
Hesslacher, Elizabeth, New York, to charity, $13,000.
Hewitt, F. C., Owego, N. Y., to charities, $253,000; Metropolitan Art Museum, $1,500,000; to library, $30,000; to Yale University, $500,000.
Hicks, Alice A., Mineola, L. I., to charities, $352,000; to Swarthmore College, $100,000.
Higgins, Milton, G., Worcester, Mass., to Memorial Hospital, $10,000; to Polytechnic Institute, $25,000; to Trade schools, $25,000.
Hill, James J., gift to McMinnville College, $50,000; library to St. Paul, Minn., $850,000.
Hillman, James, New York, gift to charity, $100,000.
Hinskamp, Mrs. H. C., Keokuk, Ia., gift to Y. W. C. A., $5000.
Historical Society, by Katherine DePeyster, $395,501.
Hitchcock, Emily H., Hanover, N. H., will to Dartmouth College, $70,000; to Hanover library, $50,000.
Hixon, Frank P., gift of school to La Crosse, Wis., $70,000.
Hobart College, will by Mary W. M. Vought, $10,000.
Hobbs, J. B., Chicago, gift to Epworth Home, $5000.
Holly, Helene H. T., Stamford, Conn., will to charity, $25,000.
Home for Aged, Brooklyn, N. Y., gift by various donors, $40,000.
Home for Boys, gift by Andrew Drumm, $550,000.
Home for Children, gift by Mary K. Gibson, $50,000.
Home for Girls, will by Cornelia Storrs, $1,000,000.
Home for Helpless and Motherless Children, Chicago, Ill., by Richard T. Crane, $1,000,000.
Hoover, Catharine, Philadelphia, Pa., to church, $6000.
Hopper, Delphine T., Philadelphia, Pa., to charity, $8100.
Hornett, Katharin, J. D., New York, to church, $18,000.
Hortenpyl, A. G., Grand Rapids, Mich., gift of park to city, $80,000.
Hospital Association in New York, gift by various donors, $20,000.
Hospital fund, Melrose, Mass., gift by various donors, $115,009.
Hospital for Deformities, gift by J. P. Morgan, $25,000; by various donors, $25,000.
Howe, George C., St. Louis, Mo., gift to city missions, $5000.
Hulbert, Henry C., New York, to charity, $50,000; to church, $25,000.
Huntley, Frances, Rochester, N. Y., gift to Y. M. C. A., $5000.
Hyde, A. H., Kansas City, Mo., gift to Y. M. C. A., $15,000.
Iden, Henry, White Plains, N. Y., to Cooper Union, $100,000; to societies, $30,000; to charity, $20,000.
Illinois Wesleyan College, gift by John D. Rockefeller, $125,000; gift by various donors, $125,000.
Illinois Western University, gift by J. B. Ayres, $10,000.
Illinois Woman's College, gift by Julius C. Strawn, $10,000.
Institute of Technology, gift by Charles H. Pratt, $750,000; gift by various donors, $200,000; gift by Thomas N. Vail, $100,000.
Iowa Wesleyan College gift by H. B. Ell, $17,000.
Irwin, Mary E., Philadelphia, Pa., to charity, $5000.
Jackson, Edward, San Angelo, Tex., to charities, $1,000,000.
Jackson, Samuel M., New York, to charity, $21,500.
Jamison, J. L., Fulton, Mo., to Central College, $5000.
Jesuit College, Stonyhurst, England, by Eugene Kelly, $10,000.

Johns Hopkins Hospital, gift by James B. Brady, $220,000.
Johnson, Orlando, New York, for Manual Training School of Scranton, Pa., $1,000,000.
Johnston, Henry I., Philadelphia, Pa., to charity, $10,000.
Julliard, Mrs. A. D., New York, gift to Colorado College, $100,000.
Kallaher, Patrick, Memphis, Tenn., to charity, $8500.
Kansas Wesleyan University, gifts by various donors, $19,500.
Keim, Mildred, gift to Wellesley College, $10,000.
Kelly, Eugene, New York, to church, $549,400; to Jesuit College, Stonyhurst, England, $10,000; to charity, $15,000.
Kennedy, Mrs. J. S., New York, gift to charity, $400,000; to Bible Teachers' Training School, $100,000; gift to University of New York, $60,000; gift to church, $6000; gift to Hartford Theological Seminary, $350,000.
Kennedy, W. L., Raleigh, N. C., gift to orphanage, $100,000.
Kenny, Charles B., Pittsburgh, Pa., to charity, $31,000; to University of America, $20,000; to Georgetown University, $20,000.
Kenosha, Wis., to cemetery association, gift by unnamed donor, $5000.
Kenwick Seminary, gift by Thomas F. Hayden, $10,000.
Kerchair, C. M., Philadelphia, Pa., to charity, $5000.
Kernan, James L., Baltimore, Md., to hospital, $40,000.
Kieltz, Anna, St. Louis, Mo., to church, $8000.
Kiley, Michael, New York, to charity, $15,000.
Kimball, Daniel A., Stockbridge, Mass., to colleges, $100,000.
Kimball, Oliver L., Newton, Mass, to church, $35,000; to charity, $90,000.
Kinberg, Edward O., Brooklyn, N. Y., to Presbyterian Hospital, $75,000.
Kingsland, Cornelius F., Riverhead, L. I., to charity, $26,000.
Knapp, Katherine, Boston, Mass., to Museum of Fine Arts, $10,000; to Berea College, $10,000; to charity, $5500; to public library, $10,000.
Knight, Robert, gift to Brown University, $25,000; gift to Y. M. C. A., $25,000.
Knox, B. C., Bloomington, Ill., gift to Lincoln College, $10,000.
Knox, S. H., Buffalo, N. Y., gift for high school at Russell, N. Y., $35,000.
Koffers, Tobias, Holland, Mich., to church, $11,520.
Kohl, Sarah, San Francisco, Cal., to charity, $22,000.
Kohn, Samuel, Philadelphia, Pa., to charity, $30,000.
LaCrosse, Wis., gift of school by Frank P. Hixon, $70,000.
Lake George, N. Y., gift of park by various donors, $10,000.
Lakewood, N. J., hospital, gift by John D. Rockefeller, $5000.
Lambert, W. S., Philadelphia, Pa., gift to Lincoln Museum, $150,000.
Lamont, Mrs. D. S., New York, gift to hospital, $5000.
Lamont, R. P., Chicago, Ill., gift to University of Michigan, $40,000.
Lampson, Isaac P., Cleveland, O., to church, $25,000.
Land, W. M., Sacramento, Cal., to charity, $250,000; park to city, $250,000.
Land, William, Sacramento, Cal., park to city, $260,000.
Lather, Jane K., Oakland, Cal., gift to University of California, $550,000.
Lathrop, Cyrus, Eaton, Mass., to charity, $15,000.
Laughlin, Henry A., Pittsburgh, Pa., gift to Brown University, $25,000.
Lawrence, Mrs. M. H., New York, will to charities, $63,000.
Lawrence, Sebastian D., New York, gift to charity, $600,000.
Lazarus, Elizabeth A., Philadelphia, Pa., to Dropsie College, $50,000.
Leahy, Mary, Louisville, Ky., to charity, $4000.
Leatherbee, George H., Dedham, Mass, to Harvard University, $20,000.
Leddy, Henry M., Buffalo, N. Y., to charities, $10,000.

Leedom, Hannah A., Philadelphia, Pa., to Swarthmore College, $10,000.
Lehman, Mrs. Meyer, New York, gift to Mt. Sinai Hospital, $100,000.
Leland, Frances L., gift to Metropolitan Museum of Art, New York, $1,020,000.
Leiewer, David, Chicago, Ill., to charity, $5000.
Lippitt, Henry F., Providence, R. I., gift to Brown University, $5000.
Leverson, Peter W., Portland, Ore., gift to Williamette Y. M. C. A., $50,000; gift to Williamette University, $100,000; gift to Williamette Y. W. C. A., $50,000.
Levy, Harry M., Cincinnati, O., gift to University of Cincinnati, $50,000.
Le y, Henry, Louisville, Ky., to charity, $9600. v
Lewisohn, Adolph, New York, gift to City College, $50,000.
Lilley, Lucius J., Tecumseh, Mich., to charity, $350,000.
Lincoln College, gift by B. C. Knox, $10,000.
Lincoln University, gift by W. S. Lambert, $150,000; by John B. Webb, $40,000.
Lincoln, William E., Pittsburgh, Pa., gift to Brown University, $5000.
Lincoln Institute, gift by Mrs. M. B. Belknap, $10,000.
Litchfield, William, Lexington, Mass., to charity, $61,000.
Little Sisters of Charity, gift by P. F. Meyer, $250,000.
Locomotor Ataxia Hospital, Chicago, gift by unnamed donor, $100,000.
Loeb, Morris, New York, to Harvard University, $500,000; to charity, $250,000.
London Y. M. C. A., gift by J. P. Morgan, $50,000.
Long, R. A., Kansas City, Mo., gift to church, $85,000.
Lopez, Calixto, New York, for girls' college in Spain, $10,000.
Louisville, Ky., gift for training schools by various donors, $6400.
Lovedale, William, to Y. W. C. A., $5000; to church, $12,500; to Y. M. C. A., $5000.
Lovelace, Mrs. Charles, Turner, Mo., gift to Baptist Theological Seminary, $5000.
Lowell, A. L., Cambridge, Mass., gift to Harvard University, $70,000.
Luther College, Deborah, Ia., gift by J. J. Hall, $50,000.
Lying-In Hospital, will by Francis Amory, $500,000; gift by various donors, Chicago, Ill., $119,500.
Lyle, John S., Tenafly, N. Y., to church, $250,000; to charity, $200,000.
Lyman, G. R., and F. W., Minneapolis, Minn., gift to charity, $27,000.
McCeney, Mary E., Washington, D. C., to charity, $52,000.
McCormick, Mrs. C. W., gift to Union Seminary, $10,000.
Mackay, Mr. and Mrs. Clarence, gift to Nevada University, $100,000.
McKean, Elizabeth W., Philadelphia, Pa., will to charity, $100,000.
Macker, Lizzie H., Medbury, Mass., to church, $15,000.
McKinley, William B., Champaign, Ill., gift to church, $50,000.
McMinnville College, gift by James J. Hill, $50,000.
McNair, Robert, Scotland, Ill., to church, $345,000.
McVilly, Thomas E., Philadelphia, Pa., will to charity, $8000.
Manday, John, Seattle, Wash., to charities, $28,000.
Mandel, Simon, Chicago, Ill., to Associated Jewish Charities, $21,000.
Manual Training School, Scranton, Pa., by Orlando Johnson, $1,000,000.
Marionville College, gift by various donors, $25,000.
March, George E., Lynn, Mass., to charity, $6000.
Marshall, Louis, New York, gift to Young Women's Hebrew Association, $5000.
Marston, Edgar L., Providence, R. I., gift to Brown University, $16,000.
Martin, J. L., New York, to charity, $40,000.
Massachusetts Institute of Technology, gift by unnamed donor, $2,500,000.
Massey, W. E. H., gift to Boston University, $10,000.
Masterton, Ann, Albany, N. Y., will to church, $10,000.

Maternal Home, Bloomington, Ill., will by Jennie E. Caldwell, $500,000.

Mate nity Hospital, gift by A. N. Brady, $100,000. r

Maxwell, J. L., Geneva, N. Y., to missions, $30,000; to charity, $5000; to Berea College, $5000.

Mayburn, Martha J., Philadelphia, Pa., to charity, $10,000.

Mayfield, Ky., gift of library by Andrew Carnegie, $20,000.

Mead, Elizabeth J., Stamford, Conn., to church, $8000; to charity, $20,000

Melrose Hospital, Melrose, Mass., by Thomas W Ripley, $5000.

Melville, George W., Philadelphia, Pa., to charity, $150,000; to University of Pennsylvania, $5000.

Memorial Hall, Richmond, Va., gift by Thomas F. Ryan, $50,000.

Memphis Associated Charities, gift by various donors, $16,000.

Memorial Hospital, gift by Milton G. Higgins, $10,000.

Memphis Associated charities, gift by various donors, $10,000.

Memphis, Tenn., gift of art gallery to city, $100,000

Menermir, Catherine M., Philadelphia, Pa., to charity, $7000

Mental Hygiene Association, New York, gift by unnamed donor, $100,000.

Mercy Hospital, Pittsfield, Mass., by Florence DeWolfe Sampson, $30,000.

Merritt, Alice, DeWitt, Ark., to charity, $5000.

Merritt, Emma L., San Francisco, Cal., gift to City of Sutro Heights, $300,000.

Meserole, Abraham, New York, to charity, $5000.

Metcalf, Stephen O., Providence, R. I., gift to Brown University, $25,000.

Metcalf, Mrs. J. H., Providence, R. I., gift to School of Design, $5000.

Metropolitan Art Museum, will by F. C. Hewitt, $1,500,000; gift by Frances L. Leland, $1,020,000.

Meyer, P. F., New York, gift to Little Sisters of Charity, $250,000.

Milerick, J. E., Boston, Mass., to charity, $20,000.

Milledgeville, Ga., State sanitarium, gift by various donors, $100,000.

Miller, Watson J., Shelton, Conn., to church, $8000.

Mills College, by James C. Tolman, $10,000.

Milwaukee, Wis., tag day, $8500; to city by Robert Nunnemacher, $17,000; gift to church by unnamed donor, $5000; gift to charity, by unnamed donor, $5000.

Minneapolis, Minn., gift of branch library by Andrew Carnegie, $125,000; tag day, $24,000.

Missionary Societies, gift by D. Matilda Douw, $50,000.

Mississippi flood fund, gift by a i us donors, New York, $36,000; by various donors, c$15,000.

Missouri Baptist Sanitarium, gift by Alanson Browne, $200,000.

Mitchell, Margaret E., New York, to charities, $26,500.

Moir, Emily H., New York, to charities, $40,000; to churches, $50,000; to colleges, $1,500,000.

Montclair State Normal School, will by Edward Russ, $50,000.

M dy Schools, gift by unnamed donor, $25,000. oo

Moorman, W. L., Lynchburg, Va., will to charity, $15,000

Morgan, J. P., gift to charity, $5000; to Lick University, $25,000; to Gottingen University, $50,000; to London Y. M. C. A., $50,000; to Hospital for Deformities, $25,000; to Peabody College for Teachers, $100,000; to St. John's Cathedral, $250,000; for church unity, $100,000; to Sailors' Home, New York, $50,000; to Titanic relief fund, $10,000; to Trinity College, $200,000.

Morris, C., Cleveland, O., to hospitals, $1,000,000.

Morton, Lydia, Quincy, Mass., to library, $5000; to charity, $6500.

Mt. Holyoke College, gift by Mr. and Mrs. N. W. Harris, $25,000; by unnamed donor, $50,000; by various donors, $250,000.

Mt. Sinai Hospital, New York, gift by Mrs. Meyer Lehman, $100,000.

Muhlenberg Hospital, Plainfield, N. J., conditional gift, $30,000.

Murphy, Mrs. George, Detroit, Mich., to church, $25,000.

Museum of Fine Arts, Boston, Mass., gift by Francis P. Bartlett, $1,481,000; by Katharine Knapp, $10,000.

Music Conservatory, gift by William Cooper, $5000; by unnamed lady, $10,000.

Musical Societies of New York, gift by A. J. Seligman, $50,000.

Muskogee, Okla., gift of library to town by Andrew Carnegie, $50,000.

Musser, John H., Philadelphia, Pa., will to University of Pennsylvania, $15,000.

Myers, Cora B., Bedford, O., will to charity, $10,000.

Nashville, Tenn., gift of branch libraries by Andrew Carnegie, $50,000.

National Academy of Designs, by Samuel Golding, $10,000.

National Association of Audubon Societies, gift by Mrs. Russell Sage, $10,000.

National Suffrage Association, gift by Mary J. Coggeshall, $15,000; by Mrs. L. L. Buckley, $30,000.

Neaton, William J., Philadelphia, Pa., to charity, $15,000.

Nebraska Wesleyan University, gift by various donors, $274,000.

Neustadter, Caroline, to Neustadter Home, $1,000,000; to other charities, $1,000,000.

Nevada University, gift by Mr. and Mrs. Clarence H. Mackay, $100,000.

New Bedford, Mass., gift by G. T. Bernard, $6000.

Newcombe, William F., Cleveland, O., to charity, $10,000.

New Kensington, Pa., gift of park by Frank M. Curtis, $10,000.

New York, unnamed donor, gift to church, $150,000.

New York Animal Hospital, gift by unnamed donor, $25,000.

New York League for Protection of Animals, gift by various donors, $55,000.

New York schools, will by Henrietta B. Andrei, $7500.

Nickerson, Samuel, Providence, R. I., gift to Brown University, $25,000.

Nikisch, Theodol H., New York, to church, $50,000.

Nixon, William, to Zion Society of New York, $1,000,000.

Northwestern University, gift of Ellen Sage estate, $8000.

Notre Dame University, gift by Max Pam, $50,000.

Noyes, LaVerne W., Chicago, Ill., gift to working girls' hotel, $50,000.

Nunnemacher, Robert, Milwaukee, Wis., to city, $17,000.

Oberlin College, gift by various donors, $172,500.

O'Brien, Kate, New York, to church, $5000.

Occidental College, gift by various donors, California, $500,000.

Ogden, Sarah M., Mt. Holly, N. J., to charity, $12,000.

Ogden, Sarah M., Jamestown, R. I., to charity, $12,000.

Ohio Northwestern University, gift by various donors, $150,000

Old Orchard, Me., various donors, gift to missions, $51,000.

Openhym, A. W., New York, to Columbia University, $91,666; to charity, $183,332.

Orange, N. J., gift of city park by various donors, $50,000; gift to playground by various donors, $44,000.

Page, Charles, San Francisco, Cal., to Yale University, $5000.

Pam, Max., Chicago, gift to Washington Catholic University, $25,000; to Notre Dame University, $50,000.

Paris School of Fine Arts, gift by James Stillman, $100,000.

Park College, by T. G. Sellew, $15,000.

Patten, Clara A. K., Bath, Me., to church $10,000.

Patten, James A. Evanston, Ill., gift to Evanston Woman's Club, $15,000; gift to hospital, $75,000.

Paul, Mrs. A. E., Chicago, Ill. to charity, $30,000.

Peabody College for Teachers, gift by J. P. Morgan, $100,000.

Pearsons, Mrs. and Mr. Samuel, Ellenburg, Wash., gift to Y. M. C. A., $5500

Pease, Jude F., Ridgewood, N. J., to library, $30,000.

Penfield, W. D., New York, to charity, $75,000.

Perry, Mary E. W., Middletown, R. I., to charity, $9000; to church, $11,000; to Bowdoin College, $10,000; to library, $50,000.

Peru, Ind., gift by E. H. Churchill, $50,000.
Peters, F. H., St. Louis, Mo., gift to missions, $5000.
Peters, F. W., St. Louis, Mo., to charities, $12,000.
Philadelphia, Pa., various donors, gift to hospital, $10,000.
Phillips Exeter Academy, will by T. W. Woodman, $5000.
Phillips, Thomas W., Newcastle, Pa., to church, $64,000.
Pinchot, Louise A. F., to charity, $11,200.
Pittsburgh, Pa., tag day, $20,000.
Plainfield, N. J., hospital, gift by various donors, $100,000.
Polytechnic Institute, Brooklyn, N. Y., gift by various donors, $115,529.
Polytechnic Institute, by Milton G. Higgins, $25,000.
Polytechnic Institute, Boston, Mass., gift by various donors, $3,000,000.
Pomona College, by Harriet S. Cousens, $5000.
Pontifical College, Columbus, O., will by Magdalena Bain, $20,000.
Porter, Henry K., Providence, R. I., gift to Brown University, $25,000.
Potter, Thomas, Peabody, Kas., gift to Emporia College, $20,000.
Poulson, Niels, New York, to charity, $484,010.
Prairie du Lac, Wis., gift of library to town by J. S. Tripp, $10,000.
Pratt, Charles H., Bost n, Mass., to Institute of Technology, $750,000. o
Presbyterian Hospital, New York, will by Cornelia Eaton, $15,000; by Edward O. Kinberg, $75,000.
Presbyterian Hospital, Pittsburgh, Pa., by unnamed donor, $50,000.
Presbyterian Ministerial Relief Board, gift by unnamed donor, $75,000.
Presbyterian Ministers' Sustentation Fund, gift by unnamed donor, New York, $50,000.
Princeton Uni e sity, gift by William C. Proctor, $300,000; by rvarious donors, $405,297; gift by Mrs. Russell Sage, $65,000.
Proctor, William C., Cincinnati, O., gift to Princeton University, $300,000.
Providence, R. I., various donors, gift to Y. M. C. A., $335,000.
Purcel, Mary B., Los Angeles, Cal., to charities, $400,000.
Quinn, Alice, New York, will to charity $14,000.
Radeke, Jesse H. and Eliza G., Providence, R. I., gift to Brown University, $25,000.
Randolph-Macon Woman's College, gift by various donors, $175,000.
Rankin, W. A., Onarga, Ill., gift to Grand Prairie Seminary, $10,000.
Rankin, William, Princeton, N. J., will to church, $5000.
Ranson, F. J., New York, to church, $200,000; will to charity, $143,000.
Red Cross Balkan Fund, gift by Mrs. Russell Sage, $5000; gift by J. D. Rockefeller, $5000.
Reid, Peter, Passaic, N. J., to charity, $340,000.
Rhinelander, Matilda F., New York, gift to St. Luke's Hospital, $85,500.
Rhodes, Eliza J., Pittsburgh, Pa., gift to charity, $7000.
Riley, James W., Indianapolis, Ind., gift to library, $70,000.
Ripley, Thomas W., Melrose, Mass., to Melrose hospital, $5000.
Ripon College, gift by Andrew Carnegie, $25,000.
Robert Mary E., New York, to charity, $9000.
Roberts, Helen B., Philadelphia, Pa., to charity, $11,000.
Robin, H. M., Philadelphia, Pa., for maternal home, $150,000.
Robinson, Laverne, Battle Creek, Mich., to Clifin College, $5000; to charity, $75,000.
Robinson, Mary, Rock Island, Ill., gift to Y. M. C. A., $15,000.
Robinson, Wallace, Boston, Mass., gift to Dartmouth College, $100,000.
Rockefeller, J. D., New York, gift to Balkan Relief Fund, $5000; gift to Brown University, $25,000; gift to church, $5000; gift to Evangelical Baptist Church, Cleveland, Ohio, $5500; gift to Lakewood, N. J., hospital, $5000; conditional gift to Illinois Wesleyan College, $125,000; gift for Preservation of Pasteur Home, Paris, $11,000; gift to Sailors' Home, New York, $50,000; gift to Technical Y. M. C. A., Atlanta, Ga., $15,000; gift to Tuberculosis Hospital, Farmington, $10,000; gift to Y. M. C. A., $15,000; gift to Young Women's Hebrew Association, $5000.
Rockefeller, J. D., Jr., gift to Brown University, $25,000.
Roebling, W. A., Trenton, N. J., gift of children's playground, $7500.
Rosenwald, Julius, Chicago, Ill., to charities, $325,000; to University of Chicago, $250,000; to Chicago Hebrew Institute, $50,000; to Social Workers' Country Club, $50,000; to Glenwood Training School, $12,500; gift to Colored Y. M. C. A., Cincinnati, $25,000; gift to public school, $10,000; gift to Colored Y. M. C. A., of New York, $25,000.
Rotch, Albert L., Dedham, Mass., to Harvard University, $50,000.
Ruddy, Thomas, Madison, Wis., to church, $5000.
Russ, Edward, Newark, N. J., to charity, $10,500; to Montclair State Normal School, $50,000.
Russell, N. Y., High School, gift by S. H. Knox, $35,000.
Russell, Sarah S., Winsted, Conn., to church, $5000.
Rutledge, Edward, Chippewa Falls, Wis., to charity, $1,000,000.
Ryan, Thomas F., New York, gift to Memorial Hall, Richmond, Va., $50,000; gift to church, $1,000,000.
Ryan, Mrs. T. F., Suffern, N. Y., gift to Convent of the Holy Child, $250,000.
Ryerson, Mrs. Arthur, Chicago, Ill., gift to Yale University, $5000.
Sacramento, Cal., will of park to city by William Land, $260,000.
Safe, Harriet F., Providence, R. I., gift to Brown University, $5000.
Sage, Ellen, estate of, gift to Northwestern University, $8000.
Sage, Mrs. Russell, New York, gift to Columbia Medical School, $25,000; gift to Princeton University, $65,000; gift to Sag Harbor Library, $122,000; gift to charity, $5000; gift to Woman's League for Protection of Animals, $10,000; gift to Chinese relief fund, $6000; gift to National Audubon Society, $10,000; gift to Syracuse University, $50,000; gift to charity, $150,000; gift to Red Cross Balkan fund, $5000; gift for relief of Turkish wounded $5000.
Sage, Mrs. R. H., Chicago, Ill., gift to Beloit College, $50,000.
Sag Harbor Library, gift by Mrs. Russell Sage, $122,000.
Sailors' Home, gift by H. C. Frick, $25,000; by J. D. Rockefeller, $50,000; by Mrs. Mary A. Harriman, $50,000; by J. P. Morgan, $50,000.
St. John's Cathedral, New York, gift by Mrs. J. J. Blodgett, $200,000; by J. P. Morgan, $250,000; by various donors, $400,000.
St. Joseph Seminary, by Mrs. Joseph Drexel, $10,000.
St. Louis, Mo., conditional bequest to college, by Samuel Cupples, $1,000,000; conditional gift for opera house, by Adolphus Busch, $50,000.
St. Louis Rescue Mission, gift by various donors, $66,410.
St. Louis Tuberculosis Hospital, gift by Helen Gould, $10,000.
St. Luke's Hospital, New York, gift by Matilda F. Rhinelander, $85,500.
St. Paul, gift of library, by James J. Hill, $850,000.
St. Paul's School, gift by Mr. and Mrs. George Armour, $50,000.
Saks, Andrew, New York, to charity, $25,000.
Solvay Process Co., Syracuse, N. Y., gift to Salvation Army, New York, gift by unnamed donor, $10,000.
Sampson, Florence De Wolfe, Pittsfield, Mass., will to Mercy Hospital, $30,000.
San Francisco, Cal., gift of library, by Andrew Carnegie, $750,000.
Savery, Elizabeth, Wareham, Mass., will to charities, $14,000.
Saybrook, Ill., gift to church, by unnamed donor, $80,000.
Schaeffer, J. H., New York, will to charity, $20,000.
Schiff, Jacob H., New York, gift to Cornell University, $100,000; to Tuberculosis Hospital, $5000; gift to Young Woman's Hebrew Association, $65,000.
Schneider, Joseph, Milwaukee, Wis., gift to University of Wurzburg, $25,000.
School of Design, gift by Mrs. J. H. Metcalf, $5000.
Schwab, Charles M., Pittsburgh, Pa., gift to church, $5000.
Seipp, W. C., Chicago, Ill., to charities, $65,000.
Sears, Roebuck & Co., Chicago, Ill., gift to Council of Grain Exchanges, $1,000,000.

Seligman, A. J., New York, to musical societies, $50,000.
Sellew, T. G., Montclair, N. J., to church, $69,000; to Cooper Union, $10,000; to Park College, $15,000.
Settlement House, gift by various donors, Baltimore, Md., $80,000.
Settlement work, New York, gift by Anna Woereshoffer, $150,000.
Shanley, John F., Newark, N. J., to charity, $10,000.
Sharpe, Henry D., Providence, R. I., gift to Brown University, $25,000.
Shea, Bartholomew, Philadelphia, Pa., to charity, $50,000.
Shedd, John G., Chicago, Ill., gift for working girls' hotel, $50,000; gift to Y. M. C. A. workingmen's hotel, $50,000; gift to Smith College, $50,000.
Sheldon, Elizabeth, Rensselaerville, N. Y., to charity, $18,500.
Sherrell, Dana, Morris, Ill., to Beloit College, $30,000.
Shevlin, Mr. and Mrs. James, gift to charity, $100,000.
Shevlin, Thomas H., Minneapolis, Minn., will to charities, $75,000.
Simons, Catherine, Boston, Mass., to charity, $6000.
Simpson, Alexander, Philadelphia, Pa., gift to church, $50,000.
Simpson, Alexander W., Philadelphia, Pa., to church, $34,000.
Sinai Temple, Chicago, Ill., gift by various donors, $340,000.
Smiley, Mrs. Joseph W., Schenectady, N. Y., will to charity, $85,000.
Smith, Mrs. Mackay, Philadelphia, Pa., gift to charities, $12,000.
Smith College, gift by John G. Shedd, $50,000; by Mr. and Mrs. D. B. Gamble, $30,000; by various donors, $23,000; by unnamed donor, $60,000.
Smith, Simeon, Bloomfield, Ind., to De Pauw University, $250,000.
Smith, William D., Reading, Pa., to charity, $30,000.
Snively, T. A., Chicago, Ill., to charity, $5000.
Snow, Clara, Brockton, Mass., to charity, $15,000.
Social Workers' Country Club, gift by Julius Rosenwald, $50,000.
Solvay Process Co., Syracuse, N. Y., gift to hospital fund, $5000.
Somerville, Mass., gift to library, by Andrew Carnegie, $80,000.
Southwell, H. S., Fort Atkinson, Wis., gift to library, $10,000.
Southwest College, will by Lizzie Graham, $14,000.
Spahr, W. J., Pittsburgh, Pa., will to church, $200,000.
Spear, Louise M., Philadelphia, Pa., will to charity, $16,000.
Speed, James B., Louisville, Ky., to charity, $20,000.
Spencer, William A., New York, to public library, $100,000.
Stanley Hall School, Minneapolis, Minn., gift by unnamed donor, $50,000.
Staterbury, Mrs. G., Washington, D. C., gift to Emergency Hospital, $10,000.
Stevens, Mrs. M. H., Sycamore, Ill., gift to hospital, $20,000.
Stillman, James, New York, gift to Paris School of Fine Arts, $100,000.
Storrs, Cornelia, White Plains, N. Y., to Home for Girls, $1,000,000; to Cancer Hospital, $1,000,000.
Straus, Isidor, New York, to charity, $85,000; to Educational Alliance, $200,000.
Strawn, Julius G., Jacksonville, Ill., gift to Illinois Woman's College, $10,000.
Sutphen, Emma E. L., New York, to charity, $5000.
Sutro Heights, gift by Emma L. Merritt, $300,000.
Swarthmore College, gift by Hannah A. Leedom, $10,000; by Alice A. Hicks, $100,000.
Syracuse, N. Y., gift to hospital, by unnamed donor, $5000; gift to hospital fund by Solvay Process Co., $5000.
Syracuse University, gift by Mrs. Russell Sage, $50,000.
Technical Y. M. C. A., Atlanta, Ga., gift by J. D. Rockefeller, $15,000.
Thalman, Ernst, New York, to charity, $30,000.
Thomas, Caroline, Germantown, Pa., to charity, $25,000.
Thompson, John D., Pittsburgh, Pa., to charities, 45,000; to Western Theological Seminary, $10,000.
Thurber, Emma, Providence, R. I., to charities, $75,000.
Titanic relief fund, gift by Andrew Carnegie, $5000; gift by Vincent Astor, $10,000; gift by J. Pierpont Morgan, $10,000.
Tobey, Susanna J., Wareham, Mass., to charities, $316,000; to church, $10,000; for town hall, $75,000.
Todd, T. J., Richmond, Va., gift to library, $15,000.
Todd, Sally, Youngstown, Pa., to church, $55,000; to charities, $155,000.
Tolman, James C., Oakland, Cal., to Mills College, $10,000.
Tomah, Wis., town of, will by Ernest R. Buckley, $20,000.
Tooley, James W., Philadelphia, Pa., to charity, $10,000.
Tourtelotte, Jacob F., Minneapolis, Minn., to school, $101,000.
Towne, Joseph H., Salem, Mass., to missions, $400,000.
Trade Schools, by Milton G. Higgins, $25,000.
Trinity College, gift by J. P. Morgan, $200,000.
Tripp, J. S., Prarie du Sac, Wis., gift of library to town, $10,000.
Tri-State Methodist Hospital, Memphis, Tenn., contributions to, $40,000.
Troy Orphan Asylum, will by Hannah M. Earl, $20,000.
Tuberculosis Hospital, Farmington, gift by John D. Rockefeller, $10,000; gift by Jacob H. Schiff, $5000.
Tucker, Mary J., Belleville, N. J., will to church, $5000.
Tuskegee Institute Hospital, gift by various donors, Boston, Mass., $50,000.
Tyrrell Mrs. M. W., Chicago, Ill., to church, $6000.
Union Theological Seminary, gift by unnamed donor, $50,000.
United Charities, Chicago, Ill., gift by various donors, $83,765.
United States Steel Corporation, gift to Y. M. C. A., Pittsburgh, Pa., $5000.
Union Seminary, gift by George W. Watts, $45,000; gift by Mrs. C. W. McCormick, $10,000.
University of America, will by Charles B. Kenny, $20,000.
University of California, gift by Michael Cudahy, $10,000.
University of Chicago, gift by Julius Rosenwald, $250,000.
University of Cincinnati, gift by Harry M. Levy, $50,000.
University of Michigan, will by J. L. Babcock, $5000; gift by R. P. Lamont, $40,000.
University of New York, gift by Mrs. John S. Kennedy, $60,000.
University of Omaha, gift by various donors, $30,000.
University of Pennsylvania, will by Mrs. Joseph Drexel, $80,000; will by George W. Melville, $5000; gift by John H. Musser, $15,000; gift by L. C. Cleeman, $50,000.
Vail, Thomas N., Boston, Mass., gift to Institute of Technology, $100,000.
Valdosta, Ga., State Normal College, gift by various donors, $21,000.
Vallejo Y. M. Institute, gift by Annie Donohoe, $100,000.
Vandegrift, C. J., Philadelphia, Pa., will to church, $20,000.
Vanderbilt family, New York, gift to Y. M. C. A., $300,000.
Vanderbilt, Mrs. Frederick, New York, gift to Girls' Home, $150,000.
Vanneck, John T., New York, to charity, $100,000.
Villa Nova College, gift by Bernard Conn, $100,000.
Vought, Mary W. M., Denver, Colo., to Hobart College, $10,000.
Vreeland, Anna H., Jersey City, N. J., gift to missions, $50,000.
Waggener, B. P., Atchison, Kas., gift to charity, $10,000.
Walden, A., Corydon, Ia., to town, $165,000.
Wallace, Mrs. James, Detroit, Mich., gift to German Wallace College, $25,000.
Walsh, Francis, New York, to charity, $5000.
Warburg family, New York, gift to Young Women's Hebrew Association, $15,000.
Ward, A. L., Fairmont, Mont., for dependent children, $150,000.
Ward, Edwin M., Montclair, N. J., to charity, $6000.
Ward, Henry C., New York to charity, $5000.
Washington Catholic University, by Mrs. Joseph Drexel, $10,000; gift by Max Pam, $25,000.

Washington University, willed by Brookins, R. S., $250,000.

Waterville, Me., will to town by Valora Chase, $5000.

Watts, George W., Durham, N. C., gift of hospital to city, $100,000; gift to Union Seminary, $15,000.

Webb, John B., Glen Ridge, N. J., to Lincoln University, $40,000.

Weinman, Moses, New York, to charity, $70,000.

Wellesley College, gift by Mildred Klein, $10,000; gift by various donors, $5000.

Wellman, Clara E., Brookline, Mass., to charity, $5000.

Wells College, gift by Andrew Carnegie, $18,000; gift by various donor, $20,000.

Wentworth, D. H., Boston, Mass., gift to library, $18,000; gift to charity, $6000.

Western Reserve University, gift by various donors, $750,000; gift by H. M. Henna, $250,000.

Western Theological Seminary, by John D. Thompson, $10,000; gift by N. W. Conklin, $100,000.

Widener, P. A. B., Philadelphia, Pa., gift of library building to Harvard University, $1,000,000; gift to Widener School for Crippled Children, $4,000,000.

Widener School for Crippled Children, gift by P. A. B. Widener, $4,000,000.

William Jewell College, gift by Alanson Browne, $100,000.

William Penn Charter School, gift by Pierre S. Dupont, $20,000.

Williamette University, gift by Peter W. Leverson, $100,000.

Williamette Y. M. C. A., gift by Peter W. Leverson, $50,000.

Williamette Y. W. C. A., gift by Peter Leverson, $50,000.

Williams, Mrs. S. A., New York, gift to charity, $10,000.

Wills, Kensel, Philadelphia, Pa., will to church, $5000.

Winchester, Ky., gift of library, by Andrew Carnegie, $15,000.

Winfield, Kas., gift of library, by Andrew Carnegie, $15,000.

Wittenberg College, by Isaac K. Funk, $10,000.

Woerrishoff, Emma C., New York, will to charity, $40,000; will to Bryn Mawr College, $750,000.

Woerishoffer, Anna, New York, gift to settlement work, $150,000.

Wolfe, Georgette E., St. Louis, Mo., will to charity, $37,500.

Wolff, Lewis S., New York, to charity, $19,500.

Wolgemut, Sarah J., Philadelphia, Pa., to charity, $65,000.

Woman's League for Protection of Animals, gift by Mrs. Russell Sage, $10,000.

Woodman, T. W., Dover, N. H., for park, $10,000; to charity, $10,200; to Dartmouth College, $5000; to Phillips Exeter Academy, $5000.

Worcester Academy, will by William H. Dexter, $40,000.

Working Girls' Hotel, Chicago, Ill., gift by Laverne W. Noyes, $50,000; gift by John O. Shedd, $50,000.

Wurzburg University, gift by Joseph Schneider, $25,000.

Yale Forestry School, endowment fund, gift by unnamed donor, $100,000; endowment fund, gift by Andrew Carnegie, $100,000.

Yale University, gift by Charles Page, $5000; gift by Francis Bacon, $400,000; by Mrs. W. C. Eggleston, $100,000; gift by Francis Bacon, $500,000; will by Matthew C. D. Borden, $250,000; will by F. C. Hewitt, $500,000; by Mrs. Arthur Ryerson, $5000; by Ciprian Brainerd, $65,000; will by Henry F. Dimock, $1,867,229; gift by Martha L. Byers, $10,000; gift by unnamed donor, $100,000.

York, Pa., gift of park to city, by A. B. Farquhar, $20,000.

Y. M. C. A., gift by Frances Huntley, $5000; gift by estate of Mrs. J. D. Boardman, $5000; Pittsburgh, Pa., gift by various donors, $20,000; by William Lovedale, $5000; gift by various donors, Ellenburg, Wash., $46,000; gift by Mr. and Mrs. Samuel Pearsons, $5500; South Bend, Ind., gift by various donors, $56,208; gift by various donors, Rock Island, Ill., $112,000; gift by Mary Robinson, $15,000; gift by Vanderbilt family, $300,000; gift by various donors, Atchison, Kas., $100,000; gift by C. P. Dodge, $5000; gift by J. D. Rockefeller, $15,000; gift by A. H. Hyde, $15,000; by Lillian Flint, $3376; Grand Island, Neb., gift by various donors, $70,000; Pittsburgh, Pa., gift by United States Steel Corporation, $5000; Portsmouth, Va., gift by Helen Gould $10,000; Providence, R. I., gift by various donors, $335,000; Providence, R. I., gift by Robert Knight, $25,000; Providence, R. I., gift by Samuel Cult $10,000; gift by Mrs. J. Chaffee, $5000; Shanghai, China, gift by various donors, $95,000.

Y. M. C. A. Training School, Chicago, Ill., gift by various donors, $50,000.

Y. M. C. A. Workingmen's Hotel, gift by unnamed donor, $25,000.

Y. M. C. A. Workingmen's Hotel, gift by John G. Shedd, $50,000.

Y. W. C. A., gift by Helen Gould, $250,000; will by William Lovedale, $5000; gift by Mrs. H. C. Hinskamp, $5000; gift by various donors, Providence, R. I., $15,000.

Y. W. C. A. for McKeesport, Pa., gift by various donors, $17,000.

Young, Reuben, York, Pa., gift to charity, $80,000.

Young, W. P., New York, will to church, $700,000.

Young Woman's Hebrew Association, gift by Jacob H. Schiff, $40,000; gift by Lewis Marshall, $5000; gift by other donors, New York, $175,000; gift by Warburg family, $15,000; gift by Jacob H. Schiff, $10,000; gift by John D. Rockefeller, $5000; gift by Mrs. Jacob H. Schiff, $5000; gift by Jacob H. Schiff, $10,000.

Young Women's Union, gift by various donors, Philadelphia, Pa., $50,000.

Youngstown, O., Hospital, gift by various donors, $160,000.

Zurbrugg, Mount Holly, N. J., will to charity, $250,000.

GILMAN, Nicholas Paine. An American sociologist, economist, and educator, died January, 1912. He was born in 1849 and received an academic education. He graduated from the Harvard Divinity School in 1871 and settled as a Unitarian clergyman over three parishes in Massachusetts in 1872. He remained here until 1884. From 1888 to 1895 he was editor of the *Literary World* and from 1895 to the time of his death was professor of sociology and ethics at Meadville Theological School. He was editor of *The New World* from 1892 to 1900. He was the author of *Profit-sharing Between the Employer and Employee* (1889); *Laws of Daily Conduct* (1891); *Socialism and the American Spirit* (1893); *A Dividend to Labor* (1899), and *Methods of Industrial Peace* (1904).

GIN. See Liquors.

GIOVANNITTI, Arturo. See Strikes.

GIPSY MOTH. See Eentomology.

GLASS. See Chemisty, Industrial.

GNÔME MOTORS. See Aeronautics.

GOITRE, Cancerous. See Carrel, Alexis.

GOLD. The production of gold in the United States from domestic ores in 1911 was 4,687,503 fine ounces, valued at $96,890,000, as compared with 4,657,018 fine ounces, valued at $96,269,100, in 1910, showing a very slight increase in the production in 1911. Of the States producing gold, California produced in 1911 the largest quantity, 964,041 fine ounces, valued at $19,928,500. Colorado produced 925,839 fine ounces, valued at $19,138,800; Montana, 875,438 fine ounces, valued at $18,096,900. The gold production of other States will be found in the paragraph *Mineral Production* under these States. In addition to the production of gold and silver from domestic smelters in 1911, the smelters and refiners produced as refined bullion from foreign ore, matte, and unrefined bullion 875,156 fine ounces.

The gold production in 1912 in the United States, as will be seen in the following table, was considerably less than that of 1911. The figures are from the *Report of the Director of the Mint*. It will be noted that California and Colorado both had decreased production in

1912 while the decrease of Nevada was nearly $5,000,000:

	1911	1912
Alabama	$ 18,335	$ 17,674
Alaska	16,002,976	17,398,943
Arizona	2,954,790	3,303,504
California	20,310,987	19,988,486
Colorado	19,153,860	18,791,710
Georgia	30,532	9,881
Idaho	1,169,261	1,303,917
Missouri	......	310
Montana	3,169,840	3,235,287
Nevada	18,968,578	13,331,680
New Mexico	639,877	604,961
North Carolina	76,693	142,760
Oregon	599,235	630,801
South Carolina	13,437	15,587
South Dakota	7,430,367	7,795,680
Tennessee	14,140	9,881
Texas	1,778	10,170
Utah	4,709,747	4,376,971
Virginia	4,300	8,755
Washington	504,537	285,044
Wyoming	18,791	22,884
Unassigned	965,247	......
Total continental U. S.	$96,757,308	$91,284,886
Philippines	130,501	400,248
Porto Rico	2,191	......
Total	$96,890,000	$91,685,134

The production of gold in the world in 1912, according to the figures gathered by the *Engineering and Mining Journal*, exceeded that of any previous year, the increase over 1911 having been $10,240,783 or 2.2 per cent. This increase is due almost entirely to the large gain in the Transvaal, which was approximately $18,225,000. The gain made in the African mines was sufficient to offset the losses in the United States, Russia, and Mexico. The Australasian mines also continued to decrease in production, and this has now extended through several years. The gold production in 1911-12, as recorded by the *Engineering and Mining Journal*, will be found in the following table:

	1911	1912
Transvaal	$170,059,273	$188,285,000
Rhodesia	12,986,000	13,375,000
West Africa	5,197,488	7,379,000
Madagascar, etc.	2,706,639	2,750,000
Total Africa	$190,949,400	$211,789,000
United States	$ 96,890,000	$ 91,685,168
Mexico	24,880,100	22,500,000
Canada	9,762,100	11,250,000
Central America, etc.	3,399,000	3,450,000
Total North America	$134,931,200	$128,885,168
Russia, inc. Siberia	$ 32,151,600	$ 27,750,000
France	1,707,100	1,825,000
Other Europe	2,584,900	2,595,000
Total Europe	$ 36,443,600	$ 32,170,000
British India	$ 11,054,100	$ 12,908,415
Brit. and Dutch E. Ind.	4,726,500	4,875,000
Japan and Chosen	6,896,900	7,115,000
China and others	3,769,600	3,750,000
Total Asia, not inc. Siberia	$ 26,447,100	$ 28,648,415
South America	$ 10,421,800	$ 11,250,000
Australasia	60,184,200	56,875,500
Total	$459,377,300	$469,618,083

For metallurgy of gold, see METALLURGY.

GOLD COAST, THE. A British crown colony, with Ashanti and the protected Northern territories situated on the Gulf of Guinea. Area of the colony, 24,200 square miles; of Ashanti, 20,000; of the Northern Territories, 35,800—total, 80,000. The census (1911) returns place the population at 1,502,899 (colony, 857,516; Ashanti, 287,814; Northern Territories, 357,569); but the figures are believed to understate the actual number of inhabitants. Accra, the capital, had (1911) 19,585 inhabitants; Coomassie, 18,853; Cape Coast Castle, 11,364; Seccondee, 7725. The chief products and exports (1910), are cacao, £866,571; gold and gold dust, £790,282; rubber, £358,876; palm kernels, £185,058; palm oil, £161,388; lumber, £148,078; kola nuts, £77,716. Cotton goods, provisions, and wine and spirits are the main imports. Total trade (1910): £3,365,641 imports, £2,697,105 exports. Revenue, £1,006,633; expenditure, £924,862. Tonnage entered and cleared, 2,599,388. A railway runs from Seccondee to Coomassie. During 1912 a railway under construction from Accra to Akwapim was opened for traffic to a temporary terminus at Pakro, about 37 miles distant. Total telegraph lines, 1424 miles. James Jameson Thorburn was governor in 1912 (Bt.-Major Herbert Bryan, acting).

GOLF. Harold H. Hilton of the Royal Liverpool Gold Club, who in 1911 came to the United States and won the National Amateur Golf Championship, not only failed to retain his title in 1912, but was put out of the running in the first round of the tournament at Wheaton, Il., by Charles G. Waldo, Jr., of Brooklawn. Jerome D. Travers of Upper Montclair captured the amateur title for the third time in his career by defeating Charles W. Evans, Jr., of Edgewater, 7 up and 6 to play in the 36-hole final round. In the gold medal contest Hilton and Evans battled to a tie, Evans winning in the play off. Travers added to his laurels by winning the metropolitan amateur tournament held at Baltusrol. The metropolitan open tournament was won by Tom McNamara, and the national open was won by John J. McDermont for the second successive year. McNamara is the first American-born player to win the metropolitan open.

Miss Margaret Curtis won the women's national championship for the third time since 1907 by defeating Mrs. Ronald H. Barlow in the final round by 3 up and 2 to play. Mrs. Barlow, however, had little trouble in winning the championship of the Women's Eastern Golf Association. The English open championship was won by Edward Ray, with Harry Vardon as runner up. John Ball captured the English amateur championship and Miss Gladys Ravenscroft the British ladies' championship. The French open championship went to Jean Gassiat, Harry Vardon finishing second. J. H. Taylor won the German open championship, Edward Ray, the English champion, taking second place.

The team championship of the Intercollegiate Golf Association for the fifth year in succession was won by Yale, which defeated Harvard in the finals by 6 matches to 3. The individual winner was F. C. Davidson of Harvard, who was the victor over J. M. Sterns of Princeton, 1 up in 37 holes. In dual college matches Yale defeated Princeton and Princeton defeated Cornell The Oxford and Cambridge contest resulted in a tie, each university winning 4 matches.

GOMEZ, J. M. See CUBA.

GOMPERZ, THEODOR. An Austrian philosopher and classical scholar, died August,

1912. He was born at Brunn in 1832 and studied at the University of Vienna, where from 1869 to 1901 he was professor of classical philology. In the latter year he entered the House of Peers. Of his many published works the most notable are: *Demosthenes der Staatsmann* (1864); *Herculanische Studien* (1865-6), and his great history of Greek philosophy, *Griechische Denker* (1893-1895). He edited the German edition of the works of John Stuart Mill (1869-1880).

GOODWIN, WILLIAM WATSON. American scholar and educator, died June 16, 1912. He was born in Concord, Mass., in 1831, and graduated from Harvard University in 1851. Until 1855 he studied in Germany at the universities of Göttingen, Berlin, and Bonn. From 1856 to 1860 he was a tutor in Harvard University. In the latter year he was appointed professor of Greek literature, serving until 1901, when he was appointed professor emeritus. He was the first director of the American School of Classical Studies at Athens, 1882-3. From 1903 to 1909 he was overseer of Harvard University. In 1903 he was president of the American Academy of Arts and Sciences. He was a member of many American and foreign learned societies. He was a Knight of the Greek Order of the Redeemer. Among his published writings are: *Syntax of the Moods and Tenses of the Greek Verb*, and a *Greek Grammar*. He edited *Demosthenes on the Crown and Against Midias*.

GORDON, JAMES. A former United States senator from Mississippi, died November 28, 1912. He was born in Monroe County, Miss., in 1855. He served in the Confederate army during the Civil War as captain of the Jeff. Davis Legion, and as colonel of the 4th Mississippi Cavalry. After the close of the war he engaged in cotton planting, in which he was successful. On December 27, 1909, he was appointed United States senator to succeed Anselm J. McLaurin. He served until February 22, 1910. Colonel Gordon made no pretense of mastering the details in the Senate and very seldom took part in its discussions. He was, however, on account of his age and his gentle and generous attitude towards certain senators who made bitter attacks on the Confederate cause, a distinguished figure in the Senate. Shortly before his retirement he delivered one of the most affecting pleas for charity and consideration on the part of the North and the South ever heard in the Senate chamber. His speech was greeted with unprecedented applause from the senators. One of the last acts of Colonel Gordon was to write a letter defending the memory of the late Senator Heyburn, whose attitude against the Confederate cause was bitter and uncompromising. Colonel Gordon pleaded that these things should be forgotten and that the better qualities of Senator Heyburn only should be remembered. Colonel Gordon had considerable literary ability and was the author of *The Old Plantation, and Other Poems.* For many years he contributed to magazines, especially to publications dealing with hunting and other sports.

GORDON, WILLIAM W. An American soldier and merchant, died September 11, 1912. He was born at Savannah, Ga., in 1834. He graduated from Yale College in 1854 and served in the Confederate army, first as second lieutenant in Stewart's cavalry and later as captain in the Confederate cavalry. He was wounded at Lovejoy's Station, Ga., and was placed upon the roll of honor for gallantry at Frederick City, Md. After the war he served in the Georgia cavalry and was four times in command of troops for riot duty. He engaged in the cotton business in Savannah and became senior partner of the firm of W. W. Gordon & Co. At the outbreak of the Spanish-American War he was appointed brigadier-general of volunteers and was a member of the Porto Rican Evacuation Commission.

GORDON-BENNETT CUP RACES. See AERONAUTICS.

GORTYNA. See ARCHÆOLOGY.

GOVERNORS' CONFERENCE. The fifth annual meeting of the governors of the States, the so-called "House of Governors," was held in Richmond, Va., in the first week in December. Many subjects of national as well as of State interest were discussed. One of the most important of these was agricultural credits, and a committee was appointed to draft a system of laws to be recommended to the State legislatures. A State income tax law and uniform divorce legislation were also discussed.

The useful work of the conference was unfortunately subordinated in the public mind by the notoriety gained through several inflammatory speeches practically defending and upholding lynching, delivered by Governor Blease of South Carolina. Governor Blease was sharply answered by several of the governors. For a more detailed account of this unpleasant episode, see SOUTH CAROLINA. The conference formed a permanent organization and elected Miles C. Riley, of the Wisconsin Legislative Reference Library, secretary. The next meeting will be held in Colorado Springs in 1913.

GRADUATE SCHOOL OF ARGICULTURE. See AGRICULTURAL EDUCATION.

GRADY, THOMAS FRANCIS. An American lawyer and politician, died February 3, 1912. He was born in New York City in 1853 and was educated in the parochial schools of that city and in Manhattan College. For a short time after graduation he worked in a publishing house in New York City, but soon took up the study of law and was for a time employed in the office of the corporation counsel. He became known as a speaker by delivering temperance lectures in New York City. He became interested in politics and was appointed recording clerk in the county clerk's office in 1874. A few years later he was elected to the State Assembly and was reëlected until 1881, when he was made State senator. He had become affiliated with Tammany Hall and was regarded as one of the most efficient politicians connected with that body. In 1883, when Grover Cleveland was governor of the State, Mr. Grady opposed many of the measures which the former wished passed by the legislature. He also assailed Cleveland in speeches and succeeded in holding up many nominations which the governor had sent to the Senate. Cleveland thereupon sent a letter to John Kelly, leader of Tammany Hall, in which he said that he did not wish Mr. Grady to be returned to the Senate, and he was, as a consequence, retired from that body. In the presidential campaign of 1884 he advocated the election of Benjamin F. Butler and made speeches in his favor throughout the United

States. In 1888, however, he advocated the reëlection of President Cleveland and in the following year was returned to the New York State Senate. For ten years he was the Democratic minority leader in the Senate, but when the Democrats obtained a majority in that body as a result of the election of 1910 he was refused the position of leader of the majority. Mr. Grady was regarded as the foremost orator connected with Tammany Hall and he became the spokesman for Richard Croker in national and State conventions. He opposed most of the reform measures advocated in the legislature during his term of service in that body.

GRAFTON, Charles Chapman. An American bishop of the Protestant Episcopal Church, died August 30, 1912. He was born in 1830 and graduated from Harvard College in 1853. In 1858 he was ordained priest. He served as rector in churches in Baltimore and Boston until 1889, when he was consecrated Bishop of Fond du Lac. He organized in England, in 1865, with the Rev. R. M. Benson, the Society of St. John the Evangelist, a religious brotherhood, otherwise known as the "Cowley Fathers." He also established the St. Margaret's Sisterhood in Boston. He was the oldest Protestant Episcopal bishop at the time of his death. He was the author of *Vocation, or Call of the Divine Master to a Sister's Life; Plain Suggestions for a Reverent Celebration of the Holy Communion; Fond du Lac Tracts; Christian and Catholic* (1905); *Catholic Atlas*, and *Roman Correspondence* (pamphlets).

Bishop Grafton was one of the foremost leaders of the High-Church section of the denomination. In 1906 a religious storm was raised by the accusations of Dr. William Austin Smith, rector of St. Paul's Church in Milwaukee, who attacked Bishop Grafton for his High-Church tendencies. He accused Bishop Grafton of polytheism. The friends of the bishop rallied to his support and an interesting theological discussion followed. He was an earnest advocate of a closer union with the Eastern Church, and with this in view made an extended trip through the East. His observations inspired him to efforts to bring about the formation of the American branch of the Anglican and Eastern Orthodox Churches' Union, whose aim was to foster intercommunion between the two bodies, as well as mutual recognition of each other's Catholic position.

GRAHAM, Charles Morice. A Roman Catholic bishop, died September 1, 1912. He was born in 1834 at Mhow, in the East Indies. He was first educated in England under the care of Protestant relatives, but at the age of ten years was placed in a Roman Catholic school and in 1851 was sent to the English College at Rome. He was appointed to serve in the diocese of Plymouth and became in succession canon and vicar-general. In 1891 he was appointed titular bishop of Cisamos and coadjutor to Bishop Clifford of Clifton. In 1902 he was appointed bishop of Plymouth. He resigned in 1911 and the Pope bestowed upon him the title of archbishop of Tiberias.

GRAND CENTRAL TERMINAL. See Architecture.

GRAND TRUNK RAILWAY. See Canada.

GRANT, Frederick Dent. An American major-general, son of Ulysses S. Grant, died April 11, 1912. He was born in St. Louis in 1850. While a boy he accompanied his father in several campaigns of the Civil War. After its close he entered the United States Military Academy, from which he graduated in 1871. In the same year he was appointed second lieutenant of the 4th United States Cavalry. From 1873 to 1881 he acted as aid to General Sheridan, having been promoted from lieutenant-colonel. In this capacity he served on the frontier in campaigns against the Indians. He resigned from the army in 1881. In 1885 he was appointed United States minister to Austria by President Harrison. From 1894 to 1898 he was police commissioner of New York City. At the outbreak of the Spanish-American War he was appointed colonel of the 14th New York Infantry and in the same year was promoted to be brigadier-general of volunteers. He saw service in the Spanish-American War and in the rebellion in the Philippines. In 1901 he was appointed brigadier-general in the United States army and major-general in 1906. He was at various times in command of districts of Southern Luzon, Northern Luzon, Department of Texas, Department of the Lakes, and the Department of the East. He was commander of the latter department at the time of his death.

GRANTLEY, Baron. See Furness, Christopher.

GRAVING DOCKS. See Docks and Harbors.

GREAT BRITAIN. The United Kingdom of Great Britain and Ireland. A constitutional monarchy. Capital, London. Great Britain consists of England, Scotland, and Wales. Attached to the United Kingdom are the Isle of Man and the Channel Islands.

Area and Population. The area of the United Kingdom, including inland water, is stated at 121,105 square miles; including the Isle of Man and the Channel Islands, 121,407 square miles. England and Wales comprise 58,340 square miles, or in land area alone 58,029 square miles; Scotland, 30,405 square miles, or in land area 29,796 square miles. By divisions the area, the population according to the censuses of April 1, 1901, and April 3, 1911, and the density per square mile in 1911, are shown in the following table (the figures for Scotland and Ireland being subject to slight revision):

	Sq. m.	Pop. 1901	Pop. 1911	Dens
England	50,874	30,813,043	34,045,290	669
Wales	7,466	1,714,800	2,025,202	271
Scotland	30,405	4,472,103	4,759,445	156
Ireland	32,360	4,458,775	4,381,951	135
U. Kingdom.	121,105	41,458,721	45,211,888	373
Isle of Man...	227	54,752	52,034	229
Channel Isls...	75	95,618	96,900	1,292
Total	121,407	41,609,091	45,360,822	374

The population figures represent persons present (population present, *de facto*, or *de fait*, as distinguished from population resident, legal, *de jure*, or *de droit*); no census of the population resident is taken in the United Kingdom, and therefore the figures above do not include British soldiers, sailors, and merchant seamen abroad.

Growth of population in Great Britain and decrease in Ireland have been as follows:

	E. & W.	Scot.	Ire.	U. K.
1841	15, 4,148	2,620,184	8,175,124	26,709,456
1871	22,[illegible]2,266	3,360,018	5,412,377	31,484,661
1891	29,002,525	4,025,647	4,704,750	41,458,721
1911	36,070,492	4,759;445	4,381,951	45,211,888

The following table shows the percentage of population in the several divisions and, in the last two columns, the percentage of increase from 1891 to 1901 and from 1901 to 1911:

	1841	1891	1901	1911	'91-'01	'01-'11
England	56.1	72.8	74 3	75 3	12.1	10.5
Wales	3.4	4.0	4.1	4 5	13.3	18.1
Scotland	9.8	10.7	10.8	10.5	11.1	6 4
Ireland	30.7	12.5	10.8	9.7	*5.2	*1.7

* Decrease.

In England and Wales, the increase per cent. by births in the period 1891-1901 was 31.57; decrease by deaths, 19.18; natural increase, 12.39; in the period 1901-11, increase by births, 28.56; decrease by deaths, 16.13; natural increase, 12.43. The actual increase per cent. in these two periods was 12.17 and 10.89, the difference between actual increase and natural increase being accounted for by excess of emigrants over immigrants.

In 1911 the number of males and females were, respectively: England, 16,421,298 and 17,-623,992 (or 1073 females to 1000 males); Wales, 1,024,310 and 1,000,892 (977 females to 1000 males); Scotland, 2,307,603 and 2,451,-842; Ireland, 2,186,804 and 2,195,147.

In England and Wales, the population of urban districts in 1901 numbered 25,058,355, and of rural districts 7,469,488; in 1911, 28,-162,936 and 7,907,556. In 1851 the percentage of population in urban districts in England and Wales was approximately 50.2; in 1881, the actual percentage was 67.9; in 1891, 72.0; in 1901, 77.0; in 1911, 78.1. The report on the 1911 census points out that the increase in the proportion of persons living in urban districts, although mainly due to an actual growth of the population within those areas as existing in the earlier census years, is also partly to be accounted for by the extension of those areas themselves, owing to the absorption of areas which were previously rural. While the general increase per cent. in England and Wales was 10.89 in the period 1901-11, the urban increase was 11.1 and the rural 10.2; in the preceding intercensal period the urban increase was 15.2 per cent., and the rural 2.9 per cent.

At the 1911 census there were in England and Wales 97 urban districts (including the administrative county of London as one district) which had a population exceeding 50,000 each. The inhabitants of these districts in 1891 numbered 13,779,848; in 1901, 15,886,874; in 1911, 17,251,009; the increase per cent. in the first intercensal period being 15.3, and in the second 8.3. London (that is, the administrative county, embracing 74,816 acres, or 117 square miles), had in 1911 4,521,685 inhabitants, as compared with 4,536,267 in 1911, or a decrease of 0.3 per cent. The City of London (comprising 675 acres) decreased in population from 37,702 in 1891 to 26,923 in 1901 and 19,658 in 1911, the decrease per cent. in the two intercensal periods being 28.6 and 27.0. The City is mainly covered by buildings used for business purposes, and the census included those persons only who passed the night of the census within the city boundaries. A special census, taken April 25, 1911, showed that within the City 364,061 persons were engaged in business during the day. "Greater London" is a term used to describe the area covered by the Metropolitan and City of London police districts; it contains, besides the administrative county of London, a wide belt of suburban towns and districts, known as the "outer ring." This outer ring had in 1891 1,405,852 inhabitants; in 1901, 2,045,135; in 1911, 2,729,673; the increase per cent. in the two intercensal periods being 45.5 and 33.5. The outer ring in 1911 embraced the following areas: Middlesex administrative county, 148,701 acres, with 1,-126,465 inhabitants; in Surrey, 80,099 acres, with 526,366 inhabitants; in Kent, 43,281 acres, with 172,327 inhabitants; in Essex, 60,-436 acres, with 849,610 inhabitants; in Hertfordshire, 36,091 acres, with 54,905 inhabitants; total, 368,608 acres, or 576 square miles, with 2,729,673 inhabitants. Greater London (that is, the administrative county plus the outer ring) embraced 443,424 acres, or 693 square miles; with 7,251,358 inhabitants, in 1911, as compared with 6,581,402 in 1901 and 5,633,806 in 1891; the increase from 1891 to 1901 being 16.8 per cent. and from 1901 to 1911 10.2 per cent.

Population, with percentage of increase over 1901 of the larger towns (after London) in England, census of 1911: Liverpool, 746,421 (6.0); Manchester, 714,333 (10.8); Birmingham, 525,833 (0.5); Sheffield, 454,632 (11.1); Leeds, 445,550 (3.9); Bristol, 357,048 (5.3); West Ham (in the "outer ring"), 289,030 (8.1); Bradford, 288,458 (3.1); Kingston-upon-Hull, 277,991 (15.7); Newcastle-upon-Tyne, 266,603 (7.9); Nottingham, 259,904 (8.4); Stoke-on-Trent, 234,534 (9.2); Salford, 231,-357 (4.7); Portsmouth, 231,141 (22.3); Leicester, 227,222 (7.4); Cardiff (in Wales), 182,-259 (10.9); Bolton, 180,851 (7.5); Croydon (in the "outer ring"), 169,551 (26.6); Willesden (in the "outer ring"), 154,214 (34.3); Rhondda (in Wales), 152,781 (34.3); Sunderland, 151,159 (3.5).

The population of Scotland from 1901 to 1911 increased 287,342. A large part of this increase was in the suburbs of Glasgow; Lanarkshire increased by 107,786 and Renfrewshire by 45,594. Most of the remaining increase was in Fifeshire, with 48,894, Dumbartonshire. 25,-966, Edinburghshire, 18,866, and Stirlingshire, 18,712. The larger municipal boroughs, with 1911 population and increase per cent. over 1901, are: Glasgow, 784,455 (1.1); Edinburgh, 320,315 (0.9); Dundee, 165,006 (1.2); Aberdeen, 163,331 (6.2); Govan, 89,725 (9.2); Paisley, 84,447 (6.4); Leith, 80,489 (3.9); Greenock, 75,140 (9.0); Partick, 66,848 (23.1); Coatbridge, 43,287 (17.0); Motherwell, 40,378 (29.6); Kirkcaldy, 39,600 (16.2).

In Ireland, the population decreased between 1901 and 1911 in all counties except Dublin, Down, Kildare, and Antrim, where the increases were 6.4, 5.2, 4.6, and 3.7 respectively. The city of Dublin had in 1911 309,272 inhabitants (increase 6.4 per cent.); with suburbs, 403,030 (7.4). The suburbs are the following urban districts: Rathmines and Rathgar, 38,-190 (17.1); Pembroke, 29,260 (13.4); Kingstown, 17,227 (0.9); and Blackrock, 9081 (4.2). The population within the Dublin Metropolitan police district was 415,866, against 392,797 in

1901. Increase of population is noted in the other large Irish towns: Belfast, 385,492 (10.4); Cork, 76,632 (0.7); Londonderry, 40,-799 (2.3); Limerick, 38,403 (0.7); Waterford, 27,430 (2.5).

The following table shows the rate, per thousand of population, of births, deaths, and marriages, i. e., persons married:

		E. & W.	Scot.	Ire.	U. K.
Births	1901	28.5	29.5	22.7	28.0
"	1910	25.1	26 2	23.3	25 0
"	1911	24.4	25.6	23.3	24.4
Deaths	1901	16.9	17.9	17.8	17.1
"	1910	13.5	15.3	17.1	14.0
"	1911	14.6	15.1	16.6	14.8
Marriages	1901	15.9	14.0	10.2	15.1
"	1910	15.0	13.0	10.1	14 3
"	1911	15.2	13.4	10.8	14.6

Arrivals and departures (exclusive of passengers from or to Europe), the last column showing the number of British passengers from and to the United States:

		British	Foreign	Total	U. S
Arrivals	1901	99,699	60,736	165,018	58,312
"	1910	164,139	134,640	298,779	58,623
"	1911	192,718	157,711	350,429	72,082
Departures	1901	171,715	124,354	302,575	104,195
"	1910	397,848	221,011	618,859	132,192
"	1911	454,527	168,898	623,425	121,814

PUBLIC EDUCATION. In England and Wales, on July 31, 1911, departments in the ordinary public elementary schools numbered 32,206; accommodations, 6,807,540; teachers, 40,909 men, 122,414 women; pupils enrolled, 3,045,074 boys, 2,987,644 girls; average attendance 89.01 per cent. On the same date there were 47 higher elementary schools, having accommodations for 12,449, with 421 teachers, 10,036 pupils enrolled (average during the year), and an average attendance of 91.3 per cent. For public secondary education there were on January 31, 1911, 971 schools recognized for grant, having full-time teachers, 5123 men and 4896 women, and full-time pupils enrolled 86,843 boys and 73,-718 girls. At evening and similar schools, pupils in 1910 numbered 763,275; in day technical classes, 10,913; at technical institutions, 2731; in art classes, 3341; at schools of art, 42,278. Teachers are trained at pupil-teacher centres, training classes, and hostels.

In Scotland, for the year ended August 31, 1911, there were 3173 public primary schools in receipt of grants, with accommodations for 1,036,784 pupils, 820,611 pupils enrolled, and 731,905 in average attendance; 196 higher grade schools in receipt or grants, with 24,444 pupils enrolled and 24,083 in average attendance; 1119 continuation classes, with 137,180 pupils. Teachers in elementary schools (primary and higher grade) numbered 5326 men and 14,786 women. There were 56 secondary schools claiming grant, with 1147 teachers, an enrollment of 20,532, and an average attendance of 19,354.

In Ireland, on December 31, 1911, public primary schools in operation numbered 8289, with accommodations for 766,002, enrollment, 684,-634, average attendance, 512,862, teachers, 13,-033.

PAUPERISM. The mean number of paupers, and the ratio per thousand of estimated population relieved on January 1 and on July 1 preceding (exclusive of casual paupers and insane), are reported as follows for England and Wales:

	Indoor No.	Indoor Ratio	Outdoor No.	Outdoor Ratio	Total No.	Total Ratio
1902	196,528	6.0	497,500	15.2	692,875	21.2
1911	256,100	7.2	503,181	14.1	758,278	21.3
1912	248,035	6.9	403,552	11.2	650,626	18.0
Of whom able-bodied adults:						
1902	35,095	1.1	59,586	1.8	94,681	2.9
1911	52,889	1.5	71,383	2.0	124,272	3.5
1912	50,884	1.4	69,333	1.9	120,217	3.3

* Deductions are made from total for paupers receiving both indoor and outdoor relief on the same day.

In parishes in Scotland, the number of poor persons of all classes receiving relief on January 15, 1911, was 67,026 paupers and 41,306 dependents; on January 15, 1912, 67,581 and 41,658. In Unions in Ireland, the number of paupers in receipt of relief at the close of the first week of January, 1911, was 80,658 (of whom 4778 were able-bodied adults receiving indoor relief); 1912, 79,636 (4609).

AGRICULTURE. The table below shows the total area in acres (including rivers and lakes, but not including foreshore and tidal waters) and the total cultivated area (in the first week in June, 1912), in Great Britain, in Ireland, and in the United Kingdom, including the Isle of Man and the Channel Islands:

		Gr. Brit.	Ireland	U. K.
Total acres		56,804,258	20,731,244	77,721,256
Cultivated	1896	32,562,359	15,195,027	47,883,008
"	1901	32,417,445	15,219,175	47,760,585
"	1906	32,266,755	14,804,182	47,196,762
"	1910	32,145,930	14,661,045	46,931,637
"	1911	32,094,658	14,707,808	46,926,500

Area in acres under the principal crops, in the first week in June, 1911 (figures for United Kingdom include the Isle of Man and the Channel Islands):

	Gr. Brit.	Ireland	U. K.
Wheat	1,906,038	45,056	1,952,422
Barley	1,597,930	158,110	1,758,842
Oats	3,010,671	1,040,185	4,071,927
Rye	46,374	9,026	55,474
Beans	311,833	1,683	313,667
Peas	167,903	301	168,311
Total corn crops	7,040,749	1,254,431	8,320,643
Potatoes	571,801	591,259	1,175,158
Turnips and swedes	1,563,390	270,805	1,842,226
Mangold	452,320	77,857	530,927
Other green crops	452,505	73,806	529,503
Total green crops	3,040,016	1,013,727	4,077,814
Rotation grass*	4,119,808	2,594,988	6,759,582
Permanent grass	17,446,870	9,763,999	27,239,778

* Including clover, etc.

The number of livestock in the first week of June, 1911, is shown below (the figures for horses include only horses used for agriculture, unbroken horses, and brood mares):

	Gr. Brit.	Ireland	U. K.*
Horses	1,480,575	543,136	2,032,216
Cattle	7,114,264	4,711,720	11,866,111
Sheep	26,494,992	3,907,436	30,479,807
Swine	2,822,154	1,415,119	4,250,013

* Including the Isle of Man and the Channel Islands.

Production of principal crops in imperial bushels, long tons, or hundredweights, and average yield per acre in 1911:

	Great Britain Production	Per acre	Ireland Production	Per acre
In bushels:				
Wheat	62,657,368	32.87	1,656,084	36.76
Barley	50,988,604	31.91	6,814,613	43.08
Oats	114,352,856	37.98	48,580,477	46.70
Beans	7,681,087	25.21	60,450	35.92
Peas	3,697,189	26.37	8,383	27.85
In tons:				
Potatoes	3,825,312	6.69	3,694,856	6.25
Turnips and swedes	16,396,948	10.49	5,273,183	19.47
Mangold	7,480,433	16 54	1,734,548	22.28
Rotation hay.	2,612,532	1.26	1,573,746	1.68
Perman't hay	4,569,372	0.91	2,900,821	1.84
In cwts.:				
Hops	328,023	9.92	....	....

MINING AND METALS. Quantity and spot value of coal and metals produced in the United Kingdom:

	1900	1905	1910
Coal, tons......	225,181,300	236,128,936	264,433,028
£......	121,652,596	82,038,553	108,377,567
Pig iron,* tons.	4,666,942	4,760,187	4,975,735
£.	19,596,910	14,992,368	17,008,812
Pig iron,† tons.	4,292,749	4,847,899	5,036,363
£.	18,025,639	15,268,619	17,216,059
Fine copper, tons	765	716	449
£	59,995	53,393	27,570
Met. lead, tons	24,364	20,646	21,522
£	418,960	286,377	283,194
White tin, tons	4,268	4,468	4,797
£	587,869	641,603	738,025
Zinc, tons......	9,066	8,880	4,168
£......	188,573	230,880	99,824
Silver, ounces..	190,850	167,569	136,665
£..	22,465	19,419	14,058
Bar gold, ounces	14,004	5,797	2,427
£	52,147	21,222	8,088

* From British ores. † From foreign ores.

Total spot value of coal and metals named above: 1900, £160,605,154; 1905, £115,552,434; 1910, £143,773,197.

FISHERIES. The value of fish (exclusive of salmon) landed on the coasts of the United Kingdom is as follows:

1910	E. & W.	Scotland	Ireland	U. K.
Fish, wet	£7,965,853	£3,100,387	£316,500	£11,382,740
Shellfish	228,424	69,760	59,130	357,314
Total	8,194,277	3,170,147	375,630	11,740,054
1911				
Fish, wet	£8,051,486	£2,978,000	£315,679	£11,345,165
Shellfish	273,012	67,355	58,406	398,773
Total	8,324,498	3,045,355	374,085	11,743,938

The most valuable fish taken in 1911 were herring, haddock, and cod, which totalled respectively £3,145,943, £1,793,260, and £1,705,-136.

COMMERCE. Total imports, imports reëxported, and net imports (that is, imports for home consumption) have been valued as follows (exclusive of specie and bullion, of foreign merchandise transshipped under bond, and of diamonds from the Cape of Good Hope):

	Total Imports	Re-exports	Net Imports
1901	£521,990,198	£ 67,841,892	£454,148,306
1906	607,888,500	85,102,480	522,786,020
1909	624,704,957	91,344,819	533,360,138
1910	678,257,024	103,761,045	574,495,979
1911	680,157,527	102,759,134	577,398,393

Value of diamonds exported from the Cape of Good Hope to the United Kingdom: 1901, £4,877,042; 1906, £9,179,333; 1909, £6,169,953; 1910, £8,480,875; 1911, £8,267,044.

Imports of gold and silver specie and bullion: 1901, £32,217,306; 1906, £63,330,653; 1909, £66,506,718; 1910, £71,422,077; 1911, £62,987,-500.

Total exports, reëxports of foreign and colonial produce, and domestic exports (that is, exports of the produce and manufacture of the United Kingdom) have been valued as follows (exclusive of specie and bullion and of foreign merchandise transshipped under bond):

	Total Exports	Re-exports	Dom. Ex.
1901	£347,864,268	£ 67,841,892	£280,022,376
1906	460,677,818	85,102,480	375,575,338
1909	469,525,166	91,344,819	378,180,347
1910	534,145,817	103,761,045	430,384,772
1911	556,878,432	102,759,134	454,119,298

Exports of gold and silver specie and bullion: 1901, £26,015,102; 1906, £61,482,552; 1909, £60,034,718; 1910, £64,724,213; 1911, £57,024,077.

Total imports of merchandise and domestic exports of merchandise in 1910 and 1911 are shown by classes in the table on page 284.

Exports reported in this table include only domestic merchandise. Reëxports (that is, exports of foreign, including colonial, merchandise), under the same classification, were as follows in 1910 and 1911 respectively: Section I., £12,873,975 and £14,311,306; Section II., £63,310,059 and £59,957,708; Section III., £27,-342,345 and £28,344,970; Section IV., £234,666 and £145,150; total £103,761,045 and £102,759,-134.

Leading imports not specified in the table were as follows in 1910 and 1911, in thousands of pounds sterling: Wheat, 44,161 and 38,010; sheep wool, 33,812 and 32,978; butter, 24,-493 and 24,601; rubber, 26,097 and 18,333; sawn fir, 16,304 and 15,147; bacon, 13,391 and 14,463; refined sugar, 13,133 and 14,353; tea, 11,381 and 12,983; unrefined sugar, 11,421 and 12,233; fresh and refrigerated beef, 11,745 and 11,134; fresh and refrigerated mutton, 9803 and 9576; broad stuffs (silk), 9398 and 9303; tin (block, etc.), 7160 and 8739; eggs, 7296 and 7968; cheese, 6812 and 7140.

Leading domestic exports not specified in the table, in 1910 and 1911, in thousands of pounds sterling: Cotton piece goods, 78,685 and 90,513; coal, 36,100 and 36,521; cotton yarn, 13,338 and 15,663; woolen tissues, 12,566 and 13,303; worsted tissues, 9958 and 9315; galvanized sheet iron, 7426 and 7614; tin plate, 6545 and 6843; textile machinery, 7614 and 6779; woolen and worsted yarn, 6549 and 6477; linen piece goods, 6115 and 5642; herring, 4034 and 4913; thread, 4193 and 3978; pig iron, 4139 and 3889; sulphate of ammonia, 3377 and 3820; war vessels, 4895 and 26.

The following table shows the value of merchandise consigned from and to foreign countries and British possessions, in thousands of pounds sterling, discriminating total imports and imports for consumption, or net imports, and total exports and domestic exports, or exports of the produce and manufacture of the United Kingdom:

	Total Imports 1910	Total Imports 1911	Net Imports 1910	Net Imports 1911
From for. c'tries...	507,807	508,898	453,893	455,508
From Br. poss.....	170,450	171,260	120,670	121,946
Total	678,257	680,158	*574,496	*577,398
	Total Exports 1910	**Total Exports 1911**	**Dom. Exports 1910**	**Dom. Exports 1911**
To foreign c'tries.	374,743	384,937	283,082	295,275
To Br. possessions.	159,403	171,941	147,303	158,844
Total	534,146	556,878	430,385	454,119

* Re-exports in excess of imports to unknown countries were about £67,000 in 1910, and about £55,000 in 1911.

SHIPPING. Total net tonnage entered and cleared, with cargo and in ballast (exclusive of the coasting trade):

	British	Foreign	Total
Entered			
1901*	31,170,534	17,210,729	48,381,263
1910	39,641,620	27,018,829	66,660,449
1911	40,777,476	28,387,039	69,164,515
Cleared			
1901*	31,099,487	17,199,144	48,298,631
1910	40,173,466	27,196,399	67,369,865
1911	41,107,978	28,636,848	69,744,826

* Exclusive of tonnage for war purposes to and from South Africa.

Total imports and domestic exports of merchandise by principal countries, in thousands of pounds sterling:

	Imports 1910	Imports 1911	Exports 1910	Exports 1911
United States	117,607	122,694	31,447	27,519
Germany	61,830	65,281	37,021	39,284
British India	42,764	45,423	45,999	52,246
Russia	43,645	43,154	12,253	13,512
France	44,283	41,631	22,463	24,283
Australia	38,584	39,096	27,652	30,881
Argentina	29,010	27,289	19,097	18,602
Canada	25,635	24,594	19,645	19,715
Egypt	21,004	21,483	8,717	10,300
Belgium	19,196	20,826	10,887	11,373
Denmark	19,672	20,794	5,581	5,478
Netherlands	18,528	18,665	12,695	13,112
New Zealand	20,943	17,850	8,653	9,869
Spain	15,351	15,146	4,893	5,497
Str. Settlements*.	13,096	14,593	4,572	5,016
Sweden	11,825	11,939	6,698	6,347
Brazil	17,497	10,864	16,427	11,938
Switzerland	9,813	10,036	3,371	3,934
Cape of G. Hope†	7,736	7,314	8,044	8,463
Italy	6,459	6,949	12,531	13,213
Aust.-Hungary ..	7,512	6,911	4,001	4,679
Ceylon	5,987	6,754	2,322	2,527
Rumania	3,184	6,583	1,827	2,710
Norway	6,631	6,251	4,033	4,850
Turkey	4,668	6,583	8,637	9,463
Java, etc.	4,029	5,334	4,076	5,460
China	5,530	4,893	9,172	12,132
Chile	5,181	4,337	5,480	6,139
Japan‡	4,327	3,382	10,122	11,869
Peru	3,688	3,151	1,315	1,392
T't'l incl. other.	678,257	680,158	430,385	454,119

* Including Federated Malay States. † Imports do not include diamonds. ‡ Including Taiwan.

	Total Imports 1910	Total Imports 1911	Domestic Exports 1910	Domestic Exports 1911
I. Food, Drink, and Tobacco:				
Grain and flour.............................£	77,298,383	£ 75,760,943	£ 3,416,637	£ 3,573,905
Meat, including animals for food........	48,878,947	49,722,183	935,958	1,023,361
Other food and drink	....	....	19,675,550	‡ 22,268,918
1. Non-dutiable	72,229,940	73,638,263	....	....
2. Dutiable	54,649,536	59,551,830	....	....
Tobacco	4,624,782	5,284,918	2,042,593	2,171,394
Total	257,681,588	263,958,137	26,070,738	29,037,578
II. Raw Materials and Articles mainly Unmanufactured:				
Coal, coke, and manufactured fuel......	34,119	29,779	37,813,360	38,447,354
Iron ore, scrap iron, and steel...........	6,261,471	5,799,162	476,863	452,614
Other metallic ores......................	8,970,272	8,859,967	71,791	110,965
Wood and timber	26,207,329	25,862,171	129,290	199,068
Raw cotton	71,711,908	71,155,614	....	....
Wool (including rags, etc.).............	37,332,470	36,037,451	4,220,443	3,901,752
Other textile materials..................	12,803,327	14,611,045	323,536	435,699
Oil seeds, nuts, oils, fats, and gums......	37,548,960	35,047,549	‡ 5,023,499	4,793,768
Hides and undressed skins	12,882,326	11,106,664	1,757,762	1,685,293
Materials for paper making.............	4,972,487	4,749,521	744,278	818,560
Miscellaneous	42,450,959	34,900,038	2,767,460	2,880,437
Total	261,175,628	248,158,861	53,328,282	53,725,530
III. Articles wholly or mainly Manufactured:				
Iron and steel and manufactures thereof	9,086,214	11,133,854	42,976,671	43,730,292
Other metals and manufactures thereof..	24,699,194	27,581,244	10,352,354	11,022,536
Cutlery, hardware, implements, instruments	4,673,473	5,273,043	6,423,695	7,395,084
Electrical goods and apparatus*..........	1,686,540	1,435,492	4,102,602	2,819,374
Machinery	4,470,898	5,568,662	29,271,380	30,960,678
Ships and boats (new)..................	27,104	64,484	8,770,240	5,663,115
Mfrs. of wood and timber (incl. furniture)	2,338,472	2,551,897	1,835,762	2,037,272
Yarns and textile fabrics:				
1. Cotton	10,874,628	11,279,717	105,871,208	120,063,355
2. Wool	9,599,286	9,586,856	37,516,397	37,239,197
3. Silk	13,521,021	13,441,249	2,278,943	2,381,528
4. Other materials	8,054,667	7,894,776	13,481,198	13,198,754
Apparel (incl. boots, shoes, and hats)....	5,107,315	5,199,932	12,717,587	13,820,465
Chemicals, drugs, dyes, and colors......	11,259,685	11,411,060	18,568,136	20,053,129
Leather and mfrs. (excl. boots and shoes)	11,824,741	12,227,521	4,686,485	4,879,175
Earthenware and glass..................	3,816,971	4,049,083	4,352,059	4,713,298
Paper	6,413,718	6,574,550	3,122,699	3,310,966
Railway carriages and trucks (not of iron), motor cars, cycles, carts, etc....	5,603,149	6,500,046	7,449,977	8,125,047
Miscellaneous	23,788,385	23,583,645	29,091,840	30,809,362
Total	156,845,461	165,557,111	342,869,197	362,222,627
IV. Miscellaneous and Unclassified†...........	2,554,347	2,483,418	8,116,555	9,133,563
Grand Total	678,257,024	680,157,527	430,384,772	454,119,298

* Other than machinery, and telegraph, and telephone wire. † Including parcel post. ‡ Refined tallow and animal fat were classified in Section II. in 1910 and in Section I. in 1911.

In 1911 entered steam 67,252,999 tons, cleared 67,844,960; total entered with cargo, 41,946,461, cleared 59,263,314. Leading foreign tonnage entered, in thousands, in 1910 and 1911 respectively: German, 6920 and 7012; Norwegian, 4360 and 4751; Dutch, 2636 and 2861; Danish, 2778 and 2787; Swedish, 2542 and 2657; French, 1587 and 1733; Spanish, 1403 and 1426. American tonnage entered was only 246,744 in 1910 and 219,541 in 1911. In 1910 and 1911, total net tonnage entered in coasting trade, 61,808,816 and 62,508,897 (57,605,740 and 58,247,243 British); cleared, 61,569,327 and 62,096,225 (57,444,022 and 57,905,596 British). Merchant marine of the United Kingdom including Jersey, Guernsey, and the Isle of Man, December 31, 1911: 12,242 steamers, of 10,717,511 tons net and 17,743,746 gross; 8830 sailing vessels, of 980,997 tons net and 1,064,713 gross; total, 21,072 vessels, of 11,698,508 tons net and 18,808,459 gross, against 21,090 of 11,555,663 tons net and 18,468,895 gross December 31, 1910.

COMMUNICATIONS. The length of railway open to traffic December 31, 1911, was 23,417 miles (13,106 double track or more, 10,311 single), compared with 23,387 at the end of 1910 and 22,078 at the end of 1901. During 1911 the total mileage in operation in England and Wales increased from 16,148 to 16,200; in Ireland an increase of a single mile is reported, from 3401 to 3402; in Scotland there was a decrease from 3838 to 3815. Total paid-up capital of railway companies in the United Kingdom December 31, 1911, £1,324,018,000 (£1,318,515,000 in 1910); average rate of dividend or interest in 1911, 3.59 per cent. (3.53 in 1910); gross receipts, £127,199,570 (£123,925,565), of which £109,189,734 in England and Wales, £13,498,609 in Scotland, and £4,511,227 in Ireland; working expenditure, £78,617,824 (£76,569,676); net receipts, £48,581,746 (£47,355,889); proportion of working expenditure to gross receipts, 62 (62). Length of tramways and light railways open at the end of 1911, 2597 miles (2562 in 1910); paid-up capital, £74,725,440; gross receipts, £13,777,001; working expenses, £8,500,941; net receipts, £5,276,060.

RAILWAYS. During the year p g ess was made with the Euston to Watford rRailway, of the London and North-Western, and the section from Willesden to Harrow and from Watford High-street to Croxley Green; and the branch to Holywell in Flintshire was opened in July. The Great Northern was completing a 15-mile line from Kirkstead to Little Steeping, to reduce the distance between Lincoln and Skegness. Considerable improvement was in progress in widening the Bytham to Stoke tunnel, south of Grantham, and improving its approaches over a distance of about 8 miles. A line from Cuffley to Hertford of 6 miles in length, and a tunnel of 2700 yards long were also started. The Great Central Railway was widening the line between Dartnall and Woodhouse and eliminating a 300-yards long tunnel at Dartnall. The Great Western Railway was reconstructing its Snow Hill station at Birmingham and completing a line in the Swansea district from Briton Ferry Road station to connect with the Llanelly-Llandilo branch. Improvements were being made at Paddington station and the extension of the Bakerloo tube to Queen's Park was contracted for. The London, Brighton and South Coast Railway extended its electrification during the year and had a total of 26 route miles in operation. New station works at Dover harbor for the South-Eastern and the Chatham lines made progress during the year, and in London considerable was accomplished at the Waterloo terminus of the London and South-Western Railway. The branch of the Shropshire and Montgomeryshire from Kinnerley to Criggion, which had not been used for 30 years, was reopened for freight traffic and a new bridge built across the River Severn, while a new and enlarged station at Letchworth was under construction. In Yorkshire the Derwent Valley Light Railway, 16 miles in length, from the Foss Islands mineral branch to Cliff Common near Selby, was under consideration, to connect two lines of the North-Eastern Railway.

The length of state telegraph lines March 31, 1911, was 61,296 miles; wire, 1,239,095 miles; postal telegraph offices, 11,451; other offices, 2508; exchange telephones, 110,796; post offices, 24,098. Letters delivered in the fiscal year 1912, in millions, 3186.8; newspapers and halfpenny packets, 1265.5; postcards, 905.5.

FINANCE. The unit of value is the pound sterling, worth $4.86656 (7.98805 grammes gold .91666 fine). For years ended March 31, the following table shows budget estimates of revenue, actual receipts into the exchequer, and the excess (+) or deficiency (—) of the actual, as compared with the estimated amounts:

	Estimates	Receipts	Difference
1902	£ 152,263,000	£152,712,089	+ £ 449,089
1907	152,590,000	155,036,486	+ 2,446,486
1910	162,590,000	131,696,456	— 30,893,544
1911	*199,791,000	203,850,588	+ 4,059,588
1912	181,621,000	185,090,286	+ 3,469,286

* Including arrears of 1909-10, estimated at £30,046,000.

For fiscal years, the table below shows budget and supplementary estimates of expenditure, actual issues out of the exchequer chargeable against revenue, and the surplus (+) or deficit (—) of actual receipts (shown in foregoing table), as compared with actual expenditure:

	Estimates	Issues	Surp. or Def.
1902	£206,651,259	£205,236,305	— £52,524,216
1907	152,636,443	149,637,664	+ 5,398,822
1910	163,171,000	157,944,611	+ 5,606,766* (1910 and 1911)
1911	174,129,000	171,995,667	
1912	181,839,000	178,545,100	+ 6,545,186

* Income and expenditure for fiscal years 1910 and 1911 were aggregated for the purpose of determining the Old Sinking Fund for 1911.

Revenue (exchequer receipts) was derived as follows, in the years ended March 31, 1911 and 1912: Customs, £33,140,000 and £33,640,000; excise, £40,020,000 and £38,380,000; estate, etc., duties, £25,452,000 and £25,392,000; stamps (exclusive of fee and patent stamps), £9,784,000 and £9,454,000; land tax, £1,220,000 and £750,000; house duty, £3,080,000 and £2,130,000; property and income tax, £61,946,000 and £44,804,000; land value duties, £520,000 and £481,000 (total from these sources, £175,162,000 and £155,040,000); post and telegraph service, £24,350,000 and £25,700,000; crown lands (net receipts), £500,000 and £530,000; receipts from Suez Canal shares and sundry loans, £1,234,350 and £1,281,497; fee and patent stamps, £1,070,000 and £1,031,000; receipts by civil departments, etc., £1,534,238 and £1,507,789; total, £203,850,588 and £185,090,286.

Expenditure (exchequer issues) chargeable against revenue in the years ended March 31, 1911 and 1912:

	1911	1912
I. Consolidated Fund Services:		
National debt services	£ 24,554,004	£ 24,500,000
(Interest of funded debt)	(15,377,321)	(15,202,702)
(New Sinking fund)	(4,111,961)	(4,447,706)
Road improvement fund, etc.	1,362,641	1,709,859
Local taxation accounts, etc.	9,881,709	9,636,399
Civil list	470,000	470,000
Annuities and pensions	299,933	317,745
Salaries and allowances	56,609	56,572
Courts of justice	514,283	523,000
Miscellaneous	323,488	325,525
Total	37,462,667	37,539,100
II. Supply Services:		
Army (incl. ordnance factories)	27,449,000	27,649,000
Navy	40,386,000	42,858,000
Civil services	43,098,000	46,001,000
(Education)	(18,744,000)	(18,983,000)
Customs and excise	2,211,000	2,297,000
Inland revenue	1,708,000	1,654,000
Post-office services	19,681,000	20,547,000
Total	134,533,000	141,006,000
Grand total	171,995,667	178,545,100

Estimated revenue for 1912-13, £187,180,000 (against receipts £185,090,286 in 1911-12); estimated expenditure chargeable against revenue, £186,885,000 (against £178,545,100).

The funded debt on March 31, 1912, stood at £602,200,092; estimated capital liability in respect of terminable annuities, £33,044,389; unfunded debt, £30,500,000 (including treasury bills to the amount of £6,400,000 temporarily paid off March 31, but renewable under the revenue act of 1906); total dead-weight debt, £674,744,481 (as compared with £685,232,459 in 1911, £729,503,545 in 1907, and £745,015,650 in 1902). Capital liabilities in addition amounted to £50,061,947; the gross debt in 1912, therefore, was £724,806,428 (as compared with £733,072,010 in 1911, £779,164,704 in 1907, and £765,215,653 in 1902). Total debt services in the fiscal year 1912, £24,500,000 (interest of funded debt, £15,202,702, of unfunded £1,158,842). Assets March 31, 1912: Estimated market value of Suez Canal shares, £44,046,000; other assets, £3,704,386 (estimated); exchequer bank balance of £11,468,591; total, £59,218,977. This amount deducted from the gross debt shows total net liabilities of £665,587,451 (as compared with £677,915,341 in 1911).

ARMY. The chief developments in the British army during the year 1912 were in the main encouraging, though criticism of the condition of the forces was not entirely absent. There was an increase in the number of candidates for commissions, and recruiting was fairly satisfactory, but owing to better conditions of trade and industry there was a shortage in the number of skilled artisans who enlisted in the more technical branches of the service. New, quick-firing howitzers were being provided for the howitzer batteries of the Royal Field Artillery, and the cavalry was being equipped with an improved sword. The lance, whose utility had figured for the past quarter of a century in discussions of mounted troops, was once more restored to the lancer regiments. A new rifle had been designed and was under test, while new ammunition with a pointed bullet was being issued to the army. This required the re-sighting of the existing rifles. The re-mount question continued to agitate the service and a plan was developed whereby trained cavalry horses could be boarded out. A Royal flying corps was organized during the year and greater attention was being paid to aviation (see MILITARY PROGRESS and AERONAUTICS). The mechanical transport service was also being developed, as in this respect the British army was held deficient, compared with the continental powers.

Few important changes in the organization and administration of the army were to be noted in 1912. Col. J. E. B. Seeley, D. S. O., succeeded Lord Haldane as secretary of state for war and thereby became head of the army council. Gen. Sir J. D. P. French became chief of the imperial general staff and first military member of the council, having under his authority the director of military operations (Brig.-Gen. H. H. Wilson), the director of staff duties (Brig.-Gen. L. E. Kiggell), and the director of military training (Brig.-Gen. D. Henderson). The other military members of the army council were the adjutant-general (Lieut.-Gen. Sir J. S. Ewart), the quartermaster-general (Maj.-Gen. J. S. Cowans), the master-general of the ordnance (Maj.-Gen. C. F. Hadden), while the parliamentary under-secretary of state was a civil member, as was also the financial secretary. Gen. Sir C. W. H. Douglass was inspector-general of the home forces, and Gen. Sir Ian Hamilton was general officer commanding-in-chief of the Mediterranean, and inspector-general of the oversea forces. The latter was authorized to examine and report upon the coast defences of the Far East in the year 1912-13. The general staff, to which appointments were made for a term of four years, was at work during the year on the general scheme of imperial defense, while a selection board to improve the character of the personnel by a more careful system of promotions was active during the year.

The British army in 1912 was organized in two lines consisting of a regular army with its reserve and special reserve and a territorial force which is a second line providing for home defense and affording an opportunity for training men who might volunteer for foreign service. The first line supplies the garrisons for India, Egypt, South Africa, and other places, besides maintaining at home a sufficiency of troops to make good the quota required for service abroad from its depot battalions. The home forces are organized to afford an expeditionary force ready to take the field, and the United Kingdom was divided into 7 commands, all under lieutenant-generals. The Aldershot, or first command, was maintained as the first force for expeditionary purposes, but the other commands were subdivided into districts on a territorial basis for the localization of the infantry. London, which does not figure in the seven commands, formed an independent district. The general officer commanding-in-chief of each district is responsible for the training, organization, efficiency, discipline, and administration.

The organization of the regular army remained essentially the same as in 1911, and service was by voluntary enlistment, the time being for eleven years, of which a portion, differing with the various arms of the service, was spent with the colors, and the rest of the time in reserve. The time spent with the colors was as follows: Cavalry, 7 years; Royal Horse Artillery and Royal Field Artillery, 6 years (5000 for 3 years); Royal Garrison Artillery, 8 years; foot guards, 3 years; light infantry, 7 years; Royal Engineers, 7 years, and for certain trades, 3 years. In a report on recruiting made in February, 1912, it was stated that in the year ending September 30, 1911, 29,452 recruits, or an increase of 3018 over the previous year, had joined the regular army, while there had been an increase in the sections of the reserve formed by those willing to join in their first year of reserve service without a general mobilization and those reëngaging in the reserve, while there was a decrease in the section of the reserve comprising those who had enlisted for short service and had discharged their active duties. There was also available on mobilization a special reserve consisting of men who were trained in the technical arms of the service and of civilians whose technical training would make them useful for military service. This latter reserve was in a rudimentary state in 1912, and there were decreases to be noted in both divisions, as the special reserve forces do not attract attention. The regular army in 1912 was made up as follows: Cavalry, 31 regiments, of which 3 were household cavalry; 7 dragoon guards; 3 dragoons; 6 lancers, and 12 hussars. There were five recruit depots for the training, posting, and drafting of men. There were four brigades with headquarters at Aldershot, Tidworth, Curragh, and Canterbury, formed of 12 regiments serving at home. The regimental establishment was 696 men and 528 horses. The horse, field, and mountain artillery was organized as 6-gun batteries, except in the case of the heavy batteries and training batteries, to which 4 guns were assigned. There were carried on the rolls 28 horse batteries, 150 field batteries, 8 mountain batteries, and 99 garrison companies, of which 12 were heavy batteries. Of these, 97 field batteries were at home, 72 belonging to the expeditionary forces, including 6 howitzer batteries while 18 were assigned to the 6 training brigades and 7 to the training of the regular reserve. The infantry of the line consisted of the brigade of guards, formed of 4 regiments with 9 battalions, and 67 regiments of infantry of the line, and 2 rifle regiments, with a total of 148 battalions. The plan of organization involves a home battalion for every one of foreign service and depot special reserve battalions for each regiment. Exclusive of India there were 85 troops of Royal Engineers, which included the various technical troops, and an aviation corps was organized during the year. The army service corps organized 80 companies for transport and supply.

The general annual report for 1912 gave the strength and distribution of the regular army or ranks on October 1, 1911, as follows:

England and Wales	96,516
Scotland	4,806
Ireland	26,438
Jersey	733
Guernsey and Alderney	970
Making a total of men at home	129,503
In the Colonies, Egypt, China, and Cyprus, there were	46,713
In Indian depots in the Colonies	323
while in India there were	77,770
Making a general total of	254,309

at home and abroad. In the army estimates for 1912-13 the total "establishments" were given as home, 134,000; Colonies, Egypt, etc., 45,700; India, 75,886, or a total of 255,866.

The territorial force which was constituted out of the former yeomanry and volunteers was in the hands of council associations, and was organized on a local basis in which the military districts of Great Britain, with the exception of London and districts Nos. 3 and 5, are divisional areas, from which a complete division in addition to other troops were to be drawn. Districts 3 and 5 were each to furnish two divisions and the London district also two divisions. The army estimates of 1912-13 gave the following statistics for the establishment and strength, excluding the permanent staff, but including all ranks, the figures for the strength being as of January 1, 1912:

	Establishment	Strength
Cavalry	26,447	24,926
Artillery	46,605	40,260
Engineers	14,817	13,128
Infantry	204,025	168,759
Army service corps	9,013	7,992
Medical corps	15,211	13,272
Veterinary service	212	90
	316,300	268,438
Officers' training corps	943	644
Total	317,273	269,082

The whole army establishments and effectives, both officers and men, are shown in the accompanying table from the Army Estimates of 1912-13:

	Establishments '12-'13	Establishments '11-'12	Effectives Jan.1,'12
Regular forces (Regimental) Home and Colonial (including regular establishment of Special reserves)	168,282	168,239	167,354
Colonial and native Indian corps	8,871	8,871	8,801
Army reserve	139,000	139,000	137,682
Special reserves (excluding regular establishment)	89,913	91,219	61,951
Militia, U. K.	.....	.....	1,446
Militia, reserve division	150	500	171
Militia, Channel Islands	3,166	3,166	3,113
Militia, Malta and Bermuda, and Bermuda volunteers	2,894	2,894	2,682
Territorial force	316,307	317,106	268,414
Isle of Man volunteers	126	126	112
Officers' training corps (officers and permanent staff)	1,008	946	708
Total Home and Colonial establishments	729,717	732,067	652,434
Regular forces (regimental) on Indian establishment	75,886	75,884	77,577
Total	805,603	807,951	729,991

NAVY. Number and displacement of warships (including colonial vessels) of 1500 or more tons, and of torpedo craft of 50 or more tons; built and building, December 1, 1912: Dreadnoughts (battleships having a main battery of all big guns, that is, 11 inches or more in calibre); built, 16 of 334,350 tons; building, 9 of 246,000 tons. Predreadnoughts (battleships of about 10,000 or more tons, whose main batteries are of more than one calibre); built, 40 of 589,-385 tons; building, none. Coast-defense vessels (including smaller battleships and monitors): none built or building. Battle cruisers (armored cruisers having guns of largest calibre in main battery): built, 7 of 142,000 tons; building, 4 of 106,300 tons. Armored cruisers: built, 34 of 406,800 tons; building, none. Cruisers (unarmored warships of 1500 or more tons): built, 73 of 374,075 tons; building, 17 of 92,660 tons. Torpedo-boat destroyers: built, 140 of 94,006 tons; building, 44 of 41,580 tons. Torpedo boats: built, 49 of 11,488 tons; building, none. Submarines: built, 70 of 26,108 tons; building, 16 of 13,400 tons. Total tonnage: built, 1,978,212; building, 499,940. Excluded from the foregoing: Ships over twenty years old unless reconstructed and rearmed within five years; torpedo craft over fifteen years old; transports, colliers, repair ships, torpedo depot ships, and other auxiliaries. See NAVAL PROGRESS and BATTLESHIPS.

The new dreadnoughts that were completed in 1912 were the *Thunderer*, *Monarch*, and *Conqueror*, launched in 1911 on February 1, March 30, and May 1, respectively; the dreadnought *Orion* and the battle cruiser *Lion* were completed late in 1911. These ships carry a battery of 13.5-inch guns, the battleships ten and the *Lion* eight. The battle cruiser *Princess Royal* (launched April 29, 1911) was completed about the end of 1912. It was expected that the dreadnoughts *King George V.* (launched October 9, 1011), *Centurion*, *Ajax* (March 21, 1912), and *Audacious* (September 14, 1912), would be completed in 1913, as well as the battle cruiser *Queen Mary* (March 20, 1912), and the colonial battle cruisers *New Zealand* and *Australia*. The dreadnoughts *Iron Duke* and *Marlborough*, both to be completed in 1914, were launched October 12 and October 24, 1912.

Officers and men in 1912, 137,222, including three admirals of the fleet, 12 admirals, 22 vice-admirals, 55 rear-admirals, and 664 captains and commanders.

GOVERNMENT. The executive authority is vested in the king, acting through his ministers. The legislative body is the Parliament, consisting of the House of Lords and the House of Commons. The peers entitled to sit in the House of Lords in 1912 (including the lords spiritual and temporal and three royal princes) numbered 636. The general election of December, 1910, returned 670 members of the Commons to the second Parliament of George V., which convened January 31, 1911. England has in the Commons 465 members, Wales 30, Scotland 72, and Ireland 103. Party representation November, 1912: Liberals, 262; Laborites, 41; Nationalists, 76; Independent Nationalists, 8; Unionists, 281; total, 668 (two seats being vacant).

The king in 1912 was George V. (born June 3, 1865), who, as second (but only surviving) son, succeeded Edward VII. May 6, 1910. The heir-apparent is Edward, born June 23, 1894, and created Prince of Wale June 23, 1910.

The ministry in 1912 was that of Mr. Asquith (Liberal), which was formed April 8, 1908. Those of the ministers who constitute the cabinet were as follows at the end of 1912: Prime minister and first lord of the treasury, Herbert Henry Asquith (appointed April, 1908); lord high chancellor, Viscount Haldane (1912); lord president of the council, Viscount Morley of Blackburn (1910); lord privy seal, Marquis of Crewe (1908-11 and 1912); first lord of the admiralty, Winston Spencer Churchill (1911). Secretaries of state: for home affairs, Reginald McKenna (1911); foreign affairs, Sir Edward Grey (1905); colonies, Lewis Vernon Harcourt (1910); war, Col. John E. B. Seely (1912); India, Marquis of Crewe (1910). Chancellor of the exchequer, David Lloyd-George (1908); secretary for Scotland, Thomas McKinnon Wood (1912); chief secretary to the lord lieutenant of Ireland, Augustine Birrell (1907); postmaster-general, Herbert Louis Samuel (1910). President of committees of the council: Board of trade, Sydney Charles Buxton (1910); local government board, John Burns (1905); board of agriculture, Walter Runciman (1911); board of education, Joseph Albert Pease (1911). Chancellor of the duchy of Lancaster, Charles Edward Henry Hobhouse (1911); first commissioner of works, Earl Beauchamp (1910). Up to 1912 the British attorney-general was not included with the cabinet ministers; but in June of that year Sir Rufus Daniel Isaacs, who became attorney-general in 1910, was appointed a member of the cabinet.

HISTORY

OPENING OF PARLIAMENT. The new session of Parliament was opened on February 14 by the king, who a short time before had returned from India. During his absence, November 11, 1911, to February 5, 1912, the crown had been represented by a special commission comprising Prince Arthur of Connaught, the Archbishop of Canterbury, the Lord Chancellor, and Lord Morley. The speech from the throne, after repeating the usual formula that the relations with foreign powers continued to be friendly, referred first to the Turco-Italian War, and the readiness of the British government to associate itself with the other powers when occasion offered for the purpose of mediating between the warring nations; second, to the situation in Persia, concerning which negotiations were going on between Great Britain and Russia as to the best means of restoring order in Persia: third, to the Chinese crisis, as to which the British government was observing the policy of strict non-intervention, while taking steps to protect British life and property; fourth, to the agreement reached at the international conference at The Hague as to the regulation of the trade in opium and other narcotics; fifth, to the recent visit of the king and queen to India, the cordial welcome accorded to them, the transfer of the capital from Calcutta to Delhi, and the changes in the administration growing out of that transfer concerning which a bill would later be laid before Parliament. As to domestic affairs, the speech from the throne, after referring to the prospective danger of disputes between employers and workmen and expressing the hope that a reasonable spirit might prevail on both sides, promised the following measures for the session: A Home Rule bill; a bill for the disestablishment of the church in Wales; amendments of the law as to franchises and registration of electors; a bill in accordance with the recommendations of the last imperial conference for the amendment and consolidation of the law regarding British nationality; and finally, measures dealing with certain social and industrial reforms.

In the debate on the address from the throne the opposition criticised the government for bringing about the important changes in the administration of India in a manner unconstitutional and indefensible. The government's course in this instance was characterized as part of its policy of doing things behind the back of the House of Commons. As to Persia, the opposition declared that the time had come when more complete information about Persia should be made public. (See PERSIA, *History.*) As to the relations with Germany, Lord Haldane's mission (see following paragraph) was characterized as "mysterious," and it was said that if such a mission were to be undertaken by anyone it should have been by Sir Edward Grey. The government was taunted with its failure to keep the promise of the preamble to the Parliament bill to reconstruct the House of Lords. The Insurance act was bitterly attacked, and the proposal of the government to carry in one session three measures of such extraordinary importance as Home Rule, Welsh disestablishment, and franchise reforms was pronounced absurd. The Liberal side retorted that the administrative changes in India should not be regarded as a reversal of the policy of the partition of Bengal, but merely a rearrangement that seemed necessary in the light of experience. As to Persia, the government still adhered to the policy as set forth by the foreign secretary in December, and had further agreed to be a party to an emergency loan to assist Persia in restoring order to its administration. As to Lord Haldane's mission, the government declared that he was going to Germany in any case, but had hastened his visit in order to engage in friendly communications with those who were responsible for the German foreign policy. The discussion would be an informal one, but would doubtless lead to results of importance and would, at all events, tend to promote friendliness between the two countries. As to Home Rule, it was conceded by everybody to be demanded by a majority of the Irish people. The disestablishment of the Welsh Church was demanded by a majority of the Welsh people. The government admitted that the task before it was one of great magnitude, but saw no reason why it should not be performed within a single session.

LORD HALDANE'S VISIT TO BERLIN. The visit of Lord Haldane to the German capital on February 9 gave rise to much discussion in the press. The object of his visit was not definitely described, but it was assumed to be the discussion of the relations between England and Germany, in order to promote a better understanding in each nation of the policy of the other. He was received with high honors by the emperor and the heads of the state. He held long conversations in the foreign office with Herr von Stumm, the head of the political department. On July 25 Mr. Asquith announced that the interchange of views which began with this visit was still continuing "in a spirit of perfect frankness and friendliness" on the part of both governments.

HOME RULE. A leading topic of discussion in connection with Home Rule during the year was the hostility of the Ulster Protestants to that measure. The movement in Ulster against Home Rule was started in 1911 and before the close of the year it had assumed serious dimensions. The wrath of the Ulster men was greatly provoked by the announcement that Mr. Winston Churchill, Mr. John Redmond, and others would hold a Home-Rule meeting at Ulster Hall, Belfast, on February 8. The standing committee of the Ulster Unionist Council held a meeting on January 16 and announced their intention to take steps to prevent this. There was much discussion of this action and even rumors that violence at Ulster Hall, the traditional gathering-place of Irish Unionists, might result if the plan for a meeting was carried out. Certain prominent Unionists went so far as to say that "bloodshed was inevitable." The campaign against Home Rule began vigorously about the middle of January, and many speeches were made on the subject both in Ireland and in England. Sir Edward Carson, the leader of the Irish Unionist party, referred openly to the possibility of a conflict with the forces of the crown, saying that the men of the North of Ireland must resist, no matter how great the cost or the suffering. He declared that Mr. Winston Churchill's plan for the Belfast meeting was merely an attempt to provoke disorder by challenging the Irish Unionists. The Unionists in the South of Ireland were not so extreme in their views, though sympathetic with the purposes of the Ulster men, for if any difficulty arose they would be the first to suffer from the reprisals of the Nationalists.

The Belfast meeting took place at the time appointed, February 8, but the plan of holding it at Ulster Hall was given up and it was held in an athletic field. The speech was heartily applauded and the convention passed off quietly without any disturbance. The speaker referred to the safeguards for the Protestants of Ireland against any oppressive laws. He said that the Irish parliament would be fully and fairly representative of the Irish nation, including Protestants as well as Catholics; that the crown would be able to withhold consent to an unjust bill; that the imperial Parliament could repeal such a bill, and that finally the Home Rule bill would contain provisions safeguarding religious freedom and rendering justice to Catholics and Protestants alike. Moreover, the privy council could throw out any law that exceeded the limits laid down by the Home Rule bill. It was thought likely that the imperial Parliament, overwhelmingly Protestant, would not fail to resent religious intolerance or interference, and the right of the imperial Parliament to take such action was unquestioned at law and equally unquestioned in fact. As to financial injury to Ulster he declared that there would be no danger of unfair taxation. There was a Home Rule demonstration at Dublin on March 31, at which about 100,000 persons were present. All during the summer the resistance of Ulster was the subject of acrimonious debate. The government blamed the opposition for trying to justify the threats of the Ulster men and the opposition took their stand on the "liberties of Englishmen." There was much talk of an "Ulster covenant" to resist Home Rule if it should ever be established.

THE ULSTER DEMONSTRATIONS. The long-expected and much-discussed demonstrations of the Ulstermen against Home Rule began with an open-air meeting at Enniskillen on September 8, attended by some 30,000 persons and presided over by Sir Edward Carson. The programme included the holding of mass-meetings of protest during a period of ten days, and the signing on September 28, known as "Ulster Day," of a "solemn covenant" to resist the Home Rule bill. The Enniskillen meeting carried a resolution reasserting the resolve of the convention of 1892, that "We will not have Home Rule." The speakers justified resistance on the ground of self-defense. The words of the opposition leader, Mr. Bonar Law, were quoted: "If the Government attempt under existing conditions to drive the people of Ulster by force from the protection of this House of Commons and British law, I can imagine no means too strong for the people of Ulster to take to prevent it." Similar meetings were held during the next ten days, culminating in the signing on Ulster Day after impressive ceremonies in Ulster Hall at Belfast of the "solemn covenant" in which the Unionists declaring that Home Rule would be disastrous to Ulster as well as to the rest of Ireland bound themselves to "stand by one another in defending for ourselves and our children our cherished position of equal citizenship in the United Kingdom, and in using all means to defeat the present conspiracy to set up a Home Rule parliament in Ireland." They further declared that if such a parliament were forced on them they would refuse to recognize its authority. On September 15 there had been a riot at Belfast, attributed to party feeling, in which about 100 persons were injured, and during the Ulster days there was a less serious riot at Londonderry, but in general the Ulster demonstrations passed off with less disturbance than had been anticipated.

Although many were disposed to belittle the Ulster movement it made a serious impression on the Liberal party, even on some of its most radical members, who admitted that Ulstermen might have a serious grievance and who urged the government to proceed slowly. It strengthened the demand for a referendum of the Government for Ireland bill. On this the Unionists insisted on the ground that the last election did not turn specifically on Home Rule and that on so important a subject the electorate must be consulted. They held that it was criminal folly to proceed to so radical a measure as the coercion of Ulster without its endorsement by the British electorate. Moreover, they declared that no plan for Home Rule should include Northeast Ulster and to the Liberal reply that no one in Ireland would accept Home Rule if it did not include Northeast Ulster they retorted that no Home Rule measure ought, therefore, to be passed. Thus between the extremists on each side matters came to an *impasse*, but many Radicals argued that it was by no means impossible to find a way of protecting the rights of the Ulster minority without sacrificing the interests of the Irish majority. Hints of a possible solution through a federal system of "Home Rule all around" were thrown out, but they took no definite shape. The arguments for excluding the four counties were ably stated by Mr. Balfour in Parliament when the bill reached the committee stage on June 11 (see below). He pointed out that to retain the four Ulster counties (Antrim, Down, Londonderry, and Armagh) against their will under a Nationalist government would leave the Nationalists precisely the same problem with which the British Parliament was struggling, for the men of the North would persistently demand Home Rule for themselves. Moreover, Ulster comprised the wealthiest and most vigorous and determined part of the population. If the British government cannot now rule Ireland on account of the opposition of the Nationalists, who are a small fraction of the population of the United Kingdom, how, he asked, could the latter expect to impose their rule on this powerful and hostile element who would insist in like manner on the right of self-government?

HOME RULE BILL. The Government of Ireland bill, as the government's Home Rule measure was officially entitled, was introduced by Mr. Asquith on April 11. Its chief features were as follows: The principle was definitely asserted that the supreme authority rested in the imperial Parliament. Under this authority Ireland was to receive real autonomy in all Irish concerns. It provided for an Irish parliament consisting of a senate and a house of commons, with power to make laws for Ireland, but certain classes of legislation were reserved from its jurisdiction. For example, Parliament could not establish or endow any religion or impose any religious disability, or make any conditions affecting the validity of marriage, or legislate in any of the following matters: Peace or war, naval or military affairs, treaties with foreign powers, titles or dignities, treason, trademarks, copyright, patents, currency, foreign commerce, and other subjects specifically excluded. The Irish constabulary was to remain under imperial control until six years after the passage of the act, when it was to be transferred to the jurisdiction of the Irish parliament. The lord-lieutenant had power to veto any act contrary to the principles of the Home Rule bill. The senate was to consist of forty members, nominated in the first instance by Great Britain, and succeeded as their terms became vacant by the appointees of the Irish executive. The house of commons was to consist of 164 members elected by Irish constituencies. Ulster was to have fifty-nine members. If the two houses disagreed they were to sit and vote together. Taxes other than post-office duties were to be collected by the imperial government and received by the imperial exchequer, and each year the latter is to transfer to the Irish exchequer the estimated contribution of Ireland. The Irish parliament was under obligation to pay the cost of the Irish services at the time of the passage of the act. Besides the Irish constabularly, the following services would be excluded from the jurisdiction of the Irish parliament for the present: The land-purchase tax, old-age pensions, national insurance, postal savings banks, and the service of public loans before the passage of the act. The Irish parliament was free to impose excise and other taxes of its own and to increase those now existing, but could levy no new customs duties or add to the imperial duties on beer or spirits. As to representation in the imperial Parliament, Ireland was to have forty-two members, according to the present plan, one for about every 100,000 of the population. The executive was vested in the king, represented by the lord-lieutenant and an Irish ministry named by the Parliament. The lord-lieutenant may name additional ministers from time to time as he finds it necessary.

The financial provisions were commonly regarded as presenting the chief difficulties. The problem was in effect how to create a budget within a budget. Ireland had hitherto been administered on a costly scale by the imperial government and the task of devising a financial system suited to her relatively small resources and of linking it with that of the United Kingdom was exceedingly difficult. Orangemen and Conservatives declared it impossible. The budget provisionally established by the new law showed a deficit of £1,515,000, due largely to the cost of old-age pensions. This burden, as well as that imposed by the Land Purchase act, would inevitably increase. To deal with financial questions arising from the new law, the plan provided for a joint exchequer board consisting of two members named by the imperial Parliament, two named by the Irish parliament, and a president appointed by the king. The plan also included the creation of a financial ministry at Dublin. The imperial exchequer, which is to continue to receive all duties for Ireland as well as for Great Britain, will, according to this plan, turn over each year to the Dublin exchequer the amount which the new exchequer board decides to be Ireland's share of the cost of government at the time of the passage of the law; also the sum of £5,000,000, which at the close of the third year after Home Rule goes into effect shall be reduced annually by £50,000 until it reaches the limit of £200,000; also a sum which in the opinion of the exchequer board equals the returns from the taxes imposed by the Irish parliament.

Among the serious questions arising from the financial clauses, was the possibility that the powers which they conferred might lead to the imposition of duties on British imports. This was regarded as one of the vulnerable points of the bill. Another question was whether the law left the British Parliament the power to raise taxes in Ireland after the creation of the Irish parliament. The bill was silent on that point save in so far as the guaranty that the supreme authority of the imperial Parliament should not be diminished might be taken to cover it. The first reading of the Home Rule bill was carried in the House of Commons on April 16 by 360 against 266, a majority of 94. In the debate on that and subsequent occasions, the arguments advanced may be briefly summarized as follows: The Unionists contended that the bill in no wise met the demands of the Irish Nationalists, while it introduced confusion, uncertainty, and injustice into the administration. They ridiculed the talk about the supremacy of the imperial Parliament. Mr. Balfour declared that there was no more reality in the claim of imperial supremacy than in the pretensions of British sovereigns during several centuries of the French rule. The bill was, he said, simply an installment of federalism. The principle would have eventually and logically to apply to England, Scotland, and Wales as well as to Ireland. "For an indefinite time we should be left with a lop-sided federal system, unworkable, and unworthy of the statesmanship of the country." The financial proposals were criticised. Fear was expressed that customs barriers would be set up between Ireland and England. The provision for forty-two Irish members at Westminster was attacked for varying reasons. The main point, however, in the opposition appeared to be the coercion of Ulster under a government to which it would be opposed. This was characterized as tyranny over the minority and as likely to result in religious persecution and even in bloodshed.

A crowded meeting of Nationalists was held at the Mansion House, Dublin, on April 23, and speeches were delivered by Mr. Redmond, Mr. Dillon, and others, to an enthusiastic audience. The convention voted confidence in the government proposals. The second reading was carried on May 9 by a vote of 372 to 271, and on June 11 it went into committee. Amendments to exclude from its operation the four Ulster counties and to strike out the provisions for an Irish senate were rejected. After Parliament had reassembled on October 7 the government proposed a motion assigning thirty-four days for the consideration of the bill, of which twenty-five days were for the committee stage, seven for the report stage and the remaining two days for the third reading. The opposition protested violently at this resort to the "guillotine." A government amendment providing for the principle of proportional representation in the election of members to the Irish senate after five years was passed on October 31 by a vote of 298 to 209. On November 11 the government was suddenly checked by an adverse vote in peculiar circumstances. The financial resolution passed the committee stage on November 7 by a majority of 121. This resolution, which was a vital part of the Home Rule measure, reached its report stage on November 11, and on that day Sir F. Banbury moved an amendment seriously changing its character. It happened that many Liberals were absent from the House, Sir F. Banbury having failed to place the amendment upon the notice paper, and after a brief debate the amendment was carried by a vote of 227 to 206. The House was immediately adjourned and for a time there was threat of a deadlock over the parliamentary question involved. On November 13 an opposition motion was rejected by a vote of 327 to 218. Disorder followed and the sitting was suspended; but on the following day it was agreed at the suggestion of the speaker that the House should adjourn till November 18 "for reflection," and upon reassembling a new financial resolution differing from the original in important respects, was carried by a vote of 318 to 207. This loss of time resulted in the abandonment of a measure regarded as very important by the government, namely, the Mental Deficiency bill (see below) which, however, the government promised to reintroduce in the next session.

Situation at the Close of 1912. The House bill was carried through the committee stage within the appointed time except for a delay of ten days caused by an adverse vote which temporarily checked the government, but which was corrected by a full majority later. It was expected that by the end of the session, March 30,

1913, the government would have carried the Home Rule and Welsh Disestablishment measures and the franchise bill abolishing plural voting. It was expected that the Home Rule bill would be rejected by the House of Lords, and then two years would have to elapse before it could be carried by the Commons alone. Toward the end of the year the government was planning to attack the land question, that is the question of breaking up the large estates which do not pay their full share of taxation. In December Mr. Lloyd-George made an address on this subject at Aberdeen denouncing the "iniquitous land laws." The large estate tended to monopoly and to drive the rural people to cities or abroad.

WELSH DISESTABLISHMENT. The long-promised bill for the disestablishment of the Church of England in Wales was introduced on April 23. It provided that on the first day of July after the passing of the act, the four Welsh dioceses should cease to be dioceses for the province of Canterbury; the ecclesiastical corporations within them would be dissolved and ecclesiastical jurisdiction would be abolished. Synods were to be held to provide for the future government of the Church. The bill provided for Welsh commissioners, three in number, for a period of three years, who should receive existing Church property and distribute it. The disestablished Church was to set up a representative body to which should be transferred all cathedrals, churches, palaces, etc. All the modern endowments were to be handed over by the commissioners to this representative body. The measure was criticised by the opposition with great bitterness, both as to its general purpose and its special features. It was denounced as a blow aimed at the Church of England as a whole, as well as at the Church in Wales. The first reading was carried in the House of Commons by a vote of 331 against 253. During the summer several mass-meetings were held to protest against the measure, including gatherings at Hyde Park, and the Albert Hall, on June 12, where addresses were made by Mr. Bonar Law and the Archbishop of Canterbury.

LABOR UNREST. The year 1912 was marked by very disturbed conditions of labor. The great textile-workers' strike in the Manchester district was in progress when the year began. In May occurred the strike of the London dockers, and toward the close of the year the North-Eastern Railway men went on strike. But by far the most serious movement of the year was the great coal-miners' strike which took place in March. A summary of this and the other labor contests will be found in the articles STRIKES and MINIMUM WAGE, but an account of the coal strike and the minimum wage law is given here because of the serious issues in national politics to which they gave rise.

THE COAL STRIKE AND THE MINIMUM WAGE. At the beginning of 1912 the agitation for a minimum wage for coal miners, which had been going on for a long time, resulted in the formulation of definite demands on the part of the miners, which the coal owners steadily opposed. These demands comprised a scale of minimum wages for the different mining districts of the United Kingdom. To meet the objections of the coal owners, the miners reduced the rate demanded in some of the districts, but still contended for the principle of the minimum wage. On January 12 the Miners' Federation referred the question of a strike to the miners, and the vote was generally in its favor. Thereupon the federation gave the employers notice that work would be stopped by the end of February. A national conference between coal owners and the miners' representatives was held in London on February 7. The revised scale of minimum wages was presented by the miners, but after consideration the coal owners passed a resolution declaring that the principle of payment in proportion to the amount of work performed was the only one that could be successfully applied. They admitted, however, that owing to exceptional conditions in the working place, certain miners, though doing their best, were unable to earn as much as they would in normal circumstances, and they declared their willingness in such cases to give the subject special consideration. The miners in reply expressed regret that the coal owners would not accept the principle of the minimum wage, which was the only condition of a settlement. Negotiations and conferences between the government and the coal owners and miners were continued, and finally, the government proposed as a basis of settlement that the principle of the minimum wage should be accepted. It declared that there were special conditions under which certain miners could not earn a reasonable minimum wage, owing to the peculiar nature of the work, and that they should receive such a wage under arrangements suited to special circumstances. It announced its readiness to confer with both parties as to the best means of carrying these principles into effect. The coal owners in the English districts accepted the proposals, but those in Scotland and South Wales rejected them. The miners, while agreeing to the general principle laid down by the government, held to the two essential points, that a concession of the individual minimum wage in each district must precede final settlement of the dispute, and that the minimum wage rates for the various districts must be those adopted by the Miners' Federation at the conference on February 7.

The miners were blamed for refusing to accept the demand of the employers that, if a minimum wage was to be guaranteed, there should be a guarantee of minimum service. Without this, what means, it was asked, would there be for dealing with those who shirked work? The miners were unyielding on this point and the government found it difficult to effect a compromise. The danger of a strike in the coal trade was especially marked in Great Britain, where coal entered so widely into the industrial life of the community that a cessation of the supply would paralyze the factories, railways, and navigation companies and threaten the means of subsistence for the entire population. The strike took place at the time appointed, February 29, and it was estimated that 760,000 men stopped work.

Early in March the miners consented to renew the negotiations, but nothing came of them. By the middle of March the number of miners on strike was placed at nearly 850,000, and of surface workers at over 200,000, while the number of the unemployed in other industries was estimated at between four and five hundred thousand. The figures were not accurate, but rough estimates placed the number of persons thrown out of employment by the strike at upwards of a million and a half. Although the strikers had gained the main point, which was the recognition of the principle of the minimum wage, they refused to admit any diminution of the scale of minimum wages that they demanded.

MINIMUM WAGE LAW. Conferences with the miners having proved unavailing, the prime minister introduced a minimum wage bill into Parliament on March 19. Save as regards the application of the minimum wage principle to certain sweated trades (see MINIMUM WAGE), such an act was unprecedented in the history of British legislation, and it gave rise to very important discussion. After the final rupture of the negotiations on March 15, the government decided on this measure as the only means of restoring peace. In the speech in which it was introduced the prime minister declared that its prompt enactment was necessary, and that the government had resorted to it only after the hope of a settlement by agreement was destroyed. The government believed that in order to meet the exceptional conditions of work in abnormal places, there must be a minimum wage on the one hand, and a guarantee on the other of adequate service. The measure was characterized as experimental. It was to be in force only for three years. The minimum wage could be recovered by civil process if it were not paid, and it could not be voided by contract. If a workingman did not comply with the conditions for the protection of owners against possible abuses, he was to lose the right to the minimum wage. Mr. Bonar Law, among others, criticised the law as likely to prove worse than the evil which it was designed to remove. What was there to prevent, he asked, the precedent of the minimum wage from being extended to other industries? It was virtually inviting every trade that has a strong organization to bring pressure upon the government to attain its object. He did not believe that the guarantees to the masters against diminished output were sufficient. When asked by Labor members what he would do in the present crisis, he replied that three courses had been open to the government. They could have taken steps before the strike to enforce arbitration, or they could have used all the force at their command to protect miners who were willing to continue work after the strike had begun, or they might have insisted that the strike should end and force the owners to open the pits and the men to go back to them. The attitude of the miners toward the bill was distinctly hostile. They demanded that the measure be amended so as to include the schedule rates that they required, and refused to accept any act of Parliament which did not provide for the payment of a minimum wage of not less than 5s. a day for workmen and 2s. a day for boys of fourteen years. The Minimum Wage bill provided for district boards to determine the rates in the different parts of the country. The miners, however, contended for the insertion in the bill of the specific figures, namely, 5s. for men and 2s. for boys as a minimum rate. This the government steadily refused on the ground that the conditions of the industry varied in different districts, and must be specially fixed in each case. The appeal of the prime minister to the miners to come to an agreement with the coal owners was unsuccessful and the bill in Parliament was hurried through its final stage. The Labor members offered an amendment to meet the demand of the miners providing for the 5s. and 2s. minimum. This amendment was rejected by a vote of 326 to 83, and the bill passed its third reading in the House by 213 votes against 48 on March 27. It went immediately to the House of Lords, where it was passed on March 28, and it received the royal assent on March 29. The discussion of the measure in Parliament brought out a division in the ranks of the Labor party, the Socialists urging that the party should abstain from voting on the third reading while the members that represented the miners wished the party to cast in its vote against it. The argument of the Socialist members was that to cast a vote against a measure embodying, for the first time, the principle of the minimum wage, would embarrass the party in future. The miners carried their point, however, and the Labor party as a whole voted against the measure. The Socialists really saw in the passage of the Minimum Wage measure a triumph for their cause. The European Socialist press expressed its exultation at the result and congratulated the miners on the firm stand that they had taken. M. Jaurès, the French Socialist, and M. Vandervelde, the leader of the Belgian Labor party, pointed to the miners' attitude in this matter as a splendid example. To the great relief of everyone the coal strike was at last declared at an end on April 6, the men having agreed to go back to work while the determination of the Minimum Wage was pending before the district boards. See MINIMUM WAGE.

SYNDICALISM. In 1911 and 1912 the term syndicalism, which had hitherto been limited to its continental application, became naturalized in Great Britain. In general, it signifies that element of unionism which aims not merely at organizing strikes for immediate ends, but at organizing a general strike for the purpose of ultimately giving the control of the means of production to the workmen of each trade. Mr. Tom Mann, the labor leader, was arrested on March 19 for having printed in the *Syndicalist* an article urging sodiers to oppose their employment against the workingmen in labor troubles, and for having made similar appeals in his speeches. The printers and publishers were also prosecuted. The matter came up in Parliament in the latter part of March in the course of a debate on the Consolidated Fund bill. The attorney-general was criticised for the prosecutions on the ground that they would tend to inflame public opinion. The working classes were already suspicious of the judiciary and it was asked whether one could not question the rightfulness of shooting working people down. In defense of the prosecutions the attorney-general said that they were in no sense an attack on the liberty of the press. If the article in the *Syndicalist* had merely urged that the soldiers should not be called upon to interfere in industrial disputes there would have been no prosecutions, but the article had tried to induce the military to disregard their duty. If soldiers refused to shoot they were liable to the severest punishment, even the death penalty. Hence the gravity of the offense in printing that open letter. The growth of syndicalism in Great Britain was thus disclosed. It was condemned by some as an anti-Social policy, based upon class warfare. At the hearing early in May Mr. Tom Mann pleaded on his own behalf that he had not attempted to seduce soldiers from lawful commands. He said that when soldiers were acting under civil law they were only citizens. He claimed his right as a man and a citizen to declare that he did not publish the letter, but he did not differ from it and would not ask mercy for his agreement with the principles of the letter. He was pronounced guilty and sentenced to six months' imprisonment, but the sentence was afterwards commuted. See SYNDICALISM.

BUDGET. The budget did not offer any new or remarkable features. No new taxes were to be levied and existing taxation was neither increased nor reduced. The chancellor of the exchequer, Mr. Lloyd-George, in his speech on the presentation of the budget in April, expressed himself in a sanguine manner as to the financial prospects and justified his former predictions. He reminded the House of the four principles that he had laid down in 1909, namely, that the taxes should not only meet the year's requirements, but should be susceptible of expansion to meet further demands; that all classes of the community should contribute; that taxation should not increase the cost of the necessaries of life, and that there should be no interference with trade, industry, and commerce. He declared that these principles had been faithfully observed. The estimated expenditure for the coming year was £186,885,000. In view of the effects of the coal miners' strike and the possible needs of naval expenditure, the chancellor declared on this occasion that the surplus amounting to about £6,500,000 could not be turned over to the sinking fund, but in June he announced that £5,000,000 would be applied to the reduction of the debt, £1,000,000 to the supplementary naval estimates, and £500,000 loaned to Uganda and the East Africa Protectorate.

WOMAN SUFFRAGE. It became evident early in the year that the suffrage question would play an important part in political discussion. The growing activities of the suffragists were met by counter-demonstrations from their opponents. The National League, formed to oppose woman suffrage, planned a monster meeting to be held at Albert Hall, February 28. It rapidly gained adherents, including many leading public men and several members of the government. The government had been long divided on the question, some of its prominent members like Mr. Lloyd-George, Sir Edward Grey, and Mr. Winston Churchill having been very active on behalf of the movement. Mr. Asquith's position on the other hand was well known. In the middle of December, 1911, he had told a deputation of suffragists that he believed the granting of the parliamentary franchise to women would be a disastrous political mistake. Lord Curzon and Lord Cromer were among its conspicuous opponents. The proposal to decide the question by referendum was much discussed during the year.

The much-heralded anti-suffrage meeting was held at Albert Hall on February 28. There were said to be 20,000 applications for seats, but the hall could seat only half that number. The meeting was addressed by several persons of prominence and demonstrated the strength of the opposition to the new movement. A few days earlier (February 23) the suffragists held a large meeting at the same place and were addressed by Mr. Lloyd-George among others. The meeting was interrupted by disorders on the part of the listeners, although Mr. Lloyd-George expressed himself strongly in favor of the suffrage. As to the proposed referendum on the suffrage, he called it a costly denial of justice. He argued that if the course indicated by Mr. Asquith were followed, the triumph of the cause was certain this year. He promised that if the woman suffrage amendment to the Reform bill were carried the government would push the amended bill through this session. On March 1 widespread rioting and window-smashing took place on several of the London streets, where many hundreds of women, armed with hammers, attacked the shops. The prime minister's house in Downing Street was among those damaged. A few days later the same window-smashing tactics were employed at Kensington, Knightsbridge, and Brompton. Hundreds of arrests were made. Many of the arrested suffragists were tried in March. In seventy-six cases the sentence was to hard labor for from four to six months.

The leaders of the suffragist movement, Mrs. Pankhurst and Mr. and Mrs. Pethick Lawrence, who had been arrested on the charge of conspiracy, were found guilty on May 22, after a hearing of six days. The jury, however, recommended mercy in view of the undoubtedly pure motives underlying the woman suffrage agitation. Justice Coleridge sentenced them to imprisonment for nine months, but after a short time they were released. An assault was made on Mr. Asquith while speaking at the Theatre Royal, Dublin, and an attempt was made to burn the building. This led to the arrest and sentence of two woman suffragists who, however, were released on license. Mrs. Pankhurst in October declared that the only way to carry out the purposes of the suffragists was to wage war on property. A Woman Suffrage bill similar to the one defeated in 1911 was introduced in 1912, but met with the same fate. A bill for the abolition of plural voting and containing a woman suffrage provision under restrictions was introduced in July, but did not reach the committee stage. An amendment to the Home Rule bill providing for woman suffrage in the elections to the Irish House of Commons was rejected on November 5.

ELECTORAL REFORM. The government introduced its Franchise and Registration bill on June 17. It provided for the abolishing of plural voting, of property qualification, and of university representation, for the reform of electoral machinery and the system of registration. It made residence or occupation the sole qualification for the suffrage and limited the qualifying period of such residence or occupation to a continuous period of six months. It reached its second reading in July, when the opposition attacked it on the ground that the government itself was not agreed as to the most important principle involved, and that it failed to remedy glaring inequalities in the representative system. It had long been contended by Mr. Asquith and by other members of the government that the question of woman suffrage would be answered in connection with this bill by offering an amendment which should provide for it. The measure as introduced was made to apply to "every male person." In July, after the second reading, several members of the House gave notice that they would offer amendment to omit the word "male." Nothing further was done with the measure during the session, but it was understood that it was the government's intention to go on with it early in the following year. The principle of proportional representation had gained many advocates in Great Britain in recent years. In 1908 a royal commission was appointed to investigate the various methods in use and its report was published in May, 1910. In 1912 the principle had gained sufficient acceptance to lead to a provision for it in the Home Rule bill in the election of members to the Irish senate. While this bill was under discussion there were vigorous efforts made by many members, both Liberals and Unionists, to extend proportional representation to the elections for the Irish house of commons as well.

MENTAL DEFICIENCY BILL. In the latter part of May Mr. McKenna presented the Mental Deficiency bill in the House of Common. This provided for a central authority of six commissioners to exercise general control over defectives and maintain institutions for such of them as are dangerous and, in general, to perform the same duties in regard to them that are performed by the commissioners of lunacy for the insane. Among its provisions was one that authorized the cessation of the prosecution for a criminal offense when the person accused was found to be feeble-minded. Another important provision forbade the marriage of defective persons.

It was dropped in November in order to give time for carrying through the Home Rule bill, but it was understood that it would be revived at the next session.

WHITE SLAVE TRAFFIC BILL. The Criminal Law Amendment bill, popularly known as the White Slave Traffic bill, provided for the arrest without warrant of anyone committing or attempting to commit the crime of procuring, and empowered the court to impose the punishment of flogging on men convicted of the offense. It passed the House of Commons on November 1. There was strong popular feeling behind the measure and it was supported in Parliament without regard to party lines.

TARIFF REFORM. In 1912 the Unionists continued to give a prominent place in their discussions to the subject of tariff reform. On February 22 a tariff reform amendment to the address from the throne was moved in the House of Commons and was rejected by a vote of 258 to 193. In the arguments on this and other occasions the Unionists laid stress on the point that tariff reform was not a return to the old policy of protection, but was a method of scientifically regulating trade and finance in the interest of the empire as a whole. They urged it as the only rational and practicable method of raising the revenue necessary for social legislation. Their opponents attacked it on the ground that it would raise the cost of production in Great Britain and limit the purchasing power of the population. They were particularly emphatic in denouncing the taxation of food which has formed an essential part of the tariff reform programme ever since Mr. Chamberlain outlined it. In regard to the food duties there was a division of opinion among the Unionists themselves and towards the end of the year it seemed evident that the larger part of the party were opposed to food duties. The majority of the party also seemed not to be in accord with their leaders on the question of the referendum. Lord Lansdowne in a speech on October 13, 1912, said that the question of tariff reform should be referred to the electorate only if the proposed measure exceeded certain limits which should be specified in advance as to the amount of protective taxation. And on December 15 Mr. Bonar Law in a speech at Ashton-under-Lyne proposed that the question of food duties should be laid before the colonies at an imperial conference, and unless the colonies decided that the food duties were absolutely essential to preference they were not to be imposed. Thus the colonies would decide the question and the proposal would not be submitted to a referendum. This speech aroused considerable opposition among those Unionists who wished for a referendum on the question of tariff reform and who were especially averse to leaving the decision as to the food duties to the colonies. While the majority of the party appeared to differ from Mr. Bonar Law in this matter, there was evidence that all were agreed in their wish that Mr. Bonar Law should retain the leadership.

NATIONAL INSURANCE. The Insurance act, which was passed in 1911, and went into effect on July 15, 1912, was one of the most extensive measures of social legislation passed in recent years. The scheme, as elaborated by Mr. William Lloyd-George, virtually attempted to carry out in a single bill what had been accomplished in the German empire by the legislation of an entire generation. It was very widely discussed in the press at home and abroad. An account of its main features and of the opposition to it will be found in the article WORKINGMEN'S INSURANCE.

NAVAL EXPANSION. While the German naval defense estimates were under discussion in the Reichstag, the British government was watching anxiously the tendency to increase the strength of the German navy. On March 18 Mr. Churchill, the first lord of the admiralty, had introduced his estimates in the House of Commons. He declared that he would adhere to his previous standard, namely, two ships a year for the next six years. This applied the principle that the British navy should be 60 per cent. in excess of the German. In May, when it became evident that the German navy would be increased, the need of supplementary estimates in Great Britain was considered. Italy's course as endangering the Mediterranean equilibrium was the cause of much anxiety (see TURCO-ITALIAN WAR). On May 22 Mr. Asquith and Mr. Churchill conferred with Lord Kitchener at Malta concerning the land and sea forces for the Mediterranean. In the latter part of July Mr. Churchill in a speech supporting the new naval estimates made comparisons between German and British naval progress, saying that these suplementary estimates were directly due to the new German navy law which aimed at increasing the striking force of the German fleet. Nearly four-fifths of their vessels would, he said, be ready for instant war. This was the fifth increase of the German navy in fourteen years. Their fleet would ultimately consist of 41 battleships, 20 large armored cruisers, 40 smaller cruisers, and a large force of torpedo-boat destroyers and submarines. The need of keeping pace with these extraordinary preparations was evident. To maintain the 60 per cent. standard a greater number of ships would have to be built within the next five years than had been estimated. The increase of the Austrian and Italian fleets would require important changes in the Mediterranean. Battleships of the *Invincible* type would replace the British vessels withdrawn and the allied force of British and French vessels in the Miditerranean would be superior to any possible combination. See paragraph above on *Navy*, also articles NAVAL PROGRESS, BATTLESHIPS, and FRANCE, *History*.

BARON VON BIEBERSTEIN. On May 14 Baron Marschall von Bieberstein (q. v.), whose record as German ambassador at Constantinople was distinguished for its remarkable successes, was appointed ambassador at London to succeed Count Wolff-Metternich. The latter had been recalled in consequence, it was said, of his failure during the Moroccan negotiations of 1911, to keep his home government informed of the actual state of British opinion. In Germany it had been believed that the British government would maintain an attitude of indifference in that affair, and the firm tone of the premier and of Mr. Lloyd-George was as unexpected as it was unwelcome. Baron von Bieberstein's policy at Constantinople had been to treat Old Turks and Young Turks simply as Turks. To his personal qualities, as well as to the lack of any especial ability on the part of his rivals, he owed his conspicuous position among the diplomats at Constantinople. His influence was impaired by the Turco-Italian War, but he had carried out his economic programme, of which the main point was the construction of the Bagdad Railway. Baron von Bieberstein died suddenly at Baden-weiler after he had held the new office only three months. He was succeeded by Prince Lichnowsky.

M. SAZONOFF'S VISIT. On September 20 M. Sazonoff, the Russian foreign minister, visited England, and on September 25 entered into conferences with Sir Edward Grey at Balmoral on the various questions of international interest. The chief purpose of the interview was said to be an agreement in regard to Persia. There was much discussion of this matter in the press and the critics of the government's Persian policy feared that it would end in more decisive measures of intervention. From the knowledge that could be gained of the conference it had no such purpose, but on the contrary, aimed to aid Persia in maintaining order with a view to hastening the withdrawal of the foreign troops. The approaching war in the Balkans, however, assumed the chief importance as a topic of discussion. It was announced that both governments were in complete accord in their desire for peace.

LABOR PARTY. The labor party held a conference in Birmingham, on January 25 and 26. Various resolutions were passed condemning the use of military in trade disputes, protesting against the repeal of the Trades Disputes act, welcoming the increasing discontent among workers, and advising trade unions to defy the law on the subject of political utterances until the Osborne judgment should be reversed. The enfranchisement of women was urged and the foreign policy of the country was attacked. A breach between the Liberal and Labor parties was threatened in June over the refusal of the former to support a Labor candidate in the election at Hanley (see SOCIALISM). The Liberal candidate received 6,647, against 5,993 Conservative and only 1694 Labor votes.

MINISTERIAL CHANGES. Early in the year Lord Crewe became lord privy seal, succeeding Lord Carrington, who had resigned. Mr. McKinnon Wood succeeded Lord Pentland as secretary for Scotland. Lord Loreburn on June 4 resigned the office of lord high chancellor and was succeeded by Lord Haldane. Col. J. E. B. Seeley succeeded to the war office, and was in turn succeeded in the office of parliamentary under-secretary by Mr. H. J. Tennant.

MISCELLANEOUS. There was much discussion in the spring of the Malecka case. Miss Kate Malecka, who had been naturalized as a British subject, was arrested while visiting in Warsaw in April, 1912, on the charge of conspiring with Polish Socialists. She denied the charge, and in England public opinion was deeply stirred. Through the influence of the British government the Russian authorities agreed that the trial should be public. It was held in May and she was sentenced to four years' penal servitude, but upon the friendly representations of the British government, the Russian government decided to release her from prison, but to forbid her to remain on Russian soil. A serious colliery accident occurred at the Cadeby coal pit in the Yorkshire mining district on July 9. An explosion early in the morning killed 30 men and later in the day while rescuers were at work a series of explosions followed, killing many more. Reports within the next few days gave the number of deaths as 81. The fifth disaster in the submarine service since 1902 occurred on October 4, when the submarine *B 2* collided with the ocean liner *Amerika* near Dover and sank with all on board. Fifteen perished, including the commanding officer. One officer was saved. The submarine *A 3* was lost with four officers and ten men in a collision with a depot ship off the Isle of Wight on February 2. In June and July, and especially in August, the weather conditions were exceedingly bad. The extraordinary rainfall in August spoiled the harvest in many parts of the country. The city of Norwich suffered particularly. A square mile was under water and the hardships and danger to the people were serious.

For notes of other matters relating to Great Britain, see ARCHITECTURE; ARBITRATION, INTERNATIONAL; CITY PLANNING; CHINA, *History*; DIVORCE; and UNEMPLOYMENT.

GREECE. A constitutional European monarchy, lying between the Ionian and Ægean seas, composed of twenty-six nomes, or departments. Athens is the capital.

AREA AND POPULATION. The area in square kilometers is 64,657 (24,964 square miles); population (1907), 2,631,952. Population of Athens, 167,479. Emigration to the United States (1910-11), 48,000.

INDUSTRIES. Agriculture is the principal industry, though the methods are antiquated; the chief crops are currants, grapes, cereals, tobacco, citrus fruits, olives, and figs. Currant crop (1910-11), 262,500,000 lbs., of which 225,130,412 lbs. were exported. The horses were estimated to number 100,000, cattle 360,000, sheep 2,900,000. Silk culture is carried on. The mineral returns for 1910 are as follows:

608,349 tons iron, 185,207 tons lead, 7000 chromite, 91 copper, 8000 emery, 35,594 manganese iron, 27,557 iron pyrites, 1500 lignite, 48,913 magnesite, 185 nickel, 51,531 sulphur, 37,108 zinc. The sale of salt is put at £118,-000. See AGRICULTUURE.

COMMERCE, ETC. In the table below is seen the trade for three consecutive years in drachmas (1 dr.=19.3 cents):

	1909	1910	1911
Imports	137,549,244	160,536,471	172,002,000
Exports	101,686,905	144,571,070	140,903,000

The chief imports are grains, textiles, coal, timber, chemical products, fish, etc. The exports for 1910 of the principal products are given below in drachmas with the share of the United Kingdom, France, Germany, and the United States in thousands of drachmas; a few only of the articles are given, and totals for each country named:

Exports	Total	U. K.	Fr.	Ger.	U. S.
Currants	40,523,474	22,497	1,064	5,189	4,876
Wine, etc.....	18,633,504	1,525	6,154	3,109	289
Olive oil	17,465,554	316	2,667	62	693
Tobacco leaf.	12,051,045	90	74	1,595	180
Figs	5,387,184	54	16	322	221
Arg. Lead....	10,110,240	1,292	2,639	.....	.....
Zinc	5,144,776	203	258	642	.....
Hematite	4,296,150	2,823	.....	513	176
Other	....	.....	.....	.....	.....
Total	144,571,070	33,084	15,468	15,097	10,540

Railways (1912), 1609 kilometers. Previous to the outbreak of the war in 1912, lines from Leontari to Gythion (70 miles) and from Olympia to near Leontari (23 miles) were under construction. The Gravia to Volo line to the Gulf of Corinth was also under way.

FINANCE. The total revenue for the year 1911 amounted to 136,277,463 drachmas, and the expenditure to 135,094,473. The budget for 1912 estimated the revenue at 144,118,645 drachmas and the expenditure at 143,326,520. The gold debt amounted, December 31, 1912, to 833,581,000 and the paper to 150,009,565 drachmas.

ARMY. The reorganization of the army which had been in progress in 1911, under the direction of General Eydoux, the French military adviser of the government, found opportunity for test in the Balkan War. On February 15, 1912, the military scheme as arranged by him was voted, and this provided for the composition of the Greek army on a war-footing as follows: 44 regular infantry battalions (36 line and 8 chasseurs) and 36 reserve battalions; 46 field and 3 heavy batteries of artillery; 16 squadrons of cavalry and 84 machine guns; affording a maximum effective of 100,500 men (80,000 rifles, 1760 sabres, and 173 guns) to which might be added 16 companies of gendarmes (147 officers, 3882 men, and 387 horses). The national guard, consisting of men between the ages of 40 and 53, amounted to about 69,-000 men.

The new law required military service from the end of the 19th year and permitted no exceptions. In addition to the main army a first reserve consisting of 14 classes and, designed ultimately to furnish some 200,000 men was provided for, while a second reserve and the territorial army were to give 250,000 men. Under the new law terms of service were as follows: With the active army 2 years; with the first reserve 12 years; with the second reserve 9 years; with the territorial army 7 years; with the territorial reserve 7 years. The new organization was not completed at the outbreak of the war, but was in active progress and the artillery was being re-armed with Schneider-Canet quick-firing guns. The new regulations provided for an active army with a peace strength of 29,000 men, which in time of war could be increased to from 120,000 to 130,-000, but in 1912 officers were not available for such a force. The 4 divisions had their headquarters at Larissa, Athens, Missolonghi and Nauplia. How well the mobilization on the outbreak of war was effected and the performance of the Greek troops in the field, will be found discussed under MILITARY PROGRESS and TURKEY AND THE BALKAN PEOPLES.

NAVY. The navy includes one Italian-built armored cruiser (*Georgios Averoff*, 10,000 tons), 3 coast-defense vessels (4800 tons each), 12 modern destroyers and torpedo boats, and some small craft. Personnel, 4941.

GOVERNMENT. The executive authority is vested in a king (1912, George I.), assisted by a responsible ministry of seven members. The legislative body consists of a single chamber of 207 members, elected by manhood suffrage. The reigning king (son of Christian IX. of Denmark) was elected king by the Greek national assembly in 1863. The ministry in 1912 was composed as follows: E. Venezelos, premier and minister of war; A. Coromilas, foreign affairs; K. Raktiván, justice; E. Repoulis, interior; I. D. Tsirimokos, worship and instruction; A. N. Diomidis, finance; N. Stratos, marine, A. Michalacopoulos, national economics.

HISTORY. The chief events of 1912 had to do with the relations with Crete and the part played by Greece in the Balkan War, and an account of them will be found in the articles CRETE, *History*, and TURKEY AND THE BALKAN PEOPLES. On January 2 the Revisionary Chamber having finished its work was dissolved, the dissolution being hastened in order that the Cretan deputies detained on the warships of the protecting powers might be set free (see CRETE). The elections, which took place in the latter part of March, resulted, despite the bitter opposition of the old parties to the premier, M. Venezelos, in the return of a large majority in his favor. Out of the 181 deputies to the new chamber, 147 were supporters of the new premier. There were some changes in the cabinet in May, the chief of which was the resignation of M. Guyparis, minister of foreign affairs, who was succeeded by M. Koromilas. The meeting of the chamber, fixed for May 4, was postponed to June 2 and on that day after the deputies were sworn it was prorogued till October. In the latter month all interest centred in the mobilization of the Greek forces, preparatory to the Balkan War. The part taken by M. Venezelos, both in the difficult question of Crete and in the events preceding the war, added greatly to his repute for statesmanship. He was credited with being the guiding spirit of the Balkan alliance. On April 8 the anniversary of the declaration of Greek independence was celebrated with a grand review of troops before the statue of Byron. In April, also, other celebrations were held in commemoration of the founding of the University of Athens, and the Congress of Orientalists held its sixteenth session. King George attended the funeral of King Frederick of Denmark in May, and was again absent in August and September, taking the cure at Aix-les-Bains. During his absence on this occasion the crown prince acted as regent.

GREEK ARCHÆOLOGICAL SOCIETY. See ARCHÆOLOGY.

GREENLAND. A Danish Arctic colony. Estimated area, 2,200,000 square kilometers (849,420 square miles). Area of settlements (colony proper), 88,100 square kilometers (34,-015 square miles). Population of colony proper in 1901, 11,893 (11,621 Eskimos and 272 Europeans); February 1, 1911, 12,968. The director (residing at Copenhagen) was I. Daugaard-Jensen in 1912.

GREENOUGH, GEORGE GORDON. An American soldier and scholar, died June 28, 1912. He was born in Washington in 1844, and was educated in private schools in Paris and in Baltimore. He graduated from the United States Military Academy in 1865 and in the same year was appointed first lieutenant in the 12th Infantry. In the following year he was transferred to the 21st Infantry, and in 1870 was assigned to the 4th Artillery. He was made a captain in 1893, major in 1898, colonel in 1903, and brigadier-general and retired in 1908. From 1868 to 1873 he was assistant professor and acting professor in French at the United States Military Academy. He served in several Indian campaigns in 1873, 1875, and 1876-77. He was one of the pioneers in range-finding work from 1892 to 1898. In the latter year he commanded the artillery defenses at Washington. He served in Cuba in the Spanish-American War, and in the Philippine Islands. He was the inventor of various devices for artillery operations.

GRENADA. The largest of the British Windward Islands colonies. Area, 133 square miles, population (1911), 66,750. Capital, St. George's (4916 inhabitants in 1911). Cacao is the most important product, the export in 1910 being valued at £259,365. Total exports (including spices) in 1910, £291,760; imports, £279,368. Revenue (1910-11), £81,413; expenditure, £75,561. Sir James Hayes Sadler, governor (1912). Attached to Grenada are some of the Grenadine Islands.

GRENADINE ISLANDS. Dependency of Grenada (q. v.).

GRIFFEN, WALTER BURLEY See CITY PLANNING, *Australian Capital.*

GRISCOM, CLEMENT ACTON. An American financier, died November 10, 1912. He was born at Philadelphia in 1841 and received an academic education. In 1857 he became clerk and, in 1863, partner in the business house of Peter Wright and Sons, shipping merchants. Soon after he had become partner in this firm he conceived the idea that the export of petroleum offered great possibilities. He was a pioneer in this trade, which was later developed by the Standard Oil Company. In 1871 he began the operation of the American line of steamships which was at that time the only line that carried the American flag in the North Atlantic Ocean. His chief ambition was to bring together under one management the greatest steamship combination in the world, and he organized the International Navigation Company, of which he was successively vice-president and president. In 1902, with the coöperation of J. Pierpont Morgan, he merged this company with the International Mercantile Marine Company, comprising the White Star, Atlantic Transport, Dominion, and Leyland lines. He was president of this company until his retirement in 1904. For forty years, almost unaided, Mr. Griscom kept the American flag in the North Atlantic Ocean and retained the interest of capital in American shipping. During these forty years his company never lost a ship, passenger, or mail bag. Although he retired from the presidency of the International Mercantile Marine Company in 1904, he accepted the chairmanship of the board of directors, remaining in active business until 1908. In addition to his shipping interests he was director and official in many important corporations, including the Pennsylvania Railroad Company and the United States Steel Corporation. For his work in the direction of safety in the construction of ships he was made an honorary member of the British Institute of Naval Architects and was at one time president of the American Society of Naval Architects.

GRISWOLD, STEPHEN BENHAM. An American librarian, died May 4, 1912. He was born at Vernon, N. Y., in 1835, and received an academic education. After studying law at the Albany Law School he was admitted to the bar in 1860. From 1868 to 1904 he was librarian of the New York City Library and from 1899 until the time of his death was a member of the faculty of the Albany Law School.

GROSSMITH, GEORGE. An English actor and entertainer, died March 1, 1912. He was born in 1847, the son of George Grossmith, a well-known journalist, lecturer, and entertainer. After studying in the North London Collegiate School he assisted his father in various fields of work. He was for a time reporter for the *Times*. He later assisted his father in miscellaneous entertainments of lecturing, reciting, imitating, etc. In the meantime he was engaged in the study of music. In 1877 he first went on the stage and joined an enterprise which was to develop into the great Gilbert and Sullivan opera. His first appearance was in *The Sorcerer*, produced in that year. For the next twelve years he was identified almost entirely with the Gilbert and Sullivan operas, although for a short time during that period he returned to entertaining. Among his best-known parts were those of "Sir Joseph Porter" in *Pinafore*, "Bunthorne" in *Patience*, the "Lord Chancellor" in *Iolanthe*, and "Ko-ko" in *The Mikado*. In 1889 he was obliged to retire from opera singing and return to entertaining along new lines. These included talking, singing and playing the piano. The entertainments were at that time unique and were very successful. He became no less popular in America and Canada than in the United Kingdom. All his songs, piano music, and humorous talks were of his own composition. Among the best-known of his songs are *The Happy Fatherland*, *The Polka and the Choir-Boy*, and *We Left the Baby on the Shore*. His talks abounded in wit and humorous satire. He composed two operas, *Cups and Saucers* and *Uncle Samuel*, and was the author and composer of over six hundred humorous and satirical songs and sketches.

GUADELOUPE. A French colony composed of islands of the Lesser Antilles. Area, 1780 square kilometers; population (1911), 212,430. Imports (1910), 16,804,000 francs; exports (sugar, cacao, coffee, tobacco, and tropical fruits), 24,053,000. The local budget balanced for 1912 at 4,559,583 francs. M. Peuvergne was governor in 1912.

GUAM. See AGRICULTURAL EXPERIMENT STATIONS.

GUANTANAMO, CUBA. See UNITED STATES, *Army*.

GUATEMALA. A Central American republic. Capital, Guatemala City.

AREA, POPULATION, ETC. One estimate of the country's area is 48,290 square miles; another, 43,641. The area cannot be definitely determined until the boundary dispute with Honduras is settled. On December 8, 1911, the boundary convention between the two countries, which would expire March 1, 1912, was extended for two years from the latter date. The census of December 31, 1903, disclosed a population of 1,842,134, about 60 per cent. Indian and most of the remainder mestizo. The vital statistics indicate that the population in 1912 had increased to over 2,000,000. Births in 1910, 74,498; deaths, 35,077; in 1911, 71,895 and 35,234. The larger towns, with estimated population, are: Guatemala City, 125,000; Quezaltenango, 34,000; Cobán, 31,000; Totanicapán, 29,000; Escuintla, Chiquimula, Zacapa, Jalapa, each 18,000; Santa Cruz del Quiche, 17,000; Jutiapa, 16,000; Antigua, Salama, and Huehuetenango, each 15,000; Amatitlan, 12,000; Sololá, 11,000.

Public primary schools in 1911 numbered 1821, with 55,685 pupils enrolled; there were 1657 students in secondary and normal schools. There are several institutions for professional and special instruction.

PRODUCTION AND COMMERCE. The principal crops are coffee, corn, sugar-cane, bananas, tobacco, and cacao. In 1911 about 880,000 acres were under coffee. There is some exploitation of cabinet woods, rubber, and chicle. Mining and manufacturing are unimportant.

Imports and exports have been valued as follows:

	1908	1909	1911
Imports	$5,811,586	$ 5,251,317	$ 6,514,421
Exports	6,756,138	10,079,219	10,981,724

Leading imports in 1911: Cotton goods, $1,848,651; woolens, $277,600; silks, $267,279; linen, hemp, jute, $272,267; iron and steel manufactures, $626,425; wheat flour, $354,155; other food products, $419,818; wines and liquors, $223,286; railway material, $311,385; agricultural and industrial machinery, $196,422; drugs and medicines, $217,635. Principal exports in 1911: Coffee, clean, 30,345 short tons, $7,282,749; coffee in parchment, 10,480 tons, $1,991,161; bananas, $526,711; sugar, $344,015; hides, $325,261; rubber, $159,621; woods, $158,178; chicle, $150,902. The United States sent imports and received exports in 1911 valued at $2,696,144 and $3,297,156 respectively; Germany, $1,592,658 and $5,851,817; United Kingdom, $1,314,202 and $1,324,721; France, $286,050 and $19,333. Of the exports to Germany, coffee amounted to $5,457,662. Entered at the ports in 1911, 623 steamers, of 1,187,800 tons, and 8 sail, of 257 tons.

COMMUNICATIONS. Railways in operation at the end of 1911 totalled 679 kilometers (422 miles). San José and Champerico, on the Pacific, are connected with Guatemala City and other towns, the lines aggregating 189 miles. From the capital a line extends to Puerto Barrios, on the eastern coast, 195 miles. During 1911 1,187,433 passengers and 252,882 tons of freight were carried; of the freight, 149,433 tons represented local freight, and 103,449 tons the freight made up of import and export. Telegraph lines, over 4200 miles; offices, 221. Post offices, 311.

FINANCE. Revenue and expenditure for fiscal years, in thousands of pesos paper:

	1906	1907	1908	1909	1910	1911
Rev. ..	30,501	35,298	37,336	49,240	51,571	62,047
Exp. ..	45,733	44,560	49,930	70,554	45,959	69,162

The approximate average value of the paper peso was 9 cents in 1906, 8 in 1907, 6½ in 1908, 6 in 1909, 7 in 1910, and 5½ in 1911. Over one-half of the revenue is derived from customs, and one-third from spirits, tobacco, etc. The budget for the fiscal year 1912 showed estimated expenditure of 37,417,217 pesos; 1913, 43,020,333 (22,000,000 for the debt; war, 5,267,268; 4,724,170 interior and justice; 3,199,035 public instruction). Debt, December 31, 1910, foreign $13,694,446 and £1,482,800, with arrears of interest £711,747; interior, 71,884,745 pesos paper.

GOVERNMENT. The president is elected by direct vote for six years and is assisted by a cabinet of six members. The legislative body is the unicameral National Assembly (69 members). The president in 1912 was Manuel Estrada Cabrera, who succeeded to the executive office in March, 1898, and subsequently was elected for terms ending March 15, 1905, 1911, and 1917.

GUGGENHEIM, BENJAMIN. An American capitalist, died at sea April 15, 1912. He was born in 1855, one of the seven sons of Meyer Guggenheim, founder of the firm of M. Guggenheim and Sons. All these sons became famous for their mining interests in many parts of the world. When twenty years of age Benjamin Guggenheim was sent by his father to Denver, Col., to take charge of some mining interests in that city. He foresaw the importance of the smelting industry and had charge of the first smelter built by the family at Pueblo, Col. He subsequently returned to the East and took charge of the smelting plant at Perth Amboy, N. J. In 1903 he erected a large plant at Milwaukee for making machinery, which became merged in the International Steam Pump Company, of which Mr. Guggenheim was elected president in 1909. With his brothers he was the ruling factor in the American Smelting and Refining Company. Mr. Guggenheim was one of the victims of the *Titanic* disaster.

GUIANA. See BRITISH GUIANA; DUTCH GUIANA; FRENCH GUIANA.

GULF OIL FIELD. See PETROLEUM.

GUN MOUNTS. See NAVAL PROGRESS, *General Progress, United States*.

GUN RUNNING. See PERSIA.

GYMNASTICS. The fourteenth annual intercollegiate gymnastic meet was won by Yale. This marked Yale's third successive victory.

Pennsylvania finished second and Princeton third. The team scores follow: Yale 24, Pennsylvania 17, Princeton 8½, Rutgers 8, New York University 4, Haverford 1, Illinois ½. The all-round championship was won by F. Callahan of Yale, who also was the victor in 1911. In dual college meets, Yale defeated Pennsylvania 28-26 and Princeton 27-26; U. S. Naval Academy defeated Princeton 25-20, Columbia 28-17, Pennsylvania 31-23, and Yale 32-22; Pennsylvania defeated Columbia 45-12, Haverford 32-22, Lehigh 44-10, and Princeton 31-23; New York University defeated Rutgers 34½-14½, and Columbia 35-16.

The club championship of the Amateur Athletic Union was won by the New York Turn Verein, which scored 24 points. The West Side Y. M. C. A., winner in 1911, was second with 13 points, and the Pittsburgh A. A. third with 11 points. Paul Krimmel, of the New York Turn Verein, for the second year in succession captured the all-round championship. The English individual championships were won by E. W. Potts of the Northampton Institute.

GYNOVAL. A colorless neutral fluid of a peculiar odor and mild oleaginous taste, having the chemical formula CH_3 CH (CH_3) CH_2 $COO.C_{10}H_{17}$. It is nearly insoluble in water, but easily dissolves in alcohol, ether, chloroform, benzol, and petroleum-benzin. It is stated to have a boiling point of 132° to 138° C., under 12 mm. pressure, and a specific gravity of 0.952 to 0.957 at 15° C.

The therapeutic action of gynoval is said to be that of a mild nervine and antispasmodic, resembling that of valerian, with the advantages of a much more agreeable odor and of being better tolerated, especially in not giving rise to unpleasant eructations. Like other valerian preparations, it is indicated in nervous headaches, nervous insomnia, nervous disorders of the climacteric, hysteria, cardiac and gastric neuroses, and neurasthenia.

HADLEY, H. S. See PRESIDENTIAL CAMPAIGN and MISSOURI.

HAGUE TRIBUNAL. See ARBITRATION, INTERNATIONAL.

HAHNKE, WILHELM VON. A German soldier, died February 8, 1912. He was born in Berlin in 1833 and received his military training as a member of the Prussian cadet corps. He entered the Prussian army in 1851 and in 1866 was on the staff of the Crown Prince, Frederick William, during the campaign in Bohemia. During the Franco-German War he was a major on the general staff in the headquarters of the crown prince. He was appointed major-general in 1881 and was given command of the first brigade of infantry guards. In 1890 he became general of infantry and from 1888 to 1901 was chief of the military cabinet. In 1899 he was appointed commander-in-chief of the Marches and governor of Berlin. He was made general field marshal in 1903.

HAINES, HENRY WILLIAMSON. An American archæologist, died February 16, 1912. He was born in Bangor, Me., in 1831, and graduated from Harvard College in 1851. He engaged in teaching for several years, after which he was admitted to the bar and for a short time practiced law. He was professor of Latin and later of Greek in the University of Vermont from 1867 to 1872. From 1873 he devoted his attention entirely to archæological research, making investigations in Europe, Egypt, and elsewhere. He received a medal and diploma from the International Congress of Anthropological Sciences, Paris, 1878. He was a member of several learned societies and was corresponding secretary to the Massachusetts Historical Society. He contributed articles on archæological subjects for scientific journals.

HAITI. A republic occupying the western part of the West Indian island of Haiti. The capital is Port-au-Prince.

AREA, POPULATION, ETC. The area is estimated at 28,676 square kilometers (11,072 square miles). Another estimate is 10,204 square miles. The number of inhabitants cannot be told with certainty. It was estimated in 1887 at 960,000; a recent estimate, based on parish registers, places it at about 2,030,000, while the figure given by the 1912 French *Annuaire Statistique* is 1,500,000 and another estimate of 1912 2,500,000. Probably nine-tenths of the people are negroes, and most of the remainder mulattoes. The principal towns include: Port-au-Prince, with perhaps 100,000 inhabitants; Cap Haïtien, 30,000; Les Cayes, 25,000; Gonaïves, 18,000. The educational system is very imperfect. There are some 400 national schools, a few private schools, and five lycées.

PRODUCTION AND COMMERCE. The leading product is coffee; other crops of some importance are sugar-cane, cacao, cotton, and tobacco. Logwood and other valuable forest products are cut for export. Mining is almost entirely undeveloped. The following statistics of production, doubtless imperfect, are reported for the year 1910-11: Coffee, 53,129,824 lbs.; cacao, 3,304,086 lbs.; logwood, 76,354,731 lbs.; roots, 8,916,800 lbs.; cotton, 5,256,573 lbs.; Dutiable imports and exports were reported at $5,880,676 and $3,479,848 for the fiscal year 1909; for the calendar year 1910, dutiable imports $7,681,746, and total exports $15,475,331. Two-thirds of the imports are from the United States, and the greater part of the exports goes to France. Weight in thousands of pounds of the chief exports in the year 1909-10: Logwood, 75,197; coffee, 51,104; cotton seed, 8058; cotton, 4198; cacao, 3228; hides, 346.

COMMUNICATIONS. There were about 64 miles of railway in 1910. In August of that year the government contracted for the construction of a system of 321 miles, and work was begun in 1911. The first section, from Cap Haïtien to La Grande Rivière, was finished in 1912, and before the end of the year the section from Gonaïves to Ennery was almost finished. Telegraph line (1910), 124 miles. There are reported 31 post offices.

FINANCE. Estimated revenue for the fiscal year 1911, $3,279,059 and 7,866,092 gourdes; estimated expenditure, $3,279,059 and 7,858,560 gourdes. The estimated revenue for 1911-12 was reported at $3,957,227 and 8,227,315 gourdes. The paper gourde fluctuates, but averages about 20 cents in value. Revenue is derived chiefly from import and export duties, and the largest item of expenditure is service of the debt. On March 31, 1911, the debt, including arrears, amounted to $26,349,510 and 10,384,300 gourdes.

GOVERNMENT. According to the constitution, the president is elected for seven years by the two chambers of the congress in joint session.

His cabinet consists of six members. The Senate consists of 39 members elected indirectly, and the Chamber of the Communes of 96 members elected by popular vote. Gen. Antoine Simon was elected president December 17, 1908, after the deposition of Gen. Nord Alexis, Simon was deposed upon the successful revolution of 1911, headed by Gen. Cincinnatus Leconte, who was elected to the presidency on August 16 as from May 15, for seven years. On August 8, 1912, General Leconte lost his life in a fire which destroyed the executive residence. His successor was chosen in the person of Gen. Tancède Auguste, for a term ending May 15, 1919. See ARBITRATION, INTERNATIONAL.

HALL, EDWARD HENRY. An American Unitarian clergyman and writer, died February 22, 1912. He was born in Cincinnati in 1831 and graduated from Harvard College in 1851. He studied theology at the Harvard Divinity School, graduating in 1855. In 1859 he was ordained to the Unitarian ministry. During the Civil War he was chaplain of the Massachusetts volunteers. He served as pastor in Plymouth, Mass., in Worcester, and in Cambridge. He was a fellow of the American Academy of Arts and Sciences, and was a member of the Massachusetts Historical Society. Among his published writings are *Orthodoxy and Heresy in the Christian Church* (1874); *Lectures on the Life of St. Paul* (1885); *Discourses* (1893); *Papias and His Contemporaries* (1899), and *Paul the Apostle* (1906).

HALOS. See ARCHÆOLOGY.

HAMBURG. See GERMANY.

HAMBURG ELEVATED RAILWAY. See ARCHITECTURE.

HAMILTON COLLEGE. An institution of higher learning at Clinton, N. Y., founded in 1812. The total enrollment in the various departments of the college in the autumn of 1912 was 185. The faculty numbered 20. There were added during the year new professors of English literature and of gymnastics and hygiene. The most notable benefaction was one of $100,000 for the new library building. The amount of productive funds was about $1,000,000 and the annual income about $75,000. The volumes in the library numbered 54,000. The college celebrated in 1912 its one hundredth anniversary with appropriate ceremonies. (See UNIVERSITIES AND COLLEGES.) President, M. W. Stryker, D. D., LL. D.

HAMMOND, JOSEPH. An English clergyman and writer, died May, 1912. He was born in 1839 and was educated at King's College, London. He served as curate and vicar of several churches in England. From 1892 to 1902 he was canon of Truro. He was chiefly known for his theological writings, principally on points of difference between the Anglicans and Nonconformists. He was also well known as a preacher. Among his published writings are *English Nonconformity and Christ's Christianity* (1893); *Seal and Sacrament* (1892); *Concerning the Church* (1896); *A Cornish Parish* (1897), and *Magister Moritur* (1910).

HAMPTON NORMAL AND AGRICULTURAL INSTITUTE. An institution for the education of negroes at Hampton, Va., founded in 1868. The total number of students enrolled in the various departments of the institute in 1912 was 1356. The faculty numbered about 200, including instructors and employees. There were no notable changes in the faculty during the year, and no important benefactions. The productive funds of the institute amount to $2,570,000. There are 30,703 volumes in the library. President, H. B. Frissell, D. D.

HANSCOM, JOHN FORSYTH. A rear-admiral, retired, of the United States navy, died September 30, 1912. He was born in Eliot, Me., in 1842, and at 16 years of age enlisted in the 62d Maine Volunteers, serving throughout the Civil War. He was then appointed draughtsman at the Norfolk Navy Yard and was later transferred to Washington and to the Boston Navy Yard in 1871. He received a commission as assistant naval constructor in 1875, serving at Chester and League Island. At the latter post he supervised the construction of the *Dolphin* and *Chicago*, and also had much to do with the construction of battleships, including the *Baltimore*, *New York*, *Columbia*, *Massachusetts*, and *Indiana*. After serving two terms on the board of inspection and survey he was on active sea service until 1903, when he was detached and appointed senior of the board of award. He was placed on the retired list with the rank of rear-admiral in 1904, but continued to act as the active head of the board of bull changes until August, 1911. He was one of the most eminent authorities in the navy on naval construction.

HANSEN, GERHARD HENRIK ARMAUER. A Norwegian biologist and physician, died May, 1912. He was born at Bergen in 1841. His early education was received in the cathedral schools of his native city. He studied medicine and became resident physician in Rigshospital at Christiania. He later spent several years as medical officer at the Lofoten fisheries. In 1868 he was appointed assistant medical officer to the Bergen Leper Hospital, of which Daniellsen was director. Under the influence of the latter, Hansen began the study of leprosy, which he continued throughout his life. His first investigation was to work out the significance of the "leper cells" of Virchow. He prosecuted his studies in various universities and then returned to Norway to resume his investigations of leprosy. These investigations pointed to the contagious and specific nature of the disease, and in recognition of the value of his work the Medical Society of Christiania voted a sum of money to enable him to continue his studies. In the course of journeys made about the country he came across cases of leprosy which were explainable only by the theory of contagion. The conclusions at which he thus arrived conformed with those of Drognat-Landré, who had studied leprosy in Surinam and had published the results of his researches. Continuing his labors, Hansen was rewarded by the discovery of a bacillus in unstained preparations. Later the microörganism was stained and became known as Hansen's bacillus. This was in 1873. In the years following he endeavored to cultivate and innoculate the leprosy bacillus, but his efforts were unsuccessful. Measures taken as a result of his work, however, have effected a marked diminution of the disease throughout Norway.

HARAHAN, JAMES THEODORE. An American railway official, killed in a railroad wreck on January 22, 1912. He was born in Lowell, Mass., in 1843, and was educated in the public schools. He began his railroad career as a switchman in 1864. He rose through various grades of promotion on different railways until in 1883 he became general superintendent of the Louisville and Nashville Railroad. Two years later he was appointed general manager of this line. In 1885 he went to the Baltimore and Ohio Railroad as superintendent of the Pittsburgh division, but returned to the Louisville and Nashville in the same year as assistant general manager. In 1888 he was appointed assistant general manager of the Lake Shore and Michigan Southern, and in 1890 was elected second vice-president of the Illinois Central, which was then controlled by Stuyvesant Fish. As a result of the famous struggle between E. H. Harriman and Stuyvesant Fish for the control of the Illinois Central, in which Harriman was successful, Mr. Harahan became president of this line, as the representative of Harriman.

HARBORS. See MUNICIPAL OWNERSHIP, and DOCKS AND HARBORS.

HARMON, JUDSON. See PRESIDENTIAL CAMPAIGN and OHIO.

HARRIMAN, E. H. See PRESIDENTIAL CAMPAIGN CONTRIBUTIONS.

HARRITY, WILLIAM FRANCIS. An American lawyer and public official, died April 17, 1912. He was born in Wilmington, Del., in 1850, and graduated from La Salle College in 1870. For a time he taught mathematics and Latin in that institution. He was admitted to the bar in 1873 in Philadelphia and practiced law in that city. He took an active interest in politics and was delegate-at-large to the Democratic national conventions of 1884 and 1896. In the latter year he received twenty-one votes for the vice-presidency. He was chairman of the Democratic national committee from 1892 to 1896. From 1885 to 1889 he was postmaster at Philadelphia, and from 1891 to 1895 was secretary of state of Pennsylvania. He was an officer and director in many important financial enterprises and institutions.

HARROD, BENJAMIN MORGAN. An American engineer, died September 7, 1912. He was born in New Orleans in 1837 and graduated from Harvard College in 1856. He served in the Confederate army as lieutenant of artillery and as captain in the engineer corps. From 1877 to 1880 he was chief State engineer of Louisiana and from 1879 to 1904 was a member of the United States Mississippi River Commission. He was city engineer of New Orleans from 1888 to 1892 and was chief engineer in charge of constructing the drainage system of that city from 1895 to 1902. From 1904 to 1907 he was a member of the Panama Canal Commission.

HARTFORD, CONN. See CITY PLANNING.

HARTLEY, JONATHAN SCOTT. An American sculptor, died December 6, 1912. He was born at Albany, N. Y., in 1845, and received his education at the Albany Academy. He took his first lessons on art in that city under E. D. Palmer. He later studied in England, where he took a medal at the Royal Academy. He later spent some time in Germany, Paris, and Rome. He made many busts of actors and actresses, including Edwin Thomas Booth, Lawrence Barrett, John Gilbert, and Ada Rehan. Among his other well-known works are the "Daguerre Monument" in Washington, the "Ericsson Monument" in New York City, the "Statue of Miles Morgan" in Springfield, Mass.; the "Statue of Alfred the Great" for the Appellate Court Building, New York City, and the "Statue of Thomas K. Beecher" in Elmira, N. Y. He also designed many other public works. His last exhibited work was a group, a boy and rabbits, called "The Cradle of Pan." Mr. Hartley was president of the Art Students' League from 1878 to 1880 and of the National Academy in 1891. He was one of the founders of the Salmagundi Club, of which he was president from 1903 to 1905.

HARVARD UNIVERSITY. The total enrollment in the university in the autumn of 1912 was 5224, which includes those in the university extension courses. The students were divided among the different departments as follows: College, 2308; graduate school of arts and science, 463; graduate school of applied science, 132; graduate school of business administration, 107; divinity school, 48; law school, 741; medical school, 290; dental school, 190. The extension students numbered 9, and those in the summer schools of 1912 numbered 1187. The officers of instruction and administration numbered 774. Of these 137 were professors, 5 associate professors, 83 assistant professors, 73 lecturers, 217 instructors, 29 Austin teaching fellows, 32 teaching fellows and fellows for research and 212 administratiors and assistants. For gifts and bequests received during the year see GIFTS AND BEQUESTS, and for other items of interest, see UNIVERSITIES AND COLLEGES.

HARTWELL, ALFRED STEDMAN. An American jurist, died August 30, 1912. He was born in Dedham, Mass., in 1836, and graduated from Harvard College in 1858. He served throughout the Civil War, receiving the brevet rank of brigadier-general of volunteers for gallantry at the battle of Honey Hill, S. C. In 1867 he was elected a member of the Massachusetts legislature and in the following year was appointed first associate justice of the Hawaiian Islands, serving until 1874, when he was elected attorney-general of the Hawaiian Islands. He was again elected to this office in 1877. In 1889-1900 he was special agent of the Republic of Hawaii. He was appointed associate justice of the Supreme Court of Hawaii in 1904 and was chief justice from 1907 to February 2, 1911, when he resigned.

HATCHER, WILLIAM E. An American Baptist clergyman, died August 24, 1912. He was born in Bedford County, Va., in 1834, and graduated from Richmond College in 1858. From 1875 to 1901 he was president of the Baptist education board of Virginia, and from 1891 to the time of his death was head of the Baptist Orphanage of Virginia. He was editor of the *Religious Herald*, the *Baltimore Baptist*, and the *Baptist Argus*. He wrote, jointly, *Life of Rev. A. B. Brown, LL.D.* (1885), and *Life of Rev. J. R. Jeter, D.D.* (1899). He wrote also *The Pastor and the Sunday School* (1902); *John Jasper* (1908), and *Along the Trail of the Friendly Years* (1910).

HAUK-WARTEGG, MINNIE. An American prima donna, died November 16, 1912. She was born in New York City in 1852. Her first appearance as a singer was made in 1865 in New Orleans, to which city her parents removed soon after she was born. Three years later she returned to New York and obtained a position as choir singer, while still continuing her studies. She made her first appearance in opera in Brooklyn, singing the part of "Norma." She later appeared in the Academy of Music in New York City and her success from that time was assured. She soon went to London and sang at the Covent Garden, where she was received with great enthusiasm. In 1870 she became the leading soprano of the Imperial Opera House in Vienna, remaining for three years. At the end of that time she went in the same capacity to the Royal Opera House in Berlin. She created the first "Carmen" heard in London and New York, and for many years she was the tradition accepted by all as to the finest embodiment of that heroine.

HAUPTMANN, GERHART. See GERMAN LITERATURE, and NOBEL PRIZE.

HAWAII. POPULATION. The population of the Territory according to the census of 1910, was 191,909, divided as follows: Japanese, 79,674; Hawaiian, 26,041; Portugese, 22,303; Chinese, 21,674; part Hawaiian 12,506; Porto Rican, 4890; Spanish, 1990; other Caucasian, 14,867; all others, including Koreans, mulattoes, negroes, and Filipinos, 7964. Of the total population, 98,157 were native born, that is, born within the United States or its possessions. By sex, 123,099 were males, and 68,810 were females. The population increased in the decade 1900-10 37,908. The population of the several islands in 1910 was as follows: Oahu, 81,993; Hawaii, 55,382; Maui, 28,623; Kauai, 23,744; Molokai, 1791; Lanai 131; Niihau, 208; Kahoolawe, 2.

IMMIGRATION. Immigration is divided into two classes, unassisted and assisted. The assisted immigration includes that induced to come to the Territory by the department of immigration and labor, and by the Hawaiian Sugar Planters' Association. Unassisted immigration includes that of Americans from the mainland of the United States. There are no accurate statistics as to the number of these, but in recent years there have been many purchases of resident lands, erection of dwelling houses, and taking up of homesteads, which indicates a comparatively large unassisted immigration. The feature of most general interest relating to unassisted immigration is that of the Japanese element in the population. For some years after annexation the arrivals of Japanese in the islands greatly exceeded the departures, but for some years now the departures have exceeded the arrivals. What increase there is among the Japanese occurs through the excess of births over deaths within the Territory. Unassisted immigration in the fiscal year 1910 included 5632 men, 2892 women, and 1313 children. The greater number of these came from Oriental countries, chiefly China, Japan, and the Philippine Islands. The departures included 3712 men, 1770 women, and 1474 children. The check in Japanese immigration is the result of an understanding between the government of the United States and Japan on the subject of the immigration of Japanese labor. The problem of securing labor is a serious one in the Territory and efforts have been made to obtain laborers from European countries, especially from Portugal and Spain, and Russians from Manchuria and Siberia. During the last five years 12,306 laborers from these countries have been induced to come to Hawaii. During 1912 the introduction of Russians from Manchuria was discontinued because of difficulties in introducing them.

AGRICULTURE. The chief industries of the islands are agricultural. Of these the most important are the sugar- and fruit-raising industries. The sugar industry outdoes all others combined. The crop of the fiscal year 1912 was 595,258 short tons, compared with 566,821 short tons for the preceding year. The crop for the fiscal year 1912-13 may be slightly smaller because of unfavorable weather conditions. Of the lesser industries that of pineapples has now reached first place and is growing rapidly. The output for 1912 is estimated at about 1,000,000 cases of two dozen cans each, besides which more or less of the fresh fruit is exported as well as juice prepared for various purposes. The area under cultivation is being continually extended and new canneries are being established. A still newer industry is that of tobacco-growing. This is now emerging from its experimental stage. Experience has resulted in better cultivation, more effective fertilization, more careful handling of the green leaves when harvesting the crop, and improved methods of curing. During 1912 a cigar factory was started and is now manufacturing cigars. The output of tobacco for 1912 on the four plantations in existence was 104,000 pounds, valued at $49,500. The area cultivated is 119 acres. New industries are constantly being started. Of these, one of the most promising is that of Bermuda onions.

The prospects for the growing of coffee, which was at one time carried on on a considerable scale in the islands, are brighter now than for some years past. The price for the last crop was 16.15 cents a pound as compared with 12.85 cents for the preceding crop. The exports of coffee in 1912 amounted to 2,127,610 pounds. Coffee is raised mostly by Chinese, Japanese, and Portuguese, although the larger estates are in the hands of Anglo-Saxons. The livestock industry is important and most of the meat is consumed in the Territory. There has been a reduction in the number of cattle in recent years, but a corresponding increase in weight and a reduction in the maturing age from about four years to about three years or less. The number of sheep has fallen off in the last few years from about 100,000 to about 80,000. This is largely due to various diseases and the overstocking of ranges. The Oriental population consumes large quantities of pork. Until two or three years ago most of this was imported from California, but the increase of prices there, due to hog cholera, gave an impetus to hog-breeding in the Territory, with the result that the local supply is sufficient for the demand.

COMMERCE. The imports and exports for the fiscal year ending June 30, 1912, aggregated $84,143,760. This is an increase of $14,692,-597 over the amount of the preceding year. The increase was chiefly in exports, although to some extent also in imports from the continental United States. The imports from foreign countries increased slightly and the exports to foreign countries increased considerably, relatively to their totals. The imports amounted to $28,-694,332, an increase of $1,181,742 over 1911. Those from the continental United States amounted to $23,095,878, an increase of $773,-757, while those from foreign countries amounted to $5,598,444, an increase of $407,995. The exports amounted to $55,449,438, an increase of $13,510,885. Those to the continental United States amounted to $55,076,165, an increase of $13,686,224, while those to foreign countries amounted to $373,273, a decrease of $357,369. The exports of sugar continued to be many times larger than all others combined. In 1912 they were $48,143,530 of raw sugar, and $1,818,006 of refined sugar. The imports and exports by countries for the fiscal years 1911-12 are shown in the following table:

	Imports		Exports	
	1911	1912	1911	1912
Australia and Tas..	$294,324	$330,263	$7,191	$7.820
Other Brit. Oceania..	929	7,618	1,227	2,562
Brit. India	552,596	623,392	....	....
Canada ...	32,829	22,788	29,171	45,579
Chile	532,376	590,589	....	....
France ...	16,530	13,786	2,126	19,651
Germany...	591,349	370,116	41,345	110,120
Hongkong..	305,176	329,814	20,081	3,704
Japan	2,022,698	2,414,346	274,744	26,845
U. Kingdom	566,198	711,602	45,955	86,719
Other for..	275,444	184,130	308,802	70,273
Total for.	5,190,449	5,598,444	730,642	373,273
U. S.......	22,322,131	23,095,878	41,207,941	55,076,165
Gr. total.	27,512,580	28,694,322	41,938,583	55,449,438

SHIPPING. During the fiscal year 1912 the tonnage entered in all the ports of the Territory amounted to 1,370,315, an increase of 26,439, and the tonnage cleared amounted to 1,359,109, an increase of 11,738. The number of American vessels entered during 1912 was 327 as compared with 313 for the preceding year. The number of all other vessels was 104 as compared with 114 for the preceding year. Although there were only about four times as many American vessels as all others, they carried about nineteen-twentieths of the freight.

On account of its isolation transportation to Hawaii from other countries has been a serious problem. Hitherto the islands have been dependent mainly upon their own demand for shipping facilities, but with the development of trans-Pacific commerce the Territory is constantly reaping in larger measure the benefits of the steamers between other countries, and the prospective opening of the Panama Canal has already resulted in orders for additional steamers, both American and foreign, in the advantage of which Hawaii will have its share. Interisland transportation is conducted almost entirely by the Interisland Steam Navigation Company. This company added during the year an additional steamer and is contemplating the construction of a 10,000-ton steamer for the bringing of coal from Australian ports to Honolulu. There are several lines of traffic between Hawaii and the mainland of Mexico. These include the American-Hawaiian Steamship Company, the Matson Navigation Company, the Oceanic Steamship Company, the Union Steamship Company, and the Associated Oil Company. A few American sailing vessels continue to carry sugar around Cape Horn. The principal railroad in the Territory is the Oahu Railway and Land Company, extending from Honolulu to the north end of the island. The only railroad of standard gauge in the Territory is the Hilo Railroad Company. There are smaller lines of railroad in some of the other islands.

PUBLIC LANDS. Sweeping changes were made in the land laws in 1910. These related chiefly to homesteading and were intended to promote genuine homesteading and prevent bogus homesteading. During the two years, 1911-12, 655 homesteads were taken up. Of these 242 were by Hawaiians, 121 by Portuguese, 76 by Americans, 7 by Russians, and 25 by Japanese. Except in a few special cases, sales of public lands for other than homestead purposes may be made only of limited area and only for a few specified objects. During the year 17 leases were made of lands aggregating 5930 acres. Of these, the larger portion was for the growing of sugar cane.

EDUCATION. The pupils enrolled in the public schools of the Territory in June, 1912, numbered 23,752. Of these 12,965 were male and 10,787 were females. The average attendance was 20,399. The teachers numbered 591, of whom 126 were male and 465 female. There were 156 schools. Of the pupils enrolled 9298 were Japanese, 4251 Hawaiian, and 4075 part Hawaiian. There is a college of agriculture and mechanic arts in Honolulu. In 1912 this was removed to a permanent site in the suburbs of the city. Its faculty was increased to 19 members and the students to 28 in the regular and 129 in special courses.

FINANCE. The receipts for the fiscal year 1912 were $3,904,503. The disbursements were $4,062,816. The cash on hand at the end of the fiscal year was $690,550. The bonded debt of the Territory at the beginning of the fiscal year was $4,004,000, which was increased during the year by an issue of $1,500,000 of 4 per cent. public improvement bonds and was decreased by the payment of $50,000 of the 1903 issue of 4 per cent. fire claims bonds, leaving a total bonded indebtedness of $5,454,000 at the close of the fiscal year. The Territory cannot incur indebtedness in excess of one per cent. of the assessed value of property in any one year or in excess of 7 per cent. in the aggregate. The bonded indebtedness at the close of the fiscal year was 3.08 per cent. of the assessed value of property.

PUBLIC HEALTH. The chief features of interest in sanitation during the year were the special rat campaign on the island of Hawaii and a special mosquito campaign on the island of Honolulu, and the steps taken to reclaim the lowlands of Honolulu. The rat campaign was undertaken on account of the plague which had become established in two districts of Honolulu. A careful study of the district led to a large increase in the number of rat catchers during the year and from 5000 to 6000 rats were caught monthly. Nearly 10,000 traps were set daily. During the year 53.841 rats and 1548 mongoose were taken, of which, during the months of February, March, and April, 79 were found to be infected with plague. In the later months no infections were found.

A campaign against tuberculosis has been carried on for several years. Special hospitals have been established in several of the islands. Radical changes have been made in recent years in the method of dealing with leprosy. Under the old system from 1904 to 1909 the number segregated annually decreased steadily from 113 to 15. Under the new system the number has increased from 15 in 1909 to 103 in 1912. This increase means not that the number of lepers has increased but that more of the lepers have been brought under control. Of the four institutions maintained in connection with this service the principal one is the leper settlement on Molokai. The United States Public Health and Marine Hospital Service has for several years been carrying on investigations in the subject of leprosy in the islands.

POLITICS AND GOVERNMENT. The governor of Hawaii in his annual report for the fiscal year 1912 makes several recommendations for needed legislation. Among these are provisions in regard to immigration. He recommends also amendments to the land laws. He urges that the United States Reclamation act be extended to Hawaii, and the creation of a park to include the largest active vocano, Kilauea, and that appropriations shouid be made to continue the work upon the harbors of the islands. During the year the large contract for the dredging of the Pearl Harbor channel was completed and the harbor was entered for the first time by a large war vessel, the *California*, the flagship of the Pacific fleet. This fleet was in Hawaiian waters for a number of months during the year and during its visit, the *West Virginia*, under Rear-Admiral W. H. H. Southerland, visited Palmyra Island for the purpose of confirming the title of the United States to it as a part of the Island of Hawaii.

OFFICERS. W. F. Frear, governor; E. A. Mott-Smith, secretary; A. Lindsay, Jr., attorney-general; D. L. Conkling, treasurer; J. D. Tucker, commissioner of public lands; M. Campbell, superintendent of public works; W. T. Pope, superintendent of public instruction; J. H. Fisher, auditor; W. E. Wall, surveyor; W. Henry, high sheriff; G. R. Clark, private secretary to governor. The delegate to Congress was J. K. Kalanianaole.

HAWLEY, EDWIN. An American railroad official, died February 1, 1912. He was born in Chatham, N. Y., in 1850. He began his business career as a boy by selling produce in his native town. He soon moved to New York City, however, and obtained work as a newsboy in a railroad freight office. He was promoted rapidly, and having saved a considerable sum of money purchased a tugboat in partnership with a friend. In a short time he had a fleet of thirty-eight tugboats. His enterprise commended him to Collis P. Huntington, who was then in active control of the Southern Pacific Railroad, and he became one of the latter's most valued employees and trusted adviser. He remained with this railroad until it was purchased by the late E. H. Harriman. Mr. Hawley soon became known as a dealer in railroads. He bought control of the Minneapolis and St. Louis, and then of the Iowa Central. He later secured control of the Colorado and Southern, which he subsequently sold to James J. Hill. He remained chiefly a buyer and seller of railroads and railroad stocks, until the death of Mr. Harriman. He then in a measure occupied the field which was left vacant. He began the acquisition of railroads with the apparent purpose of building up a great new railway system. He acquired the Chesapeake and Ohio; the Chicago, Cincinnati, and Louisville; and the Hocking Valley. He also secured control of the Chicago and Alton and later purchased a controlling share of the Missouri, Kansas, and Texas. The last important business prior to his death was the merger of the Minneapolis and St. Louis and the Iowa Central, in accordance with the plan to associate them with a railroad south from Canada and another railroad south to the Gulf of Mexico. In spite of his active business career Mr. Hawley remained to a large extent personally unknown. He left a fortune of over $25,000,000.

HAY. The world's hay crop in 1912 was favored in general by good growing weather for the grasses and other hay crops, but the harvest, particularly in Europe, was very seriously interfered with by continued heavy rains and cloudy weather. While the yield under these conditions was sufficiently large, the quality of the hay left much to be desired. In some parts of Europe the crop suffered so much from rain after the cutting that a considerable portion of it was suitable only for bedding, while in other sections the second cutting of clover and of other similar crops, after having made a most satisfactory growth, was ruined by the rains during the curing period and left upon the fields. In the United States the dry fall of 1911 and the severe winter that followed caused the failure of a large acreage of fall-sown timothy, clover, and alfalfa, but the growing season of 1912 was so favorable that the crop produced represented a yield never before equaled and of a record-breaking value. The total production amounted to 72,691,000 tons from 49,530,000 acres, as compared with the short yield of 54,916,000 tons from 48,240,000 acres in 1911. On the basis of a farm value of $11.79 per ton on December 1, 1912, the total value reached the sum of $856,695,000, exceeding the average value of the five preceding crops by nearly 20 per cent. and making corn the only crop of greater value for the year. The leading States and their yields were as follows: New York, 5,900,000 tons; Iowa, 4,952,000 tons; Pennsylvania, 4,537,000 tons; Missouri, 4,143,000 tons; Ohio, 4,026,000 tons, and California, 3,825,000 tons. The average yield for the entire country was 1.47 tons per acre, as against 1.14 tons in 1911. In the Western States, where much alfalfa is grown under irrigation, the average yield of hay per acre ranged from 3.40 tons in Arizona to 1.90 tons in Montana and Wyoming. Among the six leading States California ranked first in acre-yield, with an average of 1.53 tons.

HAYES, JOSEPH. An American soldier, died August 20, 1912. He was born in South Berwick, Me., in 1838, and graduated from Harvard College in 1855. He began service in the Civil War as major of the 18th Massachusetts Regiment, later becoming its colonel. In 1862 he was promoted to be brigadier-general. For several months he yas a prisoner in Libby Prison. In 1865 he was promoted to be major-general for his service in the Battle of the Wilderness. At the close of the war he was appointed commissioner of supplies of the seceded States. He was by profession a mining engineer.

HAYNIE, JAMES HENRY. An American newspaper correspondent and writer, died May, 1912. He was born in Winchester, Ill., in 1841, and was educated in the grammar and high schools of that city. He served in the Civil War and was for several months a prisoner in Libby Prison. He was mustered out of service in July, 1864. After the war he served as reporter on a Chicago newspaper and from 1875 to 1877 was foreign editor of the New York *Times*. In the latter year he went to Paris as a special correspondent of several American papers. Returning in 1895, he was traveling correspondent for the Boston *Herald*. From 1898 to the time of his death he devoted his attention entirely to literary work. He was a member of many clubs and associations. He was the author of *Paris, Past and Present* (1902), and *The Captains and the Kings* (1904).

HAY-PAUNCEFOTE TREATY. See PANAMA CANAL.

HAYS, CHARLES MELVILLE. An American

railway official, died at sea April 15, 1912. He was born in Rock Island, Ill., in 1856, and was educated in the public schools of St. Joseph, Mo., and Philadelphia. In 1873 he entered the railway service as a clerk in the passenger department of the Atlantic and Pacific Railroad. He served in various capacities in the offices of this line until 1877, when he was appointed secretary to the general manager of the Missouri Pacific. With this road he remained until 1884, when he filled the same position with the Wabash, St. Louis, and Pacific. In 1886 he was appointed assistant general manager of this road. Within a few years he became general manager of the Consolidated Wabash System. He left this line in 1895 to become general manager of the Grand Trunk Railway at Montreal. During his service at that post he reorganized the Central Vermont Railway Company, a subsidiary line of the Grand Trunk, completed the Victoria Jubilee Bridge across the St. Lawrence at Montreal, and replaced the old suspension bridge at Niagara Falls with a single span steel arch. Under his management the Grand Trunk Railway was double-tracked for 878 miles. On the death of Collis P. Huntington he became, in 1901, president of the Southern Pacific Railway, but in the same year resigned and returned to the Grand Trunk as its president and general manager. In 1902 he conceived the project of building the Grand Trunk Pacific Railway, extending from Moncton, N. B., to Prince Rupert, B. C., a distance of 3600 miles. In 1910 he was elected president and director of the Grand Trunk Railway and of all the subsidiary lines with a total mileage of about 14,000. In addition he was an officer and director in many industrial enterprises in the United States and Canada. Mr. Hays was one of the victims of the steamship *Titanic* disaster.

HEALTH CONDITIONS AMONG INDIANS. See INDIANS, SICKNESS AMONG.

HEALTH INSURANCE. See WORKINGMEN'S INSURANCE.

HEART STIMULATION. See CARREL, ALEXIS.

HEAT WAVES. See PHYSICS.

HEILNER, LEWIS CASS. A rear-admiral, retired, of the United States navy, died January 25, 1912. He was born in Pennsylvania in 1849 and entered the Naval Academy from that State in 1866. From 1873 to 1891 he held various grades from master to commander. In 1899 he was appointed supervisor of naval auxiliaries at the Brooklyn Navy Yard and continued in this position until his retirement in 1911. Five days prior to his retirement he was appointed rear-admiral. During the Spanish-American War he was commander of the battleship *Texas*. He served at various times in the Asiatic fleet and at the Portsmouth and Pensacola navy yards.

HEILPRIN, LOUIS. An American historical scholar and encyclopædist, died February 12, 1912. He was born in Ujhely, Hungary, in 1851. His father, Michael Heilprin, who had been an important figure in the Hungarian revolutionary government under Kossuth, came to America when his son was five years old. Michael Heilprin was one of the editors of the *American Encyclopædia* in its first edition, and in the revision of this work the son, though still a youth, assisted him not only in the general work of revision but wrote several new articles. He later revised the *Century Encyclopædia of Names* and coöperated in the editing of the *New International Encyclopædia*. His brother, the late Angelo Heilprin, prepared the last edition of *Lippincott's Gazetteer*. Mr. Heilprin was known as a man of unusual accuracy and range of knowledge. He was especially interested in matters of engineering and transportation, although his mathematical education did not go further than the elements of algebra, geometry, and trigonometry. He made occasional contributions to the *Evening Post* and the *Nation*, and was the author of *Historical Reference Book* (1884; 6th ed., 1899).

HELIOPOLIS. See ARCHÆOLOGY.

HELIOTHERAPY. The treatment of disease by exposure to direct sunlight received considerable attention during 1912. Tuberculosis of the joints and bones is particularly amenable to this form of therapy, and the result obtained in Rollier's sanatorium at Leysin, Switzerland, attracted the attention of the medical world. The sanatorium is situated at an altitude of 4000 feet above sea level. Rollier puts all new patients in bed for a few days, to insure acclimatization. After two or three days the bed is wheeled out on the gallery and the sunlight exposures begun, the disease focus being exposed three times for five minutes each the first day, ten minutes the second, until the patient is getting sunlight exposure for an hour and a half daily. At the same time the body is gradually exposed to the sunlight, at first the feet, then the legs, until the patients are able to remain all day in the open air and take the sun baths for hours at a time. During the intervals the wounds are covered with an aseptic dressing. Each patient has a gallery to himself, where he can lie exposed to the light during the day, and at night also if he wishes. Colds are unknown. Children are allowed to be up and around in winter with snowshoes and bathing trunks for their only apparel.

Collet treated patients suffering from laryngeal tuberculosis by heliotherapy, with most encouraging results. The patient, wearing a broad black hat and black spectacles, sits facing the sun, and by means of a laryngoscopic mirror placed in the throat and a hand glass in front of him directs the rays of sunlight into the larynx. This procedure is repeated at intervals during the day until a total exposure of an hour or more is attained.

Kime, of the Boulder Sanatorium, at Fort Dodge, Ia., furnished some interesting observations covering the effect upon the skin of the chemical rays obtained by filtering sunlight through various media. Direct sunlight produces *erythema solare* (sunburn), marked by extreme redness, swelling and great tenderness, with subsequent peeling of the skin. There is some tendency to the formation of blisters. Sunlight concentrated by large reflecting mirrors and passed through blue glass, thus securing the maximum effect of the chemical rays, shows a great tendency to blister, but there is little redness and swelling and practically no pain. Focusing direct sunlight through a convex lens of plain glass produces destruction of the skin and, if used with great intensity, gases form beneath the outer layers of the skin and small explosions occur. This method of using sunlight is very efficacious in the removal of warts, superficial moles, and small non-malignant growths. If the light be reflected by a concave mirror and focused, the formation of gases is not noted. Blistering is readily produced. If, after the light is focussed in either of the two ways last mentioned, it is passed through blue glass before falling on the skin, blistering is produced without destruction of the deeper layers of the skin. When a wavy, opalescent glass is employed and the sunlight is reflected with a large condensing mirror, ten feet in diameter, and passed through this opalescent glass, neither blistering nor destruction of the skin takes place, but blanching of the tissues occurs. The light used in this manner is very effective in lupus and in vascular nævi, even of very large extent. Just what the properties of the light may be that effect these various results has not been determined. It would appea., however, that some of the rays are absorbed by the reflecting mirror and others by the variously colored glasses. The wavy glass transmits the light in an irregular manner and produces results widely different and more effective, in the class of cases mentioned, than the glass with even surface.

HEMORRHAGE, CONTROL OF. See THROMBOKINASE.

HEREDITY. See BIOLOGY.

HERTEL, ALBERT. A German painter, died February 20, 1912. He was born at Berlin in 1843. He studied landscape painting in Rome from 1863 to 1867 under Fritz Greber. From 1875 to 1877 he was director of atelier at the Berlin Academy and he later had charge of a studio of instruction. Among his best-known paintings are "The Coast of Holland With Native Fishing Boats"; "A Summer Evening in Ariccia"; "Capri," and "Summer Evening From the Brandenburg Gate." He was a member of the Royal Academy of Berlin.

HESSE. See GERMANY.

HETCH HETCHY VALLEY. See WATER-WORKS.

HEWLETT, MAURICE. See LITERATURE, ENGLISH AND AMERICAN.

HEYBURN, WELDON BRINTON. United States senator from Idaho, died October 17, 1912. He was born in Delaware County, Pa., in 1852, and received an academic education. He studied law and was admitted to the bar in 1876. In a short time he removed to Shoshone County, Idaho, where he continued in the practice of law in the intervals of his senatorial duties until the time of his death. He first became prominent in politics in 1896, when he refused to follow the free silver Republicans of Idaho in their adherence to W. J. Bryan. Two years later he was a candidate for Congress and was defeated by a fusion of Democrats, Populists, and Silver Republicans. When the free silver craze subsided in Idaho he was elected to the Senate in 1903 as a Protectionist and Gold Republican. He was reelected in 1909 for the term ending 1915. Senator Heyburn was one of the most aggressive members of the Senate. He was a conservative of the old type and bitterly opposed all innovations in the government which have been advocated in recent years. He also warmly fought any effort to show favor to Confederate veterans of the Civil War, and any measure before the Senate intended to show favor to them was certain to be assailed by him in the plainest terms. He fought the proposal to permit a statue of General Robert E. Lee to be placed in the Capitol. His death was attributed largely to the strenuous part which he took in the closing days of the Sixty-second Congress. He had for months been in ill health, but insisted on taking part in the debates of the last days of the session. In particular he opposed the resolution of Senator Penrose providing for a sweeping inquiry into the campaign contributions, and for a time prevented the passage of this resolution. He was one of the most virile and able speakers in the Senate. He was the only senator who was chairman of two important committees. These were the committee on manufactures and the joint committee on the revision of the laws of the United States.

HIDES. See LEATHER.

HIGGINS, ANTHONY. Former United States senator from Delaware, died June 26, 1912. He was born at Red Lion Hundred, Del., in 1840, and graduated from Yale College in 1861. He studied law at the Harvard Law School and in 1864 was admitted to the bar, practicing in Wilmington, Del. He took an active interest in politics and in his early youth was an ardent Abolitionist. On the organization of the Republican party he became a member and supported Lincoln in his second campaign for election. He was successively appointed deputy attorney-general and United States district attorney. After the close of the war he won notice by the conduct of a case in which a negro had been convicted of a crime and sentenced to death. The Sixteenth Amendment had been added to the Constitution and Higgins raised a point that the negro had not been tried by a jury of his countrymen, inasmuch as no negroes had been included in the jury panel or the jury list. The United States Supreme Court supported his contention and the man was given a new trial, in which he was acquitted. Mr. Higgins was elected to Congress in 1863 and was largely instrumental in having the Fifteenth Amendment adopted. In 1889 he became United States senator after the Republican legislature had cast forty ballots for their man. When J. Edward Addicks gained control of the Republican legislature Senator Higgins retired to private life. He continued in bitter opposition to the rule of Addicks, and when President Roosevelt appointed an Addicks man to office Senator Higgins criticised the President at some length.

HIGH PRESSURE FIRE SERVICE. See FIRE PROTECTION.

HIGH SCHOOLS. See EDUCATION.

HILL, FRANK DAVIS. An American public official, died May, 1912. He was born in Minnesota in 1862 and was educated at the University of Minnesota. He studied law and was admitted to the bar in 1884. Entering the diplomatic service, he was appointed consul at Asunción, Paraguay, in 1887, serving until 1890. He was afterwards representative of the United States in consular capacity at Montevideo, Uruguay; La Guayra, Venezuela; Santos, Brazil; and Amsterdam, Netherlands. He was appointed consul-general at St. Petersburg in 1907. After serving here for one year he was appointed to the same office at Barcelona, Spain, and in 1910 he was appointed consul-general at Frankfort-on-Main, Germany, and held this office until the time of his death. He was a member of several learned societies.

HILL, JOHN FREMONT. An American public official and capitalist, died March 16, 1912. He was born in Eliot, Me., in 1855 and received an academic education. He studied medicine and took a degree from Long Island College in Brooklyn. After practicing medicine for a year in Boothbay Harbor, Me., he went into business. He settled in Augusta, Me., and after reading law for a short time, became a member of the law firm of Vickery & Hill, which was later a publishing house. He took an active part in the promotion of many electric railways in Maine and in Illinois. He was best known, however, as a politician. In 1889 he was elected to the Maine legislature and later served as State senator. In 1900 he was elected governor of the State and was reëlected in 1902. In 1908 he was made a member of the National Republican Committee. He was acting chairman of this committee from the time of the resignation of F. H. Hitchcock in 1908 until December, 1911, when he was elected chairman. He was one of the best known politicians in the United States.

HILL, OCTAVIA. An English philanthropist, died August 13, 1912. She was born about 1838. Early in life she showed a strong interest in sanitary science, and joined a band of workers who labored among the poor of London under the leadership of Frederick D. Maurice. She became more than ever convinced of the necessity of the employment of sanitary science among the poor, but found it impossible to put these principles into effect under the system of tenancy which prevailed. She therefore conceived the idea of herself obtaining possession of house property in the slums, of collecting her own rents and of exercising all the influence she was able in securing the transformation alike of dwellings and of tenants. She laid her proposal before John Ruskin, who advanced about $15,000 for carrying out the experiment. The experiment proved to be successful both from a financial and philanthropic standpoint. As time went on many more blocks of dwellings came under her management in different parts of London and in 1887 the Women's University Settlement was formed, and its members coöperated with Miss Hill in the erection of many courts or streets of cottages. Recognizing the comparatively limited scope of her efforts she gave active support to the Artisans' Dwellings Act of 1874, and in 1884 was one of the witnesses examined by the special commission which inquired into the question of housing for the p . To her efforts may be attributed much of the improvement that has been effected in the life of the poor in London. Among her published writings are: *Homes of the London Poor; Our Common Land*, and various articles in magazines.

HILLES, C. D. See PRESIDENTIAL CAMPAIGN.

HISTORICAL ASSOCIATION, AMERICAN. The annual meeting of this association was held in Boston, December 27-31. Additional interest was given to this meeting from the fact that Theodore Roosevelt was president, and delivered a notable address on "History as Literature." The programme of papers and conferences presented an unusual array of distinguished names. Instead of the usual programme of formal papers several of the section meetings dealt with the present condition of historical study in their respective fields. In the field of American history, Professor William E. Dodd, of the University of Chicago, and Professor Ulrich B. Phillips, of the University of Michigan, emphasized the need of a more thorough study of slavery on its economic side. Professor C. H. Van Tyne read an informing paper on "Religious Forces in the American Revolution." Professor Henry P. Biggar, of London, read a paper of much interest on "The New Columbus." This paper traversed the recent hostile criticisms of Vignaud and upheld the older view that the discovery of America was accidental. The membership of the association is about 2800. The *History Teachers' Magazine*, taken over by the association a year ago, has been so far successful that it promises to be self-supporting. The Justin Winsor prize offered by the association was awarded to Dr. A. C. Cole for an essay on "The Whig Party in the South." A report of the committee on the preparation of teachers of history in schools, headed by Professor Dana C. Munro, of the University of Wisconsin, appears in print early in 1913. The next meeting of the association will be held at Columbia and Charleston, S. C., in December, 1913. Professor William A. Dunning, of Columbia University, was chosen president.

HISTORY. See FRENCH LITERATURE, GERMAN LITERATURE, and LITERATURE, ENGLISH AND AMERICAN.

HITTITES. See ARCHÆOLOGY.

HOBBS, PERRY L. An American chemist and educator, died April 6, 1912. He was born in 1861 and graduated from the Case School of Applied Science in 1886. He afterwards studied at the University of Berlin, receiving the degree of Ph. D. In 1889 he became professor of chemistry at the Western Reserve University. He was one of the first chemists in the United States to specialize as a chemical engineer. He became widely known for experiments in the manufactures of concrete and was a prominent contributor to scientific periodicals.

HOCKEY. The Crescent A. C. again won the championship of the American Amateur Hockey League by scoring a victory over the Wanderers' Hockey Club in a play-off game. The standing of the clubs follows: Crescent A. C. won 7 lost 2; Wanderers H. C., won 6 lost 3; New York A. C., won 4 lost 4; St. Nicholas Skating Club won 4 lost 4; Hockey Club of New York won 0 lost 8.

The world's professional championship was won by the Quebec team in a series of games played at Boston and New York. The sevens taking part were all from Canada, and included, besides Quebec, the Wanderers, Canadians, and Ottawa. The totals in the final matches were: Quebec 12, Wanderers 9.

The championship of the Intercollegiate League was won by Princeton, which went through the season without being defeated. Columbia was second with 3 victories and 1 defeat. Yale won 1 and lost 3, while Dartmouth and Cornell, winner in 1911, failed to capture a game. Harvard withdrew from the league before the season opened.

Cleveland had the distinction of turning out the best amateur seven of the year, the team of the Athletic Club of the Ohio city playing a series of thirty-three games, winning twenty-five, losing seven, and tieing one. The Boston A. A. also had an excellent record.

HOFFMAN, HERMAN S. A Bishop of the Reformed Episcopal Church, died November 23, 1912. He was born in Salem, N. C., in 1841 and was educated in private schools in that State and at the Moravian Theological Seminary at Bethlehem, Pa. He was ordained to the Moravian Ministry in 1864. He founded five churches of that denomination in Philadelphia. In 1881 he united with the Reformed Episcopal Church and served as pastor in several parishes of that denomination in Philadelphia. In 1885 he founded Christ Memorial Church, and built the edifice of the Church of Our Redeemer in Philadelphia in 1893. In 1903 he was consecrated bishop of the Reformed Episcopal Church. He had in special charge the First Synod of the Dominion of Canada. In 1905 he was appointed assistant bishop in charge of New York and Philadelphia. He organized the Publication Society of the Reformed Episcopal Church and compiled a *Hymnal* and *Children's Hymns*, which have been adopted as standards in that denomination. Bishop Hoffman was a man of wealth and never accepted a salary for his religious services. He made several gifts of land on which to construct churches in Brooklyn and in the Bronx, New York City. He published *Sermons* (1886); *Life Beyond the Grave* (1898-1903), and many pamphlets on religious subjects.

HOGG, Hope W. An English scholar and educator, died February, 1912. He was born in 1863 in Cairo where his father was principal of the American College. He received his education at Edinburgh University. From 1884 to 1894 he was principal of the American College in Egypt. In the latter year he went to Oxford as a contributor of articles to the *Encyclopædia Biblica*. He entered New College and took a degree for research in Oriental history and philology. He was a member of the editorial staff of the *Encyclopædia* from 1895 until the work was completed in 1903. From 1900 to 1903 he was also lecturer in Hebrew and Arabic in Owens College, Victoria University, Manchester. In 1896 he was examiner in the Honor School of Oriental Studies in the University of Oxford. In addition to the articles contributed to the *Encyclopædia Biblica* he made several translations, including the *Diatessaron of Tatian*. He contributed many articles on Semitic subjects to classical magazines.

HOG RANCHES. See Garbage and Refuse Disposal.

HOLCOMBE, Chester. An American author and diplomat, died April 25, 1912. He was born in Winfield, N. Y., in 1844, graduating from Union College in 1861. He went to China when still a young man and became acquainted with Chinese dialects. From 1871 to 1885 he acted as interpreter and secretary of the United States Legation at Peking. In 1875-6, 1878-9 and 1881-2 he was acting minister. In 1880 he was a member of the commission for negotiating a new treaty with China and assisted in negotiating a treaty with Korea in 1882. In 1896 at the request of the Chinese authorities, he prepared in detail in Chinese and English, documents for the government loan of $100,000,000. He also developed in both languages detailed plans for construction of about 3000 miles of double track railway involving a cost of about $240,000,000. He outlined a scheme for securing the necessary funds for the establishment of schools for instructing the Chinese in railway construction and management. In 1902 he was lecturer at the Lowell Institute in Boston, Mass. He was the author of *Mental Arithmetic* (1873); *Life of Christ* (1875), *and Translation of the Declaration of Independence*, all in Chinese. He wrote in English *The Practical Effect of Confucianism upon the Chinese Nation* (1882); *Travels in Western China* (1875); *Catalogue and Handbook of Antique Chinese Porcelains* (1890); *The Real Chinaman* (1895); *The Real Chinese Question* (1899). He contributed articles on Chinese subjects to many magazines and newspapers.

HOLMES, George. An Anglican clergyman, created in 1909 bishop of Athabasca. Died February 3, 1912. He was born in 1860 and was educated in St. John's College, Winnipeg. He was ordained to the ministry in 1887. From 1886 to 1905 he was engaged in missionary work in the Northwest Territory. From 1901 to 1905 he was archdeacon of Athabasca and from 1905 to 1909 was bishop of Moosonee. He was created bishop of Athabasca in 1909.

HOLMES, Richard Sill. An American Presbyterian clergyman and author, died September 6, 1912. He was born in Brooklyn, N. Y., in 1842 and graduated from Middleburg College in 1862. He studied theology at the Auburn Theological Seminary, graduating in 1868. From 1866 to 1870 he was engaged in business in Auburn, N. Y. From 1870 to 1878 he was engaged in teaching and was again in business from 1878 to 1884. In the latter year he became registrar of the Chautauqua education work. He was ordained to the Presbyterian ministry in 1887 and in the same year became pastor in Warren, Pa. After remaining here several years he occupied the pulpit of the Shadyside Church in Pittsburgh. Here he remained until 1904 when he became president of the Holmes Press in Philadelphia. He was editor of *The Westminster* from 1904 to 1910, when it was consolidated with *The Interior* in Chicago under the name of *The Continent*. Of this journal Dr. Holmes was corresponding editor. In 1880 he acted as professor of languages in the summer school at Chautauqua. He was author of *The Maid of Honor* (1907); *The Victor*, and *The Outcome*.

HOME FLEET. See Naval Progress.

HOME RULE. See Great Britain, *History*.

HOME WORK. Clothing. See Sweating.

HONDA, Yo-ichi. A Japanese educator and bishop of the Methodist Church, died March 26, 1912. He was born at Hirosaki in 1849 and was converted to Christianity at the age of 24. He entered politics, but left on the defeat of his party in 1883. The rest of his life was devoted to religious work in Japan. He was ordained deacon in 1878 and was the first ordained Japanese minister of the Methodist Church. He visited Europe and the United States a number of times to prosecute his studies and to attend international meetings. He studied at the Drew Theological Seminary and was admitted to the Methodist ministry. In 1907 he was elected bishop. He was president of the Tokyo Aoyama Gaquin, a Christian college.

HONDURAS. A Central American republic. Capital, Tegucigalpa.

Area, Population, etc. Estimated area, 114,670 square kilometers (44,274 square miles). A census taken December 31, 1910, was not quite complete; the inhabitants of certain sections, as in La Mosquitia, were not enumerated. The census showed a population of 553,446 (270,722 male, 282,724 female), as compared with 500,-135 in 1905, 398,877 in 1895, 307,289 in 1881, and 350,000 in 1850. The bulk of the population is Indian. The larger municipalities were returned as follows: Tegucigalpa, 22,137; Santa Rosa, 10,574; Juticalpa, 10,529; Danlí, 8477; Nacaome, 8152; Choluteca, 8065; San Pedro Sula, 7820; Pespire, 7132; Cedros, 6825; Comayagüela, 6812; Ocotepequé, 6225. Movement of the population in 1909 and 1910; Marriages, 2058 and 2241; births, 19,851 and 20,994; deaths, 9219 and 10,295. There are over 850 primary schools, with about 30,000 pupils.

PRODUCTION AND COMMERCE. The leading crops are bananas and corn; sugar cane and tobacco are raised, and cabinet woods (especially mahogany), and rubber are exploited. Grazing is important, and cattle doubtless number over 500,000. Honduras is exceptionally rich in minerals, but they are not extensively worked except at the famous Rosario gold (and silver) mine (not far from Tegucigalpa).

Recent official statistics of commerce are not available. The following import and export values have been reported: 1908, 7,075,085 and 4,585,157 pesos (silver); 1909, 6,841,115 and 5,275,094; 1910, 7,548,541 and 6,429,700. Cotton goods and foodstuffs are the principal imports, while bananas, gold and silver, rubber, hides, cocoanuts, and cattle are the chief exports. The foreign trade is largely with the United States.

COMMUNICATIONS. There are about 100 kilometers (62 miles) of railway; of this, 56 miles extend from Puerto Cortés to San Pedro Sula and La Pimienta, and a continuation is projected to La Brea on the Pacific coast. In addition there are about 50 miles of light railway in the banana districts. Steamers ply the Ulua River from its mouth to Progreso. Telegraphs at end of 1910, 226 offices, with 3220 miles of line; post offices, 264.

FINANCE. The monetary unit is the silver peso, whose weight is $0.723379 oz. of fine silver, the value fluctuating with the price of the metal. For fiscal years ended July 31, revenue and expenditure are reported as follows: 1908, 3,899,287 and 4,205,995; 1909, each 3,503,215; 1910, 4,149,078 and 3,992,623. The budget for the fiscal year 1911 balanced at 4,714,065 pesos. Estimated receipts included customs 1,800,000 pesos and proceeds of monopolies 1,750,000. Preliminary estimates for 1913, revenue 13,140,415 and expenditure 13,095,101. The internal debt on August 1, 1910, was 4,053,370 pesos. The external debt on the same date consisted of four loans contracted from 1867 to 1870, amounting to £5,398,570; arrears of interest from 1872, £17,535,305; total, £22,933,875. On January 11, 1911, a convention providing for the conversion of the foreign debt was signed at Washington by the American secretary of state and a special Honduran envoy. The convention was not ratified by the American Senate.

GOVERNMENT. The president, the vice-president, and the unicameral congress of 42 members are elected by direct vote for four years. On November 11, 1911, Gen. Manuel Bonilla (a former president) was elected president for the term beginning February 1, 1912. Vice-president, Francisco Bográn.

HONDURAS, BRITISH. See BRITISH HONDURAS.

HONGKONG. An island (about 30 square miles), off the southeast coast of China, which, with a strip of territory on the mainland leased from China (376) and about four square miles of the Kowloon Peninsula, forms a British crown colony. Civil population (1911), 456,739 (Chinese, 444,664). Capital, Victoria (219,755). The island is the centre of an enormous trade. Being a free port, no returns are available, but a record of the shipping will give some idea of the extent of the trade.

Vessels	1909 No.	1909 Tons	1910 No.	1910 Tons
Brit. ocean-go'g	4,076	7,735,927	4,262	8,111,946
For. ocean-go'g	4,318	7,857,908	4,312	8,103,969
Brit. riv. steam.	5,780	3,701,754	6,483	4,009,073
For. riv. steam.	1,370	735,682	1,334	706,616
SS. under 60 t.*	3,160	140,484	3,153	136,765
Junks*	25,090	2,243,370	21,170	2,100,887
Total foreign	43,794	22,415,125	40,714	23,160,256
Steam launches, local	439,988	10,328,400	466,014	10,986,234
Junks	43,498	2,087,320	40,436	2,387,871
Total	527,280	34,830,845	547,164	36,534,361

* Foreign trade.

There is little land suitable for tillage on the island, though in the leased territory the Chinese cultivate considerable tracts. Granite quarries are worked, and various manufactories are operated. Ship-building and repairing are important industries. A railway from Kowloon to the Chinese frontier joins the line from Canton. The total revenue (one-fifth derived from the opium monopoly) for 1911 is estimated at 7,086,383 dollars. Revenue 1910, 6,960,869 dollars; expenditure, 6,907,113. Public debt, £1,485,732. Governor (1912), Sir F. J. D. Lugard.

The Hongkong University was opened on March 11. There was an outbreak of the plague about the middle of May and during one week 208 cases were reported. The number of deaths down to that date was 175.

HOOKWORM DISEASE. The second report of the Rockefeller Sanitary Commission for the Eradication of Hookworm Disease outlines the preliminary surveys of the areas of infection in the United States which have been nearly completed, and includes a report on the extent of infection in fifty-four foreign countries. Infection has been demonstrated in every county of South Carolina, in nearly every county of Virginia, North Carolina, Alabama, Mississippi, and Tennessee, and in twenty-seven out of the fifty-nine parishes in Louisiana, fifty-seven of the seventy-five counties in Arkansas, and twenty-two of the 119 counties in Kentucky. It has been found to exist in eastern Texas, Florida, California, Nevada, Oklahoma, and West Virginia, and probably in Maryland. Maps of the areas indicate that hookworm infection in these States occurs in belts or zones, the heaviest showings being in eastern Virginia and the eastern part of North and South Carolina, in central Tennessee, in the southern half of Alabama and Georgia, and in the northeastern corner and southern half of Mississippi, following the sandy plain in the seaboard States. Studies of the geographical distribution of the hookworm made through the agency of the Department of State show that the disease belts the earth in a zone about 66° wide, extending from parallel 36° N. to parallel 30° S. lat. Practically all countries in this latitude are infected. In six countries, viz., Wales, Germany, The Netherlands, Belgium, France, and Spain, the disease is confined to mines. In forty-six foreign countries, aggregating a population of about 920,000,000, the disease is general and widespread. The total population of the infected States in the United States is about 20,000,000. Together these constitute 58 per cent. of the earth's estimated population of 1,600,000,000. The degree of infection is heaviest in American Samoa, where it is found in 70 per cent. of the population; in the southern two-thirds of China, in 75 per cent. of the population; while in India from 60 to 80 per cent. of 300,000,000 population have the disease; in Ceylon, 90 per cent. in many parts; in Natal, 50 per cent. of the coolies on sugar and tea estates; in Egypt, 50 per cent. of the laboring class; in Dutch Guiana, 90 per cent. in many parts; in British Guiana, 50 per cent. of all; in Colombia, 90 per cent. of those living between sea-level and 3000 feet, which includes most of the population; and until 1904, 90 per cent. of the working population of Porto Rico were infected. The problem is thus seen to be not local, but world-wide, and, unless controlled, sanitarians believe that the disease will produce the same evil results in this country that it has in other lands, such as India, China, and Egypt, where it has undermined the physical and mental health of the population, destroying economic efficiency and preventing social development.

An important factor in the spread of hookworm disease in the United States is immigration. Every country which imports coolie laborers from India is bringing in a constant stream of heavy infection. Of 600 coolies going into Assam, only one was free from infection. The attention of the government at Durban was called in 1908 to the heavy infection among coolies on the sugar estates of Natal. The next shipload from India was examined and 93 per cent. were found infected. The situation is particularly grave in California. At Angel Island, the immigrant station of San Francisco, 1077 aliens out of 2235 examined were found to be infected. Among the Hindus 63 per cent. were found to be infected with hookworm. The number of Hindus rejected for this condition was so great as effectually to check the immigration of this class of Orientals, which was assuming embarrassing proportions.

Besides hookworm, filariasis, amœbiasis, and malarial infections are found among Orientals coming through San Francisco, and as these people settle in various agricultural communities and use the Eastern method of fertilizing the soil with human excreta, it becomes only a question of time until foci of hookworm and other infections are established at every settlement of these races in this region.

HOPS. The world's hop crop of 1912 suffered from the vicissitudes of the weather, but the production more than covered the consumption. In many European hop districts cool and wet weather interfered with crop development and harvesting, but the yield in general was satisfactory and larger than in 1911. A part of the crop was irregular in quality as a result of untoward weather conditions. In the United States the yield was large, but in certain sections the quality varied widely. The world's production for the year was estimated at 1,797,000 bales and the consumption at 1,715,000 bales of 50 kilos, or 110 pounds each. In 1911 the production for all countries was nearly a half million bales less. Official statistics placed the hop area of Germany for 1912 at 65,875 acres. The total German crop was estimated at 407,000 bales, distributed as follows: Bavaria, in the Hallertau, Gebirgs, Markt, Aischgrund, Spalt, and Kindingerland hop districts, 225,000 bales; Württemberg, 50,000 bales; Baden, 17,000 bales, Alsace-Lorraine, 100,000 bales, and Prussia, 15,000 bales. Germany consumes yearly about 300,000 bales. The crop of Austria-Hungary was estimated at 370,000 bales, of which Hungary contributed 30,000 bales. The Austrian crop by hop districts was as follows: Saaz, 190,000 bales; Auscha and Dauba, 85,000 bales; Steiermark, 32,000 bales; Galicia, 15,000 bales; Upper Austria, 8000 bales, and Moravia, 8000 bales. The annual home demand of Austria-Hungary is about 170,000 bales. The production of France was placed at 65,000 bales, Holland and Belgium 65,000 bales, Russia 85,000 bales, Great Britain 380,000 bales, and Australia 15,000 bales. The crop in the United States was distributed as follows: Oregon, 110,000 bales; California, 105,000; Washington, 30,000, and New York, 25,000 bales. A bale of hops in the United States ranges in weight from 180 to 200 pounds. In the Pacific Coast States the yield was large, but in New York only a light yield was secured and the quality was not satisfactory, only about one-fifth of the crop grading as choice.

The imports into the United States in the fiscal year ending June 30, 1912, amounted to about 3,000,000 pounds and the exports to more than 12,000,000 pounds. The successful use of hop-picking machinery was reported from California.

HORSES. See STOCK-RAISING.

HORSES, DISEASES OF. See VETERINARY SCIENCE.

HORTICULTURAL CENSUS. See HORTICULTURE.

HORTICULTURE. The year 1912 was marked by more or less serious shortages in the fruit and truck crops of nearly every country in Europe. The wine crop of Germany and the olive crop of the whole Mediterranean region suffered most severely. The world's reserve supply of olives and olive oil is low and prices are correspondingly high. The current Spanish orange crop was severely damaged by hail. In France there was a great deficiency of every kind of fruit for exportation. The prune harvest in Servia was cut short by the Balkan War. The total North American fruit crop ranged above rather than below the normal production. The Canadian fruit crop was generally good. Climatic disturbances were severe at times in the United States, but crops from the many vigorous orchards just coming into bearing went far towards swelling the total yield.

The estimated apple-crop of the United States for 1912 was 30,000,000 barrels, as compared with 36,665,000 barrels, the final figures for 1911. The severe winter reduced the California citrus crop to 40,290 cars, as compared with 46,394 cars in 1911. Florida produced a banner citrus crop of about 20,000 cars. The California fresh deciduous fruit shipments amounted to 13,325 cars and the cured fruit pack to about 239,000 tons, as compared with 12,539 cars and 197,750 tons in 1911. The raisin and prune yields were unusually heavy. The 1912 potato crop in the United States totaled over 400 million bushels, as compared with 293 million bushels in 1911. A record onion crop of over 6 million bushels was also secured. The tomato, pea, and corn packs for 1911 were 9,850,000 cases, 4,372,000 cases, and 14,301,000 cases, respectively. The packs of tomatoes and peas were again short in 1912.

EXPORT TRADE. The value of fruits exported from the United States amounted to $30,354,700, as compared with imports worth $29,549,281. Approximately one million cases of canned fruits were shipped to England. Nova Scotia exported 1,534,000 barrels of apples, as compared with 1,230,000 barrels exported from the United States. Vegetables to the value of $18,544,873 were imported, as compared with exports worth only $6,544,118. Imports of white potatoes alone amounted to $7,168,627, as against $235,847 worth in 1911. Following the public hearing at Washington in September, the Department of Agriculture declared a quarantine against many fruits and vegetables from Hawaii in order to prevent the entrance of the Mediterranean fruit-fly into this country. The Hawaiian canned pineapple trade has increased from 1893 cases in 1903 to approximately one million cases in 1912. Cuba exported 1,208,450 crates of pineapples in 1912, an increase of 218,567 crates over 1911. The value of fruit exports from Porto Rico has steadily increased from $109,101 in 1901 to $2,390,716 in 1912. Porto Rico started to export lemons to the United States in 1912. The Australian fruit industries have shown rapid expansion. Tasmania's export trade, principally of apples and pears, has grown from 218,546 bushels in 1901 to about 800 thousand bushels in 1912. Australian canned fruits are now actively competing with American canned fruits in southern India. Australia as a whole, exported almost exclusively to Great Britain in 1911 a total of 812,772 cases of apples, 61,226 cases of pears, and 3545 cases of grapes. A trial shipment of apples from Australia to the United States was unsuccessful.

HORTICULTURAL CENSUS IN THE UNITED STATES. According to the census of 1910 there were 49,435,000 tropical fruit trees of bearing age, as compared with 26,868,000 in 1900. These trees include oranges, lemons, figs, and pineapples. Deciduous fruit trees of bearing age including apples, peaches, pears, plums, cherries, apricots, and others decreased from 369,377,000 in 1900 to 301,117,000 in 1910. Grapevines of bearing age increased from 182,330,000 in 1900 to 224,104,000 in 1910. The acreage in small fruits decreased from 310,000 in 1900 to 272,000 in 1910, and cultivated nut-bearing trees increased from 3,702,000 to 5,027,000. Of trees under bearing age there were 65,792,000 apples, 42,226,000 peaches, and 8,804,000 pears. About 60 million grapevines under bearing age were reported in 1910. Florist establishments increased from 8797 in 1899 to 10,614 in 1909 and florists' products increased in value from $18,759,000 to $34,872,000. The total value of nursery products reported from 5582 establishments in 1909 was $21,051,000 as compared with $10,124,000 in 1899. There was an increase of 591 nursery establishments.

COÖPERATIVE MARKETING. The keen competition which has sprung up in recent years between the various fruit and truck districts in the United States has led to the rapid extension of local marketing associations. The movement to combine such associations into strong central organizations was active in 1912. California growers, for example, practically completed the centralized management of their big fruit industries by launching the California Associated Raisin Company and the California Cured Fruit Exchange. By a special act of the Dominion Parliament, Nova Scotia fruit growers formed a strong central organization, known as the "United Fruit Companies of Nova Scotia." A combination of Smyrna fig shippers, incorporated in London and known as "The Smyrna Fig Packers (Ltd.)," was started early in the year, with the avowed object of introducing a uniform rate of sale, economies in marketing, and more hygienic methods of packing.

CALIFORNIA FIG INDUSTRY. The United States consumes about 13,000 tons, or more than half of Smyrna's fig crop. Recent developments in California indicate that fig imports will be materially reduced in the next few years. Improved varieties have been developed and it has been demonstrated that the fig wasps, so necessary to the pollination of the Smyrna variety, can be successfully carried over severe winters by cellar storage within the caprifigs in which they make their home and breed. Several growers have recently made the discovery that the White Adriatic and other types of figs are greatly improved by pollination in the same manner as the Smyrna fig. Recent experiments by the United States Department of Agriculture have shown that fresh ripe figs of the Smyrna type, when carefully handled and quickly cooled, can be shipped successfully across the continent in refrigerator cars. California now produces about 1000 tons of the Smyrna variety and 4000 tons of other varieties.

NEW METHOD OF EXTRACTING OLIVE OIL. A new method of extracting olive oil from fresh olive pulp was recently tested in Italy with good results. Instead of using a press as in the ordinary methods of extracting olive oil, the extractor consists of 2 concentric cylinders separated by a narrow space. The outer cylinder is of sheet metal and the inner one is a metallic screen. The olive pulp is placed in the inner cylinder and kept in motion by a revolving axle furnished with aluminum pallets. By means of a suction fan attached to the lower half of the outer cylinder a slight difference of pressure is produced between the inside and the outside of the inner cylinder. The oil and water are thus extracted from the pulp. Contrary to the results secured in the ordinary press, the oil comes out more easily than the water and a greater proportion of water remains in the pulp. It is claimed that about 10 per cent. more oil is obtained from the new system and the quality of the oil is uniform and equal to, or better than, the first run from ordinary presses. The olives can be worked while fresh and the troubles and defects due to drying, molding, and rotting are avoided.

TOMATO-SEED OIL. A recent development in Italy is the production of oil from tomato seed. Dry seeds yield about 16 per cent. of an oil valued for soap manufacture. Over 300,000 pounds of tomato-seed oil, worth about seven cents a pound, are now extracted yearly in the province of Como. See CHEMISTRY, INDUSTRIAL.

PROCESSING UNRIPE PERSIMMONS. In view of recent results secured with the carbon dioxide process for removing the astringency from the large Japanese persimmons before the fruit has softened (see YEAR BOOK, 1911), the

United States Department of Agriculture now recommends this method for producing firm, tannin-freed fruit for local consumption. Treated fruit can not be successfully shipped to distant markets, but unripe fruit may be treated after shipment.

BANANA FOOD PRODUCTS. The manufacture of banana food products in Jamaica (see YEAR BOOK, 1911), was greatly increased during the year, to meet a growing demand in Europe and in the United States. In order to have a continuous supply of fruit several companies were making arrangements to grow bananas for their own use. All of the products consist of evaporated fruit prepared in different forms and sold as banana figs, cooking bananas, banana chips, flour, and meal. The present output is from 12 to 15 long tons a week.

A successful sun-drying process for strawberries, developed by a berry grower of the State of Washington, was announced during the year.

PLANT BREEDING. Investigations of the improvement of citrus fruits through bud selection have been conducted by the United States Department of Agriculture through three seasons. Careful observations on the bearing of Washington navel oranges and Marsh grapefruit show very marked difference in the yields of individual trees of the same age growing under the same conditions. The large-yielding trees have produced maximum crops and the small bearers have been consistently shy in bearing properties throughout the three seasons. This work has received wide recognition from citrus growers and is serving as a basis for the selection of propagating material, both in the establishment of new plantations and in rebudding operations. Similar investigations are being gradually extended to deciduous fruits. In connection with experiments to establish the Dutch bulb industry in the United States, the Department of Agriculture recently tested mature tulip and narcissus bulbs grown in the States of Washington and Virginia in comparison with Holland-grown bulbs. In every instance the American-grown bulbs gave stronger plants, larger and better flowers, and were a week to ten days earlier than imported bulbs of the same varieties. The tests are being continued on a broader scale. Investigations covering the improvement of the more hardy varieties of the Persian or English walnut by selection and cross-pollination are in progress at the department's experimental farm, Arlington, Va. Methods of propagation by budding and grafting and the stocks suitable for propagation in the several districts in which this nut appears to be hardy will also receive consideration. The New York State Experiment Station made an extensive study of the effect of cross-pollinating related tomato varieties on the yield of the hybrid plants. They found that the first generation seedlings gave so much higher yields than the parent forms as to warrant the production of such seed by growers and seedsmen.

TARRED ROADS INJURIOUS TO VEGETATION. As the result of an extended series of observations and experiments, a French commission appointed to investigate the subject found that many trees, shrubs, garden plants, and flowers suffer injury from the fumes given off by the tar and also from the dust arising from treated roads. The injury seems to be proportional to the distance from the road, the amount of travel, percentage of phenol in the compound, and the insolation of the plants. The effect on the plants is shown in the fading of the leaves, which are spotted and blackened.

RECENT LEGISLATION. By an act of the United States government, approved August 3, 1912, a standard apple barrel, containing 7056 cubic inches, and standard grades for apples packed in barrels were established. The act will take effect on July 1, 1913, and all sales in violation of its provisions are subject to a penalty of one dollar and costs for each such barrel sold, or offered for sale. Another measure, known as the Plant Quarantine act, August 20, 1912, provides for a system of inspection and quarantine against the importation of serious plant diseases and insect pests on nursery stock and other plants and plant products. A decision of vast importance to the orange consumers in the United States was made by Federal Judge Landis late in December. Judge Landis upheld the government authorities in the seizure of eight cars of California navel oranges which had been artificially colored by the sweating process to conceal immaturity.

An international horticultural exposition is to be held in St. Petersburg, Russia, in April, 1913. The exposition is being arranged to commemorate the three hundredth anniversary of the reign of the Romanoff dynasty.

At the Congress of Electricity in Relation to Horticulture, held at Rheims during the latter part of the year, it was decided to establish prizes for research in electro-culture, and to found an international association to be devoted to the interests of this subject. A second congress will be held in Paris in 1914.

Late in the year the governors of the South-Eastern Agricultural College, Wye, decided to establish a fruit research plantation in the southeastern district of England.

LITERATURE. The following contributions to horticultural literature appeared during the year: H. P. Hedrick et al., *The Plums of New York* (New York State Station Rpt., 1910, pt. 2), although having a special significance for New York State, is considered sufficiently broad in its scope to be offered as a record of our present knowledge of cultivated plums; P. Hubert, *Fruits des Pays Chauds, I, Etude Générale des Fruits* (Paris, 1912), is the first volume of a two-volume work dealing with the principal fruits of tropical and subtropical regions; H. N. Ridley, *Spices* (London, 1912), a handbook of information relative to the history, cultural requirements, exploitation, and uses of spices and condiments; H. C. Graham, *Coffee* (United States Dept. Agr., Bur. Statistics Bul. 79), a statistical study, by countries, of the world-production, consumption, and trade in coffee for a period of years; C. A. Reed, *The Pecan* (United States Dept. Agr., Bur. Plant Indus. Bul. 251), a practical treatise on the pecan; S. W. Moore, *Practical Orcharding on Rough Lands* (Akron, O., 1911) deals with apple orcharding on the rough hill and mountain lands in the eastern United States; L. Pichenaud, *Le Jardin Potager* (Paris, 1912), a practical treatise on amateur and market gardening; R. L. Watts, *Vegetable Gardening* (New York and London, 1912), a similar work, based largely upon commercial practices in the United States and Canada; L. H. Bailey, *Farm and Garden Rule-Book* (New York, 1911), the author's *Horticulturists' Rule-Book* is here revised to cover a much wider field; J. Kidkegaard, A *Practical Handbook of Trees, Shrubs, Vines, and Herbaceous Perennials*, (Boston, 1912), a guide to the indentification, culture, and use of hardy ornamental trees and plants; W. C. McCollom, *Vines and How to Grow Them* (Garden City, N. Y., 1911), a manual of outdoor and greenhouse climbing plants for flower, foliage, and fruit effects; E. E. Rexford, *Amateur Gardencraft* (Philadelphia and London, 1912), a popular treatise on ornamental gardening; E. Holmes, *Commercial Rose Culture* (New York, 1911), a practical guide to the modern methods of growing roses, both under glass and outdoors; A. A. Houghton, *Molding Concrete Fountains and Lawn Ornaments*, and *Molding Concrete Flower Pots, Boxes, Jardinieres, etc.* (New York, 1912).

HOSPITALS. Among the many large gifts to hospitals during the year 1912 the following may be mentioned: The Women's Hospital of Pittsburgh received $2,000,000 by the will of Thomas N. Miller; the New York Polyclinic Medical School and Hospital, $50,000 from the estate of David J. Garth; the New York Eye and Ear Infirmary, $25,000 bequeathed by John S. Lyde; Johns Hopkins Hospital, Baltimore, a donation of $220,000 from James Brady, of New York City; St. Luke's Hospital, New York City, $10,000 for the endowment of beds for actors, given by the late Mrs. Catherine E. Daly; German Hospital, Chicago, $20,000 by will of William C. Seipp; Mt. Sinai Hospital, New York City, $10,000 from Ernest Tahlman and $100,000 from Mrs. Caroline Neustadler. The latter also bequeathed $100,000 to be used for establishing the Neustadler Home for Convalescents and $20,000 to the Jewish Children's Sanatorium at Rockaway, N. Y. The Nassau Hospital, L. I., received $100,000 from Mrs. Alice A. Hicks, and the Ithaca (N. Y.) City Hospital about $100,000 from the estate of Edward M. Marshall. The endowment fund of the General Memorial Hospital, New York City, was increased by a gift of $100,000 by an unnamed donor for the maintenance of twenty beds for cancer patients. The Montefiore Home received $200,000 from four donors for the erection of a private hospital for patients having chronic diseases.

In New York City the Italian Hospital was completed at a cost of $120,000, half of which was contributed by the Italian government; the institution will accommodate 100 patients and occupies an entire block on the river front. The new Polyclinic Hospital was opened to patients on April 22 and formally dedicated June 8. The new building of the German Deaconess Hospital, Buffalo, costing about $200,000, was opened on September 1; the new $150,000 home of the Tuberculosis Preventorium for Children at Farmingdale, N. J., was opened on April 25. This institution will accommodate 700 children. The Johnson Memorial Hospital, Stafford Springs, was dedicated. The hospital cost $75,000 and will harbor thirty-five patients. It has an endowment fund of $200,000. The Collis P. Huntington Memorial Hospital, connected with the Harvard Medical School, was opened March 26. The hospital is devoted solely to the care of cancer patients and is under the charge of the cancer commission of Harvard University. To the medical buildings was added the Peter Bent Brigham Hospital, completed about November 1. The first underground emergency hospital in Illinois was opened on New Year's day in one of the mines in the Collinsville district. The hospital is built in the heart of the mine; its concrete walls are guaranteed against cave-ins and small explosions. The new St. Vincent's Hospital at Indianapolis, containing 152 rooms for patients and costing $800,000, was completed. Henry Phipps, of Pittsburgh, conveyed to the trustees of the University of Pennsylvania the Phipps Institution for the Study of Treatment of Tuberculosis. The hospital building occupies a lot with a frontage of 143 feet and a depth of 153 feet. The cost of the building is about $300,000. It is endowed in addition by the donor, the whole project representing about $1,000,000. The Babies' Hospital, organized by physicians for the free care of infants under three years of age afflicted with enteritis, opened at Wynnefield, in Fairmount Park, Pa., June 17. The Mid-Valley Hospital, Blakely, Pa., was opened May 30 to receive patients. This hospital supplies the mining district lying between Scranton and Carbondale, which has heretofore been without accommodation. It cost about $60,000. Other hospitals in Pennsylvania were opened at Rittersville and Wilkes-Barre, and the new State Hospital for the Criminal Insane at Fairview. The City Hospital of Fayetteville, Ark., erected at a cost of nearly $50,000, and with accommodations for thirty patients, was dedicated.

In foreign countries: In Guayaquil, Ecuador, often called "the pesthole of the Pacific," sanitary methods are being planned and pushed. A late number of the *Boletin de Medicina y Cirugia* of Guayaquil contains an illustrated description of the isolation hospitals for bubonic plague, yellow fever, and smallpox, in charge of W. Pareja. The buildings are constructed according to modern principles. The smallpox hospital has been closed for two years, as there has been no case of smallpox during this period. The bubonic plague boarding pavilion (*pabellion de pensionistas*) contains twenty-eight apartments, fourteen for the sick and the others for their families who may wish to accompany them. The plague pavilion proper has eighty beds. The Research Hospital was opened at Cambridge, England, as the outcome of the labors of some of the leaders of the profession, Sir Clifford Allbutt, Sir William Osler, Sir Jonathan Hutchinson, Sir Victor Horsley, and others, designed to investigate maladies which, although not immediately fatal to life, incapacitate the sufferer from active work and which in consequence of their chronicity cannot be treated for long periods and sufficiently investigated in general hospitals. The first disease taken up was rheumatoid arthritis, of which 4000 cases have been carefully recorded, observed, photographed, and chemically analyzed. A psychopathic institution for children, the first of its kind in Germany, was erected by the province of Hannover. The new institution will admit abnormal children who come under the notice of the juvenile courts and those who are not suitable for treatment in insane asylums or other existing shelters.

HOTCHKIN, SAMUEL FITCH. An American Protestant Episcopal clergyman and writer, died August 1, 1912. He was born in Sauquoit, N. Y., in 1833 and graduated from Trinity College in 1856. In 1861 he became priest in the Protestant Episcopal Church. He served as rector in several churches in Delaware and became in 1877 rector of the Church of St. Luke, the Beloved Physician, in Philadelphia. He was the author of *The Mornings of the Bible* (1893); *The Unseen Christ* (1896); *The Living Saviour* (1898); *A Splendid Inheritance* (1898). He also published *Memoirs of Bishops Stevens and Otey* (1898).

HOURS OF LABOR. See LABOR LEGISLATION.

HOUSE FLY. See ENTOMOLOGY.

HOUSE FLY AND DISEASE. See INSECTS AND THE PROPAGATION OF DISEASE.

HOUSE OF REPRESENTATIVES, RULES OF. See UNITED STATES, *Congress*.

HOUSING. See SANITATION.

HOUSING AND TOWN PLANNING ACT. See CITY PLANNING.

HOWARD UNIVERSITY. An institution of higher learning at Washington, D. C., under the direct auspices of the national government. The number of students enrolled in all departments in 1911-12 was 1409. The faculty numbered 118. Among the notable changes during the year were the opening of courses in engineering and allied subjects and the enlargement of the faculty for this purpose. The productive funds of the institution amount to $284,000 and its annual income to about $185,000. There are about 27,000 bound volumes and 19,000 pamphlets in the library. President, S. M. Newman, A. M., D. D.

HOWARD, WALTER EUGENE. An American educator, died April 12, 1912. He was born at Tunbridge, Vt., in 1849 and graduated from Middlebury College in 1871. He studied law and was admitted to the bar in Wisconsin in 1873 and in Vermont in 1878. From 1871 to 1881 he taught school. He practiced law in Fairhaven, Vt., until 1888, when he was appointed professor of political science and history in Middlebury College. In 1892 he took postgraduate courses at Oxford University. He was appointed dean of the Middlebury College in 1909. He took an interest in politics and in 1882 was a member of the State Senate. From 1883 to 1885 he was United States consul at Toronto, Canada, and at Cardiff, Wales, from 1892 to 1893. He delivered the centennial oration at the celebration of the hundredth anniversary of the founding of the Middlebury College, 1900.

HOYT, JOHN WESLEY. An American public official, formerly territorial g e n of Wyoming, died May 23, 1912. Hevwasoborn near Worthington, O., in 1821 and graduated from the Ohio Wesleyan University in 1849. He studied law at the Cincinnati Law School and medicine at the Eclectic Medical Institute in 1853. In the same year he was appointed professor of chemistry and medical jurisprudence at the latter institute. From 1855 to 1857 he was professor of chemistry at Antioch College. He took an active part in politics and was one of the organizers of the Republican Party. He also engaged in publishing, and for ten years edited an agricultural journal in Madison, Wis. He was a member of the United States Commission to the Paris Exposition in 1877 and of the Commission to the Vienna Exposition in 1873. From 1878 to 1888 he was governor of Wyoming. In 1890 he acted as chairman of the Russian Famine Relief Commission of the United States and was special representative of foreign affairs at the World's Columbian Exposition. He was the commissioner plenipotentiary of Korea to the Universal Postal Union. He took an active part in the development of Wyoming, especially in the construction of railroads. Among his published writings are: *Resources of Wisconsin* (1866); *University Progress* (1869); *Studies in Civil Service* (1878); *Agricultural Resources of Wyoming* (1892); *Histories of the Universities of Bologna, Paris, Oxford, and Cambridge during the Middle Ages* (1893-5); *Outline History of the World's Universities,—Ancient, Mediæval and Modern.* He also was the author of many reports and addresses on various subjects.

HUBBARD, ELBERT HAMILTON. An American public official, representative in Congress from Iowa, died June 4, 1912. He was born in Rushville, Ind., in 1849 and graduated from Yale College in 1872. He was admitted to the bar and took an active interest in politics, serving as a member of the House of Representatives in the 19th General Assembly of Iowa, and of the Senate in the 27th and 28th General Assemblies. He was elected to the 59th and 60th and 61st Congresses and was reëlected to the 62d Congress in 1911.

HUFF, GEORGE FRANKLIN. Former member of Congress from Pennsylvania, died April 18, 1912. He was born in Norristown, Pa., in 1842 and was educated in the public schools of Middletown and Altoona. He engaged in banking and became an officer and director in many important financial institutions. He was also an officer in several railroad and coal companies. From 1884 to 1888 he was a member of the State Senate. In 1891 he was elected to the 52d Congress and was elected to the 54th Congress in 1895. He afterwards served in the 58th and 61st Congresses, 1903-1911.

HUMBER, HARBOR IMPROVEMENT. See DOCKS AND HARBORS.

HUNGARY. See AUSTRIA-HUNGARY.

HUNTINGTON, DEWITT CLINTON. An American Methodist Episcopal clergyman and educator, died February 8. 1912. He was born at Townsend, Vt., in 1830 and graduated from Syracuse University. In 1853 he entered the Methodist Episcopal ministry and was pastor at Rochester, N. Y., from 1861 to 1871. From 1871 to 1873 he was presiding elder and from 1873 to 1876 was pastor at Syracuse. He was again pastor in Rochester from 1876 to 1879 and was for a second time presiding elder from 1879 to 1882. He occupied other pastorates at Bradford, Pa., Olean, N. Y., and Lincoln, Neb. In 1898 he was elected chancellor of the Nebraska Wesleyan University. He held this position until 1908 when he retired. He continued, however, to fill the professorship of the English Bible at that institution. He was one of the best known American clergymen in the United States. He was several times mentioned as a possible bishop. Among his published writings are: *The Cotton King, and the Rum King* (1879); *The Puritans* (1896); *Sin and Holiness* (1898); and *Half Century Messages* (1906).

HUTCHINS, STILSON. An American capitalist and newspaper proprietor, died April 22, 1912. He was born in Whitfield, N. H., in 1838 and was educated at Harvard University. In 1855 he removed to Iowa where he later founded the *Dubuque Herald*. In 1866 he founded the *St. Louis Times* and in 1877 founded the *Washington Post*. This paper became very successful under his management, but he sold it in 1889. He was one of the original promoters of the Mergenthaler Linotype and was one of the principal founders of the company which manufactures it.

HUTTON, ARTHUR WOLLASTON. An English clergyman and writer, died March 24, 1912. He was born in Spridlington in 1848 and was educated at Cheltenham College and at Exeter College, Oxford. He was rector of Spridlington from 1873 to 1876, but in the latter year was received into the Roman Catholic Church by Cardinal Newman, and in 1883 was a member of Newman's Oratorian community at Edgbaston. Following this he was appointed librarian at the National Liberal Club, holding this post from its formation in 1887 until 1899. In 1898 he returned again to the Anglican Church and served as rector and curate in several parishes. In 1907-8 he visited Canada and the United States. He wrote much on subjects relating to religion. Among his published works are: *Our Position as Catholics in the Church of England* (1872); *Cardinal Manning* in the series of "English Leaders of Religion" (1892); *Letters to Mr. Asquith and Mr. Balfour* (1894-5); *Newman's Lives of the English Saints* (1900), and *Ecclesia Discens* (1904). He also wrote encyclopædia and magazine articles.

HYDRO-AEROPANE. See AERONAUTICS.

HYDRO-ELECTRIC DEVELOPMENT. See WATERPOWER.

HYDRO-ELECTRIC POWER. See MUNICIPAL OWNERSHIP.

HYDROPLANE. See AERONAUTICS.

HYGIENE. The Fifteenth International Congress on Hygiene and Demography was held at Washington, D. C., September 23 to 28, 1912. Delegates were present from 32 foreign countries and from all the 48 States. The President of the United States was the honorary president, while the president was Dr. Henry P. Walcott, of Boston, and the secretary was Dr. John S. Fulton, of Maryland. An exhibition, lasting from September 16 to October 4, was a special feature of the gathering, and contained twelve groups, covering vital statistics, food, the hygiene of infancy and childhood, as well as of exercise, industrial and occupational, State and municipal, traffic and transportation, military, naval, and tropical and sex hygiene, as well as communicable diseases. The scientific work of the congress was divided into sections corresponding to the departments of the exhibition mentioned, and eminent men addressed the delegates upon many special topics. There were also general sections, in which medical and related topics were considered in papers and addresses. Full reports of the proceedings may be obtained in *Medical Record*, New York, September 28, to October 12, 1912; *New York Medical Journal*, same dates; *Journal of the American Medical Association*, July 13, and September 28 to October 19, 1912.

HYGIENE, INDUSTRIAL. See OCCUPATIONAL DISEASES.

ICEBERGS. See METEOROLOGY.

ICELAND. A Danish crown colony. Area about 40,456 square miles, of which 16,245 square miles inhabited; population (1911), 85,089. H. Hafstein (1912), residing at Reikjavik, is the responsible executive. The trade in 1911 amounted to 5,693,000 kroner imports and 4,901,000 kroner exports, the latter consisting of wool, dried fish, mutton, ponies, and sheep. The legislature (Althing) has 40 members, 36 elective by universal suffrage. Voting rights are exercised by men and women over 25 years of age.

IDAHO. POPULATION. According to the Census Bureau statistics issued in 1912, out of a total population in 1910 of 325,594, the foreign-born whites numbered 40,427, compared with 21,890 in 1900. The largest number, 5042, came from Germany; from Sweden, 4935; from Canada, 4496; from Norway, 2566; from Italy, 2067; and from Denmark, 2254. Other European countries were represented by smaller numbers. The negroes in the State in 1910 numbered 651 and the mulattoes, 226. The negroes in 1890 numbered 201 and the mulattoes, 101.

AGRICULTURE. The acreage, value and production of the principal crops in 1911 and 1912 are shown in the following table:

		Acreage	Prod. Bu.	Value
Corn	1912	12,000	394,000	$ 276,000
	1911	11,000	330,000	280,000
Wheat	1912	510,000	14,566,000	9,613,000
	1911	517,000	15,860,000	10,468,000
Oats	1912	348,000	17,017,000	5,956,000
	1911	331,000	14,564,000	5,826,000
Rye	1912	3,000	66,000	40,000
	1911	3,000	68,000	46,000
Potatoes	1912	35,000	6,475,000	1,878,000
	1911	29,000	5,220,000	3,393,000
Hay	1912	692,000	a1,938,000	12,209,000
	1911	525,000	a1,628,000	12,373,000

a Tons.

MINERAL PRODUCTION. During 1911 there were produced in the State 4,513,116 pounds of blister copper, compared with 6,877,515 pounds in 1910. The production since 1884 has been steady and important. At the close of 1911 it had amounted to 59,071,800 pounds. Most of the copper produced in the State comes from the Cœur d'Alène district.

The gold production of the State in 1911 was valued at $1,372,387, against $1,096,842 in 1910. Siliceous ores supplied 57.31 per cent. of the gold output; placer mines, 29.46 per cent.; copper ores, 6.76 per cent.; and lead ores, 5.78 per cent. The output of silver increased from 7,369,742 fine ounces in 1910 to 8,196,136 fine ounces in 1911. Over 86 per cent. of the silver output of the State is from the lead mines, especially from the Cœur d'Alène in Shoshone county.

MANUFACTURES. The Thirteenth Census, taken in 1910, included statistics of manufactures in the State for the calendar year 1909. The results will be found summarized in the table below. It will be seen from this that while the manufacturing interests of Idaho are not much in actual volume, they showed a remarkable increase in the five years from 1904 to 1909. The industries in which are the largest number of establishments, and the greatest capital invested, are those producing lumber and timber products. The value of these products in 1909 was $22,400,000. Flourmill and gristmill products ranked next, with a value of $10,689,000. Following are cars and general shop construction and repairs by steam railway companies, printing and publishing, manufactures of butter, cheese, and condensed milk, liquors, brick and tile. The total number engaged in manufactures in 1909 was 9909, of whom 9646 were males and 263 females. For the majority of the wage earners, the prevailing hours of labor were 60 hours a week. The following table gives a summary of the results of the censuses for the calendar years 1904 and 1909:

	Number or Amount 1909	1904
Number of establishments..	725	364
Persons engaged in industry	9,909	3,791
Proprietors and firm members	831	371
Salaried employees........	858	359
Wage earners (average number)	8,220	3,061
Primary horsepower........	42,804	16,987
Capital	$32,477,000	$9,689,000
Expenses	18,981,000	7,619,000
Services	6,482,000	2,438,000
Salaries	984,000	379,000
Wages	5,498,000	2,059,000
Materials	9,920,000	4,069,000
Miscellaneous	2,489,000	1,112,000
Value of products...........	22,400,000	8,769,000
Value added by manufacture (value of products less cost of materials)..	12,480,000	4,700,000

EDUCATION. The total number of children between the ages of 6 and 21 in the State on June 30, 1912, was 104,735. The average number of children attending school was 84,902 and the average daily attendance was 66,359. The number of teachers employed was 2710, of whom 2021 were women and 689 were men. The average monthly salary of men teachers was $87.21, and of women, $68.88. The total amount paid to teachers during the year was $1,649,648. The value of all school property in the State on June 30, 1912, was $7,090,806. The total receipts for educational purposes during the fiscal year were $3,705,792. On October 1, 1912, there was a balance on hand of $811,-876.

FINANCE. The receipts from all sources from January 1, 1911, to January 30, 1912, were $6,023,947. and the expenditures, $5,596,998. The balance on October 1, 1912, was $1,280,654, which includes the balance remaining at the beginning of the fiscal year. The chief sources of income are from taxation and the chief expenditures are for the maintenance of State departments and schools. The State indebtedness on October 1, 1912, was $2,364,250.

CHARITIES AND CORRECTIONS. The only correctional institutions in the State are the Idaho State Penitentiary at Boise, and the Industrial Training School at St. Anthony. The State maintains no charitable institutions entirely, but coöperates with the Children's Home Finding Society of Boise.

POLITICS AND GOVERNMENT. The legislature did not meet in 1912, as the sessions are biennial and the last was held in 1911. The date of the next session is January 6, 1913. Senator Weldon C. Heyburn (q. v.) died October 17, 1912, and it was necessary for the governor to appoint a successor until the legislature should meet. He appointed Judge Kirtland I. Perky. Senator Heyburn's term expired in 1915.

The political campaign in the State was of unusual interest. The Progressives were strong and Senator Borah took a conspicuous part in the deliberations of the national committee preceding the national convention. He was a strong supporter of Mr. Roosevelt and bitterly arraigned the committee for its action in refusing to seat certain of the Roosevelt delegates. Senator Borah, however, did not join the third party movement following the Chicago convention. The Republicans nominated John M. Haines for governor and the Democrats renominated James H. Hawley. On July 30 an organization of electors of the State held a convention at which delegates from a number of counties formed an organization which they designated as the Progressive party of the State of Idaho and elected delegates to attend the convention of the Progressive party in Chicago. At the same time they nominated three candidates for electors for President and Vice-President. On August 12 a committee representing this party elected a chairman and agreed upon certain persons for the nomination for State offices. The chairman caused a certificate of nomination to be prepared and circulated, nominating the persons so agreed upon for those State offices. This petition was signed by about 600 electors of the State. It asked to have the candidates mentioned in the petition appear on the final ballot under the name of the Electors' Progressive party. Action was taken by the regular Republican leaders to have this petition declared void as they alleged that the convention in which electors were nominated was contrary to the primary law of the State. The supreme court of the State decided on August 8, that the primary election law of the State forbade the recognition of such a convention and that therefore the electors nominated at that convention could not properly appear upon the ballot. As a result of this decision, the voters who wished to cast their vote for Mr. Roosevelt were obliged to write in his name on the ballot. This decision was widely criticised, both within and without the State. Mr. Roosevelt was especially bitter against the action of the supreme court and the publication of his criticisms in certain papers in Idaho resulted in the arrest of the editors of those papers for contempt of court.

The election on November 5 resulted as follows: Wilson, 33,921 votes; Taft, 32,810, and Roosevelt, 25,530. For governor, Haines, Rep., received 35,134 votes; Holly, Dem., 33,992, and Martin, Prog., 24,375. A number of amendments to the constitution were submitted at this election. Among them were those providing for the initiative, referendum, and recall. These were all carried by large majorities. In addition, the statutes relating to the bonded indebtedness of the State and taxation were also submitted and carried. Another amendment, which was carried, provided for increased membership of the legislature. The Republicans elected representatives to Congress.

STATE GOVERNMENT. Governor, John M. Haines; Lieutenant-Governor, H. H. Taylor; Secretary of State, W. L. Gifford; Treasurer, O. V. Allen; Auditor, R. Huston; Attorney-General, J. H. Peterson; Superintendent of Education, Grace Shepard—all Republicans.

JUDICIARY. Supreme Court: Chief Justice, George H. Stewart, Rep.; Associate Justices, James F. Ailshie, Rep.; Isaac N. Sullivan, Rep.; Clerk, I. W. Hart.

STATE LEGISLATURE, 1913. Senate, Republicans 20; Democrats, 4; House, Republicans, 57; Democrats, 4; joint ballot, Republicans, 77; Democrats, 8; Republican majority, Senate, 16; House, 53; joint ballot, 69.

The representatives in Congress will be found in the section *Congress*, article UNITED STATES.

IDAHO, UNIVERSITY OF. A State university for higher education at Moscow, Ida., founded in 1889, and first opened in 1892. The students enrolled in the several departments of the university in 1911-12 numbered 733. The faculty, including the members of the agricultural experiment station, numbered 79. During the year a new auditorium was completed. A summer school was inaugurated in 1912, and had an attendance of 202. The members of the Lumbermens' Association of Idaho have subscribed about $60,000 for a forestry building, the first gift of any size which the university has received outside the legislative appropriations. The university comprises the following divisions: College of letters and sciences; college of agriculture; the agricultural experiment station; college of engineering; college of law; and the summer session. The endowment of the university in 1911-12 amounted to $631,388 and the total receipts for the year to about $246,000, all of which was derived from legislative appropriations, from interest on endowment, and from the federal government. President, James Alexander MacLean, Ph. D., LL. D.

IDEALISM. See PHILOSOPHY.

IDO. See LANGUAGE, INTERNATIONAL.

IJICHI, H. A vice-admiral of the Japanese navy, died January 4, 1912. He was born in 1860 and entered the Japanese naval college in 1874. During the Chino-Japanese war he was naval attaché in Rome. In 1900 he was promoted to be captain and occupied important positions in the navy department. He was appointed captain of the *Nikasa* in 1903 and just previous to the war between Japan and Russia was made flag-captain to Admiral Togo. He was promoted to rear-admiral in 1906 and vice-admiral in 1910. Between 1906 and 1909 he was twice commander-in-chief of the Japanese training squadron and with this squadron visited Australia and the west coast of the United States. His last position was that of commander-in-chief of the naval station of the Pescadores. He was also a member of the admiralty board.

ILLINOIS. POPULATION. According to the Census Bureau statistics issued in 1912, out of a total population in 1910 of 5,638,591, 1,202,560 were foreign-born whites, compared with 964,635 in 1900. The largest proportion of these came from Germany, 318,634; from Austria, 164,966; from Russia, 149,366; from Sweden, 115,416; from Ireland, 93,381; from Italy, 72,100; from England, 60,333; from Norway, 32,896; from Canada, 37,868; from Hungary, 37,494; and from Scotland, 20,752. Other European countries were represented by smaller numbers. In the city of Chicago, with a total population in 1910 of 2,185,283, there were 781,217 foreign-born whites. Of these 181,987 came from Germany; 133,301 from Austria; 122,035 from Russia; 65,922 from Ireland; 45,111 from Italy; 63,035 from Sweden; 24,170 from Norway. There were in the State in 1910 109,049 negroes and 36,828 mulattoes. In 1890 the negroes numbered 57,028 and the mulattoes, 16,682.

AGRICULTURE. The acreage, value and production of the principal crops in 1911 and 1912 are shown in the following table:

		Acreage	Prod. Bu.	Value
Corn	1912	10,658,000	426,320,000	$174,791,000
	1911	10,150,000	334,950,000	184,222,000
Wheat ...	1912	1,183,000	9,819,000	8,641,000
	1911	2,025,000	42,000,000	37,380,000
Oats	1912	4,220,000	182,726,000	54,818,000
	1911	4,220,000	121,536,000	51,045,000
Rye	1912	48,000	768,000	538,000
	1911	52,000	874,000	708,000
Potatoes	1912	137,000	13,837,000	8,302,000
	1911	138,000	6,900,000	6,210,000
Hay	1912	2,512,000	a 3,266,000	41,152,000
	1911	2,376,000	a 1,948,000	33,116,000
Tobacco	1912	900	684,000	62,000
	1911	1,000	750,000	58,500

a Tons.

MINERAL PRODUCTION. *Petroleum.* The production of petroleum in Illinois in 1911 was 31,317,038 barrels, compared with 33,143,362 barrels in 1910. The production in the Illinios field has remained comparatively constant since 1907, when it was 24,281,933 barrels. There were 1365 wells completed in the State in 1911.

The coal produced in the State in 1911 amounted to 53,679,118 short tons with a value of $59,503,278. This is an increase of 7,778,872 tons in quantity and $7,097,381 in value over 1910. Much of the gain is due to the abnormally low production of 1910 on account of the prevailing strike. There were no labor troubles of importance in the State during 1911. The number of persons employed in the mines of the State in 1911 was 76,000.

The production of lead in the State in 1911 was 964 short tons, valued at 6760. The zinc produced amounted to 4219 short tons, valued at $480,966. The production of lead in 1910 was 373 tons, and of zinc, 3549 tons.

MANUFACTURES. The Thirteenth Census statistics are for the calendar year 1909 and were compiled in 1912. A summary of the results of the census is given in the table below:

	Number or Amount 1909	1904	P. C. of Inc. 1904-'09
Number of establishments	18,026	14,921	20.8
Persons engaged in manufactures..	561,044	447,947	25.2
Proprietors and firm members	17,357	13,990	24.1
Salar'd employees	77,923	54,521	42 9
Wage earners (average number)	465,764	379,436	22.8
Pri'ry horsepower	1,013,071	741,555	36.6
Capital	$1,548,171,000	$975,845,000	58.6
Expenses	1,733,327,000	1,281,208,000	35.3
Services	364,768,000	268,965,000	35.6
Salaries	91,449,000	60,560,000	51.0
Wages	273,319,000	208,405,000	31.1
Materials	1,160,927,000	840,057,000	38.2
Miscellaneous....	207,632,000	172,186,000	20.6
Value of products	1,919,277,000	1,410,342,000	36.1
Value of products less cost of materials	785,350,000	570,285,000	33.0

Illinios is the most important manufacturing State west of the Alegheny Mountains. As will be seen from the table in 1909, there were 18,026 manufacturing establishment giving employment to an average of 561,044 persons. Of these establishments, those devoted to printing and publishing ranked first in number, 2608. Those devoted to bread and other bakery products numbered 2099; tobacco manufactures, 1944; foundry and machine-shop products, 1178. The value of products was greatest in slaughtering and meat-packing maufactories, which numbered 109. The value of the product of these establishment was $389,595,000; foundry and machine-shop products were valued at $138,579,000; clothing establishments, $89,473,000; printing and publishing, $87,247,000; iron and steel works and rolling mills, $86,608,000. The total number of persons engaged in manufactures in 1909 was 56,104. Of these 465,139 were male and 95,905 were female. The number of persons employed under 16 years of age was 6917. The prevailing hours of labor were, for the greater proportion of those engaged in the industries, from 54 to 60 hours a week; only 8.1 per cent. worked in establishments where the prevailing hours exceeded 60 a week, and only 22.7 per cent. in establishments where they were less than 54 a week. All of the wage earners in the blast furnace industry and nearly all those in the cement and gas industries worked in establishments where the prevailing hours exceeded 72 a week, while nearly three-fifths of those in the steel works and rolling mills worked at least 72 hours a week. In Chicago were found 293,977 wage earners; in Rockford, 9309; in Joliet, 6383, and in Elgin, 6094.

FINANCE. The receipts from all sources into the State treasury during the fiscal year ending September 30, 1912, were $14,822,466, and the expenditures for the same period were $13,953,687, leaving a balance on hand at the end of the year, including the balance at the beginning of the fiscal year, of $5,499,210. The chief sources of income are from State taxes, inheritance taxes, from the Illinois Central Railway Company, and from fees from the several departments. The chief expenditures are for the support of State institutions, for education, and for the support of government offices. The State has no bonded indebtedness except such as has been called for payment.

EDUCATION. The total enrollment in the public schools of the State on June 30, 1912, was 987,379. The teachers employed numbered 30,366. The average annual salary of teachers was $634.76. The total amount expended for education during the year was $34,869,457, of which $27,324,901 was for current expenses, $6,284,242 for capital outlay, and $1,260,313 for bonds and interest. The average annual tuition per pupil enrolled for all expenses was $35.38.

CHARITIES AND CORRECTIONS. The charitable institutions under the control of the State. with their populations in 1912, include the following: Elgin State Hospital at Elgin, 1550; the Kankakee State Hospital at Kankakee, 2950; the Jacksonville State Hospital at Jacksonville, 1650; the Anna State Hospital at Anna, 1400; the Watertown State Hospital at Watertown, 1400; the Peoria State Hospital at Peoria, 2300; the Chicago State Hospital 2500; the Chester State Hospital at Chester, 280; Lincoln State School and Colony at Lincoln, 1500; the Industrial Colony for Improvable Epileptics; the Illinois School for the Deaf at Jacksonville, 411; Illinois School for the Blind at Jacksonville, 209; the Illinois Industrial Home for the Blind in Chicago, 88; the Illinois Soldiers' and Sailors' Home, Quincy, 1400; Soldiers' Widows' Home of Illinois at Wilmington, 80; Illinois Soldiers' Orphans' Home at Normal, 300; the Illinois Charitable Eye and Ear Infirmary at Chicago; the State Training School for Girls at Geneva, 450; the St. Charles School for Boys at St. Charles, 550; the Alton State Hospital, not located; Surgical Institute for Crippled Children, not located. These institutions are under the control of the State Charities Commission. The only legislation of importance relating to charities during the year was the passage of an amendment creating a State bureau of criminal statistics, making it a division of the State charities commission. The duties of this commission are to collect annual statistics of crime in Illinois. The correctional institutions of the State include the State prisons at Joliet and Chester and the reformatory at Pontiac.

POLITICS AND GOVERNMENT

There was no regular meeting of the legislature in 1912, but two special sessions were called by Governor Deneen, the more important having the primary object of passing a measure to provide for a presidential primary law. This measure was passed.

The term of Senator Cullom expiring in 1913, it was necessary to elect his successor. Although Senator Cullom was over 84 years old, and had served in the United States Senate since 1883, he announced on January 31 that he was a candidate for reëlection, and his name was placed on the primary ballot. His opponent was Lawrence Y. Sherman. On February 5 Governor Deneen announced his candidacy for the Republican renomination. The measure referred to above providing for presidential preference primary elections became a law on March 30, when it was signed by Governor Deneen. The election was appointed for April 9, and the results were awaited with greatest interest throughout the country. It was well known that the Progressive element in Illinois was strong and there was a pronounced opposition to President Taft, which had been added to by speeches made by Mr. Roosevelt and other Progressive leaders throughout the State prior to the election. In spite of this, however, the overwhelming defeat of the President was a surprise. Mr. Roosevelt received 266,917 votes, President Taft, 127,481 and Senator La Follette, 42,692. The total vote cast in the primary for these three candidates was 437,090, which may be compared with the Republican vote at the election of 1908, which was 629,932. Governor Deneen was renominated as Republican candidate for governor, and Edward F. Dunne won the Democratic nomination. In the Democratic presidential primary vote, Champ Clark defeated Governor Wilson by 142,956. Senator Cullom was defeated for renomination by Mr. Sherman, and in Chicago the voters decided by a vote of nearly two to one, against woman suffrage, on a public policy vote.

The Republican State convention for the nomination of delegates to the Republican national convention was held on April 19. Resolutions favoring initiative and referendum were emphatically rejected. The platform adopted approved the administrations of President Taft and Mr. Roosevelt, endorsed Lawrence Sherman for United States Senator and pledged the Republicans to vote solidly for him in joint assembly. The delegates at large were pledged to vote for Mr. Roosevelt. In view of the fact that Mr. Roosevelt carried the primaries for presidential candidate, Governor Deneen and the other State leaders supported him in the national convention where Governor Deneen took a leading part as a Roosevelt representative. (See PRESIDENTIAL CAMPAIGN.) After the nomination of President Taft, however, Governor Deneen refused to affiliate himself with the third party or to identify himself with the Progressive party movement. As a result of this decision the Progressive party met on August 3 and nominated Senator Frank H. Funk for governor.

The Democrats in party convention had ratified the nomination of Edward F. Dunne for governor. In the election on November 5, Governor Wilson received 405,048 votes, Mr. Roosevelt, 386,478, President Taft, 253,593, Debs, Socialist, 81,278, and Chafin, Prohibition, 15,710. For governor, Dunne received 443,120 votes, Deneen, 318,469, and Funk, 303,401. The Democrats elected 19 of the 25 representatives in Congress and among the notable defeats was that of Joseph G. Cannon, former speaker of of the House. William B. McKinley, the leader of President Taft's campaign, was also defeated for reëlection.

The election of United States senators became doubtful, the newly elected State senate having 24 Democratic, 25 Republican, and 1 Progressive members, and the House 73 Democrats, 51 Republicans, 25 Progressives, and 4 Socialists.

OTHER EVENTS. Senator Lorimer was finally deprived of his seat in the Senate on July 14. (See CONGRESS.) Governor Deneen did not appoint a successor on the ground that he had no authority to do so as a result of the conditions under which the seat was vacant, and as a result Illinois had only one representative in the Senate during the remainder of the year.

Municipal elections were held in the State on April 2. Among the interesting results was the election of Socialist aldermen in Belleville, Peoria, and Quincy.

The trial of ten accused officers of the so-called Beef Trust was concluded on March 26 by the acquittal of the defendants. They included J. Ogden Armour, of Armour and Company, Louis F., Edward F., and Charles H. Swift, of Swift and Company, Edward Morris, president of Morris and Company, and Edward Tilden, president of the National Packing Company. For a discussion of this trial and its causes, see the article TRUSTS.

The Chicago city council received a report recommending the building of a subway system, with four main lines at a cost of $131,000,000. At the end of the year public opinion was divided as to subway policy. As an alternative to the "comprehensive" subway plan, a subway for the downtown district only found support, the financing of the "comprehensive" scheme being doubtful. See SUBWAYS.

In Chicago an agreement was made between the city, the South Park commissioners, and the Illinois Central Railroad Company for the improvement of the lake shore, south of Grant Park, which is expected to result in the addition of valuable water-front land to the park system, and to give a permanent home to the Field Columbian Museum. At the election of November 5, the voters of the city approved a bond issue of $1,750,000 for the widening of Twelfth Street from South Ashland Avenue to Michigan Boulevard, an important step toward carrying out the "city beautiful" plan. The city council, August 14, passed an ordinance after a fiercely contested campaign, requiring all milk sold in the city and not coming from dairies approved by the health department to be pasteurized. Early in November, Edward W. Bemis, the city's expert, reported that a reduction in the gross income of the Chicago Telephone Company should be made of $700,000 a year, under the city's right to regulate the telephone rates, and steps were taken by the city council to make the reduction effective. Because of the large number of unemployed men in the city a commission on the unemployed was created by the city, to study ways and means of lessening the number and providing work for as many as possible. The commission had not reported by the end of the year. The movement for vocational education received an impetus through a report to the Commercial Club of Chicago, by Edwin G. Cooley, former superintendent of schools, advocating an extensive system based on German experience. A bill for the establishment of such a system throughout Illinois, drafted by Mr. Cooley, for consideration by the legislature, received the endorsement of several strong organizations, including the Chicago Association of Commerce, the Hamilton Club, and the Civic Federation of Chicago. An ordinance for the reorganization of the police force, to provide for many needed reforms, was passed by the city council in November, and the reorganization under it was begun. The most important feature of this ordinance is the creation of a civilian deputy superintendent, whose division is to be a check on the regular staff administration.

LEGISLATION. There were three special sessions of the legislature in 1912. The first of these merely passed appropriations to pay the expenses of the special session. At the second session the only measures of general importance passed were as follows: An act amending the primary law so as to provide for the appointment by each candidate of challengers in each precinct; an act providing for presidential primaries (see POLITICS AND GOVERNMENT, above); an act regulating fraternal benefit societies; an act providing for mutual insurance against liability in consequence of accident or casualty of employees or other persons. At the third special session an act was passed revising the laws of the State relating to charities, and an act was passed amending the act as to sanitary districts.

STATE GOVERNMENT. Governor, E. F. Dunne; Lieutenant-Governor, B. O'Hara; Secretary of State, Harry Woods; Treasurer, W. Ryan, Jr.; Auditor, James J. Brady; Attorney-General, P. J. Lucey; Adjutant-General, to be appointed by governor; Superintendent of Public Instruction, Francis G. Blair; Superintendent of Insurance, to be appointed by governor—all Democrats.

JUDICIARY. Supreme Court: Chief Justice, F. K. Dunn, Rep.; Associate Justices, Alonzo K. Vickers, Rep.; Wm. M. Farmer, Dem.; George A. Cooke, Dem.; John P. Hand, Rep.; James H. Cartwright, Rep.; O. N. Carter, Rep.; Clerk of the Court, J. McCan Davis, Rep.

LEGISLATURE, 1913. Republicans, Senate, 25; House, 51; joint ballot, 76; Democrats, Senate, 24; House 73; joint ballot, 97; Progressives, Senate, 2; House, 25; joint ballot, 27; Socialists, Senate, 0; House 4; joint ballot, 4.

The representatives in Congress will be found in the section *Congress*, article UNITED STATES.

ILLINOIS, UNIVERSITY OF. A State institution for higher education at Urbana-Champaign, Ill. The total number of students enrolled in all departments of the university in 1912 was 4225. The faculty numbered 543, of whom 496 were men and 47 women. There were no noteworthy benefactions received during the year and no important additions to the faculty. The university is maintained chiefly by the State. The total receipts for 1911-12 amounted to $2,305,211. In the library there were 212,700 volumes. President, E. J. James, Ph. D., LL. D.

ILLITERACY. The Thirteenth Census included investigation into illiteracy in the United States, and many interesting facts were revealed as a result. The Census Bureau treated as illiterate any persons unable to write, regardless of ability to read. The total number of persons coming under this classification in Continental United States in the census of 1910 was 5,516,693, compared with 6,180,069 in 1900, a decrease in ten years of more than 600,000 in number and a decline from 10.7 per cent. to 7.7 per cent. in the proportion of population ten years of age and over which reported.

The proportion of illiterates was less in 1910 than in 1909 in each of the nine geographic divisions into which the country is divided by the census in all but two States, Connecticut and New York. In these two States, in which the percentages were substantially the same in both censuses, the number of illiterates was larger in 1910 than in 1900, chiefly as a result of the heavy immigration into these States in the ten-year period. Owing to the same cause the number of illiterates increased in a considerable number of other States, although the proportion of illiterates in each case has decreased during the decade. The number of illiterates in each of the geographic divisions in 1909-10 was as follows: In the New England division, including Maine, New Hampshire, Vermont, Massachusetts, Rhode Island, and Connecticut, with a total population of 5,330,914, the illiterates numbered 280,806, or 5.3 per cent., compared with 272,402, or 6 per cent. in 1900. In the Middle Atlantic States, including New York, New Jersey, and Pennsylvania, with a total population of 15,446,515 in 1900, the illiterates numbered 874,012, or 5.7 per cent., compared with 704,134, or 5.8 per cent. in 1900. In the East North Central Division, including Ohio, Indiana, Illinois, Michigan, and Wisconsin, with a total population in 1910 of 14,568,949, the illiterates numbered 401,798, or 3.4 per cent., compared with 534,299, or 4.3 per cent. in 1900. In the West North Central Division, including Minnesota, Iowa, Missouri, North Dakota, South Dakota, Nebraska, and Kansas, with a total population of 9,097,311 in 1910, the illiterates numbered 263,628, or 2.9 per cent., compared with 324,023, or 4.1 per cent. in 1900. In the South Atlantic Division, including Delaware, Maryland, District of Columbia, Virginia, West Virginia, North Carolina, South Carolina, Georgia, and Florida, with a total population in 1910 of 9,012,825, the illiterates numbered 1,444,294, or 16 per cent., compared with 1,821,346, or 23.9 per cent. in 1900. In the East South Central Division, including Kentucky, Tennessee, Alabama, and Mississippi, with a total population in 1910 of 6,178,578, the illiterates numbered 1,072,100, or 17.4 per cent., compared with 1,364,935, or 24.9 per cent. in 1900. In the West South Central Division, comprising Arkansas, Louisiana, Oklahoma, and Texas, with a total population in 1910 of 6,394,043 the illiterates numbered 845,606, or 13.2 per cent., compared with 953,644, or 20.5 per cent. in 1900. In the Mountain Division including Montana, Idaho, Wyoming, Colorado, New Mexico, Arizona, Utah, and Nevada, with a total population in 1910 of 2,054,249, the illiterates numbered 140,618, or 6.8 per cent., compared with 122,901, or 9.6 per cent. in 1900. In the Pacific Division, including Washington, Oregon, and California, with a total population in 1910 of 3,496,885, the illiterates numbered 103,821, or 3 per cent., compared with 82,385, or 4.2 per cent. in 1900. It will be noted that the largest percentages of illiteracy in these divisions are: East South Central, 17.4; South Atlantic, 16; and the West South Central, 13.2. These percentages are accounted for largely by the proportion of negroes in the States of these divisions. Percentages for individual States are: Louisiana, 29; South Carolina, 25.7; Alabama, 22.9; Mississippi, 22.4; Georgia, 20.7; New Mexico, 20.2; Arizona, 20.9; North Carolina, 18.5; and Virginia, 15.2. The smallest percentage in any of the divisions is found in the West North Central Division, 2.9, and in this division is also found the smallest proportion in any of the individual States, Iowa, 1.7. Nebraska had 1.9 per cent. of illiterates; Oregon, 1.9 per cent.; Washington, 2 per cent.; Kansas, 2.2 per cent.; Idaho, 2.2 per cent; Utah, 2.5 per cent.; South Dakota, 2.9 per cent.; and California, 3.7 per cent.

The percentage of illiteracy in which a large proportion of the inhabitants are colored may be shown by figures taken from statistics dealing with those States. In the South Atlantic Division, with a total white population in 1910 of 6,018,022, the total number of illiterates among the whites was 471,743, or 7.8 per cent. The negro population in this division in 1910 was 2,986,936 and the illiterates among the negroes numbered 969,432, or 32.5 per cent. In the East South Central Division, with a total white population of 4,215,494, the white illiterates numbered 389,445, or 9.2 per cent. In this division there was a negro population of 1,960,898, and among these the illiterates numbered 681,507, or 34.8 per cent. In the West South Central Division, with a total white population of 4,881,331, the white illiterates numbered 349,218, or 7.2 per cent. This division had a negro population of 1,460,705. Of these, 483,022, or 33.1 per cent., were illiterates. Of the whole colored population in the United States, 7,318,502 in 1910, 2,228,087, or 30.4 per cent., were illiterates. There was in the decade however, a gratifying decrease in the number of illiterates among the negroes. With a total negro population in 1900 of 6,415,581, the illiterates numbered 2,853,194, or 44.5 per cent., which shows a decrease of illiteracy of 14.1 per cent. in the decade. The highest percentages of illiteracy among the colored population were: Louisiana, 48.4; Alabama, 40.1; North Carolina, 38.7; Georgia, 36.5; Mississippi, 35.6; Virginia, 30; Kentucky, 27.6; Washington, 27.3; Arkansas, 26.4; Delaware, 25.6. The highest percentage of literacy among the negroes in these States was found in Oklahoma, the percentage of illiterates being 17.7.

Illiteracy Among Children. While illiteracy among the entire population declined from 10.7 per cent. in 1900 to 7.7 per cent. in 1910, among children 10 to 14 years of age the decline in the ten-year period was from 7.2 to

4.1 per cent. In 1910 the whole number of children of the ages of 10 to 14 years who were unable to read or write was 370,120, of whom 144,659 were whites and 218,355 negroes, leaving 7106 Indians, Chinese, and Japanese. Illiteracy among the native white children fell to 1.7 per cent., and among those of foreign or mixed parentage who, for the most part, live in cities, the proportion is a low as 0.6 per cent. On the other hand as many as 18.9 per cent. of negro children were illiterate in 1910. In the northern part of the country illiteracy among children has almost entirely disappeared. In this section the proportion is considerably less than 1 per cent. of the whole number of children. See also EDUCATION.

ILLUMINATING GAS. See CHEMISTRY, INDUSTRIAL.

IMMEDIATE RESERVE. See NAVAL PROGRESS.

IMMIGRATION AND EMIGRATION. The total immigration into the United States in the fiscal year 1912 was 838,172, which was considerably less than the corresponding figures for 1911, 878,587. The largest number of immigrants came from Austria-Hungary, 178,882. In 1911 the largest number came from Italy. From Italy in 1912 came 157,134; from the Russian Empire and Finland, 162,395; from Germany, 27,788; from Greece, 21,449; from England, 40,408; from Ireland, 25,879; and from Scotland, 578. The total immigration from Europe in 1912 was 718,875. From China came 1765 immigrants; from Japan, 6114, and from Turkey in Asia, 12,788. The total immigration from Asia was 21,449. From British North America the immigration in 1912 was 55,990, compared with 56,830 in 1911. There were debarred for various reasons from the United States in 1912, 16,057 immigrants, and 2456 were deported.

EMIGRATION. For the fiscal year ending June 30, 1912, the emigrant aliens numbered 333,-263, and the non-emigrant aliens, 282.030, or a total of 615,292. The non-emigrant aliens are those who have returned temporarily to their native countries with the intention of returning again to the United States.

DESTINATION OF IMMIGRANTS. Of the immigrants arriving in 1912, 239,275 had New York as their destination, 67,118 Illinois, 70,171 Massachusetts, 109,625 Pennsylvania, 33,539 Michigan, 28,905 California, and 23,227 Connecticut.

RECENT IMMIGRANTS AND THEIR DISTRIBUTION. The Thirteenth Census taken in 1910 included investigations into the destination of recent immigrants.

The census enumerated in the United States 13,345,545 white persons of foreign birth, of whom almost exactly 5,000,000 were new arrivals who had reached this country between January 1, 1901, and the taking of the census. These figures are preliminary and subject to revision. They represent results of the inquiry made of all foreign-born residents concerning the year of their immigration to this country. For some 10 per cent. of all foreign-born whites the enumerators failed to ascertain the year of immigration, but in the figures here given these unknown cases are distributed in the same proportions as were ascertained where the facts were available.

Of these recent arrivals coming after January 1, 1901, there were 2,155,772, or 43.1 per cent. in the Middle Atlantic States (New York, Pennsylvania, and New Jersey); 1,012,417, or 20.2 per cent. in the East North Central division (Ohio, Indiana, Illinois, Michigan, and Wisconsin); and 684,473, or 13.7 per cent. in the New England States. These three divisions, comprising the States lying north of the Ohio and east of the Mississippi, contained 3,852,662, or 77.1 per cent., of the immigrants who had come to this country since the year 1900. There were only 1,147,436, or 22.9 per cent. located in the sections of the country south of the Ohio and west of the Mississippi.

The older immigrants who came to this country prior to 1901 are more widely dispersed. Of these earlier immigrants the Middle Atlantic division contained in 1910 2,670,407, or 32 per cent., as compared with 43.1 per cent. of the recent arrivals. The East North Central division had 2,054,803, or 24.6 per cent. of the earlier immigrants, but only 20.2 per cent. of the more recent ones. New England, with 1,-129,013, or 13.5 per cent. of the older immigrants, has about the same share in the older as in the newer immigration. The whole region north of the Ohio and east of the Mississippi, which contained 5,855,123 persons who came to this country before 1901, or 70.2 per cent. of the entire number, has, as previously stated, 77.1 per cent. of the newcomers.

The proportion of newcomers among the foreign whites in 1910 (37.5 per cent.) is much larger than was the case ten years before. The census of 1900 enumerated 10,341,276 foreign-born persons, of whom 2,609,173, or 25.2 per cent., had arrived in the United States after 1890. The reason for this larger proportion of newcomers in 1910 lies in the greater immigration of the decade which preceded the last census enumeration.

During the period from January 1, 1901, to April 1, 1910, the Bureau of Immigration recorded the arrival in the United States of 8.248,890 immigrants. Of these, 5,000,098, or 60.6 per cent., were accounted for as present in the United States at the census enumeration of April 15, 1910. In the period preceding the census of 1900 from January 1, 1891, to June 1, 1900, the number of immigrants reported was 3,421,184, of whom 2,609.173, or 76.3 per cent. were counted by the census enumeration of June 1, 1900. The comparison of the two periods indicates that the immigration to the United States contains a larger proportion than formerly of persons who go back instead of remaining here permanently.

RESTRICTION OF IMMIGRATION. Two bills, the Burnett bill in the House and the Dillingham bill in the Senate, which were the result of investigations carried on by a committee of Congress and concluded in 1907, were under consideration in Congress in 1912. These bills provided many restrictions, the most important of which was the literacy test, under the provisions of which immigrants were required to be able to read in some language. This provision applied to all aliens over 16 years of age. Exempt from the operation of this test were those persons who could prove that they sought admission solely to escape from religious persecution, aliens in transit through the United States, and aliens who have been lawfully admitted to the United States and who later pass from one part of the United States to another through foreign contiguous territory.

The bill passed the House of Representatives on December 12, 1912, but no action had been taken by the Senate at the end of the year.

IMMINGHAM DOCK. See Docks and Harbors.

IMPEACHMENT PROCEEDINGS. See United States, *Congress*, and Washington.

INCANDESCENT LAMPS. See Electric Lighting.

INCOME TAX. See Taxation.

INDETERMINATE SENTENCE. See Penology.

INDIA, British. British India is that part of East India governed by the British sovereign (as emperor of India) through the governor-general of India or the latter's subordinates. India, as defined by the British parliament, includes British India and those Native States under the suzerainty of the British government. The capital of British India (formally Calcutta) is Delhi (since 1912). See Architecture.

Area and Population. The area of India is stated at 1,773,168 square miles. Interprovincial transfers are not uncommon, nor transfers from Native to British territory and *vice versa*. The table below shows in detail the area of British India and of the Native States and the population according to the censuses of March 15, 1901, and March 10, 1911. The 1901 population is corrected, as far as possible, in order to allow for subsequent interprovincial transfers. The largest changes are those necessitated by the partition of Bengal. (In 1905 Bengal was divided, the eastern part being united to Assam to form the province of Eastern Bengal and Assam. See end of this section.) The population of Manipur State (284,-465), which was included under the head British territory in the 1901 census, is included under the head Native States in the 1911 census. Also the tribal areas in the North-West Frontier Province are now shown under Native States. Sikkim, which in 1901 was classed under Bengal States, is now shown separately. Areas newly included within the scope of the 1911 enumeration are as follows (the figures are estimates except for Baluchistan); in Burma: Kokang, 25,604; West Manglun, 18,562; unadministered area in Pakokku Hill tracts, 9123;—in Baluchistan: Makran (native), 71,942; Western Singrani (British), 1620;—in the Northe-West Frontier Province: agencies and tribal areas, 1,604,265;—total, 1,731,116. It should be noted that the decrease in the Baluchistan States, as shown in the table, is only apparent, as figures for 1901 were based on an estimate which now appears to be excessive.

The population of the French and Portuguese settlements is not included in the table. A French census in 1911 was carried out synchronously with the British, the provisional results being: Pondicherry, 184,840; Karikal, 56,577; Yanaon, 5033; Mahé, 10,636; Chandernagore, 25,293; total, 282,379 against 273,185 in 1901. A census of the Portuguese settlements was taken December 31, 1910, showing a provisional total of 604,930. The independent states of Nepal and Bhutan are geographically a part of India; their population is not known with certainty, but may be estimated at 3,000,000 for the former and 250,000 for the latter. Adding these totals to the 315,132,537, returned as the population of British India and Native States, we find that the inhabitants of India number about 319,270,000; or, if we exclude Burma (12,115,217), and Aden (46,-165) as not being geographically a part of India, the total is about 307,109,000. Even the approximate accuracy of these totals is in considerable doubt on account of the widely varying estimates for Nepal.

Area and population (March 15, 1901, and March 10, 1911) of British India and the Native States and agencies:

	Sq. m.	Pop. 1901	Pop. 1911
Provinces:			
Ajmer-Merwara...	2,711	476,912	501,395
Andamans and Nicobars	3,143	24,649	26,459
Br. Baluchistan..	45,804	382,106	414,412
Bengal	115,819	50,715,794	52,668,269
Bombay (Pres.)..	123,064	18,559,650	19,672,642
Burma	236,738	10,490,624	12,115,217
Central Provinces and Berar......	100,345	11,971,452	13,916,308
Coorg	1,582	180,607	174,976
Eastern Bengal and Assam.....	93,588	30,510,344	34,018,527
Madras	141,726	38,229,654	41,405,404
North-West Frontier Province...	16,466	2,041,534	2,196,933
Punjab	97,209	20,330,337	19,974,956
United Provs. of Agra and Oudh	107,164	47,692,277	47,182,044
British India...	1,085,359	231,605,940	244,267,542
Native States and Agencies:			
Baluchistan States	86,511	428,640	396,432
Baroda	8,099	1,952,692	2,032,798
Bengal States....	29,955	3,881,448	4,538,161
Bombay States...	65,761	6,908,559	7,411,675
Central India Agency	78,772	8,497,805	9,356,980
Central Provs. States	31,188	1,631,140	2,117,002
E. Bengal and Assam States..	12,542	457,790	575,835
Hyderabad	82,698	11,141,142	13,374,676
Kashmir	80,900	2,905,578	3,158,126
Madras States....	9,969	4,188,086	4,811,841
Mysore	29,444	5,539,399	5,806,193
N.-W. F. Prov. (Agencies, etc.)	......	83,692	1,622,094
Punjab States....	36,532	4,424,398	4,212,794
Rajputana Agency	127,541	9,853,366	10,530,432
Sikkim	2,818	59,014	87,920
United Provs. States	5,079	802,097	832,036
Native States...	687,809	62,755,116	70,864,995
Total India.....	1,773,168	294,361,056	315,132,537

Of the population, about 78 per cent. were in British India, and about 22 per cent. in the Native States. Males numbered 161,326,110, and females 153,806,427. The 1911 census showed the population according to the civil condition in the case of 312,643,693 persons; of these, the unmarried numbered 78,384,686 males and 52,516,947 females; married, 72,906,-881 and 73,704,162; widowed (including divorced), 8,709,755 and 26,421,262.

The larger cities, with population according to the 1911 census: Calcutta (Bengal), 896,067 (including Howrah and other suburbs, 1,222,-313); Bombay (Bombay), Madras (Madras), 518,660; Hyderabad (Hyderabad), including Secunderabad, Bolaram, and the Residency Bazars, 500,623; Rangoon (Burma), 293,316; Lucknow (United Provinces), 259,798; Delhi (Punjab in 1911, but now Delhi), 232,837; Lahore (Punjab), 228,687; Ahmedabad (Bombay), 215,835; Benares (United Provinces), 203,804; Bangalore (Mysore), including civil and military station, 189,485; Cawnpore

(United Provinces), 178,557; Allahabad (United Provinces), 171,697; Poona (Bombay), 158,856; Amritsar (Punjab), 152,756; Karachi (Sind, Bombay), 151,903; Mandalay (Burma), 138,-299; Jaipur (Rajputana), 137,098; Patna (Bengal, now in Bihar, and Orissa), 136,153; Madura (Madras), 134,130. At the time of the census, plague was prevalent in Cawnpore, and many of the inhabitants were absent. A new census taken after the epidemic had subsided showed an increase of about 17,000, the provisional total being 195,498.

The province of Eastern Bengal and Assam, formed in 1905, and the province of Bengal were reconstituted pursuant to an order of November, 1911, and three provinces were erected April 1, 1912. These provinces, the area and population of which, as newly constituted, cannot yet be given accurately, are Bihar and Orissa, Bengal, and Assam. Bengal, like Madras and Bombay, has the style "presidency." Still another new province, Delhi, was constituted October 1, 1912, out of the Punjab division of Delhi; its area is stated at 557 square miles, and population about 392,000.

RELIGION. In the census of March 10, 1911, classification by religion was made in the case of 313,523,981 persons, as shown in the following table (religion was not recorded in the case of 1,608,556 persons in the North-West Frontier Province):

	Br. India	Native States	Total
Hindus	163,621,454	53,965,466	217,586,920
Sikhs	2,171,908	842,558	3,014,466
Jains	458,578	789,604	1,248,182
Buddhists	10,644,409	77,040	*10,721,449
Parsis	86,155	13,945	100,100
Mohammedans.	57,423,866	9,199,546	66,623,412
Christians	2,492,277	1,383,919	3,876,196
Jews	18,524	2,456	20,980
Animists	7,348,024	2,947,144	10,295,168
Others and unspecified	2,347	34,761	37,108
Total	244,267,542	69,256,439	313,523,981

* Of whom, 10,384,544 in Burma.

The nine classes specified above included 313,-486,873 persons recorded by religion in 1911, out of a total of 315,132,537; the same clases in 1901 included 294,231,156, out of 294,361,-056. The recorded increase during the decade was as follows: Hindus, 10,439,894; Sikhs, 809,-136; Jains, a decrease of 85,966; Buddhists, 1,-244,690; Parsis, 5910; Mohammedans, 4,165,-335; Christians, 952,955; Jews, 2760; Animists, 1,661,020. Of the 3,876,196 Christians recorded in 1911, there were 1,490,864 Roman Catholics, 492,317 Anglicans, 413,142 Romo-Syrians, 336,-596 Baptists, 225,190 Jacobite Syrians, 218,-499 Lutherans, 181,128 Presbyterians, 171,754 Methodists, 135,264 Congregationalists, 75,848 Reformed Syrians, and 52,407 Salvationists.

EDUCATION. Literacy, as recorded by the 1911 census for 313,415,389 persons, is shown in the table in the next column.

The following comparative figures for March 31, 1901, and March 31, 1910, respectively, relate to British India (except British Baluchistan) and the Native States. Total public educational institutions, 104,884 and 130,917; scholars, 3,809,463 and 5,595,774 (of whom, females 385,284 and 764,248). Private institutions, 42,460 and 39,555; scholars, 607,959 and 616,144 (females 44,206 and 67,229). Total public and private, 147,344 and 170,469;

	Total	Literate Total	Literate Females
Hindus	217,586,445	12,037,944	814,810
Sikhs	3,014,440	201,443	17,280
Jains	1,248,182	342,705	24,120
Buddhists	10,721,228	2,451,719	317,338
Parsis	100,096	71,213	31,218
Mohammedans...	66,593,177	2,527,573	137,807
Christians	3,876,196	840,865	262,295
Animistic	10,217,544	56,820	2,987
Others and unspecified	58,081	9,296	2,908
Total, 1911.....	313,415,389	18,539,578	1,600,763
Total, 1901.....	293,414,906	15,686,421	996,341

scholars, 4,417,422 and 6,211,918 (females, 429,-490 and 831,477). Public primary schools, 98,-256 and 119,270; pupils, 3,164,269 and 4,559,-119 (females, 337,873 and 668,969). Public secondary schools, 5477 and 6443; scholars, 589,427 and 863,993 (females 44,373 and 77,-004). Public arts colleges, 142 and 137; students 16,969 and 23,184 (females 135 and 217). Expenditure on education in India (excluding British Baluchistan) in 1900-1, £2,561,529; in 1909-10, £4,588,082.

AGRICULTURE. Reported figures of production in India are not complete, as returns from some of the Native States are not available; but they cover about the same territory from year to year, and therefore have a comparative value. Some of the more important yields for 1908-9 and 1909-10 are officially estimated as follows: Rice (cleaned), 390,979,900 and 558,-480,000 cwts.; wheat, 7,616,800 and 9,587,700 tons; tea (calendar years), 247,364,750 and 258,029,232 lbs.; cotton, 4,776,000 and 5,135,-000 bales (of 400 lbs.); jute, 6,310,800 and 7,206,600 bales; linseed, 297,700 and 427,600 tons; rape and mustard, 987,500 and 1,218,400 tons; sesamum, 464,300 and 516,000 tons; groundnuts, 484,700 and 413,700 tons; indigo, 38,800 and 39,600 cwts.; cane sugar, 1,872,900 and 2,125,300 tons.

Approximate yield of rice in 1911 265,182,000 metric quintals; in 1911 and 1912, wheat, 102,-016,109 and 99,862,179 quintals (figures for about 99.8 per cent. of total reported area under wheat in India); linseed, 5,726,441 and 6,514,893 quintals (figures for 96.6 per cent. of total reported area under linseed in British India and for certain Native States).

MINERALS. The value in 1909 and 1910, and the quantity in 1910, of the chief minerals produced in British India and the Native States are shown below:

	1909	1910	1910
Coal	£2,779,866	£2,445,453	12,046,189 tons
Gold	2,092,605	2,105,944	547,746 oz.
Manganese ore	603,908	849,455	800,907 tons
Petroleum.....	910,172	835,927	214,829,647 gals.
Salt	424,828	539,600	1,485,613 tons
Mica*	154,978	188,983	42,593 cwts.
Jadestone*...	91,401	99,601	6,165 cwts.
Rubies	64,826	58,849	262,019 kts.

* Exports.

Of the coal produced in 1910, the value of £2,000,446 is credited to Bengal; of the gold, £2,105,944 to Mysore; of the petroleum, £824,-962 to Burma, as well as all the jadestone and rubies; of the manganese ore, £621,127 to the Central Provinces; of the mica, £164,428 to Bengal.

COMMERCE. The foreign trade of India, for years ended March 31, has been valued as follows, in thousands of pounds sterling:

Sea-borne Trade	1909	1910	1911	1912
Imports:				
Private mdse.....	80,844	78,038	86,236	92,383
Government stores	5,008	3,727	2,901	3,654
Total mdse......	85,852	81,766	89,137	96,037
Private treasure..	15,088	24,951	26,469	35,615
Gov't treasure....	75	65	46	33
Total treasure..	15,163	25,016	26,515	35,648
Total imports...	101,015	106,781	115,652	131,685
Exports:				
Private mdse.:				
Domestic prod...	99,905	122,891	137,218	147,813
Foreign prod....	2,114	2,259	2,841	4,018
Total	102,019	125,151	140,059	151,831
Gov't stores.......	77	55	53	96
Total mdse.....	102,095	125,206	140,112	151,927
Private treasure..	3,971	4,262	4,746	6,907
Gov't treasure....	242	4	6	9
Total treasure..	4,213	4,266	4,752	6,916
Total exports...	106,309	129,472	144,864	158,843
Net exps. mdse...	16,243	43,440	50,975	55,890
Net imps. treas..	10,949	20,750	21,763	28,732
Excess exports...	5,294	22,691	29,212	27,158

The foreign trade is largely with Afghanistan and Nepal. As registration is difficult, the statistics are of doubtful accuracy. The reported figures are as follows, for imports and exports respectively (including treasure): 1908-9, £5,525,845 and £4,640,294; 1909-10, £5,637,912 and £4,544,697; 1910-11, £6,127,000 and £4,952,000; 1911-12, £6,920,000 and £5,885,-000.

Import and export values in the year 1911-12 were the largest on record. There was a notable increase in imports of cotton good, apparel, vehicles, railway materials, raw cotton, iron and steel, provisions, hardware and cutlery, petroleum, and woolen goods; but sugar, glass, machinery, and silk goods declined. In the export trade, there were large increases in rice, raw jute, seeds, hides and skins, millet, and pulse; raw cotton declined. Values of the leading sea-borne imports of private merchandise were as follows in 1911-12, in thousands of pounds sterling: Cotton goods, 30,519; cotton yarn, 2527; metals, 9540; sugar, 7955; railway materials, 2958; machinery, etc., 2838; mineral oil, 2828; hardware, etc., 2379; apparel, 2353; woolen goods, 2272; provisions, 2127; silk goods, 1769; raw cotton, 1391; liquors, 1293; carriages and carts, 1056; glass, 1029; spices, 1029; instruments, etc., 919; jewelry and plate, 844; dyes and tans, 841; paper, etc., 785; raw silk, 706; drugs, etc., 693; chemicals, 643; matches, 584; salt, 561. Principal sea-borne domestic exports in 1911-12, in thousands of pounds sterling: Raw cotton, 10,626; rice, 19,372; seeds, 17,960; raw jute, 15,038; jute manufactures, 10,671; wheat and flour, 9430; hides and skins, 9286; opium, 8726; tea, 8631; cotton yarn and cloth, 6519; pulse, millet, etc., 5509; raw wool, 1724; lac, 1343; fodder, etc., 1140; oils, 1061; coffee, 897; manures, 770; provisions, 723; wood, etc., 634; spices, 619; coal, etc., 514; raw silk, 306.

About 65 per cent. of the trade is with Europe and about 24 per cent. with Asia. Percentages shared by the leading countries in the imports and exports of private merchandise in 1911-12: United Kingdom, 62.4 and 26.0; Germany, 6.5 and 9.8; United States, 3.8 and 7.0; China (including Hongkong), 1.8 and 8.2; Japan, 2.5 and 7.5; France, 1.5 and 6.2; Belgium, 1.7 and 6.0; Java, 6.8 and 0.8; Straits Settlements, 2.' and 3.9; Austria-Hungary, 1.9 and 3.3; Ceylon, 0.5 and 3.7; Italy, 0.9 and 2.8; Mauritius, 1.4 and 0.3; other countries, 6.2 and 14.5.

SHIPPING. Vessels entered and cleared at the ports in the foreign trade in 1910-11, 8042, of 14,984,528 tons; in 1911-12, 8868, of 16,616,-435 tons. Of the latter tonnage about 55 per cent. was from or to the United Kingdom and British possessions; and 79 per cent. of the total trade was under the British flag. The chief ports are Calcutta, Bombay, Rangoon, Karachi, Madras, and Chittagong.

COMMUNICATIONS. Nearly all the railways in India are owned by the state and administered by a railway board, though many are leased to and operated by companies. The mileage open to traffic increased from 25,365 at the end of 1900 to 32,099 at the end of 1910 and 32,839 at the end of 1911. Under construction or sanctioned, on the latter date, 2674 miles. Of the mileage in operation, about 53 per cent. is standard gauge (5 ft. 6 in.) and about 42 per cent. meter gauge. Up to December 31, 1911, the capital outlay on the lines open to traffic amounted to £338,130,000 net earnings in 1911, £14,770,000, or about 4.37 per cent. on the capital outlay (against 5.46 in 1910, 4.81 in 1909, and 5.27 in 1901). After charging to expenditure interest on capital outlay of lines under construction or provided for, the net gain to the state from the working of the railways was £2,713,000 in 1911, against £1,992,000 in 1910 and £114,000 in 1909.

Reported length of government telegraph wires, March 31, 1911, 287,940 miles; capital cost to that date, £7,412,000. Post offices March 31, 1910, numbered 18,642. The post office in 1910-10 was operated at a net loss to the government of £353; in 1910-11, at a net profit of about £42,000.

FINANCES. The standard coin is the British sovereign, par value $4.86656, but the current coin is the rupee, par value 32.444 cents (15 rupees to the pound sterling). For British India, the gross revenue and the expenditure charged to revenue, in thousands of pounds sterling, were as follows in years ended March 31 (revised estimates for 1912):

	1901	1906	1909	1910	1911	1912
Rev...	64,724	70,842	69,762	74,593	80,682	82,039
Exp..	63,054	68,750	73,499	73,987	76,746	78,946

In addition to expenditure charged to revenue, there is an expenditure on railways and irrigation charged against capital. This has been as follows for fiscal years, in thousands of pounds sterling: 1901, railways 9325, irrigation 626; 1906, 22,463 and 869; 1909, 9519 and 1463; 1910, 6335 and 1497; 1911, 8915 and 1204.

Classified receipts (revised estimates for the fiscal year 1912), in thousands of pounds sterling:

	1909	1910	1911	1912
Land revenue	19,769	21,332	20,878	20,743
Opum	5,885	5,535	7,522	5,906
Salt	3,276	3,320	3,176	3,410
Stamps	4,344	4,548	4,812	4,781
Excise	6,390	6,538	7,030	7,647
Provincial rates	534	539	554	556
Customs	4,832	4,965	6,619	6,569
Assessed taxes	1,553	1,559	1,593	1,640
Forest	1,701	1,735	1,830	1,919
Registration	431	430	426	433
Tributes from Native States	590	588	607	598
Total	49,295	51,090	55,047	54,201
Interest	987	1,184	1,465	1,448
Post Office	1,826	1,927	1,997	2,122
Telegraphs	978	903	997	1,066
Mint	103	126	196	341
Civil departments	1,146	1,146	1,211	1,207
Military department	1,048	1,137	1,221	1,333
Railways (net)	9,958	12,445	13,881	15,285
Irrigation	3,558	3,660	3,695	3,977
Grand total, including other	69,762	74,593	80,682	82,039

Classified expenditures, in thousands of pounds (revised estimates for fiscal year 1912):

	1909	1910	1911	1912
Direct demands*	8,742	8,860	8,856	8,700
Interest	1,967	2,115	2,169	2,080
Post Office	1,897	1,928	1,951	2,037
Telegraphs	1,028	992	977	1,117
Mint	192	144	92	115
Civil depts:				
Gen. adm'tration.	1,695	1,656	1,756	2,652
Law and justice	3,687	3,610	3,718	3,810
Police	4,196	4,222	4,352	4,589
Education	1,682	1,705	1,846	2,012
Medical	1,018	968	983	1,160
Political	1,008	875	1,095	969
Total, inc. other	(14,489)	(14,186)	(14,931)	(16,408)
Superannuation	3,058	3 094	3,146	3,197
Famine relief and insurance	1,645	1,000	1,000	1,000
Ry. rev. account†	11,200	11,620	11,864	12,162
Irrigation	2,949	3,064	3,110	3,176
Army services	20,651	20,249	20,487	20,962
Total, inc. other	73,499	73,987	76,746	78,946

* Direct demands on the revenue—refunds and drawback, assignments and compensations, and collection charges, including production costs in the salt and opium monopolies. † The working expenses of railways are treated, not as expenditure, but as a deduction from revenue.

Total net revenue and total net expenditure charged against revenue (in which specific receipts that are properly offsets are deducted) have been as follows, in thousands of pounds (revised estimate for fiscal year 1912):

	1901	1909	1910	1911	1912
Net revenue	41,474	45,700	49,620	55,147	56,209
Net expend	39,804	49,438	49,013	51,211	53,116
Surplus	1,670	—3,738	607	3,936	3,093

Interest-bearing debt chargeable on the revenues and outstanding March 31, 1911: Sterling debt (raised in England), £182,981,751; rupee debt (raised in India), Rs. 1,24,84,19,400 (£91,049,347; total, £274,031,098. The total on March 31, 1912, was about £276,282,000 (sterling £182,970,000, rupee £93,312,000). Interest on debt, 1909-10, £8,752,399.

Government. The king of Great Britain and Ireland is emperor of India. In England, the administration of Indian affairs is intrusted to the secretary of state for India (a member of the British cabinet), who is assisted by a council. The expenditure of Indian revenues is determined by the secretary of state in council. The secretary of state for India in 1912 was the Marquis of Crewe (from November, 1910). In India the executive power resides in the "government of India," that is, the governor-general in council. In 1912 the governor-general, who is appointed by the crown for five years, was Baron Hardinge of Penshurst, who succeeded the Earl of Minto in 1910. The council consists of six members, appointed by the crown, and of the commander-in-chief of the army in India. The governor-general's legislative council, in addition to ex-officio members, consists of 28 official and 32 non-official members (including 25 elected). There are similar legislative councils in Madras, Bombay, Bengal Bihar and Orissa, the United Provinces, the Punjab, and Burma. British India is divided into fifteen local governments and administrations: Under governors, the presidencies of Madras, Bombay, and Bengal; under lieutenant-governors, the provinces of Bihar and Orissa, the Punjab, the United Provinces of Agra and Oudh, and Burma; under chief commissioners, the Central Provinces and Berar, Assam, Ajmer-Merwara, Coorg, British Baluchistan, the North-West Frontier Province, Delhi, and the Andamans and Nicobars.

The Native States are governed by their princes, ministers, or councils, but the government of India, through British residents or agents, exercises control in varying degrees and does not permit the states to maintain external relations.

Army. The army in India includes British regular forces, Indian regular forces, various local corps, British volunteers, Indian army reserves, imperial service troops, and military police. The regular forces, both British and Indian, form the first line, while the others serve as a second line or reserve. In 1912-13 the establishment of the British regiments serving in India amounted to 75,886 and included 9 regiments of cavalry, 11 horse artillery batteries, 42 field batteries, 3 howitzer batteries, 8 mountain batteries, 21 garrison artillery companies, 6 heavy batteries, 21 ammunition columns, 52 battalions of infantry, details of the Royal Engineers, Royal Army Medical Corps, and other special branches. The Indian army consisted of 3 regiments of body guards, 39 regiments of cavalry, and the Aden troops, a corps of guides, 12 mountain batteries, 1 frontier garrison company, 26 companies of sappers and miners, 117 infantry battalions, and 20 battalions of gurkhas. The auxiliary forces forming the second line consist of 66 volunteer corps, about 35,400 in strength. 33 imperial service corps, each under the supervision of British officers and trained for service by Indian princes to the number of about 21,000 men. These militia corps aggregating about 5000, and 21 corps of military police, aggregating about 28,500, are under civil control. The total strength of the military forces available in India was approximated at 352,784. The organization of the Indian army is on the basis of 9 infantry divisions and 8 cavalry brigades, each complete with staff and supply and transport facilities. The staff officers were being trained at the staff college at Quetta and during 1912 this work was in full operation. The tendency in the Indian army was to concentrate the forces in larger garrisons along lines of railway and to improve the material especially for the field artillery. The army was divided into two great commands, the Northern army, under Lieut.-Gen. Sir James Willcocks, K.C.M.G., with divisions at Peshawur, Rawal Pindi, Lahore, Meerut, and Lucknow, and brigades at Kohat, Derajat, and Bannu, and the Southern army, under Lieut.-Gen. Sir John Nixon, G.C.B., with divisions at Quetta, Mhow, Poona, Secunderabad, and Burma, and a brigade at Aden.

History

THE REMOVAL OF THE CAPITAL. The change of the capital from Calcutta to Delhi and the administrative reorganization that grew out of it was much discussed during the early part of the year. In the British Parliament the subject came up soon after its meeting. The opposition criticised the course of the government in this matter as arbitrary. Lord Curzon declared that it was setting up an autocracy and that it broke with the precedent which required that all great changes of this nature should receive, before they went into effect, full discussion in both houses. He complained of the radical course in turning the government out of Calcutta and feared that the result would be more serious than the government supposed. The government replied that the scheme had not been rashly adopted, but had been the subject of long consideration; that the main point was the opinion of India, and there the change had been hailed with great enthusiasm. The government of India bill providing for the change of the capital received the royal assent on June 25. In September it was provided that after October 1 Delhi, with its suburbs, should constitute a small chief commissionership to be administered by an official in the civil service under the government of India.

EDUCATIONAL EXPANSION. The royal grant of £333,300 for popular education, announced at the Coronation Durbar, was afterwards increased to £400,000. It was announced in February that a teaching university would be established in Dacca, and it was proposed that universities should be established in several other important centres. Progress was made in the plan for a Hindu university at Benares and for raising the college at Aligarh to the rank of a university. A bill according the local authorities the right to adopt compulsory education was defeated.

DACCA CONSPIRACY CASE. The famous Dacca conspiracy case at its first trial in 1911 resulted in a sentence of transportation for life upon three prisoners, transportation for ten years upon seventeen, and imprisonment for seven years upon fourteen. The case was appealed and judgment on the appeal was rendered on April 2, 1912. By this decision the sentences imposed on fourteen out of the thirty-four who appealed against conviction were upheld, though the terms were reduced. The rest of the prisoners were acquitted.

OTHER EVENTS. Fourteen persons were charged in February with complicity in conspiracy and murder and the court found nine of them guilty, imposing sentences of terms varying from one to seven years. In the latter part of May a European sub-inspector and three native police officers, who had been arrested on the charge of torturing accused persons, were convicted and punished for the crime. In July a royal commission was appointed to inquire into the condition of the Indian public services. There was much agitation among the Moslems over the reverses of Turkey in the Tripolitan and Balkan wars. Mass meetings were held at Delhi and Bombay and the Pan-Islam propaganda was carried on more actively. In March the Abor expeditionary force which was dispatched in October, 1911, for the purpose of punishing the murderers of Mr. Noel Williamson returned after successfully effecting this object. The cost of the expedition and political missions sent out at the same time was placed at £124,000. See EXPLORATION, and OMAN.

INDIA, DREDGING IN. See DRAINAGE.

INDIANA. POPULATION. The Census Bureau compiled during 1912 figures giving certain characteristics of the population of the State. These include statistics of white and colored population. Of a total population of 2,700,876 in 1910, 159,322 were foreign-born whites, compared with 141,861 in 1900. Of these, 62,177 came from Germany, 11,830 from Austria, 11,266 from Ireland, 9599 from Russia, 9780 from England, and 5081 from Sweden. Other countries of Europe were represented by smaller numbers. The negroes in the State in 1910 numbered 60,320 and the mulattoes, 14,553, compared with 45,215 negroes and 13,658 mulattoes in 1890.

AGRICULTURE. The acreage, value, and production of the principal crops in 1911 and 1912 are shown in the following table:

		Acreage	Prod. Bu.	Value
Corn	1912	4,947,000	199,364,000	$83,733,000
	1911	4,850,000	174,600,000	94,284,000
Wheat	1912	1,260,000	10,080,000	9,374,000
	1911	2,337,000	34,354,000	30,575,000
Oats	1912	1,990,000	79,799,000	23,940,000
	1911	1,640,000	47,068,000	20,239,000
Rye	1912	64,000	928,000	631,000
	1911	73,000	1,000,000	800,000
Potatoes	1912	87,000	9,918,000	4,959,000
	1911	89,000	5,162,000	4,491,000
Hay	1912	1,885,000	a 2,582,000	29,435,000
	1911	1,848,000	a 1,737,000	29,182,000
Tobacco	1912	18,700	b 14,960,000	1,346,000
	1911	22,000	b 20,020,000	1,561,000

a Tons. b Pounds.

MINERAL PRODUCTION. In 1911 there were produced in the State 14,201,355 short tons of coal, valued at $15,326,808. This was a decrease from the figures of 1910 of 4,188,460 short tons in quantity and $5,486,841 in value. The production in 1910 was abnormally large, owing to the strike in most of the Mississippi Valley States. The figures for 1911, however, show a decrease of 632,904 tons, compared with the output of 1909, which was not affected by strikes. During the year 21,182 men were employed in the coal mines of the State.

The production of petroleum in Indiana in 1911 was 1,695,289 barrels, compared with 2,159,725 barrels in 1910. The production in the State, which is a part of the Lima-Indiana oil field, has decreased steadily for several years. In 1907 it was 5,128,038 barrels.

MANUFACTURES. The Thirteenth Census statistics are for the calendar year 1909 and were compiled in 1912. It will be seen from the following table that in 1909 there were in the State 7968 manufacturing establishments,

utes to compel the President to exclude sectarian garb from Indian schools, and therefore if he permits such action he is violating no law. Furthermore, there are only 51 teachers wearing such garb in the Indian schools and this number ought not to be allowed to increase. While it is true that the Indian schools are public schools and ought not to be sectarianized, the situation in this particular case is a difficult and delicate one. The simplest solution would seem to be to allow the teachers now wearing ecclesiastical garb to remain and let the practice die out of its own accord, even if it is not altogether in harmony with American institutions.

SICKNESS AMONG INDIANS. The eightieth annual report of the commissioner of Indian affairs, comprising the fiscal year 1911, gives an interesting survey of the health conditions among the American Indians and the method used to educate them in matters of health and sanitation. The Office of Indian Affairs has a medical supervisor, 100 regular and 60 contract physicians, 54 nurses and 88 field matrons. The number of Indians receiving medical care is 310,926. Most of these are in Oklahoma, California, Arizona, New Mexico, and South Dakota. Emphasis is laid on the prevention of disease, although all possible care is given to actual sickness. Physicians secure detailed information about the living arrangements of each individual by going from house to house and from camp to camp, inquiring into sanitary conditions. This quickly awakens the Indians to the dangers of contagious disease and the suggestions and instruction which are given help them toward an improvement in living conditions and in improving insanitary surroundings. The trained physician is acquiring influence and prestige at the expense of the Indian medicine men, and in some cases the medicine man has become the ally and chief assistant of the physician. Stereopticon lectures and motion pictures are employed, and simple practical talks given on outdoor exercise, ventilation, disposal of garbage, clean milk and water, tuberculosis, and trachoma. Vaccination is becoming common among the Indians, and smallpox, formerly one of their worst scourges, has decreased amazingly.

TUBERCULOSIS AND TRACHOMA. Tuberculosis offers the most serious problem. The lack of hereditary immunity, the overcrowded and unventilated houses and the insanitary habits of the Indians all contribute to a high mortality rate. In the Fort Lapwai Reservation, Idaho, practically every family in the population of over 1400 has one or more tuberculous members. The Indian Office is enlarging its four tuberculosis sanatoriums; the one at Phœnix, Ariz., now accommodates 65 patients; the one at Laguna, N. M., 25; at Fort Lapwai, Io., 120. Trachoma stands next in importance to tuberculosis. In some sections of the Southwest from 65 to 95 per cent. of the Indians are affected. The trachoma specialists of the service have visited nearly every point in the Southwest, treating existing cases and instructing the local physicians in its prevention and treatment. At the trachoma hospital in Phœnix, Ariz., over 800 patients have been operated on and treated.

Dr. I. J. Murphy investigated health conditions on the Minnesota Indian reservations, inspecting every Indian settlement on the White Earth Reservation, and reports that a large proportion of the Indians are afflicted with tuberculosis of the lungs and glands. At the Pine Point Boarding School 74 per cent. of the pupils were affected with trachoma; 21 per cent. had corneal scars; 17 per cent. had tuberculous glands; 2 per cent. were suffering with tuberculosis of the spine, and 10 per cent. had suspicious lungs. Of the 16 families at Twin Lake settlement, numbering 65 persons, 5 were found to have pulmonary tuberculosis; 5, tuberculous glands, and 13, trachoma. At Elbow Lake settlement, with 54 inhabitants, 4 had pulmonary tuberculosis; 4, glandular tuberculosis, and 13 were afflicted with trachoma. At the Wild Rice River settlement 76 were inspected. Of these, 8 had tuberculosis of the lungs; 9, tuberculosis of the glands, and 24, trachoma. At the White Earth Boarding School, with an enrollment of 140 pupils, about 25 were found to have active tuberculous processes, and about the same number were suffering from trachoma.

Statistics gathered in the fiscal year 1912 show that out of 61,500 Indians examined, 8394, or 13.6 per cent., were suffering from tuberculosis, while 9254, or 15 per cent., were suffering from trachoma. The death rate among the Indians from all causes is estimated to be 30.24 per thousand, while the average death rate in the same area among white persons is 15 per thousand. A hospital was completed during the year at the White Earth Reservation and others are in progress of construction at Wahpeton, N. D., and Zuñi, N. M. The government attempts to suppress the illegal sale of liquor to Indians, but constant difficulties are encountered. An order was issued during the year providing for absolute prohibition of the use of liquor on Indian reservations. Although this prohibition has been theoretically in force for many years, it has not hitherto been enforced. See ANTHROPOLOGY.

INDIA RUBBER. See RUBBER.

INDO-CHINA, FRENCH. See FRENCH INDO-CHINA.

INDUSTRIAL COURTS. See ARBITRATION AND CONCILIATION, INDUSTRIAL.

INDUSTRIAL DISEASES. See OCCUPATIONAL DISEASES.

INDUSTRIAL DISPUTES INVESTIGATION ACT (1907). See ARBITRATION AND CONCILIATION, INDUSTRIAL.

INDUSTRIAL INSURANCE. See INSURANCE.

INDUSTRIAL RELATIONS, COMMISSION ON. See LABOR LEGISLATION.

INDUSTRIAL WORKERS OF THE WORLD. This is the name of the most conspicuous labor organization in the United States based on the principle of industrial unionism rather than on trade or craft unionism. The idea of organization by the industry rather than by the craft was made noteworthy in the United States by the American Railway Union, which conducted the Pullman strike of 1894. During the past decade the Western Federation of Miners, another industrial union, has been conspicuous in Colorado and other Western States. The Industrial Workers of the World was formed at Chicago in 1905 by delegates from the Western Federation of Miners, the United Metal Workers, the American Labor Union, other radical industrial unions, and the Socialist Trade and Labor Alliance.

They adopted a preamble containing the following: "The working class and the employing class have nothing in common. Between these two classes a struggle must go on until the workers of the world organize as a class, take possession of the earth and the machinery of production, and abolish the wage system. We find that the centring of the management of industries into fewer and fewer hands makes the trades unions unable to cope with the ever-growing power of the employing class. The trades unions foster a state of affairs which allows one set of workers to be pitted against another set of workers in the same industry, thereby helping defeat one another in wage wars. Moreover, the trades unions aid the employing class to mislead the workers into the belief that the working class have interests in common with their employers. These conditions can be changed and the interest of the working class upheld only by an organization formed in such a way that all its members in any one industry, or in all industries, if necessary, cease work whenever a strike or lock-out is on in any department thereof, thus making an injury to one an injury to all. Instead of the conservative motto, 'A fair day's wages for a fair day's work,' we must inscribe on our banner the revolutionary watchword. 'Abolition of the wage system.' It is the historic mission of the working class to do away with capitalism. The army of production must be organized, not only for the every-day struggle with capitalists, but also to carry on production when capitalism shall have been overthrown. By organizing industrially we are forming the structure of the new society within the shell of the old." Their plan called for the forming of thirteen large unions, each to include all the workers of a group of related industries, as food products, transportation, etc.

The next year the Western Federation of Miners and some other representatives of the Socialist party withdrew. In 1908 a further split occurred whereby members of the Socialist Labor party were ejected. The organization thus came under the control of the revolutionary wing of the American Socialists. They now have headquarters at Chicago. They claim about 160 local unions, with a total membership of 70,000. They also claim national organizations in Hawaii, Australia, New Zealand, and South Africa. Being antagonistic to the closed shop and the exclusive trade union, its dues are only one dollar per month. It makes no distinction of sex, creed, or color; and it refused all alliance, direct or indirect, with political parties. Those ejected in 1908 held a convention at Paterson, N. J., and formed a second organization, which now has headquarters at Detroit. They retained the preamble adopted in 1905. The Chicago branch, however, eliminated from that preamble all reference to political action, placing their complete confidence in the principle of direct action. For this reason they were branded as anarchists by the conservative Detroit I. W. W.

While both of these organizations showed unusual energy and grew rapidly in 1912, the Chicago group was much more conspicuous. It had charge of the Lawrence and Little Falls strikes (see STRIKES AND LOCKOUTS) and of numerous disturbances on the Pacific coast, notably the free-speech controversy at San Diego, Cal. The Detroit group was in charge of the strike in the Paterson silk mills.

It is the radical branch of this organization whose social theory is most like that of syndicalism (q. v.). They favor direct action; they express bitter hostility to the methods of orthodox trade unionism, such as arbitration, profit-sharing, trade agreements, and the ballot. They denounce typical unionists as tools of the capitalists. They preach discontent and the expropriation of capital goods. They differ from the socialists in placing no confidence whatever in the election of representatives to legislative bodies or to executive positions or any other form of political action. They do not fear revolution, for they claim to have nothing to lose but wage slavery. They believe the policy of direct action to be superior both in efficiency and in educative value. The strike is their favorite weapon, but they also use sabotage and the boycott. Probably all of the Detroit Industrial Workers of the World oppose violence, as do most of the Chicago Industrial Workers of the World. Their theory is that direct action will extend and intensify the spirit of class consciousness and prepare for the final act of the present capitalist system, the general strike. Thus the Industrial Workers of the World would place an industry in the hands of its workers, as would socialism; it would organize society without any government, as would anarchism; and it would bring about a social revolution by direct action of the workers, as would syndicalism. Nevertheless, it claims to be distinct from all three.

INERT GASES. See CHEMISTRY.

INFANTILE GASTRO-ENTERITIS. See THALASSOTHERAPY.

INFANTILE SPINAL PARALYSIS. See POLIOMYELITIS.

INITIATIVE AND REFERENDUM. See ELECTORAL REFORM.

INJUNCTION. See BOYCOTT.

INJURIES, OCCUPATIONAL. See OCCUPATIONAL DISEASES.

INNES, ALEXANDER TAYLOR. A Scotch theologian, died February, 1912. He was born in Tain, Scotland, in 1833 and received his education at Edinburgh University. After studying law he was admitted to the bar in 1870. In 1881 he was advocate-depute in Scotland under Gladstone and was reappointed in several following Liberal administrations. His chief interest, however, was in theology. He wrote *Law of Creeds in Scotland* (1867); *Church and State*, a historical handbook (1890); *Studies in Scottish History* (1892); *John Knox* (1896); *Trial of Jesus Christ* (1899), and *Scottish Churches and the Crisis of 1907*.

INORGANIC ISOMERISM. See CHEMICAL PROGRESS.

INSANITY. It is asserted that the number of insane persons is increasing out of proportion to the population, especially in the more populous cities and States, and probably the assertion is true, though the increased confidence in modern public provision for the mentally diseased and the willingness of the public to avail itself of hospital facilities may account for the figures. The New York State hospital commission (formerly the State commission in lunacy) reports on September 30, 1912, the number of committed insane and voluntary cases in State hospitals and committed insane in licensed private retreats as 33,972, including 16,271 men and 17,701 women. Of this number, 1272 were inmates of Dannemora and Matteawan, the hospitals for insane criminals, and 1076 were in private retreats. There were 813 on parole from civil hospitals. The net increase for the year in these hospitals was 573, as against 653 for the previous year, and 1119 for two years ago. During the year, 1753 were deported to other States and countries, as against about 1100 the previous year. The total number admitted in the fiscal year was 7336, of which number 5742 were first admissions, and 1594 were readmissions. From the 14 civil hospitals, 1610 were discharged as recovered, 1632 as improved, and 2690 died during the year. The recoveries reached 21.96 per cent., calculated on the admissions. The amount disbursed for maintenance was $6,240,882. Upon new buildings, extraordinary repairs, or equipment, or emergencies was expended the sum of $955,-887. The annual per capita for maintenance was $203.45, omitting the cost of lodging, as against $187 the previous year. The ratio of insane to population was 1 to 282 of the estimated population of the State. The chief contributing cause is alcohol, next to heredity. Syphilis is the determining cause in a large percentage of cases and stress and strain in a somewhat smaller number.

The Massachusetts State board of insanity reported on September 30, 1911, a total of 12,-287 patients, including 6158 males, and 6129 females; besides 14 men and 284 women under family care, total, 298; as well as 113 men and 216 women, total 320, in private institutions; making a grand total of 12,914, comprising 6285 men and 6629 women. These totals show an increase of 340 for the year, as compared with 522 the previous year, and with 508, the average increase for the past five years. Of the 340 increase, 9 represents the advance in the total for licensed private houses. Court commitments numbered 2970, and there were 206 voluntary admissions, compared with 162 the previous year. Of the 3207 admissions, 2565 were first cases, and of these, 44.65 per cent. were of foreign birth, and 66.81 per cent. were born of foreign fathers. Alcohol was found to be the causative factor in 19.06 per cent. and syphilis in 6.27 per cent. of first cases. The recovery rate was 13.47 per cent., based on the admissions. The ratio to the whole population of the State was 1 to 266.

The superintendent of the sole New Hampshire State Hospital reported on September 1, 1912, a population of 499 men and 458 women, making a total of 957, an increase of 32 patients over the previous year. The death rate was 11 per cent. The recovery rate was 30 per cent., based on the admissions. Of the 301 admitted during the year, 242 were first admissions, and of these 30 per cent. are of foreign birth. Heredity operated as the cause in 25.3 per cent., alcohol in 20.5 per cent., old age in 7.3 per cent. A State care act is to go into effect on January 1, 1913, under the provision of which all insane in public care will be placed in hospitals.

On September 30, 1911, the board of State charities of Indiana reported 5629 insane in the jails, representing an increase of 136 for the five State hospitals, county poo asylums and year. There were 80 fewer in jails and poor houses than a year ago. The ratio of insane is 1 to 480 of the inhabitants of the State. The State was redistricted for insane hospital purposes in June, 1911.

The State board of charities of Connecticut, in its biennial report for September 30, 1910, enumerated 3943 patients in the institutions for the insane, of which number 370 are in private asylums, and 300 mingled with town poor. This shows an increase of 340 in two years. The ratio to population is 1 insane person to every 282.5 inhabitants.

The figures for the fiscal year ending September 30, 1910, of the board of public charities and committee on lunacy of Pennsylvania are as follows: Total number of insane patients, 16,-624, showing an increase of 53,280 in 2 years. Of the whole number, 481 are insane criminals. The Adolf Meyer (New York State) classification was adopted in 1910.

The report of the commissioners in lunacy for England and Wales for January 1, 1912, states that 135,661 insane patients were under care, an increase of 2504 over last year. Of this number 4816 men and 6320 women were called "private patients," including those in county and borough asylums, in registered establishments (including idiots), in licensed houses (including idiots), in naval military hospitals, and "private single patients." Of the total stated, 123,400 (57,455 men and 65,-945 women) were "paupers"; and 1125 (857 men and 268 women) were insane criminals, 899 of these being sheltered in Broadmoor and Parkhurst. The proportion of insane to the estimated population is 1 to 269, against 1 to 275 a year previous, and 1 to 293 in 1902, showing a tendency to an increase in the proportion of the whole class of the pauper insane. Comparsion of increases in urban and suburban districts is rendered futile by changes in the boundaries of county boroughs. The number of discharged recovered in 1911 totaled 7326; as not recovered, 2428; as died, 10,050, exclusive of idots and of 74 recertified as transfers. The recovery rate reckoned on the admissions was 33.14 per cent., or 37.59 for females and 28.92 for males.

The commissioners for Scotland reported on January 1, 1912, an aggregation of 9401 men and 9633 women, a total of 19,034 insane, including imbeciles in training schools. The increase during the year was 398 souls. In private dwellings, specially licensed for 2, 3, or 4 patients, there were 1305 men and 1712 women, total, 3017. In the criminal institution at Perth, there were 47 men and 8 women, or 55 in all, of whom 10 are new admissions this year. The recoveries reached 39 per cent. of the private patients, and 38.4 per cent. of the paupers. There are 13 poorhouses in which "lunatic wards" are maintained.

The inspectors for lunatics for Ireland report on January 1, 1912, 12,868 men and 11,787 women, or in all 24,655 insane under care, representing an increase of 261 during the year. Of the total, 606 are in private licensed houses, 168 are in Dundrum (the criminal institution), and 144 are single chancery cases and other patients in unlicensed houses. Of the total, 1583 men and 1362 women, in all 2945, represent first admissions. Alcohol is rated as the cause in 10.3 per cent. of the cases, or in 21.5 per cent. of the patients from Dublin, Louth, and Wicklow. The percentage of recoveries based on the admissions was 40.7, or 4.2 per cent. higher than the previous year. The deaths reached 1487 during the year, 759 of these being men. The ratio to population is 1 insane person to 177 inhabitants.

INSCRIPTIONS. See PHILOLOGY, CLASSICAL.

INSECTS AND THE PROPAGATION OF DISEASE. As a result of a somewhat careful study of the common cockroach, Morrell believes that this insect is able by contamination with its feces (1) to bring about the souring of milk, (2) to infect food and milk with intestinal bacilli, (3) to transmit the tubercle bacillus, (4) to disseminate pathogenic staphylococci and destructive molds. These facts, taken in conjunction with the life-habits of the insect, lead to the conclusion that the cockroach is able to, and may possibly, play a small part in the dissemination of tuberculosis and in the transmission of pyogenic organisms; that the insect is in all probability an active agent in the souring of milk kept in kitchens and larders, and that it is undoubtedly a very important factor in the distribution of molds to food and to numerous other articles, especially when they are kept in dark cupboards and cellars where cockroaches abound.

The year 1912 was marked by a country-wide, and in places almost hysterical, crusade against the house fly, which has been charged by various observers with the dissemination of a long list of diseases, including cholera and various forms of dysentery, diphtheria, erysipelas, contagious ophthalmia, cerebrospinal meningitis, anthrax, and possibly smallpox, in addition to typhoid fever. Some of these charges require further investigation. In the case of typhoid fever, at least, the evidence seems conclusive, but Torrey issued a warning against centring popular attention on one source of contagion to the exclusion of other well-proven means of dissemination, such as direct contact and water pollution. "It is probable," says Chapin, "that under certain conditions, as in military and civil camps, and in filthy communities without sewerage, insects, especially flies, may be an important factor in the spread of fecal-borne disease, but there is no evidence that in the average city the house fly is a factor of great moment in the dissemination of disease." Torrey attempted to throw some light on the question by examining the bacterial flora of the flies caught in the densely populated parts of New York City during a series of months and over a range of weather conditions which might be expected to give suggestive data. Both the bacteria occuring in the intestine and those from the surface of the insects were investigated. Flies examined in April and early in June were free from fecal bacteria and carried a homogeneous flora of coccal forms. As the summer advanced, high bacterial counts began to appear, and also an abrupt change in the character of the bacteria, the cocci giving place largely to the bacilli characteristic of fecal matter. The record counts came at the end of the two weeks of excessive heat in July. The immense number of organisms that a single insect may carry is indicated by the figures 570 to 4,400,000 for the surface contamination, and 16,000 to 28,000,000 for the intestinal bacterial content. Further facts of interest given by Torrey regarding the prevailing types of bacteria indicate that organisms such as the *Streptococcus equinus*, *fecalis*, and *salivarius* group are found in the breeding and feeding places of the house fly. There were none of the pyogenes types. The most important isolations were three cultures of *B. paratyphosus*. Since this is pathogenic for man, the findings cannot be looked upon with indifference.

See Chapin, *The Sources and Modes of Infection*, New York; and J. C. Torrey, "Numbers and Types of Bacteria Carried by Flies," *Jour. Infect. Dis.*, 1912, No. 10.

INSURANCE. STATISTICS. The 1912 report of the superintendent of insurance of New York State showed that there were engaged in insurance in that State 192 fire, 21 marine, 34 life, and 60 casualty insurance companies. These 307 companies had, on December 31, 1911, total assets of $4,715,000,000 and total risks in force of $68,358,000,000. If to these figures had been added those of [illegible], livestock, coöperative fire, Lloyds, and fraternal insurance the total of risks would have approximated $80,000,000,000. The 34 life insurance companies had assets, $3,942,000,000; total income during 1911, $754,000,000; claims paid $232,000,000, besides dividends of $80,000,000 and payments for surrendered policies of $75,700,000; expenses, $135,000,000; total disbursements, $526,742,000; and 6,621,000 policies in force, representing $12,803,000,000 of insurance. These figures did not include the policies and risks represented by industrial insurance. The 11 New York State companies were credited with slightly more than one-half of the total number of policies and slightly less than one-half of the total amount of insurance in force. Industrial insurance companies doing business in New York State included the Metropolitan, the Prudential, the John Hancock, and the Colonial. They had a total of 22,926,000 policies in force December 31, 1911, representing total insurance of $3,199,000,000. Nearly 50 per cent. of this business was credited to the Metropolitan and about 40 per cent. to the Prudential. Stock fire insurance companies authorized in New York numbered 192, with a premium income amounting to $286,000,000; assets, $594,000,000; liabilities, including capital, $421,000,000; and insurance in force, $47,390,000,000. There were in addition 174 coöperative fire insurance companies in the State, with a premium income of $2,184,000 and total insurance of $495,000,000. Marine insurance companies numbered 21, of which 18 were foreign companies. These 21 had a total premium income of $14,645,000 and a total insurance in force of $656,000,000. Casualty, fidelity, surety, and credit companies numbered 60, with a total premium income, $93,972,000; assets, $145,000,000; liabilities, including capital, $109,000,000; claims paid, $37,000,000; expenses, $53,598,000. There were also 29 assessment, life, and casualty insurance companies doing business in New York State, with a premium income of $2,658,000 and total insurance of $460,980,000. The field of Lloyds and interinsurance was represented by 15 domestic companies, with premium income amounting to $3,416,000 and total insurance of $334,000,000. Ten title and mortgage guarantee companies reported an aggregate income of $6,429,000 and assets of $50,893,000. Fraternal societies authorized to do business in New York State included 75, having a total premium income, $79,000,000; total assets, $108,600,000; total liabilities, $14,600,000; and insurance in force, $6,379,000,000.

CURRENT PROBLEMS. State insurance departments, as represented in the national convention of insurance commissioners, have united in a crusade against holding and promoting companies. Investigations have shown that numerous concerns for the promotion of life insurance companies have been organized, the object being the profits of promotion rather than the establishment of new and stable insurance undertakings. Thus thousands of investors have been induced to invest in such speculations under the prospect of great immediate profits, only to find that the insiders made away with the proceeds of stock sales. The widespread interest aroused a few years ago as to the expenses and methods of industrial insurance companies still continued. An examination made by the New York superintendent of insurance into the Metropolitan Life Insurance Company, which issues about 50 per cent. of all industrial insurance, led to the conclusion that such insurance is still expensive, although the ratio of expenses to premium income fell from 43.7 per cent. in 1905 to 36.6 per cent. in 1911; that, although lapses are very numerous, due to the weekly payment system and the classes of persons insured, nevertheless a substantial improvement in the persistence of the business had been made; that the salaries of agents and clerks were only commensurate with ability and service demanded; and that, although the company makes enormous profits, these do not go to the stockholders, except for a 7 per cent. dividend, but are distributed among the persistent policyholders. The statistics noted above showed that nearly one-fourth of the whole population of the United States holds industrial insurance in the four leading companies. Weekly premiums are usually five cents or multiples thereof; the average premium is said to be ten cents; and the average policy slightly more than $140. The fact that this is insurance for the working population makes its regulation of the greatest importance. The examiner's report declared such insurance to be a necessity, but held that the government was not yet ready in this country to assume the administration of it. On December 24 the Metropolitan declared extra bonuses to policyholders of $6,281,000 over and above dividends.

Health and accident insurance have also been given unusual attention during the last two years. Investigation by a special committee of the national convention of insurance commissioners showed that, by means of "hyper-technical construction of so-called protection clauses in the contract," policyholders were frequently exploited. Their report said: "The policyholder public of the country—particularly those who through ignorance or poverty are unable to protect themselves, and therefore are peculiarly the wards of government—has too frequently been the victim of unconscionable practices in the claim departments of the companies criticised in this report." That report was given wide publicity and companies involved were compelled to make radical changes in their claim departments. There has resulted a nation-wide movement for increased statutory regulation of such companies. Another subject receiving current attention is the supervision of salesmen. The subject of insurance rates, particularly of industrial, fire, and casualty companies, was also under discussion. In general, it was said that insurance rates must be made acceptable to the public as representing compensation received or the movement for government insurance will become irresistible. In this connection there was demand that the expenses, which in some fields amount to more than 50 per cent. of the premium, should be reduced to the lowest level consistent with efficiency; otherwise insurance through government would be introduced. An analysis of the New York report for 1912 showed that the agents' commissions of the 192 companies there summarized amounted to over 23 per cent. of the total premium income. This was believed to be excessive. Some attention was given to the investments of insurance companies, it being pointed out that even the New York law is a mass of confusion. As to the standardization of policy contracts, it was pointed out that this has been achieved in fire and ordinary life insurance, but that chaos still reigns in industrial, health, and accident insurance, as also in liability, fidelity, credit, automobile, steel boiler, sprinkler leakage, burglary, fraternal and assessment life, and marine insurance. Other matters advocated by insurance commissioners were a campaign of popular education in the various branches of insurance and the development of means to reduce the lapsation of insurance in different fields. The Association of Life Insurance Presidents began in 1906 a policy of public education and publicity. This policy was adopted in 1912 by the National Board of Fire Underwriters, by the International Association of Casualty and Surety Underwriters, by the Detroit Conference (comprising companies writing industrial accident insurance), and by the National Fraternal Congress. All these have formed bureaus for educating the public. A movement has been started for the calculation of a new mortality table through the coöperation of the National Convention of Insurance Commissioners and the Actuarial Society of America.

MASSACHUSETTS SAVINGS BANK INSURANCE. The abstract of the combined reports of the insurance departments of the savings banks of Whitman, Brockton, Berkshire County, and Pittsfield for the year ending October 31, 1912, showed that 2590 policies, representing 924,505 insurances, were issued during the year. There were in force in all four banks 6652 policies aggregating $2,528,809 besides 82 deferred annuities representing annual payments of $11,026. The assets of the four insurance departments amounted to $331,794. The Berkshire County Savings Bank began the issue of policies in August, 1911, and the City Savings Bank of Pittsfield in July, 1912. Although the rates established by the State law under which this insurance is sold are lower than those of the industrial insurance companies with which the savings banks compete, the dividends declared by the latter in 1912 were substantial, ranging from 8⅓ per cent. of the premium on policies in force one year to 20 per cent. on policies in force five years. It was stated officially that the net cost ranged from 17 per cent. to 34 per cent. less than in the private companies. This mainly represents differences in cost, as the savings banks have no solicitors, but banks, stores, Y. M. C. A.'s, high schools,

the addition of a so-called ignition oil was necessary.

GAS TURBINES. German engineers were paying greater attention to the gas turbine during 1912, as was natural in the large high-speed rotative machinery, and the opinion was advanced that where fuel oils were abandoned this machine would revolutionize power production, especially in large steel centres. An experimental gas engine of large size operated in Germany was showing good mechanical results, although much remained to be done to secure satisfactory thermal efficiency.

UTILIZATION OF INDUSTRIAL WASTE GASES. The utilization of blast-furnace gas engines in blast-furnace and steel works was being rapidly extended in Europe and the use of coke-oven gas in gas engines to generate electric power was also taking place. Various problems connected with the latter class of machinery were being solved, especially the presence of sulphur in the coke-oven gases.

German builders of gas engines were improving their machines greatly in 1912, the valve gear was being simplified and the cranking of the gas cylinders was being reduced by better design and location of materials. While in operation the gas cylinders require cleaning at regular intervals and such care adds to their life and efficiency. By building them of cast iron instead of cast steel better results were being secured. Improvements were being made also in other features of the design and in the use of better grades of steel. The cost of producing electric power in electric blast-furnace and steel plants was estimated at about $2.70 per thousand kilowatt hours, comprising $1.25 value of the raw blast-furnace gas and includes cost of gas cleaning, cost of labor, repairs and supplies of all kinds, but does not involve interest and depreciation.

INTERNAL WATERWAYS. See CANALS.

INTERNATIONAL AMERICANIST CONGRESS. See ANTHROPOLOGY.

INTERNATIONAL CONCILIATION. See ARBITRATION, INTERNATIONAL.

INTERNATIONAL HARVESTER COMPANY. See TRUSTS.

INTERNATIONAL JOINT COMMISSION. See ARBITRATION, INTERNATIONAL.

INTERNATIONAL LANGUAGE. See LANGUAGE, INTERNATIONAL.

INTERNATIONAL LAW, AMERICAN SOCIETY OF. See ARBITRATION, INTERNATIONAL.

INTERNATIONAL LAW, INSTITUTE OF. See ARBITRATION, INTERNATIONAL.

INTERNATIONAL MERCANTILE MARINE CO. See GRISCOM, CLEMENT ACTON.

INTERNATIONAL METRIC CARAT. The international metric carat for weighing precious stones and gems was adopted unanimously by representatives of the largest firms in the American jewelry trade at a meeting held in New York on October 29. The resolutions adopted provided for the use of the international carat after July 1, 1913, and requested the Secretary of the Treasury to employ this standard in levying the duty on imported diamonds and other gems. The international carat is 200 milligrams, or one-fifth of a gram (3.086 grains), and in 1912 was in use in France, Germany, and practically all countries except the United States, Great Britain, Belgium, and Holland, where various carats corresponding approximately to 205 milligrams were employed, while elsewhere in Europe and Asia at the beginning of the twentieth century 20 different carats, ranging from the Bologna carat of 188.5 milligrams to the Arabian carat of 254.6 milligrams, were in use. The international carat was established at the suggestion of dealers in precious stones in Germany in 1905, and was straightway adopted by similar interests in France and other European countries. Hitherto American jewelers had used a carat corresponding to 205.2 milligrams, or approximately that of the British Board of Trade and of the jewelry trade of Antwerp, and dealing as they did with merchants in many foreign centres of trade the diversity had often proved most annoying. With the international carat not only would this lack of uniformity be done away with, but it would be possible to employ decimal subdivisions instead of sixty-fourths, and the actual weights for the balances could be made uniform and of the highest accuracy.

INTERNATIONAL TRADE. See articles on countries, industries, and crops.

INTERPARLIAMENTARY UNION See ARBITRATION, INTERNATIONAL.

INTERSTATE COMMERCE COMMISSION. See RAILWAY ACCIDENTS.

IONIZATION. See PHYSICS.

IOWA. POPULATION. According to the Census Bureau statistics issued in 1912, out of a total population in 1910 of 2,224,771, the foreign-born whites numbered 273,379, compared with 305,782 in 1900. The largest number of these, 98,620, came from Germany; from Sweden, 26,759; from Norway, 21,890; from Ireland, 17,754; from Denmark, 17,937; from England, 16,783; from Austria, 15,962; from Holland, 11,336, and from Canada, 10,548. Other European countries were represented by smaller numbers. In 1910 there were 14,973 negroes and 3644 mulattoes in the State. In 1890 the negroes numbered 10,685 and the mulattoes 3182.

AGRICULTURE. The acreage, value, and production of the principal crops in 1911 and 1912 are given in the following table:

		Acreage	Prod. Bu.	Value
Corn	1911	9,850,000	305,350,000	$161,836,000
Wheat	1911	647,000	10,622,000	9,348,000
Oats	1911	4,950,000	126,225,000	51,752,000
Rye	1911	30,000	540,000	416,000
Potatoes	1911	174,000	12,876,000	9,399,000
Hay	1912	3,537,000	a4,952,000	47,044,000
	1911	3,240,000	a2,592,000	32,400,000

a Tons.

COAL. The total production of coal in the State in 1911 was 7,331,648 short tons, valued at $12,663,507. This was a decrease from the production of 1910 by 596,472 short tons. The number of men employed in the coal mines of the State in 1911 was 16,599.

MANUFACTURES. The Thirteenth Census included statistics of manufactures in the State. These are for the calendar year 1909 and were compiled in 1912. The most important and interesting results of the census will be found in the table below. The industry in which the largest capital was invested was slaughtering and meat packing. The value of this product was $59,045,000, and the wage earners employed numbered 4144. In the manufacture of butter, cheese, and condensed milk the value of the product was $25,850,000 and the wage earners employed numbered 1231. The foundry and machine shop products were valued at $14,064,000 and gave employment to 5103 wage earners. The largest number of persons were employed in industries relating to cars and general shop construction, 6969. The value of the product of this branch of industry was $10,269,000. Other industries in which the product was valued at over $10,000,000 were. flour-mill and grist-mill products, $12,871,000; lumber and timber products, $12,659,000; printing and publishing, $12,129,000. The total number of wage earners in the industries of the State was 61,635, of whom 51,770 were male and 9865 female. The wage earners under 16 years of age numbered 1047, of whom 405 were females. The prevailing hours of labor ranged from 54 to 60 a week for three-fourths of the wage earners employed, 14 per cent. of the total being employed in establishments operating less than 54 hours a week and only 9.5 per cent. in establishments operating more than 60 hours a week. The cities having the largest number of wage earners were Des Moines, 5383; Dubuque, 5168; Davenport, 4231; Burlington, 4190, and in Sioux City, 3750. The principal results of the census are shown in the following table, with corresponding figures for 1904 and the increase of per cent. between 1904 and 1909:

	Number or Amount 1909	1904	P. C. of Inc. 1904-'09
Number of establishments	5,528	4,785	15.5
Persons engaged in manufactures..	78,360	61,361	27.7
Proprietors and firm members.	5,323	4,758	11.9
Sala'd employees	11,402	7,122	60.1
Wage earners (average number)	61,635	49,481	24.6
Prim'y horsepower	155,384	118,065	31.6
Capital	$171,219,000	$111,427,000	53.7
Expenses	233,364,000	143,692,000	64.4
Services	43,514,000	28,945,000	50.3
Salaries	10,972,000	5,948,000	84.5
Wages	32,542,000	22,997,000	41.5
Materials	170,707,000	102,844,000	66.0
Miscellaneous ..	19,143,000	11,903,000	60.8
Value of products	259,238,000	160,572,000	61.4
Value added by manufacture (value of products less cost of materials)..	88,531,000	57,728,000	53.4

FINANCE. The receipts for the fiscal year ending June 30, 1912, amounted to $4,983,448. The expenditures for the same period were $5,224,501, leaving, together with the balance at the beginning of the fiscal year, a balance at the end of the year of $1,041,486. The chief receipts are from county taxation, insurance taxes, and fees. The chief expenditures are for education, support of State institutions, and the State government. The State has no bonded debt.

CHARITIES AND CORRECTIONS. The charitable institutions under State control, with the enrollment of each in October, 1912, are as follows:

Cherokee State Hospital (for insane), Cherokee, 980; Clarinda State Hospital (for insane), Clarinda, 1146; Independence State Hospital (for insane), Independence, 1143; Mt. Pleasant State Hospital (for insane men and women and inebriate women), Mt. Pleasant, 1093; School for the Deaf, Council Bluffs, 216; Soldiers' Orphans' Home, Davenport, 521; Institution for Feeble-minded Children, Glenwood, 1354; State Hospital for Inebriates, Knoxville, 152; Soldiers' Home, Marshalltown, 711; State Sanatorium for the Treatment of Tuberculosis, Oakdale, 110. In addition to these, 95 out of 99 counties in the State have county homes, and in these there are about 2450 insane and poor persons. There are also 27 institutions for friendless children, in which nearly 3000 children are cared for. The Mercy Hospital at Davenport, St. Bernard's Hospital at Council Bluffs, St. Joseph's Sanitarium at Dubuque, and The Retreat at Des Moines are private institutions at which insane persons are cared for. These institutions are inspected semiannually by the board of control. The correctional institutions with their population in 1912 are as follows: Industrial School for Boys at Eldora, 363; Industrial School for Girls at Mitchellville, 168; the Reformatory at Anamosa, 649; State Penitentiary at Ft. Madison, 481.

POLITICS AND GOVERNMENT

Political interest was heightened in Iowa by the fact that Senator Cummins on January 20 announced his candidacy for the Republican presidential nomination. In the convention held on April 24 for the election of delegates-at-large to the Republican national convention, the four delegates-at-large were instructed to vote for President Taft. Senator Cummins was unable to secure the full number of district delegates. President Taft was given 12, while Senator Cummins received 10. By a vote of 764 to 720 resolutions were adopted at the State convention indorsing and praising the administration of President Taft. In spite of this failure to receive a unanimous indorsement, Senator Cummins remained a candidate until the session of the national convention. Following the convention he issued a statement in which he expressed his intention to vote for Mr. Roosevelt. This was due, he said, to a careful analysis made of the election contests before the convention, by which he arrived at the conclusion that many of the delegates had been wrongfully awarded to President Taft. Although he expressed his intention to vote for Mr. Roosevelt, he said that it must be understood that he would do so protesting against the organization of a third party and dissenting from some of the doctrines of the new platform. He said: "My vote for him will indicate that I believe he desires to promote the common welfare, but will not indicate that I look upon the new party as a wise or an enduring movement in public affairs." On May 16 the Democratic State convention instructed the 26 delegates from Iowa to vote for Clark.

On June 3 a senatorial primary was held. The term of Senator Kenyon, who was elected to fill the vacancy caused by the death of Senator Dolliver in 1911, expired in 1913. Opposed to Senator Kenyon, who was a candidate for reëlection, was Senator Lafayette Young, one of the Taft leaders of the State. In this election Senator Kenyon won over Mr. Young by a plurality of about 75,000 votes. Following his defeat, Mr. Young issued a statement in which he declared that stand-patism was dead and might as well be buried. He abandoned his support of President Taft and declared that the State should support Senator Cummins.

Following the Republican national convention the Progressives in the State were for some time doubtful whether they would nominate candidates for State offices. It was finally decided to do so, and on September 4 Judge John L. Stevens was nominated for governor. The Republican nominee was Lieutenant-Governor Clark and the Democratic candidate Edward G. Dunn. The political situation was complicated by the fact that while Senator Cummins and his friends supported Mr. Roosevelt, Senator Kenyon, who was also a Progressive, declared himself for the whole Republican ticket, including President Taft, at the same time denouncing the methods by which the President secured his nomination. The election on November 5 resulted as follows: Wilson, 185,376; Roosevelt, 161,783; Taft, 119,811; Debs, 15,914 Chafin, 8437. For governor, Clark, Rep., received 184,148 votes; Dunn, Dem., 182,449, and Stevens, Progressive, 71,877. A Republican legislature was elected, making it certain that Senator Kenyon would be reelected in 1913.

STATE GOVERNMENT. Governor, G. W. Clark; lieutenant-governor, W. L. Harding; secretary of State, W. S. Allen; treasurer, W. C. Brown; auditor, J. L. Bleakly; attorney-general, George Cosson; superintendent of education, A. M. Deyoe; adjutant-general, Guy E. Logan—all Republicans.

JUDICIARY. Supreme Court: Chief justice, S M. Weaver; judges, Scott M. Ladd, E. R. Gaynor, William D. Evans, Horace E. Deemer, B. W Preston; clerk, Burgess W. Garrett—all Republicans.

STATE LEGISLATURE, 1913. Republicans, Senate, 31; House, 71; joint ballot, 102. Democrats, Senate, 17; House, 33; joint ballot, 50. Republican majority, Senate, 14; House, 38; joint ballot, 52.

IOWA, STATE UNIVERSITY OF. An institution for higher education at Iowa City, Ia., founded in 1847. The total number of students enrolled in the various departments of the university in the autumn of 1912 was as follows: Liberal arts, 1020; law, 210; medicine, 95; homœopathic medicine, 13; denistry, 174; pharmacy, 47; graduate school, 109; school of applied science, 168; fine arts, 67; nursing, 70; homœopathic nursing, 14. The faculty numbered 220, of whom 155 were actually engaged in teaching and 65 were assistants and executives. Among the noteworthy changes in the faculty was the appointment of Henry W. Dunn to succeed Austin W. Scott as dean of the College of Law; the appointment of W. A. Jessup to succeed F. E. Bolton as head of the Department of Education, and the appointment of J. A. Mars to succeed Captain M. C. Mumma. A gift of $1000 was received from George E. MacLean, former president of the university, for a fund, to be known as the student revolving loan fund. The productive funds of the university amount to $240,845, and the income from the productive funds $11,167. The library contains 98,000 volumes. President, John G. Bowman, M. A.

IPSWICH SKELETON. See ANTHROPOLOGY.

IRELAND. See GREAT BRITAIN.

IRON AND STEEL. The production of iron and steel in 1911, as noted below, is general in its nature. The production of the several States may be found in the paragraph *Mineral Production* under those States. The figures are taken from the report of the United States Geological Survey.

In 1911 there was a decided decrease in the production of iron ore, pig iron, and steel in the United States as compared with the production in 1910. This was due primarily to the fact that there was a large overproduction in 1910, and, secondarily, to a lessening in the demand. Buying on the part of railroads and for new equipment of manufacturing plants was curtailed. These conditions were foreshadowed in the last four months of 1910 and lasted well into the second half of 1911. In the closing months of that year, however, recovery was rapid and by the end of the year there was a decidedly more hopeful tone. Iron was mined in twenty-seven States during 1911. Of these, four, Idaho, Montana, Nevada, and Utah, produced ores for fluxing only. Part of Colorado's production was for fluxing and part for pig iron. In Michigan was produced a very small quantity for fluxing and a small quantity was produced in Missouri for special fluxing use. The other States produced ores for blast-furnace use. The total production in 1911 was 40,989,808 long tons, valued at $86,419,830, compared with 56,889,734 long tons, valued at $140,735,607, in 1910. As in 1910, Minnesota ranked first, with 23,398,406 long tons. This was a considerable decrease from the production of 1910, which was 31,966,769 long tons. There were produced in Michigan 8,944,393 long tons, compared with 13,303,906 in 1910; in Alabama 3,955,582 long tons in 1911, compared with 4,801.275 in 1910; in New York, 1,057,984 long tons, compared with 1,287,209 in 1910. The table below gives the production by States and the value of the product in 1910-1911:

State	1910 Quantity, in long tons	1910 Value	1911 Quantity, in long tons	1911 Value
Alabama..	4,801,275	$6,083,722	3,955,582	$4,876,106
Georgia...	313,878	482,659	207,279	315,704
Kentucky and West Virginia..	64,347	86,085	71,979	92,575
Maryland and North Carolina..	79,840	143,842	92,382	161,929
Michigan ..	13,303,906	41,393,585	8,944,393	23,808,935
Minnesota.	31,966,769	78,462,560	23,398,406	48,447,760
Missouri..	78,341	168,697	72,788	153,676
New Jersey	521,832	1,582,213	359,721	1,158,271
New York	1,287,209	3,848,683	1,057,984	2,969,009
Ohio......	22,320	35,866	16,897	30,549
Penn'vania	789,799	911,847	514,929	539,553
Tennessee	732,247	1,048,323	469,728	632,339
Texas.....	29,535	34,003	....	....
Virginia...	903,377	1,845,144	610,871	1,146,188
Wisconsin	1,149,551	3,610,349	559,763	1,386,616
Other States....	896,008	998,529	657,306	710,620
Total....	56,889,734	140,735,607	40,989,808	86,419,830

During 1911, 374 ore mines reported sales or consumption of ore; 159 mines produced over 50,000 long tons of iron ore each, compared with 191 mines in 1910. The largest quantity produced from any single mine in 1911 was 1,553,510 long tons, from the Hill mine at Marble on the Mesabi range, Minnesota. These mines in Minnesota produced more than 1,000,000 tons each.

PIG IRON. The production of pig iron in 1911 in the United States amounted to 23.257,288 long tons, valued at the furnaces at $327,234,624, as compared with 26,674,123 long tons, valued at $412,162,486, in 1910, a decrease in quantity of 3,416,835 tons and in value of $84,827,862. The average value per ton in 1911 was $14.07, as compared with $15.45 in 1910.

The quantity and value of the production in 1910-11 are shown in the following tables:

State	1910 Quantity	1910 Value	1911 Quantity	1911 Value
Alabama	1,369,770	$24,127,814	1,817,150	$17,272,171
Illinois	2,606,435	11,466,543	2,036,681	21,152,327
Kentucky	81,817	1,312,228	57,282	870,542
Michigan	297,375	5,119,071	244,664	4,572,799
N. Jersey	239,221	3,737,656	(a)	(a)
New York	1,893,413	31,593,623	1,537,201	22,924,134
Ohio	5,551,270	85,233,234	5,271,378	73,484,592
Penn	11,616,652	174,486,833	9,381,109	126,228,507
Tennessee	400,759	6,133,092	297,594	3,439,644
Virginia	402,625	5,576,509	249,789	3,898,285
Wisconsin	278,433	4,246,859	216,152	3,302,049
Other States	1,891,670	29,412,942	1,900,198	28,380,914
Total	26,674,123	412,162,486	23,257,288	327,334,624

a Included in other States.

It will be seen from this table that the largest quantity was produced in Pennsylvania, followed by Ohio, Illinois, and Alabama.

The commercial capacity of the blast furnaces of the United States on December 31, 1911, was estimated at 33,402,000 tons a year. Four new blast furnaces with a total capacity of 600,000 tons were added during 1911, compared with 13 new blast furnaces with a capacity of 1,791,000 tons in 1910. The total number of furnaces on December 31, 1911, was 466, of which 231 were in blast and 235 were out.

STEEL. The total production of steel in 1911 in the United States was 23,675,501 long tons. Of this, 7,947,819 long tons were Bessemer, 15,598,650 open hearth, 97,653 crucible, and 63,419 other steel. In the production of steel Pennsylvania occupied first place, with 9,594,911 long tons of open hearth, steel ingots and castings, and 2,338,613 tons of Bessemer ingots and castings.

IMPORTS AND EXPORTS. The quantity of iron ore imported into the United States in 1911 was 1,811,732 long tons, valued at $5,419,030, compared with 2,591,033 long tons, valued at $7,842,223 in 1910. The largest quantity was imported from Cuba, 1,147,879 long tons. Considerable quantities were brought from Sweden, Spain, Newfoundland, and Canada. The quantity of iron ore exported from the United States in 1911 was 768,350 long tons valued at $2,633,138, or $3.43 per ton. This was a slight increase over the amount exported in 1910.

IRON ORE. The production of iron ore in the United States in 1912 was much greater than in the preceding year. The year was memorable in the iron and steel industries for the rapid recovery from depression, accompanied by an increased production which raised the total outputs of nearly all forms to a higher level than had ever before been reached. The production in 1912, as given by the Engineering and Mining Journal, was as follows:

Lake Superior, 48,410,177 tons; Southern States, [illegible] tons; other States, [illegible] tons.

[illegible] The production of pig iron in the United States in 1912 was considerably in excess of that of 1911. The output in 1912 was 29,847,274 short tons, according to the *Engineering and Mining Journal*.

STEEL. Figures for the year's production of steel were not available at the end of 1912. Statistics were made up, however, for the first half of the year. The production for that period was 14,373,701 tons. The production for the second half of the year was undoubtedly greater than that of the first half, according to the estimates of the *Engineering and Mining Journal*. That authority estimates the finished rolled product of 1912 as probably exceeding 29,500,000 tons. The most notable gain was in structural steel in plates, bars, and rails. See METALLURGY.

IRON AND STEEL TARIFF. See TARIFF.

IRRIGATION. Throughout the world generally the year 1912 was one of considerable activity in the extensions of irrigation to new areas, but in the United States few new enterprises were undertaken, the extension being principally in increasing the areas irrigated under works already built. The progress of the year in different parts of the world is given in detail below:

UNITED STATES. As stated, the activity in the undertaking of new irrigation enterprises, and in the construction of new works, which has been so noticeable for a few years past, has almost ceased. The reports of the census of 1910 showed clearly that irrigation construction had far outrun settlement, and it seems likely that the next few years will be a period of adjustment in which the land under existing works will be gradually brought under cultivation. The census of 1910 showed the total acreage irrigated in the arid region of the United States in 1909 to be 13,738,458 acres, which was an increase of 82.7 per cent. over the acreage irrigated in 1899. Assuming that the same rate of increase continued, the acreage irrigated in 1912 would have been slightly more than 17,000,000 acres. In view of the decreased activity in construction, it is probable that the acreage actually irrigated in 1912 is considerably less than the figures just given. The greater part of this acreage, probably 90 per cent., is supplied with water by works controlled by the water users, either individually, or in some organized form of coöperation. The report of the United States Reclamation Service, which is building irrigation works under the law of June 17, 1902, setting aside the receipts from the sale of public lands for that purpose, for the fiscal year ended June 30, 1912, showed that this fund amounted in 1912 to $75,059,201.14, to which should be added a loan from the treasury of $20,000,000, making the total fund slightly over $95,000,000. Of this there has been expended to June 30, 1912, $74,364,767. The total acreage in reclamation projects was 3,020,689 acres, to 1,188,330 acres of which the service was ready to supply water in 1912. The acreage covered by water-right applications and rental agreements for the season of 1912 was 823,734 acres, leaving 432,328 acres to which water could be supplied in excess of the acreage covered by applications and agreements.

The decreasing activity in the undertaking of new enterprises is shown further by the limited operations under the Carey act [illegible] August

18, 1894, granting desert lands to the States on condition that they provide for their irrigation) during the year 1912. During the year ending June 30, 1912, there were applied for under this law 184,697 acres, while during the last preceding year the area applied for was 975,529 acres, and the area segregated during the year ending June 30, 1912, was but 97,917 acres, against 328,795 acres in the preceding year. The area patented in the last year was 85,596 acres, and in the preceding year 60,540 acres. The total area applied for under this law to June 30, 1912, was 7,301,037 acres, the area segregated 3,291,231 acres, and the area patented 474,000 acres.

The Philippine government is undertaking the construction of a number of irrigation enterprises and has created an "Irrigation Council," composed of the secretary of commerce and police, the chairman of the committee on agriculture of the Philippine assembly, the director of public works, and the chairman of the committee on public works of the Philippine assembly. In addition to the projects being carried out by the government, individual farmers are developing small projects.

FOREIGN COUNTRIES. In the Northwest provinces of Canada, construction of new works is much less active than it was a few years ago. The province of British Columbia is giving much attention to a revision of its laws and a general study of the organization of irrigation enterprises, with a view to providing for more successful reclamation of its arid lands. Irrigation extension in Mexico, which was receiving considerable attention from the government, which enacted laws providing for loans in aid of irrigation construction, has been halted to some extent by the unsettled conditions in that country. Notwithstanding this, some large concessions have been granted, and projects are under way. A large project taking water from the Conchos River in Chihuahua, is under construction, to provide water for about 1,000,000 acres, to be used for the growing of cotton, corn, beans, and alfalfa.

Of the South American countries, Argentina shows the greatest activity in irrigation development. A few years ago the Argentine government adopted a policy of government aid in the construction of irrigation works, and still maintains this policy. During 1912 a new project in the province of San Luis, to cost $5,000,000, was authorized, as was a new project in the province of Cordoba, to cost $1,500,000. Other projects already authorized have been delayed because bids for their construction have run far above the government estimates of cost. The Argentine g ernment is investigating the possibilities of dyrigation in Patagonia. The Chilean government is making plans for the irrigation of 172,970 acres in the central valley of Chile, at a cost of $924,000, and for another project farther north which will include 50,000 acres. The Republic of Brazil is giving considerable attention to irrigation, but without much result. Schemes for federal and state aid are proposed and bills have been introduced in the federal congress embodying these schemes, but have not become laws.

The enlargement of the Assuan Dam on the Nile, is to be completed in 1912, and should provide a largely increased supply of water for perennial irrigation in 1913. Much of this water is to be used on the Delta lands, which require drainage as well as irrigation. The Egyptian government has undertaken the drainage of these lands and has authorized the expenditure of $13,000,000 in this work. It is necessary to dike the land and pump the drainage water from the drains. The land is to be devoted to cotton. At Cairo, experiments in the use of sun-power engines for pumping water for irrigation are being conducted. The Turkish government is continuing its efforts toward the reëstablishing of irrigation in Asiatic Turkey. During the year 1912, preliminary contracts have been let for the irrigation of 1,000,000 acres in the Meander Valley, and for 1,200,000 acres in the Adana Plain. In India, the British government is increasing its expenditures for irrigation works from year to year, the amounts allotted for this purpose for the year 1911-12 being $9,310,280 for major works, and $4,152,320 for minor works. Up to March 31, 1911, the British government had spent on irrigation works in India $155,712,000, and built 58,251 miles of main and branch canals, commanding 48,000,000 acres, about 20,000,000 acres of which is cultivated. There are now under construction, awaiting sanction or under examination, fifty-five government projects, the estimated cost of which is $181,600,000. The "productive" government irrigation enterprises in India have yielded a return of 7.66 per cent. on the capital invested in them. The government of Siam is undertaking extensive irrigation works and has employed an American irrigation engineer to take charge of this work.

The first meeting of the South African Irrigation Association was held in Bloemfontein November 16, 1911. The time of this meeting was taken up principally with the discussion of a proposed law regulating the use of water from streams throughout the union. It was claimed that irrigation development was being retarded by existing laws, and the new law was designed to remove these hindrances. The South African governments are encouraging irrigation development by giving advice to farmers and by making surveys, etc., but have not yet done construction work on any large scale.

IRWIN, JOHN ARTHUR. An American physician, died June 1, 1912. He was born in Ireland in 1853 and was educated in Dublin University. He studied medicine at the College of Physicians. For a number of years he acted as surgeon in several hospitals in England. In 1882 he removed to the United States and was for ten years physician to the St. George's Society in New York City. He was president of the British Schools and Universities Club, and a member of several European and American medical societies. Among his professional writings are: *Hydrotherapy at Saratoga; Pathology of Seasickness*, etc. He was an editorial writer for the *British Medical Journal*, the London *Lancet*, the New York *Medical Record*, and the Philadelphia *Medical News*.

ISHOMOTO, SHIAROKU. A Japanese statesman, died April 2, 1912. He was born in 1854. He entered the military service and rose through successive promotions to be major-general in 1898, and lieutenant-general in 1904. In 1903 he was made vice-minister of war. For many years he was director of the Tokyo arsenal, from which he was transferred to his position in the war department.

ISOMERISM. See CHEMISTRY.

ITALIAN SOMALILAND. An Italian colony and protectorate. Area 365,400 square kilometers (141,081 square miles); population, about 300,000. Mogadisho is the seat of the civil governor (1912, Signor de Martino). Imports (1908-9), 2,788,283 lire; exports (butter, hides, timber, durrha), 1,567,760.

ITALY. A southern European constitutional monarchy, composed of the Apennine Peninsula and the islands of Sicily and Sardinia. Rome is the capital.

AREA AND POPULATION. The area, in square kilometers (according to the calculations of the Military Geographical Institute), the number of provinces in each compartimento, the population as taken at the census of June 10, 1911, and the gain or loss over the population of February 10, 1901, are given, by compartimenti, in the following table:

	Sq. kms.	P.	1911 Pop.	Increase
Piedmont	29,367	4	3,424,538	107,137
Liguria	5,278	2	1,196,853	119,380
Lombardy	24,085	8	4,786,907	504,179
Venetia	24,547	8	3,526,655	392,188
Emilia	20,701	8	2,667,510	222,475
Tuscany	24,105	8	2,694,453	145,311
The Marches.....	9,712	4	1,088,875	28,120
Umbria	9,709	1	685,042	17,832
Rome	12,081	1	1,298,142	101,233
Abruzzi e Molise	16,529	4	1,427,642	—13,909
Campania	16,295	5	3,347,925	187,477
Apulia	19,109	3	2,128,632	168,964
Basilicata	9,962	1	473,119	—17,586
Calabria	15,075	3	1,404,076	33,868
Sicily	25,739	7	3,683,380	153,581
Sardinia	24,109	2	852,934	61,180
Total	286,682*	69	34,686,683	2,211,430

* 110,688 square miles.

The population given above is the population actually present at the date of the census, the total legal (*de jure*) population on that day was 35,959,077. All the 1911 census figures here given are subject to slight revision. Rome had a communal population of 538,634; Naples, 723,208; Milan, 599,200; Turin, 427,733; Palermo, 341,656; Genoa, 272,077; Florence, 232,860; Catania, 211,699; Bologna, 172,639; Venice, 160,727; Messina, 126,172; Ferrara, 95,196; Ravenna, 71,690; Modena, 70,267. Infant, primary, normal, and secondary schools are maintained.

AGRICULTURE. In the table below are given the area in hectares sown to principal crops and the yield, in quintals (1911 and 1912), with the yield per hectare in 1911 (wheat, rye, barley, oats, corn late crop, rice, flax, sugar beets, vines, tobacco, olives:

	Hectares		Quintals		Qs.
	1911	1912	1911	1912	ha.
W.	4,751,600	4,755,400	52,362,000	45,102,000	11.0
R.	122,290	123,350	1,345,600	1,342,500	11.0
B.	247,600	244,300	2,369,400	1,829,500	9.6
O.	514,160	507,600	5,947,300	4,108,700	11.6
C.	1,550,200	1,508,000	22,832,000	23,500,000	14.7
R.	144,500	145,500	4,792,200	4,400,000	33.2
F.	14,780	18,500	86,600*	87,000*	5.9*
B.	53,120	53,000	14,404,000†	15,500,000†	271.2†
V.	4,477,200	4,455,000	42,654,100‡	43,000,000‡	9.5‡
T.	8,800	9,000	....	180,000	...
Ol.	2,344,680	....	14,100,000	1,930,000¶	...

* Seed: yield of fibre, 27,570 qs. in 1911 (1.9 qs. per ha.) and 25,000 qs. in 1912. † Beets, yield of raw sugar, 1,680,000 qs. in 1911 (31.6 per hectare of beets) and 1,700,000 qs. in 1912. ‡ Yield in hectoliters of wine. ¶ Hectoliters of oil in 1911.

Livestock (1908): 849,723 horses, 388,337 mules, 6,198,861 cattle, 19,266 buffaloes, 11,162,926 sheep, 2,714,878 goats, 2,507,798 swine. The forest products were valued in 1909 at 124,132,000 lire. See AGRICULTURAL EDUCATION.

MINING, ETC. Following are the productive mines in operation, the number of operatives, the output in metric tons, and the value in lire, in 1910:

	No.	Op.	Tons	Lire
Iron	18	1,741	551,259	7,619,031
Ferra-mang. ...	1	97	25,700	179,356
Manganese	9	174	4,200	134,793
Copper	7	1,411	68,369	1,036,674
Lead			36,540	5,303,855
Zinc	81	12,313	146,307	14,803,100
Lead and zinc..			300	3,600
Silver	1	61	32	42,400
Gold	4	92	2,147	58,730
Antimony	4	297	2,194	149,769
Mercury	9	994	87,129	3,729,352
Tin	1	52	170	41,000
F. & c. pyrites	9	1,809	165,688	2,864,531
Coal, etc........	39	3,172	562,154	4,925,950
Sulphur	396	21,201	2,815,511	32,383,409
Asphalt & bit..	20	1,712	162,669	2,326,670
Boric acid......	11	406	2,502	900,720
Graphite	26	326	12,512	354,290
Other	..	.....	......	......
Total	677	47,930	......	80,367,479

The output from the quarries was valued (1910) at 54,567,420 lire; from lime and brick kilns, at 167,988,073. Fisheries products (1909), at 3,485,000 for tunny, and 22,407,000 for other fish.

COMMERCE. The imports for consumption and exports of domestic produce, merchandise, and coin and bullion, are given below for three years, 1911 provisional (values in lire):

	1909	1910	1911
Imps. mdse..	3,111,710,447	3,245,975,961	3,358,093,630
" C. & B.*	18,000,800	31,065,700	28,896,500
Total	3,129,711,247	3,277,041,661	3,386,090,130
Exps. mdse..	1,866,889,562	2,079,977,376	2,169,312,488
" C. & B.*	54,067,700	48,116,400	42,091,900
Total	1,920,957,262	2,128,093,776	2,211,404,388

* Includes all precious metals.

Total general trade in 1910: 3,477,704,897 lire imports and 2,236,944,024 lire exports. In the next table are seen the great classes (special trade) of merchandise for two years (1911 provisional), in thousands of lire (A=beverages, spirits, and oils; B, colonial products, tobacco, etc.; C, chemical products, drugs, resins, and perfumes; D, colors, dyes, and tanning materials; E, hemp, flax, jute, and other fibrous plants, excepting cotton; F, cotton; G, wool, horsehair, etc.; H, silk; I, wood and straw; J, paper and books; K, hides and skins; L, minerals, metals, and their manufactures; M, vehicles; N, stone, earths, pottery, glass and glassware; O, rubber, etc., and manufactures; P, cereals, flour, paste, and certain vegetable products; Q, animals, animal products, and certain wastes; R, miscellaneous; T, total):

	Imports		Exports	
	1910	1911	1910	1911
A	87,667	100,601	177,987	136,775
B	76,275	81,939	10,594	15,935
C	114,227	129,176	70,376	73,525
D	38,924	37,914	8,996	8,277
E	55,728	53,894	82,478	78,670
F	368,308	397,912	173,004	217,769
G	170,419	161,003	34,667	42,649
H	210,061	211,311	555,399	492,986
I	179,778	177,180	58,599	63,523
J	44,567	48,224	23,788	26,360
K	126,041	141,107	67,049	67,237
L	547,385	566,397	69,923	81,513
M	33,477	33,910	24,245	60,398
N	340,733	360,217	89,606	100,084
O	76,396	90,683	30,084	38,657
P	475,930	466,007	320,404	371,789
Q	253,683	254,875	214,451	221,043
R	47,177	45,744	68,327	72,122
T	3,245,976	3,358,094	2,079,977	2,169,312

The export of wines in 1910 was valued at 86,481,113 lire; spirits, 13,361,500; olive oil, 66,600,468; cheese, 58,002,150; eggs and poultry, 40,942,200; almonds, 40,095,565; lemons, 28,412,175. The more important countries of origin and destination follow, with values in thousands of lire:

Imports			Exports	
1909	1910	Country	1909	1910
503,464	524,634	Germany	307,202	293,139
490,643	476,269	U. K.	167,929	210,356
390,193	362,968	U. S.	272,374	263,816
329,106	333,957	France	198,717	218,296
309,303	289,746	Austria-Hungary	155,087	164,581
209,600	265,001	Russia	33,597	50,649
120,901	97,976	Argentina	150,849	151,461
97,466	159,199	British India*	23,008	36,793
73,345	84,809	Belgium	38,781	51,458
80,498	83,916	Switzerland	216,758	216,396
71,426	57,079	Turkey	79,063	107,860

* With Ceylon.

In 1910, 142,487 Italian and 13,788 foreign vessels, with an aggregate tonnage of 51,213,-901, entered, and 142,046 Italian and 13,768 foreign vessels (51,177,007 tons) cleared at Italian ports. The merchant marine (1911) consisted of 450 steamers (987,559 tons) and 630 sailing vessels (333,094).

Open for traffic in 1911 were 10,705 miles of railway; miles of telegraph line, 33,775. Towards the end of the year work was started on the Ronco-Arquata cut on the Genoa-Milan and Genoa-Turin line. This undertaking was estimated to cost almost $1,930,000, and consisted mostly of digging two tunnels, the Galleria Borlasca, 10,875 feet long, and the Galleria Giacoboni, 2625 feet long. Besides this, there was to be a three-arch bridge across the Scrivia River at Ronco 197 feet long, and two smaller bridges. The station at Ronco was to be enlarged and, with the Scrivia bridge, was to cost $96,500, while the two tunnels were to cost $1,186,950. The line was to be double-tracked, with an expense for track work of $193,000. Work in connection with the crossing of the village of Pietra Bissara was to cost over $57,-900, and masonry along the Scrivia River and other similar work, $135,100. Progress was being made with the Rome-Naples direct railway.

FINANCE. The revenue for the year 1911-12 amounted to 2,682,640,373 lire, and the expenditure to 2,623,425,632. The budget for 1912-13 estimated the revenue at 2,645,994,671 (262,692,637 extraordinary) and the expenditure at 2,630,172,684 (498,181,504 extraordinary.) The appropriation for war was 351,-172,573 lire ordinary, and 80,350,000 extraordinary; for marine, 201,428,609 ordinary, and 15,457,560 extraordinary. The capital of the public debt in 1910 totaled 14,088,876,495 lire.

ARMY. The reorganization of the Italian army which had been in progress since 1906, was continued during 1912, and the minister of war in May asked for increased appropriations to provide for more men and material. The army consisted of the active militia, the mobile militia, and the territorial militia, the latter being almost untrained, but adding to the aggregate which would produce a total war strength of about 3,500,000 men, divided as follows:

With the colors, officers and men........	248,111
On unlimited leave, officers and men....	486,290
Mobile militia, officers and men..........	320,170
Territorial militia, officers and men......	2,275,631
Total on a war footing officers and men.	3,380,202

The above figures are normal and do not take into consideration the changes due to the war with Turkey, which involved an addition to the peace strength of some 500 officers and 10,-000 men, so that the main peace effective of 13,600 officers and 236,000 men was considerably exceeded by the large number recalled to the colors for the war. On December 15, 1912, the effective strength of the Italian army with the colors amounted to 383,000 men. The plan of organization, 12 army corps, each having 2 infantry divisions, except in the district of Rome, which had 3. The organization of the permanent army was to comprise 96 regiments of light infantry, 12 regiments of bersaglieri, making in all 318 battalions and 8 Alpine regiments, aggregating 26 battalions, 145 squadrons of cavalry formed into 29 regiments, and 24 regiments of field artillery, with 186 6-gun batteries, maintained on a peace basis of 4 guns each. There were also 1 regiment of horse artillery of 6 batteries, 2 regiments of mountain artillery with 24 batteries, 3 regiments of coast artillery, and a brigade in Sardinia, 2 regiments of fortress artillery and 5 of engineers, comprising 60 companies of technical troops. The strength of the various forces under the terms of the reoganization law varied considerably and it was found necessary to increase the annual contingent of recruits by diminishing the previous exemptions. Two years' service in the infantry was introduced, as a result of the war in North Africa. By the law of June 27, 1912, 24 infantry regiments foamed four battalions, and 3 bersaglieri regiments were also given additional battalions. New formations were made in the artillery and engineers, and an aviation battalion was formed which had practical experience during the year. The army estimates for the year amounting to 425,000,000 l. were voted on March 8, and subsequent legislation occurred during the year.

NAVY. On December 1, 1912, the number and displacement of warships, built and building, of 1500 or more tons, and of torpedo craft of 50 tons and over, were as follows: 1 battleship (dreadnought type) having a main battery of all big guns (11 inches or more in calibre), of 18,600 tons, built, and 7 of 173,268 aggregate tons, building; 8 battleships (pre-dreadnought type) with main batteries of more than one calibre of 96,100 tons, built; 9 armored cruisers (74,020 tons), built; 5 cruisers (13,090) built and 2 (7040) building; 24 torpedo-boat destroyers (8667) built and 11 (7-910) building; 48 torpedo boats (9305) built and 21 (2415) building; 18 submarines (5-055) built and 2 (840) building. Total vessels built, 113, of 224,837 tons; building, 43, of 191,473—in all, 156, of 416,310 tons. Excluded from the foregoing are ships over twenty years old, unless reconstructed and rearmed within five years; torpedo craft over fifteen years old; transports, colliers, repair ships, torpedo depot ships, or other auxiliaries. Personnel voted for 1912-13, 32,000 officers and men.

The *Dante Alighieri* (19,400 tons) was completed in August, 1912, and is the first Italian dreadnought; if her speed (24 knots) is reported correctly, she is the fastest vessel of that type afloat. The *Conte di Cavour*, the *Leonardo da Vinci*, and the *Giulio Cesare* (all dreadnoughts) are expected to be completed in 1913. Two others of the same type, the *Andrea Doria* and the *Duilio*, were laid down, one in March, the other in April, 1911. Authorized are two more, the *Morosini* and the *Dandolo*. The cruiser *Quarto* was completed in 1912 and the *Nino Bixio* and the *Marsala* were launched. The new destroyers will have a speed of 30 knots; the new torpedo boats, 26 knots. See BATTLESHIPS, and NAVAL PROGRESS.

GOVERNMENT. The king (1912, Victor Emmanuel) is the executive, acting through a responsible council of eleven ministers. The legislative authority is vested conjointly in the king and a parliament composed of a senate (318 members) and a chamber of deputies (508 members). The king is required to convoke parliament annually, but may dissolve it at will. Heir-apparent, Pince Humbert. The ministry in 1912 (constituted March 30, 1911) was as follows: G. Giolitti, premier and minister of the interior; A. (Marchese) di San Giuliano, foreign affairs; C. Finocchiaro-Aprile, justice; Gen. P. Spingardi, war; Rear-Admiral P. Leonardi-Cattolica, marine; L. Credaro, instruction; F. Tedesco, treasury; F. Facta, finance; F. S. Nitti, agriculture, etc.; E. Sacchi, public works; T. Calissano, posts and telegraphs; S. Bertolini, colonies.

HISTORY

PARLIAMENT. Parliament was reconvened on February 22. Grants were promptly made for carrying on the war with Turkey. The government at once introduced a bill for the purpose of carrying into law the decree of November 5, 1911, asserting Italian sovereignty over Tripoli and Cyrenaica. The plan was accepted with great enthusiasm and a special commission to discuss the details of such a measure was nominated. Other government measures were passed with little opposition. The chief of these were the Electoral Reform bill and an old-age pension bill providing for a state monopoly in life insurance. The Electoral Reform bill provided for almost universal manhood suffrage, rendering eligible all males over 21 years of age, save those under 30 who cannot read or write or who have not performed military service. It was estimated that the number of voters would be increased from 3,000,000 to 8,000,000. The bill also provided for the payment of deputies. It passed the Chamber on May 25 by a vote of 281 to 62. The state insurance measure passed both houses and was signed by the king in August. It placed the government in control of business in the hands of British, American, German, French, and Austrian companies, estimated at about $200,000,000, and thereby occasioned some protests from foreign governments. The new project was to be carried out by a national insurance institute organized by the government.

THE CAMORRA VERDICT. On July 9, the jury in the famous Camorra trial returned its verdict which found all the prisoners guilty on every count. The crime charged was the murder of one Cuocolo and his wife in Naples on June 5, 1906. The prosecution sought to prove the complicity of the secret criminal association known as the Camorra. Forty-one persons were implicated and the mass of evidence was enormous. The Assize Court of Viterbo which tried the case, held 300 sittings and examined 650 witnesses. The decision was as follows: Four of the accused were found guilty of the murder of Cuocolo, and two of the murder of his wife; and five were found guilty of planning and directing the murders. The rest were found guilty of membership in a criminal society. The six who executed the murders were sentenced to thirty years and the same sentence was imposed on two of the plotters of the murders, Alfano and de Marinis. The rest were sentenced to terms varying from four to twenty years.

OTHER EVENTS. On March 14, an unsuccessful attempt was made to assassinate the king by an anarchist named d'Alba, who fired two shots at the royal carriage while the king and queen were on their way to the Quirinal to attend high mass in the annual commemoration of King Humbert. The assailant was tried in October and sentenced to thirty years' imprisonment. The king received a visit from the German emperor in Venice in March. The completion of the restoration of the campanile was celebrated in April. The outstanding events of the year were in connection with the war with Turkey and the final terms of peace. See TURCO-ITALIAN WAR; ARCHITECTURE, and ARGENTINA.

IVORY COAST, THE. A French West African colony. Capital, Bingerville, with (1909) 78 European and 780 native inhabitants; other centres are: Grand Bassam, 115 and 1002; Abidjan, 110 and 613; Lahou, 63 and 6622; Aboisso, 38 and 1241; Assinie, 38 and 1135; Tabou, Tiassalé, Toumodi, etc. The railway under construction is destined to put into communication with the coast, by way of the equatorial forests, the regions of Bouaké, Kong, and Koroko. It starts at Abidjan, on the Ebrié lagoon, and is in operation as far as Dimbokro on the N'Zi, an affluent of the Bandama—a distance of 181 kilometers. There are good caravan routes, transportation by porters. Products and exports are mahogany, palm kernels and oil, rubber, dried fish, etc. G. Angoulvant was governor in 1912. See FRENCH WEST AFRICA.

JACKSON, SAMUEL MACAULEY. An American editor and educator, died August 1, 1912. He was born in New York City in 1851 and graduated from the College of the City of New York in 1870. In the following year he studied at the Princeton Theological Seminary and graduated from the Union Theological Seminary in 1873. For the next two years he studied abroad. He was ordained to the Presbyterian ministry in 1876 and from 1876 to 1880 was pastor at Norwood, N. J. In 1895 he was appointed professor of church history in New York University and held that position until the time of his death. He acted as editor and associate editor in many important undertakings. Among these were *Schaff's Bible Dictionary* (1880); *Schaff-Herzog Encyclopædia of Religious Knowledge* (1884); *Johnson's Universal Cyclopædia* (1893-95); *Cyclopædia of Living Divines* (1887); *Concise Dictionary of Religious Knowledge* (1891); *Heroes of the Reformation* (1898-1906); *New Schaff-Herzog Encyclopædia of Religious Knowledge* (1907-1912). He was one of the editors of the department of religion in the *New International Encyclopædia* (1902-4). He was also the author of *Huldreich Zwingli* ("Heroes of the Reformation Series," 1901-1903).

JAGGAR, THOMAS AUGUSTUS. An American Protestant Episcopal bishop, died December 13, 1912. He was born in New York City in 1839 and was educated in the public schools of the city and by private tutors. He began business life as a bank clerk and later prepared for the ministry and was ordained priest in the Protestant Episcopal Church in 1863. He served as rector in various parishes in New Jersey and New York and from 1870 to 1875 was rector of Holy Trinity Church in Philadelphia. In the latter year he was consecrated bishop of southern Ohio. He retired from the charge of this diocese in 1905, but retained a seat and vote in the House of Bishops. Until 1908 he was morning preacher in St Paul's Church, Boston. From the same year until the time of his death he was bishop-in-charge of the American Protestant Episcopal Churches in Europe. He was author of the *Bohlen Lectures* for 1900, and various essays, printed sermons and addresses.

JAMAICA. The largest of the British West Indies; a crown colony with dependencies as follows: TURKS AND CAICOS ISLANDS, CAYMAN ISLANDS (qq. v.), MORANT CAYS, and PEDRO CAYS. Area of Jamaica, 4207 1-6 square miles; of the dependencies, 89. Population, 831,383 (15,605 white, 163,201 colored, 630,181 black, 22,396 E. Indian). Kingston (57,379 inhabitants in 1911) is the capital and has a fine harbor. Available for cultivation, 2,612,480 acres; returned as under crops in 1910-11, 926,797 (tilled lands, 273,047 acres; guinea grass, 142,794; commons, 510.956). Area under sugar cane, 31,659 acres; coffee, 24,706; under bananas, 79,283. Imports (1910), £2,614,943; exports, £2,568,221 (bananas, £1,141,710; sugar, £261,150; coffee, £167,408; rum, £134,659; dyewoods, £77,347; pimento, £73,659; cacao, £63,017; ginger, £44,986; oranges, £52,902). Railway lines, 184 miles. Revenue (1910-11), £1,169,543; expenditure, £1,169,991. Debt (March 31, 1911), £3,909,593. Sir Sydney Olivier was captain-general and governor-in-chief in 1912.

During the serious street railway strike in February and March, there was rioting, and on one occasion the governor was stoned.

JAMES, OLLIE. See PRESIDENTIAL CAMPAIGN.

JAPAN. A Far Eastern island empire, a constitutional monarchy. Capital, Tokyo.

AREA AND POPULATION. The area of Japan proper is 24,794.36 square ri (147,657 square miles). The population, as estimated in 1912, was reported at 52,200,685. The area with dependencies is 43,458.38 square ri (258,806 square miles), and the population, as estimated in 1912, 69,148,936. If the leasehold of Kwantung (Kwanto) be added, the total area becomes 260,027 square miles, and total estimated population 69,437,025.

The 1912 estimates for the dependencies are as follows: Taiwan (Formosa), 3,443,679; Karafuto (Sakhalin), 43,273; Chosen (Korea), 13,461,299; Kwantung (area 1221 square miles), 488,089; total, 17,436,340.

The table below, derived from the official 1912 *Résumé statistique de l'Empire au Japon*, shows area in square miles and legal population December 31, 1908 (the figures for Chosen indicate resident population May 10, 1910, exclusive of Japanese and foreigners). The first column shows the area of principal islands; the second, the area of these together with adjacent small islands; and the third, total legal population:

Prin. Islands	Sq. miles Prin. Isls.	Sq. miles Total	Total Pop.
Honshiu	86,305	86,775	37,041,187
Shikoku	6,856	7,031	3,288,310
Kiushiu	13,768	15,588	7,167,148
Hokkaido	30,114	30,276	1,134,002
Chishima (31 isls.)	6,024	6,024	3,453
Sado	335	335	120,510
Oki	130	130	38,349
Awaji	218	219	210,646
Iki	51	51	40,522
Tsushima	262	266	39,264
Riukiu (55 isls.)	934	934	501,818
Ogasawara (20 isls.)	27	27	3,595
Total	.....	147,657	49,588,804
Chosen	.....	84,106	12,934,282
Taiwan	13,807	13,841	2,984,590
Hokoto (Pescadores)	23	48	52,265
Karafuto	.....	13,155	2,052
Grand total	.....	258,806	65,561,993

During the hundred and fifty years prior to the overthrow of the shogunate, the population of Japan proper was almost stationary; but the average annual increase since 1872 when the periodical census was resumed, is reported at 1.35 per cent. This change is attributed to the removal of checks and regulations imposed by the feudal system and to the establishment of free intercommunication and trade, the lack of which had often prevented famine relief. Unfortunately the urban population is increasing much more rapidly than the rural; from 1903 to 1908 the average increase in cities of over 20,000 was 20.5 per cent., while the increase for the whole country was 6.1 per cent. For 1899 the increase of population is stated at 506,640; 1903, 691,108; 1908, 769,174; 1909, 665,667. In 1909, of the legal population, there were 438,771 marriages, 59,118 divorces, 1,705,877 living births and 1,099,797 deaths (not including 161,576 still-births). The foreign population at the end of 1910 numbered 15,154 (17,537 in 1909), of whom 8462 were Chinese, 2471 British, 1665 American, 809 German, and 547 French. Resident population of the larger cities December 31, 1908: Tokyo, 2,186,079; Osaka, 1,226,647; Kyoto, 442,462; Yokohama, 394,303; Nagoya, 378,231; Kobe, 378,197; Nagasaki, 176,480; Hiroshima, 142,763; Kanazawa, 110,994; Kure, 100,679; Sendai, 97,944; Okayama, 93,421; Sasebo, 93,051; Otaru, 91,281; Hakodate, 87,875.

EDUCATION AND RELIGION. The government has established a thorough educational system, and primary instruction is compulsory. The following statistics relate to March 31, 1910: Elementary schools, 26,084, with 144,506 teachers, of whom 106,184 men, and 6,473,592 pupils; 303 middle schools (5844 teachers and 117,434 pupils); 5682 special and technical schools (7619 and 305,938); superior schools for girls, 177 (2722 and 51,440); 2348 "various" schools (7854 and 149,339); 78 normal schools (1406 and 23,422). In addition there are various special institutions, including the schools for military and naval instruction, and the three imperial universities. On March 31, 1911, the University of Tokyo had 363 teachers and 5098 students, University of Kyoto, 101 and 1375; Northeast University, 86 and 793. Expenditure on education in the year 1909-10, 76,650,922 yen, of which 57,076,003 yen was for elementary schools.

The chief religious forms are Shintoism and Buddhism. On December 31, 1909, Shintoism had 13 administrative heads of sects, 76,149 preaching priests, 14,821 monks, 171 state temples, 52,031 district temples and temples of inferior rank, and 95,239 other (non-distinguished) temples. Buddhism had 56 administrative heads of sects, 50,505 high priests, 939 high priestesses, 72,379 preaching priests, 49,118 monks, 71,976 regular temples, and 36,980 other temples. The Buddhist priesthood shows a slight increase in number, the Shinto a slight decline. The Christian priesthood, December 31, 1909, comprised 1966 ministers (1286 Japanese, 680 foreign), against 1567 in 1904; churches and chapels numbered 1219, against 1135 in 1904. In 1909 Roman Catholic churches numbered 174; Orthodox, 123; Presbyterian, 211; Congregationalist, 124; Episcopal of Japan, 199; Baptist 63.

AGRICULTURE. Of the taxed land owned by private persons and local corporations, 14,538,528 cho on January 1, 1911, 5,253,363 cho were under cultivation, 7,577,470 under forest, and 1,301,044 open field (one cho=2.4507204 acres). For cereal crops, the following table shows, in metric measure, the area harvested, the production in 1911, the estimated production in 1912, and the yield per hectare in 1911:

	Hectares 1911	Hectares 1912	Quintals 1911	Quintals 1912	Qs. ha.
Rice	2,948,516	2,961,000	73,665,208	75,044,000	25.0
Wheat	495,079	505,000	6,763,284	6,655,000	13.7
Barl.	1,255,344	1,264,000	20,691,890	20,812,000	16.5
Oats	44,602	45,700	640,862	702,000	14.4
Corn	55,000	55,000	884,000	899,000	16.1

Production in 1909 and 1910 respectively, in kwan (one kwan=8.2673297 pounds): Tea, 7,990,425 and 8,342,446; sugar cane, 183,364,834 and 187,491,859 (sugar produced, 89,990,523 and 98,024,518 kin); sweet potatoes, in 1909, 907,487,064 kwan; potatoes, in 1909, 159,637,502 kwan; peas, in 1909, 3,766,062. In 1912 about 6300 hectares of flax were harvested, 28,800 tobacco (yield about 413,000 quintals), and 2400 cotton (yield about 18,000 quintals), of cleaned cotton in 1910, 4,147,810. Livestock, December 31, 1909: Cattle, 1,350,404; horses, 1,551,156; sheep, 3411; goats, 87,338; swine, 287,107. In 1908 about 60 per cent. of the inhabitants were dependent on agriculture.

MINING. Some of the more important mineral products have been as follows:

	1904	1908	1909
Gold, ounces......	88,752	107,482	126,455
Silver, ounces.....	1,968,573	3,866,589	4,114,740
Copper, kwan*....	8,566,139	10,840,782	12,224,343
Iron, kwan	10,171,500	12,105,526	14,450,984
Pyrites, kwan	6,636,138	9,031,153	5,735,683
Lead, kwan........	480,701	776,080	914,336
Mang'se ore, kwan	1,153,234	2,968,092	2,359,280
Sulphur, kwan.....	6,823,210	8,911,856	9,839,876
Coal, tons	10,363,554	14,672,828	14,908,008
Petroleum, koku†..	1,073,640	1,641,563	1,657,036

* One kwan = 3.75 kilos, or 8.26733 pounds.

† One koku = 1.8039 hectoliters, or 39.7033 gallons.

The output of salt in the year 1908-9 was 1,038,048,628 kin, against 1,008,273,045 in 1908-9 (one kin=6 hectograms, or 1.3227727 lbs).

FISHERIES. Value of the take in 1909: Fresh fish and marine plants, 68,334,351 yen; dried fish, 18,537,155; salted, 2,198,361; fish oil, 388,391; manure, 5,709,532; other products, 8,682,027; total, 104,201,855 yen, as compared with 100,826,093 in 1908 and 75,619,443 in 1904.

MANUFACTURES. One phase of the adoption of western methods by Japan is seen in the rapid development of her manufacturing industries, especially in textiles and in iron and steel. At the end of 1909, 33,219 men and 752,919 women were employed in the textile industry. Cotton-spinning mills on that date numbered 88, with a capital of 54,377,926 yen, 89,325 employees, 1,830,755 spindles, and a yarn output for the year of 50,034,190 kwan, against 42,321,544 kwan in 1908 and 33,981,193 in 1904. Value of tissues produced in 1909: Silk, 97,780,308 yen; silk and cotton mixed, 21,207,747; cotton, 113,999,285; hemp and linen, 3,834,376; other, 4,285,450; total, 241,107,166 yen, against 221,789,054 in 1908 and 116,908,104 in 1904. In addition sash tissues were produced to a value of 5,987,909 yen. Other products in 1909: Paper, 32,377,877 yen (of which European paper 14,159,329); matches, 14,058,963; matting, etc., 10,342,219; lacquer ware, 7,520,962; porcelain and pottery, 12,357,677; vegetable oils, 11,771,565; vegetable wax, 4,235,945.

COMMERCE. The value of imports in 1911 exceeded that of any previous year, while exports showed a slight decline from the record figure of 1910. Imports of merchandise for home consumption, of total merchandise, of coin and bullion, and total imports, in yen:

	Mdse. Home Consump.	Total Mdse.	Coin and Bullion	Total Imports
1901	...252,882,610	255,816,645	.......:...	....
1906	...414,214,093	418,784,108	47,211,197	465,995,305
1909	...391,059,652	394,198,843	79,587,502	473,786,345
1910	...460,896,672	464,233,808	17,671,797	481,905,605
1911	... .	513,805,705	6,168,268	519,973,973

Exports of merchandise, domestic and total, of coin and bullion, and total exports, in yen:

	Dom. Mdse.	Total Mdse.	Coin and Bullion.	Total Exports
1901	...249,415,508	252,349,543	....	....
1906	...419,184,877	423,754,892	25,784,436	449,549,328
1909	...409,973,320	413,112,511	6,584,327	419,696,838
1910	...455,091,860	451,428,996	25,175,091	483,604,087
1911	... .	447,433,888	24,398,286	471,832,174

Leading imports in 1910 and 1911 respectively, in thousands of yen: Cotton, ginned, 157,824 and 145,455; iron and steel, 19,302 and 31,042; manures and fertilizers, 21,523 and 30,744; machinery, 15,739 and 20,070; rice, 8644 and 17,721; cotton tissues, 13,491 and 13,984; woolen tissues, 12,403 and 13,860; kerosene, 14,303 and 13,065; vehicles and vessels, 4099 and 12,270; beans, peas, and pulse, 10,830 and 11,482; dyes, pigments, and paints, 9949 and 11,460; ammonium sulphate, 9066 and 11,460; sugar, 13,140 and 9157; metal manufactures, 6764 and 8561; paper and manufactures, 8848 and 7828; phosphorite, 3838 and 6306; woolen yarn, 5951 and 4783; scientific instruments, 2881 and 4787; rubber and gutta percha, 3678 and 4044; wheat, 3338 and 3729; paraffine, 1727 and 3441.

Principal exports, in thousands of yen: Raw silk, 130,833 and 128,875 in 1910 and 1911 respectively; cotton yarn, 45,347 and 40,213; silk tissues, 32,707 and 34,335; coal and coke, 16,325 and 28,004; copper ingots and slabs, 20,806 and 20,003; cotton tissues, 20,403 and 19,680; clothing and accessories, 14,043 and 15,830; tea, 14,542 and 14,370; matches, 10,300 and 10,073; silk waste, 8417 and 7786; earthenware, porcelain and glass, 7555 and 7745; timber, lumber, etc, 7080 and 7347; sugar, 6260 and 6926; braids, 9096 and 6395; oils and waxes, 5110 and 4368; paper and manufactures, 5025 and 3977; rice, 5900 and 3940; mats and matting, 3937 and 3746; machinery, 3512 and 3640; vegetables, 3070 and 3140; metal manufactures, 3358 and 2609; dried fish, 2480 and 2576.

Imports and exports of merchandise by countries in thousands of yen:

	Imports		Exports	
	1910	1911	1910	1911
United Kingdom	94,701	111,157	25,781	23,824
British India	106,361	99,696	18,713	20,316
China	78,310	82,544	109,186	111,216
United States	54,699	81,251	143,702	142,726
Germany	43,946	56,747	11,168	11,682
Dutch East Indies	18,880	15,459	3,134	3,724
French Indo-China	4,438	9,924	341	470
Australasia	7,602	7,927	6,552	8,103
Belgium	9,409	7,737	3,465	3,178
France	5,405	5,518	44,925	43,575
Egypt	4,192	5,502	807	688
Straits Settlements	4,616	4,817	6,550	7,106
Austria-Hungary	2,782	3,083	1,160	882
Philippine Islands	788	1,329	4,411	5,996
Netherlands	919	1,183	726	427
Russia	971	1,044	4,315	5,666
Hongkong	675	702	23,460	24,522
Italy	592	665	16,835	17,895
British N. America	850	334	4,262	4,006
Chosen	8,592	....	17,450	....
Other	16,405	18,630	8,249	7,705
Total	464,234	513,806	458,429	447,434

SHIPPING. Entered at the ports in the foreign trade in 1911: Japanese, 5599 vessels, of 9,393,351 tons; British, 1939, of 6,157,930 tons; German, 384, of 1,337,871 tons; American, 179, of 1,309,917 tons; other, 908, of 1,854,500 tons; total, 9009 vessels, of 20,053,569 tons. Merchant marine January 1, 1912: Vessels of European construction, 2789 steamers, of 1,386,047 tons, and 7978 sail, of 447,307 tons; vessels of Japanese construction, 21,735 sail, of 300,931 tons.

COMMUNICATIONS. State railways March 31, 1911: In operation, 4,869.56 miles; capital invested therein, 553,154,892 yen; under construction, 652.45 miles. Private railways on the same date: In operation, 511.21 miles; capital invested therein, 32,109,409 yen; under construction, 183.06 miles. Total mileage in operation, 5380.77; under construction, 835.51. The foregoing figures are for Japan proper. Japanese railways in South Manchuria are all "private"; they aggregated, March 31, 1911, 707.02 miles in operation and 3.06 under construction; total capital invested, 66,536,631 yen. At the end of March, 1910, there were in operation in Taiwan 271,24 miles (all state), with capital invested, 28,009,115 yen; in Karafuto, 25.24 miles, 425,028 yen; in Chosen, 640.71 miles and under construction, 156.39 miles, total capital invested, 83,094,990 yen. As some of these figures are for March 31, 1911, and some for March 31, 1910, their addition shows only approximations: Total mileage in operation, 7025.38; under construction, 995.16; capital invested (exclusive of mileage under construction in Japan proper), 763,330,065 yen.

Late in 1912 it was reported that the entire track of the Kiushu division of the imperial government railways of Japan was to be relaid with 60-lb. rails except on steep gradients, where 75-lb. rails were to be used. The rails taken up were all 50-lb., and were to be used in most cases for building switches or sold to builders of light steam railways. Rapid progress was made in this work, and towards the end of the year about ±00 miles of track remained to be relaid out of a total of 660 miles.

Telegraphs (1911), 4268 offices, with 41,700 kilometers of line and 169,265 of wire. Post offices, 7717.

FINANCE. The standard of value is gold, and the monetary unit the yen; its par value is that of the Mexican dollar, or 49.846 cents. Revenue and expediture in fiscal years have been as follows, in yen:

	Ordinary	Extraordinary	Total
		Revenue	
1905	299,142,128	28,324,808	327,466,936
1909	509,862,986	285,074,274	794,937,360
1910	483,241,168	194,304,109	677,545,277
1911	491,278,823	181,542,080	672,820,903
		Expenditure	
1905	126,963,789	150,091,893	277,055,682
1909	409,245,922	227,115,171	636,361,093
1910	394,193,120	138,700,515	532,893,635
1911	412,009,179	157,144,848	569,154,027

For the fiscal year 1911, total revenue and expenditure are reported at 672,820,903 and 569,154,028 yen respectively; for 1912, 603,311,-668 and 576,201,102

The budget for the fiscal year 1913 balanced at 575,976,995 pen; estimated revenue ordinary 502,597,196 and extraordinary 73,379,799, and estimated expenditure ordinary 412,073,863 and extraordinary 163,903,132. The estimated ordinary revenue included: Excise, 127,548,636 yen; land tax, 75,407,994; monopolies, 62,132,412; posts and telegraphs, 54,161,441; customs, 49,-892,207; income tax, 32,725,282; stamps, 27,-173,962; patents, 24,595,365; forests, 10,783,-188. Estimated expenditures: Finance, 185,-674,487 yen ordinary and 41,502,664 extraordinary (including 153,526,308 yen for the public debt); war, 76,790,438 and 17,720,252; navy, 40,815,710 and 52,578,548; communications, 58,-141,658 and 20,066,160; interior, 12,407,066 and 20,888,121; justice, 12,350,337 and 778,859; agriculture and commerce, 7,626,158 and 8,412,309;

public instruction, 9,485,468 and 1,019,579; foreign affairs, 4,282,541 and 936,640; civil list, 4,500,000; total, 575,976,995.

Public debt, March 31, 1912: Internal, 1,116,255,770 yen; external, 1,437,449,203; total, 2,553,704,973, as compared with 2,770,381,215 in 1911 and 566,434,110 in 1904.

ARMY. During the year 1912 the Japanese army was maintained at its usual effective condition and the most notable events were the increases in the cavalry, which hitherto was considered a weak feature of the Japanese establishment, and the armament of the artillery with a Krupp pattern 12-pounder field gun which was being manufactured at Osaka. New light and mountain guns were also being introduced. Field Marshal Nodzu was succeeded as minister of war in April by General Jusako Ouebara, director-general of military training, but little change was made in the general scheme of organization. Japan maintained an active army with a first and second reserve, a national army with its reserve, some special forces and a militia in some of the islands. The plan was that the active army should be used for foreign service, the national army for home defense, and the militia for auxiliary operations. Military service begins at the age of 20, though 3 years earlier every Japanese is liable and is enrolled. For such as are required for the active army, or Geneki, there is 2 years' service with the colors in the case of the infantry and 3 years in the case of the cavalry, then 7⅓ years is spent with the first reserve, or Yobi, or in the case of certain classes in the Hoju or recruiting service. Ten years is then spent in the second reserve, or Kobi, and finally a period of liability to service is ended in the national army, or Kokumin. It was estimated that Japan could put into the field 1,500,000 men fully equipped and maintain them there, so complete was the system of organization and control. The army was organized with 19 divisions, and during the year an attempt was being made to increase the army by the addition of two new divisions. See below, *History*. A new .44 calibre carbine was under manufacture for the Japanese cavalry at the imperial arsenal and was to be supplied to all the cavalry regiments. It had a bayonet folded to the barrel for convenience in carrying and to be used in a mounted charge.

Much attention was being paid to the question of army transport, especially as Japan was deficient in animals, and large motor vehicles were being tested at Osaka. It was proposed to follow the example of certain European countries and subsidize large motor trucks that could be called upon for service in time of war.

NAVY. Number and displacement of warships of 1500 or more tons, and of torpedo craft of 50 or more tons, built and building, December 1, 1912: Dreadnoughts (battleships having a main battery of all big guns, that is, 11 or more inches in calibre): built, 2 of 41,600 tons; building, one of 30,000 tons. Predreadnoughts (battleships of about 10,000 tons or more whose main batteries are of more than one calibre): built, 13, of 191,380 tons; building, none. Coast-defense vessels: built, 2 of 9086 tons; building, none. Battle cruisers (armored cruisers having guns of largest calibre in main battery): built, none; building, 4 of 110,000 tons. Armored cruisers: built, 13 of 138,483 tons; building, none. Cruisers (unarmored warships of 1500 or more tons): built, 14 of 60,330 tons; building, none. Torpedo-boat destroyers: built, 58 of 22,983 tons; building, none. Torpedo boats: built, 54 of 5428 tons; building, none. Submarines: built, 11 of 2268 tons; building, 5 of 2166 tons. Total tonnage: built, 471,558; building, 142,166. Excluded from the foregoing: Ships over 20 years old unless reconstructed and rearmed within five years; torpedo craft over 15 years old; transports, colliers, repair ships, torpedo depot ships, and other auxiliaries.

In the above list the *Satsuma* and *Aki*, completed in 1910, are classified as predreadnoughts, though in some classifications they are placed with the dreadnoughts. The two dreadnoughts built are the *Kawachi*, launched in October, 1910, and the *Settsu*, launched in April, 1911, both of which were completed in 1912. The dreadnought under construction is the *Fuso*, which was begun at Kure in 1911 and will probably be completed in 1914. The four battle cruisers, of 27,500 tons each, are building at Barrow (England), Yokosuka, Nagasaki, and Kobe; they were laid down in 1911 and have received the names of *Kongo*, *Hiyei*, *Kirishima*, and *Haruna* respectively. The *Kongo* was launched May 18, 1912. See also BATTLESHIPS and NAVAL PROGRESS. Officers and men, 47,289, including one admiral of the fleet, 7 admirals, 17 vice-admirals, 45 rear-admirals, and 292 captains and commanders.

GOVERNMENT. The executive authority is vested in the emperor, who acts through a cabinet of ministers, appointed by and responsible to himself. The legislative body consists of a parliament, or imperial diet, of two chambers, the House of Peers (366 members) and the House of Representatives (379). Representatives are elected by male subjects having attained the age of twenty-five and possessing certain property qualifications. The emperor Mutsuhito died at Tokyo July 30, 1912. He was born at Kyoto November 3, 1852, and succeeded his father Komei Tenno, who died January 31, 1867. Mutsuhito was succeeded by his son Yoshihito, who was born at Tokyo August 31, 1879, and married May 10, 1900, Sadako, fourth daughter of the late Prince Kujo Michitaka. The heir-apparent is their son Hirohito, born at Tokyo April 29, 1901. The ministry of Marquis Saionji, formed August 30, 1911, was in power until December, 1912. Its composition in 1912 was as follows: Premier, Marquis Saionji Kinmochi; navy, Vice-Admiral Baron Saito Minoru; communications, Count Hayashi Tadasu; justice, Matsuda Masahisa; interior, Viscount Hara Takashi; foreign affairs, Viscount Uchida Yasuya; agriculture and commerce, Baron Makino Nobuaki; war, Lt.-Gen. Baron Uyehara Yusaku; public instruction, Haseba Sumitaka; finance, Yamamoto Tatsuo. A new ministry was formed on December 17 under Prince Katsura. See below.

HISTORY

FOREIGN AFFAIRS. Viscount Uchida, foreign minister, in a speech on foreign affairs before the Diet on January 23, announced the increasing strength of Japan's friendship and alliances with foreign powers. He referred to the good effects of the revision of the treaty between Great Britain and Japan in 1911 and to the cordial relations between Russia and Japan following the arrangements of 1907 and 1910, for the settlement of outstanding claims. As to the United States, he said that the friend-

EMPEROR MUTSUHITO
Died July 29, 1912

EMPEROR YOSHIHITO
Succeeded to the Throne, 1912

JAPAN

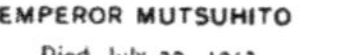

ship between the two countries was too strong to be shaken by the anti-Japanese demonstrations in certain portions of the United States. With Germany and France he reported that relations were growing more friendly and that the trade with the former country had been placed on a solid basis. As to China, Japan had coöperated with the powers to secure an early restoration of peace and order. A sharp debate arose in the Diet on January 26 over the alleged efforts of the Japanese government to prevent the abdication of the Chinese emperor. M. Uchida denied that his government had taken any part in the matter, and said that the Japanese minister at Peking in discussing the subject with Yuan Shih-kai had merely expressed his personal views. Early in July, Prince Katsura started on a tour of Europe and America, reaching St. Petersburg on July 21, but was recalled a week later by the emperor's illness. Meanwhile a supplementary agreement was made with Russia regulating their spheres of influence in Inner Mongolia and providing for their joint defense in the event of attack by other powers. Another question that appeared to have been settled by Prince Katsura was that of Russia's jurisdiction in the Sea of Okhotsk. In 1911 the Russian government attempted to extend the boundary of its territorial waters in the Sea of Okhotsk. This aroused a protest from Japan and the difference beacme so sharp in the following spring that Japanese cruisers were sent to the north. It was proposed by the Japanese government that the question should be submitted to the court of arbitration at The Hague at an early date, but after Prince Katsura's visit a settlement seems to have been reached by diplomatic negotiations, Japan admitting the Russian claim and Russia recognizing in return Japan's claims in Manchuria.

INTERNAL POLITICS. In the general elections of May for the lower house the Constitutional Unionists (Seiyukai) obtained 217 seats; the Nationalists (Kokumin-To) 96; the Independents, 37; and the Central Club, 32. As was noted in the preceding YEAR BOOK the Saionji ministry, which came into power at the end of August, 1911, were confronted with a difficult financial situation. The policy pursued was one of economy and retrenchment, but this brought them into conflict with the demands of the war office. For some time past it had been proposed that the Korean garrison should be increased by two divisions of Japanese troops. After the death of Baron Ishimoto (q. v.) in April, General Uyehara, his successor, urgently insisted upon this plan in spite of the cost, which was estimated at 26,000,000 yen. It was opposed, both on the grounds of economy and because Russia might regard it as a sign of unfriendly intentions. It was also argued that Japan could not maintain a policy involving both military and naval expansion. Dissensions in the cabinet arose, and though the war minister was supported by Count Terauchi and insisted that the measure was absolutely necessary and not in conflict with the government's policy of retrenchment, the premier opposed it. General Uyehara resigned on December 2, and the premier, finding it impossible to fill the place, resigned on December 5. A new cabinet was formed under Prince Katsura on December 17.

NAVAL PROGRESS. On February 3, Baron Saito, minister of marine, announced the irreducible minimum of naval construction to be eight battleships and eight armored cruisers of the super-dreadnought class, to be begun in 1913 and completed in 1920, at an estimated cost of about $175,000,000. Later it was announced that the programme involved the laying down of two keels a year and the building in 1920 of seven super-dreadnoughts and six very powerful cruisers.

KOREAN CONSPIRACY CASE. It was reported in February that a far-spread conspiracy had been formed in northern Korea against the governor-general, Count Terauchi, involving many of the native Christians. One hundred and twenty-three persons were accused of complicity, including Baron In-chi-ko, president of the Korean Young Men's Christian Association, and against fifty of them, all but three of whom were native Christians, evidence was secured for their prosecution. The foreign missionaries protested against the arrest of so many Christians and in certain quarters it was attributed to religious intolerance. A formal protest was presented to the governor-general by the foreign missionaries in Seoul. Count Terauchi emphatically denied that the government had any other purpose in detaining the prisoners than to make a careful examination of them. Many of them confessed to the crime, but subsequently retracted their confession, alleging that it was extorted by the fear of torture. In the examination of the prisoners early in July the judge made frequent mention of the American and English missionaries at the chief school at Syen Chyun, implying that they had incited the pupils to action. The demand of the missionaries to be heard and to offer witnesses in their own behalf was refused. Appeal was made to the supreme court for a new trial, but it refused the application. When the trial was resumed the prosecution denied emphatically that torture had been applied, and declared that the prisoners had confessed in the hope of escaping punishment. The defense did not press the matter of the alleged tortures, but argued that the confessions were untrustworthy and the prisoners deserving of leniency. Sentences were passed on 106 of the prisoners at the beginning of October, ranging from 5 to 10 years' imprisonment, and 17 were acquitted.

DEATH OF THE MIKADO. The Mikado, Mutsuhito (q. v.), died on July 29. The evidence of genuine grief among the people was remarkable. The court was ordered to go into mourning for a year. The loss was especially lamented in England where he was highly valued as a loyal ally. The crown prince, Yoshihito Harunomiya, was born in 1879, succeeded him on the throne. The funeral services of the late emperor were held on September 13 and 14. A great procession, including the military guard of honor, about 25,000 men in line, escorted the coffin through the streets which were thronged with mourners. The body was interred at Kyoto. At the moment the gun was fired to start the funeral procession on the morning of September 13, General Count Nogi, the hero of the Japanese-Russian War, and his wife committed suicide with short swords at their dwelling. In his will Count Nogi declared that he had followed the emperor into death because his services were no longer needed, that he had long wished to die, and now took the occasion of a great national calamity to end his life.

OTHER EVENTS. A serious catastrophe occurred at Osaka on January 16, when a fire, breaking out in a private house, spread rapidly to the crowded workmen's quarters and destroyed over 5000 houses, rendering some 30,000 people homeless. Asaka, Nagoya, Gifa, and Naia suffered heavily in September from a typhoon, which destroyed many million dollars worth of property and several hundred lives. A serious strike of seamen broke out in the latter part of April, interrupting the service with Europe and South America.

JAPANESE IMMIGRATION. See HAWAII.

JARROLD, ERNEST. An American writer, died March 19, 1912. He was born in Brentwood, England, in 1850 and was brought to the United States when but a year old. He was apprenticed as a typesetter in a newspaper office and in that capacity worked as compositor on the New York *Evening Post*. At the same time he wrote for newspapers and his stories attracted the attention of Garrett P. Serviss, who advised him to adopt writing as a livelihood. Before he was 18 years old he wrote a series entitled *The Mickey Finn Stories* which appeared in the New York *Sun* and became widely popular. He became known as a reciter, especially of his own stories, and in this work he found his greatest success. He was one of the best known figures in New York literary life for many years.

JAVA. See DUTCH EAST INDIES.

JETTY. See DOCKS AND HARBORS.

JEWISH AGRICULTURAL AND INDUSTRIAL AID SOCIETY. See AGRICULTURAL CREDIT.

JEWS. See JUDAISM.

JEX-BLAKE, SOPHIA. An English physician, died January 7, 1912. She was born in 1840 at Brighton. From 1858 to 1861 she was a mathematical tutor at Queen's College, London. Following a trip to the United States she became greatly interested in the movement which had been successfully started by the late Dr. Elizabeth Blackwell for the admission of women to medical degrees. Resolving to devote herself to medicine she began, in 1866, a regular course of study in Boston under Dr. Lucy Sewall. In 1868 she returned to England for the purpose of qualifying in the study of medicine in that country. She met with opposition, but finally with several other women secured the passage of regulations for the education of women in medicine at the University of London in separate classes. Here she pursued her studies for six months, but difficulties were thrown in her way and when she and her companions applied for admission to study in the wards of the Edinburgh Royal Infirmary, there was serious opposition and the lecturers finally passed a resolution which amounted to a total prohibition of the attendance of women at the classes. Attempts were made by legal proceedings to compel the lecturers to rescind this action, but this failed, and in 1874 Miss Jex-Blake returned to London. Here she took a leading part in establishing the London School of Medicine for Women. This was opened in 1874. In 1877 she became associated with the Royal Free Hospital, so that women students were at last enabled to secure both medical education and hospital experience. In the meantime she had obtained the degree of M. D. from the University of Bern in 1877, while in 1876 Parliament passed measures compelling the British examining bodies to extend their examinations and qualifications to women. Dr. Jex-Blake began to practice in Edinburgh in 1878. In 1886 she founded the Edinburgh School of Medicine for Women. She herself became dean. She continued her medical work in Edinburgh until 1899 when she retired. Among her publications are: *American Schools and Colleges* (1866); *Medical Women* (1872); *Care of Infants* (1884), and various articles contributed to magazines.

JOHN, GRIFFITH. An English missionary, died July 25, 1912. He was born in Swansea, Wales, in 1831 and was educated at Brecon College, Bedford. He began to preach in Welsh at the age of fourteen years. In 1873 he offered his services to the London Missionary Society for work in foreign countries. After spending a short time at the Missionary Academy at Bedford, he was sent to China, where he arrived in 1855. He remained in that country as a missionary for 55 years, terminating his services in 1911. The first five years in China were spent in evangelistic work in and around Shanghai. In 1861 he went to Hankow and traveled extensively in several provinces of central China, where he was the first Christian missionary. With his colleagues he established more than 100 missionary stations in the provinces of Hu-peh and Hu-nan. He acquired an intimate knowledge of Chinese literature and became the author of a number of tracts in that language. His most important work, however, was a remarkable translation of the Scriptures into Chinese. He translated the whole of the New Testament and a greater part of the Old into what is known as the *Wen-li Version*. He also rendered this translation into the Mandarin colloquial language. He was the pioneer and founder of the Protestant missions in the Yangtse valley. Here he founded the theological college for native preachers which bears his name. During his 55 years of service Dr. John returned to England only three times. In 1889 he was elected to the position of chairman of the Congregational Union of England and Wales, but he declined to serve on the ground that it was his duty to remain in China. In January, 1912, he arrived in England seriously ill and with no hope of recovery. At the time of his death he was still working on his translation of the Old Testament into Chinese. In addition to these translations he wrote a number of books and tracts for circulation among the Chinese.

JOHNS HOPKINS UNIVERSITY. An institution for higher education at Baltimore, Md., founded in 1876. The students enrolled in the various departments of the university in the autumn of 1912 were 771, of whom 403 were in the departments included in the College of Arts and Sciences and 368 in the medical school. The faculty numbered 222, of whom 202 are resident and 20 are non-resident lecturers. There were no noteworthy changes in the faculty during the year. Among the important benefactions was one of $6000 from the Peabody Education Fund for a Peabody scholarship in the Department of Education. The productive funds of the university in 1911-12 amounted to $5,270,000 and the income to $373,789. The library contained about 165,000 volumes. President, Ira Remsen, LL. D., Ph. D.

JOHNSON, HIRAM W. See PRESIDENTIAL CAMPAIGN.

JOHORE. A native state in the Malay Peninsula, under British control. Estimated area, 9000 square miles; population estimated at 200,000, mostly Chinese. Johore Bharu, the capital, has about 20,000 inhabitants. A railway connects Kuala Gemas on the Negri Sembilan border with Johore Bharu (120½ miles); constructed by the Federated Malay States Railways. Sultan (1912), Ibrahim; British adviser, D. G. Campbell.

JOLINE, ADRIAN HOFFMAN. An American lawyer and writer, died October 15, 1912. He was born in Ossining, N. Y., in 1850 and graduated from Princeton University in 1870. He studied law at the Columbia Law School and on being admitted to the bar became associated with the law firms of Butler, Hall & Vanderpoel, and Butler, Stillman & Hubbard. He was afterwards a member of the firm of Joline, Larkin & Rathbone. He early devoted his efforts as a lawyer to railway litigation and to questions pertaining to trusts, mortgages and reorganizations. He was generally recognized as a leader in these branches of legal practice. He was general counsel and chairman of the board of directors of many important railroads and financial institutions. When the Metropolitan Street Railway Company of New York City became insolvent, Mr. Joline was appointed receiver for the company. He was a notable collector of autographs and rare books, and his collection of autograph letters is believed to be among the most valuable in existence. He wrote several books, chiefly relating to autographs. These included *Meditations of an Autograph Collector* (1902); *Diversions of a Booklover* (1903); *At the Library Table* (1909), and *Edgehill Essays* (1910). Mr. Joline came into prominence at the beginning of the presidential campaign in 1912 by the publication of a letter addressed to him by Woodrow Wilson. In this letter Mr. Wilson expressed the wish that Mr. Bryan might be got rid of as a political figure (see POLITICAL CAMPAIGN).

JONES, JOHN PERCIVAL. Former United States senator from Nevada, died November 27, 1912. He was born in Herefordshire, England, in 1829 and came with his parents to the United States in his infancy. He was educated in the public schools of Cleveland, O. He went to California during the first gold discoveries in that State and engaged in mining. From 1863 to 1867 he was a member of the California State Senate. In the latter year he went to Nevada and from that time until his death he was engaged in the development of mines in that State. In 1873 he was elected to the United States Senate and served five successive terms until 1903. In that year he left the Republican party when the money question became the leading issue between the parties. He was a strong advocate of free silver. When that question ceased to be a political issue he reaffiliated himself with the Republican party.

JOURNALISM, SCHOOL OF. See UNIVERSITIES AND COLLEGES.

JUDAISM. There are no recent statistics of the number of Jews in the world or in the United States. Various estimates, however, have been made. The latest is that made in 1910 by the *American Jewish Year Book*. According to this authority, the total number of Jews was, in that year, 12,867,856. Of these, there were in the United States 2,044,762; in Austria-Hungary, 2,088,228; in Russia, 6,243,712. These were the only countries in which the Jews numbered over 1,000,000. There were in the British Empire 433,220; in Germany, 607,862; in Turkey, 463,686, of whom 78,000 were in Palestine.

JEWISH IMMIGRATION TO THE UNITED STATES. The total Jewish immigration to the United States at the end of the fiscal year 1912, was 74,854 compared with 73,187 in 1910-11. Of these, 60,038 came though the port of New York and these were divided by nationality as follows: Russians, 41,612; Austrians, 10,386; Rumanians, 1277; others, 6763.

EVENTS IN JUDAISM. The Jews continued in troubled condition in Russia during the year. Expulsions took place from many cities throughout the year, including St. Petersburg, from which many Jews were expelled in February. On February 23 the Duma agreed to the clause in the Military Service bill imposing a heavy fine upon families of Jews who evaded military service, and on the same day declined to exempt Jewish ecclesiastical authorities from military service, a privilege extended to Christian and Mussulman priests. According to the official statistics, 19,809 young Jewish recruits enrolled in the army in the early part of 1912. On May 10 the governor of Grodno ordered the expulsion of 1100 Jewish families. There were many accusations of ritual murders in the cities of the empire which led to great disorders. On June 28, the Duma adopted a motion prohibiting the Jews from accepting scholarships as medical students. See RUSSIA.

In Palestine the immigration of Jews continued during the year. The erection of a Jewish Technical Institute at Haifa was permitted by the Sultan. A conference of Judean agricultural laborers was held in January and a general organization was founded. Nathan Straus of New York, gave to the communal leaders of Jerusalem, 1000 francs a day for two months to provide food for the destitute. He also gave a large sum to the agricultural experiment station for the eradication of malaria.

In Rumania, early in January, a deputation of Jews complained to King Charles of discriminatory laws against Jews and especially against the proposed industries bill intended to drive Jews out of all industries. Appeal was made for the abolition of the oath *more Judaico*, which is still enforced in some of the law courts of the country of Rumania.

JEWISH COLONIZATION. The Ica, or Jewish Colonization Society, which is the trustee of the large fund left by Baron de Hirsch for the promotion of Jewish colonization, continued its work during 1912. The largest colony is in Argentina where nearly 4000 families are engaged in agricultural pursuits. There is also a colony in Brazil. In the United States the society loaned large amounts to Jewish farmers.

ZIONISM. There were no unusual developments in the Zionist movement in 1912, but the Zionists continued in their work of colonizing in Palestine. Several organizations are engaged in promoting agricultural developments, including the growing of olives. For a mention of the abrogation of the treaty with Russia by the United States government as a result of the discrimination against Jewish citizens of the United States, see UNITED STATES, *Foreign Relations*.

JUDICIAL DECISIONS, RECALL OF. See PRESIDENTIAL CAMPAIGN.

JUDGES, RECALL OF. See PRESIDENTIAL CAMPAIGN.

JUNGFRAU TUNNEL. See TUNNELS.

JUPITER. See ASTRONOMY.

JURISTS, CONGRESS OF. See ARBITRATION, INTERNATIONAL.

KAHN FOUNDATION. See UNIVERSITIES AND COLLEGES.

KAISER-WILHELMS-LAND. That part of German New Guinea (q. v.) which is in New Guinea island.

KAMCHATKA RIVER. See EXPLORATION.

KAMERUN. A protectorate of Germany between Nigeria and French Equatorial Africa. The area is officially estimated at 495,600 square kilometers (191,351 square miles). Colored population, 2,719,000; whites (January 1, 1911), 1455, of whom 1311 German. These figures for area and population do not take into account the rectification of the boundary pursuant to the Franco-German convention of November 4, 1911. Under this convention Germany ceded to France a portion of northwestern Kamerun, unofficially stated at 6450 square miles; and, in return for German recognition of the French potectorate in Morocco France ceded to Germany certain parts of French Equatorial Africa, greatly extending the territorial extent of Kamerun and affording German egress on the Ubangi, on the Congo, and on the Atlantic south of the Spanish colony of Río Muni. The territory thus ceded to Germany is unofficially estimated at 107,270 square miles, with a population of perhaps a million.

Imports and exports in 1909, 17,723,000 and 15,448,000 marks; in 1910, 25,481,000 and 19,924,000. Chief exports in the two years: Rubber, 7552 and 11,071 thousand marks; palm kernels, 2611 and 3553; cacao, 2854 and 3055; palm oil, 1097 and 1260; ivory, 879 and 625. In 1909 and 1910, imports from Germany, 13,774,000 and 19,991,000 marks; exports thereto, 12,874,000 and 17,248,000. Tonnage entered, 1,034,054 in 1909 and 1,290,829 in 1910. Railway in operation December 31, 1911, 160 kms.; under construction, 360 kms.; total, 520 kms. (323 miles). Fifty miles of railway were opened to traffic in 1912. The budget for 1911-12 balanced at 21,573,013 marks (including 2,313,566 marks imperial subvention and, for extraordinary expenditures, 12,300,000 marks from loan); for 1912-13, 17,634,680 marks (2,344,015 subvention, 8,050,000 loan). Governor (1912), Herr Ebermaier; seat of government, Buéa. See ANTHROPOLOGY.

KANSAS. POPULATION. According to the Census Bureau statistics issued in 1912, out of the total population, 1,690,949 in 1910, 134,716 were foreign-born whites, compared with 126,577 in 1900. The largest number came from Germany, 34,476; from Russia, 15,264; from Sweden, 13,303; from Austria, 12,122; from England, 11,256; and from Ireland, 8100. Other European countries contributed in smaller numbers. The negroes in the State in 1910 numbered 54,030 and the mulattoes, 16,131. In 1890 the negroes numbered 49,170 and the mulattoes, 13,180.

AGRICULTURE. The acreage, value and production of the principal crops in 1911 and 1912 are shown in the following table:

		Acreage	Prod. Bu.	Value
Corn	1912	7,575,000	174,225,000	$69,690,000
	1911	6,760,000	126,150,000	79,474,000
Wheat	1912	5,956,000	92,290,000	68,295,000
	1911	4,610,000	51,387,000	46,762,000
Oats	1912	1,720,000	55,040,000	19,264,000
	1911	2,000,000	30,000,000	13,500,000
Rye	1912	30,000	477,000	324,000
	1911	18,000	198,000	160,000
Potatoes ..	1912	70,000	5,740,000	4,190,000
	1911	80,000	1,760,000	1,866,000
Hay	1912	1,627,000	a 2,440,000	18,544,000
	1911	1,649,000	a 1,402,000	13,880,000

a Tons.

MINERAL PRODUCTION. The production of coal in the State in 1911 was 6,254,228 short tons valued at $9,645,572. This was an increase over the production of 1910 of 1,322,777 short tons. This, however, did not bring the total production up to the normal, for it is nearly 50,000 tons less than the average production of the preceding five years. This State suffered more than any other in the Mississippi Valley region from labor troubles in 1910. There were employed 11,695 men in the coal mines of the State.

The lead produced in the State in 1911 amounted to 2000 short tons, valued at $257,310, compared with 2412 tons valued at $212,256 in 1910. The zinc produced amounted to 10,272 tons valued at $1,171,008, compared with 13,229 tons in 1910 valued at $1,428,732.

Petroleum. The decline in the production of oil in the State, which had been marked for several years, was checked in 1911 by better prices, which stimulated new drilling. There were produced in 1911, 1,278,819 barrels, compared with 1,128,668 barrels in 1910. The oil wells drilled numbered 172 against 85 in 1910.

MANUFACTURES. The Thirteenth Census statistics are for the calendar year 1909, and were compiled in 1912. Kansas is not preëminently a manufacturing State. Its manufactures have been largely the outgrowth of its extensive agricultural resources, while in recent years they have been further stimulated by the development of rich zinc and coal mines and by the discovery of oil and gas. The table herewith shows that there were in 1909, 3435 manufacturing establishments giving employment to an average of 54,649 persons:

	Number or Amount 1909	1904	P. C. Inc. '04-'09
Number of establishments	3,435	2,475	38.8
Persons engaged in manufactures	54,649	42,057	29.3
Proprietors and firm members..	3,571	2,766	29.1
Salaried employees	6,863	3,721	84.4
Wage earners (average No.)....	44,215	35,570	24.3
Primary horsepower.	213,141	99,441	114.3
Capital	$156,090,000	$88,680,000	76.9
Expenses	305,711,000	187,955,000	62.7
Services	33,255,000	22,575,000	47.3
Salaries	7,351,000	3,692,000	99.1
Wages	25,904,000	18,883,000	37.2
Materials	258,884,000	156,510,000	65.4
Miscellaneous	13,572,000	8,870,000	53.0
Value of products....	325,104,000	198,245,000	64.0
Value of products less cost of material	66,220,000	41,735,000	58.7

In the slaughtering and meat-packing industries there were employed 10,591 wage-earners; in industries connected with railways, 7886; in printing and publishing, 3232; flour and gristmill products, 2350. The slaughtering and meat-packing industry stands first as to value of product. This amounted in 1909 to $165,-361,000. The flour-mill and gristmill products were valued at $68,467,000; railway industries $11,193,000; smelting and refining zinc, $10,857,000. The number of persons engaged in the manufacturing industries of the State in 1909 was 54,649. Of these 50,156 were male, and 4493 female. The wage-earners under 16 yea s of age numbered 235. The prevailing hours of labor among the majority of wage-earners in the State was 60 a week, and in the larger number of industries, employment was confined mainly to hours ranging from 54 to 60 a week; only 17.5 per cent. of the total being employed in establishments where the prevailing hours were less than 54 a week, and 14.8 per cent. in establishments where they were more than 60 a week. The largest number of wage-earners was in Kansas City, 12,-294; in Topeka, 4244; in Wichita, 2783, and in Leavenworth, 1311

EDUCATION. The total school population of the State at the end of the fiscal year 1912 was 510,273. Of these, 258,700 were males and 252,003 females. The enrollment in the public schools was 395,064. Of these 198,505 were male and 196,559 females. The average daily attendance was 298,128. The teachers employed numbered 14,103, of whom 2639 were males and 11,464 females. The average monthly salary paid to high school teachers was $82.94, and to teachers in graded schools, $60.20. The total average attendance in the high schools of the State during the year was 29,716. During the year 105 normal institutes were held at which 10,234 teachers were in attendance. The disbursements for all school pu p ses during the year amounted to $11,158,235o

FINANCE. There was a balance on hand at the beginning of the fiscal year 1912 of 1,423,-283. The total receipts for the year were $7,-758,025, and the disbursements $7,891,099, leaving a balance at the end of the fiscal year 1912 of $1,289,209. The chief receipts were from the general revenue fund and from the Topeka Fiscal Agency. The chief expenditures were for education, for the maintenance of State institutions, and for the expenses of the State government. The outstanding bonded indebtedness of the State at the end of the fiscal year 1912 was $370,000.

CHARITIES AND CORRECTIONS. The penal institutions of the State are under the full management, control, and supervision of a board of penal institutions. The State charitable institutions are under the control and supervision of the board of control. The charitable institutions of the State, with their populations in 1911, were as follows: Topeka State Hospital, 1417; Osawatomie State Hospital, 1339; State Hospital for Epileptics at Parsons, 420; State Home for Feeble-minded at Winfield, 476; School for the Deaf at Olathe, 233; School for the Blind at Kansas City, 76; State Orphans' Home at Atchison, 114; Boys' Industrial School at Topeka, 247; Girls' Industrial School at Beloit, 181. The penal institutions include the State Penitentiary at Lansing and the Industrial Reformatory for Young Men at Hutchinson.

POLITICS AND GOVERNMENT

There was no meeting of the legislature in 1912 as the sessions are biennial and the last was held in 1911.

CONVENTIONS AND ELECTIONS. As in the other Middle Western States, the p itical campaign was the chief interest in 1912. The campaign in Kansas included the nomination of United States senator to succeed Charles Curtis, whose term expired March 4, 1913. Governor Stubbs was a candidate for the Republican nomination, against Senator Curtis.

In the middle of March the Kansas Republican State committee decided against presidential primaries, indorsed President Taft, and called a State convention to nominate delegates-at-large. The convention in May elected delegates-at-large and instructed them for Roosevelt. The district conventions and primaries instructed their delegates for Roosevelt except in the first congressional district, where they were instructed for Taft. At the Chicago national convention the Kansas delegates therefore stood 18 for Roosevelt and 2 for Taft. The Democratic State convention for the election of delegates to the national convention instructed the delegates to vote for Champ Clark, with Governor Wilson as second choice. Primaries of all parties for the nomination of presidential electors, State and county officers, and United States senator were held on August 6. In this election Governor Stubbs (Rep.) carried 93 districts in the State, or 10 more than a majority in joint ballot in the legislature. Senator Curtis, however, had the popular vote by 1216. A Taft elector ticket and a Roosevelt ticket were opposed in the Republican party. The Roosevelt electors were chosen by majorities ranging from 34,000 to 36,000. Arthur Clapper of Topeka was nominated by the Republicans, and George H. Hodges of Olathe, by the Democrats for governor. The Democratic nominee for United States senator was Judge William H. Thompson of Garden City in the western part of the State, who defeated ex-State Senator Hugh Farrelly by legislative districts, though Mr. Farrelly received the plurality of popular votes cast.

Prior to the August primary a dispute as to the status of the Republican candidates for nomination as presidential electors of the State resulted in an argument before two Supreme Court Justices in New York City the first of August. The questions at issue were as follows: The Roosevelt Republicans in the State disputed the nomination of Taft and had submitted a ticket of Roosevelt electors for the Republican primary. The Taft men objected to these names on the primary ticket on the ground that the President was the regular nominee of the Republican party, and that electors pledged to Roosevelt could not legally run in the Republican column on the primary ballot. They therefore brought suit in the Kansas Supreme Court to prevent the names of Roosevelt electors from being printed on the Republican ticket at the primaries on the ground that this would be a wrong on the voters. The Kansas court refused to interfere, alleging that if it were a wrong it was not a wrong which the law could remedy. The remedy must not be through the court, but by political action. This decision was appealed, under the Fourteenth Amendment, to the Supreme Court of the United States and a stay was obtained, hearing to be had on October 1. Governor Stubbs thereupon telegraphed to Justice Pitney that this stay would necessarily prevent them from carrying on the Kansas primary, as the question must be decided by August 6. A hearing was therefore held in New York before Justice Pitney and Justice Vandeventer in order that a prompt decision might be reached. The justices refused to interfere, though they the left the question open for future consideration. By this decision the candidates for Roosevelt electors were allowed to remain on the Republican primary ticket, but whether, if nominated, they would be permitted to go on the ticket as the regular Republican nominees at the November presidential election was left for a later decision.

On September 16 the United States Court of Appeals, sitting at Denver, handed down an opinion in the case, which directed that the order refusing an injunction against the Roosevelt candidates be affirmed and the case be remanded to the Kansas courts with instructions to dismiss the appeal. This was a victory for the Roosevelt faction. The leaders of that faction decided on September 19, however, in order to harmonize the State ticket, that the Roosevelt electors should go on the November ballot in the independent column, permitting the Taft electors to head the Republican column. Suits filed by the two factions to keep each other off the Republican ticket were thereupon dropped.

The election of November 5 resulted as follows: For president, Wilson, 143,670, Taft, 74,844, Roosevelt, 120,123, and Debs, 26,807. For governor, Hodges, Dem., 167,540, Capper, Rep., 167,511. The Socialist candidate for governor received 24,804 votes. The Democrats obtained a majority in each branch of the State legislature, insuring the election of W. H. Thompson senator to succeed Senator Curtis. The election for governor was the closest in the history of the State. An official count was necessary before a determination could be reached. All Republican nominees for State offices were elected except governor and United States senator. On January 9, George A. Neely, Democrat, was elected to Congress from the Seventh District, succeeding the late Representative Madison.

STATE GOVERNMENT. Governor, G. H. Hodges, Dem.; Lieutenant-Governor, S. Ingalls; Secretary of State, Charles H. Sessions; Treasurer, Earl Akers; Auditor, W. E. Davis; Attorney-General, John S. Dawson; Adjutant-General, —— ——; Superintendent of Education, W. D. Ross; Superintendent of Insurance, Ike S. Lewis; Commissioner of Agriculture, F. D. Coburn—all Republicans, except Governor.

JUDICIARY. Supreme Court: Chief Justice, William A. Johnston; Associate Justices, Judson S. West, Silas Porter, Clark A. Smith, Rousseau A. Burch, Henry F. Mason and Alfred W. Bensen, all Republicans; Clerk, D. A. Valentine.

STATE LEGISLATURE, 1913. Republicans, Senate, 18; House, 50; joint ballot, 68. Democrats, Senate, 21; House, 73; joint ballot, 94. Socialists, Senate, 1; House, 2; joint ballot, 3. Democratic majority, Senate, 2; House, 21; joint ballot, 23.

The representatives in Congress will be found in the section *Congress*, article UNITED STATES.

KANSAS, UNIVERSITY OF. A State institution for higher education at Lawrence, Kan., founded in 1866. The total number of students enrolled in the various departments in 1912 was 2100. This does not include the summer school. The faculty numbered 175. There were no important changes in the faculty during the year, and as the university is supported almost entirely by the State, no noteworthy benefactions were received. The amount of productive funds was about $150,000 and the income in 1911-12 was $451,950. There were 80,000 volumes in the library. President, F. Strong, LL. D.

KANSAS-OKLAHOMA OIL FIELDS. See PETROLEUM.

KEANE, AUGUSTUS HENRY. An English etymologist and anthropologist, died February, 1912. He was born in Cork, Ireland, in 1833 and was educated privately. He traveled much and wrote extensively on many subjects. Among his writings are: *Man Past and Present; Ethnology; the Gold of Ophir; the Boer States; The World's Peoples,* and other anthropological works. He also contributed to the *Encyclopædia Britannica* and many learned publications. He received in 1897 a civil list pension of £50 for his labors in the field of ethnology. At the time of his death he was emeritus professor of Hindustani at University College, London. He received the degree of LL. D. from St. Andrews University.

KEDAH. A native state on the west coast of the Malay Peninsula, under British protection. Area, with the Langkawi group of islands, 3150 square miles; estimated population, 220,000, chiefly Malays, though there is a considerable Siamese population. Capital, Alo Star. The soil is fertile, and rice, cocoanuts, and rubber are planted. Estimated revenue for the year A. H. 1329 (January 2 to December 21, 1911), 1,444,955 Straits Settlements dollars; expenditure, 1,613,820. Native affairs are administered by the sultan (Abdul Hamid Halimshah ibni Ahmat Tajudin); British adviser (1912), W. G. Maxwell—Meadows Frost, acting. The loan (2,400,000 S. S. dollars) negotiated with the Siamese government in 1905 was taken over by the federated Malay states government upon the transfer in 1909 of the suzerainty of the state from Siam to Great Britain.

KELANTAN. A protected native state on the eastern side of the Malay Peninsula; administered by the hereditary rajah (Tuan Long Snik bin Almerhum Sultan Mohammed) under the direction of a resident British adviser (1912, J. S. Mason; J. E. Bishop, acting). The area is estimated at 5500 square miles and the population (1911) at 286,752 (268,707 Malays, 9844 Chinese, 5355 Siamese, 108 Europeans). Numbers of Chinese laborers are being brought in to work on the rubber plantations. Kota Bharu, the capital, has about 12,000 inhabitants and contains the palace of the rajah and the British residency. Other towns are Tumpat (4000 inhabitants), Bachak (2000), Tabal (2000) Pasir Puteh (2000). Rubber cultivation, cattle-raising, and fishing are principal industries; rice and paddy are exported. Gold is mined and tin is present. Roads are building, and the route is being surveyed for the railway which is to connect Kelantan with Singapore and Bangkok. The 1909-10 imports amounted to 1,175,158 Straits Settlements dollars; the exports to 1,473,413; the revenue was 370,959, and the expenditure 377,062. Kelantan was formally ceded by Siam to the protection of Great Britain, July 15, 1909.

KELP. See FERTILIZERS.

KENSICO DAM. See AQUEDUCTS.

KENTUCKY. POPULATION. According to the Census Bureau statistics issued in 1912 out of a total population of 2,289,905 in 1910, the foreign-born whites numbered 40,053, compared with 50,133 in 1900. The largest number of these, 19,346, came from Germany; from Ireland, 5913; from Russia, 3223; and from England, 2617. Other European countries are represented by smaller numbers. The city of Louisville, with a population in 1910 of 223,928, had a foreign-born white population of 17,436. In 1910 there were 261,656 negroes and 65,943 mulattoes in the State. The negroes in 1890 numbered 268,071 and the mulattoes, 51,986. It will be noted that Kentucky is the only southern State in which the number of negroes has decreased from 1890 to 1910.

AGRICULTURE. The acreage, value, and production of the principal crops in 1911 and 1912 are shown in the following table:

		Acreage	Prod. Bu.	Value
Corn	1912	3,600,000	109,440,000	$60,192,000
	1911	3,600,000	93,600,000	59,968,000
Wheat	1912	686,000	5,860,000	6,791,000
	1911	780,000	9,906,000	9,114,000
Oats	1912	150,000	4,035,000	1,775,000
	1911	170,000	3,128,000	1,564,000
Rye	1912	21,000	273,000	240,000
	1911	22,000	204,000	243,000
Potatoes	1912	51,000	5,151,000	3,451,000
	1911	52,000	2,028,000	2,170,000
Hay	1912	815,000	a 1,002,000	13,727,000
	1911	450,000	a 428,000	7,404,000
Tobacco	1912	441,000	b343,980,000	22,926,000
	1911	345,000	b303,600,000	23,377,200

a Tons. b Pounds.

MINERAL PRODUCTION. The coal production of the State in 1911 amounted to 13,706,839 short tons, valued at $13,617,217. This was a decrease from the production of 1910 of 916,480 short tons, which is accounted for largely by the abnormal figures in 1910 due to the strikes in other coal-producing States. The number of men employed in the coal mines of the State in 1911 was 21,821.

Petroleum. There were produced in the State in 1911 472,458 barrels of petroleum, compared with 468,774 barrels in 1910. The production has shown a steady decrease for several years. In 1907 it was 820,844 barrels.

MANUFACTURES. The Thirteenth Census statistics are for the calendar year 1909 and were compiled in 1912. While Kentucky is not one of the most important States in manufacturing, its manufacturing products have steadily increased at each census. From the table in the next column it will be seen that there were in 1909 4776 manufacturing establishments in the State, which gave employment to an average of 79,060 persons during the year.

The largest number of persons was employed in the lumbering and timber industries, 13,042. In industries connected with railways, employees numbered 5605; foundry and machine shop products, 4479; tobacco manufactures, 3973. The largest value of products was in the industries connected with the distillation of liquors, $44,360,000. This was followed by flour mill and grist mill products, $22,365,000; lumber and timber products, $21,381,000; tobacco

	Number or Amount 1909	Number or Amount 1904	P. C. Inc. '04-'09
Number of establishments	4,776	3,734	27.9
Persons engaged in manufactures	79,060	69,755	13.3
Proprietors and firm members	5,050	4,108	22.9
Salaried employees	8,610	5,853	41.1
Wage earners (average number)	65,400	59,794	47.1
Primary horsepower	230,224	174,625	9.4
Capital	$172,779,000	$147,282,000	17.3
Expenses	201,163,000	137,388,000	46.4
Services	37,491,000	30,310,000	23.7
Salaries	9,603,000	5,871,000	63.6
Wages	27,888,000	24,439,000	14.1
Materials	111,779,000	86,545,000	29.2
Miscellaneous	51,893,000	20,531,000	152.8
Value of products	223,754,000	159,754,000	40.1
Value of products less cost of material	111,975,000	73,209,000	53.0

manufactures, $18,598,000; foundry and machine-shop products, $9,627,000. The persons engaged in the manufacturing industries of the State in 1909 numbered 79,060. Of these 67,860 were male and 11,200 female. The number of wage earners under 16 years of age was 833. The prevailing hours of labor for the majority of those employed averaged from 54 to 60 a week; 19.5 per cent. of the total being employed in establishments where less than 54 hours a week prevailed, and 6.5 per cent. in establishments where more than 60 hours a week prevailed. The largest number of wage earners was in Louisville, 27,023. In Covington there were 3942; and in Newport 2632.

EDUCATION. The legislature of 1912 passed many important laws relating to education in the State. Among these was a compulsory attendance law, which requires children between the ages of 7 to 13 to attend school; a law creating an inspection department for inspecting all the schools and school funds of the State; a law giving the counties the right where they so desire to consolidate schools and to employ a rural supervisor and to bond itself for the purpose of building schools and extending terms.

FINANCE. The latest figures for the financial condition of the State are for the fiscal year ending June 30, 1911. The report of the treasurer showed a balance in the treasury on July 1, 1910, of $420,931. This, with the receipts for the year, left available funds amounting to $7,676,588. The disbursements for the fiscal year amounted to $7,013,330. In the general expenditure fund there was a deficit at the end of the year 1911 of $110,244. The bonded indebtedness of the State amounted at the end of the fiscal year 1911 to $2,315,627.

POLITICS AND GOVERNMENT

The legislature met in 1912 and the most important measures enacted are noted in the paragraph *Legislation* below. On January 10 the legislature elected Ollie M. James United States senator to succeed Thomas H. Paynter, whose term expired in 1913. The State Republican convention met on April 10. There was a contest between Roosevelt and Taft factions, but the Progressive delegates did not bolt the convention. President Taft was given 23 instructed votes, and one delegate from the fifth Congress district and two from the eleventh supported Mr. Roosevelt. Mass conventions throughout the State, held prior to the convention, gave the great majority of the delegates to the convention

The hottest fights were in Louisville, Frankfort, Lexington, and Shelbyville, where conventions were split up and separate delegations were elected. The Democratic delegates were instructed to vote for Champ Clark at the Democratic State convention. In county conventions held prior to the State convention an almost unanimous sentiment for Mr. Clark had been shown. In the election held on November 5, Governor Wilson received 219,584 votes, President Taft, 115,512, Mr. Roosevelt, 102,766, Debs, 11,647, and Chafin, 3323.

LEGISLATION. At the legislative session in 1912 an unusual number of important measures were passed. Among these were the following: A measure amending the laws of the State as to intoxicating liquors; an act creating a department of banking, providing for the appointment of a commissioner, etc.; an act providing for the nomination of candidates at primary elections and for placing names of candidates on the ballots to be voted for at general elections. This act provides for the nomination of party candidates for the office of United States senator, but it does not apply to certain candidates for school offices or to candidates for presidential electors. An act was passed creating and establishing a department of public roads. The school law of the State was amended in important details. An act was passed proposing to amend the constitution by allowing the employment of convict labor upon public roads and buildings. Enactments were passed providing for the protection of game and fish. A measure was enacted permitting women to vote for the election of school trustees and some other school officers, and upon school questions, and to hold common school offices such as women are disqualified from holding under the constitution. A measure was passed regulating the employment of females in order to safeguard their health. This provides, among other things, that no female under 21 years of age shall be employed or permitted to work at any gainful occupation, except domestic service and nursing, more than 60 hours in any one week or ten hours in any one day. The sale of opium was regulated. An act was passed securing compulsory education in the common schools and graded common schools. A measure was enacted providing for the creation of a commission known as the board of tuberculosis commissioners. This contemplates the establishment of sanitariums or hospitals for the treatment of tuberculosis under public authority or control. An act was passed providing for an annuity for aged, infirm, retired or disabled teachers in cities of the first class. A State board of forestry was established and other laws relating to conservation were passed. Boards of education for cities of the second class were created, and an act was passed providing for the organization of the militia.

STATE GOVERNMENT. Governor, James B. McCreary; Lieutenant-Governor, Edward J. McDermott; Secretary of State, C. F. Crecelius; Treasurer, Thomas S. Rhea; Auditor, Henry M. Bosworth; Attorney-General, James Garnett; Superintendent of Public Instruction, Barksdale Hamlett; Commissioner of Agriculture, John W. Newman; Commissioner of Insurance, M. C. Clay—all Democrats.

JUDICIARY. Court of Appeals: Chief Justice, J. P. Hobson; Justices, W. E. Settle, C. C. Turner, John M. Lassing, John D. Carroll, T. J. Nunn, Shackelford Miller; Commissioner of Appeals, William R. Clay; Commissioner of Agriculture, J. W. Newman; Clerk, Robert L. Green—all Democrats.

STATE LEGISLATURE, 1913. Democrats, Senate, 33; House, 76; joint ballot, 109. Republicans, Senate, 5; House, 24; joint ballot, 29. Democratic majority, Senate, 28; House, 52; joint ballot, 80.

The representatives in Congress will be found in the section *Congress*, article UNITED STATES.

KIAOCHOW. A German dependency on the east coast of the Chinese province of Shantung, consisting of a harbor, town, and district leased in March, 1898, for 99 years. In April, 1898, the district was declared a German protectorate. Area (exclusive of the bay), 552 square kilometers (213 square miles); population, about 165,000, exclusive of whites, who numbered (January 1, 1911) 3896, of whom 3806 German. Imports and exports at Tsingtau (the port of Kiaochow) in 1909-10, 65,464,000 and 54,732,000 marks; in 1910-11, 69,375,000 and 60,561,000. Tonnage entered (1910), 832,245. The Shantung Railway, which goes as far as Tsinan has a length of 434.4 kilometers (271 miles). The budget for 1911-12 balanced at 13,538,614 marks (including 7,703,240 marks imperial subvention); for 1912-13, 14,639,725 (8,297,565 subvention). A governor (1912, Captain Meyer-Waldeck) administers the dependency under the navy department.

KIDERLEN-WÄCHTER, ALFRED VON. A German statesman, died December 30, 1912. He was born in Stuttgart in 1852. While still a young man he entered the diplomatic service and was attached to the German embassies in St. Petersburg, Paris, and Constantinople. Through his intimacy with von Holstein, under-secretary of the foreign department, he became very influential with high government officials and he, with von Holstein and Prince Philip Eulenberg, was said to have had a remarkable influence in the councils of the emperor. In the scandals which resulted in the downfall of Prince Eulenberg, Kiderlen-Wächter was not involved. His friendship with the kaiser resulted in his appointment as minister at Copenhagen. Between 1895 and 1900 he constantly accompanied the emperor on his journeys. In this capacity it was his duty to report to the foreign office. It is said that certain of these reports found their way into the emperor's hands and their contents were such that he was for a time in disgrace and was sent to Rumania. During his stay in that country he acquired a wide knowledge of Balkan affairs and was able to supplement it by taking charge upon several occasions of the embassy at Constantinople during the absence of the ambassador. During the spring of 1908 at the time of the famous interview with the emperor published in the London *Daily Telegraph*, the foreign secretary, Baron von Schoen, was taken ill and Kiderlen-Wächter was summoned from Bucharest. His main work during his service in this office was to deal with the Casablanca incident and to prepare the Franco-German treaty of February, 1909. These negotiations were carried on with the French ambassador, Jules Cambon. Two years later Kiderlen-Wächter was appointed foreign secretary under Herr von Bethmann-Hollweg. He was largely blamed in Germany for the Agadir *coup* which greatly humiliated the German people. In their irritation many declared that he had been outplayed in the diplomatic negotiations with M. Cambon. As a result of this experience he was for a time in popular disfavor in Germany, but before his death, he succeeded in rebuilding his general reputation to a great degree and among those who had especial means of measuring his abilities he was regarded as a man of great energy and remarkable attainments.

KIDNEYS, TRANSPLANTATION OF. See CARREL, ALEXIS.

KIMURA TERM. See ASTRONOMY.

KING, HAMILTON. An American writer and diplomat, died September 2, 1912. He was born in St. John's, Newfoundland, in 1852, and graduated from Olivet College in 1878. In the following year he studied at the Chicago Theological Seminary and pursued studies abroad at Leipzig, and Athens in 1883 and 1884. From 1879 to 1898 he was principal of the preparatory department of Olivet College. He was well known as a lecturer, preacher, and political speaker. In 1898 he was appointed minister resident and consul-general to Siam. This position he held until 1903, when he was made minister to Siam. This position he continued to hold until he died. He was the author of *Greek Reader*, and *Outlines of United States History*.

KING EDWARD VII. LAND. See POLAR EXPLORATION.

KING HAAKON VII. PLATEAU. See POLAR EXPLORATION.

KIRKUP, THOMAS. An English economist, died May 3. 1912. He was born in 1844 and was educated in the village schools and at Edinburgh University. He studied also at the Universities of Göttingen, Berlin, Tübingen, Geneva and Paris. He contributed extensively on historical and economic subjects to the *Encyclopædia Britannica* and to *Chambers' Encyclopædia*. He wrote also articles for other encyclopædias and wrote and edited a large number of educational works. Among his published writings are: *An Inquiry into Socialism* (1887); *History of Socialism* (1892); *South Africa, Old and New* (1903); *Progress and the Fiscal Problem* (1905); *Primer of Socialism* (1908).

KITCHENER, SIR FREDERICK WALTER. A British administrator and lieutenant-general, died March 13, 1912. He was born in 1858, a younger brother of Field-Marshal Lord Kitchener of Khartum. After attending school at Bradfield, he obtained a commission in the 14th Foot. A year or two later he saw service in Afghanistan. He took part in the Dongola Expedition of 1896 as director of transport, and two years later participated in his brother's final advance on Khartum. In the South African War he commanded a battalion of the West Yorkshire Regiment. At the conclusion of that war he proceeded to India to take up a command. In 1908 he was appointed governor and commander-in-chief of Bermuda. General Kitchener received several medals for distinction in action. He was promoted to be major-general in 1900 and lieutenant-general in 1906.

KITCHENER, LORD. See EGYPT.

KLINGENBERG DAM. See DAMS.

KNOWLEDGE, THEORY OF. See PHILOSOPHY.

KNOX, GEORGE WILLIAMS. An American theologian and educator, died April 25, 1912. He was born in Rome, N. Y., in 1853 and graduated from Hamilton College in 1874. He studied at the Auburn Theological Seminary, graduating in 1877. In the same year he was ordained to the Presbyterian ministry. He engaged in missionary work in Japan and was for a time professor of homiletics at the Union Theological Seminary in Tokyo, and later professor of philosophy and ethics at the Imperial University of Japan. On his return to the United States he was for several years pastor at Rye, N. Y. From 1897 to 1899 he was lecturer on apologetics at the Union Theological Seminary, New York City, and from 1899 until the time of his death was professor of philosophy and the history of religion in that institution. He was Nathaniel Taylor lecturer at Yale University in 1903 and lecturer on the history of religion in 1905-6. Among his published writings are: *A Brief System of Theology, Outlines of Homiletics, The Basis of Ethics, The Mystery of Life*, all in Japanese; *A Japanese Philosopher* (1893); *The Christian Point of View* (with Professors Brown and McGiffert, 1902); *The Direct and Fundamental Proofs of the Christian Religion* (1903); *Japanese Life in Town and Country* (1904); *The Spirit of the Orient* (1906); *The Development of Religion in Japan* (1907); *The Religion of Jesus* (1909).

KOREA, or officially CHOSEN. The peninsula between the Yellow Sea and the Sea of Japan; formerly an independent monarchy, it was annexed to Japan August 29, 1910. Capital, Seoul.

AREA, POPULATION, ETC. Estimated area, 14,123 square ri (84,106 square miles). According to the census made public in 1912 the population of Korea on December 31, 1911, was 14,055,869, of whom the Japanese numbered 210,689, the Chinese 11,837, and other foreigners 967. The population of Seoul has been recently estimated at 278,958. Published estimates of the urban populations are most divergent. The following figures are officially stated for resident population December 31, 1909: Seoul, 217,391; Kyong-Syeng, 76,700; Yongsan, 50,191; Fusan, 41,081; Ping-Yang, 40,864; Hai-Syŏng, 27,640; Tai-Kou, 27,592; Chemulpo, 25,167; Jen-Ju, 17,571; Wonsan, 17,138; Ham-Heung, 17,023; Ching-Nam-Po, 15,708; Wi-Ju, 13,215; Thong-Yŏng, 12,024.

In general, the Koreans are ancestor-worshippers. Among the upper classes Confucianism prevails, and there is a considerable number of Buddhist monasteries in the country. The number of native Christians was reported at about 250,000 in 1910. The Japanese have undertaken the reorganization of the primary school system and the establishment of industrial and technical schools. In the summer of 1912 unfavorable reports were current on the general condition of the people under Japanese administration. Charges were made against the Japanese of forced labor and oppression, especially in the government salt mines, and of various outrages upon both personal and property rights.

PRODUCTION, COMMERCE, ETC. The important crops include rice and other cereals, beans, tobacco, hemp, ginseng, and cotton. Various minerals occur, including gold, copper, iron, silver, graphite, and coal, but, excepting gold, they are little worked.

Imports and exports of merchandise have been valued as follows, in thousands of yen:

	1907	1908	1909	1910	1911
Imports	40,050	41,026	36,649	39,783	54,088
Exports	17,002	14,113	16,249	18,914	18,857

Leading exports in 1910 and 1911, in thousands of yen: Rice, 6278 and 5281; beans, 5726 and 4630; cattle hides, 1005 and 1069; animals, 634 and 704; iron, 340 and 279; wheat, 361 in 1910; fish, 283 in 1911. Imports and exports by countries in 1911, in thousands of yen: Japan, 34,068 and 13,341; China, 5442 and 3009; United States, 4261 and 963; United Kingdom, 7924 and 1; Germany 1311 and 20; Russia in Asia, 49 and 1510; other countries, 1033 and 13; total, 54,088 and 18,857.

Railway in operation at the end of 1911, 1234 kilometers (767 miles); telegraphs, 6421 kms. of line and 12,457 kms. of wire; telephones, 1770 kms. of line and 18,838 kms. of wire; post offices, 465.

The branch lines of railway, the Seoul-Wusan, 140 miles in length, and the Tai-ku-Mok-pho, 175 miles in length, were under construction. The Antung-Mukden connection between Manchuria and Korea, which had been under reconstruction for some time, involving the conversion of the line of 4 ft. 8½ in. gauge, was being pushed forward and a bridge over the Yalu River at the frontier was reaching completion.

FINANCE. The monetary unit is the Japanese yen, par value 49.846 cents. For the fiscal year 1912 the budget balanced at 48,741,782 yen (including Japanese subvention 12,350,000 yen); for 1913, 52,892,209 (subvention 12,350,000 yen). Estimated ordinary revenue for the fiscal year 1912, 24,067,583 yen (including taxes 10,871,517, proceeds of government ente prises, etc., 10,962,-022; extraordinary revenue, r24,674,199 (subvention 12,350,000, loans 12,324,199). Estimated ordinary expenditure for the same year, 27,891,-437 yen; extraordinary, 20,850,345. Public debt (which has been taken over by the Japanese treasury) at the end of 1911, 29,255,335 yen.

GOVERNMENT. Formerly independent, Korea became a Japanese protectorate March 2, 1906, and was annexed to Japan August 29, 1910. The country was placed under the administration of a governor-general, Gen. Viscount (later Count) Terauchi Masakata. Civil govenor-general, Yamagata Isaburo. For history in 1912, see JAPAN, *History*.

KRYPTON. See PHYSICS.

KURIA MURIA ISLANDS. Attached to Aden (q. v.).

KWANGCHOW-WAN. A territory on the Chinese coast leased to France. See French Indo-China.

KWANTUNG, or KWANTO. A Japanese leasehold in the southern part of the Liaotung Peninsula (Manchuria). Area, 1221 square miles. Resident population at the end of 1909 (exclusive of 114 foreigners), 446,482 (251,140 male, 195,342 female); Chinese (or Manchurians) were reported to number 414,380 (232,618 male, 181,762 female) and Japanese 32,102 (18,522 and 13,580). Estimated population in 1912, 488,080. Dairen, the capital and chief port, had (1909) 41,333 inhabitants; Ryojun (Port Arthur), 15,195. Agricultural products include corn, millet, beans, wheat, rice, tobacco, and hemp. Salt is produced, and the fisheries are of some importance. The trade is chiefly with Japan. Imports and exports in 1910, 28,732,797 and 38,797,925 yen; in 1911, 42,274,722 and 47,416,-047 yen. About eighty miles of the South Manchurian Railway are in Kwantung. Estimated revenue and expenditure for the fiscal year 1912 balanced at 5,250,216 yen (including Japanese subvention 3,283,090 yen); for 1913, 5,246,887 (subvention 3,122,500). Governor-general in 1912, Gen. Viscount Oshima Yoshimara.

LABOR. The year 1912 was one of especial interest to students of the labor problem. The world-wide unrest which has been conspicuous for several years continued unabated. Throughout the western nations there was increasing evidence of the growth of class consciousness among the workers, accompanied by increasing confidence in their own strength and the justice of their demands. These features are illustrated by the record of strikes (see STRIKES AND LOCKOUTS), by the success of the British miners in securing a legal minimum wage (see MINIMUM WAGE), by the spread of theories and policies which have come to bear the name of Syndicalism (q. v.), in Great Britain and the United States, and the increasing prominence given by the trade unions of these countries to political action. (See TRADE UNIONS). At the same time the general public showed evidence of increasing concern for the welfare of children, youth, and women of the laboring classes. See CHILD LABOR, SWEATING, MINIMUM WAGE, and WOMEN IN INDUSTRY.

Other phases of the labor problem will be found under: LABOR LEGISLATION, ARBITRATION AND CONCILIATION, INDUSTRIAL; BOYCOTT; EMPLOYERS' LIABILITY, and WORKMEN'S COMPENSATION; INDUSTRIAL WORKERS OF THE WORLD; LABOR, AMERICAN FEDERATION OF; LABOR LEGISLATION; OCCUPATIONAL DISEASES; OLD-AGE PENSIONS; SOCIAL INSURANCE; SYNDICALISM; UNEMPLOYMENT; and WELFARE WORK. Other cross references will be found under these articles. Labor conditions in the United States Steel Corporation are treated under that heading.

BIBLIOGRAPHY. New books of the year included the following: F. Challaye, *Syndicalisme reformiste et syndicalisme révolutionnaire;* Ghile, *Le syndicalisme professionnel et son évolution nécessaire;* J. Goldmark, *Fatigue and efficiency: a study in industry;* G. Guy-Grand, *La philosophie syndicaliste. La philosophie nationaliste;* F. Heim, *Recherches sur l'hygiene du travail industriel;* L. Levine, *The labor movement in France; a study in revolutionary syndicalism;* Jeremiah W. Jenks and W. Jett Lauck, *The Immigration Problem;* W. Paine, *Shop Slavery and emancipation. A revolutionary appeal to the educated young men of the middle class;* W. Sombart, *Socialism and the social movement;* G. Sorel, *Réflections sur la violence. Les illusions du progrès. La décomposition du Marxisme;* A. Clay, *Syndicalism of labour; notes upon some aspects of social and industrial questions of the day;* O. Jean, *Le syndicalisme. Son origine. Son organization. Son but. Son rôle social;* E. G. Payne, *An experiment in alien labor;* I. B. Gross, *The essentials of socialism;* V. D. Scudder, *Socialism and character;* J. Spargo and G. L. Arner, *Elements of socialism;* David A. McCabe, *The standard rate in American trade unions, Finding employment for children who leave the grade schools to go to work: Report to the Chicago Woman's Club;* Mrs. Lindon W. Bates, *Mercury poisoning in the industries of New York City and vicinity;* H. Lichtenfelt, *Über die Ernährung und deren Kosten bei deutschen Arbeitern;* A. D. Lewis, *Syndicalism and the general strike: an explanation;* J. R. MacDonald, *Syndicalism;* C. Watney and J. A. Little, *The labour unrest: its aims and methods explained;* H. G. Wells and others, *What the worker wants;* E. George Payne, *An Experiment in Alien Labor.*

LABOR, AMERICAN FEDERATION OF. The most important and comprehensive body in the trade union movement in the United States is the American Federation of Labor, founded in 1881. Its fundamental principles are organization along trade lines and the greatest degree of individual trade union autonomy possible. It thus stands in direct opposition as regards the form of labor organization to the Industrial Workers of the World (q. v.). The Federation on September 30, 1912, consisted of 112 national and international unions comprising about 21,000 local unions. Its central administration included five departments: the building trades, the metal trades, railroad employees, union label trades, and mining. There were 41 State branches, 560 city central unions, 434 local trade unions, and 156 federal labor unions. The aggregate membership was 1,841,268. Unions affiliated in this organization published about 540 weekly and monthly periodicals. The official publication is the *American Federationist*, edited by the president, Samuel Gompers, and published at the Federation's headquarters in Washington, D. C.

Among the principal activities of the Federation in 1912 was the furtherance of the idea of federation not only among unions of the United States, as among the various groups of railroad employees, but also the perfection of relations between American and Canadian unions as represented in the international organizations. It carried on activities also in Porto Rico. It began a "Labor Forward Movement," designed to stimulate the organization of workers. It carried on an active campaign among the employees in the steel industry, designed to educate, uplift, and Americanize them, and enable them by concerted action to secure better labor contracts. It was active in securing eight-hour legislation. It continued to seek the enactment by Congress of a law limiting the use of injunctions in labor disputes. It continued the issue of a weekly news letter begun in 1911 as a means of furnishing accurate information to the daily press and to the labor periodicals.

LABOR EXCHANGES. See UNEMPLOYMENT.

LABOR FORWARD MOVEMENT. See LABOR, AMERICAN FEDERATION OF.

LABOR LEGISLATION. ACCIDENTS AND DISEASES. During the year 1912 fourteen States held regular legislative sessions and seven States held special sessions each of which resulted in some labor legislation. In connection with the world-wide movement for the compensation of industrial accidents (see EMPLOYERS' LIABILITY) has gone an equally extensive movement for the prevention of accidents in industry and for the reduction or elimination of diseases to which different occupations render the worker especially susceptible. In order to increase knowledge, and supply the information necessary to intelligent legislation, there have been during the last few years numerous laws for the compulsory reporting of industrial accidents and diseases. In 1912 seven States enacted legislation on the reporting of accidents. In Massachusetts and New Jersey new laws required all employers to report serious industrial accidents; in California all employers, except farmers and housekeepers, are required to report such accidents; in Rhode Island public service corporations must report any serious accidents either to employees or to the public; in Virginia accidents in coal mines must be reported; in Arizona accidents in mines and on public utilities must be reported; and in New Mexico fatal accidents in mines must be immediately reported by telegraph or telephone. Maryland and New Jersey enacted laws requiring physicians to report cases of the following occupational diseases: Anthrax, compressed-air illness, and lead, phosphorus, arsenic, or mercury poisoning. Altogether eight States, six in 1911, now require the reporting of certain occupational diseases, in all but two cases the same as those here listed. In Maryland the law especially provides that physicians must report all diseases resulting from employment. Moreover, the New York Department of Labor, under a provision of a 1911 law, requested physicians to report all occupational diseases. These reports will assist in the classification of trade diseases and open the way for effective preventive legislation.

With reference to the prevention of accidents and diseases, Massachusetts, New Jersey, New York, and Virginia passed laws relating to factories and workshops; Arizona, New Mexico, and Virginia laws relating to mines; and Arizona, Mississippi, and Congress laws relating to railroads and street cars. In addition, Congress passed a law placing a tax of 2 cents per hundred on the manufacture of poisonous white or yellow phosphorus matches. This congressional enactment included detailed rules for the manufacture and sale of such matches and for the stamping of same; imposed heavy penalties, amounting to $5000 or three years' imprisonment or both as the maximum, for failure to observe the details of the law; provided that a manufacturer defrauding or attempting to defraud the government out of the tax shall forfeit his entire business. The enforcement of this act is placed in the hands of the Commissioner of Internal Revenue, the law to become effective July 1, 1913. Certain clauses forbid the importation of white phosphorus matches after January 1, 1913, or their exportation after January 1, 1914. Provisions relating to the sale of white phosphorus matches become effective January 1, 1915.

ADMINISTRATION. Following the lead of Wisconsin, which created an industrial commission in 1911, Massachusetts in 1912 made provision for a State board of labor and industries. This was probably the most important labor legislation administrative act of the year. This board will consist of five persons and will have complete responsibility for the enforcement of nearly all labor laws of the State, including those heretofore in charge of the district police and the State board of health. This board must include one employer, one wage-earner, one physician or sanitary engineer, and one woman. Members are appointed by the governor for five years, one member retiring annually. The chairman receives $1500 and others $1000 per year. It may investigate conditions in any industry, receive complaints, employ experts, make necessary rules, and direct prosecutions. It is authorized to appoint and remove the commissioner of labor and fix his term with salary at not less than $5000 or more than $7500. Two deputy commissioners, one of whom must be a health expert, 24 inspectors and clerical assistants, at least four of whom must be women, are also provided. Arizona created a State mine inspector to be elected annually and to have power to appoint three deputies. Their powers and duties were defined in detail. Illinois, Kentucky, and Maryland provided for women factory inspectors and investigators. The latter State also increased the number of inspectors to enforce the child-labor law. New Jersey authorized the appointment of two additional factory inspectors, one to be a skilled baker, the other a skilled metal polisher and buffer. It also placed the assistant commissioner of labor and all inspectors in the competitive class of the classified civil service. New Mexico created the office of State inspector of mines to be filled by the governor. New York increased the number of factory inspectors from 85 to 125, these 40 additional inspectors being of the second grade, with salaries of $1200 each. The maximum number of women inspectors was increased from 15 to 20. The powers of the commissioner of labor were increased; the registration of factories with the labor department was required; and various provisions for the prevention of fire were laid down. The term of the factory investigating commission created in 1911 was extended for another year and $60,000 was appropriated for its use. It must report by January 15, 1913. South Carolina made certain minor changes and Virginia created the department of mines within the Bureau of Labor and Industrial Statistics, with a State mine inspector.

Hours. With reference to the hours of employment the most important legislation was the act of Congress establishing an eight-hour day for contract work done for the United States, with minor exceptions, and for letter carriers and post-office clerks in larger cities. This new legislation requires that the eight-hour provision be inserted in all contracts made by or on behalf of the United States, any Territory, or the District of Columbia. Laborers and mechanics employed by any contractor or subcontractor may not be required or permitted to work more than eight hours in any one day. A penalty of $5 for each worker for every day is imposed. Exception is made, however, of contracts for transportation by land or water, for the transmission of intelligence, for the purchase of supplies, for articles that may be bought in the open market (except armor and armor plate), for levee or other work for protection against floods. For military purposes the President may waive the provisions of the act; and he may set them aside also for any Panama Canal contract prior to January 1, 1915. Congress also provided an eight-hour day for letter carriers in the city delivery service and for clerks in first and second-class post offices. In cases of emergency overtime is allowed, but must be paid for in proportion to salaries. These eight-hour provisions become effective March 4, 1913. On August 24, 1912, a clause closing post offices of the first and second class on Sunday for public delivery of mail became effective.

The five States of Arizona, New Jersey, New Mexico, Massachusetts, and Mississippi regulated the hours of employment in private undertakings. Arizona passed an eight-hour law for mines, smelters, and similar establishments. New Jersey limited the hours of all employees in bakeries to ten a day and sixty a week, with a provision that if any part of the act be overthrown by the courts the other parts shall be unaffected. Massachusetts extended the laws regulating the hours of work of conductors and motormen to include trainmen and otherwise made minor changes in the hours of employees of street and steam railways. New Mexico regulated the hours of railway employees. Mississippi passed a most comprehensive ten-hour law making it illegal for any employer engaged in manufacturing or repairing to work his employees more than ten hours a day except in cases of emergency or where public necessity requires.

Wages. The Following States passed laws relating to wages: Arizona, Kentucky, Maryland, Massachusetts, Mississippi, New Jersey, and Virginia. Most of these related to the assignment of wages or mechanics' liens. Mississippi required payments in lawful money at least once a month, and Arizona and Virginia at least twice a month in most employments.

Miscellaneous. Arizona and Massachusetts passed laws to protect members of the militia or naval reserve from being deprived of employment on account of such membership. The Massachusetts law even imposed a penalty for dissuading any person from enlisting in militia or naval reserve by a threat of injury to him in his employment. Arizona also prohibited managers, agents, foremen, and others who hire laborers from demanding or receiving directly or indirectly any fee or gratuity as a condition of employment or continuation in employment. In Minnesota the corrupt practices act was made to prohibit employers from exercising any political influence over their employees by any threat to discharge or reduce wages. A similar law was enacted in New Mexico, which also provided that employees may have two hours off on election day. Congress made provision for cash rewards for suggestions for improvements or economies in processes or organization in the ordnance department; and also authorized the Postmaster-General to reward employees whose inventions are adopted by the postal service.

Commission on Industrial Relations. As a result of the extraordinary number of strikes in 1911, the revelations attending the Lawrence strike in 1912, and other evidences of widespread labor unrest, Congress was induced by the activities of a large and influential group of social workers and public-spirited citizens to establish a commission on industrial relations. This consists of nine persons, including three employers and three trade unionists. They are appointed by the President and receive expenses and $10 per day while actually engaged in this work. The commission has extensive powers to hold hearings and compel the giving of testimony. Its term was fixed at three years with the provision that it shall submit at least one report each year. An appropriation of $100,000 for the first year was made. The subjects into which the commission must inquire include the following: The general condition of labor in all leading industries; existing relations between employers and employees; the effect of industrial conditions on public welfare; the sanitary and safety conditions of employees; the development of associations of employers and employees, and their effects; the extent and results of collective bargaining; methods for maintaining mutually satisfactory relations between employers and employees; methods of of peacefully adjusting labor disputes; existing bureaus of labor; the smuggling of Asiatics into the United States and its insular possessions. The law provides that "the commission shall seek to discover the underlying causes of dissatisfaction in the industrial situation and report its conclusions thereon." The personnel of the commission as named by the President in December was as follows: Senator George Sutherland of Utah; George B. Chandler of Connecticut, New England representative of the American Book Company; Charles S. Barrett of Georgia, president of the Farmers' Union; Frederick A. Delano of Chicago, president of the Wabash Railroad; Adolph Lewisohn, capitalist, of New York City; Ferdinand C. Schwedtman, of St. Louis, vice-president of the National Association of Manufacturers; Austin B. Garretson of Iowa, president of the Order of Railway Conductors; and John B. Lennon and James O'Connell, important officers of the American Federation of Labor. These appointments had not been approved at the end of the year.

FRANCE. On March 30 the Chamber of Deputies passed a bill providing an eight-hour day for coal miners. This was done in response to widespread agitation among the miners and the danger of a general strike similar to that among the English miners. In July a law was passed providing a ten-hour day for employees in factories and business houses. Exceptions were made for minor and domestic industries, which were defined to include those where fewer than twenty were employed in case of hand work and fewer than ten in case machine power was used.

See CHILD LABOR; CHILDREN'S BUREAU; WOMEN IN INDUSTRY; MINIMUM WAGE; and other articles referred to under LABOR.

LABOR LEGISLATION, AMERICAN ASSOCIATION FOR. This association was formed a few years ago as the American branch of the International Association for Labor Legislation (q. v.). It has succeeded in establishing branches in New York, Massachusetts, Wisconsin, and other leading industrial States. It seeks to advance legislation designed to protect workers from exploitation, from accidents and diseases of industry, and from other abnormal economic conditions which undermine vitality and reduce the efficiency and the future prospects of the working class. One of the first subjects to which it gave extended attention was the workmen's compensation (q. v.). Largely as the result of the association's activities there has been a considerable volume of legislation replacing employers' liability by the more modern principle of fixed compensation. (See EMPLOYERS' LIABILITY.) It now seeks a federal compensation act of greatly enlarged scope. More recently it has given much attention to diseases specially incident to particular trades. (See OCCUPATIONAL DISEASES.) In connection with the compensation movement it has centred attention on the importance of accurate reports of industrial accidents and occupational diseases and the perfection of means for their prevention. (See LABOR LEGISLATION.) During 1912 it directed much attention to the subject of minimum-wage legislation, especially for women and children. This was an important subject of discussion at its annual meeting in Boston in December in connection with the American Economic Association. (See MINIMUM WAGE.) Other subjects included in the association's programme are the establishment of one day's rest in seven for all workers, and a maximum ten-hour day, preferably an eight-hour day, for women. It seeks also more efficient machinery for the administration of labor laws.

LABOR LEGISLATION, INTERNATIONAL ASSOCIATION FOR. This body met at Zurich, Switzerland, in the middle of September. Representatives were present from twenty-two different countries, there being many delegates directly representing their governments. The conference was divided into five sections. The first section devoted to general business reported the success of the international campaign against the manufacture of white phosphorus matches and recommended the coöperation of all delegates on the subjects of unemployment and workmen's insurance. The second section was devoted to the subject of industrial diseases (q. v.). Special studies of lead poisoning, ferrosilicon, caisson disease, and anthrax were recommended, as also the collection and systematization of statistics of occupational diseases and mortality. A third section studied home work. It approved minimum wage boards and outlined plans for their organization. It condemned the truck system and the imposition of fines and particularly approved methods of protecting persons engaged in embroidery-making. The fourth section approved the eight-hour shift in continuous industries, particularly in iron and steel plants; recommended a 56-hour week for glass-works with uninterrupted weekly rest of twenty-four hours; and recommended the introduction of the three-shift plan into other continuous-process industries. It determined to prosecute inquiries into means of protecting railway employees against fatigue, sickness, and accidents and for the settlement of trade disputes, especially those on public utilities. The fifth section was devoted to workingmen's insurance, child labor, and the administration of labor laws. The Saturday half-holiday was approved in principle, though the French delegates raised practical objections to it. Reports from Germany, Great Britain, and the United States on the administration of child-labor laws were uniform in showing very general lack of enforcement.

LABOR TROUBLES. See STRIKES.

LABOUCHERE, HENRY DU PRÉ. An English journalist and politician, died January 14, 1912. He was born in London in 1831 and was educated at Eton. He was the son of John Labouchere and a nephew of Lord Taunton. Following his studies at Eton he spent a short time at Cambridge, but did not take a degree. In 1854 he entered the diplomatic service, but ten years later abandoned diplomacy as a career. During this period he visited the United States, Mexico, and other foreign countries and was concerned in many adventures and escapades which made him a notable figure. These included, it is said, travel for a time with a circus and many experiences in the western part of the United States and elsewhere. He early showed ability in politics and in 1865 he was chosen to represent the borough of Windsor in the House of Commons. This seat, however, was vacated on petition in the ensuing spring. In the following year he was successful at a by-election in Middlesex. In 1868, however, he was defeated for reëlection and he suffered defeat also in 1874 when he contested Nottingham as a Liberal of advanced type. In the meantime Mr. Labouchere had become greatly interested in journalism. Just before the outbreak of the Franco-German War the *Daily News* passed into the hands of new proprietors, chief of whom were Samuel Morley, Henry Oppenheim and Mr. Labouchere. During the siege of Paris by the German army Mr. Labouchere contributed to this paper a series of letters, afterwards published under the title *Letters of a Besieged Resident*. These he sent from Paris chiefly by balloon post. He contributed much to the success of the *Daily News*, but that paper was less radical than he wished to make it and in 1874, while still retaining a dominant influence in the *Daily News*, he became associated with Edmund Yates in founding the *World*. This paper was the first success in that type which came to be known as "society journalism."

After two years' association with Yates, Labouchere, as the result of difficulties, withdrew and established under the name of *Truth* a paper on somewhat similar lines. This paper became at once successful and continued to be so. Several features attracted wide attention. Among these was the exposure of organized frauds, especially those perpetrated under the mask of charity. His fearlessness in attacking supposed or real impostors resulted in many libel suits. The heaviest judgment awarded against him was one for $5000, in the case of Dr. Dakhyl, who sued on account of allegations of quackery made in *Truth*. A new trial was ordered and *Truth* won. In ten years from 1897 to 1907, nine suits for libel were brought against Labouchere, five of which resulted in his favor. One good accomplished by the journal was its advocacy of open spaces and rights of way. In Parliament Mr. Labouchere made no great impression. He was not a powerful speaker, but in other ways had considerable influence. He is said to have been greatly disappointed that he was not invited by Gladstone to enter the cabinet after the victory of 1892, and to have considered himself largely responsible for the Liberal victory of that year.

Labouchere married in 1868 Henrietta Hodson, an actress. His interest in theatrical affairs was keen. In 1867 he managed the Queen's Theatre, at which Irving, Wyndham and Toole played.

Labouchere was perhaps best known as a conversationist and wit. As "Labby" his name was known throughout all English-reading and -speaking lands. Many anecdotes more or less authentic are related of his extemporaneous witticisms. He was perhaps more notable for his personality than for any positive accomplishment.

LABRADOR. A peninsula in the northeastern part of British America, attached partly to Newfoundland (q. v.) and partly to Canada.

LABUAN. See STRAITS SETTLEMENTS.

LACROSSE. The Crescent Athletic Club, as in former years, was the only organization in the United States in 1912 to pay much attention to lacrosse. The Crescent team defeated Carlisle 4-3, Toronto University 3-1, Mount Washington 5-2, Shamrocks of West Toronto 5-2, and the Toronto Amateur Lacrosse Club 9-3, and played a tie game with Toronto University 5-5. The United States Naval Academy was the only team to vanquish the Crescents, the score being 6-4. The victors in the Intercollegiate League were Harvard in the northern division and Swarthmore in the southern division. In the game to decide the championship Harvard defeated Swarthmore by a score of 7 to 3. Canada, the home of lacrosse, was the scene of many matches, both in the amateur and professional ranks. The Vancouver A. A. A. captured the Mann cup, while the professional New Westminster L. C. is the Minto cup holder.

LADIES' GARMENT WORKERS' UNION. See ARBITRATION AND CONCILIATION.

LAFAYETTE COLLEGE. An institution of higher learning at Easton, Pa., founded in 1832. The total enrollment for 1912 was 577. Of these, 24 were graduate students, 91 civil engineering, 68 electrical engineering, 15 mining engineering, 24 mechanical engineering, and 67 chemical. The faculty numbers 57. During the year there was completed a mechanical engineering building, an extension to the library, with a capacity for 80,000 volumes, and a student fraternity house. The income for the year 1911-12 was $125,709. The library contained about 40,000 volumes. President, E. D. Warfield, LL. D.

LA FOLLETTE, ROBERT. See PRESIDENTIAL CAMPAIGN.

LAKE MOHONK CONFERENCE. See ARBITRATION, INTERNATIONAL.

LAKE SUPERIOR REGION. See GEOLOGY.

LAMBERTON, BENJAMIN PEFFER. A rear-admiral, retired, of the United States navy, died June 9, 1912. He was born in Cumberland County, Pa., in 1844 and graduated from the United States Naval Academy in 1864. He at once saw service in the naval operations of the Civil War and after its close served in various offices. He was stationed at the Navy Yard in Boston from 1875 to 1877 and served in the Bureau of Equipment from 1879 to 1882. He was lighthouse inspector of the Sixth District from 1885 until 1888, and held the same position in the Fifth District from 1894 to 1898. In the latter year he was made chief of staff of Admiral Dewey and served in this position at the battle of Manila Bay, May 1, 1898. He was advanced seven numbers in rank for eminent and conspicuous conduct in this battle. In 1898-9 he commanded the *Olympia*, Admiral Dewey's flagship. He was a member of the Naval Examining and Retiring Board, 1900, and of the Lighthouse Board from 1900 to 1903. In 1903-4 he was commander-in-chief of the South Atlantic Squadron. He was president of the Naval War College in 1904 and in 1905-6 was chairman of the Lighthouse Board. In the latter year he retired from active service.

LANDS, PUBLIC. The question of the public lands in different phases will be found treated in the articles IRRIGATION, FORESTRY, ALASKA, HAWAII, and the PHILIPPINES. There were no developments of unusual interest in the administration of the public lands of the United States during 1912. Considerable progress was made by the field force of the general land office in the disposition of coal-land investigations in Alaska, and final disposition was made of the Cunningham coal claims (see ALASKA). There were submitted reports on 454 claims during the year, and out of 1129 coal locations before the general land office, there were only 199 which had not been investigated. Of this number 144 were either cancelled or held for cancellation for failure to submit applications for patent within the time required by law, leaving only 55 pending claims which still require some investigation. During the year adverse proceedings were directed against 188 claims. Another important work of the field force was the investigation of the California oil land. There are included in withdrawals in California over 1,500,000 acres containing valuable petroleum deposits. Of the lands withdrawn approximately 100,000 acres are covered by pending entries and selections. Much of the remainder is covered by mineral locations of oil, gypsum, and asphaltum. A number of special agents and mineral inspectors of the field service are devoting almost their entire time to the work of investigating these entries and selections, and in assisting the officials of the department of justice in suits which have been or will be instituted for the recovery of titles to a large part of these lands to which patents have issued under applications for the lands which alleged that they were non-mineral in character.

The number and acreage of applications for segregation filed under the Carey act during 1912 showed a marked decrease from 1911, due chiefly to the fact that the easiest and cheapest projects were naturally taken up first and that the field of operation was becoming more restrictive. During 1912 applications for 184,697 acres were filed, and applications aggregating 97,917 acres were approved. In applications under the act of March 15, 1910, 1,416,474 acres were applied for, applications involving 593,189 acres were rejected, 214,211 acres were withdrawn, and 1,064,572 acres were restored upon the expiration of the year granted by the act or upon relinquishment. During the fiscal year there were approved to the States and Territories an area of 181,280 acres, of which 147,988 acres were school-land selections.

An important measure was passed by Congress and approved June 6, 1912. This is known as the "three-year homestead bill." It reduces from five to three years the residence period on a homestead taken from the public domain, and otherwise improves conditions under which title to land is proven. This legislation is operative also in the Territory of Alaska.

The work of land classification was carried on during the year. The Geological Survey recommended more than one and one-fifth million acres of oil reserves and almost one and one-third million acres of phosphate reserves, based on geologic data, and more than one-third million acres of water-power sites and 60,000 acres of irrigation-reservoir sites, based upon hydrographic and topographic surveys, and 86,000 acres of public water reserves essential to the control of the public grazing lands. As regards the classification of coal lands the year was notable in that for the first time the acreage classified and restored has much exceeded that withdrawn for classification, so that at the end of the year there was a substantial reduction in the area of outstanding land withdrawals. More than 800,000 acres were classified as coal land and valued at nearly $15,000,000, while nearly 14,000,000 acres were classified as non-coal lands.

NATIONAL PARKS. There are twelve national parks under the control of the United States government, of which the Glacier National Park is the last. This was made a national reservation in 1910. The other national parks are: Yellowstone National Park, Yosemite National Park, Sequoia National Park, General Grant National Park, Crater Lake National Park, Mount Rainier National Park, Mesa Verde National Park, Wind Cave National Park, Platt National Park, Sully's Hill National Park, and Hot Springs Reservation. At the Hot Springs Reservation there were during the year 1912 135,000 visitors; at the Platt National Park in Oklahoma, 31,000; Yellowstone National Park, 22,970, and at the Yosemite Park, 10,884.

LANDSCHAFTEN SYSTEM. See AGRICULTURAL CREDIT.

LANG, ANDREW. An English man of letters, died July 20, 1912. He was born in Selkirk, Scotland, in 1844, and was educated at St. Andrews University and at Balliol College, Oxford. At Oxford he was distinguished for his knowledge of the classics. In 1868 he was made a Fellow of Merton College. Practically the whole of his life was given up to writing and he was perhaps the most prolific writer of his day, when the quality of his work is considered. His writings may be divided into three classes, although these by no means include the scope of his performance. Indeed the distinctive feature of his intellect was its extraordinary versatility. One set of his writings was concerned with the study of the literature of myths and the curious customs of primitive folk. The second of his favorite studies was that of Homer and the other Greek classics. The third was his interest in spiritualism, psychical research, and kindred subjects. He was in addition a journalist, critic, biographer, poet, scholar, historian, and parodist. His first published work was an edition of the *Ballads and Lyrics of Old France*, published in 1872. In 1880 followed a book of verse entitled *Ballads in Blue China*. This was followed in 1884 by his first serious work entitled *Custom and Myth*, an inquiry into the genesis of religions, totemism, and other savage customs. The same subjects were pursued in *Myth, Literature and Religion* (1887); *The Making of Religion; Social Origins* (1903), and *The Secret of the Totem* (1905). These, however, were but a small part of his literary output between 1894 and 1905. In addition to several volumes of verse he wrote a half dozen books of essays, edited a series of fairy tale books, and in 1893 published his first book relating to Homer entitled *Homer and the Epic*. He produced in the years following, among other works, *Life of John Gibson Lockhart* (1896); *Pickle, the Spy*, a novel (1897); *The Book of Dreams and Ghosts;* a translation of Homer's *Odyssey*, with Professor Butcher, and of the *Iliad* with Mr. Myers and Mr. Leaf; *The Homeric Hymns* (1899); *A History of Scotland from the Roman Occupation*, Vol. I.; *Prince Charles Edward* (1900); *Magic and Religion* (1901); *Alfred Tennyson* (1901); *The Mystery of Mary Stuart* (1901); *John Knox and the*

Reformation (1905); *Homer and His Age* (1906); *A Defense of Sir Walter Scott and the Border Minstrelsy* (1910).

As a translator of Homer, Mr. Lang's reputation will perhaps last longest. His translations are unmatched for fidelity and good writing. As a critic of Homer he was a steadfast upholder of the epic unity. As a critic of modern literature he did an almost unbelievable amount of work for newspapers and periodicals. He was for several years the chief reviewer of fiction for the *Times*, contributed to *Longman's Magazine*, and wrote regularly a column in the *Illustrated London News*. In addition to the three divisions of his interests mentioned above, there was a fourth, the historical, especially matters relating to Scottish history. His writings on the Stuarts in Scotland are of particular interest and value. Several years before his death he carried on an interesting controversy with Anatole France over Joan of Arc, and this was followed a biography of Joan which was designedby to counteract the somewhat derogatory biography written by M. France. Mr. Lang was, in addition to his literary activities, an ardent golfer and wrote much on the game. He was one of the most interesting figures in modern English literature and was an intimate friend of most of the writers of his generation. He received the honorary degree of Litt. D. from Oxford University. He was a Fellow of the British Academy.

LANGLOIS, Hippolyte. A French soldier and writer, died February 12, 1912. He was born at Besançon in 1839 and was educated in that city. There also he received his first military training at the École Polytechnique. In 1858 he received a commission as sub-lieutenant of artillery and was promoted to be captain in 1866 in the Franco-German War. In 1878 he was made major and in 1887, lieutenant-colonel. He was for a time professor of artillery tactics at the École Supérieure de Guerre. To this institution he returned ten years later as director with the rank of general of division. In 1901 he was appointed to the command of the famous 20th Army Corps at Nancy and in the following year was made a member of the Army Council. He retired in 1904 upon attaining the age limit. In 1906 he was elected a member of the Senate and in 1907 was chosen a member of the French Academy. He was a grand officer of the Legion of Honor.

The writings of General Langlois on military subjects were of great value. His experience in the Franco-German War revealed to him the deficiencies in artillery and he was one of the influential officers whose researches resulted in the production of the 75mm. quick-firing gun. As director of the War School and as a member of the Army Council he was able to diffuse his ideas throughout the army and this resulted in great improvement in the character and equipment of the French troops.

LANGUAGE, International. In February, 1911, a society for the creation of an international language bureau (Verband für die Schaffung einer Weltsprache Amtes) had been founded with Bern, Switzerland, as its headquarters. It issued its *Auruf* in 1912. It was due to the efforts of the Idists (see former Year Books) and the Esperantists look askance on it, not quite sure whether the bureau is going to act in a truly impartial spirit. At any rate Esperanto papers reflect not very amiably on the institution and wonder whether it is better policy to join, or to abstain. This is only one domain where it is plain that the fight between the two factions is going on. It makes not always very edifying reading for the layman. The quarrel may turn out for the real good of the cause of the International Language, forcing improvements on both sides. The Esperantists have now decided upon the creation of a "Representaro," or sort of language council, to consider, from the Esperanto point of view, what changes in the language might be acceptable while remaining true to the intangible "fundamento" adopted some years ago. Whatever it may mean ultimately, this is an admission in principle that changes *are* conceivable, the idea that the Idists have tried to impose all along.

The International Congress of the Esperantists took place in Cracow, Poland, August 11-18, a jubilee congress, which celebrated the twenty-fifth anniversaary of the first publication by Dr. Zamenhof. The inventor of Esperanto announced his retirement from active work in the cause of the International Language. His speech was significant; he asked all to work in harmony, and said that he withdrew so as not to be considered a sort of Esperantist Pope, which as a matter of fact he had never desired to be. Promptly there followed the creation of the "Representaro" just mentioned.

A movement of conciliation between Idists and Esperantists was attempted by Dr. René de Saussure, of Geneva, who started a review for the purpose: *Linguo Kosmopolita*.

As interesting contributions to the literature of the year: Couturat, "La vérité sur l'Ido" (*La Revue*, July 1), reprinted as a pamphlet; and Dr. P. Haller, "Die Vorzüge des Ido gegenüber Esperanto, und 10 Antworten dazu" (*Germano Esperantista*, December, 1912), also reprinted as a pamphlet.

LANNING, William Mershon. An American jurist, died February 16, 1912. He was born on a farm in Mercer County, N. J., in 1849 and graduated from the Lawrenceville School in 1866. He taught school for several years and at the same time studied law and was admitted to the bar in 1880. From 1883 to 1887 he was city solicitor of Trenton and from 1887 to 1891 judge of the district court in the same city. He was a member of the special commission which framed the present township laws of New Jersey and was also a member of the constitutional commission in 1894. In 1903 he was elected to the 58th Congress and resigned in June, 1904, on his appointment as United States district judge of the District of New Jersey. He served in this position until 1909 when he was appointed United States circuit judge of the 3d Circuit. In addition to his services on the bench he held a number of public positions. He was a member of the Board of Trustees of the General Assembly of the Presbyterian Church and a director of Princeton Theological Seminary.

LAOS. The largest of the territories composing the French colony of Indo-China (q. v.). Capital, Vientiane. Luang Prabang, Bassac, and Muong Sing (three protected states) are included under Laos. Teak is cut in the forests, and agriculture and mining are carried on. Georges Mahé was resident-superior in 1912.

LATHROP, Julia C. See Children's Bureau.

LAURIE, JOHN WIMBURN. An English lieutenant-general, died May 21, 1912. He was born in London in 1835 and was educated at Harrow and at Sandhurst. In 1853 he obtained his commission in the 2nd Foot. He volunteered for service in the Crimean War and took part in the siege of Sevastopol where he was twice wounded, and was mentioned in dispatches for gallant conduct. He later served in India during the Mutiny. In 1861, following the Trent affair, he was transferred to Canada, where for five years he was inspecting field officer of militia and subsequently adjutant-general of militia in Nova Scotia. He took an active part in resisting the Fenian invasions of 1861 and 1866 on the Niagara frontier. He served in the Transvaal expedition of 1881 and was a Red Cross commissioner in the Servo-Bulgarian War of 1885. During the rebellion in the Northwest Territorities he was second in command under Sir Frederick Middleton. He was retired in 1887 with the rank of lieutenant-general. In the same year he was elected to represent Shelburn County in the Dominion Parliament, but was compelled to return to England in 1891, where he turned his attention to English politics. He was defeated for election to Parliament in 1892, but was elected in 1895 and continued to hold his seat until compelled to withdraw on account of ill health in 1905. He did notable service in improving the militia forces of Canada.

LAURIER, SIR WILFRID. See CANADA.

LAW, BONAR. See GREAT BRITAIN, *History*.

LAWN TENNIS. The retirement of William A. Larned, holder of the American tennis championship, who during his career had captured the title seven times, was much regretted by all tennis followers. Larned became ill during the Davis cup matches at Christchurch, New Zealand, in January, and his recovery was so delayed that he took part in no further tournaments. Aside from this unfortunate incident the tennis season of 1912 was a most notable one, and the popularity of the sport showed a remarkable increase. From the international standpoint the defeat of the Australians, holders of the Davis cup, by the British players, was the most important tennis happening of the year. In the United States the fact that the national championships in both singles and doubles were captured for the first time by players from the Pacific Coast also was noteworthy.

M. E. McLoughlin of California won the singles title after a spirited contest with Wallace F. Johnson, while McLoughlin and T. C. Bundy, also of California, defeated the doubles champions, R. D. Little and Gustave T. Touchard. McLoughlin added to his laurels by winning the New York State Championship, the Western Championship, the Pacific States title, and the Longwood cup contest. With the exception of the matches for the Davis cup McLoughlin went through the year without defeat. Another player to enter the limelight was R. Norris Williams, who won the national clay court championship. W. C. Grant captured the indoor singles title, while F. B. Alexander and T. R. Pell successfully defended the indoor doubles title. Miss Mary Browne of California was the winner of the women's national championship, and Miss Browne, paired with Miss Dorothy Green, won the women's doubles title. Princeton won the intercollegiate championships, G. M. Church capturing the singles title, and Church and W. H. Mace the doubles event. This victory gave Princeton permanent possession of the intercollegiate trophy.

A summary of the principal championship and open tournaments held in 1912 follows:

Davis Cup Matches for world's championship, January, at Christchurch, N. Z.: Men's Singles—N. E. Brookes (Australia) defeated B. C. Wright (America) 6—3, 2—6, 6—3, 6—3; R. W. Heath, Australia) defeated W. A. Larned (America) 2—6, 6—1, 7—5, 6—2; N. E. Brookes (Australia) defeated M. E. McLoughlin (America) 6—4, 3—6, 4—6, 6—3, 6—4. Men's Doubles—N. E. Brookes and A. W. Dunlop (Australia) defeated B. C. Wright and M. E. McLoughlin (America) 6—4, 5—7, 7—5, 6—4.

Davis Cup Preliminaries, at Folkstone, England, June: Singles—C. P. Dixon (Great Britain) defeated Max Decougis (France) 6—3, 6—2, 6—4; A. H. Gobert (France) defeated A. W. Gore (Great Britain) 6—4, 4—6, 6—3, 6—3; C. P. Dixon (Great Britain) defeated A. H. Gobert (France) 4—6, 6—4, 6—2, 6—3; A. W. Gore (Great Britain) defeated Max Decougis (France) 6—3, 6—0 (defaulted). Doubles—H. Roper Barrett and C. P. Dixon (Great Britain) defeated A. H. Gobert and W. H. Laurentz (France) 3—6, 6—4, 6—1, 6—1.

Davis Cup Matches for world's championship, at Melbourne, Australia, November, 1912: Men's Singles—J. C. Parke (Great Britain) defeated N. E. Brookes (Australia) 8—6, 6—3, 5—7, 6—2; C. P. Dixon (Great Britain) defeated R. W. Heath (Australia) 5—7, 6—4, 6—4, 6—4; J. C. Parke Great Britain) defeated R. W. Heath (Australia) 6—2, 6—4, 6—4; N. E. Brookes (Australia) defeated C. P. Dixon (Great Britain) 6—2, 6—4, 6—4. Men's Doubles—N. E. Brookes and A. W. Dunlop (Australia) defeated J. C. Parke and A. E. Beamish (Great Britain) 6—4, 6—1, 7—5.

National All-comers' Championship, at Newport, R. I.: Singles—M. E. McLoughlin defeated W. F. Johnson 3—6, 1—6, 6—3, 6—4, 6—1. Doubles (challenge match) M. E. McLoughlin and T. C. Bundy defeated R. D. Little and G. F. Touchard 3—6, 6—2, 6—1, 7—5.

Preliminary National Championship Doubles Ties, at Lake Forest, Ill.: W. T. Hayes and J. H. Winston (West) defeated W. J. Clothier and G. P. Gardner, Jr. (East), 6—4, 5—7, 8—10, 6—4, 6—4; M. E. McLoughlin and T. C. Bundy (Pacific Coast) defeated C. Y. Smith and Nat Thornton (South), 6—2, 6—1, 6—1. Final—McLoughlin and Bundy defeated Hayes and Winston, 6—0, 7—5, 6—3.

Women's National Championship, at Philadelphia, Pa.: Singles—Miss Mary Browne defeated Miss Eleanora Sears, 6—4, 6—2. Doubles—Miss Browne and Miss Green defeated Mrs. Wallach and Mrs. Schmitz, 6—2, 5—7, 6—0. Mixed Doubles—Miss Browne and R. N. Williams, Jr., defeated Miss Sears and W. J. Clothier, 6—2, 2—6, 11—9.

National Clay Court Championship, at Pittsburgh, Pa.: Men's Singles—R. N. Williams, Jr., defeated W. T. Hayes, 6—3, 6—1, 8—6. Men's Doubles—Hackett and Hall defeated Winston and Whitehead, 4—6, 6—1, 6—0, 6—1. Women's Singles—Miss Sutton defeated Miss Browne, 6—4, 6—2. Mixed Doubles—Miss Sutton and Harris defeated Miss Browne and Williams, 6—3, 2—6, 6—2.

National Indoor Championship, at New York: Men's Singles—W. C. Grant defeated W. B.

Cragin, Jr., 6—1, 6—3, 6—3. Men's Doubles—F. B. Alexander and T. R. Pell defeated W. C. Grant and L. M. Burt, 9—7, 6—4, 6—0.

English Championships at Wimbledon, London: Singles—A. F. Wilding defeated A. W. Gore, 6—4, 6—4, 4—6, 6—4. Doubles—R. Roper Barrett and C. P. Dixon defeated Max Decougis and A. H. Gobert (holders), 3—6, 6—3, 6—4, 7—5. Women's Singles—Mrs. Larcombe defeated Mrs. Sterry, 6—3, 6—1, winning championship by default.

French Championship, at Neuilly-sur-Seine: Singles—A. H. Gobert defeated W. H. Laurentz, 4—2, defaulted. Doubles—Gobert and Laurentz won by default.

Western States Championship, at Chicago, Ill.: Men's Singles—M. E. McLoughlin defeated T. C. Bundy, 8—10, 6—1, 6—4, 6—4. Men's Doubles—Hayes and Winston defeated Squair and Green, 6—1, 6—3, 6—2. Women's Singles—Miss Sutton defeated Miss Browne, 6—0, 6—3. Women's Doubles—Miss Sutton and Miss Neely defeated Miss Browne and Mrs. Seymoure, 6—1, 6—3.

Pacific States Championship, at Santa Cruz, Cal.; Men's Singles—M. E. McLoughlin defeated M. H. Long by default. Men's Doubles—Bundy and Dawson defeated Gardner and Johnston, 6—4, 11—9, 7—9, 6—4. Women's Singles—Miss Florence Sutton defeated Mrs. Bruce, 6—3, 6—3. Women's Doubles—Mrs. Neimeyer and Miss Baker defeated Miss Sutton and Miss Davis, 6—2, 6—2. Mixed Doubles—Miss Sutton and Browne defeated Miss Baker and Hunt, 6—0, 6—0.

New England Championship, at Hartford, Conn.; Men's Singles—F. H. Harris defeated F. C. Inman, 6—1, 6—4, 2—6, 6—4, and in challenge match R. A. Holden, Jr., by default. Men's Doubles—Man and Peaselee defeated Harris and Currier, 7—5, 5—7, 7—5, 3—6, 6—3.

Middle States Championship, at Orange, N. J.; Singles—W. F. Johnson defeated W. M. Hall, 10—12, 1—6, 7—5, 6—1, 6—3. Doubles—Hackett and Mahan defeated Ward and Miles, 6—1, 6—2, 6—1.

New York State Championship, at Brooklyn, N. Y.; Singles—M. E. McLoughlin defeated R. N. Williams, Jr., 6—2, 6—2, 5—7, 4—6, 6—4. Doubles—McLoughlin and Bundy defeated Inman and Behr, 6—4, 6—4, 2—6, 6—4.

Metropolitan Championship, at New York: Men's Singles—R. D. Little defeated A. S. Dabney, 6—4, 6—1, 6—3. Doubles—Hackett and Hall defeated Little and Touchard, 0—6, 2—6, 6—3, 7—5, 6—4. Women's Singles—Mrs. R. H. Williams defeated Miss Marcus, 7—5, 6—4. Women's Doubles—Mrs. Williams and Miss Bunce defeated Mrs. Pouch and Miss Handy by default. Mixed Doubles—Mrs. Barger Wallach and R. D. Little defeated Miss Fenno and G. L. Wrenn, Jr., 2—6, 8—6, 6—2.

Long Island Championship, at Brooklyn, N. Y.; Singles—G. F. Touchard defeated S. H. Voshell, three sets to two. Doubles—Voshell and Baggs defeated Dr. Rosenbaum and Phillips, 3—6, 9—7, 10—8, 1—6, 6—3.

Longwood Cup Tournament, at Boston, Mass.; Singles—Maurice E. McLoughlin defeated E. P. Larned, 6—4, 6—2, 6—4. Doubles—Clothier and Gardner defeated Biddle and Williams, 6—2, 11—13, 6—4.

Intercollegiate Championship, at Haverford, Pa.; Singles—George M. Church (Princeton) defeated John G. Nelson (Dartmouth), 6—4, 5—7, 5—7, 8—6, 6—1. Doubles—George M. Church and W. H. Mace (Princeton) defeated E. H. Whitney and W. M. Washburn (Harvard), 8—10, 10—8, 6—2, 6—2.

New England Intercollegiate Championship, at Boston; Singles—C. L. Johnston, Jr., (Amherst) defeated C. E. Bacon (Wesleyan), 5—7, 4—6, 8—6, 6—3, 6—3. Doubles—C. L. Johnston, Jr., and J. A. Miller (Amherst) defeated A. Conger and H. Thurston (Williams), 4—6, 6—2, 5—7, 6—4, 6—4. See RACQUET AND COURT TENNIS.

LAWRENCE, AMORY APPLETON. An American merchant, died July 6, 1912. He was born in Boston in 1848 and graduated from Harvard College in 1870. He was a brother of William Lawrence, Episcopal bishop of Massachusetts. He engaged in the dry goods commission business and amassed a large fortune. He was director in many important financial institutions, and was noted for his philanthropic work in Boston and elsewhere.

LAWRENCE STRIKE. See STRIKES.

LAW SCHOOLS. See UNIVERSITIES AND COLLEGES.

LAWSON, THOMAS GOODWIN. An American jurist, former member of Congress from Georgia, died April 16, 1912. He was born in Putnam County, Ga., in 1835 and graduated from Mercer University in 1855. He studied law and in 1857 was admitted to the bar. For fifteen months he served as a private in the Confederate army. From 1861 to 1866 he was a member of the Georgia legislature and in 1877 was a member of the Constitutional Convention of the State. From 1879 to 1887 he was a judge in the superior courts in Georgia. He was elected to the 52d, 53d, and 54th Congresses, from 1891 to 1897.

LEA, HOMER. A soldier and writer, died November 1, 1912. He was born in Denver, Col., in 1876, and spent most of his early life in California where he was educated at Occidental College, University of the Pacific, and Leland Stanford University. While he was an undergraduate he showed an unusual interest in military affairs, especially those connected with China and was heard frequently to assert that he would become a general in the Chinese army. Shortly after the completion of his studies he went to China and came into public notice as a partisan of the Chinese in 1900 and 1901, when he undertook the relief of the Emperor, Kwang Hsu. In 1904 when the new army in China was established and put on a modern basis he raised and commanded the second army division with the rank of lieutenant-general. When the Chinese reformer, Kang Yu-wei came to New York in 1905 and spoke in behalf of the reform movement in China, General Lea accompanied him. It was said at that time that he was in command of the reform army, which was being organized by the reformers. He became an intimate friend of Dr. Sun Yat Sen, and accompanied the latter on his return to China in 1911, traveling by way of London and the Suez Canal. It was said during this journey that General Lea was to organize the military government which it was rumored was being planned by the revolutionary army. He arrived with Dr. Sun Yat Sen in Shanghai on December 24. Shortly afterwards the latter was proclaimed president of the new republic. Early in January, 1912, Gen. Lea declined to act as chief of staff of the revolutionary army as he had been notified that there was a death penalty for any foreigner participating in an insurrection. He gained an international reputation by the publication of his book, *The Valor of Ignorance*, in which he attempted to show that a Japanese invading army could capture all the Pacific coast of the United States and force the government to agree to any terms which it might dictate. Among those who highly praised the book were Lord Roberts and the Emperor of Germany. General Lea returned to the United States from China in the spring of 1912 following a stroke of paralysis. His success was obtained in spite of a physical deformity of the spine which made him a hunchback. In addition to *The Valor of Ignorance* he wrote a novel entitled *The Vermilion Pencil*, and a drama, *The Crimson Spider*. At the time of his death he was engaged in the preparation of a history of the political development of China.

LEAD. The production of primary lead in United States in 1911 showed a marked increase over that of 1910. Primary lead is that smelted from ore. The total production of such lead in 1911 was 486,975 tons compared with 470,380 in 1910, an increase of 16,595 tons, or 3.5 per cent. The production of secondary lead, which includes pig lead and lead in alloys, was 52,500 tons in 1911, compared with 55,323 in 1910. From foreign ores and base bullion there were smelted in 1911, 94,134 tons compared with 108,553 tons in 1910. The primary lead smelted or refined from ores mined in the United States in 1911 was 406,148 tons, compared with 372,227 tons in 1910. The largest quantity mined in any single State was in Missouri, 182,207 tons. From Idaho came 117,159 tons; from Utah 55,198 tons, and from Colorado, 30,621 tons. These States are the only large producers of lead.

IMPORTS. The total quantity of lead imported into the United States in 1911 was 179,903,352 pounds. Of this, by far the largest quantity, 172,633,479 pounds, came from Mexico. From South America were imported 4,778,221 pounds; from Great Britain, 401,686 pounds.

The production of lead in the United States in 1912, according to the figures of the *Engineering and Mining Journal*, was 418,224 tons of 2000 pounds. There was a large increase in the production of desilverized lead. This was due to the inauguration of smelting and refining by the International Company, which put its smeltery into operation the early part of the year and its refinery in the latter part. The production of desilverized lead was 239,264 tons. The production from southeastern Missouri was 146,038 tons and from southwestern Missouri, 22,681.

The world production of lead in 1911, according to statistics published by the *Metallgesellschaft* of Frankfurt am Main was 11,201,048 long tons. Of these, 392,842 long tons came from the United States, 189,155 from Spain, 177,801 from Germany, 132,276 from Mexico, 109,789 from Australia, and quantities varying from 2000 to 33,00 tons from Austria, Belgium, Canada, Great Britain, Greece, Italy, Japan, Sweden, and Turkey in Asia. The production in 1910, was 1,208,983 tons. The largest individual decrease was in the production in Spain, which fell off about one-sixth. The production of the United States, which was by far the largest output, more than doubled that of its nearest competitor, Spain, and constituted 32.7 per cent. of the world's production.

For metallurgy of lead see METALLURGY.

LEATHER. The hide and leather industry in 1912 suffered from a lack of supply to meet a constantly growing demand. As a result, in November, the prices for hides reached the highest level ever recorded, which was over 100 per cent. greater than in 1907. The domestic hide supply had been falling behind the increase in population and was far from meeting the demand which various industries were making for leather materials. The accompanying tables show the cattle and sheep slaughtered at the

CATTLE AND SHEEP SLAUGHTERED IN THE UNITED STATES 1912-11

	Cattle		Sheep	
	1912	1911	1912	1911
Chicago	1,681,136	1,715,379	4,880,873	4,452,831
Kansas City.	1,060,262	1,232,391	1,611,651	1,515,489
Omaha	577,138	706,415	1,572,177	1,377,578
St. Louis	884,487	758,012	938,924	881,832
St. Joseph...	297,877	312,242	561,089	550,676
Sioux City...	154,293	189,128	171,516	147,509
Fort Worth .	356,987	347,188	188,281	121,807
St. Paul	136,508	132,272	195,412	169,594
Okla. City ...	180,903	114,859	9,161	9,635
Total	5,329,591	5,507,786	10,124,084	9,226,941
Loss under 1911	178,195	......	......	......
Gain over 1911	......	......	897,143	......

great markets of the United States. There was a loss in the number of cattle slaughtered but a gain in the number of sheep slaughtered in 1912 over 1911, as there had been in the previous year, but not as marked. The high prices for domestic hides were reflected in the increased value of the exports, and the South American product was held at high figures until the early part of December. Leather prices during the year corresponded to those of hides, but an active demand was manifested.

The total cattle slaughtered in the great markets of the United States by years were as follows:

1912	5,329,591
1911	5,507,786
1910	5,762,405
1909	5,715,739
1908	5,406,144

The deficiency in the supply of native hides in part was met by increased imports. The total imports of hides and skins, raw or uncured, in 1912 were 614,966,010 pounds, valued at $121,169,395 as compared with 424,876,678 pounds valued at $81,456,323 in 1911. During the year 1912 the imports of leather and tanned skins were valued at $8,521,088 as compared with $5,897,821 in 1911 and $6,385,907 in 1910. The exports of leather in 1912 were valued at $43,836,315, of which sole leather took $10,134,457 and glazed kid, $20,163,669. The total manufactures of leather exported in 1912 were valued at $20,563,835, as compared with $17,768,295 in 1911.

In connection with the revision of the tariff, the tanners were anxious to have the duties on tanning materials which were imported reduced, so that the industry would be put on more even terms with that of Canada, where no duties were required for tanning extracts.

Considerable success attended the shoe and leather class in the Boston Continuation School, and in 1912, 15 representative shoe and leather concerns were represented in the class by young employees. This movement for limited commercial and vocational training seemed to have been a pronounced success, and a greater enrollment was looked for in future classes.

AVERAGE PRICES OF HIDES IN THE UNITED STATES

PACKER HIDES

	Heavy Native Steers	Butts	Heavy Texas Steers	Light Texas Steers	Colorado Steers	Heavy Native Cows	Light Native Cows	Branded Cows	Native Bulls	Branded Bulls	Average Price
1912	...$17.69	$16.17	$16.58	$16.14	$15.88	13.87	13.50	12.56	12.11	10.50	13.316
1911	... 14.81	13.50	14.32	13.54	13.47	$16.40	$16.30	$15.71	$14.07	$12.03	$15.697
1910	... 15.29	13.71	14.88	13.77	13.42	13.79	13.04	12.40	11.96	12.04	11.931
1905	... .	......	......	......	......	......	......	......	......	......	12.847
1900	... .	......	......	......	......	......	......	......	......	......	10.614
1896	... .	......	......	......	......	......	......	......	......	......	6.980

COUNTRY HIDES

	No. 1 Heavy Steers	Country Packer Brd Flat	No. 1 Heavy Cows	Country Brd. Flat	No. 1 Buffs	No. 1 Extremes	No. 2 Buffs	Bulls Flats	No. 1 Calfskins	No. 1 Kips	Average Price
1912	...$14.25	$13.12	$14.06	$12.33	$14.05	$14.91	$13.02	$11.22	$18.60	$16.01	$14.157
1911	... 12.24	10.72	11.82	10.02	11.82	12.80	10.79	10.01	16.34	13.23	11.979
1910	... 12.16	10.20	11.26	9.49	11.13	11.51	10.02	9.86	16.02	12.03	11.373
1905	... .	......	......	......	......	......	......	......	......	......	11.897
1900	... .	.....	......	......	......	......	......	......	......	......	9.409
1896	... .	......	......	......	......	......	......	......	......	......	6.994

LEAVITT, MARY GREENLEAF (CLEMENT). An American temperance worker and lecturer, died February 5, 1912. She was born at Hopkinton, N. H., and was educated at the State Normal School in West Newton, Mass., graduating in 1851. In 1857 she married Thomas H. Leavitt. She taught school for some years prior to her marriage, and in 1867 established and conducted a private school for young women and children. She became interested in the women's temperance crusade and helped to organize the Boston Woman's Christian Temperance Union. She was a member of the State Executive Board of this organization and later became its national lecturer. From 1883 to 1891 she was secretary of the World's Woman's Christian Temperance Union. In this capacity she traveled abroad, organizing branches of the union in Europe, Australia, Asia, Africa, and many islands. Through the aid of interpreters she spoke to the people in 51 languages. From 1891 to the time of her death she was honorary life president of the World's Woman's Christian Temperance Union. She wrote many tracts, and contributions on temperance and purity topics, and also short stories and verses for magazines

LE CONTE, JEAN JACQUES DESSALINES MICHEL CINCINNATUS. President of Haiti, killed by an explosion during a fire in the Palace at Port-au-Prince on August 8. He began his career in Haiti as school teacher in 1874. Entering politics he rose through the ranks of minor officialdom to be member of Congress. In 1880 he joined in the revolution against President Salomon and was later associated with the government of President Nord Alexis. In 1899 he became a member of the cabinet of President Simon-Sam. In February, 1911, on account of political agitation, he fled from Haiti and took refuge from political exile in St. Thomas. He remained there until July, 1911, when he returned and headed a rising and within a month had succeeded in overthrowing the government of President Simon. On August 16, 1911, ten days after he entered Port-au-Prince at the head of the successful revolutionary forces, he was sworn in as president of the republic. See HAITI.

LEEWARD ISLANDS. See ANTIGUA.

LEEWARD ISLANDS. A British colony; the most northerly group of the (British) Lesser Antilles. The five presidencies, with their area and population in 1911, are as follows:

	Sq. Miles	Pop.	Capital
Antigua*	170 1-2	32,265	St. John
Montserrat	32 1-2	12,196	Plymouth
St. Kitts and Nevis†	150 1-3	43,303	Basseterre
Dominica	304 2-3	33,863	Roseau
Virgin Islands	58	5,562	Road Town
Total	716	127,189	St. John‡

* With its dependencies, Barbuda and Redonda (62 1-2 square miles, 991 inhabitants). † Including Anguilla (35 square miles, 4075 inhabitants). ‡ Capital of the colony.

Elementary education in the islands is denominational, excepting in Dominica, the denominations receiving grants-in-aid. Government saving banks have been established in all the presidencies. There are no railway nor internal telegraphs. Cable connection exists with the continents. Statistics of trade and finance for the colony are given below for four years:

	1907-8	1908-9	1909-10	1910-11
Imports	£517,424	£567,593	£485,393	£557,817
Exports	521,509	536,312	441,728	558,165
Revenue*	152,608	154,333	149,670	164,375
Expenditure*	136,047	146,216	149,906	159,263

* Not including government grants.

Sir Ernest Bickham Sweet-Escott, the governor in 1912, was transferred to be governor of Fiji and high commissioner for the western Pacific in February, and Sir H. Hesketh Bell was appointed governor of the Leeward Islands. See articles on the separate presidencies for further details.

LEEWARD ISLANDS (ILES SOUS LE VENT). See FRENCH ESTABLISHMENTS IN OCEANIA.

LEFEBVRE, JULES JOSEPH. A French artist, died February 23, 1912. He was born at Tournon in 1836. After studying under Leon Cogniet he won, in 1861, the Prix de Rome with "The Death of Priam." He became notable as a painter of beautiful women. His works consist chiefly of single figures. They include "Caritas Romana" (1864); "Sleeping Maiden" (1865); "Reclining Woman" (1868); "Pandora" (1877); "Psyche" (1883), and "A Daughter of Eve" (1892). He also painted many portraits. In 1870 he was decorated with the Cross of the Legion of Honor and was made a member of the Académie des Beaux Arts in 1891.

LEGRAS, Gustave. An American mathematician and educator, died July 23, 1912. He was born in New York in 1858, and graduated from the College of the City of New York in 1879. In 1883 he became tutor of mathematics in the College of the City of New York and successively served as assistant professor and associate professor of mathematics in that institution. The latter position he held from 1906 until the time of his death. He was a member of many scientific societies.

LEHIGH UNIVERSITY. An institution of higher learning at South Bethlehem, Pa., founded in 1866. The enrollment in all departments of the university in the autumn of 1912 was 619, divided as follows: Arts and science courses, 113; civil engineering, 134; mechanical engineering, 123; mining engineering, 83; metallurgical engineering, 15; electrometallurgy, 16; electrical engineering, 82; chemistry, 27; chemical engineering, 26. There were 68 members of the faculty. A new course in business administration was added in the arts and science department during the year. The productive funds of the university amount to $1,200,000, and there were about 125,000 volumes in the library. President, Henry Sturgis Drinker, E. M., LL. D.

LEIGHTON, John. An English artist, died October, 1912. He was born in 1822 and was educated privately. With Roger Fenton he founded the Photographic Society and was one of the original proprietors of the London *Graphic*. He lectured on many subjects and traveled extensively, and he illustrated a large number of books. He was the founder and the vice-president of the Ex Libris Society, for which he designed many bookplates. He published, in 1881, *Suggestions in Design* under the pen-name of Luke Limner.

LEIPZIG. See Architecture.

LELAND STANFORD JUNIOR UNIVERSITY. An institution for higher education at Stanford University, Cal., founded in 1891. The enrollment in all departments of the university in 1912 was 1656. The faculty numbered 214. There were several important changes among the members of the faculty during the year. Professor Alvin S. Johnson, professor of economics, resigned to accept a similar chair at Cornell University. Professor Murray S. Wildman of Northwestern University, was chosen professor of economics to succeed Professor Johnson. The corporation of Cooper Medical College of San Francisco was dissolved during the year and all its property was placed in the hands of the trustees of Stanford University for the purposes of medical education. The university now offers a complete medical course embodying seven years of preparation and study for a degree in medicine. President, David Starr Jordan, LL. D.

LE MOINE, Sir James MacPherson. A Canadian ornithologist and historian, died February, 1912. He was born in 1856 and was educated at the Petit Seminaire de Quebec. He studied law and became a barrister in 1850. He wrote much on historical and ornithological subjects relating to Canada. Among his published writings are: *Ornithology of Canada* (1861); *Maple Leaves* (1863-1894, 6 vols.); *Quebec Past and Present* (1876); *The Scot in New France* (1879); *The Chronicles of the St. Lawrence* (1879); *Picturesque Quebec* (1882); *The Birds of Quebec* (1891); *Legends of the St. Lawrence* (1898).

LEPROSY. A survey of the prevalence of leprosy in the United States and its territorial possessions was recently made by the United States Public Health Service. Health officers of the several States, Porto Rico, Hawaii, and the Philippines were requested to submit a statement of the number of new cases reported in 1911, and of the total number on January 1, 1912. The results were incomplete, owing to the fact that in only eighteen States and in the District of Columbia is leprosy a reportable disease. A total of 146 cases was reported in the United States, of which forty were new cases first observed in 1911. In that year a commission of officers of the Public Health Service found 278 lepers in the United States. Of these, 145 were foreign-born, and 13 were of unknown nativity; 186 were believed to have contracted the disease in this country. Only 72 of the patients were isolated and cared for by local authorities. The 146 cases reported in the present survey do not indicate a decreased prevalence. California, Louisiana, and Massachusetts make provision for lepers in special hospitals. In other States varying degrees of care and isolation are provided. There are 28 known lepers in Porto Rico, while in Hawaii and the Philippines the disease constitutes an important public health problem. In the latter about 6000 lepers have been transferred to the Culion leper colony. Cebu, an island with one-tenth of the Philippine population, furnishes one-half of the cases. The Treasury Department recently amended the interstate quarantine regulations to the effect that common carriers may not transport a leper except under specified restrictions and under a special permit from the surgeon-general of the Public Health and Marine Hospital Service. A leper who violates this regulation is to be returned to the original State or to a designated federal quarantine station.

LEROY-BEAULIEU, Anatole. A French historical writer, died June 10, 1912. He was born at Lisieux in 1842, a brother of Paul Leroy Beaulieu, economist. His life was practically devoted to the study of government and politics. He is perhaps best known as the author of an elaborate work on Russia, translated into English under the title, *The Empire of the Czars*. Other well-known works are, *Papacy, Socialism, Democracy* (English trans., 1892), and *Israel Among the Nations*. The latter is the subject of an essay by Mr. W. E. H. Lecky, who characterized the author as "one of the greatest living political writers." (See the posthumous volume of Lecky's *Historical and Political Essays*, 1908.) In 1887 he was elected a member of the Academy of Political and Moral Science. He took no active part in political life beyond occupying the seat of Conseil Général of Haute Marne from 1883 to 1891.

LETTER CARRIERS AND EIGHT-HOUR DAY. See LABOR LEGISLATION, *Hours.*

LEWIS, GRACE ANNA. An American naturalist, died February 24, 1912. She was born in 1821. In 1869 she published a pamphlet showing the relation of birds to the animal kingdom. This pamphlet was the germ of a series of charts which she prepared later. These included "A Chart of the Classification of Birds," "A Chart of the Animal Kingdom," and "A Chart of Biology." She also prepared "Water-Color Paintings of Wild Flowers" and "Studies in Forestry."

LEWIS, WILLIAM H. See BAR ASSOCIATION, AMERICAN.

LIBERIA. An independent negro republic on the west African coast, covering an area estimated at about 41,000 square miles (other estimates, from thirty-five to forty thousand), and having about 1,500,000 inhabitants (or 2,000,000 according to some calculations), including about 10,000 Americo-Liberians. The indigenous negroes are mainly pagans, except the Mohammedan Mandingo tribe. There are said to be cannibals in the interior. Monrovia (with about 600 inhabitants) is the capital.

Native industries are backward, and trade is carried on under difficulties; roads being few and railroads unknown. Dense forest covers great tracks through which passage is not possible under present conditions. The imports for 1911 are estimated to have amounted to $1,025,000, and the exports to $975,000 (palm oil and kernels, plassava fibre, coffee, rubber, and ivory). Trade is mostly with Hamburg, the United Kingdom, the Netherlands, and the United States. Monrovia (since 1910) is a station on the cable route from Germany to Brazil, and beginning with 1912) a station on the French cable route to French West Africa. Revenue (1910-11), $489,656. An English source places the revenue at $471,335 and the expenditure at $470,000 for the year 1911-12. External debt (1912), $170,000. A president elected for four years (January 1, 1912-16, Daniel Edward Howard) is the executive. International financial controller, R. P. Clark (American), with G. Lange representing Germany, R. Harpe the United Kingdom, and F. Wolff, France.

HISTORY. President Daniel Howard was inaugurated on January 1, to succeed President Barclay, who had held office for eight years. The new president made especial reference in his inaugural address to the relations of Liberia to the great powers, declaring that conditions gave positive assurance of Liberia's integrity. He referred also to the satisfactory conclusion of the prolonged financial negotiations, owing to the interest of United States, Great Britain, and other powers. In March a loan agreement was concluded with American, German, British, French, and Dutch banks, subject to the settlement of outstanding claims on the Liberian government. A settlement with the German creditors was concluded in June. At the beginning of November it was announced that the German gunboat *Panther* had been ordered from her station at Kamerun Bay to the Liberian coast to protect German subjects, disturbances having arisen among the natives. The lives of Europeans and especially of Germans employed in the factories were said to be in danger.

LIBRARY ASSOCIATION, AMERICAN. A society incorporated in 1879 for the purpose of developing the public library in its bearing on American education and by coöperation to increase the efficiency of library administration. The conference of the association in 1912 was held on June 26-July 2 at Ottawa, Canada. The keynote of the meeting was the concern of the community in the awakening and development of taste in individuals. Some of the principal papers were those dealing with "The efficiency of the library staff and scientific management," "What the library schools can do for the profession," "Library publicity for the sake of information and support," "The opportunity which the open door of the library offers as a means of education and development beyond the schools," and "The relations between library assistants and the public." One of the most important events of the conference was the report submitted by a committee appointed to study the relation which the public library should bear to the municipality. The committee strongly advised against grouping the library with departments of the city which have little or nothing to do with educational work, such as parks, police departments, etc., and strongly recommended that the library either be governed by a distinctly independent board of trustees or else g uped with the other educative agencies of theocity. The committee was continued with the request that it draft a recommended library chapter for a city charter. Another important committee report dealt with the deterioration of newspaper paper, a pr · lem which has been carefully studied and experimented upon by a committee of the association for the past two years.

The publishing board of the association during 1912 issued, among other publications, a revised edition of its *List of Subject Headings* and a continuation of the *A. L. A. Catalogue,* consisting of an annotated selection of 3000 of the best books published since 1904. Officers or specially appointed delegates have attended during 1912, sixteen out of thirty-nine State library meetings as official representatives of the American Library Association. The officers for 1912 were as follows: President, Henry E. Legler, librarian of the Chicago Public Library; first vice-president, E. H. Anderson, assistant director of the New York Public Library; second vice-president, Mary F. Isom, librarian of the Portland (Oregon) Library Association; treasurer, Carl B. Roden, assistant librarian, Chicago Public Library; and secretary, George B. Utley, 78 E. Washington Street, Chicago, Ill.

LIBRARY BUILDINGS. See LIBRARY PROGRESS.

LIBRARY OF CONGRESS. At the end of the fiscal year 1912 there were in the Library of Congress 2,012,393 books, 129,123 maps and charts, 591,632 volumes and pieces of music, and 349,745 prints. The accessions during the year included 120,664 printed books and pamphlets, 34,622 volumes and pieces of music, 10,731 prints, and 5177 maps and charts. The library also contains a large number of manuscripts, but a numerical statement of this is not possible. There were many valuable gifts of printed books during the year. Chief among these were the Deinard collection of Hebraica, brought together during many years by Ephraim Deinard of Arlington, N. J. There were included in this gift 9936 volumes and pamphlets. They were presented to the library by Mrs. Jacob H. Schiff, of New York. Mrs. Henrietta Irving Bolton presented to the library the unique library of her late husband, Henry Carrington Bolton. This numbered 1631 volumes and pamphlets. These works related chiefly to the history of chemistry and bibliography on that subject. The Karow collection of works relating to Napoleon Bonaparte was presented to the library by the widow of the late Major Edward William Karow of Savannah, Ga. The collection numbered nearly 300 volumes. From the Mexican embassy at Washington came the gift of 1254 books and pamphlets, including many relating to Mexico and Central America, together with 2000 numbers of periodicals. Prince Roland Napoleon Bonaparte presented the library with 19 volumes, chiefly his own scientific publications. Perhaps the most notable purchase of books made during the year was that of the Hoes collection relating to the Spanish-American War. This numbers 43,866 pieces, and includes books, pamphlets, periodicals, and manuscripts. In the Division of Manuscripts there were many important accessions during the year. These include the Maury papers, additional Van Buren papers, Mexican Inquisition papers, the Edwin M. Stanton papers, the Louise Chandler Moulton collection, and the additional Welles papers. The Jefferson collection was enriched by the addition of 131 unedited letters. The librarian is Herbert Putnam.

LIBRARY PROGRESS, 1912. General Development. The library year of 1912 was a year of quiet growth, unmarked by such dramatic events as the catastrophe of the New York State Library fire and the New York Public Library opening, both of which made 1911 an exceptional library year. The national library conference held in Ottawa, Canada, June 26-July 2, emphasized international library interests. Library coöperation between the United States and Canada was strengthened and library interests on both sides stimulated by contact. Closer relation between the library and municipality is an encouraging indication of library progress, and the cost and administration of libraries has received more concentrated attention from librarians during the year.

Associations and Commissions. In the United States there are 34 States that have library commissions or bodies serving commission purposes. Through the activity of the State commission library facilities are extended throughout the State. Rural communities, where population is too scattered to admit of the establishment of library buildings, are thus brought into contact with books. The leading commissions publish library bulletins in which professional articles, news notes, and reading lists are printed. The League of Library Commissions is affiliated with the American Library Association and includes membership from all commissions. This association meets twice a year. Its eastern section generally meets in March at Atlantic City and its western section at Chicago in January. Important policies of commission organization and coöperation receive attention at these meetings. Of the 48 States of the Union, 36 have State organizations. The State association is distinct in organization and purpose from the State commission. Its membership is made up of the libraries and library workers of the State and through its meetings and activities it stimulates the library interests of the State. Many of the State associations hold joint meetings or conferences with one or more other State associations. At these conferences programmes are offered almost equal in value to the programmes of the national conventions. California, Wisconsin, New York, Ohio, New Jersey, and Pennsylvania have held meetings of broad scope. The Pacific Northwest Library Association is an association covering Washington, Oregon, and British Columbia, and its annual meetings in September are among the most progressive library conventions. Affiliation between the State and national associations is a current question to which librarians are giving careful consideration.

Library Buildings. The new central building of the St. Louis (Mo.) Public Library was opened January 6, 1912. This building is the result of the efforts of Frederick M. Crunden, who built up the St. Louis Library and who died in 1911. The new building was obtained through the gift of $1,000,000 from Mr. Carnegie, one-half of which was apportioned to the central building and the other half for branches of the St. Louis Public Library. Since the fall of 1909 Mr. Arthur E. Bostwick has been the librarian of the St. Louis Public Library. The City Library of Springfield, Mass., opened its new building in June, 1912. Mr. Hiller C. Wellman is librarian. The beautiful new building of the University of California at Berkeley was opened March 23, 1912. The Free Public Library of Elizabeth, N. J., and the University of Texas Library also opened imposing new buildings during the year.

Library Appointments. Changes in library personnel of considerable interest occurred during the year. Frederick W. Jenkins became librarian of the library of the New York School of Philanthropy. There were appointments of two new State librarians, Miss Sallie Dorsey in Maryland, and Herbert E. Holmes in Maine. Mr. Lawrence J. Burpee, librarian of the Ottawa Carnegie Library, resigned for work in a different field. Mr. Purd B. W ight resigned from the librarianship of the rKansas City (Mo.) Public Library, and Mr. William Watson resigned from the librarianship of the San Francisco Public Library. Mr. William F. Yust, previously of the Louisville (Ky.) Free Public Library, has become librarian of the Rochester (N. Y.) Public Library; Mr. Joseph L. Harrison, previously of the Providence (R. I.) Athenæum, has become librarian of the Forbes Library of Northampton, Mass.

Library Literature. New publications of value have been contributed as follows: Miss Hasse's new volume on Ohio in the "*Index of Economic material in documents of the States of the United States;* Frank K. Walter's *Abbreviations and technical terms used in book catalogs and in bibliographies;* F. W. Faxon's bibliography *Literary annuals and gift books;* the New York School of Philanthropy's library bulletins; E. A. Savage's *Old English libraries;* Burchard's *Guide to the law and legal literature of Germany; "Bibliothéques, livres et libraires,"* a course of nineteen lectures given during the school year 1910-11 under the auspices of the École des Hautes Études Sociales. The *Library Journal* and *Public Libraries* are the two leading library periodicals in the United States and are issued monthly.

Library Training Schools. There are eleven

library training schools in the United States. Their courses vary from one to two years and some schools admit only students who hold B. A. degrees. The schools are connected with libraries, universities, or State commissions. There are several brief summer library courses extended by library commissions or library schools with the purpose of giving systematic instruction to untrained library workers. Many libraries also give preliminary courses of training to fit applicants for work within their own grades of service.

CARNEGIE GIFTS. The total of library donations for the year was $2,112,000. In individual library benefactions Mr. Carnegie gave approximately $1,203,000, the largest gift, $750,000, being made to the San Francisco Public Library. To the Carnegie Corporation of New York, Mr. Carnegie gave $125,000,000 for the purpose of educational and library benefactions.

LIBRARY TRAINING SCHOOLS. See LIBRARY PROGRESS.

LIBYAN DESERT. See EXPLORATION.

LIEBMANN, OTTO. A German philosopher, died January, 1912. He was born at Löwenberg in 1840, and was educated at the universities of Leipzig and Halle. In 1872 he was appointed professor at Strassburg and after a service of ten years at that institution went to the University of Jena. His best known writings were as follows: *Vier Monate vor Paris*, a journal published anonymously (1871); *Kant und die Epigonen* (1865), in which, criticising the followers of Kant, he urged a return to their master and became the first of the Neo-Kantians; *Ueber die Freiheit des Willens* (1866); *Über den objektiven Anblick* (1869); and *Analysis der Wirklichkeit* (3d ed. 1900); *Gedanken und Thatsachen* (1882-99); *Klimax der Theorieen* (1884); *Geist der Transcendentalphilosophie* (1901); *Grundriss der kritischen Metaphysik* (1901).

LIFEBOATS. See SAFETY AT SEA, and TITANIC, LOSS OF.

LIFE INSURANCE. See INSURANCE.

LIGHT. See PHYSICS.

LIGHTHOUSES. There were in 1912, ending June 30, the following aids to navigation maintained by the United States Lighthouse Service.

Lighted Aids	Total
Hyper-radiant lights	1
First-order lights	57
Second-order lights	25
Third-order lights	76
Three-and-a-half-order lights	19
Fourth-order lights	338
Fifth-order lights	148
Sixth-order lights	88
Range-lens lights	23
Reflector lights	103
Lens-lantern lights	590
Post-lantern lights	2,552
Electric lights without lens	13
Light-vessel stations	51
Gas-lighted buoys	255
Gas and whistling buoys	40
Gas and aerial bell buoys	51
Float lights	92
Total	4,516
Lights on fixed aids	4,027
Lights on floating aids	489
Total lighted aids	4,516
Unlighted Aids	
Fog signals, engine power	252
Fog signals, clock-work	235
Fog signals, hand-power	22
Electric gongs	1
Submarine signals	43
Buoys, whistling (unlighted)	84
Buoys, bell (unlighted)	206
Buoys, iron	1,833
Buoys, spar (wood)	4,159
Daymarks, beacons, etc.	1,474
Total unlighted aids	8,308
Grand total	12,824

The number of lighted aids (4516) can be compared with the 4224 maintained in 1911, the increase being in all classes except light-vessel stations, the number of which was 51 as in the previous year. For light-vessels there were maintained 65 ships, 14 of which were relief vessels, and Congress in 1912 appropriated $130,000, for one light vessel for general service, and $250,000 for additional light-vessels for general service. Plans were under consideration for 4 light-vessels, one of which, a small ship, was for the Great Lakes, and one large first-class vessel, one large vessel and one small vessel for the Atlantic Coast. Of the light-vessels in service 33 had self-propelling machinery and 31 sail-power. Since the close of the fiscal year 10 additional lights were added to Alaska, making a total of 95 lights on the waterways of that Territory in November, 1912, as compared with 37 lights on January 1, 1910. There were in 1912, 265 aids to navigation as compared with 160 in 1910.

CROWN POINT LIGHTHOUSE. This light was reëstablished August 7, 1912, supplementing the old structure built in 1858, located on the northeasterly point of the peninsula of Crown Point off Port Henry, N. Y., and marking the turn of the dark, narrow channel at Chimney Point in Lake Champlain. The new tower was built to commemorate the 300th anniversary of the discovery of Lake Champlain by Samuel de Champlain, and consists of an ornamental cylindrical tower of cut granite blocks surrounded by 8 Doric columns of the same material, which rest on a conical base of rough granite. The tower and columns support an ornamental cut granite cornice, gallery, watch room, and lantern parapet on which is placed a cast-iron fourth-order cylindrical helical bar lantern with an ornamental copper roof, the focal plane of the lantern being 61 feet above grade line. On the base of the new tower was built a pyramidal pedestal capped by the prow of a canoe which supports a heroic group in bronze with Champlain as the central figure, a gift of the Republic of France. The memorial lighthouse was built by joint action of the States of Vermont and New York, and was dedicated with formal ceremonies in the summer of 1912, the French ambassador and high officials of the United States government being present.

In the fiscal year ended June 30, 1912, new lighthouses were completed at the following points: Staten Island, N. Y.; New London Ledge, Conn.; Lloyd Harbor, N. Y.; Crown Point, N. Y.; Elbow of Cross Ledge, N. J.; Split Rock, Minn.; Rock of Ages, Mich.; Livingstone Channel, Mich.; White Shoal, Mich.; Cape Hinchinbrook, Alaska; and Alcatraz, Cal.

AIDS TO NAVIGATION ON THE PANAMA CANAL. In order to provide for night navigation on the Panama Canal an elaborate system of range lights, buoys, and beacons was worked out, and the erection of the various towers and other construction was in active progress during 1912. The general scheme involves a range of two lines at each end of the longer tangents to prolong the sailing line in order that the pilot may keep his course up to the turning point. To secure these prolonged tangents it was necessary to clear a broad pathway of about 480 feet through the jungle until suitable locations were found for the lights. Where possible the various lighthouses made use of electricity, with acetylene for the floating buoys, and the towers and beacons, which were located in inaccessible places. The candle-power of the range lights varies according to the length of range from about 2500 to 15,000 candle-power, the most powerful lights naturally being those marking the sea channels at the Atlantic and Pacific entrances which are visible for between 12½ and 18 nautical miles. The beacons and gas buoys will have about 950 candle-power. The towers are of reinforced concrete construction, standardized where possible with varying forms of foundations, depending upon the site. They vary in height, depending upon their position, and owing to their isolated locations have in many instances presented difficulties of construction, as materials have had to be transported by hand.

A summary of the various aids to navigation to be used in lighting and buoying the Panama Canal is as follows:

One harbor light (west breakwater) lighted by incandescent oil vapor lamps or acetylene.

Fourteen range towers, lighted by electricity.

Eighteen range towers, lighted by acetylene gas.

Forty-six beacons, lighted by electricity.

Three beacons, lighted by acetylene gas.

Fifty-nine gas buoys, lighted by compressed acetylene dissolved in acetone.

One hundred spar buoys (unlighted).

Two gas buoys, lighted by acetylene. (Channel to terminal docks and dry dock at Cristobal.)

Seven nun buoys, unlighted. (Channel to terminal docks and dry dock at Cristobal.)

LIGHTSHIPS. During the year a lightship with a reversible 4-cylinder 2-cycle Diesel engine of 220 horsepower was placed in service at the entrance of the River Elbe from the North Sea. This vessel was 173 feet in length by 25 feet 3 inches molded beam, 12 feet 6 inches draft, and had a displacement of 720 tons. She had a fine clipper bow and was both seaworthy and well equipped. Internal-combustion engines of 35 horsepower were used to drive the dynamos and supply power for other purposes.

LILIENCRON, ROCHUS, BARON. A German author, died March, 1912. He was born in Plön, Holstein, in 1820. He studied theology, jurisprudence, and philology at the universities of Kiel, Berlin, and Copenhagen. In 1847 he became *privat-docent* at Bonn. After holding various government positions he became in 1850 professor at Kiel and two years later was appointed to the chair of German language and literature at the University of Jena. While there he published with W. Stade, *Lieder und Sprüche aus der letzten Zeit des Minnesangs* (1954). Under the direction of the Historical Commission of Munich he began in 1858 the collection of folk-songs which culminated in his *Historische Volkslieder der Deutschen vom 13.-16. Jahrhundert* (4 vols., 1865-1869). For the same commission he also edited *Allgemeine deutsche Biographie.* In 1869 he was made a foreign member in ordinary of the Bavarian Academy of Sciences, and settled in Munich. He removed to Schleswig in 1879.

LIME. The total production of lime in the United States in 1911, according to figures of the United States Geological Survey, was 3,392,915 short tons, valued at $13,689,054, compared with 3,505,954 tons, valued at $14,088,039 in 1910; a decrease of 113,039 tons. The total number of producers reported in 1911 was 1089, compared with 1126 in 1910. This decrease in the number of producers was due partly to the inactivities of small kilns operated by farmers for burning lime for local use as fertilizer, and partly to the tendency of the industry toward concentration of plants into fewer and larger units. In 1911, 44 States and Territorial possessions, including Hawaii and Porto Rico, reported production of lime, while in 1910 lime was produced in 43 States. The five leading States in 1911 in order of their production were Pennsylvania, Ohio, Wisconsin, West Virginia, and Missouri. Pennsylvania produced 841,723 short tons, valued at $2,688,374; in Ohio, 405,562 tons were produced; in Wisconsin, 250,638; in West Virginia, 179,966; and in Missouri, 158,368. Nearly half the lime manufactured in the United States is used as structural material and the remainder, amounting to 1,750,000 tons, is consumed in chemical uses. The principal uses which lime has in building operations are in lime mortars and plasters, in gaging Portland cement mortars, concrete, and gypsum plasters, and as a whitewash.

The imports of lime into the United States in 1911 amounted to 5232 short tons, valued at $55,255, and the exports were 207,232 barrels, valued at $153,212.

LIPPE. See GERMANY.

LIQUORS. The term "liquors" includes four classes of alcoholic beverages: Wines, malt liquors, distilled liquors, and cordials. Under the head of "wines" are included various fermented beverages made from different kinds of fruits, such as wine, cider, blackberry wine, etc. Under the head of "malt liquors" are those products prepared by the fermentation of a mash made from various kinds of grain, such as ale, beer, porter, stout, etc. Under the head of "distilled liquors" are classed such products as rum, brandy, gin, etc., which are made by the distillation of some fermented product. And, lastly, under the head of "cordials," are grouped those compounded preparations made from brandy or wine, with flavoring matters and sugar, the well-known examples being, in part, blackberry cordial, Benedictine, apricot cordial, and similar products.

WINE. *Le Moniteur Vinicole* publishes the table on the next page for the wine production of the world for 1911 and 1910, which probably shows more nearly the production of wine in those two years than any previous statement.

From this table it is seen that there was a much greater production of wine in 1911 than in 1910, which apparently was a bad year all over the world. The production shown for the United States, of 28,600,000 gallons, is believed to be much below the actual production. But, it is impossible to obtain accurate figures on the total production of wine in the United States, as it is not under government supervision. The estimated production of wine in France for 1912 is considerably higher than for 1911, being 1,512,034,710 gallons.

AMERICAN FORTIFIED WINE. The production of fortified wine in the United States, according to the report of the commissioner of Internal Revenue, showed a very large increase

	1911 Gallons	1910 Gallons
France	987,482,100	627,652,608
Corsica	3,441,900	3,417,012
Algeria	194,340,894	185,100,388
Tunis	3,300,000	3,300,000
Italy	930,600,000	644,446,000
Spain	368,594,400	248,235,526
Portugal	61,600,000	44,000,000
Azores, Canary Islands, and Madeira	770,000	880,000
Austria	63,800,000	22,000,000
Hungary	83,600,000	55,000,000
Germany	57,200,000	13,200,000
Russia	94,600,000	28,600,000
Switzerland	20,900,000	5,500,000
Turkey and Cyprus	26,400,000	17,600,000
Luxembourg	1,980,000	550,000
Greece	50,600,000	55,000,000
Bulgaria	28,600,000	19,800,000
Servia	11,000,000	8,800,000
Rumania	41,800,000	13,200,000
United States	28,600,000	24,200,000
Mexico	550,000	198,000
Argentine Republic	79,200,000	57,090,000
Chile	63,800,000	50,600,000
Peru	4,290,000	1,980,000
Brazil	7,700,000	5,500,000
Uruguay	4,400,000	3,080,000
Bolivia	1,540,000	440,000
Australia	4,400,000	3,520,000
Cape of Good Hope	2,640,000	2,860,010

in 1912, the increase being almost entirely confined to the State of California, which is a large producer of wines of this type.

	Tax gal. brandy used		Wine gal. fortified	
	1911	1912	1911	1912
California	4,951,640	6,153,132	18,850,166	23,467,441
Hawaii	10,190	16,598	43,593	70,884
New York	133,392	143,422	548,208	595,009
N. Carolina	5,834	7,820	53,116	54,102
Misc.	461	1,331	3,684	11,190
Total U. S.	5,101,517	6,322,303	19,498,767	24,198,626

From this table it will be seen that there were produced in 1912 4,699,859 more gallons of fortified wines than in the year 1911, and 1,220,786 more gallons of brandy used. This large increase of production was principally confined to the sherry, angelica, and muscatel types, there being practically twice as much angelica and muscatel produced in 1912 as in 1911. In 1910 there was a very considerable production of fortified sweet wines in the State of Virginia, but during 1911 and 1912 practically no wine of this type was made in that State. The production of Scuppernong wine is shown by the report of the commissioner to be confined to the fourth district of North Carolina, 54,102 gallons being produced in 1912, and 53,116 gallons in 1911.

FERMENTED LIQUORS. The production of fermented liquors during the year 1912 was 62,176,694 barrels, or a decrease of 1,106,429 barrels, as compared with the product of 1911, a decrease of 33,192,870 gallons, or, approximately one-third of a gallon per capita less. There was also a decrease in the number of breweries operating, there being 1461 breweries in 1912, or 31 breweries less than in 1911. Undoubtedly this decrease in the number of breweries operated was due to the passage of prohibition laws and the closing of breweries in certain States. As compared with 1910 the contrast is even greater, there being 197 less breweries in operation in 1912 than in 1910.

DISTILLED SPIRITS. During 1912 there were 820 distilleries in operation in the production of distilled spirts, a decrease of 103 from the previous fiscal year. The decrease in number has been steady in recent years. Four years ago there were in operation 1587 registered distilleries, or nearly twice as many as at the present time, the falling off being due very largely to the extension of the prohibition laws, especially in the southern States, where many small distilleries were in operation a few years ago. The total production of distilled spirits, exclusive of fruit brandy, in 1912, was 178,249,985 taxable gallons, as against 175,402,395.5 gallons in 1911, an increase of 2,847,589.5 gallons. Further, there was an increase of tax-paid spirits of 1,200,511 gallons during the fiscal year 1912. This increase in the amount of distilled spirits, compared with the number of distilleries in operation, shows a very marked tendency towards larger distilleries. The table given below shows the production of the various kinds of distilled spirits in the United States for the past four years. It shows that the principal increase in production during the past year was in the manufacture of commercial alcohol and neutral or cologne spirits, with a very slight reduction in the amount of production of whisky. There is still included under the head of "whisky," as has been for the past two years, a large amount of distilled spirits made from molasses, and as yet the case pending in the courts involving this question has not been brought to a decision:

Year	Rum	High Wines	Gin
1909	1,952,374	221,277	2,482,743
1910	1,730,551	206,534	2,985,435
1911	2,077,904	165,017	3,345,370
1912	2,266,063	131,001	3,577,861

Year	Whisky	Alcohol	Commercial Alcohol
1909	70,152,174	42,563,103	16,078,083
1910	82,463,894	50,703,845	15,841,370
1911	100,647,155	44,205,329	21,780,391
1912	98,209,574	45,869,685	24,492,304

The bottling of whisky in bond has not shown the same increase during the past year as has been noted in previous years, but instead, a very appreciable reduction, 9,752,486 gallons being withdrawn for this purpose during the past year, against 10,631,091 gallons in 1911. There was also a decrease in the amount of distilled spirits bottled in bond for export, 41,188.1 gallons being bottled in 1911 as against 39,775.6 in 1912.

There is still a very large amount of illicit distilling in the United States, 1443 such distilleries being seized and destroyed in 1912. Of these, 213 were in Alabama, 402 in Georgia, 90 in Kentucky, 267 in North Carolina, 162 in South Carolina, 104 in Tennessee, 151 in Virginia, and 34 in Florida. These were all small distilleries.

The table on the next page shows that the raw material used in Germany for the production of distilled spirits is quite different from that used in the United States, potatoes being the principal raw material in Germany, while corn and molasses are the principal sources in the United States. The very large production of alcohol from potatoes shows the opportunity in this country to develop this industry.

CORDIALS. The ruling of the board of food and drug inspection of the Department of Agriculture prohibiting the importation of absinthe into the United States went into effect on October 1, 1912. This ruling also prohibits its shipment in interstate commerce, on the ground

PRODUCTION OF DISTILLED SPIRITS IN GERMANY FROM VARIOUS MATERIALS

Year	Potato Gallons	Yeast Gallons	Grain Gallons	Molasses Gallons	Miscel. Gallons
1902-03	69,165,000	11,400,000	4,940,000	2,300,000	496,000
1903-04	79,460,000	11,940,000	6,114,000	2,430,000	601,000
1904-05	75,000,000	12,600,000	7,420,000	2,820,000	967,000
1905-06	91,760,000	12,600,000	6,930,000	2,170,000	810,000
1906-07	72,940,000	12,420,000	7,160,000	2,320,000	784,000
1907-08	82,280,000	12,650,000	6,380,000	2,690,000	992,000
1908-09	89,390,000	11,790,000	6,250,000	2,270,000	1,255,000
1909-10	76,800,000	9,360,000	6,090,000	1,990,000	992,000
1910-11	73,200,000	8,040,000	6,170,000	2,300,000	732,000

that it contains an added deleterious substance. As yet, no prosecution has been brought on the interstate shipment of this cordial, but its sale is practically restricted now to the States where a small amount is produced. The ruling practically means the end of the production and consumption of absinthe in the United States, and is in line with action which has been taken in other countries where its use has been found to be very harmful.

LIQUOR REGULATION. As only fourteen States held regular sessions of their legislatures in 1912 the volume of laws relating to liquor traffic was not as large as in 1911. Nearly all the legislatures in session, however, passed some measures aimed to restrict or regulate the traffic and in several of the States votes were taken on amendments to the liquor laws. A brief summary of the most important events related to the liquor regulation is given below. Additional notes will be found under the States in their regular order.

The legislature of Arkansas passed a resolution in the legislative session of 1912 submitting a prohibitory constitutional amendment to a vote of the people. This vote was taken in September and resulted in a majority against prohibition of 15,968. Under the local option law passed by the California legislature in 1911, 80 supervisal districts in California adopted no license during the succeeding 18 months, closing thereby 818 saloons in northern and central California. The vote on the question of State-wide prohibition in Colorado in November, 1912, resulted in a victory for the liquor interests. The vote under the local option law of Connecticut, which was taken in October, 1912, resulted in a victory for no license in 94½ towns and a victory for license in 73½ towns. The Tippins bill, passed by the legislature of Georgia, providing for the suppression of the near-beer establishments in that prohibition State, was vetoed by the governor. The Kentucky legislature, in the session of 1912, adopted an amendment to the county unit local option law of that State making the law apply to all counties uniformly. Heretofore the law exempted from its operation all cities having a population of 3000 or more. The amended law permits each county as a unit to vote on the liquor question, regardless of the size of any cities within the bounds of the county. In the Maine campaign of 1912 the Democratic State platform declared it "to be their purpose to use all possible endeavor to amend the constitution" by adding a local option provision. The Republican platform declared: "The people, by majority vote, have declared against the abrogation of the amendment of the constitution relating to Prohibition. We accept the verdict of the people and are emphatically opposed to all attempts to reopen this question in any form. We demand that the statutes be strictly and honestly enforced. Ours is a government of law. The law must be respected." On this platform the Republican candidate for governor was elected by a plurality of 3295 and a Republican majority in both houses of the legislature was elected.

In the 1912 session of the Maryland legislature, a local option bill was passed by the House of Representatives but defeated in the Senate by one vote. As a result of the elections under the local option law in Massachusetts, of the 33 cities of the State, 18 are under license and 15 are under no license for the year beginning May 1, 1912. Of the 320 towns of Massachusetts for the same year, 73 are under license and 247 are under no license. A number of minor provisions passed by the legislature of Mississippi makes possible the better enforcement of the prohibition law of that State. In New Mexico the lower house of the legislature of 1912 passed a prohibitory resolution by a vote of 27 to 15. The Senate, however, by a majority of 16 to 8, refused to concur in the resolution. In Pennsylvania, during 1912 the railroads of the State put into effect and operation the law prohibiting the sale of liquors on dining cars which, for a number of years, had been a dead letter. The result of the election in Tennessee in November, 1912, was an overwhelming indorsement of the State prohibition law. The vote on State-wide prohibition in West Virginia in November, 1912, resulted in a majority favorable to the amendment of 82,342, all but three countries of the State giving large majorities in favor of prohibition. The amendment goes into effect in 1914.

From a national standpoint the introduction to the so-called Kenyon-Sheppard bill in Congress was of the greatest importance. This bill is aimed to prevent the shipping of liquors for sale into States which by statute or by constitution prohibit the manufacture and sale of intoxicating liquors. The bill placed the enforcement of the law into the hands of the Interstate Commerce Commission. The measure received the support of nearly all the senators and representatives from States in which the sale and manufacture of liquors are prohibited and its passage was urged by religious organizations and societies formed to combat the liquor traffic.

The Anti-Saloon League was active in forwarding legislation for the restriction of the liquor traffic in all the States in which the legislatures were in session.

LISTER, JOSEPH, (FIRST) BARON. An English physician and scientist, died February 10, 1912. He was born at Upton, Essex, April 5, 1827. He was educated at London University, receiving the degrees of B. A. and M. B. in 1852. In the same year he became a Fellow of the

Royal College of Surgeons, England. For a short time after his graduation he acted as resident assistant in the University College Hospital. He then went on a holiday tour to Scotland and in Edinburgh saw so much that was important and instructive in relation to his profession that he obtained permission to extend his stay. He acted for a time as assistant to Professor Syme and afterwards as his house surgeon. This post he resigned in 1856 and was soon afterwards appointed assistant surgeon to the Edinburgh Royal Infirmary. He began in this position to teach as a private lecturer on surgery and continued to do this until his appointment to the chair of surgery in the University of Glasgow, in 1860. Lister had early been impressed with the great mortality which was at that time attendant upon surgical operations. Almost every operation was followed by what was known as surgical fever and even in the most successful cases the recovery was accompanied by a wound during the whole of the healing process. The probabilities of death even in the case of the most skillfully performed operation were so great that the benefit of anæsthetics was to a great extent nullified. Lister became acquainted with the great discovery of Pasteur that fermentation and putrefaction were not mere chemical changes resulting from contact with the atmosphere, but that they were due to the activities of minute living organisms and could not occur if these organisms were excluded. He at once grasped the surgical possibilities of this discovery and applied himself to the task of rendering them of practical applicability for the preservation of life. His first idea was to kill any germs which had already found admission to the wound and then to effect a protection against the entrance of more. After much consideration he selected carbolic acid as a germicide and cotton wool as a protective. The wounds were thoroughly washed out with carbolic acid and were covered with a protective dressing which was well secured by a bandage. The patients thus treated remained free from surgical fever and when the wounds were opened they were clean and free from irritation. The dressings were renewed with strict precautions against the admission of germs and the cases recovered without interruption.

The first public anonuncement of Lister's method was made in March, 1865. The next few years were devoted to efforts to simplify and bring it to perfection. His theories and expectations were received with incredulity in many quarters and in others with reasoned doubt, due largely to the stress which had been laid in some of Lister's early teaching on the necessity of excluding air as the universal germ carrier from all surgical or accidental injuries. The questions which thus arose were finally answered by Metchkinoff's discovery of what he called the "phagocytic" action of the white corpuscles of the blood, that is, of their power to envelop and destroy intruding organisms. It was rendered clear by research that the majority of floating organisms existing in the air were less dangerous to the patient than many kinds which might be derived from his own skin in the vicinity of the wound or from the hands of the surgeon or from instruments which had been imperfectly cleaned after a former operation. This resulted in the method of cleansing the skin with the greatest care, in the neighborhood of the part to be operated upon, and also in similarly treating the hands of the surgeon and his assistants. The instruments and materials used in the operation were sterilized by boiling and were lifted out of the boiling solution into a bactericide one in which they remained immersed until the moment of use. The dressings then were made sterile and impervious to micro-organisms from without.

Improvements which Lister subsequently introduced included the use of catgut as a ligature for cut arteries. These ligatures were left to be absorbed by the tissues. The actual results of these discoveries and improvements in the treatment of wounds can never be precisely known, but it was asserted in 1900 that Lister had already saved more human lives than all the wars of the preceding century had sacrificed. Claim is made for him that "in regard to the cure of disease, relief of suffering, and the saving or prolongation of life, he has been the greatest of all benefactors to the human race."

In addition to the offices held by Lister noted above he was from 1877 to 1893 professor of clinical surgery at King's College, London. He was created a baronet in 1883 and a baron in 1897. Among his published writings are: *Remarks on a Case of Compound Dislocation of the Ankle, with other Injuries, Illustrating the Antiseptic System of Treatment* (1870); *On the Effects of the Antiseptic System of Treatment upon the Salubrity of the Surgical Hospital* (1870); and *A Contribution to the Germ Theory of Putrefaction and Other Fermentative Changes* (1875).

LITERATURE, English and American. The statistics of book prouuction as given in the *Publisher's Weekly* show a curious difference in the present trend of the two countries. In Great Britain there is a continuous and rapid increase in the number of books published every year; the number having risen from 6004 in 1901 to 10,804 in 1910, and to 12,067 in 1912. In the United States, on the other hand, there has been a decline since the high-water mark of 13,470 in 1910. The figures given in the accompanying table include new editions as well as new books, and a considerable part of the literature is shared by both countries; that is, of the 10,903 books published in the United States during the past year, 7975 were by American authors anu 2928 by English and other foreign authors. Belles-lettres and poetry are apparently increasing in popularity in Great Britain and decreasing in America. In England more attention is being given to science, both pure and applied, and to educational and juvenile literature. In the list of American publications the most significant tendency is the multiplication of works in the allied fields of sociology, political economy, law and history.

Fiction. There has been a retardation in the flood of American fiction that had risen so high in previous years, but in England the increase continues. On the whole the quality has been improved by the weeding out of weak, offensive, and suggestive novels, although the year may not be signalized by the production of any one novel of the first rank. *Marriage*, by Herbert George Wells, marks a departure from the mood that has characterized his novels for several years; being a serious consideration of the question of a marriage under modern conditions and the gradual working out of a happy union through a difficult situation, not the usual

THE RIGHT HONORABLE JOSEPH (FIRST BARON) LISTER
DIED FEBRUARY 10, 1912

ENGLISH AND AMERICAN BOOK PRODUCTION

International Classification	England		United States	
	1911	1912	1911	1912
Philosophy	273	332	334	321
Religion, Theology	930	798	917	916
Sociology, Economics	725	705	653	867
Law	303	304	682	862
Education	250	311	300	254
Philology	187	206	192	294
Science	650	827	624	695
Technology	525	586	706	674
Medicine	413	440	527	495
Agriculture	169	187	240	305
Domestic Economy	99	151	95	110
Business	151	198	227	210
Fine Arts	232	.261	196	243
Music	52	83	86	93
Amusements	122	152	103	132
General Literature	345	505	919	524
Poetry	668	721	685	636
Fiction	2,215	2,464	1,024	1,010
Juvenile Publications	648	805	734	546
History	429	491	442	524
Geography, Travel	601	649	598	504
Biography, Genealogy	476	564	695	581
Encyclopædias, Bibliographies, and Miscellaneous	451	337	244	107
Total	10,914	12,067	11,123	10,903

one of illicit love, but of the press of financial and social responsibilities. Another noteworthy English novel *Mrs. Lancelot*, by Maurice Hewlett, is almost the sole exception to the general tone of English fiction. Here is not a "triangle" but a quadrilateral plot, with a wild-rose lady and three lovers to give excuse for the author's lyrical rapture over her perfection. In contrast *Mrs. Ames*, by E. F. Benson, describes a plain, elderly woman who, by sheer force of character, dominates her circle in a little English town. One of the cleverest novels of this clever author, it carries more than a suggestion of a moral and is a brilliant work of satire, as well as a masterly portrayal of a middle-aged woman equal to that of *Mrs. Thompson*, by W. B. Maxwell. Mr. Maxwell's latest novel, *General Mallock's Shadow*, is a powerful story of the effect upon an old Indian officer made by an unjust accusation of cowardice, and the devotion of his two daughters who passionately believe in toeir father's honor. *A Rogue's March*, by Evelyn Tempest, is also a story of India, and of moral obliquity; although never offensively didactic its morality is unimpeachable. *London Lavender*, by E. V. Lucas, is a wuimsical and discursive but entertaining story of a young married couple in a London lodging-house. *Manalive*, by Gilbert Keith Chesterton, is a parable of protest against conventionality. Breatrice Harraden, has equalled her early successful novel *Ships That Pass in the Night* in *Out of the Wreck I Rise*, a study of two women and a man, each of the three characters being a distinct and interesting type. William J. Locke tells in his usual engaging vein of *The Joyous Adventures of Aristide Pujol*, a sunny child of Provence, gallant and gay, unscrupulous, and yet beneficent. Miss Ethel Sidgwick is the author of three unusual novels: *Promise*, *The Gentleman*, and *Herself*, the first the boyhood of a musical genius (suggesting by piquant contrast *Jean Christophe* by Romain Roland), the second the tale of a young Scotchman in Paris, and the last, *Herself*, just issued, the life of a young Irish girl thrown on her own resources at seventeen. *Between Two Fires* is also the work of a young woman writer, Miss Clo Graves, under the pseudonym of "Richard Dehan"; the scene is that of the Crimean War and Ada Merling is a transcript from the gentle life of Florence Nightingale. *The Marriage of Captain Kettle*, by Cutliffe Hyne, continues the career of a popular hero. The romance of the verge of empire is ever attractive to Englishmen, and it has been well represented in 1912 by *Guinea Gold*, by Beatrice Grimshaw, who stages her story on Samarai, the little island off the southeastern coast of New Guinea, and in the gold fields of the interior; *The Veldt Dwellers*, by F. Bancroft, the story of an English family in the Bushveld of the northern Transvaal during the Boer war; *Twixt Land and Sea*, by Joseph Conrad; *Pike and Carronade*, by Major G. F. MacMunn, adventures on the Indian frontier, in Burma and in Africa; *The Street of the Flute-Player*, by H. de Vere Stacpoole, a story of Athens and the Athenians; *A Candidate for Truth*, by John Davys Beresford, is a continuation of the life story of Jacob Stahl, and a remarkable study of character; *Monsieur Carnifex*, by Alexander Crawford, about a troubled Balkan kingdom, with plenty of stirring incidents; *One Crowded Hour*, by Sydney C. Grier, a story of two Sicilies; *King Errant*, by Flora Annie Steel, whose hero is Zahir-uddin Mahomed, the founder of the dynasty of the Great Moguls, and *The Lost World*, in which Sir Arthur Conan Doyle not only transports the reader to South America, but to a prehistoric plateau full of survivals of Jurassic beasts! Anne Douglas Sedgwick, author of *Tante*, follows that unusual novel with *The Nest* and Eric Parker produces in *The Promise of Arden* a delightful successor to *The Sinner and the Problem* of a decade ago. *The Turnstile*, by A. E. W. Mason, is a novel of politics and Arctic exploration. *The Port of Dreams*, by Miriam Alexander, is a story of the Jacobite conspiracies of the eighteenth century in Ireland. *The Royal Road*, by Alfred Ollivant, gives the gray life history of a common London workingman in a very different style from that of *Bob, Son of Battle*. *Come Rack! Come Rope!* by Robert Hugh Benson, gives us another idealized portrait of Mary Stuart. *The Lee*, by Rose Macaulay, is the £1000 prize story in a recent London competition. A few other English novels are worthy of note: *Cynthia; a Daughter of the Philistines* and *The Man Who Was Good*, by Leonaru Merrick; *Erica*, by Mrs. Henry de la Pasture (Lady Clifford); *The Chequer Board*, by Lady Sybil Grant; *The Charwoman's Daughter*, by James Stephens; *Mary Pechell*, by Mrs. Belloc Lowndes; *The Palace of Logs*, by Robert Barr (Dublin and Canada in the days of George III.); *The Trespasser*, by D. H. Lawrence; *The Wind Among the Barley*, by M. P. Willcocks; *Three Women* by Netta Syrett; *Left in Cnarge*, by Victor L. Whitechurch, a pretty story of English village life. Eden Phillpotts brings out two novels, *The Lovers* and *The Forest on the Hill*. *The Green Overcoat*, by Hilaire Belloc, is a whimsical story of the adventures of a grave professor in a borrowed coat.

American novelists of the first rank are represented by Edith Wharton who, in a gloomy story, *The Reef*, tells of the career of a young American girl making a living for herself in Europe and snatching at happiness to a tragic end. *The Financier*, bv Theodore Dreiser, is one of the autnor's painstaking studies of an unworthy character, not unlike *Sister Carrie* and *Jennie Gerhardt* in the heavy, uncompromising method by which is built up a memorable picture of realistic power, that of a man whose life is devoted to money, its attainment, and the pleasures it will buy. Mary Johnston follows her successful novel *The Long Roll*, which has Stonewall Jackson as its central figure, with *Cease Firing*, another story of the Civil War, and Robert E. Lee is its protagonist. *The Price She Paid*, by the late David Graham Phillips, gives the career of a young woman qualifying herself for the opera. *The Streets of Ascalon*, by Robert W. Chambers, is his annual message to the richest, if not the best, American society. *The Wind Before the Dawn*, by Dell H. Munger, is a powerful story of the great Kansas prairies and of a domestic tragedy in the revolt of a generous woman against unbearable tyranny from her refined, but selfish, husband. *The Soddy*, by Sarah Comstock, is another story of the Western plains and a romance of faith in irrigation. *The Lady and Sada San*, by Francis Little, is a sequel to *The Lady of the Decoration*. *The Cry In the Wilderness*, by Mary E. Waller, is a story of life in the Canadian forest. *The Net*, by Rex Beach, is a tale of Sicily and New Orleans. *The Heroine in Bronze*, by James Lane Allen, deserts Kentucky for New York and tells a pretty story of a lovers' quarrel and misunderstanding. *Charge It*, by Irving Bacheller, is a sequel to *Keeping Up With Lizzie*, and *The Squirrel Cage*, by Dorothy Canfield, teaches the same wholesome lessons of simplicity of living. *The Voice*, by Margaret Deland, is a new Dr. Lavendar story. *A Man's World*, by "Albert Edwards" (Arthur Bullard), is a frank presentment of unpleasant phases of city life. *The Rich Mrs. Burgoyne*, by Kathleen Norris, less moving than *Mother*, is nevertheless a wholesome story. *The Penny Philanthropist*, by Clara E. Laughlin, a cheery presentment of a penny-a-day philanthropist and optimist. *Mirabel's Island*, by Louis Tracy; and *The Gate Openers*, by K. L. Montgomery, are meritorious tales.

Some of the most remarkable stories of the supernatural of recent years have been collected in *Pan's Garden*, by Algernon Blackwood; *The Moon Endureth, Tales and Fancies*, by John Buchan; *More Ghost Stories of an Antiquary*, by M. R. James; *The Stoneground Ghost Tales*, by E. G. Swan. Other short stories are: *Back Home*, by Irvin S. Cobb, delightful sketches of southern life; *The Unknown Quantity*, by Henry Van Dyke, a book of romances and some half-told tales; *Eve's Other Children*, by Lucille Baldwin Van Slyke, stories of the Syrians in Brooklyn; *May Iverson Tackles Life*, by Elizabeth Jordan, refreshingly humorous studies of girls in a convent; *Phoebe, Ernest and Cupid*, by Inez Haynes Gilmore, a picture of middle-class suburban family life in America; *Scientific Sprague*, by Francis Lynde, stories of a deductive detective; *The Red Cross Girl*, by Richard Harding Davis.

ESSAYS AND LITERARY CRITICISM. It would seem that there has been a revival of the old contemplative essay during the past few years as well as the emergence of a new sort of essay, not at all contemplative; A. C. Benson's leisurely books being an example of the former style, and G. K. Chesterton's vivacious chains of antitheses of the latter. Parody as a subtle form of criticism appears in: *A Christmas Garland*, by Max Beerbohm, in which sixteen contemporary English authors are cleverly imitated. The volume of essays entitled *The Inn of Tranquility*, by John Galsworthy, is divided into two parts: "Concerning Life," and "Concerning Letters," on both of which subjects the author speaks with ripe wisdom. *Letters From Solitude*, by Filson Young, are written from a pleasant village in Fontainebleau. *At Prior Park and Other Papers*, by Austin Dobson, are concerned with men, books, houses and works of art of the eighteenth century. *Among the Idolmakers*, by Lawrence Pearsall Jacks, is a witty and delightful bit of criticism of current fads in philosophy. *Arrested Fugitives*, by Sir Edward Russell, comprises both essays and addresses. *A Little of Everything*, by E. V. Lucas, contains sunny and genial chats upon a wide range of topics. *Studies and Appreciations*, by Darrell Figgis, includes much able and courageous literary criticism. *The Love of Nature Among the Romans*, by Sir Archibald Geikie, is sufficiently described in the title. *This, That and the Other*, by Hilaire Belloc, and *A Miscellany of Men*, by Gilbert Keith Chesterton, are alike in their power of awakening interest in everyday happenings, and the latter exhibits anew the wit, humor, and imagination that have distinguished his preceding volumes. *Walking Essays*, by A. H. Sidgwick, and *A Tramp's Sketches* by Stephen Graham, voice the joys of the open road. We note also among English essayists: Major Gambier-Parry who writes *Allegories of the Land;* Lord Rossmore who in *Things I Can Tell* gossips in a somewhat cynical way of the society of his time; William Stebbings whose second volume of *Truths or Truisms* is of unusual interest. *Men, Women and Minxes*, by Mrs. Andrew Lang, are charming essays with a prefatory note by the late Andrew Lang; *The Note-Books of Samuel Butler*, author of *Erewhon*, arranged and edited by Henry Festing Jones, are extremely interesting. *The Problem of Edwin Drood*, by Sir William Robertson Nicoll, again opens the discussion of *The Mystery of Edwin Drood*, and apparently settles for all time the fact that Drood was murdered. *English Epic and Heroic Poetry*, by W. MacNeile Dixon, professor of English poetry in the University of Glasgow, is a well-written discussion of an old-fashioned theme. *Books and Bookmen and Other Essays*, by Ian Maclaren, comprises a selection of pleasant chats on various subjects. Books by American essayists are numerous and noteworthy. Easily first is: *On Some of Life's Ideals: Three Essays*, by William James, a plea against a dull conventionality in regarding life. *The American Mind*, by Bliss Perry, considers all the printed records for 300 years a part of American literature, town-records, and diaries being included in his survey. *Time and Change*, by John Burroughs, is gently agnostic in its content and full of the serenity of a lover of woods and meadows. *Gateways to Literature and Other Essays*, by Brander Matthews, a volume of literary comment, criticises the German and some English authors for "putting the reader to unnecessary trouble." *A History of English Prose Rhythm*, by George Saintsbury, identifies quantity with accent or stress, and divides prose into feet. Other discussions are: *Humanely Speaking*, by Samuel McChord Crothers; *Is There Anything New Under the Sun?*, by Edwin Björkman; *The Provincial American and Other Papers*, by Meredith Nicholson, containing a good word for the country west of the Hudson River; *Nietzsche and Art*, by Anthony M. Ludovici, an attack on modern culture; *The Maker of Rainbows*, poetic dreams in prose by Richard Le Gallienne; *In Other Words*, by Franklin P. Adams; *The Posthumous Essays of John Churton Collins*, edited by L. C. Collins; *Morgan's Essay on the Dramatic Character of Sir John Falstaff*, edited by W. A. Gill, a most interesting reprint of a book published in 1777.

Students will find *The History of English Literature From Beowulf to Swinburne*, by the late Andrew Lang, especially valuable for its chapter on "Early Scottish Literature." Critical essays on poetry are: *Essentials of Poetry*, the Lowell lectures for 1911, by William Allan Nielson; *Poetry and Prose*, by Adolphus Alfred Jack; *Lectures on Poetry*, by John William Mackail; *A History of English Lyrical Poetry from its origins to the present time*, by Edward Bliss Reed; *Poets and Poetry*, by John Bailey; *The Greek Genius and Its Meaning to Us*, by R. W. Livingstone, treats of "Greek modernity."

DRAMA. Since plays, even the successful ones, are now being commonly published in English, the reader has at last an opportunity to make his own comparisons with contemporary foreign productions. The pessimistic and decadent plays of August Strindberg, hitherto known to most English readers by reputation alone, have many of them been translated from the Swedish during the year by Edwin Björkman and others, and besides we have equally depressing plays by the two Russian authors, Anton Tchekoff and Maxim Gorky. From the French we have a translation by Ruth Helen Davis of *The Daughter of Heaven* by Pierre Loti and Judith Gautier, a spectacular tragedy in a Chinese setting, produced at the Century Theatre in New York under the author's direction. In English drama, perhaps more courageous, certainly more robust, we have notable plays by several well-known authors: *The Terrible Meek*, a striking drama of the crucifixion, by Charles Rann Kennedy; *The War God*, a five-act tragedy, and *The Next Religion*, by Israel Zangwill; *The Pigeon*, a fantasy in three acts, and *The Eldest Son*, by John Galsworthy; *The Grey Stocking and Other Plays*, by Maurice Baring; *Milestones*, a play in three periods, *Honeymoon*, a comedy in three acts, *What the Public Wants*, a newspaper play in four acts, *Cupid and Common Sense* a play in four acts, with a preface on the "Crisis in the Theatre," *Polite Farces* for the drawing-room, all by the versatile and indefatigable Arnold Bennett. *Sherwood; or Robin Hood and the Three Kings*, poetical dramas in musical verse, by Alfred Noyes; *Five Little Plays*, by Alfred Sutro, clever society scenes; *Three Comedies*, by Ludvig, Baron Holberg; *The Nun of Kent*, a drama in five acts, by Grace Denio Litchfield; *Ginevra*, a play of medieval Florence, by Edward Doyle; *The Summons of a King*, by Philip Decker Goetz; *Plays of Protest*, by Upton Beall Sinclair; *Waters of Bitterness* and *The Clodhopper*, by S. M. Fox; *To-Morrow*, a play in three acts, and *Yankee Fantasies*, five one-act plays, by Percy MacKaye; *Embers*, one-act plays of contemporary life by George Middleton; *As a Man Thinks*, by Augustus Thomas; *Rust*, a play in four acts, by Algernon Tassin; *Jelf's*, by Horace Annesley Vachell, has been successfully staged. In dramatic criticism, we find noteworthy: *Plays and Players in Modern Italy*, by Addison McLeod; *The Elizabethan Playhouse and Other Studies*, by W. S. Lawrence; *The Evolution of the English Drama up to Shakespeare*, with a history of the first Blackfriars Theatre; a survey based upon original records now for the first time collected and published by Charles William Wallace, part IV. of "Schriften der Deutschen Shakespeare-Gesellschaft."

POETRY. The poetry of 1912 is marked by a new note, not perhaps in the many thin volumes of lyrics that come with every year, but indubitably in the dramatic poems and rhymed monologues of John Masefield and Wilfrid Wilson Gibson. The writings of both are characterized by a passion for justice and a deep sympathy with suffering, especially of the working class. *The Everlasting Mercy* and *The Widow of Bye Street*, by John Masefield, are rhymed narratives, almost novels in verse; *Womenkind*, *Daily Bread* and *Fires*, by Wilfrid Wilson Gibson are dramatic monologues written in terse and direct style, and the simplest of words, but carrying a message of indignant revolt against injustice and tender sympathy with the poor. *The Singing Man, a Book of Songs and Shadows*, by Josephine Preston Peabody (Mrs. Lionel S. Marks), author of *The Piper*, repeats the note of championship of labor and ardent love for humanity. *The Stranger at the Gate*, by John Gneisenau Neihardt is of the same order. *Heralds of the Dawn*, by William Watson; *Scum o' the Earth and Other Poems*, by Robert Haven Schauffler; *The Candle and the Flame*, by George Sylvester Viereck; *Moods, Songs, and Doggerels*, by John Galsworthy, may be mentioned in this connection, as being, in some sense, poems of protest. More purely lyrical are: *The Book of Love*, by Elsa Barker, a woman's love for a man voiced in 250 poems; *Poems*, by Gerald Gould, simple, intense and sincere; *The Lute of Life*, by James Newton Matthews, poems by a physician; *The Inverted Torch* and *Other Poems*, by Samuel John Alexander, a true poet; *Ballads and Rhymes*, by the late Andrew Lang; *Little Gray Songs From St. Joseph's*, by Grace Fallow Norton, verses of unusual quality; *The Tragedy of Etarre*, a poem by Rhys Carpenter; *Poems*, by Francis Gray Ticknor, edited and collected by Michelle Cutliff Ticknor; *A Sheaf of Poems*, translations by Bayard Taylor and Lillian Bayard Taylor Kilani; *In a Portuguese Garden*, by Cara E. Whiton Stone; *Psyche*, by Francis Coutts; *Quiet Places*, by Corlas Wupperman; *The Sailor Who Has Sailed*, by Benjamin R. C. Low; *The Vista of English Verse*, compiled by Henry S. Pancoast; *In Vivid Gardens*, by Marguerite Wilkinson; *A Little Book of Homespun Verse*, by the late Margaret E. Sangster; *Poems*, by Harriet McEwen Kimball; *An Urban Faun*, by Jean Wright; *First Love*, by Louis Untermeyer; *Youth and Other Poems*, Charles Hanson Towne; *From the Lips of the Sea*, by Clinton Scollard; *Lays of the Lake*, by John C. Wright; *Madrigali*, by Thomas A. Daly, the author of *Canzoni*, who continues his delightful lyrics in the Italian-American dialect. *Songs From Books*, by Rudyard Kipling, is a collection of the bits of verse scattered through his prose-work. *Poems*, by the late Rosamund Marriott Watson, are beautiful and sincere. *Nature and Other Poems* and *A Wiltshire Village*, by Alfred Williams, a worker in the Swindon forges, remind the reader of Whitman or Blake, but with a note of their own. We should mention also: *Uriel and Other Poems*, by Percy MacKaye; *The Unconquered Air*, by Florence E. Coates; *Poems*, by W. J. Cameron; *The Soul's Destiny*, by William Avon; *Poems, Mathematical and Miscellaneous*, by Henry Daw Ellis; and *The Lyric Year*, a collection of one hundred American poems, submitted in competition for prizes.

LITERARY BIOGRAPHY. The year has been rich in biographical studies, at least two great biographies having appeared, one on each side of the sea. *Mark Twain*, by Albert Bigelow Paine, is of unusual length, three volumes of 1700 pages each, the result of six years of arduous work. The interest of the subject, the most popular of American men of letters, for whom all the world felt a personal affection, and the honesty of the portrayal make it the leading work in this field published in the United States during the year. Much af the story is told in letters and journals. The *Letters of George Meredith*, edited by his son, fill 630 pages of intense interest to all students of literature and lovers of Meredith. A personality so vigorous and vital leaves its mark on all it touches, and especially on intimate correspondence. The letters cover fifty years of active life and disclose the fineness of the man to those who have known only the author. *The Three Brontës*, by May Sinclair, is an able characterization of the genius of the three Yorkshire sisters, and may well supplement Mrs. Gaskell's admirable *Life of Charlotte Brontë*. Another creditable work, by an Englishwoman, is: *Byron*, by Ethel Colburn Mayne, temperate in tone and scholarly in presentment; a critical, analytical, and yet sympathetic study of the poet. Two of his contemporaries are ably treated in: *Wordsworth Poet of Nature and Poet of Men*, by Prof. E. Hershey Sneath of Yale University; and in the painstaking annotations of Coleridge's poems: *The Complete Poetical Works of Samuel Taylor Coleridge*, edited by E. H. Coleridge. *George Gissing. A Critical Study*, by Frank Swinnerton, which the author calls a "record of one who failed," is pitched in the same low key as *The Private Papers of Henry Ryecroft*, by George Gissing, which appears in a new edition. *Lafcadio Hearn*, by Nina H. Kennard, contains some letters to his half-sister Mrs. Atkinson, and *Lafcadio Hearn*, by Edward Thomas, is a brief but coherent epitome of the essential facts. *Adam Lindsay Gordon and His Friends in England and Australia*, by Edith Humphries and Douglas Sladen, is the first memoir of the Australian poet published in England, although he died in 1870, and this year, too, we have the first complete editions of his work: *The Poems of Adam Lindsay Gordon*, arranged by Douglas Sladen, and *The Poems of Adam Lindsay Gordon*, edited by Frank Maldon Robb. *George Borrow, the Man and His Books*, by Edward Thomas, is a genial and pleasing biography of the author of *Lavengro*. Another *Life of George Borrow*, by Herbert Jenkins, has been compiled from unpublished documents, his works and correspondence. *Charles Dickens as Editor*, by R. C. Lehman, is chiefly composed of letters to William Henry Wills, for twenty years Dickens's sub-editor on *Household Words* and *All the Year Round*. *Robert Browning, the Poet and the Man*, by F. M. Sim, is sincere in appreciation and rich in material. *William Makepeace Thackeray*, by Sidney Dark, is a fresh and independent estimate in the series "Little Books on Great Writers." In the field of English literature we should also mention: *Letters of William Cowper*, edited and chosen by J. G. Frazer; *Keats, Shelley and Shakespeare. Studies and Essays in English Literature*, by S. J. Mary Suddard; *Great Writers of America*, by W. P. Trent and John Erskine; *Oscar Wilde*, by Arthur Ransome; *Five Types*, by G. K. Chesterton. Biographies of foreign writers are numerous as usual: *Nietzsche*, by Paul Elmer More; *Friedrich Nietzsche and His New Gospel*, by Emily S. Hamblen; *Ecce Homo, by* Friedrich Nietzsche; *Victor Hugo: His Life and Work*, by Arthur F. Davidson; *The Great Russian Realist*, by J. A. T. Lloyd, treating of Feodor Dostoieffsky whose *Brothers Karamazov* is translated by Constance Garnett; *From Ibsen's Workshop*, translated by A. G. Chater, with an introduction by William Archer, who edited a complete edition of Ibsen's works. Some unusually delightful reminiscences are: *Our House and London Out of Our Windows*, by Elizabeth Robins Pennell; *A Personal Record* by Joseph Conrad, published in England under the title *Some Reminiscences; Hail and Farewell; Salve*, by George Moore, a singular autobiography in three volumes.

GENERAL BIOGRAPHY. The most important biographical achievement of the year is the completion of the great *Dictionary of National Biography* by the third and final volume of the *Second Supplement*, edited by Sir Sidney Lee, which includes those who died in the period between the death of Victoria, January 22, 1901, and the year 1911. The whole work contains memoirs of 31,757 persons of distinction in the British empire. There are 1635 new biographies considered in the two supplements issued since the 63 original volumes were completed in 1900. The dictionary, as a whole, is remarkable for its impartiality, accuracy, and comprehensiveness, as well as for its avoidance of superfluous praise. *The Girlhood of Queen Victoria*, in two volumes, by Viscount Esher, is a selection from her majesty's diaries between the years 1832 and 1840, culled from over a hundred journals written in her own hand, and of much historic and biographical interest in their revelation of the character and the education of the queen. *The Life of David Lloyd-George*, by H. Du Parc, is to consist of four volumes, the first of which has been issued. *The Life of General Booth* is a collection of estimates by various authors, including the Rev. R. J. Campbell, Lady Francis Balfour, W. H. Beveridge, and others, who recognize his practical genius and power of organization. The second volume of William Flavelle Monypenny's *Life of Benjamin Disraeli, Earl of Beaconsfield*, covers the ten years from 1837 to 1846, perhaps the most stirring decade of his life. The death of the author leaves this important work but half done. *Portraits and Sketches*, by Edmund Gosse, includes thirteen memoirs of contemporaries and friends. *Memories*, by Sir Frederick Wedmore, reflects pleasant and discreet reminiscences. *The Life of John Henry, Cardinal Newman*, by Wilfrid Philip Ward, is an important work.

Other English biographies worthy of mention are: a new life of *Edward Irving*, by Jean Christie Root; *Arthur James Balfour as Philosopher and Thinker*, by Wilfrid Short; *The Macready Diaries*, 1833-1857, edited by William Toynbee; *A Cosmopolitan Actor, David*

Garrick and His French Friends, by Frank A. Hedgcock; *Maitland of Lethington*, by E. Russell, a study of the life and times of the minister of Mary Stuart; *Letters From Madame Du Deffand to Horace Walpole*, filling three volumes, edited by Mrs. Paget Toynbee; *Recollections of a Court Painter*, by Henry Jones Thaddeus, recalls the courts of the nineteenth century; *Family and Heirs of Sir Francis Drake*, by Lady Elliott-Drake; *Lives of the Hanoverian Queens of England*, Vol. II., by Alice Drayton Greenwood; *Life and Work of William Pryor Letchworth*, by Josephus Nelson Letchworth; *The Three Sisters of Lord Russell of Killowen*, by Matthew Russell; *Margaret and Ethel MacDonald*, by J. Ramsay MacDonald; *The Life of Henry Hartley Fowler, First Viscount Wolverhampton*, by his daughter Edith Henrietta Fowler (Mrs. Robert Hamilton); *The Letter-Bag of Lady Elizabeth Stanhope*, 1806-1873, by A. M. W. Stirling; *Lord Chatham and the Whig Opposition* by D. A. Winstanley; *The Life of Sir Joseph Banks*, president of the Royal Society, by Edward Smith; *Francis Paget*, bishop of Oxford, by Stephen Paget and J. M. C. Crum; *The Life of Sir Howard Vincent*, by S. H. Jeyes and F. D. How; *My Own Times*, by Lady Dorothy Nevill; *The Fourth Generation*, reminiscences by Janet Ross; *Unseen Friends*, by Mrs. William O'Brien; *The Battle of Life, a Retrospect of Sixty Years*, by T. E. Kebbel, an octogenarian; *Sixty Years in the Wilderness*, by Sir Henry Lucy; *Thirteen Years of a Busy Woman's Life*, by Mrs. Alec Tweedie; *Correspondence of Sarah Spencer, Lady Lyttelton*, edited by Mrs. Hugh Wyndham; *Mary Sidney, Countess of Pembroke*, Sir Philip Sidney's favorite sister, by Frances Berkeley Young; *George Frederick Watts: the Annals of an Artist's Life*, by M. S. Watts.

In foreign biography, there are a few meritorious works that should be mentioned: *William the Silent*, by J. C. Squire; *The Life of St. Francis of Assisi*, by Father Cuthbert; *St. Francis of Assisi*, by Johannes Jörgenson; *The Letters and Journals of Count Charles Leiningen Westerbury* (1848-1849), edited by Henry Marczali, written from prison and some of them in farewell under the shadow of the scaffold; *Marie Antoinette: Her Early Youth*, by Lady Younghusband; *Forty-five Years of My Life*, 1770-1815, by the Princess Louise of Prussia, edited by Princess Radziwill; *Carmen Sylva and Sketches from the Orient*, by Pierre Loti; *The Comedy of Catherine the Great*, by Francis Henry Gribble; *The Life of Michael Angelo*, by Romain Roland; *The Life and Times of Rodrigo Borgia*, by Arnold Matthew; *Caesar Borgia*, a study of the Renaissance, by John Leslie Garner; *The Life of Caesar Borgia*, by Rafael Sabatini; *Great Educators of Three Centuries*, by Frank Pierrepont Graves; *The Man Who Saved Austria: Baron Jellacic*, by M. Hartley; *Prince Talleyrand and His Times*, by Frederick Auguste Loliée; *Memoirs of Francesco Crispi; Letters and Recollections of Mazzini*, by Harriet Eleanor (Baillie-Hamilton) King; *Michael Heilprin and His Sons*, by Gustav Pollak; *Hercules Brabazon Brabazon: His Art and Life*, by C. Lewis Hind.

In American biography we have a new portrait of Lincoln in *Personal Traits of Abraham Lincoln*, by Helen Nicolay, which supplements Hay and Nicolay's History. *Washington and Lincoln, Leaders of the Nation in the Constitutional Eras of American History*, by Robert W. McLaughlin, is a comparison of the two great statesmen. *John Hancock*, by Lorenzo Sears, is the first biography that has ever been written of that famous patriot. *Marcus Alonzo Hanna: His Life and Work*, by Herbert David Croly, and *The True Daniel Webster*, by Sidney George Fisher, are worthy and readable works. Biographies of two remarkable American women are: *Frances Willard: Her Life and Work*, by Ray Strachey, and *The Life of Ellen H. Richards*, by Caroline Louisa Hunt. An arresting autobiography *The Promised Land*, by Mary Antin, tells the story of an immigrant girl in the New World. *Woodrow Wilson* by Hester E. Hosford, and *Woodrow Wilson: the Story of His Life*, by William Bayard Hall, give brief outline sketches of the President-elect. *The Story of J. Pierpont Morgan* is told by Carl Hovey, and that of *Alexander Hamilton*, by William Smith Culberson. *One Welshman: a Glance at a Great Career*, by the late Whitelaw Reid, is an able address on the life and character of Thomas Jefferson. *General Joseph Wheeler and the Army of the Tennessee*, by John Witherspoon Du Bose, is an enthusiastic tribute. Two men interested in education are discussed in: *Educational Views and Influence of DeWitt Clinton*, by Edward Augustus Fitzpatrick, and the *Life of Dr. D. K. Pearsons*, the friend of the small college, by Edward Franklin Williams. A charming autobiography is that of Yoshio Markino, *When I Was a Child*, giving an artless narrative of his home life and education in Japan. *Memories of James McNeil Whistler, the Artist*, by Thomas R. Way, gives most of its space to Whistler as a lithographer. *The Autobiography of an Individualist*, by James O. Fagan, while giving the experiences of an adventurous life, is also a plea for the open shop.

RELIGION. To the increasing interest in the problems of the moral and spiritual life the coming of Professor Rudolf Eucken to America may have contributed. Previous to his receiving the Nobel prize for idealistic literature in 1908, only one of Eucken's works had been translated into English, a volume published in 1878 with an introduction by President Noah Porter of Yale. Now we have all of his important works: *Life's Basis and Life's Ideals, Main Currents of Modern Thought, The Truth of Religion, The Problem of Human Life* and others. *The Meaning of God in Human Experience: A Philosophic Study of Religion*, by William Ernest Hocking, shows not only the equipment of a professor of philosophy, but also a sympathetic understanding of the greater mystics. *Civilization at the Cross Roads*, by John Neville Figgis, in a way the sequel or at least the supplement of his *The Gospel and Human Needs*, is courageous in its apologetic, and seeks rational foundation for religious beliefs. *Thy Rod and Thy Staff*, by Arthur Christopher Benson, tells the story of his conversion during illness from the "spectatorial" attitude toward life, looking at it through study windows, to a regenerating faith. *Within: Thoughts During Convalescence*, by Sir Frederick Younghusband, is another book produced by a severe illness. *Modern Problems*, by Sir Oliver Lodge, is mentioned here because of its ethical trend and the chapters on "The Nature of Time" and "Balfour and Bergson." *Life's Tangled Thread*, by the Right Reverend W. Boyd-Carpenter, is a defense of life against the modern pessimist. *Creative Revelation*, four lectures on the

Miraculous Christ, by J. G. Simpson, deals with miracles ably and candidly from the orthodox standpoint. *An Outline of the History of Christian Thought Since Kant*, by Edward Caldwell, continues the sketch of the reformed theology begun by Dr. Arthur McGiffert in his *Protestant Thought Before Kant*. *The Golden Bough, Part V.: Spirits of the Corn and of the Wild*, by J. G. Frazer, continues the work on magic and religion and forms a rich storehouse of legend and folk-lore. *The Autobiography and Life of George Tyrrell*, arranged with supplements by Miss M. D. Petre, is of great interest in its contribution to the history of Modernism. *The Peasant Sage of Japan*, translated by Tadasu Yoshimoto, tells of the beautiful story of the life of Sontoku Ninomiya. Some practical aspects of religious effort are considered in the series of "Catholic Studies in Social Reform." *III. The Housing Problem*, edited by Leslie A. St. Toke, and *IV. The Church and Eugenics*, by the Rev. T. J. Gerrard.

Landmarks in the History of the Welsh Church, by the Right Reverend Alfred George Edwards, Bishop of St. Asaph, has an added interest because of the present movement for the disestablishment of the church in Wales. *The Eve of Catholic Emancipation: being the History of the English Catholics During the first Thirty Years of the Nineteenth Century*, by the Right Reverend Monsignor Bernard Ward, has reached its third and concluding volume. *Studies in Early Church History*, by Cuthbert Hamilton Turner, the brilliant lecturer and inspiring teacher at Oxford, will be welcomed.

HISTORY. Perhaps the most important characteristic of the work done in history during the last few years has been the revolution in the point of view from which history is written. There has been a shifting of emphasis from the purely political to the economic and social, from the sensational and exceptional to a consideration of the permanent forces which mold society, from fields remote from the interests and problems of to-day to a careful analysis of contemporary institutions and events. These tendencies have long been apparent among the advance guard engaged in historical research, but only recently have they attained popular literary expression. The best exposition of this change of attitude on the part of modern historians and the motives which have combined to bring it about is to be found in Professor James Harvey Robinson's volume of essays, *The New History*. The most important of the coöperative histories is the *Cambridge Medieval History*, planned by J. B. Bury, edited by H. M. Gwatkin and J. P. Whitney, which worthily succeeds *The Cambridge Modern History* now completed; the first volume presenting a view of the transition from the ancient to the medieval world. Another consideration of medieval times is given by Charles Robert Leslie Fletcher, in *The Making of Western Europe* during the Dark Ages, 300-1000 A. D. *Saints and Heroes to the End of the Middle Ages*, by George Hodges, is human and entertaining. *The Story of Europe*, by Samuel Bannister Harding and Margaret Snodgrass, is wide in its scope, and well adapted to the younger students of history. *The History of the People of the Netherlands*, by Petrus Johannes Blok, reaches its fifth and final volume, treating of the eighteenth and nineteenth centuries.

English history for 1912 is varied in interest but generally marked by a desire for a broad survey of the past achievements of the English people in each of many fields of activity. The first volume of *A Modern History of the English People*, by R. H. Gretton, pictures the period from 1880 to 1898, with the promise of a second volume which shall bring the story down to the present day. *The Constitutional History of England*, by Thomas Erskine May, Baron Farnborough, is an able survey from the Whig standpoint. The older England is described in *The Romanization of Roman Britain*, by F. Haverfield. *The History of the British Nation from the Earliest Times to the Present Day*, by A. D. Innes, is a scholarly treatment of the subject in 1000 pages of careful analysis. Another topic of perennial interest is represented this year by *Puritanism in England*, by H. Henly-Henson, and *The Romantic Story of the Puritan Fathers* dealing with the English Boston and the history of the Puritans before they emigrated, by Albert Christopher Addison; *Warfare in England*, by Hilaire Belloc, is a little book on the strategical topography of England and, incidentally, of her campaigns. *The History of the British Foreign Policy from the Earliest Times to 1912*, by Arthur Hassall, is too brief for so extensive a survey, but it is accurate and gives the main events and their results. Among the histories of narrower scope we may mention *Robert Kett and the Norfolk Rising*, by Joseph Clayton, which tells the dramatic story of the revolt of the 16,000 peasants led by Kett in 1549; *The Minority of Henry the Third*, by Kate Norgate; *The History of the Royal Family of England*, by Frederick G. Bagshawe; *Studies in the History of English Commerce in the Tudor Period*, by A. J. Gerson, E. A. Vaughn, and Miss Neva R. Deardorff. Among the new books on Ireland we have a few of value: *The Beginnings of Modern Ireland*, by Philip Wilson; *The Irish Revolution*, by Michael J. F. McCarthy, vol. I treating of the murdering time from the Land League to the first Home Rule bill with an attempt at an impartial attitude; *The Land War in Ireland*, being a personal narrative of events in continuation of "A Secret History of the English Occupation of Egypt," by Wilfrid Scawen Blunt; *The Viceroys of Ireland*, by Charles O'Mahony. In Scottish history we have *The Roman Wall in Scotland*, by George Macdonald, an inquiry into the history of the Roman occupation of Britain; *Scotland and the French Revolution*, by Henry W. Meikle, an able treatment of the influence of the French Revolution upon the political and social unrest in Scotland and upon the Scottish church. We have some interesting recollections of Parliament in two books: *Letters and Character Sketches from the House of Commons*, by the late Sir Richard Temple, and *The House of Commons from Within*, by the Right Honorable Robert Farquharson. *The Decline of Aristocracy*, by Arthur Ponsonby, may be mentioned here, because of its chapters on "Lords and Commons" and on "The Aristocrat of To-day." *Cambridge and its Story*, by Arthur Grey, is a history of the evolution of the university.

In the field of French history we note with surprise that books on Napoleon are fewer than usual. *Napoleon's Last Campaign in Germany*, by F. Loraine Petre, is a partisan view; *Pitt and Napoleon*, by John Holland Rose, contains some new letters; *Joachim Murat: Marshal of France and King of Naples*, is a bit of vivid history by Andrew Hilliard Atteridge. *The Story of France*, by Mary MacGregor, extends to the Third Republic. *France of Joan of Arc*, by Andrew C. P. Haggard, is a readable narrative. *The Russian People*, by Maurice Baring, tells in an interesting way of the country and its history with special reference to recent events and present conditions. *The Outline of the Russo-Japanese War*, 1904-1906, by Charles Ross, is a military history of the conflict. *Germany in the Nineteenth Century*, by John Holland Rose and others, is a critical and scholarly volume. *Arabic Spain: Sidelights on Her History and Art*, by Bernard and Helen M. Whishaw, is an interesting work, although the authors have no knowledge of Arabic and discover no new sources. *The Common People of Ancient Rome*, by Frank Frost Abbott, discusses such modernistic topics as the cost of living and governmental control of corporations and trades unions.

TRAVEL AND CONTEMPORARY HISTORY. The memorable geographical event of the year 1912 is the discovery of the South Pole, recorded in *The South Pole*, an account of the Norwegian Antarctic Expedition in the *Fram*, 1910-1912, translated by A. J. Chater from the records of Captain Amundsen, with an introduction by Dr. Fridtjof Nansen, who also publishes *In Northern Mists*, a history of our knowledge of the Arctic regions.

Now that Africa, north and south, has been opened to the tourist, and even the interior offers no considerable adventure, the number of books aiming to throw light upon the Dark Continent is rapidly increasing. In fact Africa has displaced Italy from the position it has long held at the head of the list of books devoted to travel and description. The annexation of Tripoli by Italy and the establishment of a French protectorate over Morocco during the year have drawn attention to the northern shore of Africa and at the instigation of the steamship lines it has become in recent years the most popular part of the Mediterranean tour. Among the books of the year treating this region with varying degrees of seriousness are: *Aspects of Africa*, historical, political, colonial, by Roy Devereux; *In French Africa*, by Miss Betham-Edwards; *About Algeria*, by Charles Thomas-Stanford; *Algiers, the Sahara and the Nile*, by Rachel Humphreys; *The Last Frontier*, by E. Alexander Powell; *African Shores of the Mediterranean*, by Cyril Fletcher Grant and L. Grant; *A Motor Flight Through Algeria and Tunisia*, by Mrs. Emma Augusta Ayer; *The Land of Veiled Women*, by John Foster Fraser; *Tripoli the Mysterious* by Mabel Loomis Todd; *The Holy War in Tripoli*, by G. F. Abbott. Of the other books on Africa there is only space to mention the following: *Africa of To-day*, by Joseph King Goodrich; *The Tailed Head Hunters of Nigeria*, by A. J. N. Tremearne; *A Resident's Wife in Nigeria*, by Constance (Belcher) Larymore, describes the heart of Africa; *Alone in West Africa*, an impressionistic record of travel, by Mary Gaunt; *My Soudan Year*, by E. S. Stevens; *A Colony in the Making: or Sport and Profit in British East Africa*, by Lord Cranworth; *In the Shadow of the Bush*, by P. Amaury Talbot, life in British Nigeria; *The Life of a South African Tribe*, describing the inner life of a Bantu people, by Rev. Henri A. Junod, the result of missionary labors in Portuguese East Africa, an extremely interesting work; *Animal Life in Africa*, by James Stephenson-Hamilton, the fruit of nine years' study; *Dawn in Darkest Africa*, by John H. Harris, organizing secretary of the Anti-slavery and Aborigines Protection Society; *Among Congo Cannibals*, by the Rev. John H. Weeks; *Boyd Alexander's Last Journey*, by Herbert Alexander, containing the diary of the expedition of 1908-1910 to the Wadai-Darfur region where French and British possessions meet; *Trekking the Great Thirst*, sport and travel in the Kalahari desert, by Arnold W. Hodson.

Books on Turkey continue to abound, and we may venture the prophecy that the Balkan War will stimulate the production or the publication of many more next year. Among the volumes of 1912 dealing with the Ottoman empire and the Near East must be mentioned: Sir Edwin Pear's comprehensive discussion of racial and social questions, *Turkey and its People; Turkey and the Turks*, by Z. Duckett Ferriman; *Behind Turkish Lattices*, by Hester Donaldson Jenkins; *A Modern Pilgrim in Mecca and a Siege in Sanaa*, by A. J. B. Wavell; *Travels and Studies in the Nearer East*, vol. I, part 2, by Albert Ten Eyck Olmstead, B. B. Charles, and J. E. Wrench, in their search for Hittite inscriptions; *A Land that is Desolate*, an account of a tour in Palestine, by Sir Frederick Treves, Bart.; *To Mesopotamia and Kurdistan in Disguise*, by E. B. Soane; *Across the Roof of the World*, by P. T. Etherton; *The Strangling of Persia*, in which W. Morgan Shuster tells the story of his experience in trying to reform the finances of Persia; *Through Greece and Dalmatia*, by Emilie Isabel (Wilson) Barrington, a good acount of a six weeks' trip; *Karakoram and Western Himalaya*, 1909: an account of the expedition of H. R. H. Prince Luigi Amedeo of Savoy, by Filippo de Filippi; *Narrative of the visit to India of their Majesties King George V and Queen Mary*, and of the Coronation Durbar held at Delhi December 12, 1911, by the Hon. John Fortescue; *The Malay Peninsula*, by Arnold Wright and Thomas H. Reid; *Through Shen-Kan*, by R. S. Clark and A de C. Sowerby; *Empires of the Far East*, by Lancelot Lawton.

Japan of the Japanese, by Joseph Henry Longford; *The Japanese Nation*, by Inazo Ota Nitobé, the exchange professor from Japan; and *American-Japanese Relations*, by Kiyoshi Karl Kawakanu, are the leading books on Japan. There is a good *Story of Korea*, by Joseph Henry Longford. China, in the transition through which it is passing, evokes much comment on its precarious politics. *China and the Manchus*, and *The Civilization of China*, by Herbert A. Giles, and *The Passing of the Manchus*, by Percy H. Kent, treat of the recently deposed dynasty. Another able work is *Recent Events and Present Policies in China*, by J. O. P. Bland, joint author with E. Backhouse of *China Under the Empress Dowager*. Other important works on this subject are: *China's Revolution*, by Edwin Dingle, a succinct history of the main facts; *The New China*, by Henri Barel; *The Chinese Revolution*, by Arthur Judson Brown.

Books on continental travel are fewer than usual. On Italy, always a tourist country, we have a few important travels: *A Wanderer in Florence*, by E. V. Lucas; *My Italian Year*, by Richard Bagot, really toe result of twenty years of residence; *The Cities of Lombardy*, by Edward Hutton; *The Story of Lucca*, by Janet Ross and Nelly Erichsen. Passing to other Mediterranean cities we have: *Monaco and Monte Carlo*, by Adolph Smith, and *The Romance of Nice*, by J. D. E. Loveland. "France" usually means Paris, as we find in *Byways of Paris*, by Georges Cain; *Old Paris*, by Henry C.

Shelley; *Sensations of Paris*, by Rowland Strong; *My Parisian Year*, by Maude Annesley; but we have also *Rambles Around French Chateaux*, by Mrs. Francis M. (Parkinson) Gostling; *From the South of France*, by Thomas A. Janvier; *The Spell of France*, by Caroline Atwater Mason; *In the Heart of the Vosges*, by Mathilda Barbara Betham-Edwards; *In the Carpathians*, by Mrs. Lion Phillimore. Other European travels include: *Letters from Finland*, by Rosalind Travers; *Home Life in Norway*, by H. K. Daniels; *Two Visits to Denmark*, by Edmund William Gosse; *Germany and the German Emperor*, by Herbert Perris; *German Memories*, by Sidney Whitman; *Modern Germany*, by J. Ellis Barker (revised to 1912); *England and Germany*, by leaders of public opinion in both empires collected by Dr. Ludwig Stein, editor of *Nord und Süd*; *The Tourists' Russia*, by Ruth Kedjie Wood; *Undiscovered Russia*, by Stephen Graham; *Russia in Europe and Asia*, by Joseph King Goodrich.

The imminent opening of the Panama Canal has attracted attention to Latin America and turned the tide of tourists southward. James Bryce, now completing his term of service as British Ambassador at Washington, gives his *Observations and Impressions* of South America, opening with a vivid picture of the Panama Canal, and describing his tour down the west coast to Peru and across to Argentina and Brazil. *Panama* by "Albert Edwards" (Arthur Bullard), is an interesting account of the canal, the country, and the people. The etchings of Joseph Pennell, published in *Pictures of the Panama Canal*, show that engineering works have more beauty than artists generally allow. *Guiana: British, Dutch, and French*, by James Rodway; *Lands of the Southern Cross*, by the Rev. Charles Warner Currier; and *In the Amazon Jungle*, by Algot Lange, are descriptive books of travel in South America.

Descriptions of North America are principally of the cold regions in Canada and Alaska: *Among the Eskimos of Labrador*, by Samuel King Hutton, a series of vivid descriptions; *Through Trackless Labrador*, by Hesketh Vernon Hesketh Prichard; *Reminiscences of the Yukon*, by Stratford Haliday Robert Louis Tollemache; *Canada To-Day and To-Morrow*, by Arthur E. Copping; *The Canadian Rockies*, by Arthur P. Coleman; *Sport in Vancouver and Newfoundland*, by Sir John Godfrey Rogers; *The Wonderland of the American West*, by Thomas D. Murphy; *The Spell of the Rockies*, by Enos A. Mills; *Saddle and Camp in the Rockies*, by Dillon Wallace; *My First Summer in the Sierra*, by John Muir. *America Old and New*, by J. Nelson Fraser, is the result of a rapid trip from west to east across the United States. Three books on Australia are worthy of mention: *Across Australia*, by Baldwin Spencer; *Sport and Pastime in Australia*, by Sir George Houston Reid; *Pioneers in Australasia*, dealing largely with Australia, by Sir Harry Johnston.

Other books of the year, especially those of a technical character, will be found in the special bibliographies attached to such articles as AGRICULTURE, ANTHROPOLOGY, EDUCATION FOOD AND NUTRITION, PHILOLOGY, PHILOSOPHY, POLITICAL ECONOMY, PSYCHOLOGY, SOCIOLOGY, etc.

LITTLE FALLS STRIKE. See STRIKES.

LIVERPOOL. See DOCKS AND HARBORS, and ARCHITECTURE.

LIVESTOCK INDUSTRY. See STOCK-RAISING.

LIVINGSTONE, LEONIDAS FELIX. An American public official and member of Congress, died February 11, 1911. He was born in Newton County, Ga., in 1832, and was educated in the public schools. He served throughout the Civil War as a private, and after its close engaged in farming. He was a member of the Georgia legislature for several years. In 1891 he was elected to the Fifty-second Congress. He was reëlected and served successive terms until 1910, when he was defeated for reëlection to the Sixty-first Congress.

LI YUAN HUNG. Vice-President of the Chinese Republic, assassinated April 2, 1912. Little is known of his history previous to the outbreak of the revolution at Wuchang. He was at one time a naval officer and afterwards entered the army, becoming well versed in military affairs. He was commander-in-chief of the rebel forces at the time of the outbreak at Wuchang. He was particularly active in protecting foreigners. See CHINA.

LOAN AND TRUST COMPANIES. The report of the Comptroller of the Currency summarized the statistics for 1410 loan and trust companies with aggregate resources on June 14, 1912, of $5,107,000,000. These institutions were distributed as follows: New England States, 181, with aggregate resources of $605,038,000; Eastern States, 494, with $2,958,852,000 resources; Southern States, 271, with $251,940,000 resources; Middle Western States, 320, with $1,180,004,000; Western States, 70, with $45,886,000; and Pacific States, 74, with $65,720,000. The aggregate resources of the 81 loan and trust companies of New York City greatly exceeded those of any other community, being $1,821,889,000. The 278 loan and trust companies of Pennsylvania reported resources amounting to $750,696,000; and those of Illinois and Massachusetts ranked next in order. The principal item of resources included loans and discounts of $2,711,241,000, of which nearly one-half were based on collateral security other than mortgages; and nearly 20 per cent. on real estate, including mortgages. The investments included bonds and other securities amounting to $1,219,139,000. In this were included a small sum of United States bonds, State, county, and municipal bonds amounting to $202,293,000; railroad bonds of $380,190,000, and bonds of other public service corporations of $208,673,000. The individual deposits included $2,319,055,000 subject to check, $910,850,000 in savings accounts, $395,983,000 in certificates of deposit, and $48,688,000 in certified and cashiers' checks. The cash on hand was $282,151,000, being 7.67 per cent. of the individual deposits. Compared with 1908 there was an increase of 568 in the number of trust companies reporting to the comptroller; capital stock, which amounted to $418,985,000, not including surplus and profits of $560,741,000, had increased 50 per cent. during four years; individual deposits had increased over 96 per cent.; and aggregate resources over 78 per cent.

LOCHREN, WILLIAM. An American jurist, died January 28, 1912. He was born in County Tyrone, Ireland, in 1832. In 1834 he came with his parents to the United States. He grew up and was educated in Vermont. After studying law he was admitted to the bar in 1856, and in the same year removed to Minnesota. He served in the Civil War from 1861 to 1863. In 1869-70 he was a member of the Minnesota Senate. He was appointed judge of the first judicial district of Minnesota in 1881, serving until 1893, when he was appointed United States commissioner of pensions. In this office he remained until 1896. While commissioner of pensions he came into national prominence through his efforts to remedy many abuses in the Pension Department. In 1896 he was appointed United States district judge for the District of Minnesota. The famous Northern Securities case was before him. He was a Democrat in politics.

LOCKJAW. See TETANUS.

LOCKS. See CANALS.

LOEB, MORRIS. An American chemist and educator, died October 8, 1912. He was born in Cincinnati in 1863, and graduated from Harvard University in 1883. He studied at the University of Berlin, taking a doctor's degree from that institution. He afterwards carried on studies at the universities of Heidelberg and Leipzig. Returning to the United States he became in 1888 assistant in chemistry at Harvard University. He was *docent* in chemistry at Clark University from 1889 to 1891. From 1891 to the time of his death he was professor of chemistry at New York University and was director of the laboratory of that institution from 1895 to 1906. He was founder and sole maintainer of the Solomon and Betty Loeb Convalescents' Home, and was identified with many other philanthropic enterprises, chiefly for the benefit of those of the Jewish race. In 1911 he presented $50,000 to Harvard University for the benefit of the Walcott Gibbs Chemical Library. He was a member of the board of education of New York City. Dr. Loeb was one of the most eminent chemists in the United States and contributed many important articles on chemistry and allied subjects to technical journals.

LOLO. See ANTHROPOLOGY.

LONDON. See GREAT BRITAIN, *Area and Population*, and ARCHITECTURE.

LONDON, PORT OF. See DOCKS AND HARBORS.

LOOMIS, EBEN JENKS. An American astronomer, naturalist, and writer, died December 2, 1912. He was born in Oppenheim, N. Y., in 1828, and was educated at the Lawrence Scientific School. While he was still a student the *American Ephemeris and Nautical Almanac* was founded in Cambridge and he became an assistant in the editing of this work, and senior assistant from 1859 to 1900, when he retired. He was a member of the United States Eclipse Expedition to the west coast of Africa in 1889. In addition to his scientific work he was an accomplished naturalist and was also a specialist in English literature, particularly in the works of Shakespeare. He wrote also many poems of great merit. He was the author of *Wayside Sketches* (1894); *An Eclipse Party in Africa* (1896), and *A Sunset Idyl, and Other Poems* (1903). He contributed to various papers and periodicals.

LOOS, CHARLES LOUIS. An American scholar and educator, died February 27, 1912. He was born in Wörth, Alsace, in 1823. He came with his father to the United States when still a boy, and in 1849 he was ordained to the Christian (Disciples) ministry. In 1857-8 he was president of Eureka College, Illinois, and from 1858 to 1880 was professor of ancient languages at Bethany College. In the latter year he was chosen president of Kentucky University. He served in this position until 1897, when he resigned and became professor of Greek in that institution. He was president of the Foreign Christian Missionary Society in 1889.

LOS ANGELES. See MUNICIPAL GOVERNMENT, *Commission Plan*; GARBAGE AND REFUSE DISPOSAL.

LOS ANGELES AQUEDUCT AND WATER SUPPLY. See AQUEDUCTS.

LOTI, PIERRE. See DRAMA.

LOUISIANA. POPULATION. According to the Census Bureau statistics issued in 1912, out of a total population of 1,656,388 in 1910, the foreign-born whites numbered 51,807, compared with 51,853 in 1900. The largest number of these, 20,253, came from Italy; from Germany, 8897; from France, 5299; from England, 2056. Other European countries are represented by smaller numbers. The city of New Orleans, with a population of 339,075 in 1910, had a foreign-born white population of 27,711. In 1900 it was 29,569. The negroes in the States in 1910 numbered 715,874 and the mulattoes 152,577. In 1890 the negroes numbered 559,193 and the mulatoes 90,953.

AGRICULTURE. The acreage, value, and production of the principal crops in 1911 and 1912 are shown in the following table:

		Acreage	Prod. Bu.	Value
Corn	1912	1,805,000	32,490,000	$32,490,000
	1911	1,800,000	33,300,000	23,310,000
Oats	1912	34,000	707,000	361,000
	1911	40,000	840,000	546,000
Rice	1912	352,600	11,812,000	10,985,000
	1911	371,200	11,693,000	9,237,000
Potatoes	1912	20,000	1,460,000	1,212,000
	1911	22,000	1,518,000	1,518,000
Hay	1912	142,000	a 234,000	2,972,000
	1911	24,000	a 31,000	372,000
Tobacco	1912	500	b 150,000	45,000
	1911	500	b 225,000	69,750
Cotton	1912	......	c 361,123	......
	1911	......	c 395,000	......

a Tons. b Pounds. c Bales.

MINERAL PRODUCTION. The total production of petroleum in the State in 1911 was 10,720,490 barrels, a marked increase over the production of 1910, which was 6,841,395 barrels. By far the largest quantity was produced in the Caddo fields, 6,995,828 barrels. In the Vinton fields, which largely increased the production of 1911, were produced 2,454,103 barrels, compared with a production of only 26,701 barrels in 1910. From the Jennings fields were produced 1,180,177 barrels, a slight decrease from the production of 1910.

MANUFACTURES. The Thirteenth Census included statistics of manufactures in the State for the calendar year 1909. The industries giving employment to the largest number of wage earners in the State are those connected with the lumber and timber products. In these industries 46,072 persons were employed.

EDUCATION. The total enrollment for white pupils in the State in the school year 1911-12 was 201,297, and for colored pupils, 87,055. Of those enrolled in the white schools, 184,507 were in the elementary grades, and 16,790 in the high school grades. The total number of teachers employed was 6444, of whom 5267 were white and 1177 colored. The number of school-houses in use during the year was 3505. The average salary of male white teachers per month was $79.10 and of female teach-

	Number or Amount 1909	1904	P. C. of Inc. 1904-'09
Number of establishments	2,516	2,091	20.3
Persons engaged in manufactures...	86,563	63,735	35.8
Proprietors and firm members..	2,295	1,899	20.9
Salaried employees	8,103	5,977	35.6
Wage earners (average number)	76,165	55,859	36.4
Primary horsepower	346,652	251,963	37.6
Capital	$221,816,000	$150,811,000	47.1
Expenses	204,024,000	164,442,000	37.5
Services	42,394,000	31,360,000	35.2
Salaries	9,008,000	6,044,000	49.0
Wages	33,386,000	25,316,000	31.9
Materials	134,865,000	117,035,000	15.2
Miscellaneous ...	26,765,000	16,047,000	66.8
Value of products.	223,949,000	186,380,000	20.2
Value added by manufacture (value of products less cost of materials)	89,084,000	69,345,000	28.5

ers, $52.45. The number of white children in the rural schools was 103,852. The total disbursements for educational purposes in the State during the year was $5,382,590.

Politics and Government

There was much of political interest in the State during the year. A spirited campaign for governor was carried on for several months, which resulted in the nomination at the Democratic primary, January 23, of Luther E. Hall, candidate of the reform element of the Democratic party of the State. The total vote cast in the Democratic primary was about 120,000. In the State election in April, Hall received a vote of 50,581, compared to 4961 cast for Suthon, his Republican opponent. On August 28 the city of New Orleans voted for the commission form of government, by a vote of nearly 24,000 in the affirmative, and about 2100 against. Under this form the city will be governed by five commissioners, including the mayor. See Municipal Government.

The State legislature met in May, 1912, and on May 21, elected Joseph E. Randsell and Robert F. Broussard, Democrats, to the United States Senate, for the terms beginning 1913 and 1915, respectively.

Louisiana is so overwhelmingly Democratic that there was no doubt as to its vote for President in the election of November 5. A movement was started early in the year to hold a presidential primary for the Democratic nomination. The Democratic State central committee adopted a resolution to that effect, but it was withdrawn by the new committee, because of the unusual number of elections to be held during the year (seven, four primaries and three general elections), and the delegates to the Democratic national convention were elected at the regular convention held at Baton Rouge. The delegates were uninstructed. The delegates selected at the Republican convention were pledged to vote for President Taft. The election of November 5 resulted as follows: Wilson, 61,035; Roosevelt 9323, Taft 3834, Debs 5249. Wilson's plurality was 51,712.

The most important work of the legislature was the submission of a number of constitutional amendments, nineteen in all, most of which proposed changes in the tax and assessment system of the State, separating property for State and local taxation. These amendments were voted down, as was also an amendment allowing women to serve on school and charity boards. A subsequent investigation of the vote on the amendments in New Orleans by the grand jury showed that a majority of the tally sheets had been changed and altered. Many thousand votes were altered by the election commissioners and over a hundred and sixty of these election officers were indicted. A constitutional amendment extending "the grandfather clause," allowing illiterate white voters to register and vote, if their fathers or grandfathers could vote, was carried by a small majority. The "recall" amendment was defeated.

In the election for a new school board for New Orleans, elected at large instead of by wards, and for the city commissioners, the regular or city Democratic organization elected all its candidates, after a spirited campaign by a reform or anti-ring faction of the Democratic party.

The new commission government took charge in December, 1912, but made very few changes in the personnel of the city employees.

Other Events. The United States Treasury Department on August 22, instituted an action against the American Sugar Refining Co., of New Orleans, for the recovery of $20,000 frauds through alleged dishonest sampling methods.

An investigation of the violation of the United States neutrality laws disclosed the fact that large supplies of guns and ammunition had been sold to Mexican and Central American revolutionists in New Orleans, and led to the indictment of a number of prominent business men in the city for conspiracy to violate neutrality laws and orders issued by the President during the Mexican revolutionary troubles.

Legislation. The legislature of 1912 passed an unusually large number of important measures. Among these were the following: A joint resolution, proposing an amendment to the constitution, exempting certain classes of voters from the consequences of failure to possess the educational or property qualifications prescribed; a joint resolution ratifying the income tax amendment to the federal Constitution; a reform bill of lading act; a measure providing for a commission to prepare and recommend amendments to the constitution as to assessments and taxation. A conservation commission was created and its duties and powers defined. A commission was created for the purpose of revising and preparing amendments to the laws of the State relative to corporations. An act was passed providing for simplified pleading and practice. A measure was passed providing for a new charter for the city of New Orleans under the commission form of government, with the initiative, referendum, and recall. A measure was enacted creating a State tuberculosis commission. An elaborate act was passed governing the militia and establishing a military code. An important measure was enacted regulating the primary elections, making it compulsory that all nominations for candidates for United States senator, members of the House of Representatives, State, district, and parochial officers and members of the Senate and House of Representatives of the State, and for city and ward offices in all cities, towns, and villages shall be made by direct primary. An important conservation act was passed. An act was passed providing a form of government for certain cities of the State, the city of New Orleans excepted, which provides for the commission form of government, provided the people of the cities included shall so vote. Several important measures relating to education were enacted. An elaborate corrupt practices bill was passed. Measures were enacted defining and punishing lotteries. The laws in respect to foreign corporations doing business in Louisiana were amended.

PRESENT STATE GOVERNMENT. Governor, L. E. Hall; Lieutenant-Governor, T. C. Barrett; Secretary of State, Alvin E. Hebert; Auditor, Paul Capdeville; Treasurer, L. E. Smith; Attorney-General, R. G. Pleasant; Superintendent of Education, T. H. Harris; Commissioner of Agriculture, E. O. Bruner; Commissioner of Insurance, A. E. Hebert; Commissioner of Public Lands, Fred J. Grace—all Democrats.

JUDICIARY. Supreme Court: Chief justice, J. A. Breaux; Associate Justices, A. D. Land, Walter B. Summerville, Frank A. Monroe, O. O. Provosty; Clerk, Paul E. Mortimer—all Democrats.

STATE LEGISLATURE, 1913. Both houses Democratic.

The representatives in Congress will be found in the section *Congress*, article UNITED STATES.

LOYSON, CHARLES, known as PÈRE HYACINTHE. A French preacher and theologian, died February 9, 1912. He was born at Orleans, France, in 1827, and was educated at Pau, where his father was rector of the local academy. Convinced that his true vocation was preaching he entered the Carmelite Convent at Lyons, and after taking vows, delivered a series of advent sermons, which brought him into conflict with the ecclesiastical authorities. In 1866 as advent preacher at Nôtre Dame he delivered a sermon against *La Morale Indépendante*, and in the following year selected as his theme, *La Morale dans la famille*. As a result he was denounced to the Roman Curia by the editor of the Roman Catholic *Journal de Paris*, and in 1869 he was summoned to Rome to defend himself before Pope Pius IX. This he seems to have done, but a few weeks later in an address at a meeting of the League of International Peace he provoked a fresh controversy by describing Judaism, Catholicism, and Protestantism as the "three great religions of the civilized world." For this language he was reproved by his order and was told to discuss other topics or to keep silence. He at once replied in a famous letter to the head of the Carmelites in Rome in which he formally broke with his order. This letter came on the eve of the great Ecumenical Council at Rome, which was to proclaim the infallibility of the Pope. In spite of the pleadings of friends and enemies alike, Père Hyacinthe refused to retract and the major excommunication was pronounced against him. Notwithstanding this he declared his intention of remaining a Catholic. He resumed the name of Charles Loyson and made a lecturing tour in America, where he was received with great enthusiasm. He returned to Europe again in 1869. In 1872 he married an American woman, and the Carmelite Order immediately pronounced his "interment." He founded in 1878 the Gallican Catholic Church, which was officially recognized by the state. He assumed the title of rector. In 1905, after separation of the church and state in France, he expressed the opinion that since neither the destruction nor the transformation of the Church of Rome was possible, some *modus vivendi* was needed. He considered the ideal solution would have been a Gallican Church such as he had conceived it, but admitted that the task which he had undertaken had been beyond his unaided powers.

LUBECK. See GERMANY.

LUBLINER, HUGO VON. A German dramatist who wrote under the pen name of Hugo Burger, died in January, 1912. He was born in Breslau in 1846. His plays include: *Der Frauenadvokat* (1873), his first great success; *Die Modelle des Sheridan* (1875); *Auf der Brautfahrt* (1880); *Mitbürger* (1884); *Die armen Reichen* (1886); *Der Reignitzer Bote* (1891); *Das neue Stück* (1894); *Der schuldige Teil* (1900), and *Die lieben Feinde* (1901).

LUDDEN, PATRICK ANTHONY. An American Roman Catholic bishop, died August 6, 1912. He was born near Castlebar, Ireland, in 1836, and studied at St. Jarlath's College, Tuam, Ireland, and at the Grand Séminaire, Montreal, Canada. He was ordained a priest in 1864. He served successively as assistant at the Cathedral in Albany, N. Y., pastor at Malone, N. Y., rector at the Cathedral at Albany, and vicar-general of the diocese from 1877 to 1880. From 1880 to 1887 he was pastor of St. Peter's Church at Troy, N. Y. In the latter year he was consecrated first bishop of Syracuse. He was the author of *Church Property*.

LUDWIG, ALFRED. A German philologist, died August, 1912. He was born in Vienna in 1832, and received his education in that city and Berlin. In 1860 he became professor of comparative philology at Prague. He published many works on philological subjects, which were marked by considerable originality and by independence of commonly accepted views. They include: *Der Infinitiv im Veda* (1871); *Agglutination oder Adaption* (1873); *Die philosophischen und religiosen Anschauungen des Veda* (1875); and *Der Rigveda* (1876-88), a translation, with commentary, which advances the theory, also held by Sayce, that many verb forms are more adapted to noun cases and not compounds of verb stem and pronominal suffix, the standard from the traditional side. The last work has been augmented by *Über die Kritik des Rigvedatextes* (1889) and *Über die Methode bei Interpretation des Rigveda* (1891). He also wrote on *Platons Apologie des Sokrates und Kriton* (1856, 6th ed., 1879). He resigned his professorship in 1901.

LUTHERAN CHURCH. A religious denomination, whose membership includes the largest body of Protestants in the world. There are four general bodies and in these are embraced two-thirds of the Lutherans in the United States. The chief independent synods are the United Norwegian Synod, the Joint Synod of Ohio, and the German Iowa Synod. The statistics of the denomination given below are furnished by the authorities of the denomination. According to the census of 1910, the total number of communicants of the Lutheran faith in the United States was 2,112,494.

The church statistics of the various subdivisions are as follows: General Council—Communicants, 495,468; ministers, 1644; congregations, 2519; benevolent offerings for 1912, $597,980; receipts for local expenses, $3,820,679. The Bible schools numbered 2868, with an enrollment of 302,838. The next biennial convention of the General Council will be held in Toledo, O., September 9, 1913. General Synod—Communicants, 405,939; congregations, 1769; ministers, 1351; church property valued at $21,442,840; benevolent offerings, $494,843; receipts for local expenses, $2,729,202. The Sunday schools numbered 1710, with an enrollment of 294,193. The next convention will be held at Atchison, Kan., May 14, 1913. Synodical Conference—Communicants, 807,693; ministers, 2885; congregations, 3569; church property valued at $14,885,000; amount raised for local expenses in 1912 was $3,644,466. The Sunday schools numbered 799, with an enrollment of 158,364. This branch also maintains parochial schools, with an enrollment of 148,288. The next convention will be held in 1914. United Synod of the South—Communicants, 50,354; ministers, 247; congregations, 470; church property, valued at $2,139,588; benevolent offerings, $70,211; receipts for local expenses, $230,099. The Sunday schools numbered 397, with an enrollment of 37,430. Independent Synods—Communicants, 646,639; ministers, 2908; congregations, 5990; church property, valued at $17,089,207; benevolent offerings in 1912, $760,679; local expenses, $2,164,607. The Sunday schools numbered 2345, with an enrollment of 183,434. The grand total is 64 synods, 9062 ministers, 14,317 congregations, 2,307,877 communicants, 5868 parochial schools, with 272,812 pupils; 7366 Sunday schools, with an enrollment of 959,102. The church property is valued at $85,514,238. The receipts for local expenses in 1912 were $12,554,053 and for benevolent offerings, $2,969,948.

The most notable events in Lutheran circles in 1912 were the beginning of a movement in the Ministerium of Pennsylvania to raise an educational fund of $500,000 for the Philadelphia Theological Seminary and Muhlenberg College; the efforts of Pennsylvania College at Gettysburg to raise $300,000, and the completion of a fund of $125,000 by Augustana College at Rock Island, Illinois. The Artman legacies, amounting to about $200,000, for various educational and benevolent institutions of the church and the creation of the "Artman Memorial Home for Lutherans," with a special legacy of $100,000 and a residuary legacy, which may add $200,000 more, was a notable legacy received during the year. Two new missionary conferences, the New England and the Red River, were organized in 1912. By the legacy of a Mr. Wills, St. John's English Congregation in Philadelphia, the oldest English Lutheran congregation in the world, was endowed in the sum of about $75,000. There was a general revision of the methods of raising missionary and benevolent funds in a number of the synods.

In view of the uniting of the various Norwegian Lutheran bodies into one general body, a doctrinal conference was held by the Synodical Conference, a German body which has hitherto included one of the Norwegian bodies, to discuss the results of such a union upon itself, and a committee was appointed to urge the Norwegian body not to remain in the new union. A similar conference was held between two of the independent synods, the Joint Synod of Ohio and the Synod of Iowa.

LUITPOLD, Karl Joseph Wilhelm. Prince Regent of Bavaria, died December 12, 1912. He was born at Würzburg, Bavaria, in 1821, and at the time of his death was the oldest ruling prince in Europe. In 1844 he married the Archduchess Augusta of Austria. He fought in 1866 against Prussia, but in the Franco-German war was on the general staff of the Prussian army. He had a notable career as a soldier, and in 1886, following the death of his nephew, King Ludwig, he became prince regent of Bavaria. King Ludwig was for many years insane, and his brother, Otto, next in succession, was also insane. Luitpold was next in line of succession. He would not listen to suggestions that he assume the title of king, arguing that there was nothing in the constitution of Bavaria to warrant the barring of a prince from the throne, even on the score of madness. As a ruler, he enjoyed immense popularity and did much for the upbuilding of the resources of his country. He was particularly alert in developing the commercial and agricultural possibilities of the state and was a notable patron of the arts and crafts. During his regency, Munich, the capital, became constantly richer as an art centre. He was considered the most sagacious of the rulers of the German states and he was, in addition, a notable factor in the formation of the German empire itself. He had much to do with persuading the German rulers to offer to King William of Prussia the imperial crown. The keynote of his career as prince regent was simple straightforwardness as an administrator, and his affairs were conducted in a manner beyond criticism. On the occasion of his ninetieth birthday a costly public celebration was proposed. He refused this and expressed the wish that the public would establish a charitable fund, the income of which should be used for the common welfare instead of devoting large sums to the celebration of his birthday. His son and heir, Prince Ludwig, now more than seventy years of age, married the Archduchess Marie Thérèse of Austria d'Este, who is the "Queen Mary" of the English Jacobites.

LUNAR PETROGRAPHY. See Astronomy.

LUXEMBURG. A central European grand duchy, neutral and independent. Area, 2586 square kilometers (998 square miles); population, December 1, 1910, 259,891. Luxemburg, the capital, had 20,848 inhabitants. Roman Catholics numbered 250,543. The grand duchy belongs to the German customs union. There were 525 kilometers of railway in 1911, 701 kms. of telegraph line. Iron is mined (1,728,973 metric tons in 1911). The budget as voted April 6, 1912, estimated the revenue at 18,696,137 francs; the expenditure at 20,629,710. The debt amounts to 12,000,000 francs; annuities, 493,150. The floating debt, for public works and railway construction, is limited to 19,335,774 francs.

The reigning house of Nassau became extinct in the male line with the death of the grand duke, William, February 25, 1912. He was succeeded by his daughter, Marie Adelaide (born June 14, 1894), who attained her majority and was formally enthroned June 14, 1912. Her sister, Princess Charlotte (born January 23, 1896), is heiress-presumptive.

LYDIAN INSCRIPTIONS. See Archæology.

MACAO. A city on the Chinese island of Macao; a Portuguese dependency (with Colôane and Taipa). Total area, 4 square miles; population, 74,866.

MAC ARTHUR, ARTHUR. An American soldier, died September 5, 1912. He was born in Springfield, Mass., in 1845, and was educated in the public schools and by private tutors. He began service in the Civil War as first lieutenant in the 24th Wisconsin Infantry, and rose through various grades until he became lieutenant-colonel in 1865, and was honorably mustered out in the same year. In 1866 he was appointed second lieutenant in the 17th United States Infantry, and in the same year was transferred to the 26th Infantry, of which he was promoted to be captain. In 1870 he was assigned to the 13th Infantry. He was promoted to be major in 1896, brigadier-general of volunteers in 1898, major-general, 1898, brigadier-general in the regular army, 1900, major-general, 1901, and lieutenant-general, 1906. In 1865 he was brevetted lieutenant-colonel of volunteers for gallant service in the battles at Perryville, Stone River, Missionary Ridge, and Dandridge. He received the brevet of colonel in the same year for service in the battle of Franklin and in the Atlanta campaign. In 1890 he was awarded the congressional medal of honor for gallantry in the battle of Missionary Ridge in 1862. He participated in many of the most important engagements during the Civil War. In the Spanish-American War he commanded a brigade of the 8th Army Corps, which took part in the capture of Manila. He commanded the first brigade of the first division, 8th Army Corps, in the advance on Manila, July and August, 1898, and the battle of Manila, August 13, 1898. In 1898-99 he commanded the second division of the 8th Army Corps and was commander of the Department of Northern Luzon in 1899-1900. He commanded a division of the Philippines and was military governor, 1900-01. Returning to the United States he was in command of the Department of Colorado, 1901-02; Department of the Lakes, 1902; Department of the East, 1902; Department of the Lakes, 1902-03; Department of California, 1903; Pacific Division, 1904-07. He retired by operation of law on June 2, 1909.

MacCAMERON, ROBERT LEE. An American artist, died December 29, 1912. He was born in Chicago in 1866. After attending the public schools he went to Chicago and began to make sketches for newspapers. Soon afterwards he removed to New York and did illustrating for the newspapers of that city. In 1889 he went to Paris to study. He became a pupil of Gerôme. He became very successful as a painter of portraits. Among the best known of his are pictures of President Taft, President McKinley, Archbishop Ryan, Justice Harlan, Justice Brewer, and Madame Melba. In addition to his portraits he painted other notable pictures. These include "A Group of Friends" and "The Daughter's Return." These are at the Metropolitan Museum in New York. For his "Micarême," which was once destroyed and repainted, he received an honorable mention in the Paris Salon. For several years before his death he maintained studios in London, Paris, and New York. In 1912 he was made a Chevalier of the Legion of Honor. He was a member of several foreign and American art societies.

McCARTHY, JUSTIN. An Irish novelist, historian, and former member of Parliament, died May 1, 1912. He was born in 1830 in Cork, and was educated in that city under private tutors, chiefly for the reason that at that time no Roman Catholic in the British Isles could receive an academic degree. From 1848 to 1852 he was engaged in journalism in the city of Cork, and from 1852 to 1860 in the same profession in Liverpool. In 1864 he became editor of the *Morning Star* in London, a radical organ which especially represented the views of John Bright. This paper survived only four years, and Mr. McCarthy then became a member of the staff of the *Daily News*, to which journal he contributed both political and literary articles. He continued to take an interest in politics and in 1879 was elected to Parliament from the County of Longford. He remained in Parliament until 1900. Although he won considerable prominence as one of the Irish Nationalist party in Parliament, his services as a legislator were obscured by his fame as a writer. In 1880 he joined the Irish Land League and in the following year was registered as one of the original shareholders of the company which founded *United Ireland* and acquired the *Irishman*. In 1882 he became chairman of the Land and Labor League of Great Britain. Mr. McCarthy acted for some time as vice-chairman of the Irish Parliamentary party, and in 1890 headed the famous secession of forty-five members. He was elected chairman of the party in opposition to Parnell. This choice was in the nature of a compromise. The Irish party was at that time in close alliance with Gladstone, and it required, above all, a leader of conservative theories and respectability.

Mr. McCarthy had no great oratorical gifts, but his leadership obtained weight and authority from the very moderation of his speeches. He had nothing of the remarkable magnetism which enabled Parnell to hold together a discordant party, and intrigues and quarrels finally resulted in his abandoning the leadership. He resigned in 1896. From that time until his final resignation from Parliament he took little active part in the deliberations of that party. Mr. McCarthy's career as a novelist began early in his life. Either alone or with Mrs. Campbell Praed, he wrote many novels, which in their day were popular, but which now are little read. These included *Miss Misanthrope, Dear Lady Disdain, Maid of Athens, Mononia*, etc. His chief literary reputation rests upon his historical writings. *A History of Our Own Times*, which was completed in 1905, was perhaps the most popular English history since Macaulay's. Other historical writings include *A History of the Four Georges and William IV., Modern England*, and *The Reign of Queen Anne*. He wrote also biographies of Sir Robert Peel, Pope Leo XIII., and W. E. Gladstone. He published a volume of *Reminiscences* in 1899, a volume of sketches entitled *Portraits of the Sixties*, and *The Story of an Irishman* (1904). Mr. McCarthy was well known in the United States where he made many visits and delivered lectures. He was a contributor for many years on English political and literary topics to the *Independent*.

McCHESNEY, DORA GREENWELL. An American writer, died July 5, 1912. She was born in Chicago in 1871 and was educated privately. She made a study of historical subjects, especially relating to the English civil war and was the chronicler of Lord Strafford and Prince Rupert. Among her published writings are, *Kathleen Clare, Her Book, 1637-1641*

(1895); *Miriam Cromwell, Royalist* (1897); *Rupert by the Grace of God* (1899); *Yesterday's To-morrow*, and *Wounds of a Friend* (1908). She also contributed many short stories and reviews to magazines.

McCOMBS, WILLIAM F. See PRESIDENTIAL CAMPAIGN.

McLANE, JAMES WOODS. An American geologist, and hydrologist, died September 4, 1912. He was born in Dubuque, Ia., in 1853. He had no formal education. From ten years of age until twenty he worked on the farm of his father, and at the same time studied Latin, higher mathematics, astronomy, and surveying. He also read law and practiced in the local courts. Between the years 1874 and 1876 he worked at the forge and bench and invented a number of agricultural implements. The two succeeding years were devoted to the study of geology and archæology, and in 1877-81 he made an extensive geologic and topographic survey of northeastern Iowa entirely on his own resources. Shortly afterwards he became attached to the United States Geological Survey in charge of a division. In 1886 he surveyed and mapped out 300,000 square miles in the southeastern part of the United States. He also completed geologic maps of the country and made extensive investigations of the Charleston earthquake. In 1894-5 he explored Tiburon Island, the home of a savage tribe about whom nothing had previously been known. In 1893 he was appointed ethnologist in charge of the Bureau of American Ethnology and held this position until 1903, when he resigned to take the place of chief of the department of anthropology at the St. Louis Exposition. Here he brought together an unprecedented assemblage of the world's peoples. From 1905 to 1907 he was director of the St. Louis public museum and from 1907 until the time of his death was a member of the Inland Waterways Commission. He was also an expert in the United States Department of Agriculture and a member of the American International Commission of Archæology and Ethnology. He was senior speaker of the Department of Anthropology at the World's Congress of Arts and Sciences in 1904, and was a member of many foreign and American learned societies. He was distinguished as a lecturer and as a writer. His published writings include: *Geology of Chesapeake Bay* (1888); *The Lafayette Formation* (1892); *The Siouan Indians* (1897); *Primitive Numbers* (1901); *Outlines of Hydrology* (1908). He also wrote many scientific memoirs and over three hundred articles. He was one of the editors of the department of Anthropology in the *New International Encyclopædia*.

McGILL UNIVERSITY. An institution for higher education at Montreal, Canada, founded in 1821. The students enrolled in the university in the autumn of 1912 numbered approximately 2000, of whom 500 were in MacDonald College, which includes a school for teachers, a school of domestic science, and a school of agriculture. There were 258 members of the faculty, of whom 74 were professors, 23 assistant professors, 87 lecturers, and 74 demonstrators. A noteworthy event in the history of the university in 1912, was the successful raising of a fund of $1,600,000 by the citizens of Montreal, and a few of the graduates outside the city, for purposes of general endowment. The total value of the productive funds of the university in the collegiate year 1911-12 was $6,575,022. The annual income from all sources was $770,839. The general library contained 136,791 volumes, and the medical library about 38,000. Principal, W. Peterson.

McILVAINE, CLARENCE W. An American publisher, died December 7, 1912. He was born in Vermont in 1865, and graduated from Princeton University in 1885. Soon after his graduation he joined the staff of Harper and Brothers, of New York. In 1891 he removed to London and formed a partnership with the late James R. Osgood under the name of Osgood, McIlvaine & Co. This firm acted as the English representatives of Harper and Brothers until Mr. Osgood's death in 1892, when the business was absorbed by Harper and Brothers. Mr. McIlvaine was keenly interested in art and was a friend of Whistler, Abbey, Millet, and other famous artists. He was also in intimate relations with well-known authors, including the late William Black, Thomas Hardy, the late Theodore Watts Dunton, Henry James, and Mrs. Humphry Ward.

McKINLEY, WILLIAM B. See PRESIDENTIAL CAMPAIGN.

McLANE, JAMES WOODS. An American physician and writer, died November 24, 1912. He was born in New York City in 1839, and graduated from Yale College in 1861. He studied medicine at the College of Physicians and Surgeons, taking his degree in 1864. In 1867 he was appointed lecturer on materia medica at the College of Physicians and Surgeons, and subsequently held other chairs in that school until in 1898, when he was appointed professor emeritus of obstetrics. From 1891 to 1903 he was dean of the medical faculty and was at one time president of the College of Physicians and Surgeons. From 1905 to the time of his death he was president of the Roosevelt Hospital and was consulting physician to other hospitals in New York City. He wrote many medical treatises.

MADAGASCAR. A great island in the Indian Ocean off the east African coast; a French colony. Antananarivo (Tananarive) is the capital, with 72,000 inhabitants.

Area, 585,300 square kilometers (225,984 square miles); population (1911), 3,104,881. Fianarantsoa has about 1000 inhabitants; Tamatave, 7026; Majunga, 4600.

PRODUCTION, COMMERCE, ETC. Agriculture and cattle-raising are the chief industries; rice the principal crop. The forests contain valuable timber. The mines yield gold, silver, iron, copper, lead, and zinc. Imports and exports, in 1910, 34,595,000 and 47,883,000 francs respectively; reported in 1911 at 46,700,000 and 47,500,000 francs. Railways (1912), 272 kilometers. The main line (Brickaville to the capital) is being extended from Brickaville to Tamatave, the extension to be completed in 1913.

FINANCE AND GOVERNMENT. The local budget balanced in 1910 at 30,750,000 francs. Debt, 99,283,000 francs. A governor-general (M. Picquié in 1912) administers the colony. Dependencies are Diego-Suarez, Nosy-Bé, and Ste. Marie.

MAGDALENA BAY. See UNITED STATES, *Foreign Relations*.

MAINE. POPULATION. According to the Census Bureau statistics issued in 1912, out of a total population of 742,371 in 1910, the foreign-born whites numbered 110,133, compared with 92,535 in 1900. The largest number of these, 40,386, came from Canada, other than French Canada; from French Canada came 34,934; from Ireland, 7886; from England, 5638; from Russia, 4744; from Scotland, 2388; and from Sweden, 2564. Other European countries are represented by smaller numbers. In 1910 there were 1363 negroes and 626 mulattoes in the State. In 1890 the negroes numbered 1190 and the mulattoes, 683.

AGRICULTURE. The acreage, value, and production of the principal crops in 1911 and 1912 are shown in the following table:

		Acreage	Prod. Bu.	Value
Corn	1912	16,000	640,000	$480,000
	1911	18,000	792,000	713,000
Wheat	1912	3,000	70,000	72,000
	1911	3,000	63,000	69,000
Oats	1912	133,000	4,602,000	2,347,000
	1911	135,000	5,198,000	2,807,000
Potatoes	1912	117,000	23,166,000	12,741,000
	1911	118,000	21,240,000	16,355,000
Hay	1912	1,231,000	a 1,428,000	19,564,000
	1911	1,400,000	a 1,540,000	22,176,000

a Tons.

MANUFACTURES The Thirteenth Census statistics are for the calendar year 1909 and were compiled in 1912. Manufacturing is the leading branch of industry in the State. From the table given herewith it will be seen that there were, in 1909, 3546 establishments, employing 88,476 persons:

	Number or Amount 1909	1904	P. C. of Inc. 1904-'09
Number of establishments	3,546	3,145	12.8
Persons engaged in manufactures...	88,476	82,109	7.8
Proprietors and firm members..	3,661	3,379	8.3
Salaried employees	4,860	3,772	28.8
Wage earners (average number)	79,955	74,958	6.7
Primary horsepower	459,599	343,627	33.7
Capital	$202,260,000	$143,708,000	40.7
Expenses	154,821,000	129,208,000	19.8
Services	43,429,000	36,681,000	18.4
Salaries	5,797,000	3,989,000	45.3
Wages	37,632,000	32,692,000	15.1
Materials	97,101,000	80,042,000	21.3
Miscellaneous ...	14,291,000	12,485,000	14.5
Value of products.	176,029,000	144,020,000	22.2
Value of products less cost of materials	78,928,000	63,978,000	23.4

The largest number of wage-earners was found in industries relating to lumber and timber products, 15,086. In the manufacture of cotton goods were 14,634; in the production of paper and wood pulp, 8647; in the manufacture of woolen, worsted and felt goods, 8754; in making boots and shoes, 6626. The value of the product of paper and wood pulp industries was $33,950,000; lumber and timber products, $26,725,000; cotton goods, $21,932,000. Woolen, worsted and felt goods, $18,490,000; boots and shoes, $15,509,000. The total number of persons employed in the manufacturing industries was 88,476. Of these 68,647 were male, and 19,829 were female. Employees under 16 years of age numbered 1387. The prevailing hours of labor were for more than one-half the wage earners 60 hours a week; 28.5 per cent. were in establishments where the hours of labor were 54 a week; 11 per cent. in establishments where they were less than 54 a week, and only 8.4 per cent. in establishments where they were more than 60 hours a week. The largest number of wage-earners was in Lewiston, 6788; in Biddeford were 5076; in Portland, 4902, and in Auburn, 3452. The table above shows the general increase in manufactures in the five-year period, 1904-1909.

POLITICS AND GOVERNMENT

It was an active year in politics in Maine. As the result of elections held in 1911, the Democratic party was in power for the first time in thirty years. Although this was due largely to local issues, there was also an aggressive interest in 1912 in national politics. President Taft was strongly opposed in Maine on account of the reciprocity measure, which, it was argued, would seriously injure the farmers in the State, especially those near the Canadian border. The Progressive element in the State was very strong, and on April 10, the ten delegates selected by the Republican convention were pledged to vote for Mr. Roosevelt. The Democrats had already held their State convention on March 19. The Maine Democratic delegates are never instructed in their votes, but it was claimed that seven of the twelve were for Governor Wilson. On June 17 a primary election was held in which Edwin C. Burleigh won the Republican nomination for United States senator, and William T. Haines for governor. Senator Gardner and Governor Plaisted were renominated by the Democrats.

The election held on September 9 was of more than local interest. With Vermont, Maine is the only State which holds general elections prior to the November elections, and the results in these States are always held to forecast in a measure the results of the November elections. Local conditions, however, prevented a sharp alignment among the three parties. Although the Progressives were strong in Maine they did not desire to divide the Republican vote in the State election into two parts. An agreement was therefore made with the regular Republican party, both wings of that party voting as a whole for the Republican candidates for State offices and for the legislature. As a result of the election, William T. Haines, the Republican candidate for governor, received 70,298 votes against 60,905 cast for the Democratic nominee, Frederick W. Plaisted. In 1910 Mr. Plaisted received a plurality of 8735 votes. It was thus apparent that in two years 4758 votes had been transferred from the Democratic party column to the Republican. The Senate, as a result of the election, is strongly Republican, and the House is anti-Democratic, Republicans and Progressives having a small majority. The Republican and Progressive majority, on joint ballot, insured the election of Edwin C. Burleigh to the United States Senate, to succeed Obadiah Gardner, Democratic senator, who was appointed in 1911 to serve out the term of the late Senator Frye.

The vote for President on Nov. 5 resulted as follows: Wilson, 51,113; Roosevelt, 48,493; Taft, 26,545; Debs, 2541; and Chafin, 945.

LEGISLATION. There was no regular session of the legislature in the State in 1912, but in March a special session was called, which passed an act making some changes in the conduct of elections and the preservation of the ballots. This measure, under the referendum clause of the constitution, was voted for in the September election. At this session the legislature submitted to the people a proposition to amend the constitution, so as to empower the legislature to borrow not exceeding two millions of dollars for expenditure on the highways of the State.

STATE GOVERNMENT. Governor, William T. Haines, Rep.; Secretary of State, Cyrus W. Davis, Dem.; Treasurer, James F. Singleton, Dem.; Adjutant-General, Elliot C. Dill, Rep.; Auditor, T. F. Callahan, Rep.; Attorney General, W. R. Pattangall, Dem.; Superintendent of Education, Payson Smith, Rep.; Insurance Commissioner, A. P. Havey, Dem.; Commissioner of Agriculture, John P. Buckley, Dem.; Commissioner of Public Lands, F. E. Mace, Dem.

JUDICIARY. Supreme Judicial Court: Chief Justice, William P. Whitehouse, Rep.; Associate Justices, L. C. Cornish, Rep.; Albert M. Spear, G. E. Bird, Dem.; Albert R. Savage, Rep.; A. W. King, Rep.; George F. Huley, Dem., and George M. Hanson, Dem.; Clerk, C. W. Jones, Rep.

STATE LEGISLATURE, 1913. Republicans, Senate, 21; House, 78; joint ballot, 99; Democrats, Senate, 10; House, 73; joint ballot, 83; Republican majority, Senate, 11; House, 5; joint ballot, 16.

The representatives in Congress will be found in the section *Congress*, article UNITED STATES.

MAINE, U. S. S. The remains of the United States battleship *Maine*, which had been destroyed by an explosion in the harbor of Havana in 1898, just previous to the Spanish-American War, were towed out to sea and sunk in deep water amid appropriate ceremonies on March 16, 1912. This famous wreck had been enclosed by a cofferdam so as to permit the removal of the mud and water, and then the tangled débris of the forward part was cut away largely by the use of the oxy-acetylene torch. The after part, which remained more or less intact, was closed with a wooden bulkhead and was floated clear of the bottom and it was arranged that it should be towed out to sea beyond the three-mile territorial limit and there sunk with full naval honors. This plan was adopted from sentimental and other reasons in preference to demolition by dynamite, and the same engineering skill and foresight that attended the uncovering of the wreck were expended in arranging for the final disposal of the famous battleship. The wooden bulkhead was provided with five sluices, each about five feet high by one foot wide, to admit the sea water while in addition there were seacocks in the bottom. Provision was also made for destroying the bulkhead by the explosion of dynamite should the other devices fail to work, but its use was not necessary. The United States navy was represented by the battleship *North Carolina* and the scout cruiser *Birmingham* at the burial of the *Maine*, the former having been ordered to receive the bodies of sixty-six of the crew of the *Maine* which had been recovered during the excavation of the wreck and carry them back to the United States for burial in the National Cemetery at Arlington. After the remains of the sailors had been transferred to the battleship with full military honors the naval procession was formed and in tow of three tugs the *Maine* passed out of Havana Harbor on her last journey, followed by the American warships and four Cuban gunboats to the sound of minute guns from Cabanas Fortress. When the requisite distance off shore had been reached, a hollow square was formed, sailors boarded the wreck, and the seacocks were opened. Slowly the battleship settled in the sea with a large American flag flying from a central staff. Taps were sounded, a parting salute was fired from the warships, and thousands of roses were strewn over the watery grave of the first battleship of the new American navy. The burial of the recovered bodies took place at Arlington National Cemetery on March 23. Here it was proposed to erect the mainmast of the *Maine* as a memorial. The other mast, together with a turret and guns, was presented to the Republic of Cuba and the latter were to be combined in a memorial with a marble figure representing the Cuban Republic and various bronze tablets. The designs for this memorial were accepted by President Gomez late in the year and an appropriation of $20,000 requested for its construction.

MAINE, UNIVERSITY OF. A State institution for higher education at Orono, Me., founded in 1865. The attendance in all departments of the university in the autumn of 1912 was 953, and the faculty numbered 91. Among the new appointments during the year were those of William Edward Barrows, Jr., professor of electrical engineering and Ralph Rigby Glass, lieutenant, U. S. A., professor of military science and tactics. There was in addition a number of instructors appointed in various departments. Prof. Walter K. Ganong resigned as professor of electrical engineering and Prof. A. C. Varnum, colonel, U. S. A., resigned as professor of military science and tactics. The library contained about 48,000 bound volumes and 11,000 pamphlets. President, R. J. Aley.

MALACCA. See STRAITS SETTLEMENTS.

MALARIA. The most interesting work done recently in the study of malaria was that of Bass and Johns, who were sent to Panama by the Tulane School of Tropical Medicine to perfect a technic for the artificial cultivation of the plasmodia. The results of their work appeared in the *Journal of Experimental Medicine*, October, 1912. Bass and Johns were able to cultivate the parasites in human serum, in Locke's fluid from which calcium chlorid is omitted, and in human ascitic fluid. Positive cultures of the parasites were made in the three forms of malaria and carried as far as four generations from the parent culture. The parasites will grow only in red blood-corpuscles. When segmentation occurs and the plasmodia escape from the red blood-corpuscles, they are attacked and destroyed by leucocytes, when these are present. The blood serum is also destructive of the parasites. It is the conclusion of Bass and Johns that the plasmodium in the blood of a patient can pass from cell to cell only when the cell is in direct contact with another cell containing a segmenting parasite, and then only when the opening for the exit of merozoites occurs oposite the cell to be infected. This probably occurs frequently in the small capillaries through which the non-segmented parasite cannot pass, its protoplasm being less yielding than that of the red blood-cells. It was also discovered that blood drawn within one or two hours after a full meal was for culture media better than if drawn after fasting, which agrees with the clinical observation that the parasites will often disappear from the blood and the paroxysms will cease if the patient is put to bed and receives a purgative with a light diet. Equally interesting is the observation that calcium salts when added to the culture media caused hæmolysis of the infected as well as the non-infected cells. The authors suggest this as an explanation of malarial hæmoglobinuria, the amount of calcium salts in the blood being perhaps slightly augmented by the calcium in drinking-water or food. Only a slight excess of calcium over the normal amount is required to produce this effect. Hæmolysis from the calcium in non-infected, normal blood does not occur.

The experiments offer an interesting suggestion as to the way in which quinine acts in malaria. The authors believe that it does not directly kill the parasites, but produces permeability of the red blood-cells with destruction of the parasites of the blood serum.

MALAY STATES. See FEDERATED MALAY STATES; JOHORE; KELANTAN; KEDAH PERLIS; TRENGGANU.

MALBY, GEORGE R. A member of Congress from New York, died July 5, 1912. He was born in Canton, N. Y., in 1857, and was educated at Canton Academy and at St. Lawrence University. In 1881 he was admitted to the bar and four years later began the practice of law at Ogdensburg. In 1890 he was elected to the State Assembly and was re-elected for three successive terms. In 1894 he was chosen speaker. In the following year he was elected to the State Senate and remained a member of that body until 1907, when he was sent to Congress to succeed William H. Flack. He was reëlected to successive Congresses until 1911.

MALDIVE ISLANDS. See CEYLON.

MALE POPULATION IN THE UNITED STATES. See SEX DISTRIBUTION.

MALLET, JOHN WILLIAM. An American chemist, died November 7, 1912. He was born in Dublin, Ireland, in 1832, and graduated from Trinity College, Dublin, in 1853. He removed to the United States in the same year. In 1854 he was appointed professor of analytical chemistry at Amherst College. In 1855-6 he was chemist of the Alabama Geological Survey and was professor of chemistry in the University of Alabama from 1855 to 1860. He served in the Confederate army on the staff of General Rodes in 1861 and in the following year was transferred to the artillery and was placed in general charge of the ordnance laboratories of the Confederate States. In 1865 he was paroled as lieutenant-colonel. In the same year he became professor of chemistry in the medical department of the University of Virginia, and was professor of analytical, industrial, and agricultural chemistry in the same institution from 1868 to 1872, and of general and industrial chemistry from 1872 to 1883 and again from 1885 to 1908. In the latter year he was made professor emeritus of chemistry. In addition to his duties at the University of Virginia he lectured at Johns Hopkins University and the University of Texas and was professor of chemistry at the Jefferson Medical College, Philadelphia. He was three times a member of the United States Assay Commission. He was a member of many American and foreign scientific societies. He wrote many papers for scientific transactions and journals.

MALTA. An island (91¼ square miles) in the Mediterranean Sea; which, with the islands of Gozo (24¾ square miles), Comino (1 square mile), and Filfla and Cominotto (mere islets), forms a British crown colony. Total civil population (1911 census)) 211,473 (105,584 males). Valletta, the capital, had, April 2, 1911, 44,029 inhabitants, including suburbs (Floriana, Sliema, and St. Julien's); the Three Cities (Senglea, Cospicua, and Vittoriosa), 26,551; Citta Vecchia (the old capital), 8896; Victoria (formerly Rabat), 5655. The natives are of Punic origin, and their speech is said to be derived from the Carthaginian and Arabic languages. Valletta is a coaling station and the centre of a large transit trade. There are 7¾ miles of railway. Imports and exports of dutiable goods (1910-11), £1,026,567 and £14,408 respectively; total imports for home consumption, £2,356,043; total exports, £863,429. Total weight of goods transhipped (1910-11), 14,597 tons. Revenue (1910-11), £441,444; expenditure, £467,373. Tonnage entered and cleared, 8,667,037 (British, 4,796,133). Governor (1912), Gen. Sir H. M. Rundle (appointed 1909).

A Royal Commission was appointed in the autumn of 1911 to inquire into the administration of Malta. The report of the commission attributed the financial and economic difficulties to the rapid increase of population without a corresponding increase in the means of subsistence. It made a number of suggestions as regards taxation, education, and judicial procedure, and declared that reforms in these respects could be only palliative and that the immediate end to be attained was a plan for systematic immigration on a large scale. A commission of the British admiralty inspected the defenses of Malta on June 1.

MALTA FEVER. See VETERINARY SCIENCE.

MAMMALS. See ZOÖLOGY.

MANCHU DYNASTY. See CHINA.

MANCHURIA. A Chinese dependency, lying east of Mongolia and Chihli and between Korea and the Amur River, which separates it on the north from Siberia. Capital, Mukden.

Manchuria consists of three provinces: Heilungkiang, in the north, capital Tsitsihar; Kirin, capital Kirin; and Shengking, in the south, capital Mukden. The southern part of Shengking known as Kwantung, occupying the end of the Liaotung Peninsula and containing Dairen and Port Arthur, is held by Japan under lease acquired from Russia at the end of the Russo-Japanese War. (See KWANGTUNG). Outside of Kwangtung, Manchuria is virtually divided into Russian and Japanese "spheres of influence." The Russian sphere is much the larger, extending south to the Japanese sphere at Kwanchengtze (Changchun), the southern limit of the Russian railway, which connects with the Japanese railway from Port Arthur and Dairen. Another Japanese railway connects Mukden with Antung, on the Yalu River, which separates Manchuria from Korea. This line connects with the Korean railways. The area of Manchuria is stated at 362,483 square miles; for population, see CHINA, section *Area and Population*. Estimated population of important towns: Antung, 161,000; Mukden, 158,000; Kwangchengtze, 80,000; Newchwang (Yingtze), at the month of the Liao, 61,000; Newchwang (30 miles up the Liao), 50,000;

Liayang, 40,000; Harbin, 35,000; Tsitsihar, 30,000; Teihling, 28,500; Fenghwangcheng, 25,000; Sinminfu, 20,000.

The principal agricultural products are soy beans, kafir corn, millet, corn, barley, and tobacco. The Manchurian soy bean provides most of China's large bean export. Coal and iron are mined. Foreign trade is included in that of China. Imports and exports at the Manchurian open ports in the direct foreign trade were valued in 1910 at 46,725,156 and 58,093,583 haikwan taels respectively; in 1911, 54,052,669 and 67,954,165. These figures include the trade of Dairen (in Japanese Kwantung), which are: Imports and exports in 1910, 18,671,515 and 20,183,290 haikwan taels; in 1911, 24,012,724 and 24,184,154.

For Manchurian railways, see CHINA, section *Communications;* see also JAPAN, section *Communications.* Financial statistics of Manchuria are not available. Governor of the three provinces in 1911: Heilungkiang, Sung Hsia-lien; Kirin, Ch'ên Chao-ch'ang; Shengking, Chang Hsi-huan.

MANITOBA. A province of the Dominion of Canada. Area, 73,732 square miles. Population (census of June 1, 1911), 455,614, as compared with 255,211 in 1901. Winnipeg, the capital, had 136,035 inhabitants, as compared with 42,340 in 1901. The province is administered by a lieutenant-governor, Douglas Colin Cameron, from August 1, 1911. Premier (1912), Sir Rodman P. Roblin. The area stated above does not include a portion of the Northwest Territories annexed to Manitoba in 1912. The northern boundary of the province was advanced to the 60th parallel. See CANADA.

MANŒUVRES. See NAVAL PROGRESS.

MANUFACTURES. See UNITED STATES, *Manufactures,* and State articles.

MARATHONS. See CROSS-COUNTRY RUNNING

MARIANA ISLANDS. See GERMAN NEW GUINEA.

MARIE, Princess of Belgium, mother of King Albert of Belgium, died November 26, 1912. She was born in 1845, and on April 25, 1867, was married to Prince Philippe, Count of Flanders, brother of King Leopold of Belgium. Prince Philippe died in 1905. King Albert was the second son, the first, Prince Badouin, who was born in 1869, dying in 1891. She was of the Hohenzollern family and distantly related to Emperor William of Germany. She left, besides King Albert, two daughters, Princess Henriette, wife of Prince Emmanuel of Orleans, Duke of Vendôme, and Princess Josephine, wife of Prince Charles of Hohenzollern-Sigmaringen.

MARSDEN, SAMUEL EDWARD. Bishop of the diocese of Bristol, New South Wales. He was born in 1832, and was educated at Trinity College, Cambridge. He was ordained to the ministry in 1855, and after serving in several parishes in England was appointed bishop of Bathurst, New South Wales, in 1869. He held this post until 1885. He was appointed assistant bishop of Gloucester in 1900, honorary canon of Gloucester, and from 1906 to 1909 honorary canon of Bristol.

MARSHALL, THOMAS RYAN. Elected Vice-President of the United States, November 6, 1912. He was born in Manchester, Ind., on March 14, 1854. His father, Dr. Daniel M. Marshall, was descended from the family of Chief Justice John Marshall, the patriot and jurist of the Revolutionary period. His grandfather, Riley Marshall, came from Virginia and settled in Grant County, Ind. On his mother's side he is related to Carroll of Carrollton, one of the signers of the Declaration of Independence. His father was a physician and an uncompromising Democrat of the Jeffersonian school. After receiving instruction at home and in the public schools, his education was completed at Wabash College, from which he graduated in 1873, at the age of 19. During his term in college he gained the leadership in debates and literary activities. He began the study of law, after his graduation, in Columbia City, where his parents then lived. After his admission to the bar he began at once a career which was more than ordinarily successful. His natural eloquence, together with strong personal magnetism, combined to win him many cases before juries. Up to the time of his nomination as Democratic candidate for governor in 1909 he had held no public office. He was, however, well known throughout the State. He was elected by a plurality of about 8000. His election was due largely to the aggressive campaign of speaking which he carried on from the time of his nomination until the election. In 1895 he married Miss Lois Kinsey of Angola, Ind. The details of Governor Marshall's nomination and election will be found in the article PRESIDENTIAL CAMPAIGN.

MARSHALL ISLANDS. See GERMAN NEW GUINEA.

MARSH ISLAND PURCHASE. See ORNITHOLOGY.

MARTINIQUE. A French colony; an island in the Lesser Antilles. Area, 987 sq. kilometers (381 sq. miles); population (1911), 184,084. Fort-de-France, the capital, has about 27,000 inhabitants. Imports (1910), 19,563,000 francs; exports, 27,587,000. The local budget is said to have balanced in 1910 at 5,000,000 francs. Debt, 4,511,000 francs. M. Foureau was governor in 1912.

MARYLAND. POPULATION. According to the Census Bureau statistics compiled during 1912, out of the total population of the State in 1910, 1,295,346, the foreign-born whites numbered 104,174, compared with 93,144 in 1900. Of these the largest number came from Germany, 36,602; from Russia, 27,522; from Austria, 8291; from Italy, 6968; and from England, 5178. Other European countries were represented by smaller numbers. In the city of Baltimore, with a population of 558,485, 77,043 were foreign-born whites. Of these the largest number, 25,989, came from Germany, and 24,796 from Russia. The negroes in the State in 1910 numbered 232,250, and the mulattoes, 43,152. In 1890 the negroes numbered 221,565 and the mulattoes, 34,361.

AGRICULTURE. The acreage, value and production of the principal crops in 1911 and 1912 are shown in the table on the next page.

MINERAL PRODUCTION. There were produced in the State in 1911 4,685,795 short tons of coal, with a value of $5,197,066. This is a decrease of 531,330 short tons from the output of 1910. The product in the latter year was stimulated by the strike of miners in the Middle West. The coal mines of the State gave employment in 1911 to 5981 men.

MANUFACTURES. The Thirteenth Census included statistics of manufactures in the State. These figures cover the calendar year 1909. The

		Acreage	Prod. Bu.	Value
Corn	1912	670,000	24,455,000	$12,450,000
	1911	670,000	24,455,000	15,407,000
Wheat	1912	599,000	8,985,000	8,536,000
	1911	605,000	9,378,000	8,534,000
Oats	1912	45,000	1,350,000	608,000
	1911	46,000	1,242,000	609,000
Rye	1912	27,000	418,000	334,000
	1911	28,000	406,000	349,000
Potatoes	1912	37,000	4,144,000	2,404,000
	1911	39,000	1,755,000	1,597,000
Hay	1912	381,000	a 575,000	8,280,000
	1911	276,000	a 199,000	4,458,000
Tobacco	1912	26,000	b 17,160,000	1,373,000
	1911	26,000	b 19,110,000	1,433,250

a Tons. b Pounds.

following table gives a summary of the results of the census for the calendar years 1909 and 1904, with per cent. of increase from 1904 to 1909 and from 1899 to 1904:

	Number or Amount		Increase[1]	
	1909	1904	1904-1909	
Number of establishments.	4,837	3,852	25.6	—0.9
Persons engaged in manuf'ures	125,489	107,308	16.9	(2)
Proprietors and firm members	5,376	4,506	19.3	(2)
Salaried employees	12,192	8,624	41.4	27.9
Wage earners (average number)	107,921	94,174	14.6	(3)
Primary h. p.	218,244	165,449	31.9	25.3
Capital	$251,227,000	$201,878,000	24.4	35.2
Expenses	285,955,000	216,917,000	31.8	18.3
Services	59,053,000	44,988,000	31.3	14.6
Salaries	13,617,000	8,844,000	54.0	29.2
Wages	45,436,000	36,144,000	25.7	11.5
Materials	199,049,000	150,024,000	32.7	16.0
Miscellaneous	27,853,000	21,905,000	27.2	48.2
Value of products	315,669,000	243,376,000	29.7	15.3
Value added by manufacture (value of products less cost of materials)	116,630,000	93,352,000	24.9	14.2

1 A minus sign (—) denotes decrease. 2 Figures not available. 3 Less than one-tenth of 1 per cent.

The industry employing the largest number of wage-earners was the men's clothing industry, in which 19,184 persons were employed.

Finance. The report of the treasurer for the fiscal year ending September 30, 1912, showed a balance at the beginning of the fiscal year of $1,471,520. The receipts for the year amounted to $8,908,454, and the disbursements to $8,553,744, leaving a cash balance on hand September 30, 1912, of $1,826,229. The total debt of the State amounted at the end of the year to $13,028,095. This was an increase of $2,599,169. From this there should be deducted bonds and cash held in the sinking funds and mortgages to the value of $1,500,000. The net debt is therefore $5,826,258. The chief source of income is from taxation, and the chief expenditures are for education and for the support of State institutions.

Charities and Corrections. The institutions under State control are the Hospital for Consumptives at Eudowood, the Maryland House of Correction at Jessups, the Maryland Penitentiary at Baltimore, the Maryland Hospital for the Insane at Catonsville, the Maryland Tuberculosis Sanitarium in Frederick county, and the Springfield Hospital for the Insane at Sykesville. In addition to these, most all of the private asylums, hospitals, and homes of the State receive State aid. The reformatory institutions include the Female House of Refuge, Henry Watson Children's Aid Society, House of Good Shepherd (white), House of Good Shepherd (colored), Industrial School for Colored Girls, Maryland School for Boys, St. Joseph's House of Industry, and St. Mary's Industrial School. These are all in Baltimore.

Politics and Government

Politics in Maryland excited more than local interest during 1912 on account of the presidential primaries held on May 6, and the complications resulting from the dispute over the awarding of the Republican delegates. The bill providing for presidential primaries was passed by the legislature and was signed by Governor Goldsborough on April 4. The campaign which preceded this election was aggressively carried on by both factions of the Republican party. See Presidential Campaign.

The results of the election held on May 6 were complicated on account of the peculiarity of the Maryland law, which differs from that of any other State. At this primary delegates were elected to the State convention, while at the same time a direct vote for presidential preference was taken in each county and city legislative district throughout the State. The delegates to the national convention are elected at the State convention, the way in which the delegates vote at the State convention being determined by the preferential vote in each county and city legislative district. The delegates to the national convention are required by the primary law to carry out conscientiously the expressed wish of the voters as to the presidential nominee. In this election sixty-six Roosevelt delegates to the State convention were elected, as against sixty-three for Mr. Taft. That is, sixty-six delegates were elected from counties and districts in which the preference vote was cast for Mr. Roosevelt, although four or five of these delegates were personally favorable to Mr. Taft. For some days there was doubt as to what action would be taken by the leaders of the two factions. It was then announced by the governor of the State, who was one of the Taft leaders, and by the Taft manager, that they wished the convention to carry out in good faith the preference of the voters as expressed in the primary.

The Democratic choice of the voters was Champ Clark, and on May 6 the Democratic State convention met and endorsed Mr. Clark. The Republican State convention met on May 14 at Baltimore. Although the majority for Mr. Roosevelt had been so pronounced in the presidential primaries the convention was controlled by friends of President Taft. The delegates were divided. Eight were given to Mr. Roosevelt, six to President Taft, and one was neutral. The Progressive leaders, after the Chicago convention, were not satisfied with this result, and late in July they decided on a complete separation from the Republican party, and named a separate set of presidential electors. Sixteen delegates and as many alternates were chosen to represent the Progressives at the convention of the Progressive party, and a committee was appointed to name Progressive electors to appear on the presidential ticket. A resolution provided that no elector on the Taft ticket should be placed on the Progressive ticket until he first resigned. As a result of this action, the Republican convention reconvened on September 11 and ousted those electors favorable to Roosevelt who had been named at the first convention, electing in their place eight who were adherents to President Taft. The convention also endorsed the action of the Chicago convention in renominating President Taft and Vice-President Sherman. The results of the election held on November 5 were as follows: Governor Wilson received 112,674 votes, Roosevelt 57,789, Taft 54,956, Debs 2996, Chafin 2244, and Reimer, Socialist Labor, 322. Governor Wilson's plurality was 54,885. There was no election for State officers in 1912, as the term of Governor Goldsborough does not expire until 1916. He was elected in November, 1911, and went into office January, 1912.

An attempt to pass a local option was killed in the State Senate on March 31.

Just before the beginning of the session of Congress in December, 1912, the senior senator from Maryland, the Hon. Isidor Rayner, died and Governor Goldsborough appointed Mr. William H. Jackson, Jr., Republican, to serve until the General Assembly meets in 1914 to elect a senator to serve for the remainder of the term for which Mr. Rayner had been elected.

An important event to Maryland and the city of Baltimore in 1912 was the opening of the extension of the Western Maryland Railroad, from Cumberland, Md., to a connection with the New York Central system near Pittsburgh, Pa. This extension gives Baltimore a third trunk line to Pittsburgh and the West.

LEGISLATION. The legislative session of 1912 was an important one. At the November election in 1911 the Democrats elected a large majority of both houses of the legislature, but their candidate for governor, Arthur P. Gorman, Jr., was defeated by Phillips Lee Goldsborough, Republican. Austin L. Crothers, the outgoing governor, a Democrat, remained in office for one week after the beginning of the legislative session, and in that time the Democrats passed two bills, one repealing the so-called Wilson ballot law and the other changing the primary election law so as to provide greater safeguards in casting and counting the vote. These two laws were signed by Governor Crothers, the outgoing governor, an act almost unprecedented in the State. Several enabling acts for the amendment of the constitution of the State were passed. One of them authorizes the legislature to abolish the punishment for people who sell their votes and to put the penalty upon the vote-buyer alone. Another permits the printing of bills for final passage in the legislature, the present constitution requiring that they be engrossed. Three other amendments of minor importance were proposed and all of them will be submitted to the people for ratification in November, 1913.

Among other important laws passed was one making an appropriation of $3,170,000 to continue the work of road-making by the State, which was begun in 1908. The Haman oyster-planting law was amended with the design of further encouraging the cultivation of oysters in the Chesapeake and its tributaries. A bill creating a school of technology in the Johns Hopkins University was enacted. It provides an appropriation of $600,000 and $50,000 a year additional and requires 129 free scholarships to be granted. See also EMPLOYERS' LIABILITY.

Baltimore city was authorized to make additional loans for sewers, paving, etc., and the continuance of important works of improvement that have been in progress since the great fire of 1904.

STATE GOVERNMENT. Governor, Phillips L. Goldsborough, Republican; secretary of State, R. P. Graham, Republican; treasurer, Murray Vandiver, Democrat; adjutant-general, C. C. Macklin, Republican; attorney-general, Edgar Allan Poe, Democrat; superintendent of education, M. B. Stephens, Democrat.

JUDICIARY. Court of Appeals—Chief judge, Andrew H. Boyd; associate judges, N. Charles Burke, William H. Thomas, John R. Pattison, Hammond Urner, John P. Briscoe, Henry Stockbridge, and Albert Constable; clerk, Caleb C. Magruder—all Democrats except Stockbridge and Urner, Republicans.

STATE LEGISLATURE 1913. Senate, Democrats 19, Republicans 8; House, Democrats 60, Republicans 41; joint ballot, Democrats 79, Republicans 49. Democratic majority, Senate, 11; House, 19; joint ballot, 30.

The representatives in Congress will be found in the section *Congress*, article UNITED STATES.

MASEFIELD, JOHN. See LITERATURE, ENGLISH AND AMERICAN.

MASSACHUSETTS. POPULATION. The Census Bureau compiled in 1912 figures giving certain characteristics of the population of the State. These include statistics of white and colored population. Out of a total population of 3,366,416 in 1910 the foreign-born whites numbered 1,051,050, compared with 840,114 in 1900. The largest number of these, 222,883, came from Ireland; from Canada, other than French Canada, came 160,712; from French Canada, 134,460; from Russia, 117,248; from England, 92,411; from Italy, 85,019; from Sweden, 39,533; from Austria, 35,509; from Germany, 30,483, and from Portugal, 25,698. In the city of Boston, with a population in 1910 of 670,585, the foreign-born whites numbered 240,722, compared with 194,933 in 1900. Other European countries are represented by smaller numbers. The negroes in the State in 1910 numbered 38,055 and the mulattoes 13,956. In 1890 the negroes numbered 22,144 and the mulattoes 8036.

AGRICULTURE. The acreage, value, and production of the principal crops in 1911 and 1912 are shown in the following table:

		Acreage	Prod. Bu.	Value
Corn	1912	47,000	2,115,000	$1,629,000
	1911	47,000	2,068,000	1,716,000
Oats	1912	8,000	272,000	128,000
	1911	8,000	280,000	162,000
Rye	1911	2,000	48,000	46,000
Potatoes	1912	26,000	3,380,000	2,535,000
	1911	25,000	2,325,000	2,232,000
Hay	1912	1,010,000	a 1,515,000	12,814,000
	1911	584,000	a 631,000	14,512,000
Tobacco	1912	5,800	b 9,860,000	2,357,000
	1911	5,600	b 9,240,000	1,848,000

a Tons. b Pounds.

MANUFACTURES. The Thirteenth Census statistics are for the calendar year 1909 and were compiled in 1912. Massachusetts is one of the most important of the manufacturing States.

The table herewith shows that in 1909 there were 11,684 manufacturing establishments, which gave employment during the year to an average of 644,399 persons:

	Number or Amount 1909	1904	P. C. of Inc.[1] 1904-'09
Number of establishments	11,684	10,723	9.0
Persons engaged in manufactures...	644,399	532,481	21.0
Proprietors and firm members..	11,194	11,258	—0.6
Salaried employees	48,646	32,824	48.2
Wage earners (average number)	584,559	488,399	19.7
Primary horsepower	1,175,071	938,007	25.3
Capital	$1,279,687,000	$965,949,000	32.5
Expenses	1,320,866,000	992,294,000	33.1
Services	364,452,000	272,044,000	34.0
Salaries	63,279,000	39,655,000	59.6
Wages	301,173,000	232,389,000	29.6
Materials	830,765,000	626,410,000	32.6
Miscellaneous ...	125,649,000	93,840,000	33.9
Value of products.	1,490,529,000	1,124,092,000	32.6
Value of products less cost of materials	659,764,000	497,682,000	32.6

[1] A minus sign (—) denotes decrease.

The largest number of wage-earners were employed in the industries connected with cotton manufacture, 108,914; in the manufacture of boots and shoes, 83,063; in the manufacture of woolen goods, 53,873; and in foundry and machine-shop products, 44,179. The value of the product of the boot and shoe industry was $236,343,000; of cotton goods, $186,462,000; woolen goods, $141,967,000; foundry and machine-shop products, $86,926,000; printing and publishing, $47,445,000. The total number of persons engaged in manufactures in 1909 was 644,399, of whom 447,267 were male, and 197,132 were female. The persons under 16 years of age employed numbered 20,735. The prevailing hours of labor for a large majority of the wage-earners was between fifty-four and sixty hours a week; 27.6 per cent. of the total were employed in establishments where the prevailing hours of labor were fifty-four or less, and only 7.4 per cent. where they are sixty or more a week. In Boston the average number of wage-earners was 69,637; in Lawrence, 30,542; in Worcester, 28,221; in Lynn, 27,368; in Fall River, 37,139; in Lowell, 32,757; in New Bedford, 26,566.

Politics and Government

The legislature met in 1912, and the most important enactments will be found noted in the paragraph *Legislation* below. The year was an interesting one politically and industrially in the State. It was marked politically by the first presidential primary election, and industrially by a strike at Lawrence, which, on account of its complications, took on a national aspect. The strike and its results will be found discussed in the article Strikes. Governor Foss was inaugurated for the second time on January 4. In his inaugural address much space was devoted to national topics. Of great interest was his declaration that the Boston Railroad Holding Company must be dissolved and the New Haven, and Boston and Maine Railroads physically connected for a Greater Boston. He also advocated public ownership of docks and water terminals, and new laws providing for safety in investment. The House of Representatives on February 2 unanimously ordered a thorough investigation of all railways terminating in the city of Boston. The presidential primary bill was passed by the legislature and was signed by Governor Foss on May 15. The election itself was held on April 30.

The campaign immediately preceding the primary election held on April 30 was a very vigorous one. Both the President and Mr. Roosevelt made many addresses. In one of these Mr. Taft declared that if the presidential term were six years with no reëlection, the President would not be compelled to go on the stump and defend himself against gross misrepresentation. Mr. Roosevelt in one of his addresses insisted that the President was supported chiefly by "bosses," and that his course during his term had been marked by flabby indecision and helpless acquiescence in the wrongdoing of crooked men. The votes at the primary showed curious results. While Mr. Taft had a popular majority of about 3600, the eight Roosevelt delegates-at-large were elected on account of the rejection of many Taft ballots. These were defective because the name of an independent candidate had been added to the list and votes had been cast for nine instead of eight delegates. Mr. Roosevelt promptly declined to take advantage of these errors and urged the delegates-at-large to support Mr. Taft, but they did not accept his suggestion. Among the Democrats Champ Clark received the largest number of votes. See Presidential Campaign.

Primaries for the election of State officers and representatives in Congress were held on September 4, and resulted in the renomination of Governor Foss, Democrat, and the nomination of Joseph Walker, Republican. The Progressive party nominated as their candidate for governor Charles S. Bird, a well-known manufacturer. The Democratic and Republican State conventions, which met in October, ratified the result of the primaries.

The election of November 5 resulted as follows: Wilson received 173,408 votes, Roosevelt 142,228, Taft 155,948, Debs 12,616, Chafin 2254, and Reimer 1102. For governor, Foss received 193,184 votes, Walker 143,597, and Bird, Progressive, 122,602.

Other Events. On May 21 Senator W. Murray Crane announced that he would not be a candidate for reëlection. His term expires in 1913. Among the possible candidates as his successor were mentioned Congressman John W. Weeks, ex-Governor Draper, Curtis Guild, ambassador to Russia, and Congressman Samuel W. McCall. On May 24 the State Senate passed a bill establishing the minimum wage for women and minors in manufacturing and mercantile establishments. The Senate in May by a unanimous vote approved the constitutional amendment for the direct election of senators. This had already been approved by the House.

Legislation. The legislature of 1912 passed a number of unusually important measures. These included: A minimum wage law (see Minimum Wage), an act amending the inheritance law so that only the real estate of a deceased non-resident is taxed on the theory that the tax on his personal property at the time of his death should go to the State where he resides; an act increasing the amount recoverable from a railroad corporation for death through negligence from five to ten thousand dollars; an act prohibiting discrimination in the sale of commodities and aimed at unjust discrimination and at the creation of monopolies and combinations to destroy the trade of others. A measure was enacted regulating tenement houses in towns. A commission on economy and efficiency for the commonwealth was established, as was also a State board of labor and industries. A joint resolution of the legislature ratifying the proposed amendment to the Constitution of the United States providing that senators shall be elected by the people of the several States was passed. Resolutions were passed providing for an amendment to the constitution authorizing the referendum. This resolution was referred to the next general court. Resolutions were also passed advocating the establishment of a parcels post system by the United States government. See also CHILD LABOR and LABOR LEGISLATION.

STATE GOVERNMENT. Governor, Eugene N. Foss, Democrat; lieutenant-governor, D. J. Walsh, Democrat; secretary of State, F. J. Donahue, Democrat; treasurer, Elmer A. Stevens; auditor, John E. White; adjutant-general, G. W. Pearson; attorney-general, James M. Swift; secretary of the board of agriculture, J. Lewis Ellsworth; commissioner of insurance, Frank H. Hardison; commissioner of education, David Snedden—all Republicans except Foss, Donahue, and Walsh.

JUDICIARY. Supreme Judicial Court for the Commonwealth: Chief justice, Arthur Prentice Rugg; justices, James M. Morton, John W. Hammond, Henry Newton Sheldon, William C. Loring, Henry K. Braley, and Charles Ambrose De Courcy; clerk of the court, C. H. Cooper—all Republicans.

STATE LEGISLATURE, 1913. Senate, Republicans 27, Democrats 13, Progressives 0, Socialists 0; House, Republicans 137, Democrats 94, Progressives 8, Socialists 1; joint ballot, Republicans 164, Democrats 107, Progressives 8, Socialists 1. Republican majority, Senate, 14; House, 34; joint ballot, 49.

The representatives in Congress will be found in the section *Congress*, article UNITED STATES.

MASSACHUSETTS SAVINGS BANK INSURANCE. See INSURANCE.

MASSENET, JULIEN ÉMILE FRÉDÉRIC. A French composer, died August 6, 1912. He was born at Montaud, Department of the Loire, in 1842. He received his musical education at the Paris Conservatory, where he won praises for his pianoforte playing and for fugue-writing. His musical studies began when he was barely nine years of age. He subsequently studied under Ambroise Thomas, and in 1863 won the Grand Prix de Rome. He spent two years in that city, which he describes as the most memorable of his life. On his return to Paris his *Grand'tante* was produced at the Opéra Comique. It was not until after the Franco-German War, however, that he took first rank among French composers by the production of *Don César de Bazan*. This was followed by *Les Erinnyes* (1873); *Le Roi de Lahore* (1877); *Hérodiade* (1881); *Manon* (1884); *Werther* (1892); *Thaïs* (1894); *Sapho* (1897); *Le Jongleur de Nôtre-Dame* (1902); *Ariane* (1906), and *Thérèse*. In addition to his operas he wrote several cantatas and oratorios. He compiled many collections of songs and became famous throughout the musical world. In 1878 he was made professor of advanced composition at the Conservatory and held this post until 1896. In 1878 he was elected to the Académie des Beaux-Arts and in the same year made a successful tour of Great Britain. His musical works are notable chiefly for their instrumentation. He was a master of bizarre effects.

MATCHES, PHOSPHOROUS. See LABOR LEGISLATION.

MATES. See NAVAL PROGRESS.

MATHEWS, WILLIAM SMITH BABCOCK. An American musician and educator, died April, 1912. He was born in Loudon, N. H., in 1837, and was educated in the public schools. He studied music in Boston and became a teacher of music in 1853. He was for a time adjunct professor of music at the Wesleyan Female College, Macon, Ga., and from 1867 to 1893 he was organist of the Centenary M. E. Church, Chicago. From 1869 to 1871 he was editor of the *Musical Independent*. He was a member of the staffs of several Chicago papers from 1877 to 1887. He established in 1891 a magazine, *Music*, which, in 1903, was merged in *Philharmonic*. He wrote widely on musical subjects and among his published works are: *How to Understand Music* (1880-1888); *Music and Its Ideals* (1897); *Dictionary of Musical Terms* (1895); *The Masters and Their Music* (1898); *Popular History of Music* (1901). He also compiled many collections of music for pedagogic purposes and edited several collections of Masters of Music. He contributed articles to many musical publications.

MAURICE, JOHN FREDERICK. An English major-general, died January 12, 1912. He was born in London in 1841, the oldest son of Frederick Denison Maurice. He entered the Royal Artillery as lieutenant at the age of 20, and seven years later was appointed instructor in military history and afterwards of tactics at the Royal Military College at Sandhurst. His first active service was seen in 1873 when he accompanied Sir Garnet Wolseley to the Gold Coast as private secretary. He served throughout the Ashanti War and was mentioned in dispatches on several occasions. In 1875 he was promoted to be captain and during the Zulu war a few years later acted as deputy assistant adjutant and quartermaster-general. During the campaign in Egypt in 1882 he served on the headquarters' staff. Returning to England he was for the next five years professor of military history at the Staff College. In 1895 he was made major-general.

Although his experience in actual service was long and useful, General Maurice will be best remembered as a writer, a thinker, a student of war and of national problems. He was a clear and forcible writer and his judgment was almost invariably sound. His work *Hostilities Without Declaration of War* became almost a classic in military writing. It is an historical abstract of the cases in which hostilities have occurred between civilized powers before declaration of war, between the years 1700-1870. At the expiration of the South African War, General Maurice was appointed to prepare the official history of this campaign. He was limited within strict lines by the military authorities and thus a history which otherwise would have been of the greatest interest became little more than a colorless statement of facts. Among his writings, in addition to those mentioned, are, *Life of Frederick Denison Maurice* (1884); *Balance of Military Power in Europe* (1888); *War* (1891); *National Defenses* (1897); and *Diary of Sir John Moore* (1904).

MAURITANIA. A French West African territory, governed from St. Louis (Senegal) by a commissioner (1912, Lieutenant-Colonel Patey) under the direction of the governor-general for French West Africa (q. v. for area, population, etc.). The chief towns are Port-Etienne, Boutilimit, Aleg, Moudjeria, Kaedi, Selibaby, etc. Excepting a few groups rendered semi-sedentary by the necessity for tending the plantations of palms by which they obtain a livelihood, the Moors who constitute the larger proportion of the population are all nomads. They live in encampments, driving their flocks from pasture to pasture as the water supply fails. Travel is by caravan. Manual labor is considered dishonorable among the Moors. The negroes cultivate millet, barley, etc., gather gums for export, and catch and dry fish. Grazing is the occupation of the nomads, who raise camels, horses, cattle, sheep, and goats. Salt exists in great abundance. Lieutenant-Colonel Mouret was commissioner in 1912.

MAURITIUS. A supposedly volcanic island (720 square miles) in the Indian Ocean; a British crown colony. Total civil population (1911 census), 368,510; population inclusive of military, 370,393 (222,361 Indo-Mauritians, 35,526 other Indians, 3662 Chinese, 108,844 persons of European, African, or mixed blood). The natives of European race are in large part French creoles. Port Louis, the capital, had (1911) with suburbs, 50,060 inhabitants; Curepipe, 17,173; Mahebourg, 4068. The cultivation of sugar-cane is the staple industry. Export of sugar (1910), 215,743,242 kilos.; estimated value, Rs. 34,734,663; rum, Rs. 29,761; vanilla, Rs. 17,412; aloe-fibre, Rs. 627,501; cocoanut oil, Rs. 141,968; molasses, Rs. 510,727. Total imports and exports (1910), including shipping charges on home products heretofore excluded, Rs. 37,545,260 and Rs. 37,109,170 respectively. Revenue 1910-11, Rs. 11,129,988; expenditure, Rs. 9,578,243; customs revenue, Rs. 4,059,115. Tonnage entered and cleared (1910), 986,267 (763,786 tons British). External debt, June 30, 1911, £1,296,090. Major J. R. Chancellor (appointed November, 1911), was governor in 1912).

MAXWELL, W. H. See EDUCATION.

MAY, KARL. A German writer, died April 1, 1912. He was born in Ernsthal in 1852, and was educated at the Schoolmasters Seminary for Self-Instruction. While still a student he began to write and produced a work called *Favorite Occupations, A Study of the So-Called Inner Man.* He also wrote on immortality, world peace, development of world peoples, noblemen, knowledge, and the human soul. He wrote many stories of Indian life and translated stories from the Arabic, Turkish, Persian, and Chinese.

MAYOTTE AND THE COMORO ISLANDS. A group of islands belonging to France, administered under the government of Madagascar. Total area, 2168 square kilometers (837 square miles); population (1911), 97,750. Imports and exports (1909), 1,133,429 and 2,700,652 francs respectively. The budget for Mayotte (1909) balanced at 221,341 francs, and for Grand-Camore at 176,200. Administrator for Mayotte, M. Garnier-Mouton in 1912.

MEADE, WILLIAM EDWARD. Bishop of the Church of Ireland, died October 12, 1912. He was born in 1832, and was educated at Trinity College, Dublin. After serving in various parishes in Ireland he was appointed archdeacon of Armagh in Cork, 1885. In 1893 he was elected bishop of the United Dioceses of Cork, Cloyne, and Ross. For thirteen years he held the important office of secretary to the General Synod. He wrote *The Pastor's Inner Life* (1882) and several sermons.

MEAT PRODUCTION. See STOCK-RAISING AND MEAT PRODUCTION.

MECHANISM. See BIOLOGY.

MECKLENBURG-SCHWERIN. See GERMANY.

MECKLENBURG-STRELITZ. See GERMANY.

MEDICAL PROGRESS IN 1912. Many notable advances were made in the control of epidemic diseases and the problem of preventive medicine during 1912 (see DIPHTHERIA, HOOKWORM DISEASE, POLIOMYELITIS (Infantile Spinal Paralysis), MENINGITIS, PELLAGRA, RABIES, TETANUS, TYPHOID FEVER, OCCUPATIONAL DISEASES, SMALL-POX, and VACCINATION). Tropical diseases engaged a large share of the attention of the various countries having territorial possessions in hot climates (see BERIBERI, INSECTS AND THE PROPAGATION OF DISEASE, MALARIA, PLAGUE, SLEEPING SICKNESS). Several new drugs were introduced, among which may be noted ATOPHAN, GYNOVAL, NEOSALVARSAN, PROPERRIN, PROPAESIN, THROMBOKINASE, TYRAMINE. The quest for a cancer cure and for the means of limiting the spread of tuberculosis was perseveringly followed (see CANCER, TUBERCULOSIS). Advances in surgical technic and in the knowledge of anæsthetics were published (see ANÆSTHESIA, SURGERY). Other medical items and statistics will be found under their respective captions.

MEDICAL SCHOOLS. See UNIVERSITIES AND COLLEGES.

MEDITERRANEAN SQUADRON. See NAVAL PROGRESS.

MEIGS, ARTHUR VINCENT. An American physician and writer on medical subjects, died January 1, 1912. He was born at Philadelphia in 1850, and was educated at the Classical Academy of Philadelphia and in medicine at the University of Pennsylvania, where he took his degree in 1871. He was for many years physician to the Pennsylvania Hospital, and from 1904 to 1906 was president of the College of Physicians, Philadelphia. He was the author of *Milk Analysis and Infant Feeding* (1885); *The Origin of Disease* (1889); *A Study of the Human Blood Vessels in Health and Disease* (1907). He also contributed various articles to medical journals.

MELVILLE, GEORGE WALLACE. A rear-admiral of the United States navy, retired, died March 16, 1912. He was born in New York in 1841. He was educated in the common schools and in the Brooklyn Polytechnic Institute. He enlisted in the navy as assistant engineer in 1861, and served during the Civil War. After the war he saw service in various stations and at navy yards. In 1879 he was chief engineer of the *Jeannette* expedition to the polar regions under the command of Lieutenant-Commander De Long. He had previously taken part in a polar expedition as chief engineer on the *Tigress* in search of the *Polaris*. When the *Jeannette* was crushed in the ice Melville headed the only party of survivors which escaped from the wastes of the Lena delta. On his return to the United States be headed the expedition which recovered the records of the *Jeannette*, and the remains of De Long and his companions. In 1890 he was advanced fifteen numbers and given a gold medal by special act of Congress for bravery in the Arctic regions. He was appointed in 1887 engineer-in-chief of the navy and was reappointed to this position in 1892-96. He was made rear-admiral in 1899. He was notable as a designer, and his greatest professional successes were the triple-screw fliers, *Columbia* and *Minneapolis*. He was retired on January 10, 1903. He invented many mechanical appliances for use on ships and elsewhere. He was the author of *In the Lena Delta*.

MENDELISM. See BIOLOGY.

MENINGITIS, EPIDEMIC CEREBROSPINAL. Outbreaks of this fatal disease occurred in Kentucky, Louisiana, and Texas, and many sporadic cases were reported from other parts of the United States. Up to April 13 there were 159 cases of cerebrospinal meningitis in Louisville, with a mortality of over 42 per cent. In Shreveport, La., and vicinity there were, since December 4, 1911, 111 cases originating in the city and 19 were imported from Texas; a total of 130. Twenty-seven patients were white and 84 colored. Among the cases in the city there were 69 recoveries and 38 deaths, making the percentage of recoveries 65. Of the whites, 23, or a percentage of 85, recovered. The disease occurred most frequently among negroes between the ages of 11 and 20. The greater number of cases and higher percentage of deaths among the colored population are probably accounted for by the difference in economic and hygienic conditions. The percentage of recoveries at Shreveport is a little higher than the average in the Texas epidemic, the deaths in the latter State being between 40 and 60 per cent. In one city in Texas, where most cases occurred, the mortality in the city hospital under the serum treatment was 27 per cent., while among those treated outside of the hospital with and without serum it was 60 per cent. In a few places the death rate reached 85 per cent. The showing in favor of hospital treatment combined with the serum was remarkably good, as compared with the ordinary management of these cases.

Epidemic cerebrospinal meningitis is transmitted principally through the agency of healthy carriers. The specific germ of the malady, *Diplococcus intracellularis meningitidis* of Weichselbaum, has its natural habitat in the nose and throat. The disease is undoubtedly transmitted directly from person to person, for the *Diplococcus intracellularis* is of such low vitality that it succumbs quickly to drying, sunlight, and other noxious influences. Because of this fact individuals sufferings from the disease are decidedly restricted in their sphere of potential pathogenicity, and as only a very few of those who acquire the organism are sensitive or susceptible to it, the perpetuation and dissemination of meningitis must depend on the healthy carriers who transmit the diplococcus from one to another until an impressionable subject is reached. The number of persons who are thus made carriers during an outbreak of meningitis is far greater than the number of cases of meningitis. Nearly one-fourth of all individuals residing in the immediate vicinity of meningitis cases act as carriers, harboring the germs in the respiratory passages without displaying any evidence whatever of disease or suffering any inconvenience. In apparently the healthiest of subjects virulent diplococci have been discovered, and even the saliva has been found contaminated. In carriers the germs occur abundantly in the posterior part of the nasal chambers and in the rhinopharynx. Other persons equally exposed as carriers, but not inhabiting the same dwelling, rarely become infected. Aside from epidemic outbreaks, the germ is seldom discoverable in healthy persons; there are, however, occasional persons who, once sheltering the diplococcus in the nasopharynx, carry it permanently, thus perpetuating the disease. These chronic carriers are especially active during the periods intervening between epidemics. It appears that the *Diplococcus intracellularis* can readily obtain a foothold on the mucous membranes of the majority of individuals, but with only a comparatively small proportion of these subjects is it able to invade the tissues and manifest its pathogenic effects.

The best treatment as yet brought forward is the injection of the specific antiserum of Flexner. This investigator has examined nearly 1300 cases of this disease in which the serum was used. These cases were representative, coming from all parts of the country. Of 1249 patients, 849 recovered and 400 died, fixing the death rate at 30 per cent. The normal death rate in this disease before the discovery and use of the serum was about 70 per cent.

MENOCAL, M. G. See CUBA.

MENTAL HEALING. See PSYCHOTHERAPY.

MEREDITH, GEORGE. See LITERATURE, ENGLISH AND AMERICAN.

MERÔE. See ARCHÆOLOGY.

MERRIAM, HENRY CLAY. An American soldier, died November 18, 1912. He was born at Houlton, Me., in 1837, and at the outbreak of the Civil War was a student of Colby College. He entered the Union army in 1862 and was appointed captain in the 20th Maine Infantry. He resigned this office in the following year and was made captain of a regiment of colored troops, and to the close of the war he served with different regiments of negro soldiers, rising to the rank of lieutenant-colonel. He was mustered out of service in 1865 and in the following year was appointed major in the regular army. He rose through the different grades, becoming brigadier-general in 1897. He served as major-general of volunteers in 1898-9, and in 1901 was advanced to the rank of major-general, retired. He received brevet rank for "faithful and meritorious services during the campaign against Mobile." He was also awarded the Congressional Medal of Honor for conspicuous gallantry at Fort Blakeley. He served in numerous expeditions against the Indians in the West and commanded the Departments of Columbia and California. In this capacity he organized, equipped and forwarded troops for the Philippine expedition in 1898. In 1900 and 1901 he commanded the Department of the Colorado. He was the inventor of the Merriam infantry pack.

MERSEY IMPROVEMENT. See DOCKS AND HARBORS.

METALLURGY. The development and improvement of various metallurgical processes was fairly active in 1912, and there was the usual amount of investigation and research in progress. Many important papers in this field were presented to the International Congress of Applied Chemistry held in Washington and New York. In iron and steel metallurgy the improvement of the product, especially as regards steel rails, was under active discussion and investigation, while the advances of previous years in electro-metallurgical processes were maintained. The following paragraphs, based in large part on authoritative reviews of metallurgical progress published in the annual summary of the *Engineering and Mining Journal* (New York), indicate some of the more important developments of the year.

GOLD AND SILVER. While the application of cyanidation found increasing application during 1912, yet no remarkable discoveries were to be recorded either of a mechanical or metallurgical nature. The various ores require more or less individual study and treatment and the scientific side of the problem was more conspicuous than ever. In Colorado cyanidation had completely triumphed over chlorination, the largest plant working the latter process closing down in January, 1912. The Clancy process for treating the telluride ores of Cripple Creek was tested during the year and the Ajax mill was built for the special exploitation of this method. It was believed that the results had not altogether met the expectations of those developing the process. During the year electro-cyanide methods continued to receive study, but little more than encouragement was received from the various experiments. The metallurgy of gold and silver seemed to have reached a stage where further developments were secured by careful and economical arrangement and technical investigation, especially with a hope towards chemical improvements, rather than by the adoption of new and radical methods which for several years had not been forthcoming.

LEAD. A new lead smeltery equipped with four 100-ton Dwight-Lloyd blast-roasting machines went into blast at Tooele, Utah, during the year and was notable for the high efficiency of its mechanical equipment, eliminating the usual large number of laborers required for handling materials. A Parkes desilverizing plant to refine lead bullion was also built at Chicago and was to be in operation towards the end of the year. The record of the year seemed to be more concerned with technical progress in the line of research than with radical changes in methods of treating either lead ores or desilverizing lead bullion. At the International Congress of Applied Chemistry, R. C. Canby presented a valuable historical paper on the development of the American blast furnace, and other papers of a scientific and practical nature were read at this convention.

ZINC. In 1912 the Japanese began zinc smelting by the putting in operation at Amagasaki, near Osaka, two furnaces, each comprising 60 retorts and by erecting a plant of three furnaces of 120 retorts each near Kasaoka, on Konoshima Island, in the province of Okayama, where regenerative furnaces were installed with the Rhenish form of retorts. In American roasting furnaces attempts were being made to secure greater economies of fuel, as previously this consideration has not figured to the same extent that it has in Europe. Electric smelting of zinc received much experimental attention in 1912, both in Europe and from the Canadian Department of Mines. In the United States the experimental plant at Hartford, Conn., of W. McA. Johnson, continued in operation and a dozen tons or so of spelter were produced, while other experiments were carried on by the Butte and Superior Copper Company and the New Jersey Zinc Company. At Trollhättan and Sarpsborg electrothermic spelter was produced chemically, but in the main, progress in this field was rather limited and but little advance was being chronicled. Hydrometallurgical processes for zinc smelting, both chemical and electro-metallurgical, were attracting attention, though none had resulted in an active commercial success.

COPPER. Many new copper smelteries of large size were completed in 1912, and while radical innovations were not evident these plants showed the most modern methods for efficient operation, and in blast furnace smelting this was accomplished by first sintering all fine material so that the amount of fines in the charge was reduced to a minimum. The reverberatory furnaces built were of large size, but showed few radical departures from current practice. Progress was made during the year in the important field of fume condensation which in some places where the evil was greatest required the shutting down of copper smelteries and the removal of plants. Methods were in use whereby the dust, sulphuric acid, and sulphur trioxide contained in the escaping gases were collected and the Cottrell system found wider application for this purpose. Prof. Stuart W. Young's method, known as the thiogen process, where sulphur oxides and furnace gases are reduced to elemental sulphur by means of hydrocarbons, was installed at Campo Seco, Cal., and was found successful in collecting the reduced sulphur. During the year various hydrometallurgist processes for recovering copper from its ore were the subject of considerable experimentation. Most of these involved elaborate chemical processes, but a successful outcome of at least some of the experiments was anticipated.

IRON AND STEEL. The year 1912 was noteworthy for active attempts to improve the quality of iron and steel, particularly of steel for rails, as various defects and weaknesses had developed which were responsible for railway wrecks. Methods were being developed or investigated to eliminate pipes, blow-holes, and the segregation of solid inclosures in the ingots of cast steel from which the rails were rolled, and an elaborate inspection of manufacture and use was adopted for every rail produced. The chief difficulty in the opinion of many metallurgists was securing a sound ingot. While discarding the upper portion, as had been usual in the best practice, was recommended as the safest way, Sir Robert Hadfield, before the autumn meeting of the Iron and Steel Institute of Great Britain, proposed that the top of the ingot when cast should be heated by means of a charcoal fire, with the result that the segregation and depth of pipe were greatly diminished and correspondingly less discard was necessary. The Talbot method described during the year consisted in rolling the ingot before it had solidified inside and so obtaining the advantages of liquid compression, namely, the impoverishment of the non-ferrous elements of the centre instead of their segregation there. Dr. Hans Goldschmidt proposed that a can of thermit be introduced at the bottom of the liquid ingot so as to free it from gases, oxide inclosures, etc., by the violent stirring produced by the thermit reaction. Various methods to prevent blow-holes and slag inclosures were studied and the results published by Packer and Mars, Troubine, Stead, Austin, and other experts.

The composition of steel also attracted attention during the year and the addition of small amounts of copper for rails and steel tubes was attended with much interest, and the desire to learn of the results in service of rails was expressed. The addition of ferro-silicon and ferro-manganese was further investigated and the chemical relations of the resulting compositions duly studied. An important investigation on charcoal cast iron published by J. E. Johnson, Jr., during the year attracted wide attention. Another interesting study was of Mayari iron and steel, made from the Mayari iron ores of Cuba, which after smelting in a blast furnace produced a pig iron containing up to 3 per cent. of chromium and 1.5 per cent. of nickel. Mixing Mayari iron with other irons was said to give a superior quality of casting as regards wear, strength, finish, and closeness of grain, and the material was in demand for chilled castings and others of great strength or good finish. Blast furnace improvement during the year tended towards cheaper cost of installation and economy of operation without any radical innovations. In the open-hearth process the cost of oil fuel led to the use of tar and coke-oven gas.

There were also developed during the year new open-hearth raw materials, especially iron sponge, made by subjecting iron ore to a stream of carbon dioxide gas, which seemed to have a valuable availability for such regions as California, where the gas could be cheaply obtained from peat, oil, etc. Improvements for the making of small cast steel ingots were introduced in European and American plants, while a new process of considerable efficiency for the manufacture of charcoal iron of exceptional purity by the use of an open-hearth furnace was introduced in the United States. A large manufacturer of wrought iron introduced mechanical puddling by the Roe puddling furnace on a large scale, and other mechanical improvements were also to be recorded.

ELECTRO-METALLURGY. Electric iron and steel works were being developed during 1912 wherever waterpower was available, especially in Norway and Sweden, while at many plants electric furnaces were being used in the manufacture of special steels. An electric blast furnace was built at Domnarfvet, near Trollhätta, while a steel works with a capacity of 1500 tons of rolled steel annually was planned by the Stavanger Company, to include rolling mills and a steam-hammer plant. It was reported that in Sweden 70 electric furnaces were in active operation, including ore-smelting furnaces and furnaces for melting or refining steel. In Germany electric steel was attracting increased attention and the Remschied-Hasten works were being used for its manufacture by the Lindberg process, for which a new 25-ton furnace, said to be the largest in use, was installed during the year. This process works upon molten Thomas steel supplied from the outside steel plant and was said to be more economical than the Siemens-Martin process. In Luxemburg a large electric furnace was being operated mainly for ferro-manganese at Esch, and in Austria the Lindberg electric steel plant was being erected. The Fischer process for the electrolytic deposit of pure iron was attracting increased attention in Germany, and sheets one-fifth of an inch in thickness were obtained almost pure, with remarkable magnetic properties, notable among which was the small amount of hysteresis loss, so that it was particularly applicable for dynamo and transformer work.

In Germany the electric steel furnace has been found particularly useful for making rails and in four years' experience these have been found to be unbreakable. A less extended experience with electric rails has been had in the United States, and for two years 5600 tons were reported in service with a similar record. In the United States an electric furnace for smelting iron ore was in operation at Heroult, Cal., with a capacity of about 20 tons per day. Pig iron is here produced at a cost of about $14 per ton and of good quality, free from manganese, sulphur, and phosphorus and available for cheap conversion in the open-hearth furnace. American steel makers were using electric furnaces for the manufacture of steel castings and for the super-refining of steel from Bessemer and open-hearth furnaces, a large furnace for the latter purpose being installed by the Bethlehem Steel Company.

See also CHEMISTRY, INDUSTRIAL.

METALS, DISEASES OF. See CHEMISTRY, INDUSTRIAL.

METAPHYSICS. See PHILOSOPHY.

METEORIC SHOWER. See METEOROLOGY.

METEORITES. See METEOROLOGY.

METEOROLOGY. The summer of 1912, like that of 1911, proved to be exceptional in the annals of meteorology, but, unlike that of 1911, was characterized by the excessive rainfall and low temperatures that were experienced in many widely separated regions of the globe. The excessive temperatures of the preceding year were apparently responsible for the early and extensive breaking up of the Greenland ice field, with the result that an abnormal drift of both icebergs and ice floes was observed in the western Atlantic during the whole summer. So extensive was this drift that ice was found as far south as latitude 36°, or the latitude of the Mediterranean. The effects of this unusual condition were far more noticeable on the eastern shores of the Atlantic than on this side. Great Britain and western Europe experienced the wettest and coldest summer on record. During practically the whole of the summer high pressure areas were stationary near the Azores and between Iceland and Scandinavia, with the result that all the atmospheric disturbances arriving from the Atlantic were deflected so as to cross Great Britain and the central belt of Europe, and, in conjunction with the lowering of the temperature of the Gulf Stream by the excessive ice-drift, gave rise to the unfavorable weather conditions experienced in those countries.

West Indian Hurricanes. Dr. O. L. Fassig, in the *Journal of the Washington Academy of Sciences*, gave an interesting analysis of 135 storms recorded by the United States Weather Bureau in the West Indies from 1876 to 1910. He showed that their paths coincide closely with the two great branches of the great equatorial current of the Noth Atlantic Ocean. The path of greatest frequency lies along the track of the southern branch of this current, starting near the Windward Islands and, after running in a westerly and northwesterly direction through Jamaica, recurving and passing out towards the northeast into the Atlantic. Less frequently hurricanes are developed to the north of the Windward group and in this case they move across the Bahamas and, recurving east of Florida, pass out into the Atlantic in a northeasterly direction like the others. Ordinarily the storms of the early part of the season, which lasts from May to November, begin in the western waters of the Caribbean Sea; later in the season they originate more to the east. The mean daily progress of the storms traversing the inner track is 250 miles, while those taking the outer track move at the rate of 390 miles a day. It was found that conditions favorable to the formation of hurricanes are produced by changes in the position and intensity of the permanent areas of high and low atmospheric pressure.

Short-Period Disturbances of the Weather. In an interesting series of "Atmospheric Studies" published in the *Bulletin of the Mount Weather Observatory*, Sandström discussed the causes of the peculiar periodicity which is frequently observed in the weather phenomena at the end of a snowstorm in the mountainous regions of Sweden. This periodicity consists in alternations of hurricane winds and sunshiny calm, repeated at intervals of about 25 minutes and often lasting for a considerable period. His explanation is that the plain at the foot of the mountain is covered by a layer of air of great density, and this again by a layer of lighter air. The upper layer, being rendered heavy by the snow which permeates it, begins to rush down the mountainside and so forms an aërial cascade which pushes away the heavy layer from the base of the mountain, causing it to become heaped up at no great distance. With the deposition of the snow, the snow-laden air becomes lighter again and reascends the mountain, and the displaced heavier layer now rushes back. The cascade of snow-laden air continues, the rebounding air of the valley is again pushed back, and the cycle is repeated. The result is the institution of a series of aërial waves several hundred feet high in the region of discontinuity between the two layers. These waves are propagated in some instances to a distance of nearly 70 miles and give rise to the periodic weather phenomena over the intervening region.

Vortex Motions in the Atmosphere. In the same series of studies Sandström also discussed the hydrodynamic vortex theory in its application to meteorological phenomena. He considers that vortices in the atmosphere belong to one of two classes: rotating vortices, in which the vortex lines are nearly vertical; and "glide" vortices, in which they are very nearly horizontal. The latter kind may give rise to the former, but the reverse process has not been observed. Rotating vortices are usually circular, while "glide" vortices are unsymmetrical, the air concerned being separated into two regions by a glide plane or surface, which is usually somewhat inclined to the horizontal. The air above the glide surface is humid and has a higher temperature than the dry and heavier air below it; the pressure gradient is always directed toward the glide surface, so that the air is pressed against the surface, which is thereby accentuated in spite of the tendency of friction to obliterate it. Above and below the surface the air currents move in opposite directions, while along the surface itself there is calm. Off the west coast of Norway a dry cold east wind with fine weather is often experienced in winter. This east wind rushes down from the mountains, attaining its maximum velocity near the shore, and is bounded in the upper air by a glide surface at an altitude of about 1000 feet, above which a light west wind prevails. The altitude of the glide surface decreases to the Atlantic Ocean, and along it there takes place a conversion into wind of the heat of the Gulf Stream coming from the Atlantic. It is estimated that along a coastal belt about 300 miles long the heat energy is converted at the glide surface into the kinetic energy of wind at a rate equivalent to 22,500 millions of horsepower.

Echelon Clouds. In the *Bulletin of the Mount Weather Observatory*, Humphreys gave an explanation of the formation of certain clouds which to an observer on the surface of the earth seem to resemble a flight of stairs, and to which he has therefore given the name "echelon clouds." The appearance is produced by a series of evenly spaced cumulus clouds having plane lower surfaces at a uniform level. The conditions prevailing over the region covered by such clouds involve the uniform vertical distribution of water vapor and substantially uniform vertical temperature gradients; the amount of humidity is rather large, and vertical connection is occurring in many separate places, but nowhere with violence.

Books. Among the more important works on meteorology published in 1912 may be mentioned the following: Milham, *Meteorology, a Textbook on the Weather, the Causes of Its Changes, and Weather Forecasting;* Rotch and Palmer, *Charts of the Atmosphere for Aëronauts and Aviators*.

METHODIST EPISCOPAL CHURCH. This denomination is the largest in point of membership among the Protestant denominations in the United States. The total number of communicants in 1912 was 3,293,526, a gain of 58,891 over 1911. The churches numbered 28,433, an increase of 24, and the ministers, 18,714, an increase of 219. The Sunday schools numbered 36,014, and in them were 4,035,624 scholars and teachers. The total value of church property was $191,762,983. The denomination has mission conferences in Austria-Hungary, Bulgaria, Denmark, Finland, France, Italy, Germany, Norway, Russia, Sweden, and Switzerland. Missions are carried on in nearly all the countries of Asia and in north and central Africa and Liberia. There are missions also in South America, Hawaii, and Mexico. Missions are carried on through the board of foreign missions. The total receipts for missionary purposes during the year amounted to $1,046,113 and the disbursements to $1,546,967. Other organizations of the denomination are the Freedmen's Aid Society, the board of education, which has general charge of the educational institutions, the Methodist Book Concern, through which the publications of the denomination are issued, and the Epworth League, which is the association for the young people of the church. The women of the denomination carry on the Woman's Foreign Missionary Society, Woman's Home Missionary Society, and other benevolent and social work of the church.

Under the auspices of the denomination are maintained many universities and colleges. The largest of these are De Pauw University, Indiana, Northwestern University, Illinois, University of Southern California, Boston University, Ohio Wesleyan University, and Wesleyan University, Connecticut. Ten theological schools are maintained for white students and five for colored.

The general conference of the denomination met at Minneapolis on May 1. Eight bishops were elected: H. C. Stuntz, T. S. Henderson, W. O. Shepard, N. Luccock, F. J. McConnell, F. D. Leete, R. J. Cooke, and W. P. Thirkield. Three bishops retired. These were H. W. Warren, David H. Moore, and Thomas B. Neely. Two missionary bishops were elected for southern Asia, John Wesley Robinson and William P. Eveland. The conference passed a resolution asking Congress to pass the Kenyon-Sheppard bill, forbidding interstate traffic in liquors. The conference refused to modify the law of the denomination relating to amusements. A commission was authorized to continue negotiations with the Methodist Episcopal Church, South, and the Methodist Protestant Church for possible organic union or closer federation. Other Methodist bodies were cordially invited to join in an effort to unify the various branches of the denomination in one great Methodist Church. A plan to revise the ritual was rejected, but a commission was appointed to consider a report in 1916. Official editors in treating of biblical matters were directed to "avoid unsettled questions as far as is consistent with honesty in teaching."

METHODIST EPISCOPAL CHURCH, SOUTH. This body, which includes the greater number of Methodists in the Southern States, had in 1912, according to the official statistics of the denomination, 1,950,646 members. Of these, 29,285 were outside the United States. Traveling preachers numbered 6992 and local preachers 4749. There were 16,274 churches and the value of the church property was $50,193,598. The schools and colleges of the denomination were valued at $12,483,479, with an endowment of $3,557,315. Sunday school scholars numbered 1,381,647, of whom 31,347 were outside the United States. The officers and teachers numbered 129,575. There were paid out for foreign missions, in 1912, $445,121 and for home missions $411,453. These figures do not include contributions by the women's missionary society. For church extension there were distributed $227,229 and for superannuated preachers $281,159. For educational purposes were spent approximately $240,000.

METHODISTS, COLORED. The colored branches of the Methodist Episcopal Church include the Colored Methodist Episcopal Church, with 233,911 members, 2863 ministers and 2809 churches; the African Methodist Episcopal Church, with 858,323 members, 6920 churches, 6179 ministers; the Zion Union Apostolic Church, with 3059 members, 45 churches, and 33 ministers; the Union American Methodist Episcopal Church, with 18,500 members, 255 churches, and 138 ministers; African Union Methodist Protestant Church, 4000 members, 125 churches, and 200 ministers; Reformed Methodist Union Episcopal Church, 4397 members, 58 churches, and 72 ministers. The largest of these denominations have their chief strength in the Southern States.

METRIC SYSTEM. See INTERNATIONAL METRIC CARAT and WEIGHTS AND MEASURES.

METROLOGY. See METRIC SYSTEM, and WEIGHTS AND MEASURES.

METROPOLITAN MUSEUM OF ART. See PAINTING

METROPOLITAN OPERA COMPANY. See MUSIC.

MEXICO. A republic between the United States and Central America. Capital, Mexico.

AREA AND POPULATION. Many of the Mexican states were brought into prominence by the revolutionary movements of 1911 and 1912; all of them, together with the territories and Federal District, are named in the following table, which shows area, population (census of October 27, 1910), and density per square kilometer:

	Sq. kms.	Population	Density
Aguascalientes	7,692	120,511	15
Campeche	46,855	86,706	1.8
Coahuila	165,099	362,092	2.2
Colima	5,887	77,704	13
Chiapas	70,524	438,843	6
Chihuahua	233,094	405,265	1.7
Distrito Federal	1,499	720,753	480
Durango	109,495	436,147	4
Guanajuato	28,363	1,081,651	38
Guerrero	64,756	605,437	9
Hidalgo	22,215	646,551	29
Jalisco	86,752	1,208,855	14
México	23,185	989,510	42
Michoacán	58,594	991,880	17
Morelos	7,082	179,594	25
Nuevo León	61,343	365,150	6
Oaxaca	91,664	1,040,398	11
Puebla	31,616	1,101,600	35
Querétaro	11,638	244,663	21
San Luis Potosí	62,177	627,800	10
Sinaloa	71,380	323,642	5
Sonora	198,496	265,383	1.3
Tabasco	26,094	187,574	7
Tamaulipas	83,597	249,641	3
Tlascala	4,132	184,171	44
Veracruz	75,863	1,124,368	15
Yucatán	42,751	339,613	8
Zacatecas	63,386	477,556	8
* Baja California:			
Distrito Norte	69,921	52,272	0.3
Distrito Sur	85,279		
* Quintana Roo	48,450	9,109	0.2
* Tepic	28,371	171,173	6
Total	†1,987,201	15,115,612	‡7.6

* Territory. † 767,258 square miles. ‡ Nearly 2 per square mile.

The total in 1900 was 13,607,259, of whom 43 per cent. were of mixed blood (mostly Indian and white), 38 per cent. Indian, and 19 per cent. white. The larger cities, with population (1910 census), include: Mexico, 470,659; Guadalajara, 118,799; Puebla, 101,214; San Luis Potosí, 82,949; Monterey, 81,006; Mérida, 61,999; León, 57,722; Veracruz, 45,021; Aguascalientes, 44,800; Morelia, 39,160; Chihuahua, 39,061; Pachuca, 38,620; Oaxaca, 37,469; Orizaba, 36,189; Tacubaya, 35,830; Guanajuato, 35,147; Saltillo, 35,063; Querétaro, 35,0'1; Durango, 34,085; Toluca, 31,247; Zacatecas, 25,905; Colima, 25,148; Jalapa, 24,816; Celaya, 23,112; Irapuato, 21,281.

In 1910 there were 49,938 marriages, 435,-386 births, and 467,965 deaths; immigrants, 79,484.

EDUCATION. Primary instruction is free and nominally compulsory. Latest official figures available are for 1906: Elementary schools (primary), 8451 (with 542,539 pupils); elementary schools (superior), 354 (51,789); secondary and collegiate schools, 38 (4581); professional, 66 (8734); private, 2562 (163,020).

INDUSTRIES. In proportion to the country's capabilities, agricultural production is small. The leading crops include corn, cotton, henequen, wheat, sugar-cane, coffee, beans, and tobacco. Mining is of preëminent importance, and large amounts of foreign capital, especially American, have been invested in mineral exploitation. Many mining properties were affected disastrously in 1912 by the disturbed political conditions. The most important metals mined are silver, gold, copper, lead, antimony, and zinc. The gold and silver produced have been valued, respectively, as follows in fiscal years: 1889-90, 1,383,655 pesos and 39,156,687 pesos; 1899-1900, 15,444,666 and 70,218,914; 1904-5, 28,407,312 and 79,047,148; 1909-10, 48,295,508 and 76,371,884; 1910-11, 49,481,955 and 80,878,729. These figures show a remarkable development in the output of precious metals, especially gold; silver production reached its highest value in 1907-08, with 85,366,904 pesos. The principal manufactures are cotton and other textiles, tobacco goods, sugar, and spirits. In the year 1908-9 the mill consumption of raw cotton was 35,-434,639 kilos; 1909-10, 34,736,154; 1910-11, 34,568,212. In the last year the output was 15,090,669 bolts of piece goods and prints and 2,766,973 kilos of yarn. In 1909-10 and 1910-11 tobacco manufactures amounted to 8,972,547 and 8,874,118 kilos; alcohol, 39,352,205 and 37,-127,173 liters.

COMMERCE. For the fiscal years 1900, 1905, 1910, 1911, and 1912, ended June 30, the values of imports and exports have been as follows, in pesos:

Year	Imports	Exports Mdse.	Exports Prec. metals	Exports Total
'00	128,796,606	79,031,336	79,216,597	158,247,933
'05	178,204,962	114,634,924	93,885,527	208,520,451
'10	194,865,781	141,060,746	118,985,524	260,046,270
'11	205,874,272	150,795,273	142,958,367	293,753,640
'12	182,660,691	158,540,708	139,473,469	298,014,177

Classified imports in fiscal years 1911 and 1912: Animal substances, 17,433,251 and 16,-466,011 pesos; vegetable substances, 38,600,222 and 31,284,213; mineral substances, 52,030,587 and 46,710,312; textiles and their manufactures, 24,640,269 and 21,281,110; chemicals and drugs, 12,990,250 and 12,075,487; beverages, 6,813,346 and 6,744,083; paper, 5,608,939 and 5,120,733; machinery and apparatus, 25,811,176 and 23,383,811; vehicles, 9,095,206 and 4,604,-224; arms and explosives, 3,212,567 and 5,385,-843; miscellaneous, 9,638,455 and 9,604,859. Classified exports in the two years: Mineral products, 180,005,965 and 186,207,602 pesos; vegetable products, 91,267,202 and 83,610,345; animal products, 16,802,140 and 19,861,197; manufactures, 3,609,670 and 6,604,428; miscellaneous, 2,068,662 and 1,730,602. Leading exports in 1910-11 and 1911-12: Silver, 80,867,-861 and 89,568,354 pesos; gold, 62,090,505 and 49,905,114; copper, 26,300,228 and 33,501,873; henequen, 25,062,140 and 21,430,081; coffee, 8,623,775 and 13,563,044; rubber, 21,187,770 and 11,797,798; hides and skins, 10,773,770 and 10,509,201; guayule, 11,797,910 and 9,935,130; live animals (mostly cattle), 4,799,185 and 7,913,346; lead, 6,539,098 and 6,019,146; chick peas, 3,078,662 and 4,463,730; ixtle, 3,190,680 and 3,792,678; woods, 3,440,968 and 3,568,417; sugar, 943,366 and 3,491,404; chicle, 3,745,968 and 3,211,090; vanilla, 2,630,545 and 2,154,-164; antimony, 2,046,689 and 1,728,338; zacatón root, 2,361,120 and 1,698,614. Trade by countries, in thousands of pesos:

	Imports 1911	Imports 1912	Exports 1911	Exports 1912
United States	113,147	98,415	224,498	224,113
Germany	25,562	23,842	8,708	10,317
United Kingdom	23,969	21,469	35,882	40,200
France	18,673	15,660	9,310	8,320
Spain	5,679	5,901	1,584	2,361
Belgium	4,312	3,279	7,362	6,355
Austria-Hungary	2,187	2,091	54	208
Italy	2,377	1,951	165	157
India	2,099	1,943	....	....
Switzerland	1,452	1,565	15	....
Total, including other	205,874	182,661	293,754	298,014

For the first five months of the fiscal year 1913 imports were valued at 77,598,958 pesos, as compared with 74,163,230 pesos in the first five months of the fiscal year 1912; exports, 140,611,472, as compared with 113,992,891. The increase, therefore, in the five-months' period was 3,435,728 pesos (4.63 per cent.) in imports and 26,618,580 pesos (23.35 per cent.) in exports.

SHIPPING. In direct international navigation, there entered in the year 1910-11, 1998 vessels, of 3,727,519 tons (steam 1342, of 3,609,-823), and cleared, 1964, of 3,852,234 tons (steam 1361, of 3,746,605). Merchant marine (1911), 32 steamers, of 16,648 tons net, and 50 sail, of 8712 tons net.

COMMUNICATIONS. Railways in operation September, 1912, 25,287 kilometers (15,713 miles), of which 19,877 kms. were controlled by federal or state government; as compared with 24,717 kms. (15,358 miles) in operation in September, 1911; 24,559 kms. in 1910, and 24,161 kms. in 1909. Federal telegraph lines in 1912, 74,899 kms., with 530 offices; other lines, 8387 kms. Post offices (1911), 2858.

During 1912 it was reported that the following branch lines of railway, with a total length of 1116 miles, were under construction by the National Railways of Mexico: Durango-Canitas line and Sombrerete branch, 172 miles; Durango-Llano line, 63 miles; Penjamo-Ajuno line, 87 miles; San Andres Tuxtla branch of V. C. and T. Railway, 45 miles; Cerro Colorado branch of V. C. and T. Railway, 32 miles; Veracruz-Tampico short line and connection to Honey line, 379 miles; Tampico-Matamoros line, 264 miles; and Allende-Las Vacas line, 74 miles. The Pachuca City Electric Railway, 27½ miles in length, in the state of Hidalgo, and the Micos-Concepción, an electric railway 44 miles in length, were contracted for during the year. In connection with the recent revolution in Mexico the destruction of railway property was considerable, especially in the north, where the North-Western Railway Company suffered.

FINANCE. The monetary unit is the silver dollar, or peso, whose value is legally fixed at 0.75 gram of fine gold, or 49.846 cents. In the fiscal year 1910-11, revenue amounted to 111,142,482 pesos and ordinary expenditure to 100,913,924 pesos. The budget of 1911-12 showed estimated revenue and expenditure of 110,070,100 and 105,432,347 pesos, respectively; for 1912-13, 103,657,000 and 103,602,400. The latter budget showed estimated receipts as follows: Customs, 47,891,000 pesos; stamps (including internal revenue), 32,525,000; direct taxes, 11,150,000; posts and telegraphs, 6,800,000; taxes on mines, 2,050,000; lottery, 1,000,000; various, 2,241,000. Larger estimated expenditures: Finance and public debt, 35,054,108 pesos; war (and marine), 21,667,206; communications, 16,048,325; interior, 13,218,228; public instruction, 7,418,203; fomento, 3,993,083. Public debt, June 30, 1912: External, 302,977,624; internal, 136,726,367; floating, 482,574; total, 440,186,565. Charges on external and internal debt in fiscal year 1912, 28,952,598 pesos.

ARMY. Internal disturbances in the republic had their effects on the army and naturally interfered with the schemes of reorganization and recruitment adopted in 1910 and 1911. In fact, the active army was concerned in the effort to put down the various uprisings of the revolutionists and to maintain governmental supremacy in the Federal District, where the greater part of the state forces continued to be concentrated. In 1912 the forces were estimated to number about 30,000, having practically the same organization as in the previous year, with varying strength and efficiency on the part of the rural troops. While compulsory service was supposed to come into effect in 1912, yet it did not serve materially to increase the numbers of the army. In organization and service the unrest of the times, described below under *History*, were so apparent as to render of little service any discussion of theoretical strength and organization of the army beyond that given in previous issues of the YEAR BOOK.

NAVY. The navy in 1912 included: 2 gunboats (*Tampico* and *Veracruz*, built in 1903), of 1000 tons each; 2 gunboats (*Bravo* and *Morelos*, 1904), of 1200 tons each; one small cruiser (*General Guerrero*, 1909), of 1630 tons; one transport (*Progreso*); 2 corvettes (*Zaragoza* and *Yucatán*); 3 dispatch boats, and several small vessels of little value. Personnel (1912), 216 officers and 1240 men.

GOVERNMENT. The republic of Mexico is a federation of states, autonomous in local affairs but bound together by the constitution and fundamental laws. The constitution bears date of February 5, 1857, and received its latest modification April 25, 1912. The president is elected indirectly for six years and is assisted by a cabinet of eight members. The legislative body consists of two houses, the Senate (56 members, elected by direct vote for four years, two for the Federal District and each state) and the Chamber of Deputies (233 members, also elected by direct vote, for two years). Gen. Porfirio Diaz was president during 1877-80 and from 1884 until his resignation May 25, 1911, which was forced by the revolution under the leadership of Francisco I. Madero. Diaz was succeeded by the secretary for foreign affairs, Francisco León de la Barra, as acting president. In October, 1911, Madero was elected president and on November 6 was inaugurated for the term ending November 30, 1916 (the unexpired term of Diaz). Vice-president, José Marino Pino Suárez. Ministry in 1912: Pedro Lascurain, foreign affairs; J. Flores Magón, interior; Manuel Vásquez Tagle, justice; José Marino Pino Suárez, public instruction; Rafael Hernández, fomento, colonization, and industry; Manuel Bonilla, communications and public works; Ernesto Madero, finance and commerce; Gen. A. García Peña, war and marine.

HISTORY. The revolution of Francisco I. Madero culminated in the triumph of the revolutionists and the proclamation of peace on May 18, 1911. On June 7 General Madero entered Mexico City in triumph. During the remainder of the year the country continued to be in a disturbed condition and in the closing months the followers of Zapata were still in arms. On November 18 General Reyes, who had been a candidate for the presidency against General Madero, and who finding his election hopeless, had withdrawn from the contest and retired to Texas, was arrested by United States officials at San Antonio, Texas, on the charge of violating the neutrality laws. He was released on bail and thereupon returned to Mexico and tried to raise an army, but finding no support, surrendered to the Madero government on December 25 and was thrown into prison. It was hoped that this promised an interval of peace, but early in 1912 it was evident that the country was by no means pacified. The hostility of Zapata and his followers in the south continued to cause alarm, and in other parts of the country there were several distinct revolutionary movements, though they were not well organized. The new president was blamed for a lack of firmness in not dealing more effectually with the revolt in the first instance, and it was held that vigorous and prompt action was necessary to inspire respect for the army and the government. Warnings were addressed to President Madero by the United States government that fighting should be avoided in quarters that would endanger the lives of American citizens, and a large force of American troops was held in readiness to protect American non-combatants. During February there were frequent rumors of revolt and general indications of a widespread spirit of unrest. The American government was maintaining the same attitude toward Madero as it had toward Diaz; that is to say, it was not planning to cross the frontier unless American and foreign lives and property were menaced, but was holding its army in readiness to intervene if necessity should arise. On February 27 the capture of Juarez by the rebels was announced, but at the same time a report was issued that the rebel forces had fallen into an ambush at San Pedro and lost 237 killed and wounded. Gen. Pascual Orozco, Madero's lieutenant in the revolution of 1911, joined the rebels and became military and civil governor of Chihuahua. A great many American residents had left the disturbed region by the

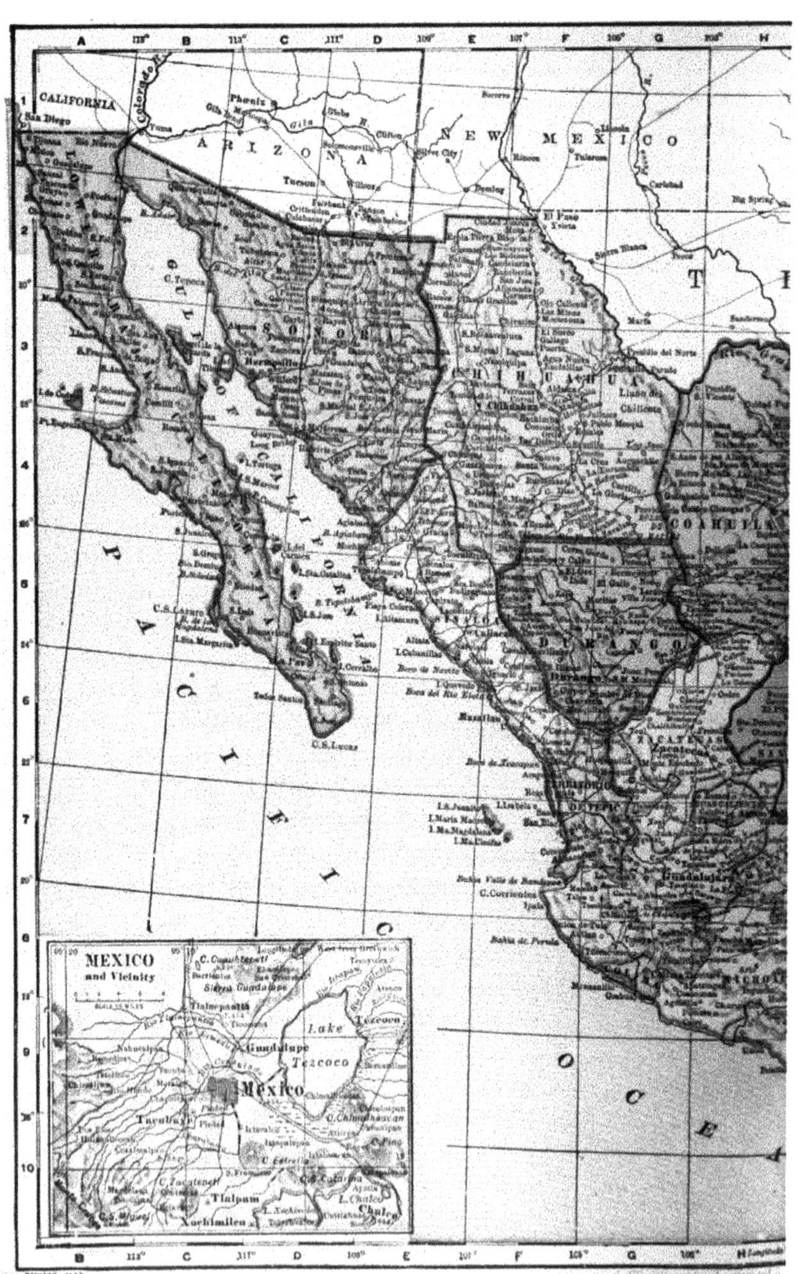
CALIFORNIA
San Diego
ARIZONA
NEW MEXICO
Phœnix
Tucson
El Paso
SONORA
CHIHUAHUA
Chihuahua
COAHUILA
DURANGO
Durango
SINALOA
ZACATECAS
Zacatecas
Guadalajara
Mazatlan
C.S.Lucas
PACIFIC
OCEAN
MEXICO
and Vicinity
Lake
Tezcoco
Mexico
Guadalupe
Tacubaya
Tlalpam
Xochimilco
Chalco
L. Chalco
Sierra Guadalupe
REVISED, 1913

MEXICO.
SCALE OF STATUTE MILES.
Capital of Country:
Capitals of States:
Railroads:
GULF OF MEXICO
Gulf of Campeche
Gulf of Tehuantepec
Delta of the Mississippi R.
Galveston
Houston
New Orleans
Mobile
Shreveport
San Antonio
Austin
Laredo
Matamoros
Tampico
Merida
Campeche
YUCATAN
BRITISH HONDURAS
GUATEMALA
HONDURAS
CHIAPAS
TABASCO
Mexico
Puebla
HIDALGO
Oaxaca

first week in March. The prospects of peace improved somewhat before the end of March, the better classes seeming to incline toward the support of the government. The United States Senate passed a resolution authorizing the President to prohibit the shipment of arms and ammunition to any American country in which they could be used for revolutionary purposes.

During the spring the reports concerning the revolutionary movement in Mexico were very confusing and indeterminate. According to President Madero, the estimates of federal losses published in foreign papers were greatly exaggerated. He said that General Orozco's troops, on the other hand, had suffered heavy losses and were unable to pursue the federal general. He said that the issue of the campaign was beyond doubt. On the other hand, it was said that the revolutionists had, on the whole, been successful in fighting around Torreon. President Taft, in order to make President Madero's task easier, made an exception in favor of the Mexican government to the proclamation against the exports of arms to Mexico.

During May, June, and July federal successes were reported at Cautro Cienagas, Comejos, Rellano, and Bachimba, and on July 9 the federals took Chihuahua, which the rebels had made their headquarters and which they abandoned as the federals came northward. The rebels made Juarez their headquarters, but abandoned this city in turn and the federals occupied it on August 20. The rebel forces of Orozco were now scattered throughout the northern part of Sonora, where they destroyed much property and caused the flight of a large number of Mormon colonists, chiefly Americans, who left their farms and sought refuge in the United States. General la Huerta was in command of the successful federal operations against Orozco. While the federals gained these advantages in the north, the southern provinces became more disturbed and it was not long before the revolution reappeared in the north again. Among the other reported engagements during the summer and autumn were the capture of Ixtapa, where the Zapatists were reported to have killed the entire garrison and a number of townsmen. At the beginning of September it was estimated that the rebel forces numbered 18,000 and that 17 states were affected, but the movement was hindered by lack of organization, being made up of separate divisions who agreed only in their desire to overthrow the Madero government. In September the Zapatists were reported to have sustained a defeat at Tenancingo. Raiding was renewed in Chihuahua in October. On October 16 General Felix Diaz, the nephew of the ex-president, who had placed himself at the head of a revolutionary body, captured the city of Vera Cruz. After a brief delay to admit of the withdrawal of non-combatants, the federal troops proceeded against the rebels and recaptured the city almost without resistance. Diaz and his staff were taken prisoners and the rebels were disarmed. Sentence of death was imposed upon Diaz and two of his officers on October 26, but the execution was postponed and he was afterwards imprisoned. The collapse of the Diaz movement seemed to improve the government's position, but at the close of the year affairs were still very threatening. On December 18 it was reported that General Orozco, who had returned to northern Mexico, had captured the town of Casas Grandes.

For further notes relating to Mexico see EXPLORATION; ARBITRATION, INTERNATIONAL, and UNITED STATES, *Foreign Relations*.

MICHIGAN. POPULATION. According to the Census Bureau statistics compiled in 1912, out of a total population of 2,810,173 in 1910 the foreign-born whites numbered 595,524, compared with 540,196 in 1900. The largest number of these, 142,713, came from Canada; from Germany came 130,538, from Russia, 38,009; from Holland, 33,470; from Austria, 31,495; from French Canada, 28,082; from Sweden, 26,373; from England, 42,721; from Finland, 31,079; from Ireland, 20,443; and from Hungary, 11,064. Other European countries were represented by smaller numbers. In the city of Detroit, which had a total population of 465,766 in 1910, there were 156,565 foreign-born whites, compared with 96,051 in 1900. The negroes in the State in 1910 numbered 17,155 and the mulattoes, 8036. In 1890 the negroes numbered 15,223, and the mulattoes, 8187.

AGRICULTURE. The acreage, value, and production of the principal crops in 1911 and 1912 will be found in the following table:

		Acreage	Prod. Bu.	Value
Corn	1912	1,626,000	56,250,000	$31,492,000
	1911	1,690,000	55,770,000	36,250,000
Wheat	1912	700,000	7,000,000	6,720,000
	1911	1,025,000	18,450,000	16,236,000
Oats	1912	1,485,000	51,826,000	17,102,000
	1911	1,500,000	42,900,000	19,734,000
Rye	1912	370,000	4,921,000	3,199,000
	1911	400,000	5,840,000	4,964,000
Potatoes	1912	350,000	36,750,000	15,068,000
	1911	330,000	31,020,000	22,024,000
Hay	1912	2,395,000	a 3,185,000	40,450,000
	1911	2,411,000	a 2,797,000	47,549,000

a Tons.

MINERAL PRODUCTION. The State ranks second in the production of iron. The quantity produced in 1911 was 8,944,393 long tons, compared with a product of 13,303,906 long tons in 1910. The value of the product in 1911 was $23,808,935, as compared with a value of the product of 1910 of $41,393,585.

The copper mines of the State produced in 1911, 497,281 fine ounces of silver against 330,500 fine ounces in 1910. The silver production is mostly from the electrolytic of the copper produced.

In connection with the mining of copper there were produced 497,281 fine ounces of silver valued at $263,559 or a total value for both metals of $27,743,572. This is a decrease in value from the output of 1910, $715,698, and is due to a slightly smaller output of copper and a little lower average price for the metal.

The production of coal in the State in 1911 was 1,476,074 short tons, valued at $2,633,803. The production in the State has decreased each year since 1907, when the maximum product, 2,035,858 short tons, was obtained. The competition of high-grade Pennsylvania coal brought by way of the lake ports is the principal factor in curtailing the output in the State.

MANUFACTURES. The Thirteenth Census statistics are for the calendar year 1909 and were compiled in 1912. The growth of the manufacturing industries of the State has been closely related to the development of transportation facilities. The rapid advance in manufactures dates from about 1825, when the Erie Canal was opened, affording connection with the eastern seaboard. The table herewith shows that in 1909 there were in tue State 9159 manufacturing establishments which gave employment to 271,071 persons.

	Number or Amount 1909	1904	P. C. of Inc. 1904-'09
Number of establishments	9,159	7,446	23.0
Persons engaged in manufactures...	271,071	200,196	35.4
Proprietors and firm members..	8,965	7,732	15.9
Salaried employees	30,607	17,235	77.6
Wage earners (average number)	231,499	175,229	32.1
Primary horsepower	598,288	440,890	35.7
Capital	$583,947,000	$337,894,000	72.8
Expenses	591,296,000	374,842,000	57.7
Services	153,838,000	98,749,000	55.8
Salaries	34,870,000	17,470,000	99.6
Wages	118,968,000	81,279,000	46.4
Materials	368,612,000	230,081,000	60.2
Miscellaneous ...	68,846,000	46,012,000	49.6
Value of products.	685,109,000	429,120,000	59.7
Value of products less cost of materials	316,497,000	199,039,000	59.0

The largest number of wage earners was employed in the industries connected with lumber and timber products, 35,627; in manufactures of automobiles, 25,444; in foundry and machine shop products, 21,649; in the manufacture of furniture and refrigerators, 16,610. The automobile industry ranks first in the value of the product, $96,651,000. This is followed by lumber and timber products, $61,514,000; foundry and machine shop products, $45,399,-000; flour mill and grist-mill products, $34,-861,000; furniture and refrigerator, $38,642,-000. The persons engaged in manufactures in the State numbered in 1909 271,071, of whom 231,915 were male and 39,156 were female. The persons employed under 16 years of age numbered 2517. The prevailing hours of labor for nearly one-half the wage earners were 60 a week. Of the remainder the majority worked from 54 hours a week to between 54 and 60 hours a week. The largest number of wage earners was in Detroit, 81,011; in Grand Rapids there were 17,590; in Flint, 7088; in Kalamazoo, 6272; in Saginaw, 5990, and in Battle Creek, 4175.

FINANCE. The receipts for the fiscal year 1912 amounted to $14,190,498, and the expenditures to $/,445,519. The balance on hand at the end of the year was $8,980,404. The chief sources of income are from the general tax, $6,788,627, and from the specific and railroad tax, $5,748,652. Later all goes to the primary school fund. There is no State debt.

CHARITIES AND CORRECTIONS. The charitable and correctional institutions under the control of the State, with their populations in 1912, are as follows: Kalamazoo State Hospital, 2015; Pontiac State Hospital, 1394; Traverse City State Hospital, 1398; Newberry State Hospital, 836; Ionia State Hospital, 439; State Psychopathic Hospital, 47; Home for Feeble-Minded and Epileptic, 981; State Prison, Jackson, 762; Michigan Reformatory, Ionia, 578; Branch Prison, Marquette, 311; Industrial School for Boys, Lansing, 779; Industrial Home for Girls, Adrian, 341; State Public School, Coldwater, 179; School for Blind, Lansing, 144; Employment Institution for Blind, Saginaw, 81; School for Deaf, Flint, 309; Soldiers' Home, Grand Rapids, 872; State Sanatorium, Howell, 66. In addition to these, there are 39 private incorporated institutions which are engaged in the business of receiving, maintaining, and placing minor children. The board of corrections and charities in the State, which has charge of these institutions, has made some important recommendations to the legislature. These include the extension of the authority of the board over city and village jails, homes for the aged and defective, and also the granting of power to the county agents of the board to visit homes in which children have been placed out. An amendment to the juvenile court law is also sugested, to provide for appeal to higher courts and for other powers in regard to this law. The board asks for legislation giving to cities or counties authority to establish houses of correction. The desirability of securing a State survey to determine the location of the centres of propagation and dspersal of mental and physical defectives, was pointed out.

POLITICS AND GOVERNMENT

The year was one of the most eventful in the political history of the State, owing largely to dissensions between the Progressive and the regular Republican wings of the Republican party. The Progressives were very strong in Michigan, and Governor Osborn was one of the seven governors who signed the appeal to Mr. Roosevelt that he should become a candidate. When President Taft was renominated Governor Osborn helped organize the third party and advocated Theodore Roosevelt's nomination, but he dissented from the third party's plan to nominate its own candidates for State, congressional, legislature, and county offices. Shortly after election he was advocating a plan to harmonize the differences between the Republican and the National Progressives.

Governor Osborn, on February 13, called a special session of the legislature for the specific purpose of enacting a presidential primary law. The legislature convened Feburary 26 and the bill passed both houses, but a two-thirds vote was necessary to give it immediate effect, so as to become operative in 1912. It did not receive this vote in the Senate, therefore it did not become operative until 90 days after the close of the session, which was too late for the 1912 conventions.

The governor, on March 16, again issued a call for a special session for the same purpose as the first. The legislature convened in special session on March 20, and again an effort to have enacted an immediately effective presidential primary bill was defeated.

The Republican State convention for the election of six delegates-at-large to the national convention met on April 11, at Bay City. The proceedings were disorderly in the extreme. Anticipating that there might be riotous doings between the Taft and the Roosevelt factions to get control of the National Guard armory, the place officially designated for the convention, national guardsmen were called to duty to see that no damage was done to the building. Both factions held conventions in the armory at the same time, and each elected six delegates-at-large to the national convention.

On the same day, and preceding the convention, the delegates met in caucus by congressional districts. Five districts elected 10 Roosevelt delegates, the remaining seven districts 14 Taft delegates. The national convention seated the six Taft delegates-at-large, so Michigan was officially represented in that convention by 20 Taft delegates and 10 Roosevelt. The 10 delegates bolted Taft's renomination along with the Roosevelt delegates of other States.

The Michigan Democrats sent an uninstructed delegation to the Baltimore convention. On the first ballot at Baltimore the delegation voted 19 for Champ Clark, 10 for Governor Wilson, and one for Governor Marshall.

The National Progressive party met at Jackson July 20, organized a State party, and elected delegates to the convention that nominated Col. Roosevelt. This was of more local interest because it was the first State convention held by that party and the platform adopted was said to have been approved by Mr. Roosevelt. Senator Dixon, the Progressives national chairman, attended the convention and participated in the framing of the platform. The platform began with denunciation of the "fraud" and "cheating" at Chicago, and of the "unholy alliance of crooked business with crooked bosses." It contained a call for the inititative and referendum, recall, direct nomination, direct election of senators, equalization of tax burdens, a parcels post, an extension of the postal savings bank system, government ownership of express and telegraph service, a physical valuation of railway property, more power for the Interstate Commerce Commission, extension of the civil service and the consular service, equal suffrage, conservation of natural resources, and "severance of the diplomatic service from such financial interests as are seeking to exploit defenseless nations." The platform opposed the currency plan of the Monetary Commission. In relation to the trusts and the tariff the platform recommended: "The federal regulation of all corporations engaged in interstate business, and the prohibition of the creation of artificial values by watered stocks and bonds."

L. Whitney Walkins, a Republican State senator, was indorsed for governor. State primary elections were held August 27. Senator Walkins was nominated by the Progressives, Amos S. Musselman by the Republicans, and Woodbridge N. Ferris by the Democrats.

At the same primaries Theodore M. Joslin was nominated for United States senator by the Progressives, William Alden Smith was renominated by the Republicans, and Alfred Lucking by the Democrats.

The Roosevelt presidential electors carried the State in November by a plurality of 66,768, it being the first time since 1852 that the Republicans failed to carry the State at a presidential election. The official vote was: Roosevelt, 219,012; Taft, 152,244; Wilson, 150,751; Debs, 23,911; Chafin, 8934; Reimer, 1252.

The Democrats carried the State for governor by a plurality of 24,054, the official vote being: Ferris, 194,017; Musselman, 169,963; Walkins, 155,372.

The Republicans elected the rest of the State ticket by pluralities around 10,000. Mr. Ferris is the second Democrat to be elected governor since 1852.

The Republicans elected 75 members of the legislature, the Democrats 40, and the National Progressives 17. This gave the Republicans a majority of eight on joint ballot.

A proposed woman suffrage amendment to the constitution was defeated at the November election. The vote was: For woman suffrage, 247,375; against, 248,135. At the election in April, 1912, 25 counties voted on local option. The drys carried 14 of the counties and the wets 11.

Of the 83 Michigan counties 35 are now dry.

Other Events. On July 26 nine aldermen and the secretary of the council committees of Detroit were arrested on the charge of accepting bribes. These men were arrested as the result of investigations carried on by William J. Burns. Among them was Thomas Glinnan, president of the council and a candidate for mayor, and E. R. Schreiter, who was also secretary of the American League of Municipalities. These arrests rose out of an effort on the part of the Wabash Railway Company to have part of a street vacated in order to make room for freight warehouses. The council opposed this application and action was delayed. Mayor Thompson suspected that an effort was being made to obtain bribes, and with the help of a citizen of means obtained the services of Mr. Burns. The latter sent to the city a detective who professed to represent the interests of the railroad. He is alleged to have been approached by Schreiter with a corrupt proposition and negotiations with several aldermen are said to have followed. The application of the railroad was then granted. When the bribers came to the office of the detective to receive their money, it was handed to them, and they were confronted with the evidence of a dictograph which had recorded their conversations with the detective. The arrest of the aldermen thereupon took place.

Legislation. At the legislative session of 1912 a number of bills of unusual importance were passed. Among these was an act authorizing the construction or purchase of detention hospitals for the care and treatment of persons afflicted with contagious or communicable diseases in cities having a population of less than five thousand inhabitants. The banking laws of the State were amended. A presidential primary act was passed (see *Politics and Government* above). An elaborate employers' liability measure was enacted. (See Employers' Liability.) This is, however, optional with the employee, under the usual coercion of being deprived of certain defenses if he does not come into this arrangement. These measures were passed at the first session of the legislature. At the second session the following measures were among those enacted: An act to amend the liquor laws of the State; an act to amend the law as to the conduct of, and preventing fraud and deception at, elections. The game laws of the State were amended. A joint resolution was adopted, proposing an amendment conferring on women the right to vote. This amendment was to be submitted at the general election in November (see above). Another joint resolution proposed an amendment relative to the amendment of the charters of cities and villages. This amendment gives a large measure of local self-government to such cities and villages.

STATE GOVERNMENT. Governor, W. N. Ferris, Dem.; lieutenant-governor, John Q. Ross; secretary of State, Frederick C. Martindale; treasurer, John C. Haarer; auditor, Oramell B. Fuller; attorney-general, Grant Fellows; adjutant-general, R. C. Vandercook; superintendent of public instruction, Luther L. Wright; commissioner of insurance, Calvin A. Palmer; commissioner of State Land Office, A. C. Carton—all Republicans, except Ferris and Vandercook.

JUDICIARY. Supreme Court: Chief justice, Joseph H. Steere; justices, John E. Bird, Joseph B. Moore, Aaron V. McAlvay, Charles A. Blair, Flavius L. Brooke, John W. Stone, Russell C. Ostrander.

STATE LEGISLATURE, 1913. Republicans, Senate, 21; House, 54; joint ballot, 75. Democrats, Senate, 5; House, 35; joint ballot, 40. Progressives, Senate, 6; House, 11; joint ballot, 17. Republican majority, Senate, 10; House, 8; joint ballot, 18.

MICHIGAN, UNIVERSITY OF. An institution of hgher learning at Ann Arbor, Mich., founded in 1837. The students enrolled in the various departments of the university in the autumn of 1912 numbered 5620. The officers of instruction and administrattion numbered 486, of whom 102 were deans and professors, 27 junior professors, 56 assistant professors, 132 instructors, 101 assistants and demonstrators. The other members of the faculty included administrative officers, members of the library staff, assistants in the museum, etc. There were few changes in the faculty in the higher grades in 1912. The following are the most noteworthy: Dr. Campbell Bonner was appointed professor of Greek language and literature in place of Martin L. D'Ooge, retired; Henry E. Riggs was appointed professor of civil engineering in place of Professor Gardner S. Williams, resigned; Professor Horace W. King was appointed professor of hydraulic engineering; William C. Hoad, professor of sanitary engineering; Lewis M. Gram, professor of structural engineering; Louis H. Boynton, professor of architecture. A number of changes were made in the medical and law schools. Graduate work heretofore conducted in connection with the department of literature, science, and the arts has been rearranged and a graduate department established, of which Dr. Karl E. Guthe has been elected dean. The management of the department is vested in an executive board, which acts together with the president of the university and the dean of the department. The university received no noteworthy benefactions during the year, although a number of small gifts were received. The amount of productive funds, which are chiefly in the form of State loans and private endowments, amounted to about $900,000 and the annual income to about $1,400,000. The library contained about 306,000 volumes, of which 235,089 were in the general library. President, Harry B. Hutchins.

MICOU, RICHARD WILDE. An American theological educator, died June 1912. He was born in 1848 and was educated in the University of Georgia. He also studied at several foreign universities and received his theological education at the General Theological Seminary. He was ordained a priest in the Protestant Episcopal Church in 1872 and served in successive pastorates at Franklin, La.; Kittanning, Pa., and Waterbury, Conn. In 1892 he was appointed professor of systematic divinity at the Philadelphia Divinity School. He remained here until 1898, when he became professor of fundamental theology and systematic divinity at the Virginia Theological Seminary. This position he retained until the time of his death.

MIKADO OF JAPAN. See MUTSUHITO.

MIKKELSEN, EJNAR. See POLAR EXPLORATION.

MILITARY PROGRESS. In spite of the efforts of peace societies, preparation for possible war has gone on unremittingly. No abatement of energy is observable in any field, whether organization, material, or increase of numbers. The leading military nations have held their manœuvres as usual. The most striking feature on the material side has been the extension of military ballooning and aviation. The Turco-Italian War dragged on until the far more dangerous situation disclosing itself in the Balkan Peninsula compelled Turkey, in October, to come to terms with her adversary, the supremacy of Italy in Tripoli being recognized. The dominating military event of the year has been the war between the allied Balkan states (Rumania excepted) and Turkey, a war that has amazed the world, and the consequences of which cannot now be fortetold with even approximate accuracy.

AVIATION AND BALLOONING. This subject has attracted the most serious attention. Every great military nation is straining every nerve to attain success in applying the "conquest of the air" to reconnaissance and information service, and to actual offensive service in war. Some idea of the growth of the subject may be had from comparing appropriations in France; in 1909, 240,000 francs for experimental purposes; in 1912, the sum asked for rose to 7,600,000 francs. The German budget for 1912 contemplated a credit of 9,000,000 marks. Our own country has done practically nothing in comparison with foreign effort. Germany has an aviation school at Döberitz and stations at other points of the empire. France has its "centres of aviation"; Russia a station at Sevastopol. The English government, early in the year, laid down conditions for a competition of military aeroplanes, in part open to all comers, in part reserved to English builders. The money prizes offered are enormous. The Italian government has done the same thing. In France military aviation is already spoken of as the "fourth arm"; its relations to the other arms of the service are being worked out. Aeroplane ballistics have been investigated and it is proved, e. g., that artillery fire can be controlled from an aeroplane, and that in any case the aeroplane can be used to indicate to batteries objectives invisible to the batteries themselves. Germany is soon to create an aviation corps. England, in April, definitely organized its aviation corps, as did Italy hers in June. With characteristic energy and thoroughness Germany is endeavoring to overcome France's lead in aeroplanes and at the same time to extend and develop her own dirigible fleet. She owned or controlled in 1912 30 dirigibles, some of which could develop a speed of over 40 miles an hour. Her military dirigible fleet proper before the end of 1912 consisted of 20 vessels, divided into cruisers of the first class, used for strategic reconnaissance and susceptible of taking the offensive, and cruisers of the second class, used for tactical reconnaissance. This fleet is further reinforced by auxiliary cruisers not included in the foregoing 20. The service of these dirigibles is completely organized: staff, personnel, "home ports," area, and terrain of operations. The value of these great aerial cruisers as offensive engines of war is no longer a matter of doubt. The German experiments have shown that, given a trained personnel and proper apparatus, it is possible to attain sufficient accuracy against troops in mass, dockyards, arsenals, etc., etc. Special guns are developed to attack the dirigibles, since beyond 1000 meters altitude the ordinary guns of an army are practically powerless.

The greatest enemy of the dirigible is the aeroplane; the Germans, to meet this danger, propose to mount a machine gun on top of their dirigibles and also to provide special armor for their upper surface as a protection against grenades, etc., thrown from an aeroplane above. The aeroplane, whether in Germany or elsewhere, is no whit behind the dirigible. As a result of the experience gained in 1912, it may be laid down that these two engines supplement each other; thus the dirigible is for strategic exploration and, later, destruction of enemies' troops, ships, camps, etc.; the aeroplane is the organ to be employed in reconnaissance. But aviators are by no means content to limit their efforts to mere reconnaissance. For the first time in the history of the aeroplane, bombs weighing 22 pounds have been used in aerial warfare in Tripoli with indifferent results on account of the great height (1000 meters) at which aviators were compelled to fly. Even at this height, the Turkish Mauser bullet has succeeded in hitting the aeroplane; better results may be expected from the "Lewis gun for aeroplanes," the invention of an American officer, Lt.-Col. I. N. Lewis, Coast Artillery Corps. This gun weighs 25½ pounds, and requires but one man to operate it. No tools are needed to disassemble or assemble it, other than the nose of its own bullet. Air cooled, it fires up to 750 shots a minute and in tests so far made has shown remarkable accuracy and facility of operation and control. (*London Engineering*, November 8, 1912.)

UNITED STATES. A considerable body of troops has been kept patrolling the Mexican border in order to maintain due observance of the neutrality laws. A state of profound peace has prevailed in the Philippines. Armed intervention in Cuba, at one time imminent, was averted. The construction of the defenses of Manila, of Hawaii, of the Panama Canal, and of Guantánamo is being continued. In the coast defense system of the United States, now taken as a model, the training of the personnel has reached such a state that, under normal conditions, the accuracy of the armament alone limits the result. Under present conditions mortar fire can be opened at 15,000 yards; the new mortar, such as will be used in the Panama defenses, will give a range of 20,000 yards. The projectile weighs 700 pounds. See UNITED STATES, *Army*.

AUSTRIA-HUNGARY. The entire army of the dual monarchy has been reorganized. Before this reorganization went into effect, the organic law of 1868, even as amended in 1889, had failed to meet the military necessities of the empire. On July 5, 1912, therefore, the emperor sanctioned a number of laws under the effect of which the available resources in trained men have been greatly increased. (See AUSTRIA-HUNGARY.) The following table shows this increase in comparison with former strength:

	Formerly No. Men	Under New Law No. Men
Army common to both kingdoms	800,000	1,360,000
Austrian landwehr	250,000	240,000
Hungarian honved	164,000	220,000
Total	1,214,000	1,820,000

GERMAN EMPIRE. The German army on October 1, 1912, under a law passed four months before, was increased by two army corps, formed by joining various elements hitherto more or less independent. Although the numerical increase of the army, due to this creation of two new corps, is not great, the step taken marks an epoch in the development of the German military power, as one of these corps is to take station on the eastern (Russian) and the other on the western (French) frontier. So placed, they strengthen very considerably the system of "cover" furnished by the German army and help on the ulterior passage to the offensive. One new "inspection," the 7th, is created, with headquarters at Saarbrücken. The new military law of 1912 completes and reinforces the quinquennate of 1911. It emphasizes the determination of the great general staff constantly to increase the offensive value of the army and to develop to the utmost its preparedness for war, its *Kriegsbereitschaft*. The increases under this law represent the greatest effort made by Germany since 1870. The statutory peace strength of the army on October 1, 1912, or shortly afterwards, was 694,000 officers, non-commissioned officers, and men. If certain other classes of men be added the enormous total reaches 710,000 men. The total increase of the army is 49,000, a part of which goes to the creation of 68 new field batteries, an increase of 288 guns. See GERMANY.

OTTOMAN EMPIRE (Turkey). A radical reformation of the Turkish army was carried out at the end of 1911. It had for its objects: (1) Modification of the high commands; (2) methodic preparation of increase of military strength; (3) endeavor to better tactical use of the army. The old organization of the army was clumsy to a degree. Under modern conditions it lent itself to the necessities of neither peace nor war. Before 1911 there were 7 commands or military regions, and 2 independent divisions spread over the face of the Ottoman empire; each of these regions comprised a variable number of infantry divisions, of cavalry, and artillery of the active army (*Nizam*) and of reserve divisions (*Redif*). The reformation contemplated in its technical aspect the so-called ternary system, under which the corps = 3 divisions = 9 regiments = 27 (or more) battalions. The grade of general of brigade disappears. Fully carried out, the Turkish army would count 527 battalions of infantry. The new régime further introduced Christian recruiting—confessedly a delicate matter, whatever the point of view, whether Christian or Mussulman. At the end of 1911 one-fourth of the recruits were Christians. We cannot here enter into the complexities of Turkish army reform. Following close upon the overthrow of the *ancien régime*, embarrassed by financial considerations and the question of Christian recruitment, valorous as the Turkish army has proved itself in the past, it was ill prepared in 1912, with its old system abandoned and its new barely begun, to undertake a war against an equally valorous but ready antagonist.

The organization of the empire provides for the mobilization of 43 active divisions, 48 *redif* divisions of the first class (instructed men), and 6 *redif* divisions of the second class (partly instructed men). The active division consists of 3 regiments of 3 battalions with one battalion of scouts, 1 regiment of artillery of two or three groups, 1 squadron of cavalry or of mounted infantry, and 1 company of the supply train (rations for three days and ammunition pack train). The army corps comprises, as usual, the corps artillery, the bridge train, the sanitary corps, etc.

BULGARIA. This country has for the past two years made serious efforts to develop and strengthen its military organization, not only for the defense of its territory, but so as to be able to intervene abroad in the interests of the Bulgar race, wherever found in the Balkan Peninsula. Thanks to the sacrifices made, Bulgaria had in 1912 a well-officered, well-instructed army, whose mobilization had been the object of methodical preparation. The men in the ranks have remarkable individual qualities, and their officers are all graduates of the Military School at Sofia. Many of them have studied in foreign schools. Mobilized, the Bulgar army has in its first line 9 divisions of infantry, containing each: 2 brigades of infantry, of 2 regiments of 4 battalions; 2 squadrons of cavalry; 9 four-gun batteries, 75 mm. rapid-fire Schneider guns; 3 to 6 six-gun batteries, Krupp; 1 four-gun battery of howitzers, rapid fire; 2 companies of pioneers, and 1 platoon of telegraph troops. Including reserve troops, etc., Bulgaria could place in the field (first line): 216 battalions or 225,000 rifles, 5000 sabres, and 800 guns. In the second line she could call upon about 150,000 men who had received military training and about 60,000 half-instructed men.

The weak points of the system are the limited ammunition supply, the shortage of horses, making the supply system in the field inadequate, and the numerous new units brought out by mobilization. The total budget of the kingdom for 1912 was 186,560,855 francs, of which 40,495,527 were to the credit of the war department.

SERVIA. This country, like Bulgaria, had made considerable progress of late years in respect of organization, instruction, and equipment. The weak points of the system are the same as those of Bulgaria to at least the same degree. In the first line Servia, in 1912, could put into the field 5 divisions of infantry, organized in time of peace and constituted, each, as follows: 4 regiments of 4 battalions; 9 four-gun batteries; 3 squadrons; and, in addition, 5 divisions of recent creation. Counting all resources, Servia could muster 127,000 rifles, 7500 sabres, 308 rapid-fire field guns, 26 howitzers, and 36 mountain guns.

GREECE. The Greek army had just undergone a process of reorganization, as a consequence of which it could take the field with 42 active battalions, 24 reserve battalions, 36 field batteries, 12 mountain batteries, 3 heavy batteries, and 1 brigade of cavalry.

MONTENEGRO. This country has no permanent army. Under the law all men fit for service are liable up to the age of 62. Theoretically, the army has a certain organization, but the deficiency of any real supply system limits the range of its offensive action

For further details see articles on the UNITED STATES, FRANCE, GERMANY, GREAT BRITAIN, and other foreign countries, and also TURKEY AND THE BALKAN PEOPLES.

MILITIA AND NAVAL RESERVE, ENLISTING IN. See LABOR LEGISLATION, *Miscellaneous.*

MILK. See DAIRYING.

MILK, INFECTION OF. See TYPHOID FEVER.

MILK, TUBERCULOUS. See DAIRYING.

MILK SUPPLY. See SANITATION.

MILLER, JAMES RUSSELL. An American clergyman and author, died July 3, 1912. He was born at Harshaville, Pa., in 1840, and graduated from Westminster College in 1862. In 1867 he was ordained to the Presbyterian ministry. From 1869 to 1878 he was pastor of the Bethany Church in Philadelphia. He afterwards filled pastorates at Rock Island, Ill., and in the Holland Memorial Church and St. Paul's Church, Philadelphia. He became pastor of the latter church in 1900 and continued in that position until the time of his death. From 1880 he was editorial superintendent of the Presbyterian Board of Publication and Sunday School Work. He was a prolific writer and produced many works, chiefly of a religious nature. They include: *Week Day Religion* (1880); *Practical Religion* (1888); *Hidden Life* (1895); *Young People's Problems* (1898); *The Inner Life* (1904); *The Gate Beautiful* (1909); *The Beauty of Every Day* (1910); *The Beauty of Self-Control* (1911). His books are translated into nearly every foreign language.

MILLET, FRANCIS DAVIS. An American artist and war correspondent, died at sea April 15, 1912. He was born in Mattapoisett, Mass., in 1846. During the war he served as drummer boy in the 60th Massachusetts Volunteers until 1864, when he was appointed acting assistant contract surgeon in the Army of the Potomac. At the close of the war he entered Harvard College, graduating in 1869. After graduation he went into the newspaper work in Boston, where he remained until 1871, when he studied art in the Royal Academy in Antwerp. Two years later he became secretary to Charles Francis Adams, commissioner from Massachusetts to the Vienna Exposition. He reported the exposition for the New York papers and at the same time studied art and assisted Mr. Adams. In 1875 he returned to the United States and assisted John La Farge in the decoration of Trinity Church in Boston. At the outbreak of the Russo-Turkish War in 1877 he became war correspondent for the New York *Herald*, the London *Graphic*, and other papers. He accompanied his descriptions of battles with sketches. For bravery under fire during this campaign he received six decorations. After the close of this war he studied art in Paris and in 1878 was a member of the Fine Arts Bureau in the Paris Exposition. For a few years following he remained in the United States, but afterwards bought a home in Worcestershire, England, where he lived for the rest of his life. In addition to the activities mentioned above, he was at different times director of decorations at the Chicago Exposition, special correspondent to the London *Times* in the Philippines, chairman of the advisory committee of the National Gallery at Washington and vice-chairman of the United States Commissioners of Fine Arts. His pictures are hung in many of the important museums in the United States and Europe. In his later years he painted mural decorations for the Court House at Newark, N. J.; the Federal Building at Cleveland, the State Capitol at St. Paul, the Custom House at Baltimore, and other public buildings. Among his best-known paintings are "The Triumph of Ceres," "A Cozy Corner," in the Metropolitan Museum of Art; "At the Inn," "Between Two Fires," in the Tate Gallery, London. In addition to his painting, Mr. Millet wrote much for magazines and was the author of the following volumes: *A Capillary Crime, and Other Stories* (1892); *The Danube, From the Black Forest to the Black Sea* (1891), and *The Expedition to the Philippines* (1899). He also translated Tolstoy's *Sebastopol*. He was for one term president of the National Academy of Design and was a member of many associations in the United States and Europe. Mr. Millet was one of the victims of the *Titanic* disaster.

MINERALOGY. The year's developments in this science included no individual researches or discoveries of extraordinary importance, but as a whole represented, nevertheless, substantial progress. An investigation which combined features of interest in both the fields of geology and mineralogy was that on the mineral sulphides of iron, published by Allen, Crenshaw, and others of the Carnegie Geophysical Laboratory. Among other results the study furnished a solution of the long-standing problem as to the chemical nature of pyrrhotite, one of the commoner vein minerals. It was shown that pyrrhotite represents really a solid solution of sulphur in ferrous sulphide, which fact accounts for the variable composition found on analysis. Experimental products obtained by decomposition of iron disulphide, or by chemical synthesis, were characterized by a considerable range of sulphur content, dependent upon the temperature and pressure of the sulphur vapor in each trial. The products all resembled the natural mineral in physical and chemical properties. It was also found that pyrrhotite is dimorphous, crystallizing in both the orthorhombic and monoclinic systems. Troilite, the monosulphide of iron, should be considered to constitute the end member of the solid solution series and can not pass hereafter as an independent species. The disulphides marcasite and pyrite reflect different conditions of occurrence, and although marcasite readily changes to pyrite by heat treatment the reaction is not reversible. The limiting temperature for marcasite is 450°C., which explains the general absence of the mineral in igneous rocks. The formation of pyrite in deep veins and hot springs involves alkaline waters, while pyrrhotite is a surface product probably formed from cold acid waters.

The present system of nomenclature for minerals was discussed by H. S. Washington, who favored the adoption of a new method which would recognize the important diagnostic features used in mineral classification. These features include chemical composition and crystal form, and on their basis a nomenclature could be constructed following the lines of the terminology of inorganic chemistry in which the word combination expresses the character of the acid and salt. The existing system has not changed essentially since the time of Pliny, when minerals were named variously accordingly to qualities, uses, or localities, the more recent innovations consisting of the introduction of proper names. An outline for a tentative scheme is given in the paper and will no doubt arouse interest in the subject, although it may not lead to such a revolutionary change as is proposed.

DIAMONDS. This interesting mineral was the subject of a monographic treatise by Fersmann and Goldschmidt, which appeared during the year. Regarding the moot question of genesis, the authors conclude that the diamond crystals were formed in a state of suspension in a molten liquid or magma. The solution from which the crystals were derived was characterized by a saturation point for carbon of extreme delicacy so that the periods of growth and reabsorption alternated in a way seldom observed in the growth of any other mineral. Derby, who has studied the diamond fields of Brazil, in a recent paper expressed the view that the conditions of extreme heat and pressure postulated in the common theory of a magmatic origin were really unessential. As an alternative hypothesis that should command serious consideration, he advocated the method known as replacement, according to which the diamond was crystallized out of a carbon-bearing solution that circulated through the rock and dissolved out the cavities in which the crystals were formed. The practical interest of the problem is chiefly in connection with the possible development of a process for the artificial production of gem stones. See CHEMISTRY, INDUSTRIAL.

Discoveries of new diamond occurrences continue to be reported from Africa, which apparently is destined to maintain its preëminence in this department of mining. The latest finds are in the Kassai district, Belgian Congo, where some 600 specimens were reported to have been secured by a Belgian-American company. The character of the deposits has not been described, but it is probable they belong to the placer type. Another new locality, in the Katanga district of northern Rhodesia, has been under exploration by a British company. A considerable quantity of gem stones has been obtained of late from placer workings in German Southwest Africa.

The second largest diamond, of which there is authentic record, was uncovered during the year in the Premier mine, the Transvaal. The stone weighed 1699 carats in the rough, but was not of first quality. The largest stone on record, the Cullinan, came from the same mine in 1905; it has since been broken up and cut.

METEORIC FALL. An event which attracted the attention of mineralogists was the great meteoric shower that occurred near Holbrook, Navajo county, Ariz., on the evening of July 19. One of its notable features was the number of individual stones, over 14,000 having been collected from an area about one-half mile wide by three miles long. In weight they ranged from a maximum of nearly 14 pounds down to one or two grains. The shower was apparently made up at first of a few large stones; these exploded when near the earth by the frictional heat developed in passing through the earth's atmosphere, a circumstance noted by local observers. The specimens that were collected all represent the type of meteorite called aeroliths or stony meteorites. They contain only a little iron, besides pyrrhotite and magnetite, the metallic minerals amounting to about four per cent. of the volume. Some specimens from the surface portion of the original masses show characteristic pitting and flowage structure from melting of the stone when in contact with the air.

NEW MINERALS. The following is a list of new species described during the year 1912. *Neocolemanite* is an allotropic form of colemanite, with which it agrees in chemical composition but differs in optical and physical properties; found near Lang, California. *Eichbergite*, a sulphide of copper, iron, antimony, and bismuth, occurs in magnesite deposits at Eichberg, Semmering, Austria. It forms masses of indistinctly crystalline structure, of metallic iron-gray color. *Fermorite* is a new arsenate and phosphate of calcium and strontium; it comes from the manganese deposits of Sitapur, India. The crystallization appears to be hexagonal, and the color is white or pinkish white. *Muthmannite* belongs to the telluride group of minerals, containing one part each of gold and silver and one of tellurium. It has earlier been referred to other compounds of tellurium. *Thorveitite* is described as a silicate of the rare-earths, orthorhombic, grayish-green, from Iveland parish, southern Norway. *Chromitite* consists of equal parts of chromic and ferric oxides; the octahedral crystals are feebly magnetic. The type locality is Mt. Zeljin, Servia. *Sheridanite* belongs to the chlorite minerals, but differs from the other representatives in the practical absence of iron; it comes from Sheridan county, Wyoming. *Voelckerite* is the name proposed by Rodgers for a variety of apatite in which oxygen takes the place of chlorine and fluorine.

MINERAL PRODUCTION. Details of the production of the leading minerals in 1911 and 1912 will be found in the articles on those minerals, as coal, copper, gold, iron and steel, etc. The table on pages 415-16 gives a summary of the production of all minerals, including metals and non-metals, in the United States in the calendar years 1910-1911:

MINES, BUREAU OF. See UNITED STATES, *Bureau of Mines.*

MINE SWEEPERS. See NAVAL PROGRESS.

MINIMUM WAGE. One of the most important parts of the programme for social standards in industry (see SOCIAL ECONOMICS) is the establishments of a living wage. This wage is such an amount as will maintain a normal standard of living, including the preservation of the health and efficiency of the worker. The demand for it is based partly upon the belief that the workers in sweated trades are exploited because of their ignorance and their lack of bargaining power, and in part upon the belief that insufficient wages must result in the perpetuation of poverty, ignorance, vice, crime, and progressive degeneracy, all of which impose upon other industries and society at large additional social burdens. The living wage is therefore demanded both in interest of the worker and in the interest of the welfare of the group as a whole. The most common objection to the establishment of minimum wage by law or by official decree is that past experience in the regulation of wages has proved futile. But it is argued that there is much difference between the establishment of general wages by official decree and the fixing of a rate below which the employer shall not go in bargaining. Moreover, a great part of the English efforts at regulation of wages was designed to keep wages down by establishing maximum rates to meet a situation where labor was scarce, whereas the minimum wage movement is designed to meet the situation where labor is relatively abundant.

The wage board for the fixing of legal minimum rates was originated as a means of destroying sweating (q. v.). Victoria first established wage boards in 1896, and they have since been adopted in England and Massachusetts. Several other American States, notably Wisconsin and Minnesota, considered their adoption in 1912. A constitutional amendment authorizing minimum wage legislation was adopted in Ohio. Moreover, the policy of "minimum wage standards for working women" was indorsed by the Progressive party; and was approved by the Democratic candidate for the presidency. In England the miners secured an act of Parliament authorizing the establishment of minimum wages in that industry. Their success led to frequent demand by radical labor leaders for the enactment of a minimum wage for all industries. Indeed some of these, with strong leanings toward syndicalism (q. v.), declared not only for a general minimum wage but for one of a very substantial sort.

VICTORIA, AUSTRALIA, AND NEW ZEALAND. The Victorian wage boards were established not only as a means of abolishing sweating and protecting the white standard of living from the undermining competitions of colored races, but also to preserve peace (see ARBITRATION AND CONCILIATION, INDUSTRIAL). The law provides for the establishment of a wage board in each trade. These boards are composed of from four to ten members, chosen equally by or in behalf of employers and workers to fix lowest legal wages not only for the sweated trades, but also for any trade, even the most highly skilled. Since 1907 there has been no limitation on the discretion of the boards, which now number nearly one hundred, in fixing minimum wages. There is, however, a court of industrial appeals, established in 1903, to which either party concerned may appeal from the decision of a board. The Victorian law is of special interest from the standpoint of social policy because it takes no account of the possibility of the destruction of an industry which cannot pay a living wage and at the same time meet outside competition. As regards wages, the Victorian boards are said to have brought about a degree of fixity, together with a massing of wages near the minima established, though this may mean only a leveling up and not a reduction of wages that were above the minima. Another effect has been a great increase in the extent and certainty of industrial peace. In the third place they have furnished much incidental protection to the standard of living.

Conditions very similar to those obtaining in Victoria are found throughout Australia and New Zealand. So general has been the resort

MINERAL PRODUCTS OF THE UNITED STATES CALENDAR YEARS 1910 AND 1911

Product	1910 Quantity	1910 Value	1911 Quantity	1911 Value
METALS				
Pig iron (a) (spot value, b) long tons (2240 lbs.)	26,674,123	$412,162,486	23,257,288	$327,234,624
Silver, commercial value (c) troy ounces	57,137,900	30,854,500	60,399,400	32,615,700
Gold, coining value (d) do.	4,657,018	96,269,100	4,687,053	96,890,000
Copper (e), value at New York City pounds	1,080,159,509	137,180,257	1,097,232,749	137,154,092
Lead (e), value at New York City short tons (2000 lbs.)	372,227	32,755,976	406,148	36,553,320
Zinc (e), value at St. Louis do.	252,479	27,267,732	271,621	30,964,794
Quicksilver, value at San Francisco flasks (f)	20,601	958,153	21,256	977,989
Aluminum (consumption since 1904) pounds	47,734,000	8,955,700	46,125,000	8,084,000
Antimony (g) short tons	....	....	....	....
Antimonial lead do.	14,069	1,338,090	14,078	1,380,556
Nickel (h), value at Philadelphia pounds	....	....	445	127,000
Tin do.	(i)	23,447	(i)	56,635
Platinum, value at New York City troy ounces	773	25,277	940	40,890
Total value of metals	....	747,790,718	....	672,179,600
NONMETALS (Spot Values b)				
Fuels:				
Bituminous coal (j) short tons	417,111,142	469,281,719	405,757,101	451,177,484
Pennsylvania anthracite long tons	75,433,246	160,275,302	80,771,488	175,189,392
Natural gas	....	70,756,158	....	74,127,534
Petroleum barrels (42 galls.)	209,557,248	127,899,688	220,449,391	134,044,752
Peat	....	140,209	....	272,114
Structural Materials:				
Clay products (k)	....	170,115,974	....	162,236,181
Cement barrels (380 lbs., net)	77,785,141	68,752,092	79,547,958	66,705,136
Glass sand short tons	1,461,089	1,516,711	1,538,666	1,543,733
Gypsum do.	2,379,057	6,523,029	2,323,970	6,462,035
Lime do.	3,505,954	14,088,039	3,392,916	13,689,054
Sand, molding, building, etc., and gravel do.	67,949,347	19,520,919	65,308,293	19,614,850
Sand-lime brick	....	1,169,153	....	897,664
Slate	....	6,236,759	....	5,728,019
Stone (l)	....	76,520,584	....	77,108,567
Abrasive Materials:				
Corundum and emery short tons	1,028	15,077	659	6,778
Abrasive quartz and feldspar do.	(m)	....	(m)	....
Garnet for abrasive purposes do.	3,814	113,574	4,076	121,748
Grindstones	....	796,294	....	907,316
Infusorial earth and tripoli short tons	....	130,006	....	147,462
Millstones	....	28,217	....	40,069
Oilstones, etc.	....	228,694	....	214,991
Pumice short tons	23,271	94,943	21,689	88,399
Chemical Materials:				
Arsenious oxide pounds	2,994,000	52,305	6,264,000	73,408
Borax do.	42,357	1,201,842	53,330	1,569,151
Bromine do.	245,437	31,684	651,541	110,902
Calcium chloride do.	10,971	74,713	14,606	91,216
Fluorspar short tons	69,427	430,196	87,048	611,447
Lithium minerals do.	....	(p)	....	(p)
Marls do.	....	....	....	....
Phosphate rock long tons	2,654,988	10,917,000	3,053,279	11,900,693
Pyrite do.	241,612	977,978	301,458	1,164,871
Sulphur do.	255,534	4,605,112	265,664	4,787,049
Sulphuric acid 60° Baume) from copper and zinc smelters short tons	....	....	438,300	2,733,696
Salt barrels (280 lbs. net)	30,305,656	7,900,344	31,183,968	8,345,692
Pigments:				
Barytes (crude) short tons	42,975	121,746	38,445	122,792
Cobalt oxide pounds	....	....	....	....
Mineral paints (n) short tons	85,304	2,141,654 }	(n) 143,350	7,842,583
Zinc oxide do.	58,481	5,238,945 }		
Miscellaneous:				
Asbestos short tons	3,693	68,357	7,604	119,935
Asphalt do.	260,080	3,080,067	360,004	2,828,751
Bauxite long tons	148,932	716,258	155,618	750,649
Chromic iron ore do.	205	2,729	120	1,629
Feldspar short tons	81,102	502,452	92,700	579,008
Fuller's earth do.	32,822	293,709	40,697	383,124
Gems and precious stones	....	295,797	....	343,692
Graphite { crystalline, pounds	5,590,592	295,733	4,790,000	256,050
Graphite { amorphous, short tons	1,407	39,710	1,223	32,415
Magnesite do.	12,443	74,658	9,375	75,000
Manganese ore long tons	2,258	22,892	2,457	24,586
Manganiferous ore do.	61,101	186,765	44,437	115,918
Mica { sheet, pounds	2,476,190	283,832	1,887,201	310,254
Mica { scrap, short tons	4,065	53,265	3,512	45,550
Mineral waters gallons sold	62,030,125	6,357,590	63,923,119	6,837,888
Quartz short tons	63,577	193,757	87,943	155,122
Talc and soapstone do.	79,006	864,213	81,521	1,032,732

MINERAL PRODUCTS OF THE UNITED STATES CALENDAR YEARS 1910 AND 1911

Product	1910		1911	
	Quantity	Value	Quantity	Value
METALS				
Talc, fibrous ....do..	71,710	728,180	62,030	612,286
Thorium minerals (monazite), and zircon ....pounds..	99,301	12,006	3,208	802
Titanium ore (rutile) ....do....	1,132,000	44,480	....	....
Tungsten ore ....short tons..	1,821	807,307	1,139	407,985
Uranium and vanadium minerals ....do....	....	(p)	....	306,500
Total value of nonmetals........	....	1,242,820,417	....	1,245,896,653
Total value of metals........	....	747,790,718	....	672,179,600
Estimated value of mineral products unspecified (p)	....	300,000	....	250,000
Grand total	....	1,990,911,135	....	1,918,326,253

(a) Production of iron ore. 1910: 56,889,734 long tons; value at mines, $140,735,607. 1911, 40,989,808 long tons; value at mines, $86,419,830. Statistics for iron ore and value of pig iron are collected by the Survey; statistics for pig iron output were furnished by the American Iron and Steel Association prior to 1910.

(b) By "spot" value is meant value at the point of production.

(c) Average price per troy ounce in 1910, 54 cents; in 1911, 53 cents.

(d) Since 1905, coining value, $20.671834625323.

(e) The product of domestic ores only.

(f) Of 75 avoirdupois pounds net.

(g) Includes antimony smelted from imported ores, and also antimony contained in hard lead.

(h) Includes nickel in copper-nickel alloy, and in exported ore and matte.

(i) In 1910, small production from Alaska, North Carolina, South Dakota, and Texas. In 1911, from Alaska and Texas.

(j) Including brown coal and lignite, and anthracite mined elsewhere than in Pennsylvania. Coke. 1910: 41,708,810 short tons; value at ovens, $99,742,701. 1911: 35,551,489 short tons; value at ovens, $84,130,849.

(k) Value of clay mined and sold as unmanufactured clay. 1910: $3,625,485. 1911: $3,480,763.

(l) Includes limestone for iron flux, but not grindstones.

(m) Included under feldspar and quartz.

(n) In 1910, also whiting; in 1911, also zinc oxide.

(p) Includes nitrate of soda, carbonate of soda, sulphate of soda, and alum clays used by paper manufacturers; and bismuth, cadmium, lithium, and selenium, valued together in 1911 at about $103,000.

TOTAL VALUE OF THE MINERAL PRODUCTS 1910-1911

	1910	1911		1910	1911
Metals	$ 747,790,718	$ 672,179,600	Unspecified	$ 300,000	$ 250,000
Nonmetals	1,242,820,417	1,245,896,653	Total	$1,990,911,135	$1,918,326,253

to wage boards, or to industrial courts which have power to fix wages, that the vast majority of principal occupations are now working under wages established by official decrees, especially in New Zealand, where official recognition of the trade unions is made. This undoubtedly is one of the chief causes for the high degree of industrial peace which prevails in these countries. Indeed it would seem that in nearly all countries there is an inevitable tendency toward governmental interference in the adjustment of wages in coal mining, in all forms of public utilities, and in those trades where sweating or obvious exploitation of labor is found. In coal mining and the public utiliti s such interference is necessary primarily in order to guarantee the continuance of the production of goods or services involved. With the increasing strength of the unions, governmental action necessitated by general welfare must take some form of fixing minimum wages.

GREAT BRITAIN. The English minimum-wage law enacted in 1909 and effective in 1910, was designed primarily to destroy sweating in industries carried on in the workers' homes. It is carried out through the medium of trade or wage boards. Such boards have been established in tailoring; in paper-box making; in finishing, mending, and darning of machine-made lace, net and lace curtains; and in certain kinds of chain-making. The law may be extended to other industries by the board of trade. Separate wage-boards are established for each industry. The members are appointed by the board of trade, by employers, and by workers. If the industry is widely scattered, local or district committees are formed. The trade-boards must fix time wages and may fix piece wages; and these may be fixed for a whole trade or any part or process, or for a special class of workers. Within six months after the first announcement of rates these become obligatory, and failure to adhere to them renders the employer liable to a fine of not more than £20; the employer must also reimburse the worker to the amount of underpay. The trade-boards may grant to any defective worker a permit enabling him to work at rates below those prescribed. Provision is also made for special consideration of beginners in a trade. Appeals may be taken from the trade-boards to the board of trade.

One effect of this minimum-wage legislation has undoubtedly been to increase the average rate of wages in the industries to which it applies. The wide diversity of wages paid for the same work has been eliminated through a process of leveling up. There has also been a stimulus to organization among both workers and employers. Along with this has gone a better organization of the trade itself, primarily through the elimination of middlemen and middlewomen and other subcontractors. Some work formerly done in homes has been transferred to factories. This is believed to be an advantage since it reduces the possibilities of sweating, increases supervision, and favors the introduction of sanitary and other regulations and the prevention of exploitation of children.

In mining a quite different turn was given to minimum-wage legislation in England, as a result of the demands of the Welsh miners for a trade-agreement guaranteeing a minimum-wage of 5s. ($1.25) per day. (See GREAT BRITAIN, *Coal Strike and Minimum Wage*.) Early in the year it was voted by the miners of Great Britain to go out in a general strike at the end of February on the refusal of operators to accede to this demand. The miners contended that they could not make a living when employed in abnormal places, as on narrow veins, making impossible a normal output. In the latter part of March the number of men out of work was estimated at a million and a half, causing a general cessation of industry and widespread misery. Prof. H. S. Jevons estimated the loss at $50,000,000 a week. Compulsory interference by the state seemed necessary and this took the form of a minimum-wage law rather than government operation of the mines. (See GREAT BRITAIN, *Minimum Wage Law*.) Wage-boards were established and their decrees made compulsory, except that either mine owners or miners may close a mine by refusal to accept the decision. The law required the fixing of minima for both men and boys, regard being had for the average wages of the district for different classes of workers. Some pits were closed by owners on the ground that they could not afford to pay the wage fixed. This development of minimum-wage legislation is very notable, especially since it was only remotely connected with the world-wide movement for a living wage. The previous English law related only to sweated home industry. The 1912 law extended state interference to a principal industry. Since freedom of contract with respect to wages has been one of the most firmly grounded doctrines of modern economic theory, this new interference with natural economic processes was described by many, both in England and America, as excessively socialistic and bound to necessitate still further state intervention. At the same time, however, it must be noted that the idea of a minimum rate had long been a factor in the collective agreements of miners and mine-owners; and that the principle of a living wage has been fully accepted by economists, publicists, and captains of industry.

UNITED STATES

There has been strong opposition among American manufacturers and publicists to the regulation of wages by law, both on general economic and on constitutional grounds. It has been thought both impossible and inexpedient to regulate wages, since they will be determined in last analysis by the supply and demand of labor. The constitutional restriction found in the fourteenth amendment and the doctrine of freedom of contract based thereon have been considered serious impediments to securing legislation which would withstand the scrutiny of the judiciary. On the other hand, most States reserved constitutional freedom of contract to men only, and it has been thought possible, therefore, to secure minimum-wage laws applicable to women and children. Moreover, the courts, both of the States and of the nation, have shown some tendency to broaden and strengthen the police-powers, and to take into account general social considerations as well as strictly legal ones. This tendency has been shown in the opinion of the highest courts of the United States and of Illinois in cases relating to hours of work for women.

MASSACHUSETTS. A minimum-wage commission was appointed by the governor of Massachusetts in 1911 to investigate the wages of women and children in confectionery factories, retail stores, laundries, and the cotton industry. This commission found that there was a wide diversity in the wages paid in the same industry for the same grade of work at different places, a condition typical of sweated trades. Taking the four industries together, they found that 40 per cent. of those employed received under $6 per week, the proportion ranging from 66.2 per cent. in candy factories to 29.5 per cent. in retail stores. In one candy factory, 53.3 per cent. received less than $5 per week, while in the other seven factories no employee of eighteen or over was receiving less than $5. On the basis of the report of this commission the legislature enacted a law instructing the governor to appoint a commission of three persons to establish a minimum-wage board for the fixing of wages of women and children in any occupation in which the wages paid to a considerable number of workers is believed to be inadequate to maintain an American standard of living, or to maintain the health of the workers. The law provides that the wage-board shall have an equal number of representatives of employers and workers, together with a smaller number of representatives of the general public, to be appointed by the governor's commission; or this latter commission may appoint all members of the board. The law forbids the payment of wages less than the minimum fixed by the wage-board. Failure to comply is to be punished by public notice in the local press, public opinion being depended upon to enforce conformity to a board's decree. This law, not being mandatory, is clearly not unconstitutional.

WISCONSIN. The Wisconsin minimum-wage bill defined the minimum-wage as such compensation for labor as would enable employees to secure for themselves and those dependent upon them the necessary comforts of life. The bill did not attempt to define "necessary comforts of life." The bill authorized the Wisconsin industrial commission to investigate, by various means, so as to ascertain and classify the oppressive employments and to fix for each underpaid employee the standard of living wage. The bill provided for the establishment of minimum wage boards after the British type, which should provisionally translate the standard-of-living wage into wage-scales adapted to the special conditions of the various sweated industries.

ADVANTAGES AND DISADVANTAGES. Among those who object to minimum wages are those who contend that there is no necessity for legislation. The promoters of minimum-wage legislation claim that such necessity is shown by the numerous investigations into wages and standards of living which have been made by Streightoff, Chapin, the Immigration Commission, the Pittsburgh Survey, the Massachusetts Commission, above referred to, and numerous smaller investigations in nearly all of the large cities of the United States. These reports uniformly showed that low wages were attended by physical deterioration of the wage-earner and his family. A second objection is that such legislation is impracticable and inexpedient, because efforts to regulate wages by law will be defeated by the operation of economic forces. This is answered by the contention that this objection does not apply to the establishment of minimum standards. It is further contended that wage-earners tend to get what they are worth; that to raise the wages of inefficient workers by law will encourage inefficiency and will prevent the elimination of the inefficient from economic life. The defenders of minimum-wage legislation contend in opposition that unskilled workers often do not get what they are worth, partly because of the oppression of some employers, and partly because they are victims of social and industrial maladjustment. Again it is contended that there are industries which cannot afford to pay a standard-of-living wage. In opposition to this there are those who say that such industries are parasitic and ought to be driven out of the country as detrimental to social welfare. It is pointed out that in the United States, workers of different standards of living either compete with each other or are finding employment in different industries. It is recognized as impossible to establish at once an American standard of payment for alien workers with much lower standards of living. This undoubtedly constitutes a practical difficulty in the United States. It is recognized also that minimum-wage legislation may throw out of employment some workers whose efficiency is so low that their employment would be unprofitable. For such workers, some freely advocate charitable support by the State; others advocate that they be granted special permit to work at less than the legal rate. The advocates and the opponents of minimum-wage legislation do not agree as to whether such legislation would tend to reduce the wages of workers who originally receive slightly more than the minimum. It seems probable, however, that with organization of the workers and publicity of conditions to prevent the depression of wages minimum-wage laws would not reduce the remuneration of any class of skilled or semi-skilled workers. See Child Labor; Arbitration and Conciliation, Industrial; Sweating; and Women in Industry.

MINING INDUSTRY. The Thirteenth Census published in 1912 its report on the mining industry, giving the statistics for the year 1909. The number of persons engaged in the mining industry on December 15, 1909, was 1,139,332, of whom 1,065,283 or 93.5 per cent. were wage-earners; 49,374 proprietors, and 24,675 were clerks. There were employed 8151 boys under 16 years of age, of whom 6968 or 85.4 per cent. were employed in the coal mining, 489 in iron, and 694 in other mining industries. Practically all the boys employed in the anthracite coal mining work above ground. In mining bituminous coal more than three-fourths work under ground.

The gross value of the products of the mines and quarries, including petroleum and natural gas wells, in 1909 was $1,238,410,322. Coal mining was the leading industry in point of value. The value of coal sold as such and of the coke produced at the mine amounted to $577,142,935, of which anthracite contributed $149,180,471; bituminous, $427,962,464. Petroleum and natural gas came next with a product valued at $185,416,684. Other industries contributing over $10,000,000 worth of products were: Copper, $134,616,987; iron, $106,947,082; gold and silver, $94,123,180; lead and zinc, $31,363,094; limestone, $29,832,492; granite, $18,997,976; phosphate rock, $10,781,192. These nine industries employed 95 per cent. of the wage-earners engaged in producing enterprises and contributed 96 per cent. of the total value of products of mining industries.

Pennsylvania ranked first in the value of its mining products, $349,059,786. Of this the coal produced was valued at $296,424,311. Other States with a product of over $25,000,000 value were: Illinois, $76,658,974; West Virginia, $76,287,889; Michigan, $67,714,479; Ohio, $63,767,112; California, $63,382,454; Minnesota, $58,664,852; Montana, $54,991,961; Colorado, $45,680,135; Arizona, $34,217,651; Missouri, $31,667,524; Oklahoma, $25,637,892. The District of Columbia and Mississippi had no mineral production in 1909.

Mining Lands. The Thirteenth Census was the first in which an inquiry was made into the amount of land controlled by producing mines, and the results obtained are of considerable interest. In 1909, the year for which the statistics were compiled, the total acreage of all land belonging to producing mines was 24,216,000 acres. Not all of this area was in actual use, as large tracts are held in reserve. The greater part of this land is mineral and oil land, but there were also 1,139,000 acres of timber land and 1,662,000 acres of other land. This includes land which had not been surveyed and whose mineral resources were still unknown, as well as some land used for building and other purposes.

Of the total area controlled by operators of mining enterprises in 1909, more than one-half (12,695,000 acres) was connected with the petroleum and natural gas industries. Of the remainder much the largest part was reported for the coal industry. Holdings connected with bituminous mines are far more extensive than those pertaining to anthracite mines, the former amounting to 7,717,000 acres and the latter to 465,000 acres. Iron mines were third in extent, the holdings amounting to 1,313,214 acres, of which 456,000 acres were in timber and 468,924 acres were reported under "other land." The proportion of reserved land was greater under this than in any other of the mining industries. The mines producing precious metals controlled 588,263 acres, of which 469,455 acres were mineral land, 33,745 timber land, and 85,063 acres other than mineral or timber land. The phosphate rock industry reported 243,221 acres of mineral land and 92,580 of timber land. The mineral land of the copper industry totaled 126,851 acres, and 57,781 acres were timber land, while the remainder was reported as "other land." The limestone quarries controlled 128,495 acres and the lead and zinc mines, 125,322 acres.

Of the total area controlled by mine operators, 38.8 per cent. was owned by the operators themselves and the remainder held under lease. In the petroleum and natural gas industry, all but 5.4 per cent. of the land is held under lease. The two industries showing the greatest percentage of land owned are the copper industry, in which the operators owned 98.6 per cent. of the land controlled, and the phosphate rock industry, in which the percentage owned was 96.2 per cent. In the coal industry, 68.1 per cent. of the anthracite land was owned, and 73 per cent. of the bituminous land. The iron industry owned 81 per cent. of its holdings, the lead and zinc operators, 81.8 per cent., and the precious metal mines 78.4 per cent. In the quarrying industries, of the lands devoted to granite quarrying, 83.6 per cent. were owned, and of the limestone industry, 74.8 per cent.

MINNEAPOLIS. See GARBAGE AND REFUSE DISPOSAL.

MINNESOTA. POPULATION. According to the Census Bureau statistics compiled in 1912, out of a total population in 1910 of 2,075,708, the foreign-born whites numbered 543,010, compared with 504,933 in 1900. Of these, the largest number, 122,511, came from Sweden; from Germany came 109,455; from Norway, 105,258; from Austria, 37,252; from Canada, 29,592; from Finland, 26,602; from Russia, 17,517; from Denmark, 16,130; and from England, 12,136. In the City of Minneapolis, with a total population in 1910 of 301,408 there was a foreign-born white population of 85,938, compared with 60,983 in 1900. The negroes in 1910 numbered 7084 and the mulattoes, 2616. The negroes in 1890 numbered 3683 and the mulattoes 1702.

AGRICULTURE. The acreage, value, and production of the principal crops in 1911 and 1912 will be found in the following table:

		Acreage	Prod. Bu.	Value
Corn	1912	2,266,000	78,177,000	$28,925,000
	1911	2,200,000	74,140,000	39,294,000
Wheat	1912	4,325,000	67,038,000	48,938,000
	1911	4,350,000	43,935,000	40,420,000
Oats	1912	2,948,000	122,932,000	31,962,000
	1911	2,948,000	67,214,000	26,886,000
Rye	1912	262,000	6,026,000	3,013,000
	1911	240,000	4,488,000	3,501,000
Potatoes	1912	245,000	33,075,000	9,261,000
	1911	225,000	25,875,000	15,008,000
Hay	1912	1,661,000	a 2,541,000	16,262,000
	1911	799,000	a 799,000	9,508,000

a Tons.

MINERAL PRODUCTION. Minnesota ranks first among the States in the production of iron ore. It produced in 1911, 23,398,406 long tons valued at $48,447,760, compared with a product of 31,966,769 long tons valued at $78,462,560 in 1910.

MANUFACTURES. The Thirteenth Census statistics are for the calendar year 1909 and were compiled in 1912. Although Minnesota is not essentially a manufacturing State, the proportion which the value of its manufactures represented of the total value of manufacturing products in the United States, increased steadily from less than two-tenths of one per cent. in 1859 to 2 per cent. in 1909. The table herewith shows that in 1909 there were 5561 manufacturing establishments in the State, which gave employment to 104,406 persons:

	Number or Amount 1909	1904	P. C. Inc. 1904-9
Number of establishments	5,561	4,756	16.9
Persons engaged in manufactures	104,406	83,301	25.3
Proprietors and firm members	5,276	4,524	18.8
Salaried employes	14,263	9,141	56.0
Wage earners (average number)	84,767	69,636	21.7
Primary horsepower	297,670	220,934	34.7
Capital	$275,416,000	$184,903,000	49.0
Expenses	376,062,000	279,924,000	34.3
Services	62,923,000	44,876,000	40.2
Salaries	15,452,000	9,033,000	71.1
Wages	47,417,000	35,843,000	32.4
Materials	281,622,000	210,554,000	33.8
Miscellaneous	31,517,000	24,494,000	28.7
Value of products	409,420,000	307,858,000	33.0
Value of products less cost of materials	127,798,000	97,304,000	31.3

In industries connected with lumber and timber products were 20,704 wage-earners; in foundry and machine shop industries, 6002; in industries connected with railways, 8232; in flour mill and gristmill industries, 4345. The flour mill and gristmill manufactories have the largest value of product, $139,136,000; lumber and timber products, $42,353,000; slaughtering and meat-packing, $25,754,000; butter, cheese, and condensed milk, $25,287,000; printing and publishing, $15,982,000; foundry and machine shop products, $15,609,000. The total number of persons engaged in manufactures in the State in 1909 was 104,406, of whom 90,058 were male and 14,348 female. The wage-earners under 16 years of age numbered 306. The prevailing hours of labor for the great majority of wage-earners were from 54 to 60 a week; only 16.7 per cent. of the total were employed in establishments where the hours were less than 54 and only 4.1 per cent. in setablishments where they were more than 60. The largest number of wage-earners was in Minneapolis, 26,962; in St. Paul, 19,339; in Duluth, 6083, and in Winona, 2032.

EDUCATION. The number of pupils in the public schools of the State in 1912 was 448,800. The teachers numbered 15,984. There were 8917 school-houses and the school property was valued at $35,331,954. The school expenditures for the year amounted to $15,346,133. There were maintained 57 agricultural and industrial schools, 211 high schools, 204 graded schools, 2362 first-class rural schools, 1394 second-class rural schools, and 81 teachers' training departments in high schools. The permanent school fund of the State is larger than that of any other State, except Texas, and is increasing at the rate of $1,500,000 a year. This is largely on account of the royalties on iron ore. Educational progress in the State in recent years has concerned itself chiefly with the furtherance of practical education, the establishment of industrial departments in the high schools and normal schools, and the improvement of rural schools and rural school teaching. The Putnam act, passed by the legislature of 1911, provided $2500 for the establishment and maintenance of industrial and agricultural departments in high schools of the State. Thirty such schools have been designated and have qualified. These schools have special intructors in agriculture, manual training, cooking, and sewing, and have demonstration plots of at least five acres. Industrial courses have also been added to the curriculum of the five normal schools of the State. Consolidation of rural schools has been effected in different parts of the State, and 65 such schools were in operation in 1912. A rural school commissioner has been added to the Department of Public Instruction to have charge of the rural schools and direct oversight in consolidation movements. The State has engaged a health expert to travel about and demonstrate to the citizens that rational conservation of the mental and physical health of children is possible and practicable with the means already at hand. Three plans are proposed: Organization with a medical officer and a nurse or nurses; organization with a school nurse or nurses only; organization by the employment of a simple, non-medical health survey on the part of the teacher only. To make it possible for every community, however small, to possess the necessary technical knowledge, the State board of health will maintain at the State capital a "clearing house of information concerning child hygiene, medical supervision, the teaching of school hygiene, and the like."

FINANCE. The receipts for the year ending July 31, 1912, were $15,805,302. The cash balance at the beginning of the year was $3,508,491. The disbursements for the fiscal year amounted to $16,321,065, and the cash balance at the end of the year was $2,992,728. The chief sources of income are railroad 4 per cent. gross earnings tax, inheritance taxes, insurance companies taxes, express companies taxes, general State taxes, and royalties on iron ore. The chief disbursements are for State institutions, general school aid, special school aid, and the expenses of the executive departments of the State.

CHARITIES AND CORRECTIONS. The charitable and correctional institutions under the control of the State, with their average population in 1912 were as follows: Anoka Asylum, 533; Hastings Asylum, 536; Fergus Falls Hospital, 1626; Rochester Hospital, 1274; St. Peter Hospital, 1117; School for the Blind, 80; School for the Deaf, 260; School for the Feeble-minded, 1332; Owatonna Orphans' Home, 242; Red Wing Industrial School, 285; Home School for Girls, 100; Reformatory, 421; Stillwater Prison, 769; Tuberculosis Sanatorium, 85; Home for Crippled Children, 91.

POLITICS AND GOVERNMENT

The chief political interest in the State, aside from the presidential campaign, was the first trial of a new primary law for the nomination of candidates for State offices. Primaries were held in May for the election of delegates to the Republican national convention. In these the Roosevelt forces were victorious. Of the 81 counties in the State, Roosevelt carried 67, Taft 9, and La Follette, 5. On May 16 the Republican State convention instructed the 24 delegates of the State to vote for Theodore Roosevelt in the national convention. The Democrats in convention for the election of delegates to the Democratic national convention instructed the delegates to vote for Woodrow Wilson. On July 30 the Progressive party held its first convention at Minneapolis, and delegates were elected to the Progressive national convention. Primaries for the nomination of State officers under the new law were held on September 17. The main State-wide contest was between Governor A. O. Eberhart, who was seeking renomination, and five other Republican candidates for the office. The Democratic candidates were C. M. Andrist and P. M. Ringdal. In the primaries Governor Eberhart was renominated by the Republicans, and Mr. Ringdal by the Democrats. The successful candidates for the United States Senate were Knute Nelson, Rep., and Daniel W. Lawler, Dem. The Progressive party on September 21 held a convention and nominated P. V. Collins for governor, and other State officers. The election of November 5 resulted as follows: For President, Roosevelt, 125,856 votes, Wilson, 106,426, Taft, 64,344, Debs, 27,505, Chafin, 7886, and Reimer, 2212. For governor, Eberhart received 129,688 votes, Ringdal, Dem., 99,659, and Collins, Progressive, 33,465.

LEGISLATION. An important measure passed at the legislative session of 1912 was the State primary election law for the nomination of all State officers. (See ELECTORAL REFORM.) This law embraces the first and second choice that is embodied in other recent legislation on this subject following a somewhat similar law in Wisconsin. The latter also provides that the justices of the supreme court, judges of the district, probate and municipal courts, county superintendents of schools, and municipal officers in cities of the first-class containing a population of more than fifty thousand, shall be nominated upon separate non-partisan ballots. An act, unusually strict in its provisions, relating to corrupt practices at primaries and elections was passed. A joint resolution was adopted ratifying the amendment to the Constitution of the United States providing for the election of senators by popular vote and also a resolution ratifying the amendment to the federal Constitution providing for an income tax. A measure was enacted amending the law as to the employment of children (see CHILD LABOR), and another measure regulating foreign fraternal benefit societies doing business in the State.

STATE GOVERNMENT. Governor, Adolph O. Eberhart; Lieutenant-Governor, J. A. Burnquist; Secretary of State, Julius A. Schmahl; Auditor, S. G. Iverson; Treasurer, Walter J. Smith; Attorney-General, L. A. Smith; Adjutant-General, Fred B. Wood; Superintendent of Education, C. G. Schultz; Commissioner of Insurance, J. A. Preus; Commissioner of Agriculture, J. S. Maxfield—all Republicans.

JUDICIARY. Supreme Court: Chief Justice, Calvin L. Brown, Rep.; Associate Justices, Andrew Holt, Rep.; C. L. Brunn, Dem.; P. E. Brown, Rep.; Oscar Hallam, Rep.; Clerk, I. A. Caswell, Rep.

STATE LEGISLATURE, 1913. Republicans, Senate, 42; House, 90; joint ballot, 132. Democrats, Senate, 20; House, 26; joint ballot, 46. Republican majority, Senate, 22; House, 64; joint ballot, 86.

The representatives in Congress will be found in the section *Congress*, article UNITED STATES.

MINNESOTA, UNIVERSITY OF. A State university for higher education, founded in

1869. The enrollment in all departments of the university in the autumn of 1912 was 6-953. Of these, 4055 were in the university courses and 2898 in secondary (agricultural) schools and extension course. The faculty numbered 499. Among the noteworthy changes in the faculty during the year were the following appointments: William R. Vance, dean of the law school; E. M. Morgan, professor of law; Dr. Margaret Sweeney, professor in the department of rhetoric and dean of women; J. Anna Norris, director of health and physical education for women; Lieut. James B. Woolnough, professor of military science; A. V. Storm, professor of agricultural education; Ernest W. Major, associate professor of animal nutrition; Arthur C. Smith professor of animal husbandry; A. B. Recknagel, professor of lumbering; and Harriet Sewall, librarian, school of agriculture. Among the resignations and retirements were the following: Henry T. Eddy, as dean of the graduate school and professor of mathematics and mechanics; Arthur E. Haynes, professor of mathematics; Willis M. West, professor of history; Major E. L. Butts, professor of military science; and Ada B. Comstock, professor in rhetoric and dean of women. The productive funds of the university amounted at the end of the collegiate year 1912 to $1,506,136. There are about 160,000 volumes in the library. President, George E. Vincent, LL.D.

MINOR PLANETS. See ASTRONOMY.

MIQUELON. See SAINT PIERRE.

MISSISSIPPI. POPULATION. According to the Census Bureau' statistics in 1912, out of a total population of 1,797,114 in 1910 the foreign-born whites numbered 9389, compared with 7625 in 1900. Of these, the largest number, 2130 came from Italy; 1663 from Germany. Other European countries were represented by smaller numbers. Mississippi has the smallest proportion of foreign-born white population of all the States. The negroes in 1910 numbered 1,009,487 and the mulattoes, 171,005. It will be noted that the negroes constitute by far the larger proportion of the population of the State; in 1890 they numbered 742,599 and the mulattoes, 85,166.

AGRICULTURE. The acreage, value, and production of the principal crops in 1911 and 1912 are given in the following table:

		Acreage	Prod. Bu.	Value
Corn	1912	3,106,000	56,840,000	$40,356,000
	1911	2,850,000	54,150,000	38,988,000
Wheat	1912	8,000	96,000	93,000
	1911	9,000	108,000	108,000
Oats	1912	113,000	1,966,000	1,180,000
	1911	130,000	2,392,000	1,555,000
Rice	1912	2,200	77,000	69,000
	1911	2,100	76,000	59,000
Potatoes	1912	10,000	890,000	801,000
	1911	9,000	747,000	859,000
Hay	1912	201,000	a 297,000	3,712,000
	1911	100,000	a 150,000	1,650,000
Cotton	1912	....	883,678	....
	1911	....	c 996,601	....

a Tons. c Bales.

MANUFACTURES. The Thirteenth Census included statistics of manufactures. These are for the calendar year 1909. The most important general results of the census are given in the table below. The most important industry in point of number of wage-earners employed and value of the product was the lumber and timber industry. In this 33,397 wage-earners were employed and the value of the product was $42,793,000. The oil, cotton seed, and cake industry gave employment to 2503 wage-earners and the value of the product was $15,966,000. There were no other industries in which the value of the product exceeded $5,000,000. In the cotton industries were employed 2645 wage-earners and the value of the product was $3,102,000. In the fertilizing industries were employed 449 and the value of the product was $2,125,000. The total number of wage-earners in the State in 1909 was 40,326, of whom 1058 were under 16 years of age. Of these, 447 were females. The prevailing hours of labor for nearly half the wage-earners of the State are 60 hours a week, and a large proportion work between 60 and 72 hours a week. In the city of Meridian was the largest number of wage-earners, 1524; in Vicksburg, 1202; in Jackson, 799; in Hattiesburg, 648, and in Natchez, 428. The following table shows the increase in manufacturing in the five-year period 1904-1909:

	Number or Amount 1909	1904	P. C. Inc. 1904-9
Number of establishments	2,598	1,520	70.9
Persons engaged in manufactures	56,761	42,966	32.1
Proprietors and firm members	2,974	1,588	87.3
Salaried employees	3,403	2,688	26.6
Wage earners (average No.)	50,384	38,690	30.
Primary horsepower	206,222	110,338	86.
Capital	$72,393,000	$50,256,000	44.
Expenses	68,707,000	49,074,000	40.
Services	22,422,000	17,417,000	28.2
Salaries	3,654,000	2,598,000	40.6
Wages	18,768,000	14,819,000	26.5
Materials	36,926,000	25,801,000	43.1
Miscellaneous	9,359,000	5,856,000	59.8
Value of products	80,555,000	57,451,000	40.2
Value of products less cost of materials	43,629,000	31,650,000	37.8

FINANCE. The report of the treasurer showed cash on hand October 1, 1911, of $572.047 The receipts for the fiscal year amounted to $4,179,307 and the disbursements to $4,500,330, leaving cash on hand October 1, 1912, of $250,999. The total bonded indebtedness of the State amounted to $1,842,899. The chief sources of revenue are State and county taxes on personal property and privilege of licenses. The chief expenditures are for State institutions, colleges, and common schools.

CHARITIES AND CORRECTIONS. The Charitable and correctional institutions of the State include: The Confederate Soldiers' Home, Beauvoir; the Deaf and Dumb Institution, Jackson; the Blind Institution, Jackson; State Insane Hospital, Jackson; the East Mississippi Insane Hospital, Meridian; the State Charity Hospital, Vicksburg; the State Charity Hospital, Natchez; and the Mattie Hersee Hospital, Meridian. In 1910 the legislature authorized the establishment of a State charity hospital at Jackson, and this institution was opened to receive patients in 1912.

POLITICS AND GOVERNMENT

The legislature met in 1912 and the most important measures enacted will be found in the paragraph *Legislation* below. On January

17, James K. Vardaman was elected senator to succeed Senator Leroy Percy. Mr. Vardaman had been previously chosen in senatorial primary. On March 5 the legislature demanded the resignation of Senator Percy, who was defeated in 1911 in the senatorial contest by Mr. Vardaman. Senator Percy refused to resign. In a letter written in reply to the request of the legislature, he declared that he had been elected by a former legislature and that the legislature had no authority to ask for his resignation nor any reason for asking it. He referred to the alleged promise which he was charged with having made that he would resign if he failed of reëlection in the primary. He explained that his pledge that he would resign had reference to his request for an extraordinary primary to be held in 1910 instead of 1911. This offer he declared was not accepted. The letter included the following statement: "I shall pay no heed to your resolution. I did not receive my commission from you; I will not lay it down at your behest; but I shall continue to do my duty to the people of Mississippi in the United States Senate as God gives me to see it, conscious that my course will meet the approval of the brain and manhood of my State." Senator Percy's resignation was asked for by the Vardaman faction of the legislature which held the power. This same majority assumed to take from the court the adjudication of a suit brought by the attorney-general against James K. Vardaman, for recovery of trust moneys, received by him when governor and unaccounted for. This suit was dismissed by the new attorney-general after the governor and the chancellor had refused to sanction dismissal.

The delegates sent by the State to the National Republican convention were pledged to vote for President Taft. Democratic preference primaries were held on May 7 and the delegates were pledged to Mr. Underwood. The Progressive convention was held at Jackson on July 31 and delegates were chosen to the National Progressive convention. Of the 150 delegates only three were white. The appearance of these delegates at the Progressive convention resulted in some friction. See PRESIDENTIAL CAMPAIGN.

There is practically no Republican party in Mississippi, and there was no question, therefore, as to the result of the election on November 5. The vote was as follows: Wilson, 57,227; Roosevelt, 3645; Taft, 1595, and Debs, 2061. Wilson's plurality was 53,582. There was no election for governor or State officers in 1912 as Governor Brewer's term does not expire until 1916.

OTHER EVENTS. The year was signalized in State and valley history by a spring flood in the Mississippi River which discharged a larger volume of water than any since the official record was established. In spite of the extensive enlargements of levees in recent years there was a break in the levee at Beulah Lake in Bolivar county which inundated large sections in that county, and half a dozen others; a number of lives were lost and hundreds of livestock drowned. The water was so late in sudsiding that much of the inundated land was not planted.

LEGISLATION. The legislature of 1912 passed an unusual number of important measures. Among these were the following: Several important laws relating to taxation; a measure providing for the commission form of government in cities which adopt the act; a measure of unusual interest prohibiting hotels, restaurants, cafés, dining cars, railroad companies, and sleeping-car companies from allowing tips to be given to employees, to prohibit all persons from giving tips and to prohibit employees from receiving them. A measure was enacted making railroad corporations liable for damages for fire set directly or indirectly by locomotives and to give such corporations an insurable interest in the property along the line of the road. A measure was passed regulating the employment of children in mills, factories, etc., providing that no male under the age of thirteen or boy under the age of twelve shall be thus employed, and no boy under sixteen or female under eighteen shall work more than 8 hours a day nor more than 48 hours a week, or at night. (See the article on CHILD LABOR.) An act was adopted abolishing Greek letter fraternities, sororities, and secret orders among students in the University of Mississippi and in all other educational institutions supported in whole or in part by the State. This is probably the first legislation of this nature ever passed. A measure was enacted providing for regular annual sessions of the legislature. The laws of the State against trusts were amended. A joint resolution was adopted providing for an amendment to the constitution to bring about a session of the legislature on the Tuesday following the first Monday in January, 1912, and every two years thereafter. Another resolution proposed an amendment that nine or more jurors in civil suits may agree on a verdict and return it as the verdict of the jury. A resolution proposing an amendment to the constitution providing for the initiative and referendum to be voted upon in the November election, was adopted (see above).

STATE GOVERNMENT. Governor, Earl Brewer; Lieutenant-Governor, Theodore G. Bilbo; Secretary of State, J. W. Power; Teasurer, P. S. Stovall; Auditor, D. L. Thompson; Superintendent of Education, J. N. Powers; Attorney-General, Ross A. Collins; Adjutant-General, Arthur Fridge; Land Commissioner, J. H. Brown; Commissioner of Agriculture, H. E. Blakeslee; Commissioner of Insurance, T. M. Henry—all Democrats.

JUDICIARY. Supreme Court: Chief Justice, S. Smith; Associate Justices, S. C. Cook and R. F. Reed; Clerk, George C. Myers—all Democrats.

STATE LEGISLATURE, 1913. The State legislature is wholly Democratic.

The representatives in Congress will be found in the article UNITED STATES, section *Congress*.

MISSISSIPPI RIVER FLOODS. In the latter part of March and early in April, 1912, occurred the most disastrous floods on record in the Mississippi River and its tributaries. The flooded area covered 15,000 square miles, or a tract larger than the combined area of the States of Maryland and Delaware or of Vermont and New Hampshire. All the States bordering on the lower Mississippi were affected by these floods. Many lives were lost and the damage to property has been estimated at nearly $45,000,000. The overflow of the river caused twelve crevasses in the levees which border it. Relief was given to the sufferers by the United States government, by the Red Cross Society, and by other agencies. Appropriations amounting to $1,240,000 were made by Congress for the purpose of providing tents, rations, and other necessities. The work of distributing this relief was organized and carried out by the quartermasters' and subsistence departments of the army, assisted by naval revenue and militia officers, by the Red Cross, and by local citizens' committees. For a considerable period of time 185,000 persons were furnished daily rations, 20,000 persons were furnished shelter, and 50,000 head of livestock were provided with forage.

The floods resulted from a series of unusual storms which visited the lower Missouri and Mississippi valleys and the pressure of the water proved too much for the levees in many places. See Red Cross Society and Mississippi.

MISSOURI. Population. According to the Census Bureau statistics compiled during 1912, out of the total population in the State in 1910, 3,293,335, there were 157,452 negroes and 44,690 mulattoes. In 1890 the negroes numbered 150,184 and the mulattoes 35,445. The total foreign-born white population of the State in 1910 was 228,896, compared with 215,775 in 1900. The largest proportion of foreign-born whites came from Germany, 88,138; from Ireland, 23,289; from Russia, 21,490; from Austria, 16,546; from England, 13,749; from Italy, 12,474, and from Hungary, 11,067. Nearly all the other countries of Europe are represented in the foreign-born population.

Agriculture. The acreage, value, and production of the principal crops are given in the following table:

		Acreage	Prod. Bu.	Value
Corn	1912	7,622,000	243,904,000	$112,196,000
	1911	7,400,000	192,400,000	115,440,000
Wheat	1912	1,900,000	23,750,000	21,375,000
	1911	2,300,000	35,110,000	31,777,000
Oats	1912	1,125,000	37,125,000	12,994,000
	1911	1,200,000	17,760,000	7,992,000
Rye	1912	15,000	222,000	178,000
	1911	16,000	226,000	190,000
Potatoes	1912	95,000	7,980,000	5,506,000
	1911	95,000	2,565,000	2,616,000
Hay	1912	3,187,000	a 4,143,000	40,601,000
	1911	2,430,000	a 1,458,000	19,391,000
Tobacco	1912	6,000	b 6,000,000	720,000
	1911	6,000	b 4,800,000	576,000

a Tons. b Pounds.

Mineral Production. The output of coal in the State in 1911 was 3,760,607 short tons, valued at $6,431,066. This is a notable gain over the product of 1910, and exceeds the output of the State in any other year except 1907. The production of 1910 was 2,982,433 tons. The remarkable decrease in that year was largely on account of labor troubles. In 1911 the industry was practically free from these disturbances, and an increased output was the result. The coal mines of the State in 1911 gave employment to 9999 men, against 9691 in 1910.

There were produced in the State in 1911, 72,788 long tons of iron ore valued at $153,676, compared with a product of 78,341 long tons valued at $168,697 in 1910.

Manufactures. The Thirteenth Census statistics are for the calendar year 1909 and were compiled in 1912. The State ranks high in manufacturing, due largely to the activity of the industries of St. Louis and Kansas City. The table herewith shows considerable increase in the manufacturing industries in the five-year period, 1904-1909:

	Number or Amount 1909	1904	P. C. Inc. 1904-9
Number of establishments	8,375	6,464	29.6
Persons engaged in manufactures	185,705	156,586	18.6
Proprietors and firm members	8,226	6,299	30.6
Salaried employees	24,486	17,119	43.0
Wage earners (average number)	152,993	133,167	14 9
Primary horsepower	340,467	247,861	37.4
Capital	$444,343,000	$379,369,000	17.1
Expenses	522,276,000	387,427,000	34.8
Services	109,837,000	85,646,000	28.2
Salaries	28,994,000	19,002,000	52.6
Wages	80,843,000	66,644,000	21.3
Materials	354,411,000	252,258,000	40.5
Miscellaneous	58,028,000	49,523,000	17.2
Value of products	574,111,000	439,549,000	30.6
Value of products less cost of material	219,700,000	187,291,000	17.3

From this table it will be seen that in 1909 there were in the State 8375 manufacturing establishments, which gave employment to an average of 185,705 persons. The largest number of persons employed in any industry was found in those relating to boots and shoes, 17,396. Those engaged in the lumber and timber manufactures numbered 13,522; in printing and publishing, 10,790; in industries connected with railways, 8121; and in the manufacture of clothing, 7994. The value of the product was largest in the slaughtering and meat-packing industries. This was $79,581,000. The value of the boots and shoes produced was $48,751,000; flour and gristmill products, $44,508,000; printing and publishing, $29,651,000; malt liquors, $27,447,000. The largest number of wage-earners was found in St. Louis, 87,371; in Kansas City, 14,643; in St. Joseph, 5390; and in Hannibal 2445. The value of the products of the industrial establishments of St. Louis was $328,495,313, and of Kansas City, $54,704,570.

Charities and Corrections. The charitable and correctional institutions of the State include thirteen separately governed charitable and penal institutions, county jails, and almshouses or infirmaries in practically all counties of the State, and special institutions of this character controlled by some of the larger cities. There is also a general system of public relief of the poor in their homes, amounting to somewhat less than $250,000 annually, and juvenile courts are established in the six largest urban districts of the State. In the thirteen State institutions about 12,000 inmates are enrolled; in the county almshouses, about 4600, and in the county jails, about 13,600. About 7000 persons receive public aid in their homes annually. In the State institutions about $6,000,000 are invested and about $3,000,000 in county jails and almshouses. The State Board of Charities and Corrections will present to the legislature in 1913, forty measures concerning the care of the unfortunates in the State. Among these are: Appropriation for a reformatory; provision for enlarging the Missouri Colony for the Feeble-minded at Marshall, and measures for bringing about a scientific, non-partisan, honest administration of the charitable and penal institutions and better supervision and care for the dependent and neglected children of the State.

POLITICS AND GOVERNMENT

The legislature did not meet in 1912 as the sessions are biennial and the last was held in 1911. The next session begins on January 8, 1913.

Missouri took a conspicuous part in the political campaign of 1912. The leading candidate for the Democratic nomination up to the holding of the national convention was Champ Clark, one of the State's representatives in Congress and Speaker of the House. Governor Hadley was one of the leading Progressive leaders in the Republican pre-convention campaign and was one of the seven governors who signed the letter urging Mr. Roosevelt to be a candidate. He was in the first days of the convention floor leader of the Roosevelt forces, and made such an impression upon the delegates that he was spoken of as a compromise candidate for President and as a candidate for Vice-President. Governor Hadley, however, did not join the movement for a new party but gave his support to President Taft in the campaign following the convention.

The Republican State convention for the nomination of national delegates was controlled by the Progressive forces and the eight delegates of the State were instructed to vote for Mr. Roosevelt. The Democratic delegates were naturally pledged to Mr. Clark and voted steadily for him at the convention until after the final vote which nominated Governor Wilson had been taken.

In spite of the fact that Governor Hadley declined to join the Progressive party it continued an aggressive campaign following the Republican national conventon, and on July 31 held a convention in which delegates were sent to Chicago to the National Progressive convention. It was decided there to hold a State convention on September 3 for the nomination of State officers. This action was largely taken through the advice of Mr. Roosevelt, who in the early part of September made a series of addresses in the State. At this convention, Judge Albert D. Nortoni of the St. Louis Court of Appeals was nominated for governor. Among the planks inserted in the platform were declarations in favor of woman suffrage, preferential presidential primaries, direct election of senators, and the initiative, referendum, and recall. Primaries for the nomination of State officers had been previously held on August 6 by the Democratic and Republican parties. In these elections Elliott W. Major was nominated by the Democrats and John C. McKinley by the Republicans. The election of November 5 resulted as follows: For President, Wilson, 330,947 votes; Taft, 207,49'; Roosevelt, 123,111; Debs, 28,145; Chafin, 5222; and Reimer, 1778. Governor Wilson's plurality was 123,456. For governor the vote was as follows: Major, Dem., 337,019; McKinley, Rep., 217,817; Nortoni, Prog., 109,146; Ward, Socialist, 28,145. The Democrats controlled the legislature by a majority of 100 on joint ballot.

OTHER EVENTS. On April 2, municipal elections were held in the State. Mayor Brown of Kansas City was defeated by Henry L. Jost, Democrat.

In July the house committee on elections of the House of Representatives by a vote of 6 to 3, held that Theron E. Catlin, Republican representative from St. Louis, should be unseated and that Patrick Gill, his Democratic opponent, should be seated in his place. The committee decided that Catlin's election was invalid because it was secured by a lavish expenditure of money. It was alleged that his father had spent $13,000 for him in the campaign. His majority was 1200. This action of the committee was upheld by the House and Mr. Catlin was unseated.

STATE GOVERNMENT. Governor, E. W. Major; Lieutenant-Governor, W. R. Painter; Secretary of State, Cornelius Roach; Auditor, John P. Gordon; Treasurer, E. P. Deal; Attorney-General, John T. Barker; Superintendent of Education, William P. Evans—all Democrats except Evans.

JUDICIARY. Supreme Court: Chief Justice, Leroy B. Valliant, Dem.; Associate Justices, Henry Lamm, Rep.; Walter W. Graves, Dem.; A. M. Woodson, Dem.; H. W. Bond, Dem.; C. B. Faris, Dem.; R. F. Walker, Dem.; John C. Brown, Rep.; Clerk, J. D. Allen, Dem.

STATE LEGISLATURE, 1913. Democrats, Senate, 25; House, 113; joint ballot, 138. Republicans, Senate, 9; House, 28; joint ballot, 37. Progressive, Senate, 0; House 1; joint ballot, 1. Democratic majority, Senate, 16; House, 84; joint ballot, 100.

The representatives in Congress will be found in the section *Congress*, article UNITED STATES.

MISSOURI, UNIVERSITY OF. An institution of higher education at Columbia, Missouri, founded 1839. The number of students enrolled in the university, including the School of Mines and Metallurgy, a division of the university, for the session 1911-12, was 3063. The members of the faculty of regular teaching grade number 238. Few changes have occurred in the faculty. The productive funds of the university amounted to $1,264,839, and the total income to about $858,768. The larger part of this appropriation was by the State. The library contains approximately 152,193 volumes. This number includes 21,000 volumes shelved in the State historical library. At Columbia new buildings for manual arts and the experimental school of education, costing $15,000 and $5000 respectively, have been completed. New buildings for physics and agricultural chemistry costing $100,000 and $60,000 respectively, are being completed and will be ready for occupancy in February, 1913. At Rolla (school of mines and metallurgy) a library and assembly hall costing $65,000 is practically completed. The enrollment for the session 1912-13 on October 15 was 2367 (includes 680 enrolled in summer session). Corresponding figures for 1911-12 were 2259. President Albert R. Hill, LL. D.

MOFFAT, GRAHAM. See DRAMA.

MOLINARI, GUSTAVE. A Belgian political economist, died January 28, 1912. He was born at Liège in 1819. He studied medicine and was for a time physician at Brussels, at the same time writing works on homeopathic medicine. He later removed to Paris, where he gained some distinction as a radical journalist, but was obliged by political conditions to return to Belgium. He was appointed professor of political economy in the Musée Royal de l'Industrie Belge. In 1874 he was elected corresponding member of the Academy of Moral and Political Sciences of the Institut de France. In 1881 he became editor of the *Journal des Économistes* at Paris. He also took part in establishing several other economic journals. Among his published writings are the following: *Questions d'économie politique et de droit publique* (2 vols., 1861); *L'évolution économique du XIXème siècle* (1880); *Les lois naturelles de l'économie politique* (1867), and *Comment se résoudra la question sociale* (1896).

MONACO. A hereditary constitutional monarchy (constitution of January 8, 1911), covering 1.5 square kilometers and having a population of 19,121. Population of Monaco (town), 2410; of La Condamine, 6218; of Monte Carlo 3794. There is no cultivation. Roman Catholicism is the only creed tolerated. The revenue, chiefly derived from the gambling concession at Monte Carlo, is spent largely for improvements. Reigning prince (1912), Albert (born 1848); heir-apparent, Prince Louis (born 1870).

MONEY TRUST. See TRUSTS.

MONGOLIA. See CHINA.

MONISTIC SYSTEM. See PHILOSOPHY.

MONOD, GABRIEL JACQUES JEAN. A French historian, died April 10, 1912. He was born in Havre in 1844. His studies were carried on at the École Normale and in Italy and Germany. In 1869 he began teaching at the École des Hautes Études, where he became director of the historical-philological section. He became in 1905 professor at the Collége de France. He was editor of the *Revue Critique* and was one of the founders of the *Revue Historique*. Among his published writings are: *Allemands et Français* (1871); *Études critiques sur les sources de l'histoire merovingienne* (1872-85); *Jules Michelet* (1875); *Bibliographie de l'histoire de France* (1888); and *Les maîtres de l'histoire, Renan, Taine, Michelet* (1894); *Portraits et souvenirs* (1897); *Souvenirs d'adolescence* (1903); *Jules Michelet* (1905).

MONOPLANE. See AERONAUTICS.

MONTANA. POPULATION. According to the Census Bureau statistics compiled during 1912, out of the total population in the State in 1910, 376,053, the foreign-born whites numbered 91,644, compared with 62,373 in 1900. Of these, the largest number 10,598 came from Canada; 8574 from Germany; 8469 from Austria; 7153 from Norway; 6408 from Sweden; 8980 from England; 9469 from Ireland; and from Finland, 4111. Other European countries are represented by smaller numbers. The negroes in the State in 1910 numbered 1834, and the mulattoes, 611. In 1890 the negroes numbered 1490 and the mulattoes, 404.

AGRICULTURE. The acreage, value, and production of the principal crops in 1911 and 1912 are shown in the table in the next column.

		Acreage	Prod. Bu.	Value
Corn	1912	24,000	612,000	$ 428,000
	1911	20,000	530,000	424,000
Wheat	1912	803,000	19,346,000	12,381,000
	1911	429,000	12,299,000	9,470,000
Oats	1912	476,000	22,848,000	7,997,000
	1911	425,000	21,165,000	8,466,000
Rye	1912	10,000	235,000	141,000
	1911	8,000	184,000	132,000
Potatoes	1912	37,000	6,105,000	2,442,000
	1911	27,000	4,050,000	2,997,000
Hay	1912	640,000	a 1,216,000	10,093,000
	1911	612,000	a 1,224,000	12,240,000

a Tons.

MINERAL PRODUCTION. The gold production of the State in 1911 was $3,710,571, a decrease of $19,915 from the production of 1910. The production from the placer mines increased, while that from dry or siliceous ores fell off. The production from copper ores remained about the same as in 1910, and that from lead and zinc ores decreased. The silver output in the State in 1911 was 11,985,196 fine ounces, against 12,161,857 fine ounces in 1910. The copper ores, mostly from Butte, produced 9,597,751 ounces in 1911 and the dry or siliceous ores 1,613,253 ounces.

The output of blister copper in the State in 1911 was 271,814,491 pounds, compared with 283,078,473 pounds in 1910. In the copper production the State is surpassed only by Arizona. At the close of 1910 the State had yielded 5,598,253,884 pounds, or 34 per cent. of the total output of the United States since 1845. This gives it first rank in total production among the copper-producing States. Three copper smelting plants were operated in 1911. These were at Butte, Anaconda, and Great Falls.

The production of coal in the State in 1911 was 2,975,358 tons, valued at $5,339,058. These figures showed an increase over the production of 1910, which was 2,920,970 short tons, valued at $5,329,322. The coal production of the State has increased steadily during the last three years, the gains being due chiefly to the development in the Bull Mountain field, which was opened in 1908 after the construction of the Chicago, Milwaukee, and Puget Sound Railway through it. Montana was the only one of the Rocky Mountain States which showed an increase in coal production in 1911. There were employed in the coal mines of the State in that year 3866 men. There were only two labor disturbances during the year and these were not important.

MANUFACTURES. The Thirteenth Census included statistics of manufactures in the State. These figures cover the calendar year 1909. The chief results of the census are summarized in the table on the next page. The principal industries of the State are mining, agriculture, and stock-raising, and the principal manufacturing industries are those supplemental to its mining interests. The largest number of persons employed in a single industry are those connected with lumber and timber products. In these industries 3106 persons were engaged. In these industries also the largest amount of capital was invested, $6,334,000.

FINANCE. The receipts for the fiscal year ending November 30, 1912, were $4,046,691. The expenditures for the fiscal year amounted to $3,568,131. The balance at the end of the year was $1,401,641. The chief source of income is the property tax, and the chief expenditure is for the support of reform and educational institutions.

CHARITIES AND CORRECTIONS. The State has three institutions which are charitable, the Soldiers' Home, Columbia Falls, where there are about 75 veterans enjoying the comforts of the home. The national government shares in

	1909	1904	P. C. Inc. 1904-9
Number of establishments	677	382	77.2
Persons engaged in manufactures	13,694	10,196	34.3
Proprietors and firm members	659	334	97.3
Salaried employees	1,380	905	52.5
Wage earners (average number)	11,655	8,957	30.1
Primary horsepower	90,402	46,736	93.4
Capital	$44,588,000	$52,590,000	—15.2
Expenses	66,830,000	55,140,000	21.2
Services	12,955,000	10,158,000	27.5
Salaries	2,054,000	1,506,000	36.4
Wages	10,901,000	8,652,000	26.0
Materials	49,180,000	40,930,000	20.2
Miscellaneous	4,695,000	4,052,000	15.8
Value of products	73,272,000	66,415,000	10.3
Value added by manufacture (value of products less cost of materials)	24,092,000	25,485,000	—5.5

the support of this home; the State Orphans' Home, Twin Bridges, where there are about 150 children, ranging in age from a few days to 16 years. The State provides generously for the maintenance and education of these children and also seeks to find homes throughout its domain for them; and, the State Industrial School, Miles City, where there are about 75 boys and 5 girls. This institution is correctional and receives children, upon commitment by the district courts, between the ages of eight years and eighteen years. It is very well equipped for industrial and manual training.

Politics and Government

The State legislature did not meet in 1912 as the sessions are biennial and the last was held in 1911. The next session begins January 6, 1913.

Political interest in the State in 1912 was increased by the fact that Senator Dixon was one of the most prominent leaders of the Progressive party and was the active campaign manager of Mr. Roosevelt throughout the campaign. See Presidential Campaign. The Republican State convention held in March elected delegates pledged to vote for President Taft. A meeting of the Progressive Republicans was held at Helena in April. The Democratic State convention on May 29 selected eight delegates to the national convention and instructed them to vote for Champ Clark for President. On July 30 the Progressive party held its first convention at Helena and elected delegates to the National Progressive convention at Chicago. The Progressive party held a convention for the nomination of State officers on September 7. Frank H. Edwards was nominated for governor. The platform adopted by the convention urged a complete reform of taxation in the State, arbitration of all labor disputes, prohibition of child labor, direct primary and direct election of United States senators. The Democrats and Republicans had already nominated candidates for State offices. These were Stewart, Democrat, and Wilson, Republican. The election on November 5 resulted as follows: For President, Wilson, 27,941 votes; Roosevelt, 22,456; Taft, 18,512; Debs, 10,855, and Chafin, 32. Governor Wilson's plurality was 5485. For governor, Stewart, Dem., received 25,375 votes; Wilson, Rep., 22,809; Edwards, Prog., 18,858, and Duncan, Soc., 12,534. The legislature is Democratic by a majority of 25 on joint ballot.

Other Events. Presidential elections were held on April 2. In Butte, where the mayor is a Socialist, the Socialists carried only one of the eight wards, and in Lewiston lost the only ward in which they were successful in 1911.

State Government. Governor, Samuel V. Stewart, Dem.; lieutenant-governor, W. W. McDowell, Dem.; secretary of state, A. M. Alderson, Dem.; attorney-general, D. M. Kelly, Dem.; treasurer, W. C. Rae, Dem.; auditor, W. Keating, Dem.; superintendent public instruction, H. A. Davee, Dem.; railroad commissioners, J. H. Hall, Dem., D. Boyle, Rep., E. A. Morley, Rep.

Judiciary. Supreme Court: Chief justice, Theodore Brantley; justices, Henry C. Smith, William L. Holloway; clerk, John T. Athey—all Republicans.

State Legislature, 1913. Senate, Democrats 16, Republicans 13, Pogressives 2; Democratic majority, 3. House, Democrats 45, Republicans 23, Progressives 16, Socialists 1; Democratic majority 22. Joint ballot, Democrats 61, Republicans 36, Progressives 18, Socialists 1; Democratic majority 25.

The representatives in Congress will be found in the section *Congress*, article United States.

MONTENEGRO. A European monarchy, hereditary and constitutional; a Balkan state. Area, 9080 sq. kilometers (3506 sq. miles); population, 285,000 (31 per sq. km.). The majority of the population belong to the Greek Orthodox church. Cettinje (5300 inhabitants) is the capital; Podgoritza has 10,053, Dulcigno 5081; Antivari, 2317. It is a mountainous, wooded country, with cultivable tracts where agriculture is carried on. The chief exports are skins (422,537 kronen in 1909), wool (364,246), horses (315,387), cattle (235,478), olive oil (230,967), sheep (63,113), etc.; total exports for the year, 2,435,550 kronen. Total imports, 6,181,369 kronen, distributed as follows: 3,063,053 kronen from Austria-Hungary, 1,384,804 from Italy, 947,521 from Turkey, 316,904 from France, 183,382 from Germany, 178,413 from the United Kingdom, 107,292 from other countries. Vessels entered (1911), 22, of 5030 tons. A railway runs from Antivari to Lake Scutari. The budget for 1912 estimates the revenue at 3,609,000 kronen and the expenditure at 4,187,126. Reigning sovereign, Nicholas I. (born 1841), father of the queen of Italy. Heir-apparent, Prince Danilo (born 1871). Premier, minister of war and of eign affairs (1912), Gen. M. Martinovitch

Army. While the army of Montenegro was organized on a militia basis, yet it takes a larger proportion of the population than any other European country, and in the Balkan War played an important part, making the first move against the Turks. Every Montenegrin is liable to military service from 18 years of age, spending two years in the recruit class, where he receives a maximum of six months' training each year, then thirty-three years in the active army, where a maximum of fifteen days' training each year is scheduled, and the remaining ten years in the reserve. The organization consisted of four divisions of infantry, three of which were composed of three brigades and one of two brigades, making a total of fifty-seven battalions. There is also a brigade of artillery, which, in addition to its armament of old-pattern guns, received some new Canet field pieces previous to the war. The field army consisted of about 60,000, but had neither cavalry nor organized transport service. The territorial headquarters were maintained at Cettinjé, Podgoritza, Niksitch, and Kolashine.

For history, see TURKEY AND THE BALKAN PEOPLES.

MONTGOMERY, THOMAS HARRISON, JR. An American zoölogist, died March, 1912. He was born in New York in 1873 and studied at the University of Pennsylvania from 1889 to 1891. He then studied in Berlin, where he received the degree of Ph. D. in 1894. From 1898 to 1903 he was professor of biology at the University of Texas. He then returned to the University of Pennsylvania, where he was professor of zoölogy from 1908 to the time of his death. He was a member of many learned societies. He contributed about eighty scientific monographs on biological subjects. He was the author of *Analysis of Racial Descent in Animals* (1906).

MONTSERRAT. A presidency of the Leeward Islands (q. v.). Plymouth, the chief town, has 1461 inhabitants. The cultivation of sugar in the island has declined, and that of limes is being yearly extended; 107,811 gallons of raw and 6270 of concentrated lime juice, 20 tons of citrate of lime, and 5670 crates of fresh limes were exported in 1910. Other fruits, cacao, and cotton are grown.

	1907-8	1908-9	1909-10	1910-11
Imports	£ 33,756	£ 40,122	£ 31,343	£ 38,106
Exports	35,103	45,304	31,569	34,393
Revenue	10,233	10,950	10,612	12,262
Expenditure	8,515	8,790	7,807	11,366
Shipping* ...	308,916	384,472	362,158	260,226

* Tonnage entered and cleared.

Customs revenue (1910-11), £8509; public debt (December 31, 1909), £11,100. Commissioner (1912), Lieut.-Col. W. B. Davidson-Houston. See LEEWARD ISLANDS.

MOOSE JAW CITY COMMISSIONER. See MUNICIPAL GOVERNMENT.

MORAL EDUCATION. See PHILOSOPHY.

MORAL EDUCATION CONGRESS. See EDUCATION.

MORAVIANS, also called UNITED BRETHREN (*Unitas Fratrum*) and the Moravian Church. An evangelical denomination first established in the United States in 1735. The communicants in 1912 numbered 18,561, the ministers 145, of whom 36 were retired on account of age or other reasons, and the churches, 122. In several of the districts of the Northern Province Synod work was commenced which took up the discussion of church government questions preparatory to the Provincial Synod to be held in 1913, at which governmental changes may be effected. Missions are carried on in Africa, Alaska, Asia, Australia, Labrador, Nicaragua, South America, West Indies, and Bohemia. Educational institutions are maintained. These include the Moravian College and Theological Seminary, the Moravian Parochial School for boys and girls, and the Moravian Seminary for girls, all at Bethlehem, Pa.; Linden Hall Seminary for Girls at Lititz; Nazareth Hall for Boys at Nazareth, Pa., and an academy for girls at Salem, N. C. The next General Synod will convene in 1914.

MORGAN, HENRY ARTHUR. An English scholar and educator, died September 2, 1912. He was born at Gothenburg, Sweden, in 1830, and was educated at Shrewsbury School and Jesus College, Cambridge. He graduated in 1853. He was ordained to the ministry in 1859 and thereafter continued in residence in Jesus College. He was appointed tutor in 1863 and held that office until 1885, when he was elected master. Under his administration Jesus College became, from one of the smallest, one of the largest of the Cambridge colleges. Among his published writings are *The Northern Circuit, or Brief Notes on Sweden, Finland, and Russia* (1862); *The Tenure of Fellowships* (1871), and *Church and Dissent in Wales* (1892).

MORGAN, J. P. See PRESIDENTIAL CAMPAIGN CONTRIBUTIONS.

MOROCCO. An African sultanate under French protection by virtue of the treaty of March 30, 1912. Area, exclusive of the Tuat and the desert, 439,240 square kilometers (169,591 square miles). Population, between four and eight millions (300,000 Jews); Europeans in 1910, 19,243. Fez (the capital) has 101,820 inhabitants. Morocco (Marakesh), 60,034; Rabat, 47,144; Tangier, 46,270; Casablanca, 31,710. There are no authoritative financial statistics; customs duties bring about ten million francs annually, and the sultan's budget is placed at about seven million. Imports and exports by countries follow (1911), values in thousands of francs:

	Imps.	Exps.		Imps.	Exps.
U. K.	29,334	19,644	U. S.......	718	758
France ...	46,359	31,373	Italy.	521	2,513
Germany .	7,861	17,429	Other.	5,170	1,971
Spain	2,871	9,180			
Belgium ..	2,245	732	Total.....	94,279	83,600

Principal exports were barley, 11,627 thousand francs; hides and skins, 7151; cattle, 6454; eggs, 5740; almonds, 5668; wool, 5263; wheat, 5203; flax, 4548; vegetables, 4278; canary seeds, 1814; slippers, 1420; corn, 1201; wax 1123. Vessels entered (1910), 3194, of 2,562,549 tons. There are no railways. Reigning sultan (1912), Mulai Yussuf, son of Mulai Hassan; proclaimed at Fez August 17, 1912, in place of his brother, Mulai Abd-el-Hafid. French resident-commissioner (1912) General Lyautey.

ARMY. The sultan of Morocco maintained a force of about 30,000 men of all arms, with mounted troops predominating, but this hardly could be called a permanent army in spite of efforts made by French officers to effect such an organization. Under General Moinier, who was engaged in this project, a mutiny developed, and General Lyautey formed four companies of infantry, sections of artillery, and engineers, and three squadrons of cavalry, from the 1200 men who refused to participate in the uprising. It had been proposed to form a shereefian guard and to organize the forces into nine battalions of infantry, five squadrons of cavalry, four mountain batteries, engineers, and other arms.

HISTORY

THE FEZ MASSACRE. The Protectorate Treaty was signed at Fez on March 30. M. Regnault having been entrusted by the French government with its negotiation (see FRANCE, *History*). A serious outbreak occurred in the city soon afterwards. On the morning of April 18 a body of Shereefian troops appeared at the sultan's palace to demand redress for certain grievances, including the holding back of part of their pay. The native garrison immediately revolted. Sixty-eight of the French were massacred, and thirty wounded. The mob then attacked the Mellah, or Jewish quarter, which they pillaged and burned. Meanwhile a body of 1500 French troops encamped outside the city hurried back and held the mutineers in check at several points, but were not in sufficient force to restore order. Soon afterward a larger force arrived from Mekinez under General Moinier and put down the revolt. Over 100 Jews were reported to have been killed and 10,000 rendered homeless. The French government was moved by this event to vest the military and civil power in a single representative, and on April 28 General Lyautey, commander of the Tenth Army Corps, was appointed the first French resident-general in Morocco. His administration was directly under the control of the foreign office.

THE ATTACK ON FEZ IN MAY. Disaffection in the Sebu and Mulua tribes, which had recently developed, came to a head after the Fez massacres and resulted in attacks upon a French reconnoitring force of some 500 men near Mekinez. The Zemmur or Zaer tribesmen fell upon the French line, but they were repulsed with heavy losses. There was great discontent among the natives with the French administration and signs of a rising of the tribes to the east and throughout the whole region between the capital and the Algerian frontier. It was also reported that the tribes in the south had risen. Throughout the entire country there were signs of unrest. Finally, on May 25 the tribesmen, reenforced by contingents from the Riff, attacked Fez on all sides, and by the following morning they had succeeded in penetrating the town on the east. It was alleged that the rebel forces in the neighborhood of the capital numbered at least 20,000. The French garrison, about 5000 strong, had difficulty in repulsing them. Peace was afterwards restored in the territory of the Sebu and on the Algerian frontier. The policy of General Lyautey was to restore to power the popular chiefs in the south and, in general, to conciliate native feeling; and to hold and consolidate the regions already occupied, but for the present to attempt no new conquests. In accordance with this policy he dispatched a strong column to operate in the regions adjacent to the capital, while another force was engaged in pacifying the territory to the west and another near the Algerian frontier. By the end of June much had been accomplished toward the restoration of order in the disturbed districts.

THE SULTAN'S ABDICATION. For some time past the sultan Mulai Hafid had made known his desire to abdicate, but the French authorities, fearing the change, succeeded in keeping him on the throne. On July 10, however, he definitely renounced the throne. The French government accepted his abdication. It was arranged that he should retire to Tangier and receive a pension of 300,000 francs. He was succeeded by his brother, Mulai Yussuf, who was proclaimed sultan on August 14.

FIGHTING AT MARRAKESH. The abdication of the sultan led to an uprising in the south, where a new pretender, El Heiba, made his appearance and was soon at the head of a formidable body of tribesmen and supported by all the powerful kaids of the region. He captured Marrakesh, the capital of southern Morocco, and then advanced northward against the troops commanded by Colonel Mangin. The French repulsed his attack, but were unable to pursue him. The fall of Marrakesh was a severe blow to French prestige. The European residents escaped in time, except nine Frenchmen, including the consul, who were held in the city as prisoners. At about the same time a French column was attacked near Fez, and lost a number of men. There was much anxiety in August over the fate of the French prisoners of Marrakesh. A slight engagement took place between the French and the pretender's force at Suk-el-Arba on August 25. The news at the end of August indicated a very disordered condition throughout the whole country from Marrakesh to Fez, and fears were expressed for the safety of European residents. On Septembe 5, however, a French flying column 4000 strong under General Mangin left the camp at Suk-el-Arba and marched on Marrakesh, fifty-five miles distant. It was preceded by a detachment of cavalry. The enemy were driven back and the French troops entered Marrakesh on September 7, the pretender, El Heiba, having meanwhile been driven out by his own followers, who turned against him on the approach of the French. The nine French prisoners, who had been in the hands of tribesmen since August 15, were rescued.

The sultan announced in June that the hitherto closed port of Mehedia, on the Atlantic coast about eighteen miles north of Rabat, would be opened to foreign trade on January 1, 1913. For further discussion of Moroccan affairs, see FRANCE and SPAIN under *History*.

MORRIS, CHARLES. An American soldier, died October 28, 1912. He was born in Charlestown, Mass., in 1844, and graduated from the United States Military Academy in 1855. In the same year he was appointed first lieutenant in the 19th Infantry. He was promoted through various grades and became colonel in 1902 and brigadier-general in 1908. He retired by operation of law in the same year.

MORRIS, THOMAS JOHN. An American jurist, died June 6, 1912. He was born in Baltimore in 1837 and graduated from Harvard College in 1856. In 1861 he was admitted to the bar and practiced in Baltimore until 1878, when he was appointed United States district judge for the district of Maryland. This position he occupied until the time of his death. He was vice-president of the American Unitarian Association, and was a trustee of Johns Hopkins University.

MORRIS, WILLIAM. See BAR ASSOCIATION.

MOSQUITO REDUCTION. See SANITATION.

MOTOR BOATING. See YACHTING.

MOTOR FIRE APPARATUS. See FIRE PROTECTION.

MOTORS. See AERONAUTICS.

MOULE, GEORGE EVANS. An English missionary bishop of the Methodist Episcopal Church, died March 3, 1912. He was born at Gillingham, Dorchester, 1828, and was educated at private schools and at Corpus Christi College, Cambridge. From 1851 to 1857 he served as curate and chaplain of the Dorset County Hospital. In the latter year he was appointed missionary to China under the auspices of the Church Missionary Society. He was first stationed at Ningpo, and thus was a witness of the great Taiping rebellion. He was the first representative of the Church Missionary Society to form a permanent mission at Hangchow. From 1866, when he first took up his residence in this city, until 1911, he did not leave the country. In 1880 he was consecrated first missionary bishop of Mid-China. He resigned the bishopric in 1908, but continued to work at Hangchow until 1911, when ill health and advancing years compelled him to relinquish his work and return to England.

MOUNT HOLYOKE COLLEGE. An institution for the higher education of women at South Hadley, Mass., founded in 1837. The students in the college in the autumn of 1912 numbered 749 undergraduates and 7 graduates. There were 84 members of the teaching staff and 44 in the administrative staff. Six members of the faculty were on leave of absence. During the year the Half-Million fund, undertaken in commemoration of the seventy-fifth anniversary of the college, was completed. A total of $553,000 was raised, of which $108,000 will be applied to the erection of a student alumnæ building, to cost $125,000, and the remainder to the general endowment. A new institution hall is also to be built, a gift of Messrs. William and Joseph Skinner of Holyoke. The chief event of the year was the celebration of the seventy-fifth anniversary of the founding of the institution. This was held on October 8 and 9, and was observed with many picturesque and imposing ceremonies. President, Mary E. Woolley, M. A.

MOUNT WILSON SOLAR OBSERVATORY. See ASTRONOMY.

MOVING PICTURES. The exhibition of moving pictures in 1912 had reached a point where, in the United States alone, judged merely as an industry, it had become a matter of striking importance. The different business interests involved were said to represent a total investment of over $200,000,000 and in one form or another moving pictures were offering employment to approximately half a million people. It was estimated that the daily receipts of the 20,000 places where moving pictures were exhibited aggregated $500,000, while in Greater New York alone some 300,000 people daily were visiting the shows. There were maintained large studios, some of which represented buildings and equipments valued at over $100,000, and in the larger establishments four or five plays a week were being produced for photographic record with all the care and elaboration of a modern melodrama. It is obvious, therefore, that the moving picture business is entitled to special consideration, involving as it does the use of real estate for exhibition halls, many of which had been specially built, the operation and maintenance of the shows, the manufacture of films and apparatus, and the provision of suitable topics for illustrations by exploration, travel, and mechanical, and other forms of enterprise. From the kinetoscope first exhibited in the form of a sort of peep-show by Thomas A. Edison in 1893 to the projection device of Lumière of Paris and Paul of London a few years later, the development and improvement of moving picture machines was rapid and constant. Mr. Edison received numerous patents and one of these, granted August 31, 1897, was the subject of a decision in the U. S. Court of Appeals handed down late in 1912, that Edison was not the pioneer inventor of the moving picture machines, but was the inventor of a special form of camera used in making the photographs on such moving films. In 1911, as described in the YEAR BOOK of that year, the Kinemacolor process, whereby moving pictures were reproduced in their original colors with a striking verisimilitude of nature, marked another advance, and in 1912 the Kinetophone of Edison, whereby moving pictures were projected synchronously with the reproduction of appropriate sound by the phonograph, represented a further practical achievement.

The curiosity first aroused by the moving pictures soon was succeeded by interest in the scenes portrayed, and straightway they became a recognized feature of vaudeville and music halls, serving to attract the better class of people to such entertainments and to raise their general tone. As the industry progressed the dramatic possibilities of the films were seen, and soon a change was made from automobile races, military parades, and similar subjects to little dramas in pantomime specially staged by competent actors with necessary stage properties and scenery under illumination by arc and mercury vapor lamps. Then came the low-priced house with its wide and direct appeal, which immediately brought substantial returns, so that in even the smaller cities and towns such exhibitions could be conducted on a profitable basis. The appetite of the people for these picture stories seemed insatiable. Tragedy, comedy, romantic drama, religious episode, historical sketches, in fact everything capable of dramatic representation in pantomime, was enacted for the moving films, and famous plays and stories were reduced to such a basis, not to mention new plays specially written. Where the scenes were out of doors an open-air setting would be selected, and often the company would be taken *en masse* to the very scene of the action.

A school of moving picture actors had been developed, trained to deliberateness of movement and plainness of facial expression and gesture, but this did not prevent such artists as Bernhardt, Réjane, Lillian Russell, Nat Goodwin, James K. Hackett, and others from appearing in film plays. Madame Bernhardt was quoted as saying that in this way she was able to immortalize her art. Several of the most powerful American managers of the legitimate drama in 1912 were providing for moving pictures, and at some of their largest playhouses, conscious of the profits thus to be reaped. In fact, these moving picture representations were making serious inroads into the business of the ordinary theatres, and their low prices and the ease with which they could be established and operated led to a remarkable development which involved as a consequence large syndicates and exchanges for the distribution and rental of films. In the cities this rapid growth led to many complicated situations. It was claimed that the shows were often demoralizing on account of the nature of the films shown and the opportunities that they offered for the young to congregate in dark halls; and in the second place, the moving pictures being exhibited too often in temporary, flimsy, and combustible structures afforded excellent opportunity for panic in case of an alarm of fire. The first series of difficulties were being met partly by legislation, as for example, local ordinances forbidding children to attend such shows without their parents or guardians and by more or less supervision or official censorship. The large producers united to maintain clean and moral films, enlisting in their aid a board of censors composed of prominent and disinterested people who passed on the suitability of the pictures. The fire and panic dangers were more serious, and in 1912 and previously a number of serious and fatal catastrophes occurred. Insurance underwriters and fire departments generally required precautions in the way of asbestos booths for the machines and varying degrees of protection of structure and exits.

Mention should be made of the use of the moving pictures to reproduce famous current events. Thus in 1912 the Balkan War, the construction of the Panama Canal, and other important circumstances were shown widely throughout the civilized world, while explorers like Shackleton and hunters like Paul Rainey exhibited moving pictures that aroused compelling interest in two continents. Pictures of wild animals in their native haunts in forest and jungle, often taken at great personal risk to the operator, attracted general as well as scientific interest. Biblical events, and classical topics, such as the Siege of Troy, were reproduced with care as to setting and costume. The moving picture industry naturally followed modern commercial methods with the inevitable tendencies toward consolidation and concentration. There resulted alleged combinations or trusts of manufactures and exchanges, which at the end of the year 1912 were receiving the attention of the Attorney-General of the United States as possible combinations in restraint of trade.

MOZAMBIQUE. See PORTUGUESE EAST AFRICA.

MUNICH. See ARCHITECTURE.

MUNICIPAL BUILDINGS. See ARCHITECTURE.

MUNICIPAL EFFICIENCY. See MUNICIPAL GOVERNMENT.

MUNICIPAL GOVERNMENT. Interest in this subject continues to be keen and there is steady progress in charter reform, including the commission plan and the short ballot; in municipal accounting and statistics; in the selection of trained administrative officers; in municipal home rule, or charter framing through local initiative, with freedom from legislative control; and a variety of other activities which are making cities and towns better living-places.

COMMISSION PLAN. To the list of some 200 cities and towns which had adopted commission government at the close of 1911 (see YEAR BOOK for 1911, pp. 471-3) there were added more than fifty in 1912. The records of the National Municipal League on November 15, 1912, showed a total of 257 commission cities, distributed geographically, in order of number, as follows: Northwestern group of States, 64; Southwestern, 59; North Central, 39; Pacific and Rocky Mountain, 32; South Central, 27; Middle, 15; Southern, 14; New England, 7. Notable additions in 1912 to the cities which have voted for the plan are New Orleans, La.; St. Paul and Duluth, Minn.; Atlantic City and Long Branch, N. J.; Salem, Mass., and Pasadena, Cal. Votes against the commission plan were reported from Los Angeles, Cal.; Savannah, Ga.; East St. Louis, Ill., and five other places. Three cities which already had commission government voted in 1912 to continue it. These were Spokane, Wash. (15,225 to 9448); Baker, Ore., and Hutchinson, Kan. The largest city operating under the commission plan to date is New Orleans (339,000 population in 1910), but there are a half dozen others with a population of 100,000 or more, and on January 1, 1914, St. Paul, Minn. (214,000 in 1910), will join the list.

The vote of more than two to one against the commission plan at Los Angeles on December 3 was a surprise, as was also the light vote cast—about 30 per cent. of the registration. The proposed charter had been framed after long deliberation by a "board of freeholders," as the home rule charter framers of California are called. The board held numerous public hearings and consulted with members of the National Municipal League and others versed in charter framing from outside the city; and at the meeting of the league held in Los Angeles in July a long session was devoted to a discussion of the charter then being framed. Among the explanations of the defeat of the Los Angeles charter are these: It was submitted to vote only four weeks after the presidential election, giving relatively little time for discussion of the completed document; the City Council refused to print the charter for circulation in pamphlet form; the *Times* and the *Examiner* both opposed it; some feared the concentration of so much power in a few hands; but the chief objection, it is said, was the fear that some of the provisions of the charter would increase taxation. The charter provided for a mayor at $7000 per annum and six commissioners at $6000 each. These, a comptroller and a board of education of seven members, would have been the only elective officers. The mayor would have been commissioner of public safety. The six other commissionerships would have been public utilities; public works; harbors and transportation; finance; welfare; and park, libraries and recreation. The initiative, the referendum, and the recall were included in the charter. An unusual, if not an original, feature was that the recall should apply to appointed as well as elected officials, but no petition for the recall of an appointed officer in the civil service could be filed unless a complaint against him had been acted upon adversely by the civil service board.

It is doubtful if any city charter previously drafted attempted to confer such sweeping powers. After authorizing the city to provide "by purchase, lease, condemnation, construction, or otherwise" everything that the most ambitious municipal socialist could ask, the proposed charter provided further that the city might own and do anything permitted by the State constitution, and in effect do almost anything within the powers of "any person, firm, or corporation whatever." Indebtedness was limited to 3 per cent. of the assessed valuation of all real and personal property, except that for revenue-producing public utilities and harbor improvements an additional 12 per cent. might be incurred. Immediately after the defeat of the Los Angeles charter two non-official committees were created to draft still another charter or else to frame amendments to the old one, which has been aptly described as a patchwork affair, long since outgrown by Los Angeles.

The commission plan charter for Duluth, adopted on December 3, 1912, to go into effect January 3, 1913, but with the first election of officers on April 1, 1913, was framed by a charter commission of fifteen members. This commission gave the following as the chief features of the charter: Elimination of party politics, bosses, and machines; nominations by petition; preferential voting; elimination of ward lines; four-year term of office, with adequate salaries; the men who make the laws will be responsible for their enforcement; the initiative, referendum and recall, and publicity features give the voters control of the city government. Each of the five commissioners is to be paid $4000 a year until the population of the city is 100,000; then $4500 until it is 150,000, and $5000 a year thereafter. The commissioners decide which one of their number shall head the following divisions: Public affairs; finance; public works; public safety and public utilities. There is to be a civil service board of three members. The recall applies only to elective officers.

SAN FRANCISCO CHARTER AMENDMENTS. Of 37 charter amendments voted on at San Francisco on December 10, 1912, 17 were carried and 20 lost. A feature of the campaign was a pre-election agreement by the Chamber of Commerce, the San Francisco Real Estate Board, and the Civic League on which amendments ought to be carried and which defeated. Of 25 amendments recommended by these three bodies, 17 were carried and 8 lost; and of 12 advised against, every one was defeated. In general, amendments which would have led to increases in the bonded debt or in the number or salaries of employees were defeated, but some propositions involving expenditures for improvements to which the city was more or less definitely committed were carried. The most popular amendment was one authorizing exchanges of land for a civic centre and the erection of buildings in that centre (see CITY PLANNING). This was carried by 50,061 against 24,290. The least popular amendments were several providing salary increases; one of these, which would have increased the salary of the chief of police from $4000 to $6000 a year, was lost by a vote of 5449 against 64,128. The creation of a two-platoon police system and the enlargement of the police force brought out a very heavy vote and was defeated by 33,721 against 46,054. Almost as heavy and far more decisive was the vote of 15,087 to 63,770 against the formation of local-option (saloon) districts of not less than 50 contiguous blocks in one voting precinct. The total vote cast on the amendments as a whole was 81,104, which was about 60 per cent. of the registration. Considerable space has been given to the San Francisco amendments here because they illustrate the extremes to which some of the cities of the far West are going in the way of home rule and direct legislation, and show that a large measure of discrimination is sometimes used in the voting. It is interesting to note that only 30 per cent. of the vote was cast on the proposed new charter for Los Angeles and double that percentage on some of the 37 amendments at San Francisco.

OHIO CONSTITUTIONAL AMENDMENTS. Of the 42 amendments to the Ohio constitution submitted to popular vote on September 3, 1912, a number made notable changes and increases in the powers of municipalities. Among the amendments which were adopted the following are pertinent here: Providing a large measure of municipal home rule, including the right of cities and villages to frame their own charters; eight-hour day on public works; preferential primaries; competitive civil service examinations. Among the amendments defeated was one which would have authorized the use of voting machines and another which would have removed existing constitutional provisions which make it impossible to regulate advertising billboards located on private property.

CITY MANAGER PLAN. A few years ago Staunton, Va., being constitutionally barred from the commission plan, appointed a city manager to run the city, subject to the policy-determining action of the City Council. In June, 1912, Sumter, S. C. (about 10,000 population), voted 3 to 1 in favor of a city manager in conjunction with the commission plan (three commissioners). The British and German practice of advertising for applicants to fill the office was followed. The advertisement stated that an engineer of standing and ability was preferred and that the appointee would hold office as long as he gave satisfaction to the commissioners, and that he would have complete administrative control of the city, subject to the commissioners. Applicants were to address the secretary of the local chamber of commerce. An engineer from another city was appointed, but he resigned to take another position at once. A town manager for Norwood, Mass., was reported in 1912, to serve as town engineer, superintendent of public works, and director of the water and lighting systems.

EXECUTIVE COMMISSIONERS IN THE CANADIAN NORTHWEST. Enterprising cities in northwestern Canada scarcely heard of until yesterday are retaining the old mayor and council system and joining with it executive or administrative commissioners something like the boards of public works in a number of American cities, except that the Canadian councils keep a tight grasp on the public purse and decide matters of policy, either originally or as a last resort. Thus Calgary, Alberta, has a mayor and a council of twelve members. The council appoints two citizens, subject to approval by popular vote, who, with the mayor serving ex-officio, are known as city commissioners. The two commissioners are paid $4000 a year and the mayor $5000. The council refers various matters to the commissioners for study and recommendation and the commissioners recommend to the council appointments to executive offices. A two-thirds vote of the council is required to override a recommendation of the commissioners. The mayor has no veto power over the acts of the council, but he can vote in council on the recommendations of the commission, of which he is an ex-officio member. A similar commission exists at Moose Jaw, Saskatchewan, a city of 20,000 to 25,000. There L. W. Rundett, for many years city engineer of St. Paul, Minn., went early in 1912 to become a city commissioner at a salary of $6000 a year. The second commissioner resigned from the city clerkship to accept the position at $3000 a year, and the mayor is the third commissioner. The "by-law" creating the commission and other interesting facts regarding the city government of Moose Jaw are given in *Engineering News* of August 1, 1912.

MUNICIPAL EFFICIENCY. A departure in municipal government is the recent creation of an efficiency division of the Civil Service Commission of Chicago. During 1912 this divison made a series of notable studies, including the distribution of wages and salaries for the year and the formulation of standards of efficiency for street cleaning and for garbage and refuse collection and removal. The Milwaukee bureau of economy and efficiency went the way of other innovations of the Socialists when they lost control of the city government at the beginning of 1912. Articles reviewing bureaus of public efficiency and research and reference bureaus up to late in 1912 may be found in the *National Municipal Review* for January, 1913. A joint committee on the selection and retention of experts in municipal office reported in 1912 to the National Municipal League and to the National Civic Service Reform League, recommending the extension of civil service examinations to govern the choice of the higher administrative municipal officials, and making various suggestions as to the qualifications of civil service commissioners.

See also CITY PLANNING; GARBAGE AND REFUSE DISPOSAL; MUNICIPAL OWNERSHIP; ROADS AND PAVEMENTS; SANITATION; SEWAGE PURIFICATION; SMOKE PREVENTION; WATER PURIFICATION.

BIBLIOGRAPHY. Prof. William B. Munro, *The Government of American Cities* and *The Initiative, the Referendum and the Recall* (New York); Prof. Charles A. Beard, *American City Government* (New York); Henry Bruére (William Sheperdson coöperating), *The New City Government* (New York), which is a study of ten commission-governed cities combined with an exposition of municipal government as viewed by the New York bureau of municipal research; John Nolen, *Replanning Small Cities* (New York), which is virtually a condensation of various city-planning reports made by the author. For British municipal data, officials, etc., *The Municipal Year Book of the United Kingdom; The Water Works Directory and Statistics*, and *The Gas Works Directory and Statistics* (all published in London).

The accompanying list of 63 cities reported as having adopted the commission plan in 1912 supplements the list of 208 cities given in the last YEAR BOOK. The lists together total 271 commission-plan cities to the close of the year.

New England (1)			
Salem, Mass.	43,697		
Middle Atlantic (7)		Longport, N.J.	118
Atlantic City, N. J.	46,150	Nutley, N.J.	6,009
Deal Beach, N.J.	273	Ridgefield Pk., N.J.	966
Long Branch, N.J.	13,298	Wildwood, N.J.	898
South Atlantic (3)		Sumter, S. C.*	8,109
Florence, S. C.	7,057	Tampa, Fla.†	37,782
South Central (12)		New Iberia, La.	7,499
Sheffield, Ala.	4,865	Natchitoches, La.	2,532
Charleston, Miss.	1,834	New Orleans, La.	339,075
Gulfport, Miss.	6,386	Lebanon, Tenn.	3,569
Jackson, Miss.	21,262	Covington, Ky.	53,270
Meridian, Miss.	23,285	Lexington, Ky.	35,099
Hammond, La.	2,942		
North Central (8)		Janesville, Wis.	13,894
St. Joseph, Mich.	5,936	Menominee, Wis.	5,036
Harvey Ill.	7,227	Rice Lake, Wis.	3,968
Marseilles, Ill.	3,291	Superior, Wis.	40,384
Portage, Wis.	5,440		
Northwestern (16)		Manhattan, Kan.	5,722
Ottumwa, Iowa	22,012	Olathe, Kan.	3,272
Duluth, Minn	78,466	Parsons, Kan.	12,463
St. Paul, Minn.	214,744	Lincoln, Neb.	43,973
Tower, Minn.	1,111	Nebraska C., Neb.	5,488
Arkansas C., Kan.	7,508	Madison, S. D.	3,137
Great Bend, Kan.	4,622	Watertown, S. D.	7,010
Holton, Kan.	2,842	Polson, Mont.	Not given
Junc. City, Kan.	5,598		
Southwestern (10)		Ada, Okla.	4,349
Bishop, Tex.	Not given	Collinsville, Okla.	1,324
Franklin, Tex.	Not given	Okmulgee, Okla.	4,176
Fankston, Tex.	Not given	Colorado City, Col.	4,333
McKinney, Tex.	4,714	Durango, Col.	4,686
Willis, Tex.	Not given		
Pacific (6)		San Mateo, Cal.	4,384
Everett, Wash.	24,814	§Phœnix, Ariz.	11,134
Pasadena, Cal.	30,291	Boise, Idaho	17,358
S. Bernard., Cal.	12,779		

* City Manager Plan. † Advisory vote. § Reported by National Short Ballot Association that governor refused to approve charter on constitutional grounds.

MUNICIPAL LEAGUE, NATIONAL. The annual meeting of the league was held in Los Angeles on July 8-12. Its keynote was "expert city management." President Foulke in his address emphasized the importance of the subject, as did the secretary in his annual review, and other speakers in the debates carried on during the meeting. The president showed in detail how the merit system could be well applied to various departments of the city government, referring to the fact that the engineers for the Los Angeles aqueduct, the auditor for Kansas City, the chief of the fire department of New York City, the superintendent of highways in Philadelphia, the librarian of the public library in Chicago, and other high officers of city administration are appointed by competitive examination. Secretary Woodruff emphasized the fact that while Los Angeles had achieved real municipal home rule and had perhaps gone further than any other city in the country in eliminating national and State party considerations from municipal affairs, and had established honesty therein, its government was still far from being efficient in a modern sense. The commission form of government came in for a large measure of attention during the meeting. It was declared to be the greatest single contribution to the cause of better municipal government in the past decade. Professor Munro of Harvard declared that, "As a protest against the old municipal régime, it has been very effective; as a policy it has, despite its incidental shortcomings, fulfilled much of what its supporters claimed for it."

Socialism in American cities was one of the most interesting subjects discussed. Secretary Woodruff in his review pointed out that there are now about 1200 Socialist officials, and that the Socialist vote is rapidly growing. An interesting paper on "Socialism in California Cities" was read by Professor Cross of Leland Stanford University. Among other subjects considered were: "The Federal Government as a Potential Contributor of Municipal Advancement"; "Home Rule in California"; "Municipal Health Problem"; "The Actual Operation of the Initiative, Referendum, and Recall"; and "The Actual Operation of Woman Suffrage in Pacific Coast Cities." The enrolled members of the league numbered 2600. On January 1, 1912, the publication of the *National Municipal Review* was begun. This takes the place of the *Proceedings of the National Municipal League*. The editor of the *Review* is Clinton Rogers Woodruff. The following officers were elected for 1913: President, William Dudley Foulke; treasurer, George Burnham, Jr.; secretary, Clinton Rogers Woodruff; vice-presidents: Miss Jane Addams, Camillus G. Kidder, A. Lawrence Lowell, George McAneny, J. Horace McFarland, Charles Richardson, Chester H. Rowell, James M. Thomson, and Dudley Tibbits.

MUNICIPAL OWNERSHIP. In December, 1912, the beginning of what it is hoped will be extensive municipal street railway systems in San Francisco, Cal., and Toronto, Ont., were put in operation. At San Francisco the municipal railway is known as the Geary Street line, and will run from Kearney Street, near the Oakland ferry, to the ocean beach. The portion put in operation extends to Golden Gate Park, a distance of about four miles. It is expected that the remaining part of the line will be ready in a few months. Under the San Francisco charter the accounts of municipally owned utilities must show all operating and capital charges, including depreciation, and the estimated taxes that would have been collected on the same property under private ownership. At Toronto the city has built nearly two miles of street railway known as the Gerrard Street line. On the completion of the Danforth and St. Clair Avenue lines the city will own about seventeen miles of single track. In some ten years the present extensive street railways now operated by the Toronto Railway Company will again come into possession of the city, as they did on expiration of a franchise some years ago.

ELECTRIC LIGHT AND POWER. The hydro-electric power commission of Ontario is now supplying 39,000 horsepower to municipalities on the Toronto circuit, of which Toronto was using about 17,000 horsepower late in 1912. The current is used for light and power. Winnipeg is going on with a municipal light and power system, for which $3,250,000 was voted in 1906, and which will ultimately cost $6,000,000. In July, 1912, a 60,000-horsepower hydroelectric plant had been built for the city, and two 60,000-volt transmission lines, seventy-seven miles long, had been built from the plant to a terminal house in or near the city. The municipal electric light plant of Seattle, Wash., reports having turned a loss of 2 per cent. on an indebtedness of $876,000 for its first year (1905) into an annual surplus, 4.7 per cent. of the debt in 1911, besides having accumulated a surplus of 11 per cent., provided a 21 per cent. depreciation revenue, and reduced rates from 20 to 6 cents per kilowatt hour.

DOCKS AND HARBORS are being built and projected by cities of the East and West at a surprising rate. These activities have been greatly stimulated by the prospective early opening of the Panama Canal. Naturally, the greatest activity, or at least the most talked about, has been on the Pacific Coast. There Seattle, Portland, San Francisco, Oakland, Los Angeles, and San Diego are all busy with extensive dock or harbor improvements. On the Atlantic seaboard Boston, New York, and Philadelphia are also engaged in extensive projects of the same general character. Kansas City, Mo., put in operation in June, 1911, a municipal wharf 50 feet wide, with a length of 526 feet on the water side and 566 on the land side; and in October, 1911, it contracted for a wharfhouse, to be completed in 120 days, which was to be provided with an improved freight-handling system. An amendment to the Ohio constitution, adopted by a heavy majority, on September 3, 1912, authorizes cities and towns to own and operate public utilities, and to sell light and power to other municipalities to the extent of half of the output of the generating plant.

MUNICIPAL POWER PLANTS. See MUNICIPAL OWNERSHIP.

MUNSEY, FRANK A. See PRESIDENTIAL CAMPAIGN CONTRIBUTIONS.

MURPHY, CHARLES F. See PRESIDENTIAL CAMPAIGN.

MURRAY, GEORGE ROBERT MILNE. An English botanist, died in January, 1912. He was born in Arbroath, Scotland, in 1858, and was educated at Strassburg University. From 1882 to 1886 he was lecturer on botany at the Medical School of St. George's Hospital. He was naturalist of the Solar Eclipse Expedition to the West Indies in 1886 and was scientific director of the National Antarctic Expedition in 1901. From 1895 to 1905 he was keeper of the department of botany at the English Museum. His publications include, *Introduction to the Study of Seaweeds* (1895), and joint authorship of *Handbook of Cryptogamic Botany* (1889). He also contributed many botanical papers to scientific periodicals.

MUSEUMS OF ART. The art year was notable for the shipment to America of the famous collections of J. Pierpont Morgan. The decision of Mr. Morgan to send his collection to the United States was reached after he had been informed, in 1911, that if portions of the collection then in the Victoria Albert Museum at South Kensington were still there at the time of his death a heavy tax would be levied against them by the British government. The value of the art objects at South Kensington was estimated at $5,000,000. Shipments of the Morgan collection commenced early in February, and continued throughout the year.

The Metropolitan Museum of Art in New York, of which Mr. Morgan is president, arranged to show thirty of the paintings as a special loan collection in January, 1913. During 1912 the museum received a gift of over $1,000,000 from Francis L. Leland, and a bequest from F. C. Hewitt, which will amount to about $1,500,000. The north wing had been completed, but was not yet ready to receive exhibitions. Important acquisitions of the year include additions to the Hearn collection of American paintings, a large early canvas by Correggio, "Four Saints," a collection of thirty-two early Italian paintings lent to the museum for a term of years by Mrs. L. C. Holden; important additions were made to the classical department; a series of ten Egyptian galleries was opened; a lecture hall seating about 500 was opened in the autumn of 1911 and is in demand for lectures to members, the public, and to teachers and pupils of the public schools. There were 3239 members; the attendance during 1912 was 690,183, and the total accessions by gift and purchase numbered 2696.

In Brooklyn the Museum of Arts and Sciences received from William T. Evans a series of twenty paintings by Otto Walter Beck, illustrating the life of Christ. A special loan collection of paintings owned in Brooklyn was shown at the institute's gallery in Montague Street, for the benefit of the "Little Italy Association." William H. Fox was appointed curator-in-chief of the museum, and took up his duties January 1, 1913.

The largest gift of the year to the Boston Museum of Fine Arts was from Francis P. Bartlett, who gave $1,500,000 for the endowment fund. In April the Evans memorial wing, which is to contain galleries of paintings, was begun. Among the important acquisitions of the year were, "Portrait of a Lady," by Lucas Cranach the elder; "Portrait by John Eld," by Gainsborough; forty-five water colors by Sargent; seventy-one objects added to the Ross Oritental collection; colonial silver; Flemish tapestries. Special exhibitions held included works by members of the "Socété des Peintres et des Sculpteurs," colonial furniture, early woodcuts, and recent acquisitions in Chinese and Japanese art. A print department has been endowed and FitzRoy Carrington was appointed on the staff of the museum as curator of the department of prints; the *Print-Collector's Quarterly* will hereafter be published by the museum.

Through the efforts of the director of the Albright Art Gallery, in Buffalo, the work by members of the "Société des Peintres et des Sculpteurs" of Paris was brought to the United States and shown first in Buffalo, and later in Chicago, St. Louis, and other cities. An exhibition of textiles was also installed. The Art Institute of Chicago is notable for its large school, where there were over 3000 students during 1911-12, and the attendance at the museum was 861,000 for the year ending June, 1912. Edward B. Butler offered to fit up a gallery for the reception of twenty paintings by George Inness, donated by him the previous year. A bequest of $50,000 was left by Daniel H. Burnham to establish an architectural library. Thirty exhibitions were held during the year.

Frederick A. Whiting was appointed director of the Heron Art Institute at Indianapolis. Mr. Whiting's connection for ten years past with the Boston Society of Arts and Crafts, placed him in a position to strengthen that side of the museum's collections, and he was also deeply interested in educational work in coöperation with the schools. The energetic campaign carried on during 1911 to raise funds for an art gallery in Minneapolis was continued during 1912. McKim, Mead, and White were appointed architects, and the permit for the new building was granted in December, 1912, the cost to be about $520,000.

The Hackley Art Gallery at Muskegon, Mich., founded by Charles H. Hackley, was dedicated June 21, 1912, under the supervision of the director, Raymond Wyer. The opening exhibition consisted of paintings of various modern schools, about two-thirds lent by collectors in different parts of the country. A permanent collection is being formed, and among the early purchases are a portrait by Sir Henry Reaburn, a landscape by Corot, "In the Surf," by Jozef Israels, and works by American painters. For many years there had been a small art society in New Orleans, but it was not until 1910 that there was a prospect of a permanent museum of art. A gift of $150,000 from Isaac Delgado led to the construction of the Delgado Museum, which was dedicated December 16, 1911. Frequent exhibitions are planned. The Louisiana State Museum, established in 1906, took possession of the old historic Cabildo, and the formal dedication was on April 30, 1912. The art collections are chiefly historical.

A new art gallery was being erected on the campus of the Rochester University, at Rochester, N. Y., at a cost of nearly $200,000, by Mrs. James S. Watson, in memory of her son, James G. Averell. While the gallery will be the property of the university, it will be maintained for the benefit of the whole city, with a separate board of directors. The Bevier Memorial Building, to house the Department of Applied and Fine Arts of the Mechanics' Institute, was dedicated during 1912.

In 1908 an act was passed in the State legislature giving all cities in the State of Missouri having over 100,000 inhabitants the right to submit the question of an art tax to any general election held in the State. As a result, the city of St. Louis voted a tax to be levied on the assessed valuation of the city, to the extent of one-fifth of a mill per dollar, which would give an income of about $125,000 a year. A State ordinance was approved Februrary 3, 1909, establishing a public museum of fine arts, which took over the property of the old St. Louis Museum, the value of which approximated $500,000. Since the death, in May, 1911, of Halsey C. Ives, who had been at the head of the museum and school since its foundation in 1881, there was no director until Robert A. Holland was appointed January 15, 1913, as director of the City Art Museum.

Elaborate plans were made for the Department of Art in connection with the Panama-Pacific Exposition, to be held in San Francisco in 1915. John E. D. Trask, director of the Pennsylvania Academy of the Fine Arts in Philadelphia, was appointed director of the Art Department; Jules Guérin is art director of color and decoration for the exhibition as a whole, and Karl Bitter and A. Sterling Calder are in charge of the sculpture. The Washington State Art Association moved from the rooms occupied in the Carnegie Library to a series of large rooms in a building nearer the heart of the city. Plans were made for the erection of a nine-story museum-auditorium building to be opened in 1913.

The Toledo Museum of Art, founded in 1901, had outgrown its quarters and a new building designed by Green & Wicks and H. W. Wachter was dedicated January 17, 1912. The opening of these galleries marks the completion of ten years of effort by the president, Edward D. Libbey, who gave the land and subscribed largely to the building fund; the director, George W. Stevens; and the towns-people, who gave in sums of from ten cents to $15,000 toward the building fund. It opens free of debt and with an endowment fund. The cost was about $500,000. At the time of the dedication there was an important loan collection of paintings, including twenty-five works by Jozef Israels.

This does not by any means include all the museums of art in the United States, but merely those which have dedicated new buildings during 1912, have had a new director whose appointment is likely to influence their growth, or have received important gifts.

MUSIC. It may not be amiss to summarize briefly the events of the five years preceding. The last year of Mr. Conried's directorship of the Metropolitan Opera House was memorable for the production of Strauss's *Salome*, which aroused such violent opposition that the work was withdrawn (1907). The following year Mr. Gatti-Casazza became the artistic manager of the famous operatic institution. By this time the Manhattan Opera House, under the management of Mr. Hammerstein, had become a formidable rival. The effect of this rivalry was particularly noted in a marked improvement of the chorus and scenic mounting at the older house (1908). As a further result of the struggle for supremacy the Metropolitan Company almost doubled its forces in all departments, and gave a series of performances at the New Theatre. A new opera house was opened at Boston. The New York Philharmonic Society was entirely reorganized under Gustav Mahler (1909). The continued keen rivalry between the Metropolitan and Manhattan companies had forced both into enormous expenses and heavy losses, so that finally Mr. Hammerstein withdrew, and sold all his interests to the rival organization. The greater part of the Manhattan company was then organized by Mr. Dippel as the Chicago Opera Company. In order to prevent a recurrence of such disastrous competition, the three great operatic institutions of New York, Boston, and Chicago came to a mutual understanding, and conceived a plan whereby they exchange their artists (1910). This exchange plan worked admirably in practice. But a more important result of this friendly understanding was the effective opposition they directed against the so-called Opera Trust. For years past the Milan publishing house of Ricordi had monopolized the rights of production of almost all Italian operas of any importance. Year after year they had raised their terms, and forced the opera houses to present works which the public did not want. When finally the trust formulated its demands, which amounted to nothing less than extortion, Mr. Dippel eliminated from his repertoire all operas controlled by Ricordi, and Mr. Gatti-Casazza greatly reduced their number in his repertoire (1911). Consult: YEAR BOOK, 1911; MUSIC, *The Opera Trust*.

THE OPERA TRUST. Although no official information has been given regarding the opposition to the Milan trust, there are unmistakable indications that the American managers have won a victory. It is known that one of the conditions demanded in 1911 was the production at the Metropolitan Opera House of Franchetti's *Cristofero Colombo*. Not only has the work not been given, but it was not even announced as one of the probable novelties. Puccini's *Girl of the Golden West* had only three performances during the pas yea , as against nine of the preceding. Mr.t Dippel firmly maintained the stand he had taken. During the season 1911-12 not a single performance of any of Puccini's works was given. That the trust must have come to an understanding with the Chicago company seems to be borne out by the fact that during the last weeks of the present year Puccini's *Manon Lescaut* was given three times.

DISCOVERIES OF MANUSCRIPTS. Closely following the discovery by Fritz Stein of a *Jena* Symphony by Beethoven (see YEAR BOOK, 1911, MUSIC, *Germany*) comes the news that Herman Abert, professor of the history of music at the University of Halle, has discovered the orchestral parts of a *Charfreitagskantate* by Beethoven. On each part is written the composer's name in Beethoven's own handwriting. The work is written for a double quartette of trombones. Seyfried added a text for male chorus, in which form the work was performed at Beethoven's funeral. The trombone arrangement found by Professor Abert was written in 1812 for Music Director F. X. Gloeggl, of Linz. In the Liszt Museum at Weimar Peter Raabe found the scores of two lost works by Liszt. The first was written originally as an instrumental work and is called *Les Morts*. Later a male chorus to the words *Beati mortui qui in Domino moriuntur* was added. The composer had expressed the wish to have this work performed at his funeral, but at that time the score could not be found. The second work is a cantata, *Hungaria*, written in 1848, in Weimar, to a text by Franz von Schober. It is for soprano, tenor, and baritone solos, and mixed chorus. This work has nothing to do with the later symphonic poem of the same name. In the *Bach Jahrbuch* Dr. Werner Wolffheim gives an account of an unpublished cantata, *Mein Herze schwimmt im Blute*, by J. S. Bach. It is written for soprano, oboe, two violins, viola, and basso continuo. D. A. Martiensson discovered this score, which is in Bach's own handwriting, among papers of Philip Emanuel Bach in the Royal Library at Copenhagen. Judging from internal evidence and the general style of the work, Wolffheim assigns the composition to the year 1714. Wasielewski, in his *Life of Schumann*, relates that at a concert given by Clara Wieck at Zwickau in 1832 a movement of a symphony in G minor by Schumann was played. But no trace of this work was ever found until last summer, when the score was discovered in Weissenborn, near Zwickau. It was immediately performed at a philharmonic concert in Zwickau.

THE UNITED STATES

ARTISTS, INSTRUMENTAL. Never did a new pianist meet with a more enthusiastic reception than Wilhelm Bachaus. He is one of those rare artists in whom one finds combined the several supreme qualities of a number of different pianists. Technique he has in abundance, but it is the last thing one admires, because he uses it solely as a means. His tone is always full and noble, capable of the subtlest *nuances*. No one can play with more sympathetic understanding of the composer's meaning. After an absence of twelve years Leopold Godowsky was heard again. He plays with greater warmth than formerly, yet he can never make the hearer forget the stupendous technique. In his case the technical execution invariably attracts more than the interpretation. Vladimir de Pachmann bade his American admirers—and they are not few—farewell forever, and they showed in no uncertain manner how they loved and appreciated his exquisite art. A young American, Arthur Shattuck, who has won his first fame abroad, proved himself a fine pianist with a brilliant technique. Gottfried Galston also was received with marked favor. Lhevinne, Bauer, Stojowsky, Ganz, Schelling, and Mmes. Goodson and Bloomfield-Zeisler are established favorites who were always greeted by large and enthusiastic audiences.

Among the violinists the incomparable Ysaye proved the greatest attraction. This artist still stands unrivaled among the host of great violinists. It is difficult to state in precise terms just what constitutes his superiority; but when listening to him, one is spellbound. Kreisler was heard only in a few concerts with the Boston Symphony Orchestra. Zimbalist, Elman, and Miss Parlow continued the success they had achieved with their initial performances. A newcomer was Louis Persinger, a native American, who made a very favorable impression.

VOCAL. The past year introduced to the American public two new liedersingers of the first rank. Elena Gerhardt has never sung in opera, and appeals only to the serious public that attends recitals. Mme. Charles Cahier, an American contralto, made her great reputation on the operatic stage in Vienna and Munich, but showed that she is equally great on the concert platform. Without Mme. Sembrich's wonderful song recitals the musical season would not be complete. Mme. Tetrazzini appeared in concerts of operatic selections; the genuine song recital seems to have no attraction for her. The Russian cantor Sirota created something of a sensation by his wonderful art of interpreting the old melodies of the synagogue. A new Italian baritone, Titta Ruffo, excited his audiences to the point of frenzy. There is no doubt that he possesses a voice of unusual range and equally unusual beauty, which he uses with consummate skill. But, besides, he has a personality that exerts a dynamic force over his hearers. Unfortunately his programmes were made to please the popular taste. Song recitals of the highest artistic merit were given by Hess, Bonci, Slezak, Warlich, McCormack, and Mmes. Schumann-Heink, Nordica, and Glück.

ORCHESTRAL CONCERTS. By his will, the late Joseph Pulitzer bequeathed $1,000,000 to the New York Philharmonic Society, one-half of which sum was to be paid as soon as the number of subscribers should have reached one thousand. At the opening of the season in the fall this condition was fulfilled. The society showed its gratitude by devoting one pair of its regular concerts to works by Mr. Pulitzer's three favorite composers, Beethoven, Wagner, and Liszt. Many changes were made in the personnel of the Boston Symphony Orchestra, especially in the strings. Several of the older members retired on a pension. The position of first 'cellist was filled by Otto Urack, who also is to act as assistant conductor. The return of Dr. Karl Muck as conductor of the famous orchestra was a source of general satisfaction. Under the leadership of Emil Oberhoffer the Minneapolis Symphony Orchestra has risen to the position of one of the best instrumental bodies in the country. A concert given in New York elicited unanimous praise for the excellence of its playing. Cincinnati seems to have bad luck with its symphony orchestra. Differences with the musical union in 1907 led to the dissolution of the original organization under van der Stucken, and for two seasons the city was without an orchestra. The new orchestra, organized in 1909, under Stokovsky, at once took its place among the great organizations and grew steadily in favor. When at the annual May festival the home orchestra was passed over in favor of the Chicago players, Mr. Stokovsky resented the action and resigned. Fortunately the board of directors kept the players together and engaged Dr. Ernst Kunwald of the Philharmonie at Berlin, under whose direction the orchestra began the new season most auspiciously. Mr. Stokovsky succeeded Carl Pohlig as leader of the Philadelphia Symphony Orchestra. An event of the first magnitude was the visit of Arthur Nikisch with the entire London Symphony Orchestra of eighty-five performers. The tour of the principal cities was a series of uninterrupted and well-deserved triumphs. It was Mr. Nikisch's first visit to America after an absence of eighteen years.

NOVELTIES. The Philharmonic Society of New York, under Stransky, introduced the much-discussed young Viennese composer, Erich Korngold, who is only 15 years of age, to the American public. The work is entitled *Overture to a Play*. It is remarkable chiefly for the treatment of the orchestral apparatus. The themes themselves are not very striking. One might characterize the style as that of the earlier Tchaikowski with some added touches of Strauss. From the same orchestra was heard a tone-poem by Delius, *In a Summer Garden*, which is distinguished by harshness and restlessness. A *Merry Overture*, by Weingartner, proved again what all his previous orchestral compositions have proved, that the eminent conductor is a splendid musician and past master of the art of instrumentation, but that he lacks all real creative ability. *Olaf's Wedding Dance*, by Alexander Ritter, is the work of a serious and sound musician, who has little to say that is of real importance. All these works were produced by the Philharmonic Society. Far more interesting, and of real musical value, were the almost unknown works of Smetana, of which Mr. Stransky produced several. Of the novelties played by the Theodore Thomas Orchestra of Chicago, under Mr. Stock, the most important was Busoni's *Fantasia Contrappuntistica* for orchestra and organ. Originally the work was written for piano, and the arrangement was made by Mr. Stock and the Chicago organist Middelschulte. The theme is taken from Bach's last composition, a fragment intended as a quadruple fugue. Mr. Stock also introduced a new overture by Georg Schumann, *Lebensfreude*, a pleasing composition. The Philadelphia Symphony Orchestra, under Stokovsky, played the introduction to Act IV. of a dramatic work written by H. Sandby upon the text of Ibsen's *Vikings of Helgoland*. The music is entirely descriptive, but scarcely sufficiently forceful for the delineation of the powerful drama. A new concerto for violin and orchestra by John Powell, produced by Efrem Zimbalist, with the assistance of Nahan Franko's orchestra, will not prove an addition to the literature of the violin. The work is hyper-modern in character, lacks decided themes, and the orchestration is far too heavy. A *Rhapsody for Clarinet and Orchestra* by Debussy was offered to the patrons of the Philharmonic Society. The work is typical of the composer's latest style. An endless surging of the orchestra, a kaleidoscopic succession of strange instrumental effects, a few detached notes from the solo instrument; nowhere any definite musical outline. In one of his piano recitals Rudolf Ganz performed the *sonata in E major, op. 2*, by Erich Korngold, whose works do not meet with the same enthusiastic reception here as in Europe. Surprising the sonata certainly is as

MME. FRIEDA HEMPEL

MLLE LUCREZIA BORI

EDWARD LANKOW

TITTA RUFFO

FOUR MUSICAL ARTISTS PROMINENT IN 1912

the work of a mere boy. It lacks logical development and spontaneity. All in all, the novelties offered during the past year were a distinct disappointment.

MUSIC FESTIVALS. The number of music festivals held during the year in the United States was legion. It is worthy of record that scarcely one festival of importance was given where Mme. Schumann-Heink was not among the soloists. The most important event of this kind was the Bethlehem Bach Festival, under the direction of Frederic Wolle. It was the first one since 1906, when Mr. Wolle went to Berkeley, Cal. The principal work was the *Mass in B minor*. Besides that four cantatas, three of which had their first pe f mance in America, were produced. The fifty-fourth annual Festival at Worcester, under the direction of Mees and Strube, brought Parker's *Hora Novissima*, Verdi's *Te Deum*, and the first performance of a new cantata, *Ruth*, by George Schumann, which proved to be a strong and beautiful work. At the biennial May Festival in Cincinnati, under van der Stucken, superb performances were given of Mendelssohn's *Elijah*, Franck's *Les Béatitudes*, Wolf-Ferrari's *La Vita Nuova*, and Berlioz's *Requiem*. A novel festival was that held at Bohemia Grove, near San Francisco. In the open air, among the giant trees of California, Henry Hadley's *The Atonement of Pan* was given under the direction of the composer. The New York Symphony Orchestra, under Walter Damrosch, and the New York Oratorio Society, under Frank Damrosch, joined forces in a four-day festival devoted entirely to the great orchestral and choral works of Brahms. *Ein Deutsches Requiem*, *Nänie*, and *Triumphlied*, and all four symphonies were performed. Bachaus played the piano concerto in B♭ and Zimbalist the violin concerto. Mme. Matzenauer contributed some of the master's most beautiful songs.

OPERA. At the Metropolitan Opera House one hundred and sixty-four performances were given from a repertoire of forty-four operas by twenty-one composers. According to nationality, these were divided as follows: German, seventeen works by seven composers totaled sixty-eight performances; Italian, seventeen works by seven composers totaled seventy-four performances; French, eight works by five composers totaled seventeen performances; American, one work by one composer totaled four performances; Bohemian, one work by one composer totaled one performance. Wagner, represented by nine works, led with thirty-four performances. Next in order came Puccini, five of whose works achieved twenty-four performances. Third ranked Verdi with five works and twenty-one performances. The works most frequently given were Puccini's *La Bohème* and Leoncavallo's *Pagliacci*, each eight times. Next came Wagner's *Walküre* and Puccini's *Madama Butterfly*, each seven times. Wagner's *Tannhäuser*, Gluck's *Orfeo*, Verdi's *Aida*, Wolf-Ferrari's *Donne Curiose*, Humperdinck's *Königskinder* and *Hänsel und Gretel* were each given six times. Three novelties were produced. Wolf-Ferrari's *Donne Curiose* (January 3), with Farrar, Jadlowker, and Didur in the principal rôles, under Toscanini, was received with great favor. In style it marks a return to the opera bouffe of Mozart and Rossini. The music is light, graceful, and sparkling. The composer employs a small orchestra. The libretto is rather poor, the chief fault being that the action is too long drawn out. Blech's *Versiegelt* (January 20), with Gadski, Jadlowker and Weil, under Hertz, in spite of excellent performances, met with an indifferent reception. Only four performances were given. Its chief fault is lack of originality. The composer has nothing new to say, and offers specimens of almost all operatic styles. Horatio Parker's *Mona* (March 14), the opera that received the $10,000 prize, with Fornia, Homer, and Witherspoon, under Hertz, was a signal failure. The composer lacks all dramatic instinct. The music impresses one as the result of cold reflection; it is deficient in sensuous charm and spontaneity. Two works were revived for the purpose of exhibiting a new singer, Frieda Hempel, of Berlin. Owing to the artist's illness the initial performance of Mozart's *Magic Flute* resulted in a splendid triumph of stage-management, which here seems to have reached the very acme of perfection. Meyerbeer's *Les Huguenots* sounds to modern ears so tedious and threadbare that it is only offered with an all-star cast. By virtue of the system of exchange with the Chicago-Philadelphia company the patrons of the Metropolitan Opera House also heard the New York premières of Massenet's *Cendrillon* and Wolf-Ferrari's *I Giojelli della Madonna*, after the American premières of both works had taken place at Chicago. Among the new singers, Frieda Hempel, the famous coloratura soprano of the Berlin Opera, had aroused the highest expectations. She made her début in Meyerbeer's *Huguenots* during the last week of the year, and was plainly showing the effects of her recent illness, so that no just estimate could be formed. Ethel Parks, another coloratura singer, proved herself an excellent artist, although her voice is not very powerful. Lucrezia Bori made a very favorable impression with her fine, clear voice, flexible coloratura, and artistic acting. Among the men only one newcomer was heard, Edward Lankow, a sterling artist with a glorious bass. All the other artists were established favorites, such as Gadski, Fremstadt, Destinn, Rappold, Farrar, Sparks, Matzenauer, Homer; Caruso, Slezak, Burrian, Jörn, Jadlowker, Martin, Weil, Griswold Witherspoon, Hinshaw, and Scotti. A very valuable addition to the corps of conductors was Giorgio Polacco, a fine musician with much temperament and authority. The other conductors were Toscanini, Hertz, and Sturani.

The Chicago-Philadelphia Opera Company gave 120 performances from a repertoire of thirty works by nineteen composers. Wolf-Ferrari, represented by two works, led with eighteen performances. Five operas of Verdi totaled sixteen performances; while Wagner ranked third, with thirteen performances of three works. Three novelties were produced. Wolf-Ferrari's *I Giojelli della Madonna* (January 16), with Caroline White, Bassi, and Sammarco, under Campanini, scored an overwhelming and genuine success. It was presented thirteen times. The music delineates wonderfully the various dramatic situations. Parelli's *A Lovers' Quarrel* (March 6), with Zepilli, Bernt, Bassi, and Sammarco, under Campanini, met with a cordial reception. It is rather light in character but full of charming melody. Goldmark's *Cricket on the Hearth* (November 7), with Teyte, Riegelmann, and Dufranne, under Winternitz, made a decidedly favorable impression. The music is very melodious, characteristic of the composer's best mood, and free from all ultra-modern touches. Of all Mr. Dippel's artists, the one that attracted the greatest attention was the Italian baritone, Titta Ruffo. Perhaps never in the history of opera in America have such frenzied demonstrations taken place as when this singer appeared in *Hamlet* and *Rigoletto*.

The Boston Opera Company gave ninety-five performances from a repertoire of twenty-eight operas by eighteen composers. Puccini led with twenty performances of four works. Next ranked Verdi, represented by five works, which achieved thirteen performances. Four performances of Wagner's *Tristan und Isolde* were given under the direction of Weingartner, while the cast was made up from the company's own artists and some stars of the Metropolitan company. For five performances of Debussy's *Pelléas et Mélisande* Mme. Le Blanc-Maeterlinck, the wife of the Belgian poet, was engaged. Mme. Nordica, one of Boston's special favorites, appeared as "Isolde" in some of the presentations of Wagner's work. No new work was produced during the year.

In the West a new operatic organization under the direction of Mario Lombardi appeared, which is known as the Pacific Coast Grand Opera Company. Among the works in its repertoire was Strauss's *Salome*. It even produced Zandonai's *Conchita* for the first time in America (September 28), thus anticipating by some months the American performance of that work announced by Mr. Dippel.

European Countries

Germany. The event of the year was the première of Richard Strauss's latest opera, *Ariadne auf Naxos*, which occurred on October 26 at Stuttgart. The composer seems determined to surprise the world with every new dramatic work. This time he has chosen one of Molière's best known comedies, *Le Bourgeois Gentilhomme*, to which he has written exquisite incidental music. "Jourdain," the principal character of the play, poses as an art Mæcenas. At an entertainment at his house *Ariadne auf Naxos*, a tragic opera, and *Zerbinetta*, a comic opera, both supposed to have been written by a protégé of his, are to be produced. As time presses, the host simply decides to have both works performed simultaneously. Thus we have not only a stage within a stage—an old device—but a comedy within a tragedy, which certainly is something new on the operatic stage. The other innovation is that the opera does not begin when the curtain rises. For two hours the audience must sit through Molière's comedy, in an adaptation by von Hoffmannsthal. In his latest work Strauss employs a very small orchestra (only thirty-six performers), but even thus this orchestral wizard offers new instrumental combinations and produces many beautiful effects. The vocal parts are of great beauty and singable, even if frequently difficult. Especially is this true of the principal aria of *Zerbinetta*, which goes up to high F sharp and is full of the most difficult coloratura work. The final duet between "Ariadne" and "Bacchus" is praised as one of the most beautiful strains in all music. Unstinted praise is bestowed upon the composer for his wonderful musical characterization of both the tragic and the comic situations. The work was conducted by Strauss himself; the principals were Jeritza (Ariadne), Siems (Zerbinetta), Jadlowker (Bacchus). In spite of its great external success, it is doubtful whether this work will gain for itself a permanent place in the repertoire. Two serious objections are pointed out by German critics. The first is that few people can adjust themselves to the frequent changes from the serious to the comic, and *vice versa;* the second, that people are tired out by being compelled to wait for two hours for the beginning of the real opera. The Stuttgart success was repeated at Dresden, while after the Cologne première hissing was heard.

A new opera, *Der ferne Klang*, by Franz Schrecker, scored a most emphatic success at its first performance in Frankfort. It is described as a work of rare beauty and pronounced individuality. Wolf-Ferrari's *Der Schmuck der Madonna* at its première in Leipzig was received with as great demonstrations as in America. A peculiar fate befell Nouguè's *Quo Vadis* after its initial performance in Berlin. The critics condemned it unanimously; the public showed its unmistakable approval. Other works that met with success at their first production were Saint-Saëns's *Déjanire* (Dessau); Busoni, *Die Brautwahl* (Hamburg); Eulambio, *Ninon von Lenclos* (Leipzig); Neitzel, *Barberine* (Crefeld). An interesting revival in commemoration of the second centenary of the birth of Frederick the Great was offered by the Royal Opera of Berlin: King Frederick's only opera, *Il Re Pastore*. The last performance of *Tristan und Isolde* directed by Dr. Muck before his departure for Boston, was made the occasion of a tremendous ovation. During the twenty years that Dr. Muck had been one of the principal conductors of the Berlin Royal Opera he conducted 1071 performances of 103 different operas, of which thirty-five were novelties. By a strange coincidence he was succeeded by Emil Paur, who conducted the Boston Symphony Orchestra from 1893-8. The first season of the Kurfürstenoper ended disastrously, so that Director Moris was obliged to retire. However, a second season under a new director, Palfi, was inaugurated. The house itself was rebuilt and many improvements made in the ensemble. At Charlottenburg the new Municipal Opera, with a seating capacity for 2200 (the largest opera house in Germany), built for the purpose of rivaling the Royal Opera, was opened with a performance of *Fidelio*. The Leipzig première of Strauss's *Feuersnot* was made the occasion of a Strauss week, when all the other operas of the master were performed. At Dresden the fortieth anniversary of Ernest von Schuch as conductor of the Royal Opera was observed in a fitting and impressive manner. The work chosen for performance in the open air in the forest near Zoppot was Humperdinck's *Hänsel und Gretel*.

The annual festival of the Allgemeiner Deutscher Musikverein was held at Dantzig. For the first time in its history a work by a woman, Gisela Selden, was performed. Of the larger works, only Noren's *Concerto for Violin and Orchestra*, played by Petschnikoff, made an impression. The chamber music was of a better quality. A string quartette, *op. 16*, by Scheinpflug and a piano quintette *op. 50*, by Juon, proved to be works of real merit. Under the auspices of the German Brahms Gesellschaft a second Brahms Festival of five concerts, under the direction of Fritz Steinbach, was given at Wiesbaden. All the great choral and orchestral works, as well as some of the chamber music, were heard. The success eclipsed even that of the first festival held at Munich in 1909. At Breslau a Bach Festival was arranged, during which only such works of the master were performed as were little known. The first Berlin performance of Mahler's *Eighth Symphony*, under Willem Mengelberg, assumed the proportions of a real festival. The chorus and orchestra numbered one thousand performers. The impression made, rather by the famous Dutch conductor (who had never been heard in Berlin) than by the work itself, was such that two extra performances had to be arranged. During the annual Mozart cycle at the Royal Opera in Munich the following works were produced: *Bastien et Bastienne, Il Seraglio, Così fan tutte, Le Nozze di Figaro, Don Giovanni*; while at the Prinzregententheater the annual Wagner festival performances were *Tristan und Isolde, Die Meistersinger, Der Ring des Nibelungen*. At Bayreuth *Die Meistersinger, Der Ring des Nibelungen*, and *Parsifal* were given.

The city of Berlin granted a subvention of 60,000 marks to the Philharmonic Orchestra on condition that it would abandon the concert tours during the summer, and remain in town giving symphony concerts at popular prices. The first summer season was successful, although the lowest admission was only 30 pfennig (8 cents). The Meiningen Court Orchestra, which was world-famous under Hans von Bülow, and later under his successor, Richard Strauss, again resumed its concert tours under the leadership of Max Reger, who proved himself but a mediocre conductor. Sam Franko's concerts of music of the eighteenth century, which he gave with the Blüthner Orchestra of Berlin, were highly appreciated. Ossip Gabrilowitsch has risen to the first rank of conductors, but his activity during the past year shows that he has no intention of relinquishing his lofty place among the greatest pianists. At one concert he played both of Brahms's piano concertos. His greatest achievement, however, is the series of six concerts in Munich, in the course of which he illustrated the historical development of the pianoforte concerto from the earliest times to the present day. In Berlin Eugen D'Albert was welcomed by crowded houses on the occasion of his reappearance, after a retirement of six years, upon the concert platform. He played with the old-time mastery which won him his enviable reputation before he began to neglect his piano in order to gather laurels as a composer. From Berlin come reports, that sound absolutely incredible, of the playing of an 11-year-old violinist, Jascha Heifetz. Nevertheless, reputable and competent critics assure us that no i ing violinist can surpass this new prodigy in the rendition of those great concertos of Brahms, Beethoven, and Bruch. Even Leopold Auer, the boy's teacher, among whose pupils are several of the greatest living violinists, declares Heifetz to be the greatest genius he has ever taught.

England. Some excitement was injected into a rather dull operatic season by the manifestos issued from time to time by Mr. Hammerstein, complaining of lack of support and berating the English for their apathy. In spite of excellent performances, the London Opera House was not patronized. After the prices of admission had been considerably reduced, larger audiences were attracted for a time, but at no time did the undertaking pay expenses. Yet Mr. Hammerstein produced three novelties: Massenet's *Don Quichotte* and *Jongleur de Nôtre Dame*, and Holbrooke's *The Children of Don* (in English). For the production of the last work no less a conductor than Nikisch was engaged. All the critics agreed that the performance was superb, but they were unable to decide whether the music was great or grotesque. When the season had been completed, Mr. Hammerstein closed his house and withdrew from London operatic affairs. Nor was the old-established opera at Covent Garden any more successful. It was remarked that the best attended performances were those at which a ballet was introduced. Only two novelties were heard: Wolf-Ferrari's *I Giojelli della Madonna* and Zandonai's *Conchita*. In the Wagner works the absence of Dr. Richter was sorely felt; Dr. Rottenburg, of Frankfort, was only a capable routine conductor. While the Moody-Manners Opera Company continued its production of grand opera in English, a dangerous rival arose for them in the Denhof Grand Opera Company, which gave, also in English, excellent representations of *The Mastersingers, Tristan, The Flying Dutchman, Orfeo*, and *Elektra* with such artists as Marie Brema, Perceval Allen, Kirkby-Lunn, Maclennan, and Balling as conductor. The London Philharmonic Society celebrated the centenary of its foundation by the performance at each concert of some work by a prominent English composer written especially for the occasion. Not one of those works made an impression. In this connection it may be recorded that perhaps nowhere, not even in Germany, are there produced so many novelties as at present in England. But very few ever get a second hearing. In spite of this fact a new "Society of Women Musicians" was organized, whose object is to perform works of its members. In connection with an exposition at Earl's Court called "Shakespeare's England," a series of concerts was arranged presenting only works inspired by the bard of Avon. Although many of the world's greatest composers, from Beethoven to Strauss, were represented, the undertaking proved a complete financial failure. At the Crystal Palace a Handel Festival was held, under the direction of F. Cowen, when *Israel in Egypt, The Messiah*, and miscellaneous works were rendered by a chorus of four thousand voices. Hereford, Birmingham, Bristol, and Brighton had their periodic music festivals. At the Hippodrome in London Mascagni drew vast audiences by conducting his *Cavalleria Rusticana*. He was followed by Leoncavallo, who conducted a new opera of his own in two acts, *I Zingari*, which failed to interest.

France. At the Grand Opéra the works of Wagner have figured more prominently than in any other year. The principal reason was the strike of the ballet. While the people in general love Wagner, fashionable society, which controls the opera house, had practically banished the works of the greatest of all dramatic composers in favor of works that introduce a ballet. The management availed itself of this strike to arrange a Wagner Festival, under the direction of Weingartner and Lohse. Massenet's last work, *Roma*, divided critical opinion, but the general impression was that the text demanded music of deep feeling and majesty, the very qualities in which Massenet is most deficient. At the Opéra Comique, Lazzari's *La Lépreuse* scored an unusual success. After the performance it was learned that this work had been sent in for a prize of 15,000 francs offered by the city of Paris. The prize was awarded to Mercier's *Elsen*, which at the Théatre de la Gaîté made a complete fiasco. At Marseilles the première of De Lara's *Les Trois Masques* called forth great enthusiasm. Under the direction of Weingartner five concerts of classical music were given in Paris. The works produced were Berlioz's *Requiem*, Handel's *Messiah*, Beethoven's *Missa Solemnis*, and several of Beethoven's orchestral works, the whole ending with a splendid performance of the *Ninth Symphony*. On this occasion the newly discovered "*Jena*" *Symphony* had its first performance in France. In a series of concerts directed by Nikisch a number of Tschaikowski's compositions were heard, which aroused unbounded enthusiasm in some quarters and equally violent opposition in others. At the age of 64 Lilli Lehmann gave two song recitals in Paris before crowded houses and evoked tumultuous applause with her masterly singing of German lieder. In recent years the Société Bach has done much to educate the French public to an appreciation of that almost unknown master's works. During the past year the famous Schola Cantorum has followed in the footsteps of the Bach Society. A few admirers of Brahms organized themselves into a Société des Amis de Bra ıms for the purpose of making propaganda for the great German master. Unfortunately their efforts have not met with success. The French public, accustomed to the hyper-modern harmonies of their national composers, absolutely refuses to have anything to do with Brahms. Word is received also of the establishment of a Société Frédéric Chopin. Among the board of directors appear the names of Chevillard, De Reszke, Ravel, and Rostand. In the prospectus we read that the object of the society is "to make known the works and preserve the honor of the composer's memory."

BIBLIOGRAPHY. Among the important books published during the year are the following:

BIOGRAPHICAL. H. Reiman, *Bach* (Berlin), completed and edited after the author's death by B. Schrader (brief, but authoritative. Profusely illustrated); M. Kalbeck, *Johannes Brahms*, vol. III., part II. (Berlin) (covers the years 1881-85); R. Schütz, *Stephen Heller, ein Künstlerleben* (Leipzig); J. Massenet, *Mes Souvenirs* (Paris) (written for his grandchildren; personal recollections from 1848 to 1912); T. de Wyzewa and G. de Saint-Foix, *W. A. Mozart, sa vie musicale et son œuvre de l'enfance à la pleine maturité*, 2 vols. (Paris) (biographical and critical, compiled from original sources, with a catalogue of the complete works in chronological order—the most complete and authoritative since Jahn); G. R. Kruse, *Otto Nicolai, ein Künstlerleben* (Berlin); W. Dahms, *Schubert* (Berlin) (the most exhaustive biography yet published. Contains thorough analyses of all important works. Profusely illustrated); F. May, *The Girlhood of Clara Schumann* (London) (an excellent study of the musical conditions from 1820 to 1840, as affecting the development of the young artist. Closes with the pianiste's marriage in 1840); M. Steinitzer, *Richard Strauss* (Berlin) (the best and most comprehensive biography yet written. Illustrated); T. San Galli, *Beethoven* (Berlin); T. San Galli, *Brahms* (Berlin); A. Weissmann, *Chopin* (Berlin). The last four belong to the same series. All are scholarly and reliable works, with excellent facsimiles and illustrations. H. S. Chamberlain, *Richard Wagner*, 2 vols. (Munich) (originally published 1895. Text not materially changed, but many new illustrations).

HISTORY OF MUSIC. M. Emmanuel, *Histoire de la langue musicale*, 2 vols. (Paris) (a treatise on the development of music as a means of emotional expression from the earliest times to the present); G. Kanth, *Bilderatlas zur Musikgeschichte* (Berlin) (contains over twelve hundred portraits and illustrations. A valuable supplement to any complete history of music); H. Kretzschmar, *Geschichte des neuen deutschen Liedes*, vol. I (Leipzig), (traces the lied from earliest beginnings in the seventeenth century to Zelter); H. Riemann, *Handbuch der Musikgeschichte*, vol. II., part II. (Leipzig) (vol. I appeared in 1904; very comprehensive; result of original research; of interest rather to the student than the general reader); B. Studeny, *Beiträge zur Geschichte der Violinsonate in achtzehnten Jahrhundert* (Munich).

AESTHETICS, CRITICISM, PHILOSOPHY. A Beyschlag: *Die Ornamentik der Musik* (Leipzig) (exhaustive and authoritative. Author had access to the vast collection of original manuscripts and first editions in the Royal Library of Berlin); E. Evans, *Handbook to the Vocal Works of Brahms* (London) (very scholarly and helpful, but too much detail); C. H. H. Parry, *Style in Musical Art* (London) (defines style as mode of expression. On this basis examines vocal, instrumental and choral style; takes up each individual art-form and traces development of national style); G. Setaccioli, *Debussy, Eine kritisch-ästhetische Studie* (Leipzig) translated by F. Spiro from the Italian into German (against Debussy's theories); R. Batka and H. Warner, *Hugo Wolf's musikalische Kritiken* (Leipzig); G. Adler: *Der Stil in der Musik*, vol I. (Vienna) (treats of principles and kinds of style).

CORRESPONDENCE. B. Scharlitt, *Friedrich Chopins gesammelte Briefe* (Leipzig) (the most complete collection; contains many only recently discovered. Translation faithful and accurate); J. Joachim and A. Moser, *Briefe von und an Josef Joachim*, vol. II. (Berlin) covers period from 1858-68); E. v. Hellmer, *Hugo Wolf, Eine Persönlichkeit in Briefen* (Berlin); G. Kaiser, *Carl Maria von Weber, Briefe an den Grafen Karl von Brühl* (Leipzig).

MISCELLANEOUS. M. B. Foster, *History of the Philharmonic Society of London* (London) (a complete record of all the programmes, soloists, conductors, etc.); L. Frankenstein: *Richard Wagner Jahrbuch*, vol. IV.; A. Schering, *Bach-Jahrbuch*, vol. VIII.

MUSSER, JOHN HERR. An American physician, died April, 1912. He was born in Strasburg, Pa., in 1856, and was educated at the Pennsylvania State Normal School. He studied medicine at the University of Pennsylvania, taking his degree in 1877. From that time until his death he practiced in Philadelphia, confining his attention chiefly to internal medicine. In 1881 he was appointed instructor in clinical medicine at the University of Pennsylvania and was successively made assistant professor and professor in that chair. He was pathologist to the Presbyterian Hospital from 1884 to 1888, and was consulting physician to several other hospitals in Philadelphia. He was a member of many medical societies. Among his published works are *Medical Diagnosis*, and contributions to medical journals and standard articles in several encyclopædias and handbooks of medicine. He edited Volume IV. of *Diseases of the Lungs, Pleura, etc.*, of Nothnagel's *Practice*.

MUTATION. See BIOLOGY.

MUTHMANNITE. See METEOROLOGY.

MUTSUHITO. Emperor of Japan, died July 29, 1912. The name Mutsuhito means simply "gentleman." He was called by the common people Tenshi Sama, "August Son of Heaven," and by the educated class, Shu-jo, "Supreme Master." He was born November 3, 1852, and according to the Japanese chronology was the 121st of his line. At the time of his birth new ideas were beginning to have an effect on the conservatism of centuries in Japan. Orders were given to Commodore Perry to sail for Japan by President Fillmore almost on the day of the emperor's birth. The future emperor was born in the mountains of Kyoto and he early learned to love nature. During his first fifteen years, or until he succeeded his father, Osahito, he lived with his mother, who had been a lady of the imperial household. He received an education which, under the circumstances, was extremely liberal, and this was superintended by his mother. When he was crowned at Osaka on October 31, 1868, the country was on the verge of being torn asunder, as a result of the bitterness, which was partly political, partly commercial, partly religious, and largely superstitious, which arose after Commodore Perry had opened Japan to the Occident. Perry had unwittingly stirred up bloody strife which followed when foreigners were granted concessions by the preceding shogun, Iyemochi, who concluded the treaty with Commodore Perry in 1854.

Mutsuhito and his advisers began immediately after his accession to formulate a political constitution, which in turn was to lead the way to the assumption by the emperor of direct personal rule. As a step in this direction, the capital was transferred from Kyoto to Yeddo, where the shogun government had been held, and the name of the new capital was changed to Tokyo, or Eastern Capital. In 1869 he returned to the old capital to marry Haruko. In the year of his marriage and after he had been crowned at Osaka he showed the sincerity of his reforms by listing a number of them and binding himself by an oath to carry them out. In a moment of patriotic exaltation his supporters among the daimios, or nobles, surrendered their estates and their feudal privileges in a large measure to the young emperor. First in his list of proposed reforms was the establishment of a deliberative assembly. He was assisted by the patriotism of the nobles, and the voluntary surrender of their privileges was the death knell of feudalism that had existed in the empire for centuries. In 1873 torture was abolished, and a judicial system founded on the "Code Napoleon" was instituted by imperial decree. About this time officials about the court began to appear in European costume. English was introduced into the curriculum of the public common schools and these schools sprung up as if by magic. The European calendar was also adopted. In 1869, as the result of a famine which made it necessary to transport large quantities of rice from the north to the south, transit facilities became a necessity, and when Sir Harry Parkes came forward with suggestions for financing a new railroad he at once received the sanction of Mutsuhito for the loan of a million pounds sterling. English engineers were secured to survey a line to run from Tokyo to Yokohama. In spite of great opposition in official as well as private circles, the emperor stood firm and the loan was granted.

The introduction of foreign innovations was bitterly opposed for years, especially in the provinces. Three times between 1876 and 1884 rebellions were started against the emperor and his attempts at modernism. The chief opponent of the emperor was the warlike clan, Satsuma, which dominated the army and navy. The emperor came into conflict with China as a result of troubles in Formosa, then claimed by the Chinese empire. Okubo, one of the most notable of the Japanese nobles, was sent alone to Peking, and there, with the backing of Mutsuhito, refused even at the risk of war to discuss the matter, according to Chinese dogma, but only in conformity with international law. China yielded and paid indemnity. It was not until 1877 that the Satsuma clan finally came under submission to the emperor. In that year, after seven months' fighting and the loss of 20,000 lives, the leader, Saigo, committed suicide. From this time forward the emperor was in supreme control in all parts of his empire. The trouble with China in 1874 caused the emperor and his advisers to give his whole time to the question of the Japanese navy and this work soon led to the building of a great fleet of warships. In 1894 came a more serious conflict with China, in which Japan was entirely victorious, but was deprived by the great powers of the fruit of victory, the possession of the great fortress, Port Arthur. This led finally to the Russo-Japanese War.

In addition to his remarkable qualities as a statesman, the emperor was one of the most productive and notable poets among his contemporaries in Japan, and much of his verse was published during his life. Characteristic of his rule was the power which he gave to his trusted servants in peace or war. He never interfered with details unless it was absolutely essential. The affection in which his subjects held him was remarkable and the great moral strength of the Japanese people came in large measure from the implicit confidence which they held in their ruler. All victories obtained by Japanese armies were ascribed to the virtue of the emperor's ancestors. A noteworthy trait was his generosity. In 1911 he gave $1,500,000 to the victims of famine, flood, disease, and war. He gave without discrimination to all sects.

Although it is sometimes assumed that the Mikado had little real power or influence, it is said by those familiar with the course of events during his reign that this was not true and that he was personally responsible for the large measure of enlightenment and power that came to Japan from his accession to his death. See JAPAN.

NANKING. See CHINA.

NANTES. See ARCHITECTURE.

NASH, Henry Sylvester. An American theologian and educator, died November 6, 1912. He was born in Ohio in 1854 and graduated from Harvard College in 1878. He studied at the Episcopal Theological School of Cambridge and at Trinity College. He was ordained priest in the Protestant Episcopal Church in 1882. Two years later he was appointed professor of literature and interpretation of the New Testament in the Episcopal Theological School at Cambridge and he remained in this chair until the time of his death. He wrote *The Genesis of the Social Conscience* (1896); *Ethics and Revelation* (1898); *History of the Higher Criticism of the New Testament* (1900), and *The Atoning Life* (1907).

NATAL. One of the four original provinces of the Union of South Africa (q. v.). Pietermaritzburg, the seat of the provincial government, had (census of 1911) 30,555 inhabitants (14,737 whites). Durban is the largest town and only port. (Population of Durban borough, 69,187; with suburbs, 89,998, of whom 34,880 whites). Ladysmith had 5595 inhabitants, and Newcastle 2886. There were in 1910 57 government schools and 501 government-aided schools, with a total attendance of 31,972. For area, population, production, and trade, see South Africa, Union of. The amount of public revenue for the eleven months ended May 30, 1910, was £4,293,728; expenditure, £3,530,349; customs revenue, £459,314; public debt, May 30, 1910, £20,895,943. Administrator (1912), C. J. Smythe.

NATCHEZ INDIANS. See Anthropology.

NATIONAL ACADEMY OF DESIGN. See Painting.

NATIONAL BANKS. According to the report of the comptroller of the currency the aggregate resources of the 7397 national banks in the United States on September 4, 1912 was $10,963,400,000. The principal item of resources included loans and discounts amounting to $6,040,000,000; or about 60 per cent. of all loanable funds. Of these loans, 9.6 per cent. were demand loans based on one or two-name paper; 16.6 per cent. demand loans secured by stocks, bonds, and other securities; 33.1 per cent. time loans secured by two-name paper; 20 per cent. time loans secured by single-name paper, and 20.6 per cent. loans based on securities. The aggregate loans were almost equally divided between the reserve cities and the country banks. New York City banks were credited with 16.1 per cent.; the banks of the central reserve cities, New York, Chicago, and St. Louis, were credited with 23.6 per cent.; and other reserve cities with 26.5 per cent. The importance of call loans for the New York City national banks was shown by the fact that the thirty-seven banks on June 14 had $326,897,000 of demand loans secured by stock, bonds, and other securities. The money rate for stock exchange call loans ranged from 1¾ per cent. at various times in January and February to 8 per cent. in October; widest variations were in March, from 2 per cent. to 5 per cent., in September from 3 per cent to 7½ per cent., and in October from 3 to 8 per cent. The time loan money rate varied from 2 to 4 per cent. during the first seven months, rising gradually to 5½ or 6 per cent. in October. Other items of the resources were $724,085,000 of United States bonds to secure circulation, $46,228,000 United States bonds to secure United States deposits, and $7,804,000 other United States bonds. Thus national banks held a total of $778,177,000 of United States bonds, or slightly more than 80 per cent. of the total bonded indebtedness of the United States. National banks also held $1,039,986,000 of other bonds, stocks, and securities. Their aggregate investments in loans and bonds were $7,708,292,000, on which the average gross earnings were 5.84 per cent. The total capital stock paid in was $1,046,012,000; surplus, $701,021,000; undivided profits, $242,735,000. The total gross earnings for the year ending June 30, 1912, were $450,043,000; deductions from this for losses, premiums, and expenses left net earnings of $149,056,000. From this latter were paid dividends amounting to 11.56 per cent. on the capital, or 6.93 per cent. on the combined capital and surplus.

The principal item of liabilities was the $4,808,937,000 of individual deposits subject to check. There were in addition $407,683,000 of demand certificates of deposit and $504,490,000 of time certificates of deposit. During the last two years the comptroller has given special attention to the savings deposits of national banks. His report showed that on September 4, 3268 national banks reported savings departments, with 2,709,000 depositors and $748,247,000 savings deposits. The law requires central reserve city banks to maintain a reserve of 25 per cent. in lawful money against all deposit liabilities. Banks in other reserve cities must maintain a reserve of 25 per cent., but one-half of this may be deposited with their agents in central reserve cities. All other banks must maintain a reserve of 15 per cent., but three-fifths of this may be deposited with their agents in reserve or central reserve cities. On September 4, the banks held $1,467,739,000 as reserves, this being equal to 20.7 per cent. of their deposit liabilities. Classification showed that the central reserve cities were slightly under the legal requirement, this being due to a deficit of New York and Chicago banks. Other reserve city banks had legal reserves of 24.92 per cent. and country banks of 16.40 per cent.; both the latter, however, had additional available reserves.

The total outstanding circulation of the national banks on September 4, was $713,823,000. This amounted to 19.5 per cent. of the general stock of money in the United States. Of the total circulation, the New York City banks were credited with $47,200,000; central reserve city banks with $77,700,000; other reserve city banks with $376,500,000, and country banks $472,600,000. Under the Aldrich-Vreeland act of 1908 incomplete notes of every bank to the extent of 50 per cent. of their capital are held in the vaults of the Treasury, the aggregate of such emergency currency being $539,164,000. Of the outstanding circulation on October 31, only $500,000 was in the form of $1 and $2 notes; $139,997,000 were in $5 notes; $330,089,000 in $10 notes; $227,332,000 in $20 notes; the remainder being in $50, $100, $500, and $1000 notes. The law requires every national bank to maintain with the Treasury a deposit in lawful money equal to 5 per cent. of its circulation. From this fund is redeemed all circulating notes presented for redemption to the Treasury of the United States. Notes that are mutilated are destroyed and replaced by new issues. In the year ending October 31,

1912, the national bank redemption agency received notes to the amount of 90 per cent. of the outstanding circulation, one-half of which was sent in from the city of New York. The cost to the national banks of maintaining their circulation amounted to $4,251,000 during the year. This included the semi-annual tax on circulation, amounting to $3,690,000, and cost of redemption of notes, $505,700. The cost of redemption was $0.78233 per one thousand dollars. Plans were matured for systematizing the designs of United States notes, silver and gold certificates, and national bank notes and at the same time reducing their size. Moreover, more artistic designs were sought as also added security against counterfeiting. The number of designs was to be reduced from 19 to 9 and the number of plates necessary for printing from 1200 to 200. It was estimated that the storage capacity of bank vaults would be increased by 25 per cent.; moreover, the reduction in size would reduce the folding and consequent wear on the notes, thus increasing their longevity. See BANKS AND BANKING; CURRENCY REFORM; FINANCIAL REVIEW; TRUSTS, *Money Trust*.

NATIONAL DRAINAGE CONGRESS. See AGRICULTURE.

NATIONAL EDUCATION ASSOCIATION, CONVENTION OF. See AGRICULTURAL EDUCATION.

NATIONAL HIGHWAYS. See ROADS AND PAVEMENTS.

NATIONAL INSURANCE. See WORKINGMEN'S INSURANCE.

NATIONAL IRRIGATION CONGRESS. See AGRICULTURE.

NATIONAL PARKS. See PUBLIC LANDS.

NATIONAL CONFERENCE OF CHARITIES AND CORRECTIONS. See PUBLIC CHARITIES.

NATIONAL PEACE CONFERENCE. See ARBITRATION, INTERNATIONAL.

NATIONAL RESERVE ASSOCIATION. See BANKS AND BANKING, *Aldrich Plan*.

NATIONAL SOIL FERTILITY LEAGUE. See AGRICULTURE.

NATIONAL SPIRITUALISTS' ASSOCIATION. See SPIRITUALISTS' ASSOCIATION, NATIONAL.

NAVAL DEFENSE REQUIREMENTS. See NAVAL PROGRESS.

NAVAL DOCKS. See DOCKS AND HARBORS.

NAVAL MILITIA. See UNITED STATES, *Navy*.

NAVAL PROGRESS. Progress in naval affairs during 1911 is here grouped under two main heads: *Aviation* and *General Progress*.

AVIATION

GREAT BRITAIN. A royal flying corps has been established, with a central flying school, and a military wing and a naval wing. The naval flying school is at Eastchurch. There were in December, 1912, two sections of the naval wing, one for aeroplanes, and the other for airships. In the military wing, there is one squadron for airships and kites, while three out of seven squadrons for aeroplanes have already been formed. On March 6, one naval hydro-aeroplane was under construction at Eastchurch, and two others were on order; experiments with this type were held at Sheerness, Lake Windermere, and Barrow. The supplementary estimates, presented in July, contained £60,000 for aircraft; it was officially stated that this "is merely the forerunner of other and larger instalments in future years." Naval airship No. 2 is building at Barrow-in-Furness. Airship No. 1 has been taken to pieces. It was officially stated in the House of Commons, December 10, that the "Royal Flying Corps possesses the following ships: Military wing, *Beta*, *Gamma*, *Delta*, and a new *Gamma* under construction, to the cost of which naval funds will contribute half; Naval wing: One experimental Willows airship which has proved satisfactory; and one Astra-Torres, and one Parseval on order." The navy has acquired a hydro-aeroplane of the French Donnet-Léveque type.

Extra rates of pay per day for naval and marine officers belonging to the Royal Flying Corps are as follows:

	Ordinary pay	Flying pay
Squadron commanders	25 s.	
Flight commanders	17 s.	8 s.
Flying officers	12 s.	

The commanding officer of the naval wing receives £800 a year with quarters. Flying pay is paid continuously to aeroplane fliers, but only on the days of ascent in the case of airships. Thirteen naval and marine officers who are qualified aviators have been appointed to the naval wing of the royal flying corps with the increased rates of pay. Four officers are serving on the staff of the central flying school with increased rates of pay. Five other officers have just graduated (December) and will be graded flying officers immediately.

GERMANY. "On October 17, the *L. I.*, the first Zeppelin airship of the German navy, was taken over by the government. The *L. I.*, built at Friedrichshaven, is about 525 feet long, 50 feet in diameter, has 706,300 cubic feet capacity; three Maybach motors, one in the front and two in the rear gondola, each of 170 horsepower; the balloon consists of eighteen gas cells. The forward aluminum propellers have two blades; and the rear ones, four blades. The horizontal steering-gear has six vertical surfaces, and the elevation steering gear eight horizontal surfaces. An observation platform of sheet aluminum is erected on the top of the balloon, which is reached by means of a shaft. In the gangway between the two gondolas is a room for officers and men, in which wireless telegraph apparatus is fitted up. Arrangements have been made for bomb-throwing in time of war. After a few trips of small extent at the beginning of the month, the airship set out from Friedrichshaven on October 13 with twenty-one persons on board, among whom were the government examining committee and Count Zeppelin, and after remaining in the air for thirty-one hours, landed at Johannisthal. The journey proceeded by way of Bielefeld to Norddeich on the North Sea, and then eastwards via Helgoland, Kiel, Lübeck, and Hamburg to Berlin, a total distance of about 1050 miles, the average speed being 33 or 34 miles an hour. The *L. I.* is stated to have successfully fulfilled all the requirements of the naval authorities." (*The Engineer*.) At the end of November tests were being held at Friedrichshaven of the first hydro-aero-biplane, *F. F. I.*, built by the Friedrichshaven-Manzell Airship Building Company. The vessel weighs 650 kilograms, has a 100-horsepower Argus motor, and carries two passengers. The tests will be continued until the conditions of the navy department are fulfilled; viz., a one-hour trip at a height of 500 meters, with two passengers. The Schütte rigid wood-frame airship made a night cruise of 16 hours on December 7. It was hoped that the army and navy would have a fleet of between fifteen and twenty airships before the end of 1912. Both departments seemed to be agreed about the aggressive value of airships, and to favor the rigid type, because it is possible to mount machine guns on top of the hulls of these vessel. It was said that the naval Zeppelin, now in service, with a surplus lifting power of three tons for armament and bombs, was likely to become a standard type. There were indications that a definite building programme had been prepared; and pressure was being exerted for a navy air-fleet law.

At the beginning of December, Germany possessed the following airships: 1 new naval Zeppelin, 9 military, including one new Zeppelin; 14 private, including two-passenger Zeppelins; but of these, 7 are under 3500 cubic meters volume, and are of little value; and one other, the *Suchard*, is built for an attempt to cross the Atlantic. The sum of $476,172 was voted in the German naval estimates, 1912-1913, for airships and experiments with airships; $702,358 is included in the German naval estimates, 1913-1914, not yet voted, for aeronautics, aviation, experiments, and special allowances. Formerly, aviation was under the office of ship-building equipment, which in turn was under the control of the dockyard bureau. A special aviation office has been established directly under the dockyard bureau. A special flying corps will be organized; for the winter half year, 199 persons, including 9 officers, were ordered to aviation duty.

FRANCE. France leads the world in aviation. "She is spending $4,886,000 this year on military aeroplanes. She is adding 300 scouting aircraft to the 200 she already owns. During the next year, and the year following, another 500 military machines will be added to her equipment; so that, at the end of 1914, she will possess an actual fleet of 1000 war-planes." (Claude Grahame-White, September 10.) There is a navy aviation headquarters on the coast of Fréjus, about halt way between Toulon and Nice. The cruiser *Foudre*, formerly a mine ship, is now an aviation ship, stationed at Fréjus. The first hydro-aeroplane accepted, a Voisin, has been hoisted in and out in three minutes. Hangars are being erected ashore. During the blockade manœuvres of the French fleet in the Gulf of Juan, a naval aeroplane obtained exact information about the disposition and movements of the blockading squadrons. Submarines had been detected navigating on the surface with evident intention of attacking the blockading force. One Nieuport (100 horse-power), three-place monoplane, and one Voisin biplane were used. The aeroplanes had neither been seen nor heard.

UNITED STATES. The winter quarters of the aviation school have been shifted from San Diego, Cal., to Guantánamo Bay, Cuba. Three areoplanes, two Curtiss and one Wright, are in use; they are now supplied with hydroplanes. Eight officers have qualified as pilots. Most of the "hydro-flying has been done at an altitude of about 500 feet. But, as scouting and reconnaisance work will require flying at an altitude of about 3000 feet, Lieutenant Ellyson has demonstrated that there will be no difficulty in flying the hydro-aeroplanes at 3000 feet or over." "There are seven different types of hydro-aeroplanes now in France, but American efforts have been confined chiefly to two distinct American types, the single boat with balancing pontoons, and the catamaran type with two pontoons. 'The Curtiss Flying Boat' is regarded as a decided advance in hydroplane design; and gives promise of extended usefulness in rough water. A simple and convenient self-starter is a practical necessity to the hydro-aeroplane before issuing it for ship use." In the navy aeroplane catapult, "compressed air is used for the power, as all ships carrying torpedoes are supplied with air compressors. The air is pumped into a receiver connected with a mall cylinder located on deck." The piston of the cylinder has a stroke of about 40 inches; and the piston rod is connected with a small wooden car by means of a wire rope purchase which multiplies the travel of the piston to any desired extent, or to any limit fixed by the travel of the car on its tracks. The aeroplane rests on the car; and when a flight takes place, both are projected from the tracks together in about 1½ seconds, the pressure being automatically and gradually accelerated during the stroke. The car drops into the water when free from the tracks; and is hauled on board by a rope attached to it." The catapult has proved very successful.

AUSTRIA. Four airships will be purchased in the first half of 1913, each to cost about $6,000,000. The budget for 1913 provides extra pay for aviators.

JAPAN. The Japanese navy has bought a Curtiss biplane in the United States; and a Farman biplane in France.

GENERAL PROGRESS

GREAT BRITAIN. The year 1912 was one of extraordinary effort in the British navy. The following are the most important developments: (1) Shooting became more practical. (2) Controlled gun fire became a reality. (3) Steaming power of the fleet increased. (4) The position of petty officers became secure and promotion better. (5) Pay of officers and men was increased. (6) Lieutenant rank was granted to a number of warrant officers. (7) The royal flying corps was established. (8) An admiralty war staff was created. (9) The fleet was reorganized; and redistributed. (10) The two-power standard was abandoned; and a standard of 60 per cent. superiority in dreadnoughts over Germany adopted. (11) A new type of ship, the light armored cruiser, was being built. (12) The rank of "mate," out of use since 1861, was revived. (13) The immediate reserve was established. (14) Work of the members of the board of admiralty was redistributed. (15) King's regulations relating to disciplinary matters in general and summary punishments in particular, were changed. (16) A royal commission was appointed to inquire into the whole question of the use of oil fuel for the naval service. (17) A remarkable parliamentary paper was issued in December, on naval defense, entitled "Memorandum on Naval Defense Requirements"; prepared by the admiralty for the government of Canada. (18) The Canadian prime minister, on December 5, introduced a naval bill proposing to give the royal navy three first-class battleships at a cost of £7,000,000. See CANADA.

Mates. The title of "mate" has been revived for the warrant and petty officers taken from the lower deck for a course of training preparatory to being granted commissioned rank. A special title was desired to distinguish these men, who will rank with sub-lieutenants, from the commissioned warrant officers on one hand, and the sub-lieutenants from Osborne on the other.

The immediate reserve. The men eligible are those under thirty-two years of age now enrolled in B class of the royal fleet reserve. Most of these men have had twelve years' service and must therefore be at least thirty years old. They are to undergo twenty-eight days' training annually, usually in June and July; and the coöperation of their employers must be obtained.

Naval war staff. The war staff will be under the general authority of the board of admiralty. The war staff must work at all times directly under the first sea lord, who has the first lord over him as the delegate of the crown. There will be three divisions: The intelligence division, the operation division, and the mobilization division. These may be shortly described as dealing with war information, war plans, and war arrrangements respectively. The divisions will be equal in status, and each will be under a director, who will usually be a captain of standing. The three divisions will be combined together under a chief of staff, a flag officer, who will be primarily responsible to the first sea lord. The creation of the staff added four executive officers to the personnel of the admiralty: One chief of staff, one director, two commanders (or lieutenants or accountant officers), and one marine officer (major or captain). A post of lieutenant-colonel of marines has been abolished.

Distribution of admiralty business. First lord: General direction of all business. First sea lord: Organization for war and distribution of the fleet. Second sea lord: Personnel. Third sea lord: Matériel. Fourth sea lord: Stores and transport. Civil lord: Works, buildings, and Greenwich Hospital. Additional civil lord: Contracts and dockyard business. Parliamentary secretary: Finance. Permanent secretary: Admiralty business.

The department formerly presided over by the controller is placed under the third sea lord and the additional civil lord. The third sea lord will have under his control a director of naval equipment, who will advise him on all naval professional questions relating to the construction of ships, whose designs have been approved by the board, and to repairs and alterations and additions to completed ships, and who will keep him informed of the progress of construction generally. He will be associated with the director of dockyards and with the superintendent of contract work in advising on questions involving considerations arising out of the building, alteration, or repair of ships. He will be responsible for the supervision of the equipment and fittings of his majesty's ships building by contract or in the dockyards.

Royal commission on the supply and use of oil fuel. This commission, under the presidency of admiral of the fleet, Lord Fisher, of Kilverston, O. M., G. C. M. G., etc., has been appointed to inquire into the whole question of the use of oil fuel in the navy. It will take a long time for the commission to make a final report; but the admiralty will take advantage of its deliberations as they proceed, and as wisdom dictates. The first results will probably be the abandonment of coal as a steam generator in the new ships of the current programme.

Fleet reorganization, dating May 1, 1912, (extract from admiralty circular letter, dated March 29, 1912). "The home fleet will be divided into the first, second, and third fleets; and ships will be classed in these fleets according to the status of commission in which they are maintained by their lordships; ships in the first fleet being in permanent commission with full crews; ships in the second fleet being in commission with nucleus crews, and receiving full complements of active service ratings on mobilization; ships in the third fleet being in commission with reduced nucleus crews, or in 'matériel reserve' and requiring reserve men on mobilization. These fleets are therefore administrative and not tactical classifications.

"The home fleet thus divided into three fleets, will comprise eight squadrons. Each squadron will consist of a battle squadron and cruiser squadron and attached ships, numbered consecutively. Four squadrons will form the first fleet, two the second fleet, and two squadrons and three additional cruiser squadrons the third fleet, as follows: First fleet: The 1st and 2nd divisions of the home fleet and the Atlantic fleet, to be in future known as the 1st, 2nd, and 3rd squadrons. A 4th squadron will be constituted within this fleet at a future date. Second fleet: The present 3rd division of the home fleet formed into the 5th and 6th squadrons. Third fleet: The present 4th division of the home fleet formed into the 7th and 8th squadrons, and the 9th, 10th, and 11th cruiser squadrons.

"The administrative grouping of the ships of the second and third fleets will usually correspond with their ports of manning and repair so far as is practicable. Upon assembly they will at once assume their organization in squadrons.

"The commander-in-chief, home fleet, will have placed under his direct command such fleets and squadrons as their lordships consider proper. In normal circumstances his command will include the whole of the first, second and third fleets. The present 4th cruiser squadron will in future be known as the 'training squadron.' The present 6th cruiser squadron will in future be known as the 'Mediterranean cruiser squadron.' The 'eastern fleet' will comprise the China squadron, the Australia squadron, and the East Indies squadron.

"Other vessels on foreign stations will continue to be designated as at present, but the vessels employed in Newfoundland, the West Indies, and on the southeast coast of South America, will, if combined, be known as the 'West Atlantic squadron.'

"The organization of the destroyer flotillas will conform to the foregoing system. 'The present 1st, 2nd, and 7th flotillas will be reorganized into four flotillas, to be known in future as the 1st, 2nd, 3rd, and 4th flotillas. The present 3rd, 4th, and 5th flotillas (nucleus crews) will be also reorganized into four flotillas, to be known in future as the 5th,

6th, 7th, and 8th flotillas. The vessels composing the present 6th flotilla will in future be included in the home-port flotillas. The 1st, 2nd, 3rd, and 4th flotillas will, in normal circumstances, be under the orders of the commander-in-chief of the home fleets. The 5th, 6th, 7th, and 8th flotillas will form the command of a flag-officer, styled 'admiral of patrols.' This officer will be under the direct orders of the admiralty.

"The submarine sections in home waters will also, from May 1, be rearranged in nine sections. They will remain under the general control of the inspecting captain of submarines, who will be responsible to the commanders-in-chief of the home ports for those sections which are assigned to port defense, and will be responsible to the admiral of patrols for the remainder."

It will take 65 ships (the flagship of the home fleet will be out of the line) to carry out this programme; and this number will not be available until the latter part of 1914.

The Mediterranean. The battleships of the Mediterranean squadron were withdrawn; and the admiralty apparently intended to keep no battleships in the Mediterranean, leaving British interests to be protected by France. Such great home opposition developed that the eight "King Edwards" were sent on a three months' cruise in the Mediterranean, to return home in January, 1913; and the battleships withdrawn are to be replaced by the *Indefatigable, Inflexible, Invincible,* and *Indomitable,* with four of the most modern and largest armored cruisers.

Important Appointments. Soon after Mr. Winston Churchill became the first lord of the admiralty Admiral Sir Arthur Wilson retired from the post of first sea lord. He refused a peerage; but he was promoted to admiral of the fleet. He was succeeded by Vice-Admiral Sir Francis Bridgman-Bridgman; who in turn was succeeded in November, by Vice-Admiral Prince Louis of Battenburg. On the retirement on August 1, of Sir Philip Watts from the office of director of naval construction, he was succeeded by Mr. E. H. Tennyson d'Eyncourt, naval architect to the firm of Messrs. Sir W. G. Armstrong, Whitworth and Company (Ltd.). Sir Philip Watts has been retained as adviser on naval construction to the board of admiralty.

Memorandum on Naval Defense Requirements. This remarkable document prepared by the admiralty for the government of Canada, in December, 1912, recited in detail the comparative development of the German and British fleets. The main points were as follows: During the last fifteen years the development of the German fleet has been the most striking feature of the naval situation. Five successive laws, namely, the fleet laws of 1898, 1900, 1906, 1908, and 1912 covered a period up to 1920.

"Whereas in 1898 the German fleet consisted of 9 battleships (excluding coast defense vessels), 3 large cruisers, 28 small cruisers, 113 torpedo-boats, and 25,000 men, maintained at an annual cost of £6,000,000, the full fleet of 1920 will consist of: 41 battleships, 20 large cruisers, 40 small cruisers, 144 torpedo-boats, 72 submarines, and 101,500 men, estimated to be maintained at an annual cost of £23,500,000. These figures, however, give no real idea of the advance, for the size and cost of ships have risen continually during the period, and, apart from increasing their total numbers, Germany has systematically replaced old and small ships, which counted as units in her earlier fleet, by the most powerful and costly modern vessels. Neither does the money provided by the estimates for the completed law represent the increase in cost properly attributable to the German navy, for many charges borne on British naval funds are otherwise defrayed in Germany; and the German navy comprises such a large proportion of new ships that the cost of maintenance and repair is considerably less than in navies which have been longer established."

This German expansion has not been provoked by British naval increases. The admiralty document goes on to show that Great Britain down to 1909 was proceeding at no such rate as to stimulate German competition. It then turns to the fifth German naval law, passed in the spring of 1912. Its main feature was not the increase of new construction, but of the striking force of ships of all classes. Instead of an active battle fleet of 17 battleships, 4 battle or large armored cruisers, and 12 small cruisers it would, in the near future consist of 25 battleships, 8 battle or large armored cruisers, and 18 small cruisers. It would not only be increased in strength, but rendered much more readily available. Ninety-nine torpedo-boat destroyers instead of 66 were to be maintained in full commission; 72 new submarines were to be built, and apparently it was intended to maintain 54 of these with full permanent crews. In short, nearly four-fifths of the entire German navy were to be maintained in full permanent commission instantly ready for war.

The first lord of the admiralty laid these facts before the House of Commons on July 22, 1912, and pointed out that in the spring of the year 1915, Great Britain would have 25 dreadnoughts and 2 Lord Nelsons to Germany's 17 dreadnoughts; and that each would have 6 battle cruisers; also that the reserve of strength would steadily diminish. Greater exertions would therefore be required by the British empire!

Light Armored Cruisers. The first lord of the admiralty, in describing the eight small armored cruisers now building, said: "They will, in fact, be the smallest, cheapest, and fastest vessels protected by vertical armour, ever projected for the British navy. They are designed for attendance on the battle fleet. They are designed to be its eyes and ears by night and day; to watch over it in movement and at rest. They will be strong enough and fast enough to overhaul and cut down any torpedo-boat destroyer afloat, and generally, they will be available for the purpose of observation and reconnaissance." It is supposed that they will displace about 4000 tons, make 30 knots speed; have a 5-inch armor belt, develop 40,000 horsepower, five of them with Parsons turbines (4 propellers) and three with Curtis turbines (2 propellers). They are to be completed in June, 1914.

GERMANY. *Naval Amendment Law,* 1912. The effect of this law is given in the British "Memorial on Naval Defense Requirements" quoted above.

Great secrecy is maintained about new material, inventions, equipment of the fleet, manoeuvres, and target practice. The press bureau has cautioned the newspapers about their indiscretions, calling attention to the fact, that,

U. S. BATTLESHIP "ARKANSAS"

IN COMMISSION 1912

for some time, the characteristics of German submarines, which ought to remain secret, have been given. *Nauticus* (1912), issued by the naval information office, and the *Taschenbuch der Kriegsflotten* (1913), by Weyer, partly from official sources, omit all armor details concerning battleships later than the 1905 programme; and give no details at all about the battleships and battle cruisers of the 1911 and 1912 programmes, or of the battle cruiser *Seidlitz* of the 1910 programme. Weyer (1913), makes public, for the first time, the displacement (700 tons) of the destroyers of the 1910-11 and 1911-12 programmes. Neither book gives any details about submarines, of which there are now 18 completed.

Ordnance. Krupp now advertises 14, 15, and 16-inch guns, of 50 cal., using 1364, 1672, and 2024 pound shells, respectively. It is now generally believed that the claim of an unusually long life for Krupp guns is unfounded. The life of the German 11-inch (28cm.) gun is 30 per cent. greater than that of the 12-inch (30.5cm.). The life of the Krupp 14-inch gun is unofficially estimated at from 80 to 90 full charges. The improved British 13.5-inch gun fires a shell weighing 1400 lbs.; and is understood to have a life of from 80 to 90 full charges.

Triple Turrets. Germany has not adopted the triple turret for heavy guns, notwithstanding the example set by the United States, Austria, and Italy. An experimental triple turret for 12-inch guns proved unsatisfactory.

Destroyers. The new destroyers (700 tons) will carry two 30 cal. 3.5-inch (8.8cm.) guns; while the British destroyers of the 1911-12 programme (920 tons) and the 1912-13 programme (1200 tons) will each carry three 4-inch guns.

UNITED STATES. *14-inch Gun.* The 14-inch 45 cal. gun for the *New York*, *Texas*, *Nevada*, *Oklahoma*, and *Pennsylvania* is far more powerful than the 12-inch 45 cal. gun on the *Delaware* and *North Dakotoa*. Muzzle energy of 14-inch gun, about 66,000 foot-tons; that of 12-inch, 49,000 foot-tons. Weight of 14-inch shell 1400 lbs.; that of 12-inch, 850 lbs. The 14-inch shell carries a much larger bursting charge of high explosive.

Gun Mounts. The triple-turret mount is to be installed on the *Oklahoma* and *Nevada;* and for the four turrets of the new battleship *Pennsylvania.* The 14-inch Mark I. mount will be used on the *New York* and *Texas*, and in the two-gun turrets of the *Oklahoma* and *Nevada.*

Powders. The principal improvement of the year is one whereby the requisite amount of diphenylamine is incorporated in the powder without variation. No smokeless powder in which diphenylamine has been incorporated has as yet shown any signs of loss of stability, the oldest lot of powder containing this stabilizer being now four years old. With regard to the use of ozokorite to reduce erosion of guns, the disadvantages more than offset the advantages.

Torpedoes. Experiences with the two new type of long-range high-speed torpedoes show that the United States is at least abreast of all foreign countries in this respect.

DESTROYERS. The eight destroyers of the *Aylwin* type, 1040 tons, five 4-inch guns, 29½ knots, ordered last year, are the most heavily armed of their class, except the six large ocean-going destroyers of the *Tomé* type, 1430 tons, six 4-inch guns, 31 knots, now building for Chile. The British *Daring* type (1912), 1200 tons, 32-33 knots, are armed with three 4-inch guns; but carry four 21-inch torpedo tubes, while the *Aylwin* carries three twin 18-inch tubes.

Submarines. *G 1 (ex-Seal)*, descended to a depth of 256 feet, and, with 12 men on board, stayed there 30 minutes 5 seconds, with no injury to the boat and no discomfort to the complement. Characteristics: length 161 ft.; beam, 13 ft.; displacement, 525 tons, submerged; 6 torpedo tubes; 10 torpedoes; speed, 14 knots on the surface, and 9.5 knots submerged.

FRANCE. *New Construction.* Chief Constructor Doyère submitted to the superior council three plans of 25,000-ton ships, 172 meters long, and 29 wide, speed, 21 knots, horsepower, about 33,000, the lines of which had been tested with success in the Paris trial-basin. Plan A provided for three quadruple turrets on the centre line; plan B, for two quadruple and two superposed twin turrets; plan C, for four quadruple turrets to contain 12-inch guns instead of 13.4-inch guns. It is claimed that the quadruple turret, in spite of its enormous weight (1500 tons) is superior to the triple turret, because it is better balanced, and can be divided into two separate and independent compartments by an armored bulkhead, which gives it the advantages of twin turrets with regard to ammunition supply and rate of fire. Owing to the weight and space saved, it permits an invulnerable armor protection. No decision has been officially announced; it seems certain that there will not be a return to the 12-inch gun. The probable design for these ships, the *L'Orient*, *Savoie*, *Gascoigne*, and *Normandie*, is: 25,387 tons, 21.5 knots speed, twelve 13.4-inch guns in quadruple turrets, and twenty-four 5.5-inch torpedo defense guns.

Submarines. France, in the *Gustave Zédé*, owns the largest submarine. Characteristics: Surface displacement, 797 tons; submerged displacement, 970 tons; surface speed, 16 knots; submerged speed, 10 knots; length, 239.5 ft.; beam, 19.6 ft.; number of torpedo tubes, 6; launched in 1912. But this type is not final, as a new design, *Q 102*, is under construction at Rochefort. Characteristics: Surface displacement. 520 tons; length, 198½ ft.; beam, 18 ft.; surface indicated horsepower, 2100; surface speed, 17½ knots; 8 torpedo tubes; complement, 3 officers and 26 men.

Redistribution of Fleet. The entire battle fleet has been concentrated in the Mediterranean; and there has been a reassignment of destroyers and submarines. Submarines are now attached to the battle fleet; though no real seagoing, so-called "squadron submarines" are yet available.

Manœuvres. This year's manœuvres have shown that superior use of gun power must be the aim of all tactics. Battle cruisers of the British *Lion* type are much favored. The attacks *en masse* by destroyers led separately against the battle line (both by day and night) would have had decisive results in warfare. Submarines were most successful; and are held to be perfect instruments of blockade, both for offense and defense. Little use was made of mines.

Powder. Large quantities of powder were destroyed and there was a time when the battle fleet was almost without powder. This critical condition no longer exists, according to the official statement of the French minister of marine.

NAVAL WAR STAFF. See NAVAL PROGRESS.

NAVY YARDS. See UNITED STATES, *Navy*.

NEBRASKA. POPULATION. According to the Census Bureau statistics compiled during 1912 out of a total population of 1,192,214 in 1910, 175,865 were foreign-born whites, compared with 177,117 in 1900. The largest number, 57,220, came from Germany; from Austria, 24,521; from Sweden, 23,194; from Denmark, 13,648; from Russia, 13,072; from Ireland, 8124; and from Canada, 6592. In the city of Omaha, with a population of 124,096, the foreign-born population numbered 27,068. Of these 4841 came from Germany, and 3789 from Sweden. The negroes in the State in 1910 numbered 7689 and the mulattoes 208. In 1890 the negroes numbered 8913 and the mulattoes 2822.

AGRICULTURE. The acreage, value, and production of the principal crops in 1911 and 1912 are shown in the following table:

		Acreage.	Prod. Bu.	Value.
Corn	1912	7,609,000	182,616,000	$67,568,000
	1911	7,425,000	155,925,000	85,759,000
Wheat	1912	3,123,000	55,052,000	37,985,000
	1911	3,098,000	41,574,000	36,169,000
Oats	1912	2,275,000	55,510,000	16,653,000
	1911	2,500,000	34,750,000	14,942,000
Rye	1912	55,000	880,000	493,000
	1911	52,000	676,000	507,000
Potatoes	1912	118,000	9,440,000	4,814,000
	1911	116,000	6,032,000	5,549,000
Hay	1912	1,150,000	a 1,552,000	13,037,000
	1911	1,350,000	a 1,148,000	11,136,000

a Tons.

MANUFACTURES. The Thirteenth Census included statistics relating to manufactures of the State. The results are given in the table below. These figures are for the calendar year 1909. While Nebraska is not preëmiently a manufacturing State, its manufacturing interests have developed considerably in the last five years, as will be seen by this table. The industries in which the largest capital is involved and whose products have the largest value are those connected with slaughtering and meat-packing. Of these there were in 1909 eighteen establishments, employing 6015 wage-earners and manufacturing products valued at $92,305,000:

	Number or Amount 1909	1904
Number of establishments	2,500	1,819
Persons engaged in manufactures	31,966	25,356
Proprietors and firm members	2,522	1,904
Saalried employees	5,108	3,192
Wage earners (average number)	24,336	20,260
Primary horsepower	64,466	46,372
Capital	$ 99,901,000	$ 80,235,000
Expenses	183,587,000	146,639,000
Services	19,439,000	14,097,000
Salaries	5,491,000	3,075,000
Wages	13,948,000	11,022,000
Materials	151,081,000	124,052,000
Miscellaneous	13,067,000	8,490,000
Value of products	199,019,000	154,918,000
Value added by manufacture (value of products less cost of materials)	47,938,000	30,866,000

EDUCATION. The total number of children of school age in the State in the school year 1911-12 was 379,028. The total enrollment in the public school was 283,602. The average daily attendance was 197,990. The teachers numbered 10,968, with an average monthly salary of $57.25. There were 7151 school houses in 7005 districts. Graduate schools numbered 543, normal training schools, 153, four-year high schools, 155, three-year high schools, 70. The total value of school district property was $17,266,334. The expenses for the support of schools was $8,045,027.

FINANCE. The report of the State treasurer for the biennial period ending November 31, 1912, showed a balance on bond on December 1, 1910, of $601,290. The receipts for the biennial period amounted to $10,862,142, and the disbursements to $10,890,121, leaving a balance, November 30, 1912, of $573,310. The principal receipts are from the general fund and the chief expenditures are for education and the support of State institutions.

POLITICS AND GOVERNMENT. There was no session of the legislature in 1912, as the sessions are biennial and the last was held in 1911. The next session convenes January 7, 1913.

Nebraska was freer from political turmoil in 1912 than most of the other western States. The Progressive party put no candidates in nomination for State offices, endorsing the Republican candidates chosen at the primaries, although they elected delegates on July 31, pledged to vote for Mr. Roosevelt at the National Progressive convention. The most interesting political event of the year was the presidential primary election held on April 10. In this Mr. Roosevelt received 46.795 votes, President Taft, 13.341, and Senator La Follette, 16,785. Champ Clark received the Democratic preferential vote. In this election Governor Aldrich was renominated by the Republicans and United States Senator Brown was defeated for renomination by Congressman Norris The Democrats nominated J. T. Morehead, for Governor, and Ashton C. Shallenbarger for United States senator.

Considerable interest was attracted in April by the action of five Populists from Osceola in placing Woodrow Wilson's name on the primary ballot as a Populist candidate for President. This drew from Wilson a request that his name be withdrawn.

Mr. Bryan took no very active part in State politics during the year. His name appeared on the presidential primary ballot on January 30, but was withdrawn. The Republican electors chosen at the State convention were pledged to vote for Mr. Roosevelt in accordance with the presidential primary vote. On October 5 six Taft electors were placed on the presidential ballot by petition. These electors replaced those men who, although on the Republican ticket, insisted on supporting Mr. Roosevelt and refused to resign from the regular ticket. The election of November 5 resulted as follows: For President, Wilson received 109.008 votes, Roosevelt, 72,678, Taft, 34,216, Debs, 10.185, and Chafin, 3383. Governor Wilson's plurality was 36,394. The vote for governor was as follows: Morehead, Dem., 123.997; Aldrich, Rep., 114.-075, Wright, Soc., 9959, Wilson, Prohib., 3662. For popular preference for United States senator George W. Norris received 126,022 votes, running on the Republican and Progressive tickets, and Ashton C. Shallenbarger had 111.-946 running on the Democratic ticket. Mr. Norris was thus assured of election by the legislature at its regular session. The legislature is Democratic by a vote of 5 on joint ballot.

.eral amendments to the conried. These included a pro-
itiative and referendum; an-
provided for a board of com-
tate institutions, and another
judges to the supreme court.
r amendment cities of 5000 and
n the privilege of framing their
instead of going to the legisla-
ht to adopt the commission form
nt was granted by the legislature

ary 17 the supreme court of the
ed an injunction against serving
f any kind in dining cars passing
the State.

GOVERNMENT. Governor, James T. ..d, Democrat; lieutenant-governor, S. R. ..il, Republican; secretary of State, Addi- ..ait; treasurer, W. A. George; auditor, W. ..oward; attorney-general, Grant G. Martin; ..rintendent of education, James E. Delzell; ..mmissioner of insurance E. C. Pierce; com- ..issioner of public lands, Frederick Beekman—..ll Republicans, except governor.

JUDICIARY. Supreme Court: Chief justice, Manoah B. Reese; justices, Charles B. Letton, Francis G. Hamer, Jacob Fawcett, William B. Rose, John B. Barnes, and Samuel H. Sedgwick; clerk, H. C. Lindsay—all Republicans.

STATE LEGISLATURE, 1913. Senate, Democrats 15, Republicans 18; House, Democrats 54, Republicans, 46; joint ballot, Democrats 69, Republicans 64. Majority, Senate, Republicans 3; House, Democrats 8; joint ballot Democrats 5.

The representatives in Congress will be found in the section *Congress*, article UNITED STATES.

NEBRASKA, UNIVERSITY OF. A State institution for higher education at Lincoln, Neb., founded in 1869. The enrollment in all departments of the university in the year 1911-12 was 3091. Of these, 1556 were in the college of arts and sciences, 157 in the teachers' college, 384 in the college of engineering, 332 in the college of agriculture, 236 in the college of law, and 162 in the college of medicine. The total enrollment in the autumn of 1912 was 3220. The faculty numbered 383. There were no changes of great importance in the faculty during the year. The university is supported almost entirely by the State and there were no noteworthy benefactions received. The income from all sources in the year 1911-12 was $911,840. The library contained about 100,000 volumes. President, Samuel Avery, Ph. D.

NECROLOGY. The following list contains the names of persons who died during 1912. An asterisk prefixed to a name indicates that there is a separate biography in proper alphabetical order, in the body of the book:

* Adam, John Noble. American merchant.
* Aehrenthal, Alois Lexa, Count von. Austro-Hungarian statesman.
* Albert, Charles Stanley. American clergyman.

Alexander, Thomas. United States commissioner. Died July 24; born, 1854.

* Alger, Philip Rounseville. American naval officer.

Allen, James Cameron. American jurist and former member of Congress from Illinois. Died January 30; born, 1822.

* Allitsen, Frances. An English composer.
* Alma-Tadema, Sir Laurence. English artist.
* Andree, Richard. A German geographer.
* Andrews, William Swain. American lawyer and public official.

Angulo, Felipe. Former Colombian minister at London. Died, March.

* Anshutz, Thomas Pollock. American artist.

Anthony, Geraldine W. American author and scientist. Died October 20.

* Arbuckle, John. American merchant and philanthropist.
* Astor, John Jacob. American capitalist.

Atwood, Charles Kellogg. Oldest graduate of Yale University. Died September 19; born, 1821.

* Austin, Henry. American lawyer.

Avery, George Alden. American architect. Died May 13; born, 1852.

* Avery, Robert. American soldier and lawyer.
* Aycock, Charles Brantley. Former governor of North Carolina.
* Ayme, Louis Henri. American public official.
* Bacon, Francis. American surgeon.
* Bacon, Henry. American artist.

Baird, Henry Carey. American publisher. Died December 31; born, 1825.

* Bang, Hermann Joachim. Danish author.
* Barr, Robert. English novelist.
* Barton, Clara. American philanthropist.

Batterman, Henry. American merchant. Died January 10; born, 1849.

Beal, Frederick Earl. American physician and educator. Died August 8; born, 1868.

* Beecher, Willis Judson. American theologian.
* Beernaert, Auguste Marie François. Belgian public official.
* Behrens, Siegfried. American musician.

Beidler, Jacob A. Former member of Congress from Ohio. Died September 13; born, 1853.

* Bent, Samuel Arthur. American lawyer.

Beruete y Moret, A. de. Spanish artist and writer. Died, January; born

Bigelow, Charles A. American comedian. Died March 12; born, 1862.

* Bingham, Henry Harrison. American public official.

Bisson, Alexandre Charles Auguste. French playwright. Died January 28; born, 1849.

Blackwood, William. English publisher. Died November 11; born, 1836.

* Blair, Charles Austin. American jurist.
* Blake, Edward. Canadian statesman.

Blaustein, David. Jewish scholar and educator. Died August 28; born, 1864.

Bleekman, George. American artist and writer on yachting. Died April 3; born, 1863.

Block, Jan. Belgian composer. Died May 26; born, 1851.

* Blodgett, John Taggart. American jurist.
* Blyden, Edward Wilmot. American negro author.
* Boas, Emil Leopold. American steamship director and philanthropist.

Boen, Haldor. Former member of Congress from Minnesota. Died July 23; born, 1850.

Boff, Felix M. Roman Catholic vicar-general. Died March 21; born, 1831.

Boisbaudra, Francis Lecoq de. French physicist. Died, June; born, 1838.

* Boise, Otis Bardwell. American music teacher.
* Boller, Alfred Pancoast. American engineer.
* Bonbright, Daniel. American educator.

Bond, Frank Stuart. American railway official. Died February 26; born, 1830.

Boniface, George C. American actor. Died January 4; born, 1824.

Bonvoisin, Maurice. Belgian caricaturist known as "Mars." Died, March; born, 1849.

* Booth, William. Commander-in-chief of the Salvation Army.

Borden, Garrick Mallory. American art director and lecturer on art. Died May 24; born, 1875.

Borden, Matthew Chaloner Durfee. American cotton manufacturer. Died May 27; born, 1842.

* Bormann, Edward. German humorist and poet.
* Bornet, Jean Baptiste Edouard. French botanist.
* Boss, Lewis. American astronomer.

Bostock, Frank C. American showman. Died October 8; born, 1862.

* Bovey, Henry Taylor. English scientist.
* Bowyer, John Marshall. Rear-admiral of the United State navy.
* Bradley, John Edwin. American educator.
* Bragg, Edward Stuyvesant. American soldier and public official.
* Brastow, Lewis Ormond. American theologian.
* Brinkley, Frank. English editor.
* Brisson, Henri. French statesman.
* Brown, Justus Morris. American soldier.
* Browne, William Hand. American writ[er]
* Browning, Robert Wiedemann Barrett, [son] of Robert Browning.
* Brush, George Jarvis. American miner[alogist]

* Buchholz, Charles Waldemar. American engineer.

* Buckhout, William A. American educator.

Bunn, Albert C. American medical missionary. Died December 24; born, 1845.

* Burnham, Daniel Hudson. American architect.

* Burt, Silas Wright. American soldier.

* Burtsell, Richard Lalor. American Roman Catholic priest.

* Butlin, Sir Henry Trentham. English physician.

* Butt, Archibald Clavering. American soldier.

* Byers, Margaret (Morrow). Irish educator.

* Byrd, Adam Monrow. American public official.

Calahan, Edward A. American inventor. Died September 12; born, 1838.

Calhoun, David Samuel. American jurist. Died November 7; born, 1827.

* Chalice, Count. Austrian diplomat.

Cameron, Agnes Deans. American author and lecturer. Died May 13; born, 1863.

* Canalejas y Mendez, José. Prime minister of Spain.

* Carey, Asa Bacon. American soldier.

* Carleton, Will. American poet.

Carlisle, Charles James Stanley Howard, Earl of. English nobleman and member of Parliament. Died January 20; born, 1868.

Carmichael, Alexander. Scotch scholar and student of folklore. Died June 6; born 1832.

Caro, Victor. Jewish rabbi and philanthropist. Died June 23;

* Carrington, Henry Beebee. American soldier.

Carson, John M. American newspaper correspondent and soldier. Died September 29; born, 1828.

* Cartwright, Sir Richard. Canadian stateman.

Caventon, Eugene. French chemist. Died February; born, 1829.

Chetwood, Farncis Barber. American clergyman and writer. Died January 14; born, 1832.

Childers, Hugh. English editor. Died August 31; born, 1862.

* Chisholm, Hugh J. American capitalist.

* Church, Alfred John. English clergyman and writer.

* Churton, Edward Townson. Anglican bishop.

* Clancy, John. Irish Roman Catholic bishop.

Clark, Alvah A. Former congressman from New Jersey. Died December 27; born, 1840.

* Clarke, William Newton. American scholar and educator.

* Cleaves, Henry Bradstreet. American public official.

* Clouston, Sir Edward Seaborne. Canadian financier.

* Collins, Loren Warren. American jurist.

* Collyer, Robert. Unitarian clergyman.

* Coman, Henry Benjamin. American jurist.

Conlon, George. French public official. Died February 20; born, 1838.

* Connell, Richard E. American public official.

Connors, Richard Stephens. American railway official. Died April 3; born, 1833.

* Coolidge, John Bacon. American chemist and dentist.

Coolidge, Horace Hopkins. American lawyer and public official. Died February 5; born, 1832.

* Cooper, Philip Henry. Rear-admiral, retired, of the United States navy.

Cooper, W. Harcourt. English engraver. Died, March; born, 1835.

* Corbett, James Francis. Roman Catholic archbishop.

* Coullié, Peter Hector. Roman Catholic cardinal.

* Countermine, John Donnan. American clergyman.

* Cox, Charles Finney. American scientist.

* Craig, John. American horticulturist.

* Crane, Richard Teller. American manufacturer.

Cromwell, Ellis. American public official, collector of internal revenue for the Philippine Islands. Died February 11; born, 1878.

* Crothers, Austin Lane. American public official.

Cruise, Sir Francis. Irish physician and scholar. Died, February; born, 1835.

Crum, William B. United States minister to Liberia. Died December 7; born, 1858.

* Cupples, Samuel. American manufacturer and philanthropist.

Currier, Mary Adams. American elocutionist and educator. Died May 2; born, 1832.

* Cutting, William Bayard. American lawyer.

* Dahlgren Charles Bunker. American soldier.

* Dahn, Felix Sophus Julius. German historian, novelist, and poet.

Dale, Richard. American financier. Died September 18; born, 1828.

* Dale, Thomas Henry. American public official.

* Dalrymple-Hay, Sir John Charles. English admiral.

Dartieu, Ferdinand. French architect. Died February 19.

* Darwin, Sir George Howard. English scientist.

* Davenport, Homer Calvin. American cartoonist.

Daumet, Honore. French architect. Died January; born, 1827.

* Dawson, Thomas Cleland. American diplomat.

Day, Edmund. American playwright. Died January 23; born, 1867.

De Beruete, Aureliano. Spanish painter and art critic. Died January 10.

Delaunay-Belleville, Louis. French engineer and inventor. Died February 10; born, 1843.

Delorme, General. French soldier. Died March; born, 1829.

D'Harcourt, Bernard, Count. French Ambassador in London, 1872-3, and in Berlin, 1874-9. Died, January; born, 1822.

* Dent, Clinton Thomas. English surgeon.

* Desclauzas, Marie. French actress.

* Despradelle, Constant Désiré. American architect.

* Detaille, Jean Baptiste Edward. French painter.

* Dewitt, David Miller. American public official.

Dick, William. American sugar refiner and financier. Died April 5; born, 1823.

* Dickens, Alfred Tennyson. Oldest surviving son of Charles Dickens.

Dickinson, Henry S. American paper manufacturer. Died June 3; born, 1863.

Dierx, Leon. French poet. Died June; born, 1838.

Dingee, Charles. American horticulturist. Died November 29; born, 1824.

* Divers, Edward. English chemist and educator.

Duane, James May. American banker and philanthropist. Died December 3; born, 1851.

* Duffield, Henry Martyn. American soldier and lawyer.

* Dunbar Ralph O. American jurist.

* Duncan, Joseph Wilson. American soldier.

* Duncan, William Butler. American capitalist.

Dyer, Charles. American artist and public official. Died February 1.

* Dykes, James Oswald. Scotch theologian and educator.

Earle, Edwin L. American educator. Died April 5; born, 1868.

Eaton, Daniel Cady. Professor emeritus of the history and cricitism of art at Yale University. Died May 18.

Egerton, Sir Robert Eyles. British colonial official. Died September 29.

* Elder, Cyrus. American lawyer and author.

Eliot, Ellsworth. American physician and genealogist. Died December 9; born, 1827.

Elwell, D. Jerome. American artist. Died December 28; born 1847.

Espinasse, Francis. Scotch writer. Died January; born, 1825.

Ettlinger, Joseph. German journalist and writer. Died February; born, 1870.

Evans, Edward C. American clergyman.

* Evans, Robley Dunglison. Rear-admiral of the United States navy.

* Everett, William Henry. Rear-admiral of the United States navy.

* Ewers, Ezra Philetus. American soldier.

Faber, Beryl. English actress. Died May 1.

* Fairbanks, Andrew Martin. English scholar.

Falt, Clarence Manning. American actor and author. Died May 13; born, 1861.

* Farley, Joseph Pearson. American soldier.

* Farnsworth, Wilson Amos. American missionary.

* Fetterolf, Adam H. American educator.

Field, Edward. English admiral and member of Parliament. Died March 26; born, 1878.

* Fife, Duke of (William George Duff).

* Finch, William Albert. American lawyer and educator.

Fischer, Hubert Antonio. Cardinal and Archbisho of Cologne. Died July 30; born, 1842.

Fischer, William Gustavus. American hymn writer. Died August 15.

Fitzgerald, Sir Gerald. English public official. Died October 11; born, 1833.

* Ford, Isaac Nelson. American newspaper correspondent.

Forestier, Antoine Clair. French sculptor. Died, January; born, 1866.

* Foster, David Johnson. American public official.

Fouillée, Alfred. French philosopher. Died July 16; born, 1937.

Franz Joseph, Duke. Bavarian prince. Died September 23; born, 1888.

* Frederick VIII. King of Denmark.

* Freer, Paul Caspar. American chemist and public official.

Frida, Emil Bohusch. Hungarian poet. Died September 9; born, 1843.

Fuller, Sidney Thomas. American engineer. Died June 2; born, 1836.

* Funk, Isaac Kaufman. American author and publisher.

* Furness, Christopher, First Baron of Grantley. English ship owner and builder.

* Furness, Horace Howard. American Shakespearean scholar.

* Futrelle, Jacques. American author.

* Gairdner, James. English historian.

Gandillot, Leon. French dramatist; died September 22; born 1862.

Ganss, Henry G. American Roman Catholic priest and author. Died December 26; born, 1855.

* Gardner, James Terry. American engineer and capitalist.

Garretson, Carleton G. American editor. Died September 2; born, 1878.

* Gates George Augustus. American educator.

George, Richard. American sculptor, son of Henry George. Died October 4; born, 1870.

Gerber H. German architect. Died January 2.

Gibbs, Heneage. American pathologist. Died July 21; born, 1832.

Gibbs, Lewis Mills. American merchant. Died July 6;

Gill, Benjamin. American classical scholar and educator. Died February 10; born, 1833.

* Gilman, Nicholas Paine. American sociologist.

Glyn, Sir John Carr. English lieutenant-general. Died, March; born, 1837.

Golden, George Fuller. American vaudeville actor. Died February 17; born 1869.

* Gompers, Theodor. Austrian philosopher.

Goodwin, Frank. American lawyer and educator.

Goodwin, John Cheever. American librettist and playwright. Died December 18; born 1850.

* Goodwin, William Watson. American scholar and educator.

* Gordon, James. American public official.

* Gordon, William W. American soldier and mechant.

Gracey, John T. American Methodist Episcopal clergyman and writer. Died January 5; born, 1832.

* Grady, Thomas Francis. American lawyer and politician.

* Grafton, Charles Chapman. American Protestant Episcopal bishop.

* Graham, Charles Morice. Roman Catholic bishop.

* Grant, Frederick Dent. American major-general.

Grant, Roland. American lecturer and writer. Died August 22; born, 1851.

* Greenough, George Gordon. American soldier and scholar.

Grignola, John. American sculptor. Died June 24; born, 1861.

* Griscom, Clement Acton. American financier.

* Griswold, Stephen Benham. American librarian.

* Grossmith, George. English actor and entertainer.

* Guggenheim, Benjamin. American capitalist.

Hackstaff, Alex. C. American railway official. Died November 28; born 1852.

* Hahnke, Wilhelm von. German soldier.

* Haines, Henry Williamson. American archæologist.

Hall, Alfred A. American jurist. Died January 21; born, 1849.

* Hall, Edward Henry. American Unitarian clergyman.

* Hammond, Joseph. English clergyman and writer.

Hancock, John. American soldier. Died October 27; born, 1829.

* Hanscom, John Forsyth. American rear-admiral of the United States navy.

* Hansen, Gerhard Henrik Armauer. Norwegian biologist.

* Harahan, James Theodore. American railway official.

Hardie, Francis H. American soldier. Died April 27.

* Harrity, William Francis. American lawyer and public official.

* Harrod, Benjamin Morgan. American engineer.

* Hartley, Jonathan Scott. American sculptor.

* Hartwell, Alfred Stedman. American jurist.

* Hatcher, William E. American Baptist clergyman.

Harvey, Margaret Boyle. American poet and historian. Died October 5; born, 1856.

* Hauk-Wartegg, Minniw. American prima donna.

Haviland, Frank. English artist. Died, April; born, 1870.

Hawkins, Erastus Corning. American civil engineer. Died April 9; born 1860.

* Hawley, Edwin. American railroad official.

* Hayes, Joseph. American soldier.

* Haynie, James Henry. American newspaper correspondent.

* Hays, Charles Melville. American railway official.

* Heilner, Lewis Cass. American rear-admiral of the United States navy.

* Heilprin, Louis. American historical scholar and encyclopedist.

Henniker-Major, Arthur Henry. British major-general. Died February 5; born, 1855.

Henning, Joseph. American Roman Catholic theologian and scholar. Died, July 3; born, 1838.

Herrick, John R. American educator. Died July 27; born, 1822.

* Hertel, Albert. German painter.

Hertford, Hugh de Grey Seymour, sixth Marquis of. English nobleman. Died March 21; born, 1843.

Herzog, Felix Benedict. American inventor and artist. Died April 16; born, 1860.

* Heyburn, Weldon Brinton. American public official.

* Higgins, Anthony. American public official.

* Hill, Frank Davis. American public official.

* Hill, John Fremont. American public official.

* Hill, Octavia. English philanthropist.

* Hobbs, Perry L. American chemist and educator.

Hodgson, Shadworth Hollway. English writer on philosophy. Died June 16; born, 1833.

* Hoffman, Herman S. American bishop.

* Hogg, Hope W. English scholar and educator.

Hoke, Robert F. Major-general of the Confederate army. Died July 3.

* Holcombe, Chester. American author and diplomat.

* Holmes, George. Anglican clergyman.

Holmes, John Henry. American newspaper publisher and editor. Died June 18; born, 1844.

* Holmes, Richard Sill. American Presbyterian clergyman.

Holstein-Lereborg, Count. Former prime minister of Denmark. Died March 1; born, 1837.

* Honda, Yo-iohi. Japanese educator.

Hope, John. American inventor. Died September 9; born, 1820.

Hopkins, Amos Lawrence. American railway official. Died April 4; born, 1844.

* Hotchkin, Samuel Fitch. American Protestant Episcopal clergyman.

* Howard, Walter Eugene. American educator.

* Hoyt, John Wesley. American public official.

* Hubbard, Elbert Hamilton. American public official.

* Huff, George Franklin. American public official.

Hume, Allan Octavian. Anglo-Indian official. Died July 30; born, 1829.

* Huntington, Dewitt Clinton. American Methodist Episcopal clergyman.

Hutchings, William Henry. Anglican clergyman. Died January 7; born, 1836.

* Hutchins, Stilson. American capitalist and newspaper proprietor.

* Hutton, Arthur Wollaston. English clergyman and writer.

Hymans, Henri. Belgian archivist and historian of art. Died, January; born 1837.

* Ijichi. Japanese vice-admiral.

* Innes, Alexander Taylor. Scotch theologian.

* Irwin, John Arthur. American physician.

* Ishomoto, Shiaroku. Japanese statesman.

* Jackson, Samuel Macauley. American editor and educator.

* Jaggar, Thomas Augustus. American Protestant Episcopal bishop.

James, Mary Ellen. American philanthropist. Died March 31; born 1834.

Jamison, Benton K. American financier. Died April 8; born, 1835.

* Jarrold, Ernest. American writer.

* Jex-Blake, Sophia. English physician.

* John, Griffith. English missionary.

Johnson, Wolcott Howe. Merchant and philanthropist. Died January 15; born, 1860.

* Joline, Adrian Hoffman. American lawyer and writer.

* Jones, John Percival. Former United States Senator from Nevada.

Justi, Karl. German philosopher. Died December; born, 1832.

* Keane, Augustus Henry. English etymologist and anthropologist.

Keller, Elizabeth C. American surgeon. Died November 29; born, 1837.

Kelly, Eugene. American banker and philanthropist. Died January 18; born, 1862.

Keppel, Friedrich. American writer and lecturer on art. Died March 7; born, 1845.

Kerwin, Michael. American soldier and public official. Died June 20; born, 1827.

Keswick, William. English administrator, merchant, and member of Parliament. Died March 9; born, 1834.

* Kiderlen-Wächter Alfred von. German statesman.

Kilburn, Edward E. American inventor. Died May 25; born, 1831.

* King, Hamilton. American writer and diplomat.

* Kirkup, Thomas. English economist.

Kirschner, Dr. K. A. Martin. German public official, formerly mayor of Berlin. Died September 13; born, 1842.

* Kitchener, Sir Frederick Walter. British administrator and lieutenant-general.

Kitchin, George William. Church of England clergyman, dean of Durham. Died October 14; born, 1827.

Kittredge, Abbott Eliot. American clergyman of the Reformed Church. Died December 17; born, 1834.

*Knox, George Williams. American theologian.

Koch, Waldemar. American physiological chemist. Died February 2; born 1876.

Kuhe, Wilhelm. Hungarian pianist. Died October 8; born, 1823.

* Labouchere, Henry Du Pré. English journalist and politician.

* Lamberton, Benjamin Peffer. Rear-admiral of the United States navy.

Lane, Edward. Former congressman from Illinois. Died October 30.

* Lang, Andrew. English man of letters.

* Langlois, Hippolyte. French soldier and writer.

* Lanning, William Marshon. American jurist.

Lassoe, Valdemar. American engineer. Died May 22; born 1836.

* Laurie, John Wimburn. English lieutenant-general.

* Lawrence, Amory Appleton. American merchant.

* Lawson, Thomas Goodwin. American jorist.

* Lea, Homer. American soldier and writer.

* Leavitt, Mary Greenleaf (Clement). American temperance worker and lecturer.

* Le Conte, Jean Jacques Dessalines Michel Cincinnatus. President of Haiti.

Lee, Christopher M. American jurist. Died May 20; born, 1855.

Leffman, Salamon. German philologist and educator. Died, January; born, 1832.

* Lefebvre, Jules Joseph. French artist.

* Legras, Gustave. American mathematician and educator.

* Leighton, John. English artist.

* Le Moine, Sir James MacPherson. Canadian ornithologist.

Lenz, Oscar Lewis. American sculptor. Died June 25; born, 1873.

* Leroy-Beaulieu, Anatole. French historical writer.

Leuche, Raval. French sculptor. Died, June; born, 1860.

Levinson, Abraham C. American Jewish scholar. Died June 8.

* Lewis, Grace Anna. American naturalist.

* Liebmann, Otto. German philosopher.

* Liliencron, Rochus, Baron. German author.

Limburg-Stirum, Count Frederick William. German political writer. Died, September; born, 1835.

* Lister, Joseph, First Baron English physician.

Little, Robbins. American librarian. Died April 13; born, 1832.

* Livingstone, Leonidas Felix. American public official.

* Li Yuan Hung. Vice-president of the Chinese Republic.

* Lochren, William. American jurist.

* Loeb, Morris. American chemist and educator.

* Loewe, Conrad. Austrian actor. Died February; born, 1856.

* Loomis, Eben Jenks. American astronomer.

* Loos, Charles Louis. American scholar and educator.

Low, Abbott Augustus. American merchant and philanthropist. Died September 25; born, 1844.

Low, Philip Burrill. Former member of Congress from New York. Died August 23; born, 1836.

* Loyson, Charles. French preacher and theologian.

* Lubliner, Hugo von. German dramatist.

* Ludden, Patrick Anthony. American Roman Catholic bishop.

* Ludwig, Alfred. German philologist.

* Luitpold, Karl Joseph Wilhelm, Prince Regent of Bavaria.

Lumley, Arthur. American artist and illustrator. Died September 27; born, 1837.

* MacArthur, Arthur. American soldier.

* MacCameron Robert Lee. American artist.

* McCarthy, Justin. Irish novelist.

* McChesney, Dora Greenwell. American writer.

McDowell, Hugh. One of the founders of the Republican party. Died June 17; born, 1827.

* McGee, WJ. American anthropologist.

McGill, John Dale. American surgeon. Died November 28; born, 1846.

McHenry, John G. Member of Congress from Pennsylvania. Died December 27; born, 1858.

* McIlvaine, Clarence W. American publisher.

McIntyre, William Watson. Former member of Congress from Maryland. Died March 30.

Mackay, Donald. American banker. Died February 29.

* McLane, James Woods. American physician and writer.

* McMahon, Stephen (Brother Justin). Roman Catholic educator. Died February 28; born, 1833

McNamara, Patrick J. Roman Catholic vicar-general of the diocese of Brooklyn. Died April 15; born, 1844.

Malabari Behramji Marwanji. Indian editor and social reformer. Died, July; born, 1854.

* Malby, George R. American public official.

* Mallet, John William. American chemist.

Mandell, Simon. American merchant. Died August 19; born, 1837.

* Marie, Princess of Belgium.

Marie Theresa. Sister of King Alfonso of Spain. Died September 23; born, 1883.

* Marriott, Watson, Rosamund (Ball). English poet.

* Marsden, Samuel Edward. Anglican bishop.

Martin, William R. H. American merchant and philanthropist. Died January 30; born, 1842.

* Massenet, Julien Émile Frédéric. French composer.

Mataafa. Former king of Samoa. Died February 14.

* Mathews, William Smith Babcock. American musician and educator.

Matsunaga, Masatoshi, Baron. Japanese lieutenant-general.

* Maurice, John Frederick. English major-general.

Maxwell, Robert Alexander. American public official. Died June 8; born, 1838.

May, Julia Harris. American writer. Died May; born, 1833.

* May, Karl. German writer.

* Meade, William Edward. Bishop in the Church of Ireland.

* Meigs, Arthur Vincent. American physician and writer.

Melcher, Frank Otis. American railway official. Died January 22; born 1864.

* Melville, George Wallace. Rear-admiral of the United States navy.

* Merriam, Henry Clay. American soldier.

Merritt, Arthur Herbert. American Greek scholar. Died June 5.

* Micou, Richard Wilde. American theological educator.
Miliutin, Dmitri Alexeivitch, Count. Former Russian minister of war. Died, February; born 1816.
Millard, Edouard. French politician. Died, May; born 1835.
* Miller, James Russell. American clergyman and author.
* Millet Francis David. American artist and war correspondent.
Milovanovich, M. G. Prime minister of Servia. Died July 2.
* Molinari, Gustave. Belgian political economist.
Monnard, Heinz. German actor. Died, July; born, 1874.
* Monod, Gabriel Jacques Jean. French historian.
* Montgomery, Thomas Harrison, Jr. American zoologist.
Moreland, Christopher Hudson. Anglican clergyman and headmaster of Christ College, New Zealand. Died March; born 1868.
* Morgan, Henry Arthur. English scholar and educator.
Morgan, William Cole. American financier. Died December 6; born, 1839.
* Morris, Charles, American soldier.
* Morris, Thomas John. American jurist.
Moss, Sir Horace Edward. English musichall promoter. Died November 25.
* Moule, George Evans. English missionary bishop.
Munch, Wilhelm. Professor of pedagogics at the University of Berlin. Died, March; born, 1843.
Murat, Prince Louis Napoleon. French nobleman. Died September 21; born, 1851.
* Murray George Robert Milne. English botanist.
* Musser, John Herr. American physician.
* Mutsuhito. Emperor of Japan.
* Nash, Henry Sylvester. American theologian.
* Neff, Stewart S. American engineer.
* Newberry, Walter Cass. American soldier.
* Newcomb, James Edward. American laryngologist.
* Nicholls, Francis Tillon. American soldier and public official.
* Nicholson, Edward William Byron. English librarian.
* Nishi, Kwanjiro, Baron. Japanese general.
* Nishi, Tokujiro, Baron. Japanese diplomat.
* Nissen Heinric,h. German archæologist.
* Nixon, George Stuart. American public official.
* Nixon, William Penn. American journalist.
* Noble, John Willock. American soldier.
* Nogi (Kiten) Marosuke, General. Japanese soldier.
Ogle, William. English educator and statistician. Died April 12; born, 1827.
Okane, T. C., American hymn-writer. Died Febuary 11; born 1830.
* Olcott, George N. American classical scholar and educator.
* Oliver, Paul Ambrose. American soldier.
Oppenheim, Henry Morris William. English financier. Died May 4; born, 1835.
* O'Reilly, Robert Maitland. American physician.
Osband, Lucy Aldrich. American chemist and educator. Died February 19; born, 1836.
* Osten-Sachen, Count Nicolai Dmitri Jevitch von der. Russian diplomat.
* Outram, Sir Francis. British soldier and administrator. Died September 23; born, 1836.
Overbeck, Charles C. Former politician and one of the founders of the Republican party. Died February 3; born, 1822.
Page, Charles Harrison. American lawyer, former member of Congress from Rhode Island. Died July 21; born, 1843.
Parkes, Albert L. American theatrical manager and writer. Died February 8; born, 1827.
* Parks, James Lewis. American Protestant Episcopal clergyman.
Pascoli, Giovanni. Italian poet. Died, April; born, 1856.
* Paine, John Alsop. American archæologist.
* Passy, Frédéric. French economist.
Patterson, John J. Former United States Senator from South Carolina.. Died September 28; born, 1830.
* Pearsons, Daniel Kimball. American physician and philanthropist.
* Peel, Arthur Wellesley, Viscount. English public official.
* Peffer, William. American public official.
Pelletan, Edouard. French publisher. Died, June; born, 1854.
Penley, William Sidney. English comedian. Died Noember 11; born, 1851.
* Perkins, Reece Wilmer. American Baptist clergyman.
* Phillips, Thomas W. American capitalist.
Pillet, J. J., Désiré. French architect.
* Pitney, Mahlon. American jurist.
* Planten, John R. Dutch public official.
* Platt, Isaac Hull. American physician and writer.
* Poincaré, Jules Henri. French mathematician.
* P te , James Davis. American public official, or r
* Potter, Louis McClellan. American sculptor.
Pratt, Henry B. American clergyman. Died, December; born, 1832.
* Preto, Ouro, Viscount. Brazilian statesman.
* Price, James L. American jurist.
Price, William S. American lawyer and writer. Died December 17; born, 1817.
Priest, Henry. American scholar and educator. Died September 27; born, 1847.
* Prime, Ebenezer Scudder. Rear-admiral of the United States navy.
* Pryor, Sarah Agnes (Rice). American writer.
Prud'Homme, Lucien Franklin. American army officer and educator. Died March 15.
Puron, Juan Garcia. Spanish author and editor. Died June 9; born, 1854.
Pyle, James Tolman. American merchant. Died February 8; born, 1859.
* Rankin, William. American lawyer.
* Ransdell, Daniel Moore. American public official.
* Rayner, Isidor. American public official.
* Reibey, Thomas. Tasmanian public official.
* Reid, Whitelaw. American diplomat.
Rendall, Isaac Norton. American educator. Died November 17; born, 1823.
* Renwick, Edward Sabine. American inventor.
* Richards, Eugene Lamb. American mathematician and educator.
* Richards, Sir Frederick William. English admiral.
* Richards, William Alford. American public official.
* Richardson, Maurice Howe. American surgeon.
Richman, Julia. American educator. Died June 25.
* Ricker, George Hodgen. American educator.
Ricordi, Giulio. Italian publisher of music. Died June 6; born, 1840.
* Ritchie, Sir Richmond. English public official.
* Robets, Ernest Stewart. English scholar and educator.
* Robie, Frederick. American public official.
* Rodenbough, Theophilus Francis. American soldier.
Rodgers, Galbraith. American aviator. Killed April 3; born, 1879.
* Rogers, Robert Cameron. American poet and author.
Romana, Alejandro Lopez de. A former president of Peru. Died May 27.
* Ropes, William Ladd. American librarian.
* Rotch, Abbott Lawrence. American meteorologist.
Runyon, Frank Willetta. American journalist. Died May 14; born, 1852.
Russell, Matthew. Irish Jesuit priest. Died September 12; born, 1834.
Ryan, Roger. Roman Catholic vicar-general of the archdiocese of Dubuque. Died January 9; born, 1837.
St. John, Florence. English actress. Died January; born ,1855.
Saks, Andrew. American dry goods merchant. Died April 8; born, 1848.
Saeilles, Raymond. French educator and professor of civil law. Died, March; born 1856.
* Salmon, Sir Nowell. English admiral.
* Sanger, Charles Robert. American chemist and educator.
* Sangster, Margaret Elizabeth. American author.
Satterlee, Charles Edward. American railway official. Died June 17; born, 1832.
Saxton, Marguerite. Shakespearean actress. Died August 18; born, 1849.
Schleyer, Johann Martin. Inventor of Volapük. Died August 20; born, 1839.
* Schreyvogel, Charles. American artist.

Schofield, William. American jurist. Died June 10; born, 1857.
* Schwab, Gustav Henry. American merchant and steamship official.
Schwarz, Rudolph. Austrian sculptor. Died, April.
* Schweighofer, Felix. Austrian comedian.
* Scobell, Sir Henry Jenner. British major-general.
* Scott, Frank Hall. American publisher.
* Scott, Robert Falcon. English explorer.
* Scruggs, William Lindsay. American diplomatist.
* Sears, Clinton Brooks. American soldier.
* Seebohm, Frederick. English historian.
Segond, Paul. French surgeon. Died, October; born, 1851.
Sercy, Hippolyte de. French minister to Luxemburg. Died, April; born, 1854.
Seyeroff, Valentine A. Russian artist. Died, January; born, 1856.
Seymour, Lobert G. American Baptist clergyman. Died September 30; born, 1843.
Shaw, Robert. American painter and etcher. Died July 18; born, 1859.
Shearer, Frederick E. American Congregational clergyman. Died July 20; born, 1838.
* Sheepshanks, John. English bishop.
Sherborn, Charles William. English bookplate artist. Died, February; born, 1832.
* Sherman, James Schoolcraft. Vice-President of the United State.
Sherman, William Watts. American banker. Died January 22; born, 1842.
Shields, Emma Barbee. American portrait painter. Died January 14; born, 1864.
Sierra, Justo. Mexican ambassador to Spain. Died September 13.
* Singer, Edmund. Hungarian violinist.
* Skeat, Walter William. English philologist and educator.
Sloane, Ulrich. American jurist. Died January 21.
* Smiley, Albert Keith. American educator and humanitarian.
* Smith, Edwin. American astronomer and geodesist.
Smith, Frederick Guest. American soldier. Died October 7; born, 1840.
* Smith, Gerritt. American organist and composer.
* Smith, John Bernhardt. American entomologist.
* Smith, William. American soldier.
Smith, William Waugh. American educator.
* Snowden, Archibald Loudon. American diplomat.
* Sorsby, William Brooks. American diplomat.
* Southwick, George W. American public official.
* Spangler, Henry Wilson. American engineer.
Spencer, John Walton. American naturalist and educator. Died October 24.
Spicker, Max. American musical composer and conductor.
* Sprague, Charles Ezra. American banker.
* Spring, Alfred. American jurist.
Stacy, Orville Briggs. American scientist and educator. Died July 12; born, 1832.
* Stahel, Julius. American soldier.
* Stanmore, Arthur Hamilton Gordon, First Baron. British administrator.
* Stead, William Thomas. English editor and publisher.
Steele, Robert William. Naval constructor. Died February 29; born, 1831.
* Steinert, Morris. American piano manufacturer.
Stephan, Friedrich. German journalist. Died, February; born, 1831.
* Stevens, Horac Jared. American copper specialist.
* Stevens, Nettie Maria. American biologist.
Stevenson, Thomas. American Methodist Episcopal clergyman. Died June 4; born, 1831.
* Stewart, Alexander. American public official.
* Stoker, Abraham. English barrister and writer.
* Stone, Charles Warren. American public official.
Stonor, Edmund. Roman Catholic Archbishop of Trebizond. Died February 26; born, 1831.
*Straus, Isidor. American merchant and philanthopist.
* Strindberg, August. Swedist novelist.
* Strong, George Augustus. American Protestant Episcopal clergyman.

Struve, Hendryk de. Russian philosopher and educator. Died, May.
* Stubbs, Charles William. Anglican bishop.
* Sumner, Edwin Vose. American soldier.
* Suvorin, Alexis Sergeievich. Russian editor.
* Sweet, Henry. English philiologist.
* Swett, Sophie Miriam. American author.
* Taft, Royal Chapin. American public official.
* Tarr, Ralph Stockman. American geographer.
* Taylor, Sir Alexander. English soldier.
* Taylor, Ezra B. American public official.
* Taylor, Robert Love. American public official.
* Taylor, Samuel Coleridge. English composer.
* Terrell, Alexander Watkins. American diplomat.
* Terrell, Joseph Meriwether. American public official.
* Terry, David Brainard. American educator.
* Terry, Edward O'Connor. English actor.
Thallman, Ernst. American banker. Died February 26; born, 1851.
Thoma, Ludwig F. American educator. Died June 22; born, 1847.
Thompson, Clifford. American soldier and editor. Died September 29; born 1834.
Thompson, Fayette L. American Methodist Episcopal clergyman. Died April 26.
Thompson, Frederick William. Canadian merchant and financier. Died, May; born, 1862.
Thurston, Gates P. American soldier and author. Died December 8; born, 1835.
Tilden, William S. American musician. Died May 15; born, 1830.
* Tillinghast, Mary Elizabeth. American artist.
* Tinel, Edgar. Belgian composer.
* Torrey, Brandford. American naturalist and writer.
* Torrey, Franklin. American sculptor.
Traeger, Christian Gottfried Albert. German writer and member of the Reichstag. Died, March; born, 1830.
* Tristram, Thomas H. English jurist and church official.
* Trotter, Lionel James. English lawyer and writer.
* Tryon, James Rufus. Rear-admiral of the United States navy.
Tucker, Seth M. American lawyer and pioneer. Died January 4; born, 1830.
Twining, Louisa. English philanthropist. Died, September; born 1820.
Ubinger, Johannes. German philosopher and educator. Died, March; born, 1855.
Varley, Henry. English evangelist. Died, March; born, 1836.
* Vernon, Frédéric. French engraver.
* Verrall, Arthur Wooligar. English scholar and educator.
Viebe, Herman Friedrich. German scientist. Died September 17; born, 1852.
Voltz, Ludwig. German painter. Died, January; born, 1826.
Wallis, Sir Frederick Charles. English surgeon. Died, April; born, 1860.
Wallot, Paul. German architect. Died August 10.
* Walton, Clifford Stevens. American lawyer and public official.
Ward, John. English Egyptologist. Died, February; born, 1833.
Ward, Rowland. English taxidermist and hunter. Died December 28.
* Warren, Henry White. American bishop.
* Wash u n, William Drew. American public official, b r
* Weaver, James B. American soldier and political writer.
Webster, H. Daniel. American sculptor. Died March 20; born, 1879.
* Weeden, William Babcock. American soldier.
Weimann, John. German editor and poet. Died January 27; born, 1848.
Welles, Benjamin Emory. American editor. Died January 4.
* Wells, Almond Brown American soldier.
Wells, Reuben. American inventor and locomotive builder. Died November 8; born, 1829.
* Wendell, Oliver Clinton. American astronomer.
Wendt, Gustav. German classical scholar and educator. Died, March; born, 1847.
Wenlock, Beilby Lawley, Third Baron. An English administrator. Died January 15; born, 1849.
* Wernher, Sir Julius. English capitalist.

* Wheeler, Charles Gilbert. American chemist and mining geologist.

* Wheelwright, Edmund March. American architect.

White, Caroline. English authoress. Died September 2; born, 1811.

* White, George Stuart. English field-marshal.

White, Henry Kirk. American missionary. Died July 19.

White, Maunsell. American metallurgist and inventor. Died October 22.

* White, Trueman Clark. American jurist.

* Wickliffe, Robert C. American public official

Widener, George D. American capitalist. Died at sea, April 15.

* Wilson, John L. American newspaper proprietor and public official.

* Wilson, Andrew. English journalist.

Wieniawski, Joseph. Polish pianist. Died November 16; born, 1838.

Wiley, Aquila. American brigadier-general, retired. Died June 5; born, 1832.

Wiley, John McClure. Former member of Congress from New York. Died August 13; born, 1842.

Willson, Sir Mildmay. English major-general. Died, March; born, 1848.

Wills, Sir Alfred. English jurist. Died August 9; born, 1828.

Winans, Ross Revillon. American capitalist. Died April 25; born, 1851.

* Wines, Frederick Howard. American statistician and penologist.

* Wing, Yung. Chinese statesman and scholar.

* Winkelmann, Hermann. German dramatic tenor.

* Wood, Henry Barnes. American educator.

Wood, Ogden. American artist. Died September 14; born, 1847.

* Woodworth, William McMichael. American zoölogist.

Wright, Ammi Willard. American capitalist and philanthropist.

* Wright, Sophie B. American philanthropist and educator.

* Wright, Wilbur. American inventor and aeronaut.

* Yeamans, Annie. American actress.

* Young, Alfred Harry. English anatomist and educator.

* Young, Lucien. Rear-admiral of the United States navy.

* Zeal, Sir William Austin. Australian public official.

NEFF, Steward S. An American engineer, died July 12, 1912. He was born in Cincinnati, O., in 1859, and was first employed by the Pennsylvania Railroad as assistant engineer, afterwards serving under James J. Hill of the Great Northern. In 1892 he became superintendent of the Lake Superior and Ishpeming Railway. In 1895 he took charge of the famous loop at Chicago and two years later organized the system. In 1900 he entered the service of the Boston Elevated Railway as consulting engineer. He was afterwards consulting engineer of the Brooklyn Rapid Transit Railway Company. This post he resigned to accept a position as general manager of a system of electric railway lines in Mexico. He returned to the United States in 1906. He was most widely known as a transit engineer in the United States

NEGRI SEMBILAN, The (Nine States). A federation of states composing a state of the protected Federated Malay States (q. v.). The area is given as 2600 square miles; population, 130,201 (96,028 in 1901). The Malays number about 65,000 and are mainly engaged in agriculture in the Kuala Pilah and Tampin districts; the Chinese work in the tin mines. Area alienated (end of 1909) for mining, 26,-677 acres; output, 4533 piculs tin and 43,537 tin ore. Area alienated for agriculture, 295-827 acres; area under rubber, (1910) 51,806 acres; rice, 33,876; cocoanuts, 19,246

Seremban is the government headquarters. Native affairs are administered by Tungku Mohamed, Yang di Pertuan of Sri Menati, and various chiefs; the British resident in 1912 was C. W. C. Parr (acting).

NEGROES, Illiteracy of. See Illiteracy.

NEMATODES. See Zoölogy.

NEOCOLEMANITE. See Meteorology.

NEON. See Physics.

NEOSALVARSAN This is a formaldehyde sodic sulphoxylate of dioxydamidoarsenobenzol. The arsenic content of three parts of neosalvarsan is approximately equal to two parts of salvarsan. Neosalvarsan is an orange-yellow powder, very unstable in the air and in solution, and readily soluble in water. Since it is merely a soluble compound of salvarsan, its actions and uses are the same as that drug. It is said to be tolerated better than salvarsan, and consequently may be employed in larger doses. Neosalvarsan may be administered by intravenous or intramuscular injection, preferably the former, but not subcutaneously. Solutions must be injected immediately after preparation. The drug is designed to replace salvarsan and to avoid the disagreeable and often dangerous by-effects of the latter remedy. Its limited trial during the short time which has elapsed since its introduction does not permit appraisal of its merits. See Salvarsan.

NERVOUS DISEASES. See Gynoval.

NETHERLANDS, The (or Holland, Kingdom of). A constitutional monarchy of western Europe, lying between Germany and the North Sea. The Hague is the capital.

Area and Population. The total area, including the rivers of Zeeland and South Holland, the Zuider Zee, the Dollart, and the Wadden (the shallows extending along the shores of Friesland and Groningen as far as the Dollart), based on a low-tide planimetric calculation, is 40,828.71 square kilometers (15,764 square miles). The land area by provinces, the population according to the census of December 31, 1909, the population as calculated December 31, 1911, and the density per square kilometer (1909 census) are given in the table below:

Provinces	Sq. kms.	Pop. 1909	1911	D.
North Brabant	4,972.84	623,079	639,507	125 30
Gelderland ...	5,024.40	639,602	654,319	127.30
South Holland	2,931.00	1,390,744	1,443,867	474.47
North Holland	2,762.01	1,107,693	1,138,421	401.05
Zeeland	1,831.75	232,515	235,007	126 93
Utrecht	1,363.21	288,514	294,930	211 64
Friesland	3,220.25	359,552	364,415	111 65
Overijssel	3,354 50	382,880	391,741	114 14
Groningen	2,283.52	328,045	333,217	143.66
Drenthe	2,662.09	173,318	178,561	65.11
Limburg	2,194.68	332,007	348,467	151.28
Total	32,600.25*	5,858,175	6,022,452	179.70

* 12,587 square miles.

Total number of males (1909) 2,899,125; females 2,959,050. According to nationality the population was divided as follows: Dutch, 2,-788,193; Germans, 37,534; Belgians, 18,338; French, 2645; English, 2102; Austro-Hungarians 1223; others 3908; not indicated, 4152. The majority of the population are Protestants. 3,334,487. There were (1911) 43,030 marriages, 174,165 births, and 86,782 deaths, including still-births, 6638 still-births; excess of births over deaths, 86,383; emigrants, 2638.

A few of the great cities (communal population as calculated December 31, 1911) are Amsterdam (580,960), Rotterdam (436,018), The Hague (288,577), Utrecht (121,317), Groningen (77,221), Haarlem (69,988), Arnhem (64,634), Leiden (59,133), Nimeguen 57,116), Dordrecht (47,304), Bois-le-Duc (35,157), Delft (34,485), Schiedam (33,235), etc.

EDUCATION. The Dutch system of education is peculiar in that the state encourages and subsidizes private primary instruction in preference to maintaining public schools, though these are provided by local taxation in the districts where other schools are inadequate. Primary instruction is compulsory between the ages of seven and thirteen. The average attendance is 95 per cent. Secondary instruction is not free. A noteworthy feature is the excellence of the special agricultural and horticultural schools. There are universities at Amsterdam, Groningen, Leyden, and Utrecht, besides a small private institution.

PRODUCTION. The area (in hectares) and the production (in quintals) for two years, and the production per hectare in 1911, are as follows:

	Hectares		Quintals		Qs.
	1911	1912	1911	1912	ha.
Wheat	57,539	57,682	1,514,826	1,254,149	26.3
Rye	225,364	225,996	4,201,114	4,146,151	18.6
Barley	28,017	26,938	780,367	862,148	27.9
Oats	138,186	136,991	2,998,003	2,148,126	21.7
Flax	15,711	14,862	94,932†	98,197†	6.0†
Beets*	55,600	62,854	20,049,630	......	360.6
Tobacco	401	405	....	......	....

* For sugar. † Fibre.

The export (1910) of bulbs, trees, and shrubs was valued at 15,156,141 guilders; vegetables, 56,700,000; fruits, 2,546,000.

From the state coal mines (mostly in Limburg) 1,292,289 metric tons were raised, valued at 8,232,000 guilders. The fisheries products (North Sea) were valued at 11,654,951 guilders in 1910 exclusive of oysters (oyster catch, 3,210,614 kilos). Number of distilleries (1910), 464; breweries, 440; sugar refineries, 12; beet-sugar refineries, 27; salt works, 34; vinegar works, 73. Export of cheese (1910), 19,491,000 guilders.

COMMERCE. The Netherlands is practically a free-trade country. The total imports for consumption and exports of domestic produce are seen below for three years (precious metals included) in guilders (1 guilder=40.2 cents):

	1909	1910	1911
Imports...	3,137,400,000	3,265,200,000	3,333,200,000
Exports...	2,454,700,000	2,632,300,000	2,732,300,000

In the following table is given the trade in 1911 by great classes, in guilders:

	Imports	Exports
Foodstuffs	869,100,000	833,500,000
Raw materials	1,312,600,000	983,500,000
Manufactures	593,400,000	517,100,000
Miscellaneous	540,100,000	377,300,000
Total merchandise.....	3,315,200,000	2,711,400,000
Precious metals.......	18,000,000	20,500,000
Total	3,333,200,000	2,732,300,000

Countries of origin and destination follow, with values in millions of guilders:

	Imps.	Exps.		Imps.	Exps.
Germany	908.5	1,358.1	Brazil	36.8	2.6
D. E. Ind.	455.7	125.5	Sweden	45.7	20.8
Russia	366.5	17.5	Norway	39.3	16.7
U. K.	339.1	554.5	France	39.4	26.3
U. S.	330.6	105.0	Turkey	11.1	19.3
Belgium	323.6	318.9	Italy	11.1	22.7
Spain	88.5	7.5	Africa	8.5	21.0
Br. E. Ind.	88.1	5.0	Other	158.6	103.0
Rumania	82.6	7.9			
			Total....	3,333.2	2,732.3

Sailing vessels entered (1911) 1278 of 1,013,996 cubic meters capacity (of which 772, of 265,853M,³ Dutch) cleared, 1578 of 51,054,738M³ (949, of 306,131M.³ Dutch). Steamers entered, 14,350, of 42,767,870M³ capacity (3751, of 11,266,122M,³ Dutch); cleared, 14,332, of 42,462,831M³ (2753, of 11,354,565M,³ Dutch). Merchant marine, January 1, 1912, 775 vessels, of 1,600,687M³ (of which, 347 steamers, of 1,480,943M³).

COMMUNICATIONS. On January 1, 1912 there were in operation 3234 kilometers of railway. The land is a network of canals and rivers. State telegraph lines, 7609 kilometers; wires, 37,867; receipts in 1911, 5,164,787 francs; expenditure, 8,729,184. Postoffices, 1511; receipts, 33,369,812 francs; expenditure, 28,025,206.

FINANCE. The 1913 budget is given below in detail:

Revenue	1000 gl.	Expenditure	1000 gl.
Excise	60,260	Internal adm....	41,083
Direct taxes.....	49,052	Interior (dept.)..	38,822
Stamps, etc......	30,075	Public debt......	38,027
Posts	17,535	War	33,364
Customs	14,826	Finance, etc.....	30,671
Telegraphs, etc...	5,237	Navy	20,130
Railways	4,188	Agriculture, etc..	11,992
Pilot dues.......	3,450	Justice	11,292
Domains	1,471	Colonial office....	2,681
Lottery	655	Foreign affairs..	1,377
Licenses	160	Civil list.........	945
Mine duties......	20	Cabinet, etc......	786
Miscellaneous ...	22,603	Miscellaneous ...	50
Total, 1913.....	209,531	Total, 1913.....	231,220
Total, 1912.....	202,068	Total, 1912.....	222,015
Total, 1910.....	199,499	Total, 1910.....	204,747

The total capital of the public debt stood (1912) at 1,156,258,450 guilders; interest, 32,504,430; amortization, 5,523,000. Between 1850 and 1911, the sum of 357,673,792 guilders has een devoted to the redemption of the public debt.

ARMY. The States-General on February 2, 1912, passed a new military law by which the total militia service was reduced from 8 to 6 years, with 5 years spent in the Landweer instead of 7, and enrollment up to the age of 40 in the Landsturm. The annual contingent of recruits was 23,000 men, and the militiamen were obtained by lot, there being variable periods of service from 4 to 18 months. The plan of organization was intended to provide a force available for ready mobilization, and the field army was organized into 4 divisions, each composed of 423 officers and 18,333 non-commissioned officers and men, with 2544 horses and 561 wagons. On a peace basis the establishment, which included the active army, the reserve cadres and the Landweer, would amount to 2900 officers and 165,000 men which could be raised to a war strength estimated at 200,000.

NAVY. The fleet (1912) included 9 armored

and 6 protected cruisers of 66,430 aggregate tons; 3 armored coast-defense vessels, of 6710; 3 river gunboats, of 1140; 12 gunboats (3 under construction), of 4000; 8 torpedo-boat destroyers (4 under construction), of 4000; 33 torpedo boats (4 under construction), of 4000; 4 mine layers (2 under construction), of 1880; 5 submarines (2 under construction), of 720.

The Dutch East India possessions contribute to the maintenance of the fleet. A bill for the construction of a new East Indian fleet was defeated in May, 1912, the proposals being considered inadequate by the majority. Upon the defeat of the bill followed the resignation of Vice-Admiral Wentholt, minister of marine. An expenditure of 12,000,000 guilders (a reduction from the 40,000,000 first proposed), was voted in July for coast-defense purposes, nearly half of which was intended for the fortifications at Flushing.

GOVERNMENT. The executive power is vested in the sovereign; the legislative, in a parliament (States-General) of two chambers acting jointly with the sovereign. Reigning sovereign in 1912, Queen Wilhelmina, born August 31, 1880; succeeded on the death of her father, November 23, 1890, under the regency of her mother; became of age and was enthroned, August 31, 1898; married, February 7, 1901, Henry, Duke of Mechlenbourg. Heiress-apparent, Princess Juliana, born April 30, 1909. The ministry, constituted February 12, 1908, was in 1912 composed as follows: Jhr. Dr. R. de Marees van Swinderen, foreign affairs; Dr. Th. Heemskerk, interior; Dr. E. R. H. Regout, justice; the minister of war, *ad int.*, marine; H. Colijn, war; Dr. M. J. C. M. Kolkman, finance; Dr. L. H. W. Regout, internal administration; A. S. Talma, agriculture, commerce, and industry; J. H. de Waal Malefijt, colonies.

HISTORY. An important debate in the spring concerned the proposals for a new fleet for the defense of the Dutch East Indies (see above, *Navy*). In September the minister of war proposed a change in the estimates that would enable him to hasten the execution of the coast-defense scheme. A preliminary credit of 1,500,000 florins was demanded. Besides the coast-defense measure, tariff reform continued to be one of the chief political issues of the year. In the speech from the throne, its necessity for the permanent increase of revenue, was specifically urged. On the day of the opening of the States-General, September 17 the Socialists, while endeavoring to force their way into the vicinity of the parliament building, came into conflict with the police, and several persons were injured, but none seriously. The queen and prince consort visited Paris in June, and Prince Henry visited London in April.

NEVADA. POPULATION. According to the Census Bureau statistics compiled in 1912, out of a total population in 1910 of 81,875, the foreign-born whites numbered 17,999, compared with 18,581 in 1900. Of these, the largest number, 2827, came from Italy; from Ireland, 1693; from England, 1793; from Germany, 1924; from Canada, 1057. Other European countries were represented by smaller numbers. The negoes in the State numbered 513 and the mulattoes 190. In 1890 the negroes numbered 242 and the mulattoes, 102.

AGRICULTURE. The acreage, value, and production of the principal crops in 1911-12 are shown in the following table:

		Acreage.	Prod. Bu.	Value.
Corn	1912	1,000	30,000	$ 29,000
	1911	1,000	30,000	27,000
Wheat	1912	39,000	1,137,000	1,137,000
	1911	36,000	1,018,000	968,000
Oats	1912	10,000	400,000	208,000
	1911	8,000	360,000	223,000
Potatoes	1912	12,000	2,136,000	1,282,000
	1911	8,000	1,280,000	1,197,000
Hay	1912	227,000	a 681,000	5,925,000
	1911	254,000	a 864,000	8,208,000

a Tons.

MINERAL PRODUCTION. The gold production of the State in 1911 was $18,193,397, compared with $18,878,864 in 1910. The great bulk of the gold output came from dry or siliceous ores and from concentrates, the small remainder being derived almost wholly from copper ores, placer gravels, and lead ores. The silver output in 1911 was 13,184,601 fine ounces, compared with 12,479,871 fine ounces in 1910. The larger part was obtained from the siliceous silver-gold ores of Tonopah.

The production of blister copper in 1911 was 65,561,015 pounds, compared with 64,494,640 pounds in 1910. At the close of 1911 the State had produced 203,500,112 pounds. It ranks eighth in the total production of copper. The only important producing district is the Ely district in White Pine county.

MANUFACTURES. Statistics relating to the manufactures of the State were included in the Thirteenth Census taken in 1910. These figures cover the calendar year 1909. The results will be found summarized in the table below. The largest number of men in any one industry are employed in the car shops of railroad companies. These number 818.

The following table gives a summary of the results of the census for the calendar years 1909 and 1904, with per cent. of increase 1904-9:

	Number or Amount 1909	1904	Increase
Number of establishments	177	115	53.0
Persons engaged in manufactures	2,650	1,016	160.8
Proprietors and firm members	137	108	26.9
Salaried employees	256	160	141.5
Wage earners (average number)	2,257	802	181.4
Primary horsepower	7,765	2,834	174.0
Capital	$ 9,807,000	$2,892,000	239.1
Expenses	11,082,000	2,632,000	321.0
Services	2,360,000	819,000	188.2
Salaries	378,000	126,000	200.0
Wages	1,982,000	693,000	186.0
Materials	8,366,000	1,628,000	413.9
Miscellaneous	356,000	185,000	92.4
Value of products	11,887,000	3,096,000	283.9
Value added by manufacture (value of products less cost of materials)	3,521,000	1,468,000	139.8

POLITICS AND GOVERNMENT

There was no regular session of the legislature in 1912, but a special session was held at which a loan of $200,000 was authorized, and provision was made for an annual State tax of sixty cents on each $100. Aside from this, no measures of general importance were enacted. There was no election for State officers in 1912. Governor Oddie's term does not expire until 1914. The death of Senator Nixon in 1912 made it necessary for the governor to appoint his successor. Governor Oddie first appointed George Wingfield, who declined the nomination, and he then appointed W. A. Massey, former chief justice of the Supreme Court of the State. The result of the election on November 5 was as follows: Wilson, 20,437; Roosevelt, 8347; Taft, 17,733; and Debs, 2859. Governor Wilson's plurality was 2704. The legislature is entirely Democratic.

STATE GOVERNMENT. Governor, T. L. Oddie; Lieutenant-Governor, G. C. Ross; Secretary of State, George Brodigan; Treasurer, William McMillan; Comptroller, Jacob Eggers; Superintendent of Public Instruction, J. E. Bray; Attorney-General, C. H. Baker—all Democrats, except Oddie, Eggers and McMillan, Republicans.

JUDICIARY. Supreme Court: Chief Justice, G. F. Talbot, Dem.; Justices, P. A. McCarran, Dem.; Frank Norcross Rep.; Clerk, Joe Josephs, Dem.

STATE LEGISLATURE, 1913. Democrats, Senate, 12; House, 31; joint ballot, 43. Republicans, Senate, 8; House, 19; joint ballot, 27. Progressives, Senate, 1; House, 1; joint ballot, 2. Socialists, Senate, 1; House, 1; joint ballot, 2. Democratic majority, Senate, 2; House, 10; joint ballot, 12.

The representatives in Congress will be found in the article UNITED STATES, section *Congress.*

NEVADA, UNIVERSITY OF. A State institution for higher education at Reno, Nev., founded in 1886. The students enrolled in the various departments of the university in the autumn of 1912 numbered 275. There were 45 members of the faculty. Three new men were added to the faculty in the department of agriculture during the year. The most notable benefaction was the endowment of the Mackay school of mines by Clarence H. Mackay, the income to be used for instruction in the school of mines. An electrical engineering building was completed during the collegiate year. Courses in dairying and soil physics were added to the curriculum and the university high school was abolished. The library contained 24,000 volumes. President, Joseph Edward Stubbs, D. D., LL. D.

NEWARK, N. J. See CITY PLANNING.

NEWBERRY, WALTER CASS. An American soldier, capitalist, and former member of Congress, died July 20, 1912. He was born in Waterville, N. Y., in 1835, and received an academic education. In 1861 he enlisted in the Civil War as a private in the 81st New York Infantry and rose successively to be captain and major of this regiment. In 1864 he became colonel and was brevetted brigadier-general in 1865 for services at Dinwiddie Court House, where he was severely wounded. After the war he settled in Petersburg, Va., and was mayor of the city in 1869. He built the reservoir water works of Richmond, Va. In 1876 he removed to Chicago, where he engaged in the mercantile business. He was postmaster of the city in 1888-89, and in 1891 was elected to the Fifty-second Congress.

NEW BRUNSWICK. A maritime province of the Dominion of Canada. Area 27,985 square miles. Population (census of June 1, 1911), 351,889, as compared with 331,120 in 1901. Fredericton, the capital, had 7208 inhabitants (7117 in 1901). The province is administered by a lieutenant-governor, Josiah Wood, appointed March 6, 1912. Premier in 1912, James K. Fleming. See CANADA.

The New Brunswick general elections gave the Conservatives a decisive majority in the assembly where, out of a membership of 48, only 2 Liberals were elected. In the House of Commons eight of the thirteen seats were retained by the Liberals. The issues were merely local, but the strengthening of the Conservatives was interpreted by the government as indicating an increasing strength of their party in the East.

NEW CALEDONIA. A French Melanesian colony. Area, with the Loyalty Islands, 19,-823 square kilometers (50,680 inhabitants); of the dependencies: Wallis Acrhipelago, 96 sq. kms. (4500); Fortuna and Alofi, 159 (1500); the Chesterfield Islands, 0.8 sq. km. Nouméa (6968 inhabitants) is the capital. Imports (1910), 12,689,000 francs (France, 5,-875,000); exports, 9,732,000 (France, 3,880,-000). The budget (1909) balanced at 3,588,000 francs, and the debt in 1910 was 10,361,000. Railways in operation, 16 kilometers; telegraph lines, 1042; wires, 1650. J. Richard was governor in 1912.

NEWCOMB, JAMES EDWARD. An American laryngologist, died August 27, 1912. He was born in New London, Conn., in 1857, and graduated from Yale College in 1880. He studied medicine at the College of Physicians and Surgeons, graduating in 1883. He began practice in New York City and continued this until the time of his death. He was lecturer on laryngology in the Cornell Medical College and was consulting laryngologist to Roosevelt Hospital. He contributed to many important medical works and edited the American edition of Grunwald's *Atlas of Diseases of the Mouth, Pharynx, and Nose.*

NEW CONSTRUCTION. See NAVAL PROGRESS.

NEWFOUNDLAND. See BERIBERI.

NEWFOUNDLAND. An island colony of Great Britain, on the northeast side of the Gulf of St. Lawrence. Area 42,734 square miles; population (as estimated December 31, 1910), 237,531. St. John's, the capital, has 31,501 inhabitants; Harbour Grace, 5184; Twillingate, 3542. Fishing, agriculture, mining, and lumbering are the chief industries. The settlements are largely on or near the coast. Paper and pulp mills have been established at Grand Falls and Bishop's Falls.

Imports (1909-10), $12,799,696; exports, $11,-824,997; shipping entered and cleared, 2,099,-698 tons; revenue, $3,447,989; expenditure, $3,-137,775. Public debt, June 30, 1910, $22,943,-197. The Trepassey Railway, an extension towards Cape Race of the colony's system, was built to within 18 miles of its terminus during 1912. Governor (1912), Sir Ralph C. Williams (appointed 1909).

Attached administratively to Newfoundland is that part of the peninsula of LABRADOR comprehended between Hudson's Strait and Blanc Sablon, including the Hamilton basin. Labrador has a 600-mile coast-line and an area of about 120,000 square miles; population (estimated December 31, 1910), 4076. See UNITED STATES, *Foreign Relations.*

NEW GUINEA. The largest of the East Indian islands. See DUTCH EAST INDIES; GERMAN NEW GUINEA; PAPUA.

NEW HAMPSHIRE. POPULATION. According to the Census Bureau statistics compiled during 1912, out of the total population in the State in 1910, 430,572, the foreign-born whites numbered 96,558, compared with 87,961 in 1900. Of these the largest number were from Canada, French, 40,752; from Canada, other, 16,-930; from Ireland, 10,608; from Russia, 4337; from England, 4861. Other European countries were represented by smaller numbers. The negroes in the State in 1910 numbered 564 and the mulattoes 208; in 1890, the negroes numbered 614, and the mulattoes, 266.

AGRICULTURE. The acreage, value, and production for the principal crops in 1911 and 1912 will be found in the following table:

		Acreage.	Prod. Bu.	Value.
Corn	1912	23,000	1,058,000	$ 794,000
	1911	23,000	1,035,000	849,000
Oats	1912	12,000	468,000	225,000
	1911	12,000	406,000	248,000
Potatoes	1912	17,000	2,380,000	1,452,000
	1911	17,000	2,125,000	1,849,000
Hay	1912	501,000	a 626,000	9,390,000
	1911	640,000	a 672,000	11,558,000
Tobacco	1912	100	b 170,000	31,000
	1911	100	b 170,000	27,200

a Tons. b Pounds.

MANUFACTURES. The Thirteenth Census included statistics of manufactures in the State. These are for the calendar year 1909. The chief results are given in the table below. The greater number of the manufacturing establishments are located in the southern part of the State which possesses marked advantages for manufacturing, among which are an abundance of water power afforded by the Merrimac River, close proximity to the markets and business centres of New England, and excellent transportation facilities. The industry whose products had the largest value in 1909 was that which included boots and shoes with cut stock and findings.

	Number or Amount 1909	1904	Increase
Number of establishments	1,961	1,618	21.2
Persons engaged in manufactures	84,191	69,758	20.7
Proprietors and firm members	2,014	1,726	16.7
Salaried employees	3,519	2,666	32.0
Wage earners (average number)	78,658	65,366	20.3
Primary horsepower	293,991	218,344	34.6
Capital	$139,990,000	$109,495,000	27.8
Expenses	149,215,000	112,888,000	32.2
Services	40,391,000	30,665,000	31.7
Salaries	4,191,000	2,972,000	41.0
Wages	36,200,000	27,693,000	30.7
Materials	98,157,000	73,216,000	34.1
Miscellaneous	10,667,000	9,007,000	18.4
Value of products	164,581,000	123,611,000	33.1
Value added by manufacture (value of produces less cost of materials)	66,424,000	50,395,000	31.8

FINANCE. The report of the treasurer shows receipts for the fiscal year ending August 31, 1912, of $2,797,894. At the beginning of the fiscal year there was on hand a balance of $293,987. The total disbursements during the fiscal year 1912 amounted to $2,514,054, leaving a balance at the end of the fiscal year of $567,-827. The chief revenue was derived from taxes of various kinds, and the chief expenditures are for education, support of State institutions, and for the support of State officers. The net indebtedness of the State on September 1, 1912, was $1,387,038. The debt was decreased during the year by the payment of $76,089.

CHARITIES AND CORRECTIONS. The charitable and correctional institutions of the State included the various State prisons and county jails, the county almshouses and the following institutions: State Industrial School, State School for Feeble-minded, the New Hampshire Soldiers' Home, the New Hampshire State Sanatorium, and several private institutions, over which the State has supervision, including the New Hampshire Orphans' Home, the Manchester Children's Home, the Dover Children's Home, the Orphans' Home at Concord, and several others. The deaf, dumb, and blind of the State receive education in institutions in other States. These are the Maine School for the Deaf, the Clark School for the Deaf at Northampton, Mass., the Perkins Institution and Massachusetts School for the Blind in Boston, and the New England Industrial School for Deaf Mutes at Beverley, Mass. There is a juvenile court law in force in the State. This was enacted in 1907 and its results have been very satisfactory. The charitable and correctional institutions are under the control of the State board of charities and corrections.

POLITICS AND GOVERNMENT

The year 1912 was an important and interesting one in the political history of the State. Besides the presidential and State elections with their unusual results, a convention was held in June to recommend amendments to the constitution, for the consideration of the voters, a two-thirds affirmative vote being necessary for ratification. The convention was in session ten days and recommended 12 amendments. A proposition to extend full suffrage to women was defeated, as was another proposing the initiative, referendum, and recall.

CONSTITUTIONAL AMENDMENTS. The amendments submitted at the general November elections were: (1) To increase the senate from 24 to 36; (2) to decrease the house membership from 410 to about 325 by changing the basis of representation; (3) to permit the classification of property for taxation; (4) to permit a grading of the inheritance tax; (5) to permit the taxation of public service corporations on income basis; (6) to strike the word "Protestant" from the bill of rights; (7) to disqualify voters convicted of certain crimes; (8) to provide that officers should be elected by plurality vote; (9) removing pension limitation as to civil officers; (10) extending jurisdiction of police courts; (11) changing basis of councilor districts from property to population; (12) giving governor veto power on separate appropriation items. Only numbers 7, 8, 10 and 11 were ratified. The chief purpose in calling the convention had been to reform the method of taxing money at interest and growing wood and timber, the present requirement being that all property taxed should be at full value and at a uniform rate. For years the money-at-interest class had been ignored and forest growth undervalued until the abuse had extended to other property and the demand for rigid law enforcement as the remedy was adopted. There was much disappointment that Nos. 2 and 3 were not ratified and a strong movement arose to reconvene the convention to resubmit those amendments, as they fell only a fraction under the necessary 66⅔ per cent. in favor. The legislature of 1913 was to be asked to make an appropriation to meet the expense of reassembling.

CONVENTIONS AND ELECTIONS. Political activity was more than ordinarily intense throughout the year, largely through the action of Governor Bass in joining in the request made by seven Republican governors to Colonel Roosevelt to be a candidate for a third term in the presidency. Although the nomination of delegates to national conventions and the nomination of presidential electors were specifically excepted from the direct primary law of 1909, Governor Bass demanded a voluntary preferential presidential vote, which was granted without opposition by the Republican State committee. It was held April 23, at the same time delegates were chosen to the Republican State convention which assembled at Concord, April 30. An active campaign was waged, but Taft won by a strong majority, both in preferential vote and number of delegates. Taft delegates were chosen by a vote of 530 to 255 for Roosevelt delegates. The preferential vote was 16,000 for Taft to 12,000 for Roosevelt. The Democratic State delegate convention was held May 14, and a resolution was adopted declaring it to be the sentiment of the convention that they should vote for Champ Clark as long as there was any chance for his nomination. The Democrats made no attempt at a presidential preference vote.

The direct primary for the nomination of State officers was held September 3. Franklin Worcester, who had been identified with the Progressive wing of the Republican party, and Samuelo D. Felker, Democrat, were the nominees, b th unopposed. Subsequent to the primary, Governor Bass issued a public address stating that a Progressive party would be formed and put in nominees for electors and for governor, congressmen, and some other State offices. This was done by petition, Winston Churchill, who had unsuccessfully sought the Republican nomination by a spectacular campaign in 1906, becoming the gubernatorial nominee. A most aggressive campaign was conducted. The election of November 5 resulted as follows: For President, Wilson, 34,724; Taft, 32,961; Roosevelt, 17,695; Debs, 1981, and Chafin, 535; for Governor, Felker, Dem., 34,203; Worcester, Rep., 32,504; Churchill, 14,401; others, about 2000.

Under the unamended constitution a majority rather than a plurality was necessary for an election, and there was no choice by the people. The election was therefore thrown into the legislature of 1913. Eleven senators were elected on the Republican ticket and nine on the Democratic, with no choice in four districts, because of the majority rule above alluded to. For the house, 208 representatives were elected as Republicans, and 197 as Democrats. Following the election, the Progressive party State committee advanced the claim that about 30 of those elected on the Republican ticket were Progressives and would not be bound to support the Republican nominees.

STATE GOVERNMENT. *Governor ——— ———; Secretary of State, ———————; Treasurer, ———————; Auditor, Frank A. Musgrove; Adjutant-General, Herbert E. Tutherly; Attorney-General, J. P. Tuttle; Superintendent of Education, Henry C. Morrison; Commissioner of Agriculture, Nahum J. Bachelder; Commissioner of Insurance, R. J. Merrill—all Republicans.

* State officers to be elected by legislature which convenes January 1, 1913; November, 1912, election not conclusive.

JUDICIARY. Supreme Court: Chief Justice, Frank N. Parsons, Rep.; Associate Justices, Robert J. Peaslee, Dem.; Reuben E. Walker, Rep.; John E. Young, Rep.; George H. Bingham, Dem.; Clerk, A. J. Shurtleff, Rep.

STATE LEGISLATURE, 1913. Republicans, Senate 12; House, 210; joint ballot, 222. Democrats, Senate, 8; House, 195; joint ballot, 203. Republican majority, Senate, 4; House, 15; joint ballot, 19.

The representatives in Congress will be found in the section *Congress*, article UNITED STATES.

NEW HEBRIDES. A group of Melanesian islands jointly administered by France and Great Britain through the French and English high commissioners for the Pacific. There were resident-commissioners, in 1912—French, M. Repiquet; English, M. King. . Vila, in the island of Efate, is the seat of government. A large proportion of the natives are cannibals, and the sale to them of arms, ammunition, and intoxicating liquors is prohibited.

NEW JERSEY. POPULATION. According to the Census Bureau statistics compiled during 1912, out of the total population, 2,537,167 in 1910, 658,188 were foreign-born whites, compared with 430,050 in 1900. The largest number of these 122,989, came from Germany; from Italy, 115,337; from Russia, 93,691; from Austria, 58,059; from England, 50,272; from Hungary, 46,006; from Ireland, 82,515; from Scotland, 17,493; and from Sweden, 10,544. Other European countries were represented by smaller numbers. In Jersey City, which had a total population of 267,779, there were 77,697 foreign-born whites. In Newark, with a population of 347,469, there were 111,658 foreign-born whites. In Paterson, with a population of 125,000 there were 46,398 foreign-born whites. The negroes in the State in 1910 numbered 89,760 and the mulattoes, 14,207. In 1890 the negroes numbered 47,638, and the mulattoes, 7202.

AGRICULTURE. The acreage, value, and production of the principal crops in 1911 and 1912 are shown in the following table:

		Acreage.	Prod. Bu.	Value.
Corn	1912	273,000	10,274,000	$7,054,000
	1911	270,000	9,936,000	7,055,000
Wheat	1912	79,000	1,462,000	1,433,000
	1911	84,000	1,462,000	1,404,000
Oats	1912	67,000	1,849,000	814,000
	1911	71,000	2,024,000	1,012,000
Rye	1912	72,000	1,260,000	995,000
	1911	72,000	1,181,000	980,000
Potatoes	1912	92,000	9,936,000	6,558,000
	1911	84,000	6,132,000	6,439,000
Hay	1912	362,000	a 521,000	10,420,000
	1911	428,000	a 449,000	9,878,000

a Tons.

MINERAL PRODUCTION. The iron ore produced in the State in 1911 amounted to 359,721 long tons, valued at $1,158,271, compared with a product in 1910 of 521,832 long tons, valued at $1,582,213.

A considerable quantity of zinc is produced in the State from Sussex county. There were treated 306,168 short tons of ore and 67,896 tons of crude ore were shipped to the smelters. Figured as metallic zinc, the total recoverable output was 154,890,900 pounds of spelter, valued at $8,828,781.

MANUFACTURES. The Thirteenth Census statistics are for the calendar year 1909 and were compiled in 1912. New Jersey is preëminently a manufacturing State and it has shown a steady increase in each census taken. The increase in the five-year period, 1904-1909, was greater than in the previous five-year period, 1889-1904. From the following table it will be seen that there were in 1909, 8817 manufacturing establishments, which gave employment to an average of 371,265 persons:

	Number or Amount 1909	1904	P. C. of Inc. 1904-'09
Number of establishments	8,817	7,010	25.8
Persons engaged in manufactures	371,265	296,282	25.3
Proprietors and firm members	8,204	6,730	21.9
Salar'd employees	36,838	23,196	58.8
Wage earners (average number)	326,223	266,336	22.5
Primary horsepower	612,293	436,274	40 3
Capital	$977,172,000	$715,060,000	36.7
Expenses	1,032,698,000	694,128,000	48.8
Services	218,046,000	157,126,000	38.8
Salaries	48,336,000	28,957,000	66.9
Wages	169,710,000	128,169,000	32 4
Materials	720,033,000	470,449,000	53.1
Miscellaneous	94,619,000	66,553,000	42.2
Value of products	1,145,529,000	774,369,000	47.9
Value of products less cost of materials	425,496,000	303,920,000	40.0

The largest number of wage-earners was employed in industries relating to the manufacture of silk and silk goods, 30,285; in foundry and machine shop production, there were 27,815; in the manufacture of woolen, worsted, and felt goods, 12,652; in the manufacture of electrical machinery, apparatus, and supplies, 11,099, and in dyeing and finishing textiles, 10,129. The greatest value of product was found in the smelting and refining industries, $125,651,000. This was followed by silk and silk goods, $65,430,000; foundry and machine shop products, $65,398,000; slaughtering and meatpacking $37,583,000; woolen, worsted, and felt goods, $33,939,000. Other industries with a value of $20,000,000 and over, were wire industries, leather industries, manufacture of electrical machinery, tobacco manufactures, chemicals, malt liquors, and bread and other bakery products. The total number of persons employed was 371,265, of whom 278,068 were male, and 92,297 female. The number of persons employed under 16 years of age was 7538. For the great majority of wage-earners the prevailing hours of labor ranged from 54 to 60 a week; 12.8 per cent. of the total were employed in establishments where the prevailing hours were less than 54 a week, and 4.8 in those where they were more than 60 a week. The largest number of wage-earners was found in Newark, 59,955; in Paterson there were 32,004; in Jersey City, 25,454; in Trenton, 18,583; in Passaic, 15,086; in Elizabeth, 12,737, and in Bayonne, 7519.

FINANCE. The report of the State treasurer for the fiscal year ending Octobe 31, 1912, showed a balance on hand November 1, 1911, of $3,309,781. The receipts for the fiscal year amounted to $9,657,366 and the disbursements to $7,696,475, leaving a balance at the end of the fiscal year of $5,270,672. The chief sources of revenue are from taxes of various kinds and the chief expenditures are for education and the support of State institutions.

CHARITIES AND CORRECTIONS. The institutions under State control, with their populations in 1912, were as follows: State Hospital for the Insane, Morris Plains, 2302; State Hospital for the Insane, Trenton, 1543; State Home for Feeble-minded Women, Vineland, 247; New Jersey State Village for Epileptics, 392; New Jersey State Prison, 1527; New Jersey Reformatory, 505; State Home for Boys, 519; State Home for Girls, 226; Soldiers' Home, Kearny, 531; Soldiers' Home, Vineland, 348; Sanatorium for Tuberculosis Diseases, 189. The legislature of 1911 provided for the appointment of a convict labor commission to study the outdoor employment of prisoners, including those confined in county penitentiaries and jails. This commission was to make a report to the legislature of 1913. The prison labor commission charged with the organization of prison industries on the "State use" system had not yet been able to accomplish any definite results owing to the absence of any appropriation for the purpose. The prison contracts in force expire in 1914, and unless favorable legislative action with a sufficient appropriation is taken during the next session of the legislature, there will be almost a certain condition of enforced idleness for practically all the 1500 prisoners in the prisons of the State.

POLITICS AND GOVERNMENT

The position of Governor Wilson as one of the leading candidates for the Democratic nomination for the presidency up to the time of the Baltimore convention and his nomination at that convention made the political year in New Jersey one of great interest. Governor Wilson's term of office had been a successful one, although he had made many enemies among the active politicians. His candidacy for President was received with enthusiasm by the great bulk of the people of the State. This was shown in the presidential primaries which were held on May 27.

The Progressive policies, advocated by Mr. Roosevelt, had large support in the State, and this too was shown by the presidential election, the results of which are noted below. An aggressive campaign was made by both Mr. Roosevelt and President Taft previous to this election. This is described in the article PRESIDENTIAL CAMPAIGN.

The law providing for this election was similar in most respects to that of Massachusetts. The voter had the opportunity to express directly his preference for the presidential candidate, and at the same time to vote for delegates to the national convention. Each candidate for delegate was permitted to have opposite his name on the ballot the name of the presidential candidate he preferred. There was therefore the same possibility in New Jersey as in Massachusetts for a confused result from the preference vote cast for one candidate and the selection of delegates committed to another candidate. No such result, however, occurred in New Jersey. Mr. Clark, the chief opponent of Governor Wilson as Democratic candidate, on April 4 sent a communication to the Secretary of State declining to allow his name to appear on the ballot. This he did out of courtesy to Governor Wilson. This action left the entire Democratic field to Governor Wilson, and was induced in some degree by the fact that Governor Wilson had made no attempt to secure delegates in Missouri.

The result of the preferential election was on the Republican side a pronounced victory for Mr. Roosevelt. He received 61,297 votes, and President Taft, 44,034. As a result, Mr. Roosevelt was given the entire 28 delegates in the national convention. The four Roosevelt delegates-at-large were elected by substantially the same plurality as in the preference vote. The vote in the State was light. Governor Wilson carried the Democratic vote by a large majority and received the Democratic delegates.

The Prohibition party on July 12 held its national convention at Atlantic City, nominating the Rev. Eugene W. Chafin of Tucson, Ariz., for President, and Aaron H. Watkins of Ada, O., for Vice-President.

After the Chicago convention the Progressive party held a convention on July 23. The platform adopted contains provisions favoring the nomination of party candidates for President and Vice-President by direct nomination; the abolition of the electoral college, and the election of President and Vice-President by popular vote; the direct election of United States senators; simpler and easier methods whereby the people may amend the constitutions of the State and the United States; the initiative, referendum and recall; the submission to the people of an amendment to the State constitution giving women the same right to vote as men; a national progressive income and inheritance tax; government ownership and operation of express, telegraph, and telephone service. The plank dealing with the tariff, called for a protective tariff limited to the difference in cost of production here and abroad, and demanding a downward revision of the present tariff. A solution of the trust problem by strict governmental regulation and control through a commission and by the abolition of all special privileges was declared for. The platform called for a revision of the patent laws and for laws providing for the government-ownership and operation of railways and all other public utilities in Alaska, together with the leasing of all coal, mineral, and timber lands in Alaska. The platform advocated a law authorizing the Interstate Commerce Commission to fix railway freight and passenger rates and to make a valuation of all physical property of railways. The establishment of a national bureau of public health was called for. The principle of the merit system of appointment to public office and the rigid enforcement and extension of the civil service laws now on the statute books was advocated, and the financial scheme of the monetary commission was opposed.

As there was no election of governor or other State officers in 1912, no nominations were made.

On September 24 senatorial primaries were held for the election of a senator to succeed Senator Briggs, whose term expires in 1913. Mr. Briggs was a candidate for renomination. The Democratic candidates were Judge William Hughes, who, a short time before, had resigned as representative in Congress, and former United States Senator James Smith. Additional interest was given to the contest between these candidate from the fact that Mr. Smih had been the most aggressive opponent of Governor Wilson, and had attempted to reverse the verdict of the preferential senatorial primary two years before when Senator Martine was elected. Judge Hughes had the active support of the governor in his candidacy. The primaries resulted in the nomination of Judge Hughes by a plurality of more than 20,000. Senator Briggs was renominated by the Republicans.

The Democratic and Republican parties both held State conventions for the nomination of presidential electors and the adoption of State platforms on October 1. Both conventions were more or less perfunctory. Representatives of the woman suffrage movement appeared at both, and the Republicans inserted a plank in their platform declaring for woman suffrage. The Democrats omitted such a plank on the ground that the calling of a constitutional convention which their platf m advocated would sufficiently cover the situation. The election on November 5 resulted as follows: Wilson, 178,289; Roosevelt, 145,410; Taft, 88,835. The legislature is Democratic, with a majority on joint ballot of 46.

Other Events. On February 20, charges were made against Senator Richard Fitzherbert of Morris county, alleging that he had solicited $5000 for his vote on certain bills abolishing the use of acetylene gas on passenger trains, and the manufacture of such gas. An investigation was held by the judiciary committee of the Senate. On March 7, by a strictly party vote of 11 Republicans and 9 Democrats, Senator Fitzherbert was adjudged guilty of conduct inconsistent with the trust and duty of a senator. In a vote taken in the Senate on March 13, the attempt to remove Senator Fitzherbert failed on account of the necessity of obtaining a two-thirds vote, which was not possible.

A remarkable condition of corruption was found in Atlantic City as a result of investigations carried on by detectives under the employ of William J. Burns. Five city councilmen confessed to taking bribes. Further investigation involved many other city officials and citizens.

Municipal elections were held in the State on May 14. The chief interest was in the vote of several cities under the commission form of government. Atlantic City voted to adopt this form of government by a majority of 122. The city of Elizabeth rejected the commission form of government by a vote of 4923 to 2829.

Legislation. The legislature of 1912 enacted an unusually large number of important measures. Among these were the following: An act making provision for the sanitary condition of bakeries, and limiting the hours of service of adults as well as of children, and forbidding children under sixteen to work at night. This measure is similar to the one which was pronounced unconstitutional by the Supreme Court of the United States in the case of Lochner vs. New York. A measure was enacted providing for a pension for the widow of a governor, for her natural life. An important measure was enacted revising the law practice. A measure was passed forbidding the employment of any woman in any mercantile or manufacturing establishment, bakery, laundry, or restaurant working more than ten hours a day or more than six days or sixty hours in any one week, with the proviso that this shall not apply to any mercantile establishment for a period shortly before Christmas or to canneries in packing perishable products such as fruits or vegetables. The power of inspection and regulation touching the composition, branding, and sale of concentrated feeding stuffs was given to the State chemists. Provision was made for the employment of inmates of penal and reformatory institutions on the State roads. A measure was enacted supplementary to the act defining motor vehicles and providing for their registration and license, regulating speed, etc. Further provision was made for the improvement and construction of State highways.

STATE GOVERNMENT. Governor, Woodrow Wilson, Dem. (to March 4, 1913); Secretary of State, D. S. Crater, Dem.; Treasurer, Daniel S. Voorhees, Rep.; Auditor, William E. Drake, Rep.; Comptroller, Edward I. Edwards, Dem.; Attorney-General, Edmund Wilson, Rep.; Adjutant-General, Wilbur F. Sadler, Jr., Rep.; Commissioner of Education, Calvin N. Kendall, Dem.; Commissioner of Insurance, G. M. La Monte, Dem.; Commissioner of Agriculture, F. Dye, Rep.

JUDICIARY. Supreme Court: Chief Justice, W. S. Gummere, Rep.; Justices, Charles W. Parker, Rep.; T. W. Trenchard, Rep.; Samuel Kalisch, Dem.; C. G. Garrison, Dem.; James J. Bergen, Dem.; Willard P. Voorhees, Rep.; James F. Minturn, Dem.; F. J. Swayze, Rep.; Clerk, J. P. Tumulty, Dem.

STATE LEGISLATURE, 1913. Republicans, Senate, 9; House, 8; joint allot, 17. Democrats, Senate, 12; House, 51; joint ballot, 63. Democratic majority, Senate, 3; House, 43; joint ballot, 46.

The representatives in Congress will be found in the section *Congress*, article UNITED STATES.

NEW MEXICO. POPULATION. According to the Census Bureau statistics compiled in 1912, out of a total population in 1910 of 327,301, the foreign-born whites numbered 22,654, compared with 13,261 in 1900. Of these, 11,912 came from Mexico; from Italy came 1958; from Austria, 1244; from Germany, 1749; and from England, 1099. The negroes in the State in 1910 numbered 1628, and the mulattoes, 439. The negroes in 1890 numbered 1956, and the mulattoes, 986.

AGRICULTURE. The acreage, value, and production of the principal crops in 1911 and 1912 are shown in the following table:

		Acreage.	Prod. Bu.	Value.
Corn	1912	93,000	2,083,000	$1,562,000
	1911	94,000	2,322,000	1,950,000
Wheat	1912	59,000	1,232,000	1,109,000
	1911	55,000	1,262,000	1,262,000
Oats	1912	53,000	1,839,000	828,000
	1911	48,000	1,862,000	1,061,000
Potatoes	1912	9,000	900,000	585,000
	1911	10,000	800,000	800,000
Hay	1912	187,000	a 436,000	3,706,000
	1911	221,000	a 575,000	7,475,000

a Tons.

MINERAL PRODUCTION. The production of blister copper in the State in 1911 was 2,860,400 pounds as compared with 3,784,609 pounds in 1910. The total production of copper since 1845 is 95,183,563 pounds. The principal production is from the districts in Grant county.

The g d production of the State in 1911 was $762,808ol compared with $482,424 in 1910. Siliceous ores from the entire State produced over 89 per cent. of the total gold output. The silver output in 1911 was 354,540 fine ounces, compared with 843,987 fine ounces in 1910. The greater part of the silver was produced in Socorro county.

The production of coal in the State in 1911 was 3,148,158 short tons, valued at $4,525,925. In common with most of the States in the Rocky Mountain region, New Mexico showed a decrease in coal production in 1911. This was due to the unusually mild weather in the winter of 1910-11, the decreased consumption by railway locomotives, and the resumption of coal-mining in the southwestern and central States, following the six months' strike in 1910. The decrease in 1911 was 360,163 short tons. The number of men employed in the coal mines of the State in 1911 was 4007.

MANUFACTURES. The Thirteenth Census included statistics of manufactures. These are for the calendar year 1909. The most important general results of the census are given in the table below. The industry in which the largest number of wage-earners was employed was that connected with cars and general shop construction, and repairs by steam railway companies. The total number was 1489 and the value of the product of the industry was $2,251,000. The only other considerable manufactuing industry in the State is that related to lumber and timber products. In this 1475 wage-earners were employed and the product was valued at $2,162,000. The total number of wage-earners in the State in 1909 was 4143. Of these 66 were under 16 years of age and of these, 3 were women. The prevailing hours of labor were 60 a week, or 10 a day for the large majority of the wage-earners. The largest number of wage-earners was in the city of Albuquerque, 587. The industries in this city comprise 9.9 of the total industrial establishments of the State. The following table shows the increase in manufacturing in the five-year period 1904-1909:

	Number or Amount 1909	1904	P. C. of Inc. 1904-'09
Number of establishments	318	199	57.3
Persons engaged in manufactures	4,766	3,891	22.5
Proprietors and firm members	288	189	52.4
Salaried employees	335	224	49.6
Wage earners (average number)	4,143	3,478	19.1
Primary horsepower	15,465	5,948	160.0
Capital	$7,743,000	$4,638,000	66.9
Expenses	7,049,000	5,081,000	38.7
Services	2,974,000	2,417,000	23.0
Salaries	383,000	264,000	45.1
Wages	2,591,000	2,153,000	20.3
Materials	3,261,000	2,236,000	45.8
Miscellaneous	814,000	428,000	90.2
Value of products	7,898,000	5,706,000	38.4
Value added by manufacture (value of products less cost of materials)	4,637,000	3,470,000	33.6

EDUCATION. The State, in 1912, contained 100,045 pupils between the ages of 5 and 21. The enrollment for the year 1911-12 was 57,436. The public school teachers numbered 1548. The total expenditure for maintaining schools for the one thousand school districts of the State in 1911-12 was $997,881. Of this amount $265,765 was expended for new buildings and improvements. The first State legislature passed twelve important school laws at its session in 1912. The revenue bill made a state-wide levy of half a mill, the proceeds from which are to go into the reserve fund for the help of weak districts. The constitution of the State provided for a minimum school term of five months in each school district and this law enables compliance with such constitutional provision. Another important measure was the industrial education bill, which provides for the teaching of domestic science, manual training, and agriculture in the elementary schools, and for the appointment of a State director of industrial education. The third bill of importance was that creating county high schools and fixing a two-mill county levy for their maintenance. The sources of revenue for education in the State are proceeds from the sale of public lands and rental from lands rented. There are aproximately eight and one-half million acres of public land to be administered in the interests of the common schools.

FINANCE. The report of the State treasurer for the fiscal year ending November 30, 1912, showed a balance in the treasury on November 30, 1911, of $568,199. The receipts for the fiscal year were $2,382,274 and the disbursements were $2,295,098, leaving a balance in the treasury on November 30, 1912, of $655,375. The chief expenditures were for education and for the support of State institutions. The principal sources of revenue were from taxation and from the income of the various funds.

CHARITIES AND CORRECTIONS. The institutions supported by the State include the Penitentiary at Santa Fé, the Asylum for the Insane at Las Vegas, the Reform School at Springer, the Deaf and Dumb Asylum at Santa Fé, and the Institute for the Blind at Alamogordo. The State also aids in the support of St. Vincent's Orphanage. There is as yet no organized department of charities and corrections in the State.

POLITICS AND GOVERNMENT

The legislature was in session in 1912 and the most important measures enacted will be found mentioned in the paragraph *Legislation* below. On January 6, New Mexico became the 47th State of the Union. On that date President Taft issued a proclamation providing for its admission. On January 15, W. C. McDonald was inaugurated governor of the State. The legislature on March 27 elected Albert B. Fall, Rep., and Thomas B. Catron, Rep., as United States senators. Senator Fall was elected for one year, while Mr. Catron received the full six-year term.

CONVENTIONS AND ELECTIONS. The Republican State convention for the choosing of delegates to the national convention met on March 9. The convention was controlled by the Taft wing of the party and eight uninstructed delegates. At the Chicago convention seven delegates voted for Taft and one for Roosevelt. The Democratic convention for the nomination of delegates instructed the delegates chosen to vote for Champ Clark for President. On June 6 Albert B. Fall was reëlected United States senator after a sharp contest. The House of Representatives for a time refused to go into joint session, but finally did so. Twenty-two members, however, refused to vote. These included all the Democrats and Progressive Republicans and three regular Republicans. The previous attempt to hold an election resulted in the arrest of four members of the House of Representatives, Julian Trujillo and J. P. Lucero of Rio Arriba County, and Manuel Cordova and Luis Montoya of Taos County. They were arrested on March 19, charged with having taken bribes of $500 each. It was alleged that these men had agreed to vote for Senator Fall for $500 each. When Senator Fall heard of this a trap was laid whereby the men were caught in the act of receiving money. An investigation was held by a committee of the House of Representatives and the accused men were exonerated.

The vote for President in the election of November 5 resulted as follows: Wilson, 20,437 votes, Taft, 17,733, Roosevelt, 8347.

LEGISLATION. The first legislative session of the State passed few measures of importance. Acts were passed relating to the bonding of the public debt and the disposition of a large body of land given to the State by the general government in the enabling act. A measure was passed providing for the prevention of corrupt practices in connection with elections, and another measure providing for the study of alcoholic drinks and their effect upon the human system.

STATE GOVERNMENT. Governor, William C. McDonald, Dem., Lieutenant-Governor, E. C. de Baca, Dem.; Secretary of State, Antonio Lucero, Dem.; Treasurer, O. N. Marron, Dem.; Auditor, W. G. Sargent, Rep.; Attorney-General, Frank W. Clancy, Rep.; Superintendent of Education, Alvan N. White, Dem.

JUDICIARY. Supreme Court: Chief Justice, Clarence J. Roberts; Associate Justices, Richard H. Hanna, and Frank W. Parker; Clerk, José D. Sena—all Republicans.

STATE LEGISLATURE, 1913. Republicans, Senate, 17; House, 33; joint ballot, 50; Democrats, Senate, 7; House, 16; joint ballot, 23; Republican majority, Senate, 10; House, 17; joint ballot, 27.

Representatives in Congress will be found in the section *Congress*, article UNITED STATES.

NEW SOUTH WALES. A state of the Commonwealth of Australia. Area, 310,372 square miles. Population (census of April 3, 1911), 1,648,448. Included in these figures are the area and population of the federal capital territory—about 900 square miles and 1714 inhabitants. The population figures do not include full-blooded aboriginals. Sydney, the capital, is the largest city of Australasia; it had 112,921 inhabitants—with suburbs, 629,503. Governor in 1912, John Napier, Baron Chelmsford (appointed May 28, 1909); to be succeeded in March, 1913, by Sir Gerald Strickland. Premier in 1912, J. S. T. McGowen. See AUSTRALIA.

A government measure for maternity endowment involving an expenditure estimated at £60,000 annually was proposed in September.

NEW STARS. See ASTRONOMY.

NEW YORK. POPULATION. According to the Census Bureau statistics compiled in 1912 out of the total population of 9,113,614 in 1910, the foreign-born whites numbered 2,929,282, compared with 1,889,523 in 1900. The largest number, 588,319, came from Russia; from Italy, 471,910; from Germany, 437,866; from Austria, 249,853; from England, 146,386; from Canada,

97,829; from Hungary, 91,542; from Sweden, 53,684; from Rumania, 33,066; from Norway, 25,981; from Scotland, 39,408. In New York City, with a population of 4,746,883 the foreign-born whites numbered 1,927,713, of whom 483,580 came from Russia, and 340,524 from Italy. The negroes in the State in 1910 numbered 134,191 and the mulattoes, 30,608. In 1890 the negroes numbered 70,092 and the mulattoes, 15,240.

MINERAL PRODUCTION. The iron ore produced in the State in 1911 amounted to 1,057,984 long tons, valued at $2,959,009, compared with a product of 1,287,209 long tons, valued at $3,848,683 in 1910.

There were produced in the State in 1911 952,515 barrels of petroleum, compared with 1,053,838 barrels in 1910. Although the production remains comparatively constant year by year there has been a slight decline in the entire production for several years.

AGRICULTURE. The acreage, value, and production of the principal crops in 1911 and 1912 are shown in the following table:

		Acreage.	Prod. Bu.	Value.
Corn	1912	512,000	19,763,000	$13,834,000
	1911	530,000	20,405,000	15,712,000
Wheat	1912	335,000	5,360,000	5,306,000
	1911	345,000	6,728,000	6,392,000
Oats	1912	1,192,000	36,714,000	16,420,000
	1911	1,310,000	38,645,000	19,709,000
Rye	1912	128,000	2,112,000	1,605,000
	1911	135,000	2,254,000	2,006,000
Potatoes	1912	360,000	38,160,000	22,133,000
	1911	375,000	27,750,000	24,975,000
Hay	1912	4,720,000	a 5,900,000	87,910,000
	1911	4,763,000	a 4,858,000	86,958,000
Tobacco	1912	4,000	b 5,200,000	655,000
	1911	3,300	b 5,054,000	525,616

a Tons. b Pounds.

MANUFACTURES. The Thirteenth Census statistics are for the calendar year 1909 and were compiled in 1912. New York holds first rank among the States in manufacturing since the completion of the Erie Canal in 1825. It will be seen from the following table that in 1909 there were in the State 44,935 manufacturing establishments, which gave employment to an average of 1,203,241 persons.

	Number or Amount 1909	1904	P. C. of Inc. 1904-'09
Number of establishments	44,935	37,194	20.8
Persons engaged in manufactures	1,203,241	996,725	20.7
Proprietors and firm members	47,569	41,766	13.9
Sal. employees..	151,691	98,012	54.8
Wage earners (average number)	1,003,981	856,947	17.2
Primary h. p.....	1,997,662	1,516,592	31.7
Capital	$2,779,497,000	$2,031,460,000	36.8
Expenses	2,986,241,000	2,191,339,000	36.3
Services	743,263,000	541,160,000	37.3
Salaries	186,032,000	111,145,000	67.4
Wages	557,231,000	430,015,000	29.6
Materials	1,856,904,000	1,348,603,000	37.7
Miscellaneous....	386,074,000	301,576,000	28.0
Value of products	3,369,490,000	2,488,346,000	35.4
Value of products less cost of materials..	1,512,586,000	1,139,743,000	32.7

The largest number of wage-earners, 98,104, was found in the manufacture of women's clothing; in the manufacture of men's clothing, 91,363; in printing and publishing, 63,120; in foundry and machine-shop products, 64,066. The greatest value of products was in the women's clothing industry, $272,518,000; in the manufacture of men's clothing, the product was valued at $266,075,000; in printing and publishing, $218,946,000; in foundry and machine-shop products, $154,370,000; in slaughtering and meat-packing, $127,130,000. Industries in which the product was valued at more than $50,000,000 were bread, and other bakery products, malt liquors, tobacco manufactures; lumber and timber products; flour and gristmill products, hoisery and knit goods, and electrical machinery. The total number of persons employed in manufacturing in the State was 1,203,241, of whom 869,434 were male, and 333,807 female. The wage-earners under 16 years of age numbered 7819. More than two-thirds of the wage-earners employed worked from 54 to 60 hours a week, while more than one-fourth were employed in establishments where the usual hours were less than 54 a week; and only 4.1 per cent. in establishments where more than 60 hours a week prevailed. The largest number of wage-earners was in New York City, 554,002; in Buffalo, 51,412; in Rochester, 39,108; in Troy, 20,020; in Syracuse, 18,148; in Schenectady, 14,931; in Yonkers, 12,711; in Utica, 13,103; and in Amsterdam, 10,284. The value of the industrial product of New York City was $2,029,692,576.

FINANCE. The total resources of the State on September 30, 1912, amounted to $171,820,570. Of this, there was included in the general fund, $50,213,405; in the canal fund, $72,677,838; in the canal debt sinking-fund, $20,890,567; in the railway improvement fund, $34,000,000. The remainder was in highway debt sinking fund, trust fund, Saratoga Springs State Reservation fund, and the Palisades interstate park fund. The balance in the State treasury at the close of the fiscal year was $16,419,334. The chief expenditures during the fiscal year were for education, $9,052,990; for curative purposes, $7,357,972; for construction, $4,534,463; for charitable purposes, $3,038,516; for legislative, $2,047,420; and for regulative, $2,331,806. The total expenditures to September 30, 1912, were $39,234,118 from the general fund. The unexpended balance of the general fund on that date was $15,978,604.

POLITICS AND GOVERNMENT. The legislature met in 1912 and the most important measures passed will be found noted in the paragraph *Legislation* below. Governor Dix in his second annual message recommended many measures for enactment by the legislature. He placed especial emphasis on the need of more economy in the administration of State government and for provision for additional revenues. Among his recommendations were those providing for the making of vote-buying a felony, the repeal of the Frawley Boxing law, provision for inspection of bakeries, good roads, and a new State office building. He also placed emphasis on the importance of changes in the primary election law. He recommended that the date of the elections for the State committee be made uniform throughout the State and that the membership of the State committee be enlarged by law so as to include a representative from each assembly district. Among other changes which he suggested were several effecting the tax laws of the State. Few of these measures were passed by the legislature.

On March 26 primary elections for delegates to the Republican State convention were held under the new primary law. In this election the Taft forces were successful and the New York delegation to the State convention was divided as follows: Taft, 83 delegates; Roosevelt, 7. On account of the size of the ballots and the difficulty of preparing them their delivery was greatly delayed and some districts in the city did not receive their supply until just before the polls closed. The delay was due in a measure to legal proceedings instituted by friends of Mr. Roosevelt in relation to the printing of names on the ballot. Samuel Koenig, chairman of the Republican county committee, was elected by a vote of 931 to 27. Mr. Roosevelt denounced the result of the election in campaign speeches made directly afterward. See PRESIDENTIAL CAMPAIGN.

CONVENTIONS AND ELECTIONS. At the Republican State convention for the election of delegates to the national convention, held at Rochester on April 9 and 10, the delegates were not instructed to vote for President Taft, but were urged in the platform to take such action. Dr. Nicholas Murray Butler, president of Columbia University, was the temporary chairman of the convention and his address was distinctly hostile to Mr. Roosevelt, although the latter's name was not mentioned. The platform declared for a "self-controlled representative democracy," the preservation of "national tradition," and the constitutional protection of citizens when "threatened by a temporary majority." It opposed the initiative, the compulsory legislative referendum, and the recall, either of public servants or judicial decisions, or "any device which impairs consistency and continuity in the expression of the popular will." The platform declared that the Sherman act should be supplemented by a definition of the offenses prohibited, and that there should be a board created to enforce the law. The platform stood for protection, holding that the duties should cover the difference in the production cost and should be adjusted upon facts ascertained by an impartial board. The Democrats were denounced for ignoring the report of the tariff board after professing to favor an inquiry by such a body. A recommendation was made for the creation of a national banking reserve association and it was declared that all justiciable international controversies should be referred to an international court of justice. The four delegates-at-large chosen were Senator Root, William Barnes, Jr., Edwin E. Merritt, Speaker of the Assembly, and William Berry.

The Democratic State convention for delegates to the national convention was held in New York City on April 11. Its work was very expeditiously done and the assembly was remarkable for its harmony. The greater part of the platform adopted related to the tariff. The Republican party and Mr. Taft were accused of grossly deceiving the people by their promises to make a fair revision. The four delegates-at-large chosen were Governor John A. Dix, Senator O'Gorman, Alton B. Parker, and Charles F. Murphy. See PRESIDENTIAL CAMPAIGN.

The Republican State convention for the nomination of State officers was held on September 27. The two prominent candidates for governor were James W. Wadsworth, Jr., and Job E. Hedges, a well-known lawyer and public speaker. Mr. Hedges received the nomination for governor and Mr. Wadsworth for lieutenant-governor. The State Democratic convention, held on September 2, nominated William Sulzer, a member of Congress from New York City, for governor. A strong effort was made previous to the meeting of the convention to bring about the renomination of Governor Dix, but this failed largely through the opposition of Charles F. Murphy, leader of Tammany Hall. Mr. Sulzer, although for many years a member of this organization, was known to be independent of its influences and was generally considered to have been the best choice under the circumstances. He had made a very creditable record in Washington in Congress and was, at the time of his nomination, chairman of the important committee on foreign affairs. The convention of the Progressive party met at Syracuse on November 5. Previous to the convention there were two conspicuous candidates for the nomination for governor, Comptroller Prendergast of New York City, and William Hotchkiss of New York City, who had had charge of the Progressive campaign in the State. The rivalry which developed between these two candidates and the bitterness engendered thereby made it impracticable for either of them to be nominated and a compromise was made by nominating Oscar S. Straus, who had been minister to Turkey for many years and was secretary of commerce and labor under President Roosevelt. Mr. Straus was permanent chairman of the convention at the time of his nomination. The campaign which followed these nominations was aggressive. All three candidates conducted speaking tours throughout the State.

The election on November 5 resulted as follows: Wilson 665,475; Taft, 455,428; Roosevelt, 390,021; Debs, 63,381; Chafin, 19,427; Reimer, 4251. For governor, Sulzer, 649,559; Hedges, 444,105; Straus, 393,183; McNicholl Prohibition, 18,990; Hall, Socialist-Labor, 4461. In New York City, including Manhattan and the Bronx, Sulzer received 159,699 votes, Hedges, 49,681, and Straus, 112,010. The entire Democratic State ticket was elected.

OTHER EVENTS. The progress of the State Barge Canal will be found noted under CANALS, and the work on the new Croton aqueduct will be found under AQUEDUCTS. In New York City the most important events of the year were concerned with the plans for new subways, which will be found discussed in the articles RAPID TRANSIT and TUNNELS, and in the graft exposures which resulted from the assassination of a gambler named Herman Rosenthal on July 16. Rosenthal, as a result of alleged persecution by the police, had declared his intention of making startling revelations which would affect the police administration of the city to the district attorney. On the night preceding the day on which he was to see the district attorney he was shot while coming out of a hotel. The murderers escaped in an automobile which, however, was soon traced. The chauffeur was captured and as a result of his confession and that of others connected with him, suspicion was directed to Charles Becker, a lieutenant of police, who had charge of the so-called "strong-arm squad" whose duty chiefly was the suppression of gambling and disorderly houses.

After skillful work on the part of the district attorney, Charles S. Whitman, Becker was indicted after a sensational trial in which startling revelations were made by gamblers and others as to police conditions. He was convicted of having instigated the murder. The actual murderers were shown to have been four notorious gamblers and "gunmen." These, after several weeks of search, were captured and were convicted and sentenced to death. It was shown at the trial of Becker that Rosenthal was in possession of valuable evidence which would have shown Becker guilty of persecution and blackmail.

As a result of these investigations and trials an aldermanic committee began an investigation into alleged conditions of corruption in New York. This had not terminated at the end of the year, but the evidence given before the committee showed corrupt conditions among the police and others connected with them.

An incident which attracted wide attention was the action of Governor Dix, of New York, in pardoning Albert T. Patrick, after what was probably the most remarkable fight ever made by a convict in the United States. Patrick was found guilty of the murder of William M. Rice in 1902 and was sentenced to death. After a series of legal proceedings which lasted for four years and seven months his sentence was commuted by Governor Higgins in December, 1906, to life imprisonment. At that time he was within three weeks of the execution of his sentence of death. Patrick devoted the years from 1906 to 1912 to efforts to secure his pardon. His case involved many difficult legal and medical complications, and Governor Dix was finally convinced that the verdict of guilty was wrongly given. Patrick was thereupon pardoned.

LEGISLATION. At the legislative session of 1912, there was passeu an unusual number of measures, some of them of first importance. The laws relating to elections were amended. In this act provision was made for the election of members of the State committee of a party at the spring primary of the year when a President is to be elected, and for the election of successors the second year thereafter; also that members of the State, county, judicial, senatorial district, Congressional district, assembly district, city, borough, aldermanic district, and municipal court district, shall be elected at primary elections at the fall primary except in a year when a president is to be elected, when they shall be elected at the spring primary. It is provided that delegates to the national convention may be elected either at State conventions held by such party or from Congressional districts, or partly by State conventions and partly by Congressional districts. A commission on barge canal operation was created, as was also a commission to investigate the conditions under which manufacture is carried on in cities of the first and second class. Amendments were made to the banking law. An appropriation of $30,000,000 to be expended in carrying out the purposes of the act for the improvement of the Erie Canal, the Oswego Canal, and the Champlain Canal was authorized. A comprehensive act amending the highway law of the State was passed. Amendments were made to the pure food law of the State. An important statute amending the act of 1891 providing for rapid transit railways in cities of over 1,000,000 inhabitants was passed. This was designed largely for the city of New York to complete contracts for new subways. The code of criminal procedure was amended in relation to the court of appeals where the sentence is death. An appropriation for an amount not exceeding $50,000,000 for the purpose of constructing State and county highways was authorized. This measure was dependent on the vote of the people at the general election. Important amendments were made to the laws relating to fish and game, and an appropriation of $6,000,000 for the improvement of the Cayuga and Seneca canals was authorized. The labor law relating to fire prevention in factories was amended. The establishment of a State reformatory for misdemeanants was authorized and provision was made for their educational, industrial, and moral instruction and training. The labor law was amenued and provision was made that no child under the age of 16 years shall be employed or permitted to work in any factory before eight o'clock in the morning or after five o'clock in the evening or for more than eight hours in one day or six days in one week. No male minor under the age of 18 years shall be employed or permitted to work in any factory for more than six days or 54 hours in any one week, nor between the hours of twelve midnight and four o'clock in the morning. No female under the age of 21, and no woman shall be employed or permitted to work in any factory before six o'clock in the morning or after nine in the evening or more than six days or 54 hours in any one week. There are, however, certain exceptions to these provisions. See CHILD LABOR, and EMPLOYERS' LIABILITY.

NEW YORK, PORT OF. See DOCKS AND HARBORS.

NEW YORK CITY. See ARCHITECTURE, and CITY PLANNING.

NEW YORK FACTORY INVESTIGATING COMMISSION. See SWEATING.

NEW YORK STATE BARGE CANAL. See CANALS.

NEW YORK SUBWAYS. See RAPID TRANSIT.

NEW YORK UNIVERSITY. An institution for higher education in New York City, founded in 1831. The attendance in all departments of the university, including the summer school, in the collegiate year 1912-13 was about 4500. The faculty numbered 381. An important event in the history of the university during the year was the opening of a department of government with Prof. J. W. Jenks as director, and Prof. F. P. Powell as assistant. No especially notable benefactions were received during the year. The productive funds of the university amounted at the end of the collegiate year 1911-12 to $1,892,000. The library contains 105,000 volumes. President, Elmer Ellsworth Brown.

NEW ZEALAND, DOMINION OF. Three principal and several smaller islands in the South Pacific; an autonomous British dependency.

AREA AND POPULATION. Area of North Island, 44,468 square miles (563,729 inhabitants, census of April 2, 1911); South Island, 58,525 square miles (444,152); Stewart Island, 665 (325)—total, New Zealand proper, 103,658 square miles; total population (including 262 on Chatham and Kermadec islands), 1,008,468.

Annexed islands, 1093 square miles (12,340 inhabitants); making a total of 104,751 square miles and 1,021,066 inhabitants exclusive of 49,844 Maoris. Total population with Maoris, 1,070,910. Wellington had 64,372 inhabitants (with suburbs, 70,729); Auckland, 82,482 (102,676); Christchurch, 53,116 (80,193); Dunedin, 41,529 (64,237).

PRODUCTION. The area of land under occupation in 1910-11 was 40,238,126 acres. Area under cereals and pulse, 1,015,822; under green crops, 713,682—a total of 1,729,504 acres under crops. In sown grasses on plowed land, 5,000,226 acres; on land not plowed, 9,214,515; in native grass and unimproved land, 23,972,236; in fallow, 209,973; in plantations, orchards, and gardens, 110,892; in vineyards, 780. Under wheat (1910-11), 322,167 acres; yield, 8,290,221 bu.; oat crop, 10,118,917 bu. Livestock, census of 1911: 23,996,126 sheep (19,826,604 in 1891), 2,020,171 cattle (831,831), 404,284 horses (211,040), 348,754 swine (308,812), 3,691,957 fowls (1,790,070). Of the foregoing, Maoris owned 486,922 sheep, 61,300 cattle, 48,222 horses, 33,290 swine.

The wool export in 1910 was 204,368,957 lbs. (value, £8,308,410); wool production 1891, 111,537,546 lbs. Frozen meat takes second place among export products, the amount shipped in 1910 being 297,269,952 lbs. (value, £3,850,777), as compared with 110,199,082 lbs. in 1891. In addition, frozen fish (£13,220), preserved meat (£146,529), salt meats (£15,855), and smoked hams, etc. (£8876), were also exported in 1910. Dairy products also are exported.

New Zealand possesses great natural mineral resources. To December 31, 1910, gold to the value of £77,437,131 was obtained; silver, to the value of £1,618,522; coal, £16,709,820. Gold produced in 1910, 478,288 oz., valued at £1,896,328; silver, 1,711,235 oz., £171,562; coal, 2,197,362 tons, £1,219,737.

COMMERCE. The imports in 1910 amounted to £17,051,583—£10,498,771 from the United Kingdom and £3,967,053 from British colonies; exports, £22,180,209—£18,633,118 to the United Kingdom and £2,468,119 to British colonies. The period for which the trade statistics are compiled embraces part of two wool clips; they do not therefore show the full effect of the fluctuations for one season as compared with another. For the year ended March 31, 1911, the imports without specie were valued at £17,385,066 (£14,774,377 in 1910); specie, £328,119 (£581,580); exports, £21,437,205 (£21,467,657); specie, £46,695 (£24,152). Tonnage entered and cleared (1910), 2,756,238 (2,672,028 tons British).

COMMUNICATIONS. There were in operation March 31, 1911, 2761 miles of government and 29 of private railways, and 192 miles under construction. Revenue from government lines for 1910-11, £3,494,182; expenditure, £2,303,272; total expenditure to 1911, £29,606,546. New construction and extension are steadily progressing. Telegraph lines, 11,316 miles, with 37,212 miles of wire.

FINANCE. The revenue for the year ended March 31, 1911, amounted to £10,297,023 and the expenditure to £9,343,106. Gross public debt on March 31, 1911, £81,078,122; accrued sinking fund, £3,380,542; net public debt, £77,697,580. Customs revenue (1910-11), £3,027,829, exclusive of beer duty, £118,100.

The Governor in 1912 was Sir John Poynder Dickson-Poynder, first Baron Islington, appointed 1910.

ARMY. By the terms of the defense act of 1909, the principle of compulsory military training was adopted and in this act and supplementary legislation provision was made for systematic military education and training, including junior cadets (12 to 14 years), senior cadets (15 to 18 years), and territorial recruits, so that eventually there would be developed a force of 65,000 men between the ages of 19 and 25 who would have had 16 days' training as recruits and yearly periods of 6 days. In 1912 the reorganization of the forces was proceeding vigorously and about 21,000 men had completed their first camp during the year. The aim was to improve the training and to secure greater uniformity with the military forces of Australia. There was to be a staff corps of 100 officers and New Zealand officers were being attached to the imperial forces for training. The territorial forces recruited from the cadet corps were to have a strength of 10,006 and were to undergo 16 days' training, 8 of which was in camp. The total peace establishment of the territorial force as projected was to number 1087 officers, 18,800 rank and file and 486 in the officers' training corps at the universities, making a total of 20,373. The rifle club movement was being actively fostered, both for the surplus men available for military training and for the youths not embodied in the territorial force. The defense estimates of 1912 carried an appropriation of £456,000, an annual item that by seven years would be reduced to a normal appropriation of £400,000.

NAVY. New Zealand is a party to the agreement between the Commonwealth of Australia and the imperial government which provides for the maintenance, by the British admiralty board, of a naval force in Australasian waters. New Zealand contributes £40,000 annually. Building for the imperial navy, at the cost of the dominion, is the armored battle cruiser *New Zealand*, laid down June 20, 1910, launched July1, 1911, to be completed early in 1913.

HISTORY. Parliament was opened on February 16. The chief features in the government's programme were: Nationalization of the iron industry and perhaps of oil fields; free education; reduction of the old-age pension limit from 65 to 55 for widows and to 60 for other women; lower railway fares for children; reduced duties on tobacco and other articles used by the working classes. The elections of December, 1911, had returned an equal number of government and Opposition members, leaving the balance of power in the hands of a few Laborites and Independents. A "no confidence" vote on February 27 resulted in a tie and the premier, Sir Joseph Ward, resigned. Parliament was prorogued on March 1. At the end of March a new cabinet was formed under the premiership of Mr. Thomas McKenzie, who held the portfolio of minister of lands. It was styled the "stop-gap" ministry, as the strength of the Opposition made it clear that it would be short-lived. It resigned after a defeat on a want of confidence motion on July 5, and was succeeded by a reform ministry under Mr. George Massey. For twenty-one years the Liberal Labor party had been in control of the government and this complete overturn caused no small astonishment among the people at large. The new ministry was distinctly imperialist in spirit.

As to its domestic programme, the principal features were: A reform of the legislative council, providing for the election of its members by a proportional system of voting; financial economy with increased governmental supervision and stricter accounting; encouragement of land settlement; removal of the public service from political influences; amendment of the conciliation and arbitration act, etc. Soon after its accession to power the new ministry appointed Mr. McKenzie, the retiring prime minister, to succeed Sir William Hall Jones as high commissioner. On meeting, the house voted an adjournment till July 31. On the reopening of parliament the budget debate was brought to a close. The Opposition was still without a leader and was unable to check the government's policy. A public service bill was introduced aiming to remove the abuses of political patronage. It provided for a commissioner who should assume control of the principal executive departments and whose decisions were subject to review by a repeal board. In October the house passed resolutions in favor of the plan to place the elections to the council on the basis of proportional representation of large electoral districts. When the session ended on November 8 the following important measures had been passed: The public service act above mentioned; a land act bestowing on a large class of crown tenants the right to purchase; and an act readjusting and increasing the graduated tax on land. See also articles on STRIKES, MINIMUM WAGE, and ARBITRATION AND CONCILIATION.

NICARAGUA. A Central American republic. The capital is Managua.

AREA AND POPULATION. The area is estimated at 49,552 square miles, and the population, which is largely Indian and mestizo, at 600,000. Reported births in 1908, 23,828; deaths, 9598; marriages, 1261 (that is, 2522 persons married). Chief towns: León, estimated population, 63,000; Managua, 40,000; Granada, 25,000; Matagalpa, 16,000; Bluefields and Masaya, 15,000 each; Jinotega, 14,000; Chinandega, 13,000. The presidential message of November 14, 1911, reported 335 schools, 3 national institutes, and a normal school.

PRODUCTION AND COMMERCE. The principal crops are coffee, bananas, and sugar-cane. The latter is grown more or less throughout the country; the coffee plantations, which are controlled largely by Americans and Germans, are in the western districts; the banana lands are chiefly in the Bluefields region. Other crops are cacao, corn, beans, and tobacco. The number of cattle is stated at about 1,200,000 There is some exploitation of the forests, which contain cabinet and other valuable wods. The mineral resources are considerable, but mining is almost restricted to gold.

Recent commercial statistics are not available. Imports in 1907 are reported at $3,224,173; 1908, $2,958,878; 1909, $2,583,257. Exports in the three years, $3,363,522, $3,647,984, and $3,989,428 respectively. The leading imports are cotton fabrics, flour, and provisions. Coffee export in 1909, about 93,640 metric quintals, valued at $1,546,919; gold, $1,037,892; woods, $415,575; rubber, $229,871. In 1909, the United States furnished imports $1,341,692 and received exports $1,677,010; United Kingdom, $625,668 and $843,453; Germany, $286,408 and $423,579; France, $131.826 and $776,429.

COMMUNICATIONS. There are reported 171 miles of railway, which are included in one line; this connects the Pacific port Corinto with Chinandega, León, Managua, Masaya, and Diriamba. Steamers ply between Granada, on Lake Nicaragua, and San Juan del Norte, on the Caribbean. In 1911, the government again assumed the administration of the railroad and the national steamers, annulling a contract (in effect January 1, 1905) with a private company which the tribunal of justice decided was against public policy. In addition to the state line, there are about 20 miles of private railway on the Atlantic coast near the Río Grande. A railway known as the Dos Bocas-Rama River was under construction in 1912. Telegraphs, 130 offices, with 3637 miles of wire; post offices, 135.

FINANCE. Revenue, in paper pesos: 1908, 13,119,503; 1909, 12,994,275; 1910, 15,182,852. Expenditure in the three years: 12,502,592, 18,639,308, and 34,573,125 pesos respectively. Of the 1910 expenditure, the sum of 12,052,848 pesos was ordinary, and 22,520,277 extraordinary, on account of the 1909 revolution. The paper peso has been worth about 16 cents, but in 1910 its value was only about 10 cents. Of the 1910 revenue, 9,793,717 pesos were derived from customs, 1,427,095 from liquor taxes, and 1,319,025 from tobacco taxes. In 1909, a loan for £1,250,000 was issued for railway construction, etc., and for conversion purposes. There is a French debt of 12,500,000 francs. Internal debt, December 31, 1910, 20,176,709 pesos paper. In 1911, a convention with the United States was signed, providing for the refunding of the foreign debt, the reform of the monetary system, and railway construction, by means of a loan to be made by American bankers and secured by a guarantee of 50 per cent. of the customs duties. Though approved by the Nicaraguan congress, the convention was not ratified by the American Senate. In 1912, Nicaragua adopted as a new monetary unit the gold córdoba, 1.67182 grams 900 fine, that is, equal in weight and fineness to the American dollar.

ARMY. Like other Central American republics the army in theory as regards its strength and organization differs materially from its actual condition and service. Nominally obligatory service is required from every male inhabitant between the ages of 17 and 55, and active service is restricted to one year with the aim of maintaining a standing army with a strength of between 2000 and 3500 in times of peace and contemplating a war strength of 40,000 on a war basis. Military affairs were in confusion in 1912 on account of the revolution.

HISTORY AND GOVERNMENT. The constitution of March 30, 1905, which was suspended (September 15, 1910) as a result of the 1910 revolution, was superseded by an instrument bearing date of March 1, 1912. On August 29, 1910, Gen. Juan J. Estrada assumed the duties of provisional president; he was the leader of the eventually successful faction in the civil war supervening upon the forced resignation of President José Santos Zelaya December 16, 1909. From September 15, 1910, to March 1, 1912, the country was administered under a provisional law promulgated by Estrada. On December 31, 1910, a national congress elected Estrada president for two years, and Adolfo Díaz vice-president. Díaz succeeded to the executive office May 11, 1911, upon the resignation of Estrada.

On October 7 following, the congress elected Gen. Luis Mena president for four years from January 1, 1913. This election was declared illegal. Mena, as secretary of war in the Diaz cabinet, refused the president's request to resign and on July 29, 1912, was deposed by force. He thereupon headed a revolt, which was suppressed with the assistance of American marines, to whom he surrendered September 25. On November 2, Diaz, as the unopposed Conservative candidate, was elected president. For further account of the revolution of 1912, see UNITED STATES, *Foreign Relations*.

NICHOLLS, FRANCIS TILLOU. An American soldier and public official, died January 5, 1912. He was born in Donaldsonville, La., in 1834, and graduated from the United States Military Academy in 1855. He took part with the 3d Artillery against the Seminole Indians and was on frontier duty in 1856 In the same year he resigned from the service and engaged in the practice of law until the outbreak of the Civil War. He served with the Confederate army throughout the war and rose to the rank of brigadier-general. He lost an arm at the battle of Winchester, Va., and a foot at Chancellorsville. After the close of the war he resumed the practice of law. He was elected governor of the State in 1887 and again in 1892. From 1893 to 1904 he was chief justice of the Supreme Court of Louisiana, and associate justice from 1904 to the time of his death.

NICHOLSON, EDWARD WILLIAMS BYRON. An English librarian, died March 17, 1912. He was born in 1849 in St. Helier, Jersey. He studied at Liverpool College and Tonbridge School and from the latter went to Trinity College, Oxford, in 1867. After taking his degree he was for a time schoolmaster, but his chief interest was in library work. On the death of H. O. Coxe, librarian of the Bodleian Library at Oxford, Mr. Nicholson was appointed to succeed him. He at once began efforts to improve the library, which continued throughout his administration. His chief aim was to make the famous collection of books more widely accessible, and before the end of his life he had the satisfaction of seeing some of his most cherished schemes carried out or inaugurated. Among these were a system of shelf classification and a subject catalogue. Beginning was also made on a revision of the general catalogue with a view to printing. The library was materially enlarged through his efforts. In addition to his interest in the library he was a strong opponent of vivisection and was an enthusiastic champion of woman suffrage. He was a prolific writer, and among his published works are: *A New Commentary on the Gospel According to Matthew* (1881); *The Bodleian Library in 1882-1887* (1888); *The Man With Two Souls, and Other Stories* (1898); *Keltic Researches* (1904); *Can We Not Save Architecture in Oxford?* (1910). He also wrote many songs and collaborated with Sir John Stainer on works relating to early Bodleian music in 1899-1902.

NIGER, MILITARY TERRITORY OF THE. A French West African territory. At the head of the administration is a commandant (1912, M. Scal) who is under the direct control of the lieutenant-governor for the Upper Senegal and Niger colony. On January 1, 1911, Zinder was made the capital, in compliance with an order (June 22, 1910) of the governor-general for French West Africa, reorganizing the Military Territory. Other cities are Timbuktu (Tombouctou), with 5127 inhabitants; Goundam (3202), Dori (3430), Niamey, and Filingué (2768). No railways traverse the country. See UPPER SENEGAL AND NIGER and FRENCH WEST AFRICA.

NILSEN EXPEDITION. See POLAR EXPLORATION.

NISHI, KWANJIRO, BARON. A Japanese general, died March, 1912. He was born in 1846 at Satsuma and entered the army while still a youth. After rising through the several grades he was made a major-general in 1889. During the Japan-China War he commanded a brigade of the 1st Army Division and fought at Port Arthur under Marshal Oyama. For his services he was created a baron. In the Russo-Japanese War he commanded the 2d Army Division and took part in the Manchurian campaigns up to the battle of Shaho. He was made a general in 1904 and was appointed commander of the garrison of Liaotung. In 1905 he was appointed inspector-general of education.

NISHI, TOKUJIRO, BARON. A Japanese diplomat, died March, 1912. He was born in Satsuma in 1847 and early in life entered the diplomatic career. From 1866 to 1896 he was minister at St. Petersburg and in 1907-8 was minister of foreign affairs. He was Japanese minister at Peking on the occasion of the Boxer outbreak and was one of those who sustained the famous siege in that city.

NISSEN, HEINRICH. A German archæologist, died in March, 1912. He was born at Hadersleben in 1839 and after studying at the Universities of Kiel and Berlin he became professor of ancient history at Marburg (1869), Göttingen (1877), Strassburg (1879), and Bonn (1884). He devoted himself especially to the critical study of early Roman history. Among his published writings are the following: *Kritische Untersuchungen über die Quellen der vierten und fünften Dekade des Livius* (1863); *Das Templum* (1869); *Pompejanische Studien* (1877); *Italische Landeskunde* (1883), and "Griechische und römische Metrologie" (1887) in Iwan Müller's *Handbuch der Klassischen Altertumswissenschaft*.

NITRATES. See CHEMISTRY, INDUSTRIAL.

NITROGEN. See CHEMISTRY, INDUSTRIAL; FERTILIZERS.

NIXON, GEORGE STUART. United States senator from Nevada, died June 5, 1912. He was born in 1860 in Placer County, Cal., and was educated in the public schools of that State. In 1887 he removed to Nevada, where he engaged in mining and ranching enterprises. He became identified with the Lovelock Land and Development Company, which reclaimed 20,000 acres of desert land in Nevada. He was also interested in cattle and sheep raising. Mining property in Goldfield, Tonopah, and other places in which he had large interests proved very profitable and he accumulated a large fortune. In addition to his other interests he edited and published the *Daily Silver State* at Winnemucca. In 1891 he served in the Nevada legislature. He was elected to the United States Senate in 1904 to succeed William M. Stewart. He was renominated without opposition and was reëlected by popular vote. The legislature, while Democratic by a majority of four, ratified his election at the primaries in 1911. In the Senate, where his term of service

CENTRAL AMERICA
SCALE OF STATUTE MILES
SCALE OF KILOMETERS
Important towns are shown in heavy face type
Railways are shown thus
GUATEMALA
HONDURAS
NICARAGUA
BRITISH HONDURAS
GULF OF HONDURAS
PACIFIC
Longitude

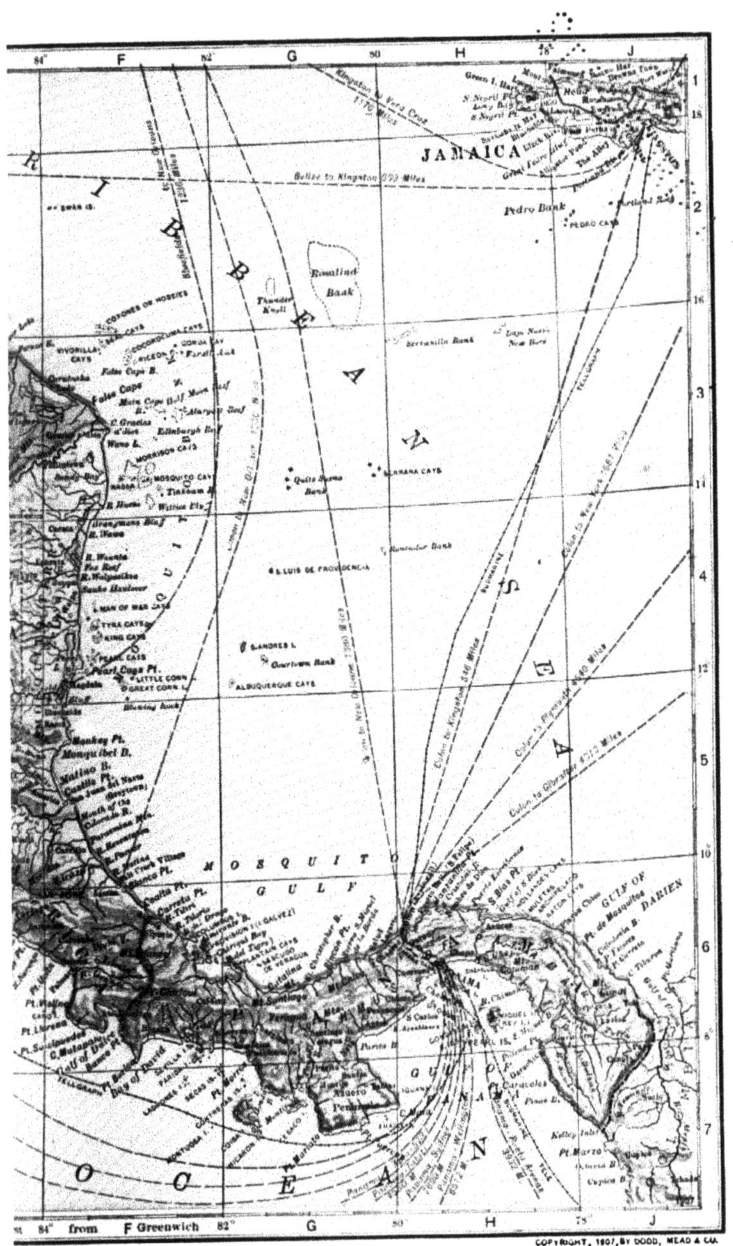

JAMAICA
Belize to Kingston 673 Miles
Kingston to Vera Cruz
Pedro Bank
PEDRO CAYS
Portland Rock
Rosalind Bank
Thunder Knoll
Serranilla Bank
Bajo Nuevo
SERRANA CAYS
Quito Sueno Bank
Roncador Bank
S. LUIS DE PROVIDENCIA
S. ANDRES I.
ALBUQUERQUE CAYS
Courtown Bank
MAN OF WAR CAYS
TYRA CAYS
KING CAYS
PEARL CAYS
Pearl Caye Pt.
LITTLE CORN
GREAT CORN I.
MOSQUITO CAYS
MORRISON CAYS
False Cape
Gracias a Dios
Bluefields
Monkey Pt.
Colon to Kingston 546 Miles
Colon to Plymouth 4540 Miles
Colon to Gibraltar 4312 Miles
Colon to New York 1981 Miles
MOSQUITO GULF
GULF OF DARIEN
Pt. de Mosquitos
S. Blas Pt.
Gulf of S. Blas
Bay of David
Azuero Peninsula
Pt. Mala
Pearl Is.
Caracoles
Kelley Inlet
Pt. Marzo
Cupica B.
Montijo
Parita B.
Chiriqui Lagoon
CARIBBEAN SEA
OCEAN
84° from F Greenwich 82° G 80 H 78° J

would have expired on March 3, 1917, he was chairman of the national banks select committee and was a member of the committees on coast defenses, irrigation, mines and mining, and the Philippines.

NIXON, William Penn. American journalist, died February 20, 1912. He was born in Fountain City, Ind., in 1833, and graduated at Farmers' College, Ohio, in 1854, and from the law department of the University of Pennsylvania in 1859. He practiced law in Cincinnati until 1868. He was a member of the Ohio legislature from 1865 to 1868. In the latter year he entered journalism as business manager of the Cincinnati *Chronicle*. He remained in this position until 1872, when he became connected with the Chicago *Inter Ocean* as business manager, publisher, manager, and editor. He served in various public positions in Chicago. In 1896 he was delegate-at-large to the Republican national convention. He was appointed collector of the port of Chicago in 1897 and was reappointed in 1901.

NOBEL PRIZES. These prizes are awarded annually from an income of $8,400,000 by the will of Dr. Alfred Bernhard Nobel. The interest from this fund is to be distributed annually to those persons that shall have contributed most materially to benefit mankind during the year immediately preceding." The value of each prize is approximately $40,000, and is given for work in chemistry, physics, medicine, literature, and for the advancement of peace. The prizes awarded from the foundation of the fund, including those of 1912, are given in the table below:

Physics

Name	Year	Nationality
Wilhelm Konrad Röntgen	1901	German
H. A. Lorentz	1902	Dutch
Pieter Zeeman	1902	Dutch
Henri Becquerel	1903	French
Pierre Curie	1903	French
Marie Sklodowska Curie	1903	Polish
Lord Rayleigh	1904	English
Philipp Lenard	1905	German
Joseph J. Thomson	1906	English
Albert A. Michelson	1907	American
Gabriel Lippmann	1908	French
William Marconi	1909	Italian
Ferdinand K. Braun	1909	German
Johannes D. van der Waals	1910	Dutch
Wilhelm Wien	1911	German
Gustav Dalen	1912	Swiss

Chemistry

Name	Year	Nationality
Jacobus H. van't Hoff	1901	Dutch
Emil Fischer	1902	German
Svante Arrhenius	1903	Swedish
Sir William Ramsay	1904	English
Adolph von Baeyer	1905	German
Henri Moissan	1906	French
Eduard Buchner	1907	German
Ernest Rutherford	1908	English
Wilhelm Ostwald	1909	German
Otto Wallach	1910	German
Marie S. Curie	1911	Polish
Paul Sabatier	1912	French
V. Grignard	1912	French

Medicine

Name	Year	Nationality
Emil von Behring	1901	German
Ronald Ross	1902	English
Niels R. Finsen	1903	Danish
Ivan Petrovich Pavlov	1904	Russian
Robert Koch	1905	German
Camillo Golgi	1906	Italian
Santiago Ramón y Cajal	1906	Spanish
Charles Alphonse Laveran	1907	French
Paul Ehrlich	1908	German
Elie Metchnikoff	1908	Russian
Theodor Kocher	1909	Swiss
Albrecht Kossel	1910	German
Allvar Gullstrand	1911	Swedish
Alexis Carrel	1912	French

Literature

Name	Year	Nationality
Armand Sully-Prudhomme	1901	French
Theodor Mommsen	1902	German
Björnstjerne Björnson	1903	Norwegian
Frédéric Mistral	1904	French
José Echegaray	1904	Spanish
Henryk Sienkiewicz	1905	Polish
Giosuè Carducci	1906	Italian
Rudyard Kipling	1907	English
Rudolf Eucken	1908	German
Selma Lagerlöf	1909	Swedish
Paul J. L. Heyse	1910	German
Maurice Maeterlinck	1911	Belgian
Gerhart Hauptmann	1912	German

Peace

Name	Year	Nationality
Henri Dunant	1901	Swiss
Frédéric Passy	1901	French
Elie Ducommun	1902	Swiss
Albert Gobat	1902	Swiss
William R. Cremer	1903	English
Institute of International Law	1904	Interna'l
Bertha von Suttner	1905	Austrian
Theodore Roosevelt	1906	American
Louis Renault	1907	French
Ernesto T. Moneta	1907	Italian
K. F. Arnoldson	1908	Swedish
M. F. Bajer	1908	Danish
d'Estournelles de Constant	1909	French
Auguste M. Beernaert	1909	Belgian
International Permanent Peace Bureau	1910	Interna'l
T. M. C. Asser	1911	Dutch
Alfred Fried	1911	Austrian
No award	1912	

For the first time since the establishment of the prize there was no award for service in the cause of international peace in 1912, because the committee was unable to discover a person who "within the year has worked most or best for the fraternization of nations, the abolition or reduction of standing armies or the calling or propagating of peace congresses." It will be noted from examination of the awards for 1912 that with the exception of two, all those who received the awards are of French birth. It is probable that the winner of the prize for literature, Gerhart Hauptmann, is the only one whose name is widely known. He has been known for many years as a leader in the advanced German school of writers. M. Carrel, a biography of whom is given under his name in another portion of the Year Book, has been known for several years among scientific men as an investigator of remarkable skill. Gustaf Dalen is noted chiefly for his achievements as a gas engineer. Professor Grignard is a member of the faculty of Nancy University, and Professor Sabatier is of the faculty of Toulouse University.

NOBLE, John Willock. An American soldier and public official, died March 22, 1912. He was born in Lancaster, O., in 1831, and graduated from Yale University in 1851. He studied law at the Cincinnati Law School, taking a degree in 1852. In the year following he was admitted to the bar in Columbus. He practiced in that city and afterwards in St. Louis and Keokuk, Ia. He was city attorney in the latter city from 1859 to 1860. He enlisted in the Union army and served throughout the Civil War in the 3d Iowa Cavalry, rising to the command of this regiment. He was brevetted brigadier-general by act of Congress for service in the field in 1865. After the war he returned to St. Louis and was engaged in practice there until the time of his death. From 1867 to 1870 he was United States district attorney and in that capacity prosecuted the whisky and tobacco frauds. He was offered the portfolio of solicitor-general by President Grant, but declined. From 1889 to 1893 he was Secretary of the Interior in the cabinet of President Cleveland. He was a member of many scientific and patriotic societies.

NOGI, (KITEN) MARESUKE, General Count. A Japanese soldier, died by his own hand at the funeral services of the Mikado of Japan on September 13, 1912. He was born in Chosu, a few miles from Tokyo, in 1849. He came from the race of the Samurai, the old nobles of Japan. Details are lacking of his earlier years, but he fought as a captain in the civil war of 1877, and his experience as a soldier seems to have been sufficient to warrant his participating in the Chino-Japanese War as the commander of a brigade. He fought at the battles of Kinchow and Port Arthur in this war. In the first of these engagements his generalship came into prominence, and at Port Arthur he placed his troops with such skill that the city fell into the hands of the Japanese almost without a struggle. In return for his services in this war he was rewarded by a peerage and was promoted to be lieutenant-general with command of the second division. He served for a short time in 1896 as governor-general of Formosa, but proved to be too strict to be popular with his subordinates. He soon returned to Japan as commander of the 11th Division. This post he resigned in 1900 and retired to civil life, where he devoted himself to the study of war books and war maps, preparing for the struggle which he knew must come with Russia. He sent his two sons to the military college to prepare for this struggle. Both these sons were killed in the Russo-Japanese War. At the outbreak of the war Nogi was given command of the Third army and was ordered to attack Port Arthur. He had previously been promoted to the rank of full general. He landed his army corps on the Liaotung Peninsula on June 1, 1904. He was in command of the 1st and 11th divisions. He gradually separated himself from Oku's army corps and brought himself into a position to take up the march to Port Arthur. The city of Dalny fell without fighting and a month was spent in preparing a base of supplies at the harbor. Nogi then marched against the Russian outposts on June 26 and drove them from a strong position. He was, however, checked seven days later by a fierce counter-attack by Stoessel, the Russian commander. By the latter part of July Nogi was in the immediate neighborhood of Port Arthur. His army had already lost 8000 men, but on July 20 he attacked with a force about equal to that of the defenders. His siege train was inadequate and he had not been correctly informed as to the strength of the defenses. The siege continued until January 2, 1905, and was marked by fighting of the utmost severity. Two forts were taken by Nogi about the middle of August and an unsuccessful attack was made by Stoessel to retake them. The Japanese lost in three weeks 16,000 men, killed and wounded. By the middle of September the fighting concentrated at 203 Meter Hill, which commanded and was a part of the western defenses of the city. The attacks on this hill continued unsuccessfully until December 5, when the Japanese finally took it. The final ten days' fighting on the slopes of this hill cost the Japanese 10,000 men and the Russians about 5000. Nogi's elder son was killed during the attempt to capture this hill. After the fall of Port Arthur Nogi led his army to take part in the final operations around Mukden, where General Kuropatkin had made his stand against the combined army corps of Japan. In the latter part of February, 1905, he enveloped the Russian right wing and was thereby instrumental in bringing about Kuropatkin's ultimate retreat and surrender. After the Peace of Portsmouth, General Nogi, at the command of the emperor, took the honorary presidency of a school for young peeresses. His direction of this institution was marked by great strictness. His chief endeavor for the rest of his life was to call back to Japan the old ideals of Spartan life from which he feared the people were falling away, and his death during the funeral of his master, the Mikado, was in strict accordance with the old traditions with which he was imbued. During time of war General Nogi gave himself entirely to military matters. His reticence was well known and his discipline was notably severe. In private he was said to have been frank and cordial.

NORGINE GLASS. See CHEMISTRY, INDUSTRIAL.

NORSE PHILOLOGY. See PHILOLOGY.

NORTH CAROLINA. POPULATION. According to the Census Bureau statistics compiled in 1912, out of a total population of 2,206,287 in 1910, the foreign-born whites numbered 5942, compared with 4394 in 1900. The largest number of these, 1073, came from Germany. Other European countries are represented by smaller numbers. The negroes in the State in 1910 numbered 697,843 and the mulattoes, 144,123. In 1890 the negroes numbered 561,018 and the mulattoes, 77,201.

AGRICULTURE. The acreage, value, and production of the principal crops in 1911 and 1912 will be found in the following table:

		Acreage.	Prod. Bu.	Value.
Corn	1912	2,808,000	51,106,000	$42,418,000
	1911	2,700,000	49,680,000	40,738,000
Wheat	1912	598,000	5,322,000	5,907,000
	1911	626,000	6,636,000	6,769,000
Oats	1912	204,000	3,794,000	2,352,000
	1911	219,000	3,614,000	2,277,000
Rye	1912	44,000	409,000	429,000
	1911	47,000	470,000	470,000
Potatoes....	1912	30,000	2,550,000	1,938,000
	1911	31,000	1,488,000	1,607,000
Hay	1912	293,000	a 381,000	6,363,000
	1911	161,000	a 169,000	2,873,000
Tobacco ..	1912	179,000	b 110,980,000	17,757,000
	1911	140,000	b 99,400,000	11,530,400
Cotton	1911	....	c 935,000	....

a Tons. b Pounds. c Bales.

MINERAL PRODUCTION. North Carolina holds first place among the eastern States in the production of gold. The amount recovered in 1911 was 3,399.89 fine ounces, valued at $70,282, an increase over the production of 1910 of 108.21 fine ounces in quantity and $2237 in value. The silver produced in the State is obtained in refining the gold produced. It amounted to 943 fine ounces in 1911, valued at $500.

MANUFACTURES. The Thirteenth Census included statistics of manufactures in the State. These are for the calendar year 1909. The most important general results of the census are given in the table below. The industry in which the largest number of wage-earners was employed, and the value of the product was the greatest, was that related to cotton goods. In this the wage-earners numbered 47,231 and the value of the product was $72,680,000. In the manufacture of tobacco 8203 wage-earners were employed and the product was valued at $35,-987,000. In the manufacture of lumber and timber products, 34,001 wage-earners were employed and the value of the product was $33,525,000. These are the only industries in the State in which the value of the product exceeded $10,000,-000. Those in which the value of the product was between $5,000,000 and $9,000,000 were oil, cotton seed and cake, flour-mill and gristmill products, furniture and refrigerators, fertilizers, leather, and hosiery and knit goods. The total number of wage-earners in the State was 121,-473. Of these, 93,787 were male and 27,686 were female. The wage-earners under 16 years of age numbered 13,698 and of these 5903 were females. The prevailing hours of labor were 60 or more a week. The cotton industry is mainly on the basis of 11 hours a day or from 63 to 66 hours a week. In the tobacco manufactures the prevailing hours are more than 54, but less than 60 a week. The largest number of wage-earners was in the city of Winston, 6708; in Charlotte, 4199; in Durham, 3718. These are the leading manufacturing cities in the State. The following table shows the increase in manufacturing in the five-year period 1904 to 1909:

	Number or Amount 1909	1904	P. C. of Inc. 1904-'09
Number of establishments	4,931	3,272	50.7
Persons engaged in manufactures	133,458	93,142	43.3
Proprietors and firm members	5,451	3,731	46.1
Salaried employees	6,529	4,072	60.3
Wage earners (average number)	121,473	85,339	42.3
Primary horsepower	378,556	216,622	74.8
Capital	$217,186,000	$141,001,000	54.0
Expenses	186,463,000	122,391,000	52.4
Services	41,259,000	25,170,000	63.9
Salaries	6,904,000	3,795,000	81.9
Wages	34,355,000	21,375,000	60.7
Materials	121,861,000	79,268,000	53.7
Miscellaneous	23,343,000	17,953,000	30.0
Value of products	216,656,000	142,521,000	52.0
Value added by manufacture (value of products less cost of materials)	94,795,000	63,253,000	49.9

CHARITIES AND CORRECTIONS. The institutions under the control of the State, with their populations on Nevember 30, 1912, are as follows: Hospital at Morganton (for insane), 1330; Hospital at Raleigh, 702; Hospital at Goldsboro (colored insane), 776; Dangerous Insane Department (at the penitentiary), 56; Epileptic Colony (State Hospital, Raleigh), 148; School for the Feebleminded at Kinston; School for the White Blind, Raleigh, 186; School for the Colored Blind and Deaf, Raleigh, 178; School for the White Deaf, Morganton, 250; Soldiers' Home (Confederate), 135; North Carolina Tuberculosis Sanatorium, 23; Stonewall Jackson Manual Training and Industrial School (Reform School for White Boys), 59; Oxford Orphanage for White Children, Oxford, 312; Oxford Orphanage for Colored Children, 235. Besides the above, which gives the charitable institutions, there are the prisons of the State: State's Prison, 87; State Farm, 435; Railroad Work, 284. In the forty county camps misdemeanants and felons number 1494. The jail population in 89 of the 100 counties is 475.

The chief discussion relating to charities and corrections in the State was in regard to the future policy to be followed on prison questions. Measures will be introduced into the legislature strengthening the child labor law. Other measures provide for the registration of births and deaths and a law for compulsory education.

POLITICS AND GOVERNMENT

The State legislature was not in session in 1912 as the sessions are biennial and the last was held in 1911. The next session began January 8, 1913. It reëlected the Hon. F. M. Simmons to the United States Senate.

CONVENTIONS AND ELECTIONS. Elections for State officers were held on November 5. The Republican party was divided into factions in North Carolina, and in March as the result of a disagreement of the two wings of the party in the State, President Taft withdrew from the Senate the nominations for ten federal officers. An attempt to harmonize the differences resulted in a conference held in Washington on March 15. This resulted in an agreement by which the leaders of the two factions agreed to support President Taft. In the State convention held on May 15, however, this agreement was upset as a result of the capture of the Republican State convention by the Roosevelt delegates. The administration of President Taft was severely attacked and the convention went on record as condemning him with "the withdrawal of appointments made, violating civil service traditions, and offering no excuse for it." The four delegates elected were pledged to vote for Mr. Roosevelt. The Democratic State convention for the choice of delegates to the national convention endorsed the candidacy of Governor Wilson. Strong effort was made to pledge the delegates to Mr. Underwood, but these failed. On September 3 primary elections for the nomination of State officers were held. These resulted in the nomination of Locke Craig by the Democrats, former Congressman Settle by the Republicans, and Iredell Mears by the Progressives. The election of November 5 resulted as follows: Wilson, 144,507; Roosevelt, 69,130; Taft, 29,139; Debs, 1025. Governor Wilson's plurality was 75,377. For governor, Craig, Democrat, received 149,975 votes, Settle, Republican, 43,625, Mears, Progressive, 49,930, and Hodges, Socialist, 944.

STATE GOVERNMENT. Governor, Locke Craig; lieutenant-governor, E. L. Daughtridge; secretary of State, J. B. Grimes; treasurer, B. R. Lacy; auditor, W. P. Wood; attorney-general, T. W. Bickett; superintendent of Education, J. Y. Joyner; commissioner of agriculture, W. A. Graham; commissioner of insurance, J. R. Young—all Democrats.

JUDICIARY. Supreme Court: Chief justice, Walter Clark, Democrat; justices, George H. Brown, Democrat; William A. Hoke, Democrat; William R. Allen, Democrat; P. D. Walker, Democrat; clerk, L. Seawell, Democrat.

STATE LEGISLATURE. 1913. Senate, Democrats 47, Republicans 1, Progressives 2; House, Democrats 104, Republicans 6, Progressives 12; joint ballot, Democrats 151, Republicans 7, Progressives 12. Democratic majority, Senate, 44; House, 98; joint ballot, 132.

The representatives in Congress will be found in the section *Congress*, article UNITED STATES.

NORTH CAROLINA, UNIVERSITY OF. An

institution for higher education at Chapel Hill, N. C., founded in 1789. The students enrolled in the various departments of the university in the autumn of 1912 numbered 818. The faculty numbered 84. There were no noteworthy changes in the faculty during the year. The most noteworthy benefaction was the gift of $40,000 for the school of education from the Peabody Educational Fund. The productive funds of the university amounted to $250,000. The income in 1911-12 amounted to $276,433. There were 65,000 volumes in the library. President, Francis P. Venable, Ph. D.

NORTH DAKOTA. POPULATION. According to the Census Bureau statistics compiled during 1912 out of the total population of 577,056 in the State in 1910, the foreign-born whites numbered 156,158, compared with 112,590 in 1900. Of these, the largest number came from Norway, 45,937; from Russia, 31,927; from Canada, 18,607; from Germany, 16,491; from Sweden, 12,155; from Denmark, 5352; and from Austria 5215. Other European countries are represented by smaller numbers. In 1910 the negroes in the State numbered 617 and the mulattoes 157. In 1890 the negroes numbered 373 and the mulattoes 220.

AGRICULTURE. The acreage, value, and production of the principal corps in 1911 and 1912 are given in the following table:

		Acreage.	Prod. Bu.	Value.
Corn	1912	328,000	8,758,000	$3,766,000
	1911	290,000	7,250,000	4,350,000
Wheat	1912	7,990,000	143,820,000	99,236,000
	1911	9,150,000	73,200,000	65,148,000
Oats	1912	2,300,000	95,220,000	20,948,000
	1911	2,180,000	51,230,000	21,004,000
Rye	1912	48,000	864,000	406,000
	1911	36,000	598,000	454,000
Potatoes	1912	52,000	6,656,000	1,864,000
	1911	42,000	5,040,000	2,772,000
Hay	1912	364,000	a 510,000	2,805,000
	1911	192,000	a 211,000	1,477,000

a Tons.

MANUFACTURES. The Thirteenth Census included statistics of manufactures in the State. These are for the calendar year 1909. The most important general results of the census are given in the table in the next column. The industry in which the value of the product was the greatest was that connected with flour-mill and grist-mill products, $11,685,000. In this industry were employed 435 wage-earners. In the manufactures related to printing and publishing 788 wage-earners were employed, and the product was valued at $1,910,000. The only other industry in which the value of the product exceeded $1,000,000 was that related to the manufacture of butter, cheese, and condensed milk. The value of these products was $1,029,000. The total number of wage-earners in the State in 1909 was 2789, and of these 2538 were male. The wage-earners under 16 years of age numbered 57, and of these 8 were female. The table shows the increase in manufacturing in the five-year period 1904-1909.

	Number or Amount 1909	1904	P.C. of Inc. 1904-'09
Number of establishments	752	507	48.3
Persons engaged in manufactures	4,148	2,545	63.0
Proprietors and firm members	723	494	46.4
Salaried employees.	636	296	114.9
Wage earners (average number)	2,789	1,755	58.9
Primary horsepower.	13,196	9,873	33.7
Capital	$11,585,000	$5,704,000	103.1
Expenses	17,290,000	8,895,000	94.4
Services	2,416,000	1,289,000	82.4
Salaries	629,000	258,000	143.8
Wages	1,787,000	1,031,000	73.3
Materials	13,674,000	7,096,000	92.7
Miscellaneous	1,200,000	510,000	135.3
Value of products	19,138,000	10,218,000	87.3
Value added by manufacture (value of products less cost of materials).	5,464,000	3,122,000	75.0

EDUCATION. There were in the State in 1912 167,326 children of school age. The number enrolled in the schools was 139,361. The average daily attendance was 99,686. The teachers numbered 7569. The average monthly salary was $55.08. The expenditures for education for the fiscal year ending June 30, 1912, were $5,597,153.

FINANCE. The receipts for the fiscal year ending November 1, 1912, amounted to $4,651,256, and the expenditures for the same period to $4,611,880. The balance on hand at the end of the fiscal year was $840,663, which includes a balance left at the beginning of the fiscal year. The chief sources of income are taxes and the chief expenditures for schools.

POLITICS AND GOVERNMENT

The legislature did not meet in 1912, as the sessions are biennial and the last was held in 1911. The present session began January 7, 1913. Politics in the State became of national interest during the year. The first presidential prima y election ever held in the State occurred on rMarch 19. Senator LaFollette had made a very aggressive campaign in the State previous to the election and largely as a result of this he received a plurality in the votes cast, which were as follows: LaFollette, 34,123; Roosevelt, 23,669; Taft, 1876. The Democratic candidate in the primary was Governor Burke, and there was no name in opposition to his on the Democratic ballot. The total vote cast in the primary was 59,668, compared with the vote in the presidential election of 1908, which was 57,680. Primaries for the nomination of State officers were held on June 27. Congressman Louis B. Hanna won the nomination for governor on the Republican ticket. Warden Frank O. Hellstrom of the State penitentiary won the Democratic nomination for governor. The Progressives on September 7 nominated Dr. C. C. Creegan, president of Fargo College, for governor, who declined, as he had not resided in the State five years as required by the State constitution. W. D. Sweet, mayor of Fargo, was then named as the Progressive candidate. The vote of the election on November 5 was as follows: Wilson, 29,516; Taft, 22,802; Roosevelt, 25,629; Debs, 6740; Chafin, 1090; Wilson's plurality, 3887; for governor, Hanna, 39,779; Hellstrom, 31,500; Sweet, 9342; Hanna's plurality, 8397.

STATE GOVERNMENT. Governor, L. B. Hanna; lieutenant-governor, A. T. Kraabel; secretary of State, Thomas Hall; treasurer, Gunder Olson; auditor, C. O. Jorginson; attorney-general, Andrew Miller; superintendent of education, E. J. Taylor; commissioner of agricultue, W. C. Gilbrath; commissioner of insurance, W. C. Taylor —all Republicans.

JUDICIARY. Supreme Court: Chief justice, B. F. Spalding; justices, Charles J. Fisk, E. T.

Burke, E. B. Goss, A. A. Bruce; clerk, R. D. Hoskins—all Republicans, except Fisk.

STATE LEGISLATURE, 1913. Senate, Republicans 44, Democrats 6; House, Republicans 104, Democrats 7; joint ballot, Republicans 148, Democrats 13. Republican majority, Senate, 38; House, 97; joint ballot, 135.

The representatives in Congress will be found in the section *Congress*, article UNITED STATES.

NORTH DAKOTA, UNIVERSITY OF. A State institution for higher education at Grand Forks, N. D., founded in 1883. The total enrollment in the autumn of 1912 was 995. Of these, 14 were in the graduate department, 189 in the college of liberal arts, 125 in the school of education, 99 in the school of engineering, 31 in the school of medicine, 89 in the law school, 134 in the model high school, and 308 in the summer session. The faculty numbered 105. Among the notable changes was the resignation of Dean A. A. Bruce, who was appointed a justice of the supreme court, and Prof. L. A. Birdsell, to become chairman of the State tax commission. The university is supported almost entirely by the State, and there were no benefactions received during the year. The amount of productive funds was $1,600,000. The income amounted to $365,000. There were 44,390 volumes in the library and 23,000 pamphlets. President, Frank L. McVey, Ph. D., LL. D.

NORTHERN BAPTIST CONVENTION. See BAPTISTS.

NORTHERN NIGERIA. A British protectorate (255,700 square miles) in western Africa. An estimate of the population made in 1911 returns 9,269,000. The Hausa population of the Fulani empire (the most densely populated region in Africa) numbers roughly eight millions. They are a highly developed Mohammedan tribe, ruled by the sultan of Sokoto. Pagan tribes are distributed along the Niger and through the Kabba country. Lokoja, the chief station, is situated at the junction of the Niger and the Benue; Zungeru is the administrative headquarters; Jebba (the capital till 1902) is the point at which the railway bridge crosses the Niger. The first train was run on the Baro-Kano Railway into Kano March 29, 1911. The line is 356 miles long and connects, through a branch to Zungeru, with the Lagos line, making a continuous route from Lagos to Kano. By means of this line the large foreign trade heretofore carried on from Kano, through French territory, by caravan to Tunis, will be diverted to Lagos, on the coast of Southern Nigeria. A branch from Zaria connects with the Buachi tin mines. The Niger valley furnishes the palm oil and palm kernels, which form a large proportion of the exports, but the climate is unhealthy. The products of higher ground are rubber, hides, ground nuts, shea butter, ivory, chillies, and medicinal plants. Tin is mined. Duties are levied on imports only; these are collected at the coast by Southern Nigeria, which contributes to the Northern Nigerian revenue. Imports and exports via Idah (returns of commercial firms only) in 1910-11, £258,600 and £308,700 respectively (£175,870 and £309,742 in 1909-10). Government returns for the calendar year 1910 give £330,506 for all imports, as compared with £1,215,084 for the previous year, attributing the decrease to the cessation of importation of railway material; imports of bullion and specie (included in the foregoing), £211,250 (£208,200 in 1909); exports, £120,652 (£406,722 in 1909). The local revenue amounted (1910-11) to £274,989; grant-in-aid, £275,000; contribution from Southern Nigeria, £70,000. Expenditure, £565,760. Sir Frederick J. D. Lugard was transferred in 1912 from the governship of Hongkong to be governor of both Northern and Southern Nigeria.

A Scottish engineer, Mr. Campbell, who was prospecting in the Ninkada District, was murdered by natives of the tribe of Mada, who were said to be cannibals, and a punitive expedition was dispatched against them.

NORTHERN TERRITORIES. See GOLD COAST.

NORTHERN TERRITORY. See AUSTRALIA.

NORTHWESTERN UNIVERSITY. An institution of higher education at Evanston, Ill., founded in 1851. The enrollment in all departments of the university in the autumn of 1912 was 4475. The faculty numbered 410. Among the important changes in the faculty were the following: Dr. Arthur I. Kendall was appointed professor of bacteriology in the medical school. He will have charge of the research work to be conducted under the Patten fund, the gift of Mr. James A. Patten, to advance scientific investigation of the cause and prevention of contagious diseases, with special attention to tuberculosis. Dr. Horace Secrist, formerly statistician for the Wisconsin industrial commission, was appointed professor of economics to succeed Prof. Murray S. Wildman, who went to Stanford University. Dr. Harlan Updegraff was appointed professor of education. Dr. Updegraff was for three years chief of the Alaska division in the United States Bureau of Education. There were no benefactions received during the year. The income was $750,000. There were 171,770 bound volumes in the libraries of the university and 92,310 pamphlets. President, A. W. Harris, LL. D.

NORTHWEST TERRITORIES. That part of Canada which is not included in any province or in Yukon Territory. Estimated area, 1,921,685 square miles. The census of June 1, 1911, returned a population of 17,196, as compared with 20,129 in 1901. The above area includes the portions of the territories annexed to the provinces of Quebec, Ontario, and Manitoba in 1912. Commissioner, Lieut.-Col. F. White.

NORWAY. A constitutional monarchy of northern Europe, occupying the western portion of the Scandinavian Peninsula. Christiania is the capital.

AREA AND POPULATION. The area and population, present (*de facto*), according to the census of December 31, 1910, are given below by amter (prefectures)—first the land area, second the total area, including fresh waters; in the third column is given the total population, and in the last the density per square kilometer:

Of the above total population, 1,123,160 were males and 1,234,630 were females. The total resident or legal population (*de jure*) numbered 2,391,782 (1,155,673 males, 1,236,109 females); in 1900, 2,240,032; in 1890, 2,000,917; in 1860, 1,608,653.

In the following list of cities the *de facto* population is given with the *de jure* population

Amter.	Sq. kil.	Sq. kil.	Pop.	D.
Smaalenene ..	3,869.51	4,144.14	150,690	38.9
Akershus	4,903.11	5,235.30	129,323	26.4
Christiania ...	16.32	16.55	242,850	....
Hedemarken ..	26,238.19	27,480.47	133,635	5.1
Christians	24,130.62	25,275.36	118,901	4.9
Buskerud	14,015.73	14,816.87	123,863	8.8
Jarlsberg and Larvik	2,244.63	2,319.58	103,333	46.0
Bratsberg	14,149.28	15,189.09	106,791	7.6
Nedenes	8,772.22	9,348.00	71,272	8.1
Lister and Mandal	6,881.17	7,264.24	77,237	11.2
Stavanger	8,671.64	9,147.15	137,581	15.9
Sondre Bergenhus	15,104.51	15,606.40	141,613	9.4
Bergen	13.03	13.55	75,888	....
Nordre Bergenhus	17,826.41	18,481.51	88,934	5.0
Romsdal	14,591.06	14,990.14	143,102	10.0
Sondre Trondhjem	17,814.65	18,612.37	147,343	8.2
Nordre Trondhjem	21,100.48	22,495.14	84,640	4.0
Nordland	37,173.34	38,646.07	161,105	4.3
Tromso	25,710.40	26,246.05	80,554	3.1
Finmarken ...	46,406.92	47,580.84	39,126	0.8
Total	309,633.22*	322,908.82†	2,357,790	7.61

* 119,549 sq. miles. † 124,675 sq. miles.

in parentheses: Christiania, 242,850 (241,834); Bergen, 75,888 (76,867); Trondhjem, 46,256 (45,335); Stavanger, 36,621 (37,261); Drammen, 24,937 (24,895); Fredrikstad, 15,481 (15,597); Christiansand, 15,408 (15,291); Christiansund, 15,891 (13,201); Aalesund, 14,785 (13,858); Skien, 12,099 (11,856); Fredrikshald, 12,023 (11,992); Sarpsborg, 10,018 (9846).

The marriages in 1910 numbered 14,566; births, 61,461; deaths, 31,856; emigrants, 18,912.

The majority of the people are Lutherans (2,329,229 in 1910 belonging to the state church and 15,287 to the Free Lutheran church); Methodists are next in numbers (10,986). All creeds are tolerated, Jesuitism excepted.

EDUCATION. Primary schools are maintained by local taxation assisted by state grants. Instruction therein is compulsory between the ages of six or seven and fourteen. There are state, communal, and private secondary schools, and special technical and industrial institutions; and a university at Christiania.

PRODUCTION. Only about one-thirtieth of the total area is cultivable; about one-third is under forest; the remainder is uncultivated pasture, barren table-lands, and uninhabitable mountains. The crops raised are not sufficient for home consumption, and the import of cereals and meats is large. Below are seen areas devoted to main crops and yield for two years, with yield per hectare in 1911:

	Hectares		Quintals		Qs.
	1911	1912	1911	1912	ha.
Wheat ...	5,021	5,021	73,513	75,147	14.6
Rye	15,056	15,056	240,615	201,930	16.0
Barley ..	35,916	35,916	584,024	712,846	16.3
Oats	106,279	106,279	1,479,373	1,640,170	13.9

The fisheries products are important, the total catch in 1910 being valued at 89,753,000 kroner. Mineral production is increasing. Export of forest produce (1910), 80,330,000 kroner (wood pulp, 39,473,000).

COMMERCE AND COMMUNICATIONS. In the table below are seen imports and exports in the 1911 trade, values in millions of kroner (1 krone=26.8 cents):

	Imps.	Exps.		Imps.	Exps.
Cereals	66.6	4.0	Metal mfrs...	29.7	2.8
Col. prods...	40.6	0.7	Wood mfrs.,	5.2	47.5
Animals	16.0	107.4	Leather mfrs.	1.5	0.5
Fruits, etc...	9.7	0.3	Paper, etc....	3.8	22.1
Spirits	8.2	0.2	Oils	32.4	13.8
Minerals	32.4	35.4	Drugs, etc...	2.7	0.5
Coal, etc.....	31.1	0.9	Various	93.9	22.4
Metals	27.2	10.8			
Hides, etc....	19.3	19.7	Total 1911.	495.7	325.4
Yarns, etc...	13.7	0.7	Total 1910.	429.3	309.7
Wood	12.3	34.2	Total 1909.	386.6	264.3
Textiles	49.4	1.7			

Countries of origin and destination follow, with value of 1911 trade in millions of kroner:

	Imps.	Exps.		Imps.	Exps.
Germany ...	148.1	67.2	France	11.9	11.6
U. K.	127.4	87.2	Spain	4.2	10.4
Sweden	57.8	20.0	Italy	3.8	9.4
Russia	35.4	11.7	Portugal	1.5	6.7
U. S.	31.1	28.5	Other	23.8	41.8
Denmark ...	22.1	7.6			
Netherlands..	16.6	11.6	Total	495.7	325.4
Belgium	12.5	11.8			

Vessels entered in the 1910 trade, 12,083, of 4,966,859 tons; cleared, 11,773, of 4,974,157. Merchant marine January 1, 1911, 3047, of 1,526,156 tons (steamers 1842, of 895,869).

Lines of railway in operation in 1911, 3085 kilometers; of state telegrapn lines, 11,013; of wires, 21,127.

FINANCE. In the table below is given in detail the budget for 1910-11:

Revenue	1000 kr.	Expenditure	1000 kr.
Finance*	77,243	Public works.....	43,926
Public works.....	37,399	Defense	21,287
Instruction, etc..	3,755	Finance	21,049
Justice, etc......	2,012	Instruction	15,106
Agriculture	1,458	Justice, etc.......	8,423
From loans.......	4,372	Agriculture	3,346
Defense	551	Commerce, etc...	2,220
Commerce, etc...	416	Council of state.	1,868
Foreign affairs...	389	Foreign affairs...	1,145
Various	64	Civil list..........	747
		Storthing	709
Total	128,280	Miscellaneous ...	240
		Total	120,108
		Extraordinary.....	798

* Customs, 50,967,393 kroner; direct taxes, 8,170,852.

The total capital of the national debt stood March 31, 1911, at 355,452,820 kroner.

ARMY. The reorganization of the army of Norway continued in 1912, following out the plan adopted by the Storthing in 1909. There was maintained a Ligne for the service of 12 years, the Landvaern with 8 years' service, and the Landstorm with enrollment up to the age of 50. The army is recruited from volunteers and men who serve compulsorily for from 72 days in the infantry to 126 days yearly in the artillery. In 1912, the contingent of recruits was increased, the infantry alone receiving 8000 men. The guard corps was being suppressed on the grounds of economy. The mountain artillery was being armed with Ehrhardt guns during the year.

NAVY. The active fleet included (1912) the following: 4 coast-defense vessels (16,300 tons), 2 monitors (3500), 3 first-class gunboats (3250), 8 second-class gunboats (2270), 2 torpedo-boat destroyers (1100), 1 torpedo dispatch boat (410), 10 first-class torpedo boats (1020), 27 second-class torpedo boats (1840), 1 third-class (30), 1 submarine (200)—all built. Building: 2 coast defense vessels, 1 torpedo-boat destroyer, 4 submarines. Personnel, about 3400.

GOVERNMENT. The king is the executive, acting through a council of state, whose members are responsible heads of departments. The legislative body is the representative Storthing, made up of the Lagthing and the Odelsthing. Reigning sovereign (1912), Haakon VII., son of the late king Frederick VIII. of Denmark. Heir-apparent, Prince Olaf. The council as constituted February 19, 1912, was as follows: J. Bratlie, president of the council and minister of state; J. Irgens, foreign affairs; E. Liljedahl, worship and instruction; F. Stang, justice and police; A. Lindvig Hovendak, commerce, navigation, and industry; E. Enge, agriculture; N. Hovdenak, public works; Fr. Konow, finance and customs.

HISTORY. A cabinet crisis occurred in the middle of February, and on February 19, the Konow ministry having resigned, a cabinet was formed under M. Bratlie, who assumed the portfolio of minister of defense. The crisis arose from a speech outside parliament by M. Konow, declaring his approval of the movement to introduce the old Norwegian language. In January the Storthing passed the bill admitting women to judicial and other public offices, except the government, state church, army, navy, and diplomatic and consular services. The October elections greatly strengthened the Left, who secured a large majority of seats.

NORWEGIAN EXPOSITION. See EXPOSITIONS.

NOVA SCOTIA. A maritime province of the Dominion of Canada. Area, 21,428 square miles. Population (census of June 1, 1911), 492,338, as compared with 459,574 in 1901. Halifax, the capital, had 46,619 (40,832 in 1901). The province is administered by a lieutenant-governor, James Drummond McGregor, appointed October 18, 1910. Premier in 1912, George H. Murray. See CANADA.

NOVELS. See FRENCH LITERATURE, GERMAN LITERATURE, and LITERATURE, ENGLISH AND AMERICAN.

NUTRITION STUDIES. See FOOD AND NUTRITION.

NYASSALAND PROTECTORATE. A British protectorate extending from German East Africa to Portuguese East Africa, between Rhodesia and Nyasa Lake, and having an area, according to the most recent survey, of 39,801 square miles. Population (March 31, 1910), 970,430: 766 Europeans, 481 Asiatics (exclusive of Sikh troops), 969,183 natives. The administrative headquarters are at Zomba; the chief town is Blantyre, in the Shiré Highlands. The cultivation of coffee has declined, that of cotton increased, 392 tons being exported in 1910-11. Total imports (1910-11), £199,710; exports, £168,911; local revenue (1909-10), £94,980; grant-in-aid, £31,451; expenditure, £112,369. There is a railway (113 miles) from Blantyre to Port Herald, to which extensions are contemplated. There are steamers on Lake Nyasa and on the rivers. Sir W. H. Manning (appointed February, 1911) was governor in 1912.

OATS. Owing to the record crops of oats in the united States and Russia, the world's production in 1912 was above the average, as these immense yields more than made up for crop shortage in other countries. In European countries, excepting Russia, the season was very unfavorable to the production of oats. Continued heavy rains through August and September interfered extensively with the harvest of the crop and much of the grain was not only discolored but even sprouted and rotted in the fields before it could be garnered. In some sections the grain did not fill out properly and was consequently light in weight. The yield and quality of the straw, which are very important items in the culture of the crop, were also largely reduced. Practically every country in Europe, except Russia and France, recorded a reduced acre-yield. In England the yield was more than 6.5 bushels under the 10-year average. Unlike her neighbors, Italy suffered from a severe drought, and among the cereal crops oats was most affected, the production being about 30 per cent. less than the crop of 1911. Russia produced in 1912 a crop of 1,067,584,650 bushels, or over 209,000,000 bushels more than the year before. Other yields, mainly estimated, were as follows: Hungary, including Croatia and Slavonia, 76,893,000 bushels; Rumania, 21,359,000 bushels; France, 375,642,000 bushels; Algeria, 12,287,000 bushels; Tunis, 2,067,000 bushels; Italy, 28,306,000 bushels; Spain, 24,461,000 bushels, and Bulgaria, 12,058,000 bushels. The crops of Argentina and Australia, harvested early in 1912, amounted to 79,924,000 and 35,828,000 bushels, respectively. Canada produced 381,502,000 bushels, an increase of more than 10,000,000 bushels over the yield of 1911.

In the United States the weather everywhere was most favorable for the crop, but at harvest time rainy weather in a number of the central States reduced the quality to some extent by staining the grain. The crop made a remarkable record and stood far above other years in total production and average acre-yield. The crop of 1912 was 1,418,337,000 bushels, or about 52 per cent. greater than the average of the preceding five years and over 40 per cent. above the crop of 1909, the largest previously produced. The area devoted to the crop was 37,917,000 acres, or 154,000 acres more than in 1911, and never before equaled. The price paid farmers December 1, 1912, was 31.9 cents per bushel, as compared with 45 cents December 1, 1911. While the price declined as a consequence of the enormous production, still the total value of the crop has never been surpassed. This value amounted to $452,469,000 and was about 16 per cent. above the average of the preceding five years. The crop ranks fifth in order of value, being within $103,000,000 of the worth of the wheat crop and of more than half the value of the entire cotton crop. The largest yields by States were as follows: Iowa, 217,818,000 bushels (a record yield for the State); Illinois, 182,726,000 bushels; Minnesota, 122,932,000 bushels; North Dakota, 95,220,000 bushels; Ohio, 93,280,000 bushels, and Wisconsin, 84,746,000 bushels. Among these States Iowa ranked first in average yield per acre with 44.2 bushels, while Idaho led all States with 48.9 bushels. The average yield per acre for the entire country was 37.4 bushels.

OBERLIN COLLEGE. An institution for higher education at Oberlin, O., founded in 1833. The total enrollment in all departments of the college for 1911-12 was 1733, divided as follows: college of arts and sciences, 998; theological seminary, 71; conservatory of music, 400, and academy, 264. The faculty numbered 153. The noteworthy changes in the faculty during the year included the retirement of Prof. F. F. Jewett of the chair of chemistry and head of that department, after 32 years of service, and the appointment of Prof. Alan W. C. Menzies of Chicago University as his successor. Professor Jewett retired under the Carnegie Foundation. The productive funds of the college amounted in 1911-12 to $3,754,400. The library contained 120,000 bound volumes, and 125,000 pamphlets. President, Henry C. King, D. D.

OCCUPATIONAL DISEASES. The marked attention which has been given recently to the subject of diseases incident to employment in certain trades continued during 1912. Though the volume of legislation was necessarily smaller than in 1911 owing to the fewness of State legislative sessions the success of the campaign for the protection of workers against industrial diseases was in some respects more striking. Especially noteworthy was the passage of the Esch bill, placing a tax on poisonous matches. (For legislation see LABOR LEGISLATION.) This campaign has been carried on by the American Association for Labor Legislation and its State branches. It has succeeded in inducing eight States to require physicians to report all cases of certain occupational diseases. Illinois has required medical examinations of workmen in a few employments where occupational diseases are most frequent. This association has also prepared reports on industrial poisoning from lead and mercury. The United States Bureau of Labor has translated the list of industrial poisons prepared by the International Association for Labor Legislation.

The second national conference on industrial diseases under the direction of the association was held at Atlantic City, in June, being attended by physicians, public health officers, medical factory inspectors, manufacturers, efficiency engineers, insurance experts, labor leaders, social workers, economists, and statisticians. At the same time the first industrial hygiene exhibit was displayed. At this conference Prof. W. Gilman Thomson of the Cornell University Medical College, classified occupational diseases and harmful substances as follows: (1) Harmful substances, as metallic poisons, toxic gases, fumes, and fluids, irritant dusts and fibres, and organic germs. (2) Harmful conditions of environment, as compressed and rarified air, excessive humidity, extreme heat or cold, and excessive light. (3) Occupational injuries, as injuries to nerves, muscles, and bones, due to strain, fatigue, cramp, blows, vibrations or pressure, injuries to eyes, to ears, to nose and throat, and to skin. Mr. John B. Andrews, secretary of the American Association for Labor Legislation, made a much more simple classification: Trades menaced (1) by specific industrial dusts, fumes, gases, vapors, and acids; (2) by compressed or rarified atmosphere; (3) by improper light; (4) by extremes of temperature and humidity; (5) by excessive strain. He laid down as the programme for advance, first, the prevention of all preventable occupational diseases; second, the reduction to a minimum of all those which we do not yet know how to prevent, and third, the compensation by some system of insurance of victims of occupational diseases. Thus the methods would be absolute prohibition, specific regulation for specific causes, such as white phosphorus in the match industry, and general regulation, such as the best sanitary conditions, and insurance against injury and compensation therefor. The conference included discussions on compressed air illness, occupational skin diseases, occupational nervous and mental diseases, occupational eye diseases, industrial poisoning, compulsory reporting of such cases by physicians, sanitary and health problems of modern industry, and the promotion of industrial hygiene by State legislation and education.

PLUMBISM. Since September 1, 1911, New York State has had a law requiring physicians to report cases of disease due to occupation, such as caisson disease, anthrax, and poisoning by lead, mercury, and arsenic. The reports are to be sent to the Department of Labor, which is charged with the duty of investigating processes or conditions which may cause industrial disease, and the administration of preventive measures to remedy such conditions. The importance of the law is shown by the reporting of a single case of lead poisoning in an employee of the Brooklyn Navy Yard. Investigation showed that this man was employed as a laborer in "scaling" lead paint in the double bottoms of battleships. Twenty men were found at the navy yard who had suffered from lead poisoning caused by work in double bottoms. Almost half the men employed on this work have been affected at one time or another by the lead; many of them had lost much time from their work on this account, and two had died. It was found that men were working in compartments four or five feet square in an atmosphere densely impregnated with dust, composed principally of red oxide of lead.

Dr. Alice Hamilton, of Chicago, has made an exhaustive study of the prevalence of industrial poisoning in the United States, the results of which were published in the *Journal of the American Medical Association* for September 7, 1912. She calls attention to the circumstance that plumbism in the United States, commonly supposed to be negligible as compared with the amount found in European countries, is really much greater here. A few comparisons may be quoted to show this. In an English white and red lead factory employing 90 men there was not one case of lead poisoning in five successive years. In an American white and red lead factory employing 85 men, 35 cases occurred in six months. Another English factory, employing 182 men, did not have a case of lead poisoning last year. An American factory, with 170 men, had 60 poisoned during this same year. Out of a group of 85 dippers, 13 men had had 16 attacks of lead poisoning in a pottery town in Ohio in one year. The English factory inspection report for 1910 states that in the Staffordshire potteries, among 786 male dippers, there were 12 cases of lead poisoning, exactly the same number as among our 85 dippers. In other words, in Staffordshire one dipper in 60 or 61 suffered from acute plumbism during one year; in Ohio, one dipper to 6 or 7.

As to the relative poisonous qualities of different lead compounds much stress is laid on dustiness as a factor. English experts believe that a less soluble lead salt may be actually more dangerous than one which is more soluble but less easily powdered. For instance, lead acetate is very soluble, but it has a disagreeable taste, so that the workman cannot swallow it unawares, and it is sticky, not powdery, so that in handling it he is not exposed to dust-laden air. On the other hand, the oxids, the basic carbonate, the chromate, sulphate, and monosilicate, are all dusty and some of them very light and fluffy. They are also almost tasteless, and the workman who handles them dry inhales into his mouth and swallows quantities without noticing it. Therefore the English authorities—Oliver, Goadby, and Legge—regard the lead salts as dangerous in proportion to their dustiness. They concentrate their efforts on the abolition of dust—and with amazing practical success. The worst of the lead compounds is probably Pb_2O, the suboxid, which forms on the surface of melted lead and is given off in fumes at high temperatures (Saeger). It is this oxid which causes poisoning in lead smelters, zinc smelters, brass molders, workers in the typographic trades, and the men employed in making lead pipe and wire, sheet lead, solder, shot and all the multitude of articles made from metallic lead. Men who handle these objects after they are made may also become poisoned, because the oxids forming on the surface of the lead rub off on their hands.

The second place would be assigned by some to the higher oxids, PbO (litharge) and Pb_3O_4, or Pb_2O_3 (red lead), or by others to the basic carbonate, white lead. The latter is decidedly more soluble and, dose for dose, more poisonous, but it is not so light and fluffy as are the oxids, and therefore Etz places it lower in the scale of industrial poisons. White lead, classed as the most dangerous of all by Lehmann, is the best known of the lead salts and probably responsible for more industrial plumbism than any, for it is white lead that poisons the majority of painters, and it is white lead that is used in the potteries and manufactured in white-lead works. The oxids, litharge and red lead, are used by makers of storage batteries; they enter into the composition of rubber, glass, varnish, certain kinds of pottery glaze, the enamel used on sanitary ware, and the paint used to cover iron and steel. Authorities are not agreed as to the size of the daily dose required to produce symptoms of lead intoxication, estimates varying from 1 mg. to 20 mg., or even more. There is a wide difference in individual susceptibility, certain workers being apparently immune, while others succumb in a few weeks. The avenue of entry is the alimentary tract, the dust being swallowed with the saliva, but absorption through the capillaries of the lungs has been experimentally proved.

SHUTTLEMAKERS' DISEASE. Shuttlemakers' disease is a rather baffling ailment found among workmen engaged in the manufacture of shuttles in Lancashire and Yorkshire, England. Numerous cases of illness among those handling the wood in these factories led to the belief that the timber used possessed a property injurious to health; and the impression went abroad that the sickness was due to some poison given off by the wood during the process of manufacture of shuttles. The symptoms complained of were "headache, sleepiness, running of the nose and eyes, chronic sneezing, giddiness, faintness, loss of appetite, shortness of breath, nausea, etc." The patients exhibited a pale, yellowish or greenish color of the skin, accompanied by a peculiar "camphor" or "Turkey rhubarb" odor from the breath and skin. Deaths were reported as due to "cardiac asthma" and cardiac incompetence. An inquiry into the details of the industry developed the fact that various woods have been used for the manufacture of shuttles, namely, Persian box, persimmon, cornel. These timbers have certain peculiarly suitable properties as cabinet woods and are capable of taking on a high polish. More recently certain other imported woods, known under the names of West African boxwood, South African boxwood, West Indian boxwood, and East London boxwood, have entered into use because of technical advantages and comparative cheapness. The sickness was most prevalent among those men who were exposed to the fine smoke-like dust given off by the saws or lathes where the inhalation of the dust or absorption in other ways was almost unavoidable, especially as the men are lightly clad and often naked from the waist up. An examination of the sawdust of supposedly toxic wood showed that an alkaloid present in the West African boxwood is a cardiac poison, inducing experimentally a gradual slowing of the heart-beat, with a cumulative effect after long exposure to its influence. The alkaloid is very soluble and probably easily absorbed. Further examinations disclosed the fact that the toxic wood variously termed West African or East London boxwood is not boxwood (*i. e.*, a species of *Buxus*) and is not identical with the South African or West Indian boxwood. It is a native of the Congo basin and the Kamerun; and Professor Gibson has at length identified it as a species of *Gonioma* which belongs to a poisonous order of tropical or subtropical plants. Thus, joint clinical, chemical, physiologic, and botanical investigations have made obvious the means of relief from a most objectionable industrial danger.

BIBLIOGRAPHY. A special bibliography on industrial hygiene has been prepared by the cooperation of the International Association for Labor Legislation, the Library of Congress, and the United States Bureau of Labor; the New York Department of Labor has published various reports on this subject, as has also the New York Factory Investigating Commission; the United States Bureau of Labor *Bulletin* number 95 contains Thomas Oliver's "Industrial Lead Poisoning"; the same *Bulletin*, number 100, publishes the list of industrial poisons and other substances injurious to health found in industrial processes, prepared by the International Association for Labor Legislation; the *American Labor Legislation Review*, Vol. II., No. 2, June, 1912, contains all papers presented at the conference above mentioned.

OCEAN DEPTHS. See EXPLORATION.

OHIO. POPULATION. According to the Census Bureau statistics compiled during 1912, out of a total population of 4,767,121 in 1910, the foreign-born whites numbered 597,245, compa ed with 457,900 in 1900. The largest number came from Germany, 175,130; from Austria, 73,162; from Russia, 48,752; from England, 43,365; from Italy, 41,581; from Ireland, 40,056; from Hungary, 84,657; from Canada, 21,068; from Sweden, 10,916; and from Scotland, 10,704. Other European countries contributed smaller numbers. In the city of Cincinnati, with a population of 364,463 in 1910, there were 56,792 foreign-born whites. Of these, 28,425 came from Germany. The city of Cleveland, with a population of 560,663, had a foreign-born population of 195,703. Of these, 41,310 came from Germany; 41,942 from Austria, and 25,499 from Russia. There were in the State in 1910, 111,452 negroes and 39,249 mulattoes. In 1890 the negroes numbered 87,113 and the mulattoes, 37,035.

AGRICULTURE. The acreage, value, and production of the principal crops in 1911 and 1912 are given below:

		Acreage.	Prod. Bu.	Value.
Corn	1912	4,075,000	174,410,000	$74,484,000
	1911	3,900,000	150,540,000	87,313,000
Wheat	1912	1,220,000	9,760,000	9,565,000
	1911	2,265,000	36,240,000	32,978,000
Oats	1912	2,120,000	93,280,000	30,782,000
	1911	1,700,000	54,570,000	24,556,000
Rye	1912	57,000	884,000	663,000
	1911	60,000	930,000	790,000
Potatoes ...	1912	186,000	20,832,000	11,041,000
	1911	190,000	12,350,000	10,374,000
Hay	1912	2,960,000	a 4,026,000	52,338,000
	1911	2,556,000	a 2,505,000	47,344,000
Tobacco ...	1912	86,200	b 79,300,000	7,217,000
	1911	88,000	b 81,400,000	6,186,000

a Tons. b Pounds.

MINERAL PRODUCTION. The production of coal in the State in 1911 was 30,759,986 short tons, valued at $31,810,123. The conditions affecting the industry in 1911 were in marked contrast to those prevailing in 1910, when the production was stimulated as a result of the strike in other States. The production in that year was 34,209,668 short tons, which is the record tonnage produced in the coal-mining history of the State. There were labor troubles in 1911, and 9530 men were on strike at one time or another during the year.

The iron ore mined in the State in 1911 amounted to 16,697 long tons, valued at $30,549, as compared with 22,320 long tons, valued at $35,866 in 1910.

The production of petroleum in 1911 was 8,817,112 barrels, which was a considerable decrease from the production of 1910, which was 9,916,370 barrels. The decrease was almost entirely in the Lima fields, which are a part of the Lima-Indiana oil field.

MANUFACTURES. The Thirteenth Census statistics are for the calendar year 1909, and were compiled in 1912. Ohio is largely a manufacturing State and the growth of the industries has been rapid and substantial. From the following table it will be seen that there were in 1909, 15,138 manufacturing establishments, giving employment to an average of 523,004 persons. The largest number of wage-earners was employed in the manufacture of foundry and machine-shop producets, 64,817; in the iron industries were employed 38,586; in industries connected with railways, 20,728; in the manufacture of pottery and clay products, 16,519; in printing and publishing, 15,756. The largest value of product was in the iron and steel industries, $197,780,000. The value of the product of the foundry and machine shops was $145,837,000; of industries connected with iron and steel, $83,699,000; slaughtering and meat-packing, $50,804,000; flour mill and grist mill products, $48,093,000. Other industries whose product was valued at more than $25,000,000 were printing and publishing, automobiles, lumber and timber products, boots and shoes, tobacco manufactures, industries connected with railways, and malt liquors. The total number of persons employed in the manufactures was 523,004. Of these, 439,811 were male and 83,193 female. Those employed under 16 years of age numbered 5244. The prevailing hours of labor among the great majority of wage-earners ranged from 54 to 60 a week; only 13.7 per cent. of the total being employed in establishments where the prevailing hours were less than 54 a week and only 7.6 per cent. in establishments where they were more than 60 a week. The largest number of wage-earners was in the city of Cleveland, 84,728. The value of the manufacturing product in this city was $271,960,833. In Cincinnati the wage-earners numbered 60,192, with a product valued at $194,515,692. Other cities whose product was over $25,000,000 were Youngstown, Akron, Toledo, Dayton, Columbus, Lorain, and Canton. The following table gives a summary of the results of the census for the calendar years 1909-1904:

	Number or Amount 1909	1904	of Inc. 1904-'09
Number of establishments	15,138	13,785	9.8
Persons engaged in manufactures	523,004	417,946	25.1
Proprietors and firm members	14,719	13,657	7.8
Sal'd employees	61,351	39,991	53.4
Wage earners (average number)	446,934	364,298	22.7
Primary h. p....	1,583,155	1,116,932	41.7
Capital	$1,300,733,000	$856,989,000	51.8
Expenses	1,282,845,000	856,206,000	49.8
Services	317,597,000	225,864,000	40.6
Salaries	72,147,000	43,435,000	66.1
Wages	245,450,000	182,429,000	34.5
Materials	824,202,000	527,637,000	56.2
Miscellaneous....	141,046,000	102,705,000	37.3
Value of products	1,437,936,000	960,812,000	49.7
Value of products less cost of materials	613,734,000	433,175,000	41.7

EDUCATION. The total daily attendance in the schools of the State in 1911-12, was 651,746. Of these, 325,986 were boys and 325,760 were girls. The total number of men teachers was 8239, and of women teachers, 18,125. The average monthly salary in elementary schools for men was $58, and for women, $47; in high schools, for men, $88, and for women, $67. The total expenditures under the common school system of the State in 1911-12 were $30,054,779. A law requiring the teaching of agriculture in the elementary schools of the State has greatly added to the value of school work. This law makes the State commissioner of schools State superintendent of agriculture, and gives him the appointment of four deputy supervisors of agriculture. This law has created a great interest in the subject, and it will largely increase the value of farms and farm products in Ohio. New laws for certification and teachers' pensions were passed in the legislature of 1911-12. Two normal schools, one at Bowling Green and one at Kent, were established during 1912.

FINANCE. The receipts for the fiscal year ending November 15, 1911, were $13,037,293, and the expenditures for the same period were $12,932,343. The balance on hand at the end of the year, including the balance at the beginning of the fiscal year, was $3,768,116. The chief sources of income are from the liquor tax, county tax settlement, excise tax, public utilities, the annual fees of corporations, and fees and taxes from insurance companies. The chief expenditures are for State institutions, for education and for State government. There is no State debt.

CHARITIES AND CORRECTIONS. The charitable and correctional institutions of the State included the Athens State Hospital, Cleveland State Hospital, Columbus State Hospital, Dayton State Hospital, Longview Hospital, the Massilon State Hospital, the Toledo State Hospital, the Ohio Hospital for Epileptics, the Madison Home, the Ohio Soldiers' and Sailors' Home, the Ohio Soldiers' and Sailors' Orphans' Home, State School for the Blind, State School for the Deaf, Institution for Feeble-minded, State Sanitarium, State Penitentiary, State Reformatory, Boys' Industrial School, Girls' Industrial School, and the Lima State Hospital, also several State farms. The juvenile court law is enforced in the State and its operation has been very satisfactory.

POLITICS AND GOVERNMENT

There is never a lack of political interest in Ohio, and the situation in the State in 1912, resulting from a number of unusual conditions, made the political history of the State during the year one of the most interesting and eventful in recent years. As President Taft is a native of the State, unusual interest centred in his campaign. Governor Harmon was, up to the time of the Democratic national convention, one of the three leading candidates for the nomination. More important than the political campaign in its lasting results was the constitution convention, which prepared an entirely new constitution for the State. This is noted at length below.

CONVENTIONS AND ELECTIONS. The Republican campaign began on the first day of the year with the organization at Columbus of the Ohio Progressive Republican League. This league was ostensibly formed to forward the nomination of Senator La Follette, but the meeting resolved itself finally into a non-committal stand for Mr. Roosevelt. This was largely due to the efforts of Gifford Pinchot, James R. Garfield, and other friends of Mr. Roosevelt. The delegates finally refused to endorse any particular person for the nomination, although the friends of Senator La Follette made an aggressive fight to have his name endorsed as the candidate of the league. The resolution to endorse Senator La Follette was defeated by a vote of 52 to 32.

On February 21, Mr. Roosevelt made his famous and long-awaited address before the constitutional convention. A summary of this is given in the article PRESIDENTIAL CAMPAIGN. Several weeks before this Governor Harmon addressed the convention. In contrast to Mr. Roosevelt he declared against the initiative and referendum, which he said were merely experiments in government, and he advised those who were making the new constitution to observe how the innovations worked in other commonwealths before adopting them. Governor Wilson was invited to address the convention, but he declined on the ground that he would not invade the territory of the State while its governor was a rival candidate for the nomination.

The first test of the relative strength of Mr. Roosevelt and President Taft in the State came in the primary election held on May 21. This, although called a presidential primary election, was not, strictly speaking, an election for the choice of the voters for President. On the ballots there appeared the name of no candidate for the presidential nomination. The voters of each party expressed their choice by voting for district delegates favorable to one candidate or another. The delegates-at-large were not voted for at this primary, but at the State convention. The campaign preceding this election was bitter and aggressive. Both President Taft and Mr. Roosevelt took part on the Republican side, while Mr. Bryan made speeches bitterly opposing Governor Harmon. The election resulted in an overwhelming victory for Mr. Roosevelt. His delegates received 165,809 votes, while those of President Taft received 118,362, and those of Senator La Follette 15,570. The total vote cast was 299,741, which may be compared with the Republican vote in the election of 1908, 572,312. The only delegates carried by President Taft were the four from Cincinnati and Mr. Roosevelt had abstained from making addresses in this city. This election may be considered the climax of the Republican campaign. The result was a bitter disappointment for President Taft, who had caused it to be understood that he would accept as conclusive the verdict of his own State.

The overwhelming victory of Mr. Roosevelt did not give him the control of the State convention. The machinery of this convention was in the hands of the Taft leaders. The convention met on June 4 and by a vote of 393½ to 359½ endorsed President Taft. The convention was riotous, and strong efforts were made to defeat the Taft majority. These failed, however, and the six delegates-at-large were given to President Taft. The action of the President in accepting these delegates after the verdict of the voters was severely criticised during the campaign. The Republican convention for the nomination of State officers was held on July 2. Edmund B. Dillon of Columbus, judge of common pleas, was nominated for governor. It was well known that Judge Dillon was favorably inclined toward Mr. Roosevelt, and he had in fact declared that he would not accept the nomination for governor. He finally consented, however, to be a candidate. After a careful study of the situation for nearly a month, Judge Dillon declined to run and resigned as a candidate. His action was not a surprise, as it was known that if the Roosevelt Republicans insisted on nominating a third candidate, or demanded that he should take a stand in favor of Mr. Roosevelt for President, he would decline to run. The State committee, in whose hands lay the selection of a new candidate, met on August 10 and nominated Gen. R. B. Brown of Zanesville, who had previously been the nominee for lieutenant-governor. Walter F. Brown, chairman of the State committee and leader of the Progressive party in the State, resigned, following the nomination of General Brown. He was followed by eight other Roosevelt men on the committee. In the following week the committee nominated other candidates for State offices. The Progressive party held a convention on September 4 and nominated Arthur L. Garford for governor, and other State officers. James R. Garfield was temporary chairman.

The Democratic campaign, while not so spectacular as the Republican, had features of great interest. The attacks made upon Governor Harmon by Mr. Bryan are referred to above. To these attacks Governor Harmon replied at length. He declared that although he had been the candidate of his party for five years, he had never yet disappointed it. He declared that, although Mr. Bryan had predicted certain defeat in November if he (Harmon) should be nominated for the presidency, he did not think Mr. Bryan had the qualifications for picking a successful candidate.

Mr. Harmon carried the primary election on May 21, winning a majority of the district delegates to the national convention though Mr. Wilson polled a heavy vote and was generally successful in northern Ohio. The State convention was controlled by Governor Harmon, elected six delegates-at-large in his interest, and then after a bitter fight, voted to apply the unit rule to the Ohio delegation as a whole. That was to make it impossible for the Wilson district delegates to support the New Jersey man in the Baltimore convention. The Wilson adherents, however, refused to abide by the decision of the State convention, took their fight to the floor at Baltimore and won. See PRESIDENTIAL CAMPAIGN.

The Democrats on July nominated Congressman James M. Cox for governor. The result of the election on November 5 was as follows: For President, Wilson received 423,152 votes, Taft 277,066, Roosevelt 229,327, Debs 89,930, Chafin 11,459, and Reimer, Socialist Labor, 2623. Governor Wilson's plurality was 146,086. For governor, Cox, Democrat, received 439,323 votes, Brown, Republican, 272,500, Garford, Progressive, 217,903, Ruthenberger, Socialist, 87,709, Poling, Prohibitionist, 16,607, and Kircher, Socialist Labor, 2689. The legislature is Democratic by a majority of 72 on joint ballot.

CONSTITUTIONAL CONVENTION. The fourth constitutional convention of the State concluded its reports on June 7, 1912. It prepared forty-two amendments to the constitution, which were submitted to the people on a single ballot, and arranged in the order in which they would appear, if adopted, in the constitution, except the amendment relating to the liquor traffic, which was placed by itself on the ballot.

This constitutional convention met primarily as a result of the desire of the State board of commissioners to replace the general property tax with classification of property. The efforts of this board to bring about the convention were seconded by the liquor interests, which believed that through a convention they might succeed in securing a license clause in the organic law of the State. These two bodies of advocates were joined by the friends of the initiative and referendum, who wished to make the State thoroughly progressive by placing legislative power in the hands of the people. The three proposals advocated by these various bodies occupied nearly one-third of the time of the entire session of the convention.

The agitation for a change in relation to taxes was brought about by the fact that for sixty years the State has had a general property tax. In 1905, by amendment to the constitution, municipal bonds were exempted from taxation, this being the only exemption for individuals, except personal property to the extent of $200 for each person. The proposal adopted by the convention restores State, city, village, county, and township bonds issued after the going into effect of the proposal, if it should be ratified by the people, to taxation, but increases the $200 exemption to $500. It also gives to the legislature authority to provide for inheritance taxes, income taxes, excise, and franchise taxes, and taxes upon the production of coal, oil, gas, and other minerals. It prohibits any indebtedness of the State or a political subdivision of the State, unless provision is made for payment of part of the principal together with the interest each year. The proposal was considered by many of the delegates too conservative. But the fact that a 1 per cent. tax law was passed by the State legislature in 1911 and had been found to work satisfactorily brought about the result that most of the people, particularly the farmers, felt favorably toward the general property tax.

Second in importance were the measures relating to the liquor traffic. The State had been a no-license State since 1851, the date of the adoption of the constitution. That instrument contains this paragraph: "No license to traffic in intoxicating liquors shall hereafter be granted in this State; but the General Assembly may, by law, provide against the evils resulting therefrom." Under the latter part of this provisions a body of laws was passed at various times by the legislature. The liquor proposal adopted by the constitutional convention provides for license and it safeguards all the liquor laws previously on the statute books. It further provides that license shall be granted only to persons of good moral character, who are interested in the business nowhere else and who are citizens of the United States. It also provides that applicants for license must be the only persons interested in the business for which the license is asked, that conviction for a second offense against the liquor laws of the State shall revoke a license, and that licenses shall be limited to one for every 500 population in townships and municipalities. Under municipal home rule, municipalities will have the right to restrict further the number of saloons within their corporate limits.

The measures relating to the initiative and referendum resulted in one of the bitterest fights of the convention. The delegates were divided into those who were opposed to the initiative and referendum altogether or unless well safeguarded; those who favored the indirect initiative with reasonably high percentages, being bitterly opposed to the direct initiative in any form; and those who favored only the direct initiative with low percentages. The proposal passed was a compromise. It provides for the direct initiative for constitutional amendments only, with a requirement of 10 per cent. of the electors on petition, and the indirect initiative for all laws, with a requirement of 3 per cent. of the electors on petition. If a proposed law is ignored by the General Assembly or is passed in its original or in an amended form it is subject to the referendum, though it can be referred only on a petition signed by a supplementary 3 per cent. of the electors, which petition shall state the form of the law asked to be referred, whether the original or an amended form. Laws proposed by the initiative petition shall not be subject to the veto power of the governor.

Important proposals were passed having to do with Congress and judicial procedure. These provided that in civil cases the General Assembly may authorize the rendering of a verdict by not less than three-fourths of the jury. Provision was also made for the removal of occasions for the law's delay, making the administration of the law less expensive to litigants and the State. Other measures provided for the regulation of the use of expert witnesses and expert testimony in criminal trials and proceedings.

Proposals relating to labor were important. Nearly all the proposals asked for by the labor delegates were granted. These included measures authorizing the legislature to pass laws regulating the hours of labor, limiting a day's work to eight hours, and a week's work to 48 hours on all public work of the State, establishing a minimum wage, providing for the comfort, health, and safety of employees, providing for workmen's compensation, providing that no injunction shall issue in any controversy involving the employment of labor, except to preserve property from injury or destruction, and securing for persons charged with violating an injunction in such controversy a trial by jury as in criminal cases. (See EMPLOYERS' LIABILITY.) A measure was passed providing that prison labor and prison-made goods shall not enter into competition with other labor and goods, and the limit on the amount of damages recoverable for death by wrongful act or neglect of another, was removed. Mechanics, artisans, laborers, and material men were secured by a direct lien upon property upon which they have bestowed labor or furnished material. A proposal was passed providing for a bond issue of $50,000,000 to build an inter-county system of wagon roads. An important proposal was that relating to conservation of national resources and the conservation of the water power of the State. A woman suffrage proposal was passed, as well as a proposal authorizing the appointment of women to positions in those institutions of the State where the interests of women and children are involved. The word "white" was eliminated from the elective franchise article of the constitution, by request of the negroes of the State.

Important proposals providing for the removal from office of officers for misconduct involving moral turpitude or other causes were passed, and provision was made for primary elections, except in villages and townships of less than 2000 population. A civil service provision for the State and all subdivisions was passed.

Two important proposals relating to education were passed. One of these made the superintendent of public instruction an appointive office. The other provided for the organization, administration, and control of the public school system of the State, giving each city school district powers, by referendum vote, to determine for itself the number of members and the organization of its board of education.

Perhaps the most radical proposal adopted by the convention was that giving home rule to municipalities. This proposal provides that municipalities may choose their own form of government and exercise all powers within their corporate limits that are not prohibited by the general laws of the State. It provides further that municipalities may acquire public utilities and may operate them, and sell, without the corporate limits, the product of service of the utilities to the extent of 50 per cent. of the product or service of the utilities used within the corporate limits, or that they may acquire property beyond their needs and sell the excess. Municipalities are also permitted by a vote of two-thirds of the council or on petition of 10 per cent. of the electors, to create a charter commission of 15 members, who shall prepare a charter to be submitted to the people, which is to go into effect on the approval of the electors.

Capital punishment was abolished.

The convention consisted of 119 delegates, divided politically into 65 Democrats, 48 Republicans, 3 Independents, and 3 Socialists. Several important addresses were delivered from time to time by distinguished men. These included Judge Lindsay of Denver, who spoke on the initiative and referendum. President Taft delivered a short address. Governor Harmon addressed the convention, and frankly stated his ideas on a number of subjects. He expressed his disapproval of the initiative and referendum, and recommended that a clause licensing the liquor traffic be embodied in the constitution. The address of President Roosevelt is noted in full in the article PRESIDENTIAL CAMPAIGN. Governor Johnson of California advocated the initiative and referendum, the recall of judges, and woman suffrage. William J. Bryan also advocated these reforms and included the guarantee of bank deposits. Senator Burton and former Senator Foraker delivered forcible addresses against the initiative and referendum.

The 42 amendments were voted on at a special election on September 3, 34 being adopted and 8 defeated. Among the lost amendments was one establishing woman's suffrage, another to abolish capital punishment, and another to encourage good roads through a $50,000,000 State bond issue. On the other hand, the 34 amendments adopted establish what is generally considered one of the most progressive constitutions in the Union. They accept the initiative and referendum in a mandatory form, permit the adoption of minimum wage legislation, broaden the workingmen's compensation laws, establish the eight-hour day on all public work, facilitate the removal of State officials, radically modify the judicial system of the State, limit the veto power of the governor, compel State-wide primaries and State-wide civil service, establish a "blue sky" law, and greatly broaden the freedom of local municipalities to govern themselves as they choose. The new legislature to meet in January will have as its chief duty the carrying out of the mandates of the new constitution. Already in several cities of the State steps have been taken to revise their forms of government for the establishment of home rule.

For the decision of the Supreme Court on control of sewage disposal and water-supplies by State boards of health, see SANITATION.

OTHER EVENTS. The trial of members of the legislature indicted for bribery in 1911 was continued during 1912. On March 13, Senator L. R. Andrews was convicted of accepting a bribe for legislative favors. On May 23, Senator Isaac E. Huffman was convicted. On December 4, Senator G. K. Cetone was found guilty. All are now in the penitentiary. On October 9, Representative George B. Nye pleaded guilty to the charge of soliciting a bribe of $1000. He subsequently made confession of everything that he knew of the legislative graft to Attorney-General Hogan. Proceedings were at once begun looking towards the indictment of persons and corporations mentioned in this confession.

STATE GOVERNMENT. Governor, J. M. Cox; Lieutenant-Governor, Hugh L. Nichols; Secretary of State, Charles H. Graves; Treasurer, J. M. Brennan; Auditor, V. Donahey; Attorney-General, Timothy S. Hogan; Adjutant-General not appointed; Commissioner of Insurance, Edmond H. Moore; Superintendent of Education, Fank W. Miller—all Democrats.

JUDICIARY. Supreme Court: Chief Justice, John A. Shauck, Rep.; Associate Justices, James G. Johnson, Maurice H. Donohue, J. F. Wilkin; O. Newman—all Republicans; R. M. Wanamaker, Ind.; Clerk, Frank McKean, Republican.

STATE LEGISLATURE, 1913 Republicans, Senate, 7; House, 32; joint ballot, 39. Democrats, Senate, 26; House, 88; joint ballot 114. Progressives, House, 3; joint ballot, 3. Democratic majority, Senate, 19; House, 53; joint ballot, 72.

The representatives in Congress will be found in the section *Congress*, article UNITED STATES.

OHIO RIVER DAM. See DAMS.

OHIO STATE UNIVERSITY. The students enrolled in all departments of the university in the autumn of 1912 were 3608. The faculty numbered 274. During the year a graduate school was organized with Prof. William McPherson, Ph. D., as dean. Henry Adam Weber, professor of agricultural chemistry, died July 14, 1912. Dr. Frederick Arps, Ph. D., of the University of Illinois, was appointed professor of psychology, and Forrest Kizer Pence was appointed professor of ceramic engineering. The productive funds of the university at the end of the collegiate year 1911-12 amounted to $950,004, and the income to $1,029,958. There were in the library 118,654 bound volumes, and about 10,000 pamphlets. President, W. O. Thompson, D. D., LL. D.

OHIO UNIVERSITY. An institution of higher learning at Athens, O., founded in 1804. The total enrollment in all departments of the university in the autumn of 1912 was 1832. The faculty numbered 75. There were no noteworthy benefactions received during the year. Among the additions to the faculty made during the year were the following: C. M. Douthitt, director of indoor athletics; Clinton N. Makinnon, assistant professor of English, and Elizabeth H. Bohm, principal of the school of domestic science. The income of the university is about $252,000 annually. The library contained 41,000 volumes. President, Alston Ellis, Ph. D., LL. D.

OHIO WESLEYAN UNIVERSITY. An institution for higher education at Delaware, O., under the auspices of the Methodist Episcopal Church, founded in 1842. The enrollment in all departments of the university in 1912 was 1041. The faculty numbered 65. There were no noteworthy changes in the faculty during the year and no notable benefactions. The productive funds amounted to $555,000, and the gross income to about $200,000. The library contained 63,000 volumes. President, Herbert Welch, D. D.

OIL ENGINES. See INTERNAL COMBUSTION MOTORS.

OKLAHOMA. POPULATION. According to the Census Bureau statistics compiled during 1912, out of the total population, 1,657,155, in the State in 1910, 40,084 were foreign-born whites, compared with 20,390 in 1900. Of these, the largest number, 10,084, came from Germany; from Russia, 5850; from Austria, 3908; from Canada, 2498. Other European countries were represented by smaller numbers. The negroes in the State in 1910 numbered 137,612, and the mulattoes 39,342. In 1890 the negroes numbered 21,609 and the mulattoes 817.

AGRICULTURE. The acreage, value, and production of the principal crops in 1911 and 1912, are given below:

		Acreage.	Prod. Bu.	Value.
Corn	1912	5,448,000	101,878,000	$41,770,000
	1911	5,675,000	36,888,000	25,822,000
Wheat	1912	1,570,000	20,096,000	15,072,000
	1911	1,122,000	8,976,000	8,258,000
Oats	1912	936,000	23,494,000	7,988,000
	1911	909,000	8,181,000	3,927,000
Rye	1912	4,000	48,000	42,000
	1911	4,000	38,000	40,000
Potatoes ...	1912	29,000	1,740,000	1,618,000
	1911	30,000	540,000	670,000
Hay	1912	385,000	a 481,000	3,559,000
	1911	810,000	a 648,000	5,184,000
Cotton	1911	......	c 915,000	....

a Tons. c Bales.

MINERAL PRODUCTION. There were produced in the coal mines of the State in 1911, 3,074,-242 short tons, valued at $6,291,494. This is a considerable gain over the figures of 1910, 2,-646,226 short tons, valued at $5,867,947. It did not, however, equal the tonnage mined either in 1909 or 1907, which was less than the average production of the preceding eight years. The decrease in the production is largely due to the competition of fuel oil and natural gas from the Louisiana and mid-continent fields, and of coal from other States where mining conditions are more favorable. There were 27 men killed by accidents in the coal mines of the State during 1911.

The production of lead and zinc for 1911 was valued at $812,190, a decrease of $132,-506, compared with the production in 1910. The production of lead was 2501 short tons, and of zinc, 5150 short tons, compared with a production of 288 short tons of lead and 6394 tons of zinc in 1910.

Petroleum. The State ranks second in the production of petroleum, being surpassed only by California. The production has shown a steady increase for several years. In 1911 it was 56,069,637 barrels, compared with 52,028,-718 barrels in 1910. The most significant factor in the increase of 1911 was the development of the Barnsdall and Sinclair pools near Osage Junction where wells of 1000 to 3000 barrels in daily yield kept the production of the pool in tne neighborhood of 20,00 barrels a day. The value of the product in 1911 was $26,451,767, compared with a value of $19,-922,660 in 1910. In 1911 there were 4087 wells completed, of which 3294 produced oil.

MANUFACTURERS. The Thirteenth Census statistics are for the calendar year 1909 and were compiled in 1912. The manufacturing industries in the State have increased rapidly in importance, although many are still in their infancy. From the table on the next page it will be seen that in 1909 there were in the State 2310 manufacturing establishments, giving employment to 18,034 persons.

The largest number of wage-earners was found in industries connected with lumber and timber, 3175; in printing and publishing were employed 1698; in flour and gristmill products, 842; and in the manufacture of brick and tile, 730. The greatest value of product was in the flour and gristmill manufactures, $19,144,000. The product of oil, cottonseed, and cake manufactures was $5,187,000; lumber and timber

	Number or Amount 1909	1904	P. C. of Inc. 1904-'09
Number of establishments	2,310	1,123	105.7
Persons engaged in manufactures....	18,034	7,456	141.9
Proprietors and firm members...	2,698	1,187	127.3
Salaried employees	2,193	813	169.7
Wage earners (average number)..	13,143	5,456	140.9
Primary horsepower	71,139	29,608	140.3
Capital	$38,873,000	$16,124,000	141.1
Expenses	47,216,000	21,383,000	120.8
Services	9,285,000	3,517,000	164.0
Salaries	2,045,000	718,000	184.8
Wages	7,240,000	2,799,000	158.7
Materials	34,153,000	16,394,000	108.3
Miscellaneous	3,778,000	1,472,000	156.7
Value of products..	53,682,000	24,459,000	119.5
Value of products less cost of materials	19,529,000	8,065,000	142.1

products, $4,439,000. The total number of persons engaged in manufactures was 18,034. Of these, 17,071 were male and 963 female. The prevailing hours of labor for the majority of the wage-earners was 60 or more a week; 56.3 per cent. were employed in establishments where those hours prevailed, and 43.7 per cent. in establishments where less than 60 hours a week prevailed. The largest number of wage-earners was found in Oklahoma City, 1398; in Shawnee were 1014; in Tulsa, 462; in Muskogee, 381, and in Chikasha, 364.

EDUCATION. The total number of pupils of school age in the State in 1911 was 556,852. Of these, 509,577 were white and 47,275 were colored. The white males numbered 261,730 and the white females 247,847. The colored males numbered 23,634 and the colored females 23,641. The total enrollment in the schools of the State was 443,227. Of these, 405,873 were white and 37,354 colored. The average daily attendance was 260,-018. The teachers numbered 10,020. The number of schools taught during the year was 5981. The total amount of money spent on the public schools was $6,759,412. The total number of school-houses was 6222.

POLITICS AND GOVERNMENT

The legislature did not meet in 1912 as the sessions are biennial and the last was held in 1911. The next session was scheduled to convene January 7, 1913.

There was no election for governor or other State offices in 1912, as the term of Governor Cruce does not expire until 1913. Interest therefore centred in the presidential campaign. The first Republican congressional district convention held in the country was convened at Colgate on January 23. This convention endorsed President Taft. The Republican State convention for the election of delegates to the national convention was held at Guthrie on March 14. It was controlled by the Progressives and the ten delegates were instructed to vote for Mr. Roosevelt. The Oklahoma delegates were among the most aggressive partisans of Mr. Roosevelt at the Republican national convention.

The Democratic State convention met at Oklahoma City on February 23. The delegates were divided, ten each being given to Woodrow Wilson and Champ Clark. An attempt to endorse Champ Clark was defeated by 314 votes to 289. These delegates each had half a vote, and if their candidate withdrew from the convention they were instructed to cast all their votes for the remaining candidate. Roosevelt electors did not appear on the ballots, therefore all the Republicans in the State voted for President Taft. The result of the election was as follows: Wilson, 119,156 votes; Taft, 90,786; Debs, 42,262; Chafin, 2185. Governor Wilson's plurality was 28,370. The legislature is Democratic by a majority of 89 on joint ballot.

STATE GOVERNMENT. Governor, Lee Cruce; Lieutenant-Governor, J. J. McAlester; Secretary of State, Benjamin F. Harrison; Treasurer, Robert Dunlop; Auditor, Leo Meyer; Attorney-General, Charles West; Commissioner of Insurance, P. A. Ballard; Commissioner of Education, R. H. Wilson; President Board of Agriculture, G. T. Bryan—all Democrats.

JUDICIARY. Supreme Court: Chief Justice, John B. Turner; Associate Justices, Mathew J. Kane, Robert L. Williams, Jesse J. Dunn and Samuel W. Hayes; Clerk of the Court, W. H. L. Campbell—all Democrats.

STATE LEGISLATURE, 1913. Republicans, Senate, 8; House, 19; joint ballot 27. Democrats, Senate, 36; House, 80; joint ballot, 116. Democratic majority, Senate, 28; House, 61; joint ballot, 89.

The representatives in Congress will be found in the section *Congress*, article UNITED STATES.

OLCOTT, GEORGE N. An American classical scholar and educator, died March 1, 1912. He was born in Brooklyn, N. Y., in 1869, and graduated from Columbia University in 1893. After pursuing post-graduate studies he was, in 1897-8, fellow of the American School of Classical Studies in Rome. From 1898 to 1904 he was lecturer on Roman archæology at Columbia University. From 1901 to 1904 he was assistant in Latin at the same institution, and from 1905 to the time of his death was professor of Latin. He contributed many articles on numismatics to the *American Journal of Archæology* from 1898 to 1905. He was the author of *Studies in the Word Formation of the Latin Inscriptions* (1898); *A Dictionary of the Latin Inscriptions in Rome* (1904).

OLD-AGE PENSIONS. During the past few years, old-age pensions have been established by governmental action in England, France, Australia, and New Zealand, and Germany has recodified her insurance and pension laws. There were no new foreign developments in 1912. In Great Britain the cost of about a million pensions exceeded $60,000,000. In the United States, old-age pensions thus far have been provided, either by the traditional form of insurance annuities, by fraternal societies, by trade unions, or by the corporations. Few American unions have developed this policy. The corporation schemes are now very numerous, all the principal railroads and the leading industrial trusts have introduced them and recently leading banks of New York have taken up the idea. State action thus far has been limited to civil service employees. Twenty-six of the leading railroads now have their own systems of retirement pensions. Twenty-three of these roads, employing more than 850,000 workers, had about 8500 pensioners in 1912. The most extensive system is that of the Pennsylvania Railroad, which had 2505 pensioners and which makes an annual appropriation of $850,000 to its pension fund.

In addition, the Pennsylvania lines west of Pittsburgh had 875 pensioners and appropriated $222,500. The New York Central, with 800 pensioners, appropriated $450,000; the Chicago and Northwestern with 521 pensioners $200,000; and the Southern Pacific with 503 pensioners, $191,326. As a rule these pensions are based on wages and length of service. Usually, at least ten years of consecutive service are required, but in some cases fifteen or twenty years are required, and on the Pennsylvania Railroad even thirty years' continuous service are required. The pension system is usually accompanied by an age limit for new employees. This is most frequently forty-five years, though a number of roads refuse to take men more than thirty-five years of age. Retirement is optional, customarily at the age of sixty-five, but in a number of cases at the age of sixty or sixty-one, and on the Grand Trunk at the age of fifty-five. Retirement is usually compulsory at the age of seventy, but in a few cases at the age of sixty-five or even sixty. These corporation schemes are, in nearly all cases, non-contributory. Thus the cessation of service by an employee for any reason destroys his claim upon the pension fund. This is vigorously objected to by some labor leaders on the ground that after an employee has worked a number of years he is literally "tied to his job" by the prospective benefits of the retirement system; this prevents his striking for better conditions.

For a complete account of schemes in force in this country, see Squier's *Old-age Dependency in the United States.*

LEGISLATION. There was very little legislation in the United States relating to old-age pensions. The Maryland legislature passed a joint resolution urging Congress to appoint a national commission to investigate the subject. In Massachusetts, where the investigation of this subject was begun in 1907, where a law of 1910 provided for the establishment of voluntary retirement pension systems by the cooperation of private employers and employees, and for the establishment of similar pensions for their civil service employees by cities and towns, and where an act of 1911 established a system of retirement pensions for State civil service employees, a new law authorized cities and towns, other than Boston, to retire and pension laborers. If the voters of any city or town approve, the local authorities may retire and pension laborers who have been in their employ not less than twenty-five years, are at least sixty years of age, and have become physically or mentally incapacitated for labor; they may also similarly pension laborers who have been employed for not less than fifteen years and have become incapacitated because of injuries received while at work. If the law is approved the retirement of laborers who have been employed for as many as twenty-five years and have reached the age of sixty-five is made compulsory. New Jersey established a pension scheme for employees of penal institutions and reformatories who have been employed for twenty years and have become incapacitated. The pension is to equal one-half the salary at the time of retirement but may not be less than $50 per month.

THE BREWING INDUSTRY. One of the most liberal and comprehensive compensation schemes yet instituted by private initiative in this country was that begun by the employers and union workers in the brewing industry, effective January 1, 1913. (See EMPLOYERS' LIABILITY.) Their plan provides that pensions should be paid out of a fund to which employers contribute three-fourths and employees one-fourth. Any man of the age of 60 who has served 25 years may retire on a weekly pension equal to one-half his average weekly wage during the six months preceding. A man may be retired at any time on a similar pension if he is incapacitated. The scheme provides that cessation of work for 12 months for any cause will not interfere with a man's record of continuous employment; furthermore, a man may change from one brewery to another without spoiling his record. A general board of award is to be composed of three representatives of the Brewers' Association and three from the Brewery Workers' Union. There will also be local boards of award. On the employers' side fully two-thirds of those engaged in the industry in the United States are included, and their workers number about 70,000.

BANK PLANS. Shortly before Christmas the National City Bank announced the introduction of a non-contributory pension system for its 450 employees beginning January, 1913. The first important financial institution to undertake the payment of pensions and death benefits was the First National Bank of New York City, which introduced its system in January, 1911. Its plan was contributory, the employees subscribing sums amounting to 3 per cent. of their salaries. Both of these plans provided for retirement pensions equal to 2 per cent. of the average salary during the preceding two or three years, multiplied by the number of years of service. The maximum pension was to be $5000 per year; moreover, no pension could exceed 60 per cent. of the average salary for three years before retirement in the case of the National City Bank plan, nor 35/50ths of the average salary for two years preceding in the First National Bank plan. Both plans provided death benefits for both employees and pensioners. The beneficiaries of employees would receive two years' salary and those of pensioners twice the annual pension. It was stated that several other banks were expecting to introduce similar systems at once.

For the American Telephone and Telegraph scheme, see WORKINGMEN'S INSURANCE.

OLDENBURG. See GERMANY.

OLIVE OIL. See HORTICULTURE.

OLIVER, PAUL AMBROSE. An American soldier and manufacturer, died May 18, 1912. He was born at sea on his father's ship in 1831 and was educated in Germany. He was appointed second lieutenant in the 12th New York Infantry in 1861 and in 1864 became captain of that regiment. In the same year he was transferred to the 5th New York Infantry. In 1865 he was brevetted brigadier-general of volunteers. He was awarded the Congressional medal of honor in 1892 for gallantry in service. From 1870 until the time of his death he was a powder manufacturer.

OLYMPIC GAMES. The fifth Olympiad was held at Stockholm, Sweden, from July 6 to 15 and resulted in an overwhelming triumph for the United States athletes. Through funds raised by popular subscription the American team was taken to Stockholm in a specially chartered steamer, the *Finland*, and thus had an opportunity to do considerable training aboard ship during the trip. The Americans, with the exception of the Marathon runners, also lived on the vessel during the games. Although the scope of the Olympiad was most broad, including practically every test in which athletic skill counts, the track and field events attracted the greatest interest. It was in this department that the Americans showed marked superiority, scoring more than twice as many points as any other nation. Finland's athletes finished second, and those representing the British empire took third place. Sweden ranked fourth. The points scored by each of the various countries on track and field follow: United States, 85; Finland, 27; British empire, 24; Sweden, 21; Greece, Germany, and France, 4 each; Norway, 2; Hungary and Italy, 1 each. Twenty-seven countries in all were represented in the games. Of the points scored by the British empire, Canada and South Africa contributed one-half of the total.

A large number of new Olympic and world's records were made in the track and field events, the Americans showing up especially well in this regard. The most import of these were: 100-meter dash, trial heat, D. Lippincott (United States), 10⅗ seconds, equaling world's record and establishing new Olympic record; 800-meter run, J. E. Meredith (United States), 1 minute, 51 9-10 seconds, new world's and Olympic record; 1500-meter run, A. N. S. Jackson (Great Britain), 3 minutes, 56⅕ seconds, new Olympic record; 5000-meter run, H. Kolehmainen (Finland), 14 minutes, 36⅗ seconds, new world's and Olympic record; 10,000-meter walk, G. Goulding (Canada), 46 minutes, 28⅗ seconds, new Olympic record; 400-meter run, trial heat, J. E. Meredith (United States), 48 seconds, new world's and Olympic record; Marathon run, K. K. McArthur (South Africa), 2 hours, 36 minutes, new Olympic record; running high jump, A. W. Richards (United States), 6 feet 3¾ inches, new Olympic record; 16-pound shot, best hand, P. McDonald (United States), 50.32 feet, new world's and Olympic record; javelin, best hand, E. Lemming (Sweden), 198.4 feet, new world's and Olympic record; javelin, both hands, J. J. Saaristo (Finland), 358.11 feet, new world's and Olympic record; pole vault, H. S. Babcock (United States), 12 feet, 11½ inches, new Olympic record; running broad jump A. L. Gutterson (United States), 24 feet, 11 inches, new Olympic ord; javelin, both hand, J. J. Saaristo (Finland), 148 feet, 1½ inches, new world's and Olympic record; hammer throw, M. J. McGrath (United States), 180 feet, 5 inches, new Olympic record.

A full summary of the track and field events follows:

100-meter Dash—R. Craig (U. S.), winner; A. T. Meyer (U. S.), second; D. Lippincott (U. S.), third. Time, 10 4-5.

400-meter Run—C. R. Reidpath (U. S.), winner; H. Braun (Ger.), second; E. F. Lindberg (U. S.), third. Time, 48 1-5.

200-meter Dash—R. Craig (U. S.), winner; D. Lippincott (U. S.), second; W. R. Applegate (G. B.), third. Time, 21 7-10.

800-meter Run—J. E. Meredith (U. S.), winner; M. Sheppard (U. S.), second; I. N. Davenport (U. S.), third. Time, 1:51 9-10.

1500-meter Run—A. N. S. Jackson (G. B.), winner; A. R. Kiviat (U. S.), second; N. S. Taber (U S.), third. Time, 3:56 4-5.

5000-meter Run—H. Kolehmainen (Fin.), winner; J. Bouin (Fr.), second; E. W. Hutson (G. B.), third. Time, 14:36 3-5.

10,000-meter Run—H. Kolehmainen (Fin.), winner; L. Tewanima (U. S.), second; Stauroos (Fin.), third. Time, 31:20.

8000-meter Cross-country—Sweden, winner; Finland, second; Great Britain, third. Team race.

10,000-meter Walk—G. Goulding (Can.), winner; E. J. Webb (G. B.), second; F. Altimani (It.), third. Time, 46:28 2-5.

110-meter Hurdles—F. W. Kelly (U. S.), winner; J. J. Wendell (U. S.), second; M. W. Hawkins (U. S.), third. Time, 15 1-10.

400-meter Relay—Great Britain, winner; Sweden, second. Time, 42 4-10.

3000-meter Team Race—United States, winner; Sweden, second; Finland, third.

1600-meter Relay—United States, winner; France, second; Great Britain, third. Time, 3:16 3-5.

Marathon Run—K. K. McArthur (S. Afr.), winner; G. W. Gitshaw (S. Afr.), second; G. Strobino (U. S.), third. Time, 2:36.

Pentathlon—J. Thorpe (U. S.), winner; F. R. Bie (Nor.), second; A. Brundage (U. S.), third. Five events.

Decathlon—J. Thorpe (U. S.), winner; H. Wieslander (Swd.), second; C. Lomberg (Swd.), third. Ten events.

Running High Jump—A. W. Richard (U. S.), winner; Lische (Ger.), second; G. L. Horine (U. S.), third. Height, 6 ft. 3¾ in.

Standing Broad Jump—C. Tsiclitiras (Gr.), winner; P. Adams (U. S.), second; B. Adams (U. S.), third. Distance, 11 ft. 7-10 in.

Sixteen-pound Shot (best hand)—P. McDonald (U. S.), winner; R. Rose U. S.), second; L. A. Whitney (U. S.), third. Distance, 50.32 ft.

Sixteen-pound Shot (both hands)—R. Rose (U. S.), winner; P. McDonald (U. S.), second; E. Niklander (Fin.), third. Distance, 90 ft. 5½ in.

Javelin (best hand)—E. Lemming (Swd.), winner; J. J. Saaristo (Fin.), second; M. Kovacs (Hung.), third. Distance, 198 4 ft.

Javelin (both hands)—J. J. Saaristo (Fin.), winner; Sukaniomi (Fin.), second; Peltonen (Fin.), third. Distance, 358 ft. 11 in.

Running Broad Jump—A. L. Gutterson (U. S.), winner; C. D. Bricker (Can.), second; G. Aberg (Swd.), third. Distance, 24 ft. 11 in.

Pole Vault—H. S. Babcock (U. S.), winner, 12 ft. 11½ in.; M. S. Wright (U. S.) and F. T. Nelson tied for second place at 12 ft. 10 in.

Discus (best hand)—A. R. Taipale (Fin.), winner; R. L. Byrd (U. S.), second; J. H. Duncan (U. S.), third. Distance, 148 ft 1½ in.

Discus (both hands)—A R. Taipale (Fin.), winner; E. Niklander (Fin.), second; Magnusson (Swd.), third. Distance, 271 ft 9¾ in.

Standing High Jump—P. Adams (U. S.), winner; B. Adams (U. S.), second; C. Tsiclitiras (Gr.), third. Distance, 5 ft. 4 in.

Hammer Throw—M. J. McGrath (U. S.), winner; D. Gillis (Can.), second; C. C. Childs (U. S.), third. Distance, 180 ft. 5 in.

Hop, Step and Jump—Lindblom (Swd.), winner; G. Aberg (Swd.), second; Almlolf (Swd.), third. Distance, 48 ft. 5 1-10 in.

Of the track and field contests, the Marathon and the all-around events—the pentathlon and decathlon—proved the most popular. The United States had an unusually good squad of distance runners entered in the Marathon and it was confidently expected by those who had looked after the training of these athletes that victory was assured. South Africa, however, upset America's hopes by capturing both first and second places, McArthur, the winner, also succeeding in establishing a new record. The United States athletes had to be content with third place, but at the same time among the first fifteen runners to finish the United States was represented by more than all other countries combined.

James Thorpe of the Carlisle Indian School (United States) was the hero of the games. He won both the pentathlon and the decathlon against a big field by a wide margin and stamped himself the greatest athlete of all time. The king of Sweden gave him special audience, complimenting him on his athletic prowess, and calling him "the most wonderful athlete in the world."

Taking the Olympic events of every sort into consideration, Sweden scored more points than any other nation, the United States ranking second, and Great Britain third. A summary of the total number of points made by each country follows: Sweden, 133; United States, 129; Great Britain, 76; Finland, 52; Germany, 47; France, 32; Denmark, 19; Hungary, Norway, and South Africa, 16 each; Italy, Australia, and Canada, 13 each; Belgium, 11; Russia and Austria, 6 each; Greece, 4; Holland, 3.

OMAN. A Mohammedan state (independent) in southeastern Arabia. Area, about 82,000 square miles; population about 500,000. Muscat (25,000 inhabitants) is the capital. Dates are the chief food of the people; also the main article of export, besides pearls, limes, mother-of-pearl, fruits, fish, hides and skins. Imports and exports in 1910-11, Rs. 5,917,238 and Rs. 4,065,512 (dates, 1,978,115) respectively. The Indian government subsidizes the sultan (1912, Seyyid Feysal bin Turki) and retains a political agent (1912, Maj. S. G. Knox) at his court, with power to restrain the cession of territory to any power other than Great Britain.

GUN-RUNNING. For years past the illicit trade in arms on the Persian coast between Mekran and Muscat has occasioned the British authorities much concern, and has continued in spite of measures for its suppression. In the spring of 1912, however, Admiral Slade, to whom the duty of suppressing the gun-running was entrusted, succeeded in carrying out what proved to be effective measures. The guns were designed for the troops on the northeastern frontier of India, who employed them against their British rulers. They were brought in by way of Muscat, where the trade was protected under a commercial treaty of long standing between the French government and the sultan of Oman. France refused to give up her treaty right and there seemed no way of preventing the trade, but in 1912 the sultan decided that all imports of arms should be stored in a bonded warehouse, not to be released until certificates as to their destination were received, and no certificates were to be issued from the region of Mekran. The sultan's regulations were issued on June 4 and were to come into effect after September 1. Soon after the latter date a shipload of arms consigned to a French firm was confiscated. The French consul thereupon protested.

ONTARIO. A province of the Dominion of Canada. Area, 260,862 square miles. Population (census of June 1, 1911), 2,523,274, as compared with 2,182,947 in 1901. Toronto, the capital and, excepting Montreal, the largest city of Canada, had 376,538 inhabitants (208,040 in 1901). The province is administered by a lieutenant-governor, Col. Sir John Morison Gibson, appointed September 22, 1908. Premier in 1912, Sir James P. Whitney. The area stated above does not include the portion of the Northwest Territories annexed in 1912. The northwestern part of the province now extends to Hudson Bay. See CANADA.

OPERA. See MUSIC.

OPIUM TRADE. See CHINA.

ORANGE FREE STATE, THE. One of the four original provinces of the Union of South Africa (q. v.). Bloemfontein, the seat of the provincial government, had, according to the census of 1911, 26,925 inhabitants (14,720 whites); Jagersfontein, 9019; Harrismith, 6799; Kroonstad, 5700; Ladybrand, 3323. In 1910 the white pupils enrolled at town and country schools numbered 19,131; the mission schools had about 10,000 native scholars. For area, population, production, and trade, see SOUTH AFRICA, UNION OF. Public revenue for the eleven months ended May 30, 1910, £952,890; expenditure, £957,741; customs revenue, £342,337; public debt, May 30, 1910, £1,250,000. Administrator (1912), Dr. A. E. W. Ramsbottom.

ORCHESTRA. See MUSIC.

ORDNANCE. See NAVAL PROGRESS.

ORE DEPOSITS. See GEOLOGY.

OREGON. POPULATION. According to the Census Bureau statistics compiled during 1912, out of the total population of 672,765 in 1910, 103,001 were foreign-born whites, compared with 53,861 in 1900. The largest number of these came from Germany, 17,904; from Canada, 11,149; from Sweden, 10,099; from Norway, 6841; from Italy, 5520; from England, 7092, and from Austria, 5249. Other European countries were represented by smaller numbers. In the city of Portland, with a population of 207,214, the foreign-born whites numbered 43,780, compared with 17,734 in 1900. The largest number of these came from Germany, 7466. The negroes in the State in 1910 numbered 1492 and the mulattoes 434. In 1890 the negroes numbered 1186 and the mulattoes 629.

AGRICULTURE. The acreage, value, and production of the principal crops in 1911 and 1912 are given below:

		Acreage.	Prod. Bu.	Value.
Corn	1912	20,000	630,000	$472,000
	1911	20,000	570,000	456,000
Wheat	1912	842,000	21,018,000	15,132,000
	1911	796,000	16,726,000	12,545,000
Oats	1912	359,000	13,714,000	5,622,000
	1911	359,000	12,457,000	5,481,000
Rye	1912	22,000	352,000	246,000
	1911	18,000	351,000	316,000
Potatoes	1912	65,000	10,075,000	3,123,000
	1911	46,000	5,980,000	4,007,000
Hay	1912	790,000	a 1,738,000	14,425,000
	1911	452,000	a 949,000	9,110,000

a Tons.

MINERAL PRODUCTION. The gold production of the State in 1911 was $633,407, compared with $679,488 in 1910. The silver output was 45,221 fine ounces, compared with 35,978 fine ounces in 1910.

The value of the mining product of gold, silver, and copper of 1911, according to the United States Geological Survey, was $669,016, compared with a value of $700,676 in 1910. The production of gold decreased from $679,488 in 1910 to $633,407 in 1911. The value of the silver production increased from $19,428 in 1910 to $23,967 in 1911. The copper ore shipped to smelters in 1911 amounted to 4205 tons, yielding 93,136 pounds of copper, valued at $11,642.

MANUFACTURES. The Thirteenth Census statistics are for the calendar year 1909 and were compiled in 1912. Although Oregon is increasing in importance as a manufacturing State, the growth of its manufacturing industries during the past sixty years has not kept pace with that of its population. It will be seen from the following table that in 1909 there were 2246 manufacturing establishments, which gave employment to an average of 28,750 wage earners.

	Number or Amount 1909	1904	P. C. of Inc. 1904-'09
Number of establishments	2,246	1,602	40.2
Persons engaged in manufactures....	34,722	22,018	57.7
Proprietors and firm members...	2,499	1,726	44.8
Salaried employees	3,473	1,769	96.3
Wage earners (average number)..	28,750	18,522	55.2
Primary horsepower	175,019	81,348	115.1
Capital	$89,082,000	$44,024,000	102.3
Expenses	82,124,000	48,360,000	69.8
Services	23,949,000	13,577,000	76.4
Salaries	4,047,000	2,133,000	89.7
Wages	19,902,000	11,444,000	73.9
Materials	50,552,000	30,597,000	65.2
Miscellaneous	7,623,000	4,186,000	82.1
Value of products..	93,005,000	55,525,000	67.5
Value of products less cost of materials	42,453,000	24,928,000	70.3

The greatest number of wage earners was employed in the manufacture of lumber and timber, 15,066; in printing and publishing, 1459; in foundry and machine-shop products, 1055. The value of the lumber and timber products was $30,200,000; of flour and grist-mill products, $8,891,000; of slaughtering and meat-packing, $5,880,000; printing and publishing, $5,041,000. The total number of persons engaged in the manufacturing industries in 1909 was 34,722, of whom 31,849 were male and 2873 female. The number of persons under 16 years of age employed in the manufacturing industries was 98. The prevailing hours of labor for the majority of wage earners averaged from 54 to 60 a week; only 14.5 per cent. of the total being employed in establishments where less than 54 a week prevailed, and only 6.3 per cent. employed in establishments where the hours of labor were more than 60 a week. Portland and Salem are the only cities in which there are extensive manufactures. In Portland there were 12,214 wage earners and in Salem 597. The value of the product in Portland was $46,860,767 and in Salem $2,208,031.

Education. The total enrollment in the public schools of the State in 1912 was 112,057. The total number of persons of school age between 4 and 20 years was 189,425. The teachers employed in 1912 numbered 5189, of whom 4190 were female and 999 male. The average salary of male teachers per month was $82.11 and of female teachers $59.96. The total value of school property in the State was $12,389,307. The total amount of school funds was $8,643,700.

Charities and Corrections. The charitable and correctional institutions under the control of the State, with their populations in 1912, are as follows: Oregon State Tubercular Sanatorium, 48; Oregon School for the Deaf, 93; Oregon Institute for the Blind, 30; Oregon School for the Feeble-minded, 191; Oregon State Training School, 101; Oregon State Insane Asylum, 1735; and Oregon State Penitentiary, 720.

Politics and Government

The legislature did not meet in 1912, as the sessions are biennial and the last was held in 1911. The next session convenes on January 13, 1913. There was no election for governor or any of the principal State officers, as their terms do not expire until 1915. The chief political interest in the State centred in the presidential primary held on April 19, which was the first presidential primary held in the State. At the same time votes were cast for the nomination of United States senator. Senator Bourne was the Republican candidate for the nomination. He was opposed by Ben Selling, a merchant of Portland. The presidential primary election resulted as follows: Roosevelt, 28,905; Taft, 20,517, and La Follette, 22,491. The total vote cast was 71,913, which may be compared with the vote cast at the Republican national convention in 1908, 62,530. Senator Bourne was defeated for the Senate. Governor Wilson was given the Democratic presidential primary vote and Harry Lane received the Democratic senatorial nomination. The delegates to the Republican and Democratic national conventions therefore were pledged to vote for Mr. Roosevelt and Governor Wilson. The vote for President on November 5 resulted as follows: Wilson, 47,064; Roosevelt, 37,600; Taft, 34,673; Debs, 13,329, and Chafin, 4360. Governor Wilson's plurality was 9464. Several important constitutional amendments were voted for at this election. The most conspicuous of these was one providing for equal suffrage for women. This was carried by a vote of 61,265 for, to 57,104 against. Other amendments relating to taxation were passed. Another amendment gave the railway commission power to regulate all public service corporations in the State. Ober amendments related to matters of local interest.

Other Events. On February 19 the United States Supreme Court refused to declare the provisions of the initiative and referendum in the Oregon constitution unconstitutional. The decision did not discuss the question which was raised as to whether the organic law of the State established not a republican form of government as guaranteed by the constitution but a pure democracy. The Supreme Court simply denied jurisdiction, asserting that the question was political, not judicial. The decision ended the long litigation carried on by the Pacific States Telephone and Telegraph Company against the State of Oregon.

State Government. Governor, Oswald West, Dem.; secretary of State, Ben W. Olcott, Rep.; State treasurer, Thomas B. Kay, Rep.; superintendent of public instruction, L. R. Alderman, Rep.; adjutant-general, W. E. Finzer, Dem.; attorney-general, A. M. Crawford, Rep.; commissioner of insurance, J. W. Ferguson, Dem.

Judiciary. Supreme Court: Chief justice, Robert Eakin; justices, Thomas A. McBride, Frank A. Moore, Henry J. Bean, and George H. Burnett; clerk, J. C. Moreland—all Republicans.

State Legislature, 1913. Republicans, Senate, 28; House, 48; joint ballot, 76. Democrats, Senate, 2; House, 5; joint ballot, 7. Republican Progressive, House, 6; joint ballot, 6. Democrat Progressive, House, 1; joint ballot, 1. Republican majority, Senate, 26; House, 36; joint ballot, 62.

The representatives in Congress will be found in the section *Congress*, article United States.

OREGON, University of. A State institution of higher learning at Eugene, Ore., founded in 1876. The enrollment in all departments of the university in the autumn of 1912 was 1260. The faculty numbered 116. The only noteworthy change in the faculty during the year was the appointment of Fred C. Ayer, Ph. D., to succeed Dr. C. J. C. Bennett as head of the department of education. The annual income of the university was about $150,000. The library contained about 40,000 volumes. President, Prince L. Campbell, B. A.

O'REILLY, Robert Maitland. An American physician and soldier, died November 3, 1912. He was born at Philadelphia in 1845 and graduated from the medical department of the University of Pennsylvania in 1866. He was appointed medical cadet in the United States army in 1864. In 1867 he became assistant surgeon and was promoted through various grades until in 1902 he became brigadier-general and surgeon-general of the United States army. He retired with the rank of major-general in 1909. During the Spanish-American War he served with the volunteers as lieutenant-colonel and chief surgeon. He was a close friend and the medical adviser of Grover Cleveland, whose companion he was on many hunting and fishing trips.

ORNITHOLOGY. Purchase of Marsh Island. The most important ornithological event of the year was the purchase as a bird reservation of Marsh Island, La., by Mrs. Russell Sage, at a cost of $150,000. The island is on the Gulf coast, southwest of New Orleans; is about 18 miles long and 9 miles wide, and contains about 75,000 acres. It has long been famous as a winter feeding ground for ducks and geese and has been one of the most popular resorts for market hunters in the South. Mrs. Sage proposed to maintain this island as a breeding ground for birds, but the details of the plan had not been published at the end of the year. According to Hornaday, 4,265,-585 game birds were officially reported as having been killed in Louisiana during the year 1909-1910, and this does not take into consideration the number of robins and other song-birds killed by negroes and poor whites for food.

Food of Birds, etc. The United States Biological Survey published during the year a number of bulletins dealing with the food of birds, especially of woodpeckers. According to their conclusions, woodpeckers in general are beneficial, but the sapsuckers do much damage by boring holes in trees. They may be killed by the application of arsenic to the trees, either by putting it in the holes already made, or by smearing various arsenical mixtures around the bark of the trees just above the upper rows of holes. Around orange groves, however, other woodpeckers may do much damage by puncturing the fruit in order to get the juice. Contrary to the usual supposition, humming-birds live largely on an insect diet.

William Brewster recorded observations on the flight of herring gulls, which off the coast of Ireland kept pace with the progress of a steamship without any apparent movement of their wings, though headed almost directly into a wind blowing approximately thirty-five miles an hour. The only conclusion he could reach was that their movement was a resultant of the force of gravity and the force of the wind acting on the long flight quills and thus keeping the bird in motion. Forbush investigated the starling, which is getting a strong foothold in the eastern United States, and decided that it does much more harm than good, because it drives away the house wrens, bluebirds, etc., by appropriating their nesting places, and that it does no compensating good to the farmer. Hodge and others continued the offer of a reward for the discovery of an undisturbed nest of the passenger pigeon, but no announcements were made of the discovery of any birds. Julian Huxley reported to the London Zoölogical Society concerning the courtship of the red-shank, *Totanus salidris*. While only one male courted any one female, in fully 90 per cent. of the cases the male was rejected and flew away.

OSIREION. See Archæology.

OSTEN-SACHEN, Nicolai Dmitri Jevitch von der, Count. A Russian diplomat, died May 22, 1912. He was born in 1831 and entered the diplomatic service in 1853. He remained in Sebastopol throughout the Crimean War and was created a count for gallantry displayed during the siege. He was appointed successively to The Hague as secretary of the legation, to Madrid as chargé d'affaires, and to the legations of Bern (Switzerland) and Turin, capital of the Kingdom of Piedmont. Before the Franco-German War he was appointed Russian minister-resident in Darmstadt, where he remained until transferred to Munich, eleven years later. After two years in that city he returned to Russia, and for two years served in the Foreign Office, afterwards returning to Darmstadt and Munich as minister. In 1895 he was appointed Russian ambassador to the German Empire and retained that post for seventeen years, in spite of a paralytic stroke in 1909.

OSTIA. See Archæology.

OTTOMAN EMPIRE, The. See Turkey.

OXFORD. See Architecture.

PAGASAE. See Archæology.

PAINE, John Alsop. An American archæologist, died July 23, 1912. He was born in Newark, N. J., in 1840, and graduated from Hamilton College in 1859. He studied theology at Andover Theological Seminary, graduating in 1862. In 1867 he was ordained to the Congregational ministry. From 1862 to 1867 he was employed by the Board of Regents to enlarge the flora of the State of New York. From 1867 to 1869 he was professor of natural science at Robert College, Constantinople. In 1870-71 he was professor of natural history and German at Lake Forest University. In the following year he acted as associate editor of the *Independent*. He was archæologist for the first expedition of the Palestine Exploration Society East of the Jordan and Dead Sea from 1872 to 1874. From 1882 to 1884 he edited and published the *Journal of Christian Philosophy*. In 1888 he was a member of the staff of the *Century Dictionary* and from 1890 to 1906 was curator at the Metropolitan Museum of Art. He was the author of *Catalogue of Plants Found in Oneida County and Vicinity* (1865); *Handbook of Sculptural Plaster Casts and Bronze Reproductions in the Metropolitan Museum of Art*, and contributed many articles on Oriental and scientific subjects to magazines.

PAINTING. Mural Decoration in the United States. During 1912 a series of decorations was completed for the Wisconsin State capitol at Madison. These are by Edwin H.

General Washington Watching the Assault on Fort Washington

DECORATION FOR THE HUDSON COUNTY COURT HOUSE, JERSEY CITY

BY C. Y. TURNER

DECORATION FOR THE WISCONSIN STATE CAPITOL

By EDWIN HOWLAND BLASHFIELD

Blashfield, Kenyon Cox, and Hugo Ballin. A series of panels for the Hudson County Court House at Jersey City, N. J., have been executed by C. Y. Turner. The designs by Will H. Low have been accepted for thirty-two panels in the rotunda of the Department of Education at Albany. Albert Herter has completed decorations for the Library and Supreme Court Building at Hartford.

The principal awards for painting have been as follows: National Academy of Design, eighty-seventh annual exhibition—Clarke prize to Charles Bittinger, for "Getting Ready for the Ball"; Inness gold medal to Albert L. Groll, for "Lake Louise"; Saltus medal to Bruce Crane, for "The Hills"; Shaw memorial to M. Jean McLane, for "Portrait Group"; first Hallgarten prize to Charles Rosen, for "A Rocky Ledge"; second, to Everett L. Warner, for "Along the River Front"; and third, to Ben Ali Haggin, for "Girl in Black Gown." Pennsylvania Academy of the Fine Arts—Temple gold medal to Emil Carlsen, for "Open Sea"; Seanan medal to Willard L. Metcalf, for "Spring Fields"; Beck medal to Joseph de Camp, for "Portrait of Francis I. Amory"; Mary Smith prize to Elizabeth Sparhawk-Jones, for "In the Spring"; Lippincott prize to Edward W. Redfield, for "The Laurel Brook." Carnegie Institute of Pittsburgh—Medal of the first class and $1500 to Charles Sims, for "Pastorella"; medal of the second class and $1000 to Paul Dougherty, for "A Freshening Gale"; third class and $500 to Henri Martin, for "Portrait of My Son." The special exhibit of the year consisted of thirty-five pictures by John Lavery. Corcoran Art Gallery, Washington—Clark gold medal and $2000 to Childe Hassam, for "A New York Window"; silver medal and $1500 to Daniel Garber, for "Wilderness"; third and $1000 to Gardner Symons, for "The Dragging of the River Ice"; honorable mention and $500 to Carl J. Nordell, for "Femme Nue." Art Institute of Chicago—The most important of the prizes awarded at the annual exhibition of American paintings and sculpture were the Potter Palmer gold medal and $1000 to Daniel Garber, for a landscape, "Towering Trees"; the Norman Wait Harris silver medal and $500 to John C. Johanson for the painting, "The Village Rider"; and the same donor's bronze medal with $300 to Margaret F. Richardson, for "Portrait of Asa H. Paige." At the annual exhibition of works by Chicago artists prizes were awarded to Anna L. Stacey, Frank C. Peyraud, and Charles Francis Browne for painting, and to Nellie V. Walker for sculpture.

Art Societies in the United States. The American Federation of Arts, with headquarters at Washington, D. C., has grown during the past year from 120 chapters to 171. These chapters consist of art societies, each one being entitled to send delegates to the annual convention which is held during May in Washington.

The Michigan State Federation of Art was organized in October, 1912, in which the following cities were represented: Grand Rapids, Saginaw, Jackson, Kalamazoo, Alina, and Muskegon. The special purpose is to arrange a circuit of art exhibitions for the State.

In New York City three new societies came into existence during 1912: The Association of American Painters and Sculptors, which will hold a large international exhibition of modern paintings in the 69th Regiment Armory, opening February 17, 1913. The National Association of Portrait Painters held its first exhibition in New York in March, and the pictures were shown later in Chicago. The Museum of French Art, organized with the coöperation of the Institute de France, held an exhibition at the American Fine Arts Building in May, 1912; in October it opened permanent rooms, where art magazines and treasures of French art are available for the use of members and students; an exhibition of the work of Albert Besnard will be held early in 1913. The American Institute of Arts and Letters and the American Academy of Arts and Letters were incorporated by act of Congress during December, 1912. Art commissions were established in the cities of Pittsburgh, Philadelphia, and Milwaukee.

Foreign Art—In the United States. In addition to the international exhibition held in Pittsburgh, a group of paintings by members of the Société des Peintres et des Sculpteurs was circulated in the large cities, appearing first in Buffalo. The exhibition of Scandinavian art, organized by the American Scandinavian Society, was shown in New York in December, and went thence to Buffalo and other large cities.

France. The Luxembourg received a bequest from Edmond Davis of fifteen pictures by modern British painters, to form the nucleus of a British room. The following are the principal awards made at the Paris Salon: Medal of honor to Paul Chabas, for "Matinée de Septembre" and "Portrait de Mme. Aston Knight"; medals of the first class to Monchablon and to Roganeau; 10,000-franc prize to Pierre Gourdault. The Rome scholarship was awarded to M. Girodon.

London. The winter exhibition of the Royal Academy contained twenty-two paintings by Reynolds and works by the Italian, Dutch, and French masters and English painters of the eighteenth century. The central hall and three large galleries were devoted to a memorial exhibition to Edwin A. Abbey, the American painter. A memorial exhibition of the work of Alma-Tadema forms the special exhibition during the winter of 1912-13. Works by the late Alphonse Legros, the naturalized Englishman, were shown at the Tate Gallery for three months.

Holland and Belgium. A memorial exhibition of the work of Jozef Israëls was held at The Hague under the auspices of the Artists' Association. An important exhibition of miniatures was opened in Brussels March 5, 1912, and continued for three months.

Paintings at Auction. During the year ending October, 1912, 3634 paintings were sold at auction in the United States for $1,160,119, according to the records published in the *American Art Annual*. Of this number, 2265 brought $50 or over. The highest price was $85,000, paid for "Lake Nemi," by Corot, in the Newcomb sale, January 24, 1912. Among the important sales in Paris was the Doucet sale, which brought over $2,750,000; the Roussel sale brought over $200,000; the Rouart sale over $900,000. In Berlin the collection of Edward P. Webber was sold for over $1,125,000, and included the "Virgin and Child" by Andrea Mantagne, which brought $150,000, the highest price for a single picture during the year. The most important sale in London was that of Charles Wertheimer, for a total of more than $500,000.

ART CONGRESSES. An International Art Congress was held in Paris, June 14-16. The Congress of Decorative Arts was held at Dijon, France, in August. The International Congress of the History of Art was held in Rome, October 16-21. The Fourth International Congress on Art Education was held in Dresden, August 12-18.

PAHANG. A state (the easternmost) of the protected Federated Malay States (q. v.). It has an area of 14,000 sq. miles. The figure (approximate only) for population in 1911 was 117,933 (84,113 in 1901). Tin and gold are mined; agriculture is carried on. Output (1909), 11,654 piculs tin and 31,490 tin ore; gold, 14,887.6 ounces. Area planted to rubber (1909), 20,271 acres; to rice, 36,793; to cocoanuts 15,735; tapioca, 2262. A line of railway from Gemas in the Negri Sembilan to Kuala Semantan in central Pahang (70 miles) was completed in June, 1911, and is being extended to the Kelantan frontier. Roads are in process of construction. State revenue (1910), 1,017,-801 dollars; expenditure, 1,755,128. Kuala Lipis is the administrative headquarters. The sultan (Ahmad Maätham Shah bin Almerhum Ali) resides at Pekan, as does also the regent, The Tungku Besar. British resident, E. J. Brewster.

PALESTINE. See ARCHÆOLOGY.

PANAMA. A republic on the Isthmus of Panama, formerly a department of Colombia. It declared its independence November 4, 1903. Capital, Panama.

AREA AND POPULATION. Estimated area, 33,-776 square miles. A boundary dispute with Costa Rica has been submitted to the arbitration of the chief justice of the United States. By the treaty of November 18, 1903, the United States guaranteed the independence of Panama, and the latter granted to the United States, in perpetuity and with sovereign rights and powers therein, a strip of land (the Canal Zone) extending to a width of five miles on either side of the centre of the Panama Canal. The area of the Canal Zone is 474 square miles. Population of the republic (1911), 336,742, of whom 191,933 mixed bloods, 48,967 negroes, 47,606 Indians, and 46,323 whites. There were reported 267,736 Roman Catholics, 26,829 Protestants, 2088 Buddhists, 505 Jews, and 36,096 pagans. The population of the Canal Zone, not included above, was about 75,000. The city of Panama was reported to have 37,505 inhabitants, and Colón 17,748. These cities are not included in the Canal Zone, but in both of them and in their harbors complete jurisdiction is granted to the United States in respect of sanitation and quarantine. For the town of David were reported 15,079 inhabitants; Bocas del Toro, 9759. Movement of the population in 1910: 1299 marriages, 5876 births, 5177 deaths, 28,215 immigrants, 14,910 emigrants.

Public schools are reported to number 294, with 18,645 pupils. In 1911 the National Institute (high school, college of commerce and language and normal school) was opened in the city of Panama.

PRODUCTION, COMMERCE, ETC. Only a small part of the country is under cultivation. The leading crop is bananas, and other products include sugar-cane, cacao, coffee, rice, corn, yams, and sweet potatoes. Mining is little developed.

Imports, exclusive of non-dutiable supplies for the Panama Canal, and exports are shown below. The figures are for calendar years, except those for 1911, which are for the fiscal year ended June 30; the trade for the last six months of 1910 is included under both 1910 and 1911.

	1908	1909	1910	1911
Imps.	$7,806,812	$8,756,308	$10,056,994	$10,020,070
Exps.	1,827,050	1,502,475	1,769,330	1,754,056

Principal classified imports in fiscal year 1911: Vegetable products, $2,836,568; textiles, $1,766,459; animal products, $1,623,932; mineral products, $919,080; liquors (including mineral waters), $858,955; drugs and chemicals, $406,839; machinery and apparatus, $274,224. Of the exports, bananas were valued at $1,030,-885; bar gold, $119,830; ivory nuts, $118,408; cocoanuts, $112,827; rubber, $111,143. Imports from the Unted States amounted to $5,652,653, and exports thither $1,508,422; United Kingdom, $2,166,989 and $165,273; Germany, $966,-151 and $93,669; France, $307,982 and $1966.

The Panama Railway crosses the isthmus from Colón to Panama, 48 miles; branch to Balboa, three miles. Light railways in the territory about Bocas del Toro, principally for the banana industry, 151 miles. Telegraph and post offices, about 40 and 100, respectively.

FINANCE. The unit of value is the balboa, equivalent to the American dollar. The republic has $6,300 000 invested in the United States. Revenue in 1909, $2,846,297; in 1910, $3,370,-511; in 1911, $3,366,470. Expenditure in 1911, $3,359,588. Import duties in 1911, $1,785,866; liquor licenses, $161,377; lotteries, $122,800; interest, $335,505. Disbursements in 1911 were as follows, by departments: Interior and justice, $1,087,259; fomento, $908,379; public instruction, $684,744; treasury, $438,309; foreign affairs, $240,897; total, $3,359,588. In 1913 Panama will receive the first annual payment of $250,000 from the United States on account of the construction of the Panama Canal.

GOVERNMENT. The president is elected by popular vote for four years and is assisted by a cabinet of five members. The legislative body is the unicameral National Assembly (32 members). Three *designados* are elected by the assembly to succeed, in order, to the residency in case of vacancy. José Domingo de Obaldía, president for the term ending October 1, 1912, died March 10, 1910. He was succeeded by Carlos Antonio Mendoza, the second *designado* (the first *designado* having died in 1909). On September 14, 1910, the assembly elected as first *designado* Pablo Arosemena, who thus became acting president for Obaldía's unexpired term. In the summer of 1912 the Liberal candidate, Dr. Belisario Porras, was elected president; he was inaugurated October 1, for the four-year term. *Designados:* Rodolfo Chiari, first; Ramón Valdez, second; Aristides Arjona, third.

PANAMA (City), MUNICIPAL IMPROVEMENTS IN. See PANAMA CANAL.

PANAMA, AIDS TO NAVIGATION. See LIGHTHOUSES.

PANAMA CANAL. Public interest in the Panama Canal in 1912 was concerned more with the future of the great enterprise than with the actual work of construction being carried on. From the statements of the chief engineer, it was evident that the canal would be open to navigation in 1913 and that its completion at that time was merely a matter of routine of construction and excavation. This fact made it imperative that Congress should pass laws relating to the navigation of the canal and such laws, as will be noted below, were passed. The President in November issued a proclamation fixing the tariff tolls on vessels passing through the canal. This also is noted in the paragraphs below.

THE CANAL BILL. The prospective completion and opening of the Panama Canal some time in 1913 brought about the necessity of passing laws providing for its operation and a declaration of the general policy of the United States in regard to its own rights and the rights of foreign countries in the canal. President Taft repeatedly urged the passage of such laws, but p siti e action was not taken by Congress until Mayy 1912. On May 23 the Panama Canal bill was passed by the House of Representatives. That bill admitted American-owned ships to free passage in the canal and fixed a toll of not more than $1.25 per net registered ton on foreign ships. (Compare, however, paragraph on *Canal Tolls* below.) It debarred entirely vessels owned directly or indirectly by railroads from using the canal. The bill then went to the Senate, and on July 11 that body received a protest from Great Britain against the provisions of the bill which permitted American ships to use the canal free of tolls. The British government declared that such measures were in direct contradiction of the terms provided in treaties between the governments of United States and Great Britain. This contention was based on the interpretation given by the British government to articles contained in the Clayton-Bulwer treaty ot 1850 and the Hay-Pauncefote treaty of 1902, which superseded the Clayton-Bulwer treaty. Article 1 of the Clayton-Bulwer treaty read as follows: "The governments of the United States and Great Britain hereby declare that neither the one nor the other will ever obtain or maintain for itself any exclusive control over the said ship canal; agreeing that neither will ever erect or maintain any fortifications commanding the same, or in the vicinity thereof, or occupy, or fortify, or colonize, or assume or exercise any dominion over Nicaragua, Costa Rica, the Mosquito Coast, or any part of Central America; nor will either make use of any protection which either affords, or may afford or any alliance which either has or may have, to or with any state or people for the purpose of erecting or maintaining any such fortifications."

When it became evident that the United States, on the failure of the French company, intended itself to build the canal, Great Britain waived the rights set forth in the Clayton-Bulwer treaty and bound itself by the terms of a new treaty made in 1902 and known as the Hay-Pauncefote treaty. Section 1 of article III. of this treaty reads as follows: "The canal shall be free and open to the vessels of commerce and of war of all nations observing these rules, on terms of entire equality so that there will be no discrimination against any such nation, or its citizens or subjects, in respect of the conditions or charges of traffic, or otherwise. Such conditions and charges of traffic shall be just and equitable." Upon this section Great Britain based its objection to the discrimination in favor of American-owned ships contained in the bill passed by the House of Representatives, and upon this point turned the course of the debates in the Senate during the discussion of the bill. The senators who insisted that a strict interpretation of the Hay-Pauncefote treaty meant an absolute identity of the treatment of the vessels of all nations, including the United States, included Senators Root of New York and Burton of Ohio, and these senators made strong speeches urging their conviction as to this interpretation.

The senators who favored the admission of American ships free of toll claimed that the section under the Hay-Pauncefote treaty should read as applying to the ships of all nations except those of the United States. They argued that the United States is the absolute owner of the canal and of the Canal Zone, and could therefore make whatever rules she wished for the administration of the canal provided that they did not discriminate between vessels of other countries. They pointed out also the custom of foreign countries to pay in the form of subsidies the tolls of vessels passing through the Suez Canal and that these governments were prepared to undertake the same measures for vessels passing through the Panama Canal. If, therefore, the United States required tolls from American vessels, they would be placed at a disadvantage with the vessels of other countries, the tolls for which had been paid or would be paid by these governments. Advocates of this interpretation of the Hay-Pauncefote treaty insisted that the action of Great Britain resulted from protests made by Canadian ship-owners, who claimed that they would suffer if American coatswise vessels were allowed to pass through the canal free.

The other point in the treaty most warmly debated in the Senate was that relating to the admission or exclusion of vessels owned by railroads, and it was finally decided that such vessels should not be admitted for passage through the canal. On August 7 the Senate refused to strike from the bill the provision exempting American coastwise ships from the payment of tolls, and two days later passed the bill. It was at once signed by the President. The most important features of the bill in its final form are as follows: The President is authorized when, in his judgment, the construction of the canal shall be sufficiently advanced toward completion to render the further service of the Isthmian Canal Commission unnecessary, to discontinue the commission and to complete, govern, and operate the canal and the Canal Zone through a governor of the Panama Canal and such other persons as the may deem competent to discharge the duties. If any of the persons employed for these duties shall be in the military or naval service of the United States, the amount of the official salary paid to him shall be deducted from the amount of salary or compensation provided under the terms of this act. The governor of the Panama Canal is to be appointed by the President, by and with the advice and consent of the Senate. He is commissioned for a term of four years and is to receive a salary of $10,000 a year. All other persons needed for the completion, care, and management of the canal are to be appointed by the President or by his authority and are removable at his pleasure. He has power to fix salaries, but they shall not in any case exceed by more than 25 per cent. the salary paid for the same or similar services to persons employed by the government in continental United States. The President is authorized to prescribe and from time to time to change the tolls which shall be levied by the government of the United States for the use of the Panama Canal. Six months' notice, however, must be given of such change. No toll shall be levied upon vessels engaged in the coastwise trade of the United States. The rate of tolls is not to exceed $1.25 per registered net ton.

The President is authorized to cause to be erected, maintained, and operated, subject to the international convention and the act of Congress to regulate radio communication, at suitable places along the canal and the coast adjacent to its two terminals, such wireless telegraph installations as are found necessary. He is also authorized to establish, maintain, and operate dry docks, repair shops, yards, and such other facilities as are found necessary for the repairing of vessels passing through the canal. Money received in payment for such repairs or for actual purchases at the canal on which a profit is made is to be expended and reinvested for such purposes without being covered into the treasury of the United States. The governor of the canal is given exclusive control and jurisdiction over the Canal Zone and is to perform all duties in connection with the civil government of the Canal Zone, which is to be held, treated, and governed as an adjunct of the Panama Canal. The President is authorized to determine or cause to be determined what towns shall exist in the Canal Zone and subdivide and from time to time resubdivide the Canal Zone into subdivisions, to be designated by name or number. Provision is made for the setting up in each town such courts as are necessary, and for other agents of civil government. The governor is given the right, after the canal has been completed and opened for operation, to make such rules and regulations, subject to the approval of the President, as are necessary to establish the right of any person to remain upon or pass through any part of the Canal Zone.

Section XI., which has for its object the exclusion of vessels owned by railroad companies through the canal, reads as follows: "From and after the 1st day of July, 1914, it shall be unlawful for any railroad company or other common carrier subject to the act to regulate commerce to own, lease, operate, control, or have any interest whatsoever (by stock ownership or otherwise, either directly, indirectly, through any holding company, or by stockholders or directors in common, or in any other manner) in any common carrier by water operated through the Panama Canal or elsewhere with which said railroad or other carrier aforesaid does or may compete for traffic or any vessel carrying freight or passengers upon said water route or elsewhere; and in case of the violation of this provision each day in which such violation continues shall be deemed a separate offense."

Jurisdiction is conferred on the Interstate Commerce Commission to determine questions of fact as to the competition or possibility of competition, on the application of any railroad company or other carrier. The paragraph further reads: "No vessel permitted to engage in the coastwise or foreign trade of the United States shall be permitted to enter or pass through said canal, if such ship is owned, chartered, operated or controlled by any person or company which is doing business in violation of the provisions of the act of Congress approved July 2, 1890, entitled 'An act to protect trade and commerce against unlawful restraints and monopolies,' or the provisions of sections 73 to 77, both inclusive, of an act approved August 27, 1894, entitled 'An act to reduce taxation, to provide revenue for the government, and for other purposes,' or the provisions of any other act of Congress amending or supplementing the said act of July 2, 1890, commonly known as the Sherman Anti-Trust act, and amendments thereto, or said sections of the act of August 27, 1894. The questions of fact may be determined by the judgment of any court of the United States of competent jurisdiction in any cause pending before it to which the owners or operators of such ships are parties. Suit may be brought by any shippe or by the Attorney-General of the United States."

The Interstate Commerce Commission is given jurisdiction over the transportation of all property from point to point in the United States by rail and water through the Panama Canal or otherwise, when the transportation is made by a common carrier and not entirely within the limits of a single State. It is also given power to establish physical connection between the lines of the rail carrier and the dock of the water carrier by directing the rail carrier to make suitable connection between its line and a track or tracks which have been constructed from the dock to the limits of its right of way, or by directing either or both the rail and water carrier individually, or in connection with one another, to construct and connect with the lines of the rail carrier a spur track or tracks to the dock. The commission was also given authority to determine the terms and conditions upon which these connecting tracks when constructed, shall be operated. It is also given power to establish through routes and maximum joint rates between and over such rail and water lines, and to establish maximum proportional rates by rail to and from the ports to which the traffic is brought, or from which it is taken by the water carrier, and to determine to what traffic and in connection with what vessels and upon what terms and conditions such rates will apply.

These paragraphs of section XI., which were designed to eliminate from the canal vessels owned by railroad companies and to establish competition between railroad companies and steamship companies where, on account of monopolies or otherwise, it has ceased to exist, are in the form of amendments to the act of February 4, 1887, which was an act to regulate commerce.

Section XIII. of the law provides: "That in time of war in which the United States shall be engaged, or when, in the opinion of the President, war is imminent, such officer of the army as the President may designate shall, upon his order, assume and have exclusive authority and jurisdiction over the operation of the Panama Canal, including the entire control and government of the Canal Zone, and during a continuance of such condition the governor of the Panama Canal shall, in all respects and particulars as to the operation of the canal, and all duties, matters and transactions affecting the

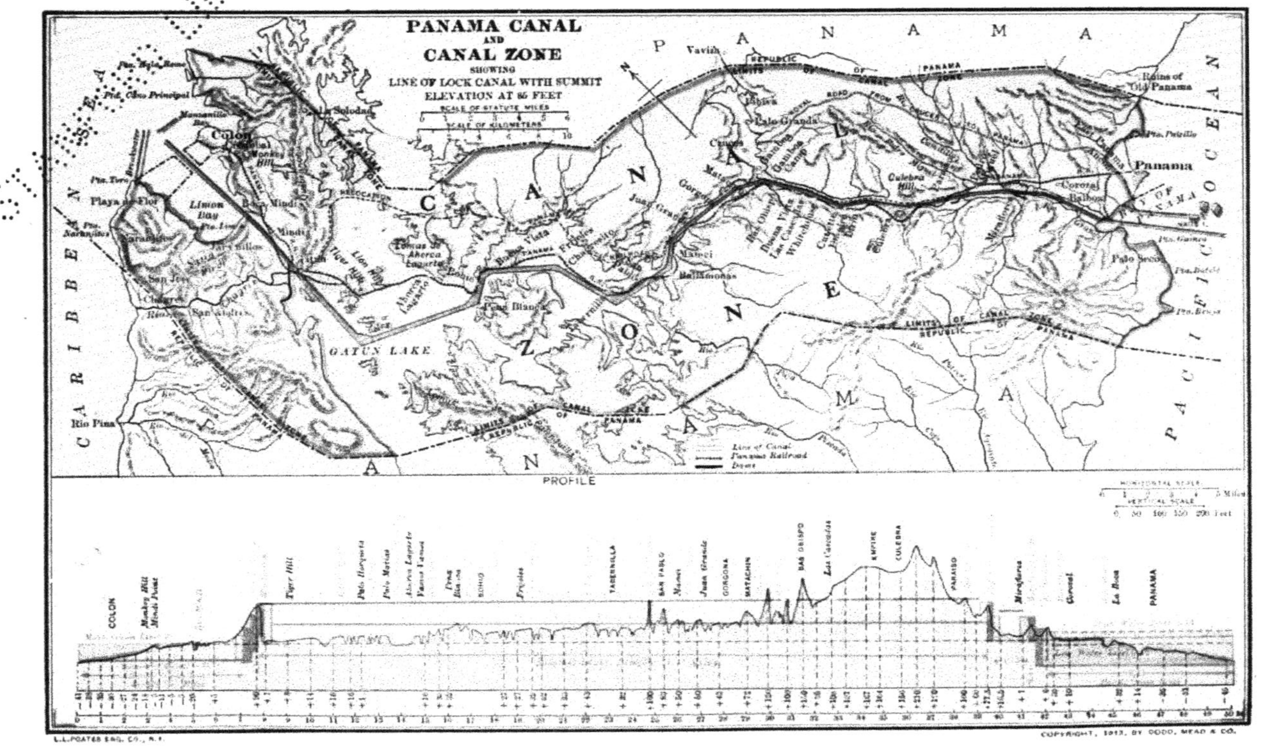
PANAMA CANAL
AND
CANAL ZONE
SHOWING
LINE OF LOCK CANAL WITH SUMMIT
ELEVATION AT 85 FEET
SCALE OF STATUTE MILES
SCALE OF KILOMETERS
CARIBBEAN SEA
PACIFIC OCEAN
CANAL ZONE
PANAMA
GATUN LAKE
Colon
Limon Bay
Playa de Flor
Pta. Toro
Manzanillo Bay
Monkey Hill
Mindi
Gatun
Lion Hill
Tiger Hill
Ahorca Lagarto
Pena Blanca
Frijoles
Bohio
Matachin
Gorgona
Juan Grande
Mamei
Bas Obispo
Las Cascadas
Culebra
Culebra Hill
Empire
Miraflores
Corozal
Balboa
Panama
Ruins of Old Panama
Palo Seco
Rio Pina
Vavish
LIMITS OF CANAL ZONE
REPUBLIC OF PANAMA
Line of Canal
Panama Railroad
Dams
PROFILE
COLON
Monkey Hill
Mindi Point
Tiger Hill
Palo Horquita
Palo Matias
Ahorca Lagarto
Pena Blanca
BOHIO
Frijoles
TABERNILLA
SAN PABLO
Mamei
Juan Grande
GORGONA
MATACHIN
BAS OBISPO
Las Cascadas
EMPIRE
CULEBRA
PARAISO
Miraflores
Corozal
La Boca
PANAMA
HORIZONTAL SCALE
VERTICAL SCALE
0 50 100 150 200 Feet
5 Miles
L. L. POATES ENG. CO., N. Y.
COPYRIGHT, 1913, BY DODD, MEAD & CO.

Canal Zone, be subject to the order and direction of such officer of the army."

On August 24 the President signed the Panama Canal bill after a long conference with members of his cabinet. At the same time he sent to Congress a statement of his views in relation to the controverted features of the bill. He said: "After full examination of the treaty and of the treaty which preceded it, I feel confident that the exemption of the coastwise vessels of the United States from the tolls, and the imposition of tolls on vessels of all nations engaged in foreign trade, is not a violation of the Hay-Pauncefote treaty, but distinguished lawyers in the House and Senate differ from this construction and the Secretary of State has received an informal protest from the British government that the contemplated legislation is a violation of her treaty rights. I am sure that it is not the intention of Congress to violate the Hay-Pauncefote treaty or to enact anything inconsistent with its provisions, and that it certainly is not its purpose to repeal by subsequent enactments, the treaty, in so far as it represents the law of the land. It is of the highest importance, however, that this attitude should be made clearly known to the nations of the world, and that we should avoid any apparent justification for criticism." In order to make clear the position of Congress and the government, the President recommended that Congress pass an addition to the act or a supplementary resolution declaring that nothing in the act shall be deemed a violation of the treaty or an impairment of any rights under the treaty, and that any alien who considers the charging of tolls a discrimination can bring suit against the United States in the United States courts, with appeal to the Supreme Court. Congress took no action on these suggestions.

The President also issued a public statement defending his action in signing the bill. In this statement he argued that there was nothing in the treaty which prevented Great Britain and other nations from extending such favors to their own ships passing through the canal as they see fit. He said: "The British protests lead to the absurd conclusion that this government in constructing the canal, maintaining the canal and defending the canal, finds itself shorn of its right to deal with its own commerce in its own way, while other nations using the canal in competition with American commerce enjoy that right and power unimpaired. The British protest, therefore, is a proposal to read into the treaty a surrender by the United States of its right to regulate its own commerce in its own way and by its own methods, a right which neither Great Britain herself nor any other that may use the canal has surrendered or proposes to surrender. While the bill here in question seems to vest the President with discretion to discriminate in fixing tolls in favor of American ships and against foreign ships engaged in foreign trade within the limitation of the range from 50 cents a ton to $1.25 a net ton, there is nothing in that to compel the President to make such a discrimination. The policy of exempting coastwise trade from all tolls really involves the question of granting a government subsidy for the purpose of encouraging that trade in competition with the trade of the transcontinental railroads. I approve this policy. It is in accord with the historical course of the government in giving government aid to the construction of transcontinental roads. It is merely giving government aid to a means of transportation that competes with these transcontinental roads. I believe the bill to be one of the most beneficial that has passed this or any other Congress, and I find no reason in the objection made to the bill which should lead me to delay until another session of Congress provisions that are imperatively needed now in order that due preparation by the world may be made for the opening of the canal."

On December 9, James Bryce, the British ambassador, presented to the Secretary of State a formal demand from the British government that the government of the United States either repeal the act of Congress granting free passage through the Panama Canal to American ships engaged in the coastwise trade or submit the matter to arbitration. The statement, which was signed by Sir Edward Grey, was an amplification of the original note of protest presented on July 8. It endeavored to establish by argument the soundness of the British contention that the legislation favoring American ships is in violation of the treaty rights of Great Britain with regard to the Panama Canal. The note gave warning that another protest would be forthcoming from Great Britain if it was held by the government of the United States that the disbarment from the use of the canal of ships in which any railroad under the jurisdiction of the Interstate Commerce Commission has an interest and ships whose owners may be adjudged guilty of violating the Sherman anti-trust law, applies to British ships. The note states that the British government assumes that these two clauses do not apply to or affect British ships.

In regard to arbitration the note stated that the British government had taken cognizance of the fact that many persons of note in the United States "whose opinions are entitled to great weight" hold that the act of Congress in question does not infringe the treaty obligations of the United States and therefore it is declared that the British government is perfectly willing to submit the question to arbitration if the United States prefers. This sentence was added: "Such arbitration would be rendered unnecessary if the government of the United States should be prepared to take such steps as would remove the objections to the act which his majesty's government have stated."

Sir Edward Grey in the note denied that the British government is attempting to deny the right of the United States to grant subsidies to its shipping and thus deprive it of the rights enjoyed by other nations which will send subsidized vessels through the Panama Canal. It was carefully stated, however, that the British government does not concede the right of the United States to favor by subsidy a special class of American shipping in such a way as to place such shipping at an advantage in the use of the canal as compared with British shipping. The British arguments rested chiefly on the interpretation of the Hay-Pauncefote treaty and the Clayton-Bulwer treaty and upon the argument that if any American ships are granted the free use of the canal, British ships using the canal will be forced to bear more than a proper share of the burden of the cost of the upkeep of the canal and interest charges on the cost of construction. This, it is claimed, is in violation of the Hay-Pauncefote treaty, which declares that all charges made by the United States for the use of the canal shall be just and equitable.

TOLL RATES. On November 13 President Taft issued a proclamation announcing the rates to be paid by ships passing through the canal. The basis of these rates was a report submitted by Professor Emory R. Johnson of the University of Pennsylvania, who, as a special commissioner, devoted a year to the task. The rate fixed by the President is $1.20 per net ton for passenger vessels carrying cargo or passengers or both, each 100 cubic feet of earning capacity to be counted as a ton; 40 per cent. less, or 72 cents per ton for vessels in ballast, without passengers; 50 cents for each displacement ton of warships; $1.20 per net ton for army or navy transports, colliers, hospital ships, and supply ships. There is no per capita charge for passengers carried on vessels. The rates declared by the President are practically the same as the rates which went into effect on the Suez Canal on January 1, 1913. The former rates on the Suez Canal were $1.25 per ton. Professor Johnson's estimates of the financial results of the operation of the canal were as follows: The estimated cost is $375,000,000, which includes the payment to the French company and the Republic of Panama. Thus, to make the canal self-supporting, a revenue of about $19,250,000 annually will be required, to be divided as follows: Operation and maintenance, $3,500,000; sanitation and government of the zone, $500,000; annual payment to Panama, $250,000; interest on the investment, at 3 per cent., $11,250,000; 1 per cent. in a sinking fund for ultimate amortization, $3,750,000. Professor Johnson estimates that the toll revenue will rise from about $12,000,000 in the first year to about $20,000,000 in 1925. In his report he opposed the exemption of American coastwise shipping on the ground that this shipping does not need such aid; that if it should pay tolls the steamship and railroad rates would not be appreciably increased. He declared that there is already an American monopoly of coastwise trade and that this trade will be increased by the canal. Such subsidies, he said, as are giving to the American merchant marine should be paid to vessels in the foreign trade. President Taft in his proclamation, however, did not recommend a repeal of the act exempting coastwise shipping.

SUMMARY OF CANAL WORK. As the completion and opening of the canal are assured in 1913, it may be of interest and value to present a general résumé of the chief features of gigantic task which is probably the greatest engineering feat of which there is a record in history.

The elevation of the summit of the canal is 85 feet above sea level. The summit will be reached by a flight of three locks located at Gatun on the Atlantic side and by one lock at Pedro Miguel, and a flight of two locks at Miraflores on the Pacific side. These locks are all made in duplicate, that is, they have two chambers side by side. The usable length of each lock will be 1000 feet and its width 110 feet. The summit level of the canal which extends from Gatun to Pedro Miguel, about 31.5 miles, is regulated between 82 and 87 feet above sea level by means of the spillway in the dam at Gatun. The Gatun Lake, which has an area of 164.23 square miles, is maintained by earth dams at Gatun and Pedro Miguel. Into this lake empty the Chagres River and other streams. Another small lake about two miles in area, with a surface elevation of 55 feet has been formed between Pedro Miguel and Miraflores, the valley of the Rio Grande being closed by an earth dam on the west side and a concrete dam with a spillway on the east side at Miraflores. The approaches from deep water to the Gatun locks on the Atlantic side and from deep water to the locks at Miraflores on the Pacific side are sea level channels about seven and eight miles in length respectively, and each 500 feet wide.

From deep water in the Caribbean Sea to deep water in the Pacific Ocean the canal is about 50 miles in length. The distance from deep water to the shore line in Limón Bay on the Atlantic side is about 4½ miles, and from the Pacific shore line to deep water, about 4 miles. The total length of the canal from shore to shore, therefore, is approximately 41½ miles. The channel from the beginning of the canal in the Caribbean Sea to the north end of the Gatun locks, about 7 miles, is 500 feet wide; from the south end of Gatun locks to a distance of 23½ miles it is 1000 feet wide; for the next three miles, 800 feet wide; for the next half mile, 700 feet wide; for the next four and a quarter miles, 500 feet wide, and from this point to Pedro Miguel lock, about 8 miles, is 300 feet wide. From the Pedro Miguel locks to Miraflores locks and from Miraflores locks to deep water in Panama Bay, it is 500 feet wide. The average width of the canal is 649 feet and its minimum width is 300 feet. It has a minimum depth of 41 feet. The most spectacular feature of the canal, without doubt, is the Gatun dam which holds in place the waters of Gatun Lake and the Chagres, and other rivers. This dam is about 800 feet long, including the spillway, and is 2100 feet wide at its greatest width. The crest of the dam is at an elevation of 115 feet above sea level, or 30 feet above the normal level of Gatun Lake, and is 100 feet wide. Its width at the normal level of the lake, that is, 85 feet above sea level, is about 388 feet. The central part of the dam was filled by hydraulic process, protected by rock toes on both sides. The upper slope on the lake side is further protected by a 10-foot thickness of rock. The other parts were filled with available material from canal excavation.

The course of a vessel entering the canal from the Atlantic side is as follows: It will pass from deep water in Limón Bay to Gatun locks, a distance of 6.9 miles, through a channel 500 feet wide. Passing into the locks which are .78 of a mile in length the ship will be carried to an elevation of 85 feet above sea level in three lifts to the level of the water in Gatun Lake; thence for a distance of 16 miles the channel will be 1000 feet or more in width. This carries the vessel about 24 miles into the canal. Passing into the Pedro Miguel lock, which is .37 of a mile in length, the vessel will be lowered to the level of Miraflores Lake, 55 feet above mean tide to Miraflores locks, which is 41.72 miles from the Atlantic opening of the canal. Through the two Miraflores locks,

GATUN SPILLWAY, VIEW LOOKING SOUTHWEST, SHOWING DOWN STREAM FACE OF OGEE DAM, JUNE 6, 1912

VIEW OF THE PEDRO MIGUEL LOCKS, SOUTH END OF EAST CHAMBER, SHOWING CONSTRUCTION OF SAFETY AND LOWER GATES, June 3, 1912

PANAMA CANAL

which are .58 of a mile in length, the vessel will be lowered to tide level and proceed through a channel 500 feet wide to deep water in the Pacific, a distance of 50.5 miles from the beginning of the journey on the Atlantic side. It is estimated that the time required for the passage of a ship of medium size through the entire length of the canal will be from 9½ to 10 hours, and for larger vessels, from 10½ to 11 hours.

WORK ON THE CANAL IN 1912. Progress in excavation and in the construction of the locks and dams continued uninterruptedly in 1912. Detailed plans were made for the operation and maintenance of the canal after its opening. Work was also carried on on the fortifications, for which $2,000,000 was appropriated by Congress in 1911. On January 1, 1912, the work on the fortifications was consolidated and placed in charge of Col. George W. Goethals, chief engineer.

The work of the canal is in four divisions, all under the authority of the chief engineer.

The first division, under Colonel H. F. Hodges, has charge of the design of the locks, dams, regulating works, and accessories; the design and construction of aids to navigation; and the inspection of the manufacture and erection of the lock gates, operating machinery, etc. During the year in this division the general plans for the lower portion of the lower locks at Gatun and Miraflores were completed, and work was carried on on the rising stem gate valves. During the year the drawings for all the different heights of gates were completed and approved. On June 30, 1912, the work of erecting the gates on the Isthmus was in progress on 23 gates, or exactly half the total number on the canal. The general features of lock illumination, both exterior and interior, were fixed during the year. For exterior lighting, concrete lamp standards will be erected on the coping of the locks approximately 100 feet apart, throughout the entire length of each wall. The work of erecting the lock machinery was carried on during the year. To enable the pilot of a vessel to keep his course up to the turning point it is necessary to have a range of two lights at each end of the longer tangents in prolongation of the sailing line. It was necessary for the prolongation of these tangents to cut down heavy growths of brush and timber during the year. A total of 809.85 acres was cleared. Construction work was carried on on the range towers at the Pacific entrance during the year. These towers, which are of concrete, are constructed by means of steel forms. Eleven towers were completed at the end of the fiscal year. In these towers will be placed powerful lights for the guidance of navigators.

The Atlantic division, which embraces the construction of the locks and dam at Gatun, the quarry at Porto Bello, the excavation between the locks and deep water in the Caribbean, the municipal improvements in Colón and the various settlements, is in charge of Lieut.-Col. William L. Sibert. During the year the work of construction of Gatun dam went forward steadily. Work on the upper or south approach pier was continued throughout the year. The total amount of masonry, which includes concrete and large stone laid during the year, was 451,025 cubic yards. Plans which were prepared for the hydroelectic power plant below the spillway in the dam were approved, and excavation work was started in May, 1912. The total amount excavated during the year was 72,119 cubic yards. In the channel between Gatun locks and the Atlantic Ocean excavation in the dry was continued through the Mindi Hills and, with the exception of the dike separating the cut from the French canal, was completed in February, 1912. Work was carried on in the breakwater extending out from Toro Point, which is intended for the protection of the harbor and the shelter of vessels against northern winds. During the year 5514 lineal feet of double track and 48 lineal feet of single track trestle were completed, making a total length of trestle on July 14, 1912, of 10,927 feet.

The Central division embraces all the excavation between the Gatun dam and Pedro Miguel locks. It also includes the construction of the Naos Island breakwater and municipal improvements in the various settlements included within the division limits, and such sanitary engineering work in the same area as is prescribed by the sanitary department. The work is in charge of Lieut.-Col. D. D. Gaillard. The Culebra cut is included in this division. During the fiscal year 16,476,769 cubic yards of material were removed from this cut and from estimates 11,863,540 cubic yards remain to be removed in order to complete this section of the canal. Several slides occurred during the year which involved a considerable amount of extra labor. The total amount of material due to slides during the work removed up to the end of the fiscal year was 16,671,000 cubic yards, and about 4,000,000 cubic yards remained to be removed. The Naos Island breakwater extends from the shore of East Balboa to Naos Island, a distance of 3.29 miles. It is constructed for the purpose of cutting off silt-bearing currents from the excavated channel in the Pacific, thereby reducing the cost of maintenance and making the navigation of the channel easier by eliminating the cross currents. In constructing the breakwater a pile trestle was driven towards the island from which material was dumped. During the year this trestle was extended 1360 feet, giving a total length of 16,051 feet, or about 3 miles at the end of the year.

The work on the Pacific division includes the construction of the locks and dam at Pedro Miguel, the locks and dams at Miraflores, and sanitary work which comes within its boundaries. The excavation necessary to prepare for work on the division, including coaling stations, dry docks, and machine shops, is also included in the work of this division. The work is in charge of Mr. S. B. Williamson. The excavation for the Pedro Miguel locks was practically completed at the end of the fiscal year 1911, and at the beginning of the fiscal year 1912 the construction plant was removed to Miraflores. The total amount of concrete laid during the year at Pedro Miguel was 182,870 cubic yards. At Miraflores 624,747 cubic yards were excavated from the lock pit. The total amount of concrete placed in the Miraflores lock at the end of the year was 751,540 cubic yards. The total amount of concrete laid in the Pacific division locks at the end of the fiscal year 1912 was 1,874,029 cubic yards. There remained to complete the locks, 51,150 cubic yards at Pedro Miguel and 386,729 cubic yards at Miraflores. Excavation of the channel by steam shovels between Pedro Miguel and Miraflores, and south of the latter was continued during the year and 864,475 cubic yards were removed.

MUNICIPAL IMPROVEMENTS IN COLÓN AND PANAMA. These improvements are carried on in accordance with a treaty made between the United States and Panama in 1906. The sum of $800,000 was authorized in 1909. This was to be defrayed by water rents from the two cities. A large number of water mains and sewer pipes were laid during the year at Colón. In Panama plans were made for developing new districts of the city and for laying water mains and sewer pipes.

LABOR. At the end of the fiscal year 1912 there were approximately 45,000 employees on the isthmus on the rolls of the commission and of the Panama Railroad Company. Of these about 5000 were Americans. On September 25 there were 35,861 men actually employed. Of the 29,571 men working for the commission, 4166 were on the gold roll, which includes mechanics, skilled artisans, clerks, and higher officials, the remainder on the silver roll, which includes common laborers. These are practically all foreigners.

COSTS AND APPROPRIATIONS. The total estimated cost of the canal is $325,201,000, which includes $20,053,000 for sanitation and $7,382,000 for civil administration. These figures do not include the $50,000,000 paid to the French Canal Company and to the Republic of Panama. It is therefore estimated that the total cost of the canal to the United States will approximate $375,000,000. The total appropriation for the construction of the canal, for the administration of the civil government, and for the purchase of canal rights to June 30, 1912, including collections and salvage, was $304,336,744. In addition $3,000,000 was appropriated for fortifications. The disbursements in all departments of the work to the end of the fiscal year 1912 amounted to $275,435,971, leaving a balance available on June 30, 1912, of $28,900,802.

FORTIFICATIONS. The project for the defense of the canal contemplates: Strong fortifications at each terminus; adequate submarine defense; construction of defensive line of field fortifications for the protection of the more vulnerable portions of the canal from injuries by raiding parties; the necessary filling, clearing, and drainage to secure healthful surroundings for the troops detailed for the defense of the canal; and the establishment of the necessary communications for the prompt employment of the mobile garrison against any force which may land at a distance from the coast fortifications. Plans for most of the batteries of the primary armament have been completed; the excavations or foundations of over 50 per cent. of these have been undertaken and the concrete construction of about one-half was already under way. The armament for these batteries is being manufactured, and the first delivery of guns and carriages is expected in June, 1913.

RECORD OF EXCAVATION. Excavations to January 1, 1913, are recorded in the next column. On that date there remained to be excavated in the Culebra cut 5,351,419 cubic yards, and in the entire canal proper 24,223,826 cubic yards.

PANAMA-PACIFIC EXHIBITION. See ARCHITECTURE.

By French companies		78,146,960
French excavation useful to present canal		29,908,000
By Americans:		
Dry excavation	116,428,685	
Dredges	71,851,627	
Total		188,280,312
May 4 to December 31, 1904	243,472	
Jan. 1 to Dec. 31, 1905	1,799,227	
Jan. 1 to Dec. 31, 1906	4,948,497	
Jan. 1 to Dec. 31, 1907	15,765,290	
Jan. 1 to Dec. 31, 1908	37,116,735	
Jan. 1 to Dec. 31, 1909	35,096,166	
Jan. 1 to Dec. 31, 1910	31,437,677	
Jan. 1 to Dec. 31, 1911	31,603,899	
Jan. 1 to Dec. 31, 1912	30,269,349	

Totals by Divisions and Amount to Be Excavated

Divisions	Amount excavated	Remaining to be excavated
Atlantic—		
Dry excavation	8,702,997	211,120
Dredges	34,021,280	4,936,380
Central—		
Culebra Cut	88,531,237	5,351,419
All other points	12,384,655	150,000
Pacific—		
Dry excavation	6,998,035	3,312,704
Dredges	37,642,108	10,212,203
Grand total	188,280,312	24,223,826

PAPER. See CHEMISTRY, INDUSTRIAL.

PAPER. The paper industry in the United States, while fairly prosperous, was in a rather abnormal condition during the year 1912, due to uncertainty and anxiety regarding tariff and other legislation. This industry represented capital amounting to over $400,000,000, and gave employment to 80,000 or more people, to whom wages exceeding $40,000,000 were annually distributed. The yearly production amounted in value to almost $300,000,000. In 1912 the increase in production of previous years was maintained in the news print, book paper, and writing paper divisions, which represent the greater part of the paper industry. In news print the entire year's total was stated at 1,426,921 tons, compared with 1,366,609 tons for 1911 and 1,278,002 tons for 1910. The imports from Canada were 84,630 tons in 1912 and 54,484 tons in 1911. The total production of book paper for 1912 was 1,387,568,000 pounds, or greater than that of 1911 by 84,428,000 pounds. In 1912 the total production of writing and other fine paper was 348,118,000 pounds, as against 324,240,000 pounds in 1911. During the year there was a certain amount of labor trouble, as at Kalamazoo, Mich., floods and other difficulties, but in the main the political situation was largely responsible for the feeling of uncertainty. Paper manufacturers claimed that while the tariff on paper had been lower there had been no corresponding reduction of the import duty on the supplies required, which put other manufacturers, especially those of Canada, at a distinct advantage. In fact, the paper and pulp industry during 1912 was in a somewhat singular condition owing to developments that had followed the tariff legislation of the previous year. It will be recalled that in the act passed July 26, 1911, it was provided that irrespective of the acceptance of the reciprocity agreement by Canada that wood pulp of all kinds, news print paper, and other paper and pulp to the value of 4 cents per pound, would be admitted into the United States free of

PEDRO MIGUEL LOCKS, BIRDSEYE VIEW FROM HILL ON EAST BANK, JULY 28, 1912

PANAMA CANAL

duty, but only such pulp and paper were to be so admitted upon which there were no export restrictions or duties. This measure was duly passed by Congress, but the reciprocity agreement was rejected by Canada, so that the owners of private woodland in Canada secured a decided advantage in the markets of the United States, while those whose supplies of pulp were obtained from the crown forests were correspondingly handicapped. This led to serious dissatisfaction in Canada as well as in the United States, and throughout the year the entire situation was canvassed actively. With changed political conditions alterations in the tariff were anticipated. Toward the end of the year the British government removed the export restrictions from certain forests in Quebec, while from the western part of the Dominion pulp from crown lands imported into the United States was made a subject of controversy in the collection of duties, and the case was being argued before the general board of appraisers, with a strong probability of review by the courts. Furthermore, the importers of pulp from Europe claimed that they were being discriminated against under the most favored nation clause of the treaties which their governments enjoyed with the United States, and they accordingly made claim for the admission of their product on the same terms as the Canadian. This the United States government declined to concede, and the position was sustained in a decision by the board of general appraisers handed down on April 23. The decision was appealed to the Customs Court, but the hearing set for October was postponed.

The question, as in previous years, resolved itself into a contest between the newspaper publishers on the one side and the paper men on the other, and it was anticipated that in the tariff legislation of 1913 the paper and pulp schedules would be vigorously discussed.

The result of the passage of the McCall bill in July, 1911, was seen in increased activity in Canada, and not only were existing plants extended, but new ones were constructed, and during 1912 an increased amount of paper made its way into the United States so that at the end of the year 1912 the rate of importation from Canada was estimated at about 125,000 tons per year, of which 75 per cent. paid no duty. It was remarked by *The World's Paper Trade Review*, of London, in an editorial:

"Should the present tariff system existing between Canada and the United States continue, the outlook for the Canadian export trade is very rosy. United States paper men are pointing with alarm to the fact that between January and September 75,000,000 pounds of paper came into the Republic from Canada, free of duty; it is certain that every month of the coming year will only render this condition more pronounced."

In the United States Department of Agriculture at Washington, laboratory experiments in connection with the testing and investigation of paper and pulp materials were continued during the year. Greater standardization than ever was effected in the specifications for the paper used by the government and new processes were being studied. R. E. Doolittle, active chemist of the Department of Agriculture, in his annual report referring to the utilization of the waste long leaf pine for the making of paper and the recovery of wood turpentine, resin oil, and wood creosote, stated that the results so far obtained confirmed the opinion previously expressed by the bureau that the waste pine lumber of the South from the cut-off land could be utilized with profit, and would furnish one of the most promising fields of industrial development for the future.

PAPER TRUST. See TRUSTS.

PAPUA, TERRITORY OF (formerly British New Guinea). Part of the island of New Guinea, forming, with a number of small islands lying mostly to the southeast, a dependency of the Commonwealth of Australia. The area of the dependency is 90,540 square miles. The population, June 30, 1911, numbered 1032 (771 adult males); colored (other than Papuans), 450; half-castes, 280. The native population is estimated at between four and five hundred thousand. Port Moresby is the capital. The local industries are not numerous, but they are becoming more diversified. The soil is favorable to agriculture. On March 31, 1911, there were 167 plantations, with 9513 acres under cocoanuts, 2889 under rubber, 2332 under sisal hemp, 132 under coffee, and 1015 under various crops. The six government plantations cover 229 acres. About 350,000 acres have been planted to cocoanuts under the ordinance which obliges the natives to plant for food supply. About 400,000 superficial feet of log timber were exported to Australia in 1910-11. Pearl-fishing is followed; export of pearl-shell (1910-11), £1445; bêche-de-mer, sandal wood, rubber, copra, etc., are produced for export. Gold-mining is the chief occupation of the European population; yield (1910-11), 18,497 ozs. (£68,803). Pearl exports (1909-10), £4290. Imports (1910-11), £202,910; exports, £117,410; shipping entered and cleared, 300,244 tons. Revenue (1910-11), £45,972; expenditure, £70,699. J. H. P. Murray was lieutenant-governor in 1912. See ANTHROPOLOGY.

PARAGUAY. A South American republic bounded by Bolivia, Brazil, and Argentina. The capital is Asunción.

AREA AND POPULATION. The estimated area is 97,722 square miles. There is an unsettled boundary dispute with Bolivia. Population, census of 1899, 643,852; estimate of December 31, 1908, 715,841. An estimate of 1910 is 752,000, but it is not unlikely that this figure is too high; some authorities believe that on account of political disturbances, the population has decreased since 1904. The population is largely a mixture of Spanish, Guarani, and negro. The larger towns: Asunción, about 84,000 inhabitants; Villa Rica, 30,000; Concepción, 25,000; Carapeguá, 15,000; Luque, 15,000. Immigrants in 1909-10, 634; in 1910-11, 418.

In 1911 there were 485 public schools, with 861 teachers and about 45,000 pupils, and 57 private schools. The state religion is Roman Catholicism.

PRODUCTION AND COMMERCE. Paraguay is a country of exceptional natural resources, but internal conflicts have retarded progress. Unfortunately also much of the land has been alienated to foreign capitalists and syndicates. Stock-raising has become an important industry; the number of cattle probably exceeds 5,500,000. The leading agricultural products include yerba, maté, tobacco, corn, alfalfa, beans, manioc, and various fruits, especially oranges. The quantity of domestic tobacco marketed in 1909 is reported at 10,694,371 lbs.; in 1910, 12,396,031 lbs.; in 1911, 14,187,395 lbs. Promising industries are the cultivation of cotton and sugar. See AGRICULTURE.

Imports and exports have been valued as follows in gold pesos (worth 96.5 cents): 1906, 6,267,194 and 2,695,139; 1909, 3,787,951 and 5,136,639; 1910, 6,067,459 and 4,744,826. Leading exports in 1909 and 1910, in thousands of pesos: Hides, 1135 and 1178; timber, 980 and 1038; quebracho extract, 634 and 782; tobacco, 534 and 572; yerba maté, 554 and 522. Imports and exports by countries in 1910, in thousands of pesos: United Kingdom, 2601 and 15; Germany, 1101 and 873; Argentina, 672 and 2758; Italy, 333 and 83; France, 286 and 25; United States, 308 and 2; Uruguay, 44 and 513; other, 720 and 476.

COMMUNICATIONS. In 1911 there were 373 kilometers (232 miles) of railway. Asunción is connected with Encarnación, which is on the Paraná River opposite the Argentine town Posadas. Formerly the journey from Asunción to Buenos Aires, by river steamer, required about five days; it is now made by rail in about 53 hours. Telegraph, over 60 offices, with nearly 2500 miles of line; post offices, 385.

FINANCE. Revenue in 1910, 1,480,615 pesos gold and 22,002,226 pesos paper; estimated expenditures, 710,552 pesos gold and 27,094,948 paper. (The gold peso is valued at 96.5 cents, and the paper between 7½ and 8 cents.) For 1911, estimated revenue, 2,738,000 pesos gold and 9,190,500 paper; estimated expenditure, 999,412 pesos gold and 32,687,228 paper. On December 31, 1910, the English funded debt amounted to 3,920,717 pesos gold; floating debt, 600,000 gold; paper money (1908), 35,000,000.

GOVERNMENT. The constitution provides for the election of a president and vice-president by indirect vote for four years. Five members constitute the cabinet. The congress consists of the Senate and the Chamber of Deputies, members of both houses being elected directly.

HISTORY. In December, 1910, Manuel Gondra was inaugurated president. He was forced to resign in the following month, and Col. Albino Jara, the minister of war, assumed office as acting president. On July 5, 1911, Jara was seized by officers of the garrison at Asunción and compelled to resign, and on the next day Liberato Rojas, president of the Senate, was elected provisional president by the congress. Disturbed political conditions, amounting at times to civil war, continued for many months. In succession to Rojas, Pedro Pena assumed the presidency March 1, 1912. On the 22d of the same month revolutionists captured Asunción, Pena and his cabinet took refuge on foreign war vessels. On the 25th Emiliano González Navero became provisional president. The latter served as president in 1908-10; he was elected vice-president for the term beginning in 1906, but in 1908, as the result of a revolutionary movement, he superseded the president, Gen. Benigno Ferreira. On April 27, 1912, civil war was renewed. The revolutionists suffered defeat near Asunción on May 13, and on July 19 Eduardo Schaerer was elected president and Pedro Bobadilla vice-president for the four-year term beginning August 15, 1912. Ministry: J. Montero, interior; Eus. Ayala, foreign affairs; Jer Zubizarretta, finance; F. Paiva, justice, worship, and public instruction; Manuel Gondra, war.

PARCEL POST. For a considerable number of years there has been in the United States a general demand that the government establish a parcel post as an integral part of the post office department. The political parties have approved the establishment of such a system in their party platforms for more than a decade, but public opinion solidified slowly. There were a variety of proposals and time was needed to effect general agreement as to the wisest plan of procedure. Among the proposals were the following: The extension of the rural free delivery service, making possible the sending of parcels weighing up to eleven pounds; the purchase of the express companies by the government and their unification into a single public-owned and operated system; the organization of a government fast-freight system; and the introduction of a general system of parcel post such as is found in most European countries. One of the strongest arguments for the establishment of such a system was found in the high express rates and other causes of dissatisfaction with the express service. Comparison between the cost of transporting parcels of moderate weight in this country and in England and Germany showed the American cost to be five to ten times greater. The chief opposition to the introduction of the system was found in various trade and merchants' associations and the country storekeepers, who were feeling the competition of the retail mail-order houses of Chicago, New York, Philadelphia, and other large cities. The political power of the express companies was also a serious block to progress of the movement.

So strong, however, was the public demand for a general system that a bill establishing it was passed in Congress with almost no debate on the principle; indeed the press of the country for the most part, contented itself with explaining the provisions of the proposed law. As finally enacted in August the bill provided for the plotting of the country into units fifty miles square. The rates were to be determined by weight and distance, the country being divided into eight zones. The maximum weight allowed is eleven pounds. For city and suburban rural route delivery the rate will be five cents for the first pound and one cent for each additional pound, making a total charge of fifteen cents for the maximum weight of eleven pounds. Otherwise the zones and charges are as follows:

	First pound	Each additional pound	Eleven pounds
50-mile zone	$.05	$.03	$.35
150-mile zone	.06	.04	.46
300-mile zone	.07	.05	.57
600-mile zone	.08	.06	.68
1000-mile zone	.09	.07	.79
1400-mile zone	.10	.09	1.00
1800-mile zone	.11	.10	1.11
Over 1800 miles	.12	.12	1.32

The law provided that the parcels to be received should include all fourth class mail matter and "all other matter, including farm and factory products not now included in other classes of mail matter"; but no parcels should include matter likely to perish before the normal time required for delivery, or that might injure postal employees or damage other

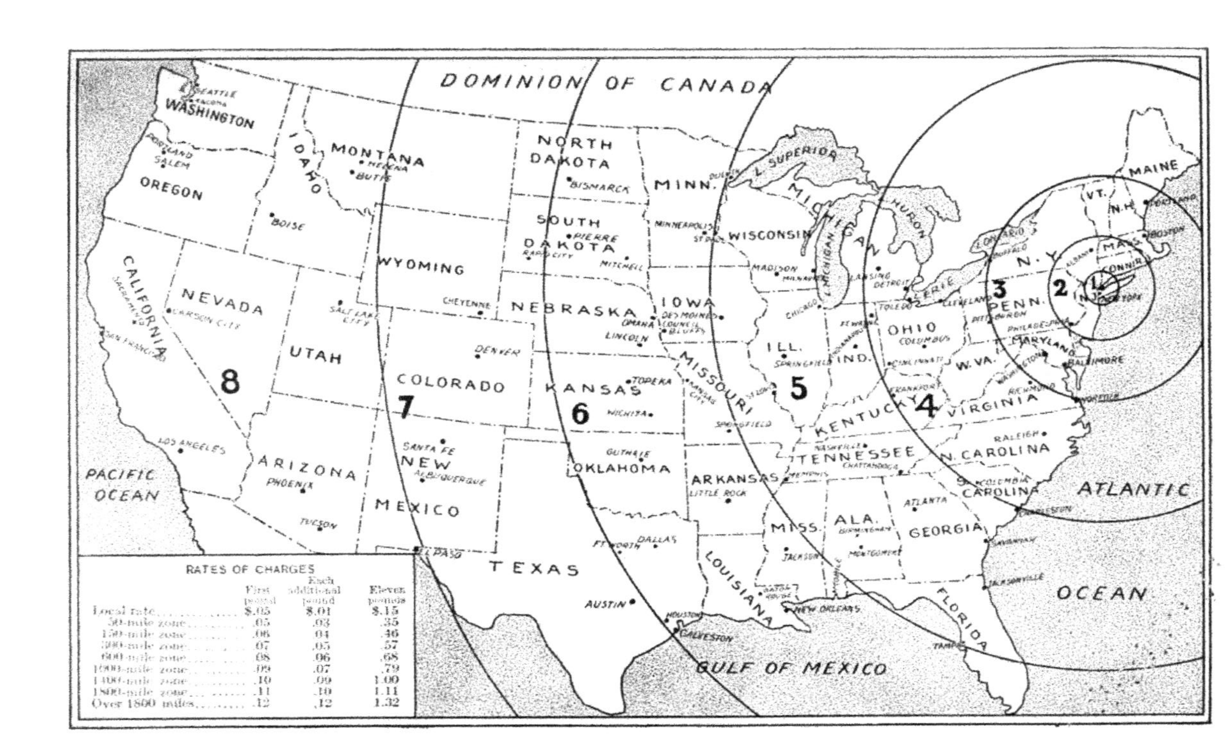

RATES OF CHARGES

	First pound	Each additional pound	Eleven pounds
Local rate	$.05	$.01	$.15
50-mile zone	.05	.03	.35
150-mile zone	.06	.04	.46
300-mile zone	.07	.05	.57
600-mile zone	.08	.06	.68
1000-mile zone	.09	.07	.79
1400-mile zone	.10	.09	1.00
1800-mile zone	.11	.10	1.11
Over 1800 miles	.12	.12	1.32

PARCEL POST RATE ZONES FROM NEW YORK CITY

THE UNITED STATES IS DIVIDED INTO DISTRICTS EACH FIFTY MILES SQUARE FROM THE CENTRE OF WHICH A SIMILAR ARRANGEMENT OF ZONES IS ESTABLISHED

mail matter. Articles excluded include intoxicants; poisons, other than medicinal; poisonous animals; inflammable articles, as matches and benzine; revolvers; live or dead animals, except stuffed specimens. Morever, the size of the package was limited to seventy inches in length and girth combined. The law provides that the Postmaster-General may change zone boundaries; and a congressional committee will keep special oversight of the operation of the system during its first year. Special red stamps for all fourth class matter and parcels are to be used as a means of determining the volume of business done. These stamps, labeled "U. S. Parcel Post," will be in twelve denominations ranging from one cent to one dollar. Special green postage due stamps are also provided. Parcels will not be received at drug store stations, but will be handled through central and branch offices, and sub-stations. A parcel may be insured against loss to the amount of $50 for ten cents.

Members of the Postal Progress League, which was largely instrumental in securing the passage of the law, were disappointed with the complicated system of charges. They declared that several country post offices must become the centre of an almost endless system of bookkeeping; that large maps differing for each zone would have to be provided; and that the post office officials would make numerous mistakes and cause many delays through the difficulty of understanding the system. In answer to this it was declared by prominent postal authorities that any parcel post rate could be determined in a few moments. During the last two months of the year extensive preparations were made for establishing the system on an efficient and nation-wide basis on January 1. Postmasters everywhere were given thoroughgoing instructions as to the rules and the organization of the system and united in gathering information as to the probable extent of its use. While the system was expected to prove of great advantage to the great mail-order houses, the zone system was expected to protect the smaller local merchants and even to increase their trade. It was estimated that about twenty million people who do not now have the services of any express company would be reached by tne parcel post. Department stores planned to make extensive use of the system.

Of special interest in connection with the establishment of the parcel post was the issuance of an order early in the fall by the Interstate Commerce Commission ordering the thirteen express companies of the country to show cause why they should not adopt a new schedule of charges. The commission had made an extensive inquiry covering 600,000 different express rates and an equal number of waybills and receipts. The order contained an elaborate system of proposed charges whereby the whole country was divided into blocks of fifty miles square, all the points in each block to be common, except as to adjacent blocks, rates to be scaled according to weights from one to 100 pounds, as well as distance, and to be posted in each office. Rates in general were directed to be reduced, and the companies were ordered to send packages by the most direct route. The same order also endeavored to meet complaints of over-charges and especially of duplicate charges by providing vari-colored waybills, receipts, and labels. These latter suggestions were at once adopted. Postmaster-General Hitchcock on December 28 declared that in his view the introduction of the parcels system would force the express companies to offer themselves for sale to the government. He favored such a purchase on a fair basis just as soon as the new system was well started. He pointed out that the rates established while higher than would probably be necessary were lower than express rates and would force a reduction in the latter. At the same time the parcel post rates were based on the principle of averages, so that they were quite low for long hauls but relatively high for short hauls. Government ownership of the express companies would make possible a new scale of short-distance rates.

PARIS. See ARCHITECTURE.

PARKER, ALTON B. See PRESIDENTIAL CAMPAIGN.

PARKS, JAMES LEWIS. An American Protestant Episcopal clergyman, died February 18, 1912. He was born in New York in 1838 and graduated from the General Theological Seminary in 1871. He was ordained to the priesthood in 1872 and served as rector in Oakland, Cal.; Middletown, Conn., and Philadelphia, and from 1896 to 1910 in Calvary Church, New York City.

PARSEVAL AIRSHIPS. See AERONAUTICS, and NAVAL PROGRESS.

PARTICLES. See PHYSICS.

PASADENA. See GARBAGE AND REFUSE DISPOSAL.

PASSY, FRÉDÉRIC. A French economist and peace advocate, died June 12, 1912. He was born in Paris in 1822. He was educated as a lawyer, but entered the government service as auditor of the Council of State. From 1881 to 1889 he was a member of the Chamber of Deputies. During the same period and until his retirement in 1902 he was professor of political economy in several colleges. He always took a profound interest in the cause of general peace and was one of the founders of the International and Permanent League of Peace, which was organized in 1867. He became permanent secretary of the society. In 1888 with M. W. Randal-Cremer he founded the Interparliamentary Union for Arbitration and Peace. He was also a member of the International Bureau of Peace at Bern, Switzerland. In 1901 he received the Nobel peace prize and was the first recipient of that prize. He was commander of the Legion of Honor and a member of the Moral and Political Science Academy of the French Institute. He wrote several books on economics and philosophy and also published a volume of verse.

PATENT MONOPOLY. See TRUSTS.

PATENTS. See UNITED STATES, and TRUSTS.

PATERSON STRIKE. See STRIKES.

PAVEMENTS. See ROADS AND PAVEMENTS.

PAYNE-ALDRICH LAW. See TARIFF.

PEABODY MUSEUM OF HARVARD UNIVERSITY. An institution for anthropological and archæological research, founded in 1866 by George Peabody. The most important event in the history of the museum in 1912 was the appointment, by the Corporation of Harvard University, of a committee to raise money for the completion of the University Museum Building. This one remaining section of the building will belong to the Peabody Museum and will give the much-needed space and facilities for the proper development of the museum. Several important explorations were carried on under the direction of the museum. During the year, Dr. Charles Peabody, in charge of the European section, gave to the museum a very important collection of bone and stone objects from the Cavern of Espélugues, at Lourdes, France. Dr. Peabody was in Europe during the summer of 1912, and represented the museum at several European anthropological congresses, and also carried on investigations in prehistoric archæology of England and France. Explorations were also carried on for the museum in the Delaware Valley by the continuation of the extended research of Mr. Ernest Volk for traces of glacial man in America; in the southwest by Mr. A. V. Kidder, among the ruined pueblos and cliff-houses, where he continued his special study of types of pottery and their distribution; in the Charles River Valley, Massachusetts, where Mr. S. J. Guernsey discovered and examined several rock shelters and caches of stone implements; at Martha's Vineyard, where Mr. Guernsey located prehistoric burial places, village sites, and shell heaps; and in Douglas County, Nebraska, where Mr. F. H. Stearns explored several prehistoric habitation sites with interesting results. The Central American Expedition was in the field in 1911-12 and a number of ancient sites were discovered in Southern Yucatan, north of the Rio Hondo.

In the Division of Anthropology, Assistant Professor R. B. Dixon was granted leave of absence in the year 1912-13 to travel in the Far East. He is carrying on researches in the ethnology and linguistics of the Hill tribes of India. A new course on the Ethnography of Asia has been added to the courses in this division. The officers of the museum in 1912 were: President, Abbott Lawrence Lowell; honorary curator, Frederic W. Putnam; librarian, Roland B. Dixon; secretary, Frances H. Mead.

PEACE, INTERNATIONAL, CARNEGIE ENDOWMENT FOR. For the establishment of this endowment Mr. Andrew Carnegie gave in 1911 $10,000,000. Its general purpose, as its title indicates, is the promotion of international peace. For administrative purposes the work is divided into three divisions: Division of Intercourse and Education, directed by Nicholas Murray Butler, president of Columbia University; Division of International Law, directed by Dr. James Brown Scott; and Division of Economics and History, directed by Professor John Bates Clark. The president of the executive committee is Elihu Root. The most important event in connection with the endowment in 1912 was the world tour made by Dr. Charles W. Eliot, formerly president of Harvard University. The general purpose of Dr. Eliot was to test the sentiment in foreign countries as to the best methods for the solution of the problem for the amelioration of which the endowment was organized. During his visit in Ceylon, Dr. Eliot was ill for some time with appendicitis but fortunately recovered. Under the auspices of the endowment Dr. Inazo Nitobe, of Japan visited the United States in 1912.

The endowment has financial charge of the American branch of the Association for International Conciliation, of which Dr. Butler is the American head and Baron D'Estournelle de Constant is president-general.

PEACE MOVEMENT. See ARBITRATION, INTERNATIONAL.

PEARL HARBOR DRY DOCK. See DOCKS AND HARBORS.

PEARSONS, DANIEL KIMBALL. An American physician and philanthropist, died April 27, 1912. He was born in Bradford, Vt., in 1820, and was educated in the public schools of that State. His first days were spent on a farm and he was prevented by poverty from obtaining a college education. He spent one year at Dartmouth College, but was unable to continue. After several years spent in saving he studied at the Medical School at Woodstock, Vt., and received his degree in 1842. Until 1857 he practiced medicine in Chicopee, Mass. In that year he removed to Illinois and ultimately settled at Hinsdale, near Chicago. He saw profits in real estate investment, and giving up the practice of medicine engaged in the business of buying and selling land. He was successful at this and later removed to Chicago. After the Chicago fire he accumulated a large fortune. In 1873 he retired from active business, but remained the director in several financial institutions. He was greatly interested in the work of the American colleges and, as he had no relatives, he resolved to distribute his fortune to such of these institutions as needed and deserved assistance while he was still alive. He continued this distribution until within a year of his death, when he had practically given away his entire fortune. He is known to have given assistance to forty-four colleges, and in addition to a dozen or more societies and other institutions. The amounts given were, for the most part, comparatively small. His largest benefaction was $600,000. This was to Beloit College, Wisconsin. His total donations to colleges and charities aggregated over $4,000,000. These included $280,000 to the Chicago Theological Seminary, $150,000 to Mount Holyoke College, and $100,000 to Lake Forest University. With each gift was coupled the requirement that a larger sum must be raised from other sources before his gift became available. The colleges which he assisted were chiefly in the Middle West, the South, and the Far West. The larger universities did not receive help from him, as he declared they were abundantly provided for from other sources.

PEAT. See CHEMISTRY, INDUSTRIAL.

PEEL, ARTHUR WELLESLEY, Viscount. An English public official, died October 24, 1912. He was born in 1829, the youngest son of the famous Sir Robert Peel. He was educated at Eton and Balliol, Oxford, taking his degree in 1852. In 1865 he began his career of thirty years in the House of Commons as Liberal member from Warwick. He represented that town until 1885, and from 1885 to 1895 the joint boroughs of Warwick and Leamington. In 1868 when Mr. Gladstone formed his first ministry, which remained in power for more than five years, Peel served as parliamentary secretary to the Poor Law Board, as secretary to the Board of Trade, and as patronage secretary to the Treasury. The last position is the official title of the "whip" of the party. Except for a few months of office in 1880 as under secretary to the Home Department, these were his only official appointments. In 1884 he was nominated speaker of the House of Commons to succeed Sir Henry Brand and he was unanimously elected. The speech which he delivered on the occasion of his election was a memorable one in the modern history of the House of Commons.

He assumed the duties of speaker at a time when, as a result of disturbances created by Irish members, the speakership was invested with powers and duties that had not formerly accompanied that office. He was three times reëlected speaker and retired in April, 1895. The eleven years of his speakership covered an exciting and eventful period. They saw the end of the Gladstone government of 1880, the beginning and the end of Lord Salisbury's administration, the last administration of Gladstone, and the whole of Lord Randolph Churchill's official career. They also included special commission debates, the beginning and end of two home rule bills, and the disruption of the Liberal party. On his retirement in 1895 Mr. Peel became Viscount Peel. After his retirement as speaker he held several civic offices. He was chairman of the British commission to the St. Louis Exposition.

PEFFER, WILLIAM. Former United States senator from Kansas and founder of the Populist party, died October 7, 1912. He was born in Cumberland County, Pa., in 1831. He taught school when he was fifteen years of age and between terms worked on his father's farm. At the age of twenty-one he removed to the West and in the second year of the Civil War enlisted as a private in the 83d Regiment of Illinois Volunteers He served throughout the war and was mustered out with the rank of lieutenant. After the close of the war he removed to Clarksville, Tenn., and there began the practice of law. Soon after he removed to Kansas, where he lived for the rest of his life. He established two country newspapers and in 1874 was elected to the State Senate. He was Republican presidential elector in 1880. In 1891 a wave of Populism arose in the West, and Peffer was elected to the United States Senate as a Populist. Seven years later, when he had retired from the Senate, he was Prohibition candidate for governor. From that time until his death his time was occupied in writing. Senator Peffer was one of the first persons in public life to attack Wall Street. He fought "intrenched capital" and "vested interests" with the greatest vigor. He was a striking figure in the Senate during his period of service. His beard, which covered his face and extended half way to his waist, became famous throughout the country and furnished abundant material for cartoonists and humorists. He introduced many bills covering the contentions of Populism while he was in the Senate, but none of these were passed. For some time before his death he had been engaged upon a history of Populism, which was to have been kept in the archives of the Kansas State Historical Society. In order that he might live long enough to complete this work he suffered the amputation of a leg a few months before his death. He wrote, in 1900, *The Rise and Fall of Populism in the United States*, and he contributed several articles on the subject to magazines.

PEKING. See CHINA.

PELLAGRA. The National Association for the study of pellagra held its triennial meeting at Columbia, S. C., October 3 and 4, to discuss the disease, which has become a subject of grave concern, particularly in the South. While its exact etiology is still underdetermined and no definite form of treatment has been devised, the tendency of opinion is toward a hopeful prognosis when treatment is begun before the disease is too far advanced. After 200 years of study in European countries, the pellagra problem still awaits elucidation.

Three theories have been advanced as to the cause of the disease: (1) The zeistic theory of Ballardini, dating from 1845, giving corn poison from excessive use of corn products as the cause, supplanting the old theory of faulty metabolism; (2) the cotton seed products poison theory of Mizell, in 1911, and (3) the sand-fly theory of Sambon, dating from 1910. The first two rest on malnutrition, the last on the action of a parasite. Sambon's investigations were made in Italy and his conclusions were so well grounded that, the spoiled-maize theory having failed to find sufficiently strong supporting evidence in this country, attempts were made to substantiate Sambon's findings here. The grounds on which Sambon based his conclusions may be outlined as follows: (1) The endemic centres of pellagra in Italy have remained the same since the disease was first described; (2) the pellagra season coincides with the season of the appearance of the full-fledged sand-fly, even to the extent that if the spring is early or late the sand-fly is early or late in appearing, and pellagra cases are correspondingly early or late in their appearance; (3) in centres of pellagra infection whole families are attacked simultaneously; (4) in non-pellagrous districts the disease does not spread with the advent of a pellagrin from a pellagrous district; (5) where a family has removed from a pellagrous to a non-pellagrous district the children born in the former districts are pellagrins, while the children born subsequent to removal do not develop the disease; (6) the disease is not hereditary, although infants a few months old may become infected, especially if taken to the fields where their mothers work during the sand-fly season; (7) pellagra is not contagious, but is transmitted to each individual by an infected sand-fly.

As noted in the last YEAR BOOK, Roberts, of Georgia, found conditions in his section of the country similar to those described by Sambon in Italy. A like investigation in Kansas was later undertaken by Prof. S. J. Hunter, whose work is not yet completed, but the evidence thus far obtained points to the sand-fly as a probable cause. The only species of sand-fly found in Kansas thus far is *Simulium vittatum*. *Simulium reptans* is the species referred to by Sambon, reported on this continent from Greenland only. *Simulium vittatum* is distributed in Kansas along Turkey Creek, a tributary of the Kaw, in Wyandotte County; along the Marais des Cygnes in Franklin County; along the Neosho and its tributaries in Labette County, and along the Arkansas in Sedgwick County. Cases of pellagra have been reported in Allen, Chautauqua, Labette, Meade, and Montgomery counties. All are in the sand-fly territory. None of the patients have been out of the State, so it seems that the cause is local.

BIBLIOGRAPHY. *A Preliminary Study of Kentucky Localities in Which Pellagra Is Prevalent. Having Reference to the Conditions of the Corn Crop and to the Possible Presence of an Insect or the Other Agent by Which the Disease Spreads* (Bulletin 159, Kentucky Agricultural Experiment Station of the State University); *Pellagra, an American Problem*, by George M. Niles, M. D. (Philadelphia, 1912), and *Pellagra*, by E. J. Wood, M. D. (New York, 1912).

PENANG. See STRAITS SETTLEMENTS.

PENNSYLVANIA. POPULATION. According to the Census Bureau statistics compiled in 1912, out of the total population in 1910, 7,665,111, the foreign-born whites numbered 1,438,719, compared with 982,543 in 1900. The largest number, 252,083, came from Austria; from Russia, 239,262; from Italy, 196,040; from Germany, 194,829; from Hungary, 122,471; and from England, 109,172. All the other countries of Europe contributed to the foreign-born white population. In Philadelphia, with a population in 1910 of 1,549,008, the foreign-born white population numbered 382,578. Of these, 89,094 came from Russia; 83,073 from Ireland, and 61,235 from Germany. In Pittsburgh, with a population of 533,905, the foreign-born whites numbered 140,436. Of these, 29,438 came from Germany and 26,271 from Russia. The negroes in the State in 1910 numbered 193,919 and the mulattoes 37,154. In 1890 the negroes numbered 107,596 and the mulattoes 25,710.

AGRICULTURE. The acreage, value, and production of the principal crops in 1911 and 1912 are given in the table below:

		Acreage.	Prod. Bu.	Value.
Corn	1912	1,449,000	61,582,000	$38,797,000
	1911	1,435,000	63,858,000	43,423,000
Wheat	1912	1,240,000	22,320,000	21,204,000
	1911	1,289,000	17,402,000	16,010,000
Oats	1912	1,099,000	36,377,000	14,915,000
	1911	1,121,000	31,724,000	15,862,000
Rye	1912	282,000	4,935,000	3,800,000
	1911	285,000	4,304,000	3,443,000
Potatoes	1912	265,000	28,885,000	16,464,000
	1911	270,000	15,120,000	14,062,000
Hay	1912	3,173,000	a 4,537,000	70,777,000
	1911	3,148,000	a 3,148,000	62,960,000
Tobacco	1912	44,200	b 64,090,000	5,448,000
	1911	46,000	b 65,320,000	6,205,400

a Tons. b Pounds.

MINERAL PRODUCTION. The production of iron ore in 1911 was 514,929 long tons, valued at $539,553, compared with 739,799 long tons produced in 1910, with a value of $911,847.

The production of anthracite coal in the State in 1911, according to the United States Geological Survey, broke all previous records except the maximum output in 1907. The returns for 1911 showed a total production of 80,732,015 long tons, valued at $174,852,843. This was an increase over the output of 1910 of 5,298,607 long tons in quantity and $14,577,541 in value. The greater production of anthracite in 1911 was probably due to the increased activity in anticipation of a possible coal strike in April. The extremely severe weather of the winter 1910-11, however, practically exhausted any accumulated coal before the termination of the three-year period of wage agreements on March 31, 1912.

The production of bituminous coal in the State in 1911 was 144,721,303 short tons, valued at $146,311,930. This was a decrease of 5,800,223 short tons from the production of 1910. The decrease was almost entirely in that portion of the product used for the manufacture of coke. Except for this the coal trade in 1911 was well maintained and indicates that general industrial conditions were satisfactory. The number of men employed in the coal mines of the State in 1911 was 341,126, of whom 168,541 were engaged in soft coal mining.

The total production of petroleum in the State in 1911 was 8,247,728 barrels, compared with 8,794,662 barrels in 1910. The production in the State has shown a decerase for several years. In 1907 it was approximately 10,000,000 barrels. Several new wells were drilled with successful results in 1911, but the increase resulting from these was not sufficient to prevent a decrease in the production of the State.

MANUFACTURES. The Thirteenth Census statistics are for the calendar year 1909 and were compiled in 1912. Pennsylvania is one of the leading States in manufacturing. It holds second place, being surpassed only by New York. The growth of manufactures has been steady since their beginning in 1849, when the first authoritative census was taken. From the following table it will be seen that in 1909 there were in the State 27,563 manufacturing establishments, which gave employment to an average of 1,002,171 persons.

	Number or Amount 1909	1904	P. C. of Inc. 1904-'09
Number of establishments	27,563	23,495	17.3
Persons engaged in manufactures	1,002,171	855,392	17.2
Proprietors and firm members	29,743	26,029	14.3
Sal'd employees	94,885	66,081	43.6
Wage earners (average number)	877,543	763,282	15.0
Primary h. p.	2,921,547	2,302,398	26.9
Capital	$2,749,006,000	$1,995,837,000	37.7
Expenses	2,355,385,000	1,751,440,000	34.5
Services	566,524,000	441,230,000	28.4
Salaries	110,897,000	73,269,000	51.4
Wages	455,627,000	367,961,000	23.8
Materials	1,582,560,000	1,142,943,000	38.5
Miscellaneous	206,301,000	167,267,000	23.3
Value of products	2,626,742,000	1,955,551,000	34.3
Value of products less cost of materials	1,044,182,000	812,608,000	28.5

The largest value of products was in manufactures of iron and steel, $500,344,000; foundry and machine-shop products were valued at $210,746,000; iron and steel blast furnaces, $168,578,000; leather, $77,926,000; woolen, worsted, and felt goods, $77,447,000. Other manufactures in which the value of the product was more than $50,000,000 were industries connected with railways, printing and publishing, silk and silk goods, lumber and timber products, petroleum, slaughtering and meat-packing, manufacture of coke, and tobacco manufactures. The total number of persons engaged in manufactures in the State in 1909 was 1,002,171. Of these, 802,548 were male and 199,623 were female. The number of persons under 16 years of age employed was 29,107. The prevailing hours of labor for the majority of wage earners ranged from 54 to 60 a week; only 12.3 per cent. of the total being employed in establishments where less than 54 hours a week prevailed, and only 11.4 per cent. in establishments where the hours of labor were more than 60 a week. The largest number of wage earners was in Philadelphia, 251,884; in Pittsburgh, 67,474; in Reading, 24,145; in Scranton, 12,851; in Allentown, 11,481, and in Johnstown, 10,574. The value of the products in Philadelphia was $746,075,659, and in Pittsburgh $243,453,693.

EDUCATION. There were on June 30, 1912, 1,322,254 pupils of school age in the State. The average number of pupils in daily attendance was 1,061,673. There were 36,945 teachers employed, of whom 8154 were males and 28,791 females. The average salary of male teachers per month was $65.04 and of female teachers $48.41. There were 35,719 schools, with 15,207 schoolhouses. The first-grade high schools numbered 155, the second-grade high schools 259, and the third-grade high schools 442. The expenditure for teachers' wages was $21,137,685. For schoolhouses there was expended $7,309,527. The total expenditures amounted to $42,557,986.

FINANCE. The report of the State treasurer showed a balance in the treasury at the beginning of the fiscal year 1912 of $12,923,370. The total receipts for the fiscal year ending December 31, 1912, amounted to $32,374,890 and the total disbursements to $35,516,410, leaving a balance in the treasury on December 1, 1912, of $9,781,850. The principal receipts are from taxes on corporations, taxes on personal property, and taxes on collateral inheritance. The chief disbursements are for State institutions, for public schools, and for the maintenance and construction of highways. The total public debt at the end of the fiscal year was $659,160. The sinking fund assets amounted to $785,510, leaving a net surplus in the sinking fund of $126,350.

CHARITIES AND CORRECTIONS. The charities and corrections of the State are under the control of the Board of Public Charities. During 1912 two new State institutions for the care of the insane were established. These were the Homœopathic State Hospital for the Insane at Rittersville and the State Hospital for the Criminal Insane at Farview. There were also two new State hospitals, the State Hospital of Coaldale in Schuylkill County and the State Hospital of Nanticoke in Luzerne County. These hospitals were private institutions prior to 1912.

POLITICS AND GOVERNMENT

The political year in Pennsylvania was one of the most remarkable in the history of the State. The Republican party was rent into factions and nominally, a new State leader was created. The State, always strongly Republican, had for years given its support to the Republican candidate for President under the guidance of the party machine, controlled by Senator Penrose, which, till the rise of the Progressive wing of the party in the State, had been considered invulnerable. In the case of the Democratic party, too, the old order was changed and the party went through a "reorganization" led by antagonists of James M. Guffey, who had previously held the predominating power over the Democratic party in the State.

Among the first advocates of the candidacy of Mr. Roosevelt for a third term was E. A. Van Valkenburg, editor of the *Philadelphia North American*. He was joined in his efforts by William Flinn, for twenty years known as the political "boss" of Pittsburgh. An aggressive campaign throughout the State was carried on by these leaders and others in behalf of the Progressive element of the party prior to the primary election for delegates to the national and State conventions, held on April 13. The result of this primary was a surprise even for those who had been confident of the success of the election of Roosevelt delegates. Out of the total number of 76 national delegates, which included 12 delegates-at-large, 67 were elected by Mr. Roosevelt's supporters. Aside from its national significance the most important result of the election was the wresting of control of the Republican organization from Senator Penrose, who since the death of Senator Quay had been the Republican leader of the State. The election apparently placed Mr. Flinn in almost absolute power as political dictator of the State.

The Republican State convention held at Harrisburg on May 1, instructed the delegates-at-large of the State to vote for Mr. Roosevelt for President, indorsed his policies, nominated the anti-Penrose State ticket, and practically turned the party machinery over to Mr. Flinn and Mr. Van Valkenburg. The rout of the old Republican organization was complete. The only roll call was on the office of State treasurer and this, by a vote of 244 to 208, nominated the candidate of the Progressive wing. The followers of Senator Penrose made no other efforts to stand against the heavy odds and the prearranged programme of the Roosevelt wing went through without change. The State officers nominated at this convention were Robert K. Young for State treasurer and Archibald W. Powell for auditor-general. The convention also nominated four congressmen-at-large. The platform adopted was a radical one. Among its demands were direct presidential primaries, direct election of United States senators, a definition of the purposes for which money may be contributed and spent in general and primary elections and a limit for total expenditure, the public utilities law, employers' liability and workmen's compensation act, and immediate State appropriations for the Lake Erie and Ohio River ship canal. Declaration was also made for the recall of judges and similar plans advocated by Mr. Roosevelt.

The victory of the Roosevelt faction in the primary and in the State convention gave rise to complications. Taft and Sherman being nominated by the Republican national convention, their names were to stand at the head of the Republican column on the ballot to be voted at the general election in November. The electors-at-large nominated by the State convention and the district electors chosen at the primary by the Roosevelt-Flinn wing declared they would vote for Roosevelt and Johnson in the electoral college, despite the fact that Roosevelt and Flinn both had betaken themselves out of the Republican party and had joined in forming the Progressive party. Republicans demanded that the Progressive electors withdraw from the Republican ticket, permitting them to nominate for electors men who would support Taft in the electoral college. The Progressives, meantime, had filed nominations under three party titles—Bull Moose, Roosevelt Progressive, and Washington party—the last named being the designation officially chosen by the leaders of the new organization. The Progressives persisting in their determination to keep their electors in the Republican column though declaring their intention to vote against Taft, a plan was proposed by Philadelphia Republicans that the regular Republicans place a ticket of their own in the field with a view to defeating the Progressive State ticket. This division of the Republican forces might have given the Democrats the control of the State. The Roosevelt wing was anxious to avoid such a possibility. A proposal was made by Mr. Flinn that the electors should vote for Mr. Taft or for Mr. Roosevelt, their action depending upon the popular majority cast for one or the other. Mr. Roosevelt refused to consider this suggestion and declared that he would not assent to any agreement which recognized Mr. Taft as a candidate of the Republican party. He said: "I claim that in every primary State where the primaries were carried for me and where electors have been nominated, that as a matter of the highest moral obligation these men are bound to vote for me, for I am the nominee of the overwhelming majority of the rank and file of the Republican party, and Mr. Taft's nomination represents nothing but the successful dishonesty of the Barnes-Penrose-Guggenheim machine and is not binding on any honest Republican. In certain of these primary States, as I understand it, there is now a contest on in the primaries to see whether my name or that of Mr. Taft was to be put on the regular ticket instead of being nominated by petition, it being the intention of the party beaten in the primary to nominate its electors by petition. This is all right and proper; but so far as I have any say in the matter, I shall not assent to any arrangement by which, under any circumstances, my supporters, or electors supported by them, shall cast their votes for Mr. Taft." After a consultation between the leaders of the Progressive and Republican campaigns a compromise was finally arrived at by which the 27 presidential electors who were for Mr. Roosevelt withdrew from the Republican ticket and the Republican State committee replaced their names with 27 Taft men. At the same time it was agreed that no new party ticket should be put in the field.

In the Democratic primary held on April 13, Governor Wilson had practically no opposition. Both the old organization under the control of James M. Guffey, and the reorganization faction of the party indorsed him for the presidential nomination. In the Democratic State convention held on May 7, the control of the party machinery, as noted above, was wrested from Mr. Guffey and his associates by a combination headed by Congressman A. Mitchell Palmer, George W. Guthrie, former mayor of Pittsburgh, and Vance C. McCormick, former mayor of Harrisburg. As a result of these conditions Mr. Palmer was elected national committeeman to succeed Mr. Guffey. William H. Berry was nominated for State treasurer and Robert E. Cresswell for auditor-general. Four nominees for congressman-at-large were also nominated. Twelve delegates-at-large were elected to the national convention and were instructed to vote for Woodrow Wilson as long as his name should be before the convention. The platform adopted contained a plank calling for an immediate referendum in the State on the subject of votes for women. The platform declared that the three great issues of the day are the restoration of representative government, the restraining of the judiciary to its proper office, and the revision of the tariff. The initiative and referendum were indorsed and also the separation of judicial and legislative functions "so that courts shall cease their interfering with the legislature in the exercise of the police power and shall be relieved of all executive functions."

The election on November 5 resulted as follows: Wilson, 395,619; Roosevelt, 447,426; Taft, 273,305; Debs, 80,915; Chafin, 19,533; and Reimer, 704. The Republicans and Progressives combined elected the four congressmen-at-large the State treasurer, and auditor-general. The State legislature is Republican on joint ballot by a majority of 65.

OTHER EVENTS. In June Mayor Blankenburg of Philadelphia appointed a committee of 21 prominent residents, four of whom were women, to make an investigation concerning vice in Philadelphia. On September 25 there was celebrated at Altoona a semi-centennial of the meeting of the fourteen loyal governors who pledged to President Lincoln their support. President Taft was present and took part in the ceremonies.

STATE GOVERNMENT. Governor, John K. Tener; lieutenant-governor, John M. Reynolds; secretary of the commonwealth, Robert R. McAfee; treasurer, C. F. Wright; auditor-general, A. E. Sisson; adjutant-general, Thomas J. Stewart; attorney-general, John C. Bell; superintendent of public instruction, N. C. Schaeffer; insurance commissioner, C. Johnson; commissioner of agriculture, N. B. Critchfield—all Republicans, except Schaeffer, Democrat.

JUDICIARY. Supreme Court: Chief justice, D. Newlin Fell; associate justices, J. Hay Brown, William P. Potter, John Stewart, Robert Von Moschzisker, S. L. Mestrezat, and John P. Elkin—all Republicans, except Mestrezat. Prothonotary, eastern district, James T. Mitchell; prothonotary, middle district, William Pearson; prothonotary, western district, George Pearson.

STATE LEGISLATURE, 1913. Democrats, Senate, 15; House, 56; joint ballot, 71. Republicans, Senate, 34; House, 127; joint ballot, 161. Progressives, Senate, 1; House, 24; joint ballot, 25. Republican majority, Senate, 18; House, 47; joint ballot, 65.

The representatives in Congress will be found in the section *Congress*, article UNITED STATES.

PENNSYLVANIA STATE COLLEGE. An institution of higher learning at State College, Pa., founded in 1855. The enrollment in all departments of the university in the autumn of 1912, was 1914. The faculty numbered 190. The position of dean of the faculty was created at the beginning of the collegiate year 1912-13. Dr. Arthur Holmes of the University of Pennsylvania was appointed to fill this position. Other new chairs were those of biblical literature, which was filled by Rev. Robert Rush Reed of Princeton, and that of music, to which Prof. C. C. Robinson of Oklahoma University was elected. Dr. J. A. Moyer was appointed professor of mechanical engineering; and W. H. Tomhave, professor of animal husbandry. The only noteworthy benefaction during the year was a legacy of $8000 to the college Y. M. C. A. The productive funds amount to $567,000, and the total income to $725,596. The library contained 46,188 volumes.

PENNSYLVANIA, UNIVERSITY OF. The

enrollment in all departments of the university in the autumn of 1912 was about 5100. The faculty numbered 549. A radical change in the faculty and curriculum of the university was made in September, 1912. Under this readjustment the Wharton School of Finance and Commerce was given self-government, and James E. Young, formerly director, was replaced by Roswell Cheney McCrea, formerly of the New York School of Philanthropy. Dr. McCrea had previously been teaching in the university for about five months. The Towne scientific school was placed in charge of all the technical courses of the university, and Dr. John Frazer was made dean. Dr. Arthur Hobson Quinn was made dean of the college department, embracing the departments of arts and science, with the summer and post-graduate courses. Robert Heywood Fernald was placed at the head of the mechanical engineering course. In the medical school, Dr. William Pepper was appointed dean to succeed Dr. Allen J. Smith, who will devote his time to his professorship in pathology. Two new professors to fill the vacancies caused by the deaths of Dr. Thomas H. Montgomery, professor of zoölogy, and Dr. Henry M. Spangler, professor of mechanical engineering, were appointed. These were Dr. Clarence E. McClung, to succeed Dr. Montgomery, and Dr. Robert H. Fernald, to succeed Dr. Spangler. Dr. Eric Doolittle was appointed professor of astronomy to succeed his father, who resigned on account of advanced age. Prof. Clarence D. Childs was appointed to fill the chair of English comparative philology, made vacant by the resignation of Dr. Morton W. Easton. Prof. David W. Amram was appointed to fill the vacancy in the chair of practice in the law school, made vacant by the resignation of John W. Batton, and William G. Lloyd and Ralph Baker were appointed assistant professors of law. There were, in addition, many minor changes in the faculty. The provost is Edgar F. Smith, Ph. D.

PENOLOGY. Concurrently with the shift of emphasis in social theory from individual responsibility to social responsibility there have gone on changes in theories of criminology and in theories of punishment. Coördinated with the theory that the individual was solely responsible for a criminal act was the theory that society should take revenge on the individual for his unsocial conduct. With the development, however, of the doctrine that the criminal is due largely to bad social conditions there has grown up the theory that he should not be punished in a revengeful manner, but put through a process of character reconstruction. Consequently old types of prisons with dark cells, excessive isolation of the prisoner, and ingenious methods of inflicting torture are being replaced by new types of prisons with more open and brighter cells, and new methods of management, designed to reform the character, build up self-respect, and raise the economic efficiency of the convict. Along with the reformatory, with its new ideas of prison labor, have come the systems of parole and probation. These are designed to place the convict who is deemed worthy on his own responsibility in society, but under the temporary guidance of skilled official advisers. The indeterminate sentence also is being widely adopted on the ground that society desires not to punish the convicted person, but rather to restore in him normal social traits and to protect itself from abnormal conduct. Not only are modern prisons made sanitary and wholesome humane treatment with provision for recreation introduced, but prison schools with cultural and vocational training are being developed. In Oregon, Washington, Oklahoma, Kansas, Arizona, and some other States prisoners have been placed upon their honor in greater and greater numbers. This policy has been applied not only to prisoners within the walls, but also increasingly to the larger numbers now being employed in the building of highways and public institutions. In Canada, and also now in the United States, prison farms are coming to be extensively used. Moreover, in the more advanced prisons the inmates are now paid moderate sums for their labor, these wages being sent to his family, if he be married, or saved for him until his release. Released convicts are being assisted by various bodies to regain a normal social status. One of the most important movements is that for the reform of the county jail in the United States and the local prisons in Europe. This involves the separation of the sexes; and special facilities and methods for the treatment of delinquent boys and girls. Special courts and reform institutions are being developed for wayward girls and women. Very recently about eight States have assented to the principle of sterilization of certain classes of congenital criminals.

STATISTICS. The latest general statistics of prisoners in the United States showed that on January 1, 1911, there were in American prisons 113,579 persons. The total number of commitments during the preceding year was 479,-763. This number included persons convicted of every class of offense, from vagrancy to murder in the first degree. The numberof prisoners per 100,000 population was 125; it ranged from 48 in South Dakota to 353 in Nevada. The number of commitments per 100,000 population ranged from 123 in North Carolina to 2992 in Arizona. The differences were explained as due primarily to differences in laws and in the vigor of police enforcement and not as indicating differences in degrees of criminality in the population.

PRISON LABOR. Probably the most important question of penology in 1912, in the United States dealt with the best method of utilizing the labor of convicts. Methods found in this country may be classed as private management or State management systems. The systems of private management include the lease and contract systems; the others, the public account and State use systems. The convict lease system was, until recently, extensively employed in the southern States, but has been almost eliminated. By it convicts are leased or hired to contractors, who work them in mines, quarries, lumber camps, or otherwise under conditions mainly prescribed by the contractors. The per capita price to the State was small, but often aggregated a considerable addition to State income. In practice, however, this system amounted to a form of peonage or slavery in many respects much worse than that preceding 1860. The contract system, while often much superior, is often even worse. By this system the contractor is supplied at the prison with factory room, storage facilities, heat, light, and power. He hires the prisoners on a per head per diem basis, usually of 40 to 60 cents, or at a piece price rate. Here again the prisoners become the contractor's slaves. They are employed in the manufacture of hollow-ware, shirts, overalls, chairs, boots and shoes, brushes, mats, and brooms. Their product thus competes with the product of free labor in the open market; and the prisoner usually does not learn a trade which provides him a secure economic status when released. He often is forced to compete with the women and children of the unskilled class while a prisoner; and he continues to compete with these persons and with prisoners after release. During the year considerable rivalry developed between the governors of Arkansas and South Carolina in pardoning convicts because of the unwholesome conditions in the prison factories of those States. See ARKANSAS and SOUTH CAROLINA. Everywhere control by the State is replacing the systems of private lease or contract. Under the State account and State use systems prisoners may be employed in manufacturing articles to be used by the State or its minor civil divisions or in highway and park construction and the building of State institutions.

A special committee of the American Prison Association, after a year's investigation, reported itself as strongly in favor of the State use and State account systems, and in opposition to the other systems. It declared that the private contract system involves the use of State power to encourage unfair competition with law-abiding citizens; moreover, the State loss control over the reconstructive agencies that should surround the prisoner and over his economic training and the quality of his work. It reported that in the Minnesota binder-twine plant the prisoners earned from 10 to 50 cents per day, but the profit to the State had exceeded $1,600,000 in 20 years. It declared the State use system was possible in every State with a population of 2,000,000 or more. In New York alone, investigation had shown that $20,000,000 worth of goods needed by State and city departments and charitable and correctional institutions could be made by State prisoners. At least $35,000,000 worth of such goods could be used in all the States. The committee believed it possible under this system to fit the work to the qualifications of the prisoners, some being employed at farm work, some at road-building or other outside work, and others in various kinds of manufacturing. The committee contended that the p is ne has a right to work. It reported that the Maryland penitentiary has a well-developed contract system, under which the inmates in 24 years have earned about $500,000,000 annually. About 93 per cent. of all the prisoners were on contract, only 7 per cent. being employed in the upkeep of the institution, as compared to 10 per cent. to 20 per cent. where the State use system prevails. It condemned the contract system on account of the lack of restrictions as to hours, the absence of sanitation, and other normal conditions of work. Other investigations of Maryland penal institutions showed that they were not only hot beds of tuberculosis, but also were undoubted sources for the spread of contagious disease.

LEGISLATION. The tendency which has been very noticeable during the past few years for the States to discard the convict leasing and other systems for the private employment of State prisoners and to extend the State use system continued during 1912. Kentucky authorized the submission of a constitutional amendment allowing the employment of convict labor on public roads and bridges. Maryland provided that prisoners in the county jail of Garrett county, committed for less than one year, may be sentenced to hard labor on county roads under official direction for not more than ten hours per day. Massachusetts required prison commissioners to so organize prison industries that articles and materials used by the public offices and institutions, State, county, cities and towns, shall be produced by prison labor. In Mississippi the convicts on the penitentiary farms in four counties who are between 18 and 50 years of age may be required to work on county roads 15 days per year. New Jersey authorized the appointment of a convict commission to devise a scheme for the employment of convict labor on public roads, in public parks, forestry, and otherwise not in competition with free labor. The law also makes it possible for counties to secure prisoners for work on roads by application to this commission. New Mexico increased by ten days per month the extra good-record time granted to mechanics acting as foremen or trusties in the penitentiary. New York authorized the conservation commission to employ prisoners in propagating trees. Virginia established a convict time board for the employment of prisoners in quarrying limestone and oyster shells. This board is given full authority to establish a complete industry and dispose of the product.

One of the most important legislative advances of the year was the passage by the House of Representatives of the Boober bill. This declared that all convict-made goods transported into any State or Territory should upon arrival become subject to the laws of such State or Territory regulating the disposition of goods similarly manufactured. The States of New York, Illinois, Iowa, Louisiana, South Dakota, and perhaps other States which have adopted exclusively the State use system and prohibit the sale of any goods made in their own prisons in the open market still received convict-made goods from other States. In this way the manufacturers and free labor are still subjected to the competition of prison workers and convict labor. It is believed that the enactment of this law would encourage many other States to prohibit the sale of convict goods in the open market.

The National Committee on Prison Labor, organized in 1910, aims particularly to establish better conditions of prison labor. It has made numerous investigations and revelations, and has been active in stimulating advanced legislation. During the year its secretary, E. Stagg Whitin, published *Penal Servitude*, an authoritative work dealing with the entire subject.

PENROSE, BOIES. See PRESIDENTIAL CAMPAIGN CONTRIBUTIONS.

PENSIONS. See UNITED STATES, *Pensions*.

PENSIONS, OLD-AGE. See OLD-AGE PENSIONS.

PEPTIDS. See CHEMISTRY.

PERAK. A state (the most northerly) of the Federated Malay States protectorate (q. v.).

Area, 7900 square miles, population (1911), 494,123. Tin was discovered in Larut about 1850 and the mines have become the chief source of wealth in the country. The chief mining districts are Larut, Kinta, Batang Padang, and Klian Intan (in Reman). In 1909 the output was 115,376 piculs tin and 346,289 tin ore. Gold output, 1279 ounces. Rubber is an important product. In 1909 the area under rubber was 68,278 acres; under rice, 75,346; under cocoanuts, 63,225; under sugar-cane, 7000.

The state is traversed by the main line of railway from Penang. Length of metalled roads, 750 miles; unmetalled, 66; paths, 843. Taiping is the government headquarters, Ipoh the commercial centre. The sultan is (1912) Idris Mersid-el-Aazam Shah, and the British resident H. C. Belfield.

PERCEPTION. See PSYCHOLOGY.

PÈRE HYACINTHE. See BOYSON, CHARLES.

PERFUMERY. See CHEMISTRY, INDUSTRIAL.

PERIM. A dependency of Aden (q. v.).

PERKINS, GEORGE W. See PRESIDENTIAL CAMPAIGN CONTRIBUTIONS.

PERKINS, REECE WILMER. An American Baptist clergyman and educator, died July 2, 1912. He was born at Brandywine Summit, Delaware County, Pa., and graduated from Bucknell University in 1872. He studied theology at the Crozier Theological Seminary and was ordained to the Baptist ministry in 1877. He filled pastorates in Camden, N. J., and Lock Haven, Pa., until 1901, when he was chosen president of Leland University, New Orleans. He was founder of the Lock Haven Hospital and the Lock Haven Chorus. He was a member of several historical and theological societies.

PERSIA. An Asiatic monarchy (constitutional) extending from the Caspian Sea to the Gulf of Oman. Capital, Teheran.

AREA AND POPULATION. Area (estimate), 1,645,000 square kilometers (635,135 square miles); population, about 9,500,000, of whom about 2,500,000 are nomads. Population of Teheran, 280,000; Tabriz, 200,000; Meshed, 130,000; Ispahan, 70,000.

PRODUCTION AND COMMERCE. The agricultural products include cereals, cotton, sugar, opium, and tobacco. The country possesses valuable mineral resources—petroleum, coal, iron, copper, and lead; but exploitation on a considerable commercial basis is hindered by lack of transportation facilities. Silk and carpets are manufactured. The trade by countries for 1910-11 is shown in the next column in thousands of krâns, the krân being equal in that year to about 9 1/6 cents.

	Imps.	Exps.		Imps.	Exps.
Russia	219,559	262,226	Italy	2,782	3,975
U. K.	134,014	15,342	Oman	2,376	4,780
Brit. Ind.	55,651	22,070	China	408	2,337
Turkey	15,268	40,003	U. S.	292	5,040
Germany	13,977	2,089	Other	1,857	2,397
France	13,674	12,244			
Aus.-Hun.	10,448	49	Tl. 10-11	484,508*	375,427†
Belgium	8,137	456	" 09-10	442,428	371,526
Afgh'stan	4,126	2,411	" 08-09	372,484	326,207

* Cottons, 139,076,000 krâns; sugar, 120,596,000; silver, 42,467; tea, 24,822,000; cotton yarn, 11,145,-000; woolens, 9,725,000; iron manufactures, 7,061,-000; petroleum, 6,998,000.

† Raw cotton, 70,380,000 krâns; fruits, 62,507,-000; carpets, 46,693,000; rice, 29,210,000; skins, 21,-349,000; silk and cocoons, 17,601,000; opium, 13,-170,000; gums, 11,959,000; wool, 10,483,000.

Vessels entered at Persian gulf ports, 4492, of 1,443,838 tons (1096, of 1,151,822 tons, British); at Caspian ports (all Russian), 2755, of 718,765 tons.

COMMUNICATIONS The Russo-German convention of August 19, 1911, binds Germany to seek no railway, road, navigation, or telegraph concessions north of an imaginary boundary drawn from Kasri-Shirin to the Afghan border. Russia was to seek a concession to build a railway from Teheran to Khanikin, to be begun two years after the completion of the Sadidje-Khanikin line and to be finished within four years. Other agreements concern international traffic on the projected Khanikin-Teheran and the Khanikin-Bagdad lines, and the facilitation of extensions under construction. A Belgian light railway extends south from Teheran about six miles. A branch of the Transcaspian Railway, to run from Askhabad to Meshed, is projected. Trade is carried on over the great caravan routes. These are infested with brigands with whom the Persian government is powerless to deal adequately, and the danger and uncertainty incident to transportation have given rise to protest and threats of intervention by Great Britain in the south and Russia in the north.

ARMY. The plan of reorganization adopted in 1905, was still the underlying basis for the reform and organization of the army, whose peace strength was estimated at 115,000, exclusive of the irregular cavalry. In 1912 the reorganization of the gendarmerie was proposed.

FINANCE AND GOVERNMENT. The revenue (about half of which is derived from taxes levied in kind or in cash upon the laboring classes) fluctuates between seventy and one hundred million krâns; no statement of expenditure can be made, except that it regularly exceeds the revenue. The Russian debt of 1900 amounts to 22,500,000 rubles at five per cent., payable in 75 years and guaranteed upon the customs receipts other than those of the province of Fars and of the Persian Gulf ports; debt of 1902, 10,000,000 rubles at 5 per cent. British loan of 1911: £1,250,000, at 5 per cent. Floating debt, 104,870,000 krâns; annuities, 14,000,000 krâns. See *History* below.

The country is divided into thirty-three provinces administered by governors-general appointed by the shah; but the nomad tribes are ruled by their own chiefs so far recognized by the central government as to be held responsible for the collection of the tribal revenue.

The long-existing conflict between Russia and Great Britain for supremacy in Persia has resulted in complete financial demoralization and obstruction of transportation and other progress. Persia became a party in 1912, to the Anglo-Russian convention of August 31, 1907, by which each of the two contending powers agrees to confine its political and commercial operations to definite regions not overlapping; Persia agrees to respect these rights and to reorganize her army to suit the two powers. The Mejliss (a national assembly provided for in the constitution of June, 1909) was dissolved in December, 1911, and no elections has since been held. The ruler in 1912 was Ahmed Shah Kajar (born 1898); regent, Abou'l Kassim

Khan Nasr-el-Mulk. The heir-presumptive is the shah's second brother, Mohammed Hassan Mirza (1899).

History

Mr. Shuster's Criticisms. Mr. W. Morgan Shuster, whose administration as financial adviser had involved him in difficulties with Russia and Great Britain during 1911, and made him a conspicuous figure on the stage of international politics, left Teheran on January 11. His successor was M. Mornard, a Belgian. The criticism of Russia on the strength of Mr. Shuster's representations continued and gave much offense to friends of the government at St. Petersburg. The latter complained that the critics, forgetful of the enormous common frontier of Russia and Persia and the preponderance of Russian interests in Persian trade, did not appreciate that good government in Persia was more important to Russia than to any other country. According to the Russian view the dispatch of troops was necessary to protect her own interests. The reports of cruelties perpetrated by the Russian troops were characterized as calumnious. The attacks on the Russian military ignored, they said, the fact that the Turks were systematically advancing in Urumiah, thus turning the flank of the Caucasus defenses.

Upon arriving in the United States, Mr. Shuster repeated his charges against the Russian and British policy in Persia. He pronounced the condition in Persia to be one of anarchy and said that the country was in the control of seven Persian officials, who were without character or honesty, and who were despised by the people. Their continuance in power was, he said, wholly due to the support of the British and Russian governments. He held that Great Britain had made a serious mistake in not holding Russia to the promise of the Anglo-Russian agreement, as that would have checked Russia's action and might have prevented the serious trouble that now threatens the country. England alone, he said, could check the encroachment of Russia. On the other hand, on behalf of Great Britain, it was said that its policy was necessarily one of conciliation. It was argued that the British government could not intervene in particular disputes which concerned Russia and Persia alone, for its general policy was to prevent Russian influence, which had for a long time existed in the north of Persia, from being extended in directions prejudicial to India.

In a later speech of Mr. Shuster's, delivered in London toward the end of January, he said, after reviewing the incidents of his administration in detail, that there was only one of two conclusions to be reached, either that the Russian and British governments, especially the former, must have meant through their consular officials in Persia to follow out a plan that would destroy all hope of Persia's regeneration through the efforts of the people themselves; or that those two governments must have been constantly and grossly misinformed as to what was happening. He said that in certain quarters he had been charged with a lack of *finesse* and with failing to understand that diplomatic agreements did not always mean precisely what they seemed to mean. His reply to this was that if the agreements between the countries concerned contained such inner meanings he should have been informed of the secret code by which they were to be translated. He said he was constantly in communication with the legations and in the pleasantest relations with their members. He sympathized with the movement in Great Britain to get fair treatment for Persia and he declared that it was his hope that the meeting which he was addressing marked the awakening of interest in Great Britain to the needs of the "weakened, war-cursed country of Persia." There was much criticism of the British policy in Persia during the year and no small part of it came from the government's supporters. It will be found briefly summarized, along with the government's explanation, in a succeeding paragraph.

Anglo-Russian Loans. Negotiations were carried on between the Russian and British governments after the December crisis for the purpose of developing a joint policy for the restoration of settled conditions in Persia in order that the British and Russian troops might safely be withdrawn. One object of the negotiations was to arrange a joint loan to strengthen the Persian finances. M. Mornard, the new treasurer-general, reported that the finances were in great disorder. He complained of "foreign machinations" and called the attention of the Belgian government to the injurious effects of what he described as "the English campaign." The British and Russian governments sent a joint note to the Persian government saying that Russia would require the ex-shah to leave Persia provided Persia would grant him a pension and his followers amnesty.

The terms of the Anglo-Russian note as to the joint loan to Persia were made public on February 19. It was provided that the British and Russian governments should each loan Persia £100,000, for immediate expenses, which sum was to be disbursed under the supervision of the treasurer-general with the approval of the British and Russian legations. In return the Persian government was to undertake to conform to the principles of the Anglo-Russian convention, to dismiss the irregular troops and the fedais from the army as soon as the ex-shah left Persia, and to confer with the legations as to the organization of the regular effective army and finally to make arrangements for the departure of the ex-shah and for a pension to him and an amnesty to his followers. It was stated that the British loan was to be mainly applied to the restoration of order on the southern routes. Persia accepted the loans on the attached conditions in March. Another joint loan to an equal amount was announced on September 4.

The Russian Occupation. Toward the close of 1911, Russian troops advanced as far as Kazvin and reinforcements were pushed forward toward the Persian frontier. There was fighting between Russians and the tribesmen at Tabriz, Resht, and Enzeli. In January, 1912, the Russian troops were in force throughout the province of Azerbaijen and in northeastern Khorassan. Inquiries and protests on this subject were frequent among the British partisans of the liberties of Persia. The Russians were charged with the commission and permission of the grossest cruelties, and the British government was blamed for its subservience to Russian influence. The charges of

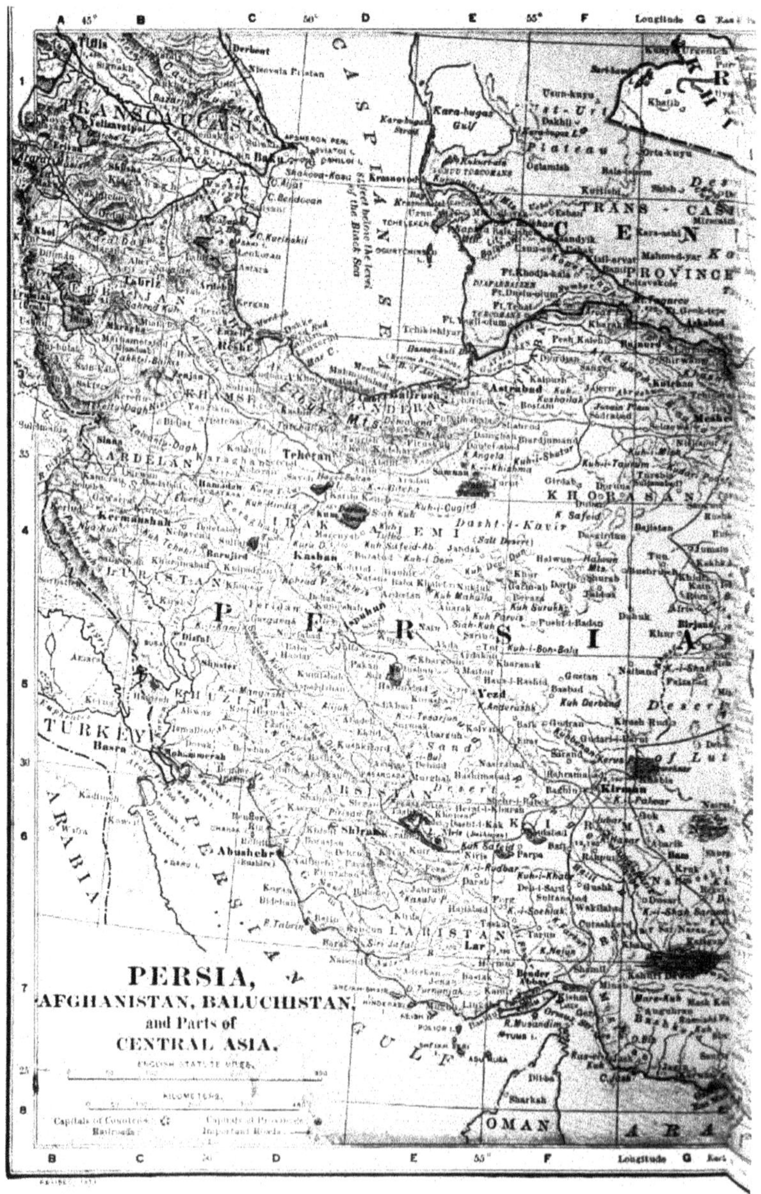
PERSIA,
AFGHANISTAN, BALUCHISTAN,
and Parts of
CENTRAL ASIA.
ENGLISH STATUTE MILES
KILOMETERS
Capitals of Countries
Railroads
Capitals of Provinces
Important Roads
CASPIAN SEA
Surface below the level of the Black Sea
TRANSCAUCASIA
PERSIA
TURKEY
ARABIA
PERSIAN GULF
OMAN
Teheran
Tabriz
Kermanshah
Ispahan
Yezd
Kirman
Shiraz
Abushehr
Basra
Longitude

60° from H Greenwich J 65° K L 70° M N
AFGHANISTAN
BALUCHISTAN
BOKHARA
Herat
Kabul
Kandahar
Quetta
Kelat
Merv
Bokhara
Samarkand
Tashkend
Khokan
Peshawur
PUNJAB
Karachi
SEA
60° from H Greenwich J 65° K L 70 M

cruelty were denied by the Russian government, which furthermore protested that it had no designs on Persian independence and declared the troops would be withdrawn as soon as order was restored. On February 14, Mr. Asquith stated that a considerable part of the troops had already been withdrawn and that the government understood that the removal of the rest would soon follow.

SIR EDWARD GREY'S EXPLANATION. The policy of the British government toward Persia was outlined by Sir Edward Grey in the course of a debate on the Anglo-Russian agreement on February 21. He declared that the strategic interests of Great Britain had not been injured in any way by Russia. The dispatch of troops was not intended as a permanent occupation, and some of the troops had already been withdrawn. He drew attention to the fact that Russia was entitled to take steps to defend her interests against Turkish troops, which had been concentrated on the frontier. As to the ex-shah, the government had taken a strong position and would not recognize him again. In general, the policy of Great Britain toward Persia involved the principle that British intervention must be based on British interests; that the British government could not act as arbiter when disputes arose between other countries; that the foreign minister ought not to be expected to pronounce judgment from day to day on the events that took place in the north of Persia. While the situation was difficult and would continue to be so, the Anglo-Russian agreement tended to remove difficulties in the way of restoring order. Without it the situation would be aggravated by jealousies and suspicions. "If there had not been confidence between Russia and Great Britain we might have been forced to assert our authority in Persia in order to safeguard our Indian frontiers. Then indeed, we should have come near to the partition of the country."

THE INTERNAL SITUATION. On March 11, Mohammed Ali, the ex-shah, left Persia for Russia, arrangements having been made for paying off his followers. He proceeded to Odessa to rejoin his family. His chief supporter, Salar-ed-Dowleh, remained, and gave the government much concern. His violent course at Kermanshah, where he was reported to have closed the banks and other business houses and executed prisoners, led to protest, and finally he was requested through the British and Russian consuls to leave the country. This he refused to do. He also rejected the offer of a pension and persisted in claiming authority over western Persia in the name of the shah. Upon the entry of the government troops at Kermanshah he took to flight, but continued to cause trouble throughout the year. Reports in the summer indicated that the internal situation was far from promising. The regent resigned on June 11, leaving the way open to new rivalries and intrigues. The government was disorganized and it was feared that the ex-shah, who still had many supporters in Persia, would take advantage of the confusion to renew his attempts. Meanwhile it was alleged that conditions on the southern trade routes, which had been the subject of the British note of October, 1910, threatening intervention, had not improved. A body of troops under Yar Mohammed sent out by Prince Firman Firma, governor of Kermanshah, on an expedition to Senna in August mutinied and demanded the revival of the Mejliss. They deserted to Salar-ed-Dowleh, who promised to restore constitutional government. These troops were routed near Fermanshah on October 7, and Yar Mohammed was killed. Meanwhile the affairs of government were in great confusion. The regent, Nasr-el-Mulk, remained in Paris and showed no intention of returning. With a boy ruler on the throne, a regent who refused to govern, ministers who shirked responsibility, and provisional governors who would not enforce their authority, the administration seemed to have completely broken down, and lawless bands of the tribesmen were harrying the country.

ANGLO-RUSSIAN POLICY. The friends of the new régime in Persia feared that Russia would take advantage of these disturbed conditions to advance her interests, that in fact she was already preparing a more aggressive course in Persia on the assumption that the constitutional experiment was a failure and that the strong hand was necessary. Many of the British Radicals took the government to task for inertness in the matter. On July 17, Sir Edward Grey announced in answer to a question that the Russian troops in Persia numbered about 12,000, most of them being in Azerbaijan and Khorassan. M. Sazonoff, the Russian foreign minister, visited London on September 20 mainly for the purpose of discussing Persian affairs with the British foreign office. His visit was the occasion of a pronouncement of the British Persian committee against what it called the present British government's "policy of drift," which would surely lead to a coterminous frontier with Russia in Persia. They objected to the proposal that British troops be sent into southern Persia to "restore order" on the southern routes, these routes being in the neutral sphere, for they held that this policy would lead to the partition of that neutral region and would equally bring about a coterminous Russo-British frontier. They blamed Russia for the present disorganization in Persia, especially for its interference with the recent efforts of Mr. Shuster, which gave promise of success. They accused the British government of disregarding its pledge that Persia should have a chance to work out her own salvation, and they urged a loan of £5,000,000 to Persia for the increase of its present gendarmerie and for the establishment of a small army. It was feared that M. Sazonoff's visit aimed at new understanding still more unfavorable to the constitution aspirations of Persia. From the official account, however, it appeared that instead of seeking a new arrangement in regard to Persia, the interview aimed at finding some means of restoring order in the country in conformity with the spirit of the Anglo-Russian agreement, that neither power had any desire for partition, and that they were both considering how to strengthen the Persian government in maintaining order and safety with a view to expediting the withdrawal of the foreign troops.

TRANS-PERSIAN RAILWAY PROJECT. The creation at Russia's instance of a commission known as the Société d'Études to study the question of a trans-Persian railway led to much comment in the British press and the British government was blamed for not opposing the scheme by many who regarded it as a dangerous departure from the policy hitherto pursued for the defense of India. The government, on the other hand, denied that it had committed itself to any such scheme and declared that it had merely not imposed an absolute veto on the investigation of the subject by the Société d'Études.

PERSIMMONS. See HORTICULTURE.

PERU. A republic of South America, on the Pacific coast south of Ecuador and Colombia. The capital is Lima.

AREA AND POPULATION. Estimates vary considerably in respect of both the territorial extent of Peru and the number of its inhabitants. There are boundary disputes with Ecuador and Colombia. The area given by the Lima Geographical Society is 1,769,804 square kilometers (683,335 square miles); this figure does not include the area of Tacna department, which appears to be definitely attached to Chile. (In 1912 Peru agreed to postpone the plebiscite on the Tacna question for twenty-one years.) An estimate of 1896 placed the population at 4,559,550, but it is believed that this figure was too high, and probably remains too high, since there seems to be some doubt as to whether the population of Peru is increasing. About one-half of the population is Indian, and most of the remainder mestizo. The larger towns include Lima (estimated population about 141,000), Arequipa (35,000), Callao (34,500), Cuzco (30,000), Ayacucho (20,000), and Iquitos (20,000).

EDUCATION. Primary instruction, though nominally free and compulsory, is received by only a minority of the children. Few recent statistics are available, but the number of public primary schools reported at the beginning of 1909 was 2339, with 3105 teachers and 162,298 pupils. In 1911, there were 27 national "colleges," with 4674 students enrolled, of whom 2077 were in the preparatory and 2597 in the higher courses. In 1910 the University of San Marcos (founded 1551) at Lima was enlarged, and the university at Cuzco, for a time inactive, was reopened. The state religion is Roman Catholicism. The fact that the public exercise of other religious forms is unlawful became prominent when, in the summer of 1912 it was proposed in England and the United States to establish a Protestant mission in the region of the Putumayo River, the scene of most infamous atrocities practised on the Indians by agents of a British rubber company. See *History* below.

PRODUCTION AND COMMERCE. Peru's extensive mineral deposits have been its chief source of wealth. Copper and silver are the most important metals worked, and to some extent gold, lead, coal, and petroleum are exploited. The leading agricultural products are sugar-cane, cotton, rice, and coffee. Some coca and cacao are produced, and rubber has become a valuable product in the northeast. The production of wool, from sheep, alpacas, and llamas, is a developing industry.

Imports and exports are reported as follows, in soles: 1909, 42,986,270 and 64,926,700; 1910, 49,806,970 and 70,740,760; 1911, 63,713,880 and 74,220,280. The leading imports are cotton and woolen goods, and machinery and metal wares. Principal exports in 1909 in thousands of soles: Minerals and metals, 16,380; cotton, 12,460; sugar 11,600; rubber, 11,370; rice, 5990; wool, 3940; spirits, 3790; guano, 1550. In the foreign trade the United Kingdom is first, the United States second, and Germany third.

COMMUNICATIONS. Railways in operation at the beginning of 1911, 2665 kilometers (1656 miles). Reported length in operation September 24, 1912, 2766 kms. (1719 miles). Several extensions and new lines have been surveyed, and on some of them construction was in progress in 1912. The construction of the Ucayali railway was begun in 1912; that of the Madre de Dios railway was contracted for; and the survey of the branch line to Puerto Werthemann was completed. About three-fourths of the mileage is operated by the Peruvian Corporation, Ltd. This corporation owns and operates a line of steamers on Lake Titicaca, by which, together with the Guaqui-La Paz railway in Bolivia (bought by the corporation in 1910), direct communication is maintained between La Paz and the corporation's line which reaches the coast at Mollendo.

Telegraphs at the end of 1910, 254 offices and 11,381 kilometers of line; during 1911, 733 kms. of line were added. Wireless telegraph stations have been established at Callao, Lima, and Iquitos; operation of the Lima-Iquitos service (across the Andes) was begun June 16, 1912. Post offices, 664.

FINANCE. The monetary standard is gold, and the unit of value the libra, which is equivalent to the British sovereign ($4.86656) and is divided into ten soles. In 1910, revenue and expenditure amounted to 27,957,750 and 26,853,220 soles respectively. Customs receipts were 12,435,720 soles, and taxes 10,507,450 soles; of the ordinary expenditure, war and marine required 5,438,310 soles, administration 5,134,720, finance and commerce, 4,126,490, and justice and public instruction, 3,745,210. Estimated revenue for 1911, 32,274,170 soles; estimated expenditure, 32,410,850; for 1912, 32,092,370 and 28,799,240 soles respectively. Reported foreign debt, £1,200,000 at 5½ per cent. interest (amortization, £37,240). The internal debt, in July, 1911, stood at 26,606,450 soles at one per cent. interest and 11,425,850 soles without interest.

ARMY. Under the direction of Colonel Clément and other French officers, the reorganization of the Peruvian army was undertaken, and there were maintained 6 battalions of infantry, numbering about 160 officers and 23,000 men; 6 squadrons of cavalry, 72 officers and 750 men; 3 batteries of artillery armed with Schneider guns; an independent section and a mixed battalion of foot artillery, including 50 officers and 800 men. An army of 24,000 men could be mobilized, it was believed, and in addition, reserves and a territorial force with but little military training and discipline.

GOVERNMENT. The president is elected by direct vote for four years, and is ineligible for the following term. Responsible to him are the members of his cabinet, six in number. There are two vice-presidents. The legislative body consists of the senate (52 members), and the house of representatives (116), all members being elected directly. For the term ending September 24, 1912, the president was

Agusto B. Leguia. He was succeeded on that date by Guillermo Billinghurst; first vice-president, Roberto Leguia; second vice-president, Miguel Echenique. Premier and minister of the interior, El. Malpartida.

History

The Putumayo Atrocities. For two years past there had been rumors that conditions resembling those which prevailed in the Congo under the late King Leopold existed in the Putumayo rubber industry, especially in the region exploited by the Peruvian Amazon Company. The British government made it the subject of an official investigation, appointing Sir Roger Casement for that purpose. The latter's report, published on July 13, fully confirmed these rumors, declaring that the rubber traders forced the Indians into bondage and treated them with the utmost cruelty. Floggings, he said, were the least of the tortures inflicted. For failing to bring in the required amount of rubber, Indians were mercilessly flogged and any attempt at flight was followed by still more brutal punishment or even murder. The region in which this condition prevailed was wider than the Putumayo and part of it was in dispute between Colombia and Peru. The investigation was conducted with thoroughness and the testimony of many eye-witnesses was taken. The United States government declared itself ready to coöperate with Great Britain in securing reform, and communications on the subject passed between the governments of Great Britain, and United States, and Peru, during 1911 and 1912. Sir Roger Casement's report was at once sent to the Peruvian government. A judicial investigation appointed by the Peruvian government substantiated its findings, but though Peru made frequent promises of reform, little was accomplished.

The force of the long-established usage in the rubber regions, their remoteness and the consequent difficulty in enforcing the law were the chief obstacles. In the summer of 1912 a plan of reform submitted to the Peruvian government by the Peruvian commissioner was under consideration. The publication of the British report and the comments of the press upon it, gave occasion to expressions of ill-will on the part of certain German journals which declared the atrocities to be the work of white employees on the rubber plantations, mostly Englishmen. A United States special agent was dispatched to the rubber country in July to ascertain how far Peruvian promises to remove the abuses had been redeemed. This report confirmed Sir Roger Casement's findings and was submitted to the United States Congress. In his message to the Peruvian congress toward the end of July, President Leguia announced that a commission had been appointed to investigate the conditions in the rubber districts, to bring offenders to justice, and to prepare a plan of reform. Early in August the Peruvian commissioner of Putumayo and the Peruvian minister to the United States issued a joint statement to the effect that the Peruvian Amazon Company was to blame for the atrocities. In England the four English directors were subjected to sharp criticism on the ground that they had delayed investigation when the charges were brought to their attention and that their negligence had permitted the outrages. It was also pointed out that the present liquidator of that company, Sñnor Julio Cesar, Arana, had been the original employer of the rubber gatherers and the organizer of the inhuman system. The Anti-Slavery Aborigines Protection Society issued an appeal to stockholders of the company for his removal.

In August a sharp controversy took place between the English directors of the company and Canon Hensley Henson, who, in a sermon on August 4, had charged them with being "guilty of unknowing connivance" at the crimes. They characterized his statements as slanders and absolute untruths, but he declined to withdraw them. In September the Peruvian Chamber of Deputies passed a resolution protesting against the attitude of the United States and British governments and demanded an investigation of the alleged atrocities and the punishment of the guilty. At the same time the prefect of the Putumayo district informed the United States minister to Peru that the abuses had been removed and that the Indians were receiving protection and pròper wages. On December 17 the arrest of Arana was ordered and other arrests were reported.

Other Events. It was announced in November that friendly relations between Peru and Chile, long interrupted by the dispute over the provinces of Arica and Tacna, had been resumed. The special arbitral tribunal of The Hague decided in favor of Peru in the Canevaro case. See Arbitration, International.

PETROLEUM. The marked increase in the production of petroleum which has characterized the industry from 1906 was continued in 1911, when the production of the previous year was increased by 10,892,143 barrels, or more than 5 per cent. The total production in 1911 was 220,449,391 barrels compared with 209,-557,248 barrels in 1910. The increase was caused chiefly by the gain in California where, in spite of efforts to limit the production, which is more than the present demand, the consumption increased to 81,134,391 barrels, compared with 73,010,560 barrels in 1910. Increased supplies also came from Louisiana. The field of high-grade oil at Electra in northern Texas became important at the end of the year, and new discoveries substantially increased production in the mid-continent field. The increases in this field, however, were offset by declines in Illinois and States farther east. As a whole, it may be said that fuel oil has increased in production and refined oil has declined. It will be seen from the table below, which gives the production and value of the oil-producing States, that California not only led in quantity of product but produced nearly half as much again as Oklahoma, the second State in rank. Omitting the mid-continent field, California produced as much oil as all the rest of the United States put together, and omitting the United States, it produced more oil than any other nation. California, Illinois, and Oklahoma form a class by themselves in the production of oil. These three States produce three-fourths of the entire output. The second division is formed by Louisiana, West Virginia, Texas, Ohio, and Pennsylvania. In 1911, Louisiana passed to the head of the second division, surpassing the production of West Virginia, Texas, and Ohio, which in previous years had led Louisiana. The table below shows the rank of the States in the production of petroleum and the quantity and value of the production in 1911:

	1910		1911	
State	Quantity	Value	Quantity	Value
Cal.	73,010,560	$35,749,473	81,134,391	$38,719,080
Col.	239,794	243,402	226,926	228,104
Ill.	33,143,362	19,669,383	31,317,038	19,734,339
Ind.	2,159,725	1,568,475	1,695,289	1,228,835
Kan.	1,128,668	444,763	1,278,819	608,756
Ken.	468,774	324,684	472,458	328,614
La.	6,841,395	3,574,069	10,720,420	5,668,814
Mich. } Mo. }	3,615	4,794	7,995	7,995
N. Y.	1,053,838	1,414,668	952,515	1,248,950
Ohio	9,916,370	10,651,568	8,817,112	9,479,542
Okla.	52,028,718	19,922,660	56,069,637	26,451,767
Penn.	8,794,662	11,908,914	8,248,158	10,894,074
Texas	8,899,266	6,605,755	9,526,474	6,554,552
Utah } Wyo. }	115,430	93,536	186,695	124,037
W. Va.	11,753,071	15,723,544	9,795,464	12,767,752
Total	209,557,248	127,899,688	220,449,391	134,044,752

FUEL OIL. The most important feature developed by the oil industry of 1911 was the realization of a supply of fuel large enough to be reckoned on as a national asset in power production. Prophecies made during 1910 that fuel oil in sufficient quantity existed on the Pacific coast to justify great trade and manufacturing expansion were justified. Oil has been already adopted as fuel on the northern transcontinental railways for considerable portions of their lines. The introduction of oil as fuel as far north as Alaska, without bringing the consumption up to the level of the present production, has given assurance of permanency of the supply sufficient for the industrial needs of the whole Pacific slope. The bringing about of similar conditions on the Atlantic Coast was made p a e by the great development of oil suppliesbihl Mexico. The quantity of oil which Mexican fields are now ready to furnish is estimated at from 6,000,000 to 12,000,000 barrels a month. Improvements in engines, which make it no longer necessary to convert the oil into power by burning it under boilers, have greatly raised the efficiency of oil for power. These engines are of the Diesel type, and in them a great variety of oils can be injected directly into the cylinders of the internal combustion engine. The quantity of oil consumed by railways in 1911 was 27,774,821 barrels, and this included most of the important railways in the north and southwest of the United States. Large quantities of oil are also used as fuel in manufacturing and other industries. Experience with fuel oil in the United States navy has been so satisfactory that its use will be extended as rapidly as is permitted by considerations of supply and cost. During 1911 the navy used 15,000,000 gallons of fuel oil, and it is estimated that in 1912 21,000,000 gallons of fuel oil were used. A considerable quantity is also used in the merchant marine for fuel.

The chief foreign countries producing petroleum are Canada, Mexico, Russia, Austria, and Rumania. The production of the oil wells of the world for 1907-1911 will be found in the table in the next column.

The production in Russia, which is second to the amount produced in the United States, showed a decline in 1911. This decline occurred

Country	1907	1910	1911
United States...	166,095,335	209,557,248	220,449,391
Russia	61,850,734	70,336,574	66,183,691
Mexico	1,000,000	3,332,807	14,051,643
Dutch E. Indies	9,982,597	11,030,620	12,172,949
Rumania	8,118,207	9,723,806	11,101,878
Galicia	8,455,841	12,673,688	10,485,726
India	4,344,162	6,137,990	6,451,203
Japan	2,010,639	1,930,661	1,658,903
Peru	756,226	1,330,105	1,398,034
Germany	756,631	1,032,522	995,764
Canada	788,872	315,895	291,096
Italy	59,875	42,388	71,906
Other (estimated)	30,000	30,000	200,000
Total	264,249,119	327,474,304	345,512,185

in the fields of Baku, and although fields in other parts of the country showed an increase it was not sufficient to make up for the loss in the Baku fields. In Rumania, where a considerable amount of oil is obtained, the highest point of production ever known was reached in 1911, 11,101,878 barrels.

The production of crude petroleum in the United States in 1912 is given in the table below, as estimated by the *Engineering and Mining Journal*. The figures indicate a slight increase in the oil production of the country. The increase in California and the smaller producing States was sufficient to offset the declines in the mid-continental and Illinoián fields:

Field	In barrels of 42 gal.	Field	In barrels of 42 gal.
California ...	84,823,992	Mid-conti'tal[1]	52,771,603
Colorado	200,000	Ken.-Tenn.....	500,000
Gulf—Texas..	11,778,324	Appalachian[2].	26,000,000
—La. ..	(a)9,791,896	Wyoming[3]....	500,000
Illinois	28,400,000	Others	5,000
Lima—Indiana.	1,200,000		
—Ohio....	3,000,000	Total	218,970,815

[1] Kansas and Oklahoma. [2] Pennsylvania, New York, West Virginia, and eastern Ohio. [3] Includes Utah. a Includes Marion County, Texas.

PHARMACY, SCHOOLS OF. See UNIVERSITIES AND COLLEGES.

PHILIPPINE ISLANDS. AGRICULTURE. Dr. George E. Nesom, director of agriculture, resigned on September 13, 1911, and Mr. Frederick W. Taylor was appointed to fill the vacancy.

During 1912 the islands were visited by a prolonged drought which affected the growth of all staple crops and caused suffering and want in localities where the people depend for their welfare upon the success of a particular product. The long, dry season was accompanied by unusually large swarms of locusts and other pests, because of the failure of their customary food. It was particularly severe in its effect on the rice crop, which was probably 40 per cent. less than that of the preceding year. The failure of the rice crop resulted in a large increase in corn planting. See AGRICULTURE.

On October 15 a severe typhoon passed over the island and City of Cebu and adjacent places, with casualties estimated at about 500, and doing damage to some two and one-half million dollars' worth of property. In addition to the loss of life and the wreckage of property, great damage was done by the storm to the sugar, rice and hemp crops. It was reported that various vessels were sunk in the harbor and hundreds of small craft were driven to shore by a great tidal wave, the damage being such as to leave possibly one-half of the population homeless.

COMMERCE. The commerce throughout the islands showed steady advancement during the year. The value of imports and exports amounted to $104,869,816 as compared with $89,612,351 in 1911, an increase of 17 per cent. The increase of the exports of $10,541,207 was largely due to copra. For the first time since American occupation, copra was at the head of the list of exports, and hemp, which heretofore has always held first place among exported articles, dropped into second place. The sugar exports were 128,926 tons, valued at $7,144,755 in 1911, while during the year 1912, the exports were 161,783 tons, valued at $9,142,833. The slump in the cigar trade with the United States seems to have ended and 63,808,000 cigars were shipped into the United States as compared with 42,472,000 in 1911. The customs receipts amounted to $9,347,647.50.

During the fiscal year 1912, the value of imports amounted to $54,549,980, an increase of $4,716,258 over that for 1911, due largely to the increased importation of rice, which amounted to $4,009,319. The export trade amounted to $39,778,629 as compared with $39,778,629 for 1911.

RAILROADS. The total length of railroad lines authorized by law to be constructed in the Philippine Islands is 1785.9 kilometers; of this 1034.9 kilometers have been constructed and are in operation, 16.3 kilometers constructed but not in operation, leaving about 734.7 kilometers to be constructed. Contracts have been signed with the Manila Railroad Company for the construction of a line to Baguio, to be built within two years. Construction work has been commenced.

POSTS AND TELEGRAPHS. There were 587 post offices in the Philippines on June 30, 1912. Free delivery letter carrier service was established at 101 additional post offices outside of the city of Manila, making a total of 397 offices at which such service is in operation. Money order service was established at 46 additional post offices and closed at 2, leaving a total of 253 money order offices. The value of money orders issued was $7,425,173.70. The total amount of money sent out of the islands by means of money orders was $1,832,972.85.

The total length of telegraph and cable lines was 9010.84 kilometers. The number of telegraph offices, 267. A Telefunken wireless station was erected at Davao, Moro province, and opened for business on March 6, 1912, and construction work was begun on wireless stations at Cuyo and Puerto Princesa, Palawan. On June 30, 1912 the bureau of posts operated wireless stations at 4 points: Davao, Jolo, Malabang, and Zamboanga, all in the Moro province.

The business of the postal savings banks continued to grow and showed an increase in both the number of offices and depositors. The total number of accounts on June 30, 1912, were 35,802, an increase of 6998, or 24 per cent. Of these, 29,555, or 82.55 per cent., were Filipinos. The amount on deposit was $2,388,986.42. The number of banks in operation was 437, an increase of 23.

On October 1 the inter-island parcel post went into effect. The maximum weight allowed for a package is 11 pounds.

PUBLIC WORKS. *Roads and Bridges.* There was expended for the construction, maintenance, and improvement of roads and bridges during the past 12 months, $2,193,523.21. There are now about 2000 kilometers of hard-surfaced road in the islands. There was constructed during the year 291.4 kilometers of first-class roads, 101 kilometers of second-class, 95 kilometers of third-class, and 40 kilometers of trail.

WATER SUPPLY. One of the most important projects executed during the year was the water-supply system for the city of Cebu, which has been named in honor of the speaker of the Philippine Assembly. The construction work was commenced on February 17, 1911, and finished February 19, 1912, with a cost of $263,000. Its storage reservoir has a capacity of 330,000,000 gallons and its distributing reservoir a capacity of 4,000,000 gallons. The main pipe system is 51.2 kilometers long, and the total length of pipe in the distributing system within the city is 21 kilometers.

EDUCATION. At the close of the schools in the month of March, 1912, there were in operation 3364 primary, 283 intermediate, and 38 secondary public schools, with 664 American and 7696 Filipino teachers. During the year 529,655 pupils were enrolled, with an average daily attendance of 329,073.

Some industrial instruction is now given in practically all schools. In February, 216,290 boys and 125,203 girls, representing 91 per cent. of the monthly enrollment, were engaged in industrial work, such as regular manual training and trade work, school gardening and farming, housekeeping, lace-making and embroidery, the making of hats and mats, and the study of basketry. The finished product which is turned out by the children of the public schools is remarkable both for its quality and diversity. The dainty laces and embroideries, beautiful baskets, hats, pottery, furniture and other products were eagerly sought for at the exhibit held by the bureau of education in connection with the carnival in February.

The school of household industries was opened during the year with an attendance of some 150 women, who are receiving a thorough training in lace-making and embroidery.

Arrangements have also been made to give a course in seamanship in the Philippine School of Arts and Trades and a practical training on inter-island steamships.

There were 1400 students registered in the University of Porto Rico, a gain of 180 over last year. Students from all provinces in the islands are taking courses in the colleges of agriculture and forestry.

The first class to complete the entire medical course was graduated this year and a member of it was a Filipino woman, the first to secure a degree of M. D.

Athletics play an important part in the work of the public schools. There is hardly a school in the islands which does not have a baseball team. A great many field meets were held during the past year which were attended by large and enthusiastic crowds. During the carnival an interscholastic meet was held in Manila, at which the provinces which had won the interprovincial meets were represented. The crack Waseda University team of Tokyo was brought to Manila for the carnival, and was defeated by some of the local amateur organizations.

HEALTH AND SANITATION. Although the health conditions in China and other surrounding countries have been very unsettled and they have been suffering from epidemics of plague and cholera, which have seriously threatened the islands, the health conditions are better than at any time since American occupation. Cholera has been generally absent; smallpox, through the vigorous vaccination campaign of the health officers, has been largely reduced, and but two cases of plague were reported. Since the opening of the new water supply for the city of Manila there has been a decrease of more than 60 per cent. in the number of cases of dysentery. Owing to the efficient quarantine and the well-organized district health service the scourges of Asiatic cholera, bubonic plague and smallpox have been successfully combated, and generally speaking, eradicated. The new Southern Islands Hospital at Cebu was completed in 1912, but owing to the failure of the legislature to pass an appropriation bill, no provisions have been made for its maintenance. In the mountain province a fine hospital, with dispensaries in the near-by districts, was opened and is doing much good. The demand for better water by drilling artesian wells and constructing municipal water systems continues to gain strength. Nearly 700 successful wells have already been drilled, and this pure water movement is followed by a wonderful decrease in the mortality statistics of the districts affected. The collection and segregation of lepers continue. Since the leper colony was founded in 1905, almost 7000 lepers have been collected.

A modern 30-bed hospital of brick, with ample facilities for the treatment of outpatients, has been opened at Bontoc, among the wild tribes. This institution has been doing wonderful work among people who, prior to the American occupation, were absolutely without medical or surgical assistance of any kind. See BERIBERI.

POLITICS AND GOVERNMENT

ELECTIONS. Heretofore elections have been held on the first Tuesday after the first Monday in November, the day when federal elections are held in the United States, but by act of Congress approved February 15, 1911, the term of office of delegates to the Philippine Assembly was made four years, beginning October 16, 1912, and the legislature was given the right to fix the date of its annual sessions. The legislature selected October 16 as the date and also fixed the date for future elections as the first Tuesday in June, every four years. By the same act the terms of office of elective provincial and municipal officers were made the same as those of delegates.

Elections were held on June 4, 1912, for delegates to the Philipine Assembly, and provincial and municipal elective offices in all the regularly organized provinces and for two members of the municipal board in the city of Manila. The election passed off quietly and peaceably.

OTHER EVENTS. In response to a resolution sent by Congress to the President in July asking for a statement of expenditures on account of the Philippines, President Taft sent in a special message in which he said that the islands had actually paid for themselves, and that there was a balance in their favor in all items except in the increased cost of the army and the navy, which could not be accurately determined. The direct expenditures for the islands, he said, amounted to $3,451,925, and against this was $4,975,747 expended out of Philippines revenue in the execution of the military purposes of the United States, for which the islands had not been reimbursed. The President said: "Aside from the direct appropriation of Congress, the expenditures incident to military and naval operations and the support of the United States forces in the archipelago, the Philippine Islands have been in no way a charge against the United States treasury. In other words, the Philipines government has been entirely self-supporting. Moreover, it has been throughout self-supporting in a larger sense than any other territorial possession of the United States. All expenses attached to the collection of revenues, to the administration of the Post Office Department, and of course to the survey of the islands, to the conservation of their resources, and to the improvement of their rivers and harbors, and to all similar works which elsewhere, as in Porto Rico, Alaska, and the Hawaiian Islands are a charge against the national treasury, are, and have been paid from the revenue of the Philippine Islands."

There was a notable demonstration in Manila on November 11 in celebration of the election of Mr. Wilson to the presidency. In a parade in which 10,000 Filipinos took part, banners were carried bearing the words "immediate independence" and a mass meeting was attended by 20,000 persons. Addresses were made by Manuel Quezon, delegate to Congress, Speaker Osmena and Emilio Aguinaldo, former leaders of the insurgent forces. The speakers expressed their confidence in the fulfillment of the promises made in the Democratic platform for the immediate independence of the Philippines.

LEGISLATION. The second regular session of the second Philippine legislature convened October 16, 1911, and continued in session until February 1, 1912. A special session was called by proclamation of the governor-general which lasted from February 2 to 6 inclusive.

The legislature again failed to pass the appropriation bill for current expenses of the government for the fiscal year 1913, so it was necessary to pay the expenses of the government in accordance with the provisions of section 7 of the organic act.

Among the more important acts passed were an act authorizing the purchase of rice for sale to prevent its price rising above a reasonable rate. This action was prompted by the shortage of the crop, not only in the Philippines, but throughout the Orient. The legislature also passed an act affecting the gold standard fund; it granted a franchise to form a mortgage bank with a capital of $2,000,000; it amended the charter of the Spanish Filipino Bank, and passed an act amending the distribution of the internal revenue between municipal, provincial, and the insular governments.

Changes were also made in the corporation law, and there was passed an act to regulate the issuance of warehouse receipts, another governing water rights and irrigation projects, and $250,000 was appropriated for a Philippine exhibit at the Panama-Pacific Exposition.

The assembly at its last session passed a bill postponing the use of the English language as the official language of the courts until January 1, 1917. The Philippine commission amended the bill leaving to the discretion of the court whether the English or Spanish language should be used in making up its record after January 1, 1913, until January 1, 1917. The bill as amended failed in conference, so the English language remains the official language of the courts after January 1, 1913, as provided by law.

PHILLIPS, THOMAS W. An American capitalist, former member of Congress from Pennsylvania, died July 21, 1912. He was born in Mount Jackson, Pa., in 1835. In 1861 he engaged in the petroleum industry and became one of the largest individual producers in the United States. He was interested in philanthropic work and was a member of various benevolent and religious boards. He took an interest in State and local politics and was the originator of the campaign text book, which was first used in the Garfield campaign of 1880. He was elected to the Fifty-third and Fifty-fourth Congresses and introduced the bill which created the Industrial Commission. He was a member of this commission and presided at most of its meetings as vice-president. At the conclusion of the report of the commission in 1902 he made a supplementary report which attracted wide attention and from which was evolved the law creating the bureau of corporations.

PHILLPOTTS, EDEN. See LITERATURE, ENGLISH AND AMERICAN.

PHILOLOGY, MODERN. In this department of linguistics relatively little of far-reaching importance was done in 1912. As has generally been the case in recent years, the attention of modern philologists was directed chiefly to the editing of texts and to the investigation of special linguistic phenomena; and perhaps the most interesting studies have been those of the modern dialects. As in former YEAR BOOKS, the present review will include such books as appeared too late to be recorded in the previous year.

GERMANICS. The most important work here is the continuation of the *Reallexikon der Germanischen Altertumskunde*, edited by J. Hoops, of which two fascicles have thus far appeared. The difficult problem of the weak preterite receives fresh light in H. Collitz's *Schwaches Präteritum und seine Vorgeschichte* (Göttingen, 1912) and S. Krüer's *Der Bindervokal und seine Fuge im schwachen deutschen Präteritum bis 1150* (Berlin, 1912), while B. Delbrück discusses the position of the verb in the second part of his *Germanische Syntax* (Leipzig, 1911). Here, too, may be placed F. Kluge's *Wortforschung und Wortgeschichte* (Leipzig, 1912), A. Schirmer's *Zur Geschichte der deutschen Kauffmannssprache* (Leipzig, 1911), and R. Kleinpaul's *Ortsnamen im Deutschen* (Leipsiz, 1912).

OLD AND MIDDLE HIGH GERMAN. The sole contribution of general interest in Old High German was J. Schneiderhan's *Roswitha von Gandersheim, die erste deutsche Dichterin* (Paderborn, 1912); while studies of specific problems in Old High German authors were contributed in E. Och's *Lautstudien zu Notker von St. Gallen* (Freiburg, 1911), and F. Köhler's *Zur Frage der Entstehungsweise der Althochdeutschen Tatianübersetzung* (Leipzig, 1911).

Among the general treatises dealing with Middle High German special mention should be made of C. von Krauss's *Mittelhochdeutsches Uebungsbuch* (Heidelberg, 1912), the second part of G. Brockstedt's *Von mittelhochdeutschen Volksepen französischen Ursprungs* (Kiel, 1912), F. Konziella's *Volkstümliche Sitten und Bräuche im mittelhochdeutschen Volksepos* (Breslau, 1912), and H. Mangold's *Studien zu den ältesten Bühnenverdeutschungen des Terenz* (Halle, 1912). Considerable interest was evinced in the editing of texts, these including two volumes of *Mittelhochdeutsche Novellen* by L. Pfannmüller (Bonn, 1912), *Konrad von Megenberg's Deutsche Sphaera* on the basis of Munich manuscript by O. Matthaei (Berlin, 1912), *Wernher der Gaertnaere's Meier Helmbrecht* by F. Panzer (Halle, 1911), the German version of the *Seven Wise Masters* on the basis of two Heidelberg manuscripts (Jena, 1912), and the poetical version of *Daniel* edited from the Stuttgart manuscript by A. Hübner (Berlin, 1911) as the third volume of the *Dichtungen des deutschen Ordens* in which latter connection it may be noted that the language of the documents of the Teutonic Knights was studied by A. Weller in his *Sprache der ältesten deutschen Urkunden des deutschen Ordens* (Breslau, 1911). Turning to more restricted themes, we may note K. Herold's *Der Münchener Tristan: Ein Beitrag zur Ueberlieferungsgeschichte und Kritik des Tristan Gottfrieds von Strassburg* (Strassburg, 1911), H. G. Klinkott's *Ulrich von dem Türlin als Nachahmer Wolframs von Eschenbach* (Griefswald, 1911), P. Claus's *Rhythmik und Metrik in Sebastian Brandts Narrenschiff* (Strassburg, 1911), E. Dornfeld's *Textkritische, sprachliche und metrische Untersuchungen zu Gottfried Hagens Reimchronik der Stadt Köln* (Marburg, 1911), F. Stütz's *Die Technik der kurzen Reimpaare des Pamphilus Gengenbach* (Strassburg, 1912), R. Koenig's *Stilistische Untersuchungen zur Braunschweigischen Reimchronik* (Halle, 1911), and A. Weller's *Die frühmittelhochdeutsche Wiener Genesis nach Quellen, Uebersetzungsart Stil, und Syntax* (Berlin, 1912).

MODERN GERMAN DIALECTS. This branch contains, in some respects, the most permanently valuable results of Germanic philology in 1912. The great German dialect dictionaries continued to make steady progress, the *Siebenbürgisch-sächsisches Wörterbuch*, edited by A. Schullerus and F. Hofstädter reaching the second fascicle of the second volume the *Schweizerisches Idiotikon* its seventieth fascicle, H. Fischer's *Schwäbisches Wörterbuch* its thirty-eighth, and K. Müller-Fraureuth's *Wörterbuch der obersächsischen und erzgebirgischen Mundarten* its fifth, while K. Hentrich issued a *Wörterbuch der nordwestthüringischen Mundart des Eichfeldes* (Göttingen, 1912). Among grammatical treatises on modern German dialects were F. Wenzel's *Studien zur Dialektgeographie der südlichen Oberlausitz und Nordböhmens* (Marburg, 1911), P. Meynen's *Ueber die Mun-*

dart von Homberg-Niederrhein (Leipzig, 1911), H. Batz's *Lautlehre der Bamberger Mundart* (Erlangen, 1911), B. Capesius's *Die Vertreter des alten ī ū ü im Siebenbürgisch-Sächsischen* (Berlin, 1912), A. Schwaederle's *Vorgermanische Fluss- und Bach-Namen im. Elsass* (Colmar, 1912), E. Beck's *Enleitung zu einer Grammatik der oberen Markgräfler Mundart* (Heidelberg, 1911), K. Schlemmer's *Die Ortsnamen der Kreise Kolberg-Körlin und Griefenberg in Pommern und ihre Bedeutung für die Heimatkunde* (Treptow, 1912), E. Döring's *Beiträge zu einer Laut- und Wortlehre der Sondershauser Mundart* (Sondershausen, 1912), and T. Schörnborn's *Das Pronomen in der schlesischen Mundart* (Breslau, 1912). Finally, in his little *Deutsche Mundarten* (Leipzig, 1912), H. Reis has given the first preliminary survey of the modern German dialects as a whole.

NORSE, ANGLO-SAXON, AND ENGLISH. *In* Norse philology the only important contribution was the first two parts of A. Kock's *Umlaut und Brechung im Altschwedischen* (Lund, 1911-12). Studies of Anglo-Saxon culture were put forth in H. Jacob's *Namen der profanen Wohn- und Wirtschaftsgebäude und Gebäudeteile im Altenglischen* (Kiel, 1911); and the relations between Anglo-Saxon and Old High German received attention in C. Leydecker's *Ueber Beziehungen zwischen althochdeutsche und angelsächische Glossen* (Bonn, 1911), and in H. Michaels's *Altenglisches in den altdeutschen Glossen* (Bonn, 1911), and *Ueber englische Bestandteile altdeutscher Glossenhandschriften* (Bonn, 1912).

In Middle English K. Rosskopf edited for the first time the Cambridge manuscript of the *Cassamus*, a fragment of the cycle of Alexander the Great (Munich, 1911) and T. Spira reprinted the fifteenth century *Maistre d'escole anglois* (Halle, 1912), while A. Müller wrote upon *Mittelenglische geistliche und weltliche Lyrik des dreizehnten Jahrhunderts* (Halle, 1911). H. Price was the author of *A History of Ablaut in the Strong Verbs from Caxton to the end of the Elizabethan Period* (Bonn, 1912), and Middle English dialects were considered in J. Sixtus's *Sprachgebrauch des Dialekt-Schriftstellers Frank Robinson zu Bowness in Westmoreland* (Berlin, 1912). G. Wendt contributed the first part of a *Syntax des heutigen English* (Heidelberg, 1911), dealing with morphology.

LOW GERMAN. The principal monument of Old Saxon was discussed in J. Jostes's *Heimat des Heliand* (Münster, 1912), and a phase of the history of Low German hymnology received attention in R. Möllencamp's *Jüngere Ebstorfer Liederhandschrift* (Kiel, 1911). A rather unusual amount of interest in Frisian was manifested, as is shown by the first part of L. Hahn's *Eindringen der neuhochdeutschen Schriftsprache in Ostfriesland* (Halle, 1911), dealing with the history of the chancery language; by E. König's edition of Johannes Cadovius Muller's *Memoriale linguæ Frisicæ* (Norden, 1911); and by A. Dunkmann's *Ostfriesisch-plattdeutsches Dichterbuch* (Aurich, 1911), which is prefaced by a history of the Low German language and literature in East Frisia.

ROMANCE. Within the sphere of romance philology in general W. Myer-Lübke's *Romanisches etymologisches Wörterbuch* reached its fifth fascicle, extending as far as *mel*, and L. Alexander made a study of *Participial Substantives of the -ata Type in the Romance Languages, with Special Reference to French* (New York, 1912).

OLD FRENCH. Here the most important activity was manifested in the editing of texts. H. Sommer's edition of *The Vulgate Version of the Arthurian Romances* reached the third part of *Le Livre du lac* (Washington, 1912), and H. Bubringer's *Altfranzösischer Prosaroman von Lancelot del Lac* was extended to the second part of *Les Enfances Lancelot* and the first of *La doloreuse Garde* (Marburg, 1912). The other principal editions of Old French texts were the following: Krappe, *Christi Leben von seiner Geburt bis zur Geschichte von der Samariterin*, on the basis of Arsenal Manuscript 5204 and Bibliothèque Nationale f. fr. 9588 (Greifswald, 1912); C. Iburg, *Ueber Metrum und Sprache der Dichtungen Nicole de Margivals nebst einer kritischen Ausgabe des Ordre d'Armour von Nicole* (Rostok, 1912); F. Reuter, *Die Bataille d'Arleschant des altfranzösischen Prosaromans Guillaume d'Orange* (Halle, 1911); A. Ott, *Das altfranzösische Eutachiusleben (Histoire d'Eustachius) der Pariser Handschrift Nat. Bibl. fr. 1374* (Erlangen, 1912); C. Zipperling, *Das altfranzösische Fabel du Vilain Mire* (Halle, 1912); G. Rosenthal, *Die altfranzösische Version von Alain Chartiers Dialogus familiaris* (Rossleben, 1912); A. Barth, *Le Lai du Conseil; ein Altfranzösisches Minnegedicht* (Zurich, 1912); J. Longon, *Chronique de Morée* (1204-1305) (Paris, 1912); P. Aubry and A. Jeanroy, *Le Chansonnier de l'Arsenal*, a phototypic reproduction of Arsenal Manuscript 5198 (Paris, 1912); and A. Langfors, *Huon de Roi, Le Vair Palefroi, avec deux versions de La Male Honte par Huon de Cambrai et par Guillaume* (Paris, 1912); while A. de la Sale wrote *La Petit Jean de Saintré* (London, 1911). More technical problems are discussed in C. Sostmann's *Formenbau des Nomens und Verbums in dem Fragment von Gormond et Isembart* (Kiel, 1912); G. Schad's *Die Wortstellung in der Chanson de Guillaume und ihrer Fortsetzung, der Chanson de Rainvart* (Halle, 1912); F. Müller-Marquart's *Die Sprache der alten Vita Wandregiseli* (Halle, 1912); A. Graf's *Die beiden engeren Fassungen der altfranzösischen Dichtung in achtsilbigen Reimpaaren über Christi Höllenfahrt und Auferstehung* (Griefswald, 1912), and K. Bardenwerfer's *Die Anwendung fremder Sprachen und Mundarten in den französischen Farcen, Sottien, Moralitäten und Sermons joyeux des Mittelalters* (Halle, 1912). Old French dialects are considered in C. de Boer's *Pyrame et Thisbé, texte normand du douzième siècle* (Amsterdam, 1912) and A. Porschkes *Laut- und Formenlehre des Cartulaire de Limoges, verglichen mit der Sprache der Uebersetzung des Johannesevangeliums* (Breslau, 1912).

MODERN FRENCH. A. Tobler published the fifth part of his *Vermischte Beiträge zur französischen Grammatik* (Leipzig, 1912), and J. Sanneg's *Dictionnaire étymologique de la langue française* reached its fifth fascicle (Hanover, 1912). General interest also attaches to E. Winkler's *Doctrine grammaticale française d'après Maupas et Oudin* (Halle, 1912); and grammatical problems were discussed in A. Schardt's *Vollständige hypothetische Satzgefüge mit der Konjunktion si im Französischen* (Göttingen, 1911); P. Fay's *Elliptical Partitive*

Usage in Affirmative Clauses in French Prose of the Fourteenth, Fifteenth and Sixteenth Centuries (Paris, 1912); A. Höring's *Zur Geschichte des Possessivpronomens im Französischen* (Heidelberg, 1912), and J. Schoch's *Perfectum historicum und Perfectum præsens im Französischen von seinen Anfängen bis 1700* (Halle, 1912). The interesting subject of French slang is discussed in the two volumes of L. Sainéan's *Les Sources de l'argot ancien* (Paris, 1912), and in A. Niceforo's *Génie de l'argot, essai sur les languages spéciaux, les argots et les parlers magiques* (Paris, 1912).

MODERN FRENCH DIALECTS. Here less has been done than in German dialects. Yet among the dialect texts mention should be made of L. Zéliqzon and G. Thiriot's *Textes patois recueillis en Lorraine* (Metz, 1912); E. Philipon's *La Piedmonteyza, poème en dialecte bressan, par Bernardin Uchard, de Pont-de-Veyle* (Paris, 1911); A. Dubut's *Din la doublo. Lou Doublaou Milon, counté patois* (Ribérac, 1911), and P. Delesques's *Poèmes normands. Récits cauchois du pé Malandrin* (Caen, 1912).

Among strictly philological discussions were K. Fester's *Satzphonetik im wallonischen Dialekt Malmedys* (Erlangen, 1911); J. Marichal's *Mundart von Gueuzaine-Weismes* (Bonn, 1912); J. Gilliéron's *L'Aire de Clavellus d'après l'Atlas linguistique de la France* (Neuveville, 1912); E. Vey's *Le Dialecte de Saint-Etienne au dix-septième siècle* (Paris, 1911); J. Daniel's *Eléments de grammaire périgourdine* (Périgueux, 1911); R. de Beaucoudrey's *Le Langage normand au début du vintième siècle. Noté sur place dans le canton de Percy (Manche)* (Paris, 1912); W. Bederlich's *Die lexicographischen Eigentüm lichkeiten des Franko-Provenzalischen nach dem Atlas linguistique de la France* (Bonn, 1912).

PROVENÇAL, ITALIAN, SPANISH, CATALAN. In Provençal E. Levy's *Supplementwörterbuch* of that language reached its thirtieth fascicle (Leipzig, 1912), and E. Portal edited an *Antologia provenzale* (Milan, 1911). In Italian the most important work was G. Capponi's *Raccolta di proverbi toscani*, based on the older work of Giusti (Florence, 1911). For Spanish A. Martinez Abellán wrote a *Diccionario de ortografia, homologia y régimen de la lengue española* (Madrid, 1911); while J. Pujal y Serra was the author of a *Diccionario catalan-castellano y castellano-catalan* (Barcelona, 1911), and A. Rubió y Lluch published in Catalan a series of lectures on Ramon Lull (Barcelona, 1912).

RUMANIAN, RHÆTO-ROMANCE. Two fascicles of the official Rumanian dictionary, the *Dicționarul Limbii Române*, published at Bucharest, appeared, and H. Tiktin's *Rumänisch-deutsches Wörterbuch* issued at Leipzig, reached its nineteenth fascicle. Another work of importance was R. Lovera and A. Jacob's *Grammaire roumaine* (Heidelberg, 1912), and R. Weidelt published *Die Nominalkomposition im Rumänischen*. In Rhæto-Romance the most noteworthy production was the fourth volume of C. Decurtin's *Rätoromanische Chrestomathie* (Erlangen, 1911).

CELTIC, SLAVIC, ALBANIAN. In Celtic, besides the two general treatises of T. Rolleston, *Myths and Legends of the Celtic Race* (New York, 1911), and A. Tedeschi, *Ossian l'Homère du nord, en France* (Milan, 1911); E. Ernault wrote *L'Ancien Vers Breton* (Paris, 1912), although the most important production was *O'Connell's Grammar of Old Irish* (Dublin, 1912). In the Slavic field E. Berneker's *Slavisches etymologisches Wörterbuch*, published at Heidelberg, reached its ninth fascicle, extending to *likŭ*, and another work of importance was A. Doritsch's *Beiträge zur litauischen Dialektologie* (Tilsit, 1911).

In the outlying field of Albanian N. Jokl's *Studien zur albanesischen Etymologie und Wörtbildung* (Vienna, 1911) is by all odds the most important work on this language since 1891.

PHILOLOGY, CLASSICAL. The feature of work in classical philology in 1912, of most interest to the general public, is seen in the translation of Greek and Latin authors; this tendency, exemplified for some years in many ways, e. g., in the Oxford Library of Translations, culminated last year in the appearance of the first volumes of the Loeb Classical Library. The scope and the purposes of this collection of translations of Greek and Latin authors were set forth fully in the last YEAR BOOK. Fifteen volumes have appeared, giving translations of the whole or of parts of the following authors: Greek—Appian, Apollonius Rhodius, Euripides, Philostratus, Sophocles, Theocritus, Bion, and Moschus (the three Greek bucolic poets in the one volume), and the Apostolic Fathers; Latin—Cicero, Propertius, Terence, St. Augustine. In accordance with the general plan of the library, existing translations (e. g., Horace White's of Appian, A. S. Way's of Euripides), have been utilized, but in revised form. The library has attracted much attention; its purpose and general plan have been commended. But one or two of the volumes thus far issued seem to betray haste in translation and printing; it is to be hoped that later volumes will be less open to criticism in these respects. It has been warmly urged, further, that the use of verse translations for the poets will in large measure defeat the purposes of the library.

The project of devising a system of uniform grammatical terminology is still attracting much attention. The American Commission of Fifteen, mentioned in the last YEAR BOOK as considering this difficult problem, hopes to publish a preliminary report in 1913. References may be made to a report of a *Symposium on Uniform Grammatical Terminology*, held at Ann Arbor, in 1911, and described in *The School Review* for November, 1911, and January, 1912. The Oxford University Press has published A *New Latin Grammar*, by E. A. Sonnenschein, "based on the recommendations of the Joint Committee on Grammatical Terminology." For the report of the English Joint Committee see the YEAR BOOK for 1910.

To the teaching of the classics, especially Latin, much attention is constantly given, particularly in England and America. In both these countries a small but earnest group is advocating the "direct method" of teaching Latin: see *The Classical Weekly, passim*, in particular VI., 34-37, 42-45, 50-53, 58-62, 70. Books intended to illustrate this method are beginning to pour from the press. The third volume of the *Cyclopedia of Education* edited by Paul Monroe, contains important articles on the teaching of Latin and Greek, by Professors T. D. Goodell and G. Lodge. The book on *The Teaching of Latin and Greek*, by Professor C.

E. Bennett and G. P. Bristol, reached its second edition in 1911.

That the year 1912 was one of extraordinary activity in classical philology, covering a wide field, may be seen by a mere glance at the titles of the articles in the periodicals published in this country, and in Europe. Their contents are entirely too varied and their themes for the most part too special to find record here. As in other years, however, mention will be made of some of the articles which appeared in the two chief repositories of American work in classical philology, *The American Journal of Philology* and *Classical Philology*. In the former journal appeared "Apollonius and Cyzicus," by E. Fitch (an argument that in writing the portion of his *Argonautica* which deals with the Cyzican adventure Apollonius had his eye on a definite locality—one might almost say, wrote with a map before him—so that his account has a higher topographical value than has heretofore been accorded to it); "Phœnix in the Iliad," J. A. Scott; "The Johns Hopkins *Tabulæ Defixionum*," W. S. Fox (an elaborate discussion of certain curse-tablets: the author thinks the curses were written at Rome, shortly before 40 B. C.); "The Sceptical Assault on the Roman Tradition Concerning the Dramatic Satura," C. Knapp; "Horace and Tibullus," B. L. Ullman; "Latin Inscriptions at the Johns Hopkins University: Series VII.," H. L. Wilson; "The Dative with Prepositional Compounds (in Latin)," E. B. Lease; "Submerged *Tabellæ Defixionum*," W. S. Fox; "Lucilius on *ī* and *ei*," E. W. Fay; an elaborate review of various books on Propertius, by B. O. Foster; "Contributions to the Study of Homeric Metre," G. M. Bolling; "Imagination and Will in *μή*," T. D. Goodell; "Usque Recurrent *μή*," B. L. Gildersleeve; "On the Use of *ὅταν* with Causal Implication," A. C. Pearson, which Professor Gildersleeve considers in the same number in his usual illuminating fashion, in a review of M. P. Nilsson's "Die Causalsätze im Greichischen bis Aristoteles. I. Die Poesie."

From *Classical Philology* we note "The Position of 'Deferred' Nouns and Adjectives in Epic and Dramatic Verse," H. W. Prescott; "Roman Satire; Its Early Name," J. W. D. Ingersoll; "The Manuscripts of Pliny's Letters," Dora Johnson; "The New Metric," by P. Shorey, a masterly translation of O. Schrader's important discussion, in German, of this theme; "On the Origin of Roman Satire," R. H. Webb; "Recent Homeric Literature," A. Shewan, an admirable survey of the more important books and articles on Homer since 1900; "On Anaximander," W. A. Heidel; "The Tacitean Tiberius: A Study in Historiographic Method," T. S. Jerome; "Patronymics as a Test of the Relative Age of Homeric Books," J. A. Scott; "Notes on Latin Etymologies," F. A. Wood; "The Homeric Augment," A. Shewan, a review of an elaborate paper on this subject by J. A. J. Drewitt, published in *The Classical Quarterly* (1912); Studies in Greek Noun-Formation: Labial Terminations III.," E. H. Sturtevant; "Satura as a Generic Term," A. L. Wheeler, an answer to the paper by G. L. Hendrickson, "Satura—The Genesis of a Literary Form," mentioned in the last YEAR BOOK; "Evidence in the Areopagus," R. J. Bonner.

As in other years much excellent work has been contributed to both journals in the way of reviews, especially by Professor Gildersleeve in "Brief Mention," a feature of each issue of *The American Journal of Philology*, and by Professor Paul Shorey, managing editor of *Classical Philology*. In the United States, again, much valuable work appears in the volumes of "studies" published under the auspices of various universities, and in *The Transactions and Proceedings of the American Philological Association* (the leading association of classical scholars). From the forty-second volume of the *Transactions*, published late in 1912, we may mention the following: "The Mind of Herodotus," M. Hutton; "Notes on the Character of Greek and Latin Accent," E. H. Sturtevant; "Latin *Mille* and Certain Other Numerals," R. G. Kent; "Altars on the Roman Comic Stage," Catharine Saunders. Klussmann's *Bibliotheca Scriptorum Classicorum et Græcorum et Latinorum*, mentioned last year, was advanced by the publication of part 1 of volume 2, giving a conspectus of books and articles on Latin authors (Ablavius to Lygdamus) from 1878 to 1896. Here too should be named *The Year's Work in Classical Studies*, published annually for The Classical Association of England and Wales; the book consists of fifteen to twenty articles, by various scholars, on the work done in the preceding year in various fields of classical philology; volume 6, covering 1911, appeared early in 1912.

In the field of inscriptions we note first useful summaries of the work done in 1910-1911: *Bulletin Annuel d'épigraphique grecque* (3e *Année*), A. J. Reinach; *Année (L) épigraphique relative à l'antiquité romaine*, published by Leroux (Paris). Important, too, are *Inscriptiones Græcæ*, giving the inscriptions of Delos, published at Berlin, under the direction of the Royal Prussian Academy; *Christian Epigraphy. With a Collection of Ancient Christian Inscriptions, mainly of Roman Origin*, a translation from the Italian of Orazio Marucchi, by J. A. Willis; *Greek Inscriptions from Sardes I.*, by W. H. Buckler and D. M. Robinson, published in *The American Journal of Archæology*, an elaborate discussion of a long inscription belonging to the end of the fourth century B. C., found in the new excavations at Sardis under the direction of Professor Howard Crosby Butler (see ARCHÆOLOGY, in the YEAR BOOK, for 1910, 1911, 1912). The inscription is most interesting; it is the only extant specimen of a certain type of mortgage; it prescribes the conveyance of the property, in the event of the mortgagor's failure to pay the debt involved in the mortgage. In the course of these excavations many other inscriptions, both Greek and Lydian, have been found; the number of Lydian inscriptions is very large, and it is hoped that one inscription, a bilingual document in Greek and Lydian, may give a clue to the decipherment of the Lydian inscriptions. Volume 2, Fasciculus 1 of the *Corpus Inscriptionum Etruscarum*, by O. A. Danielsson and G. Herbig, must also be noted.

Two works on coins are to be mentioned: *Receuil général des Monnaies grecques d'Asie Mineure*, Volume 1, Fasciculus 4, by E. Babelon and Th. Reinach, a revision and completion of the work by W. H. Waddington; *Numismatique Constantinienne*, Volume 2, by Jules Maurice, a book that throws much light on both secular and ecclesiastical history; through the study of the coins, reinforced by the documentary anthorities, "we can follow the process," says G. Macdonald in *The Classical Review* 26.190, "by which the representative upon earth of Hercules became transformed first into a champion of the solar cult, then into a Christian."

In the field of palæography striking activity was shown in the reproduction of manuscripts. Of prime interest and importance are three additions, Volumes XV.-XVII., to the great series of photographic reproductions of Greek and Latin manuscripts published by A. W. Sitjhoff, at Leyden. These volumes give, respectively, the "Codex Palatinus" and the "Codex Parisinus" of the *Anthologia Latina*, the "Codex Guelferbytanus Gudianus 224 (*olim* Neapolitanus)" of Propertius, and the "Codex Heinsianus (Leidensis 118)" of Cicero's *De Natura Deorum*. Important also are *Exempla Codicum Græcorum Litteris Minusculis Scriptorum. Vol. I.: Codices Mosquenses*, by G. Ceretelli and S. Sobolevski; *Specimina Codicum Latinorum Vaticanorum*, F. Ehrle and P. Liebaert, a collection of fifty photographs giving good examples of practically all the main styles of handwriting in manuscripts from the fourth to the fifteenth century, especially of early capital and minuscule manuscripts; *Papyrus Grecs (de Lille)*, Volume 2, Fasciculi 2, 3, 4; *Proben aus Griechischen Handschriften und Urkunden*, F. Steffens (Trier); *Griechische Papyri in Museum zu Giessen*, Volume 1, Heft 3, edited by E. Kornemann and P. M. Meyer; *Griechische Papyri der kaiserlichen Universitäts- und Landesbibliothek zu Strassburg im Elsass*, Volume 1, Heft 3, edited by F. Preisigke; *Oxyrhynchus Papyri*, Part IX., A. S. Hunt.

In the field of religion must be mentioned Mr. Fox's work on the *Tabellæ Defixionum* (see above); *The Thunder-Weapon in Religion and Folklore*, C. Blinkenberg; *Geburt, Hochzeit, und Tod: Beiträge zur vergleichenden Volkskunde*, Ernst Samter (see *Classical Philosophy* 7.124); *Themis. A Study of the Social Origins of Greek Religion*, Jane Harrison (a book to be used with caution; see *Classical Philology* VII., 359). An important book, which gains special interest from the fact that it consists of lectures delivered under the auspices of the American Committee for Lectures on the History of Religions, is *Astrology and Religion Among the Greeks and Romans*, by F. Cumont.

Of the work done in the kindred fields of syntax · linguistics, and rhetoric, only a few titles can be mentioned. Brief, but of great value, is Hoffmann's *Geschichte der Griechischen Sprache* (in the Sammlung Göschen). A. Thumb's second edition of his *Handbook of the Modern Greek Vernacular: Grammar, Texts, Glossary* was translated into English by S. Angus. R. Kühner's *Ausführliche Grammatik der lateinischen Sprache* is undergoing revision: Volume I., dealing with "Formen- und Wortlehre," and Part 1 of Volume 2, treating "Satzlehre," appeared in 1912. The new edition is a severe disappointment; the revision has not been careful and thorough-going and the book is far behind the times. Other specimens of syntactical work are *Beiträge zur lateinischen Syntax*, W. A. Baehrens; *Die Nebensätze in den Griechischen Dialektinschriften*, E. Hermann; *Case Usage in Livy. III. The Accusative*, R. B. Steele; *Grammatica Militans*, P. Cauer, fourth edition. To be named also is *Sophistik und Rhetorik*, H. Gomperz.

In lexicography the most notable event of the year is the publication of the first fascicle of an *Epitome Thesauri Latini*, compiled by F. Vollmer and E. Bickel; this work is intended to make accessible, in brief and handy form, the substance of the vast collections of material found in the great *Thesaurus Linguæ Latinæ*. The latter work itself made progress in 1912. A useful *English Greek Lexicon* was published by G. M. Edwards. It will be convenient to note here that Volume 7 of Pauly-Wissowa's *Encyclopädie der Classischen Altertumswissenschaft* (Fornax to Helikeia) appeared in 1912, under the editorship of W. Kroll.

Some books in the field of comparative philology must be named. These are *Elementarbuch der Phonetik*, O. Jespersen; *Grundriss der vergleichenden Grammatik der Indo-Germanischen Sprachen*, second edition (Part 2, Volume 2, which appeared in 1912, treats the inflection of nouns, the stems and inflection of pronouns, and, finally, adjectives, adverbs, and prepositions); *Introduction à l'Etude Comparative des Langues Indo-Européennes*, A. Meillet, third edition ("as an introduction to the comparative study of the historic Indo-European languages without a serious rival"); *Beiträge zur Indogermanischen Wortforschung*, a monumental work of 1111 quarto pages, the first and larger part of which consists of a collection of etymological articles dealing with all the Indo-Germanic languages. Of importance, too, to classical scholars is Meyer-Lübke's *Romanisches Etymologisches Wörterbuch;* this is to be arranged on virtually the same plan as Körting's *Lateinisch-romanisches Wörterbuch*, and will supersede that work.

More closely connected with classical philology are *Comparative Grammar of the Greek Language* J. Wright; *Untersuchungen über die Natur der griechischen Betonung*, H. Ehrlich (the book combats the recent theory that classical and pre-classical Greek had a stress accent strong enough to affect the vocalism of the language); *Against the Stress Accent in Latin*, R. L. Turner (see *The Classical Review* 26.147); *Studien zur Lateinischen und Griechischen Sprachgeschichte*, Emil Thomas.

In the fields of classical history and Greek and Roman life we may note first revisions of important books: *Aristotle's Constitution of Athens*, edited by J. E. Sandys; *The Romanization of Roman Britain*, F. Haverfield; *C. Iulius Cæsar. Sein Leben nach den Quellen kritisch darstellt*, E. G. Sihler (a revision of the *Annals of Cæsar*, noted in the last YEAR BOOK); *Technologie und Terminologie der Gewerbe und Künste bei Griechen und Römer*, Volume I.; *Geschichte der sozialen Frage und des Sozialismus in der antiken Welt*, Volumes 1-2, R. v. Pöhlman. Here, too, may be mentioned the second edition of *Formæ Urbis Romæ Antiquæ*, by H. Kiepert and Ch. Hülsen. New books in this field were: *A History of the Eastern Roman Empire from the Fall of Irene to the Accession of Basil I.* (A. D. 802-867), J. B. Bury; *Prehistoric Thessaly*, A. G. B. Wace and M. S. Thompson; *A Companion to Roman History*, H. Stuart Jones; *Wahrheit und Kunst Geschichtschreibung und Plagiat im klassischen Altertum*, H. Peter; *Greece and Babylon*, L. R. Farnell; *The Periplus of the Erythræan Sea. Travel and Trade in the Indian Ocean, by a Merchant of the First Century. Translated from the Greek*, W. H. Schoff; *Antike Schlachtfelder*, by

G. Veith (dealing with ancient battles in Africa; the book forms Volume 3, Part 2, of J. Kromayer's well-known work); *Excavations in the Island of Mochlos*, R. B. Seager ("our best source for the beginnings of Bronze Age Culture in Greece"); *Der Hellenismus in Klein Africa*, W. Thieling (see *The Classical Review*, 26.126); *The Outdoor Life in Greek and Roman Poets*, Countess Evelyn Martinengo-Cesaresco; *A Source Book of Ancient History*, G. W. Botsford. Most important is the periodical known as *Klio; Beiträge zur alten Geschichte*, edited by C. F. Lehman-Haupt and E. Kornemann; Volume 12 appeared in 1912. In the field of law we have space only to mention *Problems of the Roman Criminal Law*, 2 volumes, J. L. Strachan-Davidson, intended to supplement Mommsen's *Römische Strafrecht; Apulejus von Madaura und das römische Privatrecht*, F. Norden; *Etudes Historiques sur le Droit de Justinien*, P. Collinet; *Das Attische Recht und Rechtsverfahren*, J. H. Lipsius (new edition of Volume 2, second half).

Mention was made above of Professor Shorey's translation of O. Schrader's article on *The New Metric*. In *The Verse of Greek Comedy* Prof. John Williams White champions the (so-called) new metric, taking issue with the received views of Westphal, Schmidt, Christ, etc. A book on a kindred theme is *Aristoxenian Theory of Musical Rhythm*, C. F. Abdy Williams.

Turning to the field of Greek and Latin literature we note first new editions of several books: *Select Epigrams from the Greek Anthology*, J. W. Mackail (third edition); *Plautinische Forschungen*, F. Leo; *The Rise of the Greek Epic*, G. Murray; *Die Griechische und Lateinische Litteratur und Sprache*, by Wilamowitz, Krumbacher, etc.; *Einleitung in die Altertumswissenschaft*, by Gercke and Norden; *A Companion to Greek Studies*, edited by L. Whibley. Important additions were made to the Oxford Classical Text Series and to the Teubner Series of Classical texts; the most interesting of the former, perhaps, is that of the text of Isidorus, by W. M. Lindsay, which now for the first time makes that author accessible to everyone. An important annotated edition is that of the *Satires of Horace*, by P. Lejay. Attention must be directed also to *The Vitality of Platonism and Other Essays*, J. Adam; *Platonische Aufsätze*, O. Apelt; *Sprachliche Forschungen zur Chronologie der Platonischen Dialoge*, H. von Arnim; *The Greek Genius and its Meaning to Us*, R. W. Livingstone; *Das Plagiat in der Griechischen Litteratur*, E. Stemplinger; *English Literature and the Classics*, a collection of essays by various English scholars; *Troy. A Study in Homeric Geography*, W. Leaf, in which the author, on the basis of a careful study of the topography of the Troad, concludes that the Iliad describes a real war, at the back of which lay commercial and economic considerations; *Aristotle's Researches in Natural Science*, T. E. Jones; *The Love of Nature among the Romans*, A. Geikie; *Mathematik und Astronomie im klassischen Altertum*, E. Hoppe.

Of special interest, finally, are several volumes by American scholars: The Classical Papers of Mortimer Lamson Earle, who died in 1905 (Professor Earle was an expert in text criticism, especially in the Greek dramatists); *Greek Literature*, a collection of ten lectures on various departments of Greek literature delivered in 1911 at Columbia University by as many American scholars; *Harvard Essays on Classical Subjects*, papers on "Roman Art," "Alciphron," "Plato," "Ovid," "Greek Conceptions of Immortality," etc., by members of the Classical Department of Harvard University; *The Greek Romances in Elizabethan Prose Fiction*, a dissertation by S. L. Wolff; *The Common People of Ancient Rome*, F. F. Abbott. (Halle, 1912).

PHILOSOPHIC SOCIETY, WESTERN. A learned society, founded in 1900. The twelfth annual meeting of the association was held at the University of Chicago, April 5-6, 1912. In pursuance of the plan adopted by the executive committee, the morning and afternoon sessions of the first day were devoted to ethics and the discussion of ethical problems. The special topic of the afternoon was "The Teaching of Ethics." The morning of the second day was given to a joint session with the Western Psychological Association, in which five papers were read and discussed. Officers for 1912 were elected as follows: President, J. E. Boodin; vice-president, V. H. Bode; secretary and treasurer, H. W. Wright.

PHILOSOPHY. NEW TENDENCIES. Characteristic features in recent modern thought are the antagonism to rationalistic monistic systems, mechanistic and idealistic, to the so-called block-universe with its alleged fatalism, and the plea for methods and interpretations that will satisfy both the head and the heart and bring philosophy into closer touch with life. Doubts are raised against the competence of the intellect to reach a satisfactory world-view, and it is proposed either to confine its operations and jurisdiction to the physical world or to conceive it as an instrument in the service of the will, or to judge its truth-value by its utility, or to regard its conclusions as mere conventions, as symbols, or as approximations to truth. Those who do not discourage all attempts at constructing systems of metaphysics find in feeling, belief, immediate experience, or intuition the sources of a surer knowledge than in the discursive understanding, and would substitute pluralism, pragmatism, intuitionism, voluntarism, and theism for the traditional monism, rationalism, and idealistic pantheism. William James and Henri Bergson are the chief figures in this anti-intellectualistic movement which harks back to the Romanticism of the nineteenth century. These antagonistic currents in contemporary philosophy are not moving without resistance from the older intellectualistic conceptions, which refuse to admit the inadequacy of rational thinking either in natural science or in metaphysics; while other schools insist on reconstructing philosophical thought upon a rationalistic and realistic basis. Instead of rejecting natural science as utterly incapable of interpreting reality, some thinkers demand that philosophy employ scientific methods, others that it leave to natural science itself the task of solving the world-riddle, while still others relegate metaphysics to the realm of poetry and religion. The formation of a Positivistic Society in Germany, with the avowed purpose of developing a world-view on a scientific basis, and the coöperation of a small group of realists in the United States for similar ends are symptoms of protest against Romanticism in philosophy. The reader is referred to *The New Realism* by Holt, Marvin, Montague, Perry, Pitkin, and Spaulding. The

Proceedings of the First Monistic Congress (edited by Blossfeldt in coöperation with Ostwald and Riess) likewise gives evidence of a trend towards a universal theory based on natural science. The discord prevailing in the field of contemporary philosophy has suggested the need of some sort of philosophic platform; and the American Philosophical Association at its Christmas meeting, held at Columbia University, debated the question: Is a continuous progress towards unanimity among philosophers on the fundamental philosophical issues desirable and attainable? Ranzoli, *Il linguaggio dei filosofi*, points out the need of coöperation and particularly of a common vocabulary. Further information is given in the articles of Kemp Smith, Pitkin, and K. Schmidt in *J. of Phil.*, IX. 26. However undesirable disagreement may be, it cannot be denied that the conflict between the schools has had many wholesome effects; it has intensified the interest in philosophical study not only among the specialists but in other fields of learning (particularly in natural science and mathematics), as well as among the educated public; it has led to the reconsideration of all the vital problems, especially in the theory of knowledge; and it has made necessary a clearer and less one-sided restatement of the older rationalistic system. See YEAR BOOK of 1911.

LITERATURE OF THE NEW SCHOOLS. English translations of Bergson's *Matter and Memory* and *Introduction to Metaphysics*, a collection of James's *Essays in Radical Empiricism*, and Schiller's *Formal Logic* have appeared during the year. Keyserling's *Metaphysische Wirklichkeit* and Vogel's *La religion de l'évolutionisme* show the influence of Pragmatism and Bergsonism. Among the books discussing modern currents of thoughts and the new thinkers are: Alliotta, *La reazione idealistica contro la scienza;* Ruggiero, *La filosofia contemporanea;* Perry, *Present Philosophical Tendencies* (an extended discussion of this book by Lovejoy in *Journal of Phil.*, IX. 23); Eucken, *Main Currents of Modern Thought* (translation); Flournoy, *La philosophie de W. James* (best account of James's philosophy); Boutroux, *W. James* (French and English); Balsillie, *An Examination of Bergson's Philosophy; Le Roy, Une philosophie nouvelle, H. Bergson;* Elliot, *Modern Science and the Illusions of Professor Bergson;* Solomon, *Bergson;* Benda, *Le Bergsonisme;* Gagnebin, *La philosophie de l'intuition;* Wilbois, *Devoir et durée.*

METAPHYSICS. The large number of works published in this field shows a growing interest in ultimate questions. The realists are represented in the persons of B. Russel (*Problems of Philosophy*), Fullerton (*The World we Live in*), and Marvin (*Introduction to Metaphysics*). In his *Sources of Religious Insight* Royce offers an application of his voluntaristic idealism to the problem of religion. Other idealistic systems are presented in the following books: Boutroux, *The Beyond that is Within;* F. J. Schmitt, *Der philosophische Sinn;* Braun, *Grundrisz einer Philosophie des Schaffens;* Radulescu-Motru, *Eléments de métaphysique.*

Naturalistic systems (monistic and materialistic) are given by J. G. Vogt, *Der absolute Monismus;* Gilbert, *Neue Energetik;* Bardonnet, *L'universe-organisme.* The mechanical conception of life is upheld by Professor Schæfer in his inaugural address before the British Association of Science on *The Chemical Creation of Life* and by J. Loeb in his book, *The Mechanical Conception of Life.* The student of metaphysics will find the following helpful: Poincaré, *Leçons sur les hypothèses cosmogoniques;* Hartmann, *Philosophische Grundfragen der Biologie;* Joussain, *Philosophie de la nature;* G. Richter, *Bewegung, die vierte Dimension;* Driesch, *Ordnungslehre.* Le Dantec, *Contre la métaphysique,* opposes all metaphysics as poetry, and claims that we must look for the solution of our problems to natural science, which is wholly impersonal.

LOGIC and THEORY OF KNOWLEDGE. Ever since the revival of the critical philosophy of Kant during the latter half of the nineteenth century, the theory of knowledge has formed one of the main subjects of study in philosophy, (see YEAR BOOK, 1908), especially among the Germans, who are doing thorough work in this field under the leadership of Cohen and Natorp (the Marburg school), Schuppe, Husserl, Rickert, Meinong, and others. Consult the article on "Kant and the Marburg School," by Natorp in *Kant-Studien*, XVII., 3, and the treatise of Lanz, *Das Problem der Gegenständlichkeit in der modernen Logik;* also the yearly articles by Ewald in the *Philosophical Review* on German Philosophy. It is to be noted, however, that a large part of the year's books has been produced by scholars of other countries and that many of them are valuable contributions. We mention: Hegel, *Doctrine of Formal Logic* (translated by Macran); Bosanquet, *Logic*, second edition, two volumes; Baldwin, *Thoughts and Things*, vol. III.; Coffey, *The Science of Logic;* Mercier, A *New Logic;* Sheffield, *Grammar and Thinking; Logik*, by Windelband, Royce, Couturat, Croce, Enriques, Losskij (vol. I. of *Encyclopädie der philosophischen Wissenschaften*); Stadler, *Logik;* Döring, *Grundlinien der Logik;* Frischeisen-Köhler, *Wissenschaft und Wirklichkeit;* Kraft, *Weltbegriff und Erkenntnissbegriff;* Schlesinger, *Geschichte des Symbols;* Gallinger, *Das Problem der objektiven Wirklichkeit;* Ostler, *Die Realität der Aussenwelt;* Lask, *Die Lehre vom Urteil;* Pickler, *Möglichlichkeit und Widerspruchslosigkeit;* Meyerson, *Identité et realité;* Padoa, *La logique deductive;* Roberty, *Les concepts de la raison et les lois de l'univers;* Brien, *La méthode générale et scientifique;* Le Bon, *Les opinions et les croyances;* Honigswald, *Die Grundlagen der Mathematik;* Brunschvigg, *Les étappes de la philosophie mathematique;* Bachelier, *Calcul des probabilités;* Carvallo, *Le calcul des probabilités;* Varisco, *Conosci te stesso;* Levi, *Studi logici;* Botti, *L'infinito.*

ETHICS. There is continued interest in the study of ethics, as one might expect from the prominence of moral questions in contemporary public affairs. The large number of books in this field deal not only with basal principles, but with practical social problems, with morality in its relations to economics, law, politics, and education. Attention is also paid to the evolutionary study of moral ideas and practices, but no works of this character have appeared during the year equalling in importance those of Westermarck, Hobhouse, Dewey, and Tufts, which were so favorably received a number of years ago. See YEAR BOOK, 1908.

THEORIES and SPECIAL PROBLEMS. Wundt, *Ethik*, in four parts (sociological, historical, theoretical, and social), fourth edition; G. E.

Moore, *Ethics* (a clear and forceful discussion of fundamental principles); Vogel, *La religion de l'évolutionisme. Essai d'une synthèse ethique moderne;* Höffding, *Principles of Personality;* Bax, *Problems of Men, Mind, and Morals;* Lagrésille, *Le monde moral;* Steudel, *Alte und neue Tafeln;* Furtmüller, *Psychoanalyse und Ethik* (application of the psychological theories of Adler to ethics); Duprat, *La morale theoric psycho-sociologique;* Sollier, *Morale et moralité;* Novicow, *La morale de l'intéret* (an ethics based on enlightened self-interest); Bauer, *La conscience collective et la morale;* Bayet, *Le mirage de la vértu;* Horne, *Free Will;* Orelli, *Die philosophische Auffassung des Mitleids;* Terraillon, *L'honneur;* Pagano, *L'individuo nel etica e nel diritto;* Witherspoon, *Lectures on Moral Philosophy* (reprint); Jeffs, *Concerning Conscience. Studies in Practical Ethics.*

History of Ethics and Ethical Ideals. Mitchell, *The Ethics of the Old Testament;* Friedlander, *Rabbinic Philosophy and Ethics;* Benz, *Die Ethik des Apostel Paulus;* Terraillon, *La morale de Geulincx;* Reisner, *Egyptian Conception of Immortality;* Dahlke, *Buddha als Weltanschauung;* Wallis, *Sociological Study of the Bible;* Chatterton-Hill, *Sociological Value of Christianity;* Abbott, *Society and Politics in Ancient Rome;* Macaggi, *Les origines de la déclaration des droits de l'homme de 1789;* Drouilly, *Les problèmes sociaux du temps présent;* Lodge, *Modern Problems;* Verghaegen, *Vingt-cinq années d'action sociale;* H. S. Wells and others, *The Great State.*

Social Philosophy. Many of the books mentioned in the preceding section as throwing light on the history of moral progress are of value to students of social philosophy, just as many books placed under this head will prove helpful in the study of the evolution of morals. Urwick, *A Philosophy of Social Progress* (a criticism of sociological methods); Engert, *Teleologie und Kausalität* (a philosophy of history); Duckworth, *Prehistoric Man;* Wundt, *Elemente der Völkerpsychologie;* Dupréel, *Le rapport social;* Pelletier, *Justice sociale;* Palante, *Les antinomies entre l'individu et la société;* Arréat, *Génie individuel et contrainte sociale.* The student of ethics will also be interested in Ellwood's *Sociology in its Psychological Aspects* and McDougall's *Psychology, The Study of Behavior,* as well as in the following books on religion: Stratton, *Psychology of Religious Life;* Leuba, *Psychological Study of Religion;* Hocking, *The Meaning of God in Human Experience;* Watson, *Interpretation of Religious Experience;* Durkheim, *Les formes élémentaires de la vie religieuse;* Cremer, *Le problème religieux dans la philosophie de l'action;* Hügel, *Eternal Life;* Schmidt, *Ursprung der Gottesidee;* Harrison, *Themis: A Study of the Social Origins of Greek Religion.*

Practical Social and Legal Questions. Müller, *Die Keuschheitsideen;* Müller-Lyer, *Die Familie;* Forsyth, *Marriage: Its Ethics and Religion;* Lofthouse, *Ethics and the Family; Report of the Royal Commission on Divorce and Matrimonial Causes;* Haynes, *Divorce Problems of To-day; Problems in Eugenics* (Papers of the First Eugenics Congress); H. Ellis, *Task of Social Hygiene;* Brugeilles, *Le droit et la sociologie;* Castelein, *Droit naturel;* Miceli, *Lezioni di filosofia del diritto,* vol. II., III.; Breuer, *Der Rechtsbegriff auf Grundlage der Stammlerschen Socialphilosophie;* McConnell, *Criminal Responsibility and Social Restraint.*

Moral Education. Papers of the Second Moral Education Congress held at The Hague, July, 1912; Paulsen, *Pädagogische Abhandlungen;* Marceron, *La morale par l'Etat;* Dugas, *L'éducation du caractère;* Kerschensteiner, *Characterbegriff und Charactererziehung;* Whitehouse, *Problems of Boy-Life.* The Western Philosophical Association devoted one of its meetings to the discussion of the teaching of ethics in colleges; the papers have been published in the *Journal of Philosophy.*

History of Philosophy. Cornford, *From Religion to Philosophy* (an attempt to find the origins of Greek philosophy in primitive religion); Stöckl, *Handbook of the History of Philosophy,* vol. I. (translation); Drews, *Geschichte der Philosophie;* Sortais, *Histoire de la philosophie* (throughout the Renaissance); Boutroux, *Historical Studies in Philosophy;* Brochard, *Études de philosophie ancienne et moderne;* Windelband, *Geschichte der antiken Philosophie,* third edition; Messer, *Geschichte der Philosophie im Altertum und Mittelalter;* de Wulf, *Histoire de la philosophie mediévale,* fourth edition; Brett, *A History of Psychology, Ancient and Patristic;* Baumann, *Neues zu Sokrates, Aristoteles, Euripides;* Apelt, *Platonische Aufsätze;* Wilson, *Aristotelian Studies;* Brentano, *Aristoteles' Lehre vom Ursprung des menschlichen Geistes;* Jones, *Aristotle's Researches in Natural Science;* Jaeger, *Enstehungsgeschichte der Metaphysik des Aristotles;* Colle, *La métaphysique d'Aristote* (translation and commentary); Husik, *Matter and Form in Aristotle;* Gentile, *Telesio;* Höffding, *Brief History of Modern Philosophy,* translated; Seth, *English Philosophers;* Stock, *English Thought for English Thinkers;* Stöcker, *Problem der Methode bei Descartes;* Tönnies, *Hobbes,* second edition; Bellange, *Spinoza et la philosophie moderne;* Maire, *L'œuvre scientifique de B. Pascal* (bibliography); Fabre, *Les pères de la révolution. De Bayle à Condorcet;* David, *Berkeley;* Lewin, *Die Lehre von den Ideen bei Malebranche;* Thomsen, *David Hume;* Lévy-Bruhl, *Préface à Hume;* Kofink, *Lessing's Anschauungen über die Unsterblichkeit,* etc.; Uebele, *Tetens;* Hensel, *Rousseau,* second edition; Meynier, *Rousseau;* Fabre, *Rousseau;* Grand-Carteret, *Rousseau;* Tiersot, *Rousseau;* Liebmann, *Kant und die Epigonen,* second edition; Stadler, *Kant;* Bowne, *Kant and Spencer;* Kuntze, *Die Philosophie Maimons;* Kastil, *Fries' Lehre von der unmittelbaren Erkenntniss;* Wilm, *Philosophy of Schiller;* Rosalewski, *Schiller's Aesthetik;* Kronenberg, *Geschichte des deutschen Idealismus,* vol. II.; Bréhier, *Schelling;* Walzel, *Deutsche Romantik,* second and third edition; Phalén, *Das Erkenntnissproblem und Hegel's Philosophie;* Cross, *The Theology of Schleiermacher;* Armendola, *Maine de Biran;* Saulze, *Le monisme matérialiste en France;* L. Secrétan, *C. Secrétan;* Flügel, *Herbart's Leben und Lehre,* second edition; Seillière, *Schopenhauer;* Parisot, *Spencer;* Schwarze, *Spencer;* Schumann, *Wundt's Lehre vom Willen;* Schlumke, *Rickert's Lehre vom Bewusstsein;* A. H. Stirling, *J. H. Stirling, His Life and Work; La Philosophie allemande au XIXe siècle,* by a number of French and Belgian scholars.

DICTIONARIES OF PHILOSOPHY, TRANSLATIONS, ETC. Mauthner's *Wörterbuch der Philosophie* (which has been appearing serially, is now complete in two volumes); M. Schmidt, *Philosophisches Wörterbuch*. Translation of part of Hegel's *Logic* by Macran; translation of Rosmini-Serbati's *Theodicy* in three volumes. Selections from psychological works (translations) in Rand's *Classical Psychologists*. New editions of the works of Kant, Fries, Fichte, Schelling, Hegel, Schleiermacher, Schopenhauer, Lotze, Nietzsche, Avenarius, Spir, and others.

PHIOGEN PROCESS. See METALLURGY.

PHONGAS. See ANTHROPOLOGY.

PHONOLITH. See CHEMISTRY.

PHOSPHATE. The production of phosphate rock in the United States, according to the United States Geological Survey, has increased steadily in the last ten years. The production in 1911 was 3,053,279 long tons, valued at $11,900,693. In 1910 the output was 2,654,988 tons, valued at $10,917,000. Since the beginning of phosphate mining in the United States in 1867 162,629,275 tons of phosphate rock have been mined. Florida in 1911 continued to lead in the production, with 2,436,248 long tons. Tennessee was second with 437,370 long tons, and South Carolina third, with 169,156 long tons. The production in the West was small. The exports of phosphate rock during 1911 amounted to 1,246,577 long tons, valued at $9,235,388. See FERTILIZERS.

PHOSPHORUS MATCHES, WHITE OR YELLOW. See LABOR LEGISLATION, *Accidents and Diseases*.

PHOTO-ELECTRIC EXPERIMENTS. See PHYSICS.

PHYSICS. The progress during the year 1912 has been along much the same lines as in the past two or three years. There has been a certain amount of what might be called routine work in the way of checking up the values of previously determined constants, and in certain lines some decidedly new and interesting work has been done. The most fruitful field of research has been in the domain of radioactivity and discharge through gases. The realm of theoretical physics has received its full share of attention, but from the mathematical nature of these articles it is often almost impossible to give any adequate idea of their content.

GENERAL. The study of extreme conditions has long been one of the most fascinating provinces of the physicist. For a number of years P. W. Bridgman has been investigating the phenomena observed when substances are subjected to high pressures. Of necessity his earlier work consisted largely in perfecting his apparatus and in devising means for measuring his results. During the past year or two he has begun to reap the fruits of this work of preparation, and several very interesting papers have been published from his laboratory. In one of these he discusses the behavior of water and ice when subjected to pressures up to 20,000 atmospheres —approximately 300,000 pounds per square inch. Among the results of this work are the discovery of two new forms of ice in addition to the three already described by Tammann. These results are of great theoretical interest in the light that they throw on the possibility of compressing the molecules themselves rather than the spaces between them. Bridgman has also studied the effects of high pressures—in some cases as much as 450,000 pounds per square inch—on the collapse of tubes and the breaking strengths of various materials. These results promise to be of great value in certain lines of engineering.

In the 1911 YEAR BOOK, the low temperature investigations of Kamerlingh Onnes were mentioned. This work has been continued in several directions. The paramagnetic properties of a number of substances have been investigated at very low temperatures. The results are important in showing that in all probability there is a region of low temperature in which all substances show marked variations from Curie's law that the paramagnetic susceptibility is inversely proportional to the absolute temperature.

During the year 1901, Sir William Ramsay published several articles dealing with the properties of the rare gases of the atmosphere—neon, krypton, and xenon. He stated that these were probably all monatomic gases, but the difficulty of preparing pure samples in any but the minutest quantities left the matter open to doubt. During the past year he has succeeded in preparing relatively large equantities of these gases in a very pure form. By determining the ratio of the specific heats at constant pressure and at constant volume he has fully confirmed his earlier predictions.

Among the most useful achievements of the year is the work of Dr. Gaede in perfecting a new form of vacuum pump. By applying the principle of the difference in pressure on the two sides of a rotating cylinder, he has succeeded in producing vacua far beyond anything heretofore attained. Moreover, the action of the "molecular air-pump" is very rapid after the preliminary vacuum is established. The perfection of this easy and rapid means of producing the very highest vacua places a new tool at the service of the investigator, and this should prove of great assistance in certain lines of research.

RADIATION QUANTUM. This theory, to which reference was made in the 1910 and 1911 YEAR BOOKS, has continued to be the subject of considerable discussion. Early in the year, papers by Planck and by Poincaré were published, in which mathematical treatments of the theory of black body radiation were given. The relation of the light quantum hypothesis to the photo-electric effect has been discussed by O. W. Richardson. He has called attention to the point that the confirmation by Compton's experiments of his theory of the photo-electric effect does not necessarily carry with it the truth of the light quantum hypothesis.

RELATIVITY THEORY. In the 1911 YEAR BOOK a general outline and résumé of the relativity theory was presented. The work of the past year has in general been along the lines indicated in that discussion. In addition to new applications of the theory, several investigators have devoted themselves to clearing up the relations between the fundamental postulates and assumptions. Among the articles that have appeared along this line, one by Carmichael is worthy of mention. As generally stated, the theory of relativity requires that the mass of a body—viewed as its inertia—with respect to forces acting in the direction of its motion shall be different from its "mass" with respect to forces at right angles to its motion. This has introduced many complications in certain problems. In a recent paper, Tolman has shown that it is possible to use the "transverse" mass for longitudinal as well as transverse collision. J. D. van der Waals, Jr., by making certain assumptions about the variation of mass with velocity, has shown that the results of the relativity theory may be derived directly from the classical mechanics. The problem of gravitation has received considerable attention from some of the leaders in this line. Abraham and Einstein have each published papers dealing with this question. D. L. Webster has discussed the various theories of gravitation and their relation to the relativity theory. It has generally been considered that acceptance of the relativity principle destroyed all need for or possibility of an ether. It is interesting to note that there have recently appeared several objections to this view. Ehrenfest has shown that Einstein's theory presents difficulties in the way of regarding the ether as superfluous. Helm has gone farther and maintains that only on the relativity principle is a thoroughgoing hypothesis of the ether possible.

RADIOACTIVITY. In the 1911 YEAR BOOK, Rutherford and Geiger's table was reproduced. This gave the order of the products of the three radioactive families and the data concerning their half-value periods and radiations as far as then determined. The work of the past year has filled in one or two of the gaps in this table. From studying the loss of activity of Vesuvian cotunnite, Rossi has concluded that the half-value period of radium D is about 17 years. The work of Geiger and Nuttall—see below—has shown that uranium probably consists of two products, uranium I. and uranium II. Barratt has found that the range of the α particles from thorium A is 5.4 cm. By studying the rate of diffusion of radium A, Eckmann has shown that, while an atom of radium A is originally positively charged, it may become neutral, or even negatively charged in the presence of strong ionization. The coefficient of diffusion of radium A in air was found to be very close to the value for radium emanation as determined by Rutherford. It was also shown that the atomic weight of radium A was approximately the same as that of radium emanation.

In the 1911 YEAR BOOK, the failure of Weiss and Piccard to detect any influence of a strong magnetic field on radioactive transformations was noted. In some recent work by Rutherford and Chadwick, it was observed that a strong magnetic field had no appreciable effect on the γ ray activity of a radium preparation. Rutherford has also shown that the rate of decay of radium emanation is independent of the concentration and that it is the same at the temperature of liquid air as at ordinary temperatures. Russell has attempted to detect some influence of temperature on radioactive disintegration, but his results were entirely negative. All these results are in line with the accepted theory that the radioactive changes occur within the atoms themselves, and are therefore only very slightly susceptible to external influences. The discoverey of some method of influencing the rate of radioactive transformations would prove an immense aid in the study of the real nature of the processes.

Barratt and Marsden have continued their study of the emission of α particles by the various radioactive products. Their results on the branching of thorium B into thorium C_1 and thorium C_2 have been confirmed by some work of Hevesy on the electrochemical behavior of thorium C. Barratt has followed up the work of Geiger and Marsden (see 1911 YEAR BOOK), by determining the relative number and the ranges of the α particles emitted by the disintegration products of thorium. His results may be summarized as follows: thorium emanation emits 100 particles of 5.0 cm. range; thorium A emits 100 particles of 5.4 cm. range; thorium C_1 emits 35 particles of 4.8 cm. range; thorium C_2 emits 65 particles of 8.6 cm. range.

In 1911, Fajans and Makower showed that radium C_2 was not in the direct line of disintegration products of the radium series, but was a sort of side branch. That is, radium C_1 may disintegrate so as to give either radium D or radium C_2. This is similar to the behavior of thorium C_1 noted above. (See also 1911 YEAR BOOK.) The investigation of the transformation of radium B into radium C_1 and of radium C_1 into radium C_2, or radium D, has been continued by Fajans and Makower. Their chief results are as follows: (1) The α rays as well as the greater part of the β rays from radium C belong to radium C_1. (2) The ionization due to the β rays from radium C_2 is too small to be detected in comparison with that due to the β rays from radium C_1. (3) The β rays from radium B can be divided into two parts, one of which has a coefficient of absorption seven times as great as that of the other. This group produces only 1½ per cent. of the total ionization due to radium B. The γ radiation from radium B was studied by Mosley and Makower. They prepared radium B by recoil from radium A (see YEAR BOOKS for 1910 and 1911) and made corrections for the γ radiation from the radium C in equilibrium with radium B. Their results show that radium B gives no *hard* γ rays and that, if radium C_2 emits any γ rays at all, the quantity is too small to be detected by the ordinary methods.

As already noted Geiger and Nuttall have shown that the transformation of uranium into uranium emanation takes place in two steps, each of which is accompanied by the loss of an α particle. Their method consists in plotting the ionization against the ranges of the α particles for uranium, ionium, and polonium, making certain corrections for impurities, leak, etc. It is known that the atoms of ionium and polonium give off one α particle each on disintegrating. The curves for these two were found to be in complete agreement. The curve for uranium, however, while of the same general type as the others, differed from them decidedly in the position of the maximum and the rate of decrease from the maximum. Geiger and Nuttall showed that this curve could be obtained by combining two "pure" curves (such as ionium or polonium) for α particles whose ranges are 2.9 and 2.5 cm. The value of the range of the α particles from uranium previously given, viz., 2.72 cm., is evidently the mean value for these. According to this theory, uranium I. has a half-value period of 5×10^9 years and emits α particles of range 2.5 cm. (in air at 760 mm. and 15°C.) and is thus transformed into uranium II. This has a half-value period of 2×10^6 years and emits α particles of range 2.9 cm. These two products should differ in atomic weight by 4, and must be very similar in chemical properties since thus far it has been found impossible to separate them by chemical process. It has been calculated that there is about one milligram of uranium II. in each gram of pure uranium. Geiger and Nuttall have also shown that in the radium, thorium, and actinium series, the logarithm of the range of the α particles is a linear function of the logarithm of the transformation constant. This result has proved to be of considerable theoretical importance. The characteristics of the β rays from the various products of the radium series have been investigated by Danysz, and by Danysz and Götz. The method consisted in determining the deflection produced when the rays were subjected to the action of a strong magnetic field. As the deflection for a given field depends upon the velocity, the particles of different speeds are sorted out, thus forming a "magnetic spectrum." In this way Danysz showed that there were at least 23 groups of β particles whose speed varied from 0.615 to 0.998 times the velocity of light. Von Baeyer, Hahn, and Meitner have made a similar study of the "magnetic spectrum" of the β rays from thorium.

Parallel with the work of experimental investigation, several papers have been published, which develop more or less completely the theory of the effects. Among these are a paper by Darwin, on the absorption and scattering of α rays. He assumed that when α particles pass through matter they exert a force on the electrons according to the inverse square law tending to pull the electrons out of the atoms. From this he developed the relation between the velocity and the distance from the source. The experimentally determined "velocity curves" for a number of substances agree with this relation. These deductions give us a means of estimating the number of electrons in an atom. This was found to lie between the atomic weight and half that number. H. A. Wilson has suggested that the kinetic energy of the α particles may be regarded as a sort of "atomic temperature" determining the internal state of the atom. Its influence on the rate of radioactive decomposition would then be similar to that of temperature on the velocity of chemical reaction. By assuming that the work done by an α particle in escaping from an atom is practically the same in all cases, he developed an equation connecting the rate of transformation with this "atomic temperature." The results of Geiger and Marsden (see 1911 YEAR BOOK) agree with this theory. From the data on helium, Wilson has calculated that the work necessary for the escape of one gram-molecule of electrons in radioactive emission is about 10^6 times as great as that necessary to liberate one gram-molecule of electrons from hot platinum in thermionic emission.

One of the most important of the theoretical contributions is a paper by Rutherford on the origin of the β and γ rays from radioactive substances. The disintegration of each atom of radium B and radium C has been shown to furnish about one β particle. The work of Barkla and Sadler, and their associates (see 1911 YEAR BOOK and below) has shown that under certain conditions each element emits one or more definite types of X-radiation, which are characteristic of the element. By comparing the data on the absorption of this characteristic X-radiation from bodies of lower atomic weight, Rutherford was led to the conclusion that the penetrating γ radiation from radium C may be regarded as the *characteristic* radiation from that element due to the escape of the β particles. The relationships between the energies of some of the groups of β particles from radium B and radium C, as given by Danysz (see above) were also considered. Rutherford showed that these could be explained to some extent by the assumption of two definite units of energy, but the phenomena were too complicated to be fully explained with the meagre data at hand. Rutherford's idea of the matter is suggestive. He regards the atom as consisting of a small, central, positively-charged nucleus, surrounded by electrons in motion. There are some reasons for believing that the electrons are in rings rotating in one plane. The instability of the atom, to which radioactive properties are due, would then be of two kinds, though these would not necessarily be independent of each other. Instability of the central nucleus would give rise to the emission of α particles, while instability of the electronic distribution would give rise to β and γ radiation. If we think of a β particle expelled from one of the inner rings, its passage through each of the outer rings might be accompanied by a loss of energy and the production of a particular type of γ rays.

IONIZATION AND GENERAL DISCHARGE IN GASES. The work of Barkla, Sadler, and others on the nature of the secondary X-rays produced when a beam of X-ray falls on a polished metal surface (See 1911 YEAR BOOK) has been continued with very interesting results. Barkla and Collier have shown that there is one "fluorescent" spectrum characteristic of all the elements; the only differences for the different elements being in the absorbability of the radiation. For this radiation from various elements, the absorption curves referred to aluminum seemed to show that the effects in the elements studied were identical. The discovery of this homogeneous secondary X-radiation has been of great assistance in investigations on the nature of the action of the X-rays, since heretofore the radiation from any available source was far from homogeneous. Sadler and Mesham have shown that when a homogeneous beam is scattered by a substance of low atomic weight, it is transformed into a "softer" type of radiation, and that the "harder" the exciting beam, the greater is the intensity of the scattered radiation, and the greater is the change in quality produced by the scattering. Barkla and Simons have studied the ionization due to the homogeneous Röntgen radiation emitted by elements when exposed to ordinary primary Röntgen radiation. (See YEAR BOOKS for 1911 and 1912.) They showed that the ionization produced is not purely an atomic phenomenon, but depends to some extent on the chemical combination of the elements in the gases. Equal absorptions of X-rays or their secondary rays by different gases were not always accompanied by equal ionizations, though in general ionization was found to be roughly proportional to absorption. Similar results were obtained for the absorption of the electronic radiation by different gases. The results point to the conclusion that the relative ionizations in different gases when Röntgen radiation is totally absorbed are identical with the ionizations produced by electronic and α radiations.

It has long been a matter of speculation whether the X-rays are similar to ultra-violet light of extremely short wave-length or are corpuscular in nature. Recent experiments of Laue at Munich, promise to throw light on this question. A cylindrical beam of X-rays was passed through a crystal of zinc blend on to a photographic plate. Upon development, this showed a pattern similar to that which would be produced by diffraction if the "wave-lengths" of the rays were comparable to the distances between the molecules. Naturally this has provoked a lively discussion, and the advocates of a corpuscular theory have suggested explanations based on reflection. Apparently the question is by no means settled, and we shall probably in the immediate future see much work along this line.

J. J. Thomson has given a theoretical discussion of the process of ionization by moving particles. His assumptions are (1) "Cathode or positive rays when they pass through an atom repel or attract the corpuscles (electrons) in it and thereby give them kinetic energy." (2) "When the energy imparted to a corpuscle (electron) is greater than a certain definite value—the value required to ionize the atom—a corpuscle (electron) escapes from the atom, and a free corpuscle (electron) and a positively charged atom are produced." From these assumptions and various experimental data, Thomson shows that, in the case of cathode rays, the number of ions produced per centimeter should be inversely proportional to the kinetic energy of the moving particle. Glasson's experimental results (1911) confirm this view. From Townsend's calculation of the energy required for ionization, Thomson concludes that the number of electrons per atom is probably not more than two or three times the atomic weight. The recombination of the electrons with the ions would produce a radiation which would ordinarily be "very far" into the ultra-violet. On the assumption that the atoms also contain electrons requiring a much greater force for ionization, Thomson shows that this theory accounts for pulses similar to the X-rays. Since this radiation would owe its character primarily to the properities of the atom which produced it, it would resemble very strongly the homogeneous (characteristic) Röntgen radiation studied by Barkla and his associates. Thomson also shows that this radiation would probably be divided into definite units or "quanta." The actual mechanism of ionization has also been considered by several others, both experimentally and theoretically. Gill and Pidduck have found some very interesting effects in helium. Four years ago these investigators showed that the minimum spark potential was lower in helium than in other gases. The sample used at that time contained various impurities. Their latest results were obtained with very pure helium. They found that in pure helium the minimum spark potential was 156 volts, while the presence of 1 per cent. of impurity increased this to 187 volts. This extremely low spark potential they ascribed to ionization by collision.

The ionization in closed vessels by Röntgen rays and by γ rays has been studied by Eve. His results show that the ionization produced by these agents is really due to electrons projected with velocities of the order of magnitude of the cathode rays or the β rays of radium C. In the case of Röntgen rays, these electrons come from the gas in the vessel, while in the case of γ rays these electrons come chiefly from the walls of the containing vessel. This was shown by working with electroscopes contained in very thin walled cases. The ionization due to Röntgen rays in the case of iron or zinc vessels with ½ millimeter walls was only about 15 per cent. of the ionization in free air, while that due to γ rays was about 40 per cent. greater than that in free air.

The work of C. T. R. Wilson in photographing the path of an ionizing particle in a gas was mentioned in the 1911 YEAR BOOK. During the past year he has perfected the details of this method and has brought out several new points of decided interest. One of the most noteworthy facts concerns the path of an α particle. This has generally been regarded as a straight line. The photographs in general confirm this, but in many cases an abrupt bend occurs within the last few millimeters of the path. Some plates showed evidence that this was due to the phenomenon of recoil.

Pohl and Pringsheim have continued their investigations on the selective photo-electric effect, mentioned in the 1911 YEAR BOOK. Previous results obtained for rubidium, potassium, and barium agreed exactly with Lindemann's calculated values, but the results of their recent experiments on sodium and lithium show departures of from 12 per cent. to 20 per cent. from the theoretical values. Elster and Geitel have determined the minimum luminous energy necessary for the production of an electronic current in a potassium photo-electric cell. To produce a current of about 10^{-15} amperes per square centimeter, they found that it required approximately 10^{-7} ergs per second per square centimeter.

J. Robinson's work on the photo-electric properties of thin metallic films indicates that for very thin films the velocity of the emitted electrons is greater when produced by emergent than by incident light, while for thicker films the reverse is the case. Robinson has also studied photo-electric fatigue, showing among other things that fatigue occurs when a metal is exposed to ultra-violet light, but that recovery begins as soon as the light is shut off and is completed in a few minutes. He has suggested that Allen's results, which differ from these, were probably due to the presence of occluded gas. The theoretical bearings of the photo-electric effect have been discussed by O. W. Richardson and Compton. The general agreement between Richardson's theory and the experimental results seems to be very good, and the theory fits in well with the theory of other allied effects. Compton has pointed out that the electrons moving between emitting and receiving plates are subject to a force due to the contact difference of potential, as well as to that due to the external field. When corrected for this effect, his results indicate that, under the action of a given beam of ultra-violet light, the different metals give off electrons with practically equal velocities.

In some respects, one of the most interesting and suggestive discoveries of the year is one made by R. W. Wood, incidental to his work on long heat waves. He found that the electrical conductivity of a thin film of silver, deposited on glass or quartz, was not greatly affected by a number of cross-cuts, providing that these cuts were not more than 0.0003 millimeter in width. The original resistances of the films were about 10 ohms each, and this was increased by the cross-cuts in some cases to only 13 or 15 ohms, while in others it was found to be as great as 300 or 400 ohms. Apparently this variation was due to slight differences in the width of the cuts. When the width of the cross-cuts was increased to about 0.0006 millimeter, the resistance became practically infinite. Other experiments of a different nature seemed to show that this was a real effect. Wood has suggested the novel explanation that this may be due to the "presence of an atmosphere of electrons in the immediate proximity of metallic surfaces." Some recent work by Anderson and Morrison on electric currents in air at ordinary pressure seems to be in harmony with this explanation.

δ RAYS. The production and nature of δ rays—slow moving β particles excited by a beam of α rays—have been studied by several investigators, notable among whom are Norman Campbell and H. A. Bumstead. Campbell's results show that the initial velocity of the δ rays is not as great as has been heretofore supposed, and that it is probably independent of the nature of the material in which the δ rays are excited. The number of δ particles emitted under the influence of a given beam of α rays is independent of the nature of the surface. Campbell seems to favor the view that the ionization produced in a gas by an α particle is an indirect result, the energy of the α particle being primarily expended in some process other than ionization. Pound has shown that the occluded gas at the surface of the plate exerts a large influence on the production of the secondary rays excited when α rays fall on a polished metal surface. In the case of a carbon plate, the production of secondary rays was increased by cooling to liquid air temperature, since this increased the amount of occluded gas.

The experiments of Bumstead and MacGougan indicate that the number of δ particles emitted under given conditions depends upon the speed of the exciting α particles in much the same manner as the number of ions produced in a gas. The fact that the rate of production of δ rays decreases for some time after the establishment of the vacuum was ascribed to the influence of gas absorbed by the walls of the vessel. It was found that polonium and the active deposit of thorium emitted a radiation which consisted of two parts. The primary part was not appreciably affected by an electric field; the secondary part consisted of electrons whose velocity was greater than that of the δ rays and less than that of the β rays. This secondary radiation was also emitted by any metal upon which the α rays were incident. Bumstead and MacGougan found that at least part of the δ rays were due to the action of these secondary rays and their experiments were "not adverse to the view that the whole of the δ ray effect was produced in this way."

THERMIONS. The emission of electrons and positively charged particles from heated metals and oxides has been the subject of investigation for several years. O. W. Richardson and his students have devoted a great deal of attention to it, and Richardson has developed a formula giving the relation between the temperature and the number of electrons emitted. During the past year, several investigations bearing on this subject have been published. The value of e/m for the positive ions from various salts of barium, strontium, calcium, magnesium, and zinc, has been determined by Davisson. His results indicate that the characteristic positive ions from these salts consist of single atoms of the metals, each of which has lost a single electron. This agrees with Richardson's previous results.

The investigation by Pring and Parker of the ionization produced by hot carbon, indicates that the pressure of the surrounding gas and the impurities in the carbon exert a great influence. Their investigation was carried up to temperatures as great as 2000°C. Their results differ widely from those calculated by Richardson's formula. Their conclusion is that the relatively large currents obtained by previous investigators should be ascribed to an emission of electrons due to a chemical reaction between the hot carbon or its impurities and the surrounding gas, rather than to a direct emission of electrons by the carbon itself. The results of Fredenhagen on the emission of electrons from a hot lime cathode confirm this view. When the cathode was heated in an electric furnace, the emission of electrons was only about 1 per cent. of that found at the same temperature when the cathode was heated by the passage of a current. As the hot lime conducts electrolytically, this would indicate that the emission of electrons was not primarily due to the temperature. It would seem from these rather conflicting results that there is need of considerable investigation along this line, both experimental and theoretical.

LIGHT. In the 1911 YEAR BOOK, reference was made to the work of Wood on "resonance spectra," and some account was given of the results obtained with sodium and iodine vapors. This work has been continued and extended during the past year by Wood and others. Some of the results obtained are very striking. Wood has found that mercury vapor at ordinary temperatures gives this resonance spectrum when illuminated by a beam of ultra-violet light of the same wave length as its so-called absorption line ($\lambda = 2536$). This investigation, of course, was made entirely by photography, the vapor being contained in a quartz tube, which is transparent to ultra-violet light. The results obtained by a study of this effect are in accord with Planck's theory of absorption. It was found that with mercury vapor in a high vacuum, there was no true absorption, but only a scattering of the light. However, when a small quantity of air or other gas was admitted, true absorption occurred, that is, the energy was partially converted into heat. The ratio of the amount of energy scattered to the amount absorbed was found to be a function of the pressure of the gas mixed with the mercury vapor. When the scattered radiation from a directly illuminated tube was allowed to fall on a second quartz tube containing mercury vapor, it was found that the vapor in the second tube gave out an extremely homogeneous radiation, which was called "secondary resonance radiation." In this way a "resonance lamp" was constructed. The light from this lamp was extremely sensitive to the presence of the mercury vapor in the air, being very easily absorbed by it. A layer of mercury vapor 5 millimeters thick at a pressure corresponding to room temperature—approximately 1/76000 of an atmosphere—was sufficient to cut down the intensity one-half. In one experiment, a quartz bulb, in which mercury had been heated, was afterwards cleaned with nitric acid and distilled water and then heated almost to redness. Even after this treatment it cast an almost totally black shadow when photographed by the light from the resonance lamp.

A continuation of the work on iodine vapor (see 1911 YEAR BOOK) with a 40-foot spectrograph gave results which are full of suggestion for future work. For example, with the high resolving power of this instrument the absorption spectrum of iodine was found to contain many thousand lines—Wood estimates the number at 50,000. In the region covered by the green line of mercury, $\lambda = 5460.7$, no less than seven distinct lines were found. These were comprised within a difference of wave length of less than 0.4 of an Ångström unit. In the red, orange, and yellow parts of the spectrum, the lines were found to be even more closely crowded together. In Wood's previous work, he showed that the resonance spectra of iodine when excited by the mercury arc consisted of three superposed series of lines—one excited by the green line and the other two by the two yellow lines. By using suitable absorbing screens, he has succeeded in separating the effect of the green line from the other two. This spectrum was found to consist of a series of thirty-seven double lines, the differences in *frequency* being approximately constant, and two lines of the series being missing. This result is somewhat similar to his previous results for sodium vapor, except that in that case it was the differences in *wave length* which were constant. The series excited by the two yellow lines were somewhat similar, though the relation between the members of the series were so complex that no relation between frequencies or wave lengths was apparent.

While Wood has been the leader in this line of investigation, the researches of Dunoyer on sodium vapor and of Franck and Hertz on iodine vapor have added considerable to our knowledge of these very complicated effects. Franck and Hertz studied the fluorescence of iodine vapor under the influence of polarized light and showed that in the direction perpendicular to the plane of polarization of the exciting light, the intensity of the fluorescence was 16 per cent. smaller than in the plane of polarization. The question whether the radiation from a luminous gas is due primarily to its temperature is one of great importance in the theory of radiation. An equation has been deduced on theoretical grounds giving the width of a spectrum line as a function of the wave length, the absolute temperature, and the mass of the vibrating particle. The width of the spectrum line can be measured by interference methods, and hence the temperature of the radiating particle can be deduced. Using this as the method of attack, Fabry and Buisson studied the spectra of the rare gases—helium, neon, and krypton—when subjected to an alternating current discharge. The discharge tubes were surrounded by a water bath at room temperature, and it was assumed that the temperature of the gas in the tube was the same as the temperature of the surrounding bath. Measurements were also taken with the tube immersed in liquid air. The results at room temperature agreed with the theoretical results within 1 per cent. The results at liquid air temperature differed from the calculated results by less than 10 per cent., the deviation being such as would result if the temperature of the gas were slightly greater than that of the liquid air. These results are in general accord with the principles of the kinetic theory of gases. They indicate that the mass of the luminous particles is of the same order of magnitude as that of the atoms, and that the temperature of the luminous gas is not very much different from that of its surroundings. Hence the luminosity of the gas cannot be due primarily to high temperature.

Following up this line still further, Fabry and Buisson have made approximate determinations of the temperatures of various sources of light. In the case of the Cooper-Hewitt lamp, the maximum temperature possible was calculated to be 1200°C. This is undoubtedly too high, since the effect of impacts between the luminous particles in this case is certainly not negligible, as is implicitly assumed in the calculations. Experiment also gives a much lower value for this temperature. Hence in this case also the temperature cannot be the sole cause of the radiation. The temperature of the arc between iron electrodes was calculated to be 2400°C. Here the effect of impacts is very slight. This line of attack promises excellent results for the future.

PIG IRON. See IRON AND STEEL.

PIGGERIES. See GARBAGE AND REFUSE DISPOSAL.

PITNEY, MAHLON. An American jurist, appointed on February 19, 1912, associate justice of the Supreme Court of the United States. He was born in Morristown, N. J., in 1858, and graduated from Princeton University in 1879. He studied law and was admitted to the bar in 1882, practicing at Morristown, N. J. He was elected to the Fifty-fourth and Fifty-sixth Congresses, 1895-1899, and resigned his seat on January 10, 1899. From that year until 1901 he was a member of the New Jersey Senate and its president in 1901. In 1901 he was appointed associate justice of the Supreme Court of the State and served in this position until 1908, when he was made chancellor for the term expiring 1915. See UNITED STATES, *Federal Judiciary*.

PITTSBURGH, PA. See CITY PLANNING.

PITUITARY GLAND. See SURGERY.

PLAGUE. Bubonic plague made its appearance in the West Indies in 1912, giving rise to some alarm and causing a stiffening of quarantine precautions in the seaports of the United States. Up to August 6, 47 cases had been reported in Porto Rico, 23 of which were fatal. Three cases were also reported from Havana and others from the island of Trinidad. The rat is the main factor in the spread of plague, but other rodents may act as carriers and serve as a reservoir in certain localities, as, for example, the ground squirrel in California and a species of marmot, called tarbagan, in Manchuria. Attention has of late been directed to the mongoose, an animal allied to the rat and squirrel by nature and habits, which swarms in Porto Rico, where it is said to have been introduced to kill off the rats. It has been proved that this rodent does become infected with the *Bacillus pestis* and that it is a possible if not probable carrier. Since 1904, when the present pandemic began, plague has circled the globe. From south-central China, where it has been endemic for centuries, the disease first invaded Canton, Hongkong, Amoy, and Macao. It then spread to India, Japan, and Asiatic Turkey; to Russia, Austria, and Portugal in Europe, and to a number of localities in Africa; then in 1899 to Hawaii, New Caledonia, and to various countries in South America; in 1909 to Australia, New Zealand, the Philippines, Germany, Great Britain, and California. By 1911 the plague had invaded those countries having the most extensive maritime commerce. In the western hemisphere, by 1907, plague had been reported in Argentina, Brazil, Chile, Mexico, Panama, Paraguay, Peru, Trinidad, and Uruguay, and in the United States in the States of California and Washington. The cases recently reported in Porto Rico and Cuba are the first known to have occurred in either place during the present pandemic. See VITAL STATISTICS.

PLANETS. See ASTRONOMY

PLANT BREEDING. See HORTICULTURE; BIOLOGY.

PLANT CANCER. See CANCER.

PLANT DISEASES. See BOTANY.

PLANTEN, JOHN R. A Dutch public official, consul-general for the Netherlands in New York City, died December 8, 1912. He was born in Amsterdam in 1834 and removed to New York with his parents at the age of ten. He was educated in the public and private schools of New York City and entered the manufacturing firm of his father. In 1874 he was appointed vice-consul of the Netherlands in New York, and in 1883 consul-general. From time to time he had charge of the consular interests of the Grand Duchy of Luxemburg. He acted as chargé d'affaires of the Netherlands at Washington during the absence of the ambassador. He received many honors from foreign countries during his years of service. He was a member of many foreign and American historical societies.

PLANT PHYSIOLOGY. See BOTANY.

PLANT QUARANTINE. See HORTICULTURE; and AGRICULTURAL LEGISLATION.

PLASMODIA. See MALARIA.

PLATFORMS, POLITICAL. See PRESIDENTIAL CAMPAIGN.

PLATINUM. The entire output of crude platinum in the United States is obtained from placer mines in Oregon and California. These mines also produce gold. The production in the United States increased slightly in 1911. This was due undoubtedly to the higher prices paid for the metal. There were mined in 1911 628 troy ounces, an increase of 238 ounces compared with the output in 1910. The value of the product of 1911 was $18,137, an average price per ounce of $28.87. Of the total output California produced 511 troy ounces and Oregon 117.

IMPORTS AND EXPORTS. The total amount of platinum imported into the United States in 1911 was 122,751 troy ounces, valued at $4,886,207. This includes platinum ore or crude platinum, ingots, bars, sheets and wire, and manufactured products. The total output of crude platinum in the world in 1911 was 314,323 troy ounces. Of this by far the larger quantity came from Russia, where, it is estimated by the United States Geological Survey, 300,000 troy ounces were produced. In Colombia were produced about 12,000, and small quantities in New South Wales and Canada.

PLATT, ISAAC HULL. An American physician and writer, died August 16, 1912. He was born in Brooklyn, N. Y., in 1853, and was educated at the Brooklyn Polytechnic Institute. He was admitted to the bar in Alabama in 1875. Two years later he studied at Columbia University and was admitted to the New York bar in 1877. He afterwards studied medicine and obtained the degree of M. D. in 1883. From 1886 to 1897 he practiced medicine at Lakewood, N. J., and following the latter date he traveled extensively. He was an ardent advocate of the Baconian authorship of Shakespeare's plays. He wrote *Bacon Cryptograms in Shakespeare, and Other Studies* (1905), and *Walt Whitman*, in "Beacon Biographies Series."

PLUMBISM. See OCCUPATIONAL DISEASES.

POETRY. See FRENCH LITERATURE; GERMAN LITERATURE, and LITERATURE, ENGLISH AND AMERICAN.

POINCARÉ, JULES HENRI. A French mathematician and physicist, died July 19, 1912. He was born in Nancy in 1854 and studied at the École Polytechnique and in the École des Mines. In 1879 he became an engineer and in the same year received the degree of doctor of science. He was called to Paris in 1881, where, in 1886, he became professor of mathematical physics and the calculus of probabilities in the Faculty of Sciences. After the death of Tisserand in 1896 Poincaré succeeded to the chair of celestial mechanics. In 1887 he became a member of the Academy of Sciences in Paris and after 1893 was a member of the Bureau of longitudes, of which, after 1898, he was president. He obtained the prize awarded by King Oscar of Sweden for a work on the problem of the three bodies in 1889. He carried on some of the most important researches and investigations in the modern history of mathematics. His work included a study of the various laws of the theory of functions and research in the domain of physics. He introduced into mathematics a new class of transcendents, which he named the "Fuchsian functions." He contributed to the theory of non-Euclidean geometry, to the theory of differential equations, and the various branches of higher algebra. His written contributions in mathematical subjects are of great importance. The most important of these are: *Les méthodes des nouvelles de la méchanique céleste* (3 vols., 192-99); *Electricité et optique* (2 vols., 1890-91); *Cours de physique* (13 vols., 1890). He also published important memoirs on mathematics and physics in the leading mathematical journals of France and Germany. He was a cousin of Raymond Poincaré, French premier, and was a member of the French cabinet.

POINCARÉ, RAYMOND. See FRANCE, *History*.

POISONING, INDUSTRIAL. See OCCUPATIONAL DISEASES.

POLAND. See RUSSIA.

POLAR EXPLORATION. ANTARCTIC. Captain Roald Amundsen reached the South Pole on December 16, 1911. The YEAR BOOK recorded last year the arrival of his party on the *Fram* at the Bay of Whales, an indentation in the Great Ice Barrier, on January 14, 1911, the landing of the stores, their transportation to the top of the barrier ice, and the building of "Framheim," the house that served as quarters for the expedition. The ship with a crew of 9 men, including Captain Nilsen, then started north, leaving 9 men in the land group. On February 10, Amundsen with 3 men, 18 dogs, and 3 loaded sledges started south to establish the first provision depot. For traveling and for hauling power Amundsen placed his whole trust in skiis and Eskimo dogs, and the results justified his choice. Sledging rapidly over a smooth, white snow plain, they reached 80°S. on February 14. They had covered 99 miles, and after caching 1300 pounds of provisions, returned to camp in two days. They left the station again on February 22 to plant supplies as far south as p ssi e. Five days later, the party reached 81°S. parallel, where they left 1150 pounds, and on March 8 reached 82°S., where they left 1375 pounds of food. Before winter began more supplies were added to the first station, or a total of 6700 pounds of advanced provisions in three caches. To insure finding the depots, rows of signs and flags were planted on opposite sides of each of them, extending at right angles across the N-S. route of March and five miles from the caches. It was proven later that the depots could easily be found even in a dense fog. Before the sun disappeared the seals killed weighed 132,000 pounds, an ample supply both for men and dogs.

The winter passed comfortably and all enjoyed the best of health. Experience had shown that the sledges were heavier than need be, and they, and other items of equipment, were reduced in weight. Meteorological observations were taken incessantly. The weather, on the whole, was fine. During the year at the station there were only two moderate storms. It was very cold, however, and the mean annual temperature of 26°C. was perhaps the lowest ever recorded. On October 20 the spring season was so well established that it was deemed safe to begin the southern march. The party numbered 5 men with 52 dogs and 4 sledges. The sledding was fine till 81°S. was passed, when, for nineteen miles, very dangerous crevasses had to be crossed. The supplies were in good condition at the two depots. Beginning at 80°S., a line of 150 snow pillars were erected along the route, as guides on the return, and they served so well that the return was made on exactly the same road. The ice was very even south of 82°, and rapid progress was made. At every unit parallel of advance a supply of provisions was cached. At 83°S., South Victoria Land was seen in the southwest. From day to day, new mountains from 10,000 to 16,000 feet high came into view. On November 11 they saw land directly south, and it was soon evident that a mountain range in about 86°S. and 163°W. crosses South Victoria in an easterly and northeasterly direction. The route had been directly south from headquarters when, on November 17, they left the ice to pursue their journey on the land. This was in 85°7'S. and 165°W.

The ascent to the lofty plateau of the continent was begun between the high peaks of South Victoria Land. This was not difficult till glaciers became the only highway to the south, and their steep and rugged surface offered the most formidable difficulties. Twenty dogs were sometimes required on a single sledge in spite of the greatly reduced loads. Dogs were killed to eke out the diminishing supplies, and the party was considerably delayed by snow gales. They finally reached the great interior plateau, and found themselves, on December 6, at an elevation of 11,024 feet above the sea. The land now sloped very gently towards the south, the going was good, but there was plenty of time, and the average advance a day was only about 17 miles. On December 15 a round of observations seemed to show that their latitude was 89°55'S. Next day, they moved their tent the remaining 5¾ miles south, and the observations they took in the next 24 hours are now in the hands of the University of Christiania. Amundsen had with him a small tent to be erected at the South Pole. He left the Norwegian flag floating above the tent, named the place "Polheim," and the land enclosing the South Pole, "King Haakon VII. Plateau."

He had covered 863 miles on his journey to the pole, his mean daily marches being fifteen miles. After an absence of ninety-nine days, he reached headquarters again on January 25, 1912, making an average of 22.1 miles a day. He found that two ranges unite in one mighty mountain range in 86°S., which extends in a southeasterly direction. Lieutenant Prestrud and two men reached King Edward VII. Land, but were not able to ascertain its limits. The *Fram*, before returing, made a voyage from Buenos Ayres to Africa and back, and took oceanographical observations at sixty stations.

No news was received from Capt. R. F. Scott's British expedition in Antarctica till March 31, 1912. In the late summer of 1911 he established supply depots for his expedition to the South Pole. Long excursions were also made by members of the scientific staff to the mainland of South Victoria Land. The winter was spent in camp at McMurdo Sound. Scott started south early in November, 1911, for the Pole. The weather was bad and snowstorms frequent. Sledging was so difficult after the party reached Beardmore Glacier (which Shackleton in December, 1908, ascended to the continental plateau), that the explorers could advance only about five miles a day. On January 4, 1912, Lieutenant Evans and some of Scott's sledgemen turned back, leaving the advance expedition at 87°35'S., at an altitude of 9800 feet. Scott had a month's provisions for the advance march, and as he had attained the smooth plateau where travel was easy, he was able to reach the South Pole on January 18, where he found Amundsen's tent and records. On the return journey the whole party perished. (See SCOTT, ROBERT F.) During the second summer season a great deal of research was carried on, and it is expected that the scientific results of this expedition will be especially important.

The Australasian Antarctic Expedition under the leadership of Dr. Douglas Mawson successfully landed on the coast of Wilkes Land early in January, 1912. Dr. Mawson set up his first station at Point Alden, the eastern part of Adelie Land. Meanwhile Captain Davis, master of the *Aurora*, which had taken the party south, proceeded along the coast to the westward. No expedition for seventy-two years, since Wilkes was in these waters, had approached this forbidden land. The vessel skirted the coast, or the barrier ice that fronted parts of it, for about 1200 miles, proving the exist-

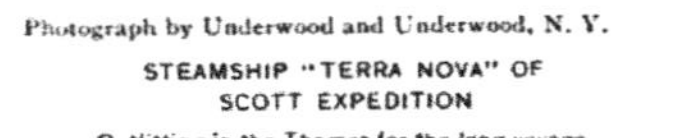

Photograph by Underwood and Underwood, N. Y.

STEAMSHIP "TERRA NOVA" OF SCOTT EXPEDITION

Outfitting in the Thames for the long voyage

ROALD AMUNDSEN

DISCOVERER OF THE SOUTH POLE

OSCAR WISTING AND HIS DOGS AT THE SOUTH POLE

From "The South Pole," by Roald Amundsen

Copyrighted, 1913, by Lee Keedick

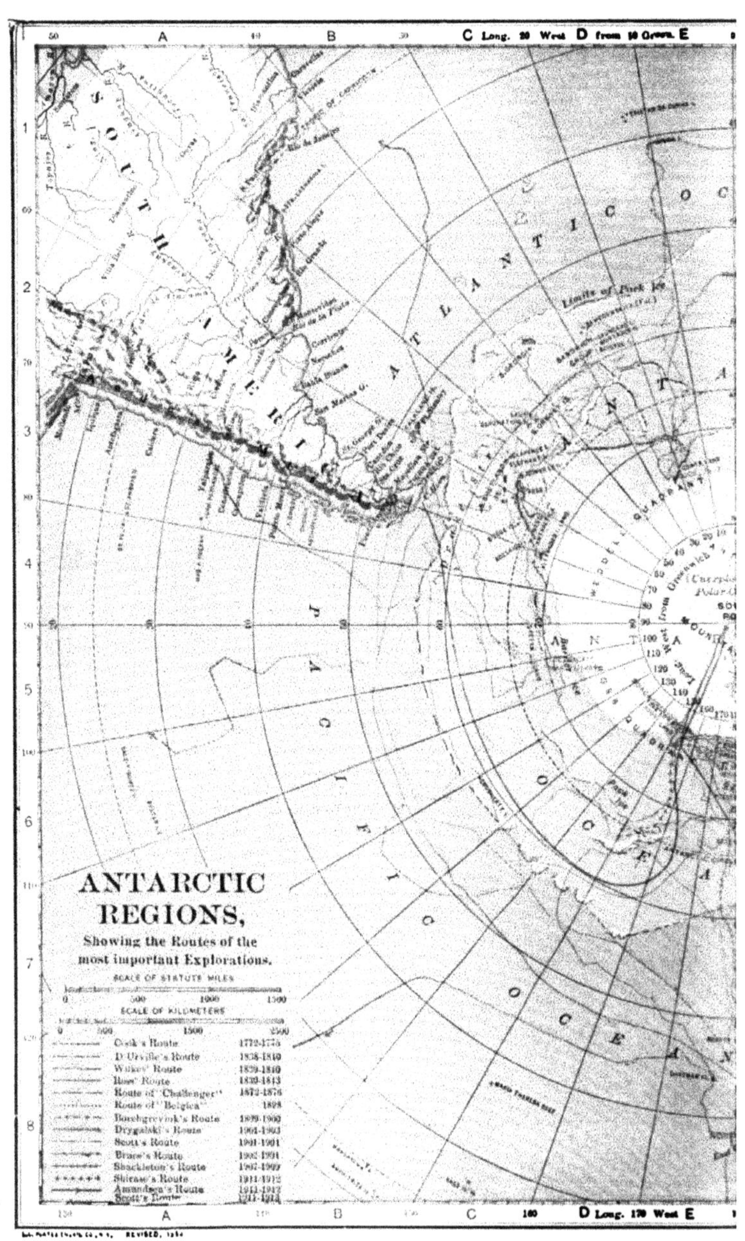
ANTARCTIC
REGIONS,
Showing the Routes of the
most important Explorations.
SCALE OF STATUTE MILES
0 500 1000 1500
SCALE OF KILOMETERS
0 500 1500 2500
Cook's Route
D'Urville's Route 1838-1840
Wilkes' Route
Ross' Route
Route of "Challenger" 1872-1876
Route of "Belgica" 1898
Borchgrevink's Route
Drygalski's Route
Scott's Route
Bruce's Route
Shackleton's Route
Shirase's Route
Amundsen's Route
Scott's Route
ATLANTIC
PACIFIC
OCEAN
SOUTH AMERICA
Limits of Pack Ice
Long. 20 West from 10 Green.
Long. 170 West

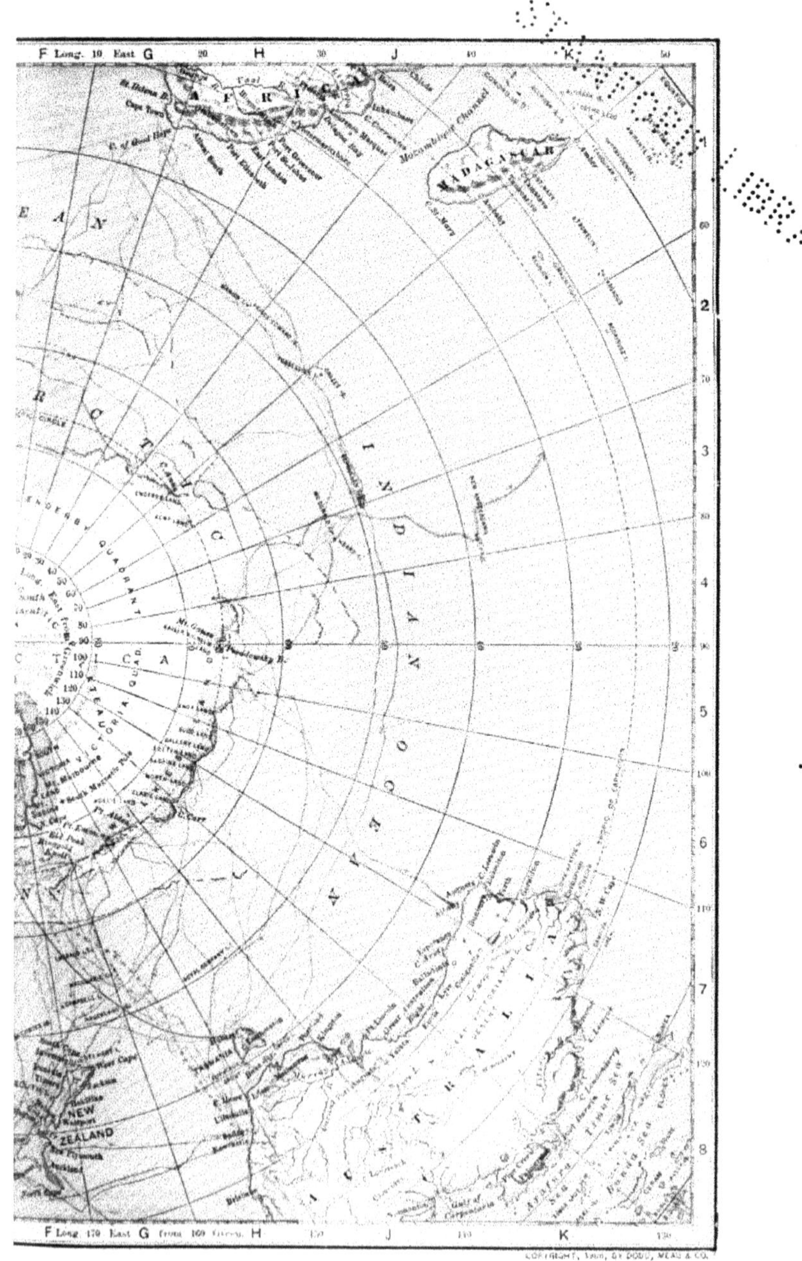
F Long. 10 East G 20 H 30 J 40 K 50
AFRICA
St. Helena B.
Cape Town
C. of Good Hope
Mozambique Channel
MADAGASCAR
C. St. Mary
INDIAN OCEAN
ANTARCTIC
ENDERBY QUADRANT
VICTORIA QUADRANT
Mt. Melbourne
South Magnetic Pole
Mt. Gauss
Posadowsky B.
C. Carr
AUSTRALIA
Gulf of Carpentaria
Arafura Sea
Timor Sea
Banda Sea
NEW ZEALAND
New Plymouth
F Long. 170 East G from 160 Green. H 150 J 140 K 130

ence of Wilkes Land, which since the days of Capt. James Ross had been disputed by some foreign geographers. The voyage of the *Aurora* thus did much to support the theory of there being one continental land mass round about the South Pole. Dr. Mawson had with him, at Point Alden, fourteen men, and expected to spend the Antarctic winter in scientific investigations.

On December 10, 1911, Dr. Filchner, the leader of the German Antarctic Expedition, sailed from South Georgia, intending to take a course due south till he reached the northern edge of the pack ice, which he would then follow to the east till he found an opening to the region of Coats Land. Nothing more was heard from the expedition until just after the close of the year, when it was announced that Filchner had returned with a part of his expedition, had discovered new land which he named "Prince Regent Luitpold Land," and new barrier ice, which is regarded as a sure indication of continental land behind it. He expected to return to the eastern part of the Antarctic next season.

ARCTIC. Mr. V. Stefansson returned from the American Arctic in the fall of 1912. His work there covered the years 1908-1912. His main geographical results were outlined in the YEAR BOOK for 1911 (p. 574). His sledge routes covered several thousand miles along the north coast of Alaska and Canada, between Point Barrow and Coronation Gulf, including long journeys along the Barter, MacKenzie, Horton, Dease, and Lower Coppermine Rivers, and a northern trip into the southwestern part of Victoria Island to the middle region of Prince Albert Sound. He and his companion, Dr. R. M. Anderson, made large ethnological and zoölogical collections. He visited and studied thirteen groups of Eskimos in the region east of Cape Bathurst. One of Stefansson's discoveries was the Horton River, which is probably about 200 miles in length and is 350 to 400 yards wide, over fifty miles from the sea. The Horton empties into the Arctic Ocean between Liverpool and Franklin Bays.

Captain Ejnar Mikkelsen and his companion, Engineer Iversen, were found on the coast of East Greenland by the Norwegian fishing vessel *Söblomsten*, and safely returned to Denmark. For more than a year they had lived chiefly upon the game they were able to kill. Mikkelsen accomplished the purpose that took him to East Greenland. He found various records and the diary of Mylius Erichsen, who, with his two companions, Brönlund and Hagen, perished after completing the mapping of the unknown coast of Northeast Greenland.

According to Erichsen's reports, Peary Channel does not extend from Robson Sea to the Greenland Sea, and therefore is not entirely the northern boundary of Greenland.

Mr. Ernest De K. Leffingwell spent the summer in continuing his study of the north coasts of Alaska, and will return there to resume his work next summer.

Dr. M. A. Quervain, a Swiss meteorologist, crossed the inland ice of Greenland from Holstenborg, in West Greenland, to Angmagsalik, on the east coast.

POLIOMYELITIS, EPIDEMIC. INFANTILE PARALYSIS. Important advances in our knowledge of this disease were made in 1912. Several observers had already demonstrated the virus of poliomyelitis in the nasopharyngeal mucosa and tonsils of monkeys and human beings infected with the disease; but attempts to demonstrate the virus in the secretions of the nasopharynx and intestines had failed until Kling, Wernstedt, and Pettersson presented their work, in which they showed, for the first time, the infectiousness of the secretions of the nasopharynx and intestines of persons who had died of poliomyelitis. At the International Congress of Hygiene and Demography in Washington Pettersson presented a summary of the more recent investigations of Kling, Wernstedt and himself, in which the virus of poliomyelitis was shown for the first time to exist not only in the buccal and intestinal secretions of persons in the acute stage of the disease but convalescents, persons suffering from clinically obscure infections of poliomyelitis, and apparently healthy persons in the immediate vicinity of poliomyelitis patients. Most important was the report by Dr. Pettersson that he and his colleagues had succeeded in demonstrating the virus in the buccal and intestinal secretions of persons who gave no history of recent illness but who had been in intimate contact with other persons in their own families sick with poliomyelitis. "Virus carriers" were found in six families. It was thought that such carriers were common during epidemics of poliomyelitis, probably exceeding the number of persons with clinically recognizable infections. The work of these men would seem almost to justify the conclusion that the infection is disseminated by transfer of the virus directly from person to person, "virus carriers" and abortive cases accounting to a large extent for the spread of the disease.

The possibility that an insect carrier might be implicated in the spread of poliomyelitis has also received considerable attention. Dr. Richardson, of the Massachusetts State board of health, had summarized the investigations of the disease made in that State from 1907 to 1912, in which the evidence was strongly in favor of fly transmission. Impressed with this evidence, Dr. Rosenau, in coöperation with the State board of health, undertook experiments to determine whether the stable fly, *Stomoxys calcitrans*, could transmit poliomyelitis. Dr. Rosenau stated that six out of twelve monkeys exposed daily for several weeks to the bites of large numbers of *Stomoxys*, which were also daily allowed during this time to bite monkeys experimentally infected with poliomyelitis, had developed symptoms of the disease. Sections of the spinal cord from one of the dead monkeys showed lesions characteristic of poliomyelitis, while the cords of the others showed degenerative changes which, in the absence of infiltrative lesions, were not considered sufficiently typical to justify a diagnosis. At present the question remains undecided as to whether the disease is directly contagious, whether a biting fly is a necessary factor in its transmission, or whether it may be conveyed in more than one way. If the stable fly should prove to be the chief or only means of transmitting the disease, its prevention and eradication will be a comparatively easy matter. A campaign of destruction against this species of fly should be much more easily conducted than those which have been waged against the mosquito and other insects which have been shown to be transmitters of disease.

POLITICAL ECONOMY. A considerable number of articles will be found elsewhere treating various problems and movements of economic interest. A general survey of business conditions during the year is given under FINANCIAL REVIEW. In the article on LABOR will be found references to the various topics treating different aspects of the labor problem. The article on BANKS AND BANKING, which includes statistics of all banks in the United States and the proposals for banking reform, is supplemented by articles on the several kinds of banking institutions, CURRENCY REFORM, and AGRICULTURAL CREDIT. Other articles related to the general subject of economics are INSURANCE, PARCEL POST, OLD-AGE PENSIONS; PRICES; SOCIAL ECONOMICS, and subjects there referred to; TARIFF; TAXATION; TRUSTS, and UNITED STATES STEEL CORPORATION.

AMERICAN ECONOMIC ASSOCIATION. The twenty-fifth annual session of this body was held in Boston, December 27-31. During the year the association increased considerably in membership, a special effort being made to this end by the secretary, Prof. T. N. Carver of Harvard University. The association members met first with the American Sociological Society and the American Statistical Association for the presidential addresses of these bodies, and, on the evening of December 27, with the American Historical Association to hear the address of its president, Theodore Roosevelt. In joint session with the Association for Labor Legislation, the "Theory of the Minimum Wage" was discussed by Henry R. Seager of Columbia, John R. Commons of Wisconsin, and a number of others. The necessity of minimum-wage legislation was well established; it was argued that the administration of such legislation should be placed in the hands of an administrative bureau rather than left to the courts; it was also brought out that minimum-wage legislation is only one phase of the movement for establishing minimum social standards in all aspects of industry, being thus comparable to sanitary legislation and limitation of hours. Prof. Irving Fisher of Yale, in discussing the "Rising Cost of Living," showed that this phenomenon is being experienced everywhere, that it will probably continue for many years, and that the most effective remedy is standardization of the purchasing power of the dollar. For a brief statement of his theory see PRICES. Prof. Frank A. Fetter, president of the association, in his address on "Population or Prosperity," developed the idea that unrestrained immigration will inevitably check the advance in the general level of economic welfare. He thought the optimistic theory of population commonly held in the United States should be revised. The subject of "Banking Reform" was discussed by Prof. E. W. Kemmerer of Princeton, Prof. J. H. Hollander of Johns Hopkins, Prof. O. M. W. Sprague of Harvard, and others. Other subjects discussed were "Economic Theory: Theories of Distribution," by Prof. Simon N. Patten of Pennsylvania; "Agricultural Economics: Farm Management," by Prof. H. C. Taylor of Wisconsin, Professor Carver, and others; and finally the "Economics of Governmental Price Legislation," by Prof. J. M. Clark of Amherst, C. W. Wright of Chicago, and others. The 1913 session will be held at Minneapolis.

The Hart Schaffner and Marx Company of Chicago offer several annual prizes for the best papers on a selected list of economic subjects. In 1912 the first prize of $1000 was awarded to Albert H. Leake, inspector of technical education for Ontario, Canada, for "Industrial education, its problems, methods and dangers." A second prize of $500 was awarded to Harry E. Smith, Ph. D., instructor in Cornell University, for "The United States federal internal tax history from 1861 to 1871."

BIBLIOGRAPHY. Below is a classified list of some of the principal works of the year. In addition to these references, lists will be found under SOCIAL ECONOMICS, LABOR, SOCIOLOGY, TAXATION, and WOMEN IN INDUSTRY.

ECONOMIC THEORY. Joseph Schumpeter, *Theorie der wirtschaftlichen Entwicklung;* Irving Fisher, *Elementary Principles of economics;* J. A. Hobson, *The Science of Wealth;* C. Colson, *Organisme économique et désordre social;* F. A. Fetter, *Source book in economics;* P. Clerget, *Géographie économique. L'exploitation rationelle du globe.*

HISTORY. H. Allsopp, *An introduction to English industrial history;* S. Salmon, *An introductory economic history of England;* Oliver Merton Dickerson, *American Colonial Government, 1696-1765. A Study of the British Board of Trade in its Relation to the American Colonies, Political, Industrial, Administrative;* S. L. Mim, *The commercial policy of Colbert toward the French West Indies.*

BUSINESS. C. N. Fay, *Report of the Commissioner of Corporations on Water-Power Development in the United States; Big Business and Government;* H. A. Foster, *Engineering valuation of public utilities and factories;* C. L. King, *The regulation of municipal utilities;* C. R. Van Hise, *Concentration and control: a solution of the trust problem in the United States;* C. Carpenter, *Copartnership in industry; with notes on over 200 British copartnership and profit-sharing schemes, 1829-1912;* H. Emerson, *The twelve principles of efficiency;* E. Garcke, *Factory accounts; their principles and practice;* F. A. Parkhurst, *Applied methods of scientific management;* J. B. Clark, *The control of trusts;* F. B. Gilbreth, *Primer of scientific management;* J. Hartness, *Human factor in works management;* J. Moody, *How to analyze railroad reports;* edited by Clyde Lydon King, *The Regulation of Municipal Utilities;* M. Neumann, *Das Reichsmonopol für Petroleum;* D. Knopp, *Principles and methods of municipal trading;* Walter H. Lyon, *Capitalization: A book on corporation finance.*

MONEY. J. R. Cummings, *Natural money, the peaceful solution;* W. J. Ashley, *Gold and prices;* D. Barbour, *The Standard of Value;* W. T. Layton, *An introduction to the study of prices; with special reference to the history of the nineteenth century;* W. W. Carlile, *Monetary economics;* W. Ashley, *The rise in prices and the cost of living. An inquiry into its extent and causes;* M. Sefourmantelle, *Agricultural credit;* edited by J. Laurence Laughlin, *Banking Reform.*

TRANSPORTATION. J. F. Strombeck, *Freight and Classification;* J. C. Hemmeon, *History of the British post office;* Samuel O. Dunn, *The American Transportation Question;* Charles Lee Raper, *Railway Transportation.*

POLITICAL PLATFORMS. See PRESIDENTIAL CAMPAIGN.

POLO. No international matches for the

Challenge Cup were held in 1912, and interest was chiefly centred in the championships decided at Narragansett Pier. Cooperstown won the open championship, defeating the Bryn Mawr team in the final match by 9¾ goals to 5¼. The winning four included F. S. Von Stade, C. C. Rumsey, C. P. Beadleston and Malcolm Stevenson, and the losing team was made up of Alex Brown, H. W. Harrison, R. E. Strawbridge and C. R. Snowden. The Cooperstown players also captured the junior championship, winning the final match against Piping Rock by 11 to 6¾, and were victors in the matches for the Governors' Cups at Cedarhurst, defeating Great Neck's first team by 11 to 8½. The senior championship was won by the Meadow Brook four, which defeated Bryn Mawr 15 to 3¼. The Meadow Brooks comprised Foxhall Keene, Lawrence Waterbury, J. M. Waterbury and E. S. Reynal. Harry Payne Whitney, who has been selected as the captain of the American team for the international challenge matches to be held this year, played in only one of the 1912 cup contests. This was in the match for the Westbury challenge cups, in which Meadow Brook defeated Great Neck by 11 to 6¾. Playing with Whitney were Harrison Tweed, J. A. Rawlins, A. S. Burden and J. M. Waterbury. The Great Neck four were Lawrence Waterbury, W. R. Grace, Hamilton Hadden and J. G. Milburn, Jr. Much interest was taken in polo in army circles in 1912, and several new clubs joined the national association. The army championship was decided in matches played at Washington.

POOL. See BILLIARDS.

PORTER, JAMES DAVIS. An American public official, formerly governor of Tennessee, died May 18, 1912. He was born in Paris, Tenn., in 1828, and graduated from the University of Nashville in 1846. After studying law he began its practice in 1850. From 1859 to 1861 he was a member of the Tennessee legislature. He served as adjutant-general on the staff of Major-General Cheatham, C. S. A. In 1870 he was a delegate to the Tennessee Constitutional Convention, and in the same year was appointed Judge of the Twelfth Judicial Circuit. He served as governor of Tennessee from 1874 to 1878. For several years after he was president of the Nashville and Chattanooga Railway Company and from 1885 to 1889 was assistant secretary of State. He was appointed minister to Chile in 1893, serving until 1897. From 1901 until the time of his death he was chancellor of the University of Nashville. He was president of the Tennessee Historical Society. He wrote a Confederate military history of Tennessee.

POMPEII. See ARCHÆOLOGY.

PORTLAND CEMENT. See CEMENT.

PORTO RICO. POPULATION. The population of Porto Rico, according to the Thirteenth Census taken in 1910, was 1,118,012, compared with 953,233 in 1900. The chief cities with their population in 1910 are as follows: San Juan, 48,716; Ponce, 25,005; Mayaguez, 16,563; Caguas, 10,354; Arecibo, 9612; and Aguadilla, 6315.

AGRICULTURE. The chief industries of the island are those connected with agriculture. The conditions during the fiscal year 1912 were favorable to these pursuits, and the output of all products was substantially increased. The acreage under cultivation on the island was largely extended, as has been the case each year in recent years. The scientific study of agriculture, stimulated by federal and private experimental stations, and the board of education, established during the year, all contributed to the improvement of agricultural conditions. See AGRICULTURAL EXPERIMENT STATIONS. Increased production of sugar, which has marked that industry since the removal of the tariff restrictions in 1911, was again marked in 1912. The production in that year was 367,000 tons, compared with 323,000 tons in 1911. The growth of these industries is shown by the fact that in 1901 the exports of sugar were less than 7000 tons. The growth of the tobacco industry is shown by the fact that the output of cigars in 1912 was more than fourteen times greater than in 1901. In the fiscal year 1911-12 the output of cigars reached 281,000,000, an increase of 75,000,000 over the preceding year. Of these, 170,000,000 were consumed in the United States. Less than one-fourth of the tobacco crop is shipped in the leaf, the remainder being shipped in manufactured form. The growing of coffee continues to be an industry of increasing importance in the island. The crop of 1912 was the largest yet produced, and it was sold at profitable prices. The value of the coffee sold abroad during 1911-12 was $6,754,913. The growing of coffee is being extended throughout the mountains of the island, the soil and climate of which are especially adapted to the successful culture of the highest grades of coffee to be found in the world. The government of Porto Rico has established a commercial agency for the exploitation of Porto Rican coffee in New York City. The shipment of fruit for foreign markets increased in value during the year, amounting to $2,377,762. Fruits most successfully raised are oranges, pineapples, and grapefruit. These find ready sale in the United States. Fruit-raising in Porto Rico is rapidly becoming one of the principal industries of the Territory. Much attention is being given to the production of cocoanuts. The value of shipments during 1912 showed a continuation of the gradual increase they have received during recent years, when they reached $300,000. The industries mentioned comprise the leading agricultural activity of the island.

COMMERCE. The commerce in the fiscal year 1912 between Porto Rican and other points aggregated $92,631,886, of which $49,705,413 was exports and $42,926,473 imports. The imports in 1911 amounted to $38,786,997 and the exports to $39,918,367. The total trade with the United States amounted to $80,297,946, compared with $69,437,367 in 1911. Sugar was the most valuable of the exports. There were exported in 1912 367,145 tons, valued at $31,544,063. Next in importance were manufactured and unmanufactured tobacco, the value of which is noted in the paragraph above. Other imports of considerable value included sea island cotton, $59,342; hides and skins, $93,243, and molasses, $700,981. The most important imports were those of rice, $4,894,747. Other important imports were manufactures of iron and steel, $4,445,396, cotton and cotton cloths, $2,933,194; other manufactures of cotton, $2,642,448; leather $1,599,047; pork, $1,346,333.

COMMUNICATIONS. During the year 69 kilometers of highway were completed. The total length of the insular road system was increased to 1069 kilometers. Road construction during the past two years, a considerable portion of which has been done by convict labor, has averaged in cost $5500 per kilometer.

HARBORS AND DOCKS. The scarcity of adequate accommodations for vessels in the ports of the island has been a matter of much concern and study ever since the American occupation. Important progress toward the solution of existing defects has been made. A private company has completed a large and commodious dock and warehouse system at San Juan and a franchise was granted during the year to the American Railway Company under which work on anotner pier has been commenced. The Legislative Assembly in 1912 passed an act creating a harbor for the port of San Juan and authorizing a $500,000 bond issue to be used in the construction of water-front improvements. A $300,000 pier of modern type was in course of construction at Ponce at the end of the year. This will provide necessary facilities for handling cargo for many years to come. Plans for improving the port of Arecibo were under consideration during the year, as were improvements required at other ports on the island.

IRRIGATION. Plans for irrigating the dry zone between the foothills and the southern coast, a strip of land approximately forty miles in length and averaging two in width, made great progress as the result of favorable weather conditions in 1912. All the contracts except two have been completed. The canals, syphons, power stations, etc., that form a part of this project were nearing completion at the end of the year.

EDUCATION. The average number of pupils in daily attendance in public schools during 1912 was 114,834, which is approximately 10 per cent. of the total population of the island. The pupils enrolled numbered 160,657, an increase of 15,000 over the enrollment for 1911. Since the plan of universal education was first inaugurated in Porto Rico in 1900, the enrollment has increased from 20,000 to over eight times that number. The educational facilities at present afforded are far from sufficient. It is estimated that there are not less than 350,000 children of school age in Porto Rico and with the present accommodations and number of teachers, not half of them can be reached. The attention of the Department of Education has been concentrated upon so extending the school system as to give some education to the greatest number of children. Much thought is being given at the present time to the character of the instruction given, especially to the importance of gradually including in the course of study, trade or vocational training. There are at present manual training and domestic science courses. Instruction in agriculture is given by means of practical demonstration and work. High schools are maintained at San Juan, Ponce, Mayaguez, and Arecibo. The educational system of the island is completed by the University of Porto Rico, where a college of liberal arts, an agricultural and a training school for teachers are maintained. The total expenditures for school purposes during the fiscal year 1912 was $980,375 by the insular government, and $386,434 by the local government.

HEALTH AND SANITATION. A campaign was carried on during 1912 for the reduction of the mosquitoes in San Juan. This was in charge of Major Noble, who had formerly been engaged in this work in the Panama Canal Zone. As a result of these efforts, San Juan, formerly infested with mosquitoes, was made practically free from this pest, and their number was greatly diminished in the suburbs of the city. Their complete reduction could not be accomplished on account of the absence of sewers, poor surface drainage, and adjacent swamp lands. Mosquito work was also carried on in other municipalities. There was a material decrease in the number of cases of typhoid fever during the year due to the strict enforcement of sanitary rules. The number of deaths from tuberculosis has drawn the attention of the health authorities to the urgent necessity of improving the faulty housing conditions of the various municipalities. The work of the anemia or hookworm service progressed throughout the island during the year. Each health officer maintained a dispensary where persons suffering from this disease are treated and their condition observed. On June 14, 1912, the sanitary authorities of the island learned that an individual having symptons of bubonic plague had died in San Juan and an immediate investigation was made. The fact of plague was established and prompt and effective measures were immediately adopted to check infection and prevent a general epidemic. The total expenditures of the sanitation service during the year were $639,029.

CHARITIES AND CORRECTIONS. The charitable and correctional institutions of the island include an insane asylum, an asylum for the blind, a boys' charity school, a girls' charity school, several penitentiaries, and a reform school for boys. There were in the prisons of the island on June 30, 1912, 1585 prisoners.

FINANCE. The receipts of the island from all sources during the fiscal year aggregated $6,665,348. This was the largest revenue in the history of the island. The disbursements amounted to $4,880,669.

POLITICS AND GOVERNMENT

The following changes in personnel took place in 1912: Walter H. Pitkin, Jr. was appointed attorney-general April 21, and Allen H. Richardson, treasurer January 25. Foster V. Brown, attorney-general, resigned on April 20, 1912. Edwin Grant Dexter, commissioner of education, resigned June 30, 1912, and Samuel D. Gromer, treasurer, on January 24, 1912.

LEGISLATION. The sixth legislative Assembly of Porto Rico convened in second session on January 8, 1912, in accordance with the law, remaining in session 60 days. As several matters of importance had not been disposed of on March 7 at the close of the regular session, a special session was called and continued until the work of the legislature had been satisfactorily completed on March 14. During this session 85 laws and 19 joint resolutions were enacted. Of special importance are the sanitation law, the law providing for a bureau of labor and the act providing for minority representation in the House of Delegates. The election law was so amended as to insure the secrecy of the ballot, provide for minority representation in the House of Delegates, and correct various minor deficiencies. The bill providing for citizenship for the people of Porto Rico, the bill to substitute the original organic act of Porto Rico, the bill providing for a substitute judge in the United States district court, and the bill to authorize the exchange of certain insular government property for portions of the federal military reservation, are still awaiting final action in Congress. The most importance of these bills is that providing for citizenship. The people of Porto Rico have waited for more than ten years to be admitted to American citizenship without action by Congress having been taken. The governor in 1912 was George R. Colton.

PORTSMOUTH, ENGLAND. See DOCKS AND HARBORS.

PORTUGAL. A European republic occupying the western coast of the Iberian Peninsula. Capitol, Lisbon.

AREA AND POPULATION. Area of continental Portugal, 88,740 square kilometers; of the Azores, 2388; of the Madeiras, 815—total, 91,943 square kilometers (35,499 square miles). Total population, December 1, 1900, 5,423,132 (Azores, 256,291; Madeiras, 150,574). Population of Lisbon, 356,009; Oporto, 167,955; Braga, 24,202; Funchal (Madeira), 20,844; Ponta Delgada (Azores), 17,620; Portalegre, 11,820.

Primary education is theoretically compulsory, but over 70 per cent. of the population over 6 years of age remain illiterate. All creeds are now tolerated. The law of 1911 for the separation of church and state discarded the Roman Catholic as the national faith.

PRODUCTION. Three-fifths of the population are engaged in agriculture. Of the total area 26.2 per cent. is under crops and pasture, 3.5 per cent. under vineyards, 3.9 per cent. under orchards, 17.3 per cent. under forest, 43.1 per cent. barren or uncultivable. Wine, olive oil, and fruits are produced for export; cattle, sheep, and goats are raised. There are valuable mineral deposits, but little worked. In 1910, 239,745 metric tons of sulphur were mined, 3768 tons of copper precipitate, 17,630 of copper pyrites, 1991 of copper ore, 947 of wolfram, 6 of silver ore, 919 of lead ore, 138 of uranium, 9 of tin ore, 8149 of anthracite, 3360 of iron, and 974 of arsenic.

COMMERCE, ETC. In the table below is given the trade for two years in contos (1000 milreis):

	Imports 1909	Imports 1910	Exports 1909	Exports 1910
Raw materials.....	28,404	30,513	6,866	7,495
Foodstuffs	18,662	16,060	15,462	19,129
Yarns and textiles.	6,582	7,828	2,177	3,064
Various manufrs..	5,246	5,063	2,098	2,461
Machinery, etc....	4,694	5,848	149	134
Live animals......	2,859	3,456	4,142	3,534
Tare	124	148	.....	.....
Total mdse.......	66,607	69,816	30,894	35,727*
Coin and bullion	36	299	905	602
Total	66,643	70,155	31,799	36,329

* Wine, 12,416,000 milreis (1 milrei is equal to $1.08); cork, 4,618,000; cotton textiles, 2,645,000; fish, 2,424,000; tropical fruits, 1,845,000; copper, 942,000; timber, 909,000; olive oil, 702,000.

Vessels entered (1910), 11,560, of 20,615,688 tons. The merchant marine included (1911) 66 steamers (70,193 tons), and 259 sailing (43,844).

Railways in operation January 1, 1911, 2894 kilometers (state, 1081). Telegraph lines (1907), 9431 kilometers; wires, 21,404.

FINANCE. An English source gives the estimated revenue and expenditure for the year 1911-12 at £15,247,495 and £15,637,625 respectively, as compared with £14,160,775 and £14,699,976 in 1910-11. The regular excess of expenditure over revenue during many years has added to the national debt. Foreign debt, 181,039,200 milreis; internal, 629,215,224, including 82,530,995 floating debt at 6 per cent. A recent decree alters the name of the monetary unit from milreis to escudo. The escudo has the same value as the milreis, but is divided into 100 centavos, whereas the milreis represents 1000 reis. The centavo equals 10 reis.

NAVY. The fleet includes 1 armored coast defense vessel of 3030 tons (the *Vasco da Gama*, remodeled in 1902), 4 cruisers (9410 tons), 6 gunboats of date 1895-1909 (2573), 11 gunboats of date 1874-90 (4300), 1 torpedo gunboat (535), 4 torpedo boats of date 1880-1886 (252)—total, 27 vessels of 22,100 aggregate tons; besides training ships, yachts, etc.

ARMY. The army law passed in 1911 by the National Assembly provided for active, reserve, and territorial forces organized on a militia basis, with every citizen liable for military service from his 16th to 45th year. At 20 years of age there was liability to compulsory service, which in the infantry was made 4 months and for the mountain troops 8 months. In May, 1912, the annual contingent would have been 46,000 men, but lack of barrack accommodations and other facilities, as well as financial conditions, made it necessary to reduce the number to 35,000, and 10,000 were accordingly excluded on a stricter medical examination, the rejected young men paying a fine for inefficiency. The republic was divided into 8 large recruiting areas, each of which support an active division and 2 reserve infantry brigades, as well as a necessary formation for the territorial forces. In 1912 there were 4 divisions of the active army, garrisons at Madeira and the Azores, and the troops of the reserve, while in the colonies an army of about 10,000 was maintained.

GOVERNMENT. The president, elected for four years, is the executive. The legislative power is exercised by a congress composed of a chamber of deputies (164 members) and a senate (71 members). President August 24, 1911-1915, Manoel de Arriaga. The ministry as constituted June 16, 1912, was composed as follows: Dr. Duarte Leite, premier and minister of the interior; Aug. de Vasconcellos, foreign affairs; F. Correia de Lemos, justice; Vicente Ferreira, finance; A. da Costa Ferreira, public works; Col. A. X. Correira Barreto, war; F. Fernandes Costa, marine; J. B. Cerveira Sousa, colonies.

HISTORY

CHURCH AND STATE. The government proceeded vigorously against the hierarchy for its refusal to accept the separation law. The attitude of the higher clergy toward the new government led to the arrest and trial of several bishops, including the Patriarch of Lisbon, two archbishops and six bishops. By the end of February all the higher ecclesiastics except the bishops of Evora and Braganza, had incurred the displeasure of the Republican government, and during that month the archbishops of Portalegre and Braga and the bishop of

Lamego were expelled for two years. Many of the poorer priests accepted at first the stipends offered by the government, but eventually refused them on account of the steady opposition of the clergy generally to accepting state aid from a government that in their view was guilty of gross injustice toward the church. Many of the priests were imprisoned as political offenders. Although the government maintained a legation at the Vatican "to defend national interests," relations with the Holy See were virtually suspended.

CABINET CRISIS. Parliament was in session till July, and passed a large number of measures, including bills for the payment of senators and deputies, for relief of disabled workmen and for the reward of those who had played a prominent part in the late revolution. In consequence of the dissensions between the Democrats under Dr. Costa, and the Unionists under Dr. Comacho, the two party groups that constituted the main support of the cabinet, the government resigned early in June. A coalition cabinet was formed under Dr. Duarte Leite, premier and minister of the interior, with Senhor Vasconcellos as foreign minister.

THE GOVERNMENT AND THE GENERAL STRIKE. A strike at Evora resulted in the closing of the workingmen's associations there and of the arrest of a number of strikers. On January 29 the Workingmen's Federation of Lisbon declared a general strike and demanded that the workingmen's associations at Evora be reopened and the strikers released. At the first show of violence at Lisbon, the government took energetic measures, declaring the city in a state of siege and suspending constitutional guarantees. The streets were placed under the control of the troops and the authorities arrested a large number of disorderly and suspicious characters. Conditions rapidly improved and after a day or two the trouble was pronounced to be at an end. An important debate took place in the first week of March upon a motion of the leader of the Conservative Republicans for general amnesty to the recent strikers and to political prisoners, and to the Royalists under Captain Couceiro, with the exception of the leaders. The premier declared that such an amnesty was at the present time inopportune and the motion was rejected by a vote of 63 to 22. Disturbances arose in May and June over a street railway strike in Lisbon.

THE ROYALISTS. At a conference between the ex-king, Manoel, and Dom Pedro, the pretender, at Dover on January 22, the latter renounced his claim to the throne. At the beginning of May there were signs of a design on the part of the followers of Captain Couceiro to resume their Royalist raids. A small band of Royalists at that time attacked the customs post at Monaco, and afte seizing some of the guns, returned to Spanish soil. During June there were continued reports of Royalist activities, and finally in the first week of July the *émigrés* crossed the border in four columns, each about 200 strong, three in the neighborhood of Verin and the fourth near Minho, but they were defeated and driven back. The Monarchists in Portugal did not join the movement as its leaders had expected. The government called out its reserves and according to official accounts the invasion was an utter failure. Captain Couceiro in command of 300 or 400 men continued in camp on the frontier but was held in check by the Republicans.

Early in July another Monarchist outbreak was threatened at Torres Vedras, but was prevented by the prompt action of the authorities, who made many arrests. Many of the Royalists surrendered owing to lack of provisions. In August the Royalist prisoners were tried by court-martial and sent to the Lisbon penitentiary, which was reported to be so unsanitary and so rigidly administered that few who were confined were likely to survive. A large number of suspects arrested and subjected to severe hardship afterwards proved their innocence.

Difficulties with Spain over the Royalist *émigrés* were finally amicably settled in September, Spain agreeing to the expulsion of Royalist leaders from her territory and to certain measures in regard to future conspiracies against the Portuguese government. Despite the frequent assertions of the authorities that conditions were now quiet and satisfactory, there was evidence of serious disturbance in commerce and industry. Recent events had frightened away capital and the moneyed classes were not sufficiently assured of security to return. There was much complaint of slackness of business.

THE NEW PARLIAMENTARY SESSION. Parliament reassembled in November. There was much criticism of the new Republican government for its failure to redeem the promises which it made at the time of the revolution, and many declared that political conditions were no better than under the monarchy, while economic conditions were distinctly worse. Friends of the government retorted that the Royalists and their sympathizers were largely to blame. The new government had been obliged to devote to the repression of disloyal movements energies which it would have applied to carrying out reforms. Among the important measures to come before it was that for electoral reform.

PORTUGUESE EAST AFRICA, or MOZAMBIQUE. A Portuguese colony in Africa, covering an area of 293,860 square miles and having 3,120,000 inhabitants. Lorenzo Marques (10,000 inhabitants) is the capital. The trade is divided among the state territories, the Mozambique Company and the Nyassa Company. There are about 300 miles of railway. Budget (1910-11), 5,418,332 milreis revenue and 5,118,832 milreis expenditure. Governor-general (1912) Dr. A. de Magalhães.

PORTUGUESE GUINEA. A Portuguese colony in western Africa. Area, 13,940 square miles; population, 820,000. Bolama is the capital. Trade 1908: 875,155 milreis imports and 492,238 milreis exports. The budget (1910-11) balanced at 309,900 milreis. The islands of Bolama and Bijagoz belong to the colony. Governor (1912), Lieut. C. A. Pereira.

Because of the rising at Cacheo, reported at the end of February, five Portuguese native soldiers were killed. The rising was attributed to the enforced collection of the hut tax.

Acts of brigandage were attempted by the natives of Satary, who rebelled after the garrison had been diminished by sending a number of the troops to Macao, and the government was obliged to take severe measures to restore order.

POSTAL SAVINGS BANKS. The following table from the report of the Comptroller of the Currency gives the latest statistics of postal savings banks of all countries:

Country	Number of Depositors	Deposits	Average Deposit
Austria[2]	2,261,658	$ 46,317,746	$ 20.48
Belgium[1]	2,384,511	157,150,474	65.90
Bulgaria[1]	280,775	9,129,433	32.52
Finland[1]	59,723	1,396,856	23.39
France[1]	5,786,035	329,974,970	57.03
Hungary[1]	775,970	21,894,118	28.22
Italy[1]	5,160,008	324,279,617	62.84
Netherlands[1]	1,510,033	66,039,592	43.73
Russia[3]	2,691,361	192,456,530	70.02
Sweden[2]	565,759	12,645,957	22.35
Great Britain[2]	12,370,646	859,027,319	69.44
Bahamas[1]	2,186	132,602	60.66
Canada[3]	146,310	42,683,232	291.73
British Guiana[1]	18,004	738,175	41.00
Dutch Guiana[1]	9,478	337,925	35 65
British India[1]	1,378,916	51,478,416	37.33
Ceylon[1]	85,954	932,236	10.85
Straits Settlements[1]	4,312	382,667	88.74
Federated Malay States[1]	5,312	330,431	62.20
Dutch E. Indies[2]	91,898	3,616,685	39.36
Japan[3]	11,950,158	91,896,942	7.69
Formosa[2]	100,819	955,592	9.48
Cape of Good Hope[1]	105,369	10,411,974	98.81
Gold Coast[2]	3,137	169,262	53.96
Orange Free State[1]	7,646	868,291	113.56
Rhodesia[1]	3,306	435,299	131.67
Sierra Leone[2]	6,002	485,735	80.93
Transvaal[1]	71,185	8,769,798	123.20
Egypt[1]	104,095	2,255,664	21.67
Tunis[1]	5,701	1,288,268	225.97
New South Wales[1]	368,306	73,926,126	200.72
Victoria[2]	595,424	84,065,980	141.19
Queensland[2]	127,219	31,033,520	243.04
Tasmania[1]	24,403	3,401,304	139.40
Western Australia[2]	99,017	19,916,171	201.14
New Zealand[1]	380,714	68,641,934	180.30
Philippine Ids.[3]	35,802	1,177,435	32.89
United States[3]	300,000	28,000,000	93.33

[1] 1910; [2] 1911; [3] 1912.

For notes on the operation of the postal savings banks in the United States see UNITED STATES, *Post Office.*

POST OFFICE, SUNDAY CLOSING OF. See LABOR LEGISLATION, *Hours.*

POTASH. See FERTILIZERS; and CHEMISTRY, INDUSTRIAL.

POTATOES. While statistics on the potato crop are not so regularly furnished by all countries as are data on cereal production, the yields and the crop conditions reported by the principal potato-growing countries, particularly Russia and Germany, indicated a world's normal crop, which ranges from about 5 to 5½ billion bushels. Yields in parts of Europe were reduced by an unusually cool and wet season, but the injury resulting to the crop from these unfavorable weather conditions was not nearly so great as the damage sustained by the cereal and forage crops. In many sections, particularly in Austria and Ireland, the fields were so wet when the tubers had matured that harvesting was delayed and the percentage of sound tubers as well as the keeping quality was reduced. The best yields in general were secured on light, dry, sandy soils, which were less affected by the rains than the heavier clayey lands. In the United States and Canada the crop contended with late planting on account of unfavorable spring weather, a brief drought in early summer which temporarily checked growth, and with rainy weather during the latter part of the growing season, especially in many of the Northern States, which furnish a large percentage of the total yield. The total production of Russia, which is generally outranked only by Germany, was 1,398,950,000 bushels, or about 232,625,000 bushels more than in 1911. The Hungarian crop was estimated at 185,369,000 bushels, and the Irish crop at 2,546,700 bushels, as compared with 3,694,850 bushels the year before. The production of England and Wales amounted to 83,762,000 bushels, or about 22,643,000 bushels less than the preceding crop. Official estimates placed the total yield of Prussia at 1,249,000,000 bushels. Canada in 1912 produced 81,343,000 bushels on 472,400 acres, and in 1911 66,023,000 bushels on 459,100 acres.

The total production of the United States in 1912 amounted to 420,647,000 bushels, an excess of 127,910,000 bushels over the short crop of 1911. The yield secured in 1912 is the highest to date, but the total value of the crop was exceeded the year before. The price paid farmers on December 1, 1912, was only 50.5 cents per bushel, as compared with 79.9 cents a year before, and on this basis the two crops had a total value of $212,550,000 and $233,778,000, respectively. The average yield per acre, 113.4 bushels, as given by the Department of Agriculture, is also the highest on record and greater by 32.5 bushels than the preceding average acre-yield. The yields reported for the different States ranged from 125,000 bushels for Arizona to 38,160,000 for New York. The States ranking next to New York in production were: Michigan, 36,750,000 bushels; Wisconsin, 34,920,000 bushels; Minnesota, 33,075,000 bushels; Pennsylvania, 28,885,000 bushels, and Ohio, 20,832,000 bushels. In Maine, the Aroostock County crop was reported short by about 25 per cent., but the crop in the central part of the State was about 25 per cent. above normal. In 1912 every State, except Louisiana, reported an increase in yield over 1911. In the nineteen leading potato-growing States about one-third of the crop grown for market in 1911 was in the hands of the producers on January 1, 1912.

POTATO ROT. See BOTANY.

POTTER, LOUIS MCCLELLAN. An American sculptor, died August 29, 1912. He was born in Troy, N. Y., in 1873, and graduated from Trinity College in 1896. He studied painting under Charles N. Flagg and Montague Flagg and afterwards spent four years in Paris in the *ateliers* of Luc Olivier Merson and Jean Dampt. He decided, however, that modeling and not painting was his peculiar talent. From Paris he went to Tunis, where he made a study of Oriental types, living in the Arab quarter and making friends with Bedouins and negroes. The government of France chose his work to represent Tunisian types at the Paris Exposition. After a year spent in Africa he came to the United States, where he spent two or three years in executing various commissions. He then went to Alaska, where he spent some time studying primitive types. Later he returned to New York. His work shows a great variety of conception. His earlier works were inclined toward realism, but his later works became more symbolic. Among his best-known works are "The Call of the Spirit" and "The Dance of the Wind Gods." He made a bust of Mark Twain, whom he had never seen, and the result was wonderfully true to life. He designed a memorial to Horace Wells of Connecticut, which was erected in 1909.

POULTRY. See STOCK-RAISING.

POULTRY, DISEASES OF. See VETERINARY SCIENCE.

POULTRY ASSOCIATION, AMERICAN See STOCK-RAISING.

PRAGMATISM. See PHILOSOPHY.

PREHISTORIC MAN. See ANTHROPOLOGY, and GEOLOGY.

PRESBYTERIAN CHURCH IN THE UNITED STATES OF AMERICA. The official title of that branch of the Presbyterian Church popularly known as the Northern Branch in distinction from the Presbyterian Church in the United States (see above). According to statistics gathered by officials of the denomination, the communicants in 1912 numbered 1,380,058. The ministers numbered 9274, the churches, 10,030. For governmental purposes there are 37 synods with 292 presbyteries. There were added to the number of communicants during 1912 79,432. In the Sabbath schools of the denomination were enrolled 1,274,458 pupils. The contributions for all sources during the year amounted to $25,-798,615, divided as follows: Home missions, $1,818,345; foreign missions, $1,437,660; education, $159,055; Sabbath school work, $190,562; church erection, $223,598; relief fund, $186,-091; freedmen, $187,083; colleges, $465,068; temperance, $126,131; general assembly, $173,-361; for congregational purposes, $18,653,574; and for miscellaneous purposes, $2,178,087. The missionary work of the denomination is under the control of the board of home missions, which has control of the domestic missions, and of the board of foreign missions, which conducts the work in foreign countries. There were in operation during the year 26 foreign missions with 162 stations, 1082 missionaries, 5041 native helpers, 636 fully organized churches, 115,976 communicants, 1707 schools with 55,982 pupils, 155,667 pupils in the Sabbath schools and 167 hospitals and dispensaries in which 463,782 patients were treated. During the year 135,963,274 pages of Christian truth were printed in over twenty languages. The educational work of the denomination is conducted by the board of education. Other important boards are those of publication and Sabbath school work, church erection, relief, ministerial sustentation fund, missions for freedmen, college board, committee on temperance, and committee on vacancy and supply. There is held annually a general assembly. This met in May, 1912, at Louisville, Ky. The most important acts of the assembly were as follows: A synod of Arizona was created; delegates were appointed to the Second Federal Council of Church Coöperation and Union; a synod of New England was created, including the presbyteries of Boston, Connecticut Valley, Newburyport, and Providence, and several important changes in polity were adopted. Among these was a provision giving the presbytery the right to determine for itself whom it will receive into menbership. It was decided that it was inexpedient for the presbytery to receive women as candidates for the ministry. It was decided that any presbytery that ordains to the ministry men who deny the teachings of God's word as interpreted by the standards of the church, is guilty of perjury. Persons having a part in the manufacture and sale of alcholic stimulants are not to be admitted to the church membership. Perhaps the most interesting action taken by the assembly, from the general point of view, was the adoption of a new catechism called the "Intermediate Catechism." This was the final result of an attempt to qualify and change the old catechism which has been carried on for many years. In 1902 the general assembly approved "A Brief Statement of the Reformed Faith." This was adopted in 1903. The "Intermediate Catechism," approved in 1912 virtually supplants the famous "Shorter Catechism." In the new form all speculative and scholastic teaching is omitted. The first question of the old "Catechism," "What is the chief end of man?" is supplanted by "What do we most need to know?" The thirty-seven questions and answers of the "Shorter Catechism" relating to the Ten Commandments are condensed to three. Room is thereby made for New Testament principles and precepts. Most of the work of the assembly was devoted to denominational interests and enterprises. The sum of $3,250,000 was asked for 1913. The officers of the general assembly in 1912 were as follows: Moderator, Mark A. Matthews, D. D.; vice-moderator, James Yereance; stated clerk, William Henry Roberts; permanent clerk, William Brown Noble; assistant clerk, James M. Hubbert.

PRESIDENTIAL CAMPAIGN OF 1912. The presidential campaign of 1912 was, in many of its features, the most extraordinary in the history of the United States. It saw, among other things, the disruption of the Republican party as the result of the candidacy of a former Republican President, who made his campaign for the nomination an attack on the policy of his successor. It was a campaign marked by a bitterness of attack and defense for which comparisons are to be sought only in campaigns early in the history of the nation. It saw, finally, the defeat of the Republican party, as a result of internal dissension, by a Democratic vote which was less than the vote cast in the presidential election of 1908.

Unique interest was also added to the campaign by the inauguration, for the first time, of a system for registering the people's choice, known as the preferential presidential primaries. These were held in a number of States, in some cases as the result of legislative action and in others by direction of the State committees, who were authorized in this course by the Republican national committee, which met in December, 1911, and by the Democratic national committee, which met in January, 1912.

It is impossible, and unnecessary, to relate in detail all the events and episodes which filled this campaign from its actual beginning in January, 1912, to the election on November 5. It is only possible here to set down the more important facts in an attempt to make clear the main causes and results. The Democratic campaign for the nomination did not differ materially from other campaigns, while the Republican campaign differed widely and radically from any other campaign ever carried on by that party. It is inevitable therefore that the greater part of the space in this article should be devoted to a record of the Republican campaign, with an attempt to minimize as much as possible such elements of it as were merely temporary and superficial.

A detailed discussion of the State campaigns, as distinguished from the national, will be found under the headings of the various States. The details of these are mentioned in this article only in such a way as to produce a consecutive narrative.

The campaign will be discussed under the following sub-divisions: I. PRE-CONVENTION CAMPAIGN. II. THE CONVENTIONS. III. POST-CONVENTION CAMPAIGN. IV. THE ELECTION. V. THE PARTY PLATFORMS.

PRE-CONVENTION CAMPAIGN, REPUBLICAN

REPUBLICAN CANDIDATES. The dawning of the year 1912 found two declared Republican nominees for the presidency. These were President Taft and Senator La Follette. The great question, however, in the public mind was: "Will Mr. Roosevelt be a candidate for a third term?" Upon this hinged a discussion which filled the public press. Mr. Roosevelt's own attitude up to a little before the beginning of the year was non-committal. It was well known that he was being urged by prominent Progressive opponents to President Taft to accept the leadership of the Progressives and to be a candidate for a third term. On the other hand, stood his declaration, made in 1904 and repeated in 1907, that "under no conditions" would he be a candidate for a third term. This was the situation at the beginning of the year.

Senator La Follette's campaign for the nomination for the presidency was begun in 1911. An organization known as the National Progressive Republican League was established early in that year with the avowed purpose of bringing about the nomination of Senator La Follette as the leading representative of Progressive policies. (See also OHIO.) Senator La Follette began the campaign by the delivery of two speeches in Ohio in December, 1911, and he followed these with a speech-making tour which included cities in Michigan, Indiana, and Illinois. There was no doubt, therefore, as to his active candidacy for the nomination. President Taft, too, made it clear that he would be a candidate for the nomination. On January 3, he declared, in a statement made to friends, that nothing but death would keep him out of the fight. Pressure continued to be placed on Mr. Roosevelt to define his position, and, although he would as yet make no formal declaration, it was learned early in February that his supporters were preparing for an active campaign and that George W. Perkins had become one of his most active advisers. It was learned, too, that Ormsby McHarg, who had been conspicuous in previous campaigns as an organizer, was engaged in work in the South for the advancement of Mr. Roosevelt's candidacy. Senator Beveridge of Indiana was known to be another aggressive supporter of and worker for Mr. Roosevelt.

MR. ROOSEVELT'S CANDIDACY. One of the first positive statements as to the probable candidacy of Mr. Roosevelt was contained in an article published about the middle of January in the Pittsburgh *Leader*, the editor of which was A. P. Moore, one of the earliest advocates of Mr. Roosevelt as a candidate. Mr. Moore asserted that Mr. Roosevelt had bade him tell his readers that he would not desert the Progressive cause and that they would find him fighting side by side with them to the finish.

Mr. Roosevelt's attitude toward his previous declaration in regard to the third term was indicated in an interview published by the Chicago *Evening Post* on January 30. He said:

"I used language which simply stated that I paid heed to the essence and not the form of the wise custom of our forefathers; the essence of course being that the custom applies just as much when my first term was the filling out of the unexpired term of my predecessor as if it had been an elective term, but that on the other hand, it had no application whatever to the candidacy of a man who was not at the time in office whether he had or had not been President before. Men at once began to ask me whether my refusal was held to apply to 1912 or 1916, to which I, of course, responded that it would be preposterous to answer any such question one way or another."

Early in February, Mr. Roosevelt accepted an invitation to address the Ohio constitutional convention on February 22. On February 10, seven governors and delegates from 28 States met at Chicago and formed a permanent organization to advocate his candidacy. Delegates to this meeting favored presidential primaries in all the States. At this meeting a letter was addressed to Mr. Roosevelt, signed by the seven governors. These were the governors of West Virginia, Nebraska, New Hampshire, Wyoming, Michigan, Kansas, and Missouri. This letter urged him to accept the nomination and was as follows:

"We, the undersigned Republican governors, assembled for the purpose of considering what will best insure the continuation of the Republican party as a useful agency of good government, declare it our belief, after a careful investigation of the facts, that a large majority of the Republican voters of the country favor your nomination, and a large majority of the people favor your election, as the next President of the United States.

"We believe that your candidacy will insure success in the next campaign. We believe that you represent, as no other man represents, those principles and policies upon which we must appeal for a majority of the votes of the American people, and which, in our opinion, are necessary for the happiness and prosperity of the country.

"We believe that, in view of this public demand, you should soon declare whether, if the nomination for the presidency come to you, unsolicited and unsought, you will accept.

"In submitting this request we are not considering your personal interests. We do not regard it as proper to consider either the interests or the preference of any man as regards the nomination for the presidency. We are expressing our sincere belief and best judgment as to what is demanded of you in the interests of the people as a whole. And we feel that you would be unresponsive to a plain public duty if you should decline to accept the nomination, coming as the voluntary expression of the wishes of a majority of the Republican voters of the United States through the action of their delegates in the next national convention.

"Yours truly,

"William E. Glasscock, Chester H. Aldrich, Robert P. Bass, Joseph M. Carey, Chase S. Osborn, W. R. Stubbs, Herbert S. Hadley."

A few days later Mr. Roosevelt stated that he would, after his address before the Ohio constitutional convention, reply to this letter. Meanwhile an article had appeared in *The Outlook* in which it was explained that Mr. Roosevelt's declaration against a third term meant only a third consecutive term.

THE COLUMBUS SPEECH. On February 22, Mr. Roosevelt made the eagerly awaited address before the Ohio constitutional convention at Columbus, O. It was generally understood that this address would contain the principles upon which his candidacy, now generally assumed, would be based. This assumption proved to be correct and in addition to the principles for which it was well known that Mr. Roosevelt stood, he advanced an entirely new proposal, which included the recall of judicial decisions under certain conditions. A résumé of this address will be found at the end of the section *Pre-Convention Campaign, Republican.*

MR. ROOSEVELT'S CANDIDACY ANNOUNCED. On February 25, Mr. Roosevelt made formal announcement of his candidacy for the nomination to succeed Mr. Taft. This took the form of a reply to the letter of the seven Republican governors, who two weeks previously had asked him to issue a frank statement of his intentions. Mr. Roosevelt's reply in full was as follows:

"Gentlemen—I deeply appreciate your letter, and I realize to the full the heavy responsibility it puts upon me, expressing as it does the carefully considered convictions of the men elected by popular vote to stand as the heads of government in their several States.

"I absolutely agree with you that this matter is not one to be decided with any reference to the personal preferences or interests of any man, but purely from the standpoint of the interests of the people as a whole. I will accept the nomination for President if it is tendered to me, and I will adhere to this decision until the convention has expressed its preference. One of the chief principles for which I have stood and for which I now stand, and which I have always endeavored and always shall endeavor to reduce to action, is the genuine rule of the people; and therefore I hope that so far as possible the people may be given a chance, through direct primaries, to express their preference as to who shall be the nominee of the Republican presidential convention.

"Very truly yours,
"Theodore Roosevelt."

LA FOLLETTE'S CAMPAIGN. Rumors to the effect that Senator La Follette would withdraw his candidacy were denied early in January by the directors of his campaign. He made a series of addresses in Illinois and Indiana in the early part of the month.

In these speeches Senator La Follette applied the fundamental principles of the Progressive movement to the trust question, finance, the tariff, party nominations, conservation, and other political and administrative questions. He declared that the great issue before the American people was the control of their own government, and he asserted that the present Progressive movement represented a conflict as old as the history of man, the fight to maintain human liberty, the rights of the people against the encroachment of a powerful few. He declared that a great power had grown up, strong enough at times to nominate the candidates of both political parties and to rule in the organization of legislative bodies and of committees which form legislation. The purpose of the Progressive movement, he declared, was to destroy this power, restore the popular sovereignty, and so to modify and reform, wherever it was found necessary, the constitution, statutes, courts, and all the details of government, that they may be made to carry out and express the well-formulated judgment and the will of the people. In regulation of the trusts, he asserted that Congress should prohibit specifically all methods which make unfair competition possible and which operate as unreasonable restraints of trade. He would have a commission created which should investigate and prohibit all such unreasonable restraints of trade as might be discovered, and to this commission he would give power to ascertain the physical value of the property of any corporation, as well as the value which its intangible property, such as good will, would have under conditions of fair competition. As regards the tariff, he approved the Republican principle of protective duties based upon the difference in the cost of production in the United States and competing countries, and he advocated the creation of a permanent non-partisan, scientific tariff commission. He declared his belief that the direct primary for the selection, not only of candidates for local offices, but of delegates to the presidential convention, and a presidential preference primary by which voters may directly express their choice for presidential candidates, were indispensable pieces of machinery for carrying out Progressive principles. He favored also the initiative, referendum, and recall, including the recall of judges. In the later speeches which Senator La Follette made he, to a large extent, reiterated the subject matter of these addresses.

On January 22 he addressed an audience in Carnegie Hall, New York. This was his first appearance in that city. His address followed in general the lines which he had taken in his speeches in the West. He was greeted by a large and enthusiastic audience. Among other speakers of the same evening were Regis Post, former governor of Porto Rico, and Gifford Pinchot. Shortly after his speech in New York, Senator La Follette, as a result of the strain of the campaign, suffered a nervous breakdown which necessitated a rest of several weeks. On the evening of February 2, he delivered an address in Philadelphia in which he made a savage assault upon the "money trust" and followed it with an attack upon newspapers. The character of some of the remarks included in this address indicated to the friends of Senator La Follette that he was suffering under great nervous strain, and following its delivery he retired from active work in the campaign for several weeks. Even before this, however, it was evident that his cause had been losing ground in favor of Mr. Roosevelt.

Although he was for a time compelled to abandon the activities of his campaign, Senator La Follette refused formally to withdraw as a candidate. Many of his supporters, however, including Gifford Pinchot, now became advocates of the candidacy of Mr. Roosevelt, partly on the ground that Mr. La Follette had not the political strength to be a successful candidate and partly on the ground of his physical and mental condition. On February 14, a statement was issued from the headquarters of Senator La Follette in the form of a telegram addressed by the latter to a newspaper in Fargo, S. D., which had inquired whether he had withdrawn from the contest. In this statement Senator LaFollette declared that the reports that he had withdrawn were false and that the statements in regard to his health were gross misrepresentations. He asserted that they were the result of a pressure brought to bear to force him from the contest.

As the purpose of Mr. Roosevelt to become a candidate grew clearer, Senator La Follette and his supporters showed signs of bitter disappointment. Senator La Follette's campaign manager issued a statement which included the following: "La Follette became a candidate because Roosevelt urged him to make the race. Then Roosevelt began insidiously and secretly to undermine La Follette's organization. Some people are already realizing that if this is the sort of square deal Roosevelt stands for, they do not want his kind." Senator La Follette continued to repeat his refusal to withdraw as a candidate.

La Follette's Platform. On March 13, Senator La Follette issued at Madison, Wis., a campaign platform, reiterating his belief in the policies for which he stood, including "the adoption of graduated income and inheritance taxes, parcel post, government ownership of express companies, and government operation at cost." He said that he would have a commission created to investigate legal actions on the part of trusts and combinations with power to make a physical valuation of their properties. He favored the creation of a properly empowered tariff commission and opposed the Aldrich currency scheme. He favored also government ownership and operation of the Alaskan railways and coal mines and of an Alaskan steamship line by way of the Pacific ports and Panama to New York. He opposed reciprocity with Canada. He pointed out that during Mr. Roosevelt's term of office as President the total stock and bond issues of combinations and trusts rose from $3,784,000,000 to $31,672,000,000, "more than 70 per cent. of which was water."

President Taft's Candidacy. During these incidents the campaign for President Taft's nomination had been actively begun. In a speech on January 30, at Columbus, O., the President expressed the utmost confidence in the victory of the Republican party in November. He declared there were three reasons why the party should return to power: First, the administration had done reasonably and fairly well and deserved a vote of confidence; second, the administration was progressive, and would put in operation all necessary legislation that is progressive; and third, that the administration was not chasing chimeras and unsettling the foundations of the government. He declared that his administration had been attacked because it enforced the trust laws and thereby "forfeited the support of business." Speeches in a similar vein were made at Akron and other cities in Ohio. In a long address, delivered in Cleveland in February, the President defended his administration at great length.

To conduct his campaign, William B. McKinley of Illinois was chosen on February 8, and headquarters were opened in Washington. Mr. McKinley at once issued a statement that President Taft would have 780 votes in Chicago on the first ballot. Early in February the Colorado State central committee voted by 105 to 10 to send delegates to the convention pledged to Mr. Taft. Delegates pledged to him were also elected in Alaska, in the Eighth Virginia District, and in Florida.

In a speech delivered before the New York Republican Club on Lincoln's birthday, President Taft made a general statement of the policy up n which he proposed to be a candidate for renomination. This statement included a severe attack upon attempts of those men who had charged the administration with being affiliated with corrupt influences. He declared that "there are those who look upon the present situation as one full of evil and corruption, and as the tyranny of concentrated wealth." Those people, he affirmed, undertook to pull down the pillars of the temple of freedom and representative government and to reconstruct society upon new principles without any understanding of the constitutional results to be attained. He denounced these men as "political emotionalists and neurotics." He was particularly emphatic in denouncing the recall of judicial officers, which he had declared would bring about conditions similar to those which were prevalent during the French Revolution or during the anarchy of South American republics. He declared that his administration had been steadily progressive in every sense of the word. He admitted that there were faults in the administration of judicial functions, which included tardiness, technicality, and expense involved in procedure, but these defects, he declared, could be removed by means already at hand. He declared that the Republican party "will stand with its face like flint against any constitutional change in it to take away from the high priests, upon whom we depend to administer justice, the independence that they must enjoy of influence, of powerful individuals, or of powerful majorities."

Nine Republican Governors. A statement was issued from the headquarters of the Taft committee in Washington on February 27, to the effect that messages endorsing the administration and assuring the President of their support and confidence had been received from nine Republican governors. These governors were, Eberhart of Minnesota, Hay of Washington, Carroll of Iowa, Penniwill of Delaware, Tener of Pennsylvania, Hooper of Tennessee, Goldsborough of Maryland, Spry of Utah, and Pothier of Rhode Island. Mr. Taft had already been promised the support of Governors Oddie of Nevada and Mead of Vermont.

National Roosevelt Committee. Senator Dixon of Montana, on February 29, was chosen to head the executive committee of the national Roosevelt committee. Immediately after his appointment Senator Dixon issued a statement which had been approved at a conference which Mr. Roosevelt attended. In this statement he said: "The lack of positive leadership during the past three years has turned a Republican majority of 60 in the House of Representatives into an adverse Democratic majority of 70; has changed a two-thirds vote in the Senate into a bare political control of that body, and temporarily has lost control of a dozen Republican States of the North and West. The lack of leadership, of statesmanship, has produced a condition of business bewilderment which has halted the prosperity of the whole country. There can be no cure for this industrial stagnation unless we can substitute a policy of progressive and constructive legislation which shall meet modern conditions with modern laws." In the same statement, Mr. Dixon charged that the only hope left to those Republicans who opposed the nomination of Mr. Roosevelt was to control, through the prostitution of Federal patronage, delegates from the South, together with the delegates from some

Eastern States where they are named in conventions largely controlled by political bosses.

PRESIDENT TAFT'S REPLY TO MR. ROOSEVELT. On March 8, the President delivered an address at Toledo which was designed to be to some extent a reply to Mr. Roosevelt's proposals in his Columbus speech. The President severely criticised the proposal for the recall of judicial decisions. He said of it that it was "a remarkable suggestion so contrary to anything in government hitherto proposed that it is hard to give it the serious consideration which it deserves because of its advocates and the conditions under which it was advanced." The President did not refer directly to Mr. Roosevelt, but said of his programme that it lays "the axe at the foot of the tree of well-ordered freedom and subjects the guarantees of life, liberty, and property without remedy to the fitful impulse of a temporary majority." The President, while be welcomed the progress made toward securing greater equality of opportunity, and destroying the undue advantage of special privilege and accumulated capital, urged that human progress should be advanced without recourse to "feverish, uncertain and unstable" votes upon judicial decisions. "Such a proposal," he said, "is without merit or utility and instead of being progressive is reactionary; instead of being in the interest of all the people and of the stability of popular government is sowing the seed of confusion and tyranny." He declared the defects in our judicial decisions are due, not to the corruption of judges, but to faulty procedure and the difficulties which judges have in aiding juries to reach just decisions. He declared that corrupt judges may be impeached and that if the apparatus for impeachment is too cumbersome, it should be simplified.

PREFERENTIAL PRIMARIES. In the early part of March the directors of Mr. Roosevelt's campaign complained of the activity of federal office-holders in behalf of President Taft and challenged Mr. McKinley to support real primary bills and come out for preferential presidential primaries. Mr. McKinley replied that the plan suggested amounted to the recall of conventions. He declared that he favored properly conducted primaries, but that all but seven States had already made provision for holding primaries or conventions and that he did not favor "changes in the rules of the game while the game is in progress."

MR. ROOSEVELT'S NEW YORK ADDRESS. On March 20, Mr. Roosevelt made an important address in New York City. This was awaited with much interest as it was assumed that he would reply to President Taft's speech at Toledo, which in turn was regarded in some measure as an answer to Mr. Roosevelt's speech at Columbus before the Ohio constitutional convention. Mr. Roosevelt, in this address, made an aggressive attack on President Taft and his administration, and in addition amplified, and to some extent modified, his utterances made at Columbus relating to the recall of judicial decisions. An abstract of this address will be found at the end of the section *Pre-Convention Campaign, Republican.*

ADDRESSES BY PRESIDENT TAFT. During the week of March 21, President Taft visited Boston and several towns in New Hampshire. His chief address was made in the State House on election day, when he addressed the legislature on the recall and the presidential primary. He declared that he favored the latter "wherever full and fair notice of the election can be given; wherever adequate election safeguards can be thrown around to protect it; and wherever the constitution of the State permits its being made applicable to the present election." He added that "a voluntary primary outside the law—known from its informal character as a 'soap-box' primary—is worse than none." He affirmed that a primary of this sort opened the way to fraud and violence. The President said further in the course of his speech:

"This is a government based on popular control. We all concede that the operations of election and the operations of government are not perfect . . . and that it is the part of patriotism to remove as far as possible, the obstacles which prevent honest primaries, honest elections and the honest administration of the government in the interest of the people, but the continued iteration and reiteration of the proposition 'let the people rule,' if it has any significance at all and is intended otherwise than to flatter the people, is intended to be a reflection on the government that we have had down to the present time. Now, in spite of all the corruption, in spite of all the machine politics, in spite of every defect in the operation of our government that can be pointed out, I do not hesitate to say that the history of the last one hundred and thirty-five years shows that the people have ruled."

In a speech delivered in Philadelphia on March 30, Mr. Taft said: "Some call themselves Progressives, and there are others just as progressive but who do not say so much about it. I am glad to express my gratification that this surface noise and lecturing does not represent the true sentiment of the people of this country. We are ready for progress on conservative principles. We have not the time to refute all the theories that noisy so-called reformers are advocating without having worked out their half-baked plans. A progressive is one that makes progress in the right direction." He declared that he was in favor of a movement for reform provided that it was "sound and not affected with fads and a disposition to disturb those things which have been useful to us for a hundred years."

NEW YORK PRIMARIES. As time drew near for the first of the elections, interest in the campaign, which up to this time had been centred chiefly in the personality of the two Republican candidates, became concerned more with their respective strength before the voters in the different States. A primary for the election of delegates to the convention was held in New York on March 26. The election was carried on under a new election law which provided new and distracting conditions for voting. Among these were a cumbersome ballot. As a result of the late decision of the court which was passing on the question of the position of the Roosevelt candidates on the ballot, it was found impossible to have the ballots printed early enough before the election to insure each voter a ballot wherewith to vote. As a result, voters in Kings, Queens, and Richmond counties were largely disfranchised, because no ballots were delivered until after the polls were closed. The result of the balloting was, for the Taft delegates, 67, and for the Roosevelt delegates, 7. Mr. Roosevelt was greatly incensed at the result of the balloting in New York, and in a series of speeches, denounced the New York primaries as "an infamy unmatched even by the kindred infamies perpetrated in behalf of President Taft in Indianapolis and Denver."

NORTH DAKOTA. On March 19, the first of the presidential preference primaries was held. This was in North Dakota, where an aggressi e campaign had been made by Senator La Follette and no particular attempt had been made to influence the voters for the other candidates. In this election Senator La Follette received 28,600 votes, Mr. Roosevelt, 19,100, and President Taft, 1500.

ILLINOIS, WISCONSIN, PENNSYLVANIA, ETC. The month of April Mr. Roosevelt spent in speechmaking in the Middle West. On April 8 at Ft. Wayne, Ind., he made his first declaration on reciprocity. He declared that he opposed the administration's reciprocity measure without reserve. He had reached this conclusion, he said, after a careful study of the measure, following his first approval of it. While Mr. Roosevelt was engaged in making this series of speeches, several important elections were held. On April 6, presidential preference primaries were held in Wisconsin. In these Senator La Follette received 131,920 votes, and President Taft 47,630. Mr. Roosevelt's name did not appear on the ballots in Wisconsin. On April 9, a presidential preference primary was held in Illinois, which was the first of the great popular victories gained by Mr. Roosevelt over President Taft. In these primaries Mr. Roosevelt received 115,000 more votes than the President. For details of this vote, see ILLINOIS. Regular primaries held earlier in the month gave to Mr. Taft delegates in Nevada, West Virginia, and Kentucky. On April 13 the presidential primary held in Pennsylvania resulted in a victory for Mr. Roosevelt greater even than attained by him in Illinois, as the 76 delegates to the convention were pledged to Mr. Roosevelt. See PENNSYLVANIA.

MR. ROOSEVELT ON POPULAR RIGHTS. During the week of April 20 Mr. Roosevelt made a number of speeches in Nebraska. In the course of his address at Omaha he spoke of two issues in the campaign which he termed the issue between the boss and the people and the issue between the man and the dollar. In the course of his remarks on the second of these issues, he said:

"Some time ago I stated that the creed of the Progressives was that they stood for both the man and the dollar, but that if they had to choose between them they stood for the man rather than the dollar; in other words, that we were for both human rights and property rights, but that in the rare cases where they conflicted we were for human rights. Referring to this statement President Taft said: 'The next time a demogogue mounts the platform and says he is for the man rather than the dollar, ask him what he means by it.' The humorous side of this comes in the fact that Mr. Taft was evidently ignorant of the fact that I was merely quoting Lincoln's letter which he wrote to some Boston correspondent in 1859. 'The demagogue on the platform,' of whom he spoke was Abraham Lincoln! As for what Lincoln meant by it he simply meant that he was for the human right of the slave as against the property right of the master when the two could not be reconciled. In the same way I am for the human right of the overworked girl, or of the crippled workingman or workingwoman against the so-called property right of the employer. I am for the right of the workman against the factory-owner or mine-owner who runs company-stores; I am for the right of the legislature to prohibit men, women, and children being huddled like pigs in a tenement-house room as against the property right of the owner of the tenement house, which the Illinois Supreme Court held to override all other considerations in such a case."

MASSACHUSETTS PRIMARY. The presidential primary election in Massachusetts, on April 30, was of peculiar interest as possibly indicating the relative strength of Mr. Roosevelt and President Taft in New England. In the elections in the other States where State primaries had been held efforts were made to explain the results on the ground of local issues. For example, in Illinois the defeat of President Taft was attributed to the feeling against Senator Lorimer, with whom it was alleged President Taft was in sympathy. In Pennsylvania, likewise, it was alleged that hostility toward Senator Penrose on the part of the voters had resulted in the defeat of the party machine. In Massachusetts, however, there were no such local issues. In this campaign Mr. Taft, for the first time, took active part.

The decision of the President to take this action was the result of a series of sharp attacks which had been made upon him by Mr. Roosevelt, and his speech in Boston on April 25 was a reply to these attacks and an aggressive defense of his administration. The address had been carefully considered by the cabinet before its delivery. A few days before, on April 21, Representative Gardner of Massachusetts telegraphed to Mr. Roosevelt a series of charges in which he asserted that the latter had sought to mislead the public in regard to the President's attitude towards Senator Lorimer, and had made favorites of certain financial and industrial interests. He challenged Mr. Roosevelt to produce the report of Commissioner Herbert Knox Smith relating to the Harvester Trust. President Taft dealt with this matter in his address, and also criticised Mr. Roosevelt's attitude on reciprocity, and read certain letters which had been exchanged between them which indicated that Mr. Roosevelt had heartily supported the measure when it was first placed before him by the President. The President also defended himself against the charges made by Mr. Roosevelt and others, that he had been favorable towards Senator Lorimer.

Replying to the charges made by Mr. Roosevelt that he had affiliated himself with Speaker Cannon, the President declared that his predecessor had most earnestly advised him to make agreements with the former speaker. Speaking of the tariff, Mr. Taft asked whether Mr. Roosevelt had ever condemned the Payne tariff revision. The closing paragraph of the President's address showed a deep feeling on account of the attitude of Mr. Roosevelt toward him. After quoting the promise made by the latter in regard to the third term, he said:

"If he had frankly announced that he had changed his mind no one would be disposed to hold him to a promise of that sort merely because he had made it. The promise and his treatment of it only throw an informing light on the value that ought now to be attached to any promise of this kind he may make for the future. . . . There is not the slightest reason if he secures a third term, and the limitation of the Washington, Jefferson, and Jackson tradition is broken down why he should not have as many terms as his life will permit. If he is necessary now to the government why not later? One who so lightly regards constitutional principles, and especially the independence of the judiciary, one who is so naturally impatient of legal restraints and of due legal procedure, and who has so misunderstood what liberty regulated by law is, could not safely be intrusted with successive presidential terms."

The facts relating to the Harvester Trust episode will be found summarized at the end of the section *Pre-Convention Campaign, Republican.*

As a test, the result of the Massachusetts primaries was of little value. While Mr. Taft had a popular majority of 3600 votes, the 8 Roosevelt delegates-at-large were elected as the result of the rejection of many Taft ballots. These were defective because the name of an independent candidate had been added to the list and votes had been cast for 9 instead of 8 delegates. Mr. Roosevelt promptly declined to take advantage of these errors and urged the delegates-at-large to support Mr. Taft.

MARYLAND PRIMARIES. The next State in which presidential primaries were held was Maryland, and both the President and Mr. Roosevelt took an active part. The vote was close, and in the election held on May 6, Mr. Roosevelt received 29,124 votes and President Taft about 26,000. Supporters of Mr. Taft, however, controlled the State convention, but later when it met, they decided to yield to Mr. Roosevelt's delegates on account of the popular majority. (See MARYLAND.) On the day of the election in Maryland, Mr. Roosevelt published a long statement, attacking the President.

OHIO AND NEW JERSEY PRIMARIES. Following the election in Maryland, interest in the campaign was transferred to Ohio in the second week of May. Here both the President and Mr. Roosevelt made a series of speeches. In an address made at Portsmouth, Mr. Taft said: "I am up against the wall. I am being hit below the belt and I am here to fight."

The campaign in this State was bitter in the extreme. Both the President and Mr. Roosevelt in their addresses made sharp attacks. The President asserted that Mr. Roosevelt was an egotist and a demagogue, and Mr. Roosevelt replied with equal acerbity. All the assertions which had been made by the two in other States were repeated with additional emphasis. Certain statements which Mr. Roosevelt made at this time were regarded as indicating his purpose to bolt the nomination of Mr. Taft, for although the former President repeatedly claimed that he, himself, had so many delegates that he was certain to be nominated on the first ballot, he declared that the President was striving to win by fraud and that if he should so win, honest Republicans could no longer respect the action of the convention. He declared that a nomination gained in this way would mean the ruin of the Republican party. On May 20, Mr. Taft published a statement in which he declared that the certainty of Mr. Roosevelt's defeat must be a source of congratulation to all patriotic citizens who could see "the utter wreck he would have made of the party if nominated, and the great danger to which the country would have been exposed if there had been any chance of his election for a third term." He charged that Mr. Roosevelt's contests for delegates would be found without merit and that they had been brought about by sheer premeditation without the slightest reason.

The election in Ohio was not, strictly speaking, a presidential preference primary, because on the Republican ballot there appeared the name of no candidate for presidential nomination. The voters of the Republican party expressed their choice by voting for delegates known to be favorable to one candidate or another. In this election two delegates were chosen from each congressional district. The delegates-at-large were not voted for at this primary but at the State convention. As a result of the voting, Mr. Roosevelt defeated President Taft by more than 20,000 votes, electing 34 of the district delegates. The result of this election was a bitter blow to President Taft because he had expressed the utmost confidence that Ohio, his native State, would give him her delegates. He still expressed himself, however, as confident of the nomination and took part with unabated vigor in the campaign in New Jersey, which followed next. In the election in this State, held on May 16, Mr. Roosevelt carried the State by a plurality of over 13,000, losing only two of the twenty-four counties.

LA FOLLETTE CAMPAIGN FUND. Senator La Follette, who had been active in the campaign in Ohio preceding the presidential primary, published several days before that election a list of contributors to his campaign fund. This list showed that a total of $53,500 had been contributed, and among those who had given were Gifford Pinchot, Amos R. Pinchot, and William Kent, $10,000 each, and William Flinn of Pittsburgh, $1000. These sums were all given in the early part of the senator's canvass and before Mr. Roosevelt announced his candidacy for the presidency. Later all these contributors became supporters of Mr. Roosevelt. During his campaign in Ohio, Senator La Follette declared his belief that a fund of not less than $1,000,000 had been contributed for Mr. Roosevelt's primary canvass by George W. Perkins of the Harvester Trust, Judge Gary of the Steel Corporation, Daniel R. Hanna of Ohio, and others. He said: "I call upon Colonel Roosevelt to publish a complete list of contributors to his campaign fund before I leave this State. I make affidavit to the accounts of and the donors to my campaign fund. I ask that Colonel Roosevelt be equally frank with the people."

CALIFORNIA AND SOUTH DAKOTA PRIMARIES. New Jersey was the last of the States in which the rival candidates took active part in the campaign previous to the presidential primaries. Two States remained in which primaries were to be held, California and South Dakota. It was generally assumed that Mr. Roosevelt would carry California, where Governor Johnson was one of the most aggressive of the Progressive leaders and where the voters had, wherever opportunities offered, indicated a pronounced Progressive sentiment throughout the State.

Secretary Knox made an address at Los Angeles on May 9, defending the President and attacking Mr. Roosevelt. He characterized the latter as "a man of whims, imperious ambitions, vanities, and mysterious antipathies," and who "would break any rule of his party and his country, and his own solemn word to gain the seat of his friend." Mr. Roosevelt's comment on this assertion was: "I could not expect Senator Penrose's representative in the cabinet to take any other attitude." The anticipation of the Progressives were abundantly realized at the primary held on May 14, when Mr. Roosevelt carried the State by a plurality of over 70,000 votes over Mr. Taft, and by a plurality of over 25,000 over Mr. Taft and Senator La Follette combined. Mr. Taft did not carry a single county in the State. Mr. Roosevelt ran second in only one county, which voted for Senator La Follette by a small margin. The last of the States holding presidential primaries was South Dakota. The vote was taken in this State on June 4. Mr. Roosevelt received over 33,000 votes, Senator La Follette over 18,000, and President Taft about 10,000.

Republican political interest was now transferred from the active campaign in the field to the convention. In the early part of June, the national committee convened and began the preliminary work of preparing the temporary roll of the convention.

ANALYSIS OF REPUBLICAN PRESIDENTIAL PRIMARIES. Below is summarized the popular vote received by each of the three candidates for the Republican nomination in the presidential primaries. These primaries were held in eleven States. The results were as follows:

State	Total Vote	Roosevelt	Taft	LaFollette
Illinois	437,090	266,917	127,481	42,692
Maryland	55,133	29,124	26,009	....
Massachusetts	171,879	83,099	86,722	2,058
Nebraska	76,921	46,795	13,341	16,785
New Jersey	108,795	61,297	44,034	3,464
North Dakota	59,66	23,669	1,876	34,123
Ohio	299,741	165,809	118,362	15,570
Oregon	71,914	28,905	20,517	22,491
Pennsylvania	492,025	298,962	193,063	....
South Dakota	63,301	35,637	9,843	17,821
Wisconsin	181,496	628	47,514	133,354

The total vote cast in these primaries for each of the candidates was: For Roosevelt, 1,179,405; for Taft, 758,107; for La Follette, 33,423. The total popular vote cast in these presidential primaries was 2,284,163. The total popular vote cast in these States in the presidential election of 1908 was 3,372,173. In these States, with the exception of Oregon, California, and South Dakota, the votes cast in the presidential primary ranged from about 40 to about 75 per cent. of those cast in the presidential election of 1908.

SUMMARY OF THE COLUMBUS SPEECH OF MR. ROOSEVELT. As is noted in another portion of this article, Mr. Roosevelt delivered an address before the Ohio constitutional convention on February 21. As this was one of the most important addresses delivered by Mr. Roosevelt during the year, a summary of its most important features seems advisable.

He began with an assertion of his belief in a pure democracy together with the right of the people to rule. He declared that the battle which was now being waged was against privilege on behalf of the common welfare. After an emphatic statement of his belief in constitutional government, he declared that constitutions must be interpreted and administered so as to fit human rights. He emphatically dissented from the view that it was either wise or necessary to try to devise methods which under the Constitution would automatically prevent the people from deciding for themselves what governmental action they think just and proper. This he said is precisely what is done in every case where the State permits its representatives whether on the bench or in the legislature or in executive office to declare that it has not the power to right grave social wrongs. He then entered upon a discussion of the struggle between labor and capital and followed this with an exposition of his theories as to the proper manner of controlling "big business," which he declared was responsible for much of the special privilege which has become characteristic of the national life. He emphasized the fact that while the administrative department must play an important part in regulating combinations the legislature and the judiciary have an equally important part. He then turned his attention to the machinery by which these ends are to be achieved. He declared that each community has an absolute right to determine for itself what that machinery shall be, subject only to the fundamental law of the nation as expressed in the Constitution of the United States. He then declared his belief in various methods for improving the machinery of government, including the short ballot, direct nomination by the people, direct preferential primaries, election of United States senators by direct vote, the initiative and referendum, and with qualifications, the recall. Thus far Mr. Roosevelt had only recited his well-known opinions on these topics. His next recommendation, however, was for the most part unanticipated both by his friends and his opponents. This was his advocacy of the recall, under certain conditions, of judicial decisions. After speaking of the caution which should be employed in recalling judges, he said: "We should hold the judiciary in all respect, but it is both absurd and degrading to make a fetish of a judge or of anyone else." He quoted Abraham Lincoln as to limitation of the proper authority of courts. He then said: "What the Supreme Court of the nation decides to be law binds both the national and the State courts and all the people within the boundaries of the nation, but the decision of a State court upon a constitutional question should be subject to revision by the people of the State. . . . When the Supreme Court of the State declares a given statute unconstitutional because in conflict with the State or national Constitution, its opinion should be subject to revision by the people themselves. Such an opinion ought always to be treated with great respect by the people and unquestionably in the majority of cases would be accepted and followed by them. But actual experience has shown the vital need of the people for reserving to themselves the right to pass upon such opinion. If any considerable number of the people feel that the decision is in defiance of justice, they should be given the right by petition to bring before the voters at some subsequent election, special or otherwise as might be decided, and after the fullest opportunity for deliberation and debate, the question whether or not the judges' interpretation of the Constitution is to be sustained." The remainder of the address was given to an elaboration of this proposal, together with a recital of some decisions of the Supreme Court which he considered oppressive and wrong.

SUMMARY OF THE NEW YORK ADDRESS. The speech delivered in New York City on March 20 contains an elaboration and, to some extent, a modification of Mr. Roosevelt's previous utterances on the recall of judicial decisions. In this speech he also replied with some bitterness to President Taft's comments on the proposals.

He began the address with an affirmation of his belief in the right of the people, expressed in majorities, to rule, but declared that for the last twenty years the government had been not by a majority, but by a minority, composed largely of political leaders. He then followed with a statement of the proposals which the Progressives of the Republican party had formulated for a change of form in the State government. These included the recall of judges and judicial decisions. In answer to criticisms made by President Taft and others upon the latter, he recited certain decisions in which he declared that the courts had set aside the will of the majority of the people. He asserted that these proposals did not anticipate anything in connection with the Supreme Court of the United States or with the federal Constitution; that he was not proposing anything having any connection with ordinary suits, civil or criminal, as between individuals; that he was not speaking of the recall of judges; that he was proposing merely in a certain class of cases, involving police power, when a State court had set aside as unconstitutional a law passed by the legislature for the general welfare, the validity of the law should be submitted for final determination to a vote of the people taken after due time for consideration. He then replied to the criticism made by President Taft in which the latter had said that the proposal was "utterly without merit or utility, and, instead of being . . . in the interest of all the people and of the stability of popular government, is sowing the seeds of confusion and tyranny." Roosevelt declared this criticism to be really less a criticism of his proposal than a criticism of all popular government. He said: "Mr. Taft's position is the position that has been held since the beginning of our government, although not always so openly held, by a large majority of reputable and honorable men who, down at bottom, distrust popular government, and when they must accept it, accept it with reluctance, and hedge it around with every species of restriction and check and balance, so as to make the power of the people as limited and as ineffective as possible. Mr. Taft fairly defines the issue when he says that our government is and should be a government of all the people by a representative part of the people. This is an excellent and moderate description of an oligarchy. It defines our government as a government of all the people by a few of the people." The remainder of the address was given to further criticisms of the President's comments and especially of the use of Mr. Taft's expression "the fitful impulse of a temporary majority." Mr. Roosevelt declared that if this were true, all presidents, including Mr. Taft, had been elected by "the fitful impulse of a temporary majority," and that the constitutions of the States and the Constitution of the nation with its amendments had been adopted by such an impulse. He declared that the doctrine advocated by Mr. Taft had tended to create a bulwark for privilege, a bulwark unjustly protecting social interests against the rights of the people as a whole. He finally recapitulated his stand in the speech at Columbus and his quotations from William Draper Lewis, dean of the law school of the University of Pennsylvania, in defense of his proposal for the recall of judicial decisions.

The Harvester Trust Episode. This episode, which resulted in some of the most bitter charges and recriminations made in the campaign, first came to the public eye on April 21, when Representative Gardner of Massachusetts telegraphed to Mr. Roosevelt a series of charges in which he asserted, among other things, that the latter had made favorites of certain powerful financial and industrial interests. He challenged Mr. Roosevelt to produce the report of Commissioner Herbert Knox Smith concerning the Harvester Trust. On the following day, Representative Campbell of Kansas, made a speech, in which he asked Mr. Roosevelt to say whether he, while he was President, had sent a note to the Department of Justice, directing the suspension of action against this trust. On April 24, in response to a resolution introduced by Senator Johnston of Alabama, a mass of political correspondence relating to the Harvester Trust was sent to the Senate. From this correspondence it appeared that in August, 1907, Mr. Perkins had called upon President Roosevelt with certain papers and asked that no action against the Harvester Trust be taken before the completion of the investigation then being made by Commissioner Smith. He made the argument that the company had sought to obey the law and to meet the requirements of the government. On August 22, Mr. Roosevelt wrote to Attorney-General Bonaparte referring to the visit of Mr. Perkins and his arguments, and said: "Please do not file the suit until I hear from you." The trust was not prosecuted under the administration of Mr. Roosevelt. Among other papers sent to the Senate in response to its request was a long letter from Commissioner Smith, dated September 23, 1907, commenting upon the Sherman act and the course taken by the Harvester company. This letter did not favor the prosecution of the company, but pointed with approval to the attitude of the company and other allied corporations toward the government. "It is a practical question," he said, "whether it would be well to throw away now the great influence of the so-called Morgan interests." It was indicated in the context that he had in mind the influence of these corporations in favor of publicity and regulation. Following the appearance of this correspondence in the Senate, Mr. Roosevelt published a statement, in which he said that his note to Mr. Bonaparte had been in accord with his custom in such cases, and pointed out the fact that President Taft had not prosecuted the company. He asserted emphatically that his action had been approved by his entire cabinet, including President Taft, and that the latter had heartily concurred. On April 29, however, the President published a statement saying that he had never heard the matter discussed in the cabinet and that neither Secretary Root nor Secretary Wilson heard any discussion relating to the matter or knew of the commissioner's letter. He also asserted that the dates showed that he (Mr. Taft) had been out of the country at the time when Mr. Roosevelt asserted he had taken part in the cabinet meeting.

The publication of the matter relating to the Harvester Trust, and Mr. Roosevelt's criticisms of President Taft, led to a sharp exchange of personalities between the friends of the two. Mr. Taft insisted that he had no knowledge of the action of the former President and Mr. Roosevelt repeated his assertion that it had been approved by Mr. Taft. Among the former members of Mr. Roosevelt's cabinet there was a division of opinion. Mr. Root, former Secretary of State, and Mr. Wilson, Secretary of Agriculture, supported Mr. Taft's contention, while Mr. Bonaparte, former Attorney-General, upheld Mr. Roosevelt, and remarked that Mr. Taft was no longer worthy to hold office. A long statement was published by George W. Perkins, in which he declared that he had contributed large sums in the campaigns of Mr. Bannard for mayor of New York City, Mr. Taft for President, and Mr. Stimson for governor of New York, and that at the end of the national campaign in 1908, he had made good the campaign committee's deficit of $15,000, which had never been repaid. He urged that his support could not have been less objectionable at that time as he was more closely identified with Mr. Morgan and certain trust interests than he was at the time when his money was given to aid Mr. Roosevelt. He asserted that the publication of the Harvester Trust correspondence was a "scurrilous attack upon Mr. Roosevelt."

He declared that Mr. Taft had not only been present at a cabinet discussion of the Harvester Trust case, but also had repeatedly and emphatically approved the course actually taken in private conversations. He said that it was utterly impossible for Mr. Taft to have forgotten this and that it was impossible to reconcile his present position with any standard of honorable conduct. He also attacked the President's action in relation to the activities of federal office-holders and said that the President knew well that delegates elected for him in Kentucky, Indiana, New York City, and elsewhere represented barefaced frauds. He said: "He stands guilty of connivance at and condonation of these frauds; he stands guilty of approving and encouraging fraud, which deprives the people of their right to express their will."

Pre-Convention Campaign, Democratic

Democratic Candidates. As was indicated in the beginning of this article, the Democratic campaign for the presidential nomination did not differ in essentials from other Democratic campaigns for the presidency. There were, at the beginning of the year, four avowed prominent candidates for the nomination. These were Governor Woodrow Wilson of New Jersey, Champ Clark, Speaker of the House of Representatives, Governor Harmon of Ohio, and Congressman Oscar W. Underwood of Alabama. As the campaign developed other names were mentioned as possible candidates. These included Governor Foss of Massachusetts, Governor Marshall of Indiana, Joseph W. Folk, former governor of Missouri, and Mayor Gaynor of New York City. The chief contest, however, was between Governor Wilson, Mr. Clark, and Governor Harmon, with Governor Harmon throughout the campaign stronger theoretically than practically. Together with Mr. Underwood, Governor Harmon had the disadvantage of having the bitter hostility of Mr. Bryan to contend with. Mr. Bryan denounced them both as conservatives and reactionaries and lost no opportunity of assailing them.

Mr. Bryan's Attitude. Mr. Bryan at no time throughout the campaign appeared himself as an avowed candidate; indeed, early in January he issued a statement in which he said: "I cannot conceive any condition that could arise which would make me a candidate this year." His influence with the party, however, remained the strongest single element, and it was generally assumed that the candidate whom he openly favored would receive the nomination. That Mr. Bryan was not without opposition in his party, however, was shown in the meeting of the Democratic national committee, early in December, when he was overwhelmingly defeated in two test votes which were forced by himself, one in Alabama and one in Pennsylvania. This vote was taken in an attempt by Mr. Bryan to prevent the filling of vacancies from Alabama and Pennsylvania in the national committee. In the case of Alabama he was defeated by a vote of 34 to 13, and in the case of Pennsylvania, where he attempted to prevent the seating of his ancient foe, James M. Guffey, he was defeated by a vote of 30 to 18. At this meeting of the national committee it was decided that the convention should be held in Baltimore, beginning June 25, 1912. The most important act of the committee, aside from its selection of the convention city, was the passage of a resolution for presidential primaries. This resolution declared that delegates and alternates may, if not otherwise directed by law, be elected directly if, in the opinion of the respective members, it is deemed desirable and possible. An effort by Mr. Bryan to have the committee pass a resolution declaring for preference primaries without reservation of any kind was defeated. The two leading candidates for the nomination began an active campaign early in January, 1912.

Governor Wilson's Candidacy. The beginning of 1912 found Governor Wilson an avowed and active candidate for the Democratic nomination. On January 2, Governor Wilson made an address before the National Democratic Club of New York City, on the general question of the tariff. In this speech he attacked the protective policy, asserting that the tariff was "the most critical question of a campaign which must decide the policy of our government, not only in this, but in respect to a score of things which touch the general adjustments of our life." The settlement of the tariff question, he said, could not be avoided or postponed. He declared that the control of prices and the shutting down of competition must be abolished; that protection is a system of favoritism under which the beneficiaries will never be satisfied or the oppressed ever content to submit. He asserted that one bad effect of the system was the encouragement of a system of paternalism, which looked upon the government as an instrument of gain instead of one for the promotion of the well-being of all.

Alleged Attempts to Discredit Governor Wilson. Coincident with Governor Wilson's appearance in the political arena as an avowed candidate was the beginning of what his supporters declared to be a conspiracy on the part of his enemies to discredit him. The fight against him in New Jersey was headed by former Senator James Smith, whom he had caused to be defeated for the United States Senate in 1911. A letter written by Governor Wilson in 1905, while he was still president of Princeton University, and addressed to Adrian H. Joline, a lawyer of New York, was published early in January, in which among other things he exclaimed of Mr. Bryan as follows: "Would that we could do something at once dignified and effective to knock Mr. Bryan into a cocked hat." This letter was written shortly after the defeat of Judge Parker for the presidency. As the letter was published at a time when relations between Governor Wilson and Mr. Bryan were especially cordial, it created much comment. Mr. Bryan declared it was of little importance.

Several days after the publication of Governor Wilson's letter relating to Mr. Bryan, came an incident which, for a time, occupied the attention of the public press. For several years the most enthusiastic advocate of Mr. Wilson as a presidential candidate had been *Harper's Weekly*, edited by Colonel George Harvey, and the name of Mr. Wilson had been carried at the head of the editorial pages of this periodical as its choice for the presidency. Suddenly in the middle of January this heading disappeared and rumors at once arose that a disagreement had arisen between Governor Wilson and Colonel Harvey. For a time the latter refused to make any comment or explanation, but after several weeks published a note in which he stated that his advocacy of Governor Wilson's candidacy had ceased as a result of the latter's assertion that the support of *Harper's Weekly* was injurious to him. This action of Colonel Harvey followed a conference held between him, Governor Wilson, and Colonel H. W. Watterson, editor of the Louisville *Courier-Journal*, and in the details of this conference, which came out several weeks after it had been held, it appeared that Colonel Harvey asked Governor Wilson the direct question whether he believed the support of *Harper's Weekly* was doing him injury, and Governor Wilson to this frankly replied that he thought it was. The affair naturally created much comment, which was increased by the publication of a long statement by Colonel Watterson, in which he attacked Governor Wilson and charged him with ingratitude and discourtesy. With the consent of both Governor Wilson and Mr. Harvey an exchange of letters relating to the controversy was published. These letters showed that while Colonel Harvey had been hurt by the episode, there was no feeling of hostility between the two men.

The basis of the objection of Governor Wilson to the support of *Harper's Weekly* appears to have been the opinion, more or less general, especially in the western part of the country, that *Harper's Weekly* is the organ of, and is largely supported by, the large financial interests of the country. The supporters of Governor Wilson in this controversy claimed that his action in severing his relations with Colonel Harvey and Colonel Watterson was the result of an attempt made by them to seek large financial support for his candidacy from Thomas F. Ryan, and that Governor Wilson refused to have "tainted money" used in the furtherance of his cause. It was denied by Colonel Harvey that he had made any effort to secure money from Mr. Ryan, but Colonel Watterson made a practical admission that he had attempted to do so.

Other Candidates. Governor Harmon had made several addresses in January, including one at St. Louis and one in Chicago. In the former city he declared that economy and tariff revision would be the issues of the campaign. He asserted that the prospects for Democratic success were bright and that there were no indications of party disunion. He declared at Chicago that the present tariff law "sticks out like a sore thumb." Early in February, Joseph W. Folk, former governor of Missouri, withdrew as an active Democratic candidate for the nomination and asked his friends to support Champ Clark.

Governor Wilson's Campaign. Governor Wilson, on February, 1912, opened his speaking campaign by an address in Chicago. With the chief candidates in the field the campaign proceeded quietly, and as compared with the Republican campaign attracted little attention. In the primaries held in the different States, Mr. Clark carried the States of New Hampshire, Vermont, Massachusetts, Maryland, Virginia, Kentucky, Illinois, one-half of Wisconsin, Iowa, Kansas, Nebraska, Montana, Wyoming, Colorado, New Mexico, Washington, Idaho, Arizona, Nevada, and California. Governor Wilson carried the primaries in New Jersey, in which there was really no contest as the other candidates refused to have their names appear on the ballots, three-quarters of Pennsylvania, North Carolina, South Carolina, one-half of Wisconsin, Minnesota, one-half of Oklahoma, Texas, Utah, one-half of Louisiana, and Oregon. Representative Underwood carried the primaries of Georgia, Florida, Alabama, and Mississippi. The votes of other States were either given to "favorite sons" or had no choice. Details of the votes in these State will be found in the political history under those States.

National Convention, Republican

Meeting of the National Committee. The meeting of the Republican national committee which precedes the assembling of the convention by about a week has been in previous elections little more than a formality. The functions of the committee are chiefly to select presiding officers of the convention and to decide disputed contests for delegates. The meeting of the committee on June 6, 1912, was, however, anticipated with the greatest interest. On their decision as to delegates in dispute depended, to a large extent, the majority of either of the candidates in the convention, for although the decisions of the committee are passed upon by the committee on credentials after the convention has formally organized, such action is hardly more than a formality, for the decisions of the national committee usually stand without change.

Temporary Chairman. Prior to its formal convening the committee had offered the temporary chairmanship of the convention to Senator Root. This appointment was at once opposed by Mr. Roosevelt on the ground that he was too conservative in type and too thoroughly identified with the policies of President Taft. The candidate of the Progressives was Senator Clapp of Minnesota. Several days later, however, the opposition of Mr. Roosevelt was withdrawn. In a statement he said that he had been advised by delegates that the matter was of little importance. After a conference held with George W. Perkins, Gifford Pinchot, and others, however, Mr. Roosevelt published, on June 3, a long statement, in which he declared that Senator Root should be opposed by every Progressive. In this statement he declared that Senator Root "stands as the representative of the men and the policies of reaction. He is put forward by the bosses and the representatives of special privileges." Thus the first contest of the strength of the convention was destined to come in the selection of the temporary chairman.

Organization of the Committee. It was decided that the rules for decisions of disputed delegates should be the same as those of the meeting of the committee in 1908. On June 3, President Taft sent a letter to the committee in which he asked that the sessions should be open to the public, and although this was contrary to precedent, it was decided that the hearings should be public. Representatives of the five press associations of the United States were admitted. Friends of Mr. Roosevelt on the committee offered an amendment for the admission of about 200 additional reporters, but this was lost by a vote of 13 to 9. The chairman of the committee was Victor Rosewater of Nebraska, and the chief spokesman for Mr. Roosevelt was Senator William E. Borah of Idaho. Each side was allowed counsel. Charles Dick, former United States senator of Ohio, was the leading counsel for the Taft delegates whose seats were disputed, and

Ormsby McHarg acted in a similar capacity for the Roosevelt delegates who claimed seats in the convention.

By the rules under which the national committee did its work in 1908, votes were taken *viva voce*, and a roll call could not be had except at the request of twenty members. At the first session of the committee, Senator Borah submitted an amendment whereby a roll call could be had at the request of eight members of the committee. Senator Borah supported his amendment in an aggressive speech, but the amendment was defeated by a large majority.

DISPUTED SEATS. There were in dispute about 260 seats. Most of these were in the South and concerned chiefly the negro delegates from the southern States. There were, however, important contests in several of the northern States, including Indiana, California, and Washington. The States were taken in alphabetical order, but the contests in Arizona and California were postponed for a week on account of the impossibility of the persons interested arriving in Chicago before that date. The contests in Alabama were the first heard. In this State there were contests in the first, second, fifth, sixth, and ninth districts. In all but the ninth district, however, the contests were trivial and were decided in favor of the Taft delegates by a unanimous vote of the committee. In this contest the committee divided by a vote of 38 to 15 in favor of the Taft delegates. This was the first decisive trial of strength. This action of the committee was bitterly opposed by the Roosevelt members and was denounced by Senator Dixon as "a cold-blooded, premeditated theft." Mr. Roosevelt, in a statement made on the following day said that he had expected only two delegates from Alabama.

On the second day of the hearing of these contests, 48 cases were decided and these were all in favor of seating the Taft delegates. The only test case was the fifth Arkansas district, in which by a vote of 42 to 10 the Taft delegates were seated. This test vote came on a compromise motion to admit the Taft and Rosevelt delegates with half a vote each. Mr. Roosevelt, on June 8, issued an appeal, which followed a denunciation of the action of the national committee in unseating his two delegates in the ninth Alabama district. He declared that a nomination obtained by a vote of delegates seated in utter defiance of justice, as were those two Alabama delegates, was worthless to the man obtaining it.

All the contests from the State of Georgia were decided in favor of delegates for President Taft. The 12 contested delegates from Indiana, including four delegates-at-large, were given to President Taft. A bitter struggle was anticipated in these Indiana cases, but on the question of seating the delegates-at-large every member of the national committee voted in favor of seating the Taft delegates. Taft delegates also were seated from the first district and from the third district. In the fourth district the Roosevelt contestants withdrew. The only contest from Indiana on which a test vote was taken was in the thirteenth district, and in this instance the Taft delegates were seated by a vote of 36 to 13. The cases for the Roosevelt delegates of California were presented by Francis J. Heney, who conducted them with such aggressiveness that he was in frequent difficulties with the members of the committee. On June 10 it was finally decided that all of the 26 delegates from California except two in the fourth contest district, should be placed upon the temporary roll. During the progress of these contests Mr. Roosevelt had issued statements attacking the action of the committee, and he declared in an editorial in *The Outlook* that in many cases the Taft delegates to the convention "represented absolutely nothing but fraud as vulgar as brazen and as cynically open as any ever committed by the Tweed régime in New York forty odd years ago." This editorial also contained a bitter attack upon the methods of electing the national committee and indirectly upon President Taft as willing to benefit by dishonest practices in the seating of his delegates.

On June 11, 18 contests from Kentucky were heard by the committee and 17 Taft delegates and one Roosevelt delegate were seated. The Roosevelt delegate was from the eleventh Congress district where the two Roosevelt delegates were the regular delegates, while the two Taft delegates were contested. The committee voted to split the delegates between the Taft and Roosevelt factions on the ground that while the Roosevelt supporters controlled the Congress district convention, they violated the rule of the Republican party in organizing a convention. Colonel Roosevelt issued another statement in which he said: "The question at Chicago becomes clearer with every vote of the national committee. It is simply whether the people have the right to nominate whomever they wish for the highest office in their gift, or whether, by deliberate theft and fraud, certain machine leaders, acting in the interest of special privilege, are to be permitted to deprive people of this right." He made further attack upon the "bosses," who, he claimed, were unscrupulously setting themselves to bring about the renomination of President Taft.

On June 12, the committee disposed of the contests in Arizona, California, Louisiana, Michigan, and part of Mississippi. All of these contests, involving forty seats were decided in favor of Taft delegates. The only roll call in these contests was in that of the fourth California district. The Taft delegates were seated by a vote of 37 to 16. In the course of these contests Mr. Heney read a note from Governor Johnson of California, in which the latter refused to appear before the committee on the ground that he would not submit to "a trial of a title of property by the thief who steals it." On June 13, the committee gave to Mr. Taft 11 Congress district delegates in Mississippi, and 6 district delegates in Missouri. To Colonel Roosevelt were given one district delegate in Mississippi, four delegates-at-large and four Congress delegates in Missouri, and four Congress district delegates in North Carolina.

On June 15, Mr. Roosevelt arrived in Chicago to take active lead in his own campaign for the nomination. He was greeted with the greatest enthusiasm, and on his arrival at a hotel addressed the people from the balcony on the text "It is a naked fight against theft and the thieves will not win." On the same day the national committee finished the contests, giving 26 in Texas, 20 in Virginia, 14 in Washington, and 2 in the District of Columbia to

President Taft; and 4 in Texas, and 2 in North Carolina to Mr. Roosevelt.

COLORED DELEGATES. It was evident at this time that the balance of power in the convention rested in the hands of the colored delegates from the South. The results of the contests before the national committee gave Mr. Taft 555 votes, or enough for the nomination if these votes could be held. The withdrawal of 60 or 70 colored delegates from his support to that of Mr. Roosevelt would prevent the President's nomination. The strongest possible effort was, therefore, made by the Taft leaders to hold the negro votes, while the Roosevelt leaders were no less aggressive in their efforts to win them away from President Taft. Rumors of attempts to corrupt delegates were frequently made, but were not substantiated. The completed work of the national committee gave to Mr. Taft 234 disputed delegates and to Colonel Roosevelt 20. On the completion of its work the committee adjourned to pass out of existence. A new committee is chosen by each convention.

CONDITIONS PRECEDING THE CONVENTION. On the eve of the convention, President Taft had on paper seven more delegates than enough to nominate. He lost five delegates from Mississippi, and seven from Georgia withdrew from his support, as did Timothy L. Woodruff of Brooklyn. Four New York delegates previously counted for him declared that they would vote for Justice Hughes and two Taft delegates in Illinois declared for Robert T. Lincoln. Colonel Roosevelt on paper was 61 votes short of a plurality. There were 540 votes necessary for a choice and on the eve of the convention an unofficial poll of the delegates resulted as follows: William H. Taft, 547; Theodore Roosevelt, 479; Robert M. La Follette, 36; Albert B. Cummins, 10; Charles E. Hughes, 4; and Robert T. Lincoln, 2; total, 1078.

MR. ROOSEVELT'S ATTITUDE. Mr. Roosevelt spent the hours prior to the convention in conference with his leaders. Rumors had arisen that he would bolt the convention if he did not receive the nomination, but these were denied by him. He issued a statement in which he called attention to the difference in composition between the delegates who would vote for him and those who would vote for Mr. Taft. He said: "Of Mr. Taft's delegates, over half come from Territories and from States that have never cast a Republican electoral vote since the days of reconstruction. Among these the only delegates really for Mr. Taft are those who are controlled by the use of federal patronage in his interest. Over half of the remainder are boss-picked delegates from northern States where there have been no open primaries. Contrast this with the votes of the delegates who are for me. Thirty-three States cast electoral votes for me in 1904. Of these thirty-three States at the recent primaries, I carried twenty-one, Senator La Follette two, Senator Cummins divided one with Mr. Taft, and nine went in whole or in part to Mr. Taft." He reiterated his claim that his failure to receive the nomination would be the result of fraud and theft on the part of the national committee. On the night of June 17, Mr. Roosevelt made an address in the Auditorium Theatre. In this he denounced the Republican national committee as thieves and robbers, and demanded that the temporary roll call of the convention made by the committee should be smashed at the outset. He declared that the contesting delegates seated by the committee should not be allowed to vote on anything until after the uncontested delegates in the convention had passed upon their credentials. He also said that it was the duty of the convention to refuse to sanction the choice of the committee for temporary chairman, no matter who he might be and without regard to his past services and reputation. He again attacked President Taft as a tool of the "bosses" and declared that they had won for him all the delegates that he had.

OPENING OF THE CONVENTION. The convention was called to order by William Hayward, secretary of the national committee, who read the official call for the election of delegates. Governor Hadley of Missouri was floor manager for the Roosevelt delegates, and James E. Watson of Indiana, former member of the House of Representatives, acted in the same capacity for the Taft delegates.

CONTEST ON THE TEMPORARY ROLL. The first effort of the Roosevelt faction in the person of Governor Hadley was to prevent the seating of the delegates on the temporary roll of the convention, and on the conclusion of the reading of the temporary roll by Secretary Hayward, Governor Hadley rose to a point of order. He inquired as to whether the national committee had prepared a list of delegates and alternates claiming seats in the convention and had placed this in the hands of its secretary for the consideration of the convention as a temporary roll. Mr. Watson thereupon made a point of order that prior to the organization of the convention no business of any character could be done. Victor Rosewater, presiding officer and temporary chairman of the national committee, replied that Governor Hadley's point of order was not well taken unless he could present good reasons in opposition. Governor Hadley thereupon addressed the convention on the point of order. He moved that the list of delegates prepared by the national committee and placed in the hands of the secretary known as the temporary roll be amended in the following particulars: That the names of certain delegates should be removed from the temporary roll and another list substituted and that the temporary roll when thus amended be considered the temporary roll of the convention for the consideration of its business. This motion in effect provided that the contested delegates should not be allowed to take part in the business of the convention until action of the convention had been taken upon them.

Mr. Watson, at the conclusion of Governor Hadley's remarks, renewed his point of order that no business could be done by the convention until it had organized. Each side was then given 20 minutes for a discussion of the question. Mr. Hadley first addressed the convention. He asserted that the question presented was: Whether the national committee of the Republican party has the absolute power to prepare a list of delegates or temporary roll, which can be changed by the convention only through the representative of the committee on credentials and the acceptance or rejection of that report of that committee, or whether the list of delegates prepared by the national committee is in the nature of a recommendation of those upon that list, that they shall adopt it as the basis of the organization of the convention. He asserted that if the former contention were true a political oligarchy was the result. He quoted precedents in support of his contention that the national committee had no absolute power to select delegates. He reviewed the work of the committee and asserted that while some of the charges made against its rulings might not be true, others unquestionably were true. He said: "We contend that this convention should not proceed to the transaction of any business until it either disproves the charges of fraud and dishonesty that have been made against this roll of delegates or until it sustains that charge and purges the roll of this convention of the names that 15 high-minded and honorable men have stated do not belong there at all."

Governor Hadley was followed by J. Franklin Fort, former governor of New Jersey, who supported his contention. Representative Sereno E. Payne of New York defended the action of the committee in a brief speech, and Mr. Watson then spoke at greater length. He stated that his contention was that at that time, and until after the convention had been regularly organized under the customary preliminary procedure, no business was in order because there was no convention, no presiding officer, and no person duly accredited to whom an appeal could be made. He declared that the national committee was not a part of the national convention, but that since 1868 it had always made the roll of the convention because there must be some authoritative body which shall prepare the temporary roll of the convention; otherwise chaos would result. He said that the national chairman, because of his position as national chairman, had simply called the convention to order and had no further power. He declared that if Governor Hadley's amendment prevailed the convention would then proceed to take up every contested case before it had been organized, and that it would not be necessary to have a committee on credentials in the convention for the purpose of determining these questions. He appealed to the convention, in the name of orderly procedure and precedent, to sustain the ruling of the chairman. He then moved to lay Governor Hadley's appeal on the table. Mr. Rosewater then after citing precedents made his ruling. He declared that until the convention had organized under its temporary presiding officer it was simply an assembly of individuals gathered under the rule to hold a convention. That in such bodies it had been the rule that the delegates in accordance with the general preliminary law, as laid down in Cushing's *Manual*, should first effect a temporary and then a permanent chairman, and that the first business of the convention was to appoint a committee to receive the credentials of the delegates in the proper way. After citing the duties of this committee, he said: "It is not within the powers of this assemblage to pass upon the credentials and they are not in any sense before it, but they are in the custody of the secretary of the national committee where the rules require them to be lodged." He said that any proposition like an investigation of the credentials was out of order before the organization of the convention. He thereupon sustained Mr. Watson's point of order and held that the motion of Governor Hadley to amend the roll was out of order. Governor Hadley appealed from the decision of the chair, and on motion of Mr. Watson, the appeal was laid on the table.

Mr. Rosewater then said: "I have the honor to present the name of the Hon. Elihu Root, a delegate from the State of New York, as temporary chairman of this convention and invite other nominations." Henry F. Cochems of Wisconsin nominated, as the candidate of the Roosevelt faction, Governor Francis E. McGovern of Wisconsin. The nomination of Senator Root was seconded by Job E. Hedges of New York, and that of Governor McGovern by Governor Hadley of Missouri and Governor Johnson of California.

Vote for Temporary Chairman. The vote on the temporary chairmanship was the first actual test of the strength of the convention. It resulted in Mr. Root receiving 558 votes, and Governor McGovern, 502. W. S. Lauder of North Dakota received 9 votes from the Wisconsin delegation, Walter S. Houser of Wisconsin, 3, and Senator Gronna of North Dakota, 1.

Senator Root's Address. Senator Root in his address as temporary chairman defended the administration of President Taft while he stood for affirmative, constructive policies for the betterment and progress of the country. He declared that the President had carried out faithfully all the policies of President Roosevelt. He outlined the position of the Republican party on the tariff and noted its accomplishment under President Taft, praised the work of the tariff board, and contrasted the policy of the Democratic party in regard to the tariff, which he said would result in business disaster. He praised the proposed system for currency reform, and the income tax amendment, dwelt upon the successful trust prosecutions carried on by President Taft's government, reviewed legislation on employers' liability, and for the improvement of labor, and laid stress upon great reforms which had been made in economy in the public service as the result of a commission on economy and efficiency appointed by the President. He emphasized the growing efficiency of the navy and contrasted the action of the Democratic and Republican parties in Congress on the question of new battleships. He reviewed the foreign relations of the United States and pointed out the great increase of commerce under the Republican administration. The portion of his address which excited the most interest was that concerned with the discussion of the more radical policies advocated by President Roosevelt. This he treated in a general way as follows: "We will maintain the power and honor of the nation, but we will observe those limitations which the Constitution sets up for the preservation of local self-government. This country is so large and the conditions of life are so varied that it would intolerable to have the local and domestic affairs of our home communities, which involve no national rights, controlled by majorities made up in other States thousands of miles away or by the officials of a central government." He declared that however wise, able and patriotic a Congress or government might be, if things should be done by them by usurping the powers confided to another department or another officer, the door would be open for the destruction of liberty. He quoted the pledge given to the American people by the last Republican national convention: "The Republican party will uphold at all times the authority and integrity of the courts, State and federal, and will ever insist that their powers to enforce their process and to protect life, liberty, and prosperity shall be preserved inviolate." "We must," he said, "be true to that pledge, for in no other way can our country keep itself within the straight and narrow path prescribed by the principles of right conduct embodied in our Constitution."

Attempt to Bar Contested Delegates. The second day of the convention, June 19, was given over almost entirely to an attempt on the part of the Roosevelt followers to bar from the convention the contested delegates who had been seated by the national committee. Again Governor Hadley of Missouri led the fight in behalf of Mr. Roosevelt, while James E. Watson of Indiana directed the struggle on the part of the Taft adherents. Shortly after the convention had been called to order by Senator Root, Governor Hadley introduced a resolution which substituted the roll of the Roosevelt delegates for that prepared by the members of the national committee. Mr. Watson thereupon moved to amend by referring the resolution to the committee on credentials, when it had been appointed. To this amendment, Governor Deneen of Illinois offered an amendment that no delegate whose seat was contested should have voice in the proceedings of the committee on credentials or should have a vote on the floor of the convention in determining the merits of the contestants. Mr. Watson moved to lay Governor Deneen's motion on the table, and it was on this motion that the storm raged throughout the day. The contested seats numbered 78, and included delegates-at-large from Arizona, Michigan, Texas, and Washington, and delegates from the Congress districts in Alabama, Arkansas, California, Indiana, Kentucky, Oklahoma, Tennessee, Texas, and Washington. It was obvious that upon the decision rendered in regard to those delegates depended the nomination. For the uncontested delegates pledged to President Taft and Mr. Roosevelt were so evenly numbered that the votes of those contested delegates were sufficient to determine the result.

An agreement was reached whereby Governor Hadley and Mr. Watson each were to have an hour in which to present the respective cases. Governor Hadley spoke first. His address contained a severe criticism of the decisions of the national committee and also of the decision of the chairman of the convention, made on the previous day, whereby his motion to substitute the Roosevelt delegates for the temporary roll prepared by the national committee, was declared out of order by the chairman. He read the list of members of the national committee who had signed a report to the effect that the contested delegates were not entitled to sit in the convention. These names were those of William E. Borah of Idaho, George A. Knight of California, John G. Capers of South Carolina, C. E. Loose of Utah, T. C. DuPont of Delaware, Cecil A. Lyon of Texas, Sidney Bieber of the District of Columbia, Thomas Thorson of South Dakota, Pearl Wight of Louisiana, M. C. Mundy of Tennessee, and A. R. Burnham of Kentucky. He then reviewed the California and Texas cases.

Governor Hadley's address was delivered with great eloquence and spirit, and at its close there broke out a remarkable demonstration for him which lasted for forty minutes. Many of the Taft men joined in the personal tribute which was paid to him. From this time on Governor Hadley was frequently mentioned as a possible compromise candidate for President or Vice-President. Following Governor Hadley, W. T. Dovell of Seattle, Wash., argued the Washington contests in opposition to Governor Hadley's motion. Mr. Dovell was the contesting Taft delegate-at-large. He contended that the Taft delegates were elected regularly and no questions were ever raised as to their regularity. The Roosevelt delegates, he said, were elected at a mass meeting. Henry J. Allen of Kansas then spoke in support of Governor Hadley's motion. He summed up the cases for the Roosevelt delegates in Washington and the fifth district of Missouri. James Hemenway of Indiana then spoke against the motion. The Indiana contests he said were paper contests made only as a pretext for appealing to the convention. There then followed George L. Record of New Jersey, who spoke in support of Governor Hadley's motion, explaining the details of the contests in Arizona and Indiana. Judge Robert E. Morrison of Arizona defended the action of the national committee in regard to Arizona, and Thomas H. Devine, chairman of the committee on credentials, spoke in opposition to Governor Hadley's motion. He dealt especially with the Texas case.

After several other delegates had spoken for and against the motion, James E. Watson of Indiana made the chief argument in opposition to it. He insisted that the contests before the national committee had been fairly and impartially heard, and declared that the convention was not in a condition to judge upon the merits of the contests, because in the case of many of them, not one word of evidence had been heard. Mr. Watson concluded his speech by moving that the whole matter be referred to the committee on credentials when appointed, and Governor Deneen, as noted above, moved to amend this by adding that no man should be allowed to have a vote in the selection of that committee whose seat was to be affected by the contests taken before it, or should be allowed to vote on the report. This motion Mr. Watson moved to lay on the table, and on this the only vote of the day was taken. It resulted in 556 votes in support of Mr. Watson's motion and 510 votes against it, four delegates not voting. This concluded the active work of the convention for the day.

MEETING OF THE COMMITTEE ON CREDENTIALS. As soon as the convention adjourned, the committee on credentials, which was to pass upon the contests already decided by the national committee, went into session. On this committee the Taft members numbered 33 and the Roosevelt, 19. The Roosevelt States represented were California, Idaho, Illinois, Kansas, Maine, Maryland, Minnesota, Missouri Nebraska, New Jersey, North Carolina, Ohio, Oklahoma, Oregon, Pennsylvania, South Dakota, West Virginia and Wisconsin. After a session of several hours the Roosevelt members of the committee left and refused to take part further in the deliberations on the ground that the committee had passed a resolution limiting the hearing in all contests, to five minutes each, with ten minutes permitted for arguments in general contests. Later, however, on the advice of Mr. Roosevelt, these bolting members of the committee returned and took part in the hearing of the contests.

THE QUESTION OF BOLTING. In the meantime the question most discussed was whether or not Mr. Roosevelt's followers would bolt the convention, following an adverse report of the committee on credentials. A conference was held at which were present Colonel Roosevelt, William Flinn of Pennsylvania, James R. Garfield, Amos Pinchot, Governor Johnson, Governor Stubbs of Kansas, Governor Hadley, Senator Borah, and former Governor Fort of New Jersey. The proposition to bolt hinged on the seating of 72 delegates from California, Arkansas, Washington, Arizona, Oklahoma, Texas, Alabama, Kentucky, Michigan, Indiana, and Tennessee. It was contended that that number of seats had been taken by the Republican national committee from Roosevelt and given to Taft. It was practically decided at this conference that if the Roosevelt followers were defeated in their fight in the convention to seat their contested delegates there should be a bolt following the report of the committee on credentials, if it were unfavorable. Senator Borah, Governor Hadley, and several other prominent Roosevelt supporters opposed the idea of bolting the convention and refused to enter into any such plan. The Roosevelt delegates from several States voted not to follow Colonel Roosevelt in a bolt from the convention. Among these were 20 of the 46 delegates of Missouri. Governor Hadley, addressing this delegation, said: "We came here to vote for Roosevelt, not to leave the Republican party for any third party movement. We are instructed for Roosevelt, but we are not instructed to bolt the Republican party." Representatives from Kansas, Michigan, Massachusetts, Illinois, and other States took action similar to that of Missouri. The Illinois Roosevelt delegates, by a vote of 30 to 2, decided not to follow Colonel Roosevelt in any bolt or in any movement looking to a superseding convention. Governor Deneen of Illinois said, "This decision does not mean that we are abandoning Colonel Roosevelt. We have been instructed by tne Republicans of Illinois to support the former President for the presidential nomination. It is obvious that he can win that nomination only in a Republican convention."

STATEMENT BY MR. ROOSEVELT. The committee on credentials passed upon the disputed cases in Alabama, Arizona, and Arkansas, and upheld the action of the national committee. It became obvious to Mr. Roosevelt that the national committee's action in the other contests would be adverse, and on June 20, he gave up hope of being nominated in the regular Republican convention. He issued a long statement in which he said that he would accept a nomination from the "honestly elected majority of the Republican convention, or a nomination made by such Progressives as may stand together and formulate a progressive platform." He said:

"The time has come when I feel that I must make certain statements, not merely to honestly elected members of the Republican convention, but to the rank and file of the Republican party and to the honest people of the entire nation."

He then reviewed the course of the pre-nomination campaign, pointing out his successes in the States in which primaries had been held, declaring that in those States he had obtained six delegates to Mr. Taft's one. He said:

"Mr. Taft's strength as indicated by the two roll calls already taken, consisted chiefly (aside from the ninety stolen delegates) of nearly the solid delegations from the Territories and from the Southern States in which there is no general Republican party, and of Northern States, like New York, where the people had no chance to express themselves at primaries, and where the delegates were controlled by the bosses. In spite of these odds against me I obtained a clear majority of all the delegates elected to the convention. In my campaign I again and again stated that if the people decided against me I would have nothing to say, but if they decided for me and the politicians then robbed me of the victory I would not silently and tamely acquiesce. It was evident that my opponents, with Mr. Taft's encouragement, intended to beat me by foul means if they could not do so by fair means."

He then criticised the action of the national committee in making up the temporary roll call and declared that it showed a cynical contempt of the most ordinary rules of decency in unseating ninety fairly elected Roosevelt delegates and substituting for them ninety Taft delegates who in the convention represented nothing whatever but successful fraud. He declared that the votes taken in the convention by which Mr. Root was elected temporary chairman, and Governor Deneen's motion was rejected, were due to the votes of those ninety fraudulent delegates.

After further criticising the action of the convention as constituted he said:

"I decline any longer to be bound by any action it may take. I decline to regard as binding any nomination it may make. I do not regard successful fraud and deliberate political theft as constituting a title to party regularity, or a claim to the support of any honest man of any party. I hope that the honestly elected majority will at once insist on the purging of the roll in its entirety and not piecemeal by the convention. If this is not accomplished I hope the honestly elected delegates will decline all further connection with a convention whose action is now determined and has hitherto been determined by a majority which is made a majority only by the action of the fraudulent delegates whom the convention has refused to strike from the rolls. . . . If the honestly elected majority of the convention choose to proceed with business and nominate me as a candidate of the general Republican party, I shall accept. If some among them fear to take such a stand and the remainder choose to inaugurate a movement to nominate me for the presidency as a Progressive on a progressive platform, and if in such event the general feeling among Progressives favors my being nominated, I shall accept."

DECISIONS BY THE CREDENTIALS COMMITTEE. As no work could be transacted by the convention until after the report of the committee on credentials, there was no business of importance transacted on the third day, June 20. The committee on resolutions was busy preparing its draft of a platform, but interest centred about the work of the committee on credentials. Hearings were held on the Ninth Alabama District contest and on the contests in Arizona. In each instance the committee endorsed the action of the national committee in seating the Taft delegates, in the Alabama case by a vote of 34 to 13, and in the Arizona case by a vote of 33 to 15. When the Fourth California District was reached, no one appeared for the Roosevelt delegates, and the Taft delegates were accordingly seated. The action of the national committee in the case of the twelve delegates from Florida was not opposed by Roosevelt representatives and they, too, were seated.

The most notable occurrence on this day in the convention was the demonstration in favor of Mr. Roosevelt, which lasted forty minutes.

VOTE ON CREDENTIALS COMMITTEE REPORT. On the third day of the convention, June 21, occurred the first test on the part of the convention as a whole as to whether or not it would support the action of the national committee and the committee on credentials in regard to disputed delegates. The work of the committee on credentials was so delayed on account of the exhaustive hearings of the cases that at the end of the first day of these deliberations it had reached only the disputed cases in Alabama, Arizona, Arkansas, and California. In these, as is noted above, the action of the committee had followed that of the national committee, and these delegates had been given to President Taft. Ordinarily the work of the convention is delayed until the committee on credentials reports in full, but as there was no prospect of the conclusion of the committee's report for several days, Senator Root insisted that reports be made on cases already settled, and that the convention be permitted to vote on these. The majority and minority reports were therefore prepared on the Ninth Alabama District contest, the first in alphabetical order. The majority report upheld the national committee giving the delegates to President Taft. The minority report protested against the seating of the two Taft delegates. Governor Hadley, leader of the Roosevelt forces, then moved that the tentative minority report be substituted for the majority report. This was in the nature of a prepared statement, and was read by R. R. McCormick of Illinois. Following the reading of this statement, Governor Hadley read the following resolution:

"Resolved, That in the vote upon the adoption of the minority report of the committee on credentials, the delegates nominated in the list attached hereto, and whose names are upon the temporary roll of this convention and whose seats are contested, shall not vote upon the report until the right of any contestant named therein to a seat in this convention shall be determined in his favor by a majority vote of the uncontested delegates to this convention."

The list to which this resolution referred contained the names of 72 delegates, whose seats in the convention were protested by 14 members of the national committee. James W. Wadsworth, Jr., of New York, objected to Governor Hadley's resolution on the ground that it was identical in substance with Governor Deneen's amendment to Governor Hadley's resolution of July 18, which had been defeated in the convention by a vote of 564 to 510. By the defeat of Governor Deneen's amendment the convention had refused to permit the contestants to vote in the convention on their own contests, but gave them the right to vote on all other contests. Mr. Watson then moved that Governor Hadley's resolution be laid on the table and this was seconded. Senator Root, however, decided to permit Governor Hadley's resolution to go to a vote. It was defeated by a vote of 569 to 499, ten delegates not voting. Thus this resolution was defeated by six more votes than Governor Deneen's on the previous occasion. The convention then voted to lay the minority report of the Alabama cases on the table by a vote of 605 to 464. This was the first vote taken by the convention on the contested cases, and it showed a substantial majority for the Taft delegates. In this vote eight Roosevelt delegates from Idaho voted for the Taft delegates, as did also 25 Wisconsin delegates accredited to La Follette. The convention then adopted the majority report. In the Arizona contest the Taft delegates were seated by a vote of 564 to 497, seventeen not voting. In the contest for the delegates in the Fifth Arkansas Congress district there was no roll call, the majority report seating the Taft men being adopted by a *viva voce* vote. The California contest, which came next in alphabetical order, resulted in a sharp struggle. The minority report of the committee on credentials protested against the "tyrannical overthrow of the will of the people of California as expressed by a plurality of 77,000 at the presidential preferential primary." Twenty minutes were given for discussion on each side.

Francis J. Heney argued in favor of the adoption of the minority report. He declared that the question involved was the right of a sovereign State to say how its delegates should be elected. His address, which was aggressive, was interrupted by expressions of disapproval on the part of the Taft delegates. Sereno E. Payne of New York supported the action of the majority of the committee. He declared that the sole question was whether the law of the State of California should control the law of the Republican national convention. He said that the convention of 1880 had settled that question forever in formulating the rule that congressional districts should be represented by delegates elected by the district.

James E. Watson of Indiana also favored the majority report. The debate was closed by Governor Johnson of California. He said that the question was, Shall the people rule? "Four years from now," he said in conclusion, "you will find the people in every State selecting delegates, and selecting them just as California has done. If he leaves no other heritage than that all the people have the right to rule in this nation, that will be a priceless privilege to Theodore Roosevelt."

The result of the roll call on the California contests was on the adoption of the majority report, ayes, 542; noes, 529. This was the closest vote taken on any contest. The Taft contested delegates were seated from Georgia, Indiana, Kentucky, and Louisiana. In the case of Georgia the four delegates-at-large were seated by unanimous vote, and in the other cases the vote was *viva voce*, roll calls not being deemed necessary. On the conclusion of the Louisiana cases the convention adjourned for the day.

The result of the votes of the convention on the contested cases made it evident to the leaders of the Roosevelt forces that they had no chance of controlling the convention or of nominating their candidate. The plan of bolting the convention following the first unfavorable action of the delegates on the report of the committee on credentials, was abandoned, although some of the aggressive supporters of Mr. Roosevelt still favored such action. This decision resulted largely from the refusal of important State delegations pledged to Mr. Roosevelt before the convention, to follow him in a bolt. While the convention was voting upon contested delegates, Mr. Roosevelt remained quietly in his hotel holding occasional conferences with his leaders.

Much favorable sentiment developed during this day of the convention in favor of Governor Hadley of Missouri for Vice-President. Governor Hadley had made an excellent impression upon the conservative delegates by his self-restrained attitude in the face of a difficult situation, and it was felt that he would materially strengthen the ticket if he were nominated as Vice-President.

PRESIDENT TAFT'S NOMINATION ASSURED. On Saturday, June 22, the last day of the conven-

pyright, Harris and Ewing, Washington, D. C.

SENATOR ELIHU ROOT

Copyright, Pach Bros., N. Y.

SENATOR WILLIAM MURRAY CRANE

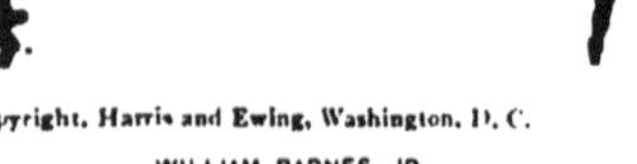

pyright, Harris and Ewing, Washington, D. C.

WILLIAM BARNES, JR.
New York Member Republican National Committee

Copyright, Harris and Ewing, Washington, D. C.

CHARLES D. HILLES
Chairman Republican National Committee

FOUR PROMINENT WORKERS IN THE REPUBLICAN CAMPAIGN, 1912

tion, the renomination of President Taft was practically assured. The convention met and passed upon the remaining contested delegates, and the Taft delegates were seated. These included contests in Mississippi, Washington, and Texas, and in all cases the majority report of the committee on credentials, which upheld the decisions of the national committee, was supported by a majority of the delegates. Majority and minority reports were presented in the cases of Washington and Texas. The acceptance of these reports concluded the permanent organization of the convention. Action had been completed on all disputed cases at 2:45 in the afternoon. The committee on permanent organization then reported, nominating Senator Root as permanent chairman. This was received and adopted by the convention amid cheers from the Taft delegates. Senator Root then asked the unanimous consent for some remarks from Henry J. Allen of Texas, who had succeeded Governor Hadley as the representative of Mr. Roosevelt in the convention. Mr. Allen read the following statement from Mr. Roosevelt:

Final Statement of Mr. Roosevelt. "A clear majority of the delegates honestly elected to this convention were chosen by the people to nominate me. Under the direction and with the encouragement of Mr. Taft the majority of the national committee by the so-called 'steam roller' methods and with scandalous disregard of every principle of elementary honesty and decency stole eighty or ninety delegates, putting on the temporary call a sufficient number of fraudulent delegates to defeat the legally expressed will of the people and to substitute a dishonest for an honest majority.

"The convention has now declined to purge the roll of the fraudulent delegates placed thereon by the defunct national committee and the majority which thus endorsed fraud was made a majority only because it included the fraudulent delegates themselves, who all sat as judges on one another's cases. If these fraudulent votes had not thus been cast and counted the convention would have been purged of their presence. This action makes the convention in no proper sense any longer a Republican convention representing the real Republican party. Therefore I hope the men elected as Roosevelt delegates will now decline to vote on any matter before the convention. I do not release any delegate from his honorable obligation to vote for me if he votes at all; but under the actual conditions I hope that he will not vote at all.

"The convention as now composed has no claim to represent the voters of the Republican party. It represents nothing but successful fraud in overriding the will of the rank and file of the party. Any man nominated by the convention as now constituted will be merely the beneficiary of this successful fraud; it would be deeply discreditable to any man to accept the convention's nomination under these circumstances, and any man thus accepting it would have no claim to the support of any Republican on party grounds and would have forfeited the right to ask the support of any honest man of any party on moral grounds."

Following the reading of this statement Mr. Allen addressed the delegates, bitterly attacking the action of the national committee and declaring that the Roosevelt delegates felt that they could no longer share in the responsibility for the acts of the convention. He concluded as follows:

"We do not bolt, we merely insist that you, not we, are making the record and we refuse to be bound by it. We have pleaded with you ten days, we have fought with you five days for a square deal; we fight no more, we plead no longer, we shall sit in silent protest, and the people who sent us here shall judge us."

Vote on the Platforms. Following the remarks of Mr. Allen the regular programme of the convention was resumed. First came the report of the committee on rules. This was temporarily laid on the table. Charles W. Fairbanks of Indiana then read the platform prepared by the majority of the committee on resolutions. Senator Owen of Wisconsin read the platform prepared by Senator La Follette containing the latter's well-known doctrines. On motion of Mr. Fairbanks the La Follette platform was laid on the table. William Barnes of New York then demanded a roll call upon the platform prepared by the majority of the committee. When California was reached in the roll of States, Governor Johnson rose and said, "California declines to vote." This was greeted with cheers from the Roosevelt delegates. Senator Root ordered the California delegates to be polled, but there was no answer to the names called until the names of the two contested Taft delegates were read. They voted aye. The delegates from Maine refused to vote. The Roosevelt delegates refusing to vote were the following: Alabama, 2; California, 24; Illinois, 9; Indiana, 7; Kansas, 18; Maine, 12; Maryland, 6; Massachusetts, 14; Michigan, 8; Minnesota, 24; Mississippi, 3; Nebraska, 16; New Jersey, 28; New York, 5; North Carolina, 12; Ohio, 34; Oklahoma, 15; Oregon, 2; Pennsylvania, 63; South Carolina, 3; South Dakota, 10; Tennessee, 1; Texas, 8; Vermont, 2; Virginia, 1; West Virginia, 16; Wisconsin, 26. The number of delegates who did not vote on the resolution was 343, with 16 absent. Those voting for the resolution numbered 666.

Nomination of Candidates. On the completion of this vote the next business in order was the nomination of candidates for President. The States were called in their alphabetical order, and no nominations were made until Ohio was reached. Warren G. Harding then nominated President Taft in a speech which, after reviewing President Taft's record and deprecating the movement against his renomination, concluded as follows:

"I present to you to-day a leader who is a composite of the virtues of all those deservedly enshrined in our party pantheon—William Howard Taft—as wise and patient as Abraham Lincoln, as modest and dauntless as U. S. Grant, as temperate and peace-loving as Rutherford B. Hayes, as patriotic and intellectual as James A. Garfield, as courtly and generous as Chester A. Arthur, as learned in the law as Benjamin Harrison, as sympathetic and brave as William McKinley, and as progressive as his predecessor, with a moral stamina, breadth of view, and sturdy manhood all his own.

At the first mention of President Taft's name in Mr. Harding's address there was a demonstration lasting twenty minutes. His nomination was seconded by John Wanamaker of Pennsylvania and Dr. Nicholas Murray Butler of New York. Senator La Follette was nominated by Michael B. Oelrichs of Wisconsin and was seconded by Robert M. Pollock of North Dakota. There were no other nominations. On the roll call which followed the formal nomination, the same scenes were enacted as accompanied the roll calls on the platform. California delegates again refused to vote, and their example was followed by delegates from other States which had been pledged to Mr. Roosevelt. Idaho gave 7 votes to Senator Cummins of Iowa, who had not been placed in nomination. Ten delegates from Iowa also voted for Senator Cummins. When the turn of Massachusetts was reached a poll was demanded when the Roosevelt men refused to vote. Senator Root called for the alternates amid cries of protest. One of the Massachusetts delegates, rising, said, "Massachusetts is a law-abiding State and refuses to have its vote stolen." Senator Root replied: "If any delegate sent to this convention from the State of Massachusetts refuses to perform his duty as a delegate, his alternate will be called and will have an opportunity to do it." This was the first case in which the alternates had been called upon to vote when the regular delegates had refused to do so. Protest was made and Senator Root explained his action on the ground that the vote had been challenged, so that it was necessary to call an individual roll. The protesting delegate from Massachusetts appealed from the decision of the chair and defied the convention to make him vote for any man. By calling the alternates in the Massachusetts delegation, Mr. Taft received a gain of two votes. The delegates from Minnesota refused to vote, as did the Roosevelt delegates in the Missouri delegation. The Nebraska delegates did not vote, and all but two of the delegates from New Jersey refused. These voted for Mr. Roosevelt. The New York delegates cast 76 votes for President Taft and 8 for Mr. Roosevelt, 6 not voting. Thirty-four Roosevelt men from Ohio refused to vote. Pennsylvania gave 2 votes to Charles E. Hughes, 2 for Roosevelt, 9 for Taft, and 62 not voting. The South Dakota delegation cast 5 votes for La Follette and 5 for Roosevelt. The President was nominated when Washington was reached. This State gave him the 540 necessary for nomination. The West Virginia delegates refused to vote.

NOMINATION OF TAFT AND SHERMAN. The result of the balloting was announced at 9:35 P. M. It was as follows: Taft, 561; not voting, 344; Roosevelt, 107; Hughes, 2; Cummins, 17; La Follette, 41; absent, 6. Senator Root then made the following announcement: "William Howard Taft, having received a majority of the votes, is declared to be renominated for the presidency of the United States. There was no motion to make the nomination unanimous, which was unprecedented in a Republican convention. Mr. Root then called for nomination for Vice-President. On the call for candidates, Alabama yielded to New York, and Representative J. Van Vechten Olcott presented the name of Vice-President Sherman for renomination. There were no other nominations. The balloting for Vice-President resulted as follows: James S. Sherman, 597; Herbert S. Hadley, 14; Howard Gillette, 1; Senator William E. Borah, 21; Charles G. Merriam, 20; Albert J. Beveridge, 2; present, but not voting, 352; absent, 71. A resolution giving the national committee power to fill all vacancies and to declare the seat of any member vacant who it may be decided does not support the ticket, was adopted. The convention adjourned at 10:30 P. M.

The balloting for President Taft by States is shown in the table in the next column.

La Follette received 41 votes in North and South Dakota and Wisconsin. Roosevelt received 107 votes from Illinois, Indiana, Kentucky, Maryland, Michigan, Nebraska, New Jersey, New York, North Carolina, Oklahoma, Oregon, South Dakota, and Tennessee. Charles

	Taft	Not Voting
Alabama	22	2
Arizona	6	0
Arkansas	17	1
California	2	24
Colorado	12	0
Connecticut	14	0
Delaware	6	0
Florida	12	0
Georgia	28	0
Idaho	1	0
Illinois	2	2
Indiana	20	7
Iowa	16	0
Kansas	2	18
Kentucky	24	0
Louisiana	20	0
Maine	0	12
Maryland	1	5
Massachusetts	20	16
Michigan	20	1
Minnesota	0	24
Mississippi	17	3
Missouri	16	20
Montana	8	0
Nebraska	0	14
Nevada	6	0
New Hampshire	8	0
New Jersey	0	26
New Mexico	7	0
New York	76	6
North Carolina	1	22
North Dakota	0	0
Ohio	14	34
Oklahoma	2	15
Oregon	0	2
Pennsylvania	9	62
Rhode Island	10	0
South Carolina	16	1
South Dakota	0	0
Tennessee	23	0
Texas	31	8
Utah	8	0
Vermont	6	2
Virginia	22	1
Washington	14	0
West Virginia	0	16
Wisconsin	0	0
Wyoming	6	0
Alaska	2	0
District of Columbia	2	0
Hawaii	6	0
Philippines	2	0
Porto Rico	2	0
Total	561	344

E. Hughes polled 2 votes in Pennsylvania. Cummins received 17 votes in Iowa and Idaho. Six delegates were absent.

PROGRESSIVE NOMINATING CONVENTION. Directly after the adjournment of the convention the Roosevelt delegates assembled at Orchestra Hall and organized an informal nominating convention. The convention was called to order by Governor Johnson of California. All the leaders of the Roosevelt forces attended. In his opening remarks Governor Johnson outlined the purpose of the assemblage as follows: "We, the delegates from all parts of the United States, representing a majority of legally elected delegates to the Republican convention, propose to do here and now what we were prevented from doing there." He declared further that the meeting had been called to give to Theodore Roosevelt the nomination of which he had been robbed. This was the first indication that such a purpose was intended, and it was greeted with great outbursts of cheers. Following Governor Johnson's address, Senator Clapp of Minneapolis offered the following resolution:

"We, delegates and alternates to the Republican convention, representing a clear majority of the voters of the Republican party in the United States, and representing a clear majority of the delegates and alternates legally elected to the convention in meeting assembled, make the following declaration:

"We were delegated by a majority of the Republican voters of our representative districts and States to nominate Theodore Roosevelt in the Republican national convention as the candidate of our party for President and thereby carry out the will of the voters as expressed at the primaries. We have earnestly and conscientiously striven to execute the commission entrusted to us by the party voters. For five days we have been denied justice in the national convention. This result has been accomplished by the action of the now defunct national committee in placing upon the preliminary roll of the convention and thereby seating upon the floor of the convention a sufficient number of fraudulently elected delegates to control the proceedings of the convention.

"These fraudulent delegates once seated have, by concerted action with one another, put themselves upon the permanent roll where they constitute an influence sufficient to control the convention and defeat the will of the party as expressed at the primaries.

"We have exhausted every known means to head off this conspiracy and to prevent this fraud upon the popular will, but without success.

"We were sent to this convention bearing the most specific instructions to place Theodore Roosevelt in nomination as the candidate of our party for President, and we therefore deem it to be our duty to carry out those instructions in the only practicable and feasible way remaining open to us.

"Therefore, be it resolved that we, representing the majority of the voters of the Republican party and of the delegates and alternates legally elected to the national Republican convention, in compliance with our instructions from the party voters, hereby nominate Theodore Roosevelt as the candidate of our party for the office of President of the United States; and we will call upon him to accept such nomination in compliance with the will of the party voters

"And, be it further resolved, that a committee be appointed by the chair to forthwith notify Colonel Roosevelt of the action here taken and request him to appear before us in this hall as soon as convenient."

The reading of this resolution was followed by another tremendous outburst of cheers and calls for Mr. Roosevelt. He appeared in the hall directly after the nominating resolution had been adopted. In accepting the nomination thus offered to him, he made an address, a part of which was as follows:

ADDRESS OF MR. ROOSEVELT. "Gentlemen—I thank you for your nomination, and in you I recognize the lawfully elected delegates to the Republican convention who represent the overwhelming majority of the voters who took part in the Republican primaries prior to the convention, and who represent the wish of a majority of the lawfully elected members of the convention. I accept the nomination subject to but one condition. This has now become a contest which cannot be settled merely along the old party lines. The principles that are at stake are as broad and as deep as the foundations of our democracy itself. They are in no sense sectional. They should appeal to all honest citizens, East and West, North and South; they should appeal to all right thinking men, whether Republicans or Democrats, without regard to their previous party affiliations. I feel that the time has come when not only all men who believe in progressive principles, but all men who believe in those elementary maxims of public and private morality which must underlie every form of successful free government should join in one movement. Therefore I ask you to go to your several homes, to find out the sentiment of the people at home, and then again to come together, I suggest in mass convention, to nominate for the presidency a progressive candidate on a progressive platform, a candidate and a platform that will enable us to appeal to Northerner and Southerner, Easterner and Westerner, Republican and Democrat alike, in the name of our common American citizenship." He declared that if the sentiment of the progressives was that he make a fight he would do so, if only one State supported him. "The only condition I impose," he said, "is that you shall feel entirely free when you come together to substitute any other man in my place if you deem it better for the movement, and in such case I will give him my heartiest support." He then attacked the methods of the convention and the national committee and declared that the delegates had been stolen from him by the bosses. He said: "I am in this fight for certain principles and the first and most important of these goes back to Sinai and is embodied in the commandment: 'Thou shalt not steal.'" He concluded as follows: "As for the principles for which I stand I have set them forth fully in the many speeches I have made during the last four months while making an active contest for the nomination which I won and out of which I have been cheated by the men who feared to see the principles reduced to action.

"Fundamentally, these principles are, first, that the people have the right to rule themselves and can do so better than any outsiders can rule them, and second, that it is their due so to rule in a spirit of justice toward every man and every woman within our borders, and to use the government so far as possible as an instrument for obtaining not merely political but industrial justice.

"We do not stand for these principles as mere abstractions any more than we stand for honesty and fair play as mere abstractions. We seek to apply them practically in every relation of life where we have power. We stand for honesty and fair play. We practically apply the commandment, 'Thou shalt not steal,' and we wish to give a square deal to every citizen of the republic so that he may have a chance to show the stuff there is in him, unhelped by privilege and unhampered by privilege for others

"I hold that we are performing a high duty in inaugurating this movement, for the permanent success of practices such as have obtained in the fraudulent convention that has just closed its sitting would mean the downfall of this republic, and we are performing the most patriotic of duties when we set our faces like flint against such wrong."

Following the address of Mr. Roosevelt the convention adjourned. On the morning of June 23, 300 Roosevelt delegates assembled to inaugurate the formal temporary organization of the new party. Governor Johnson presided, and with him were Medill McCormick, James R. Garfield, and Senator Clapp of Minnesota. An address was made by Governor Johnson, who declared that the Progressives were about to "begin on the road that is to lead to political freedom." On motion of Mr. Garfield, a resolution was passed giving to Governor Johnson the power to select seven men who, after a conference with Mr. Roosevelt, would be able to present to the convention a plan of action and organization that would make it possible to carry on the movement. This motion was carried and Governor Johnson remarked, "Gentlemen, this is the birth of a new party." After addresses by several of the delegates the meeting adjourned. Mr. Roosevelt returned to his home at Oyster Bay on June 25. On his arrival in New York City, in reply to the question as to how he felt, he said that he felt "like a bull moose." From this reply originated the phrase "Bull Moose Party," which was the popular designation of the National Progressive party during the campaign.

NATIONAL CONVENTION, DEMOCRATIC

While the Democratic national convention lacked, to a great extent, the intensity and bitter feeling which characterized the Republican convention, there was no lack of dramatic situations. These were brought about almost entirely by Mr. Bryan, who, although not a candidate himself for the nomination to the presidency, was the dominating figure in the convention, and it was generally believed that the nomination of Governor Wilson was brought about by his tacit but powerful assistance.

There were no important disputed cases of delegates to the convention, and the preliminary work of the national committee was devoted almost entirely to the organization of the convention and the selection of a temporary chairman. Previous to the meeting of the convention one of the leading candidates for the nomination had a sufficient number of votes pledged to him to insure his choice. The rule of Democratic conventions called for a two-thirds vote of the delegates to nominate the candidates for President and Vice-President, and not a plurality or majority vote, as in the case of the Republican convention. This rule complicates the choice of candidates and makes it comparatively easy for the convention to fall into a deadlock which can be broken only when a compromise is made on some one candidate.

MR. BRYAN'S ATTITUDE. As is intimated above, Mr. Bryan had not committed himself prior to the convention to any candidate. He had expressed friendly feeling, however, toward Governor Wilson and Champ Clark, but which of these he preferred was not known. There was a well-marked line of cleavage among the delegates between those who wished to eliminate entirely the influence of Mr. Bryan from the deliberations and those to whom he was still the strongest man in the Democratic party and the logical leader of the Democratic forces in the convention.

FIGHT FOR TEMPORARY CHAIRMAN. The fight between these two elements had its first outbreak in the choice of a temporary chairman. This choice fell upon the committee of arrangements, a sub-committee of the national committee. A majority of this committee, representing the more conservative element of the party selected Judge Alton B. Parker, of New York as temporary chairman. Mr. Bryan, who was at the time in Chicago, reporting the Republican convention for a New York newspaper, in a telegram sent to the members of the committee heartily protested against the selection of Judge Parker, which he said would be nothing short of a crime. He based his objection on the ground that Judge Parker was a conservative and a reactionary and that the choice of him for temporary chairman would stamp the convention as non-progressive and committed to a non-progressive candidate.

Notwithstanding Mr. Bryan's objections the majority of the committee on arrangements insisted on the selection of Judge Parker. On June 22, Mr. Bryan sent from Chicago a telegram to all the Democratic candidates for President except Governor Harmon of Ohio and Congressman Underwood, inviting them to join with him in a fight against the selection for temporary chairman of Alton B. Parker. The candidates thus addressed were Champ Clark, Governor Wilson, Governor Burke of North Dakota, Governor Foss of Massachusetts, Governor Baldwin of Connecticut and Mayor Gaynor of New York City. Governor Wilson replied at once to Mr. Bryan's telegram informing the latter that he was ready to support a progressive candidate for temporary chairman. Mr. Clark was much more guarded in his reply and argued for harmony and against the fight on Judge Parker. This action of Mr. Bryan was construed by many of the delegates as a move against the candidacy of Speaker Clark, who, it was alleged, had been gradually turning from Mr. Bryan in an effort to capture delegates from so-called conservative ranks and was, in a measure, pledged to the election of Judge Parker as temporary chairman. It was said also that the managers of the Clark campaign had been exacting a pledge from their delegates that they would not vote for Mr. Bryan under any circumstances. It was claimed also that the Clark managers were arranging with Charles F. Murphy of New York, with a view to throwing their votes in support of Judge Parker in exchange for the 90 delegates from New York State. These charges were denied by the Clark managers. Whether any truth was contained in them or not, it was plain that the action of Mr. Bryan in calling for direct opposition to Judge Parker placed Speaker Clark in an embarrassing position, and Mr. Bryan's action was strongly resented by the Clark delegates. The telegram sent by Mr. Bryan read as follows: "I shall be pleased to join you and your friends in opposing his [Judge Parker's] selection by the full committee or by the convention. Kindly answer here."

On June 23 Mr. Bryan arrived in person in Baltimore. He avowed his intention of continuing the fight on Judge Parker and declined to listen to any suggestion that would bring about the latter's election as temporary chairman. Mr. Bryan's candidate for the position was Ollie James of Kentucky. On the same day the Wilson delegates began an aggressive fight against the election of Judge Parker and their friendliness with Mr. Bryan gave color to the belief that Mr. Bryan favored the nomination of Governor Wilson.

On June 24 the Democratic national committee upheld the action of the committee on arrangements and chose Judge Parker as temporary chairman of the convention. Judge Parker received 31 votes against 20 votes cast for Ollie James of Kentucky and 2 votes cast for Senator O'Gorman of New York. Members from fifteen States whose delegations were pledged to Speaker Clark for the presidency voted for Judge Parker, while those from nine States pledged to Mr. Clark, voted for Mr. James. Following the nomination by the committee Mr. Bryan made an attack on Parker in which he declared that the predatory interests were at work as they were in Chicago, and he himself would go into the convention and nominate a progressive to oppose Judge Parker. He said that he himself would be a candidate if no one else were willing to appear in opposition to Judge Parker.

As a result of these conditions the opening of the convention on June 25 was awaited by the delegates with no little anxiety. Mr. Bryan's chief opponent in these preliminary details relating to the temporary chairmanship and indeed throughout the convention, was Charles F. Murphy, who headed and practically controlled the New York delegation. He had thrown the weight of the delegation on the side of Judge Parker's selection. Mr. Bryan bitterly resented this action and his attitude toward the New York delegation throughout the convention was of uncompromising hostility.

OPENING OF THE CONVENTION. The convention was called to order at 12:21 June 25, by Norman E. Mack, chairman of the national committee. After prayer by Cardinal Gibbons, the list of officers chosen by the national committee, including Alton B. Parker for temporary chairman, was read to the convention. Mention of Mr. Parker's name was greeted with cheers from the New York delegation, but it was poorly received by the others. Mr. Bryan at once raised a point of order. He then placed the name of Senator John W. Kern of Indiana in nomination in opposition to Judge Parker.

SPEECH OF MR. BRYAN. In support of this nomination he delivered a speech. He said:

"I rise to place in nomination for office of temporary chairman of the convention the name of John W. Kern of Indiana, and in thus dissenting from the judgment of our national committee as expressed in recommendations, I recognize that the burden of proof is on me to overthrow the assumption that the committee can say that it represents the wishes of the convention and of the party of the nation."

He declared that the rules drafted and recommended by the committee were not final, and that the convention had the right to accept or reject its action. "If anyone of you ask for my credentials," he said; "if any of you inquire why I, a mere delegate to this convention from one of the sovereign States, ask you to accept it in face of the name they presented, I beg to tell you, if it need to be told, that in three campaigns I have been the champion of the Democratic party's principles and that I have received the votes of 6,000,000 Democrats. If that is not proof of a party's confidence I shall not attempt to furnish proof." He declared that from the day of his first nomination he had fought the enemies of his party, and that he believed himself still worthy of the support of the party.

After detailing the political history and services of Senator Kern, he said: "The delegates to this convention must not presume on the ignorance of those people who did not come because they did not have enough money to become delegates to this convention. And the people now know of the influence that dominated Chicago and made effective there a farce, and they know the same influences are at work here and more brazenly than they were at Chicago." After declaring that he did not impeach the good intent of Judge Parker, he declared that not every man of high character or good intent is a fit man to sound the keynote of a progressive campaign. "I remind you," he said, "that this is not a question where personal ambition or personal compliments are uppermost. We are writing history to-day. We need not deceive ourselves that that which is done in a national convention is done in secret. . . . It seems to me that now when the hour of victory arrives the song of victory should be sung by one whose heart has been in the fight." He declared that John W. Kern was such a man. Mr. Bryan concluded as follows: "Progressive Democracy has been the pillar of fire to lead the people by night. Delegates, I pray that now the dawn has come, you do not rob the people of the right to have it as the cloud to lead by day."

ELECTION OF TEMPORARY CHAIRMAN. As Mr. Bryan took his seat among the delegates, Senator Kern took the speaker's stand. After referring to Judge Parker in complimentary terms, he appealed to him to retire in the interest of harmony and to make place for any one of a number of eminent Democrats, whose selection as temporary chairman would create no friction. He named Senator O'Gorman of New York, Senator Culberson of Texas, Senator Shively of Indiana, Representative Henry D. Clayton of Indiana, Senator Lea of Tennessee, and James E. Campbell of Ohio. It was apparent that Senator Kern was unwilling to take up the fight against Judge Parker and Mr. Bryan again ascended the speaker's platform. He said:

"I tried to get the committee to agree upon a Progressive, and when it did not agree upon a Progressive I went to the man who received the largest number of votes. I urged Senator-elect James to lead in the fight. He said that conditions were such that he did not feel that he could accept the obligation. Then I went to Senator O'Gorman and urged him to accept this leadership. I stand ready to accept any Progressive, but if no Progressive appears, I shall accept the leadership and you shall accept or reject the advocacy of what we have been fighting for for sixteen years."

Theodore A. Bell of California then spoke in favor of Judge Parker, but such was the uproar in the convention that he was heard by but few delegates. Congressman Fitzgerald of New York endeavored to speak in favor of Judge Parker but the convention would not hear him. The chairman of the convention then closed the debate. Mr. Bryan rose to a point of order, and Senator Lea made a motion to allow each side fifteen minutes. This motion was lost. The chairman then ordered a vote telling the assemblage that there were only two candidates, Alton B. Parker and William J. Bryan. There was great confusion during the voting. The New York delegation cast its 90 votes for Parker and the 67 votes of Pennsylvania were given to Bryan. The votes of most of the other States were split. The vote resulted in 578 for Judge Parker and 506 votes for Mr. Bryan, with six delegates absent. Following the nomination of Judge Parker the convention adjourned until evening, as the temporary chairman was not prepared to make his address until that time.

ADDRESS OF JUDGE PARKER. Judge Parker's address delivered at the evening session was received coolly by the delegates.

He began by alluding to the Republican convention at Chicago and designated it as a brutal brawl. He urged, using Colonel Roosevelt's candidacy as an example, the necessity of limiting the presidential term to one term, and declared that Colonel Roosevelt's lust of power alone had broken the tradition hitherto observed since the beginning of the government. He discussed the high cost of living, attributing it to the tariff statutes and to combinations restraining trade and competition created for the purpose of wringing from the public everything which the tariff statutes make possible. He asserted that the Republican party favored the few at the expense of the many and that protection is purchased from that party by corporations. He declared that the failure of the executive and legislative branches of the government, both federal and State, to protect the people from the special privilege hunters and graft-seekers is deeply rooted in a corrupt alliance between the latter and the leaders of the Republican party. "For their crimes against American citizenship," he said, "the present leaders of the Republican party should be destroyed. For making and keeping the bargain to take care of the tariff-protected interests in consideration of campaign funds, they should be destroyed. For encouraging the creation of combinations to restrain trade and refusing to enforce the law, for a like consideration, they should be destroyed. For the lavish waste of the public funds; for the fraudulent disposition of the people's domain and for their contribution toward the division of the people into classes, they should be destroyed. For the efforts to seize for the executive department the federal governmental powers rightfully belonging to the States, they should be destroyed. And destruction will be theirs this very year if we but do our duty."

On the conclusion of Judge Parker's address the convention adjourned until the following morning.

SECOND DAY OF THE CONVENTION. The morning session of the second day of the convention, June 26, was devoted chiefly to routine matters. The committee on credentials was not ready to present its report and no other business was transacted. Almost the entire time of the session was devoted to hearing addresses by many eminent Democrats. Among those who spoke were Joseph W. Folk, former governor of Missiouri, Senator Rayner of Maryland, Henry D. Clayton of Alabama, and Senator Gore of Oklahoma. The convention then adjourned until evening.

The committee on credentials sat during the afternoon on the cases of contested delegates. Of these the most important were the contests from Illinois, which involved the question of regularity of credentials between two sets of delegates. The committee in each case sustained the finding of the national committee when it made up the temporary roll.

THE UNIT RULE. The night session was marked by the return of the progressive element as a dominating power in the convention. The question was on the unit rule applied to delegations which had hitherto been in force in Democratic conventions. The issue involved related to the Ohio convention and the question was as to whether the instruction given by the State convention bound simply the delegates-at-large from Ohio or whether it applied to district delegates who were elected under instructions from their representative districts. Of the 46 delegates from Ohio, 19 elected from congressional districts were chosen under instruction to vote for Governor Wilson. The remainder of the 46 delegates, including the delegates-at-large, were elected as Harmon delegates. The State convention sought to apply the unit rule and vote the entire 46 delegates for Governor Harmon. This effort was resisted and an appeal was made to the national committee, which refused to consider the matter. Newton D. Baker, mayor of Cleveland, who resisted the action of the State convention after the convening of the convention, took up the matter with the committee on rules.

This committee by a vote of 22 to 16 decided that Governor Harmon's friends were right and that the unit rule did apply. The majority and minority reports of this committee were submitted to the convention and on the acceptance of one of these reports came the test vote of the relative strength of the conservative and progressive elements. The majority vote was submitted to the convention by Representative J. Harry Covington of Maryland, a member of the committee on rules, and was defended by E. H. Moore, personal manager in the convention of Governor Harmon's candidacy. It was opposed by Representative Henry of Texas, Senator Williams of Mississippi, and Mayor Baker of Cleveland. The debate continued for two hours and then by a vote of 555½ against 495⅓ the convention rejected the report of the committee on rules, declaring the unit rule imposed by the Ohio convention did not bind the 19 Wilson delegates and that they were free to vote for Governor Wilson. This vote was regarded as an indication of a development of strength for Woodrow Wilson and the Byran forces.

ELECTION OF PERMANENT CHAIRMAN. The convention in this session decided almost unanimously to defer the adoption of a platform until after the nominees for president were named. This resulted through Mr. Bryan, who, by his efforts carried the motion through the committee on resolutions by a vote of 41 to 11. Ollie James of Kentucky was selected by the committee on organization for the permanent chairmanship. The chairmanship of the committee on resolutions was offered to Mr. Bryan, but he declined on the ground that he wished to have his hands free to conduct any fight that he deemed necessary. The committee on resolutions took up the work of drafting a platform and a tentative draft was presented by the New York delegation. This was drawn by Senator O'Gorman.

REPORT OF CREDENTIALS COMMITTEE. The third day of the convention, June 27, was filled with important and sensational happenings. It was marked by the first test vote which indicated the relative strength of Governor Wilson and Mr. Clark, by an attempt by Mr. Bryan to have August Belmont of New York and Thomas F. Ryan of Virginia, expelled from the convention as delegates, and by the beginning of nominations for presidential candidates. The first business of the day was the submission of the minority report from the committee on credentials in opposition to a majority report brought in by the chairman of the committee. The most important issue turned on the case of the South Dakota delegates. In that State delegates had been instructed for Governor Wilson. The committee on credentials, however, displaced these and substituted delegates for Mr. Clark. There were ten delegates.

The debates on this report were begun by W. A. McCorkle, former governor of West Virginia, who defended the action of the majority of the committee in seating the Clark delegates. The minority report was defended by Senator Lea of Tennessee. Theodore A. Bell of California then attacked the Wilson men and charged them with sharp practices. Mr. Bryan in the course of his speech mentioned the name of Governor Wilson. This was the signal for a great Wilson demonstration. The Wilson delegates paraded about the hall carrying banners and the business of the convention was obliged to suspend. An attempt was made to offer a counter-demonstration in favor of Mr. Clark. This did not succeed. When the convention again came to order, the roll call of the States was ordered on the adoption of the minority report of the credentials committee. There was great surprise when Roger Sullivan, chairman of the Illinois delegation, rose and cast the 58 votes of that delegation in favor of the minority report, or for Governor Wilson's delegates. Charles F. Murphy also voted the 90 delegates from New York for the minority report. The vote of the convention on the minority report was 633¼ for and 437 against. The Wilson delegates from South Dakota were therefore seated. These were the only important disputes between the rival delegations decided by the convention.

SPEECH OF MR. JAMES. The chairman of the committee on permanent organization, reported that Ollie James of Kentucky had been nominated for permanent chairman. The nomination was ratified with enthusiasm. Mr. James addressed the convention in a speech which aroused great enthusiasm.

He attacked the record of the Republican party and declared that it was flushed with many victories, imperious as a tyrant, and unheeding of the demands of the people. He declared that its promises in regard to revising the tariff had been broken and contrasted the action of the Democratic house in passing the tariff bills which actually reduced the tariff, and he bitterly arraigned President Taft for vetoing these bills. He declared that the Republican platform adopted at Chicago in regard to the tariff and trust questions was a puzzle absolutely meaningless to the American people. He concluded as follows: "The progressive spirit that sweeps this country now is called by some the principles of the progressives, by others the doctrine of the insurgents; but back yonder when a voice in the western wilderness cried out for them they were called the vagaries of Bryan the dreamer. However much we may differ in national conventions upon minor questions, all just men must admit that the one living American whose name will shine in history, studded by a thousand flaming stars, alongside those of Jefferson and Jackson, is that of William Jennings Bryan of Nebraska."

After the conclusion of Mr. James's address, a motion to proceed to the nomination of a candidate for President was defeated, and the convention took a recess until 8 P. M.

MR. BRYAN'S ATTACK ON BELMONT AND RYAN. The evening session was given over almost entirely to an attempt of Mr. Bryan to unseat August Belmont and Thomas F. Ryan as delegates. As soon as the session had convened Mr. James asked for unanimous consent to Mr. Bryan's reading of a resolution which he had prepared. Mr. Bryan accordingly read the following resolution:

"Resolved, That in this crisis in our party's career and in our country's history this convention sends greeting to the people of the United States and assures them that the party of Jefferson and of Jackson is still the champion of popular government and equality before the law. As a proof of our fidelity to the people we hereby declare ourselves opposed to the nomination of any candidate for President who is a representative of or who is under any obligation to J. Pierpont Morgan, Thomas F. Ryan, August Belmont, or any others of the privilege-hunting or favor-seeking class; be it further

"Resolved, That we demand the withdrawal from this convention of any delegate or delegates constituting or representing the above-named interests."

The greatest confusion followed the introduction of this resolution. The point of order was raised that the resolution be referred to the committee on resolutions, which was overruled. Mr. Bryan then moved that the rules be suspended and that the convention proceed to a consideration of the resolution. He then made an address lasting twenty minutes. He opened with a savage attack on August Belmont, Thomas F. Ryan and Charles F. Murphy. He said:

"There has never been a more brazen, insolent, and impudent effort to control the action of a Democratic convention than has been going on here. I do not intend that the representative of the predatory interests shall dominate this convention and stifle the will of 6,500,000 Democrats.

"The control of the money trust is ruthless. It is time that we gave notice to the people of the country that this convention is not under the thumb of the interests represented by Morgan, Ryan, and Belmont.

"I am not willing that Belmont and Ryan shall come here with counsel and seek to control this convention. No false sense of fairness shall stop me from protecting my party. I cannot speak for you delegates. You must take the responsibility for driving these men from our midst. The time for action has arrived.

"One of these men sits with New York and the other with Virginia. I make you this proposition: If the State of New York will take a poll of its votes and a majority of them—not all, but a majority—and if New York will on roll call, where her delegates can have their names reported and printed, ask for the retention of Mr. Belmont, and if Virginia will on roll call protest against the withdrawal of Mr. Ryan, I will then withdraw the last part on the request of the States in which these gentlemen sit, but I will not withdraw the first part that demands that our record be free from entanglements."

Congressman Flood of Virginia followed Mr. Bryan in a defense of Mr. Ryan. He said: "In the name of the sovereign State of Virginia, I accept the insolent proposition made by the only man in this convention who would dare to make it." This declaration was greeted with cheers and before they had died away, Charles F. Murphy and the leaders of the New York delegation entered the convention. They had been absent during the introduction of the resolution by Mr. Bryan. After several others had spoken for and against the resolution, Mr. Bryan again took the platform. He demanded if New York asked for the withdrawal of the last part of the resolution. The New York delegates answered him by cries of "Withdraw it yourself." Mr. Bryan again asked the question and there was no response. Congressman Flood of Virginia again defended Mr. Ryan, declaring that the latter had offered to withdraw and that the other delegates had refused to accept his withdrawal.

Following Mr. Flood's speech, Mr. Bryan arose and modified his resolution. He said that he would withdraw the last part of the resolution so that nobody could hide behind it, but that the delegates would have a chance on roll call to show what they thought of the first part. Lewis Nixon of the New York delegation said that the New York delegates did not ask for the withdrawal of any part of the resolution and made a point of order that part of the resolution could not be withdrawn. This was overruled by the chairman. The vote on the motion to suspend the rules and pass the resolution was then taken. This required a two-thirds vote or the votes of 725 of the delegates. The vote was taken amid the greatest confusion. The resolution was carried by 888 in the affirmative and 196 in the negative. The New York delegation voted in favor of the resolution.

The adoption of this resolution, which is unprecedented in national conventions, was conceded to establish Mr. Bryan as the dominant figure of the convention.

NOMINATION FOR PRESIDENT. Following the adoption of the resolution the chairman called for nominations for President.

The vote on the first ballot was as follows: Clark, 440½; Wilson, 324; Underwood, 170½; Harmon, 148; Marshall, 31; Baldwin, 22; Bryan, 1. Twelve ballots were taken on June 28 in an endeavor to break the deadlock between the three leading candidates. On the twelfth ballot the vote stood as follows: Clark, 549; Wilson 354; Underwood, 123; Harmon, 29; Marshall, 29. This was the last ballot of the day and the convention adjourned.

DECLINE OF CLARK STRENGTH. On June 29, the fourth day of the convention, balloting continued throughout the day, but it was interrupted by a bitter attack made by Mr. Bryan upon the New York delegation.

On the fourteen ballots taken during the day, Mr. Clark's strength was reduced from 549 to 463, a loss of 85½ votes. Governor Wilson, on the other hand, gained on the fourteen ballots 53½ votes, increasing from 354 to 407½. The standing on the 26th ballot, the last taken on this day, was as follows: Clark, 463½; Wilson, 407½; Underwood, 112½; Foss, 43; Marshall, 30; Harmon, 29; and Bryan, 1. The impression become general among Democratic leaders that Mr. Clark's chances for the nomination had vanished. He lost strength on practically every ballot during this day. The States of California, Idaho, Kansas, Massachusetts, and Montana, whose delegates were instructed for him, changed to Governor Wilson. Mr. Clark and Governor Wilson were the only two candidates whose nomination was deemed a possibility. Governor Harmon received, for the greater part of the votes, only the 29 votes from his own State. On the 22d ballot these votes were given to Mr. Clark, it is said on the request of Governor Harmon himself. After voting twice for Mr. Clark, the Ohio delegates again returned to Governor Harmon.

Mr. Bryan's Attack on Tammany. The revolt of the States which seceded from Mr. Clark's support was led by Mr. Bryan, who took the platform and announced that as an instructed delegate from Nebraska he could no longer support Mr. Clark, because of the latter's alliance with Charles F. Murphy and Tammany Hall. He added that he would not support any candidate in the convention whose nomination could not be brought about without the support of the 90 delegates from New York, whose votes he declared in effect to be tainted. He declared that as cast under the unit rule they did not represent "the intelligence, the virtue, the democracy, or the patriotism of the 90 men of the delegation." He declared that the votes of the delegates from New York represented the will of Charles F. Murphy, who, he said, represented the influences that dominated the Republican convention at Chicago and were endeavoring to dominate this convention. Mr. Bryan announced that on account of these considerations he would turn from Mr. Clark and would support the second choice of Nebraska, Woodrow Wilson. This announcement was greeted by one of the greatest demonstrations thus far witnessed in the convention.

Mr. Clark on being informed of the charges made by Mr. Bryan that he had affiliated himself with the interests in the hope of obtaining the presidential nomination, wrote a letter to Senator William J. Stone, who had charge of his interests in Baltimore, in which he denied the charges and made a sharp attack on Mr. Bryan. He said:

"It would be unbecoming to one holding my present official position to express the indignation which I feel at these veiled aspersions upon my character. I will say only this, that I am ashamed and humiliated as never before in my life, that one who has known me and my acts for a quarter of a century could find it in his heart to impugn my integrity before thousands of my fellow citizens. As a Democrat, moreover, jealous of my party's reputation and anxious for its success, I regret more than I can tell that political or personal exigencies should have induced such an assault from such a source upon a Democratic Speaker of the House of Representatives." He denied that he knew any of the persons with whom Mr. Bryan declared him to be in affiliation. He declared that his name would remain before the convention, subject to no trade or dicker, until two-thirds of the delegates should ratify or refuse to ratify the actions of the majority.

Mr. Bryan's Compromise Proposal. As the deadlock continued throughout July 30, the convention adjourned until the following Monday, July 1. On Sunday Mr. Bryan proposed a compromise candidate, suggesting the names of five men. These were Senator John W. Kern of Indiana, Senator-elect Ollie James of Kentucky, Senator Culberson of Texas, Senator Rayner of Maryland, and Senator O'Gorman of New York. The statement in which this compromise was suggested, contained another denunciation of what he termed the Ryan-Belmont-Murphy combine and he repeated that no candidate must accept the 90 votes of New York in order to obtain the necessary two-thirds. He insisted that the candidate for Vice-President must be equally as trustworthy as the candidate for President, because the Progressives would not be satisfied with only one life between a progressive administration and reactionary control. He also attacked Governor Harmon, and Mr. Underwood, as chief of the reactionaries.

Mr. Bryan's attitude toward Mr. Clark's candidacy aroused the bitterest feeling among the Clark leaders and delegates. For sixteen years Mr. Clark was one of the most loyal and aggressive Bryan men in the Democratic party. He stumped the country in behalf of Mr. Bryan in the three campaigns in which the latter was a candidate and frequently spoke in his defense on the floor of the House. The bitterness which the delegates felt was aggravated by the conviction, resulting from the voting, that Mr. Clark was gradually losing strength, and this they charged chiefly to the attitude taken by Mr. Bryan.

There was bitter feeling, too, in the New York delegation. As a result of Mr. Bryan's attack upon the delegates a conference was held as to whether a reply should be made by some delegate, but it was decided that no answer was called for on the part of the New York delegation.

Renewal of Balloting. The voting was continued on July 1, and the convention was in session until 12:30 a. m., July 2. Fifteen ballots were taken on this day and in the balloting Governor Wilson continued throughout the day to add to his strength. On the 27th ballot, the first taken on July 1, Mr. Clark had 469 votes, Governor Wilson, 406½; Mr. Underwood, 112; Governor Harmon, 29; Governor Marshall of Indiana, 30. On the 41st ballot, the last taken, Mr. Clark had 424, Governor Wilson 499½, Mr. Underwod 106, and Governor Harmon 27. Delegates from five States pledged to Mr. Clark in the course of this day's voting voted for Governor Wilson. These included delegates from Indiana, Florida, Michigan, Iowa, and Arizona.

Wilson Passes Clark. On the 30th ballot, taken on July 1, Governor Wilson had overtaken and passed Mr. Clark in the race for the nomination and from that ballot until the end of the balloting on this day his vote steadily increased. During the day's voting there was indication of the bitterest feeling toward Mr. Bryan on the part of the Missouri delegation, and he narrowly escaped personal assault from Missouri delegates when he appeared on the floor near them. There were two sessions of the convention on this day. The 90 votes of

rright, Harris and Ewing, Washington, D. C.
JOSEPHUS DANIELS
Member Democratic National Committee

Copyright, Pach Bros., N. Y.
GOVERNOR JUDSON HARMON

Copyright, Pach Bros., N. Y.
WILLIAM G. McADOO

New York continued to be thrown steadily for Mr. Clark.

THE NEW YORK DELEGATION ANSWERS MR. BRYAN. A reply was made to the charges made by Mr. Bryan against the New York delegation by John B. Stanchfield, one of the New York delegates. It was one of the most pointed and acrimonious speeches ever heard in a national convention. Mr. Stanchfield characterized Mr. Bryan as "a money-grabbing, selfish, favor-hunting, publicity-seeking marplot." He charged him with double-dealing, with playing Mr. Clark against Governor Wilson and Governor Wilson against Mr. Clark for the sole purpose of bringing about his own nomination through a deadlock convention. Mr. Stanchfield made his speech in explaining his vote for Governor Wilson after a poll from the New York delegation had been demanded. This poll disclosed 0 votes for Wilson, 78 for Clark, and 2 for Underwood. The convention adjourned at 12:30 A. M. until the following day.

The increase of Governor Wilson's strength and the steady falling off of the delegates voting for Mr. Clark made it apparent that it was only a question of time when Mr. Wilson would receive the necessary two-thirds vote required for the choice. The Clark leaders, however, persisted in their claim that Mr. Clark would ultimately be nominated. The opening ballot taken at the reconvening of the convention on July 2, however, made it evident that their claims had no foundation.

STAMPEDE TO GOVERNOR WILSON. On this ballot, the 43d of the convention, a stampede to Governor Wilson began, which ended in his nomination. On this ballot the 58 delegates from Illinois changed from Clark to Wilson, and this was followed quickly by the swing to the latter of West Virginia's delegation of 16, and the 24 votes from Virginia. Other scattered votes were given to Governor Wilson on this ballot, which brought his total to 602, a gain of 108, while Mr. Clark had lost 101 votes, and received a total of 329. After this first ballot the Wilson forces swept everything before them. On the second vote of the day they gained 27 votes, while Mr. Clark lost 23. In the third ballot of the session Governor Wilson gained only 4, while Mr. Clark held his own at 306. He had fallen already, however, far below the 363 necessary to block the nomination under the two-thirds rule. Mr. Clark depended now for his support almost entirely upon the 97 delegates who had been pledged to Mr. Underwood and who continued to vote for him.

The Clark leaders pleaded with Mr. Underwood's managers to stand with them against the movement for Governor Wilson, but Senator Bankhead, the Underwood leader, declined to be a leader to any coalition designed to thwart the will of a large majority of the convention. He therefore took the platform and released the Underwood delegates from their pledges. Senator Stone, the Clark leader, announced that Missouri would stand by Mr. Clark to the end, but that the nominee, whoever he might be, would have Mr. Clark's support. Mayor Fitzgerald of Boston then withdrew the name of Governor Foss, who had received 27 votes from Massachusetts throughout the balloting. John J. Fitzgerald, from New York, then pleaded for harmony and moved that the roll call be dispensed with, and Governor Wilson be nominated by acclamation. Senator Reed of Missouri objected because Missouri wished to vote for Clark to the end.

The name of Governor Harmon was withdrawn and the roll call on the 46th and last ballot was resumed. On this ballot Mr. Clark received only 84 votes, including the 36 votes from Missouri.

NOMINATION OF GOVERNOR WILSON. Governor Wilson received 990; Governor Harmon 12, and 2 were absent. Only 726 votes were necessary for a choice. Senator Stone immediately moved that the nomination be made unanimous by acclamation. This was carried with cheers, and at 3:33 o'clock the nomination of Governor Wilson was announced amid great uproar. The convention then took a recess until nine o'clock in the evening for the purpose of preparing nominations for Vice-President. The following table shows the total number of votes received by each of the principal candidates on each ballot:

No of Ballot	Clark	Wilson	Underwood	Harmon
a First	440½	324	117½	148
a Second	446½	339¼	111¼	141
a Third	441	345	114½	140½
a Fourth	443	349½	112	136½
Fifth	443	351	119½	141½
Sixth	445	354	121	135
Seventh	449½	352½	123½	129½
b Eighth	448½	351½	123	130
Ninth	452	352½	122½	127
Tenth	556	350½	117½	31
Eleventh	554	354½	118½	29
Twelfth	549	354	123	29
Thirteenth	554½	356	115½	29
Fourteenth	553	361	111	29
Fifteenth	552	362½	110½	29
Sixteenth	551	362½	112½	29
Seventeenth	545	362½	112½	29
Eighteenth	535	361	125	29
Nineteenth	532	358	130	29
Twentieth	512	388½	121½	29
Twenty-first	508	395½	118½	29
Twenty-second	500½	396½	115	0
Twenty-third	497½	399	114½	0
Twenty-fourth	496	402½	115½	0
Twenty-fifth	469	405	108	29
Twenty-sixth	463½	407½	112½	29
c Twenty-seventh	469	406½	112	29
d Twenty-eighth	468½	437½	112½	29
d Twenty-ninth	468½	436	112	29
d Thirtieth	455	460	121½	19
d Thirty-first	446½	475½	116½	17
d Thirty-second	446½	477½	119½	14
d Thirty-third	447½	477½	103½	29
d Thirty-fourth	447½	479½	101½	29
d Thirty-fifth	433½	494½	101½	29
d Thirty-sixth	434½	496½	98½	29
d Thirty-seventh	432½	496½	100½	29
d Thirty-eighth	425	498½	106	29
d Thirty-ninth	422	501½	106	29
d Fortieth	423	501½	106	28
d Forty-first	424	499½	106	27
e Forty-second	430	494	104	27
e Forty-third	329	602	98½	28
Forty-fourth	306	629	99	27
Forty-fifth	306	633	97	25
f Forty-sixth	84	990	0	12

a—For Baldwin 22, 14, 14, 14.
b—For Gaynor 1; for James 1.
c—Not voting 1½.
d—Absent ½.
e—James 1, Gaynor 1, Lewis 1, Bryan ½.
f—Absent 2.

The table on page 568 shows the vote by States on the 46th or final ballot, which resulted in the nomination of Governor Wilson.

NOMINATION OF VICE-PRESIDENT. The nomination for Vice-President was offered to Mr. Clark but he refused it. Agreement was then quickly reached on Governor Thomas R. Marshall of Indiana, and on the reconvening of

State	No. of Votes	Clark	Wil-son	Under-wood	Har-mon	Foss
Alabama	24	....	24	....	....	....
Arizona	6	....	6	....	....	....
Arkansas	18	....	18	....	....	....
California	26	24	2	....	....	....
Colorado	12	....	12	....	....	....
Connecticut	14	....	14	....	....	....
Delaware	6	....	6	....	....	....
Florida	12	5	7	....	....	....
Georgia	28	....	28	....	....	....
Idaho	8	....	8	....	....	....
Illinois	58	....	58	....	....	....
Indiana	30	....	30	....	....	....
Iowa	26	....	26	....	....	....
Kansas	20	....	20	....	....	....
Kentucky	26	....	26	....	....	....
Louisiana	20	2	18	....	....	....
Maine	12	....	12	....	....	....
Maryland	16	....	16	....	....	....
Massachusetts	36	....	36	....	....	....
Michigan	30	....	30	....	....	....
Minnesota	24	....	24	....	....	....
Mississippi	20	....	20	....	....	....
Missouri	36	36	....	....	....	....
Montana	8	....	8	....	....	....
Nebraska	16	....	16	....	....	....
Nevada	6	6	....	....	....	....
New Hampshire	8	....	8	....	....	....
New Jersey	28	4	24	....	....	....
New Mexico	8	....	8	....	....	....
New York	90	....	90	....	....	....
North Carolina	24	....	24	....	....	....
North Dakota	10	....	10	....	....	....
*Ohio	48	1	33	....	12	....
Oklahoma	20	....	20	....	....	....
Oregon	10	....	10	....	....	....
Pennsylvania	76	....	76	....	....	....
Rhode Island	10	....	10	....	....	....
South Carolina	18	....	18	....	....	....
South Dakota	10	....	10	....	....	....
Tennessee	24	....	24	....	....	....
Texas	40	....	40	....	....	....
Utah	8	....	8	....	....	....
Vermont	8	....	8	....	....	....
Virginia	24	....	24	....	....	....
Washington	14	....	14	....	....	....
West Virginia	16	....	16	....	....	....
Wisconsin	26	....	26	....	....	....
Wyoming	6	....	6	....	....	....
Alaska	6	....	6	....	....	....
Dis of Columbia	6	6	....	....	....	....
Hawaii	6	....	6	....	....	....
Porto Rico	6	....	6	....	....	....
Totals	1088	84	990	....	12	....

* Absent, 2:

the convention in its last session at 9 P. M., Governor Marshall was unanimously nominated. After the reading of the platform, which had been prepared largely under the direction of Mr. Bryan, the convention adjourned.

The success of the effort to bring about the nomination of Governor Wilson who, at the opening of the convention, had far fewer votes pledged to him than had Mr. Clark, was due largely to the skillful management of those who had charge of his campaign. These included, first of all, William F. McCombs, the chairman of the committee which conducted the preliminary campaign; Josephus Daniels, head of the publicity department; Senator Gore of Oklahoma, and others. Mr. McCombs had been advocating and working for the nomination of Governor Wilson for two years prior to the actual beginning of the campaign. He was a newcomer in politics and previous to the active candidacy of Governor Wilson had not been heard of outside his own immediate circle of friends.

National Convention, Progressive

Call for the Convention. The call for a convention to form the proposed new party was issued on July 8 and the date set for the convention was August 5. The signers of the call represented 40 States and it was addressed to "the people of the United States without regard to past political differences." Among those whose names were attached to the call were James R. Garfield of Ohio, William Flinn and Gifford Pinchot of Pennsylvania, Cecil Lyon of Texas, Senator Poindexter of Washington, Governor Carey of Wyoming, Judge Lindsey of Colorado, Medill McCormick of Illinois, Henry J. Allen of Kansas, Charles J. Bonaparte of Maryland, Matthew Hale of Massachusetts, Senator Dixon of Montana, Everett Colby, George L. Record, and former Governor Fort of New Jersey; Governor Johnson of California, Leslie Coombs of Kentucky, Governor Vessey of South Dakota, and William A. Prendergast, Oscar S. Straus, and Timothy L. Woodruff of New York. The call appealed to those who "realize that the power of the crooked political bosses and of the privileged classes behind them is so strong in the old party organizations that no helpful movement in the general interest of the country can come out of either; to those who believe in the right and capacity of the people to rule, and to those who believe that government by the few has become government by the sordid influences that control the few; that only through the proposed movement can legislation demanded by modern evolution be obtained, and that the commandment "Thou shalt not steal" applies to politics as well as to business.

Organization of the Convention—Negro Delegates. In response to this call, about 2000 delegates assembled at Chicago on August 5. A provisional national committee, including a committeeman from each State, had previously been appointed. Its only important action prior to the convening of the convention was its refusal to seat negro delegates from certain southern States. This was in accordance with a declaration made several days before by Mr. Roosevelt in a letter written to Julian Harris, in which he outlined his attitude toward negro delegates. These delegates were excluded on the ground that they came from States which had never cast a Republican vote and had never elected a colored man to office, and that the delegates from southern States sent to previous Republican conventions had reflected discredit upon the Republican party and upon the race itself. Delegates from northern States regularly elected in State conventions were admitted as delegates to the convention. The action of the Progressive committee was severely criticised, but its action was upheld by the committee on credentials. Mr. Roosevelt in an address made before the convention (see below) defended his attitude toward these delegates from the southern States.

Opening of the Convention. The convention met in its first session on August 5. Including delegates, there were present in the Auditorium nearly 15,000 people. It was in many respects the most remarkable political assemblage ever gathered together. Its dominant feature was an enthusiasm which at times resembled religious zeal. This appearance of a religious gathering was increased by the singing of hymns and a general devotional attitude on the part of the delegates. Another conspicuous feature was the presence of many women delegates, including Jane Addams and other well-known advocates of woman suffrage.

The convention was called to order by Senator Dixon of Montana. He made a short address, in which he told those assembled that they were about to erect a new milestone in the political history of the United States. The call of the provisional committee of the party was then read by the secretary, Oscar King Davis. When the names of the signers of the call were read each State delegation rose and cheered. Among the names were some of the best-known leaders of the Progressive party, including Governor Johnson of California, Judge Ben D. Lindsey of Colorado, and James R. Garfield of Ohio.

SENATOR BEVERIDGE MADE TEMPORARY CHAIRMAN. Albert J. Beveridge, formerly United States senator from Indiana and the Progressive candidate for governor of that State, had been selected for temporary chairman. His address is generally conceded to be one of the most notable pieces of oratory ever delivered in a national convention. He said in part:

"We stand for an undivided nation. . . . We stand for social brotherhood as against savage individualism. . . . We stand for representative government that represents the people. . . . We Progressives believe in this rule of the people. . . . Who knows the people's needs so well as the people themselves? Who so wise to solve their own problems? To-day these problems concern the living of the people. . . . We have more than enough to supply every human being beneath the flag. . . . Hunger should never walk in these thinly peopled gardens of plenty. . . . We mean to remedy these conditions. . . . To make human living easier, to free the hands of honest business, to make trade and commerce sound and healthy, to protect womanhood, save childhood, and restore the dignity of manhood—these are the tasks we must do. . . . The Progressive party believes that the Constitution is a living thing, growing with the people's growth . . . permitting the people to meet all their needs as conditions change. . . . The first words of the Constitution are, 'We, the people,' and they declare that the Constitution's purpose is to form a more perfect union and to promote the general welfare. To do just that is the very heart of the Progressive cause."

Senator Beveridge's address was received with the greatest enthusiasm by the delegates and the spectators and on its conclusion the convention adjourned until noon of the next day. The interim was devoted to the settlement of three questions of importance.

PROCEEDINGS OF PROVISIONAL COMMITTEE. One of these questions concerned the status of certain of the delegates from the South, referred to above. In issuing the call for delegates, the provisional chairman for Florida had, it appeared, led two groups, one white and the other colored, to believe that each was authorized to hold a State convention and choose delegates. The provisional national committee before whom the conflicting claims were presented declared that neither convention was authoritative and that both could be excluded. The case was appealed to the credentials committee of the convention. Another dispute arose as to the delegates sent from Mississippi. In that State the call for the State convention used the term "white." In protest some negroes assembled and chose two of their race to act as delegates. The provisional national committee decided that the negro meeting was without any authority, and that, therefore, although the use of the term "white" was not authorized or approved, there was no ground for sustaining the contest.

The second question pertained to the platform. This was the problem of formulating the Progressive faith in a document which would be short, specific, and comprehensive. Among those who labored on this platform were Dean Lewis of the Law School of the University of Pennsylvania, chairman of the committee; Professor Kirchwey, of Columbia University; Gifford Pinchot; William Allen White, of Kansas, and Herbert Knox Smith.

The third question related to the rules of the convention. It was desired to avoid the evils created by the rules hitherto observed in Republican conventions, and the task was to avoid these evils and not create others as serious. The reports of these committees were later unanimously accepted by the convention with the exception of the modification of one of the rules. This change referred to the name of the party. The rule as reported designated the party as a Progressive party. The modification provided that in those States where the law made it necessary or desirable that a different name be used, the name chosen would be recognized as official.

MR. ROOSEVELT'S ADDRESS. On the second day of the convention Mr. Roosevelt, by invitation, addressed the delegates. Before he was permitted to begin, however, a demonstration occurred which lasted precisely one hour. Mr. Roosevelt's address he designated as his "confession of faith." It consumed an hour and a half in delivery and was about 20,000 words in length. Although most of the questions considered in this address had been previously discussed by Mr. Roosevelt, it was generally considered to be one of the greatest speeches delivered by him during his political career. The address dealt primarily with the "right of the people to rule," which consisted, Mr. Roosevelt pointed out, in preserving a check on every branch of public service, including the courts.

He declared that his aim was "to control business and not to strangle it." This control, he emphasized, should be through national, not State, channels. He urged "social and industrial justice to wage-earners," and promised that if elected he would institute an immediate investigation of conditions with a view to obtaining minimum-wage standards.

Among other things, he favored the revival of the country life commission and the creation of a new commission to deal with the tariff question. He also proposed an inquiry into the high cost of living. Referring to the currency, he advocated reform that would be free from manipulation by "Wall Street or the large interests." It is impossible to undertake a complete summary of this address, which may be considered the platform of the National Progressive party. Note will be made, however, of Mr. Roosevelt's utterances on the questions most in dispute. On the tariff he said: "I believe in a protective tariff, but I believe in it as a principle, approached from the standpoint of the interests of the whole people and not as a bundle of preferences to be given to favored individuals. . . . It is not merely the tariff that should be revised, but the method of tariff-making and of tariff administration. Whenever an industry is to be protected it should be on the theory that such protection will serve to keep up the wages and the standard of living of the wage-worker in that industry with full regard for the interest of the consumer. . . . The practice of undertaking a general revision of all the schedules at one time, and of securing information as to conditions in the different industries and as to rates of duties desired chiefly from those engaged in the industries, who themselves benefit directly from the rates they propose, has been demonstrated to be not only iniquitous but futile. The first step should be the creation of a permanent commission of non-partisan experts whose business shall be to study scientifically all phases of tariff-making and of tariff effects. This commission should be large enough to cover all the different and widely varying branches of American industry. . . . It should examine into the wages and conditions of labor and life of the workmen in any industry. . . . This commission would be wholly different from the present unsatisfactory tariff board which was created under a provision of law which failed to give it the powers indispensable if it was to do the work it should do." On the question of trusts, he said: "Our aim is to control business and not to strangle it—and, above all, not to continue a policy of make-believe strangle toward big concerns that do evil, and constant menace toward both big and little concerns that do well. . . . It is utterly hopeless to attempt to control the trusts merely by the anti-trust law, or by any law the same in principle, no matter what the modifications may be in detail. . . . What is needed is the application to all industrial concerns and all co-operating interests engaged in interstate commerce in which there is either monopoly or control of the market of the principles on which we have gone in regulating transportation concerns engaged in such commerce.

The anti-trust law should be kept on the statute books and strengthened so as to make it genuinely and thoroughly effective against every big concern tending to monopoly or guilty of anti-social practices. At the same time, a national industrial commission should be created which should have complete power to regulate and control all the great industrial concerns engaged in interstate business—which practically means all of them in this country. This commission should exercise over these industrial concerns like powers to those exercised over the railways by the Interstate Commerce Commission and over the national banks by the Comptroller of the Currency, and additional powers if found necessary."

A considerable portion of this address was devoted to an exposition of Mr. Roosevelt's creed on the right of the people to rule, and it included also a sharp attack on the machines of both parties. He re-stated in effect his views as to the relation of the courts to the people. He declared that he did not question the general honesty of the courts and pointed out that his purpose was not to impugn the courts, but to emancipate them from a position where they stand in the way of social justice, and to emancipate the people in an orderly way. Mr. Roosevelt's general attitude toward the courts will be found in abstracts of his speeches in Columbus, Ohio, and New York City, noted above. He spoke briefly on the importance of conservation and upon the development of Alaska. He declared his belief in a strong navy and in the fortification of the Panama Canal. He concluded as follows:

"Now, friends, this is my confession of faith. I have made it rather long because I wish you to know just what my deepest convictions are on the great questions of to-day, so that if you choose to make me your standard-bearer in the fight you shall make your choice understanding exactly how I feel—and if after hearing me you think you ought to choose someone else, I shall loyally abide by your choice."

At the conclusion of this, his main address, Mr. Roosevelt, in response to questions asked from the floor by delegates, made a supplemental speech in which he discussed the question of the negro delegates to the convention. He said:

"As soon as the Progressive party was formed I at once set about, as many other men in different States did, securing from the northern States themselves an ample recognition of the colored man in these States, so that as a matter of fact there is in this convention a representation from the Republican States of colored men such as there never has been before anything like in any convention in the country. . . . I propose to take toward the southern States the exact attitude that we have taken to West Virginia and Maryland. And I believe that in adopting that action we shall naturally and spontaneously see from those southern States a repetition of the conditions in West Virginia and Maryland, so that in future Progressive national conventions you will see colored delegates come from the South Atlantic and Gulf States precisely as they now come from West Virginia and from Maryland. . . . Now, I have taken the action which, as far as I am able to judge my own soul, I believe with all my heart is the only action that offers any chance to the black man in the South, to the white man in the South, and which offers a better chance to the black man in the North, which has already given to the black man in the North a better chance than he ever had before. And if I had advocated the following of any other action I should have been in the position of insincerely advocating for purposes of temporary political advantage a course of action which has been followed for forty-five years in the Republican party."

Resolution of Credentials Committee. The committee on credentials ratified the decision of the provisional national committee on the contests of the southern negro delegates. The committee appointed reported the following resolution, which was unanimously adopted by the convention:

"Resolved, That we recognise the constitutional and inherent right of each and every State to determine the qualifications and manner of election of its delegates to the national convention to nominate a President and Vice-President.

"Resolved, further, That the certificate of election of the State official authorized to issue the same in States having laws on the subject, the certification of election by the highest governing body of the party in the State, shall be the conclusive evidence of the right of the delegates named therein to seats in the national convention."

Nomination of Candidates. Previous to the convening of the session of the third and last day, Hiram W. Johnson, governor of California, had been selected as candidate for Vice-President. Other names considered were those of John M. Parker of Louisiana and Judge Ben B. Lindsey of Colorado. When the convention met, the nominating speeches for President and Vice-President were at once begun. William A. Prendergast of New York presented the name of Mr. Roosevelt. This was followed by cheering which lasted half an hour. Among those who seconded the nomination was Jane Addams. After alleging her belief in the platform of the Progressive party, she said: "I second the nomination of Theodore Roosevelt because he is one of the few men in our public life who has been responsive to modern movement. Because of that, because the programme will require a leader of invincible courage, of open mind, of democratic sympathies, one endowed with power to interpret the common man and to identify himself with the common lot, I heartily second the nomination." General Horatio C. King seconded the nomination in behalf of the old soldiers, and among others who spoke were General McDowell, chairman of the Tennessee delegation; Colonel Lloyd, a former Confederate soldier, and Henry J. Allen, of Kansas. The platform was then read by Dean William Draper Lewis of the Law School of the University of Pennsylvania and was adopted on the motion of Governor Carey of Wyoming. The rules were then suspended and Theodore Roosevelt was nominated by acclamation. Governor Johnson was then nominated for Vice-President by Judge M. Parker of Louisiana. The nomination was seconded by Judge Lindsey. He moved that the nomination be made unanimous. A committee of notification was at once appointed and Mr. Roosevelt and Governor Johnson made brief speeches of acceptance. The convention then adjourned.

OTHER CONVENTIONS. The national convention of the Socialist party was held at Indianapolis on May 12. The report of the national secretary showed that the membership of the party in the early part of 1912, as shown by the average dues received, was 125,823, but that a great many voters who were not in active affiliation with the Socialist party were in sympathy with its political propaganda was shown by the vote received by Mr. Debs in the election of November 5. Mr. Debs received over 900,000 votes, as will be noted in the table given in the section *Elections* in this article. Eugene V. Debs was again nominated for President and Emil Seidel for Vice-President. About 300 delegates attended the convention, of which Morris Hillquit was elected chairman. The platform adopted by the convention will be found in the section *Party Platforms*.

The national convention of the Prohibition party was held at Atlantic City, N. J., on July 10-11. The platform adopted will be found in the section *Party Platforms*. Eugene W. Chafin of Arizona was nominated for President and Aaron S. Watkins of Ohio for Vice-President.

The Socialist Labor party nominated for President Arthur E. Reimer and for Vice-President August Gillhaus. The chief articles in the platform of the party are the abolition of the wage system and the establishment of industrial self-government of the workers for the workers by the workers. The total vote received by the candidates for this party will be found in the section *Elections* in this article.

POST-CONVENTION CAMPAIGN, REPUBLICAN

The Republican campaign following the nominating convention was slow in starting and was throughout lacking in enthusiasm. In spite of the professed confidence of President Taft in his reëlection, the general impression prevailed not only at large but among the Republican leaders themselves that the President's chances for reëlection in the face of a divided party were small. The President took little active part in the campaign. He made several addresses, reference to which is made below, but for the most part he contented himself with interviews and with public letters.

ORGANIZATION OF THE CAMPAIGN. Charles D. Hilles, private secretary to the President, was, at the latter's request, appointed chairman of the national committee, with active charge of the campaign. Senator Penrose of Pennsylvania, Senator Crane of Massachusetts, and Senator Smoot of Utah assisted Mr. Hilles in the prosecution of the work of the committee. George R. Sheldon was appointed national treasurer.

ATTITUDE OF REPUBLICAN LEADERS. The result of the nominating convention, and especially the mooted question of the disputed election cases, and the establishment of the third party, resulted in the defection of many of the well-known leaders of the Republican party in the various States to the Progressive party. In those States in which the popular vote was cast in large majorities for Mr. Roosevelt in the preferential primaries most of the political leaders became identified with the Progressives. Several, however, who had been prominent in their advocacy of Mr. Roosevelt's nomination at Chicago declined to join the third party movement. These included Governor Hadley of Missouri (see MISSOURI), Governor Deneen of Illinois (see ILLINOIS), and Senator Cummins of Iowa. The attitude of Senator Cummins toward the third party is noted below.

PRESIDENT TAFT'S SPEECH OF ACCEPTANCE. On August 1 the President was formally notified of his nomination. The ceremonies took place in the East Room of the White House and were accompanied with little formality. The address of notification was delivered by Senator Root. In this he declared that there was no just ground for impeaching the honesty and good faith of the decision by which that convention was constituted and that both the making up of the roll of delegates and the rights accorded to persons on that roll were in accord with "the rules of law governing the party and founded upon justice and common sense." Speaking directly to the President, he said: "Your title to the nomination is as clear and unimpeachable as the title of any candidate of any party since political conventions began." In response to this speech of notification the President delivered a long address, which may be summarized as follows:

He began by stating that the issue presented to the Republican national convention made a crisis in the life of that party. He said: "A faction sought to force the party to violate a valuable and time-honored national tradition by entrusting the power of the presidency for more than two terms to one man, and that man one whose recently avowed political views would have committed the party to radical proposals involving dangerous changes in our present constitutional form of representative government and our independent judiciary." He then summarized the legislative enactments for which the Republican party had been responsible during recent administrations. These included the pure food law, employers' liability law, establishment of a federal mining bureau, the creation of a children's bureau, passage of a white slave act, railroad legislation, parcel post, and conservation.

Referring to the popular unrest which characterized the times, he spoke as follows: "In the work of arousing the people to the danger that threatened our civilization from the abuses of concentrated wealth and the power it was likely to exercise, the public imagination was wrought upon and a reign of sensational journalism and unjust and unprincipled muck-raking has followed in which much injustice has been done to honest men. Demagogues have seized the opportunity offered to inflame the public mind and have sought to turn the peculiar conditions to their advantage. . . . In the ultimate analysis, I fear the equal opportunity which is sought by many of those who proclaim the coming of so-called social justice involves a forced division of property, and that means socialism." Referring directly to Mr. Roosevelt and Governor Wilson, he said: "I do not say that the two gentlemen who now lead, the one the Democratic party and the other the former Republicans who have left their party, in their attacks upon existing conditions and in their attempt to satisfy the popular unrest by promises of remedies are consciously embracing socialism. The truth is that they do not offer any definite legislation or policy by which the happy conditions they promise are to be brought about; but if their promises mean anything they lead directly toward the appropriation of what belongs to one by another. The truth is, my friends, both those who have left the Republican party under the inspiration of their present leader and our old opponents, the Democrats, under their candidate, are going in a direction they do not definitely know and toward an end they cannot definitely describe, but with one chief and clear object, and that is, of acquiring power for their party by popular support through the promise of a change for the better. What they clamor for is a change. They ask for a change in the government so that the government may be restored to the people, as if this had not been a people's government since the beginning of the Constitution. I have the fullest sympathy with every reform in governmental and election machinery which shall facilitate the expression of the popular will, such as the short ballot and the reduction in the number of elective offices to make it possible. But these gentlemen propose to reform the government, whose present defects, if any, are due to the failure of the people to devote as much time as is necessary to their political duties, by requiring a political activity by the people three times that which thus far the people have been willing to assume; and thus their remedies instead of exciting the people to further interest and activity in the government will tire them into such an indifference as still further to remand control of public affairs to a minority."

After attacking Mr. Roosevelt's plan for the recall of judges and the provision in the Democratic platform forbidding the use of the writ of injunction, he declared that the Republican party stood for none of these innovations. "The Republican party," he said, "stands for the Constitution as it is, with such amendments adopted according to its provisions as new conditions thoroughly understood may require. We believe that it has stood the test of time, and that there have been disclosed no really serious defects in its operation." The President followed with a review of the work of his administration. He called attention to his efforts to bring about greater economy and efficiency in government offices, referred to the Panama Canal, reviewed foreign relations, declared for a steady increase in the navy and deplored the ill-advised policy proposed by the Democratic party of holding before the Philippine people independence as a prospect of the immediate future. He then defended the action of the Republican party on the tariff, declaring that the Payne-Aldrich bill had vindicated itself, as was shown by increased revenues and the restoration of prosperity. He declared that the policy of the Democratic party toward our great protected industries would postpone the coming of prosperity and tend to cause a recurrence of the hard times which the country suffered in the decade between 1890 and 1897.

The President denied that the high cost of living could be attributed in any degree to the Payne-Aldrich tariff law. He then discussed the anti-trust law. He defended the dissolution of the American Tobacco Company and the Standard Oil Company. He concluded as follows: "May we not hope that the great majority of voters will be able to distinguish between the substance of performance and the fustian of promise; that they may be able to see that those who would deliberately stir up discontent and create hostility toward those who are conducting legitimate business enterprises, and who represent the business progress of the country, are sowing dragons' teeth? Who are the people? They are not alone the unfortunate and the weak; they are the weak and the strong, the poor and the rich, and the many who are neither, the wage-earner and the capitalist, the farmer and the professional man, the merchant and the manufacturer, the storekeeper and the clerk, the railroad manager and the employee—they all make up the people and they all contribute to the running of the government and they have not any of them given into the hands of anyone the mandate to speak for them as peculiarly the people's representative. Especially does not he represent them who, assuming that the people are only the discontented, would stir them up against the remainder of those whose government alike this is? . . . So may we not expect in the issues which are now before us that the ballots cast in November shall show a prevailing majority in favor of sound progress, great prosperity upon a protective basis and under true constitutional and representative rule by the people?"

Mr. Sherman was officially notified of his nomination as Vice-President at Utica, N. Y., on August 21. The most important address made by Mr. Taft during the campaign was at Columbus, O., on August 29. This was chiefly a defense of his action on the tariff bills passed by Congress.

Vermont and Maine. Elections in Vermont and Maine early in September gave the first indication of the possible result on November 5. The vote in Vermont indicated that the Republican party had been practically cut in two. The election in Maine was not conclusive because the Progressives and Republicans had united in the support of State officers against the Democratic party. See Maine and Vermont.

Decision of Senator Cummins. Early in September, Senator Cummins of Iowa, who had up to that time adhered to the Republican presidential candidates, declared that he would not vote for President Taft. He issued a statement explaining his attitude, of which the following is a part:

"The renomination of President Taft was opposed by an overwhelming majority of the Republicans throughout the country simply because in his administration he had not done nor said the things which the great body of the people believed he should have done and said. . . . The reason the Republicans were so largely against the renomination of Mr. Taft was their profound conviction that he is not a Progressive, and does not believe, in a proper sense, that the people should rule the country. . . . Theodore Roosevelt was the manifest choice of the great number of Republicans who expressed a choice for president. He is appealing to the moral and progressive forces of the people and I expect to vote for him; but it must be understood that I will do so protesting against organization of a new party, and dissenting with some of the doctrines of his platform. My vote for him will indicate that I believe he desires to promote the common welfare, but will not indicate that I look upon the new party as a wise or enduring movement in public affairs."

Reorganization of the National Committee. On September 18 four members of the Republican national committee who favored Colonel Roosevelt for President were expelled from the committee and three others who were in favor of Mr. Roosevelt were allowed to resign. In each case the accusation was disloyalty to the party and President Taft. The four committeemen ousted were Russ Avery of California, Borden D. Whiting of New Jersey, Richmond Pearson of North Carolina, and William S. Edwards of West Virginia. The three whose resignations were accepted were G. C. Priestly of Oklahoma, Walter F. Brown of Ohio, and J. A. Casewell of Minnesota. This action was taken at a meeting of the committee held in New York City. The places thus made vacant were filled by committeemen favorable to President Taft.

Statement of the President. In the latter part of September President Taft issued a long statement treating the issues of the campaign. He defended the protective tariff, while calling for revision to keep prices from being exorbitant. He opposed the third party plan for trust regulation, discussed the monetary problem, the Nicaraguan situation, the recall, immigration, etc. He declared that suffrage for women was an issue to be decided by the States. In an address delivered at Beverley on September 28 he attacked the Democratic tariff programme and the third party, which he declared to have split off from the Republican party, "not for any one principle, or indeed for any principle at all, but merely to gratify personal ambition and vengeance." He attacked the Progressive platform as a "crazy quilt" and stated that the movement would collapse if its standard bearer should be removed. He declared that there was not the slightest chance for the success of the third party.

Death of Mr. Sherman. Vice-President

Sherman died suddenly at Utica, N. Y., on October 30. He had been ill for several years. No effort was made to fill his place on the Republican ticket.

The last few weeks of the campaign were marked with an increase of confidence among the Republican leaders, and President Taft just prior to the election issued a statement asserting his confidence that he would be elected.

POST-CONVENTION CAMPAIGN, PROGRESSIVE

ORGANIZATION. The Progressive party lost no time in effecting its organization after the nomination of Mr. Roosevelt on August 7. Senator Dixon remained in charge of the campaign as chairman of the national committee. In general the organization of the new party was based on that of the regular Republican party, with State, congressional, and county committees. Elon H. Hooker of New York was made national treasurer and general appeals for funds were circulated throughout the country.

BEGINNING OF THE CAMPAIGN. On August 16 Mr. Roosevelt began a series of campaign speeches at Providence, R. I. In these addresses he attacked the bosses and denounced both the old parties. In the course of remarks upon the tariff he referred to reports that the present schedule relating to cotton goods had been written by Senator Lippitt of Rhode Island, a cotton manufacturer. In the course of these remarks he said:

"If the Democratic platform were carried out in good faith the factories would have to close altogether, for that proposal is to prevent Mr. Lippitt from prospering by the simple process of preventing everyone from prospering. The Republican proposal is only to give prosperity to the Mr. Lippitts and then to let it trickle down according as they may condescend to permit such trickling. Our proposal is to keep the factories open, to see that the Mr. Lippitts receive full justice, and to see also that they do justice as well as get it: that they do justice to the wage workers whom they employ and to the customers whom they serve, and make their own profits only as an incident of thus rendering service to the advantage of the public as a whole."

Mr. Roosevelt made four speeches in Boston. In these he referred particularly to the tariff paragraph of the platform of the Progressive party. He declared that Mr. Perkins and Mr. Flinn had come to him declaring that they desired to support a movement for improving the relations of capital and labor in order that the country might be a good place for their children.

ATTACKS BY SENATOR LA FOLLETTE. In the early part of July, before the Progressive convention, Senator La Follette published a long article in which he severely attacked Mr. Roosevelt. He declared that the latter at Chicago was backed by money derived from the stock-watering operations of the Steel Trust and the Harvester Trust, and that previous to the convention the money obtained from these trusts had been spent in organizing fake contests as to nearly 200 delegates in order to control the convention and secure Roosevelt's nomination. He declared that Mr. Roosevelt had the power, had he so wished to have nominated a real Progressive, such as Governor Hadley of Missouri, but, he added, "He would have no one but himself. He was there to force his own nomination or to smash the convention. He was not there to preserve the integrity of the Republican party and make it an instrument for the promotion of progressive principles and the restoration of government to the people. He gagged his followers in the convention without putting on record any facts upon which the public could base a definite and intelligent judgment regarding the validity of Taft's nomination. He submitted no suggestions as to a platform of progressive principles. He clamored loudly for purging the convention roll of tainted delegates without purging his own candidacy of his tainted contests and his tainted trust support. He offered no reason for a third party except his own overmastering craving for a third term."

Senator La Follette continued his attacks on Mr. Roosevelt throughout the campaign. In *La Follette's Magazine* he made repeated accusations against Mr. Roosevelt, in which he charged him with double dealing in his relations with trusts and in connection with his candidacy for the presidency. In the Senate on August 17 he announced his allegiance to the Republican party and again bitterly attacked Mr. Roosevelt. He declared that during the latter's administrations the trusts were increased from 140 to 1020. Mr. Roosevelt treated these attacks as the outcome of personal feeling against him on the part of Senator La Follette.

MR. ROOSEVELT'S SPEECHES. Mr. Roosevelt took part in the campaign in Vermont and on September 2 started west for a month's tour of the Pacific Coast and the Western States.

On September 9 he addressed 5000 women voters in Spokane, Wash. He announced that he had become a suffragist through association with women who had advocated woman suffrage. A number of regular Republican speakers, including John N. Harlan of Chicago, J. Adam Bede, former congressman from Minnesota, and others, followed Mr. Roosevelt through Idaho, Utah, Nevada, California, and Colorado, seeking to counteract the effect of his speeches in those States.

On September 17, at Tucson, Ariz., Mr. Roosevelt announced that if reëlected President he would make Washington a model city for other municipalities to copy. He declared that if elected he would call an extra session of Congress "to be devoted exclusively to putting into federal law every provision recommended in the plank dealing with social and industrial justice." At Denver on October 17 he declared for the recall of Presidents for misconduct or inefficiency. "Third term talk which refers to a nonconsecutive terms is an utter absurdity," he said.

Early in October, after his return from the West, he made a tour through the South, including the States of Missouri, Oklahoma, Arkansas, Louisiana, and Georgia. In Atlanta on September 28 he charged Governor Wilson with making misstatements as to his position on the question of trusts. After this tour he went directly to New York.

In his addresses and interviews during this period Mr. Roosevelt showed that he felt keenly the assertions of Governor Wilson as to his attitude on trusts, tariff, and other matters.

CONTROVERSY WITH GOVERNOR DENEEN. He engaged in a controversy with Governor Deneen of Illinois. The latter who, as noted above, had refused to join the third party movement and had come out in support of President Taft in Ohio, asserted that Mr. Roosevelt's attitude toward the stolen contests was largely insincere. He declared that Mr. Roosevelt had told him (Governor Deneen) that there were only thirty-four serious contests in the Chicago convention. Mr. Roosevelt denounced this assertion as an absolute falsehood and attacked Governor Deneen for double dealing in the Chicago convention.

SHOOTING OF MR. ROOSEVELT. On October 14, while he was on his way to deliver an address, Mr. Roosevelt was shot in front of his hotel in Milwaukee by one John Schrank, who was well known in certain circles in New York City and was believed to be mentally unbalanced. Mr. Roosevelt had just entered his automobile and was bowing in response to the cheers of the people around him when the bullet, fired at close range, struck him in the breast. Elbert H. Martin, one of Mr. Roosevelt's stenographers, who was with him, seized Schrank and prevented him from firing a second shot. In spite of the efforts of those about him to have him go at once to a hospital, Mr. Roosevelt insisted on proceeding to the hall in which the address was to have been delivered. He was able to appear on the platform, and when he announced that he had narrowly escaped assassination and displayed sheets of manuscript through which the bullet had penetrated, there was wild excitement. Mr. Roosevelt succeeded in delivering the greater part of the address which he had intended to make. Following this he was taken to the Mercy Hospital in Chicago, where he remained until October 21, when he was taken to his home in New York, fully recovered.

This deplorable incident halted the campaign for a time. Governor Wilson, who was the only active opponent to Mr. Roosevelt, decided to cancel his campaign engagements as far as possible, and did so. Mr. Bryan, who was campaigning for Governor Wilson in Indiana, declared that, while he had the greatest sympathy for Mr. Roosevelt, personal feeling should not determine the conduct of a great campaign. With this statement Mr. Roosevelt agreed.

CONTINUATION OF THE CAMPAIGN. The principal engagements made by Mr. Roosevelt were now filled by Albert J. Beveridge, Progressive candidate for governor of Indiana and former senator from that State. Governor Johnson of California transferred his campaign activities from the Western to the Eastern States and became in a measure the spokesman of Mr. Roosevelt. On October 30 Mr. Roosevelt was so far recovered as to be able to address a great meeting in Madison Square Garden in New York. A great demonstration of cheering took place at this meeting. He appeared also at a second meeting a few days later. In each of these meetings he made addresses which constituted his final message to the Progressives before election. He declared that even though the party might be defeated, it had won a moral victory. Just before the election Senator Dixon issued a statement in which he expressed his conviction that Mr. Roosevelt would be elected.

POST-CONVENTION CAMPAIGN, DEMOCRATIC

ORGANIZATION. At the suggestion of Governor Wilson a system for carrying on the Democratic campaign was devised which in many ways differed from the procedure which had marked previous campaigns. Instead of the usual custom of having the campaign conducted by the national committee as a whole, with its chairman and secretary as actual directors, a board of directors as an ordinary corporation was formed, with William F. McCombs as chairman. A directorate was created, half of whom were members of the national committee. On all questions except those on which the candidate had a pronounced opinion a majority vote of the committee was final. There were no subcommittees to divide authority or responsibility. At a meeting of the national committee in Chicago on July 15 this plan was adopted. Joseph E. Davies of Wisconsin was appointed secretary, and Rolla Wells, formerly mayor of St. Louis, treasurer. Other members of this directing committee were Senator O'Gorman of New York, Senator Gore of Oklahoma, Congressman Albert S. Burleson of Texas, Congressman Robert S. Hudspeth of New Jersey, Josephus Daniels of North Carolina, Congressman A. Mitchell Palmer of Pennsylvania, and William G. McAdoo of New York.

GOVERNOR WILSON'S SPEECH OF ACCEPTANCE. The official notification to Governor Wilson of his nomination was made at Sea Girt, N. J., on August 7. The address of notification was made by Ollie M. James of Kentucky. Mr. Wilson, after expressing his appreciation of the nomination and declaring that he accepted it with a deep sense of its unusual significance, made an address which may be summarized as follows:

He declared that the nation was awakened and had become impatient of partisan make-believe, and that it was never more susceptible to unselfish appeals and to the high arguments of sincere justice. He said that the country stood face to face not with questions of party or with contest for office, but with great questions of right and of justice. "The forces of nature," he said, "are asserting themselves against every form of special privilege and private control, and are seeking bigger things than they have ever heretofore achieved. They are sweeping away what is unrighteous in order to vindicate once more the essential rights of human life." "There are," he said, "two great things to do. One is to set up the rule of justice and of right in such matters as the tariff, the regulation of the trusts and the prevention of monopoly, the adaptation of our banking and currency laws to the various uses to which our people must put them, the treatment of those who do the daily labor in our factories and mines and throughout all our great industrial and commercial undertakings, and the political life of the people of the Philippines, for whom we hold governmental power in trust, for their service, not our own. The other, the additional duty, is the great task of protecting our people and our resources and of keeping open to the whole people the doors of opportunity through which they must, generation by generation, pass if they are to make conquests of their fortunes in health, freedom, in peace, and in contentment." Speaking then of the tariff, he said: "The tariff question as dealt with in our time, at any rate, has not been business. It has been politics. Tariff schedules have been made up for the purpose of keeping as large a number as possible of the rich and influential manufacturers of the country in good humor with the Republican party, which desired their constant financial support. The tariff has become a system of favors, which the phraseology of the schedule was often deliberately contrived to conceal. . . . Our own clear conviction as Democrats is that in the last analysis the only safe and legitimate object of tariff duties, as of taxes of every other kind, is to raise revenue for the support of the government. We denounce the Payne-Aldrich tariff act as the most conspicuous example ever afforded the country of the special favors and monopolistic advantages which the leaders of the Republican party have so often

SENATOR JOSEPH DIXON

GOVERNOR HIRAM JOHNSON

SENATOR ALBERT S. BEVERIDGE

G. W. PERKINS

FOUR MEN PROMINENT IN THE PROGRESSIVE CAMPAIGN, 1912

shown themselves willing to extend to those to whom they looked for campaign contributions. . . . There should be an immediate revision and it should be downward, unhesitatingly and steadily downward. It should begin with the schedules which have been most obviously used to kill competition and to raise prices in the United States, arbitrarily and without regard to the prices pertaining elsewhere in the markets of the world; and it should, before it is finished or intermitted, be extended to every item in every schedule which affords any opportunity for monopoly, for special advantage to limited groups of beneficiaries, or for subsidized control of any kind in the markets or the enterprises of the country; until special favors of every sort shall have been absolutely withdrawn and every part of our laws of taxation shall have been transformed from a system of governmental patronage into a system of just and reasonable charges which shall fall where they will create the least burden. When we shall have done that, we can fix questions of revenue and of business adjustment in a new spirit and with clear minds." Referring to the Republican claim of prosperity throughout the country, he declared that although wages had increased the majority of the people were poorer, and that while the nation had grown immensely rich and was growing richer, the majority of the people continued to grow poorer, even though wages were slowly increasing. He said that prices were not fixed by the competition of the market or by the law of supply and demand, but by private arrangements, and that the high cost of living is arranged by private understanding. He then passed to a consideration of the trusts. After declaring that the period of infant industries had passed, he said: "I am not one of those who think that competition can be established by law against the drift of a world-wide economic tendency. Neither am I one of those who believe that business done upon a great scale by a single organization—call it corporation or what you will—is necessarily dangerous to the liberties, even the economic liberties, of a great people like our own, full of intelligence and of indomitable energy. I am not afraid of anything that is normal. I dare say that we shall never return to the old order of individual competition, and that the organization of business upon a great scale of co-operation is, up to a certain point, both normal and inevitable. . . . Big business is not dangerous because it is big, but because its bigness is an unwholesome inflation created by privileges and exemptions which it ought not to enjoy." He said that the general terms of the anti-trust law, forbidding combinations in restraint of trade, had apparently proved ineffectual, inasmuch as under its ban trusts have grown up very luxuriantly and have established virtual monopolies without serious let or hindrance. He said that the problem and the difficulty were much greater than were provided for by existing laws. In addition to great trusts and combinations, there are, he asserted, vast confederacies of banks, railways, express companies, insurance companies, manufacturing corporations, mining corporations, power and development companies, all bound together by the fact that the ownership of their stock and the members of their boards of directors are controlled and determined by comparatively small and closely interrelated groups of persons who could control both credit and enterprise. The existence of such combinations, he declared, gives rise to the suspicion of a "money trust," a concentration of the control of credit which may at any time become infinitely dangerous to free enterprise. He declared that means must be devised to prevent this, and that laws must be passed to safeguard the welfare of the working people, who are the backbone of the nation. He followed this with the declaration that the Philippines are held merely in trust for the people who live in them and that it is our duty as trustees to make whatever arrangement of government will be most serviceable to their freedom and development. He dwelt upon the necessity of husbanding natural resources and the development of merchant marine for carrying American goods. He pointed out the provision of the Democratic platform relating to the duty of the government in promoting agricultural, industrial, and vocational education in every way possible within its constitutional powers. No other platform, he said, had given this intimate vision of the party's duty. Concluding, he said: "What is our cause? The people's cause. That is easy to say, but what does it mean? The common as against any particular interest whatever? Yes, but that, too, needs translation into acts and policies. We represent the desire to set up an unentangled government, a government that cannot be used for private purposes, either in the field of business or in the field of politics; a government that will not tolerate the use of a great organization of a great party to serve the personal aims and ambitions of any individual, and that will not permit legislation to be employed to further any private interest. . . . I could not have accepted a nomination which left me bound to any man or group of men. No man can be just who is not free; and no man who has to show favors ought to undertake the solemn responsibility of government in any rank or post whatever, least of all in the supreme post of President of the United States. . . . Should I be intrusted with the great office of President I would seek counsel wherever it could be had upon free terms. I know the temper of the great convention which nominated me; I know the temper of the country that lay back of that convention and spoke through it. I heed with deep thankfulness the message you bring me from it. I feel that I am surrounded by men whose principles and ambitions are those of true servants of the people. I thank God and will take courage."

GOVERNOR WILSON'S CAMPAIGN. Governor Wilson began his campaign in the middle of August, and on August 15 addressed 2500 farmers of New Jersey. His remarks were devoted largely to the tariff. He declared that the present tariff was one of the greatest impositions upon the farmer that had ever been devised. He charged that the President's veto of the steel tariff bill had affected the cost of the farmers' tools. He said that business enterprises should stand on their own bottoms and not be propped by taxes which all were compelled to pay. He spoke of the protective tariff as a great dam running around all our coasts. He said:

"I would prefer to call it the restrictive tariff. I would prefer to call it the tariff that holds us back. I should prefer to call it the tariff that hems us in, the tariff that chokes us, the tariff that smothers us, because the great unhatched energy of America is now waiting for a field greater than America itself in which to prove that Americans can take care of themselves. . . . You people own a big house, but you have let the other fellow live in it. It is time to turn him out. What I modestly suggest is that you proceed to break into your own house and live in it. The tenants who have lived in it a long time have been making you pay the rent instead of paying rent to you. You have paid the money that enabled them to live in your own home and dominate your own premises. Turn them out."

He spoke to an assemblage of farmers in Pennsylvania in the same month. In this address he attacked the tariff and defended the tariff bills which had been vetoed by President Taft. In response to criticisms which had been made on portions of his writings in relation to immigration, he expressed himself as in favor of "as liberal unrestricted immigration as any man with common sense and with love for America could desire," but was opposed to immigration stimulated in an unnatural way.

NEW JERSEY PRIMARY. The New Jersey primary held on September 24 was noted with interest throughout the country on account of the candidacy of former Senator James Smith of the United States Senate as a Democrat. Mr. Smith was strongly opposed by Governor Wilson, whose controversy with him in the autumn of 1910 resulted in the defeat of Mr. Smith and the election of Senator Martine, who had received a majority of votes in the senatorial primary held in 1910. A notable feature of the primary was the small total of the votes cast. The Democratic primary vote on the preferential ballot for United States senator was less than 30 per cent. of the vote cast for Woodrow Wilson as governor in 1910. In spite of the smallness of the vote, however, the defeat of Mr. Smith was emphatic. His opponent, William Hughes, was nominated by a plurality of about 25,000 in a total vote of about 76,000. Other details of the election will be found in the article NEW JERSEY. In the same week a primary election was held in Massachusetts, and, as in the case of New Jersey, there was a marked falling off from that cast at the previous primary election. The total primary vote was less than half the vote for governor cast in 1911. While it did not differ materially from the vote cast at the preferential primary in April, the Democratic vote rose from about 28,000 in April to about 99,000 in September, while the Republican vote fell from about 172,000 in April to about 97,000 in September. Further details will be found in the article MASSACHUSETTS.

FURTHER SPEECHES OF GOVERNOR WILSON. Governor Wilson made an address on September 9 in New York City. In this he attacked the attitude of both Republican and Progressive platforms toward the tariff. During a visit to Syracuse, N. Y., at the State Fair on September 12, an effort was made by Charles F. Murphy of Tammany Hall to make political capital out of Governor Wilson's presence in company with Governor Dix. Governor Wilson issued a statement announcing that his visit was without political significance. On September 15 he started on a tour of the Western States, including Iowa, South Dakota, Minnesota, Wisconsin, Illinois, and Michigan. The addresses delivered in these States were largely given up to explanations of his attitude on the tariff and the regulation of trusts and to attacks on the positions of Mr. Roosevelt and President Taft on these questions. In Ohio he was greeted by Governor Harmon and with him opened the State campaign in Columbus. In speeches delivered in Minneapolis and Detroit, he attacked the bosses in politics. After his return from this tour an attempt was made by Democratic leaders in New York to identify him with factional disputes in the party. He refused to take sides in this issue. In the early part of October he made another tour in the West. Speaking at Pueblo, Col., on October 7, he attacked Mr. Roosevelt's record in the prosecution of the steel corporation, and made the charge that the latter's campaign had the support of this corporation. His attacks during this tour were directed more emphatically against Mr. Roosevelt than President Taft, and Mr. Roosevelt replied to these sharply.

On Columbus Day, October 12, Governor Wilson made an address in New York City. This was devoted chiefly to the part played in America by Italian immigrants, and was designed to offset criticisms made against his former writings criticising immigration from southern Italy. An address made at Pittsburgh on October 18 was devoted chiefly to an explanation of his attitude on the tariff.

Following the shooting of Mr. Roosevelt, Governor Wilson made few addresses in accordance with his desire that no advantage be taken of this occurrence. The last address of the campaign was delivered at Madison Square Garden. It was greeted with a remarkable demonstration which lasted over an hour.

MR. BRYAN'S PARTICIPATION IN THE CAMPAIGN. Mr. Bryan took an active part in the campaign for the election of Governor Wilson. His original plan was to follow up Mr. Roosevelt in the various States and answer his assertions and arguments. This, however, was abandoned. His speeches were devoted chiefly to an attack on the third term proposal and Mr. Roosevelt's attitude on the regulation of trusts and the tariff.

THE ELECTION

Detailed results of the election on November 5 are shown in the table on page 577. An analysis of this vote shows many interesting and several surprising facts. The total popular vote of all candidates was 14,045,292. This was hardly more than the total popular vote in the election of 1908, which was 14,888,442, and this in spite of the fact that the population of the country had greatly increased in the four-year period. Even greater significance is seen in the number of votes cast in 1912, when it is noted that according to the Thirteenth Census taken in 1910 the number of males of voting age in the continental United States was 26,999,151. According to these figures, therefore, nearly half the voting population did not vote in the election of 1912.

The votes for President Taft and Mr. Roosevelt showed that the Republican party was divided into two fairly equal parts and that the combined vote of President Taft and Mr. Roosevelt exceeded the vote of Mr. Wilson by 1,410,682. It may also be noted that the vote for Governor Wilson was less than that cast for Mr. Bryan in 1908. Mr. Bryan's vote was 6,328,601. The total vote cast for President Taft in 1908 was 7,811,143, which was greater than the combined vote cast for President Taft and Mr. Roosevelt in 1912. The electoral vote cast for Mr. Wilson, however, was greater than that cast for President Taft in 1908, which was 321. The electoral vote for Governor Wilson in 1912 was 435.

It will be noted from this table that the only States carried by President Taft were Utah and Vermont, with eight electoral votes. Mr. Roosevelt carried the electoral votes of the States of California, Michigan, Minnesota, Pennsylvania, South Dakota, and Washington, with 88 electoral votes. In addition to carrying two States, President Taft ran second in 15 other States. Mr. Roosevelt ran second in 26 States. The contest in several of the States was so close that an official count was required. This was true of California and Idaho. President Taft was defeated in his own State of Ohio, although he received more votes than Mr. Roosevelt.

Governors were elected in 35 States, in 21 of which the Democrats were successful. For details of these elections see the articles on the STATES.

As a result of the election the 63d Congress will be composed of 291 Democrats and 144 Republicans. One of the notable features of the election was the increase in the Socialist vote.

POPULAR AND ELECTORAL VOTE FOR PRESIDENT IN 1912

States	Popular Vote: Wilson, Dem.	Taft, Rep.	Roosevelt, Prog.	Debs, Soc.	Chafin, Proh.	Reimer, Soc. L.		Plurality	Electoral Vote: Wilson, D.	Taft, R.	Roosevelt, P.
Alabama ...	82,439	9,731	22,689	3,029	....	....	....	59,750 D	12	...	...
Arizona	10,324	3,021	6,949	3,163	265	....	....	3,375 D	3	...	...
Arkansas ...	68,838	24,297	22,673	8,153	898	....	....	44,541 D	9	...	...
California ..	283,436	3,914	283,610	79,201	23,366	....	....	174 P	2	...	11
Colorado ...	114,223	58,386	72,306	16,418	5,063	475	....	41,917 D	6	...	...
Connecticut .	74,561	68,324	34,129	10,056	2,068	1,260	....	6,237 D	7	...	...
Delaware ...	22,631	15,998	8,886	556	623	....	....	6,631 D	3	...	...
Florida	36,416	4,279	4,535	4,806	1,854	....	....	31,611 D	6	...	...
Georgia	93,171	5,190	22,010	1,014	147	....	....	71,161 D	14	...	...
Idaho	33,921	32,810	25,530	11,942	....	....	....	1,111 D	4	...	...
Illinois	405,048	253,613	386,478	81,278	15,710	4,066	....	18,570 D	29	...	...
Indiana	281,890	151,267	162,007	36,931	19,249	3,130	....	119,883 D	15	...	...
Iowa	185,376	119,811	161,783	16,967	8,440	....	....	23,593 D	13	...	...
Kansas	143,670	74,844	120,123	26,807	....	....	....	23,047 D	10	...	...
Kentucky ..	219,584	115,512	102,766	11,647	3,233	956	....	104,072 D	13	...	...
Louisiana ..	61,035	3,834	9,323	5,192	....	....	....	51,637 D	10	...	...
Maine	51,113	26,545	48,493	2,541	945	....	....	2,660 D	6	...	...
Maryland ...	112,674	54,956	57,786	3,996	2,244	322	....	54,888 D	8	...	...
Massac's'tts .	173,408	155,948	142,228	12,616	2,754	1,102	....	17,460 D	18	...	...
Michigan ...	150,751	152,244	219,012	23,216	8,934	1,252	....	62,340 P	...	...	15
Minnesota ..	106,426	64,344	125,856	27,505	7,886	2,212	....	19,430 P	...	...	12
Mississippi .	57,227	1,595	3,645	2,017	....	....	....	53,537 D	10	...	...
Missouri ...	330,947	207,491	123,111	28,466	5,380	1,778	....	122,925 D	18	...	...
Montana	28,230	18,404	22,448	10,828	....	....	....	5,782 D	4	...	...
Nebraska ...	108,109	34,216	72,678	10,219	3,419	....	....	36,333 D	8	...	...
Nevada	7,986	3,190	5,605	3,263	....	....	....	2,381 D	3	...	...
New Hamp..	34,724	32,927	17,794	1,981	535	....	....	2,097 D	4	...	...
New Jersey..	178,289	88,835	145,410	15,801	2,878	1,321	....	32,879 D	14	...	...
New Mexico.	20,437	17,733	8,347	2,859	....	....	....	2,704 D	3	...	...
New York...	655,475	455,428	390,021	63,381	19,427	4,251	....	200,047 D	45	...	...
N. Carolina .	144,507	29,139	69,130	1,025	117	....	....	75,377 D	12	...	...
N. Dakota ..	29,516	22,802	25,629	6,966	1,243	....	....	3,829 D	5	...	...
Ohio	423,152	277,066	229,327	89,930	11,459	2,623	....	146,086 D	24	...	...
Oklahoma ..	119,156	90,786	....	42,262	2,185	....	....	28,370 D	10	...	...
Oregon	47,064	34,673	37,600	13,343	4,360	....	....	9,464 D	5	...	...
Penna.	395,619	273,305	447,426	83,164	19,533	704	....	51,807 P	...	...	38
Rhode Id. ...	30,142	27,703	16,878	2,049	616	236	....	2,709 D	5	...	...
S. Carolina .	48,355	536	1,293	164	....	....	....	47,062 D	9	...	...
S. Dakota ..	48,942	....	58,811	4,662	3,910	....	....	9,869 P	...	...	5
Tennessee ..	135,399	60,634	53,986	3,493	825	....	....	70,891 D	12	...	...
Texas	221,589	28,853	26,755	25,743	1,738	442	....	192,736 D	20	...	...
Utah	36,579	42,100	24,174	9,023	....	....	....	5,521 R	...	4	...
Vermont	15,350	23,305	22,070	928	1,154	....	....	1,235 R	...	4	...
Virginia	90,332	23,288	21,777	820	709	50	....	67,044 D	12	...	...
Washington.	86,840	70,445	113,698	40,134	9,810	1,872	....	26,858 P	...	...	7
West Virgin.	113,197	56,754	79,112	15,248	4,517	....	....	34,085 D	8	...	...
Wisconsin ..	164,409	130,878	58,661	34,168	8,467	698	....	33,531 D	13	...	...
Wyoming ..	15,310	14,560	9,232	2,760	434	....	....	750 D	3	...	...
Total ..	6,293,857	3,484,960	4,124,579	901,725	206,395	28,750	....	....	435	8	88

Popular Vote, Wilson over Roosevelt 2,174,278
Popular Vote, all others combined, over Wilson 2,447,578
Electoral Vote, Wilson over Taft and Roosevelt 339
Total Popular Vote, all candidates 15,045,292

The above was compiled from the highest vote received by the electors.

This vote almost doubled in the four years from 1908. The vote for Debs in the latter year was 448,453. The Prohibition vote decreased in 1912. In 1908 it was 241,252. The Socialist Labor vote increased slightly in 1912. In 1908 it was 15,421.

AFTER THE ELECTION. While the Progressive party was defeated in the election, the organization was continued and steps were taken to make it permanent. On November 19 Mr. Roosevelt made an address in New York in which he advised against all combination or fusion with other parties. On December 10 a national conference of members of the party was held in Chicago. At this were present over 1500 persons, representing every State in the Union. Plans were promoted for the national organization and for publicity. National headquarters were established in New York and Washington. A legislative reference bureau was created to be under the direction of experts, and a committee of seven was authorized to visit Europe and study the operation of social laws in European countries.

Leaders of the Republican party took definite steps toward reorganization, and on December 7, Republican governors from twelve States who had been in attendance at the conference of governors, held a consultation in Washington. The principal subject of discussion was the advisability of calling a meeting of the Republican national committee with a view to calling, prior to the congressional campaign in 1914, a national convention of the party for the purpose of agreeing upon a platform upon which both the Progressives and Conservatives could unite.

PARTY PLATFORMS

In the following pages are given in full the platforms of the parties, adopted at their national conventions in 1912:

DEMOCRATIC

We, the representatives of the Democratic party of the United States in national convention assemled, reaffirm our devotion to the principles of Democratic government formulated by Thomas Jefferson and enforced by a long and illustrious line of Democratic Presidents.

Tariff Reform. We declare it to be a fundamental principle of the Democratic party that the federal government under the Constitution has no right or power to impose or collect tariff duties except for the purpose of revenue, and we demand that the collection of such taxes shall be limited to the necessities of government honestl; and economically administered.

The high Republican tariff is the principal cause of the unequal distribution of wealth; it is a system of taxation which makes the rich richer and the poor poorer; under its operations the American farmer and laboring man are the chief sufferers; it raises the cost of the necessaries of life to them but does not protect their product or wages. The farmer sells largely in free markets and buys almost entirely in the protected markets. In the most highly protected industries such as cotton and wool, steel and iron, the wages of the laborers are the lowest paid in any of our industries. We denounce the Republican pretense on that subject and assert that American wages are established by competitive conditions and not by the tariff.

We favor the immediate downward revision of the existing high and, in many cases, prohibitive tariff duties, insisting that material reductions be speedily made upon the necessaries of life. Articles entering into competition with trust-controlled products and articles of American manufacture which are sold abroad more cheaply than at home should be put upon the free list.

We recognize that our system of tariff taxation is intimately connected with the business of the country and we favor the ultimate attainment of the principles we advocate by legislation that will not injure or destroy legitimate industry.

We denounce the action of President Taft in vetoing the bills to reduce the tariff in the cotton, woolen, metals, and chemical schedules and the farmers' free list bill, all of which were designed to give immediate relief to the masses from the exactions of the trusts.

The Republican party, while promising tariff revision, has shown by its tariff legislation that such revision is not to be in the people's interest, and having been faithless to its pledges of 1908 it should no longer enjoy the confidence of the nation. We appeal to the American people to support us in our demand for a tariff for revenue only.

High Cost of Living. The high cost of living is a serious problem in every American home. The Republican party in its platform attempts to escape from responsibility for present conditions by denying that they are due to a protective tariff. We take issue with them on this subject and charge that excessive prices result in a large measure from the high tariff laws enacted and maintained by the Republican party and from trusts and commercial conspiracies fostered and encouraged by such laws, and we assert that no such substantial relief can be secured for the people until import duties on the necessaries of life are materially reduced and these criminal conspiracies broken up.

Anti-Trust Law. A private monopoly is indefensible and intolerable. We therefore favor the vigorous enforcement of the criminal as well as the civil law against trusts and trust officials and demand the enactment of such additional legislation as may be necessary to make it impossible for a private monopoly to exist in the United States.

We favor the declaration by law of the conditions upon which corporations shall be permitted to engage in interstate trade, including among others the prevention of holding companies, of interlocking directorates, of stock watering, of discrimination in price, and the control by any one corporation of so large a proportion of any industry as to make it a menace to competitive conditions.

We condemn the action of the Republican administration in compromising with the Standard Oil Company and the tobacco trust and its failure to invoke the criminal provisions of the anti-trust law against the officers of those corporations after the court had declared that from the undisputed facts in the record they had violated the criminal provisions of the law.

We regret that the Sherman anti-trust law has received a judicial construction depriving it of much of its efficiency and we favor the enactment of legislation which will restore to the statute the strength of which it has been deprived by such interpretation.

Rights of the State. We believe in the preservation and maintenance in their full strength and integrity of the three co-ordinate branches of the federal government—the executive, the legislative, and the judicial—each keeping within its own bounds and not encroaching upon the just powers of either of the others.

Believing that the most efficient results under our system of government are to be attained by the full exercise by the States of their reserved sovereign powers, we denounce as usurpation the efforts of our opponents to deprive the States of any of the rights reserved to them and to enlarge and magnify by indirection the powers of the federal government.

We insist upon the full exercise of all the powers of government, both State and national, to protect the people from injustice at the hands of those who seek to make the government a private asset in business. There is no twilight zone between the nation and the State in which exploiting interests can take refuge from both. It is as necessary that the federal government shall exercise the powers delegated to it as it is that the States shall exercise the powers reserved to them, but we insist that federal remedies for the regulation of interstate commerce and for the prevention of private monopoly shall be added to and not substituted for State remedies.

Income Tax and Popular Election of Senators. We congratulate the country upon the triumph of two important reforms demanded in the last national platform, namely, the amendment of the federal Constitution authorizing an income tax and the amendment providing for the popular election of senators, and we call upon the people of all the States to rally to the support of the pending propositions and secure their ratification.

We note with gratification the unanimous sentiment in favor of publicity before the election of campaign contributions—a measure demanded in our national platform of 1908 and at that time opposed by the Republican party—and we commend the Democratic House of Representatives for extending the doctrine of publicity to recommendations, verbal and written, upon which presidential appointments are made, to the ownership and control of newspapers and to the expenditures made by and in behalf of those who aspire to presidential nominations, and we point for additional justification for this legislation to the enormous expenditures of money in behalf of the President and his predecessor in the recent contest for the Republican nomination for President.

Presidential Primaries. The movement toward more popular government should be promoted through legislation in each State which will permit the expression of the preference of the electors for national candidates at presidential primaries.

We direct that the national committee incorporate in the call for the next nominating convention a requirement that all expressions of preference for presidential candidates shall be given and the selection of delegates and alternates made through a primary election conducted by the party organization in each State where such expression and election are not provided for by State law. Committeemen who are hereafter to constitute the membership of the Democratic national committee and whose election is not provided for by law shall be chosen in each State at such primary elections, and the service and authority of committeemen, however chosen, shall begin immediately upon the receipt of their credentials respectively.

Campaign Contributions. We pledge the Democratic party to the enactment of a law prohibiting any corporation from contributing to a campaign fund and any individual from contributing any amount above a reasonable maximum.

Term of President. We favor a single presidential term, and to that end urge the adoption of an amendment to the Constitution making the President of the United States ineligible to reelection, and we pledge the candidate of this convention to this principle.

Democratic Congress. At this time, when the Republican party, after a generation of unlimited power in its control of the federal government, is rent into factions, it is opportune to point to the record of accomplishment of the Democratic House of Representatives in the Sixty-second Congress. We indorse its action and we challenge comparison of its record with that of any Congress which has been controlled by our opponents. We call the attention of the partriotic citizens of our country to its record of efficiency, economy, and constructive legislation.

It has among other achievements revised the rules of the House of Representatives so as to give to the representatives of the American people freedom of speech and of action in advocating, proposing, and perfecting remedial legislation.

It has passed bills for the relief of the people and the development of our country; it has endeavored to revise the tariff taxes downward in the interest of the consuming masses and thus to reduce the high cost of living.

It has proposed an amendment to the federal Constitution providing for the election of United States senators by the direct vote of the people.

It has secured the admission of Arizona and New Mexico as two sovereign States.

It has required the publicity of campaign expenses both before and after election and fixed a limit upon the election expenses of United States senators and representatives.

It has passed a bill to prevent the abuse of the writ of injunction. It has passed a law establishing an eight-hour day for workmen on all national public work.

It has passed a resolution which forced the President to take immediate steps to abrogate the Russian treaty.

And it has passed the great supply bills which lessen waste and extravagance and which reduce the annual expenses of the government by many millions of dollars.

We approve the measure reported by the Democratic leaders in the House of Representatives for the creation of a council of national defense which will determine a definite naval programme with a view to increased efficiency and economy. The party that proclaimed and has always enforced the Monroe Doctrine, and was sponsor for the new navy, will continue faithfully to observe the constitutional requirements to provide and maintain an adequate and well proportioned navy sufficient to defend American policies, protect our citizens and uphold the honor and dignity of the nation.

Republican Extravagance. We denounce the profligate waste of the money wrung from the people by oppressive taxation through the lavish appropriations of recent Republican Congresses, which have kept taxes high and reduced the purchasing power of the people's toil. We demand a return to that simplicity and economy which befit a democratic government, and a reduction in the number of useless offices, the salaries of which drain the substance of the people.

Railroads, Express Companies, Telegraph and Telephone Lines. We favor the efficient supervision and rate regulation of railroads, express companies, telegraph and telephone lines engaged in interstate commerce. To this end we recommend the valuation of railroads, express companies, telegraph and telephone lines by the interstate commerce commission, such valuation to take into consideration the physical value of the property, the original cost, the cost of the production, and any element of the value that will render the valuation fair and just.

We favor such legislation as will effectually prohibit the railroads, express, telegraph, and telephone companies from engaging in business which brings them into competition with their shippers or patrons, also legislation preventing the overissue of stocks and bonds by interstate railroads, express companies, telegraph, and telephone lines, and legislation which will assure such reduction in transportation rates as conditions will permit, care being taken to avoid reductions that would compel a reduction of wages, prevent adequate service, or do injustice to legitimate investments.

Banking Legislation. We oppose the so-called Aldrich bill, or the establishment of a central bank and we believe our country will be largely freed from panics and consequent unemployment and business depression by such a systematic revision of our banking laws as will render temporary relief in localities in which such relief is needed, with protection from control or dominion by what is known as the money trust.

Banks exist for the accommodation of the public and not for the control of business. All legislation on the subject of banking and currency should have for its purpose the securing of these accommodations on terms of absolute security to the public and of complete protection from the misuse of the power that wealth gives to those who possess it.

We condemn the present methods of depositing government funds in a few favored banks, largely situated in or controlled by Wall Street, in return for political favors, and we pledge our party to provide by law for their deposit by competitive bidding in the banking institutions of the country, national and State, without discrimination as to locality, upon approved securities and subject to call by the government.

Rural Credits. Of equal importance with the question of currency reform is the question of rural credits or agricultural finance. Therefore we recommend that an investigation of agricultural credit societies in foreign countries be made, so that it may be ascertained whether a system of rural credits may be devised suitable to conditions in the United States; and we also favor legislation permitting national banks to loan a reasonable proportion of their funds on real estate security.

We recognize the value of vocational education and urge federal appropriations for such training and extension teaching in agriculture in co-operation with the several States.

Waterways. We renew the declaration in our last platform relating to the conservation of our natural resources and the development of our waterways. The present devastation of the lower Mississippi Valley accentuates the movement for the regulation of river flow by additional bank and levee protection below and the diversion, storage, and control of the flood waters above and their utilization for beneficial purposes in the reclamation of arid and swamp lands and the development of water power, instead of permitting the floods to continue, as heretofore, agents of destruction.

We hold that the control of the Mississippi River is a national problem. The preservation of the depth of its water for the purpose of navigation, the building of levees to maintain the integrity of its channel and the prevention of the overflow of the land and its consequent devastation, resulting in the interruption of interstate commerce, the disorganization of the mail service, and the enormous loss of life and property, impose an obligation which alone can be discharged by the general government.

To maintain an adequate depth of water the entire year and thereby encourage water transportation, is a consummation worthy of legislative attention and presents an issue national in its character. It calls for prompt action on the part of Congress, and the Democratic party pledges itself to the enactment of legislation leading to that end.

We favor the co-operation of the United States and the respective States in plans for the comprehensive treatment of all waterways, with a view of co-ordinating plans for channel improvement, with plans for drainage of swamp and overflowed lands, and to this end we favor the appropriation by the federal government of sufficient funds to make surveys of such lands, to develop plans for draining the same, and to supervise the work of construction.

We favor the adoption of a liberal and comprehensive plan for the development and improvement of our inland waterways, with economy and efficiency, so as to permit their navigation by vessels of standard draught.

Post Roads. We favor national aid to State and local authorities in the construction and maintenance of post roads.

Rights of Labor. We repeat our declarations of the platform of 1908 as follows:

"The courts of justice are the bulwark of our liberties, and we yield to none in our purpose to maintain their dignity. Our party has given to the bench a long line of distinguished justices, who have added to the respect and confidence in which this department must be jealously maintained. We resent the attempt of the Republican party to raise a false issue respecting the judiciary, an unjust reflection upon a great body of our citizens to assume that they lack respect for the courts.

"It is the function of the courts to interpret the laws which the people enact; and if the laws appear to work economic, social, or political injustice it is our duty to change them. The only basis upon which the integrity of our courts can stand is that of unswerving justice and protection of life, personal liberty and property. As judicial processes may be abused we should guard them against abuse.

"Experience has proved the necessity of a modification of the present law relating to injunction, and we reiterate the pledges of our platform of 1896 and 1904 in favor of a measure which passed the United States Senate in 1896 relating to contempt in federal courts and providing for trial by jury in cases of indirect contempt.

"Questions of judicial practice have arisen, especially in connection with industrial disputes. We believe that the parties to all judicial proceedings should be treated with rigid impartiality and that injunctions should not be issued in any case in which an injunction would not issue if no industrial dispute were involved.

"The expanding organization of industry makes it essential that there should be no abridgment of the right of wage-earners and producers to organize for the protection of wages and the improvement of labor conditions to the end that such labor organizations and their members should not be regarded as illegal combinations in restraint of trade.

"We pledge the Democratic party to the enactment of a law creating a department of labor represented separately in the President's cabinet, in which department shall be included the subject of mines and mining."

We pledge the Democratic party, so far as the federal jurisdiction extends, to an employees' compensation law providing adequate indemnity for injury to body or loss of life.

Conservation. We believe in the conservation and the development for the use of all the people of the natural resources of the country. Our forests, our sources of water supply, our arable and our mineral lands, our navigable streams, and all other material resources with which our country has been so lavishly endowed constitute the foundation of our national wealth. Such additional legislation as may be necessary to prevent their being wasted or absorbed by special or privileged interests should be enacted and the policy of their conservation should be rigidly adhered to.

The public domain should be administered and disposed of with due regard to the general welfare. Reservations should be limited to the purposes which they purport to serve and not extended to include land wholly unsuited therefor. The unnecessary withdrawal from sale and settlement of enormous tracts of public land upon which tree growth never existed and cannot be promoted tends only to retard development, create discontent, and bring reproach upon the policy of conservation.

The public land laws should be administered in a spirit of the broadest liberality toward the settler exhibiting a bona fide purpose to comply therewith to the end that the invitation of this government to the landless should be as attractive as possible, and the plain provisions of the forest reserve act permitting homestead entries to be made within the national forests should not be nullified by administrative regulations which amount to a withdrawal of great areas of the same from settlement.

Immediate action should be taken by Congress to make available the vast and valuable coal deposits of Alaska under conditions that will be a perfect guaranty against their falling into the hands of monopolizing corporations, associations, or interests.

We rejoice in the inheritance of mineral resources unequaled in extent, variety, or value and in the development of a mining industry unequaled in its magnitude and importance. We honor the men who in their hazardous toil underground daily risk their lives in extracting and preparing for our use the products of the mine so essential to the industries, the commerce, and the comfort of the people of this country. And we pledge ourselves to the extension of the work of the Bureau of Mines in every way appropriate for national legislation with a view of safeguarding the lives of miners, lessening the waste of essential resources and promoting the economic development of mining, which, along with agriculture, must in the future even more than in the past serve as the very foundation of our national prosperity and welfare and our internal commerce.

Agriculture. We believe in encouraging the development of a modern system of agriculture and a systematic effort to improve the conditions of trade in farm products so as to benefit both the consumers and producers. And as an efficient means to this end we favor the enactment by Congress of legislation that will suppress the pernicious practice of gambling in agricultural products by organized exchanges or others.

Merchant Marine. We believe in fostering by constitutional regulation of commerce the growth of a merchant marine which shall develop and strengthen the commercial ties which bind us to our sister republics of the south, but without additional burdens upon the people and without imposing bounties or subsidies from the public treasury.

We urge upon Congress the speedy enactment of laws for the greater security of life and property at sea, and we favor the repeal of all laws and the abrogation of so much of our treaties with other nations as provide for the arrest and imprisonment of seamen charged with desertion or with violation of their contract of service. Such laws and treaties are un-American and violate the spirit if not the letter of the Constitution of the United States.

We favor the exemption from tolls of American ships engaged in coastwise trade passing through the Panama Canal.

We also favor legislation forbidding the use of the Panama Canal by ships owned or controlled by railroad carriers engaged in transportation competitive with the canal.

Pure Food and Public Health. We reaffirm our previous declarations advocating the union and strengthening of the various governmental agencies relating to pure foods, quarantine, vital statistics, and human health. Thus united and administered without partiality to or discrimination against any school of medicine or system of healing, they would constitute a single health service, not subordinated to any commercial or financial interests, but devoted exclusively to the conservation of human life and efficiency. Moreover, this health service should co-operate with the health agencies of our various States and cities, without interference with their prerogatives or with the freedom of individuals to employ such medical or hygienic aid as they may see fit.

Civil Service Law. The law pertaining to the civil service should be honestly and rigidly enforced to the end that merit and ability shall be the standard of appointment and promotion rather than service rendered to a political party; and we favor a reorganization of the civil service, with adequate compensation commensurate with the class of work performed, for all officers and employees; we also favor the extension to all classes of civil service employees of the benefits of the provisions of the employers' liability law.

We also recognize the right of direct petition to Congress by employees for the redress of grievances.

Law Reform. We recognize the urgent need of reform in the administration of civil and criminal law in the United States and we recommend the enactment of such legislation and the promotion of such measures as will rid the present legal system of the delays, expense, and uncertainties incident to the system as now administered.

The Philippines. We reaffirm the position thrice announced by the Democracy in national convention assembled against a policy of imperialism and colonial exploitation in the Philippines or elsewhere. We condemn the experiment in imperialism as an inexcusable blunder which has involved us in enormous expense, brought us weakness instead of strength, and laid our nation open to the charge of abandonment of the fundamental doctrine of self-government. We favor an immediate declaration of the nation's purpose to recognize the independence of the Philippine Islands as soon as a stable government can be established, such independence to be guaranteed by us until the neutralization of the islands can be secured by treaty with other powers. In recognizing the independence of the Philippines our government should retain such land as may be necessary for coaling stations and naval bases.

Arizona and New Mexico. We welcome Arizona and New Mexico to the sisterhood of States and heartily congratulate them upon their auspicious beginning of great and glorious careers.

Alaska. We demand for the people of Alaska the full enjoyment of the rights and privileges of a territorial form of government, and we believe that the officials appointed to administer the government of all our Territories and the District of Columbia should be qualified by previous bona fide residence.

The Russian Treaty. We commend the patriotism of the Democratic members of the Senate and House of Representatives which compelled the termination of the Russian treaty of 1832, and we pledge ourselves anew to preserve the sacred rights of American citizenship at home and abroad. No treaty should receive the sanction of our government which does not recognise the equality of all of our citizens, irrespective of race or creed, and which does not expressly guarantee the fundamental right of expatriation.

The constitutional rights of American citizens should protect them on our borders and go with them throughout the world and every American citizen residing or having property in any foreign country is entitled to and must be given the full protection of the United States Government, both for himself and his property.

Parcel Post and Rural Delivery. We favor the establishment of parcel post or post express and also the extension of the rural delivery system as rapidly as practicable.

Panama Canal Exposition. We hereby express our deep interest in the great Panama Canal Exposition to be held in San Francisco in 1915 and favor such encouragement as can be properly given.

Protection of National Uniform. We commend to the several States the adoption of a law making it an offense for the proprietors of places of public amusement and entertainment to discriminate against the uniform of the United States similar to the law passed by Congress applicable to the District of Columbia and the Territories in 1911.

Pensions. We renew the declaration of our last platform relating to a generous pension policy.

Rule of the People. We call attention to the fact that the Democratic party's demand for a return to the rule of the people expressed in the national platform four years ago has now become the accepted doctrine of a large majority of the electors. We again remind the country that only by a larger exercise of the reserved power of the people can they protect themselves from the misuse of delegated power and the usurpation of governmental instrumentalities by special interests. For this reason the national convention insisted on the overthrow of Cannonism and the inauguration of a system by which United States senators could be elected by direct vote. The Democratic party offers itself to the country as an agency through which the complete overthrow and extirpation of corruption, fraud, and machine rule in American politics can be effected.

Conclusion. Our platform is one of principles which we believe to be essential to our national welfare. Our pledges are made to be kept when in office as well as relied upon during the campaign, and we invite the co-operation of all citizens, regardless of party, who believe in maintaining unimpaired the institutions and traditions of our country.

REPUBLICAN

The Republican party, assembled by its representatives in national convention, declares its unchanging faith in government of the people, by the people, for the people. We renew our allegiance to the principles of the Republican party and our devotion to the cause of Republican institutions established by the fathers.

The Tariff. We reaffirm our belief in a protective tariff. The Republican tariff policy has been of the greatest benefit to the country, developing our resources, diversifying our industries, and protecting our workmen against competition with cheaper labor abroad, thus establishing for our wage earners the American standard of living. The protective tariff is so woven into the fabric of our industrial life that we cannot afford to have a tariff that would destroy many industries and throw millions of our people out of employment. The products of the farm and of the mine should receive the same measure of protection.

We hold that the import duties should be high enough while yielding a sufficient revenue to protect adequately American industries and wages.

Some of the existing import duties are too high and should be reduced. Readjustment should be made from time to time to conform to changing conditions and to reduce excessive rates, but without injury to any American industry. To accomplish this correct information is indispensable This information can best be obtained by an expert commission, as the large volume of useful facts contained in the recent reports of the tariff board has demonstrated.

The pronounced feature of modern industrial life is its enormous diversification. To apply tariff rates justly to these changing conditions requires closer study and more scientific methods than ever before. The Republican party has shown by its creation of a tariff board its recognition of this situation and its determination to be equal to it. We condemn the Democratic party for its failure either to provide funds for the continuance of this board or to make some other provision for securing the information requisite for intelligent tariff legislation We protest against the Democratic method of legislating on these vitally important subjects without careful investigation.

We condemn the Democratic tariff bills passed by the House of Representatives of the Sixty-second Congress as sectional, as injurious to the public credit, and as destructive of business enterprise.

Cost of Living. The steady increase in the cost of living has become a matter not only of national but of world-wide concern. The fact that it is not due to the protective tariff system is evidenced by the existence of similar conditions in countries which have a tariff policy different from our own, as well as by the fact that the cost of living has increased while rates of duty have remained stationary or been reduced.

The Republican party will support a prompt scientific inquiry into the causes which are operative both in the United States and elsewhere to increase the cost of living. When the exact facts are known it will take the necessary steps to remove any abuses that may be found to exist in order that the cost of the food, clothing, and shelter of the people may in no way be unduly or artificially increased

Monopoly and P ivilege. The Republican party is opposed to special privilege and to monopoly. It placed upon the statute books the interstate commerce act of 1887 and the important amendments thereto, and the anti-trust act of 1890, and it has consistently and successfully enforced the provisions of these laws. It will take no backward step to permit the re-establishment in any degree of conditions which were intolerable.

Experience makes it plain that the business of the country may be carried on without fear or without distrust and at the same time without resort to practices which are abhorrent to the common sense of justice. The party favors the enactment of legislation supplementary to the existing anti-trust act which will define as criminal offenses those specific acts which uniformely mark attempts to restrain and monopolize, to the end that all who obey the law may have a guide for their action and ,that those who aim to violate the law may the more surely be punished. The same certainty should be given to the law prohibiting combinations and monopolies that characterizes other provisions of commercial law in order that no part of the field of business may be restricted by monopoly or combination, that business success honorably achieved may not be converted into crime and that the right of every man to acquire commodities, and particularly the necessaries of life, in an open market uninfluenced by the manipulation of trust or combination may be preserved.

Campaign Contributions. We favor such additional legislation as may more effectually prohibit corporations from contributing funds, directly or indirectly, to campaigns for the nomination or election of the President, the Vice-President, senators, and representatives in Congress. We heartily approve the recent act of Congress requiring the fullest publicity in regard to all campaign contributions, whether made in connection with primaries, conventions, or elections.

Republican Administration. We challenge successful criticism of the sixteen years of Republican administration under Presidents McKinley, Roosevelt, and Taft. We heartily reaffirm the indorsement of President McKinley contained in the platforms of 1900 and 1904 and that of President Roosevelt contained in the platforms of 1904 and 1908.

We invite the judgment of the American people on the administration of W. H. Taft. The country has prospered and there was peace under his presidency.

We appeal to the American electorate upon the record of the Republican party and upon this declaration of its principles and purposes. We are confident that under the leadership of the candidates here to be nominated our appeal will not be in vain; that the Republican party will meet every just expectation of the people whose servant it is; that under its administration and its laws our nation will continue to advance; that peace and prosperity will abide with the people and that new glory will be added to the great republic.

Republican Accomplishment. The approaching completion of the Panama Canal, the establishment of a bureau of mines, the institution of postal savings banks, the increased provision made in 1912 for the aged and infirm soldiers and sailors of the republic and for their widows, and the vigorous administration of the laws relating to pure food and drugs, all mark the successful progress of Republican administration and are additional evidences of its effectiveness.

The Navy. We believe in the maintenance of an adequate navy for the national defense and we condemn the action of the Democratic House of Representatives in refusing to authorise the construction of additional ships.

Efficiency in Government. We commend the earnest effort of the Republican administration to secure greater economy and increased efficiency in the conduct of government business. Extravagant appropriations and the creation of unnecessary offices are an injustice to the taxpayer and a bad example to the citizen.

Federal Trade Commission. In the enforcement and administration of federal laws governing interstate commerce and enterprises impressed with a public use engaged therein there is much that may be committed to a federal trade commission, thus placing in the hands of an administrative board many of the functions now necessarily exercised by the courts. This will promote promptness in the administration of the law and avoid delays and technicalities incident to court procedure.

Banking and Currency. The Republican party has always stood for a sound currency and for safe banking methods. It is responsible for the resumption of specie payments and for the establishment of the gold standard. It is committed to the progressive development of our banking and currency system. Our banking arrangements to-day need further revision to meet the requirements of current conditions. We need measures which will prevent the recurrence of money panics and financial disturbances and which will promote the prosperity of this country by producing constant employment.

We need better currency facilities for the movement of crops in the West and South. We need banking arrangements under American auspices for the encouragement and better conduct of our foreign trade. In attaining these ends the investments of individual banks, whether organized under national or State charters, must be carefully protected, and our banking and currency system must be safeguarded from any possibility of domination by sectional, financial, or political interests.

It is of great importance to the social and economic welfare of this country that its farmers have facilities for borrowing easily and using the money. It is important that financial machinery be provided to supply the demand of farmers for credit. Therefore we recommend and urge an authoritative investigation of agricultural credit societies and corporations in other countries and the passage of State and federal laws for the establishment and capable supervision of organizations having for their purpose the loaning of funds to farmers.

Rivers and Harbors. We favor a liberal and systematic policy for the improvements of our rivers and harbors. Such improvements should be made upon expert information and after a careful comparison of cost and prospective benefits.

Flood Prevention in Mississippi Valley. The Mississippi River is the nation's drainage ditch. Its flood waters, gathered from thirty-one States and the Dominion of Canada, constitute an overpowering force which breaks the levees and pours its torrents over many million acres of the richest land in the Union, stopping mails, impeding commerce, and causing great loss of life and property.

These floods are national in scope and the disasters they produce seriously affect the general welfare. The States unaided cannot cope with this giant problem, hence we believe the federal government should assume a fair proportion of the burden of its control so as to prevent the disasters from recurring floods.

Integrity of the Courts. The social and political structure of the United States rests upon the civil liberty of the individual, and for the protection of that liberty the people have wisely, in the national and State constitutions, put definite limitations upon themselves and upon their government officers and agencies. To enforce these limitations, to secure the orderly and coherent exercise of governmental powers, and to protect the rights of even the humblest and least favored individual are the functions of independent courts of justice.

The Republican party reaffirms its intention to uphold at all times the authority and integrity of the courts, both State and federal, and it will ever insist that their power to enforce their process and to protect life, liberty, and property shall be preserved inviolate.

An orderly method is provided under our system of government by which the people may when they choose alter or amend the constitutional provisions which underlie that government. Until these constitutional provisions are so altered or amended in orderly fashion it is the duty of the courts to see to it that when challenged they are enforced.

That the courts, both federal and State, may bear the heavy burden laid upon them, to the complete satisfaction of public opinion, we favor legislation to prevent long delays and the tedious and costly appeals which have so often amounted to a denial of justice in civil cases and to a failure to protect the public at large in criminal cases.

Since the responsibility of the judiciary is so great, the standards of judiciary action must be always and everywhere above suspicion and reproach. While we regard the recall of judges as unnecessary and unwise, we favor such action as may be necessary to simplify the process by which any judge who may be found to be derelict in his duty may be removed from office.

Reclamation. We favor the continuance of the policy of the government with regard to the reclamation of arid lands, and for the encouragement of the speedy settlement and improvement of such lands we favor an amendment to the law that will reasonably extend the time within which the cost of any reclamation project may be repaid by the landowners under it.

Conservation Policy. We rejoice in the success of the dictinctive Republican policy of conservation of our national resources for their use by the people without waste and without monopoly. We pledge ourselves to a continuance of such a policy.

We favor such fair and reasonable rules and regulations as will not discourage or interfere with actual bona fide homeseekers, prospectors, and miners in the acquisition of public lands under existing laws.

Merchant Marine. We believe that one of the country's most urgent needs is a revived merchant marine. There should be American ships, and plenty of them, to make use of the great American interoceanic canal now nearing completion.

Safety at Sea. We favor the speedy enactment of laws to provide that seamen shall not be compelled to endure involuntary servitude and that life and property at sea shall be safeguarded.

The Public Health. The Republican party is now, as always, a party of advanced and constructive statesmanship. It is prepared to go forward with the solution of those new questions which social, economic, and political development have brought into the forefront of the nation's interest. It will strive not only in the nation but in the several States to enact the necessary legislation to safeguard the public health, to limit effectively the labor of women and children, and to protect wage earners engaged in dangerous occupations; to enact comprehensive and generous workmen's compensation laws in place of the present wasteful and unjust system of employers' liability, and in all possible ways to satisfy the just demands of the people for the study and solution of the complex and constantly changing problems of social welfare.

The Civil Service. We reaffirm our adherence to the principles of appointment to public office based on proved fitness and tenure during behavior and efficiency.

The party stands committed to the maintenance, extension, and enforcement of the civil service law, and it favors the passage of legislation empowering the President to extend the competitive service as far as practicable. We favor legislation to make possible the equitable retirement of disabled and superannuated members of the civil service in order that a higher standard of efficiency may be maintained.

We favor the amendment of the federal employees' liability law so as to extend its provision to all government employees as well as to provide a more liberal scale of compensation for injury and death.

Philippines Policy. The Philippines policy of the Republican party has been and is inspired by the belief that our duty toward the Filipino is a national obligation which should remain entirely free from partisan politics.

Arizona and New Mexico. We congratulate the people of Arizona and New Mexico upon the admission of those States, thus merging in the Union in final and enduring form the last remaining portion of our continental territory.

Alaska. We favor a liberal policy toward Alaska to promote the development of the great resources of that district, with such safeguards as will prevent waste and monopoly.

We favor the opening of the coal lands to development through a law leasing the lands on such terms as will invite development and provide fuel for the navy and commerce of the Pacific Ocean.

Protection of American Citizenship. We approve the action taken by the President and the Congress to secure with Russia, as with other countries, a treaty that will recognize the absolute right of expatriation and that will prevent all discrimination of whatever kind between American citizens, whether native born or alien, and regardless of race, religion, or previous political allegiance. The right of asylum is to be neither surrendered nor restricted.

Parcel Post. In the interest of the general public, and particularly of the agricultural or rural communities, we favor legislation looking to the establishment under the proper regulations of a parcel post, the postal rates to be graduated under a zone system in proportion to the length of carriage.

Republican Record. The Republican party looks back upon its record with pride and satisfaction and forward to its new responsibilities with hope and confidence. Its achievements in government constitute the most luminous pages in our history.

Our great advance has been made during the years of its ascendancy in public affairs. It has never been either stationary or reactionary.

It has gone from the fulfillment of one great pledge to the fulfillment of another in response to the public need and to the popular will. We believe in our self-controlled representative democracy, which is a government of laws, not of men, and in which order is the prerequisite of progress. The principles of constitutional government, which make provision for orderly and effective expression of the popular will, for the protection of civil liberty and the rights of men and for the interpretation of the law by an untrammelled and independent judiciary, have proved themselves capable of sustaining the structure of a government which after more than a century of development embraces one hundred millions of people scattered over a wide and diverse territory but bound by common purpose, common ideals and common affection for the Constitution of the United States.

Under the Constitution and the principles vitalized by it, the United States has grown to be one of the great civilized and civilizing powers of the earth. It offers a home and an opportunity to the ambitious and the industrious from other lands. Resting upon a broad basis of a people's confidence and a people's support, and managed by the people themselves, the government of the United States will meet the problems of the future as satisfactorily as it has solved those of the past.

PROGRESSIVE

Declaration of Principles. The conscience of the people, in a time of grave national problems, has called into being a new party, born of the nation's awakened sense of injustice.

We of the Progressive party here dedicate ourselves to the fulfillment of the duty laid upon us by our fathers to maintain that government of the people, by the people, and for the people whose foundations they laid.

We hold, with Thomas Jefferson and Abraham Lincoln, that the people are the masters of their Constitution to fulfill its purposes and to safeguard it from those who, by perversion of its intent, would convert it into an instrument of injustice. In accordance with the needs of each generation, the people must use their sovereign powers to establish and maintain equal opportunity and industrial justice, to secure which this government was founded and without which no republic can endure.

This country belongs to the people who inhabit it. Its resources, its business, its institutions, and its laws should be utilized, maintained, or altered in whatever manner will best promote the general interest. It is time to set the public welfare in the first place.

The Old Parties. Political parties exist to secure responsible government and to execute the will of the people. From these great tasks both the old parties have turned aside. Instead of instruments to promote the general welfare, they have become the tools of corrupt interests, which use them impartially to serve their selfish purposes. Behind the ostensible government sits enthroned an invisible government, owing no allegiance and acknowledging no responsibility to the people. To destroy this invisible government, to dissolve the unholy alliance between corrupt business and corrupt politics, is the first task of the statesmanship of the day.

The deliberate betrayal of its trust by the Republican party, the fatal incapacity of the Democratic party to deal with the new issues of the new time, have compelled the people to forge a new instrument of government through which to give effect to their will in laws and institutions.

Unhampered by tradition, uncorrupted by power, undismayed by the magnitude of the task, the new party offers itself as the instrument of the people to sweep away old abuses, to build a new and nobler commonwealth.

Covenant With the People. This declaration is our covenant with the people, and we hereby bind the party and its candidates in State and nation to the pledges made herein.

Rule of the People. The Progressive party, committed to the principle of government by a self-controlled democracy expressing its will through representatives of the people, pledges itself to secure such alterations in the fundamental law of the several States and of the United States as shall insure the representative character of the government. In particular, the party declares for direct primaries for the nomination of State and national officers, for nationwide preferential primaries for candidates for the presidency, for the direct election of United States senators by the people; and we urge on the States the policy of the short ballot, with responsibility to the people secured by the initiative, referendum, and recall.

Constitution Should Be Easily Amended. The Progressive party, believing that a free people should have the power from time to time to amend their fundamental law so as to adapt it progressively to the changing needs of the people, pledges itself to provide a more easy and expeditious method of amending the federal Constitution.

Nation and State. Up to the limit of the Constitution, and later by amendment of the Constitution, if found necessary, we advocate bringing under effective national jurisdiction those problems which have expanded beyond reach of the individual States.

It is as grotesque as it is intolerable that the several States should by unequal laws in matter of common concern become competing commercial agencies, barter the lives of their children, the health of their women, and the safety and well-being of their working people for the benefit of their financial interests.

The extreme insistence on States' rights by the Democratic party in the Baltimore platform demonstrates anew its inability to understand the world into which it has survived or to administer the affairs of a union of States which have in all essential respects become one people.

Social and Industrial Reform. The supreme duty of the nation is the conservation of human resources through an enlightened measure of social and industrial justice. We pledge ourselves to work unceasingly in State and nation for:

Effective legislation looking to the prevention of industrial accidents, occupational diseases, overwork, involuntary unemployment, and other injurious effects incident to modern industry.

The fixing of minimum safety and health standards for the various occupations, and the exercise of the public authority of State and nation, including the federal control over interstate commerce and the taxing power, to maintain such standards.

The prohibition of child labor.

Minimum wage standards for working women, to provide a "living scale" in all industrial occupations.

The prohibition of night work for women and the establishment of an eight-hour day for women and young persons.

One day's rest in seven for all wage workers.

The eight-hour day in continuous twenty-four hour industries.

The abolition of the convict contract labor system; substituting a system of prison production for governmental consumption only and the application of prisoners' earnings to the support of their dependent families.

Publicity as to wages, hours and conditions of labor; full reports upon industrial accidents and diseases, and the opening to public inspection of all tallies, weights, measures, and check systems on labor products.

Standards of compensation for death by industrial accident and injury and trade diseases which will transfer the burden of lost earnings from the families of working people to the industry, and thus to the community.

The protection of home life against the hazards of sickness, irregular employment, and old age through the adoption of a system of social insurance adapted to American use.

The development of the creative labor power of America by lifting the last load of illiteracy from American youth, and establishing continuation schools for industrial education under public control and encouraging agricultural education and demonstration in rural schools.

The establishment of industrial research laboratories to put the methods and discoveries of science at the service of American producers.

We favor the organization of the workers, men and women, as a means of protecting their interests and of promoting their progress.

Regulation of Interstate Corporations. We believe that true popular government, justice and prosperity go hand in hand, and, so believing, it is our purpose to secure that large measure of general prosperity which is the fruit of legitimate and honest business, fostered by equal justice and by sound progressive laws.

We demand that the test of true prosperity shall be the benefits conferred thereby on all the citizens, not confined to individuals or classes, and that the test of corporate efficiency shall be the ability better to serve the public; that those who profit by control of business affairs shall justify that profit and that control by sharing with the public the fruits thereof.

We therefore demand a strong national regulation of interstate corporations. The corporation is an essential part of modern business. The concentration of modern business, in some degree, is both inevitable and necessary for national and international business efficiency. But the existing concentration of vast wealth under a corporate system, unguarded and uncontrolled by the nation, has placed in the hands of a few men enormous, secret, irresponsible power over the daily life of the citizen—a power unsufferable in a free government and certain of abuse.

This power has been abused in monopoly of national resources, in stock watering, in unfair competition and unfair privileges, and, finally, in sinister influences on the public agencies of State and nation. We do not fear commercial power, but we insist that it shall be exercised openly, under publicity, supervision, and regulation of the most efficient sort, which will preserve its good while eradicating and preventing its evils.

To that end we urge the establishment of a strong federal administrative commission of high standing, which shall maintain permanent active supervision over industrial corporations engaged in interstate commerce, or such of them as are of public importance, doing for them what the government now does for the national banks, and what is now done for the railroads by the Interstate Commerce Commission.

Such a commission must enforce the complete publicity of those corporate transactions which are of public interest; must attack unfair competition, false capitalization and special privilege, and by continuous trained watchfulness guard and keep open equally to all the highways of American commerce. Thus the business man will have certain knowledge of the law and will be able to conduct his business easily in conformity therewith, the investor will find security for his capital, dividends will be rendered more certain and the savings of the people will be drawn naturally and safely into the channels of trade.

Under such a system of constructive regulation legitimate business, freed from confusion, uncertainty, and fruitless litigation, will develop normally in response to the energy and enterprise of the American business man.

Commercial Development. The time has come when the federal government should co-operate with manufacturers and producers in extending our foreign commerce. To this end we demand adequate appropriations by Congress and the appointment of diplomatic and consular officers solely with a view to their special fitness and worth, and not in consideration of political expediency.

It is imperative to the welfare of our people that we enlarge and extend our foreign commerce. We are pre-eminently fitted to do this because, as a people, we have developed high skill in the art of manufacturing; our business men are strong executives, strong organizers. In every way possible our federal government should co-operate in this important matter.

Anyone who has had opportunity to study and observe at first hand Germany's course in this respect must realize that their policy of co-operation between government and business has in comparatively few years made them a leading competitor for the commerce of the world. It should be remembered that they are doing this on a national scale and with large units of business, while the Democrats would have us believe that we should do it with small units of business, which would be controlled, not by the national government, but by forty-nine conflicting sovereignties. Such a policy is utterly out of keeping with the progress of the times and gives our great commercial rivals in Europe—hungry for international markets—golden opportunities of which they are rapidly taking advantage.

The Tariff. We believe in a protective tariff which shall equalize conditions of competition between the United States and foreign countries, both for the farmer and the manufacturer, and which shall maintain for labor an adequate standard of living. Primarily the benefit of any tariff should be disclosed in the pay envelope of the laborer. We declare that no industry deserves protection which is unfair to labor or which is operating in violation of federal law. We believe that the presumption is always in favor of the consuming public.

We demand tariff revision because the present tariff is unjust to the people of the United States. Fair dealing toward the people requires an immediate downward revision of those schedules wherein duties are shown to be unjust and excessive.

We pledge ourselves to the establishment of a non-partisan scientific tariff commission, reporting both to the President and to either branch of Congress, which shall report, first, as to the costs of production, efficiency of labor, capitalization, industrial organization and efficency, and the general competitive position in this country and abroad of industries seekng protecion from Congress. Second, as to the revenue-producing power of the tariff and its relation to the resources of government; and, thirdly, as to the effect of the tariff on prices, operations of middlemen, and on the purchasing power of the consumer.

We believe that this commission should have plenary power to elicit information, and for this purpose to prescribe a uniform system of accounting for the great protected industries. The work of the commission should not prevent the immediate adoption of acts reducing these schedules generally recognised as excessive.

We condemn the Payne-Aldrich bill as unjust to the people. The Republican organization is in the hands of those who have broken, and cannot again be trusted to keep, the promise of necessary downward revision. The Democratic party is committed to the destruction of the protective system through a tariff for revenue only—a policy which would inevitably produce widespread industrial and commercial disaster.

Reciprocity With Canada. We demand the immediate repeal of the Canadian reciprocity act.

High Cost of Living. The high cost of living is due partly to world-wide and partly to local causes; partly to natural and partly to artificial causes. The measures proposed in this platform on various subjects, such as the tariff, the trusts, and conservation, will of themselves remove the artificial causes. There will remain other elements, such as the tendency to leave the country for the city, waste, extravagance, bad systems of taxation, poor methods of raising crops, and bad business methods in marketing crops. To remedy these conditions requires the fullest information and, based on this information, effective government supervision and control to remove all the artificial causes. We pledge ourselves to such full and immediate inquiry and to immediate action to deal with every need such inquiry discloses.

Improvement of the Currency. We believe there exists imperative need for prompt legislation for the improvement of our national currency system. We believe the present method of issuing notes through private agencies is harmful and unscientific. The issue of currency is fundamentally a government function and the system should have as basic principles soundness and elasticity. The control should be lodged with the government and should be protected from domination or manipulation by Wall Street or any special interests.

We are opposed to the so-called Aldrich currency bill because its provisions would place our currency and credit system in private hands, not subject to effective public control.

Conservation of Natural Resources. The natural resources of the nation must be promptly developed and generously used to supply the people's needs, but we cannot safely allow them to be wasted, exploited, monopolized, or controlled against the general good. We heartily favor the policy of conservation and we pledge our party to protect the national forests without hindering their legitimate use for the benefit of all the people. Agricultural lands in the national forests are, and should remain, open to the genuine settler. Conservation will not retard legitimate development. The honest settler must receive his patent promptly without hindrance, rules, or delays.

We believe that the remaining forests, coal and oil lands, water powers, and other natural resources still in State or national control (except agricultural lands) are more likely to be wisely conserved and utilized for the general welfare if held in the public hands.

In order that consumers and producers, managers and workmen, now and hereatfer, need not pay toll to private monopolies of power and raw material, we demand that such resources shall be retained by the State or nation and opened to immediate use under laws which will encourage development and make to the people a moderate return for benefits conferred.

In particular we pledge our party to require reasonable compensation to the public for water power rights hereafter granted by the public. We pledge legislation to lease the public grazing lands under equitable provisions now pending which will increase the production of food for the people and thoroughly safeguard the rights of the actual homemakers. Natural resources whose conservation is necessary for the national welfare should be owned and controlled by the nation.

Waterways. The rivers of the United States are the natural arteries of this continent. We demand that they shall be opened to traffic as indispensable parts of a great nation-wide system of transportation in which the Panama Canal will be the central link, thus enabling the whole interior of the United States to share with the Atlantic and Pacific seaboards in the benefit derived from the canal.

It is a national obligation to develop our rivers, and especially the Mississippi and its tributaries, without delay, under a comprehensive general plan covering each river system, from its source to its mouth, designed to secure ith highest usefulness for navigation, irrigation, domestic supply, water power and the prevention of floods. We pledge our party to the immediate preparation of such a plan, which should be made and carried out in close and friendly co-operation between the nation, the State, and the cities affected.

Under such a plan the destructive floods of the Mississippi and other streams, which represent a vast and needless loss to the nation, would be controlled by forest conservation and water storage at the headwaters, and by levees below, land sufficient to support millions of people would be reclaimed from the deserts and swamps, water power enough to transform the industrial standing of whole States would be developed, adequate water terminals would be provided, transportation would revive, and the railroads would be compelled to co-operate as freely with the boat lines as with each other.

The equipment, organization, and experience acquired in constructing the Panama Canal soon will be available for the Lakes-to-the-Gulf deep waterway and other portions of this great work, and should be utilized by the nation in co-operation with the various States, at the lowest net cost to the people.

Panama Canal. The Panama Canal, built and paid for by the American people, must be used primarily for their benefit. We demand that the canal shall be so operated as to break the transportation monopoly now held and misused by the transcontinental railroads by maintaining sea competition with them; that ships directly or indirectly owned or controlled by American railroad corporations shall not be permitted to use the canal, and that American ships engaged in coastwise trade shall pay no tolls.

The Progressive party will favor legislation having for its aim the development of friendship and commerce between the United States and Latin-American nations.

Alaska. The coal and other natural resources of Alaska should be opened to development at once. They are owned by the people of the United States and are safe from monopoly, waste or destruction only while so owned. We demand that they shall neither be sold nor given away except under the homestead law, but while held in government ownership shall be opened to use promptly upon liberal terms requiring immediate development.

Thus the benefit of cheap fuel will accrue to the government of the United States and to the people of Alaska and the Pacific Coast; the settlement of extensive agricultural lands will be hastened; the extermination of the salmon will be prevented, and the just and wise development of Alaskan resources will take the place of private extortion or monopoly.

We demand also that extortion or monopoly in transportation shall be prevented by the prompt acquisition, construction, or improvement by the government of such railroads, harbor, and other facilities for transportation as the welfare of the people may demand.

We promise the people of the Territory of Alaska the same measure of local self-government that was given to other American Territories, and that federal officials appointed there shall be qualified by previous bona fide residence in the Territory.

Woman Suffrage. The Progressive party, believing that no people can justly claim to be a true democracy which denies political rights on account of sex, pledges itself to the task of securing equal suffrage to men and women alike.

Corrupt Election Practices. We pledge our party to legislation that will compel strict limitation of all campaign contributions and expenditures, and detailed publicity of both before as well as after primaries and elections.

Publicity and Public Service. We pledge our party to legislation compelling the registration of lobbyists; publicity of committee hearings, except on foreign affairs, and recording of all votes in committee; and forbidding federal appointees from holding office in State or national political organizations or taking part as officers or delegates in political conventions for the nomination of elective State or national officials.

Popular Review of Judicial Decisions. The Progressive party demands such restriction of the power of the courts as shall leave to the people the ultimate authority to determine fundamental questions of social welfare and public policy. To secure this end, it pledges itself to provide:

First—That when an act passed under the police power of the State is held unconstitutional under the State constitution by the courts, the people, after an ample interval for deliberation, shall have an opportunity to vote on the question whether they desire the act to become law, notwithstanding such decision.

Second—That every decision of the highest Appellate Court of a State declaring an act of the legislature unconstitutional on the ground of its violation of the federal Constitution shall be subject to the same review by the Supreme Court of the United States as is now accorded to decisions sustaining such legislation.

Administration of Justice. The Progressive pa ty, in order to secure to the people a better administration of justice, and by that means to bring about a more general respect for the law and the courts, pledges itself to work unceasingly for the reform of legal procedure and judicial methods.

We believe that the issuance of injunctions in cases arising out of labor disputes should be prohibited when such injunctions would not apply when no labor disputes existed.

We also believe that a person cited for contempt in labor disputes, except when such contempt was committed in the actual presence of the court or so near thereto as to interfere with the proper administration of justice, should have a right to trial by jury.

A Department of Labor. We pledge our party to establish a department of labor, with a seat in the cabinet, and with wide jurisdiction over matters affecting the conditions of labor and living.

Country Life. The development and prosperity of country life are as important to the people who live in the cities as they are to the farmers. Increase of prosperity on the farm will favorably affect the cost of living and promote the interests of all who dwell in the country and all who depend upon its products for clothing, shelter, and food.

We pledge our party to foster the development of agricultural credit and co-operation, the teaching of agriculture in schools, agricultural college extension, the use of mechanical power on the farm and to re-establish the country life commission, thus directly promoting the welfare of the farmers and bringing the benefits of better farming, better business, and better living within their reach.

National Health Service. We favor the union of all the existing agencies of the federal government dealing with the public health into a single national health service, without discrimination against or for any one set of therapeutic methods, school of medicine, or school of healing, with such additional powers as may be necessary to enable it to perform efficiently such duties in the protection of the public from preventable disease as may be properly undertaken by the federal authorities, including the executing of existing laws regarding pure food; quarantine and cognate subjects; the promotion of appropriate action for the improvement of vital statistics and the extension of the registration area of such statistics, and co-operation with the health activities of the various States and cities of the nation.

Patents. We pledge ourselves to the enactment of a patent law which will make it impossible for patents to be suppressed or used against the public welfare in the interest of injurious monopolies.

Interstate Commerce Commission. We pledge our party to secure to the Interstate Commerce Commission the power to value the physical property of railroads. In order that the power of the commission to protect the people may not be impaired or destroyed, we demand the abolition of the Commerce Court.

Good Roads. We recognize the vital importance of good roads, and we pledge our party to foster their extension in every proper way, and we favor the early construction of nationa highways. We also favor the extension of the rural free delivery service.

Inheritance and Income Tax. We believe in a graduated inheritance tax as a national means of equalizing the obligations of holders of property to government, and we hereby pledge our party to enact such a federal law as will tax large inheritances, returning to the States an equitable percentage of all amounts collected. We favor the ratification of the pending amendment to the Constitution giving the government power to levy an income tax.

Peace and National Defense. The Progressive party deplores the survival in our civilization of the barbaric system of warfare among nations, with its enormous waste of resources even in time of peace, and the consequent inpoverishment of the life of the toiling masses. We pledge the party to use its best endeavors to substitute judicial and other peaceful means of settling international differences.

We favor an international agreement for the limitation of naval forces. Pending such an agreement, and as the best means of preserving peace, we pledge ourselves to maintain for the present the policy of building two battleships a year.

Protection of American Citizens Abroad. We pledge our party to protect the rights of American citizenship at home and abroad. No treaty should receive the sanction of our government which discriminates between American citizens because of birthplace, race or religion, or that does not recognize the absolute right of expatriation.

Immigration. Through the establishment of industrial standards we propose to secure to the able-bodied immigrant and to his native fellow workers a larger share of American opportunity.

We denounce the fatal policy of indifference and neglect which has left our enormous immigrant population to become the prey of chance and cupidity. We favor governmental action to encourage the distribution of immigrants away from the congested cities, to rigidly supervise all private agencies dealing with them, and to promote their assimilation, education, and advancement.

Pensions. We pledge ourselves to a wise and just policy of pensioning American soldiers and sailors and their widows and children by the federal government.

And we approve the policy of the Southern States in granting pensions to the ex-Confederate soldiers and sailors and their widows and children.

Parcel Post. We pledge our party to the immediate creation of a parcel post, with rates proportionate to distance and service.

The Civil Service Law. We condemn the violations of the civil service law under the present administration, including the coercion and assessment of subordinate employees, and the President's refusal to punish such violation after a finding of guilty by his own commission; his distribution of patronage among subservient congressmen, while withholding it from those who refuse support of administration measures; his withdrawal of nominations from the Senate until political support for himself was secured, and his open use of the offices to reward those who voted for his renomination.

To eradicate these abuses we demand not only the enforcement of the civil service act in letter and spirit but also legislation which will bring under the competitive system postmasters, collectors, marshals, and all other non-political officers, as well as the enactment of an equitable retirement law, and we also insist on continuous service during good behavior and efficiency.

Government Business Organization. We pledge our party to readjustment of the business methods of the national government and a proper coordination of the federal bureaus which will increase the economy and efficiency of the government service, prevent duplications, and secure better results to the taxpayers for every dollar expended.

Supervision Over Investments. The people of the United States are swindled out of many millions of dollars every year through worthless investments. The plain people, the wage earners, and the men and women with small savings, have no way of knowing the merit of concerns sending out highly colored prospectuses offering stock for sale, prospectuses that make big returns seem certain and fortunes easily within grasp.

We hold it to be the duty of the government to protect its people from this kind of piracy. We therefore demand wise, carefully thought-out legislation that will give us such governmental supervision over this matter as will furnish to the people of the United States this much needed protection, and we pledge ourselves thereto.

Conclusion. On these principles and on the recognized desirability of uniting the progressive forces of the nation into an organization which shall unequivocally represent the progressive spirit and policy, we appeal for the support of all American citizens, without regard to previous political affiliations.

SOCIALIST

The representatives of the Socialist party in national convention at Indianapolis declare that the capitalist system has outgrown its historical function, and has become utterly incapable of meeting the problems now confronting society. We denounce this outgrown system as incompetent and corrupt and the source of unspeakable misery and suffering to the whole working class.

Under this system the industrial equipment of the nation has passed into the absolute control of a plutocracy which exacts an annual tribute of millions of dollars from the producers. Unafraid of any organized resistance, it stretches out its greedy hands over the still undeveloped resources of the nation—the land, the mines, the forests, and the water powers of every State in the Union.

In spite of the multiplication of labor-saving machines and improved methods in industry which cheapen the cost of production, the share of the producers grows ever less, and the prices of all the necessities of life steadily increase. The boasted prosperity of this nation is for the owning class alone. To the rest it means only greater hardship and misery. The high cost of living is felt in every home. Millions of wage workers have seen the purchasing power of their wages decrease until life has become a desperate battle for mere existence.

Multitudes of unemployed walk the streets of our cities or trudge from State to State awaiting the will of the masters to move the wheels of industry.

The farmers in every State are plundered by the increasing prices exacted for tools and machinery and by extortionate freight rates and storage charges.

Capitalism Denounced. Capitalist concentration is mercilessly crushing the class of small business men and driving its members into the ranks of propertyless wage workers. The overwhelming majority of the people of America are being forced under a yoke of bondage by this soulless industrial despotism.

It is this capitalist system that is responsible for the increasing burden of armaments, the poverty, slums, child labor, most of the insanity, crime and prostitution, and much of the disease that afflicts mankind.

Under this system the working class is exposed to poisonous conditions, to frightful and needless perils to life and limb, is walled around with court decisions, injunctions and unjust laws, and is preyed upon incessantly for the benefit of the controlling oligarchy of wealth. Under it, also, the children of the working class are doomed to ignorance, drudging toil, and darkened lives.

In the face of these evils, so manifest that all thoughtful observers are appalled at them, the legislative representatives of the Republican and Democratic parties remain the faithful servants of the oppressors. Measures designed to secure to the wage earners of this nation as humane and just treatment as is already enjoyed by the wage earners of all other civilized nations have been smothered in committee without debate, and laws ostensibly designed to bring relief to the farmers and general consumers are juggled and transformed into instruments for the exaction of further tribute. The growing unrest under oppression has driven these two old parties to the enactment of a variety of regulative measures, none of which has limited in any appreciable degree the power of the plutocracy, and some of which have been perverted into means for increasing that power. Anti-trust laws, railroad restrictions and regulations, with the prosecutions, indictments and investigations based upon such legislation, have proved to be utterly futile and ridiculous.

Nor has this plutocracy been seriously restrained or even threatened by any Republican or Democratic executive. It has continued to grow in power and insolence alike under the administrations of Cleveland, McKinley, Roosevelt, and Taft.

In addition to this legislative juggling and this executive connivance, the courts of America have sanctioned and strengthened the hold of this plutocracy as the Dred Scott and other decisions strengthened the slave power before the Civil War.

We declare, therefore, that the longer sufferance of these conditions is impossible, and we purpose to end them all. We declare them to be the product of the present system in which industry is carried on for private greed, instead of for the welfare of society. We declare, furthermore, that for these evils there will be and can be no remedy and no substantial relief except through socialism, under which industry will be carried on for the common good and every worker receive the full social value of the wealth he creates.

Society is divided into warring groups and classes, based upon material interests. Fundamentally, this struggle is a conflict between the two main classes, one of which, the capitalist class, owns the means of production, and the other, the working class, must use these means of production on terms dictated by the owners.

The capitalist class, though few in numbers, absolutely controls the government—legislative, executive, and judicial. This class owns the machinery of gathering and disseminating news through its organized press. It subsidizes seats of learning—the colleges and schools—and even religious and moral agencies. It has also the added prestigo which established custom gives to any order or society, right or wrong.

The working class, which includes all those who are forced to work for a living, whether by hand or brain, in shop, mine, or on the soil, vastly outnumbers the capitalist class. Lacking effective organization and class solidarity, this class is unable to enforce its will. Given such class solidarity and effective organization, the workers will have the power to make all laws and control all industry in their own interest.

All political parties are the expression of economic class interests. All other parties than the Socialist party represent one or another group of the ruling capitalist class. Their political conflicts reflect merely superficial rivalries between competing capitalist groups. However they result, these conflicts have no issue of real value to the workers. Whether the Democrats or Republicans win politically, it is the capitalist class that is victorious economically.

Socialism the Expression of the Workers. The Socialist party is the political expression of the economic interests of the workers. Its defeats have been their defeats and its victories their victories. It is a party founded on the science and laws of social development. It proposes that, since all social necessities to-day are socially produced, the means of their production and distribution shall be socially owned and democratically controlled.

In the face of the economic and political aggressions of the capitalist class, the only reliance left the workers is that of their economic organizations and their political power. By the intelligent and class-conscious use of these, they may resist successfully the capitalist class, break the fetters of wage slavery, and fit themselves for the future society, which is to displace the capitalist system. The Socialist party appreciates the full significance of class organization and urges the wage earners, the working farmers, and all other useful workers everywhere to organise for economic and political action, and we pledge ourselves to support the toilers of the fields as well as those in the shops, factories, and mines of the nation in their struggles for economic justice.

In the defeat or victory of the working class party in this new struggle for freedom lies the defeat or triumph of the common people of all economic groups, as well as the failure or the triumph of popular government. Thus the Socialist party is the party of the present-day revolution, which marks the transition from economic individualism to socialism, from wage slavery to free co-operation, from capitalist oligarchy to industrial democracy.

Working Programme. As measures calculated to strengthen the working class in its fight for the realization of its ultimate aim, the Co-operative Commonwealth, and to increase its power of resistance against capitalist oppression, we advocate and pledge ourselves and our elected officers to the following programme:

Collective Ownership. First: The collective ownership and democratic management of railroads, wire and wireless telegraphs and telephones, express service, steamboat lines and all other social means of transportation and communication and of all large-scale industries.

Second: The immediate acquirement by the municipalities, the States or the federal government of all grain elevators, stock yards, storage warehouses, and other distributing agencies, in order to reduce the present extortionate cost of living.

Third: The extension of the public domain to include mines, quarries, oil wells, forests, and water power.

Fourth: The further conservation and development of natural resources for the use and benefit of all the people:

(a) By scientific forestation and timber protection.

(b) By the reclamation of arid and swamp tracts.

(c) By the storage of flood waters and the utilization of water power.

(d) By the stoppage of the present extravagant waste of the soil and of the products of mines and oil wells.

(e) By the development of highway and waterway systems.

Fifth: The collective ownership of land wherever practicable, and in cases where such ownership is impracticable, the appropriation by taxation of the annual rental value of all land held for speculation or exploitation.

Sixth: The collective ownership and democratic management of the banking and currency system.

Unemployment. The immediate government relief of the unemployed by the extension of all useful public works. All persons employed on such works to be engaged directly by the government under a work day of not more than eight hours and at not less than the prevailing union wages. The government also to establish employment bureaus; to lend money to States and municipalities, without interest, for the purpose of carrying on public works, and to take such other measures within its power as will lessen the widespread misery of the workers caused by the misrule of the capitalist class.

Industrial Demands. The conservation of human resources, particularly of the lives and well-being of the workers and their families:

First: By shortening the work day in keeping with the increased productiveness of machinery.

Second: By securing to every worker a rest period of not less than a day and a half in each week.

Third: By securing a more effective inspection of workshops, factories and mines.

Fourth: By forbidding the employment of children under sixteen years of age.

Fifth: By abolishing the brutal exploitation of convicts under the contract system and prohibiting the sale of goods so produced in competition with other labor.

Sixth: By forbidding the interstate transportation of the products of child labor, of convict labor and of all uninspected factories and mines.

Seventh: By abolishing the profit system in government work, and substituting either the direct hire of labor or the awarding of contracts to co-operative groups of workers.

Eighth: By establishing minimum wage scales.

Ninth: By abolishing official charity and substituting a non-contributory system of old-age pensions, a general system of insurance by the State of all its members against unemployment and invalidism and a system of compulsory insurance by employers of their workers, without cost to the latter, against industrial diseases, accidents, and death.

Political Demands. First: The absolute freedom of press, speech, and assemblage.

Second: The adoption of a graduated income tax, the increase of the rates of the present corporation tax, and the extension of inheritance taxes, graduated in proportion to the value of the estate and to nearness of kin—the proceeds of these taxes to be employed in the socialization of industry.

Third: The gradual reduction of all tariff duties, particularly those on the necessities of life. The government to guarantee the re-employment of wage earners who may be disemployed by reason of changes in tariff schedules.

Fourth: The abolition of the monopoly ownership of patents and the substitution of collective ownership, with direct rewards to inventors by premiums or royalties.

Fifth: Unrestricted and equal suffrage for men and women.

Sixth: The adoption of the initiative, referendum, and recall and of proportional representation, nationally as well as locally.

Seventh: The abolition of the Senate and the veto power of the President.

Eighth: The election of the President and Vice-President by direct vote of the people.

Ninth: The abolition of the power usurped by the Supreme Court of the United States to pass upon the constitutionality of the legislation enacted by Congress. National laws to be repealed only by act of Congress or by a referendum vote of the whole people.

Tenth: The abolition of the present restrictions upon the amendment of the Constitution, so that that instrument may be made amendable by a majority of the voters in a majority of the States.

Eleventh: The granting of the right of suffrage in the District of Columbia with representation in Congress and a democratic form of municipal government for purely local affairs.

Twelfth: The extension of democratic government to all United States territory.

Thirteenth: The enactment of further measures for general education and particularly for vocational education in useful pursuits. The Bureau of Education to be made a department.

Fourteenth: The enactment of further measures for the conservation of health. The creation of an independent Bureau of Health, with such restrictions as will secure full liberty to all schools of practice.

Fifteenth: The separation of the present Bureau of Labor from the Department of Commerce and Labor and its elevation to the rank of a department.

Sixteenth: Abolition of all Federal District Courts and the United States Circuit Courts of Appeals. State courts to have jurisdiction in all cases arising between citizens of the several States and foreign corporations. The election of all judges for short terms.

Seventeenth: The immediate curbing of the power of the courts to issue injunctions.

Eighteenth: The free administration of justice.

Nineteenth: The calling of a convention for the revision of the Constitution of the United States.

Such measures of relief as we may be able to force from capitalism are but a preparation of the workers to seize the whole powers of government, in order that they may thereby lay hold of the whole system of socialized industry and thus come to their rightful inheritance.

PROHIBITION

The Prohibition party of the United States of America in convention at Atlantic City, N. J., July 11, 1912, recognizing God as the source of all governmental authority, makes the following declaration of principles:

The alcoholic drink traffic is wrong, the most serious drain upon the nation's wealth and resources, detrimental to the general welfare, destructive of the inalienable rights of life, liberty, and the pursuit of happiness, and, therefore, all laws taxing or licensing a traffic that produces crime, poverty, and political corruption and spreads disease and death should be repealed. To destroy such a traffic there must be elected to power a political party which will administer the government from the standpoint that the alcoholic drink traffic is a crime and not a business, and we pledge that the manufacture, importation, exportation, transportation, and sale of alcoholic beverages shall be prohibited.

We favor:

The election of United States senators by direct vote of the people.

Presidential terms of six years, and one term only.

Uniform marriage and divorce laws.

The extermination of polygamy and the complete suppression of the traffic in girls.

Suffrage for women upon the same terms as to men.

Court review as to post office and other departmental decisions and orders; the establishment of postal savings banks, the extension of the rural delivery and the establishment of an efficient parcel post, and add the following planks:

The protection of one day in seven as a day of rest.

The absolute protection of the rights of labor without impairment of the rights of capital.

The settlement of all international disputes by arbitration.

The initiative, referendum, and recall.

The tariff is a commercial question and should be fixed on the basis of accurate knowledge secured by a permanent omnipartisan tariff commission with ample powers.

The abolition of child labor in the mines, workshops and factories, with the rigid enforcement of laws now flagrantly violated.

Equitable graduated income and inheritance taxes.

Conservation of our mineral and forest reserves, reclamation of arid and waste lands and we urge that all mineral and timber lands and water powers now owned by the government be held perpetually and leased for revenue purposes.

Clearly defined laws for the regulation and control of corporations transacting an interstate business.

Greater efficiency and economy in government service.

To these fundamental principles the National Prohibition party renews its long allegiance and on these issues invites the co-operation of all citizens to the end that the true object of popular government may be attained; i. e., equal and exact justice to all.

PRESIDENTIAL CAMPAIGN CONTRIBUTIONS. A thorough investigation into the subject of contributions to political campaigns was carried on during the summer and fall of 1912 by a committee of the Senate composed of Senator Clapp of Minnesota, chairman, and Senators Jones of Washington, Oliver of Pennsylvania, Paynter of Kentucky, and Pomerene of Ohio. The investigation resulted from charges of corruption in the campaign of 1904 and the scope of the investigation was originally limited to that campaign. As a result of conditions thereafter developed, as noted below, the scope of the committee was broadened to include also the campaign of 1912. The most important results derived from this investigation as related to the different political parties, are noted herewith.

REPUBLICAN CAMPAIGN CONTRIBUTIONS, 1904. George W. Cortelyou, chairman of the Republican national committee in 1904, testified early in July that all the vouchers and official records relating to Republican contributions in 1904 had been destroyed. From his recollection, however, he testified that the election of President Roosevelt in 1904 cost in round numbers, $1,900,000 and that the election of President McKinley in 1900 cost twice as much, or $3,800,000. Mr. Cortelyou testified that he knew of no contributions having been made directly by J. Pierpont Morgan or H. H. Rogers, and that he knew nothing of the contribution of $260,000 made by E. H. Harriman and others until certain letters were printed in the newspaper controversy which followed the charges made by Mr. Harriman in 1906. He declared that there was not the slightest ground for the charges that he had used the knowledge acquired by him as Secretary of Commerce and Labor to obtain contributions from corporations.

The publication of certain letters in *Hearst's Magazine* in August, 1912, aroused public interest in the investigations of the committee. These letters were alleged to have been written by John D. Archbold of the Standard Oil Company to Senator Penrose of Pennsylvania and others. The first of these letters was published under the heading "Startling Revelations in Standard Oil Letters." It was dated October 13, 1904, and read as follows:

"My Dear Senator:

"In fulfillment of our understanding it gives me pleasure to hand you herewith certificate of deposit to your favor for $25,000, and with good wishes, I am,

"Yours truly,
"John D. Archbold."

This letter was marked "personal." Opponents of Senator Penrose, in Pennsylvania, took advantage of the appearance of these and other letters from Mr. Archbold to make an attack upon him. They demanded that he be expelled from the Senate on the ground that he had been the paid agent of the Standard Oil Company for many years. On August 21, Senator Penrose, on the point of privilege, addressed the Senate and undertook to explain the transaction. He admitted that the amount mentioned in Mr. Archbold's letter had been received, but claimed that it was part of a fund of $125,000 which was contributed by the Standard Oil Company through Mr. Archbold as its agent to the Republican campaign of 1904. He stated that $100,000 of this amount was given directly to Cornelius N. Bliss, who was at that time treasurer of the national campaign committee, of which the chairman was George B. Cortelyou. Senator Penrose intimated that this gift from the Standard Oil Company was known to President Roosevelt, and that later an additional sum of $150,000 was asked for from the Standard Oil Company by members of the national committee. The inference to be drawn from Senator Penrose's statement was that the subsequent prosecution of the Standard Oil Company by President Roosevelt's administration was the indirect result of the refusal of that company to give the additional amount asked for. Senator Penrose stated that while Mr. Archbold wished to make this contribution he was overruled by his associates in the Standard Oil Company. He further declared that he, himself, had been present at interviews between Mr. Archbold and Mr. Bliss and that Mr. Bliss had assured Mr. Archbold that President Roosevelt knew about the actual contribution and appreciated it. This statement, he claimed, was the result of the insistence of Mr. Archbold that the President should be personally notified that this sum had been contributed by the Standard Oil Company. On August 22, Senator Penrose continued the explanation of this transaction and made further attacks upon Mr. Roosevelt.

Directly following these charges made by Senator Penrose, Mr. Roosevelt, who was then campaigning in Pennsylvania, denounced the aspersions as false and produced letters written by him in October, 1904, to Mr. Cortelyou insisting that if any money had been received from the Standard Oil Company it must be at once returned. Both Mr. Cortelyou and Mr. Loeb, who was in 1904 Secretary of the Treasury, denied through the newspapers that they knew anything of the alleged gift of $100,000 by the Standard Oil Company. On August 23 Mr. Archbold appeared before the Senate committee which was investigating campaign fund contributions. His testimony, in all essentials, agreed with statements made by Senator Penrose as to the circumstances of the alleged gift.

Mr. Roosevelt asked the privilege of being allowed to testify directly following Mr. Archbold's appearance before the committee, but as the Senate was on the point of adjourning, and the members of the committee were so scattered, that the chairman was not able to bring them together, this was found impossible. It was, however, arranged by the Senate that these particular charges should be investigated together with those relating to recent political expenditures, including those of the campaign of 1912, and it was decided that the committee should convene for this investigation on September 30.

Mr. Roosevelt wrote to Senator Clapp a long letter in which he reviewed, in detail, the circumstances covering the period under investigation, denying the charges wholly and making a vigorous assault upon his enemies.

When the committee reassembled on September 30, George R. Sheldon, former treasurer of the Republican national committee, testified that corporations contributed 73½ per cent. of the Republican campaign fund in 1904. Mr. Morgan testified that he had contributed $100,000, and later had added $50,000. The latter sum, according to his recollection, was spent wholly or largely in New York as a part of the $240,000 which was raised by Mr. Harriman a week before the election.

On October 4 Mr. Roosevelt testified before the committee. His testimony, in effect, followed the contents of his letter previously addressed to the committee. He denied that he had asked Mr. Harriman to raise money for the Republican party in 1904. He also denied that he knew until October 3, 1912, that money had been contributed by the Standard Oil Company in 1904, and he declared himself without knowledge of contributions of Messrs. Gould and Morgan He also made denial of the allegation that Ormsby McHarg had been sent to the South previous to the Republican national convention to purchase delegates to the Republican convention. Mr. McHarg also denied this charge.

Mr. Roosevelt said that he had sent for Messrs. Harriman and Morgan in the fall of 1904, but not to discuss politics. He declared that he knew of the contribution made by Mr. Frick, but did not regard it of especial moment. He said that he did not regard Mr. Morgan's contribution of $150,000 as of greater consequence than that of $1 sent to him in 1912 by a veteran of the Soldiers' Home. Mr. Roosevelt was on the stand before the committee for nearly five hours. His testimony is covered chiefly by the summary above. His testimony was corroborated, in certain points, by William Loeb, Jr., his former secretary. Mr. Loeb wrote a letter which he read to Mr. Sheldon, Republican treasurer, on September 21, 1908, advising against certain contributions from Mr. Archbold or Mr. Harriman to President Taft's campaign. The reply made by Mr. Roosevelt to Senator Paynter, who asked him whether, as a "practical" man, he did not think some of the contributions, by corporations, to the campaign fund of 1904 were made with the expectation that the corporations would receive favors, was received with applause. Mr. Roosevelt said: "As a practical man of high ideals, who has always endeavored to put his high ideals in practice, I think any man who would believe that he would get any consideration from making any contribution to me was either a crook or a fool."

On October 18, Elmer Dover, who, in 1904, was secretary of the Republican committee, produced at the investigation a list of the contributors in that year. This list had been copied from a private memorandum book of Cornelius N. Bliss, at that time treasurer of the Republican national committee, with Mr. Bliss's consent. The total contributions, according to this tabulation, amounted to $2,280,018. Among the contributors were E. H. Harriman, $150,000; J. P. Morgan & Co., $150,000; George J. Gould, $100,000; Chauncey M. Depew, $100,000; George W. Perkins, $160,000; and Whitelaw Reid, $30,000. One group of contributions, in which there were thirteen names, appeared to have been those collected by Mr. Harriman after his visit to President Roosevelt in 1904.

Republican Campaign Contributions, 1912. From the investigations carried on by the committee and from reports received in accordance with the law providing for the publicity of campaign contributions, it was shown that the total receipts of the Republican national campaign committee for the campaign of 1912 were $904,828, and the expenditures, $900,363. Charles P. Taft of Cincinnati, the half-brother of President Taft, testified before the committee that he had contributed in 1912 about $372,000. Other contributors were F. L. Leland, who gave $50,000, Andrew Carnegie, $35,000, and J. P. Morgan & Co., $25,000.

Democratic Contributions, 1904. Thomas Taggart, chairman of the Democratic national committee in 1904, testified before the committee in July that the books of the Democratic national committee had been burned, and that he had little recollection of the expenditures. August Belmont stated that, in his judgment, the fund amounted to between $600,000 and $700,000. W. F. Sheehan, also a member of the national committee in 1904, testified that approximately $1,000,000 was contributed for the Democratic campaign of 1904, and that of this sum the national committee itself handled about $800,000. Thomas F. Ryan testified that he had contributed $50,000 at the beginning of the campaign, and that within a short time he had added $50,000, and after the campaign collapsed he contributed $350,000, a sum sufficient to pay off the debts of the national committee to save the Democratic organization.

Democratic Contributions, 1912. Testimony from several witnesses showed that there had been spent for the nomination of Governor Wilson, $208,565. Of this sum $85,500 was contributed by a small group of men who were classmates of Governor Wilson or were trustees of Princeton University. Mr. Ryan testified that he had contributed $75,000 for the benefit of Governor Harmon in 1912, and about $35,000 for the fund of Mr. Underwood.

The total receipts of the Democratic national committee in the election of 1912 were $1,159,446.

Progressive Party Contributions. Testimony in regard to the campaign contributions for the carrying on of the Progressive campaign of 1912 was of particular interest, as it showed that the larger part of the sum spent had been contributed by several men prominent in the new party. William Flinn of Pennsylvania testified that $325,000 had been spent in Pennsylvania and New York county alone previous to the election and that the national organization had spent about $144,000 more. The sums contributed by different persons to this fund were as follows: William

Flinn, $144,308; George W. Perkins, $130,000; Frank A. Munsey, $33,000, and Dan R. Hanna, $25,000. The total receipts of the Progressive national committee were $676,672 and the expenditures, $666,500.

PRESIDENTIAL PRIMARY ELECTIONS. See PRESIDENTIAL CAMPAIGN and ELECTORAL REFORM.

PRETO, OURO, Viscount. A Brazilian statesman and writer, died February 22, 1912. He occupied many important offices in Brazil under the last emperor, Dom Pedro. He was for a time minister of finance, but at the time of the war between Brazil and Paraguay in 1864-68 he was minister of marine, and to his services are said to have been largely due the Brazilian victories. When the empire was overthrown by the Republicans, Preto was premier. After the establishment of the republic his loyalty to the dethroned emperor and his heirs prevented him from accepting any of the positions offered to him by the republic. He took up the practice of law and devoted much of his time to writing.

PREVENTION. See PUBLIC CHARITIES.

PRICE, JAMES L. An American jurist, died March 11, 1912. He was born in New Hagerstown, O., in 1840, and was educated in the public and high schools of that city. He was admitted to the bar in 1862 and until 1865 practiced at Carrollton, O., and afterwards at Lima. In 1895 he was appointed judge of the Circuit Court of Ohio, serving until 1901, when he became associate justice of the Supreme Court of the State. In 1908-9 he was chief justice of the court.

PRICES. One of the most universal subjects of discussion in recent years has been the rise of prices or the increased cost of living. This upward movement, which began in 1895 or 1896, continued to the close of 1912 with recessions of greater or less degree at different times. As indicated by Bradstreet's index number, which is the total sum of the wholesale prices of 96 commodities, the price level December 1, 1912, was 9.5462. This compared with 8.9824 on December 1, 1911, an increase of 6.2 per cent.; and reached the highest level in many recent years. It was 8.5 per cent., 4.6 per cent., 16 per cent., 12 per cent., 7 per cent., and 21.8 per cent. above the level on December 1, 1910, 1909, 1908, 1907, 1906, and 1903 respectively. During the year 65 of the 96 commodities advanced in prices, 13 remained unchanged, and 28 declined. Breadstuffs, oils, naval stores, chemicals, and drugs were the groups declining, while livestock, provision, fruits, hides and leather goods, textiles, metals, coal and coke, and building materials increased. The average of the index numbers of the first days of the twelve months of 1912 was 9.1867. The average index numbers of other years were as follows: 1911, 8.7132; 1910, 8.9881; 1909, 8.5153; 1908, 8.0094; 1907, 8.9045; 1906, 8.4176; 1905, 8.0987; 1900, 7.8839; 1896, 5.9124. This indicated a rise of 53 per cent. since 1896. See FINANCIAL REVIEW.

FOREIGN. The rise of prices in foreign countries was not so marked as in the United States, but was universally felt. Statistical inquiries were made in nearly every European country, Japan, and Australia, and revealed everywhere the upward movement. This was very frequently made responsible for the world-wide unrest in both the industrial and political spheres. Radical labor movements have been noticeable in the last few years in England, Germany, France, Austria, Hungary, Italy, Australia, and America. Food riots have been common in various parts of Europe, leading to governmental action in various ways; the establishment of public fish, meat, and vegetable markets and bakeries; the reduction or temporary relaxation of tariff duties on food products, as in Germany. A report of the merchant elders of Berlin showed that prices of all food products had advanced rapidly since 1901, the advances ranging from 20 to 50 per cent. During the year hundreds of public meetings throughout Germany petitioned for complete or partial suspension of taxes on foodstuffs; the matter was a subject of continuous debates in municipal councils and other public works. The continued rise was held to constitute a danger to the government, as it greatly strengthened the Socialist ranks. In Japan the rising prices were reported to have greatly increased the unrest by aggravating the hardships of the laboring poor; desertions of wife and family had greatly increased, as had also the demands for charitable aid and the amount of crime.

According to the Department of Labor for Canada, the index number of prices for January was 131.4; it rose steadily t 136.9 for June, fell gradually to 132.5 for September, and rose again to 134.3 for November. The London *Economist's* figures began at 2.613 for January; rose continually to 2.746 for July, except for a slight recession for April; fell to 2.722 for August; rose to 2.740 for September; and fell to 2.721 for November. Sauerbeck's index average for 1878-87 was 79; for 1890-99, 66; 1902-11, 74. Its lowest point was that for 1896, when it was 61; it rose to 75 for 1900; fell to 69 for 1903; rose to 80 for 1908; fell to 74 for 1909, and 78 for 1910, but rose to 80 for 1911. Its highest level in recent years was 86.7 for September, 1912, which may be compared with 88 for the year 1880. In general it may be said that there has been a rise of from 45 per cent. to 60 per cent. since 1896, and that it continues unabated, but that the general level is still considerably below the general level of the 70's.

In the Argentine Republic conditions similar to those in the United States were reported. Great stress was laid on increasing extravagance as the most obvious factor. Among the remedies advocated were sanitary housing of the poor in cities at low rents; lowering of the tariff; reservation of land near cities and towns for free farms; encouragement to small farmers; small banks; coöperative stores; and checking the exportation of cereals and meats.

CAUSES. Although a great multiplicity of causes for the increased cost of living is here and there assigned, it has come to be generally conceded that the principal cause is the increased production of gold. In 1890 the world's output of gold was only $118,000,000; in 1896 it had risen to $202,000,000; in 1899 to $396,000,000; in 1906 to $401,000,000; and since 1909 it has averaged more than $450,000,000 per year. Fundamentally, prices are but the ratios between the value of gold and the values of other things. Consequently this enormous increase in gold production has cheapened gold relatively so that more gold is needed to buy given quantities of other things. Of the same character is the action of the increase in the facilities for business credit. With the steady improvement in banking methods and an enormous increase in the use of checks, drafts, and other credit instruments, it has become possible to transact a much larger volume of business on the basis of a given quantity of gold than ever before. Undoubtedly also the protective system, as found in the United States and Germany, has the effect of increasing the prices of certain articles. This is also true of trusts and monopolies in some cases. This period of rising prices seems also to have been a period of rising standards of living, attended by demand for a greater variety and higher quality of goods. Among other conditions which might affect one or more particular commodities are the following: Cold storage; trade unions; shorter hours and increased wages of labor; pure food laws; advertising; unreasoning extravagance; military expenditures. When, however, one centres attention on the fact that this is a world-wide phenomenon, he is forced to conclude that the most important causes must be the increased supply of gold and increased use of credit in trade.

INTERNATIONAL COMMISSION. It was the world-wide character of this movement that led to the proposition by Professor Irving Fisher that an international commission be created to inquire into the facts, the causes, the remedies, and the probable future of the rise. This proposal was approved by numerous economists, publicists, and boards of trades in the United States and Europe. It received the hearty endorsement of President Taft, who urged upon Congress the authorization of such a commission. At the close of the year it seemed highly probable that Congress would pass the bill for its creation.

REMEDIES. Naturally, the remedies suggested have been determined by the explanations. Those who have laid stress upon the tariff, or the trusts, or cold storage, or farming methods, have found in a change of these the principal means for reducing the cost of living. Other suggestions included the coöperative movement; the elimination of middlemen; the repeal of the taxes on oleomargarine, and other food taxes; the use of vacant city lots for gardens; the establishment of public municipal markets; increased efficiency in business organization and labor; increased simplicity of living; and currency reforms.

It seemed evident, however, that the only way to effect the general movement was to deal with gold, by whose value the values of all other things are measured. Professor Irving Fisher brought forward a proposal to give the dollar uniform purchasing powers. It has long been understood that the index numbers of prices measure the rise and fall in the purchasing power of the gold dollar, pound, or whatever constitutes the standard of value. By resorting to the old method of a seignorage charge on the coinage of gold the amount of bullion required to make a dollar could be made to vary as much as desired. Professor Fisher therefore proposed that the index number be made to serve as a guide for the amount of the seignorage charge so that, although the legal weight of the gold dollar would vary, its purchasing power would be made as stationary as statistical calculation permitted. Thus any loss in purchasing power as shown by a rising index number would be offset by virtually putting more gold into the dollar. Such readjustment could be made by a public bureau at intervals, and its operation, in the proposer's claim, would soon become automatic. It was quite clear, however, that such a proposal could not be adopted without international agreement, as any one nation adopting it would suffer inconvenience in its foreign exchanges. Furthermore, the rise in prices is not at the same rate in different countries. It varies also for different commodities and hence the proposal for a stable dollar might, if adopted, bring about serious new disturbances.

HIGHER PRICES AND CROP PRODUCTION. It has been commonly asserted that one of the causes of rising prices of food products was the reduction in the per capita production. That this statement is unfounded was asserted by the Secretary of Agriculture and supported by evidence presented in the *Crop Reporter* for April. It was shown that for fifteen years considerable increases in the prices of agricultural products have occurred in every important country; but that the world's production of staple food products has increased faster than the population. Thus in wheat-growing the average annual increase during the ten years 1900-1909 inclusive was 2.5 per cent. This was due, in part, to increased acreage and in part to a better yield per acre. In corn production the average annual increase was 2.8 per cent; in oats 2.7 per cent; in barley 3.8 per cent; in rye 0.7 per cent; in rice 1.7 per cent; in sugar 4 per cent; in potatoes 3 per cent. During the five years 1905-1909, the flax-seed crop increased 13 per cent; the cotton crop 12 per cent., and tobacco 6 per cent. These eleven articles were said to constitute three-fourths of the acreage and 70 per cent. of the value of all agricultural products. Similarly with reference to meat production, the report showed that in the United States the numbers of cattle, sheep, and swine had increased materially between 1905-1910, some of this increase being attributed to better data. In 26 countries outside of the United States it was estimated that the number of cattle had increased 13 per cent. between 1899 and 1909, the number of sheep 7 per cent., and of swine 11 per cent.

PRIMARY ELECTIONS, PRESIDENTIAL. See PRESIDENTIAL CAMPAIGN and ELECTORAL REFORM.

PRINCE EDWARD ISLAND. An insular province of the Dominion of Canada. Area, 2184 square miles. Population (census of June 1, 1911), 93,728, as compared with 103,259 in 1901. Charlottetown, the capital, had 11,198 inhabitants (12,080 in 1901). The province is administered by a lieutenant-governor, Benjamin Rogers, appointed June 1, 1910. Premier in 1912, John A. Mathieson. See CANADA.

PRINCETON UNIVERSITY. Among the important changes in the faculty during the year were the following: George B. McClellan, formerly mayor of New York City, was appointed for the year professor of economic history, conducting a senior course. Deans Henry B. Fine of the school of science and E. G. Elliot of the college were granted leave of absence for the year, and Prof. W. F. Magie and Prof. Howard McClenahan were elected to fill their respective places. Prof. Archibald A. Bowman, of the University of Glasgow, was elected to the chair of logic, comprising many of the courses formerly taught by Dr. Hibben. William Franklin Willoughby, formerly assistant director of the United States census, was appointed to the McCormick professorship of jurisprudence, the chair formerly held by Woodrow Wilson. Dr. Edwin Walter Kemmerer, formerly of Cornell University, was appointed professor of economics and finance. Work progressed during the year on the new graduate college, and many of the buildings approached completion.

PRISON ASSOCIATION, American. See Penology.

PRISON FARMS. See Penology.

PRISON LABOR. See Penology.

PRISON POPULATION. See Penology.

PRIVATE BANKS. The report of the Comptroller of the Currency estimated that there were more than 4000 private and brokerage banking houses in the United States. Only 1110 of these furnished reports to the comptroller, of which nearly three-fourths were in the middle western States. From Illinois alone 295 reported, from Indiana 194, from Ohio 149, and from Iowa 107. The aggregate resources of these 1110 private banks were $196,940,000. Included in this were loans and discounts amounting to $129,784,000. Their individual deposits were $152,494,000.

PRIME, Ebenezer Scudder. A rear-admiral, retired, of the United States navy, died April 27, 1912. He was born in New York City in 1847 and graduated from the United States Naval Academy in 1863. He served throughout the remainder of the Civil War. In 1874 he was made lieutenant and rose through successive grades until he became rear-admiral in 1905. He was retired in the same year at his own request. He served in the Spanish-American War as lieutenant-commander.

PROBATION ASSOCIATION, National. See Public Charities.

PROFERRIN. This is a compound of iron and milk casein containing iron equivalent to about 10 per cent. elementary iron, and phosphorus equivalent to about 0.5 per cent. elementary phosphorus. It is prepared by treating an alkaline solution of casein with a solution of an iron salt and precipitating with acetic acid. Proferrin is a brown powder, almost odorless and tasteless, insoluble in water and dilute acids, slowly soluble in alkalies. Proferrin acts as a ferruginous tonic and as a means of restoring the iron and phosphorus waste of the body. It undergoes very little change in the stomach, but is said to be quickly digested and absorbed in the intestines. Its hematogenous actions resemble those of other organic iron preparations.

PROFESSIONAL SCHOOLS. See Universities and Colleges.

PROGRESSIVE NATIONAL CONVENTION. See Presidential Campaign.

PROGRESSIVE PARTY. See Presidential Campaign.

PROHIBITION PARTY. See Presidential Campaign.

PROMOTION OF INSURANCE. See Insurance.

PROPAESIN. (Propyl Aminobenzoate Paramidobenzoic Acid Propyl Ester). Propaesin, $C_6H_4.NH_2COO\ (C_3H_7)$, 1:4, is the propyl ester of paraminobenzoic acid, $C_6H_4.NH_2.COOH$, 1:4. It is prepared by esterification of paraminobenzoic acid with propyl alcohol and is a fine, white or colorless, odorless, nearly tasteless powder, which produces numbness when placed on the tongue. Propaesin is very slightly soluble in water and is not readily wetted by this solvent. It is soluble in alcohol, benzene, chloroform, and ether. Propaesin is a local anæsthetic and analgesic. It is astringent and is said to be practically non-toxic, and to be useful in the treatment of gastralgia, gastric ulcer, and other painful diseases of the mouth, esophagus, and stomach. Externally, it reduces the sensibility of the mucous membranes of the nose, ear, and larynx, and induces local anæsthesia. It is therefore of value in all painful wounds and ulcers of the mucous membranes and of the skin, and for relieving pain in dental operations.

PROTESTANT EPISCOPAL CHURCH. The communicants in 1912, including those in the United States and foreign missions, numbered 986,021, compared with 963,097. The clergy numbered 5678, and the parishes and missions, 8164. In the Sunday schools of the denomination were 454,495 scholars and 51,138 teachers. The total contributions from all sources for the work of the denomination during 1912 were $18,802,183. The communicants in the United States proper numbered 970,451. The denomination comprises in the United States 68 dioceses and 28 missionary districts, including those in Alaska and insular possessions. In addition, there are 12 foreign missionary districts. There was contributed for missions, including domestic and foreign missions during the year, $1,010,944. There were five consecrations to the episcopate during the year and one bishop died, Bishop Charles Chapman Grafton (q. v.) Dr. James H. Van-Buren, Missionary Bishop of Porto Rico, and Dr. William M. Brown, Bishop of Arkansas, resigned during the year. Rev. George Biller, Jr., was elected Missionary Bishop of South Dakota, and Rev. Herman Page Missionary Bishop of New Mexico. Mr. Biller accepted, but Dr. Page subsequently resigned. The House of Bishops also elected Rev. Henry St. George Tucker Missionary Bishop of Kyoto, Japan, and Rev. Daniel Trumbull Huntington Missionary Bishop of Wuhu. There was no general convention of the denomination in 1912, as the conventions are triennial and the last was held in Cincinnati, O., in 1910. The Church Congress held its sessions in 1912 in St. Louis. Among the most discussed questions were, "Modern Psychic Phenomena and Demonology"; "The Possibility of Unity in Church Government"; "The Sanctity of Marriage"; "Official Censorship in the Interest of Morals"; "The Good and Evil in Trade Unions"; "Music as an Aid to Religion"; and "Conversion as a Christian Experience." The social work of the church has been actively prosecuted during recent years. The Christian Social Union at its annual meeting in January voted that the joint commission on social service, appointed at the last general convention, made continuation of their work as an organization unnecessary. The general conference on faith and order continued its work during the year. In June a deputation consisting of the Bishop of Chicago, president of the commission, the Bishop of Southern Ohio, chairman of the house of bishops, the Bishop of Vermont, and the Rev. William T. Manning, D. D., visited Great Britain and secured promise of the appointment of coöpera-

commissions by the Church of England in England, by the Episcopal Church of Scotland, and by the Church of Ireland.

PROTOZOA. See ZOÖLOGY.

PRUSSIA. See GERMANY.

PRYOR, SARAH AGNES (RICE). An American writer, died February 15, 1912. She was born in Halifax County, Va., in 1830. In 1848 she married Roger Atkinson Pryor and became one of the most prominent agitators for secession in the South. She was the author of *The Mother of Washington and Her Times* (1903); *Reminiscences of Peace and War* (1904); *Birth of a Nation* (1907); *My Day* (1909), and *The Colonel's Story* (1910). Mrs. Pryor's reminiscences of war times are among the most interesting and valuable of those written by observers of conditions in the South.

PSYCHICAL RESEARCH. To those interested in this field of human inquiry the sudden death of Andrew Lang on July 20 came with no small degree of surprise and sorrow. The *Athenæum* (July 27) says, with reference to this brilliant litterateur, that he "was intensely interested in spiritualism, crystal-gazing, and psychical research generally, and was one of the founders and a past-president of the [British] Psychical Research Society; and no one could tell a ghost-story better." Preceded in the chair by men eminent in their several walks of life, men whose names scientists, philosophers, and statesmen conjure with, he showed for the first time how well a man of high literary ideals and achievements could sympathize with the efforts of those interested in psychic phenomena. The presidential address of his successor, the Rt. Rev. Bishop Carpenter (in *Proceedings* of the Society for Psychical Research, 26), points out the significance of the conception of the self as a growing, dynamic entity, inheriting the experiences of past selves and capable of contributing its share to selves which are to come. To quote, "And may it not be that our present life compared with the future life is an embryonic life? May there not be faculties and powers which are now being formed, whose full significance and value will only be evident when we pass into a life of new conditions?" That, in spite of the clever deceptions practised on the society by mediums, the work of culling the wheat from the chaff goes steadily on, is indicated by the advice: "While being strictly vigilant against fallacious representations of phenomena, vigorous in examining all facts and circumstances brought to notice, it ought to hold a mind open enough to welcome hints and helps from every quarter; it ought to be as stern in rejecting what is irrelevant as it should be keen to perceive the importance which lurks in what is insignificant."

The results obtained from "experiments" have been questioned by able critics. Tuckett (*Bedrock*, 1, p. 18) says that "the Will to Believe has made them [Barrett and Lodge] ready to accept evidence obtained under conditions which they would recognize to be unsound if they had been trained in experimental psychology. Sidgwick (1895) believed the chief work of the Society for Psychical Research has been the exposure of impostors and that their best results were mainly negative." Hill and Lodge (*Bedrock*, 1, pp. 333, 342) maintain, however, that some phenomena, such as telepathy, are entitled to respectful consideration and that there is some virtue in quantity of results over against quality. The subject of "automatisms" or automatic writing, is responsible for considerable discussion. A series of "automatisms" recorded for about a month "seems to have resulted in the production not only of cross-correspondence" between mother and daughter without normal means of communication, "but of statements, subsequently verified, about events [normally] unknown to the automatists." This "experiment" is similar to a case reported in Piddington's well-known paper, "A series of concordant automatisms," entitled "the Latin message." In Podmore's last book, *The Newer Spiritualism,* this reported "experiment" fared ill under the destructive criticism of the author, and has led, since that time, to a series of apologetic explanations of "faults in the experimentation," and of the possibility of the subjects actually seeing without consciously noticing" references which later figured in the concordance of "automatic phenomena." Maxwell, in reviewing the "experimental" methods involved in investigating "scripts" of this sort, indicates two sources of error, aside from all prevalent possibility of conscious or unconscious fraud: (1) The difficulty of proving what a medium does not know; and (2) the ascription of "automatic phenomena" to a "supernormal force" when it can very easily be a matter of cryptomnesia, or subconscious memory. That interest in psychical research is not on the wane is manifested by the appearance, in its thirty-fourth edition (85th thousand), of the popular book on hypnotism, spiritism, and mental therapeutics, by Hudson, called *The Law of Psychic Phenomena.*

PSYCHOLOGICAL ASSOCIATION, AMERICAN. See PSYCHOLOGY.

PSYCHOLOGY. The tendency which directed psychological investigation toward applied fields of research (cf. YEAR BOOK, 1911, p. 590) has steadily continued to make itself felt. A second tendency toward a thorough examination of phychological methods is increasingly manifest, both in America and in Europe. A perusal of the output of the laboratories and of the subjects of discussion at the annual conferences of psychologists in both continents, gives ample evidence of the first tendency, and the theoretical papers that have appeared in a number of psychological journals bear witness to the second. Were these two operating principles, application and self-examination, equipotent in the progress of psychology as a science, the combination would doubtless be of incalculable value to the firmer establishment of the discipline. The appearance of these two tendencies is significant in a dual way: (1) It is indicative of a basic supply of well-established phenomena; and (2) it is symptomatic of a healthy and normal growth of the science. When experimenters have time and inclination to attack problems in applied fields of investigation, it means that they have an adequate kit of psychological tools ready at hand with which to work. Then, if these workmen, operating under slightly different conditions, find their tools not wholly fit, and if, under these circumstances, they carefully examine the tools and the way in which they were in the habit of using them, that is, if they hesitate to use their implements wrongly and take time to think about right methods, then there is assurance that the science is not over-hasty but normally progressive. So we find, on the one hand, the instilling of a self-conscious factor, a check on a too rapid and too clumsy application of facts and methods, and, on the other, the contribution of interrogations from the field of applied psychology becoming a guide to further examination of the premises, both in the matter of subject and of method, of psychology. Of the twenty-nine theses (an increase of six over last year) presented in connection with the requirements of the Ph. D. degree in our American colleges this year, a little over one-half were on subjects of an applied nature; several of the remainder dealt with the investigation of psychological method—remarkable, even if the number be small, when one remembers that theoretical discussions are usually the product of minds older than that of the average candidate for a doctor's degree, and more adequately trained in psychological perspective.

The American Psychological Association met at Cleveland under the presidency of E. L. Thorndike on December 30, 31, and January 1, in conjunction with affiliated sections of the American Association for the Advancement of Science. The Association of Experimental Psychologists met at Clark University, Worcester, Mass., on April 15-17. By sheer coincidence, the Congress for Experimental Psychology was held at about the same time at Berlin, Germany, on April 16-19. Several new psychological journals have appeared. Among these are *Psiche*, in Italy, under the editorship of Assagioli; *Imago*, edited at Vienna by S. Freud, and devoted to the application of psychoanalysis; and *Fortschritte d. Psychologie u. ihren Anwendung*, edited by K. Marbe, at Würzburg. W. Wundt, the pioneer experimentalist, a knight of the Prussian order *pour le mérite*, celebrated his 80th birthday on August 16, on which occasion he was the recipient of a fund of 7000 marks, presented to him by about 60 of his friends and former students. The obituary of the year is fortunately short: we have to record only the death, on July 16, of Alfred Fouillée, editor and writer of topics related to social psychology.

General Books and Treatises. An unusually large number of general texts and treatises have come from this year's press. The current trend toward a revision of psychological principles appears this year in the large systematic work *Grundzüge der Psychophysiologie* by A. Lehmann of Copenhagen; Lehmann considers theory, explanation, to be the most pressing need in psychology. He points to the rapid advance of physical science under the atomic theory of matter and he declares that mental science stands in want of a corresponding theory of mind. He proposes the doctrine of psychical energy. Mental processes are bound up, so he maintains, with a special form of energy which appears in the transformation within the central nervous system of chemical energy and which is subject to the general laws of energetics. A decade of experimental work has convinced Lehmann that his doctrine is fruitful within psychology, and he proceeds therefore to apply it to the several problems of mind. The volume is divided into four parts: (1) Mind and Body; (2) Psychophysics (analysis into elementary processes); (3) Psychodynamics (neural facilitation and inhibition, and the mental activities); and (4) Mental Complexes. Less extensive use of the principle of energetics in psychology has been made by other writers. Lehmann himself gave an intimation of its use in his earlier *Elemente der Psychodynamik* (1905). Further evidence of this trend is given in Wirth's new book on *Psychophysik, Darstellung d. Methoden d. experimentellen Psychologie*. There are two subdivisions: (1) Mathematical Methods; (2) Experimental Arrangements. Appearing as part of a text-book on the methods of physiology, it includes all of the methods of experimental psychology, which, however, are woven into a texture colored by the theory of psychometric functions.

Wundt's little elementary text-book, which recently appeared, has now been translated into English by R. Pintner, *An Introduction to Psychology*. The work presents in simple language, without technical detail, much of the material already accessible in the *Outlines*. It begins with the general delineation of consciousness, it proceeds to the description of the elements and of the associative and apperceptive forms of combination, and it closes with the general laws of mental life. The English of the *Introduction* is not always felicitous; but it renders with a fair degree of success the difficult sentences of the original. The translation will help junior students unfamiliar with the larger works toward an understanding of the main principles of Wundt's psychology. A. Kröner, in his *Elemente d. Völkerpsychologie v. W. Wundt*, has, in an independent and simplified way, condensed Wundt's larger work, so that it is now not in the form of a series of scholarly lectures, but in the less attractive guise of a text-book. Ebbinghaus's *Abriss d. Psychologie* has this year passed into its fourth edition. Calkin's *First Book in Psychology* appeared in a third and revised edition in which the author has aimed "to emphasize the essential social nature of the conscious self, to accentuate the fact that the study of the self, as thus conceived, involves a study of behavior, and, finally, to prune the book of expressions which lend themselves to interpretation in terms of an atomistic psychology." On the whole, it still clings very firmly to the notion of the self which James had when he wrote his *Principles of Psychology* (1890). *A System of Psychology*, written by K. Dunlap is designed to give "as consistent a sketch as possible of the general field of normal human psychology." The work lays a good deal of emphasis upon psychological theory. The author extends his theory in a controversial manner in a subsequent article (*Psychol. Rev.*, 19, pp. 415-46), in which he argues in favor of the addition of "relational elements" to the list of simple mental processes. A neurology written partly for the use of students of psychology was published during the year in England (*The Nervous System*, by J. D. Lickley). It contains many good figures and many useful descriptions; but its psychology is, unfortunately, both crude and antiquated. Other systematic text-books are W. Schmied-Kowarzik's *Umriss einer neuen analytischen Psychologie* and S. Radhakrishnan's *Essentials of Psychology*. A book reminiscent in subject and style is G. S. Hall's *The Founders of Modern Psychology*, a collection of lectures recently delivered at Columbia University. The layman who is interested in the scope and the achievements of psychology will profit from the inspection of J. R. Angell's *Chapters from Modern Psychology*, a series of eight lectures devoted to General, Physiological, Experimental, Individual and Applied, Social and Racial, Animal, and Genetic Psychologies, and the Psychology of the Abnormal. In a compact form, B. Rand has gathered together excerpts from the writings of some of *The Classical Psychologists*, from Anaxagoras to Wundt. This book is similar to collections of the writings of the moralists and the philosophers which have already been prepared by the author. The choices are usually happy as far as material is concerned, although one wonders why Stumpf is included and Ebbinghaus is omitted. Now that Dessoir's biographical *Outlines of the History of Psychology* has been translated by Fisher, the psychologist is waiting for the translation of Klemm's *History of Psychology*, a topical presentation of the historical development of the science, promised us by Wilm, to use as a companion volume. Brett has also issued a *History of Psychology; Ancient and Patristic*.

SENSATION AND PERCEPTION. *Vision.* Important investigations in vision, somewhat controversial in nature, have been reported from laboratories at Bryn Mawr and Cornell. Ferrée and Rand (*Psychol. Rev.*, 19, pp. 195-239) claim that under proper conditions, especially when the degree of brightness favors color saturation in the after-image, a colored after-image can be sensed in the peripheral field of vision when no color is sensed in the stimulus. Day (*Am. Jour. of Psychol.*, 23, p. 576) claims that these "anomalous" results occur more frequently with colorless than with colored stimuli, but that "previous stimuli were found to influence the hue of succeeding sensations, as well as succeeding after-images." Rand, in a paper on "the effect of changes in the general illumination of the retina upon its sensitivity to color" (*Psychol. Rev.*, 19, pp. 463-90) shows that the color-sensitivity of the retina is influenced by changes in the illumination of the visual field, "particularly when the stimulus is surrounded by a white field," and points out the absolute necessity, in the standardization of comparative results, "of keeping the general illumination of the room constant." "The relative legibility of different faces of printing types" is the title of a paper by Roethlein (*Am. Journal of Psychol.*, 23, pp. 136) which ought to be taken seriously by those engaged in the publishing business. A great many cards of various fonts of type were presented, as in the ordinary legibility tests modified to suit the experiment, and the number of correct readings were tabulated. It was discovered that legibility is, in the main, a product of five factors: The form and size of the letter, the heaviness of the face, the width of the white margin surrounding the letter, the position of the letter in the letter-group, and the shape and size of the adjacent letters. Relatively heavy-faced types are more legible than the light-faced types. For greater ease in reading, the initial position of a letter in a group is the most favorable, the final less, and the intermediate the least favorable. That quality and texture of the paper on which the printed type is presented are much less significant than is generally supposed, and that modification of the "lower case" letters *s*, *x*, *e*, *a*, *w*, and o is needed, are conclusions drawn from the results of this important experiment. The geometrical illusions still claim their share of interest. Tichý finds (*Zeit. f. Psychol.*, 60, pp. 267-79) that the Poggendorff illusion does not depend on binocular vision, freedom or fixity of fixation, knowledge or ignorance of the phenomena, while Valentine (*Brit. Journal of Psychol.*, 5, pp. 8-35) found, on the other hand, that the horizontal-vertical illusion was increased with practice, that it differs for each of the two eyes, and that it reaches its maximum effect at a definite length of line. Rice has compiled a great number of instructive statistics in his *Visual Acuity with Lights of Different Colors and Intensities*.

METHODS. One of the chapters of G. E. Müller's *Zur Analyse d. Gedächtnistätigkeit u. d. Vorstellungsverlaufes* (*cf.* YEAR BOOK, 1911, p. 591) gave a real impetus to the present theoretical discussion of psychological methods noted elsewhere. The fact that the report of "meaning" was distinguished by two observers in an article by Titchener (*Am. Journal of Psychol.*, 23, pp. 165-82) as logical, non-psychological, and non-introspectible, in contrast to the report of process as a psychological description, called for further delineation of method. This plea was emphasized by Dodge (*Am. Journal of Psychol.*, 23, pp. 214-29), who entered a protest against the limitation of psychological methods to introspection. He claimed that neurological and pathological facts, reports of animal behavior, investigations of mental work and fatigue, should be admitted into the records in addition to introspective data. Titchener, in two consecutive studies of introspection (*Am. Journal of Psychol.*, 23, pp. 427-48; and also pp. 485-508), claims that introspection is the most important of psychological methods and is its own test. Introspection, while it does not furnish a psychological system, "always presupposes the point of view of descriptive psychology, and the introspective methods thus do us the same service in psychologizing that 'observation and experiment' do in natural sciences."

SOCIAL PSYCHOLOGY. *Religion.* To the large number of books dealing with this phase of psychological study must be added, this year, the comprehensive and important work by J. H. Leuba, entitled *The Psychological Study of Religion, Its Origin, Its Function, and Future*. Religion is viewed by this author as one of the manifestations of human behavior. Having taken his "stand against the opinion that psychology, since the transcendental is beyond its ken, can have nothing to say upon the existence of the God of Christianity," he finds the "origin of the ideas of unseen things from apparitions, feeling of obligation, sleep, trances, motor and sensory abnormalities." "The Gods of religion are inductions from experience." He calls upon anthropology, sociology, psychology, results of questionaries, and the data of private correspondence, for the facts to support these assertions. Coming at the same time, J. Watson's *The Interpretation of Religious Experiences*, though not a psychological study, adds its share to the data already gathered. It appears in two large volumes, the one "historical," the other "constructive," and comprises the Gifford Lectures for 1910-1912. In the second volume the point is made that psychophysical parallelism, if accepted, leads to agnosticism. That, naturally, is a debatable question, and furthermore, still more naturally, not at all a question for the psychologist but for the philosopher. C. A. Ellwood's recent book on *Sociology in Its Psychological Aspects* bases its claims on a consciousness that "does work, does function, and as such has a survival value in the life process," and in so doing opens itself to all the criticisms that have been urged against this "teleological aspect" of functional psychology. Many other psychological interpretations of religion have appeared, notably in W. E. Hocking's "Mysticism as Seen Through Its Psychology" (*Mind*, 21, pp. 38-61); J. Morse's "The Psychology and Pedagogy of Doubt" (*Journal of Religious Psychol.*, 5, pp. 418-28); and J. B. Pratt's "The Psychology of Religion" (*Journal of Religious Psychol.*, 5, pp. 383-94).

INDIVIDUAL PSYCHOLOGY. *Mental Efficiency.* Applied psychology very often runs into channels of "mental tests." It is, of course, impossible to cite in a short résumé all the work done in this field this year. In E. B. Huey's *Backward and Feeble-minded Children* a summary of the results obtained is given in a non-technical yet scientific manner calculated to interest the average reader. Seashore (*Journal of Ed. Psychol.*, 3, p. 50), Terman and Childs (*Journal of Ed. Psychol.*, 3, pp. 61-74), and Town (*Psychol. Clinic*, 5, pp. 239-44) deal more specifically with the well-known Binet-Simon tests compiled to give an index of the "mental age" of the subject. There is a plan on foot to revise and extend these tests so that they can be applied to ages beyond 13 and 14 years. Thorndike's "curve of work" (*Psychol. Rev.*, 19, pp. 165-94) attempts to trace the efficiency of various "mental functions." He finds that two hours or less of continuous exercise of a function at maximum efficiency, so far as the worker can make it so, produce a temporary negative effect, curable by rest, of not over 10 per cent.—most functions produce less. There is a 4 per cent. rise near the end of the work when the date of the end is known. Several traditions are overthrown. That an increase in efficiency occurs at first, or a few moments after the efficiency is slackened, is not verified. The "curve of work" does not drop when the work becomes boresome, except when the work is intermittent. Less satisfaction in the continuous learning process accounts for the looseness of "bonds" of association. Hollingworth has traced the effects of caffein on both work and sleep (*Psychol. Rev.*, 19, pp. 66-73, and *Am. Journal of Psychol.*, 23, pp. 89-100). In the first case, work was measured by the "speed and quality of performance in typewriting" Ruskin's *Sesame and Lilies*. Some of his results are: Typewriting was quickened by small doses of caffein alkaloid (1-3 gr.) and retarded by large doses (4-6 gr.). In general, caffein produced superior quality of typewriting. In the case of sleep, the results are taken from the reports of observers. He found that small doses of caffein alkaloid (¼ gr.) do not in general produce sleep disturbances; larger doses (6 gr.) produce marked sleep impairment. Caffein has its greatest effect on subjects previously or subsequently without food, and it does not depend for its effect on age, sex, or previous habits. Bischoff (*Arch. f. d. gesam. Psychol.*, 22, pp. 423-52) attempted to get correlations between mental and physical efficiency and fatigue. His observers added for ten minutes, with five-minute pauses, on the first day, and thereafter on twelve mornings without pauses, during which time the physical strength of the hand was tested. Although there were differences in persons, he concludes that practice and confidence lessen fatigue, while there is no relation between practice in psychical work and fatigue of body. Those who are interested in studying this sort of investigation will find further material in B. R. Simpson's *Correlations of Mental Abilities* and C. H. Bean's *The Curve of Forgetting*, both of which were published this year.

ÆSTHETICS. A growing field of investigation is that of the mental response to the beautiful in poetry, music, and painting. Kallen (*Journal of Philos., Psychol.*, etc., 9, pp. 253-65) questions the propriety of examining æsthetic experiences on the ground that there is inevitable distortion of the experience. In his words, "private, concrete, elusive, in itself neither mental nor amental, beauty is the optimal mode of that positive, intrinsic value-relation which binds the mind to its object in such wise that the two are completely and harmoniously adapted to each other in the very act of apprehension." Weld, who studied the effect of music produced by a gramophone on the minds of a number of observers, reports (*Am. Journal of Psychol.*, 23, pp. 245-308) that in addition to well-known physiological effects, such as variation in the distribution of blood-supply, increase in the heart-rate, irregularity or respiration, and muscular reactions, his observers reported images of movement, when the enjoyment was purely "emotional," and auditory images, when the enjoyment was of the "intellectual" type. He groups his observers, as the result of their experiences, into "analytic," "motor," "imaginative," and "emotional." Groos (*Arch. d. gesam. Psychol.*, 22, pp. 401-22) made an analysis of Wagner's *Ring des Nibelungen* and found words denoting both visual and auditory experiences, with a predominance of the visual. While the expressions of vivid colors are surprisingly few in this dramatic poem, over one-half of the visual material pertains to glosses, sheens, and glows. In comparison with Goethe's and Schiller's works, this investigator finds more auditory-vocal material in Wagner. It seems fair to argue that, however much an analytical study of the writings of an author may contribute to the knowledge of the effect produced on the reader, it may not give a correct index of the writer's mental life. Together with other material, gathered when the author is engaged in a non-professional description of his experiences, a study of this kind may be of service. Rignano (*Scientia*, 11, pp. 71-87) claims that affective experiences or inclinations give rise, in their conflict, to attention, and that the choice of memories really depends upon these affective elements. Sartorius (*Psychol. Stud.*, 8, p. 1) in Wundt's laboratory returns to the defense of the classical tridimensional theory of affection, and illustrates his defense with diagramatical curves of breathing corresponding to the six primary affective experiences. Other interesting studies of these problems are Lee and Anstruther's *Beauty, Ugliness, and Other Studies in Psychological Æsthetics*, and Downey's *The Imaginal Reaction to Poetry, the Affective and the Æsthetic Judgment*.

ANIMAL PSYCHOLOGY. The *Journal of Animal Behavior*, which appeared for the first time last year (YEAR BOOK, 1911, p. 563), has established itself as a useful, interesting, and flourishing publication. With the appearance of the fifth *Behavior Monograph* (S. B. Vincent, "The Function of the Vibrissæ in the Behavior of the White Rat"), the first volume of the series is complete; the second volume, soon to be published, will contain as its first number a paper by H. M. Johnson on "Some Sensory Responses in Dogs." Discussion of the general behavior of animals when stimulated, especially by light, still occupies a large place in the literature. S. O. Mast's book, *Light and the Behavior of Organisms* (YEAR BOOK, 1911, p. 563), reviewed last year in the *Journal*, gave a summary of results obtained up to that time. The reviewer, G. H. Parker, could not understand why so little emphasis was laid on the "selection" of a particular orientation of movement, after a number of preliminary trials had been made. The earthworm, for example, "selects," according to this reviewer, a trial in a pa ticu a direction, which "through the stimulation of rsymmetrical points on its body has been found to be most favorable for orientation." The author replies, in this year's *Journal* (p. 209), that "the organism retains a given direction of locomotion not because of continuous action of light, but because it tends to move in a direct course in the absence of external stimuli." He cites instances, such as earthworms and fire-flies following a given direction in darkness after a flash of light has been given. R. M. Yerkes (*Journal*, p. 351) found that earthworms could direct their movements in accordance with associations formed between two or more stimuli. C. H. Turner (*Biological Bulletin*, 23, p. 371) has experimented on the "apparent reversal of the response to light of the roach" and finds that, by applying disagreeable electric shocks to roaches, organisms which prefer the dark, he can train the male species more readily than the female to avoid dark chambers. J. S. Szymanski (*Journal of Animal Behavior*, 2, p. 81) also taught male roaches to avoid the dark by the same "method of punishment." E. G. Boring, in a "Note on the negative reaction under light adaptation in the planarian" (*Journal*, 2, p. 247), concludes that these simple organisms can become "light-adapted on one side during the exposure to directive light" and, consequently, later, when the light is turned off, "turn consistently in the direction from which the light first came." M. F. Washburn and E. Abbott (*Journal*, 2, p. 145) report work done "on the brightness value of red for the light-adapted eye of the rabbit" in which it was found that rabbits can discriminate saturated red paper from gray. F. S. Breed (*Journal*, 2, p. 280) found that chicks depend to a large extent on the difference in the brightness of colored stimuli for their reactions. There is a discussion among entomologists as to whether flowers, which are vividly contrasted in color with respect to the background of leaves, do not attract more bees and other pollen-distributing insects than do flowers of less color-contrast. *Die neue Tierpsychologie*, by G. Bohn, is a German edition of a French prize essay based upon a biological theory of psycho-chemical activities. K. Krall in *Denkende Tiere* gives an interesting account of the performances of the "thinking" horse, Hans, and his successors. A number of other experiments on singing mice, albino rats, wasps, bloodsucking insects of tropical Africa (v. *Bulletin of Entomological Research*, 3, p. 275), tree-frogs, and may-flies have been performed. All shed light on the degrees of "intelligence" displayed in the lower forms of animal life. The relation of this "intelligence" to human intelligence, as well as the applicability of these experiments to the interpretation of "consciousness," still remains to be worked out.

PSYCHOTHERAPY. Suggestion, as a cure for a certain type of ailment, still occupies the minds of physicians, and a movement is under way to bring psychology into closer touch with medicine. Külpe has described in his *Psychologie u. Medizin* the way that psychology can be of service to the physician. At last year's meeting of the American Psychological Association a conjoint session was held with men professionally interested in therapeutics at which the possibilities of coöperation were considered. The discussion turned upon psychological courses for medical schools. This year Jacoby, a man eminent in medicine, has written a book on *Suggestion and Psychotherapy*. While, in its attempt to reduce some of the data of psychology to simple terms, it discusses them in a crude and antiquated manner, it gives, nevertheless, a coherent account of the way in which the mind works. The author shows the commonness of "suggestion" and its importance in our mental lives. In the second part of the work, he illustrates how, in the hands of a skillful physician, this agent may work wonders in the organism; but he sanely warns the reader not to expect miracles to be wrought. "Suggestive possibilities, however, have distinct limitations, set by the laws of nature. We can produce false concepts and sensory deceptions, with their accompanying sensations, or remove such concepts by awakening contrary conceptions, but we cannot bring about any organic change by means of suggestion (p. 149)... But, as we have shown before, psychotherapy can have for its object only the cure of functional diseases and functional symptoms, diseases of the imagination, which, despite their immaterial basis, are perceived as actual diseases" (p. 222). Jones (*Rev. of Neurol. and Psychiat.*, 10, p. 1) includes under the term "suggestion" all conscious and unconscious processes, but confines it later to the transference of an emotional attitude, usually unconscious, to an object, viz., the physician. MacDougall (*Journal of Abnormal Psychol.*, 6, p. 368) traces the development of suggestion from the extreme slavish imitation of the "subjective" individual to "persistent and meaningless opposition to all suggestion," and cites instances of typical reactions for verification of the various grades. The Freudian school (*cf.* YEAR BOOK, 1911, p. 574) is well represented in this year's literature by its adherents and by its opponents. A number of examples of pictorially symbolic forms experienced in hallucinations, dreams, and ordinary life are given and interpreted by Siberer (*Jahrbuch f. psychoanalytische u. psychopathologische Forschungen*, 3, p. 661), and Bertschinger (*ibid.*, p. 69) shows a variety of symbolic drawings made during hallucination. While many followers of the Freudian school are still to be found, there are indications in places that the system of psychoanalysis needs modification. A paper to this effect by Taylor (*Journal of Abnormal Psychol.*, 6, p. 449) suggests that the "anxiety type" of neurosis can be cured at a single sitting and without making any "inquiry as to his sexual life, or to his social relations in general." Much attention still centres about the dream consciousness. The second volume of Vold's *Über den Traum* came out this year. Coriat (*Journal of Abnormal Psychol.*, 6, p. 367) says that "dreams take place because the brain is somewhat active; in deep sleep where the brain is completely at rest it is doubtful if dreams occur at all." During the summer of this year, at a meeting of leading physicians of New York City, Freud's character was severely assailed, and the results of his method questioned. In general, however, and especially abroad, his school is still respectfully recognized, and his investigations are considered important contributions to this special field of research.

PUBLIC CHARITIES. One of the most conspicuous features of recent social history is the great expansion of charitable and philanthropic activities. Bequests for charitable purposes have been unusually frequent and generous; numerous organizations have come into existence and annual conferences of many bodies are now held. Not only has the scope of charitable and philanthropic activities greatly expanded, but the very purpose and nature of charities are changing. The traditional subjects of poor relief and care of the criminal have been supplemented by attention to the neglected, the delinquent, the defective, the helpless, the aged, the epileptic, the feeble-minded, the tubercular, the vagrant; child life in all its aspects and the labor of women in mills and factories are given earnest and intelligent attention. But most notable is the change of emphasis from relief to prevention. Modern charity aims to become scientific. It would discover the causes of poverty, of misery, of maladjustment in all their forms, and by removing causes stamp out these impediments to social welfare. Both voluntary agencies and public assistance have expanded; there is an increase in public supervision of both State and private activities; and there is an even finer classification of persons dealt with.

The conferences noted below give an intimation of the present problems of charitable agencies. Reference should also be made to CHILD LABOR, CHILDREN'S BUREAU, MINIMUM WAGE, OCCUPATIONAL DISEASES, PENOLOGY, OLD-AGE PENSIONS, SWEATING, WOMEN IN INDUSTRY, WELFARE WORK, WIDOWS' PENSIONS, WORKINGMEN'S INSURANCE, and WORKINGMEN'S COMPENSATION.

NATIONAL CONFERENCE OF CHARITIES AND CORRECTIONS. The thirty-ninth annual session of this conference was held at Cleveland in June. There were more than 2000 registered delegates, besides hundreds of other interested auditors, it being more largely attended than any preceding conference. The subjects of discussion included immigration, with special reference to its distribution and assimilation; sex hygiene, including discussion of sex problems encountered in social work, sex education, venereal diseases in children, international traffic in vice, eugenics, and the relation of the medical profession and hospitals to the hygiene of sex; standards of living and labor, under which was presented a platform of industrial minimums, including a living wage, an eight-hour day, a six-day week, ample provision for health and safety, for housing, for compensation for accidents and diseases of occupation, for old-age and unemployment insurance, and for the protection of women, children, the unemployed, and the unemployable; children; housing and recreation; medical and social work; courts and prisons; families and neighborhoods; and public supervision and administration.

It was decided to hold the 1913 session at Seattle, Wash. Mr. Frank Tucker of New York was chosen president and Mr. Alexander Johnson of Angola, Ind., was continued as general secretary. The following committees for that conference were named: children; church and social work; distribution and assimilation of immigrants; families and neighborhoods; health and productive power; probation, prisons, and parole; public supervision and administration; relation of commercial organizations to social welfare; and standards of living and labor.

OTHER CONFERENCES. In conjunction with the above national conference there were held at Cleveland ten other charitable and philanthropic conferences. The *Seventh Biennial Conference of Jewish Charities* was devoted primarily to the subject of wife desertion. A bureau organized in 1911 showed that it had located 561 out of 869 deserters reported to it. The subject of Palestinian Charities was also discussed and a plan for pensioning social workers presented. The National Federation of Settlements, Federated Boys' Clubs, National Association of Societies for Organizing Charity, and the Commission on Church and Social Service of the Federal Council of the Churches of Christ in America also held sessions.

The *National Federation of Remedial Loan Associations* held its third annual conference with representatives of sixteen of the twenty-five member societies present. These societies are engaged in a war against the loan shark.

The *National Probation Association* demanded that Congress pass a probation law for the federal courts, emphasized its belief that the juvenile courts and probation officers should coöperate with all constructive agencies in the community; and agreed that special detention homes or shelters for children awaiting trial are desirable. It decided to give greater publicity to its activities and with this in view authorized an assistant secretary. The *American Red Cross* session was devoted to a review of the relief work in connection with the Mississippi River flood and the *Titanic* wreck. A plan whereby more than 3000 graduate nurses have been enrolled under the Red Cross was described; as were also the results of the sale of the Red Cross Christmas stamps.

The *National Association of Public Relief Officials* was devoted to a study of the methods now in vogue in the United States for the relief of poverty by public agencies, the official programme for the prevention of mental defectiveness and insanity, and the present status of the public almshouse.

The *Conference for the Education of Backward, Truant, Delinquent, and Dependent Children* was devoted to the methods and efficiency of institutional vocational training, the opportunities for encouraging the agricultural movement of the country, institutional administration, and the study of individual children both within and outside of institutions.

In addition to the foregoing there are now about thirty State conferences of charities and corrections, at which similar problems are discussed and where the workers of the State receive inspiration and knowledge. These are important factors in the education of public opinion in their respective States.

The *National Conference of Catholic Charities* met in Washington, D. C., during the last week of September. Some forty pape s and addresses were presented dealing with needy families, defective childen, the protection of immigrants from those who prey upon them; the visitation, treatment, and relief of the chronic sick; and coöperation. There was formed a federation of Catholic women's charitable societies, representatives being present from all principal cities.

The *American Federation of Catholic Societies* met in Louisville, Ky., the latter part of August. In addition to discussions and resolutions on a great variety of other subjects resolutions were passed urging the abolition of unnecessary Sunday work, and the religious care and humane treatment of prisoners; demanding a living wage, reasonable hours of labor, abolition of child labor, prevention of accidents and their just compensation, proper moral and sanitary provisions in home, shop, mine, and factory; and recommending assistance to handicapped members of society, the immigrant, and the unorganized worker.

The *Southern Sociological Congress* met at Nashville, Tenn., May 7-10, at the call of Governor B. W. Hooper. It was attended by two representatives from each State and the District of Columbia. After lengthy discussion it was determined to effect a permanent organization and to hold annual conferences; whenever possible these will be in conjunction with the national conference. This was not due, however, to the belief that certain problems are peculiar to the Southern States, but rather because of the stimulating effect of such a conference and the much larger attendance of Southern workers made possible. Governor Hooper was made president, and A. J. McKelway and Kate Barnard, vice-presidents. Standing committees on public health, courts, prisons, child welfare, organized charities, the negro problem, and the church and social service, were created. The organization committee drafted a programme containing resolutions for the adoption of modern methods of prison reform; for juvenile courts and reformatories; for uniform laws on marriage, divorce, vital statistics, child labor, and school attendance; for the suppression of prostitution; for proper care of defectives, the blind, the deaf, the insane, the epileptic, and the feeble-minded; for a spirit of helpfulness and equal justice in the solution of the race problem; and for coöperation between the church and all social agencies.

PUBLIC DEBT. See articles on countries.

PUBLIC LANDS. See LANDS, PUBLIC, and HAWAII.

PUBLIC SCHOOLS. See EDUCATION.

PUGET SOUND DRY DOCK. See DOCKS AND HARBORS.

PUJO COMMITTEE. See BANKS AND BANKING.

PULP. See PAPER.

PUMP, VACUUM. See PHYSICS.

PUMPING MACHINERY. The Humphrey Gas Pump described in the YEAR BOOK for 1910 found wider application during 1912, and the metropolitan water board of London decided to install five of these pumps, four of 40,000 gallons per day capacity and the fifth of 20,000. It was reported that larger units had been designed for the Egyptian government for use in irrigation work at the pumping station at Mex. One of these was to have a capacity of 100,000 gallons per day with a lift of nineteen feet. See also FIRE PROTECTION.

PUNISHMENT OF CRIMINALS. See PENOLOGY.

PURDUE UNIVERSITY. A State institution of higher education at Lafayette, Ind., founded in 1869. The total enrollment in all departments of the university for the year 1911-12 was 2066. This includes the enrollment in the summer school. The faculty numbered 160. There was received a gift from W. C. Smith of Williamsport, Ind., of $100,000. The annual income, including that for the agricultural experiment station was in 1912, $578,483. The funds of the university are derived mainly from federal and State appropriations. The productive funds amounted to $240,000. The library contained 30,800 volumes. President, W. E. Stone.

PURE FOOD LAW. See FOOD AND NUTRITION.

PUT-IN-BAY EXPOSITION. See EXPOSITIONS.

PUTUMAYO ATROCITIES. See PERU, *History*.

PUZZOLAN CEMENT. See CEMENT.

PYGMIES. See ANTHROPOLOGY.

PYRRHOTITE. See MINERALOGY.

QUADRUPLE TURRETS. See NAVAL PROGRESS.

QUAKERS. See FRIENDS.

QUEBEC. A province of the Dominion of Canada. Area, 351,873 square miles. Population (census of June 1, 1911) 2,002,712, as compared with 1,648,898 in 1901. The city of Quebec, the capital, had 78,190 inhabitants (68,840 in 1901). The province is administered by a lieutenant-governor, Sir François Langelier, who was apointed May 5, 1911, upon the death of Lieut.-Gov. Sir Charles Alphonse Pantaléon Pelletier. Premier in 1912, Sir Lomer Gouin. The area stated above does not include the portion (the former district of Ungava) of the Northwest Territories annexed to Quebec in 1912. See CANADA.

HISTORY. In the general elections the Liberal government secured a large majority. Only seventeen Conservatives were elected as against sixty-four Liberals, the latter having the support of the Nationalists, who resented the Borden government's refusal to create Roman Catholic schools in Keewatin when it was added to Manitoba, its rejection of the Nationalist policy as to naval defense, and its failure to meet the Nationalist demands as to the dismissal of certain public officials. There was, moreover, general satisfaction with the Liberal administration of Quebec under Sir Lomer Gouin.

QUEENSLAND. A state of the Commonwealth of Australia. Area, 670,500 square miles. Population (census of April 3, 1911), 605,813, exclusive of full-blooded aboriginals. Brisbane, the capital, had 35,491 inhabitants; with suburbs, 139,480. Governor in 1912, Sir William MacGregor; premier, D. F. Denham. See AUSTRALIA.

HISTORY. The Queensland general elections toward the end of April resulted in a majority of eighteen for the government as against eight in the former Parliament. The issue of the election, according to the government, was that between a parliamentary government and a syndicalism which aimed at a general strike. The Labor party gained in the city of Brisbane, but lost in the country and mining districts. The press interpreted the result as a complete victory over syndicalism. The strike at Brisbane resulted in many acts of violence and in a speech on March 29, the premier, in reviewing the history of the affair, condemned the strike committee for its cruelty and stupidity. He praised the police and law-abiding citizens, however, for restoring order. In June the government introduced a bill providing for secret ballot of persons concerned in a proposed strike and compulsory fortnight's notice before striking.

QUIMBY, HARRIET. See AERONAUTICS.

QUIPUS. See ANTHROPOLOGY.

RABIES. A comparison of the figures obtained by the Public Health and Marine Hospital Service in 1911 with those of 1908 show that rabies is apparently on the increase in the United States. In 1911 cases were reported from 1381 localities, as against 534 in 1908. There were 98 deaths in 1911, as compared with 111 deaths in 1908. This is accounted for probably by the large increase in the number of institutions in which treatment could be obtained and by the fact that victims availed themselves of this treatment. In 1908 there were 23 institutions in the country where antirabic treatment was administered; in 1911 there were at least 42. A number of laboratories supply material for inoculations to practicing physicians. The number of persons known to have taken the treatment in 1908 was about 1500; in 1911 it was 4625. The figures for 1911 show that the period of incubation in 19 out of 65 cases was between 21 and 30 days. Three cases occurred over twelve months after the injury. The average incubation period of all cases, excluding those over one year, was 49.25 days. The main facts brought out in this report are the wider distribution of the infection, its spread to the Pacific Coast, which in 1908 seemed to be free from the disease, and the decreased death rate, owing to better facilities for early treatment and better distribution of the antirabic virus.

RACING. Nearly sixteen hundred trotting meetings were held in the United States and Canada in 1912 in which about 15,000 horses took part and more than $6,000,000 in purses and stakes was distributed. The Grand Circuit comprised thirteen cities, and there were fifteen weeks of continuous racing. Twenty world's records were broken, some of them of long standing. The biggest winner during the season was W. R. Cox, who gathered in $54,885 in purses. Others to win large amounts were T. W. Murphy, $44,338; E. F. Geers, $41,730; A. McDonald, $37,226, and A. S. Rodney, $37,015. The winning trotters of the year were: Baden, with $35,775 and Esther W., with $20,520. Joe Patchen II. led the pacers with $23,450, followed by Knight Onwards, with $10,495. Baden captured 12 firsts, 1 second, 1 third, and 1 fourth. Joe Patchen II. in thirteen races was first 12 times and second once. T. W. Murphy held first place among the drivers, finishing first 26 times, second 27, third 21, fourth 14, and unplaced 41. W. R. Cox was second, with 25 firsts, and E. F. Geers third, with 19 firsts.

Uhlan, by trotting the fastest mile in the history of light-harness racing, carried off the season's laurels. His time in the open was 1:58, which shattered the record of 1:58½ made by Lou Dillon in 1903 with a wind shield. Another horse to gain distinction was Airedale, a yearling colt, who lowered the record from 2:19½ to 2:15¾. The world's record for the fastest four-heat race was broken by Dudie Archdale, who clipped an average of half a second for each heat off the former record. Grace won the world's fastest five-heat race by capturing the third, fourth, and fifth heats in a race at Columbus in 2:04¾, 2:08½, and 2:06¾. The world's trotting team record of 2:07¾, made by The Monk and Equity in 1904, was reduced by Uhlan and Lewis Forest to 2:03¼. Another record to go by the board was in the two-year-old filly class, Nowaday Girl trotting a mile on a half-mile track in 2:16½. The former record was 2:19¾. In pacing, too, several new records were established. Impetuous Palmer paced a mile in 2:05¼, lowering by a quarter of a second the time made by Klatawah in 1898 and equaled by Jim Logan in 1909. Braden Direct reduced the record for four-year-olds from 2:04 to 2:03¾. The old record was established by Online in 1894. Evelyn W. was another pacer to break records. She paced the world's fastest two-heat and five-heat races. Mino Heir and George Gano established a new team record of 2:02, lowering the best previous time made by Hedgewood Boy and Lady Maud C. in 1909 by three-fourths of a second.

RACQUETS AND COURT TENNIS. The national amateur racquet championship tournament was held at Boston in February. In the final round Reginald Fineke, the title-holder, defeated J. Gordon Douglas 15—7, 15—11, 11—15, 9—15, 15—3. Q. A. Shaw and G. R. Fearing won the doubles championship from M. S. Barger and Payne Whitney by default. J. Gordon Douglas captured the gold racquet trophy for the second successive year by defeating H. F. McCormick 15—5, 15—6, 17—15. Charles Williams, who in 1911 had won the world's professional championship, retained his title by defeating George Standing 2—15, 15—9, 15—9, 15—11. The military singles championship was decided at London, A. H. Muir defeating A. C. G. Luther, the title-holder, 14—17, 14—18, 18—15, 15—8, 15—12. E. M. Baerlein, holder of the English singles championship, retired in 1912, and the title passed to B. S. Foster through his defeat of G. G. Kershaw 12—15, 17—14, 15—8, 15—1. The Oxford-Cambridge doubles tournament was won by Cambridge. C. Hutchins won the United States amateur championship at squash racquets by defeating F. B. Smith 15—10, 15—10, 15—18, 17—15. The national squash tennis championship went to Alfred Stillman, 2d, who defeated John W. Prentiss 15—3, 15—10, 15—9, 15—8.

Jay Gould successfully defended his title as amateur court tennis champion by defeating Joshua Crane 6—3, 6—1, 6—0. Gould and W. H. T. Huhn captored the doubles title in a match with G. R. Fearing and Crane 6—4, 5—6, 6—2, 3—6, 6—4.

RADIATION QUANTUM. See PHYSICS.

RADIOACTIVITY. See PHYSICS.

RADIOTHERAPY (RÖNTGEN RAYS). The discussions of these therapeutic agencies were characterized by a somewhat pessimistic tone during 1912. Ravogli enumerated the untoward results reported from treatment by X-ray exposures, which include, beside skin burns and ulcers, the occurrence in many instances of malignant tumors after the ray had been used for benign affections. Another real danger is that malignant growths, under the influence of radiation, are apt to be stimulated to metastatic activity. In other words, a localized tumor may be "scattered" and set up other growths in various parts of the body, resulting in the early death of the patient.

RADIUM. As to radium, Kronka, at the congress for balneology in Berlin made the statement that this substance had so far not shown any certain success in any single disease. Nevertheless, radium is being largely used, and radio-activity is being discovered in the springs of many watering places needing exploitation. New radium institutes were established in Berlin and Vienna. It cannot be said, however, that any definite advance was made in 1912 in our knowledge of the therapeutic value of this substance.

RADIUM. See CHEMISTRY, and RADIOTHERAPY.

RAIFFEISEN BANKS. See AGRICULTURAL CREDIT.

RAIL FAILURES. See RAILWAY ACCIDENTS.

RAILWAY ACCIDENTS. The question of safety in railway travel throughout the United States was especially prominent in the year 1912 on account of a succession of serious accidents and a general awakening of public opinion and discussion. The winter of 1911-12 had been unusually severe and this was in large part responsible for a number of derailments, due primarily to defects developing in track and roadbed. At the same time the weights carried by the wheels had been increased and high speeds maintained without a proper understanding in all cases of the strength of the track. Accordingly there were wrecks of fast trains on railway lines supposed to be maintained in the best possible manner, with all protection of automatic block signals and other safety devices. Failures of rails under service were conspicuous to a greater degree than ever before, while the human factor became prominent through accidents caused by negligence, carelessness, or disobedience of various railway employees. There were also the usual number of wrecks due to lack of block signals and improper condition of maintenance and operation, but these were not as provocative of the general discussions as those which followed losses of life and injuries on the best equipped and maintained lines. In fact, it was found necessary for the two eighteen-hour trains between New York and Chicago on the New York Central and Pennsylvania lines to lengthen their schedules by two hours, following several accidents to these trains, while in other cases, notably on the New York, New Haven and Hartford Railroad, accidents resulted from undue speed at certain points on the line where the trains were using switches or crossovers at too high a rate of speed. The more serious accidents served to bring before the public more prominently than ever the annual accident report of the Interstate Commerce Commission and to emphasize the great number of casualties that seem to accompany railway operation in the United States. These casualties are given in the accompanying table from the twenty-sixth annual report of the commission, which under the provisions of the law of May 6, 1910, receives a "Monthly report under oath of all collisions, derailments, or other accidents resulting in injury to persons, equipment, or roadbed arising from the operation of such railroad." This law gives the commission "authority to investigate all collisions, derailments, or other accidents resulting in serious injury to person or to the property of a railroad occurring on the line of any common carrier engaged in interstate or foreign commerce by railroad."

	1912		1911	
	Killed	Injured	Killed	Injured
Passengers:				
In train accidents	139	9,391	142	6,722
Other causes	179	6,995	214	6,711
Total	318	16,386	356	13,433
Employees on duty:				
In train accidents	596	7,098	630	8,601
In coupling accid.	192	3,234	209	2,966
Overhead obstructions, etc.	77	1,523	76	1,510
Falling from cars	573	13,874	539	12,989
Other causes	1,482	23,391	1,427	21,782
Total	2,920	49,120	2,871	45,848
Total passengers and employees on duty	3,238	65,506	3,227	59,281
Employees not on duty:				
In train accidents	20	156	13	174
In coupling accid.	....	2	.....	......
Overhead obstructions	1	12	2	13
Falling from cars	53	312	49	367
Other causes	241	477	228	410
Total	315	959	292	964
Other persons:				
Not trespassing—				
In train accidents	13	277	11	175
Other causes	1,185	4,746	1,143	4,898
Total	1,198	5,023	1,154	5,073
Trespassers:				
In train accidents	91	151	81	141
Other causes	5,343	5,536	5,203	5,473
Total	5,434	5,687	5,284	5,614
Total accidents involving train operation	10,185	77,175	9,957	70,932
Industrial accidents to employees not involving train operation	400	92,363	439	79,227
Grand total	10,585	169,538	10,396	150,159

COLLISIONS AND DERAILMENTS ON AMERICAN RAILWAYS

	1912	1911	1910	1909
Collisions	5,483	5,605	5,861	4,411
*Damage to cars, engines, and road	4,330	4,302	4,629	3,109
Killed in collisions	378	436	433	342
Derailments	8,215	6,260	5,918	5,259
*Damage to cars, engines, and road	7,197	6,550	5,195	4,372
Killed in derailments	394	349	340	264
Total collisions and derailments	13,698	11,865	11,779	9,670
*Damage	11,527	9,852	9,824	7,480
Killed	772	785	773	606

* Damage in thousands of dollars.

The reports of these investigations were to be published, but were not admissible as evidence in any damage suits arising out of an accident. Under this the Interstate Commerce Commission, through its inspectors of safety appliances, made a series of investigations, and up to September 1, 1912, they had made a critical examination of 81 of the more serious accidents, 49 of which were collisions, 31 derailments, and one a grade-crossing accident. It was found that in the case of the derailments 14 were either directly or indirectly caused by bad track, but that in 5 of these excessive speed in violation of existing speed restrictions had been maintained. In 3 cases investigated track conditions were found obviously unsafe, and in one of these the derailment took place at ordinary speed. Forty-eight of the 49 collisions investigated were caused by mistakes on the part of employees and 33 occurred on roads operated under train-order system. The report made by the inspectors of the commission stated these various accidents in detail and in connection with the condition of track and roadbed. The assistance of James E. Howard, engineer-physicist of the United States National Bureau of Standards, was enlisted and he made a number of tests of rail which indicated conditions of weakness and lack of power to resist the stresses caused by heavy trains moving at high speed.

While these reports were made by the government, and in many cases there were similar investigations by State railway or public service commissions, there was corresponding activity on the part of the railways themselves. The question of rails received much attention, and it was found that there was need of maintaining the most rigorous specifications and insisting that only the best portion of the cast steel ingot should be used in their manufacture. (See METALLURGY.) Speeds were reduced on many lines, and in some cases speed recorders were placed in the cabs of the locomotives. The provision of automatic train stops was also discussed and the satisfactory use of these devices on elevated and subway lines urged in their behalf.

The question of discipline came prominently to the front, as it was found that many rules were disobeyed and that tendencies to overrun signals were developed. Surprise tests were prosecuted with vigor on many lines and the "safety committee" movement, which had been organized in 1910 on the Chicago and Northwestern with the aim of securing the interest and coöperation of the employees, was extended over a large number of lines. This plan involved the formation of representative committees on each division from the various classes of employees who were charged with the duty of investigating accidents and using their influence towards arousing a more general appreciation of the serious effects of carelessness, taking of chances, and disobedience of orders, and in their bringing home to the employees the fact that they were the ones to suffer by loss of life and injuries rather than the stockholders and operating officials. On the Chicago and Northwestern, where this plan had been in operation for almost two years, a great improvement was observed and which involved a striking decrease in the loss of life among employees and passengers, notwithstanding the unfavorable operating conditions. In the winter of 1911-12 large safety rallies were held in Kansas City, Buffalo, Jersey City, and other points and the interest of both officials and employees was genuine and spontaneous. Safety committees by the end of the year had been formed in some railroad companies.

In connection with the question of discipline there was considerable discussion, as it was claimed that the strength of organized labor interfered with the maintenance of satisfactory operating conditions and failed to bring about the elimination of unfit employees. This view was taken by a number of railroad operating men, and also by J. O. Fagan, the railway signal man who had distinguished himself as an author. On the other hand, the railway brotherhoods combated this position, maintaining that they had raised the standard of labor and individual efficiency on American railway lines and that it was largely due to their influence that it was maintained at its present point of efficiency.

It was of interest to note in this connection the effects of government control, as in no single industry in the United States has government interference been as active as in the case of the railways. This has involved many efforts to secure increased safety, such as various safety appliance acts, the hours of service law, the inspection of locomotives law, compulsory reporting of all accidents and provision for their inspection, and other statutes and regulations of the commission having the same end in view. These unquestionably have brought about better conditions in American railroading and have secured a uniformity of practice that has been distinctly beneficial.

Railway safety in the United States can hardly be compared with railway conditions in Europe, as there are fundamental differences which render impossible any just comparison. The railway lines of the United States have an aggregate length of some 240,000 miles, as compared with 200,000 miles for all Europe, and in many cases go through regions thinly settled. This makes much more difficult the task of supervision, and at the same time the country itself, often rugged and mountainous, must be considered. The more concentrated traffic of Europe permits a more stable track and conditions of maintenance, and the comparison may be effected with a system of suburban lines around a great city as contrasted with transcontinental lines where there is much less traffic but greater difficulty in arranging for it. Furthermore, the military training and habits of obedience to law, both on the part of employees and the general public, make for greater safety, as infractions of rules are punished with severity in most cases.

In any comparison of statistics considerable allowance must be made for differences of method of classification and definition, and the accompanying tabular statement for all Europe is compiled from the best official statistics available, but its deficiencies are manifest. It should be noted that any comparison made should be between the collected railway lines of the United States and those of all Europe rather than between separate countries.

That the dereliction of employees producing railway accidents was not confined to the United States was shown by the derailment occurring on the London and North-Western Railway on September 17, in which 15 persons, including both engineer and fireman, were killed and 40 injured, 8 seriously. This accident occurred to a train passing from the fast to the slow line at Ditton Junction, and was caused by the ignorance of the engine-driver, who failed to slacken speed when the signals indicated that the train

TABULAR STATEMENT OF CASUALTIES ON THE RAILWAYS OF EUROPE

Compiled from Official Statistics contained in the Statistical Abstract for the Principal and Other Foreign Countries of Great Britain.

Country	Year	Total Length of Miles	Passengers Killed	Passengers Injured	Employees Killed	Employees Injured	Other Persons Killed	Other Persons Injured	Total Killed	Total Injured
Russia in Europe	1908	33,385	198	980	645	2,962	1,866	1,928	2,709	5,870
Great Britain	1910	23,387	121	4,080	420 •	25,137	580	893	1,121	30,110
Norway	1910	1,831	1	2	5	14	7	12	13	28
Sweden •	1909	8,366	6	7	32	161	59	23	97	191
Denmark †	1910-11	3,438	1	2	...	.....	25	31	26	33
German Empire	1909	58,216	121	567	533	1,348	338	307	992	2,222
Netherlands	1909	2,208	3	17	20	59	9	22	32	98
Belgium	1910	2,931	11	359	77	535	80	84	168	978
France	1909	25,017	8	283	351	648	333	211	692	1,142
Switzerland	1909	2,875	12	76	39	1,369	25	45	76	1,490
Spain	1907	8,961	25	141	64	2,191	213	207	302	2,539
Italy	1908-9	10,425	26	821	174	2,138	93	185	293	3,144
Austria	1909	13,847	34	479	154	2,081	125	301	313	2,861
Hungary	1910	12,821	24	135	140	276	189	162	353	573
Rumania	1908-9	1,979	13	28	22	58	53	50	88	136

• Including suicides. † Accidents on State Railways.

was being turned from the fast to the slow line. In the investigation of this accident by the Board of Trade inspectors, it was brought out that there was practically no method of testing an engine-driver's knowledge of the roads over which he is to travel beyond his own assertion over his signature that he knows the section of the line. The danger in the case of extra or casual drivers operating trains was found to be considerable, and indicated a lack of care and forethought on the part of the railway companies whose good management in all matters of operation previously had been studied.

The discharge of an engine-driver for intoxication produced a strike in England during the year and brought up anew the discussion of safety on railways and the discipline required of railway servants.

On May 19 there occurred a wreck at Paris, France, in which 17 people were killed, and on July 31 there was a disaster on the Central Railroad of Brazil, with 100 fatalities. On October 22, 200 persons were killed in a railroad wreck at Smyrna. See BELGIUM.

Possibly, however, the best indication of relative safety is the number of passengers carried one mile to each person killed in a train accident. The figures for 1910 of 119,772,207 passengers carried one mile to one killed in a train accident, and for 1909 of 115,056,611 passengers carried one mile to one killed in a train accident, are perhaps significant in comparison with the figures immediately following, the first being perhaps a fair average for the past twenty years. Now, taking the figures given in the British Statistical Abstract, it is found that in Sweden in 1909 for each passenger killed, 243,943,702 passengers were carried one kilometer (151,489,040 passengers carried one mile); in Holland, 422,929,000 (262,638,909 passengers carried one mile); in Belgium, 395,638,840 (245,548,249 passengers carried one mile); in France, 2,042,835,920 (1,268,601,106 passengers carried one mile to one killed in a train accident); in Switzerland, 173,868,654 (107,972,404 passengers carried one mile), and in Hungary, 183,558,970 (113,990,120 passengers carried one mile) were carried one kilometer to each passenger killed; in Japan on company railways 179,811,266 passengers were carried one mile to each one killed.

RAILWAY ENGINEERS. See ARBITRATION AND CONCILIATION, INDUSTRIAL.

RAILWAYS. In a plea for higher rates at almost the beginning of the campaign, which the railways started in 1907 and which ended in failure in 1911, President Mellen of the New York, New Haven, and Hartford pointed out that there was an economic fallacy somewhere in a demand for a higher price for transportation at a time when the supply had not only overtaken the demand but was rapidly exceeding it. This condition of excess of supply over demand for transportation continued through 1908, 1909, 1910, 1911, and the first half of the calendar year 1912. With an abruptness that is comparable to the rapidity with which business fell off in 1907, business began in 1912 to make demands on the transportation plant of the country in excess of the possible output of this plant. Although even the so-called granger roads have a tonnage, furnished by products of agriculture, amounting to but 25 per cent. of their total tonnage, and revenue derived from this source alone of not over 15 per cent. of their total revenue, nevertheless crop conditions have an effect on railway gross earnings out of all proportion to the importance of the actual tonnage of these products carried. The shoe manufacturer or the piano manufacturer is affected directly by crop conditions, because a part of the added wealth from large crops is spent on his product, but the effect on railways is twofold. The railway gets the revenue both from transporting the articles bought with the added wealth and from transporting the crops themselves. The demand on railway facilities in a season of large crops and resulting activity is correspondingly heavy. During the years since 1907 there have been two powerful forces at work restricting railway expenditure on railway facilities and rolling stock. The decreased gross business and the increased unit price of labor have left smaller net earnings available for improvements, and the system of accounts prescribed by the Interstate Commerce Commission and in effect since June 30, 1907, has provided for a restriction of the term "expenses" to cover only replacing in kind for maintenance. The traditional inclination of American railroad operating officers is to put back into the property each year in the form of betterments a certain part of net earnings, and in the past many roads have charged these betterments to expenses when they were not evidently improvements which would add earning power. The commission's rules for accounting provide that such expenditures should be charged to capital account, and since this rule was promulgated at a time when retrenchment became necessary, it has been instrumental in causing the abandonment by railroad directors of a policy which has always been considered peculiar to American railroading and synonymous with good business.

The advantages that have accrued to railways through the necessity of cutting down on expenses can hardly be overestimated. Some of the reports of roads for the fiscal year ending June 30, 1912, show astounding increases in operating efficiency. The Baltimore and Ohio showed an increase in its average trainload of revenue freight of over 100 tons, or more than 25 per cent.; the average trainload being 544 tons in 1912. As a corollary of this attempt to reduce expenses is a recognition of the value to railroad companies of the services of competent general officers. The pay of railroad officers has been low, and is low to-day, and although a number of the railroad presidents in the United States have worked up from the ranks, yet the owners—those who have made fortunes from the development of railroads—are not in a great number of cases railroad men. The value and importance of men of the type of Daniel Willard at the head of railroad managements is being more and more recognized, and an important instance of this is the extension of the authority of B. F. Bush, who was made president of the Missouri Pacific in 1911, over the Denver and Rio Grande, the Western Pacific, and other Gould roads; the election of W. J. Harahan as president of the Seaboard Air Line, and the election of C. E. Schaff as president of the Missouri, Kansas and Texas.

Almost at the end of 1912 James J. Hill made an address before the Railway Business Association in which he made a new plea for increased railway rates based on the theory that the railways of this country could not handle the business that this country has to offer with a property worth no more than $60,000 per mile. The year 1912, therefore, makes, in a way, both a justification for the commission's refusal to grant increases in rates at a time of business depression, which is really a recognition of a general economic principle, and a new starting point in which higher rates will be justified, if they are to be justified at all, upon the principle of supply and demand for transportation. There have been certain tendencies which have crystallized during 1912 that may be either the foundation on which railroad officers base their beliefs that higher rates are necessary, or manifestations of more fundamental facts of which Mr. Hill's speech is simply another manifestation. In 1912 there was less new railroad built than in any one of the past fifteen years. There was more equipment ordered than in any year since 1906, there was very little permanent financing done, even by the stronger railroad companies, and the only two large independent projects for new railroad building that have been started within the last dozen years both went into the hands of receivers.

RECEIVERSHIPS AND FORECLOSURES. The Denver, Northwestern and Pacific, for which a receiver was appointed, was projected from Denver, Col., to Salt Lake City, Utah, thus paralleling the Union Pacific and the Denver and Rio Grande; in other words, threatening competition with both the Gould interests and the Harriman interests. The route selected is generally understood to be better than that followed by the Denver and Rio Grande, although it involves one very long and very expensive tunnel through the Continental Divide. The project naturally had the enthusiastic support of a great many people in Colorado, and the financial arrangements were made by David H. Moffatt, president of the First National Bank of Denver, Col. Up to 1912, 211 miles of road from Denver west to Steamboat Springs had been built and the company had outstanding $11,288,609 funded debt and $10,940,700 stock. Even before Mr. Moffatt's death, which took place in the latter part of 1911, further extension of the road had been stopped and operation was carried on on the most modest scale. Attempts were made to get the financial backing of the State of Colorado. After Mr. Moffatt's death it was found necessary to refinance notes falling due and bearing his personal guarantee. An Eastern banking firm gave some help, already having been interested in the proposal, and an attempt was made to persuade the voters of Colorado to agree that the State should issue bonds to pay for at least part of the cost of the tunnel through the Continental Divide This proposal was not ratified at the elections in November, 1912, but difficulty in refinancing the short term notes had already led to the appointment of a receiver. Mr. Moffatt was at one time a rich man, but he had not only done his best to finance the building of the Denver, Northwestern, and Pacific through local capital which he, as president of the First National Bank of Denver, was in a remarkably good position to interest, but had largely invested his own fortune in the plan. Regardless of whether or not his original idea had been to force the Harriman or Gould interests to buy him out, he appealed to the local capitalists of Colorado on the ground that not only would the building of this line help to develop Colorado, but that railroad building itself was still a profitable undertaking in which to invest new capital. In this plea he failed.

The Kansas City, Mexico, and Orient, which went into the hands of a receiver in 1912, was projected to run from Kansas City southwest through the United States and Mexico to a port on the Gulf of California. There was a real economic reason for building this road. It not only developed new territory, but it will form a new route when completed that, while it will compete in certain instances with existing roads, will also supply transportation that was not heretofore available. Unlike the Denver, Northwestern, and Pacific, the project was hardly open to even the suspicion that it might have been undertaken to force some other existing railroad company to buy. There is here the distinction between forcing an existing railroad company to buy new property and making it desirable for them to do so. There are at least four railroad systems which might find the Kansas City, Mexico, and Orient worth buying and developing. E. A. Stilwell very largely raised the money to build the 764 miles of road that had been completed in 1912. A part of it was raised in the United States, entirely from private investors, and a part in Europe. Mr. Stilwell's consistent aim was to keep the road independent and himself in control. Since he was not himself a capitalist—he was a former insurance man—it was necessary that no bank or group of bankers be called on to furnish any large proportion of the money needed to build the road and Mr. Stilwell relied on interesting enough small investors to carry out his project. With 764 miles built, $21,146,000 outstanding funded debt and about $25,000,000 stock, the company found itself unable to raise more capital in the way in which the money already invested has been raised. That the project as a railroad undertaking had real merit there can be little doubt. A study of traffic conditions leads almost inevitablyo to this conclusion, and the personnel of the b ndholders' committee, which was formed when the road was put into the hands of a receiver, shows conclusively that Mr. Stilwell was able to interest in his project a very shrewd class of investors. There is, therefore, exemplified in the receivership of this road, even more strikingly than in that of the Denver, Northwestern, and Pacific, the failure of an attempt to interest the small investor in new railroad building regardless of the inherent soundness of the undertaking.

The Père Marquette, with 2331 miles of road, $63,672,000 of funded debt, and $26,186,590 stock, was put into the hands of a receiver in 1912. The fact that this receivership took place in 1912 has little or no bearing on contemporary railroad history. The road had a rather top-heavy capitalization. An attempt was made a few years ago to have the Cincinnati, Hamilton, and Dayton take it over, but it proved an impossible burden for this company, and J. P. Morgan and Company, who had control of both roads, sold the Cincinnati, Hamilton, and Dayton to the Baltimore and Ohio, and in 1912 apparently allowed the Père Marquette to fall into a receivership through its own weight. The immediate cause of the receivership was the refusal of the Michigan Railroad Commission to grant authority to the Père Marquette to issue certain new securities. For statistics, see FINANCIAL REVIEW.

CONSTRUCTION IN 1912. The receivership of the Denver, Northwestern, and Pacific and the Kansas City, Mexico, and Orient did not stop new construction on these roads in 1912 simply because new construction had been stopped previously. There was, however, no existing road which was making extension on any very large scale, and this, combined with the fact that railroad companies were not pursuing a policy of building branch lines into new territory, made the record of new construction, which record is compiled each year by the *Railway Age Gazette* from a very thorough canvass of the chief engineers of all roads that are doing new work, one of the smallest for any year during the twenty that this record has been kept. There were 2997 miles of first track built in 1912, comparing with 3066 miles built in 1911, and 2109 miles built in 1897, the next previous smallest year. In 1895 but 1420 miles of new first track were built, which is the smallest of any year in the record. Last year was a culmination of a period of restriction in new railroad building, but the end of the year saw work begun on a very considerable mileage of new roads and plans made for an even larger mileage. In the beginning of 1913 there were 2500 miles under construction and over 2800 miles additional are definitely projected. In a sense, therefore, the construction situation is analogous to the equipment situation.

CARS AND LOCOMOTIVES ORDERED. Up to 1912 and during the early part of the year the equipment market had been extraordinarily dull. Even with a sudden revival in orders there was a lack of confidence on the part of builders that induced them to take new business on a very narrow margin of possible profit. As the prospect for very large crops became more assured and the adequacy of railroad equipment under present methods of loading and terminal handling became more and more plainly apparent, premiums were offered for immediate delivery and equipment builders began to take business not only on a profitable basis but as rapidly as they could desire. These large orders and the pressure for immediate delivery continued through the entire second half of 1912. The total number of locomotives ordered in 1912 was 4515, comparing with 2850 ordered in 1911 and 5642 ordered in 1906, the next previous year in which as large orders were placed. There were 234,758 freight cars ordered in 1912, comparing with 133,117 ordered in 1911 and 310,315 ordered in 1906. There were 3642 passenger cars ordered in 1912, comparing with 2623 ordered in 1911. The American Railway Association's latest bi-weekly bulletin of freight car surpluses and shortages shows a total surplus for the two weeks ending November 30, 1912, of 26,135 freight cars of all kinds, and a shortage of 62,536. The shortage is a little less and the surplus a little greater than shown for the previous two weeks period, but nevertheless the shortage is greater by over three times than in any corresponding period since 1907. This shortage of equipment is particularly interesting in the light of the fact that the average mileage per car per day for all freight cars varies from about 20 to 25 miles and the average loading per loaded car is between 19 and 21 tons. Among the questions that the *Railway Age Gazette* asked railway presidents and vice-presidents at the end of the year was one as to whether or not they believed a real shortage of equipment existed, and it is a significant fact that there was a wide difference of opinion, even in some cases as between a president and a vice-president on the same road. It is, of course, easier for a railroad officer to say that he needs more equipment than for him to acknowledge that he is not making effective use of the equipment that he has, but not by any means all of the railroad presidents who answered this question took the easier way. And in the explanations why more effective use was not made of equipment the blame was distributed as between shippers' methods of using freight cars as warehouses and congestion at terminals. Two further contributing causes might properly have been mentioned: The laxity of railroad officers themselves, especially in the case of equipment detained by large shippers, and the opposition, to a certain extent, of labor to new methods which have the appearance of getting more work with less expenditure of labor.

WAGE DISPUTES. The enginemen on 52 Eastern roads, totaling about 30,000 employees, made demands for increases in pay and changes in working conditions which, after being refused by railroad managements, were eventually decided by an arbitration board. This board was made up of Daniel Willard, president of the Baltimore and Ohio; P. H. Morrissey, former grand master of the Brotherhood of Railroad Trainmen; Oscar S. Straus, of New York; Charles R. Van Hise, president of the University of Wisconsin; Albert Shaw, editor of the *Review of Reviews;* Frederick N. Judson, of St. Louis, former member of the Hadley Securities Commission, and Otto M. Eidlitz, former president of the Building Trades Association of New York City. The board awarded the enginemen certain increases in rates, stating its belief that the enginemen not only should be paid a fair compensation but that the majority of railroads in the territory affected could afford to pay the enginemen a fair compensation. A minimum wage of $4.25 for 100 miles or less for enginemen in passenger service, and a minimum of $4.75 per day of 100 miles or less for enginemen in freight service, was granted, and all rates higher than these minima were contained in effect. As a matter of fact, the award gave the enginemen about the wages paid by the roads paying the highest wages in the territory affected. Even more important than the award of the board in regard to wages were certain recommendations that the board made. They found that the Erdman act, providing for voluntary arbitration of wage disputes, does not adequately protect the rights of the public, and this arbitration board, composed of admittedly able and strong men, suggests the creation of national and State wage commissions which should exercise functions regarding labor engaged at work in public utilities analogous to those now exercised with regard to capital by the public service commissions already in existence. The expressions of railroad presidents in answer to a question about this suggestion of the arbitration board were naturally guarded, some, however, coming out frankly with the opinion that the Interstate Commerce Commission, since it now has power to fix rates, should also have power to pass on questions involving rates of wages. There was a general agreement among railroad men whose opinions have been recorded that the present methods of settling disputes between railroads and their employees are not satisfactory to the public. The Sherman anti-trust law specifically exempts labor combinations in restraint of trade from its provisions, but there was a strong expression of opinion on the part of the board of arbitration that some legislation should be passed which would prevent the possibility of a labor dispute between railroads and their employees resulting in a general tie-up of all industrial activities dependent on railroad transportation.

LEGISLATION. Since the finding of this arbitration board, which was made public in November, there has, of course, not been an opportunity for the introduction of any such legislation as that impliedly recommended. On the other hand, the more important legislation affecting railroads passed during 1912 had to do with placing further restrictions on the railroad companies in their dealings with their employees. Woodrow Wilson, in his annual message as governor of New Jersey, strongly recommends an act requiring railroads operating in New Jersey to provide trains with "adequate crews." In Massachusetts, however, Governor Foss refused to sanction a full-crew law which, in his opinion, was unjustified. A bill was introduced in Congress in March, 1912, providing for compensation for accident injuries to employees of interstate railroads. The bill was discussed, but never became a law.

LEGAL DECISIONS. Three very important interpretations of the Sherman anti-trust law as applied to railroads were made by the Supreme Court of the United States in 1912. Control of the Southern Pacific by the Union Pacific was found to be an illegal combination in restraint of trade under the meaning of the act. The Terminal Railroad Association of St. Louis and the fourteen railroads entering the city and owning the Terminal Company were found to be a combination in violation of the Sherman law. The present arrangements between anthracite coal carriers and the methods of handling the anthracite coal business were held to be not an unlawful combination or conspiracy in restraint of trade under the meaning of the act. While these three decisions of the Supreme Court contain numerous points in the interpretation of the act on which the court has thrown a good deal of light, they demonstrate one fact quite conclusively, namely, that the court will consider and does consider each case brought before it under the Sherman law as a separate question to be decided purely on the facts in that particular case, and on the facts rather than on the law. (For an account of the Union Pacific and anthracite coal cases see the article TRUSTS.) In the St. Louis case, Judge Lurton, who wrote the opinion concurred in by all the justices, specifically pointed out that it was not contended that every terminal company in every city was a violation of the Sherman law, but that the St. Louis topographical conditions made it impossible for any road to reach the city without using the Terminal Company's facilities and under these circumstances the form of the Terminal Company was in violation of the Sherman law.

Passing upon the jurisdiction by the Interstate Commerce Commission, the Supreme Court held that its authority extended to Alaska, the commission having previously itself held that its jurisdiction did not cover Alaska. The Commerce Court in passing on an appeal from a case in which the Interstate Commerce Commission had refused to reduce rates, held that it did not have the power to overrule a negative decision of the commission's. In other cases, however, the Commerce Court held that it was proper for it to receive new evidence not submitted heretofore to the commission. The opinions, however, of the Commerce Court, while legally binding until overruled by the Supreme Court, are of less importance in a review of contemporary railroad history than they would otherwise have been because Congress refused in 1912 to include an appropriation for the expenses and salaries of this court. The practical result of this refusal appears to be the abolishment of this court. The court had not been popular from the start, and the fact that one of the judges of this court, Judge Archbald, was being tried before the United States Senate on impeachment charges made by the House of Representatives, on the ground that he used his official position as judge to obtain personal favors from railroads who were possible litigants before the Commerce Court, unquestionably had its influence in deciding Congress to permit the abolishment of the court.

INTERSTATE COMMERCE COMMISSION. While the majority of opinions handed down by the commission have continued during the past year to favor rate reductions in certain specific instances and the commission has been very free to use its new power to refuse advances in rates, there has been a growing disposition on the part of railroad officers on the one side and the interstate commerce commissioners on the other to have a greater respect for each other's work. The commission has corrected a great number of petty abuses which the railroads should have corrected for themselves, and railroad officers are more generally recognizing this fact. The most important case that the commission decided during the year was the question brought up in the so-called tap-line cases. The tap lines are short railroads owned or controlled by industrial companies, these industrial companies furnishing the greater part of the business for the short railroads. The commission decided that in a great majority of the cases that it investigated, mainly the industrial roads of lumber companies, the tap line was in reality a plant facility and not a common carrier, and that, therefore, a division of the through rate between the connecting railroads and the tap lines was not legal. The railroads were, therefore, ordered to discontinue making these differences of rates. The commission also decided the case of the differentials to the Atlantic seaboard. This question of differentials has been discussed for years without any particular result, and the commission's decision does not change, apparently, the arrangements that have been in force from time to time. Baltimore and Philadelphia are allowed differentials under New York, while Boston is put on a par with New York.

RAILROAD FINANCING AND DIVIDEND CHANGES. Railroads, as well as other companies and municipal corporations, found it difficult to sell securities bearing a low rate of interest. The Canadian railways continued to find no difficulty in raising large amounts of new capital, but there were comparatively few roads in the United States issuing long term low interest securities. The issue of $20,000,000 3 year 4½ per cent. notes by the New York Central and Hudson River was typical of the financing done by the stronger companies. It is a noteworthy fact that the Pennsylvania Railroad did no new financing during 1912, although there were $6,000,000 "Pennsylvania" car trust certificates issued. In January the New York, New Haven, and Hartford issued $30,000,000 one year 4 per cent. notes, and in December $40,000,000 one year 5 per cent. notes. Even a company with the strong credit of the Illinois Central found it more advantageous to issue notes than bonds, issuing $15,000,000 secured 4½ per cent. notes due 1914. There were a number of smaller companies that increased their dividends or paid dividends in 1912 where they had paid no dividends in 1911, and the only reductions in dividends of any importance were in the case of the New York, Ontario, and Western, which passed its annual 2 per cent. dividend entirely, and the Colorado and Southern, which reduced its dividend from 2 per cent. annually to 1 per cent. annually. On the other hand, the Southern Railway increased its dividends on the preferred stock from 2 per cent. paid in 1911 to an annual rate of 5 per cent., paying 4¼ per cent. total in 1912. The Reading Company, the holding company for the Philadelphia and Reading, increased its dividends from an annual rate of 6 per cent. paid in 1911 to 8 per cent. in 1912, and the Buffalo, Rochester, and Pittsburgh increased its dividends from an annual of 5 per cent. in 1911 to 6 per cent. in 1912.

CHANGES IN OWNERSHIP AND CONTROL AND NEW OFFICERS. There were no important changes in the ownership and control of railways in 1912, except the changes mentioned in connection with the receiverships of the Denver, Northwestern, and Pacific and the Kansas City, Mexico, and Orient. In 1912 James McCrea, who had been president of the Pennsylvania Railroad since the death of A. J. Cassatt in 1907, retired, and Samuel Rea, who had been first vice-president, was elected president. Mr. Rea is, in some senses, more truly a successor to Mr. A. J. Cassatt than to Mr. McCrea. Mr. McCrea was president of the "lines west" before Mr. Cassatt's death, and one of the reasons urged for his election in 1907 was his reputation for conservatism, and during, especially the latter part of his administration. Mr. Rea, who had been a close associate with Mr. Cassatt, shared to a quite considerable extent in the management of the road.

NEW ENGLAND SITUATION. In sharp contrast to a general better feeling between the public and railroad officers is the attack that has been made on Charles S. Mellen and his management of the New York, New Haven, and Hartford. Under Mr. Mellen's management the New Haven had established a monopoly of the transportation facilities in New England, and there was a series of events that happened in 1912 that resulted in a bitter and quite violent attack both in the courts and in the newspapers against the New Haven management. Three serious accidents were followed closely by the announcement that the Grand Trunk had abandoned its extension, which it had been building for three or four months, from a connection with the Central Vermont, its subsidiary, to Providence, R. I. Mr. Mellen and President Chamberlin of the Grand Trunk have been indicted for conspiracy in restraint of trade in this connection. The real foundation for newspaper attacks and the feeling in New England appears to be not that the New Haven is a monopoly but that the railroad company has not furnished what is considered adequate service.

RAILWAY EARNINGS. The trend of railway earnings in 1912 was sharply upwards. The average gross earnings per mile went from about $930 in January to over $1300 in October, and while expenses increased to some extent, net earnings per mile per month increased from $200 in January to about $475 in October. See also RAILWAY ACCIDENTS.

RANKIN, WILLIAM. An American lawyer, died October 20, 1912. He was born in Elizabeth, N. J., in 1810, and graduated from Williams College in 1831. After graduation he studied law in the office of William Pennington, once governor of New Jersey. He was admitted to the bar in that State and then removed to Cincinnati, where he entered the law office of William Henry Harrison, former president of the United States. He afterwards went into partnership in Cincinnati with Salmon P. Chase and continued in that association until 1850. Mr. Rankin took great interest in church affairs and held important positions of trust in religious organizations. He was elected treasurer of the Board of Foreign Missions of the Presbyterian Church in 1850, retiring from that office in 1887. He was the oldest living alumnus of Williams College and probably the oldest college graduate in the United States.

RANSDELL, Daniel Moore. Sergeant-at-arms of the United States Senate, died November 28, 1912. He was born in Indianapolis in 1842 and was educated at Franklin College. He enlisted in the Civil War in 1862 as private and served until the close of the war. He lost his right arm at the battle of Resaca in 1864. After the war he taught school for one year. He was deputy recorder of Marion County in 1866-67 and city clerk of Indianapolis from 1867 to 1871. After serving in other offices in Indianapolis he was appointed marshal of the District of Columbia in 1889. He served in this position until 1894. In 1900 he was appointed sergeant-at-arms of the United States Senate.

RAPID TRANSIT. New York Subways. During 1912 progress was being made in the construction of the various additions to the present subway system of the city of New York and in the development of plans for carrying out the so-called "Dual System" of rapid transit for that city. The legal and financial complications involved naturally were great, and at the end of the year the contracts had not been signed, as various modifications were proposed, and the entire scheme was receiving the public consideration and criticism which its magnitude deserved. This dual system provided for the construction of new subways by the city, or jointly by the city and the contracting companies, the extension to present lines and the third-tracking and extension of the elevated lines and the use of the previously completed Steinway tunnel under the East River between Manhattan and Long Island City. In this manner there would be secured a practical doubling of the existing lines in Greater New York, so that there would be accommodations for some 3,000,000,000 passengers a year, as compared with 798,281,850 passengers in the year ended June 30, 1911.

The mileage of this dual system is shown by the table in the next column.

While the contracts for construction and operation were most elaborate and, as said before, had not been signed at the end of the year, these provided that the city should furnish a part of the funds necessary for the construction of the various subways, but the money for their equipment, both of subways and elevated roads, as well as for the reconstruction and extension of existing elevated roads, was to be furnished by the companies. The city was to supply funds to the amount of about $150,000,000, while the Interborough Rapid Transit Company was to contribute $56,000,000 for con-

For Operation by the Interborough Rapid Transit Company		
Existing subway	73.00	
Existing elevated lines	118.00	
Subway and elevated lines for construction jointly by city and company	146.80	
Elevated railroad extensions to be constructed by company	10.40	
Third-tracks on elevated roads to be constructed by company	10.50	
Total		358.70
For operation by Brooklyn Rapid Transit Company		
Existing elevated lines	105.00	
Subway and elevated lines for construction jointly by city and company	110.41	
Elevated extensions for constructions by company	46.29	
Third-tracking and reconstruction by company	9.30	
Total		271.00
Grand total—Dual System		629.70

struction and $21,000,000 for equipment for new subways or subway extensions, in addition to paying for the extensions and third-tracking of the elevated railroads. The Brooklyn Rapid Transit Company was to contribute about $60,000,000 towards the dual system, and of this about $13,000,000 was to be supplied on account of the construction of city-owned lines, $21,000,000 for the extension and third-tracking of the existing elevated lines, and about $26,000,000 for new equipment. The total cost of the new dual system of rapid transit for Greater New York, therefore, would amount to about $347,000,000. The condition of the contract was the continuous ride, with transfers, for five cents on each company's system, and the operating contracts to run for a period of 49 years, the leases of the original subway entering into the new arrangement. The city was to share in the profits of operation, according to a detailed plan, for apportioning expenses, rentals, net earnings, fixed charges, etc., and a provision was made for the city taking over the lines any time after ten years of operation.

Physical Features of the New Subways. The engineers of the Public Service Commission made many improvements in planning the new subways. All curved platforms were eliminated, and as far as possible sharp curves requiring a decrease in speed. The new subways were to have separate tunnels so that each train would act as a piston, driving the air out as it progressed and causing an incoming of fresh air at the rear. Less waterproofing was to be used, with the aim of reducing the heat, while there was to be an increase in size. The express stations were to be large enough to accommodate 10-car express and 6-car local trains. Reinforced concrete was to be used more extensively in the construction, and for the Lexington Avenue line a double-deck form, with express tracks on a lower level, was to be employed. In the new tunnels in the East River and Harlem River footpaths were to be added in case of accident stalling the train under the river. The engineers further provided for the more ornamental design of the elevated structures to be erected, and as these lines to be built in the outlying districts are usually on broad streets, they will be far from the disfigurement that many of the older elevated lines in Brooklyn and Manhattan were.

During the year the dual system of subway construction, as prepared by the Public Service Commission and accepted by the Interborough Rapid Transit Company and the Brooklyn Elevated, received the approval of the Board of Estimate and Apportionment, representing the municipal government of the city of New York. In both bodies a minority favored municipal ownership, but the plans in the main received the approval of the majority of the civic organizations and of citizens at large. There were expressions of discontent on the part of certain real estate interests, who believed that their sections were failing to secure adequate treatment, and at the close of the year a political feeling against the signing of the contracts was developing. The entire project, however, seemed to represent the best that could be done to satisfy existing conditions and to provide for the future developments of the city, where transport facilities had been far behind the needs of the hour, not to mention provision for the future.

On December 31, 1912, the city of New York had expended for rapid transit within the city $87,808,238, of which amount $55,625,231 had been spent for the existing subways and $32,-183,006 had been paid out under the contracts previously awarded for the construction of the new subways for the dual system, viz., the Lexington Avenue and Centre Street Loop subways in Manhattan and the Fourth Avenue subway in Brooklyn. The total construction work under contract on the subway system on December 31, 1912, was $71,214,127.

CHICAGO. During the year the Harbor and Subway Commission of the city of Chicago reported in reference to a plan for a system of subways or underground railways for rapid transit which would be municipally owned and would radiate to outlying sections of the city from the business centre. That there was a need of such provisions of accommodations was shown by the fact that the seating capacity of the lines in use in Chicago in 1912 amounted to but 85,000 passengers during the rush hour and the number actually handled aggregated about 160,000, so that double the seating capacity, as advocated by the opponents of the subway project, would do but little to solve the problem which the increase of population, amounting to about 500,000 in ten years, is making serious. The subway lines as designed would give a seating capacity of 180,000 per hour and would cut down by over half the time required by the present surface lines and express trains on the elevated railways. The estimated capital cost of the proposed subway, including equipment, was given at $13,000,000, and it was figured that the basis of estimated population to be served by the territory through which the subways would pass was such as to afford adequate traffic. The entire project was under discussion during the year, but no decision as to its adoption was reached.

BOSTON. On March 31, 1912, the subway from Park Street, Boston, to Harvard Square, Cambridge, was opened and continued in successful operation throughout the year. Trains were operated over a length of track of 3.2 miles, and running time of eight minutes between Harvard Square and Boston was maintained.

SAN FRANCISCO. The transportation problem of San Francisco attracted attention during 1912 and several reports were made by Bion J. Arnold, engineer, for a rapid transit tunnel under Twin Peaks extending to the region of the city from Market Street. The plan provided for several types of construction which local conditions seemed to require, as well as considerations of cost. It was also proposed that a Mission Street tunnel crosstown tube frm Market Street to Golden Gate Park, passing under the southern edge of Buena Vista Park, should be constructed for vehicles and car traffic. Mr. Arnold proposed that such a tunnel be combined with a branch of the rapid transit line just mentioned and that the car lines be run at a lower level beneath the roadway, the tunnel being used by both subway and surface cars. These plans were under consideration at the end of the year.

LONDON. In London the electrification of the East London Railway proceeded during the year and various improvements of the Metropolitan line at Baker-street were under way. The Bakerloo extension to Paddington was also in progress and will have its terminus below the Great-Western Station, which will be reached by an escalator. The Central London extension to Liverpool-street was opened in July and added an important link in the London railway system. At Moorgate Station a subway for foot passengers was opened, connecting the Metropolitan, City and South London, and Great Northern and City railways. The Charing Cross to Hampstead tube was being extended to connect by escalator with the District Railway at the former point, while the latter line had begun a deviation at Earls Court on the same level as the Wimbledon and Ealing trains.

RATIONALISTIC SYSTEM. See PHILOSOPHY.

RAYNER, ISIDOR. United States Senator from Maryland, died November 25, 1912. He was born in Baltimore in 1850, and was educated at the University of Maryland and the University of Virginia. In 1871 he was admitted to the bar. Within two years he had won recognition in that State as a brilliant pleader in law cases. In 1878 he was nominated by the Democrats for the State legislature and was elected. His oratorical powers at once won for him a commanding position in party councils and attracted national attention. He resigned after having served one term and resumed the practice of law. In 1886 he was elected to the State Senate and in the same year to the national House of Representatives. He was reëlected to the Fifty-second and Fifty-third Congresses, 1891 and 1895. While in Congress he served as a member of the committee on foreign affairs, the committee on weights and measures, and the commerce committee. His career in the House of Representatives was marked by energetic service and he was considered one of the most useful members of that body. After the completion of his service in Congress he was elected attorney-general of Maryland in 1894. He made a national reputation as counsel for Admiral Schley in the naval inquiry which followed the battle of Santiago. In 1905 he was elected to the United States Senate and at once became one of the most prominent Democratic senators. He early took a stand as one of the most severe critics of President Roosevelt. He delivered many speeches in which he declared that Roosevelt had usurped powers which belonged to Congress, and had set a precedent which would result in great harm. When Colonel Roosevelt delivered his speech on "The Charter of Democracy" before the Ohio State Constitutional Convention Senator Rayner was one of the first men in public life to attack the doctrines enunciated therein. In a speech delivered in the Senate he declared that Colonel Roosevelt's utterances constituted "the most dangerous doctrine ever brought forward by anyone who has the slightest regard for the stability of our institutions, and whose opinion is entitled to weight and respect." Senator Rayner had a deep and thorough knowledge of the Constitution and was always a quick defender of any alleged encroachments on the part of the executive or legislative branches. He took a strong stand for State rights and in a stirring address delivered on April 23, 1908, denounced the Federal government's encroachments on these rights. He was one of the most eloquent speakers in the Senate and his addresses were always listened to with marked attention. He was chairman of the Indian depredations committee of the Senate, and was a member of the civil service and retrenchment committee, the committee on education and labor, the judiciary committee, committee on foreign relations, and several less important committees.

RECALL. See ELECTORAL REFORM.

RECALL OF JUDGES AND JUDICIAL DECISIONS. See PRESIDENTIAL CAMPAIGN.

RECIPROCITY, CANADIAN. See TARIFF.

RECLAMATION. See IRRIGATION, and DAMS.

RED CROSS, AMERICAN NATIONAL. The American Red Cross Society found an abundant field for work in 1912. Its national relief board assisted the needy in the strike of the textile workers of Lawrence, Mass. (see STRIKES), rendered aid at two mine disasters, did efficient service in furnishing succor in the Mississippi River floods, took an active part in the relief of the survivors of the *Titanic* disaster, and gave aid to American refugees from Mexico and wounded Mexicans in El Paso, Texas. The most important work was that carried on in connection with the Mississippi River floods. Relief work was begun on April 6. The Red Cross coöperated with the United States army and took charge of the actual organization of camps, their administration and sanitation, the distribution of supplies and later of the breaking up of the camps and the return of the camp population to its homes as the waters subsided. The greater part of the relief work lay in Louisiana and a small part of Mississippi. The expenditures of the Rred Cross for this work were approximately $110,000. For the relief of the *Titanic* survivors a fund of over $160,000 was contributed to the Red Cross.

The total of all relief funds contributed to the Red Cross for the relief of sufferers in 1912 was approximately $276,000. This does not include very considerable sums contributed through local relief committees direct and expended in conjunction with the Red Cross fund and in accordance with the Red Cross methods of administration and accounting.

INTERNATIONAL RELIEF WORK. Six foreign fields called for assistance from the American Red Cross during 1912. Although this was three less than the number in 1911, the funds expended in relief work more than doubled its expenditures in the previous year. In 1911 a total of about $94,000 was expended, while the expenditures for 1912 amounted to $244,000. The causes for which it was given in 1912 were the following: The Chinese famine, the Persian relief, relief in Mexico, relief in Turkey, relief in Nicaragua, and relief on account of the Balkan War. For the Chinese famine $169,000 was contributed to the Red Cross. In Persia over 2000 persons were aided during the period of suffering caused by disturbed governmental conditions and poor harvests. The relief in Mexico was undertaken for the benefit of American citizens and was in response to a request received by the United States through the State Department. For this relief $3500 was appropriated from the contingent fund. A contribution of $2000 was made to relieve suffering in Nicaragua caused by the revolutionary outbreak. The total expenditures of the Red Cross on account of the Balkan War in 1912 was $61,156.

The eighth annual meeting of the society was held on December 12, 1912, in Washington. The officers in 1912 were the following: President, William H. Taft; vice-president, Robert W. De Forest; treasurer, Lee McClung; counselor, William Marshall Bullitt; national director, Ernest E. Bicknell, and secretary, Charles L. Magee. See BARTON, CLARA.

REFERENDUM. See ELECTORAL REFORM.

REFORM BUREAU, INTERNATIONAL. An organization formed to promote all moral reforms in all lands, incorporated in 1896. It grew from a course of lectures on sociology, delivered by Rev. Wilbur F. Crafts, Ph. D., at Princeton University. Among the social evils which the bureau was formed to combat were intemperance, impurity, Sabbath breaking, and gambling. Its work is carried on through legislation, by letters, by lectures, and by literature. Its four fields of work are local, State, national, and international. The most important event in the history of the bureau during the year 1912 was the recognition of the effectiveness of the bureau's Oriental secretary, Rev. E. W. Thwing, in his leadership of the anti-opium crusade and other reforms by Sun Yat Sen and Yuan Shih-kai in China. Dr. Thwing was appointed official adviser of the Opium Commission, and also of the new Bureau of Education, in which he secured the establishment of a department of social service. He has organized branches of the Internationl Reform Bureau in Shanghai with the coöperation of missionaries of many nations and denominations, and in Peking with the coöperation of President Yuan. The second important event was a two months' campaign for prohibition, made by the president of the bureau, Rev. Wilbur F. Crafts, in Maine, in August and September, 1911. He also made a four months' campaign for the enforcement of anti-alcohol educational work in the South, followed by campaigns in New England and the West to promote work by men for boys in "safeguarding adolescence." Dr. Henry N. Pringle was elected assistant superintendent of the bureau. For eleven years he was secretary of the Maine Civic League.

REFORMED CHURCH IN AMERICA (Dutch). A Protestant religious denomination known until 1867 as the Reformed Protestant Dutch Church of North America. The last general synod of the Reformed Church in America was held in June, 1912, at Grand Rapids, Mich. There are connected with the church 4 particular synods, 35 classes, 681 churches, 739 ministers, 118,564 communicants, 782 Sunday schools with an enrollment of 120,815. Contributed during the year for benevolent objects, $498,303; congregational, $1,657,006; total, $2,155,309. There are connected with the church the foreign missionary board, women's foreign missionary, domestic missionary, women's domestic missionary, board of education, board of publication, two theological seminaries, and several other educational institutions.

The next general synod is to meet at Asbury Park, N. J., June 5, 1913.

The president of the general synod is Rev. William P. Bruce, D. D., of Yonkers, N. Y.; vice-president, Rev. Evert J. Blekkink, D. D., Holland, Mich.; stated clerk, Rev. William H. De Hart, D. D., Plainfield, N. J.; permanent clerk, Rev. Henry Lockwood, East Millstone, N. J.

REFORMED CHURCH IN THE UNITED STATES, GERMAN. This denomination, known also as the German Reformed Church, had in 1912, 300,147 communicants, 1737 churches, and 1200 ministers. The communicants increased in 1912, 2318; the churches decreased 22, and the ministers, 41. The denomination is divided for administrative purposes into eight district synods and 59 classes corresponding to the presbyteries in the Presbyterian bodies. In the Sunday schools are 240,000 scholars, and 25,000 teachers. Mission work is carried on in practically the entire United States and portions of Canada. Foreign missions are also carried on in Japan, and China. The theological institutions are the Eastern Theological Seminary at Lancaster, Pa., and the Central Theological Seminary of the Reformed Church in the United States at Dayton, O. The colleges maintained by the denomination include Franklin and Marshall College and Heidelberg College at Tiffin, O. Colleges for women are maintained at Frederick, Md., and Allentown, Pa.

REFORMED EPISCOPAL CHURCH. This denomination in 1912 had 10,400 communicants, 80 churches, and 94 ministers. There was a gain of 790 communicants over 1911. There are six bishops at the head of the church. Domestic mission work is carried on among colored people in South Carolina and foreign missions are maintained in India. The theological seminary of the denomination is in Philadelphia, and the official organ of church is the *Episcopal Recorder*, published in the same city.

REFORMED PRESBYTERIANS. The general name given to several religious bodies of Presbyterian doctrine, founded by members of the Covenanted or Reformed Presbyterian Church of Scotland. Included in the title are: The Synod of the Reformed Presbyterian Church of North America; the Reformed Presbyterian Church in North America, General Synod; the Reformed Presbyterian Church, Covenanted; and the Reformed Presbyterian Church in the United States and Canada. The Synod of the Reformed Presbyterian Church in North America is the largest of these bodies. It has about 10,000 communicants, with 100 churches, and 125 ministers. The Reformed Presbyterian Church of North America, General Synod, has about 3700 communicants, 27 churches, and 22 ministers. One American missionary was sent by this body to Northern India in 1912. The next general meeting of the General Synod will be held in Cincinnati, O., on the third Wednesday of May, 1913. The other two bodies are small. The General Synod maintains a theological seminary at Philadelphia and a college at Cedarville, O.

REIBEY, THOMAS. A Tasmanian public official, died February 1912. He was born in 1821 and was educated at Trinity College, Oxford. He was for a time in holy orders, but removed to Tasmania, where he took an active part in politics. He became a member of the Executive Council in 1876 and in 1877-8 was the leader of the Opposition. From 1876 to 1877 he was premier and colonial secretary. He also served as colonial secretary in 1878-9. From 1887 to 1891 he was speaker of the House of Assembly and held office without portfolio in the Braddon government from 1894-99. He was a member of the House of Assembly from 1874 to 1903.

REID, WHITELAW. An American diplomat and editor, died December 15, 1912. He was born near Xenia, O., in 1837. Both his parents were of Scottish blood. As they were poor, a kinsman, Dr. Hugh McMillan, undertook to fit Whitelaw Reid for college, and under his uncle's instruction the youth was so well grounded in Latin that at the age of fifteen he entered Miami University as a sophomore. In 1856 he graduated with scientific honors. He became principal of the graded schools in South Charleston, O., where he taught French, Latin, and the higher mathematics. Through prudent management he was able to save enough money to repay his uncle for the cost of his education and, in addition, to buy a newspaper called the Xenia *News*, thus beginning his journalistic career, for which he had planned in his earliest years. As editor of this paper he attracted the attention of the leaders of the newly formed Republican party in Ohio. He made speeches for Frémont in 1856 and wrote political articles which had much influence. Four years later he advocated the nomination of Abraham Lincoln and was a powerful spokesman in Lincoln's campaign. He soon outgrew the opportunities offered him in Xenia and removed to Cincinnati, where he became city editor of the *Gazette* of that city. At the outbreak of the Civil War he joined the staff of General Morris in West Virginia and later the staff of General Rosecrans. He also acted as war correspondent for the Cincinnati *Gazette*, writing over the nom-de-plume *Agate*. His descriptions of the campaign, particularly the report of the battle of Gettysburg, attracted widespread attention because of their clearness and accuracy. At this time he made the acquaintance of John Hay, then one of President Lincoln's secretaries, and of Edmund Clarence Stedman and William Dean Howells. At the battle of Shiloh he was the only correspondent who witnessed the entire action and his account in ten columns of the Cincinnati *Gazette* was widely copied. Shortly after this, as the result of a disagreement with General Halleck, he ceased to act as war correspondent. In 1862 he became the Washington correspondent of the Cincinnati *Gazette* and at the same time purchased an interest in that newspaper. With his share of the profits for the first year he laid the foundations of his fortune. His work at Washington attracted the attention of Horace Greeley, who invited him to join the staff of the New York *Tribune*. At this time, however, he declined this offer. In 1865, after a visit to the South, he published *After the War; a Southern Tour*. This was the first of his many contributions to literature. In the following year he made an experiment at cotton planting in the South, but this was a failure. He published another book, entitled *Ohio in the War*, and then returned to journalism as a leader writer on the *Gazette*. He reported the impeachment proceedings against President Johnson and in the same summer accepted a position on the political staff of the New York *Tribune*. His position was that of leading editorial writer, with responsibility only to Mr. Greeley. He wrote many of the editorial leaders throughout the campaign which resulted in the election of General Grant. He was soon advanced to the position of managing editor of the *Tribune*, and in this position retained the affection and confidence of Mr. Greeley. By a bold expenditure of money in 1870 he enabled the *Tribune* to cover thoroughly the Franco-German War and from that time on gradually reorganized and strengthened the entire staff of the paper. In 1872, after the nomination of Greeley for President, Mr. Reid was made editor-in-chief of the *Tribune*, and on the defeat and retirement of Greeley Mr. Reid borrowed enough money to acquire control of the paper. He then devoted his energies to making it profitable, which it had ceased to be during Greeley's political experiments. The circulation and income of the paper increased rapidly and soon he was able to pay back out of the earnings the money which he had borrowed. In 1881 he married a daughter of D. Ogden Mills of California, who had inherited half of the immense estate of her father. President Hayes offered in 1878 to make Mr. Reid minister to Germany. This offer, however, was declined, as was also an offer of the same position by President Garfield. In March, 1889, he was offered and accepted the post of minister to France. Largely through his efforts the French decree prohibiting the importation of American meat was repealed. He also assisted in negotiating reciprocity and extradition treaties between France and the United States. In 1892 he resigned the office and in the summer of that year was nominated for vice-president by the Republican party on the ticket with Benjamin Harrison, with whom he suffered defeat. He was appointed special ambassador to represent the United States at the Queen's Jubilee in London in 1897 and in the following year was a member of the commission which negotiated the treaty of peace with Spain. In 1892 he was special ambassador to represent the President at the coronation of King Edward VII. He became chancellor of the University of the State of New York in 1904 and early in the following year was made American ambassador to Great Britain by President Roosevelt. His great wealth enabled him to entertain lavishly and he became a conspicuous social figure in London, although personally his tastes were of the simplest. He held office during the administration of President Roosevelt and the administration of President Taft. His diplomatic career in London was successful. He was in great demand as an after-dinner speaker and delivered addresses before many learned societies and in different cities of the United Kingdom. He was honored with degrees by several universities in the United States and in foreign countries. King Victor Emanuel of Italy decorated him with the Grand Order of the Crown of Italy. Among his published writings, in addition to those mentioned above, are: *Schools of Journalism* (1870); *Newspaper Tendencies* (1874); *Introduction to English Edition of Thackeray's Memoirs* (1881); *Our New Duties* (1899); *A Continental Union* (1900); *Problems of Expansion* (1900); *The Monroe Doctrine* (1903); *Greatest Fact in Modern History* (1906); *How America Faced its Educational Problem* (1906). He delivered notable addresses on Edmund Burke, Byron, Abraham Lincoln, Thomas Jefferson, and on the Scots and Ulster Scots in America.

REINFORCED CONCRETE. See ARCHITECTURE.

REINFORCED CONCRETE BRIDGE. See BRIDGES.

REINHART, MAX See DRAMA.

RELATIVITY THEORY. See PHYSICS.

RELIGION. See LITERATURE, ENGLISH AND AMERICAN.

RELIGIOUS DENOMINATIONS AND MOVEMENTS. Information in regard to the principal Protestant denominations, the Jews and the Roman Catholics will be found elsewhere in this volume in proper alphabetical order. In the following table, which was compiled by Dr. H. K. Carroll and was printed in the *Christian Advocate*, the membership of the principal denominations is shown for the years 1890 and 1912:

Denominations	Rank in 1912	Communicants	Rank in 1890	Communicants
Roman Catholic........	1	12,888,466	1	6,231,417
Methodist Episcopal..	2	3,293,526	2	2,240,354
Regular Baptist (So.)	3	2,475,609	4	1,280,066
Meth. Epis., South..	4	1,919,873	5	1,209,976
Regular Bapt. (Col.)	5	1,912,219	3	1,348,989
Presbyterian (North.)	6	1,368,150	7	788,244
Disciples of Christ...	7	1,340,887	8	641,051
Regular Baptist (No.)	8	1,175,923	6	800,450
Protestant Episcopal.	9	970,451	9	532,054
Lutheran Syn. Confer.	10	807,693	12	357,153
Congregationalist	11	742,350	10	512,771
African Meth. Epis...	12	620,234	11	452,725
Afr. Meth. Epis. Zion	13	547,216	13	349,788
Lutheran Gen. Council	14	473,295	14	324,846
Lutheran Gen. Synod	15	316,949	20	164,640
United Brethren......	16	301,448	16	202,474
Reformed (German)..	17	300,147	15	204,018
Latter-Day Saints....	18	296,000	21	144,352
Presbyterian (South.)	19	292,845	18	179,721
German Evan. Synod.	20	258,911	17	187,432
Colored Meth. Epis...	21	234,721	24	129,383
Spiritualists	22	200,000	39	45,030
Methodist Protestant.	23	183,318	22	141,989
Greek Orth. (Cath.).	24	175,000	138	100
United Norweg. Luth.	25	169,710	26	119,972
United Presbyterian..	26	139,617	27	94,402
Luth. Synod of Ohio.	27	132,316	33	69,505
Reformed (Dutch)....	28	118,564	28	92,970
Orthodox Friends.....	29	100,568	31	80,655

Certain smaller denominations are not given in this table. Of these the most important are the following: Christian Scientists, communicants, 85,096; Unitarians, 70,542; and Universalists, 51,716. These statistics are for the United States only. The statistics of the Ro-

RHODESIA. A country (named for Cecil Rhodes) under the administration of the British South Africa Company; a British protectorate, which is divided into Northern Rhodesia (estimated area, 291,000 square miles; estimated population 1,001,400) and Southern Rhodesia (148,575 square miles, 769,471 inhabitants).

NORTHERN RHODESIA includes the two provinces of Barotseland, or North-Western Rhodesia and North-Eastern Rhodesia. It was constituted a single British sphere in 1911. Lewanika, the native king, resides at Lealui; L. A. Wallace, residing at Livingstone, was administrator of the company in 1912.

SOUTHERN RHODESIA includes the provinces of Mashonaland (European population, 12,543) and Matabeleland (11,039). Chief towns: Salisbury (the capital), with 3479 white inhabitants; Umtali, and Victoria, in Mashonaland; Bulawayo (5200 white inhabitants), Gwelo, and Tuli, in Matabeleland. The country is well adapted to stock-raising and agriculture. Gold has been mined in Rhodesia supposedly from the time of the Phœnicians. From 1890, the date of the occupation by the South Africa Company, to September, 1898, the gold production was 6470 ounces; in 1902 the value of the yield (bullion) was estimated at £687,096; in 1905, £1,449,985; 1908 (fine gold), £2,526,007; 1911, £2,647,896. Coal mined in 1911, 212,529 tons; silver, 187,641 ounces; lead, 639 tons. Diamonds are found. Trade and financial statistics follow:

*	1907-8	1908-9	1909-10	1910-11
Imports ...	£1,450,174	£1,818,372	£2,214,014	£2,786,321
Exports ...	2,474,236	2,735,685	3,178,416	3,199,956
Revenue ..	554,209	564,399	620,243	784,908
Expend. ..	543,597	535,150	614,405	684,683

* Trade for calendar, finance for fiscal years.

Sir William Milton was the company's administrator in 1912.

RAILWAYS. The total mileage of the Rhodesian Railway systems (including the Beira line) was, at the end of 1911, 2357. Through connection exists between Cape Town and the Congo border, a total distance of 2149 miles; and between Cape Town and Beira, over 2000 miles. Branches extend to the mining districts and to the burial-place of Cecil Rhodes in the Matopos. There was considerable railway extension in 1912. The branch from Salisbury, built by the Brinkwater Railway Company, which had been finished to the Jumbo mine in December, 1911, was being carried on to Kimberley, whence it was to run to the Shamva mines.

RHODES SCHOLARSHIPS. See UNIVERSITIES AND COLLEGES.

RICE. Data on rice production in 1912 were available for only a few countries, and in fact many important rice-producing countries do not collect statistics relating to the crop. British India, which is the leading rice country of the world, yielded in 1912, as estimated, 1,300,000,000 bushels, which is about 20 per cent. below the normal yield. Italy's yield amounted to more than 20,000,000 bushels on an area of about 360,000 acres. The area devoted to the crop in Japan was 7,317,000 acres and the normal annual production is about 330,000,000 bushels. The early rice crop of Siam was almost a complete failure and in parts of the country there was such a dearth of seed grain that the government appropriated money for the introduction of seed paddy. The 1912 rice crop of the United States amounted to 25,054,000 bushels, produced on 722,800 acres, the corresponding figures for 1911 being 22,934,000 and 696,300, respectively. The farm value on December 1, 1912, was 93.5 cents per bushel, and the total value of the crop was estimated by the Department of Agriculture at $23,423,000, the highest value ever recorded for the crop. Among the ten producing States Louisiana ranked first, with a yield of 11,812,000 bushels, Texas second with 9,429,000 bushels, and Arkansas third with 3,405,000 bushels. South Carolina, which stood fourth, produced only 200,000 bushels, and California, which produced only 6000 bushels in 1911, had a yield of 70,000 bushels and an average acre-yield of 50 bushels in 1912. The average yield per acre was 33.5 bushels in Louisiana, 35.5 bushels in Texas, and 37.5 bushels in Arkansas.

RICE INSTITUTE. See WILLIAM MARSH RICE INSTITUTE.

RICHARDS, EUGENE LAMB. An American mathematician and educator, died August 5, 1912. He was born in Brooklyn, N. Y., in 1838 and graduated from Yale College in 1860. He was successively tutor in mathematics, assistant professor, professor, and professor emeritus. He retired from active work in 1906. From 1892 to 1902 he was director of the Yale gymnasium. His published writings include *Plane and Spherical Trigonometry, with Applications* (1879); *Elementary Navigation and Nautical Astronomy* (1902).

RICHARDS, SIR FREDERICK WILLIAM. An English admiral, died September 28, 1912. He was born in 1833 and entered the navy in 1848. He was appointed flag lieutenant in 1859 and in the following year was given command of the sloop, *Vixen*. During 1862-1865 he commanded the *Dart* on the west coast of Africa. In 1866 he was promoted to be captain. Four years later he was given command of the Indian troopship, *Jumna*. On this vessel he served for three years and in 1873 was appointed to command the *Devastation*, the first sea-going turret ship which had been designed without any auxiliary sail-power. He took part in the fighting in South Africa in 1880-1881 and was present at the battle of Gingihlovo and the relief of Eshowe. He was also present at the action of Laing's Nek in 1881. The following year he was promoted to the rank of rear-admiral and for three years served as junior lord of the Admiralty. He then became commander-in-chief of the East Indies, which position he occupied for three years. On his return home he acted on several important naval commissions. In 1888 he was promoted to the rank of vice-admiral and in November, 1890, he was appointed commander-in-chief in China. He held this position until June, 1902, when he was appointed second naval lord of the Admiralty. He succeeded Sir Anthony Hoskins as senior naval lord in 1893 and continued to hold this position until 1899. He had been appointed admiral in 1893, and by special Order in Council was made admiral of the fleet in 1898. He was retained on the active list of the navy until he had reached the age of 70.

In 1904 he received the honorary degree of D. C. L., from Oxford University.

RICHARDS, WILLIAM ALFORD. An American public official, former governor of Wyoming, died July 26, 1912. He was born in Hazel Green, Wis., in 1849 and was educated in the public schools of that town and at Galena, Ill. From 1889 to 1893 he was surveyor-general of Wyoming and was governor of that State from 1895 to 1899. He was assistant commissioner of the general land office from 1889 to 1903 and was commissioner from 1903 to 1907. From 1909 to the time of his death he was commissioner of taxation of the State of Wyoming.

RICHARDSON, MAURICE HOWE. An American surgeon, died July 31, 1912. He was born in Atbol, Mass., in 1851 and graduated from Harvard College in 1873. In 1882 he was appointed demonstrator of anatomy in the medical school of Harvard College; in 1883 assistant in surgery; in 1887 assistant professor of anatomy; in 1895 assistant professor of clinical surgery, and in 1903 professor of clinical surgery. From 1907 to the time of his death he was Mosely professor of surgery. In 1886 he was appointed visiting surgeon to the Massachusetts General Hospital and was also consulting surgeon to hospitals in Boston and elsewhere. He was one of the most eminent surgeons in the United States. He contributed to *Park's Surgery by American Authors*, and *Dennis' System of Surgery*.

RICKER, GEORGE HODGEN. An American educator, died April 27, 1912. He was born in 1821 and graduated from Dartmouth College in 1845. He was for many years a teacher in seminaries in New Hampshire and in Maine, and was for several years professor in Greek in Hillsdale College, Mich. He afterwards was principal of the Fryeburg Academy, at Fryeburg, Me. He retired from active teaching several years before his death after he had been engaged in educational work for 55 years.

RITCHIE, SIR RICHMOND. An English public official, died October 14, 1912. He was born in 1854 and was educated at Eton and at Trinity College, Cambridge. He left Cambridge and entered the India office in 1877. In 1883 he was appointed private secretary to the parliamentary under-secretary of state. He held this office under successive chiefs until 1892. He afterwards rose to be principal private secretary to the secretary of state and in 1902 was appointed secretary in the political and secret department. In 1909 he was appointed by Lord Morley, permanent under-secretary of state, one of the most important positions in the English cabinet. He held this position until the time of his death. In 1887 he married the eldest daughter of William M. Thackeray.

RIVERS, STANDARD OF PURITY FOR. See SANITATION.

ROADS AND PAVEMENTS. Never in the history of the United States was so much road and street improvement work in progress or projected as in 1912.

ROADS. Until within a few years past little was done outside the cities and a few States to provide other than dirt roads or at best roads surfaced with gravel. Massachusetts and New Jersey led the way in State aid, and one by one the other States have followed—generally a long way behind. Counties have also taken up the work, either alone or in conjunction with the States, and the same is true in lesser degree of towns and townships in the older and more thickly settled parts of the country. A number of years ago the federal government began to consider road improvements, confining its efforts to investigations and reports. Later on the office of public roads was established in the United States Department of Agriculture. The work of investigation was continued in the office, the laboratory, and the field, and finally short sections of experimental improved roads were built to test different types of surfacing and different modes of construction. In the year ending June 30, 1912, the office of public roads built the equivalent of 88 miles of 14-foot roadway at a cost of $91,877. With the exception of two experimental roads these were known as object-lesson roads. For many years strong efforts have been made to get Congressional authorization and appropriations for extensive federal road improvements. In fact, an organization, known as the National Highway Association (Charles Henry Davis, South Yarmouth, Mass., president), has gone so far as to publish a map of the United States showing "a broad and comprehensive system of national highways to be built, owned, and maintained by the national government," comprising a total of no less than 51,025 miles. An editorial writer in *Engineering News* of May 16, 1912, estimates that this system—since it is designed primarily for automobile traffic and would be built under difficulties in many of its parts—would cost an average of, at least, $13,000 a mile, or a total of $663,-000,000, and that allowing 10 per cent. for maintenance and repairs and only 4 per cent. for capital charges the annual cost would be $92,000,000. This project is mentioned to show how rapidly federal road construction would run into the billions, once it was begun on a "comprehensive" plan. Few of the road enthusiasts have gone quite so far as this, but fewer yet have seriously counted the cost. As a result of various, more or less ambitious, proposals for federal aid, Congress appropriated $500,000 for road construction in the several States, in conjunction with either State or local governments, the latter to provide two dollars for each one dollar of federal money. This money is to be expended by the Secretary of Agriculture in coöperation with the Postmaster-General. It is to be used to improve "the condition of roads selected by them over which rural delivery is or may hereafter be established." Congress also appropriated $25,000 for the use of a joint Congressional committee investigation "of federal aid in the construction of post roads." The obvious intent of the act was that the $500,000 fund should be divided as equally as may be among the 48 States of the Union. This would give a little over $10,000 to each State, and with State or local appropriations would give $30,000. Obviously this will do little more than provide a few miles of object-lesson dirt or gravel and experimental roads in each State, or two or three miles of macadam; but it is equally obvious that it will stimulate local interest in good roads and that the bill may prove to be an opening wedge through which hundreds of millions of road money may yet flow from the federal treasury.

An interstate road project, to be carried out

by the various States or counties traversed, is what is known as the Meridian Road, extending from Winnipeg, Man., to the Gulf of Mexico. An automobile reconnaissance of the portion of this road lying in South Dakota, as well as projects for several other trunk lines across that State, was described by Samuel H. Lea, State engineer, in the *Municipal Journal* for September 26, 1912. The same author described in *Engineering News* of October 10, 1912, the construction, or improvement, in two days' time of the portion of the Meridian Road extending across Codington County, South Dakota, a distance of 24 miles. Under a prearranged plan the business men of Watertown, S. Dak., and residents of other communities along the road, turned out and regraded and shaped up the highway as well as could be done with local materials along the route. Such spectacular and spasmodic efforts give results of relatively temporary value, except in the way of education and stimulus. The real progress now being made in high-class road construction in the United States, other than necessary work of investigation and education, is due chiefly to State and county highway improvement. Only the latter can be given further mention here except to note that New Jersey, on one side of the continent, and California on the other, afford notable examples of highway construction by counties—although in New Jersey most of the county work has the assistance of State funds and general State engineering supervision. California, of late, has been spending millions through county highway commissions, besides the large amount of work which the State is doing.

Of the 48 States of the Union, 26 had done more or less in the way of State aid for road construction up to the early part of 1912. This had ranged all the way from the $50,000,000 of bonds authorized (and largely spent) in New York, to small annual appropriations. Another $50,000,000 of State aid in New York was made possible by a constitutional amendment adopted by popular vote in November, 1912. Among the 42 Ohio constitutional amendments submitted to popular vote on September 3, 1912, one increasing the bond limit for inter-county roads to $50,000,000 was lost, having been voted down in 48 counties, although the total majority against it was less than 2000 out of a total of 550,000 votes. Pennsylvania has entered on a State highway network project, under legislation of 1911, which will presumably cost $50,000,000 or more. California has authorized $18,000,000, and Maryland $5,000,000 for such work.

A large mass of statistical and other data on State road aid and State highway administration resulting from a special investigation may be found in *Engineering News* of March 28, 1912. Reviews of State highway work in Massachusetts, New Jersey, Connecticut, and California appeared in the *Engineering Record* for September 28, 1912, and still more information on the California work in the *Municipal Journal* for September 26, 1912.

No marked change in materials and methods of road construction occurred during the year. Water-bound macadam continued to give place to bituminous-bound where the traffic demanded and the public purse could afford it. For years to come, dirt or at best gravel will continue to form the wearing surface and foundation of by far the larger part of the hundreds of thousands of miles of roads of the country. There were 2,199,000 miles of public roads in the United States proper in 1909, of which only 190,467, or 8.66 per cent., had been improved or graded, drained and provided with a hard surface. Much of the unimproved mileage could be vastly improved at an expense well within the means of the localities directly concerned by simple means of drainage, grading, and cross-sectional shaping, whereas even the least expensive macadam construction, if extensively gone into, would bankrupt thousands of rural communities.

PAVEMENTS. Growth of heavy traffic is increasing the need of substituting the more permanent wearing surfaces for macadam. Bituminous concrete, asphalt, brick, creosoted-wood blocks, some of the harder sandstones and, for the heaviest traffic, granite, are the principal kinds of pavement now used. Portland cement concrete is gaining in use. The organization of city officials for standardizing paving specifications is continuing its works with promising results, as is also the American Society of Municipal Improvements.

REFERENCES. During the year new editions appeared of George W. Tillson's *Street Pavement and Paving Materials* (New York) and Prof. F. P. Spalding's *A Text-Book of Roads and Pavements*. New books in this field were: Francis Wood, *Modern Road Construction* (London and Philadelphia), a British book; L. W. Page, *Roads, Paths and Bridges* (New York), a small popular book, and W. G. Harger and E. A. Bouney, *Handbook for Highway Engineers* (New York).

ROBERTS, ERNEST STEWART. An English scholar and educator, died June 17, 1912. He was born at Swineshead, Lincolnshire, in 1847 and was educated at Boston, England, and at Caius College, Cambridge. In 1870 he became a fellow at Caius College, and six years later was appointed tutor. In 1885 he was made senior tutor, and in 1894 president of Caius College. In 1903 he was chosen master to succeed Ferrers. In addition to his service in this college he was equally active in the university. He was for a time university lecturer in comparative philology, and held the office of proctor in 1876 and 1884. He was vice-chancellor from 1906 to 1908 and served on the council of the senate continuously from 1904 to the time of his death.

ROBIE, FREDERICK. An American public official, former governor of Maine. He was born in Gorham, Me., in 1822, and graduated from Bowdoin College in 1841. He studied medicine at the Jefferson Medical College in Philadelphia and practiced as a physician until the outbreak of the Civil War. He served throughout the Civil War and was brevetted lieutenant-colonel of volunteers for gallantry in service in 1865. After the close of the war he engaged in business in Portland, also taking an active interest in politics. He was at various times member of the State legislature and from 1883 to 1887 was governor of the State. He was a member of the boards of directors of many State institutions and held office in several banks and insurance companies in Portland.

RODENBOUGH, THEOPHILUS FRANCIS. An American soldier, died December 19, 1912. He was born at Easton, Pa., in 1838 and was educated at Lafayette College At the outbreak of the Civil War he was engaged in the mercantile business. He was appointed second lieutenant in the Second United Dragoons in 1861 and within two months was promoted to be first lieutenant. In 1862 he was made captain. He took part in the battle of Gaines' Mills and the Peninsular campaign of 1862. He was captured at the battle of Manassas and was shortly afterwards exchanged. At the battle of Beverly Ford in June, 1862, he was wounded. At Gettysburg he had command of his regiment. He was again wounded at Trevilian Station in 1864. While leading his regiment at the battle of Opequan in September, 1864, he lost his right arm. He was granted leave of absence and on his recovery was made colonel of the 18th Pennsylvania Volunteer Cavalry. By direction of the President he was especially assigned to command a brigade of regulars and volunteers in the district of Clarksburg, W. Va. He received a medal of honor for gallant conduct at Trevilian Station and was given five brevets for his war service. For gallantry at the battle of Cold Harbor he was made brigadier-general. In the winter of 1865 he served as inspector-general in Kansas and later with the Second Cavalry. He was major of the 47th Infantry, serving in the northern part of New York until December 15, 1870, when he was put on the retired list with the rank of colonel. He then became governor of the Soldiers' Home at Washington, holding that position for one year. From 1890 to 1901 he was chief of the Bureau of Elections in the City of New York. He was one of the founders, and from 1878 until the time of his death, secretary of the Military Service Institution. He was the author of *From Everglade to Cañon with the Second Dragoons* (1875); *Afghanistan and the Anglo-Russian Dispute* (1885); *Uncle Sam's Medal of Honor* (1886); *Autumn Leaves from Family Trees* (1892); *Sabre and Bayonet* (1897). In 1896 he edited *The Army of the United States*, and in 1899 was editor of the *Journal of the Military Service Institution*. He was editor of the Military Department in the *New International Encyclopædia*.

ROGERS, H. H. See PRESIDENTIAL CAMPAIGN CONTRIBUTIONS.

ROGERS, ROBERT CAMERON. An American poet and author, died April, 1912. He was born in Buffalo in 1862 and graduated from Yale University in 1883. He engaged in journalism and became editor of the Santa Barbara (Cal.) *Morning Press*. He contributed verses to many magazines. Among his published writings are *Wind in the Clearing, and Other Poems; Will o' the Wisp; Old Dorset; Chronicles of a New York Country Side; For the King, and Other Poems* (1899); *The Rosary, and Other Poems* (1906).

ROMAN CATHOLIC CHURCH. Church statisticians estimate the Catholic population of the world in 1912 at 292,787,085 and of this total, 29,000,000 are in English-speaking countries. In round numbers there are 1754 Catholic bishops in the world; 11 apostolic delegates; 155 vicars apostolic; and 68 prefectures apostolic. As appointments now average the whole hierarchy of the world is renewed about every fifteen years. The religious orders and congregations of men number 116.

There are 15,015,569 Catholics in the continental United States according to the 1912 edition of *The Official Catholic Directory*, an increase of 396,808 over the figures of the preceding year. This 15,015,569 does not deduct 15 per cent. for children and infants, as was done by the government in its census of 1906-09. The Catholic population shows a gain of 4,038,812 for the decade.

There are 17,491 priests. Of these 4495 are members of religious orders, a gain of 407 priests. Four hundred and seventy-eight additional churches are recorded, and the general summary shows 13,939 Catholic churches. Of these 9256 have resident priests, the other 4683 being mission churches, that is, attended from neighboring parishes.

There are 17 archbishops, each of the 14 archiepiscopal sees being occupied. Three archbishops are cardinals, and three are titular archbishops, Bonzano, Keane, and Spalding. There are 84 bishoprics. All told there are 101 bishops, 17 of these being coadjutor and auxiliary bishops. In addition, there are two arch-abbots and 15 abbots.

Eighty-three seminaries are located in various parts of the country, with 6000 students. There are 229 colleges for boys and 701 academies for girls, and more students in the 229 colleges for boys than there are in the 701 academies for girls. In 5119 parishes schools are open, with an attendance of 1,333,786. Besides the parochial schools there are 289 orphan asylums, in which 47,111 orphans are taken care of. Counting the children in parochial schools, the number of young ladies and young men in academies and colleges, and including the orphans and children in other charitable institutions, there are under Catholic care in the United States 1,540,049 young people. The five States having the largest number of Catholics rank as follows: New York, 2,778,076; Pennsylvania, 1,616,920; Illinois, 1,447,400; Massachusetts, 1,381,212; Ohio, 745,271.

The Catholics in the British Empire number 12,968,814, an increase of 392,559 over the total for 1911. The totals for the sub-divisions of the empire are: England and Wales, 1,793,038; Scotland, 547,336; total for Great Britain, 2,340,374; Ireland, 3,242,670; total for British Empire in Europe 5,800,526; in British America, 3,105,916 (of these Canada has 2,824,558); in Australasia, 1,184,500; in Asia, 2,288,898 as compared with 1,975,305; Africa, 489,965 (in 1911, 380,105). These figures are officially computed for the *English Catholic Directory* for 1913.

ITALY. In spite of repeated rumors concerning his ill-health Pope Pius X. continued during the year to give public manifestation of his physical and mental ability to govern the Church, by repeated audiences, and the promulgation of many decrees and letters on matters of legislation and discipline. Among these documents of special importance were the letter to the South American bishops on the condition of the native Indians; the decrees on the establishment of a special department of the Consistorial Congregation for spiritual care of emigrants; defining the duties of the Third Order of St. Francis; the establishment of the Ruthenian Rite in Canada; the settlement of the controversy over membership in Catholic and in non-sectarian labor unions in Germany and the censure of a syndicate of five Catholic dailies in Italy for lax opinions o·

the question of the temporal power of the Pope and the integrity of the Papal state. The first part of the new code of canon law was sent to the bishops of the world for study and instruction. It will take two years to complete the work. The higher criticism writings of the Dominican Father LaGrange, director of the Biblical School at Jerusalem and editor of the *Revue Biblique*, were condemned as unfit for reading or consultation in Catholic seminaries. He resigned both these positions. A consistory was held December 2 at which Bishop Charles de Hornig of Veszprem, Hungary, was created a cardinal and the red hat was given to five of the cardinals created at the previous consistory (November 27, 1911); Nagl, Bauer, Vico, Cos y Macho, and Almaraz y Santos. The number of cardinals in 1912 was 61 (the full number of the sacred college is 70) divided nationally as follows: From Italy, 33; Austria-Hungary, 5; France, 6; Spain, 6; United States, 3; Germany, England, Belgium, Ireland, Brazil, Holland, and Portugal, one each. Of the whole number, 33 have been appointed by the present Pope Piux X. Cardinals Fischer, Samassa, Couillié, and Copecelatro died during 1912, making 38 deaths during the pontificate of Piux X. A committee was named by the Pope to invite the Catholics of the world to join, during 1913, in a general celebration of the edict by which, in 313, Constantine gave peace to the Christian Church.

FRANCE. Catholicism showed many evidences of vigor in France, in spite of the rupture of the Concordat, in the building of new churches in the neglected quarters of large cities, the erection of new schools, and the inauguration of works of benevolence in the interest of the working classes. Under the appeals of Maurice Barrés protests were made against the government policy of letting the churches, many of them national monuments, fall into decay. Since 1902, 20,000 schools belonging to religious congregations have been closed by the government. Of these, according to a report made by Canon Laude for the Société d'Education, 8000 have been reopened by lay teachers or secularized religious and Catholics have voluntarily contributed 45,000,000 francs for the support of these schools. Of this amount, 30,000,000 francs went to pay the salaries of 8000 men and 25,000 women teachers.

GERMANY. The activity of German Catholics was specially manifested at the Marial Congress at Treves (August 4-6); during the Catholic Day gatherings at Aachen (August 12-15), and at the various Windthorst centenary celebrations (January). The Centre party successfully aroused the indignation of the country in an agitation against duelling in the army, begun over the dismissal of a Catholic officer who refused a challenge on conscientious grounds. The repeal of the anti-Jesuit laws was strongly urged. Four priests were sentenced to six months' confinement because their request to be excused from service as military reservists was judged a breach of military discipline. The Pope's decree on the question of Catholics joining non-Catholic labor unions was well received. See GERMANY.

UNITED STATES. Mgr. John Bonzano, rector of the College of the Propaganda, was appointed apostolic delegate to the United States, and consecrated Archbishop of Mitylene March 3, and assumed the duties of his office in February. Extraordinary public demonstrations of welcome marked the return in January from Rome of Cardinal Farley to New York and Cardinal O'Connell to Boston. Two new dioceses were created during 1912: Corpus Christi, Texas, from the vicariate of Brownsville, and Kearney, Neb., from the former boundaries of the diocese of Omaha. The Rev. James Albert Duffy was appointed Bishop of Kearney. The pallium was imposed on Archbishop James J. Keane of Dubuque (January 21), and Archbishop Edmond F. Prendergast of Philadelphia (January 31). These bishops were appointed: Denis O'Connell, Richmond, Va.; P. A. McGovern, Cheyenne; Austin Dowling, Des Moines; John G. McCort, auxiliary of Philadelphia; Joseph H. Conroy, auxiliary of Ogdensburg; Edward A. Hanna, auxiliary of San Francisco. Bishop P. A. Ludden of Syracuse, N. Y., died and was succeeded by his coadjutor, Right Rev. John Grimes. Bishop Carroll of Nueva Segovia, P. I., resigned and returned to parish work in Philadelphia.

The 400th anniversary of the creation of the diocese of San Juan, Porto Rico, the senior diocese of all America, was commemorated (August). During this period it has had 51 bishops, the present one being Bishop Jones, formerly of Philadelphia, Pa.

CONGRESSES AND MEETINGS. The twenty-third international Eucharistic Congress drew to Vienna (September 12-15) more than a hundred thousand visitors. Cardinal von Rossum was the Pope's delegate, and three other cardinals and 4000 prelates and priests from all over the world attended. The grand procession at the close, in spite of a downpour of rain, was participated in by the venerable Emperor Francis Joseph of Austria, the nobility and clergy. The first week of September also, the third convention of the International Federation of Catholic Women met in Vienna, 24 nations being represented. The social conditions of women, their betterment, and the religious education of children were among the chief topics of discussion.

The third national Catholic Congress was held at Norwich, England (August 2-5), and was marked by the distinct advance in boldness with which the social and religious Home Missions, Women's League, trade conditions, and other topics were treated. It was the first general meeting of bishops, clergy, and laity since the division of England into three ecclesiastical provinces and the establishment of the archdioceses of Liverpool and Manchester.

ROMANCE. See PHILOLOGY.

ROME. See ARCHITECTURE.

RÖNTGEN RAYS. See RADIOTHERAPY.

ROOSEVELT, THEODORE. See PRESIDENTIAL CAMPAIGN.

ROOT, ELIHU. See PRESIDENTIAL CAMPAIGN.

ROPES, WILLIAM LADD. An American librarian, died October 14, 1912. He was born in Newton, Mass., in 1825, and graduated from Harvard College in 1846. He taught for several years in the public Latin School of Boston, and was then ordained to the Congregational ministry. From 1853 to 1862 he was pastor of the first church at Wrentham, Mass. From 1866 to 1905 he was librarian at the Andover Theological Seminary. In the latter year he retired and was appointed librarian emeritus.

ROTCH, ABBOTT LAWRENCE. An American

meteorologist, died April 5, 1912. He was born in Boston in 1861 and was educated in private schools in Boston and in European cities. In 1884 he received the degree of S. B. from the Massachusetts Institute of Technology. He established in 1885 the Blue Hill Meteorological Observatory near Boston, which became famous for investigations of the clouds and for the use of kites to record meteorological data. From 1896 to the time of his death he was professor of meteorology at Harvard University. Professor Rotch observed the three solar eclipses of 1887, 1889, and 1893 for meteorological purposes. The first of these was in Russia, the second in California, and the third in Chile. He was a member of several international commissions and congresses and was decorated by various foreign universities and governments. In 1905-6 he collaborated with Teisserenc de Bort in sending a steam yacht to explore the tropical atmosphere. He also took part in several scientific expeditions in the United States, South America, Europe, and Africa. From 1886 to 1896 he was associate editor of the *American Meteorological Journal*. He delivered lectures before the Lowell Institute of Boston in 1891 and 1898. He was librarian of the American Academy of Arts and Sciences. Among his published works are: *Sounding the Ocean of Air* (1900); *The Conquest of the Air* (1909). He also edited *Observations and Investigations at Blue Hill*, published since 1887 in the *Annals* of the Harvard College Observatory. Numerous articles were contributed by him to scientific journals.

ROUSSEAU BI-CENTENARY. See FRENCH LITERATURE.

ROWING. Cornell still reigns supreme in the college rowing world, having made a clean sweep of the races in the intercollegiate regatta held on the Hudson River, near Poughkeepsie. Cornell also defeated Harvard and Princeton in a two-mile race on the Charles River. In the intercollegiate regatta Cornell scored its fourth consecutive victory in the 'varsity eight oars and also won the four-oared and freshmen eight-oared events. Wisconsin finished second in the 'varsity eight oars, Columbia third, Syracuse fourth, and Pennsylvania fifth. Leland Stanford University which, for the first time, took part in the regatta, had to be content with last place.

The Cornell 'varsity eight consisted of C. H. Elliott, bow; E. S. Bates, 2; B. A. Lunn, 3; W. O. Kruse, 4; G B. Wakely, 5; B. C. Spransy, 6; C. B. Ferguson, 7, and W. G. Distler, stroke. With one exception the make-up of the crew was the same as in 1911. The winner's time for the four miles was 19 minutes, 31⅗ seconds. The record for the event, 18 minutes, 53⅕ seconds, was made by Cornell in 1901. The times of the other crews in 1912 were: Wisconsin, 19:35⅘; Columbia, 19:41; Syracuse, 19:47; Pennsylvania, 19:55, and Stanford, 20:25. In the 'varsity four-oared event (2 miles) Cornell's time was 10:34⅕; Columbia's, 10:41⅕; Syracuse's, 10:58⅗, and Pennsylvania's, 11:23⅗. The winning four included C. W. Brown, bow; G. P. McNear, 2; L. Chapman, 3, and E. L. Dole, stroke. Cornell, also the winner of the freshman eight oars, covered the two miles in 9 minutes 31⅗ seconds. Wisconsin was second in 9:35⅗; Syracuse third in 9:42⅗; Pennsylvania fourth in 9:46⅗, and Columbia last in 9:47. The winning eight were E. Ornelas, bow; S. V. Hiscox, 2; E. L. Pollard, 3; L. F. Cramer, 4; E. S. Craft, 5; W. W. Butts, 6; J E. O'Brien, 7, and W. V. Ellms, stroke.

Harvard for the fifth year in succession was triumphant over Yale in the annual races held on the Thames River, near New London. The Cambridge oarsmen made a clean sweep of the three events for the third time since 1909. Harvard's time in the 'varsity eight-oared event was 21 minutes 43½ seconds and Yale's 22 minutes 4 seconds. The winning eight comprised G. H. Balch, bow; M. Eager, 2; Q. Reynolds, 3; A. M. Goodale, 4; L. H. Mills, 5; A. Strong, Jr., 6; G. P. Metcalf, 7, and G. F. Nettleton, stroke. In the 'varsity four oars Harvard's time was 11 minutes, 24 seconds and Yale's 11 minutes, 55 seconds. The winning four included G. F. Stratton, bow; F. H. Trumbull, 2; E. D. Morgan, 3, and L. S. Chanler, stroke. The most exciting race was that between the freshmen eights, the Harvard crew's time, 10:52, being only 2½ seconds better than Yale's, 10:54½.

In the Pacific Coast intercollegiate 'varsity race over a three mile course, Leland Stanford finished first, Washington second, and California third. The winner's time was 16 minutes, 10 seconds. Stanford also won the freshman event over a two-mile course with California second. In dual college regattas the United States Naval Academy defeated Pennsylvania, and Syracuse defeated the Naval Academy.

The Canadian oarsmen carried off the laurels at the fortieth annual regatta of the National Association of Amateur Oarsmen held at Peoria, Ill., by winning eight of the ten most important events. The Winnipeg Rowing Club triumphed in the crew races, capturing the senior eight-oared shells, senior four-oared shells, and the senior international four-oared shells. H. H. Phinney of the Winnipegs won the intermediate single sculls, while Phinney and Punshen captured the intermediate double sculls event. The senior single sculls went to A. F. Culver of the Winnipegs. E. B. Butler of the Argonaut Rowing Club of Toronto, repeated his victories of 1911, by winning both senior sculls championships at 1¼ miles and the ¼-mile dash. The only important events won by the United States oarsmen were the intermediate four-oared shells and the intermediate eight-oared shells. The four oars were won by the Grand Rapids Boat and Canoe Club and the eight oars by the Duluth Boat Club, whose crew established a new world's record by rowing the 1¼ miles in 6 minutes, 16 seconds. The old record was 6:19⅕.

The tenth annual regatta of the National Rowing Association, popularly known as the American Henley, was held on the Schuylkill River, over a course of 1 mile, 550 yards The winners of the main events were: First four-oared shells, Puritan Cup, University Barge Club of Philadelphia; first eight-oared shells, Columbia University Rowing Club; junior collegiate eight-oared shells, New England Cup, Harvard; first four-oared sculls, Union Boat Club of Boston; first single sculls, Farragut Cup, Walter Stokes of the University Barge Club.

At the Henley regatta, held on the Thames, England, the Sydney Rowing Club of New South Wales won the Grand Challenge Cup.

Eton College, for the second successive year, captured the Ladies Challenge Plate. New College, Oxford, won the Steward's Challenge Cup. The sixty-ninth annual Oxford-Cambridge regatta was won for the fourth successive year by Oxford in the slow time of 22 minutes, 3 seconds. The record for the event, 18:29, was made by Oxford in 1911. R. Arnst of New Zealand, who won the world's professional sculling championship in 1908, lost his title to Ernest Barry in a 4¼-mile race on the Thames, England.

ROYAL COMMISSION ON DIVORCE. See DIVORCE.

ROYAL COMMISSION ON OIL FUEL. See NAVAL PROGRESS.

ROYAL COMMISSION ON SEWAGE DISPOSAL. See SEWAGE PURIFICATION.

ROYAL FLYING CORPS. See NAVAL PROGRESS.

RUBBER. Much attention was aroused in 1912 by the discussion of practical methods for the production of synthetic or artificial rubber, as is fully discussed below. Whether the synthetic product would enter into competition with the native material was, of course, a matter of speculation and opinions differed, some holding that, as in the case of artificial indigo, the plantation supply would be seriously cut into, while others believed that with practically an unlimited territory in the tropics available for cultivation, improved methods of rubber culture in which due economy was considered, would be fully able to insure an ample supply, the processes of nature, all things being considered, being the most economical.

The constantly increasing use of rubber is shown in the statistics of production and consumption. These figures, as compiled by Arthur Lampard, chairman of the Rubber Plantations Investment Trust in December, 1912, give the following estimates of the world's production and consumption in 1912:

PRODUCTION

	December Estimate Tons
South America (East Coast)	40,700
South America (West Coast)	2,000
Central America and Mexico	5,000
Africa	15,000
Assam, Rangoon, and Borneo	2,500
Guayule and Jelutong rubber	10,000
Plantation	28,500
All other sources	1,000
Total tons	104,700

CONSUMPTION

	December Estimate Tons
America	48,000
Great Britain	17,250
Germany	16,000
France	10,000
Russia	7,000
Belgium	2,000
Other countries	8,000
Total tons	108,250

During the year the visible supply of rubber at the markets of the world constantly decreased, and it was stated that the United States alone was able to absorb the entire world's supply of this material. This fact accounts for the conclusion reached in the above table that the year's consumption, 108,250 tons, was 3550 tons in excess of the production for the year. It is of interest to note that the supply of plantation rubber is constantly increasing and Mr. Lampard estimated that in 1913 this amount would increase from 28,500 tons to 40,000 tons.

In Hawaii during the year there were under cultivation about 1500 acres of rubber, of which 1200 acres were planted in Ceara and 300 in Hevea. The principal part of the industry is controlled by five large companies operating with local capital, whose names and acreage are given in the accompanying table:

	Established.	Capital.	Rubber acreage planted (approx.)
Nahiku Rubber Co.	1905	$150,000	480
Hawaii American Co.	1905	50,000	245
Koolan Rubber Co.	1906	30,000	275
Nahiku Sugar Co.	1906	......	250
Pacific Development Co.	1907	80,000	250
Total			1,500

The organized planting was begun in 1905, and the best results have been found where the trees have been carefully cultivated. The trees are tapped when about two years of age and in 1912 some 50,000 trees were tapped. The preference of the growers is in favor of Ceara rubber, though large experimental plantations of Hevea rubber have been made.

As further illustrating the wonderful increase in the consumption of rubber the official estimates of the State of Pará which are compiled annually show that the world's production in 1895 amounted to 58,277 tons, of which the Amazon region furnished 20,700 tons and Africa, Central America, and Malaysia, 37,577 tons. By 1911 this amount had increased to 88,000 tons, of which the Amazon districts supplied 42,800 tons, and Africa, Central America, and Malaysia, 32,980 tons, and Indian plantations, which only began to figure in statistics at the beginning of the century, had reached 12,220 tons.

The Pará government estimate of the production of Amazonian rubber for the calendar year 1911, from the various republics and districts, follows:

	Tons.
Federal Territory	10,580
State of Amazonas	10,420
State of Pará	10,300
Republic of Bolivia	2,950
Republic of Peru	2,490
State of Matto Grosso	2,100
Republic of Venezuela	50
Republic of Colombia	30
* States of Ceara, Bahia, Maranhao	3,900
Total	42,820

* Also including Manicoba, Mangabeira, and Soria. The exports of rubber from South America show that New York is the chief destination for the product and that Pará is the leading port of export. The figures of shipments for the year ending June 30, are as follows:

Shipments from	'10-11 Tons.	'11-12 Tons.	Shipped to	'10-11 Tons.	'11-12 Tons.
Para	14,972	21,577	New York	13,596	20,613
Manaos	16,142	16,664	Liverpool	16,522	15,529
Iquitos	2,372	2,498	Hamburg	777	690
Itaquatiara	108	166	Havre	2,615	3,914
			Antwerp	84	155
Total	33,594	40,905	Vigo	...	4
			Total	33,594	40,905

SUMMARY OF NEW YORK RUBBER PRICES FOR 1912

Average Prices in Cents

	Upriver. Fine.	Upriver. Coarse.	Island. Fine.	Island. Coarse.	Cameta. Coarse.
1912	111¾	89½	105⅓	59	63¾
1911	118¼	95	110¼	64	70½
1910	201¼	136¼	189¾	90	100

Statistics of Pará Rubber.

In tons.	1912	1911	1910
World's visible supply, December 31	4,527	5,852	3,891
Pará receipts, July 1 to December 31	15,655	14,635	13,400
Pará receipts of caucho, same dates	2,790	1,760	2,370
Afloat from Pará to U. S., December 31	1,379	1,300	435
Afloat from Pará to Europe, December 31	1,379	720	1,080

An India Rubber Exposition was held at the Grand Central Palace in New York City from September 23 to October 3, 1912, and in addition to exhibits showing the various stages of the industry from the raw material to the many finished products, a conference was held at which a number of important technical papers were presented by the various delegates, many of whom came from abroad.

The annual sales of manufactures of rubber in the United States in 1912 were estimated at $225,000,000 to $250,000,000, of which pneumatic tires took some $100,000,000. In the early part of the year it was proposed to place an import tax on raw rubber on the ground that it would be effective in producing revenue and that it would concern principally automobile tires used by the wealthy. Little definite, however, was heard of this proposal, which many thought was injudicious. In the calendar year 1912 the imports of unmanufactured India rubber into the United States were valued at $111,158,015 as compared with $87,941,338 in 1911 and $110,408,359 in 1910. The imports of manufactured India rubber amounted in 1912 to $1,177,680 as compared with $867,629 in 1911, and $1,050,875 in 1910. The total exports of India rubber manufactures in 1912 were valued at $13,540,835 as against $12,701,202 in 1911 and $11,224,936 in 1910. See AGRICULTURE and for Putumayo Atrocities PERU, History.

RUBBER, SYNTHESIS OF. Chemists, conscious of the possibility of reproducing by laboratory methods products similar to natural compounds, as shown by the successful synthesis of alizarin in 1869, and indigo in 1880, have sought, since the increasing demand for rubber and the decreasing sources of supply in recent years, to build up a synthetical rubber. Chemists in Germany and in England have made reports from time to time (see YEAR BOOKS for 1910, p. 153, and for 1911, p. 166) concerning their progress in obtaining the desired product, but it was not until June 17, 1912, that Dr. W. H. Perkin, of Manchester, at a meeting in London of the Society of Chemical Industry, made the definite announcement of his success in obtaining the much-sought after product. Earlier investigators, notably W. A. Tilden, of England, and G. Bourchardat, of France, had clearly pointed out that isoprene, an oily volatile hydrocarbon that may be obtained from oil of turpentine, was the important ingredient of rubber. This isoprene under given conditions was converted into a substance analogous to caoutchouc. The problem, therefore, was to derive isoprene from abundant raw materials and then to effect its conversion into rubber through the medium of plentiful and cheap reagents. Dr. Perkin in studying these problems associated with him Dr. E. Fernbach of the Pasteur Institute, Dr. F. E. Matthews, and others. A cheap source of isoprene was sought, and coal, petroleum, wood, sugar, and starch were considered. Starch may be converted into acetone or fusel oil by fermentation. These substances can then readily be converted into isoprene. Fernbach found a germ capable of changing the starch into the ingredients mentioned, thus solving the first part of the problem. Isoprene when brought into contact with metallic sodium, according to Matthews, became converted into solid rubber. In consequence of these two discoveries, Dr. Perkin announced that "there can now be no doubt that rubber may actually be obtained synthetically by the polymerization of isoprene, and its homologues, and that the synthetic product is really rubber and strictly comparable with natural rubber."

Meanwhile, at the great Farbenfabriken-Bayer Company of Elberfeld, in Germany, the process had been worked out along similar lines, using coal as a starting point and polymerizing the resulting isoprene by heat. Dr. Carl Dulsberg, president of the Elberfeld plant, showed at a meeting of the Congress of Applied Chemistry, held in New York in September, two synthetic rubber automobile tires, made in his works, which had run over 4000 miles. He said: "The stone is rolling and we will see to it that it reaches its destination. The end in view is this, that artificial rubber may soon play as important a rôle in the markets of the world as does natural rubber. Synthetic rubber, let me say, will surely not appear on the market in the immediate future."

So far as is known, the German synthetic rubber has met all of the exacting tests and analyses of other German chemists. On the other hand, it is said that the English artificial rubber is not chemically identical in its atomic makeup with natural caoutchouc, and the critics declare that this artificial substitute will not meet all of the requirements. As is usual with new products, much work both in the laboratory and in the factory will have to be done before synthetic rubber can be placed on the market, but Perkin in his lecture claimed that the new rubber could be produced at 60 cents a pound, as against $1.35, the price given by him as that of Para rubber. The "synthetic rubber scare" over the possibility of successfully marketing the artificial product seriously depressed rubber shares in England and almost precipitated a panic, but it was soon shown that the increasing rate of demand, the reduced plantation output, as well as the possible future of synthetic rubber, were sufficient to counteract any disastrous results. At the third international rubber and allied trades exhibition, held in New York in September, Dr. L. E. Weber said: "By the time the synthetic chemists will achieve what they are after—and they will achieve it in time, we have absolutely no doubt—the output of plantation rubber will be so great and the cost of plantation rubber will have been so reduced, that synthetic rubber can't meet the figures."

Announcement is made that a factory has been established at Gmuiden, at the mouth of the North Sea Canal, to produce artificial rubber. The process is secret, but the principal ingredient is said to be fresh sea fish. According to report, 15 to 16 per cent. of natural rubber is added to the fish, and the result is a substance as flexible and elastic as rubber, but much cheaper. This artificial rubber can be vulcanized in a short time, is benzine-proof, and can resist the effect of heat.

Meanwhile factories for the reclaiming of rubber are increasing both in this country and abroad. No ideal process has as yet been discovered, but essentially the treatment involves the following steps: (1) The grinding of the waste rubber; (2) its solution in some solvent, such as naphtha or xylol; (3) heating for the liberation of the sulphur used in vulcanization; (4) the separation from the solution of mineral and other insoluble ingredients; (5) the separation of the rubber by precipitation, as with alcohol, or by filtration, leaving the rubber on the filter.

See *The Production and Polymerization of Butadiene, Isoprene and Their Homologues*, by W. H. Perkin, *Journ. Soc. Chem. Industry*, vol. 31, p. 616, July 15, 1912. Recent books are: *The Chemistry of the Rubber Industry*, by Harold E. Potts, and *Rubber, Its Production and Industrial Uses*, by P. Schidrowitz.

RUBBER, WORLD'S PRODUCTION OF. See AGRICULTURE.

RUM. See LIQUORS.

RUMANIA. A European constitutional monarchy, bordering on the Black Sea and composed of the former principalities of Moldavia and Wallachia, with the territory of the Dobruja. Bucharest is the capital.

AREA AND POPULATION. Area of the 32 districts which compose the kingdom, 131,353 square kilometers (50,715 square miles). Population (estimated at end of 1911), 7,086,796. Marriages (1911), 74,542; births, 290,870; deaths, 170,076; still-births (not included in the foregoing), 8144; excess of births over deaths, 120,794. Population (1911) of Bucharest, 295,213; Jassy, 79,680; Galatz, 66,507; Braila, 60,901; Ploeshti, 49,256; Craiova, 45,-780.

EDUCATION. In spite of progress, educational facilities remain inadequate. Primary instruction is technically compulsory between the ages of 7 and 14. Although improvement has been made, nearly 60 per cent. of the population are returned as illiterate. Secondary schools are well attended; special schools are mainly agricultural There are universities at Bucharest and Jassy. The religion of the country is the Greek Orthodox.

PRODUCTION. Agriculture is the leading industry, and has progressed notably in the last forty years. In 1866 (the first year of the present reign), the area under sown crops was but 2,230,000 hectares; while in 1906 it was 5,-520,000 hectares. Forests cover 17.5 per cent. of the total area, 7.8 per cent. is under pasture, 3.8 under natural grasses, 1.4 under orchards, 46.1 under sown crops and fallow—representing 76.6 per cent. of the total area of the kingdom. In a year of good crops the value of the entire agricultural output is approximately nine hundred million lei; in a year of excellent crops, over a billion. The country amply feeds itself and is able to export grain and fruits and vegetables in great quantities

Wheat has shown the greatest increase, in 1866 about 238,360 metric tons, valued at 54,-892,000 lei, having been exported, as compared with 1,716,000 tons, valued at 251,342,000 lei, in 1905. Viniculture has declined by reason of the phylloxera ravages, but replanting is proceeding rapidly. Plum orchards cover about 72,000 hectares; counting an average of 600 trees per hectare, this gives a total of 43,000,-000 trees. In the following table are seen areas devoted to main crops and yield for 1911 and 1912, with the yield per hectare in 1911:

	Hectares		Quintals		Qs.
	1911	1912	1911	1912	ha.
Wh.	1,930,164	2,069,420	26,033,561	24,334,331	13 5
Rye	131,796	107,244	1,274,721	915,447	9.7
Bar.	507,201	499,885	5,686,522	4,600,000	11.2
Oats	401,415	381,785	4,016,454	3,100,000	10 0
Corn	2,085,251	2,078,526	30,041,407	22,500,000	14 4
Flax	21,124	31,761	142,289*	182,332*	6 7*
Beets†	13,603	14,363	2,630,518	3,200,000	193 4
Vines	71,438	70,429	993,437‡	1,250,000‡	13 9‡
Tobacco	9,992	9,284	93,030	....	9.3

* Seed. † For sugar. ‡ Hectoliters.

The cultivation of forage plants, formerly extensive, has declined with the cattle-raising industry—an industry which has steadily lost ground since the closing, in 1882, of the Austro-Hungarian frontier to the export of live animals. While during the year 1866-7 the export of cattle alone was between forty and sixty thousand head, it had fallen, in 1882, to two thousand. The only class of livestock whose numbers have increased since 1866, is horses; cattle have remained stationary, sheep have not gained materially; and hogs, of which 178,000 head were exported in 1881, are raised only in sufficient numbers to supply the country's own needs.

On the other hand, the fishing industry has grown. In place of the large importation common in former years, there is now an annual export valued at about 2,790,000 lei. The state forests yield an average revenue of 30,000,000 lei In 1886 the petroleum output was 5370 tons; in 1905, 682,000; in 1910, 1,352,300. In 1905 the export of crude petroleum was 52,000 tons; of refined, 120,000; of mineral oils, 90,-000; of benzine, 49,000. The total export in 1910 of petroleum and bitumens was 586,151 tons, valued at 38,897,169 lei; of which France took 140,159 tons (13,105,317 lei) and the United Kingdom 125,687 (6,610,839).

COMMERCE. Trade for four years is shown below in lei (1 lu=19.3 cents):

	1907	1908	1909	1910
Imps.	430,590,115	414,058,479	368,300,099	409,715,576
Exps.	554,018,631	379,430,871	465,056,619	616,504,872

The chief imports (1910) were metals, minerals, and their manufactures, 98,072,000 lei; vegetable fibre textiles, etc., 66,185,000; machinery, 30,219,000; wool, hair, and their manufactures, 36,246,000; silk and its manufactures, 14,982,000; skins, etc., 14,920,000; vehicles 11,289,000; drugs and chemicals, 8,279,000; building stone, etc., 5,194,000; glassware, 4,-870,000; clocks and watches, 3,170,000.

The largest export was cereals and cereal derivatives, 489,821,008 leï in 1910, compared with 357,587,891 leï in 1909 (3,230,235 tons against 2,187,763 tons). Of these the most important are shown for 1910 compared with 1909, in thousands of leï:

Exports	1909	1910	Exports	1909	1910
Wheat..	178,402	329,619	Rye........	8,872	16,015
Corn....	102,716	69,597	Flour......	6,504	12,509
Barley..	37,442	41,185	Millet......	1,729	1,679
Oats....	20,338	17,041	Bran.......	1,189	1,482

Petroleum export, 38,897,160 leï (36,268,546 leï in 1909), of which 17,694,368 refined petroleum, 16,676,140 benzine, 3,696,105 crude petroleum and residue—in tons, 337,036, 126,-334, and 118,931.

Legumes, seeds, flowers, and parts of plants, 34,730,967 leï, of which 21,700,078 leï oil seeds, 10,784,983 peas and beans, 897,002 other seeds, 609,529 tobacco. Wood and timber, 25,102,207 leï (29,445,651 leï in 1909). Live animals, only 2,693,473 leï in 1909, rose to 5,951,725 in 1910, the principal customers being Russia (4,-660,946 leï) and Italy (776,560). Animal foods, 4,826,201 leï (5,782,356 in 1909), of which 3,428,813 leï eggs, the remainder fish.

Countries of origin and destination (1910 trade) follow, values in millions of leï:

	Imps.	Exps.		Imps.	Exps.
Germany....	138.2	24.3	Russia.......	11.8	6.3
Aus.-Hun...	98.1	37.3	Switzerland..	8 5	....
U. K........	56.8	33.5	Netherlands.	5.8	99 1
France......	25.6	46.9	Egypt.........	.2	8.8
Italy.........	21.7	68.7	Gibraltar....	...	31.7
Belgium....	14.1	226 2	Other.........	15.3	9.7
Turkey.....	13.9	19.0	Total	409.7	616.5

Vessels entered (1911), 37,985, of 11,707,-631 tons; cleared, 37,849, of 11,739,333. Merchant marine, January 1, 1912: 96 steamers, of 22,202 tons; sailing, 497, of 150,739.

COMMUNICATIONS. In 1876 the tonage transported by rail was 574,000, in 1905, 6,723,000; passengers carried (1876), 742,000 and 6,590,000 in 1905. The 916 kilometers in operation in 1876 earned 12,800,000 leï and the expenditure was 10,000,000 (excess of revenue over expenditure, 3032 leï per kilometer); in 1905 the 3179 kilometers in operation earned 71,000,000 leï and expended 37,500,000 (10,516 per km.). In operation September 1, 1912, 3690 kilometers, of which 3473 kilometers were state-owned. State telegraph lines (1911), 7321 kilometers; wires, 20,841.

FINANCE. The budget for 1912-13 is given in detail below:

Revenue	1000 leï	Expenditure	1000 leï
Public service....	133,439	Finance	207,010
Indirect taxes....	85,100	Public works.....	95,828
Monopolies	72,360	War	74,428
Finance	69,946	Instruction	48,219
Direct taxes.....	49,280	Interior	47,417
Stamps, etc......	29,461	Justice	11,029
Domains	28,875	Agriculture, etc..	9,630
Subventions	23,272	Ind. and com....	3,762
Instruction	5,265	Foreign affairs..	3,142
Interior	4,396	Council	836
Other	*	Extraordinary....	5,100
Total	505,647	Total	505,647
1910-11 †	583,358	1910-11 †	524,709

* Justice, 1,868,000; industry and commerce, 1,496,000; war, 536,780; foreign affairs, 180,000; agriculture and domains, 138,000; public works, 34,6000. † Actual revenue and expenditure.

The public debt stood April 1, 1912, at 1,-565,954,115.

ARMY. The reorganization of the Rumanian army based on the budgetary law of 1911-12 and previous legislation came into effect on October 1, 1912. This organization was considered advanced and effective, and resulted in greater centralization. The plan of organization included a central administrative bureau which included the general staff and 5 army corps and 5 reserve divisions. The infantry consisted of 9 rifle battalions, of which 32 are divided into 2 battalions of 4 companies and 8 into 3 battalions of 4 companies each, with an equal number of reserve battalions. The cavalry consisted of 1 regiment of Royal Guards divided into 3 active squadrons and 1 depot squadron, 10 regiments of Roshiori, each consisting of 4 active squadrons and 1 depot squadron, 10 regiments of Calarashi, each of 4 active squadrons and 1 depot squadron, the latter being formed from the old Schimbul, a form of militia which was being eliminated under the new law. The artillery consisted of 20 regiments of field artillery of 6 batteries each, and 4 horse batteries, and 2 regiments of fortress artillery. The engineers included 5 battalions of pioneers, each comprising 3 companies, and 1 telegraph company, 3 companies of fortress pioneers, 4 companies of pontoon troops with 1 depot company, 4 active companies of railway troops with 1 depot company, an aeronautic section, and other technical troops. The annual recruit contingent in Rumania was about 28,000 men out of 100,000 who reach the age of eligibility, when they are liable to 7 years' service in the regular army and first reserve. The peace strength of the army consisted of about 70,-000 men, but on a war basis this could be raised to 200,000, with 13,200 cavalry, and 496 guns, with 100,000 trained men still available to make good the losses in the field. The Rumanian army was well trained and its participation in any general Balkan movement would have been important.

NAVY. The effective fleet included (1912), one protected cruiser (date of 1888), of 1320 tons, 1 dispatch boat (130 tons), 5 gunboats (607), 1 training ship (350), 1 torpedo depot (104), 3 gunboats date of 1882 (135), 4 torpedo gunboats (128), 3 torpedo boats (150), 4 police boats (2720), 8 torpedo vedettes (360) —in all, 31 vessels of 6004 aggregate tons; besides police launches, etc.

GOVERNMENT. The executive authority is vested in a king, assisted by a council of eight members. A senate and a chamber of deputies compose the legislative body. Reigning sovereign (1912), Charl s I., born April 20, 1839, elected to the princeship in 1866, crowned king May 10, 1881. The ministry as constituted October 14, 1912, was composed as follows: T. Maiorescu, premier and minister for foreign affairs; Al. Marghiloman, finance; T. Jonesco, interior; C. G. Dissesco, worship and instruction; N. Filipesco, agriculture and domains; M. G. Cantacuzene, justice; Al. Badarau, public works; Gen. C. Herjeu, war; N. Xenopol, commerce and industry.

HISTORY. On April 10, M. Carp, premier and minister of finance, resigned office and the minister of war and minister of public works laid down their offices at the same time. The premier's resignation was attributed to the hostility of the Opposition, who alleged that the methods of the government were unconstitutional. The new government was formed under M. Titu Maiorescu, who was foreign minister in the Carp government and who retained that portfolio. The November elections gave the new Conservative Democratic party under the leadership of M. Take Jonesco the preponderance in the Chamber, and the ministry was reconstituted to provide for its proper representation.

RUMANIAN PHILOLOGY. See PHILOLOGY.

RURAL CREDIT. See AGRICULTURE.

RURAL SCHOOL SUPERVISION. See EDUCATION.

RUSSIA. A vast empire that includes a large part of eastern Europe and northern Asia; it extends from the Baltic to the Bering seas and from central Europe and Asia to the Arctic Ocean. St. Petersburg is the capital.

AREA AND POPULATION. The first Russian census was taken January 28, 1897. The results of that census and the population as calculated January 1, 1910, together with the area, exclusive of the great internal waters, in square versts (1 sq. verst=.439408 sq. mile), are shown below:

	Sq verste	1897	1910
Europ'n Russia	4,238,711.7	94,215,400	118,690,600
Poland	111,554 2	9,455,900	12,129,200
Caucasus	412,310.8	9,248,700	11,735,100
Siberia	10,940,644 7	5,699,000	8,220,100
Central Asia...	3,110,623 7	5,724,700	9,973,400
Finland	286,041.8	2,555,500	3,030,400
Total	19,099,886.9*	126,896,200	163,778,800

* 8,392,643 square miles.

As calculated for January, 1911, the total population was 167,003,400, distributed as follows: European Russia, 120,588,000; Poland, 12,467,300; Caucasus, 12,037,200; Siberia, 8,719,200; Central Asia, 10,107,300; Finland, 3,084,400.

The density for the empire (1910) is 8.5 per sq. verst. The Polish provinces are the most densely populated, Piotrkov having 179.6 to the sq. verst; Siberia is the most sparsely populated, Yakoutsk having but 0.1. In European Russia, Podolia (101.4) has the greatest and Arkhangel (0.6) the fewest inhabitants per sq. verst; in the Caucasus, Koutais (53.5) and the Black Sea government (17.2); in Siberia, Tomsk (4.3) and Yakoutsk (0.1), and Kamchatka has but 0.03; in Central Asia, Samarkand (19.3) and Zacaspian (0.8). The urban population is placed at 22,506,800, and the rural at 141,272,000. Slavs (including Great, Little, and White Russians, Poles, etc.) form 91.8 per cent. of the population of the empire; Letts and Lithuanians, 3.1. The Kalmuks of the Astrakhan steppes are Mongols. Tatar tribes inhabit southern Siberia. The Cartvelian tribes form 14.5 per cent. of the entire population of the Caucasus, and Turko-Tatars 20.2 per cent. Cossacks are found only in the Cossack provinces—Don, Orenburg, Amur, etc. To the Orthodox Greek Catholic Church belong 69.90 per cent. (Russians, Rumanians, most Cartvelians, some Turko-Tatars) of the total population; to Islam, 10.83 (most Turko-Tatars, and the mountain tribes of the Caucasus); to the Roman Catholic Church, 8.91 (Poles and Lithuanians); Finns, Germans, and some Lithuanians are Protestants, and the Armenians belong to the Gregorian Church. Jews constitute 4.05 per cent. of the total. Divided according to social status, 771 per 1000 of the inhabitants are peasants, 107 burgesses, 15 nobles, 5 clergy, 5 privileged merchants, etc.; Cossacks, members of wild tribes, gypsies, etc., make up the remainder.

POPULATION of St Petersburg (1910), 1,907,708; Moscow, 1,481,240; Warsaw, 855,900; Odessa, 478,900; Kiev, 446,800; Lodz, 395,670; Riga, 324,720; Kharkov, 219,600; Saratov, 198,600; Baku,* 217,900; Vilna, 186,200; Tashkent*, 192,000; Rostov-on-Don, 121,300; Ekaterinoslav, 148,870; Astrakhan, 149,630; Kazan, 167,400; Tula, 133,700; Kishinev, 118,610; Samara, 120,980; Irkutsk,* 85,800; Minsk, 109,300; Vladivostak*, 90,160; Orenburg, 91,240; Tomsk*, 105,620; Nizhni-Novgorod, 103,860; Nikolayev, 95,400; Kokand,* 112,800; Namangan.* 85,500; Dvinsk, 80,310; Orusk,* 90,200; Elisavetgrad, 75,480. The cities marked with an asterisk are in Asiatic Russia. In 1862 there were but five cities (St. Petersburg, Moscow, Warsaw, Odessa, and Riga) with over 100,000 inhabitants; there are now thirty-two.

The birth rate and the death rate are high. In the period 1901-5 the number of births averaged 47.6 per thousand of the population; deaths, 31.0. The marriages averaged 8.7 per thousand.

EMIGRATION. Many emigrants abroad escape from Russia without passports, and their number can be calculated only approximately from the immigration returns of other countries. Far the greater number go to the United States. Jews average about half the emigrants; next in order are Poles, Germans, Letts and Lithuanians, and Finns. Few Russians properly so-called emigrate.

Figures for the migration into Siberia are incomplete. The figures which follow are given by the board of emigration. During the period 1896-1910, emigrating peasants (into Asia) numbered 2,920,626; the forerunners (men who preceded the colonists to search out sites) numbered 696,367—total, 3,616,993. In 1910 the emigrants numbered 316,163, the forerunners 36,787, and the total, 352,950. The year 1908 shows the largest number: 664,777 emigrants, 94,035 forerunners—total, 758,812; 1909, with a total of 707,463, is not far behind. In each case the exodus was due to bad crop years in European Russia; 1910, on the contrary, shows a great decrease, due to a favorable season. Poltava and Chernigov stand first and second among the governments from which the emigrants originate.

EDUCATION. Primary education is in the hands of the minister of public instruction and of the holy synod, and to the holy synod is entrusted the expenditure of a large part of the appropriation devoted to education. Instruction is totally inadequate, and in many of the rural districts nominal only; while many of the teachers are without proper qualification. The total primary attendance in 1911 was said to be only 6,000,000 for the empire. These remarks are not applicable to Finland, which has an admirable school system, with which, however, the Russian government seems disposed to interfere.

There are secondary schools in the central districts; special schools are few and inferior. The universities have a total attendance of about 41,000.

AGRICULTURE. In the table below are given (official) figures for the distribution of agricultural lands (1909), in dessiatines (1 dessiatine=2.7 acres) by great divisions:

	Under crops	Pasture	Forest
Europ. Russia*..	74,880,300	23,549,600	139,543,700
Poland	5,163,700	867,700	2,177,200
Caucasus	7,546,300	1,953,100	4,967,200†
Siberia	5,273,600	5,568,500	228,189,100†
Central Asia.....	1,733,600	2,597,900	15,370,700†

* Fifty governments. † Forests administered by the forestry department.

Little attention having been paid by timber-exploiting companies to that part of their contract requiring replantation of depleted areas, and the government being negligent or unable to enforce its demands, the profitable forests have declined (from 1887 to 1905) from four to thirty-five per cent. in the various governments. The net profits (1907) from the forests of the various parts of the empire, as given in the preceding table, are as follows: European Russia, 40,906,000 roubles; Poland, 6,010,000; Caucasus, 218,000; Siberia, 983,000; Central Asia 164,000—total, 48,281,000.

In the following table are given areas under main crops and production for two years (1012 preliminary), with production per hectare in 1911:

	1000 hectares 1911	1000 hectares 1912	Quintals 1911	Quintals 1912	Qs. ha.
Wheat *a*	25,786	24,512	121,663,668	169,763,320	4.7
" *b*	4,092	4,342	17,000,067	28,105,429	4.2
Rye *a*..	28,666	28,468	188,568,891	256,802,204	6.6
" *b*..	974	1,046	5,000,250	8,401,538	5.1
Barley *a*	11,367	11,351	88,001,794	99,263,950	7 7
" *b*	353	334	2,181,926	2,683,611	6 2
Oats *a*..	17,241	16,581	115,085,443	141,096,204	6.7
" *b*..	2,015	1,947	9,508,251	13,862,784	4 7
Corn *a*..	1,593	1,645	20,810,834	20,221,350	13.1
" *b*..	9	9	91,648	86,816	10.1
Flax 1*a* }	1,388	1,403	....	5,218,375	3.8
" 2*a* }			....	4,688,315	3.4
" 1*b* }	113	92	....	225,244	2.3
" 2*b* }			....	220,475	1.9
Beets *	779	753	130,127,016	89,589,955	167.1

a European Russia (63 govts.). *b* Asiatic Russia (10 govts.). Flax 1, seed (production); 2, fibre * For sugar (empire).

The sugar-beet production for 1912 is final; preliminary figures gave 131,755,820 quintals, but frost destroyed part of the crop.

A telegraphic dispatch from the Russian government gives final figures for production of winter cereals for 1912, in Russia in Europe (63 govts.) and 24 Asiatic governments and provinces. To these in the table below are added the preliminary figures for spring cereals (63 European anu 10 Asiatic govts.), and the resulting totals:

	Wheat	Rye	Barley
Europe 1.........	66,340,863	255,698,981	819,023
" 2.........	103,354,478	1,156,624	98,375,965
Total	169,695,341	256,855,605	99,194,988
Asia 1............	9,500,667	6,879,793	2,293,264
" 2............	27,985,197	1,960,413	2,678,697
Total	37,485,864	8,840,206	4,971,961

1—winter grain. 2—spring grain.

The 1911 agricultural year was considered a bad season, the results at harvest not fulfilling early estimates; final figures for 1912 show much better results, and the autumn sown grains promised well for 1013, being, in October, in better than the normal average condition.

The following (unofficial) figures are given for production (1910) for other than the great cereal crops (63 European and 10 Asiatic govts.): 1,207,870 tons buckwheat, 2,596,740 tons millet, 35,729,700 tons potatoes.

Official returns for livestock, giving number on July 1, 1912, compared with July 1, 1911, show a notable decrease of all classes:

	Europe * 1911	Europe * 1912	Asia † 1911	Asia † 1912
Horses ...	24,795,151	23,860,178	7,194,538	6,865,878
Cattle ...	37,317,182	34,547,348	8,319,074	7,381,247
Sheep and goats ..	45,988,702	42,735,567	17,165,204	16,257,736
Swine ...	12,422,966	11,944,568	1,132,537	918,634

* 63 govts. † 10 govts.

For notes in regard to drainage of lands see DRAINAGE.

MINING AND METALS. The average annual coal output is estimated at 24,200,000 tons. The import of foreign coal and coke into Russia in 1910 was 4,032,000 metric tons. Coal mined in 1910, 24,409,583 metric tons. From the Donetz basin (a region in Ekaterinoslav, covering about 16,000 sq. miles) comes a large proportion of Russia's coal—12,697,700 tons in 1910; it is mostly consumed by the railways, iron works, sugar refineries, etc. Poland has an output of over 5⅔ million tons. A poor quality of coal is abundant in Siberia, which is nearly all locally consumed. Other important producing regions include the Urals, the Eskibastus district south of Omsk, the Kousnetski basin (Tomsk), and the Tkviboulski district (Caucasus). A new field has been discovered about eighty miles north of Rostov-on-Don, near Alexander-Grushevski. In Russian Sakhalin the coal fields are worked by convicts.

In 1910, 22,000 tons of copper were raised (in 1909, 18,180; 1908, 16,550), the principal producing regions being the Urals, Caucasus, Siberia and the Altai mountains.

Gold (mainly derived from alluvial deposits in the Urals and Siberia) was reported at 48,723 kilos for 1909; asbestos (1910), 10,936 tons; iron (1909), 2,622,419 tons; salt, 2,264,699. Petroleum output 1910, 9,193,458 tons; 1909, 8,435,072. Output (1910) of cast iron, 184,600,000 poods; pig-iron, 185,595,000; T-beams and sleepers, 11,800,000; heavy rails, 30,000,000; assorted iron, 63,400,000; roof iron, 22,900,000. The iron syndicate (Prodamet) was dissolved automatically January 14, 1912, and was expected to be renewed for another three years.

MANUFACTURES. Cottons are manufactured, chiefly in Poland; other manufactures are flax and silk, sugar, tobacco, hemp, paper, flour, furniture, etc. Distilling is a government monopoly. Agricultural machinery is now made on a large scale, and peasant industries (wood carving, metal working, etc.), are important. Prohibitive impost duties protect the manufacturer, but the high cost of fuel and inadequate transportation facilities are at present insurmountable obstacles to the proper development of home industries.

FISHERIES. Total catch 1911, 708,000 tons,

valued at more than 97,000,000 roubles. The fish carried westward on the Siberian Railway are consumed principally in the Ural, Perm, and Zlatoust districts. The inland seas and lakes and the great rivers are practically inexhaustible sources.

COMMERCE. In the table below is shown the total external trade of the empire for four successive years, in thousands of roubles (1 rouble = 51.5 cents).

	1907	1908	1909	1910
Imps.: mdse...	847,365	912,659	906,336	1,084,446
" p. m.*..	10,937	28,226	46,284	71,281
Exps.: mdse...	1,053,010	998,250	1,427,675	1,449,085
" p. m.*..	13,108	18,914	26,806	32,158

* Precious metals.

The countries of origin and destination in the total trade of the empire are given below, with value of trade for two years in thousands of roubles:

	Imports		Exports	
	1909	1910	1909	1910
Germany	363,263	449,794	387,119	390,640
United King.	127,946	153,847	288,885	315,476
China	74,607	78,813	21,782	20,158
U. S.	57,854	74,441	11,496	9,489
France	49,547	60,972	89,061	93,646
Persia	31,579	36,702	32,302	37,904
Finland	32,974	35,992	51,802	42,821
Aus.-Hun.	27,315	35,026	60,875	49,735
Netherlands	18,068	20,444	189,198	195,982
Italy	12,060	16,916	67,785	75,196
Turkey	8,824	10,836	27,682	27,859
Egypt	9,979	10,144	3,129	3,310
Denmark	7,936	7,719	36,728	26,534
Sweden	7,620	7,615	11,033	8,907
Belgium	6,726	7,093	64,392	66,515
Norway	8,798	6,522	8,092	6,154
Rumania	1,892	2,312	15,783	15,049
Greece	780	1,587	16,554	18,331
Spain	1,323	444	4,456	7,007
Other	57,245	67,227	39,521	38,382
Empire	906,336	1,084,446	1,427,675	1,449,085

The principal articles of import for consumption and of export of domestic produce follow, for 1910, with values in thousands of roubles:

Imports	1000 r.	Exports	1000 r.
Cotton	129,608	Cereals & flour	723,273
Machinery	113,996	Timber	138,205
Tea	59,444	Flax and tow	73,908
Woolens	54,365	Eggs	63,694
Metal mfrs.	47,151	Butter	51,294
Rubber	39,871	Seeds	36,759
Coal and coke	34,067	Oil cake	31,562
Metals	30,403	Live animals	30,120
Silks	28,685	Petroleum, etc.	29,723
Fish	28,157	Sugar	25,930
Paper, etc.	23,447	Cotton textiles	25,159
Hides*	23,153	Bran	24,679
Woolen yarn	22,669	Metals	19,978
Plants and seeds	21,292	Hides and skins	17,938
Chemical prods.	20,313	Hemp and tow	11,539

* Prepared; in addition, raw hides to the value of 16,988,000 roubles were imported.

Nearly all the exports show some advance over the preceding year; both were exceptionally good harvest years, and exports increased from 998,250,000 in 1908 to 1,427,675,000 in 1909. Imports declined slightly from 912,659,000 roubles in 1908 to 906,336,000 in 1909; and increased materially in 1910, owing partly to the increased purchasing power of the peasants, due to the exceptionally good harvest, and partly to increased prices.

The tables which follow relate to the trade passing by way of the European and Black Sea (Caucasus) frontiers and to and from Finland.

Trade by great classes, values in thousands of roubles:

	Imports		Exports	
	1910	1911	1910	1911
Foodstuffs	121,430	134,134	907,203	988,547
Raw materials*	515,918	517,046	430,357	473,486
Animals	3,068	3,437	22,808	25,831
Manufactures	312,124	368,062	23,507	25,873
Total	952,540	1,022,699	1,383,875	1,513,737

* Including half raw.

The cereal export in 1910 was much greater in quantity than in 1909 (847,084,000 poods, against 760,746,000), but the total value was somewhat less. The principal details of the cereal export are given below:

	1000 poods		1000 roubles	
	1909	1910	1909	1910
Wheat	314,259	374,560	384,173	405,170
Rye	35,499	40,537	34,130	29,867
Barley	219,159	244,578	165,868	158,445
Oats	74,652	83,904	61,750	63,665
Corn	41,142	27,417	31,143	19,164
Wheat flour	5,369	6,186	10,488	11,481
Rye flour	6,933	5,474	7,663	5,672
Bran	38,976	37,337	26,501	24,500

The principal articles of export across the Asiatic frontier are sugar and cotton goods; imports, rice and raw cotton.

SHIPPING. Vessels and tonnage entered and cleared in the total foreign trade of the empire (1910) are shown in the following table:

	Entered		Cleared	
Ports	No.	Tons	No.	Tons
White Sea	1,130	830,000	1,079	828,000
Baltic	7,446	5,547,000	7,525	5,629,000
Black and Azov	5,335	7,554,000	5,220	7,425,000
Pacific Coast	672	955,000	635	879,000
Total	14,583	14,886,000	14,459	14,761,000

Merchant marine, January 1, 1912: White Sea, 476 vessels, of 34,916 tons (net); Baltic, 957, of 186,086; Black and Azov, 1249, of 269,471; Pacific Ocean, 38, of 22,949; Caspian Sea, 811, of 229,380—total, 3531 vessels, of 742,802 tons.

COMMUNICATIONS. Total railways in operation January 1, 1912, 69,432 versts (74,061 kilometers), of which 15,957 versts in Asiatic Russia, and in European Russia 53,475 (35,075 state, 16,273 private, and 2128 local).

During the year ending June, 1912, the department for railways and the commission under the finance ministry for the construction of new railways considered sixty-nine new railway projects, which comprised an aggregate of 14,855 versts (about 9860 miles), entailing an expenditure of more than 1000 millions of roubles (about $500,000,000). Nine projects had been approved by the commission, but not further advanced; while three schemes had met with the disapproval of the commission, and five were disapproved of by the ministerial council. For one project—the Bui-Rybinsk Railway at the middle of the year—the decision of the ministry had not been reached; for two projects—the Orsk-Troizk and the Mobilev-Ljgov schemes

—the authorities considered further survey necessary, and two, it was held, should be built for state reasons. Of the remaining thirty-nine projects which had been laid before the ministerial council, two—the Kazan-Ekaterinburg and the Nizhni-Novgorod-Kotelnitch—had still to be laid before the second department of the council of state, while the other thirty-seven schemes had already been passed by this department. These thirty-seven railway projects referred to an aggregate length of 5418 versts (3600 miles), the calculated aggregate cost being 389,318,000 roubles.

A railway which extends the Koltshuginsk-Barnaul-Pavlodar line for the Altai district, in southern Siberia, has been approved by the Russian government. This new line will enable coal from the Koltshuginsk coal mines, which, while containing millions of tons of the finest coal, had been shut down for several years, to be shipped for the Altai Railway to those parts of the Altai district, where fuel is lacking on account of the absence of forests.

Total telegraph lines (1910), 203,677 kilometers; wires, 714,220. Post offices, 15,701.

FINANCE. The standard of value is gold, and the monetary unit the rouble, par value 51.456 cents. Revenue and expenditure, ordinary and extraordinary, have been as follows, in roubles (1912 budget):

	1910	1911	1912
Rev. ord....	2,780,987,000	2,951,782,684	2,896,519,261
" extraord.	24,249,000	2,567,906	105,400,000
Total	2,805,236,000	2,954,350,590	3,001,919,261
Exp. ord...	2,473,157,000	2,535,995,758	2,669,941,806
" extraord	123,503,000	309,694,698	331,977,455
Total	2,596,660,000	2,845,690,456	3,001,919,261

The foregoing figures are compared with those of earlier years as follows, in thousands of roubles: 1909, revenue 2,689,085 (2,526,341 ordinary and 162,744 extraordinary), expenditure 2,607,452 (2,451,424 and 156,028); 1906, revenue, 3,355,781 (2,271,670 and 1,084,111), expenditure 3,212,697 (2,061,134 and 1,151,563); 1901, revenue 1,963,373 (1,799,457 and 163,916), expenditure 1,874,257 (1,664,887 and 209,370).

Sources of estimated revenue and items of estimated expenditure as shown in the budget for 1912, are given in the table in the adjoining column. Included in the estimated revenue from state property is 646,154,695 roubles from railways, while the "various" revenue includes annuities from railway companies 18,113,472 roubles. The ordinary expenditure for public debt includes 375,061,670 roubles interest, 27,893,326 amortization, and 966,550 exchange; for finance, 100,729,481 roubles pensions, etc., and 195,461,647 sale of spirits; for interior, 69,247,121 roubles posts, telegraphs, and telephones, and 59,410,459 police.

The public debt amounted to 9,014,141,796 roubles on January 1, 1911, and 8,941,640,620 roubles on January 1, 1912.

ARMY. The reorganization of the Russian army as a result of the war with Japan had been practically effected by 1912, and three new army corps formed in European Russia—one in the Caucasus and two in Siberia and the Far East—were practically organized. This made 27 army corps in Europe, 3 in the Caucasus, 2 in Turkestan, and 5 in Siberia and the

Revenue	1000 rs.	Expenditure	1000 rs.
Direct taxes....	230,645	Holy Synod.....	40,130
Indirect taxes:		Imperial House.	16,360
Customs	325,000	Higher state in-	
Beverages ...	46,881	stitutions ..	8,148
Tobacco	66,070	Communications	553,616
Cigaret. paper	4,465	War	492,933
Petroleum ...	45,036	Finance	426,861
Beet sugar...	128,430	Public debt.....	404,522
Matches	19,016	Interior	172,394
Stamps, regis-		Navy	159,146
tration, etc.	191,847	Pub. instruction	117,537
Royalties:		Agriculture	116,636
Mining	374	Justice	82,616
Mint	8,129	Commerce and	
Posts	71,531	industry ...	49,236
Telegraphs,		Audit	11,035
telephones...	34,900	State stud......	2,204
Sale of spirits	763,990	Other	10,000
State property..	831,011		
Redempt. pay'ts.	806	Total ord.....	2,669,942
Reimbursements.	51,613	Extraordinary:	
Various	76,774	Ry. construct.	110,215
		Army	70,000
Total ord.....	2,896,519	Jap War.....	410
Extraord.	105,400	Amortization..	149,146
		Other	2,206
Total	3,001,919		
		Total	3,001,919
Total, 1913....	3,208,407	Total, 1913....	3,208,407

Far East, forming virtually independent armies which might be termed the European, the Caucasian, the Turkestan, and the Amur forces, divided into thirteen greater military districts exclusive of the Transcaspian region and the territory of the Don Cossacks.

Figures for the peace strength of the Russian army were mainly estimates and varied between 1,200,000 and 1,400,000 men, including some 60,000 in Turkestan and Semiryetschenk and 280,000 in Siberia, or in round numbers a million men in Europe and the Caucasus and the remainder in Asiatic Russia. The total mobilizable strength on a war basis was estimated at 5,400,000 men.

Each male inhabitant is liable for personal service between the 21st and 43d years and the annual quota of recruits available is about 1,300,000 men (1,308,712 in 1910), from whom an annual contingent of about 457,000 is voted. Less than this number (435,283 in 1910) were actually embodied in the ranks. The recruits joining the active army serve three years in the infantry and artillery and five years in the other arms, then pass into the reserve for thirteen years, and finally conclude their service in the opoltchénié, or militia. The reserve and the opoltchénié are also filled from those not required for service with the colors. The Cossacks, who are an important element in the Russian army, have special service liability, which begins with the 18th year and involves three years spent in local service and then twelve years spent either with the colors in the first ban or with the second or third bans, which are on unlimited leave. The Cossacks on a peace basis number over 50,000, which in time of war could be increased threefold.

The training of officers and men has improved greatly since the Japanese war and a large aviation corps has been formed.

NAVY. On December 1, 1912, the number and displacement of warships, built and building, of 1500 or more tons, and of torpedo craft of 50 tons and over, were as follows: 7 battleships (dreadnought type), having a main battery of all big guns (11 inches or more in calibre), of 158,450 aggregate tons—all building; 8 battleships (predreadnought type) with main batteries of more than one calibre, of 112,050 tons, built; 2 coast-defense vessels, of 10,380 tons, built; 6 armored cruisers (63,500 tons) built; 9 cruisers (52,845) built; 98 torpedo-boat destroyers (39,375) built, and 9 (9450) building; 14 torpedo boats (2132) built; 31 submarines (6648) built, and 8 (4377) building. Total vessels built, 168, of 286,930 tons; building, 24, of 172,277—in all, 192, of 459,207 tons. Excluded from the foregoing are ships over twenty years old, unless reconstructed and rearmed within five years; torpedo craft over fifteen years old; transports, colliers, repair ships, torpedo depot ships, or other auxiliaries. Number of men voted for 1911, 46,655.

Four of the dreadnoughts reported as building are for the Baltic fleet (the *Sevastopol*, the *Petropavlovsk*, the *Gangut*, and the *Poltava*); three are for the Black Sea (the *Emperor Alexander III.*, the *Empress Marie*, and the *Yekaterina*). A programme in accord with the bill of July, 1911, was sanctioned by the Duma June 19, 1912. (See below under *History*.) An expenditure of 502,000,000 roubles was voted to cover this programme. Several million roubles will be required in addition for the adaptation of Sveaborg as the base of the future dreadnought fleet. See BATTLESHIPS and NAVAL PROGRESS.

GOVERNMENT. Nicholas II. succeeded Alexander III. as "emperor of all the Russias" November 1, 1894. He was born May 18, 1868. He married Princess Alix of Hesse-Darmstadt November, 1894, and was crowned at Moscow May, 1896. The health of the eight-year-old heir-apparent, Alexis, has latterly been the cause of much anxiety.

The third Duma sat from November 1, 1907, to June 21, 1912; the fourth Duma was elected September, 1912. The heads of departments were, 1912: V. N. Kokovtsov, premier and minister for finance; A. A. Makarov, interior; V. B. (Baron) Fredericksz, minister of the imperial household; S. D. Sazonov, foreign affairs; Gen. V. A. Sukhomlinov, war; Vice-Admiral I. K. Grigorovitch, marine; J. G. Stcheglovitov, justice; S. I. Timachev, commerce and industry; S. V. Rukhlov, communications; A. V. Krivocheyn, agriculture; P. A. Kharitonov, state comptroller; Dr. L. A. Casso, instruction; V. K. Sabler, procurator-general of the Holy Synod.

HISTORY

GENERAL POLITICAL SITUATION. In 1912 as the election of a fourth Duma was approaching there was much discussion of the recent political history of Russia and of the outlook for the future. Opposing views are held as to the condition of affairs since the revolution. To English-speaking readers the unfavorable view is the more familiar. It may be briefly summarized as follows: The rights wrested from autocracy in October, 1905, by the threat of revolution were either canceled or gradually reduced as soon as the fear of a popular rising was allayed. Government officials have controlled the elections in the interest of the central authorities. They have numerous ways of getting rid of an objectionable candidate, one simple and effective method being to expel him until after the election. A Duma chosen in that manner is in no sense a parliamentary assembly. The government has left it no real power. It cannot remove the ministers and if it refuses to pass a law the government may carry it into effect during the recess of the Duma by simple decree. Autocracy and bureaucracy have little by little regained all the powers that they had for the moment lost.

The other side has recently been set forth by a French traveler in the following words: "Such criticisms are much exaggerated and very unjust. Between Russia of to-day and Russia as she was before the war with Japan, under the Von Plehve ministry, the difference is, whatever people say, enormous. Public liberties are infinitely greater; the journals say nearly what they wish; the Duma, even with its reduced prerogatives, exercises by its mere presence an appreciable influence upon the acts of public officials; parliamentary discussion is free; and the sharpest and bitterest criticism is leveled against the governors, the ministers, and sometimes even the members of the imperial family. . . . The pretended reformers of the first and second Dumas with their extreme and chimerical notions, their absolute ignorance of the mentality and the real needs of the peasants, that is to say of nine-tenths of the Russian population, led the country toward anarchy and chaos. Reforms can be made only in a slow and gradual manner. In a country so vast, peopled by millions of moujiks, who a half-century ago were still serfs, it is impossible to introduce by a single stroke the political system of England or France."

ATTITUDE TOWARD THE POLES. The Nationist measure proposed by M. Stolypin, gave great offense to the Poles, whose opposition finally led to an important modification of it. One clause provided that the new province of Kholm established by the bill was no longer to form a part of the kingdom of Poland. An amendment rejecting this clause was passed by the House in March by a vote of 150 to 105, the government's representatives raising no objection. This action was welcomed as a sign of a more conciliatory attitude on the part of the government; but later, at the third reading, this amendment was modified. The Polish problem seemed as far from solution as ever. With the growth of Russian nationalist sentiment during the last few years it has become more acute. Throughout the kingdom of Poland proper, where the great majority are Poles, the government has not ventured on a policy of complete Russification, but though according the natives some concessions it has pursued an inconsistent and harassing course. Since 1905 instruction in the private schools may be given in Polish, but public schools remain essentially Russian and the University of Warsaw is attended mainly by Russians and Jews. Young Poles attend foreign universities, especially that of Cracow. Under the régime of Governor-General Skalone a number of Polish schools have recently been closed. As a result of this policy the number of illiterates has greatly increased. Another grievance is the fact that the promise of self-government has not been carried out to the satisfaction of the natives, who desire a Diet like that in Galicia. But the problem of Poland proper is complicated by the conflicting interests of races in the mixed zone extending between western Russia and the kingdom of Poland. Here the bulk of the population is Lithuanian, Little Russian, and White Russian, but for centuries the country had belonged to Poland, and the Polish landed aristocracy, though reduced considerably under Russian rule, still held the majority of the large estates, and under the electoral system, representatives of this class were sent to the Imperial Council. The Russian nationalists objected to this Polish representation of a region whose population was mainly Russian, but they were unwilling to adopt the obvious remedy which was to establish a more democratic basis for the local representative bodies (zemstvos) which chose the members of the Council.

To solve the problem of suppressing the Poles without elevating the democracy, M. Stolypin had recourse to his ingenious device of national "curias," which went into effect in 1907. Under this system the electors are divided into two "curias," according to their nationality, and the Russian "curia" chooses the number of delegates. It is analogous to the class system employed in Prussia and elsewhere, but differs from it in aiming at the dominance of race and not of a social class. M. Stolypin's measure for placing the zemstvos of the western provinces on this electoral basis, though approved by the Duma, was strongly opposed in the Imperial Council, and led to the constitutional crisis of March, 1911, when, as noted in our preceding YEAR BOOK, he resorted to arbitrary means and forced it through in spite of the resistance of the upper chamber. The zemstvos measure was obviously designed, not for the purpose of extending the principle of self-government in those provinces, but in order to eliminate the Poles. The nationalist policy now went even further and sought to increase the territory under this system at the expense of Poland proper. In certain parts of the governments of Lublin and Siedlce the majority of the population speak Little Russian, but a good many of these Little Russians in Poland have gone back to Catholic orthodoxy since the decree of 1905 on liberty of conscience, being "Uniates," who down to that time had been kept from Catholic "Union" only by the arm of the law. Thus the race and religious questions are interwoven. To strict, conservative Russians, members of the Catholic Church in Poland are virtually Poles, and they wish to see these Little Russian "Uniates" brought back to Greek orthodoxy. These extremists hold that Russia can change at will the limits of Poland as fixed by the Congress of Vienna in 1815, and they have urged the formation of a new government out of these Little Russian districts with Kholm as capital, to be united with the government of Kiev or placed under the ministry of the interior. Great indignation was aroused by this plan, which was characterized as the "fourth partition of Poland." If the frontier was to follow strictly linguistic lines, the western part of the government of Grodno should be restored to Poland, but the nationalists had no idea of doing that. The subject was under discussion in the Duma during the early part of 1912 and an amendment refusing to separate the new Kholm government was at first carried, but later modified (March, 1912), as noted above. The question was still unsettled.

END OF THE THIRD DUMA. The third Duma came to an end on June 21, having passed the navy bill the day before. The vote on this most important measure was 228 to 71. It provided for the expenditure of 502,000,000 roubles on the building of vessels and ports between the years 1912 and 1917. Its specific features were as follows: The construction of 4 armored cruisers, 8 small cruisers (4 for the Baltic, 2 for the Black Sea, and 2 for the Pacific station), 36 destroyers for the Baltic, and 18 submarines; the enlargement and improvement of the present naval dockyard; and the equipment of the ports of Kronstadt, Reval, Sveaborg, Sebastopol, Nicolaieff, and Vladivostok; the dreadnoughts proposed or in process of construction to have a coal capacity sufficient for service either in the North Sea or in the Mediterranean. It meant nothing less than the revival of Russia's sea power, for which various reasons were assigned, including the relations between Russia and Germany, and the danger of a foreign coalition against Russia. Other important measures passed by the Duma were laws relating to workingmen's insurance, to the reform of the local administration of justice, and to military recruiting. The czar in his prorogation speech congratulated the Duma on its passage of the navy bill and commended it for the attention it had bestowed during the last five years on questions of the highest importance, namely, the organization of peasant farming, workingmen's insurance, the care of workingmen's families, popular education, and national defense On the other hand, he lamented the acrimony shown in debate on various occasions.

THE FOURTH DUMA. The elections for the fourth Duma began in October and were concluded early in the following month. They resulted in the complete triumph of the Right, which secured an absolute majority of seats. The electoral law of June 3, 1907, was designed to assure the preponderance of the great landed proprietors and to p e en democratic or revolutionary elements from gaining control. It allowed the government a free hand in interfering with elections. The ministry took full advantage of it in the elections for the fourth Duma. Opponents of the government accused the authorities of gross unfairness and withdrew from the contest in many districts. Under the law of 1907 the government manipulated the complex "curia" or electoral class system (see above paragraph) in its own interest, particularly as regards the clergy, who moreover were organized by the higher ecclesiastical authorities into an active campaigning body. The vote of ecclesiastics was made practically compulsory and in some governments nearly every member of the clergy cast a vote. On the other hand the bureaucracy did all that was possible to check the activities of the opposition by refusing to permit the publication of platforms, by prohibiting or breaking up their meetings, by exiling to another part of the empire electors suspected of holding adverse opinions, etc. The electioneering of the clergy occasioned much adverse comment not only among the parties of the Left, but among the great landed proprietors who found their own political influence menaced by it. The party that suffered the heaviest loss was the Octobrists or Liberal Conservatives, who had supported the policy of M. Stolypin, but who had offended the reactionaries by their fight for religious liberty and the preponderance of the civil authority. Their number was reduced from 132 in the third Duma to 90 in the fourth.

The fourth Duma, which met on November 28, was divided approximately as follows: Right,

60; Nationalists, or moderate Right, 125; Octobrists, 90; opposition groups, 160. M. Rodzianko, an Octobrist, was elected president.

FOREIGN AFFAIRS. The new foreign minister, M. Sazonoff, made his first speech in the Duma on April 26. He referred to the undiminished strength of the alliance with France and the entente with Great Britain and expressed hope of a reconciliation between England and Germany and a better understanding with Austria-Hungary and with Italy. Apropos of the Persian crisis he commented on the excellent effects of the Anglo-Russian understanding. He expressed the firm determination of the government to safeguard Russian interests in Mongolia and Northern Manchuria. An interview between the czar and the German emperor and their respective foreign ministers and chancellors took place at Port Baltic on July 4. These meetings have become a matter of custom, having been held in 1902, 1905, 1907, 1909, and 1910. They seem to have had no definite effect upon the general foreign policies of the two countries, although they have given rise to much speculative comment in European journals, especially in France and England. Early in August the French premier, M. Poincaré, paid a visit to the czar, which was followed by the usual expressions of renewed international amity. A supplementary naval clause to the Franco-Russian military convention was reported to have been signed on this occasion, thus completing the alliance by assuring the coöperation of the two powers on sea as well as on land. The actual text was kept secret. The interview occasioned much conjecture in the press, and many declared that Russia's ulterior motive in forming this naval convention was to secure the opening of the Dardanelles. This was emphatically denied by M. Sazonoff, who characterized M. Poincaré's visit as "a happy but normal event." On July 23 an interview took place between the czar and the king of Sweden. For further discussion of Russia's foreign relations, see PERSIA, GREAT BRITAIN, UNITED STATES, and CHINA, under *History*, and TURKEY AND THE BALKAN PEOPLES.

ARMENIAN REVOLUTIONARY TRIAL. In the spring of 1912 146 Armenians were tried on the charge of belonging to a secret society and seeking to bring about a political revolution in order to establish a Caucasian federated republic. After two months' trial, four of the 146 prisoners were sentenced to penal servitude for varying periods, 26 to exile, 21 to fortress imprisonment, and the others were acquitted.

THE LENA STRIKE. A strike of about 3000 men in the Lena gold fields region in Siberia led to a conflict with the Rural Guard April 22. As the crowd of strikers were advancing, they were ordered to stop by the captain of the rural guard, but being pressed on by those behind, were unable to do so, whereupon the troops fired and killed 190 and wounded 210 others. Public indignation was expressed at this action of the authorities, who were accused of deliberately provoking bloodshed. One Russian paper remarked that while in England a strike of 5,000,000 had not cost a single drop of blood, in Russia a strike of 3000 people cost hundreds of lives. The explanations of the ministry in reply to the criticisms of the press were not regarded as satisfactory. One of the ministers held that the movement at Lena was of a political nature, and that the troops were obliged to fire in self-defense, and another, in contradiction to his colleague, claimed that the men's grievances were of an economic nature. One consequence of the affair was a strike of 100,000 workingmen in St. Petersburg as a protest against the massacre of strikers at Lena.

ANTI-SEMITISM. The long-standing and frequently repeated charge against the Jews of ritual murder was revived in the city of Kiev in 1912 and arrests were made for the murder of a boy named Yuschinsky, which was attributed to religious motives. The authorities harbored a suspicion that a certain secret sect of the Jews were responsible for the crime, which was virtually a ritual murder. Many believed the accusations to be baseless and merely to reflect the hatred of the Jews. The hearing in the case was postponed until the autumn. In March, during a debate on the reform of the judicial administration, a motion was carried in the Imperial Council rendering Jews ineligible to the office of justice of the peace.

OTHER EVENTS. A British delegation of members of Parliament, university men, merchants, etc., visited Russia in January and received a cordial reception at St. Petersburg in the closing days of the month. King George expressed the thanks of the government and people for the cordial welcome accorded to the deputation by the Russian government and nation. In January the czar granted a pension of $5000 a year to the widow of Tolstoy. During the summer there was evidence of revolutionary propaganda in the navy and 300 sailors of the Black Sea fleet were arrested and sent ashore for trial by court-martial. Eleven of the mutineers were shot in November. The funeral of M. Alexis Suvorin was held on August 27 amid thousands of spectators. See FINLAND.

RUST. See BOTANY.

RUTGERS COLLEGE. An institution of higher education at New Brunswick, N. J., founded in 1766. The number of students enrolled in all departments of the college in the autumn of 1912 was 510, of whom 380 were in the full courses leading to a degree and 130 in the short courses in agriculture. The faculty and instructors numbered 60. The new appointments for 1912 include Alexander James Inglis, Ph. D., professor of the science of teaching; Melville Thurston Cook, Ph. D., professor of plant pathology; and Thomas J. Headlee, Ph. D., professor of entomology. The only notable benefaction during the year was one of $20,000 from Miss Susan Y. Lansing. The productive funds of the university amounted to $727,000 and the income to $288,000. The library contained 66,990 volumes. President, W. H. S. Demarest, D. D.

RYAN, THOMAS F. See PRESIDENTIAL CAMPAIGN.

RYE. The world's crop of rye in 1912 was normal in quantity and quality. While in Europe an unusually wet harvest season was injurious to the cereal crop in general, the time of harvesting and other conditions so favored the rye crop that among the cereals it sustained the least injury. Any reduction in yield in Europe was more than offset by the remarkable crop harvested in Russia, which amounted to 1,043,982,356 bushels and surpassed the yield of 1911 by 281,773,302 bushels. In France also the yield was better in 1912 than the year before, the production for the two years being about 51,000,000 and 48,000,000 bushels, respectively. The crop of Hungary, including Croatia and Slavonia, was estimated at about 57,000,000 bushels; that of Spain, where it was the best among the cereals, at 25,755,000 bushels; of Italy at 5,285,000 bushels; of Rumania at 3,622,000 bushels; the production of Bulgaria at 12,402,000 bushels, and that of Germany at 456,608,000 bushels. The Canadian rye production in 1912 was 3,086,000 bushels, an increase of over 400,000 bushels as compared with the previous yield.

In the United States the growth of the crop after a cold winter and a late spring was favored by suitable weather and by a small margin a record crop was produced, although the acreage as compared with that of 1911 was somewhat decreased. Rye is one of the stationary crops and the area devoted to it does not change much from year to year. The production of 1912 in the United States was 35,664,000 bushels, or 2,545,000 bushels more than in the previous year. The total acreage was 2,117,000, which was 10,000 acres less than in 1911. The average yield was 16.8 bushels per acre, the highest on record. The price paid farmers on December 1, 1912, was 66.3 cents per bushel, while in 1911 on the corresponding date the price was 83.2 cents. On this basis the total value of the crop for the year was $23,636,000, as against $27,557,000 the year before. The leading rye-producing States and their yields were as follows: Wisconsin, 6,240,000 bushels; Minnesota, 6,026,000 bushels; Pennsylvania, 4,935,000 bushels; Michigan, 4,921,000 bushels; New York, 2,112,000 bushels, and New Jersey, 1,200,000 bushels. All other States produced less than a million bushels. The acreage and yield of Michigan have been steadily decreasing for several years. Among the leading States Minnesota ranked first in average acre-yield, with 23 bushels.

SABATIER, PAUL. See NOBEL PRIZE

SAFETY AT SEA. Largely as a result of *Titanic* disaster, the board of supervising inspectors of the Department of Commerce and Labor amended a number of the general rules and regulations under the authority conferred upon them by Congress. These regulations as amended up to September 25, 1912, received the approval of the Secretary of the Department of Commerce and Labor and thus acquired the force of law. Due provision was made for the construction and inspection of various forms of lifeboats, life-rafts, davits, and other appliances, including the equipment of lifeboats with the necessary appliances, food and distress signals, all of which were duly specified. The most important change was that providing for the number of lifeboats or life-rafts which represented an advance over previous requirements.

The new regulations provided that all ocean steamers carrying passengers must be equipped with lifeboats to accommodate at one time all persons on board, but that one-half of such equipment might be in approved life-rafts or collapsible boats. Coastwise steamers must make similar lifeboat provision for all persons on board, except in the case of vessels navigating only between May 15 and September 15, when accommodations for at least 60 per cent. of all persons on board are required. In the case of lake, bay, and sound passenger steamers the same provision holds good, except that for summer boats 30 per cent. accommodation is demanded, and that in case the regular route lies within a distance of five miles from land or over water whose depth is not sufficient entirely to submerge the vessel in case of disaster but 10 per cent. accommodation is demanded as a minimum. For lake, bay, and sound passenger steamers navigating the waters of the lakes, bays, and sounds tributary to the Pacific coast, the Atlantic coast south of the 33rd parallel of North Latitude and the Gulf of Mexico, lifeboat accommodations for at least 30 per cent. of all persons on board is demanded, except for vessels whose routes lie at all points within five miles of land or other shallow waters, when accommodations for at least 10 per cent. is the minimum. Three-fourths of the lifeboat capacity for lake, bay, and sound steamers may be in approved life-rafts or collapsible boats. River passenger steamers must be equipped with lifeboat accommodations for at least 10 per cent. of all persons on board, three-fourths of which equipment may be in approved life-rafts or collapsible boats.

An important statute requiring efficient apparatus and at least two operators for radio-communication on ocean steamers was enacted by the Sixty-second Congress and was approved July 23, 1912. This law amended and extended previous legislation on this subject and provided "that from and after October 1, 1912, it shall be unlawful for any steamer of the United States or of any foreign country navigating the ocean or the Great Lakes and licensed to carry, or carrying, fifty or more persons, including passengers or crew or both, to leave or attempt to leave any port of the United States unless such steamer shall be equipped with an efficient apparatus for radio-communication, in good working order, capable of transmitting and receiving messages over a distance of at least one hundred miles, day or night."

The act was to go into effect on the Great Lakes on April 1, 1913, and for ocean cargo steamers on July 1, 1913. In the case of the latter it was provided that, in lieu of the second operator, "there may be substituted a member of the crew or other person who shall be duly certified and entered in the ship's log as competent to receive and understand distress calls or other usual calls indicating danger, and to aid in maintaining a constant wireless watch so far as required for the safety of life."

Another important act to harmonize the national law of salvage with the provisions of the international convention for the unification of rules, with respect to assistance and salvage at sea was also passed by the Sixty-second Congress and was approved August 1, 1912. This act provided "that the master or person in charge of a vessel shall, so far as he can do so without serious danger to his own vessel, crew, or passengers, render assistance to every person who is found at sea in danger of being lost; and if he fails to do so, he shall, upon conviction, be liable to a penalty of not exceeding one thousand dollars or imprisonment for a term not exceeding two years, or both.

"That salvors of human life, who have taken part in the services rendered on the occasion of the accident giving rise to salvage, are entitled to a fair share of the remuneration awarded to the salvors of the vessel, her cargo, and accessories.

"That a suit for the recovery of remuneration for rendering assistance or salvage services shall not be maintainable if brought later than two years from the date when such assistance or salvage was rendered, unless the court in which the suit is brought shall be satisfied that during such period there had not been any reasonable opportunity of arresting the assisted or salved vessel within the jurisdiction of the court or within the territorial waters of the country in which the libelant resides or has his principal place of business."

The Sixty-second Congress also passed an act requiring a license granted by the Secretary of Commerce and Labor for the use of apparatus for radio-communication between the several States or with foreign nations, or upon vessels of the United States, and any person or corporation using or operating such apparatus in violation of this act was liable to punishment by a fine not exceeding five hundred dollars and the forfeiture of the apparatus. The act provided further for the supervision of all persons so licensed and for the use of a normal wave length that shall not exceed 600 meters, or that shall exceed 1600 meters. Every coast station shall be required to receive messages of such wave length as are required by the Berlin convention and every ship station shall with certain limitations conform to its provisions. The act specifies the various lengths and form of the wave, nature and form of the signal of distress, provides for reduced powers for ships near a government station, for the intercommunication of various stations, for the division of time between government and private stations, for various restrictions of power, for communication from ships to the nearest shore stations, for the limitation of further installation in the vicinity of government stations, and for the secrecy of messages. Penalties were provided for the violation of the various regulations and especially for the uttering or transmitting of a false signal of distress. This act, which was approved on August 13, 1912, did not apply to the Philippine Islands, and was to take effect four months from its passage.

A committee of the British Admiralty which had the question of lifeboat accommodations under consideration made a report recommending that provisions should be made for every passenger on a steamship. This was brought to the attention of Parliament and a bill to that end was introduced which, while not passed in the year 1912, was expected to be enacted in the subsequent year so that it would go into effect by March, 1913. The report of the Bulkhead committee which had to do with the revision of the Admiralty regulations for steamship construction and was expected to involve a thorough study of the subject in view of the discussion and criticism aroused by the *Titanic* disaster, was not presented up to the close of the year. See TITANIC, LOSS OF THE.

SAFETY COMMITTEES. See RAILWAY ACCIDENTS.

SAFETY ON RAILROADS. See RAILWAY ACCIDENTS.

ST. ANDREW, BROTHERHOOD OF. An organization for the spread of religious faith among young men of the Protestant Episcopal Church. The brotherhood is divided into senior and junior chapters. In 1912 there were 912 senior chapters and 543 junior chapters. The membership of the brotherhood is about 15,000, and the organization maintains four field secretaries. An important part of the brotherhood's work is what is known as its follow-up department. This is a bureau through rectors and parents to follow up young men who move to new places for business employment or to enter college or boarding school. In the national convention held in Chicago in 1912 there were 900 delegates present from all parts of the United States. Other meetings of importance during the year were the New England convention, the Connecticut State convention, the Tri-Diocesan convention, and the New York State convention at Albany. The twenty-eighth national convention of the brotherhood will meet in New York City August 1-5, 1913, just prior to the meeting of the general convention in that city.

ST. HELENA. An island in the south Atlantic Ocean; a British possession (47 square miles, 3477 inhabitants). The capital and only town is Jamestown (1439 inhabitants). Imports (1910), £37,350; exports, £9234; shipping entered and cleared, 172,358 tons; revenue, £9306; expenditures, £9596. Capt. H. E. S Cordeaux, governor in 1912.

ST. KITTS (or ST. CHRISTOPHER) **AND NEVIS.** A presidency of the Leeward Islands (q. v.), consisting of the islands of St. Kitts, Nevis, and Anguilla, with their dependencies. Basseterre, the capital, on St. Kitts, has 8469 inhabitants; Charlestown, the principal town in Nevis, about 1500. The main industry of the islands is the production of sugar, molasses, and rum, about 17,000 acres being under sugarcane in 1910 and 5000 under cotton; 12,323 tons of sugar, 2521 puncheons of molasses, 18,489 gallons of rum, and 302,039 pounds of sea-island cotton were exported during the year. Salt also is exported.

	1907-8	1908-9	1909-10	1910-11
Imports	£180,347	£184,002	£172,220	£195,277
Exports	189,903	180,539	182,446	205,693
Revenue	50,385	47,913	48,112	52,748
Expenditure	47,170	46,443	48,689	49,872
Shipping*	620,435	638,751	593,932	625,636

* Tonnage entered and cleared.

Customs revenue (1910-11), £32,408; public debt, £50,003. T. L. Roxburgh was administrator in 1912. See LEEWARD ISLANDS.

ST. LAWRENCE TUNNEL. See TUNNELS.

ST. LOUIS. See ARCHITECTURE.

ST. LOUIS MUNICIPAL BRIDGE. See BRIDGES.

ST. LUCIA. A British West Indian island; one of the Windward Islands colonies (233 square miles; 48,637 inhabitants, census of 1911.) The capital is Castries, with 8000 inhabitants; Soutrière has about 2300. The chief products are sugar, cacao, logwood, spices, rubber, and limes. The island has a much exaggerated reputation for unhealthiness and for a superabundances of reptiles.

*	1907-8	1908-9	1909-10	1910-11
Imports ..£	310,309	£289,775	£266,227	£277,208
Exports ..	264,402	252,668	250,674	238,955
Revenue ..	67,351	65,694	65,739	65,066
Expend. ..	64,840	65,038	64,446	67,285
Shipping†.	2,627,218	2,186,591	2,515,914	2,792,359

* Trade figures are for calendar, financial for fiscal years. † In tons entered and cleared.

Resident administrator in 1912, E. J. Cameron.

SAINT-PIERRE AND MIQUELON. A French colony of the southeastern coast of Newfoundland, including some smaller islands. Area, 241 square kilometers (93 square miles); population, 6482. Imports and exports (1910), 5,114,000 and 9,394,000 francs respectively. In 1910 the local budget balanced at 489,000 francs. M. Marchand was administrator in 1912.

ST. THOMAS. See SÃO THOMÉ AND PRINCIPE.

ST. VINCENT. A British West Indian island, one of the Windward Islands colonies (140 or 150 square miles, 41,877 inhabitants). Part of the Grenadines are attached to St. Vincent. Kingstown (4300 inhabitants) is the capital. The chief products are sugar, rum, cacao, arrowroot, and cotton. The island is of volcanic origin.

*	1907-8	1908-9	1909-10	1910-11
Imports ....£	96,554	£113,713	£ 87,810	£ 97,737
Exports	94,265	94,739	88,698	101,180
Revenue	28,456	31,395	28,440	30,125
Expenditure	24,653	27,200	31,331	30,343
Shipping†	305,978	339,983	322,994	290,917

* Trade figures are for calendar, financial for fiscal years. † In tons entered and cleared.

C. Gideon Murray was resident administrator in 1912.

SAKHALIN. An island off the eastern coast of Siberia (16,370 square miles and 12,000 inhabitants, administered by Russia and 13,155 square miles and 20,000 inhabitants by Japan). The Japanese territory is called Karafuto.

SALINAN INDIANS. See ANTHROPOLOGY.

SALMON, SIR NOWELL. An English admiral, died February 14, 1912. He was born in 1835 and received his early education at Marlborough. In 1847 he entered the navy. After being promoted to a lieutenancy in 1856 he served on the *Shannon*, visiting China and India. In the latter country he served with the celebrated *Shannon* Brigade, which took part in the relief of Lucknow. As the result of his bravery on this occasion he received the Victoria Cross and was promoted to the rank of commander. After promotion through various grades he became rear-admiral in 1879 and from 1882 to 1885 was commander-in-chief at the Cape of Good Hope. In 1885 he was made a vice-admiral, and on the occasion of Queen Victoria's Jubilee in 1887, a K. C. B. From 1888 to 1891 he was commander-in-chief in China. In the latter year he became admiral and in 1899 was promoted to the rank of admiral of the fleet. He retired from active service in February, 1905.

SALVADOR. A Central American republic on the Pacific coast. Captial, San Salvador

AREA AND POPULATION. The area of Salvador, the smallest and, with the exception of Haiti, the most densely populated of the American republics, is variously stated, but a recent planimetric calculation indicates that the superficial extent is approximately 21,160 square kilometers (8170 square miles). The estimated population January 1, 1912, was 1,161,425. Although the people are largely mestizo and Indian, the republic shows a considerable degree of government stability and economic progress. In 1910 and 1911: Births, 46,866 and 49,179; deaths, 27,353 and 26,472. The larger towns include: San Salvador, about 60,000 inhabitants; Santa Ana, 50,500; San Miguel, 25,000; Ahuachapán, 20,600; Chalchuapa, 20,400; San Vicente, 20,400; Zacalecoluca, 20,000; Nueva San Salvador (Santa Tecla), 19,000.

EDUCATION. Primary instruction is free and nominally compulsory. Of the 173,495 children of school age in 1911, only 21,569 were enrolled in the public primary schools. These schools numbered 486, of which 203 were for males, 200 for females, and 83 mixed; teachers 851 (382 male). Besides a number of private schools, there are several institutions for secondary and special instruction.

PRODUCTION AND COMMERCE. In 1912, 166,000 acres were planted in coffee, the leading crop, and the estimated yield was about 70,000,000 lbs. In the past ten years the average production has been 70,530,000 and the average export 60,553,000 lbs. Other products include cacao, tobacco, indigo, rubber, sugar, and bananas. Mining is of increasing importance.

In 1910 and 1911, imports amounted to $3,745,249 and $5,390,370, respectively; exports, 18,245,590 and 19,779,551 pesos. The average value of the silver peso was about 40 cents in 1910 and 42.5 cents in 1911, so that in gold the export values may be placed at $7,297,836 and $8,406,309. Leading imports in 1911: Cotton cloth and manufactures, $1,758,585; hardware, $345,861; drugs and medicines, $287,615; flour, $263,714; boots and shoes, $247,558; cotton yarn, $178,139; machinery, $108,735; wines, $108,406. Principal exports in 1910 and 1911: Coffee, $5,128,761 and $5,835,439; gold in bars, $601,319 and $760,413; gold and silver amalgams, etc., $167,800 and $700,256; sugar, $279,107 and $391,796; indigo, $314,843 and $261,031; silver in bars, $487,063 and $160,702; balsam, $81,120 and $87,683. In 1911 the United States sent imports and received exports valued at $1,924,652 and $2,908,312; United Kingdom, $1,644,238 and $523,020; Germany, $534,130 and $1,571,042; France, $393,991 and $2,138,532; Italy, $186,915 and $438,034.

COMMUNICATIONS. At the end of 1910, 156 kilometers (97 miles) of railway were in operation. On July 6, 1912, a railway was opened to traffic between the port of La Unión and San Miguel (62 kilometers). This line connects a rich agricultural, mining, and stock-raising section with the southernmost port of the country. In 1911, there were 2573 miles of telegraph wire and 2112 miles of telephone wire. Post offices, 101.

FINANCE. The silver peso fluctuates in value; it was worth about 40 cents in 1910 and 42.5 in 1911. In the fiscal year 1910-11, revenue amounted to 13,251,626 pesos (ordinary 10,620,865, extraordinary 2,630,761); expenditure, 13,206,248. For 1911-12, estimated revenue 13,129,750 pesos, estimated expenditure 13,206,248; for 1912-13, 13,140,415 and 13,095,101 respectively. Estimated receipts, 1912-13: Import duties, 7,343,140 pesos; export duties, 1,478,000; liquor tax, 2,800,000; other, 1,519,275; total, 13,140,415. The larger estimated expenditures, 1912-13: Public debt, 3,900,000 pesos; war and marine, 2,399,690; interior, 1,590,068; fomento, 1,510,510; public instruction, 1,045,397. Public debt, as reported for December 31, 1911: Foreign, 8,039,257 pesos gold; internal, 2,627,330 pesos gold and 2,587,331 pesos silver; treasury bonds, 3,619,728 pesos silver.

ARMY. During 1912 attempts were being made to improve the organization of the army of the republic, which was maintained with a strength of about 3000 men, with 18,000 militia in addition, though all inhabitants of the republic were liable for military service. A headquarters staff was being organized under the control of the war minister. This included four sections as follows: 1. Recruiting, organization, and distribution of units, mobilization, concentration, and schemes of operation. 2. Instruction of officers, manœuvres, military schools, inspection of troops, regulation, and technical establishments. 3. Armament, clothing, equipment, regulations for carriages and animals, feeding of troops, medical service, and transport. 4. Foreign armies, geographical service, statistics, and cryptography.

GOVERNMENT. The president is elected by popular vote for four years and is assisted by a cabinet of four members. The National Assembly is a unicameral body of forty members. The president in 1912 was Manuel Enrique Araujo, who was inaugurated March 1, 1911, succeeding Gen. Fernando Figueroa; vice-president Onofre Durán.

SALVAGE. See SAFETY AT SEA.

SALVARSAN (ARSENO-BENZOL; "606"). This interesting drug continued to excite lively discussion during 1912 and an approximate estimation of its actual value seems to have been reached. In spite of the fact that the early claims for it have not been realized; that it does not cure syphilis at a single dose; that its use is not without danger, and that recurrences take place after its exhibition, those having the greatest experience with the drug hold it in high regard. Woldovar of Vienna reported 2000 cases treated with salvarsan without a death; 7 patients, however, developed paralysis of the peroneus muscle; in about 0.5 per cent. symptoms of arsenical poisoning (diarrhœa, vomiting, nausea, dryness of the mouth, loss of appetite) occurred. Other observers have reported fatal cases. Rovant had 9 patients who developed intense headaches, or *tinnitus aurium*, one facial paralysis, and one optic neuritis after injection. Lesser reported a case of epileptiform seizures eight weeks after salvarsan treatment and found 17 similar cases in the literature. Witt records 9 cases of complications affecting the acoustic nerve, and advises expert examination of the ear before applying salvarsan in treatment. If a tendency is found to progressive otitis and catarrh, otosclerosis or acoustic neuritis, or if there is an inherited tendency to deafness, he urges careful weighing of the pros and cons before starting a treatment which may localize the relapse in this organ, even if it does not exert a toxic action on it. Similar reports embracing hundreds of cases found their way into medical literature. One observer noted two cases of actual reinfection following treatment with this drug. To obviate these disadvantages the manufacturers of salvarsan have put forward an improved product which they call neosalvarsan. See NEOSALVARSAN.

SALVATION ARMY. According to statistics gathered by Dr. H. K. Carroll, the total number of communicants in the Salvation Army in 1912 was 26,909. The associations corresponding in other denominations to churches numbered 852. The officers corresponding to minister, 2935. The statistics of communicants are no indication of the actual number of adherents to the body. The army is divided in the United States into 870 corps and outposts. The outdoor attendance at meetings was over 8,000,000. Over eighty hotels are conducted, accommodating over 7000 people. The army operates over one hundred industrial homes and five children's homes. The most important event in the history of the Salvation Army in 1912, was the death of its commander, William Booth (q. v.). His son, Bramwell Booth, succeeded him as the supreme authority of the organization. Evangeline Booth continued to be the head of the American branch of the army.

SAMOS. An Anatolian island; a principality tributary to the Porte in the sum of 200,000 piasters annually. Area, 468 square kilometers (181 square miles); population (October, 1902), 53,424, besides 15,000 natives of Samos residing on the Anatolian shore. Vathy (about 8000 inhabitants) is the capital. Imports (1911), 37,036,352 piasters; exports, 19,741,212 (wine, 8,595,000; tobacco, 2,875,000; leather, 2,764,000; cigarettes, 1,492,000). The receipts (budget estimate 1910) amounted to 3,651,660 piasters and the expenditure to 3,627,496. Debt, 2,570,500 piasters. Begleris Bey was named in 1912 by the Porte to be prince of Samos.

The prince-governor of Samos, Kopassis Effendi, was assassinated by a Greek in the latter part of March. Kopassis, who had been appointed governor in 1901, incurred the hostility of the Greeks in the following year by his attitude toward the popular party under Sophoulis. The trouble at that time caused the Porte to send troops to his assistance, and bloodshed resulted. The town was bombarded by Turkish warships. The popular leader, Sophoulis, fled, and after his departure he was condemned to death and his property was confiscated. The Greeks of Samos and of Greece generally, continued to bear resentment for this course, and the murder was attributed to this feeling.

SAMOS. See ARCHÆOLOGY.

SAND FLY AND DISEASE. See PELLAGRA.

SAN DIEGO. See ARCHITECTURE.

SAN DIEGO EXPOSITION. See EXPOSITIONS.

SANDWICH ISLANDS, THE. A dependency of the Falkland Islands.

SAN FRANCISCO. See WATER WORKS.

SAN FRANCISCO. See MUNICIPAL GOVERNMENT, *Commission Plan;* GARBAGE AND REFUSE DISPOSAL.

SAN FRANCISCO, CHARTER. See MUNICIPAL GOVERNMENT.

SAN FRANCISCO EXPOSITION. See EXPOSITIONS.

SAN FRANCISCO HIGH-PRESSURE FIRE SERVICE. See FIRE PROTECTION.

SANGER, CHARLES ROBERT. An American chemist and educator, died February 24, 1912. He was born in Boston in 1860 and graduated from Harvard University in 1881. He was assistant in chemistry in that institution in 1881, 1882, and again from 1884 to 1886. From 1886 to 1892 he was professor of chemistry in the United States Military Academy and from 1892 to 1899 occupied the same chair at Washington University. In the latter year he returned to Harvard as assistant professor of chemistry.

He retained this position until 1903, when he was made professor and director of the chemical laboratory. He was a member of several chemical and other societies.

SANGSTER, MARGARET ELIZABETH (MUNSON). An American author, died June 4, 1912. She was born in New Rochelle, N. Y., in 1838 and was educated in private schools. Her first book, *Little Jennie*, was written when she was but 17 years of age. This was published by the Presbyterian Board of Education. This was followed by several books which were written for and given to the American Sunday Schools Union. In 1858 she married George Sangster. Shortly after the close of the Civil War she became one of the most popular of American poets. Her poems, *Elizabeth Aged Nine*, and *Are the Children at Home?* were read and recited all over the United States. In 1871 she became associate editor of *Hearth and Home*. She was associate editor of *Christian at Work* from 1873 to 1879 and of the *Christian Intelligencer* from 1879 to the time of her death. She was editor of *Harper's Bazaar* from 1889 to 1899 and was a staff contributor to several woman's magazines. Among her published works are: *Poems of the Household; Easter Bells; Little Knights and Ladies; Eleanor Lee; Lyrics of Love; Little Kingdom of Home* (1905); *Fairest Girlhood* (1906); *The Joyful Life* (1907); *From My Youth Up* (1909). The greater part of her books were written for children.

SANITATION. The continued fall of the general death rate raises an interesting question as to the part which sanitation has played in this reduction. To answer this in specific terms and in small compass is impossible, because it would first be necessary to discuss the various senses in which the word sanitation is used, and choose among them or make up a new definition; and, that done, the most careful analysis of the general death rate would not show definitely what portion of it from year to year is due to insanitary conditions and what to other causes. The one certain fact is that the death rate of that part of the United States (known as the registration area), which has trustworthy mortality records shows a steady general decrease, and the same thing is true in other civilized countries. The general death rate of New York City for 1912 (subject to slight correction), was 14.11 per 1000. Although this is slightly above the London rate of two or three years ago, it is the lowest rate ever recorded for New York and a notable decrease as compared with years not long past. Chicago, Philadelphia, Washington, and Boston had also reported reductions in the 1912 death rate over earlier years, prior to the time this YEAR BOOK went to press, and there was reason for believing that many other cities would soon do the same.

If we define sanitation, for present purposes, as environmental conditions subjected to human control, which conditions affect the health of man, and limit the definition still further to city conditions more or less thoroughly under municipal control, we may conclude, though the argument cannot be given here, that the chief sanitary undertakings which reduce the general death rate are housing control, water-supply, the collection and removal of sewage, supervision of the milk-supply, sanitary factory inspection, and, in some localities, the suppression or reduction of various insect and animal pests, which serve as a vehicle of infection; such as the mosquito for malaria and yellow fever, and the rat, which carries the flea which carries the germ of the plague. Garbage collection and disposal and plumbing inspection have heretofore been classed as sanitary undertakings vitally affecting the public health, but the scientific evidence is against such an assumption, particularly as regards communicable diseases. Still, for the present, they may be classed under sanitation, like all other works of cleansing. The nearest we can as yet come to measuring the health benefits of any single one of these sanitary undertakings in terms of vital statistics would be to cite the many reductions in typhoid death rates which seem to be attributable to the introduction of sewers and to the substitution of pure for impure water; and we can also point to numerous epidemics of typhoid fever due to impure water or milk and to outbreaks of scarlet fever, diphtheria, and septic sore throat which careful investigation has charged against milk supplies. The Mills-Reincke theorem and the Hazen formula, together with studies by Sedgwick and McNutt, point also to a reduction in the general death rate coincident with marked declines in typhoid, due to improved water-supplies. Doubtless other measurable death rate reductions directly related to a single sanitary improvement might be cited, but with less certainty, for, in general, falling total death rates are due to a combination of many causes not separable and measurable, or at least not yet properly separated and measured by municipal and State agencies It should be stated that in this discussion the work of boards of health in the location, isolation, and control of persons suffering from communicable diseases has purposely been omitted as not coming under the head of sanitation, as here used.

HOUSING, as related to health, has had comparatively little attention in the United States, beyond varying amounts of plumbing and nuisance inspection in most cities of size, and outside the work of the New York City and the New Jersey State tenement house departments (see their annual reports); and forming also private organizations, the most conspicuous of which is the National Housing Association (q. v.). In striking contrast British cities have spent millions in the construction of houses for the working classes, while in 1909 Parliament passed the notable Housing and Town Planning act, which not only gives local authorities more control over housing, but also gives the central agency, known as the local government board, control over local authorities in this and allied important respects. Reviews of municipal housing outside the act just named and also under it were published by the board in 1912.

MILK SUPPLY. The health department of New York City put in effect during 1912, regulations for grading milk into four classes, according to quality, and ordered that all milk sold should be labeled according to its grade. The Chicago health department, after one defeat and then a hard struggle in which it was backed by some other city officials, various civic associations, and at least a portion of the press, was again authorized by the city council to supervise the milk supply, after the city attorney had declared the whole milk ordinance void because the legislature had passed an act (aimed at

Chicago) prohibiting any municipality in Illinois to require that all milk sold within its limits must be from cows shown by the tuberculin test to be free from tuberculosis (see also Bulletin 13, Milwaukee Bureau of Efficiency, January 30, 1912, on the milk supply of that city, report of milk inspector of Boston, Mass., for 1911-12, and health reports of other cities).

MOSQUITO REDUCTION. Acting under new legislation several New Jersey counties created and financed mosquito committees in 1912. An appropriation of $75,000 was granted to the Essex County commission. The county was inspected at frequent intervals, and breeding places were abated or else sprayed with oil. The board of health of Montclair, N. J., had six mosquito inspectors at work during the summer, some of whom were finally paid by the Essex County mosquito commission. Property owners were held responsible for maintaining mosquito breeding places. Mosquitos were relatively few in the town during the season, but the experience of several years will be necessary to settle whether mosquito reduction work can be made continuously efficient where the mosquitos are, for the most part, a pest rather than a menace to health, and where thorough work is demanded in many municipalities. That mosquitos can be kept below the danger limit and excluded from habitations where otherwise yellow fever or malaria would prevail has been abundantly proved in various parts of the world.

WATER POLLUTION. The power of the Ohio State Board of Health to compel cities to build sewage treatment plants under the Bense act of 1908 (sec. 1249 et seq. 1, General Code of Ohio) was upheld on demurrer by the Supreme Court of Ohio, early in 1912 (see *Engineering News*, July 12, 1912; also April 9, 1908, for the act in full). A summary by Paul Hansen of responses to a letter sent to 120 engineers and sanitarians asking for their opinions on the principles which should govern water pollution was read before the Illinois Society of Engineers and Surveyors early in the year (see *Proceedings*; also "Conclusion" in *Engineering News* for May 2, 1912). At a water pollution conference held at Cleveland, Ohio, in October, 1912, Mr. Hansen carried his studies to a more specific personal though tentative conclusion. At the same meeting George C. Whipple, professor of sanitary engineering at Harvard University, presented an important committee report on "Standards of Purity for Rivers and Waterways" (*Engineering News*, October 31, 1912), in which was embodied the growing consensus of opinion among sanitary engineers that sewage disposal by dilution (discharge into water) is often permissible under proper control; that where treatment is required the standard should depend on local conditions, and that so far as water supplies are concerned reliance should be placed on water purification rather than sewage treatment. Reference to new British standards is made under SEWAGE PURIFICATION. (See *Sewage Pollution of Interstate and International Waters, with Special Reference to the Spread of Typhoid Fever*, by Allan T. McLoughlin: a bulletin of the U. S. Public Health and Marine Hospital Service. An earlier bulletin dealt with Lake Erie. Also *Sewage Polluted Oysters as a Cause of Typhoid Fever*, by George W. Stiles, a 1912 bulletin of the U. S. Department of Agriculture dealing with numerous cases of typhoid among persons who partook of a banquet at Goshen, N. Y., in 1911.)

GENERAL. A great range of sanitary topics was discussed at the International Congress of Hygiene Demography held at Washington, D. C., in September, 1912, including ventilation from physiological and engineering viewpoints, cold storage, State and municipal health administration, and all or nearly all the subjects touched upon in this article. The *Transactions* of the Congress, in six volumes, will appear in 1913 (address Dr. John S. Fulton, secretary-general, Senate Annex, Washington, D. C.). Many sanitary topics were also discussed at the meeting of the American Public Health Association, held at Washington the previous week, and some at the International Congress of Applied Chemistry, held at New York City in September, 1912. See also GARBAGE; SEWAGE PURIFICATION; SMOKE ABATEMENT; STREET CLEANING, *Water Purification;* HYGIENE.

SANTO DOMINGO. See DOMINICAN REPUBLIC, and ARBITRATION, INTERNATIONAL.

SÃO THOMÉ AND PRINCIPE. Two islands off the coast of French Equatorial Africa, composing a Portuguese colony. Area, 939 square kilometers (363 square miles); population (1909), 68,221. Cacao is the principal product of the islands, their output constituting a large part of the world's supply. Owing, however, to foreign interferences in the matter of the prevailing system of coercion of indentured laborers, the trade fell off in 1909-10. Total imports (1909), 2,912,033 milreis; exports, 8,150,632. Revenue (1909-10), 931,429 milreis; expenditure, 703,315. M. Martins was governor in 1912.

SARAWAK. The northwestern portion of the island of Borneo; a British protectorate (about 42,000 square miles; population, about 500,000—no census has ever been taken). The capital is Kuching (25,000 inhabitants); Sibu has a large Chinese population, mostly traders, and the Rejang River has a raft population of some 90,000. Chinese are employed in the gold mines of Paku and the Batang Lupar Residency. Gold export, 1910, 951,119 Straits Settlements dollars; 1909, 1,139,440 dollars; 1906, 1,415,470; 1903, 1,784,600. Coal output (1910), 32,073 tons. Export (1910) of timber, 25,241 dollars. Statistics below are in Straits Settlements dollars (shipping in tons entered and cleared):

	1907	1908	1909	1910
Imports	7,321,766	6,456,326	7,811,556	10,115,298
Exports	8,220,896	7,331,722	8,098,142	10,711,039a
Revenue	1,441,195	1,269,482	1,346,962	1,407,360b
Expenditure.	1,359,274	1,248,643	1,152,727	1,263,063
Shipping ...	110,726	112,242	111,907	121,470

a Manufactured gutta-percha, 1,855,773 dollars; jelatong, 1,089,274; pepper, 1,531,246; sago flour, 1,148,572; gutta-percha and rubber, 653,704; gambier, 134,149; rattans, 92,781.

b Customs, 503,501 dollars; gambling, arrack, and pawn farms, 385,070; Dyak and Malay exemption tax, 84,979.

Rajah, Sir Charles Johnson Brooke (born 1829); acting, Charles Vyner Brooke (Rajah Muda), the heir (born 1874).

SARDIS. See ARCHÆOLOGY.

SASKATCHEWAN. A province of the Dominion of Canada. Area, 251,700 square miles

Population (census of June 1, 1911), 492,432, as compared with 91,279 in 1901. Regina, the capital, had 30,213 inhabitants (2249 in 1901). The province is administered by a lieutenant-governor, G. W. Brown, appointed Oct. 5, 1910. Premier in 1912, Walter Scott. See CANADA.

The general elections were a triumph for the Liberal party who secured about five-sixths of the seats in the new legislature. The chief issue in the campaign was a national one with which the provincial legislature had nothing to do, namely, "low tariff and larger markets." The Liberals appealed to the interests of the grain growers with this shibboleth, urging them to demand above all things a reduction of the customs duties and access to United States markets. Many Americans have recently settled in Saskatchewan and they appeared to be solidly against the Conservatives for their blocking of the reciprocity measure. The campaign was exceedingly bitter, the tone of the press was discreditable and intimidation, bribery, and election frauds were openly charged. The election was regarded as significant of the alignment of the two great parties on the tariff question. The Liberals contended that if the people did not stand by the Scott administration (Liberal) the Liberal party throughout Canada would take it as a sign that the issue of a low tariff and reciprocity might be given up. After the election the Liberal press throughout Canada took the stand that the widening of the markets and the removal of the taxation of foodstuffs would thenceforth be the leading issue.

SAULT SAINTE MARIE CANAL. See CANALS.

SAVINGS BANKS. Savings banks in the United States are of two classes, mutual and stock. Mutual savings banks, while less numerous, are immensely more important from the standpoint of depositors and aggregate deposits. The report of the comptroller of the currency showed that on June 14, 1912, there were in the United States 1922 savings banks with 10,010,304 depositors having aggregate deposits of $4,451,816,000, the average deposit account being $444.72. The average per capita deposit for the entire population was $46.53. The number of banks and aggregate deposits nearly doubled since 1900. In that year there were 1002 with 6,107,000 depositors having $2,449,547,000 of deposits. Even compared with 1908 the aggregate deposits showed an increase of more than 21 per cent. By geographical divisions the banks with the numbers of their depositors and the amount of deposits were as follows: New England States, 417, with 3,464,000 depositors and $1,426,805,000 deposits; Eastern States, 244, with 4,193,000 depositors and $2,070,306,000 deposits; Southern States, 179, with 366,000 depositors and $84,539,000 deposits; Middle Western States, 852, with 1,206,000 depositors and $410,778,000 deposits; Western States, 58, with 67,600 depositors and $14,378,000 deposits; and Pacific States, 172, with 711,800 depositors and $445,010,000 deposits. New York State alone had 140 savings banks with 3,024,000 depositors and $1,633,495,000 deposits. Massachusetts far exceeded all other States with 193 such banks having 2,179,973 depositors and $824,778,000 deposits. California showed aggregate deposits of nearly half those of Massachusetts; and Connecticut had savings deposits of nearly $300,000,000, there being only five other States, New Jersey, Pennsylvania, Maryland, Ohio, and Iowa, with more than $100,000,000 of savings deposits.

Mutual savings banks are practically confined to the New England and Eastern States, being apparently connected with the development of manufacturing centres. Only 21 out of a total of 630 mutual savings banks were reported outside of those groups of States. The aggregate deposits of all mutual savings banks on June 14 were $3,608,000,000; depositors numbered 7,851,000; the average deposit account was $459.62. All the banks above credited to Massachusetts, New York, and Connecticut were mutual savings banks. The loans aggregated $1,920,000,000, about 90 per cent. of which were secured by real estate. Their investments in bonds and other securities aggregated $1,778,000,000, including State, county, and municipal bonds to the amount of $733,000,000, railroad bonds of $770,000,000, and other public service corporation bonds of $110,000,000. Their total cash on hand was only $16,186,000 or less than one-half of 1 per cent. of aggregate deposits. The average rate of interest paid by mutual savings banks was 3.9 per cent. Stock savings banks numbered 1292. Only 52 of these were found in New England and Eastern States; 178 were in the Southern States; 833 in Middle Western States; 58 in Western States; and 171 in Pacific States. Iowa alone had 728 and California had 131. Their loans aggregated $669,000,000, of which somewhat more than one-half were secured by real estate, including mortgages. Their investments in bonds and other securities were $144,877,000. Their depositors numbered 2,158,000, of whom 412,000 had commercial accounts. Their deposits aggregated $842,897,000, of which $178,127,000 were commercial deposits. The interest paid on deposits by stock savings banks ranged from 2.94 per cent in Wisconsin to 4.5 per cent. in New Mexico.

The table on the following page from the comptroller's *Report* shows the condition of all classes of savings banks of all countries at recent dates. For separate table of statistics of postal savings banks see POSTAL SAVINGS BANKS.

SAVINGS BANKS, POSTAL. See POSTAL SAVINGS BANKS.

SAVOFF, MICHAEL. A Bulgarian general who held chief command in the Bulgarian armies in the Turco-Bulgarian War. He was born in Eastern Rumelia in 1857. His early education included instruction in a Bulgarian school at Gabrovo, and for a brief period in Robert College, Constantinople. At the age of 21 he entered the military school at Sofia, and within a year he received the rank of lieutenant-general of the Eastern Rumelian army. From 1881 to 1885 he studied in the Academy of the General Staff in St. Petersburg. He returned to Philippopolis in 1885 and took part in the revolution which resulted in the union of Eastern Rumelia with Bulgaria. He first attracted general attention during the Servo-Bulgarian War, chiefly by distinguished service at Slivnitza, where he commanded the left wing of the Bulgarian forces. He received a wound in this action. He was given the order for bravery by Prince Alexander for gallantry in the field. Following the Servo-Bulgarian War General Savoff filled various military appoint-

Statistics of Savings Banks

Countries	Population	Date of report	Form of Organization	Number of depositors	Deposits	Average [illegible] account	Average deposit per inhabitant
Austria	28,572,000	Dec. 31, 1909	Communal and private savings banks	4,119,295	$1,161,149,241	[illegible]88	$40.64
		Dec. 31, 1910	Postal savings banks, savings department	2,205,703	46, [illegible]89	21.14	1.63
		...do...	Postal savings [illegible], [illegible] department	102,574	79,682,452	776.83	2.79
Belgium	7,501,000	Dec. 31, 1911	Government savings banks	2, [illegible]953	194,534,158	67.04	25.93
		Dec. 31, 1910	Communal and private savings banks	6,[illegible]97	11,679,721	248 52	1.56
Bulgaria	4,285,000	....do....	Postal savings ban[illegible]ks	280,775	9,129,423	32.52	2.13
Chile	3,415,000	June 30, 1910	[illegible]a de ahorros	268,731	10,543,275	39 23	3.09
Denmark	2,757,000	[illegible]. 31, 1910	Communal and [illegible]ate savings banks	1,166,607	174,182,302	149.28	63.18
Egypt	11,626,000	Dec. 31, 1910	[illegible] savings banks	104,095	2,255,664	21.67	.19
France	39,602,000	Dec. 31, 1911	Private savings banks	8.411,791	754,255,333	89.67	19.05
		[illegible]. 31, 1910	[illegible] savings banks	5,786,035	329,974,970	57.03	8.33
Algeria	5,232,000	Dec. 31, 1908	Municipal savings banks	19,301	[illegible]380	48.41	.18
Tunis	1,923,000	Dec. 31, 1910	Postal savings banks	5,701	1,288, [illegible]8	225.97	.67
Germany	64,432,000	...d.	[illegible]lic and corporate savings [illegible]	21,534,034	3,993,775,184	185.46	61.98
[illegible]burg	246,000	...do...	State savings banks	69,202	11,863,592	171 43	48.23
[illegible]ngary	20,886,000	...do...	Postal [illegible] banks, [illegible] department	775,970	21,894,118	28.22	1.05
		...do...	Postal savings banks, [illegible]	20,716	20,075,888	969.10	.96
Italy	34,687,000	June 30, 1911	Communal and corporate savings banks	2.294,063	472,879,910	206.13	13.63
		June 30, 1910	Postal savings [illegible]	5,160,008	324,279,617	62.84	9.35
Japan	51,547,000	[illegible]. 31, 1910	Private savings banks	7,500,470	73,106,674	9 75	1.42
		Mar. 31, 1912	Postal savings [illegible]	11, [illegible]858	91,896,942	7.69	1.78
Formosa	3,341,000	Dec. 31, 1910	Private savings banks	6,779	[illegible]327	17.90	.04
		[illegible]h. 31, 1911	Postal savings banks	100,819	955,592	9.48	.28
China and Korea	....	...do...	Postal [illegible] banks	207,195	3,098,571	14.95	......
Netherlands	5,945,000	[illegible]c. 31, 1909	Private savings banks	433 209	41,718,485	96 30	7.02
		Dec. 31, 1910	[illegible] savings [illegible]	1, [illegible]3	66,039,592	43.73	11.11
Dutch East Indies	37,717,000	...do...	Private savings banks	13,228	2,887,566	218.29	.08
		Dec. 31, 1911	Postal savings banks	91,898	3,616,685	39.36	.10
Dutch Guiana	86,000	[illegible]c. 31, 1910	Postal savings banks	9,478	337,925	35.65	3.86
Norway	2,393,000	... d.	[illegible] and private savings banks	1, [illegible]810	135,886,457	135.71	56.78
Rumania	6,866,000	July 1, 1910	Government savings banks	218,690	11,616,820	53.12	1.69
Russia	163,779,000	June 30, 1912	State, including postal savings banks	8,189,734	784,117,885	95.74	4.79
Finland	3,120,000	Dec. 31, 1910	Private savings banks	291,603	44,068,779	151.13	14.12
		...do...	Postal savings banks	9,[illegible]23	1,396,856	23.39	.45
Spain	19,588,000	Dec. 31, 1910	Private savings banks	495,772	46,931,094	94.66	2.40
Sweden	5,522,000	Dec. 31, 1910	Communal and trustees savings banks	1,560,317	216,755,326	138.92	39.25
		Dec. 31, 1911	Postal savings banks	[illegible]659	12,645,957	22.36	2 29
Switzerland	3,647,000	Dec. 31, 1908	Communal and private savings banks	1,899,332	303,196,216	159.63	83.14
[illegible]t Britain	45,289,000	Nov. 20, 1911	Trustee savings banks	[illegible]43	258,083,128	139.58	5.70
		Dec. 31, 1911	Postal savings banks	12,370,646	859,027,319	69.44	18.97
British India	244,127,000	Mch. 31, 1910	Postal savings banks	1, [illegible]916	51,478,416	37.33	.21
Australia, Co[illegible]mealth	4,425,000	1910-11	Government, trustee, and joint-stock savings banks	1,600,112	289,039,353	180 64	65.32
New Zealand	1,008,000	[illegible]c. 31, 1910	Postal savings banks	380,714	68,641,934	180.30	68.10
		...do...	Private savings banks	51,508	7,375,302	143.19	7.32
Canada	7,205,000	June 30, 1912	Postal savings banks	146,310	42,683,232	291.73	5.92
		...do...	Dominion government savings banks	35,031	14,171,966	404 55	1.97
British South Africa	6,745,000	1909-10	Government, post office, and private savings banks	222,772	25,103,835	112.69	3.72
British West Indies	1,679,000	1909-10	Government and post office savings banks	91,881	6,301,465	68.58	3.75
British colonies, n. e. s.	20,427,000	1909-10	Government and post office savings banks	[illegible]967	12,921,863	58.74	.63
Total foreign countries	859,620,000			109,725,758	11, 0[illegible] 223 [illegible]47	101.13	12.91
United States	95,411,000	Nov. 30, 1912	Postal savings banks	300,000	[illegible]00	93.33	......
		June 14, 1912	Mutual and stock savings banks	10,010,304	4,451,818,523	444.72	46.66
Philippine Islands	8,460,000	June 30, 1912	Postal savings banks	35,802	1,177,435	32.89	.14

ments which involved the reorganization of the Bulgarian army. The establishment of the present military school came under his supervision. He made radical changes in the veterinary and commissary departments and in the rearmament of the infantry and cavalry. From 1891 to 1894 the purchase of artillery, munitions of war, and other supplies was practically under his control. During these years he was minister of war under Stambouloff. His obstinacy and lack of tact brought about frequent quarrels with Stambouloff, but an open break did not take place until 1897. As a result Savoff was sent to command the garrison at Shumla. His qualities as an organizer gained for this division praise as the premier unit in the country. He was next appointed chief of the Military Academy in Sofia and here he became widely known as a teacher of military science and as a strict disciplinarian. Conditions in the army became unsatisfactory and Savoff was, for a second time, called to increase its efficiency. As minister of war in 1903 when Turkey threatened an invasion he prepared a plan of campaign which was practically the same as that carried out in 1912. It was as a result of his efficiency in organization that the Bulgarian peasants were brought from their farms to the front in so short a time as to fill the world with amazement in 1912. Through his efforts the famous military law of 1904 was passed. It has in effect transformed the entire nation into a fighting machine. For three years following the passage of the law, which is considered the crowning point of his career as a military organizer, he coped with a stupendous task. He placed the engineering troops on a sound footing, established a training school for reserve officers, and made radical changes in the armament. He is responsible for the use of the Creusot gun which proved so effective in the hands of the Bulgarian artillery. His conduct of operations in the war showed that his skill as a commander in the field was as great as his ability as an organizer and disciplinarian. See TURKEY AND THE BALKAN PEOPLES.

SAXE-COBURG-GOTHA. See GERMANY.

SAXE-MEININGEN. See GERMANY.

SAXE-WEIMAR. See GERMANY.

SAXONY. See GERMANY.

SCHAUMBURG-LIPPE. See GERMANY.

SCHNITZLER, ARTHUR. See GERMAN LITERATURE.

SCHOOL OF JOURNALISM. See UNIVERSITIES AND COLLEGES.

SCHOOLS. For facts concerning elementary and secondary schools, see EDUCATION, and for professional and technical schools see UNIVERSITIES AND COLLEGES and AGRICULTURAL EDUCATION.

SCHREYVOGEL, CHARLES. An American artist, died January 27, 1912. He was born in New York in 1861 and was educated in the public schools of that city. He served an apprenticeship to a gold engraver, then to a diesinker and later to a lithographer. From 1886 to 1889 he studied at Munich. Returning to the United States he devoted his talents chiefly to depicting scenes in Western life, and he shared with Frederic Remington the distinction of being the foremost American painter of such scenes. His most famous picture, perhaps, is the one entitled "My Bunkie." This obtained the Thomas B. Clarke prize in the National Academy of Design in 1900. He received medals at the Paris Exposition in 1900, the Buffalo Exposition in 1901 and the St. Louis Exposition in 1904. He was an associate of the National Academy of Design.

SCHULTZE-DELITZCH BANKS. See AGRICULTURAL CREDIT.

SCHÜTTE. See NAVAL PROGRESS.

SCHWAB, GUSTAV HENRY. An American merchant and steamship official, died November 12, 1912. He was born in 1851 in New York City and was educated privately and at the Gymnasium at Stuttgart, Germany. When he was eighteen years of age he entered the mercantile business at Bremen. After spending half a year at Liverpool, England, learning English business methods, he returned to the United States and entered the office of his father's firm, Oelrichs & Company. In 1876 he was made a member of this firm, which was general agent for the North German Lloyd Steamship Company. Mr. Schwab took an active interest in municipal affairs and was chairman of the canal committee of the New York Produce Exchange. He was also chairman of the canal improvement State committee, formed by New York and Buffalo business interests in the campaign for the enlargement and improvement of the Erie Canal, which resulted in the so-called One Thousand Ton Barge Canal. He was a director and official in many important financial enterprises. Decorations for services were given him by the king of Italy and the German emperor.

SCHWABEN. See AERONAUTICS.

SCHWARZBURG-RUDOLSTADT. See GERMANY.

SCHWARZBURG - SONDERSHAUSEN. See GERMANY.

SCHWEIGHOFER, FELIX. An Austrian comedian, died January, 1912. He was born at Brünn in 1842 and in early life began a mercantile career. He later became an employee on the street railroad. His tastes, however, were for the stage, and after singing for a time in opera he turned his attention to farce. His earlier appearances were on the smaller stages in Austria. He went to Vienna in 1871 and there achieved distinction. He remained for many years first at Strompfer, and afterwards at the Theater an der Wien and the Carl Theater. He was a comedian of exaggerated methods, but he was an artist in working out every detail of his characterizations. For several years before his death he had lived in retirement.

SCIENCES, NATIONAL ACADEMY OF. A society organized for the purpose of examining and investigating any subject of science or art and for making reports of such investigations at the call of the United States government. The actual expenses of such examinations and reports are paid out of an appropriation made for that purpose. The society was incorporated in 1863. Annual meetings are held each year in Washington, and autumn meetings are held in different cities of the United States. The autumn meeting in 1912 was held in Worcester, Mass., November 12-13. About fifty members were in attendance and twenty-one papers were read, nearly all of which had to do with geological or biological subjects. Among these were the following: Dr. William M. Davis, of Harvard University, read a paper entitled "Physiographic Evidence in Favor of the Subsidence Theory of Coral Reefs." In this he gave arguments for the theory which was proposed many years ago by Dana, and which had received scant attention from naturalists since that time. A paper entitled "Restorations of Tertiary Mammals" was read by Dr. William B. Scott, of Princeton University. In this was given an interesting explanation of the processes of such restorations and reconstructions. Dr. Henry F. Osborn, of the American Museum of Natural History, in a paper on "The Geologic Correlation of Upper Paleolithic Faunas of Europe and America," described a recent visit to the paleolithic caverns of Italy, southern France, and Spain. In a paper entitled "On the Fertilization of the Egg of Invertebrates With Blood," Dr. Jacques Loeb, of the Rockefeller Institute, described some of the ways in which artificial parthenogenesis may be brought about. Other papers included "Cell Division and Differentiation," by Dr. Edwin G. Conklin, of Princeton University; "Heredity of Skin Color in Negro-White Crosses," by Dr. Charles B. Davenport, of the Carnegie Institution; "New Data on the Influence of Heredity and Environment Upon the Bodily Form of Man," by Dr. Franz Boas, of Columbia University; and "The Problem of the Asteroids," by Dr. Ernest W. Brown, of Yale University. Dr. Robert W. Wood, of Johns Hopkins University, contributed a paper describing some of the results obtained with the most powerful spectrograph in the world. He also read a second paper on "The Possibility of Photographing Molecules." The officers of the Academy for 1913 are as follows: President, Ira Remsen; vice-president, C. D. Wolcott; home secretary, Arnold Hague; treasurer, Whitman Cross.

SCOBELL, Sir Henry Jenner. A British major-general, died February 1, 1912. He was born in 1859 and received his early education at Eton. After leaving this school he entered the army, joining the Scots Greys. His chief military service was performed in the Boer War where he went with his regiment as a major. He performed brilliant service as a scout and in attacks against the Boer intrenchments. He narrowly escaped death and capture in the disaster at Silikat's Nek, where a British force of 240 men was overwhelmed under De la Rey. Two months later, however, he captured Barberton. Throughout the remainder of the war he distinguished himself as a cavalry officer and was said by authorities to be one of the ablest cavalry leaders that the Boer War produced. He received rapid promotion, becoming major-general in 1903, and inspector of cavalry in 1907. He received many decorations for bravery in battle.

SCOTLAND. See Great Britain, and Child Labor.

SCOTT, Frank Hall. An American publisher, died November 25, 1912. He was born in Terre Haute, Ind., in 1848 and was educated in the public schools of that State and in the Pennsylvania Military Academy. After finishing his education at the latter institution, he engaged in business in Indiana. He soon removed to New York and entered the business department of Scribner & Company in 1870. When *Scribner's Monthly* became the *Century Magazine* in 1881, Mr. Scott remained with it as treasurer. In 1893 he became president of the Century Company. He was prominently identified with the publishing interests in the United States and was at one time president of the American Publishers' Association. He was also founder and former president of the Aldine Club, a club composed of those engaged in publishing and kindred pursuits. He was given the honorary degree of L. H. D. from Marietta College in 1894.

SCOTT, Robert Falcon. An English Antarctic explorer and naval officer, died from privation in company with three companions while returning from the South Pole on March 29, 1912.

Captain Scott was born at Outlands, Devonport, England, on June 6, 1868. After attending school at Stubbington House, Fareham, he became a naval cadet on the *Britannia* in 1881. Two years later he was appointed midshipman and served on the Cape Station, in the Channel squadron, and in the training squadron. In 1887 he became an acting sub-lieutenant. After passing his examination for the rank of lieutenant, taking a first-class certificate in four out of five subjects, he was appointed to this rank in 1889 while serving on the Pacific Station. He devoted especial attention to the study of torpedoes, and in 1891 was appointed torpedo lieutenant. After serving for a time on the *Vulcan*, a torpedo depot ship, he became a staff officer on the *Defiance*, a torpedo school ship. In 1896 he again went to sea as torpedo lieutenant of the battleship *Empress of India* and in the following year served in a similar capacity on the *Majestic*. He served on this ship for three years and in 1900 was promoted to the rank of commander. He became greatly interested in the subject of Antarctic exploration and in 1900 headed an expedition known as the National Antarctic Expedition into the regions surrounding the South Pole. He remained for four years, and on his return to England in 1904 was given a reception which was enthusiastic beyond measure. He was awarded a royal medal and a special Antarctic medal. He was promoted to the rank of captain in recognition of his services, but did not return to active service in the navy until 1906, when he was appointed flag captain on the *Victorious*. He served in this post for twelve months. In 1908 he commanded the *Essex*, which he left to become flag captain of the *Bulwark*. In March, 1909, he was appointed naval assistant to the second sea lord of the Admiralty. He was the first holder of this appointment. This was his last official position in the Admiralty. He resigned in 1909 to prepare for a second expedition to the Antarctic. This expedition was known as the British Antarctic Expedition.

Captain Scott sailed from Port Chalmers, New Zealand, on his vessel, the *Terra Nova*, on November 29, 1910, and reached his proposed headquarters near the foot of Mt. Erebus, South Victoria Land, near the end of that year. Included in his party were Dr. E. A. Wilson, zoölogist; T. J. Taylor and W. G. Thompson, geologists; G. C. Simpson, meteorologist and physicist; Lieut. H. L. Pennell, student of magnetic phenomena, and Dr. E. L. Atkinson, bacteriologist. No definite news of the results of the expedition was received until March 31, 1912 (see Polar Exploration). In December, 1912, a report was widespread that Captain Scott had discovered the South Pole. This proved erroneous and a few days later the news of the discovery of the pole by Captain Amundsen was received.

Photograph by Underwood and Underwood, N. Y.

CAPTAIN ROBERT F. SCOTT, R. N.

ANTARCTIC EXPLORER, PERISHED MARCH, 1912

No particular anxiety was felt from the failure of Captain Scott to send news to the outer world, because it was well understood that no tidings of him could be expected until he was reached by the *Terra Nova*, which in the latter part of 1912 was sent to bring him and his party home. The tidings brought by the *Terra Nova* shocked the world. A message signed by Commander Evans, who was second in command of the party, told that the members of the advance party which had reached the pole on January 18, 1912, on their return had been overtaken by a blizzard and had perished. Captain Scott, Dr. Wilson, and Lieutenant Bowers died from exposure on March 29. Edgar Evans, petty officer, died on February 17 at the foot of Beardmore Glacier. His death was accelerated by concussion of the brain sustained while traveling over the rough ice some time before. Details of the death of Captain Oates were found in the statement left by Captain Scott. From this it was learned that, on March 17, Captain Oates, knowing that it would be impossible for him in his physical condition to proceed with his comrades, had deliberately walked away into the blizzard and perished. Captain Scott, Dr. Wilson, and Lieutenant Bowers were found dead in the tent, which they had erected as their last camping-place. This disaster was doubly tragic from the fact that a base of relief was only eleven miles distant.

In the meantime a relief party had been dispatched to assist the southern party commanded by Captain Scott, whose return was expected about March 10. This relief party reached One Ton Depot, which was within eleven miles of the spot at which Scott and his party perished, on March 3, and was compelled to return on March 10, owing primarily to the failing supply of food for the dogs, and also to the poor condition of the dogs after the strain of a hard season's work. Other efforts to reach the southern party were made, but these, too, failed. On October 30 a searching party organized by Surgeon Atkinson, consisting of two divisions, finally reached One Ton Camp. This was found to be in order and well provisioned. Proceeding along the road taken by Captain Scott, the tent which contained the bodies of the explorers was found on November 12.

Captain Scott had written his diary up to the day of his death. In this was found also a message to the public, and this gave the causes of the disaster. Captain Scott's statement in part is as follows: "The causes of this disaster are not due to faulty organization, but to misfortune in all risks which had to be undertaken. First, the loss of pony transport in March, 1911, obliged me to start later than I had intended and obliged the limit of stuff transported to be narrowed. Second, the weather throughout the outward journey, and especially the long gale in 83° South stopped us. Third, the soft snow in the lower reaches of the Glacier again reduced the pace. We fought these untoward events with a will and conquered; but it ate into our provisions reserve. . . . The advance party would have returned to the Glacier in fine form and with a surplus of food, but for the astonishing failure of the man whom we had least expected to fail. Seaman Edgar Evans was thought the strong man of the party, and the Beardmore Glacier is not difficult in fine weather. But on our return we did not get a single completely fine day. This, with a sick companion, enormously increased our anxieties. . . . But all the facts above enumerated were as nothing to the surprise which awaited us on the Barrier. . . . On the summit in Lat. 85° to Lat. 86° we had minus 20 to minus 30. In Lat. 82°, 10,000 ft. lower we had minus 30 in the day and minus 47 at night pretty regularly, with a continuous head wind during our day marches. It is clear that these circumstances came on very suddenly, and our wreck is certainly due to this advent of severe weather. . . . I do not think human beings ever came through such a month as we have come through, and we should have got through in spite of the weather but for the sickening of a second companion, Captain Oates, and a shortage of fuel in our dépots for which I cannot account, and finally but for the storm which has fallen on us within 11 miles of this dépot, at which we hoped to secure the final supplies. . . . We arrived within eleven miles of our old One Ton Camp with fuel for one hot meal and food for two days. For four days we have been unable to leave the tent, a gale blowing about us. We are weak; writing is difficult; but for my own sake I do not regret this journey, which has shown that Englishmen can endure hardship, help one another and meet death with as great a fortitude as ever in the past. We took risks—we knew we took them. Things have come out against us, and therefore we have no cause for complaint, but bow to the will of Providence, determined still to do our best to the last. But if we have been willing to give our lives to this enterprise, which is for the honor of our country, I appeal to our countrymen to see that those who depend on us are properly cared for. Had we lived I should have had a tale to tell of the hardihood, endurance, and courage of my companions which would have stirred the heart of every Englishman. These rough notes and our dead bodies must tell the tale, but surely, surely, a great rich country like ours will see that those who are dependent upon us are properly provided for."

Records and diaries kept by members of the party were found in the tent. The searching party made efforts to find the body of Captain Oates, but these failed. A memorial was erected in the neighborhood of the place of his death.

SCRUGGS, William Lindsay. An American diplomatist and lawyer, died July 18, 1912. He was born near Knoxville, Tenn., in 1836 and was educated at Strawberry Plains College, Tenn. In 1858 he was admitted to the bar. From 1862 to 1866 he was chief editor of the Columbus, Ga., *Daily Sun*, and from 1870 to 1872 was editor of the Atlanta *New Era*. From 1872 to 1877 and again from 1882 to 1887 he was minister to Colombia. From 1878 to 1882 he was consul-general in China and was minister to Venezuela from 1889 to 1893. He was legal adviser and special agent of the Venezuelan government, charged with the settlement of the Anglo-Venezuelan boundary dispute from 1894 to 1898. He brought this case to arbitration in 1897. He was one of the founders of the Atlanta public school system. He wrote *British Aggressions in Venezuela or the Monroe Doctrine on Trial* (1894); *Official History of the Guiana Boundary Dispute* (1895), *Lord Salisbury's Mistakes* (1896); *The Colom-*

bian and Venezuelan Republics (1905); *Evolution of American Citizenship* (1901); *Origin and Meaning of the Monroe Doctrine* (1902); *Evolution of the Fourteenth and Fifteenth Amendments*. He also contributed to historical, economic, and legal reviews.

SCULPTURE. During the early part of the year a bronze statue of Lincoln, by F. Edwin Elwell of New York, was unveiled at East Orange, N. J., and in October the Lincoln statue by Daniel Chester French was dedicated at Lincoln, Neb. The State of Massachusetts dedicated two battlefield monuments at Petersburg, Va., and at Valley Forge Park. On April 11, the State of South Carolina unveiled the first monument erected to the women of the State; it is by F. Wellington Ruckstuhl and cost $20,000, of which $7500 was appropriated by the State legislature and the balance by popular contribution. The Iowa State Memorial at Vicksburg, by Henry H. Kitson, was completed in May. In Potomac Park, Washington, D. C., the John Paul Jones memorial by Charles H. Niehaus, with a pedestal by Thomas Hastings of New York, was unveiled. A $12,000 memorial was dedicated by the Elks at New Orleans in June. On September 16, the Illinois Centennial Memorial by Charles J. Mulligan was unveiled at Edwardsville, Ind. Two famous groups for the entrance to the Pennsylvania Capital at Harrisburg, the work of George Grey Barnard, were dedicated on the fifth anniversary of the State House. In celebration of the ter-centenary of Champlain's voyage, Rodin's "France" was dedicated at Lake Champlain in May, 1912.

SCULPTURE ABROAD. A bronze statue of Washington by Pompeo Coppini, the gift of American residents of the City of Mexico in commemoration of the centennial of the Mexican Republic, was unveiled February 22, 1912, in Mexico City.

The "Bourgeois de Calais," by Rodin, was erected in London, between the Tate Galleries and the Houses of Parliament. It was purchased by the National Art Collection Fund, and a replica will be erected at Calais. An important dedication in London was that of George V.'s memorial to Queen Victoria, by Sir Thomas Brock, and the architect Sir Aston Webb, R. A., which consists of a white marble shaft, surmounted by a bronze "Victory," with symbolic groups below. In Dublin, the Parnell monument, one of the last and greatest works of the American, Augustus Saint-Gaudens, was unveiled in the middle of 1912.

NECROLOGY. In the field of sculpture, the death roll includes J. Scott Hartley, secretary of the National Sculpture Society, who died at his home in New York, Dec. 6, 1912, and Mathurin Moreau, who died in Paris at the age of 91.

SEARS, CLINTON BROOKS. An American soldier, educator, and writer, died February 16, 1912. He was born in Penn Yan, N. Y., in 1844 and after attending the Ohio Wesleyan University until 1862 entered the United States Military Academy, from which he graduated in 1867. In 1862-1863 he served as a private in the 95th Ohio Infantry. At the close of the Civil War he was appointed to the United States Engineers as a second lieutenant. He was made captain in 1880 and, after various promotions, colonel in 1907. He served in the United States and Philippine Islands in constructing river and harbor works, fortifications, dams, etc. From 1876 to 1877 he was assistant professor of civil and military engineering at West Point, and until 1882 acted successively as professor of geography, history and ethics, mechanics, acoustics, and optics and astronomy in that institution. In 1891-2 he was instructor in submarine mining at the United States Engineering School. From 1901 to 1903 he was chief engineer of the Division of the Philippines. He served as a member of the Mississippi River Commission and was president of the special board to report upon the 14-foot water-way project from Chicago to the Gulf. He was retired with the rank of major-general in 1908. He was the author of numerous official reports and of *Principles of Tidal Harbor Improvements*. He also compiled a history of the Ransom Genealogy.

SEATTLE. See ARCHITECTURE; GARBAGE AND REFUSE DISPOSAL; DOCKS AND HARBORS; and CITY PLANNING.

SECONDARY SCHOOLS. See AGRICULTURAL EDUCATION, and EDUCATION.

SECRET SOCIETIES IN HIGH SCHOOLS. See EDUCATION.

SEEBOHM, FREDERICK. An English historian, died February 5, 1912. He was born in 1833 of Quaker parentage. After attending the Quaker school at York he went to London to study law. He was called to the bar and practiced for a short time, but in 1857 went into business as a banker, settling at Hitchin, Herts. He was successful in business, but his more notable activities were along the lines of self-government and social progress. In his younger years he took an important part in the politics on the Liberal side, but dissatisfaction with the Gladstone Home Rule bill and other measures advocated by Gladstone led to his joining the free-trade wing of the Liberal-Unionist group. His chief reputation, however, comes from his writings in the field of social science. His work was of great originality and brilliancy. Among his writings are: *The Oxford Reformers; The Era of the Protestant Revolution; The English Village Community; The Tribal System of Wales;* and *Tribal Custom in Anglo-Saxon Law*. He received the degree of LL. D. from Edinburgh University, Litt. D. from Cambridge, and the same degree from Oxford.

SEED CORN WEEK. See AGRICULTURE.

SEISMOLOGY. See EARTHQUAKES.

SELANGOR. A state on the western shore of the Malay Peninsula; one of the protected Federated Malay States (q. v.). It has a coast line of about 125 miles and an estimated area of 3200 square miles (population 294,014). Kuala Lumpur (46,718 inhabitants, census of 1911) is the capital of the state and the administrative headquarters for the federation. Chief port, Port Swettenham (aggregate tonnage registered in 1909, 1,182,284). Import duties are levied on opium and spirits only.

Tin mining is the main industry, the output in 1909 being 49,022 piculs tin and 216,984 tin ore. Area actually under rubber in 1909, 100,637 acres; alienated for rubber cultivation at end of 1910, 225,013 acres, of which 113,114 were planted. Area (1909) under cocoanuts, 24,294 acres; under rice, 9112; gambier, 39,060; coffee, 10,645; pepper, 1250. The value of the tin export (1909), was 18,068,479 S. S. dollars. Area alienated for mining, 76,110 acres; Chinese miners employed, 62,-

SOLDIERS AND SAILORS MONUMENT, ALBANY, N. Y
H. A. MacNeil

"MEMORY"
For the Marshall Field Monument
By Daniel Chester French

374. Value of rubber export (1910), 26,269,-569 S. S. dollars.

Miles of metaled roads, 560; unmetaled, 54; paths, 233. The sultan is Suleiman bin Almerhum Raja Musa, and the British resident, R. G. Watson.

SELECTION. See BIOLOGY.

SELENIUM-EOSIN. See CANCER.

SENATE, DISPUTED SEATS IN. See CONGRESS.

SENEGAL. A French West African colony. Capital, Saint-Louis, with (1909) 22,093 inhabitants. Dakar (the capital of French West Africa) had 24,914; Rufisque, 12,457; Tivaouane, 3403; Thiès, 2404; Louga, 1726; Gorée, 1131. The Dakar-Saint-Louis Railway has a development of 264½ kilometers, nearly all in the Cayor region. Starting from Dakar, it runs east to Thiès (91 kms.), then north along the coast to Louga (193), then to the terminus, Saint-Louis (264). This line uniting the two chief towns of the colony was begun from a strategical, rather than a commercial, motive; but since the pacification of Cayor the region has become the principal field for peanut cultivation—one of the important industries. From Thiès a railway, having for ultimate destination Kayes, is now in operation to Guinguino. Travel into the interior is on horseback, and goods are carried by donkeys, oxen, and camels. Besides peanuts, millet, rice, corn, manioc, cotton, indigo, etc., are raised. Rubber and gums are gathered. Horses are plentiful and of good quality; camels are numerous during the dry season, but are sent north of the river by their owners (mostly Moors) for the wet season as they die in great numbers if exposed to the long rains. Cattle, goats, and sheep are raised. Minerals are found in abundance. Henri Cor was lieutenant-governor in 1912. See FRENCH WEST AFRICA.

SENSATION. See PSYCHOLOGY.

SERUM. See TYPHOID FEVER.

SERVIA. A constitutional monarchy in southern Europe—one of the Balkan states; previous to 1878 an autonomous Turkish dependency. Belgrade is the capital.

AREA AND POPULATION. The table below shows area by departments, population according to the census of December 31, 1910, population calculated December 31, 1911, and density (9111) per square kilometer:

Department	Sq. kms.	1910	1911	D.
Belgrade*	12	89,876	92,288	123
Belgrade	2,025	155,815	158,378	
Kraguyevats	2,295	189,025	192,124	84
Krayina	2,909	112,142	113,128	39
Krushevats	2,710	167,371	170,353	63
Morava	2,900	203,638	206,547	71
Nish	2,558	198,768	201,762	79
Ushitse	3,288	146,763	149,112	45
Pirot	2,419	112,314	114,115	47
Podrinye	3,351	238,275	242,029	68
Posharevats	4,157	259,906	262,203	63
Rudnik	1,569	85,340	87,137	56
Smederevo	1,277	143,216	144,829	119
Chachak	3,798	138,911	141,267	37
Timok	3,196	149,538	150,965	47
Toplitsa	2,839	110,218	112,610	40
Valyevo	2,458	157,648	160,873	65
Vranya	4,342	252,937	257,087	59
	48,303†	2,911,701	2,957,207	61

* City. † 18,650 square miles.

According to religions the censused population was divided into Greek Catholics (2,881,220), Roman Catholics (8435), Mohammedans (14,-335), Jews (5997), Protestants (799), and other religions (915). The marriages in 1911 numbered 30,453, births 107,229, deaths 64,-415. Belgrade had (1910) 89,876 inhabitants; Nish, 24,919; Kraguyevats, 18,376; Lescovats, 14,266; Pozharevats, 13,613; Shabats, 11,541; Pirot, 10,737; and Vranya, 10,487.

While primary instruction is nominally compulsory, actual attendance is less than 25 per cent. More than 80 per cent. of the adult population is illiterate. On the other hand, nearly every peasant occupies and cultivates his own freehold, varying from 10 to 30 acres, and there is practically no pauper population necessitating alms-houses.

PRODUCTION. Agriculture is practically the only industry, and stock-raising (particularly swine), the most remunerative branch. The area (1910) under main crops and the yield (1911) are reported as follows: 385,584 hectares under wheat, 4,167,000 quintals; barley, 107,523 hectares and 1,003,000 quintals; rye, 435,000 quintals; oats, 108,101 hectares and 733,000 quintals; corn, 585,226 hectares and 6,739,000 quintals; flax, 1723 hectares and (1910) 9944 quintals; vines, 35,210 hectares producing (1911) 154,000 hectoliters of wine. Plum orchards cover over 130,000 hectares and the fruit is preserved in large quantities for export as well as distilled for spirits. Livestock reported (from a German source) December 31 1910: 965,208 cattle, 3,808,815 sheep, 152,617 horses, 836,544 swine, 627,427 goats.

Worked forests cover over 135,000 hectares and unworked 167,000.

The mineral resources include coal and lignite, the output being valued in 1910 at 12,-802,548 dinars. The manufactures include milling, brewing, distilling, sugar refining, carpet weaving, etc.

COMMERCE AND COMMUNICATION. Imports for consumption and exports of domestic produce follow, values in thousands of dinars (1 dinar=19.3 cents):

	Imps.	Exps.		Imps.	Exps.
Foodstuffs, etc.	22,769	103,776	Stone, etc.	1,619	132
Metals	20,304	9,657	Glass	1,520	.....
Minerals	6,936	718	Machinery	12,350	28
Drugs, etc.	7,573	288	Other mdse.	1,041	43
T'xtiles, etc.	31,416	2,143	Total '11.	115,425	116,916
Hides, etc.	4,575	87	Total '10.	84,697	98,388
Luxuries	2,809	66	Total '09.	75,535	92,982
Paper	2,513	28			

Countries of origin and destination follow, with values in thousands of dinars:

	Imps.	Exps.		Imps.	Exps.
Aus.-Hun.	47,448	48,433	Belgium	2,081	6,142
Germany	31,347	28,933	Switzerl'd.	1,553	258
U. K.	9,524	87	Rumania	1,539	6,141
France	5,746	3,841	Bulgaria	697	2,802
Italy	4,861	4,394	Greece	325	110
Turkey	3,814	11,984	Bosnia	220	112
Russia	3,391	53	Other	742	17
U. S.	2,136	3,609			
			Total	115,425	116,916

Railways are lacking for the p pe development of the country. At the end of 1911 there were 949 kilometers open for traffic. The Danube, the Save, and the Drina are the navigable rivers. The roads are badly in need of repair, many being nearly impassable. Telegraph lines, 4350 kilometers; wires, 8289.

FINANCE. The 1912 budget estimated the revenue at 130,764,713 dinars (31,655,698 from monopolies, 30,613,000 from direct taxes, 16,000,000 from state railways, 14,500,000 from customs, 9,001,000 from excise, 8,402,000 from fines, 5,547,485 from domains, 4,100,000 from posts and telegraphs, 5,093,365 extraordinary); expenditures, 130,764,713 (32,394,550 for the service of the debt, 29,527,571 war, 17,329,254 public works, 12,875,195 finance, 9,630,384 worship and instruction, 5,358,829 agriculture and commerce, 5,302,193 interior, 4,807,366 pensions and subventions, 4,834,542 extraordinary). The debt stood, January 1, 1912, at 663,617,000 dinars.

GOVERNMENT. The legislative authority is vested in a king assisted by a cabinet of eight responsible heads of departments. After the murder of Alexander I. (Obrenovitch) May 29, 1903 (o. s.), Peter Karageorgevitch, grandson of the celebrated Kara George and son of Alexander Karageorgevitch, was elected king (June 2, 1903 o. s.) under the name Peter I. He was born June 29, 1844 (o. s.), married (1883) Princess Zorka of Montenegro, and has two sons: George (born 1887), who was forced in 1909 to renounce his right of succession on account of incompetence and violence, and Alexander (born 1888), the heir-apparent. The Narodna-Skupscntina (160 members) is the legislative body. In November, 1912, Servia recaptured from Turkey her old capital, Uskűb.

There are three political parties, of which the Radicals and the Liberals are pro-Russian, and the Progressives, pro-Austrian.

The ministry as constituted September 12, 1912, was as follows: N. P. Pashitch, premier and minister for foreign affairs; Dr. L. Patchou, finance; S. M. Protitch, interior; Colonel Djoravitch, war; L. Jovanovitch, worship and instruction; Dr. M. Politchevitch, justice; K. Stoyanovitch, commerce, etc.; I. P. Ivanovitch, public works.

ARMY. The effect of the reorganization which had taken place in the Servian army previous to 1912 was shown in its service in the Balkan War. The Servian army, in which compulsory service is required from the age of 21, was maintained on a skeleton basis with an average peace strength of about 24,000 officers and men, which is increased in the summer months by about 10,000 men. In 1911 the peace establishment amounted to about 36,000. Ten years are spent enrolled in the first line, including the active army and the reserves, and then in the second and third lines of the national army, but on the average, hardly more than 6 months is spent with the colors in the case of the infantry, a somewhat greater period with the cavalry and artillery, where two years is the nominal service, and 18 months in the other branches. The organization is one of cadres which were to be filled on mobilization, the country being divided into 5 divisional areas, with headquarters at Nish, Belgrade, Valyevo, Kraguyevats, and Zayechar. Each of these should supply 8 battalions of infantry, 9 4-gun batteries, and a regiment of divisional cavalry. These 5 divisions theoretically when mobilized for war should furnish a total of 110,000 men, which number might be increased to nearly 200,000 officers and men available for the field, but without requisite experience and training. The armament consisted of the Mauser rifle (model '99) for the first line troops, and the Berdan and a modified Mauser for the others, while modern quick-firing guns from the Schneider works had been supplied to the artillery. The results of the mobilization of the Servian army and the part it played in the Balkan War, will be found discussed under MILITARY PROGRESS and TURKEY AND THE BALKAN PEOPLES.

HISTORY. The general elections on April 15 gave the government a majority of one vote. Upon the refusal of the king to dissolve the Skupschtina the cabinet resigned, and the leader of the Young Radicals, M. Stoynovitch, was summoned by the king to form a new cabinet by a coalition of the Old and Young Radicals. M. Milanovitch, president of the council, died June 30. The ministry resigned in September and was succeeded by a cabinet consisting of Old Radicals under M. Pashitch. The main events in the history of Servia during the year will be found treated at length under TURKEY AND THE BALKAN PEOPLES. See also the article on MILITARY PROGRESS.

SEVENTH DAY ADVENTISTS. See ADVENTISTS.

SEWAGE DISPOSAL, STATE CONTEST OF. See SANITATION.

SEWAGE PURIFICATION. Many engineers now feel that sewage treatment would be better than sewage purification to designate the various processes used to fit sewage for discharge into water where the volume of water and other conditions make is unwise to depend upon disposal by dilution alone. The facts are that but few sewage works are either designed or operated with the object of purifying sewage, as these two words are commonly understood. Purification would mean restoring the large volumes of water which convey plumbing wastes to their original state of purity. As a rule, sewage treatment works are operated to produce an effluent which will not offend the eye or nose, or give rise to objectionable deposits on the bed of the water which receives it. Rarely is an attempt made to remove all the bacteria from sewage. Where public water-supplies are endangered by this condition the sewage effluent should either be discharged into some other water or else the water should be purified before it is used. The view just outlined was set forth at length in a paper entitled "Sewage Treatment vs. Purification," read by George C. Whipple before the American Public Health Association in September, 1912 (see *Engineering News*, October 3, 1912).

A notable sewage treatment event of the year was the publication of the eighth report of the Royal Commission on Sewage Disposal (London, Eng.). The report was devoted wholly to the subject of standards for sewage treatment and to a standard for discharging sewage without treatment, in both cases for discharge into fresh water. For effluents from treatment works three standards were set up, corresponding with "complete" or a high degree of treatment, where screens, tanks and filter beds would be required, and to less complete works, where either chemical precipitation or else plain sedimentation in septic or ordinary settling tanks would suffice. The volume of diluting water was the main factor in determining each standard, and the standards themselves were the amounts of suspended solids in the effluent and of dissolved oxygen that would be taken up by the effluent, the latter during a period of five days. For abstract of the report and for the standards see *Engineering News*, January 9, 1912.

During the year the first of three sewage treatment plants for Atlanta, Ga., was put in operation, including Imhoff tanks for sedimentation and sludge reduction and sprinkling filters for final treatment. Imhoff tanks were completed or put under construction in perhaps a half-dozen other American cities and their number was increased in Germany, where originated this modification of the Travis or Hampton tank, which is in itself a modification of the septic tank. It should be noted that none of the types of tanks mentioned are "systems" of sewage treatment, as is commonly supposed; they merely effect a partial removal of suspended solids from sewage, leaving the tank effluent subject to further treatment, if the work done by the tank is not sufficient to meet local conditions.

A large sewage testing or experiment station was built by the city of Columbus, O., late in 1912, in order to determine the means of sewage treatment best suited to the particular needs of that city. It was also announced that a sewage experiment station was to be installed by the engineering department of the University of Michigan. The Massachusetts State board of health continued its sewage treatment studies at its experiment station at Lawrence. These studies were begun in 1887. See also SANITATION.

SEX DETERMINATION. See BIOLOGY.

SEX DISTRIBUTION OF THE POPULATION OF THE UNITED STATES. The Thirteenth Census included statistics of sex distribution and the results show that in 1910, out of a total population of 91,972,266 there were 47,332,277 males and 44,639,989 females, or 106 males to every 100 females. In 1900 the per cent. was 104.4 males to every 100 females. The excess of males in the United States is due mainly to the extensive immigration, a much larger proportion of the immigrants being males than females. In the foreign-born white population there are 129.2 males to 100 females. In the native white population, however, there is also a slight excess of males, the ratio being 102.7 to 100. In the negro population the males are outnumbered by the females in the ratio of 98.9 to 100. Among the Chinese, males outnumbered females by more than 14 to 1, and among Japanese by about 7 to 1. The Indian population showed a small excess of males, 103.5 to 100 females.

The preponderance of males in the aggregate population of the United States is most marked in the Pacific and Mountain divisions (the far western States), with ratios of 129.5 and 127.9 males to 100 females respectively. The proportion of males is lowest in New England, this being the only geographic division in which there is a slight excess of females over males. There are only five States in which females outnumber males: Massachusetts, Rhode Island, Maryland, North Carolina, and South Carolina. In the decade 1900-1910 males increased more rapidly than females in the United States. The increase of the former was 21.9 per cent., and of the latter, 20.1 per cent. There was little change in the sex ratio for the native population, but among the foreign-born whites the number of males per 100 females increased from 117.4 in 1900 to 129.2 in 1910.

IN URBAN AND RURAL COMMUNITIES. Of the aggregate urban population of Continental United States in 1910, 21,496,181 were males, and 21,127,202 females, the number of males per 100 females being 101.7. Of the aggregate rural population 25,836,096 were males and 23,512,787 females, the number of males per 100 females being 109.9. Of the 50 cities having over 100,000 inhabitants there were 28 in which the males outnumbered the females. The number of males per 100 females was the greatest in Seattle, where it was 136.2. Nashville showed the smallest proportion of males with a ratio of 89.6 per 100 females. Of the eight cities having 500,000 or more inhabitants, Baltimore had the lowest number of males per 100 females, 92.4, and Cleveland the highest, 106.6 The table below shows the proportion of male to female population in each of the States in 1910:

Division and State	Total population	Males	Females	Males to 100 fem.
United States[1]	91,972,266	47,332,277	44,639,989	106.0
New England:				
Maine	742,371	377,052	365,319	103.2
New Hampshire	430,572	216,290	214,282	100.9
Vermont	355,956	182,568	173,388	105.3
Massachusetts	3,366,416	1,655,248	1,711,168	96 7
Rhode Island..	542,610	270,314	272,296	99.3
Connecticut...	1,114,756	563,642	551,114	102.3
Middle Atlantic:				
New York.....	9,113,614	4,584,597	4,529,017	101 2
New Jersey...	2,537,167	1,286,463	1,250,704	102.9
Pennsylvania..	7,665,111	3,942,206	3,722,905	105.9
East North Central:				
Ohio	4,767,121	2,434,758	2,332,363	104.4
Indiana	2,700,876	1,383,295	1,317,581	105.0
Illinois	5,638,591	2,911,674	2,726,917	106 8
Michigan	2,810,173	1,454,534	1,355,639	107.3
Wisconsin	2,333,860	1,208,578	1,125,282	107.4
West North Central:				
Minnesota	2,075,708	1,108,511	967,197	114.6
Iowa	2,224,771	1,148,171	1,076,600	106.6
Missouri	3,293,335	1,687,813	1,605,522	105.1
North Dakota.	577,056	317,554	259,502	122.4
South Dakota.	583,888	317,112	266,776	118.9
Nebraska	1,192,214	627,782	564,432	111.2
Kansas	1,690,949	885,912	805,037	110.0
South Atlantic:				
Delaware	202,322	103,435	98,887	104.6
Maryland	1,295,346	644,225	651,121	98 9
Dist. of Col..	331,069	158,050	173,019	91.3
Virginia	2,061,612	1,035,348	1,026,264	100.9
West Virginia	1,221,119	644,044	577,075	111.6
North Carolina	2,206,287	1,098,476	1,107,811	99.2
South Carolina	1,515,400	751,842	763,558	98.5
Georgia	2,609,121	1,305,019	1,304,102	100.1
Florida	752,619	394,166	358,453	110.0
East South Central:				
Kentucky	2,289,905	1,161,709	1,128,196	103 0
Tennessee	2,184,789	1,103,491	1,081,298	102.1
Alabama	2,138,093	1,074,209	1,063,884	101.0
Mississippi ...	1,797,114	905,760	891,354	101.6
West South Central:				
Arkansas	1,574,449	810,026	764,423	106.0
Louisiana	1,656,388	835,275	821,113	101.7
Oklahoma	1,657,155	881,578	775,577	113.7
Texas	3,896,542	2,017,626	1,878,916	107.4
Mountain:				
Montana	376,053	226,872	149,181	152.1
Idaho	325,594	185,546	140,048	132.5
Wyoming	145,965	91,670	54,295	168.8
Colorado	799,024	430,697	368,327	116.9
New Mexico..	327,301	175,245	152,056	115.3
Arizona	204,354	118,574	85,780	138 2
Utah	373,351	196,863	176,488	111.5
Nevada	81,875	52,551	29,324	179.2
Pacific:				
Washington ..	1,141,990	658,663	483,327	136.3
Oregon	672,765	384,265	288,500	133.2
California	2,377,549	1,322,978	1,054,571	125.5

[1] Exclusive of Alaska, Hawaii, Porto Rico, and other noncontiguous possessions.

SHAKESPEARE, VARIORUM EDITION. See FURNESS, HORACE HOWARD.

SHAW, GEORGE BERNARD. See DRAMA.

SHEEP. See STOCK-RAISING AND MEAT PRODUCTION.

SHEEPSHANKS, JOHN. An English ecclesiastic, former bishop of Norwich, died June 3, 1912. He was born in London in 1834 and was educated in the grammar school at Coventry and at Christ's College, Cambridge. He became interested in the missionary work of the church and having been ordained as a priest, he went in 1859 to be rector of New Westminster and chaplain to the Bishop of Columbia. Here he remained for eight years and carried on efficient work among the lumbermen, miners, and agriculturists of British Columbia. Before his return to England he made a tour of the Pacific islands, China, and Siberia, studying the missionary work and the ancient religions of the countries which he visited. He returned to England in 1868 and became rector of Bilton. He afterwards served as rector in Liverpool. Here he took a practical interest in the development of middle-class schools and other educational efforts. In 1893 he was appointed by Gladstone bishop of Norwich. The appointment was in the nature of a surprise, as Bishop Sheepshanks was at that time little known throughout England. He continued in this office until 1910, when he resigned on account of ill health. Among his published writings are: *Confirmation and Unction of the Sick; Charge, Eucharist and Confession* (1902); *My Life in Mongolia and Siberia* (1903); and *The Pastor in His Parish* (1908).

SHELDON, EDWARD. See DRAMA.

SHELDON, GEORGE R. See PRESIDENTIAL CAMPAIGN CONTRIBUTIONS.

SHERIDANITE. See METEOROLOGY.

SHERMAN, JAMES SCHOOLCRAFT. Vice-President of the United States, died October 30, 1912. He was born in New Hartford, a suburb of Utica, N. Y., October 24, 1855. His father was General Richard U. Sherman. He was educated in the public schools of New Hartford and at Hamilton College, from which he graduated in 1878. Although his father and his two brothers were Democrats and he himself was a member of that party in his early years, he joined the Republican party when still a young man. After his graduation from college he studied law and in 1880 was admitted to the bar. He was elected to the office of mayor of Utica in 1884, the youngest man who ever held that position. In 1887 he was elected to the 50th Congress and was reëlected to serve in the 51st, 54th, 55th, 56th, 57th, 58th, 59th, and 60th Congresses. He was a delegate to the Republican national convention in 1892, and was chairman of the Republican State conventions of 1895, 1900, and 1908. In Congress he soon made an impression as a strong figure. He became a close friend of Thomas B. Reed during the latter's speakership, and presided over the House of Representatives more frequently than any other member. He was also for many years a firm friend and admirer of Theodore Roosevelt. In 1900 he was offered the office of secretary of the Senate, while he was still a member of the House of Representatives. He declined this offer and a little later President McKinley urged him to accept a post as one of the appraisers of the port of New York. Mr. Sherman's constituents in the Oneida-Herkimer district held a mass meeting and asked him to continue to represent them in Congress. He therefore declined the President's offer. In the same year, while he was chairman of the State convention, he was for several days a close rival of Theodore Roosevelt for the nomination to the Vice-Presidency. In the autumn of 1902 he was a candidate for speaker of the House of Representatives, but when Sereno E. Payne of New York also became a candidate, Mr. Sherman withdrew.

In Congress he was identified with the conservative wing of the Republican party and with former Speaker Cannon, Congressman Dalzell of Pennsylvania, and Congressman Payne of New York, formed a group which for years practically controlled the legislative procedure of the House. He was also chairman of the Republican Congressional committee in charge of the campaign of 1906, and in this capacity originated the scheme of dollar contributions from the people. During this campaign he was obliged for the first time to make a strong fight to retain his seat in Congress. Strong opposition had been organized both within and outside the Republican party. The anti-organization men had with them Samuel Gompers of the American Federation of Labor, the United Labor party and the Independence League. In spite of this opposition he was elected by a vote of 24,027 against 19,757 for his Democratic opponent. His most important appointments while in Congress were to the chairmanship of the Indian affairs committee and as a member of the committee on rules. Certain charges made against him as to the use of his position in Congress to further his business interest were not substantiated. In 1908 Mr. Sherman received practically a unanimous nomination for the Vice-Presidency. In the struggle for the control of the Republican party in New York which occurred in 1910, Mr. Sherman broke his friendship with Theodore Roosevelt and allied himself with the latter's opponents at the Republican State convention at Saratoga. He contested with Roosevelt for the temporary chairmanship of the convention and was defeated. He received a decisive defeat in his attempt to secure the 23 delegates of his county for this convention. He failed even to carry his own ward against the Progressive element.

SHIPBUILDING. The annual report of shipbuilding in various countries compiled by Lloyd's *Register* and giving the tonnage of merchant ships exceeding 100 tons launched in all countries shows that the total output of the world for 1912 was 1719 merchant vessels, of 2,901,760 tons This represents a total increase in the world's production of merchant ships of 251,629 tons; but this did not constitute a record, for 1906, when 2,919,763 tons were launched, still holds an advantage of 17,994 tons. Of the 1912 aggregate, 712 vessels were launched in the United Kingdom, representing 1,738,514 tons—practically 60 per cent. of the total. Germany ranks second with only 165 vessels, representing 375,317 tons, or a quota of 13 per cent. The United States comes third with 90,000 tons for ships built on the great lakes, making a total of 174 vessels of 284,223 tons launched during the past year This proportion is 9.8 per cent. France takes fourth place with 80 vessels, of 110,734 tons, a proportion of 3.8 per cent.; and Holland, with 112 vessels, of 99,439 tons, contributes 3.43 per cent. of the total; Japan, which comes next, launched 168 vessels, of 57,755 tons.

Accordingly, it is apparent that Great Britain was still preëminent in shipbuilding, and its proportion for 1912 was up to the average, though in 1911 this was 68 per cent.; while in 1907, the last year of great activity, the ratio was 58 per cent., and in 1906, 63 per cent. Germany's proportion for 1912 was 13 per cent. as compared with 9.7 per cent. in 1911; and in 1906, when also there was great activity, it was 11 per cent.; in 1904-8 it was over 10 per cent. In 1912, therefore, Germany considerably improved its relative position. In the case of the United States the proportion was considerably more than in 1911, when, however, the total was abnormally low—namely, 6½ per cent. In 1910, on the other hand, it was 17 per cent. The French total was less than in the previous years, their 3.8 per cent. for 1912 comparing with 4.75 and 4.13 per cent. in the two previous years. Holland's proportion was practically the same as in the previous year, when it was 3½ per cent., and 3.63 per cent. in 1910.

TONNAGE OF MERCHANT AND WAR VESSELS (OVER 100 TONS) LAUNCHED IN EACH MARITIME COUNTRY

Austria-Hungary	29,297	58,105	88,742
Belgium	6,226	7,563	18,542
British Colonies......	26,343	·19,662	34,790
China	3,942	2,189	8,681
Denmark	12,371	19,651	26,262
France	105,114	184,184	169,889
Germany	210,367	387,477	477,742
Holland	71,761	93,670	101,642
Italy	52,078	92,719	40,060
Japan	53,316	81,790	88,731
Norway	37,481	35,535	50,358
Russia	4,395	96,264	15,663
Spain	3,234	6,598	21,580
Sweden	9,869	9,852	13,968
United States	361,605	287,550	349,496
Other countries	150	120	....
Total foreign and colonial	990,893	1,384,379	1,506,147
Total for the U. K.	1,277,814	2,034,630	1,930,251
Total for world....	2,268,707	3,419,009	3,436,398

Lloyd's figures for the displacement tonnage of warships exceeding 100 tons, launched for the various navies showed that the abnormal output of 1911 was not maintained during 1912, though the total was only second to the figures then recorded. The decrease—234,240 tons—was attributable largely to Great Britain and Germany and would be regarded with some degree of satisfaction were the figures indicative of any lessening of the competition in naval strength and armaments, but an examination of the facts does not justify any such feeling of optimism. It will be noted that the total output is 174 vessels, of 534,629 tons. This makes the aggregate for 1911 and 1912 therefore over 1,300,000 tons, equal to an average of 650,000 tons, which is nearly 40 per cent. higher than the largest total for any previous year. The British proportion of the total for the two years was 30 per cent., which, against the proportion of 60 per cent. of the world's merchant tonnage launched was thought by British naval authorities to constitute matter for reflection. The German total was 18¼ per cent., which compared with her proportion of 13 per cent. of the world's merchant shipping output. The United States added 5000 tons to the displacement of their warships launched in 1912, as compared with the previous year; France, 2000 tons; Japan, 19,000 tons; and Austria-Hungary, 29,000 tons. The British total was 58,343 tons less; the Italian total, 60,079 tons less; and the Russian total, 92,768 tons less. No significance need be attached to such increases or decreases, because the figures from year to year must fluctuate. In the case of Russia, for instance, there was greater activity in the building of warships in 1912 than in 1911, and in other states the tendency was distinctly towards increased production of warships. See BATTLESHIPS, and NAVAL PROGRESS, also tables on page 650.

SHIPBUILDING IN AMERICAN COAST YARDS. In addition to a number of warships for various nations, the American coast shipyards were filled with important vessels under construction, and with the opening of the Panama Canal increased business was looked for. The New York Shipbuilding Company at Camden, N. J., was building the steel Chinese cruiser *Fei Hung*, 322 feet length over all and 2600 gross tons' displacement, the steel first-class battleship *Moreno*, 594 feet, 7 inches over all and 27,600 gross tons' displacement, for Argentina, a steel collier 332 feet, 1 inch over all, for coast service, a steel passenger and freight steamer 442 feet, 6 inches over all for the Pacific Coast Steamship Company, a steel freight steamer 344 feet over all for the Old Dominion Steamship Company, and two steel bulk oil steamers 343 feet, 4 inches over all for the Standard Oil Company. The Maryland Steel Company at the Sparrow's Point yards, Maryland, had under construction six freight steamers, 429 feet, 2 inches over all for the American-Hawaiian Steamship Company, each of 6600 gross tonnage, and two passenger steamers 277 feet over all for the Chesapeake Steamship Company, of Baltimore, Maryland. A steel freight steamer 314 feet, 7½ inches over all was building at the Fore River yards, Quincy, Mass., for the Union Sulphur Company, as was also a steel oil steamer 436 feet over all, for the Standard Oil Company. The Newport News Shipbuilding and Dry Dock Company had under construction several large freight and passenger steamers, oil steamers, and oil barges, and at the yards on the Atlantic coast a large and varied programme of construction was under way. The Pacific shipbuilders also shared in this activity and while no very large work was reported from that coast, yet most of the plants were exceedingly active.

The large side-wheel steamer *Washington Irving*, for the Hudson River Day Line, was launched from the New York Shipbuilding Company's yard at Camden, N. J., on December 7. This vessel was to be licensed to carry 6000 passengers and was 416 feet, 6 inches in length over all, molded beam 47 feet, beam over guard 86 feet, 6 inches, depth 14 feet, 6 inches. The engines were three cylinder compound inclined type supplied with steam from four single and two double-ended Scotch boilers.

The accompanying table from Lloyd's *Register* shows the tonnage of vessels of 100 tons gross and upwards, exclusive of warships, launched in the principal countries of the world from 1908 to 1912:

business at times of reduced activity, it would seem as if the competition with the coast yards was becoming greater. The number of bulk freighters under construction showed a decrease for the year, and tne 7 under construc-

Year	U. K. tons	Aus.-Hun. tons	Brit. Cols. tons	Denmark tons	France tons	Germany tons	Holland tons	Italy tons	Japan tons	Norway tons	United States tons	Other c'tries tons	No.	Totals tons
1908	929,669	23,502	34,181	19,172	83,429	207,777	58,604	26,864	59,725	52,839	304,543	32,981	1405	1,832,286
1909	991,066	25,006	7,461	7,508	42,197	128,696	59,106	31,217	52,319	28,601	209,604	19,276	1063	1,602,057
1910	1,143,169	14,304	26,343	12,154	80,751	159,303	70,945	23,019	30,215	36,931	331,318	29,401	1277	1,957,853
1911	1,803,844	37,836	19,662	18,689	125,472	255,532	93,050	17,401	44,359	35,435	171,569	27,291	1599	2,650,140
1912	1,738,514	34,790	38,831	26,103	110,734	375,317	99,439	25,196	57,755	50,255	284,223	60,633	1719	2,901,769

The attached table from Lloyd's *Register* shows the number and tonnage of warships launched by Great Britain and other countries from 1908 to 1912:

Year	United Kingdom No.	United Kingdom Tons	Abroad No.	Abroad Tons
1908	36	74,186	91	235,503
1909	42	126,230	109	278,245
1910	45	134,645	77	176,209
1911	50	230,786	119	533,083
1912	30	101,737	141	342,892

The following table from Lloyd's *Register* shows the number and displacement of warships of 100 tons and upwards launched for the various navies from 1908 to 1912:

tion would have a capacity of 62,000 gross tons of ore on a single trip, so that when they are completed, the carrying capacity added to the lake fleet of bulk freighters in eleven years, would have been increased by 43,298,000 tons.

The launchings on the great lakes in American yards during 1910 amounted to 35 vessels, of which 11 were bulk freighters (6 for the coast), 6 package freighters (3 for the coast), 3 oil barges for coast service, 3 passenger boats, 1 conveyor boat, 1 sand steamer, 1 oil steamer, 2 scows, 1 car ferry, 1 bridge pontoon, 1 floating dock, 1 barge, and 1 stern wheel steamer for Kootenay Lake.

During the year the Detroit Shipbuilding Company, at its Wyandotte yard, launched a large passenger steamer, built for the Cleve-

Year	British tons	American (U. S.) tons	Austro-Hung. tons	French tons	German tons	Italian tons	Japanese tons	Russian tons	Other Flags tons	No.	Total tons
1908	49,560	52,850	16,153	21,600	97,660	29,400	2,245	8,800	31,421	127	309,689
1909	98,790	48,639	22,217	95,740	99,116	2,088	875	1,246	36,264	151	404,475
1910	133,525	30,287	14,993	24,063	49,024	19,374	23,100	......	16,488	122	310,854
1911	221,430	57,526	20,269	53,995	128,340	75,018	37,071	93,260	81,960	169	768,869
1912	163,087	62,673	49,361	55,965	99,810	14,939	56,085	492	32,267	174	534,629

The following table shows the ships built and documented in the United States for the calendar year ending December 31, 1912, from the report of the Bureau of Navigation:

land and Buffalo Transit Company for service on the great lakes. This was the largest sidewheel steamship in the world, being 477 feet in length over all, 96 feet, 6 inches extreme

	Wood Sail No.	Wood Sail Gross	Wood Steam No.	Wood Steam Gross	Wood Unrigged No.	Wood Unrigged Gross	Steel Sail No.	Steel Sail Gross	Steel Steam No.	Steel Steam Gross	Steel Unrigged No.	Steel Unrigged Gross	Total No.	Total Gross
Atlantic and Gulf ...	67	17,221	427	18,510	149	42,432	3	2,040	46	86,401	10	5,890	702	171,494
Porto Rico..	7	91	4	115	...	......	..	.....	..	......	..	.....	11	206
Pacific	6	726	333	18,263	127	10,778	..	.....	13	7,728	..	.....	478	37,496
Great Lakes	3	24	239	4,060	62	4,178	2	4,456	33	61,369	6	2,316	345	76,403
Western Rivers...	..	......	146	3,872	28	482	..	.....	14	1,245	3	1,281	191	6,880
Total	86	18,062	1149	44,820	366	57,870	5	6,496	105	155,743	19	9,486	1727	292.477

Shipbuilding on the Great Lakes. During 1912 the shipyards of the great lakes on both sides of the boundary had 52 vessels under construction for 1913 delivery. These included 7 bulk freighters, 3 passenger steamers, 2 package freighters, 3 oil steamers, 3 oil barges, 1 car ferry, 15 barges, 3 lighters, 9 dredges, 1 floating dry dock, 1 lighthouse tender, 1 tug, 1 tunnel launch, 1 machine boat, and 1 scow. It was worthy of note that 24 of these vessels were for salt-water service, 6 being for the Standard Oil Company and 18 for coastwise trade. The construction of vessels for coast service by the shipyards on the great lakes was showing a steady increase, and while the builders have been looking for such

breadth over guards and 23 feet, 6 inches molded depth of hull. The engines were of 8000 horsepower and were designed to give a speed of 22 miles an hour from dock to dock. Elaborate and luxurious accommodations were arranged for passengers, of which some 6000 could be accommodated, there being a total of 510 staterooms, while 1500 tons of freight could be carried on the main deck of the vessel. The vessel was provided with a bow rudder for use in the tortuous channels at both Buffalo and Cleveland. The electric equipment, including a complete wireless plant, was exceedingly elaborate, and unusual facilities for fire protection were installed.

Great Britain. In Great Britain there were

HAMBURG-AMERICAN LINE STEAMSHIP "IMPERATOR"
LAUNCHED 1912

fewer small craft and fewer moderate-sized ships built in 1912, but a greater number of vessels between 6000 and 10,000 tons register—60, as compared with 34 in 1911. Seventeen merchant ships exceeded 10,000 tons, which was one less than in 1911, but the largest was only 18,500 tons, tnough several vessels of extraordinary size were being constructed for launching during 1913.

The following table (from *Engineering*, London), shows the notably large merchant steamers launched during the year in British yards:

Name	Tons	I.H.P.	Builders
White Star liner Ceramic	18,500	8,370	Harland & Wolff, Ltd., Belfast.
Canadian Pacific liners Empress of Asia and Empress of Russia....	16,850	.....	Fairfield Co., Ltd., Glasgow.
Nestor	14,500	8,000	Workman, Clark and Co., Ltd., Belfast.
Union Steamship Co. of New Zealand liner Niagara.	13,500	.....	John Brown & Co., Limited, Clydebank.
Desna, Darna and Drina...	11,500	5,960	Harland and Wolff, Ltd., Belfast.
P. and O. liners Beltana and Benalla	11,120	9,000	Caird & Co., Limited, Greenock.
Spanish Transatlantic liner Reina Victoria Eugenia	10,840	11,000	Swan, Hunter and Wigham Richardson, Ltd., Newcastle.
Hawkes Bay...	10,650	5,200	Workman, Clark and Co., Ltd., Belfast.
Makarini	10,624	5,200	Do. Do.
Vestris	10,494	7,000	Do. Do.
Vauban	10,421	7,000	Do. Do.
Holt liner Ixion	10,220	5,500	Scotts' Co., Limited, Greenock.
Spanish Transatlantic liner Infanta Isabel de Bourbon..	10,020	11,000	Denny, Dumbarton.

The following table from *Engineering*, London, gives the aggregate shipbuilding in the United Kingdom in the year 1912, as compared with 1911:

	1912 Tons	1911 Tons
Steam tonnage*	1,924,320	1,985,184
Sailing tonnage	129,680	47,874
Totals	2,054,000	2,033,058
His Majesty's dockyards....	54,230	55,600
Grand totals	2,108,230	2,088,658
Foreign-owned tonnage......	471,600	400,000
Per cent. of total...........	22.4	20.0
Total merchant tonnage**...	1,911,535	1,858,624
Per cent. of steam tonnage to total merchant tonnage	93.2	97.5
Horsepower of engines......	2,271,775	2,241,500
Per cent. of all naval tonnage to merchant tonnage	10.3	13.6

* Includes warships built in private yards.
** Excludes British and foreign warships.

The above table includes vessels smaller than the 100 ton limit observed by Lloyd's *Register* and floating dry docks.

GERMANY. In 1912 Germany achieved the record total of 200 vessels of 477,742 tons. The merchant shipping output showed an increase of nearly 120,000 tons over 1911, and the total increase, reckoning all ships, was 90,265 tons, the difference being due to the smaller number of warships built. The figures, however, did not take into account the large number of river craft launched at yards situated in inland waters. The list included the largest vessel built during the year, the *Imperator*, of about 52,000 tons, launched by the Vulcan Company at Hamburg. Five of the vessels built, representing 18,258 tons, were fitted with internal-combustion engines, the largest being an oil-carrying steamer of 5810 tons. There were 10 other vessels, averaging 271 tons, fitted with oil engines. There were under construction a turbine-steamer of about 58,000 tons, also at the Vulvan Works at Hamburg, a steamer of about 35,000 tons, three between 20,000 and 25,000 tons (one of them to be fitted with turbines), two between 10,000 and 15,000 tons, and 30 other vessels of between 5000 tons and 10,000 tons, including 11 to carry oil in bulk, three of which were to be fitted with Diesel engines.

FRANCE. The 1912 output, 108 vessels, of 169,889 tons, constituted a better record for France than for several years, except 1911, when the total was 14,295 tons greater. Regarding the purely merchant work, however, there was a decrease of nearly 15,000 tons. The output included six vessels of over 5000 tons; the largest was the *Mississippi*, of about 7000 tons, and a turbine Channel steamer *Rouen*, of 1656 tons, was designed for a speed of 22 knots. The merchant work on hand (175,000 tons) considerably exceeded the output of 1912, and four of the vessels were between 12,000 tons and 15,000 tons. Two of these were to be fitted with combination turbines and reciprocating machinery.

NETHERLANDS. The total output of all Dutch shipping was greater than in previous years, the 117 vessels launched making up 101,642 tons. As regards the merchant work, the total was 6400 tons above the output of 1911, and was the largest ever recorded in such return. As in the case of Germany, there were not included the vessels for river navigation, of which more than 90,000 tons were launched in 1912. The larger vessels launched were three, of between 6000 and 7000 tons. Here, again, the internal-combustion engine is making headway, two large vessels and 17 small vessels having been fitted with such machinery, while on hand there are two cargo steamers, each of 4500 tons, to be propelled by Diesel engines.

JAPAN. The total merchant and war tonnage produced included 174 vessels of 88,731 tons, which is about 7000 tons more than in the previous year. The merchant tonnage consisted almost entirely of small vessels, with the exception of two steamers of about 6500 tons. The increase in the merchant total, it will be seen, was about 13,400 tons.

AUSTRIA-HUNGARY. This country showed an increase of 30,637 tons. Part of this, however, was due to activity in warship-building, the increase in merchant work being only 3000 tons. The output was made up almost entirely of vessels between 5000 and 8000 tons. In progress there are new ships of 57,000 tons.

NORWAY. The Norwegian total, composed entirely of merchant vessels, with the exception of one warship of 103 tons, represented 50,358 tons, the measurement of 90 vessels, nearly all small craft. This was nearly 15,000 tons more than in the previous year.

BRITISH COLONIES. The output, of course, did not include any warships, and was 15,000 tons more than in 1911. Only a small proportion of the increase was due to sea-going tonnage.

DENMARK showed an increase of less than 7000 tons, and there were included in the output two vessels of 4934 tons and 3716 tons, fitted with Diesel engines. This method of propulsion was recorded by Lloyd's *Register* as being adopted by several cargo vessels of considerable size building in Copenhagen.

In the table below are given the steam and sailing vessels of over 100 tons, number, and net and gross tonnage of the several countries of the world, as recorded in Lloyd's *Register* for 1912-13:

depth far above the water line. The [illegible] machinery consisted of turbines of propulsion power.

The *Aquitania*, whose tonnage was stated at 45,000 tons, was also fitted with steam turbines which were adopted for two other ocean liners of 16,000 tons, and four steamers, of a total tonnage of 4150 tons. Including the *Britannic*, of 50,000 tons, there were nine steamers, with a total gross tonnage of 194,380 tons, to be fitted with a combination of steam turbines and reciprocating engines. One of these, of 32,500 tons, was for the Holland-Amerika Line; another, of 27,000 tons, for the Red Star Line; two Royal Mail liners, of 29,900 tons; two vessels, of 31,200 tons, for the Pacific Steam Navigation Company; one of 14,980 tons; and another of 8800 tons.

	Steam			Sail		Total	
British:	Number	Net tons	Gross tons	Number	Net tons	Number	Tonnage
United Kingdom	8,524	10,784,104	17,730,940	755	482,680	9,279	18,213,620
Colonies	1,490	858,972	1,471,830	675	188,910	2,165	1,660,740
Total	10,014	11,643,076	19,202,770	1,430	671,590	11,444	19,874,360
American (United States)							
Sea	1,171	1,174,378	1,797,929	1,558	1,050,900	2,729	2,848,829
Lakes	588	1,707,689	2,262,480	34	96,854	622	2,359,334
Philippine Islands	77	29,020	47,440	14	2,884	91	50,324
Total	1,836	2,911,087	4,107,849	1,606	1,150,638	3,442	5,258,487
Argentinian	228	102,066	171,631	66	32,720	294	204,351
Austro-Hungarian	392	560,695	902,704	3	363	395	903,067
Belgian	152	168,536	267,131	8	4,553	160	271,684
Brazilian	370	177,608	290,887	64	14,443	434	305,330
Chilean	98	69,191	108,834	42	36,418	140	145,252
Chinese	65	55,978	87,242	..	......	65	87,242
Cuban	60	38,289	62,236	7	1,083	67	63,319
Danish	548	413,122	703,520	281	54,079	829	757,599
Dutch	602	681,257	1,104,220	99	25,686	701	1,129,906
French	932	942,598	1,638,501	559	414,017	1,491	2,052,518
German	1,908	2,603,655	4,276,191	306	352,792	2,213	4,628,983
Greek	346	407,137	648,667	87	19,563	433	668,230
Haitian	5	2,017	3,387	...	....	5	3,387
Italian	536	677,209	1,119,121	554	279,461	1,090	1,398,582
Japanese	960	855,709	1,344,991	..	....	960	1,344,991
Mexican	41	22,480	36,813	14	3,129	55	39,942
Norwegian	1,495	1,019,987	1,695,321	637	597,275	2,132	2,292,596
Peruvian	19	13,142	25,346	38	16,916	57	42,262
Portuguese	105	50,982	85,481	100	26,603	205	112,084
Rumanian	22	14,884	28,539	1	285	23	28,824
Russian	690	440,519	754,627	517	181,964	1,207	936,591
Sarawak	4	2,015	3,373	..	....	4	3,373
Siamese	12	7,955	12,936	..	....	12	12,936
Spanish	526	461,571	756,136	64	15,849	590	771,985
Swedish	1,006	509,152	866,853	403	103,090	1,409	969,943
Turkish	141	70,591	120,412	175	60,645	316	181,057
Uruguayan	46	36,230	58,915	14	12,098	60	71,013
Venezuelan	8	2,420	4,232	5	679	13	4,911
Other countries: Bulgaria, Colombia, Costa Rica, Ecuador, Egypt, Honduras, Liberia, Nicaragua, Oman, Panama, Persia, Salvador, Samos, Zanzibar, etc.	50	16,766	29,311	20	6,561	70	35,872
Total	23,217	24,977,920	40,518,177	7,079	4,082,500	30,316	44,600,677

NOTABLE STEAMSHIPS. The year 1912 was noteworthy for the building of three steamships larger than any previously built—the Hamburg-American liner *Imperator*, the Cunard liner *Aquitania*, and the White Star liner *Britannic*. The *Imperator* was 919 feet long, 96-foot beam, and of over 50,000 tons displacement, being some 5000 tons larger than the *Olympic*. This vessel, which had been under construction since June 18, 1910, was launched from the Vulcan Shipbuilding Works at Hamburg. She weighed 27,000 tons when launched, and was the first four-screw turbine steamship of the German mercantile fleet. The ship was supplied with both longitudinal and transverse bulkheads and a double bottom, the longitudinal bulkhead in the engine room extending from the bottom 50 feet upward to the second

In 1912 eight commercial ships with oil engines were put into commission, as against three such vessels in 1911, the horsepower amounting to 3350, and averaging 1660 per ship. The three pioneer vessels made successful records during the year, and two of them made extensive trips to the Far East. Most of the new construction for the year was being built in the works of Holland, Denmark, and Germany, while an English Diesel combination was established at Glasgow during the year.

Two vessels, of between 3000 and 4000 tons each, along with a number of small craft, were being fitted with internal-combustion engines. Attention, however, was called to the fact that with forty steamers, of a total tonnage of about 231,000 tons, being built to carry oil in bulk, this number of motor-ships seemed small; because if marine engineers and ship-owners were satisfied with the reliability of the oil-engine, oil-carrying ships presented a most favorable opportunity for the application of the system, as commercial conditions were favorable. No better scope for the application of the system could be found. But British firms were obviously indisposed, with the great demand for tonnage manifested during the year, to risk experiments on such a scale.

SHIPPING. See SHIPBUILDING.

SHOES. See BOOTS AND SHOES.

SHOOTING. The United States carried off the honors in shooting in 1912 by winning the most important events in three international matches. These contests were held at Buenos Ayres, Argentina, Ottawa, Canada, and at the Olympic games in Stockholm. In the competition at Buenos Ayres there were five marksmen on a side, each man firing 120 shots—40 standing, 40 kneeling, and 40 prone—at a range of 350 meters. Out of a highest possible score of 6000 points, the U. S. team made 4729 and Argentina 4598. The individual championship was won by Capt. Stuart W. Wise of Massachusetts. In the matches for the Palma Trophy at Ottawa, the U. S. defeated Canada by 1720 points to 1712 at 800, 900 and 1000 yard ranges. For a summary of the shooting matches at Stockholm, see OLYMPIC GAMES.

The principal rifle matches held in the U. S. during the year were those held under the auspices of the National Rifle Association at Sea Girt, N. J. The individual military championship was won by Corporal C. B. Long, of the Massachusetts Volunteer Militia, with a score of 235. Other events and winners were: Wimbledon Cup (1000 yards, 20 shots), A. L. Briggs, U. S. A., 497; Leech Cup (800, 900, and 1000 yards, 7 shots), Sergeant F. H. Keene, Massachusetts Volunteer Militia, 104; Marine Corps (600 and 1000 yards, 15 shots), Capt. G. H. Emerson, Ohio National Guard, 194; Regimental Team match, First Infantry District of Columbia National Guard, 754; Company Team match, Company K, First Infantry, D. C. N. G., 354; Revolver Team match, First Squadron, New York National Guard, 1031.

The outdoor championship matches of the U. S. Revolver Association were held throughout the various States from September 28 to October 6. The winners of the more important events were: Target revolver, A. M. Poindexter, Denver, 467; target pistol, L. P. Castaldini, Springfield, Mass.; military revolver and military record matches, Dr. J. H. Snook, Columbus, Ohio; military revolver team match, Denver Revolver Club. The Association was represented in the Olympic Games (q. v.)

The world's amateur championship at trap shooting was won by George L. Lyon, who defeated L. S. German at Wilmington, Del. German, however, retained his championship title in the professional matches. The world's amateur team championship went to J. R. Graham and R. W. Clancy. B. M. Higginson captured the national amateur championship.

The intercollegiate indoor championship of the U. S. (rifles) was won by the Massachusetts Agricultural College, and the outdoor championship by Harvard.

SHUTTLEMAKERS' DISEASE. See INDUSTRIAL DISEASE.

SIAM. An independent kingdom of southeastern Asia, extending approximately from the 6th to the 20th degree of north latitude and from the 97th to the 106th degree of east longitude; ength from north to south, approximately 1020 miles, and greatest breadth, 480. Coast line, 1300 miles; total area, about 198,-900 sq. miles.

POPULATION, ETC. The country is divided into 17 monthons (circles), subdivided into 79 muangs (provinces), which are again subdivided into 409 amphurs (districts); these are in turn made up of 3993 tambons (villages), divided into mu bans (hamlets). According to an official report issued in November, 1910, the population of the kingdom was 7,561,977; of whom lay males numbered 3,707,466 and lay females 3,729,021, and persons in holy orders numbered 142,636. The racial figures for the Bayap and Isarm monthons are not yet available. In the remaining monthons the Siamese numbered 4,419,506 (639,920 in Bangkok monthon); Chinese, 370,134 (197,918); Malays, 363,756 (20,764); Cambodians, 83,762; Mohns, 27,260; Karens, 17,512; Annamites, 6647. There are upwards of 2000 Europeans and Americans resident in Siam, mostly in Bangkok.

The ministry of public instruction is generally responsible for all government schools. It has drawn up a plan of education for the entire country, which is now partly in operation. There are besides government-aided private schools, and several missions. The religion of the court is Buddhism, and large educational powers are in the hands of the Buddhist monks.

PRODUCTION. Agriculture is carried on under primitive conditions. Wooden plows are used, drawn by water buffaloes in the stiff lowland clays and by bullocks on the sandier highlands. Irrigation is practiced, and rice is the leading crop. Many of the varieties grown are considered by experts to be among the finest in the world. The production next in importance after rice is teak. The forests in which this species occurs are situated for the most part in the monthons of Bayap, Nakonsawan, and Pitsanulok, and are leased to private companies for a term of years, usually 15. Teak is worked by girdling the trees, leaving them standing for two years to season, and felling them; they are then dragged, mostly by elephants, to the nearest streams, down which they are floated to the duty station at Paknampoh, where they are measured and the duty is collected before they are sent to Bangkok. Before the organization of a government forestry department the teak forests were ruthlessly exploited, all the more accessible tracts having been so overworked that they will supply no more teak for another fifty years. Rosewood and other valuable timbers are found in lower Siam, and efforts are being made to work them upon a commercial basis.

The only minerals worked on a commercial scale are tin and wolfram. Seven-eighths of the tin comes from the Puket monthon (70,718 piculs in 1910-11). The output from the east coast is small, though it is hoped that the new railway will develop the industry there. Since the cession to the French of the Pailin district (1907) the gem industry has ceased to be of importance; gems are found near Krat and elsewhere, but their value is negligible.

COMMERCE. In the table below are seen imports and exports for 1909-10 and 1910-11, with the five-year average from 1905-1910, in ticals (1 tical=about 36.5 cents):

	1909-10	1910-11	Average
Imports:			
3% goods*	58,818,199	58,389,400	61,219,028
Liquors	1,452,786	1,416,979	1,618,909
Gold leaf	3,129,306	3,206,972	5,906,350
Opium	2,341,250	2,109,747	1,916,932
Treasure	4,070,070	3,082,230	3,589,856
Total	69,811,711	68,205,328	74,251,075
Exports:			
Rice†	85,078,585	91,060,879	81,021,633
Teak	6,975,057	7,624,092	11,896,244
Treasure	1,618,588	223,140	982,830
Misc.‡	7,548,658	8,549,231	7,989,429
Re-exports	1,349,546	1,450,479	1,287,149
Total	102,570,434	108,907,821	103,177,285

* Cotton goods in the 1910-11 trade, 11,808,211 ticals; silk goods, 3,744,304; gunny sacks, 3,453,391; provisions, 4,775,442; oil, 3,636,652; machinery, hardware, etc. † 17,588,349 piculs in 1910-11. Buffalo- and cow-hides (1910-11), 1,267,940 ticals; bullocks, 248,820; buffalo horns, 190,571; other horns, 39,732; hogs, 226,923; fish (platoo), 849,613; other fish, 729,723; dried mussels, 460,012; pepper, 689,070; rough rubies, 30,000; tin oxide, 15,943; etc.

Total imports 1911-12, 73,139,000 ticals (U. K., 17,971,000; Singapore, 11,078,000; China, 10,024,000; Hongkong, 8,741,000; British India, 5,034,000; Germany, 4,783,000; Dutch possessions, 3,026,000); total exports, 84,634,000 (through Singapore, 40,111,000; Hongkong, 25,618,000). Rice exports 1911-12, 65,841,000 ticals; teak, 6,113,000. Vessels entered 1911-12, 735 steamers, of 624,608 tons. Merchant marine, 1912, 29 steamers, of 8725 tons, and 91 sailing, of 7442.

RAILWAYS. The total length (April, 1911) of state and private railways was 1093 kilometers, of which 106 kms. were privately owned narrow-gauge lines and 987 belonged to the state, as follows: Bangkok to Korat, 264 kms.; the Lopburi line, 42 kms., which constitutes a section of the projected Northern Railway; the Southwestern, 151.5 kms., from Bangkok via Nakonchaisi to the Mekong, thence south to Petchaburi; another section of the Northern, 118 kms., Lopburi to Paknampoh, with extension to Pitsanulok, 138 kms. The first section of the Eastern line, from Bangkok to Petriu, 63 kms., was opened in January, 1908; the section of the Northern, from Pitsanulok to Ban Dara, 67.7 kms., on November 11, 1908; the section Ban Dara, Utaradit, Pang Ton Phung, 52.5 kms., August 15, 1909, together with a branch from Ban Dara to Sawankalok, 29 kms.

The Pang Ton Phung to Meh Puak line, 19 kms., was opened June 1, 1911, and replaces the caravan route from Utaradit to Phrae over the Kao Plung pass. The first section of the Southern line, Petchaburi to Ban Cha Am, 36 kms., was completed June 19, 1911, and a further section of 24 kms. to Hua Hin before the end of the year.

Under construction on the Northern is the short section of 5 kms. from Meh Puak to Dene Chai, the temporary terminus until the extension to Chiengmai is authorized. The ultimate terminus of the Southern Railway is the Kelantan boundary by an extension from Trang, a total distance of 970 kms (distance from Petchaburi to Trang, 676 kms.). The line will serve a population of over 1¼ millions, and open up fertile tracts; it will also develop the mining districts and accelerate the mail service to Europe.

FINANCE. The estimated revenue in 1911-12 was 62,321,000 ticals. Ordinary expenditure, 62,235,539; for railway construction, 9,660,670; for irrigation, 2,014,399—total extraordinary, 11,675,069; making a total estimated expenditure of 73,910,608. The public debt (1911) stood at £7,000,000; paper currency, March 31, 1911, 18,770,220 ticals. The reserve fund established under the Gold Standard act now stands at £945,941, held entirely in gold, and reserved absolutely for the purpose of maintaining the stability of exchange.

ARMY. A standing army of about 25,000 is maintained, and under the terms of the law of 1905 a system of universal military training was in force. The troops are armed with Mannlicher and Mauser rifles.

GOVERNMENT. The government is an absolute monarchy, and succession is limited to the princes of the blood ranking highest among the king's sons. The present ing being without male issue, the succession passes presumptively through the line of the queen-mother's sons according to their respective ages. Reigning king, (Somdetch Phra Paramindr) Maha Vajiravudh; born January 1, 1881, proclaimed successor and crown prince 1895, and succeeded to the throne October 23, 1910. He was educated at Oxford and has traveled extensively. Bangkok is the seat of government.

It was announced early in March that documents had been discovered revealing a widespread conspiracy at Bangkok involving officers of the army and navy, in both of which branches of the service a mutiny had been brought about. This discovery led to the arrest of many persons. They were tried by court-martial, which sentenced three to imprisonment for life and twenty to twenty years.

SIBERIA. See RUSSIA, and EXPLORATION.

SIERRA LEONE. A British colony and protectorate (32,110 sq. miles; 1,400,000 inhabitants, as estimated December 31, 1910); a country on the west coast of Africa. The capital, Freetown, had (1911) 34,090 inhabitants. The colony proper contained (census of 1911) 75,370 inhabitants (40,896 males); of whom 702 were white (640 males) and 74,668 (40,256 males) colored. The death rate in Freetown in 1910 was 27 per thousand.

	1907	1908	1909	1910
Imports	£ 988,022	£ 813,700	£ 978,807	£1,162,470
Exports	831,259	736,755	981,466	1,249,367a
Revenue	359,104	321,000	361,326	425,215
Expend.	345,567	341,871	326,746	361,222
Shipping*	1,890,531	2,046,152	2,191,123	1,994,290

* Tonnage entered and cleared.
a Palm kernels, £644,684; kola nuts, £191,942; silver, £185,965; palm oil, £62,852; coal, etc., £62,434; ginger, £33,288; raw rubber, £7666.

The main railway (the first to be opened in British West Africa) extends from Freetown to Baima, 220¼ miles. Branch lines run to the Hill Station (6 miles) and to government wharves, etc. A branch line from Boia to the Rokell River was under construction in 1912. Telegraph lines, 298 miles. Sir E. M. Merewether was governor in 1912.

SILK. The silk industry in 1912 suffered from various developments in world politics. The revolution and the new republic in China disturbed business conditions in that country, while the war between Italy and Turkey involved two important silk-producing nations. Likewise the Balkan War had its effect upon raw silk production, for in the silk production for 1911-12 European Turkey and the Balkan States were responsible for 7,034,747 kilograms of cocoons or 603,000 kilograms of silk, which production was divided into 375,000 kilograms produced by Salonica and Adrianople and 228,000 by the Balkan States and Greece. The production of France and Italy, however, increased during the year, and a greater amount of raw silk was handled in the European conditioning works than in 1911, while European mills were busy throughout the year, though with a less active demand near its close. The imports from Japan to the United States were greater in 1912 than in 1911, but to Europe less, while the shipments from Shanghai to the United States were also greater in 1912 than in 1911, Canton, however, showing a small decrease in 1912 from the figures for 1911. Italy made shipments in the last three months of 1912 to the United States more than double those of 1911. Of the old crop, 54 per cent. of the total exports of the Asiatic market was sent to the United States, as against 39 per cent. taken by Europe, the balance going to India and the Eastern markets.

SILK CROP ESTIMATE. The world silk crop for 1912-1913 at the end of the year was estimated at about 24,000,000 kilograms (52,910,000 pounds), or an excess over the season of 1911-1912 of about 6 per cent. The reports from almost all of the silk-producing countries showed an increase over the previous year's crop, except in the Levant, where a shortage of about 10 per cent. from the previous year was estimated, due to a deficiency in the yellow cocoon of Syria and of the white cocoon in Bruti and Adrianople. Italy's crop for 1912 was estimated at about 15 per cent. in excess of that for 1911. France showed an increase of about 30 per cent. Hungary and Spain were approximately the same, as was also Japan, while Canton, where the 1911 production was abnormally small, showed an increase of about the normal average. The accompanying table from the *American Silk-Journal* gives the estimated totals of the different countries compared with the results for the two years previous, the quantities being in kilograms.

Europe	5,050,000	4,330,000	4,700,000
Levant	2,550,000	2,800,000	2,800,000
Japan	9,300,000	9,320,000	8,930,000
China	4,700,000	4,300,000	3,510,000
Canton	2,100,000	1,680,000	2,630,000
India	300,000	220,000	230,000
	24,000,000	22,650,000	22,800,000

This table does not include the tussah raw silk, the estimated production of which, in the season 1912-13, was given at 8,439,000 pounds.

It was reported that the secretaries of agriculture and commerce in France were preparing a bill to make compulsory the indelible marking of each and every article containing artificial silk as such, in order to maintain the quality of the French silk products and protect natural silk against the invasion of the artificial product. Nevertheless, in Europe artificial silk continues to make headway and a number of large factories are now at work on its production. Many of the leading makers, however, failed to show a profit and several concerns reported a net loss on the year's business. On the other hand an English concern operating in the United States was reported as paying 35 per cent. in dividends, while a German factory at Elberfeld paid 36 per cent. These concerns, however, were considered the most successful manufacturers in the business, and it was the general opinion that taking the industry as a whole the gains and losses would about balance.

The silk industry in the United States was not particularly concerned with tariff questions during the year, but at its close, it was anticipated that changes more or less radical would be made in Schedule L.

Silk manufacturers of the United States were busy throughout the year, but with varying degrees of prosperity, as in many cases it was thought that the manufacturing business has been conducted upon too close a margin. Nevertheless, the use of silk greatly increased and silk and silk fabrics were favored by fashion. However, the actual consumption of silk fabrics during the year was restricted by the fashion which continued to decree narrow skirts and limited material. This was offset in some degree by the use of more costly and elegant silks and their continuance in general favor.

The total number of silk manufacturers in the United States in 1912 as given by *Davison's Directory of the Silk Trade* (1913) was stated at 1552, an increase of 97 mills over the number in 1911. In New Jersey there were in 1912 380 as against 382 in 1911, and of these 293 were in Paterson, as compared with 300 in 1911. The State of New York had 375 in 1912, as compared with 348 in 1911, or a gain of 27, while Pennsylvania had 473 in 1912, as compared with 420 in the previous year. There were 394 broad silk mills in 1912, as against 387 in 1911, 25 more ribbon mills and 32 more mills manufacturing webbing and narrow fabrics. In 1912 there were 199 throwing and spun silk mills, or 3 less than in 1911, while the knit goods mills using silk were 340, as against 250 in the earlier year. The number of dyers and finishers of silk and silk mixed goods at the end of 1912 was 133, as compared with 123 in 1911, while there were seven more mills devoted to cotton and silk, and worsted and silk mixtures.

SILK, ARTIFICIAL. See CHEMISTRY, INDUSTRIAL.

SILK, WORLD'S PRODUCTION OF. See AGRICULTURE.

SILOXYD GLASS. See CHEMISTRY, INDUSTRIAL.

SILVER. See METALLURGY.

SILVER. The production of silver in the United States as a whole and by States is shown in the table on page 656, prepared by the director of the mint. It will be seen from this table that the production in the continental United States was slightly larger in 1912 than in 1911:

WORLD PRODUCTION. The silver production of the world in 1911-12 is shown in the table on page 656, which is taken from the *Engineering and Mining Journal*. It will be seen from this table that Mexico continues to be the chief producer of silver, with the United States second and Canada third:

UNITED STATES SILVER PRODUCTION

(Fine Ounces)

	1911	1912
Alabama	174	237
Alaska	275,691	516,224
Arizona	1,594,428	3,456,989
California	2,737,336	1,255,192
Colorado	7,530,940	8,350,316
Georgia	225	65
Idaho	7,507,802	7,703,721
Illinois	4,648	3,740
Maryland	....	201
Michigan	507,234	542,360
Missouri	56,228	25,311
Montana	11,116,278	12,338,589
Nevada	10,651,571	13,042,118
New Mexico	1,142,337	1,251,412
North Carolina	2,227	3,783
Oregon	69,116	79,896
South Carolina	....	40
South Dakota	106,188	200,796
Tennessee	126,683	109,773
Texas	442,486	420,994
Utah	12,679,633	12,795,072
Virginia	45	7,974
Washington	142,196	258,152
Wyoming	1,009	298
Unassigned	3,601,542	....
Total, Contin'tal U. S.	60,396,017	62,364,253
Philippine Islands	3,383	5,650
Total	60,399,400	62,369,903
Total value	$32,195,296	$37,942,773

SILVER PRODUCTION OF THE WORLD

(Fine Ounces)

	1911	1912
Mexico	79,032,440	76,500,000
United States	60,399,400	62,369,903
Canada	32,740,748	35,250,000
Australasia	16,578,421	17,950,000
Other countries	36,621,835	37,500,000
Total	225,372,844	229,569,903

EXPORTS AND IMPORTS. The total imports of silver into the United States in 1912 amounted to $44,402,933. The total exports to $64,343,-611. The exports from the United States are chiefly to Great Britain, though in 1912 there were considerable sales to France for coinage purposes.

MARKET IN 1912. The monthly average price of silver in New York in 1911-12 is shown in the table below, which is taken from the *Engineering and Mining Journal:*

. MONTLHY PRICE OF SILVER

Month	1911	1912
January	53.795	56.260
February	52.222	59,043
March	52.745	58.375
April	53.325	59.207
May	53.308	60.880
June	53.043	61.290
July	52.630	60.654
August	52.171	61.606
September	52.440	63.078
October	53.340	63.471
November	55.719	62.792
December	54.905	63.365
Year	53.304	60.835

New York quotations, cents per ounce troy, fine ounce, sterling silver, 0.925 fine.

SINGAPORE. See STRAITS SETTLEMENTS.

SINGER, EDMUND. A Hungarian violinist, died January 26, 1912. He was born at Fort Totis, Hungary, in 1831. He studied music under Ellinger at Budapest and later with Ridley Kohne. At the same time he appeared in public in concerts in Austria and Germany. He later studied at the Paris Conservatory. In 1846 he became first violinist of the Budapest Opera and ten years later was conductor at Vienna. From that time until his death he was one of the conductors of the Royal Opera at Stuttgart and professor of the Conservatory in that city. He was regarded as a brilliant concert master and a fine teacher. He composed a variety of compositions for the violin and was the author of a method which became popular. Shortly before his death his reminiscences were published.

SKATING. The international outdoor skating championships were held at Saranac Lake in February, R. M. McLean, of Chicago, and R. L. Wheeler, of Montreal, winning a majority of the events. McLean finished first in the mile and three miles, while Wheeler won the quarter-mile, half-mile, and two miles. L. Roe, of Toronto, captured the 220-yard dash. In the international indoor championships held at Boston, McLean won the half-mile, mile, and two miles; H. B. Kaad, of Chicago, won the quarter-mile, and O. B. Bush, of Vancouver, the 220-yard dash. Edmund Lamy and Morris Wood met at Saranac Lake to decide the American professional championship, Lamy winning the half-mile, three-quarter-mile, mile, and two miles, and Wood capturing the 220-yard dash and quarter-mile. Abroad, O. Mathiesen, of Christiania, established three new world's amateur records. He skated 500 meters in 44⅕ seconds, 1500 meters in 2 minutes, 20⅗ seconds, and 10,-000 meters in 17 minutes, 46 3/10 seconds.

The winners of the various roller-skating championships held in the United States were: 1-mile world's professional, H. Davidson, St. Paul, Minn.; 2-mile world's professional, R. Peters, St. Louis; 1-mile world's amateur, L. Kimm, Chicago; 1-mile eastern professional, W. Blackburn, New York; 2-mile eastern professional, W. Blackburn; 3-mile eastern professional, W. Blackburn; 4-mile eastern professional, F. J. Clarke, New York; 5-mile, W. Blackburn; 1-mile eastern amateur, J. Timney, Newark; 2-mile eastern amateur, F. J. Clarke, New York; 3-mile eastern amateur, W. Burke, Brooklyn; 4-mile eastern amateur, W. Burke; 5-mile eastern amateur, J. Timney.

SKEAT, WALTER WILLIAM. An English philologist and educator, died October 7, 1912. He was born in London in 1835 and was educated at Christ's College, Cambridge. In 1860 he was elected a fellow of this college. In the same year he was ordained to the ministry and held curacies at East Dereham and at Godalming. Owing to an affection of the throat he was obliged to abandon the ministry. He returned to Cambridge and resumed studies of English, philology, and literature. In 1873 he assisted in the foundation of the English Dialect Society, becoming its first director and afterwards its president. He had already begun the editing of the Middle English texts for the Royal English Text Society which had been established by F. J. Furnival. In 1878 he was appointed the Elrington and Bosworth professorship of Anglo-Saxon at Cambridge and in 1883 was reëlected a fellow at Christ's College. He was a very voluminous writer on philological subjects and was one of the most eminent philologists living at the time of his death. He covered in his writings almost all of Chaucer, and wrote several dictionaries of words used at various periods. Among his published writings are: *Launcelot of the Laik* (1865); *Piers the Plowman* (1865-1884); *Etymological Dictionary of the English Language* (1879-1884); *Notes on English Etymology* (1901); *Primer of Classical and English Philology* (1905); *Proverbs of Alfred* (1907); and *Early English proverbs* (1910).

SKYSCRAPERS. See TALL BUILDINGS.

SLEEPING SICKNESS. The activities of the British Sleeping Sickness Commission, appointed by the Colonial Office under the general direction of Sir David Bruce, were centred on discovering how large a part the fly *Glossina morsitans* had in the transmission of the trypanosomes and to what extent wild and domestic animals served as reservoirs of infection. Until 1911 the tsetse fly, *Glossina palpalis*, was believed to be the sole carrier of sleeping sickness; but the occurrence of cases in regions where this fly did not exist (Rhodesia and Nyasaland) made further study imperative. Drs. Kinghorne and York, working in the Luangwa Valley, northern Rhodesia, found that *Glossina morsitans* transmits, in nature as well as in laboratory experiments, the human trypanosomes of that region, and that wild animals are naturally infected. Ninety-eight wild animals were examined, 77 antelopes and 8 wild pigs. In 7 antelopes and 1 pig human trypanosomes were found. It was also shown that in other parts of Africa cattle and other domestic animals may harbor human trypanosomes without detriment to health. Consequently, it is possible that domestic animals, subject to the bites of *Glossina morsitans*, also harbor the human trypanosomes in Rhodesia and Nyasaland. This will greatly complicate the p em, because it is out of the question to decide the destruction of all the domestic animals in Nyasaland. Similarly, it follows that the destruction of all or the greater number of the wild animals, which has been advocated, would be useless. It is possible that if this were done the fly, unable to obtain the blood of these animals, would attack man and the domestic animals to a greater extent. The work done and conclusions reached by the investigators in Northern Rhodesia are summarized as follows: (1) The human trypanosomes in the Luangwa Valley are transmitted by *Glossina morsitans*; (2) approximately 5 per cent. of the flies may become permanently infected and capable of transmitting the virus; (3) the period which elapses between infection and outbreak is fourteen days; (4) an infected fly retains the power of transmitting the disease during its life and is infective at each meal (5) mechanical transmission does not occur if a period of twenty-four hours has elapsed since the infecting meal; (6) there is some evidence that in the interval between the infecting feed and the date on which transmission becomes possible the parasites found in the flies are non-infective; (7) certain species of buck have been found to be infected with the human trypanosome; (8) a native dog has been found infected.

SMALL-POX AND VACCINATION. Dr. R. L. Dixon states that during the first three months of 1912 there were reported 283 cases of small-pox in Michigan. The vaccination histories of these cases are as follows: 17 patients were vaccinated between 1 and 10 years previously; 5 between 10 and 20 years previously; 1 between 20 and 30 years previously; 2 as far back as between 50 and 60 years previously, and several "in childhood," "years ago," "doubtful, if ever," etc.; but 245 had never been vaccinated. It costs Michigan $150,000 a year to take care of indigent small-pox patients and to protect the unvaccinated. Dixon believes that these figures constitute as powerful an argument for thorough vaccination and could well be advanced.

In a recent bulletin, issued by the Public Health and Marine Hospital Service the laws and regulations of the several States relating to vaccination have been compiled and analytically compared. There is a marked lack of uniformity; legal requirements for compulsory vaccination exist only in Kentucky, the Philippine Islands, and Porto Rico. In Kentucky, the law requires that children shall be vaccinated within twelve months after birth. All minors and adults are also to be vaccinated. Persons coming into the State to reside must be vaccinated within six months. But there seems to be no penalty for violation of the law and the statute has not been enforced. In the Philippine Islands, every child three months of age must be vaccinated. Persons not furnishing satisfactory evidence of immunity to small-pox must be vaccinated as often as required by the health authorities. In Porto Rico, the board of health requires that every person shall possess a certificate of vaccination. Arizona, Hawaii, Maryland, New Mexico and North Dakota have laws requiring the vaccination of children, which, enforced, would in time produce a population of which large proportion would have been vaccinated at least once. In Hawaii, every child is to be presented for vaccination within six months after birth. In Maryland, it is made the duty of parents and guardians to have children under their care vaccinated within twelve months after birth or as soon thereafter as practicable. Guardians are also to have other persons under their control, and not previously vaccinated, vaccinated prior to November 1. In New Mexico, it is the duty of the county school superintendents to see that all children of school age in their respective counties are vaccinated or have been vaccinated within a year. In North Dakota, parents or guardians are to cause minors or other persons under their care or custody to be vaccinated.

Although small-pox has been widely prevalent in the United States for years, it has, probably because of its general extreme mildness, received less attention than should have been given to it. In many sections it has been so mild that the death rate has been as low as 0.2 per cent. In most countries, the death-rate varies from 15 to 40 per cent., and this was apparently true in the United States previous to 1898. The mildness of the present form of small-pox does not show that the people of this country are peculiarly immune or resistant to the disease, as has been proved by repeated local outbreaks of the virulent form. See VITAL STATISTICS.

SMILEY, ALBERT KEITH. An American educator and humanitarian, died December 2, 1912. He was born at Vassalboro, Me., in 1828 and graduated from Haverford College in 1849.

He was an instructor in that institution until 1853. In that year, with his brother, he founded and became principal of the English and Classical Academy at Philadelphia, remaining in this position until 1857. He became in 1858 principal of the Oak Grove Seminary at Vassalboro, Me., and two years later was chosen principal of the Friends' Boarding School at Providence, R. I. Here he remained until 1879. In 1869 he purchased property at Lake Mohonk, Ulster County, New York, which by subsequent additions ultimately included 5500 acres. Here in 1870 he built a hotel as a summer resort. From 1882 to 1904 he yearly invited to this place about 200 persons as his personal guests for four days to discuss the Indian question. From 1904 onward the question of other dependent peoples (Philippines, Porto Rico and Hawaii) was included. During each spring since 1894 a similar conference was held in the interest of international arbitration. To this about 300 personal guests were invited for four days. In 1889 Mr. Smiley purchased jointly with his brother a large property at Redlands, Cal. This property was thrown open to the public and is visited yearly by many tourists. In 1898 he presented to the city of Redlands a public library and an adjoining park at a cost of $60,000. He was a member of the board of trustees of Brown University and was a member of the original board of trustees of Bryn Mawr College. He was a member of many philanthropic and humanitarian societies and organizations. The reports of the conferences on international arbitration have been published each year and have contained valuable data bearing on the subject.

SMITH COLLEGE. An institution for the higher education of women at Northampton, Mass., founded in 1871. The enrollment in all the departments of the college in the autumn of 1912 was 1523. The actual teaching faculty numbered 110. There were 30 others, instructors and assistants. During the year Professor H. M. Tyler and Professor B. K. Emerson retired, and Miss Ada M. Comstock, A. M., Litt. D., was appointed dean of the college. A conditional pledge of $200,000 was made by the general education board. The productive funds of the college amounted in 1911-12 to $1,227,-821, and the income to $376,401. The library contained 40,300 volumes. President, Marion L. Burton.

SMITH, Edwin. An American astronomer and geodesist, died December 2, 1912. He was born in New York City in 1851 and graduated from the College of the City of New York in 1871. He carried on private studies in astronomy and geodesy and in 1870 entered the United States Coast and Geodetic Survey, of which he was appointed assistant in 1874. In the same year he was astronomer in charge of a party to observe the transit of Venus at the Chatham Islands in the South Pacific Ocean. He had charge of a party for the same object at Auckland, New Zealand, in 1882. He determined the force of gravity at Auckland, Singapore, Sydney, Tokyo, San Francisco, and Washington. From 1879 to 1894 he was in charge of the instrument division of the United States Coast and Geodetic Survey. During this time he also carried on observations for the variation of latitude at Rockville, Md. In 1895 he left the Coast and Geodetic Survey and was with the New York State Land Survey until 1897, when he was again appointed assistant in the Coast and Geodetic Survey. In 1899 he established the International Geodetic Association Latitude Observatory at Gaithersburg, Md., and made observations for variation of latitude from October, 1899, to January, 1901. From the latter date until the time of his death he was engaged on astronomical, magnetic, and geodetic work of the Survey. He was a member of many learned societies and was one of the founders of the Cosmos Club, Washington. He contributed several papers, published as appendices to Coast and Geodetic Service Reports.

SMITH, Gerritt. An American organist and composer, died July 21, 1912. He was born in Hagerstown, Md., in 1859. He was educated at Hobart College and studied music and architecture abroad. He was successively organist at St. Paul's Cathedral, Buffalo, St. Peter's Church, Albany, and the Old South Church, New York. This position he held from 1895 to the time of his death. He was professor of music at the Union Theological Seminary and was professor of theory at the Master School, Brooklyn. In this city he gave over three hundred free organ recitals. He was the founder and for six years the president of the Manuscript Society of Composers and was at one time honorary president of the American Guild of Organists. He was well known as a composer and writer on musical topics. Among his compositions are: *King David*, a cantata; *Song Cycle;* and over seventy-five songs, numerous piano pieces, carols, and church anthems.

SMITH, John Bernhardt An American entomologist and educator, died March 12, 1912. He was born in New York City in 1858 and was educated in the public schools. After studying law he was admitted to the bar in 1879. In 1884 he acted as special agent of the entomological division of the United States Department of Agriculture. He was appointed assistant curator of the United States National Museum in 1886. In 1898 he was appointed State entomologist of New Jersey. He acted as professor of entomology at Rutgers College and entomologist of the New Jersey Agricultural College Experiment Stations from 1889 to the time of his death. He did notable service in checking the mosquito pest. He was a member of many learned societies and contributed many articles to government and technical publications. He was the author of *Economic Entomology for the Farmer and Fruit Grower* (1896), and *Our Insect Friends and Enemies.*

SMITH, William. An American soldier, died January 17, 1912. He was born in Orwell, Vt., in 1831 and graduated from the University of Vermont in 1854. He served throughout the Civil War as paymaster and as regimental officer. He was brevetted lieutenant-colonel in 1865. After the close of the war he was appointed major and paymaster in the United States army and was promoted to various grades until he became brigadier-general and paymaster-general in 1890. He was retired by operation of law in 1895.

SMITH, William Waugh. An American educator, died November 29, 1912. He was born in Warrenton, Va., in 1845 and served in the Confederate army from 1862 to 1865. He was twice wounded. After the war he studied at Randolph-Macon College. In the same year he became associate and later senior principal of Bethel Academy. In this position he remained until 1878, when he became a professor in the Randolph-Macon College. In 1886 he was chosen president of this institution and in 1897 chancellor. He raised large sums to build and endow the Virginia institutions organized into the Randolph-Macon System. He was founder of the Randolph-Macon Woman's College at Lynchburg, Va. He was the author of *Outlines of Psychology* (1880); *A Comparative Chart of Syntax of Latin, Greek, German, French and English* (1882), and numerous educational tracts, magazine articles, and poems.

SMITHSONIAN INSTITUTION (The). A learned institution in Washington, D. C., established in 1846 under the terms of the will of James Smithson of England, who bequeathed his fortune "to the United States of America, to found at Washington, under the name of the Smithsonian Institution, an establishment for the increase and diffusion of knowledge among men." This bequest, which eventually amounted to $541,379.63, was formally accepted by the United States, and the institution was established by an act of Congress, approved August 10, 1846. The original endowment has been increased by gifts and bequests from Thomas G. Hodgkins and others, to a total permanent fund, June 30, 1912, of $986,918.69. The interest on this amounted to $58,375.12, and with various other funds provided by friends of the institution for special purposes, made available a total of $107,168.31 for carrying on the operations and activities of the institution for the year ending June 30, 1912. For the maintenance of the six government branches under the direction of the Smithsonian, Congress appropriated $742,000.

The statutory members of the institution are the President of the United States, the Vice-President, the chief justice, and the heads of the executive departments. A governing body, known as the board of regents, and consisting of the Vice-President of the United States, the chief justice, three members of the Senate, three members of the House of Representatives, and six citizens selected by joint resolution of Congress, administers the affairs of the institution. This board elects a chancellor as its presiding officer. The present incumbent is the chief justice of the United States. The roll of the regents at the close of the year 1912 was as follows: Edward D. White, chief justice of the United States, chancellor; Shelby M. Cullom, member of the Senate; Henry Cabot Lodge, member of the Senate; Augustus O. Bacon, member of the Senate; John Dalzell, member of the House of Representatives; Scott Ferris, member of the House of Representatives; Irvin S. Pepper, member of the House of Representatives; Andrew D. White, citizen of New York; Alexander Graham Bell, citizen of Washington, D. C.; George Gray, citizen of Delaware; Charles F. Choate, Jr., citizen of Massachusetts; John B Henderson, Jr., citizen of Washington, D. C., and Charles W. Fairbanks, citizen of Indiana.

The executive officer is the secretary of the institution, who is elected by the board of regents. Dr. Charles D. Walcott has served in this capacity since 1907. There are also two assistant secretaries: Dr. Richard Rathbun, in charge of the National Museum, and Dr. Frederick W. True, in charge of the Library and Exchanges.

The institution administers the United States National Museum (q. v.), including the National Gallery of Art; the Bureau of American Ethnology; the National Zoölogical Park; the Smithsonian Astrophysical Observatory; the International Exchange Service; and the Regional Bureau for the United States of the International Catalogue of Scientific Literature.

Explorations and Researches. During the past year several scientific exploration and research parties have been conducting field operations under the direction of the institution so far as its limited income and the generosity of its friends have permitted, and opportunity has recently been offered for participating in a number of privately-organized hunting and exploring enterprises, whereby scientific collections of great importance have been obtained for the National Museum.

Paleontological. The secretary, Dr. Walcott, continued in 1912 his studies and collected Cambrian fossils from the famous fossil locality above Burgess Pass, north of Field, British Columbia, on the main line of the Canadian Pacific Railway, and made a reconnaissance survey of the geological section from Moose Pass to the summit of Mount Robson, for the comparison of the Cambrian section there with that of the Canadian Pacific Railway line.

Biological. One of the private expeditions in which the institution was invited to participate was that organized by Mr. Paul J. Rainey, which operated in British East Africa and southern Abyssinia for a year. All the natural history collections were offered to the Smithsonian, and Mr. Edmund Heller, late of the Smithsonian African expedition, was designated as the representative of the institution to accompany the expedition. The results were excellent, totaling some 4700 skins of animals, birds, and reptiles. Among the specimens are the series of lions secured by Mr. Rainey with his hounds, as described in his public lectures.

The institution was also represented in the expedition to Africa conducted and financed by Mr. Childs Frick, of New York, whose object was to secure a collection of animals from the territory north of that visited by Colonel Roosevelt in 1910-11, covering at the same time certain parts of Abyssinia, northern British East Africa, and the country about Lake Rudolf. Dr. Edgar A. Mearns of the original Smithsonian expedition was chosen as the naturalist of the party. About 5000 specimens of birds donated by Mr. Frick to the institution have been received, and promise to materially enrich the African bird collections of the National Museum.

In 1910 the institution, with the coöperation of several of the government departments, organized a biological survey of the Panama Canal Zone. This survey was continued in 1912, and the work accomplished thus far has added greatly to the scientific knowledge of this region. Fine collections of the mammals, birds, fishes, reptiles, and plants have been made, while special studies have been carried on concerning the microscopic plant and animal life in the fresh waters of the Zone.

Through the liberality of Dr. Theodore Lyman, of Cambridge, Mass., the institution has been enabled to participate in a zoölogical expedition to the Altai Mountain region of the Siberia-Mongolian border, Central Asia, an excellent territory from the standpoint of the hunter and collector, and one from which the National Museum has at present no collections. Mr. N. Hollister, a museum naturalist, was detailed to accompany the party, the expenses of which were provided for by Dr. Lyman, who has offered to present the natural history specimens obtained to the National Museum. Although this expedition had not completed its work at the close of the fiscal year, it is anticipated that it will result in adding to the museum collections large numbers of mammals and birds, especially specimens of the wild sheep and the ibex, the principal big game animals of this locality.

Dr. W. L. Abbott, of Philadelphia, has placed funds at the disposal of the institution for continuing the explorations he began personally some time ago in Borneo. The field-work is being done by Mr. H. C. Raven, who is collecting in eastern Dutch Borneo, the natural history of which is practically unknown. The museum will be fortunate to secure a collection from this country, and it is hoped that the characteristic mammals, such as orangs, deer, and wild pigs, and possibly specimens of the rhinoceros and tapir, may be secured.

ANTHROPOLOGICAL RESEARCHES. The institution has planned to coöperate with the authorities of the Panama-California Exposition of San Diego, to carry on researches bearing on the origin of the American Indian. In this connection Dr. Ales Hrdlicka, of the National Museum, was authorized to trace in a preliminary way the remnants of the stock of people from which, in all probability, the American race sprang. He departed on May 16 for Siberia and such parts of Mongolia and Turkestan as the time available would allow. In these places he was to study the native types which are regarded as bearing a striking resemblance to the Indian, securing not only data, but, when possible, photographs, casts and material objects. Returning from his Siberian trip, Dr. Hrdlicka will proceed to Peru, where he will study the collections there existing and make observations on the living natives, furthering his former investigations there in regard to the distribution of the various types of man in Peru.

Dr. Riley D. Moore, also of the museum, will make a trip to St. Lawrence Island, Alaska, where he intends to make a scientific study of the Eskimo tribe which dwells there. The data and material gathered are to be introduced in the exhibits for the exposition above mentioned. A large amount of anthropological work is carried on annually by the Bureau of American Ethnology.

PUBLICATIONS. In "the diffusion of knowledge among men," no agency of the institution does more than its publications, which include the "Smithsonian Contributions to Knowledge," the "Smithsonian Miscellaneous Collections," and the Smithsonian Annual Report, besides other publications. In all, about 150 new publications were issued by the Smithsonian and its branches during the year. Of these, a total of 100,231 copies was distributed to libraries and scientific institutions. These publications relate to all branches of natural and physical science.

LIBRARY. The library of the Smithsonian Institution is deposited in the library of Congress, and comprises about 265,000 publications consisting chiefly of the transactions of learned societies and scientific periodicals. The library of the National Museum has a total of 42,000 volumes and 70,000 pamphlets. The library of the Bureau of American Ethnology contains about 21,000 volumes.

BUREAU OF AMERICAN ETHNOLOGY. This bureau is maintained by the government for the purpose of carrying on ethnological researches among the American Indians and the natives of Hawaii, and is also charged with the excavation and preservation of archeological sites and remains, under the direction of the Smithsonian Institution. Special attention is paid to the history, languages, manners, and customs of the Indians. The results of these studies are published as soon as completed in the reports and bulletins. Since its organization under the institution in 1879, the bureau has published 27 annual reports, and more than 50 bulletins.

During the year just passed much work has been done on an annotated bibliography of the Pueblo Indians by Mr. F. W. Hodge, ethnologist in charge of the bureau. He was also in the field and made a brief visit to the archæological sites of Rito de los Frijoles, and to El Morro, or Inscription Rock, where he made squeezes of the early Spanish inscriptions. Later he accompanied Dr. Edgar L. Hewett, of the American School of Archæology, to the ruined pueblo of Kwasteyukwa in the Jemez Valley, to make investigations and collections.

Dr. J. W. Fewkes conducted field investigations among the Pueblo Indians of Arizona, and made photographs and notes of many new and interesting discoveries in other parts, which are to be printed in a report of the bureau. He is also preparing a report relating to "Designs on Prehistoric Hopi Pottery," and making a further study in anthropology in the West Indies.

Other investigations were carried on by the various representatives of the bureau among the east Cherokee of western North Carolina; the "Croatan" Indians of southeastern North Carolina; the Tewa tribes of New Mexico; the Fox Indians near Tama, Iowa; the Sauk, the Creek, the Shawnee and the Osage Indians of Oklahoma; the Kickapoo of Mexico; and the Winnebago Indians of Wisconsin; and studies were made in the music of the Chippewa and Sioux, while considerable progress was made on manuscripts and texts in the course of preparation for publication.

ASTROPHYSICAL OBSERVATORY. The Smithsonian Astrophysical Observatory was founded for the purpose of investigating solar radiations and other phenomena, and is under the supervision of Mr. Charles G. Abbot, director. The year was notable for expeditions to Algeria and California to test the supposed variability of the sun by making simultaneously, at two widely separated stations, spectrobolometric determinations of the solar constant of radiation. The measurements made at Bassour, Algeria, agree with earlier ones at Washington and on Mount Whitney, California, and indicate that Mount Wilson values are systematically a little low. Apart from this systematic error the average accidental differences between Algerian and Mount Whitney determinations were only 1.2 per cent, indicating an average accidental error of a single solar constant determination at one station of only 0.9 per cent. So far as yet reduced, high solar constant values obtained in Algeria coincide with high values at Mount Wilson and vice versa. Many values remain to be computed, but it can hardly be doubted that the outcome will prove conclusively the irregular short-period variability of the sun. Progress also has been made in the dissemination of standards of pyrheliometry and on the absorption of radiation by atmospheric water vapor.

INTERNATIONAL EXCHANGES. This is the office of the International Exchange Service for the United States, and is conducted in accordance with the terms of a convention entered into between the United States and various other countries for the free interchange of scientific, literary, and governmental publications between governments, learned institutions, and investigators. Packages were delivered to 12,608 institutions and individuals during the first half of 1912. This bureau has handled since its establishment over 3,300,000 packages; during the last year 315,492 packages, having a total weight of 568,712 pounds. Shipments have been made to 72 different countries.

INTERNATIONAL CATALOGUE OF SCIENTIFIC LITERATURE. The institution has charge of the United States regional bureau of the International Catalogue of Scientific Literature, which, as its name implies, is a classified catalogue in book form, of current publications relating to all branches of science. Bureaus have been established in 32 different countries, with a central bureau in London. Since its inception in 1901, this international scientific catalogue has been published annually in the form of 17 separate volumes, each relating to a separate branch of science. The regional bureau for the United States is supported by an annual appropriation by Congress, and is engaged in collecting references of all current scientific publications issued in this country. The number of references forwarded to the Central Bureau last year was 27,201, or about 13 per cent. of the total for the world.

SMOKE ABATEMENT. This, or smoke reduction, is a better term than the more common American term, smoke prevention, since after all smoke cannot be wholly prevented. Abatement is widely employed in Great Britain. A review of the status of the subject in the United States was published in 1912 as *Bulletin 49*, U. S. Bureau of Mines: *City Smoke Ordinances and Smoke Abatement*, by Samuel B. Flagg. A new British book is Julius B. Cohen's *Smoke: A Study of Town Air* (London and New York, 1912). Of some 240 cities of less than 50,000 inhabitants "only 12 reported having either a smoke ordinance or an official charged with smoke inspection"; of replies from 60 cities of from 50,000 to 200,000 population, "17 are making more or less vigorous efforts to suppress the nuisance"; and of 28 cities having more than 200,000 it appears that 23 are making some effort to reduce smoke, while of 5 that "are making practically no effort," 3 use fuel oil almost exclusively. The seventh annual meeting of the International Association for the Prevention of Smoke was held at Indianapolis in September, 1912.

SNOWDEN, ARCHIBALD LOUDON. An American diplomat, died September 7, 1912. He was born in Cumberland County, Pa., in 1837 and graduated from Jefferson College in 1856. He studied law at the University of Pennsylvania. In the Civil War he served as lieutenant-colonel in the Pennsylvania volunteers and participated in several battles. After the war he served as register and later chief coiner of the United States Mint. From 1877 to 1879 he was postmaster at Philadelphia and from 1879 to 1895 was superintendent of the United States Mint in that city. He twice declined the directorship of all United States mints, which was tendered to him by President Hayes. From 1889 to 1891 he was minister-resident and consul-general of Greece, Rumania, and Servia. He was minister to Spain from 1891 to 1893. He was well known as an orator and a writer, and was an authority on coins and coinage. He wrote many papers on these subjects. He received several decorations from foreign rulers for his diplomatic services.

SOCIAL CENTRES. One of the most interesting and promising of social movements of the day is that known as the social or civic centre movement. This is an outgrowth of the agitation for a wider use of school buildings and for the development of the spirit of community coöperation. During the past ten years there has been a gradual increase in the utilization of school houses for recreation centres, branch libraries, public lectures, and debating, musical, and dramatic clubs. The social centre movement is a logical result. It would have school houses constructed with a view to their use for a large number of recreational, amusement, and civic activities, instead of day instruction of children merely. Thus the civic centre school house will require an auditorium, library and reading rooms, and movable school desks. Then under the control of the educational authorities there will be organized in each community games and dancing for young and old; gymnastic and bathing opportunities; singing societies, orchestras, glee clubs, and other musical efforts; literary, debating, and civic clubs; and public lectures on matters of civic and general scientific interest. Moreover, the school house as the civic centre would be used for political meetings during campaigns, for polling places on election day, and as headquarters for political or civic improvement associations looking to the betterment of the political and social life of the community, State and nation.

Though the social centre has been approached for some years by the multifarious activities of the New York and other city departments of education, it is only within the past three years that it has become a widespread propaganda. One of the first cities to adopt the idea was Rochester in 1907. This was achieved through the leadership of Edward J. Ward, since then connected with the extension division of the University of Wisconsin. Chicago followed in December, 1910, and has to-day developed the idea on an extensive scale. Under the leadership of Col. E. P. Holland, the Southwestern Social Centre Conference was held at Dallas, Tex., February, 1911, and resulted in an astonishingly rapid and widespread use of school houses for libraries, amusement centres, and civic-betterment activities in city and country in Texas and Oklahoma. The first national conference was held at Madison, Wis., in October, 1911, under the auspices of the extension division of the State University. There resulted The Social Centre Association of America, with Josiah Strong president and Edward G. Ward secretary, and headquarters at 80 Bible House, New York City. The school department of Boston has just undertaken the organization of four social centres under a special supervisor. Under a new State law authorizing cities to levy a tax of two cents per $100 assessed valuation for the wider use of school houses, Milwaukee has voted this tax and begun the organization of centres. Numerous other cities which had previously provided playgrounds or other organized recreation, have extended these activities, usually under a special supervisor, until they approach the civic centre. Perhaps the most complete centre is that organized in September, 1912, by the New York Social Centre Committee at Public School 63, on the lower East Side. This has committees in finance, dramatics, moving pictures, music, dancing, debating, public meetings, clubs, festivals, outings, neighborhood social welfare, gymnastics, and lectures. A very striking feature of this movement is that the universities of Kansas, Missouri, Oregon, Texas, Virginia, and Washington have followed that of Wisconsin in leading the development of centres in their respective States.

The second national conference on civic and social centre development was held at Lawrence, Kan., toward the close of the year.

LITERATURE. The Division of Recreation of the Russell Sage Foundation publishes various pamphlets describing wider uses of school houses; Clarence A. Perry of that division has written *Wider Use of School Plants*, covering the entire subject, including evening schools, vacation schools, school playgrounds, public lectures and entertainments, recreation and social centres, athletics, dancing, and games. *The Survey* frequently gives information of the progress of this movement; a new periodical, *The Social Centre*, appeared in November, Ossian Lang, editor, Mount Vernon, N. Y.

SOCIAL ECONOMICS. Within the past few years a new department of economic study has been differentiated under the name of social economics. It studies the social aspects of industrial conditions. It is practical, reformative, and socially constructive in its aims. It seeks to establish such conditions for industry as are justifiable from the standpoint of the social welfare of workers and the community. It thus places the human elements in economic life above profits for the employer. Much attention is therefore given to the protection of workers from exploitation through child labor, excessive hours or bad conditions of women workers, unnecessary accidents, insufficient compensation for industrial injuries, occupational diseases, and other conditions. One of its most important principles is the establishment of minimum standards in industry. Thus the social economists favor a minimum wage for women and children; ultimately also for men. Its establishment would raise the plane of competition to a fair and reasonable level; prevent the grasping and conscienceless employer from making profits by exploiting his workers; give the employer who prefers to pay fair wages a better chance; and throw the balance of industrial opportunity in favor of the *entrepreneur* who has superior organizing ability. This same principle applies to almost the entire field. Phases of this subject will be found treated under CHILD LABOR; CHILDREN'S BUREAU; INSURANCE, paragraphs dealing with *Industrial Insurance;* LABOR LEGISLATION; LOAN SHARKS; MINIMUM WAGE; OCCUPATIONAL DISEASES; OLD-AGE PENSIONS; SOCIAL CENTRES; SWEATING; WOMEN IN INDUSTRY; WELFARE WORK; WIDOWS' PENSIONS; WORKINGMEN'S INSURANCE; WORKMEN'S COMPENSATION.

SOCIAL STANDARDS FOR INDUSTRY. At the 39th National Conference of Charities and Corrections the committee on standards of living and labor presented an outline of living and working conditions considered socially justifiable. Finding that a larger and larger percentage of the population is engaging in industry, the committee insisted that more and more public regulation is necessary in order to protect life, health, and efficiency. It insisted that the community has a right to complete knowledge of industrial conditions and their social effects, in order to establish minimum occupational standards as regards wages, hours, housing, health, and other phases of the relation of labor to industry. Their programme as to wages included a living wage for all engaged in industrial pursuits. Such a wage must provide education, recreation, care for immature members of the family, sickness, and a reasonable provision for old age. Minimum-wage commissions should be established for those industries where women, children, and immigrant men are employed at wages insufficient to maintain a normal standard of living. Moreover, all employers should be required to make detailed public reports of their wage scales, their systems of fining, their bonuses, and all modifications therein. As to hours, this platform provided an 8-hour day for all men engaged in continuous industries, and for women and minors in all industries. It included a six-day week and a weekly rest period of 40 consecutive hours; the prohibition of night work for minors and women, and its minimization for men. As regards safety and health, it provided for a federal investigation into every phase of industrial accidents and occupational diseases, with a view to the establishment of intelligent regulations; and the establishment of such regulations and thorough-going inspection. As to housing, the committee's report declared that the highest social welfare includes for a family the right to a home which shall be safe and sanitary in all respects, and shall cost in rental not to exceed 20 per cent. of the family income. It would transfer a share of the taxes from dwellings to land held for speculative purposes, would abolish home-work and tenement manufacture. As to the term of working life, this programme would prohibit the employment of children under 16, would greatly restrict the employment of women, would introduce supervision and regulation of seasonal trades, and would provide more efficient industrial training. Finally the programme included provision for compensation for industrial accidents and trade diseases; and insurance for old age and unemployment.

BIBLIOGRAPHY. F. A. Ogg, *Social Progress in Contemporary Europe;* Carlton Hayes, *British Social Politics;* Lee Welling Squire, *Old Age Dependency in the United States;* George F. Kenngott, *The Record of a City. A Social Survey of Lowell, Mass.;* L. A. S. Toke, National Housing Association, Proceedings of the First National Housing Conference held in New York, June 3, 5, and 6, 1911, *The Housing Problem;* Havelock Ellis, *The Task of Social Hygiene;* T. Hertzka, *Das soziale problem;* G. Kerr, *The Path of Social Progress;* G. H. Knibbs, *Social Insurance;* B. Emminghaus, *Das Versicherungswesen;* A. Manes, *Sozialversicherung;* F. M. Leavitt, *Examples of Industrial Education;* S. P. Breckenridge and E. Abbott, *The Delinquent Child and the Home;* E. T. Devine, *The Spirit of Social Work;* C. Cora, *Essai sur l'extinction du paupérisme;* C. F. Dole, *The Burden of Poverty: What to Do;* F. W. Van Eeden, *Happy Humanity;* J. B. Haldane (Ed.), *Social Workers' Guide;* Jane Addams, *A New Conscience and an Ancient Evil;* E. R. A. Seligman (Ed.), *Social Evil;* Josephine Goldmark, *Fatigue and Efficiency.*

SOCIAL INSURANCE. See WORKINGMEN'S INSURANCE.

SOCIAL INSURANCE IN GREAT BRITAIN. See WORKINGMEN'S INSURANCE.

SOCIALISM. SOCIALISTS AND WAR. During the Balkan War, when it was feared that the great European powers might be drawn into the struggle, the International Socialist Bureau at Brussels issued an appeal to the Socialist organizations of all European countries to arrange for a concerted demonstration on behalf of peace in the capitals and leading cities on November 17. The plan was successfully carried out. The leading Socialist orators addressed meetings in their own and other countries. French and English orators spoke in Berlin, and Russian, Belgian, and German leaders addressed a large gathering of Parisian Socialists, communists, and anarchists. The French Syndicalists, however, as represented by the General Confederation of Labor, took no official part in this demonstration, being opposed to any sort of alliance with Socialists. On November 24 a great International Socialist Congress was held at Basle for the purpose of considering the best means of preventing a general European war. It was attended by 500 delegates representing 21 European countries. The same divergence of views was manifest as in the preceding conferences of Stuttgart and Copenhagen, the French Socialists favoring an anti-militarist programme and a general strike, and the Germans holding that such measures were impracticable, since patriotism would, in the event of war, outweigh all other considerations. The Congress of Basle, which lasted ten days, voted an eloquent resolution against war, but it was couched only in general terms, and like the previous declaration of the Congress of Stuttgart, refrained from urging the specific measures desired by the French, namely, an insurrection of the working classes and a general strike as a protest against war. These measures were not acceptable to the German and Austrian delegates. The view of the latter was that the Socialists were at present not strong enough to prevent war and that the threat of a general strike was foolish. It was idle to suppose that theoretical considerations of remote social advantage would govern men when their country was actually threatened by a hostile invasion. On the other hand, it was argued that if Socialists confined themselves to peace demonstrations and parliamentary protests they would accomplish nothing to the end of averting war. To emphasize the difference between Syndicalists and Socialists the French General Confederation of Labor called a meeting on the same day (November 24) and declared that they were the party of action, not of words. They frankly urged a general strike in case of war, recommended sabotage in the transport and military supply services, and advised men to refuse to obey the call to the colors. They summoned to the Congress workers in the marine, in powder works, arsenals, on the railways, and in other services indispensable to the government in the event of war. Finally they fixed on December 16 as the date for a twenty-four hours' strike as a foretaste of what would happen if war broke out. The strike took place at the time appointed, but was of little importance. There were no disturbances except at Lyons, and the interruption of work was not serious.

GERMANY. SOCIALISTS IN THE REICHSTAG. Between the years 1881 and 1903 the number of Socialist deputies in the Reichstag rose from 12 to 81. As a result of von Bülow's policy of uniting Liberals, Radicals, and Conservatives against the Socialists and Centre, the number of Socialist deputies fell to 43 in 1907, but this unnatural grouping of parties into a government *bloc* could not survive the dissensions occasioned by the project of fiscal reform. It fell to pieces and the von Bülow government was overthrown, failing to carry through the imperial succession tax. The "blue-black" *bloc* of von Bethmann-Hollweg followed, consisting of the two reactionary groups—Conservatives and Catholic Centre. Indirect taxation was increased. Discontent with this reactionary policy and the high cost of living strengthened the Socialists as the extreme party of opposition, and in the partial elections down to the beginning of 1912 they gained ten seats. Then came the general election of January, 1912 (see GERMANY, *Elections*), which increased their strength beyond their expectations, giving them a representation in the Reichstag of 110. The popular vote was 4,250,329, a gain of a million votes since 1907. It was an unprecedented victory. It showed that one-third of the entire electorate supported them. Their success was due in part, however, to the help of the Liberals, who for the first time made common cause with them. In the separate Diets the number of Socialist deputies increased from 110 to 224. Although there was great rejoicing among the rank and file of Socialists, their more thoughtful leaders realized that this new-found power seemed greater than it really was. They had drawn to their side temporarily a large number of malcontents of all shades of political opinion, who were certain eventually to fall away, and who were in no sense collectivists. Moreover, there was little unity of view. The party's success was due merely to its gathering to itself those who favored a progressive liberalism. The specific planks in the Socialist platform at the elections were: Democratization of the state and the army, rights of association, professional inspection, popular schools, suppression of indirect taxes, and progressive taxation of incomes, property, and inheritance.

The attitude of the German Socialists toward war was illustrated in 1912, as it had been in the preceding year during the Moroccan negotiations, by the speech of Herr von Vollmar, leader of the Bavarian Socialists in the Bavarian Diet, in August. He said that while the Social Democrats sought always to maintain peace, nevertheless, if their efforts were of no avail, they would surely cast in their lot with the defenders of the Fatherland, postponing all other considerations. The party had been treated by the German government as an enemy, and it refused to express confidence by voting the army estimates, but if occasion arose it would not be found lacking in patriotism.

THE CHEMNITZ CONGRESS. Of the many resolutions presented to the Socialist Congress which met at Chemnitz on September 15, abou* one-half concerned domestic matters, as for example the creation of a new presiding body in place of the present one, which was alleged to be unresponsive to the demands of the masses. Others condemned the alliances with the Radicals in the recent elections, declared the hostility of the Socialists to the Church and to religious education, and urged the enlightening of the people by a campaign in the press which should show the incompatibility of religion with scientific truth. The figures presented at the Congress showed an extraordinary increase during the year. The active, enrolled membership in 1912 was reported at nearly a million, an increase of 16 per cent. over 1911, and the number of their daily journals at 86, with 1,500,000 subscribers, an increase of 170,000 over 1911. The great increase in the Reichstag and in the Diets of the empire is noted above. There was a corresponding increase in the municipal governments. The Congress narrowly escaped a break between the Orthodox and Revisionist wings of the party. There was a sharp debate over the heresy of the prominent Socialist, Herr Hildebrandt, who in a recent volume on industrialism had expressed a doubt as to the possibility of nationalizing all production without exception. He was expelled from the party. Herr Bebel was reëlected president.

GREAT BRITAIN. COAL MINERS' STRIKE; SOCIALISM AND SYNDICALISM. The miners' strike at the beginning of March (see GREAT BRITAIN and STRIKES), the most serious movement in recent industrial history, aimed apparently at a war of labor against the state. It showed plainly the influence of French Syndicalism and had nothing in common with Socialism. The English Syndicalists, like the French, were bitterly hostile to the parliamentary Socialists. The Labor party were their sworn foes. Mr. Lloyd-George declared that the best policeman for the Syndicalist is the Socialist. A new Syndicalist paper was published in England in January under the title of the *Industrial Syndicalist*, edited by Mr. Guy Bowman and Mr. Tom Mann, of whom the former had lived in France and had translated into English M. Hervé's book *Leur Patrie*, and the latter was a well-known labor leader. For mention of their arrest for inciting soliders to mutiny, see GREAT BRITAIN, *History*. From the point of view of the Syndicalists, the miners' strike was the first step toward the general strike. Coal being the essential of all industries, its stoppage would paralyze industrial activity. There was talk of a sympathetic railway strike, and attempts were made to bring about an international movement. A German strike of miners was threatened, but it was merely local and soon put down. French miners planned a strike of 24 hours, and there were other signs of European Syndicalist sympathies. Both wings of the British Socialists, namely, the British Socialist party and the Independent Labor party, attacked Syndicalism at their respective congresses. The Trades Unions (q. v.) in their congress at Newport in September also condemned it. At the British Socialist congress at Manchester, Mr. Hyndman, the leader, reproached both the Labor group and the Syndicalists. He blamed the former for submitting to Liberal domination in Parliament, and for not fighting the battles of class. As to the trade unions, their hope lay not in the path of Syndicalism, with its contempt for parliamentary action, but in a course that would lead to the conquest of political powers. The ballot, said he, is a more effective instrument than strikes. Socialism, he declared, favored the unions, but its main purpose was to organize the working class into a political party to wrest from capital the control of legislation. Syndicalism, which held aloof from parliamentary action, was denounced by another speaker as merely anarchism under another name. The same views were expressed by the Independent Labor party in its congress at Merthyr. Here, too, it was averred that the ballot was the key to economic liberty and Syndicalists who, like Tom Mann, professed to regard political action as resulting only in measures to deceive the working classes, were condemned. As matters stood it appeared that it was only by allying themselves with the Liberals that the Socialists could hope to maintain their position in Parliament. This was illustrated by the Hanley election in 1912, held for the choice of a successor to Mr. Edwards, a Socialist candidate who had been supported by the Liberals and received over 8000 votes. Now, however, the Liberals and Socialists each put up their candidate, and the Liberals won, the Socialists casting less than one-fourth of the Liberal vote and less than one-third of the Conservative. The London dock strike, whose chief promoter was Ben Tillet, a member of the British Socialist party, was terminated unsuccessfully at the end of July. In the November municipal elections the Socialist parties gained 40 seats.

FRANCE. The ninth annual Congress of the Unified Socialists was held at Lyons February 18-22, 1912. The number of paying members of the party had not increased much and the conditions were not encouraging. The membership of the eighty-six federations was 63,657. The principal issues were: Anti-semitism, free masonry, the agrarian question, the municipal question, and the organization of the young. The chief of these were the agrarian and municipal questions, of which the former presented the usual insoluble problem of reconciling the interests of peasant proprietors and industrial wage-earners. It was deferred to the next congress. As to free masonry, although it was opposed by a number of Socialists as exerting an adverse influence, the congress decided to leave Socialists free to join if they chose. Similarly in regard to the Jews and the Catholics the congress, true to the Marxist principle that religion was a private affair, did not commit itself either to anti-semitism or anti-clericalism. There was some sharp discussion of the proper attitude to take toward the General Confederation of Labor. In December, 1911, two members of the party had denounced in unmeasured terms the methods of the General Confederation of Labor, direct action, sabotage, and violence. There was bitter hostility between French parliamentary Socialists and the Syndicalists, the latter regarding the parliamentary group as merely self-seekers who posed as champions of the proletariat. In general the congress showed sympathy with the deputies who had denounced the General Confederation of Labor in the Chamber, but did not pass any formal vote of approval. It compromised on a vote that left the matter ambiguous, apparently approving, but essentially condemning. The old line of cleavage between the Guesdists and the party of reform continued. The latter, represented by such men as Jaurès and Vaillant, favored all measures of reform, whether violent or moderate, as likely to undermine the present social system. On the other hand, the Guesdists, doctrinaire and imbued with German notions, regard all reforms as useless in a capitalistic society and aim solely at a political revolution. Hence they desire the conquest of political powers by the ballot, by discipline, recruiting, stirring up the masses, and the subordination of the General Confederation of Labor. The two groups are apparently irreconcilable. The congress did nothing to bring them together and was in other respects as well rather barren of results. The hostility of the Syndicalists toward the Socialists was as bitter as ever and was shown on many occasions. Syndicalists who had taken part with M. Hervé in founding his journal, the *Social War*, accused him of treason in inclining too far toward Socialism. The General Confederation of Labor, the great central organ of Syndicalism, issued a manifesto declaring its hostility to Socialists, whether followers of M. Jaurès or M. Hervé.

ITALY. As was noted in the YEAR BOOK for 1911, Italian Socialists were divided on the question of the war with Turkey and on the question of supporting the Giolitti ministry when it came into power. A branch of the party favored participation in the government, despite the vote of the Socialist Congress against it, and Signors Bissolati, Cabrini, and Bonomi would have accepted portfolios in the new cabinet had it not been for the opposition of the majority. Although the Socialists in the Chamber voted unanimously against the government's decree annexing the North African provinces, a considerable portion of the party declared in favor of the war, and many Socialists holding office in the municipalities subscribed to funds in aid of the war and took part in patriotic demonstrations on its behalf. The thirteenth congress of the Italian Socialists was held at Reggio Emilia in the summer of 1912. Signor Bissolati favored a programme of gradual conquest of political power by active participation in government. To this Signor Turati and the other reformers of the Left who remained in the party were opposed, contending that changes should be brought about by popular pressure without compromising with a capitalist government. They corresponded to the Guesdist group in France. The preponderant element in the original party consisted of revolutionists who differed from Signor Turati on the question of electoral alliances. The new Socialist group began an active campaign and won many adherents. In the Chamber thirteen deputies joined the new party, while twelve remained faithful to the old. The question of the status of the dissident deputies immediately arose and they finally decided to send a circular letter to the electors asking whether they continued to regard them as their representatives. The executive committee of the old party referred the matter to the International Socialist Bureau at Brussels, declaring that the new group had split off on principles at variance with those of the International, were endangering the unity of the proletariat, etc.

BELGIUM. The defeat of the Liberal Social alliance in the elections of June has been noted under BELGIUM, *History*. The reverse was complete and unexpected and was characterized by Belgian Socialist journals as a blow at free thought and international socialism. The Socialists refused to acknowledge their defeat as an expression of the popular will, contending that under the present electoral system the majority did not represent the people. Soon after the elections the Walloon coal miners in the region of Charleroi went on strike. The Socialists discouraged the movement as premature, but held a congress at Brussels July 3-9 for the purpose of organizing a general strike to force the hand of the government if it refused to submit to the Chamber in November an amendment to the constitution providing for universal suffrage and for the abandonment of the system of plural voting. The congress was attended by 1500 delegates, including 20 deputies and 4 senators. It decided upon a general strike, leaving its date uncertain in order to take the government by surprise. It was marked by unanimity and enthusiasm, and its programme was carried out in an orderly fashion. Great stress was laid on the necessity of regarding the law and abstaining from all acts of violence. Trades unions, coöperative societies, and other workingmen's bodies were urged to side with the Socialists and to supply the sinews of war. Commissions of the general strike were formed, local committees promptly came into existence, and a national subscription was opened. Monster meetings were held and addressed by prominent Socialist orators, like MM. Vandervelde, Anseele, Destrée, and others. The national committee on the electoral law and the general strike circulated a million copies of a manifesto to the effect that the plural vote reduced the working classes to a minority, that the country really desired universal suffrage, that the Clericals would not dare to combat it openly, etc. It also declared that the strike to be successful must last five or six weeks. The enormous losses this would entail on the working population were plainly pointed out, but it seemed not to dampen their ardor. Much alarm was felt lest, despite the efforts of its organizers, the strike should degenerate into a riot.

OTHER COUNTRIES. In Spain the Socialist party has recently made rapid progress. In 1888 it comprised only 16 associations. In 1912 the number of these bodies had risen to 216 without counting the 55 associations of the so-called Young Socialist party. They published fifteen journals. In Denmark, where the Social Democrats are the largest political group, there were reported to be one thousand Socialists on the provincial council in 1912. They gained another seat in the Copenhagen municipal election of that year, giving them exactly half of the seats in the council. The party published thirty-two newspapers. In the Netherlands the membership of the Social Democratic party was reported at 13,398 in 1912, a considerable increase over the previous year. In Norway the Socialists had 23 seats in Parliament after the general election of November, a gain of 13, and their popular vote rose from 91,000 to 126,000. In Russia the Social Democratic party showed increasing strength in 1912, although owing to the rigid measures taken by the government (see RUSSIA, *History*) they elected only twelve members to the fourth Duma.

For an account of the Socialist strength in the United States see PRESIDENTIAL CAMPAIGN paragraph *Elections*, and for the Socialist programme see the same article, paragraph *Platforms;* for municipal elections see MONTANA and WISCONSIN under *Politics and Government;* and for Socialism in American cities, see MUNICIPAL LEAGUE, NATIONAL.

SOCIALIST PARTY. See PRESIDENTIAL CAMPAIGN.

SOCIAL SERVICE, AMERICAN INSTITUTE OF. An organization founded in 1898 for the purpose of gathering and disseminating information on all branches of social thought and service. It supplies information and advises as to methods by correspondence. Its publications, lectures, and special reference library are open to the public. Its service is free except when special investigations are required. Series of illustrated lectures on industrial problems prepared especially for use in churches are being widely circulated. *The Gospel of the Kingdom*, published monthly by the institute, containing studies in the application of Christian principles to present-day problems, is used by classes in churches, Y. M. C. A.'s, etc., in all parts of the United States and Canada. For the 1913 series, containing special articles and bibliographies in the "What To Do" department, the following subjects were selected for treatment: Poverty, Wealth, Socialism, Eugenics, Euthenics, The Unfit, Rural Communities, the Mormon Menace, The Coming Church, Moral Training in the Public Schools, The Unemployed, and Peace.

SOCIOLOGICAL SOCIETY, AMERICAN. See SOCIOLOGY.

SOCIOLOGY. Various articles of sociological interest will be found under their respective headings. Matter relating to the condition of labor is referred to under LABOR; of special interest to the sociologist are CHILD LABOR, MINIMUM WAGE, WOMEN IN INDUSTRY, OCCUPATIONAL DISEASES, INDUSTRIAL WORKERS OF THE WORLD, SYNDICALISM, WELFARE WORK, and WORKINGMEN'S INSURANCE. Renewed interest in divorce during the year was due to the report of the English commission, for which see DIVORCE. Under PENOLOGY is a brief summary of changes occurring in the treatment of prisoners. See also the topics referred to under SOCIAL ECONOMICS.

THE AMERICAN SOCIOLOGICAL SOCIETY. The seventh annual meeting of this society was held at Boston, December 27-31, in connection with the American Economic Association, the American Statistical Association, and other bodies of kindred interest. The various papers on the programme of the society centred about the changes which have been wrought in the various social sciences as a result of the development of the social idea. The president, Albion W. Small of Chicago, read a paper on "The Present Outlook of Social Science." The unity of the programme is shown by the list of other papers: "Social Phases of Psychology" by President G. Stanley Hall of Clark University; "Social Aspects of Educational Theory," by Paul Munroe of Teachers College; "Social Phases of the Historical Method," by Carl L. Becker of the University of Kansas; "The Outlook for a Régime of Social Politics in the United States," by C. E. Merriam, of the University of Chicago; "Legislation as a Social Function," by Roscoe Pound of Harvard Law School; "Social Implications of Remedial and Preventive Legislation in the United States," by E. R. James of the University of Wisconsin Law School; "Social Ideals Implied in Present American Programmes of Voluntary Philanthropy," by Edward T. Devine of Columbia University; "The Socialization of Religion," by Francis G. Peabody of Harvard Divinity School; a symposium on "The Social Presuppositions of English and American Economic Theory"; and a round table meeting on "How far is it possible to go in constructing a platform of social theory acceptable to all American sociologists?" Following the custom of the society of a two-year term for its officers, Albion W. Small was reelected president and S. E. W. Bedford, also of Chicago University, secretary-treasurer.

BIBLIOGRAPHY. The volume of distinctively sociological literature put out in 1912 was unusually small. Among books of interest were the following: G. Richard, *La sociologie générale et les lois sociologiques;* H. Webster, *Rest days: a sociological study;* Thomas Nixon Carver, *The Religion Worth Having;* E. J. Urwick, *A philosophy of social progress;* F. Consentini, *Sociologia: genesi ed evoluzione dei fenomeni sociali;* S. B. Kitchin, *A history of divorce;* J. Q. Sealey, *The family in its sociological aspects;* Lucien Arreat, *Génie individuel et contrainte sociale;* S. N. Patten, *The social basis of religion;* G. Chatterton-Hill, *Sociological value of christianity; Papers and proceedings* of the sixth annual meeting of the American Sociological Society at Washington, D. C., 1911; C. A. Elwood, *Sociology in its psychological aspects;* F. S. Granger, *Historical sociology;* Walter Rauschenbush, *Christianizing the social order;* J. G. Frazer, *The golden bough*, 3d ed.

EUGENICS. W. E. Kellicott, *The social direction of human evolution;* Castle and others, *Heredity and eugenics;* C. B. Davenport, *Heredity in relation to eugenics*, (1911); Papers communicated to the First International Eugenics Congress held at the University of London, July 24-30, 1912, *Problems in eugenics;* K. Pearson, *Social problems; their treatment, past, present and future;* W. Bateson, *Biological fact and the structure of society;* O. C. Beale, *Racial decay;* M. S. Iseman, *Race suicide;* W. C. D. and C. D. Whetham, *An introduction to eugenics;* Arthur Newsholme, *The declining birth-rate: its national and international significance* (1911); René Worms, *La sexualité dans les naissances françaises;* Henry H. Goddard, *The Kallikak family;* L. H. Baker, *Race improvement;* G. E. Dawson, *Right of the child to be well-born;* C. W. Saleeby, *Methods of race-regeneration;* Vernon L. Kellogg, *Beyond War.*

SOIL ORGANISMS. See BIOLOGY.

SOILS. There is evidence that the influence of the comprehensive and consistent study of soils in the United States is having an effect on practice for, as Secretary Wilson says in his last report (1912), "beginnings have been made in a production increasing faster than the natural increase of population."

SOIL SURVEYS. The proper basis for the improvement of methods of soil management is an accurate and comprehensive soil survey. Such surveys are now available for all parts of the United States. Up to June 30, 1912, the total area surveyed and mapped by the United States Bureau of Soils was 622,595 sq. m., or 398,460,800 acres. "It is probable that all the widely distributed and important soils in the country have been encountered and identified in one or more places." Interest and activity in soil surveying is becoming quite general throughtout the world and work of this kind was reported in 1912 from Russia, Australia, New Zealand, Java, Africa, South America, and Cuba, but in no case was the work as systematic and comprehensive as that in the United States.

As the work of soil surveying extends, questions of soil classification become increasingly important and are engaging more and more attention. Congress at its last session passed a law providing for a practical application of such work in the classification of the lands included within the national forests, with a view to delimiting those of agricultural value.

SCIENTIFIC INVESTIGATIONS. That the study of soils is engaging the attention of an increasing number of scientific men is shown by the fact that a large number of papers dealing with various scientific aspects of soil problems were presented at the Eighth International Congress of Applied Chemistry, held during the year at New York. These papers emphasized especially the complex composition of soils and the delicate balance which must be maintained between soil constituents in order to insure fertility. See also FERTILIZERS.

The United States Bureau of Soils added some twenty new compounds to the fifteen which it had already isolated from the organic matter of the soil. These represent nearly every chemical class of organic substance. Progress was also made in studying the effect of these compounds on the growth of plants and on the biochemical changes which take place in soils. Jodidi of the Iowa Experiment Station made further important contributions to the transformation of the organic nitrogenous compounds of the soil. Studies of these compounds, as well as of various mineral constituents usually occurring in relatively small amounts and hitherto considered of minor importance, are beginning to throw light upon many problems of soil fertility and of the use of fertilizers. They show that comparatively small variations in amount or relative proportion of the soil constituents may have a profound effect upon the productiveness of the soil as determined by physical, chemical, and biological properties. The investigations of the past year emphasize the close relation between bacterial activities and crop-producing power of soils. They show more clearly than ever before that soil constituents are transformed, absorbed, and fixed by bacterial action as well as by chemical and physical action. Stoklasa has shown, for example, that a large amount of carbon dioxid is produced in fertile soils by the respiration processes of soil bacteria and that this exerts a pronounced influence on the physical condition and the chemical composition of the soil. That these processes are most active in fertile soils supports Hall's conclusion that high productiveness is accompanied by high waste, the latter being due largely to bacteria which attack the nitrogen compounds of the soil and liberate free nitrogen. The wasteful processes can apparently be partly controlled by partial sterilization, by heat or antiseptics, and possibly by other means. A practical problem of great importance, therefore, is to devise methods of sterilization which can be economically applied in large scale field operations. Practical methods applicable to greenhouses and other small scale operations have been in use for some years. It has been shown that by use of sterilization (heating to 200° F.) the expensive process of renewing green house soils may be obviated, the productiveness increased, and the danger from disease reduced.

Investigations reported during the year emphasize the important fact that there is considerable bacterial activity even in frozen soils, although the growth is confined largely to one group, which, however, includes those of most importance from the standpoint of soil fertility. The investigations of Hilgard and Loughridge, showing that soils of arid regions differ from those of humid regions, in the greater uniformity in physical and chemical composition of the former to a great depth, have recently been supplemented by work by C. B. Lipman, of the California Experiment Station, and others, indicating that bacteria are more active and occur to a greater depth in soils of the arid regions than in those of humid regions, a fact which doubtless accounts in part for the greater fertility of the arid soils. Lipman has also shown that the common alkali salts have a toxic effect on the ammonifying, nitrifying, and nitrogen-fixing organisms of the soil. W. P. Kelley found that 5 to 10 per cent. of manganese oxid in Hawaiian soils had no effect upon ammonification or nitrification, although causing pronounced chlorosis in pineapples. Since, according to Hall, the problem of maintaining soil fertility is largely a matter of preventing loss of nitrogen and insuring a high nitrogen content of the soil, it is important to know that the practice in China and Japan and experiments conducted by the Illinois and Rhode Island stations and by others show that the nitrogen supply of the soil may be maintained without recourse to fertilizers. In experiments at the Rhode Island station soils gained one ton of nitrogen per acre in five years, with a rotation including such leguminous plants as cowpeas, soy beans, and vetch.

LITERATURE. The most important recent contribution to the permanent literature of soils is *The Black Soils, or Chernozem of Russia*, by P. Kossovich, which deals in detail and with great thoroughness with these noted soils analogous in many respects with much of the prairie and dry lands of the western United States. The Bureau of Soils has undertaken a series of monographs which will summarize for each group and type of soil all the information secured by its soil surveys.

SOKOTRA. A dependency of Aden (q. v.).

SOLAR ECLIPSES. See ASTRONOMY.

SOLAR RADIATION. See ASTRONOMY.

SORSBY, WILLIAM BROOKS. An American diplomat, died March 27, 1912. He was born in Panola, Miss., in 1858 and was educated in private schools and at the Mississippi College. He engaged in journalism and edited several country newspapers in that city. In 1884 he became part owner of the Mobile *Morning Telegram*. In 1893 he became interested in gold mining in Ecuador. He was consul-general in that country from 1889 to 1893. From 1897 to 1901 he was consul at San Juan del Norte, Nicaragua, and at Kingston, Jamaica, in 1901-2. In the latter year he was appointed United States minister to Bolivia. He retained this office until 1909 when he resigned and left the diplomatic service.

SOUTH, UNIVERSITY OF THE. An institution for higher education at Sewanee, Tenn., under the auspices of the Protestan Episcopal denomination, founded in 1857. The enrollment in the various departments of the university in the autumn of 1912 was 246. The faculty numbered 27. Among the important changes in the faculty were the resignation of the Rev. Henry R. Gummey, professor of ecclesiastical history and polity, and the appointment as his successor of the Rev. Thomas Allen Tidball, and the appointment of Thomas Nottingham Ware, professor of modern languages, in the place of Glen Levin Swigget. Professor Gummey was elected professor emeritus. The benefactions received during the year amounted to $17,437. The productive funds of the university amount to $351,383. The income for 1911-12 was $84,916. The library contains 33,731 volumes. Vice-chancellor, William B. Hall.

SOUTH AFRICA, UNION OF. A British colony; a legislative union, under one government, of four Britisn provinces. Their areas according to latest returns, total population (census of May 7, 1911), and their white population (census 1911) are shown in the following table:

	Sq. miles.	Total pop.	Whites
Cape of Good Hope	206,860	1,563,630	546,162
Bechuanaland	51,524	99,553	14,917
Transkeian Territories:			
East Griqualand	7,594	249,088	7,950
Tembuland.	4,129	236,086	8,138
Transkei	2,552	188,895	2,189
Pondoland	3,906	234,637	1,383
Walfish Bay	430	637	32
Total Cape Province	276,995	2,564,965	582,377
Natal	24,866	974,437	95,994
Zululand	10,424	219,606	2,120
Total Natal	35,290	1,194,043	98,114
Transvaal	110,426	1,686,212	420,562
Orange Free State	50,389	528,174	175,189
Total Union of South Africa	473,100	5,973,394	1,276,242

Of the total population, 3,069,392 were males, 2,904,002 females; of the total whites (who numbered 21.37 per cent. of the total population), 685,164 were males and 591,078 females. The Bantus numbered 4,019,006 (2,022,949 males and 1,996,057 females), or 67.28 per cent. of the total population; mixed and other colored, 678,146, or 11.35 per cent. Density per square mile for the Union, 12.63 (Cape of Good Hope, 9.26; Natal, 33.83; Transvaal, 15.27; Orange Free State, 10.48). The total population in 1904 was 5,175,824.

The South Africa act provided that elementary education shall remain under the jurisdiction of the several provincial councils for "five years and thereafter until Parliament otherwise provides."

MINING. The Union of South Africa stands first among the countries of the world in the production of gold and diamonds. Other mineral products are coal, copper, tin, asbestos, graphite, magnesite, zinc, lime, salt, etc. The number of white and colored laborers employed (December 1910) and value of the output for the year 1910 are shown by provinces in the following table:

	Laborers White	Laborers Colored	Output £
Transvaal	27,891	219,610	35,426,586
Cape Province	5,034	17,455	5,777,910
Orange Free State	1,473	11,966	1,667,902
Natal	579	9,901	710,535
Total Union	34,977	258,932	43,581,933

Gold. The gold produced in the Transvaal amounted (1910) to more than one-third of the world's supply. Of the 26,198 whites employed in the gold mines of the Union in June, 1911, 26,159 were in the Transvaal, 25 in Natal, 12 in the Orange Free State, and 2 in the Cape province; of the 208,182 colored laborers, 207,907 were in the Transvaal, 216 in Natal, 46 in the Orange Free State, and 13 in the Cape province. The total output for the Union in 1910 was £31,991,295 (world's output 1910, £93,500,000), of which the Transvaal furnished £31,973,123 (from the Witwatersrand mines, £30,653,933), or 7,527,108 fine ounces. The total output for 1909 was £30,994,905, of which £30,987,650 came from the Transvaal (contribution of the Witwatersrand mines, £29,787,569).

Diamonds. In June, 1911, 4723 whites were employed in the diamond mines (Cape, 2830; Orange Free State, 1096; Transvaal, 797) and 39,884 colored (Cape, 18,004; Transvaal, 11,254; Orange Free State, 10,626), besides several thousand individual diggers. The output for the year 1910 was 5,456,557 carats, valued at £8,101,363 (Cape, 2,586,294 kts., £5,267,659; Orange Free State, 780,195 kts., £1,505,074; Transvaal, 2,090,068 kts., £1,328,630). The value of the stones obtained from the Cape and Orange Free State mines is greatly in excess of that of the Transvaal diamonds, the latter selling at one time for 13 shillings per carat when the former were averaging from 42s. to 36s.

Coal. White and colored labor employed in coal mines in June, 1911, 1237 and 23,440, respectively (Natal, 517 and 11,248; Transvaal, 504 and 9399; Orange Free State, 101 and 1600; Cape, 115 and 1193). The output in 1910 and the pit's mouth value of the total production to the end of 1910 are given below:

	1910 Tons	1910 £	Total £
Transvaal.	3,974,376	987,260	11,722,988
Natal	2,570,115	688,424	6,849,285*
O. F. S.	469,762	131,728	887,498
Cape	93,280	59,808	2,131,307
Total Union	7,107,533	1,867,220	21,591,078

* From 1903 only.

The Cape province, having less competition, obtains higher prices than the other provinces. Better qualities are found in Natal and the Transvaal. Most of the supply from Natal is bunkered at Durban or exported, while the mines, railways, and other local industries consume much of that produced by the other provinces.

Other Minerals. Of the other mining products, only tin and copper are exploited in commercial quantities, largely in the Transvaal and Cape provinces. Output of tin in 1910, £326,352 (Transvaal, £324,559; Cape, £1793); of copper, £477,381 (Cape, £401,206; Transvaal, £76,175). Value of cement, bricks, pottery, etc., produced in 1910, £489,268; of silver contained in export of gold bullion, £90,790. A total of 582 whites and 7058 colored were employed in the miscellaneous mines in June, 1911.

OTHER INDUSTRIES. There is an efficient agricultural department, which has established agricultural colleges and experiment stations. Ostrich and sheep farming are important industries. Corn was produced for export in 1910 to the value of £693,413 (178,000 tons); wool, £3,830,914 (121,672,255 lbs.); tea, 2,092,000 lbs.; sugar, 82,000 tons; whale oil (from the whaling station at Durban), £60,000; wattle bark, £219,433 (41,344 tons). The ostrich-feather production had a selling value of about £6,000,000. Manufactures are making progress.

COMMERCE AND COMMUNICATIONS. For 1910 statistics of trade by provinces are not available; as, in consequence of the formation of the Union (May 31, 1910), only the totals were given in the original returns. The total imports (including bullion and specie) into the Union of South Africa, together with Swaziland, Basutoland, and Bechuanaland Protectorate, during the year 1910 were valued at £41,-430,037 (of which £4,703,207 bullion and specie); £24,002,537 was from the United Kingdom. The total exports were valued at £56,-428,455 (£34,608,381 bullion and specie), of which exports to the United Kingdom were valued at £49,998,413. Preliminary returns place the imports and exports for 1911 at £36,925,384 and £57,024,000, respectively, exclusive of specie.

The table below gives trade by provinces (or, as they were previous to 1910, colonies) for three years, including bullion and specie. Figures for bullion and specie are given separately for 1909 in the last column.

	1907	1908	1909	B. & S.
Nat. a	£ 7,737,750	£ 7,034,422	£ 8,225,792	£ 601,192
Nat. b	2,292,875	3,159,523	3,951,092	1,135,991
Cape. a	15,599,655	13,767,158	14,831,153	212,229
Cape b	44,536,729	42,140,459	46,598,993	32,201,958
O.F.S. a	3,672,591	2,945,860	3,662,696	238,307
O.F.S. b	3,751,049	3,558,373	4,777,126	72,833
Trans. a	15,760,987	16,196,692	19,643,615	2,178,703
Trans. b	31,268,276	33,323,590	34,128,956	30,999,649

a = imports; b = exports.

The government in 1910 owned and operated 7041 miles of railways, and 545 miles were owned and operated by private companies. The receipts from government lines amounted to £12,036,871 and the working expenditure to £6,597,011. Construction proceeded on the following lines during 1912: Port Elizabeth to Avontuur; Ceres Road to Ceres; George to Oudtshoorn; Lady Grey to Gairtney; Llewellyn to Franklin; India Junction to Alberton; Coomatipoort to Tzaneen; Umlaas Road to Mid Illovo; and on the Howick Railway. These for the most part were short lengths. During 1912 the connection between Zeerust and the Rhodesian system at Mafeking was under construction, reducing the distance between Johannesburg and Bulawayo by 250 miles. There are 47,421 miles of telegraph wires and 38,832 of telephone wires; telegraph offices, 1231. There is cable connection with Europe, Australia, India, and the Far East; two wireless stations have been established, one at Cape Town and one at Durban. Railway lines under construction, 859 miles.

SHIPPING. Shipping entered 1909, 9,857,081 tons; 1910, 11,494,855 tons.

ARMY. An energetic campaign, as a result of the Defense act of 1912 prepared by General Smuts, with the advice of Lord Methuen, was undertaken with the aim of "establishing in South Africa an adequate system of national defense, which will recognize the application of the citizen to take part in the defense of his country." This act provided for liability to military service in any part of South Africa upon the whole white male population up to the age of 60, and the formation of an Active Citizen Force of 20,000 to 25,000 men, with a reserve up to the age of 45. This was being organized so that it would come into existence by July 1, 1913. Every youth must undergo military training as a cadet, except upon conscientious objections, and in the rural districts they must join rifle associations and get some military training in that way. The Active Citizen Force arranged to provide for four annual trainings of about 50 per cent. of the young men between the ages of 21 and 25, and every effort was being made to increase volunteering in the joining of rifle clubs. The permanent force for the Union was to consist of 2500 mounted riflemen, divided into 5 regiments, many of whom were already on police duty, and 5 field batteries. The men on police duty would be relieved by a reserve. On July 1, 1912, a military school was opened at Bloemfontein for the instruction of future district officers and adjutants. The first class was composed of 40 staff officers, all of whom had war experience. The course was to last for six months.

FINANCE AND GOVERNMENT. Financial statistics are given separately in the articles on the various provinces.

The four original provinces form a legislative union under one head—a governor-general appointed by the crown, who, with an executive council (whose members are chosen by him), administers the country as the governor-general in council. Forty members make up the Senate (eight nominated by the governor-general in council; thirty-two elected, eight for each province). Fifty-one members from the Cape of Good Hope, 17 from Natal, 36 from the Transvaal, and 17 from the Orange Free State compose the House of Assembly. Pretoria (Transvaal) is the capital and administrative headquarters; Cape Town, the seat of the legislature. The governor-general in 1912 was Viscount Gladstone of Lanark. General Louis Botha, premier since May 31; 1910, resigned December 14, 1912, on account of dissensions between the Dutch and the British on naval and other matters.

HISTORY

THE PARLIAMENTARY SESSION. The Union Parliament was opened on January 26. In the speech from the throne the government policy was briefly outlined as including the necessity of adequate defense legislation, of customs revision, of the promotion of local industries, and of legislation as to the regulation of railway and other public services, land settlement, irrigation, the establishment of a Union land bank, railway development, agricultural development, a national university, restriction of immigration, etc. A comparatively small portion of this programme had been carried out at the close of the session toward the end of Jur

The chief measures passed were the Defense act, the Railway Service act, the Miners' Phthisis act, the Public Services act and the measures dealing with land settlement, irrigation, and a land bank. The Immigration Restriction bill, though pressed by the government early in the session, failed of passage, as did the Financial Relations bill and the University bill. In outlining the government's policy as to lands, General Botha declared that the crown lands should first be used for settlement, and that then other land would be purchased for that purpose. The government would also render aid to the poor whites in South Africa and would then use what money was left over for assisting immigration. He denied that immigration was in any way discouraged. The Defense bill was substantially the same as had been anticipated in the previous year. Its chief defect, according to the opposition, was the danger of arbitrary action on the part of the government in view of the great power that it conferred upon it. Other critics expressed the fear that the citizens' force might be engaged outside South Africa, and officered from outside, that the period of training might be unduly prolonged, and that the compulsory cadet system might be applied in the thinly settled districts. The government met these objections by saying that they arose from a misunderstanding of the measure. In its final shape, however, it was as much the work of the opposition as of the government. This was true also of the Irrigation and the Miners' Phthisis bills. The session revealed a lack of harmony and consequent weakness in the ministry, and on June 26, to avert a cabinet crisis, the portfolios were redistributed.

RACE QUESTIONS. The Immigration Restriction bill mentioned above had been framed after a long correspondence between the imperial and Union governments and was designed to meet the objections of the home government and of the Indians to the existing methods of restriction. The immigration bill of the previous year, whose chief feature was the replacing of the racial qualifications by an educational test, had been withdrawn for lack of time, but the government had promised the Indians to bring in a new measure and meanwhile to relax their restrictions. The new bill was introduced in May, 1912, but failed of passage. In October the leader of the Indian Progressives, Mr. Gokhale, visited South Africa for the purpose of studying on the spot the question of the treatment of the Indians. Another racial question concerned the so-called "black peril." There was much discussion of this in the early part of the year owing to the frequency of outrages on white women committed by the negroes in recent years. Conditions resembling those prevailing in some of the Southern States of the United States were reported, and early in May the government decided to appoint a commission of inquiry. Finally the old question of the language to be used in teaching in the schools continued to absorb attention. The provincial councils of the Cape, Transvaal, and the Orange Free State passed ordinances establishing equality between the English and Dutch languages in the schools, but providing for instruction in the mother tongue in the "junior standard." These ordinances were ostensibly based on the compromise proposed in the parliamentary report of 1911, but the Unionists declared that they had been so greatly modified as to depart altogether from the spirit of that compromise. On this ground a similar ordinance in Natal was projected.

THE MINISTRY. The conciliatory policy toward the government was abandoned by the leader of the opposition, Sir Starr Jameson, who early in the year strongly opposed the government's plan for reorganizing the civil service. In April he was succeeded in the leadership by Sir Thomas Smartt. The government was also embarrassed by differences among its own members. In May Mr. Hull, the minister of finance, resigned on account of differences with Mr. Sauer, minister of railways, and when the affair was discussed in parliament it brought the government to the verge of a crisis and led to a redistribution of portfolios on June 26, as noted above. In the latter part of the year differences between General Botha and General Hertzog, the anti-imperialist leader, led to the resignation of the former on December 14. He was at once asked, however, to form a new cabinet.

SOUTH AFRICAN IRRIGATION ASSOCIATION. See IRRIGATION.

SOUTH AUSTRALIA. A state of the Commonwealth of Australia. Area, 380,070 square miles. Population (census of April 3, 1911), 408,558, exclusive of full-blooded aboriginals. Adelaide, the capital, had 42,294 inhabitants; with suburbs, 189,646. Governor in 1912, Admiral Sir Day Hort Bosanquet; premier, A. H. Peake. See AUSTRALIA.

SOUTH CAROLINA. POPULATION. According to the Census Bureau statistics compiled during 1912, out of a total population of 1,515,400, 6054 were foreign-born whites, compared with 5371 in 1900. Of these foreign-born whites, 1739 came from Germany, 785 from Russia, 675 from Ireland, 504 from England. Other European countries are represented by smaller numbers. The negroes in the State in 1910 numbered 835,843 and the mulattoes 134,381. In 1890 the negroes numbered 688,934 and the mulattoes 67,153. It will be seen from these figures that the negro and mulatto population in the State exceeds the white.

AGRICULTURE. The acreage, value, and production of the principal crops in 1911 and 1912 are shown in the table below.

		Acreage	Prod. Bu.	Value
Corn	1912	1,915,000	34,272,000	$29,126,000
	1911	1,790,000	32,578,000	29,646,000
Wheat	1912	79,000	727,000	865,000
	1911	83,000	946,000	1,164,000
Oats	1912	324,000	6,966,000	4,598,000
	1911	345,000	7,038,000	5,067,000
Rye	1912	3,000	28,000	41,000
	1911	3,000	30,000	44,000
Rice	1912	8,000	200,000	186,000
	1911	10,000	117,000	88,000
Potatoes	1912	....	....	....
	1911	10,000	700,000	854,000
Hay	1912	194,000	a223,000	4,014,000
	1911	64,000	a69,000	1,173,000
Tobacco	1912	35,000	b24,500,000	2,670,000
	1911	13,600	b11,016,000	1,358,016
Cotton	1912	....	....	....
	1911	....	c1,480,000	....

a Tons. b Pounds. c Bales.

MANUFACTURES. The Thirteenth Census included statistics of manufactures in the State. These are for the calendar year 1909. The most important general results are shown in the table below. The industries in which the largest number of wage earners were employed and the value of product greatest were those connected with cotton goods. In these industries the wage earners numbered 45,454 and the product was valued at $65,930,000. Next in point of importance were the industries connected with lumber and timber products. In these, 14,604 wage earners were employed and the product was valued at $13,141,000. The only other two industries of great importance were those connected with oil, cottonseed and cake, and fertilizers. The total number of wage earners in the State in 1909 was 73,046. Of these, 9405 were under 16 years of age, 3989 of these being females. For the great majority of wage earners in the State the prevailing hours of labor are 60 a week. The largest number of wage earners are in Charleston, 2874; in Columbia, 2522; in Spartanburg, 1773, and in Greenville, 1182.

	Number or Amount 1909	1904	P. C. of Inc. 1904-09
Number of establishments	1,854	1,399	32.5
Persons engaged in manufactures	78,040	63,071	23.7
Proprietors & firm members	1,737	1,241	40.0
Salaried employees	3,257	2,389	36.3
Wage earners (average No.)	73,046	59,441	22.9
Primary horsepower	276,378	197,479	40.0
Capital	$173,221,000	$113,422,000	52.7
Expenses	97,371,000	72,206,000	34.9
Services	24,117,000	16,224,000	48.6
Salaries	3,756,000	2,355,000	59.5
Wages	20,361,000	13,869,000	46.8
Materials	66,351,000	49,969,000	32.8
Miscellaneous	6,908,000	6,013,000	14.8
Value of products	113,236,000	79,376,000	42.7
Value added by manufacture (value of products less cost of materials)	46,885,000	29,407,000	59.4

FINANCE. The total receipts during the fiscal year 1911 amounted to $3,208,790. There was a cash balance December 31, 1910, of $648,730. The expenditures for the fiscal year amounted to $3,132,164, leaving a cash balance at the end of the fiscal year, December 31, 1911, of $725,356. The chief receipts were from general taxes, from insurance license fees, and from the fertilizer tax. The chief expenditures were for the support of State institutions, education, and the administration of State government.

CHARITIES AND CORRECTIONS. The institutions under the control of the State are the State Hospital for the Insane, the South Carolina Industrial School, the Infirmary for Colored Veterans, the deaf, dumb, and blind institutions, and the State prisons.

POLITICS AND GOVERNMENT

The legislature was in session in 1912 and the most important enactments will be found in the paragraph *Legislation* below. Elections for governor and other State officers and senatorial primaries were held during the year. The full Democratic State, county, and federal tickets were elected by the usual majorities.

The Democratic State convention on May 16 indorsed Woodrow Wilson for President. The Republican delegates-at-large were instructed for President Taft, the district delegates being divided. On July 24 the national Progressive party held a convention in which nine delegates were elected to the national Progressive convention in Chicago.

Governor Coleman L. Blease was much in the public eye during 1912. In his annual message to the legislature he took a strong stand against negro education and urged a law to prevent white persons teaching negroes. He also indirectly defended lynching and recommended the adoption of a law prohibiting negroes from secret societies. Investigations carried on by detectives during the year on behalf of the investigating committee of the legislature resulted in the publication of charges of corruption against Governor Blease. These charges related to pardons, and it was alleged that Governor Blease had received large sums for pardoning convicts. It was also alleged that Blease's appointee as liquor constable in Charleston was transmitting "graft" to men higher up. On July 20 Governor Blease replied in detail to the charges made against him, denying them and expressing contempt for those who brought them. In spite of an apparently strong feeling against him throughout the State he was renominated for the second term on August 28. He was opposed by Ira B. Jones, a former chief justice of the State Supreme Court, who had resigned his position on the bench for the purpose of contesting the nomination against Governor Blease. The result of the election (held August 27) was 67,240 votes for Blease and 64,072 for Jones. Senator Tillman was renominated at this election. A committee of the legislature conducted an investigation into the returns of the election, chiefly to determine whether the charges of fraud could be sustained. The committee at the same time investigated the general charges of corruption against Governor Blease. The executive committee of the Democratic party examined into the charges of fraud in the primary election, but found the evidence insufficient to vitiate the choice of Governor Blease as a candidate for reëlection. On August 24 Senator Tillman issued an appeal to defeat Governor Blease for the second term. He said: "I have become convinced of the unfitness of Blease to be governor. The State has been disgraced in the eyes of the world and its good name made a by-word and a hissing. No one can redeem it except its own people. I implore the people to take care of the State's good name next Tusday."

On September 4 the Democratic State committee met to canvass the returns of the primary and decided to make a thorough and sweeping investigation of all the charges of fraud and irregularity. On October 1 this committee reported that the allegations of fraud could not be sustained and Governor Blease was thereupon made the Democratic candidate, which was equivalent to election. Governor Blease won still more notoriety by addresses delivered before the governors' conference in Virginia in the first week of December. He made bitter speeches against negroes and again defended lynching under certain conditions. His addresses were bitterly resented by the other governors present at the conference. Later in the month Governor Blease pardoned or paroled seventy-nine convicts. He had declared at the governors' conference his intention of pardoning at least 800. His total for pardons and paroles, including the 79 issued the day before Christmas, reached 506 in the two years of his first administration. The result of the election on November 5 was as follows: For President. Wilson received 48,355 votes, Roosevelt 1293, Taft 536, and Debs 164. Wilson's plurality was 47,064. For governor, Blease received 44,122, and Britton, Socialist, 208. There was no Republican candidate as the Republican party practically does not exist in South Carolina.

LEGISLATION. The legislative session of 1912 was marked by disagreement between the legislators and the governor. As a result of this, while 301 acts and joint resolutions were passed by the General Assembly, the governor approved only 15. Several measures were passed over his veto, but the majority became effective without his signature. Among these measures were the following: A liquor act; an act amending the law establishing the insurance department of the State; a measure providing for electrocution as a method for capital punishment; a measure creating a State warehouse commission and providing for operating a State warehouse system for storing cotton and other commodities; a measure providing for a State commission with authority to make and enforce rules and regulations to eradicate or prevent the introduction or dissemination of injurious insects and plant diseases; a measure providing that only citizens may vote at primary elections, although citizens of the United States who have been residents of South Carolina for one year with a bona fide intention of becoming citizens of that State may vote at such election. Provision was made for elections in any city of over 4000 inhabitants upon the question of adopting a commission form of government, and for the adoption of that form of government in cities of over 10,000 and less than 25,000, and cities of over 50,000 and less than 100,000 inhabitants. A similar act was passed relating to cities and towns of not more than 10,000 and not less than 4000 inhabitants. The regulation and supervision of investment companies was provided for.

STATE GOVERNMENT. Governor, Coleman L. Blease; Lieutenant-Governor, C. A. Smith; Secretary of State, R. M. McCown; Attorney-General, J. F. Lyon; Treasurer, S. T. Carter; Comptroller-General, A. W. Jones; Superintendent of Education, J. E. Swearingen; Adjutant-General, W. W. Moore; Commissioner of Agriculture, E. J. Watson; Commissioner of Insurance, F. H. McMaster—all Democrats.

JUDICIARY. Supreme Court: Chief Justice, Eugene B. Gary; Justices, C. A. Woods, D. E. Hydrick, R. C. Watts, and Thomas B. Fraser; Clerk, U. R. Brooks—all Democrats.

STATE LEGISLATURE, 1913. Democrats, Senate, 43; House, 124; joint ballot, 167.

The representatives in Congress will be found in the section *Congress*, article UNITED STATES.

SOUTH DAKOTA. POPULATION. According to the Census Bureau statistics compiled during 1912, out of the total population in 1910, 583,888, the foreign-born whites numbered 100,638, compared with 88,329 in 1900. Of these the largest number came from Germany, 21,543; from Norway, 20,918; from Russia, 13,160; from Sweden, 9998; from Canada, 5894; from Denmark, 5038, and from England, 4024. Other European countries were represented in smaller numbers. The negroes in the State in 1910 numbered 817 and the mulattoes 276. In 1890 the negroes numbered 541 and the mulattoes 231.

AGRICULTURE. The acreage, value and production of the principal crops in 1911 and 1912 are shown in the following table:

		Acreage	Prod. Bu.	Value
Corn	1912	2,495,000	76,347,000	$28,248,000
	1911	2,310,000	50,820,000	26,935,000
Wheat	1912	3,675,000	52,185,000	36,008,000
	1911	3,700,000	14,800,000	13,468,000
Oats	1912	1,550,000	52,390,000	13,098,000
	1911	1,540,000	11,396,000	4,900,000
Rye	1912	16,000	312,000	162,000
	1911	13,000	130,000	99,000
Potatoes ..	1912	62,000	6,510,000	2,344,000
	1911	56,000	4,032,000	2,822,000
Hay	1912	460,000	a672,000	4,099,000
	1911	459,000	a252,000	2,142,000

a Tons.

MINERAL PRODUCTION. The production of gold in the State in 1911 was $7,439,874, compared with $5,402,257 in 1910. The output in 1911 was exceeded by that of only one year, 1908, when gold to the value of $7,657,376 was produced. The bulk of the output is obtained from the Homestake mines of Lawrence County. The silver production in the State in 1911 was 203,755 fine ounces, as compared with 118,000 fine ounces in 1910. The silver is obtained mainly from refining gold mill bullion.

The total value of the product of gold, silver, and lead in the State in 1911 was $7,550,758. This yield is only slightly below that of the record output of 1908 and is an increase of $2,083,727 over the value of the output for 1910. The production of gold was 359,903 fine ounces, valued at $7,439,874, or almost 99 per cent. of the total value of the mineral production. The increase in gold for the year was 98,569 fine ounces. The yield of silver increased from 118,800 fine ounces to 203,755 in 1911. There were produced 64,311 pounds of lead, compared with 14,136 pounds in 1910. The greater portion of the production of coal comes from the Homestake mine. This mine, which suffered from labor troubles in 1909-10, was again operating at its full capacity in 1911.

MANUFACTURES. The Thirteenth Census, taken in 1910, included statistics of manufactures in the State. These are for the calendar year 1909. The results of the census will be found summarized in the table below:

	Number or Amount 1909	1904
Number of establishments...	2,020	686
Persons engaged in manufactures	5,226	3,582
Proprietors and firm members	942	649
Salaried employees	682	441
Wage earners (average number)	3,602	2,492
Primary horsepower	17,666	11,154
Capital	$13,018,000	$7,585,000
Expenses	15,787,000	11,246,000
Services	2,914,000	1,716,000
Salaries	616,000	294,000
Wages	2,298,000	1,422,000
Materials	11,476,000	8,697,000
Miscellaneous	1,397,000	833,000
Value of products............	17,870,000	13,085,000
Value added by manufacture (value of products less cost of materials)........	6,394,000	4,388,000

As will be seen from this table, the number of manufacturing establishments showed a marked increase in the five-year period, 1904 to 1909. The capitalization in that period nearly doubled. The greatest number of manufacturing establishments, 825, were those connected with printing and publishing. The largest amount invested, however, was in establishments connected with flour-mill and grist-mill products.

FINANCE. The report of the treasurer for the fiscal year ending June 30, 1912, showed a balance on hand July 1, 1911, of $421,156. The receipts for the fiscal year amounted to $3,779,-652, and the expenditures to $3,208,519, leaving cash on hand June 30, 1912, amounting to $992,289. The chief source of revenue is taxation, and the chief expenditures are for education and the support of State institutions.

CHARITIES AND CORRECTIONS. The charitable and correctional institutions of the State, with their populations in 1912, are as follows: State Insane Asylum, Yankton, 950; State Penitentiary at Sioux Falls, 225; State Training School, Plankinton, 75; State School for the Blind, Gary, 25; State School for the Deaf, Sioux Falls, 80; Sanatorium for Tuberculosis, Custer, 17; Northern Hospital for the Feebleminded, Redfield, 220. The State Board of Charities and Corrections has general supervision over these institutions.

POLITICS AND GOVERNMENT

No legislative session was held in 1912. The session for 1913 convenes January 7, 1913. The most important political event in the State during 1912 was the primary election held on June 10. It resulted in the selection of Roosevelt delegates to the Republican national convention. His vote was 35,637; Taft, 9843; La Follette, 17,821. The Democratic party was likewise divided, Wilson-Bryan delegates getting 4694 votes; Wilson-Clark-Bryan, 4275; Champ Clark, 2722.

In the November election the Republican ticket was elected so far as State officers are concerned. Part of the State officers were regular Republicans and pa t progressive. The Democrats nominated E. S. Johnson for governor, and although the State was normally 30,000 Republican, Johnson lacked less than 4000 of defeating Frank M. Byrne. For the first time congressmen were elected by district: C. H. Dillon in the first, C. H. Burke in the second, and E. W. Martin in the third, the last two being holdover representatives at large. The vote for presidential electors gave Roosevelt 58,811, Wilson 48,942, Chafin 3910, and Debs 4,662.

The vote for governor was: Byrne, 57,160; Johnson, 53,850; Lovett, Socialist, 3578; Butterfield, Prohibition, 3486. At the November election a new primary law, known as the Richards primary, was adopted. This is far different from anything of its kind heretofore adopted in any State or country, and practically does away with all party organizations. Five other laws and amendments to the constitution were submitted and all were adopted by overwhelming votes. The most important besides the new primary law was a measure requiring locomotives to be equipped with electric headlights.

STATE GOVERNMENT. Governor, Frank M. Byrne; Lieutenant-Governor, E. L. Abell; Secretary of State, Frank Glasner; Treasurer, A. W. Ewart; Superintendent of Instruction, C. G. Lawrence; State Land Commissioner, F. F. Brinker; Attorney-General, Royal C. Johnson; State Auditor, Henry B. Anderson—all Republicans except Governor Byrne, Progr.

JUDICIARY. Supreme Court: Presiding Judge, Ellison G. Smith; Justices, Dick Haney, Charles S. Whiting, S. C. Polley, and J. H. Gates; Clerk, Frank Crane—all Republicans.

STATE LEGISLATURE, 1913. Republicans, Senate, 35; House, 89; joint ballot, 124. Democrats, Senate, 10; House, 11; joint ballot, 21. Republican majority, Senate, 15; House, 78; joint ballot, 103.

The representatives in Congress will be found in the section *Congress*, article UNITED STATES.

SOUTH DAKOTA, UNIVERSITY OF. A State institution of higher learning at Vermillion, S. D., founded in 1882. The enrollment in all departments of the university in the autumn of 1912 was 370, divided as follows: Arts and sciences, 212; law, 80; engineering, 40; medicine, 13; music, 25. There are about 50 members of the faculty. There were no notable gifts during the year. An important event in connection with the curriculum was the adoption of type or standard courses based upon a schedule of recitations, worked out with respects to majors and minors, the group system, and other graduation requirements. The library contains about 16,000 volumes. President, Franklin B. Gault, Ph. D.

SOUTHERN COMMERCIAL CONGRESS. See AGRICULTURE.

SOUTHERN NIGERIA. A British colony and protectorate on the Gulf of Guinea. Area, 79,880 square miles; population (1911), 7,836,-189. Lagos, the capital and chief port, in the Lagos province, has about 102,190 inhabitants; other towns of the Lagos province are Ibadan (341,875 inhabitants), Abeokuta (264,723), Oyo (217,583), Ijebu Ode (131,326). Towns of the Central province: Warri (64 Europeans, 141,-614 natives), Onitsha (399,916), Asaba (200,-262), Benin City (84,340), etc. Of the Eastern province: Calabar (57,544), Degema (127,-237), Brass (90,171), etc. The country is generally unfit for habitation by Europeans.

*	1907	1908	1909	1910
Imports ..	£4,438,907	£4,284,830	£4,962,544	£5,857,335
Exports .	4,202,704	3,409,288	4,169,161	5,304,186a
Revenue .	1,459,553	1,387,975	1,361,891	1,933,235
Expend. ..	1,217,337	1,357,763	1,648,680	1,989,978
Shipping†	....	....	1,513,014	807,220

* Trade statistics include goods in transit to and from Northern Nigeria. † Tons entered and cleared. a Palm kernels; £2,450,814; palm oil, £1,742,234; rubber, £311,691; cacao, 101,151; cotton, £78,479; tin ore, £72,660; wood and timber, £60,191; nuts, £43,510; specie, £45,734.

The government contributes £70,000 annually to the administration of Northern Nigeria. The greater part of the Lagos-to-Kano railway is in Northern Nigeria, but the line is controlled by the Southern Nigeria government. A. G. Boyle administered the country in 1912, under the governorship of Sir Walter Egerton.

SOUTHERN PACIFIC RAILWAY. See TRUSTS.

SOUTHERN SOCIOLOGICAL CONGRESS. See PUBLIC CHARITIES.

SOUTH GEORGIA. A dependency of the Falkland Islands (q. v.).

SOUTH ORKNEY ISLANDS. A dependency of the Falkland Islands (q. v.).

SOUTH POLE. See Polar Exploration.

SOUTH VICTORIA LAND. See Polar Exploration.

SOUTHWICK, George N. An American public official and writer, died October 17, 1912. He was born at Albany, N. Y., in 1863 and graduated from Williams College in 1884. He entered the Albany Law School where he remained for one year. He then joined the staff of the Albany *Morning Express* as a reporter. In 1889 he was made managing editor of that paper and then accepted the same position on the Albany *Evening Journal*. In 1895 he received the Republican nomination to the House of Representatives and was elected. He remained in the House from 1895 to 1899, and again from 1901 to 1911. He was chairman of the Republican State convention in 1896. He contributed several articles on political subjects to the *North American Review* and other periodicals.

SPAIN. A constitutional European monarchy, occupying the eastern part of the Iberian Peninsula. Capital, Madrid.

Area and Population. The Spanish provinces, with their area in square kilometers and population according to the census of December 31, 1910, are as follows:

Alava	3,045	96,993
Albacete	14,863	264,363
Alicante	5,660	497,616
Almería	8,704	365,016
Avila	7,882	208,817
Badajoz	21,894	564,131
Baleares	5,014	326,023
Barcelona	7,691	1,141,626
Biscaya	2,165	349,969
Burgos	14,196	346,694
Cáceres	19,863	395,499
Cádiz *	7,342	470,068
Canarias	7,273	447,688
Castellón	6,465	322,210
Ciudad-Real	19,608	380,565
Córdoba	13,727	498,782
Coruña	7,903	674,830
Cuenca	17,193	269,634
Gerona	5,865	319,679
Granada	12,768	522,517
Guadalajara	12,113	209,352
Guipúzcoa	1,885	226,385
Huelva	10,138	309,672
Huesca	15,149	248,257
Jaén	13,480	532,368
León	15,377	395,430
Lérida	12,151	284,974
Logroño	5,041	188,235
Lugo	9,881	477,239
Madrid	7,989	877,819
Málaga	7,389	523,429
Murcia	11,537	607,786
Navarra	10,506	312,235
Orense	6,979	411,573
Oviedo	10,895	685,131
Palencia	8,434	196,031
Pontevedra	4,391	496,292
Salamanca	12,510	330,633
Santander	5,460	303,152
Saragossa	17,424	448,995
Segovia	6,827	167,744
Seville	14,062	597,194
Soria	10,318	156,354
Tarragona	6,490	334,535
Teruel	14,818	254,998
Toledo	15,257	413,648
Valencia	10,751	884,298
Valladolid	7,569	285,211
Zamora	10,615	273,045
Total	504,517†	19,611,334

* With Ceuta. † 194,794 square miles.

The greatest density per square kilometer is found in Biscaya—162; in Barcelona it is 148, in Guipúzcoa 120, in Pontavedra 113, in Madrid 109. Huesca and Cuenca show least density, with 16 to the sq. km.; Teruel has 17, Albacete 18, and Cáceres 20. The mean density for the kingdom is 40. Provisional figures for the movement of population in 1911 give 142,119 marriages, 625,172 births, 463.678 deaths (161,494 surplus of births), 175,587 emigrants, 105,055 immigrants. Some of the principal cities, with their communal population, census of 1910, are Madrid, 599,807; Barcelona, 587,284; Valencia, 233,348; Seville, 158,336; Málaga, 136,365; Murcia, 125,243; Saragossa, 113,729; Carthagena, 102,519; Bilbao, 93,536; Granada, 80,511; Lorca, 72,795; Valladolid, 71,066; Palma (Baleares), 67,544; Cádiz, 67,306; Santa Cruz de Tenerife, 65,615; Santander, 65,209; Córdoba, 64,407; Las Palmas, 63,947; Jerez, 61,250; Alicante, 55,300.

Lack of Progress. A report of the minister of the interior occasioned by an order for an investigation into the progress of the country in recent years shows 4500 villages without roads or railroads, 30,000 villages and towns without schools, and nearly two-thirds of the population as unable to read or write. Many private schools are under clerical control, though recent legislations has made attempts to provide for some control of their curricula, condition, and faculties. Public schools are maintained by local taxation. Secondary instruction is provided by one high school in each province, but the curricula are imperfect; special schools are few. There are ten universities.

The struggle of the state against church encroachment still goes on, without notable successes. In December, 1910, a temporary bill was passed seeking to restrain the establishment of additional religious orders until a more comprehensive act could be drafted and passed. Toleration within certain limits is accorded Protestant worship.

Production. Of the total area, 79.65 per cent. is returned as "productive" (33.8 per cent as under sown crops and gardens, 3.7 under vineyards, 1.6 under olives, 19.7 under natural pasture, and 20.8 under orchards). As a matter of fact, according to the report of the minister of the interior, although the soil is fertile and conditions favorable to agriculture, 60 per cent. of the land is uncultivated and 38 per cent. is entirely without irrigation. Tropical fruits thrive. The vine is grown in every province, sherry and tent wines coming from Jerez, malaga and alicante from the southeast. In the table below are given areas under main crops and yield for two years, with yield per hectare in 1911:

	Hectares		Quintals		Qs.
	1911	1912	1911	1912	ha.
Wheat	3,927,892	3,851,472	40,414,186	30,594,820	10.3
Rye	804,460	804,460	7,340,311	6,542,204	9.1
Barley	1,443,689	1,318,621	18,896,974	12,759,956	13.1
Oats	513,305	490,724	4,914,592	3,556,514	9.6
Corn	463,402	466,357	7,297,780	6,600,106	15.7
Rice	38,248	38,858	642,408	1,748,100	16.8
Flax *	1,585	1,180	5,135	8,600	3.2
Beets †	33,234	43,075	8,749,550	10,789,738	263.3
Vines ‡	1,289,977	1,264,005	14,747,051	14,000,000	11.4
Sugar cane	....	7,242	....	2,732,760	....

* Yield in table is for seed; yield of fibre, 1911, 15,584 quintals; 1912, 6810. † For sugar. ‡ Yield in hectoliters of must.

Livestock December 31, 1911: 546,035 horses, 904,725 mules and hinnies, 836,741 donkeys.

2,541,112 cattle, 15,725,882 sheep, 3,369,624 goats, 2,472,416 swine, 3398 camels.

In the spring of 1912, 7500 hectograms of silkworm eggs were placed for hatching and the production of cocoons was estimated at 1,175,000 kilograms, as compared with 1,250,000 kms. obtained in 1911. Cotton goods, paper, cork, and glass are manufactured.

Rich mineral deposits exist, but almost the only efficient exploitation is by foreign enterprise employing foreign capital.

In 1909, 3,622,573 metric tons of coal (valued at 47,345,231 pesetas) were raised; 8,786,020 of iron (45,503,256); 2,955,253 of copper (35,407,181); 161,496 of argentiferous lead (30,619,076); 137,049 of lead (18,780,025); 163,521 of zinc (7,388,293); 37,397 of mercury (5,082,425); 265,019 of lignite (3,269,094); 21,749 of sulphur (149,127). Value of fisheries products, between forty and sixty million pesetas; of the output of the sardine factories, about sixteen million pesetas.

COMMERCE. The special trade is given in pesetas below, for three successive years (1 peseta=19.3 cents):

	1909	1910	1911
Imports......	956,976,672	1,000,036,564	1,065,822,000
Exports......	925,930,062	970,519,366	965,794,000

Imports for consumption and exports of domestic produce follow, with values in thousands of pesetas, for 1911: Foodstuffs, 170,259 imports, 388,187 exports; cotton and cotton mfrs., 159,440 and 56,118; drugs and chemical products, 149,474 and 38,765; machinery, 134,383 and 4625; minerals and ceramics, 113,037 and 152,306; animals and animal products, 85,080 and 52,949; metals and their mfrs., 60,912 and 139,092; timber, 61,984 and 69,050; silk and its mfrs., 22,469 and 5212; wool and woolens, 21,803 and 10,226; other textiles, 21,068 and 3449; paper, 16,846 and 12,424; various, 24,475 and 9943; special imports, 21,468; packing, 1886; total merchandise, 1,064,584 imports and 951,348 exports; precious metals, 1238 and 14,446; totals, 1,065,882 and 965,704.

The principal countries of origin and destination follow, values in thousands of pesetas:

	Imps.	Exps.		Imps.	Exps.
U. K......	168,012	235,433	Argentina	27,111	68,530
France ...	131,123	193,901	Switz.....	20,857	8,129
U. S......	129,621	57,710	Italy.....	15,806	38,324
Germany..	127,271	60,357	Norway..	15,524	2,496
Brit. Ind..	57,009	916	Neth.....	14,989	58,060
Russia ...	43,570	4,849	Phil. Is..	14,825	6,723
Portugal..	39,237	34,829	Sweden...	14,358	1,594
Belgium...	33,788	46,399	Brazil....	13,049	2,835

SHIPPING. Vessels entered during 1911, 20,766, of 20,900,576 tons (11,358, of 7,948,303 tons, Spanish); cleared, 18,157, of 20,338,480 tons (9069, of 7,475,300 tons, Spanish). Total coasting vessels entered, 57,668, of 15,347,923 tons. Merchant marine January 1, 1912, 582 steamers, of 750,081 tons, and 301 sailing, of 44,325.

COMMUNICATIONS. In 1912 (January 1) there were in operation 14,805 kilometers of railway and 42,553 of telegraph lines (wires, 93,432). Madrid has now a shorter and better connection with Paris by way of the tunnel through the Pyrenees, which was completed in November, 1912.

FINANCE. The budget for 1912 is detailed below in thousands of pesetas:

Revenue	1000 ps.	Expenditure	1000 ps.
Direct taxes...	474,875	Debt	408,236
Customs	159,100	War	188,257
Stamps, etc.....	87,500	Agriculture† ...	103,341
Salt tax........	58,000	Interior	81,966
Sugar tax.......	38,000	Pensions	75,216
Transport	27,200	Marine	70,188
Alcohol	15,000	Instruction	61,255
Other indirect..	10,600	Worship	41,359
Tobacco	160,000	Tax dept.......	38,294
Lottery	36,500	Justice	19,985
Matches	11,500	Finance	18,537
Explosives	3,700	Civil list.......	8,900
Other	2,520	Foreign affairs.	6,567
Domains	23,350	Colonies	1,900
Treasury	25,863	Judiciary	1,027
		Council	685
Total, 1912...	1,133,208	Total, 1912...	1,128,363
" 1910*..	1,071,240	" 1910*..	1,028,214
" 1909*..	1,065,704	" 1909*..	1,100,936

* Actual revenue and expenditure.
† Agriculture, industry, commerce, and public works.

The public debt stood, January 1, 1912, at 9,407,724,977 pesetas.

ARMY. Compulsory personal military service was established for all Spaniards by the law of June 29, 1911, and the young men declared fit for military service in each annual contingent are divided by law into two groups, the first being incorporated in the active army, usually for three years' service, and the other receiving partial instruction in varying amounts under specified conditions. Service in the reserve amounts to 6 years and territorial service will complete a total period of 18 years. Under the terms of the law of December 26, 1907, an effective strength of 80,000 men was maintained, but this may be increased by the minister of war to 100,000 at certain times, provided a corresponding and compensating reduction is made at others. In 1912 the effective strength was 115,440 men, which number the minister was authorized to increase if necessary. The Spanish war budget for 1913 provided for the abolition of the headquarters staff and of the consultative committees of the various branches of the service and for the transfer and centralization of these powers in the war department, the abolition of the general inspection of the military instructional establishments and industries, the transformation of the captaincy-general of Melilla into a military command, the grouping of the Morocco occupational troops into mixed independent brigades, the increase of the peace effective from 114,000 to 121,000 men, and the formation of a fourth mountain artillery regiment of 2 groups of 2 batteries, and of a telegraph regiment. Accordingly, on December 2, 1912, the minister of war was authorized by the king to present to the Spanish Chamber a proposed law fixing the effective strength of the permanent army at 121,065 men.

NAVY. The navy, exclusive of non-effective vessels, is composed of 1 second-class battleship (9890 tons), 3 first-class protected cruisers (25,133), 1 second-class (5871) and 2 third-class (4083), 4 torpedo-boat destroyers (1845), 1 torpedo boat (127) of the first and 4 (284) of the second class, 8 first-class gunboats (6925) and 8 second- and third-class (3202)—in all, 32 vessels, of 57,360 aggregate tons.

Building are 3 battleships, 4 gunboats, 3 destroyers, and 24 torpedo boats.

GOVERNMENT. The constitution vests the executive power in the king, acting through a responsible cabinet of ministers appointed by himself. The Cortes, conjointly with the king, exercises the legislative authority; there are two houses—a senate (360 members, partly hereditary, partly appointive, and partly elective) and a congress of deputies (431 members, elective). Reigning sovereign (1912), Alfonso XIII. Heir-apparent, Prince Alfonso, born 1907. The assassination of the prime minister, José Canalejas y Mendez (November 12, 1912), leader of the anti-clerical party in the Cortes, in large part author of the Franco-Spanish treaty signed two days after his death, an eminent statesman, and a man feared and hated in many quarters, fulfilled the anarchist prediction persistently reiterated since the execution, in 1909, of Francisco Ferrer. His place was filled November 14 by the appointment of the president of the Chamber of Deputies, Count Alvarado de Romanones, to be prime minister. The rest of the ministry, constituted February 9, 1910, was composed at the end of 1912 as follows: A. Barroso y Castillo, interior; M. García Prieto, foreign affairs; Arias Miranda, worship and justice; Lieut.-Gen. de Luque, war; J. Pidal Rebollo, marine; J. Navarro Reverter, finance; S. Alba, instruction and arts; M. Villanueva, agriculture, industry, commerce, and public works.

HISTORY

THE MINISTRY. In September, 1911, during the general strike, rioters in Cullera brutally murdered a local magistrate and two court officers. Seven men were charged with the murders and six of them were sentenced to death by a military court. At the beginning of 1912 the case was tried before the Supreme Council of War and Marine, which condemned all seven. Public opinion was deeply stirred on behalf of the prisoners, and the premier early in January recommended that clemency should be exercised in the case of six, but that the sentence against the seventh should stand. Later the government was induced to recommend that a reprieve be granted to the seventh as well, the king having expressed his desire that this be done. On January 10 Premier Canalejas tendered the resignation of the cabinet as a matter of form, but resumed office immediately. This act was characterized by certain journals as a "false crisis" and a "political farce." A similar "false crisis" followed a few days later. Upon the opening of the Cortes on January 19 a Republican deputy, Zulueta, attacked the government for its course during the recent strikes, for the execution of the *Numancia* mutineers, for the conduct of the Melilla campaign, and for the "false crisis" just passed. This was followed by attacks by the Radical Albornoz and the Socialist Pablo Iglesias. The premier replied to these varied accusations, which, though violent, seemed in no wise to impair the strength of the ministry, but to the surprise of all he again went to the king to offer the resignation of the cabinet (January 24). There were diverse rumors as to his reasons, but no adequate explanation was given. The king expressed his wish that the present cabinet should continue in office, and again the crisis passed. On March 12 Señor Gasset, finding himself in disagreement with some of his colleagues, resigned the portfolio of public works and the premier took advantage of the occasion to reconstitute his cabinet, as noted above under *Government*. During this interruption of the session the cabinet worked on the budget, their delay in presenting it having been one of the chief points in the criticism by the opposition, and on the reopening of the Cortes on May 1 the new minister of finance, Señor Reverter, submitted his project in detail. It embodied certain measures of economy which the finance minister had previously outlined to the press, as follows: "After 1907 expenditures increased from year to year to such an extent that our financial resources could not long have borne the burden. It was necessary to go to the root of the difficulty. That is what I have tried to accomplish for the budget of 1913. I have not been willing to appear before parliament without an honest budget—a budget of order and liquidation. It is not a political problem, as people have just now been saying, for all the ministers are in accord as to the plans of economy which I have proposed. It is necessary to tell the country the truth. The present state of the finances does not frighten me. I have seen several times as many millions leave the treasury for colonial wars. We may have to resort to extraordinary loans, but only for the moment." The budget placed the receipts at 1,167,400,000 pesetas, the expenditures at 1,146,-900,000 pesetas. It provided for a number of retrenchments, including the suppression of the office of captain-general in Melilla, for a temporary sur-tax on certain imports, for a tax on salt and for a tax on timber. The weak point in it was the low estimate for expenses in Morocco, only 50,000,000 pesetas, which indicated the government's intention to have recourse to the improvident expedient of borrowing. Nevertheless it was well received by the Chamber. A scandal was occasioned by the revelations of Señor Gasset in support of his charges against Señor Barroso, his successor in the ministry of public works. He accused the latter of using his authority when minister of justice to check legal proceedings against one of his relatives for election frauds. Señor Barroso denied the charges, but certain documents read by his accuser created a feeling of suspicion both in regard to Barroso and in relation to the ministry in general. Nevertheless, the position of the ministry seemed secure. Though the anti-monarchist groups were loud in their reproaches, accusing the ministry of a total failure to redeem the pledges they had given on coming into power more than two years before, they were apparently not eager to push their opposition to extremes, for they feared still more the return of Señor Maura and the Conservatives to power. On the close of the debate on the ministerial policy the Chamber voted confidence by 180 against 73 (May 11).

THE OPPOSITION. In September, 1911, the groups opposed to the Canalejas ministry seemed irreconcilable. Republicans and Socialists united in attacking the government, angered by its course in the suppression of the general strike, the suppression of constitutional guarantees, the sending of troops to Melilla, the judgments against Republican newspapers, and the dissolution of trades unions. Moreover, its policy had deeply offended the extreme right. At the beginning of 1912 it seemed destined to a short tenure of office. But its moderation in the Cullera affair tended to appease the anti-monarchist groups. Both the Socialist and Radical leaders displayed unexpected moderation in their criticism of the ministry. On one point, however, the anti-constitutional groups found themselves heartily in agreement in their opposition to the government. This was the Moroccan War. Radicals and Socialists alike condemned the Moroccan adventure as altogether wicked and wasteful. Despite the government's declaration that it was not embarking on a war of conquest but merely enforcing the application of its treaties, public and secret, and upholding the honor of Spain, the Republicans and Socialists persisted in their denunciations. "Why," exclaimed a member of the opposition, "have we gone into the Riff region? I have never seen a country so poor and destitute. Our troops have to take with them fuel and water. They go unwillingly. Some of them remind me of the convicts they used to send to Ceuta. The same means were employed to prevent their escape. Nobody wants the war. The expedition will add nothing to our prestige. It is only a question of boundaries. So long as Gibraltar stands, our frontier will be the limit of the range of the British batteries." He went on to remind the government that the cost of the expedition had reached the figure of 250,000,000 pesetas. To this the premier replied simply, "I cannot accept the responsibility of abandoning the only territory available for the expansion of Spain." The opposition were not satisfied with this plea or with the previous one, that Spain's honor was involved.

THE WAR IN MOROCCO. In general the Spanish public seemed weary of the long negotiations with France and of the government's campaign in Melilla. As to the latter, Señor Canalejas himself, speaking informally at a dinner, expressed the wish that "this accursed war" would end as soon as possible. Many of the leading newspapers showed their disgust with it. The news from the seat of war was not encouraging. The positions at Samar and Tumiat held by the Spaniards in October and November, 1911, were evacuated, and there was fighting within the zone of military occupation. Mass meetings were held in protest against the war, and at Toledo the Republicans made an especially vigorous demonstration (March 31). In carrying on the war the government was accused of a blind and servile obedience to the caprice of the king. The war was characterized as a wasteful and inglorious adventure, a useless drain on the treasury, and discreditable to the Spanish army. As the campaign dragged on and news of Spanish reverses reached the country, the opposition grew more bitter and the Radicals made common cause with the Republicans in demanding that the war should cease.

THE DECENTRALIZATION BILL. During the summer the chief subject of discussion was the government measure for regional decentralization. It granted, under certain reservations of state control, autonomous government to the departments of the local and provincial administrations. While the Catalans welcomed it, it was attacked both by the Conservatives and by many of the Liberal supporters of the government. The latter pronounced it inconsistent with the policy of their party and an undue concession to the regionalist spirit. It was passed by the Chamber by a large majority in July and was awaiting ratification by the Senate when the Cortes was adjourned on July 9. During the vacation it was vehemently discussed in the press.

OTHER EVENTS. At the end of September a strike on the railways in Catalonia was ordered, and the men finally decided upon a general strike on all the Spanish railways to be begun on October 8. They demanded increased wages and reduced hours. The revolutionary element rallied to the movement and the affair assumed serious dimensions. The government's policy followed the same line as that of Premier Briand in France during the great railway strike of 1910. It declared that it would resort to all legitimate means to suppress it and the premier issued a mobilization order calling railway servants to the colors. When the men reported for duty they were permitted to go home, but on the understanding that they were soldiers subject to military discipline. They received extra pay. This action, together with the government's promise of laws to redress their grievances led the men to suspend the strike until it could be seen what course the government would take on their behalf. Upon the assembling of the Cortes on October 15 legislation was immediately introduced providing for a settlement of labor disputes. On November 12 Señor Canalejas (q. v.) was killed in the streets of Madrid by an anarchist, and on the following day his body was buried with public honors. He was succeeded, as noted above under *Government*, by Count de Romanones. King Alfonso visited London in August. As to the negotiations and treaty with France concerning Morocco, see FRANCE, under *History*.

SPANGLER, HENRY WILSON. An American engineer, died March 16, 1912. He was born in Carlisle, Pa., in 1858 and graduated from the United States Naval Academy in 1878. He acted as engineer of the navy from 1878 to 1889 and again in 1898. From 1881 to 1884 he was assistant professor in mechanical engineering at the University of Pennsylvania and from 1889 until the time of his death was full professor. He was a member of many engineering societies. He was the author of *Valve Gears, Notes on Thermodynamics, Graphics*, and was coauthor of *Elements of Steam Engineering*.

SPIRITUALISM. See PSYCHICAL RESEARCH.

SPIRITUALISTS' ASSOCIATION, NATIONAL. An organization of various spiritualistic societies in the United States into one general association for the purpose or mutual aid and coöperation in benevolent, charitable, educational, and other purposes. The society in 1912 numbered 800, the State associations, 22, edifices for meeting, 200, and the membership of avowed spiritualists, 200,000. The number of public mediums was 2000, and private mediums, many thousands. The ordained ministers numbered 500. The convention of the association was held October 6-13 in Dallas, Tex. Much was accomplished looking toward the extension of edifices for meeting places, especially of a national temple in Washington, D. C. Active effort was being put forth to prevent unjust legislation and local laws against the exercise of mediumship. The president of the association in 1912 was F

George B. Warne; vice-president, Joseph P. Whitwell; secretary, George W. Kates, and treasurer, Cassius L. Stevens. The next annual convention will be held in Chicago in October, 1913.

SPOROTRICHOSIS. A disease caused by a fungus, *Sporotrichium*, which invades the tissues through small skin wounds, or scratches. The sporothrix on finding lodgment produces a hard lump, which breaks down into an abscess or ulcer; making its way through the lymph channels, the infection results in a series of such lesions, which heal very slowly, sometimes taking several months. Like other granulomas, the disease may become systemic, and all the tissues of the body be invaded. Farmers and other workers in rural districts are usually attacked, and the malady is believed to be often mistaken for glanders, tuberculosis, syphilis, blastomycosis, or actinomycosis, which produce similar chronic ulcerative lesions. This confusion in diagnosis probably accounts for the comparative rarity with which cases are reported, only 200 cases being on record throughout the civilized world, 58 of them occurring in the United States since 1898. The diagnosis of sporotrichosis depends on a consideration of the following details: its occurrence in farm workers; a history of slight traumatism succeeded by the slow development of small subcutaneous nodules, following the course of the deep lymphatic channels and softening into cold abscesses and ulcers; and the protracted course of the disease, with little pain and no temperature, or other effect on the general health. Diagnosis is confirmed by finding the sporothrix in the discharges, under the microscope.

SPRAGUE, Charles Ezra. An American banker and etymologist, died March 21, 1912. He was born in Nassau, N. Y., in 1842 and graduated from Union College in 1860. He served in the Civil War, becoming brevet-colonel in the New York Volunteers. He was wounded and disabled at the battle of Gettysburg. After the war he became a public accountant and was president of the board of examiners for public accountants in New York City from 1896 to 1898. He was connected with the Union Dime Savings Bank in New York from 1870 and was its president from 1892 until his death. He acted for a time as professor of accountancy in New York University. He was the inventor of many devices and systems for saving banks. He was the author of *Handbook of Volapük* (1888); *The Accountancy of Investment* (1904); *Extended Bond Tables* (1905); and *The Philosophy of Accounts* (1907). He also wrote many articles on language and bookkeeping. He was the first American advocate of Volapük.

SPRING, Alfred. An American jurist, died October 22, 1912. He was born at Franklinville, N. Y., in 1851. He attended the University of Michigan for two years and in 1875 was admitted to the bar. He was elected surrogate of Cattaraugus County, N. Y., in 1880, serving until 1892. In 1895 he was appointed justice of the supreme court of the State and was elected for the terms 1895 to 1909, and 1910 to 1921. From 1899 to the time of his death he served as a justice of the appellate division. He contributed on legal and other subjects to several magazines.

STABLE FLY AND DISEASE. See Poliomyelitis.

STAGE CHILDREN, EMPLOYMENT OF. See Child Labor.

STAHEL, Julius. An American soldier, died December 4, 1912. He was born in Hungary in 1825. He took part in the struggle for Hungarian independence under Louis Kossuth in 1848, and was wounded, and decorated for gallantry. In 1856 he removed to the United States and was engaged in newspaper work in New York City until the outbreak of the Civil War. He was appointed lieutenant-colonel of the Eighth New York Infantry in 1861 and a few months later was made colonel. In the same year he was appointed brigadier-general of volunteers. He reached the rank of major general of volunteers in 1863. He resigned from the regular army in 1865. In 1893 he was awarded the medal of honor for leading his division after he was severely wounded, and turning the enemy's flank at Piedmont, Va., June 5, 1864. At the first battle of Bull Run he covered the defeat of the Union army. He commanded the defense column of General Fremont's army in the Shenandoah Valley and commanded a brigade of the first division at the second battle of Bull Run. In 1863 he was placed in command of the Eleventh army corps and later in the same year he was sent for by President Lincoln and assigned to a command in front of Washington. In 1884 he was appointed consul at Yokohama, Japan, and consul-general at Shanghai, China. In the following year he resigned this office on account of ill-health.

STANCHFIELD, John B. See Presidential Campaign.

STANDARD OIL. See Presidential Campaign Contributions.

STANDARD TIME. See Time, Standard.

STANMORE, Arthur Hamilton Gordon, First Baron. A British administrator, died January 30, 1912. He was born in 1829 and was educated at Cambridge University, where he took the degree of M. A., in 1851. In the following year he became private secretary to the prime minister, his father, Earl of Aberdeen. In this position he served until 1854, when he was elected to Parliament. This seat he held until 1857 when he was defeated. In the following year he accompanied Gladstone as secretary on his mission as lord high commissioner to the Ionian Islands. In 1867 he began a career as colonial administrator, which lasted for thirty years. He was governor of New Brunswick from 1861 until 1866; of Trinidad from 1866 to 1870; of Mauritius from 1871 to 1874; of Fiji from 1875 to 1880; of New Zealand from 1880 to 1882; and of Ceylon from 1883 to 1890. In 1887 he was also made high commissioner for the Western Pacific. In this office he performed efficient service. He was the first governor of Fiji and the first high commissioner of the Western Pacific. In both capacities he laid down principles of administration which have been followed without substantial departure. On his retirement from administrative work he devoted himself to literary, and particularly to public and financial, work in London. He was raised to the peerage in 1893. Among his published works are: *Wilderness Journeys in New Brunswick* (1864); *Story of a Little War* (1879); *Life of Lord*

Aberdeen (1893); *Memoir of Sidney Herbert* (1906); and various pamphlets and articles in magazines.

STATE AID FOR ROADS. See ROADS AND PAVEMENTS.

STATE BANKS. The report of the comptroller of the currency showed that there were in the United States, June 14, 1912, a total of 13,381 State banks. Their aggregate resources were $3,897,770,000, including $2,549,-323,000 of loans and discounts, $341,797,000 bonds and other securities, and $241,756,000 cash on hand. Of the loans, 22 per cent. were secured by real estate, and 22 per cent. by other collateral, the remaining 56 per cent. being secured by personal paper. The bonds were composed very largely of State and municipal bonds; but included also a large amount of railroad and other public service corporation bonds.

The total capital stock of these banks was $459,067,000, to which should be added a surplus of $177,307,000 and undivided profits of $94,066,000. Their individual deposits amounted to $2,919,977,000, of which $657,477,000 represented savings deposits and $610,207,000 represented certificates of deposit; practically all of the remainder being deposits subject to check.

STATE BOARD OF HEALTH OF OHIO, CONTROL OVER SEWAGE DISPOSAL AND WATER-SUPPLIES. See SANITATION.

STATE CONTROL OF SEWAGE DISPOSAL AND WATER-SUPPLIES. See SANITATION.

STATISTICS, RAILWAYS. See RAILWAYS AND RAILWAY ACCIDENTS.

STAUNTON, VA. See MUNICIPAL GOVERNMENT.

STEAD, WILLIAM THOMAS. An English editor and publicist, died at sea April 15, 1912. He was born at Embleton, England, in 1849 and was educated at Silcoates School at Wakefield. At the age of fourteen he was apprenticed to a merchant, but his tastes were for journalism and he became in 1871 editor of *The Northern Echo* at Darlington. He continued in this position until 1880 when he became an assistant on the *Pall Mall Gazette*, of which in 1883 he became editor. He continued in the editorship of this paper until 1889. He was imprisoned for three years for the publication of sensational articles relating to crime against children and women. The agitation started by him resulted in the passing of the Criminal Amendment act of 1885. In 1891 he left the *Pall Mall Gazette* to found the *Review of Reviews*. The *Australian Review of Reviews* was founded in 1894. In 1895 he began the publication of a series called "Masterpiece Library of Penny Poets, Novels, and Prose Classics." He became greatly interested in the movement for world peace and after a visit to the Czar of Russia in 1898, started on a peace crusade. He founded and published a weekly paper called *War Against War*. At the first Hague Conference which he attended he strongly opposed the war with the Transvaal and edited the weekly paper of the Stop the War Committee. In 1890 he proposed the formation of the Union International to combat militarism and to secure the adoption of the recommendations of The Hague Conference. He began in the same year the publication of portfolios of pictorial masterpieces. In 1907 he visited the United States to be present at the founding of the Carnegie Institute in Pittsburgh, and to further the cause of world peace in America. After this visit he published a book entitled *If Christ Came to Chicago*, which created a profound sensation both in the United States and in England. In addition to his other interests he became a student of, and a convert to, spiritualism. In 1909 he declared that he was receiving daily letters from his son who had died the year before. Among his many publications, in addition to those mentioned above, are: *The Truth About Religion* (1888); *The Pope and the New Era* (1899); *The Labor War in the United States* (1894); *Her Majesty, The Queen* (1897); *Satan's Invisible World* (1897); *The United States of Europe* (1899); *Last Will and Testament of Cecil John Rhodes;* and many articles in magazines and newspapers. Mr. Stead was one of the victims of the disaster to the *Titanic*, on which he was a passenger on his way to the United States.

STEAMBOAT INSPECTION. See SAFETY AT SEA.

STEAMBOAT TRUST. See TRUSTS.

STEAM ENGINE. No radical innovations in the design of the steam engine were to be found in 1912. Through active studies, increased economy was made and some attention was being paid to flue-gas analysis and combustion recorders so that the fire of the boilers could be improved. This was found to be an important consideration in many plants where fuel economy was greatly increased. The use of superheated steam in some turbines and locomotives suggested its availability for reciprocating engines and during the year progress was made in overcoming the various difficulties involved. In connection with the use of superheated steam it was found necessary to employ separators to obviate the effects of local condensation and to eliminate moisture, as this last element, especially in the case of turbines, caused blade erosion. The most general use of superheated steam was at a temperature of from 100° to 150°. The American uniflow steam engine, which had been developed in 1911, was put on the market during the year and other machines of the same type were developed. This differs from the German Stumpf engine in that it has Corliss instead of poppet valves, but by reducing the loss due to initial condensation secures the same greater economy and has a large overload capacity. This type of steam engine was said to be particularly useful where the load was subject to large variations.

STEAMSHIPS. See SHIPBUILDING.

STEAM TURBINE. The success of the 20,000 kilowatt turbo-generators at the Water Side station in New York City and at the Northwest station of the Commonwealth Edison Company of Chicago, led the latter company in 1912 to contract for a still larger unit of this type for its Fisk Street station. This machine, which had a maximum rating of 25,000 kilowatts, was to be the most powerful combined prime mover and generating unit ever built. The generator was to develop 4500 volts and to it was to be connected a step-up transformer raising the potential to 9000 volts. The turbine was of the Parsons type and was being built in Great Britain.

In Europe the Brown-Boveri Company had

constructed a 25,000 h. p. group in the great St. Denis plant at Paris, to supplement the 100,000 h. p. in turbo-generators previously installed, making this the largest turbine station in Europe. The remarkable economy of space of the turbo-generator was shown by the fact that the new group accupied no more floor space than the 10,000 h. p. groups which had been used. The rotary part of this new Paris turbine weighed 40 tons and the outer part 42 tons. A larger turbine of 24,000 h. p. was installed at the Chorzow station in Silesia. It was built by the Allgemeine-Gesellschaft and has a capacity of 24,000 h. p. The Rhenish-Westphalia station at Essen in Germany was supplied with a Zoelly turbine built by the Escher-Wyss Company of Switzerland, which was stated to have a capacity for a momentary load of 30,000 h. p. This turbine, whose rotor and shaft weighed 30 tons, was coupled to a 65-ton Siemens-Schuckert alternator. The growth of the use of the turbine is shown by the fact that of the Zoelly turbine alone, some 500,000 h. p. had been built up to 1912.

Steam turbines in the form of 8000 kilowatt turbo-generators were to be substituted for each of four 3500 kilowatt reciprocating engine sets at the Greenwich station of the tramway system of the London County Council, increasing the station capacity from 34,000 to 52,000 kilowatts, with sufficient economy in the coal expenditure to more than provide the interest on the new capital charges. In Great Britain the Curtis turbine was reported to be finding its way into vessels where previously the Parsons type was regarded as preëminent. This was due, in part, to the use of the helical gear connection between the turbine and the propeller.

STEEL. See IRON AND STEEL.

STEEL CORPORATION, UNITED STATES. See UNITED STATES STEEL CORPORATION.

STEEL TARIFF. See TARIFF.

STEFANSSON, V. See POLAR EXPLORATION.

STEINERT, MORRIS. An American piano manufacturer and musician, died January 21, 1912. He was born in Scheinfeld, Bavaria, in 1832. He removed to the United States when he was fifteen years of age and became a member of Theodore Thomas's orchestra. He later went to Georgia, but removed to New Haven in 1862. In 1892 he founded the New Haven Symphony Orchestra and was for several years associated with Professor Horatio W. Parker in its leadership. He was a notable collector of musical instruments, and in 1890 took to Vienna his collection of harpsichords and spinets to illustrate a lecture on "The Old Art of Music." He later lectured on the same subject at the World's Fair in Chicago. He owned the largest collection of keyboard instruments and musical manuscripts in the world. The greater part of this was given to Yale University. He founded three scholarships in the Yale School of Music. He was the founder of the M. Steinert Piano Company.

STELLAR AND NEBULAR PARALLAXES. See ASTRONOMY.

STEVENS, HORACE JARED. An American copper specialist, died April 21, 1912. He was born in Coneango, N. Y., in 1866 and was educated in the common schools. He taught school for a time and afterwards served in various capacities in the copper mines in Michigan. Entering journalism he became manager and owner of the *Penninsular News Bureau*, and from 1901 to the time of his death was editor and publisher of the *Copper Handbook*, an annual devoted to the copper interests of the world. He was for two years editor of the Michigan *Mineral Statistics*, published by the State, and contributed to annual reviews on the copper industry.

STEVENS, NETTIE MARIA. An American biologist and educator, died May 4, 1912. She was born in Cavendish, Vt., in 1861 and graduated from Leland Stanford University in 1899. She was appointed reader in experimental morphology at Bryn Mawr College in 1904, serving in that position for one year, when she was appointed associate professor in the same branch. She was research assistant in Carnegie Institution from 1903 until the time of her death. Her chief interest was in the study of regeneration and in the connection of the germ cells with the problems of heredity. She carried on studies in these branches in Naples and in Germany and read many monographs in relation to them. She was one of the most eminent women scientists in the United States.

STEWART, ALEXANDER. An American public official, formerly member of Congress from Wisconsin, died May 24, 1912. He was born in York County, New Brunswick, Canada, in 1829, and was educated in the common schools of that county. In 1849 he removed to Wisconsin and engaged in the lumbering business in which he was very successful. In 1884 he was a delegate to the Republican national convention and was a member of Congress from 1895 to 1901, representing the 9th Wisconsin district.

STOCK EXCHANGE. See FINANCIAL REVIEW.

STOCK-HOLDINGS. See FINANCIAL REVIEW.

STOCK-RAISING AND MEAT PRODUCTION. The year 1912 was an eventful one in the livestock industry, owing to a number of causes, the chief of which was the completion of the liquidation of cattle which had been in progress for several years. Though the number of cattle received at the principal markets was about normal the weight of those arriving was below the average, for the mature beef stock had been cleaned up in 1911. There was no great increase in price until early in the summer, when the shortage became apparent. The rise continued until August, when the price of cattle on the hoof in Chicago exceeded that of the high prices of the spring of 1865, which had previously been the highest ever recorded at that market. This upward movement was accentuated by the promises of a good corn crop, which caused a heavy demand for stockers and feeders, a large number of which were shipped from Chicago in the spring to distant points in the West, there being a shortage of pastures near Chicago because the high price of corn had caused many farmers in the central part of the Corn Belt to plow up their pastures and plant corn.

For many years the movement of livestock, both on the hoof and in the refrigerator cars, has been from west to east, but areas of excessive production and limited consumption are rapidly disappearing and the increase of population in the Mississippi Valley has changed to some extent the method of distribution.

During the year, Virginia sent cattle to Pennsylvania; Tennessee has been sending them to Chicago; and Chicago has sent more stock cattle west than ever before. This is the beginning of a more even production of meat animals throughout the country and in the future it will be produced near points where it is packed or consumed.

About 25,000 acres of land in the Southern States was released from quarantine during the year, making a total of 164,000 sq. m., which have been cleared of the Texas fever tick. The farmers in the South are improving their stock and will soon contribute materially to the meat supply. The value of animals sold and slaughtered on farms was estimated to be worth about $1,930,000,000, and the total value of animal products for 1912 $3,395,000,000. The number of cattle on farms in the United States in 1912 was less than 60,000,000, a decrease of 20 per cent. in the last 5 years. The cattle imports during the fiscal year ending June, 1912, were heavier than ever before, while exports dropped to a low ebb. The number imported was 318,372 as against 105,506 exported; whereas in 1902 exports were four times greater than imports, but the value of the exported cattle was much greater per head than those imported, the latter being mainly Mexican stockers, while the cattle exported were finished steers. The value of the cattle imported was $4,805,574, as compared with $8,870,975 at which the exports were valued. Had not the Mexican insurrection handicapped traffic across the Rio Grande even more cattle would have been imported. The exports of mutton amounted to only a few hundred thousand dollars in value, but this represents a slight increase. The exports of lard and cured pork hams, which declined in 1910 and 1911, were very nearly restored to figures of earlier years. Exports in eggs have been rising very rapidly and amount to more than three times the average figures between 1900 and 1909. There was an increase in imports of wool and packinghouse products, including hides and skins.

There was an unusually heavy loss of animals in the United States from exposure and diseases. The number estimated for the year ending April 1, 1912, was: cattle, 2,497,581; sheep, 3,834,702; swine, 5,834,456. The highest losses of cattle from exposure occurred in Louisiana, Wyoming, Colorado, Florida, Mississippi, and Montana. The highest loss of cattle from exposure was 80 head per 1000 in the first three mentioned States. The heaviest loss of sheep occurred in Wyoming, Colorado, and Arizona. The heaviest loss among swine was mainly due to hog cholera.

Meat and Meat Inspection. The Committee on Markets of the New York State Food Investigation Commission in their study of wholesale cost price and retail selling price found the cash margin to be as follows: Beef hind quarters, 70 per cent.; beef fore quarters, 35.5 per cent.; pork and hams, 45.45 per cent.; lamb, 31.1 per cent.; bacon, 33.33 per cent.; live fowls, 25 per cent.; frozen roasters, 24.15 per cent.; western eggs, 19.47 per cent.; sample White Leghorn eggs, 43.43 per cent.

There has been considerable agitation throughout the country to establish municipal markets similar to those in European cities in order to lower this high cost of distribution. At the close of the year a number of distributing centres in Philadelphia, Chicago, and Boston for the sale of eggs were opened for the purpose of bringing the consumer and producer of eggs nearer together and temporarily it reduced the price of eggs. Several suits were conducted by the government against the so-called "Beef Trusts" and the corporation known as the National Packing Company was compelled to dissolve and parcel its property out among the different packing interests which held stock in it.

The government meat inspection was conducted at 940 establishments located in 259 cities and towns. There were inspected at the time of slaughter 59,140,019 animals, an increase of over 6,000,000 compared to the preceding year, the greatest increase being in hogs, 5,000,000 more being slaughtered than the previous year. There was a slight decrease in the number of cattle. There was a total of over 600,000 carcases condemned, wholly or in part. Tuberculosis was the cause of a proportion of the condemnations of cattle and hogs. There were also over 18,000,000 pounds of meat condemned on reinspection after slaughter. Inspection certificates issued for exports of meat and meat-food products covered more than 10,000,000,000, a slight increase over the preceding year. Nearly 27,000 samples of various products were examined in meat inspection laboratories for the purpose of detecting preservatives, coloring matter, adulterants, or impurities. The results showed products singularly free from preservatives and coloring matters. Farmers, retail butchers and dealers, unless they make interstate shipments of meat, are exempt from inspection by law, but it is estimated that federal inspection covers about 60 per cent. of the meat slaughtered in this country. The success of meat inspection since the new law has been in effect has stimulated sentiment for the establishment of abattoirs for the inspection of meats intended for purely local consumption.

Sheep. The marketing of sheep has been heavy at the principal western markets, so that mutton has been relatively cheap as compared with beef and pork, except for a brief period in the spring. This extra supply of mutton undoubtedly prevented a meat famine, and, in spite of the scarcity of beef and pork, mutton would have been nearly unsalable if packers had not used the surplus for canning and making sausages. But the liquidation in sheep was over at the end of the year.

The trade in wool was heavy throughout the year, and in spite of a record clip in Australia the supply of raw wool is somewhat short of normal. The amount of the clip in the United States amounted to 318,548,000 pounds, having a farm value of $55,500,000. The flocks in Australia and New Zealand now contain 117,110,654 head, a slight increase over the previous year, but there was a general improvement in the character of the flocks. The cost of wool production was also slightly increased. The over-sea shipments of wool amounted to 662,845,907 pounds from Australia and 169,915,939 pounds from New Zealand. The quality of Australian wool has gradually become less fine and soft than formerly, as the coarser breeds have been found to be more profitable. About 76 per cent. of the Australian clip was sold at colonial centres and the balance on th [illegible] market. A heavy drought causing a [illegible] 5,000,000 or 6,000,000 sheep and about [illegible] cent. of the lambs will reduce materially the Australian clip for the coming year. There was a decline in shipments of wool from Argentina, as sheep are being replaced by cattle. There has been great activity in the sheep industry in Canada, due in part to the measures taken by the government to promote the industry. According to *Dalgety's Review* the total number of sheep in all the principal sheep countries of the world amounts to 616,229,372 head, an increase of about 100,000,000 since 1895.

HORSES. The work of the United States government in breeding Morgan horses in Vermont, carriage horses in Colorado, and gray draft horses in Iowa has been continued, and the average excellence of the foals produced was considerably above that of previous years. A large practical horse-breeding plant has been established at the Tuskegee Institute in Alabama, largely by gift of stallions and standard-bred mares.

POULTRY. The poultry industry, as usual, has continued to increase until now it is valued at $570,000,000. On October 31, the yearly egg-contest conducted by the Connecticut and Missouri Experiment Stations came to a close. The Connecticut contest was won by a flock of five White Leghorns, which laid a total of 1071 eggs; the highest number of eggs laid by a single hen was 254, by a Rhode Island Red. In the Missouri contest the best hen was a White Plymouth Rock, which laid 281 eggs in 12 months. The leading pen consisted of five rose-comb Rhode Island Reds, that laid an average of 208 eggs per hen. The 655 hens in the contest laid an average of over 134 eggs each. These contests show that both utility qualities and standard-bred points may be combined in the same fowl, as the best laying hen in the Missouri contest during the first eight months was a pure-bred fowl from a pure-bred male and female, both of which had been prize winners at poultry shows. These contests have emphasized the fact that there are both good and poor layers in all breeds of fowls. On April 1, there was finished a decade of annual egg contests at the Hawkesbury Agricultural College in New South Wales. During the decade there was an improvement in the type of breed and the average number of eggs laid per hen per year was raised from 131 to 184.

The eggs exported from the United States in 1912 were valued at $3,400,800, an enormous increase over recent years. The studies of the Department of Agriculture have been a great help towards improving conditions under which eggs are marketed. During the year a traveling refrigerator was made by the installation of mechanical refrigeration in a refrigerator car. This permits the taking of improved methods into rural districts, where it is otherwise impossible to convince the people what good handling, combined with refrigeration, can do for the producer. Better methods have been devised for handling dressed poultry, marketing fresh eggs, and for the preparation of frozen and dried eggs.

The American Poultry Association, which is the largest livestock association in the world, held its thirty-seventh annual meeting at Nashville, Tenn., the first time it was ever held in the South. The association is doing much to promote investigation and the development of the poultry industry. The International Association of Poultry Instructors and Investigators was organized in London in July, the object being to interchange knowledge and experience among those engaged in poultry teaching throughout the world. A new method of preserving eggs has been reported from France, which consists of packing them in a specially constructed metal box, in which they are treated with carbonic acid and nitrogen.

The experiment stations have been active in finding economical methods of feeding and finishing all kinds of livestock for market. They have demonstrated that the silo is as advantageous for making beef and mutton as for milk production. The feeding tests conducted during the year at the stations in Alabama, North Carolina, and other southern States have shown conclusively that a combination of silage and cotton-seed meal makes excellent beef at a comparatively low price, which means that in the future the South is going to be a greater factor in beef production than in the past.

LIVESTOCK INDUSTRY IN FOREIGN COUNTRIES. In South America the grain-growing area is being extended, so that the beef industry has not been increasing as rapidly as it otherwise would. The grazing land is increasing in value, so that the jerked beef industry is being supplanted by freezing establishments as jerked beef can be prepared at a profit only when the cattle are grazed at a low cost. Argentina has passed a law providing for a premium to be paid for the first establishment for frozen meat. Uruguay has extended its cattle raising and the annual production is increasing because of improvement in the grade of cattle and the use of silage and improved pastures. The government has made grants to livestock shows and subsidies have been given to breeders' associations. The Brazilian government is establishing stud farms, which will give special attention to the improvement of indigenous breeds of cattle and the improvement of a type of horse suitable for remounts in the army.

Great Britain's supply of beef, formerly obtained from the United States, is now being sent from Argentina. Arrangements have been made for the enlargement of cold storage facilities on the Thames and for the increase in the amount of frozen and chilled meat imported. Livestock returns from England and Wales show a decrease in all species of domestic animals.

The necessity for improving the remounts in the English armies led the government to take steps towards encouraging the industry of light horse breeding.

Besides an unusually large number of experiment station publications, popular articles, and other publications on animal production, the following books have been issued during the year: E. Lavalard, *L'Alimentaton du Cheval* (Paris); J. Collier, *The Pastoral Age in Australasia* (London and Melbourne); E. Molier, *L'Equitation et le Cheval* (Paris); Richard Lydekker, *The Horse and its Relatives;* Richard Lydekker, *The Ox and Its Kindred;* Richard Lydekker, *The Sheep and Its Cousins* (London); F. T. Barton, *Horses and Practical Horse Breeding* (London); P. Dechambre, *Traité de Zootechnie. I, Zootechnie Générale* (Paris); J. T. Critchell, and J. Raymond, *A History of the Frozen*

Meat Trade (London); F. Kleinheinz, *Sheep Management* (Madison, Wis.); H. C. Dawson, *The Hog Book* (Chicago); J. H. Robinson, *Principles and Practice of Poultry Culture* (Boston, New York and London); C. Kronacher, *Grundzüge der Züchtungsbiologie* (Berlin); C. S. Valentine, *The Beginner in Poultry* (New York); D. H. Doane, *Sheep Feeding and Farm Management* (Boston, New York and London); W. A. Dryden and W. T. Ritch, *The Sheep Industry in Canada, Great Britain and the United States* (Canada Dept. Agr., Branch Live Stock Comr., Spec. Rpt., 1911, Nov.); A. Kraemer, *Das Schönste Rind* (Berlin); D. Meyer, *Handbuch der Futtermittel and Getreidetrocknung* (Leipsic); *Hides and Skins* (Chicago); *Origin and History of all Breeds of Poultry* (Chicago); T. Allen, *Profitable Pig Breeding and Feeding* (London); R. S. Matthews, *The Retail Butcher* (Memphis, Tenn.); T. E. Quisenberry, *The Poultryman's Guide* (Mountain Grove, Mo.); J. E. Richelet, *The Meat Industry of Argentine* (An. Soc. Rural Argentine, 46 (1912), No. 2, pp. 160-201, figs. 28); G. Wilsdorf, *Tierzüchtung* (Leipzig); H. Werner, *Die Rinderzucht* (Berlin); C. Correns, *Die Neuen Vererbungsgesetze* (Berlin); H. Kraemer, *Aus Biologie, Tierzucht und Rassengeschichte. Gesammelte Vorträge und Aufsätze* (Stuttgart); J. Rostafinski, *Die Tierzucht Ungarns* (Vienna and Leipzig); C. W. Burkett, *First Principles of Feeding Farm Animals* (New York and London); C. S. Plumb, *Beginnings in Animal Husbandry* (St. Paul, Minn.); H. Draeger, *Die Fleischschafzucht* (Hannover).

STOKER, ABRAHAM (better known as "BRAM"). An English barrister and writer, died April 18, 1912. He was born in Dublin in 1847 and was educated at Trinity College, Dublin. He was admitted to the bar and was for a time inspector of petty sessions in the Civil Service. He later engaged in journalism and worked as literary, dramatic, and art critic for various newspapers. In 1876 he met Henry Irving and two years later became his manager and confidential secretary. He retained this position until the time of Irving's death. Among the many books he wrote are: *Under the Sunset* (1882); *The Shoulder of Shasta* (1895); *Dracula* (1897); *Miss Betty* (1898); *The Jewel of the Seven Stars* (1903); *The Man* (1905); *Snowbound* (1909); and *The Lady of the Shroud* (1909). His best known work, however, is *Personal Reminiscences of Henry Irving* (1906-1907).

STONE, CHARLES WARREN. An American public official, former Congressman from Pennsylvania, died August 15, 1912. He was born in Groton, Mass., in 1843, and graduated from Williams College in 1863. He studied law and was admitted to the bar in 1866, practicing in Warren, Pa. He also became interested in oil producing and farming. In 1870-71 he was a member of the State House of Representatives and of the State Senate in 1877-78. From 1879 to 1883 he was lieutenant-governor of the State, and from 1887 to 1890 was secretary of State. He was elected to the Fifty-first Congress in 1890 to fill the unexpired term of L. F. Watson, and was reëlected to the Fifty-second and Fifty-fifth Congresses, 1891-9. He was a member of several learned societies.

STRAITS SETTLEMENTS. A British crown colony composed as follows: Singapore (206 square miles), Penang (107), and Malacca (659). Attached to Singapore are Labuan, Christmas Island (Indian Ocean), and the Cocos (or Keeling) Islands; to Penang, Province Wellesley and the Dindings. Total area, between 1630 and 1650 square miles; population (census of 1911), 714,069 (1891, 512,342). The city of Singapore (the capital) had 193,089 inhabitants in 1901. No duties are levied on imports or exports. Tapioca, rice, rubber, and sugar are produced in the colony, and coal is mined in Labuan.

*	1908	1909	1910
Imports	316,395,939	313,358,427	364,470,653
Exports	273,818,124	281,183,021	324,189,786
Revenue	8,969,015	8,795,001	9,336,328
Expenditure ...	9,837,624	8,542,731	7,532,242
Shipping	21,750,245	22,192,354	23,429,495

* Trade and financial statistics in Straits Settlements dollars; shipping in tons entered and cleared.

Beginning January 1, 1912, the railways of the Straits Settlements came under the management of the Federated Malay States government. The terms called for a lease of 21 years at an annual rental of $95,200, subject to septennial revision. It was later proposed to sell the railways to the Federated Malay States government and a joint committee during the year was considering the question of the amount to be paid.

Sir Arthur Henderson Young (appointed 1911), was governor in 1912.

STRAUS, ISIDOR. American merchant and philanthropist, died at sea April 15, 1912. He was born in Rhenish Bavaria in 1845, and removed to the United States with his parents in 1854. He was educated in the Collingsworth Institute, Talbotton, Ga. In 1863 he went abroad as foreign representative of a mercantile house in Columbus, Ga. Returning to the United States he joined his father in 1866 in forming the firm of L. Straus and Sons, importers of pottery and glassware. In 1888, with his brother Nathan, he became a partner in the department store of R. H. Macy and Co., and also in the firm of Abraham and Straus, Brooklyn. Mr. Straus took an active interest in politics in New York City, although he was at no time a candidate for public office. At a special election in 1893 he was appointed to fill the unexpired term of Ashbel P. Fitch in the House of Representatives. Here he became the friend of William L. Wilson and assisted him in the preparation of schedules of the Wilson tariff bill. He was a profound student of economic questions, especially those relating to tariff and trade expansion. He was a warm friend of Grover Cleveland and took a prominent part in the election of the latter for the presidency. Cleveland offered him the portfolio of Postmaster-General, but he declined. He is said to have been largely instrumental in the action of President Cleveland in convening an extraordinary session of Congress for the consideration of tariff measures. When William J. Bryan came into control of the Democratic party, Mr. Straus retired from active participation in public affairs, but in 1908 he served as head of the National Democratic Business Men's League. Mr. Straus was conspicuous for his works of charity and was an ardent supporter of every enterprise to improve the condition of immigrants in New York Ci'

He was president of the American Educational Alliance and was a member of boards of many philanthropical institutions. He was one of the most successful merchants of the United States and gave much of his wealth to charitable institutions. Mr. Straus was one of the victims of the *Titanic* disaster, and one of the touching incidents of the wreck of that vessel was the refusal of Mrs. Straus to leave her husband when there was an opportunity for her to be saved.

STREET CLEANING. The use of various kinds of pick-up sweepers is increasing, and naturally the newer of these machines are motor-driven, as is increasingly true of street-cleaning apparatus generally. Washing, rather than sweeping, appears to be a growing practice where conditions favor it. A significant study of street-cleaning methods, with a view to determining efficiency standards and cost, was made during 1912 by the Efficiency Division of the Civil Service Commission of Chicago. The study also included garbage and refuse collection and haulage to the point of disposal. See pamphlet *Report on Appropriations and Expenditures Bureau of Streets* of Chicago; also reports of departments of street cleaning for: (1) Boroughs of Manhattan, Bronx, and Brooklyn, and (2) Richmond, for descriptions of methods used and for statistics. The Richmond borough report contains important suggestions for reforms in budget appropriation methods, designed to put the appropriations on a work-quantity and unit-cost basis. The general plan suggested was adopted for this borough for the 1913 budget.

STREET RAILWAYS. See MUNICIPAL OWNERSHIP.

STREET-TRADES, REGULATION OF IN ENGLAND. See CHILD LABOR.

STRIKES. The year 1912 witnessed some of the most extensive and significant labor disturbances of recent years. Probably the most conspicuous of these was the strike of the British coal miners. For the American public the most significant was the strike of the textile workers in the woolen mills at Lawrence, Mass. Dr. W. A. MacDonald, writing in the Boston *Evening Transcript*, estimated the total strike losses for the world during the year ending October 1, at about one billion dollars. He estimated the loss resulting from the British coal strike at $250,000,000; from the British dock strike, $15,000,000; from the American anthracite strike, $50,000,000; from the strike of the employees on the Harriman railway lines $26,000,000; from the Lawrence textile strike, $5,000,000. His list included the following strikes: Baggage porters at Cherbourg; revolutionary labor disturbances at Bilboa, Spain; the general strike at Valencia, Spain; the Irish railway strike; the strike of 30,000 laborers at Madrid; the six months' coal strike in western Canada; the 6000 taxicab drivers in London; the 31,000 tailors throughout Prussia; the 300,000 coal miners of Germany; the Havana dock strike; the Belgian riots; the Budapest riots in which 50,000 laborers participated; the strike of the freight handlers of Ontario, Canada; and that of the cigar makers at Manila. The evidence showed that the labor unrest is world-wide. May and June, 1912, were months of excessive disturbance in Great Britain. Thus 69 strikes began in June. In Great Britain 135,900 men and women were thrown out of work, and the total of 1,505,000 days work was lost.

LAWRENCE MILLS. The most spectacular strike of the year in this country was that of the Lawrence textile workers in January. The first outbreak occurred in the Lawrence Duck mill on January 1, and complete work was not resumed for nearly eleven weeks thereafter. This strike aroused the active interest of the entire country and led to debate and investigation by Congress. It was notable for the appearance for the first time in the Eastern States of industrial unionism or syndicalism (q. v.), the most radical form of the labor movement. It was due primarily to a law effective January 1 reducing the hours of women and children employed in factories from 56 to 54 per week and followed by a corresponding reduction in wages. By January 12 the strike had spread so that it involved some 4000 workers in the cotton mills, and some 29,000 workers in the woolen mills of the city. Not all of these were out at any one time, the proportion of actual strikers varying from 40 per cent. to 70 per cent. The Industrial Workers of the World (see SYNDICALISM) already had small organizations among the English-speaking and the Italian-speaking workers. On January 12, Joseph J. Ettor, a member of the executive board of the I. W. W., arrived in Lawrence, and a strike that would probably have collapsed in a few days because of financial weakness and lack of leadership soon became determined. Ettor, a Syro-Italian of only 26 years, had been a leader in labor disputes at Paterson, Brooklyn, McKee's Rocks, and elsewhere. He succeeded in inspiring the polyglot workers of seventeen nationalities with a sense of the righteousness of their cause and of social solidarity. Troops were sent to the city, by early February there being more than a dozen companies of infantry and two of cavalry on hand.

The strikers presented their formal demands as follows: 15 per cent. increase in wages; abolishment of the premium or bonus systems; double pay for overtime; and no discrimination against strikers. Certain other grievances dealt with speeding up of machinery, fining, and the payment of higher wages to native than to foreign help for the same work. The strikers claimed that they had been induced to come to America and to Lawrence by deceptive posters. The premium system was said to act as a powerful stimulus on account of the low wages and often to lead the workers to sacrifice their health for small increases in pay. Attempts were made to bring about conferences by the State board of arbitration and conciliation; Governor Foss urged the legislature to investigate, and in an open letter urged the strikers to return for thirty days pending an inquiry; and a special committee of the legislature held many hearings. Though the militia had been sent to the scene on January 15 and though there was little violence, a woman, Anna Lopizzo, was shot on January 29. The next day Ettor and his assistant, Giovannitti, were arrested on a charge of being accessories to the murder. A few days previously William D. Haywood arrived on the scene. Early in February the United Textile Workers, a part of the American Federation of Labor, of which a few small unions in Lawrence were members, entered the field. The opposition between craft unionism and industrial unionism was most bitter. Late in February attempts to send children to Philadelphia and New York were resisted by the military and police authorities, thus arousing universal demand for governmental intervention and leading to investigations by Massachusetts officials, by the United States District Attorney, and by the United States House of Representatives. Later several hundred children were sent to these cities and to Barre, Vt.

On March 1 notices were posted in mills announcing wage increases ranging from 5 per cent. to 11 per cent. and averaging 7 or 8 per cent. The largest increases applied to the lowest wages. The strike leaders, however, resisted settlement. It was afterwards charged, and in part shown, that this resistance was due to a desire on the part of the leaders to take advantage of large contributions coming in from socialist organizations of the country. Work was resumed by larger numbers of strikers on March 15 when the strike was practically ended. It was estimated that the strike cost the mill owners and strikers from one to five million dollars and imposed upon the State and city extra police expenses of nearly $300,000. The sequel to this memorable labor disturbance had several phases. Strikes occurred almost simultaneously at Lowell and Clinton, Mass., Barre, Vt., Passaic, N. J., and various places in Pennsylvania, partly as a result of imitation and partly as a result of the programme of the labor leaders. In all these places wage advances were secured. Moreover, other textile centres, such as Fall River and New Bedford, felt the pressure for higher wages. In New England it was estimated that more than 200,000 textile workers secured wage advances of five to twelve per cent. Total wage increases estimated at $10,000,000 per year were followed by a slight advance in the price of goods.

Much more significant, however, than the wage advances was the publicity of certain phases of the labor problem which the agitation secured. The low wages and exploitative conditions revealed in an industry conceded to be dependent on the protective system strengthened the belief that the protective system with unrestricted immigration is developing economic inequality in American industrial centres. Some of the mills were highly capitalized and yet ordinarily paid good dividends. The argument that the tariff must be maintained in order to enable the manufacturer to pay high wages was declared to be manifestly false. The fact that the mill owners had at first refused to grant any increase in wages but later granted considerable increases was said to be due to their fear that obstinacy on their part would surely result in congressional reduction of the tariff on textile products. The radical character of the leaders of the I. W. W. was also calculated to arouse public attention. The fact that numerous nationalities were readily brought into coöperation, that evidence of class consciousness among the mill workers all over the eastern States was shown, also forced the public to recognize that the conditions producing the strike at Lawrence were not purely local. The class consciousness of the workers was further accentuated by the long detention of the accused leaders, so that the necessary basis for the spread of radical unionism was greatly broadened.

One of the investigations undertaken was that ordered by the Senate and made by the Commissioner of Labor. It showed that three-fourths of the 85,892 inhabitants of Lawrence were directly dependent upon the mills. The investigation covered 21,922 operatives. The average wage of all these was found to be 16 cents an hour; 23.3 per cent. of them earned less than 12 cents an hour; and 20.4 per cent. earned 20 cents an hour or over. Almost exactly one-third, or 7275 employees, of whom 5294 were over 18 years of age, earned less than $7 a week. Of these 5294, 36 per cent. were males. The inquiry showed that the normal family of five must send at least two wage-earners into the mills in order to secure the necessities of life. Where there was no child of at least 14, it thus became necessary for the wife to become a mill worker. These wages brought forcefully to the attention of the public the necessity of minimum wage legislation in order to prevent the undue exploitation of ignorant unskilled workers.

Ettor and Giovannitti, as well as a mill worker, Joseph Caruso, all charged with being accessories to the murder of the Lopizzo woman, were detained in jail, bail being refused. Their trial began about October 1, and continued until late in November. Early in October many thousands of mill workers at Lawrence went on strike for a few days as a protest against this long imprisonment. The case brought out much conflicting testimony as to the cause of death and the attitude of the leaders toward industrial peace. At the very close of the evidence Ettor made a notable speech to the jury. A verdict of not guilty was rendered November 26.

On February 2, John W. Breen, an undertaker and a member of the Lawrence school committee, was arrested on a charge of conspiracy to place dynamite on the premises of strikers, especially in the Syrian quarters. On August 30, William M. Wood, president of the American Woolen Company, and Dennis Collins were indicted on a charge of having instigated the conspiracy. It was alleged that the dynamite had been secured by Ernest W. Pitman, a building contractor, and taken to Lawrence by Collins and Breen, and put by the latter in such places as would discredit the strikers. The evidence sustained this theory, it being shown that special police, previously informed, followed Breen's course, "discovered" the dynamite and arrested a number of Syrians on a charge of having dynamite on their premises.

LITTLE FALLS. A strike in the Phœnix Knitting Mills at Little Falls, N. Y., began early in October. It was due to a reduction of pay following the enforcement of a law reducing the hours of women from 60 to 54 per week. It was thus comparable to the Lawrence, Mass., strike. Socialist and I. W. W. agitators and leaders put themselves in charge. Mayor George R. Lunn, the Socialist mayor of Schenectady, was arrested, with others, for speaking in a strike district, a permit having been refused. The speakers had purposely designed to test their rights of free speech and assembly. Application was made to the governor for protection and the attorney-general rendered an opinion sustaining the rights of free speech and assembly so long as no disorderly acts were committed. On December 17, Mayor Lunn was indicted on a charge of inciting to riot in an October speech. The New York board of mediation and arbitration began inquiries into the situation on December 27. It was brought out that conditions similar to those at Lawrence existed: a large mass of foreign workers from central, southern, and southeastern Europe, newly organized by radical labor leaders, were found to be working at grievously low wages. It seemed likely that the efforts of the board would bring the strike to a close at the beginning of the year.

Among other American strikes of the year were the following: In February and March a strike involving 7000 workers in Paterson silk mills for higher pay; in March and April about 3000 strikers in the cotton mills near Utica, N. Y., for higher pay and better conditions, being attended by riots and a call for troops; in March and April a strike of 900 cotton mill workers in West Warren, Mass., resulting in increased pay; about the same time a strike of 800 weavers at Passaic, N. J. In April occurred also a strike of 15,000 carpenters for an increase of five cents per hour at Chicago and near-by cities; in May a strike of newspaper pressmen and stereotypers on the Hearst and other papers at Chicago, followed by sympathetic strikes on Hearst papers in New York, San Francisco, Atlanta, and Los Angeles, resulting in failure primarily because other printers' unions refused to break contracts. In May occurred also a strike of 5000 freight handlers at Chicago, and 2000 laborers at Newark demanding an 8-hour day and a $2 wage. On May 31 began a strike of about 5000 waiters in restaurants and hotels in New York for better pay and recognition of the union, the strike collapsing on June 25; a similar waiters' strike followed in Boston, being attended by the efforts of Mrs. Rose Pastor Stokes to organize the female employees. In June occurred an extensive strike among the elevated and street railway employees in Boston, accompanied by violence and greatly impeding traffic; about 1000 mill operatives near Middletown, Conn., organized by the I. W. W., engaged in so much rioting that a troop of cavalry was sent to the scene; over 3000 cablemakers quit at Perth Amboy, N. J., demanding higher pay and shorter hours, the strike being attended by rioting resulting in fatalities; a strike of about 5000 foreign laborers near Newark, N. J., was attended by the shooting of several officers and the killing of four strikers and a high school student, 21 of the strikers being afterward sent to the penitentiary. In July a big strike in Atlantic ports, involving 30,000 persons, on a demand for higher wages and better conditions led to rioting and some fatalities. In August, 2500 weavers at Adams, Mass., demanded a closed-shop, and 15,000 street railway employees in Chicago secured wage advances. In September strikes were in progress in coal mining communities in West Virginia and Colorado, in fire arms works at Hartford, Conn., among the trackmen on the Pittsburgh and Lake Erie Railroad, and among the 6000 Greek and Cretan workers in copper, lead, and silver mines at Bingham, Utah; a one-day strike of 1500 street car men at Detroit for better pay; a one-day strike of 12,000 mill operatives at Lawrence in protest against the long imprisonment of Ettor and Giovannitti; and the successful termination of a strike of 9000 miners at Panther Creek Valley, Pa., demanding the discharge of two non-union men. In October 35,000 employees in copper mining at Ely, Nev., struck for higher pay; striking trainmen on the Georgia railroad agreed to submit their case to arbitration under the Erdman act. In November and December occurred a strike of 1000 yard trainmen in the Homestead, Braddock, and other plants of the United States Steel Corporation at Pittsburgh, for higher wages and the right to circulate petitions, the strike causing much anxiety because of activities of I. W. W. leaders; but it was overcome by the steadfast refusal of the companies to hear complaints of workers collectively. In the Christmas season a strike of express drivers at Newark was attended by violence and great congestion of traffic. On December 30, began a strike of the employees in the men's and children's ready-made clothing industry of New York and vicinity involving at least 100,000 workers who demanded better pay. (See RAILWAYS.)

FOREIGN STRIKES. Among strikes abroad not described above may be noted the following: In January and February strikes of railway and dock workers in the Argentine Republic; of various groups of workers at Brisbane, Australia, in a general sympathetic strike, and of street railway men at Wellington, New Zealand. In April and May a strike of stevedores and harbor engineers at Havana with sympathetic strikes at other Cuban ports. In May great strikes of street railway employees at Lisbon, Portugal; and a general strike in Hungary as a political manifestation following the election of Count Tisza as speaker of the lower house of the Hungarian Parliament; much property was destroyed and several deaths resulted. In June the most important strike was that of the French seamen, beginning at Havre and spreading to other French ports; the strikers demanded increased pay; a number of them were sentenced to fifteen days' imprisonment for desertion; they yielded on August 2, after seriously crippling traffic for six weeks; they gave notice, however, that they were determined to obtain satisfaction and sent delegates to Paris to present their claims. Following the success of the clerical party in June, 100,000 miners, mill workers, glass workers, and railway employees in the Walloon provinces struck as a protest, the strike being attended by much rioting requiring the calling out of reserves; a strike of marine engineers crippled the coastal traffic of Norway; 15,000 miners in the Asturia district of Spain engaged in rioting, the disturbance being largely political in character; a general strike of seamen and transport workers at Palermo, Sicily, of a political character. In October a strike on Spanish railways was met by the government in the same manner as France met the railroad strike in 1910, the army reserves to the number of 60,000 being mobilized. In December a strike of shop employees on the national railways of Mexico resulted in several deaths; on December 31, taxicab drivers of London, estimated at 6000, voted to strike.

GREAT BRITAIN. The year was notable for its large labor disturbances and the radical character of new labor movements. It opened with the strike of 160,000 textile operators in the Manchester district which had begun on December 28, 1911. This strike was due primarily to the refusal of weavers to work with nonunionists; they also demanded an increase in wages. It was compromised about the middle of January. The most important strike of the year was that of the coal miners for a legal minimum wage, for which see MINIMUM WAGE.

In May began another extensive strike of the dock workers, led by the Amalgamated Society of Watermen, Lightermen, and Watchmen, comparable to the transport workers' strike of 1911 in numbers engaged, but not so extensive in scope or serious in effects. More than 200,000 men were out; there was considerable violence, and great quantities of goods were destroyed. The strike closed abruptly on July 27. The cause was the refusal of unionist workmen to work with a non-unionist. The men and the employers each accused the other party of violating the trade agreement. Sir Edward Clarke was called upon to investigate the case and found that on this point the union was, in the main, correct. At the same time, however, much dissatisfaction was expressed in English labor circles because men had gone on strike before seeking an arbitration of the dispute. The workers were accused of an effort to starve the nation in order to secure slightly better conditions for themselves. Shortly after the strike was begun the transport workers drew up a new and extensive list of demands, including a closed shop in all dock work, and an increase of wages with shorter hours. On the one hand there were papers that accused the government of cowardice in not dealing with the situation with stern repression. On the other, Tom Mann, former president of the International Transport Workers' Federation, declared that it was useless to depend on parliament and government for betterment of conditions since little had been done in a generation. He declared "labor runs the machine and labor will stop the machine until its demands are met." This strike apparently was not well organized. It was precipitated before coöperation of other unions had been worked out and had not been in progress long before funds were lacking for the payment of strike benefits. The men having no individual resources were forced to yield. Nevertheless the growth of labor class sympathy was shown by the fact that before the strike closed steps were being taken to bring into active coöperation the miners, the railway men, and the transport workers. On December 7, 3000 men on the North-Eastern Railway went out on account of a reduction of a main-line locomotive engineer, Knox, to the rank of pilot driver in consequence of his conviction by a local magistrate for drunkenness while off duty. Many of the men struck in spite of a trade agreement. They claimed that only recently the directors had condoned a glaring case of drunkenness of a higher official and that there should be one law for rich and poor alike. Settlement was effected on December 14 on condition that Knox be reinstated, provided investigations by the Home office showed he was not legally convicted, men breaking contracts were to be fined six days' pay.

STRINDBERG, AUGUST. A Swedish novelist, dramatist, and essayist, died May 14, 1912. He was born in Stockholm, January 22, 1849. His father was a small tradesman who had failed in business just before the birth of his son, and his mother was a barmaid in one of the inns of Stockholm. Strindberg's early youth was spent in poverty. A 18 years of age he left Stockholm to attend the university at Upsala. During his first term he was so poor that he could not only buy no books, but could not purchase wood necessary to heat the garret in which he lived. He soon returned to Stockholm and endeavored to teach in one of the public schools. During this time he began writing. His first attempts were in verse and he soon had written a comedy which, however, has not survived. He then wrote a one-act play which was accepted by the Royal Theatre and was produced with some success. His next play was *The Outlaw,* which brought him the personal good will and financial support of King Charles XV., although it was spurned by critics and the public. Strindberg now returned to the university with the thought of taking a degree. He made no attempt to follow the courses and quarreled with the professors. On the sudden death of the king the small pension which had been granted him ceased and he again returned to Stockholm.

During the next two years he studied medicine and appeared for a short time on the stage as an actor and conducted a trade journal. He also did hack writing for various obscure newspapers. This life he has depicted in his first important novel, *The Red Room.* Finally, at the age of 23, he completed a five-act play called *Master Olof.* This play was greeted with indifference which so disappointed Strindberg that he did not recover from the shock for years. In the meantime he had obtained a position in the Royal Library which gave him a living and free access to all the books. He made researches in philology, including the study of the Chinese language. At this time he wrote a monograph which was accepted by the French Institute. Gradually, however, he renewed his interest in modern affairs. He read and studied modern scientists, philosophers, and novelists. Of the latter, Hugo and Dickens were among his favorites.

At the age of 26 he met a woman who afterwards secured a divorce from her husband and married him. Their married life began happily. He began now to experience his first taste of success. His novel, *The Red Room,* was produced in 1879 and became comparatively popular. He threw himself into the study of Swedish history and the result of this was *The Swedish People,* which is said to be, next to the Bible, the most read work among the Swedes at the present time. He also wrote a series of short stories on historical themes which is named *Swedish Events and Adventures.* About the same time he wrote a volume of satirical essays on social conditions, entitled *The New Kingdom.* During this period he wrote also several plays, including *The Secret of the Guild* and *King Bengt's Lady. The Wanderings of Lucky-Per,* a play written for children, also dates from this time. He resigned from the Royal Library and retired to Switzerland for the purpose of devoting all his time to writing. A volume of short stories entitled *Marriage* led to the first turning point in his artistic career. It was a severe criticism on the marriage state. The book was confiscated by the authorities and criminal proceedings were brought against its publisher on the ground that it spoke offensively of sacred rites. Strindberg returned home and became a defendant in this suit. He was acquitted and became the leader and spokesman of the youth of the country. This experience embittered him and its results are shown in his later writings.

In 1885 he published a volume of short stories entitled *Real Utopias*. This achieved for him a reputation in Germany, where he was at the time living. The second part of *Marriage*, issued in 1886, formed a protest against the modern movements with which women were identified. Perhaps the best known of his plays, a three-act tragedy, *The Father*, was produced in 1887. This was followed by *The Comrades*, a four-act comedy, and by *Miss Juliet*, a realistic drama. Other plays during this period from 1885 to 1894 included eight one-act plays and a fairy play, *The Keys to Heaven*. At the same time he wrote a series of novels and short stories, and five autobiographical novels. Three of these are collectively known as *The Bondwoman's Son*. This treated of his life up to the time of his marriage. In *A Fool's Confession* he laid bare the tragedy of his first marriage, which had been dissolved in 1891.

After the divorce from his wife, Strindberg went to Germany, where his works had been making steady headway. While in Berlin he met a young woman writer of Austrian birth who soon after became his second wife. This marriage lasted only a few years and while it was not as unhappy as the first, it aided in bringing on a mental crisis which resulted in a cessation of his literary labors. He plunged into scientific speculation and experimentation. He began to take great interest in psychic phenomena and was deeply influenced by the writings of Swedenborg. He gradually rejected all the orthodox and established rules of living and became a mystic. This experience finally led to his being placed in a private sanitarium, where he remained until 1896.

In the following year he resumed his writing and soon produced the autobiographical novels, *Inferno* and *Legends*. The former is a remarkable study in abnormal psychology. He next wrote *The Link*, another one-act play. In 1898 he produced the first two parts of a play, *To Damascus*. The last part of this trilogy was not added until 1904.

The next ten years of his life was a period of amazing productivity. Most of his works at this time were of a symbolic nature. They included a play, *The Great Highway*, and a series of plays dealing with historical events in Sweden. These included *Gustavus Vasa*, *Eric XIV.*, *Gustavus Adolphus* and *Charles XII.* In these plays he achieved a higher reputation than he had hitherto attained in Sweden. During the same period he was busy with another group of plays characterized by realistic symbolism. Among these were, *There are Crimes and Crimes*, *Christmas*, *Easter*, and *Midsummer*. Related to this group is *The Dance of Death*, which is considered by many critics as Strindberg's greatest play. He became interested in the project of establishing a theatre in Stockholm and for this project wrote the five dramas which he called "Chamber Plays." In this period of ten years he completed twenty-nine dramatic works in addition to novels, volumes of autobiography, collections of short stries, collections of poems, and three volumes entitled *The Blue Books* which contained his scientific speculations. Besides this he wrote many pamphlets and satirical studies of contemporary social and literary conditions. From his return to his native country in 1897 Strindberg's life was outwardly quiet. He married for a third time in 1901 and this was dissolved three years later. His last years were spent in Stockholm, where he busied himself chiefly with philological studies.

Strindberg's reputation in the United States is by no means as great as in Europe. This is due largely to lack of knowledge of his works.

STRONG, GEORGE AUGUSTUS. An American Protestant Episcopal clergyman and educator, died March 7, 1912. He was born in Norwich, Conn., in 1832. He graduated from Kenyon College and after working for some years in a bank, entered the Virginia Theological Seminary, where he was a classmate of Phillips Brooks. He was rector in several churches in Pennsylvania. In 1867 he was appointed to the chair of English literature in Kenyon College. Here he remained for eleven years, then becoming rector of Christ Church in New Bedford, Mass. In 1888 he retired from the active ministry.

STUBBS, CHARLES WILLIAM. Church of England bishop of Truro, died May 6, 1912. He was born in Liverpool in 1845, and was educated at the Royal Institution School, Liverpool, and Sidney Sussex College, Cambridge. After holding several minor positions in the church he was appointed in 1894 dean of Ely, on the recommendation of Gladstone. From 1881 to 1895, and again in 1901, he was select preacher at Cambridge, and from 1898 to 1899 at Oxford. In 1906 he was appointed bishop of Truro. He became distinguished as a scholar and militant Broad Churchman, a historical and sociological writer, and a pulpit orator. He wrote many books, among them: *Christ and Democracy* (1883); *The Land and the Laborers* (1890); *Christ and Economics* (1893); *Historical Memorials of Ely Cathedral* (1897); *In a Minister's Garden* (1901). He also edited *Matthew* and *Mark* in the *Temple Bible*. He wrote several volumes of verse, including *Castles in the Air*, *Poems Old and New* (1903). He was the author of a book on Cambridge, entitled *Cambridge and Its Story* (1904). *Cornish Bells, Carols, and Verses* was published in 1910. He lectured in 1900 in the United States. Among the subjects which he treated were "Shakespeare as a Religious Teacher," "Milton and the Puritans," "Shelley," "Tennyson," "James Russell Lowell," and "Chivalry."

STUTTGART. See ARCHITECTURE.

SUBIG BAY. See UNITED STATES, *Army*.

SUBMARINES. See NAVAL PROGRESS.

SUBWAYS. See TUNNELS AND RAPID TRANSIT.

SUCHARD. See NAVAL PROGRESS.

SUDAN, THE ANGLO-EGYPTIAN. An African country, south of Egypt, under the joint administration of the British and the Egyptian governments. Area, 984,520 square miles; population (1909 census), 2,500,000 (estimated, 1911, at approximately 3,000,000). The capital is Khartum, with (1909) 18,235 inhabitants; Omdurman had 42,779; Khartum North, 35,285. Pupils in all schools (1911), 4118. Total cultivated area (1911), 1,426,497 feddans (116,556 artificially irrigated, 1,192,265 under rain crops, 117,676 flood irrigation). The shortage of unskilled labor is an undiminished hindrance to cultivation. Vast irrigation schemes are projected; sites have been located and plans drawn up. Imports in 1911 £E2,-273,940 (£E1,931,426 in 1910); specie imports £E287,289 (£E126,128); exports, £E1,376,958 (£F977,621); transit and reëxports, £E128,-610 (£E104,386). The export of dura amounted to 17,794 tons, valued at £E86,657, compared with 32,377 tons (£E118,064) in 1910. The decrease is due to the ruling high prices, as Sudan dura can find a footing in foreign markets only when the price is low enough to enable it to compete on a point of economy. Livestock export in 1911: 21,611 cattle (5646 in 1910), valued at £E129,375 (£E47,491); 97,-752 sheep and goats (63,919), valued at £E86,-606) (£E62,947). Export of gum, 13,929 tons; cotton (lint and seed), 12,330 tons; millet, 17,-147 tons; ivory, 74,061 kilograms. Railways in operation (1911), 1500 miles; telegraph lines, 4965 miles; number of post and telegraph offices, 63. Estimated revenue 1912, £E1,375,-600 (1911 actual, £E1,305,000); contribution by the Egyptian government, £E335,000 (£E360,-000); estimated expenditure, £E1,538,600 (£E1,351,000); paid to Egyptian government for army in the Sudan, £E172,000 (£E172,000). Sirdar of the Egyptian army and governor-general of the Sudan, in 1912, Lieut.-Gen. Sir Reginald Wingate.

In Kordofan the notorious ex-meg of Tagoi was arrested, tried by a governor's court, and, having been proved guilty of several murders, was hanged April 11, 1912.

SUGAR. The steady progress in the production of beet sugar in the United States is indicated by the yield of nearly 700,000 short tons in 1912, a gain of about 100,000 tons over 1911, which was the record crop up to that time. Thirteen years ago, in 1899, the census showed a production of 81,729 short tons; by 1905 it had increased to 312,921, and in the census year 1909, to 501,682 tons. The present crop is about one-fifth of the national sugar consumption. If the by-products of the beet sugar manufacture are combined with the factory value of the sugar, the total value of the crop of 1912 is about $67,000,000. There are now in operation in the United States 66 factories in 17 States, which required and used the past season over five million tons of sugar beets from 473,877 acres.

Floods due to the overflow of the Mississippi river severely injured the crop of sugar cane, making the production of sugar from cane the lowest since 1899. The value of the product, including molasses and sirup, was only about $34,000,000, as compared with $45,000,000 in 1911. The world's production of cane sugar for 1912-13 is estimated by Willett and Gray (December 26) at 9,028,000 tons, as compared with 9,023,216 tons in 1911-12, and the European beet sugar crop is estimated by F. O. Licht at 8,420,000 tons, as compared with 6,-346,000 tons in 1911. This gives a combined estimated production of cane and beet sugar, allowing 625,000 tons for the American beet sugar crop (Willet and Gray), of 18,073,000 tons, an increase of 2,163,000 tons over 1911.

The production in the principal sugar-growing countries was as follows: West Indies and Lesser Antilles 278,000 tons; Cuba, 2,250,000 tons; Hawaii, 500,000 tons; Porto Rico, 320,-000 tons; Louisiana and Texas, 170,000 tons; Mexico, 160,000 tons; Central America, 25,-000 tons; Brazil, 249,000 tons; Argentina, 145,000 tons; Peru, 140,000 tons; other South American countries, 106,000 tons; British India, 2,400,000 tons; Java, 1,300,000 tons; Philipppine Islands (exports), 200,000 tons; Formosa, 112,000 tons; Australia and Fiji Islands, 205,000 tons; Africa, 428,000 tons; Spain, 20,-000 tons; and other countries in Europe (beet sugar), 8,420,000 tons.

The Brussels Sugar Convention met during the year to arrange a basis of agreement as to sugar exports. Subsequently the governments of Great Britain and Italy notified the Belgian government that from September 1, 1913, they would cease to be parties to the convention.

LITERATURE. H. C. Prinsen Geerligs, *The World's Cane Sugar Industry, Past and Present* (an English translation of volume 4 of *Handbökten dienste van de Suikerriet-Cultuur en de Rietsuiker-Fabricage*) (England, 1912); C. A. Browne, *A Handbook of Sugar Analysis* (New York and London, 1912); G. E. Nesom, H. S. Walker, et al., *Handbook on the Sugar Industry of the Philippine Islands; The American Beet Sugar Industry in 1910 and 1911* (United States Department of Agriculture, Bureau of Plant Industry, Bul. 260, 1912).

SUGAR TARIFF. See TARIFF.

SULPHUR. Sulphur was produced in the United States in 1911 in Louisiana, Utah, and Wyoming. Nevada, which had hitherto produced on a small scale, reported no production during the year. The admission of Japanese sulphur free of duty undoubtedly affected somewhat the sulphur market in certain of the western States. The production of Louisiana continued to be the chief factor in the domestic industry, and in both Utah and Wyoming the output was greater than during 1910. The total production in 1911 amounted to 265,-664 long tons, valued at $4,787,049 as compared with 255,534 long tons, valued at $4,605,112 in 1910, an increase in quantity of 10,130 tons and in value of $181,937. The production of 1911 was the largest since 1908, when 369,444 tons were produced.

There were imported in 1911 29,144 long tons of sulphur. This includes all varieties, crude, refined, flowers of sulphur, and other kinds. The imports were valued at $532,836. The amount imported was slightly less than for 1910, which was 30,833 long tons. The great bulk of sulphur imported into the United States comes from Japan and it is consumed chiefly on or near the Pacific coast. From Italy were imported 8031 tons, and small quantities were imported from Great Britain and other countries. The exports of sulphur in 1911 amounted to 37,142 long tons, valued at $736,928, compared with 30,742 long tons, valued at $552,941 in 1910. The excess of imports over exports amounted in 1911 to only 1041 long tons in quantity. This increase indicated that the United States is providing ample sulphur for domestic demand.

SUMNER, EDWIN VOSE. An American soldier, died August 24, 1912. He was born in Carlisle, Pa., in 1835. He joined the volunteer service in the Civil War as first sergeant of the Henry Clay Guards, Washington. He was later made second lieutenant, and assigned to the First United States Cavalry. He served as aid on the staff of General Stoneman, chief of the cavalry of the Army of the Potomac and in a short time was made first lieutenant. In 1863 he was promoted to be captain in the regular army and in the following year was appointed colonel of the 1st New York Mounted Rifles. He was brevetted brigadier-general in 1865, and was appointed brigadier-general in the regular army in 1899. As a member of General Stoneman's staff he took part in the closing battles of the Maryland campaign. He also took part in the raid on Richmond and was three times brevetted for gallantry. After the war he served for fourteen years on the Pacific Coast, taking part in many important Indian campaigns. He afterwards served in Kansas, Indian Territory, and Oklahoma. He retired from active service in 1899.

SUMTER. See MUNICIPAL GOVERNMENT, *Commission Plan.*

SUN. See ASTRONOMY.

SUNDAY CLOSING OF POST OFFICES. See LABOR LEGISLATION.

SUNLIGHT TREATMENT OR BATHS. See HELIOTHERAPY.

SUN SPOTS. See ASTRONOMY.

SUN YAT SEN. See CHINA.

SUPERHEATED STEAM. See STEAM ENGINE.

SURGERY. Several methods of reaching the pituitary gland, long considered inaccessible to surgical attack, have recently been devised. This gland is situated at the base of the brain, nearly in the centre of the skull, and exercises an important function with regard to growth and development, by means of its internal secretion. Tumors, cysts, and other disorders of the gland give rise to profound and fatal disturbances of the human organism. Surgeons have reached the pituitary body through the nose, but this route has been unsatisfactory, on account of the bleeding, impossibility of maintaining asepsis, and the permanent damage done to the nasal framework. The method proposed by McArthur is to make an incision through the shaved eyebrow, to trephine the frontal bone just above the middle of the supraorbital arch, and to follow the roof to the orbit back to the region of the pituitary body. Here the covering of dura mater is incised and the necessary surgical work done on the gland. In order to secure room enough for instruments the frontal lobe of the brain is retracted upward and the eyeball displaced downward.

Alexis Carrel's brilliant work at the Rockefeller Institute in the preservation and transplantation of animal tissues, the artificial cultivation of malignant tumors and the anastomosis of blood vessels is already largely familiar to the public, and has been noted in previous numbers of the YEAR BOOK. Some of his later work, dealing with the preservation of animal tissues and their transplantation, is reviewed in the *Journal of the American Medical Association*, August 17, 1912. His experiments had in view two general objects: preservation of tissues in latent life outside the animal organism, and their preservation in active life. A tissue is in latent life when its metabolism becomes so slight that it can hardly be detected, or when its metabolism is completely suspended. Latent life was discovered two centuries ago by Loewenhoeck, who resurrected *Milnesium tardigradum*, which had been completely dried for a long time, by moistening it with water. In 1840, Doyère also studied the peculiarities of latent life of *Milnesium tardigradum*. He dried some of these animals, heated them to a temperature of 100°C., and, on moistening them, observed that they lived again. These observations were important because *Milnesium tardigradum* is highly organized and contains muscular fibres, nerves, nervous ganglia, etc. Paul Bert, in several famous experiments, preserved in latent life the tissues of mammals, and succeeded in transplanting rats' tails, kept for several days in a small quantity of confined air at a temperature of 12° C. In 1907-08 Carrel transplanted vessels preserved for days or weeks in cold storage in a condition of unmanifested actual life. See CARREL, ALEXIS.

A tissue isolated from the organism can be kept in active life if it is given artificially a normal nutrition. The possibility of the active life of a tissue outside of the organism was demonstrated in 1907 by Harrison, in the anatomic laboratory of Johns Hopkins University. Harrison transplanted the central nervous system of a frog embyro in a drop of fluid taken from the lymph sac of an adult frog. He then observed, during a few days, the growth of the axis cylinders. In 1910, with the collaboration of Dr. Burrows, Carrel observed the growth of tissues of mammals in plasma. In 1912, he found that the permanent active life of the tissues outside of the organism was possible: a piece of a chick's heart pulsated strongly one hundred and four days after its extirpation, and connective tissue was growing actively during the fifth month following its removal from the organism. The success with which tissues can be preserved depends largely upon their character. Highly specialized tissues, such as brain substance and glands, disintegrate so rapidly that a few minutes of blood deprivation suffices for irreparable damage; while skin, bone, and connecting tissue will resist molecular death for long periods if properly conserved: in the case of latent life, in cold storage; in nutrient serums when preservation in active life is desired.

The practical object of all this experimental work is to have on hand vital tissues ready for use in various branches of plastic surgery. For example, Dr. Tuffier, in 1910 and 1911, preserved in petrolatum and in a refrigerator pieces of fat, bone, cartilage, and peritoneum which he had removed from amputated limbs. He also used lipomas and fragments of ovaries and of peritoneum which had to be extirpated during certain operations. These tissues were kept in cold storage for as long as two months. Grafts of lipoma and omentum were inserted by Tuffier between the pleura and the thoracic wall in several cases of pleurisy and intrapulmonary abscesses. In the reconstruction of joints, Dr. Tuffier used pieces of omentum, peritoneum and cartilage. In resection of the elbow he covered the cut surface of the bone with cartilage preserved for five days in cold storage. After seventeen months the patient was examined and the result found excellent. In another case Tuffier covered the ends of the bones with fragments of omentum preserved for one month in cold storage. Ten days afterward the elbow-joint could be moved easily. Ten operations of similar character were successful.

In 1911, Dr. Magitot of Paris, enucleated the eye of a patient suffering with glaucoma. The eye was placed in a tube containing human serum, and kept for eight days in a refrigerator at a temperature of + 4° C., during which time the cornea remained transparent. Magitot resected the anterior part of the cornea of a man who had been burned by alkali. A large scar had developed on the cornea and the patient was blind. In the opening, a flap of cornea from the eye preserved in cold storage was inserted. The graft lived, and seven months after the operation the transplanted cornea was still transparent and the patient could see through it.

I. S. Haynes, working in collaboration with S. Kopetsky, on the nature and surgical relief of infective meningitis, devised an operation for draining the brain cavities of cerebrospinal fluid, without invading brain tissue, as had previously been done in tapping the ventricles in similar cases. Haynes's operation consists in draining the *cisterna magna*, at the base of the brain. Access to this region is obtained by cutting down upon the occipital bone in the mid-line to the edge of the *foramen magnum* and the first vertebra. A triangular piece of bone, its base including the margin of the *foramen magnum*, is removed by means of a trephine and bone forceps, and the brain coverings opened and retracted. The space immediately underneath is called the *cisterna magna*, which communicates with the ventricles of the brain and the spinal canal. By this means the excess of cerebrospinal fluid, always present in meningitis, is drained off and pressure symptoms relieved. See Lister, Joseph, and Tetanus.

SUSSEX MAN. See Anthropology, and Geology.

SUVORIN, Alexis Sergeievich. A Russian editor, died August 24, 1912. He was born in 1835, and at an early age was sent to the military school at Veronezh, and in 1853 obtained his commission in the engineers. He left the army and tried unsuccessfully to enter the university. As he had no other means of livelihood he became a schoolmaster in his native village. Here in 1888 he produced his first literary work, the translation of Beranger's *Captive*. This was followed by a series of humorous sketches of country life which appeared in the Moscow magazines. In 1860 he became a tutor in the high school at Veronezh, where he came in touch with local literary circles. Thereafter he was a constant contributor to the Moscow journals and magazines. In 1863 he removed to St. Petersburg. For twelve years he was chief sub-editor of the St. Petersburg *Viedomosti* and became well known as an editor. In 1876 he acquired the right of publishing the *Novoe Vremya*. The first issue of this journal was brought out on February 29 of that year. It was the time of the Serbo-Turkish War, and Suvorin proceeded as correspondent for his own paper to the Balkans, visiting Constantinople, Bucharest, and Servia. Letters written to his journal during this time gave it a predominant standing in Russia. It soon acquired and continued to hold first place among Russian political organizations and became one of the best known papers in the world. It strongly supported the constitutional régime and was national in its home politics.

SWAMP LANDS. See Drainage.

SWAZILAND. A British protectorate (6536 square miles; 1083 white and 98,876 colored inhabitants, census of 1911) in south Africa. Gold was mined in 1910-11 to the value of £57,530 and tin £42,250. Swaziland is included for customs purposes with the Union of South Africa and no trade statistics are now kept. Revenue (1910-11), £68,722; expenditure, £62,257. Debt, £100,000. Mbabane (Embabaan) is the capital. Railway construction was in progress during 1912. Paramount chief, Sobhuza (regent, Nabotsibeni). Resident commissioner in 1912, R. T. Coryndon.

SWEATING. This is a term applied to those industries usually carried on in homes at unduly low piece-rate wages, thus requiring excessively long hours of labor. It is usually associated with insanitary housing, though this is undoubtedly largely dependent on low wages. Various schemes have been tried for its elimination. Organization of the workers has been found impracticable, both on account of their own character and the character of the work. Licensing of the premises and of the workers, with official inspection and supervision, has been tried, but with only moderate success. Consumers' leagues and the use of union labels have likewise had some, though slight effect. The difficulty with this latter scheme lies in the education of the public and the retailers, and in the difficulty of holding them to the scheme in spite of economic disadvantage. The London County Council adopted a set of minimum piece rates for making uniforms for city employees as a means of preventing the use of sweated labor on city contracts. But this law was generally circumvented. Reform has been tried from within through the formation of associations by the clothiers in London. This also failed because those who refused to join undersold those who adhered to higher wage scales. It would seem that where effective organization of workers is impossible sweating can be remedied only by the establishment of a legal minimum wage for the industries involved. See Minimum Wage.

Home Work. That phase of the employment of women and children which is most universally condemned is home work. Sweating has been largely abolished in factories through sanitary regulations and inspection, and restrictions of hours through legislation. It still thrives, however, in the tenements and homes of the poor. Its abolition has been resisted primarily on the ground that poverty would thereby be increased, since many of the poorest families are wholly dependent on it for support. The national *Report on the Condition of Women and Child Wage-Earners* showed that poverty in varying degrees is correlated with home work, particularly in the families of the foreign-born. It often happens, however, that the men of such families do not work because their wives, mothers, sisters, or children are able to eke out a bare subsistence by doing home finishing. This report severely condemned home work because of the lack of sanitary conditions, ventilation, and light. The hours of work, were all found to be bad. Moreover, small children, often as young as five years of age, are employed by the home workers in spite of child labor laws. This report pointed out that the driving of home work into the factories would have the effect of raising the wages of the workers. Thus married shop finishers all earned more than $2 a week, while of the married home finishers 15 per cent. earned less than that amount; 55 per cent. of the married shop finishers earned $5 or more, and only 7 per cent. of the married home finishers earned that much. It was found also that many home workers are now dependent, in part, upon outside relief. Home work favors seasonal work. This has the effect of excessive labor during rush periods and complete idleness and a tendency to degeneration during other periods. During the rush periods children are taken out of schools. The federal investigators of the men's ready-made clothing found that 15 per cent. of the children of school age in families doing home work were out of school unlawfully. It is pointed out that, although the abolition of home work would increase the hardships in some families during the period of transition from home to factory, such families could be relieved by charitable organizations and by school scholarships. It is believed by many that home work does not relieve poverty, but rather fosters it and that it is a serious menace to the public health.

New York. The National Child Labor Committee employed six trained investigators for five weeks on an inquiry into tenement house home work in New York City. See *Annual Report* under Child Labor. They found that home manufacture in city tenements becomes more complicated and difficult of investigation with every increase in congestion. Their inquiry showed that the factories, contract shops, and contractors spring up with marvelous rapidity in nearly every new tenement house section. They found 108 child helpers under legal factory age in 131 families making artificial flowers; of these children 60 per cent. were of ages 3 to 10. Of all children found engaged in home work 36 per cent. were under the legal age of 14. Among families doing home work school attendance is proverbially irregular. They found numerous abuses amounting to heartless exploitation of ignorant workers. The investigators found that only 12 per cent. of families doing home work had widowed, separated, or deserted mothers, and only 3 per cent. had invalid or incapacitated fathers, showing that poverty is not always the cause of home work. Indeed, they were inclined to believe that home work is often due to excessive thrift coupled with ignorance and lack of wholesome standards of life. They found a reduction of the father's responsibility in home work just as noted in the federal *Report* above mentioned. They emphasized the menace to public health due to the very unsanitary conditions of tenement homes, heightened by the complete ignorance of the workers of the relation of dirt and bacteria to disease. They insisted that all home work should be prohibited and the industries driven to the factories.

The New York Factory Investigating Commission was engaged at the close of the year in an inquiry into home work in the metropolis. The number of outside or home workers in the city was estimated at 125,000. Evidence was submitted showing that more than 7 per cent. of tenements where artificial flowers and clothing were made were unlicensed; that many of the places were very unsanitary; and that the work was injurious to the workers and a serious menace to the public health. See Child Labor; Minimum Wage; and Women in Industry.

SWEDEN. A constitutional monarchy of northern Europe, occupying the eastern part of the Scandinavian Peninsula. Stockholm is the capital.

Area and Population. The area in square miles and the population according to the census of December 31, 1910, are given by prefectures in the table below:

Prefs.	Sq. m.	Pop.	Prefs.	Sq. m.	Pop.
Stockholm*	13	342,323	Skaraborg	3,274	241,260
Stockholm	3,016	229,165	Värmland	7,461	260,149
Uppsala	2,051	128,171	Örebro	3,523	207,034
Söder'land	2,630	178,577	Väst'land	2,602	155,925
Öster'land	4,265	294,177	Kop'berg	11,525	233,874
Jönköping	4,449	214,460	Gafleborg	7,615	253,775
Kronoberg	3,826	157,968	Väst'mor.	9,856	250,517
Kalmar	4,457	228,150	Järntl'd	19,680	118,117
Gottland	1,220	55,217	Väst'bot.	22,777	161,372
Blekinge	1,164	149,377	Nörr'ten	40,881	161,093
Krist'stad	2,488	228,321			
Malmöhus	1,865	457,247	Total prefs.	169,403	5,522,474
Halland	1,900	147,231	Vänern †	2,150	....
Göteborg and Bohur	1,949	381,279	Vättern †	733	....
Älfsborg	4,915	287,700	Mälaren †	449	....
			Hjälmaren †	155	....
			Total..	172,920	5,522,474

* City. † Lakes.

The total land area is 158,692 square miles. Total number of male inhabitants, 2,699,107; female, 2,823,367. Total population as estimated December 31, 1911, 5,561,799. Number of marriages in 1910, 33,162; births, 138,976; deaths, 80,563; still-births (included in foregoing), 3351; emigrants, 27,816; immigrants, 8142. Population of Stockholm (1911 estimate), 346,599; Göteborg, 170,606; Malmö, 89,719; Norrköping, 46,629; Gäfle, 35,719; Hälsingborg, 33,225.

Education. Primary instruction is free and compulsory, and the schools are maintained by local taxation with state aid. The system is efficient, the schools are well attended, and illiteracy is uncommon. There are well-developed secondary and special schools, and universities at Lund and Uppsala, besides private faculties. The Lutheran is the national creed, but all others are tolerated. The expulsion, however, of all proselytizing Mormon elders was decided upon, July 20, 1912, by the government.

Production. Forest products are a valuable asset. The yield in metric quintals of the principal crops has been as follows in successive years:

	1909	1910	1911	1912
Wheat	1,881,000	2,047,619	2,241,070	2,122,060
Rye	6,338,000	6,237,350	6,270,240	5,861,480
Barley	3,037,000	3,385,320	3,199,720	3,082,150
Oats	11,728,000	12,876,680	11,025,770	12,739,260
Potatoes ...	15,696,000	....	....	....
Beets*	....	....	8,211,230	9,901,842

* For sugar.

The livestock report of December 31, 1911, returned 588,485 horses, 2,592,609 cattle, 945,709 sheep, 66,136 goats, 951,164 swine; a decline in comparison with December 31, 1910, of 154,917 cattle, 58,272 sheep, 3043 goats, and 5064 swine; and a gain of 1650 horses.

The mineral wealth is considerable. Output (1910) of iron ore, 5,552,678 tons; 2700 tons of silver and lead ore, 3638 of copper ore, 49,453 of zinc ore, 5752 of manganese ore, 25,445 of sulphur pyrites, 302,786 of coal. Production of gold (1910), 1.846 kilograms, 30.2 of silver, 355,436 of lead, 3,110,778 of copper, 558,484 of zinc, 603,939 tons of pig-iron, 431,722 tons of bar iron.

In 1909 there were 1200 saw and planing mills employing 35,576 people; value of output 130,795,580 kronor; joinery and furniture factories, 515, employing 10,004 people; output valued at 23,913,784 kronor; wood-pulp mills, 159, employing 11,986 people, value of output 70,841,807 kronor; flour mills, 1403, with 4064 employees, output valued at 111,435,844 kronor.

COMMERCE. The trade, including precious metals, by countries for 1910 and totals for four years, is given in the following table in thousands of kronor (1 krona=26.8 cents):

	Imps.	Exps.		Imps.	Exps.
Germany	231,036	124,483	Argentina	6,624	5,183
U. K.	164,481	190,656	Italy	4,675	2,609
U. S.	52,672	22,582	Africa	3,150	18,347
Russia	47,253	27,745	Spain	2,726	7,563
Denmark	45,086	55,146	Portugal	2,170	1,852
France	28,095	42,352	Other	13,510	27,085
Norway	21,141	28,765			
Netherl'ds	18,379	16,092	Tot. '10	671,633	592,864
Brazil	12,639	1,256	" '09	616,806	472,980
Belgium	9,145	16,770	" '08	608,932	482,017
Brit. Ind.	8,251	4,478	" '07	682,105	524,663

The principal articles of import and export in the 1910 trade are as follows, with values in thousands of kronor:

Imports	1000 kr.	Exports	1000 kr.
Coal	56,133	Timber	169,623
Cereals	54,971	Wood pulp	72,681
Coffee	30,161	Iron	54,765
Hides	30,117	Butter	44,152
Cotton	27,525	Iron ore	43,125
Vegetable oils	23,415	Machinery	34,798
Machinery	20,096	Paper	32,228
Petroleum	18,577	Iron mfrs.	14,304
Oil cake	17,778	Stone	12,961
Iron mfrs.	17,389	Matches	11,854
Copper	15,414	Wooden wares	10,552
Fish	14,910	Hides	10,207
Wool	13,608	Live animals	9,474
Iron	13,604	Fish	8,078

Vessels entered in the 1910 trade, 35,435, of 11,031,000 tons; cleared, 35,407, of 11,064,000. Merchant marine, January 1, 1911, 1635 sailing, of 176,912 tons, and 1214 steamers, of 593,073—total, 2849, of 769,985.

COMMUNICATION. There were, at the end of 1911, 13,972 kilometers of railway open to traffic, of which 4460 were operated by the state and 9512 by private companies. State telegraph lines, 10,273 kilometers; railway telegraph lines, 10,468.

FINANCE. The budget for 1913 balanced at 263,027,200 kronor, the main sources of revenue being customs and excise, 110,000,000 kr.; tax on income, invested capital, etc., 51,700,000; revenue-earning administrations, 36,029,700; from loans, 44,805,300; state bank profits, 6,311,000; etc. Main branches of expenditure: Army, 48,850,280 kr. ordinary, 6,274,820 extraordinary; navy, 20,223,450 and 5,822,965; worship and instruction, 26,250,550 and 4,514,050; finance 14,682,949 and 3,129,151; interior, 12,074,046 and 7,083,254; administration of State enterprises, 33,142,300 and 6,969,600; etc. The total debt stood January 1, 1912, at 606,096,173 kr., contracted in large part on account of railway construction.

ARMY. Progress was made during 1912 in the scheme of reorganization which was to be completed by 1914. Personal service is required, but the time spent with the colors is short, consisting of 8 months for the infantry and 1 year for the cavalry and artillery. The obligation, however, is for 8 years in the first line of the Beväring, 4 in the second line, and 8 in Landstorm. The organization of the army consisted of 28 regiments of infantry of various strengths, aggregating 81½ battalions; 8 regiments of cavalry, amounting to 50 squadrons; 60 batteries of artillery, including 3 horse batteries; 4 heavy batteries; 7 fortress batteries, and technical troops. In 1912 the reorganization of the artillery took place and 20 additional batteries of light field howitzers were provided. During the year an additional battery was added to the heavy artillery and also a battery of machine-guns. The fortress artillery was comprised of 2 regiments. The peace strength of the army was estimated at about 28,000 men, of whom 22,000 were actually serving, while those joining for short repeating exercises and duly enrolled would bring the total up to about 64,000, including the Landstorm. An approximate war strength of about 450,000 would be available, which with the plan of the new scheme, would be raised to 600,000 men. On September 10, 1912, a surprise mobilization occurred.

NAVY. The effective fleet (1912) contained 93 vessels of 68,100 aggregate tons, as follows: 12 coast defense vessels (42,600 tons), 1 armored cruiser (4100), 10 protected monitors (7200), 5 torpedo gunboats (4000), 4 gunboats (1850), 8 destroyers (3450), 31 first-class torpedo boats (3100), and 22 second-class (1300), besides submarines, school-ships, dispatch boats, etc. Building are 1 coast-defence vessel, 5 torpedo boats, and several submarines, the exact number not being officially disclosed.

GOVERNMENT. The king is the executive, acting through an executive council. The legislative body is the Riksdag, composed of an upper chamber (150 members elected for six years) and a lower chamber (230 members elected for three years). Reigning sovereign (1912), Gustaf V. (born 1858). Heir-apparent, Prince Gustaf Adolf (born 1882). The ministry, constituted October 7, 1911, was composed in 1912 as follows: Karl A. Staaff, minister of state; Dr. J. J. A. (Count) Ehrensvärd, foreign affairs; Gustaf Sandström, justice; Dr. David K. Bergström, war; Jacob L. Larsson, marine; P. Axel V. Schotte, interior; A. T. (Baron) Adelswärd, finance; Dr. F. Berg, worship; P. Alfred Petersson, agriculture; B. A. Petrén, Karl J. Stenström, without portfolio.

HISTORY

GENERAL POLITICAL SITUATION. Before the last general elections to the Riksdag in 1911 the Left controlled the majority in the lower house and the Right in the upper house. In 1909 the new electoral law established universal suffrage for elections to the lower house, but the property qualification was retained, though lowered, for the election of senators. For a long time past the Conservative Lindman ministry had remained in power despite the adverse majority in the lower chamber. Against this state of affairs the Liberals who desired to advance to a purely parliamentary system, protested, and in the last electoral campaign, M. Staaff, the chief of the Liberal party, insisted that constitutional reform was the main point in the Liberal programme. M. Lindman and the Conservatives, on the other hand, stood by the constitution and opposed any further extension of parliamentarism. In a sense the Swedish ministry conformed to the principles of parliamentary government, despite the complaint of the Liberals that it governed against the wishes of a majority of the popular representatives; for on two important classes of questions, namely those of subsidies and taxes, the joint vote of both houses is required, and the majority in the total vote was Conservative owing to the great preponderance of Conservatives in the upper house. Hence the ministry could say that after all it rested on a majority in Parliament. Moreover, for some years past it had become the custom for the king to appoint the ministry chosen by the majority in Parliament. Thus there was in Sweden virtually a responsible ministry, though not necessarily depending on a majority in the lower house. The elections for that body in 1911 gave the Left a still larger majority, 102 Liberals, and 64 Socialists against 64 Moderates or Conservatives, and a Liberal ministry under M. Staaff assumed the government. On accepting office M. Staaff received the king's assurance that the upper chamber would be dissolved and new elections held before the next meeting of the Riksdag on January 15, 1912. The Liberals hoped to gain enough seats in that body to control a majority in joint session. If they did not, they talked of constitutional reform, which would remove the power of the upper house to oppose the wishes of a majority of the popular representatives. The recent course of the British Parliament in abolishing the veto power of the House of Lords was frequently cited with approval by Liberals, who have long regarded the British parliamentary system with admiration. But the present need of such a radical programme was removed by the successful outcome of the elections which gave them a strong enough minority in the upper house to place them in the majority when both houses voted together.

PARLIAMENT. On the opening of the Riksdag on January 16, the king in the course of his address announced that the time had come when justice required that the suffrage should be extended to women and that therefore a bill would be laid before Parliament during the coming session giving the parliamentary vote to women under the same conditions as to men. Referring to the recent measures of electoral reform removing distinctions based on wealth and to the great extension of the suffrage, the king reminded his hearers that they were now more truly representative of the people than ever before. The suffrage bill was presented on April 2. It gave women the right to vote and to hold office on the same terms as men, but denied the suffrage to married women whose husbands had paid no taxes for three years.

An important debate occurred in the Riksdag toward the end of May, when the Social Democrats introduced their bill for neutralization. The bill was referred to a special committee, which decided against it. In the course of the debate, the foreign minister, Count Ehrensvärd, declared that while Sweden was firm in her allegiance to her traditional policy of neutrality and intended to be so in future, she would not refuse to defend by all the means in her power any violation of her neutrality. The bill was rejected without being put to a vote.

The popularity of the Conservative scheme of naval defense was illustrated in May by the offer by a deputation to the king of a popular subscription of 12,000,000 kronor to build a battleship for the navy. The king in accepting the gift applauded the patriotism and generosity of the people.

SWEET, HENRY. An English philologist and educator, died April 30, 1912. He was born in London in 1835, and was educated at King's College, London, Heidelberg University, and Balliol College, Oxford. From boyhood he was interested in the study of alphabets, and he early adopted philology as his life work. In two branches, phonetics, and later, Old English philology, he early obtained a position in the first rank of European scholars. The teaching of English pronunciation in Germany is based almost entirely on his work. In addition to studies in these branches he made researches into Arabic and Chinese, and on the science of language in all its aspects he was a profound and original thinker. From 1901 until the time of his death he was University Reader in Phonetics at Oxford University. He wrote many works on philology. These include, *A History of English Sounds*, *Primer of Phonetics*, *A History of Language*, and *The Practical Study of Languages*. He also edited many editions of Old and Middle English texts, and contributed many papers on philological subjects to reviews and journals of learned societies.

SWETT, SOPHIE MIRIAM. An American author, died November 12, 1912. She was born in Brewer, Me., and was educated in the private and public schools of Boston. She was at one time associate editor of *Wide Awake* and was the author of many short stories and juvenile books. The first of these was *Captain Polly*, published in 1899. Among others were, *Stories of Maine* (1899); *The Young Shipbuilder* (1902); *Princess Wiela* (1908), and *The Six Little Pennypackers* (1911).

SWIMMING. Many new records were established in 1912, the fact that some of the figures set by Charles M. Daniels of the New York A. C. were bettered being especially notable. It was the opinion of the experts that Daniels's marks would stand for a much longer period than they did. Duke Kahanamoku of Honolulu, Kenneth Huszagh of Chicago, Perry McGillivray of Chicago, and L. B. Goodwin of New York all had a hand in the recork-breaking performances of the year. Kahanamoku created a world's record for the 100 meters over a straightaway course at the Olympic games, covering the distance in 1 minute 2⅗ seconds and lowered Daniels's time for the 220 yards, open water, from 2 minutes, 40⅘ seconds to 2 minutes, 40 seconds. McGillivray smashed another Daniels's mark by swimming 440 yards in a 60-foot pool in 5 minutes, 23⅘ seconds. Goodwin's chief feat of the year was to swim a mile in tidal water in 25 minutes, 36⅕ seconds, lowering the record made by James H. Reilly in 1911 by 4⅗ seconds. The showing made by the Americans entered in the Olympic swimming events was very creditable considering the few who were able to make the Stockholm trip. See OLYMPIC GAMES.

The championships of the Amateur Athletic Union were held in several different cities at various times during the year. The winners of the principal events were: Indoor—50 yards, Philip Mallen, Chicago A. A.; 100 yards, D. Kahanamoku; 220 yards, P. McGillivray, Illinois A. C.; 500 yards, J. H. Reilly, New York A. C.; 440-yard relay, City A. C. (R. E. Frizell, J. C. Eddy, Jr., H. R. Adae, and R. M. Ritter); springboard diving, G. W. Gaidzik, Chicago A. A. Outdoor—440 yards, R. E. Frizell, City A. C.; 880 yards, L. B. Goodwin, New York A. C. (1911 winner); 1 mile, L. B. Goodwin; high diving, J. F. Dunn, New York A. C.

Pennsylvania won the intercollegiate indoor team championship with a total of 30 points. Yale was second, with 23 points. Shryock of Pennsylvania won the 50-yard event and Palmer of Yale the 220 yards. Sharp of Pennsylvania in the 100-yard race established a new record of 58⅕ seconds. Yale won the 200-yard relay in the record time of 1 minute, 48⅗ seconds. Willis of Pennsylvania captured the plunge for distance, with 74 feet, 6 inches. Later in the year the same swimmer went 80 feet, thereby breaking the record of 75 feet, 11 inches held by M. Kaiser. The Conference College Championships in the West were won by Illinois. Northwestern finished second. The Annual Mississippi Marathon (10 miles) was won by C. Heath, who covered the distance in 1 hour, 39 minutes, 2⅕ seconds. J. H. Taylor won the English long-distance championship (5 miles, 60 yards) in 1 hour, 5 mintes, 7⅗ seconds.

SWITZERLAND. A federal republic of central Europe. Capital, Bern.

AREA AND POPULATION. The area and *de facto* population (census of December 31, 1910) by cantons are given in the following table:

	Sq. kms.	Pop.		Sq. kms.	Pop.
Zürich	1,724.76	503,915	Appenzell A.-Rh.	242.49	57,973
Bern	6,844.50	645,877	Appenzell I.-Rh.	172.88	14,659
Lucerne	1,500.80	167,223	St. Gall	2,019.00	302,896
Uri	1,076.00	22,113	Graubünden	7,132.80	117,069
Schwyz	908.26	58,428	Aargau	1,404.10	230,634
Obwalden	474.80	17,161	Thurgau	1,011.60	134,917
Nidwalden	290.50	13,788	Tessin	2,800.90	156,166
Glarus	691.20	33,316	Vaud	3,252.00	317,457
Zug	239.20	28,156	Valais	5,224.49	128,381
Fribourg	1,674.60	139,654	N'chatel	807.80	133,061
Solothurn	791.51	117,040	Geneva	282.35	154,906
Basel-Stadt	35.76	135,918			
Basel-L'dt.	427.47	76,488			
Schaffhausen	294.22	46,097	Total	41,323.99	3,753,293

Total *de jure* population, 3,765,123. Protestants numbered 2,108,642, Roman Catholics 1,590,832. Speaking German as their native tongue were 2,599,194; French, 796,220; Italian, 301,323; Romansh, 39,912; other languages, 28,172. Marriages in 1911 27,800; births, 94,082; deaths, 62,168; still-births (included in foregoing), 2855. In the same year 5512 Swiss citizens emigrated—4196 to North America, 1145 to South America, 15 to Central America, 80 to Australia, 40 to Asia, and 36 to Africa. Bern (communal population estimated 1912) 80,900 inhabitants; Zürich, 192,200; Basel, 135,500; Geneva, 132,800; Lausanne, 69,100; St. Gall, 62,400; Lucerne, 40,900; Chaux-de-Fonds, 38,600; Winterthur, 25,700; Bienne, 23,900; Neuchâtel, 23,600.

EDUCATION. There is no federal direct control of education, authority being vested in the cantons and communes. Primary instruction is free and in the Protestant cantons attendance is enforced. Secondary schools are amply provided and well attended. There are excellent special schools and seven universities.

PRODUCTION. In the valleys agriculture is carried on. About one-sixth of the area of the country is forest. The area under main crops and yield for two years, with yield per hectare in 1911, are shown below:

	Hectares 1911	Hectares 1912	Quintals 1911	Quintals 1912	Qs. ha.
Wheat....	42,365	42,200	959,200	865,000	22.6
Rye.......	24,254	24,500	464,321	433,000	19.1
Barley....	5,182	5,000	98,800	93,000	19.1
Oats......	32,644	33,000	704,000	583,000	21.6
Corn.......	1,330	1,330	30,800	27,000	23.2
Vines*....	23,700	23,700	854,770	903,000	36.1
Tobacco..	290	320	5,590	5,500	19.3

* Yield in hectoliters of wine.

The quantity of silkworm eggs placed for hatching in the spring of 1912 was 188 hectograms; production of cocoons, 31,200 kilograms, compared with 42,835 kilograms in 1911. Livestock 1911: 144,000 horses, 1,443,000 cattle, 160,000 sheep, 340,000 goats, 569,000 swine. The dairy industry comprehends several distinct branches—the manufacture of butter, cheese, condensed milk, and milk chocolate. The timber industry and pisciculture are important, as are also salt mining, and the manufacture of cement and alcoholic liquors. Outside of the big business plants, house industries employ large numbers of both men and women; watches and clocks, gloves, and other leather goods, pottery, tobacco, and snuff, etc., are thus produced. The silk and cotton industries employ in the neighborhood of sixty thousand persons.

COMMERCE. The imports and exports of merchandise by countries of origin and destination in the 1911 trade are set forth in the table below, in thousands of francs:

	Imps.	Exps.		Imps.	Exps.
Germany	581,395	274,879	Arg'tina	29,232	28,405
France	339,633	132,627	Brazil	18,550	18,152
Italy	180,629	85,234	Colombia	11,055	1,517
Aus.-Hun.	113,884	85,045	Oth.S.A.	16,388	19,568
U. K.	99,857	212,920	Asia	48,144	47,135
Neth.	23,993	9,871	Africa	32,732	15,298
Belgium	38,926	25,226	Australia	13,188	14,396
Spain	24,772	22,800	Unstated	.....	8,099
Rumania	32,346	9,056	Other	250,237	319,282
Russia	89,580	48,064			
Oth. Europe	27,177	32,305	Tot. '11	1,802,359	1,257,309
U. S.	75,085	142,228	" '10	1,745,021	1,195,872
Canada	11,863	24,486	" '09	1,602,140	1,097,666

Imports and exports of coin and bullion in 1911, 41,484,208 and 31,528,813 francs respectively; in 1910, 42,890,821 and 28,258,200—making total trade, in 1911, 1,843,843,263 francs imports and 1,288,838,217 francs exports; in 1910, 1,787,911,832 and 1,224,130,331. The principal articles of the 1911 trade are given in the table on page 696.

COMMUNICATIONS. There were January 1, 1912, 5112 kilometers of railway in operation. Most of the railways have been nationalized, but the state lines do not show a uniform working profit nor, in some cases, any profit at all.

Imports	1000 fr.	Exports	1000 fr.
Cereals, etc.	199,400	Cottons	242,400
Silk	148,500	Watches	164,000
Coal	94,300	Silks	158,400
Animals	73,400	Machinery	84,400
Cottons	68,300	Cheese	63,200
Chemicals	62,200	Spun silk	58,000
Precious metals	61,100	Chemicals	57,700
Woolens	60,300	Raw silk	47,400
Iron	57,300	Chocolate	47,100
Cotton	52,400	Milk	41,500
Wine	48,800	Cotton yarn	24,400
Meat	47,700	Hides	20,000
Machinery	45,700	Iron mfrs.	17,300
Sugar	40,000	Straw mfrs.	17,200
Timber	38,000	Woolens	15,600
Iron mfrs.	36,400	Jewelry	14,400
Wool	26,600	Woolen yarn	13,100
Leather	24,800	Animals	12,600

During the year the question of the electrification of the state railways assumed considerable importance, as the annual fuel bill approximated $5,000,000 and the coal must be imported from abroad. Several commissions investigated the matter of general electrification, using water power under government control, and it was proposed that this should be done in stages, beginning with the sections which were most easily convertible. Accordingly a state generating station was to be erected at Amsteig in the Uri canton and electrification was to be begun on the St. Gothard line with its steep grades and many tunnels. The total expense involved in electrifying the whole Swiss federal system was estimated at $100,000,000. It was proposed to use single phase alternating current with a pressure of 15,000 volts on the overhead wires. Electric railway construction in Switzerland, which had been particularly active during 1912 and the years immediately preceding, has resulted in the completion of the following lines in the canton of Tessin: Locarno-Bignasco, 17 miles; Bellinzona-Mesocco, 16 miles; Biasca-Acquarossa, 9 miles; Capolago-Chiasso, 8 miles; Lugano-Ponte Tresa, 8 miles; Lugano-Tesserete, 5 miles; Lugano-Cardo-Dino, 5 miles.

Several important though short lines of railway were completed in Switzerland during the year 1912, among which the following are worthy of mention: Bernina Pass line, 37 miles, connecting the Engadine with the Italian railway system at Terano; the Davos branch of the Rheatisch road, which also traverses the Engadine valley; and the Sweisimmen-Leuk branch of the Montreux-Oberland railway, which passes through one of the most beautiful sections of the Bernese Oberland range. The latter is a link in the chain of mountain roads financed by the canton of Bern at a cost of $26,000,000. Progress continued on the extension of the Jungfrau line, and the tunnel to Jungfraujoch was pierced in February (see TUNNELS); but the complete line to the summit was not expected to be finished for several years. Progress was made also with the Lotschberg tunnel, which is over nine miles long and establishes a new and important traffic outlet for Switzerland. It shortens the distance between London and Milan and other points in northern Italy by several hours, and when completed and equipped with electric motive power, according to the plans, will prove an important branch of the transportation system of Switzerland.

The Swiss railways give employment to 42,000 people, 35,200 of whom work on the state lines and 6800 on private railways. These figures are exclusive of the tramways or funiculars, which for the most part are common to the municipalities or the cantons. Receipts of the state railways for 1911 were as follows: Passenger traffic, $15,001,890; freight traffic, $21,263,988; other receipts, $1,458,926; a total of $37,724,804. Expenditures were $22,664,762, making a balance in favor of the government of $15,060,042.

State telegraph lines (1911), 3575 kilometers; wires, 26,306.

FINANCE. The details of (actual) revenue and expenditure in 1911 are seen in the following table:

Revenue	1000 fr.	Expenditure	1000 fr.
Customs, etc.	80,948	Military	44,778
Investments	4,459	Interior	16,867
Military	4,405	Ind. and agri.	14,976
Posts and rys.	3,833	Customs, etc.	8,516
Real property	1,993	Debt charge	7,108
Ind. and agr.	1,249	Justice, etc.	2,030
Interior, etc.	1,028	Administration	1,415
Administration	99	Political	1,108
Political	24	Posts and rys.	54
Miscellaneous	81	Miscellaneous	96
Total	98,044	Total	98,296

The debt stood, January 1, 1912, at 255,130,031 francs.

ARMY. The federal forces are organized as a national militia rather than as a standing army, and liability to service involves thirteen years in the auszug or elite, twelve years in the landwehr, and six in the landsturm, but previously the young men and boys have undergone gymnastic and military training in schools and cadet corps, so that they are prepared for military service and can avail themselves of the recruit course in the first year of service, which amounts to 92 days for the cavalry, 77 days for the artillery, and 67 days for the infantry, with repetition courses of 13 days every year, so that there is an aggregate service during the time spent in the auszug of 141 days in the infantry, 146 in the engineers, 160 in the cavalry, and 163 in the artillery. In 1912 special orders were issued for the landsturm, defining their service as principally for frontier and communications guard. Under the provisions of the law of 1907, the organization of the army came into effect April 1, 1912, whereby staffs were provided for the eventual formation of three army corps with the requisite divisions, brigades, and other subdivisions. There were thus composed six divisions and mountain and fortress troops. Each division was given a sapper battalion and a company of telegraphists bearing the same numeral as the division. The sapper battalions consisted of four companies and in each of them the fourth company was organized as mountain troops. In addition three pontoon battalions were organized with six bridging equipments, a photo-electric company attached to the foot artillery, two army telegraph companies, two balloon companies, and a company of signalers. The auszug was made up of thirty-six infantry regiments, eight companies of cyclists, six companies of infantry for communications, six groups of gui es, four brigades of cavalry, six brigades of artillery, with technical and other troops. The auszug and landwehr embraced three corps of foot artillery, three battalions of bridge builders, aviation corps, and other troops. The landwehr was divided into six infantry brigades, of seventy-two battalions, six battalions for communications, twelve squadrons of guides, cyclists, machine-gun companies, engineers, and other technical troops. The field army was estimated at over 200,000, of which 140,000 were in the auszug and the remainder in the landwehr, while the landsturm consists of about 300,000 men. The application of the law of 1907 brought about a substantial increase in the army budget for 1912, while the army factory at Bern and other military works were also responsible for increases in the national expenses.

GOVERNMENT. The constitution of May 29, 1874, entrusts the executive authority to a federal council (seven members) presided over by a president and a vice-president elected annually. The council is elected for three years by a federal assembly composed of a national council (167 members, directly elected for three years by popular vote) and a council of states (44 members, directly elected in some of the cantons and in others by the legislative authorities). Ecclesiastics alone are ineligible for office among Swiss citizens over twenty years of age.

The principles of the referendum and recall are in force. To the federal government alone is given power to make treaties and to declare war, and in its control are the army and the postal, financial, and customs departments. The treaty of Vienna (1815) guarantees the neutrality of Switzerland. The president in 1912 was Dr. Louis Forrer (elected December 14, 1911); and the vice-president, E. Müller, who was elected December 12, 1912, to be president for the ensuing year.

HISTORY

WORKINGMEN'S INSURANCE. As was said in the 1911 YEAR BOOK the elections for the National Council were held on October 29, 1911. They renewed the representation in the council for three years, and the distribution of parties among the 189 deputies was as follows: Radicals, 113; Catholic Conservatives, 38; Liberals of the Centre, 14; Socialists, 15; Democrats, 5; belonging to no party, 4. Owing to changes in the electoral districts and to the dispute between Radicals and Liberals, the Socialists who, in the old National Council, had numbered only 5, now numbered 15, and their activity and influence in parliamentary affairs was more than proportionate to their number. They carried on a very vigorous campaign against the customs tariff, aiming at ultimate free trade. Public attention, however, at the begining of the year was concentrated on the insurance law which, pursuant to a demand for referendum, was to be submitted to popular vote on February 4, 1912. This law for the insurance of workmen against sickness and accident had been under discussion for several years and was very carefully framed in order to meet the necessities of all concerned. Its chief features as regards sickness insurance were, the subvention of private and mutual insurance companies that already existed or might be formed in future, provided they conformed to certain rules, and the provision that while sickness insurance was not arbitrary, the cantons and communes should have authority to make it so within their jurisdiction. As to accident insurance, employers were required to insure in a private or mutual insurance company, which was to be under the control of the Federal Council. The chief objections of the opponents to the measure were that it would establish a state monopoly and by the insurance of non-professional risks would impose a heavy and indeterminate financial burden. The law was favored by the Radicals, the Catholic Conservatives, and the Socialists. The Liberal party was divided on the question. Meetings to discuss the measure were held in all parts of the country and its merits and defects were thoroughly canvassed. Every elector received a copy of the bill. The referendum on February 4 gave the measure a large majority, 285,037 against 238,694.

SYNDICALISM. This is the name commonly applied to the most radical form of the modern labor movement. The name and to a large extent the social theory of the movement is derived from the French unions or *syndicats*. (See TRADE UNIONS, *France*.) It is a logical development of the revolutionary wing of socialism and the "Internationale" as represented by Baunin as against the evolutionary socialism of Marx and Engels. The term, however, has come to be indiscriminately applied to almost all labor movements that are inimical to peace and order. In its original French meaning the term applies to a movement of the organized workers in each industry to obtain control of that industry. It differs from socialism in that the latter would bring all industries under the common direction of the state. It agrees with socialism in desiring to get rid of the employer: it is even more extreme than socialism as to the productivity of capital, holding narrowly that labor produces all. See SOCIALISM. It would organize the workers industrially, that is, by industries rather than by trades or crafts; and it would get possession not by political means, that is, through parliamentary action or governmental control, but more directly. It holds that labor representatives in government are even worse than useless, for this leads to compromise, to a sacrifice of principles, and to false hopes of emancipation. It contends that the propertied class and the "intellectuals" will always control government; these latter, though not always biased, take a philosophical view of the class war and are content with mere reforms, with gradual progress. Syndicalism rejects reform because it does not go to the root of social ills; and it detests government because it is an instrument for the exploitation of the workers. It thus differs from political and evolutionary socialism which seeks control of parliamentary and administrative machinery by ordinary methods, which prides itself on its fruitfulness in social and industrial reforms, and which would make the state the controlling agency of all industries. In theory syndicalism ignores the existence of the state; it thus approximates philosophical anarchism. But in practice it finds the state as great an enemy as the employer and attacks both by its favorite devices. In England a most common meaning of syndicalism is such labor union activity as requires the intervention of the government in behalf of community welfare.

Syndicalism would gain control of an industry by direct action. This may be peaceful, as by the adoption of labor coöperation, or more forceful, as by the strike, sabotage, boycott, label, and other means designed to render an industry unprofitable to an employer, forcing him to abandon it to the workers. The use of the general strike is identified with the syndicalist movement, the term being used in the double sense of a strike of all workers in a given industry or a strike of all workers in all industries. The general strike, however, is more of an ideal than a practical policy even with the syndicalists; it is a final culmination, a day of deliverance, for which workers must be in readiness. The irritation strike designed to continually annoy the employer has been adopted in Australia. Sabotage means the obstruction of the processes of manufacture by destruction of materials, by slow or bad work, and by crippling the machines; for example, by disturbing the regularity of railway traffic, scratching the varnish of furniture or placing emory powder in machinery bearings. The principle of direct action has come to be the distinguishing trait of syndicalism in the public mind. Its primary function in the syndicalist theory is to develop and maintain the spirit of aggressive class consciousness among the workers. It is in the struggles of the industrially organized workers with employers that they will learn their weakness and their strength and develop the cohesion and experience needed to manage industries themselves. In England the principle of direct action met with wide acceptance in labor circles during 1912. Though retaining the policy of political action the unionists were far from unanimous in rejecting the adoption of direct action. (See TRADE UNIONS.) In the transport workers' strike (see STRIKES AND LOCKOUTS) the theory of direct action was frequently expressed. Tom Mann and Ben Tillett, two radical labor leaders, were thoroughly imbued with revolutionary doctrines. The former said: "Labor runs the machine and labor will stop the machine until its demands are met." It was frequently noted that the appearance of syndicalism made socialism appear quite acceptable; but it may also be noted that syndicalism is by many looked upon as socialism's most bitter enemy. Not only does it scornfully reject the results of decades of socialist efforts and the present power of socialist members in legislative bodies throughout the world, but it draws to itself the most aggressive of the radical leaders whenever it appears. Two papers started in England are *The Industrial Syndicalist*, edited by Tom Mann, and *The Syndicalist Railwaymen*, edited by Charles Watkins. Mann, his publishers, and a contributor were convicted and sentenced on a charge of inciting to mutiny to terms of imprisonment, afterwards commuted. (See GREAT BRITAIN, *Syndicalism*.)

Both in England and Australia the syndicalists took advantage of the minimum wage movement. In England they declared that the profits of industry would warrant the payment of £2 per week to every worker regardless of capacity or output. In New South Wales the miners demanded 8s. per day and a 7-hour day for all men in and about mines. The granting of these was to be followed by higher demands and the constant use of the irritation strike until the employers gave up in despair and the workers came into full control of the industry.

In America the Industrial Workers of the World (q. v.) represent the nearest approach to syndicalism. They were prominent in the Lawrence and Little Falls strikes (q. v.). The dynamiting of the Iron Workers' Union (see TRADE UNIONS) was an extreme form of direct action, but was contrary to syndicalist policy, since it involved destruction of life. Moreover, the McNamaras sought not the overthrow of the present industrial system but the establishment of the orthodox trade-union policy of the closed shop.

SYNTHESIS OF FOODSTUFFS, ARTIFICIAL. See CHEMISTRY.

SYRACUSE UNIVERSITY. An institution for higher education at Syracuse, N. Y., founded in 1870. The total enrollment in all departments of the university in the autumn of 1912 was 3530 and the faculty numbered 260. Among the noteworthy changes in the faculty during the year were the appointments of Hugh B. Baker, M. F., Ec. D., as dean of the New York State College of Forestry; F. W. Howe, M. S., as director of the division of agriculture. The most important benefaction received during the year was a gift of $83,000 from Mrs. Russell Sage for the division of agriculture. The productive funds of the university amounted to about $2,000,000. The income from all sources in 1912 was $547,600. The library contained 87,705 bound volumes and 41,627 pamphlets.

SYRIA. See ARCHÆOLOGY.

TAFT. ROYAL CHAPIN. Former governor of Rhode Island, died June 4, 1912. He was born in Northbridge, Mass., in 1823, and was educated at Worcester Academy. In 1849 he engaged in the business of manufacturing cotton and woolen goods and afterwards acquired large interests in several mills. He was president of many important financial institutions in Providence and elsewhere and was a director of the New York, New Haven and Hartford Railroad. He was for several years a member of the Providence city council, and was elected to the State House of Representatives in 1880, serving until 1884. He was elected governor of the State in 1888 and declined renomination to that office.

TAFT, W. H. See PRESIDENTIAL CAMPAIGN and UNITED STATES. *Administration.*

TALL BUILDINGS. The approaching completion of two skyscrapers of record-breaking height and capacity in New York and the filing of plans for a new building of large dimensions to take the place of the Equitable building destroyed by fire during the year, gave unusual interest in 1912 to this field of architecture and structural engineering. The practical problems in regard to the construction and maintenance of these huge structures by this time had been well understood and mastered, and, in New York City at least, the matter was one rather to be considered on the score of economy and expediency in view of their erection on narrow streets without adequate daylight illumination and the concentration of business interests on limited ground areas and restricted districts. The evolution of the skyscraper in America has been rapid and along practical lines, the keynote always being utility. The architect has set conditions for the engineer and especially the elevator manufacturer to realize, so that the triumph is one rather of engineering than of design. As regards ornament, this naturally is restricted and the best practice is considered to confine it in large measure to ground floors and entrances and to the attic stories, as here any original or monumental treatment is visible for great distances and gives the individual character to the building, rising as it does to great heights above or among its neighbors. Likewise the ornate entrance and entrance halls establish the character of the building to the man on the street and attract people by the degree and general nature of their decoration, these being in fact supplemental highways to the main street.

The skyscraper structurally is a skeleton construction of steel carried on a firm and massive foundation properly subdivided so that each vertical column will be properly supported. These vertical columns are cross connected by beams carrying the floors, adequate wind bracing is provided, and the whole metal structure is properly fireproofed. The exterior walls of brick or stone are carried by the main structure and are independent of the foundations. An efficient and adequate elevator system for vertical transportation is provided and then conveniences for the safety and ease of the tenants are provided in varying degree.

The primary structural consideration is the foundation, and in fact the engineering below the ground is quite as important and almost as costly as that which stands above it. That this must be firm to support the immense weight of the structure is manifest, and therefore it must be founded on bed rock or be of sufficient area to provide adequate bearing surface. Thus the New York City building code provided that "when foundations are carried down through the earth by piers of stone, brick, or concrete caisson the loads on same shall be not more than fifteen tons to the square foot when carried down to rock; ten tons to the square foot when carried down to firm gravel or hard clay; eight tons to the square foot in open caissons or sheet pile trenches when carried down to rock." For such a structure as the fifty-five-story Woolworth building in New York City with an estimated weight of 125,000 tons the foundations consisted of piers which necessarily were carried to bed rock reached at a distance of 110 feet below the sidewalk. This, as in the case of similar foundations, was possible by the use of pneumatic caissons such as are used for bridge construction where excavating under compressed air and loading the caissons they could be worked down to the solid rock and filled with concrete.

In another notable case, the New York Municipal building, the solid rock was considerably in excess of 115½ feet below tide level at which the limiting pressure of fifty pounds set by New York statute for compressed air-workers was encountered. Accordingly here no foundations were sunk below 112 feet, 1 inch below tide level and where rock failed a broad concrete foundation was built with the bearing surface so spread out that a maximum pressure of six tons to the square foot was obtained.

From the foundation pier each column or pair of columns rises, being supported on ribbed bases of cast iron laid directly on the concrete or on a grillage of steel beams or a cantilever structure of girders. The columns are built up of steel, successive lengths being riveted on as they are hoisted into place as they come from the storage yard. Each section has been carefully trimmed and punched at the factory and the task of erection proceeds rapidly. To the columns are riveted the girders and to these in turn the floor beams, the temporary bolts being replaced by rivets which are set in place by pneumatic or electric hammers. Braces connect columns, girders, and beams while wind bracing, especially in tower buildings, is provided after careful computation to withstand stresses; these being figured usually on a maximum wind pressure of 30 pounds to the square foot. The entire structure therefore is firmly united into a homogeneous skeleton of adequate strength and the steel forms an appreciable fraction of the entire weight carried by the foundations.

Mention might be made of the steel itself which is fabricated in the special shapes and sizes desired at the mills, built up into columns and girders, accurately trimmed, fitted and punched and then stored at some convenient point to the place of erection. Most large cities do not permit the use of the streets for the storage of materials, and consequently it must be transported to the building as needed, hoisted into position and then bolted with a minimum expenditure and waste of time. This is done by steam or electric cranes which are mounted successively on upper floors as the building progresses and are able to handle the material rapidly and efficiently.

Given the skeleton the next consideration is making it fireproof, for the steel unprotected yields readily to heat, and failure in any single part can impair the entire structure. Likewise the spaces between the beams must be filled with brick, tile, or concrete, in order to finish the floors while the exterior walls, of brick or stone, which are mainly for ornament, must be added. The protection of the columns, girders, and beams may be secured by enclosing them completely in hollow tile, brick, or concrete, or by coating them with the more recent cement gum.

The relative merits of these and other methods of fireproofing, as well of course as the construction of the floors either by tile or brick filling or by reinforced concrete, are matters of controversy, but the opinion of disinterested engineers who have examined buildings exposed to conflagration dangers is that quality of work is more important than any particular kind of construction. This subject in 1912 formed an important topic of discussion in connection with the adoption of the new building code for the city of New York, as the various interests were in conflict as regards the rules governing the use of different materials and no decision was reached by the end of the year.

With frame and floors constructed the next question is the enclosure of the building. This is where the architect is permitted to have the predominant influence. The material and its ornamentation naturally make for the appearance of the building. It may be of brick, tile, or stone, and the effect is usually of solidity so that a tower, for example, rises as a massive monument. By some architects this is not considered appropriate, as they believe that the material and treatment should more accurately represent the actual construction and that lightness rather than massive appearance should be sought. Furthermore, in case of fire it is the stone and the carving and ornamentation that suffers most, as it will be cracked and spalled even while resisting heat. But be that as it may, we find skyscrapers built of various materials, from brick to limestone and the more costly marble. These exterior walls are carried in curtain form on the main steel structure, and while they diminish in thickness as the height increases they are independent of foundation walls.

Within the building the means of access plays an important part. A city street virtually is swung around to a vertical position and of course there must be adequate transportation facilities, some of the larger buildings housing as many as 10,000 tenants, not to mention those coming and going for business or other purposes. Accordingly vertical transportation must be arranged and must be considered in the earliest plans. Elevators must be provided and distributed to handle the traffic speedily and economically, and these must be arranged with regard to certain vertical columns for their support and guide rails. These elevators are enclosed in fireproof and independent shafts with wire glass doors and panels on the sides, where they give access to the floors and must be independent of the stairways, which in a tall building are considered rather for emergency use than as a practical means of communication. But it is the elevators that make the tall building possible and it is the elevator engineer who has to realize the demands of architects and builders. So far every exaction has been met and with the succesfsul development of electric machines, notably of the traction pattern, the various heights have been reached. The traction elevator consists essentially of a car whose cable after passing around a sheave on an electric motor is connected to a balancing counterweight. As the weight of the cable is compensated by a flexible chain the only work for the motor in addition to moving the system is to raise or lower the load provided by the passengers. This can be done at a speed of 700 feet per minute, so that express cars can be run to the highest floors in a minute or less, this time being the practical limit from the standpoint of renting availability. With the elevators provided and suitably protected a tall building requires proper subdivision of the floor space. The stairways in a separate fireproof shaft must be cut off at each floor by fireproof doors so as to avoid being a chimney to carry fire through a building. Floor space must be restricted to suitable fireproof partitions and all trim, doors, etc., must be made of metal, the tenants supplying, as it is, far too much combustible material in the way of furniture, books, records, etc. For the fire danger is always present and there must be adequate standpipes constantly under pressure for instant use. In addition sprinklers and fire alarms must be installed and the vast network of wires required for light, power, and communication must be carried in suitable conduits and distributed from proper panels and switchboards. Water supply and plumbing of a most elaborate character extend throughout a modern skyscraper and a heating system susceptible of exact regulation. In fact the maintenance and economy of such a building is no small problem and the superintendent is in most cases a mechanical engineer graduate from a leading technical school.

The skyscraper, aside from its structural and insurance features, is furnishing a great problem to American cities. It tends to concentrate business interests and thus prevent the more even distribution that many claim would benefit real estate at large. It deprives the owners of adjoining property of air and daylight, as such buildings are usually constructed on the narrow and older streets of a city. It has been proposed that the area covered by any portion of a building rising to extreme height should be limited by law so as to restrict the aggregate amount of high buildings, yet permit of lofty towers. While extreme examples of tall buildings are seen in New York City, the tendency is general throughout the United States, and many large corporations even in smaller cities have erected such buildings, securing not only adequate returns therefrom, but also the valuable asset of the prestige associated with the occupation and ownership of such a structure. In fact many of the large life insurance companies owning these lofty and monumental structures esteem their advertising value of the highest importance.

Five of the tallest buildings in the world at the end of 1912 were in New York City: Woolworth building, 775 feet; Metropolitan Life Tower, 700 feet; Singer building, 612 feet; New York City Municipal building, 580 feet; Bankers Trust Company building, 540 feet; The L. C. Smith building in Seattle, and the Union Central Life Insurance building in Cincinnati are also notable buildings.

TAMMANY HALL. See PRESIDENTIAL CAMPAIGN.

TANAGRA. See ARCHÆOLOGY.

TARIFF. Ever since the enactment of the Payne-Aldrich law of 1909 the tariff has been a foremost subject of political and economic discussion. So general has been the demand for reduction that almost no conspicuous political leaders have openly defended the existing rates. The Republican party in its political platform, however, argued mainly for the protective system, though admitting that "some of the existing import duties are too high and should be reduced." It contended that reductions should be gradual and on the basis of accurate information. The Democratic platform declared tariff duties unconstitutional and denounced the contention that the tariff system is favorable to labor. It declared protection to be "the principal cause of the unequal distribution of wealth"; it favored an immediate downward revision, but in such manner as not to injure or destroy legitimate industry. The Progressive party platform declared in favor of the protective system, but demanded tariff revision. Like the Republican party it pledged itself for a non-partisan scientific tariff commission. Much attention was given to the subject in Congress, but no legislation affecting duties resulted. The tariff board, for which President Taft had valiantly contended throughout his administration, was eliminated because the House Democrats refused an appropriation for its continuance. The various bills and reports noted below were introduced, but the efforts of all three groups to gain political advantage, before the country, assisted by the President's vetoes, checkmated each other effectually. In general the conservative Republicans either refused to do anything or took an attitude of indifference, while the Progressive Republicans favored reductions, but to a less degree than did the Democrats.

PRESENT TARIFF. The import duties as established by the Payne-Aldrich tariff of 1909 were classified under fourteen schedules, A to N inclusive. These schedules contain 480 paragraphs each relating to a group of articles or a single article. Schedule A includes chemicals, oils, and paints. Among the articles there included are drugs, with a duty of 1¼ cents a pound and 10 per cent. ad valorem; glue; castor oil; olive oil; whale oil; opium; phosphorus; perfumery, and cosmetics; and soap. A majority of the duties are specific, but many are a combination of both specific and ad valorem as illustrated by drugs. Schedule B includes earths, earthenware and glassware; these comprise also cement, marble, sponges, etc. Most of these have only ad valorem duties. Schedule C, including metals and manufactures of metals, contains iron ore; iron in pigs and bars; automobiles and parts; horseshoe nails, copper plates; pens; table and kitchen utensils; tin plates; pins; and manufacturers of iron. Nearly all of these have specific duties, though manufactured articles are likely .to have ad valorem duties. Schedules D includes wood and its manufacturers; and schedule E, sugar, molasses, and their manufactures. Sugar pays duties according to weight and degrees of quality as shown by the polariscope test. Its rates are the same as under the Dingley act of 1897, being aproximately one cent per pound. Schedule F includes tobacco and manufactures of tobacco, the duties on manufactured tobacco ranging from $1.85 to $2.50 per pound, on snuff 55c per pound, and on cigars and cigarettes $4.50 per pound plus 25 per cent. ad valorem. Schedule G, agricultural products and provisions, includes cattle, horses, mules, barley, oats, rice, rye, butter and cheese, eggs, hay, honey, hops, potatoes, fish, fruits, and salt. Nearly all of the rates of this schedule are specific. Schedule H includes spirits and wines. Proof alcohol pays $2.60 per gallon; brandy, gin, whisky, and cordials, proof, pay the same; wines, including champagne, $9.60 per dozen quarts; still wines pay much less; and malt liquor 45 cents per gallon. Schedule I includes cotton manufactures. It is made very complex not only by frequent combinations of both specific and ad valorem duties, but also by the classification of articles according to number of threads, their coloring, and other qualities. Thus the duties on cotton thread, colored and bleached, range according to numbers from 6 cents per pound to 67 cents per pound. Cotton handkerchiefs pay duties of 4½ cents per square yard and 10 per cent. ad valorem; cotton hosiery, 70 cents to $2.00 per dozen pairs plus 15 per cent. ad valorem; cottonshirts and drawers from 60 cents per dozen pairs plus 15 per cent. ad valorem to $2.25 per dozen pairs plus 35 cents ad valorem. Schedule J comprises flax, hemp, jute, and their manufactures. Schedule K includes wool and woolens. Wool is divided into three classes with subdivisions, the rates ranging from 33 cents to 3 cents a pound; dress goods pay duties ranging from 7 cents per square yard plus 50 per cent. ad valorem to 11 cents a square yard plus 55 per cent. ad valorem; blankets, 22 cents a pound plus 30 per cent. ad valorem to 44 cents a pound plus 55 per cent. ad valorem; clothing and carpets have similar combinations of both specific and ad valorem duties. Schedule L covers silk and silk goods; schedule M includes pulp, paper, and publications; and schedule N includes sundries. Among the latter are agricultural implements, beads, brushes, bristles, bituminous coal, coke, toys, feathers, prepared furs, human hair, manufactures of leather, gutta-percha, musical instruments, paintings and statuary, and umbrellas.

The law of 1909 placed 236 articles on the free list. Among the articles on this list are the following: Animals for breeding, exhibition, or racing; birds, land, and water fowl; books, maps, music, and publications issued for subscribers or exchanges by scientific and literary associations or academies or publications for gratuitous private circulation; public documents of foreign governments; books and pamphlets in raised print; books, maps, and music especially imported in very limited numbers for the use of a religious, philosophic, educational, or scientific society; rough or uncut diamonds or other precious stones; undressed furs; guano; hides of cattle; india rubber; models of invention; needles; petroleum, crude or refined, and its products; crude paper stock; philosophic and scientific apparatus for cultural uses; crude potash; professional books, implements, and instruments; tobacco stems; woods when in logs; and works of art.

TARIFF BOARD. Throughout his administration President Taft stood for revision of the tariff on the basis of the findings of a tariff board or commission. His principle in the campaign of 1908 had been that protective duties should be made on the basis of differences in cost of production at home and abroad. Consequently he from the first demanded a board of investigation to determine relative costs. The Payne-Aldrich act authorized such a board; and against much oposition appropriations for its work were secured for 1910-11 and 1911-12. The House Democrats, however, refused further appropriations and the life of the board terminated in June, 1912. The press of the country accepted this outcome calmly, partly because it was expected that the functions of the board would be transferred to a new bureau of foreign and domestic commerce in the Department of Commerce and Labor. It was quite widely conceded that the board had done faithful and valuable work; that it had shown the necessity of revision downward; but that the task assigned it of determining differences of cost of manufacture was insuperable. Democratic opposition was due to their belief that the board had been made an excuse for preventing tariff legislation. Nevertheless the board did much to show that high costs and high wages do not uniformly go together; and to bring into question the traditional Republican argument that protection is the cause of the high wages of American labor.

RECIPROCITY. The Canadian reciprocity treaty which was passed by a special session of Congress in 1911, but not accepted by Canada, provided that whether Canada approved the agreement or not, print paper and wood pulp upon which there were no export restrictions should be admitted free from Canada. Following the enactment of that provision,

Norway, Sweden, Denmark, Germany, and Austria claimed that their paper and wood pulp should likewise be admitted free under the "most favored nation" clause of their commercial treaties. In 1911 Germany sent to the United States 70,000 tons of wood pulp valued at $3,000,000. Moreover, Germany took occasion to admit steel from Sweden at rates more favorable than those imposed upon American steel, defending her action on the ground that she was dealing with Swedish steel as Congress dealt with Canadian wood pulp. Such facts as these made urgent either the repeal of the provision or the extension of a similar privilege to all countries desiring to export wood pulp and print paper. Nothing, however, was done, in spite of considerable agitation.

IRON AND STEEL. The Democrats of the House had intended to deal with the wool schedule first, but on account of the report of the tariff board submitted late in December they turned to the metals schedule as most available for immediate revision. On January 26 the committee on ways and means of the House reported a bill reducing rates on iron and steel products by 30 to 50 per cent. This was passed by the House three days later. It put iron ore on the free list, as also various products controlled by monopolies, including sewing machines, cash registers, and linotype machines. It also placed on the free list agricultural implements and various articles of common use such as nails and barbed wire. It placed duties of 8 per cent. on pig iron and 10 per cent. on steel rails, and made large reductions in the duties on structural shapes and other heavy products. Cutlery was given a rate of 35 per cent. These reductions were supported by various reports, especially that of the Commissioner of Corporations on the steel industry, which had just been issued, but also by the reports of the immigration commission and the Bureau of Labor dealing with the steel industry and by hearings before committees of the House. The figures of international trade, showing the ability of American producers to compete in foreign markets, were used to show that reductions were warranted. When the measure reached the Senate it met the opposition of both wings of the Republicans. The conservatives took refuge behind the fact that a tariff board report on the industry had not been made. The Progressive Republicans brought forward a measure on April 29 intermediate in its proposals. The House bill shifted the basis of the duties from specific to ad valorem rates, the average being estimated at 19 to 22 per cent.; existing rates average about 33 to 37 per cent.; the Progressive Republican bill averaged about 25 per cent. Moreover, the latter bill retained the specific duties used in the existing law. A compromise bill was passed by both houses, but vetoed by the President on the ground that the tariff board had made no report on the steel schedule, and that the proposed duties furnished insufficient protection. This veto was overridden in the House by a vote of 173 to 83, but sustained in the Senate on August 16 by a vote of 32 to 39.

CHEMICAL SCHEDULE. On February 16 the committee on ways and means reported a bill for the revision of the chemical schedule with a view to increased revenues. This was the first general revision of that schedule since 1883 and required the rearrangement of paragraphs, and the renaming of numerous commodities. The rates were considerably altered. Contrary to Democratic rule, ad valorem duties, however, were used only to a small extent, owing to the more ready application of specific rates. Chemicals cannot be readily tested at time of importation, with the result that ad valorem duties encourage the importation of high grades under the guise of low grades. The report accompanying the bill showed that, between 1900 and 1910, 4068 patents relating to chemical industries were issued by the Patent Office, of which 62 per cent. were secured by foreigners. Foreign holders of American patent rights are not required to manufacture their products in this country; they thus have a monopoly of their products sold here. Consequently the tariff on such products in no way benefits the American producer, who cannot compete for lack of patent rights. Moreover, the industry was found to be closely organized so that prices generally were not on a competitive basis. For these reasons large reductions were believed warranted. The House bill failed to pass in the Senate.

WOOL. A report of the tariff board on wool and woolens in four volumes was transmitted to Congress by President Taft December 21, 1911. It was commended as summarizing a vast amount of information, but criticised for duplicating material already available elsewhere. Opinion varied widely as to the value of cost estimates contained in it. After an extensive study of this report the ways and means committee of the House filed on March 27 a thorough criticism of it. This criticism began by rejecting the cost of production theory upon which the tariff board had operated. It declared that costs, meaning thereby expenses of production, do not show accurately the competitive power of different countries. Moreover, tho difficulties of ascertaining true money costs were held to be insuperable. Besides the House Democrats declared that the tariff board had not separated the cost of producing wool from that of producing mutton nor presented any satisfactory method of treating the joint cost of these two products. The cost estimates of cloths were shown to be few in number and largely conjectural. They were ascertained by procuring sample fabrics abroad which were then sent to American manufacturers for estimates of cost of production. Extensive variations in cost due in part to faulty statistical methods were shown to undermine the validity of the cost of production basis of comparison. Though the board's report seemed to warrant the conclusion that raw wool should be free, the committee found evidence to warrant a duty of 20 to 25 per cent. ad valorem. In other respects also the committee found that the duties proposed in the Underwood bill of 1911 were largely sustained by the board's report.

The House Democrats therefore reënacted the Underwood bill of 1911. In the Senate a substitute bill proposed by Mr. Penrose was passed in the committee of the whole on July 25, this bill having, it was said, been approved by the President. Senator La Follette moved the enactment of his bill of 1911 and it was accepted. There followed a conference between House and Senate leaders and the enactment by both houses of a bill substantially the same as that passed in 1911. This, however, was vetoed by President Taft on the ground that it authorized reductions greater than the board's report justified. He declared, however, that he would approve a bill making less excessive reductions. The original bill was passed over the President's veto on August 13 by the House by a vote of 174 to 80, twenty-one Republicans voting in the affirmative. In the Senate the vote was only 39 for to 36 against, the veto thus being sustained.

COTTON. On March 26, the report of the tariff board on cotton manufactures was sent to Congress by the President. In an accompanying message he found that it would warrant very considerable reductions of duties and urged action to that end. This report made no study of raw materials, that being considered unnecessary. It made some estimates of the costs of yarns in the United States and in Lancashire mills. Also efforts were made to determine the cost of producing sample fabrics, the results being based on the estimates of manufacturers. It found the differences in the costs of yarns to equal about three to fifteen per cent. of the mill costs of producing such yarns in Great Britain. It set forth certain practices of jobbers and dealers whereby prices are maintained; thus notwithstanding the fact that the costs of production in American mills sometimes are less than costs abroad, selling prices here are uniformly higher. The report warranted the conclusion that in all but the very finest grades of cotton goods no protection was needed.

In June the House committee on ways and means presented a criticism of this report. The committee declared the report incomplete because it dealt with only one-third of the schedule; and therefore it was impossible as a basis for revision. The committee laid special stress on the absence of accurate figures of cost of manufacture here and abroad. It contended that the estimates of cost for yarns were not authoritative. It found that the board had actually abandoned the idea of comparative costs for that of comparative wholesale prices as a basis for rate making. Thus the selling prices of samples were obtained in Great Britain; these samples were then submitted to American mills for estimates. The committee contended that the report showed the difference in yarn costs to be slight; that cheaper grades cost no more to manufacture here than in Great Bratain; but that on fancy cotton cloths, knit goods, underwear, and hosiery some protection was warranted. A bill carrying out these ideas was passed by the House and about the middle of August by the Senate. It, however, was vetoed by the President.

SUGAR. The Democratic leaders of the House sought to place sugar on the free list. They succeeded with the aid of 24 Republicans in passing a bill on March 15 to this effect. The resulting loss of more than $50,000,000 in revenue was made up by a new excise tax passed four days later. (See TAXATION.) The Senate, however, substituted a bill providing for only moderate reduction of duties together with alterations in the mode of application. No agreement being reached in conference, both the Free Sugar bill and the Excise bill were lost.

TARKHAN. See ARCHÆOLOGY.

TARR, RALPH STOCKMAN. An American geographer and educator, died March 21, 1912. He was born in Gloucester, Mass., in 1864, and graduated from the Lawrence Scientific School in 1891. In 1882 he was assistant to the United States Fish Commission and Smithsonian Institution. He was assistant geologist in the Texas Geological Survey in 1888 and 1891. In 1890 and 1891 he was assistant in geology at Harvard University. From 1892 to 1906 he was a member of the faculty of Cornell University as assistant professor of geology and professor of dynamic geology and physical geography. From 1906 until the time of his death he was professor of physical geography at Cornell. He acted also as special field assistant of the United States Geological Survey. He wrote widely on geological and geographical subjects. Among his published works are: *Economic Geology of the United States* (1893); *Elementary Physical Geography* (1895); *Elementary Geology* (1897); *First Book of Physical Geography* (1897); *Tarr and McMurry Geographies* (1900, 1902); *Physical Geography of New York State* (1902); *New Physical Geography* (1904). He also wrote many monographs on geographical and geological topics. He was associate editor of the *Journal of Geography*.

TASMANIA. An island south of Victoria, constituting a state of the Commonwealth of Australia. Area, 26,215 square miles. Population (census of April 3, 1911), 191,211, exclusive of full-blooded aboriginals. Hobart, the capital, had 27,526 inhabitants; with suburbs, 39,937. Governor in 1912, Maj.-Gen. Sir Harry Barron, appointed to be governor of Western Australia in 1913; premier, A. E. Solomon. See AUSTRALIA.

A new cabinet was formed in June under Mr. A. E. Solomon as premier.

TAXATION. The development of the taxation in recent years has tended to take more and more the direct forms of income, inheritance, and land increment taxes. At the same time the traditional general property tax is being generally superseded by the taxation of realty separately and the extension of taxes on corporations. Nevertheless Ohio, in its new constitutional reform retained the general property tax. In Germany, England, Oregon, Washington, the Canadian Northwest, and China the movement for the taxation of the unearned increment of land has received wide acceptance and increasing adoption. In New York City this policy was actively discussed during the year, particularly as a means of relieving congestion of population as well as the burdens of the poor. The proposal for income taxation gained wider acceptance; the propaganda for the uniform inheritance tax law which New York adopted in 1911 was carried forward; and administrators and scientific students of taxes continued the discussion of the problem of separating national, State, and local taxes and forming them into a just and supplementary whole.

INCOME TAX AMENDMENT. A joint resolution of Congress adopted in 1909 proposed an amendment to the Constitution authorizing Congress to levy a tax on income "from whatever source derived, without apportionment among the several States, and without regard to any census or enumeration." This had been approved at the close of 1912 by the following

34 States: Alabama, Arizona, Arkansas, California, Colorado, Georgia, Idaho, Illinois, Indiana, Iowa, Kansas, Kentucky, Louisiana, Maine, Maryland, Michigan, Minnesota, Mississippi, Missouri, Montana, Nebraska, Nevada, New York, North Carolina, North Dakota, Ohio, Oklahoma, Oregon, South Carolina, South Dakota, Tennessee, Texas, Washington, Wisconsin. Only 4 States had finally rejected the amendment: Connecticut, New Hampshire, Rhode Island, and Utah. The ratification of 36 States was necessary for its adoption.

CORPORATION TAX. The federal corporation tax law of 1909 provided that insurance companies should pay excise taxes equal to one per cent of their annual net income exclusive of dividends from the stock of other corporations. The law defined in particular the methods of determining the net income. Suit was brought early in 1912 by the Mutual Life Insurance Company of New Jersey in the United States District Court on the grounds that the law was wrongly interpreted when dividends paid to its policy holders were included within the net income. The court decided in favor of the company, holding that dividends are not "income received," and that expenditures for replacing furniture, etc., are expenses and not investments. It was the lay opinion that the court thus exempted insurance companies from the burden which Congress probably sought to place upon them, but that in so doing it had reasoned logically from the nature of the corporation tax.

DEMOCRATIC INCOME TAX PROPOSAL. A bill known as the Excise bill, presented by the House committee on ways and means in February, provided that the loss in revenue resulting from the proposed removal of the duty on sugar should be made up by a federal income tax. This tax assumed the form of an excise tax to make it harmonize with the ruling of the Supreme Court on the corporation tax in 1911. This decision upheld that tax as "an excise on the privilege of doing business as a corporation." The new proposal therefore was to levy a "special excise upon doing business by copartnerships or individuals." All incomes of $5000 and less were exempted; as were also incomes affected by the corporation tax. The old method of self assessment rather than the stoppage-at-source method was retained. The rate was one per cent. The tax was estimated to yield $60,000,000, but Republican Congressmen declared it would yield less than half that sum. Though passed by the House, and by the Senate with various encumbrances, it was a part of the unfinished business at the close of the session.

WISCONSIN. In 1911 Wisconsin enacted a progressive income tax law. This exempted all personal property, except farm animals and merchants' and manufacturers' stock; applied the principle of stoppage-at-source; authorized the taxation of corporations under a separate set of progressive schedules; and made the following exemptions: For an individual $800, for a husband and wife $1200; for each child under 18 or other dependent person $200. The constitutionality of this law was upheld by the Supreme Court of the State on every point. The court denied the soundness of the arguments that the progressive features were unreasonably discriminating, led to double taxation, and deprived citizens of the equal protection of the laws. It found progressive taxation specifically authorized by the State constitution, which provides that "taxes may also be imposed on incomes, privileges, and occupations, which taxes may be graduated and progressive, and reasonable exemptions may be provided." The court held the progressive features not only constitutional, but also economically sound. Similarly it held the exemption features to be not only essentially reasonable, but well within legislative discretion. Finally the separate rates for corporations were held justified because of the privileges which corporations exclusively hold and the differences between a corporation and an individual in business

BIBLIOGRAPHY. Among the new books were the following: *State and local taxation.. Addresses and proceedings*, fifth annual conference under the auspices of the National Tax Association, held at Richmond, Va., September 5-8, 1911: J. Orr, *Taxation of land values as it effects landowners and others;* L. F. Post, *Outlines of lectures on the taxation of land values;* Paul Leroy-Beaulieu, *Traité de la science des finances;* W. V. Marshall, *Curb to predatory wealth;* Vineberg, *Provincial and local taxation in Canada;* P. V. Ross, *Inheritance taxation;* C. F. W. Dasslar, *Treatise on the law of taxation*. Mention should be made also of articles by Professor E. R. A. Seligman on "Recent tax reforms abroad" in the *Political Science Quarterly* for September and December.

TAYLOR, SIR ALEXANDER. An English soldier, engineer, and educator, died February 24, 1912. He was born in 1826. He entered the army, and in 1845 went to Calcutta as a subaltern of the Bengal Engineers. He took part in several battles from 1845 to 1849, chiefly in the capacity of engineer. In 1857 he joined the force before Delhi as second-in-command of the engineers. On several occasions he penetrated alone and in daylight through the enemy's outpost and made a detailed study of the defenses. His plan of attack was finally adopted. During this siege he was severely wounded. Following the relief of Delhi he was employed in quieting the surrounding districts. He commanded the Bengal Engineers in the siege and capture of Lucknow, where he was again wounded. He also commanded the engineers in the Umballa campaign of 1863. In 1865 he was appointed chief engineer and secretary to the Punjab government and in the last two years of his Indian service was deputy inspector-general of military works and president of the Indian defense committee. From 1890 to 1896 he was president of the Royal Indian Engineering College. This institution was abolished several years before his death. He was made a general in 1878. He received several medals and decorations for gallantry in action.

TAYLOR, EZRA B. An American public official, former member of Congress from Ohio, died January 29, 1912. He was born in Nelson, O., in 1823, and received an academic education. He was admitted to the bar in 1845 and served as prosecuting attorney for Portage County. From 1877 to 1880 he was judge of the court of common pleas. He was elected to the Forty-sixth Congress in 1880 for the unexpired term of James A. Garfield and was reelected to the Forty-seventh and Fifty-second Congresses inclusive (1881-1893).

TAYLOR, ROBERT LOVE. United States

Senator from Tennessee, died March 31, 1912. He was born in Carter County, Tenn., in 1850. His early days were spent on the farm of his father, but even at the outset of his career politics were his chief interest. In 1878 he was elected to the Forty-sixth Congress. He made a unique campaign for election during which he played the violin and sang the old folk songs of the mountains. By this means he won the title of "Fiddling Bob," which clung to him for life. After serving in the House of Representatives for one term he became pension agent at Knoxville, Tenn. He was elected governor of Tennessee in 1886 and was re-elected in 1888. He was again elected governor in 1896. In this campaign he pursued the same tactics which had proved so popular when he was elected to Congress. For several years he retired from politics and appeared on the lecturing platform. His most popular lecture was entitled "The Fiddle and the Bow." This he delivered hundreds of times in all parts of the United States. In the Democratic primary election in 1906 he was nominated for the United States Senate and was elected to this office in January, 1907, by an almost unanimous vote of the legislature.

TAYLOR, Samuel Coleridge. An English composer, died August, 1912. He was born in London in 1875. His father was a doctor of medicine, a native of Sierra Leone, and his mother an English woman. In 1891 he entered the Royal College of Music as a student of the violin, studied composition with Sir Villiers Stanford, and in 1893 gained a composition scholarship. In 1898 the first part of his Hiawatha trilogy, *Hiawatha's Wedding Feast*, was produced at the Royal College. The second part, *The Death of Minnehaha*, was brought out at the North Staffordshire Festival in 1899, and the third, *Hiawatha's Departure*, by the Royal Choral Society in 1900. In the May following the overture for the whole trilogy was heard for the first time. He wrote incidental music for many of the plays produced by Sir Herbert Beerbohm Tree. This included accompaniments to the dramas, *Herod*, *Ulysses*, *Nero*, and *Faust*, all by Stephen Phillips. In 1904 he became conductor of the London Handel Society. He was best known in the United States through his choral work. He was the most important of colored musical composers and one of the best known of modern composers.

TELEGRAPHY. The deferred message form of day and night service inaugurated in 1910 has stimulated the use of telegraphic facilities to a marked degree. The number of messages of this class handled in 1912 was in excess of 20,000,000. There has been an extensive introduction of switching devices whereby operators are enabled to switch their table instruments from circuit to circuit in response to lamp signals. These have been extensively utilized in the British service and in the London main office save the daily repetition of 18,000 through messages. In America the transmission of 90 per cent. of all messages is done manually, despite the development of a number of types of automatic and printing devices. In cable telegraphy transmission is largely accomplished by perforated strips of paper and mechanical senders.

TELEGRAPHY AND TELEPHONY, Wireless. See Wireless Telegraphy and Telephony.

TELEPHONY. Telephonic progress has turned from the direction of new appliances to the more efficient use of existing facilities. Important aspects of this progress in 1912 were the great extension in the use of Pupin loading coils, the completion of a loaded network of high transmission efficiency connecting all important centres east of the Rocky Mountains, and the unification of telephone and telegraph circuits. The radius of long distance transmission still reaches from the Atlantic seaboard to Denver, but plans for the extension of the circuits point to transcontinental transmission in 1914. The automatic systems have made little advance in direct use, but the Bell interests have acquired extensive patent rights in this field and are making preparations for a considerable use of semi-automatic operation, particularly in handling incoming trunking calls, that is calls for connection to an exchange other than the one to which the calling party is connected. Automatic systems have received more attention in Europe than in America, as government ownership tends to make the elimination of the operator more important than here.

The 450-mile cable system between Boston and Washington was practically completed during the year. The cables represent the highest advance in phantom operation, or the employment of a pair of basic metallic circuits as a third circuit, giving three circuits from four wires. This installation was undertaken primarily to eliminate the interruption of service on overhead lines attendant upon accidents and adverse weather conditions. The new French cable crossing the English Channel is an interesting example of continuous loading. The main conductors are surrounded by a close helical layer of fine iron wire, so distributed as to completely compensate for the electrostatic capacity of the cable. Its working results have been excellent. The tendency of the American telephony industry to become concentrated entirely under the Bell system has continued unabated. The most noteworthy transfer of control in 1912 was in the case of the extensive Bay Cities Home Telephone Company operating in the San Francisco district. An important aspect of telephone progress was the establishment of a complete pension and sick benefit system by the Bell interests. A fund of $10,000,000 was set aside for the purpose and 175,000 employes are included in its benefits.

The following table shows the number of telephones and miles of wire on January 1, 1912:

	Telephones Jan. 1, '12			Wire Jan. 1, '12		
	Number (partly est'd.)	P.C. inc. over Jan. 1, '11	P.C. to T'l.	Miles (partly est'd.)	P.C. inc. over Jan. 1, '11	P.C. to T'l.
U. S.	8,362,000	10	67.1	18,179,000	9	61.5
Canada	336,000	18	2.7	788,000	11	2.6
Europe	3,239,000	9	26.0	9,461,000	8	32.0
All other countries	517,000	21	4.2	1,138,000	32	3.9
Total	12,453,000	10	100.0	29,566,000	9	100.0

TEMPERATURE. See Physics.
TEMPLEHOF. See Architecture.
TEMPLE IRON COMPANY. See Trusts.

TENANT FARMING. See AGRICULTURE.

TENEMENT-HOUSE WORK IN NEW CITY. See CHILD LABOR.

TEN-HOUR LAW IN MASSACHUSETTS. See LABOR LEGISLATION, *Hours*, and MASSACHUSETTS, *Legislation*.

TENNESSEE. POPULATION. According to the Census Bureau statistics compiled during 1912 out of the total population, 2,184,789, the foreign-born whites numbered 18,479, compared with 17,586 in 1900. Of these, the largest number, 3870, came from Germany; from Russia, 2494; from Ireland, 2281; from Italy, 2025; and from England, 2036. Other European countries were represented by smaller numbers. The negroes in the State in 1910 numbered 473,088 and the mulattoes, 118,697. In 1890 the negroes numbered 430,678 and the mulattoes, 74,463.

COAL. The production of coal in the State in 1911 was 6,433,158 short tons, valued at $7,209,734. This was a decrease from the output of 1910, which was 7,121,380 short tons, valued at $7,925,350. The output in 1911, however, was larger than that in 1909, and exceeded that in any preceding year except 1907.

The production of blister copper in the State in 1911 was 18,965,143 pounds, compared with 16,691,777 pounds in 1910. The entire output was from the Ducktown district, located in the extreme southeastern part of the State. This district was one of the earliest large producers in the country. At the close of 1911 the total output was approximately 230,660,000 pounds.

The production of iron ore in the State in 1911 amounted to 469,728 long tons, valued at $632,339, compared with a product of 732,247 long tons valued at $1,048,323.

AGRICULTURE. The acreage, value, and production of the principal crops in 1912 are given in the following table:

		Acreage	Prod. Bu.	Value
Corn	1912	3,332,000	88,298,000	$53,862,000
	1911	3,400,000	91,120,000	55,583,000
Wheat	1912	674,000	7,077,000	7,077,000
	1911	720,000	8,280,000	7,949,000
Oats	1912	258,000	5,599,000	2,632,000
	1911	315,000	6,142,000	3,071,000
Rye	1912	17,000	196,000	192,000
	1911	19,000	226,000	224,000
Potatoes	1912	38,000	3,344,000	2,341,000
	1911	38,000	1,558,000	1,683,000
Hay	1912	888,000	a 1,154,000	18,233,000
	1911	400,000	a 400,000	6,680,000
Tobacco	1912	110,000	b 72,600,000	5,155,000
	1911	77,000	b 62,370,000	5,301,450
Cotton	1911	......	c 420,000	....

a Tons. b Pounds. c Bales.

MANUFACTURES. The Thirteenth Census statistics are for the calendar year 1909, and were compiled in 1912. Tennessee is preëminently an agricultural and mining State, and its manufactures are based largely on its rich mineral resources. From the table in the next column it will be seen that in 1909 there were 4609 manufacturing establishments, giving employment to 87,672 persons.

The value of the product was largest in the lumber and timber industries, $30,457,000; in the manufacture of flour-mill and grist-mill products, $29,070,000; in foundry and machine-shop products, $9,190,000; in printing and publishing, $7,173,000; in industries connected with railways, $6,777,000. The total number of persons employed in manufacturers in 1909 was

	Number or Amount 1909	1904	P. C. of Inc. 1904-'09
Number of establishments	4,609	3,175	45.2
Persons engaged in manufactures	87,672	69,287	26.5
Proprietors and firm members	5,415	3,805	42.3
Salaried employees	8,417	4,910	71.4
Wage earners average number)	73,840	60,572	21.9
Primary horsepower	242,277	175,780	37.8
Capital	$167,924,000	$102,439,000	63.9
Expenses	158,980,000	119,328,000	33.2
Services	37,438,000	27,886,000	34.3
Salaries	9,186,000	5,080,000	80.8
Wages	28,252,000	22,806,000	23.9
Materials	104,016,000	79,352,000	31.1
Miscellaneous	17,526,000	12,090,000	45.0
Value of products	180,217,000	137,960,000	30.6
Value of products less cost of materials	76,201,000	58,608,000	30.0

87,672, of whom 77,277 were male and 10,395 female. The prevailing hours of labor for more than one-half the wage-earners were 60 a week. Nearly one-fourth of the total worked from 54 to 60 hours a week; 7.6 per cent. were employed in establishments where the prevailing hours of labor are less than 54 a week, and 15 per cent. in establishments where they are more 60 hours a week. The largest number of wage-earners was employed in Nashville, 9721; in Memphis were 7927, and in Chattanooga 6410. The value of the manufactures of Memphis was $30,241,519; of Nashville, $29,649,697.

EDUCATION. The school population of the State on June 30, 1912, was 756,966. Of these, 587,156 were whites and 169,810 were colored. The pupils enrolled numbered 539,991, of whom 438,603 were white and 101,309 were colored. In the elementary schools there were enrolled 441,163 pupils; in county high schools, 7546, and in city schools, 91,202. The total number of teachers was 11,367. Of these, 3220 were white male teachers, 5928 white female teachers, and the colored male teachers numbered 574 and colored female teachers, 1364. The average monthly salary of teachers was $48. The total expenditures for schools was $5,537,029.

POLITICS AND GOVERNMENT

There was no session of the legislature in 1912 as the sessions are biennial and the last was held in 1911. The date for the next session is January 6, 1913.

Elections were held for State officers on November 5. The Democratic State convention on May 6 elected 24 delegates to the national convention. Resolutions not to instruct the delegates were adopted. The convention also named 8 delegates-at-large who had been agreed upon by the campaign managers of Clark, Wilson, Harmon, and Underwood. Each of these delegates had half a vote. Governor Hooper was the Republican candidate for reëlection and was indorsed by the Independent Democrats, while the Democratic candidate for governor was Benton McMillin. The Hon. M. R. Patterson was nominated by the regular Democrats for United States senator, but later withdrew. The election of November resulted as follows: For President, Wilson received 135,390, Taft 60,674, Roosevelt 53,986, Debs 3482, and Chafin 834. Wilson's plurality was 74,720. For governor, McMillin, Dem., received 111,973 votes,

Hooper, Rep., 120,078, Poston, Soc., 4464, and Harold, Pro. 2702. The legislature contains 59 regular Democrats, 29 independent Democrats, 33 Republicans, and 11 Shelby County Democrats.

As the result of the death of Senator Robert L. Taylor (q. v.) it was necessary for Governor Hooper to appoint a successor to fill out his term. On April 2 he appointed Newell Sanders, a prominent manufacturer of Chatanooga, and chairman of the Tennessee Republican committee.

STATE GOVERNMENT. Governor, Benjamin W. Hooper, Rep.; Secretary of State, H. W. Goodloe, Dem.; Treasurer, George T. Taylor, Rep.; Commissioner of Agriculture, George Peck, Rep.; Superintendent of Education, J. W. Brister, Dem.; Comptroller, Frank Dibrell, Dem.; Adjutant-General, Frank Maloney, Rep.; Attorney-General, Charles T. Cates, Jr., Dem.; Commissioner of Insurance, George T. Taylor, Rep.

JUDICIARY. Supreme Court: Chief Justice, John K. Shields; Justices, A. S. Buchanan, Grafton Green, M. M. Neil, and D. L. Lansden; Clerk, Joseph J. Roach—all Democrats.

STATE LEGISLATURE, 1913. Democrats, Senate 18, House 57, joint ballot 75; Republicans, Senate 6, House 22, joint ballot 28; Progressives, Senate 0, House 3, joint ballot 3; Independents, Senate 9, House 17, joint ballot 26. Democratic majority, Senate 3, House 15, joint ballot 18.

The representatives in Congress will be found in the article UNITED STATES, section *Congress*.

TENNESSEE, UNIVERSITY OF. An institution of higher learning at Nashville, Tenn., founded in 1874. The enrollment in all departments of the university in the collegiate year 1911-12 was 1541. There were 150 members of the faculty. There were no noteworthy changes in the faculty during the year and no important benefactions were received. The productive funds of the university amounted at the end of the collegiate year 1911-12 to $636,036. There were 34,596 volumes in the library. President, Brown Ayres, Ph. D., LL. D.

TERRELL, ALEXANDER WATKINS. An American diplomat, died September 10, 1912. He was born in Patrick County, Va., in 1827, and was educated at the University of Missouri. In 1849 he was admitted to the bar and began practice in St. Joseph, Mo. He removed to Texas and was appointed judge of the district court in that State in 1857, serving until 1862. During the Civil War he was colonel of cavalry in the Confederate army. He was a member of the Texas House of Representatives for four years and of the senate for ten years. In 1893 he was appointed United States minister to Turkey. He held this position until 1897.

TERRELL, JOSEPH MERIWETHER. American public official, former governor of Georgia, died November 17, 1912. He was born in Greenville, Ga., in 1861, and was educated in the common schools. He studied law and was admitted to the bar in 1882. During 1884-1886 he was a member of the Georgia House of Representatives and in 1890-1892 was State senator. From 1892 to 1902 he was attorney-general of the State. He resigned this office in 1902 to accept the nomination for governor, to which office he was elected. He served two terms until 1907 and was succeeded by Hoke Smith. In 1910 he was appointed United States Senator to fill the vacancy caused by the death of Senator Clay. A few months after his arrival in Washington he had a stroke of paralysis which eventually caused his death. Ill though he was he returned home and endeavored to have the legislature confirm his appointment to the Senate. The election, however, resulted in the choosing of a legislature which was opposed to him. Following this defeat he retired from politics and resumed the practice of law in Atlanta.

TERRESTRIAL MAGNETISM. See CARNEGIE INSTITUTION.

TERRY, DAVID BRAINERD. An American educator, died May 21, 1912. He was born in Worcester, Mass., in 1839, and graduated from Yale College in 1863. In 1871 he was a tutor at Yale and in 1872 was ordained to the Congregational ministry. In the following year he was appointed acting president and professor of Latin and Greek at Doane College, serving until 1881, when he was chosen president and professor of psychology. This position he retained until the time of his death.

TERRY, EDWARD O'CONNOR. An English actor, died April 1, 1912. He was born in London in 1844. He made his first appearance on the stage at the age of 19 in small local theatres. He later played in Douglas, Isle of Man, where in 1865 he was in the same company with Henry Irving. He made his first success at Manchester and shortly afterwards went to London. For seven years he took leading parts at the Strand Theatre, now demolished. He then went to the Gaiety, where he formed one of the famous quartette of actors including, besides himself, Royce, Nellie Farren, and Kate Vaughan. Here he remained six years playing burlesque parts. In 1887 he opened his own theatre in the Strand with *The Churchwarden*, and produced among other famous plays, *Sweet Lavender*, in which he played the leading part 670 times. He became one of the best known and most popular actors in England. Among the other well-known plays in which he took a prominent part were: *The Times*, and *In Chancery*, by Pinero. In addition to his activities in the theatre, he was a great traveler and a prominent Freemason. He wrote several farces and published several magazine articles.

TETANUS. The *Journal of the American Medical Association's* tenth annual summary of Fourth of July injuries showed a very gratifying reduction in the number of injuries and cases of tetanus compared with previous years. Only 7 cases of lockjaw were reported, as compared with 18 last year, and 17 in 1909. Six patients died in from 7 to 10 days after receiving the injury. All of the cases developed from blank-cartridge wounds. Besides the cases of lockjaw due directly to the use of fireworks, it is interesting to note also those occurring during the Fourth of July season which were due to penetrating wounds from other causes, such as nails or splinters, to crushing injuries, etc. Instead of a reduction in these cases this year there was an increase; 43 cases being reported during this Fourth of July season, or 14 more than last year, when 29 cases were reported. The fact that tetanus germs were apparently fully as prevalent if not more so this year than in 1911 makes the marked reduction of cases from Fourth of July injuries all the more significant. In addition to the 6 deaths due to tetanus, 35 persons were killed by various forms of fireworks, making a total of 41 deaths, 16 less than last year, 90 less than 1910, and 174 less than in 1909. This is the lowest number of deaths from such causes during the ten years covered by *The Journal's* statistics. In 1912, 9 persons were killed outright by firearms, 7 by explosions of powder, bombs, or torpedoes, 2 by cannon, 2 by giant firecrackers, and 7 by various causes, as blood-poisoning, explosions of chemicals, etc. There were 8 victims also, mostly little girls, who were burned to death by fire from fireworks, some of these being the so-called harmless varieties, including very small firecrackers and sparklers.

The number of casualties shows a continuation of the remarkable decrease of the last few years, which unquestionably is the result of the efforts to secure more intelligent methods of celebration. This is evident from the fact that the most marked decreases are in the States in which the agitation for restrictive measures has been strongest. For example, the total casualties in Illinois this year are 39 as against 218 last year, 285 in 1910 and 546 in 1909; Massachusetts had 45 casualties this year as compared with 27 last year, 63 in 1910 and 430 in 1909; Ohio had only 55 casualties this year, as compared with 105 last year, 166 in 1910 and 323 in 1909; New York has 115 this year, as compared with 237 last year, 327 in 1910 and 897 in 1909; Wisconsin had only 38 this year, as compared with 52 last year, 171 in 1910 and 157 in 1909. Even in Pennsylvania, which has had the largest number of casualties for each of the last five years, there has been a marked improvement, clearly the result of a powerful campaign which has been carried on in that State, and particularly in Philadelphia, for more enlightened methods of celebration. That State has 265 casualties this year, as compared with 442 last year, 623 in 1910 and 986 in 1909. Altogether there were only 988 casualties this year, 615 less than last year, 1935 less than in 1910 and 4319 less than in 1909. There were 947 non-fatal injuries. Eight persons were totally blinded, 21 lost one eye each, 13 lost legs, arms and hands, and 43 lost one or more fingers. Although there has been a marked reduction in the total number of non-fatal injuries, the totals of these more severe injuries are about the same as reported for the two previous years. The giant firecracker continues to hold the first place as a cause of lacerated wounds and is responsible for most of the losses of eyes, hands and fingers. This year 362 injuries, including 2 deaths, were due to the giant firecracker. Firearms caused 157 accidents, including 9 killed. Of the total number thus injured nearly half were orderly persons who were struck by stray bullets from the reckless use of firearms by others, and 6 deaths resulted. The use of cannon caused 75 injuries, including 2 killed. In the ten years, a total of 40,117 people were killed or injured in the celebration of the Fourth of July.

Kocher has injected a solution of magnesium sulphate into the spinal canal in three cases of tetanus with success. He used Meltzer's technic except that a 15 per cent. instead of a 25 per cent. solution was employed; as high as 10 c. c. of fluid, corresponding to 0.03 per kilogram of body weight were injected. The greater susceptibility of children to the toxic action of this drug must be borne in mind in treating a child; 2 c. c. would be the maximal dose for a child weighing 10 kilograms (about 22 pounds). Special care is taken in repeating the dose; an interval of twenty-four hours seems to be sufficient. If the dose is repeated sooner there is danger of cumulative action. After injection of 7 c. c. and five hours later of 10 c. c. of a 15 per cent. solution one patient reacted with deep sleep and stertorous respiration. Antitetanic serum may also be used, but the two methods should not be used together. Time must be allowed for the action of one drug to pass off before injecting the other.

TETANUS IN ANIMALS. See VETERINARY SCIENCE.

TEXAS. POPULATION. According to the Census Bureau statistics, compiled during 1912 out of the total population in the State in 1910, 3,896,542, the negroes numbered 690,059, and the mulattoes, 124,695. In 1890 the negroes numbered 488,171 and the mulattoes, 65,724. The foreign-born white population in 1910 was 240,001, compared with 177,581 in 1900. Of these, the larger proportion came from Mexico, 123,817; from Germany, 44,796; from Austria, 20,583; from Russia, 5805; from Italy, 7190, and from Ireland, 5360. Other countries in Europe are represented by smaller numbers.

AGRICULTURE. The acreage, value, and production of the principal crops in 1911 and 1912 are given below:

		Acreage	Prod. Bu.	Value
Corn	1912	7,300,000	153,300,000	$98,112,000
	1911	7,300,000	69,350,000	55,480,000
Wheat	1912	735,000	11,025,000	10,253,000
	1911	700,000	6,580,000	6,588,000
Oats	1912	865,000	31,140,000	12,290,000
	1911	737,000	18,499,000	9,989,000
Rye	1912	2,000	33,000	36,000
	1911	2,000	20,000	21,000
Rice	1912	265,600	9,429,000	8,862,000
	1911	238,300	8,174,000	6,539,000
Potatoes ...	1911	50,000	2,850,000	3,591,000
Hay	1912	387,000	a 542,000	5,637,000
	1911	606,000	a 606,000	7,311,000
Tobacco	1912	200	b 140,000	24,000
	1911	300	b 195,000	39,000
Cotton	1912	....	c 4,369,600	....
	1911	....	c 4,280,000	....

a Tons. b Pounds. c Bales.

MINERAL PRODUCTION. The total production of the petroleum in 1911 was 9,526,474 barrels, compared with a total of 8,899,266 barrels in 1910. This increase is the first in the history of petroleum production in the State since 1905, when the production was 28,136,187 barrels.

The amount of coal mined in the State in 1911 was the greatest in the history of the industry. The total output was 1,974,393 long tons, valued at $3,273,398, an increase over 1910 of 82,417 tons in quantity and $112,323 in value. The State produced both bituminous and lignite coals. The increase in production was in bituminous coal. The increase is due chiefly to the growing population, and industrial development of the State, which consumes not only its own product, but also considerable quantities brought in from Arkansas, Oklahoma, Colorado, and New Mexico. Coal-mining in 1911 was free from labor troubles.

MANUFACTURES. The Thirteenth Census included statistics of manufactures in the State. These are for the calendar year 1909 and were compiled in 1912. The manufactures of the

State depend largely for their raw material upon the stock-raising, agricultural, and mineral products, and have been greatly stimulated in recent years by the rapid increase in the production of these materials. From the following table it will be seen that there were in 1909 4588 manufacturing establishments, which gave employment to an average of 84,575 persons.

	Number or Amount 1909	1904	P. C. of inc. 1904-'09
Number of establishments	4,588	3,158	45.3
Persons engaged in manufactures....	84,575	57,892	46.1
Proprietors and firm members...	4,496	3,073	46.3
Salaried employees	9,849	5,753	71.2
Wage earners (average number)..	70,230	49,066	43.1
Primary horsepower	282,471	164,637	71.6
Capital	$216,876,000	$115,665,000	87.5
Expenses	244,873,000	134,406,000	82.2
Services	48,775,000	30,587,000	59.5
Salaries	10,868,000	6,118,000	77.6
Wages	37,907,000	24,469,000	54.9
Materials	178,179,000	91,604,000	94.5
Miscellaneous :...	17,919,000	12,215,000	46.7
Value of products..	272,896,000	150,528,000	81.3
Value of products less cost of materials	94,717,000	58,924,000	60.7

The value of the product was largest in the industries connected with slaughtering and meat-packing, $42,530,000; in flour and gristmill products, $32,485,000; lumber and timber products, $32,201,000; oil, cottonseed, and cake products, $29,916,000; industries connected with railways, $13,359,000; printing and publishing, $11,587,000. The total number of persons engaged in manufactures in the State in 1909 was 84,575, of whom 79,696 were male and 4879 female. Those under 16 years of age employed numbered 1256. The prevailing hours of labor for the majority of wage-earners averaged from 54 to 60 a week; 12 per cent. of the total being employed in establishments where less than 54 hours a week prevailed, and 21.8 per cent. in establishments where more than 60 a week prevailed. The largest number of wage-earners was in Houston, 5338; in Dallas, 4482; in San Antonio, 3105; in Fort Worth, 2059, and in Galveston, 1094. The value of the manufacturing industries in Dallas was $26,958,664, and in Houston $23,015,556.

Education. The total number of children of school age in the State in 1912 was 1,017,133. Of these, 684,248 were American white children and 204,237 were colored. There were 79,491 Mexican children of school age and 29,345 Germans.

Finance. The report of the State treasurer for the fiscal year ending August 31, 1912, showed a cash balance at the beginning of the fiscal year of $413,124. The receipts for the year amounted to $18,119,072 and the disbursements to $17,973,122, leaving a balance on hand September 1, 1912, of $793,417. The chief sources of revenue are from taxation and the chief expenditures are for education and the support of State institutions.

Charities and Corrections. The charitable and correctional institutions under the control of the State include the State prisons, the Blind Asylum, the State Lunatic Asylum, the Orphans' Asylum, the Deaf and Dumb Asylum, the North Texas Insane Asylum, the Southwestern Insane Asylum, and the State Epileptic Colony.

Politics and Government

There was no meeting of the legislature in 1912 as the sessions are biennial and the last was held in 1911. The next session convened January 14, 1913. Elections for governor and other State officers were held during the year. The contest for delegates to the Republican National convention resulted in the most spirited struggles before the national committee and later before the national convention. This is discussed fully in the article Presidential Campaign, paragraph *Disputed Elections*. Precinct conventions were held in the State on May 4 for the election of delegates to the State convention. The Roosevelt forces won a majority. Governor Wilson received a majority of the Democratic votes, with Governor Harmon second. Primaries for the nomination of State officers were held on July 22. Governor Colquitt was renominated by a majority of about 40,000. His opponent for the nomination was Judge W. F. Ramsey. Congressman Morris Sheppard received the senatorial nomination to succeed Senator Bailey, who had announced his purpose to resign at the end of the present term. Mr. Sheppard made his campaign as an outspoken Prohibitionist and defeated Jacob F. Wolters, who opposed him on the anti-prohibition issue.

The election on November 5 resulted as follows: For President, Wilson received 221,435 votes, Taft 28,688, Roosevelt 26,740, Debs, 25,742, and Chafin 1738. Wilson's plurality was 192,767. For governor, Colquitt, Dem. received 233,013 votes, Johnson, Rep., 22,914, Lasater, Prog., 15,741, Andrews, Soc., 25,258, Houston, Pro., 2353, and Choate, Soc. Labor, 398. The legislature is Democratic by an overwhelming majority.

Other Events. On February 22, a fire in the city of Houston did damage to the amount of $5,000,000. The burned area covered 57 city blocks. Many factories were destroyed and St. Patrick's Roman Catholic Church was among the important edifices burned.

State Government. Governor, O. B. Colquitt; Lieutenant-Governor, William H. Mays; Secretary of State ; Attorney-General B. F. Looney; State Treasurer, J. M. Edwards; Comptroller, W. P. Lane; Superintendent of Public Instruction, F. M. Bralley; Land Commissioner, J. T. Robinson; Commissioner of Agriculture, E. R. Kone—all Democrats.

Judiciary. Supreme Court: Chief Justice, Thomas J. Brown; Associate Justices, N. Phillips and W. E. Hawkins; Clerk, F. T. Connerly—all Democrats.

State Legislature, 1913. Democrats, Senate 30, House 108, joint ballot 138; Republicans, Senate 1, House 1, joint ballot 2. Democratic majority, Senate 29, House 107, joint ballot 136.

The representatives in Congress will be found in the article United States, section *Congress*.

TEXAS, University of. A State institution for higher education at Austin, Tex., founded in 1883. The total enrollment in all departments of the university in the autumn of 1912 was 2250. The faculty numbered 130, which does not include tutors and student assistants. There were no noteworthy changes in the faculty during the year and no important benefactions were received. The institution is supported almost entirely from State appropriations. The productive funds amounted at the end of the year 1911-12 to $449,728. The library contained about 80,000 bound volumes and 27,500 pamphlets. President, Sidney E. Mezes, Ph. D.

TEXAS FEVER. See STOCK-RAISING AND MEAT PRODUCTION.

TEXTILE MANUFACTURING. During 1912 the manufacture of textiles proceeded vigorously, notwithstanding various conditions tending to disturb markets and prices. The year was not one of great profits for the manufacturers, but it was one of considerable activity, and except where harassed by strikes the various plants were in the most part operated to capacity, and where this was not the case it was often due to a lack of labor or disinclination on the part of local wage earners to avail themselves of employment. The price of cotton advanced soon after the beginning of the year and those manufacturers who had not purchased future cotton in the speculative markets were compelled to pay high prices for the raw material. The sales of cotton goods were large and the exports, both in value and yardage, were greater than in the two years immediately preceding, notwithstanding the fact that the business was conducted with smaller profits. The strike in the woolen and cotton mills at Lawrence, Mass. (see STRIKES), involved a bitter struggle and was followed by labor controversies at other manufacturing centres, which were settled by increased wages and concessions as to work, hours, etc. As manufacture was not efficiently conducted and controlled, a scarcity of goods developed during the year, notwithstanding the impending revision of the tariff. It was the general consensus of opinion of those working in the textile industries that the revision of the tariff on raw materials as well as on the finished products could be undertaken with advantage if it were done according to some consistent plan and with expert knowledge of the conditions involved. The newer manufactories in the United States were well equipped and organized, capable of handling a large volume of business, and in many cases the protection given in the Payne-Aldrich tariff law was considered unnecessary. The following official figures, compiled by the ways and means committee of the House of Representatives in regard to the various tariff schedules on textiles, are of interest as showing the general trend of the discussion and the basis on which the majority of the committee was working at the close of 1912:

Tariff schedule and description	Estimated consumption (000 omitted)	Consumers' tax (000 omitted) Revenue	Protection
I—Cotton manufactures	$ 1,408,000	$ 12,325	$ 210,251
J—Flax, hemp, etc.	373,000	47,053	23,578
K—Wool	1,442,000	28,982	323,326
L—Silk	273,000	16,053	54,653
All others	16,873,000	196,168	1,294,620
Total	$20,369,000	$309,581	$1,916,428

The amount of estimated protection was based on the assumption that the goods consumed in the United States were raised in price above what they would have been under free trade equal in percentage to the foreign tax.

MILL CONSTRUCTION, 1912. The annual report of new textile mill construction for 1912, compiled by the *Textile World Record* of Boston, stated that 265 new textile mills of various kinds were built in the United States during the year, this number being almost exactly equal to the annual average (269) for the preceding ten years. This was considered to indicate a healthy development of the industry and a gratifying freedom from depression or an equally undesirable boom. Equally satisfactory was the report of enlargements and improvements, showing that manufacturers had been active in strengthening their plants by extensions and improvements..

COMPARISON OF NEW MILL CONSTRUCTION FOR FIVE YEARS

	1912	1911	1910	1909	1908
Cotton	37	32	67	80	47
Woolen	24	20	31	47	23
Knitting	122	92	113	106	94
Silk	46	38	34	37	33
Miscellaneous	36	26	29	20	25
Total	265	208	274	289	222

As regards new cotton mills, the Southern States led, with 21 of the total of 37 mills, 437,000 spindles out of a total of 533,000 installed in new mills, and 6650 looms out of a total of 9774, making 1912 about an average year. The Carolinas, with 293,000 spindles, represented two-thirds of the southern total and 55 per cent. of the total number of new spindles for the United States. New England had 94,400 of the new spindles, showing a decided slackening in the development of the cotton industry in the older manufacturing section. The decrease in new mill construction in the leading manufacturing centres means a wider distribution of the industry throughout the United States, a condition that brings with it many advantages.

NEW COTTON MILLS, 1912

	No.	Spindles	Looms
New England States:			
Maine	1	75,000	2,000
Massachusetts	5	4,400	700
Rhode Island	4	15,000	358
Southern States:			
Alabama	1	35,000	900
Georgia	1	14,000	300
North Carolina	10	153,000	2,000
South Carolina	5	140,000	2,250
Tennessee	2	10,000	.....
Texas	1	10,000	200
Virginia	1	75,000	.....
Middle States:			
New Jersey	1	....	.....
Pennsylvania	5	1,700	66
Total	37	533,000	9,774

COMPARISON OF SPINDLES IN NEW COTTON MILLS FOR THREE YEARS

	1912	1911	1910
New England	94,400	170,500	462,714
Southern States	437,000	172,000	214,028
Middle and Western	1,700	4,920	12,500
Totals	533,100	347,420	696,242

In the knitting industry just one-half of the 112 new mills were built in Pennsylvania, the Middle States accounting for 82, or about three-quarters of the total for the entire country. In 1911 the new construction was 113 mills, as compared with 104 in 1910 and 92 in 1909.

NEW KNITTING MILLS

New England:	1912	Western States:	1912
Connecticut	1	Michigan	3
Maine	3	Minnesota	2
Massachusetts	7	North Dakota	1
Rhode Island	1	Ohio	4
Middle States:		Washington	1
Delaware	1	Wisconsin	4
Maryland	2	Southern States:	
New Jersey	3	Georgia	1
New York	20	North Carolina	2
Pennsylvania	56	Tennessee	1
Western States:		Virginia	1
California	2		
Illinois	3	Total	112
Indiana	3		

The silk industry claimed 47 new mills, as compared with 38 for 1911 and an annual average of 40 for the preceding seven years. There was a marked tendency exhibited toward concentration in silk manufacturing in New Jersey and Pennsylvania.

NEW SILK MILLS

Connecticut:	1912	Underwear	1
Broad silks	1	Pennsylvania:	
Braids	1	Broad	2
Illinois:		Ribbon	2
Neckwear	1	Throwing	7
New Hampshire:		Narrow silk	3
Ribbon	1	Braids	2
New Jersey:		Silk plush	1
Broad silks	16	Winding	1
Throwing	2	Rhode Island:	
Veilings	1	Broad silks	1
New York:			
Broad	3	Total	47
Trimmings	1		

In woolen and worsted manufacturing there were constructed 23 new mills, as compared with an annual average of 35 for the preceding eight years. Among the 23 for 1912 there were six small plants with worsted and woolen spinning machinery, the others being weaving mills or equipped for felts, wadding, and other wool goods.

NEW WOOLEN AND WORSTED MILLS, 1912

New England:	1912	Pennsylvania	9
Connecticut	1	Southern States:	
Maine	1	Virginia	1
Massachusetts	5	Tennessee	1
Rhode Island	2	Western States:	
Middle States:		Wisconsin	1
New Jersey	1		
New York	1	Total	23

The production of woolens and worsteds was stated to be the largest on record in the United States, in spite of the fact that here impending changes in the tariff were concerned, as the wool schedule figured preëminently in the discussions. (See TARIFF.) The strikes in the spring and the increased value of raw materials also contributed to the higher prices for the finished products, which continued, nevertheless, in good demand. Notwithstanding the limited yardage required for women's dresses, there was a compensating demand for materials for cloaks and suits, while in cloths for men's clothing business was particularly active during the year. The use of domestic materials was constantly increasing and the importation of women's dress goods and cloths was considerably less than in 1912. New plants were being built in the United States, especially in Passaic, N. J., and vicinity. Here a group of worsted and woolen mills, founded by German capital and managed by German manufacturers, had grown up, and these, along with other mills built by English and French capital and managed by foreign experts in other parts of the United States, were becoming important features of the industry. It was admitted that the cost of building and equipping such plants was greater than in Europe, and also that the cost of raw materials was higher, but with a proper adjustment of duties and other conditions it was believed that the foothold gained by such industries would be maintained and business extended.

THALASSOTHERAPY. Mace and Quinton continued their reports on the treatment of infantile gastro-enteritis by subcutaneaus injection of "marine plasma," as they call the sterilized sea-water they use for the purpose. Milk feeding is begun immediately and continued during the treatment; the children are transformed by the injection so that they are able to take care of milk. The amounts of sea-water to be injected vary with the nature of the trouble. With enteritis causing constipation, they inject from 10 to 30 c. c. twice a week, feeding the child with from one-eighth to one-sixth of its weight. With athrepsia and ordinary diarrhea, they inject from 30 to 100 c. c. two or three times a week, and feed from one-seventh to one-fifth of the weight. Photographs show the recovery of almost moribund children under this regimen. In 1905 a series of experiments was made, including 2592 days of tests, to determine the superiority of sea-water over ordinary salt solution for these injections in infants. It was found that infants increased in weight twice as fast under sea-water, and this increase was not due to the weight of the sea-water, being out of proportion to the amount of sea-water ingested. In severe cases 200 or 300 c. c. of sea-water is injected night and morning. From the start the child is given from six to eight bottles of milk a day, each representing 100 gm. of milk, to which 20 gm. of water have been added. A bottle of pure water between the feedings completes the treatment, as much water being given as the child will drink. This is kept up for a week and then one injection a day is sufficient. The sea-water almost invariably restores the digestive capacity in less than two hours so that the infant stretches out its hands for the bottle it previously rejected.

THEATRE. See DRAMA.

THEOLOGICAL SCHOOLS. See UNIVERSITIES AND COLLEGES.

THERMIONS. See PHYSICS.

THERMO-RADIOTHERAPY. See CANCER.

THORIUM. See PHYSICS.

THORIUM. See CHEMISTRY.

THORVEITITE. See METEOROLOGY.

THROMBOKINASE. The idea that the tissue juices might furnish a body which would hasten clotting, and that this might be of more service than fresh blood serum in the control of hemorrhage, led Strong to prepare, following the method of Batelli, an extract of sheep's lungs after the following technic: Sheep's lungs are taken direct into sterile towels, and the larger bronchi are removed to avoid as many bacteria as possible. The lungs are then ground in a meat grinder and soaked in twice their volume of sterile water for an hour; 1.5 c. c. glacical acetic acid for every liter of extract is then added, drop by drop, with constant stirring. A white flocculent precipitate results, which is immediately collected by centrifuging. The free acetic acid is removed by washing thoroughly with salt solution. The centrifuge tubes are then filled with alcohol and the mixture is again centrifuged thoroughly, when the alcohol may be decanted and the nearly dry precipitate may be spread on crystallizing dishes and rapidly evaporated at a low temperature in vacuo. Dryness will be secured within twelve hours. The resultant brownish powder is scraped off and sealed in sterile tubes. Several preliminary tests showed that rabbit's blood, in test tubes containing a few flakes of the powder, clotted more rapidly than blood alone, and that the powder contains a body which in the moist state is inactivated at 70° C. for thirty minutes. It is this evidence of a ferment body which leads to the use of the term thrombokinase for the powder. Similar preparations were made from spleen, liver, bone marrow, endocardium and aorta. Experimentally, these did not work as well as preparations from the lungs. The powder is said to have been used clinically with success by many operators in nose and throat work.

TIBET. A central Asian Chinese dependency. Area, 756,000 square miles; population, estimated, 2,000,000. Capital, Lhasa, with an estimated population of from fifteen to twenty thousand. Many Buddhist monks are included among the inhabitants, the city being the home of Buddhism. Two Chinese ambans, previous to the outbreak of the Chinese revolution, administered the country; but the non-Chinese tribes subsequently declared their independence, and during the ensuing mutiny the ambans abdicated. The Dalai Lama, who has spent the last few years fleeing to India and returning thence, made his way back in June, 1912, after an absence of about a year. The Chinese garrison having received orders from Peking in October not to vacate the capital, their general was imprisoned in the Tenyeling monastery.

TICK FEVER. See VETERINARY SCIENCE.

TIDES, MECHANICS OF. See DARWIN, SIR GEORGE HOWARD.

TILLINGHAST, MARY ELIZABETH. An American artist, died December, 1912. She was born in New York City and studied in Paris under Carolus Duran and Henner, studying also in New York under John La Farge. Her work was almost entirely in stained glass. She was awarded a gold medal at the Chicago Exposition in 1893 and a gold medal at the Cotton States Exposition in 1895. Among her best known works are mosaic glass windows in the Home of the Friendless, for Mrs. Russell Sage, in honor of Miss Helen Gould: an astronomical and classic window in the New Allegheny Observatory; "Revocation of the Edict of Nantes" in a window of the New York Historical Society Building, and mural decorations in the café of the Savoy Hotel, New York City. She also executed memorial windows in churches in Terre Haute, Ind., and Washington, D. C.

TIME, STANDARD. The twenty-four hour system of time notation was adopted for the French army in an order to the chief of the general staff to obviate the use in military correspondence and reports of A. M. and P. M. This system has been adopted by the French railways, post office, and telegraph systems, which are allied to the military service and in the interests of harmony and convenience. Under the new system 11:30 P. M. will be 23:30.

RADIOTELEGRAPHIC TIME SIGNALS. An International Time Signal Conference was held at Paris on the invitation of the French government, October 15 to 23, to organize a radiotelegraphic time signal service to cover the entire globe so that even the most remote points might receive at least two signals every 24 hours. These signals were being transmitted from the Eiffel Tower, Paris; Halifax, Nova Scotia; Norddeich, North Germany, and Washington. The extent of the time service proposed may be appreciated from the fact that Africa was to have stations at Massauah in Erythrea, Mogadiscio in Somaliland, and Timbuctoo, while in America there would be a station at San Francisco, in South America at San Fernando in Brazil, and on the Pacific at Honolulu, Samoa, Guam, and Manila. The signals were to be sent out from the great national observatories near the principal stations and the control of the service was to be under an international bureau at Paris. Official support was to be furnished by 16 states taking part in the conference and the service was to begin in July, 1913. Storm and weather signals were also to be transmitted and the plan was considered to promise great assistance to mariners, as it would enable them daily to correct their chronometers and would increase the accuracy of their observations for position. Many interesting developments of the scheme were anticipated.

TIMOR. An island (the largest) of the Lesser Sunda group, divided between the Netherlands and Portugal. Area (estimated), 12,-593 square miles, of which 7330 belong to Portugal; population, 400,000, of whom 200,000 are Portuguese subjects. Capital of the Portuguese portion, Dilli.

TINEL, EDGAR. A Belgian composer and director, died October 28, 1912. He was born in Sinay, Belgium, in 1854, and received his musical education at the Brussels Conservatory. He won the Prix de Rome for a cantata. In 1889 he was made inspector of music in the state schools and in 1896 succeeded Kufferath as professor of counterpoint at the Brussels University. His oratorio, *Franciscus*, won for him a reputation outside of his own country and attracted so much attention that it was produced at the Cardiff Festival in 1895. In 1909 he was appointed director of the Royal Conservatory of Music at Brussels. He was the author of a book on Gregorian chants, and among his compositions in addition to those mentioned are: The opera *Godoleva; Katharina*, a sacred opera; and several works for chorus and orchestra.

TISSUES, PRESERVATION OF. See SURGERY.

TITANIC, Loss of the. The Royal Mail steamship *Titanic* of the White Star Line, sailing on her maiden voyage from Southampton to New York, with 2223 passengers and crew, was lost at sea by collision with an iceberg on the night of Sunday, April 14, 1912, and 832 passengers and 685 of the crew perished, the remainder being rescued from lifeboats by the Cunard steamship *Carpathia*. The *Titanic* was the largest vessel in the world at the time of the disaster. She was built for the White Star Line at Belfast, Ireland, by Harland and Wolff for service between Southampton and New York, being a sister ship of the *Olympic* of the same line, and costing about $7,500,000. The keel was laid on March 31, 1909; she was launched on May 31, 1911, and on March 31, 1912, at Belfast, she was inspected and passed by the officials of the British Board of Trade.

The registered dimensions of the *Titanic* were as follows: Length, 852.5 feet; beam, 92.5 feet; depth from top of keel to the lowest point of the highest deck extending continuously from bow to stern, 73 feet, 3 inches; displacement, at 34 feet, 7 inches, 52,310 tons; gross tonnage, 46,328; net registered tons, 21,831. She was a three-screw vessel with Parsons low-pressure turbines for the centre propeller, and reciprocating engines for the wing propellers, some 50,000 or more horsepower being developed, which was sufficient to drive the vessel at a speed of 21 knots an hour. There were 29 boilers and 159 furnaces. There were seven principal steel decks and a cellular double bottom 5¼ feet deep between the inner and outer skins. The vessel was divided by 15 transverse water-tight bulkheads into 16 compartments reaching well above the water line. There were, however, no longitudinal bulkheads, nor were there coal bunkers along the side so cut off as to serve a similar function in case of exterior injury. In fact, the arrangement of the bottom plating did not conform so closely to warship design as did that of the *Mauretania* and other ships built under Admiralty specifications with the idea of possible use as cruisers in the naval service, where the danger of torpedo attack had to be considered. That these were real defects may be judged from the fact that the *Olympic*, the sister ship of the *Titanic*, was withdrawn from service to be changed by the introduction of an inner skin throughout the ship well above the water line, this skin being three feet within the outside hull of the ship and in a portion of it it was proposed to store fuel oil for the boilers. A larger ship under construction was considerably modified in its plans to secure similar advantages.

The *Titanic* was provided with 14 wooden lifeboats, each 35 feet long and capable of holding 65 persons; two wooden cutters 25 feet long, constructed to carry 40 people each, and 4 Engelhardt collapsible life-rafts with a capacity of 47 persons each. There were 3560 life-belts in cabins and berths. The crew numbered 899, of whom 494, including 23 women, were stewards, cooks, etc.; 70 were in the deck or navigating department, 327 were engineers, oilers, stokers, etc., in the engineering department, and 8 formed the band.

The fateful voyage was begun on April 10, 1912, the Titanic leaving Southampton shortly after noon in command of Captain E. J. Smith, an experienced and careful officer. She proceeded to Cherbourg, where passengers and mails were taken aboard and the voyage resumed to Queenstown, leaving that port about 1:30 P. M. on Thursday. Steady progress was made until Sunday night, when, at 11:40, ship's time, most of the passengers having retired, an almost imperceptible shock occurred and the engines were stopped. The *Titanic* had struck an iceberg obliquely on the starboard side. The ice had been seen by the lookout at the crow's nest, who gave the usual signal and telephoned the officer of the watch; but despite the fact that the helm was put hard to starboard and the engines were reversed, it was too late, for the ship was moving at a speed of over 20 knots, or 300 feet in less than 10 seconds. So early as 5 o'clock the *Titanic* had been warned by wireless of the presence of icebergs in her track, and an active lookout had been maintained without slackening speed. The ship, moving with high velocity, struck the iceberg, whose jagged points below the water pierced the plating on the starboard side at the bilge, or about 10 feet above the level of the keel, and broke and ripped away the plates form about the forepeak aft, the damage extending a distance of some 300 feet. Six compartments were immediately opened to the sea and in these the water rose steadily, driving the stokers out. The shock was sufficient to bring Captain Smith to the bridge, and the seriousness of the situation was soon realized. At about 12:05 orders were given to uncover the lifeboats and about a quarter of an hour later came the order to swing out the boats. In the meantime the position of the ship, 41° 46′ N. lat. and 50° 14′ W. long., had been worked out and given to the wireless operator, with orders to send out the international distress signal. At about 12:30 came the order, "All passengers on deck with life-belts on," and the hastily clad and assembled passengers were grouped while the boats were prepared for loading and lowering. The women and children were separated from the men, but the chance distribution of passengers enabled some of the latter to be saved simply by their being in proximity to boats whose capacity was not reached. From 12:45 to 2:05 the 16 lifeboats and two of the collapsible boats were launched successfully, the remaining two collapsible boats floating off as the ship sank at 2:20. The main promenade deck was under water when the last boat left the davits. The vessel seemed to go down by the stem and finally to sink in an almost vertical position, with propellers out of water. The lights burned until the submergence of the dynamo room, and the band played on the deck as the ship went down. Captain Smith and all of the engineer staff perished at their posts, but a few of the ship's officers who clung to wreckage were subsequently picked up. In addition to the wireless, which was kept constantly in operation, signals of distress were fired and these, subsequent investigation seemed to show, were seen by the steamship *Californian* from a distance of about 10 miles, but were unheeded.

To the *Carpathia*, on her way from New York to Gibraltar and Genoa, with 720 passengers and a crew of 325, fell the lot of picking up the survivors in the boats. This Cunard vessel received the *Titanic's* wireless call for

reached port in safety. Nor has increase in speed increased the risk of the traveler at sea. According to statistics presented by Sir Alfred Chalmers, late adviser to the Board of Trade, in the decade 1892-1901 three an a quarter millions of passengers made the transatlantic trip, and of these, 73 perished as the result of accidents in British ships. In the ten years 1902-1911 the number of travelers had risen to six million and the loss of life in British ships had fallen to nine. In American vessels the proportion of casualties has been one death to 800,000 passengers carried. Therefore, any conclusions from this great disaster can be drawn only after considering the abnormal conditions prevailing, which might not be repeated for centuries, and this was most apparent in the recommendations of the two national commissions charged with the investigation of the matter. Popular criticism and comment, while abundant, were far from pertinent or constructive. In England more than in the United States the calamity formed the subject of serious essays and articles from noted men of letters and students of affairs as well as naval men. Two interesting volumes were published dealing with the disaster: *The Loss of the Titanic*, by Lawrence Beesly, one of the survivors, and *An Unsinkable Titanic*, by J. Bernard Walker, editor of the *Scientific American*, in which the various structural and engineering questions connected with the wreck are discussed. That the disaster would have a most healthy effect on transatlantic navigation was evident very early, for the lines of their own volition instituted a number of reforms, but the number of radical innovations necessary or desirable were comparatively few.

TOBACCO. The tobacco crop of the United States in 1912 was 962,855,000 pounds, which was 7 per cent. above the average of the preceding five years. The average price was the highest in many years, making the total value of the crop $104,063,000, which is the largest on record. The production and value of the crop by types and districts were as follows:

Cigar Type	Acreage Acres	Prod. 1000 Pounds	Value 1000 Dollars
New England 1	23,500	39,950	9,589
New York 2	4,000	5,200	655
Pennsylvania 3	44,200	64,090	5,448
Ohio—Miami Valley 4	54,000	53,460	4,277
Wisconsin 5	42,200	54,438	5,958
Georgia and Florida 6	4,500	3;766	1,130
Chewing, Smoking, Snuff, and Export Types			
Burley 7	228,000	196,080	21,569
Kentucky and Tennessee Dark 8	384,000	268,040	18,686
Virginia sun cured 9	15,000	9,750	780
Virginia dark 10	75,000	49,500	3,861
Bright yellow (Va., N. C., and S. C.) 11	310,000	187,540	29,202
Maryland and Eastern Ohio export 12	31,000	22,010	1,783
Perique (La.) 13	500	150	45
Scatterings	9,900	8,881	1,050

Price paid farmers, in cents: 1 24; 2 12.6; 3 8.5; 4 8; 5 11; 6 30; 7 11; 8 6.2-7.8; 9 8; 10 7.8; 11 15.2-16.1; 12 8.1; 13 30.

The small yields of tobacco in some of the export and manufacturing tobacco districts have been demonstrated to be due to the continued growing of clean-cultured humus-depleting crops on the tobacco lands, with little or no attention to soil-improving crops. Rotations for tobacco are being advocated. The growing of winter cover crops has been shown to be highly beneficial to tobacco.

The report of the commissioner of internal revenue for the year ending June 30, 1912, shows that tax was collected on 7,256,390,303 cigars (an increase of nearly four and a half million over 1911), 1,093,728,800 little cigars (a decrease of 10 per cent.), 11,239,535,803 cigarettes (a gain of 15 per cent.), 30,079,482 pounds of snuff (a gain of 7 per cent.), and 393,785,146 pounds of smoking and chewing tobacco. The manufacture of cigarettes was the largest on record. The total revenue collected on all lines of tobacco manufactures was the largest ever received, amounting to $70,590,151.60, an increase over the previous fiscal year of $3,584,201.04, or 5.35 per cent. In the 50 years in which revenue has been collected on tobacco and its manufactures these taxes have aggregated the colossal sum of $1,853,699,379.79. In 1911 the United States imported 48,203,288 pounds of tobacco, mainly filler and other leaf, valued at $27,865,565. It exported in that year 255,327,072 pounds, but the price was much lower than that of the imported, its total value amounting to $39,255,320.

As a result of the charge that five foreign governments have taken steps to discriminate against American tobacco, a commission was provided by Congress to investigate the conditions surrounding the sale of American-grown tobacco to foreign markets. A bill has been introduced in Congress greatly increasing the taxes on tobacco and bringing them up to the rates of 1879, the increase being justified by its proposed use for building great trunk lines of highways to connect the capitals of the several States with the national capital. This, it is estimated, could be done in a period of five years.

A treatise on the *Import and Manufacturing Tobaccos of the United States, with Brief References to the Cigar Types, by* E. W. Mathewson, was published by the Department of Agriculture during the year.

TOBACCO TRUST. See TRUSTS.

TOGO. A German West African protectorate between Dahomey and the Gold Coast. Estimated area, 87,200 square kilometers (33,668 sq. miles). Estimated population, 1,000,000; whites (January 1, 1911), 363, of whom 327 German. Lome is the seat of government and chief port. Imports and exports in 1909, 11,235,000 and 7,372,000 marks; in 1910, 11,466,000 and 7,222,000. Imports from Germany in 1909 and 1910, 6,678,000 and 6,298,000 marks; exports thereto, 4,532,000 and 4,526,000. Chief exports in the two years: Palm kernels, 1635 and 2034 thousand marks; silver coin, 1545 and 1401; palm oil, 912 and 1233; rubber, 969 and 1147; cotton, 417 and 456; corn, 979 and 290. Tonnage entered (1910), 576,639. Railways in operation at the end of 1911: Lome-Anecho (Little Popo), 44 kilometers; Lome-Palime, 119; Lome-Atakpame, 160; total, 323 kms. (201 miles). The budget for 1911-12 balanced at 3,343,700 marks (including 127,500 marks loan); for 1912-13 at 3,175.510 (24,900 loan). Governor (1912), Duke Adolf Friedrich of Mecklenburg-Schwerin.

TOLL-RATES. See PANAMA CANAL.

TOMATO SEED OIL. See HORTICULTURE, and CHEMISTRY, INDUSTRIAL.

TONGA (or FRIENDLY) **ISLANDS.** A British protectorate; a group of islands (390 sq. miles, 21,695 inhabitants in 1910) in the southern Pacific. Most of the islands are of coral formation; some contain active volcanoes. Tongatabu contains the capital, Nukualofa. Imports (1910), £160,543; exports, £245,946; revenue (1910-11), £33,600; expenditure, £42,852. There is a native king (Jioaji Tubou II.), and a British agent and consul (in 1912, W. Telfer Campbell).

TONGKING. The northernmost division of the French colony of Indo-China (q. v.). Hanoi (103,238 inhabitants) is the capital, and the capital of French Indo-China. Rice is the chief crop cultivated; sugar-cane, cotton, cardamoms, etc., are also raised. There are cotton, silk, and sugar mills.

TONICS. See PROFERRIN.

TORONTO, CANADA. See MUNICIPAL GOVERNMENT.

TORONTO, ONTARIO. See MUNICIPAL OWNERSHIP.

TORONTO, UNIVERSITY OF. An institution for higher education, founded in 1827 as Kings' College, at Toronto, Canada. The enrollment in the various departments of the university in the autumn of 1912 was 4136, divided as follows: Arts, 2352; medicine, 519; applied science, 793; household science, 134; education, 305; forestry, 33. The faculty numbered 430. Dr. F. J. W. Ross, professor of gynecology, died during the year, and Dr. B. P. Watson of Edinburgh, Scotland, was appointed his successor. Professor Ramsay Wright, professor of biology, and Professor Henry Montgomery, museum curator, retired. Dr. G. A. Guess was appointed professor of metallurgy. Among the important gifts during the year was the sum of $10,000 for the establishment of the James H. Richardson research fellowship in anatomy. The George N. Peters scholarship was established with a fund of $2500. The valuation of the assets of the university, including lands, building, and equipment on June 30, 1912, was $5,568,537. The income in the collegiate year 1911-12 was $863,556. The library contained 127,317 bound volumes and 39,392 pamphlets.

TORRES STRAITS, PEOPLE OF. See ANTHROPOLOGY.

TORREY, BRADFORD. An American naturalist and writer, died October 6, 1912. He was born at Weymouth, Mass., in 1843, and was educated in the public schools of that town. He engaged in literary and journalistic work for the greater part of his life. From 1886 to 1901 he was an editor of *Youth's Companion*. Most of his writings deal with natural history. Among them are, *Birds in the Bush* (1885); *A Rambler's Lease* (1889); *The Foot-Path Way* (1892); *A Florida Sketch-Book* (1894); *Spring Notes from Tennessee* (1896); *Every-Day Birds* (1900); *The Clerk of the Woods* (1903); *Nature's Invitation* (1904), and *Friends on the Shelf* (1906). He edited Thoreau's *Journal*.

TORREY, FRANKLIN. An American sculptor, died November 17, 1912. He was born in 1829. Early in his youth he went to Italy and studied sculpture and he remained in that country practically for the remainder of his life. He became the owner of the Carrara Marble Works in Florence and was for a time United States consul at Genoa. The American Church at Florence was built largely by his munificence. Some of his works in sculpture are in the United States.

TOTEMISM. See ANTHROPOLOGY.

TOWN PLANNING. See CITY PLANNING, GREAT BRITAIN.

TRACHOMA. See INDIANS, SICKNESS AMONG.

TRADE UNIONS. The year 1912 was of special interest in the trade union movement primarily because of the radical character of many union activities in various countries. In the United States, syndicalism (q. v.), represented in the Industrial Workers of the World (q. v.), appeared for the first time in the eastern manufacturing section; in England also the syndicalistic agitators were especially active. (See STRIKES AND LOCKOUTS.) In general trade unions in the United States showed a greater tendency toward political action and those of Great Britain became more decidedly Socialistic; while on the Continent, particularly in France, Radical movements gained in power.

UNITED STATES. The principal trade union organization in this country is the American Federation of Labor (see LABOR, AMERICAN FEDERATION OF). This was an off-shoot from the Knights of Labor, an industrially organized body. The Knights of Labor still exist, but with a relatively small membership. Other national unions not affiliated with the American Federation of Labor include the following: American Flint Glass Workers Union; Bricklayers and Masons International; Brotherhood of Locomotive Engineers; Brotherhood of Locomotive Firemen and Enginemen; Brotherhood of Railroad Trainmen; and the Order of Railway Conductors. Other important features of the trade union history in the United States were the progress of the boycott case against the Hatters' Union, described under BOYCOTT, and the criminal suits described below.

DYNAMITERS. The destruction of the *Los Angeles Times* building, involving the slaughter of 21 persons in October, 1910, proved to be only one of about a hundred dynamitings by members of the International Association of Bridge and Structural Iron Workers. These hundred cases of destruction were a part of the warfare which this union was carrying on against employers who refused to accede to the demands for a closed shop. This warfare began with a strike in 1905 and had not been terminated at the close of 1912. The first dynamiting case occurred in 1906. In May, 1911, J. J. McNamara, secretary of the Iron Workers, and his brother, J. B. McNamara, were arrested. They pleaded guilty. (For details of this celebrated case, see preceding YEAR BOOK.) Meanwhile the federal government and the National Erectors' Association, composed of employers, had employed numerous detectives on the case under the direction of William J. Burns. Grand jury proceedings were begun at Indianapolis early in the year, evidence regarding about 113 dynamitings of bridge, viaduct, and building construction work in various parts of the country being presented. On January 17, Ortey McManigal, who had been employed with J. B. McNamara under the direction of J. J. McNamara to do dynamiting, gave to the jury the details of his activities. Early in February, 54 labor leaders were arrested, 32 of them simultaneously in widely separated parts of the country following telegraphic signals. Much difficulty was met in securing talesmen for the jury to try the accused iron workers, but the trial was begun October 1. Meanwhile 7 defendants were discharged; McManigal pleaded guilty, as did Edward Clark, leaving 45 defendants for trial. Four of these were discharged on December 2. The momentous character of the case was shown by the employment of more than a dozen attorneys, including Senator Kern of Indiana, by the defense. The evidence showed that the executive board of the Iron Workers' Union had granted McNamara $1000 per month, which he was allowed to expend without rendering any account. Letters written by various officers indicated that a "dynamiting crew" was employed as a regular part of the campaign against open-shop employers. It was on these facts that the government showed all the indicated officials to be linked together in guilt. The most important witness for the government was McManigal, who detailed 21 explosions which he personally caused. Altogether 549 witnesses were examined, their testimony covering 25,000 pages. These witnesses were brought from all parts of the country, one from Hawaii and one from Panama; they included mechanics, engineers, railway station check-boys, hotel clerks, detectives, stenographers, contractors, and telephone operators. Although the technical charge against the defendants was illegal transporation of explosives, all other evidence relative to the destruction of property by dynamite and nitro-glycerine was allowed as showing the motives for transportation. In his testimony McManigal declared that he was induced to perform his first dynamiting job in 1907 by Herbert S. Hockin, former secretary of the Iron Workers' Union. For this he received $75. He declared that the McNamaras had planned to blow up the Panama Canal locks, the Frick Building in Pittsburgh, the Los Angeles aqueduct, and also a sleeping car in which was a woman stenographer formerly employed by them who knew of the dynamite plots and whose testimony might be used against them. On December 27, after more than 30 hours deliberation, the jury returned a verdict of guilty in the case of 38 of the defendants. Frank M. Ryan, president of the Iron Workers' Union, was sentenced on December 30 to 7 years' imprisonment; John T. Butler, vice-president, to 6 years; Herbert S. Hockin, former secretary, to 6 years; Olaf A. Tvetmoe, of San Francisco, to 6 years; Eugene A. Clancy, of San Francisco, secretary of the California building-trades council; Philip A. Cooley, of New Orleans; Michael J. Young of Boston; J. E. Munsey, of Salt Lake City, and Frank C. Webb, of New York, to 6 years each. Two others were sentenced to imprisonment for 4 years; 12 others for 3 years; 4 for 2 years; and 6 for 1 year and 1 day. All terms of imprisonment were to be served in the Federal Penitentiary at Leavenworth, Kan. Six, including Edward Clark, who confessed, were given suspended sentences, and two were set free.

At the time of imposing sentence Judge Anderson stated that many of the accused were guilty of murder; but since they were not then charged with that crime he could not sentence them for it. In speaking of the motive which had actuated the defendants he said: "Everyone of these explosions was upon the work of open-shop concerns. Since the arrest of the McNamaras and McManigal the explosions have ceased. This system of destruction was not carried on for revenge or in obedience to any other human passion, but for the deliberate purpose, by a veritable reign of terror, to enforce compliance with the demands of the Iron Workers upon the open and closed shop question." It was widely believed that the outcome of this most important of all criminal cases in the labor history of the United States would serve in part to discredit the whole union movement in the minds of the American people. Many believed it would force upon trade unions better systems of organization and control and more reasonable methods in the conduct of trade disputes. But there were those who held that this experience would intensify the class consciousness of the working class, serve to embitter the feelings of class hatred, and prove to be a forerunner of radicalism in the American labor movement.

The Darrow Trial. Growing out of the trial of the McNamara brothers for conspiracy in blowing up the *Los Angeles Times* building were charges that Clarence Darrow, the attorney for the defense, had connived at efforts to bribe jurors. In November, 1911 Bert H. Franklin, chief detective of the McNamara defense, was arested on a charge of bribing a juror named Lockwood. About February 1, Franklin confessed that he had bribed Robert F. Bain, another juror, and had attempted to bribe five others, including Lockwood. On January 29 Darrow was indicted for alleged bribing of Bain and Lockwood. Trial on the Lockwood indictment was begun May 15, and continued thirteen weeks and two days. Evidence was presented designed to show that Darrow furnished the money to intermediaries with which to do the bribing. The defense, however, alleged that the McNamaras had pleaded guilty before the alleged bribing of Lockwood and that therefore there was no reason for corrupting jurors. On August 17 a verdict of acquittal was rendered. There remained the second indictment for bribing the juror Bain which was called to begin at Los Angeles January 20, 1913.

Legislation. Only a few laws were enacted in 1912 relating to trade unions and trade disputes. Arizona prohibited blacklisting; it defined carefully the term black list, making it include any name or list of names whether written, printed, or spoken, given with an agreement that the receiver will discharge or refuse employment. Massachusetts has heretofore provided that an employer in whose plants a strike or lockout existed must so state in his advertisements for employees; this provision was made inoperative after the State board of arbitration and conciliation has declared that the employer's business is being carried on in the normal manner and to the usual extent. The Mississippi legislature passed a concurrent resolution expressing sympathy for the striking employees of the Illinois Central Railroad and expressing the hope that organized capital may be compelled by public opini n to recognize organized labor. New Mexico forbade employers from in any way preventing or bindering a discharged employee from obtaining employment elsewhere.

Probably the most interesting trade-union legislation of the year was that portion of the post office appropriation act which provided that membership in an organization of postal employees seeking better conditions of labor for its members shall not be a cause for unfavorable discrimination. The law stated, however, that this shall be true on condition that the union of postal employees shall not be affiliated with any other organization imposing an obligation to participate in a strike or assist in any strike against the United States. Moreover, the postal employees may not be penalized for petitioning Congress or any member of Congress or for furnishing information to them. Trade union publications are to be admitted as second-class mail matter.

GREAT BRITAIN. The year 1912 was notable for the strikes of the transport workers and the miners (see STRIKES AND LOCKOUTS), the enactment of a minimum wage law for the miners (see MINIMUM WAGE), for the growth of mutual understanding and the policy of concerted action among unionists, and for the increasing evidence of the acceptance of syndicalist policies by the radical labor leaders (see SYNDICALISM). The total membership of all trade unions was estimated at nearly 3,000,000; they numbered 2,435,704 in 1910. The seamen's union more than trebled its membership; the unions representing canal, dock, and riverside workers increased by 187 per cent. during the year ending September 1; railway unions increased decisively; and there was a considerable increase in the organization of unskilled laborers.

There were many evidences of a great extension of the idea of federation or amalgamation among trade-union leaders. The growth of combinations among employers which goes on steadily could be met in no other way than by wider and wider unions of workers. Thus the seamen, dockers, and carters have realized the great advantage of an amalgamation into one transport workers' union. Their unsucessful strike of the summer (see STRIKES AND LOCKOUTS) showed the advantage of their alliance with the railway men. Similarly other trade disputes have taught the various railway unions and unions in the iron and steel industries the advantage of federation. Another stimulus to the same end was the success of the Miners' Federation in winning a minimum wage by legislative action. The tendency toward a grand federation of all unions was shown by the active negotiations under way for the amalgamation of the Trades Union Congress and the General Federation of Trade Unions.

A board of trade report on the hundred principal unions comprising about 60 per cent. of the total trade union membership showed their total income in 1910 to have been £2,691,000 and total expenditures about the same. Owing to the depression following 1907 and consequent great increase in benefits paid the total funds on hand decreased £520,000 from 1908 to 1910. Thus the unemployment benefits paid during 1908 and 1909 aggregated nearly £2,000,000. Superannuation benefits have also been increasing steadily during the past few years.

The British Trades Union Congress held its annual conference at Newport, December 2. It was attended by 502 delegates representing 1,967,000 members. This was an increase in membership of 305,000 over 1911. The deliberations of the congress considered 32 resolutions. These included the proposal for a general eight-hour bill to be presented to the House of Commons; the simultaneous demand on the part of all trade unionists for an increase of $1.25 per week in wages for all grades of workers on account of the increased cost of living; the question of political action and direct action, involving resort to the general strike; the amalgamation of all existing trade unions by industries, as, for example, the organization of one central industrial association out of the seventy-odd unions now existing in various branches of the building trades; the half-time system in certain machine trades. Without abandoning its policy of seeking ends through political action, as by parliamentary representation, the congress refused by a vote of 1,123,000 to 550,000 to condemn and oppose syndicalism, or direct action. *The Daily Citizen* in both London and Manchester, in the interest of labor, was begun in the late fall. It was financed primarily by the unions, the board of directors including members of trade unions of the Labor party, and of Socialist organizations.

GERMANY. At the close of 1911 the total average membership of all trade unions was found to be 3,042,000, being an increase of 354,000 over the preceding year. These members were included in 137 national unions and a few local unions. Of the national unions 51 were affiliated with the General Commission of Trade Unions, including 2,321,000 members; 23 with the Federation of Christian Trade Unions, a group which favors a close connection between the labor movement and the churches, especially the Catholic Church, comprising 341,000 members; 18 national unions and 7 local unions affiliated with the Hirsch-Duncker Trade Unions, aggregating 108,000 members. Some 40 local unions comprised 272,000 members. The membership of the Hirsch-Duncker unions decreased 12 per cent., the other groups increasing about 15 per cent. Among the general commission unions, the miners, furriers, shipwrights, and wood-engravers experienced slight decreases in membership, whereas the building trades unions, the metal workers, the transport workers, and the general factory workers unions increased decisively. The national unions comprised 11,669 local branches, of which 1051 were in the building trades, 874 among wood-workers, 816 among miners, 738 among carpenters, 724 among painters, and 542 among general factory workers. The organization of women workers progressed rapidly, membership reaching 191,332, or 8.2 per cent. of the total membership. The total income of the 51 national unions affiliated with the general commission was $17,164,000; their expenditures, $14,292,000. Their total funds on hand January 1, 1912, amounted to $14,787,000. The principal expenditures included $4,120,000 for strike and lockout benefits, $5,089,000 for benevolent benefits, $583,000 for official publications, $1,800,000 for unemployment benefits, and $2,500,000 for sick benefits.

FRANCE. The principal organization of labor in France is the *Confédération Générale du Travail* organized in 1895. Its membership at its annual convention at Havre, September 17-22, was placed at 600,000. It is composed of representatives from about 150 labor exchanges (*Bourses du Travail*) and the trade unions proper known as *Fédérations de Syndicats*. The former are subsidized by the various cities but have come largely under the control of the radical trade union leaders. The *Syndicats* represent the aggressive organizations among the French unionists. The most active committee of the General Confederation is the committee on strikes, including the general strike. It is through this committee that the philosophy of Syndicalism, which derives its name from *Syndicats*, has made itself manifest in the labor movement and in trade disputes. See SYNDICALISM.

At its 1912 convention the General Confederation of Labor considered the following subjects: The English week, including the Saturday half-holiday and the eight-hour day; anti-militarism; working-class pensions; and the high cost of living. Probably the most interesting session of the convention was that involving a discussion of the principles of Syndicalism which were reaffirmed by a vote of 1057 to 35. The resolution adopted included the following: "Syndicalism aims at the coördination of the workers' efforts, the improvement of the welfare of the workers by the realization of ameliorations, such as reduction of hours and increase of wages." As concerns the organization, the congress declared that, "In order that 'Syndicalism' shall attain its maximum effect, economic action ought to be aimed directly against the employing class, the confederated organizations not having, as syndical groups, to occupy themselves with parties or sex which, otherwise, may pursue, in full liberty, the social transformation." The discussion was marked by vituperative epithets directed against the Marxists and those trade unionists who would seek relief through political action.

TRADE UNIONS LIABLE FOR DAMAGE. See BOYCOTT.

TRAINING SQUADRON. See NAVAL PROGRESS.

TRAIN STOPS. See RAILWAY ACCIDENTS.

TRANSMISSION OF ELECTRIC POWER. The tendency to increase the upper limit of transmission pressure continues without abatement. The number of 100,000 volts systems has increased markedly in 1912 and experience indicates that the difficulties in sustaining continuous operation are not sensibly greater at this voltage than at the pressures previously employed. During the year the Au Sable Electric Company put into service a 140,000 volt line 250 miles long, establishing a new record for operating voltage. The Pacific Gas and Electric Company in California has under construction lines for 150,000-volt operation. The present tendency in American plants is to use an average voltage of about 750 per mile of line. There would appear to be no physical barrier to the use of much higher voltages whenever economic conditions warrant. There is gradual progress in the evolution of insulators toward a type which will resist the tendency to puncture when subjected to abnormal voltage until the strain is removed by flash-over or the discharge of lightning arresters. An important practical advance in line protection is afforded by the arcing-ground suppressor which places a momentary ground on the line at the power station when an arcing ground occurs on the line, thus affording an important measure of protection to line insulators. In the design of waterpower stations there is a marked tendency to introduce water-wheels of very large capacity. Units of 10,000 horsepower for low heads and of 16,000 to 24,000 horsepower for high heads are frequently used. In some cases the efficiency obtained at best load approaches 85 per cent. There is also gradual progress in improving the efficiency at fractional loads. In overhead transmission a uminum conductors have increased greatly in popularity in Europe and in Canada, while in the United States they have been sparingly introduced. Through the artificial control of its market price in America due to tariff protection the economic advantage of about 35 per cent. is eliminated, when the higher cost of erection and handling is taken into the account.

A large number of projects of unusual importance were begun in 1912. It was decided to proceed with the development of an extensive chain of plants in connection with the Los Angeles reservoir and aqueduct system. Seven power plants are planned, the first of these to be 40 miles north of Los Angeles, with three 7500 kilowatt units of immediate and six of ultimate capacity. The system is to be gradually extended to a total of 90,000 kilowatts. The transmission is to be at 100,000 volts over several duplicate lines to guarantee reliability. By reason of the extensive hydraulic plant with which it is to be associated the cost is estimated at the unusually low figure of $80 per kilowatt. The returns from the electric system, it is predicted, will suffice to meet the interest and refunding of the entire bond issue for the combined project. The proposed Hetch-Hetchy water supply system for San Francisco involves the possibility of three plants of a combined capacity of 160,000 horsepower under unusually favorable conditions as to low cost and reliability. The Big Creek project under construction in Central California involves the development of 60,000 kilowatts in two plants utilizing a total fall of 4000 feet. Transmission to Los Angeles will be at 150,000 volts and the distance 275 miles. It is planned to finally extend this system to 120,000 kilowatts. The Appalachian Power Company has installed two plants aggregating 29,000 horsepower in the New River coal district of Virginia and is extending the system to five plants aggregating 75,000 horsepower. At Niagara there have been extensions in the Canadian plants which when completed will make use of the full volume of water permitted by the existing treaty. The amount in use on the American side is already at the limit permitted by the War Department.

The most important project ever undertaken in the Central States is the development of the Mississippi River at Keokuk. The installation is to comprise fifteen 7500 kilowatt units. Of the product, 90,000 horsepower is to be transmitted a distance of 140 miles to St. Louis over two 3-phase lines operated at 110,000 volts. This plant is expected to prove a great stimulus to the development of manufacturing interests in the adjacent region. In the realm of underground cable transmission the greatest advances of late have been made in Germany. The Prussian state railways are operating sections of cable at 60,000 volts, while in Berlin an extensive network at 30,000 volts has been installed. The latter cables are paper insulated and were tested as high as 250,000 volts without failure. The Brazilian government has granted to a syndicate for a period of 70 years the right to develop waterpower on the São Francisco River. An initial capacity of 200,000 horsepower is provided for, while ultimate extensions to 1,300,000 horsepower are planned.

Statistics show the present waterpower development in the United States to have exceeded 6,000,000 horsepower, of which more than one-half is associated with long-distance electric transmission.

TRANSVAAL. One of the four original provinces of the Union of South Africa (q. v.). Pretoria, the seat of the provincial government, had, according to the census of 1911, 48,607 inhabitants; with suburbs, 57,674 (35,942 whites); Johannesburg, 237,104 (119,953 whites); Krugersdorp, 55,144; Germiston, 54,325; Boksburg, 43,628; Benoni, 32,560; Roodepoort-Maraisburg, 32,578; Premier, 12,608. There were, in 1910, 735 schools for white and 13 for colored and native children, with an average aggregate attendance of 42,531. There are three normal schools. For area, population, production, and trade, see SOUTH AFRICA, UNION OF. Public revenue for the eleven months ended May 30, 1910 (exclusive of one-half the government's share of profits derived from the diamond mines, reserved for the redemption of loans), £5,585,637; expenditure, £5,909,811; customs revenue, £1,680,203; public debt, May 30, 1910, £40,000,000. Administrator (1912), J. Rissik.

TRAVEL. See LITERATURE, ENGLISH AND AMERICAN.

TREATIES. See ARBITRATION, INTERNATIONAL.

TRENGGANU. A native state on the east coast of the Malay Peninsula; a British protectorate (6000 square miles). Population (census March, 1911), 154,073 (10 Europeans, 149,379 Malays, 4169 Chinese, 61 Indians, 454 of other races). Kuala Trengganu (13,991 inhabitants) is the capital and is built on both banks of the mouth of the Trengganu River. The following articles are produced for export (value in Straits Settlements dollars, 1910)—fish, SS$ 464,288; tin ore, 313,177; copra, 281,813; paddy, 174,295; black pepper, 152,707; rattans, 28,039; rice, 24,746; rawhides, 14,946; dammar torches, 12,251. A British agent (W. D. Scott in 1912) administers the state; native sultan, Sir Zainal Abdin ibni Almerhum Ahmad.

TRINIDAD AND TOBAGO. A British colony, composed of the West Indian islands of Trinidad (1754 sq. miles) and Tobago (114). Total population (1911 census), 330,093 (86,373 East Indians). Capital, Port of Spain (1911 census, 59,658); San Fernando (8607) is thirty miles south of the capital. Under cultivation, about 423,600 acres.

	1907-8	1908-9	1909-10*	1910-11
Imports	£3,374,824	£2,682,702	£3,288,826	£3,343,011
Exports	3,907,503	2,500,195	3,218,092	3,467,588a
Revenue	871,201	834,745	853,565	948,383
Expendit.	781,038	855,050	863,254	927,033
Shipping †	1,798,810	1,987,252	2,404,143	2,771,364

* Beginning with 1909 trade figures are for calendar years. Tonnage entered and cleared.

a Cacao, £1,230,097; domestic produce (£1,407,814 total); asphalt, £180,865; raw sugar, £723,949; balata, £261,105; hides and skins, £105,331; raw rubber, £58,168; cocoanuts, £72,557; coal, etc., £44,370; spirits (bitters), £33,521; molasses, £10,433; specie (gold), £80,601.

Total railways open, 81½ miles (all government lines). Extensions are projected to Siparia from San Fernando (16¼ miles) and from Tabaquite to Poole (13). The latter was begun September 30, 1911. Sir G. R. Le Hunte was governor in 1912.

TRINITY COLLEGE. An institution for higher education at Hartford, Conn., founded in 1823. The number of students enrolled in the various departments of the college in 1912 was 253. The faculty numbered 22. The most noteworthy change in the faculty during the year was the appointment of Professor George B. Viles to the chair of Romance languages to take the place of Professor John C. Gill, retired. In the latter part of October the announcement was made that Mr. J. Pierpont Morgan had given the sum of $100,000 for the building of a new library and administration building for the college. The productive funds at the end of 1911 amounted to $1,210,106 and the income for 1911-12 was $76,653. The volumes in the library numbered 65,000. President, F. S. Luther, LL. D.

TRIPLE TURRETS. See NAVAL PROGRESS, and BATTLESHIPS.

TRIPLEX GLASS. See CHEMISTRY, INDUSTRIAL.

TRIPOLI. A country bordering on the Mediterranean coast of Africa, between Tunis and Algeria on the west and Egypt on the east, and bordered on the southeast and south by the Sahara. As a result of the Turco-Italian War, Tripoli, hitherto a vilayet of the Ottoman empire, was proclaimed at Rome, November 5, 1911, together with Cyrenaica, a province of the kingdom of Italy. The area, with Cyrenaica (or Bengazi, or Barca), is estimated at 405,800 square miles, and the population at about one million. Tripoli, with 40,000 inhabitants, is the capital of Tripoli; Bengazi, with 25,000, of Bengazi, both Mediterranean ports.

The trade stream flows through these ports, and is fed by the caravan routes across the Sahara, which are the natural outlet by which Sudanese trade reaches the sea. As certain of the oases which make practicable the most traversed of these routes are in the territory long disputed by Turkey with France in behalf of Tunis, and with Great Britain in behalf of Egypt, the delimitation of Tripoli is now imperative and will undoubtedly be the source of much diplomatic discussion by the three powers involved. As this southern commerce becomes increasingly important it is probable that railway construction will be undertaken (a short line from Tripoli to Ainzara was under construction in 1912); but for the present the measures indicated are pacification of the hinterland tribes and an effective policing of the existing routes. Caravans now cross the Sahara in from three to five months, according to the route taken and the number and strength of robber bands to be overcome.

The total commerce of the country is reported for 1909 as follows: 10,941,605 lire imports, 5,934,151 lire exports (esparto, hides and skins, ostrich feathers, sponges, live animals, wool, cereals, etc.). The revenue has been derived from taxation on the wealth of the individual and from tithes.

No civil governor had been appointed by Italy at the end of 1912. The final draft of the treaty of peace between Italy and Turkey was signed October 18 by the delegates at

Ouchy, Switzerland. It provides for complete Italian sovereignty in "Libya" (Tripoli and Cyrenaica) without formal recognition by Turkey; for the caliph's retention of free religious authority; for the withdrawal of Turkish troops; for the reëstablishment of former diplomatic and commercial relations, etc. With the withdrawal of Turkish troops, however, hostility to Italian occupation is not ended. The fierce and fanatical Mohammedan tribes of the hinterland remain to dispute every inch of their territory with the invader. See TURCO-ITALIAN WAR.

TRIPOLITANIA. See EXPLORATION.

TRISTRAM, THOMAS H. An English jurist and church official, died March 8, 1912. He was born in 1825 and was educated at Durham School and Lincoln College, Oxford. In 1855 he became an advocate of Doctors' Commons. His first appearance in connection with clerical cases was in behalf of Mr. Mackonochie in the first appeal to the Privy Council in 1868. In the various stages of this famous case Dr. Tristram was retained. The case related to charges made for alleged ritual offenses and was followed by the passage of the public worship regulation act of 1874. In 1888 an appeal was made to the archbishop of Canterbury for a citation against a bishop for alleged ritual offenses. The archbishop dismissed the petition and the petitioners thereupon appealed to the Privy Council. Dr. Tristram, then a Queen's counsel, appeared, with two other advocates. A board of five bishops allowed the appeal. Thus began the great suit of "Read against the bishop of Lincoln." Dr. Tristram had many official appointments. He was commissary of the city and diocese of Canterbury, and chancellor of the dioceses of London, Hereford, Ripon, Wakefield, and Chichester. Though a layman, letters patent appointing him chancellor entitled him to issue marriage licenses and other canonical dispensations as vicar-general of the bishop. In 1903 he offered to license the marriage of divorced persons, but the bishop of London formally disowned his chancellor's action and pronounced his licenses of doubtful validity. The chancellor, however, continued to issue such licenses to the end. He was the last member of that historic body of practitioners who were known as advocates of Doctors' Commons, whose qualifications were not those belonging to one of the four Inns of Court, but the possession of a degree in law of one of the universities. He twice stood for parliament, as a Conservative candidate in 1880 and in 1885. He was both times defeated.

TROILITE. See MINERALOGY.

TROPICAL DISEASES. See BERIBERI, LEPROSY, PLAGUE, SLEEPING SICKNESS, and VITAL STATISTICS.

TROTTER, LIONEL JAMES. An English lawyer and writer, died May, 1912. He was born in 1827 at Calcutta, and was educated in the Charterhouse School and at Merton College, Oxford. He went to India in 1847 as a cadet of Bengal infantry and served in the British army until 1862, retiring in that year with the rank of captain. He wrote much on Indian subjects. Among his published writings are, *Studies in Biography and British Empire in India* (1865), biographies of Warren Hastings, Dalhousie, and John Nicholson, *History of India* (1874), and *The Bayard of India* (1903). He also contributed to several Indian and English newspapers.

TRUSTS. The amount of attention given to the trust problem in 1912 was probably equal to that of any preceding year. Not only did it figure prominently in the political campaign, but the numbers of prosecutions completed, of new ones begun, and of those advanced, were unusually numerous. Its prominence in the political campaign led to an unusual volume of newspaper and periodical literature dealing with the subject. A summary representing all the different views, based on a report of a session of the American Academy of Political and Social Science, is given below. The principal suits terminated during the year included those against the Aluminum Trust, the Beef Trust, the Wallpaper Trust, the Bathtub Trust, the Harriman lines, the anthracite coal roads, the St. Louis Terminal Railroad Association, and the criminal suit against officers of the American Sugar Refining Company. Suits were begun against ten steamship companies engaged in trade between Atlantic ports and the Far East; four steamship lines alleged to have monopolized American traffic with Brazil; the National Cash Register Company; the United Fruit Company; the Atlantic steamship lines on account of a compact for the transportation of steerage passengers; the Motion Picture Patents Company and the General Film Company, constituting the Moving Picture Trust and including ten corporations; the Elgin Board of Trade, known as the Butter Trust; the Brazilian valorization scheme, known as the Coffee Trust; the Kellogg Toasted Cornflake Company for dictating prices of retailers; the Harvester Trust; the United States Steel Corporation; various corporations known as the Horseshoers' Trust at Detroit; and the Candy Trust, or the Philadelphia Jobbing Confectioners' Association. Investigation of the New Haven Railroad for monopolization of traffic in New England by checking the extension of the Grand Trunk Railroad and control of trolley and seaboard transportation was under way at the close of the year; the presidents of these two railways were indicted under the criminal sections of the Sherman law by the Federal Grand Jury at New York on December 23.

The Harvester Trust suit was brought at St. Paul on April 11 against the International Harvester Company, including seven corporations and eighteen individuals. The government charged that this trust controlled 90 per cent. of the harvester trade, 75 per cent. of the trade in mowing machines, and was seeking to monopolize the production of all kinds of agricultural implements; that it had absorbed competing companies, then pretended that they were still independent; and that it used unfair methods in driving other competitors out of the field and otherwise in the conduct of its business. The capital of the trust was placed at $140,000,000. This suit acquired special interest through the fact that Mr. George W. Perkins, a large contributor to the expenses of the Roosevelt campaigns, was a prominent director. Hearings were being held also in Chicago and St. Louis at the close of the year. On November 20 the president of the company admitted that it had reduced prices to drive out rival companies.

Shortly after the suit against the Butter Trust in December the Elgin board reorganized and amended its rule of seventeen years' standing, whereby prices had been arbitrarily fixed by its quotation committee, and adopted the plan of allowing actual sales of butter as related to its supply to determine the price.

Suits that were merely advanced during the year included those against the Key-Stone Watch Company, or Watch Trust; against the United Shoe Machinery Company, the American Sugar Refining Company, and the Lumber Trust. A committee of the House of Representatives under the chairmanship of Representative Pujo prosecuted an inquiry into the alleged Money Trust.

Late in April the Supreme Court declared the St. Louis Terminal Association, which controls railroad entrance to the city and passage across the Mississippi River, a monopoly in restraint of trade. The decree permitted a reorganization under specific conditions. In May the government and the Powder Trust agreed upon a decree for dissolution. Late in May the suit against the Wallpaper Trust at Cleveland was terminated, the eight defendants being acquitted. By mutual agreement the Aluminum Company of America, or the Aluminum Trust, was enjoined from using unfair methods, the company promising to reorganize in lawful form. In March several officers of the American Sugar Refining Company were brought to trial under the penal division of the Sherman act. On November 31 the jury failed to agree and the defendants were discharged. The weakness of the suit was due to insufficient evidence available under the statute of limitations. The government finally dismissed the criminal indictments in December. This, however, did not terminate the civil suit for the dissolution of the Sugar Trust, hearings in which were being held in Philadelphia at the close of the year.

Opinion. The most comprehensive and authoritative discussion of the trust problem during the year occurred at the meeting of the American Academy of Political and Social Science in March. As reported in the *Annals* of the Academy for July, nearly ever phase of the problem of "competition versus combination" was presented. With reference to the effect of combination on labor several labor leaders, especially those in the steel industry, contended that conditions had been better before combination; but representatives of manufacturers endeavored to show that "the labor conditions in the large factory are better than in the small one," as regards wages, sanitation, protection from machinery and fire, rate of work, and fairness of the management. See United States Steel Corporation, paragraph *Labor Conditions*, and Welfare Work.

The majority opinion strongly favored competition as a better basis for industrial progress. Prof. John Bates Clark of Columbia, though assenting to the need for a government bureau with power to charter corporations doing interstate business, presented clearly the necessity and advantage of preserving competition, at least in its potential form, as a regulator of prices, a stimulus to industrial progress and, in general, a protection of the public. Prof. Bruce Wyman of Harvard pointed out the unfair competitive methods of the monopolistic corporation, including railroad rebates, the abuse of patent laws, the establishment of bogus competing concerns, bribery of competitors' employees, factors' agreements, local competition, and various other devices for price-control. Prof. E. S. Meade of the University of Pennsylvania declared that the supposition that the trust, as a type of business organization, is superior to the individual concern is a fallacy, as shown by comparison of the United States Steel Corporation, a huge unnatural composite, with the Pennsylvania Railroad, a single united naturally evolved business organization. Some speakers were inclined to point to the increase in international trade as evidence of the economic superiority of the trust, while others declared this expansion had been secured largely at the expense of the American public since higher prices were charged at home than abroad.

Other Countries. Some time was devoted to the discussion of the policies of different countries, particularly Canada, England, France, and Germany towards combination. Mr. Francis Walker of the Bureau of Corporations classified the legal attitudes as follows: (1) Complete legality of combinations, as in Germany; (2) invalidity of combinations when they are of the nature of conspiracy under the civil law, as in England; (3) probibition under the criminal law, as in Canada and the United States. In Germany the cartels are encouraged by the government, as a rule, but this must be connected with the policy of extending government ownership and enterprise. The German law hinders financial excesses and promotes publicity, the states and nation own the railroads, and most of the state governments produce such raw materials as coal, lumber, and potash. In England the judicial attitude is that the ordinary trade or industrial combination is not a conspiracy at common law and therefore not illegal. Moreover, opinion and the government hold that although there are numerous combinations in existence, some of which are doubtless injurious to public welfare, yet the existence or free trade with the ease of foreign competition prevents serious evil to the English pubiic. In Canada the Combines Investigation act of 1910 has been a check upon unfair combinations. This provides for public investigation of an alleged combine and relies upon public opinion to give due force to the finding of an impartial inquiry. Moreover, other laws place restrictions on the patent rights of combinations and provide for a reduction of tariff duties on goods produced by a trust. Austria-Hungary follows the plan of England, namely, encouragement of competition and relative indifference as yet to the tendency to combine. Most other countries where the problem has arisen have taken the attitude of decisive opposition shown in the United States and Canada.

Combination vs. Competition. The conference brought out characteristic differences as to the naturalness of large combinations and as to the effect of the Sherman law. Some held that the great combinations of 1898-1902 were made in obedience to an inevitable tendency of economic evolution and others that they were the result of a mania for promotion and stock manipulation. Some pointed to the undoubted economies of combination and others were inclined to stress the inefficiencies of management as compared with the small, closely organized and personally supervised organization. Professor Seager of Columbia, though recognizing the economies of combination, showed by a statistical study of some thirty leading trusts that about half had succeeded, some of them brilliantly, and about half had failed, some of them ignominiously. He was thus inclined to consider competition a sufficient regulator of prices provided it be fair and attended by the publicity which a federal licensing system would introduce. He, however, advocated governmental regulation of prices wherever a combination secured monopoly, just as we to-day have regulation of railroad rates. Moreover, with the perfection of public administration he thought public ownership of railroads and industrial monopolies would be reasonable and proper. Speaking on the question of a constructive trust policy, President Taft and Attorney-General Wickersham both declared strongly for the continued enforcement of the Sherman law and the creation of a federal licensing system. Commissioner of Corporations Herbert K. Smith said that whether one would rely on competition or prefer to permit combination, experience shows the necessity of a federal authority similar to the present Bureau of Corporations but with greatly enlarged powers to secure information and publicity. Throughout the discussion the need of publicity and the consequent formation of an intelligent public opinion was reiterated. Mr. James M. Beck of New York declared that the courts do not understand what is meant by restraint of trade and that the Supreme Court in the Standard Oil and Tobacco decisions has plunged the whole subject "into a fathomless morass." He favored the Canadian method of reliance on an informed public opinion.

Proposed Bills. Two of the speakers presented outlines of bills before Congress designed to cure the existing evils of the trust situation. Congressman Ernest W. Roberts's bill was copied largely after the Massachusetts corporation law, but in addition provided for more complete publicity. It prohibited the watering of stock; required all capital to be paid in before business was begun; prohibited the issue of stock or scrip dividends; required that all issues of stocks and bonds after the first be approved by the commissioner of corporations; and provided joint fine and punishment for violations. It aimed to prevent the formation of boards of interlocking directors by forbidding a director of one corporation to serve as a director in more than four others. The scope of this proposed law was limited to those interstate corporations whose total valuation exceeds five million dollars. Senator John Sharp Williams of Mississippi found the chief source of present evils in the multiplicity and liberality of State legislation. He held that all the great evils of combination have grown out of the law-conferred or law-permitted privileges granted in State charters. He, however, opposed federal incorporation because it would tend to governmental and industrial centralization; he also opposed the federal license idea because that would tend to bureaucracy, a government of men and not of laws. His remedy, therefore, would be a congressional enactment refusing the privilege of interstate commerce to those corporations that are now permitted by State charters to exercise evil methods or exert injurious powers, such as ownership of stock of competing concerns, factors' agreements, and other unfair methods.

Anthracite Coal. The suit begun in 1907 in the circuit court for the Eastern District of Pennsylvania against the Reading, the Lackawanna, the Lehigh Valley, the Central Railroad of New Jersey, the Erie, and the New York, Susquehanna, and Western railroads and their nine subsidiary companies for maintaining a combination in the mining and transportation of anthracite coal was ended by the decision of the supreme court on December 16. The decision of the circuit court in this suit rendered December 8, 1911, was in the main favorable to the defendants, but found that the Temple Iron Company, whose stock was owned by these roads, constituted a violation of the Sherman law. The case was considered an important one in its bearing upon further elucidation of the significance of the anti-trust law. The evidence showed that shortly after 1900 when numerous contracts between the coal-carrying roads and independent mine operators were expiring, plans were made for the construction of an independent railroad to be called the New York, Wyoming, and Western. The defendant road then formed the Temple Iron Company for the purpose of preventing the construction of this road. They thus retained, in their own hands, control over all transportation for the anthracite fields. and indirectly retained considerable power over the independent operators. Although the supreme court held that the government's allegation that there existed a general combination in the nature of a pooling arrangement among the six roads was indefinite and not sustained, it did declare the Temple Iron Company unlawful and ordered its discontinuance. The coal-carrying roads produced in their own mines about 75 per cent. of the total output of anthracite coal; independent mines produced only 25 per cent. Furthermore, by means of contracts known as the 65 per cent. contracts by which independents producers had bound themselves to deliver the output of their mines to the railroads for 65 per cent. of the average tide-water market price, the roads had acquired a virtual monopoly in the handling of anthracite coal. The court held these contracts invalid because in violation of the anti-trust law. Finally the court reiterated a declaration made in the Standard Oil case that the anti-trust act does not "forbid or restrain the power to make normal and usual contracts to further trade by resorting to all normal methods whether by agreement or otherwise."

A new inquiry was begun in December at the Attorney-General's direction, to determine whether there remained a basis for another suit against the anthracite coal interests.

Union Pacific-Southern Pacific. On February 1, 1908, suit was begun in the United States circuit court for the District of Utah against the Union Pacific, Oregon Short Line, Oregon Railroad Navigation, the Southern Pacific, San Pedro, Los Angeles and Salt Lake, and the Atchison, Topeka and Sante Fé companies, and certain individuals for combination and conspiracy in violation of the Sherman act through the formation of a railway system in restraint of competition. On June 23, 1911, the circuit court rendered a decision dismissing the suit on the ground that the government had not shown the Union Pacific and Southern Pacific railroads to have been competing lines. Judge Hook dissented from that decision. The case was argued before the supreme court early in the year, decision being rendered on December 2. By a unanimous decision the court declared the combination to be in violation of the trust statute. It ordered the dissolution of the merger and required that plans for accomplishing this end should be presented within three months; otherwise the court declared its intention to proceed by receivership and sale, if necessary, to dispose of stock so as to dissolve the unlawful combination. This case grew out of the acquisition of 46 per cent. of the stock of the Southern Pacific Company by the Union Pacific Railway. The court held that, although in a small corporation a minority interest might not amount to control, nevertheless such a large minority holding as 46 per cent. in a large corporation with many scattered stockholders is ample to control the operations of the corporation. The court also declared that the trust law makes no difference between stock control acquired by means of a holding company, as in the Northern Securities case, and control by outright purchase of the stock of one corporation by another. It found that domination and the power to suppress competition are acquired in either case. It also found evidence to show that real competition had existed between the parallel lines of the Southern Pacific and the Union Pacific before the merger. The court even declared that mere ability to stifle competition is practically the same as engaging in such stifling. In December this case again came before the supreme court on a motion to determine whether the stock of the Southern Pacific held by the Union Pacific should be sold to stockholders of the latter road only or to those of both roads. The plan for dissolution had not been worked out at the close of the year, although the Attorney-General had declared that the government would not accept the plan for direct distribution of stock to Union Pacific stockholders.

Minor Court Decisions. On December 2, the supreme court reaffirmed a previous decision declaring unconstitutional the corporation law of Kansas closing the courts of that State to foreign corporations which had not secured certificates to do business in that State. The law was declared unconstitutional as a burden on interstate commerce. On the same date the supreme court affirmed the constitutionality of the South Dakota anti-monopoly act of 1907. This law makes it a crime to sell a commodity in general use to a dealer in one place at a rate lower than to dealers in other places in the State with the intent to ruin competition. Laws similar to this, designed to destroy local competition, have been enacted in various northwestern States and are considered one of the most rigorous and effective anti-monopoly devices yet formulated.

Patent Law. One of the most important judicial decisions of the year and one giving rise to national discussion of "patent monopoly," was that handed down by the United States Supreme Court in the case of Henry vs. The A. B. Dick Company. The latter company manufactured a rotary mimeograph sold "with the license restriction that it may be used only with the stencil paper, ink, and other supplies made by the A. B. Dick Company." A Mr. Henry sold ink to a purchaser of one of these mimeographs, knowing the purchaser's intention to use it with the latter. The supreme court, by a vote of 4 to 3, declared Henry's act to constitute contributory infringement of the Dick Company's rights under the patent law. The point at issue was whether such a restriction as the Dick Company sought to impose—that is, a regulation of the materials that might be used in connection with its patent—was a right under the patent law or merely a contract between buyer and seller. In the former case the rights of the manufacturer of an article would be enormously extended. The majority opinion, based on a long line of decisions, held that the intention of the patent law is to give an exclusive monopoly during a limited period, and therefore, if the purchaser of a patented article knows in advance of the restriction on its use, any limitation whatever may be imposed by the patentee. The opinion also held that if this interpretation be injurious to the public interest, remedy lies in congressional action. Chief Justice White, in a dissenting opinion, held that the decision would destroy a large part of the judicial authority of the State courts, and extend, to an unwarranted degree, that of the federal courts. He held that the principle laid down in the majority opinion was "as broad as society: capable of operating upon every conceivable subject of every human interest or activity." On the basis of numerous decisions he objected to the reasoning of the court whereby the patent law is made to include unpatented articles; this he declared to be judicial legislation of a most dangerous kind. He held that the patent law extended only to the machine and that any control of material used therewith was merely a private contract. Though this decision was rendered by a divided court and less than a full bench, application for a re-hearing was denied on April 8.

United Shoe Machinery Company. Suit was begun in the United States district court at Boston against this company on five counts, four of which charged criminal conspiracy in restraint of trade. These four counts were dismissed on March 2. There remained only the charge of monopoly through a system of leases of patented machinery. In the fall the court ruled that hearings in this suit should be secret, thus arousing public comment and special condemnation from Attorney-General Wickersham. This fifth charge was finally dismissed by the court on the ground that its interpretation of the patent law showed no violation of the Sherman act. The government, however, took the case to the supreme court on December 22. Its contention was that the patent lease agreements whereby this company manufactured and retained control of 80 per cent. of the business in its line resulted in the maintenance of an illegal monopoly. This case appeared to be quite similar to the Dick patent case noted above.

Bathtub Trust. Civil suit at Baltimore and criminal suit at Detroit were begun in the circuit courts against the Standard Sanitary Manufacturing Company and numerous other defendants in 1910. In the criminal suit against certain individuals decision in which was rendered early in 1912 the jury failed to agree. Near the close of the year it was announced that a retrial of this case would be begun at Detroit, February 3, 1913. The defendants in the civil suit included the above company and 49 other parties, one-half of whom were other companies manufacturing 85 per cent. of the sanitary enameled ware made in this country. These concerns were licensed to use a patented dredger in spreading enamel upon an iron base on signing the following patent license agreement: to abide by an established price list, not to sell to jobbers who bought of independents nor in certain territory, and not to sell "seconds." They forced retailers to sell at fixed prices. Moreover, the manufacturers assenting to the license agreement were punishable by a system of fines if they broke any part of it. The circuit court in 1911 held that the ownership of a tool gave no monopoly right over the products made therewith. In a unanimous decision in November, the supreme court declared that there could be no monopoly in the unpatented product of a patented machine. The defendants put their main reliance on the opinion of the supreme court in the Dick patent case above noted. The court, however, did not find the cases comparable. These defendants really sought to effect a monopoly of trade by control of unpatented articles; they sought to fix the price not of a patented article, or of materials believed necessary to the use of such article, but rather of unpatented products.

The suit was one of the most important yet terminated under the Sherman act. This combination commenced operations in June, 1910. The Attorney-General commenced proceedings in July, 1910. Following the circuit court decision of 1911 prices of the defendants' products fell from 25 to 40 per cent. It has become more and more common for manufacturing concerns to endeavor to control the retail price of products by some sort of patent license agreement. Numerous cases having shown the trust plan and the holding company plan of combination to be illegal, refuge is taken behind the patent laws.

Beef Trust. A criminal suit was begun against the National Packing Company and others in September, 1910. The defendants included the ten principal owners of the Swift, Armour, and Morris Packing companies, who were charged with violating the Sherman law by a conspiracy in restraint of interstate commerce. Trial of the case began in December, 1911. The government traced the history of the combinations of the beef packers; exposed their system of p ice making; set forth the operations of pooling agreements by which territory and business were divided, and traced the history of price wars to drive out competitors and of absorptions of the more successful competitors. The defense claimed that the National Packing Company did not fix prices or control trade; that its function had been mainly to prevent an over-supply of fresh meat; and that there were several hundred competitors who transacted about one-third of the domestic trade. On March 26 a verdict of not guilty was rendered. The suit cost the government $100,000 and the defendants $500,000. In June, 1912, the National Packing Company announced that it would voluntarily dissolve. The Attorney-General thereupon announced that further proceedings to compel dissolution would be held in abeyance. The New York *Journal of Commerce* stated that this company was used to acquire control by holding stock of about 350 principal packing plants in St. Louis, Omaha, Kansas City, and other western and eastern cities, including the New York Butchers' Dressed Meat Company, the Stock Yards Warehouse Company, the Anglo-American Refrigerator Car Company, and the Fowler Canadian Company. The announcement of voluntary dissolution was not taken seriously by the press as it was not expected to affect concerted control or to lower prices.

Tobacco Trust. The dissolution of the American Tobacco Company in 1911 did not prove satisfactory to the independents and to certain members of Congress. It was alleged that control was unaltered and that competition was not restored. In April the supreme court refused to review the dissolution decree. At once efforts were made in Congress to secure the passage of the Cummins bill giving the independents the right to appeal to that court. About the same time the United States district court at New Orleans punished, by fine, the American Tobacco Company for conspiring to injure an independent company by unfair business methods. In December damage suits under the Sherman act at New York against the American Tobacco Company and other tobacco concerns were unsuccessful. The court, however, declared that without doubt the defendants did constitute an illegal combination, but that no injury to complainant company was shown. Appeal was taken. In December the dividends declared by the various constituents of the former trust aggregated about $6,000,000 less than during the two or three years preceding, the total for 1912 being about $10,000,000. This was, in part, due to the actual division of property and separation of commercial operations effected by the dissolution, and in part to the accumulation of additional capital out of earnings by some of the companies.

Coffee Trust. Suit was begun in the circuit court at New York in May against eight persons, mostly foreigners, identified with the Brazilian valorization plan. This was a plan to regulate the price and market supply of coffee and grew out of the low price some years ago due to a large crop. The state of São Paulo and the Brazilian government bought 10,000,000 bags of coffee, borrowing thereon $65,000,000 from European bankers and $10,000,000 from a Morgan syndicate. The wholesale price of coffee thereafter rose from 7½ cents in 1906 to 14¾ cents in 1912. The coffee purchased under this plan has been gradually sold during years of small crops under the direction of an international supervising committee representing the money lenders. The United States government sought to enjoin the exportation of 950,000 bags of this coffee stored in New York and to secure authority for its confiscation and sale. It failed. The court held that the Sherman act did not extend to goods thus imported. In his annual report the Attorney-General demanded a law authorizing the seizure of goods imported for unlawful combination.

Money Trust. In February, by an almost unanimous vote, the House of Representatives ordered its committee on currency and banking to inquire into the existence of an alleged money trust. The matter was taken up by a sub-committee headed by Representative Pujo. Mr. Samuel Untermyer of New York was employed as counsel. Hearings were begun in April and continued until mid-summer. At the outset steps were taken to secure from the 25,000 or more banks answers to questions designed to bring out the extent of their affiliations. Many banks refused. Hearings were resumed again early in December. The first subject then taken up was the clearing house association at New York, its membership, and its power over smaller banks. It was the belief of the committee that refusal to permit the Oriental Bank to enter the clearing house in 1907 was responsible for its failure. Evidence was presented showing that an effort was being made to bring about a working agreement between the clearing house associations of Pittsburgh, Cleveland, Columbus, Cincinnati, Indianapolis, and Louisville, in order to regulate charges for collecting out-of-town checks and drafts, as also the rate of interest to be paid on deposits. This was believed to be a combination in violation of the Sherman Anti-Trust law. Evidence was presented justifying the charges of New York banks for collecting out-of-town checks and drafts; and also showing that the associations of Boston and Philadelphia did not make similar charges on the ground that they were expenses similar to clerk hire and lighting bills.

Several days were spent in investigating the stock exchange. Evidences of manipulation and stock juggling were presented. It was shown that the stock transactions in Reading had equalled 44 times the capitalization of the Reading Railroad in a single year. In other cases ratios of 9, 12, 17, and even 30 times the capitalization had been reached. The manipulation of the stocks of the Columbus and Hocking Valley Coal and Railroad companies by James R. Keene in 1909 was brought out in detail; as also the Rock Island fiasco of 1909, and other similar transactions. The ethics of the "short sale" were discussed, witnesses universally agreeing that it was reprehensible. The relation between the banks and the stock exchange was also investigated. It was shown that 35 New York City banks had 19,015 out-of-town correspondents. Nearly one-half of the deposits of these correspondents, or $240,480,000, had been loaned by these correspondents on stock exchange securities. This was due to the fact that the call money rate in New York was as high as 8, 10, 15, and even 20 per cent. in November, whereas the rate on loans on commercial paper or securities in the various communities represented by these banks was only 5 to 6 per cent. (see BANKS AND BANKING). It was reported that the committee would recommend to Congress the federal incorporation of the New York and other stock exchanges as the only means of protecting the public against manipulations. At the very close of the year the governors of the New York exchange were engaged in working out reforms to meet objections of the committee.

Probably the most striking bit of evidence presented to the committee was that bearing on the existence of a system of interlocking directorates headed by the firm of J. P. Morgan and Company. It was declared that 18 firms with 180 leading members held directorships to the number of 746 in at least 134 industrial, financial, and transportation corporations, with an aggregate capital of $25,325,000,000. The firm of J. P. Morgan and Company was credited with 33 directorships in 39 corporations with a total capitalization of $10,036,000,000; the First National Bank of New York with 103 directorships in 49 corporations with $11,542,000,000 capital; the Guarantee Trust Company with 160 directorships in 76 corporations with $17,342,000,000 capital; the Bankers Trust Company, with 113 directorships in 56 corporations with $11,184,000,000 capital; the National City Bank with 86 directorships in 47 corporations having $13,205,000,000 capital; the National Bank of Commerce with 149 directorships in 82 corporations having $18,165,000,000 capital; the Chase National Bank with 69 directorships in 48 corporations having $11,527,000,000 capital; and the Astor Trust Company with 74 directorships, in 47 corporations with $12,408,000,000 capital. Other firms included in the list of 18 were: Kuhn, Loeb and Company; the Hanover National Bank; Blair and Company of New York; Speyer and Company of New York; the Continental and Commercial National Bank; the First National Bank of Chicago; the Illinois Trust and Savings Bank of Chicago; Kidder, Peabody and Company of Boston; and Lee, Higginson and Company of Boston. Among the principal corporations in which 180 directors of these 18 banking houses were represented as having an important influence were: The American Telephone and Telegraph Company; the Consolidated Gas Company of New York; the Inter-Boro Metropolitan Company; the Inter-Boro Rapid Transit Company; the electric railway companies of Boston, Brooklyn, Chicago, Philadelphia, and St. Louis; the Amalgamated Copper Company; the American Sugar Refining Company; the following trusts: Tobacco, woolen, beef, leather, powder, electric, rubber, harvester, nickel, paper, biscuit, oil, shoe machinery, and steel; the four principal express companies; 32 railway systems with a total of 167,200 miles, or about two-thirds of the total mileage of the country; 13 leading insurance companies; and 46 principal banks in Boston, Chicago, Philadelphia, Pittsburgh, Providence, St. Louis, Washington, and New York City. The aggregate capitalization of the public utilities corporations included in the list was $4,440,000,000, and their gross income, $477,000,000; the capitalization of the industrial companies was $3,883,000,000 and their gross income more than $1,300,000,000. These 18 financial institutions were believed to constitute the money trust. On the other hand, Mr. J. P. Morgan in his testimony on December 19 declared a monopoly of credit and money to be impossible. He said that credit is a personal thing being based on character. It was expected that further hearings would be held and that the committee would finally formulate constructive legislation designed to restrain cupidity, to equalize the opportunity for securing business credit, and to induce local banks to render larger service to the business needs of their respective communities. The committee endeavored to induce the comptroller of the currency to gather information for them. Following an opinion of Attorney-General Wickersham, President Taft authorized the comptroller to deliver any information already in his possession, but not to undertake the collection of additional data. See RAILWAYS.

TRYON, JAMES RUFUS. A rear-admiral, retired, of the United States navy, died March 20, 1912. He was born in Coxsackie, N. Y., in 1837, and graduated from Union College in 1858. In 1863 he entered the United States navy as assistant surgeon, and in this capacity was present at the battle of Mobile Bay. After the war he had charge of the Naval Hospital in Boston and in 1871 was in charge of the temporary smallpox hospital in Yokohama. He served during the yellow fever epidemic in 1873 at Pensacola. He later saw service in Uruguay and Venezuela. The latter country conferred a decoration upon him for his service in caring for the wounded in one of the revolutions. In 1893 he was appointed surgeon-general of the United States navy, and in 1897 he was made chief of the Bureau of Medicine and Surgery. As surgeon-general he did much to bring the service up to a high standard and the result of his efforts was shown in the small mortality in the navy during the Spanish-American War. He was retired as rear-admiral in 1899, and for six years following was in charge of the hospital at Sailors' Snug Harbor, S. I.

TUBERCULOSIS. The sputum of the tuberculous patient is usually considered the single important factor in spreading infection, although it has been recognized that the bacilli find their way into many of the body fluids. That the perspiration of tuberculous subjects not only contains tubercle bacilli, but is markedly infectious, seems to be proved by recent researches. In March, 1912, Professor Poncet of Lyons presented before the Académie de Médecine a study of the subject of the virulence and contagiousness of the perspiration of tuberculous patients, by Dr. Piery, who attended a number of consumptives, most of whom lived in lodgings, each, in many instances, consisting of a single room used by the patient with the patient's wife or husband and numerous children. Dr. Piery was impressed by the absence of tuberculous infection in the children surrounded by ideal conditions of contamination, and by the frequent infection of the patient's husband or wife, who was apparently equally exposed, but capable of taking prophylactic precautions unknown to the children. He endeavored to trace the cause of this apparent contradiction. The researches of Professor Poncet and his pupils with regard to the septicity of the perspiration of the hands and the infection of surgical wounds by perspiration from the hands of the surgeon suggested the idea of investigating the possible virulence of the perspiration of the tuberculous patient as a cause of the frequency of conjugal tuberculosis. It appears from his investigation that the perspiration of a tuberculous patient is virulent in 30.76 per cent. of cases (surgical lesions, tuberculous arthritis, and tuberculous peritonitis, that is to say, in securely closed and slowly progressing lesions). In 41.66 per cent. of tuberculous cases the perspiration may be the vehicle of tubercle bacilli. This elimination of the tubercle bacillus through perspiration seems an argument in favor of the frequent septicemic nature of tuberculous infection. The heavy sweats of the tuberculous may be considered as crises of elimination of the bacillus. At all events, perspiration is one means of contagion, dangerous in itself, directly or indirectly, and should be guarded against by disinfection of clothing and other objects soiled by such perspiration and by isolation of the patient by at least the use of a separate bed.

The extent to which tubercle bacilli circulate in the blood was studied by Rumpf, who declared that his own and others' researches have confirmed beyond question that tubercle bacilli exist far more often than hitherto supposed in the circulating blood, not only of the tuberculous but also of the healthy. More delicate bacteriologic technic has disclosed their presence with startling frequency. But at the same time inoculation of animals with blood containing the bacilli does not seem to transmit tuberculosis to the animals. Thirty-five guinea-pigs were inoculated with blood containing the bacilli from several patients with advanced tuberculosis, from some with the disease in an incipient form and from three clinically healthy physicians, who all had tubercle bacilli in their blood. Only three of the animals developed tuberculosis and one had dubious lesions. None of the others displayed any symptoms, and when the animals were killed and examined thirty-one weeks later, no tuberculous lesions were found in them. Rumpf suggests that either the bacilli are not viable, or the blood vehicle in which they were injected protected the animal against them. Other experiments in which the bacilli were cultivated in pure cultures from the blood and the animal inoculated with the cultures alone, all resulted positively. Kennerknecht found bacilli in the blood in 91 per cent. of 120 children examined, including 74 per cent. of 31 children supposedly entirely free from tuberculosis. He inoculated guinea-pigs with the bacilli, with positive results.

The rapid spread of tuberculosis in certain parts of South Africa, led to the appointment of a commission by the government to investigate the subject. This commission reported an alarming increase, particularly among the colored races. The primary factor seems to be its introduction into many centres previously free from it by the immigration of consumptive persons who come to South Africa to obtain the benefits of the climate. As a result, stringent regulations are likely to be enforced against the admission of emigrants suffering from open tuberculosis or any form likely to develop into that stage. Tuberculous emigrants may be admitted only at certain ports of entry, under permit to remain in the country for a definite period, under conditions of strict sanitary surveillance, restricted residence, and periodical examination by district surgeons appointed by the government. See INDIANS and AGRICULTURAL EXPERIMENT STATIONS.

TUMOR. See CANCER.

TUNIS. A French protectorate in North Africa lying between Algeria and Tripoli. Capital, Tunis, with 227,519 inhabitants. Total area, 167,400 square kilometers (64,600 square miles); population (1910): 1,706,830 indigenous Arabs, Berbers, Moors, etc.: 49,245 Jews, and about 149,000 Europeans. Population figures are estimates.

PRODUCTION, COMMERCE, ETC. In the mountainous regions are fertile valleys where grazing is carried on; in the lowlands agriculture is practiced and cereals, olives, vines, etc., are grown. In the table on page 728 are shown areas under main crops and yield for two years, with yield per hectare in 1911.

Livestock, December 31, 1911: 39,441 horses, 80,951 donkeys, 13,289 mules and hinnies, 110,707 camels, 191,450 cattle, 686,730 sheep, 468,828 goats, 17,898 swine. The mines yield coal, copper, lead, zinc, and iron.

The 1911 trade follows, with countries

	Hectares		Quintals		Qs.
	1911	1912	1911	1912	ha.
Wheat	..567,500	511,000	2,350,000	1,150,000	4.1
Barley	..482,900	446,000	2,900,000	1,050,000	6.0
Oats	 60,000	50,000	675,000	300,000	11.2
Corn	 20,000	20,000	69,000	81,947	3.4
Vines *	.. 15,761	17,427	454,700	250,000	28.8

* Yield in hectoliters of wine.

origin and destination, values in thousands of francs:

	Imports	Exports
France	69,288	73,575
United Kingdom	13,076	20,370
Algeria	12,011	5,967
Italy	5,234	17,366
Germany	2,892	3,233
United States	2,620	117
Belgium	2,015	7,244
Austria-Hungary	1,583	1,059
Switzerland	1,311	9
Turkey	1,098	118
Tripoli	1,085	1,949
Malta	246	1,284
Egypt	233	2,455
Netherland	167	3,355
Russia	23	303
Other countries	6,941	5,257
Total, 1911	121,685	143,661
Total, 1910	105,497	120,401

Leading exports in 1911—cereals, 46,184,000 francs; phosphates, 38,485,000; lead, 5,705,000; iron, 4,353,000; zinc ore, 4,127,000; esparto, 4,069,000; wine, 3,840,000; olive oil, 3,750,000; woolens, 3,643,000; animals, 3,625,000; fish, 3,168,000; skins, 2,758,000; sponges, 2,695,000.

Railways (1910) 1532 kilometers; extensions are projected. Telegraph lines, 4630 kilometers; wires, 16,004.

FINANCE AND GOVERNMENT. The 1911 budget estimated the revenue at 108,832,148 francs and the expenditure at 108,821,131.

By the treaty of 1881, French control over Tunis is to obtain until the local government is declared by both sides entirely capable of orderly administration. A French resident-general (since 1907, G. F. Alapetite) governs the country under the direction of the foreign office. The reigning bey (1912, Sidi-Mohammed en Nasser) receives an annuity of 940,000 francs; in addition, 750,000 francs are granted to the royal princes.

TUNNELS. Aside from the schemes for municipal subway systems (see RAPID TRANSIT) and the improvement of existing tunnels, but little important work was being undertaken by American railways during the year 1912. On the Pacific Coast active plans were under way still further to eliminate coal burning locomotives where possible and to substitute therefor electricity derived from hydro-electric stations in the mountains, or adjacent power plants. Important tunneling was being carried on in connection with the New York aqueduct (see AQUEDUCTS), especially its distribution system extending under the city of New York and this, both in size and length, represented work quite comparable with a railway structure. Two important pressure tunnels were completed during the year by the United States Reclamation Service. These were the Yama siphon under the Colorado River, 15 feet in diameter and 1000 feet in length, and the Strawberry tunnel in Utah, 19,200 feet in length. The LaSalle street tunnel under the Chicago River, at Chicago, was opened on July 21. This tunnel is composed of a double tube section of steel, lined with concrete, between bulkheads under the river. These sections were built in the dry dock and towed to position and then sunk and joined. The tunnel was for the Chicago railways. The contract for a subaqueous tunnel connecting Montreal with the south shore of the St. Lawrence and involving four miles of construction, including approaches, was let during the year to Sir John Jackson, Limited. The estimated cost was about $7,500,000.

JUNGFRAU TUNNEL. On February 21 the tunnel piercing the Mönch and terminating at Jungfraujoch was completed to a point 11,410 feet above sea evel. This point, which affords a station for the mountain railway to the summit of the Jungfrau, lies between the two great mountain peaks, the Jungfrau and Mönch, and is 4620 feet above Kleine Scheidegg, the starting point of the railway. The construction of the tunnel involved no serious difficulties and only once did the temperature fall below zero. The material traversed was hard gneiss for the most part with occasional layers of softer granite of a brownish color. In order to secure adequate ventilation and to discharge the spoil from the blasting, a side gallery leading to the southeastern slope of the Mönch at a height of about 11,000 feet was pierced about 1.4 miles from Eismeer station, which hitherto had been the end of the line. This side gallery affords a magnificent view of the mountain. The section from Eismeer to Jungfraujoch was scheduled for 18 minutes' running time and consists of both adhesion and rack railroad, the last 1550 feet before reaching Jungfrau station being operated as a rack road with a gradient of 25 per cent. At the Jungfraujoch station the tunnel was widened into a vast platform from which a shaft 82½ feet long leads to a waiting room with a restaurant and hotel accommodations, while a gallery about 330 feet in length, affords not only a grand view but access to the higher points of the mountains and opportunity for winter sport. No less than six Alpine peaks more than 13,000 feet in height can be reached from this point, which promises to become an important centre for mountain climbers.

The new tunnel through the Cote d'Or mountains in France being driven as a part of the cut-off on the main railway line from Paris to Italy by way of Lausanne, Switzerland, and the Simplon tunnel, received a notable check in its progress on December 23, when an underground river was pierced by the advance heading. The workmen barely escaped with their lives and the flow from the tunnel increased so rapidly that the rivers in the neighborhood were being swollen to a dangerous degree. It was thought at the end of the year that the tunnel might have to be abandoned unless the exhaustion of the source occurred.

The French minister of public works in December, 1912, approved a project for a tunnel between Thillet and Giromagny under the Ballon d'Alsace, a high mountain forming the southern spur of the Vosges, obviating the round-about route to the Est Railway between Epinal and Belfort, and not only shortening the line but developing the Vosges district.

ARTHUR'S PASS TUNNEL. This tunnel, 5¼ miles in length, was under construction through the Southern Alps range to afford access for a new line of the New Zealand government railway in the South Island. The new line will give connection between the east and west sections of the island which are separated by the mountain range and afford access to the coal lands in the province of Westland. Work on the tunnel was commenced in May, 1908, and was to be completed in four years, the contract price being about $3,000,000. The tunnel is at a height of 2400 feet above sea level or about 600 feet below the level of a pass crossing the mountains, and was being built for a single line track of 3½ feet gauge, the New Zealand government standard. It is 5 miles, 1660 feet long all on tangent with a 3 per cent. grade from the west end to the summit at the east portal. American methods and machinery were used in the excavation which, however, was being carried on by the English bottom heading system. Concrete blocks were being used for the lining on top of sidewalls of concrete. The tunnel is 16 feet, 9 inches in clear height above subgrade and has a maximum width of 15 feet.

TURCO-ITALIAN WAR. International Difficulties. At the beginning of 1912 it was announced that attempts of foreign powers to mediate between Italy and Turkey had all failed. In Italy this was attributed to the obstinacy of Turkey in holding out against the indispensable condition proposed by the Italian government, namely, Italy's absolute sovereignty in Tripoli and Cyrenaica. The German and Austrian press were blamed by Italy for the publication of false news of Turkish successes, which naturally had a marked effect on Turkish public sentiment. On January 17 France was stirred by the report of the seizure of the French mail boat, *Carthage*, and further anger was aroused by the seizure on the following day of another mail steamer, the *Manouba*. The former vessel was taken because it carried an aeroplane consigned to Tunis, which the Italians believed was intended for the use of the Turkish troops in Tripoli. The *Manouba* was stopped because it had on board 29 Turks whom the Italians believed to be army officers. The French government made inquiry into both affairs. As to the *Carthage*, it was released after five days, evidence having been given that the aeroplane would not be placed at the service of the belligerents. As to the *Manouba* affair, on January 26 the Italian government agreed to submit the status of the Turkish prisoners to a French commission of inquiry, which promptly authorized 27 of them to proceed to Tunis and Tripoli. One was seriously ill. One was regarded as doubtful, and not permitted to resume his journey. The questions of law involved in the case were referred to the Hague tribunal.

Engagements on Land.. Fighting was reported between the Italians and a mixed force of Turks and Arabs on January 18 at the Gargaresh oasis, where the Italians were building redoubts for the protection of the stone quarries. The Italians encountered a severe resistance from the enemy, but succeeded finally in driving them back. The Italian casualties were placed at 50. The loss of the Turks and Arabs was not reported. Some 400 Bedouins made a vigorous attack on a small fort at Bengazi on January 30, but were driven back by the garrison with considerable loss.

On March 3 a fierce attack on the Italian position near Derna was repulsed, and serious losses were inflicted on the enemy. Admiral Aubry, in command of the Mediterranean squadron, died suddenly on March 4, and was succeeded by Admiral Farrabelli.

On March 11 a force of Turks and Arabs attacked Tobruk, but were driven back by banner troops. The Italian losses were given as 12 soldiers and one officer killed, and three officers and 70 soldiers wounded. On the same day seven battalions of infantry with mountain and field batteries attacked a force of the enemy estimated at 6000, and according to Italian accounts inflicted a loss of 1000. The engagement occurred in the two oases that lie to the northeast of Fogat.

Naval Actions. On January 1 an Italian squadron engaged a Turkish naval force in the Red Sea and sank seven gunboats. The Italians later bombarded Hodeida. The war entered on a new phase toward the end of February when it was learned that two Italian warships had entered the port of Beirut, and receiving no answer to the demand for the surrender of the Turkish gunboat and torpedo boat, had fired upon them and sunk them. From the time of the action at Preveza at the beginning of the war in October, 1911, the Italians had abstained from activities in Turkish waters and the new turn of affairs was regarded with apprehension in Europe as likely to complicate the situation in the Balkans. On April 16 the powers again addressed the Porte on the subject of mediation. Two days later an Italian squadron of 20 torpedo craft, ironclads, and transports appeared in the Dardanelles and bombarded the forts in the neighborhood of Kun Kalek for a period of two hours, after which the fleet withdrew. On April 23 the Porte replied to the communication from the powers in respect to mediation that it could accept mediation only on the condition that the sovereign rights of Turkey should be maintained and that Tripoli should be evacuated by the Italians. To prevent further Italian depredations in the Dardanelles the Turkish government closed the Straits on April 19, but on May 1 the council of ministers, on the pressing demand of the powers, especially of Russia, decided to open them to navigation until further notice.

Seizure of the Ægean Islands. On May 4 the Italian forces occupied the island of Rhodes without opposition and captured the Turkish garrison. As a retaliatory measure, the council of ministers at Constantinople resolved on the expulsion of all Italian residents from the vilayet of Smyrna and its dependencies.

By the middle of June twelve of the Ægean islands had been occupied by Italy. Their inhabitants chose delegates to an assembly on the Island of Patmos at which an address was voted to the Italian government saying that the inhabitants desired union with Greece, but if that could not be accorded, they hoped that Italy and the European powers would accord autonomy to all the islands of the Ægean. The Italian press generally held the opinion that it was Italy's right to decide when the islands should be restored to Turkey and pointed out that when under Italian protectorate they had once tasted the blessings of western civilization they ought not to be placed again under the Turkish yoke. During June there were no military occurrences of importance, and the two powers seemed to be at a deadlock. Italy's seizure of the islands raised the question of the balance of power in the Mediterranean. The British government, taking note of the new posture of affairs, considered the question of strengthening the Mediterranean squadron, which had been diminished to supplement the naval forces in the Atlantic and the North Sea against Germany. The navies of Austria and Italy had greatly increased. The growing power of the Triple Alliance in the Mediterranean threatened to disturb the equilibrium and caused grave anxiety both in England and in France. Certain British journals even began to agitate for the turning of the *entente* between France and England into an offensive and defensive alliance. In July there was much discussion of a possible diplomatic solution of the question between Italy and Turkey, the long-protracted war having led to no decisive result.

PEACE NEGOTIATIONS AND THE END OF THE WAR. In the latter part of August officially recognized representatives of Italy and Turkey engaged in pourparlers for the restoration of peace. The meetings were held at Ouchy, Switzerland. The chief difficulty arose from Italy's decree of annexation (November 5, 1911) which Turkey was unwilling to accept. The Italian government, on the other hand, declared it could not recall its decision. Nevertheless it expressed its willingness to accept Turkey's mere recognition of the fact and to concede to the Sultan as the religious head of Islam a nominal and spiritual authority over the Moslems in Tripoli. It was understood from the beginning that Italy had no intention of exacting the payment of a war indemnity. The Italian envoys were the Hon. Pietro Bertolini, the Hon. Guido Fusinato, and Commander Giuseppe Volpi; the Turkish were Naby Bey and Fahr-ed-din Bey, who were afterwards joined by Reshid Pasha, the former ambassador to Rome. Finally the plenipotentiaries agreed on a formula that avoided the difficulty in regard to Turkish recognition of annexation. It provided for the autonomy of the provinces without requiring the express recognition by Turkey.

While the negotiations were pending the war in Tripoli was still going on and the prospects of peace were not definitely assured till the war in the Balkans made further Turkish resistance in the Tripolitaine hopeless. On July 8 the Italians captured the town of Misurata to the east of Tripoli, completely routing the enemy according to Italian official reports and suffering a loss of 9 killed and 121 wounded. On the night of July 18 a squadron of Italian torpedo-boats succeeded in penetrating into the Dardanelles though their position was revealed by searchlights and they were subjected to a heavy fire. After reconnoitring the straits they effected their escape, sustaining only slight damage. On September 17 fighting took place at Derna, where, after an eight-hour engagement, the Italians, according to their own report, defeated the enemy, inflicting a loss of 1000 killed and many wounded. Their own losses were placed at 61 killed and 113 wounded.

TREATY OF LAUSANNE. On October 15 on the receipt of the joint note from Bulgaria, Servia, and Greece, Turkey immediately agreed on the terms of peace, and on the evening of that day the plenipotentiaries at Ouchy signed the preliminaries. The terms were as follows:

1. Italy maintains absolutely the decree in which she declared her full sovereignty over Libya, *i. e.*, the Tripolitaine and Cyrenaica.

2. Italy does not require Turkey to recognize expressly the annexation—and thus transgress the letter of the Koran, which forbids the cession to the infidel of lands belonging to the Caliph.

3. Turkey engages to recall her troops, to cease supplying the Arabs with munitions of war and money. In return Italy offers pardon to all the Arabs who are willing to submit, though she will treat as rebels those who do not lay down their arms.

4. Italy engages to restore to Turkey the Ægean Islands occupied by her troops, but on the condition that a general amnesty shall be granted to their inhabitants, that local autonomy be respected, and that public liberty be guaranteed.

If Turkey fails to fulfill these conditions, Italy reserves to herself the right of taking action against her, and the islands are not to be restored until the agreement respecting them is loyally carried out.

5. Italy accepts a clause like that in the Austro-Hungarian treaty in regard to Bosnia-Herzegovina, recognizing the religious authority of the Caliph in the Tripolitaine, but expressly excluding any sort of political authority.

6. No war indemnity is required by either belligerent. Italy engages, however, to pay that portion of the Ottoman public debt which is guaranteed by the revenues of the Tripolitaine and Cyrenaica.

7. The diplomatic and commercial relations between the two countries shall be restored to the same status as before the war.

TURKEY. The TURKISH or OTTOMAN EMPIRE is an absolute monorchy, with possessions in southeastern Europe, southwestern Asia, and northeastern Africa (Egypt). Capital, Constantinople.

AREA AND POPULATION. At the end of 1912, with Tripoli definitely surrendered to Italy and much of her European territory occupied by the armies of the Balkan allies, it would be idle to attempt a calculation of Turkey's actual area and population. If, with the sanction of the great powers, the Balkan allies succeed in making good their threat to drive Turkey out of Europe, and Great Britain makes a protectorate of Egypt, the area of the empire will be less than 900,000 square miles and its population under eighteen millions. The table on the next page gives area in square kilometers, estimated population, and density per square kilometer, by vilayets and (six) mutessarifats (marked *) at the outbreak of the Balkan War and exclusive of Tripoli and Bengazi.

Total Turkey in Europe, 169,300 square kilometers (65,367 square miles) and 6,130,200 inhabitants; Asia Minor, 501,400 (193,591) and 9,089,200; Armenia and Kurdistan, 186,500 (72,008) and 2,470,900; Syria and Mesopotamia, 637,800 (246,255) and 4,288,600; Arabia, 441,100 (170,309) and 1,050,000. Asir, Nejd, and El Hasa and El Katr, in Arabia, are regarded as belonging to Turkey, but are inhabited by tribes whose subjection is merely nominal. Anatolia is another name for Asia Minor; the name Albania is given to an indeterminate

Turkey in Europe:	Sq. Kil.	Pop.	D.
Constantinople	3,900	1,203,000	308
Tchataldja *	1,900	600,000	32
Adrianople	38,400	1,028,200	27
Salonika	35,000	1,130,800	33
Monastir	28,500	849,000	29
Kossovo	32,900	1,038,100	31
Scutari	10,800	294,100	28
Janina	17,900	527,100	30
Asia Minor:			
Archipelago	6,900	322,300	47
Ismid *	8,100	222,700	27
Bigha *	6,600	129,500	20
Brussa	65,800	1,626,800	25
Smyrna	55,900	1,396,500	25
Konia	102,100	1,069,000	10
Adana	39,900	422,400	11
Angora	70,900	932,800	13
Kiastamuni	50,700	961,200	18
Sivas	62,100	1,057,500	17
Trebizond	32,400	948,500	29
Armenia and Kurdistan:			
Erzerum	49,700	645,700	13
Mamuret-ul-Aziz	32,900	575,200	17
Bitlis	27,100	398,700	15
Diarbekr	37,500	471,500	13
Van	39,300	379,800	9
Syria and Mesopotamia:			
Aleppo	86,600	995,800	11
Beirut	16,000	533,500	33
Lebanon *	3,100	200,000	65
Jerusalem *	17,100	341,600	20
Syria	95,900	719,500	8
Zor *	78,000	100,000	1
Bagdad	111,300	614,000	5
Mosul	91,000	351,200	4
Basra	138,800	433,000	3
Arabia:			
Hejaz	250,000	300,000	1
Yemen	191,100	750,000	4
Total empire	1,926,100†	23,028,900	12

* Mutessarifat. † 747,528 square miles.

area embracing the vilayets of Scutari and Janina with portions of Kossovo and Monastir; Macedonia comprehends the vilayet of Salonika, the eastern (and larger) part of Monastir, and southeastern Kossovo. The Turks are estimated to number about 11,000,000; Greeks, Arabs, Albanians, Bulgarians, Servians, Vlachs, Kurds, Armenians, Jews, Syrians, Circassians, and other races are scattered over the empire. Reliable population figures are unobtainable—the eleven million Turks being merely a guess. In a country so disorganized not much attention has been paid to the compilation of accurate statistics; foreign statisticians have attempted numerous calculations, which all disagree. Mohammedans form the majority of the population. Christians (Orthodox Greek) predominate in some districts, notably in Macedonia, and Gregorians in Armenia. There are also Roman Catholics, Jews, Nestorians, etc.

Public education, in the Western sense, is almost unknown, except in non-Moslem institutions, which are not as a rule interfered with. Moslem instruction, theoretically obligatory and in all cases free, is confined mainly to the reading of the Koran and is largely in the hands of the priests.

In the following list of principal cities a reliable authority is quoted for population figures. No accurate official census having been taken, they must be regarded as estimates. Population of Constantinople, 942,900 (1,200,000 with suburbs); of Salonika, 144,200; Adrianople, 123,000; Prisrend, 60,000; Monastir, 60,000; Serres, 32,000; Scutari (Albania), 30,000—all in Europe. Population of Damascus, 250,000; Smyrna, 250,000; Aleppo, 200,000; Beirut, 140,000; Bagdad, 125,000; Erzerum, 120,000; Jerusalem, 84,000; Brussa, 80,000; Mosul, 80,000; Sivas, 78,000; Mecca, 70,000; Basra, 60,000; Trebizond, 60,000; Adana, 50,000; Homs, 50,000.

Production. Following are the statistics of production (1910) in "29 provinces and districts": 44,845,000 quintals of wheat, 4,773,000 of rye, 29,005,000 of barley, 4,478,000 of oats, 11,246,000 of corn, 1,019,000 of rice. Cotton, tobacco, opium, and other crops are raised; olive oil, wool, and mohair are valuable exports; rugs are manufactured. There are rich mineral deposits which are not worked, and fertile tracts through which no railroads run. The labor problem is acute in Turkey.

Commerce. Trade statistics are incomplete. A reliable German source gives the following as the trade by countries of origin and destination for the year ended February 28, 1911, in thousands of pounds Turkish (£T1 = $4.40):

	Imps.	Exps.		Imps.	Exps.
U. K.	8,480	5,370	Rumania	1,070	529
Aus.-Hun.	7,663	2,194	Netherlands	822	334
France	3,930	4,403	Persia	691	446
Germany.	3,897	1,310	U. S.	648	1,009
Italy	3,649	1,480	Servia	463	304
Russia	2,798	912	Greece	250	382
Bulgaria.	2,003	797	Other	1,434	158
Brit. Ind.	1,937	255			
Belgium.	1,670	614	Totl	42,556	22,080
Egypt	1,164	1,584	1909-10.	33,283	18,199

In thousands of pounds Turkish are given import and export values for the year 1909-10, showing great classes: Agricultural and forest products, including animals, foodstuffs, and beverages, 12,388 imports and 7865 exports; textiles and raw materials. 12,012 and 5525; hides and leather, 936 and 779; machinery and vehicles, 782 and 6; paper and books, 683 and 54; stone, pottery, and glassware, 683 and 29; articles of luxury, 466 and 28; minerals, including petroleum, 2961 and 743; drugs, chemicals, etc., 1662 and 2435; rubber manufactures, 142 and 1; other merchandise, 567 and 732.

Vessels entered (1910) at the port of Constantinople, 20,268, of 19,153,951 tons, of which 11,684 steamers, of 18,554,116 tons; at Smyrna, 6655, of 2,477,733 tons, of which 2661 steamers, of 2,400,333 tons. The merchant marine included (1911) 120 steamers (66,878 tons) and 963 sailing (205,641).

Communications. Railways 1910: 1994 kilometers in European Turkey, 2372 in Asia Minor, 2294 in Syria and Arabia; a total of 6660 kilometers, or 4138 miles. Reported in 1912 to be 4230 miles, divided as to ownership as follows: Hejaz line (1000 miles), Turkish; Salonika-Constantinople (320), Smyrna-Kassaba (330), Syrian (370), Jaffa-Jerusalem (60)—all French lines; Salonika-Monastir (140), Anatolian (to Angora, 360; to Konia, 300; to Adabazar 50), Bagdad-Bulgurli-(130), Mersina-Adana (50)—all German; Oriental railways (800), Austro-German; Smyrna-Aidin (320), British. The line which runs from Smyrna via Aidin to Dinar had in hand the Egerdir extension, but it was reported that war had interfered with its progress. On the Bagdad Railway, the laying of rails for the section east of Aleppo began in February, 1912, and the section from Konia to Kishla, a distance of 150 miles, had been opened. Later this was extended ninety miles from Dorak to Marmoret, though between these sections there are twenty miles of very difficult work which was in progress. Previous to the outbreak of the war a line from Derven to Gidu was also in course of construction.

Telegraph lines (1910), 45,466 kilometers; wires, 76,738; stations, 1202. Post offices (1910-11), 929.

FINANCE. The 1912-13 budget is given below in detail:

Revenue	£T	Expenditure	£T
Direct taxes...	14,870,381	Public debt †..	14,709,937
Ind. taxes.....	5,692,728	War	8,948,705
Monopolies	3,621,373	Administrat.‡ .	4,166,053
Stamps, etc...	1,361,886	Justice, etc.‖..	1,690,104
Pensions	1,178,513	Pub. works....	1,217,521
Tribute *	893,877	Marine	1,276,000
Various	1,724,770	Posts & tels...	732,800
		For. affairs § ..	678,833
Total	30,514,159	Civil list......	505,880
		Sheikh-ul-Islam	19,170
		Total	34,590,561

* Egypt, Cyprus, Mount Athos, Samos. † And finance. ‡ Senate, Chamber, council, gendarmerie, court of accounts, etc. ‖ And worship and instruction. § And agriculture, mines, and forests.

The public debt stood, September 24, 1912, at £T118,745,378. The piaster, worth about 4.4 cents, is the unit of value, 100 piasters being equal to one pound Turkish.

ARMY. The Turkish army at the beginning of 1912 was organized on the basis of obligatory service, the divisions and terms of service being as follows:

Active army (nizam), 3-4 years; reserve (ikhtiat), 5-6 years; landwehr (redif), 9 years; and mustafiz (territorial reserve), 2 years. The reserve training was very perfunctory, but the redif formations were frequently called into service at times of domestic disorders. The numerical strength of the entire army either on a peace or war basis in 1912 would be more or less a matter of conjecture, but its organization and distribution at the beginning of the year are indicated below, while under MILITARY PROGRESS and TURKEY AND THE BALKAN PEOPLES, its activity and service are described.

The reorganization of the Turkish army under Izzet Pasha, which had begun in 1911, involved the adoption of the 33-battalion organization with three regiments and a machine-gun company to a division, three divisions (with corps troops) to an army corps, etc. There was also in process of formation a field army composed exclusively of nizam elements, with proper complements of fortress and coast-defense troops, and separate redif divisions were also planned, modeled upon those of the nizam army. This reorganization was still in progress in 1912 and was given the test of war, though in fact the theoretical organization and grouping were broken up even before the outbreak of actual hostilities in the Balkans. Both officers and recruits in many cases were new to their work in the nizam, while in the redif formations there was a lack of commissioned officers.

Class 1 of the redif consisted of men who had completed their time with the nizam and class 2 consisted of all troops not serving with the nizam, class 1 of the redif, or the mustafiz.

The total theoretical strength of the Turkish infantry was as follows: 79 nizam regiments of four battalions of four companies each; 20 separate chasseur battalions of four companies; 4 special chasseur battalions (on Bulgarian frontier), or a total of 340 battalions in the first line.

In the second line were 96 redif regiments, class 1, of four battalions each, or a total of 384 battalions. The projected strength of redif class 2 was: 172 regiments of four battalions each, or a total of 688 battalions. This class was reported as completed in Turkey in Europe at 40 regiments of four battalions each—a total of 160 battalions.

The Turks claimed a total war strength of infantry battalions as follows:

Special chasseurs, 26 officers, 800 men, 650 rifles. Nizam, 24 officers, 700 men, 650 rifles. Redif, 1st, 24 officers, 900 men, 850 rifles. Redif, 2d, 24 officers, 800 men, 750 rifles. Mustafiz, 8 to 15 officers, 400 to 600 men, 400 to 600 rifles.

The above would give a grand total of: Officers, 37,008; men, 1,222,200; rifles, 1,158,600.

The infantry was armed with the Mauser rifle as a rule (models 1887-1890), of which 1,120,000 were issued or in store, with 510,000 Martini-Henry rifles in reserve.

The Turkish cavalry consisted of the "Cavalry of the Guard"—one regiment ertogrul, two of hussars, and one of lancers, and 38 regiments nizam, all of 5 squadrons each, or 190 squadrons in all, and 12 regiments redif of 4 squadrons each, or 48 squadrons. The redif cavalry was attached to the first three army corps or "ordus." On a war basis a squadron would number 6 officers, 100 men, 80 horses (ertogrul, 140 men, 135 horses). The nizam cavalry was incorporated with the first six ordus, one division of three brigades of two regiments each being appointed to each ordu. The total war strength was 54 regiments (210 squadrons); 1580 officers, 26,800 men, 21,900 horses. The cavalry was armed with repeating carbines and sabers.

The Turkish artillery was all nizam, there being no second line.

Military reports current in 1912 gave the total strength of the artillery at 198 field-batteries (1188 guns), 18 horse-batteries (108 guns), 40 mountain batteries (240 guns), and 12 howitzer batteries (72 guns); total, 268 batteries (1608 guns). These were all of various Krupp types. The ammunition train counted 1254 wagons. On a war footing the strength of the artillery was 1032 officers and 29,380 men.

Technical troops were organized into battalions of railway and telegraph troops, sappers, and miners, etc.; in all 11 battalions ([illegible] companies), numbering 245 officers and 10,47[illegible] men. Other non-combatant troops as medical corps, military train, etc., were undergoing reorganization before the outbreak of the war. Colonel Brose, late of the information department of the German general staff, estimated the number available for war as 600,000 of all arms, and this estimate was considered liberal by military men. For other notes on the army of Turkey see MILITARY PROGRESS.

NAVY. No reliable figures can be quoted for the number and displacement of vessels composing the Turkish navy at the end of 1912, the exact damage sustained during the Balkan War being unascertainable. In April, 1912, Rear-Admiral H. P. Williams was succeeded

NICHOLAS I
King of Montenegro

FERDINAND I
Czar of the Bulgars

GEORGE I.
King of Greece

PETER KARAGEORGEVITCH
King of Servia

as naval adviser to the government by Rear-Admiral A. H. Limpus. The British foreign secretary has declared that British naval officers now in the service of Turkey will not be recalled so long as they refrain from active engagement in hostilities.

GOVERNMENT. Both temporal and spiritual authority rest with the sulten, who appoints a grand vizier to form a cabinet. A senate and a chamber of deputies constitute the legislative body. At the head of ecclesiastical affairs is the Sheikh-ul-Islam, under the direction of the sultan. Reigning sovereign (1912), Mohammed V., born 1844, brother of the deposed Abdul Hamid, whom he succeeded April 27, 1909.

In July, 1912, the minister of war, Mohammed Shevket Pasha, having been severely criticised for harsh measures in Albania, resigned; and with him resigned also the minister of marine. Unable to fill the vacancies, Saïd Pasha followed suit. Upon the refusal of Tewfik Pasha to head a new ministry, Ghazi Ahmed Mukhtar Pasha was prevailed upon to accept the post. On the twenty-ninth of October he resigned and the aged Kiamil Pasha became grand vizier. See below under *History*.

HISTORY

INTRODUCTION. The chief interest in Turkey during 1912 centred in the Balkan War and the events that led up to it and in the Turco-Italian War. These subjects are discussed under the titles of TURKEY AND THE BALKAN PEOPLES and TURCO-ITALIAN WAR. The present article deals only with the internal affairs of the empire.

DISSOLUTION OF PARLIAMENT. On December 30, 1911, as narrated in the last YEAR BOOK, the cabinet resigned on account of party differences, but a few days later (January 3, 1912) Saïd Pasha was reappointed premier and the cabinet was reconstituted with only a few changes. The point at issue was an amendment to the constitution which empowered the sultan to dissolve the Chamber in war time without the consent of the Senate. The opposition to the representatives of the committee of union and progress had steadily increased and before the end of 1911 a parliamentary coalition, under the name of the Union and Liberty party, had been formed against it. The new party regarded the proposed constitutional amendment as a manœuvre of the government to bring about the dissolution of Parliament and order the elections at a time advantageous to itself. The measure failed of the requisite two-thirds majority. Under the new cabinet it was reintroduced on January 13, but was again rejected. Parliament was dissolved nevertheless, the Senate giving its consent apparently for fear lest the government would otherwise secure the required majority by the creation of new senators. Thus terminated the first session of the Turkish Parliament under the constitutional régime (January 18).

THE ELECTIONS. The results of the elections, which became known in April, were a clean sweep for the committee of union and progress. Despite the severe criticism of the committee for its blunders and even crimes, the people took little interest. The government was accused of intimidation and of threatening officials with dismissal if they voted against it, of striking names of hostile voters off the registers, etc. Places known to be centres of opposition voted for the government nevertheless. Opposition papers were suppressed. Gerrymandering, suppression of free speech, etc., were common. But the chief reason for the victory was the fact that the committee of union and progress was organized and the opposition was not. The opposition was completely blotted out, while the committee of union and progress seemed stronger than ever.

The chief criticism of the committee of union and progress was directed against its course in the Hauran, in Yemen, and especially in Macedonia and Albania. It was blamed for its ruthless policy of Ottomanizing the empire, which had raised up enemies on all sides. Macedonia was declared to be in a worse condition than it had been in under Abdul Hamid. On the other hand, it was urged on behalf of the committee that under its administration the country had been allowed to develop, the army strengthened, the roads made secure, and the finances brought into some sort of order.

MACEDONIA AND ALBANIA. There were many signs of disturbance in Macedonia at the beginning of the year. At the close of 1911 the Bulgarian revolutionary body known as the "Internal Organization" was revived on the ground that conditions in Macedonia were as bad as they had been under the Hamidian régime. The massacre of Bulgarians at Ishtib in December, 1911, and the slowness of the authorities in bringing the culprits to justice led to savage reprisals. A similar outrage took place at Kotchana in August and again the authorities delayed in punishing the murderers. Almost at the same time another massacre was reported at Berane on the Montenegrin frontier. Meanwhile the long-threatened revolt in Albania had broken out in May and the government was further embarrassed by a mutiny of its own troops on June 22. Since these were among the events which led to the Balkan War they will be discussed further in the article on TURKEY AND THE BALKAN PEOPLES, paragraphs on *Macedonia* and *Albania*.

POLITICAL CRISES. The hostility between the Military League and the committee of union and progress continued. The announcement by the new ministry of its policy on July 30 responded to the demands of the league in promising to dissolve the recently elected Chamber. The hostility to the Young Turk party in certain quarters has been frequently mentioned in previous YEAR BOOKS. Their organ, the committee of union and progress, with headquarters at Salonika, had become the real, though secret source of all authority, the power behind the government. But the committee's power in turn rested on the army, whose officers during the past four years had, in spite of the government's efforts to prevent it, concerned themselves with political affairs. Dissensions developed in military circles and a group of officers opposed the minister of war, Mahmud Shevket Pasha, and prominent members of the committee. These attacks led finally to the resignation of the committee and of the minister of war. The occasion closely resembled the beginning of the revolution in 1908. Now, as then, there was a serious outbreak in Albania and a military mutiny in

Macedonia. It was soon found that the disaffection among the troops was not confined to Macedonia, but extended to other parts of the empire. The grounds of this discontent were not easy to determine. Some officers accused the authorities of leaving Tripoli without defense. The war minister, Mahmud Shevket Pasha, was blamed for arbitrary conduct. He resigned on July 9, giving as his reason that "having lately caused a law to be voted forbidding army officers to engage in politics, he judged it more expedient and wise to leave to another the task of applying that law." Little importance was attached to this declaration since military officers had constantly participated in political discussion and election contests for four years past. The only difference now was that they were against the policy of Mahmud Shevket instead of for it. This was followed by the fall of the Saïd ministry on July 17. Two days later the sultan addressed the army, reminding it of its oath of allegiance to the constitution. On July 22 a new cabinet was formed under Ghazi Muktar Pasha, a well-known general of the Russo-Turkish War, with Kiamil Pasha as foreign minister.

On August 5 the Muktar Pasha ministry pronounced the dissolution of the Chamber. Meanwhile the committee of union and progress had endeavored to organize a movement of resistance and for the moment there was fear of conflict, but the army did not support them, even the garrison of Salonika siding with the government. There was much dissension and the internal situation was very critical while the danger from outside gathered. The cabinet itself was divided, the majority demanding the dismissal of the committee of union and progress and the governors of the provinces, while the grand vizier and Hilmi Pasha opposed this and urged a conciliatory policy. The latter resigned, as did his opponent, Zia Pasha. Many partisans of the committee of union and progress were dismissed from office. Army officers were forbidden to take part in politics.

On October 29, Ghazi Muktar Pasha resigned and was succeeded on the following day by Kiamil Pasha, who for the fifth time formed a cabinet. He retained a number of the old ministers, including Nazim Pasha, minister of war.

THE BAGDAD RAILWAY. Work on the section of the Bagdad Railway eastward from Aleppo was begun on February 10. Negotiations between Turkey and Great Britain concerning the construction of the Persian section of the Bagdad Railway were discussed in March and it was arranged that they should be conducted in London. The main question was whether the British government should consent to the increase of the Turkish customs desired by the Turkish government. The purpose of the British government was to reach an understanding with Turkey as to the status of questions concerning the Persian Gulf. It was expected in 1912 that the rail head would reach Bagdad by 1918. On October 31 Sir Edward Grey announced in Parliament that the sections from Konia to Kishla and from Dorak to Mamouret were already open to traffic.

OTHER EVENTS. On July 10, 1911, Zeki Bey, chief secretary of the Public Debt Administration, was shot and killed. He had been an active journalist and foremost in attacking the policy of the committee party, and his murder was attributed to political reasons. In the latter part of May, 1912, the High Court of Constantinople sentenced to fifteen years' imprisonment at hard labor the two persons accused of the crime. On June 3 a fire broke out in Stamboul, destroying over a thousand houses and public buildings. On August 9 a disastrous earthquake occurred on the shores of the Dardanelles and the Sea of Marmora, destroying many towns and villages. The loss of life was estimated at 3000; some 6000 persons were injured, and 40,000 rendered homeless.

For other notes on Turkey, see ARBITRATION, INDUSTRIAL; EARTHQUAKES, and for recent books on Turkey, see LITERATURE, ENGLISH AND AMERICAN, *Travel and Contemporary History*.

TURKEY AND THE BALKAN PEOPLES. On September 30, 1912, came the news that Bulgaria, Servia, Montenegro, and Greece were mobilizing their troops with great rapidity and that unless the great powers took strong measures to prevent it war was inevitable. Some crisis of this sort in the Balkans had been predicted on the outbreak of the Turco-Italian War and signs of its approach were manifest in the summer and early autumn months. A review of the situation will be given here. For supplementary information, see TURCO-ITALIAN WAR, TURKEY, GREECE, CRETE, BULGARIA, AUSTRIA-HUNGARY, and MILITARY PROGRESS.

The immediate causes of the c isis were the Albanian revolt and the irregular fighting in Macedonia and Thessaly and on the borders of Servia, Bulgaria, and Montenegro. But since conditions in Macedonia and Albania had been for many years preparing for this event, it is necessary to review them briefly. The following paragraphs outline the course of events in these parts of the empire down to the final outbreak of war in October, 1912.

MACEDONIAN REFORMS. Macedonia was ceded by Turkey to Bulgaria in 1878 pursuant to the treaty of San Stefano, but the Congress of Berlin in the same year revised this treaty and through the insistence of Great Britain and Austria restored the province to Turkey. In Article XXIII. of the treaty of Berlin, however, the signatory powers bound themselves to establish an organic law providing for good government in Macedonia and to see that it was applied. During the thirty-four years that followed this promise was unfulfilled, despite the frequent complaints of the Christian peoples—Bulgars, Greeks, and Serbs—of Turkish misgovernment and atrocities. It was only when the Balkan states constituted themselves protectors of Macedonia and threatened war against Turkey that the powers began to act in the matter. At the end of 1902 Austria and Russia, in view of the increasing disorder in Macedonia, demanded of Turkey a moderate plan of reform, while they urged Servia, Bulgaria, and Greece to observe patience and self-restraint. With an inspector-general appointed by the sultan were associated two civil agents, one a Russian and the other an Austrian. This was the first measure of reform. Europe was at least represented in the Macedonian administration. The other powers, especially France and England, next obliged the Porte to accept other foreign agents with special functions—namely, four financial advisers and thirty-six officers whose duty it was to reorganize the Ottoman gendarmerie in Macedonia. Thus Bu-

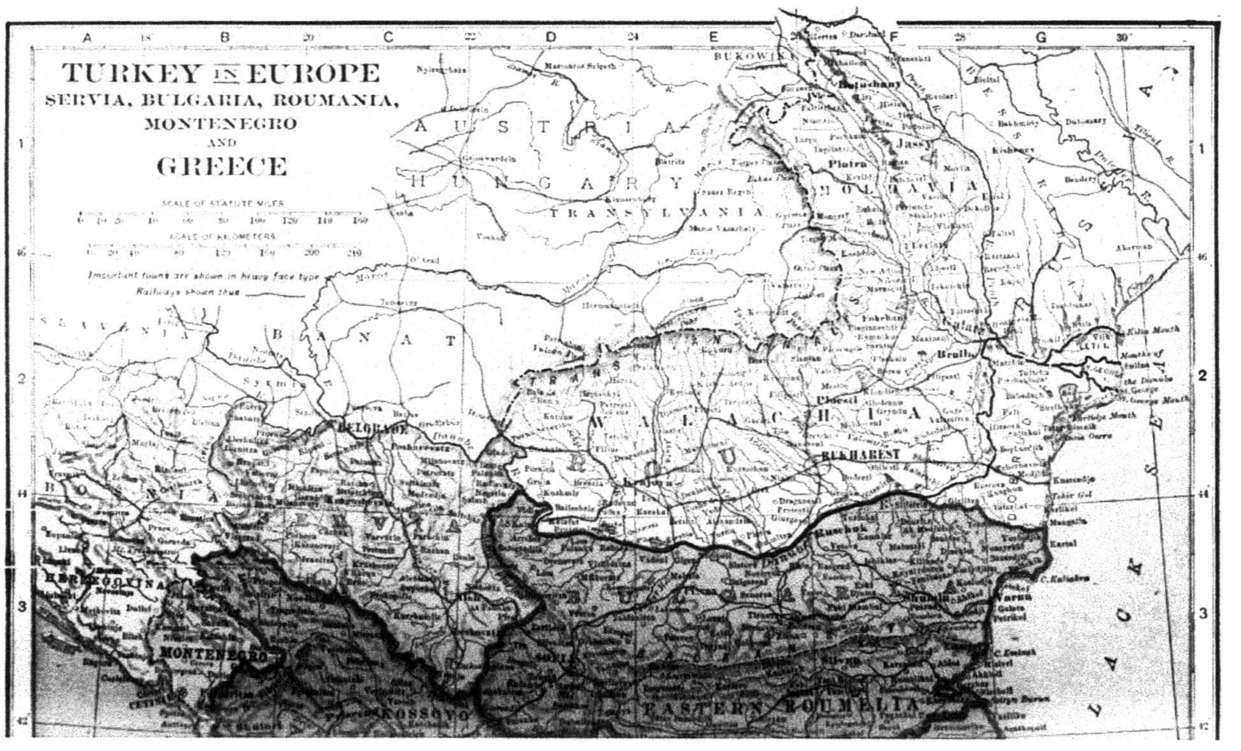

TURKEY IN EUROPE
SERVIA, BULGARIA, ROUMANIA,
MONTENEGRO
AND
GREECE
SCALE OF STATUTE MILES
SCALE OF KILOMETERS
Important towns are shown in heavy face type
Railways shown thus
AUSTRIA
HUNGARY
TRANSYLVANIA
BUKOWINA
MOLDAVIA
WALACHIA
BANAT
SLAVONIA
BOSNIA
HERZEGOVINA
MONTENEGRO
SERVIA
BULGARIA
EASTERN ROUMELIA
KOSSOVO
DOBRUDJA
BLACK SEA
BELGRADE
BUKHAREST
Jassy
Piatra
Braila
Ploesti
Ruschuk
Varna
Shumla
Kilia Mouth
St. George Mouth
C. Kaliakra
C. Emineh
Danube

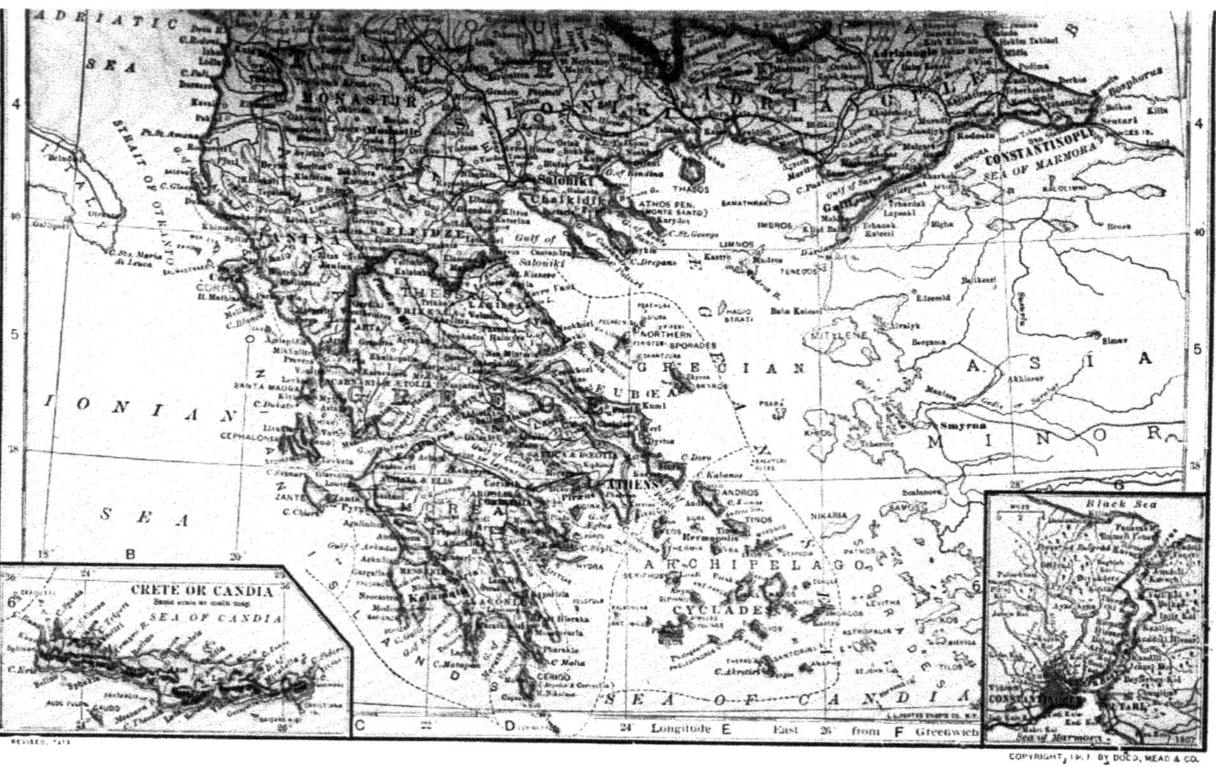
ADRIATIC SEA
IONIAN SEA
STRAIT OF OTRANTO
ITALY
MONASTIR
SALONIKI
ADRIANOPLE
CONSTANTINOPLE
SEA OF MARMORA
Bosphorus
Saloniki
Chalkidike
ATHOS PEN.
THASOS
SAMATHRAKI
IMBROS
LIMNOS
TENEDOS
Gulf of Saloniki
THESSALY
JANINA
CORFU
SANTA MAURA
CEPHALONIA
ZANTE
ARTA
EUBŒA
NORTHERN SPORADES
GRECIAN ARCHIPELAGO
ATHENS
ATTICA & BŒOTIA
MOREA
ACHAIA & ELIS
ARGOLIS & CORINTH
CYCLADES
ANDROS
TINOS
NIKARIA
SAMOS
KOS
MITYLENE
KHIOS
Smyrna
ASIA MINOR
Gulf of Arkadia
Kalamata
C. Matapan
CERIGO
C. Malia
HYDRA
SEA OF CANDIA
CRETE OR CANDIA
Same scale as main map
SEA OF CANDIA
C. Krio
C. Sidero
GAUDO
Black Sea
Sea of Marmora
B
C
D
E
F
Longitude East from Greenwich
15°
20°
22
24
26
28°
4
5
6
38
40
36
REVISED, 1913

ropean powers gained the right of supervision in the three important departments of the gendarmerie, the finances, and the civil administration, but the system was incomplete and there was little harmony between the powers. Germany wished to meddle as little as possible with the administration of a Turkish province. England, on the other hand, supported by Russia, wished to go further, following the logic of the situation. It was argued that there could not be a reform of the gendarmerie without a reform of justice, that financial reforms called for administrative reforms, etc. Accordingly, in 1907 the British ministry proposed a new plan, including the reorganization of justice under the direction of European agents, and King Edward VII. and the czar met at Reval with their respective foreign ministers and agreed on a thorough programme of reforms.

MACEDONIA UNDER THE YOUNG TURKS. Then came the Young Turk revolution of 1908, which, having the principles of equality and liberty before the law as its basis, promised to bring about the reforms of itself. The European powers believed in the good faith of the Young Turks and in their ability to remove the Macedonian abuses. This confidence was shared by the subject races of Macedonia themselves. Bands of Bulgars, Serbs, and Greeks laid down their arms and fraternized with the Turks. But these hopes were short-lived. It soon became evident that the Young Turk revolution was directed not only against the tyranny of the Hamidian régime, but against its feeble foreign policy, which permitted the powers to interfere in the internal affairs of the empire. The revolution aimed at nationalization and centralization quite as much as at liberalism. It has been said in fact that the meeting at Reval itself was the immediate occasion of the revolution, so averse were the Young Turks to foreign intervention in Macedonia.

The elections immediately following the revolution proved that the Young Turks had no intention of carrying out the policy of equality for the different races and confessions. The programme of the committee of union and progress pronounced Turkish the official language and declared that education must be uniform for all citizens. The policy of "Turkification" was made clear from the first. Still, it was hoped that eventually matters would mend, and the powers agreed to the request of the new government that they give up their policy of reform. The Christians of Macedonia continued loyal to the revolutionary movement and on the attempted counter-revolution in 1909 they were among the first to march on Constaninople. After the fall of Abdul Hamid and the accession of Mohammed V. the way was open to the reconciliation of the alien races in the empire, but the Young Turk party did not improve the opportunity. On the contrary they insisted rigidly on that policy of centralization and assimilation which has kept the empire in a state of ferment during the last four years. While requiring Christians to serve in the army they excluded them from civil functions. The disarmament of the Christian population was the occasion of worse atrocities than in the time of Abdul Hamid. Many concealed their weapons and armed bands began to appear in the country as before. The Christians were further incensed by the policy of planting Moslem colonies in Macedonia, with a view to readjusting the balance of the population in favor of the Turks. The constitutional privileges accorded to the subject races were curtailed. Public meetings were forbidden. The constitutional clubs were suppressed. The effect of this was to drive the malcontents to the use of lawless methods. The execution of native chieftains who had returned to their homes, relying upon the promise of amnesty, added to the discontent. At the end of the first year under the new régime conditions in Macedonia were said to be nearly as bad as they were under Abdul Hamid. In general, the discontent in Macedonia, as elsewhere, arose from the efforts of the Young Turks to efface national distinctions and abolish local privileges, pursuant to their policy of Ottomanizing the empire. In Macedonia, where race feelings are strong, this had the effect of driving the people into secret rebellion. Lawless bands infested the country. Political assassinations were common. The repressive measures of the Turks served only to bring new recruits to the outlaws. The Bulgarian "Internal Organization" was revived in the autumn of 1911 and continued its revolutionary activities during 1912. Its aim was Macedonian autonomy through international intervention. Among the various features of Turkish misrule as reported in the press during the last three years are the following: The suppression of the political liberties promised by the new régime; the disarmament of the natives in 1910 in circumstances of great brutality; the inhuman extension of the punishment for brigandage to the families and friends of the insurgents; the harrying of the country by lawless bands under the auspices of the committee; the colonizing of Christian districts by Moslem immigrants; and the violent or corrupt methods employed in the last election of April, 1912. (See TURKEY, *History*.) A very significant effect of these mistakes was to draw the nationalities together in a common hatred of the Turks. From 1902 to 1908 the Serb, Bulgar, and Greek bands were as likely to massacre one another as to massacre Turks. Now they laid aside their rivalries. By the close of 1910 the Bulgars and Greeks in Macedonia who had long been the bitterest and most active in their hostility became fully reconciled, and this was followed by close and friendly relations between the governments of Bulgaria and Greece. During 1912 events occurred which further angered the Balkan states and drew them together in a common policy against Turkey.

THE KOTCHANA MASSACRE. While crowds were gathered in the market-place of Kotchana in August a bomb was suddenly exploded and another explosion followed within fifteen minutes. Attributing the outrage to the Bulgars the Turks attacked and killed a large number of them and arrested many more. The incident greatly excited the Bulgars on both sides of the frontier and there were many popular demonstrations on behalf of immediate war with Turkey for the liberation of Macedonia from the Turk. The Bulgars asserted that the bomb-throwers were not of their race and accused the Turks of having instigated the crime. An official investigation was at once begun. According to some accounts of the affair, the bomb explosions were followed immediately by a rush of 200 Turkish troops from the garrison who fired into the crowd, and then fell upon them, bayoneting them or clubbing them to death. Later the soldiers went to the houses of Bulgars and arrested all whom they could find. The official inquiry established the guilt of several officers, many of the garrison troops, and some of the civil officials. Orders were given that the accused should be tried by court-martial. The authorities, however, did not bring any of the guilty persons to justice and their delay greatly intensified ill-feeling in Bulgaria, where the memory of the massacre of Ishtib in December, 1911, was still fresh. See TURKEY, *History*.

At about the same time as the Kotchana atrocity, a massacre of Christians by Turkish soldiers was reported at Berane on the Montenegrin frontier.

THE ALBANIAN DIFFICULTY. Similar results followed the government's treatment of the Albanians, who had been the hereditary allies of Turkey and her main support in the Balkan peninsula. On four occasions they rose in revolt. The uprisings of 1910 and 1911 were not put down till armies of 60,000 to 70,000 took the field. The Albanians were incensed by the government requirements that the Arabic should be used instead of the Latin alphabet and still more by the flogging of some of their chiefs at the time of the disarmament in 1910. For their loyalty to the sultan they had long enjoyed the right of bearing arms. The attempt to deprive them of it caused them to revolt and the excesses of the Turkish soldiery under Torgut Pasha left them in a vengeful temper. In the campaigns of 1911 Montenegrin irregulars fought on the side of the Albanians against the Turks. The policy of the government brought about a reconcilation between the Albanians of the north with both Montenegrins and Serbs.

The influence of Montenegro in northern Albania continued to be paramount. It was said that King Nicholas resorted to every means to retain his influence over the Malissori and that Montenegrin agents were active throughout northern Albania. In Macedonia the Bulgarians and Greeks formed a compact to join forces in the coming elections against the Young Turk party. The long expected disturbances began to assume serious character in the latter part of May, 1912. There had already been signs of insurrection and as these grew more serious the Turkish forces were increased to thirty battalions in northern Albania. In the latter part of May the Albanian demands were set forth in a memorandum to the great powers and to the Turkish authorities. They included the fixing of the boundaries of Albania, the recognition of its flag, the appointment of a governor-general from the old ruling family of Albania, the appointment of Albanians in place of the Turkish-speaking officials, the adoption of Albanian as the official language, and the guarantee of these reforms by the great powers. Early in August the Albanians submitted their programme of reform to the Turkish government. It included: A special system of administration of justice; Albanian military service in time of peace to be confined to the European vilayets; civil functionaries to employ the national language; the establishment of agricultural schools; an increased number of schools for science and religion; the teaching of the several languages in the schools; road-making and railway building; the unrestricted right to create private schools; the impeachment of the Hakki Pasha and Said Pasha cabinets; a general amnesty and restitution of arms. It was announced soon afterwards that the government accepted this programme except as it regarded the impeachment of ministers and the restoration of arms. On the latter point they offered as a compromise to arm the people on the frontiers and the shepherds and forest workers. The government dispatched a mission to inquire into the Albanian grievances. It was announced on August 20 that the Albanian chiefs, assembled at Prishtina, had accepted the government's terms, that the malcontents were returning to their homes, and that the country was virtually pacified. In the early part of September, however, fighting with the Malissori was reported and both that tribe and the Mirdites were said to be preparing for a general uprising.

MUTINY IN ALBANIA. On June 25 came the news of the mutiny of the officers and men in a battalion of the 49th Regiment at Monastir. Reports of disaffection among the troops of the Monastir army corps had been circulated for some time past, and this was attributed largely to growing hostility to the régime of the committee of union and progress. The deserters, seizing such ammunition and supplies as they could find, repaired to the hills near the spot where four years before the revolt of a small body of soldiers against the Hamidian despotism had marked the beginning of the Young Turk revolution. Simultaneously with this news came the report of a new outbreak in western Albania, where the Malissori had again taken up arms. Within a few days additional desertions were announced and it became evident that the disaffection had spread widely among the troops. Dispatches were censored, but the demands of the mutineers were said to include the resignation of the ministry, the cessation of the committee's interference with the executive, and the impeachment of certain members of the cabinet. The government hurried a large body of reinforcements into the region, but did not proceed vigorously against the mutineers. On July 9 the experienced and able minister of war, Mahmud Shevket Pasha, resigned from the cabinet. This was followed on July 17 by the resignation of the grand vizier, Saïd Pasha, and the entire cabinet, in spite of a nearly unanimous vote of confidence from the Chamber two days before. See TURKEY, *History*.

INTERNATIONAL ASPECTS. Behind the immediate issues between Turkey and her Christian populations and their natural protectors, the Balkan states, was the play of greater European forces, arising from racial and national ambitions. On the one hand was the Pan-Slavist movement, and Russia's dream of a union of the Balkan Slavs with Greece, which would give her access to the southeastern ports. On the other, was Austria's desire to preserve the *status quo*, which was attributed to her hope of eventually gaining more Slav territory to be united with her own Slavic dominions. Count Berchtold, who succeeded Count Von Aehrenthal as foreign minister in February, 1912, began at once to work for peace on a basis favorable on the whole to Turkey. He proposed that the war between Italy and Turkey should cease on the understanding that while Italy should retain the occupied territory in

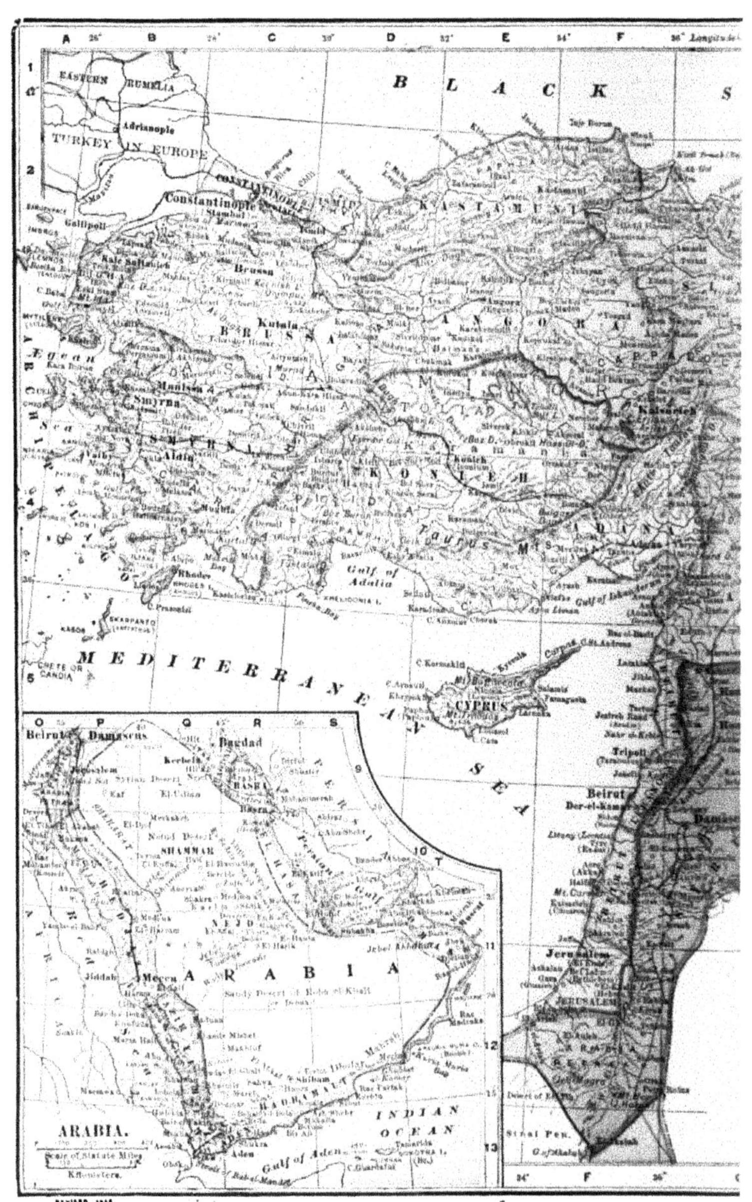

REVISED, 1916

Caucasus Mountains
Caspian Sea
Tiflis
Baku
Tabriz
Erzerum
Bitlis
Van
Urumiah
Diarbekir
Urfa
Aleppo
Mosul
Kerkuk
Kermanshah
Bagdad
Kerbela
Basra
PERSIA
TURKEY IN ASIA.
Capital of Empire
Capitals of Vilayets
Ruins
Railroads
Ancient names ... PAMPHYLIA
Scale of Statute Miles
Kilometers
THE MATTHEWS-NORTHRUP WORKS, BUFFALO, N.Y.
Longitude East from Greenwich

north Africa, Turkey was to be in a stronger position than ever in Europe and the Levant. Turkey, which was passing through a political crisis, did not accept this solution and it provoked resentment in the Balkans, where it was regarded as too much in the Ottoman interest, and in Greece, where the fear of a return of the twelve Ægean Islands to Turkey caused public demonstrations in protest. Russia on this occasion showed her sympathy with Italy. Nethertheless there were signs of improved relations between Russia and Austria-Hungary early in the year, and the new Russian foreign minister, M. Sazonoff, in a speech in the Duma in April, declared the two governments agreed on the following principles: The maintenance of the *status quo* in the Balkans, the independence and peaceful development of the Balkan states, and the support of the new régime in Turkey. In August Count Berchtold endeavored to unite the European governments in a policy that should secure peace and the maintenance of the *status quo* in the Balkans. He invited the powers to coöperate in encouraging the Ottoman government in a policy of moderate decentralization along racial lines and to try and win the Balkan peoples to acquiescence, without, however, going so far as actual intervention. His specific proposal was for a court of arbitration consisting of three representatives of the powers and two of Turkey to decide the points at issue between the latter and the Balkan kingdoms, and that meanwhile a plan for "progressive decentralization" should be carried out in Macedonia and Albania. This was taken as indicating Austria's intention of taking the initiative in Balkan affairs and was regarded with suspicion by the Balkan states and with apprehension by the Turks. The latter declared it a step toward dismemberment. The powers accepted it provisionally, but awaited an explanation of what was meant by "progressive decentralization." In Russia there was much talk of Austria's intrigues to have Turkey support her policy of Slav expansion. Russians favored a policy of strengthening the Balkan states at the expense of Turkey, while Austria aimed at keeping them overawed by maintaining the Ottoman power.

THE BALKAN ALLIANCE. The Turco-Italian War offered an opportunity of taking Turkey at a disadvantage. From the beginning of that war the danger of concerted action on the part of the Balkan states against Turkey had been imminent. It was enhanced by the Albanian revolts in 1911 and 1912, which not only further drained the resources of the Ottoman government, but by their final success in wresting from it the desired reforms spurred on the Balkan powers to demand a new system for Macedonia. In addition to all this was the exasperation caused by the accounts of the Turkish massacres of Christians—at Ishtib in 1911, at Berane, Kotchana, and elsewhere in 1912. Nevertheless peace was expected till the last moment because it seemed incredible that the great powers could not, if they seriously united in the attempt, prevent the war. It was clear that they could do so if they once made it evident that they stood ready to back up their demands by force. But mutual distrust and jealousy made that course impossible. The aims of Austria and Russia were too far apart to admit of a union of the powers in such direct coercive action as would prevent the war. Therefore they merely threatened. The Balkan states realized this weakness, and paid no attention to the threats. A definite understanding was reached in February by the governments of Bulgaria, Servia, Greece, and Montenegro. Owing, it is said, largely to the statesmanship of M. Venezelos, the Greek premier, jealousies and conflicting interests were not permitted to divide the states or keep them from their central purpose. An alliance was formed to free the men of their religion and race from Turkish rule and to press on to the overthrow and dismemberment of Turkey in Europe. The events mentioned above in Macedonia and Albania during the year angered the people of the Balkan states and held their governments together.

Greece, Bulgaria, and Servia naturally sympathized with the men of their race in Macedonia. In Bulgaria, where public opinion was greatly agitated by the report of the Kotchana massacre, a mass meeting was held at Philippopolis on August 21 and the immediate liberation of Macedonia demanded. In Montenegro the war feeling was aroused by the repeated conflicts between Turks and Montenegrins on the border. As stated in the preceding YEAR BOOK, Montenegro sympathized with the Albanian rebels. Many of the latter had found refuge within her borders and the Turks complained of the frequent attacks by Montenegrins on the border. As to Servia, one of the many incidents that angered the people was the massacre of Christians, mostly Serbs, by Musulmans in the town of Senitza in Novibazar in July. Novibazar, having been evacuated by Austria under the terms of her annexation of Bosnia-Herzegovina, was left a prey to Turkish raids. As to Greece, reports of Turkish atrocities in Thessaly stirred the popular wrath.

THE BEGINNING OF THE WAR. On September 30 Bulgaria ordered the mobilization of her troops, raising the strength to about 400,000 men. Mobilization orders were issued at the same time by Servia, Montenegro, and Greece. Turkey retorted immediately by a similar order of mobilization. The neutral powers at once began to bring pressure on both sides to prevent hostilities, but without avail. The four Balkan states had determined to act together and to insist on taking advantage of Turkey's distressed internal condition and her war with Italy and secure an autonomous government for Macedonia pursuant to article XXIII. of the Berlin Treaty. To this Turkey was unalterably opposed. It was seen from the first that unless the neutral powers proceeded to the extreme of using force they could not bring about a plan for settlement. The immediate cause of war, as alleged by the Bulgarian government to the powers, was the threatening attitude of Turkey on the frontier. The Turks had ordered manœuvres of their troops in the neighborhood of Adrianople, and when the ambassadors of the powers protested the Turkish government replied that the manœuvres were of annual occurrence and in no wise a threat against Bulgaria. In the case of Servia it was the detention by the Turks at Salonika and Uskub of ammunition destined for the Servians. Meanwhile conferences had taken place between Count Berchtold and the German chancellor at Buchlau, September 8; between M. Sazonoff and Sir Edward Grey later in the month, and finally between M. Sazonoff and the French premier, M. Poincaré. At the instance of M. Poincaré it was proposed that Russia and Austria should act as mandatories of the powers in the Balkan capitals and that the powers should act collectively at Constantinople. This was accepted. On October 8 the Austro-Hungarian and Russian ministers delivered a joint note to the Balkan states declaring that the powers would energetically reprove any measures tending to break the peace, that they would proceed on the basis of article XXIII. of the Treaty of Berlin and undertake to realize the reforms in the administration of Turkey in Europe, but that these reforms would not violate the integrity of the Ottoman empire or the sovereignty of the sultan; that if war should break out they "would not permit at the end of the conflict any modification of the territorial *status quo* in European Turkey." This came too late. On the same day Montenegro formally declared war, and on the following morning (October 9) the Montenegrin army began the war with an attack on the Turkish position at Podgoritza. After a four hours' artillery engagement the Turks evacuated the heights and the Montenegrins then advanced to attack them in their fortified position at Detchich. On October 9 King Nicholas of Montenegro issued a proclamation summoning his people to a "holy war" in which they would have the sympathy of the civilized world, of the Serb people, and of the Slav race, and the loyal support of Bulgaria, Servia, and Greece. He called on them to come to the aid of their brothers in Old Servia, where men and women were being massacred by the Mussulmans. Meanwhile the Turkish government had submitted a plan of reform for Macedonia, but it was regarded by the Balkan states as altogether inadequate. On October 13 Bulgaria, Servia, and Greece dispatched an identical note to Turkey requiring the establishment of Macedonian autonomy under European governors within six months. The autonomy was to be complete and would exclude the Porte from all control of the administration. Upon receipt of the note Turkey immediately recalled her representatives from their respective capitals. Another consequence was the signing of the preliminary peace with Italy on October 15. (See TURCO-ITALIAN WAR.) Regarding this note as an ultimatum, Turkey announced to the powers on October 16 that it had severed diplomatic relations with the three governments. The latter thereupon issued their declaration of war (October 17). Estimates of the available strength of the respective states on the eve of the war differed widely. According to some authorities they were as follows: Turkey, 500,000; Bulgaria, 400,000; Servia, 150,000; Greece, 80,000; Montenegro, 50,000. Toward the close of the year the following estimate was published: Turkey, 400,000; Bulgaria, 300,000; Servia, 200,000; Greece, 150,000; Montenegro, 40,000.

THE WAR IN OCTOBER. Within less than three weeks from the beginning of the war the four armies of the Balkan allies had crossed their respective frontiers, advanced into Macedonia, driving the Turks before them, captured Prishtina and Kumanovo, routed the Turks at Kirk-Kilisse, invested Adrianople, and rolled back the main body of the Turkish army in the direction of the Tchatalja forts, the last main line of defenses on the way to Constantinople. A little later in the three days' battle of Lule-Burgas (October 28-30) the Bulgarians gained a decisive victory over the Turks, who were now forced to retire behind the Tchatalja defenses. The first act of the war occurred on October 9, and by the end of the month the allies had practically possessed themselves of Macedonia and the Bulgarians were holding the main Turkish force behind a fortified line within fifty miles of Constantinople, and seemed in a fair way to force that position and enter the city itself. This extraordinary and rapid success caused the greatest surprise in Europe, where the press had for years overestimated the military strength of Turkey and belittled that of the Balkan states. The following outline presents the movements a little more in detail.

GENERAL PLAN OF CAMPAIGN. The military plans of the four Balkan powers seem to have been well coördinated and directed to a common purpose. The chief objective of the Montenegrin campaign was Scutari. The Servians aimed at overthrowing the Turkish forces in Macedonia in coöperation with the Montenegrins in the west and the Greeks in the south and then to dispatch a force to seize a port at Durazzo on the Adriatic. The Greek attack was directed to the capture of Salonika. The Bulgarians, whose forces were the strongest, were to perform the chief task of overwhelming the Turks in Thrace and pushing them back to Constantinople. Thus the Turks were attacked at the same time in four separate regions and were unable to concentrate and act on the offensive. Their commander-in-chief was Nazim Pasha, who was appointed on October 3. It was soon seen that in the face of the vigorous and rapid assault of the Balkan armies the Turkish military organization had fallen into a deplorable state of inefficiency and unreadiness.

THE MONTENEGRIN CAMPAIGN. The Montenegrin forces were divided into three armies, one to operate against Berane, the other two having for their objective, Scutari. On October 9 they entered Albania on the northwest. The northern army, constituting the left wing, occupied Berane on October 16, rapidly took possession of several other places in the sandjak of Novi Bazar, and then captured Ipek and Djakova. The main force reduced Detchitch and Tuzi, and on October 26 began the investment of Scutari. Meanwhile they had found the Turks in a strong position at Tarabosh, which they bombarded and several times attempted to storm, losing considerable numbers. They were unable to accomplish the main purpose of capturing Scutari, which was still holding out when hostilities were suspended on December 3. At that time, however, they were occupying San Giovanni di Medua on the Adriatic, which was one of the important objects of their campaign.

THE SERVIAN OPERATIONS. The commander-in-chief of the Servian forces was General Putnik. The first and strongest Servian army formed the centre and was commanded by the crown prince. The second, constituting the left wing and including the Bulgarian contingent, was under the command of General Stepanovitch. The Turkish troops in Macedonia were commanded by Zekki Pasha. The Servians began active operations on October 18, when the centre, under the crown prince, crossed the frontier near Vrania and advanced along the road to Uskub. This and Kumanovo were its

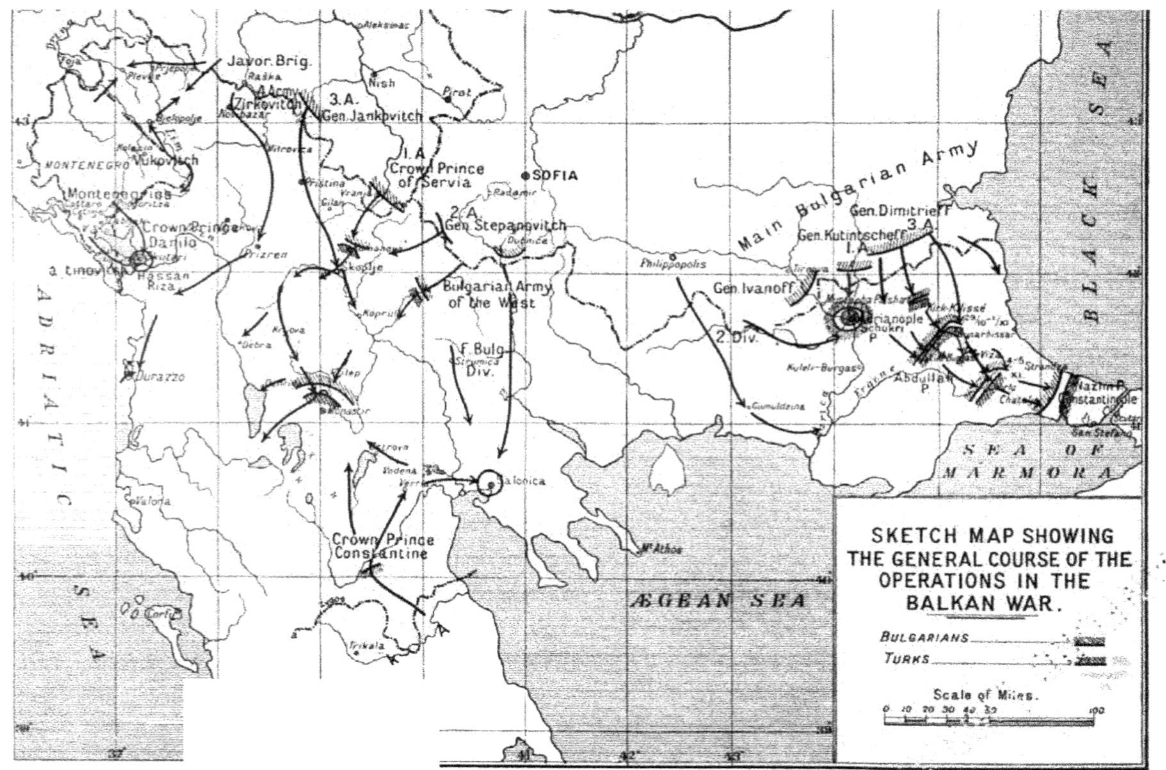
SKETCH MAP SHOWING THE GENERAL COURSE OF THE OPERATIONS IN THE BALKAN WAR.
BULGARIANS
TURKS
Scale of Miles.
BLACK SEA
SEA OF MARMORA
ÆGEAN SEA
ADRIATIC SEA
Main Bulgarian Army
Gen. Dimitrieff
3.A.
Gen. Kutintscheff
I.A.
Gen. Ivanoff
2. Div.
Philippopolis
Kuleli-Burgas
Abdullah P.
Nazim P.
Constantinople
San Stefano
SOFIA
2.A.
Gen. Stepanovitch
Dubnica
Bulgarian Army of the West
F. Bulg. Div.
I.A.
Crown Prince of Servia
3.A.
Gen. Jankovitch
Nish
Pirot
Javor. Brig.
Zirkovitch
Montenegro
Vukovitch
Crown Prince Danilo
Hassan Riza
Prizren
Durazzo
Valona
Crown Prince Constantine
Salonica
Trikala
Corfu

objectives. The left wing was to operate against Uskub by way of Egri-Palanka, while to the west of the first, or main body, was a force of 32,000 men which was to operate in the plain of Kossovo. The last named, under General Yankovich, captured Prishtina on October 22 and Novi Bazar on the following day. The fighting at the latter place was severe. The Turkish forces under Zekki Bey, whose numbers were variously reported at from 30,000 to 80,000, were employed against the main Servian army. But though they fought desperately they were unable to check the advance. In a severe engagement which lasted some 60 hours they were defeated at Kumanovo with an estimated loss of 5000, and fled in disorder. A second defeat followed on the road between Kumanovo and Uskub and again the retreat became a rout, the Turks abandoning a large quantity of ammunition and many guns, and leaving their dead and wounded on the field. On October 26 the Servians entered Uskub in triumph. Many of the Turks scattered in panic, but the main body withdrew toward Monastir. On October 27, the Servians, after driving the Turks back with heavy losses from Kotchana and Ishtib, captured Kuprulu. The Turks came to a stand in a narrow defile of the mountains between Kuprulu and Perlepe, whence the Servians tried to dislodge them on November 3. This was accomplished, but only after a long battle, in which the Servians suffered heavily. Meanwhile, one portion of their army had been dispatched in the direction of Scutari to coöperate with the Montenegrins, another toward the coast at Durazzo, and the third to join the Greeks in the neighborhood of Salonika. But the main body advanced to Monastir, which, after two days of desperate fighting, was captured on November 18. The last important success of the Servians was the capture of Durazzo on November 28. The victorious advent of Servia on the Adriatic coast gave rise to international complications noted in a paragraph below.

THE BULGARIAN CAMPAIGN. The brunt of the war fell on Bulgaria, whose army was by far the strongest and was known to be well equipped and trained. For years past, preparations had been made for such an emergency and in 1912 General Savoff, the organizer of the Bulgarian forces, had announced that they were completely ready for war and were able to defeat the Turks. The war strength of Bulgaria was estimated at 330,000 men. Bulgaria had completed her organization while radical changes in the Turkish military system were still going on. At the beginning of October Turkey had discharged her time-expired men and filled their places with new men, many of whom were Christians. Bulgaria had kept with the colors some of the time-expired men for the ostensible purpose of participating in the manœuvres. Turkey, moreover, was greatly hampered by the scattering of her forces and could count on little help from the troops in Asia, not only on account of the distances to be covered, but because the Greeks controlled the situation at sea, being ready to intercept transports from Asia Minor or the Islands. After Montenegro declared war, Bulgaria mobilized her infantry in five days. Owing to the lack of horses the artillery and supply trains were delayed until the eleventh day. A few days later their position was, according to the military authorities, as follows: Chief grouping, 8 active divisions, 5 reserve brigades, and one cavalry division, all constituting the army of the Maritza and concentrated in the zone Tirnovo-Seimen-Stara-Zagora on both sides of the Maritza, comprising in all 225,000 men; secondary grouping, about 75,000 men which, with the addition of 2 active Servian divisions, formed the army of Kustendil. On the declaration of war (October 17), the Bulgarian forces immediately crossed the frontier in three corps. Mustapha Pasha was captured on October 19. One body then proceeded eastward by rail toward Adrianople. The generals in command of the three Bulgarian armies were General Kutincheff, General Ivanoff, and General Dimitrieff. The commander-in-chief of the Turkish army was Nazim Pasha, while directly in command of the third corps and engaged in the fighting around Kirk Kilisse was Mahmud Mukhtar Pasha.

THE BATTLE OF KIRK KILISSE. The attacks on the Turkish positions in the neighborhood of Adrianople began on October 22. The accounts of the battle are conflicting. Owing to the extreme severity of the censorship, the correspondents had small chance of reporting the military operations, and few of them were permitted to ascertain what was going on. It appears, however, that on October 23 there was heavy fighting all along the line. Several of the fortified positions were carried by bayonet charges and a counter-attack of the Turks to the northeast was repulsed with heavy loss. On the night of October 23 the Bulgarians captured several positions in the north and mounted artillery on the heights. On the following morning, October 24, they began to bombard Kirk Kilisse, which was soon in flames. At the same time the infantry advanced along the battle front and by 10 o'clock the Bulgarians had forced their way into the town, whence, after an hour's fierce street fighting, the enemy was driven out with a considerable loss and in some disorder.

According to Lieutenant Hermenegild Wagner, the special correspondent of the Vienna *Reichspost*, in his volume *With the Victorious Bulgarians*, about 1500 Turks were taken prisoners at Kirk Kilisse. He places the total strength of the Turks in the battle at about 70,000 men, of whom, however, a large number were either in action only for a short time or took no part in the fighting.

LULE BURGAS. The operations of the Bulgarian armies were now directed to cutting off the retreat of the Turks, but the latter in the course of some severe fighting effected a change of front. The Turkish left wing was withdrawn to Lule Burgas, under the command of Abdullah Pasha. On October 29 began the sanguinary battle of Lule Burgas-Bunar Hissar, the chief battle of the war, which extended along a front of about 22 miles. During the engagement reserves were brought up by General Kutincheff from Adrianople. Three attacks on the Turkish centre were repulsed and the position was only carried after a hand-to-hand conflict. The Bulgarian generals did not restrain the ardor of the troops, and movements, especially infantry charges, involving great sacrifices of life were carried out with remarkable heroism. The losses on each side were very heavy. The Turks were ill-supplied with food and ammunition and suffered also from defective leadership. The well-directed Bulgarian artillery fire wrought havoc among them. At last they began to retreat, but without panic, and the fighting did not actually cease till November 2. The strength of the Turkish army was placed at 150,000. The estimates of their loss in killed and wounded vary from 25,000 to 40,000 and in prisoners from 2000 to 2800. A rough estimate placed the loss of the Bulgarians at 15,000.

The Turks now fell back on Tchorlu and a little later withdrew behind the Tchatalja lines. The investment of Adrianople was now complete. Leaving some 20,000 reservists there and taking all the troops available, the Bulgarians advanced against the Tchatalja forts, the last line in defense of Constantinople, hoping to carry it and reach the city. On November 12 they began the attack, but the Turks successfully stood their ground. To carry the strong defenses involved heavy loss, and it was hoped that the cholera, which had broken out among the Turks, would lead them to surrender. The Turks opened negotiations for an armistice on November 13, and operations were suspended, but when the allies presented their terms on November 20, they were at once rejected. On November 25, however, a meeting was arranged between General Savoff of the Bulgarians and Nazim Pasha, the Turkish commander-in-chief and minister of war, and three days later the negotiations were definitely resumed at Tchatalja between General Savoff, Dr. Daneff, and King Ferdinand's private secretary on the one hand, and Nazim Pasha and two members of his cabinet on the other. Finally, on December 3, a protocol was signed for an armistice which was to last until the end of the peace negotiations.

Mr. Ellis Ashmead Bartlett, who accompanied the Turkish army and published an account of his experiences in a volume entitled *With the Turks in Thrace*, declared, in common with many others, that the responsibility for the disaster should not be laid on the Turkish soldier. He says:

"The responsibility rests solely on the administrative classes and high officials, who, eaten up with pride and self-confidence, and regarding all the Balkan states with the utmost contempt, believed the Turkish army to be invincible. The army was caught utterly unprepared for war, and the military authorities remained blind in their belief that mere numbers set forth on paper and published broadcast in the press would win the day against an army smaller in numbers, but which had been carefully organizing and preparing for war for twenty-five years."

"It is impossible for me to describe severely enough the utter state of chaos, mess, muddle, and make-believe, which exists throughout all branches of the army. Had the Turkish soldier been supplied with even one biscuit a day he might have held his ground against the invader, and I am convinced that he has been defeated more by sheer starvation than by any other single factor."

"Looking back to the great tragedy, it is almost impossible to understand how the wretched private soldier existed for three days without a scrap of food, without shelter, and yet covered himself with glory. The most splendid material has been sacrificed on the altar of stupidity, conceit, self-satisfaction, and the grossest ineptitude."

GREEK CAMPAIGN. On the eve of the war, Greece seems to have concentrated the main body of her forces, 56 battalions, in the region of Larissa and the remainder in the region of Arta. Immediately after the declaration of war on October 17, the main body under the crown prince advanced with the ultimate object of reaching Salonika while the smaller army began to move from Arta against the Turks at Janina. The Turkish forces under Hassan Tahsi, withdrew before the advance of the crown prince, and on October 20 the Greeks captured Elassona without much opposition. They won a decisive victory over the Turks at Selfidje on October 23. After capturing a number of other towns in the region and defeating a Turkish force of considerable strength, which was sent to attack their rear, they advanced at the end of October on Monastir and Salonika. On November 1 the column marching on Salonika was temporarily repulsed, but soon recovered its lost ground and forced its way on. The condition of the Turks in the defense of Salonika was deplorable and they were unable to offer effective resistance. After a two-days' investment the town was surrendered on November 8. The number of the Greeks was placed at about 60,000 and of the Turks at about 25,000. The capture of Salonika was hailed with enthusiasm throughout all Greece as the recovery of the ancient heritage of Hellas after Ottoman domination for 470 years. The officer immediately in command of the Greek army at Salonika was General Kleomenes. A Bulgarian division and a Servian regiment entered Salonika on November 9 and there were rumors of jealousies among the allies. It was reported, in fact, that the Greek commander-in-chief objected to the entry of the Bulgarians and that the Bulgarian government had overcome this opposition only by firm insistence. There were again signs of discord between Greece and the other allies when the armistice of December 3 was announced. Greece rejected the terms of the armistice and continued operations on land and sea, but without important results. Greek troops had been landed on the Island of Lemnos on October 21.

INTERNATIONAL ASPECTS OF THE WAR. Meanwhile, the European powers had continued their effortsl for peace. M. Poincaré, whose first proposa for joint action on the part of Russia and Austria-Hungary has been noted above, offered another proposal early in November to the effect that the powers should pledge themselves to "territorial disinterestedness," but this did not meet with favor among the members of the Triple Alliance, of whom Austria-Hungary occasioned the chief apprehension. Her government had several times announced its purpose of taking all the necessary steps to protect its own vital interests. It was known to be hostile to any movement that would bring Servia to the Adriatic or, by imposing a barrier of Slavic states, cut Austria off from the road to Salonika. Toward the end of November Sir Edward Grey proposed that representatives of the respective powers should be authorized to confer on the Balkan question at one of the European capitals. This was accepted and London was designated as the place for the conference. Soon after the appearance of the Bulgarians before the Tchatalja lines, Turkey had asked the powers to mediate and had received a reply that no terms unacceptable to all the belligerents would be forced upon them. There was a suspension of hostilities during the exchange of views between Turkey and the allies concerning the terms of

Photograph, Underwood and Underwood, N. Y.

THE BALKAN-TURKISH PEACE PLENIPOTENTIARIES WHO WERE ENTERTAINED AT STAFFORD HOUSE, LONDON, ENGLAND JUST BEFORE THE CONFERENCE

Seated left to right: M. VENEZELOS (Greece), ANDRA NIKOLICS (Servia), STOYAN NOVAKOVITCH (Servia), M. MIJOUSKOVITCH (Montenegro), DR. DANEFF (Bulgaria), M. MADJAROFF, Bulgaria), MUSTAPHA RESHAD PASHA (Turkey), LIEUT.-COL. POPOVITCH (Montenegro), DR. MILERKO VISNITCH (Servia). On the left of the centre row, M. SCOULOUDIS (Greece). Second Man in centre row on left: LORD HALDANE (The Lord Chancellor). Centre of centre row: M. GENNADIUS (Greece). Next man is SIR EDWARD GREY, then MRS. ASQUITH on the left of her husband, MR. ASQUITH (English Premier), who stands on the extreme right of the centre row

an armistice, but the conditions required by the allies were too severe and hostilities were accordingly renewed. Then came the armistice of December 3, declaring hostilities suspended in order that negotiations for peace might go on.

PEACE NEGOTIATIONS. The original demand of the allies included the withdrawal of Turkish troops from Tchatalja, the surrender of Adrianople, and practically the abandonment of the Turkish domain in Europe. The peace conference in London began on December 16, after some delay on account of the unwillingness of Turkey to treat with the Greek representatives while their government was not a party to the armistice. The regular discussion of the terms of peace began on December 23. Meanwhile, the exchange of views between the representatives of the foreign powers in London as proposed by Sir Edward Grey was going on, and the outcome of these informal conferences was announced on December 20 to be the recommendation of the ambassadors to their governments of the acceptance of the principle of Albanian autonomy and of a guarantee to Servia of commercial access to the Adriatic. The agreement of the powers on these two important points quieted the apprehension that had long prevailed as to the danger of a general European war. But the delegates to the peace conference could not agree. The allies demanded terms which Turkey regarded as too humiliating. They included the surrender of all Turkey in Europe except a small strip in the neighborhood of Constantinople. Turkey proposed, on the other hand, the retention of the province of Adrianople and the Ægean Islands, and of her sovereignty over Macedonia and Albania, which were to be autonomous provinces; and the withdrawal of the Cretan question from the discussion as it involved only Turkey and the great powers. At the close of the year there seemed little prospect of a settlement. The principal figures in the negotiations for peace were Dr. Daneff, the president of the Bulgarian Sobranje, and M. Venezelos, the premier of Greece. The head of the delegation from Turkey was Mustafa Reshid Pasha.

The Austro-Servian difficulty mentioned above arose from Servia's insistence on her right to retain Durazzo and a small strip of the adjacent Albanian coast and from her objection to the autonomy of Albania. Austria-Hungary's opposition to the access of Servia to the Adriatic finally took the form of actual preparations of war. Before the armistice she had begun the mobilization of her troops throughout the empire. The menacing attitude of Austria-Hungary led to a series of declarations by the powers which indicated an alignment of the two great groups, namely, the Triple Entente and the Triple Alliance, on the question, and led to fears of a general European war. On November 9, the British premier, Mr. Asquith, declared that public opinion in his country was unanimously opposed to a policy that should rob the victors of their spoils. Later in the same month, the German chancellor declared that if the other members of the Triple Alliance were attacked by a third power while they were maintaining their interests, Germany would take their part. On December 6 the French premier declared that France would stand by her allies and her friendships. The official announcement of the representatives of the powers in London on December 20 of the acceptance in principle of the Albanian autonomy and of the commercial access of Servia to the Adriatic, quieted the fears of a European war and public opinion was reassured by the report before the close of the year that Austria-Hungary and Servia had come to an agreement whereby the latter was to have access to the Adriatic but was to recognize Albanian autonomy.

TURKS AND CAICOS ISLANDS. British islands of the West Indies, dependent upon Jamaica (169 sq. miles, 5615 inhabitants), census of 1911). Grand Turk is the principal island and the government seat. Imports (1910), £27,916; exports, £24,461; revenue, £8645; expenditure, £6827; shipping entered and cleared, 280,735 tons. Commissioner (1912), F. H. Watkins.

TUSKEGEE NORMAL AND INDUSTRIAL INSTITUTE. An institution for the industrial and higher education of negroes, at Tuskegee, Ala., founded in 1881. The number of students enrolled in the various departments of the institute in the autumn of 1912 was 1645. The faculty numbered 181. There were no noteworthy changes in the faculty during the year and no notable benefactions were received. The productive funds of the institute at the close of the year 1911 amounted to $1,859,015, and the income for the year 1911-12 was $75,963. There were about 45,000 volumes in the library. President, Booker T. Washington, LL. D.

TUTTLE'S COMET. See ASTRONOMY.

TYPHOID FEVER. See INSECTS AND THE PROPAGATION OF DISEASE, and SANITATION.

TYPHOID FEVER. Several recent outbreaks of typhoid fever have been traced to "carriers," one of which, showing at what distances these people may operate in disseminating infection, may be cited. Bolduan and Noble, of the New York City health department, while searching for the cause of an apparently unexplainable epidemic of typhoid which appeared in certain districts of the city, finally narrowed the source down to the milk supply. On tracing the source of infection back through the wholesale dealer to the shipping station in the country, it was found that the infected milk came from Camden, N. Y. The former manager of the creamery there had typhoid fever at the time of inspection, but judging from the date of onset he was apparently one of the victims of the infection and not the cause of it. There had also recently been a case of typhoid fever on the dairy farm of X., one of the three local milk dealers of the village, but not a patron of the creamery. Further inquiry showed that there had been an undue prevalence of typhoid fever in Camden for years; in fact, it was called by several physicians "Camden fever" and believed not to be typhoid fever at all. It is estimated that the number of cases of typhoid in the village had not averaged less than fourteen or fifteen each year, which is at the rate of fifty or sixty per 10,000 of population. The rate for New York City during this time ranged from six to ten per 10,000. A tabulation of all the cases occurring in the village in 1908 and 1909, twenty-seven in number, showed that twenty received milk from Dairy X. Investigation of the dairy and home of Dairyman X. showed both to be exceptionally clean and well kept. This man had come to Camden in 1866, a year or two after he had recovered from typhoid. Several cases of illness had occurred in his own family or employees during the succeeding years, all of them believed to have been typhoid fever. Examination of his excreta gave an almost pure culture of typhoid bacilli. This dairyman had been selling most of his milk in Camden, but a few quarts a day were added to a neighbor's supply, which was shipped to New York, and thus started what would doubtless have been a serious epidemic had not the facts been discovered and the infected milk cut off.

The value of the Widal test in detecting typhoid carriers is not fully agreed upon. Bigelow states that most carriers may be detected by an examination of the blood after this method, and cites a number of instances where it proved serviceable. One case is cited to show that the excreta may be apparently free from bacilli and yet react positively to the Widal test. In the family of a man dead from typhoid several other cases occurred. In this same family was a man who had had an attack of typhoid eighteen months previously, followed by necrosis and abscess formation about the sternum. In spite of an operation a year previously, he still had two small pus-discharging sinuses over the sternum leading down to the bone bare of periosteum. His blood gave a positive Widal reaction. On three different examinations his urine and feces were found negative for typhoid bacilli, but the pus from the sinuses over the sternum was positive on each of these occasions.

Prophylactic vaccination against typhoid has now been practiced long enough to enable us to estimate the duration and degree of immunity conferred by this measure. From the rich experience of the British army in India, Colonel Firth concludes that immunity begins to diminish in about two and one-half years after inoculation. His tables also show that even after four and five years, the maximum period of observation, the rate per thousand among the inoculated is, roughly speaking, only one-fourth that of unprotected troops. It is known that the immunity is not absolute, for in 1911, among 80,000 persons vaccinated in the United States army, there were twelve cases of typhoid with one death, and in 1910 there occurred six cases among the vaccinated, with no fatalities. Had it not been for the prophylactic immunization there would have occurred, at the prevailing rates of incidence, about 250 cases. The fact that the immunity is not absolute is no objection to the use of vaccine, but is rather an argument for its repetition at intervals to be determined in the future as the lessons of experience become clear, just as we now do in the case of smallpox. It is the present practice to revaccinate against both smallpox and typhoid at the beginning of each three-year period of enlistment. The failure to secure absolute protection in these few cases may be due to inefficiency of the vaccine, to exposure of the patient to exceptionally large quantities of infectious material, or inability of the individual to respond to immunization with the usual antibodies; and this failure can best be interpreted as a personal idiosyncrasy.

TYRAMINE. Tyramine is para-hydroxy-phenyl-ethyl-amine hydrochloride ($OH.C_6H_4.CH_2.CH_2.NH_2.HCL$), the hydrochloride of the para-hydroxy-phenyl-ethyl-amine ($OH.C_6H_4.CH_2.CH_2.NH_2$), obtained synthetically. The base para-hydroxy-phenyl-amine was first isolated by Barger from ergot and also prepared synthetically by him by the reduction of para-hydroxy-acetonitrile with sodium in alcoholic solution. It is chemically and physiologically related to epinephrine. Tyramine is a white crystalline powder, easily soluble in water, forming a neutral solution. Taken internally or injected subcutaneously, tyramine increases the blood pressure; for this reason it can be used in shock or collapse; it is also claimed to be valuable for producing post-partum contraction of the uterus. It is useless as a local hemostatic. The action is similar to epinephrin, being weaker and slower, but lasting longer. It is given subcutaneously.

UGANDA PROTECTORATE. A British possession in east Africa (estimated, 117,681 sq. miles, exclusive of lake area) made up of five provinces—Rudolph, Eastern, Northern, Western, and Buganda. Population, between two and three millions. Neither area nor population can be accurately stated, no survey having been completed and no complete census taken. Mengo is the native, Entebbe the British capital. Malaria, spirillum fever, dengue fever, and sleeping sickness are prevalent, and the country is not suited for European habitation.

	1907-8	1908-9	1909-10	1910-11
Imports *	£371,567	£419,303	£403,400	£549,153
Exports *	178,608	174,413	225,258	340,326a
Revenue	111,883	102,572	165,145	287,094
Expenditure ...	195,528	256,337	240,241	276,157

* Including transit.

a £306,609 exclusive of re-exports. Export of ginned cotton, £120,664; unginned, £44,748; ivory, £35,674; hides, £20,544; skins, £26,691; chillies, £30,-492; rubber, £13,559.

The so-called Uganda Railway lies entirely in the East Africa Protectorate. In 1911 the line from Jinja to Kakindu (over 54 miles) was completed. The king of Uganda is Daudi Chua (born August 8, 1896); regent, Sir Apolo Kagwa. Governor and commander-in-chief, F. J. Jackson.

ULSTER MOVEMENT. See GREAT BRITAIN, *History*.

ULTRA-VIOLET LIGHT. See PHYSICS.

UNDERWOOD, OSCAR W. See PRESIDENTIAL CAMPAIGN.

UNEMPLOYMENT. Since the industrial depression of 1907-8 an unusual amount of attention has been given to the problem of unemployment in the United States and western Europe. This problem arises from the existence of considerable numbers of able-bodied and efficient workers who, although often on the verge of poverty, can find no remunerative work. The various policies for solving this problem include vocational training and guidance on a comprehensive, if not universal, scale; the distribution of the construction work of cities, towns, and States so as to dovetail with the fluctuations of private industry; the better organization and regularizing of such seasonable trades as clothing manufacture, millinery, dressmaking, and mining; efforts at the decasualization of those trades where the demand for labor is intermittent, as in freight handling in maritime ports; various forms of employment insurance; and a better distribtuion of population and industries, especially all policies for the relief of city congestion.

In the United States there have been passed in Indiana, Missouri, Massachusetts, Michigan, and Montana laws establishing and regulating public employment bureaus. Numerous other States have enacted legislation regulating private employment agencies with the view to eliminating their exploitation of the unemployed. The National Employment Exchange was organized in New York City in 1909 as a private but non-profit making bureau for locating men in mercantile and manual work. Though it has succeeded in placing some thousands of men, its experience indicates that the problem of unemployment in the great cities is exceedingly difficult. This is largely owing to the fact that the demand for labor declines in the winter at the very time that detached laborers from the surrounding country are gravitating toward the metropolis.

GREAT BRITAIN. The problem has been unusually acute in the British Isles in recent years. The cities have endeavored to meet the situation by providing public work on parks and highways. This, however, was very inadequate. The government therefore began the establishment in 1910 of exchanges throughout the entire country. Early in 1912 the number of these exchanges approximated 250 in ten districts of Great Britain and one district in Ireland. All local offices are connected with a central district office by telephone and telegraph and the district offices are similarly connected with the central office in London.

This system of labor exchanges is to be supplemented by a comprehensive scheme of insurance against unemployment. This insurance programme has been begun by provision for unemployment insurance in the engineering trades. See WORKINGMEN'S INSURANCE.

In their intensive study of unemployment in the city of York, England, Messrs. Rowntree and Lasker showed the close relation of this problem to the lack of vocational training and to "dead-end" or "blind-alley" trades. They insisted, therefore, on vocational training and guidance. They found in the irregular and casual workers men who had been neglected or unfitted for industry in their youth. Their programme for reform included the following: Better training for youths; regulation of work of public bodies; afforestation; decasualization of labor; insurance; and decentralization of town population.

LIVERPOOL DOCK LABORERS. One of the most trying problems connected with the alleviation of unemployment grows out of the economic conditions of the casual worker. For many years the status of the Liverpool dock workers has been studied from this point of view. In recent years more than 27,000 dock laborers have been available where not more than 16,000 could hope to find work on any one day. An important step in the decasualization of this labor was made during the summer when a new clearing house system was established. This plan does away with the nearly 100 booths where laborers have been hired daily and substitutes clearing houses in definite areas. All clearing houses communicate with the central office. Men are required to register at these clearing houses. The plan is expected to reduce the influx of destitute and undesirable workers and to distribute uniformly the available work among the much reduced suppy of workers. The expenses of these clearing houses are borne by the Board of Trade, the work being done by officials of the government labor exchanges. The machinery thus established also serves as a more convenient means of paying wages and as a means of arranging for the payment of the compulsory weekly contributions under the national insurance act. It was only by some system of registration that casual workers could be brought under that scheme. Through misunderstanding the introduction of the plan precipitated a short strike, although the dockers' union officials were favorable to the system.

THE INTERNATIONAL COMMITTEE ON UNEMPLOYMENT met in Zurich, Switzerland, in September. Seventeen countries, including all the principal countries of Europe and the United States, were represented. Topics of discussion included the preparation of schedules and methods for uniform and scientific collection of facts in regard to employment; public works in their relation to unemployment; emigration and immigration. The American delegates presented plans for the formation of an American section of the International Association on Unemployment. The next congress of this association will meet in Ghent in 1913.

INSURANCE. The belief steadily gains ground that some form of insurance is necessary to prevent the evil social consequences of unemployment. Various plans are now in operation. The British trade unions generally and the American unions in some instances pay out-of-work benefits. The chief objection to this plan is that no provision is made for the great mass of unorganized laborers who have smaller economic resources and are therefore more likely to suffer poverty and degradation from periods of unemployment. The cities of the Continent have developed two plans of public municipal insurance. One of these involves the payment from the public treasury of a subsidy to unions paying unemployment benefits. The other provides for an insurance fund to which any citizen may contribute stated amounts for a minimum number of weeks and receive out-of-work benefit for a proportionate time. The city usually subsidizes such a fund. A similar fund is sometimes created and operated by a voluntary citizens' organization. In Germany, where these forms of municipal insurance against unemployment have been widely developed, there is a strong demand for a comprehensive and compulsory system as a part of the imperial plans for workingmen's insurance. For the British plan see WORKINGMEN'S INSURANCE.

UNIFORM LAWS. UNITED STATES COMMISSION ON. See CHILD LABOR.

UNION COLLEGE. An institution of higher learning at Schenectady, N. Y., founded in 1795. The enrollment in all departments of the college in the autumn of 1912 was 338. The faculty numbered 32. There were no noteworthy changes in the faculty during the year and no important benefactions were received. The productive funds at the end of the collegiate year 1911-12 amounted to $843,730, and the approximate income from all sources was $42,200. The library contains about 40,000 volumes. President, C. Richmond, D. D.

UNION PACIFIC RAILWAY. See TRUSTS.

UNION PACIFIC-SOUTHERN PACIFIC MERGER. See TRUSTS.

UNITARIANS. The distinctive feature of this denomination is the acceptance and adoption of the principles of freedom and progress in religious thought. The American Unitarian

Association is the administrative body of the church. Its headquarters are in Boston. According to statistics gathered by Dr. H. K. Carroll, the Unitarians in 1912 numbered 70,542 communicants, 476 churches, and 527 ministers. The denomination is active in distributing its literature and in organizing conferences for the promulgation of Unitarian thought. It has considerable strength in Great Britain, where there are 375 ministers and 370 congregations. The divinity schools are at Cambridge, Mass.; Meadville, Pa., and Berkeley, Cal. Missionary work is carried on at many points among Icelandic, Norwegian, and Swedish immigrants of the United States. Among the more important publications are the *Christian Register*, published in Boston; the *Unitarian Advance*, published in New York, and the *Pacific Unitarian*, published in San Francisco. The president of the American Unitarian Association is the Rev. Samuel A. Eliot and the secretary the Rev. Lewis G. Wilson.

UNITED KINGDOM. See GREAT BRITAIN.

UNITED PRESBYTERIAN CHURCH OF NORTH AMERICA. This denomination was formed in 1853 by a union of associate and associate reformed churches. The general assembly met in Seattle, Wash., on May 22, 1912. The boards and institutions reported a successful year. The returns show a decided increase in the missionary spirit and a marked enlargement of the evangelistic work. The church cultivates the most cordial relations with other evangelical denominations and seeks coöperation with them, but does not as yet see the way clear for organic union. A communication was received from the general assembly of the Presbyterian Church in the United States that it had appointed a committee to confer with a similar committee on the subject of the union of the two assemblies. In response to this, a committee of conference was appointed to ascertain whether a practicable basis of union can be found and to report to the next general assembly. It was also agreed to hold the next meeting of the assembly at Atlanta, Ga., at the same time with the meetings of the assemblies of other Presbyterian churches.

STATISTICS. Synods, 13; presbyteries, 72; congregations, 1127; licentiates, 44; students of theology, 98; communicants, 178,601, of whom 38,984 (22 per cent.) are in the mission fields in the Punjab, India, Egypt, and the Sudan. Contributions: For the boards of the church, $579,462; for all purposes, $2,644,848; average per member, $18.78; average salary of pastors, $1241; average cost of churches erected, $9000; of parsonages, $2971.

UNITED SHOE MACHINERY COMPANY. See TRUSTS.

UNITED STATES. POPULATION. The Thirteenth Census included statistics of population of the United States by nationalities. These were made public in 1912. For the States these figures will be found under the titles of the different States. The table given below is for the whole country. Of a total population of 91,972,266 in 1910, 68,389,104 were born in the United States and 13,343,583 were born in foreign countries. Those whose parents were both natives of the United States numbered 49,488,441. Those whose parents were both foreign born numbered 18,900,663. By race, the white population numbered 81,732,687; negroes, 9,828,264; Indians, 265,683, and Mongolians, 142,666. The urban population was 42,623,383, and the rural population 49,348,883. The urban population in 1910 was 46.3 per cent., compared with 40.5 per cent. in 1900. The rural population in 1910 was 52.7 per cent., compared with 59.5 per cent. in 1900. The nationality of foreign-born citizens in 1900 and 1910 is given in the following table:

	1900 Number	1910 Number
Austria	275,907	1,190,200
Bohemia	156,891	....
Canada (English)*	784,741	1,198,000
Canada (French)*	395,066	
China	81,534	....
Denmark	153,805	181,500
England	840,513	875,400
France	104,197	117,100
Germany	2,663,418	2,499,200
Holland	104,931	120,000
Hungary	145,714	468,500
Ireland	1,615,459	1,351,400
Italy	484,027	1,341,800
Mexico	103,393	218,800
Norway	336,388	403,500
Poland	383,407	....
Russia	423,726	1,577,300
Scotland	233,524	263,400
Sweden	572,014	665,500
Switzerland	115,593	124,800
Wales	93,586	82,600
Other countries	273,442	....

* Includes Newfoundland.

Statistics of sex distribution of population will be found in the article SEX DISTRIBUTION IN THE UNITED STATES. The comparative figures of illiteracy in 1900-1910 will be [illegible] in the article ILLITERACY. See also the article IMMIGRATION AND EMIGRATION.

AGRICULTURE. Statistics of agriculture relating to the United States and its dependencies will be found in the articles dealing with agriculture and agricultural products. The State production in 1911-12 will be found under the States. Statistics of foreign countries will be found under the titles of those countries. See also AGRICULTURE, articles on crops, and IRRIGATION.

MANUFACTURES. Statistics of manufactures in the separate States will be found in the State articles. The Census Bureau issued during 1912 a bulletin containing a summary of manufactures for the United States. These figures are for the calendar year 1909. The most important results of the census will be found in the table on page 745, which contains also the percentage of increase from 1904 to 1909. It will be seen from this table that the total number of wage earners in the United States in 1909 averaged 6,615,046.

The value added by manufacture in 1909, namely, the difference between the cost of materials and the total value of products, was $8,530,261,000. This figure best represents the net wealth created by manufacturing operations, because the gross value of products includes the cost of the materials used, which are either the products of non-manufacturing industries, such as agriculture, forestry, fisheries, and mining, or else are themselves the product of manufacturing establishments. The value of products derived from this latter class of materials involves a duplication, inasmuch as the value of these materials has already figured in the value of products reported for the establishments manufacturing them in the first instance; in some cases, indeed, where a given product has passed through several distinct stages of manufacture in different establishments before reaching its final form, this duplication may be repeated several times. All such duplications, as well as the original value of materials, are, however, eliminated in the figures for value added by manufacture. This value covers salaries and wages—which represent over one-half of the total—overhead charges, depreciation, interest, taxes, and other expenses attendant upon the manufacturing operations, as well as the profits of the undertaking.

Statistics of manufactures by industries in 1909, with the percentage of increase in the ten-year period, are given in the table below.

In this table the industries are arranged in the order of their gross value of products. Some of the industries which hold a very high rank in gross value of products rank comparatively low in the average number of wage-earners employed and in the value added by manufacture. Where this is the case it indicates that the cost of materials represents a large proportion of the total value of products, and that therefore the value added by manufacture, of which wages constitute usually the largest item, is not commensurate with the total value of products. Thus the slaughtering and meat-packing industry, which ranks first

SUMMARY FOR THE UNITED STATES FOR 1909 *

	Census 1909	1904	P. C. of Inc. 1904-'09
Number of establishments.	268,491	216,180	24.2
Persons engaged in manufactures	7,678,578	6,213,612	23.6
Proprietors and firm members	273,265	225,673	21.1
Salaried employees ..	790,267	519,556	52.1
Wage earners (average number) ...	6,615,046	5,468,383	21.0
Primary h. p...	18,680,776	13,487,707	38.5
Capital	$18,428,270,000	$12,675,581,000	45.4
Expenses	18,453,080,000	13,138,260,000	40.5
Services	4,365,613,000	3,184,884,000	37.1
Salaries	938,575,000	574,439,000	63.4
Wages	3,427,038,000	2,610,445,000	31.3
Materials	12,141,791,000	8,500,208,000	42.8
Miscellaneous..	1,945,676,000	1,453,168,000	33.9
Value of products	20,672,052,000	14,793,903,000	39.7
Value added by manufacture (value of products less cost of materials)	8,530,261,000	6,293,695,000	35.5

MANUFACTURES BY INDUSTRIES *

Industries.	Average Number of Wage Earners.	Value of Products	Value Added by Manufacture	Per Cent. Increase in Ten Years (a)	(b)
Slaughtering and packing..............	89,728	$1,370,568,000	$168,740,000	29.5	73.8
Foundries and machine shops..........	531,011	1,228,475,000	688,464,000	24.4	53.9
Lumber and timber....................	695,019	1,156,129,000	648,011,000	36.6	51.9
Iron and steel, steel works............	240,076	985,723,000	328,222,000	31.0	65.1
Flour and grist mills.................	39,453	883,584,000	116,008,000	22.4	76.2
Printing and publishing...............	258,434	737,876,000	536,101,000	32.4	86.7
Cotton goods	378,880	628,392,000	257,383,000	25.1	85.3
Clothing, men's	239,696	568,077,000	270,562,000	52.1	75.4
Boots and shoes	198,297	512,798,000	180,060,000	31.1	76.8
Woolen, worsted, and felt goods.......	168,722	435,979,000	153,101,000	29.1	75.2
Tobacco	166,810	416,695,000	239,509,000	25.9	58.0
Car shops	282,174	405,601,000	206,188,000	62.5	86.0
Bread and bakeries	100,216	396,865,000	158,831,000	66.5	126.3
Iron and steel, blast furnaces.........	38,429	391,429,000	70,791,000	†2.1	89.3
Clothing, women's	153,743	384,752,000	175,964,000	83.6	141.5
Copper, smelting and refining.........	15,628	378,806,000	45,274,000	38.0	129.4
Liquors, malt	54,579	374,730,000	278,134,000	38.3	58.2
Leather.	62,202	327,874,000	79,595,000	19.4	60.7
Sugar and molasses, not including beet.	13,526	279,249,000	31,666,000	†4.3	16.5
Butter, cheese, and milk..............	18,431	274,558,000	39,012,000	44.0	109.9
Paper and wood pulp..................	89,492	267,657,000	102,215,000	53.0	110.2
Automobiles	75,721	249,202,000	117,556,000	3278.9	5148.6
Furniture	128,452	239,887,000	131,112,000	41.8	83.6
Petroleum refining	13,929	236,998,000	37,725,000	14.2	91.2
Electrical machinery	87,256	221,309,000	112,743,000	107.7	139.4
Liquors, distilled	6,430	204,699,000	168,722,000	72.8	111.5
Hosiery and knit goods...............	129,275	200,144,000	89,903,000	54.5	108.8
Copper, tin, and sheet iron...........	73,615	199,824,000	87,242,000	92.1	155.0
Silk and silk goods...................	99,037	196,912,000	89,145,000	51.4	83.6
Lead, smelting and refining...........	7,424	167,406,000	15,443,000	†10.8	4.6
Gas, illuminating and heating.........	37,215	166,814,000	114,386,000	65.7	120.3
Carriages and wagons..................	69,928	159,893,000	77,942,000	†5.3	15.6
Canning and preserving................	59,968	157,101,000	55,278,000	5.2	58.2
Brass and bronze	40,618	149,989,000	50,761,000	49.5	69.2
Oil, cottonseed	17,071	147,868,000	28,035,000	55.1	151.8
Agricultural implements	50,551	146,329,000	86,022,000	8.5	44.6
Patent medicines	22,895	141,942,000	91,566,000	20.3	59.9
Confectionery.	44,638	134,796,000	53,645,000	66.2	122.3
Paint and varnish	14,240	124,889,000	45,873,000	46.8	79.5
Cars, steam railroad..................	43,086	123,730,000	44,977,000	28.8	36.7
Chemicals	23,714	117,689,000	53,567,000	24.7	87.6
Marble and stone work.................	65,603	113,093,000	75,696,000	57.4	77.6
Leather goods	34,907	104,719,000	44,692,000	19.2	73.3
All other industries..................	1,634,927	4,561,002,000	2,084,399,000	46.9	100.7
All industries, total.................	6,615,046	$20,672,052,000	$8,530,261,000	40.4	81.2

* In the year 1909. (a) Increase in average number of wage-earners, 1899-1909. (b) Increase in value of products, 1899-1909. † Decrease.

in gross value of products, and the flour-mill and grist-mill industry, which ranks fifth in that respect, both hold a comparatively low rank with regard to number of wage-earners or to the value added by manufacture. The blast-furnace industry, the smelting and refining of copper, the manufacture and refining of sugar and molasses, the manufacture of butter and cheese and condensed milk, the refining of petroleum, and the smelting and refining of lead, are other industries which rank much higher in gross value of products than in the number of wage-earners or the value added by manufacture.

TABLE I

VALUE OF IMPORTS AND EXPORTS, BY COUNTRIES, CALENDAR YEARS 1911 AND 1912

Countries	Imports 1911	Imports 1912	Exports 1911	Exports 1912
Europe	Dollars	Dollars	Dollars	Dollars
Austria-Hungary	16,202,300	18,212,467	21,083,336	24,048,325
Belgium	37,326,398	42,648,251	50,002,923	62,552,352
Denmark	2,224,245	3,467,351	15,392,808	15,942,678
France	121,765,074	133,933,485	128,303,274	155,212,669
Germany	165,636,669	186,042,644	294,847,562	330,450,830
Greece	3,412,135	3,739,559	847,927	966,136
Italy	46,365,923	51,817,947	61,153,592	73,874,013
Netherlands	34,125,347	37,072,289	106,392,194	110,322,134
Norway	8,294,349	8,381,489	7,868,133	8,059,945
Portugal	5,561,572	7,377,810	2,591,383	2,778,793
Russia in Europe	14,726,509	26,279,295	24,151,483	26,099,092
Spain	21,009,070	22,221,201	23,678,960	31,671,556
Sweden	8,549,734	10,452,650	9,121,424	10,504,151
Switzerland	24,832,952	23,305,201	729,627	853,192
Turkey in Europe	8,817,145	9,504,163	2,893,500	2,280,891
United Kingdom	250,122,175	312,934,838	538,810,316	606,975,989
Total Europe	770,393,236	899,956,944	1,293,072,862	1,467,453,571
North America				
Bermuda	581,568	635,519	1,392,214	1,551,915
British Honduras	1,299,267	1,542,437	1,540,862	1,535,097
Canada	93,923,757	120,851,025	299,100,457	376,162,489
Central American States				
Costa Rica	4,441,601	3,777,296	3,502,536	3,615,568
Guatemala	2,621,919	2,717,378	2,155,520	3,579,830
Honduras	2,770,015	3,043,409	2,396,920	2,682,020
Nicaragua	1,460,341	1,354,492	2,729,594	2,575,031
Panama	3,859,129	4,278,823	20,650,070	24,724,538
Salvador	1,447,922	1,510,573	2,186,240	2,626,698
Total Central American States	16,600,927	16,681,971	33,620,880	39,803,685
Mexico	57,311,622	76,767,931	53,454,407	55,029,708
Newfoundland and Labrador	1,299,907	1,085,302	4,729,633	4,642,301
West Indies				
British:				
Barbados	360,690	322,764	1,484,603	1,589,826
Jamaica	6,750,589	6,165,472	4,701,359	5,245,378
Trinidad and Tobago	4,705,754	4,585,715	3,380,964	3,263,414
Other British	1,215,410	1,363,689	2,757,050	3,017,858
Cuba	106,098,026	137,890,004	62,280,509	65,228,061
Danish	476,422	57,314	831,636	915,743
Dutch	385,065	697,638	819,926	1,075,558
French	22,274	92,731	1,485,516	1,619,688
Haiti	813,101	841,786	6,656,093	7,246,057
Santo Domingo	4,419,845	4,186,414	4,143,301	5,314,096
Total West Indies	125,247,176	156,203,527	88,540,957	94,515,679
Total North America	296,320,121	373,809,916	482,[illegible]38,006	573,297,541
South America				
Argentina	28,487,431	34,007,864	50,140,438	51,170,397
Bolivia	140	9,829	1,031,125	992,527
Brazil	103,464,111	132,957,326	28,853,819	40,591,519
Chile	20,230,463	22,401,492	14,934,955	15,302,738
Colombia	9,894,431	14,284,781	5,220,248	6,685,010
Ecuador	3,257,722	3,607,285	2,360,090	2,311,861
Falkland Islands	....	....	1,570	258
Guiana—British	1,191,816	118,970	1,932,963	1,782,495
Dutch	1,255,633	729,005	756,328	723,544
French	47,630	63,753	333,676	248,494
Paraguay	35,937	13,485	171,329	123,740
Peru	8,940,895	10,614,221	5,944,196	5,964,619
Uruguay	1,976,406	3,476,533	5,953,313	7,322,726
Venezuela	8,673,489	11,551,691	4,102,554	5,724,002
Total South America	187,456,104	233,836,235	121,736,604	138,944,936

TABLE I—*Continued*

Asia	Imports 1911 Dollars	Imports 1912 Dollars	Exports 1911 Dollars	Exports 1912 Dollars
Aden	1,564,783	1,896,217	1,553,029	2,010,183
China	31,768,838	34,147,181	23,366,505	19,799,556
Chosen (Korea)	416,055	8,575	889,395	1,363,258
East Indies—British				
British India	47,243,621	59,283,163	11,733,101	14,868,671
Straits Settlements	23,601,314	26,941,554	2,295,462	3,181,824
Other British	8,768,584	11,427,669	374,807	467,696
Dutch	13,720,879	5,891,677	2,984,839	3,224,907
Hongkong	2,813,788	3,352,505	9,772,730	9,730,878
Japan	78,022,980	87,418,042	44,103,802	57,519,654
Persia	1,197,728	1,632,807	23,798	118,487
Russia—Asiatic	1,172,749	2,067,573	1,306,550	1,216,045
Siam	78,863	85,090	386,140	456,417
Turkey in Asia	10,889,782	11,011,939	1,503,401	890,005
Other Asia	69,498	132,137	144	....
Total Asia	222,076,910	246,279,758	101,312,594	116,382,338
Oceania				
British:				
Australia and Tasmania	8,659,604	11,748,556	40,172,346	41,050,329
New Zealand	2,456,714	3,078,805	7,967,826	8,474,765
All other	77,232	60,085	236,702	360,043
French Oceania	936,249	1,217,627	727,865	717,244
German Oceania	15,291	68,056	144,231	161,237
Guam	....	....	....	....
Philippine Islands	20,212,917	22,437,356	20,928,753	24,685,931
Total Oceania	32,358,007	38,610,485	70,177,723	75,449,549
Africa				
British West Africa	124,740	314,906	2,201,060	3,165,268
British South Africa	2,285,546	2,557,328	12,858,951	13,567,263
British East Africa	1,120,100	923,536	587,868	899,084
French Africa	699,669	737,310	1,704,430	4,301,025
German Africa	265,622	419,215	298,573	416,202
Morocco	144,079	93,949	57,306	23,051
Portuguese Africa	224,306	92,178	2,793,837	2,152,740
Turkey in Africa—Egypt	18,597,252	20,080,161	2,348,867	1,421,146
Tripoli	82,751	176,728	452	219,492
Total Africa	23,754,782	25,640,017	23,788,957	27,690,064
Grand total	1,532,359,160	1,818,133,355	2,092,526,746	2,399,217,993

MINERAL PRODUCTION. A complete tabular summary of the mineral production of the United States in 1911 will be found under the title MINERAL PRODUCTION. The production of different minerals and metals in 1911 and in 1912, when available, is given under the separate headings of these articles, as GOLD, SILVER, COAL, COPPER, IRON AND STEEL, etc.

EDUCATION. For an account of educational matters in the United States in 1912 see the article EDUCATION IN THE UNITED STATES. For notes of higher education see UNIVERSITIES AND COLLEGES. For notes of educational progress in the different States see the paragraph *Education* under those States.

RELIGION. For an account of the changes and growth of the various religious denominations during the year, see the articles on the respective denominations. A summary is also given under the article RELIGIOUS DENOMINATIONS AND MOVEMENTS.

FOREIGN COMMERCE

In the tables on pages 746, 747, and 748 is given a summary of the foreign commerce of the United States for the calendar and fiscal year 1912. The summary for the calendar year 1912 is given in detail by countries. This is Table No. I. Table No. II. gives a general summary of the commerce for the fiscal year, and Tables III. and IV. give the chief articles of import and export for the fiscal years 1911 and 1912. From the detailed summary of the calendar year given in Table No. I. it will be seen that the total foreign trade, including both imports and exports, was $4,217,351,348, compared with a total of $3,624,885,906 in 1911 and $3,429,-163,045 in 1910. The total foreign trade in 1912 greatly exceeded that of any other year. Of the total, $2,399,217,993 represented exports and $1,818,133,355 imports, leaving a balance in favor of exports, or a balance of trade of $581,084,638. The balance of trade in 1911 was $560,167,586 and in 1910 $303,354,753. The total exports in 1911 were $2,092,526,746, and in 1910 $1,866,258,904. The total imports in 1911 were $1,532,359,160, and in 1910 $1,-562,904,151. Of the imports in 1912, $992,376,-460, were free of duty and $825,756,895 were dutiable. Of the foreign exports $21,741,237 were free of duty and $14,780,700 were dutiable.

An examination of the detailed table will show that the largest total trade, including both export and import, was with the United Kingdom. The imports from the United Kingdom in 1912 were $312,934,838, compared with $250,122,175 in 1911. The exports in 1912 were $606,975,989, compared with $538,812,316 in 1911. The European country with which trade was second in value was Germany. The imports from that country in 1912 were $186,-042,644, compared with $165,636,669 in 1911, and the exports $330,450,830 in 1912, compared with $294,847,562 in 1911. Ranking next in order of importance were France, Italy, Belgium, Netherlands, Russia, Switzerland, and Spain, in imports; in exports, France, Netherlands, Italy, Belgium, Austria-Hungary, Spain, and Russia. The imports from Canada in 1912 amounted to $120,851,025, compared with $93,923,757 in 1911, and the exports to Canada in 1912 amounted to $376,162,489, compared with $299,100,457. The total imports from South American countries in 1912 amounted to $233,836,235, compared with $187,456,104 in 1911. The exports to South American countries were considerably less than the imports. The total exports were $138,944,930 in 1912, compared with $121,736,604 in 1911. The largest import trade was with Brazil, $132,957,326 in 1912, compared with $103,464,111 in 1911. The export trade with Brazil in 1912 was $40,591,519, compared with $28,853,819 in 1911. Next in order of importance in the import trade were Argentina, Chile, Colombia, Venezuela, and Peru. In export trade Argentina stands first, with $51,170,397, compared with $50,140,438 in 1911. Following in order are Brazil, for which figures are given above, Chile, Uruguay, Colombia, and Venezuela. The largest import trade with Asiatic countries, as will be seen from the table, is with Japan. This in 1912 amounted to $87,418,042, compared with $78,022,980 in 1911. The total trade with the British possessions in India, however, was greater than with Japan, $97,652,386 in 1912, compared with $79,613,519 in 1911. The total imports from China in 1912 amounted to $35,126,226, compared with $32,516,281 in 1911. The exports to Japan in 1912 amounted to $57,519,654, compared with $44,103,802 in 1911; to the British possessions, $18,518,191, compared with $14,403,360 in 1911; to China, $21,040,546, compared with $24,127,683 in 1911.

COMMERCE WITH NON-CONTIGUOUS TERRITORIES. The exports to Alaska in 1912 amounted to $21,322,536, compared with $14,693,588 in 1911. The imports from Alaska in 1912 were valued at $23,385,437, compared with $18,345,844 in 1911. The exports to Hawaii in 1912 amounted to $28,029,240, com-

TABLE II.

FOREIGN COMMERCE, BY GRAND DIVISIONS, FISCAL YEARS 1911 AND 1912

	Europe	North America	South America	Asia and Oceania	Africa	Total
	Imports					
1911 ....$	768,167,760	$305,496,793	$182,623,750	$243,724,182	$27,213,620	$1,527,226,105
1912	819,585,326	334,072,039	215,089,316	261,932,365	22,585,888	1,653,264,934
	Exports					
1911	1,308,275,778	457,059,179	108,894,894	151,483,241	23,607,107	2,049,320,199
1912	1,341,732,789	516,837,671	132,310,451	189,398,074	24,043,424	2,204,322,409

TABLE III

CHIEF ARTICLES OF IMPORT FISCAL YEARS 1911 AND 1912

Articles	Imports 1911	1912
Art works	$ 22,495,842	$ 36,092,595
Automobiles	2,250,759	1,619,150
Chemicals, drugs and dyes.	95,101,006	92,029,625
Coal	5,534,113	3,711,479
Copper and manufactures of	32,013,562	35,843,537
Coffee	90,567,788	117,826,543
Cotton, manufactures of.	66,996,551	65,152,785
Earthen, stone, and chinaware	11,411,665	9,997,698
Fibres:		
Manufactures of........	54,765,999	59,659,843
Unmanufactured	30,752,250	34,462,866
Fish	14,939,314	14,553,347
Fruits, including nuts...	41,515,067	45,377,259
Furs and manufactures of	8,267,947	8,533,029
Hides and skins other than fur skins.......	70,504,980	102,476,327
India rubber and gutta-percha crude.........	92,910,513	105,037,506
Iron and steel, and manufactures of..........	34,205,968	26,551,040
Precious stones..........	40,623,137	41,297,759
Leather, and manufactures of..............	14,636,720	16,166,706
Oils	33,023,687	31,348,602
Silk:		
Manufactures of........	31,900,054	27,204,364
Unmanufactured	74,924,004	69,541,672
Spirits, wines, and malt liquors	18,004,908	19,334,605
Sugar	96,691,096	115,515,079
Tea	17,613,569	18,207,141
Tin, in bars, blocks, or pigs	37,935,978	46,214,198
Tobacco, unmanufactured.	27,855,996	31,918,670
Wood, and manufactures of	52,931,803	52,502,131
Wool:		
Manufactures of........	18,569,791	14,912,619
Unmanufactured	23,228,005	33,078,342

TABLE IV

CHIEF ARTICLES OF EXPORT, FISCAL YEARS 1911 AND 1912

Articles	Exports 1911	1912
Agricultural implements.$	35,973,298	35,640,005
Animals	19,048,653	15,447,987
Breadstuffs	124,913,530	123,979,715
Cars, carriages, and other vehicles	30,534,936	25,657,294
Chemicals, drugs, dyes, and medicines........	23,007,414	25,117,217
Coal	45,013,436	52,648,750
Copper, and manufactures of..............	98,705,308	108,875,117
Cotton:		
Manufactures of........	24,387,099	31,388,983
Unmanufactured	585,318,869	565,849,271
Fertilizers	10,721,132	10,873,908
Fish	7,698,321	8,640,938
Fruits, including nuts...	24,498,465	30,963,638
Iron and steel, and manufactures of, not including ore	230,725,351	268,154,262
Leather, and manufactures of..............	53,673,057	60,756,772
Mineral oils	98,115,516	112,472,100
Meat and dairy products	149,389,737	156,260,876
Naval stores	25,022,720	26,754,987
Oil cake and oil cake meal *	19,631,121	28,096,173
Paper, and manufactures of	19,215,499	19,458,050
Paraffin and paraffin wax	7,378,736	8,123,486
Seeds	2,475,066	2,398,302
Tobacco:		
Manufactures of.........	4,383,584	5,053,125
Unmanufactured	3?,255,320	43,251,857
Vegetable oils............	19,806,232	26,908,931
Wood, and manufactures of	92,255,951	96,782,186

* Not including corn oil cake.

pared with $21,917,747 in 1911. Imports from Hawaii amounted to $50,356,851 in 1912, compared with $47,334,271 in 1911. To Porto Rico the exports in 1912 amounted to $33,991,-622, compared with $35,872,109 in 1911. The imports from Porto Rico were valued at $41,-183,009 in 1912, compared with $35,138,365 in 1911. The exports to the Philippine Islands in 1912 amounted to $24,659,150, compared with $20,896,829 in 1911. The imports from the Philippines amounted to $22,355,310 in 1912, compared with $20,104,446 in 1911.

INTERNAL COMMERCE

DOMESTIC COMMERCE ON THE GREAT LAKES. The total vessel passages through the Sault Ste. Marie Canal for the nine months ending December, 1912, were 22,778. Of these, 14,916 went through the United States canal and 7862 through the Canadian canal. The total registered tonnage of these vessels was 56,736,807 and the passengers carried numbered 66,877. The principal articles carried in this traffic were as follows: East bound—Copper, 116,954 tons; grain, 69,024,446 bushels; flour, 8,652,153 barrels; iron ore, 46,293,423 short tons; lumber, 667,542 M. feet; wheat, 174,086,456 bushels; general merchandise, 238,865 short tons. West bound—Coal (hard), 2,142,485 short tons; coal (soft), 12,789,109 short tons; manufactured iron, 629,060 short tons; salt, 660,991 barrels; general merchandise, 1,425,918 short tons.

Through the Portage Lake canals passed 1583 steamships and 697 tugs and tow barges, or a total tonnage of 2,393,856. The principal commodities carried through these canals in the nine months to December 31, 1912, were: Bituminous coal, 1,111,983 tons; wheat, 3,159,983 bushels; flour, 1,747,415 barrels; iron ore, 74,308 short tons; iron manufactures, 119,656 short tons; salt, 168,977 barrels; shingles, 183,802 M.; general merchandise, 170,689 tons. The total commerce passing through these canals was 2,428,578 tons. The traffic passing through Sturgeon Bay and the Lake Michigan Ship Canal for the season ending December 31, 1912, was 550,169 short tons. The vessels passing through numbered 2134, with a total tonnage of 1,267,695. The chief articles of traffic were coal, grain, lumber, posts, and railroad ties.

RECEIPTS AND DISBURSEMENTS. The following table, compiled from figures given by the Secretary of the Treasury, shows the receipts and disbursements of the federal government for the fiscal years 1911 and 1912:

Receipts	1911	1912
Customs	$314,497,071.24	$311,321,672.22
Internal revenue:		
Ordinary	289,012,224.20	293,028,895.93
Corporation tax	33,516,976.59	28,583,303.73
Sales of public lands	5,731,636.88	5,392,796.75
Miscellaneous	58,614,466.08	53,451,796.74
Ordinary receipts	701,372,374.99	691,778,465.37
Panama Canal receipts *	18,102,170.04	33,189,104.15
Public debt receipts	40,232,555.00	20,537,645.00
Total, exclusive of postal	759,707,100.03	745,505,214.52
Postal revenue	237,879,823.60	246,744,015.88
Total, including postal	$997,586,923.63	$992,249,230.40

* Proceeds of bonds.

Disbursements	1911	1912
Civil and miscellan.	$173,838,599.04	$172,256,794.41
Postal deficiency	....	1,568,194.88
War Department	160,135,975.89	148,795,421.92
Navy Department	119,937,644.39	135,591,955.72
Indians	20,933,869.44	20,134,839.80
Pensions	157,980,575 01	153,590,456.26
Int. on public debt	21,311,334.12	22,616,300.48
Ordinary disbursements	654,137,997.89	654,553,963.47
Panama Canal disbursements	37,063,515.38	35,327,370.66
Public debt disbursements	35,223,336.35	28,648,327.53
Total, exclusive of postal	726,424,849.57	718,529,661.66
Postal expenditures	237,879,823.60	246,744,015.88
Total, including postal	$964,085,555.05	$965,273,677.54
Excess of receipts	33,501,368.58	26,975,552.86

The receipts and disbursements for the fiscal year ending June 30, 1913, are estimated by the Secretary of the Treasury in this annual reports as follows:

Receipts	
Customs	$328,000,000.00
Internal revenue	297,000,000.00
Corporation tax	29,000,000.00
Miscellaneous	57,000,000.00
Total ordinary receipts	$711,000,000.00
Disbursements	
Civil establishment	$177,000,000.00
War Department	158,000,000.00
Navy Department	130,000,000.00
Indian service	18,000,000.00
Pensions	165,000,000.00
Interest on the public debt	22,800,000.00
Total ordinary disbursements	670,800,000.00
Surplus for 1912 in ordinary receipts	40,200,000.00
Panama Canal disbursements	42,000,000.00
Miscellaneous redemptions of the public debt	150,000.00
Total estimated deficit	1,800,000.00

COINAGE. The coinage executed at the mints of the United States during the calendar year 1912 was as follows:

	1912	
Denomination	Pieces	Value
Double eagles	149,824	$ 2,996,480.00
Eagles	705,083	7,050,830.00
Half eagles	1,182,144	5,910,720.00
Quarter eagles	616,197	1,540,492.50
Total gold	2,653,248	17,498,522.50
Half dollars	5,221,500	2,610,750.00
Quarter dollars	5,108,700	1,277,175.00
Dimes	34,530,700	3,453,070.00
Total silver	44,860,900	7,340,995.00
Five cents	34,948,714	1,747,435.70
One cent	82,995,060	829,950.60
Total minor	117,943,774	2,577,386.30
Total coinage	165,457,922	$27,416,903.80

Coinage for government of Philippine Islands

Silver—Pesos	680,000	pieces
20 centavos	750,000	"
10 centavos	1,010,000	"
1 centavo	3,001,000	"

Coinage for Costa Rica

10 centimes	267,783	pieces
5 centimes	535,565	"

	General Stock Jan. 2, 1913	‡ Held in Treas. Jan. 2, 1913	Money in Circulation Jan. 2, 1913	Jan. 2, 1912
Gold coin (including bullion in Treasury)	*$1,878,577,122	$170,983,732	$622,159,221	$614,026,906
† Gold certificates	....	128,747,197	955,686,972	906,944,367
Standard silver dollars	565,481,020	165,022	74,628,998	74,538,591
† Silver certificates	....	12,814,458	477,972,542	478,027,234
Subsidiary silver	** 174,538,163	17,814,855	156,723,308	147,773,018
Treasury notes of 1890	2,797,000	10,115	2,786,885	3,078,614
United States notes	346,681,016	6,995,837	339,685,179	337,950,300
National bank notes	750,972,246	30,787,771	720,184,475	705,236,242
Total	$3,719,046,567	$368,318,987	$3,350,727,580	$3,267,575,322

Population of continental United States January 2, 1913, estimated at 96,496,000; circulation per capita, $34.72.

* A revised estimate by the Director of the Mint of the stock of gold coin was adopted in the statement for August 1, 1907. There was a reduction of $135,000,000.

** A revised estimate by the Director of the Mint of the stock of subsidiary silver coin was adopted in the statement of September 1, 1910. There was a reduction of $9,700,000.

† For redemption of outstanding certificates an exact equivalent in amount of the appropriate kinds of money is held in the Treasury, and is not included in the account of money held as assets of the government.

‡ This statement of money held in the Treasury as assets of the government does not include deposits of public money in national bank depositaries to the credit of the Treasurer of the United States, amounting to $33,261,598.08. Fora full statement of assets, see Public Debt statement.

National Debt. The amount and classification of the United States national debt at the end of the calendar years 1910, 1911, and 1912, were as follows:

	Dec. 31, 1910	Dec. 31, 1911	Dec. 31, 1912
Interest-bearing debt at from 2 to 4 per cent. and redeemable from 1908 to 1961, inclusive	$ 913,317,490.00	$ 963,359,390	$ 964,621,630.00
Debt on which interest has ceased since maturity	1,995,045 26	1,821,830	1,695,070.36
Debt bearing no interest	387,919,402.43	379,794,799	374,732,081.90
Gross debt	$1,303,231,937.69	$1,344,976,020	$1,341,059,782.16
Cash balance in general fund	89,393,472.14	126,925,992	143,576,381.22
Net debt	$1,213,838,465.55	$1,218,050,138	$1,197,483,400.94

Army

Strength of the Army. On June 30, 1912, the actual strength of the regular army was 4470 officers and 77,835 enlisted men, a total of 82,305. This was an increase over July 30, 1911, of 189 officers and 7834 enlisted men. There were, in addition, Philippine scouts numbering 180 officers and 5480 enlisted men. The geographical distribution of the army, including the Philippine scouts, on June 30, 1912, was as follows: In the United States, 61,584; in Alaska, 1232; in the Philippines, regular army 10,970, Philippine scouts 5660; in China, 1256; in Porto Rico, 614; in Hawaii, 3969; in the Canal Zone, 821; troops en route and officers at other foreign stations, 1859. During the fiscal year 395 second lieutenants were appointed in the army. Of these, 177 were graduates from the United States Military Academy, 29 were from among the enlisted men in the army, and 189 were from civil life. These appointments left 134 vacancies of second lieutenancies in the line on October 15, 1912, and 20 vacancies in the corps of engineers.

The actual strength of the army on June 30, 1912, was about 4½ per cent. below its authorized strength. There were during the year 158,917 applicants for enlistment and reënlistment. Of these only about 25 per cent. were accepted, a smaller percentage than during the preceding year and indicating a continued maintenance of the existing standards of care of selection. The percentage of desertions was about 3 of the whole number of enlistment contracts in force during the year and rose from 2.28 for the preceding year, a percentage lower, with one exception, than in any other year during the past 90 years.

Army Reorganization. During the year an important general scheme for army reorganization was perfected by the war college division of the general staff. This plan is the result of a system of post-graduate education which is being carried on at service schools at Leavenworth, Fort Monroe, and the war college at Washington. In general scope and purpose the plan is a constructive application to modern American conditions of the principles of military policy carefully worked out by General Upton in his exhaustive studies of military policy soon after the Civil War. The scheme is too complicate for detailed discussion in this place. A summary of its principle features, however, may be noted. It deals, first, with the general relations between the land and naval forces; second, with the relation between the land forces at home and abroad, including the detachments on foreign service; third, with the land forces within the territorial limits of the United States, including the time required to raise armies, relations of the two classes of citizen soldiers, organized and unorganized, the relation of the regular army to the nation's war power, and the joint use of regulars and citizen soldiery; fourth, the plan deals with the peace administration of the regular land forces, including the relations between the coast artillery and the mobile army and the division and administration of the forces in the continental United States; fifth, it deals with the reserve system and outlines a plan for a regular army reserve, unorganized reserves, special reserves, and reserves for the citizen soldiery. Other details considered in this plan are the tactical organization of mobile troops, the relation of promotion to organization, a suggestion as to initial tactical organization for the mobile army with a programme of gradual expansion into a field army, plans for raising and organizing the national volunteer forces, and considerations determining the strength, composition, and organization of the land forces of the United States. The final suggestion in this plan of organization concerns a council of national defense, this to include: The President; the secretaries of State, War, and Navy; the chairmen of the committees on appropriations, foreign affairs, military affairs, naval affairs, in the Senate; the chairmen of the committees on appropriations, foreign affairs, military affairs, and naval affairs in the House of Representatives; the chief of the general staff of the army; an officer of the navy not below the rank of captain; the president of the army war college; and the president of the navy war college.

There is especial need of the reorganization of foreign garrisons on account of the approaching completion of the Panama Canal and the new readjustment of conditions in the Philippines. A garrison of troops will be necessary at the canal in order that the fortifications may be properly manned and for other purposes. It is estimated by the Secretary of War that not less than 6500 should compose this garrison. The plan of readjustment of conditions in the Philippines, begun in 1911, was carried out in 1912. The former garrison of 12 regiments of infantry and cavalry at reduced strength was replaced by a garrison of 6 regiments of full strength. The six regiments which were thus relieved from Philippine service were returned to the United States and are available to furnish the Panama and Hawaiian garrisons. In addition to this reorganization of foreign troops, steps were taken during the year to organize the army within the United States on a tactical basis. Hitherto the army has been administered according to a purely geographical organization, and the mobile troops were scattered in about 40 posts situated in 24 different States, containing an average strength of less than 700 men at each post. Plans were practically completed at the end of the year under which these dissociated units will be united into a tactical organization of three infantry divisions, each consisting of two or three brigades of infantry, and so far as practicable of a proper proportion of divisional cavalry and artillery. In addition there will be several separate brigades of cavalry available for the formation of a cavalry division.

LEGISLATION. The army appropriation bill passed October 21, 1912, contained many important provisions relating to the administration of the army. It provided for the consolidation of office establishments of the quartermaster-general, the commissary-general, and the paymaster-general of the army into one bureau of the War Department, to be known as the "quartermaster's bureau"; and the consolidation of the quartermaster's, the subsistence, and pay departments of the army into a single department, to be known as the "quartermaster corps of the army." James B. Aleshire, formerly quartermaster-general, was appointed chief of the new quartermaster corps. The act also provided for a general service corps of enlisted men to do for the army such work as that of clerks, engineers, firemen, carpenters, teamsters, etc., which work was heretofore performed by a large force of civilian employees and soldiers detailed on extra duty. By a third provision of the same act the detachment of officers below the grade of major from duty with their companies, troops, or batteries was restricted under severe penalty, unless they shall have been present for duty with such organizations for at least two out of the preceding six years.

On February 15 Major-General Frederick C. Ainsworth was removed from his office as adjutant-general of the United States after 37 years of service. He entered the army in 1874 as a surgeon. General Ainsworth was removed by order of the Secretary of War, who charged him with insubordination the next day on his own application. In removing General Ainsworth, Mr. Stimson alleged that he had "impugned the fairness and intelligence of the Secretary of War, under whose authority the proposition in question [the proposal of the general staff to make changes in the form of the muster roll] was submitted to you. You also criticised and impugned the military capacity of the officers of the general staff and the war college. This is not an isolated instance of insubordination and impropriety." General Ainsworth and General Wood, chief of staff, had long been at odds on the question of the proper conduct of their respective duties.

On February 16 the House of Representatives adopted an amendment to the army bill providing for consolidation of the office of army-general and inspector-general with that of chief of staff. The House also adopted a measure abolishing five of the fifteen cavalry regiments and indorsed the action which it had taken on the previous day in advancing the terms of enlistment from three to five years. This proposal was strongly opposed by General Wood, by Secretary Stimson, and President Taft.

When this bill came to the Senate objections were made to the amendment abolishing five of the cavalry regiments, as well as to other amendments which were new legislation. A conference committee of the two houses was appointed and on May 27 the bill was again submitted to Congress. It had been greatly changed, several of the old amendments had been struck out and others even more radical had been added. One of these was made with the plain intention of preventing the further service of General Leonard Wood as chief of staff. It provided certain conditions of service under which not only General Wood but many of the other general officers who were in direct line for appointment as chief of staff would have been ineligible. The conference report was adopted by the Senate on June 10 and by the House on June 13. The President promptly vetoed the bill, largely on account of the provision relating to the chief of staff. The President's action left the War Department without funds and it was necessary for Congress to pass three special resolutions continuing the appropriation act of 1912. The appropriation bill with the objectionable elements eliminated was finally signed by the President on August 9.

THE NATIONAL GUARD. Secretary Stimson in his annual report made recommendations in regard to legislation relating to the national guard with the object of bringing these organizations under more direct control of the government when war is threatened. At the present time the use of the national guard by the federal government is limited to the comparatively narrow functions of executing the laws of the Union, suppressing insurrection, and repelling invasion. It cannot be used outside the limits of the United States. It thus cannot be used for general military purposes. The recommendations included payment of the members of the national guard and provisions that should make it possible for the organization to be transferred and made available as a general military force, and not militia, in time of war. He urged the necessity of providing these bodies with adequate training so that they would be useful as volunteers in emergencies. He said that an attempt to use them in war as a militia would be to disregard some of the most costly and bloody experiences of our history. A militia pay bill was introduced in Congress, but no action was taken. Mr. Stimson also recommended the passage of the volunteers' bill, providing the necessary legislation under which, in time of war, a force of national volunteers can be created without delay. Even if the militia were organized as indicated above, there would be available only about 100,000 men, which would be an entirely inadequate force under serious conditions. A bill giving the government power to organize national volunteers was pending in Congress.

MILITARY OPERATIONS. The active operations of the army during the year were confined to the Philippines and to the Mexican frontier. In the Philippines there was less trouble from outlaws and from *ladrones* than in former years. The only affair of serious character was an attack made on Capt. Ephraim G. Peyton's command, Troops A and C, Second Cavalry, and Thirty-fourth and Fifty-second companies, Philippine Scouts, by a band of Moro outlaws on January 14, 1912, in the island of Jolo. One officer and one enlisted man were wounded in the engagement, and 20 Moros were found dead after the conflict.

The outbreak of the revolution in Mexico during 1912 made it necessary to patrol the frontier so as to enforce neutrality. The Second Cavalry was sent to Fort Bliss, El Paso, and the Fourteenth Cavalry to Forts Clark and McIntosh. On September 7, 1912, owing to border raids by Mexicans, formerly part of Orozco's rebel army, the Ninth Cavalry was ordered from Fort D. A. Russell to Douglas, Ariz., and the Thirteenth Cavalry was ordered to El Paso, Tex., from Fort Riley. These troops assisted in Texas in the suppression of General Reyes' attempt to instigate an insurrection against Madero's government, and later, after the passage of the joint resolution of Congress authorizing the President to prevent the importation of arms and munitions of war into Mexico, they assisted in the enforcement of that legislation, which was primarily responsible for the unsuccessful end of the insurrection led by General Orozco in Chihuahua. After the rebel forces had been broken up or scattered and were raiding the border, there was considerable active patrol duty performed by United States troops to prevent raids upon American ranches in Texas and Arizona. Brig.-Gen. Joseph W. Duncan was in command of the Department of Texas, and in charge of these operations until his death, on May 14, 1912, after which Brig.-Gen. E. Z. Steever succeeded him. At the end of the year there were on duty on the Mexican border six regiments of cavalry, a regiment and a half of infantry, a battery of field artillery, two companies of coast artillery, and one company of signal corps troops. The approximate total strength of these troops was 6754 officers and enlisted men.

ERECTION OF COAST FORTIFICATIONS. Work continued on fortifications for the defense of Honolulu and Pearl Harbor during 1912 and it was expected that by the end of the fiscal year 1913 they would be advanced to approximately 90 per cent. of completion.

The fortifications of Subig Bay in the Philippine Islands were completed. The fortifications of Manila Bay were about three-fourths completed, and with the funds already appropriated could be advanced about 90 per cent. towards completion.

At Guantánamo, Cuba, some emplacements were provided for medium and rapid-fire guns. About $285,000 was expended for that purpose and for the erection of structures for the mining system.

NAVY

NAVAL AIDS. The experiment of detailing four naval aids to assist the Secretary of the Navy in his conduct of naval affairs, first inaugurated by Secretary Meyer, has been so successful that Mr. Meyer in his annual report for 1912 recommended that these four aids be legalized. He said that during a trial extending over three years he had become convinced that efficient administration of the navy cannot be accomplished by the secretary without some sort of a board or council made up of expert advisers. The four aids appointed by Secretary Meyer are as follows: Aid for operations of the fleet; aid for personnel; aid for material; and aid for inspections. These officers are without executive authority, but have a supervisory function and serve in an advisory capacity. The "aid for operations" gives his entire time to the operations of the fleet. He works in conjunction with the war college and the general board on war-plans and strategical matters. The "aid for personnel" is instrumental in coördinating the work of the bureau of navigation, the bureau of medicine and surgery, the marine corps, offices of naval militia, naval reserve, aviation, radio-telegraphy, and of the judge-advocate-general. The "aid for material" acts largely as referee when differences of opinion arise between heads of the different bureaus making up the division of material. The "aid for inspections" is especially charged with the supervision of the work of the two permanent department inspection boards, the one for ships and the other for shore stations. All four aids recommend the assignments of flag officers and captains.

THE FLEETS. The vessels of the navy are divided into the Atlantic fleet, the Pacific fleet, the Asiatic fleet, the Atlantic torpedo fleet, the Pacific torpedo fleet, and unattached vessels in active service.

Throughout the fiscal year 1912 the Atlantic fleet, under the command of Admiral Hugo Osterhaus, carried on exercises, manœuvres, and fleet training. In the winter of 1911-12 the usual visit was made to Guantánamo Bay, where there was target practice and other exercises. No foreign cruises were made by the fleet during the year. One squadron of the fleet welcomed the German fleet which called at Hampton Roads and New York in June, 1912. In the latter part of May it became necessary to employ one squadron of the fleet in the waters of Cuba and vicinity because of the disturbed conditions existing in that republic, but by the end of June conditions had so improved as to permit of the release of these vessels and their return to their usual exercises.

The Pacific fleet, consisting of two divisions of armored cruisers, three in the first division and two in the second, was until March 7, 1912, under the command of Rear-Admiral Chauncey Thomas. On that day he was succeeded by Rear-Admiral W. H. H. Southerland. The early part of the year was spent by this fleet in overhauling, docking, and target practice. But in November, 1911, conditions made it desirable for the fleet to base at Honolulu. About three and a half months were spent in the Hawaiian Islands, with Honolulu as a base. On March 18 six vessels sailed for the naval station at Olongapo, Philippine Islands, and operated in that vicinity until the latter part of June, when they crossed to China and Japan and the voyage home was started.

The Asiatic fleet, under the command of Rear-Admiral Joseph B. Murdock, throughout the fiscal year continued operations on the Asiatic station. During the revolution in China in the winter of 1911-12 very valuable services were rendered, and all available strength, including the destroyers, was concentrated in Chinese waters. Rear-Admiral Reginald F. Nicholson succeeded Rear-Admiral Murdock in July, 1912. The submarines of the Asiatic fleet made a very successful cruise to the Philippine Islands in April, 1912. The vessels of this fleet were ordered to Nicaragua during the revolution under General Mena and through their efforts order was established in that country. See UNITED STATES, *Foreign Relations*.

The Atlantic torpedo fleet of destroyers and submarines continued their valuable and instructive exercises in developing the offensive and defensive tactics of torpedo boats, working in conjunction with the Atlantic fleet whenever opportunity offered. This fleet ceased to exist as a separate organization in March, 1912, when the destroyers with their tenders were attached to the Atlantic fleet as the torpedo flotilla thereof, and nine submarines and their three tenders were constituted as the Atlantic submarine flotilla, a separate organization which will be attached to the fleet whenever joint exercises are possible.

The Pacific torpedo fleet, consisting of twelve destroyers and torpedo boats and two submarines with tenders, also carried out tactical and strategical exercises of an advanced nature and valuable information was obtained from their operations. Shortage of personnel made it necessary to place most of these vessels in reserve so that at the end of the fiscal year 1912 only one group of five destroyers remained on active service, together with two new submarines that took the place of two older ones placed in reserve.

MOBILIZATION OF THE FLEETS. The second mobilization of the Atlantic fleet took place in the North River, New York City, beginning October 14, 1912. Simultaneously there was a mobilization of the Asiatic fleet in Manila Bay, and arrangements were made to have the Pacific fleet mobilized at San Francisco. The vessels of the Atlantic fleet assembled at New York on October 14 and were inspected on the forenoon of that day by the Secretary of the Navy. In the afternoon of the same day the President inspected the fleet and on the following day reviewed it, as the ships passed out of the harbor in fleet formation. At this review there were 31 battleships, 4 armored cruisers, and 88 smaller vessels, representing a total displacement of 720,486 tons. There were attached to these vessels 1300 officers, 27,464 enlisted men of the navy and marine corps. Among the battleships were the *Arkansas* and the *Wyoming*, each of 26,000 tons; the *Utah* of 21,825 tons, and the *Delaware* and *North Dakota*, of 20,000 tons each. The total displacement of battleships was 478,508 tons. There were in this review 25 vessels in addition to those in the review held the previous year. Of these, 11 were completed, commissioned, and added to the active fleet since the date of the previous review.

NEW CONSTRUCTION. During the fiscal year 1912 the two largest battleships heretofore constructed were completed. These are the *Wyoming* and the *Arkansas*, each of 26,000 tons displacement and 21 knots designed speed. Each of the vessels on trial much exceeded the designed speed and they have been characterized as the fastest battleships in the world. Each carries twelve 12-inch 50-calibre guns in six turrets on the centre line, permitting all guns to be fired on a broadside. They are protected by eleven inches of the most efficient armor. They are driven by Parsons turbines with four shafts and the boilers are fitted to burn both coal and oil. They were in 1912 the largest battleships in service in any navy, in addition to being the fastest. The three battleships *Texas*, *Nevada*, and *Oklahoma* were under construction in 1912, as well as a number of smaller vessels.

The Secretary of the Navy in his annual report pointed out the necessity of a continuing annual building programme. He declared it necessary that the navy shall include a total of 41 battleships, with a proportionate number of other fighting and auxiliary vessels, in order to place the United States on a safe basis in its relation with the other world powers. The general board of the navy will recommend at the session of the Sixty-third Congress the construction of 4 new battleships, 2 armored cruisers, 16 destroyers, and a number of transports, submarines, and gunboats.

NAVY YARDS. The work of coördinating the work at the navy yards, undertaken by Secretary Meyer, continued during 1912. A uniform system of modern management has been inaugurated at these yards and a uniform system of shop stores has been formulated and put into operation. The subject of protection for yard workmen from accidents has been thoroughly investigated and instructions have been issued to all yards to bring about a monthly inspection of all shops expressly to maintain safety devices at all points showing necessity therefor. In the matter of improving and unifying the system of shop management at the yards progress has been made with a view to securing results of permanent value. In pursuance of the policy of the department of dispensing with such navy yards and stations as are not necessary, the naval stations at Pensacola, New Orleans, San Juan, Porto Rico, Culebra, and Sitka were closed during the year. The coaling stations at Frenchmans Bay, Me., and New London, Conn., were shut down with a view to ultimate abandonment and disposal of the land.

PERSONNEL. The Secretary of the Navy repeated his recommendations made in previous years as to the necessity of creating the rank of "admiral" and "vice admiral." At the present time no provision is made except for the lowest grade in flag rank, that of rear-admiral. The great battle fleet of the American navy is commanded by a rear-admiral and four other rear-admirals are under his orders. This is contrary to the system maintained by other great naval powers. Nineteen of the navies of the world include at least vice-admirals, nine of them admirals, and Japan, Germany, and England have admirals of the fleet, in addition.

NAVAL MILITIA. The naval militia organizations of a number of the States volunteered for active service in the fleet during the naval review in New York in October, 1912. Seventy-eight officers and 567 men of the naval militia took part in the manœuvres. These materially assisted in the movement of the reserve ships. The Secretary of the Navy urged legislation to increase the strength and efficiency of the naval militia. He also pointed out the necessity of establishing a naval reserve of 50,000 men in order to properly man ships in time of emergency.

Statistics in regard to the strength of the United States navy in comparison with the strength of foreign powers will be found in the article NAVAL PROGRESS.

POST OFFICE

The surplus in the administration of the Post Office Department, which for the first time was attained in 1911, was not repeated in 1912 on account of the extraordinary amount of franked matter mailed in the political primaries. This produced a deficit up to the end of the fiscal year. After its close, however, the income of the department again outstripped expenses. During the administration of Mr. Hitchcock as postmaster-general the reports of income and expense in the department indicated an aggregate saving of about $45,000,000. During his administration 4765 new post offices were established, delivery by carrier was provided in 80 additional cities, and 3043 new rural routes, aggregating 73,191 miles, were authorized. To insure prompt and accurate handling of the mails by reason of this extended service, the force of postal employees was increased by more than 12,000.

The most notable event of the year in connection with the Post Office Department was the inauguration of the parcel post. This will be described in the article PARCEL POST.

POSTAL SAVINGS SYSTEM. The work of establishing postal savings depositories at presidential post offices was completed early in the fiscal year 1911. During 1911-12 the system was extended to include 4004 fourth-class post offices, as well as 645 branch offices and stations in the larger cities. At the end of the fiscal year 1912 there were 12,812 depositories at which patrons of the system may open accounts. The depositors numbered about 300,000 and the deposits amounted to approximately $28,000,000, not including $1,314,140, which is the sum withdrawn by depositors for the purpose of buying postal savings bonds. These bonds had been rendered particularly attractive by the announcement that the board of trustees will purchase them at their face value whenever their holders desire to convert them into cash.

The postal savings funds deposited at each post office are required by law to be redeposited in local banks. State and national banks to the number of 7357 had qualified at the end of the fiscal year as depositories for these funds. The deposits in such banks are secured by bonds aggregating $54,000,000. Of this amount, $37,000,000 represents municipal bonds, the market ability of which has been greatly increased by the establishment of the postal savings system. It is estimated that by the end of the fiscal year ending June 30, 1912, the gross income of the postal savings system will amount to $700,000 and the interest payable to depositors to $300,000. It is expected that when the deposits shall have increased to $50,000,000 the system will be self-sustaining.

READJUSTMENT OF POSTAGE RATES. In accordance with a joint resolution passed by Congress on March 4, 1911, a commission was appointed by the President to investigate the subject of the readjustment of the postage rates. The commission included Mr. Justice Hughes of the Supreme Court, President Lowell of Harvard, and Mr. Harry A. Wheeler of Chicago. After granting an extensive hearing the commission prepared an exhaustive report and submitted it to the President on February 3, 1912. It was found that the cost of handling and transporting second-class mail was approximately six cents a pound. The recommendation of the Post Office Department that as a step toward the prope adjustment of postage charges the rate be increased from one to two cents a pound on all second-class publications, except those mailed for delivery in the county of publication, was approved by the commission. On February 22, 1912, the report of the commission was transmitted to Congress by the President, who urged favorable consideration. At the end of the year no action had been taken by Congress.

SHIPMENT OF PERIODICALS BY FREIGHT. The plan of shipping monthly, semi-monthly, and bi-weekly periodicals in fast freight trains, which was undertaken in one of the four contract sections of the country in 1912, resulted in a saving during the year of more than a million dollars. After the close of the fiscal year 1912 this method of transporting periodicals was extended to another contract section, but Congress forbade the further application of the policy in the two remaining sections.

CLASSIFICATION OF POSTMASTERS. On October 15, 1912, President Taft issued an order classifying fourth-class postmasters in the United States who had not already been classified under a previous order. In 1908 postmasters of the fourth class in the fourteen States lying east of the Mississippi River and north of the Ohio River had been placed in the classified service by executive order. These postmasters numbered about 15,000. By the executive order of October 15, 1912, over 36,000 postmasters were affected. By the terms of this order fourth-class post offices are divided into two groups, A and B. Group A embraces all post offices at which the compensation of postmasters is $500 or more, and Group B includes all offices at which the compensation of postmasters is less than $500. Appointments to offices in Group A are made by selecting one of three names certified by the Civil Service Commission after competitive examination. Appointments to the offices in Group B are made on the recommendation of post office inspectors, with the approval of the Civil Service Commission, after personal investigation by the inspectors.

FINANCIAL SUMMARY. The total revenues of the Post Office Department from all sources for the fiscal year ending June 30, 1912, amounted to $246,744,015. The expenditures amounted to $248,525,450, leaving an excess of expenditures over revenues of $1,781,434. The chief source of revenue was the sale of stamps, stamped envelopes, newspaper wrappers, and postal cards. The amount received from this source was $221,563,619. For second-class postage the revenue amounted to $9,399,140, and for third- and fourth-class postage paid in money, to $5,444,615. The largest expenditure was for transportation of mails on railroads, $47,095,984; for compensation to assistant postmasters and clerks in post offices was paid $42,484,457; for the expense of rural delivery, $41,840,910; for city delivery, $34,162,562; for compensation to postmasters, $28,647,776; and for the railway mail service, $20,711,675.

PENSIONS

A new pension act was passed by Congress in 1912, becoming operative on May 11. This act provides that any person who served for 90 days or more in the military or naval service of the United States during the Civil War, who was honorably discharged therefrom, and who has reached the age of 62 years or over, shall, upon making proof of such facts, be placed upon the pension roll and be entitled to receive a monthly pension in accordance with the following table (this act includes those who have served also in the War with Mexico):

LENGTH OF SERVICE

Age	90 days	6 mos.	1 year	1½ years	2 years	2½ years	3 years
62....	$13.00	$13.50	$14.00	$14.50	$15.00	$15.50	$16.00
66....	15.00	15.50	16.00	16.50	17.00	18.00	19.00
70....	18.00	19.00	20.00	21.50	23.00	24.00	25.00
75....	21.00	22.50	24.00	27.00	30.00	30.00	30.00

Up to June 30, 1912, 406,048 applications for pensions under this act had been received.

The total number of survivors of the Civil War on the pension roll at the close of the fiscal year 1912 was 497,263, a net decrease of 32,621. The number of survivors whose names were dropped from the roll during the year on account of death was 33,891 and the number of new names added to the roll was 1513. The number of individuals in the military and naval service of the United States during the Civil War is estimated at 2,213,365. It is therefore evident that 75 per cent. or more of those who rendered service in the Civil War are deceased. The annual death rate of the survivors is nearly 7 per cent. and the average age is approximately 71 years. In addition to the Civil War pensioners there were on the rolls at the end of the fiscal year 239 widows of the War of 1812; 1387 survivors and 2629 widows of the Indian wars; 1639 survivors and 5982 widows of the War with Mexico; 23,383 invalids of the War with Spain, and 13,757 invalids of the regular army. The total number of persons on the roll from all wars in the fiscal year 1912 was 860,294, a decrease of 51,188 during the year. The amount disbursed for pensions during the fiscal year was $152,986,433. The total amount paid as pensions from 1866 to 1912 is $4,286,922,719. The total amount paid for pensions since the beginning of the government, including pensions for all wars, is $4,383,368,163. Of this sum, it is estimated that $70,000,000 has been paid to survivors of pensioners of the War of the Revolution. The total number of pension certificates issued during the fiscal year was 90,922. Of these, 22,777 were original applications. There were pending at the close of the fiscal year 422,464 claims for pensions. There are now no pensioners from the War of the Revolution on the pension rolls. The last widow pensioner of that war was Esther S. Damon of Plymouth Union, Vt., who died November 11, 1906, aged 92 years. The last survivor of the War of the Revolution was Daniel F. Bakeman, who died at Freedom, N. Y., April 5, 1869, aged 109 years, 6 months, and 8 days. The last surviving soldier of the War of 1812 was Hiram Cronk of Ava, N. Y., who died May 13, 1905, aged 105 years and 16 days.

PATENTS

During the fiscal year ended June 30, 1910, there were received 69,236 applications for mechanical patents, 1775 applications for designs, 195 applications for reissues, 7238 applications for trade marks, 941 applications for labels, and 362 applications for prints. There were 35,539 applications for patents granted. The number of patents expiring was 19,634. The need for a new building for the United States Patent Office becomes each year more obvious. Valuable models and papers are stored in places which have no adequate fire protection. A bill will be introduced into Congress providing for the construction of a new Patent Office building.

BUREAU OF MINES

The general purpose of this bureau is to conduct, in behalf of the public welfare, fundamental inquiries and investigations concerning the mining industry. The two phases of the industry that are of the greatest national importance are safety and efficiency, and it is with these that the bureau is chiefly concerned. The investigations conducted by the bureau during 1912 were confined mainly to two groups: The study of fuels belonging to or used by the government and inquiry into the causes of accidents in mines and the most feasible means for preventing such accidents. The first of these investigations has to do chiefly with the purchase, for the use of the government, of coal aggregating in cost about $8,000,000, chiefly for the use of the navy. In addition to investigations of coal, the bureau tested and analyzed a large number of samples of fuel oil now used to determine the suitability of the oils for use as fuel on naval vessels or at government power plants. The investigations into the causes and means of prevention of mine accidents were continued and extended during the year, but as yet they have not progressed as far as the needs of the coal-mining industry. In order to provide facilities for exploring mines immediately after disasters, while the mines are still full of poisonous explosive gases so that an examination may be made while the evidence of the disaster is still fresh, the bureau maintains six safety stations, one each at Pittsburgh, Pa.; Knoxville, Tenn.; Birmingham, Ala.; McAlester, Okla.; Urbana, Ill., and Seattle, Wash. The bureau is also equipped with seven mine-safety cars, which are provided with mine rescue and fire-fighting apparatus.

Diplomatic Service

There were several changes of importance in the diplomatic service of the United States in 1912. Three new ambassadors were appointed. These were Edwin V. Morgan, appointed ambassador to Brazil to succeed Irving B. Dudley, who died in 1911; Myron T. Herrick of Ohio to succeed Robert Bacon as ambassador to France, and Larz Anderson to succeed Charles Page Bryan. Whitelaw Reid (q. v.), American ambassador to Great Britain, died on December ; and his successor had not been appointed at the close of the year. There were many important changes among the ministers to foreign countries, especially to Central and South American countries. John W. Garrett was appointed minister to the Argentine Republic to succeed John Ridgely Carter; Theodore Marburg succeeded Larz Anderson as minister to Belgium; Jacob G. Schurman, president of Cornell University, was appointed minister to Greece and Montenegro, to succeed George Moses; Cyrus E. Woods was appointed minister to Portugal to succeed Edwin V. Morgan, who became ambassador to Brazil; and Fred W. Carpenter became minister to Siam to succeed Hamilton King.

Among the ambassadors accredited to the United States the most important event was the announcement that James Bryce, ambassador from Great Britain, would retire and would be succeeded by Sir Cecil Arthur Spring-Rice. Konstantin Theodor Dumba was appointed ambassador from Austria to succeed Baron Hengelmüller von Hengebar, who had served since 1902. Viscount Sutemi Chinda was sent from Japan as ambassador, succeeding Viscount Uchida Yasuya. Señor Don Manuel Calero succeeded Don Gilberto Crespo y Martinez as ambassador from Mexico. As noted in the table below, there were no ministers from the Argentine Republic, Colombia, Dominican Republic, Guatemala, Haiti, Honduras, Panama, Peru, and Siam in 1912.

Federal Judiciary

There was one appointment to the bench of the United States Supreme Court in 1912. Mahlon Pitney (q. v.) of New Jersey received on the bench the place made vacant by the death of Justice Harlan in 1911. The Supreme Court in 1912 was made up as follows, with dates of appointment given in parentheses: Chief Justice, Edward D. White of Louisiana (1910); Joseph McKenna, California (1898); Oliver W. Holmes, Massachusetts (1902); William R. Day, Ohio (1903); Horace Lurton, Tennessee (1909); Charles A. Hughes, New York (1910); Willis Van Devanter, Wyoming (1910); Joseph R. Lamar, Georgia (1910); Mahlon Pitney, New Jersey (1912). The strong opposition which developed in Congress against the Commerce Court resulted in legislation which practically abolished that court after March , 1913. See Railways.

The impeachment trial of Robert W. Arch-

Ambassadors

Country	Accredited by United States		Accredited to United States	
Austria-Hungary	Richard C. Kerens, Mo.,	1909	Konstantin Theodor Dumba	1912
Brazil	Edwin V. Morgan, N. Y.,	1912	Domicio da Gama	1911
France	Myron T. Herrick, O.,	1912	J. J. Jusserand	1903
Germany	John G. A. Leishman, Pa.,	1911	Johann Heinrich, Count von Bernstorff	1908
Great Britain			James Bryce	1907
Italy	Thomas J. O'Brien, Mich.,	1911	Marchese Cusani-Confalonieri	1910
Japan	Larz Anderson, D. C.,	1912	Viscount Sutemi Chinda	1912
Mexico	Henry L. Wilson, Wash.,	1911	Don Manuel Calero	1912
Russia	Curtis Guild, Mass.,	1911	George Bakhméteff	1911
Turkey	W. W. Rockhill, D. C.,	1911	Youssouf Zia Pasha	1910

Ministers Plenipotentiary

Country	Accredited by United States		Accredited to United States	
Argentine Republic	J. W. Garrett, Md.,	1912	Rómulo S. Naón	1911
Belgium	Theodore Marburg, Md.,	1912	E. Havenith	1911
Bolivia	Horace G. Knowles, Del.,	1910	Ignacio Calderón	
Chile	Henry P. Fletcher, Pa.,	1909	Eduardo Suarez	1911
China	William J. Calhoun,	1909	Chang Yin Tang	1909
Colombia	James T. DuBois, Pa.,	1911	Don Julio Betancourt	1912
Costa Rica	Lewis Einstein, N. Y.,	1911	Joaquin Bernardo Calvo	1899
Cuba	Arthur M. Beaupré,	1911	Antonio Martin Rivero	1911
Denmark	Maurice F. Egan, D. C.,	1907	Count Moltke	1908
Dominican Republic	W. W. Russell, D. C.,	1910	Emilio C. Joubert	1909
Ecuador			Rafael M. Arizaga	1910
* Greece	Jacob G. Schurman, N. Y.,	1912	L. A. Coromilas	1909
Guatemala	R. S. Reynolds Hitt,	1905	Joaquin Antonio Mendez	
Haiti	Henry W. Furniss, Ind.,	1911	Solon Ménos	1911
Honduras	Charles Dunning White, N. J.,	1910	Dr. Alberto Membreno	1912
† Netherlands	Lloyd Bryce, N. Y.,	1911	Jonkherr J. Loudon	1908
Nicaragua	George T. Weitzel, Mo.,	1911	Salvador Castrillo, Jr.	1911
Norway	Laurits S. Swenson, Minn.,	1911	Bryn	1910
Panama	Percival Dodge, Mass.,	1911	Ramon M. Valdés	1912
Persia	Charles W. Russell, D. C.,	1909	§ Mirza Ali Kuli Khan	1910
Peru	Clay Howard, Ky.,	1911	Federico A. Pezet	1912
Portugal	Cyrus E. Woods, Pa.,	1912	Viscount de Alte	1902
‡ Rumania	John B. Jackson, N. J.,	1911		
Salvador	William Heimke, Kan.,	1909	Federico Mejia	1907
Siam	F. W. Carpenter, Cal.,	1912	Prince Traidos Prabandh	1912
Spain	Henry C. Ide, Vt.,	1909	Juan de Riaño y Gayangos	1910
Sweden	Charles H. Graves, Minn.,	1905	W. A. F. Ekengren	1912
Switzerland	Henry S. Boutell,	1911	Paul Ritter	1909
¶ Uruguay	Nicolay A. Grevstad,	1911	Carlos María de Pena	1911
Venezuela	Elliott Northcote, W. Va.,	1911	P. Ezequiel Rojas	1909
Minister and Resident Consul to Liberia, W. D. Crum, S. C., appointed				1910

* Accredited also to Montenegro. † Accredited also to Luxemburg. ‡ Accredited also to Servia and Bulgaria. ¶ Accredited also to Paraguay. § Chargé d'Affaires.

bald, a member of this court, is described under the section *Congress.* President Taft made one appointment in the Circuit Court of the United States, Joseph B. McPherson of Pennsylvania, who was appointed judge of the third circuit.

The most important decisions handed down by the Supreme Court are noted in various articles in the YEAR BOOK, notably TRUSTS and RAILWAYS.

An interesting decision because of the relation of the Court of Commerce to the Supreme Court was handed down by the latter in June. The case was that of a soap company, which had been appealed from the Commerce Court to the Supreme Court. The decision of the Supreme Court was delivered by Chief Justice White. In this he used strong language in regard to the functions of the Commerce Court. He said in the course of his opinion that "to give to the act creating the Commerce Court the meaning affixed to it by the court below would be virtually to overthrow the entire system which had arisen from the adoption and enforcement of the act to regulate commerce." The case was one in which the Interstate Commerce Commission denied the relief for which the soap company had petitioned. The commission declared that the rules of the railway concern which the soap company complained of conformed to the act regulating commerce and tended to prevent discrimination. Upon receipt of this decision the soap company appealed to the Commerce Court, complaining of the decision of the Interstate Commerce Commission. The commission challenged the right of the court to hear the complaint, inasmuch as there was no affirmative order of the commission upon which the court could pass. In spite of this, the court decided to go on and hear the merits of the case, and upon hearing them the court decided that the commission was right on the merits of the question. The soap company thereupon appealed to the Supreme Court, and this court in the decision of Justice White decided that the Commerce Court exceeded its powers in attempting to take up the question at all. Stated in brief, the point is that it is the business of the commission to administer the law and the business of the court not to enforce its conceptions of the meaning of the interstate law, but simply to decide whether the affirmative orders of the commission are contrary to law. Justice White pointed out in this decision that the purpose of creating the Commerce Court was "not to create a court with new and strange powers destructive of the previous well-established administrative authority of the Interstate Commerce Commission."

DISTRICT OF COLUMBIA

The results of the census of manufactures in the District, taken in 1910, were published in 1912. The number of establishments was 518, compared with 482 in 1904. The wage earners numbered 7707, compared with 6299 in 1904. The capital invested was $30,553,000, compared with $20,200,000 in 1904. The value of the product was $25,289,000, compared with $18,359,000 in 1904. The most important industries were those connected with printing and publishing. In these 1565 wage earners were employed and the product was valued at $4,899,000. Other important industries were the making of bread and other bakery products, the brewing of malt liquors, and foundry and machine shop products. Of the 7707 wage earners 828 were women. Those under 16 years of age numbered 19, of whom 18 were male. The prevailing hours of labor did not exceed 54 a week. A large proportion of the wage earners of the District are employed by the federal government in operations similar to those carried on in manufacturing establishments conducted under private ownership. These establishments numbered 11. They included four plants for engraving and printing, one for manufacture of professional and scientific instruments at the Smithsonian Institution, a naval gun factory at the United States Navy Yard, three government printing offices, and two other industries. The wage earners employed in these government industries numbered, in 1909, 10,657. The capital invested amounted to $28,479,599.

Several bills for improvements in the District were introduced in the Sixty-second Congress. These included a new memorial bridge across the Potomac and additions and improvements to Rock Creek Park. Final action had not been taken upon these measures at the end of the year.

The commissioners of the District in 1912 were Cuno H. Rudolph (Republican), John A. Johnson (Democrat), and Major W. V. Judson (non-partisan) of the corps of engineers, United States army; secretary, William Tindall.

CONGRESS

The Sixty-second Congress convened in its first regular session on December 4, 1911. In a special session which had met on April 4, 1911, at the call of President Taft, for the immediate purpose of taking action on the Canadian reciprocity measure, the organization of both houses had been perfected and this organization remained practically unchanged in the regular session. The Sixty-second Congress presented many features of unusual interest. For the first time in sixteen years the House of Representatives was strongly Democratic, while the Senate, though nominally Republican by a majority of eight, as the result of the division of the Republicans into Progressives and Conservatives, could not be depended upon to give Republican majorities; in fact, throughout the special and regular sessions the majority of the Republican vote in the Senate was cast quite as often against measures favored by the President as for them.

The leader of the Democratic majority in the House was Oscar W. Underwood, chairman of the ways and means committee. Other Democrats who took an important part in the work of the House were: John J. Fitzgerald of New York, chairman of the committee on appropriations; Henry D. Clayton of Alabama, chairman of the Interstate Commerce Commission, and William Sulzer of New York, chairman of the committee on foreign affairs. The Republicans of the House chose James R. Mann of Illinois as leader. He declined to serve on any committee and gave his whole energy to the minority leadership. At a Republican caucus held prior to the special session he was authorized to assign to Republican members the minority places left for them on the various committees by the Democratic caucus. The most important of these appointments were those of Sereno E. Payne of New York as the leading Republican member of the ways and means committee, and former Speaker Cannon as the chief Republican on the appropriations committee. In preparing his assignments Mr. Mann gave full recognition to the Republican insurgents of the House.

In the Senate there was no aggressive Republican leadership, due largely to the fact that the Republican forces were divided and the divisions were continually opposing each other, and secondarily to the fact that while there were many senators of ability in each wing of the party, there was none who showed the aggressive force necessary to a leader. Senator Penrose of Pennsylvania succeeded to the nominal leadership as chairman of the finance committee, formerly held by Senator Aldrich of Rhode Island, but he did not at any time assume the rôle of leader of the majority. The Democrats, too, were divided into the regular element, composed, in the main, of older senators, and the progressive element, comprising most of the newly elected senators. Senator Martin of Virginia was chosen nominal leader on the Democratic side.

WORK OF THE SPECIAL SESSION. While the special session was called by President Taft for the single purpose of acting upon the reciprocity measure the Democratic leaders took advantage of the opportunity offered them and introduced a number of tariff and other bills in addition to the reciprocity measure. The reciprocity bill was passed by the Senate on July 22, and on the following day was signed by the President. The tariff measures included bills amending the wool and cotton schedules of the Payne-Aldrich tariff, and another called the farmers' free list bill, which aimed to make up to the farmers whatever losses they were supposed to have incurred from the reciprocity measure. All these measures were vetoed by the President.

A committee was appointed to reopen the investigation into the election of Senator Lorimer. A bill providing for the direct election of senators, which was introduced into the Sixty-first Congress and lost, was reintroduced into the Sixty-second Congress and was passed by the vote of both houses. The session closed, however, before final action could be taken by a committee of conference of both houses. A bill provided for the publicity of campaign expenditures and was signed by the President. Bills providing for the admission of Arizona and New Mexico were passed and became laws. A number of investigations were authorized during the session of this Congress. Among these were: The investigation of the United States Steel Corporation; investigation of the operation of the sugar trust; investigations into the conduct of various departments of the government; investigations into the postal service, and investigation into the affairs of the Civil Service Commission.

SECOND SESSION, OR FIRST REGULAR SESSION. There were few changes in the personnel of the Senate and House when Congress reconvened in the first regular session on December 4, 1911. In the Senate, a new senator from Maine, Obadiah Gardner, took the place of the late William P. Frye. Failure to choose a senator from Colorado to succeed Senator Hughes, who died between the special and regular sessions, left the total number of members in the Senate, 91, of whom 49 were Republicans and 42 Democrats. In the House there were 390 members, of whom 227 were Republicans and one Socialist. There was one vacancy in the membership of the House. The session of Congress preceding the Christmas holidays is usually given to the routine business and the introduction of bills. In those first days of the Sixty-second Congress, however, business of much importance was transacted before Congress adjourned for the holidays.

The President's message to Congress at the opening of the session was, as has been the custom of President Taft, devoted to a single subject. It was the notable message on the phases of the Anti-Trust statute. The President analyzed the judicial decisions and the judicial interpretations of the Sherman law, dwelling at length on the legal aspect of the question. He defended the action of the courts in the Standard Oil and Tobacco Trust cases. The President suggested the enactment of a law which would describe and denounce unfair methods. He suggested, in addition, federal incorporation under the control of an executive bureau or commission. He urged that corporations which have been incorporated with federal charters should be subjected to rigid supervision by this bureau or commission, which should also supervise the issue of stocks and bonds, and bring about effective publicity. The Pension bill, known as the Sherwood Pension Service bill, was introduced in the House on December 12 (see paragraph *Pension Bill* below). On December 20 the President sent to Congress a message dealing with tariff reform, together with a summary of the report of the tariff board. At the same time he sent a special message in which he approved the main features of the report of the national monetary commission. He renewed, at this time, his recommendation for legislation fixing tolls and the government of the Canal Zone.

The most important action taken by Congress in these first days of the session was that which led to the abrogation of the treaty of 1823 with Russia (see *Foreign Relations*). Congress reassembled after the holidays on June 3, 1912. The most important work done until its adjournment on August 26, 1912, is discussed in the following paragraphs.

RULES OF THE HOUSE. By action of the Democratic majority in the House of Representatives on February 3, the action taken in the previous Congress by which the Speaker was largely deprived of power, was, to a great extent, nullified. The most important change made in the previous session related to the calling of bills from the committee to which they had been referred. Up to the time of the change in 1910, it had been comparatively easy to allow any bill, no matter what its merits or importance, to die in committee, as if the committee was unfriendly it could refuse to report and nothing could be done. The only way in which such a bill could be called from committee was in securing the consent of the Speaker, so that, as a matter of fact, the whole question rested with the Speaker of the House and the committee which had been appointed by him. The revolt against Speaker Cannon in 1910 brought about the adoption of a rule which made it possible to let the House vote on the question whether a bill should be called from committee or not without it being necessary to obtain the consent of the Speaker. This change was brought about by the Democrats and insurgent Republicans acting in combination. When the Democrats came into power in the House they found this rule an inconvenient one. They, therefore, on February 3, 1912, changed the procedure so that the calling of a bill out of committee cannot be secured until other business which depends on the Speaker is concluded. This makes it possible for the Speaker to prevent bills being called out and gives to that officer a portion at least of the power which he had before the rules were changed.

TARIFF BILLS. The tariff bills passed in the regular session of the Sixty-second Congress are discussed in detail in the article on TARIFF. Here is given only a chronological summary of the passage of these bills through Congress and their final disposition. The first measure introduced by Representative Underwood was a bill revising the steel and iron schedule of the tariff. This was passed in the House on January 29, by a vote of 210 to 109. On February 19, a bill revising the chemical schedule of the tariff was introduced and discussion was begun upon it. The bill passed the House on February 21. It was passed almost entirely by Democratic votes, only two Republicans voting for it. In the Democratic caucus held on March 1, Chairman Underwood stated that a unanimous agreement of the members of the ways and means committee had been made to the proposal to revise the tariff duties and upon a new form of income tax which was to be levied through the extension of the p esent corporation-tax law to individuals and copartnerships, the rate being one per cent. on the net income of the individual or copartnership from business sources. This tax was to apply only to net incomes of over $5000. Mr. Underwood estimated that this tax would bring in a revenue of $60,000,000. The object of levying this tax was to offset the loss of $53,000,000 in customs revenues on sugar, which would have resulted from the passage of the measure eliminating duty on sugar. The caucus voted to support these measures and on March 19, by a vote of 250 to 40, the House passed this bill. It had already passed on March 13, by a vote of 198 to 103, a bill placing sugar on the free list. On March 26 the President sent to the House the report of the tariff board on the cotton schedule. In this message he urged a considerable reduction of duties in this schedule. The report of the tariff board suggested such a reduction, possibly averaging 30 per cent. On March 29, Mr. Underwood introduced a bill revising the wool schedule of the tariff, and on April 2, by a vote of 129 to 92, this bill passed the House. This measure provided for a duty of 20 per cent. on raw wool, a reduction of 50 per cent. It was approximately the same as the bill which was passed by the House and Senate at the previous session, and had been vetoed by the President. This concluded the introduction of tariff bills in the House and the direct action of that body thereon. In the Senate the wool bill was brought to a vote on May 31 and was passed by a coalition of Democrats and insurgent Republicans. The bill revising the chemical schedule of the tariff, which was brought to a vote on July 3, was rejected by the Senate. On July 25, action was taken by the Senate on several of these tariff measures by a vote of 34 to 20. The annual appropriation for the tariff board, proposed by the President, was passed. All the Democratic senators, with the exception of three, voted against the appropriation. The Senate also adopted an amendment requiring the board to submit an annual report to Congress. Senator Penrose, on behalf of the finance committee, proposed a substitute for the wool bill passed by the House and the substitute was passed in the committee of the whole by a vote of 34 to 32. It was supported by the Progressives. After its passage, however, Senator La Follette moved as an amendment his bill which was passed in the previous session and was vetoed by the President. This bill passed the Senate by a vote of 40 to 26, the majority being composed of the Democrats and ten Republican insurgents. This bill made the duties 35 per cent. on raw wool and from 40 to 55 per cent. on manufactured wool. On July 26, the so-called Excise bill, which had already passed the House, was passed by the Senate by a vote of 37 to 18, those voting for it being again a combination of Democrats and Insurgents. Amendments were placed on the bill which were designed to include idle holders of stocks and bonds, and excluding labor, agricultural, benevolent, and building loan associations. Another amendment providing for a permanent tariff commission, introduced by Senator Cummins, was also attached to the bill together with a provision repealing the Canadian reciprocity measure. On July 27 the Senate passed a substitute for the House sugar bill. This bill was proposed by Senator Lodge and amendments were added to it by Senator Bristow. This bill eliminated the differential and revised the main duties on raw and refined sugar by about 16 per cent. It was passed by a vote of the united Republican senators. The bills which had been passed by both houses thereupon went to conference for the purpose of reconciling amendments made in the Senate. On August 3, however, the amendment to the wool bill, which repealed the Canadian reciprocity act, was withdrawn in the Senate. The conference report on the wool-tariff bill was accepted by the Senate on August 5 by a vote of 35 to 28 and the bill was sent to the President. It was vetoed by him on August 9 on the ground that the rates in the bill were too low and that they would be unjust to the wool growers as well as to the manufacturers and would throw thousands of employees out of work. He said, however, that he would be glad to sign a bill making whatever reductions in the tariff the report of the tariff board would permit. On August 13, the House again passed this bill over the President's veto by a vote of 174 to 80. Sixty Republicans were absent from the chamber and 21 were counted with the Democrats in the affirmative. In the Senate, however, the bill was not passed over the veto, the vote in that body being 39 to 36 against passage. The President had also vetoed the steel-tariff bill. This was passed over his veto in the House by a vote of 173 to 83, 16 Republican representatives voting for its passage. In the Senate the veto was sustained by a vote of 32 to 29 by a strictly party vote. The bill revising the cotton schedule of the tariff, previously passed by the House, was passed by the Senate on April 14. This bill was vetoed by the President. This concludes the record of tariff bills in the first session of the Sixty-second Congress.

THE ARBITRATION TREATIES. The proposed arbitration treaty with Great Britain is discussed in detail in the article ARBITRATION, INTERNATIONAL. The following paragraphs are a summary of the action taken by Congress. Discussion of the treaty began in the Senate on January 4, when Senator Hitchcock of Nebraska attacked the treaty, making the charge that the administration was plunging into an "entangling alliance." He declared that the plan for the nomination of commissioners to a high court of arbitration was revolutionary and dangerous. The debate continued until March 7. The chief defenders of the measure were Senators Lodge of Massachusetts, Root of New York, and Burton of Ohio. It was strongly opposed by Senator Bacon of Georgia, Senator Reed of Missouri, and others. Amendments were added which struck from the treaties the vital paragraph relating to the joint high commission, and other amendments which, to a large extent, vitiated the results of the treaty. These amendments were made by a vote of 42 to 40. The failure of the measure to pass in its original form was due practically to the vote of the Democratic senators, supported by several Progressive Republicans, and one or two of the regular Republicans. In their changed form the treaties were passed with only three dissenting votes. These were cast by Senator Lorimer of Illinois, Senator Martine of New Jersey, and Senator Reed of Missouri.

PENSION LEGISLATION. A new Pension bill was introduced in the House on January 30 by Representative Sherwood of Ohio. This was the so-called "One Dollar a Day Pension" bill, and it made provision for pensions to be paid to practically every survivor of the Civil War. This bill involved additional expenditure for pensions of about $75,000,000. In the Senate the committee on pensions voted to report the bill unfavorably by a vote of 10 to 4. A substitute bill, or compromise measure, was suggested by Senator Smoot of Utah and was voted for by the committee by 12 to 2. This bill carried an annual appropriation of about $24,000,000. It was passed by the Senate and after receiving some modifications in the conference committee of the two houses, was signed by the President on May 11. See PENSIONS.

DISPUTED SEATS IN THE SENATE. A special committee of the Senate committee on privileges and elections, appointed to reconsider the evidence in the case of Senator Lorimer of Illinois, made its report on May 20. The committee presented two reports, those of the majority and the minority. Five senators, Dillingham, Campbell, and Jones, Republicans, and Fletcher and Johnston, Democrats, joined in the report which declared that all the rules of law, judicial procedure, and justice required that the former judgment of the Senate in Senator Lorimer's favor be regarded as final and conclusive. They said that in the new investigation no additional substantial evidence had been produced. The minority members of the committee, comprising Senators Kern and Lea, Democrats, and Kenyon, Republican, asserted in their report that the new evidence was broader and more far-reaching than that which had preceded it and that it proved that at least ten of the votes cast for Mr. Lorimer were procured by corruption and that his election therefore was invalid. A vote was taken in the Senate on July 13 and by 55 to 28 the senators adopted the resolution declaring that corrupt methods and practices had been employed in the election of William Lorimer and that his election was therefore invalid. This action was preceded by a remarkable debate of seven days, three of which were occupied by Mr. Lorimer himself, who spoke in his own defense. In the course of these speeches he denounced President Taft, Colonel Roosevelt, and many others who had opposed him, especially those connected with newspapers in Chicago, which he declared had been responsible for all the charges brought against him. This action of the Senate finally terminated the Lorimer case and at the conclusion of the vote Mr. Lorimer was no longer a senator. This left the State of Illinois with but one representative in the Senate chamber.

The committee appointed to inquire into the right of Senator Stephenson of Wisconsin to retain his seat, reported on February 28, "The majority report exonerates Senator Stephenson," and this report was accepted by the Senate.

On February 26 a resolution was introduced by Senator Reed of Missouri, calling for investigation into the election of Senator Du Pont of Delaware on the ground that his election was secured through corruption. On the following day Senator Du Pont denied the charges and a committee was appointed to investigate them and report to the Senate.

IMPEACHMENT PROCEEDINGS. There was begun in the second session of the Sixty-second Congress the unusual procedure of a trial for impeachment. This was against Judge Robert W. Archbald, a member of the United States Commerce Court. Early in the year, rumors of charges against Judge Archbald were widely circulated, and on April 25, the House of Representatives took cognizance of these allegations by sending a resolution to the President asking for any information in the hands of the executive department bearing on them. The President, on May 3, replied in a message in which he stated that in February, 1912, certain charges of improper conduct on the part of Judge Archbald had been brought to his attention by Commissioner Meyer of the Interstate Commerce Commission. These charges the President transmitted to the Attorney-General with instructions to investigate and confer with Mr. Meyer. The Attorney-General made a careful investigation of the charges, and, as a result, advised the President that in his opinion the papers should be transmitted to the committee on the judiciary of the House of Representatives, to be used by them as a basis for an investigation of the facts involved in the charges. These papers were accordingly laid before this committee. A resolution for an investigation by the committee on judiciary was at once passed in the House, and on May 7 hearings on the charges and the taking of testimony was begun by the committee in the open session and continued from day to day until June 4, 1912. At these hearings witnesses were sworn and examined and Judge Archbald was present in person and was represented by counsel in accordance with his request made to the committee. His counsel was permitted to cross-examine the witnesses.

As a result of the hearings the House of Representatives on July 11, with a single dissenting vote, which was that of a member representing Judge Archbald's district in Pennsylvania, voted to accept the articles of impeachment prepared by the investigating committee. These articles numbered thirteen, each of which was an allegation of misconduct on the part of Judge Archbald. Article 1 declared that on or about March 31, 1911, he entered into a partnership agreement with Edward J. Williams of Scranton, Pa., for the purchase of a certain culm dump in Lackawanna county, for the purpose of disposing of this property at a pecuniary profit to themselves. It was alleged that Judge Archbald used his official position as judge of the Commerce Court to induce improperly and influence the officers of certain corporations who owned this bank to sell it for a sum much less than its actual value. It was further charged that Judge Archbald and Williams secured an option to purchase this property for $3500, whereas it was worth, according to the appraisal of engineers, nearly $50,000. Article 2 alleged that Judge Archbald entered into an agreement to sell stock of the Marian Coal Company to the Delaware, Lackawanna, and Western Railway Company while litigation was in progress between the coal company and the railway company and while the causes at issue between the two companies were pending before the Interstate Commerce Commission, whose decision was subject to review by the Commerce Court. It was asserted that Judge Archbald attempted to induce the officers of the Delaware, Lackawanna, and Western Railway Company to enter into an agreement to settle the case then pending before the Interstate Commerce Commission and purchase the stock of the Marian Coal Company at a highly exorbitant price. It was asserted also that it was his expectation to receive a part of the fee in the event that a settlement would be effected.

Article 3 charged that on August 11, 1911, Judge Archbald endeavored to induce the officers of the Lehigh Valley Coal Company to relinquish the right of that company to operate a culm dump containing approximately 472,670 gross tons, and that while these negotiations were in progress the Lehigh Valley Railroad Company was a party litigant in two suits pending before the Commerce Court. The coal company did relinquish these rights, and it was asserted by the committee that these were relinquished because of influence exercised upon them through Judge Archbald's position as a member of the Commerce Court.

Article 4 charged Judge Archbald with improper conduct as a judge during litigation between the Louisville and Nashville Railway Company and the Interstate Commerce Commission, which case was argued on April 2 and 3, 1911, before the Commerce Court. It was charged that on April 22, 1911, Judge Archbald wrote to Helm Bruce, attorney for the railway, requesting him to confer with the traffic manager of the road who had given material testimony before the Interstate Commerce Commission and to advise the judge whether the witness intended to give an affirmative answer as appeared from the record, or whether he intended to give a negative answer to the question propounded to him by the chairman of the commission. Bruce, after consultation with the traffic manager, advised Judge Archbald that the witness intended to give a negative answer. It was alleged that on January 10, 1912, Judge Archbald again wrote to Bruce calling attention to certain conclusions reached by another member of the court which it was claimed refuted statements and contentions advanced in Bruce's original brief and sustaining the action of the Interstate Commerce Commission with respect to certain features of the case. In this, Judge Archbald asked Bruce whether he would still affirm the position taken in his brief and if so, upon what theory it could be sustained, assuming that the conclusions of the other member of the court were correct. This was followed by other questions concerning the testimony and replies from Bruce. On February 28, 1912, this case was decided by the Commerce Court in favor of the railway company, Judge Archbald writing the opinion of the majority which followed the views expressed by Bruce. It was charged that the Interstate Commerce Commission were given no opportunity to examine and answer the arguments advanced by the attorney for the railway company in his communication with Judge Archbald, nor were they informed that such correspondence had taken place. In the opinion of the committee this conduct of Judge Archbald was a misbehavior in office and unfair and unjust to the parties defendant in the case.

Article 5 related to the alleged negotiations with the Philadelphia and Reading Coal and Iron Company relative to a culm dump near Lorberry, Pa. It was alleged that in 1904 a two-thirds interest in an operating lease of this land was purchased by Frederick Warnke of Scranton. The land was owned by the Philadelphia and Reading Coal and Iron Company and the entire stock of this company was owned in turn by the Reading Company. Warnke's operations were carried on at a loss on account of unfavorable conditions and he applied to the Reading Company for the mining maps of the land covered by his lease. He was informed that the lease under which he claimed had been forfeited two years previous to its assignment to him and his application was therefore denied. He attempted to exchange this lease for a lease of other property owned by the company, but the officials of the company refused to accede to his request. It was alleged that in the latter part of November, 1911, Judge Archbald called upon the vice-president and general manager of the Philadelphia and Reading Coal and Iron Company and attempted to influence the latter's refusal to accede to the proposition made by Warnke. The officials of the road continued their refusal. In December, 1911, while Warnke was considering the advisability of purchasing a culm fill near Pittston, Pa., it was charged that he was advised that Judge Archbald was familiar with the title to the property and the rights of way of certain railroads through it. In pursuance of this assurance, Warnke is alleged to have consulted Judge Archbald, who advised him that the title was clear. The charge was made that he promised to pay to Judge Archbald $500 for the information which he had received. Shortly afterwards this property was purchased by Warnke and several associates, and in March, 1911, Warnke drew a promissory note for $500, which was delivered to Judge Archbald. The committee found that Judge Archbald was guilty of misbehavior in office in attempting to use his influence as a member of the Commerce Court with the officials of the Philadelphia and Reading Coal and Iron Company for the purpose of securing a lease of the culm bank. It was charged also that the $500 given in the guise of compensation for legal advice was, in fact, in the nature of a reward for favors previously shown in connection with the judge's efforts to bring about an acceptance of Warnke's proposition to the Philadelphia and Reading Coal and Iron Company.

Article 6 charged that in December, 1911, or January, 1912, Judge Archbald entered into an agreement with James R. Dainty of Scranton, Pa., to open negotiations with the Lehigh Valley Coal Company and the Everhart estate for the purpose of effecting the sale of two tracts of land near Wilkesbarre, Pa. It was charged that Judge Archbald attempted to use his official influence as a member of the Commerce Court to affect the action of the general manager of the Lehigh Valley Coal Company with respect to the purchase of this property.

Article 7 dealt with transactions relating to the discounting of a note made by W. W. Rissinger which Judge Archbald had indorsed. The latter had presided at a litigation between the Old Plymouth Coal Company and the Equitable Fire and Marine Insurance Company. Mr. Rissinger was the controlling stockholder of the plaintiff-company. The litigation ended in a compromise by which the plaintiff recovered about $28,000. Several days after it was alleged that Judge Archbald entered into a deal with Rissinger for the purchase of an interest in a gold mining project in Honduras, and in order to finance the transaction it was claimed that a promissory note for $2500 was signed by Rissinger and was indorsed by Judge Archbald. It was charged that an attempt was made to discount this note a few days after the settlement of the suit by compromise and the committee charged that the evidence tended strongly to indicate that Judge Archbald had entered into negotiations with Rissinger while litigation was pending before the United States District Court, of which he was judge.

Articles 8 and 9 also referred to the discounting of a note. In the fall of 1909 the case of John W Peale against the Marian Coal Company, which involved a considerable sum of money, was opened before the United States District Court at Scranton, over which Judge Archbald presided. This coal company, which is the same as that referred to in the previous article, was principally owned and controlled by Christopher G. Boland and William P. Boland, and it was charged that this fact was well known to Judge Archbald. In the latter part of November or the early part of December, 1909, for the purpose of raising funds to invest in a timber project in Venezuela, which was being promoted by one John Henry Jones of Scranton, Judge Archbald is alleged to have drawn and indorsed a promissory note for $500, payable to himself, which note was signed by Jones as promisor. It was charged that Judge Archbald agreed and consented that Edward J. Williams should present this note to Christopher G. Boland or William P. Boland or either of them for discount, and that the note was presented to each of them and that they refused to discount it on the ground that it would be highly improper for them to do so under the existing circumstances. After the refusal of a bank in Scranton to discount the note it was finally discounted by Jones in a Providence bank, a small State bank in a suburb of Scranton. The president of this bank was C. H. Van Storch of Scranton, an attorney who had prevailed as a party in interest in litigation before Judge Archbald within a year prior to the date of the discount of the note. It was alleged that Judge Archbald advised Van Storch that he would consider it a great favor if the discount should be granted. The charge was made by the committee, that the note had never been paid although the bank had made, at least, one call for payment. The committee charged that Judge Archbald had used his influence as a judge to secure this loan from parties litigant before his court, and failing in this used his influence to secure the loan through an attorney who was then practicing before his court and who had but a short while before received favorable judgment in his suit adjudicated therein.

Articles 10 and 11 charged the wrongful acceptance of money by Judge Archbald on the occasion of a pleasure trip to Europe. It was alleged that he allowed Henry W. Cannon of New York City to pay his entire expenses on a pleasure trip to Europe. Mr. Cannon, it was charged, was and is a stockholder and officer in various interstate railroad corporations and corporations engaged in the business of mining and shipping of coal. While it was claimed that Mr. Cannon is a distant relative of Judge Archbald's wife, the committee declared it improper for a judge to thus obligate himself to an officer of numerous corporations likely to become directly or indirectly involved in litigation before his court, or before other courts over which he might be called to preside from time to time. It was further alleged that two officials of the United States District Court of Scranton raised a fund of more than $500, which was presented to Judge Archbald on his departure. The contribution, it was alleged, was made by certain attorneys practicing before the United States District Court, some of whom had cases then pending before that court. The committee regarded the acceptance of this fund as improper, and held that it was subversive of the confidence of the public in the judiciary for a judge to place himself in this manner under obligations to attorneys practicing before his court. Article 12 charged that Judge Archbald, in 1901, appointed one J. D. Woodward of Wilkesbarre, Pa., as jury commissioner in the district court over which Judge Archbald presided, while Woodward was general attorney for the Lehigh Valley Railroad. The committee declared that the appointment of a legal representative of a large railroad corporation which was likely to become directly or indirectly involved in litigation before the United States District Court was misbehavior in office calculated to bring the federal judiciary into disrepute.

Article 13 dealt in a general way with the alleged misbehavior of Judge Archbald. It declared that the testimony in the whole case tended to show such misbehavior. The testimony failed to disclose any case in which Judge Archbald invested any actual money of his own in any of these enterprises, but it was alleged that it did show that he used his personal influence as a judge in consideration of which he received or was to receive his share or interest in the property or his profits in the deal.

The articles of impeachment were forwarded to the Senate, which has charge of the trial of impeachment cases, and on July 16 that body organized itself into a court of impeachment. Judge Archbald appeared before it on July 19 and was given until July 29 to prepare his answer to the articles of impeachment. On that date the Senate, sitting as a court of impeachment, received his formal answer which was, in general, a denial of all charges made against him. This concluded the proceedings of this session of Congress. Postponement of the actual trial was made until the succeeding session.

Judge Archbald was appointed United States District Judge for the middle district of Pennsylvania by President McKinley on March 29, 1901. The appointment was to last only during vacation, but after the convening of Congress he was duly commissioned a judge of the same district by President Roosevelt. He was appointed an additional circuit judge of the United States and was designated a judge of the United States Commerce Court by President Taft. The appointment was confirmed by the Senate, and he received his commission on January 31, 1911.

SIXTY-SECOND CONGRESS, THIRD SESSION. The Sixty-second Congress met in its third and last session on December 3, 1912. During the interval which had elapsed between the two sessions three senators had died, Heyburn of Idaho, Rayner of Maryland, and Nixon of Nevada. Three temporary successors were appointed to fill out the terms of these senators until other successors should be elected at the meeting of the State legislatures. Kirtland I. Perky succeeded Senator Heyburn, William P. Jackson succeeded Senator Rayner, and W. A. Massey succeeded Senator Nixon. See IDAHO, MARYLAND, and NEVADA.

In accordance with the custom which prevailed during his administration, President Taft sent his message to Congress in the form of installments. The first message sent on December 3, dealt chiefly with the foreign relations of the United States. He discussed his policy in connection with the diplomatic and consular offices and detailed the reorganization of the State Department which has taken place under his direction. He urged that the merit system be made to apply more fully in the consular and diplomatic corps. That he himself had followed out this plan as fully as possible he showed by pointing that of the ten ambassadors appointed by him, five were by promotion from the rank of minister. Of the thirty ministers appointed, eleven were promoted from the lower grades of the foreign service or from the Department of State. Of the nineteen missions in Latin America, fifteen chiefs of missions appointed were service men. The thirty-seven secretaries of the embassies were chosen for appointment after passing successfully the required examination. The President urged larger provision for embassies and legations and for other expenses of foreign representatives of the United States government. The substance of the President's allusions to foreign relations will be found in the section *Foreign Relations* in another part of this article.

On December 6 the President sent a second message, which was more in the nature of a general message than the first. His principal recommendations were the following: The plan of currency reform outlined by the monetary commission; an amendment to the law to lessen the penalty when corporations inadvertently disobey the corporation tax law; congressional approval of the plan of army reorganization prepared by the war college; the passage of the military bill increasing compensation to militia in the field; citizenship without statehood for Porto Ricans; regulation of water power grants so that navigable streams may be improved by water power companies; the elevation of Col. G. W. Goethals, builder of the Panama Canal, to a generalship; a return to the policy of two battleships a year by appropriation for three battleships in 1913; and authority to the United States Supreme Court to make rules of procedure in common law cases in federal courts to expedite and lessen the cost of litigation. The President emphatically disapproved the project for immediate independence of the Philippines. He declared that the true course in regard to those islands is to "pursue steadily and courageously the path we have thus far followed; to guide the Filipinos into self-sustaining pursuits; to continue the cultivation of sound political habits through education and political practice; to encourage the diversification of industries and to realize the advantages of their industrial education by conservatively approved coöperative methods, at once checking the dangers of concentrated wealth and building up a sturdy, independent citizenship." He declared further that a present declaration even of future independence would retard progress by the dissension and disorder it would arouse. On December 19 the President sent a third message which was, in effect, a defense against the charge that he had been instigated by political motives in placing 36,000 fourth-class postmasters under the operation of the civil service law (see CIVIL SERVICE and *Post Office*, earlier in this article). The President said: "Nothing could be further from the truth. The order was made before the election and in the interest of efficient public service. I have several times requested Congress to give me authority to put first, second, and third class postmasters and all other local officers, including internal revenue officers, customs officers, United States marshals, and the local agents of the other departments under the classification of the civil service law by taking away the necessity for confirming such appointments by the Senate." In the same message the President advocated legislation permitting members of the cabinet to sit in Congress with the right of debate but without votes. He also urged the adoption of the plan of the Postmaster-General for the readjustment of the compensation allowed to railroads for carrying the mails, and he recommended the revision of the land laws to secure and regulate conservation, and legislation affecting Alaska and the registry of mineral lands. He pointed out the necessity of further pure food legislation and requested Congress to make provision for a government building at the San Francisco Panama-Pacific International Exposition. He asked also for an appropriation for beautifying Washington and the establishment of a public utilities commission at the capital and the extension of the suffrage to citizens of the District of Columbia.

The work of Congress in the first weeks of the session directly preceding the holidays is usually more or less perfunctory. Some important measures, however, were acted upon in the first weeks of this session. The house committee on ways and means provided for hearings on tariff revision to begin January 6, 1913. By a vote of 141 to 101 the House refused to adopt the proposed rule providing for the immediate consideration of the Senate concurrent resolution favoring the purchase, by the government, of "Monticello" the home of Thomas Jefferson. By a vote of 153 to 118 the House declared that Charles C. Bowman, Rep., of the Eleventh Pennsylvania district, was not entitled to be seated, and by a vote of 181 to 118 it declined to seat his Democratic opponent, George R. McLean. Both seats were rejected on the ground of corrupt practices. Before adjournment for the holidays the House passed by a vote of 178 to 52 the Burnett bill for the regulation of immigration (see IMMIGRATION).

The Senate continued to sit as a court of impeachment in the trial of Judge Archbald. The House managers concluded their presentation of the case before the holiday recess. The Democratic senators in caucus decided that confirmation of President Taft's appointments, with the exception of those in the army and navy, would be opposed and, if possible, prevented.

CONGRESSIONAL APPROPRIATIONS. The table below shows the appropriations of Congress for the various purposes in the sessions held during 1912. It will be noted that the appropriations in the first and second sessions of the Sixty-second Congress form a somewhat smaller total than those made in the third session of the Sixty-first Congress. The total expenses of the government for 1913 are estimated by the Secretary of the Treasury at $670,800,000 for the administration of the regular departments of the government. For the Panama Canal, $42,000,000, and for miscellaneous redemption of the public debt, $150,000. The total estimated deficit at the end of 1913 was estimated at $1,800,000.

	61st Congress 3d session 1912	62d Congress 1st-2d sessions 1913
Deficiencies	$ 10,028,526.84	$ 8,506,587.25
Legislative, executive, and judicial......	35,378,149.85	34,245,356.75
Sundry civil..........	135,241,935.34	102,538,934.40
Support of the army	93,374,755.97	90,958,712.98
Naval service.........	126,405,509.24	123,151,538.76
Indian service........	8,842,136.37	8,920,970.66
Rivers and harbors.	30,883,419.00	40,559,620.50
Forts and fortifications	5,473,707.00	4,036,235.00
Military Academy...	1,163,424.07	1,064,668.26
Post Office Dept.....	Indefinite	Indefinite
Pensions	153,682,000.00	165,146,145.84
Consular and diplomatic	3,988,516.41	3,638,047.41
Agricultural Depart.	16,900,016.00	16,648,168.00
District of Columbia	12,056,786.50	10,675,833.50
Reclamation fund....	....	....
Reliefs and misc....	1,130,678.81	7,292,359.03
Totals	$634,549,561.40	$617,382,178.34

THE SIXTY-THIRD CONGRESS. The election of November 5, 1912, resulted in important changes in the Senate. Several of the best known Republican senators were defeated for renomination in the senatorial primaries and their places will be taken in the Sixty-third Congress by Democratic senators. These were Senators Curtis of Kansas, Dixon of Montana, and Bourne of Oregon. Democratic senators who were defeated for renomination included Senators Paynter of Kentucky, Foster of Louisiana, Percy of Mississippi, Watson of West Virginia, and Gardner of Maine. Senator Gardner, who was appointed by a Democratic governor of the State to fill out the unexpired term of Senator Frye will be succeeded in the Sixty-third Congress by Edwin C. Burleigh. In addition to the senators who were defeated for renomination several retired voluntarily, declining to become candidates for another term. These were Senators Crane of Massachusetts, Guggenheim of Colorado, and Bailey of Texas. Below is given a list of the senators in the Sixty-third Congress, which includes those whose terms expire in 1915, 1917, and 1919, together with those whose election by State legislatures in 1913 was assured by senatorial primaries held in 1912. The membership of the House in the Sixty-third Congress is also given in accordance with the returns of the election of November 5. It will be noted that Illinois has no senators on this list. Senator Lorimer was deprived of his seat in the Senate and Senator Cullom was defeated for renomination. Indications were that Lawrence Y. Sherman, his successful competitor, would be elected as Republican senator by the legislature of 1913, and that James H. Lewis would be chosen as the Democratic senator.

The names of Republican senators and representatives are in Roman and the names of Democrats in italics. An asterisk following the name of a representative indicates that he served also in the Sixty-second Congress.

ALABAMA.

SENATORS.

Term expires.

1915—*Joseph F. Johnston.*

1919—*John H. Bankhead.*

REPRESENTATIVES.

*George W. Taylor.**
*S. H. Dent, Jr.**
*Henry D. Clayton.**
*F. L. Blackmon.**
*J. Thomas Heflin.**
*Richmond P. Hobson.**
*John L. Burnett.**
*William Richardson.**
*Oscar W. Underwood.**

At Large.

J. W. Abercrombie.

ARIZONA.

SENATORS.

1915—*Marcus A. Smith.*

1917—*Henry F. Ashurst.*

REPRESENTATIVES.

Carl Hayden.*

ARKANSAS.

SENATORS.

1915—*James P. Clarke.*

1919—*Jefferson Davis.*

REPRESENTATIVES.

T. H. Carraway.
*W. A. Oldfield.**
*John C. Floyd.**
O. T. Wingo.
*H. M. Jacoway.**
S. M. Taylor.
*W. S. Goodwin.**

CALIFORNIA.

SENATORS.

1915—George C. Perkins.

1917—John D. Works.

REPRESENTATIVES.

William Kent.
*J. E. Raker.**
Chas. F. Curry.
Julius Kahn.*
J. I. Nolan.
Joseph R. Knowland.
D. S. Church.
Everis A. Hayes.*
C. W. Bell.
William D. Stephens.*
William Kettner.

Copyright, Pach Bros., N. Y.

SENATOR HENRY CABOT LODGE
Massachusetts

Copyright, Harris and Ewing, Washington, D.C.

SENATOR JAMES A. O'GORMAN
New York

Copyright, 1909, by Moffett Studio, Chicago

SENATOR THOMAS P. GORE
Oklahoma

Copyright, Harris and Ewing, Washington, D.C.

SENATOR A. B. CUMMINS
Iowa

FOUR UNITED STATES SENATORS PROMINENT IN 1912

COLORADO.

SENATORS.

1915—*Charles S. Thomas.*
1919—*John F. Shafroth.*

REPRESENTATIVES.

George Kindel. *H. H. Seldomridge.*

At Large.

*Edward T. Taylor.** *Edward Keating.*

CONNECTICUT.

SENATORS.

1915—Frank B. Brandegee.
1917—George P. McLean.

REPRESENTATIVES.

Augustus Lonergan. *Jeremiah Donovan.*
B. F. Mahan.
*Thomas L. Reilly.** *Wm. Kennedy.*

DELAWARE.

1917—Henry A. Du Pont.
1919—*A Democrat.*

At Large.

Franklin Brockson.

FLORIDA.

SENATORS.

1915—*Duncan U. Fletcher.*
1917—*Nathan P. Bryan.*

REPRESENTATIVES.

*Stephen M. Sparkman.**
*Frank Clark.**
Emmett Wilson.

At Large.

Claude L'Engle.

GEORGIA.

SENATORS.

1915—*Hoke Smith.*
1919—*Augustus O. Bacon.*

REPRESENTATIVES.

*Charles G. Edwards.** *Gordon Lee.**
*S. A. Roddenbery.** *S. J. Tribble.**
C. R. Crisp. *Thomas M. Bell.**
*William C. Adamson.** *Thomas W. Hardwick.**
*W. S. Howard.** *J. R. Walker.*
*Charles D. Bartlett.** *D. M. Hughes.**

IDAHO.

SENATORS.

1915—A Republican.
1919—William E. Borah.

REPRESENTATIVES.

Burton L. French.* Addison T. Smith.

ILLINOIS.

SENATORS.

1915— —— ——
1919— —— ——

REPRESENTATIVES.

Martin B. Madden.* *Claude U. Stone.**
James R. Mann.* *Louis FitzHenry.*
George E. Gorman. *Frank T. O'Hair.*
*James T. McDermott.** *Chas. M. Borchers.*
*A. J. Sabath.** *H. T. Rainey.**
James McAndrews. *J. M. Graham.**
*Frank Buchanan.** *W. N. Baltz.*
*Thomas Gallagher.** *M. D. Foster.**
Fred A. Britten. *H. R. Fowler.**
Chas. M. Thomson. *R. P. Hill.*
Ira C. Copley.*
Wm. Hinebaugh.
John C. McKenzie.
C. H. Tavenner.
Stephen A. Hoxworth.

At Large.

W. E. Williams.
L. B. Stringer.

INDIANA.

SENATORS.

1915—*Benjamin F. Shively.*
1917—*John W. Kern.*

REPRESENTATIVES.

Chas. Lieb. *John A. M. Adair.**
*William A. Cullop.** *Martin A. Morrison.**
*W. E. Cox.** *J. B. Peterson.*
*Lincoln Dixon.** *George W. Rauch.**
*Ralph W. Moss.** *Cyrus Cline.**
*F. H. Gray.** *Henry A. Barnhart.**
*Charles A. Korbly.**

IOWA.

SENATORS.

1915—Albert B. Cummins.
1919—William S. Kenyon.

REPRESENTATIVES.

C. A. Kennedy.* S. F. Prouty.*
*I. S. Pepper.** H. M. Towner.*
Maurice Connolly. W. R. Green.*
Gilbert N. Haugen.* Frank P. Woods.*
James W. Good.* George C. Scott.
S. Kirkpatrick.

KANSAS.

SENATORS.

1915—Joseph L. Bristow.
1919—*Wm. H. Thompson.*

REPRESENTATIVES.

Dan'l R. Anthony, jr.* *G. T. Helvering.*
*Joseph Taggart.** *J. R. Connelly.*
*Philip P. Campbell.** *Geo. A. Neeley.**
Dudley Doolittle. Victor Murdock.*

KENTUCKY.

SENATORS.

1915—William O. Bradley.
1919—*Ollie M. James.*

REPRESENTATIVES.

A. W. Barkley. *J. Campbell Cantrill.**
*Augustus O. Stanley.** *Harvey Helm.**
*R. Y. Thomas, jr.** *W. J. Fields.**
*Ben Johnson.** J. W. Langley.*
*Swagar Sherley.** Caleb Powers.*
*A. B. Rouse.**

LOUISIANA.

SENATORS.

1915—*John R. Thornton.*
1919—*Joseph E. Ransdell.*

REPRESENTATIVES.

*Albert Estopinal.** *J. W. Elder.*
*H. Garland Dupre.** *L. L. Morgan.*
*Robert F. Broussard.** *L. Lazaro.*
*John T. Watkins.** *J. B. Aswell.*

MAINE.

SENATORS.

1917—*Charles F. Johnson.*
1919—E. C. Burleigh.

REPRESENTATIVES.

A. C. Hinds.* Forrest Goodwin.
*D. J. McGillicuddy.** Frank E. Guernsey.*

MARYLAND.

SENATORS.

1915—*John W. Smith.*
1917—William P. Jackson.*

REPRESENTATIVES.

*J. Harry Covington.** *J. C. Linthicum.**
*Joshua F. C. Talbott.** *J. F. Smith.*
*George Konig.** *D. J. Lewis.**

WISCONSIN.

SENATORS.

1915—Isaac Stephenson.
1917—Robert M. La Follette.

REPRESENTATIVES.

Henry A. Cooper.*	John J. Esch.*
*M. E. Burke.**	E. E. Browne.
John M. Nelson.*	*T. F. Konop.**
William J. Cary.*	James A. Frear.
William H. Stafford.*	Irvine L. Lenroot.*
M. K. Reilly.	

WYOMING.

SENATORS.

1917—Clarence D. Clark.
1919—Francis E. Warren.

REPRESENTATIVE.

Frank W. Mondell.*

ALASKA.

REPRESENTATIVE.

James Wickersham.*

HAWAII.

REPRESENTATIVE.

Jonah K. Kalanianaole.*

PORTO RICO.

REPRESENTATIVE.

Name of Representative not given in official list.

PHILIPPINE ISLANDS.

REPRESENTATIVES.

Manuel Quezon. *Manuel Earnshaw.*

In the House, Democrats, 291; Republicans, 144; whole number, 435. In the Senate, Democrats, probably, 49; Republicans, 45; total, 94, with two vacancies to be filled.

ADMINISTRATION

The history of Presidents Taft's administration in 1912 in its larger aspects is told in other parts of this volume. The chief interest of course centred in the presidential campaign, which is described under its title. Events which relate to the chief departments of the government and legislation will be found in other sections of this article. Other important articles which have to do directly or indirectly with the administration are TRUSTS, TARIFF, PUBLIC LANDS, and TAXATION. In this section are noted only such events as do not properly fall within any of the other logical divisions of the YEAR BOOK.

COMMISSION ON ECONOMY AND EFFICIENCY. On January 17 the President sent to Congress a message dealing with the work of the Commission on Economy and Efficiency, which was appointed in 1910 to make an investigation of the business methods of the departments of the government. As a result of the work of the commission the President informed Congress that there was necessity of a reorganization of the government departments, and the consolidation or weeding out of bureaus which performed a duplicate work. Many so-called local offices throughout the country should be abolished, and hundreds of appointees made for political purposes should be taken off the pay-roll. The personnel of government employees should be improved through the introduction of civil service in practically every field. The same business methods should be applied to the administration as are used in large corporations. The commission recommended the abolition of the revenue cutter service, which would mean a saving of $1,000,000 a year. Great savings also could be made in the handling of the mail in the various departments. It is possible to bring about economies in traveling expenses in which the government expends about $12,000,000 a year. Tests made by the commission showed that a saving in this item alone of over half of one cent a mile could be effected. Perhaps the most radical proposal advanced by the President was that administrative officers of the government in the departments at Washington and in the field should be put under the civil service rules and be removed from the hands of politics, and that their terms of office should not be limited, as at present, to four years.

A second message on the work of the commission was sent to Congress on April 4. In this the President again urged the passage of legislation which would allow the classification of local offices in the departments of the treasury, justice, interior, post office, and commerce and labor. The President declared that the results of the inquiry had shown that the loss caused by the fact that work which should be done by one person was done by two or more amounted easily to $10,000,000. He stated that if the postmasters of the first and second class were placed in the classified service the saving in alaries alone would amount to $4,500,000.

President Taft continued his efforts to economize the administration of government by directing in September that all department heads should appoint representatives to confer with the Economy and Efficiency Commission. The ultimate wish of the President as stated by him was that the government should prepare a budget or proper statement of governmental incomes and expenses in accordance with the usage of other governments. The method of making appropriations which are based upon estimates submitted by the various departments under a law which makes no provision for executive review the President declared both "haphazard and wasteful." He added: "Authority is granted for the expenditure of a billion dollars each year, without any thought as to where money is coming from. This is done on the theory that there will be no deficit. . . . While the Constitution makes Congress responsible for money-raising as well as for appropriations, responsibility for borrowing has been shifted to the President, by empowering him to procure loans to meet deficits." Some time previous to this President Taft had sought to correct the method of estimating for appropriations by directing the heads of departments to send their estimates to him before they were printed, so that a certain uniformity or standard might be exercised over all of them. This order reduced the initial estimates by millions of dollars. A part of the work of the Economy and Efficiency Commission is to summarize the statements sent by the heads of departments so as to coördinate them and to bring about a statement of necessary coming expenses which will not exceed the balance in the treasury.

Such officers he declared should not be appointed by the President with the necessity of confirmation by the Senate, but upon merit. In effect, the recommendations of the President were that the government should be conducted along strictly business principles.

Measures in accordance with the recommendations of the President had been introduced in

JOHN J. FITZGERALD
New York

ARSÈNE P. PUJO
Louisiana

WILLIAM SULZER
New York

A P GARDNER
Massachusetts

FOUR MEMBERS OF THE HOUSE OF REPRESENTATIVES PROMINENT IN 1912

Congress, but no action had been taken at the end of the year.

ADMINISTRATIVE OFFICES. There was no change in the membership of the cabinet during the year. Among the minor officials Harvey W. Wiley, chief chemist of the Department of Agriculture, resigned on March 15, indicating that he was prompted to do so by conditions within the Department of Agriculture. Dr. C. L. Alsberg, chemical biologist in the bureau of plant industry, was appointed to succeed Dr. Wiley. Herbert Knox Smith, commissioner of corporations, resigned on account of his sympathy with the Progressive party and Mr. Roosevelt. He took an active part in Mr. Roosevelt's campaign and was nominated by the Progressive party for governor of Connecticut. Luther Conant, Jr., was appointed to succeed Mr. Smith. The President appointed W. M. Bullitt solicitor-general to succeed Frederick W. Lehmann, who died in 1911. On July 3 A. Piatt Andrew resigned as Assistant Secretary of the Treasury. At the same time he made public letters in which he questioned the methods of the Treasury Department and the efficiency of Secretary MacVeagh. James F. Curtis of Massachusetts was appointed assistant secretary to succeed Mr. Andrew. As the result of an act of Congress changes were made in the Department of Commerce and Labor, whereby the bureau of statistics was abolished and a bureau of foreign and domestic commerce was established. O. P. Austin retired as chief of the bureau of statistics and A. H. Baldwin was appointed chief of the new bureau.

FOREIGN RELATIONS

The year 1912 was an especially exacting period in the foreign relations of the United States. This was caused chiefly by the disordered conditions in Cuba, Mexico, and several of the Central American states. It required the highest exercise of diplomacy and caution to avoid complications involving the active participation of the United States in the affairs of those countries, and in one case, Nicaragua, the American government was forced to take an active hand.

CANADA. The relations with Canada were devoid of unusual incident in 1912.

The organization of the international joint commission created by the United States and Great Britain to adjust differences between the United States and Canada over the uses of the boundary waters was perfected early in January. On January 18 at a meeting of the American section of the commission, James A. Tawney was named chairman to succeed the late Thomas H. Carter of Montana. The other American commissioners are George Turner of Washington, and Frank S. Streeter of New Hampshire. The Canadian commissioners are Thomas C. Casgrain, Henry A. Powell, and Charles A. Magrath. Among the problems which will be considered by this commission are the application of the Lake Champlain and St. Lawrence Ship Canal Company to construct a canal wholly within Canadian territory, regulating works to be erected in the Richelieu River, which will impound the flood waters of Lake Champlain and raise the level of that lake on the American side of the line; and the application of the Long Sault Development Company for permission to construct a dam across the Long Sault in the St. Lawrence River to improve the navigation of that river and develop water power.

On July 20 an agreement was concluded between the United States and Great Britain adopting, with different modifications, the rules and method of procedure recommended in the award rendered by the North Atlantic Coast Fisheries Arbitration Tribunal on September 7, 1910, for the settlement hereafter, in accordance with the principle laid down in the award, of questions arising with reference to the exercise of the American fishing liberties in Article I of the treaty of October 20, 1818, between the United States and Great Britain. This agreement received the approval of the Senate on August 1, 1912, and was formally ratified by the two governments on November 15. The rules and methods of proceedure embodied in the award provided for determining by an impartial tribunal the reasonableness of any new fishery regulations on the treaty coasts of Newfoundland and Canada before such regulations could be enforced against American fishermen exercising their treaty liberties on those waters, and also for determining the delimitation of bays more than ten miles wide in accordance with the definition adopted by the tribunal of the meaning of the word "bays" as used in the treaty. In the subsequent negotiations between the two governments undertaken for the purpose of giving practical effect to these rules and methods of procedure, it was found that certain modifications therein were desirable from the point of view of both governments, and these negotiations finally resulted in the agreement mentioned above by which the award recommendations as modified by mutual consent of the two governments were finally adopted and made effective, thus bringing this century-old controversy to a final conclusion.

An incident occurring in connection with the presidential campaign in the United States caused considerable discussion, and not a little ill feeling in Canada (see PRESIDENTIAL CAMPAIGN). In the course of a speech delivered in Massachusetts, President Taft read a letter from Mr. Roosevelt in which the latter strongly approved the President's proposal for reciprocity. In the letter which the President had written asking for Mr. Roosevelt's opinion occurred the following passage: "The amount of Canadian products we would take would procure a current of business between Western Canada and the United States which would make Canada only an adjunct of the United States. It would transfer all their important business to Chicago and New York, with their bank credits and everything else, and it would increase greatly the demand of Canada for our manufactures. I see this is an argument made against reciprocity in Canada and I think it is a good one." The publication of the President's frank opinion that Canada would be only an "adjunct" of the United States if the reciprocity measure were passed, created great resentment in Canada, and it was generally conceded to have been an unwise and impolitic act on the part of the President to have given the letter to the public.

MEXICO. The conditions of disorder and revolution existing in Mexico during 1912 were the greatest source of anxiety to the administration of President Taft. Complaint received by American citizens in Mexico compelled the President on February 3 to issue a warning to President Madero to protect American interests near the border, and in the two days following four additional regiments of United

States troops were sent to the border. A request of the Mexican government to allow Mexican troops to pass through Eagle Pass at El Paso in order to reach Juarez, then in the hands of the rebels, was declined. On February 24 a regiment of United States infantry and two batteries of artillery were sent to El Paso to protect American interests near the border. In response to a complaint made by President Madero that Mexican insurgents were importing military supplies from the United States, he was informed by the State Department that such importation could not be prohibited under the laws of the United States. On March 14, however, at the request of President Taft, a joint resolution was passed by both houses of Congress, which had an important bearing on the exportation of arms from the United States.

The resolution declared that "whenever the President shall find that in any American country conditions of domestic violence exist which are promoted by the use of arms or munitions of war procured from the United States and shall make proclamation thereof it shall be unlawful to export, except under such limitations and exceptions as the President shall prescribe, any arms or munitions of war from any place in the United States to such country until otherwise ordered by the President or by Congress." Hitherto under the principles of international law, while it is forbidden to citizens of one country to prepare an expedition or raise armed forces with a view to invasion of another country, there has not been any recognized prohibition against the sale of arms in the regular course of commerce by the citizens of one country to the citizens or subjects of another, and this without any regard to the question whether the purchasers are or are not in arms against their government. Therefore, while it had been within the right of the Mexican government to seize arms intended for the insurrectionists when found within the borders of Mexico, it had not been the duty of the United States to prevent passage of arms from one country to another in the regular course of commerce. By the passage of this resolution Congress in effect took the stand that the relation of the United States to the smaller republics on this side of the Atlantic is radically different from the relation of the United States to the European countries, chiefly on account of the responsibility placed on the United States by the Monroe Doctrine. Immediately following the passage of the resolution, President Taft issued a proclamation in accordance with its provisions.

On March 24 this regulation was so modified as not to apply to the Mexican government. The situation of Americans in Mexico became so grave that on March 29 the War Department sent 1000 rifles to the American Legation in the city of Mexico for the protection of American citizens.

On April 14 the State Department sent a note of warning to President Madero. In this attention was called to the great property losses suffered by Americans in Mexico and to the personal violence which American citizens in some cases had suffered. It also stated that lives of American citizens had been taken contrary to the conditions which governed many civilized nations. In view of these facts the government gave notice that, "It expects and must demand that American life and property within the Republic of Mexico be justly and adequately protected, and that this government must hold Mexico and the Mexican people responsible for all wanton or illegal acts sacrificing or endangering American life, or damaging American property or interests there situated." A specific demand was made for just treatment for American citizens who might be taken prisoners as participants on one side or the other of the existing disturbance, and insistence was made that they be dealt with in accordance with humanity as well as international law. A similar note was sent to General Orozco, the most prominent of the insurgent leaders. The immediate result of this note was a reply from President Madero, which was not altogether conciliatory in tone. He affirmed with some resentment the adherence of Mexico to humane principles and the rules of international conduct. He said: "The Mexican government is perfectly acquainted with its duty. Neither word nor deed warrants doubt of our sincerity or our adherence to international privileges."

The policy of President Taft in dealing with the difficult Mexican problem received almost universal commendation. The general policy which he adopted is outlined as follows in his message on foreign relations sent to Congress in December. He said: "For two years revolution and counter-revolution have distraught the neighboring republic of Mexico. Brigandage has involved a great deal of depredation upon foreign interests. There have constantly occurred questions of extreme delicacy. On several occasions very difficult situations have arisen on our frontier. Throughout the trying period, the policy of the United States has been one of patient non-intervention, steadfast recognition of constituted authority in the neighboring nation and the exertion of every effort to care for American interests. I profoundly hope that the Mexican nation may soon resume the path of order, prosperity, and progress. To that nation in its sore troubles, the sympathetic friendship of the United States has been demonstrated to a high degree. There were in Mexico at the beginning of the revolution some thirty or forty thousand American citizens engaged in enterprises contributing greatly to the prosperity of the republic and also benefiting the important trade between the two countries. The investment of American capital in Mexico has been estimated at one billion dollars. The responsibility of endeavoring to safeguard those interests and the dangers inseparable from propinquity to so turbulent a situation have been great, but I am happy to have been able to adhere to the policy above outlined, which I hope may be soon justified by the complete success of the Mexican people in regaining the blessings of peace and good order."

Magdalena Bay. In April the Senate adopted a resolution calling upon the President to transmit to them "any information in the possession of the government relative to the purchase of land at Magdalena Bay by the Japanese government or by a Japanese company." This resolution was introduced by Senator Lodge.

In reply to a resolution in the Senate requesting information relating to Magdalena Bay, Mr. Taft sent on May 1 a brief message, accompanied by the report of Secretary Knox. In this Mr. Knox said there was nothing on file in the department to justify any inference that the Mexican government or the Japanese government had been "occupied with any disposition of land near Magdalena Bay, by which the latter government would acquire land there for any purpose." He said that owing to rumors in circulation the Japanese ambassador had, with the authorization of his government, made an unreserved and categorical denial of the reported purchase of land by the government or by a Japanese company, saying that his government had never directly or indirectly attempted or contemplated the acquisition of any land at Magdalena Bay for any purpose. Mr. Knox said that the rumors were due to the efforts of an American syndicate to sell the land in the vicinity of the bay to Japanese citizens. In response to a request from the owners of these lands as to the attitude of the United States government, the department had informed them that such a sale would be regretted by the government. Following this no further action had been taken by the owners as far as information had been received by the Department of State.

Following the President's message, a committee of the Senate was appointed to take evidence in relation to the matter. This committee having examined the facts reported that it found no evidence tending to show that the government of Japan was involved in negotiations concerning Magdalena Bay, and added: "It appears from the evidence that the corporations or persons who have, or claim to have, title to the lands surrounding Magdalena Bay, have made efforts to form a syndicate and to p m te the sale of these lands upon the basisroofothe existence of some national value to a foreign nation in Magdalena Bay as distinct from any commercial value which that bay and the adjoining territory might possess. The fact that such an idea has formed the basis of negotiations between the possessors of title to land about Magdalena Bay and citizens, subjects, or corporations of a foreign power, seems to the committee on foreign relations to afford an appropriate occasion for an expression of the view of the Senate regarding this and similar cases." As a direct result of the recommendation made in the last sentence of this report, a resolution was introduced into the Senate on July 31 and was passed three days later by a vote of 51 to 4. The purpose of the resolution is to broaden or extend the Monroe Doctrine, and it reads as follows: "Resolved, that when any harbor or other place in the American continents is so situated that the occupation thereof for naval or military purposes might threaten the communications or the safety of the Uinted States, the government of the United States could not see without grave concern the possession of such harbor or other place by any corporation or association which has such a relation to another government, not American, as to give that government practical power or control for national purposes."

CUBA. As the result of disturbances in Cuba brought about by conflict between the Veterans' Association and the administration of President Gomez (see CUBA), Secretary Knox on January 16, following reports received from the United States minister at Havana, sent the following note of warning to the Cuban government: "The situation in Cuba, as now reported, causes grave concern to the government of the United States. That the laws intended to safeguard free Republican government shall be enforced and not defied is obviously essential to the maintenance of the law, order, and stability indispensable to the status of the Republic of Cuba, in the continued well-being of which the United States has always evinced and cannot escape a vital interest. The President of the United States looks to the president and government of Cuba to prevent a threatened situation which would compel the United States, much against its desires, to consider what measures it must take in pursuance of the obligations of its relations to Cuba."

A negro uprising in Cuba in May in protest against the failure of the government to recognize the political status of negroes in proportion to their numbers throughout the island was a source of anxiety to the American government, and on May 23, on account of threatening conditions, two battalions of United States marines were sent to protect American interests. On May 25 a fleet of nine United States war vessels with extra marines were ordered to assemble at Key West for possible service in Cuba. President Taft, however, informed the president of Cuba that the mobilization of the fleet was not intended as a step toward intervention. On May 28, 700 American marines were landed at Guantánamo, and on June 7 the batteships *Ohio* and *Minnesota* arrived at that port. This display of energy and force on the part of the American government, together with the death of General Estenoz, the leading spirit of the revolution, enabled the Cuban government to end the disorders without difficulty. That there was a feeling of bitter hostility toward Americans among certain elements in Cuba was shown on August 27, when Hugh S. Gibson, chargé d'affaires, was attacked and severely beaten in Havana. Mr. Gibson had been in conference with the Cuban cabinet, asking for the prompt payment of the Reilly claim for $557,000 due an American citizen for the construction of waterworks at Cienfuegos. Objection was made to paying the debt, but Mr. Gibson insisted, having been instructed to do so. He declined a check offered in payment and received cash. That evening as he was entering a restaurant he was attacked and knocked down by Enrique Maza, a reporter, who resented, he said, the humiliation of Cuba. Maza was arrested, but when taken before a magistrate was discharged, although he admitted the assault. Mr. Gibson protested against the release of Maza and thereupon the latter was again arrested and was released upon a bond of $500. The United States government then protested and Maza was arrested for a third time and sent to jail. In the meantime the Havana papers were printing columns of abuse of Mr. Gibson, attacking his public and private life. Maza was made a popular hero and subscriptions for his benefit were suggested. The government officials, however, made prompt apologies to Gibson, and on September 1 President Gomez sent a long cable message to President Taft in which he expressed regret and indignation for this assault. He promised that Maza should be justly punished and that the newspapers should be prosecuted for libel. He appealed for a friendly settlement, fearing, he said, that the United States government might be misled because of exaggerated reports.

Following the attack on Mr. Gibson, the diplomatic representatives of other governments held a conference and sent a note to President Gomez asking what measures had been taken to protect them. The Secretary of State thereupon called together the editors of newspapers of Havana and warned them that such attacks as those upon Mr. Gibson might result in international complications. They promised to heed the warning and all but one paper ceased to abuse Mr. Gibson. President Gomez also sent his secretary to Mr. Gibson to present what was virtually an apology for the assault made upon him.

COLOMBIA. In the early part of the year the announcement was made that Secretary Knox would visit the Latin-American republics bordering on the Caribbean Sea. Shortly after, a statement was given out by General Pedro nel Ospina, Colombian minister, and formerly commander of the Colombian army, in which he described the proposed visit of Mr. Knox to Colombia as "inopportune." He based his action on the non-acknowledgment by the State Department of a letter which, three months previous, had been submitted by him requesting an arbitration of pending questions between the United States and Colombia. In the statement referred to above he appealed the Colombian case from the State Department to the public, alleging that Colombia was the only nation with which the United States refuses to submit to an arbitral court questions referring to the interpretation of treaties. This communication of the Colombian minister was followed by his prompt recall by the Colombian government.

MR. KNOX'S VISIT. On February 23 Mr. Knox left Key West for the purpose of making this tour of visits. He was warmly welcomed on February 28 at Panama. He visited Costa Rica on March 3, Nicaragua on March 5, Honduras on March 8, San Salvador on March 11, Guatemala on March 15, Venezuela on March 22, and Havana on April 11. At all the places at which he stopped he was received with the greatest enthusiasm. It was hoped that the visit of Mr. Knox would so ameliorate conditions in Central America that the threatened disturbances in several of the countries would not take place. This hope, however, was not realized.

HONDURAS. Conditions in Honduras, which resulted largely through the failure of the United States Congress to authorize the loan negotiations for the refunding of the foreign debt by J. P. Morgan & Co., compelled the landing of marines for the protection of American property on February 9. This was the result of the act of President Bonilla in seizing a pier and a railroad which had been leased to American citizens. The Honduran government suspended all traffic on the railway, whereupon the marines withdrew after notice had been given by the United States government that Honduras would be held responsible for any violation of the rights of American citizens.

DOMINICAN REPUBLIC. During the summer of 1912 the revolution against the administration which followed the assassination of President Carceres of the Dominican Republic in 1911 brought the republic to the verge of administractive chaos. In pursuance of the treaty relations of the United States with the Dominican Republic, which were threatened by the necessity of suspending the operation under American adminitsration of the custom houses on the Haitian frontier, it was found necessary to dispatch special commissioners to the islands to reëstablish the custom houses and with a guard sufficient to insure needed protection to the customs administration. The efforts which were made resulted in the restoration of normal conditions throughout the republic and the good offices which the commissioners were able to exercise were instrumental in bringing the contending parties together.

At a conference held in December between the United States commissioners and General Vasquez, leader of the revolutionists in Santo Domingo, it was agreed that President Victoria and the members of the council at the capital should resign at once and that a provisional government should be proclaimed, with Archbishop Nouel as president. A new cabinet was formed and assurance was given that the electoral laws would be improved and that a convention would be held to amend the constitution.

NICARAGUA. From August to November Nicaragua was in a state of revolution, which, as it imperiled the lives and property of American citizens, led to the intervention of the United States. On July 29 President-elect Mena, who had been chosen by the legislature in October, 1911, for the four years beginning January 1, 1913, headed an insurrection, in which he was joined by a part of the government troops. The ground of his action, as reported, was his insistence on assuming office without the preliminary of a popular election which had been agreed upon. Leaving the capital, Managua, he took possession of Granada and seized railway property and vessels on Lake Nicaragua which belonged to an American syndicate, whereupon the United States minister appealed to President Diaz for the protection of American citizens. President Diaz, declaring his government unable to offer the necessary protection, appealed to the United States for assistance and a body of American marines from the *Annapolis* was landed at Corinto and proceeded to Managua on August 4.

On August 11 Managua was bombarded by a body of rebels under General Zeledon, former member of Zelaya's cabinet, and many of the inhabitants and government troops were killed. On August 19 they captured Leon and cut to pieces a body of government troops numbering about 500. During the bombardment of Managua the 100 bluejackets from the *Annapolis* protected American citizens and acted as a legation guard. It had, in the meantime, become advisable to send the *Tacoma* to Bluefields, on the east coast of Nicaragua, and this vessel remained there from August 6 to October 19, a landing force of about 50 men being ashore most of the time in order to insure protection of American life and property in case of disaster. In addition, a force of 350 marines from the Canal Zone was brought north in the collier *Justin* and at once proceeded to Managua, arriving there on August 15 and reinforcing the legation guard. On August 10 the *Denver* was diverted from a projected cruise to the Mexican coast and was ordered to Nicaragua. Affairs continued to grow so serious, with increasing menace to the railroad and other American properties, that on August 21 it was decided to send an additional regiment of marines and the armored cruiser *California* to the scene. The *Glacier*, with provisions, and the *Prometheus* and *Saturn*, with coal, were also dispatched there, followed finally by the *Colorado* and *Cleveland*, thus bringing the force to a satisfactory strength for keeping open communication with Managua and Granada, for protecting the lives and property of Americans and other foreigners, and for maintaining an adequate legation guard. On August 28 Admiral Southerland, chief of the Pacific fleet, arrived at Corinto and took complete charge of the military forces in the western part of Nicaragua, controlling the land operations of the bluejackets and marines, as well as the duties performed by the ships in patrolling the coast and preventing filibustering.

On the arrival of the *Cleveland* at Corinto on September 14 her landing force was at once sent ashore, bringing the number of bluejackets and marines ashore in Nicaragua to about 2350. These combined forces were used in opening the railroad from Corinto to Managua and their effective services assisted in restoring tranquillity to Nicaragua and in relieving the deplorable conditions of privation and hunger that resulted in several localities from the operations of the rebel forces. It became necessary to use armed force in order to dislodge a band of revolutionists from the Barranca, a fortified position consisting of two islands near Masaya, between which the railroad passes and from which the revolutionists controlled and threatened the railroad and held Masaya in a state of great destitution. A short assault succeeded in overcoming the resistance of the rebels, but in this assault four Americans were killed and five wounded. This occurred on October 4 and on the same day five marines were slightly wounded in a skirmish at Chichigalpa.

On October 6, while an American detachment was entering Leon to occupy the town, some resistance was encountered and three Americans were killed and three wounded. With the surrender of General Mena to Admiral Southerland and his deportation from the country, followed by the death of General Zeledon, the revolutionary movement quickly subsided and by the latter part of October practically normal conditions obtained throughout the country, although it was deemed prudent by the United States government to keep a considerable force ashore for the time being. The removal of the American troops began on October 25, and after December 1 there remained only the legation guard of 100 marines at Managua. In the elections of November 2 Adolfo Diaz, the provisional president, was chosen president for the four years beginning January 1, 1913, and Fernando Salorzano was chosen vice-president.

There was a considerable amount of criticism in the United States against an active American intervention in Nicaragua. President Taft in his message in December, 1912, declared that the loss of life and suffering in Nicaragua might have been averted had the Department of State, through approval of the loan convention by the Senate, been permitted to carry out its policy of encouraging the extending of financial aid to weak Central American states with the primary object of avoiding just such revolutions by assisting those republics to rehabilitate their finances, to establish their currency on a stable basis, to remove the custom houses from the danger of revolutions by arranging for their secure administration, and to establish reliable banks. He declared that the actual and immediate cause of the landing of American marines and bluejackets and their participation in hostilities was the result of the admission of the government of Niçaragua that it was unable to protect American life and property against acts of sheer lawlessness on the part of the malcontents and its request to the United States government to assume that office. The note presented to the Nicaraguan government on December 18 by the Department of State clearly outlined the policy of the American government. It declared: "The policy of the government of the United States in the present Nicaraguan disturbances is to take the necessary measures for an adequate legation guard at Managua, to keep open communications, and to protect American life and property."

"In discountenancing Zelaya, whose régime of barbarity and corruption was ended by the Nicaraguan nation after a bloody war, the government of the United States opposed not only the individual but the system, and this government could not countenance any movement to restore the same destructive régime. . . . The revolt of General Mena in flagrant violation of his solemn promises to his own government and to the American minister, and of the Dawson agreement, by which he was solemnly bound, and his attempt to overturn the government of his country for purely selfish purposes and without even the pretense of contending for principle, make the political rebellion in origin the most inexcusable in the annals of Central America. The nature and methods of the political disturbances, indeed, place them in the category of anarchy rather than ordinary revolution."

Friendly Relations. Not all the relations of the American government with Central and South American countries were of an aggressive nature. The government took part in several arbitrations and mediations and through the efforts of American diplomacy wars were prevented. In association with the Argentine Republic and Brazil a successful mediation was concluded between Peru and Ecuador. A boundary dispute between Panama and Costa Rica was settled through peaceable arbitration by the United States. Threatened war between Haiti and the Dominican Republic was stayed. The government of the United States was thanked for its influence toward the restoration of amicable relations between the Argentine Republic and Bolivia. In the disagreements between the governments of Chile and Peru on account of the famous Tacna-Arica dispute the United States government exerted her friendly influence and pacific counsel.

Chile. In the last part of August a payment was made of the long drawn-out Alsop claim, which for years has occupied the attention of the governments of the United States and Chile and at one time threatened friendly relations between the two countries. The claim arose through the loss suffered by the firm of Alsop & Company, doing business in Peru, Bolivia, and Chile before the war between these three countries. The company complained against the three governments and Bolivia and Peru made settlements, but Chile would not do so on the ground that the claim had to do with certain lands which, in the meantime, had been ceded by Bolivia to Chile. Alsop & Company thereupon appealed to the United States government. Arbitration at The Hague was suggested, but this was not agreed to by the Chilean government. It was finally agreed to refer the claim to Edward VII., as arbitrator, and on his death the dispute was submitted to his successor, George V. In August, acting on the report of the commissioners whom he designated to study the case, King George pronounced his award, assigning a sum about one-third as much as the original amount of the claim to the Alsops in full settlement.

EUROPE. With the countries of Europe the relations of the United States were pleasant and amicable during 1912. Under a special agreement entered into between the United States and Great Britain on August 18, 1910, for the arbitration of outstanding pecuniary claims, a schedule of claims and the terms of submission were agreed upon by the two governments, and together with the special agreement were approved by the Senate on July 19, 1911, but in accordance with the terms of the agreement they did not go into effect until confirmed by the two governments by the exchange of notes, which was done on April 26, 1912. At the end of the year negotiations were still in progress for a supplemental schedule of claims.

The wars in the Near East during 1912 made it necessary for the dispatch to Turkish waters of a special service squadron consisting of two armored cruisers.

No action was taken by Russia as a result of the abrogation of the treaty of 1832 in December, 1911. This treaty was abrogated as the result of alleged discrimination toward American citizens of Jewish birth who wished to visit and travel in Russia. Under the terms of the treaty the American government maintained that the action of Russia in preventing the entrance of American citizens of Jewish birth into that country was contrary to the terms of that treaty.

CHINA. The political disturbances in China in the autumn and winter of 1911-12, which resulted in the abdication of the Manchu rulers and the formation of a provisional republican government, occasioned some anxiety for American citizens in China. In view of the seriousness of the disturbances and their general character, the American minister at Peking was instructed at his discretion to advise American citizens in the affected districts to concentrate at such centres as were easily accessible to foreign troops or men-of-war. Nineteen American naval vessels were stationed at Chinese ports and other measures were taken for the protection of American interests. The American government, in common with the other great powers, took no active part in the Chinese affairs, on the assumption that independent action by foreign governments in their own individual interests would add further to a situation already complicated.

On February 3 Secretary Knox forwarded to the German ambassador an important communication relating to the policy of foreign nations in China. After calling attention to the unanimous action of the powers thus far shown, he said: "It is therefore evident to this government that all the powers have up to the present, by common consent, not only refrained from independent action and from intervening in China's internal affairs, but have acted in full accord with their mutual assurances that they would respect its integrity and sovereignty.

"There happily has thus far been no reason for interference on the part of foreign powers, inasmuch as both imperialists and republicans have guaranteed the lives and property of the foreign population, and the latest reports tend to strengthen the belief that it is improbable that future developments will necessitate such interference. If, however, contrary to all expectations, any further steps should prove necessary, this government is firm in the conviction that the policy of concerted action after full consultation by the powers should and would be maintained in order to exclude from the beginning all possible misunderstandings.

"Moreover, this government has felt it to be a corollary of the policy of strict neutrality hitherto pursued by common accord with respect to loans to China to look with disfavor upon loans by its nationals unless assured that such loans would be of neutral effect as between the contending factions, as it has also felt that the present was an occasion where there might be invoked with peculiar appropriateness the principle of the lending governments deterring their nationals from making loans not approved as to their broad policy by their own governments in consultation with the other interested powers."

The action is said to have been taken on account of the discovery by the German secret service that Japanese troops had been mobilized on the Manchurian frontier.

The Chinese Republic had not been recognized by the United States government at the end of the year. The Chinese loan, participation in which was attained for American capital by prompt and effective action on the part of American officials, was not consummated in 1912, as it had up to the end of the year proved unacceptable to the provisional government. The loan agreement was promulgated in June, 1912, and it included representative banking groups of the United States, France, Germany, Great Britain, Japan, and Russia. See CHINA, section *History*.

JAPAN. The death of the Mikado of Japan made it necessary for the United States government to send a representative to the funeral, and in August Mr. Knox, Secretary of State, was created special ambassador to Japan, charged with the mission of bearing to the imperial family, the government, and the people of that empire a sympathetic message of the American commonwealth on the occasion of the death of the emperor. The kindly reception everywhere accorded to Mr. Knox showed that his mission was deeply appreciated by the Japanese nation.

LIBERIA. As the result of the efforts of the United States government to place the government of Liberia in a position to pay its outstanding indebtedness and to maintain a stable and efficient government, negotiations for a loan of $1,700,000 were successfully concluded and it is anticipated that the payment of the old loan and the issuance of the bonds of the 1912 loan for the rehabilitation of the finances of Liberia will follow early in 1913, when the new receivership will go into active operation. This receivership will consist of a general receiver of customs, designated by the government of the United States, and three receivers of customs designated by the governments of Germany, France, and Great Britain, which countries have commercial interests in the republic of Liberia.

For treaties negotiated with foreign countries during 1912, see ARBITRATION, INTERNATIONAL.

UNITED STATES CENSUS. The Census Bureau continued the collation of statistics gathered in the Thirteenth Census, and published many bulletins containing the results during the year. The census covered four main branches: Population, agriculture (including irrigation), manufactures, and mines. The results relating to these subjects are published first in the form of advance bulletins, which appear from time to time as the data relating to any given topic or any given State become available. Abstract bulletins will be issued relating to the four main branches. State bulletins will be issued only for the three subjects. Up to the end of 1912 there had been issued under the main subject of population an abstract of statistics of the number and distribution of the inhabitants of the United States; abstracts of race nativity, parentage, sex, State of birth, and males of voting age and militia age; abstract of statistics of school attendance and illiteracy; an abstract of statistics of age and marital condition, and an abstract of statistics of country of birth. In the branch of agriculture there had been issued abstracts of statistics of farms and farm property, statistics of livestock on farms and elsewhere, statistics of crops for 1910, statistics of tenure, mortgage indebtedness, color and nativity of farmers and size of farms, and statistics of livestock products. Under irrigation there had been issued an abstract of the statistics of irrigation. In the branch of manufactures there had been issued an abstract of statistics of manufactures for States and by industries, and in the branch of mines an abstract of the statistics of mining industries. Statistics relating to each of the States, giving data in all the four main branches, had also been issued. In addition, several special bulletins had been prepared. These related to population and gave the population of counties and equivalent subdivisions, the total population and area by States and Territories, and the population of cities. The data and text published in advance bulletins and the abstract and special bulletins will be brought together in the final reports of the census. Because of the size and number of the volumes the distribution of complete sets will be necessarily restricted. They will be sent generally to important libraries and institutions of learning, and to certain selected social, civil, industrial and economic associations, and to persons engaged in statistical research work or having special occasion to use detailed results of the census for all States covering any one or all main branches of the census.

The general statistics of agriculture for the United States will be found in the article AGRICULTURE. Statistics of manufactures in the States will be found in the articles on each of the States. A summary of the manufactures of the United States is given in the article UNITED STATES. A brief summary of the foreign-born population of the different States will be found in the paragraph *Population* in the articles on the different States. General statistics of mining are covered in the article MINING INDUSTRY. Data on illiteracy and statistics relating to sex distribution in the United States will be found under the respective titles.

COST OF THE CENSUS. The annual report of E. Dana Durand, director of the census, for the fiscal year ending June 30, 1912, shows the total expenditure from July 1, 1909, to June 30, 1912, to be $15,171,593, of which $7,223,385 was expended for field work, including the salaries of supervisors and enumerators; $6,271,446 for compilation and publication of statistics, and $1,676,762 for annual and other investigations of the permanent bureau not connected with the decennial census. The total census force on December 31, 1912, numbered 813, with 740 additional special agents stationed in the southern States to collect statistics of cotton.

UNITED STATES MILITARY ACADEMY. The enrollment in the academy on September 1, 1912, was 538, and the faculty numbered 138. The changes in the faculty during the year included the retirement of Professor Samuel E. Tillman of the department of chemistry and the appointment of Professor Wirt Robinson as his successor. Professor Charles W. Larned (q. v.) of the department of drawing died June 19, 1911, and Professor Edwin R. Stuart was appointed to succeed him in this chair. The superintendent in 1912 was Col. C. P. Townsley.

UNITED STATES NATIONAL MUSEUM. The United States National Museum, the legal depository of all national collections, is a museum of record, research, and education. It is especially rich in the natural history, ethnology, and archæology of America, but has also very extensive collections pertaining to the zoölogy, botany, geology, paleontology, archæology, and ethnology of other parts of the world. All the natural history collections, including those of anthropology and archæology, are contained in a new building, recently completed at a cost of $3,500,000. The National Gallery of Art is also temporarily housed in this building. The larger portion of the older museum building is occupied by the collections and exhibits of the industrial arts. It also contains extensive exhibits illustrative of American history, including many unique objects of national importance and interest, and collections of laces and embroideries and other art textiles. The main hall of the Smithsonian building contains comprehensive exhibits of graphic arts.

The publications of the National Museum consist of the Proceedings, the Bulletins, and the Annual Reports. The first two of these series are devoted mainly to technical articles on various branches of science, based on, or descriptive of, the collections of the museum. In 1912 the museum was open to the public on Sundays. This measure has been long advocated for all the buildings, but as yet the practice concerns only the new building.

In the fiscal year ending June 30, 1912, the additions to the collections of the museum comprised about 238,000 specimens and objects, of which about 168,000 were biological, 63,000 geological and paleontological, and 7000 anthropological.

A large number of valuable temporary additions, in the form of loans, were made to the National Gallery of Art, to the collections of art textiles and to the division of history.

UNITED STATES NAVAL ACADEMY. The enrollment in the academy in the autumn of 1912 was 785. Among the additions to the academy for the academic year 1912-13 were the following: Commander H. O. Stickney was appointed head of the department of marine engineering and naval construction; Lieutenants T. F. Caldwell and J. G. H. Bowdey were appointed assistants in mathematics and mechanics; Lieutenant G. F. Neal was appointed assistant instructor in physics and electrical engineering; Lieutenants E. G. Oberlin and I. C. Schulte were appointed instructors in the school of marine engineering; and First Lieutenant A. A. Cunningham and Second Lieutenant B. L. Smith were appointed to aviation duty at the engineering experiment station. The superintendent is Captain John H. Gibbons, U. S. N., and the commandant is Commander G. W. Logan, U. S. N. The productive funds of the academy amounted to $625,720. The library contained 63,261 volumes.

UNITED STATES STEEL CORPORATION. The year was an eventful one for this concern. Early in the year a committee of the House of Representatives under the chairmanship of Representative Stanley began an extensive investigation into the organization and methods of the trust. On May 6, hearings were begun in the suit of the United States government to dissolve the corporation. Evidence was being taken in this case at the close of the year. The reports of the Stanley committee were not submitted to the House, but various bills were recommended by members of the committee. One of these, approved by 4 of the 5 members, would make the control of 30 per cent. of an industry presumptive evidence of unlawful restraint of trade; and would place upon the corporation the burden of proving its innocence. There were four other bills all favoring federal control and regulation with variations, some of them approving the proposal to empower the government to fix maximum prices. None of these bills were acted upon.

EARNINGS. A statement issued December 18 showed that the capacity of the corporation had increased from 7,700,000 tons in 1901 to 14,200,000 in 1912. The production had increased from 8,197,000 tons in 1902 to about 12,300,000 tons in 1912. Nevertheless the net earnings had fallen from $133,300,000 in 1902, or an average of $16.25 per ton, to $108,000,000, or an average of $8.86 per ton, in 1912. The ratio of net earnings to tonnage output had declined steadily from $15.24 in 1907 to $11.00 in 1911. The statement declared that about $500,000,000 had been spent in new construction and acquisitions, almost all of which had been met from surplus earnings. Thus the fixed charges represented by preferred dividends and interest remained about the same as at the time of organization. The decline of net earnings in spite of an increase of 50 per cent. in production was explained by advanced wages, increased taxation, the profit-sharing and pension systems, and lower prices of steel. It was claimed that the advances in wage rates added between $20,000,000 and $30,000,000 to the pay-roll per year; that taxes paid had risen from $2,391,000 in 1902 to about $10,000,000 in 1912; and that welfare work was costing nearly $5,000,000 a year.

LABOR CONDITIONS. Ever since the Pittsburgh Survey the conditions of labor in the plants of the corporation have been given a great deal of public attention. The points about which public discussion centred were the seven-day week, with a long shift of twenty-four hours when night and day shifts changed; the twelve-hour day; speeding of the workmen by bonuses to superintendents and foremen and a system of rate-cutting of piece-wages; and the repression of the men by an autocratic rule which destroyed initiative and capacity for good citizenship. In 1910, Mr. Charles M. Cabot of Boston began a movement to secure an investigation of labor conditions. Such an investigation was authorized in April, 1911. Mr. Cabot also sought the privilege of mailing to each of the 15,000 stockholders copies of an article by Mr. John A. Fitch, who had investigated labor conditions in the Pittsburgh Survey. Judge Gary refused to give Mr. Cabot a mailing list of the stockholders and the matter was taken into the courts. Before final decision was made, however, an agreement was reached on the basis of which letters from Judge Gary and Mr. Cabot, together with a twenty-page pamphlet by Mr. Fitch, were mailed to the stockholders in March, 1912.

Meanwhile an investigation by a stockholders' committee had been authorized by Judge Gary. This committee made a ten-days' tour of the mills in April. It found that, with the exception of two or three plants, the seven-day week had been discontinued. With reference to the twelve-hour day, it found that 25.7 per cent. of the 175,700 workmen were employed twelve hours per day. In the rolling mills, open hearths, and blast furnaces the number of employees working twelve hours varied from 50 to 60 per cent. The committee pronounced this long day bad from the standpoints both of the individual worker and of society. As to speeding, though the committee favored retention of the bonus system and piece-wages, it favored the introduction of means for checking those officials guilty of imposing excessive strain upon their men; and it favored also the distribution of bonuses to all workers rather than to foremen and superintendents only. The repression of the workers was found to be due largely to the policy of the corporation toward unionism. The committee did not pronounce itself in favor of the restoration of union conditions, but expressed a hope that the day might come "when employer and employees shall enter into a common administration of industrial interests." The finance committee of the corporation, headed by Judge Gary, took steps toward the complete elimination of the seven-day week and the long 24-hour turn. It also determined to reduce the 12-hour day in so far as was "reasonable, just, and practicable."

Early in the summer Congress passed an eight-hour law which applied extensively to steel companies, especially as regards armorplate. See LABOR LEGISLATION, *Hours*.

The report of the Stanley committee gave considerable attention to labor conditions. The majority report showed that the increase in the average daily wage from $1.89 in 1902 to $2.09 in 1909 had been attended by a decline in labor-cost per ton from $1.25 in 1902 to 82 cents in 1909. It criticised with great severity the hours and wages of steel laborers and condemned the company for its apparent favor for foreign labor and its attitude toward unions.

Finally there was much unrest among the steel workers themselves. Two brief strikes occurred in various plants at Pittsburgh, both by unorganized laborers. At the same time representatives of the American Federation of Labor and of the Industrial Workers of the World carried on open and vigorous campaigns of organization. The presence of the latter caused general public uneasiness. The federation's plan was systematic and thorough-going. It was to culminate in simultaneous meetings of the workers in the steel mills of the entire country at the same time to effect general organization and prevent the playing of one mill against another or one company against another by the associated employers.

For the betterment programme of the corporation, see WELFARE WORK.

UNIVERSAL PEACE CONGRESS. See ARBITRATION, INTERNATIONAL.

UNIVERSALISTS. The most distinctive tenet of this denomination is the final salvation of all men. According to statistics gathered by Dr. H. K. Carroll, there were in 1912 51,716 communicants, 709 churches, and 702 ministers. The Sunday schools have a membership of about 50,000 and the value of church property is about $12,800,000. The denomination carries on foreign mission work in Japan and China and sustains domestic missions in fifteen churches. Its institutions of higher education include Tufts College at Medford, Mass.; St. Lawrence University at Canton, N. Y.; Buchtel College at Akron, O., and Lombard College at Galesburg, Ill. The next session of the general conference of the denomination will be held at Chicago, Ill., in October, 1913.

UNIVERSITIES AND COLLEGES. ATTENDANCE. For the year ending June, 1911, 581 universities, colleges, and technological schools reported to the commissioner of education 111,449 men and 61,265 women in collegiate and 7577 men and 3281 women in resident graduate work. This was a total of 183,572 students. Thirty-seven per cent. of these were enrolled in the 89 public institutions. Five institutions enroll more than 10 per cent. of the entire number of students. These institutions (Columbia, California, Harvard, Cornell, and Chicago) have 28 per cent. of the total endowment, 16 per cent. of the books, and about 14 per cent. of the scientific apparatus of all colleges, universities, and technological schools in the United States. They have nearly 10 per cent. of all the collegiate instructors and grant more than 20 per cent. of the scholarships. In the professional departments of universities, colleges, and technological schools there were 36,275 men and 1389 women. The five States having the largest number of students in these institutions are New York, 26,458; Illinois, 22,300; Massachusetts, 16,458; Ohio, 15,687, and Pennsylvania, 15,270. Eighty per cent. of the resident graduate students are in the Eastern Atlantic and Northern Central divisions of States. The following table, which shows the registration in twenty-eight of the leading institutions on November 1, 1912, and on the corresponding date for 1911 was prepared from data gathered by Professor Rudolph Tombo, Jr. (*Science*, December 27, 1912):

Institution	Attendance Nov.1 1912	Attendance Nov.1 1911	Institution	Attendance Nov.1 1912	Attendance Nov.1 1911
California	6457	5724	Northwestern	3632	3438
Chicago	6351	6062	Ohio State	3608	3567
Columbia	9007	7938	Pennsylvania	4843	5220
Cornell	5412	5609	Pittsburgh	1833	....
Harvard	5729	5426	Princeton	1568	1543
Illinois	4315	4929	Stanford	1670	1648
Indiana	2234	2154	Syracuse	3529	3307
Iowa	1944	1967	Texas	3016	2539
Johns Hopkins	1088	1238	Tulane	2249	2040
Kansas	2403	2265	Virginia	799	781
Michigan	5620	5452	Washington University	958	859
Minnesota	5063	4548	Western Reserve	1378	1331
Missouri	2871	2780	Wisconsin	5141	5015
N. Y. Univer.	4543	4055	Yale	3265	3224

The following table shows the number of professional schools reporting to the Bureau of Education in 1911, the number of students, the graduates, and the percentage of students who were college graduates in 1905 and in 1911:

Class	Schools	Students	Graduates 1911	P. C. students with deg. 1905	P. C. students with deg. 1911
Theology	193	10,834	1,877	34.9	30.2
Law	116	19,615	3,901	22.0	21.3
Medicine	122	19,146	4,048	11.4	10.3
Dentistry	55	6,961	1,764	2.5	1.7
Pharmacy	77	6,131	1,743	1.5	1.4
Vet. Medicine	21	2,571	706	1.1	.7

Schools of dentistry show an increase of students over the previous year amounting to over 6 per cent. There was also a slight increase of students of law. There was a decrease in schools of veterinary medicine of 5 per cent., and small decreases in both theology and pharmacy. The most pronounced decline was in the schools of medicine. The number of students decreased by 2248, or 11 per cent. Thirteen medical schools closed their doors during the year. The largest number of medical students ever enrolled in American institutions was in 1903, when there were 27,062. The registration in 1910-11 was 19,146, showing a decline of over 36 per cent. in 8 years. This decline is due to several causes, chief of which has been overcrowding of the profession and the thorough exposure of the methods and low standards of certain medical schools by the report on medical education issued by the Carnegie Foundation. It has been claimed that the schools are raising their standards. If this were true, it ought to appear in an increased percentage of college graduates among the students, but there was a somewhat smaller percentage of such students in 1911 than in 1905. During these years students seem to have been about equally successful in pursuing their work, for there has been a decrease of less than half of 1 per cent. in the ratio of students to graduates. The decline of college graduates among the students of the professional schools is noteworthy. It has been greatest among the theological schools, but it is evident in all.

The variation in the per capita investment in the different professional schools based on student registration is remarkable. For each student in theology there is invested in grounds and buildings in round numbers $2000, ten times the per capita investment for law students, twice the investment for each student in medicine, and nearly twice the per capita investment for grounds, buildings, scientific apparatus, and dormitories in colleges and universities. For each student in pharmacy, dentistry, and veterinary medicine there is invested respectively $338, $280, and $250.

RESOURCES. Productive funds aggregating $299,347,272 were reported by the 581 universities, colleges, and technological schools, including colleges for women, for 1911. Their scientific apparatus, machinery, and furniture were valued at $38,280,589, buildings at $194,183,339, dormitories at $31,099,277, and grounds at $81,053,420. The total receipts for the year, exclusive of addition to endowment, were $80,902,571. Of this amount $18,493,120 was from tuition and other educational sources, $13,293,446 from productive funds, $14,707,243 from State and city, $3,469,739 from private benefactors for current expenses, and $5,875,185 from the United States government. There was received for endowment, $13,769,870. From 1900 to 1911 the productive funds of these institutions increased 93 per cent., but the income from them was increased 108 per cent., which shows that the funds are invested and managed to better advantage than in 1900. The rate of tuition has not been greatly changed. The increase in students since 1900 has been 66 per cent., the increase in amount received from tuition 73 per cent. Buildings and grounds are more economically employed, for while the increase of students as stated was 66 per cent., the increase in value of buildings and grounds was only 48 per cent. During these 11 years the total income of these institutions has increased 235 per cent., the value of scientific apparatus, machinery, and furniture 126 per cent., the number of volumes in the library 80 per cent., but the number of scholarships and fellowships has not kept pace with the increase in students. The number of scholarships increased 46 per cent., and fellowships 35 per cent.

DEGREES. The total number of degrees conferred on examination during 1910-11 was 27,319, of which men received 18,524 and women 8106. The total includes 2520 post-graduate degrees. Fifty-three per cent. of the first degrees were bachelor of arts, 26.5 per cent. bachelor of science, and 4.6 per cent. bachelor of philosophy. In 1900, 56 per cent. were bachelor of arts, 21 per cent. were bachelor of science, and 8 per cent. bachelor of philosophy. A considerable specialization is shown in the number of degrees granted in the different States. Massachusetts leads in the number of bachelor of art degrees; Pennsylvania in the number of bachelors of science; Connecticut in the number of bachelors of philosophy; New York in the number of civil and mechanical engineering degrees, and Ohio in electrical engineering degrees.

A complete list of the doctorates conferred on examination by American universities in 1911-12 was printed in *Science* (August 2, 1912). There were 492 such degrees, showing a gain of 55 over the previous year. The eight universities conferring the largest number of doctor's degrees were, Columbia 81, Chicago 57, Harvard 41, Pennsylvania 34, Cornell 33, Johns Hopkins 32, Yale 31, and Wisconsin 27. It will be noticed that these eight institutions conferred more than two-thirds of all the doctorates. Two hundred and seventy-three of the degrees were in the natural and exact sciences. Degrees in these subjects are increasing more rapidly than in other subjects. Seventy-eight doctorates were given in chemistry, 34 in English, 30 in physics, 30 in botany, 29 in psychology, 26 in economics, and the others were distributed among 33 subjects.

BENEFACTIONS AND APPROPRIATIONS. The commissioner of education reports an aggregate of gifts and bequests, excluding grants by the United States and different States for 1910-11 amounting to $22,963,145. This was an increase of $4,226,006 over the preceding year. Fifty institutions reported gifts of $100,000 or over. Columbia reported $2,535,064, Harvard $1,745,438, University of Chicago $1,358,951, New York University $928,445, and Yale, $1,134,385. Thus these five institutions received one-third of the entire amount. The most important new legislative appropriations were the voting of $600,000 and an annual grant of $50,000 by the legislature of Maryland to establish and maintain a school of technology in connection with the Johns Hopkins University, and an appropriation by the Massachusetts legislature of $50,000 annually for five years to the Worcester Polytechnic Institute.

NEW PRESIDENTS. Among the institutions which elected new presidents during 1912 were, Amherst College which elected Dr. Alexander Meiklejohn, professor of philosophy and dean of the faculty of Brown University; the University of Oklahoma which elected Stratton D. Brooks, former superintendent of the Boston public schools; the University of Maine which elected E. T. Fairchilds, former State superintendent of public instruction for Kansas, and president of the National Educational Association; and the University of Wyoming which elected Dr. C. A. Dunaway, former president of the University of Montana. Dr. Ira Remsen tendered his resignation as president of Johns Hopkins University. He will remain professor of chemistry which he has been since the opening of the university in 1876.

NEW BUILDINGS. The building activities of the various institutions have been extensive. The most important building completed during the year is the William Rainey Harper Memorial Library at the University of Chicago. The cost of this building was $800,000. A new library building at the Ohio State University costing $200,000 has been practically completed. The University of Pennsylvania and Princeton University have each begun work on new graduate schools. In each case the buildings involve an expenditure of about $500,000. Columbia has under construction a building for the school of journalism. The corner stone of the new Germanic Museum at Harvard, for which Mr. Adolphus Busch contributed $250,000, was laid June 9, 1912. The University of Illinois is constructing a school of commerce building. Regent Hill's bequest of $200,000 to the University of Michigan has made possible the building of a new auditorium which will have a seating capacity of 5500. The following are some of the more important building undertakings of the various institutions: University of California, a new agricultural hall costing $200,000; Harvard University, the new T. Jefferson Coolidge, Jr., memorial laboratory; Cornell University, five agricultural buildings and three veterinary buildings; University of Missouri a building for the department of physics costing $100,000, and another for the department of chemistry at a cost of $60,000; University of Iowa, a new physics building costing $225,000; Sheffield Scientific School, a building costing about $115,000; University of Illinois, a transportation building, mining building, ceramics building, locomotive-testing laboratory, and several buildings for the school of agriculture. The leading institutions which have built or planned dormitories during the year are Cornell, Columbia, Ohio State University, Yale, Illinois, and Pennsylvania.

CARNEGIE FOUNDATION. The sixth annual report of the Carnegie Foundation for the Advancement of Teaching, covering the year ending September 30, 1911, shows that the endowment of the foundation was $12,123,000, its income for the year $590,000, and $526,000 was expended for retiring allowances and pensions. The number of allowances and pensions in force

STRATTON D. BROOKS
President University of Oklahoma

C. A. DUNIWAY
President University of Wyoming

ALEXANDER MEIKLEJOHN
President of Amherst College

TALCOTT WILLIAMS
Director of School of Journalism, Columbia University

was 373. The average annual payment was $1631. Fifteen recipients of allowances died and 31 retiring allowances and 17 widows' pensions were granted during the year. Seventy-two universities, colleges, and schools of technology are on the accepted list, the University of Virginia being the only one added during the year. President Pritchett urged upon the colleges themselves a sense of obligation to their old and disabled professors at least equal to that shown by business corporations. The foundation conducted an exchange of teachers which sent 9 American teachers to Prussia and brought 9 Prussian teachers here during the year. The report states that the increase in number and size of post-graduate schools has been greater than the natural need.

In June, 1912, the foundation published a bulletin "Concerning Medical Education in Europe," by Dr. Abraham Flexner. President Pritchett says, "Three-fourths of the medical schools in America would be driven out of existence if the lowest terms upon which medical schools can exist abroad were applied in this country." In spite of serious defects, which are frankly pointed out, the author finds medical education in Germany still leading the world, both because the medical sciences are highly developed in the laboratories and institutes of German universities, and because clinical teachers in the German university are univeristy professors.

New Institutions and Departments. The most important new institution to be opened during the year is Rice Institute at Houston, Tex. The endowment of this institution, amounting to about $10,000,000, is the gift of the late William Marsh Rice. The formal dedication of the institute took place in October, 1912. Dr. Edgar Odell Lovett of Princeton is the first president. It is the aim of this institute to occupy a position in the South similar to that occupied by the Massachusetts Institute of Technology in the North. The New York legislature, in 1911, established a State college of forestry in connection with Syracuse University. Professor H. T. Baker of Pennsylvania State College has been chosen as the dean and director of the college. The college proposes to offer extension work in forestry to the high schools of the State. In September, 1913, there will be offered a four-year course for the training of city foresters. Dr. Talcott Williams, associate editor of the *Philadelphia Press*, was appointed director of the Pulitzer School of Journalism at Columbia University. About 100 students were admitted to the school in September. Men of experience and ability are admitted without examination, and after two years of work are eligible to the degree offered after completion of the course. The four-years course is divided between studies in history, law, government, party organization, economics, unions, trusts, literature, training in reporting, and training in writing. About one-third of the time is devoted to training in writing. Students are expected to do about as much writing each week as the average man in the newspaper office. As nearly as possible, newspaper conditions are introduced in the school in order to train the newspaper men.

Aims and Methods. Recently President Butler has called attention to the wasteful duplication of work in universities and colleges. He believes that the time has come when the large institutions should concentrate on the work they are best able to do. While the movement toward specialization is not well defined, it is becoming more pronounced each year. One of the most important steps in this direction was the action taken by Amherst College in 1911. Briefly stated, the "Amherst idea" is a return to the cultural subjects in distinction to the technological courses that are offered in the universities. This involves an increased emphasis on the classical studies. Four years of Latin will be required of all for entrance and two years of an ancient language and two years of science are now required in the college course instead of one year each in classics and science as in the past. "Amherst does not look on any man as educated unless he has been taught to interpret the problems of his own day through the lessons of the past and has received a knowledge of classic literature, philosophy, and civilization, gaining discipline in the expression of his own tongue through the mental process of translation. Neither does Amherst look on any man to-day as fully trained for modern life who has not learned the methods of the laboratory and laid a secure foundation in science." The degree of bachelor of science will not be offered to classes entering after 1913, but only the one degree of bachelor of arts. It should be noted that this change seems to have been called forth by an address to the trustees by the class of 1885.

In October, 1912, the board of trustees of Hamilton College determined to keep that college on a strictly classical basis. Unlike the conditions at Amherst, this change seems to be due, not to the judgment of the alumni, but rather against it. Earlier the trustees had voted "that a special commission should consider the curriculum and entrance requirements and report their findings." The commission had for its chairman G. P. Bristol, professor of Latin at Cornell University, and included E. L. Stevens of the New York City board of superintendents, and Calvin N. Kendall, commissioner of education in New Jersey, all Hamilton men. The commission, after a year of work which included much testimony and counter-testimony, recommended, among other things, that the degree of A. B. should be given at Hamilton without Greek, and that not even Latin should be required as an entrance to the non-Greek course. The recommendations of this committee in so far as they concerned Latin and Greek were rejected by the board of trustes. Four years of Latin and three years of Greek are to be required for admission to the classical course and four years of Latin and two years of a modern language for admission to the Latin-Scientific course. The degree of bachelor of arts will be conferred only upon those who have done all the required work of the classical course in both Latin and Greek. These changes become operative with the entering class in 1913, except that provisions will be made for those who began their preparation to meet the older requirements of admission and are now unable to offer all the required subjects. The effect of this change will be watched with interest. The trustees of Amherst, while asserting their belief in the value of Greek, regretted that the requirement of Greek could not be made, since so few preparatory schools teach it. The faculty of the College of Arts and Sciences in the University of Maine have abolished the requirement of ten hours in the classical department for the bachelor of arts degree, and hereafter neither Latin nor Greek will be required for admission or for the degree.

In some respects the most radical changes from conventional college methods and aims are to be found in Reed College, Portland. President Foster frankly purposes to take full advantage of the freedom from traditions and customs which is to be found in the new institution. Many of the methods he has introduced would be strongly opposed if they were to be tried in older institutions. The institution is to conduct only college work in the liberal arts and sciences until such a time as increased endowment will permit of more advanced work. Particular emphasis is placed upon the teaching ability of the instructors. The requirements for admission to the college are scholarship, health, and character. As regards the first, candidates for admission must have completed a four years high school course of standard grade or its equivalent. This means fifteen units of work. There is no minimum age for entrance, no prescriptions whatever are to be offered concerning the subjects for admission. No students are admitted on condition, nor are there to be any special students. There are no fraternities, no sororities, no inter-collegiate athletics, and few of those outside activities that have often interfered with the supreme objects of higher education. The college purposes to select its students. The fact that of the 263 candidates who applied for admission to the first class, all but 50 were declined, shows how rigidly the college is enforcing its methods.

The faculty of arts and sciences of Harvard has recommended to the governing boards of the university a further limitation of the elective system which is now in operation in that institution. If this recommendation is accepted, a student may continue to take his courses in the parts of the subject which most interest him, but he will be compelled to supplement them by enough other study to see how the parts which he has mastered are related to each other. He will also have to keep in mind what he learns in the early part of the course in order to employ it in his senior year. There would be a continuous pressure on the student to do some independent comparing of facts. The resolution adopted by the faculty is as follows: "That the division of history, government, and economics be authorized to require of all students whose field of concentration lies in this division, in addition to the present requirements stated in terms of courses for the bachelor's degree, a special final examination upon each student's field of concentration, and that the passing of this examination shall be necessary in order to fulfill the requirements for concentration in this division."

Columbia College has under consideration what is termed a "conference programme" for students of the junior and senior years. "Two years' residence will be necessary for a degree, there being no provision for advanced standing. The course of study is to be arranged not on departmental lines, but the aim will be to represent among the teachers the principal divisions of knowledge. A certain number of professors have already offered to conduct, in addition to their present programmes, one three-hour course continued through two years. None of these courses are to be elementary, the students being expected to familiarize themselves, by private study, with the elementary parts of the subject not already covered by their previous collegiate work. Each student is to appear at least twice a year before a conference of all the instructors and students of the group and to present, by means of an essay or otherwise, evidence of the progress of his studies. This conference which, in plan, is not unlike the disputations of the medieval universities, is to be held weekly. It is designed to be the educational centre of the programme, it being the expectation that participation in and preparation for the conferences will take up a considerable part of the students' time and energies. Each student is to present to the faculty, not later than April 15 of the year of his graduation, an essay on a topic proposed by himself and approved by the committee in charge at least one year before graduation. The essay must show mastery of the topic with which it deals.

The trustees of Rutgers College have adopted a recommendation of the faculty committee on graduate degrees by which the master's degree in that college is to be regarded as a degree to be given after extended liberal study. To this end the subjects studied by the candidate constitute a distinct course consisting of three subjects, not differing essentially from senior elective courses, to be pursued for two years. The committee urged that there were an increasing number of men and women graduating from colleges who were not fitted and did not desire to do the research work for a doctor's degree, but who did desire to pursue further some college subjects. The smaller colleges which are unable to offer proper facilities to candidates for the doctorate may be able to offer abundant opportunities for a continuation of liberal studies.

CHANGE IN ORGANIZATION. The University of Chicago has set aside a fund of about two million dollars to be used in paying retiring allowances to professors or their widows. The statute provides that any person in the service of the university sixty-five years of age and who has been in the service of the university for at least fifteen years in a rank not lower than assistant professor, may retire or be retired with an annual allowance computed as follows: "(a) For fifteen years' service, 40 per cent. of the average annual salary received during the five years immediately preceding the time of retirement. (b) For each year of service beyond fifteen years, 2 per cent. of the said average annual salary. But no annual allowance shall exceed 60 per cent. of the said average annual salary, nor shall it exceed $3000." The widow of any person in receipt of or eligible to a retiring allowance will receive one-half the amount of this allowance during her widowhood.

ANNIVERSARIES. Among the anniversaries that received particular attention during the year were: the seventy-fifth anniversary of the founding of Mt. Holyoke College, the seventy-fifth anniversary of the founding of the University of Michigan, the centennial celebration of the founding of Hamilton College, and the one hundred and twenty-fifth anniversary of the founding of the University of Pittsburgh.

EXCHANGE AND VISITING PROFESSORS. The exchange professors from abroad are: Kaiser Wilhelm Professor at Columbia, Dr. Felix Krueger of the University of Halle; visiting professor at Harvard, Dr. Rudolph Eucken, of the University of Jena; visiting French professor at Columbia, Dr. Henri Bergson of the University of Paris; Hyde lecturer at Harvard, Dr. Émile Legouis of the Sorbonne; and the first Japanese exchange professor at Harvard, Dr. Inazo Nitobe, president of the First National College of Tokyo. The Harvard exchange professor at the University of Berlin is Dr. Charles S. Minot of Harvard, and the Theodore Roosevelt Professor at the University of Berlin is Dr. William M. Sloane of Columbia University. Dr. Paul Shorey of the University of Chicago has been appointed Roosevelt Professor for 1913. Among the representatives of foreign universities who have lectured in this country during the year are: Prof. Israel Abrams of Cambridge University, Prof. Émile Borel of the University of Paris, Prof. Guenther Jacoby of the University of Greifswald, Prof. Giovanni Luzzi of the Waldensian School in Florence, Italy, Prof. Wilhelm Paszowski of the University of Berlin, Sir William Ramsay of the University of London, Prof. Ludwig Sinzheimer of the University of Munich, and Prof. Hugo de Vries of the University of Paris.

THE KAHN FOUNDATION. A recent benefaction by M. Albert Kahn of Paris makes it possible for college and university professors to travel freely for a year in order to see the world and in this way broaden their intellectual horizon and widen their sympathies. Two traveling fellows are appointed each year. The fellowship amounts to $3000 each with an additional $300 for the purchase of souvenirs, books, etc. No stipulation is made regarding the routes, countries visited, or subjects to be studied. The foundation is administered by E. D. Adams, N. M. Butler, and H. F. Osborn, of New York City; Charles W. Eliot of Cambridge, Mass.; Charles D. Walcott of Washington, D. C.; and Frank D. Franckenthal, secretary of Columbia University, as secretary of the board. The fellows for this year are, Dr. William E. Kellicott, professor of biology in Goucher College, and Ivan M. Linforth, professor of Greek in the University of California.

ATTENDANCE IN FOREIGN UNIVERSITIES. The following table shows the number of students in all foreign universities which report more than five hundred. Unless otherwise indicated the figures are taken from *Minerva Jahrbuch der Gelehrten Welt* for the years specified.

Universities	Attendance 1900-01	1901-02	1910-11	1911-12
Africa:				
Algiers	433	......	1,442	......
Cairo, Azhar School	10,003	......	10,450*	......
Argentina:				
Buenos Ayres	2,665	......	4,650	......
Australia:				
Adelaide	494	......	663	......
Melbourne	647	......	1,150	......
New Zealand	1,244	......	1,800*	......
Sydney	853	......	1,342	......
Austria-Hungary:				
Budapest	.....	5,339	7,548	......
Czernowitz	......	543	971	......
Gratz	.....	1,760	2,073	......
Innspruck	.....	1,001	1,298	......
Klausenburg	.....	1,592	2,359	......
Krakow	.....	1,711	3,380	......
Lemberg	.....	1,412	4,704	......
Prague (Karl-Ferdinand - Universitat)	.....	1,116	1,844	......
Prague (C. K. Ceska Universitat Karlo - Ferdinandova)	.....	3,459	4,432	......
Vienna	.....	4,810	7,148	......
Belgium:				
Brussels	.....	1,060	1,250*	......
Ghent	.....	804	1,176	......
Liège	.....	1,644	2,790	......
Louvain	.....	2,011	2,630	......
Canada:				
Kingston (Queens)	.....	672	1,612	......
Montreal (McGill)	1,111	......	2,426	......
Montreal (Université Laval)	.....	793	1,063	......
Toronto	.....	1,624	4,166	......
Chile:				
Santiago	.....	......	1,000	......
Cuba:				
Havana	.....	......	1,017(g)	......
Denmark:				
Copenhagen	.....	......	3,000*	......
England and Wales(a)				
Birmingham	677	......	984	.....
Bristol	677	563	980*	......
Cambridge	2,958	......	.....	3,781(r)
Durham	590	......	1,049	......
Leeds	1,165	......	933	......
Liverpool	.....	700	......	833(r)
London	6,889	......	9,263	......
Manchester	2,404	......	1,554	......
Oxford	3,481	......	......	3,995(r)
Sheffield	.....	......	886	......
Wales	1,428	......	1,552	......
France (b):				
Aix-Marseilles	950	......	1,236	......
Bordeaux	2,119	......	2,552	......
Caen	646	......	826	......
Dijon	699	......	992	......
Grenoble	566	......	1,156	......
Lille	1,110	......	1,779	......
Lyon	2,458	......	2,922	......
Montpellier	1,610	......	1,965	......
Nancy	1,027	......	1,899	......
Paris	12,289	......	17,602	......
Poitiers	821	......	1,299	......
Rennes	1,139	......	2,029	......
Toulouse	2,040	......	2,828	......
Alger	771	......	1,442	......
Germany (c):				
Berlin	5,431	......	......	9,829
Bonn	2,240	......	......	3,998
Breslau	1,770	......	......	2,702
Erlangen	977	......	......	1,202
Freiburg	1,766	......	......	2,466
Giessen	916	......	......	1,272
Göttingen	1,409	......	......	2,506
Greifwald	820	......	......	1,124
Halle	1,713	......	......	2,879
Heidelberg	1,464	......	......	2,231
Jena	772	......	......	1,738
Kiel	1,040	......	......	1,586
Königsberg	923	......	......	1,505
Leipzig	3,517	......	......	5,170
Marburg	1,231	......	......	1,968
Munich	4,494	......	......	6,797
Münster	791	......	......	2,126
Rostock	549	......	......	852
Strassburg	1,118	......	......	2,138
Tübingen	1,489	......	......	1,852
Würzburg	1,108	......	......	1,458
Greece:				
Athens	....	......	2,800*	......
Ireland:				
National Univ.	....	......	......	1,435
Queens Univ.	....	......	618	......
Italy:				
Bologna	1,469(d)	......	2,000*	......
Catania	981(e)	......	1,160*	......
Genoa	1,351	......	1,325	......
Naples	5,165(e)	......	6,600*	......
Padua	1,525(r)	......	1,447(r)	......
Palermo	.....	......	1,590	......
Pavia	1,029(e)	......	1,600*	......
Pisa	1,074(r)	......	1,024(r)	......
Rome	2,685(f)	......	3,882	......
Turin	2,700	......	2,204	......
Japan:				
Kyoto	.....	498	1,042	......
Tokyo	.....	3,213	5,355	......

	Attendance			
Netherlands:	1900-01	1901-02	1910-11	1911-12
Amsterdam	......	1,332	1,139	......
Leyden	......	1,027	1,195	......
Utrecht	......	1,003	1,082	......
Norway:				
Christiania	......	......	1,500*	......
Philippine Islands:				
Manila	......	......	2,119(g)	......
Portugal:				
Coimbra	1,181	......	1,262(g)	......
Rumania:				
Bukharest	4,313	......	3,898(g)	......
Jassy	......	782	900*	......
Russia:				
Helsingfors	2,558	......	2,830	......
Jurjews	1,790	......	2,901	......
Kazan	873	......	2,955	......
Kharkof	1,384	......	4,602	......
Kief	2,316	......	3,000*	......
Moscow	......	4,691	9,940	......
Odessa	......	1,116	2,699	......
St. Petersburg	......	3,775	9,586	......
Warsaw	1,122	......	1,911	......
Scotland:				
Aberdeen	905	......	1,300*	......
Edinburgh	......	2,920	3,421(r)	......
Glasgow	......	2,059	2,726(r)	......
St. Andrews	......	269	510(r)	......
Servia:				
Belgrade	......	403	1,025	......
Siberia:				
Tomsk	......	......	1,300*	......
Spain:				
Barcelona	1,887*	......	1,900*	......
Granada	......	......	1,000*	......
Madrid	5,118	......	5,675(g)	......
Oveido	234	......	900*	......
Salamanca	......	......	1,200*	......
Valencia	1,728	......	1,700	......
Valladolid	......	......	4,600*	......
Sweden:				
Lund	675	......	1,162	......
Stockholm	337	......	562	......
Upsala	1,384	......	2,261	......
Switzerland:				
Basel	......	529	806	......
Bern	......	1,344	1,664	......
Freiburg	......	420	620	......
Geneva	......	1,247	1,438	......
Lausanne	......	708	1,227	......
Zurich	......	924	1,452	......
Uruguay:				
Montevideo	......	......	700*	......

* Estimate of attendance based on last available report. (a) The figures for England and Wales are taken from the "Report of the Commissioner of Education," 1911, p. 554. (b) The figures for France are taken from the "Report of the Commissioner of Education," 1911, p. 565. (c) The figures for Germany are taken from "Deutscher Universitäts Kalender" for the years named. (d) For the year 1897-98. (e) For the year 1899-1900. (f) For the year 1902-03. (g) For the year 1909-1910. (r) Taken from the report of the institution concerned.

BIBLIOGRAPHY. Among the books dealing with higher education published in 1912 are: *Professional Distribution of College and University Graduates*, by Bailey Burritt; *Medical Education in Europe*, by Abram Flexner; *The Essentials of Liberal Education*, by President John G. Hibben; *The Rhodes Scholarships*, by George R. Parkin, and *Why Go to College*, by Clayton C. Sedgwick.

UPPER SENEGAL AND NIGER. A French West African colony. Bamako, the capital, has 6539 inhabitants; Bobo-Dioulasso, 7788; Ségou, 6255; Kayes, 5932; Djenné, 4904. About a million and a half of the population are Mussulmans; the remainder are fetichists and polygamists of a low type. The railway from Kayes to Kowlikoro (553 kilometers) reaches the Niger at Bamako. A branch (12 kms.) joins Médine to Kayes; another (44 kms.) connects Kayes with Ambidédi. Cotton is grown, as well as rice, corn, millet, peanuts, sesame, manioc, tobacco, etc. Rubber and gums are gathered, and the forests abound in valuable timbers. Horses, donkeys, cattle, dromedaries, and ostriches are raised in great numbers. Gold is mined. A lieutenant-governor (in 1912, M. Clozel) administers the colony and controls the government of the military territory of the Niger, being himself under the direction of the governor-general for French West Africa. See FRENCH WEST AFRICA.

URANIUM. See PHYSICS.

URIC ACID. See ATOPHAN.

URUGUAY. See AGRICULTURE.

URUGUAY. A South American republic on the Atlantic coast between Brazil and Argentina. The capital is Montevideo.

AREA AND POPULATION. The area of Uruguay is stated at 186,925 square kilometers (72,172 square miles), and the population at the census of October 12, 1908, was 1,042,686. The department of Montevideo, with 664 square kilometers (256 square miles), had 309,231 inhabitants. Of the total, 50.88 per cent. were males; 82.62 per cent. Uruguayans; 17.38 per cent. foreigners. Of the foreigners, Italians numbered 62,357, Spaniards 54,885, Brazilians 27,789, and Argentines 18,600 The population of the cities and chief towns was: Montevideo, 291,465; Paysandú, 20,953; Salto, 19,788; Mercedes, 15,667; Minas, 13,345; Melo, 12,355; San José, 12,297; Rocha, 12,200; Florida, 10,606; Durazno, 10,597. Population of the republic calculated for December 31, 1911, 1,177,560 (Montevideo department, 338,175). Recently estimated population of Montevideo city, 308,710. In 1910 and 1911 respectively, marriages, 6818 and 6967; births, 35,927 and 37,530; deaths, 16,515 and 16,552; vegetative increase, 19,412 and 20,978. Immigrants and emigrants in 1910, 119,684 and 105,683; in 1911, 141,224 and 123,934. In 1912 a law was enacted for the encouragement of immigration, particularly that of a good class of farm laborers.

INDUSTRIES AND COMMERCE. The principal industry is grazing. The 1908 livestock census returned 8,192,602 cattle, 26,286,296 sheep, 556,307 horses, 17,671 mules, 4428 asses, 180,099 swine, and 19,951 goats. Only a small part of the country is under cultivation. The principal crop is wheat; others of some importance are linseed, corn, oats, barley, tobacco, olives, and grapes. Mining and manufacturing are little developed.

The special trade has been valued as follows, in thousands of gold pesos:

	1907	1908	1909	1910	1911
Imports	37,471	38,730	37,157	40,814	47,412
Exports	34,912	40,296	46,150	40,801	46,051

Comparative figures for trade details for 1910 and 1911 are not available, but for the first six months of these two years the following export values by classes are reported: Grazing and meat industry, 27,341,316 and 25,531,595 pesos; agriculture, 700,556 and 601,006; miscellaneous industries, 969,724 and 1,036,287; ships' supplies, 155,621 and 56,179; other, 44,605, 57,986; total, 29,211,822 and 27,283,053. For the six months of 1911, the exports of animals and their products included: Live animals, 451,257 pesos; meats and extracts, 4,474,534; hides and skins, 4,684,594; grease and tallow, 610,965; wool, 15,010,897; the agriculture exports included oil seeds valued at 306,795 pesos and flour 186,280. Imports from and exports to the principal countries in 1910, in thousands of pesos: United Kingdom, 12,128 and 2772; Germany, 6841 and 6900; United States, 4344 and 3890; France, 3842 and 8889; Italy, 2943 and 1586; Belgium, 2811 and 4156; Argentina, 2772 and 8474. In 1910 there entered 5240 vessels, of 9,333,144 tons, and cleared 5206, of 9,230,930 tons. Merchant marine (1911): 30 steamers, of 23,960 tons net, and 62 sail, of 27,178 tons net.

COMMUNICATIONS. The reported length of railways in operation at the end of 1911 was 2512 kilometers (1561 miles); under construction, 610 kilometers (379 miles). It was announced towards the close of 1912 that a branch of the Central Uruguay Railway from Rivera to Santa Ana, where it connects with the Rio Grande do Sul railways of Brazil, would soon be opened to traffic. Other construction was in progress during the year, including the Pietra Sala-Tres Arboles line, 38 miles in length. Among several projected lines is one from Montevideo to Artigas, on the northern frontier.

Reported telegraph lines (1910), 7804 kilometers (4849 miles), with 319 offices. Post offices (1911), 1031.

FINANCE. The standard of value is gold, and the monetary unit the peso, par value $1.03424. Estimated revenue and expenditure for the fiscal year 1910, 21,079,880 and 21,075,330 pesos; for 1911, 35,142,360 and 35,133,812. About one-half the revenue is derived from customs. Larger items of estimated expenditure for the fiscal year 1911: National obligations, 17,110,-911 pesos; war and marine, 4,710,491; interior, 3,351,754; industry, 3,219,641; finance, 2,157,-732; public instruction, 1,487,765; public works, 1,385,340. Public debt December 31, 1911: External consolidated, 122,561,041 pesos; international, 2,387,000; internal, 6,909,500; total, 131,-857,541. Debt charges in 1910, 7,573,447 pesos.

ARMY. A small standing or active army was maintained and a national guard. The recruitment of the army is mainly voluntary and involves two to five years' service with reëngagements up to the age of forty-four. The government believed that an efficient standing army was a guarantee of internal peace and accordingly $5,000,000 of the budget for 1912-1913 was allotted to the ministry of war and marine. The active army was made up of 4 battalions of rifles, 9 cavalry regiments, 2 field batteries, and fortress artillery, with a peace strength of about 4000. In time of war it was estimated that a field army with three divisions amounting to about 12,000 men could be organized. There was also a police force of about 5000.

NAVY. Vessels in commission in 1912 included the following: One armored cruiser, of 2200 tons (*Montevideo*, built in 1887); one torpedo cruiser, of 1500 tons (*Uruguay*, 1910); one gunboat, of 300 tons (*18 de Julio*); one schoolship, of 300 tons (*Suárez*); three dispatch boats. The personnel comprises about 60 officers and 600 men.

GOVERNMENT. The president is elected by the General Assembly for four years and is not eligible for a consecutive term. He is assisted by a responsible ministry of seven members. The General Assembly consists of the Senate (19 members, elected for six years indirectly) and the House of Representatives (90 members, elected for three years by direct vote). The president in 1912 was José Batlle y Ordóñez. He was president in 1903-7 and on March 1, 1911, again assumed the executive office, succeeding Claudio Williman.

Authentic current statistics of Uruguay have been difficult and often impossible to obtain. In 1912 the Statistical Office was reorganized, and it is hoped that hereafter more consistent and accurate reports will be made public.

UTAH. POPULATION. According to the Census Bureau statistics compiled during 1912, out of a total population of 373,351 in 1910, 63,408 were foreign-born whites, compared with 52,804 in 1900. Of these, 18,082 came from England; 7227 from Sweden; 8295 from Denmark; 3117 from Italy; 2850 from Scotland; 2304 from Norway; 3956 from Germany, and 3991 from Greece. Other European countries were represented by smaller numbers. The negroes in the State in 1910 numbered 1144 and the mulattoes 290. In 1890 the negroes numbered 588 and the mulattoes 209.

AGRICULTURE. The acreage, value, and production of the principal crops in 1911 and 1912 are shown below:

		Acreage	Prod. Bu.	Value
Corn	1912	9,000	270,000	$202,000
	1911	8,000	280,000	227,000
Wheat	1912	236,000	6,059,000	4,544,000
	1911	225,000	5,025,000	3,518,000
Oats	1912	91,000	4,222,000	2,069,000
	1911	87,000	3,889,000	1,828,000
Rye	1912	6,000	90,000	61,000
	1911	5,000	78,000	55,000
Potatoes	1912	19,000	3,515,000	1,722,000
	1911	15,000	2,100,000	1,785,000
Hay	1912	368,000	a1,023,000	8,184,000
	1911	380,000	a950,000	8,550,000

a Tons.

MINERAL PRODUCTION. The gold production of the State in 1911 was $4,696,998, compared with $4,032,085 in 1910. The increase was due to the larger output of copper ores in Salt Lake County and of siliceous ores in Juab County. The silver output in 1911 was 12,473,-787 fine ounces, compared with 10,466,971 fine ounces in 1910. The larger part of the production was from the lead-silver ore produced in Juab, Salt Lake, Summit, Utah, and Wasatch counties.

The production of copper in 1911 was 142,-340,215 pounds, compared with 125,185,455 pounds in 1910. The marked increase was due to the production from the Bingham district. The total recorded output of the State at the close of 1911 was 797,044,788 pounds. In its total output the State ranks fourth among the copper-producing States. Two copper-mining plants were operated during 1911.

The production of coal in the State in 1911 was 2,513,175 short tons. This production was about the same as in 1910, the difference being less than 5000 tons. The value of the output, however, showed an increase of $24,110. That the decrease was not larger was due to developments in Emery County, which nearly trebled its production of 1910. There were employed in the coal mines of the State in 1911 3060 men.

MANUFACTURES. The Thirteenth Census included statistics of manufactures in the State. These are for the calendar year 1909, and the most important general results are shown in the following table, together with the percentages of increase from 1904 to 1909:

	Number or Amount 1909	1904	P. C. of Inc. 1904-09
Number of establishments	749	606	23.6
Persons engaged in manufactures	14,133	9,650	46.5
Proprietors and firm members	688	619	11.1
Salaried employees	1,660	979	69.6
Wage earners (average number)	11,785	8,052	46.4
Primary horsepower	42,947	19,397	121.4
Capital	$52,627,000	$26,004,000	102.4
Expenses	54,207,000	32,601,000	66.3
Services	10,366,000	6,195,000	67.3
Salaries	1,966,000	1,038,000	89.4
Wages	8,400,000	5,157,000	62.9
Materials	41,266,000	24,940,000	65.5
Miscellaneous	2,575,000	1,466,000	75.6
Value of products	61,989,000	38,926,000	59.2
Value added by manufacture (value of products less cost of materials)	20,723,000	13,986,000	48.2

The industry in which the largest number of wage earners was employed was that connected with cars and general shop construction and repairs by steam railroad companies, 1731. In printing and publishing were 967; in manufacture of confectionery, 586; in canning and preserving, 396; in lumber and timber products, 431. The most important industries in point of value of product were flour-mill and gristmill products, $3,131,000; in car construction the product was valued at $2,740,000; in printing and publishing, $2,405,000; in the manufacture of butter, cheese, and condensed milk, $1,971,000; in the manufacture of confectionery, $1,952,000. Other important industries were slaughtering and meat-packing, and the brewing of malt liquors. The total number of wage earners was 11,785, of whom 1223 were females. The wage earners under 16 years of age numbered 110, of whom 18 were women. The prevailing hours of labor for about one-half the wage earners employed ranged from 54 to 60 a week, although 25.2 per cent. of the total number were employed in establishments where less than 54 hours a week prevailed, and 17.1 per cent. in establishments where more than 60 hours a week prevailed. The largest number of wage earners was found in Salt Lake City, 4287; in Ogden were 1323. These were the only two important manufacturing centres in the State.

CHARITIES AND CORRECTIONS. There is no department having direct charge of the charitable and correctional institutions of the State. Previous to 1912 the only organized charitable society was one in Salt Lake City, which was supported by private subscriptions, and the work supervised by a secretary. The ladies of the Mormon Church have women's relief societies in practically every ward and precinct in the State, under one general head, with headquarters in Salt Lake City. The association was newly organized in 1912 to replace the old Salt Lake Charitable Society. The primary object of this organization is to afford immediate relief pending investigation, and to avoid any oversight or duplication of charitable work. In a number of counties throughout the State infirmaries and poor farms are maintained by public funds, and in all counties relief and aid are given to indigents from a fund raised by annual levy of one mill taxed against all assessable property. The State maintains a State Mental Hospital at Provo, which averages about 400 inmates; a State Industrial School at Ogden, with an average of about 100 to 125 inmates; and a School for the Deaf and Blind at Ogden, with an enrollment of from 100 to 125. The State has a juvenile court which has done excellent service in the last few years.

POLITICS AND GOVERNMENT

The legislature did not meet in 1912, as the sessions are biennial and the last was held in 1911. The next session convenes January 13, 1913. State officers were elected November 5.

Utah was one of the two States carried by President Taft in the presidential election. The Progressive movement has made little or no headway in the State and the Republican machine, headed by Senators Smoot and Sutherland, has retained full control. The delegates to the Republican national convention were pledged to President Taft, while the Democratic delegates were uninstructed. The Republicans renominated William Spry for governor. The Progressives nominated N. L. Morris, and the Democrats John Franklin Tolton. The election on November 5 resulted as follows: For President, Taft received 42,013 votes; Wilson, 36,579; Roosevelt, 24,174; Debs, 8989; and Reimer, Socialist Labor, 509. President Taft's plurality was 5434. For governor, Spry (Rep.) received 42,552 votes; Tolton (Dem.), 36,076; Morris (Prog.), 23,591; Burt (Soc.), 8797; and Battell (Soc. Labor), 479. The vote for representatives in Congress was: Joseph Howell (Rep.), 43,133; Jacob H. Johnson (Rep.), 42,049; T. D. Johnson (Dem.), 36,640; Mathonihah Thomas (Dem.), 37,192; Stephen Love (Prog.), 22,358; Lewis Larson (Prog.), 21,931; William M. Knerr (Soc.), 8953; Murray E. King (Soc.), 8971; Elias Anderson (Soc. Labor), 555; Harry S. Joseph (independent), 187.

The legislature is Republican by a majority of 29 on joint ballot.

STATE GOVERNMENT. Governor, William Spry; Secretary of State, D. Mattson; Treasurer, J. D. Jewkes; Auditor, L. G. Kelly; Attorney-General, A. R. Barnes; Superintendent of Education, A. C. Nelson; Commissioner of Insurance, Willard Done—all Republicans.

JUDICIARY. Supreme Court: Chief Justice, W. M. McCarty; Justices, J. E. Frick and Daniel N. Straup; Clerk, H. W. Griffith—all Republicans.

STATE LEGISLATURE, 1913. Democrats: Senate, 2; House, 14; joint ballot, 16. Republicans: Senate, 16; House, 31; joint ballot, 47. Republican majority: Senate, 14; House, 17; joint ballot, 31.

The representatives in Congress will be found in the section *Congress*, article UNITED STATES.

VACCINATION. See SMALL-POX AND VACCINATION.

VACUUM PUMP. See PHYSICS.

VANDERBILT UNIVERSITY. An institution for higher education at Nashville, Tenn., founded in 1872. The students enrolled in the various departments of the university in the collegiate year 1911-12 were 1120. The faculty numbered 123. Professor Edward Mims, formerly of the University of North Carolina, was appointed to fill the chair of English. There were no noteworthy benefactions during the year. The productive funds of the university amount to about $1,750,000 and the income to about $200,000. The library contained about 50,000 volumes. Chancellor, J. H. Kirkland, LL. D., D. C. L.

VANIMAN, MELVIN. See AERONAUTICS.

VARIATION OF LATITUDE. See ASTRONOMY.

VASSAR COLLEGE. An institution for the higher education of women at Poughkeepsie, N. Y., founded in 1861. The total enrollment for the degree of A. B. in the autumn of 1912 was 1042. The limit for admission to the college is about 1000. The faculty numbered 110. There were no noteworthy changes in the faculty during the year. Among the important benefactions were gifts of $28,000 from the alumnæ, and $75,000 additional from Mrs. Russell Sage for a new residence hall. The productive funds of the college amount to $1,472,514. There are 76,123 volumes in the library. President, James M. Taylor, D. D., LL. D.

VÉDRINES, JULES. See AERONAUTICS

VEILLER, BAYARD. See DRAMA.

VEINS, TRANSPLANTATION OF. See CARREL, ALEXIS.

VENEZUELA, UNITED STATES OF. A republic lying east of Colombia on the northern coast of South America. Capital, Caracas.

AREA AND POPULATION. Under the constitution of August 5, 1909, Venezuela is organized into twenty states, two territories, and a federal district. The area, as officially stated, is 1,020,400 square kilometers (393,976 square miles); according to an unofficial planimetric calculation, 942,300 sq. kilometers (363,822 sq. miles). The area cannot be definitely fixed until the settlement of the boundary dispute with Colombia. No census has been taken since 1891, when a population of 2,323,527 was returned, 2.27 per square kilometer. On the basis of this census and the political division of 1909, the Federal District had a density per square kilometer of 58.65; Carabobo state, 36.42; Nueva Esparta, 31.65; Trujillo, 19.80; Miranda, 17.79; Aragua, 16.96; Yaracuy, 12.09; Lara, 9.58; Táchira, 9.16; Sucre, 7.80. The territory of Amazonas, with an area of 281,700 square kilometers, had an average of only 0.16. The total population as calculated for 1906 was 2,647,624, and for 1911 2,743,841. It is estimated that about 70 per cent. of the people are mestizos, about 10 per cent. whites, and the remainder negroes and tribal Indians. Movement of population in 1910 and 1911: Marriages, 8120 and 8017; births, 82,487 and 83,758; deaths, 55,436 and 54,428; arrivals, 8420 and 9204; departures, 7374 and 7219. Principal towns, with estimated population: Caracas (in Federal District), 73,000; Maracaibo (Zulia), 50,000; Valencia (Carabobo), 40,000; Barquisimeto (Lara), 32,000; Puerto Cabello (Carabobo), 14,000; La Guaira (Federal District), 12,000.

EDUCATION. It is probable that at least 60 per cent. of the inhabitants are entirely illiterate. Pupils receiving elementary education in the last quarter of 1909 numbered 48,148; of these, 31,850 were in the national schools (1004), 4723 in the federal schools (146), 7564 in the municipal schools (225), and 4011 in private schools (150). In 1911 a reorganization of the elementary school system was undertaken. For secondary and higher instruction there are reported 34 national and 63 private colleges. There are two universities, at Caracas and Mérida, and a few institutions for special or technical instruction.

PRODUCTION AND COMMERCE. The crops include coffee, sugar cane, cacao, and cereals. Among the forest products are rubber, balata, copaiba, and vanilla. Stock-raising is important, and the number of cattle probably exceeds 2,000,000. Mining is not highly developed; the unsettled political conditions to which the country has been subject have repelled foreign investments in mining and transportation enterprises. Large mineral resources exist, however, including gold, silver, copper, iron, asphalt, and petroleum.

Total imports and exports have been valued, in bolivars, as follows, for years ended June 30:

	1909	1910	1911	1912
Imp.	49,180,485	56,640,971	80,178,932	105,677,096
Exp.	83,145,316	86,419,582	96,920,228	133,323,961

Exclusive of specie, the imports of 1911-12 were valued at 89,773,572 bolivars and the exports at 131,347,134; the specie imports included over 7,780,000 bolivars for coinages executed in France. The leading import is cotton goods. Leading exports, in the fiscal years 1911 and 1912, in thousands of bolivars:

	1911	1912		1911	1912
Coffee	43,111	79,314	Aigrettes	....	1,636
Cacao	18,605	15,937	Goat skins	2,367	....
Balata and rubber	14,461	11,631	Asphalt	1,013	1,587
Hides	4,520	10,271	Horned animals	942	1,152
Gold	2,914	5,253			

Trade by countries in the fiscal years 1910 and 1912, in thousands of bolivars:

	Imports		Exports	
	1010	1912	1910	1912
United States	18,451	32,309	30,976	43,387
United Kingdom	15,242	27,167	9,682	10,696
Germany	10,661	16,314	8,306	22,590
France	3,760	13,895	28,580	39,397
Netherlands	3,911	7,641	4,283	4,858
Spain	2,757	4,403	3,240	8,068
Italy	1,489	3,397	169	1,275
Cuba	14	14	619	634
Other	356	717	464	2,419
Total	56,641	105,677	86,420	133,324

Vessels entered at the ports in the year 1911-12, 1950, of 1,570,399 tons. Merchant marine (1911), 8 steamers, of 2046 tons net, and 15 sail, of 2432 tons net.

COMMUNICATIONS. Railways extend from the coast into the interior; but as they are not connected to form a system, they afford only inadequate transportation facilities. Lines in operation in 1911 aggregated 925 kilometers (575 miles). The gross receipts for that year are reported at 10,790,190 bolivars, and gross expenditures at 6,219,525 bolivars. A contract was let for a 3 ft. 2 in. gauge line from Caracas eastward through Guareras to Quatire. There is a large amount of internal navigable waterway. Reported length of telegraph lines in 1911, 7598 kilometers, with 181 offices; post offices, 284.

FINANCE. The monetary unit is the bolivar, with a par value of 19.295 cents. Revenue and expenditure in the year ended June 30, 1909, 50,410,133 and 47,668,810 bolivars; in 1910, 48,-

552,857 and 52,337,125. The budget for the fiscal year 1912-13 balanced at 52,500,000 bolivars, the estimated expenditure including 5,066,666 extraordinary. Estimated receipts: Customs, 22,000,000 bolivars; surtax, 12,292,500; stamps and revenue from salt and spirits, 13,200,000; other, 5,007,500; total, 52,500,000. Estimated ordinary expenditures: Finance and public debt, 15,372,804 bolivars; interior, 11,440,815; war and marine, 9,500,000; public works, 3,605,763; public instruction, 3,250,832; fomento, 3,210,720; foreign affairs, 1,052,400; total, 47,433,334. Public debt December 31, 1911: Foreign, 123,204,254 bolivars; internal, 62,587,001; credit of the mixed commissions, 3,507,283; total, 189,298,538.

ARMY. The active army was composed of 20 battalions of infantry, each of 400 men, and 8 batteries of artillery, each of 200 men.

NAVY. The navy in 1912 included three gunboats, a torpedo boat, a dispatch boat, a transport, a tug, and the old Spanish warship *Isla de Cuba*. The latter was purchased in 1912 from the United States government.

GOVERNMENT. The present constitution, which bears date of August 5, 1909, vests the executive authority in a president elected for four years. The legislative body is composed of a senate (40 members) and a chamber of deputies. The president in 1912 was Gen. Juan Vicente Gómez, whose term of office began April 19, 1910. Council of government: President, Gen. José Ignacio Pulido; first vice-president, Gen. Alejandro Ibarra; second vice-president, Gen. Mariano García; secretary, Dr. A. Borjas. Council of ministers (formed April 29, 1912): Interior, Cesar Zumeta; foreign affairs, Dr. J. L. Andara; finance, Manuel Porras; war and marine, Gen. Ismael Pereira Álvarez; public works, R. R. Álvarez; public instruction, D. Arreaza Monagas; fomento, Pedro Emilio Coll.

VENICE, CAMPANILE OF. See ARCHITECTURE.

VERMONT. POPULATION. According to the Census Bureau statistics compiled in 1912, out of a total population in 1910 of 355,956 the foreign-born whites numbered 49,861, compared with 44,694 in 1900. Of these the largest number, 14,624, came from French Canada; from other parts of Canada, 11,354; from Ireland, 4936; from Italy, 4591; from Scotland, 2615; and from Russia, 2454. The negroes in the State in 1910 numbered 1621, and the mulattoes 436. In 1890 the negroes numbered 937 and the mulattoes 416.

AGRICULTURE. The acreage, value, and production of the principal crops in 1911 and 1912 are given below:

		Acreage	Prod. Bu. •	Value
Corn	1912	45,000	1,800,000	$1,296,000
	1911	46,000	1,886,000	1,509,000
Wheat	1912	1,000	25,000	24,000
	1911	1,000	28,000	28,000
Oats	1912	77,000	3,311,000	1,589,000
	1911	76,000	2,660,000	1,569,000
Potatoes	1912	26,000	3,640,000	2,002,000
	1911	26,000	2,730,000	2,157,000
Hay	1912	1,010,000	a1,515,000	21,210,000
	1911	930,000	a1,209,000	16,926,000
Tobacco	1912	100	b170,000	31,000
	1911	100	b170,000	37,200

a Tons. b Pounds.

MANUFACTURES. The results of the census of manufactures taken in 1910 are shown in general in the following table, together with the percentage of increase from 1904-1909:

	Number or Amount 1909	1904	P. C. of Inc. 1904-09
Number of establishments	1,958	1,699	15.2
Persons engaged in manufactures	38,580	37,015	4.2
Proprietors and firm members	2,113	1,856	13.8
Salaried employees	2,679	2,053	30.5
Wage earners (aver. number)	33,788	33,106	2.1
Primary horsepower	159,445	140,616	13.4
Capital	$73,470,000	$62,659,000	17.3
Expenses	59,851,000	54,677,000	9.5
Services	20,075,000	17,324,000	15.9
Salaries	2,803,000	2,103,000	33.3
Wages	17,272,000	15,221,000	13.5
Materials	34,823,000	32,430,000	7.4
Miscellaneous	4,953,000	4,923,000	0.6
Value of products	68,310,000	63,084,000	8.3
Value added by manufacture (value of products less cost of materials)	33,487,000	30,654,000	9.2

The chief manufacturing industry is marble and stone quarrying. In this, 10,411 wage earners were employed and the value of the product was $12,395,000. In lumber and timber products were employed 4790 wage earners and the value of the product was $8,598,000; in the manufacture of butter, cheese, and condensed milk 519 were employed and the product was valued at $8,112,000; in woolen, worsted, and felt goods manufactures were employed 2294, and the product was valued at $4,497,000. Flour-mill and grist-mill products gave employment to 156 wage earners, with a product valued at $4,133,000. Other important manufactures, with the value of their product, were paper and wood pulp, $3,902,000; foundry and machine shop products, $3,775,000; hosiery and knit goods, $1,746,000; furniture and refrigerators, $1,618,000; patent medicines and compounds, $1,290,000; men's clothing, $1,274,000; car construction, $1,135,000; and printing and publishing, $1,039,000. The total number of wage earners was 23,783, of whom 4098 were women. The wage earners under 16 years of age numbered 211, of whom 67 were women. The prevailing hours of labor for the great majority of wage earners ranged from 54 to 60 a week, only 17.7 per cent. being employed in establishments where the employees worked less than 54 a week, and 1.9 per cent. in establishments where the employees worked more than 60 hours a week. The largest number of wage earners was in Burlington, 2371; in Barre, 2340; in Rutland, 1636. These are the three largest manufacturing centres in the State.

FINANCE. The receipts for the fiscal year 1912 amounted to $2,303,734. There was at the beginning of the fiscal year a balance on hand of $566,141. The total disbursements for the fiscal year were $2,350,508, leaving a balance on hand at the end of the year of $519,388. The chief sources of income were taxation of railroads, savings banks and trust companies, telephone and telegraph companies, and insurance companies. The chief expenditures were for education, support of State institutions, and for the State government. The State debt is $346,631, including $135,500 in bonds and $211,131 due the school fund.

POLITICS AND GOVERNMENT

The State legislature met in 1912 and the most important measures enacted will be found in the paragraph *Legislation* below. The election for State officers was held on September 3. See below.

A convention for the election of delegates to the Republican national convention was held on April 10 and the delegates were instructed to vote for President Taft. The delegates to the Democratic national convention were pledged to vote for Governor Wilson. On June 27 the State convention for the nomination of State officers nominated Allan M. Fletcher for governor. The Democrats nominated Harland B. Howe, and the Progressives, Fraser Metzger. State elections in Vermont are held on September 3 and in the presidential year they are of the greatest national interest because they furnish a possible criterion for results in November. The voting revealed the fact that the Republican party had been practically cut in two when no candidate received a majority of the votes. The figures were as follows: Fletcher, Rep., 26,237; Howe, Dem., 20,001; Metzger, Prog., 15,629. Mr. Fletcher had a plurality of 6183 over Howe, Democrat, but he lacked the majority required for election by the Vermont constitution. It was necessary, therefore, to carry the election to the legislature. This body met in joint session and elected Mr. Fletcher governor. This was the first defeat of the Republican party in the State in twenty years. To the aggressive campaign made in the State by Mr. Roosevelt previous to the election was generally attributed the heavy Progressive vote. The result of the election of November 5 was as follows: For President, Taft received 23,305 votes; Roosevelt, 22,070; Wilson, 15,350. Vermont was one of the two States carried by President Taft.

STATE GOVERNMENT. Governor, Allan M. Fletcher; Lieutenant-Governor, F. E. Howe; Secretary of State, Guy W. Bailey; Treasurer, Edward H. Deavitt; Auditor, Horace F. Graham; Attorney-General, R. E. Brown; Adjutant-General, Lee S. Tillotson; Superintendent of Education, Mason S. Stone; Commissioners of Insurance, E. H. Deavitt and Guy W. Bailey; Commissioner of Agriculture, O. L. Martin—all Republicans.

JUDICIARY. Supreme Court: Chief Justice, John W. Rowell; Assistant Justices, Loveland Munson, John H. Watson, Seneca Haselton, George M. Powers; Clerk, L. C. Moody—all Republicans except Haselton.

STATE LEGISLATURE, 1913. Republicans, Senate, 27; House, 164; joint ballot, 191. Democrats, House, 57; joint ballot, 57. Progressives, Senate, 3; House, 22; joint ballot, 25. Republican majority, Senate, 24; House, 85; joint ballot, 109.

The representatives in Congress will be found in the article UNITED STATES, section *Congress*.

VERMONT, UNIVERSITY OF. A STATE institution for higher education in Burlington, Vt., founded in 1791. The students enrolled in the autumn of 1912 numbered approximately 550. There were 102 members of the faculty. Professor Frederick W. Stone assumed directorship of athletic and gymnasium instruction in the university on September 1, 1912. There were no important changes in the faculty during the year. Several noteworthy benefactions were received during the year. The productive funds of the university amount to about $1,000,000 and the annual income to about $200,000. The library contained about 85,000 volumes. President, Guy Potter Benton, D. D.

VERNON, FRÉDÉRIC. A French engraver, died October 28, 1912. He was born in Paris in 1858, and was educated at the Beaux Arts, and the School of Decorative Arts. In 1887 he won the Prix de Rome for engraving. His subject was "Jason and the Golden Fleece." Among his best known works are medals commemorative of the centenary of the "Marseillaise," and of the arrival of the Czar at Cherbourg. He was one of the foremost of French engravers.

VERRALL, ARTHUR WOOLLGAR. An English scholar and educator, died June 16 1912. He was born in Brighton, England, in 1851, and was educated at Wellington College and Trinity College, Cambridge, graduating from the latter in 1873. He was made a fellow following his graduation and remained a fellow of Trinity until his death, becoming in course of time a tutor. He studied law and in 1877 was called to the bar. His classical studies, as far as his published work is concerned, lay chiefly with the Greek dramatists. An edition of *Medea* appeared in 1881 and was followed at intervals by editions of Æschylus and Euripides. His translations are notable as combining human interest with accuracy of scholarship.

VETERINARY MEDICINE, SCHOOLS OF. See UNIVERSITIES AND COLLEGES.

VETERINARY SCIENCE. The year 1912 was notable for a serious outbreak of a disease among horses which became epidemic in Kansas during the third week in August and spread to the neighboring States, resulting in the loss of many millions of dollars. It is estimated that in Kansas alone 30,000 horses died during the period between July 15 and October 1, while Nebraska and Colorado lost heavily. The indirect loss, due particularly to farm work undone on account of the scarcity of horses, is estimated at twice the direct loss. The disease, which presented a variety of symptoms, many of which resembled those of the so-called "blind staggers" and indicated a derangement of the central nervous system, was characterized by its sudden onset, rapid course, epizoötic nature, and high rate of mortality. A bacteriological study of brains showing well-defined lesions resulted in the isolation of micro-organisms which bear a remarkable similarity, both morphologically and culturally, to the diplococcus described as being present in the Borna disease of Europe, said to be a serous cerebrospinal meningitis, but no pathogenic properties were shown by inoculations made on experiment animals.

In reviewing the advances made during the year in the field of animal diseases and therapeutics, special mention should be made of the work with infectious abortion in cattle, the application of the complement fixation test as a reliable means for diagnosing additional diseases, including contagious abortion, dourine, Malta fever, and hemorrhagic septicemia, of the application of Ehrlich's "606," which is placed on the market under the trade name of Salvarsan, in treating contagious pleuropneumonia of equines, lymphangitis, canine piroplasmosis, etc., and of the preparation by Ehrlich of a new drug, known as "914," or Neosalvarsan, which is even more toxic to trypanosomes than is Salvarsan. The translation from the German of Hutyra and Marek's large two-volume quarto work on the pathology and therapeutics of the diseases of domestic animals, edited by Doctors J. R. Mohler and A. Eichhorn, which appeared during the year, has done much for the advancement of the veterinary profession in an educational way.

TUBERCULOSIS. Investigations of the tubercle bacilli in 70 cases of bone and joint tuberculosis in children were reported by Fraser of the research laboratory of the Royal College of Physicians, Edinburgh. The bovine type was present in 41 cases, the human type in 26 cases, and both the bovine and human types in 3 cases. Fraser reports that there can be no doubt that milk was the medium through which the infection occurred. Fresh evidence was obtained to prove that bovo-vaccination, or the injection of living tubercle cultures of an insufficient degree of virulence to cause progressive tuberculosis in cattle, is a practice that should be emphatically condemned as unfit for use in the control and eradication of bovine tuberculosis. The work of eradication of bovine tuberculosis in the District of Columbia commenced in the fall of 1909 and continued in 1912, by the systematic retesting of cattle within the area and the testing of cattle brought ino the District from various States for dairy and breeding purposes, has reduced the percentage from 18.87 at the time the work was commenced to 1.29. But 3.61 per cent. of the premises was found to be infected, against 18.35 per cent. in 1909.

INFECTIOUS ABORTION. From the viewpoint of economic importance, infectious abortion ranks second only to tuberculosis, and in certain sections of the country even supersedes the latter in the monetary loss it occasions. The direct loss reaches into the millions, while the potential loss is enormous and practically inestimable. During the year it was shown that the bacillus found by Schroeder and Cotton in 1911 to be of common occurrence in milk from apparently healthy cows is no other than that of infectious abortion, namely *Bacillus abortus*. In investigations conducted by the federal bureau of animal industry the bacillus was found in the tonsils of children, presumably as a result of drinking infected milk. It has been found that cows may continue to expel the abortion bacillus with their milk continuously for several years without giving evidence of their infected condition by aborting or in any other known manner. Studies of ordinary market milk indicate that infectious abortion is a more common disease in dairy herds than it was formerly believed to be, that its frequency is increasing, and that vigorous measures should be taken against its further spread. Whether the abortion bacillus has the power to injure human health still remains unknown.

TICK FEVER AND TICK ERADICATION. The tick eradication work carried on by the federal bureau of animal industry in coöperation with authorities of various southern States resulted in the release from quarantine of 22,827 square miles of territory, distributed among 11 States. The total area released since the work was commenced in 1906 amounts to 162,648 square miles, or an area equal to more than the combined areas o. Georgia, Alabama, and Mississippi, and nearly one-fourth of the total area infested at the time of beginning the work. The outlook is bright for the eventual control of this parasite, the presence of which has been a great handicap to cattle-raising in the South.

HOG CHOLERA. This serious disease of hogs, though the source of great loss, was not so prevalent as in 1911. Experiments seem to prove quite definitely that pigs from immune or hyperimmune sows are themselves immune against hog cholera at birth and that this immunity lasts for at least three weeks. Thirty States are now engaged in distributing anti-hog-cholera serum, a vast majority of which are manufacturing the serum. Investigations made by the bureau of animal industry led to the estimate that considerably more than one million doses of anti-hog-cholera serum were manufactured and applied in all the various States combined. The outlook for the ultimate control and possibly the complete eradication of hog cholera is now brighter than it has been at any time since the disease reached its present state of severity in this country.

TETANUS. In investigations conducted with a view to determining the smallest quantity of antitoxin which will protect a horse against a positive infection of tetanus, it was found that 500 American units is a sufficient dose for use as a prophylactic even in cases where the infection has occurred for days prior to the injection of the antitoxin.

MALTA FEVER. Further investigation of this disease in Texas and New Mexico, where it is also locally known as "mountain fever" and "slow typhoid fever," has shown that it has existed in these States for at least 25 years. Reports indicate that the disease also occurs among goats in Arizona.

FOOT-AND-MOUTH DISEASE. This highly contagious disease of cattle and other cloven-footed animals, transmissible to man particularly through milk from affected animals, was much less prevalent in European countries than in 1911. The several outbreaks which occurred in Great Britain, including one in Ireland, resulted in the holding of the Royal Agricultural Show without cattle, sheep, or pigs. A departmental committee of 12 appointed by the president of the board of agriculture and fisheries to inquire into the disease made its report in the latter part of the summer. A German investigator, J. Siegel, isolated and cultivated a cytorhycte coccus, which appears to be the causative organism and to which the name *Cytorhyctes aphtharum* has been given.

DOURINE. The complement fixation test as applied to this disease, which was perfected during the year by the federal bureau of animal industry, makes it possible to diagnose dourine in a comparatively short time. Suspected cases in eastern Montana reported late in June were diagnosed in the Washington laboratory upon the receipt of blood sera from the suspected animal, four or five horses being found to have the disease. The occurrence of dourine in Brazil, where it is known as "mofo," was reported for the first time.

FOWL SPIROCHETOSIS. Hindle reported finding that when once the fowl tick becomes infected with *Spirochæta gallinarum*, the cause of the highly fatal disease of fowls known as spirochetosis, its offspring of the first generation is infective in all its stages, and, moreover, that infection is transmitted to the second generation.

ONCHOCERCIASIS. The infestation of the flanks and briskets of Australian beef cattle by the nematode *Spiroptera reticulata*, which forms the so-called "worm nests," became of considerable importance with the increase in the quantity of frozen meat exported to England.

BIBLIOGRAPHY. Some of the books or larger contributions that appeared during 1912 are as follows: H. Baum, *Das Lymphgefässystem des Rindes* (Berlin, 1912); F. Hutyra and J. Marek, *Special Pathology and Therapeutics of the Diseases of Domestic Animals* (Chicago, 1912, two volumes), a first English translation of the third edition of *Spezielle Pathologie und Therapie der Haustiere;* J. Marek, *Lehrbuch der klinischem Diagnostik der inneren Krankheiten der Haustiere* (Jena, 1912); V. A. Moore, *Principles of Microbiology: A Treatise on Bacteria, Fungi, and Protozoa Pathogenic for Domesticated Animals* (Ithaca, N. Y., 1912); M. Neveu-Lemaire, *Parasitologie des Animaux Domestiques: Maladies Parasitaires non Bactériennes* (Paris, 1912); and D. H. Udall, *Veterinarian's Handbook of Materia Medica and Therapeutics* (Ithaca, N. Y., 1912).

VICTOR EMMANUEL MONUMENT. See ARCHITECTURE.

VICTORIA. See MINIMUM WAGE.

VICTORIA. A state of the Commonwealth of Australia. Area, 87,884 square miles. Population (census of April 3, 1911), 1,315,551, exclusive of full-blooded aboriginals. Melbourne, the capital and temporary capital of Australia, had 103,593 inhabitants; with suburbs, 588,971. Governor in 1912, Sir John Michael Fleetwood Fuller (from May 24, 1911); premier, W. A. Watt. See AUSTRALIA.

VIRGINIA. POPULATION. According to the Census Bureau statistics compiled during 1912, out of the total population, 2,061,612 in the State in 1910, 26,628 were foreign-born whites, compared with 19,068 in 1900. Of these, the largest number, 4361, came from Russia; 4221 from Germany; 2450 from Ireland; 3676 from England, and 1604 from Austria. Other European countries are represented by smaller numbers. The negroes in the State numbered 671,096 and the mulattoes 222,910. In 1890 the negroes numbered 635,438 and the mulattoes 122,441.

AGRICULTURE. The acreage, value, and production of the principal crops in 1911 and 1912 are given below:

		Acreage	Prod. Bu.	Value
Corn	1912	1,980,000	47,520,000	....
	1911	1,980,000	47,520,000	$34,690,000
Wheat	1912	741,000	8,596,000	8,682,000
	1911	750,000	9,000,000	8,640,000
Oats	1912	175,000	3,885,000	2,020,000
	1911	194,000	3,880,000	2,095,000
Rye	1912	48,000	600,000	510,000
	1911	48,000	552,000	491,000
Potatoes	1912	95,000	8,265,000	5,372,000
	1911	95,000	4,275,000	4,104,000
Hay	1912	741,000	a889,000	13,513,000
	1911	437,000	a280,000	5,740,000
Tobacco	1912	187,000	b112,200,000	13,464,000
	1911	160,000	b128,000,000	12,288,000

a Tons. b Pounds.

MINERAL PRODUCTION. The iron ore mined in the State in 1911 amounted to 610,871 long tons with a value of $1,146,188, as compared with a product of 903,377 long tons in 1910 with a value of $1,845,144.

The coal production of the State in 1911 was 6,864,667 short tons valued at $6,254,804, compared with a product of 6,507,997 short tons valued at $5,877,486 in 1910. All the important producing counties in the State, except Lee County, showed increases in production, the principal gains being due to developments in Russel County, following the completion in 1910 of the Carolina, Clinchfield, and Ohio Railroad and the opening of transportation from the mines to the South Atlantic seaboard.

MANUFACTURES. The Thirteenth Census statistics are for the calendar year 1909 and were compiled in 1912. Although the State does not rank among the first in manufactures, there has been a considerable advance during recent years. The following table shows that there were in 1909, 5685 establishments, employing 120,797 persons:

	Number or Amount 1909	1904	P. C. of Inc. 1904-'09
Number of establishments	5,685	3,187	78.4
Persons engaged in manufactures	120,797	88,898	35.9
Proprietors and firm members	6,570	3,643	80.3
Salaried employees	8,551	4,970	72.1
Wage earners (average number)	105,676	80,285	31.6
Primary horsepower	283,928	176,998	60.4
Capital	$216,392,000	$147,989,000	46.2
Expenses	196,246,000	130,870,000	50.0
Services	47,255,000	32,818,000	44.0
Salaries	9,101,000	4,875,000	86.7
Wages	38,154,000	27,943,000	36.5
Materials	125,583,000	83,649,000	50.1
Miscellaneous	23,408,000	14,403,000	62.5
Value of products	219,794,000	148,857,000	47.7
Value of products less cost of materials	94,211,000	65,208,000	44.5

The largest value of product was in the manufacture of lumber and timber, $35,855,000; tobacco manufacturers were valued at $25,385,000; flour and gristmill products, $17,598,000; industries relating to railways, $9,956,000; manufactures of leather, $8,267,000. The total number of persons engaged in manufactures in the State in 1909 was 120,797, of whom 104,662 were male and 16,135 female. The number of persons employed under 16 years of age was 3622. The prevailing hours of labor for 77 per cent. of the total number of wage-earners ranged from 54 to 60 a week; only 9.6 per cent. being employed in establishments where less than 54 a week prevailed, and 13.4 per cent. in those where they were more than 60 a week. The largest number of wage-earners was in Richmond, 14,849; in Norfolk, 4749; in Lynchburg, 4026. The value of the manufactures of Richmond was $47,357,985; of Norfolk, $10,341,321; and of Lynchburg, $10,188,136.

FINANCE. The report of the treasurer for the fiscal year ending September 30, 1912, showed a balance on October 1, 1911, of $350,601. The receipts for the fiscal year amounted to $7,052,190 and the disbursements to $707,178,395, leaving a balance on hand October 1, 1912, of $224,396. The chief receipts are from taxation and the principal expenditures are for education and the maintenance of State institutions.

CHARITIES AND CORRECTIONS. Several important measures relating to charities and corrections were passed at the legislative session of 1912. Among these was a measure putting into effect a very thorough vital statistics law. Money was appropriated to establish a State institution for the custodial care of feeble-minded children, and a law was passed providing surgical aid and treatment for indigent, crippled, and deformed persons. Woman and child labor laws were improved and the juvenile and adult probation laws were extended to include small towns and magisterial districts, and the State board of charities and corrections was given authority to place certain juvenile delinquents in family homes under supervision. All the State institutions were somewhat improved and the tuberculosis sanatorium was provided with funds for a well-equipped infirmary. During the year Richmond opened the first juvenile court in the State and the city charter has been amended so as to provide a workhouse to take the place of the old city jail. During the year several new private philanthropies came into existence. Among these was a movement on the part of the federated colored women's clubs to establish a much-needed reform school for colored girls. A housing commission in Richmond was planning to conduct a thorough survey of the city with recommendation for a more stringent housing code and its enforcement.

Politics and Government

The legislature met in 1912 and the most important measures enacted will be found noted in the paragraph *Legislation* below. There was no election for governor and other State officers in 1912, as Governor Mann's term does not expire until January 31, 1914. He was elected in 1909, assuming office February 1, 1910, and the term of the governor of Virginia is four years.

A legislature (members of house) will be chosen in November next to begin its duties in January, 1914.

On March 2, the senate refused to pass the Jordan bill providing for referendum of the State-wide prohibition question to the vote of the people upon petition of 25 per cent. of the voters who cast their votes in the last gubernatorial election. The opposition to the bill was on the ground that it vested in a minority of the voters the question of State policy on public matters. The Republican convention for the election of delegates to the national convention met on February 19. The Republican party was divided into factions, and as a result, there were two conventions, one of which passed resolutions endorsing President Taft and elected delegates pledged to vote for him. The other faction declined to participate in the convention of the Republican regulars and held another convention at the same time. Uninstructed delegates were chosen. A majority of the Democratic delegates favored Governor Wilson, but the State convention refused to instruct for him.

The election on November 5 resulted as follows: Wilson, 90,332; Taft, 23,288; Roosevelt, 21,777; Debs, 820; Chafin, 709; and Reimer, 50. Governor Wilson's plurality was 67,061.

Other Events. On March 14 a band of mountaineers shot and killed the judge, prosecutor, and sheriff at Hillsville, county seat of Carroll, just after the judge had pronounced sentence upon one of their number who had been found guilty of a felony. The band dispersed to the hills, but finally all of its members were captured after a search which lasted for months. The participants in the shooting were all tried during the year and two, Floyd and Claude Allen (father and son), were sentenced to death and four others received terms of imprisonment ranging from 15 to 37 years.

Legislation. An unusual number of important measures was passed at the legislative session of 1912. Among these were the following: Amendments to the law relating to corporations; the proposal of an amendment to the constitution as to special legislation for the organization of government of cities and towns; measures relating to the employment of convicts; amendments to the law relating to the sanitary arrangements in factories, workshops, etc.; an act to facilitate the development of the resources of the State by providing ways of ingress and egress for mining, manufacturing, and timber-cutting, and to authorize proper passways, tram-roads, and other means of transportation over the lands of others; an act to prohibit unauthorized hypnosis; an act to amend an act of the general assembly constituting a united agricultural board to coördinate the Virginia College of Agriculture and Polytechnic Institute and the Virginia Agricultural Experiment Station, the commissioner of the board of agriculture and the State board of education in coöperation with the United States Department of Agriculture for the betterment of agricultural, experimental, and demonstration work; an act to provide for the designation by cities and towns of segregation districts for the residence of white and colored persons; an elaborate drainage act; an act amending the general banking laws of the State; an act establishing a department of mines; a measure establishing a feeble-minded colony on the farm of the State epileptic colony; measures relating to taxation of railway and canal corporations; measures relating to the selling of liquor, providing for license, etc.; an act amending the act regulating the hours of labor in factories and manufacturing establishments, by providing that no female and no child under 14 years of age shall work as an operative in any factory, workshop, or any manufacturing establishment of the State for more than ten hours in any one day of 24 hours; an amendment to the act imposing upon railroad corporations liability for injuries to their employees in certain cases; an act providing for the holding of primary elections and for preventing and punishing corrupt practices in connection therewith. This act includes a primary for the nomination of United States senators and State officers, members of the house of delegates, and county and city officers, but does not extend to presidential electors. A measure was enacted dealing with the militia of the State. The law relating to the admission of children to the public schools was revised. A measure was passed providing for submission to the people of a proposed amendment to the section of the constitution as to special legislation for the organization and government of cities and towns.

State Government. Governor, William H. Mann; Lieutenant-Governor, J. T. Ellyson; Secretary of Commonwealth, B. O. James; First Auditor, C. Lee Moore; Treasurer, A. W. Harman, Jr.; Superintendent of Instruction, J. D.

Eggleston, Jr.; Attorney-General, Samuel W. Williams; Adjutant-General, W. W. Sale; Commissioner of Agriculture, George W. Koiner; Commissioner of Insurance, Joseph Button—all Democrats.

JUDICIARY. Supreme Court of Appeals: President, James Keith; Justices, S. G. Whittle, John A. Buchanan, George M. Harrison, and Richard H. Cardwell; Clerk of the Court, H. Stewart Jones—all Democrats.

STATE LEGISLATURE, 1913. Democrats, Senate, 35; House, 90; joint ballot, 125. Independents and Republicans, Senate, 5; House, 10; joint ballot, 15. Democratic majority, Senate, 30; House, 80; joint ballot, 110.

The representatives in Congress will be found in the section *Congress*, article UNITED STATES.

VIRGINIA, UNIVERSITY OF. A State institution of higher learning at Charlottesville, Va., founded in 1819. The enrollment in the various departments of the university on October 15, 1912, was 805. The faculty numbered 75. Several important changes in the faculty occurred during the year. Professor Ormond Stone of the chair of astronomy and Professor Milton W. Humphreys of the chair of Greek retired on the Carnegie Foundation. Professor R. H. Webb was appointed to the professorship of Greek, and Professor C. N. Wunder to the chair of astronomy. There were no noteworthy benefactions received during the year. The productive funds amounted at the close of the year 1911-12 to $2,005,299. The income at the end of the year amounted to $92,094. There were about 75,000 volumes in the library. President, E. A. Alderman, D. C. L., LL. D.

VIRGIN ISLANDS. A presidency of the Leeward Islands (q. v.). Tortola is the largest island (there are about 32); Road Town (in Tortola), the chief town, has 410 inhabitants. Cotton and some sugar are grown.

	1907-8	1908-9	1909-10	1910-11
Imports	£ 7,009	£ 8,629	£ 7,579	£ 8,717
Exports	5,951	7,150	7,519	6,684
Revenue	2,335	2,278	2,371	6,091
Expenditure	2,050	2,251	2,334	5,964
Shipping *	13,796	14,422	12,853	12,770

* Tonnage entered and cleared.

Commissioner (1912), T. L. H. Jarvis. See LEEWARD ISLANDS.

VITALISM. See BIOLOGY.

VITAL STATISTICS. According to the commonwealth statistician of Australia, that country is the healthiest in the world, with the exception of New Zealand. In Australia, the death rate has steadily decreased from 15.75 per 1000 in 1884, to the present rate of 10.5. New Zealand has a still lower death rate, 9.75 per thousand. Infant mortality has shown a still more striking fall. In 1880 there were 130 deaths per 1000 births, as against the present rate of 71.

The latest available statistics from England, France, and Germany show a continued falling off in the number of births. The registrar-general's summary for 1911 indicates a fall in the birth-rate in England and Wales. The marriages registered last year numbered 274,577; corresponding to a rate of 15.2 per thousand of population. The number of births was 881,241, or 24.4 per thousand, and deaths numbered 527,864, or 14.6 per thousand. The marriage-rate was 0.2 per thousand above that in the previous year, but 0.3 below the average for the preceding ten years. A decline of 0.7 per thousand is recorded in the birth-rate when compared with that of 1910, which was the lowest on record; and last year's rate was 2.8 below the average of the preceding ten years. The death-rate was 1.1 above that in 1910, but was 0.8 below the average for the preceding ten years. Infantile mortality, measured by the proportion of deaths under one year to registered births, was 130 per thousand, or twenty-five above the rate in 1910 and three above the ten years' average. Deaths attributed to violence numbered 20,103, a rate of 0.26 per thousand of population.

The *Journal Officiel* published very discouraging statistics on the French population in 1911. In 1911, there was an excess of 34,869 deaths, while the year before there was an excess of 71,418 births. The difference is due to the diminution of births (742,114 infants reported living in 1911, against 774,390 in 1910), and, to the increase in the number of deaths (74,011 greater in 1911 than in 1910). The deaths have been more numerous in 1911 than in 1910 in almost all the departments, but notably in Normandy. The increase in the proportional number of deaths in France as compared with other countries is attributed partly to the great number of aged people, but chiefly to the small birth-rate in recent years. Although the birth-rate is low, the number of marriages is relatively large. In 1911, 307,788 marriages were registered. The number of divorces reached 13,058, slightly more than in 1910.

A summary given by the German imperial bureau of statistics shows that the births for 1910, including still births, amounted to 1,982,836, as compared with 2,038,357 in 1909, and 2,076,660 in 1908. While the births fell in 1909 by 38,300, the reduction in 1910 was by 55,500. For the first time since 1897 the number of births has fallen below two millions. In 1910 there were 30.7 births per 1000 inhabitants. The rate has never been so small in the last sixty years; it has been sinking for a long time after reaching its highest point in the seventies. From 1851 to 1860, the birth-rate for the present area of the German empire was 36.8 per 1000 inhabitants, from 1861 to 1870, 38.8, from 1871 to 1880, 40.7 (with a maximum of 42.6 in the year 1876), from 1881 to 1890, 38.2, from 1891 to 1900, 37.4, from 1901 to 1910, 34.0. The reduction in the last decade has been marked. In 1908 the rate was 33, in 1909, 31.9. The rate of illegitimate births has been rising since 1903, following a previous fall; in 1903 there were in 100 births 8.3 illegitimate, in 1909, 9, and in 1910, 9.1. With the reduction in births, however, there has also been a reduction in deaths; in 1910 there were 1,103,723 as compared with 1,154,296 in 1909 and 1,197,098 in 1908. As compared with the population the mortality of 17.1 per 1000 has never been so low. In 1909 the rate was 18.1, in 1908, 19, and in the decade from 1901 to 1910 it was 19.5, as compared with 23.5, 26.5, 28.8, 28.4, and 27.8 in the preceding five decades.

The following statistics as to contagious diseases throughout the world have been compiled from the United States Marine Hospital Service reports. While in many instances incomplete and misleading, they are the best obtainable:

SMALLPOX. Algeria, 153 cases, 3 deaths; Arabia, 23 cases, 12 deaths; Argentina, 44 deaths; Austro-Hungary, 146 cases, 1 death; Brazil, 1122 deaths; British East Africa, 16 cases, 3 deaths; Canada, 653 cases, 4 deaths; Ceylon, 4 cases; Chile, 1193 cases, 412 deaths; China, 844 cases, 616 deaths; Cuba, 2 cases; Dutch East Indies, 283 cases, 106 deaths; Egypt, 37 cases, 13 deaths; France, 164 cases, 25 deaths; Germany, 10 cases; Great Britain, 26 cases, 2 deaths; Honduras, 37 cases; India, 2446 cases, 1360 deaths; Indo China, 71 cases, 18 deaths; Italy, 3078 cases, 944 deaths; Japan, 39 cases, 3 deaths; Mexico, 1242 cases, 675 deaths; Portugal, 175 cases; Russia, 1172 cases, 372 deaths; Siam, 2361 deaths; South Africa, 135 cases, 4 deaths; Spain, 558 cases, 374 deaths; Straits Settlements, 73 cases, 33 deaths; Switzerland, 20 cases; Teneriffe, 54 deaths; Turkey in Asia, 1733 cases, 124 deaths; Turkey in Europe, 570 deaths; Uruguay, 26 cases, 4 deaths; Venezuela, 16 cases, 2 deaths; Zanzibar, 5 cases, 4 deaths.

PLAGUE. Algeria, 8 cases, 8 deaths; Arabia, 3 cases, 2 deaths; Azores, 35 cases, 21 deaths; Brazil, 47 cases, 36 deaths; British East Africa, 69 cases, 14 deaths; Chile, 69 cases, 28 deaths; China, 2062 cases, 1747 deaths; Dutch East Indies, 595 cases, 527 deaths; Ecuador, 325 cases, 123 deaths; Egypt, 845 cases, 423 deaths; Hawaii, 5 cases, 5 deaths; India, 368,017 cases, 306,748 deaths; Indo China, 171 cases, 82 deaths; Japan, 191 cases, 144 deaths; Mauritius, 247 cases, 147 deaths; Persia, 988 cases, 629 deaths; Peru, 50 cases, 13 deaths; Philippine Islands, 23 cases, 22 deaths; Porto Rico, 56 cases, 29 deaths; Russian Empire, 298 cases, 266 deaths; Siam, 8 deaths; South Africa, 28 cases, 23 deaths; Straits Settlements, 52 cases, 40 deaths; Turkey in Asia, 26 cases, 17 deaths; Venezuela, 11 cases, 6 deaths; West Indies, 10 cases, 8 deaths.

CHOLERA. Arabia, 22 cases, 12 deaths; Austro-Hungary, 75 cases, 17 deaths; Bahrein Islands, Persian Gulf, 260 deaths; China, 113 deaths; Dutch East Indies, 626 cases, 510 deaths; India, 4770 deaths; Indo China, 2538 cases, 1856 deaths; Italy, 196 cases, 95 deaths; Japan, 13,555 cases, 139 deaths; Malta, 6 cases, 6 deaths; Montenegro, 9 cases, 5 deaths; Persia, 38 deaths; Philippine Islands, 5 cases, 5 deaths; Rumania, 154 cases, 18 deaths; Servia, 6 cases, 4 deaths; Siam, 2811 deaths; Straits Settlements, 109 cases, 98 deaths; Tunis, 80 cases, 35 deaths; Turkey in Asia, 4169 cases, 3253 deaths; Turkey in Europe, 330 cases, 126 deaths; Zanzibar, 155 cases, 125 deaths.

YELLOW FEVER. Brazil, 164 deaths; Chile, 1134 cases, 391 deaths; Ecuador, 347 cases, 174 deaths; Mexico, 81 cases, 35 deaths; Peru, 43 deaths; Venezuela, 54 cases, 14 deaths.

VIVISECTION. The report of the Royal Commission on Vivisection appointed in 1906 and consisting principally of eminent British physicians and lawyers, to inquire into and report on the law relating to vivisection and its administration, was published early in 1912. More than seventy meetings were held, at which a large number of witnesses were examined. The commission was freely accessible to all persons who were or believed themselves to be in a position to criticise the practice of vivisection. The allegations of a number of active anti-vivisectionists were examined and found to have no basis in fact. The commissioners believe that the holders of licenses and certificates for vivisection, with rare exceptions, have endeavored, with loyalty and good faith, to conform to the provisions of the law, and that the harrowing descriptions and illustrations of operations on animals, are calculated to mislead the public, so far as they suggest that the animals are not under an anæsthetic. Twenty-five pages of the report are devoted to the recent history of the progress of medical science in connection with experiments on animals, and to the question whether or not these give valuable results in the prevention and cure of disease. The commissioners point out that in recent years the value of the experimental method has largely been recognized by the public, as well as by various public bodies, as is shown by the foundation of schools of tropical medicine and the appointment of research expeditions to investigate on the spot various tropical diseases, the foundation of an imperial research fund for the purpose of investigating cancer and the appointment of a royal commission to study tuberculosis by experimental methods.

On the question of the morality of vivisection, the commissioners conclude that experiments on animals, adequately safeguarded by law, are morally justifiable. A number of recommendations are made, with which the anti-vivisectionists express some satisfaction: (1) Further limitation with regard to curare, during the use of which an inspector should be present, and see that the animal is in a state of complete anæsthesia; (2) stricter provision as to the definition and practice of pithing, which should be performed only by a licensed person and under an adequate anæsthetic; (3) additional restrictions regulating the painless destruction of animals which show signs of suffering after experiments; (4) the keeping of special records by experimenters in certain cases; (5) an inspector should have the power to order the painless destruction of any animal after experiment which shows signs of obvious suffering, even though the object of the experiment has not been attained. A minority report is made by three of the commissioners, who recommend that the administration of an anæsthetic shall be obligatory in all experiments likely to cause pain, or, if the nature of the investigation render this impossible, then on the supervention of real or obvious suffering, the animal shall be killed.

VOCATIONAL EDUCATION. See EDUCATION.

VOCATIONAL GUIDANCE. See CHILD LABOR.

VOCATIONAL TRAINING. See EDUCATION.

VOELCKERITE. See METEOROLOGY.

VOISIN. See NAVAL PROGRESS.

VOLCANISM. See GEOLOGY.

VOLCANOES. There were few volcanic outbursts in 1912 that involved any very remarkable features or widespread damage to life and property. In the Mediterranean region, the scene of considerable activity during the few preceding years, conditions generally were normal, so far as they have been reported. Mt. Etna, after its display of 1911, resumed its usual state, but Stromboli developed great energy during the latter part of September and for a time threatened to lay waste the island on which it is situated. The upper slopes of the volcano were buried beneath a thick ash mantle and some agricultural lands were damaged badly, but no casualties were reported. Taal volcano, in the Philippines, remained quiescent; this crater in 1911 wrought great destruction upon the district to the south of Manila. The most forcible eruption of the year was that of Katmai volcano in Alaska, a crater not previously known to have been active and considered by the natives as extinct. The volcano, which is situated on the coast of Alaska Peninsula, near the base, suddenly displayed violence on June 6, without any warning unless the earthquakes reported from Alaska earlier in the year were premonitory of the outbreak. For two days dust, ashes, and steam clouds poured out unceasingly, shrouding the region for miles around in total darkness. The village of St. Paul and other settlements on the island of Kodiak, across Shelikof strait from the volcano, were damaged by the fall of ashes that accumulated to a depth of several feet. The principal loss was involved in the destruction of vegetation and the injury to the fishing industry through pollution of the streams by the acid ejecta. Mt. Wrangell, the most noted of the Alaskan volcanoes, was reported in eruption in September.

WAGE, Minimum. See Minimum Wage.

WAGES, Legislation Affecting. See Labor Legislation.

WAINWRIGHT COMPENSATION ACT. See Employers' Liability, *New York Law.*

WALDECK. See Germany.

WALES. See Great Britain, and Architecture.

WALTON, Clifford Stevens. An American lawyer, author, and public official, died in May, 1912. He was born in Chardon, O., in 1861, and was educated at the United States Military Academy and at the University of Madrid, Spain, where he studied law. He became proficient in international law and served as attorney for and against the United States in several international law matters, including controversies between the United States and Chile, Peru, Salvador, etc. In 1898-9 he was major of the United States volunteers on the staffs of Major-Generals Brooke and Ludlow in Porto Rico and Cuba. He was for several years consul-general of the United States in Portugal. He was a member of many patriotic and legal associations. Among his writings on international law were: *The Civil Law in Spain and Spanish America* (1900); *Commercial and Maritime Laws of Spanish America* (1907). He also contributed articles on law to law journals and wrote several sketches of Spanish life. He was said to be the only native American lawyer who was a licentiate in Spanish law.

WARREN, Henry White. An American bishop of the Methodist Episcopal Church, died July, 1912. He was born in Williamsburg, Mass., in 1831, and graduated from Wesleyan University in 1853. For several years he taught science and languages and in 1855 was ordained to the ministry. He filled pastorates at Worcester, Boston, Lynn, Cambridge, Brooklyn, and Philadelphia. In 1880 he was elected bishop. He was the author of *Sights and Insights* (1874); *Studies of the Stars* (1878); *Recreations in Astronomy* (1879); *The Bible in the World's Education* (1892); *Among the Forces* (1898), and many articles in newspapers and reviews.

WASHBURN, William Drew. An American flour miller and former United States Senator from Minnesota, died July 29, 1912. He was born in Livermore, Me., in 1831, and graduated from Bowdoin College in 1854. In 1857 he removed to Minnesota and engaged in the practice of law. He became largely interested in flour manufacture and lumber enterprises and was for years interested in the Washburn and Crosby flouring mills, and later stockholder and director in the Pillsbury-Washburn Company. He was promoter and president for many years of the Minneapolis and St. Louis Railway and was also projector and builder of the Minneapolis, St. Paul and Sault Ste. Marie Railway, of which he was president until 1889. He was twice a member of the Minnesota House of Representatives and was surveyor of the State from 1861 to 1865. He was a member of the Forty-sixth and Forty-eighth Congresses and was United States Senator from Minnesota from 1889 to 1895.

WASHINGTON. Population. According to the Census Bureau statistics compiled during 1912, out of the total population in 1910, of 1,141,990, the foreign-born whites numbered 241,237 compared with 102,125 in 1900. Of these, the largest number, 35,271 came from Canada; from Sweden, 32,011; from England, 19,397; from Norway, 28,363; from Austria, 12,725; from Italy, 13,114. Other European countries contributed in smaller numbers. In the city of Seattle, with a population of 237,194, the foreign-born whites numbered 60,825. In Spokane, with a population of 104,402, the foreign-born whites numbered 21,260. The negroes in the State in 1910 numbered 6058 and the mulattoes 1840. In 1890 the negroes numbered 1602 and the mulattoes, 558.

Agriculture. The acreage, value, and production of the principal crops in 1911 and 1912 are shown below:

		Acreage	Prod. Bu.	Value
Corn	1912	31,000	846,000	$ 651,000
	1911	30,000	855,000	675,000
Wheat	1912	2,285,000	53,728,000	36,535,000
	1911	2,230,000	50,661,000	35,969,000
Oats	1912	284,000	13,689,000	5,476,000
	1911	281,000	14,528,000	6,538,000
Rye	1912	9,000	180,000	117,000
	1911	8,000	176,000	141,000
Potatoes	1912	68,000	11,356,000	4,088,000
	1911	59,000	9,440,000	6,419,000
Hay	1912	776,000	a 1,707,000	17,241,000
	1911	400,000	a 960,000	11,520,000

a Tons.

Mineral Production. The gold production of the State in 1911 was $847,677, compared with $788,185 in 1910. This is the largest output since 1903. The output and increase are mainly due to the Republic district of Ferry County. The silver output of the State in 1911 was 243,781 fine ounces, compared with 205,345 fine ounces in 1910. The production was mainly from siliceous smelting ores from Ferry County and copper and lead ores from Stevens County.

The production of coal in the State in 1911 was 3,572,815 short tons valued at $8,174,170. Washington is the only one of the Pacific coast States in which coal-mining is an industry of any importance. The output of 1911 showed a decrease from that of 1910 by

339,084 tons in quantity and $1,590,295 in value. The decrease is due almost entirely to the increased use of oil for fuel. The number of men employed in the coal mines of the State was 6498. There were 25 men killed in the coal mines of the State in 1911.

The value of the gold, silver, copper, lead, and zinc produced in the State in 1911 was $1,056,017, compared with a value of $968,249 in 1910. The production of gold was $847,677, which is the largest output for many years. The silver product in 1911, 243,781 fine ounces, was larger than the output of any year since 1903, and exceeded the production of 1910 by 38,436 ounces. The copper production increased from 86,918 pounds in 1910 to 318,207 pounds in 1911. The output of lead was 848,584 pounds, a decrease of 473,703 pounds from the production of 1910.

MANUFACTURES. The chief results of the census of manufactures, taken in 1910, are shown in the following table, together with the percentage of increases from 1904-1909:

	Number or Amount 1909	1904	P. C. of Inc. 1904-'09
Number of establishments	3,674	2,751	33.6
Persons engaged in manufactures ..	80,118	51,459	55.7
Proprietors and firm members...	3,264	2,602	25.4
Salaried employees.	7,734	3,658	111.4
Wage earners (average number)..	69,120	45,199	52.9
Primary horsepower	297,897	168,342	77.0
Capital	$222,261,000	$ 96,953,000	129.2
Expenses	196,275,000	111,381,000	76.2
Services	59,593,000	34,180,000	74.4
Salaries	9,827,000	4,093,000	140.1
Wages	49,766,000	30,087,000	65.4
Materials	117,888,000	66,166,000	78.2
Miscellaneous	18,794,000	11,035,000	70.3
Value of products..	220,746,000	128,822,000	71.4
Value added by manufacture (value of products less cost of materials)	102,858,000	62,656,000	64.2

The chief manufacturing industries of the State are those relating to lumber and timber products. In these, 43,749 wage-earners were employed in 1910 and the value of their product was $89,155,000; in flour-mill and gristmill products 644 wage-earners were employed and the product was valued at $17,853,000; in slaughtering and meat-packing, 828 wage-earners were employed and the product was valued at $15,654,000; in canning and preserving, 2029 persons were employed with a product valued at $9,595,000; in printing and publishing, 2624 persons were employed with a product valued at $9,286,000; in foundry and machine shop products, 2439 persons were employed, with a product valued at $7,988,000. Other industries, the value of whose product was more than $5,000,000, were the manufacture of butter, cheese, and condensed milk, and the brewing of malt liquors. The total number of wage-earners in the State in 1909 was 69,120, of whom 2859 were women. The wage-earners under 16 years of age numbered 266, and of these 47 were females. For over 70 per cent. of the wage-earners employed the prevailing hours of labor were 60 a week. This large percentage was explained by the general prevalence of 60 hours a week in the predominant lumber industry. The largest number of wage-earners was in Seattle, 11,331, and the value of the manufactured products was $50,569,198; in Tacoma were 5765 wage-earners and the value of the products was $22,449,979; in Spokane, 3989 wage-earners were employed and the products were valued at $18,879,591. Other important manufacturing centres were Everett, Bellingham, Aberdeen, Walla Walla, and North Yakima.

EDUCATION. The number of children of school age in the State on May 1, 1912, was 283,141. The enrollment in the public schools was 224,405, and the average daily attendance was 170,036. The teachers employed numbered 8041, of whom 6496 were females, and 1545 males. The average salary paid to male teachers per month was $87.25 and to female teachers, $67.80. The high schools numbered 410.

FINANCE. The receipts for the biennial period ending September 30, 1912, amounted to $16,911,514, and the expenditures to $15,711,107, leaving, with the balance on hand at the beginning of the fiscal year, a balance of $2,446,247 at the end of the fiscal year. The general fund of the State has no debts. The State owns in bonds belonging to six permanent irreducible funds, $9,920,020, which nets the State in interest $1250 a day for each day in the year.

POLITICS AND GOVERNMENT

The legislature did not meet in 1912, as the sessions are biennial and the last was held in 1911. The next session convenes January 8, 1913. Elections for State officers were held in 1912. The contest over the Washington delegates was one of the most bitterly fought before the national committee at Chicago at the Republican national convention. It will be found fully described in the article PRESIDENTIAL CAMPAIGN. The delegates from the State were finally awarded to President Taft. The Democratic delegates were instructed to vote for Governor Wilson. Governor Hay was renominated by the Republican party for governor, and the Progressives nominated Robert D. Hodge. The Democratic nominee was Ernest Lister. These were nominated in the State primaries held on September 10. The election of November 5 resulted as follows: Roosevelt, 111,797; Wilson, 87,674; Taft, 71,252; Debs, 39,555; Chafin, 7467; and Reimer, 1872. Roosevelt's plurality was 24,123. For governor, Lister, Dem., received 97,239 votes; Hay, Rep., 96,613, and Hodge, Prog., 77,873. The Democrats, Republicans, and Progressives each elected one congressman-at-large. The next State legislature will contain 27 Democrats; 77 Republicans; 33 Progressives; and 1 Socialist.

MUNICIPAL POLITICS. The application of the principle of recall furnished the chief local political interest in the State during 1912, aside from the presidential and gubernatorial campaigns. On February 20, Hiram C. Gill was nominated for mayor of Seattle. He had been elected mayor in 1910 and was recalled before he had served a year, although in the primaries for nomination he received 24,630 votes, while his closest competitor had 14,221. The Socialists polled in this election about 10,841 votes. Although Mr. Gill had received the nomination by a substantial majority, in the election held on March 6 he was defeated by George F. Cotterill by a majority of 804 votes.

The defeat of Mr. Gill was attributed to the vote of the women. He had been bitterly opposed by women's clubs and by the church element of the city. Mr. Cotterill ran on the platform of municipal ownership and single tax. Nevertheless, the single tax amendment to the charter, which was printed on the same ballot, was overwhelmingly defeated. The total vote for Cotterill was 32,086 and for Gill, 31,281. An attempt was made in March to bring about the recall of the mayor of Tacoma, but this met with failure. A complaint was filed, but it was found impossible to secure a sufficient number of names to bring about the election for the recall. The League of Washington Municipalities met in convention at Wenatchee, December 12-14, and defined a home rule programme for the next session of the legislature.

THE OLESON CASE. The decision rendered by Judge C. H. Hanford of Washington, revoking the citizenship papers of one Leonard Oleson on the ground that he was a Socialist, attracted wide attention and resulted in the introduction of a resolution in Congress by Mr. Berger, the Socialist member of Congress, for the impeachment of Judge Hanford. Judge Hanford subsequently resigned his office and therefore it was not necessary to bring the charges to an issue. In a statement of his defense given to the press, Judge Hanford declared that the reason for his ruling was not to be found in the character of Oleson or in any alleged misdeeds done by him. He said that "Oleson admitted that he is a Socialist and a frequenter of assemblages of Socialists in which he participates as speaker, advocating a propaganda for radical changes in the institutions of the country." He further affirmed that Oleson was affiliated with a party whose main object is "the complete elimination of property rights in this country." Furthermore, Oleson insisted that all the land, buildings, and industrial institutions should become the common property of all the people, that when this is done through the ballot there will be no more use for the political government of the country. Judge Hanford added that "those who believe in the propagation of crude theories hostile to the constitution are barred" and the privilege of becoming naturalized is restricted to "those whose sentiments are compatible with genuine allegiance to the existing government as defined by the oath which they are required to take." He concludes his statement as follows: "In order to secure a certificate of naturalization he intentionally made representations to the court which necessarily deceived the court, or his application for naturalization would have been denied. Therefore, by the petition which he was required to file and his testimony at the final hearing of his application, and by taking the oath which was administered to him in open court, he perpetrated a fraud upon the United States and committed an offense for which he may be punished as provided by law. The case, therefore, comes clearly within the provision of the law requiring the court to set aside and cancel his certificate of naturalization, and it was so decreed." Judge Hanford's decision was widely criticised and Attorney-General Wickersham expressed his opinion that Oleson had been unjustly treated.

STATE GOVERNMENT. Governor, Ernest Lister; Lieutenant-Governor, Louis Hart; Secretary of State, I. M. Howell; Treasurer, Edward Meath; Auditor, C. W. Clausen; Superintendent of Education, J. P. Preston; Attorney-General, V. W. Tanner—all Republicans except the governor.

JUDICIARY. Supreme Court: Chief Justice, R. O. Dunbar; Associate Justices, O. G. Ellis, H. D. Crow, M. A. Fullerton, W. Mount, M. F. Gose, S. J. Chadwick, George E. Morris and Emmett N. Parker—all Republicans, except Chadwick; Clerk, C. S. Reinhart.

STATE LEGISLATURE, 1913. Republicans, Senate, 27; House, 48; joint ballot, 75. Democrats, Senate, 7; House, 18; joint ballot, 25. Progressives, Senate, 7; House, 30; joint ballot, 37. Republican majority, Senate, 13; joint ballot, 13.

The representatives in Congress will be found in the article UNITED STATES, section *Congress*.

WASHINGTON ACADEMY OF SCIENCES. A society organized for the assistance of research and the prosecution of any business pertinent to an academy of sciences, founded in 1898. It acts as a federal head for the affiliated societies, which, with their vice-presidents in 1912, were as follows: Anthropological Society, F. W. Hodge; Archæological Society, Mitchell Carroll; Biological Society, E. W. Nelson; Botanical Society, W. R. Maxon; Chemical Society, J. A. Le Clerc; Engineers Society, G. W. Littlehales; Entomological Society, A. L. Quaintance; Foresters Society, H. S. Graves; Geographic Society, Henry Gannett; Geological Society, David White; Historical Society, James Dudley Morgan; Medical Society, John B. Nichols; Philosophical Society, E. B. Rosa. Three scientific meetings were held during 1912. These dealt with sound waves, the recent work of the *Carnegie*, the total solar eclipse of April 28, 1911, and with an exhibit of new and interesting apparatus from the United States government and other scientific laboratories of Washington. The president in 1912 was F. V. Coville. The society publishes the *Journal of the Washington Academy of Sciences.*

WASHINGTON UNIVERSITY. An institution for higher education at St. Louis, Mo., founded in 1853. The total number of students in all departments of the university in the autumn of 1912 was 1326. The faculty numbered 147. There were no noteworthy changes in the faculty during the year and no noteworthy benefactions. The productive funds of the university amounted to $6,697,590 and the income to $598,963. The library contained about 130,000 volumes. Chancellor, David F. Houston.

WASHINGTON, UNIVERSITY OF. A State institution of higher education at Seattle, Wash., founded in 1861. The number of students enrolled in the various departments of the university in the collegiate year 1911-12 was 2632. The faculty numbered 143. Among the noteworthy changes in the faculty during the year were the following: Professor Frederick E. Bolton of the University of Iowa was appointed head of the department of education in place of Dr. E. O. Sisson, resigned; Dr. Edwin J. Vickner of Gustavus Adolphus College was appointed head of the department of Scandinavian languages; Miss Effie I. Raitt, formerly of Northwestern University, was appointed head of the department of home economics; Dr. Samuel L. Boothroyd, formerly of Cornell University, was appointed to the chair of astronomy in place of Associate Professor James Gould, resigned; Associate Professor Lee

Emerson Bassett, formerly of Stanford University, was given charge of public speaking and debate. During the year an extension division was established, with Professor Edwin A. Start in charge. The largest gift during the year was a set of chimes, consisting of 12 bells, costing $12,500, presented by Colonel Alden J. Blethen, a former regent of the university. The income of the university is derived from 100,000 acres of land, with a minimum selling price fixed by law of $10 an acre, $1,000,000, and a tract of land in the business district of Seattle valued at $2,000,000. The amount furnished by the State annually for the support of the university is about $475,000. The library contains 51,163 volumes. President, Thomas F. Kane, Ph. D.

WASHINGTON AND LEE UNIVERSITY. An institution for higher learning at Lexington, Va., founded in 1749. The students enrolled in the autumn of 1912 numbered 470, divided as follows: Academic department, 263; engineering department, 59; law department, 149. The faculty numbered 26. Professor R. M. Withers was appointed to the Bradford chair of international and constitutional law in the law school. The university received $10,000 under the will of Frank T. Howard, an alumnus, of New Orleans, La. The productive funds of the university amounted at the end of the year 1911-12 to $893,979. The annual income is about $95,000. There were 50,000 volumes in the library. President, George H. Denny, LL. D., Ph. D.

WASSERMAN'S EXPERIMENTS. See CANCER.

WATER POLLUTION. See SANITATION.

WATER PURIFICATION. The use of hypochlorite of lime (bleaching powder or chloride of lime) or else hypochlorite of soda for water disinfection continues to make marvelous progress. The practice was begun a few years ago, chiefly as an emergency measure in case of typhoid outbreaks due to unfiltered, polluted water. It was continued as a temporary protection against typhoid pending the construction of filters. Then it was taken up as an adjunct to mechanical filtration and gradually as supplementary to slow sand filtration, and then to sedimentation as well. Rapidly the larger cities of the United States, and also the smaller ones, are coming to disinfect their water-supplies by this means, when those supplies are from surface sources. Minneapolis, Minn., virtually completed a large water mechanical filter plant, with provision for using hpyochlorite, in 1912. The use of ozone for disinfection is slowly extending in Europe, but is making little headway in this country. The cost is still high, the working of the apparatus somewhat uncertain, and as a rule, the water must be filtered before the ozone is applied. The ultra-violet ray process is as yet in its infancy.

WATER SUPPLIES, STATE CONTROL OF. See SANITATION.

WATER SUPPLY. See AQUEDUCTS.

WATERWAYS, STANDARD OF PURITY FOR. See SANITATION.

WATER-WORKS. Important studies of water waste were made at Chicago and a water conservation exhibition, designed to educate the public against the almost criminal waste of water at Philadelphia, were features of the year. Baltimore and San Francisco installed special high-pressure water-works systems for fire protection. Aside from its high-pressure system, San Francisco still depends on a private company for water, after every other large city has built or bought works. The San Francisco project for a great municipal gravity water-supply from the headwaters of the Tuolumne River, involving a huge dam in the Hetch Hetchy Valley and a long and large aqueduct, is still in abeyance. A large engineering report on the project, presenting a scheme of greater magnitude than the earlier ones, was made by John R. Freeman, and published by the city. The Spring Valley Water Company issued two volumes designed to show that its present and projected works are all sufficient for scores of years to come. Opponents of flooding the Hetchy Valley, which lies in the Yosemite National Park, had their innings in November, 1912, before Secretary of the Interior Walter Fisher, to whom the reports already mentioned were made. The secretary, aided by a board of advisory engineers (U. S. army), will decide in 1913 whether San Francisco's need of the Hetch Hetchy supply is great enough to warrant the flooding of the valley, for which a conditional, but deferred, permit was granted by ex-Secretary Garfield a few years ago. See SANITATION, *Sewage Purification*.

WATSON, JAMES E. See PRESIDENTIAL CAMPAIGN.

WATSON, ROSAMUND (BALL) MARRIOTT. An English poet, died January, 1912. She was born in 1863 and was the wife of H. B. Marriott Watson, the English novelist. Among her publications are: *The Ballad of the Bird-Bride, and Other Poems; A Summer Night, and Other Poems; The Art of the House* (1896); *After Sunset* (1903); and *The Heart of a Garden* (1905). She was a contributor of poetry to many magazines.

WEATHER CONDITIONS. See METEOROLOGY.

WEAVER, JAMES B. An American soldier and political writer, died February 6, 1912. He was born in Dayton, O., in 1833, and his early education was obtained from the public schools. He studied law and in 1854 was admitted to the bar. At the outbreak of the Civil War he had joined the Iowa volunteers as a private, and when the war began he was made a colonel of this regiment. He attained the rank of brigadier-general. After the war he resumed the study of law and entered politics. In 1866 he was elected district-attorney of the second judicial district of Iowa and served in this office for four years. In 1867 he became assessor of internal revenue for the first district of Iowa, holding this office for four years. He was for several years editor of the *Iowa Tribune*. In 1879 he was elected to the Forty-sixth Congress as a Greenbacker. He was also elected to the Forty-ninth and Fiftieth Congresses in 1885-89. He was the candidate for the presidency on the Greenback ticket in 1880, and was again candidate for the presidency in 1892 by the People's party. He received twenty-two electoral votes. From 1904 to 1906 he was mayor of Colfax, Ia.

WEEDEN, WILLIAM BABCOCK. An American soldier, manufacturer, and writer, died March 28, 1912. He was born in Bristol, R. I., in 1834, and studied at Brown University from 1848 to 1850. In 1851 he engaged in the business of manufacturing woolens. At the outbreak of the Civil War he enlisted as first lieutenant of artillery in the United States volunteers. He participated in many battles and rose to be chief of artillery in the 1st division of the 5th Corps. He resigned from the service in August, 1862, and resumed business in Providence. He retired from active business in 1902. He was the author of *Morality of Prohibitory Liquor Laws* (1875); *Social Law of Labor* (1882); *Economic and Social History of New England, 1620-1789* (1890), and *War Government, Federal and State* (1906).

WEEVIL. See Cotton.

WEIGHTS AND MEASURES. United States Legislation. In 1912 the legislature of the State of New York passed a bill which became Chapter 81 of the Laws of 1912, relating to the sale of commodities. This gave what is said to be one of the broadest weights and measures laws in existence anywhere. It applied to all commodities and provided that whoever sells any commodity whatsoever must make a written representation of the quantity. The statute provided that the State superintendent of weights and measures, with the cooperation of the chief and principal weights and measures officials of first-class cities, should establish tolerances, rules, and regulations for carrying out the provisions of the act, and a board so established during the year issued the preliminary regulations and requirements demanded under the act. The laws of 1912 also contained statutes dealing with the method of selling meat products and butter, and prescribed the sizes of the containers for various vegetable products and fruit. This act required the net contents of containers to be indicated on the outside, and provided for the immunity from prosecution of any person who could show a guarantee signed by a wholesaler, jobber, or manufacturer from whom the commodity was purchased, to the effect that the person guaranteeing in the first instance then became amenable to prosecution, fines, and other penalties. The attorney-general of the State of New York decided that it was not legal under the terms of the new statute for a dealer to place on his package in connection with the statement of the weight of its contents, the word "average," with or without other qualifying clause.

Metric System; Recent Progress. Successful progress was made in 1912 in the adoption of the metrical system of weights and measures either as an obligatory or permissive system. On April 1, the law of Denmark, promulgated on May 4, 1907, went definitely into effect. Henceforth the metric units are exclusively to be employed in that country except for the agricultural measures for which the application is still deferred. The new system has been employed without detriment and to general satisfaction. A convention signed at Tegucigalpa February 3, 1910, by the delegates of the five republics, Costa Rica, Guatemala, Honduras, Nicaragua, and Salvador, provided for the complete application on January 1, 1912, of the metric system. As to the methods of the reform information, unhappily, was lacking. In the kingdom of Siam metric units had already been adopted for certain applications, notably in public works, and it is interesting to note that according to a report addressed to the government of Lord Salisbury, the English engineers in the service of the Siamese government at that time declared themselves invariably well satisfied with its use and did not desire to return to the British system of weights and measures. In 1910 the Siamese government decided to adopt the metrical system for all uses and successively to render it obligatory in each of the provinces according as the machinery should be created for its application. Since it has taken that position the government of Siam has made great efforts to hasten the moment when the system may be applied throughout the whole country. In 1908 the imperial Chinese government decided upon the adoption of a system of measures that was, in great part decimal, and in which the unit of length was by definition equal to 32 centimeters, showing thus its intention of preparing by an intermediate stage for complete metrical reform. Such reform is in process of realization. The government of the Chinese Republic presented in effect to the Chambers a bill providing for the immediate and obligatory employment of the metric system. Without waiting for a vote on that bill the Peking government began preparatory studies in order to take a definite step in the reform. The British colonies have not remained behind in the movement for the adoption of decimal measures. At Malta the complete application of the metric system was decided upon in December, 1910, to become effective at the beginning of January, 1912. On the latter date, however, it was deferred until July, 1912, and finally to July 1, 1913. On August 4 the Australian house of representatives decided to propose to the imperial conference the obligatory employment of the metric system in all the British Empire and if this result could not be obtained, to agree with New Zealand to adopt it without delay. The Imperial conference did not see fit to follow the suggestions of the Australian parliament and it seemed probable that the second part of the decision of the house would soon go into effect. The Union of South Africa has taken an equally important step toward the adoption of the metric system by the elaboration of a bill published on February 10, 1912, in the *Union Gazette Extraordinary* and of which the first article is couched in the following language: "From a date to be fixed by the governor-general by proclamation in the *Gazette*, the lawful and standard measures of weight capacity (or volume), length, superficial area and cubic content shall, throughout the Union, be those described in the second schedule to this act and no other." The second schedule provided in the first place for metric measures; in the second place, for British measures and those of the Dutch colonists. Thus it is the undisguised intention of the legisalture to give preponderance to the metric system.

Besides these accessions either actual or in preparation which have just been enumerated, it is interesting to note that there have been other adoptions of the metric system of which the most important are those in Bosnia-Herzegovina and Belgian Congo. The adherents to the metric system already make a long list, which is as follows: Austria, Argentina, Belgium, Brazil, Bulgaria, Chile, Colombia, Costa Rica, Cuba, Denmark, France, Germany, Guatemala, Honduras, Hungary, Italy, Luxembourg, Mexico, Montenegro, Netherlands, Nicaragua, Norway, Peru, Rumania, Salvador, Servia, Spain, Sweden, Switzerland, and Uruguay. The inclusion of Siam and China in this list is a question only of a short time. The metric system is practically permissive in the United States (obligatory for the medical departments of the national government), in Greece, in the United Kingdom, in Russia (obligatory in military medicine), in Egypt (obligatory in public works and in government transactions), in Turkey, in Bolivia, and in Paraguay. The obligatory adoption of the metric system rejected in the United Kingdom by a vote in the House of Commons by a majority of 32 votes on March 22, 1907, will certainly be hastened by the vigorous movement in its favor in the British colonies. The British government has, in fact, instituted a royal commission charged with the study of measures designed to increase the commerce of the mother country with the colonies and with foreign countries. The question of the reform of weights and measures is one of the first on the programme of the commission. Parallel to this reform, the application of the metric system has been adopted in certain international branches of commerce. For example, the trade in precious stones, in which the carat, differing in the respective countries, was nowhere a simple submultiple of the gram. (See INTERNATIONAL METRIC CARAT.) Besides these accessions to the principles of the system, it is interesting to note a marked tendency toward extending the principle of legal uniformity to other measures than those of space and quantity of material to which it had hitherto been limited. Dynamic and thermal quantities, such as energy in all its forms, have become the subjects of constant change and their use demands their own special measures just as in the case of those quantities whose units have been for a long time defined in the laws. For the expression of these units the C. G. S. system, whose fundamental units have been loaned to the metric system, gives a code of measures universally adopted in the sciences and from which the electrical industries have equally profited. A more complete elaboration of the rational systems of measures beginning with the fundamental units of the meter or kilogram and the second, is about to be carried out. It attracts the close attention of scientists and technicians, and equally concerns the law-makers. The Hungarian law of January 10, 1907, gives a large place to the rational units for the measure of energy. The Bulgarian law of April 10 has sanctioned a similar measure of progress and the definite form under which definitions must be given is laid down in the laws that are in preparation in Argentina and France. The application of rational principles led to the joule and the watt as units for energy and power. The employment of these units by electricians in all countries will shortly result in imposing them upon all the industries. This will be a new and important conquest for the metric system.

WEIHAIWEI. The territory leased by China to Great Britain, situated on the northeast coast of the Shantung Peninsula and composed of the island of Liukung, all the islands in Weihaiwei Bay, and a strip of mainland ten miles wide along the entire coast line. Total area, 285 square miles; population (census of 1911), 147,177. Port Edward is the chief port and the residence of the commissioner (1912, Sir J. H. Stewart Lockhart).

WELFARE WORK. During the past few years there has been a very striking extension of the activities and expenditures of employers designed to better the health and increase the efficiency and contentment of their workers. This welfare work has taken a great variety of forms extending all the way from clean factory yards to old-age pension systems. One of the most active agencies in the promotion of welfare work is the National Civic Federation, which has a special department devoted to it. Among the features of such work promoted by this department are: More sanitary work places; recreation opportunities and facilities; educational advantages; rental or sale of houses to employees; and provident funds for loans to employees, sickness insurance, and other normal expenditures, as well as provision for old age. Thus the introduction of sanitary science into factory construction and management has resulted in better air and light, more healthful temperature, pure water, lavatory facilities, clean and cheery lunch rooms, rest rooms, and hospital rooms with attendant nurses for the injured or temporarily sick. Recreational and educational advantages have similarly been developed more or less elaborately, depending on the character of the industry and the enthusiasm of the employer. The construction of model towns or suburbs for employees has not been carried as far in this country as in England, but is becoming a conspicuous feature of the efforts to improve the conditions of workers. Those of recent construction embody the best ideas of city planning with provision for gardens, parks, playgrounds, gymnasium, and recreation centre, library, and civic centre. There are now numerous companies that have regularly employed welfare experts who organize and supervise the industrial betterment activities in all respects. One of the new features of such work is instruction of the workers in personal hygiene; especially is attention being given to the instruction of girl and women workers in the care of their bodies. So also there are instances of regular instruction in domestic science at the employer's expense in plants employing many young women. This looks forward to the time when many of them will be wives and mothers.

Many employers have enlisted in the campaign against the loan shark. There is scarcely an employer of labor some of whose employees do not find themselves unexpectedly in urgent need of money as a result of accident, sickness, surgical operation, funeral expenses, unemployment, and other common incidents. These have furnished the loan shark's opportunity and he has loaned at exorbitant rates and under hard conditions. Thus the money-lender fattened upon human misfortune. Welfare work to remedy this evil has taken the form of loans by employers at low rates of interest or even without interest; this is usually accompanied by a deposit system whereby the employer pays more than savings-bank interest on deposits of his own employees. This stimulates thrift and provides the worker with a fund of his own in case of any unexpected need. See LOAN SHARKS.

One of the most extensive plans of welfare work is that instituted by the United States Steel Corporation in the latter part of 1911. This is under the immediate supervision of Dr.

Thomas Darlington, formerly health commissioner of New York City. The estimated cost in 1912 was $5,000,000. In the first place should be mentioned the comprehensive plans for accident prevention and compensation, for retirement pensions, and for profit-sharing. Thus the campaign for accident prevention cost over $2,500,000 and now entails an annual cost of $750,000; the plan of compensation for accidents, including hospitals, and medical, and surgical attendance, costs about $2,000,000 annually; for old-age pensions there has been provided a permanent fund of $12,000,000. More than 1600 employees have been retired on pensions varying from $12 to $100 per month at an annual cost to the corporation of $700,000. The new departure has undertaken an extensive plan for sanitation and welfare costing in the first year $1,250,000. Among these activities are: Perfected sewage disposal; pure water in plants and company houses; drainage, fly prevention; weed cutting and garbage collection; installation of wash rooms; shower baths and swimming pools; playgrounds for employees' children; and provision of lunch-rooms, waiting-rooms, better light, and ventilation. Not all of these have been undertaken by all the companies. The corporation has announced its belief that "following in the wake of betterment of conditions in the steel industry, there will naturally come a shortening of the hours of labor, which will tend toward increase of efficiency and resourcefulness in the working population." See UNITED STATES STEEL CORPORATION, paragraph *Labor Conditions*.

Many trade-union leaders continued to look with suspicion on the various kinds of welfare work, including old-age pension and accident compensation systems. Their fear is that by these means the workers will be so tied to their jobs that all effective means of bettering their conditions, as by strikes, will be made impossible, or at least extremely difficult. Mr. Louis D. Brandeis, speaking before the organized labor of Massachusetts in September, declared that these schemes "create a new form of peonage." Moreover, many workers prefer to get their betterments in the form of higher wages which they may then devote as they individually choose to higher standards of living. They strongly resent the element of tutelage involved in having social betterment plans handed down to them from higher authorities. Thus between merely enlightened selfishness on the employer's part and thankless acceptance on the laborer's part, welfare work does not seem destined to solve the labor problem.

WELLAND CANAL. See CANALS.

WELLESLEY COLLEGE. An institution for the higher education of women at Wellesley, Mass., founded in 1875. The total enrollment in the autumn of 1912 was 1424. The faculty numbered 173. The following promotions among the members of the faculty are important: Associate Professors Eva Chandler, mathematics, Margaret Pollock Sherwood, English literature, and Alice Robertson, zoölogy, were appointed professors in their respective departments. A number of instructors became associate professors, and several assistants became instructors. The most noteworthy benefaction received during the year was a scholarship of $10,000. The productive funds at the end of the collegiate year 1912, amounted to $940,814, and the income was $59,969. The library contained 73,100 volumes. Dean, Ellen F. Pendleton.

WELLS, ALMOND BROWN. An American soldier, died September 7, 1912. He was born in New York City in 1842. In 1863 he was appointed first lieutenant of the first battalion of Nevada Cavalry, and was promoted to be captain in the following year. He was honorably mustered out of service in 1865 and in 1866 was appointed second lieutenant of the 8th United States Cavalry. He rose through the different ranks of service until he became brigadier-general in 1903, and in the same year was retired from active service at his own request, after thirty years spent in the army. This included service in Cuba during the Spanish-American War, in China during the Boxer Rebellion, and in the Philippine Islands.

WELLS, H. G. See LITERATURE, ENGLISH AND AMERICAN.

WELSH DISESTABLISHMENT. See GREAT BRITAIN, *History*.

WENDELL, OLIVER CLINTON. An American astronomer, died November 8, 1912. He was born in Dover, N. H., in 1845, and graduated at Bates College in 1868. In the same year he became an assistant in the Harvard Observatory. For the ten years following 1869 he was a civil and hydraulic engineer. In the latter year he again became assistant in the Harvard Observatory, remaining in that position until 1898, when he was appointed assistant professor. During his term at the observatory he had charge of the reductions and calculations for the *Annals of the Observatory* and was also orbit calculator. He made upward of 1000 observations. He achieved distinction by his discoveries of several stars. He was a contributor to journals of astronomy.

WERNHER, SIR JULIUS. An English capitalist, died May 22, 1912. He was born in Darmstadt in the Grand Duchy of Hesse in 1850. His commercial career was begun in a banking house in Frankfort, but early in 1870 he removed to London as a clerk in an Anglo-German firm. He returned to Germany at the outbreak of the Franco-German War and served throughout that conflict. After the war he engaged in business for a short time in Paris, but at the close of 1871 he went to South Africa, where the diamond fields had recently been discovered and the city of Kimberley had just been founded. His mission to South Africa was the purchase and exportation of diamonds. He remained in Kimberley for nearly ten years and laid the foundations of his great fortune. He became the South African representative of a great French diamond house and in 1880 was transferred to London as English partner in the firm of Porges and Wernher. In 1884 he returned to Kimberley and remained there for the year. During this visit he formed a connection with the late Alfred Beit, who became the Kimberley representative of the firm. Two years previously the firm of H. Eckstein and Co. had been founded at Johannesburg as a branch of the business of Porges and Wernher. This branch was formed as a result of the discoveries of gold in the Witwatersrand in 1886. From that date the fortunes of the firm began to increase greatly. In 1888 as a result of the amalgamation of the diamond mines of Kimberley by the late Cecil Rhodes and Alfred Beit, Wernher became the life governor of the De Beers corporation. Before the close of the following year Mr. Porges retired from business and the firm assumed the name under which it became famous, Wernher, Beit, and Co. The partners in this firm formed a combination of extraordinary strength and amassed a great fortune. Besides playing a great part in the government of De Beers, Wernher was a director of the Rand Mines, and chairman of the Central Mining Investment Corporation. A few years before his death his name was before the public in connection with the prosecution of a Frenchman named Lemoine, who had obtained from him large sums of money on the pretense of having discovered a process for the manufacture of diamonds. Lemoine was subsequently sentenced to six years' imprisonment for fraud. Wernher was created a baronet in 1905. At the time of the South African War he, with his partner, provided the funds which enabled the citizens of Johannesburg to raise a volunteer regiment. He was much interested in education and in February, 1911, was awarded the gold medal of the Institute of Mining and Metallurgy in recognition of his services to the advancement of technological education. A short time before this he gave $50,000 to the National Physical Laboratory for the extension of the metallurgical department. The greatest monument to his munificence, however, will be the new South African University, to which he and his partner, Alfred Beit, made large gifts. He was well known as an art collector and was conspicuous in philanthropic and social movements.

WESLEYAN METHODIST CONNECTION OF AMERICA. This denomination was founded in 1843 by members of the Methodist Episcopal Church who strongly opposed the institution of slavery. In 1912 there were 18,510 members or communicants, 613 ministers and 519 churches. The church property is valued at approximately $650,000. Among the educational institutions maintained are Houghton Seminary at Houghton, N. Y., Miltonvale College at Miltonvale, Kan., and Central College at Central, S. C. The official journal of the denomination is the *Wesleyan Methodist*, published at Syracuse, N. Y. The highest authority is the quadrennial general conference. The last meeting of this body was held in October, 1911. The denomination carries on missions in Sierra Leone, West Africa, and in India.

WESLEYAN UNIVERSITY. An institution of higher education at Middletown, Conn., founded in 1831. The enrollment in all departments of the university in the autumn of 1912 was 405. The faculty numbered 40. Durant Drake, Ph. D., was appointed associate professor of ethics and religion. During the year an endowment fund of $1,000,000 was completed largely through the efforts of the alumni of the university. The productive funds amounted on June 30, 1912, to $1,814,150. The income from investments amounted to $84,226, and from other sources, $59,223. There were about 90,000 volumes in the library. President, William A. Shanklin, D. D.

WESTERN AUSTRALIA. A state of the Commonwealth of Australia. Area, 975,920 square miles. Population (census of April 3, 1911), 282,114, exclusive of full-blooded aboriginals. Perth, the capital, had 35,767 inhabitants; with suburbs, 106,792. Governor in 1912, Sir Gerald Strickland, who was appointed to be governor of New South Wales in 1913, when Maj.-Gen. Sir Harry Barron, the governor of Tasmania, would succeed him as governor of Western Australia. Premier in 1912, John Scadden. See AUSTRALIA.

WESTERN PHILOSOPHIC SOCIETY. See PHILOSOPHIC SOCIETY, WESTERN.

WESTERN RESERVE UNIVERSITY. An institution for higher education at Cleveland, O., founded in 1826. The number of students enrolled in the various departments of the university in the autumn of 1912 was 1380. The faculty numbered 242. There were no noteworthy changes in the faculty during the year. During the year a special endowment fund of $1,000,000 for the medical department of the university was completed. The productive funds amounted to about $3,500,000, and the income to about $170,000 annually. The library contained about 100,000 volumes. President, Charles F. Thwing, D. D.

WEST INDIAN HURRICANES. See METEOROLOGY.

WEST VIRGINIA. POPULATION. According to the Census Bureau statistics compiled during 1912 out of the total population of 1,221,119 in 1910, 57,072 were foreign-born whites, compared with 22,379 in 1900. Of these the largest number, 17,223, came from Italy; from Germany, 6316; from Austria, 8582; from Hungary, 5707; from Russia, 5142. Other European countries were represented by smaller numbers. The negroes in the State in 1910 numbered 64,173 and the mulattoes 20,879. In 1890 the negroes numbered 32,690 and the mulattoes 9354.

AGRICULTURE. The acreage, value, and production of the principal crops in 1911 and 1912 are shown below:

		Acreage	Prod. Bu.	Value
Corn	1912	725,000	24,505,000	$15,928,000
	1911	707,000	18,170,000	13,391,000
Wheat	1912	233,000	3,278,000	3,412,000
	1911	238,000	2,737,000	2,792,000
Oats	1912	111,000	3,108,000	1,461,000
	1911	110,000	2,420,000	1,355,000
Rye	1912	17,000	221,000	186,000
	1911	17,000	187,000	168,000
Potatoes	1912	47,000	5,264,000	3,264,000
	1911	44,000	1,980,000	2,059,000
Hay	1912	745,000	a 1,028,000	15,420,000
	1911	648,000	a 428,000	8,560,000
Tobacco	1912	15,800	b 12,008,000	1,321,000
	1911	15,000	b 11,250,000	900,000

a Tons. b Pounds.

MINERAL PRODUCTION. The total production of petroleum in the State in 1911 was 9,795,464 barrels, compared with a production of 11,753,071 barrels in 1910. The product of 1910 was the largest ever obtained in the State. Several important oil fields were discovered during the year. There were 1191 wells completed in the State in 1911.

The production of coal in West Virginia in 1911 was 59,831,580 short tons, valued at $53,670,515. Since 1909 the State has ranked second in the coal-producing States. It stands alone in the low average price which its coal, some of it the highest grade bituminous, brings to the producer. In 1911 the average price per ton was 90 cents. The production in 1911 showed a decrease from that of 1910 by 1,839,439 tons. The production of 1910, however, was above the normal on account of strikes in other coal-mining regions. The number of men employed in the coal mines of the State in 1911 was 66,350.

The value of the brick and tile, pottery, and other clay products in 1911 was $4,333,420, an increase of $335,375, compared with the figures for 1910.

MANUFACTURES. The Thirteenth Census statistics are for the calendar year 1909 and were compiled in 1912. While West Virginia is more a mining than a manufacturing State, it is especially well adapted to the development of manufactures on account of the vast deposits of coal, the abundance of petroleum and natural gas, abundant timber, and gasoline, and waterpower facilities. It will be seen from the following table that the number of manufacturing establishments in 1909 was 2586, which gave employment to 71,463 persons.

	Number or Amount 1909	1904	P. C. of Inc. 1904-'09
Number of establishments	2,586	2,109	22.6
Persons engaged in manufactures ..	71,463	48,880	46.2
Proprietors and firm members...	2,599	2,230	16.5
Salaried employees.	4,971	2,892	71.9
Wage earners (average number)..	63,893	43,758	46.0
Primary horsepower	217,496	138,578	56.9
Capital	$150,923,000	$86,821,000	73.8
Expenses	144,666,000	86,738,000	66.8
Services	38,710,000	24,052,000	60.9
Salaries	5,710,000	2,899,000	97.0
Wages	33,000,000	21,153,000	56.0
Materials	92,878,000	54,419,000	70.7
Miscellaneous	13,078,000	8,267,000	58.2
Value of products..	161,950,000	99,041,000	63.5
Value of products less cost of materials	69,072,000	44,622,000	54.8

The largest value of product was in industries connected with lumber and timber, $28,758,000; iron and steel products were valued at $22,435,000; leather products, $12,451,000; glass, $7,779,000; flour and gristmill products, $7,696,000. The total number of persons employed in manufactures in the State in 1909 was 71,463, of whom 66,121 were male and 5342 female. The number of persons employed under 16 years of age was 1053. The prevailing hours of labor for 49.3 per cent. of the wage earners were 60 a week; only 16.2 per cent. of the total working in establishments where the prevailing hours were less than 54 a week, and 12.9 per cent. in those where they were more than 60 a week. The largest number of wage-earners was in Wheeling, 7809; in Huntington, 3156; in Parkersburg, 1495; and in Martinsburg, 1420.

FINANCE. The receipts for the fiscal year 1912 from the State fund amounted to $4,625,212, and from the general school fund to $797,186. The expenditures for the fiscal year amounted to $4,486,307, leaving a balance in the treasury at the end of the fiscal year of $1,616,515, to which should be added the invested portion of the irreducible school fund, $973,200, making a total balance of $2,589,715. The chief expenditures were for education, for the maintenance of charitable and correctional institutions, and for the salaries of State officers. There is no State debt.

CHARITIES AND CORRECTIONS. The charitable and correctional institutions of the State, with their populations on September 30, 1912, were as follows: West Virginia Hospital for the Insane, 1002; Second Hospital for the Insane, 500; West Virginia Asylum, 535; Miners' Hospital No. 1, 72; Miners' Hospital, No. 2, 24; Miners' Hospital, No. 3, 24; West Virginia Penitentiary, 1128; West Virginia Reform School, 285; West Virginia Industrial Home for Girls, 77; West Virginia School for the Deaf and Blind, 184; West Virginia Colored Orphans' Home and Industrial School, 78; Children's Home, 52. The Colored Orphans' Home and Industrial School and the West Virginia Children's Home are institutions which have been recently established by the State legislature. The legislature also established a State tuberculosis sanitarium, which was ready for patients on December 1, 1912.

POLITICS AND GOVERNMENT

The legislature did not meet in 1912, as the sessions are biennial and the last was held in 1911. The next session convenes January 9, 1913. Elections for governor and other State officers were held on November 5.

On May 16 the Republican State convention instructed sixteen of the State delegates to vote for Roosevelt at the national convention. The Democratic delegates were instructed to vote for Champ Clark. The Republican State primary for the nomination of State officers nominated Henry D. Hatfield for governor. The Democrats nominated William R. Thompson. The Progressive party had no candidates for State officers in the field. This party held its first convention on July 30 and chose delegates to the National Progressive convention. The election on November 5 resulted as follows: Wilson 113,048, Roosevelt 78,819, Taft 56,667, Debs 15,346, and Chafin 4534. Wilson's plurality was 34,227. For governor, Hatfield, Republican, received 127,942 votes, Thompson, Democrat, 119,173, Hilton, Socialist, 14,900, and Jackson, Prohibition, 5816.

STATE GOVERNMENT. Governor, H. D. Hatfield; Secretary of State, Stuart F. Reed; Superintendent of Free Schools, M. P. Shawkey; Auditor, John S. Darst; Commissioner of Agriculture, Howard E. Williams; Attorney-General, A. A. Lilly; Treasurer, E. L. Long; Adjutant-General, Charles D. Elliott; Secretary State Board of Agriculture, J. M. Millan—all Republicans.

JUDICIARY. Supreme Court of Appeals—President, L. Judson Williams; Associate Justices, George Poffenbarger, Ira E. Robinson, Charles W. Lynch, Henry Miller; Clerk, W. B. Mathews—all Republicans.

STATE LEGISLATURE, 1913. Senate, Democrats 16, Republicans 14; House, Democrats 33, Republicans 53; joint ballot, Democrats 49, Republicans 67. Democratic majority in Senate 2. Republican majority in House 20; on joint ballot 18.

The representatives in Congress will be found in the article UNITED STATES, section *Congress*.

WEST VIRGINIA UNIVERSITY. A State institution for higher education at Morgantown, W. Va., founded in 1867. The enrollment in the colleges of the university in the autumn of 1912 was 476, and in the various schools 103. The faculty numbered 65. Several new members of the faculty were appointed during the year. These include Prof. George F. Wells, who succeeded Professor Willey of the law department, who retired after twenty-four years of service. Prof. R. E. Hunt was appointed to the head of the department of animal husbandry in the department of agriculture. Dr. J. E. Hodgson was appointed associate professor of mathematics, and Prof. Alexander P. Moore was appointed assistant professor of French. An important change in the college administration was the division of the school year into semesters, instead of three terms as formerly. There were no noteworthy benefactions received during the year. The library contained about 46,000 volumes. President, Thomas E. Hodges.

WHARTON, Edith. See Literature, English and American.

WHEAT. The world's wheat crop of 1912 was not uniformly good, but was somewhat irregular as a result of unfavorable climatic conditions. In nearly all European countries the crop suffered from a cool and backward season and later from rainy and cloudy weather during harvest. Yield and quality were both reduced by these conditions, the reductions in yield being large enough to increase perceptibly the requirements of most wheat-importing countries. In Italy the wheat yield was reduced by a long and serious drought during the growing season. Drought also menaced the wheat crop of Russia early in the season, but timely rains more than offset the injury and the production was about normal and nearly 50 per cent. greater than the yield of 1911, a year of extreme shortage. In the southern hemisphere the crop harvested late in 1911 and early in 1912 was satisfactory in Argentina, but short in Australia, being about 25 per cent. less than the e us yield. The import requirements of all countries were estimated at 622,400,000 bushels in 1912, as compared with 530,400,000 bushels in 1911. The greatest increase in import requirements was recorded for the United Kingdom, the quantity being 25,600,000 bushels, or about one-eighth of the total imports the year before. Germany's requirements were 80,000,000 bushels and Italy's 60,000,000 bushels, as against 57,600,000 and 40,000,000 bushels respectively in 1911. The import requirements of the world supplied by the export countries were distributed as follows: Russia, 136,000,000 bushels; Canada, 112,000,000 bushels; United States, 96,000,000 bushels; Balkan States, 56,000,000 bushels; India, 48,000,000 bushels; and Argentina, Australia, and Chile together, 176,000,000 bushels.

In the United States, climatic conditions were unfavorable to the winter wheat crop through the fall and winter, and the acreage of wheat winter-killed has probably never been greater. The fall of 1911 was very dry, the following winter was of unusual severity, and the spring exceptionally late. After the opening of spring, however, the season was most favorable and the excellent growth of the crop largely overcame the losses due to the extensive winter-killing of the fall-sown grain.

The principal wheat-producing countries of the world in 1912 and their yields were as follows: United States, 730,627,000 bushels; Russia, 727,011,000 bushels; British India, 366,370,000 bushels; France, 334,871,000 bushels; and Canada, 205,685,000 bushels. According to statistics furnished by the Department of Agriculture, the United States produced 399,919,000 bushels of winter wheat from 26,571,000 acres, this production being about 30,000,000 bushels less than in 1911, when the area was greater by 2,591,000 acres. This reduction in acreage was to a large extent the result of the severe winter. The spring wheat yield amounted to 330,348,000 bushels from an area of 19,243,000 acres, as compared with 190,682,000 bushels and 20,381,000 acres in 1911. The farm value per bushel on December 1, 1912, was 76 cents, the average price for spring and winter wheat, while a year before it was 87.4 cents, and two years before 88.3 cents. The total value of the crop in 1912 was $555,280,000, or only $12,217,000 greater than in 1911, when the total production was about 109,000,000 bushels less. This value was exceeded only by the value of the crops of 1908, 1909, 1910. The farm value of winter wheat December 1, 1912, was 80.9 cents, and that of spring wheat 70.1 cents per bushel.

The leading winter wheat States in 1912 were: Kansas, producing 91,450,000 bushels; Nebraska, 50,850,000 bushels; Washington, 27,269,000 bushels; Missouri, 23,750,000 bushels; Pennsylvania, 22,320,000 bushels; and Oklahoma 20,096,000 bushels. In 1911 the leading States in decreasing order of production were: Kansas, Illinois, Nebraska, Ohio, Missouri, and Indiana; and the range in yield was from 51,030,000 to 34,354,000 bushels. The average yield of winter wheat was 15.1 bushels per acre as against 14.8 bushels in 1911. Among the leading States Washington ranked first, with an average yield of 27.6 bushels per acre, while Oklahoma produced only 12.8 bushels. Spring wheat in 1912 was produced in 19 States, of which 15 also produced winter wheat. The leading States and their yields were as follows: North Dakota, 143,820,000 bushels; Minnesota, 67,038,000 bushels; South Dakota, 52,185,000 bushels; and Washington, 26,459,000 bushels. In all other States the production was under 8,000,000 bushels. The average acre-yield of spring wheat for the United States in 1912 was 17.2, as compared with 9.4 bushels in 1911. Among the leading spring wheat States Washington ranked first, with an average acre-yield of 20.4 bushels. The durum wheat production of the country was estimated at over 40,000,000 bushels, of which North Dakota produced 17,884,000 bushels; South Dakota, 14,343,000 bushels; and Minnesota, 2,334,000 bushels.

On March 1, 1912, about 122,025,000 bushels of wheat were in farmers' hands, or 19.6 per cent. of the crop of 1911, as compared with 162,705,000 bushels, or 25.6 per cent. of the crop of 1910 on March 1, 1911. The wheat exports of 1912 exceeded those of recent years, the quantities sent abroad being mainly from the crop of the year and shipped to offset European shortage in the cereal.

WHEELER, Charles Gilbert. An American chemist and mining geologist, died February, 1912. He was born in London, Canada, and graduated from Harvard College in 1858. He studied in foreign universities and in 1886 was appointed professor of chemistry in the University of Chicago. In 1869 he invented the Babcock chemical fire extinguisher. He acted as geologist and interpreter on the commission to examine the route of the Nicaragua canal in 1899.

WHEELWRIGHT, Edmund March. An American architect, died August 16, 1912. He was born in Roxbury, Mass., in 1854, and graduated from Harvard College in 1876. He studied architecture at the Massachusetts Institute of Technology and later in Europe. On his return to the United States he was employed in the offices of Peabody and Sterns in Boston, and in firms in New York and Albany. In 1883 he started a business of his own and afterwards became a member of the firm of Wheelwright and Haven, and later, Wheelwright, Haven, and Hoyt. He was city architect of Boston from 1891 to 1895. He with R. Clipston Sturgis designed the new Museum of Fine Arts in Boston. He also designed Jordan Hall and the Boston Opera House. He was chief designer of the Cambridge Bridge in 1900. Other works include the Cleveland Museum of Art and the Massachusetts General Hospital. He was the designer of the new Hartford bridge, which cost $2,000,000.

WHISKY. See LIQUORS.

WHITE, Sir GEORGE STUART. An English field marshal, died June 24, 1912. He was born in White Hall, County Antrim, Ireland, in 1835. He enlisted in the army at the age of 18. In 1863 he was made captain and in 1873 major. He became lieutenant-colonel of the Gordon Highlanders and military secretary to the Viceroy of India in 1881. Four years later he participated in the expedition to the Nile. He reached the rank of colonel in 1885, and lieutenant-general in 1895. From 1893 to 1898 he was commander-in-chief of the forces in India. He took a prominent part in the Boer War and conducted the notable defense of Ladysmith, which made his name famous throughout the world. He twice won the Victoria Cross, first in 1879 for conspicuous bravery in the action against the Afghans, and in 1880 in an action also against the Afghans. He took part in Lord Roberts' famous march to Candahar.

WHITE, TRUEMAN CLARK. An American jurist, died February 7, 1912. He was born at Perrysburg, N. Y., in 1840, and was educated at the Springville Academy. He enlisted as a private on the first call for troops in the Civil War and served throughout the conflict, rising to the rank of first lieutenant. After the war he practiced law in Buffalo and became judge of the superior court of that city. He was later appointed judge of the supreme court of the State. His term expired December 31, 1910. Judge White presided at the trial of Leon Czolgosz, who assassinated President McKinley.

WHITE MOUNTAINS. See FORESTRY.

WICKLIFFE, ROBERT C. Representative in Congress from Louisiana, died as the result of accident, June 11, 1912. He was born at Bardstown, Ky., in 1874, and was educated in the public schools of St. Francisville, La., and at Centre College, Ky., graduating from the latter institution in 1895. He studied law at Tulane University, taking a degree in 1887. He then began the practice of law at St. Francisville in 1898. He was a member of the constitutional convention which framed the present constitution of Louisiana. He served throughout the Spanish-American War, and after this resumed the practice of his profession. In 1900 he was elected district-attorney of the 24th judicial district of the State. In 1908 he was a candidate in the Democratic primaries for the nomination to Congress from the 6th district and received the nomination. He was elected to the Sixty-first Congress and reëlected to the Sixty-second.

WIDOWS' PENSIONS. See WELFARE WORK.

WIDOWS' PENSIONS. The frequent objection to child labor legislation, that it inflicts hardship upon widows of the working class who have children thrown out of employment thereby, has finally resulted in widows' pensions as a means of meeting this undoubtedly difficult situation. A number of cities in recent years have established scholarship funds from which children of poor widows affected by advanced child labor laws have been paid small weekly sums in lieu of possible earnings. The children have thus been enabled to attend school and the economic status of the family has remained unchanged. Beginning in 1911 five States have now determined to handle this problem by governmental action. Illinois, Michigan, Missouri, Ohio, and Oklahoma in 1911 made legal provisions whereby the courts or other public authority should pay regular sums to any widowed mother of good character who needs aid. In some cases relief is granted through the school authorities; in some cases it is in the form of textbooks, clothing, and meals, and in others in the form of money. This plan is actively advocated by the National Probation League and the Widowed Mothers' Fund Association of New York. It has been approved by the New York City Commission on Congestion of Population, adopted by the juvenile courts of Chicago and Milwaukee, and was being investigated in 1912 by commissions in Massachusetts and Ohio. One form of solving the problem is the boarding of dependent children with their mothers instead of caring for them in public institutions or in other homes. The courts of California have authorized the "boarding out" of children with their own parents. Similarly the Cook County Juvenile Court had in the summer of 1912 provided for the care of 327 mothers with 1200 children. The cost per child was $5.65 per month, as compared with about $10 under the older plans of institutional care or boarding in homes of strangers. The city of Indianapolis has even gone to the length of building a number of small cement houses which are let, rent free, to working women with children. A free nursery and kindergarten are also provided. The argument is made that it is better for the community that the mother devote her time to the rearing of her children in normal circumstances than that she neglect them in order to earn a small wage for her support. It is pointed out that statistics of the Elmira Reformatory show that 60 per cent. of the inmates were brought up in institutions. Consequently the additional cost to the State is expected to be offset by a decrease in expenditures for criminal prosecutions. Moreover, there will be a lessening of criminal and other pathological social conditions. Since it is clear that a mother cannot both work and at the same time give her children the full services of motherhood, and since the mother may be expected to care more conscientiously for her offspring than strangers, it is believed to be wholly justifiable for the State to assume the responsibility of moderate support. In Massachusetts a committee of the legislature was appointed to investigate the subject and recommend legislation to the 1913 session.

WILLIAM MARSH RICE INSTITUTE, now RICE INSTITUTE. An institution of liberal and technical learning, incorporated in 1891, in Houston, Tex., as the William M. Rice Institute for the Advancement of Literature, Science, and Art. Its founder was William Marsh Rice, a resident of Houston, who had amassed a large fortune. In accordance with the wish of Mr. Rice, the elaboration of plans for the development of the institute were postponed until after his death. This occurred in 1901 under circumstances which led to the charge of murder against Albert J. Patrick (see NEW YORK) and which involved the estate in long years of litigation. When the trustees came into possession of the foundation, which then amounted to about $10,000,000, they invited Dr. Edgar Odell Lovett of Princeton University to assist them in formulating and executing the educational programme of the institute and elected him its president. Dr. Lovett undertook a year's journey of study which extended from England to Japan, and on the completion of this investigation, a site of 300 acres was secured at Houston, and the task of designing a general architectural plan consistent with the programme which had been adopted for the institute was undertaken.

In 1911, on the seventy-fifth anniversary of Texan independence, the corner stone of the administration building was laid by the trustees. This building, together with the first wing of the engineering quadrangle, the mechanical laboratory, and power house, and the first residential hall for men, neared completion at the end of 1912. The initial building schedule includes also special laboratories for instruction and investigation in physics, chemistry, and biology, and in the application of these sciences to the arts of industry and commerce.

The academic work of the institute began on September 23, 1912, and on October 10, 11, and 12 imposing ceremonies of inauguration accompanied the formal opening. Distinguished scholars and scientists from America and foreign universities participated in the proceedings. Among these were Prof. Rafael Altamira y Crevea, of Madrid, Spain, Prof. Emile Borel of Paris, France, Prof. Hugo de Vries, of Amsterdam, Holland, Prof. Sir Henry Jones of Glasgow, Scotland, Baron Dairoku Kikuchi, formerly Japanese minister of education, Prof. Wilhelm Ostwald, formerly professor of chemistry in the University College, London. All these scholars read or presented inaugural lectures, and a poem was read by Dr. Henry Van Dyke. The visiting scholars were welcomed by the governor of Texas, the mayor of Houston, and the board of trustees of the institute.

Tuition and matriculation at the institute are free. The endowment of the institute, approximately $10,000,000, makes it seventh in rank in amount of endowment among American universities.

The initial staff of the institute was organized in 1912 in the faculty of science and the faculty of letters. At the end of the year the following members of the faculty of science had been chosen: Prof. Percy John Daniell, research associate in applied mathematics; William Franklin Edwards, formerly president of the University of Washington, lecturer in chemistry; Griffith Conrad Evans, Ph. D., assistant professor of pure mathematics; Julian Sorell Huxley, formerly of Oxford University, research associate in biology; Francis Ellis Johnson, instructor in electrical engineering; Edgar Odell Lovett, Ph. D., formerly professor of mathematics in Princeton University and later head of the department of astronomy, professor of mathematics; William Ward Watkins, D. Sc., instructor in architectural engineering; Harold Albert Wilson, formerly of McGill University, professor of physics. The faculty of letters had not been established at the end of the year. The subjects of instruction which will first be established are mathematics, physics, chemistry, biology, engineering, architecture, ancient languages, modern languages, history and politics, philosophy and psychology, economics and sociology, and art and archæology.

WILLIAMS COLLEGE. An institution of higher education at Williamstown, Mass., founded in 1793. The total enrollment in the college in the autumn of 1912 was 517. The faculty numbered 56. There were several important changes in the faculty during the year. These included the resignations of Assistant Professor James Percival King of the German department, who became professor of German at the University of Rochester, and Assistant Professor Clyde Shepherd Atchison to become professor of mathematics at Washington and Jefferson College. The following were added to the staff of instruction: Prof. Robert Longley Taylor, assistant professor of Romance languages at Dartmouth College, to be professor of Romance languages in place of Prof. Karl Ephraim Weston, who was transferred to the chair of the history of art and civilization. Prof. P. G. Wright was appointed instructor of economics during the absence of Assistant Professor David Taggart Clark. Several additional instructors were appointed in other departments. The total productive funds of the college on March 31, 1912, amounted to $3,183,468 and the annual income is about $225,000. The library contained about 75,000 volumes. President, Harry A. Garfield, LL. D.

WILSON, ANDREW. An English journalist and lecturer, died September 25, 1912. He was born in Edinburgh in 1852, and was educated at Edinburgh University and Medical School. In 1876 he was appointed lecturer on zoölogy and comparative anatomy at the Edinburgh Medical School and was for several years editor of *Health* and examiner on the faculty of medicine at the University of Wisconsin. Among his publications are: *Studies in Life and Sense; Leisure Time Studies; Chapters on Evolution; Leaves from a Naturalist's Notebook; Brain and Nerve;* and *The Modern Physician*. He was also an extensive contributor to magazine literature and contributed "Science Jottings" to the *Illustrated London News*.

WILSON, BUTLER H. See BAR ASSOCIATION, AMERICAN.

WILSON, JOHN L. An American newspaper proprietor and former United States Senator from Washington, died November 6, 1912. He was born in Crawfordsville, Ind., in 1850, and graduated from Wabash College in 1874. In 1880 he was elected a member of the Indiana House of Representatives. He removed to Washington and in 1882 was appointed receiver of public moneys at Spokane Falls, Wash., remaining in this position until 1886. In 1889 he was elected to the Fifty-first Congress and was reëlected to the Fifty-second and Fifty-third Congresses. He resigned from the latter in 1895. In February of the same year he was appointed United States Senator to fill the unexpired term of John B. Allen, Republican. He was the first member of Congress from the new State of Washington. Previous to his election to the House of Representatives he had served as delegate to Congress from the then Territory of Washington. He was proprietor of the *Seattle Post Intelligencer* of Seattle, Wash.

WILSON, (THOMAS) WOODROW. Elected President of the United States November 6, 1912. He was born in Staunton, Va., on December 28, 1856, of Scotch-Irish stock. His paternal grandfather, James Wilson, came to the United States from Ireland about 105 years ago, and settled in Philadelphia, where he engaged in the newspaper business with William Duane. He married Anne Adams, an Irish girl, who came over on the same ship. James Wilson did not remain long in Philadelphia, but afterwards established papers in several other cities of Pennsylvania. He died during the cholera epidemic of 1857, leaving four sons. The youngest son, Joseph Ruggles Wilson, father of Woodrow Wilson, was born in 1822. He learned the printing trade, but his inclinations were for the church. After studying at Washington and Jefferson College and at the Western Theological Seminary and Princeton Theological Seminary, he was ordained to the Presbyterian ministry. In 1849 he married Janet Woodrow, whose forebears were Scotch ministers and Covenanters. Joseph Ruggles Wilson became a professor in rhetoric in Jefferson College immediately after his marriage, and afterwards served as professor of chemistry in Hampden-Sidney College. He was called to a pastorate in Staunton in 1855, and there his son, Woodrow Wilson, was born. His parents removed to Augusta, Ga., in 1858, and thereafter, until he left to attend Princeton College, his home was in the South. His early education was received in Augusta, Ga. In 1870 the family removed to Columbia, S. C., where the father had been appointed professor in the Southern Presbyterian Theological Seminary. Woodrow Wilson was sent to Davidson College, at Davidson, N. C., where he remained for only one year when, on account of illness, he was obliged to return home. In the following year, 1875, he entered Princeton College, graduating in the class of 1879. Among his classmates were Mahlon Pitney, now a justice of the supreme court, Dr. A. S. Halsey, secretary of the Presbyterian board of foreign missions, Robert Bridges, an editor of *Scribner's Magazine*, and several other persons who afterwards became notable.

His career as a scholar at Princeton was not especially brilliant. His standing at graduation was forty-first in a class of 122. He was, however, prominent in other phases of intercollegiate life. He was editor of the *Princetonian*, an active member of the American Whig Debating Society, and also organized a debating society among his friends. His interest in public life and the study of government was strong even in those early days, and it was said that at that time he made a resolution to support himself as a publicist. After his graduation he went to the Law School of the University of Virginia, where he remained until January 1, 1881. While he was at the law school he was awarded the medal in oratory given by the Thomas Jefferson Literary Society. He was obliged to cut short his law studies on account of illness and returned to his home, which was then at Wilmington, N. C. In 1882 he was admitted to the bar and entered into partnership with E. I. Renick at Atlanta, Ga. He soon found that the active practice of law was not attractive and he began the writing of *Congressional Government*, the success of which later decided him against law as a profession.

In 1883 he decided to return to his studies and entered Johns Hopkins University for a post-graduate course in the science of government. He received the degree of Ph. D. from Johns Hopkins in recognition of his thesis on *Congressional Government*, which was published in 1885. It at once attracted wide attention and became the standard textbook in many high schools and colleges. James Bryce in his *American Commonwealth* acknowledged his obligation to Woodrow Wilson. The publication of this work brought to its author calls to the chairs of several colleges, and he finally accepted the position of associate professor of history and political economy at Bryn Mawr College in 1885. In the same year he married, at Savannah, Ellen Louise Axson, daughter of the Rev. S. Edward Axson.

In 1886 Dr. Wilson lectured at Johns Hopkins University and in 1888 was appointed professor of history and political economy at Wesleyan University. While serving in this chair he received the appointment of professor of jurisprudence and political economy at Princeton University where he entered upon his duties in 1890. He soon became one of the most popular members of the faculty. While at Wesleyan University his textbook, *The State*, had been published. This book has the distinction of serving as the accredited textbook in more than one hundred universities, including Oxford University. During his professorship at Princeton he published, *Division and Reunion*, *An Old Master and Other Political Essays*, *Mere Literature*, and *Life of Washington*. His most comprehensive work, *The History of the American People*, was published in 1902. In the same year he was unanimously elected president of Princeton University to succeed President Patton, who had resigned. He at once undertook measures of reform in the curriculum and administration of the university. His first work was to systematize four well defined courses leading to distinct degrees. He also brought about higher standards of admission and of routine scholarships. His most notable service at Princeton, however, was the establishment of a preceptorial system, which was at this time an innovation in the college administration. By this plan sixty-five new professors were added to the faculty and to each of them groups of students, numbering from two to five were assigned for personal supervision. These reforms were not made without opposition. His next attempt to bring about radical reform failed. This was the proposal to introduce the quadrangle system, and its purpose and effect would have been largely to abolish the upper class clubs, which are a distinctive feature of the social life at Princeton University. Dr. Wilson's plan was not to destroy these clubs, but to reorganize them on a basis of democracy where all students might enjoy their advantages. This he proposed to do by making the clubs a part of the university. This plan when first presented to the board of trustees was adopted almost unanimously, but in the summer following the wealthy members of the university alumni clubs, who had been members of the exclusive upper class clubs, brought so much pressure to bear upon the university board that Dr. Wilson was requested to withdraw the quadrangle plan. These and other attempts to bring about more democratic conditions at Princeton won for him, to a certain extent, the hostility of the alumni of the university, especially the younger alumni.

During his administration at Princeton he had continued to write and lecture on political and social questions, and he became widely known throughout the country. As early as 1906 suggestions were made that he be a candidate for public office, but it was not until 1910, when conditions in New Jersey indicated the possibility of electing a Democratic governor, that serious thought was given to Dr. Wilson as a candidate for high office. James Smith, Jr., former United States Senator from New Jersey and the dominant figure in Democratic politics in the State, conceived the idea that Dr. Wilson would be an excellent candidate for governor. After a conference with other leading members of the Democratic party he was offered the nomination and accepted it. Conditions in New Jersey at that time were such as to call for severe and immediate reforms. The State was practically under the control of the large transportation companies which crossed it. After a stirring campaign in which Dr. Wilson took an active and prominent part, he was elected. He at once began to urge upon the legislature the necessity of passing measures leading to radical reforms. Before he had been governor for two weeks he came out for direct primaries, and it was largely through his influence that a law providing for them passed the legislature. He also brought about in a short time a direct primary for the selection of a successor to John Kean, United States Senator, and in that vote James E. Martine received the most votes among the Democratic candidates. This brought about a split between Governor Wilson and former Senator Smith, who himself had been a candidate for the nomination, but had received fewer votes than Mr. Martine. In spite of the efforts of Mr. Smith to annul the results of the direct primary vote, Governor Wilson remained firm and Martine was elected senator by the legislature.

Governor Wilson's administration was not popular with the political leaders of his party, but he soon obtained and held throughout office the support and approval of the people. His success as a Democratic governor in a normally Republican State made him early in 1911 a conspicuous candidate for the Democratic presidential nomination. He had, in fact, even before his election as governor, been frequently mentioned as a strong candidate, especially by Colonel George Harvey, editor of *Harper's Weekly* and the *North American Review*. While in his writings on American government he had taken rather a conservative point of view in his judgment of measures urged by the more radical wing of the Democratic party under W. J. Bryan—such measures as the initiative, referendum, and recall—during his term as governor he avowed his belief in these measures under the proper conditions. He thus made himself acceptable not only to the conservative but to the progressive element of the party. The details of his campaign for the nomination and election will be found in the article PRESIDENTIAL CAMPAIGN.

During Governor Wilson's term in office in New Jersey there were passed, largely through his efforts, a direct primary law, a public utilities law, an employers' liability law, a corrupt practices act, a measure providing for the substitution of indeterminate sentences, the reorganization of the State school system, the abolition of contract labor in penal institutions, measures for the regulation of the age, employment, safety, health, and working hours of persons employed in mercantile establishments, a law extending the civil service to employees of the State, county, and municipalities, and an optional commission form of government act for cities, under what was originally known as the Galveston plan.

WINDWARD ISLANDS. The British West Indian colonies of St. Lucia, St. Vincent, and Grenada, together with the Grenadines, attached partly to Grenada and partly to St. Vincent. Each colony retains its separate institutions. See the articles under the separate titles. Sir James Hayes Sadler was governor and commander-in-chief in 1912, residing at St. George's, in Grenada. Geographically the Windward Islands include Barbados, Trinidad, and Tobago.

WINE. See LIQUORS.

WINES, FREDERICK HOWARD. An American statistician and penologist, died January 31, 1912. He was born in Philadelphia in 1838, and graduated from Washington College in 1857. He afterwards studied theology at the Princeton Theological Seminary, but was obliged to discontinue his course on account of weakness of the eyes. He was licensed by the presbytery of St. Louis in 1860. He served in the Civil War from 1862 to 1864 as chaplain in the Federal army. He afterwards returned to Princeton Theological Seminary, graduating in 1865. In the same year he was ordained to the Presbyterian ministry. From 1865 to 1869 he was pastor of the first church of Springfield, Mass. In the latter year he was appointed secretary of the Illinois State board of commissioners of public charities. He served in this position until 1893 and again from 1897 to 1899. In the latter year he was appointed assistant director of the United States Census. He held this office until 1902 and in the following year was appointed secretary of the New Jersey State Charities Aid Association, where he remained for one year. From 1909 until the time of his death he was statistical secretary of the Illinois State board of administration of public institutions. He was special lecturer on penological subjects at the Lowell Institute, Boston, and at Harvard, Charleston, Johns Hopkins, and other universities. In 1878 he was a member of the International Prison Conference and was president of the National Conference of Charities and Corrections in 1883. He served also as president of the National Prison Association. He was the author of *Defective, Dependent, and Delinquent Classes in the United States* (a volume of the Tenth Census); *Crime, Pauperism, and Benevolence* (a volume of the Eleventh Census); *Punishment and Reformation* (1895); *The Liquor Problem in Its Legislative Aspects* (1897-98).

WOODROW WILSON

ELECTED PRESIDENT OF THE UNITED STATES, 1912

He also published numerous pamphlets on charities and on penology.

WING, Yung. A Chinese statesman and scholar, died April, 1912. He was born in China in 1828 and was one of the first of the group of Chinese youth sent to the United States for education. He graduated from Yale College in 1854. In 1872-4 he brought 120 Chinese youths to the United States to be educated. In 1898 when the empress dowager obtained control of the government he became allied with the reform party. Most of his time, however, was spent in the United States. He received the degree of LL. D. from Yale in 1876. In 1910 he edited a volume of *Reminiscences*.

WINKELMANN, Hermann. A German dramatic tenor, died January, 1912. He was born in 1845 at Brunswick. He did not adopt the profession of singer until he had reached manhood. He began his career at Sondershausen and then went to Darmstadt and Hamburg. In 1882 he became identified with Wagnerian drama, taking the part of "Parsifal" at Bayreuth. He was so successful that he was engaged for the Imperial Opera at Vienna. Here he sang in Wagner's operas with Madame Materna and Herr Scaria. This trio made a tour of the United States in 1884.

WINNIPEG, Man. See Municipal Ownership.

WIRELESS TELEGRAPHY. See Safety at Sea.

WIRELESS TELEGRAPHY AND TELEPHONY. Public interest in wireless communication was developed to an unprecedented degree as a result of the *Titanic* disaster. Federal regulations were established which enforce the installation of an efficient auxiliary transmitter and the carrying of two operators on passenger vessels, require all operators commercially engaged in interstate and foreign work to obtain a federal license, and forbid the establishment of radio stations within fifteen miles of certain important naval plants. The federal government has determined upon the erection of a chain of powerful stations connecting the new Arlington station with the Canal Zone and the Philippine Islands. The former is already complete and in use. It is said to have received clear transmission from Honolulu and to possess a sending radius of 3000 miles. Important developments in sending and receiving apparatus include a duplex arrangement whereby telegraphic messages may be sent and received at a station simultaneously. There has been marked progress in the direction of the use of the high-frequency alternator for sending purposes. Machines of small size have been developed for frequencies of 100,000 and 200,000 cycles, which considerably exceed the necessary limit for wireless use. It is predicted that suitable machines of a few hundreds of kilowatts will soon be available and will supplant the existing arc type of transmission, thereby greatly increasing the range and the independence of atmospheric conditions.

Announcement has been made of the successful use of the wireless detector in predicting the approach of storms by Professor Tourpain at his experimental post at La Rochelle, France.

An international conference on time agreed to the establishment of a central bureau at Paris, whence time is to be signaled officially from the Eiffel Tower station.

Experiments in wire-directed aerial telephony made by its inventor, Major Squier, have demonstrated the practicability and importance of tuning the line to resonance at both the receiving and transmitting end, using the Audion detector and the high-resistance telephone receiver. The range of practicable frequencies extends from 10,000 to 100,000 cycles per second. A system of wireles telephony developed by Moretti and Vanni was tried successfully in Italy between Rome, Palermo, and other points over a range of about 250 miles with excellent communication. Bethenod announced that he has succeeded in increasing the length of the wave given off by the antennæ by combining a new system of induction coils with a new form of antennæ and a double-phase generator, all sparks and intermediary apparatus being suppressed. The arrangement facilitates to a marked degree the tuning of the receiver and transmitter. The inventor claims that his system brings wireless telephony close to a commercial basis and greatly extends its possible range of distance.

WISCONSIN. Population. According to the Census Bureau statistics during 1912 out of a total population of 2,333,860 in 1910, 512,569 were foreign-born whites, compared with 515,705 in 1900. The largest proportion came from Germany, 233,018; from Norway, 56,948; from Austria, 38,862; from Russia, 29,786; from Sweden, 25,676; from Canada, 16,875; from Denmark, 16,454; from Ireland, 14,047; and from England, 13,959. Other European countries were represented by smaller proportions. In the city of Milwaukee, with a total population of 373,857, there were 111,456 foreign-born whites. Of these, 64,720 were from Germany. The negroes in the State in 1910 numbered 2900 and mulattoes 1143. In 1890 the negroes numbered 2444 and the mulattoes 1437.

Agriculture. The acreage, value, and production of the principal crops in 1911 and 1911 are shown in the table below:

		Acreage	Prod. Bu.	Value
Corn	1912	1,632,000	58,262,000	$29,714,000
	1911	1,600,000	58,080,000	34,848,000
Wheat	1912	188,000	3,564,000	2,958,000
	1911	195,000	3,097,000	2,788,000
Oats	1912	2,272,000	84,746,000	27,119,000
	1911	2,250,000	67,050,000	30,172,000
Rye	1912	341,000	6,240,000	3,806,000
	1911	355,000	6,025,000	5,069,000
Potatoes	1912	291,000	34,920,000	11,873,000
	1911	280,000	26,600,000	10,108,000
Hay	1912	2,250,000	a 3,600,000	43,560,000
	1911	2,079,000	a 2,495,000	38,922,000
Tobacco	1912	42,200	b 54,438,000	5,988,000
	1911	41,000	51,250,000	5,125,000

a Tons. b Pounds.

Mineral Production. The production of iron ore in the State in 1911 amounted to 559,763 long tons valued at $1,386,616, as compared with 1,149,551 long tons valued at $3,610,349 in 1910.

The lead produced in the State in 1911 amounted to 3353 short tons valued at $301,770, compared with 4413 short tons valued at $388,344 in 1910. The zinc produced amounted to 28,774 tons valued at $3,280,236, compared with 25,927 tons valued at $2,800,116 in 1910.

Manufactures. The Thirteenth Census statistics are for the calendar year 1909 and were compiled in 1912. While Wisconsin is largely an agricultural State, the advance in relative importance of its manufacturing industries has been marked. While in 1849 it ranked nineteenth among the States in manufactures, in 1909 it occupied eighth place. It will be seen from the following table that in 1909 there were 9721 manufacturing establishments, giving employment to 213,426 persons.

	Number or Amount 1909	1904	P. C. of Inc. 1904-'09
Number of establishments	9,721	8,558	13.6
Persons engaged in manufactures ..	213,426	173,572	23.0
Proprietors and firm members...	8,556	7,961	7.5
Salaried employees.	22,287	14,220	56.7
Wage earners (average number)..	182,583	151,391	20.6
Primary horsepower	554,179	440,234	25.9
Capital	$605,657,000	$412,647,000	46.8
Expenses	525,747,000	359,899,000	46.1
Services	119,642,000	86,970,000	37.6
Salaries	25,737,000	15,498,000	66.1
Wages	93,905,000	71,472,000	31.4
Materials	346,357,000	227,255,000	52.4
Miscellaneous	59,748,000	45,674,000	30 8
Value of products..	590,306,000	411,140,000	43.6
Value of p oducts less cost of materials	243,949,000	183,885,000	32.7

The largest value of product was in the lumber and timber industries, $57,969,000; foundry and machine shop products, $54,124,000; butter, cheese, and condensed milk, $53,843,000; leather, $44,668,000; malt liquors, $32,126,000. Other industries whose product was valued at more than $10,000,000 were flour and gristmill products, slaughtering and meat-packing, paper and wood pulp, furniture and refrigerators, industries relating to railroads, boots and shoes, printing and publishing, automobiles, agricultural implements, and the manufactures of iron and steel. The total number of wage-earners in the State was 213,426, of whom 186,350 were male and 27,076 were female. The prevailing hours of labor for more than five-sixths of the wage-earners ranged from 54 to 60 a week; only 9 per cent. of the total being employed in establishments where they were less than 54 a week, and only 6.7 per cent. in those where they were more than 60 a week. The largest number of wage-earners was in Milwaukee, 59,502; in Racine were 8381; in Kenosha, 6449; in Oshkosh, 5778. The value of the manufacturing industries of Milwaukee was $208,323,630.

FINANCE. The receipts for the fiscal year 1912 amounted to $14,626,753, and the expenditures to $13,985,248. The balance on hand at the end of the year was $3,161,512. The chief sources of income were the railroad and corporation taxes and inheritance taxes. The chief expenditures were for educational purposes, charitable and penal institutions, for the State government, and for the new capitol. The State debt, which is the amount the State owes its trust funds at the end of the fiscal year, was $2,251,000.

POLITICS AND GOVERNMENT

The legislature did not meet in 1912, as the sessions are biennial and the last was held in 1911. The next session convenes January 8, 1913.

There was much political interest in the State during the year, both on local and national issues. Senator La Follette up to the time of the Republican national convention, was an aggressive candidate for the Progressive nomination. (See PRESIDENTIAL CAMPAIGN.) He received strong support in his native State and in the presidential primary held on April 2 he carried the State by a large plurality of votes. He received 131,920 votes, and President Taft 47,630. Mr. Roosevelt did not appear as a candidate on the ballots in this election. At the national convention he contested the temporary chairmanship with Senator Root.

In accordance with the vote at the presidential primary the Wisconsin delegation was instructed to vote for Senator La Follete. In these primaries Governor Wilson received a majority of the votes for presidential candidate and the Democratic delegates were accordingly instructed to vote for him at the Democratic State convention. On September 3 Governor McGovern was renominated and Judge John C. Karel was chosen as the Democratic nominee. The Progressive party had no candidate in the field for State offices. The result of the election on November 5 was as follows: Wilson 164,228, Taft 130,695, Roosevelt 62,460, Debs 33,481, Chafin 8526, and Reimer 522. Governor Wilson's plurality was 33,533. For governor, McGovern, Republican, received 179,360; Karel, Democrat, 167,316; Thompson, Socialist Democrat, 34,468; Hill, Prohibition, 9433; Curtis, Socialist Labor, 3253.

OTHER EVENTS. A sub-committee of the Senate committee on privileges and elections, appointed in 1911 to inquire into the charges of corruption in the election of Senator Stephenson, agreed on January 18 upon a report in which it was held that the charges of bribery and corruption had not been proved. On February 10 the full committee ordered, by a vote of 8 to 5, a report exonerating Senator Stephenson. Five members of the committee, three Republicans and two Democrats, signed the majority report holding that the admitted expenditure of $107,000 to obtain the nominaton raised a presumption of guilt which had not been removed by the evidence. On March 26 the Senate by a vote of 29 to 27, refused to declare Senator Stephenson's seat vacant, and on the following day by a vote of 40 to 34 it declared that the charges against him had not been proved and that he was entitled to the seat. The vote for Stephenson was 28 Republicans and 12 Democrats, while against him were 18 Democrats and 16 Republicans.

Municipal elections were held in Milwaukee on April 2. These resulted in the defeat of the Socialist candidate for mayor, Emil Seidel, who had been mayor for two years. Mr. Seidel was defeated by Dr. G. A. Bading, candidate of the combined Republican and Democratic parties. Dr. Bading's majority was about 13,000. Over 80,000 votes were cast, as against 60,000 in the previous municipal election.

The income tax law enacted by the legislature of 1911 was held constitutional by the Supreme Court of the State on January 9.

The measure for the control of water power was declared unconstitutional January 31.

STATE GOVERNMENT. Governor, F. C. McGovern; Lieutenant-Governor, Thomas Morris; Secretary of State, John S. Donald; Treasurer, Henry Johnson; Attorney-General, W. C. Owen; Superintendent of Education, C. P. Cary; Commissioner of Insurance, H. L. E. Kern; Commissioners of Public Lands, Secretary of State, Attorney-General, and State Treasurer—all Republicans.

JUDICIARY. Supreme Court — Chief Justice, John B. Winslow, Democrat; Associate Justices, William H. Timlin, Democrat; R. G. Siebecker, Democrat; A. J. Vinje, Republican; Rouje D. Marshall, Republican; J. C. Kerwin, Republican; John Barnes, Democrat; Clerk, Clarence Kellogg, Republican.

STATE LEGISLATURE, 1913. Senate, Democrats 6, Republicans 23, Socialist 1, Nonpartisans 3; House, Democrats 24, Republicans 57, Socialists 6, Nonpartisans 13; joint ballot, Democrats 30, Republicans 80, Socialists 7, Nonpartisans 16. Republican majority, Senate 13, House 14, joint ballot 27.

The representatives in Congress will be found in the article UNITED STATES, section *Congress*.

WISCONSIN, UNIVERSITY OF. A State institution for higher education at Madison, Wis., founded in 1848. The total enrollment in the autumn of 1912 was 4014, which does not include the summer session for 1912 or the total for the short courses which begin December 1. The division among the departments of the university was as follows: College of letters and science, 2329; school of music, 60; college of engineering, 655; law school, 160; college of agriculture, 802; medical school, 65; Wisconsin library school, 36. The faculty numbered 595. During the year Prof. Eugene Kühnemann of Breslau, Germany, was appointed the first Carl Schurz memorial professor; Prof. Heinrich Keidel was appointed Prussian exchange professor, and Thomas Wood Stevens was appointed lecturer in art. The art department was newly created in 1912. The university is supported chiefly by the State. Its productive funds amounted at the end of the year 1912 to $665,885, and the income from the productive funds to $31,134. The library contains 185,079 bound volumes and about 60,000 pamphlets. President, Charles R. Van Hise, Ph. D.

WOMAN SUFFRAGE. In 1912 votes for women became a political question in the United States. Miss Jane Addams of Hull House spoke before the resolutions committee of the Republican national convention at Chicago and Dr. Anna Howard Shaw, president of the National American Woman Suffrage Association, addressed the resolutions committee of the Democratic national convention at Baltimore. Mrs. Florence Collins Porter and Mrs. Elizabeth Blaney of California were delegates to the Republican convention; Mrs. W. W. Pitzer of Colorado (sister of Champ Clark, Speaker of the House of Representatives) and Mrs. Mary Arkwright Hutton of the State of Washington were delegates to the national Democratic convention. A number of women were delegates to the national Socialist convention at Indianapolis and to the Progressive convention at Chicago. Jane Addams seconded the nomination of Theodore Roosevelt as Progressive candidate for President.

The American people were greatly impressed by the dignity and intelligence of the women who took part in these great conventions and also aided their parties in the campaigns succeeding them. Equal suffrage was made a plank in the platform of three of the national parties —Progressive, Socialist, and Prohibition—and, in a number of States, was endorsed by all five parties. At the November elections an equal suffrage amendment was submitted in six States. This amendment passed in Arizona, Kansas, and Oregon. Each one of these States is adjacent to a State which had previously granted equal suffrage, the list being California (1911), Washington (1910), Iowa and Utah (1896), Colorado (1893), Wyoming (1869). The amendment was lost in Wisconsin and Ohio. In Michigan the majority against woman suffrage was only 760. The charge of election frauds was very freely and generally made, but in spite of the strong evidence of illegality it was decided wiser to resubmit the amendment in 1913, rather than go through the tedious and expensive process of proving fraud in the courts.

In all of the States where the amendment was submitted active campaigns were carried on during the summer. Many interesting forms of peaceful propaganda were developed. The most striking feature of these campaigns was, however, their economy, the average cost where the amendment carried being only 3 cents per woman. Two million women of the United States are now eligible to vote at all elections on the same terms as men.

The number of enrolled and dues-paying members of the National American Woman Suffrage Association on January 1, 1912, was about 100,000. This was increased to approximately 250,000 by January 1, 1913. At the annual convention of the National Association, in Philadelphia, November 21-26, there were delegates from practically all of the States of the United States. No hall in Philadelphia was large enough to hold the crowds which tried to attend the open meetings of the convention.

The most conspicuous demonstration of the year was the torchlight parade in New York on November 9 to celebrate the victories of the fall elections. Ten thousand women marchers represented the various States of the United States, the foreign countries where women are enfranchised, and the occupational and professional openings to women. There were also parades in Baltimore, at the time of the Democratic convention; in Columbus, Ohio, at the close of the suffrage campaign in that State, and in New York in May to impress on the legislature of that State the strong demand for equal suffrage. That the suffragists of the United States do not depend on spectacular demonstrations alone is shown by the fact that the National Association published and sold 3,000,000 pieces of suffrage literature in the year 1912. A votes for women moving-picture play, written and acted by suffragists, was shown all over the United States. The most prominent men and women in the country are constantly in demand for suffrage speeches. The question is now considered one of great intellectual and social importance as well as of political expediency.

Delegates have been appointed from the United States to the Congress of the International Suffrage Alliance in Budapest, June 15-20, 1913. They are Dr. Anna Howard Shaw, Miss Jane Addams, Mrs Joseph Bowen, Mrs. Stanley McCormick (all officers of the National Association), Mrs. Emma B. Sweet, Mrs. Frederick Nathan, Mrs. Tod Helmuth, Mrs. Minnie Rutherford, Mrs. Henry Villard, Miss Ruutz-Reese, Miss Anna Maxwell Jones, and Mrs. O. H. P. Belmont. Mrs. Carrie Chapman Catt, president of the Alliance, has recently returned from a two years' trip around the world, in which she organized for suffrage the women of many countries, including Burmah, India, China, South Africa, and Hawaii. Delegates from twenty-six countries will be present at the congress. The International Conference of Men's Leagues for Woman Suffrage will take place in Budapest while the woman's congress is in session. See GREAT BRITAIN, *History*.

WOMEN IN INDUSTRY. The most extensive and thoroughgoing investigation of the employment of women and children in industry, at any rate, in the United States, is contained in the *Report on Condition of Women and Child Wage-Earners in the United States*, which was issued during 1910-11-12 by the Department of Commerce and Labor. This report comprises nineteen volumes, of which the titles and authors, where specialists were employed, are as follows: "Cotton textile industry," 1044 pp.; "Men's ready-made clothing," 878 pp.; "Glass industry," 970 pp.; "Silk industry," 592 pp.; "Wage-earning women in stores and factories," 384 pp.; "Beginings of child labor legislation," by Elizabeth Lewis Otey, 225 pp.; "Conditions under which children leave school to go to work," 309 pp.; "Juvenile delinquency and its relation to employment," 177 pp.; "History of women in industry in the United States," by Helen L. Sumner, 277 pp.; "History of women in trade unions," by John B. Andrews and W. D. P. Bliss, 236 pp.; "Employment of women in the metal trades," by Lucian W. Chaney, 107 pp.; "Employment of women in laundries," 121 pp.; "Employment of women and infant mortality"; "Causes of death among women and child cotton-mill operatives"; "Relation of occupation to criminality of women," by Mary Conyngton, 119 pp.; "Family budgets of typical cotton-mill workers," by Wood F. Worcester and Daisy Worthington Worcester, 225 pp.; "Hookworm disease among cotton-mill operatives"; "Employment of women and children in selected industries"; "Labor laws and factory conditions."

Every phase of the employment of both women and children was covered in this report, and incidentally much light was thrown on the employment of men in various industries. The cotton, the men's ready-made clothing, the glass, and the silk industries were chosen for special investigation because of the large number of women and children employed. Thus in the cotton industry such workers constitute 53.4 per cent. of all workers employed, there being altogether 60 per cent. more women than in any other manufacturing industry and more children than in any other four industries combined. The ready-made clothing industry ranks second in number of women employed and is worthy of special attention because much of it is home work. The silk industry similarly is specially dependent on women and children, who constituted in 1905 two-thirds of all wage-earners. All of the investigations were made in a thoroughgoing maner and constitute models of completeness and freedom from bias. Nevertheless the material relating as it does to the year 1908 became in many respects antiquated before the reports were published. As a whole this investigation showed clearly the immense social waste due to existing conditions of woman and child labor. Nearly everywhere the investigators found conditions undermining the health of the present generation and reducing the vitality of the next; unnecessary risk of accidents and disease; a reduction of industrial vigor due to insufficient wages and consequent insufficient standard of living; the loss of future welfare through the haphazard drifting of children into unsuitable occupations, where ambition was soon stifled. The report showed that many factors enter into the determination of the difference between the wages of men on the one hand and women and children on the other. These wages are really fixed in different markets. The immaturity of the workers and their consequent employment in unskilled trades, the brevity of their industrial careers and their lack of organization are all causes of the low wage level for women. The report emphasizes the youthfulness of the typical woman wage-earner. Thus, in southern cotton mills 61 per cent. of the women employed were under 21; in Pennsylvania silk mills 74.2 per cent. of the women employed were under 21, 51.7 per cent. being in the age group 16-20; and fully one-half of the women in the clothing industry were under 21. Another interesting and surprising conclusion was that the girl who goes into industrial work for the sake of pin money is very rare. In the New York stores 84.3 per cent. of the women employed who lived at home contributed their entire earnings to family support; in New York factories the percentage was 88.1. The report presents clearly the viciousness of home work and recommends the abolition of home finishing on the ground that its regulation is impossible, and that its existence is a danger to the public health.

An example of the character of material and conclusions in these volumes is furnished by volume four treating of the Silk Industry in New Jersey and Pennsylvania. A limited number of mills in each State was studied intensively. In Pennsylvania mills visited, 67.8 per cent. of all the employees were found to be women, and 23.2 per cent. children, leaving only 9 per cent. men. These figures contrasted with 49.6 per cent. women, 6 per cent. children, and 44.4 per cent. men in New Jersey silk mills. Many children were found working at ages below the legal limit; and most of the mills failed to keep affidavits of children as required by law. Moreover, multitudes of false affidavits were found; so that in New Jersey silk manufacturing districts 4.7 per cent. and in Pennsylvania 16.8 per cent. of children of ages 6-13 were at work. Nightwork was found to be common in Pennsylvania, one-fifth of the mills having it. There was a sharp contrast between the wages of New Jersey and Pennsylvania operatives. The weekly wages in throwing mills in the former State were distributed as follows: For women over 16 years, 8.7 per cent. received less than $4, 15.8 per cent. received $4 to $6, and 75.5 per cent. received over $6; for girls under 16 years the percentages for the same wage groups were 40.1, 41, and 18.9 respectively. In Pennsylvania the percentages for the same wage groups among women over 16 years were 57.2, 37.1, and 5.7 respectively and among girls under 16 years, 91.6, 7.6, and 0.8. Thus the silk industry, particularly in Pennsylvania, revealed many of the characteristics of a parasitic industry with its large proportion of woman and child labor, the absence of labor organizations, and wages below normal standards of even poorly paid industries.

LEGISLATION. The most important law relating to the employment of women in industry was the Massachusetts minimum-wage law. (See MINIMUM WAGE.) Other legislation relating to women in industry was enacted in Arizona, Kentucky, Maryland, Massachusetts, New Jersey, New York, and Virginia. Arizona prohibited employment of women in occupations in which they must remain standing or in or about any mine, quarry, or coal breaker. Kentucky prohibited the employment of women under 21 for more than 10 hours a day or 60 hours per week, except for domestic service and nursing. Women of any age may not be employed more than that length of time in laundries, bakeries, factories, workshops, stores, hotels, restaurants, telephone exchanges, telegraph offices, or mercantile, manufacturing, or mechanical establishments. The new Kentucky law also requires all employers of women to provide seats for them when not necessarily engaged in active work; all stores must provide at least one seat for every three females employed; and must provide wash and toilet rooms. Maryland similarly prohibited the employment of any woman in any manufacturing, mercantile, or mechanical establishment, printing office, bakery, or laundry more than 10 hours a day or 60 hours a week. If a woman is employed before 6 A. M. or after 10 P. M. she may not work more than 8 hours a day, and no woman may work more than 6 hours continually without an interval of at least one-half hour. Exception as to hours is made for Allegany County, where women may be employed as many as 12 hours per day during rush seasons, provided the average length of day for the year does not exceed 9 hours. Massachusetts directed the State board of health to investigate rooms where women are employed and to make rules regulating them. It also strengthened the law requiring the provision of seats for women employees. New Jersey limited to 10 hours a day, or 60 hours a week, the employment of women in manufacturing and mercantile establishments, bakeries, laundries, and restaurants, but mercantile establishments are excepted for six working days before Christmas; nor does the law apply to canneries. New York forbade the employment of a woman in a factory, mercantile establishment, mill, or workshop within four weeks after she has given birth to a child. It reduced the hours of factory women from ten to nine per day and from sixty to fifty-four per week; but more than nine hours a day is permitted in order to secure a short day or holiday on Saturday. Moreover, this limitation of hours does not apply to women and children over 16 in canning or preserving establishments between June 15 and October 15. Virginia prohibited the employment of women in coal mines. The ten-hour law was extended to include not only factories and manufacturing establishments but also workshops and mercantile establishments; exceptions were made of bookkeepers, stenographers, cashiers, or office assistants in fruit and vegetable packing establishments from July 1 to November 1, in mercantile establishments in towns of less than 2000 inhabitants, and in mercantile establishments on Saturdays.

BIBLIOGRAPHY. Besides the government reports above noted the following new books appeared: *Saleswomen in mercantile stores, Baltimore, 1909*, by E. B. Butler; *Fatigue and Efficiency*, by Josephine Goldmark; *Making a business woman*, by A. S. Monroe; *Woman and social progress*, by S. and N. M. Nearing; and a series of pamphlets by the Women's Educational and Industrial Union of Boston on *Medical social service, Organized charity, Settlement Work*, and *Social service for children* as vocations for women.

WOOD FROM STRAW. See CHEMISTRY.

WOOD, HARRY BARNES. An American educator, died April 22, 1912. He was educated at Williams College and at Hamilton College. After graduating from the latter institution he taught in several places and received a master's degree from Hamilton in 1899. In the same year he was appointed professor of Latin in that college and remained there until 1911, with the exception of a few years spent in study in Germany. In the autumn of 1911 he became a teaching fellow in Latin at the University of Wisconsin.

WOODWORTH, WILLIAM MCMICHAEL. An American zoölogist and educator, died May 28, 1912. He was born in San Francisco, Cal., in 1864, and graduated from Harvard College in 1888. He was assistant in microscopic anatomy in Harvard from 1889 to 1891; inspector from 1891 to 1897, and assistant in charge of the Museum of Comparative Zoölogy from 1898 to 1900. He was keeper of this museum from 1900 to 1905. He was editor of the *American Naturalist*. He was a member of many learned societies and associations.

WOOL. See TEXTILE MANUFACTURING, and STOCK-RAISING AND MEAT PRODUCTION.

WOOL TARIFF. See TARIFF.

WOOLWORTH BUILDING. See ARCHITECTURE.

WORKINGMEN'S INSURANCE. The past few years have seen a very comprehensive movement for the provision of insurance against sickness, invalidity, old-age, unemployment, and industrial accidents, and diseases throughout the world. In Germany the government has long given attention to the subject; more recently England, France, and Switzerland have taken it up. In the United States provision is being made through State action for insurance against and compensation for industrial accidents and diseases. (See EMPLOYERS' LIABILITY and WORKMEN'S COMPENSATION.) Insurance for sickness, invalidity, and old age are still in this country in the control of voluntary organizations, as the industrial insurance companies and fraternal societies. (See INSURANCE.) Massachusetts has provided industrial insurance by State action. (See INSURANCE.) Numerous corporations now provide retirement pensions as do many cities and some States for civil service employees. (See OLD-AGE PENSIONS.) The most comprehensive schemes yet instituted by corporations are described below.

AMERICAN TELEPHONE AND TELEGRAPH COMPANY. This corporation and its associated companies, the Western Union Telegraph and the Western Electric, announced in November that it would make available January 1, 1913, a fund of ten million dollars for old-age pensions, sick benefits, compensation for accidents, and life insurance. The companies involved employed 175,000 workers, all of whom were to share in the benefits, at an annual cost to the employers of $1,000,000. The fund was to be added to by annual appropriations. The plan did not call for any contributions from the employees themselves. As to retirement pensions the plan provided that male employees of 60 years of age or over who have been 20 years or more in the service of one of the companies may retire on a pension. The company may retire any employee at 55 after 25 years of service. Women employees reach pensionable age 5 years younger than men. Any employee may be pensioned after 30 years of service regardless of age. The amount of the pension will be one per cent. of the average annual wage for 10 years multiplied by the number of years of service; but no pension will be less than $20 a month. Compensation for accidents occurring in the performance of work for the company will be paid at the rate of full pay for 14 weeks and half pay for the remaining period of disability, but not beyond 6 years. Employees disabled by sickness or accidents not occurring in the course of regular employment who have been employed at least 10 years will receive full pay for 13 weeks and half pay for 39 additional weeks; those employed less than 10 years, but more than 5, will receive full pay for 13 weeks and half pay for 13 weeks; those employed from 2 to 5 years will receive full pay for 4 weeks and half pay for 9 weeks. Those employed less than 2 years may receive some sick or disability benefit at the discretion of the heads of departments.

Perhaps the most unique feature of this scheme is the payment of death benefits not only in cases of fatal accidents while on duty, but also in cases of death from sickness or accident at other times. In case of death from an accident while on duty a payment equal to 3 years' wages, but not exceeding $5000, will be paid to the victim's dependents. In case of death from sickness or accident outside of duty this payment will equal one years' wages for those employees who have served 10 years or more, and one-half of one year's wages for those who have served from 5 to 10 years, the maximum payment being $2000. If in any State the provisions of this plan should be less liberal than those required by workmen's compensation laws the latter will be followed. The funds for the payment of these various benefits will be administered by committees of five to be appointed by the board of directors for each company.

Wisconsin. In December plans were formulated for the presentation in the Wisconsin legislature of a bill providing for sickness insurance for working men and women. The administration was to be in the hands of the State industrial commission and was to be correlated with that of the workmen's compensation law. It provided for contributions by employers and employees, but not by the State. The industrial commission was given discretionary power to decide the amount to be paid on claims.

Abroad. The Association on Social Insurance met in Zurich, Switzerland, during the second week in September. The following topics were discussed: The extension of obligatory insurance to persons other than workmen; supplementary insurance through voluntary organization; the financial burden of social insurance; international statistics of industrial accidents; petty accidents. It was generally agreed that wage-earners and all other persons who need insurance should be either required to take advantage of State insurance schemes or be permitted to do so; if excluded from compulsory insurance plans such persons should be actively assisted in securing some voluntary form of insurance. There was no general agreement as to the relative scope of compulsory and voluntary insurance.

Great Britain. By far the most comprehensive and far-reaching social insurance legislation of recent years is the national insurance act passed December, 1911, by the British Parliament and effective July 15, 1912. This act occupies nearly eighty large closely printed pages, being divided into three parts and an appendix. Part 1 deals with health insurance; Part 2 with unemployment insurance; and Part 3 with general provisions. In the first part insurance against sickness is made compulsory upon all employed persons sixteen years of age or over, except those in the military and naval services, those employed by public authorities for whom provision has been made otherwise, and certain employees of railways, teachers, and a few others who are provided for by other acts. Any of these persons excepted may be brought under the compulsory provision at the discretion of the insurance commissioners. Provision is made also for the voluntary insurance of persons not subject to the compulsory provisions who are engaged in a regular occupation and wholly or mainly dependent on their own earnings; but no person may be a voluntary contributor whose annual income exceeds £160 ($778.64), unless he has been previously insured for at least five years. The act makes no discrimination as to sex or citizenship, residence only being required.

Health Insurance. The administration of the health insurance is entrusted in the first place to a central body of insurance commissioners with extensive powers. Under their authority an insurance committee is to be set up in every county, with a membership of from 40 to 80 persons, some of whom must be women. These county committees are authorized to subdivide counties into districts over which district insurance committees shall have supervision. These latter must make reports on the health of insured persons and sanitary conditions of their territory and must disseminate information. In cases of excessive sickness these district committees may make investigations at the expense of persons charged with neglect or otherwise with causing unhealthful conditions.

The normal premium for health insurance is 14 cents for men and 12 cents for women, made up of contributions from employer, employee, and the public funds. These contributions are proportioned to wages. Thus, if wages equal or exceed 60.8 cents, the employer pays 6.1 cents, male employees 8.1 cents, and female employees 6.1 cents per week. If wages fall between 49 cents and 61 cents a day, the employer pays 8 cents for male employees and 6 cents for female employees and the employee pays 6 cents. If wages fall between 37 cents and 49 cents a day, the employer pays 10 cents for men and 8 cents for women per week, while the employee pays 2 cents and the public funds contribute 2 cents. If wages do not exceed 37 cents a day the employer pays 12 cents for men and 10 cents for women per week, the employee pays nothing, and the public funds contribute 2 cents. These rates apply to all employees at least 21 years of age. Special provision is made for younger employees and certain rules are laid down regarding the contributions of persons who have reached the age of 70. Special rates are also provided for voluntary contributors.

The benefits of the health insurance consist of medical attendance, medicines, and appliances; and a special weekly sick benefit. This benefit amounts to 10s ($2.43) per week for men and 7s 6d ($1.83) for women during the first 26 weeks. If sickness continues beyond this period the benefit is technically known as disablement or invalidity benefit and amounts to 5s ($1.22) per week for either sex during the continuance of incapacity. Special maternity benefits are provided. The payments to unmarried minors, to some persons above 50 years of age, and to married women are smaller. If insured persons are entitled to compensation or damages under compensation or liability acts the sick benefit is reduced so that the total shall not exceed the amount provided in the insurance act, unless the benefit from other sources is greater than the sick benefit, when no sick benefit at all shall be paid. Persons supported in workhouses, hospitals, asylums, and elsewhere by public funds receive no sick, disablement, or maternity benefits. A special fund of $7,500,000 the first year and large annual additions are set aside for the establishment of sanitoria and other facilities for the cure and prevention of tuberculosis.

The administration is extremely complex, the Local Government Board, the Board of Education, the Home Office, the Board of Trade, and the County, Borough, and District Councils all being given authority to promote public health in various ways. Extensive use is made of approved societies. These include the friendly societies, trade unions, provident societies, associations of persons insured in industrial insurance companies and other similar groups. These societies receive the contributions of their own members. Persons who are not members of such societies pay through the post office, by means of stamps, these contributions being under the direct control of the insurance committees.

UNEMPLOYMENT INSURANCE. The second division of the act provides for compulsory insurance against unemployment in the engineering trades. These include building, the construction of railroads, docks, harbors, canals, etc.; shipbuilding, mechanical engineering, iron founding, the construction of vehicles, and woodworking. The funds for this benefit are provided by workmen, employers, and the public treasury. Workmen and employers each contributed 5d (10c) weekly per workmen and the public treasury adds to this sum an amount equal to one-third of it. The employer is expected to make the contribution for both himself and his workers, deducting the latter's share from wages. In order to receive unemployment insurance the worker must show that he has been employed in an insured trade for not less than a part of twenty-six different weeks during the preceding five years, that he is capable of working but unable to find suitable employment, and that he has not exhausted his right to employment benefits. In order to obtain employment a workman is not required to accept employment in a community other than that of his residence or at a lower rate than is customary for the given trade in any district. In case, however, loss of employment results from a trade dispute, no employment benefits shall be paid, unless the worker obtains employment elsewhere in an insured trade. Workers who lose their jobs through misconduct or leave them without just cause will receive no benefits for six weeks after the date of such loss of employment. Otherwise benefits begin after the first week of unemployment and amount to 7s ($1.70) per week, unless some other rate is fixed upon. Benefits are not payable for more than 15 weeks in any period of 12 months, nor in general will benefits exceed one week's benefit for every 5 weekly contributions paid. The act makes provision for the determination of claims and the arbitration of differences under both health and unemployment sections and also includes many exceptions and other conditions made necessary by existing institutions and varying social conditions. See UNEMPLOYMENT.

THE DOCTORS' OPPOSITION. Even before the act passed, the doctors, organized in the British Medical Association, had united in opposition. They succeeded in effecting some changes. They were, however, not satisfied and the association's opposition continued to the close of the year. Although 27,400 members of the association signed a pledge in 1911 not to accept the terms of the chancellor, a poll in the fall of 1912 brought out only 10,000 against working under the act. One of the original objections of the doctors raised was that well-to-do persons would come in under the act and thus a principal source of income would be cut off. This was met by fixing an income limit of £160 for insurable persons. A second objection dealt with the administration. The administration of the medical benefit was placed in the hands of local insurance committees under the general supervision of the insurance commissioners. The doctors objected to control by lay or non-professional committees. This was answered by showing that the act provided for the enrollment, known as a panel, of all doctors willing to serve in various districts; for the right of free choice from such list by the insured person; for payment according to certain general rules; and for participation of the local committee of medical men in all gene a questions effecting the administration of medil cal benefit.

The principal objection dealt with the amount of remuneration. The government was willing to grant 6s per capita of insured persons, but later agreed to grant 7s for the doctor, 1s 6d for drugs, and an additional 6d for drugs, if needed, otherwise to be added to the doctor's fee. The doctors at first demanded 10s, but agreed to compromise on 8s 6d as their per capita fee, not including medicines. The existing colliery and works systems already in existence were to be continued. Moreover, special payment for extras was provided. The reason for lack of agreement was largely the difference of opinion as to the average amount of attendance per head of insured persons that would be required. Investigations covering the incomes of medical men in five cities were variously interpreted. Other statistical tables were prepared from the experience of contract physicians and likewise variously interpreted. Late in the year the chancellor, by way of showing the utmost reasonableness, appointed a commission to investigate, the question of increased remuneration to be determined upon its report. Opinion was sharply divided as to whether the demands of the doctors were excessive or not. On the basis finally granted by the government a physician having 2000 insured persons on his list would have a gross income of $4500 per year. This would include the cost of medicines and other expenses. However, many thought 2000 a larger number than efficient services would permit. The health provisions were to become effective January 15, 1913. At the close of the year it was reported that about 10,000 doctors had accepted the government's terms, there being a sufficient number in all of the 121 insurance areas, except in parts of London and the Manchester district, both Unionist strongholds.

GERMANY. In 1911 the numerous laws, regulations, and judicial interpretations bearing on the various systems of national insurance were codified. These systems are three: Sick insurance, accident insurance, and invalidity insurance, which includes old-age insurance for workmen at least seventy years of age. The sick insurance system includes some 23,000 local societies with nearly 14,000,000 members. About 45 per cent. of the members receive sick aid annually. Sickness insurance covers illness for periods less than six months; funds are derived from equal contributions by employers and employees. Invalidity insurance includes sickness for periods longer than six months and old-age pensions. Nearly 16,000,000 persons are insured under it, receiving pensions of $3.00 to $3.50 per month. Funds are contributed equally by employers and employees. The accident system provides definite compensation for injuries. Employers have combined into mutual insurance societies, of which there are about fifty for agriculture and nearly seventy for industry and trade. Funds are provided by assessments upon employers varying according to trade risks. The total annual revenues for all three systems preceding 1912 were about $210,000,000, and the total expenditures about $165,000,000. The new law extended the system of sick insurance to farm laborers, domestic servants, and casual laborers; extended the pension system to include widows and orphans of insured laborers; and increased the scope of the accident system. As a result the total expenditures were expected to increase by $32,000,000. In addition to these three systems of workmen's insurance the imperial government began, under the law of 1911, an independent system for other persons having incomes less than $1200 per year.

The 1911 changes revived the problem of the relation of the doctors to the sickness societies. This had, as in 1912 in Great Britain, caused much friction when the system of sickness insurance was established in the early eighties. Previous to the revision of 1911 the income limit of persons insurable under the sickness system was about $500; the new law raised the limit to about $625. The doctors manifested special opposition to treat on ordinary insurance terms persons who were enabled to take insurance by this extension of the income limit. The doctors preferred payment in proportion to services rendered, whereas the sickness societies preferred to pay in a lump sum, usually so much per member per annum. Though not entirely settled, compromises in some places were reached by a society or federation of societies and the association of doctors on the basis of a capitation fee. The total payment by the society was to be divided among the doctors by their own association. This obtained at Leipzig, where the sickness society had 200,000 members, and also at Munich, Frankfurt-am-Main, and Stuttgart. Such an arrangement permits special payment for special services and does not include hospital treatment. This plan allows for free choice of doctor and renders control of the doctors by the societies easier. That is, the welfare of the societies requires that the doctors be not too lenient in giving certificates of inability to work; but, on the other hand, the doctors must be unhampered by ignorant persons. In Germany primary control of the doctors is exercised through committees of their own association to which the society makes complaints. There is a conciliation committee composed of representatives of the society and of the doctors' association to settle disputes and other matters of common interest, and an arbitration committee with an impartial chairman as a court of final appeal. In addition, societies are at liberty to have special medical advisers in their exclusive employ.

SWITZERLAND. A new sickness and accident insurance law was enacted by the Federal Council of Switzerland on July 13, 1911, and approved by a referendum vote of the Swiss people on February 14, 1912. By this law the confederation will grant subsidies to recognize sick insurance funds. Sickness insurance may be made compulsory by the cantons, either generally or for special classes of persons. Public funds may be established for such insurance, and though employers are not themselves obliged to contribute they must oversee the payments of their employees whenever the latter are compulsorily insured in such funds. Sick benefits consist of medical care and medicines; a daily indemnity for loss of time of not less than one franc (19.3 cents); benefits must be provided for at least 180 days each year. Special provision is made for women during confinement.

For accidents the confederation granted a subsidy of five million francs ($965,000) as working capital and an equal amount as a reserve fund for the national accident insurance fund. The confederation also pays part of the expense of administration; each canton is entitled to one agency of this fund. Accident insurance is made compulsory for all employees in the transportation and postal services, in factories, in the building trades, engineering works, telegraph and telephone construction and maintenance, in the operation of mines, quarries, and gravel banks, and in industries which produce or use explosives. Insurance is given against accidents, whether occupational or otherwise. An occupational accident is one occurring to a worker while actually employed. Diseases essentially due to employment in designated classes of work are considered accidents within the meaning of the law. The benefits of the accident insurance include medical attendance, medicine, indemnity for loss of time, whether temporary or permanent, and death annuities. The indemnity for disability amounts to 80 per cent. of the earnings, but no earnings above 14 francs ($2.70) per day are considered. If the disability be permanent the total annuity equals 70 per cent. of the annual earnings. For partial disability proportionate deductions are made, no annual earnings in excess of 4000 francs ($772) being considered. An annuity may be revised at any time within three years and afterwards at the expiration of the sixth and ninth years. In case of death the annuity to a widow or to an infirm or permanently disabled widower equals

30 per cent. of the annual earnings. On remarriage a widow is allowed a lump sum equal to three times her annuity. In addition, each legitimate child receives 15 per cent. of the annual earnings of the insured person until 16 years of age. Provision is made also for other relatives, but the total of all annuities cannot exceed 60 per cent. of the earnings of the insured person. Employments are classified according to risk, occupational accident premiums being paid entirely by the employer. For non-occupational accidents the insured pays three-fourths and the confederation one-fourth of the premium. In all cases the employer acts as the collector. Any person not subject to the provisions of compulsory insurance may insure voluntarily.

WORKMEN'S COMPENSATION. This is a term used to designate that form of compensation for industrial accidents which has come to replace employer's liability. Under the older system the employer was required to compensate a workman injured while in employment only when the employee could show in a suit at law that the employer had been grossly negligent, that the worker had not been negligent, and that the accident was not due to the carelessness of a fellow employee. Under the common law the employer was securely entrenched behind the rules of assumed risks, contributory negligence, and the fellow-servant doctrine. Employers' liability laws gradually reduced the employer's security by modifying these doctrines in various respects, but still imposing on the injured worker the necessity of bringing suit in court. The employers at the same time insured themselves against such suits in employers' liability insurance companies, which assumed the obligation of fighting the employees' suits and of paying penalties imposed. Thus the worker was forced to assume the costs of repeated law suits before he could secure any damages. Statistics showed that not more than 45 per cent. of the premiums paid by employers to insurance companies were finally paid to injured workers. Moreover, actual statistical investigation showed that between 60 per cent. and 70 per cent. of injured workers received no compensation whatever. Even when compensation was secured, the expenses involved so reduced it that the remainder was wholly inadequate to offset the economic loss involved in the injury itself. Thus many families were permanently reduced to a lower standard, even to permanent poverty, by industrial accidents. The compensation principle introduced into England and continental countries fifteen to twenty years ago has within the past two years found extensive adoption in the United States. Because most of the American legislation still takes the form of employers' liability laws, the subject is treated more comprehensively under EMPLOYERS' LIABILITY.

The advantages of the compensation principle may be briefly summarized as follows: (1) It furnishes certain, prompt, and reasonable compensation to injured workers and their dependants; (2) it removes from the courts the numerous cases growing out of employers' liability litigation; (3) it relieves charity of the poverty due to uncompensated accidents; (4) it is more economical, since the costs of lawyers, witnesses, insurance companies, and court trials are eliminated, and because it gives to the worker a much larger proportion of the cost to employers; (5) it increases good will and stimulates accident prevention; (6) it furnishes a basis for accurate statistical knowledge of phases of industrial and social life heretofore neglected.

WORLD PEACE FOUNDATION. See ARBITRATION, INTERNATIONAL.

WORLD'S FAIR IN TOKYO. See EXPOSITIONS, *Japan*.

WRESTLING. Several professional matches were held in 1912, but Frank Gotch had no difficulty in retaining his title of world's champion. The only one whose showing during the year makes him a possible contender for the highest honors is S. Zybszko and a match between him and Gotch will doubtless take place in 1913. Of international interest were the bouts held at the Olympic games (q. v.), in which Finland's wrestlers showed marked superiority. The winners of the national championships held under the auspices of the Amateur Athletic Union were: 105-pound, G. Taylor, National Turn Verein, Newark; 115-pound, W. Strobach; 125-pound, Gus Bauer, National Turn Verein; 135-pound, E. Halikman, Educational Alliance; 145-pound, Gus Peterson, Harlem Y. M. C. A.; heavyweight, E. Kaino, Finnish-American A. C. Cornell won the intercollegiate championships. Princeton was second, Pennsylvania third, and Columbia fourth. The winners of the main bouts follow: 112-pound, T. I. S. Boak, Cornell; 125-pound, J. D. Matchat, Cornell; 135-pound, H. H. Ormond, Princeton; 145-pound, J. H. Frantz, Princeton; 158-pound, R. D. Shaw, Cornell; 175-pound, S. Bame, Cornell; heavyweight, J. L. Collins, Cornell.

WRIGHT. See NAVAL PROGRESS.

WRIGHT, SOPHIE B. American philanthropist and educator, died June 10, 1912. She was born in 1886 in New Orleans and when she was three years old she fell and hurt her back and hips so badly that for six years she was strapped to a chair. She was able to attend school, however, and at the age of fourteen opened a school for girls, which she conducted in the forenoons, while in the afternoons she taught in a normal school to pay for home lessons in languages. Observation of the ignorance of many of the boys of the city gave her determination to establish means of giving them some education. She soon established the Home Institute, which had for its especial duty the care of poor boys in the city of New Orleans. She also started a night school. She was obliged to close her school in 1897 on account of yellow fever, but she reopened it as a depot of supplies for the sick and with her teachers went through the city giving help. The attendance at her night school increased so rapidly that within a year there were 1000 pupils in attendance, and her work as a moral agent on the boys of the city had remarkable results. After many years she began to receive financial assistance from wealthy men of the city. She then established a hospital for crippled children of the city and engaged in many other branches of charitable work. Societies throughout the State combined to raise money to pay off mortgages which threatened to ruin her enterprises. She became known throughout the country as a leader of education and one of the deepest thinkers among the women of the

South. She was one of the promoters of "Rest Awhile," the home of the King's Daughters, where many mothers and children are entertained throughout the summer. She was for years before her death so afflicted with asthma that she was scarcely able to sleep. In spite of this she continued her work. Her night school and home institute became one of the most successful among the schools of the South.

WRIGHT, Wilbur. An American aeronaut and inventor, died May 30, 1912. He was born near Millville, Ind., April 16, 1867. He was the son of Milton Wright, a bishop of the Church of the United Brethren. His formal education was obtained from the public and high schools of Dayton, Ohio. Wilbur Wright and his brother, Orville D., early developed a talent in mechanics, and at the time of the popularity of the bicycle they conducted a small shop in Dayton, Ohio, for repairing and building bicycles. The brothers became interested through the experiments carried on by Professor Langley, Octave Chanute, and others, in the science of aeronautics and began experiments at Dayton in flying with kites and afterwards with a device known as gliders.

In the experimental work and in the final results which crowned the efforts of Orville and Wilbur Wright with success, the portions contributed by the two brothers are so closely related that it is impossible to speak of the definite accomplishments of one without also including those of the other. Those who knew them both well have said that to Orville Wright should be credited the larger part of the theoretical work, while to Wilbur, who was of a more practical turn of mind, must be credited the greater share of bringing these theories into actual practice. There is, however, no definite proof of this. The brothers would not at any time discuss the relative share of each in their inventions.

The two brothers found their experiments at Dayton hampered by the physical contour of the country and by the too pressing curiosity of their neighbors. Accordingly in 1903 they began carrying on experiments at Kittyhawk, N. C. By this time their experiments had advanced to such a point that they had produced a machine in which they could remain in the air a minute at a time. This machine was equipped with a 12-horsepower motor. The first flight in this aeroplane covered half a mile in distance and it was made in 59 seconds. This formed the first actual success of a practical air machine. Up to this time the experiments of the Wright brothers had been regarded by the public with an incredulity and in some quarters with ridicule. The final attainment of flying, however, changed this into a serious consideration of their work. Soon after came their invention of warping planes by which the making of air curves and safe steering became possible. In 1905 they constructed a larger machine and with this a flight of 24¼ miles was made. During this flight the machine remained in the air thirty minutes.

In 1906 they built several additional machines. In 1908 Wilbur Wright went to France, where his achievements and those of his brother had received much more recognition than in the United States. His brilliant work in France was acclaimed by European authorities as the successful solution of the problem of mechanical flying. It was admitted that his skill in the manipulation of the aeroplane and his complete knowledge of the conditions involved in its use were far in advance of the best French work. On September 21, 1908, he made a continuous flight of 1 hour and 31 minutes, and in the trial for the Michelin prize of $4000, was in the air continuously for 1 hour, 53 minutes, and 59 seconds, covering a distance of 61½ miles at a speed of 36 miles an hour. This was by far the most successful flight made up to this time. The success of Mr. Wright's experiments in France enabled the brothers to dispose of the French patent rights for $100,000. On December 31, 1912, Mr. Wright made a flight from Le Mans lasting 2 hours and 18 minutes, and covering 76 6/10 miles. While Wilbur Wright was in France making these exhibitions, his brother, Orville, had conducted similar trials prior to the acceptance of the Wright aeroplane for the United States army. On September 17, 1908, the aeroplane in which were Mr. Wright and Lieut. T. E. Selfridge, fell, and Lieutenant Selfridge was killed and Mr. Wright seriously injured. The trials were renewed in July, 1909, and resulted in the acceptance of a Wright machine by the United States army at a price of $30,000.

During the Hudson-Fulton celebration in New York City in October, 1909, Wilbur Wright flew from Governor's Island, New York Bay, over the Hudson River as far as Grant's Tomb and returned.

Following the practical solution of flying, Mr. Wright and his brother devoted the greater part of their attention to improving and perfecting their designs with the object of making safety in flight as nearly attainable as possible. Personally they did not take part in exhibitions of flying, which was such a feature of the years 1910-11. Representatives of their company, however, flew at these meetings and in nearly every case demonstrated the superiority of the Wright machines. Mr. Wright and his brother consistently discouraged feats of flying which called for unusual displays of courage and skill. In 1910 they produced a new machine which was marked by several improvements.

In 1911 the brothers returned to the scene of their original notable experiments at Kittyhawk, N. C., where they made trials with a motorless glider, with the object of perfecting flying in the face of the wind. These experiments were conducted chiefly by Orville Wright. Alleged infringement of their patents, both in the United States and in foreign countries, resulted in the bringing of suits by the Wright brothers against a large number of aviators. The greater number of these suits had not been finally decided at the time of the death of Wilbur Wright.

Although several other experimenters had nearly reached the point of successful flying at the time when the Wright brothers actually reached it, it is generally conceded that they were the pioneers in actual flying in heavier-than-air machines. It was not, however, until Wilbur Wright made his successful exhibitions in France, which were succeeded by other trials in other countries of Europe, than the American public awoke to a real conception of the value and importance of their achievements. This was due partly to the fact that there was in the United States no such interest in flying as prevailed in some countries of Europe, but more especially to the character of the two brothers. Wilbur Wright, especially, was extremely reticent and owing to his disinclination to speak of the experiments until they had succeeded little was actually known of the results until the flights of Wilbur Wright in France and of Orville Wright at Fort Myer, Va., gave them the first place among the aeronauts of the world. In 1909 Wilbur Wright was awarded a gold medal by the French Academy of Sciences and he received many honors from scientific societies both in the United States and foreign countries. These honors he accepted with a modesty which amounted almost to diffidence. Mr. Wright died after a long illness of typhoid fever.

WÜRTTEMBERG. See GERMANY.

WYOMING. POPULATION. According to the Census Bureau statistics compiled during 1912, out of the total population, 145,965 in 1910, 27,146 were foreign-born whites, compared with 16,582 in 1900. Of these the largest number, 4013, came from Austria; 2984 from England; 2293 from Sweden; 2629 from Germany. Other European countries were represented by smaller numbers. The negroes in 1910 numbered 2235 and the mulattoes 293. In 1890 the negroes numbered 982 and the mulattoes 251.

AGRICULTURE. The acreage, value, and production of the principal crops in 1911 and 1912 are shown in the table below:

		Acreage	Prod. Bu.	Value
Corn	1912	16,000	268,000	$ 236,000
	1911	12,000	195,000	148,000
Wheat	1912	76,000	2,181,000	1,745,000
	1911	69,000	1,794,000	1,687,000
Oats	1912	205,000	8,569,000	3,171,000
	1911	190,000	6,655,000	3,278,000
Rye	1912	3,000	57,000	37,000
	1911	2,000	40,000	26,000
Potatoes	1912	11,000	1,540,000	924,000
	1911	10,000	420,000	588,000
Hay	1912	452,000	a 859,000	7,387,000
	1911	330,000	a 693,000	7,138,000

a Tons.

MINERAL PRODUCTION. The value of the production of gold, silver, and copper in the State in 1911, according to the United States Geological Survey, was $34,407, an increase of $2173 over the value of these metals for 1910. The output of gold was valued at $19,200, an increase of $16,001. The production of copper in 1911 was 118,584 pounds, valued at $14,823. This was a decrease of 103,755 pounds from the production of 1910. This was due chiefly to the idleness of the Penn-Wyoming mine and smelter in Carbon County. The decrease in the copper output caused a decline in the smelter production from 1478 ounces in 1910, valued at $798, to 725 ounces, valued at $384, in 1911.

The coal production of the State in 1911 was 6,744,864 short tons, valued at $10,508,863. As in most of the other States in the Rocky Mountain region, the coal production of Wyoming was considerably smaller than in 1910, when a record output was obtained. The output in 1911 showed a decrease of 788,224 short tons in quantity and of $1,197,324 in value.

The production of petroleum in the State in 1911 was 186,695 barrels, a marked increase over the production of 1910, which was 115,430 barrels. This increase included the production of Utah.

MANUFACTURES. The most important general results of the manufacturing census, taken in 1910, together with the percentage of increase from 1904 to 1909, are as follows:

	Number or Amount 1909	1904	P. C. of Inc. 1904-'09
Number of establishments	268	169	58.6
Persons engaged in manufactures	3,393	2,163	56.9
Proprietors and firm members	263	150	75.3
Salaried employees	263	179	46.9
Wage earners (average number)	2,867	1,834	56.3
Primary horsepower	7,628	3,604	111.7
Capital	$6,195,000	$2,696,000	129.8
Expenses	5,594,000	3,189,000	75.4
Services	2,392,000	1,467,000	63.1
Salaries	311,000	206,000	51.0
Wages	2,081,000	1,261,000	65.0
Materials	2,608,000	1,301,000	100.5
Miscellaneous	594,000	421,000	41.1
Value of products	6,249,000	3,523,000	77.4
Value added by manufacture (value of products less cost of materials)	3,641,000	2,222,000	63.9

The State has as yet few manufacturing industries. The most important in point of number of wage earners and value of product were the industries connected with cars and general shop construction and repairs by steam railroad companies. In these industries were employed 1690 persons and the product was valued at $2,337,000. In the lumber and timber products were employed 648 wage earners, and the product was valued at $751,000. Other industries were flour and gristmill products, printing and publishing, manufacture of butter, cheese, and condensed milk, manufacture of bread and other bakery products, and the brewing of malt liquors. The wage earners in the State in 1909 numbered 2867, of whom 46 were women. The wage earners under 16 years of age in the State numbered 12 and of these, 11 were boys. The prevailing hours of labor for the great majority of the wage earners ranged from 60 to 72 a week, only 16.9 per cent. being in establishments operating less than ten hours a day. Of the total number of wage earners, 58.9 per cent. were employed in the railroad repair shops, and practically all of these operate between 60 and 72 hours a week. The only important manufacturing centre is Cheyenne, and in this city were 853 wage earners in 1909.

FINANCE. The receipts for the fiscal year ending September 30, 1912, were $1,178,000, and the expenditures for the same period were $895,748. Including the balance on hand at the beginning of the fiscal year, there was a balance at the end of the year of $1,185,047. The chief sources of income are from State taxes and land rentals. The chief expenditures are for the maintenance of the State government and State institutions. The State debt amounts to $117,000.

POLITICS AND GOVERNMENT

The legislature did not meet in 1912 as the sessions are biennial and the last was held in 1911. The next session, known as the Twelfth Legislature, convenes January 14, 1913. There was no election of State officers in 1912. Governor Joseph M. Carey was elected in November, 1910, and inaugurated January, 1911, for a term of four years. The next general State election will be held in November, 1914. The Republican State convention on May 13 instructed six delegates of the State for President Taft. The Democratic delegates were pledged to vote for Champ Clark. The election on November 5 resulted as follows: Wilson, 15,310; Taft, 14,560; Roosevelt, 9232; Chafin, 434; Wilson's plurality was 750. Agriculturally, the year 1912 was one of the most prosperous in the history of the State. Crops with and without irrigation were unprecedented.

STATE GOVERNMENT. Governor, Joseph M. Carey; Secretary of State, F. L. Houx; Treasurer, J. L. Baird; Auditor and Commissioner of Insurance, R. B. Forsyth; Adjutant-General, M. C. Barkwell; Attorney-General, Douglas A. Preston; Superintendent of Public Instruction, Rose Baird—Houx, Baird, and Preston, Democrats; Carey, Progressive; rest Republicans.

JUDICIARY. Supreme Court: Chief Justice, R. H. Scott; Associate Justices, Cyrus Beard, Charles N. Potter; Clerk, W. H. Kelly—all Republicans.

STATE LEGISLATURE, 1913. Republicans, Senate, 15; House, 31; joint ballot, 46. Democrats, Senate, 12; House, 26; joint ballot, 38. Republican majority, Senate, 3; House, 5; joint ballot, 8.

The representatives in Congress will be found in the article UNITED STATES, section *Congress*.

WYOMING, UNIVERSITY OF. A State institution for higher education at Laramie, Wyo., founded in 1886. The total enrollment in all departments of the university in the autumn of 1912 was 317. The faculty numbered 41. The university consists of the colleges of liberal arts, agriculture, engineering, the normal school, departments of commerce, home economics, and music, university extension, and a preparatory school. During the year a new agricultural hall, to cost $100,000, was begun. This will make the seventh building on the campus of the university, which contains 54 acres. In addition it has two farms adjacent to the city, containing 1100 acres. The university owns, scattered throughout the State, about 130,000 acres of land. By constitutional provision these lands cannot be sold for less than $10 an acre, and the money so realized is to form an endowment fund, the interest of which is to be used for current expenses, but the principal of which cannot be touched. The library contained about 30,000 volumes. President, Charles O. Merica, LL. D.

YACHTING. The year 1912 was a banner one in yatching, and the interest in motorboating also showed a marked increase. Among the large schooners to distinguish themselves during the year were M. F. Plant's *Elena* and E. W. Clark's *Irolita*. The *Elena* won the Astor Cup during the cruise of the New York Yacht Club and the *Irolita* captured the Commodore's Cup. In the sloop class G. M. Pynchon's *Istalena* won the Astor Cup for sloops, while E. T. Hall's *Winsome* was victor in the King's Cup race. The *Aurora*, owned by Cornelius Vanderbilt, also captured several valuable prizes during the season. To determine the superiority among these three sloops a special race was sailed, which the *Istalena* won. In class P, H. C. Smith's sloop *Corinthian* and W. H. Child's *Joyant* made the best showings. E. Randolph's *Helen II.* carried off the laurels in the schoonerette class, P. V. Griffin's *More Joy* in class Q, C. Mallory's *Cliphora* in the American raceabout class, and G. G. Fry's *Toutog* in the American yacht dory class. The best percentage of the season was attained by G. Corry's *Little Dipper* of the star class, which captured 10 firsts and 1 second out of 12 starts. The Richardson International Cup for the supremacy of the Great Lakes was won by the *Patricia* of Canada. The longest ocean race was from Los Angeles to Honolulu, 2600 miles. It was won by Captain Harris' schooner, the *Lurline*, in 335 hours, 16 minutes.

In motorboating, the record-breaking performances of J. S. Blacton's *Baby Reliance II.* and *Baby Reliance III.* were especially noteworthy. The *Baby Reliance III.*, driven by a 12-cylinder engine in a mile trial against time, covered the distance in 1 minute, 7 seconds, or at the rate of 53.73 knots an hour. Equipped with an 8-cylinder engine, the same boat did 35 miles in 47 minutes, 39 seconds. The *Baby Reliance II.* in the international race at Huntington, which was won by E. M. Edgar's British boat, the *Maple Leaf IV.*, did one lap of 7¼ miles in 11 minutes, 43 seconds. The *Baby Reliance II.* also added another wonderful performance in winning the E. R. Thomas interlake championship trophy, by covering 35 miles at an average speed of 46.15 knots.

YALE UNIVERSITY. The total enrollment in all departments in the autumn of 1912 was 3282, divided as follows: Graduate school, resident, 392; non-resident, 82; college, 1127; Sheffield Scientific School, 1107; art school, 43; music school, 103; forest school, 40; department of theology, 90; department of medicine, 43; department of law, 138. The faculty numbered 539, of whom 128 were professors, 93 assistant professors, 134 instructors, 78 assistants in instruction, and 106 assistants in administration. Among the new appointments in the faculty were the following: Ralph Waldo Gifford, formerly of Fordham University, was appointed professor of testamentary law in the law school; Julius Petersen of the University of Munich was appointed professor of German; John Woolman Churchman, formerly of Johns Hopkins University, was appointed professor of surgery in the medical school, and Henry Gray Barbour was appointed assistant professor of pharmacology. The beginning of the collegiate year saw the completion of the new Wright dormitory, which, for the first time, makes it possible for every member of the college to live on the campus. This is the culmination of the task undertaken a quarter of a century ago by Dean Henry Parks Wright, who planned that at some time in the future a sufficient number of buildings should be provided on the campus to house all the students. The building of dormitories has steadily progressed since that time until the completion of the dormitory named in his honor, which provides accommodation for the last of those remaining outside the campus. In addition to this new dormitory, two other buildings were completed during the year and were opened in September, 1912. These were the Sloane physics laboratory, erected at a cost of $400,000 by William D. Sloane and Henry T. Sloane of New York City, and the Day mission library, erected from the bequests of Professor George E. Day, formerly of the divinity school faculty. It is the only building of its kind in America devoted exclusively to a library of foreign missions. The university laboratory of biology and zoölogy approached completion at the beginning of the collegiate year. The annual report of the treasurer showed that bequests during 1911-12 amounted to $1,164,715, as compared with $1,-134,385 in 1910-11.

YASS-CANBERRA. See CITY PLANNING.

YEAMANS, ANNIE. An American actress, died March 1, 1912. She was born in 1835 in the Isle of Wight, and was taken by her parents while still a child, to Sydney, New South Wales. She played in Australia for two seasons in the circus and in 1853 married Edward Yeamans. Her first appearance in New York was in *Cendrillon*. She also appeared in *The Ticket of Leave Man*. She played for a short time in Daly's Theatre, which she left to enter upon a long engagement with Harrigan and Hart at the Theatre Comique. Here she became notable for her impersonation of Irish characters. When Harrigan's dramas ceased to be given Mrs. Yeamans appeared under many managements and in a great variety of plays both in England and the United States. She was one of the oldest actresses on the stage, and was for half a century a favorite with the playgoing public.

YOSHI-HITO, HARUNOMIA. Emperor of Japan, succeeding at the death of his father, Mutsuhito (q. v.). The name Yoshi-Hito signifies "good man." He was born August 31, 1879, the son of Princess Yanigawara, one of the eight princesses of noble blood, who became members of the household of the emperor. His two older brothers died soon after birth. He was nominated as heir-apparent on his eighth birthday and he at that time received the decoration of the Grand Order of Merit and a commission as a colonel in the Imperial Royal Guards. He was educated at the school for members of the imperial royal family at Tokyo. It comprised modern training as well as the old Japanese studies. The emperor speaks English, French, and German. In 1900 he married Princess Sada, his cousin. Yoshi-Hito was a lieutenant-colonel in the army and vice-admiral in the navy. Although his disposition is said to be toward liberal and modern ideas, he is also said to display a desire to maintain so much of ancient tradition as will not interfere with the real progress of his country. The emperor and empress have three children, Princes Michi, Atsu, and Teru. The first-named is the heir-apparent and is the first son to have been born to either an empress or a crown princess in many generations.

YOUNG, ALFRED HARRY. An English anatomist and educator, died February 24, 1912. He was born in Warrington and graduated in medicine at Edinburgh University in 1876. He was appointed demonstrator of anatomy in the Medical School of that university, and in 1877 removed to Manchester to take a similar position in Owens College. In 1885 he was elected to the chair of anatomy in that institution and was at the same time dean of the medical school. He was connected with the Salford Royal Hospital until 1903, when he resigned and was appointed honorary consulting surgeon. In 1902 he resigned as dean of the medical school. He continued to lecture until 1909, when he vacated the chair on account of ill health. He was then made professor emeritus. He contributed to numerous papers and to medical journals and was the editor of *Studies in Anatomy from the University of Manchester*, and was also a former editor of the *Medical Chronicle*.

YOUNG, LUCIEN. A rear-admiral of the United States navy, died October 2, 1912. He was born in Lexington, Ky., in 1852, and graduated from the United States Naval Academy in 1873. In the same year he was made a midshipman. While still a midshipman serving on the *Alaska*, he jumped overboard on July 23, 1873, and rescued a seaman while the ship was under way at sea. The act received mention by the Secretary of the Navy in general orders, and Midshipman Young was awarded a gold medal by the New York Benevolent and Live Saving Institution, and a certificate by the Humane Society of Massachusetts. He was one of the officers on board the *Huron*, which was wrecked off Nag's Head, N. C. Here he distinguished himself in the rescue of members of the ship's company, only twelve of whom were saved. On this occasion he received the thanks of the Secretary of the Navy and a gold medal from the United States Live-Saving Service. He was presented with a sword by the Kentucky legislature and was made an honorary member of that body. He was also advanced to the rank of master by special act of Congress at the nomination of the President. In 1878 he was sent on special duty to the Paris Exposition. While in that city he declined a medal from the Legion of Honor. He afterwards declined a medal offered by the king of Portugal for heroism in saving five persons from a wreck off the mouth of the Tagus River. In 1877, after serving on various ships and in the Bureau of Equippment, he became instructor in the Naval War College. For much of the time in the few years following he was in the Bureau of Equippment, the office of the Secretary of the Navy, and the War Records office. During the revolution in Hawaii he was in service there and he severely attacked Queen Liliuokalani before the Senate committee which investigated that revolution. At the outbreak of the Spanish-American War he was on sick leave, but he was called back to active service and put in command of the gunboat *Hist*. He was advanced three numbers for meritorious conduct in that war. From 1899 to 1900 he was commander of the port of Havana and was then made commandant of the United States naval station at Havana. For services rendered during a severe storm which occurred while at this post he received a commendatory letter from the mayor and City Council of Havana. After two years spent in the lighthouse service he was given command of the *Bennington* and was in command of this vessel when its boilers exploded off San Diego, Cal., in July, 1905. Commander Young was court-martialed in connection with this accident, but was vindicated, the court finding the boilers defective and that Commander Young had so reported them before the accident. At the time of the San Francisco earthquake he was commander of the Mare Island Navy Yard and his work of relief received mention by the Secretary of the Navy. From Mare Island he was transferred to Key West. In 1910 he was promoted to the rank of rear-admiral. He was the author of a standard work on navigatioo, *Archæological Researches in Peru*, and *The Real Hawaii*.

YOUNG MEN'S CHRISTIAN ASSOCIATION. The international committee of the Y. M. C. A. in its present form was created by the international convention of 1866. It now consists of 70 members and 22 advisory members, resident in the United States and Canada, who are elected by delegates sent from the local associations to the triennial conventions. Its headquarters are at 124 East 28th Street, New York City, with branch offices in Chicago, Montreal, and other important centres. The committee employs a force of 111 executive, traveling, and office secretaries on the North American field, besides a staff of 128 secretaries engaged in planting the American type of association work in the important centres of the non-Christian world. The present chairman of the international committee is Alfred E. Marling of New York City, and at the head of the committee's secretarial staff are Richard C. Morse, who has been the general secretary since 1869, and John R. Mott, who, as associate general secretary, has general charge of the student work and work in foreign lands. The international committee exists, not as an end in itself, but solely to aid and strengthen the local associations through a service of counsel and coöperation. The next triennial convention of the Young Men's Christian Associations will be held in Los Angeles, May 8-12, 1913.

In 1912 there were 8612 associations in the world, of which 2192 were in North America. The total membership of the American associations was 563,479. These associations occupy 756 buildings of their own and have 570 libraries. In the evening educational classes were 67,417 young men as students, and in the physical departments 300,590. In the Bible classes were 103,599 students. The general secretaries and other paid officials numbered 3633. The expenditures for current expenses amounted to $11,302,547.

YOUNG WOMEN'S CHRISTIAN ASSOCIATION OF THE UNITED STATES OF AMERICA, NATIONAL BOARD OF. Affiliated with the national board of this association are 208 city and town associations, 660 in colleges and schools, and 7 in counties, or 875 in all, a total membership of 253,406. The national board opened in September, 1912, at Fifty-second street and Lexington avenue, New York City, a new building for the administrative offices and for the national training school, which offers a one-year post-graduate course for the association secretaryships. The national board conducted in 1912 eleven city and student conferences in which over 4000 young women were given ten days of rest, recreation, and grounding in Christian fundamentals.

YUAN SHIH-KAI. See CHINA.

YUKON. A territory of the Dominion of Canada. Area, 207,076 square miles. Population (census of June 1, 1911), 8512, as compared with 27,219 in 1901. Dawson, the capital, had 3013 inhabitants (9142 in 1901). Commissioner, George Black.

ZANZIBAR. An island (640 square miles—the largest coralline island on the African coast) which, with Pemba (380 square miles) and several other small islands, constitutes a British protectorate. Population (census 1910), 197,199 (300 Europeans, about 10,000 Arabs, and about 20,000 Indians). The bulk of the population is Swahili. Mohammedanism is the prevailing religion. Imports (1910), £993,031; exports, £1,033,467 (cloves, £253,470; copra and chikichi, £219,369; grain, £50,385; ivory, £60,844; gum copal, £11,802; hides and skins, £10,050; bullion and specie, £55,507). Revenue (1910) £181,705; expenditure, £192,925; debt, £75,573. British agent and consul-general, Edward Clarke, residing at Zanzibar. Sultan, Seyyid Ali.

ZAPATA, EMILIANO. See MEXICO.

ZEAL, Sir WILLIAM AUSTIN. An Australian public official, died March, 1912. He was born in Westbury, Wiltshire, England, in 1830, and was educated privately. In 1852 he went to Australia, where for a time he was engaged as a railway engineer and subsequently in farming. He became a member of the Legislative Assembly of Victoria, 1864, and a member of the Legislative Council for the Northwest provinces in 1881 and of the North Central provinces in 1882. In 1892 he was postmaster-general and from 1892 to 1901 was president of the Legislative Council of Victoria. He took a prominent part in the federal movement and was a member of the national convention which framed the Commonwealth constitution in 1897-8. He was elected to the first Commonwealth Senate for Victoria in 1901. He was made a K. C. M. G. in 1895.

ZEPPELIN. See NAVAL PROGRESS.

ZEPPELIN AIRSHIP. See AERONAUTICS.

ZINC. The production of primary spelter, which is the ore of zinc, from domestic ores in 1911 was 271,621 short tons, valued at $30,964,794 compared with 252,479 short tons, valued at $27,267,732 in 1910. The total production of spelter from both domestic and foreign ores in 1911 was the greatest in the history of the zinc-smelting industry in the United States, being 286,526 short tons compared with 269,184 tons in 1910, a gain of 17,342 tons or 6.4 per cent. Together with the increase in the production, there was a large increase in the consumption, which was nearly 10,000,000 tons greater than the abnormal consumption of 1909. The largest quantity of spelter was produced in Missouri, 127,540 tons. This State surpassed all others in production. In Colorado, 42,233 tons were mined; in Montana, 22,115; in Wisconsin, 31,809, and in New Jersey, 15,128. There are the only States in which spelter is produced in large quantities. The exodus of zinc spelters from Kansas which began in 1910, continued in 1911. Of 16 plants which were in existence in 1910, but 10 were left at the close of 1911. The total amount of crude ore mined in 1911, including zinc ore, zinc lead ore, and all other ore, was 44,141,005 tons. From this was recovered 345,260 short tons of zinc content.

The zinc imported into the United States in 1911 was valued at $110,123. This included block or pigs, sheets, and old zinc. The exports were valued at $1,935,677. These included zinc ore, plates, sheets, pigs or bars, and zinc dross.

WORLD PRODUCTION. The world's production of spelter in 1911 was 978,695 short tons. Of this, the largest quantity, 286,526 tons, was produced in the United States. In Germany 276,006 tons were produced, and in Belgium, 215,050. Other countries producing quantities ranging from 18,000 to 73,000 tons were Austria, France, Spain, Great Britain, Holland, and Poland.

The production of zinc in the United States in 1912 was 347,922 short tons. Of this amount 110,724 tons were produced in Missouri and Kansas, 94,886 in Illinois, 77,524 in Oklahoma, and 56,083 in the eastern States. These figures are taken from the *Engineering and*

Mining Journal. See also METALLURGY, and CHEMISTRY, INDUSTRIAL.

XENON. See PHYSICS.

ZOOLOGY. Zoölogical research in 1912, as in previous years, was conducted along both observational and experimental lines. A good deal of this work had distinctly an economic importance. See ENTOMOLOGY, FISH AND FISHERIES, and BIOLOGY.

A standing committee of the International Congresses of Zoölogy is one on nomenclature, appointed to devise some remedy for the present chaotic condition of zoölogical nomenclature. Much controversy was excited during the year by the report from this committee that they propose to apply in all cases the rule of priority, a procedure that may make it necessary to change some long established usages. See YEAR BOOK for 1907. Zoölogists whose work is mainly systematic seem in favor of applying the priority rule, while others apparently prefer not to give up familiar names, and suggest that the committee prepare an official list, which need not in all cases follow the priority rule.

PHYLOGENETIC SPECULATION. While much in vogue some twenty or more years ago, phylogenetic speculation has received of late very little attention from zoölogists. An important book of the year along this line is Patten's *The Evolution of the Vertebrates and Their Kin*, in which the author develops a theory as to the origin of the vertebrate phylum. Patten's theory, upon which he has been working since 1884, and which has been outlined in a number of earlier papers, is that the vertebrates have descended from the arachnids, including the trilobites and *Limulus* in this group. The fossil *Ostracodermata* he regards as a connecting link between the arachnids and the true vertebrates.

PROTOZOA. The question as to the meaning of conjugation in the protozoa was apparently still unsettled. Woodruff reported results in agreement with those of his earlier papers. See YEAR BOOK for 1911. A pedigreed culture of *Paramœcium*, which he had kept through 3029 generations, was still in good condition, though there had been no conjugation during that time. From these results he concluded that the protoplasm of a single cell may be sufficient to reproduce itself indefinitely under favorable environmental conditions, without recourse to conjugation. Senescence and need of fertilization are not primary attributes of living matter. Baitsell studied *Stylonychia*, and concluded that conjugation periods are a result of a peculiar stimulation due to external conditions, and have no relation whatever to a "life-cycle."

CŒLENTERATES. Annandale recorded a case where sea anemones had been kept in an aquarium for over fifty years, indicating that the normal life of these animals must be even longer than this.

NEMATODES. Loos, in *Records of School of Medicine*, published by the Ministry of Education in Egypt, on the life history of the hookworm, *Ankylostoma duodenalis*, and the American form, *Necator americanus*, reported that in both cases thirty days elapse between the time of infection and the time when the eggs appear in the feces of the victim.

ANNELIDA. Shearer stated that in *Dinophilus gyrociliatus* the immature females are fertilized while still within the egg capsule, the sperm being recognizable in the body of the female before any eggs have appeared. When these latter arise, they enter into such relations with the spermatozoa, that the nucleus of the oögonium is of double nature, one portion being derived from the sperm, the other from the oögonium itself. Later divisions are such that in some cells the female part of the compound nucleus divides before the male, so that of the two daughter cells, one has all of the male, and half of the female nucleus, while the other has only female. The former gives rise to a female adult, the latter to a male. If the nucleus divides equally, the resulting cells degenerate. Whitney stated that the rotifer *Hydatina senta*, if forced to breed parthenogenetically for 384 generations, showed a gradual decrease in the rate of reproduction, but that cross fertilization of such weakened races caused a sudden increase in the reproduction rate of the ensuing race.

CRUSTACEA. Megusar, experimenting on the chromatophores of decapod crustacea, found that light exerts a direct influence in that a certain amount of light is essential, for the appearance of the color. The eyes also are of importance in producing the color variations, blinding of the animals being followed by a complete loss of color. Color disappears if the animal is kept in the dark, the loss being greater if it be blinded at the same time.

FISH. See FISH AND FISHERIES.

AMPHIBIA. Kammerer discovered interesting correlations between the environment and the structure of the blind amphibian, *Proteus anguinus*. If kept below 15° C. it is viviparous. If above 15° C. it lays eggs, one and the same female being either oviparous or viviparous according as it is kept at the lower or the higher temperature. In the dark the animal is colorless, but becomes pigmented if kept in daylight, the change being greater the brighter the light, the higher the temperature, the longer it is exposed to it, and the younger and better nourished the animal is. Offspring of the pigmented forms are pigmented, whether born in the dark or in the light. The eye is imperfect and soon degenerates in the embryo, though if kept in the light this degeneration soon ceases. Smith studied the embryology of *Cryptobranchus alleghenienis*. Egg laying takes place in August and September, the eggs being laid in definite nests. The male guards the nest after the eggs are laid, possibly to protect the eggs, though both male and female will eat them. Smith suggested that possibly the male eats fewer of them than does the female.

MAMMALS. The Stefansson-Anderson expedition in Arctic America returned in 1912, having covered the coast region of Alaska east of the Colville River, and the Barren Grounds of the Yukon and Makenzie districts east to Coronation Gulf. Large collections of birds and mammals were reported, of especial importance being caribou material, and a series of 17 specimens of the little known, Barren Ground bear, a form not yet thoroughly studied, but apparently related to the grizzly. Baker reported that experiments in breeding black bear have been successfully carried on for the past 21 years at a private park near Akron, O. Sixty-eight or sixty-nine cubs have been produced during this time, of which only one died. Contrary to the usual assumption, the bear is quite fat when it emerges from its winter hibernation.

Townsend reported that the elephant seal, *Macrorhinus angustirostris*, formerly much hunted for oil, but which has seldom been seen since 1852, is still to be found at Guadalupe, a small island 140 miles from Lower California. The proboscis is not capable of inflation and apparently appears only at the time of sexual maturity. The males have a length of 16 feet with a girth of 11 feet, while the females are about 11 feet long. The Mexican government has taken steps to protect this herd. The discovery of a shrew, *Microscolex winnemana*, from Virginia, was announced in 1912. The specimens measured 76 and 86 mm. respectively, making it the smallest mammal yet described from North America. In 1911 the first natural history collection ever made in the Mount Robinson region of the Canadian Rockies resulted in the discovery of four new mammals, a chipmunk, a manteled ground squirrel, and two bats, which have since been described by Hollister.

ZULULAND. A province of Natal (q. v.).

THE END

Lightning Source UK Ltd.
Milton Keynes UK
UKHW020100140219
337249UK00009B/475/P

9 781528 138994